ATHL

2016

THE INTERNATIONAL TRACK AND FIELD ANNUAL

BY PETER MATTHEWS

ASSOCIATION OF TRACK & FIELD STATISTICIANS

Published by SportsBooks Ltd

SportsBooks Limited
9 St Aubyns Place
York
YO24 1EQ
United Kingdom
Tel: 01904 613475
e-mail randall@sportsbooks.ltd.uk
Website www.sportsbooks.ltd.uk

This publication incorporates the ATFS Annual.

Photographs supplied by Mark Shearman OBE, 22 Grovelands Road, Purley, Surrey, CR8 4LA.
Tel: 0208 660 0156: mark@athleticsimages.com

British Library Cataloguing in Publication Data

Athletics: the international track and
field annual – 2016
1. Athletics. Track & Field events –
Serials
1. International athletics annual (London)
796.4'2'05

ISBN 9781907524516

Cover design: Kath Grimshaw

Printed arranged by Jellyfish Solutions, UK

CONTENTS

Introduction 5
Abbreviations 6
Acknowledgements 9
ATFS & Web Sites 10

Review of 2015
Diary of the year by *Peter Matthews* 11
Athletes of the year – Men by *Peter Matthews* 23
Athletes of the year – Women by *Peter Matthews* 32
Junior athletes of the year by *Peter Matthews* 40

Cross-country 44
Road race review *by Marty Post* 46
Marathon review *by Marty Post* 49
Marathon Majors 53
Ultramarathon review *by Andy Milroy* 53

Major Championships 2015
World Championships 55
IAAF World Relays 67
World Youth Championships 68
IAAF Hammer Throw Challenge 69
IAAF World Race Walking Challenge 69
World University Games 70
IAAF World Combined Events Challenge 71
All-Africa Games 71
African Junior Championships 72
Arab Championships, Asian Championships 73
Balkan Championships 74
Commonwealth Youth Games, European Cup Winter Throwing 75
European Team Championships 75
European Cups: Combined Events, Race Walking, 10,000m 77
European U23 Championships 77
European U20 Championships 78
Small States of Europe, Gulf, NACAC and Oceania Championships 80
Pacific Games, Pan-American Games 81
Pan-American Junior Championships 82
Pan-American Race Walking Cup, South American Championships 83
South American Junior Championships, South East Asia Games 84
World Military Games 84
IAU 50km, 100km and 24 Hours World Championships 85
IAAF Diamond League 85
IAAF Continental Cup 2014 86

IAAF World Athletics Tour – Major Meetings 2015–2016 90
Major international events 2016–20 91

Early 2016 Championships
IAAF World Half Marathon 85
World Indoor Championships 93
Asian Indoor Championships 94

Preview of 2016 Olympic Games 95
World Junior Championships 97

Obituary 99
Drugs bans 114, 592

How British Steeplechasers prepared 60 years ago *by Bob Phillips* 116

World Lists Trends – 10th and 100th bests on world lists 119

Corrections to ***Athletics 2015*** (year lists 2014) - and earlier years 121
Reference Books 2015/2016 123
Hall of Fame 127

National champions and Biographies
National champions 2015 and biographies of leading athletes 137

Introduction to World lists and indexes 255
Records
World and Continental records - men 257
World and Continental records - women 262
World bests - non-standard events 268
World long distance bests 269
World Indoor Records 270
World indoor junior records 271
World Veterans/Masters records 272
World and Continental Records set in 2015 274
World and Continental Records set in Jan-Mar 2016 276
World Records superlatives 277

All-time Lists
Men 278
Women 316
Junior men 349
Junior women 354

2015 World Lists
Men 360
Women 444
Men's Index 527
Women's Index 561

2016 World Indoor lists 594

Miscellany
Retirements announced, top women athletes giving birth in 2015 43
Miscellany 66, 98
Marriages of athletes in 2015 114
Transfer of national allegiance 114
Women's name changes 114

INTRODUCTION

IT IS SADLY the case that athletics has come into increasing disrepute over the past year with more and more stories of drug abuse and, most disturbing of all, of corruption at the heart of our sport.

I hate having to rewrite history. Yet it has been necessary in recent years in athletics, with the steady stream of retrospective drugs disqualifications. Many of these mean changing championship results and both year and all-time lists not only for the athlete concerned but also to change the positions of other finishers in events in which the disqualified athlete has competed. This has substantially increased with the introduction of the IAAF's biological passport programme that has caught many athletes. Each year I include a lists of drugs bans in this Annual, and also show changes major changes to results and effects on lists in my Amendments pages.

For many years the IAAF has led the way in a greater testing programme than for any other sport, and yet in 2015 in particular the sport came into disrepute due to the number of positives, especially of top Russian athletes, and, even more so ironically, because it was alleged that such positive tests were being covered up. Media coverage was headed by the German TV station ARD and the British newspaper *The Sunday Times*. Impressions given by them were often misleading for the general public but the upshot was that WADA set up an Independent Commission 'to conduct an independent investigation into doping practices; corrupt practices around sample collection and results management; and other ineffective administration of anti-doping processes that implicate Russia, the IAAF, athletes, coaches, trainers, doctors and other members of athletes' entourages; as well as the accredited laboratory based in Moscow and the Russian Anti-Doping Agency (RUSADA).' This culminated in two damning reports, the suspension of Russia from international athletics until it could be seen that the Russian authorities were complying with the WADA Code, and the decision at the IAAF Council meeting in March 2016 that it was implementing an action plan to monitor compliance to IAAF Rule 30.6 with respect to the federations of Ethiopia, Morocco, Belarus, Kenya and Ukraine. Meanwhile The IAAF's recently retired President, Lamine Diack, was arrested and questioned by French police about allegations that he took bribes to suppress positive doping tests and also under investigation were Diack's legal adviser Habib Cissé and the former director of the IAAF's anti-doping department Gabriel Dollé. The IAAF Ethics Commission recommended that disciplinary charges be brought against Papa Massata Diack (Lamine's son and former consultant to the IAAF), Valentin Balakhnichev (former President of ARAF and IAAF Treasurer), Aleksey Melnikov (former Russian Chief Coach for walkers and distance runners) and Dollé for various alleged breaches of the IAAF code of ethics. In January 2016 the IAAF announced life bans for P M Diack, Balakhnichev and Melnikov for multiple breaches of anti-doping rules relating to Liliya Shobukhova (who had apparently been blackmailed to cover up her doping violations) and a five-year ban for Dollé. Appeals were lodged with the CAS contesting the life bans.

Despite the above there has been much terrific athletics over the past year reviewed in this Annual, and most particularly a great and highly enjoyable World Championships in Beijing and a most enjoyable World Indoor Championships in March 2016 in Portland. The increasingly universal nature of the sport has helped to produce a noticeable increase in standards at many events.

Meanwhile we have another great summer of the sport to look forward to, with the main emphasis being on the Olympic Games in Rio de Janeiro. It will probably be too much to hope for, but it would be good if the majority of media interest could actually be on the competition rather than on yet more doping issues.

Peter Matthews

ABBREVIATIONS

The following abbreviations have been used for meetings with, in parentheses, the first year that they were held.

AAU (USA) Amateur Athletic Union Championships (1888) (later TAC)
Af-AsG Afro-Asian Games (2003)
AfCh African Championships (1979)
AfG African Games (1965)
Af-J African Junior Championships (1994)
AmCp America's Cup (World Cup Trial) (1977)
APM Adriaan Paulen Memorial, Hengelo
AsiC Asian Championships (1973)
AsiG Asian Games (1951)
Asi-J Asian Junior Championships (1990)
ASV Weltklasse in Köln, ASV club meeting (1934)
Athl Athletissima, Lausanne (1976)
Balk Balkan Games (1929), C - Championships
Barr (Cuba) Barrientos Memorial (1946)
BGP Budapest Grand Prix (1978)
Bisl Bislett Games, Oslo (1965) (Bergen 2004)
Bol G Bolivar Games (1938)
BrGP British Grand Prix
CAC Central American and Caribbean Championships (1967)
CAG Central American and Caribbean Games (1926)
C.Asian Central Asian Championships
CAU Inter-counties, GBR (1934)
CG Commonwealth Games (1930)
C.Cup Continental Cup (2010)
Déca Décanation, Paris (C) (2005)
DL Diamond League (2010)
DNG DN Galan, Stockholm (1966)
Drake Drake Relays (1910)
EAF European Athletics Festival, Bydgoszcz (2001)
EAsG East Asian Games (1993)
EC European Championships (1934)
ECCp European Clubs Cup (1975)
EChall European Challenge (10,000m 1997, Throws 2001); see ET
ECp European Cup - track & field (1965), multi-events (1973)
EI European Indoor Championships (1970, Games 1966-9)
EICp European Indoor Cup (2003)
EJ European Junior Championships (1970)
ET European Team Championships (replaced European Cup, 2009)
EU23 European Under-23 Championships (1997) and European Under-23 Cup (1992-4)
FBK Fanny Blankers-Koen Games, Hengelo (formerly APM) (1981)
FlaR Florida Relays (1939)
FOT (USA) Final Olympic Trials (1920)
Franc Francophone Games (1989)
Gaz Gaz de France meeting, FRA (was BNP) (1968)
GGala Golden Gala, Roma (from 1980), Verona (1988), Pescara (1989), Bologna (1990)
GL Golden League (1998-2009)
GNR Great North Run – Newcastle to South Shields, GBR (1981)
GP Grand Prix
GPF IAAF Grand Prix Final (1985)
GS Golden Spike, Ostrava (1969)
Gugl Zipfer Gugl Grand Prix, Linz (1988)
GWG Goodwill Games (1986)
Gyulai István Gyulai Memorial, Budapest (2011-13), Székesfehérvár (2014-16)
Hanz Hanzekovic Memorial, Zagreb (1958)
Herc Herculis, Monte Carlo, Monaco (1987)
IAAF International Association of Athletics Federations
IAC IAC meeting (1968), formerly Coca-Cola
IAU International Association of Ultrarunners
IbAm Ibero-American Championships (1983)
ISTAF Internationales Stadionfest, Berlin (1921)
Jenner Bruce Jenner Classic, San Jose (1979)
Jerome Harry Jerome Track Classic (1984)
Jordan Payton Jordan U.S. Track & Field Open, Stanford (2004)
JUCO Junior Colleges Championships, USA
KansR Kansas Relays, Lawrence (1923)
Kuso Janusz Kusocinski Memorial (1954)
Kuts Vladimir Kuts Memorial (1978)
LGP London Grand Prix, Crystal Palace
LI Loughborough International (1958)
MAI Malmö Al Galan, Sweden (1958)
Mast Masters pole vault, Grenoble (1987), Donetsk
MedG Mediterranean Games (1951)
Mill Millrose Games, New York indoors (1908)
ModR Modesto Relays (1942)
MSR Mt. San Antonio College Relays (1959)
NA Night of Athletics, Heusden (2000) formerly Hechtel
NACAC North American, Central American & Caribbean Ch (2003)
NC National Championships
NC-w National Winter Championships
NCAA National Collegiate Athletic Association Championships, USA (1921)
NCAA-r NCAA Regional Championships (2003)
NCp National Cup
Nebiolo Memorial Primo Nebiolo, Torino (2000, originally 1963)
NG National Games
Nik Nikaïa, Nice (1976)
NM Narodna Mladezhe, Sofia (1955)
N.Sch National Schools
Nurmi Paavo Nurmi Games (1957)
NYG New York Games (1989)
OD Olympischer Tag (Olympic Day) (1963)
Oda Mikio Oda Memorial Meeting, Hiroshima (1967)
Odlozil Josef Odlozil Memorial, Prague (1994)
OG Olympic Games (1896)
OT Olympic Trials
Owens Jesse Owens Memorial (1981)
PAm Pan American Games (1951)
PArab Pan Arab Championships (1977) (G-Games 1953)
Pedro Pedro's Cup, Poland (2005)
PennR Pennsylvania Relays (1895)
PTS Pravda Televízia Slovnaft, Bratislava (1957) (later GPB)
Pre Steve Prefontaine Memorial (1976)

RdVin	Route du Vin Half Marathon, Luxembourg (1962)
RomIC	Romanian International Championships (1948)
RWC	Race Walking Challenge Final (2007)
SACh	South American Championships (1919)
SAsG	South Asian Games (1984)
SEAG	South East Asia Games (1959)
SEC	Southeastern Conference Championships
SGP	IAAF Super Grand Prix
Skol	Skolimowska Memorial (2010)
Slovn	Slovnaft, Bratislava (formerly PTS) (1990)
Spark	Sparkassen Cup, Stuttgart (indoor) (1987)
Spart	(URS) Spartakiad (1956)
Spitzen	Spitzen Leichtathletik Luzern (1987)
Stra	Stramilano Half marathon, Milan (1972)
Super	Super Meet, Japan (Tokyo, Shizuoka, Yokohama, Kawasaki)
TexR	Texas Relays (1925)
Tsik	Athens Grand Prix Tsiklitiria (1998)
USOF	US Olympic Festival (1978)
VD	Ivo Van Damme Memorial, Brussels (1977)
Veniz	Venizélia, Haniá, Crete (1936)
WAC	Western Athletic Conference Championships (1962)
WAF	World Athletics Finals (2003)
WCh	World Championships (1983)
WCM	World Challenge Meeting (2010)
WCp	World Cup - track & field (1977), marathon (1985) Walking – Lugano Trophy – men (1961), Eschborn Cup – women (1979)
WCT	World Championships Trial
WG	World Games, Helsinki (1961)
WI	World Indoor Championships (1987), World Indoor Games (1985)
WJ	World Junior Championships (1986)
WK	Weltklasse, Zürich (1962)
WMilG	World Military Games
WRly	World Relays (2014)
WUG	World University Games (1923)
WY	World Youth Championships (1999)
Zat	Emil Zátopek Classic, Melbourne
Znam	Znamenskiy Brothers Memorial (1958)

-j, -y, -23 Junior, Youth or under-23

Dual and triangular matches are indicated by "v" (versus) followed by the name(s) of the opposition. Quadrangular and larger inter-nation matches are denoted by the number of nations and -N; viz 8-N designates an 8-nation meeting.

Events

CC	cross-country
Dec	decathlon
DT	discus
h	hurdles
Hep	heptathlon
HJ	high jump
HMar	half marathon
HT	hammer
JT	javelin
LJ	long jump
Mar	marathon
Pen	pentathlon
PV	pole vault
R	relay
SP	shot
St	steeplechase
TJ	triple jump
W	walk
Wt	weight

Miscellaneous abbreviations

+	Intermediate time in longer race
=	Tie (ex-aequo)
A	Made at an altitude of 1000m or higher
b	date of birth
D	Made in decathlon competition
dnf	did not finish
dnq	did not qualify
dns	did not start
exh	exhibition
h	heat
H	Made in heptathlon competition
hr	hour
i	indoors
kg	kilograms
km	kilometres
m	metres
M	mile
m/s	metres per second
mx	Made in mixed men's and women's race
nh	no height
O	Made in octathlon competition
P	Made in pentathlon competition
pb	personal best
Q	Made in qualifying round
qf	quarter final (or q in lists)
r	Race number in a series of races
sf	semi final (or s in lists)
w	wind assisted
WIR	world indoor record
WR	world record or best
y	yards
*	Converted time from yards to metres: For 200m: 220 yards less 0.11 second For 400m: 440 yards less 0.26 second For 110mh: 120yh plus 0.03 second

Countries

(IAAF membership now stands at 214). IAAF and IOC abbreviations are now identical.

AFG	Afghanistan
AHO	Netherlands Antilles #
AIA	Anguilla
ALB	Albania
ALG	Algeria
AND	Andorra
ANG	Angola
ANT	Antigua & Barbuda
ARG	Argentina
ARM	Armenia
ARU	Aruba
ASA	American Samoa
AUS	Australia
AUT	Austria
AZE	Azerbaijan
BAH	Bahamas
BAN	Bangladesh
BAR	Barbados
BDI	Burundi
BEL	Belgium
BEN	Benin
BER	Bermuda
BHU	Bhutan
BIH	Bosnia Herzegovina
BIZ	Belize
BLR	Belarus
BOL	Bolivia
BOT	Botswana
BRA	Brazil

BRN Bahrain
BRU Brunei
BUL Bulgaria
BUR Burkina Faso
CAF Central African Republic
CAM Cambodia
CAN Canada
CAY Cayman Islands
CGO Congo
CHA Chad
CHI Chile
CHN People's Republic of China
CIV Côte d'Ivoire (Ivory Coast)
CMR Cameroon
COD Democratic Republic of Congo
COK Cook Islands
COL Colombia
COM Comoros
CPV Cape Verde Islands
CRC Costa Rica
CRO Croatia
CUB Cuba
CUR Curaçao
CYP Cyprus
CZE Czech Republic
DEN Denmark
DJI Djibouti
DMA Dominica
DOM Dominican Republic
ECU Ecuador
EGY Egypt
ENG England
ERI Eritrea
ESA El Salvador
ESP Spain
EST Estonia
ETH Ethiopia
FIJ Fiji
FIN Finland
FRA France
FRG Federal Republic of Germany (1948-90)
FSM Micronesia
GAB Gabon
GAM The Gambia
GBR United Kingdom of Great Britain & Northern Ireland
GBS Guinea-Bissau
GDR German Democratic Republic (1948-90)
GEO Georgia
GEQ Equatorial Guinea
GER Germany (pre 1948 and from 1991)
GHA Ghana
GIB Gibraltar
GRE Greece
GRN Grenada
GUA Guatemala
GUI Guinea
GUM Guam
GUY Guyana
HAI Haiti
HKG Hong Kong, China
HON Honduras
HUN Hungary
INA Indonesia
IND India
IRI Iran
IRL Ireland
IRQ Iraq
ISL Iceland
ISR Israel
ISV US Virgin Islands
ITA Italy
IVB British Virgin Islands
JAM Jamaica
JOR Jordan
JPN Japan
KAZ Kazakhstan
KEN Kenya
KGZ Kyrgyzstan
KIR Kiribati
KOR Korea
KOS Kosovo
KSA Saudi Arabia
KUW Kuwait
LAO Laos
LAT Latvia
LBA Libya
LBR Liberia
LCA St Lucia
LES Lesotho
LIB Lebanon
LIE Liechtenstein
LTU Lithuania
LUX Luxembourg
MAC Macao
MAD Madagascar
MAR Morocco
MAS Malaysia
MAW Malawi
MDA Moldova
MDV Maldives
MEX Mexico
MGL Mongolia
MKD Former Yugoslav Republic of Macedonia
MLI Mali
MLT Malta
MNE Montenegro
MNT Montserrat
MON Monaco
MOZ Mozambique
MRI Mauritius
MSH Marshall Islands
MTN Mauritania
MYA Myanmar
NAM Namibia
NCA Nicaragua
NED Netherlands
NEP Nepal
NFI Norfolk Islands
NGR Nigeria
NGU Papua New Guinea
NI Northern Ireland
NIG Niger
NMA Northern Marianas Islands
NOR Norway
NRU Nauru
NZL New Zealand
OMA Oman
PAK Pakistan
PAN Panama
PAR Paraguay
PER Peru
PHI Philippines
PLE Palestine
PLW Palau
PNG Papua New Guinea
POL Poland
POR Portugal
PRK North Korea (DPR Korea)
PUR Puerto Rico
PYF French Polynesia
QAT Qatar
ROU Romania
RSA South Africa
RUS Russia
RWA Rwanda
SAM Samoa
SCG Serbia & Montenegro (to 2006)
SCO Scotland
SEN Sénégal
SEY Seychelles
SIN Singapore
SKN St Kitts & Nevis
SLE Sierra Leone
SLO Slovenia
SMR San Marino
SOL Solomon Islands
SOM Somalia
SRB Serbia
SRI Sri Lanka
SSD South Sudan
STP São Tomé & Principé
SUD Sudan
SUI Switzerland
SUR Surinam
SVK Slovakia
SWE Sweden
SWZ Swaziland
SYR Syria
TAN Tanzania
TCH Czechoslovakia (to 1991)
TGA Tonga
THA Thailand
TJK Tadjikistan
TKM Turkmenistan
TKS Turks & Caicos Islands
TLS East Timor
TOG Togo
TPE Taiwan (Chinese Taipei)
TTO Trinidad & Tobago
TUN Tunisia
TUR Turkey
TUV Tuvalu
UAE United Arab Emirates
UGA Uganda
UKR Ukraine
URS Soviet Union (to 1991)
URU Uruguay
USA United States
UZB Uzbekistan
VAN Vanuatu
VEN Venezuela
VIE Vietnam
VIN St Vincent & the Grenadines
WAL Wales
YEM Republic of Yemen
YUG Yugoslavia (to 2002)
ZAM Zambia
ZIM Zimbabwe

ceased to exist as a separate territory in 2010, and absorbed into the Netherlands.

ACKNOWLEDGEMENTS

ONCE AGAIN I would like to thank all those who have helped me to compile this Annual – whether in a major way or just with a few items of information. As they have throughout the 65-year history of the ATFS Annual, the annual world lists provide the essential core of the book and I have worked up these lists from original compilations by Richard Hymans and Mirko Jalava with reference to those of many other experts. I refer all who want to follow the results of the sport closely to Mirko's superb web site www.tilastopaja.net. I am indebted to Pino Mappa for work on men's lists, Carlos Fernández for his expertise on the road lists and to Ray Herdt for the walks. I circulate draft lists to a number of ATFS experts and receive much valuable information from a worldwide circle of correspondents, most of whom have helped with information from their nations for many years. Of the great Spanish group Juan Mari Iriondo and Miguel Villaseñor checked the biographies and obituaries. Børre Lilloe provided much index data and Ken Nakamura checked distance lists. Bob Phillips has again provided an article, keeping up his long association with the Annual.

Both for this annual and throughout the year with *Athletics International* that I produce with Mel Watman, Winfried Kramer helps with widespread probing for results as do the area experts: *Africa*: Yves Pinaud, *Asia*: Heinrich Hubbeling, *Central and South America*: Eduardo Biscayart and Luis Vinker, and specialists: *Records* György Csiki, *Road racing*: Marty Post, *Ultrarunning* Andy Milroy, *Indoors* Ed Gordon, *Multi events:* Hans van Kuijen, *Pole vault* Kenneth Lindqvist, *800m:* Nejat Kök.

Australia: Paul Jenes and David Tarbotton; *Austria*: Dr Karl Graf; Belgium: André de Hooghe and Alain Monet; *Bulgaria*: Aleksandar Vangelov; *Canada*: Andrew Cameron; *China*: Mirko Jalava; *Cuba*: Alfredo Sánchez; *Czech Republic*: Milan Urban; *Denmark*: Erik Laursen; *Dominican Republic*: Arisnel Rodríguez; *Estonia*: Erlend Teemägi and Enn Endjärv; *Finland*: Juhani Jalava, Mirko Jalava, Mikko Nieminen and Matti Hannus; *France*: Alain Bouillé, Carles Baronet and Patricia Doilin; *Greece*: Thomas Konstas and Nikos Kriezis; *Hungary*: György Csiki; *India*: Ram. Murali Krishnan; *Ireland*: Pierce O'Callaghan and Liam Hennessy; *Israel*: David Eiger; *Italy*: Raul Leoni; *Japan*: Yoshimasa Noguchi, Akihiro Onishi and Ken Nakamura; *Latvia*: Andris Stagis; *Lithuania*: Stepas Misiunas; *Luxembourg*: Georges Klepper; *Malaysia*: Jad Adrian, *Montenegro*: Ivan Popovic; *New Zealand*: Murray McKinnon and Steve Hollings; *Norway*: Børre Lilloe; *Poland*: Zbigniew Jonik and Janusz Rozum; *Portugal:* Manuel Arons Carvalho; *Puerto Rico*: Pedro Anibal Diaz; *Russia*: Sergey Tikhonov; *Serbia*: Ozren Karamata and Olga Acic; *Slovakia*: Alfons Juck; *Slovenia*: Zdravko Peternelj; *South Africa:* Danie Cornelius, Riël Hauman , Clyde Kinloch and Richard Mayer; *Spain*: José Luis Hernández, Carles Baronet and the AEEA team; *Sweden*: Jonas Hedman and Peter Larsson; *Switzerland*: Alberto Bordoli and Antonin Hejda; *Trinidad:* Bernard Linley, *Turkey*: Nejat Kök, *Ukraine*: Ivan Kachkivskiy; *UK*: Tony Miller and Ian Hodge; *USA*: Tom Casacky, Garry Hill, Mike Kennedy, Sieg Lindstrom, Glen McMicken, Marty Post, Jack Shepherd and *Track Newsletter*. Also various national federation lists and to those who post results or ranking lists to various web sites.

Also to Marco Buccellato, Mark Bsutler, Ottavio Castellini (IAAF), Carole Fuchs, José Maria García, Grzegorz Gladzikowski, Stan Greenberg, Alan Lindop, Rooney Magnusson (obituaries), Bill Mallon, Pino Mappa, David Monti, Jiri Ondrácek (European U23), Bob Phillips, Zdenek Procházka (hammer), Priit Tanava, Miguel Villaseñor and Rob Whittingham.

My apologies to anybody whose name I may have missed or who have corresponded with other key ATFS personnel, but all help, however small is deeply appreciated.

Keep the results flowing

DURING THE YEAR Mel Watman and I publish marks to ATFS standards (150-200 deep on world lists) in *Athletics International*, of which there are over 35 issues per year by email. This serves as a base from which the lists in this book can be compiled, together with information from web sites, especially Mirko Jalava's *Tilastopaja, Track & Field News* (USA) with its email results spin-off *Track Newsletter* and newsletters, especially Alfons Juck's *EME News* and Carles Baronet's *Track in Sun*.

In order to ensure that the record of 2016 is as complete as possible I urge results contribution worldwide to AI, and then in turn our lists in *Athletics 2017* (if there is one) will be as comprehensive as we can make them.

Peter Matthews

THE ASSOCIATION OF TRACK & FIELD STATISTICIANS

The ATFS was founded in Brussels (at the European Championships) in 1950 and ever since has built upon the work of such key founding members as Roberto Quercetani, Don Potts and Fulvio Regli to produce authoritative ranking lists in the International Athletics Annual and elsewhere.

Current Executive Committee
President: Paul Jenes AUS
Vice-President: A.Lennart Julin SWE
Treasurer: Tom Casacky USA
Secretary: Michael J McLaughlin AUS
Past Presidents: Rooney Magnusson SWE, Dr Roberto Quercetani ITA
Committee: Eduardo Biscayart ARG/USA, Riël Hauman RSA, Nejat Kök TUR, Bernard Linley TRI, Giuseppa Mappa ITA, Peter J Matthews GBR, Yoshimasa Noguchi JPN, Yves Pinaud FRA

Website: www.afts.org

Internet – Websites

IAAF	www.iaaf.org
IAU	www.iau-ultramarathon.org
Africa (CAA)	www.webcaa.org
Asian AA	athleticsasia.org
CAC Confederation	www.cacacathletics.org
European AA	www.european-athletics.org
NACAC	www.athleticsnacac.org
Oceania AA	www.athletics-oceania.com
South American Fed.	www.consudatle.org
WMRA	www.wmra.info
World Masters	www.world-masters-athletics.org
Marathon Majors	www.worldmarathonmajors.com
Africa	www.africathle.com
Andorra	www.faa.ad
Argentina	www.cada-atletismo.org
Australia	www.athletics.com.au
Austria	www.oelv.at
Bahamas	www.bahamastrack.com
Belarus	www.bfla.eu
Belgium	www.val.be
Bermuda	www.btfa.bm
Bosnia Hercegovina	www.asbih.org
Brazil	www.cbat.org.br
Bulgaria	www.bfla.org
Canada	www.athletics.ca
Chile	www.fedachi.cl
China	www.athletics.org.cn
Costa Rica	www.fecoa.org
Croatia	www.has.hr
Cyprus	www.koeas.org.cy
Czech Republic	www.atletika.cz
Denmark	www.dansk-atletik.dk
Dominican Republic	www.fedomatle.org
England	www.englandathletics.org
Estonia	www.ekjl.ee
Finland	www.sul.fi
France	www.athle.com
Germany	www.leichtathletik.de
Great Britain	www.britishathletics.org.uk
deep statistics	www.topsinathletics.info
	www.thepowerof10.info
Greece	www.segas.gr
Hong Kong	www.hkaaa.com
Hungary	www.masz.hu
Iceland	www.fri.is
India	www.indianathletics.org
Indonesia	www.indonesia-athletics.org
Ireland	www.athleticsireland.ie
Israel	www.iaa.co.il
Italy	www.fidal.it
Jamaica	www.trackandfieldja.com
Japan	www.jaaf.or.jp
running news	japanrunningnews.blogspot.co.uk
Kazakhstan	www.kazathletics.kz
Kenya	www.athleticskenya.or.ke
Latvia	www.lat-athletics.lv
Lithuania	www.lengvoji.lt
Luxembourg	www.fla.lu
Macedonia	www.afm.org.mk
Malaysia	www.maf.org.my
results	www.adriansprints.com
Mexico	www.fmaa.mx
Moldova	www.fam.com.md
Monaco	www.fma.mc
Montenegro	www.ascg.co.me
Morocco	www.moroccanathletics.com
Netherlands	www.atletiekunie.nl
New Zealand	www.athletics.org.nz
Northern Ireland	www.niathletics.org
Norway	www.friidrett.no
Peru	www.fedepeatle.org
Poland	www.pzla.pl
Portugal	www.fpatletismo.pt
	www.atletismo-estatistica.pt
Puerto Rico	www.atletismofapur.com
	www.pedroanibaldiaz.com
Romania	www.fra.ro
Russia	www.rusathletics.com
Scotland	www.scottishathletics.org.uk
	www.scotstats.net
Serbia	www.ass.org.rs
Singapore	www.singaporeathletics.org.sg
Slovakia	www.atletikasvk.sk
Slovenia	www.atletska-zveza.si
South Africa	www.athletics.org.za
Spain	www.rfea.es
Sweden	www.friidrott.se
Switzerland	www.swiss-athletics.ch
Taiwan	www.cttfa.org.tw
Trinidad & Tobago	www.ttnaaa.org
Turkey	www.taf.org.tr
Ukraine	www.uaf.org.ua
Uruguay	www.atlecau.org.uy
USA	www.usatf.org
collegiate results	www.ustfccca.org
Wales	www.welshathletics.org
	athleticsstatswales.webeden.co.uk

Other recommended sites for statistics and results

AIMS	www.aimsworldrunning.org
ARRS	www.arrs.net
British historical	www.gbrathletics.com
	www.athlos.co.uk
DGLD (German stats)	www.ladgld.de
French history etc.	http://cdm.athle.com
Marathons	www.marathonguide.com
Masters Track & Field	www.mastersathletics.net
Mirko Jalava	www.tilastopaja.org
NUTS/Track Stats	www.nuts.org.uk
Rankings etc	www.all-athletics.com
Runners World	www.runnersworld.com
Tracklion (NED/BEL)	sportslion.net/tracklion.html
Track & Field News	www.trackandfieldnews.com
Track in Sun results	trackinsun.blogspot.co.uk
Ultra marathon stats	statistik.d-u-v.org/index.php
World juniors	www.worldjuniorathleticsnewsnzl.co.nz
Olympic Games	www.aafla.org
	www.sports-reference.com

DIARY OF 2015
by Peter Matthews

A chronological survey of highlights in major events in the world of track and field athletics.
See Championships or National sections for more details. DL = Diamond League, WCM = World Challenge Meeting.

January

3 **Xiamen**, China. Mare Dibaba improved her course record from 2:21:36 to 2:19:52, tying her pb, and Moses Mosop ran his fastest time since 2012, 2:06:19 to win the men's marathon.

23 **Dubai**, United Arab Emirates. 16th Standard Chartered Marathon. Hayle Lemi Berhanu was a surprise winner in 2:05:28; his only previous marathon was 2:10:40 to win in Zürich in April 2014. Ethiopians took the top 12 places, including ten men under 2:10. Aselefech Mergia was the women's winner (as in 2011-12) in 2:20:02 in her first marathon since the 2012 Olympic Games. Gladys Cherono 2:20:03 and Lucy Kabuu 2:20:21 were 2nd and 3rd with 4th-placer Shure Demise setting a world junior record of 2:20:59. Both winners won $200,000.

24 **Rouen**, France. Renaud Lavillenie cleared 6.00 at the Elite PV tour meeting for his first 6m clearance since his world record a year earlier.

24 **Torun**. Konrad Bukowiecki added 3cm to the world junior indoor record set by David Storl with the 6kg shot with 22.38, but this could not be ratified as there was no drugs control.

25 **Osaka**, Japan. 34th Women's Marathon. Tetyana Hamera-Shmyrko won for the fifth successive year in 2:22:09, but this was later annulled due to a positive drugs test.

29 **Düsseldorf**, Germany. PSD Bank meeting. Kim Collins beat James Dasaoulu 6.511 to 6.514, his 6.52 being a world age-38 best.

31 **Karlsruhe**, Germany. IAAF Permit. After 30 editions of the meeting at the Europahalle, there was a new venue – the Messe-Arena (6-lane track), Sifan Hassan ran a Dutch 1500m record of 4:02.57.

31 **New York (Armory)**, USA. A US team of Matthew Centrowitz 2:49.47 1200m, Mike Berry 46.40 400m, Erik Sowinski 1:47.60 800m and Pat Casey 3:56.48 1600m took nearly 6 seconds off the world best for the distance medley relay with 9:19.93.

February

1 **Moscow**. Russian Winter meeting (IAAF Permit). Kim Collins improved his over-35 world 60m best to 6.48. Triple jumper Yekaterina Koneva improved her long jump pb to 6.82.

4 **Banská Bystrica**, Czech Republic. Mutaz Essa Barshim jumped an Asian indoor high jump record of 2.40.

7 **Boston (Roxbury)**, USA. New Balance GP. Jenny Simpson ran an American 2 miles indoor record with 9:18.35, and, although outkicked by Dejen Gebremeskel 7:48.19, Bernard Lagat smashed the world M40 record with 7:48.33. Nick Willis set an Oceania record 3:51.61 to win the 1 mile and there was a women's world best for the distance medley as a New Balance team ran 10:42.57: Sarah Brown 3:15.54, Mahogany Jones 53.59, Megan Krumpoch 2:05.68, Brenda Martinez 4:27.77.

13 **Ra's Al Khaymah**, United Arab Emirates. Mary Keitany was the women's winner of the annual half marathon in 66:02 from Mamitu Daska, Ethiopian record 66:27. Men's winner was Mosinet Geremew in 60:05 after a slow start.

14 **Berlin**, Germany, ISTAF meeting. Renaud Lavillenie produced his third 6m vault of 2015 with 6.02 before trying a would-be world record 6.17. Dafne Schippers took 0.05 off her 60m pb with a 7.09 win.

14 **New York (Armory)**, USA. 108th Millrose Games. Bernard Lagat ran easily the fastest ever mile by a 40 year-old with 3:54.91 (3:40.20 M40 world best en route) for 4th. Matthew Centrowitz won in 3:51.35 from Nick Willis 3:51.46 (Commonwealth and Oceania record).

14-15 **UK Indoor Championships**, Sheffield. With 1.97 Katarina Johnson-Thompson added 1cm to the British high jump record that she had set the previous year.

15 **Barcelona**, Spain. Florence Kiplagat repeated her 2014 feat of setting a world record for the half marathon in the Mitja Marató. She took 3 seconds off with 65:09 and set world records en route at 15k 46:14 and 20k 61:54.

17 **Lódz**, Poland. Pedros Cup. Kim Collins improved his world M35 60 record to 6.47 and Orlando Ortega ran a world-leading 7.45 for 60m hurdles.

17-19 **Russian Indoor Championships**, Moscow. Top marks came at pole vault from Aleksandr Gripich pb 5.81 and Anzhelika Sidorova 4.75. Yekaterina Koneva won an excellent LJ/TJ double with 6.79 and 14.44.

18 **Athlone**, Ireland, Mutaz Essa Barshim improved his Asian indoor high jump record to 2.41.

19 **Stockholm**, Sweden. XL Galan. After smashing the world indoor record for 3000m in 2014 Genzebe Dibaba returned to the Ericsson Globe arena to take the 5000m record, taking 5.51 off Meseret Defar's 2009 mark here with 14:18.86. Dibaba's 1000m splits were 2:53.3, 5:44.8, 8:37.22, 11:31.8 and a final kilometre in 2:47.1.

21 **Birmingham**, GBR. IAAF Permit Meeting. Mo Farah ran his first ever world best time, with 8:03.40 for 2 miles (and a UK record 7:33.1 at 3000m); he had negative mile splits of 4:03.9 and 3:59.5. Katarina Johnson-Thompson added 4cm to the UK indoor long jump record with 6.93, beating Christabel Nettey 6.84 and Ivana Spanovic 6.75.

21-22 **French Indoor Championships**, Aubière. Highlight was Renaud Lavillenie's 6.01 pole vault.

21-22 **German Indoor Championships**, Karlsruhe. David Storl returned form injury to win the shot with 21.26.

21-22 **Polish Indoor Championships**, Sopot. Kamila Licwinko cleared 2.02 for a national high jump record.

21-22 **Spanish Indoor Championships**, Antequera. Ruth Beitia (35) won her 14th national indoor title with 1.95.

22 **Tokyo Marathon**, Japan. Endeshaw Negesse 2:06:00 and Berhane Dibaba 2:23:15 made it an Ethiopian double. Second and third in the men's race were Stephen Kiprotich in a Ugandan record 2:06:33 and the 2014 winner Dickson Chumba 2:06:34. 34,029 finished.

25 **Malmö**, Sweden. Sharika Nelvis completed a series of wins and pbs with the year's fastest 60m hurdles time of 7.83.

27 **Russian Winter Walks Championships**, Sochi. Elmira Alembekova went to the top of the world all-time list for women's 20k walk with 1:24:47, but, as usual, lack of sufficient numbers of international judges prevented recognition of this as a world record. Marina Pandekova 1:25:03 went to 5th and Svetlana Vasilyeva 1:25:04 to 6th on the all-time list.

27-Mar 1 **US Indoor Championships**, Boston (Roxbury). Casimir Loxsom, who had run an American record for 600m with 1:15.58 at Albuquerque on January 24, improved that mark to 1:15.33 to make him the fourth fastest ever man indoors at the distance. Shannon Rowbury won both 1 and 2 miles.

March

6-8 33rd **European Indoor Championships**, Prague, Czech Republic. The O2 Arena provided a splendid setting – but not for many of the spectators (52,284 over the three days) who found the sight lines far from ideal. Hugely enthusiastic spectators were rewarded with magnificent Czech victories by Pavel Maslák at 400m and Jakub Holusa at 1500m. Maslák's 45.33 was one of three men's Championship records, the others being Renaud Lavillenie's 6.04 pole vault (adding 1cm to his 2011 mark and a fourth successive title,) and the 3:02.87 European 4x400m record by Belgium (with the three Borlée brothers). Katarina Johnson-Thompson was the women's star as she scored 5000 points in the pentathlon, just 13 short of Nataliya Dobrynska's world record. World leading marks for the year came from Lavillenie, Johnson-Thompson, Ilya Shkuryenov, 6353 heptathlon, Michel Tornéus, 8.30 long jump, Yekaterina Koneva, 14.69 women's triple jump, and Dafne Schippers with 7.05 in a closely-contested 60m with six women at 7.11 or better. In second place Dina Asher-Smith tied the UK record with 7.08, also a world age 19 best. *For leading results see Athletics 2015 p. 87-8.*

8 **Arles**, France. Yohann Diniz set a world record for 20km walk with 1:17:02 (38:40 at 10k), to add to his 2014 50k mark.

13-14 **NCAA Indoor Championships**, Albuquerque, USA. Oregon men's and Arkansas women's teams were clear winners. Shawn Barber set his fourth Collegiate pole vault record of the year at 5.91, while Marquis Dendy had a splendid double, LJ 8.28 and TJ 17.37, and there were the fastest 200m times of the year – men Trayvon Bromell 20.19 (a world age-19 best) and women Jenna Prandini 22.52 in a heat before she was beaten in the final by Tyra Jefferson. Omar McLeod matched the 60m hurdles year's best of 7.45, a Jamaican record. Kendell Williams set a collegiate record for women's pentathlon with 4678 points.

14-15 15th **European Cup Winter Throwing**, Leiria, Portugal. Fine depth of performance was led by Krisztián Pars, hammer 79.24 from Pawel Fajdek 76.24, Martin Kupper, 66.67 discus, and Nadine Müller, 65.27, her fourth win at discus.

15 **Asian Walks Championships**, Nomi, Japan. Yusuke Suzuki took 26 secs off the week-old world 20k walk record with 1:16:36 (national record 38:06 for 10k en route).

15 **Lugano**. Switzerland. Just a week after his world record, Yohann Diniz won by over 4 minutes in the EA Permit 20k race in 1:17:24.

20-21 **Chinese Walks Trials**, Beijing. Lu Xiuzhi set a women's Asian 20k walk record, 1:25:13 well clear of Liu Hong 1:27:39.

21 **Melbourne**, Australia (WCM). Tom Walsh produced an Oceania shot record with 21.37 and there was a terrific duel in the women's javelin, won by Sunette Viljoen 66.62 from Kim Mickle 66.57.

21 **Dudince**, Slovakia. Matej Tóth went to third on the world all-time list for 50k with a

brilliant win in 3:34:38 in the 34th edition of this walks meeting.

23 **Lisbon**, Portugal. Mo Farah set a European half marathon record with 59:32 (and 56:27 for 20k) on the day before his 32nd birthday.

23-28 **European Masters Championships**, Torun, Poland. Germany headed the medal table with 101 gold, 82 silver and 70 bronze, from Britain 59-55-41 and Poland 56-58-48.

25-28 88th **Texas Relays,** Austin, USA. A plethora of fast wind-aided sprint times were headed by Yoshihide Kiryu 9.87w, Trayvon Bromell 9.90w, Anaso Jobodwana 19.87w and Michelle-Lee Ahye 10.87w. Shawn Barber maintained his indoor form by setting Canadian pole vault records outdoors at 5.80 and 5.90.

26-29 **Australian Championships**, Brisbane. Sally Pearson won her seventh 100m hurdles title in 12.59, Kim Mickle won her tenth javelin title (although beaten by South African Sunette Viljoen) and Dani Samuels her tenth in eleven years at discus.

28 **World Cross-Country Championships**, Guiyang, China. Kenya and Ethiopia won all four individual and team races (5-3 in Kenya's favour) and collected 7 silver and 4 bronze medals plus a bronze from Eritrea. Geoffrey Kamworor (junior champion in 2011 and world half marathon champion in 2014) won the men's individual title from Bidan Karoki and Muktar Edris with the first 23 places going to East Africa-born athletes. There was a similar story in the senior women's race, won by Agnes Kirop of Kenya who was followed 2-4 by Ethiopians. *For leading results see Athletics 2015 p. 89-90.*

April

3-4 **Florida Relays**, Gainesville, USA. Michelle-Lee Ahye clocked a remarkable 10.97 for 100m into a 2.5m wind.

3-4 **Stanford**, USA. Gelete Burka had a successful 10,000m track debut beating Shalane Flanagan 31:08.16 to 31:09.02 with 11 of the first 13 setting pbs and similar results in other top races: 13 of the first 15 in the men's 5000m, 18 of the first 21 at 10,000m and 13 of 14 in the top women's 5000m.

6 **Paris Marathon**, France. Mark Korir won in 2:05:49 from a previous best of 2:07:08, while Meseret Mengistu made a massive break–through to win the women's race in 2:23:26, taking almost six minutes off her best in a thrilling finish to beat Amane Gobana by 4 secs. This was Europe's biggest marathon with 40,173 finishers (30,618 men and 9,555 women).

11 **Kingston**, Jamaica, Usain Bolt won his first 200m race of 2015 in 20.20 and Elaine Thompson improved her 100m best from 11.10 to 10.92.

11 **Los Angeles (Westwood)**. Rafer Johnson/JJK Invitational. Joe Kovacs lengthened his shot pb from 22.03 to 22.35.

11-12 **IAU 24 Hours World Championships**, Turin, Italy. Winners were Florian Reus with 263,899k and Katalin Nagy 244,495k.

12 **Rotterdam Marathon**, Netherlands. Abera Kuma won the 35th running of this race in 2:06:47, but was disappointed that strong wind prevented him from taking his pb down from 2:05:56.

16-18 57th **Mt SAC Relays**, Walnut, California, USA. There were fine sprint doubles from Jenna Prandini in 10.92 and 22.42 and Andre De Grasse, 9.87w and 20.16 (tying Canadian record) and Christabel Nettey long jumped 6.98 (but the wind gauge was not working on this). Jeff Henderson took just one long jump, a pb 8.50.

17-18 **South African Championships**, Stellenbosch. Rushwal Samaai improved his long jump best from 8.13 to a world-leading 8.38. Stephen Mokaka won the 10,000 and returned the next day to win the 5000m in 13:11.44, a time that broke the 20 year-old national record.

20 119th **Boston Marathon**, USA. The 2013 winner Lelisa Desisa won again, in 2:09:17, and Caroline Rotich won the women's race in 2:24:55 by 4 secs from Mare Dibaba in cold weather and into a headwind for much of the race. Both winners won $150,000.

23-25 121st **Penn Relays**, Philadelphia, USA. The USA had four wins and Jamaica two in the annual relays match. It was cold throughout the three days but the total attendance was 110,587 including 48,920 for the final day.

24-25 106th **Drake Relays**, Des Moines, USA. Kirani James won the 400m in 44.22 despite cold and windy conditions, with LaShawn Merritt only fifth in 45.27. Jasmin Stowers made a huge breakthrough, wining the 100m hurdles in 12.40, clear of Dawn Harper Nelson 12.71. There were world bests in both shuttle hurdle races. A men's team of Jason Richardson, Aleec Harris, Aries Merritt and David Oliver ran 52.94 and two women's teams ran 50.50: Kristi Castlin, Queen Harrison, Dawn Harper Nelson and Brianna Rollins (50.495), and Jacqueline Coward, Sharika Nelvis, Tiffany Porter GBR, and Stowers (50.500); the previous best being 50.78.

24-27 **Arab Championships**, Manama, Bahrain. 12 championships records were set.

26 Virgin **London Marathon**, GBR. Kenyans took the first four places in the men's race, headed by Eliud Kipchoge 2:04:00, whose win was his fourth in five marathons, from Wilson Kipsang 2:04:47, Dennis Kimetto 2:05:50 and Stanley Biwott 2:06:41. Tigist Tufa was a surprise women's winner, beating Mary Keitany by 18 secs in 2:23:22. Paula Radcliffe, at 41, made an emotional appearance and came 20th in 2:36:55 in her final race. There were a record 37,675 finishers from 38,020 starters.

May

2 **Stanford**, USA. Payton Jordan Invitational. Excellent depth of distance times included 15 men, led by Andy Vernon 27:42.62, under 28 minutes and 14 women, led by Susan Kuijken 31:31.97, under 31:50 in the top 10,000m races.

2-3 **IAAF World Relays**, Nassau, Bahamas. As in 2014 this was a huge success with the Thomas A. Robinson Stadium again packed both days. A very strong US team won seven of the ten events and set world records in the newly recognised distance medley relays. The men's team of Kyle Merber 2:53.56, Brycen Spratling 45.95, Brandon Johnson 1:44.75, Ben Blankenship 3:51.24 ran 9:15.50 from Kenya 9:17.20, and the women's of Treniere Moser 3:18.38, Sanya Richards-Ross 50.12, Ajeé Wilson 2:00.08, Shannon Rowbury 4:27.92 for 10:36.50, each sharing $50,000 prize money for first place and the $50,000 world record bonus. A couple of the Kenyans set off at an absurd pace on the third and fourth legs of the men's race: Ferguson Cheruiyot ran the first half of his 800m in 47.84 but still held on for 1:44.49 and Timothy Cheruiyot ran 51.96 to 400m, but ran 3:52.75, After Kenya had held a big lead, Blankenship judged the race perfectly and came past and drew clear from the bell. More times that remained 2015 bests were: men 4x200m Jamaica 1:20.19 heat, 4x800m USA 7:04.84, women 4x200m Nigeria 1:30.52, 4x800m USA 8:00.62. The US men's 4x100m team of Mike Rodgers, Justin Gatlin, Tyson Gay and Ryan Bailey equalled the North American record of 37.38 with an encouraging win over Jamaica, for whom Usain Bolt ran the anchor, 37.68, but it was the other way round in the women's 4x100m. Despite Chris Brown running 44.17 on the final leg, the Bahamas could not quite overcome the US team in the 4x400m, running 2:58.91 behind the USA 2:58.43. Richards-Ross ran a scintillating third leg in 48.79 in the women's 4x400m, won by the USA in 3:19.39.

8-11 **Asian Youth Championships**, Doha, Qatar. Inaugural event. China with 16 gold, 11 silver and 5 bronze medals was easily the most successful nation.

9 **Manchester**, GBR. Great City Games. L J van Zyl equalled the world best of 22.10 for 200m hurdles on a straight track and Dina Asher-Smith beat Dafne Schippers 16.82 to 16.95 in a straight 150m. Jessica Ennis-Hill was third in the 100m hurdles in 13.14 in her first race since 27 July 2013 and the birth of her son in 2014.

9 **Kingston**, Jamaica (WCM). Outstanding sprinting and hurdling was a feature of the Jamaica International Invitational. Asafa Powell ran his quickest 100m time for four years with 9.84 a metre clear of Ryan Bailey's 9.93, and Elaine Thompson had a clear-cut 10.97 victory over Blessing Okagbare and Allyson Felix. Shaunae Miller won the women's 200m in 22.14 from Tori Bowie 22.29 and Shelly-Ann Fraser-Pryce 22.37, Sanya Richards-Ross the 400m in 49.95, and Jasmin Stowers improved her world-leading 100mh mark to 12.39 while Aleec Harris matched his at 110mh with 13.16.

9-10 **Pan-American Race Walking Cup**, Arica, Chile.

10 **Kawasaki**, Japan (WCM). Bohdan Bondarenko opened his season with a clearance of 2.37 at the Seiko Golden Grand Prix.

10 **Wiesbaden**, Germany. With elder brother Robert missing the whole season through injury, Christoph Harting threw a world-leading discus mark of 67.53 in the Werfer Cup.

14-16 **Collegiate Conference Championships**, USA. The Southeastern Conference (SEC) was, as ever, a powerhouse for sprinting, including 19.99 for 200m by Dedric Dukes and 44.42 400m Deon Lendore, and for women 22.39 at 200m by Kyra Jefferson, 12.50 for 100mh Kendra Harrison and 54.68 for 400mh by Shamier Little. Marquis Dendy completed a notable double with LJ 8.19w and TJ 17.35. Andre De Grasse had set a world-leading 200m mark of 20.03 (also a Canadian record) the day before Dukes's 19.99, before going on to win a 100m/200m double in 9.97 and 20.05 at the Pac 12 meeting in Westwood. There was strong wind assistance for the sprints at many of the venues, although it was only just over the limit at +2.1 for Tevin Hester 9.87w at the Atlantic Coast Conference. 20 year-old Shakima Wimbley had a great double with 200m in 22.43 and 400m in 50.84.

15 **Doha**, Qatar. For the first time two men beat 18m in a triple jump competition, a thrilling contest being won by Pedro Pablo Pichardo with a CAC record 18.06 from Christian Taylor, pb 18.04. As usual perfect conditions at the Qatar Sports Club helped impressive performances throughout the range of events of the first IAAF Diamond League meeting of 2015. Allyson Felix won the 200m in 21.98, her fastest since the 2012 Olympics, Jasmin Stowers improved again, to 12.35 for 100mh, Tianna Bartoletta long jumped 6.99 followed by Shara Proctor, Christabel Nettey and Lorraine Ugen all over 6.90, Bershawn Jackson won the 400mh in 48.09, and Justin Gatlin was another to hit the headlines, with 9.74 for 100m far ahead of Mike Rodgers 9.96. Hagos Gebrhiwet showed Mo Farah a clean pair of heels over the last lap of the 3000m to win by 0.14 in 7:38.08, Farah's first loss on then track for almost two years.

16 **Clermont**, USA. There were again exceptional sprint times at this venue, including 9.82w and 19.75w by Isiah Young and 10.87w by Carmelita Jeter.

16-17 **Halle**, Germany. 41st Werfertage. Christoph Harting improved at the discus to 67.93 and further top marks came from David Storl, shot 21.72, and Pawel Fajdek, hammer 82.76.

17 **Shanghai**, China (DL). Almaz Ayana had a runaway victory in the women's 5000m, running the third-fastest time ever of 14:14.32. Her kilometre splits were 2:53.84, 2:54.90, 2:47.79, 2:50.22 and 2:47.57, so she covered the last 3000m in 8:25.58! Viola Kibiwot was a distant second in 14:40.32. Mutaz Essa Barshim did not try higher after clearing 2.38 in the high jump while Bohdan Bondarenko was 2nd at 2.32 before failing at 2.28 and 2.41.

17 **European Race Walking Cup**, Murcia, Spain. The women's 20k was won in a meeting record 1:26:15 by Elmira Alembekova, with three of the top seven setting national records. Russia won three of the five team titles. Miguel Ángel López won the men's 20k in 1:19:52, heading the two fastest ever 50k walkers Matej Tóth 1:20:21 and Yohann Diniz 1:20:37.

20 **Beijing**, China (WCM). Christina Schwanitz, who had lost in her first competition since knee surgery, 19.94 to 20.23 by Gong Lijiao in Shanghai, was well ahead here with 20.22 and 20.38 before a fifth round 20.77, a mark that remained the best of the year, as Gong managed only 19.50. Anita Wlodarczyk landed all six throws beyond 74m and made her best ever start to a season with 77.73 in the hammer. David Oliver followed a 13.17 win with 13.15 in the 110m hurdles.

22-23 **Dakar**, Sénégal (WCM).

23 **Ponce**, Puerto Rico (WCM). Machel Cedonio had a notable win over LaShawn Merritt, 44.97 to 45.42.

24 **Hengelo**, Netherlands. 33rd Fanny Blankers-Koen Games (WCM). Dafne Schippers ran 10.94 for 100m, the fastest by a European for ten years and way inside her own Dutch record of 11.03. In the women's 1000m Sifan Hassan set a Dutch record of 2:34.68, the world's fastest for six years.

25-26 **Ostrava**, Czech Republic. 54th Golden Spike (WCM). In his first 200m race since August 2013, Usain Bolt won in 20.13, a decent time on a cold and wet evening, but David Rudisha pulled up injured very early in the 600m won by Adam Kszczot in 1:16.02. Polish athletes won both the men's and women's IAAF World Hammer Challenge events the previous day, Pawel Fajdek with 80.75 and Anita Wlodarczyk 76.61. Julius Yego set a Kenyan record of 86.88 to win the javelin from a top-class field.

26-28 **Havana**, Cuba. The Copa Cuba (national championships) was combined with the Barrientos Memorial. Denia Caballero improved her discus pb from 67.87 to a mighty 69.51 and Pedro Paulo Pichardo continued his superb triple jumping with 17.93 and 18.08, his only two efforts, the latter adding 2cm to his Doha mark. This was a CAC record, as was Roberto Janet's 78.02 hammer throw.

28-29 **Russian Team Championships**, Sochi. Top marks were 17.42 triple jump by Andrey Fyodorov, a pb by 23cm, and a world-leading 1:58.75 for 800m by Anastasiya Bazdyreva.

28-30 **NCAA Qualifying**, USA. Preliminary rounds for the NCAA Championships were held in Eastern and Western sections at Jacksonville and Austin. Fast sprint times were a feature. At the East meeting, Dedric Dukes clocked 20.14 for 200m and Kyra Jefferson lowered her pb to 22.26, while in the West 19 year-old Trayvon Bromell registered just windy times of 9.94 and 9.93 plus a 200m pb of 20.13. Stronger winds blew Jasmine Todd to 100m times of 10.89 and 10.88. Jamaica's Omar McLeod missed his 110m hurdles pb by 0.01 with 13.22.

29-30 **Eugene**, USA. 41st Prefontaine Classic (DL). Again a super meeting. In the pole vault Renaud Lavillenie sailed over on his first attempt at 6.05 before ending with a narrow failure at 6.16. This and Mutaz Essa Barshim's high jump 2.41 remained the best marks of 2015. Tyson Gay won the men's 100m in 9.88 and six women bettered 10.90 in the two 100m races with English Gardener and Elaine Thompson 1-2 in the B race, both 10.84, and the main race won by Shelly-Ann Fraser-Pryce in 10.81 from Muriel Ahouré 10.81, Tori Bowie 10.82 and Blessing Okagbare 10.87. At 200m Justin Gatlin equalled his pb of 19.68 and at 400m Kirani James won in 43.95, 5m clear of LaShawn Merritt 44.51 and Chris Brown's world masters record of 44.54. Genzebe Dibaba went through 3000m in a track record 8:33.33, but missed the world record for 5000m with 14:19.76. Tianna Bartoletta long jumped 7.11w, the longest of her career, and Christabel Nettey a legal 6.99 for the Canadian record, and the top two women triple jumpers finished Caterine Ibargüen 15.18w for her 24th consecutive win and Yekaterina Koneva 15.04. These marks came in ideal conditions after a much cooler Friday evening when there were world-leading marks at 5000m,Yomif Kejelcha 13:10.54, and Mo Farah, 10000m 26:50.97 from Paul Tanui 26:51.86 and Geoffrey Kamworor 26:52.55, and a US all-comers 3000m steeplechase record 8:01.71 by Ezekiel Kemboi.

29-31 **South American Junior Championships**, Cuenca, Ecuador (A).

30-31 **Götzis**, Austria. Winners at the 41st Hypo Meeting were Kai Kazmirek 8492 decathlon, after the late withdrawal of Ashton Eaton, and Brianne Theisen-Eaton heptathlon 6808, adding 167 points to her Canadian record of 6641 with three pbs. Jessica Ennis-Hill returned to multi-event action with a fine fourth place 6520 score. Dafne Schippers was second with 5690 points until she scratched from the 800m due to a sore knee resulting from hitting a hurdle in a race two weeks earlier.

30-31 **European Clubs Cup**, Mersin, Turkey. There was a Spanish double with Playas de Castellón men's champions and Valencia Terra i Mar retaining their women's title.

June

3-7 **Asian Championships**, Wuhan, China. Femi Ogunode smashed the championship record twice in the 100m, first with 9.97 in his semi-final and then with 9.91 to take the Asian title, and completed a double with 20.32 for 200m. Li Ling added 1cm to her Asian record with a 4.66 vault clearance and Kemi Adekoya set a Bahrain and Championships 400m hurdles record with 54.31.

4 **Rome**, Italy. Golden Gala Pietro Mennea (DL). Yomif Kejelcha, amazingly still only 17, beat a strong 5000m field to win in 12:58.39 with Paul Tanui 12:58.69 and Hagos Gebrhiwet 12:58.69 also under 13 minutes. More world-leading marks came from Mohammed Aman, 800m 1:43.56, Jenny Simpson, 1500m 3:59.31, and Hyvin Jepkemoi, 3000m steeple 9:15.08. Justin Gatlin reinforced his status as the world's leading sprinter of the year, breaking Usain Bolt's meeting record of 9.76 with 9.75, just 0.01 shy of his pb from Doha. Jasmin Sawyers pulled up in the 100m hurdles after hitting hurdle six, and Sharika Nelvis won in a pb 12.52.

6 **European Cup 10,000m**, Chia-Pula, Italy. Kenyan-born Polat Kemboi Arikan of Turkey won as he had in 2012 and 2014 and Ethiopian-born Trihas Gebre was the women's winner, like Arikan finishing well clear of the rest of the field. Hosts Italy won the men's team prize and Great Britain the women's.

6 **La Coruña**, Spain. Liu Hong clocked 1:24:38 to remove as the world record not only the recognised 1:25:02 set by Yelena Lashmanova at the 2012 Olympics but also unratified marks (due to lack of international judges) of 1:24:50 by Olympiada Ivanova and 1:24:54 by Olga Kaniskina. In near-perfect conditions Liu was timed in 42:38 for the first 10k and then speeded up to 1:03:41 at 15k and a second half in 42:00. There was a Chinese 1-2-3 in the men's race, won by Wang Zhen in 1:18:00 and a great standard in depth.

7 **Birmingham**, GBR (DL). Julius Yego improved the African record from 89.21 to 91.39 with his final throw that flew over to the right-hand side but beyond the sector line that extended only to 87m. Originally ruled a no throw, that decision was later reversed. Second was Vitezslav Vesely 88.18 and third Keshorn Walcott a TTO record 86.43. Other notable field event wins included 69.23 discus by Sandra Perkovic for her third DL victory of the season, 17.40 triple jump by Christian Taylor and 4.72 vault by Fabiana Murer, with a home win 8.24 long jump by Greg Rutherford. Adam Gemili ran 10.00 in his 100m heat and then 9.97 behind Marvin Bracy 9.93 in the final, but his season was ended with a hamstring injury as he crashed to the track at the finish. A very close race in the women's 200m resulted in a win for Jenneba Tarmoh in 22.29 from Allyson Felix 22.29 and Dina Asher-Smith 22.30 (from a previous best of 22.61). Wayde van Niekerk impressed with an African record 31.63 for 300m.

8 **Prague**, Czech Republic. 20th Josef Odlozil Memorial.

9-12 28th **South East Asia Games**, Singapore. 11 new Games records, 42 national records and 15 national junior records were set at these biennial Games. Eric Cray won an unusual double as he set a Philippines record of 10.25 for 100m and a Games 49.40 record for 400m hurdles. Nguyen Thi Huyen won triple gold – at 400m, 400m hurdles and 4x400m – and Maria Londa defended her long and triple jump titles, the former at 6.70, perhaps the top mark of the Games. James Rittidet won his fourth successive title at 110m hurdles and for the fourth time broke the Games record (13.69).

10-13 **NCAA Championships**, Eugene, USA. A new format had men's and women's events split onto separate days. Oregon were again clear winners of the men's title with 88 points from Florida 56 and Arkansas 53, and also took the women's title with 59 from Kentucky 50 and Texas A&M 47. Andre De Grasse achieved a brilliant sprint double with 9.75w (after a legal 9.90 semi) and 19.58w, clear of Trayvon Bromell 9.88w and Dedric Dukes 19.86w and more top windy times came from Marquis Dendy 8.43 long jump and 17.71 triple (with legal marks at 8.34 and 17.50), Omar McLeod 13.01 at 110mh, and Quanesha Burks 6.91 long jump. Jenna Prandini won the 100m in 10.96w but had to settle for 2nd at 200m in 22.21 behind Dezerea Bryant's 22.18 (big pbs for both) and long jump pb 6.80. Shamier Little took her 400m hurdles best down from 54.68 to a world-leading 53.74. Anthony Rotich achieved a third successive win at steeple. *See USA section for winners.*

11 **Oslo**, Norway (DL). 50th anniversary Bislett Games. The high jump was touted as an attempt at a world record but neither Mutaz Essa Barshim nor Bohdan Bondarenko was able to clear higher than 2.33 as victory went to Zhang Guowei with 2.36 on his final attempt while Marco Fassinotti was 2nd with 2.33. Another record attempt 'failed' as Genzebe Dibaba slowed from being on schedule at 3000m in 8:39.41 to finish the 5000m in 14:21.29, 10.14 secs slower than her big sister Tirunesh's record in this stadium seven years earlier. Memories of Tom Byers's 1500m win in 1981 were kindled as Laura Muir bravely escaped from the pack for a lead at the bell of almost 40m, and she held on to win in 4:00.39 from Faith Kipyegon 4:00.94. There was a fourth Dream Mile for Asbel Kiprop

who sprinted home in 3:51.45 ahead of arch-rival Silas Kiplagat.

12-14 49th **South American Junior Championships**, Lima, Peru. Eight new championship records were set and Déborah Rodríguez won a notable double with 2:01.46 for 800m and 56.33 for 400mh, both Uruguay records.

13 **New York (Randall's Island)**, USA. adidas GP (DL). Usain Bolt was the star attraction in a non-DL 200m, but only just won the race, that he described as one of the worst of his career, in 20.29 from Zharnel Hughes 20.32. Wayde van Niekerk, South African record 44.24, and Francena McCorory 49.86 won fast 400m races, and David Rudisha returned to form with an 800m win in 1:43.58.

14 **Rabat**, Morocco (WCM). Out on her own after the first kilometre, Almaz Ayana ran an Ethiopian outdoor record of 8:22.22 for 3000m, with Vivian Cheruiyot second in 8:39.75. Pawel Fajdek notched up his seventh consecutive victory, once again beating arch-rival and Olympic champion Krisztián Pars, 79.90 to 77.81.

17 **Hengelo**, Netherlands. The Ethiopian 10,000m trials for the Worlds were held here. Men's winner was Muktar Edris in 27:17.18 with seven men under 27:23, and the women's Gelete Burka 30:49.48 from Alemitu Haroye, on her 10,000m track debut, 30:50.83 with five women under 31 minutes.

17 **Gold Coast**, Australia. One of the greatest and most respected of athletes, Ron Clarke died at the age of 78.

20 **Shoreline**, USA. 16 year-old Candace Hill ran 10.98 for 100m, by far the best ever by a Youth (U17) as the previous best was 11.10 by Kaylin Whitney USA in 2014.

20-21 **European Team Championships**, Cheboksary, Russia. Russia regained the team title, beating Germany by 22 points with France just edging out Poland for fourth. Anita Wlodarczyk, hammer 78.28, and Silke Spiegelburg, pole vault of 4.75, were marks equal or superior to anything in the combined history of the European Cup and these degraded Team Champs. Russia's women jumpers were in fine form with wins from Yekaterina Koneva, triple jump 14.98w and legal 14.87, Darya Klishina, long jump 6.95, and Mariya Kuchina, a strongly contested high jump with 1.99. The First League in Iráklio, Greece was won by the Czech Republic, the Second League in Stara Zagora, Bulgaria by Denmark and the Third League in Baku, Azerbaijan by Slovakia.

25 **Turku**, Finland. 53rd Paavo Nurmi Games. Tero Pitkämäki threw the javelin 89.09, his best since 2007, and his ninth successive win.

25-28 **Jamaican Championships**, Kingston. There was as usual superb sprinting with 100m wins going to Asafa Powell 9.84 leading four men under 10 secs, and Shelly-Ann Fraser-Pryce 10.79. Omar McLeod ran a world-leading 12.97 at 110m hurdles.

25-28 **US Championships**, Eugene. Another great meeting included world leading marks for the year from winners: Justin Gatlin, 200m pb 19.57, Trey Hardee, decathlon 8725, Jenn Suhr, outdoor pole vault, 4.82, and Tianna Bartoletta, long jump 7.12 (for her first ever US title). Also from Sherika Nelvis, 12.34 in her heat and 12.37 in her semi before only just making the Worlds team with 12.59 in third place at 100m hurdles, and in their semis English Gardner ran 100m in 10.79 and Francena McCorory 400m 49.48. While Gardner followed with second to Tori Bowie 10.81 in the final, McCorory was surprisingly only fourth in the final won by Allyson Felix in 50.19. Suhr's was her 16th national title (9 outdoors, 7 indoors), Michelle Carter put 20.02 for her ninth at shot (6 out, 3 in) and Chaunté Lowe her seventh outdoor high jump. Galen Rupp won the 10,000m for the seventh successive year. Other highlights includes 8.68w long jump by Marquis Dendy, 2.37 high jump by Erik Kynard, 9:15.59 steeplechase by Emma Coburn, 53.83 400mh by Shamier Little, and 21.84 shot by Joe Kovacs. Teenager Trayvon Bromell qualified with 9.84 and 9.76 but had to settle for second in the 100m final in 9.96 behind Tyson Gay 9.87.

26-27 **Bahamas Championships**, Nassau. 19 year-old Steven Gardiner ran 44.27 for 400m. That took the national record from Chris Brown, but the remarkable 38 year-old improved his pb from 21.05 to 20.58 for 2nd at 200m.

26-28 **Trinidad & Tobago Championships**, Port of Spain. The 100 metres finals provided the headlines, with Keston Bledman timed at 9.86 and Kelly-Ann Baptiste 10.84.

27 **Wroclaw**, Poland. Anita Wlodarczyk threw the hammer 79.83, but the conditions of the throwing area by the River Oder were irregular as regarding record ratification. Pawel Fajdek maintained his supremacy over Krisztián Pars, 81.91 to 78.68.

27-28 **Ratingen**, Germany. Winners were Michael Schrader, 8419 decathlon, and Anouk Vetter, 6387 pentathlon.

July

1 **Tomblaine**, France. At the Meeting Pro Athlé de Nancy Taoufik Makhloufi ran 2:13.08 for 1000m, the fastest time at the event for 16 years, to take him to fourth on the world all-time list.

1 **Velenje**, Slovenia. 20th Miners; Day Meet. The South African sprinter Akani Simbine broke 10 seconds for the first time with 9.99 and the Amel Tuka made a dramatic improvement as he took his Bosnian record for 800m from 1:46.12 to 1:44.19.

3-5 **UK Championships**, Birmingham. Tom Bosworth, 19:00.73 for 5000m walk, and Isobel Pooley, 1.97 high jump, set national records.

4 **European Mountain Running Championships**, Porto Moniz, Madeira, Portugal. Italy achieved their 20th men's team win in the 21 years of the event (19th successive). Andrea Mayr was the women's champion for the third successive year (with a previous win in 2005).

4 **Saint-Denis**, France. Areva meeting (DL). Jairus Birech won the steeplechase in 7:58.63 but was led to the final barrier by Evan Jager, who had kicked away over the last 600m, only to catch his toe on that barrier and crash to the track; he still came second in a North American 8:00.45, but that could so easily have been well under 8 minutes. Wayde van Niekerk became the first African to beat 44 secs for 400m as he won the 400m in 43.96 ahead of Kirani James 44.17, and the highlight for French fans came from Jimmy Vicaut as he tied the European record of 9.86 when second to Asafa Powell 9.81. Year's bests were run by Shelly-Ann Fraser-Pryce 10.74 for 800m from Blessing Okagbare 10.80, and Eunice Sum 800m with a pb 1:56.99. At 1500m Silas Kiplagat outkicked Ayanleh Souleiman 3:30.12 to 3:30.17 with Ronald Kwemoi 3rd 3:30.43 and Taoufik Makhloufi 4th 3:30.50, and the standard was such that 11th in 3:32.85 was the best ever for that place. Genzebe Dibaba and Almaz Ayana had another crack at the world 5000m record. Almaz did most of the work but came 2nd in 14:21.97 (the fastest ever non-winning time) as Dibaba streaked away over the last lap to return 14:15.41. After Renaud Lavillenie managed only 5.71 for fifth equal, Konstadínos Filippídis won the vault with a Greek record of 5.91, matching the achievement of Nikoléta Kiriakopoúlou who broke her own Greek record with a world-leading 4.83. Valerie Adams returned from shoulder and elbow operations, but 5th with 18.79, far behind Christina Schwanitz 20.31, meant that her five-year win streak ended at 56. Zuzana Hejnová continued a successful return from injury with 53.76 in the 400m hurdles from national records by Sara Petersen 53.99 and Kemi Adekoya 54.12.

4-5 **European Cup of Combined Events**. Russia, led by Ilya Shkuryenov who had a clear decathlon victory with 8378 points, retained their title in the Super League at Aubagne, France. Alina Fyodorova won the heptathlon with 6278. At Inowroclaw, Poland the First League was won by Switzerland and the Second League by Finland. In the latter Laura Ikaunice-Admidina had the top heptathlon score with 6470 points.

5 **La Chaux-de-Fonds**, Switzerland. Isaac Makwala again took full advantage of the 997m altitude and regained his African record for 400m with 43.72 from the exciting 18 year-old talent from Qatar, Abdelilah Haroun 44.27.

6-7 **Székesfehérvár**, Hungary. 5th István Gyulai Memorial Meeting. Pawel Fajdek extended his world lead at hammer to 83.12.

7-8 **Barcelona (Serrahima)**, Spain. Genzebe Dibaba took 1.19 off the African record with 3:54.11 for 1500m, the world's fastest since 1997, and Ayanleh Suleiman won the 800m in 1:43.08.

8-12 **World University Games**, Gwangju, Korea. Three new Games records came from Akani Simbine, 100m 9.97, and two women Yekaterina Sokolenko, 3000m steeplechase 9:25.77, and Anisya Kirdyapkina, 20k walk 1:28:18. Russia, with 11 gold, 8 silver and 8 bronze medals, was easily the most successful nation. Pawel Fajdek, hammer, and Yekaterina Koneva, triple jump, won third consecutive WUG titles.

9 **Lausanne**, Switzerland. Athletissima (DL). In another terrific triple jump clash Christian Taylor beat Pedro Paulo Pichardo 18.06 to 17.99, Anna Chicherova high jumped a 2015 best of 2.03, Keshorn Walcott became the latest 90m javelin thrower with 90.16 and David Storl won the shot with a pb 22.20 from Joe Kovacs 21.71. On the track Nijel Amos beat David Rudisha 1:43.27 to 1:43.76 and Mo Farah used a 54.4 last lap to beat Yomif Kejelcha at 5000m in 13:11.77 in his first race since being subjected to a media furore over allegations against his coach Alberto Salazar. Allyson Felix beat Dafne Schippers 22.09 to 22.29 at 200m and Justin Gatlin remained in prime form with a 9.75 100m win over Asafa Powell 9.92. Viktoriya Zyabkina won the women's sprint treble.

9-12 **European Under 23 Championships**, Tallinn, Estonia. Rebekka Haase became the first athlete in the history of the event to win triple gold with both 100m and 200m and a leg on the dominant German 4x100m team, and Ali Kaya simply ran away from the field in first the 10,000m and then the 5000m, winning by margins of 60.56 and 34.17 secs respectively, smashing the championship records with 13:20.16 and 27:53.38. The best of six more championships records were from Alexandra Tavernier, 72.98 in hammer qualifying before 72.50 in the final, Christine Hussong, 65.60 javelin, and Mariya Ponomaryova, 1:27:17 for 20k walk by just 8 secs from Anezka Drahotová.

10-12 **French Championships**, Villeneuve d'Ascq. Top mark was 9.92 for 100m by Jimmy Vicaut.

11 **Madrid**, Spain (WCM). Taking advantage of the 640m altitude the 100m races were won by Mike Rodgers in 9.88 and Elaine Thompson 10.90.

14 **Luzern**, Switzerland. The 29th Spitzen

Leichtathletik meeting included 19.94 for 200m by Wayde van Niekerk, who beat Alonso Edward 20.03, and 9.88 for 100m by Asafa Powell, his 88th sub-10 sec time. Katharina Molitor set pbs at 65.40 and 66.40 in the javelin.

15-19 **World Youth (U17) Championships**, Cali, Colombia (1046m altitude). There were championship records in nine men's and five women's events. These included sprint doubles by Candace Hill, 11.08 and 22.43, and Abdul Hakim Sani Brown, 10.28 and 20.34. Niklas Kaul's decathlon score of 8002 was a world youth best with the current implements, and the 45.27 by Christopher Taylor was just 0.13 off the world youth best, and the best ever by a 15 year-old. Norman Grimes impressed with 49.11 for 400m (84m) hurdles and took a second gold on the US 4x400m team. Best in the field was 84.91 with the 5kg hammer by Hlib Piskunov.

16-19 **European Junior Championships**, Eskilstuna, Sweden. Championship records were set by Konrad Bukowiecki who put the 6kg shot out to 22.62, Nazim Babayev, triple jump 17.04, Bartlomiej Stoj, 1.75kg discus 68.02, and Bence Halász 6kg hammer 79.60. Alina Reh achieved a distance double at 3000m and 5000m, and other highlights included a brilliant display of race walking by the Russians headed by Klavidya Afanasyeva 43:36.88, Caroline Agnou adding 401 points to her Swiss junior heptathlon record with 6123, and Florentina Marincu, 6.78w long jump. Britain was easily the most successful nation with 11 gold medals.

17 **Herculis, Monaco** (DL). One of the greatest performances of the modern era was achieved at this marvellous meeting as Genzebe Dibaba ran the 1500m in 3:50.07 to sweep away one of those controversial Chinese world records from 1993. Chanelle Price led through 400m in 60.31 and 800m in 2:04.52 from Dibaba 60.5 and 2:04.77, and then Dibaba went on to the bell in 2:50.3 and a last lap of 59.79, 300m in 45.45. There were great times behind her: Sifan Hassan European record 3:56.06, Shannon Rowbury 3:56.29, Jenny Simpson 3:57.30, Laura Muir Scottish record 3:58.66, and Maureen Koster 3:59.79. Asbel Kiprop won a great men's 1500m in 3:26.69 for third on the world-all time list, and the world's best since 2001, from pbs by Taoufik Makhloufi 3:28.75 and Abdelaati Iguider 3:28.79. Then came Mo Farah 3:28.93 heading the fastest ever times for positions 4-6 and 8-10 as ten under 3:31 beat the previous record of seven at this meeting in 2014. Joe Kovacs threw 22.56 in the shot, the best since 1990 apart from 22.67 by Kevin Toth (later drugs banned) in 2003. Fast-improving Amel Tuka was the biggest surprise winner as he took his Bosnian record down to 1:42.51, and other world-leading marks came from Francena McCorory, 400m 49.83, Habiba Ghribi, 3000m steeple 9:11.28,and Caleb Ndiku, outdoor 3000m 7:35.13. But the standard was terrific in every event, including the third triple jump clash of the year between Taylor and Pichardo, with Taylor winning 17.75 to 17.73.

18 **Heusden-Zolder**, Belgium. KBC Night of Athletics. Depth of distance running, such as 17 men under 13:20 in the A 5000m, headed by Dejen Gebremeskel 13:05.38, was as usual the feature here.

18-19 **Zhukovskiy**, Russia. 57th Znamenskiy Memorial.

18-26 **Pan-American Games**, Toronto, Canada. Although the USA topped the medal table with 13 gold, 15 silver and 13 bronze, the host nation enjoyed their most successful Pan-Ams with 8 men's and 3 women's winners, including championship records (there were 15 in all) by Damien Warner, 8659, and Shawn Barber, 5.80 pole vault, and Andre De Grasse won a superb sprint double in 10.05 (9.97w heat) and 19.88 Canadian record. Caterine Ibargüen won the triple jump with 15.08w, O'Dayne Richards the shot with a CAC record 21.69 and there was also a world leading 4.85 vault by Cuba's Yarisley Silva in defeating Fabiana Murer 4.80 and Jenn Suhr 4.60.

19-21 **Polish Championships**, Kraków. Tomasz Majewski (20.80) won his 13th shot title in 14 years and Piotr Malachowski (65.80) his tenth in 11 years at discus. Hammer throwers Pawel Fajdek and Anita Wlodarczyk produced the top marks with 79.74 and 78.24 respectively

24-25 **London (Olympic Stadium)**, GBR. Sainsbury's Anniversary Games (DL). Usain Bolt had his first competition for six weeks with a pair of 9.87 times for 100m. Mo Farah was imperious as he won the 3000m in 7:34.66, his outdoor best, and Jessica Ennis-Hill was delighted to run 12.79 for fifth place in the 100m hurdles won by Jasmin Stowers 12.47. The 200m win in 20.05 by Zharnel Hughes, newly-qualified for Britain, took him to third on the UK all-time list. Renaud Lavillenie went over 6.03 with Shawn Barber second in a Canadian record 5.93 in the pole vault moved to the Saturday due to heavy rain on day one. Dina Asher-Smith (19) became the first British woman to crack 11 sec for 100m as she improved her own UK record from 11.02 to 10.99 in a heat before 4th in 11.06 in the final won by Dafne Schippers, Dutch record 10.92. Another UK record was set by Shara Proctor, 6.98 long jump. Asbel Kiprop coasted to an Emsley Carr Mile victory in 3:54.87, all 15 finishers breaking 4 minutes.

24-26 **German Championships**, Nuremberg. Raphael Holzdeppe returned to top form to win the pole vault with 5.94. Betty Heidler threw the hammer 75.34 for a tenth hammer title and Verena Sailer won her eighth 100m title. Katharina Molitor maintained her recent supremacy in the women's javelin beating Christina Obergföll and Linda Stahl 65.40 to 64.11 and 62.57.

24-26 **Italian Championships**, Turin. Chiara Rosa won her eleventh successive shot title and Fabrizio Donato his 8th at triple jump.

30 **Stockholm**, Sweden. Bauhaus Meeting (DL). Chilly weather and rain held back performances, but Shelly-Ann Fraser-Pryce beat Tori Bowie by over a metre in 10.93 for 100m, Greg Rutherford long jumped 8.34 and 8.32, and Yarisley Silva won a closely-contested pole vault with 4.81 from Nikoléta Kiriakopoúlou 4.76 and Fabiana Murer 4.71.

30-Aug 2 **Finnish Championships**, Pori. Tero Pitkämäki took the lead in the first round of the javelin with 87.82, but Antti Ruuskanen retained the title by throwing 88.98, a pb by 97cm, in the final round.

31- Aug 1 **Kenyan Trials**, Nairobi. There was a superb set of times at 10,000m as Geoffrey Kamworor won in 27:11.89, the best ever achieved at high altitude, from Bidan Karoki 27:15.33 and Paul Tanui 27:18.45. There was an upset in the 800m as Ferguson Cheruiyot beat David Rudisha 1:43.60 to 1:43.89 and Nicholas Bett improved his pb for 400m hurdles from 49.03 to 48.29.

31-Aug 2 **Eberstadt**, Germany. Derek Drouin won the annual high jump competition at 2.37, but that height was also cleared by Gianmarco Tamberi, for an Italian record. Marie-Laurence Jungfleisch was the women's winner at 1.96.

31-Aug 2 **Pan-American Junior Championships**, Edmonton, Canada. Yulenmis Aguilar set a world junior record for javelin with 63.86 and Vashti Cunningham tied the world youth high jump record with 1.96. The USA won 30 gold, 14 silver and 14 bronze medals and Harrison Williams set US junior decathlon record with 8037 points.

August

1 **Cetniewo**, Poland. Anita Wlodarczyk became the first women to throw the women's 4k hammer over 80 with her fourth world record, 81.08. Pawel Fajdek 82.07 had another decisive win over Krisztián Pars 79.91 and in the discus Pawel Malachowski opened with a world-leading 68.29.

1-2 **Spanish Championships**, Castellón. Ruth Beitia won her eleventh title (10 in succession) at high jump with 1.98.

1-2 74th **Balkan Championships**, Pitesti, Romania. In her first competition after her two-year drugs ban Zalina Marghieva set a Moldovan women's hammer record of 73.97 (she had thrown over 74m in 2012-13 but those results were annulled). Romania won both men's and women's team competitions.

2 **Beckum**. Germany. Yarisley Silva added a centimetre to her CAC pole vault record with 4.91, a world's best for 2015.

3-5 **Russian Championships**, Cheboksary. Tatyana Tomashova, who served a two-year drugs ban 2008-10, won the 1500m title in 4:04.48; now aged 40 she had won previously in 2001-03. The best mark was perhaps a 2.00 high jump by Anna Chicherova in beating Mariya Kuchina 1.97. The Crimean athlete Vera Rebryk, who transferred from Ukraine to Russia, won the javelin with 64.93, her best for three years.

7-9 **Hungarian Championships**, Székesfehérvár. Krisztián Pars won his 11th successive hammer title, and there was a ninth title overall (from 2001) for Zoltán Kövágó, while Anita Márton won her tenth successive shot title and eighth successive discus, and Éva Orbán her ninth at hammer.

7-9 **NACAC Open Championships**, San José, Costa Rica. Held at 1122m altitude, previous NACAC Championships had been for under-23 athletes, but these were open to all ages and winners could qualify for the World Championship without necessarily having qualifying standards. Individual winners who doubled up at both Pan-American Games and here were Andrew Wheating (1500m), Ashley Higginson (3000mSt) and Levern Spencer (HJ). Top performances included Quanesha Burks, 6.93 long jump, and the 200m wins by Rasheed Dwyer 20.12 and Kyra Jefferson 22.50.

8 **Kuortane**, Finland. Thomas Röhler threw a javelin pb of 89.27.

9 **Szczecin**, Poland. The 61st Kusocinski Memorial included two world-leading and national record throws by Pawel Fajdek with 83.83 and 83.93.

22-30 15th **World Championships**, Beijing, China. Ashton Eaton's decathlon world record of 9045 points headed performances. That earned him the IAAF bonus of $100,000 as well as his first place prize money of $60,000. His amazing 45.00 for the 400m was easily a best ever in a decathlon. Championship records were set in four more events: women's 200m, 5000m, hammer and 4x100m. The USA headed the points table, but their 18 medals was down from 25 in 2013 and a significant number of their team underperformed or even met with disaster, and their six gold medals was headed by seven for both Kenya and Jamaica. Kenyans starred as usual in the distance events but their range was extended by the brilliant victories of Julius Yego in the javelin and Nicholas Bett in the 400m hurdles, while Jamaica's sprinters were marvellous. Usain Bolt was, as ever, the super-star, overcoming his reduced preparation with yet another superb treble (including 100m in 9.79 and 200m in 19.55 his fifth best ever), to take his World Champs record medal collection to 13 (11 golds and two silvers) as well as his 6 Olympic golds. Also extending her record tally of World golds to 10 (plus 2 silver and a bronze) was Allyson Felix, who followed her expected 400m win with the fastest 400m relay leg ever seen in World Champs, 47.72. Supreme racer Mo Farah won both 5000m and 10,000m for his fifth major championship double and in all Moscow 2013 winners repeated in 13 events.

September

3 **Zürich**, Switzerland. Weltklasse. 16 Diamond Race titles were decided here, but the over-close proximity to the World Championships affected many and a lot of results were contrary to usual form. The top clash came at the women's 3000m where Almaz Ayana beat Genzebe Dibaba 8:22.34 to 8:26.54, but Dibaba took the DL prize of $40,000. Another to win the Diamond Race from 2nd here was Tianna Bartoletta, her 6.97 taking the lead in the final round only for Ivana Spanovic to jump a Serbian record 7.02. Asbel Kiprop lay well back in the 1500m, tenth at the bell, before sprinting down the home straight to win and LA Shawn Merritt with 44.18 beat both Kirani James 44,28 and Wayde van Niekerk 44.35 in the 400m. The pole vault, won by Shawn Barber 5.92, was held on the previous evening in the Main Railway Station (indoors).

6 **Berlin**, Germany. 74th ISTAF (WCM). Some consolation for missing out on World finals were achieved by wins from Nijel Amos, 1:43.28 800m, Lynsey Sharp, Scottish record 1:57.71 800m, and Dawn Harper Nelson, 12.82 100m hurdles. Virginia Nyambura ran 6:02.16 for the best time ever in a women's 2000m steeplechase race (although Gulnara Galkina had a split of 6:01.20 in her 3000m record); the 1-7 here went to 1-2-4-6-13-20-25 on the world all-time list.

7-8 **Zagreb**, Croatia. 65th Boris Hanzekovic Memorial (WCM). Records came in the shot with Tom Walsh improving his Oceania mark to 21.62 and in third place Konrad Bukowiecki setting world junior outdoor bests of 20.75 and 20.78. Croatia's own Sandra Perkovic won the discus with 69.88, her longest since she opened her season with 70.08 in March

7-9 **Commonwealth Youth Games**, Apia, Samoa.

11 **Brussels**, Belgium. 39th Van Damme Memorial. Performance of the night at this DL final meeting came from Habiba Ghribi, 3000m steeplechase in 9:05.36, the world's best since Gulnara Galkina's world record in 2008. Faith Kipyegon ran an African and Commonwealth record 4:16.71, the fastest in the world for 19 years, to beat Sifan Hassan, Dutch record 4:18.20, in the women's mile in which there were best ever times for places 7-11. The men's 5000m, won by the 18 year-old Yomif Kejelcha 12:53.98 from Hagos Gebrhiwet 12:54.70 with Abdelaati Iguider and Thomas Longosiwa also under 13 minutes, was the fastest of the year. Dafne Schippers won the 200m in 22.12 but second in 22.22 was enough for Allyson Felix to win the Diamond League race. Renaud Lavillenie cleared 5.95 in the pole vault and became the only athlete to have won the Diamond Race every year since its inception in 2010, and Sandra Perkovic beat Dania Caballero 67.50 to 65.77 to win the DL for the fourth successive year. Winning for the third year were Justin Gatlin at 100m and Caterine Ibargüen, whose triple jump 14.60 was her 30th successive win. Mariya Kuchina could not quite catch Ruth Beitia in the high jump Race, but she won here with 2.01.

12 **IAU World 100k Champs**, Winschoten, Netherlands. After placing second in four of the last five championships, Jonas Buud won, his 6:22:44 taking 6:14 off his Swedish record; he won by more than 13 minutes after going clear from 63k and he also led Sweden to the men's team title. Camille Herron won the women's title in 7:08:35 for fourth on the world all-time list and led the USA to team victory. Second was Kajsa Berg, who took the concurrent European title and went to eighth on the all-time list with a Swedish record 7:20:48.

12-13 **Finland v Sweden**, Stockholm. Sweden's men beat Finland 231-179 but Finland's women won 213.5 to 193.5 in the annual Finnkampen.

12 **Rieti**, Italy. Pawel Fajdek sealed the men's IAAF Hammer Throw Challenge with 80.96, his 11th competition of 2015 over 80m and 16th successive win.

13 **Rieti**, Italy (WCM). Francine Niyonsaba produced the highlight of the 45th edition of the Rieti Meeting, the last leg of the IAAF World Challenge, as she won the 800m in 1:57.62 from Faith Kipyegon, who ran a pb 1:58.02.

13 **Copenhagen**, Denmark. Bidan Karoki ran a pb 59:14 to win the half marathon in which Kenyans took the first nine places.

13 34th **Great North Run, Newcastle to South Shields**, GBR. Mo Farah 59:22 outsprinted Stanley Biwott 59:24, although the usual drop of 30.5m overall and point-to-point course meant that this was not eligible as a European record. As in 2014 Mary Keitany was a runaway winner of the women's race in 67:32. There were 40,895 starters.

13 **Paris (Charléty)**, France. The USA had an eighth successive win in the annual DécaNation (ten men's and ten women's events) meeting with 131.5 points from Russia 120.5 and France 86.

13 **Warsaw**, Poland. Poland's three World champions all won at the 6th Kamila Skolimowska Memorial meeting: hammer

throwers Pawel Fajdek 81.99 and Anita Wlodarczyk 78.16, and Piotr Malachowski, discus 63.71.

13-17 **All-Africa Games.** , Brazzaville, Congo. Five new Games records were set at men's events. Ihab Abdelrahman added nearly 7m to the javelin record with 85.37, and the others were by Getaneh Tamire at 5000m, Antonio Alkana at 110m hurdles and Frank Elemba at shot as well as the Kenyan 4x400m team, who ran 3:00.34. Marie Josée Ta Lou took 0.01 off the Games record for 100m and won by a huge margin, 11.02 to 11.47 here and in her 200m win in 22.57. Further women's Games records came at pole vault, hammer, 20k walk and from Alice Aprot, who made a brilliant debut at 10,000m to win in 31:24.18. More top marks came at 400m from Isaac Makwala 44.35 and Kabange Mupupo 50.22, at 400mh Abdelmalik Lahoulou 48.67, and three men, headed by Tebalu Zawude 27:27.19, under 27:30 in the 10,000m.

19 31st **WMRA World Mountain Running Championships**, Betws-y-Coed, Wales, GBR. Fred Musobo won the men's race, the fourth man from Uganda to do so and third in succession, and another Ugandan Stella Chesang, junior winner in 2014, became the first African woman to win at these Championships since their inauguration in 1985.

19-20 **Talence**, France. Décastar. Winners were Willem Coertzen, decathlon 8187, and Györgyi Zsivoczky-Farkas, pentathlon 6306.

27 BMW **Berlin Marathon**, Germany. Eliud Kipchoge maintained his place as the world's top marathoner with 2:04:00 despite his insoles slipping from the 8th kilometre and thus getting blisters, and he had his fifth win in six races at the distance. The lead pack went through halfway in 61:53 before Kipchoge accelerated away from the 32nd kilometre. Eliud Kiptanui was 2nd in 2:05:21. In only her second marathon Gladys Cherono won in 2:19:25 to move to seventh on the world all-time list from Aberu Kebede 2:20:48. There were 36,820 finishers (27,897 men and 8923 women).

October

4-8 **World Military Games (CISM)**, Mungyeoung, Korea. Two world champions, Mariya Kuchina, high jump 1.95, and Sergey Shubenkov, 110m hurdles 13.43, won, but another, Piotr Malachowski, was well beaten in the discus by Zóltan Kövágó, 66.01 to 62.12. Also taking a silver medal was Marina Arzamasova behind Nataliya Lupu at 800m. Zhang Wenxiu, with 74.87, won the hammer title for an extraordinary fourth time, following previous successes in 2003, 2007 and 2011. This was one of eleven championship records.

11 38h **Chicago Marathon**, USA. With strong winds and no pacemakers, Dickson Chumba 2:09:25 and Florence Kiplagat 2:23:33 were the winners. There were 37,182 finishers (20,144 men + 17,038 women).

18 **Amsterdam Marathon**, Netherlands. Bernard Kipyego repeated his win of 2014 and improved his best by 3 secs to 2:06:19. The women's winner was Joyce Chepkirui in a pb 2:24:11.

18 **Valencia**, Spain. Abreham Cheroben repeated his 2014 win as he won the half marathon in 59:10.

25 **Frankfurt-am-Main**, Germany. Sisay Lemma ran a pb to win the men's race in 2:06:26 with Arne Gabius in fourth place running a German record 2:08:33, and three Ethiopian women broke 2:24, headed by Gulume Tolesa 2:23:12 from a previous best of 2:29:40.

November

1 **New York City Marathon**, USA. Mary Keitany defended her title in fine style, crossing the line in 2:24:25, while the men's race went to Stanley Biwott in 2:10:34, 14 secs ahead of Geoffrey Kamworor. There were 49,330 finishers (28,686 men and 20,644 women).

4 It was announced that the French police had opened a criminal investigation into former IAAF President, **Lamine Diack**, for alleged corruption and money-laundering.

28 **Machida**, Japan. The terrific depth of Japanese distance running was demonstrated when, including their East African team members, 17 men broke 28 minutes for 10,000m, 45 ran under 28:30 and 79 men broke 29 minutes in five races of the Hachioji Distance Carnival in this Tokyo suburb. Kenyan William Malel Sitonik won the A race in a pb 27:22.12 from Kota Murayama who ran a Japanese record 27:29.69.

29 **New Delhi**, India. Birhanu Legesse led five men under 59:30, beating Mosinet Geremew by a second in 59:20, and Cynthia Limo 68:35 just held off her Kenyan compatriots Helah Kiprop 58:35 and Gladys Chesire 58:36 at the Airtel Delhi Half Marathon.

December

4 **IAU World 50k Champs**, Doha, Qatar.

6 **Fukuoka**, Japan. Patrick Makau won the 69th Fukuoka International Marathon in 2:08:18, four seconds quicker than in his 2014 win.

6 **s'Heerenberg**, Netherlands. Meseret Defar won the 20th Montferland Run in her first race since her second place in the Great North Run on 15 September 2013 and the birth of her daughter on 23 June 2014.

13 **European Cross-Country Championships**, Hyères, France. The British team was again much the most successful nation overall with three gold, four silver and two bronze medals. The senior individual titles went to distinguished African-born runners: Ali Kaya and Sifan Hassan.

ATHLETES OF 2015

By Peter Matthews

Male Athlete of the Year

ASHTON EATON NOT only achieved the world record in the decathlon, but he also did so on the biggest possible stage, in the World Championships in Beijing. His 400m in 45.00 to close the opening day was, on its own, a strong candidate for the top individual performance of the year. That was his only decathlon of the year as he had to miss Götzis though injury. Having excelled at 400m hurdles in 2014, the hurdles remained a strength for him, as he set a pb at 60m hurdles indoors with 7.51 for 3rd at the Millrose Games and he ran 13.30 for 110mh, and he also got close to his bests at 100m with 10.23 and 10.20w. The only other world records at standard men's events were those for 20k walk by Yohann Diniz and Yusuke Suzuki in March.

The main challenge to Eaton for the best performance of the year was the 18.21 triple jump by Christian Taylor in Beijing after a marvellous season in which his clashes with Pedro Paulo Pichardo provided highlights from the Doha Diamond League meeting in which, for the first time, two men went beyond 18m. We almost take their exploits for granted, but perennial favourites Usain Bolt and Mo Farah continued to sweep up gold medals. Farah achieved his third successive global 5000m and 10,000m double and was undefeated at these events, two competitions each, and also in his two half marathons, setting European bests in both races. He also won at 2 miles indoors and once at 3000m outdoors, but was 2nd in his other 3000m race. He was also 4th at 1500m in Monaco, but there ran an amazing 3:28.93 to demonstrate again just what a fantastic range he has.

My selection of the top 10 athletes of 2015 together with the lists compiled by international experts polled by *Track & Field News* and those of *Athletics International* readers:

	PJM	*TFN*	*AI*
Ashton Eaton	1	1	1
Christian Taylor	2	2	4
Usain Bolt	3	3	2
Mo Farah	4	4	3
Pawel Fajdek	5	5	5=
Justin Gatlin	6	8	11
Eliud Kipchoge	7	9	9
Asbel Kiprop	8	6	8
Wayde van Niekerk	9	7	7
Renaud Lavillenie	10		12
Julius Yego			5=
Joe Kovacs		10	
Matej Tóth			10

IAAF: Eaton; Shortlist: Bolt, Taylor

Other World champions who were unbeaten at their events, but only in limited competition, were Usain Bolt in 3 events at 100m and 4 at 200m, Matej Tóth who won both his races at 50k, and Eliud Kipchoge won his two marathons in the two fastest times of the year. The greatest domination of world lists was by Pawel Fajdek, who had the top 12 performances in the hammer. He also won 16 of 17 competitions.

Most successful in the Diamond League was five wins by Justin Gatlin at 100m.

100 Metres

JUSTIN GATLIN HAD one of the greatest seasons ever for a sprinter. At 100m he ran the five fastest times of the year (9.74 to 9.78) and won six of his seven 100m competitions, four in the Diamond League. The average winning margin of his five races prior to the Worlds was 0.17. Afterwards he only just held off Femi Ogunode, as both ran 9.98 in Brussels. But by far the most significant race of the year was for the World title, and indeed this was most keenly anticipated of all the races in Beijing, as Gatlin faced Usain Bolt, who had just three races in the year to then, running 10.12 in Rio and 9.87 twice in London. But Bolt beat Gatlin. The margin was but 13/1000ths (9.784 to 9.797), and was such a narrow win enough to gainsay Gatlin's superb overall season? The Worlds are so much the biggest event that I think it can be, provided of course that the relevant athletes were fit and that the competition was truly run and held in decent conditions – that was the case here, with all to play for.

The greatest depth of times in 2015 were by Mike Rodgers and Asafa Powell, but they were 5th and 7th respectively at the Worlds, where Andre De Grasse and Trayvon Bromell tied for bronze over a metre behind the big two. De Grasse and Bromell were 1-2 at the NCAAs and as US collegians missed the DL season apart from Bromell's false start disqualification in Monaco. But Bromell was 2-0 v Rodgers; he was 2nd and Rodgers 3rd at the US Champs. Tyson Gay was the winner there and 6th at the Worlds, 3-1 v Rodgers, 1-1 v Powell (in the same time in each race) and 2-1 v Bromell. Powell closed in on 100 sub-10 times (now 93 plus 7w and

1 while banned) with another 10 but, despite his five sub-9.90 times and winning 12 of his 15 100m competitions, his ability only to run 10.00 for 7th in the World final has to affect his ranking; he was 3-2 v Rodgers, who only won three of 18 events, but was ultra-consistent. After Adam Gemili pulled up injured when 2nd in Birmingham to Marvin Bracy (whose season also ended prematurely), Jimmy Vicaut was easily the top European and was 8th in the Worlds and 4-2 v Rodgers, but well behind the American on times. Ogunode was just edged out of the World final, but won the Asian title and four of five post-Beijing races in Europe. Kemar Bailey-Cole was 3rd in the Jamaican Champs behind Powell and Neville Ashmeade (World semis) and also 3rd in London behind Bolt and Rodgers, but missed the Worlds through injury.

The evergreen Kim Collins (39 in April) had a decent outdoor season after he had run five of the six fastest times run indoors at 60m headed by a CAC record 6.47.

Most times at 10.00/10.05 or faster: Rodgers 15+1w/18+1w, Powell 11/18, Gatlin 7+1w/8+1w, Vicaut 7/11, Ogunode 7+2w/9+3w, Bromell 6+6w/8+6w, de Grasse 6+3w/8+4w, Gay 6+2w/6+2w, Bolt 5/5, Bracy 3+1w/3+1w, Carter 3/6, Simbine 3/4+1w, Collins 2+1w/5+1w, Bailey-Cole 2/4, Fisher 1/5, I Young 1+4w/1+4w, Bledman 1+3w/5+3w, B J Lee 1+3w/1+4w, Ujah 1/4+1w, Ronnie Baker 0+3w/1+4w, Harvey 0/4, Remontay McClain 0+4w/0+4w.

1. Bolt, 2. Gatlin, 3. De Grasse, 4. Bromell, 5. Gay, 6. Powell, 7. Rodgers, 8. Vicaut, 9. Ogunode, 10. Bailey-Cole

200 Metres

AS IN THE 100m the World final was decisive, Bolt beating Gatlin, but clearly here 19.55 to 19.74. Both had four competitions at the event, but Gatlin's other races were of a much higher quality with six sub-20 times in all topped by 19.55 to win the US title, while Bolt had three wins in 20.13 to 20.29 prior to Beijing, where he was also sub-20 in his semi-final. The World 3-4-5 were Anaso Jobodwana, Alonso Edward and Zharnel Hughes. They were closely matched with Edward ahead on times but beaten 3-2 by Jobodwana and 2-1 by UK champion Hughes, who were 2-2 in their clashes. Edwards had three DL wins and Hughes won both his races. Andre De Grasse did not run the 200 at the Worlds but he completed an NCAA double in 19.58w and also had a significant win over Rasheed Dwyer at the Pan-Am Games. Dwyer ran 19.80 in his Pan-Am semi but was only 5th at the Jamaican Champs, won by Nickel Ashmeade from Warren Weir and I rank him behind the men who came in 6-7-8 at the Worlds: Ramil Guliyev, Femi Ogunode (Arab and Asian champion, who ran an Asian record 19.97 to win in Brussels) and Ashmeade. Just missing the top ten are Isiah Young, 2nd at the US Champs, but who went out in his World heat and was 7th in the DL final in Zürich behind Edward, Dwyer, Jobodwana, Ashmeade and Miguel Francis, Dedric Dukes (2nd NCAA, 5th US) and Julian Forte (3rd Jamaican). Trayvon Bromell was 3rd in the NCAAs, having won the indoor title in the world indoor fastest of the year, 20.19.

Most times at 20.10/20.30 or better: Edward 7/8, Gatlin 6+1w/7+1w, De Grasse 4+1w/8+2w+1i, Jobodwana 4/10+1w, Guliyev 3/6, Dukes 2+1w/8+1w, Young 2+1w/5+1w, Dwyer 2/9, Bolt, Hughes 2/6; Spearmon 2/5+1w, Ogunode 2/5, Skyers 2/4+1w, Bromell 1+1w/5+1w, Francis 1/4+1w, Forte, Tsákonas 1/4, Ashmeade 5, Lee 4+1w, Lemaitre, Rodney 4.

1. Bolt, 2. Gatlin, 3. Jobodwana, 4. Edward, 5. Hughes, 6. De Grasse, 7. Guliyev, 8. Ogunode, 9. Ashmeade, 10. Dwyer

400 Metres

AFTER FOUR YEARS in which Kirani James and LaShawn Merritt had contested the top two rankings, both were upstaged in 2015 by Wayde van Niekerk, who set an African record of 43.48 to win the World title. The South African won his first six 400m competitions before his only loss, 3rd in the DL final in Zurich behind Merritt and James. James beat Merritt 3-2 and had five big race wins to Merritt's two, but Merritt was ahead in the two races (above) that mattered most. Overall there were 8 sub-44 and 125 (by 33 men) sub-45 sec. times compared to 4 and 59 (by 17 men) in 2014 so a huge recovery in standards exemplified by the astonishing first round at the World Champs when 21 men broke 45 and Youssef Al-Masrahi and Rusheen McDonald ran 43.93, Asian and Jamaican records respectively. The remaining places 4-8 in the World final were: 4 Luguelín Santos, 5 Isaac Makwala, 6 Rabah Yousif, 7 Machel Cedenio, and 8 Al-Masrahi. Of these men Santos won the World Universities and Pan-Am titles, Makwala the African, and Al-Masrahi the World Military. But there was conflicting data on win-loss between those ranked from 4th. For instance Al-Masrahi beat Santos 2-1 and was 2-2 v Merritt and Makwala, but he was beaten 2-0 by David Verburg (3rd semi Worlds, 1st US) and 2-1 by Abdelilah Haroun, the hugely promising 18 year-old Asian champion (well ahead of Al-Masrahi), who had to miss the Worlds through injury. Santos, 4th in the DL final ahead of Yousif, Verburg and Makwala, was 2-1 v Makwala and 2-2 v Cedenio, who was 2nd at the Pan-Ams. Close to a ranking were Jamaican champion Javon Francis, 4th in his semi at the Worlds, and Chris Brown who, at the age of 36, improved his own World over-45 record to 44.54 and was 7th in his World semi as was the 19 year-old Steven Gardiner.

Most sub-45.00 times: Merritt 11, James 9, van Niekerk, Verburg 8, Haroun 7, Al-Masrahi, Makwala, Cedenio 6, Santos, Gardiner, Francis, McDonald, L Gordon 5; Norwood, Brown, J Borlée, Quow 4.

1. van Niekerk, 2. Merritt, 3. James, 4. Santos, 5. Makwala, 6. Verburg, 7. Cedenio, 8. Haroun, 9. Al-Masrahi, 10. Yousif.

800 Metres

THE WORLD 800m final was in many ways an unsatisfactory one. The first lap was run in a pedestrian 54.17 before David Rudisha showed total control to add the title to World 2011 and Olympic 2012 gold as he sped to victory with finishing 100m splits of 13.0, 12.2 and 12.1. Adam Kszczot was runner-up but he had been trapped on the inside for too long. Third placer Amel Tuka was the revelation of the season, running consistently well as he improved during the year from 1:46.12 to 1:42.51 for his win in Monaco when the second and third fastest times of the year were run by Nijel Amos and Ayanleh Souleiman. Rudisha had three wins and three second places prior to Beijing and 4th in Zürich afterwards, behind Kszczot, Taoufik Makhloufi and Mohammed Aman. What helped make the World final a disappointment was that the 2014 1-2 Amos and Aman went out in the semis, 3rd in a dawdling race and disqualified for pushing respectively. Aman mixed wins in Eugene and Rome with 8th in Lausanne and Monaco and 9th in Doha before ending with 3rd in Zürich and Berlin and that 4th in Brussels. Amos, however, had an otherwise excellent year, with the 2nd, 5th and 6th fastest times and beating Rudisha 2-1 and Kszczot 6-1 with wins in Birmingham, Lausanne, London, Berlin and at the African Games and 2nd in Eugene, Rome, Monaco and Brussels. Souleiman only ran three 800m races but had big wins in the 1:43s in Doha and Barcelona and Makhloufi had just four races but good win-loss against top men. Ferguson Rotich Cheruiyot won the Kenyan Trials and was 4th in the Worlds, with a 3-3 record against Aman. Pierre-Ambroise Bosse was 5th in the Worlds but beaten 3-0 by Marcin Lewandowski and 4-1 by Alfred Kipketer (World 8th). Kipketer also had a 4-1 advantage over compatriot Job Kinyor, but both were beaten 2-1 by World 6th placer Abdulrahman Musaeb Balla.

Most times sub-1:45.0: Cheruiyot, Kszczot 7, Rudisha 6, Amos 5, Aman, Tuka, Kipketer 4, Bosse, Kinyor , Lewandowski 3.

1. Amos, 2. Rudisha, 3. Kszczot, 4. Tuka, 5. Souleiman, 6. Cheruiyot, 7. Aman, 8. Lewandowski, 9. Kipketer, 10. Balla

1500 Metres

ASBEL KIPROP CONSOLIDATED his position as the current miling king with his fifth top ranking and eighth successive year in the top three. Sometimes he treats his opponents with seeming disdain as he hangs well back before coming through with his great long strides, but this year, apart from 3rd in Eugene to Ayanleh Souleiman (3:51.10, the year's fastest) and Matt Centrowitz, he had seven wins in 8 races at 1500m or 1 mile. These included just one superfast race, as he recorded a pb of 3:26.69 in Monaco, In the rest he unleashed his finish after a more gentle pace. including the Worlds when he took gold ahead of Elijah Manangoi, Abdelaaati Iguider. Taoufik Makhloufi, Silas Kiplagat, Nick Willis, Timothy Cheruiyot and Centrowitz. Souleiman did not finish, injured, in his heat. The year's seven fastest times and 10 of the top 12 came in that Monaco race, in which Kiprop was followed by Makhloufi, Iguider, Mo Farah (his only 1500m), Willis and Manangoi under 3:30, with Robert Biwott, Wote, Collins Cheboi and Centrowitz just outside. Manangoi was the biggest improver of the top men, from 3:35.0A in 2014 to 3:29.67; he was Kenyan champion and 3rd in their trials and also 2nd in the DL final in Zürich behind Kiprop with Biwott 3rd and Iguider 4th. The second fastest race was at Saint-Denis, won by Silas Kiplagat in 3:30.12 from Souleiman, Ronald Kwemoi, Makhloufi, Biwott, Iguider, James Magut, Cheboi, Wote, Iham Özbilen and Henrik Ingebrigtsen, 11 men to 3:32.85, a time achieved only in these two fast races. Makhloufi was 2-1 v Iguider, but both he and Willis only had four events at 1500/1M. Kwemoi beat Cheboi 4-0.

Most times sub-3:35.0 or 3:52.0M: Kiplagat 6, Kiprop 5, Manangoi, Biwott 4, Iguider, Makhloufi, Souleiman 3.

1. Kiprop, 2. Manangoi, 3. Makhloufi, 4, Iguider, 5. Kiplagat, 6. Souleiman, 7. Willis, 8. Biwott, 9. Centrowitz, 10. Kwemoi

3000 Metres/2 Miles

THERE WAS MORE action indoors than out, with Mo Farah topping the rankings with his 7:33.1 en route to his world indoor 2 miles best of 8:03.40. Farah also ran the fastest time for 3000m outdoors with 7:34.66 in London, followed in the lists by Caleb Ndiku and Yenew Alamirew in Monaco. Bernard Lagat set world over-40 records three times to 3000m (to 7:37.92) and at 2 miles (8:17.05) indoors and at 3000m (7:42.75) outdoors.

5000 Metres

MO FARAH COMPLETED his third successive global double with a last 800m in c.1:48.6 but his time of 13:50.38 was the slowest in World Champs history. Apart from his World heat of 13:19.44, his only other 5000m race of the year was a win in Lausanne in 13:11.77, good for only 31st on the world list. But that form was enough for top ranking (his fourth) as he beat Yomif Kejelcha, who tumed 18 on 1 August), in both these races. Kejelcha was 2nd in Lausanne, 4th at the Worlds and won his other four races including at Brussels, where his 12:53.98 was the year's fastest as he was followed under 13 minutes by Hagos Gebrhiwet, Abdelaaati Iguider (also 10th at Lausanne) and Thomas Longosiwa. The 13 fastest times of the year were set either here or in Rome, where Kejelcha won in 12:58.39 from Paul Tanui, Gebrhiwet, Imane Merga, Longosiwa (five under 13 min), Muktar Edris, Ali Kaya and Dejen Gebrmeskel. Caleb Ndiku was 5th in Brussels and had been only 11th in Lausanne, but he was the only man able to offer a real challenge to Farah at the Worlds, where following were Gebrhiwet 3rd, and 5-7 the US trio of Galen Rupp, Ben True and Ryan Hill (who were then 10th, 7th and 8th in Brussels and had been 3-2-1 at the US Champs) with 8-10 Isiah Koech, Kaya and Edwin Soi. Longosiwa missed the Worlds after 4th at the Kenyan Trials behind Soi, Emmanuel Kipsang and Koech, but had a consistently good set of results. Soi was 3rd in Lausanne and 14th in Brussels with 2-3-4 places in other DL races. Conflicting form or limited races, such as only two races for Iguider and Edris, made ranking this event very difficult.

Most times under 13:15: Kejelcha 4, Longosiwa, Koech 3.

1. Farah, 2. Kejelcha, 3. Gebrhiwet,
4. Longosiwa, 5. Ndiku, 6. True, 7. Tanui,
8. Rupp, 9. Hill, 10. Soi

10,000 Metres

THE THREE FASTEST times of the year were at the Prefontaine Classic in Eugene as Mo Farah, Paul Tanui and Geoffrey Kamworor all broke 27 minutes. Three months later these three men ran the next three fastest times of 2015 as they took the medals in the World Champs, Farah's finish proving too much for the Kenyans who tried to race as a team at a decent pace but still could not prevent Farah winning with a last kilometre of 2:28.81 with Kamworer 2nd and Tanui 3rd. Bidan Karoki completed a Kenyan 2-3-4 at the Worlds, having been 2nd in the Kenyan Trial behind Kamworor, who ran a remarkable high altitude 27:11.89 ahead of Tanui, Vincent Yator, Leonard Barsoton and Geoffrey Kirui; nine men under 28 minutes. Tanui was the most prolific, with three wins (27:08.21 to 27:46.36) in Japan in addition to the above three races. The Kenyans who had been 4-5-6 at the Trials were given their opportunity at the African Games, and Barsoton was 2nd, Yator 4th and Kirui 5th in a race won by Tabalu Zawude with Adugna Takele 3rd as these men had been 4th Takele and 5th Zawude in the Ethiopian trial at Hengelo that had been won by Muktar Edris from Imane Merga and Mosinet Geremew, who were 10th, dnf and 11th at the Worlds. US champion Galen Rupp was 5th at the Worlds, followed by Abrar Osman (also 1st in Leiden), Ali Kaya (1st at Turkish and European U23 Champs), Timothy Toroitch and Joshua Cheptegei, the last two 12th and 8th respectively at Eugene. Cam Levins was 4th at Eugene and 14th at the Worlds, El Hassan El Abbassi 7th at Eugene, 12th Worlds and 1st World Military Games, and Yator, 19th at Eugene was also Kenyan champion.

1. Farah, 2. Kamworor, 3. Tanui, 4. Karoki,
5. Rupp, 6. Kaya, 7. Edris, 8. Zawude,
9. Barsoton, 10. Takele

Half Marathon

JUST AS IN 2014 the fastest half marathon of the year was run at Valencia by Abreham Cheroben, in 59:10; he was 3rd at Berlin in 59:49 in his other race at the distance. Bidan Karoki won in Copenhagen in 59:14 and third fastest time of the year was 59:20 for wins in The Hague by Stanley Biwott and in New Delhi by Birhanu Legesse. The last, with six men under 59:40, had the best depth of times and Legesse had earlier won in Berlin in 59:45. The other men to break 1 hour twice were Simon Cheprot, 4th at Copenhagen in 59:32 and 2nd to Robert Chemosin at Ostia in 59:49, and three of the Delhi top men: Mosinet Geremew 2nd 59:21, Edwin Kiptoo 4th 59:26 and Geoffrey Kirui 6th 59:38. Multiple world champion Zersenay Tadese was 3rd in 59:24. Mo Farah set a European record with 59:32 to win at Lisbon and improved that on the slightly downhill Great North Run course when he beat Biwott 59:22 to 59:24.

Marathon

FOR ONCE THE decision as to who was the world's top marathon runner of the year was easy as Eliud Kipchoge recorded the two fastest times of the year, winning major races in London 2:04:42 and Berlin 2:04:00. Full marks to 19 year-old Ghirmay Ghebreslassie for winning in the heat and humidity of Beijing to take the world title, but frankly such conditions and the fact that most of the world's best were not there made those results less relevant for world rankings, even though the top names Wilson Kipsang and Dennis Kimetto, who had been 2nd (in 2:04:47) and 3rd in London and Kipsang later 4th in New York, did not finish. Ghebreslassie's other race was 2nd to Lucas Rotich in Hamburg, and the World silver medallist Yemane Adhane, was also 2nd in Boston and 5th in New York. Other winners in the World Marathon Majors series were Endeshaw Negesse in Tokyo, Dickson Chumba in Chicago (after 3rd in Tokyo), Stanley Biwott in New York (after 4th London), and Lelisa Desisa at Boston; he was also 2nd in Dubai, 7th

Worlds and 3rd New York. Hayle Lemi won in Dubai in 2:05:28 and also won in Warsaw before 15th at the Worlds. Second in Berlin in 2:05:21, the fourth fastest time of the year, was Eliud Kiptanui (also 7th in Seou). Sammy Kitwara had two good major results: 6th in London and 2nd in Chicago and Deriba Robi was 3rd in Dubai and Prague and 2nd in Eindhoven, just behind Stephen Chebogut, who had been 3rd in Hamburg, with both men under 2:06 in Eindhoven,

1. Kipchoge, 2. Biwott, 3. Desisa, 4. Kipsang, 5. Chumba, 6. Kiptanui, 7. Lemi, 8. Ghebreslassie, 9. Adhane, 10. Robi

3000 Metres Steeplechase

EZEKIEL KEMBOI MAKES a mockery of attempts at world rankings as he simply plays around in so many of his races, but when it comes to what really matters he shows himself to be the world's greatest ever. So he did as the complete master at the World Champs, leading a Kenyan 1-2-3-4 as he took his fourth world title to add to his two Olympic triumphs plus three World silvers and four Commonwealth Games medals. Kemboi had started with a win in Eugene in 8:01.71 for the third fastest time of the year and there he was followed home by Jairus Birech, Conseslus Kipruto and Evan Jager. Kemboi's other races were 10th Oslo, 4th Kenyan Trials (behind Birech, C Kipruto and Brimin Kipruto but assured of his World place due to a wild card as defending champion) and, after Beijing, 14th in Zürich.

At the Worlds the order 2nd to 7th was C Kipruto, B Kipruto, Birech, Dan Huling, Jager and Brahim Taleb. The top man of 2014 Birech again had the best series of results and times, with 6 wins in his 10 competitions, including three DL wins, and 5 of the 11 sub-8:10 times. Jager took the US title from Donn Cabral and Huling, and had his finest result with a US record 8:00.45 at Saint-Denis. That would surely have been sub-8 minutes but for his fall at the final hurdle and he could have beaten Birech, the winner in 7:58.83, as they ran the two fastest times of the year. Well behind them C Kipruto was 3rd and B Kipruto 4th with Clement Kemboi 5th and Paul Kipsiele Koech 6th. As usual Koech could not cope with the altitude of Nairobi as he was 9th in the Kenyan Trials but otherwise he ran consistently well and his one win was in the DL final in Zürich with Birech 2nd and Jager 3rd. Koech beat C Kemboi, 6th Kenyan Trials, 4th Zürich and 1st African Games, 4-3. Jonathan Ndiku and Hillary Yego made it eight Kenyans (and two Americans) in the world's top ten fastest.

Most times under 8:15: Birech 7, C Kipruto, P Koech 6, Jager 3.

1. Birech, 2, E Kemboi, 3. C Kipruto, 4. Jager, 5. Koech, 6. B Kipruto, 7. C Kemboi, 8. Ndiku, 9. Yego, 10. Huling

110 Metres Hurdles

FOUR MEN RAN sub-13 second times: one each by Orlando Ortega, who, having applied for Spanish nationality was not eligible to run at the Worlds, Omar McLeod, David Oliver and Sergey Shubenkov. The last, whose 12.98 Russian record came in his World Champs victory, started with 5th places at Shanghai and Eugene but had an overall record of 8 wins in 12 competitions. David Oliver hit too many hurdles too hard, even with his power, to come in 7th in the World final, but was 3-3 v Shubenkov, won the US and Pan-Am titles and was 2nd to Shubenkov in the DL final as well as having the most top-level times. He was 5-3 v Ortega, who was 4-2 v Shubenkov and 3-3 v Aries Merritt, who was 3rd in the Worlds, a wonderful achievement considering the announcement that he had made just prior to the Championships that he needed a kidney transplant. The surprise World silver medallist in 13.03 was Hansle Parchment, who had a more limited campaign than any of his rivals and did not run in the Diamond League. He was also beaten 12.97 to 13.08 in the Jamaican Champs by Omar Macleod, NCAA champion and World 6th. Pascal Martinot-Lagarde was generally well down on his 2014 form, but was 4th at the Worlds in which the other finalists were also Frenchmen: Dmitri Bascou 5th and Garfield Darien 8th, with Darien ahead 4-2 on win-loss. Ronnie Ash was 2nd at the US Champs with Aleec Harris 4th and Jason Richardson 6th, but Richardson was best on win-loss, 3-2 v Ash and 4-2 v Harris, with Ash and Harris 3-3, and Richardson was also 3-1 v Martinot-Lagarde. Darien was 2-1 v Ash and 2-1 v Harris, who had better times then the Frenchmen.

Indoors US champion Omo Osaghae won the 60mh World Indoor title in 7.45 from Martinot-Lagarde 7.46 and Garfield Darien 7.47, and Martinot-Lagarde had five of the 9 times at 7.50 or better, sharing the world lead with 7.45.

Most times under 13.30: Oliver 15+1w, Shubenkov 11, Merritt, Harris 9, McLeod 8+2w, Martinot-Lagarde 8, Darien 7, Ortega 6, Bascou, Richardson 5; Parchment, Ash, S Brathwaite, O'Farrill, Porter 4.

1. Shubenkov, 2. Oliver, 3. Ortega, 4. Merritt, 5. Parchment, 6. Martinot-Lagarde, 7. McLeod, 8. Richardson, 9. Darien, 10. Harris

400 Metres Hurdles

BERSHAWN JACKSON HAD much the best record before Beijing with eight wins and a 2nd, heading the rankings from his 48.09 win in Doha. But then came a shocker at the Worlds as he messed up the final hurdle and was 7th in his heat. In stark contrast Nicholas Bett had a modest season, 49.09A for 2nd at the Kenyan Champs being his best from nine races, five over 50secs, before a breakthrough 48.29A at the Kenyan Trials. Then in Beijing he was fastest in the heats with 48.37, ran 48.54 in his semi and finally an amazing 47.79 from lane 9 in the final. But how to rank him? World champion in the fastest time of the year would normally be enough but he had so many poor races and ended with 49.90 for 7th in Brussels, the DL final won by Jeffery Gibson from Jackson and Kariem Hussein. Denis Kudryavtsev ran pbs in each round at the Worlds to take the silver medal in 48.05 but only ran one DL race (3rd in Lausanne behind Jackson and L.J. van Zyl). Gibson made it national records for each of the medallists with his 3rd at the Worlds. Then Kerron Clement was 4th, but he had a patchy season having been 3rd to Jackson and Johnny Dutch at the US Champs and 4th at the Pan-Ams behind Gibson, Javier Culson and Roxroy Cato. Dutch was 5th in his World semi, but was 3-0 v Clement and 3-2 v Tinsley. Michael Tinsley was another American below par with 8th at the Worlds but was 4-1 v Culson, NACAC champion and 5th semi at the Worlds. Kenyan champion Boniface Muchuru Tumuti was 5th, Yasmani Copello 6th and European U23 champion Patryk Dobek 8th at the Worlds. Both Dutch and Tinsley were beaten 2-0 by Dobek, who only ran one DL race but that was a good 2nd in Monaco to Jackson and ahead of Dutch, Tinsley and van Zyl. Hussein, 3rd in his semi at the Worlds, just misses a ranking, as does Thomas Barr, 4th World semi and World Universities champion. NCAA champion Michael Stigler was 4th at the US Champs but was 7th in Monaco and 4th in London in his two DL races.

Most times to 49.00: Jackson, Gibson, Dutch 9; Stigler 7, Clement, Culson, Tinsley, Hussein 5; Bett, Kudryavtsev, Dobek, Tumuti, Barr, van Zyl, Annsert Whyte 4; Copello 3.

1. Jackson, 2. Bett, 3. Gibson, 4. Kudryavtsev, 5. Dobek, 6. Dutch, 7. Clement, 8. Tumuti, 9. Tinsley, 10. Culson

High Jump

AFTER THE SPECIAL year for men's high jumping in 2014, standards fell a little although still above previous years. This time only Mutaz Essa Barshim jumped over 2.40, with 2.41 and 2.40 indoors and 2.40 outdoors. He won all his four indoor competitions but after a good start his form fell away outdoors when he had five wins (3 in the DL) in 11 events. However 3-1 records against Bohdan Bondarenko and Derek Drouin, who both only competed outdoors, was enough for top ranking. Drouin won the World title at 2.34 after a tense three-way jump-off with Bondarenko and Zhang Guowei who with 4th placed Barshim cleared 2.33. Bondarenko. although troubled by a foot injury, was 3-1 v Drouin and 3-1 (1 tie) v Zhang. Drouin won with 2.37 at the Pan-Am Games and at Eberstadt, but was 2-3 v Zhang, whose best was 2.38 behind Barshim's 2.41 at Eugene. The only other men to better 2.34 were Erik Kynard, who won the US title with 2.37 and was 3-2 v Drouin and Gianmarco Tamberi, 2nd at Eberstadt with 2.37, but both were only 8= at the Worlds with 2.25 and both beaten 2-1 by Daniyil Tsyplakov, the Russian and World Universities champion and 5th Worlds. Tsyplakov also won the European Indoor title. Michael Mason and Donald Thomas (6th Worlds) were 2nd and 3rd at the Pan-Am Games, but Mason, whose best result was 3rd at Eberstadt at 2.33, was a non-qualifier at the Worlds as was JaCorian Duffield after winning NCAA titles indoors and out and 2nd US Champs. Marco Fassinotti had six 2.30 plus events but was unfortunate to miss the Worlds through injury, and, although without such good heights as others, Jaroslav Bába was 7th at the Worlds, 5= at the European Indoors and 2-0 v Duffield.

Most competitions over 2.35/2.30m (outdoors+in): Barshim 3+2i/7+4i, Zhang 3/10+1i, Bondarenko, Drouin 2/8, Kynard 2/3+2i, Tamberi 1/3, Fassinotti, Tsyplakov 4+2i; Thomas 4+1i, Onnen 4, Mason 3+1i, Duffield 3, Protsenko 2+2i, Bába 2+1i, Dmitrik, Ukhov, Mástoras 1+2i

1. Barshim, 2. Bondarenko, 3. Drouin, 4. Zhang, 5. Kynard, 6. Tsyplakov, 7. Tamberi, 8. Thomas (9), 9. Fassinotti (8), 10. Mason. (Including indoors).

Pole Vault

RENAUD LAVILLENIE WAS top for the sixth successive year. Although he tied for third with Piotr Lisek and Pawel Wojciechowski at the Worlds behind Shawn Barber and Raphael Holzdeppe, he was ahead of all his rivals on win-loss apart from the fast improving Barber with whom he went 3-3. Lavillenie had five competitions over 6m indoors and the three best marks outdoors with 6.05, 6.03 and 5.95, while Barber set five Canadian records indoors from 5.79 to 5.91 and three outdoors from 5.90 to 5.93. In all indoors and out Lavillenie won 18 (4 DL) of his 24 competitions and Barber 24 of his 31. Holzdeppe had a slow start to recapture his form but came through to clear 5.90 at the Worlds; he was beaten 6-5 outdoors by Konstadínos Filippídis, but the Greek, who had two DL wins, failed at the Worlds by doing only 5.55 in qualifying. However, after that he recovered to 5.80 for 3rd at the DL final in Brussels, behind the big two and 15cm ahead of 4th placed Sam Kendricks (9= Worlds). Filippídis was also 6-2 outdoors v Wojciechowski, while Lisek was 6-4 v Filippídis outdoors but 6-0 indoors. Kendricks was 3-3 v Wojciechowski, 4-1 v Lisek and 2-1 v Thiago Braz da Silva, who was 5-2 v Lisek and 4-1 v Kévin Menaldo (World 6th). The European

Indoors was won by Lavillenie from Aleksandr Gripich (dnq 17= Worlds), Lisek, Robert Sobera (15 Worlds) and Filippídis. The Polish rivalry went 7-5 (2 tied) for Wojciechowski over Lisek (0-1 indoors) and the Czechs Jan Kudlicka and Michel Balner were closely matched, with the former 6-4 ahead outdoors (and 1-0 indoors), and both had win-loss advantage over Carlo Paech, who was 9-3 (1-2 indoors) v World 7= Scherbarth, who, however, beat Menaldo and Kudlicka on win-loss but had less good marks. The excellent indoor form of Lisek moves him up, but Sobera and Gripich was perhaps not enough to move them up in the rankings, given that they were all down on win-loss outdoors.

Most competitions over 5.75m (outdoors/in): Barber 11/10, Lavillenie 11/9, Filippídis 9/1, Holzdeppe 7, Kendricks 5/3, Wojciechowski, Braz da Silva 5; Lisek 4/8; Menaldo, Paech 3, Sobera 0/3.

1. Lavillenie, 2. Barber, 3. Holzdeppe (5), 4. Filippídis, 5. Wojciechowski (6), 6. Kendricks (7), 7. Braz da Silva (8), 8. Lisek (3), 9. Menaldo, 10. Kudlicka. (Including indoors).

Long Jump

IN 2014 IT was hard to judge between Greg Rutherford and Jeffrey Henderson for top ranking, but, while they remained the top two, Rutherford was clearly the best, a class apart at the Worlds in his season's best of 8.41 and winning 8 of his 10 competitions, including 4 DL wins. After big jumps at the US Champs, Marquis Dendy 8.68w, Henderson 8.44 and Mike Hartfield 8.42w, the Americans disappointed at the Worlds, as Henderson was 9th and Hartfield had no jumps in the final and Dendy failed to qualify (21st). But Dendy also won the NCAA titles with 8.43w outdoors and indoors with 8.28, won in London with 8.38, followed by Zarck Visser and Rutherford, and was 2-1 v Henderson, who was at his best at the Pan-Am Games with 8.54w/8.52. The Americans were also back in form at the DL final in Zürich as Dendy was 2nd at 8.32 and Henderson 4th at 8.22 when Rutherford won with 8.32 and Fabrice Lapierre was 3rd in his year's best of 8.27. Lapierre had shown modest form until he surprised with 2nd at the Worlds, when he was followed by the Chinese trio of Wang Jianan, Gao Xinglong and Li Jinzhe. Li had a 3-2 advantage over both Wang and Gao, with Wang 3-1 v Gao.

In 28th place in the world list with 8.13 is Marquise Goodwin, but that best legal jump of the year disguises two amazing competitions by the American Footballer who had not long jumped since 2012, as he was 4th at the US Champs with 8.37w and 2nd at the Pan-Ams with 8.27w; but that was probably too little for a top ten ranking. Similarly Jarrion Lawson was 5th at the US Champs with 8.36w and was 2nd at the NCAAs outdoors with 8.34 and indoors with 8.27. Without achieving previous distances Aleksandr Menkov was a solid 6th at the Worlds, followed by Kafétien Gomis and Sergey Polyanskiy with Tyrone Smith 10th. Khotso Mokoena was 8-1 v compatriot Visser and 3-3 v Hartfield, but beaten 3-0 by Smith (4th Pan-Ams). In turn Smith was beaten 2-0 by Gomis, who had several poor competitions, but was 2nd at Saint-Denis to Hartfield and ahead of Lapierre, Menkov and Smith. Michal Tornéus had the best indoor jump, 8.30 to win the European Indoor title, but was held back by injury to just one 8m plus jump outdoors.

Most competitions over 8.10m: Rutherford 8+1i, Henderson 7+1w, Li 7+1i, Dendy 5+1w+1i, Lapierre, Hartfield 4+1w; Visser 4, Gao 3+2i, Mokoena 3+1w, Menkov, Wang, Heinle 3, Gomis 2+1i, Lawson 1+1w+1i.

1. Rutherford, 2. Dendy, 3. Henderson, 4. Lapierre, 5. Menkov, 6. Li, 7. Wang, 8. Hartfield, 9. Gao, 10. Gomis

Triple Jump

CHRISTIAN TAYLOR AGAINST Pedro Pichardo is developing into one of the world's great track and field rivalries. In 2014 they shared the best 13 performances of the year and won all the DL meetings. They met five times, with Taylor winning 4-1. Their first meeting in Doha was the first time ever that two men had bettered 18m in the same competition, Pichardo winning 18.06 to 18.04. Then Taylor won in Lausanne 18.06 to 17.99, Monaco 17.75 to 17.73, Worlds 18.21 to 17.73 and Brussels 17.59 to 17.06. These were Pichardo's only losses (with six wins) while Taylor had six wins and two seconds, also finishing behind Will Claye at the Drake Relays. Omar Craddock, Nelson Évora and Marquis Dendy followed on the world list at 17.53 to 17.50. Évora was 3rd and Craddock 4th at the Worlds, but overall Craddock had a 3-1 advantage. Lyukman Adams was 5th in the World final, followed by Marian Oprea, Dmitriy Sorokin and Tosin Oke.

The 2014 number one Benjamin Compaoré was 12th, but Alexis Copello, seeking to switch from Cuba to Spain could not compete. In the DL final 3rd to 7th were Adams, Craddock, Évora, Oke and Sorokin with Compaoré no jumps. Dendy won the NCAA titles indoors (17.37) and outdoors (17.71w) and was 3rd at the US Champs behind Craddock and Claye, but was only 6th in Monaco in his only European outing and Claye only competed in the five meetings in the US before these two Americans did not qualify for the Worlds final, Dendy 13th and Claye 19th – but they did have some much longer jumps than the top Europeans. Sorokin was 2nd to Adams in the Russian Champs and won WUG and World Military titles, He was 3-1 v Aleksey Fyodorov, 5th and 2nd at those two international events. Fyodorov was 2-0 v Oprea. Another Russian Dmitriy Chizhikov was an impressive winner of the European U23 title. Oke was the African champion and was 2-2 v Compaoré who beat Dendy 2-0. European Indoor medallists were Évora, Pablo Torrijos and Oprea. Teddy Tamgho missed another year after rupturing his left Achilles in Doha, where he was 3rd with 17.24.

Most competitions over 17.00: Pichardo 11, Taylor 8, Évora 5+2i, Craddock, Sorokin 5; Chizhikov 4, Oprea 3, Dendy 2+1w+2i, Copello 2+1w+1i, Tsonov 2+1w

1. Taylor, 2. Pichardo, 3. Craddock, 4. Évora, 5. Adams (6), 6. Dendy (5), 7. Claye (7), 8. Copello, 9. Sorokin, 10. Fyodorov. (Including indoors).

Shot

JOE KOVACS WAS the only man with a positive win-loss record against all his rivals and although David Storl had more top marks, Kovacs had the two best throws of the year, 22.56 and 22.35 to Storl's 22.20, and crucially beat Storl 21.93 to 21.74 to win the World title. While Storl was ahead at Doha (1st to 4th) and at Lausanne, Kovacs also came out ahead at Eugene and Brussels, where these top men were 3rd to 4th in the DL final behind Tom Walsh and O'Dayne Richards. Overall Kovacs won 10 of his 15 competitions and Storl 11 (inc. 2 indoors) of his 16 and each had three DL wins. Although Richards was 3rd and Walsh 4th at the Worlds, Walsh was 6-1 ahead overall. Even though only 4th at the US Champs behind Kovacs, Christian Cantwell and Jordan Clarke, Reese Hoffa ranks in his World position of 5th, although Cantwell, US indoor champion, beat him 3-2 but was unable to take part after qualifying for the World final. Ryan Whiting had the best indoor throw of the year, 21.80, and although only 7th at the US Champs, he was 5th in the DL final and beat Clarke (dnq 13th Worlds) 4-3. Asmir Kolasinac was sixth on the world list with 21.58 and while that and his next best of 21.01 came in minor meetings he was consistent and was 1-1 v Clarke and 3-2 v Tomas Majewski, who was a place ahead of him 6th to 7th at the Worlds. Those positions were, however, reversed in the DL final. Ryan Crouser was good indoors and started with 21.11 outdoors, but his form fell away thereafter.

Most competitions over 20.80: Storl 16+3i, Kovacs 13, Walsh 12, Richards, Hoffa 8; Cantwell 7+1i, Whiting 6+4i, Kolasinac 3+2i, Clarke 3, Crouser 3+1i.

1. Kovacs, 2. Storl, 3. Walsh, 4. Richards, 5. Hoffa, 6. Cantwell, 7. Whiting, 8. Kolasinac, 9. Majewski, 10. Clarke.

Discus

AFTER SIX SUCCESSIVE years at the top Robert Harting was side-lined by a knee injury, and after nine years in the top six, Piotr Malachowski ranks top for the first time. He topped the year list with 68.29, had easily the best depth of top marks and his 13 wins in 18 competitions included the World title and four in DL competition. Philip Milanov made a big improvement to rank for the first time. His busy season included the World Universities title and World silver, and he was 4-3 against the World bronze medallist Robert Urbanek, who in turn beat the World 4th placer Gerd Kanter 7-5. While he lacked the distances of other men (only once over 64m, 64.73 for 5th at the Worlds) Daniel Ståhl fared well on win-loss, but he was 1-2 v Christoph Harting and 1-1 v Vikas Gowda, 8th and 9th at the Worlds but with substantially better marks. Ståhl was also 2-0 v Zoltán Kővágó, who was 2-1 v Gowda and also had good marks but slipped to dnq 18th at the Worlds. The Jamaican champion Fredrik Dacres did not compete in the Diamond League but won at the Pan-American Games and was 7th at the Worlds, a place behind Apostolos Parellis, who lost 2-1 to Benn Harradine, who was 10th at the Worlds. Martin Wierig had six competitions over 64m, Daniel Jasinski five and Andrius Gudzius four, although none of this trio qualified for the World final.

Most competitions over 65m: Malachowski 12, Milanov, Urbanek, Kővágó, Dacres 4, C Harting, Gowda, Gudzius 3.

1. Malachowski, 2. Milanov, 3. Urbanek, 4. Kanter, 5. C Harting, 6. Gowda, 7. Ståhl, 8. Kővágó, 9. Parellis, 10. Dacres

Hammer

FOR THE PAST three years Krisztián Pars and Pavel Fajdek have been vying for supremacy in world hammer throwing. This year, Fajdek, over seven years younger than his Hungarian rival, was clearly the best as he had the 12 best performances of the year, all over 80m and 15 of the top 17, topped by 83.93. Of his 17 competitions, he won all but the first, a loss to Pars at the European Winter Throws. For only the second time in 12 years Pars did not exceed 80m, but although 4th at the Worlds, when Dilshod Nazarov was 2nd and Wojciech Nowicki 3rd, he ranked second with a 4-2 record v Nazarov, who beat Nowicki 7-0. Mostafa Al-Gamal, 7th at the Worlds, was just 1cm behind Pars for 2/3 on the World list at 79.90 and beat Nowicki and Sergey Litvinov 3-1. Russian champion Litvinov's World 5th and slightly better set of marks just gives him precedence over Marcel Lomnicky, 8th at the Worlds, and Nick Miller, who won the European U23 title and took the 31 year-old British record, but although Miller was 2-1 v both of them his 11th place at the Worlds with 72.94 let him down (after 77.42 in qualifying). Lomnicky was 4-3 v Litvinov to emphasise how close these men were, There was then a gap before the top ten is filled out by David Söderberg and Ashraf Amjad El-Seify, 6th and 9th at the Worlds, but neither having too much to back this up. Just missing out was Roberto Janet, 12th Worlds, NACAC champion and 2nd to Kibwe Johnson (dnq 16th Worlds) at the Pan-Am Games.

Most competitions over 78m: Fajdek 17+1u, Pars 8, Nazarov, Nowicki 3.

1. Fajdek, 2. Pars, 3. Nazarov, 4. Al-Gamal, 5. Nowicki, 6. Litvinov, 7. Lomnicky, 8. Miller, 9. Söderberg, 10. El-Seify

Javelin

JULIUS YEGO SET four Kenyan records and his last two, massive efforts of 91.39 at Birmingham and 92.72 to win the World title, were also African and Commonwealth records. Although he only won four of his ten competitions, that was more than enough to ensure him top ranking. On win-loss he was 4-4 against both Tero Pitkämäki and Vitezslav Vesely, who were 3rd and 8th at the Worlds, and 5-3 against Thomas Röhler, 4th Worlds. Ihab Abdelrahman El Sayed took the World silver medal, but was beaten 7-1 by Pitkämäki, 5-2 by Vesely and 5-3 by Röhler. Also Vesely beat Röhler 6-3 to settle the order of the top five. Antti Ruuskanen was 5th at the Worlds and, although he failed at the Worlds (dnq 26th), Keshorn Walcott had good marks, was Pan-Am champion and 3rd in the DL final at Brussels behind Pitkämäki (third DL win of 2015) and Röhler and ahead of Yego, Johannes Vetter, Vesely, Andreas Hofmann and Abdelrahman. So the top seven were the same as in 2014 although in a different order. Vetter beat Hoffmann 4-1, although they were 7th and 6th respectively at the Worlds. Both these men had win-loss advantage over Jakub Vadlejch, who had good marks and was 2-1 v Ari Mannio, but disappointed with dnq 20th at the Worlds. Andreas Thorkildsen sat out the season following hip surgery.

Most competitions over 84m/82.50m: Pitkämäki 10/15, Röhler 8/14, Ruuskanen 8/10, Yego, Vadlejch 6/9; Vesely 5/9, Walcott 5/8, Abdelrahman 4/7, Hofmann 3/5, Arai 3/4, Vetter 2/6, Mannio 1/6, Wirkkala 1/4, Laanmäe 0/4.

1. Yego, 2. Pitkämäki, 3. Vesely, 4. Röhler, 5. Abdelrahman, 6. Ruuskanen, 7. Walcott, 8. Vetter, 9. Hofmann, 10. Vadlejch.

Decathlon

ASHTON EATON CONTESTED just one decathlon – but what a performance he gave, winning the World title with a world record 9045 that was set up by his fantastic 45.00 for 400m at the end of the first day. The second highest score of the year was 8725 by Trey Hardee to win the US title but he sustained a back injury in the long jump and did not finish at the Worlds; this makes him hard to rank. Damien Warner was only 14th in Götzis due to no throws in the shot, but then set Canadian records of 8659 at the Pan-Ams and 8695 for the World silver. Rico Freimuth did not finish at Ratingen, but was 4th at Götzis and 3rd at the Worlds and others who did well at both these major contests were Ilya Shkurenyov 5/4 (also 1st European Cup, 3rd Talence), Kai Kazmirek 1/6 (dnf Ratingen) and Michael Schrader 2/7 (1st Ratingen). Kevin Mayer was sixth on the world list with 8469, but injury prevented any more decathlons. Larbi Bouraada was 5th at the Worlds in his only decathlon, and Willem Coertzen did not finish in Beijing but had three good results: 3rd Götzis, 2nd Ratingen and 1st Talence. Kurt Felix was 8th, Oleksiy Kasyanov 9th and Maicel Uibo 10th at the Worlds with Felix 2nd at the Pan-Ams, Kasyanov 2nd at the European Cup and Talence, and Uibo over 8300 points twice (to win SEC and NCAA titles) in the USA.

The top indoor heptathlon score was 6353 by Shkurenyov to win the European title.

1. Eaton, 2. Warner, 3. Freimuth, 4. Shkurenyov, 5. Kazmirek, 6. Schrader, 7. Hardee, 8. Coertzen, 9. Bouraada, 10. Uibo

20 Kilometres Walk

THE WORLD ROAD record was broken in successive weeks in March, first by Yohann Diniz and then by Yusuke Suzuki in the Asian Championship race on a weekend when Diniz also recorded the year's third best mark of the year before missing the rest of the year with a groin injury. Suzuki had been 2nd in the Japanese Championships to Eiki Takahashi but later failed to finish at the Worlds. The one other 20k race for Diniz was 3rd at the European Cup behind Miguel Ángel López and Matej Tóth, whose other 20ks were 2nd to Christopher Linke and dnf Rio Maior. López, however, went on to win the World title after a great race against Wang Zhen, who had earlier won the Chinese Trial race and at La Coruña, when he was followed by Chen Ding, Cai Zelin, López, Dane Bird-Smith (8th Worlds and 1st WUG) and Takahashi (47th Worlds). López and Wang were the two men to have three sub-1:20 races and Cai and Chen had been 2nd and 3rd at the Chinese trials and were 5th and 9th at the Worlds. Other top placers at the Worlds were Ben Thorne, 3rd (and 2nd WUG, but down the field in earlier races including 23nd at La Coruña), Igor Hlavan, 4th (5th European Cup, 6th WUG, 20th La Coruña), and the most prolific racer Caio Bonfim 6th; his 11 races also included 3rd Pan-Ams, 8th La Coruña, 2nd Pan-Am Cup and 3rd to 4th in four big European races. Eider Arévalo won at Rio Maior and was 7th Worlds. Kim Hyun-sub was 10th Worlds after 2nd Asian Champs and 3rd Taicang (won by Chen).

1. López, 2. Wang Zhen, 3. Diniz, 4. Suzuki, 5. Cai Zelin, 6. Chen Ding, 7. Bird-Smith, 8. Bonfim, 9. Arévalo, 10. Kim Hyun-sub.

50 Kilometres Walk

MATEJ TÓTH HAD a perfect year as he won at Dudince in 3:34:38, the third fastest of all-time, and then the World title in 3:40:31. The year's second fastest was Hiroki Arai, Japanese champion in 3:40:20. To that he added 4th at the Worlds behind the other medallists Jared Tallent (only 50k of 2015) and Takayuki Tanii, who had been 2nd to him in the Japanese race. Mikhail Ryzhov and Ivan Noskov were 1st and 2nd at the European Cup, but did not contest the Worlds as the doping enquiries into Russian walking continued and they were both suspended, so are not ranked. Next best at the Worlds with their other races were: 5 Robert Heffernan (4th Dudince), 6 Zhang Lin & 7 Yu Wei (2nd and 1st in the Chinese trial), 8 Andrés Chocho (2 Chihuahua, 1st Pan-Ams). Ninth was the amazing Jesús Ángel García at his record 12th World Championship (dq European Cup). At the Pan-Am Games 2nd was Erick Barrondo, who did not finish at the Worlds, and 3rd Horacio Nava, who competed at 20k at the Worlds, but won the Pan-Am Cup. Rafal Augustyn was only 26th at the Worlds but 2nd at Dudince, where Lukasz Nowak was 3rd and eight men broke 3:50, the second best depth of the year to the 12 who did so in Beijing. In December Evan Dunfee (12th Worlds) improved the North American record.

1. Tóth, 2. Tallent, 3. Tanii, 4. Arai, 5. Heffernan, 6.Zhang, 7. Yu, 8. Chocho, 9. Dunfee, 10. Nava

Woman Athlete of the Year

TOP WOMEN'S PERFORMANCE of 2015 was the marvellous world record 3:50.07 for 1500m run by Genzebe Dibaba at Monaco. She won her three competitions at 1500m including the World Championship when she ran an amazing long drive for the tape such that her last 800m was an amazing 1:56.94. She had started the year with a world indoor record for 5000m with 14:18.86 at Stockholm and at this distance ran three brilliant times before finding trying to double back from the 1500m too much at the Worlds, as unable to cope with the searing pace set by Almaz Ayana, she fell back to third. Then she was beaten by Ayana in the DL final for 3000m in Zürich. Meanwhile Anita Wlodarczyk won all her eleven hammer competitions, with the eight best marks of the year, headed by a world record 81.08 and complete domination at the Worlds with two more 80m throws. It is a close call between these two women for athlete of the year but perhaps the sheer brilliance of that run to break the 22 year-old 1500m record just shades it in Dibaba's favour. The other standard event at which the world record was broken was the women's 20k walk, at which Liu Hong, later world champion, recorded 1:24:38 at La Coruña.

Other athletes who were unbeaten are headed by Caterine Ibargüen, who won all her nine triple jump competitions maintaining an unbeaten record from 2012. The other world champions who went through the year undefeated at that event in limited competition were Allyson Felix, four finals at 400m, and Vivian Cheruiyot, who won her three races at 10,000m.

Shelly-Ann Fraser-Pryce was undefeated in seven events at 100m after 5th in her first race of the year (and won one of two at 200m) and Ayana lost just once in two finals at 3000m and three at 5000m – to Dibaba over 5000m in Saint-Denis. Dafne Schippers, concentrating in 2015 on the sprints rather than multi-events, showed her exciting talent headed by gold at 200m and silver at 100m at the Worlds. In all her finals she won 4 of 5 (one dq) at 60m, including the European Indoors, 7 of 9 at 100m and 5 of 7 at 200m, plus a 2nd at 150m. Ibargüen and Sandra Perkovic (DT) each had six wins in the Diamond League, while Christina Schwanitz SP) and Eunice Sum (800m) had five each.

Selections for World Top Ten

	PJM	TFN	AI
Genzebe Dibaba	1	1	1
Anita Wlodarczyk	2	2	2
Caterine Ibargüen	3	5	4
Dafne Schippers	4	3	3
Almaz Ayana	5	4	7
Shelly-Ann Fraser-Pryce	6	6	6
Allyson Felix	7	7	5
Liu Hong	8	8	9
Sandra Perkovic	9		-
Tianna Bartoletta	10		10
Christina Schwanitz		9	
Zuzana Hejnová		10	
Jessica Ennis-Hill	-		8

Note Track & Field News excludes cross-country and road (apart from marathon) races

IAAF: Dibaba; Shortlist: Schippers, Wlodarczyk

100 Metres

SHELLY-ANN FRASER-PRYCE ran three of the four 100m times under 10.80 in 2015, the other being 10.79 by English Gardner. Fraser-Pryce was only 5th in her opening race in Shanghai, but won the remaining seven and had a 0.05 margin in taking the World title from Dafne Schippers, who in turn was 0.05 ahead of Torie Bowie. Schippers had seven wins and just one other loss – 4th at Saint-Denis, where Fraser-Pryce ran the year's fastest time of 10.74, followed by Blessing Okagbare and Gardner. Bowie, Gardner and Jasmine Todd were 1-2-3 at the US Champs, followed under 11 secs by Jeneba Tarmoh, Tianna Bartoletta and Jenna Prandini (NCAA champion). Bowie, with five sub 10-90 times plus 10.72w, was 3-0 v Veronica Campbell-Brown, 4th at the Worlds, and 2-0 v Okagbare, who was only 8th at the Worlds, although running 11.02, but 2-1 v VCB and 2-2 v Bowie. Michelle Lee Ahye and Kelly-Ann Baptiste were 5th and 6th at the Worlds after 1st and 2nd at the Trinidad Champs. Elaine Thompson was undefeated, but her only DL appearances were in B races and she was just beaten by Gardner at Eugene in a rare clash against the top women. Murielle Ahouré did well in four DL races but, like Gardner, went out in the semis in the Worlds. Also close to the top ten were Natasha Morrison (2nd Jamaican, 7th Worlds) and Candyce McGrone. Overall standards were very high with 57 sub-11.00 times by 17 women (plus 15 wind-assisted times). In 2014 there were just 15 such times by 6 women (and 4 wind assisted).

At 60m indoors Schippers (European Indoors) and Ahouré (Millrose Games) head the world list with 7.05. Schippers had four and Ahouré three times at 7.10 or better,

Most times under 11.00/11.10: Fraser-Pryce 8+1w/8+1w, Okagbare 6/10, Schippers 5+1w/9+2w, Bowie 5+2w/9+2w, Gardner 4+2w/6+2w, Thompson 4/6, Ahye 4+2w/5+2w, Prandini 3+2w/4+3w, Baptiste 3/8+2w, Campbell-Brown 3/7, Ahouré 2/6, Tarmoh 2+1w/3+1w, Todd 1+4w/1+5w, Bartoletta 1+2w/4+2w, Pierre 1+1w/5+2w, Morrison 1/4, Asher-Smith 1/3, Jeter 3w/2+3w, Ta Lou 1w/4+1w, Bryant 1w/2+3w, Henry-Robinson 1w/2+2w, R Santos 5+1w.

1. Fraser-Pryce, 2. Schippers, 3. Bowie,
4. Okagbare, 5. Campbell-Brown, 6. Ahye,
7. Gardner, 8. Baptiste, 9. Thompson, 10. Ahouré

200 Metres

DAFNE SCHIPPERS WENT to third on the world all-time lists when her dip finish took her to the World title in 21.63 from Elaine Thompson, whose 21.66 was the fastest ever non-winning mark. Schippers lost twice in seven events, to Allyson Felix in Lausanne and to Candyce McGrone in Monaco. Felix ran just four 200m races, winning also at Doha and second to Jeneba Tarmoh in Birmingham and to Schippers in Brussels, where, in the DL final, Thompson was 3rd, McGrone 4th, Tarmoh 5th and Sherone Simpson 6th. Veronica Campbell-Brown was beaten by Thompson and Simpson at the Jamaican Champs, but was 3rd and McGrone 4th at the Worlds. There the 19 year-old British star, Dina Asher-Smith, who broke UK records at 60m, 100m and 200m, was 5th, a place ahead of Tarmoh, who however, beat her in both their other clashes. As usual many of the top women sprinters competed sparingly at this distance. Tori Bowie for instance had four races but a big win in New York and was 2-0 v McGrone and Simpson, and Murielle Ahouré had three races. Jenna Prandini, busy in US collegiate action at 100m and long jump as well as 200m, was 22.21 for 2nd in the NCAAs, 0.03 behind Dezerea Bryant and then won the US title ahead of McGrone and Tarmoh with Kaylin Whitney and Bryant 4th and 5th. 17 year-old Whitney went on to win the Pan-Am title. Kyra Jefferson won the NCAA indoor title and ran a prolific series of fast times in the US outdoors, including when 4th at the NCAAs, 6th US Champs, 2nd Pan-Ams and 1st NACAC.

Most times under 22.70: Jefferson 9+1w+1i, McGrone, Bryant 9+1w; Schippers 9, Thompson, Tarmoh 8; Simpson 6, Asher-Smith, Whitney 5; Prandini 4+2w+1i, K Brown 4+2w, Felix, Bowie, Campbell-Brown 4; Ahouré, Lalova 3.

1. Schippers, 2. Thompson, 3. Felix,
4. Campbell-Brown, 5. McGrone, 6. Tarmoh,
7. Asher-Smith, 8. Prandini, 9. Bowie, 10. Simpson

400 Metres

THE TWO FASTEST times of the year came at the Worlds, when Allyson Felix won clearly from Shaunae Miller and Shericka Jackson became the fifth women to break 50 secs in 2015. The other two were Francena McCorory, who most surprisingly faded to 4th at the US Champs, and Sanya Richards-Ross, who did not make it beyond the US semis. McCorory still had four DL wins and was 1-1 v Miller. Apart from her surprise World bronze, Jackson ran only at Kingston, but there was 2nd in the Jamaican Champs to Christine Day (World 4th) and ahead of Stephenie Ann McPherson. Another Jamaican Novlene Williams-Mills did not run in that race but came 6th at the Worlds and was 5-3 v Day and 3-1 v Phylis Francis, US 3rd placer and World 7th. Natasha Hastings was 5th in her World semi and was beaten 6-1 by McPherson, but was ahead on win-loss of the other Jamaicans: 1-0 v Jackson, 6-1 v Day, and 6-3 v Williams-Mills. Former World and Olympic champion Christine Ohuruogu was 8th at the Worlds and just misses a ranking.

Most times under 50.80: McCorory 10, Miller, McPherson 8; Felix 6, Jackson, Day, Francis 5; Hastings, Richards-Ross 4; P George 3.

1. Felix, 2. Miller, 3. McCorory, 4. Richards-Ross,
5. McPherson, 6. Jackson, 7. Hastings, 8. Day,
9. Williams-Mills, 10. Francis

800 Metres

THE WORLD CHAMPIONSHIPS races were of a high standard with 17 women breaking 2 minutes in the semis and all eight in the final, but the result was far from predictable, and the form of many of the top women at the event in 2015 was most variable. Eunice Sum stood out in ranking first for the third successive year; although beaten by Maryna Arzamasova and Melissa Bishop at the Worlds, she won all her other seven races, six of them DL races and topping the world list with 1:56.99 at Saint-Denis. The next three fastest times were from

Bishop, Arzamasova and Sum in their World semi. Arzamasova only won one other race, the BLR Champs, and did not break 2 minutes until Beijing, but ran 1:58s for 3rd at Berlin and 4th at Rieti afterwards. Similarly Bishop excelled in the second half of the season but was beaten 4-1 by compatriot Fiona Benson in the first part. Selina Büchel made a big impression with six wins and 3rd at Saint-Denis in her first seven races, but just missed the World final, and Lynsey Sharp disappointed with 8th in her World semi but was another with good second half results and 3-1 v Arzamasova and 2-1 v Büchel, but beaten 3-0 by Bishop. Sharp was 2nd to Sum in the DL final in Zürich and ran her fastest, 1:57.71, in her last race to win in Berlin. Rabab Arrafi was 4th at the Worlds, but she only had three other moderate 800m races, and Shelyane Oskan-Clarke made a fine breakthrough to make the World final and place 5th but did not otherwise break 2 minutes, while the World 6th to 8th: Nataliya Lupu, Joanna Józwik and Rénelle Lamote showed more good form as did German champion Fabienne Kohlmann; they were closely matched. Ajee' Wilson ran 1:57.87 for 2nd in Eugene and won in New York, but had to miss the Worlds through injury. Sifan Hassan was quickest when 5th in her World semi, but had good results with 2nd in London and 4th in Zürich.

Most times under 1:59.8: Sum 8, Kohlmann, Sharp 6; Arzamasova 5, Bishop, Büchel, Almanza, Ludlow 4; Lupu, Józwik, Lamote, Price 3.

1. Sum, 2. Arzamasova, 3. Bishop, 4. Sharp, 5. Lamote, 6. Büchel, 7. Lupu, 8. Kohlmann, 9. Józwik, 10.Wilson.

1500 Metres

GENZEBE DIBABA HAD set four world indoor records, but her first outdoor one was very special, as she improved from her 2014 best of 3:55.17i to 3:50.07 at Monaco, thus removing one of those incredible times set at the Chinese National Games of 1993 (3:50.46 by Qu Yunxia). Dibaba only had two other 1500m races – 3:54.11 African record at Barcelona and her win at the World Champs. Sifan Hassan had the next two fastest times, 3:56.05 and 3:56.33mx, but was beaten 2-1 by Faith Kipyegon, including 2nd to 3rd at the Worlds and 1st and 2nd in the year's fastest mile, the DL final at Brussels when Kipyegon ran 4:16.71 to Hassan's 4:18.20. Jennifer Simpson was 11th at the Worlds when her shoe was ripped off in a clash, but had wins in Eugene and Rome (Hassan 2nd) and was 3rd in Lausanne and 4th in Monaco and Brussels. Shannon Rowbury was a place ahead of her in the last and 3rd in Monaco, and 3-2 ahead overall including World 7th but ranks behind the World 4-5 the junior Dawit Seyaum and Laura Muir, who won in Oslo from Kipyegon and Seyaum. In Rome Seyaum was 3rd and Muir 4th. In the DL final 5th was Mercy Cherono, 6th Abeba Aregawi (also World 6th after being held back by a thigh injury) and 7th Rabab Arrafi (World 9th and beaten 3-0 by Aregawi), while after the top seven the only other woman who broke 4 minutes for 1500m was Maureen Koster when 6th in Monaco, but she went out in her semi at the Worlds. Anna Mishchenko started well with three wins in four races and three times sub-4:03 but after 10th in Rome ended her season with a poor run at home; she beat Arrafi and Koster 2-1 and would have taken the final ranking spot but her results from 2012 were annulled in February 2016.

Fastest indoors at 1500m was Hassan with 4:00.46 and 4:02.57 and at 1 mile Rowbury with 4:22.56. Axumawit Embaye was second fastest at both distances in 4:02.92 and 4:23.50.

Most times under 4:04 (or 4:23.6M): Hassan 8+2i, Kipyegon, Simpson 5, Mishchenko 4, Rowbury 3+1i, Dibaba, Seyaum, Aregawi, Muir 3, Embaye 1+2i.

1 .Dibaba, 2. Kipyegon, 3, Hassan, 4. Simpson, 5. Seyaum, 6. Muir, 7. Rowbury, 8. Cherono, 9. Aregawi, 10. Arrafi.

3000 Metres

THERE WAS LESS action than usual at this event. Almaz Ayana won in Rabat in 8:22.22 and in Zürich in 8:22.34 from Genzebe Dibaba 8:26.54 and the next three women on the world list: Senbere Teferi, Jenny Simpson and Mercy Cherono in 8:34-8:35 times with Vivian Cheruiyot 6th (as well as a distant 2nd in Rabat), Shannon Rowbury 7th and Viola Kibiwot 8th.

5000 Metres

GENZEBE DIBABA STARTED the year by taking 5.51 secs off the world indoor record with 14:18.86 at Stockholm. Outdoors she tried hard to get older sister Tirunesh's world record of 14:11.15, but could not quite do it although her 14:19.76 at Eugene, 14:21.29 at Oslo and 14:15.41 at Saint-Denis all went into the top ten performances of all time. She beat Almaz Ayana (14:21.97) at Saint-Denis after Ayana had moved to third on the world all-time list with 14:14.32 at Shanghai. The showdown came in Beijing with Dibaba the favourite, but having won the 1500m five days earlier, she had to yield to Ayana from three laps to go and ended up well beaten and indeed passed in the finish by Senbere Teferi. The third fastest women was Faith Kipyegon, 14:31.95 for 2nd at Eugene, well clear of 3-7: Vivian Cheruiyot (her only 5000m), Sally Kipyego, Alemitu Haroye, Irene Cheptai and Viola Kibiwot. But Saint-Denis had the greatest depth with eight women under 14:45. Placing 3-8 there were Mercy Cherono, Kibiwot, Teferi, Gelete Burka, Kipyegon and Haroye. At the Worlds Kibiwot was 4th, Cherono 5th, Janet Kisa 6th and Cheptai 7th. Kibiwot and Teferi were 2nd and 3rd at Shanghai and 3rd and 2nd at Oslo, so 2-2 on win-loss, while Cherono won in London. Kipyego had a win in Stanford, while Burka was 9th in Shanghai and 4th in Oslo.

Most times under 15:10: Kibiwot 5, G Dibaba, Ayana, Teferi, Cheptai 4; Cherono, Haroye 3.

1. Ayana, 2. G Dibaba, 3. Teferi, 4. Kibiwot, 5. M Cherono, 6. Kipyegon, 7. Kipyego, 8. Haroye, 9. Burka, 10. Cheruiyot

10,000 Metres

THE ETHIOPIAN TRIAL race at Hengelo provided the fastest seven women in the world in 2015 with Gelete Burka, Alemitu Haroye, Belaynesh Oljira, Mamitu Daska and Wude Ayalew all breaking 31 minutes. Burka also won at Stanford (3 April) in 31:08.16 from Shalane Flanagan and Jip Vastenburg, but Vivian Cheruiyot outkicked her to win the World title in a slower race and won her other two races, a virtually solo 31:13.29 at Brussels in July and the Kenyan Trials. Molly Huddle beat Flanagan for the US title and they were 4th and 6th at the Worlds, but in that race Huddle was surprised on the line for the bronze by Emily Infeld, who had been 6th at Stanford (2 May race) and 3rd in the US Champs. Sally Kipyego was 6th and Betsy Saina 8th at the Worlds after Saina had been 2nd and Kipyego a non-finisher at the Kenyan Trials. Haroye was 7th and Oljira 9th at the Worlds with Susan Kuijken 10th and European U23 champion Vastenburg 11th. Alice Aprot won the African Games title from Gladys Chesire, Burka and Ayalew, but had no other 10,000m races. Only three of the 2014 top ten are in this year.

1. Cheruiyot, 2. Burka, 3. Huddle, 4. Flanagan, 5. Infeld, 6. Kipyego, 7. Haroye, 8. Saina, 9. Oljira, 10. Aprot

Half Marathon

JUST AS IN 2014 Florence Kiplagat set a world record at Barcelona in February, improving from 65:22 to 65:09, and taking her intermediate 20k record from 61:56 to 61:54. Next fastest was Mary Keitany with 66:02 at Ra's Al-Khaymah from Mamitu Daska 66:27 and Cynthia Limo 67:02. Keitany had two more important wins, 66:38 at Olomouc and 67:32 in the Great North Run. Gladys Cherono was the other women under 67 mins, as she won in Istanbul in 66:38, and the most prolific racer at top level was Worknesh Degafa with four times at 68:37 or better, topped by a win in Prague in 67:14 after she had been RAK 5th in 70:45. Flomena Cheyech beat Limo and Daska in Luanda and also beat Degefa at Yangzhou, and Limo won in New Delhi in 68:35.

Marathon

TWO WOMEN BROKE 2:20 in 2015, Gladys Cherono 2:19:25 in Berlin, and Mare Dibaba 2:19:52 in Xiamen. Dibaba was 2nd to Caroline Rotich in Boston and beat a good field to win the World title. Cherono was 2nd in Dubai in 2:20:03 in what was easily the top race for depth of times, as the winner Aselefech Mergia ran 2:20:02. They were followed by Lucy Kabuu 2:20:21, Shure Demise in a world junior record 2:20:59, and then Aberu Kebede, Mulu Seboka, and four more under 2:24. Tigist Tufa was a non-finisher in Dubai, going on to win in London, 6th Worlds and 3rd in New York. Mary Keitany was 2nd in London and won in New York, while Mergia was 4th and 2nd in these two races. Other Marathon Major winners were Florence Kiplagat at Chicago (also 5th London) and Birhane Dibaba at Tokyo (also 3rd Chicago). Kebede was 2nd in Berlin in 2:20:48 and 7th in Boston, Demise 8th in Boston and 1st in Toronto, Seboka 5th in Chicago. The one women to run three sub-24 times was Yebrqual Melese, winner in Houston and Prague and 2nd in Chicago. 2nd to 4th at the Worlds were Hellah Kiprop (2nd Tokyo), Eunice Jepkirui (1st Nagoya) and Jemina Jelagat (6th London).

1. M Dibaba, 2. Cherono, 3. Keitany, 4. Mergia, 5. Tufa, 6. Kebede, 7. F Kiplagat, 8. Melese, 9. B Dibaba, 10. Kiprop

3000 Metres Steeplechase

EASILY THE MOST impressive run at the event was 9:05.36 by Habiba Ghribi in winning the DL final at Brussels when second to her was Hyvin Jepkemoi in 9:10.15. Ghribi had also beaten Jepkemoi 9:11.28 to 9:12.51 at Monaco and these were the four fastest times of the year. But Ghribi's only other race was at the Worlds when Jepkemoi beat her for the gold by 0.13, while Jepkemoi contested eight events with four wins, three seconds and one third. Virginia Nyambura made a huge breakthrough as from a previous best of 9:58.08 (2013), she ran nine races at 9:33.69A or better with three under 9:20 and three DL wins, although 7th at the Worlds. As in 2014 Hiwot Ayalew and Sofia Assefa were close rivals with Assefa 3-2 up on win-loss including 4th to 6th at the Worlds, Assefa 1st and Ayalew 2nd at the African Games, and 3rd and 4th at the DL final behind the big two, followed by Purity Kirui, Nyambura, Stephanie Garcia and Emma Coburn. Nyambura was ahead of both Assefa and Ayalew on win-loss but behind in the two biggest races. Gesa-Felicitas Krause was much the best European with 3rd at the Worlds, two places ahead of US champion Coburn. Kirui was 2nd to Jepkemoi at the Kenyan Champs but missed the Worlds as she was 4th at the Trials, but she ran sub-9:18 for 5th at Monaco and Brussels. 9-11 at the Worlds were Garcia, Salima El Ouali Alami and Ruth Chebet, the Arab and World Military champion who was 3-1 v Tigist Mekonnen, who was 2-0 v Lydia Chepkurui. The 2013 world champion Milcah Chemos was prevented from competing by a hamstring injury.

Most times under 9:30: Ayalew, Nyambura 8, Jepkemoi 7, Assefa, Coburn 5; Ghribi, Garcia 4; Alami, Chebet, Chepkurui, Krause, Quigley 3.

1. Ghribi, 2. Jepkemoi, 3. Nyambura. 4. Assefa, 5. Ayalew, 6. Krause, 7. Coburn, 8. Kirui, 9. Chepkurui, 10. Garcia

100 Metres Hurdles

THIS WAS A fascinating year for the event with five US athletes sharing the 18 fastest wind-legal times of the year (12.55 or better). Yet none of them took a medal at the Worlds, where the upset medallists were Danielle Williams, Cindy Roleder and Alina Talay with the sixth fastest US runner Brianna Rollins (competing on a wild card as defending champion) in 4th place followed by Tiffany Porter. Sharika Nelvis and Jasmin Stowers shared the seven fastest times with Nelvis heading the world list with 12.34 in a US Champs heat followed by 12.37 in her semi. However, Nelvis slowed to 3rd in 12.59 in the final behind Dawn Harper Nelson and Kendra Harrison. The topsy-turvy form at the Worlds included Harper Nelson crashing out in her semi-final, K Harrison false-starting in hers and Nelvis clobbering the first hurdle to come in last in the final. The Americans dominated on times and normal service was resumed in the DL final in Brussels, where Harper Nelson won from Nelvis, Stowers, Porter, Roleder, Noemi Zbären and Talay. Win-loss guided me to rank them: Harper Nelson beat Nelvis and Stowers 5-4, Nelvis was 4-3 v Stowers, 4-2 v Rollins and 7-1 v Porter, Stowers was 4-1 v Rollins and 5-1 v Porter, who was 1-1 with K Harrison. Apart from Nelvis who went 3-3 with her, all had the advantage over Queen Harrison, 4th in the US Champs and Pan-Am Games champion. The surprise world champion Williams also won the Jamaican and WUG title but only contested one DL race (3rd in New York) and was well down on times. Sally Pearson started the year with four wins, but after 4th in Doha her season ended prematurely when she broke her left forearm in a fall in Rome. Lolo Jones did not finish in the US final but was 3-0 v Talay and 1-2 v Roleder.

At 60m indoors Nelvis headed the world list with 7.83 and lost only once in eight finals; she beat Stowers, who won the US title, at the Millrose Games. Talay was European champion and lost just once, to Nelvis in Malmö. Kendra Harrison won her two events, taking SEC and NCAA titles.

Most times at 12.70 or faster: Nelvis 12+1w, Porter 10, Stowers 9+2w, K Harrison 9+1w, Harper Nelson 9, Rollins 6, Q Harrison 5+1w, Pearson 3, L Jones 2+2w.

1. Harper Nelson, 2.Nelvis, 3. Stowers, 4. Rollins, 5. Porter, 6. K Harrison, 7. Williams, 8. Q Harrison, 9. Roleder, 10. Jones

400 Metres Hurdles

ALTHOUGH NOT AS dominant as in 2013, Zuzana Hejnová was clearly number one, winning 7 of her 9 competitions, including the World title in the year's best of 53.50 and four DL races. Second fastest was Shamier Little with 53.74 at the Worlds; she also won US and Pan-Am titles and her only loss was when 2nd at the Worlds (her pre-2015 best was 55.07). Sara Peterson made a notable advance, as at the age of 28 she ran 12 times under her previous best of 55.68 (2012); her four Danish records were topped by 53.99 and she was 4th at the Worlds and was 3-1 on win-loss over the World 3rd placer Cassandra Tate. Tate was 2nd and Kori Carter 3rd at the US Champs, but Carter had little to back that up and did not finish her semi at the Worlds. Georganne Moline was unfortunate to be a non-finisher at the US Champs but had a strong season and was 4-0 v Janeive Russell and 5-0 v Eilidh Child, who were 5th and 6th at the Worlds, where the other finalists were Wenda Nel 7th and Kaliese Spencer 8th, Spencer, however, had three DL wins in the 54s and Nel was also ahead of Russell and Child on win-loss. At the DL final in Zürich Hejnová won from Petersen, Moline, Spencer, Tate, Nel and Russell. The top ten is completed by Tiffany Williams, 5th US and NACAC champion. Kemi Adekoya was disqualified in her World heat but won the Asian and World Military titles.

Most times under 54.0/55.0: Hejnová 3/7, Little 3/6, Petersen 1/6, Tate 9, Moline, Nel 7, Child 6, Spencer, Williams 4; Russell 3.

1. Hejnová, 2. Little, 3. Petersen, 4. Tate, 5. Spencer, 6. Moline, 7. Nel, 8. Russell, 9. Child, 10. Williams

High Jump

CLOSELY MATCHED RIVALS, Anna Chicherova headed the world list with 2.03 at Lausanne and Mariya Kuchina's best was 2.01 when she won both the World title and at the DL final in Brussels. Blanka Vlasic and Chicherova also cleared 2.01 for silver and bronze at the Worlds, but Vlasic, with knee and Achilles problems, only contested two other events, 2nd with 1.97 in Rome and New York. Kuchina won 6 of her 8 competitions indoors and 10 of 15 outdoors; she beat Chicherova 4-1, the only loss being at the Russian Champs, where Chicherova won 2.00 to 1.97. Chicherova won 3 of her 7 events; she was 3-1 (1 tie) v Ruth Beitia, who beat Vlasic 2-1. Kamila Licwinko was best indoors where she set Polish records at 2.00, 2.01 and 2.02, although 3rd with 1.94 at the European Indoors behind Kuchina and Alessia Trost, but was also consistent outdoors and 4th at the Worlds, beating Beitia on countback at 1.99.

That height was also achieved by Marie-Laurence Jungfleisch in 6th place after she had a big win at Eberstadt with 1.96. Beitia beat Licwinko 4-1, but it was 2-0 to Licwinko indoors. Ana Simic, consistent at 1.91-1.94 outdoors, after 1.95 and 1.94 indoors, was 5-0 v Levern Spencer, who won Pan-Am and NACAC titles and was 2-1 v her St. Lucian compatriot NCAA champion Jeanelle Schepper, who was, however, ahead at the Worlds, 7th to 12=. Eleanor Patterson was unbeaten in Australia, but her 8th at the Worlds was her only other competition. She had better heights outdoors than Airine Palyste, who just missed the World final but was 2-0 v Erika Kinsey and had a good win in Doha and 4= in Monaco; she was much better indoors where she twice cleared 1.98. Just missing the top ten were Kinsey, Isobel Pooley, Asian champion Svetlana Radzivil, and Justyna Kaprzycka. Trost did well indoors but her summer campaign was ended by an Achilles injury as was that of the 2013 world champion Svetlana Shkolina, who jumped 1.95 indoors and only had three outdoor competitions, but beating Pooley and Jungfleisch 2-0 in these.

Most competitions over 2.00/1.96m outdoors (+indoors): Kuchina 4/6 + 0/4i, Beitia 1/7 + 0/1i, Chicherova 3/5, Vlasic 1/3, Licwinko -/7 + 3/4i, Trost 0/3i.

1. Kuchina, 2. Chicherova, 3. Beitia, 4. Vlasic (5), 5. Licwinko (4), 6. Jungfleisch, 7. Simic, 8. Spencer (-), 9. Schepper (-), 10. Patterson (-). Trost (8), Palsyte (9), Shkolina (10). (Including indoors)

Pole Vault

YARISLEY SILVA STRUGGLED for form at the start of the season, but came through for the top two marks of the year, 4.91 at Beckum and 4.90 to win the World title. Fabiana Murer matched her South American record with 4.85 for World silver when bronze went at 4.80 to Nikoléta Kiriakopoúlou, who was, however, ahead on win-loss, 5-2 v Silva and 4-3 v Murer and also won the DL final in Zürich, with the World 1-2 tying for second. Jenn Suhr had a thin season, competing only in North America before her World 4= (with Angelika Bengtsson and Sandi Morris). Crucially at the US Champs Suhr beat the two women who enlivened the US Collegiate season, Morris, who improved during the year from 4.55 to 4.76, and Demi Payne, who made an even bigger advance, from 4.29 to 4.75i/4.71.

Morris was NCAA champion indoors and Payne outdoors, but Payne managed only 4.30 in World qualifying. Apart from her no height in the World final, Russian champion Anzhelika Sidorova had a strong season and was 3-1 v Morris, but she was even better indoors, where she won Russian and European Indoor titles, her 4.80 at the last making her one of the five women to clear that height in 2015. Ekateríni Stefanídi (dnq 15th Worlds) and Bengtsson won silver and bronze in that event. Bengtsson was better indoors than out but 3-1 outdoors v Stefanídi, achieving her best (4.70) at the two major championships. Lisa Ryzih no heighted at the European Indoors but had a solid outdoor season, 12th Worlds and 2-1 v Stefanídi and 4-2 v Martina Strutz (World 8th), whom she beat for the German title. Silke Spiegelburg was the German 3rd and did not reach her usual heights, apart from 4.75 to win at the European Teams, and did not qualify for the World final, but was 4-1 v Bengtsson. Nicole Büchler just misses out, as does Li Ling, whose 4.66 at the Asian Champs and 4.60 at 8th at the Worlds were her only competitions over 4.50; she also won WUG and Chinese titles.

Most competitions over 4.60m (outdoors + in): Kiriakopoúlou 11+6i, Murer 9+3i, Silva 9, Morris 7+4i, Suhr 6+3i, Sidorova & Payne 5+5i; Stefanídi 4+6i, Ryzih 4+2i, Büchler, Strutz, Spiegelburg 4; Bengtsson 3+6i, Boyd 3, Krasnova 1+7i, Bauer 1+2i, Fiack 4i.

1. Silva, 2. Kiriakopoúlou, 3. Murer, 4. Suhr, 5. Sidorova, 6. Morris (7), 7. Bengtsson (8), 8. Ryzih (9), 9. Stefanídi (6), 10. Spiegelburg (-). Payne (10). (Including indoors)

Long Jump

TIANNA BARTOLETTA recaptured her World title ten years on from her win in Helsinki. For the first time since 1991 three women exceeded 7m at the Worlds as there were national records from Shara Proctor 7.07 and Ivana Spanovic 7.01 behind Bartoletta's last round 7.14. Excellence in depth had Christabel Nettey 4th with 6.95 followed by Lorraine Ugen 6.85, Malaika Mihambo 6.79 and Khaddi Sagnia 6.78. Bartoletta was also over 7m at Eugene and the US Champs and her nine long jump competitions were six firsts and three seconds: to Nettey in New York, and to Spanovic in Monaco and Zürich, where the Serbian improved to 7.02. Proctor, however, had a 3-2 advantage over Spanovic. Nettey was over her pre-2015 best three times indoors and eight times outdoors, and Ugen also found a new level of consistency; both these women were way down in the final big meetings at Zürich and Berlin, but these events were both too soon and too anti-climatic after Beijing. Sosthene Moguenara managed only 6.23 in World qualifying as her form fell away after an excellent indoor season, where she was over 6.80 twice including for the European Indoor silver behind Spanovic, and 3rd places outdoors in Rome 6.80 and European Team 6.79.

She also beat Mihambo, the European U23 champion, 2-1. Brittney Reese, was 2nd at US Champs with 6.97 but only jumped 6.39 in World qualifying and an even better set of marks was achieved by Quanesha Burks, who won the NACAC title with 6.93A and NCAA with 6.91, but whose ranking prospects were marred by 6th at the US Champs and 8th at the Pan-Ams. Better was Janay DeLoach, who had changed her take-off foot two years ago, 3rd US Champs, 8th Worlds and 4-0 v Darya Klishina, who had a best of 6.95 to win the European Team event and won in Rome with 6.89, but had modest form thereafter, including World 10th place. For Katarina Johnson-Thompson it was a case of what might have been with her narrow no jumps in the World heptathlon, and although she came back for 11th in the World final she was best indoors with a 6.93 at Birmingham (beating Nettey and Spanovic) and 6.89 in her European Indoor pentathlon. A knee injury prevented Éloyse Lesueur, top ranked in 2014, from competing outdoors after four events indoors.

Most competitions over 6.70m (outdoors/in): Bartoletta 9, Nettey 8+1w+3i, Proctor 8+1w, Ugen 6+1w, Spanovic 6+5i, Sagnia 6. Mihambo 5, Reese, Stuart 4+1w; Moguenara 4+4i, Klishina 4, Rotaru 3+1i, Burks 3+1w, Pidluzhnaya 3, Johnson-Thompson, Jimoh 1+2i; Koneva 3i

1. Bartoletta, 2. Proctor, 3. Spanovic, 4. Nettey, 5. Ugen, 6. Mihambo, 7. DeLoach (8), 8. Klishina (9), 9. Reese (-), 10. Moguenara (7). Johnson-Thompson (10). (Including indoors)

Triple Jump

CATERINE IBARGÜEN HAD her third successive unbeaten season. her nine wins (inc. six DL) taking her unbeaten run to 30. Of the 15 wind-legal competitions at 14.68 or better, she had 7 (plus 15.18w and 15.08w), Yekaterina Koneva 6 (two indoors), and Hanna Minenko and Olga Rypakova 1 each. While Koneva had clearly the second best set of marks, she disappointed with 7th at the Worlds and was beaten 2-1 by World runner-up Minenko, although she won the European Indoor title with Gabriela Petrova 2nd and Minenko 3rd. The Worlds order: 3 Rypakova, 4 Petrova, 5 Kimberley Williams and 6 Olha Saladukha is confirmed by their win-loss records as is Kristin Gierisch, also 4th European Indoors, for her World place of 8th. The World 9-10-11 were Jeanine Assani Issouf, Yorsiris Urrutia and Keila Costa, but Jenny Elbe, who missed the Worlds but was 2nd at the German Champs and World Universities, was 1-0 v Issouf and Costa, who had the best set of marks of this group.

Most competitions over 14.30m: Minenko 10+2i, Ibargüen 9+1w, Koneva 8+5i, Petrova 7+2i, Rypakova 7; Saladukha 5, Gierisch 1+1w+2i.

1. Ibargüen, 2. Minenko, 3. Koneva, 4. Rypakova, 5.Petrova, 6. Williams, 7. Saladukha, 8. Gierisch, 9. Elbe, 10. Costa. (Including indoors)

Shot

JUST THREE WOMEN exceeded 20m in 2015. Christina Schwanitz was much the most prolific with 9 such marks and winning 15 times (five DL) and 2nd twice in her 17 competitions. Both losses were to Gong Lijiao who pushed her hard at the Worlds and went over 20m four times in six competitions (two 1st, four 2nd). The World bronze medallist Michelle Carter threw 20.02 to win the US title. After the big three the best mark was 19.48 for 4th at the Worlds by Anita Márton, behind 16 at 19.50 plus by Schwanitz, 6 by Gong and 3 by Carter. Another three women went over 19m outdoors: Cleopatra Borel (twice), Gao Yang (when 5th at the Worlds) and Tia Brooks, after Brittany Smith and Yuliya Leontyuk just reached that level indoors. Gao is difficult to rank as her second best mark was 18.65, but she was the World Military champion and 2nd at the Asian and Chinese champs. BLR champion Alyona Dubitskaya was 6th at the Worlds and Leontyuk 7th. although she had generally better form indoors including 2nd to Márton at the Europeans. Several Americans vied for final places in the rankings, with little to choose between them. At the US Champs the order 1-5 was Carter, Brooks, Jeneva Stevens, Jill Camarena-Williams and Brittany Smith and at the Worlds Stevens was 10th and Brooks dnq 13th. Overall Smith was 5-4 v Brooks, and Stevens 3-2 v both Brooks and Smith (also 1-0 indoors). Camarena-Williams was 0-5 v Brooks but 3-2 v Stevens (including 2nd to 6th at the Pan-Ams won by Borel, and beating Stevens clearly at the NACAC) and 3-1 v Smith. Valerie Adams, so dominant over the past decade, returned from injury, but after four competitions in July in the 18.59 to 18.79 range decided that she could not compete as she would like at the Worlds, but she had positive win-loss records against all but the big three, for instance 3-1 v Borel.

Most competitions over 19m: Schwanitz 18, Carter 10+1i, Gong 8.

1. Schwanitz, 2. Gong, 3. Carter, 4. Márton, 5. Borel, 6. Adams, 7. Gao, 8. Dubitskaya, 9. Smith (10), 10. Brooks (-). – Leontyuk (9). (Including indoors).

Discus

FOR THE FOURTH successive year Sandra Perkovic ranks as number one; but she was beaten by Denia Cabellero at the Worlds, and while both had a throw over 70m in 2015, Cabellero heads the list with 70.65. Perkovic won 9 of her 11 competitions, including, as in 2014, six Diamond League meetings and was 3-1 v Caballero, who won 9 of 13 events, both losing at Lausanne to Yaimí Pérez at Lausanne, where Perkovic was 2nd and Cabellero 3rd. Caballero, Pérez and Gia Lewis-Smallwood (World 11th) were the 1-2-3 at the Pan-Am Games. Germany had four contenders for ranking places with the order at their champs being Julia Fischer, Nadine Müller, Shanice Craft and Anna Rüh, the latter two being 1st and 2nd at the Europeans U23s, and Craft 2-1 v

Rüh. Müller was 3rd, Fischer 5th and Craft 7th at the Worlds. Müller was 3-2 v Pérez although the Cuban had, just, the better marks. Dani Samuels was 6th at the Worlds and 2-2 v Pérez and Fischer. Asian champion Su Xinyue was 8th and US runner-up Whitney Ashley 9th at the Worlds but overall their records were inferior to the 10th Mélina Robert-Michon and 11th Lewis-Smallwood (US champion). The top ten are the same as in 2014, although in a different order.

Most competitions over 63m: Caballero, Perkovic 12; Samuels 11, Pérez, Fischer 9; Müller 8, Robert-Michon 5, Craft 4, Lewis-Smallwood, Rüh 3.

1. Perkovic, 2. Caballero, 3. Müller, 4. Pérez, 5. Samuels, 6. Fischer, 7. Robert-Michon, 8. Craft, 9. Lewis-Smallwood, 10. Rüh

Hammer

ANITA WLODARCZYK HAD a brilliant season to retain her top ranking, well clear of the rest. She won all her 11 competitions and had the eight best performances of the year, headed by a world record 81.08 at Cetniewo and 80.85 and 80.27 at the World Champs. Zhang Wenxiu was second on the world list with 76.33 for her World silver but Betty Heidler had the second best set of marks, with five competitions over 75m compared to ten by Wlodarczyk and one by Zhang. Heidler disappointed, however, with only 7th at the Worlds and 4th at the European Throws Cup although otherwise she had six wins and five second places. Alexandra Tavernier beat Heidler 2-1, 3rd at both European Throws and Worlds, but her best throws were three in the 74s. Zhang was also over 74m three times, also in winning the Chinese and World Military titles, but did not compete outside Asia.

Wang Zheng was 2nd in the Chinese Champs and 5th at the Worlds, a place behind Sophie Hitchon, who set two British records there and was 1-1 v Wang, 3-2 v Kathrin Klaas (World 6th) and 3-1 v Martina Hrasnová, who slipped to dnq 16th at the Worlds. Rosa Rodríguez, Amber Campbell and Sultana Frizell took the Pan-American Games medals and at the World Champs were respectively 11th, no throws in final, and dnq 13th. Campbell was 2-1 v Hrasnová, who was 3-1 v Frizell and 5-3 v Joanna Fiodorow (2nd WUG and dnq 17th Worlds). Amanda Bingson was 3rd at the US Champs and 9th at the Worlds, a place behind Zalina Marghieva, who, however, only had three competitions, and one ahead of Alena Soboleva, who was 2nd to Tavernier at the European U23s.

Most competitions over 72.50m: Wlodarczyk, Heidler 11; Wang Z 8, Tavernier 6, Zhang 4, Hrasnová 3.

1. Wlodarczyk, 2. Zhang, 3. Heidler, 4, Tavernier, 5. Wang, 6, Hitchon, 7. Klaas, 8. Rodríguez, 9. Campbell, 10. Hrasnová

Javelin

WHILE THERE WAS not a clear-cut world number one this year, winning the World title with the best throw of the year, 67.69, was enough to give this to Katharina Molitor. She also had two other competitions over 65m, in Luzern and at the German Champs, although with Bottrop these were her only wins from 11 events. Barbora Spotáková was the only other woman over 65m three times and, although only 9th at the Worlds, she had five major wins including at the DL final in Zürich and was 3-1 v Molitor and Lu Huihui, and 4-2 v Sunette Viljoen. Lu and Viljoen were 2nd and 3rd at the Worlds and Lu was 3-2 in their clashes although Viljoen had a better series of marks. Kimberley Mickle was only 22nd at the Worlds and was 2-2 v Lu and 2-1 v Li Lingwei (World 5th but little else) and Liz Gleadle (World 11th), but only contested seven events.

Christina Obergföll was the hardest to rank; she had a generally modest season but was over 64m twice, firstly when second at the German Champs ahead of Linda Stahl and then for a fine World 4th place; however, only 7th to 10th at 58-59m at Saint-Denis, Zürich and Berlin held her back. Christin Hussong was similarly inconsistent but excelled to win the European U23 tile with 65.60, and after 4th at the German Champs was 6th at the Worlds; 2-3 v Obergföll. Gleadle was 11th at the Worlds and 3-1 v Obergföll, 5-2 v Madara Palameika (dnq 13 Worlds) and 5-3 v Kara Winger (8th Worlds); she was crucially 2nd at the DL final when followed by Molitor, Palameika, Hussong, Stahl, Lu, Obergföll, Winger and Viljoen. Winger (US champ, 2nd to Gleadle at Pan-Ams) was 3-2 v Stahl (10th Worlds). Margaryta Dorozhon, dnq 16 Worlds, was 3-1 v Obergföll and 3-3 v Palameika.

Most competitions over 62m: Viljoen 10, Spotáková 8, Stahl, Gleadle, Palameika 7; Molitor, Lu 6; Obergföll, Mickle, Winger, Dorozhon 5; Li, Hussong, Ratej 4; Roberts 3.

1. Molitor, 2. Spotáková, 3. Lu Huihui, 4. Viljoen, 5. Gleadle, 6. Palameika, 7. Obergföll, 8. Hussong, 9. Mickle, 10. Stahl

Heptathlon

BRIANNE THEISEN-EATON recorded the top score of the season with 6808 at Götzis, but was beaten 6669 to 6554 at the Worlds by Jessica Ennis-Hill, who made a marvellous return to competition after the birth of her son in 2014 but was 388 points down on the Canadian when 4th at Götzis. Further Götzis/World placings were: Carolin Schäfer 2/dnf, Nadine Broersen 3/4, Nadine Visser 5/8, Anouk Vetter 6/12, Claudia Rath 7/5, Laura Ikauniece-Admidina 8/3, Nafissatou Thiam 9/11, Anastasiya Mokhnyuk 12/7, Xénia Krizsán 13/9, Györgyi Zsivoczky-Farkas dnf/6. At Ratingen the order was: Vetter, Jennifer Oeser (10 World), Rath with

Schäfer dnf and at Talence: Zsivoczky-Farkas, Mokhnyuk, Visser, dnf Broersen. Admidina was the only woman with three scores over 6400, including when she won the European Cup 2. Barbara Nwaba (11 Götzis) and Sharon Day-Monroe were 6th and 8= on the world lists with 6500 and 6458 at the US Champs but 27th (fell 100mh) and 14th at the Worlds. Katarina Johnson-Thomson crashed out of the World Champs with three no jumps in the long jump, all better jumps by far than anybody else but all just over the board denying her a likely medal; she also failed to finish in Talence in an unhappy injury-ridden season.

Easily the best indoor pentathlon score was 5000 by Johnson-Thomson at the European Indoors, where Thiam was 2nd, Eliska Klucinová 3rd and Yana Maksimova (earlier second best of the year with 4742) 4th.

1. Ennis-Hill, 2. Theisen-Eaton, 3. Ikauniece-Admidina, 4. Broersen, 5. Rath, 6. Zsivoczky-Farkas, 7. Visser, 8. Schäfer, 9. Vetter, 10. Mokhnyuk

20 Kilometres Walk

THE CONTINUING SCANDAL of the Russian walkers meant that none was chosen to compete in the Worlds. That left the Chinese as clear favourites and Liu Hong and Lu Xiuzhi duly delivered gold and silver to cheer home supporters. Lu had beaten Liu at the Chinese Trials but Liu clearly retained her IAAF World Race Walking Challenge title with further wins at Rio Maior and La Coruña (in a world record 1:24:38 with a final kilometre in 4:05). The next three fastest times of the year had come at the Russian Winter Championship from Elmira Alembekova, Marina Pandakova and Svetlana Vasilyeva with Vera Sokolova 4th for sixth on the world list behind Lu. Anisya Kirdyapkina was 5th, but went on to 2nd in the Russian Champs to Sokolova and to win the World Universities title from Pandakova.

The top race for depth of performance was at the European Cup with eleven women under 1:30. Alembekova won in 1:26:15 from Eleonora Giorgi (1st Dudince and 2nd Rio Maior), Vasilyeva, Anezka Drahotová (8th Worlds), Pandakova, Sokolova, Lyudmila Olyanovska, Elisa Rigaudo and Ana Cabecinha (4th Rio Maior, La Coruña and Worlds). Giorgi and Rigaudo were disqualified at the Worlds, where Antonella Palmisano (3rd Dudince) was the top Italian in 5th place. Olyanovska was 2nd at Dudince, 3rd at the European U23s behind Mariya Ponomaryova and Drahotová, and then 3rd at the Worlds. After 4th in the Chinese Trials, Qieyang Shenjie was 2nd at La Coruña and won the Chinese title. In the Challenge: Giorgi was 2nd and Erica de Sena (4th Dudince, 3rd La Coruña and 6th Worlds) 3rd. Brigita Virbalyte (1st Podébrady, 14th European Cup, 7th Worlds) was 2-1 v Drahotová. So overall there was a rather muddled situation, particularly as at the end of the year Alembekova and Sokolova were suspended and are left out of my rankings.

1. Liu Hong, 2. Lu Xiuzhi, 3. Giorgi, 4. Vasilyeva, 5. Olyanovska, 6. Kirdyapkina, 7. Pandakova, 8. Qieyang Shenjie, 9. Cabecinha, 10. Palmisano

Note abbreviations: DL = Diamond League, WUG = World University Games.

JUNIOR ATHLETES OF 2015

Men

Juniors to make the world (senior) top ten merit rankings were Abdelilah Haroun at 400m, Alfred Kipketer 800m, Robert Biwott 1500m, Yomif Kejelcha 5000m and Wang Jianan LJ.

100m: Jaylen Bacon ran the fastest time of 10.10, but perhaps the most significant result was Reynier Mena's win over Noah Lyles, 10.17 to 10.18, at the Pan-American Juniors after they had run 10.08w and 10.07w respectively in the heats.

200m: Noah Lyles ran 20.18 to win the US Junior title for 7= on the world all-time list and he also won the Pan-Am Juniors with 20.27. There were 16 wind-legal times under 20.50 with most 5 by Reynier Mena (2nd Pan-Am-J) and 3 by Lyles, Michael Norman (2nd US-J 20.24) and Abdul Hakim Sani Brown, who was the IAAF Rising Star of 2015 after winning the World Youth title in 20.34A.

400m: Abdelilah Haroun improved during the year from 45.74 to 44.27, second to Steve Lewis on the world junior all-time list. He ran the seven fastest junior times of 2015 to 44.85 (and five of the 20 world's best ever by juniors) as the next fastest was 17 year-old Akeem Bloomfield with 44.93. Christopher Taylor, at the age of 15, ran 45.30A and 45.27 when he won the World Youth title.

800m: Although Robert Biwott was easily the fastest junior with 1:43.56 (7th all-time), Alfred Kipketer was clearly the top man with 8 of the top 12 times from 1:44.07A to 1:45.45 (he was faster in 2014 at 1:43.95 when he won the World Junior title).

1500m: The 2013 World Youth champion Robert Biwott's 3:30.10 at Monaco was the second best ever by a junior and he ran the four fastest and six of the seven fastest times. 16 year-old Kumari Taki won the World Youth title in 3:36.38A.

5000m: Yomif Kejelcha, with three Diamond League wins and the African Junior title as well as World 4th, was the top junior star and also topped the junior list at 3000m 7:39.99. His 12:53.98 took him to seventh on the world junior all-time list. Japan-based Kenyan Hiram Ngatia had two wins and a second in Japanese races, all under 13:24.

10,000m: Joshua Cheptegei was easily the fastest at 27:27.57 and was 9th at the Worlds and the African Junior champion.

Mar: Edwin Kibet 2:08:17 and Tola Shure 2:08:53 went to 4th and 7th on the world junior all-time list.

3000mSt: Nicholas Bett was fastest at 8:19.26 and ran the top three and 4 of the best 5 times. Hailemariyam Aamare, who was 3rd in the African Games and 12th at the Worlds, had 4 of the best 11 times, but he was only 3rd at the African Juniors, won by Abraham Kibiwot, the second fastest junior of the year at 8:22.10, with Wogene Sebisibe (4th African Games, 2nd World Youths) 2nd. World Youth champion at 2000mSt was Vincent Kipyegon.

110mh: Fastest man over the 99cm hurdles was Misana Viltz with 13.21 to win the US junior title – and he also won the Pan-Am Juniors.

400mh: Jaheel Hyde moved up to 14th on the all-time list with his Jamaican Schools time of 49.01 and he ran 4 of the 5 best times. He also won a Carifta Games double at 110mh and 400mh. 17 year-old Norman Grimes won the Pan-American Juniors and won the World Youth title in 49.11, the fastest time over the 84cm hurdles; he also ran 36.10 for 300mh.

HJ: No stand-out this year with two men at 2.28 heading the lists.

PV: Adam Hague topped the rankings with 5.60 outdoors and 5.55 indoors, and won the European Junior title with 5.50. His four competitions at 5.50 or better was exceeded by Huang Bokai with six at 5.50.

LJ: Wang Jianan topped the list with 8.25 (5th on the world all-time junior list) for 3rd in the Shanghai DL and 8.18 for the World bronze medal. Maykel Massó jumped 8.12 (3rd all-time for youths) in Havana on the day after his 16th birthday and went on to win the World Youth title.

TJ: Two men dominated as they went over 17m while the third best junior was at 16.55. Nazim Babayev won the European Junior title with 17.04 and Lázaro Martínez had a best of 17.02 and the next three best marks. Leslie Caesar won the Pan-Am Juniors with 16.83w from Mártinez 16.52w.

SP: Konrad Bukowiecki, who remained a junior in 2016, was a super-star. With the 7.25kg shot he had 17 performances at 19.40 or better, topped by a world junior record 20.79 (although behind the unratified indoor 21.05 by Terry Albritton in 1974) and he also set European junior indoor records (twice) at 20.46. He now has 4 of the top 7 junior performances of all-time. With the 6kg shot he had four performances over 22m: 22.62 to win the European Juniors (a mark ever exceeded by just two juniors, David Storl and Jacko Gill), 22.21 and 22.12 outdoors and 22.38 indoors. Mohamed Hamza took the African Games silver medal with 19.78 and the next best man with the senior shot was Andrei Toader 19.11. With the 6kg shot John Maurins won the US Junior title with 21.90 for fifth on the all-time list.

DT: Top spot was closely contested. Matt Denny had the 2kg best with 62.58 for 2nd at the World University Games and Martin Markovic threw 62.43; these two marks ranking 6th and 8th on the world junior all-time list. Markovic topped the 1.75kg list with 68.48, but he was beaten, 68.02 to 67.11, by Bartlomiej Stój at the European Juniors, and these men are now 2nd and 3rd on the all-time list, Markovic moving up a place from the 66.94 with which he won the World Junior title in 2014, while Denny had a best of 66.66 with this implement (ranking sixth all-time from his 66.81 in November 2014).

HT: The best senior throw of 71.10 by Humberto Mansilla put him 80th on all all-time list. With the 6kg hammer three men went over 80m, Joaquin Gómez, South American record to win the S.American Junior title, 80.48 Matt Denny, Oceania record, and Humberto Mansilla, 80.21 to win the Pan-American Junior title. Bence Halász had a best of 79.86 and won the European Junior title with 79.60.

JT: On the very last day of the year Neraf Chopra threw an Indian junior record 81.04 for the only 80m throw by a junior in 2015, tenth on the world all-time list and a big improvement from his previous best of 77.67 to win India's senior title. Next best was 79.20 that Matija Muhar threw to win the European Junior title. Of the 15 performances over 77m, Muhar and Chopra had three each, but most was four by Ioánnis Kiriazís (best 78.41).

Dec: Harrison Williams had the top two scores with the senior specification, 7806 and 7679, and also the two scores over 8000 with the junior implements, 8037 to win the Pan-American Juniors and 8001 for the US Junior title. Next came the European Junior 1-2, Jan Dolezal 7929 and Karsten Warholm 7764 (a performance that he amazingly interrupted to win the 400m silver).

10,000m walk: Toshizaku Yamanishi's 39:29.83 took him to fourth on the junior all-time list. After the three fastest times were by Japanese, Diego García was an impressive winner at the European Juniors and he also recorded 1:21:35 at 20k.

20kW: Tomohiro Noda had the best two times, 1:20:08 (12th world all-time) and 1:20:59.

Women

Juniors to make the world (senior) top ten merit rankings were Dawit Seyaum (1500m) and Eleanor Patterson (HJ).

100m: The phenomenal Candace Hill, at 16 the new world youth record holder at 10.98, became the World Youth champion at 100m and 200m, and was the IAAF female Rising Star of the Year. She was undefeated in 17 100m competitions and went to third on the world junior all-time lists and Ángela Tenorio to fourth with 10.99 for 2nd at the Pan-American Games. That was Tenorio's only loss of the year at 100m.

200m: Hill won all her 12 200m competitions, and, as at 100m, set a world youth record, 22.43 at the World Youths. Tenorio ran four times sub-23 secs, headed by 22.59w and 22.84A; she was 4th at the Pan-Ams as well as completing a 100/200 double at the South American Juniors. But while Hill had the fastest time, Kaylin Whitney had the next seven fastest wind-legal 200m times, and had set two world youth records at the US Champs, at which she was 4th in the final in 22.47. Gina Lückenkemper won the European Junior title in 22.41w.

400m: Tosin Adeloye had the fastest time of 51.24 and five of the top eight times, but Salwa Eid Nasser had perhaps the most impressive results as, at 17, she won the World Youth and World Military titles.

800m: Raevyn Rogers improved from 2:01.67 to 1:59.71 to win the NCAA title, and that was by 1.3 sec the best junior time of the year; she also won the US and Pan-Am Junior titles. Anita Henriksdóttir ran 2:01.01 in a heat of the Worlds and had the best depth of times, but disappointed with 3rd at the European Juniors, won by Renée Eykens. Hinriksdóttir did not improved her 2013 pb, but went to 5th on the all-time list at 1000m with 2:36.63.

1500m: Dawit Seyaum had an outstanding season, a best of 3:59.76, 4th at the Worlds, and winning African senior and junior titles with Besu Sado second in both those races. With 4:00.65 Sado went to 11th on the junior all-time list. A third Ethiopian Gudaf Tsegay had six times under 4:07.0.

5000m: Alemitu Hawi had the two fastest times, 15:13.16 and 15:17.52, and was also fastest at 3000m, 8:51.23.

Marathon: Shure Demise ran a world junior record 2:20:59 for 4th at Dubai and was also 8th in Boston in 2:27:14 and the winner in Toronto in 2:23:37.

2000mSt: Outstanding times by Tigist Mekonnen 6:14.34, Sandra Tuei 6:16.19, Celphine Chespol 6:17.18 and Ann Gathoni 6:18.12 took them to 4-6-8-10 on the world junior all-time list. Chespol beat Tuei at the World Youths.

3000mSt: Tigist Mekonen ran 9:20.65, third best ever by a junior and just 0.28 off the world junior record. Ruth Chebet was a place behind Mekonen in Monaco in 9:21.40, slightly slower than her 2014 best but the fifth fastest ever by a junior. Chebet ran five times under 9:35, Mekonen three and Rosefline Chepngetich, the Keyyan Trials third placer, one (in her heat at the Worlds). Chebet was ahead of Mekonen, 4th to 5th in Lausanne, and at the World Military Games, 1st to 3rd.

100mh: Dior Hall, who had been 2nd in the World Youths in 2013 and in the World Juniors in 2014, set a world junior record of 12.74 when 3rd at the NCAAs. She ran four (inc. 1 wa) of the five sub-13 sec times by juniors in 2015 and was a clear winner of the Pan-Am Juniors. The other sub-13 was a Jamaican junior record of 12.97 by Daeshon Gordon.

400mh: Sydney McLaughlin (16 on 7 Aug 2015) ran 55.28 to win the US junior title; this took her to 11th on the world junior all-time lists and 2nd on the world youths (record 55.20) and she remains a youth for 2016. She was unbeaten at any event and her nine 400mh races included the four fastest and six of the best eight times in the world.

HJ: Eleanor Patterson and Vashti Cunningham, nearly two years younger, were the stand-out competitors. Both had bests at 1.96. Patterson, 8th at the Worlds, had 8 competitions over 1.90, to three by Cunningham and Morgan Lake, European Junior champion with a best of 1.94. Cunningham's 1.96 at the Pan-Am Juniors tied the world youth record.

PV: Eliza McCartney was 2nd in the World University Games with 4.40 in July, and then made great progress, with 4.50 in November and a world junior record 4.64 in December. The world junior all-time list was transformed as Alyona Lutkovskaya went to 3rd with a Russian Junior record 4.61, Rosbeilys Peinado to 4= with a South American junior record at 4.60 and Nina Kennedy to 7th as she tied the 4.59 Oceania junior record. But Lutkovskaya was surprisingly beaten for the European Junior title by Angelica Moser 4.35 to 4.20.

LJ: Kate Hall topped the rankings with an amazing 6.83, but her next bests were 6.38i/6.22, and the top junior was surely Florenta Marincu, who was 3rd in European Indoors with 6.79 and outdoors had nine performances 6.51-6.66 (and 6.78w to win the European Junior title 6.62w).

TJ: Keturah Orji, who was also third in the long jump list at 6.63, was top ranked at TJ with 14.15, her US junior record to win the NCAA title. She was also 2nd at the NCAA indoors and 3rd at the US Champs. A longer, wind-assisted jump was recorded by Núbia Soares, 14.16w to win the Pan-American Junior title from Liasagmis Povea 14.18 and Povea had two more 14m performances.

SP: Raven Saunders set four indoor (to 18.66) and four outdoor (to 18.35) US junior records and was the double NCAA champion and won the US and Pan-American Junior titles. She had five 18m plus competitions and Emil Dereli, two, topped by 18.40 at the European Juniors. These two were far ahead of the next best (17.23).

DT: Claudine Vita, with a best of 62.31 (26th world all-time juniors), had the best 12 marks of the year, including winning the European Junior title (plus silver at shot), with Xie Yuchen at 57.08 next best.

HT: Réka Gyurátz became the first junior woman ever to throw the discus over 70m with 70.39. She had the top four marks and 12 competitions over 67m, to 5 by Audrey Ciofani (best 69.25) and one by Beatrice Nedberge Llano, but was only 3rd with 62.94 at the European Indoors behind Ciofani and Llano.

JT: Yulenmis Aguilar set a CAC junior record with 59.18 in May but then made a massive improvement to a word junior record 63.86 to win the Pan-American Junior title in August. She also threw 60.52 in World qualifying and the other 60m throwers of 2015 were Maria Andrejcazk 62.11 (4th all-time) and 60.77 and Anete Kocina 60.01. The last two were 1-2 at the European Juniors, 59.73 to 58.88.

Hep: Caroline Agnou headed the rankings with a 6123 score to take the European Junior title, a 401 improvement on her previous Swiss record; she also scored 5866 at the Worlds. That was the only change to the world top 100 junior lists.

10,000m walk: The Russian walkers gave a superb exhibition of race walking at the European Juniors with a clean sweep of the medals, and the top five track times of the year came in this race, won by Klavdiya Afanasyeva in 43:36.88. A quicker road time was recorded by Yang Jiayu in winning the Chinese Junior title in 43:19.

The **longest current win streak** by a top athlete is 30 by Caterine Ibargüen with 30 finals from November 2012 (her last loss was at the 2012 Olympic Games to Tatyana Lysenko). 2012- 1, 2013- 9, 2014- 11, 2015- 9. Anita Wlodarczyk as 18 (2014- 7, 2015- 11); her last loss was 2nd at Ostrava to Betty Heidler. Adding 100m and 200m together Usain Bolt has 9 successive wins at 100m (last loss to Justin Gatlin on 6 June 2013) and 10 at 200m (last loss to Yohan Blake on 1 July 2012).

The **greatest dominance by individuals in 2015** were by the Polish hammer throwers. Anita Wlodarczyk had the top eight women's performances of the year and, including all in a series had the best 21 throws of the year plus another four in the irregular competition at Wroclaw (ahead of the next best, 76.33 by Zhang Wenxiu). She put six marks into the all-time top 30 performances so that she now has 15 of these, and with ancillary marks now has 30 of the 46 throws over 77.50 (including the top four). Pawel Fajdek had the top 13 performances from 80.06 to 83.93 and the best 24 throws (23 over 80m ahead of the next best Krisztían Pars 79.91). He had less impact on the all-time list, however, as his Polish record 83.93 made him tenth.

Renaud Lavillenie matched Wlodarczyk in having the top eight pole vault performances of the year(5.95 to 6.05). Next on the list of athletes who dominated in 2015 world lists were: Men: Justin Gatlin five at 100m, Women: Christina Schwanitz four at shot.

Asafa Powell now has 93 sub 10.00 times for 100m (plus 7w and 1 while banned). His breakdown: 2004- 9, 2005- 4, 2006- 12, 2007- 8, 2008- 15, 2009- 12, 2010- 5, 2011- 9, 2012- 6, 2013- 0 (drug dq 9.88), 2014- 3, 2015- 10.

At Beijing in 2015 Greg Rutherford joined the elite four British athletes to have **won Olympic, World, European and Commonwealth titles**:

Linford Christie 100m: OG 1992, WCh 1993, EC 1986/90/94; CG 1990/94

Jonathan Edwards OG 2000, WCh 1995, EC 1998, CG 2002,

Sally Gunnell 400mh OG 1992, WCh 1993, EC 1994; CG 1990/94

Daley Thompson Dec OG 1980/84, WCh 1983, EC 1982/86, CG 1978/82/86.

Winning **Olympic, World, Africa and Commonwealth titles**:

Ezekiel Kemboi KEN 3000mSt OG 2004/12, WCh 2009/11/13/15, AfG 2003, CG 2006

Maria Mutola MOZ 800m OG 2000, WCh 1993/2001/03, AfCh 1990/93/98/2002, AfG 1991/95/99; CG 1998/2002

Winning **Olympic, World, Pan-American (or Asian) and Commonwealth titles**: None

Top women athletes who gave birth in 2015 included

Nia Ali USA, Jéssica Augusto POR, Karolina Jarzynska-Nadolska POL, Anna Jesien POL, Cathrine Larsåsen NOR, Tatyana Lysenko RUS, Tatjana Mirkovic (née Jelaca) SRB, Hellen Obiri KEN, Yuliya Pechonkina RUS, Bianca Perie ROU, Jana Pittman AUS, Mariya Savinova-Farosova RUS

Retired in 2015/16

Men: Marvin Anderson JAM, Richard Buck GBR, Adrien Deghelt BEL, Sebastian Ernst GER, Jan Fitschen GER, Ryan Hall USA, Periklís Iakovákis GRE, Primoz Kozmus SRB, Liu Xiang CHN, Norman Müller GER, Niclas Sandells FIN, Silvio Schirrmeister GER, Alexander Straub GER, Matt Tegenkamp USA, Stef Vanhaeren BEL

Women: Elisa Cusma Piccione ITA, Antonietta Di Martino ITA, Naide Gomes POR. Natalya Kholodilina RUS, Maurren Maggi BRA, Verena Sailer GER, Myriam Soumaré FRA, Adonía Steryíou GRE

CROSS-COUNTRY - NATIONAL CHAMPIONS 2015

	Men (long distance)	*Women (long distance)*
Argentina	Joaquin Arbe	Sandra Amarillo
Australia	Liam Adams	Courtney Powell
Austria	Valentin Pfeil	Martina Brunder-Winter
Belarus (Oct)	Sergey Platonov	Nina Savina
Belgium	Isaac Kimeli	Louise Carton
Brazil	Gilberto Silvestre Lopes	Nonata Cruz
Bulgaria (Nov)	Ivan Sirakov	Silvia Denkova
Canada	Ross Proudfoot	Natasha Wodak
China	Zhu Renxue	Zhang Xinyan
Croatia (Nov)	Danijel Fak	Matea Matosevic
Czech Republic	Lukás Kourek	Lucie Sakanová
Denmark	Abdi Hakim Ulad	Sara Sig Møller
England	Charlie Hulson	Lily Partridge
Eritrea	Abrar Osman	Nazret Woldu
Estonia	Roman Forsi	Liina Luik
France	Hassan Chahdi	Sophie Duarte
Germany	Manuel Stockert	Maya Rehberg
Greece	Dímos Maggínas	Konstadína Kefalá
Hungary	Lászlo Gregor	Viktoria Gyurkes
India	Deepak Kumar	Swathi Gadhave
Ireland	Michael Clohisey	Maria McCambridge
(Nov)	Michael Clohisey	Fionnuala McCormack
Israel	Almeru Almeya	Azawant Teka
Italy	Andrea Lalli	Sara Dossena
Korea	Kang Soon	Kim Sung-eun
Lithuania (spring)	Paulius Bieliunas	Milda Vilcinskaite
(autumn)	Vitaliy Shafar UKR	Milda Vilcinskaite
Luxembourg	Christian Thielen	Charline Mathias
Moldova (Oct)	Nicolae Gorbusco	Lilia Fisicovici
Netherlands	Khalid Choukoud	Ruth van der Meijden
New Zealand	Malcolm Hicks	Lucy Van Dalen
Northern Ireland	Declan Reed	Teresa Doherty
Norway (Oct)	Henrik Ingebrigtson	Kristin Stormer Steira
Poland	Arkadiusz Gardzielewski	Dominika Napeiraj
Portugal	Rui Pinto	Dulce Félix
Russia	Aleksandr Novikov	Gulshat Fazlitdinova
Scotland	Andrew Butchart	Madeleine Murray
Serbia	Nemanja Cerovac	Amela Terzic
Slovakia (Nov)	Peter Durec	Katarina Beresová
Slovenia	Rok Puhar	Marusa Mismas
South Africa	Samuel Matsepe	Glenrose Xaba
Spain	Toni Abadia	Gebre Trihas
Sweden (Oct)	Adhamom Abraham	Sara Holmgren
Switzerland	Christian Kreienbühl	Fabienne Schlumpf
Trinidad & Tobago (Nov)	Matthew Hagley	Tonya Nero
UK	Andrew Butchart	Lily Partridge
Ukraine	Ruslan Savchuk	Tetyana Vernyhor
Ukraine (Nov)	Dmytro Lashyn	Darya Mykhaylova
Welsh	Dewi Griffiths	Ffion Price
Balkan (Nov)	Hasan Pak TUR	Ancuta Bobocel ROU
Nordic (Nov)	Olle Walleräng SWE	Johanna Peiponen FIN
Pan-American Cup	Maksim Korolev USA	Gladys Tejeda PER
Southern Africa	Kefasi Kasiteni MAW	Olivia Chitate ZIM

Short course winners	**Men**	**Women**
Austria	Christian Steinhammer	
Belarus (Oct)	Artyom Logish	Olga Rulevich
Czech Republic	Peter Vitner	
Denmark	Mads Valentin Tærsbøl	Sara Sig Møller
Estonia	Andi Noot	Jekaterina Patjuk
Germany	Benedikt Karus	
Lithuania	Mykola Yuhimchuk	Diana Lobacevske
Norway	Erik Udø Pedersen	Heidi Mårtensson
Poland	Tomasz Osmulski	
Portugal	Rui Pinto	Catarino Ribeiro

Russia	Ilgizar Safiulin	Dina Aleksandrova
Scotland (Nov)	Andrew Butchart	Laura Muir
Slovenia	Lucijan Zalokar	Alenka Radej
Sweden (Oct)	Jonas Leandersson	Sarah Lahti
Switzerland	Marco Kern	Florence Peguiron
Ukraine	Pavlo Oliynyk	Mariya Khodakivska
Ukraine (Nov)	Roman Rostykus	Viktoriya Pohorelska

Winners of EAA and IAAF Permit Cross-Country Races 2015

4 Jan	Amorebieta (EA)	Timothy Toroitich UGA	Magdalene Masai KEN
6 Jan	San Giorgio su Legnano (IAAF)	Dathan Ritzenhein USA	Janet Kisa KEN
10 Jan	Edinburgh (IAAF)	Chris Derrick USA	Emilia Gorecka GBR
11 Jan	Villa Lagarina (EA)	Andrew Mangata KEN	Silvia La Barbera ITA
18 Jan	Santiponce (IAAF)	Teklemariam Medhin ERI	Emily Chebet KEN
25 Jan	Elgóibar (EA)	Teklemariam Medhin ERI	Mimi Belete BRN
25 Jan	Hannut (EA)	Dame Tasama ETH	Louise Carton BEL
1 Feb	Belgrade (EA)	Lászlo Gregor HUN	Amela Terzic SRB
8 Feb	Diekirch (IAAF)	Benedikt Karus GER	Simret Restle-Apel GER
8 Feb	Chiba (IAAF)	Charles Ndirangu KEN	Zoe Buckman AUS
14 Feb	Nairobi (IAAF)	Bidan Karoki KEN	Faith Kipyegon KEN
15 Feb	San Vittore Olana (IAAF)	Muktar Edris ETH	Violet Jelagat KEN
22 Feb	Albufeira (IAAF)	Roman Prodius MDA	Dominika Nowakowska POL
14 Mar	Antrim (IAAF)	Thomas Ayeko UGA	Birtukan Fente ETH
17 Nov	Burgos (Atapuerca) (IAAF)	Imane Merga ETH	Belaynesh Oljira ESP
22 Nov	Tilburg (EA)	Richard Ringer GER	Sifan Hassan NED
22 Nov	Soria (EA)	Timothy Toroitich UFA	Linet Masai KEN
29 Nov	Alcobendas (EA)	Tamirat Tola ETH	Linet Masai KEN
29 Nov	Leffinckroucke (EA)	Alfred Ngeno ETH	Dera Dida ETH
29 Nov	Roeselare (EA)	Alex Kibet KEN	Louise Carton BEL
	Venta de Baños (EA)	Ayeke Ayalew BRN	Alemitu Haroya ESP
22 Dec	Brussels (IAAF)	Dane Tasama ETH	Fionnuala McCormack IRL

European Cross-Country Championships 2015

At Hyères, France, December 15

Senior Men (10.117k)
1. Ali Kaya TUR 29:20
2. Alemayehu Bezabeh ESP 29:31
3. Adel Mechaal ESP 29:51
4. Ayad Lamdassem ESP 29:57
5. Illas Fifa ESP 30:02
6. Florian Carvalho FRA 30:06
7. Roberto Alaiz ESP 30:20
8. Yohan Durand FRA 30:20
9. Mourad Amdouni FRA 30:24
10. David Nilsson SWE 30:25
11. Abdi Hakin Ulad DEN 30:28
12.Timothée Bommier FRA 30:31
13. Vasyl Koval UKR 30:33
14. Olle Walleräng SWE 30:35
15. Tom Lancashire GBR 30:36

73 of 78 finished.
Teams: 1. ESP 14, 2. FRA 35, 3. GBR 78, 4. ITA 99, 5. NED 103, 6. DEN 105, 7. NOR 143, 8. UKR 151, 9. TUR 154, 10. BEL 177, 11. IRL 181.

Under-23 Men (8.087k)
1. Jonathan Davies GBR 23:32
2. Carlos Mayo ESP 23:35
3. Amanal Petros GER 23:39
4. Marc Scott GBR 23:39
5. Djilali Bedrani FRA 23:41
6. Lorenzo Dini ITA 23:41
7. Hassim Hassaous ESP 23:47
8. Napoleon Solomon SWE 23:49

61 of 69 finished.
Teams: 11. ESP 39, 2. GBR 41, 3. FRA 59, 4. ITA 77, 5. GER 81, 8 teams completed.

Junior Men (5.947k)
1. Yemaneberhan Crippa ITA 17:39
2. Fabien Palcau FRA 17:45
3. El Madhi Lahoufi ESP 17:46
4. Jimmy Gressier FRA 17:48
5. Said Ettaqy ITA 17:49

88 of 90 finished.
Teams: 1. FRA 27, 2. ITA 29, 3. GBR 67, 4. ESP 87, 5. BEL 12, 13 completed

Senior Women (8.087k)
1. Sifan Hassan NED 25:47
2. Kate Avery GBR 25:55
3. Karoline Bjerkell Grøvdal NOR 25:57
4. Fionnuala McCormack IRL 26:00
5. Ancuta Bobocel ROU 26:07
6. Stephanie Twell GBR 26:08
7. Clémence Calvin FRA 26:17
8. Gemma Steel GBR 26:25
9. Maureen Koster NED 26:28
10. Johanna Peiponen FIN 26:34
11. Trihas Gebre ESP 26:35
12. Esma Aydemir TUR 26:40
13. Lizzie Lee IRL 26:41
14. Veerle Dejaeghere BEL 26:41
15. Anna Sofie Baumeister DEN 26:41

67 of 69 finished.
Teams: 11. GBR 33, 2. FRA 78, 3. IRL 83, 4. ESP 95, 5. ITA 118, 6. ROU 129, 7. UKR 238.

Under-23 Women (5.947k)
1. Louise Carton BEL 19:46
2. Jip Vastenburg NED 19:46
3. Amela Terzic SRB
4. Laura Muir GBR 19:53
5. Vittoria Kushnir BLR 20:05
6. Sarah Lahti SWE 20:06
7. Federica Del Buono ITA 20:12
8. Emma Oudiou FRA 20:14

50 of 50 finished.
Teams: 1. GBR 41, 2: FRA 71, 3. ITA 82, 4. UKR 127, 5. TUR 140, 6. POR 18.

Junior Women (4.157k)
1. Konstanze Klosterhalfen GER 13:12
2. Harriet Knowles-Jones GBR 13:16
3. Alina Reh GER 13:20
4. Célia Antón ESP 13:27
5. Bobby Clay GBR 13:29

80 of 81 finished.
Teams: 1. GER 20, 2. GBR 40, 3. DEN 62, 4. FRA 77, 5. ESP 108, 11 completed.

Overall medals: GBR 3 gold- 4 silver-2 bronze, ESP 2-2-2, GER 2-0-2, FRA 1-4-1, ITA 1-1-1, NED 1-1-0, TUR & BEL 1-0-0, NOR. IRL. SRB & DEN (first ever team medals for both) 0-0-1

2015 WORLD ROAD RACE REVIEW

By Marty Post

ANYONE SCANNING ATHLETICS headlines on February 15, 2015 might have thought the following was a mistake: "Florence Kiplagat sets world record at the Mitja Marato de Barcelona Half-marathon." Was this an error in that Kiplagat had done this in 2014 and the news story was a reference to that race? No it was not as the Kenyan star indeed managed to slice another three seconds from the mark she had set there twelve months earlier. She sped through the first 5k in 15:39, followed by 10k in 31:02, 15k at 46:14 and 20k at 61:54, to reach the finish in 65:09. (In 2014 she had splits of 15:50/31:09/46:36/61:56). Kiplagat's faster start in 2015 also enabled her en route to set world records for 15k and 20k.

Kiplagat may have been the fastest but countrywoman Mary Keitany was the best as she dominated the top end of the year half marathon list with three of the top ten performances. She won the most competitive race of the year at Ra's Al-Khaymah in 66:02 (the number 2 time) as well as Olomouc (66:38, = #4) and South Shields (67:32, #10). For her career Keitany has eight sub-67s with no other woman posting more than three.

Mamitu Daska was the runner-up to Keitany at the RAK half-marathon in 66:27, a significant a mark as it was the best time ever by an Ethiopian on a record quality course. (Meseret Defar had run 66:09 at the slightly downhill 2013 Great North Run). There were a couple of other sub-70 minute national records in 2015, 69:33 by Diane Nukuri, Burundi (28 March, Prague), and 69:37 by Eunice Jepkirui Kirwa, Bahrain (17 May, Gifu).

Four women broke 31 minutes at 10k in 2015 led by Gladys Chesire whose 30:41 at Berlin, October 11 made her the ninth fastest women in history. Ethiopian Sutume Asefa became just the third sub-1:22 runner in a 25k race, running 1:21:55 at Berlin, May 10. Genzebe Dibaba, the world champion bronze medalist at 5000m (and gold medalist/world record-holder at 1500m) made a rare excursion on the road at Carlsbad, California on March 29. She set the year-leading time for 5k at 14:48, a mere two seconds off the acknowledged world best set by Defar there in 2006.

No man managed to break 59 minutes for the half-marathon in 2015, with Abreham Cheroben's 59:10 at Valencia on October 18, the standard bearer for the year. Cheroben's 15k split (42:01), along with the same time for Matthew Kisorio, were the world leaders. In a somewhat surprising result, the New Delhi half-marathon was the highest quality men's race with half of the top ten 2015 times. Zersenay Tadese of Eritrea was third (59:24), extending his all-time career record for most sub-60 minute times (11).

Cheroben managed the feat of not only repeating as world leader for the half-marathon in 2014 and 2015, but also did so at 25k (1:12:31 at Berlin). Another Kenyan, Stephen Sambu repeated his lead at 10k, his 27:30 (Manchester) edging Cheroben (27:35 at Utrecht).

Special recognition goes to Bernard Lagat. The Kenyan-born American celebrated his 40th birthday in December 2014 and last year smashed the veteran's world road bests at 5k (13:40) and 10k (27:48).

WINNERS OF LEADING 2015 ROAD RACES

4 Jan	Adana HMar	Barselius Kipyego KEN 60:51	Rose Chelimo KEN 68:53
11 Jan	Egmond aan Zee HMar	Azmeraw Mengist ETH 63:01	Purity Cherotich KEN 71:40
11 Jan	Maia 10k	Rui Pedro Silva POR 28:59	Ana Dulce Felix POR 31:25
18 Jan	Santa Pola HMar	Vincent Yator KEN 60:15*	Georgina Rono KEN 71:02
18 Jan	Houston HMar (US Ch)	Diego Estrada USA 60:51	Kim Conley USA 69:44
31 Jan	Modena 13.1k	Thomas Lokomwa KEN 38:33	Viola Jelagat KEN 44:17
1 Feb	Granollers HMar	Wilson Kipsang KEN 62:39	Olga Kotovska UKR 73:21
1 Feb	Marugame HMar	Paul Kuria KEN 59:47	Eloise Wellings AUS 70:41
7 Feb	Edinburgh USA 10k	Julius Kogo KEN 28:05*	Risper Gesabwa KEN 33:05
8 Feb	San Blas 10k	Levy Matebo KEN 64:13	Rose Chelimo KEN 71:40*
13 Feb	R'as Al-Khaymah HMar	Mosinet Geremew ETH 60:05	Mary Keitany KEN 66:02
15 Feb	Barcelona HMar	Tadesse Abraham SUI 60:42	Florence Kiplagat KEN 65:09
15 Feb	Yamaguchi HMar	Charles Ndirangu KEN 60:18	Michi Numata JPN 69:27

1 Mar	Rome-Ostia HMar	Robert Chemosin KEN 59:37	Amane Beriso ETH 68:43
1 Mar	San Juan 10k	Sammy Kitwara KEN 28:51	Belaynesh Olijara ETH 31:57
8 Mar	Den Haag HMar	Stanley Biwott KEN 59:20	Maja Neuenschwander SUI 71:08
8 Mar	Paris HMar	Vincent Yator KEN 60:12	Yebrgual Melese ETH 69:50
8 Mar	Taroudant 10k	Amos Mitei KEN 28:02	Malika Asahsah MAR 31:30*
15 Mar	Jacksonville 15k (US Ch)	Ben True USA 44:03	Amy Cragg USA 50:18
15 Mar	New Orleans 8k	Julius Kogo KEN 22:29	Buze Diriba ETH 24:58
15 Mar	New York HMar	Leonard Korir KEN 61:06	Molly Huddle USA 68:31*=
21 Mar	Kerzers 15k	Temesgen Daba ETH 43:49	Sutume Asefa ETH 50:35
21 Mar	Laredo 10k	Dawi Fikadu ETH 28:04	Malika Asahssah MAR 31:00*
22 Mar	Lisbon HMar	Mo Farah GBR 59:32	Rose Chelimo KEN 68:22
22 Mar	Reading HMar	Amos Kiplagat KEN 63:10	Lily Partridge GBR 70:32
22 Mar	Venlo HMar	Alfers Lagat KEN 60:33	Jane Moraa KEN 70:41
28 Mar	Charleston 10k	Dominic Ondoro KEN 29:22	Cynthia Limo KEN 32:18
28 Mar	Mobile 10k	John Muritu KEN 28:34	Susan Jerotich KEN 33:43
28 Mar	Praha HMar	Daniel Wanjiru KEN 59:51	Worknesh Degefa ETH 67:14
29 Mar	Brunssum 10k	Nicodemus Kipkurui KEN 28:29	Marianne Wanjiru KEN 32:21
29 Mar	Berlin HMar	Birhanu Legese ETH 59:45	Cynthia Kosgei KEN 70:52
29 Mar	Bratislava HMar	Hilary Kimaiyo KEN 62:33*	Rebecca Korir KEN 73:34
29 Mar	Carlsbad 5k	Lawi Lalang KEN 13:32	Genzebe Dibaba ETH 14:48
29 Mar	Chicago 8k	Stephen Sambu KEN 23:03	Alexi Pappas USA 26:32
29 Mar	Madrid HMar	Alex Cherop KEN 62:30	Linah Cheruto KEN 70:38
29 Mar	Milano HMar	Thomas Lokomwa KEN 60:33	Rebecca Chesire KEN 68:21*
29 Mar	Tarsus HMar	Evans Kiplagat KEN 62:15	Purity Changwony KEN 71:35
29 Mar	Warszawa HMar	Kiprop Limo KEN 60:52	Amane Beriso ETH 70:54
4 Apr	New Orleans 10k	John Muritu KEN 28:56	Hiwot Aleyu ETH 31:55
4 Apr	Paderborn 10k	Homiyu Tesfaye GER 27:54	Sutume Asfefa ETH 31:49
4 Apr	Paderborn HMar	Abraham Yano KEN 61:06	Maryanne Wanjiru KEN 71:12
6 Apr	Dongio 10k	Victor Chumo KEN 28:20	Mary Wanjohi KEN 35:31
11 Apr	Dublin 10k	Japheth Korir KEN 28:15	Gemma Steel GBR 33:03
12 Apr	Washington DC 9.4M	Stephen Sambu KEN 43:20	Mary Wacera KEN 48:35
18 Apr	Boston 5k	Ben True USA 13:22*	Molly Huddle USA 14:50*
19 Apr	Genova HMar	Edwin Kipkorir KEN 63:55	Hellen Jepkurgat KEN 71:52
19 Apr	Hilversum 10k	Isaac Langat KEN 28:14	Susan Tanui KEN 32:28
19 Apr	Vancouver 10k	Luke Puskedra USA 28:53	Risper Gesabwa KEN 32:28
19 Apr	Verbania HMar	Solomon Yego KEN 60:47	Sutume Kebede ETH 69:07
19 Apr	Vitry-sur-Seine HMar	Norbert Kigen KEN 61:02	Buzunesh Gudeta ETH 71:41
19 Apr	Yangzhou HMar	Mosinet Geremew ETH 59:52*	Flomena Cheyech KEN 68:36
25 Apr	Lausanne 20k	Temesgen Daba ETH 59:51	Sutume Asefa ETH 66:49
26 Apr	Istanbul HMar	Evans Kiplaget KEN 60:13	Gladys Cherono KEN 66:38
26 Apr	Nice HMar	James Rungaru KEN 60:12	Ednah Kimaiyo KEN 70:45
26 Apr	Warszawa 10k	Hillary Kimaiyo KEN 28:45	Dominika Napieraj POL 32:46
26 Apr	Würzburg 10k	Japhet Korir KEN 27:47	Caroline Chepkemoi KEN 32:36
1 May	Puy-en-Velay 15k	Daniel Chebii KEN 43:57	Sutume Asefa ETH 49:35
2 May	Indianapolis HMar	Elisha Barno KEN 62:31	Sarah Kiptoo KEN 73:09
3 May	Piacenza HMar	Thomas Lokomwa KEN 60:41*	Viola Jelagat KEN 69:27*
3 May	Spokane 12k	Lani Rutto KEN 34:22	Cynthia Limo KEN 39:27
8 May	Aschaffenburg 7.9k	Abraham Kipyetich KEN 21:47	Fate Tola ETH 25:03
9 May	Grand Rapids 25k (US Ch)	Jared Ward 1:14:47	Lindsey Scherf 1:26:36
10 May	Berlin 25k	Abreham Cheroben KEN 1:12:31	Sutume Asefa ETH 1:21:55
10 May	Manchester 10k	Stephen Sambu KEN 27:30	Betsy Saina KEN 31:49
17 May	Bangalore 10k	Mosinet Geremew ETH 28:16	Mamitu Daska ETH 31:57
17 May	Cape Town 12k	Emmanuel Bett KEN 33:32	Vivian Cheruiyot KEN 38:22
17 May	Cleveland 10k	Najim el Quady MAR 29:08	Ann Wanjiru KEN 33:00
17 May	Gifu HMar	James Rungaru KEN 62:12	Eunice Kirwa BRN 69:37*
17 May	San Francisco 12k	Isaac Mwangi KEN 35:25	Jane Kibii KEN 40:04
23 May	Göteborg HMar	Richard Mengich KEN 60:44	Worknesh Degefa ETH 68:13*
23 May	Karlovy Vary HMar	Elijah Serem KEN 61:01*	Mulu Seboka ETH 69:11*
23 May	Ottawa 10k	Nicholas Bor KEN 27:55	Gladys Cherono KEN 30:56*
24 May	Lisboa 5k	*women only*	Priscah Jeptoo KEN 15:47
24 May	London 10k	Andy Vernon GBR 28:38	Jo Pavey GBR 32:56

25 May	Boulder (A) 10k	Belete Assefa ETH 29:05	Meskerem Assefa ETH 33:32
25 May	Mobile 10k	Julius Kogo KEN 29:30	Tigist Jabore ETH 33:35
30 May	Albany 5k	*women only*	Emily Chebet KEN 15:38
30 May	New York 10k	Ben True USA 28:13	Joyce Chepkirui KEN 32:33
31 May	San Diego HMar	Jordan Chipangama ZAM 62:24	Eri Hayakawa JPN 70:47
31 May	Wien 5k	*women only*	Jessica O'Connell CAN 15:33
7 Jun	Casablanca 10k	Daniel Chebii KEN 28:20	Viola Jepchumba KEN 32:09
7 Jun	Ceske Budejovice HMar	Abreham Cheroben KEN 61:24	Rose Chelimo KEN 72:01
12 Jun	Oelde 10k	Richard Mengich KEN 28:24	Tola Fate ETH 32:57
13 Jun	Green Bay 10k	Allan Kiprono KEN 29:01	Risper Gesabwa ETH 32:50
13 Jun	Langueux 10k	Simon Cheprot KEN 28:05	Gladys Yator KEN 31:40
13 Jun	New York 10k	*women only*	Mary Keitany KEN 31:15
13 Jun	Zwolle HMar	Richard Mengich KEN 61:22	Janet Rono KEN 71:10
20 Jun	Olomouc HMar	Josphat Kiptis KEN 60:21	Mary Keitany KEN 66:38*
20 Jun	Peoria 4M	Moses Kikosgei KEN 18:19	Sarah Boyle CAN 20:51
21 Jun	Boston 10k	Daniel Salel KEN 28:09	Mary Wacera KEN 32:07
21 Jun	Hamburg HMar	Merhawi Kesete ERI 60:52*	Agnes Mutune KEN 71:27*
4 Jul	Atlanta 10k	Daniel Salel KEN 28:43	Shalane Flanagan USA 32:05
4 Jul	Cedar Rapids 8k	Abraham Chelanga KEN 23:32	Abigael Wanjiku KEN 26:55
11 Jul	Kingsport 8k	Cleophas Ngetich KEN 22:28	Cassie Graves USA 29:31
12 Jul	Utica 15k	Eliud Ngetich KEN 43:31	Mary Wacera KEN 48:49
17 Jul	Buffalo 4M	Teshome Mekonen ETH 18:01	Mary Wacera KEN 20:20
25 Jul	Davenport 7M	Leonard Korir KEN 33:06	Cynthia Limo KEN 36:57
26 Jul	Bogotá (A) HMar	Stanley Biwott KEN 63:15	Amane Gobena ETH 73:44
26 Jul	Capitola 6M	Sam Chelanga KEN 27:25	Risper Gesabwa KEN 31:19
1 Aug	Cape Eliizabeth 10k	Stephen Kibet KEN 28:29	Wude Ayalew ETH 31:56
9 Aug	Sydney 14k	Brad Milosevic AUS 42:09	Cassie Fien AUS 46:32
15 Aug	Schortens 10M	Charles Cheruiyot KEN 46:40	Winnie Jepkorir KEN 53:55
15 Aug	Parkersburg HMar	Kimutai Cheruiyot KEN 62:54	Buze Diriba ETH 72:56
16 Aug	Falmouth 7M	Stephen Sambu KEN 32:17	Diane Nukuri BDI 36:47
22 Aug	Flint 10M	Leonard Korir KEN 47:00	Caroline Rotich KEN 53:06
23 Aug	Amatrice 8.5k	Joshua Mongusho UGA 24:07	Mercyline Chelangat UGA 27:53
23 Aug	Klagenfurt HMar	Laban Korir KEN 61:52	Lisa Nemec CRO 71:04
30 Aug	Arras 10k	Abraham Niyonkuru FRA 30:14	Christelle Daunay FRA 32:23
30 Aug	Rio de Janeiro HMar	Edwin Rotich KEN 62:25	Nancy Kiprop KEN 72:37
5 Sep	Lille HMar	Stephen Chebogut KEN 60:19	Peninah Arusei KEN 68:56
5 Sep	Prague 10k	Daniel Chebii KEN 27:42	Peres Jepchirchir KEN 30:55
6 Sep	Hamburg 10k	Geoffrey Koech KEN 28:29	Margaret Muringi KEN 33:29
6 Sep	Luanda HMar	Sammy Kitwara KEN 60:25	Flomena Cheyech KEN 68:18*
6 Sep	Sarnen HMar	Edwin Koech KEN 59:54*	Maja Neuenshcwander SUI 72:25*
6 Sep	Tilburg 10M/10k	Bernard Koech KEN 45:21	Genet Ayalew ETH 30:58
7 Sep	New Haven 20k (US Ch)	Jared Ward USA 59:24	Molly Huddle USA 66:26
12 Sep	Ústi nad Labem HMar	Merhawi Kesete ERI 60:58	Peris Jepchirchir KEN 67:17*
13 Sep	Bologna HMar	Cosmas Kipchoge KEN 62:28	Peninah Arusei KEN 71:43
13 Sep	Bristol HMar	Morris Gachaga KEN 61:32	Teresiah Omosa KEN 73:48
13 Sep	København HMar	Bedan Muchiri KEN 59:14	Purity Rionoripo KEN 68:29
13 Sep	Newcastle/S.Shields HMar	Mo Farah GBR 59:22	Mary Keitany KEN 67:32
13 Sep	Wachau HMar	Bernard Bett KEN 61:34	Viola Jelagat KEN 69:57
20 Sep	Amsterdam/Zaandam 10M	Edwin Kiptoo KEN 45:19	Joyce Chepkirui KEN 51:30
20 Sep	Bogotá (A) 10k	*women only*	Belaynesh Oljira ETH 33:57
20 Sep	Porto & Gaia HMar	Emmanuel Bor KEN 61:06	Monica Jepkoech KEN 70:26
20 Sep	Providence 5k (US Ch)	David Torrence USA 13:56	Molly Huddle USA 15:12
20 Sep	Udine HMar	Solomon Kirwa KEN 60:04	Viola Jepchumba KEN 69:29
27 Sep	Paris/Versailles 16k	Dawit Fikadu ETH 47:42	Sutome Asefa ETH 54:20
27 Sep	Remich HMar	Paul Kipkorir KEN 62:04	Yeshi Chekole ETH 72:17
27 Sep	San Jose USA HMar	Jordan Chipangama ZAM 63:00	Aliphine Tuliamuk-Bolton KEN 71:26
27 Sep	Utrecht 10k	Abraham Cheroben KEN 27:35	Yasmin Hillebrink NED 34:36
4 Oct	Breda HMar	Philip Langat KEN 61:06	Elizabeth Cherono KEN 70:10
4 Oct	Cardiff HMar	Ben Siwa UGA 62:07	Lenah Jerotich KEN 71:31
4 Oct	Glasgow HMar	Moses Kipsiro UGA 62:18	Edna Kiplagat KEN 68:21
11 Oct	Arezzo HMar	Paul Sugut KEN 1:01:55	Ruth Chebitok KEN 72:57

11 Oct	Berlin 10k	Joshua Cheptegei UGA 27:50	Gladys Chesire KEN 30:41
11 Oct	Boston HMar	Daniel Salel KEN 60:56	Mary Wacera KEN 70:21
11 Oct	Groningen 4M	Yomif Kejelcha ETH 17:21	Viola Kibiwot KEN 19:42
11 Oct	Paris 20k	Stephen Ogari KEN 59:11	Nancy Kimaiyo KEN 66:03
12 Oct	Boston 10k	*women only*	Molly Huddle USA 31:21*
18 Oct	Cremona HMar	Solomon Kirwa KEN 61:33	Alice Kimutai KEN 71:14
18 Oct	Lisboa HMar	Nguse Amlosom ERI 62:38	Beatrice Mutai KEN 69:50
18 Oct	Valencia HMar	Abreham Cheroben KEN 59:10	Netsanet Gudeta ETI 67:31*
25 Oct	Marseille/Cassis 19.6k	Edwin Kipyego KEN 57:18	Peres Jepchirchir KEN 66:01
25 Oct	Southsea/Portsmouth 10M	Moses Kipsiro UGA 46:00	Vivian Cheruiyot KEN 51:17
25 Oct	Saint-Denis HMar	Lengurisi Loitarakwai KEN 62:08	Alice Mogire KEN 71:45
31 Oct	Philadelphia HMar	Tim Ritchie USA 61:23	Maegan Krifchin USA 69:51
31 Oct	Tulsa 15k	Elisha Barno KEN 44:28	Monicah Ngige KEN 52:34
1 Nov	Laayoune HMar	Albert Kangogo KEN 62:44	Violah Jepchumba KEN 72:35
8 Nov	Monterrey HMar	Elisha Barno KEN 63:04	Kara Goucher USA 71:13
15 Nov	Alexandria 12k (US Ch)	Sam Chelanga USA 34:35	Molly Huddle USA 38:36
15 Nov	Istanbul 15k	Bernard Sang KEN 43:29	Ruti Aga ETH 49:45
15 Nov	Nijmegen 15k	Joshua Cheptegei UGA 42:39	Yenesh Tilahun ETH 50:05
22 Nov	Philadelphia HMar	Eliud Ngetich KEN 63:40	Aliphine Tuliamuk-Bolton KEN 69:49
26 Nov	Manchester USA 4.75M	Will Geoghegan USA 21:34	Diane Nukuri BUR 24:19
26 Nov	San Jose 5k	Eliud Ngetich KEN 13:55	Buze Diriba ETH 15:43
29 Nov	Kosa 10M	Karemi Thuku KEN 45:19	*Men only*
5 Dec	Geneve 7.25k/4.79k	Tadesse Abraham SUI 21:01	Helen Bekele ETH 24:28
6 Dec	's-Heerenberg 15k	Abreham Cheroben KEN 42:54	Meseret Defar ETH 50:04
12 Dec	Sion 7.35k/5.25k	Tadesse Abraham SUI 19:42	Helen Bekele ETH 16:03
13 Dec	Zürich 9k/6.6k	Tadesse Abraham SUI 25:01	Martina Strähl SUI 21:54
23 Dec	Okayama HMar	*women only*	Selly Chepyego KEN 68:17
31 Dec	Bolzano 10.05k/5.05k	Tamirat Tola ETH 28:29	Netsanet Gudeta ETH 15:58
31 Dec	Luanda 10k	Alex Oloitiptip KEN 28:45	Jemima Sumgong KEN 32:15
31 Dec	Madrid 10k	Kaan Kigen Ozbilen TUR 27:35*	Linet Masai KEN 31:38
31 Dec	Peurbach 6.8k/5.1k	Victor Chumo KEN 19:16	Alice Aprot KEN 15:42
31 Dec	São Paulo 15k	Stanley Biwott KEN 44:31	Wude Ayalew ETH 54:01
31 Dec	Trier 8k/5k	Haymanot Alew ETH 22:59	Meskerem Amare ETH 15:35

** course record*

MARATHON REVIEW – 2015

By Marty Post

MANY OF HISTORY'S greatest marathon runners have had sensational starts to their careers and in 2015 the Kenyan Eliud Kipchoge furthered the case for being included in this highest echelon. He had won his debut in 2:05:30 (Hamburg, 2013) and added two other wins in 2:05:00 (Rotterdam, 2014) and 2:04:11 (Chicago, 2014). He suffered his only setback when he ran 2:04:05 for second at Berlin in 2013 and it took a world record from Wilson Kipsang to beat him. In April 2015 Kipchoge won at London in 2:04:42, prevailing over one of the greatest fields ever assembled, one that included Kipsang (the course record holder), Dennis Kimetto (the current world record-holder) and Stephen Kiprotich (the defending Olympic and World Champion). He proceeded to make it five victories in six races at Berlin five months later, finishing in 2:04:00, despite running most of the race with inserts that were flopping out of the rear of his shoe.

Kipchoge's total time of 4:08:42 in 2015 was the best ever in one year over two record-quality courses (Geoffrey Mutai totaled 4:08:08 in 2011 when one of the races was the tailwind-aided Boston Marathon.) Moreover, Kipchoge was the first man since Haile Gebrselassie in 2008 to have the top two world-leading times for the calendar year. Kenyan men also swept arguably the most important races in October (Chicago, Dickson Chumba), November (New York City, Stanley Biwott) and December (Fukuoka, Patrick Makau).

Another Kenyan, Kenneth Mburu Mungara, won at Milan, Italy in April and achieved something not done in more than 42 years as he crossed the finish line in 2:08:44, slicing four seconds off the world veteran's record that had stood since September 2008. This was the first time this record had been set in a winning effort since Jack Foster at Kyoto in February 1973. Mungara wasn't finished though. He lowered the world age-40 plus mark to 2:08:42 at Gold Coast in July, again in first place becoming the first man to achieve an overall victory/world veterans record twice. However, Mungara's reign may be short-lived. On October 11 at Eindhoven, Mark Kiptoo finished in 2:06:00. At the age of 39 years 112 days Kiptoo – who ran 2:06:16 at 37 and 2:06:49 at 38 – became the oldest man to run under 2 hours 7 minutes.

More records fell to one of the most prolific world-class marathoners in history, Yuki Kawauchi of Japan. The indefatigable 28-year-old competed in 12 marathons (and a 50k) in 2015 and at year's end held all-time career records for most sub-2:13s (28), sub-2:14s (34), sub-2:15s (36), sub-2:16s (41), sub-2:17s (46) and sub-2:18s (50). Men's national records from four continents were broken in 2015 including those from Iran (2:17:41, Mohammad Jafar Moradi), Jordan (2:17:24, Hamad Maarouf Methkal), Uganda (2:06:33, Stephen Kiprotich), Chad (2:19:34, Ahmat Abdou Daouad), Peru (2:11:01, Raul Pacheco), Sri Lanka (2:13:47, Anuradha Cooray), Georgia (2:16:17, Daviti Kharazishvili) and Germany (2:08:33, Arne Gabius).

Like their male counterparts, African women dominated marathon running in 2015. They swept the events comprising the Abbott World Marathon Majors series, extending a Kenyan/ Ethiopian winning streak to 37 consecutive AWMM events. Mare Dibaba of Ethiopia was the champion at the most competitive race of the year, the World Championships. The differences between first and second (one second), first and third (four seconds) and first and fourth (seven seconds) were the closest in World Championships history.

Dubai also provided a fight to the finish as Aselefech Mergia prevailed in 2:20:02 to 2:20:03 over Gladys Cherono whose time was the third fastest debut in history. Cherono went on to run the fastest time in the world for 2015, 2:19:25 at Berlin and her 2015 total of 4:39:28 made her the only woman besides Paula Radcliffe to have a sub-4:40 one year double. At the same Dubai race Shure Demise ran 2:20:59, the fastest time ever by a junior (the IAAF does not recognize a marathon world junior record).

Another Ethiopian Aberu Kebede had an unprecedented accomplishment as her 2:20:48 second place at Berlin made her the first woman with 11 lifetime sub-2:25s. Women's national records continued to tumble, including Belarus (2:23:06, Aleksandra Duliba), Turkey (2:24:44, Sultan Haydar), Sri Lanka (2:40:07, Niluka Rajasekara Geethani), Bahrain (2:22:08, Eunice Kirwa), Mongolia (2:33:36, Munkhzaya Bayartsogt), Paraguay (2:36:01, Carmen Martínez), Burundi (2:27:50, Diane Nukuri), Colombia (2:32:32, Kelly Arias) and Uganda (2:34:54, Adero Nyakisi), Switzerland (2:26:59,Maja Neuenschwander) and India (2:37:29, Orchatteri P Jaisha).

Unfortunately doping-related disqualifications invalidated some notable results. At Nagoya a 2:22:27 woman's veterans' record by Mariya Konovalova was a casualty as was the 2:22:09 winning performance at Osaka by Tetyana Hamera.

Nonetheless one of the great female legends of the sport had a high note moment in 2015. Paula Radcliffe, who redefined the notion of how fast 26.2 miles could be run by a woman, retired with one last competition at London on her favorite course. London was where Radcliffe ran her epochal 2:15:25 in 2003, still the world record and a surrealistic 3 minutes, 12 seconds (2.36 percent) better than the next fastest women's marathon time. London was also the site of her all-women's competition record (2:17:42) and debut record (2:18:56). Radcliffe still holds the World Championships record of 2:20:57. After many years of frustrating injury the 41-year-old Englishwoman kept up a sub-six minute per mile pace throughout the non-elite race and crossed the line as the winner in 2:36:55. "London is about giving the best on the day," she said afterwards. "There's magic about it."

WINNERS OF 2015 INTERNATIONAL MARATHONS

3 Jan	Xiamen	Moses Mosop KEN	2:06:19*	Mare Dibaba ETH	2:19:52
9 Jan	Tiberias	Hailu Mekonnen ETH	2:12:31	Riki Salem ISR	2:54:02
18 Jan	Houston	Birhanu Gedefa ETH	2:08:03	Yebrqual Melese ETH	2:23:23
18 Jan	Mumbai	Tesfaye Abera ETH	2:09:46	Dinknesh Mekasha ETH	2:30:30
23 Jan	Dubai	Hayle Lemi ETH	2:05:28	Aselefech Mergia ETH	2:20:02
25 Jan	Hong Kong	Sentayehu Merga ETH	2:13:00	Kim Hye-gyong PRK	2:31:46
25 Jan	Marrakech	Workneh Tiruneh ETH	2:08:51	Worknesh Edesa ETH	2:31:06
25 Jan	Osaka	*women only*		Jelena Prokopcuka LAT	2:24:07¶

1 Feb	Beppu-Oita	Tewelde Estifanos ERI	2:10:18	Chiyuki Mochizuki JPN	2:41:28
8 Feb	Nobeoka	Hasinori Kitajima JPN	2:12:28	Yuko Hakoyama JPN	2:39:34*
15 Feb	Ahmedabad	Melaku Belachew ETH	2:13:43	Berhan Aregawi ETH	2:39:11
22 Feb	Sevilla	Lawrence Cherono KEN	2:09:39	Filomena Costa POR	2:28:00
22 Feb	Tokyo	Endeshaw Negesse ETH	2:06:00	Birhane Dibaba ETH	2:23:15
27 Feb	Tel Aviv	William Kiprono Yegon KEN	2:10:30	Azeb Welde ETH	2:51:24
1 Mar	Otsu	Samuel Ndungu KEN	2:09:08	*men only*	
1 Mar	Torreón (A)	Erick Mose KEN	2:14:38	Misiker Mekonnin ETH	2:37:28
8 Mar	Nagoya	*women only*		Eunice Jepkirui BRN	2:22:08*
15 Mar	Barcelona	Philip Kangogo KEN	2:08:16	Aynalem Kassahun ETH	2:28:18
15 Mar	Santa Monica (dh 122m)	Daniel Kiprop Limo KEN	2:10:36	Olga Kimaiyo KEN	2:34:10
15 Mar	Seoul	Wilson Loyanae KEN	2:06:11	Guteni Shone ETH	2:26:22
22 Mar	Rome	Abebe Degefa ETH	2:12:23	Meseret Kitata ETH	2:30:25
29 Mar	Zhengzhou	Julius Kiplimo Maisei KEN	2:14:17	Elizabeth Rumokol KEN	2:35:49
5 Apr	Daegu	Girmay Birhanu ETH	2:07:26	Meselech Melkamu ETH	2:27:24
12 Apr	Brighton	Duncan Maiyo KEN	2:10:15	Pennina Wanjiru KEN	2:34:25
12 Apr	Debno	Felix Kangogo KEN	2:14:28	Rebecca Jepchirchir KEN	2:44:52
12 Apr	Gunsan	Felix Keny KEN	2:09:05	Jung Hyung-sun KOR	2:38:29
12 Apr	Milano	Kenneth Mungara KEN	2:08:44	Lucy Karimi KEN	2:27:35
12 Apr	Paris	Mark Korir KEN	2:05:49	Meseret Mengistu ETH	2:23:26
12 Apr	Pyongyang	Ri Yong-ho PRK	2:16:04	Kim Hye-song PRK	2:29:12
12 Apr	Rotterdam	Abera Kuma ETH	2:06:47	Asami Kato JPN	2:26:30
12 Apr	Santiago de Chile	Luka Lobuwan KEN	2:11:53	Inés Melchor PER	2:28:18*
12 Apr	Wien	Sisay Lemma ETH	2:07:31	Maja Neuenschwander SUI	2:30:09
18 Apr	Beograd	Silas Sang KEN	2:14:42	Abebu Adugna ETH	2:33:14
19 Apr	Enschede	Evans Cheruiyot KEN	2:09:40	Mireille Baart NED	2:51:48
19 Apr	Hannover	Jacob Cheshari Kirui KEN	2:09:32	Souad Ait Salem ALG	2:27:21
19 Apr	Linz	Anthony Maritim KEN	2:09:39	Sarah Jebet KEN	2:32:52
19 Apr	Lódz	Albert Matebor KEN	2:11:49	Monika Stefanowicz POL	2:29:28
19 Apr	Nagano	Henry Chirchir KEN	2:11:39	Beatrice Toroitich KEN	2:34:02
19 Apr	Padova	Robert Kiplimo Kipkemboi KEN	2:09:32	Nancy Waigumo KEN	2:41:28
19 Apr	Rabat	Justus Kimutai KEN	2:10:38	Pamela Rotich KEN	2:30:25
19 Apr	Zürich	Edwin Kemboi Kiyeng KEN	2:11:35	Yoshiko Sakamoto JPN	2:37:47
20 Apr	Boston (dh 136m)	Lelisa Desisa ETH	2:09:17	Caroline Rotich KEN	2:24:55
26 Apr	Dongying	Ernest Ngeno KEN	2:11:47	Helah Kiprop KEN	2:31:38
26 Apr	Düsseldorf	Marius Ionescu ROU	2:13:19	Annie Bersagel USA	2:28:29
26 Apr	Hamburg	Lucas Rotich KEN	2:07:17	Meseret Hailu ETH	2:25:41
26 Apr	Madrid	Ezekiel Chebii KEN	2:12:00	Monica Jepkoech KEN	2:33:42
26 Apr	London	Eliud Kipchoge KEN	2:04:42	Tigist Tufa ETH	2:23:22
26 Apr	Warszawa	Hayle Lemi ETH	2:07:57	Fatuma Sado ETH	2:26:25*
3 May	Genève (dh 46m)	Peter Kiplagat KEN	2:11:18	Jane Kiptoo KEN	2:35:44
3 May	Praha	Felix Kandie KEN	2:08:32	Yebrqual Melese ETH	2:23:49
10 May	Mainz	Tola Bane ETH	2:11:28	Tizita Terecha ETH	2:33:25
17 May	Riga	Haile Tolossa ETH	2:12:29*	Eshetu Deme ETH	2:37:04
17 May	São Paulo	Asbel Kipsang KEN	2:15:14	Caroline Komen KEN	2:35:49
24 May	København	Hassane Ahouchar MAR	2:15:25	Nancy Jebet Koech KEN	2:33:45
24 May	Ottawa	Girmay Berhanu ETH	2:08:14	Aberu Zennebe ETH	2:25:30
30 May	Luxembourg	John Komen KEN	2:13:57	Naomi Tuei KEN	2:34:24
30 May	Stockholm	Yekeber Bayabel ETH	2:18:22	Isabellah Andersson SWE	2:34:14
13 Jun	Lanzhou (A)	Abeyneh Ayele ETH	2:10:10	Rael Kiyara KEN	2:31:22
14 Jun	Caen	Keneni Muleta ETH	2:12:57	Workitu Gurmu ETH	2:38:14
20 Jun	Duluth	Elisha Barno KEN	2:10:38	Jane Kibii KEN	2:32:06
5 Jul	Gold Coast	Kenneth Mungara KEN	2:08:42*	Risa Takenaka JPN	2:28:25
5 Jul	Guiyang (A)	Marius Kimutai Kipserem KEN	2:10:02	Melka Muru Diro ETH	2:39:14
26 Jul	Rio de Janeiro	Willy Kimutai KEN	2:14:21	Caroline Komen KEN	2:37:46
30 Aug	Sapporo	Arata Fujiwara JPN	2:16:49	Yui Okada JPN	2:32:10
30 Aug	Mexico City (A)	Daniel Aschenik ETH	2:19:24	Shewarge Amare ETH	2:41:08
6 Sep	Münster	Josphat Kiprono KEN	2:12:18	Nancy Koech KEN	2:30:25
20 Sep	Beijing	Mariko Kipchumba KEN	2:11:00	Betelhem Moges ETH	2:27:31

20 Sep	Cape Town	Shadrack Kemboi KEN	2:11:41	Isabella Ochichi KEN	2:30:20
20 Sep	Sydney	Hisanori Kitajima JPN	2:12:44	Miriam Wangari KEN	2:34:38
26 Sep	Hengshui	Ernest Ngeno KEN	2:07:57	Agnes Kiprop KEN	2:25:46*
27 Sep	Berlin	Eliud Kipchoge KEN	2:04:00	Gladys Cherono KEN	2:19:25
27 Sep	Warszawa	Ezekiel Omullo KEN	2:09:19	Ruth Wanjiru KEN	2:29:39
4 Oct	Kosice	Samuel Kosgei KEN	2:07:07	Mulu Diro ETH	2:35:33
4 Oct	Lyon	Nixon Machichim KEN	2:10:15	Emily Rotich KEN	2:39:59
4 Oct	Odense	Julius Karinga KEN	2:11:21	Mulunesh Zewedu ETH	2:34:10
4 Oct	St. Paul	Dominic Ondoro KEN	2:11:16	Serkalem Abrha ETH	2:31:40
4 Oct	Torino	Alex Saekwo KEN	2:15:29	Silvia Weissteiner ITA	2:32:35
11 Oct	Buenos Aires	Jonathan Chesoo KEN	2:12:24	Abeba Gebremeskel ETH	2:30:33
11 Oct	Chicago	Dickson Chumba KEN	2:09:25	Florence Kiplagat KEN	2:23:33
11 Oct	Eindhoven	Stephen Chebogut KEN	2:05:52	Els Rens BEL	2:38:16
11 Oct	Gyeongju	Wilson Loyanae KEN	2:07:01	Lee Sook-jung KOR	2:39:21
11 Oct	Poznan	Emil Dobrowolski POL	2:13:50	Irene Chepkirui KEN	2:32:48
11 Oct	Zagreb	Gadissa Birhanu ETH	2:13:10	Stella Barsosio KEN	2:38:34
18 Oct	Amsterdam	Bernard Kipyego KEN	2:06:19	Joyce Chepkirui KEN	2:24:11
18 Oct	Lisboa	Asbel Kipsang KEN	2:09:26	Purity Rionoripo KEN	2:25:09
18 Oct	Toronto	Ishmael Bushendich KEN	2:09:00	Shure Demise ETH	2:23:37
25 Oct	Casablanca	Jonathan Yego KEN	2:10:42	Alem Mokonnin ETH	2:32:03
25 Oct	Chuncheon	Adugna Takele ETH	2:09:40	Lee Yeon-jin KOR	2:41:53
25 Oct	Frankfurt	Sisay Lemma ETH	2:06:26	Gulume Tollesa ETH	2:23:12
25 Oct	Hefei	Marius Kipserem KEN	2:09:21	Meselech Tsegaye ETH	2:33:21
25 Oct	Ljubljana	Limenih Getachew ETH	2:08:19*	Melkam Gizaw ETH	2:25:42
25 Oct	Nairobi (A)	Joshua Kipkorir KEN	2:13:25	Elizabeth Rumokol KEN	2:29:32
25 Oct	Rennes (dh 65m)	Marius Kipserem KEN	2:09:14	Netsanet Achamo ETH	2:27:14
25 Oct	Venezia	Julius Rotich KEN	2:11:08	Ehite Bizuayehu ETH	2:35:19
26 Oct	Dublin	Alemu Gemechu ETH	2:14:01	Nataliya Lehonkova UKR	2:31:08
1 Nov	New York City	Stanley Biwott KEN	2:10:34	Mary Keitany KEN	2:24:25
1 Nov	Seoul	Tebalu Zawude ETH	2:08:46	Park Ho-sun KOR	2:36:30
8 Nov	Beirut	Jackson Limo KEN	2:11:04*	Kaltoum Bouaasayriya MAR	2:36:05
8 Nov	Nice to Cannes	Barnabas Kiptum KEN	2:10:43	Rose Chepchumba KEN	2:36:02
8 Nov	Shanghai	Paul Lonyangata KEN	2:07:14	Rael Kiyara KEN	2:26:23
8 Nov	Xichang	Gosa Tefera ETH	2:12:55	Ayantu Abera ETH	2:37:40
15 Nov	Istanbul	Elijah Chelimo KEN	2:11:17	Amane Gobena ETH	2:31:58
15 Nov	Saitama	*women only*		Atsede Baysa ETH	2:25:44
15 Nov	Valencia	John Mwangangi KEN	2:06:13*	Beata Naigambo NAM	2:26:57*
27 Nov	Alger	Shume Hailu ETH	2:11:34	Aberash Fayesa ETH	2:32:30
29 Nov	Firenze	Tujuba Megersa ETH	2:09:54	Priscah Cherono KEN	2:31:34
29 Nov	La Rochelle	Norbert Kigen KEN	2:09:25	Bekelech Daba ETH	2:32:11
6 Dec	Castellón	Chalachew Asmamaw ETH	2:12:04	Berhan Aregawi ETH	2:36:31
6 Dec	Fukuoka	Patrick Makau KEN	2:08:18	*men only*	
6 Dec	Guangzhou	Sentayehu Merga ETH	2:09:57	Tizita Terecha ETH	2:28:02
6 Dec	Macau	Vitaliy Shafar UKR	2:14:44	Olena Shurkhno UKR	2:33:24
6 Dec	Sacramento (105m dh)	Elisha Barno KEN	2:12:12	Serkalem Abrha ETH	2:31:50
6 Dec	Singapore	Julius Kiplimo Maisei KEN	2:17:26	Doris Changeywo KEN	2:44:26
13 Dec	Honolulu	Filex Kiprotich KEN	2:11:43	Joyce Chepkirui KEN	2:28:34
20 Dec	Danzhou	Gilbert Chepkwony KEN	2:14:45	Caroline Kilel KEN	2:35:11
20 Dec	Hofu	Arata Fujiwara JPN	2:11:50	Hisae Yoshimatsu, JPN	2:35:46*
20 Dec	Taipei	William Chebor KEN	2:16:15	Nancy Rotich KEN	2:36:42

¶ race day winner subsequently disqualified; *A = altitude over 1000m; * course record*

World Marathon Majors

The World Marathon Majors competition began in 2006 wherein elite marathoners would earn points based on their finish position in a series of the most significant 42.2km events around the globe. The man and woman with the most points at the conclusion of a two-year cycle would each win a prize of 500,000 US dollars.

In 2013 the Tokyo Marathon was added to the roster of Big City races, Boston, London, Berlin, Chicago and New York City. (The World Championships and Olympic Games marathons were also part of the program in the years they were run). Abbott Laboratories, an American world-wide health care company, became the title sponsor in October 2014 and in December a full-time general manager was hired.

Significant changes were announced early in 2015. A switch was made from the two-year scoring system to a rotating one-year system, with the series beginning and ending at one of the six annual city races in two consecutive years. The competition entitled Series IX began at Tokyo 2015 and ended at Tokyo 2016. The next series spans Boston 2016 to Boston 2017. The scoring was also changed from 25-15-10-5-1 to 25-16-9-4-1 but each athlete could only accumulate points from the best two finishes.

Eliud Kipchoge won Series IX with his victories at the 2015 London and Berlin Marathons. Three women led the women. The tie was settled by a vote by the leaders of the six AbbottWMM member races in favour of Mary Keitany, who had a victory at the New York City Marathon and a second-place at the London Marathon in 2015.

Top 5 men: 1. Eliud Kipchoge KEN 50 points; 2= Dickson Chumba KEN, Feyisa Lilesa ETH, Lelisa Desisa ETH 34, 5. Yemane Tsegay ETH 32

Top 5 women: 1. Mary Keitany KEN 41, 2= Mare Dibaba ETH, Helah Kiprop KEN 41; 4= Dirhane Dibaba ETH, Tigist Tufa ETH

REVIEW OF ULTRARUNNING 2015

by Andy Milroy

THERE WERE SOME interesting developments in the sport in 2015 with runners emerging from countries new to Ultrarunning; the involvement of Kenyans and Ethiopians in the 100k event has threatened for some time. In 2010 Erick Wainaina KEN ran 6:39:52 at Lake Saroma in Japan but thus far that has been the extent of the serious "invasion". In 2015, however, an Ethiopian finished second in the biggest ultra in the world, the Comrades and there was also the emergence of runners from China, setting new national records at 24 hours and making the world annual rankings for the event for the first time. North Africans have occasionally figured in the ranking lists and a Moroccan runner made the 24 hour rankings, the first such mark for some years.

There were new best performances in the most extreme distance race on the road, as well as major crossover marks with current world champions conquering a major point-to- point event in the same year. This had been achieved in 2014 when Ellie Greenwood won both the Comrades and World 100k. In 2015 double wins in the World 24 and another classic point to point event were achieved by male and female runners. There was also a continuation in interest in running traditional intermediate ultras – the 100 miles and the 12 hours at a high level.

The World 100k was held in Winschoten in the Netherlands and the men's event was won by Jonas Buud of Sweden, for whom it must have been especially sweet, as this remarkably consistent runner had previously finished second in the event four times! His 6:22:44 on the very fast, flat course was by far the fastest time in the world in 2015. Asier Cuevas of Spain was second in 6:35:49 with the former winner Giorgio Calcaterra third in 6:36:49. The fastest man in the field on paper, Vasiliy Larkin was fourth in 6:38:48. Buud led the Swedish team to the World and European team titles in a combined time of 19:59:40 from Italy 20:32:29 and France 20:37:43. The women's race was also won in the fastest time of the year. American Camille Herron ran a strong 7:08:35 to finish well clear of Kajsa Berg of Sweden 7:20:48 and Croatian Marija Vrajic 7:27:11. Herron was the strong favourite to win, already holding the world lead with 7:26:24, and she led the American women to the team title with 22:39:35 from Sweden 22:51:06 and Russia 23:30:05, led by Marina Zhalybina's 7:34:09. The European title went to Sweden, from Russia with Croatia third 23:37:13, Buud and Herron were clear World No. 1s.

Zach Bitter broke his US 100 mile track record with 11:40:55 and only the former world record marks of Don Ritchie and Cavin Woodward, along with the Russian marks of 11:28:03 and 11:29:32 of Oleg Kharitonov and Denis Zhalybin, set in 2002 in London, are ahead of him on the world all-time list. Another Briton Mark Perkins also came close to running a 100 miles in 12 hours when at Crawley he covered 160.157k.

The 2015 World 24 hour event was held in Turin in Italy. The German Florian Reus won a close race with 263.899k from Pole Pawel Szynal 261.181k and the British runner Robbie Britton 261.140k. Great Britain won the men's team event with 770.777k from Australia 752.665k and Germany 745.075k. The USA women's team was very strong, and as with the World 100k it was a battle with the Swedes. The former Hungarian, now USA, Katalin Nagy won with 244.495k, well clear of her team mate Traci Falbo's 239.740k. Maria Jansson SWE took third with 238.964k. Fourth by Maggie Guterl 235.811k ensured the US team took the team title with 720.046k – the best combined distance on record, surpassing their own previous world best set in 2013. Sweden were second 684.981k and Poland third 678.468k. GBR totalled 770.777k to win the European men's title from Germany 745.075k and France 736.237k. Women's champions were Sweden with 684.981k from Poland 678.468k and GBR 668.305k. Reus and Nagy are clear No.1s in the event and the nearest challenger to Reus in terms of distance covered was newcomer Pete Kostelnick (USA) who ran 263.418k for the best track mark of 2015.

It was a mixed year in the 48 hour event. The best male mark by Frenchman Christian Mauduit was a unspectacular 382.182k. However 376.939k by Torill Fonn SWE was the best ever by a European woman.

The top 6 day mark, Joe Fejes's 975.654k, was an USA amateur best, (still some way short of the 1000.613k set by professional James Albert Cathcart in 1888). In contrast, the female best mark of 744.488k by Silke Gielen GER was some 30k shy of Cornelia Bullig's national record. As has happened several times in recent years, the best 1000 miles marks of the year were set en route in the New York 3100 mile race. Pekka Aalto (FIN) ran a solid 12:17:19:40 first thousand miles for the fastest mark of the year and the Austrian Paula Mairer ran the fastest female mark of 16:07:47:46 as her opening split. Aalto is an experienced veteran of the race but has not been so successful in recent years. However in 2015 he came back to set a new record of 40 days 9:06:21 with Paula Mairer completing the distance in 49 days 7:52:01. Unusually the runners have the opportunity to continue on to 5000k and Aalto's 40:12:30:26 is the best on record ever for the distance, as was Mairer's female mark of 49:10:39:01.

Within the sport of Ultrarunning there is a dichotomy between the standard events recorded above, that offer direct international comparability, and the classic roots of the sport in the running journey of the point-to-point course. The oldest such race still held is the Comrades Marathon in South Africa, with its 90th in 2015. For the first time in 23 years, South Africans won both the men's and women's titles. In the 87.7k Up run from Durban to Pietermaritzburg the winner was Gift Kelehe in 5:38:36 from the Ethiopian Mohammed Teman in 5:46:14 and a second South African, Hatiwande Nyamande 5:48:19. Teman had previously run the Two Oceans race, also in RSA, recording in 8th place a 50k split of 2:53:01. A 2:12:45 marathon pb suggests that the Ethiopian could be a serious threat if he stays with ultrarunning. In the women's race Caroline Wostmann beat not only last year's winner Britain's Ellie Greenwood, but also the redoubtable Russian twins Yelena and Olesya Nurgaliyeva who had dominated the women's events for several years. In second place was another South African Charne Bosma, running 6:33:24 to the winner's 6:12:22, with Yelena Nurgaliyeva third in 6:40:36. There were some 22,000 starters.

It is difficult for the winner of a World 24 hour event, held usually on a small, flat loop course, to make the transition to the demands of a mountainous point to point course like the Spartathlon, so it was remarkable that Reus and Nagy achieved double wins. Reus won the Spartathlon, convincingly running from Athens to Sparta in emulation of Pheipiddies, in 23:17:31 well ahead of the Britain Dan Lawson 23:53:32 and the Dane Kim Hansen in 23:54:37. Then Nagy matched his feat when she won in 25:07:12 from her fellow country woman Alyson Venti 26:50:51 with three time winner Szilvia Lubics some way back in third with 29:18:44.

The longest stage race held in 2015 was Le Tour de France Footrace which started and finished in Paris. The 43-stage race covered 2741k with the stages varying between 46-86k in length each day. The winner, in an elapsed time of 263hr 28:00, was the Japanese Takazumi Senoo, from the Australian Martin Fryer 281:23:00 and Christian Fatton of France 304:21:00. The women's event was dominated by the Dutch; Wilma Dierx won with an elapsed time of 332:55:00 from Jannet Lange 363:10:00 and Jenni de Groot in the same time.

Picking the most significant highlight among the Ultra feats of 2015 is not easy. However arguably it is the second place by Teman in the Comrades. He won the Beirut Marathon twice and seems young (at 25 in 2015) to have made the transition to the ultras, but, with runs in the Ethiotrail Shashamane trail marathon in Ethiopia and the 33k road/trail Kinabalu Climbathon, obviously alternatives to marathons appeal to him.

WORLD CHAMPIONSHIPS 2015

August 22-30, Beijing, China

HOT WEATHER AND the heat of intense competition provided excellent conditions for a high-performance meeting. While the magnificent Birds Nest Stadium was never completely full, the crowds were excellent, far exceeding pessimistic predictions, and they were hugely supportive of the athletes, in particular of course, the Chinese, whose nine medals exceeded their previous World Champs best of eight by their controversial team in 1993. The heat and high humidity was, however, unhelpful to the distance athletes, particularly in the men's marathon despite its 7:34am start.

Championship bests were set in five events and many best ever marks for place were achieved. All were headed by the great world record by Ashton Eaton, who added six points to his 2012 decathlon mark. Some of the greatest names in the history of the sport added to their championships successes, above all Usain Bolt, who despite limited preparation had yet another superb treble to take his World Champs record medal collection to 13 (11 gold and 2 silver) as well as his 6 Olympic golds. Shelly-Ann Fraser-Pryce won at both 100m and 4x100m as in 2009 and 2013 and now has 6 World golds and 2 silvers, Allyson Felix followed her expected 400m win with the fastest 400m relay leg ever seen in World Champs and now has 9 World golds plus 3 silver and a bronze, and LaShawn Merritt now has 8 gold and 3 silver medals, including six in succession at 4x400m. Ezekiel Kemboi won his fourth successive steeplechase gold following three silvers.

There was a fascinating mix of expected and surprise champions. Moscow 2013 winners repeated in 13 events, including Mo Farah, who once again completed the 5000m and 10,000m double, holding off all that the Kenyans could throw at him, and Asbel Kiprop maintained his 1500m supremacy with a third title. But few would have predicted the wins by Danielle Williams at 100m hurdles or Nicholas Bett at 400m hurdles.

Jamaica and Kenya both had terrific success and headed the list of gold medal winners with seven apiece, while the USA had to settle for six golds. Although well ahead on points, the US tally was far below their 2011 and 2013 figures as was their 18 medals as a significant number of their team underperformed or even met with disaster. Russia declined hugely.

Medals and Points Table

Points: 8 for 1st to 1 for 8th place. 68 nations placed athletes in top eight, 43 won medals, and 19 won gold.

Nation	*G*	*S*	*B*	*Pts*	*2013*	*2011*
USA	6	6	6	211.5	282	251
KEN	7	6	3	173	139	174
JAM	7	2	3	132	100	191
GER	2	3	3	112.5	101.5	83
GBR	4	1	2	94	79	70
CHN	1	7	1	93.5	42	60.5
ETH	3	3	2	83	97	66
POL	3	1	4	66	43.5	44
CAN	2	3	3	64.5	41	12
RUS	2	1	1	60	182	200.5
FRA	-	-	2	41	50	45
CUB	2	1	-	30	32	48
UKR	-	1	1	28.5	51	33
NED	1	1	1	28	24	4
RSA	1	-	2	22	18	34
TTO	0	1	1	22	13	16
BLR	1	-	1	20	5	25
AUS	-	2	-	19	27	34
BAH	-	1	1	16	8	11
MAR	-	-	1	15	0	23
CRO	-	2	-	14	8	7
CZE	1	-	-	13.5	37.5	24
BRA	-	1	-	13	18.5	13
JPN	-	-	1	13	31	18
FIN	-	-	1	13	10	0
SWE	-	-	-	13	12	9
HUN	-	-	-	13	8	7
ESP	1	-	-	12	23.5	11
ERI	1	-	-	11	1	5
BEL	-	1	-	11	9	10
POR	-	-	1	11	6	13
ITA	-	-	-	11	18.5	17
COL	1	-	-	10	8	12
UGA	-	-	1	10	8	3
BRN	-	-	1	10	3	6
QAT	-	-	-	10	7	3

SVK (1G), EGY (1S), ALG, NZL 9; SRB (1B), LAT (1B), TUR 8; ISR, TJK, TUN (all 1S), GRN (1B), BUL 7; BIH, GRE, KAZ (all 1B), NGR 6; DEN, DOM, EST, PAN 5; BOT, IRL 4; ANT, CYP, ROU, SUI 3; LCA, LTU 2; ECU, IND, KSA, MDA 1

MEN

100 Metres *(prelim, h 22nd, sf, F 23rd -0.1)*

1. Usain Bolt JAM	9.79
2. Justin Gatlin USA	9.80
3= Andre De Grasse CAN	9.92
3= Trayvon Bromell USA	9.92
5. Mike Rodgers USA	9.94
6. Tyson Gay USA	10.00
7. Asafa Powell JAM	10.00
8. Jimmy Vicaut FRA	10.00
9. Su Bingtian CHN	10.06

GATLIN CAME TO Beijing with a series of superb runs in 2015, but Bolt, from a very limited racing programme, prevailed in this most keenly anticipated final. Gatlin led most of the way but had to yield to Bolt's strength as he won by 0.13, 9.784 to 9.797. Well behind, the US collegiate rivals De Grasse and Bromell tied for the bronze ahead of more fancied men. Eight bettered 10 secs in the heats with Gatlin 9.83w, Bromell 9.91 and Vicaut 9.92 fastest (Bolt 9.96) and in the semis all the finalists did so, headed by Gatlin 9.77 and Rodgers 9.86 with Bolt winning his race in 9.96 after stumbling in the first 10m. Su Bingtian tied the Chinese record with 9.99 and although he was last in the final the times by 8th and 9th were the fastest ever for these places. Femi Ogunode just missed the final after 9.99 in his heat and 10.00 (equalling the fastest ever non-qualifying time) in his semi.

200 Metres *(h 25th, sf 26th, F 27th -0.1)*

1. Usain Bolt JAM	19.55
2. Justin Gatlin USA	19.74
3. Anaso Jobodwana RSA	19.87
4. Alonso Edward PAN	19.87
5. Zharnell Hughes GBR	20.02
6. Ramil Guliyev TUR	20.11
7. Femi Ogunode QAT	20.27
8. Nickel Ashmeade JAM	20.33

GATLIN WAS FASTER than Bolt in heats and semis with 20.19 and 19.87 to 20.28 and 19.93, but there was never any doubt about Bolt's supremacy as he took his sixth global 200m title by two metres with his fifth fastest ever time. Jobodwana ran a South African record for bronze, just 0.02 ahead of Edward, whose 19.87 was the fastest ever fourth place (as was also the 8th place). Hughes set a pb in fifth. Guliyev, with a Turkish record 20.01, was fastest in the heats, and Ogunode ran a Qatari record 20.05 in the semis, in which the 20.14 run by Miguel Francis ANT was the fastest ever non-qualifying time.

400 Metres *(h 23rd, sf 24th, F 26th)*

1. Wayde van Niekerk RSA	43.48
2. LaShawn Merritt USA	43.65
3. Kirani James GRN	43.78
4. Luguelín Santos DOM	44.11
5. Isaac Makwala BOT	44.63
6. Rabah Yousif GBR	44.68
7. Machel Cedenio TTO	45.06
8. Youssef Al-Masrahi KSA	45.15

IN AN EXTRAORDINARY first round 18 men broke 44 seconds and the fastest ever first round time of 43.93 came from Al-Masrahi (Asian record) and Rusheen McDonald of Jamaica. McDonald managed 44.86 in his semi but it needed 44.64 or better to make the final, with winners Makwala 44.11, James 44.16 and van Niekerk 44.31. Merritt (44.51 and 44.34 in qualifying) was out fastest in the final, but van Niekerk took command down the back straight to reach 200m in 20.7 from Merritt 20.8 and continued to pull away so that at 300m they clocked 31.4 and 31.6 from James 31.7. Van Niekerk held on to smash the African record with 43.48 and was followed by the best ever times for 2-3-4, including a pb for Merritt and a Dominican Republic record for Santos (also a record 44.26 in his semi).

800 Metres *(h 22nd, sf 23rd, F 25th)*

1. David Rudisha KEN	1:45.84
2. Adam Kszczot POL	1:46.08
3. Amel Tuka BIH	1:46.30
4. Ferguson Cheruiyot KEN	1:46.35
5. Pierre-Ambroise Bosse FRA	1:46.63
6. Musaeb Abdulrahman Balla QAT	1:47.01
7. Nader Belhanbel MAR	1:47.09
8. Alfred Kipketer KEN-J	1:47.66

RUDISHA USED UNUSUAL tactics in the final to add to his 2011 World and 2012 Olympic titles, as after reaching 200m in 25.06 he slowed the pace right down to 400m 54.17, and it was not until 500m that the pace picked up. Rudisha then sped to 100m splits of 13.0, 12.2 and 12.1 to take him clear. Kszczot was a clear second entering the finishing straight and held that position (51.74 last lap) while Tuka (51.58 lap) overtook Cheruiyot for Bosnia & Herzegovina's first ever World Champs medal. Cheruiyot had run the fastest heat with 1:45.83 and was second fastest in the semis with 1:44.85 behind Tuka 1:44.84, and Kszczot won his semi in 1:44.97, but there were big name casualties as Mohammed Aman was disqualified for obstruction (3rd in semi one 1:45.01) and Nijel Amos came from too far back and just missed out with third in semi two.

1500 Metres *(h 27th, sf 28th, F 30th)*

1. Asbel Kiprop KEN	3:34.60
2. Elijah Manangoi KEN	3:34.63
3. Abdelaati Iguider MAR	3:34.67
4. Taoufik Makhloufi ALG	3:34.76
5. Silas Kiplagat KEN	3:34.81
6. Nick Willis NZL	3:35.46
7. Timothy Cheruiyot KEN	3:36.05
8. Matthew Centrowitz USA	3:36.13
9. Charlie Grice GBR	3:36.21
10. Leonel Manzano USA	3:37.26
11. Robby Andrews USA	3:38.29
dnf. Aman Wote ETH	–

KENYANS DID MUCH of the work with Cheruiyot and Manangoi taking turns in the lead while Kiprop held back to be 10th at the bell in 2:42.87 before moving up to fifth before the final turn and striding clear with an impressive finish of 25.6 200m, 51.53 400m and 1:50.0 last 800m to take his third title. Manangoi finished fastest of the rest and Iguider dived past Makhloufi for the bronze. Ayanleh Souleiman dropped out injured in his heat.

5000 Metres *(h 26th, F 29h)*

1. Mo Farah GBR	13:50.38
2, Caleb Ndiku KEN	13:51.75
3. Hagos Gebrihwet ETH	13:51.86
4. Yomif Kejelcha ETH-J	13:52.43
5. Galen Rupp USA	13:53.90
6. Ben True USA	13:54.07
7. Ryan Hill USA	13:55.10
8. Isiah Koech KEN	13:55.98
9. Ali Kaya TUR	13:56.51
10. Edwin Soi KEN	13:59.02
11. Albert Rop BRN	14:00.12
12. Mohammed Ahmed CAN	14:00.38
13. Imane Merga ETH	14:01.60
14. Richard Ringer GER	14:03.72
15. Tom Farrell GBR	14:08.87

DESPITE FARAH ALREADY having run the 10,000, the three fresh Kenyans made no attempt to make this race fast. Farah had qualified in much the fastest of the two heats, 13:19.44 behind Kejelcha's 13:19.38, and in the final was in last place (3:04.40) in a desperately slow first kilometre (3:02.04). 2000m was reached in 6:00.90 before Merga was the first to increase the pace but it was still slow at 3000m 8:47.28 with Farah now up to second and Ndiku only 12th. Farah moved ahead with four laps to go and Ndiku took over with 58.39 for the 11th lap. He ran 28.16 to reach the bell 4m clear, and 26.08 for the first 200m of that final lap. But Farah could not be shaken off and sprinted past the Kenyan with 80m to go. Farah's finishing splits were 26.59, 52.67, c. 1:20.8, c.1:48.6 and 2:19.22 for 1000m and he is the only man to have completed the 5/10 double at three successive Olympics/Worlds. Three Americans took places 5-6-7.

10,000 Metres *(22nd)*

1. Mo Farah GBR	27:01.13
2. Geoffrey Kamworor KEN	27:01.76
3. Paul Tanui KEN	27:02.83
4. Bidan Karoki KEN	27:04.77
5. Galen Rupp USA	27:08.91
6. Abrar Osman ERI	27:43.21
7. Ali Kaya TUR	27:43.69
8. Timothy Toroitich UGA	27:44.90
9. Joshua Cheptegei UGA-J	27:48.89
10. Muktar Edris ETH	27:54.47
11. Mosinet Geremew ETH	28:07.50
12. El Hassan El Abbassi BRN	28:12.57
13. Nguse Tesfaldet ERI	28:14.72
14. Cameron Levins CAN	28:15.19
15. Hassan Mead USA	28:16.30

FOLLOWING A SLOW first kilometre of 2:52.22 (Farah 2:54.26), the Kenyan trio took turns to lead at a fast pace. The second kilometre took 2:39.89 (Farah 2:40.33), followed by 2:43.02 (2:43.33), 2:42.49 (2:41.30) and 2:43.21 (2:42.79). At halfway the times were Karoki 13:40.83, Kamworor 13:41.01, Tanui 13:41.08, Merga 13:41.16, Kaya 13:41.50, Rupp 13:41.69, Farah 13:42.01. The Kenyans continued to tick off the laps in 64/65 sec, Kamworor usually in front, and sixth to ninth kilometres were 2:42.09 (Farah 2:41.74), 2:43.42 (2:42.84), 2:43.65 (2:43.66) and 2:42.31 (2:42.07). Farah went ahead with 500m to go, momentarily stumbled passing some lapped runners, but held all at bay with a 54.14 last lap and 13:19.12 for his second 5000m.

Marathon *(22nd)*

1. Ghirmay Ghebreslassie ERI	2:12:28
2. Yemane Tsegay ETH	2:13:08
3. Solomon Mutai UGA	2:13:30
4. Ruggero Pertile ITA	2:14:23
5. Shumi Dechasa BRN	2:14:36
6. Stephen Kiprotich UGA	2:14:43
7. Lelisa Desisa ETH	2:14:54
8. Daniele Meucci ITA	2:14:54
9. Amanuel Mesel ERI	2:15:07
10. Jackson Kiprop UGA	2:15:16
11. Pak Choi PRK	2:15:44
12. Alphonce Simbu TAN	2:16:58
13. Javier Guerra ESP	2:17:00
14. Tsepo Ramonene LES	2:17:17
15. Berhanu Lemi ETH	2:17:37

GHEBRESLASSIE BECAME AT 19 the youngest ever global marathon champion and the first Eritrean gold medallist. Despite a 7:34 am start conditions were sweltering and 25 of the 67 starters failed to finish, including the biggest names Denis Kimetto and Wilson Kipsang (both before 35k), and Kenya had just one finisher, Mark Korir 22nd.

3000m Steeplechase *(h 22nd, F 24h)*

1. Ezekiel Kemboi KEN	8:11.28
2. Conseslus Kipruto KEN	8:12.38
3. Brimin Kipruto KEN	8:12.54
4. Jairus Birech KEN	8:12.62
5. Daniel Huling USA	8:14.39
6. Evan Jager USA	8:15.47
7. Brahim Taleb MAR	8:17.73
8. Matthew Hughes CAN	8:18.63
9. Krystian Zalewski POL	8:21.22
10. Donald Cabral USA	8:24.94
11. Hamid Ezzine MAR	8:25.72
12. Hailemariyam Amare ETH-J	8:26.19
13. Bilal Tabti ALG	8:29.04
14. Hicham Bouchicha ALG	8:33.79
15. Tolosa Nurgi ETH	8:44.81

KEMBOI, WHO HAD been fastest in the heats with 8:24.75, won his fourth consecutive world title as he followed a very slow tempo set by his teammates (C Kipruto 2:49.50 and 5:36.77) with a sensational last lap of 56.81 despite easing up and veering into lane three for his victory celebrations. C Kipruto stuttered badly at the last hurdle but Kenya took the first four places for an unprecedented sweep.

110m Hurdles *(h 26th, sf 27th, F 28th 0.1)*

1. Sergey Shubenkov RUS	12.98
2. Hansle Parchment JAM	13.03
3. Aries Merritt USA	13.04
4. Pascal Martinot-Lagarde FRA	13.17
5. Dmitri Bascou FRA	13.17
6. Omar McLeod JAM	13.18
7. David Oliver USA	13.33
8. Garfield Darien FRA	13.34

IN THE FIRST round Ronnie Ash USA was disqualified for a false start with Oliver fastest at 13.15, and the semis were won by Shubenkov 13.09, Merritt 13.08 and Bascou 13.16. Aleec Harris ran the fastest ever non-qualifying mark of 13.29. Merritt, who had only just revealed that he suffered from a rare kidney disorder and was to have a transplant after the Championships, got out well in the final with McLeod and Bascou, but Oliver hit early hurdles hard and was never in contention as Shubenkov came through strongly to take the title and lower the Russian record by 0.08. A late charge by Parchment brought him silver 0.01 ahead of Merritt.

400m Hurdles *(h 22nd, sf 23rd, F 25th)*

1. Nicholas Bett KEN	47.79
2. Dennis Kudryavtsev RUS	48.05
3. Jeffrey Gibson BAH	48.17
4. Kerron Clement USA	48.18
5. Boniface Mucheru KEN	48.33
6. Yasmani Copello TUR	48.96
7. Patryk Dobek POL	49.14
8. Michael Tinsley USA	50.02

THERE WAS A major upset as Bett won from lane 9 in the world's fastest time for two years. The other medallists Kudryavtsev and Gibson also set national records. Tinsley had gone out hard but made mistakes and Kudryavtsev led until the final hurdle but had no answer to Bett's speed on the run-in. Bett had also run in lane 9 when he ran much the fastest time of the heats 48.37, and Kudryavtsev ran pbs of 48.51 and 48.23, the fastest time in the semis in which all eight finalists ran 48.54 (Bett) or better with national records from Gibson 48.37 and Copello 48.46. Kariem Hussein was the fastest non-qualifier with 48.59.

High Jump *(Q 2.31 28th, F 30th)*

1. Derek Drouin CAN	2.34
2= Bohdan Bondarenko UKR	2.33
2= Zhang Guowei CHN	2.33
4. Mutaz Essa Barshim QAT	2.33
5. Daniyil Tsyplakov RUS	2.29
6. Donald Thomas BAH	2.29
7. Jaroslav Bába CZE	2.29
8= Erik Kynard USA	2.25
8= Gianmarco Tamberi ITA	2.25
10. Trevor Barry BAH	2.25
11. Dimitrios Hondrokoukis CYP	2.25
12= Eike Onnen GER	2.25
12= Brandon Starc AUS	2.25
14. Konstadínos Baniótis GRE	2.20

AN EXCITING COMPETITION was decided by a three-man jump off. Four men cleared 2.33 but failed at 2.36. Barshim had one failure earlier so took fourth and then the three medallists, who all had clean cards up to 2.33, failed on their extra leap at 2.36 before Drouin was the one to go over 2.34. Ten men qualifying at 2.31 matched the all-time record and 2.29 by Ghazal, Duffield and Protsenko was the best-ever non-qualifying height.

Pole Vault *(Q 5.70m 22nd, F 24th)*

1. Shawn Barber CAN	5.90
2. Raphaël Holzdeppe GER	5.90
3= Renaud Lavillenie FRA	5.80
3= Pawel Wojciechowski POL	5.80
3= Piotr Lisek POL	5.80
6. Kévin Menaldo FRA	5.80
7= Michal Balner CZE	5.65
7= Tobias Scherbarth GER	5.65
9= Germán Chiaraviglio ARG	5.65
9= Ivan Horvat CRO	5.65
9= Sam Kendricks USA	5.65
9= Augusto Dutra de Oliveira BRA	5.65
13= Jan Kudlicka CZE	5.50
13= Robert Renner SLO	5.50
15. Robert Sobera POL	5.50
nh. Ivan Gertleyn RUS	–

THE BIG FAVOURITE Lavillenie had to settle for a fourth World medal (but no gold) as he tied with Wojciechowski and Lisek for bronze at 5.80, a height also cleared by Menaldo. Barber went over 5.60, 5.65, 5.80 and 5.90 on his first attempts and defending champion Holzeppe cleared 5.90 on his third, before both found 6.00 too much. A record 16 men competed in the final by clearing 5.70 and that and 24 men at 5.65 were all-time records. Missing the final, however, were Brad Walker 5.65 and Konstadínos Filippídis 5.55.

Long Jump *(Q 8.15m 24th, F 25th)*

1. Greg Rutherford GBR	8.41/0.3
2. Fabrice Lapierre AUS	8.24/0.7
3. Wang Jianan CHN-J	8.18/0.0
4. Gao Xinglong CHN	8.14/1.2
5. Li Jinzhe CHN	8.10/0.2
6. Aleksandr Menkov RUS	8.02/-0.5
7. Kafétien Gomis FRA	8.02/0.1
8. Sergey Polyanskiy RUS	7.97/0.0
9. Jeffrey Henderson USA	7.95/-0.6
10. Tyrone Smith BER	7.79/0.0
11. Radek Juska CZE	7.57/-0.4
nj. Mike Hartfield USA	–

A SILLY QUALIFYING standard of 8.15 was achieved by only two men: Henderson 8.36 and Rutherford 8.25, and indeed by only three in the final. Rutherford rose above the overall modest standard with 8.29 in the second round and 8.41 in the fourth for a clear win, and Lapierre took a surprising silver with 8.20 and 8.24 as his last two jumps. The Chinese excelled to come 3-4-5. Henderson missed the top eight although his 7.95 was 8.22 from take-off.

Triple Jump *(Q 17.05m 26th, F 27th)*

1. Christian Taylor USA	18.21/0.2
2. Pedro Pablo Pichardo CUB	17.73/0.2
3. Nelson Évora POR	17.52/0.3
4. Omar Craddock USA	17.37/0.2
5. Lyukman Adams RUS	17.28/0.3
6. Marian Oprea ROU	17.06/0.4
7. Dmitriy Sorokin RUS	16.99/0.4
8. Tosin Oke NGR	16.81/0.4
9. Khotso Mokoena RSA	16.81/0.3
10. Leevan Sands BAH	16.68/0.3
11. Jonathan Drack MRI	16.64/0.1
12. Benjamin Compaoré FRA	16.63/0.2

TAYLOR AND PICHARDO had another great clash, their fourth of 2015. After 17.28 and 17.43 respectively, the top qualifiers, Pichardo took an early advantage with a first-round 17.52 in the final with Taylor jumping 17.49 in the second and both doing 17.60 in the third. Taylor led with a fourth-round 17.68 and then both produced their best in the last round. Taylor's 18.21 was the second longest ever legal mark and his assisting wind of only 0.2m/sec compared to 1.3 for Edwards on his WR jump. Taylor took off with 11.5m to spare on the board so he actually travelled 18.32! He hopped 5.96, stepped 5.84 and jumped 6.41. Pichardo's response of 17.73 was 6.53, 4.96 and 6.24. Evora's final round 17.52 (his best for six years) overtook Craddock's 17.37 for the bronze.

Shot *(Q 20.65m & F 23rd)*

1. Joe Kovacs USA	21.93
2. David Storl GER	21.74
3. O'Dayne Richards JAM	21.69
4. Tomas Walsh NZL	21.58
5. Reese Hoffa USA	21.00
6. Tomasz Majewski POL	20.82
7. Asmir Kolasinac SRB	20.71
8. Jacko Gill NZL	20.11
9. Germán Lauro ARG	19.70
10. Jan Marcell CZE	19.69
11. Inderjeet Singh IND	19.52
dns. Christian Cantwell USA	

IN QUALIFYING KOVACS edged Storl 21.36 to 21.26 with Hoffa next with 20.75. In the final Kovacs opened with 21.23 with Storl 21.46 in round two. But then Richards duplicated his CAC and Jamaican record 21.69 to take the lead in r3 and Walsh produced an Oceania record 21.58 in R4, in which Kovacs advanced to 21.67. Then Kovacs went to 21.93 followed by Storl 21.74 in r5 to seal the issue.

Discus *(Q 65.00m 27th, F 29th)*

1. Piotr Malachowski POL	67.40
2. Philip Milanov BEL	66.90
3. Robert Urbanek POL	65.18
4. Gerd Kanter EST	64.82
5. Daniel Ståhl SWE	64.73
6. Apostolos Parellis CYP	64.55
7. Fedrick Dacres JAM	64.22
8. Christoph Harting GER	63.94
9. Vikas Gowda IND	62.24
10. Benn Harradine AUS	62.05
11. Mauricio Ortega CHI	62.01
12. Julian Wruck AUS	60.01

MALACHOWSKI NEEDED THREE throws to reach a qualifying distance but then his 65.59 matched the best of the round by Dacres, and in the final he won with a second round 67.40, backed by four more throws over 64m to take gold after silvers in 2009 and 2013 plus the 2008 Olympics. Milanov came second with a Belgian record in the third round and Urbanek third ahead of Kanter, whose fourth place followed a gold, two silver and two bronze World medals.

Hammer *(Q 77.00m 22nd, F 23rd)*

1. Pawel Fajdek POL	80.88
2. Dilshod Nazarov TJK	78.55
3. Wojciech Nowicki POL	78.55
4. Krisztián Pars HUN	77.32
5. Sergey Litvinov RUS	77.24
6. David Söderberg FIN	76.92
7. Mostafa Al-Gamal EGY	76.81
8. Marcel Lomnicky SVK	75.79
9. Ashraf Amjad El-Seify QAT	74.09
10. Tuomas Seppänen FIN	73.18
11. Nick Miller GBR	72.94
12. Roberto Janet CUB	72.50

FAJDEK FULFILLED HIS favourite's status with 78.38 in qualifying (from Miller 77.42 and Litvinov 76.79) and top throws of 80.64, 80.88 and 79.34 in rounds 3-5 of the final. Silver and bronze went at 78.55 with Nazarov ahead from a second best 78.06 to Nowicki's 77.20, Pars, the 2011 winner, was only fourth.

Javelin *(Q 83.00m 24th, F 26th)*

1. Julius Yego KEN	92.72
2. Ihab Abdelrahman EGY	88.99
3. Tero Pitkämäki FIN	87.64
4. Thomas Röhler GER	87.41
5. Antti Ruuskanen FIN	87.12
6. Andreas Hofmann GER	86.01
7. Johannes Vetter GER	83.79
8. Vitezslav Vesely CZE	83.13
9. Ryohei Arai JPN	83.07
10. Braian Toledo ARG	80.27
11. Kim Amb SWE	78.51
12. Risto Mätas EST	76.79

IN WINDLESS CONDITIONS Yego became the first Kenyan to win a global field event title with a mighty Commonwealth record 92.72

in the third round to move up to third on the world all-time list. In the first round Röhler led with 86.68 from Abdelrahman 86.07 and the latter then threw 88.99 in the second round. That sealed silver but both Pitkämäki and Röhler threw over 87m twice and Ruuskanen once. Pitkämäki added bronze to his 2007 gold and 2013 silver.

Decathlon *(28-29th)*

1. Ashton Eaton USA	9045*
2. Damian Warner CAN	8695
3. Rico Freimuth GER	8561
4. Ilya Shkurenyov RUS	8538
5. Larbi Bouraada ALG	8461
6. Kai Kazmirek GER	8448
7. Michael Schrader GER	8418
8. Kurt Felix GRN	8302
9. Oleksiy Kasyanov UKR	8262
10. Maicel Uibo EST	8245
11. Adam Sebastian Helcelet CZE	8234
12. Pieter Braun NED	8114
13. Bastien Auzeil FRA	8093
14. Thomas Van Der Plaetsen BEL	8035
15. Zach Ziemek USA	8006

THE STANDARD WAS good with eight men over 8300 points, pbs for 1-5 and 8 and national records for Canada and Grenada and an African record by Bouraada, but Eaton was a class apart as he retained his title and added 6 points to his 2012 world record. After a superb start of 10.23 for 100m, two factors were particularly significant – his brilliant 400 metres to conclude day one when his 45.00 (previous pb 45.55) was far ahead of the previous best ever in a decathlon, Bill Toomey's high altitude 45.68 in 1968, and that he had an excellent 1500m runner to key off at the end as, needing 4:18.25 for the record; Eaton followed Bouraada 4:16.61 with 4:17.52. Warner also competed brilliantly – pbs at long jump 7.65 and shot 14.44 with 10.31 for 100m and 13.63 for 110mh at his best events.

4 x 100m Relay *(h, F 29th)*

1. JAM	37.36	Carter, Powell, Ashmeade, Bolt (ht: 3. Dwyer, 4. Ashmeade)
2. CHN	38.01	Mo Youxue, Xie Zhenye, Su Bingtian, Zhang Peimeng
3. CAN	38.13	Brown, de Grasse, Rodney, J Warner (ht: 1. Warner, 4. Brown)
4. GER	38.15	Reus, Knipphals, Kosenkow, Menga
5. FRA	38.23	Biron, Lemaitre, Anouman, Vicaut
6. ANT	38.61	Walsh, D Bailey, Jarvis, Francis
dq. USAdq	(37.77)	Bromell, Gatlin, Gay, Rodgers
dnf. GBR	–	Kilty, Talbot, Ellington, Ujah

THE FAVOURITES JAMAICA 37.41 and USA 37.91 won their heats, with excellent times also by France 37.88, China, Asian record 37.92, and Antigua, national record 38.01. The experienced Jamaicans, anchored by Bolt, won the final but this was (once again!) a disaster for both the USA and Britain. Rodgers crossed the line in second place for the Americans, but he was beyond the zone when taking the baton from Gay, who was in the lead at the time, and Ujah set off much too early for Britain at the final change so that the incoming Ellington could not get the baton to him. This left China to take a surprising second place. It was the seventh time in the last 13 Worlds that the USA was disqualified or failed to finish.

4 x 400m Relay *(h 29th, F 30th)*

1. USA	2:57.82	Verburg 45.2, McQuay 44.2, Nellum 44.38, L Merritt 44.18 (Clemons & Norwood ran in heat)
2. TTO	2:58.20	Quow 44.9, L Gordon 44.1, Lendore 44.85, Cedenio 44.47 (Solomon ran in heat)
3. GBR	2:58.51	Yousif 45.1, D Williams 44.6, Dunn 44.98, Rooney 43.97
4. JAM	2:58.51	Matthews 45.3, Chambers 45.3, McDonald 44.56, Francis 43.52
5. BEL	3:00.24	J Borlée 45.5, Venderbemden 45.3, K Borlée 43.98, Gillet 45.95
6. FRA	3:00.65	Anne 45.4, Venel 44.4, Hanne 45.62, Jordier 45.31
7. CUB	3:03.05	Collazo 46.2, Acea 45.4, Chacón 46.63, Lescay 44.93
8. RUS	3:03.05	Denmukhametov 46.8, Trenikhin 45.9, Alekseyev 45.05, Ivashko 44.41

ALL EIGHT FINAL teams broke 3 minutes in the heats plus Botswana running the fastest ever non-qualifying time of 2:59.95 and Bahamas 2:59.24 only to be disqualified. Many fast splits were headed by K Borlée 43.78, Lalonde Gordon 43.82 and Soriano DOM 43.8. Only four teams broke 3 mins in the final, but it was an exciting race and Jamaica ran the fastest ever fourth place time. Quow gave Trinidad a first-leg lead and Gordon retained that with a 44.1 leg. The US was in hot pursuit and Nellum took them into the lead after three legs before Merritt pulled away on the final leg to ensure his sixth successive World relay gold medal. 19 year-old Cedenio ensured Trinidad's silver and national record as Rooney's 43.97 anchor for Britain almost (just 0.004 behind) caught him. A great third leg by Kevin Borlée had taken Belgium to third but then they slipped back to fifth.

20 Kilometres Walk *(23rd)*

1. Miguel Angel López ESP	1:19:14
2. Wang Zhen CHN	1:19:29
3. Benjamin Thorne CAN	1:19:57
4. Ihor Hlavan UKR	1:20:29
5. Cai Zelin CHN	1:20:42
6. Caio Bonfim BRA	1:20:44
7. Eider Arévalo COL	1:21:13
8. Dane Bird-Smith AUS	1:21:37

9. Chen Ding CHN	1:21:39
10. Kim Hyun-sub KOR	1:21:40
11. Lebogang Shange RSA	1:21:43
12. Evan Dunfee CAN	1:21:48
13. Isamu Fujisawa JPN	1:21:51
14. Iñaki Gómez CAN	1:21:55
15. Eder Sánchez MEX	1:21:56

AFTER THE LEADERS had reached halfway in 40:20/22, Wang Zhen opened up a significant lead to reach 15k in 59:53, 11 sec ahead of López, but he had two warnings and could not match the finish of the Spaniard, who had 5k splits of 20:13, 20:08, 19:43 and 19:10 to end with a pb. Thorne was an unexpected bronze medallist with a last 5k in 18:47 and a North American record. There were 50 finishers from 61 starters and world record holder Yusuke Suzuki dropped out soon after halfway.

50 Kilometres Walk *(29th)*

1. Matej Tóth SVK	3:40:32
2. Jared Tallent AUS	3:42:17
3. Takayuki Tanii JPN	3:42:55
4. Hiroki Arai JPN	3:43:44
5. Robert Heffernan IRL	3:44:17
6, Zhang Lin CHN	3:44:39
7. Yu Wei CHN	3:45:21
8. Andrés Chocho ECU	3:46:00
9. Jesús Ángel García ESP	3:46:43
10. Quentin Rew NZL	3:48:48
11. Adrian Blocki POL	3:49:11
12. Evan Dunfee CAN	3:49:56
13. Chris Erickson AUS	3:51:26
14. Wu Xianlong CHN	3:51:35
15. Ivan Banzeruk UKR	3:52:15

THE FAVOURITE TÓTH took the lead as early as 600m and steadily widened his advantage all the way to the finish, leading by 27 sec at 10k (45:22), 50 sec at 20k (1:29:24), 1:09 at 30k (2:13:14). Tallent was second for his sixth global medal, Chocho set a South American record and Jesús Ángel García, the 1993 champion, came 9th in his record 12th World Championship. 38 finished from 53 starters.

WOMEN

100 Metres *(h 23rd, sf, F 24th -0.3)*

1. Shelly-Ann Fraser-Pryce JAM	10.76
2. Dafne Schippers NED	10.81
3. Tori Bowie USA	10.86
4. Veronica Campbell-Brown JAM	10.91
5. Michelle-Lee Ahye TTO	10.98
6. Kelly-Ann Baptiste TTO	11.01
7. Natasha Morrison JAM	11.02
8. Blessing Okagbare NGR	11.02

FRASER-PRYCE RAN 10.88w in her heat, with Bowie 10.88, Marie Josée Ta Lou 10.95w and Ahye 10.98 also under 11 secs, and was the fastest semi-final winner in 10.82, the others being Schippers, Dutch record 10.83, and Bowie 10.87, before taking her fifth global 100m title in 10.75, half a metre ahead of Schippers, who took another 0.02 off her Dutch record. Fraser-Pryce's reaction time was only 0.161 but she was very quickly into her running and then led all the way. All eight finalists broke 11 secs in their semis as did Murielle Ahouré, whose 10.98 was the fastest ever non-qualifying mark. English Gardner was a surprise non-qualifier with only 11.16 heat and 11.13 semi.

200 Metres *(h 26th, sf 27th, F 28th 0.2)*

1. Dafne Schippers NED	21.63
2. Elaine Thompson JAM	21.66
3. Veronica Campbell-Brown JAM	21.97
4. Candyce McGrone USA	22.01
5. Dina Asher-Smith GBR	22.07
6. Jeneba Tarmoh USA	22.31
7. Ivet Lalova-Callio BUL	22.41
8. Sherone Simpson JAM	22.50

SCHIPPERS SHOWED THAT her decision to leave the heptathlon for the year to concentrate on the sprints was correct as she won the final in the world's fastest time for 17 years, taking 0.4 off her 2014 Dutch record. Thompson was also brilliant as she improved her best by 0.44 to finish just 0.03 down on Schippers and go to fifth on the world all-time list while VCB ran her fastest time for seven years and took her 19th global medal. Pbs were also run by McGrone and Asher-Smith, whose 22.07 was the fastest ever fifth place time with pbs in each round, heading 17 women under 23 secs in the heats with 22.22 and being fastest in the semis at 22.12 with Thompson 22.13 and McGrone 22.26 nex.

400 Metres *(h 24th, sf 25th, F 27th)*

1. Allyson Felix USA	49.26
2. Shaunae Miller BAH	49.67
3. Shericka Jackson JAM	49.99
4. Christine Day JAM	50.14
5. Stephenie Ann McPherson JAM	50.42
6. Novlene Williams-Mills JAM	50.47
7. Phyllis Francis USA	50.51
8. Christine Ohuruogu GBR	50.63

AFTER A MASS of sprint medals, Felix won her first global title at 400m. She ran an easy 50.60 heat and was fastest in the semis at 49.89 before going off hard in the final, making up from lane 6 the stagger on defending champion Ohuruogu (l7) within a few seconds, going through 100m in 11.4 and 200m in 23.3, so that slowing to 35.6 at 300m and a last 13.7 to the finish meant that she was never threatened as she had built up such a commanding lead. Miller (200m 23.7 and 300m 36.1) passed Jackson (23.4 and 36.1) for silver as Jamaicans took places 2-3-4-5. Ohuruogu (50.16 in her semi) worked too hard to try to catch Felix with 23.7 at 200m but faded and was passed by the rest of the field.

800 Metres *(h 26th, sf 27th, F 29th)*

1. Marina Arzamasova BLR	1:58.03
2. Melissa Bishop CAN	1:58.12
3. Eunice Sum KEN	1:58.18
4. Rababe Arrafi MAR	1:58.90
5. Shelayna Oskan-Clarke GBR	1:58.99
6. Nataliya Lupu UKR	1:58.99
7. Joanna Józwik POL	1:59.09
8. Renelle Lamote FRA	1:59.70

THERE WAS TOPSY-TURVY form here, with the favourite Sum coming third and several leading contenders, including Büchel, Sharp, Kohlmann, Martinez and Almanza, not making the final. Arzamasova 1:58.69 and Sharp 1:58.98 ran the fastest heats and then the semis were hot with 11 women under 1:59 and 17 under 2 minutes. Bishop, with a Canadian record 1:57.52, was quickest in semi 3 from Arzamasova 1:57.54 and Sum 1:57.56, with other winners Arrafi 1:58.56 and Oskan-Clarke 1:58.86. The final started fast, 27.3 at 200m, before Sum slowed to 400m in 59.08. Arzamasova challenged to lead at 600m in 1:28.87 and Sum fought hard but could not get past as Bishop finished fastest to split them.

1500 Metres *(h 22nd, sf 23rd, F 25th)*

1. Genzebe Dibaba ETH	4:08.09
2. Faith Kipyegon KEN	4:08.96
3. Sifan Hassan NED	4:09.34
4. Dawit Seyaum ETH-J	4:10.26
5. Laura Muir GBR	4:11.48
6. Abeba Aregawi SWE	4:12.16
7. Shannon Rowbury USA	4:12.39
8. Angelika Cichocka POL	4:13.22
9. Rabab Arrafi MAR	4:13.66
10. Tatyana Tomashova RUS	4:14.18
11. Jennifer Simpson USA	4:16.28
12. Malika Akkaoui MAR	4:16.98

DIBABA RAN REMARKABLE last laps of 59.33 to win her heat in 4:02.59 and 58.00 for her semi in 4:06.74. 17 women ran under 4:07.09 in the first round, but the final was much slower. At least it was to start with as the opening lap took 1:17.05. Then at 700m Dibaba took off and ran a sensational third lap in 57.22 and her last 800m in an extraordinary 1:56.95 to win by 6m from Kipyegon (1:57.54), who overtook Hassan (1:57.15) in the finishing straight. Seyaum (1:58.55) was fourth and Muir (1:59.95) fifth. Simpson had a shoe partially ripped off in the scramble to catch Dibaba and then lost it 200m later.

5000 Metres *(h 27th, F 30th)*

1. Almaz Ayana ETH	14:26.83*
2. Senbere Teferi ETH	14:44.07
3. Genzebe Dibaba ETH	14:44.14
4. Viola Kibiwot KEN	14:46.16
5. Mercy Cherono KEN	15:01.36
6. Janet Kisa KEN	15:02.68
7. Irene Cheptai KEN	15:03.41
8. Susan Kuijken NED	15:08.00
9. Ayuko Suzuki JPN	15:08.29
10. Eloise Wellings AUS	15:09.62
11. Mimi Belete BRN	15:17.01
12. Stephanie Twell GBR	15:26.24
13. Nicole Tully USA	15:27.42
14. Misaki Onishi JPN	15:29.63
15. Jennifer Wenth AUT	15:35.46

THE FAVOURITES, AYANA 15:09.40 and Dibaba 15:20.82 won their heats, but in the final Ayana was far too strong for Dibaba, who, of course, had already run three rounds of 1500m races. The opening pace was slow, Onishi leading at 1000m 3:01.56 and Suzuki at 2000m 6:06.27, but then Ayana kicked in laps of 68.06, 67.60 and 65.85 through 3000m in 8:55.63 (Dibaba 8:55.84, Cherono 8:56.34, Kibiwot 8:58.41 and Teferi 8:58.69) and then 66.30 before seeing off Dibaba with a tenth lap of 64.52 so that she was 40m clear at 4000m in 11:39.25. Although slowing a little, a last kilometre in 2:47.58 brought Ayana home 100m ahead, and the tired Dibaba was passed by Teferi for the silver, their last kilometres 2:49.27 and 2:59.50. Ayana's last 3000m was an astonishing 8:19.91.

10,000 Metres *(24th)*

1. Vivian Cheruiyot KEN	31:41.31
2. Gelete Burka ETH	31:41.77
3. Emily Infeld USA	31:43.49
4. Molly Huddle USA	31:43.58
5. Sally Kipyego KEN	31:44.42
6. Shalane Flanagan USA	31:46.23
7. Alemitu Haroye ETH	31:49.73
8. Betsy Saina KEN	31:51.35
9. Belaynesh Oljira ETH	31:53.01
10. Susan Kuijken NED	31:54.32
11. Jip Vastenburg NED	32:03.03
12. Sara Moreira POR	32:06.14
13. Kasumi Nishihara JPN	32:12.95
14. Brenda Flores MEX	32:15.26
15. Kate Avery GBR	32:16.19

HAVING MISSED THE 2013 and 2014 seasons, Cheruiyot regained the title from 2011 by closing with a spectacular final kilometre of 2:48.30. There was a gentle early pace by Takashima and Ohara of Japan to 5000m 16:11.99 (Cheruiyot 16:13.48). Then Moreira led at 6k, Haroye at 7k, Cheruiyot at 8k and Huddle at 9k, when ten women remained in contention from the 25 starters. Huddle pushed on and still led at the bell from Burka and Cheruiyot but the latter prevailed with a last lap of 31.3 and 29.3. Huddle made the mistake of easing off a stride or two before the line and Infeld flashed past on her inside; the US women came 3-4-6.

Marathon *(30th)*

1. Mare Dibaba ETH	2:27:35
2. Helah Kiprop KEN	2:27:36
3. Eunice Jepkirui BRN	2:27:39

4. Jemima Jelagat KEN	2:27:42
5. Edna Kiplagat KEN	2:28:18
6. Tigist Tufa ETH	2:29:12
7. Mai Ito JPN	2:29:48
8. Tirfi Tsegaye ETH	2:30:54
9. Kim Hye-song PRK	2:30:59
10. Serena Burla USA	2:31:06
11. Rasa Drazdauskaite LTU	2:31:23
12. Filomena Costa POR	2:31:40
13. Sairi Maeda JPN	2:31:46
14. Risa Shigetomo JPN	2:32:37
15. Alina Prokopyeva RUS	2:32:44

JUST FOUR SECONDS covered the medallists with Dibaba's finishing sprint earning her the victory. The race was run on the last and coolest day of the Championships, but it was still pretty warm and 13 of the 65 starters failed to finish. So the pace was cautious to start with and halfway was reached in 1:15:16. The 5k to 35k was run in 17:14 and that reduced the leading pack to five before 16:34, easily the fastest 5k of the race, to 40k. Kiplagat was the first to drop back and finally Jelagat, leaving the others to battle to the line.

3000m Steeplechase *(h 24th, F 26th)*

1. Hyvin Jepkemoi KEN	9:19.11
2. Habiba Ghribi TUN	9:19.24
3. Gesa Felicitas Krause GER	9:19.25
4. Sofia Assefa ETH	9:20.01
5. Emma Coburn USA	9:21.78
6. Hiwot Ayalew ETH	9:24.27
7. Virginia Nyambura KEN	9:26.21
8. Lalita Babar IND	9:29.64
9. Stephanie Garcia USA	9:31.06
10. Salima El Ouali Alami MAR	9:32.15
11. Ruth Chebet BRN-J	9:33.41
12. Colleen Quigley USA	9:34.29
13. Özlem Kaya TUR	9:34.66
14. Fadwa Sidi Madane MAR	9:41.45
15. Rosefline Chepngetich KEN	9:46.08

FOURTEEN WOMEN RAN under 9:30 in the heats, headed by Jepkemoi 9:24.38. After a very slow start Babar, who in her heat had reduced her Indian record from 9:34.13 to 9:27.86, sped away to open up a big lead by 1000m in 3:09.96. She was still ahead at 2000m in 6:22.27 but dropped back to eighth during a very speedy final kilometre of 2:56.84. At the final water jump Ghribi and Jepkemoi (a poor technician) were just about level, with Krause in close attendance, but Assefa came to a complete stop before climbing over the barrier. Krause held a slim advantage over the last hurdle, but on the run-in she was passed by both Jepkemoi and Ghribi in a very close finish.

100m Hurdles *(h 27th, sf, F 28th -0.3)*

1. Danielle Williams JAM	12.57
2. Cindy Roleder GER	12.59
3. Alina Talay BLR	12.66
4. Brianna Rollins USA	12.67
5. Tiffany Porter GBR	12.68
6. Noemi Zbären SUI	12.95
7. Shermaine Williams JAM	12.95
8. Sharika Nelvis USA	13.06

THIS EVENT PROVIDED the biggest surprises of the Championships as few would have predicted any of the eventual medallists to have been in contention. The US fielded four athletes, each a possible winner with times in 2015 between 12.34 and 12.56 … and yet only two reached the final, and they placed 4th and 8th. In the semis Dawn Harper Nelson failed to finish and Kendra Harrison was disqualified for a false start. Defending champion Rollins was fastest in the heats with 12.67, and ran 12.71 in her semi, fourth fastest behind Williams who ran a pb 12.58, Nelvis 12.59 and Talay 12.70. In the final Williams improved further to 12.57, just 0.2 ahead of Roleder, whose pre-meeting best was 12.80, and Talay, who ran a Belarus record.

400m Hurdles *(h 23rd, sf 24th, F 26th)*

1. Zuzana Hejnová CZE	53.50
2. Shamier Little USA	53.94
3. Cassandra Tate USA	54.02
4. Sara Petersen DEN	54.20
5. Janieve Russell JAM	54.64
6. Eilidh Child GBR	54.78
7. Wenda Nel RSA	54.94
8. Kaliese Spencer JAM	55.47

HEJNOVÁ RETAINED her title in a season's best time from Little, who completed a terrific season in her first year as a senior athlete, and Tate, whose 54.01 was just 0.01 outside her best after having a big lead early on. Tate was fastest in the heats with 54.27 and Hejnová 54.24, Tate 54.33 and Petersen 54.34 in the semis. Spencer ran 54.45 in her semi but clobbered the second hurdle in the final.

High Jump *(Q 1.95 15th, F 17th)*

1. Mariya Kuchina RUS	2.01
2. Blanka Vlasic CRO	2.01
3. Anna Chicherova RUS	2.01
4. Kamila Licwinko POL	1.99
5. Ruth Beitia ESP	1.99
6. Marie-Laurence Jungfleisch GER	1.99
7. Jeanelle Scheper LCA	1.92
8. Eleanor Patterson AUS-J	1.92
9= Ana Simic CRO	1.88
9= Svetlana Radzivil UZB	1.88
9= Mirela Demireva BUL	1.88
12= Doreen Amata NGR	1.88
12= Levern Spencer LCA	1.88

THE STANDARD WAS good as six women cleared 1.99, a record for the World Champs and equalling the 2008 Olympics for depth. Three went over 2.01 before failing at 2.03, with Kuchina winning due to a clean card to 2.01, Vlasic taking silver with one failure (at 1.92) and Chicherova bronze with a second-time clearance at 2.01. 13 women made the final by clearing 1.92 in qualifying.

Pole Vault *(Q 4.60m 24th, F 26th)*

1. Yarisley Silva CUB	4.90
2. Fabiana Murer BRA	4.85
3. Nikoléta Kiriakopoúlou GRE	4.80
4= Jennifer Suhr USA	4.70
4= Sandi Morris USA	4.70
4= Angelica Bengtsson SWE	4.70
7. Holly Bradshaw GBR	4.70
8. Martina Strutz GER	4.60
9. Li Ling CHN	4.60
10. Minna Nikkanen FIN	4.60
11. Alana Boyd AUS	4.60
12. Lisa Ryzih GER	4.60
nh. Anzhelika Sidorova RUS	–
nh. Michaela Meijer SWE	–

THERE WERE RECORD numbers of 14 women over 4.55 and 18 over 4.45 in qualifying, and in the final seven at 4.70 beat the previous record of five, and 10th-12th in 4.60 also set new all-time records. Four women failed at 4.80 after clearing 4.70, but Kiriakopoúlou cleared first time and Silva and Murer on their second attempts, with the later having the advantage as Silva had needed three tries at 4.70. Both Murer, tying her South American record, and Silva went over 4.85 first time, while Kiriakopoúlou failed there and twice at 4.90, at which the medals were settled as Silva cleared on her final attempt.

Long Jump *(Q 6.75m 27th, F 28th)*

1. Tianna Bartoletta USA	7.14/1.2
2. Shara Proctor GBR	7.07/0.4
3. Ivana Spanovic SRB	7.01/0.6
4. Christabel Nettey CAN	6.95/0.9
5. Lorraine Ugen GBR	6.85/0.7
6. Malaika Mlhambo GER	6.79/0.3
7. Khaddi Sagnia SWE	6.78/1.3
8. Janay DeLoach USA	6.67/0.6
9. Anastasiya Mironchik-Ivanova BLR	6.66/0.6
10. Darya Klishina RUS	6.65/1.2
11. Katarina Johnson-Thompson GBR	6.63/0.6
12. Erica Jarder SWE	6.48/0.4

TEN YEARS AFTER she won the world title as Tianna Madison and some years concentrating as a sprinter, Bartoletta won again. In the first round Nettey jumped 6.95 followed by Spanovic, Serbian record 7.01, and then Bartoletta moved to third with 6.95 in round 2. Proctor took the lead with a British record 7.07 in r3, followed by 7.01, and then in the last two rounds Bartoletta went out to 6.94 and a pb 7.14 and Spanovic 6.98 and 7.01 again. Olga Sudareva's 6.65 was the best ever non-qualifying mark in a competition in which Spanovic set her first Serbian record in Beijing of 6.91 followed by Ugen 6.87 and Mihambo 6.84.

Triple Jump *(Q 14.25m 22nd, F 24th)*

1. Caterine Ibargüen COL	14.90/0.1
2. Hanna Minenko ISR	14.78/-0.1
3. Olga Rypakova KAZ	14.77/0.1
4. Gabriela Petrova BUL	14.66/0.4
5. Kimberly Williams JAM	14.45/0.0
6. Olha Saladukha UKR	14.41/0.4
7. Yekaterina Koneva RUS	14.37/0.0
8. Kristin Gierisch GER	14.25/0.1
9. Jeanine Assani Issouf FRA	14.12/0.0
10. Yosiri Urrutia COL	14.09/-0.3
11. Shanieka Thomas JAM	14.08/0.2
12. Keila Costa BRA	13.90/0.2

IBARGÜEN CONTINUED HER three-year win streak, taking the lead with 14.80 in round two and improving to 14.90 in r4. while Minenko set a national record in r2 to become the first woman to win a World medal for Israel, and Rypakova passed Petrova to take bronze in the final round. Koneva disappointed with seventh place.

Shot *(Q 18.30m & F 22nd)*

1. Christina Schwanitz GER	20.37
2. Gong Lijiao CHN	20.30
3. Michelle Carter USA	19.76
4. Anita Márton HUN	19.48
5. Gao Yang CHN	19.04
6. Alyona Dubitskaya BLR	18.52
7. Yuliya Leontyuk BLR	18.25
8. Natalya Mikhnevich BLR	18.24
9. Natalia Ducó CHI	17.98
10. Jeneva Stevens USA	17.84
11. Paulina Guba POL	17.52
12. Cleopatra Borel TTO	17.43

THREE WOMEN WENT over 19m in qualifying, Schwanitz 19.39, Carter 19.22 and Gong 19.11, and these three took the medals ahead of Martón's Hungarian record. Schwanitz opened with 19.80 and then the crowd delighted as Gong put 20.30. Gong threw 20.05 and 20.25 in the next two rounds as Schwanitz responded with 20.00 and then the decisive 20.37 in the third round. Carter's 19.67 came in the second round and she ended with 19.71.

Discus *(Q 63.00m 24th, F 22nd)*

1. Denia Caballero CUB	69.28
2. Sandra Perkovic CRO	67.39
3. Nadine Müller GER	65.53
4. Yaimí Pérez CUB	65.46
5. Julia Fischer GER	63.88
6. Dani Samuels AUS	63.14
7. Shanice Craft GER	63.10
8. Su Xinyue CHN	62.90
9. Whitney Ashley USA	61.05
10. Mélina Robert-Michon FRA	60.92
11. Gia Lewis-Smallwood USA	60.55
12. Nataliya Semenova UKR	59.54

CABALLERO 65.15, PERKOVIC 64.51 and Müller 64.39 were best in qualifying and finished

in that order in the final. Perkovic had a 7-0 record over Caballero before the event, but the Cuban opened with 69.28 and that took the gold as Perkovic was just out of the medals with 65.37 before her final throw but then managed 67.39 for the silver.

Hammer *(Q 73.00m 26th, F 27th)*

1. Anita Wlodarczyk POL	80.85*
2. Zhang Wenxiu CHN	76.33
3. Alexandra Tavernier FRA	74.02
4. Sophie Hitchon GBR	73.86
5. Wang Zheng CHN	73.83
6. Kathrin Klaas GER	73.18
7. Betty Heidler GER	72.56
8. Zalina Marghieva MDA	72.38
9. Amanda Bingson USA	72.35
10. Alena Soboleva BLR	70.09
11. Rosa Rodríguez VEN	67.78
nt. Amber Campbell USA	–

AFTER LEADING THE qualifiers with 75.01 from Tavernier 74.39 and Wang 73.06, Wlodarczyk took the lead with the second throw of the final, 74.40, and was never headed as she improved to 78.52 and championship records of 80.27 and 80.85, ending with 79.31 and a no throw. Behind such domination Zhang had the next two best throws of 75.92 and 76.33, and 21 year-old Tavernier took bronze with her opening 74.02. Hitchon, fourth, set two British records, 73.65 and 73.86.

Javelin *(Q 61.50m 28th, F 30th)*

1. Katharina Molitor GER	67.69
2. Lu Huihui CHN	66.13
3. Sunette Viljoen RSA	65.79
4. Christina Obergföll GER	64.61
5. Li Lingwei CHN	64.10
6. Christin Hussong GER	62.98
7. Sinta Ozolina LAT	62.20
8. Kara Winger USA	60.88
9. Barbora Spotáková CZE	60.08
10. Linda Stahl GER	59.88
11. Elizabeth Gleadle CAN	59.82
12. Brittany Borman USA	58.26

THE TOP FOUR qualifiers were Hussong with 65.92 and then Borman 64.20, Oberföll 64.10 and Gleadle 64.02, but none of them won a medal. Chinese hopes were high in the final as Li 64.10 and Lu 63.80 led in the first round. Lu improved to 64.72 in round three but lost the lead on the following throw as Molitor went 2 cm further. Viljoen took over in r4 with 65.79 but Lu threw an Asian record 66.13 in r5. It looked as if that would win, until, with the very last throw of the competition, Molitor produced a world-leading and pb 67.69.

Heptathlon *(22/23rd)*

1. Jessica Ennis-Hill GBR	6669
2. Brianne Theisen-Eaton CAN	6554
3. Laura Adminina LAT	6516
4. Nadine Broersen NED	6491
5. Claudia Rath GER	6441
6. Györgyi Zsivoczky-Farkas HUN	6389
7. Anastasiya Mokhnyuk UKR	6359
8. Nadine Visser NED	6344
9. Xenia Krizsán HUN	6322
10. Jennifer Oeser GER	6308
11. Nafissatou Thiam BEL	6298
12. Anouk Vetter NED	6267
13. Eliska Klucinová CZE	6247
14. Sharon Day-Monroe USA	6246
15. Grit Sadeiko EST	6213

RETURNING ENNIS-HILL, with a strong set of performances throughout, regained the title that she had won in 2009 as Theisen-Eaton could not quite match the form that she had shown earlier in the year at Götzis. At the end of the first day the top scores were Ennis-Hill 4005, Katarina Johnson-Thompson 3925, Visser 3871 and Theisen-Eaton 3865, but KJT met with disaster in the long jump – she had clearly the best jumps of anyone, but all three were narrow fouls and her probable medal chance had gone. Broersen, with a fine 53.52 javelin, was second to Ennis-Hill with just the 800m to come, but in that was overtaken by both Theisen-Eaton and Admidina. who took silver and bronze. Fittingly Ennis-Hill won that final event in 2:10.13 to complete the triumph after the birth of her son 13 months earlier.

4 x 100m Relay *(h & F 29th)*

1. JAM	41.07*	Campbell-Brown, Morrison, Thompson, Fraser-Pryce (ht: 1 Simpson, 3 Stewart)
2. USA	41.68	Gardner, Felix, Prandini, Todd
3. TTO	42.03	Baptiste, Ahye, Thomas, Hackett (ht: 4 St. Fort)
4. GBR	42.10	Philip, Asher-Smith, J Williams, Henry (ht: 2 J Williams, 3 B Williams)
5. GER	42.64	Haase, Burghardt, Lückenkemper, Sailer
6. CAN	43.05	Emmanuel, Hyacinthe, Fofanah, Bingham
dnf. RUS	–	Panteleyeva, Ryzhova, Demirova, Kukushkina
dq, NED	(42.33)	Visser, Schippers, Sedney, Samuel

THERE WERE FAST heat wins from Jamaica 41.84 and the USA 42.00 with national records from Trinidad 42.24, Netherlands 42.32 and Canada 42.60. Jamaica brought in their best sprinters Campbell-Brown and Thompson for the final in which VCB ran a brilliant turn on the first leg to set up the team to win as on the anchor leg Fraser-Pryce stretched a 1m lead to 6m in the second fastest time ever (behind USA 40.82 in 2012). The US team's 41.68 was their fastest for two years and Trinidad & Tobago snatched bronze in another national record of 42.03. The British team excelled with a UK record of 42.10, the fastest ever time for fourth place.

4 x 400m Relay *(h 29th, F 30th)*

1. JAM	3:19.13	Day 50.5, Jackson 49.4, McPherson 50.19, Williams-Mills 49.14 (Le-Roy and Gordon ran ht)
2. USA	3:19.44	Richards-Ross 51.5, Hastings 50.4, Felix 47.72, McCorory 49.93 (Francis and Beard ran ht)
3. GBR	3:23.62	Ohuruogu 51.3, Onuora 51.0, Child 50.61, Bundy-Davies 50.84 (McAslan ran heat)
4. RUS	3:24.84	Kotlyarova 51.8, Zadorina 51.2, Ryzhova 51.12, Aksyonova 50.82
5. NGR	3:25.11	R George 52.4, Oladoye 50.9, Adeloye 51.14, P George 50.76
6. UKR	3:25.94	Zemlyak 52.1, Lupu 51.6, Pyhyda 51.47, Lyakhova 50.89
7. FRA	3:26.45	Perrossier 52.0, Gayot 50.6, Raharolahy 53.95, Guei 49.95
8. CAN	3:27.69	Muir 52.1, Stiverne 51.9, Watson 51.37, Jean-Baptiste 52.38

SANYA RICHARDS-ROSS ran a poor opening leg for the USA and then a 49.4 leg by Shericka Jackson took Jamaica to a 20m lead. The race was transformed, however, by a wonderful 47.72 third leg for the US by Allyson Felix, the third fastest ever split, to take the US into a 4m lead. Finally Novlene Williams-Mills hunted down Francena McCorory, who tied up in the finishing straight, and Jamaica won by 0.31. Well behind, Britain ran solidly for the bronze.

20 Kilometres Walk *(28th)*

1. Liu Hong CHN	1:27:45
2. Lu Xiuzhi CHN	1:27:45
3. Lyudmyla Olyanovska UKR	1:28:13
4. Ana Cabecinha POR	1:29:29
5. Antonella Palmisano ITA	1:29:34
6. Erica de Sena BRA	1:30:06
7. Brigita Virbalyte LTU	1:30:20
8. Anezka Drahotová CZE	1:30:32
9. Alejandra Ortega MEX	1:31:04
10. María José Poves ESP	1:31:06
11. Nadiya Borovska UKR	1:31:18
12. Mirna Ortíz GUA	1:31:32
13. Rachel Seaman CAN	1:31:39
14, Raquel González ESP	1:32:00
15. Viktória Madarász HUN	1:32:01

RUSSIA SENT NO walkers to Beijing after so many had been caught for drugs offences, and that left the way clear for the Chinese 1-2 here, with Liu and Lu dominating the race. They went though 5k in 22:24, 10k in 44:19 and 15k in 66:24 before speeding home with a final 5k in 21:21, Liu prevailing by a metre. Fourth at the last two Olympics, Liu now has a full set of World Champs medals after bronze in 2009 and 2013, silver in 2011. At halfway the top two were followed by Olyanovska (who also finished fast, in 21:28) and the Italians Elisa Rigaudo and Eleonora Giorgi, both of whom were disqualified during the final 5k. 42 of the 49 starters finished.

Prize money

Individual Events: Winner: US $60,000, 2nd $30,000, 3rd $20,000, 4th $15,000, 5th $10,000, 6th $6000, 7th $5000, 8th $4000.

Relays: Winners $80,000, 2nd $40,000, 3rd $20,000, 4th $16,000, 5th $12,000, 6th $8000, 7th $6000, 8th $4000.

Miscellany

The **Weeks twins** (b.20 Nov 1996) set US High School records in 2015: indoors Tori 4.37 and outdoors Lexi 4.46.
265 men broke 66 minutes for the half marathon at the Japanese University Championships in March 2015.
Diamond League: The scoring system changed in 2016 season to top six (10-6-4-3-2-1).

ALL-TIME LISTS – notes on changes in 2015

Men

3000m: only change to outdoor all-time top 100 Farah 7:34.66 at 90th
3000mSt: Only change to top 100: Evan Jagar moving up to 13th with 8:00.45. Next Clement Kemboi to 107th with 8:12.68
DT: first change 68.19 Jason Morgan to 54th
HT: Pawel Fajdek up from 11th to 9th only change in top 100. Next Serghei Marghiev up to 145th with 78.72.

Women

800m: Only change in top 100: 1:56.99 Eunice Sum to 72nd
400mh- top performance (53.50) was only 148=
SP: only change in top 100; 20.77 Schwanitz from 51st to 39th, Next Márton 19..44 to 118th
Most change: 5000m: 5 marks in all-time top 10 performances

CHAMPIONSHIPS 2015

IAAF World Relays

At Nassau, Bahamas 2-3 May

Men

4x100 metres (a)

1, USA (Mike Rodgers, Justin Gatlin, Tyson Gay, Ryan Bailey) 37.38*
2. JAM (Nesta Carter, Kemar Bailey-Cole, Nickel Ashmeade, Usain Bolt) 37.68
3. JPN (Kazuma Oseto, Kenji Fujimitsu, Yoshihide Kiryu, Kotaro Taniguchi) 38.20
4. BRA (de Barros, V dos Santos J, Gomes da Silva, Vides) 38.63
5. FRA (Vincent, Lemaitre, Pessonneaux, Biron) 38.81
6. SKN (Rogers, Lawrence, Roland, Adams) 38.85
7. TTO (Bledman, Burns, Sorrillo, Thompson) 38.92
8. GER (Menga, Knipphals, Kosenkow, Domogala) 39.40

B final: 1, GBR (Robertson, Talbot, Ellington, Kilty) 38.67
2. BAR (Cadogan, Gittens, Deshong, Burke) 38.70
3. DOM (Montas, Andujar, Del Carmen, Martínez) 38.98

4x200 metres (b)

1. JAM (Nickel Ashmeade, Rasheed Dwyer, Jason Livermore, Warren Weir) 1:20.97
2. FRA (Teddy Tinmar, Christophe Lemaitre, Pierre-Alexis Pessonneaux, Ben Bassaw) 1:21.49
3. GER (Robin Erewa, Sven Knipphals, Alex-Platini Menga, Alexander Kosenkow) 1:22.65
4. POL 1:22.85, 5. BAH 1:22.91, 6. SKN 1:22.92, 7. SUI 1:24.37; dq, USA (Spearmon, I Young, Mitchell, Gatlin)

4x400 metres (a-b)

1. USA 2:58.43 (David Verburg 44.91, Tony McQuay 44.00, Jeremy Wariner 44.80, LaShawn Merritt 44.72)
2. BAH 2:58.91 (Ramon Miller 45.66, Michael Mathieu 44.50, Steven Gardiner 44.58, Chris Brown 44.17)
3. BEL 2:59.33 (Dylan Borlée 45.57, Julien Watrin 45.36, Jonathan Borlée 44.39, Kévin Borlée 44.01)
4. JAM 3:00.23 (McDonald 45.74, Steele 45.49, Chambers 45.00, Francis 44.00)
5. BRA 3:00.96 (de Oliveira 45.55, Cardoso 45.97, Estefani 44.44, H Souza 45.00)
6. GBR 3:01.50 (C Williams, Yousif, J Green 45.22, Caddick 45.04)
7. TTO 3:03.10, 8. BOT 3:03.73

B final: 1, POL 3:03.23, 2. CUB 3:03.73, 3. GER 3:04.90

4x800 metres (a)

1. USA 7:04.84* (Duane Solomon 1:47.60, Erik Sowinski 1:44.75, Casimir Loxsom 1:45.59, Robby Andrews 1:46.90)
2. POL 7:09.98 (Karol Konieczny 1:48.28, Kamil Gurdak 1:48.17, Marcin Lewandowski 1:46.80, Adam Kszczot 1:46.73)
3. AUS 7:16.30 (Jared West 1:48.50, Joshua Ralph 1:49.74, Ryan Gregson 1:47.81, Jordan Williamsz 1:50.25)
4. MEX 7:22.61, dq. KEN (7:09.66) (Alfred Kipketer 1:47.62, Nicholas Kipkoech 1:47.70, Timothy Kitum 1:47.34, Jeremiah Mutai 1:47.00).

Distance Medley (b)

1. USA 9:15.50* (Kyle Merber 2:53.56, Brycen Spratling 45.95, Brandon Johnson 1:44.75, Ben Blankenship 3:51.24)
2. KEN 9:17.20 (Abednego Chesebe 2:54.68, Alphas Kishoyan 45.28, Ferguson Cheruiyot 1:44.49, Timothy Cheruiyot 3:52.75)
3. AUS 9:21.62 (Ryan Gregson 2:53.15, Alex Beck 45.83, Jordan Williamsz 1:45.64, Collis Birmingham 3:57.00)
4. POL 9:24.07 (Demczyszak 2:54.85, Krawczuk 46.45, Kszczot 1:46.04, Lewandowski 3:57.08)
5. GER 9:24.37 (Keiner 2:54.50, Plass 46.39, Schembera 1:45.75, Orth 3:57.38
6. PNG 10:50.63

Women

4x100 metres (b)

1. JAM (Simone Facey, Kerron Stewart, Schillonie Calvert, Veronica Campbell-Brown) 42.14
2. USA (Tianna Bartoletta, Allyson Felix, Kimberlyn Duncan, Carmelita Jeter) 42.32
3. GBR (Asha Philip, Ashleigh Nelson, Bianca Williams, Margaret Adeoye) 42.84
4. CAN (Emmanuel, Hyacinthe, Davis, Bingham) 42.85
5. TTO (Durant, Ahye, Thomas, Selvon) 42.88
6. BRA (V dos Santos, Silva, Krasucki, R Santos) 42.92
7. NGR (Asumnu, Okagbare, Duncan, Uko) 42.99
8. SUI (Kambundji, Sprunger, Lavanchy, Humair) 43.74

B final: 1. ECU 44.14, 2. BAH 44.14, 3. VEN 44.17

4x200 metres (a)

1. NGR (Blessing Okagbare, Regina George, Dominique Duncan, Christy Udoh) 1:30.52
2. JAM (Samantha Henry-Robinson, Veronica Campbell-Brown, Shericka Williams, Sherone Simpson) 1:31.73
3. GER (Rebekka Haase, Christina Haack, Nadine Gonska, Josefina Eisler) 1:33.61
4. CHN 1:34.89, 5. IRL 1:36.90; dq, BAH; dnf, USA & FRA

4x400 metres (a-b)

1. USA 3:19.39* (Phyllis Francis 51.40, Natasha Hastings 49.93, Sanya Richards-Ross 48.79, Francena McCorory 49.27)

2. JAM 3:22.49 (Anastasia Le-Roy 51.88, Novlene Williams-Mills 50.02, Christine Day 50.46, Stephenie Ann McPherson 50.13)
3. GBR 3:26.38 (Eilidh Child 52.82, Anyika Onuora 50.94, Kelly Massey 51.00, Seren Bundy-Davies 51.62)
4. FRA 3:26.68 (Guion-Firmin 53.27, Gayot 50.74, Diarra 51.44, Guei 51.23)
5. POL 3:29.30 (Ptak 52.98, Holub 51.75, Linkiewicz 52.23, Swiety 52.34)
6. CAN 3:29.65 (Sassine 53.79, Dorr 52.13, Muir 51.77, Jean-Baptiste 51.96)
7. AUS 3:30.03 (Rubie 52.32, Gulli 53.03, Mitchell 52.09, Pekin 52.59)
8. BRA 3:31.30 (Sousa 53.01. de Lima 54.02, Barbosa 52.86, Coutinho 51.41)

B final: 1. CUB 3:30.94, 2. JPN 3:34.65, 3. BAH 3:35.01

4x800 metres (b)

1. USA 8:00.62* (Chanelle Price 2:01.30, Maggie Vessey 2:00.92, Molly Ludlow 1:59.50, Alysia Montaño 1:58.90)
2. POL 8:11.36 (Syntia Ellward 2:02.44, Katarzyna Broniatowska 2:03.64, Angelika Cichocka 2:00.90, Sofia Ennaoui 2:04.38)
3. AUS 8:13.97 (Abbey de la Motte 2:02.43, Kelly Hetherington 2:03.49, Selma Kajan 2:05.68, Brittany McGowan 2:02.37)
4. CUB 8:15.84 CAC (Almanza 2:00.45, Thaureaux J, Casanova, Diago)
5. JAM 8:16.04 (McDonald, Campbell, Goule, James)
6. CAN 8:16.27 (Belleau-Béliveau, Francois, Whelan, Aubry)
7. MEX 8:30.56, 8. KEN 8:33.15

Distance Medley (a)

1. USA 10:36.50* (Treniere Moser 3:18.38, Sanya Richards-Ross 50.12, Ajeé Wilson 2:00.08, Shannon Rowbury 4:27.92)
2. KEN 10:43.35 (Selah Busienei 3:18.96, Joyce Zakari 52.59, Sylivia Chesebe 2:03.32, Virginia Nyambura 4:28.48)
3. POL 10:45.32 Eur (Katarzyna Broniatowska 3:19.87, Monika Szczesna 54.12, Angelika Cichocka 2:01.06, Sofia Ennaoui 4:30.27)
4. AUS 10:46.94 (M Duncan 3:19.78, Lind J 53.31. McGowan 2:03.15, See 4:30.70)
5. GER 11:06.14, 6. FRA 11:06.33

Team Standings for Golden Baton (8-7-6-5-4-3-2-1) 1. USA 63, 2. JAM 46, 3. POL 34, 4. AUS 25, 5. GER 21, 6. FRA 19, 7. KEN 15, 8. GBR 15, 9. BRA 13, 10. BAH 11, 11. CAN 11, 12. NGR 10.

Prize money: 1st $50,000, 2nd $30,000, 3rd $20,000, 4th $12,000, 5th $10,000; 6th $8000, 7th $6000, 8th $4000; World record $50,000 bonus.

IAAF World Youth Championships

At Calí, Colombia 15-19 July

Men

100m (-0.4) 1. Abdul Hakim Sani Brown JPN 10.28*
2. Derick Silva BRA 10.49
3. Rechmial Miller GBR 10.59

200m (-0.4) 1. Abdul Hakim Sani Brown JPN 20.34*
2. Kyle Appel RSA 20.57
3. Josephus Lyles USA 20.74

400m 1. Christopher Taylor JAM 45.27
2. Josephus Lyles USA 45.46
3. Keshun Reed USA 45.96

800m 1. Willy Tarbei KEN 1:45.58
2. Kipyegon Bett KEN 1:45.86
3. Luis Pires BRA 1:48.61

1500m 1. Kumari Taki KEN 3:36.38*
2. Mulugeta Asefa ETH 3:41.10
3. Lawi Kosgei KEN 3:41.43

3000m 1. Richard Yator KEN 7:54.45
2. Davis Kiplangat KEN 7:54.52
3. Tefera Mosisa ETH 7:55.04

2000mSt 1. Vincent Kipyegon KEN 5:27.58
2. Wogene Sebisibe ETH 5:29.41
3. Geoffrey Rotich KEN 5:30.16

110mh (-1.2) 91.4cm 1. Matteo Ngo FRA 13.53
2. Joseph Daniels CAN 13.54
3. Isaiah Lucas USA 13.54

400mh 84cm 1. Norman Grimes USA 49.11
2. Ryusei Fujii JPN 50.33
3. Masaki Toyoda JPN 50.53

HJ 1. Stefano Sottile ITA 2.20
2. Dmytro Nikitin UKR 2.18
3. Darius Carbin USA 2.16

PV 1. Armand Duplantis SWE 5.30
2. Vladyslav Malykhin UKR 5.30
3. Emmanouil Karális GRE 5.20

LJ 1. Maykel Massó CUB 8.05/0.5
2. Darcy Roper AUS 8.01/0.5
3. Eberson Silva BRA 7.76/0.1

TJ 1. Cristian Nápoles CUB 16.13/-3.1
2. Du Mingze CHN 16.02/0.0
3. Julio César Carbonell CUB 15.70/0.2

SP 5kg 1. Adrian Piperi USA 22.00
2. Szymon Mazur POL 21.77
3. Wictor Petersson SWE 21.56

DT 1.5kg 1. Werner Visser RSA 64.24
2. Wang Yuhan CHN 60.33
3. George Evans GBR 60.22

HT 5kg 1. Hlib Piskunov UKR 84.91
2. Myhaylo Havrylyuk UKR 78.93
3. Ned Weatherly AUS 77.60

JT 700gm 1. Paul Botha RSA 78.49
2. Niklas Kaul GER 78.05
3. Vladislav Polyunin UZB 76.77

Dec 1. Niklas Kaul GER 8002* (11.59/-0.2, 6.76/1.1, 16.08, 2.05, 51.20, 15.44/-0.7, 44.09, 4.70, 78.20, 4:42.29)
yth imps 2. Ludovic Besson FRA 7678
3. Hans-Christian Hausenberg EST 7657

10,000W 1. Sergey Shirobokov RUS 42:24.41
2. Zhang Jun CHN 42:33.68
3. Federico González MEX 42:54.55

4x400m mixed relay 1. USA (Keshun Reed, Lynna Irby, Norman Grimes, Samantha Watson) 3:19.54
2. RSA 3:23.60
3. CAN 3:23.60

Women

100m 1. Candace Hill USA 11.08*

(0.0) 2. Khalifa St Fort TTO 11.19
3. Jayla Kirkland USA 11.41
200m 1. Candace Hill USA 22.43*
(-0.7) 2. Lauren Rain Williams USA 22.90
3. Nicola de Bruyn RSA 23.38
400m 1. Salwa Eid Nasser BRN 51.50
2. Lynna Irby USA 51.79
3. Catherine Reid GBR 52.25
800m 1. Samantha Watson USA 2:03.54
2. Gadese Ejara ETH 2:03.67
3. Marta Zenoni ITA 2:04.15
1500m 1. Bedatu Hirpa ETH 4:12.92
2. Dalilah Gosa BRN 4:13.35
3. Joyline Cherotich KEN 4:15.20
3000m 1. Shuru Bulo ETH 9:01.12
2. Emily Kipchumba KEN 9:02.92
3. Sheila Chelangat KEN 9:04.54
2000mSt 1. Celphine Chespoi KEN 6:17.15
2. Sandra Tuei KEN 6:19.61
3. Agrie Belachew ETH 6:34.68
100mh 1. Maribel Caicedo ECU 13.04
(0.1) 2. Brittley Humphrey USA 13.22
76.2cm 3. Sarah Koutouan FRA 13.29
400mh 1. Sydney McLaughlin USA 55.94*
2. Xahria Santiago CAN 56.79
3. Brandeé Johnson USA 57.47
HJ 1. Michaela Hrubá CZE 1.90
2. Ieva Turke LAT 1.82
3. Lada Pejchalová CZE 1.82
PV 1. Elienor Werner SWE 4.26
2= Chen Qiaoling CHN 4.05
2= Phillipa Hajdasz AUS 4.05
LJ 1. Tara Davis USA 6.41/0.3
2. Kaiza Karlén SWE 6.24/-0.2
3. Maja Bedrac SLO 6.22/0.3
TJ 1. Georgiana Anitei ROU 13.49/0.3
2. Zeng Rui CHN 13.04/0.3
3. Yanna Armenteros CUB 13.04/-0.3
SP 3kg 1. Julia Ritter GER 18.53
2. Sophia Rivera USA 17.93
3. Kristina Rakocevic MNE 17.49
DT 1. Alexandra Emelianov MDA 52.78
2. Kristina Rakocevic MNE 51.41
3. Samantha Peace AUS 50.59
HT 3kg 1. Sofiya Palkina RUS 67.82
2. Deniz Yaylaci TUR 67.01
3. Shang Ningyu CHN 66.84
JT 500g 1. Haruka Kitaguchi JPN 60.35*
2. Stella Weinberg NOR 57.11
3. Laine Donane LAT 56.15
Hep 1. Géraldine Ruckstuhl SUI 6037
yth imp (13.93/0.7, 1.73, 14.25, 25.83/-0.5, 5.71/0.0, 52.87, 2:17.58)
2. Sarah Lagger AUT 5992
3. Alina Shukh UKR 5896
5000W 1. Ma Zhenxia CHN 22:41.08
2. Olga Yeliseyeva RUS 22:45.09
3. Ayainesh Dejene ETH 22:48.25

Medal and Points Table

Points (1st- 8, 2nd- 7, to 8th- 1)

Nation	*1*	*2*	*3*	*Pts*
USA	8	5	6	163
KEN	5	4	4	100
ETH	2	3	3	90
CHN	1	5	1	71.5
JPN	3	1	1	70.5
GBR	-	-	3	62.5
RSA	2	2	1	62
FRA	1	1	1	57
GER	2	1	-	51
CUB	2	-	2	51
RUS	2	1	-	42.5
SWE	2	1	1	41
UKR	1	3	1	39
CAN	-	2	1	36
AUS	-	2	2	32
BRA	-	1	2	29
ITA	1	-	1	29
POL	-	1	-	26.5
MEX	-	-	1	26
CZE	1	-	1	23
JAM	1	-	-	20
TUR	-	1	-	20

BRN (1G, 1S) 17, LAT & MNE (1S, 1B) 13, ROU (1G) 11, AUT & NOR (1S) 11, ESP & HUN 11, GRE 1B (10), BAR & BLR 10, ECU, MDA & SUI (1G) 8, COL 8, TTO (1S) 7, EST, SLO & UZB (1B) 6, CAY, CHI, IRQ, KOR, POR & PUR 5; BEL, BOT, DEN, EGY, SRI & UGA 4, ARG, CRO, SRB & TUN 3, BOL & KAZ 2, IND 1.5, DOM, KGZ & PER 1. 20 countries won at least one gold medal; 36 at least one medal and 63 scored at least 1 point

IAAF Hammer Throw Challenge

Final standings, top three of 14 meetings to score. Prize money from $30,000 for 1st to $500 for 12th.

Men: 1. Pawel Fajdek POL 248.01, 2. Dilshod Nazarov TJK 236.20, 3. Krisztián Pars HUN 234.75, 4. Sergey Litvinov RUS 231.15, 5. Mostafa Al-Gamal EGY 231.04, 6. Marcel Lomnicky SVK 230.14, 7. Wojciech Nowicki POL 230.04, 8. Nick Miller GBR 226.05, 9. Ashraf Amjaf El Seify QAT 233.14, 10. Lukás Melich CZE 222.90.

Women: 1. Anita Wlodarczyk POL 235.28, 2. Betty Heidler GER 222.28, 3. Martina Hrasnová SVK 222.20, 4. Wang Zheng CHN 221.50, 5. Kathrin Klaas GER 217.76, 6. Sophie Hitchon GBR 216.28, 7. Sultana Frizell CAN 215.83, 8. Amanda Bingson USA 214.03, 9. Joanna Fiodorow POL 212.95, 10. Gwen Berry USA 212.60.

IAAF World Race Walking Challenge

Results of walks at 12 meetings qualified. Walkers needed to compete at three or more of these to qualify and positions were based on the best positions from these races, with a sliding scale of points from three categories. Prize money: 1st $30,000, 2nd $20,000, 3rd $14,000, 4th $9000, 5th $7000, 6th $6000, 7th $4500, 8th $4000, 9th $3000, 10th $2000, 11th $1000, 12th $500.

Final standings: **Men**: 1. Matej Tóth SVK 29, 2. Miguel Ángel López ESP 25, 3. Chen Ding CHN 24, 4. Andrés Chocho ECU 24, 5. Caio Bonfim BRA 18, 6. Jared Tallent AUS 17, 7. Eider Arévalo COL 16, 8. Dane Bird-Smith AUS 14, 9. Eder Sánchez MEX 14, 10. Cai Zelin CHN 14. **Women**: 1. Liu Hong CHN 40, 2. Eleonora Giorgi ITA 27, 3. Erica de Sena BRA 25, 4. Ana Cabecinha POR 22, 5. Lyudmyla Olyanovska UKR 18, 6. Inês Henriques POR 16, 7. Anezka Drahotová CZE 12, 8. Alejandra Ortega MEX 12, 9. Kimberly García PER 10, 10. Viktoria Madarász HUN 10.

World University Games

At Gwangju, Korea 8-12 July

100m (0.0)
1. Akani Simbine RSA 9.97*
2. Kemarley Brown JAM 10.12
3. Ramil Guliyev TUR 10.16

200m (-2.5)
1. Wilfried Koffi CIV 20.41
2. Bryce Robinson USA 20.51
3. Ramil Guliyev TUR 20.59

400m
1. Luguelín Santos DOM 44.91
2. Gaone Maotoanong BOT 45.63
3. Jan Tesar CZE 45.73

800m
1. Shaquille Walker USA 1:49.05
2. Abdellatif El Guesse MAR 1:49.29
3. Ryhardt van Rensburg RSA 1:49.30

1500m
1. Aleksey Kharitonov RUS 3:39.13
2. Abdelali Razyn MAR 3:39.20
3. Staffan Ek SWE 3:39.68

5000m
1. Hayle Ibrahimov AZE 13:44.28
2. Zouhair Talbi MAR 14:02.06
3. Rinas Akhmadiyev RUS 14:05.88

10,000m
1. Igor Maksimov RUS 29:15.30
2. Nicolae Soare ROU 29:18.71
3. Keisuke Nakatani JPN 29:19.30

HMar
1. Yusuke Ogura JPN 64:41
2. Tadashi Isshiki JPN 64:52
3. Yuta Takahashi JPN 65:29

3000mSt
1. Martin Grau GER 8:31.55
2. Kaur Kivistik EST 8:32.23
3. Yuriy Kloptsov RUS 8:33.09

110mh
1. Greggmar Swift BAR 13.43
2. Konstantin Shabanov RUS 13.57
3. Genta Masuno JPN 13.69

400mh
1. Thomas Barr IRL 48.78
2. Abdelmalik Lahoulou ALG 48.99
3. Ivan Shablyuyev RUS 49.04

HJ
1. Daniyil Tsyplakov RUS 2.31
2. Matus Bubeník SVK 2.28
3. Hsiang Chun-Hsieng TPE 2.28

PV
1. Nikita Filippov KAZ 5.50
2. Ilya Mudrov RUS 5.50
3. Robert Sobera POL 5.50

LJ
1. Pavel Shalin RUS 8.29w/6.5
2. Vasiliy Kopeykin RUS 8.13w/4.4
3. Roelf Pienaar RSA 7.98w/4.0

TJ
1. Dmitriy Sorokin RUS 17.29/0.2
2. Fabrice Zango Hugues BUR 16.76/0.4
3. Xu Xiaolong CHN 16.76/0.8

SP
1. Inderjeet Singh IND 20.27
2. Andrei Gag ROU 19.92
3. Aleksandr Bulanov RUS 19.84

DT
1. Philip Milanov BEL 64.15
2. Matt Denny AUS 62.58
3. Andrius Gudzius LTU 62.54

HT
1. Pawel Fajdek POL 80.05
2. Pavel Boreysha BLR 75.75
3. Sergey Kolomoyets BLR 74.68

JT
1. Tanel Laanmäe EST 81.71
2. Huang Shih-Feng TPE 81.27
3. Zigismunds Sirmais LAT 79.37

Dec
1. Thomas Van Der Plaetsen BEL 7952
2. Bastien Auzeil FRA 7913
3. René Stauss GER 7791

4x100m
1. JPN 39.08
2. POL 39.50
3. AUS 39.71

4x400m
1. DOM 3:05.05
2. JPN 3:07.75
3. POL 3:07.77

Women

100m (0.4)
1. Viktoriya Zyabkina KAZ 11.23
2. Shimayra Williams JAM 11.46
3. Yelena Chernyayeva RUS 11.47

200m (-0.8)
1. Viktoriya Zyabkina KAZ 22.77
2. A'Keyla Mitchell USA 22.95
3. Kedisha Dallas JAM 23.24

400m
1. Justine Palframan RSA 51.27
2. Malgorzata Holub POL 51.93
3. Yang Huizhen CHN 51.98

800m
1. Angie Petty NZL 1:59.06
2. Simoya Campbell JAM 1:59.26
3. Fabienne Kohlmann GER 1:59.54

1500m
1. Dorcus Ajok UGA 4:18.53
2. Gabriela Stafford CAN 4:19.27
3. Kristina Ugarova RUS 4:19.78

5000m
1. Kristina Mäki CZE 16:03.29
2. Camille Buscomb NZL 16:03.72
3. Daria Maslova KGZ 16:04.09

10,000m
1. Alla Kulyatina RUS 32:52.27
2. Gulshat Fazlitdinova RUS 32:55.35
3. Zhang Yingying CHN 32:56.60

HMar
1. Zhang Yingying CHN 75:06
2. Nanako Kanno JPN 75:24
3. Ayumi Uehara JPN 75:35

3000mSt
1. Yekaterina Sokolenko RUS 9:25.77*
2. Natalya Vlasova RUS 9:35.99
3. Özlem Kaya TUR 9:37.79

100mh (0.1)
1. Danielle Williams JAM 12.78
2. Nina Morozova RUS 12.83
3. Michelle Jenneke AUS 12.94

400mh
1. Joanna Linkiewicz POL 55.62
2. Emilia Ankiewicz POL 56.55
3. Irina Takuntseva RUS 56.57

HJ
1. Airine Palsyte LTU 1.84
2= Elizabeth Boyer USA 1.80
2= Madara Onuzane LAT 1.80

PV
1. Li Ling CHN 4.45
2. Eliza McCartney NZL 4.40
3. Chloé Henry BEL 4.40

LJ
1. Yuliya Pidluzhnaya RUS 6.79/0.4
2. Anna Jagaciak POL 6.57/-1.1
3. Naa Anang AUS 6.55/1.3

TJ
1. Yekaterina Koneva RUS 14.60/0.3
2. Jenny Elbe GER 13.86/0.1
3. Anna Jagaciak POL 13.81/-0.1

SP
1. Lena Urbaniak GER 18.00
2. Paulina Guba POL 17.94
3. Brittany Crew CAN 17.27

DT
1. Yuliya Maltseva RUS 59.37
2. Marike Steinacker GER 58.83
3. Stefania Strumillo ITA 58.22

HT
1. Hanna Skydan AZE 70.67
2. Joanna Fiodorow POL 69.69
3. Julia Ratcliffe NZL 67.54

JT
1. Tatyana Kholodovich BLR 60.45
2. Lina Muze LAT 60.26
3. Irena Sedivá CZE 59.89

Hep (a/b)
1. Anna Maiwald GER 5965
2. Ida Marcussen NOR 5865
3. Anna Petrich RUS 5795

IAAF World Combined Events Challenge 2015

Based on the sum of the best scores achieved in any three of the 13 designated competitions during the year.

Men Decathlon

1	Ilya Shkurenyov	25,259	8343 Götzis	8378 Eur Cup	8538 Worlds
2	Michael Schrader GER	25,252	8415 Götzis	8419 Ratingen	8418 Worlds
3	Damian Warner CAN	25,247	7893 Götzis	8659 Pan-Am G	8695 Worlds
4	Willem Coertzen RSA	24,926	8398 Götzis	8341 Ratingen	8187 Talence
5	Oleksiy Kasyanov UKR	24,410	8105 Eur Cup	8262 Worlds	8043 Talence
6	Bastien Auzeil FRA	24,153	8147 Götzis	7913 W.Universities	8093 Worlds
7	Yordani García CUB	24,082	8186 Götzis	7977 P.Am Cup	7919 Pan-Am G
8	Kurt Felix GRN	23,866	8269 Pan-Am G	8302 Worlds	7295 Talence

Women Heptathlon

1	Laura Ikauniece-Admidina LAT	19,422	6436 Götzis	6470 Eur Cup II	6516 Worlds
2	Claudia Rath GER	19,189	6458 Götzis	6290 Ratingen	6441 Worlds
3	Anouk Vetter NED	19,112	6458 Götzis	6387 Ratingen	6267 Worlds
4	Nadine Visser NED	19,068	6467 Götzis	6344 Worlds	6287 Talence
5	Anastasiya Mokhnyuk UKR	18,959	6331 Götzis	6359 Worlds	6269 Talence
6	Eliska Klucinová CZE	18,744	6349 Götzis	6148 Kladno	6247 Worlds
7	Yorgelis Rodríguez CUB	18.496	6096 Götzis	6068 P.Am Cup	6332 Pan-Am G
8	Xénia Kriszán HUN	18,406	6116 Götzis	6322 Worlds	5968 Talence

Prize Money: 1st $30,000, 2nd $20,000, 3rd $15,000, 4th $10,000, 5th $8000, 6th $7000, 7th $6000, 8th $5000.

Best of three scores at qualifying meetings.

20kW 1. Anisya Kirdyapkina RUS 1:28:18*
2. Marina Pandakova RUS 1:29:52
3. Hou Yongbo CHN 1:32:42

4x100m 1. KAZ 44.28
2. USA 44.95
3. THA 45.03

4x400m 1. POL 3:31.98
2. RUS 3:32.46
3. USA 3:37.20

Medal and points table

Nation	G	S	B	Points
RUS	11	8	8	249
POL	3	6	3	104.5
JPN	2	3	5	100
USA	1	4	1	95.5
CHN	2	-	4	76
GER	3	2	2	69.5
AUS	1	1	3	57.5
NZL	1	2	1	51.3
JAM	1	3	1	51
CAN	-	-	1	50
RSA	2	-	2	47
KAZ	4	-	-	39
BEL	2	-	1	36
LTU	1	-	1	34
CZE	1	-	2	31
MAR	-	3	-	30
TUR	-	-	3	30
TPE	-	1	1	29
BLR	1	1	1	26
EST	1	1	-	24.3
LAT	-	2	1	23.5
DOM	2	-	-	23
KOR	-	-	-	22
ITA	-	-	1	20
FRA	-	1	-	19.5
SVK	-	1	-	19.5
THA	-	-	1	18
IND	1	-	-	18

ROU (2S) 17, AZE (2G) 16, NOR (1S) 14.3, UGA (1G) 12, IRL (1G), BOT (1S), SWE (1B) 11; FIN 10.2; DEN, CYP 9; BAR (1G), CIV (1G), UKR, HUN 8; ALG (1S), BUR (1S), SRB, MDA 7; KGZ (1B), POR 6; BRA, MAS, HKG, SUI, MGL 5; MNE 4.5; MEX, KEN 4; AUT 3; NED, CRO, BUL 2; SEN 1. Note: sharing points for ties.

11th All-Africa Games

At Brazzaville, Congo September 13-17

100m (-2.1) 1. Ben Youssef Meité CIV 10.04
2. Egwero Ogho-Oghene NGR 10.17
3. Wilfried Koffi CIV 10.23

200m (-1.2) 1. Wilfried Koffi CIV 20.42
2. Divine Oduduru NGR 20.45
3. Tega Odele NGR 20.58

400m 1. Isaac Makwala BOT 44.35
2. Boniface Mweresa KEN 45.01
3. Onkabetsa Nkobolo BOT 45.50

800m 1. Nijel Amos BOT 1:50.45
2. Taoufik Makhloufi ALG 1:50.72
3. Job Kinyor KEN 1:50.79

1500m 1. Mekonnen Gebremedhin ETH 3:45.73
2. Abdi Waiss Mouhyadin DJI-J 3:45.98
3. Salim Keddar ALG 3:46.31

5000m 1. Getaneh Tamire ETH 13:21.88*
2. Leul Gebrselassie ETH 13:22.13
3. Thomas Longosiwa KEN 13:22.72

10,000m 1. Tebalu Zawude ETH 27:27.19
2. Leonard Barsoton KEN 27:27.55
3. Adugna Takele ETH 27:28.40

HMar 1. Zersenay Tadese ERI 63:11
2. Luka Kanda KEN 63:27
3. Hizkel Tewelde ERI 63:39

3000mSt 1. Clement Kemboi KEN 8:20.31
2. Hillary Kemboi KEN 8:22.96
3. Hailemariyam Amare ETH-J 8:24.19

110mh **(0.5)** 1. Antonio Alkana RSA 13.32*
2. Lyès Mokdel ALG 13.49
3. Ty Akins NGR 13.54

400mh 1. Abdelmalik Lahoulou ALG 48.67
2. Miloud Rahmouni ALG 49.27
3. Mohamed Sghaier TUN 49.32
HJ 1. Kabele Kgosiemang BOT 2.25
2. Ali Mohamed Younes Idris SUD 2.22
3. Chris Moleya RSA 2.22
PV 1. Hichem Cherabi ALG 5.25
2. Jordan Yamoah GHA 5.20
3. Mohamed Amine Romdhana TUN 5.10
LJ 1. Ndiss Kaba Badji SEN 7.74/-0.3
2. Mamadou Guèye SEN 7.69/-0.1
3. Romeo N'tia BEN 7.44/-0.6
Drugs dq (1) Samson Idiata NGR 7.83/-1.1
TJ 1. Tosin Oke NGR 17.00/0.5
2. Olu Olamigoke NGR 16.98/0.9
3. Mamadou Chérif Dia MLI 16.55/0.3
SP 1. Frank Elemba CGO 20.25*
2. Mohamed Hamza EGY-J 19.78
3. Jaco Engelbrecht RSA 19.55
DT 1. Russel Tucker RSA 60.41
2. Essohounamondom Tchalim TOG 52.72
3. Frank Elemba CGO 50.30
HT 1. Mostafa Hicham Al-Gamal EGY 74.92
2. Chris Harmse RSA 73.49
3. Nicholas Li Yun Fong MRI 59.36
JT 1. Ihab Abdelrahman EGY 85.37*
2. John Ampomah GHA 82.94
3. Phil-Mar van Rensburg RSA 76.85
Dec 1. Guillaume Thierry MRI 7591
2. Atsu Nyamadi GHA 7478
3. Friedrich Pretorius RSA 7186
20kW 1. Lebogang Shange RSA 1:26:43
2. Samuel Gathimba KEN 1:26:44
3. Wayne Snyman RSA 1:27:32
4x100m 1. CIV (Naliali, Koffi, Cissé, Meité) 38.93
2. NAM 39.22
3. GHA 39.71
4x400m 1. KEN (Kibet 45.5, Sampao 45.6, K Kosgei 45.4, Mweresa 43.8) 3:00.34*
2. BOT (Nkobolo 45.3, Amos 45.6, Maotoanong 45.6, Makwala 44.5) 3:00.95
3. ALG 3:03.07

Women
100m (0.6) 1. Marie Josée Ta Lou Gonorie CIV 11.02*
2. Eunice Kadogo KEN 11.47
3= Kadidiatou Traoré BUR 11.49
3= Adeline Gouenon CIV 11.49
200m (-1.1) 1. Marie Josée Ta Lou Gonorie CIV 22.57
2. Ngozi Onwumere NGR 23.24
3. Lauretta Ozoh NGR 23.37
400m 1. Kabange Mupopo ZAM 50.22
2. Patience George NGR 50.71
3. Tjipekapora Herunga NAM 51.55
800m 1. Caster Semenya RSA 2:00.97
2. Annet Mwanzi KEN 2:01.54
3. Chaltu Shume ETH-J 2:01.59
1500m 1. Dawit Seyaum ETH-J 4:16.69
2. Besu Sado ETH-J 4:18.86
3. Beatrice Chepkoech KEN 4:19.16
5000m 1. Margaret Chelimo KEN 15:30.15
2. Rosemary Wanjiru KEN 15:30.18
3. Alice Aprot Nawowuna KEN 15:31.82
10,000m 1. Alice Aprot Nawowuna KEN 31:24.18*
2. Gladys Chesire KEN 31:36.87
3. Gelete Burka ETH 31:38.33
HMar 1. Mamitu Daska ETH 72:42
2. Worknesh Degefa ETH 72:42
3. Yebergara Melesse ETH 72:42
3000mSt 1. Sofia Assefa ETH 9:51.30
2. Hiwot Ayalew ETH 9:51.94
3. Purity Kirui KEN 9:52.54
100mh (-0.1) 1. Amusan Oluwatobeloba NGR 13.15
2. Gnima Faye SEN 13.28
3. Lindsay Lindley NGR 13.30
400mh 1. Amaka Ogoegbunam NGR 55.86
2. Joke Odumosu NGR 57.63
3. Lilanne Klaasman NAM 58.68
HJ 1. Lissa Labiche SEY 1.91
2. Doreen Amata NGR 1.85
3. Julia du Plessis RSA 1.80
PV 1. Sirine Ebondo TUN 4.10
2. Dorra Mahfoudhi TUN 4.10
3. Alima Quattara CIV 3.40
LJ 1. Joëlle Mbumi Nkouindjin CMR 6.31/-0.5
2. Romaissa Belbiod ALG 6.30/0.2
3. Lissa Labiche 6.25/-0.3
Drugs dq (1) Chinazor Amadi NGR 6.31/-0.8
TJ 1. Joëlle Mbumi Nkouindjin CMR 13.75/0.1
2. Blessing Ibrahim NGR 13.52/0.0
3. Nadia Eke GHA 13.40/-0.1
SP 1. Auriole Dongmo CMR 17.21
2. Claire Uke NGR 16.64
3. Sonia Smuts RSA 15.92
DT 1. Claire Uke NGR 54.25
2. Ischke Senekal RSA 50.53
3. Julia Agawu GHA 49.08
HT 1. Laëtitia Bambara BUR 66.91*
2. Amy Sène SEN 63.64
3. Jennifer Batu CGO 62.13
JT 1. Kelechi Nwanaga NGR 52.70 jnr
2. Mary Zuta Nartey GHA 50.93
3. Jo-Ané van Dyk RSA-J 50.52
Hep 1. Uhunoma Osazuwa NGR 5892
2. Odile Ahouanwanou BEN 5734
3. Marthe Yasmine Koala BUR 5664
20kW 1. Grace Njue KEN 1:38:28*
2. Aynalem Eshetu ETH 1:39:49
3. Askale Tiksa ETH 1:42:25.
4x100m 1. NGR (Francis, Okagbare, Onwumere, Ozoh) 43.10
2. GHA 43.72
3. CIV 43.98
4x400m 1. NGR (Ossai, Oladoye, Adeloye, P George) 3:27.12
2. BOT 3:32.84
3. KEN 3:35.91

Medal table leaders: NGR 8G-9S-4B, ETH 6-5-6, KEN 5-9-6, CIV 5-0-4, RSA 4-2-8, BOT 3-2-1, ALG 2-4-2, CMR 3-0-0, EGY 2-1-0; 25 nations won medals.

11th African Junior Championships

At Addis Ababa, Ethiopia (A) 5-8 March

Men: **100m/ 200m**: Divine Oduduru NGR 10.44/21.22, **400m**: Karabo Sibanda BOT 46.33, **800m**: Patrick Kiprotich Rono KEN 1:50.21, **1500m**: Anthony Kiptoo KEN 3:43.98, **5000m**: Yomif Kejelcha ETH 14:31.03, **10,000m**: Joshua Cheptegei UGA 29:58.70, **3000mSt**:

Abraham Kibiwot KEN 8:47.43, 99cm **110mh**: Bashiru Abdullahi 13.99, **400mh**: Larry Lombaard RSA 51.80, **HJ**: Hicham Bouhanoun ALG 2.12, **PV**: Seifeddine Mehri TUN 4.40, **LJ**: Mohcine Khoua 7.45, **TJ**: Heitham Sebbat ALG 15.39, 6kg **SP**: Hamza Mohamed EGY 20.66*, 1.75kg **DT**: Johan Scholtz RSA 57.57, 6kg **HT**: Ahmed Tarek Ismael EGY 74.46, **JT**: Bahaa Abdelwareth EGY 70.09, **4x100m**: NGR 39.99, **4x400m**: BOT 3:11.00, **10000mW**: Mahmoud Mohamed Abdelfattah EGY 48:47.90. **Women**: **100m**: Tamzin Thomas RSA 11.69, **200m**: Praise Idamadudu NGR 23.76, **400m**: Tosin Adelote NGR 54.09, **800m**: Chaltu Shume ETH 2:09.20, **1500m**: Dawit Seyaum ETH 4:15.94, **3000m**: Meina Nigussie ETH 9:31.37, **5000m**: Etagenne Woldu ETH 17:02.71, **3000mSt**: Stella Jepkosgei KEN 10:22.47, **100mh**: Amusan Oluwatobeloba NGR 14.26, **400mh**: Gizelle Magerman RSA 59.41, **HJ**: Marelize Higgins RSA 1.80, **PV**: Kaityln Sparks RSA 3.40*=, **LJ/TJ**: Ese Brume NGR 6.33*/13.16, **SP**: Monique Wagner RSA 13.96, **DT**: Leandri Geel RSA 46.76, **HT**: Mostafa Mhamed Esraa EGY 57.85, **JT**: Jo-Ané van Dyk RSA 49.47, **Hep**: Rebecca Oshinbajo NGR 4765, **4x100m/4x400m**: NGR 44.83*/3:38.94, **5000mW**: Yehualye Belete ETH 24:49.11. **Medal table**: NGR 12G-8S-7B, RSA 9-7-7, ETH 6-12-10, EGY 5-5-3, ALG 2-1-2, BOT 2-1-0, MAR 1-1-3; 16 nations won medals (10 gold).

19th Arab Championships

At Manama, Bahrain 24-27 April

Men: **100m/200m**: Femi Seun Ogunode QAT 10.04w/20.52w, **400m**: Abdelilah Haroun QAT 44.68*, **800m**: Musaeb Abdulrahman Balla QAT 1:46.74, **1500m**: Fouad El Kaam MAR 3:46.54, **5000m**: Ayanleh Souleiman DJI 13:17.97*, **10000m**: El Hassan El Abbassi BRN 28:23.11*, **HMar**: Shumi Dechasa BRN 62:50, **3000mSt**: Hamid Ezzine MAR 8:30.57, **110mh**: Abdulaziz Al-Mandeel KUW 13.35w, **400mh**: Ali Khamis Abbas BRN 50.10, **HJ**: Mutaz Essa Barshim QAT 2.19, **PV**: Mouhcine Cheaouri MAR 5.00, **LJ**: Saleh Al-Haddad KUW 7.96w, **TJ**: Issam Nima ALG 16.78w, **SP**: Mustafa Amer Ahmed EGY 19.22*, **DT**: Essa Mohamed Al-Zankawi KUW 63.22, **HT**: Mostafa Al Gamal EGY 74.81, **JT**: Ihab Abdulrahman Al-Sayed EGY 80.72*, **Dec**: Mohamed Al-Qaree KSA 7568w, **4x100m**: KUW 39.75, **4x400m**: QAT 3:04.93, **20kmW**: Hassanine Sbai TUN 1:28:09. **Women**: **100m**: Hajer Al-Ameeri BRN 11.65w, **200m**: Adedoyin Odiong BRN 22.98w, **400m**: Kemi Adekoya BRN 54.06, **800m**: Malika Akkaoui MAR 2:05.77, **1500m**: Amina Bakhit SUD 5:22.27, **5000m**: Mimi Belete BRN 16:50.90, **10000m**: Alia Mohamed Saeed UAE 32:16.97*, **HMar**: Eunice Jepkirui Kirwa BRN 71:02*, **3000mSt**: Ruth Chebet BRN 9:39.61*, **100mh/400mh**: Lamiae Lhabz MAR 13.53w/56.64*, **HJ**: Besnet Mohamed EGY 1.75, **PV**: Sirini Ebondo TUN 4.11*, **LJ**: Romaissa Belabiod ALG 6.37w, **TJ**: Jamaa Chnaïk MAR 13.51, **SP**: Noora Salem Jassem BRN 14.97, **DT**: Amina Moudden MAR 48.99, **HT**: Zouina Bouzebra ALG 60.06, **JT**: Norhan Mohamed EGY 49.58, **Hep**: Houda Mohamed Atef EGY 5404, **4x100m/4x400m**: BRN 46.40*/3:36.77*, **10000mW**: Chahine Nasri TUN 50:34.4. **Medal table**: BRN 12G-9S-10B, MAR 8-6-6, QAT 6-6-2, EGY 6-5-7, KUW 4-1-2, ALG & TUN 3-4-4, KSA 1-2-2, SUD 1-2-1, UAE 1-1-2, DJI 1-1-1, OMA 0-4-0, IRQ 0-1-4.

Asian Championships

At Wuhan, China 3-7 June

100m	1. Femi Ogunode QAT 9.91*
(1.8)	2. Zhang Peimeng CHN 10.15
	3. Reza Ghasemi IRI 10.19
200m	1. Femi Ogunode QAT 20.32
(1.0)	2. Fahad Al-Subaie KSA 20.63
	3. Dharambir Singh IND 20.66
400m	1. Abdelilah Haroun QAT 44.68
	2. Youssef Al-Masrahi KSA 45.14
	3. Kentaro Sato JPN 46.09
800m	1. Abdulrahman Musaeb Balla QAT 1:49.40
	2. Jinson Johnson IND 1:49.69
	3. Sho Kawamoto JPN 1:50.50
1500m	1. Mohamed Al-Garni QAT 3:41.42
	2. Mohammed Tiouali BRN 3:42.43
	3. Belal Mansour Ali BRN 3:43.67
5000m	1. Mohamed Al-Garni QAT 13:34.47*
	2. Albert Rop BRN 13:35.26
	3. Govindan Lakshmanan IND 13:36.62
10,000m	1. El Hassan El Abbassi BRN 28:50.71
	2. Govindan Lakshmanan IND 29:42.81
	3. Andrey Petrov UZB 30:20.68
3000mSt	1. John Koech BRN 8:27.03
	2. Hashem Abbas QAT 8:36.02
	3. Evans Chematot BRN 8:42.76
110mh	1. Xie Wenjun CHN 13.56
(-0.6)	2. Abdulaziz Al-Mandeel KUW 13.67
	3. Kim Byung-jun KOR 13.75
400mh	1. Yuta Konishi JPN 49.58
	2. Chen Chieh TPE 49.68
	3. Kazuaki Yoshida JPN 49.95
HJ	1. Takashi Eto JPN 2.24
	2. Hsiang Chun-Hsien TPE 2.24
	3. Mutaz Essa Barshim QAT 2.20
PV	1. Zhang Wei CHN 5.60
	2. Seito Yamamoto JPN 5.50
	3. Huang Bokai CHN 5.50
LJ	1. Gao Xinglong CHN 7.96/-1.1
	2. Ted Hooper TPE 7.80/-0.5
	3. Tang Gongchen CHN 7.79/-0.3
TJ	1. Kim Duk-hyung KOR 16.86/-0.1
	2. Cao Shuo CHN 16.77/-0.1
	3. Roman Valiyev KAZ 16.67/-0.3
SP	1. Inderjeet Singh IND 20.41*
	2. Chang Ming-Huang TPE 19.56
	3. Tian Zhizhong CHN 19.25
DT	1. Vikas Gowda IND 62.03
	2. Essa Al-Zankawi KUW 61.67
	3. Mahmoud Samimi IRI 59.78
HT	1. Dilshod Nazarov TJK 77.68
	2. Ashraf Amjad El-Seify QAT 76.03
	3. Wan Yong CHN 73.40
JT	1. Huang Shih-Feng TPE 79.74
	2. Bobur Shokirjonov UZB 79.09
	3. Yukifumi Murakami JPN 79.05
Dec (d/e)	1. Akihiko Nakamura JPN 7773
	2. Guo Qi CHN 7289
	3. Hu Yufei CHN 7042
4x100m	1. CHN (Chen Shiwei, Mo Youzue, Su Bingtian, Zhang Peimeng) 39.04
	2. HKG 39.25

	3. TPE 39.35
4x400m	1. QAT (F Ogunode, A M Balla, M Mohamed, A Haroun) 3:02.50*
	2. KSA 3:02.62
	3. JPN 3:03.47
Women	
100m (2.5)	1. Chisato Fukushima JPN 11.23w
	2. Viktoriya Zyabkina KAZ 11.34
	3. Wei Yongli CHN 11.46
200m (0.4)	1. Viktoriya Zyabkina KAZ 23.09
	2. Olga Safronova KAZ 23.46
	3. Srabandi Nanda IND 23.54
400m	1. Yang Huizhen CHN 52.37
	2. Machettira Poovamma IND 53.07
	3. Anastasiya Kudinova KAZ 53.41
800m	1. Tintu Luka IND 2:01.53
	2. Zhao Jing CHN 2:03.40
	3. Liyanarachchi Nimali SRI 2:03.94
1500m	1. Betlhem Desalegn UAE 4:29.39
	2. Zhao Jing CHN 4:29.40
	3. Maya Jino JPN 4:32.90
5000m	1. Betlhem Desalegn UAE 15:25.15
	2. Alia Mohamed Saeed UAE 15:28.74
	3. Daria Maslova KGZ 15:42.82
10,000m	1. Alia Mohamed Saeed UAE 31:52.29*
	2. Eunice Chumba BRN 32:22.29
	3. Michi Numata JPN 32:44.57
3000mSt	1. Lalita Babar IND 9:34.13*
	2. Li Zhenzhu CHN 9:41.43
	3. Zhang Xinyan CHN 9:46.82
100mh (-0.4)	1. Wu Shuijiao CHN 13.12
	2. Anastasiya Pilipenko KAZ 13.33
	3. Ayako Kimura JPN 13.41
400mh	1. Kemi Adekoya BRN 54.31*
	2. Manami Kira JPN 57.14
	3. Xiao Xia CHN 57.69
HJ	1. Svetlana Radzivil UZB 1.91
	2. Wang Yang CHN 1.88
	3. Zheng Xingjuan CHN 1.84
PV	1. Li Ling CHN 4.66*
	2. Xu Huiqin CHN 4.30
	3. Tomomi Abiko JPN 4.20
LJ	1. Lu Minjia CHN 6.52/-0.4
	2. Jung Soon-ok KOR 6.47/0.8
	3. Xu Xiaoling CHN 6.46/-0.3
TJ	1. Wang Wupin CHN 13.76/-0.8
	2. Li Yanmei CHN 13.57/0.2
	3. Wang Rong CHN 13.44/-0.7
SP	1. Guo Tianqian CHN 18.59
	2. Gao Yang CHN 17.98
	3. Bian Ka CHN 17.78
DT	1. Su Xinyue CHN 63.90
	2. Tan Jian CHN 62.97
	3. Lu Xiaoxin CHN 62.30
HT	1. Liu Tingting CHN 68.24
	2. Luo Na CHN 64.97
	3. Akane Watanabe JPN 59.39
JT	1. Liu Shiying CHN 61.33*
	2. Yang Xinli CHN 59.24
	3. Risa Miyashita JPN 54.76
Hep (a/b)	1. Yekaterina Voronina UZB 5689
	2. Liksy Joseph IND 5554
	3. Purnima Hembran IND 5511
4x100m	1. CHN (Tao Yujia, Yuan Qiqi, Lin Huijun, Wei Yongli) 43.10*
	2. JPN 44.14
	3. THA 44.73
4x400m	1. CHN (Huang Guifen, Cheng Chong, Chen Jingwen, Yang Huizhen) 3:33.44
	2. IND 3:33.81
	3. KAZ 3:35.14

Medal and points table

Nation	G	S	B	Points
CHN	15	13	13	422
JPN	4	3	11	208
IND	4	5	4	148
QAT	7	2	1	86
KAZ	1	3	3	76
BRN	3	3	2	67
TPE	1	4	1	61
UZB	2	1	1	57
KOR	1	1	1	50
IRI	0	0	2	43
SRI	0	0	1	38
UAE	3	1	0	31
KSA	0	3	0	30
KGZ	0	0	1	21
THA	0	0	1	20
KUW	0	2	0	19

HKG 15 (1S), MAS 15, PRK 12, TJK 11 (1G), OMA 8, SYR 4, NEP 3, TKM, PLE 2, IRQ 2, INA 1.

Marathon: *At Hong Kong 25 January.* **Men**: Shingo Igarashi JPN 2:14:20; **Women**: Kim Hye-gyong PRK 2:31:46.

Walks: *At Nomi City, Japan 15 March.* **Men 20k:** 1. Yusuke Suzuki JPN 1:16:36*, 2. Kim Hyun-sub KOR 1:19:13, 3. Baljinder Singh IND 1:22:58; **Women 20k**: 1. Hou Yongbo CHN 1:29:25, 2. Kumiko Okada JPN 1:29:46, 3. Jeon Young-eun KOR 1:30:35.

67th Balkan Championships

At Pitesti, Romania 1-2 August

Men: **100m**: Jak Ali Harvey TUR 10.11, **200m**: Ramil Ganiyev TUR 20.59, **400m**: Luka Janezic SLO 46.39, **800m**: Zan Rudolf SLO 1:50.10; **1500m**: Konstadínos Nakópoulos 3:48.82, **5000m**: Dino Bosnjak CRO 14:12.20, **3000mSt**: Mitko Tsenov BUL 8:29.73, **110mh**: Milan Trajkovic CYP 14.23, **400mh**: Yasmani Copello Escobar TUR 50.19, **HJ**: Dimítrios Hondrokoúkis CYP 2.24, **PV**: Robert Renner SLO 5.65, **LJ**: Loúis Tsátoumas GRE 7.90. **TJ**: Georgi Tsonov **BUL 17.01**, **SP**: Ab]ndrei Gag ROU 20.96; **DT**: Filip Mihaljevic CRO 60.74, **HT**: Esref Apak TUR 76.82, **JT**: Vedran Samac SRB 77.92, **Dec**: Mihail Dudas SRB 7720, **4x100/ 4x400**: TUR 39.35/3:06.55; **Women**: **100m**: Maja Mihalinec SLO 11.34, **200m**: Mária Belibasáki GRE 23.23, **400m**: Bianca Razor ROU 52.26, **800m**: Florina Pierdevara 2:03.14, **1500m**: Luiza Gega ALB 4:08.74, **5000m**: Esma Aydemir TUR 15:51.27, **3000mSt**: Silva Danekova BUL 9:33.41, **100mh**: Andrea Ivancevic CRO 13.00, **400mh**: Angela Morosanu ROU 57.88, **HJ**: Mirela Demireva BUL 1.91, **PV**: Tina Sutej SLO 4.20, **LJ**: Florentina Marincu ROU 6.65, **TJ**: Petia Dacheva BUL 13.67, **SP**: Emel Dereli TUR 17.39, **DT**: Hrisoúla Anagnostopoúlou GRE 54.8, **HT**: Zalina Marghieva MDA 73.97, **JT**: Martina Ratej SLO 59.19; **Hep**: Serpil Koçak TUR 5119, **4x100**: CRO 45.71, **4x400**: ROU 3:33.07.

Half Marathon *at Apatin,Serbia 18 October*. **Men**: Medeni Demir TUR 66:58; **Women**: Burcu Büyüik-

bezgin TUR 77:51; **Marathon** *at Podgporica, Montengro.* **Men**: Drako Zivanovic SRB 2:35:05; **Women**: Olivera Jevtic SRB 2:39:32.
Walks *at Ayvalik, Turkey 18 April.* **Men 20k**: Sahin Senoduncu TUR 1:27:30, **Women 20k**: Andreea Arsine ROU 1:39:36.

Commonwealth Youth Games

At Apia, Samoa 7-9 September

Men: **100m/200m**: Tiotliso Gift Leotlela RSA 10.20*/20.56w, **400m**: Karabo Sibanda BOT 45.83*, **800m**: Willy Tarbei KEN 1:46.05*, **1500m**: Kumari Taki KEN 3:39.80*, **3000m**: Davis Kiplangat KEN 7:59.78, 91.4cm **110mh**: Mpho Katlego Tladi RSA 13.50, 84cm **400mh**: Rivaldo Leacock BAR 51.12*, **HJ**: Tejasswin Shankar IND 2.14*, **LJ**: Richard Seklorwu GHA 7.67w, 5kg **SP**: Kevin Nedrick JAM 20.12*; 1.5kg **DT**: Werner Visser RSA 60.94, **700g JT**: Mohd Hadeesh IND 79.29, **4x100m**: BOT 41.94, **4x200m**: NGR 1:28.35, **4x400m**: JAM 3:13.45; **Women**: 100m: Abolaji Omotayo Oluwaseu NGR 11.59, **200m**: Idamadudu Praise Oghenef NGR 23.30w, **400m/400mh**: Junelle Bromfield JAM 53.09/60.78, **800m/1500m**: Any Harding-Delooze AUS 2:06.84/4:18.02*, **3000m**: Sheila Chelangat KEN 9:10.12, 76.2cm **100mh**: Taylon Bieldt RSA 13.18*, **HJ**: Niamh Emerson ENG 1.80, **LJ**: Renate van Tonder RSA 6.26w, 3kg **SP**: Grace Robinson AUS 16.39*, **DT**: Kristina Moore AUS 46.95, 500g **JT**: Emma Hamplett ENG 49.57, **4x100m/4x200m/4x400m**: NGR 45.86/1:28.35/4:02.75.

14th European Cup Winter Throwing

At Leiria, Portugal 14-15 March

Men: **SP**: 1. Borja Vivas ESP 20.15, 2. Leif Arrhenius SWE 20.09, 3. Carlos Tabalina ESP 20.04; **DT**: 1. Martin Kupper EST 66.67, 2. Andrius Gudzius LTU 65.51, 3. Viktor Butenko RUS 65.44; **HT**: 1. Krisztián Pars HUN 79.24, 2. Pawel Fajdek POL 76.19, 3. Serghei Marghiev MDA 73.84; **JT**: 1. Valeriy Iordan RUS 83.00, 2. Thomas Röhler GER 81.83, 3. Fatih Avan TUR 81.45; **Women**: **SP**: 1. Yuliya Leontyuk BLR 18.56, 2. Anita Márton HUN 17.59, 3. Chiara Rosa ITA 17.38; **DT**: 1. Nadine Müller GER 65.27, 2. Mélina Robert-Michon FRA 64.75, 3. Irina Rodrigues POR 63.25; **HT**: 1. Anna Bulgakova RUS 72.06, 2. Joanna Fiodorov POL 70.90, 3. Alexandra Tavernier FRA 70.45; **JT**: 1. Martina Ratej SLO 62.43, 2. Linda Stahl GER 62.12, 3. Katarina Molitor GER 62.08. **Team:** Men: 1. RUS 4438, 2. ITA 4175, 3. EST 4143, 4. ESP 4123, 5. UKR 4120, 6. POR 3936; Women: 1. GER 4339, 2. FRA 4221 3. RUS 4189, 4. ITA 4055, 5. BLR 4054, 6. CZE 3960, 7. UKR 3880, 8. EST 3570.

European Team Championships

Super League at Cheboksary, Russia 21-22 June

1. RUS 368.5, 2. GER 346.5, 3. FRA 319.5, 4. POL 317, 5. GBR 291, 6. ITA 288, 7. UKR 281.5, 8. ESP 230.5, 9. BLR 217, 10. SWE 187, 11. FIN 149.5, 12. NOR 121

100m	1. Christophe Lemaitre FRA 10.26
(-1.7)	2. Richard Kilty GBR 10.35
	3. Sven Knipphals GER 10.50
200m	1 (1B). Serhiy Smelyk UKR 20.45
(-0.2/-0.9)	2 (1A). Danny Talbot GBR 20.62
	3 (2B). Enrico Demonte ITA 20.67
400m	1. Jarryd Dunn GBR 45.09
	2. Mame-Ibra Anne FRA 45.26
	3. Aleksandr Linnik BLR 45.43
800m	1. Giordano Benedetti ITA 1:45.11
	2. Pierre-Ambroise Bosse FRA 1:45.14
	3. Adam Kszczot POL 1:45.84
1500m	1. Valentin Smirnov RUS 3:52.03
	2. Marcin Lewandowski POL 3:52.06
	3. Oliver Aitchison GBR 3:52.33
3000m	1. Richard Ringer GER 8:34.35
	2. Roberto Alaiz ESP 8:35.07
	3. Andrew Butchart GBR 8:35.75
5000m	1. Mourad Amdouni FRA 14:04.63
	2. Jesús España ESP 14:05.09
	3. Andrew Vernon GBR 14:05.85
3000mSt	1. Krystian Zalewski POL 8:37.51
	2. Nikolay Chavkin RUS 8:39.39
	3. Yuri Floriani ITA 8:40.47
110mh	1. Sergey Shubenkov RUS 13.22
(-2.6)	2. Pascal Martinot Lagarde FRA 13.42
	3. Lawrence Clarke GBR 13.64
400mh	1. Denis Kudryavtsev RUS 48.66
	2. Patryk Dobek POL 49.04
	3. Leonardo Capotosti ITA 49.93
HJ	1. Daniyil Tsyplakov RUS 2.33
	2. Marco Fassinotti ITA 2.28
	3. Mateusz Przybylko GER 2.25
PV	1. Renaud Lavillenie FRA 5.85
	2. Rafael Holzdeppe GER 5.85
	3. Piotr Lisek POL 5.80
LJ	1. Aleksandr Menkov RUS 8.26/2.0
	2. Kafétien Gomis FRA 8.26/0.4
	3. Alyn Camara GER 8.11w/2.1
TJ	1. Fabrizio Donato ITA 17.11w/3.3
	2. Aleksey Fyodorov RUS 16.92/1.6
	3. Simo Lipsanen FIN 16.62w/2.3
SP	1. David Storl GER 21.20
	2. Tomasz Majewski POL 20.23
	3. Pavel Lyzhyn BLR 20.15
DT	1. Robert Urbanek POL 63.03
	2. Martin Wierig GER 60.23
	3. Frank Casañas ESP 60.01
HT	1. Pawel Fajdek POL 81.64
	2. Nick Miller GBR 75.91
	3. Yevhen Vynohradov UKR 75.91
JT	1. Tero Pitkämäki FIN 84.44
	2. Johannes Vetter GER 78.97
	3. Valeriy Iordan RUS 78.32
4x100m	1. GBR (Kilty, Talbot, Ellington, Robertson) 38.21
	2. FRA (Vincent, Lemaitre, Pessonneaux, Biron) 38.34
	3 (1B). ITA (Ferraro, Demonte, Manenti, Obou) 38.71
4x400m	1. FRA (Anne, Venel, Hanne, Jordier) 3:00.47
	2. GBR (Yousif, D Williams, C Williams, Buck) 3:00.54
	3. POL (Krawczuk, Pietrzak, Omelko, Dobek) 3:01.24

Women

100m (-1.4)	1. Asha Philip GBR 11.27 2. Nataliya Pohrebnyak UKR 11.29 3. Ewa Swoboda POL 11.48
200m (0.5)	1. Nataliya Pohrebnyak UKR 22.76 2. Bianca Williams GBR 23.16 3. Yekaterina Smirnova RUS 23.29
400m	1. Floria Guei FRA 51.55 2. Mariya Mikhailyuk RUS 51.59 3. Libania Grenot ITA 51.82
800m	1. Renelle Lamote FRA 2:00.18 2. Joanna Józwik POL 2:00.30 3. Anastasiya Tkachuk UKR 2:00.72
1500m	1. Anna Shchagina RUS 4:15.22 2. Karoline Bjerkeli Grøvdal NOR 4:16.22 3. Rhianwedd Price GBR 4:16.59
3000m	1. Sofia Ennaoui POL 9:20.39 2. Maren Kock GER 9:20.82 3. Yelena Korobkina RUS 9:20.93
5000m	1. Renata Plis POL 15:49.29 2. Olga Mazuronak BLR 15:51.89 3. Clémence Calvin FRA 15:53.28
3000mSt	1. Gesa-Felicitas Krause GER 9:46.49 2. Lennie Waite GBR 9:59.75 3. Emma Oudiou FRA 10:01.02
100mh (0.4)	1. Alina Talay BLR 12.80 2. Nina Morozova RUS 12.85 3. Cindy Roleder GER 12.92
400mh	1. Eilidh Child GBR 54.46 2. Anna Titimets UKR 54.75 3. Yadisleidy Pedroso ITA 55.18
HJ	1. Mariya Kuchina RUS 1.99 2. Ruth Beitia ESP 1.97 3, Kamila Licwinko POL 1.97
PV	1. Silke Spiegelburg GER 4.75* 2. Anzhelika Sidorova RUS 4.70 3. Angelica Bengtsson SWE 4.60
LJ	1. Darya Klishina RUS 6.95/1.6 2. Olga Sudareva BLR 6.86/0.6 3. Sosthene Moguenara GER 6.79/0.4
TJ	1. Yekaterina Koneva RUS 14.98w/2.3 2. Kristin Gierisch GER 14.46w/3.5 3. Simona La Mantia ITA 14.22/2.0
SP	1. Christina Schwanitz GER 19.82 2. Irina Tarasova RUS 18.51 3. Alyona Dubitskaya BLR 18.38
DT	1. Mélina Robert-Michon FRA 62.24 2. Zaneta Glanc POL 58.92 3. Sanna Kämäräinen FIN 58.53
HT	1. Anna Wlodarczyk POL 78.28* 2. Betty Heidler GER 75.73 3. Alexandra Tavernier FRA 74.05
JT	1. Christina Obergföll GER 61.69 2. Tatyana Kholodovich BLR 61.08 3. Jenni Kangas FIN 55.33
4x100m	1. UKR (Strohova, Pohrebnyak, Kashcheyeva, Stuy) 42.50 2. RUS (Panteleyeva, Ryzhova, Demirova, Smirnova) 42.99 3. GER (Kwadwo, Pinto, Haase, Burghardt) 43.21
4x400m	1. RUS (Mamina, Zadorina, Ryzhova, Mikhailyuk) 3:24.98 2. FRA (Diarra, Raharolahy, Sananes, Guei) 3:28.84 3. (1B). UKR (V Tkachuk, Lohvynenko, Bibik, Zemlyak) 3:29.79

First League *at Iráklio, Greece 21-22 June*

1.CZE 351, 2. GRE 327, 3. NED 299.5, 4. BEL 276.5, 5. POR 270.5, 6. IRL 261.5, 7. TUR 259.5, 8. SUI 239, 9. ROU 227, 10. EST 215.5, 11. LTU 214.5, 12. LAT 169.5

Winners: **Men**: **100m/200m**: Likoúrgos-Stéfanos Tsákonas GRE 10.32/20.44, **400m**: Pavel Maslák CZE 45.57, **800m/1500m**: Ilham Tanui Özbilen TUR 1:47.97/3:38.03, **3000m**: Halil Akkas TUR 8:12.00, **5000m**: Bashir Abdi BEL 15:17.47, **3000mSt**: Tarik Langat Akdag TUR 8:44.53, **110mh**: Konstadínos Douvalídis GRE 13.58, **400mh**: Rasmus Mägi EST 49.59, **HJ**: Jaroslav Bába CZE 2.30, **PV**: Konstadínos Filippídis GRE 5.80, **LJ**: Loúis Tsátoumas GRE 7.77, **TJ**: Nelson Évora POR 16.34, **SP**: Tomás Stanek CZE 19.67, **DT**: Philip Milanov BEL 62.02, **HT**: Lukás Melich CZE 74.84, **JT**: Tanel Laanmäe EST 82.67, **4x100m**: SUI 40.00, **4x400m**: CZE 3:04.52. **Women**: **100m/ 200m**: Dafne Schippers NED 11.12/22.45, **400m**: Nicky van Leuveren NED 52.04, **800m**: Selina Büchel SUI 2:00.56, **1500m**: Claudia Bobocea ROU 4:14.58, **3000m**: Sara Moreira POR 9:01.67, **5000m**: Jip Vastenburg NED 15:36.32, **3000mSt**: Özlem Kaya TUR 9:43.07, **100mh**: Anne Zagré BEL 13.03, **400mh**: Zuzana Hejnová CZE 55.11, **HJ**: Oldriska Maresová CZE 1.88, **PV**: Nikoléta Kiriakopoúlou GRE 4.65, **LJ**: Karin Melis Mey TUR 6.53, **TJ**: Paraskeví Papahrístou GRE 13.99, **SP**: Emel Dereli TUR 17.47, **DT**: Zinaida Sendriuté LTU 60.51, **HT**: Tereza Králová CZE 64.52, **JT**: Barbora Spotáková CZE 62.56, **4x100m**: GRE 43.80, **4x400m**: CZE 3:32.37.

Second League *at Stara Zagora, Bulgaria 21-22 June*

1. DEN 224, 2. BUL 218, 3. HUN 202.5, 4. SRB 179.5, 5. CRO 167, 6. ISL 156.5, 7. CYP 151, 8. SLO 127.5.

Winners: **100m/200m**: Denis Dimitrov BUL 10.34/21.38, **400m**: Nick Ekelund-Arenander DEN 46.32, **800m**: Andreas Bube DEN 1:50.38, **1500m/3000mSt**: Mitko Tsenov BUL 3:46.31/9:07.37, **3000m**: Mads Tærsbøl DEN 8:29.09, **5000m**: Thijs Nijhuis DEN 14:28.66, **110mh**: Andreas Martinsen DEN 13.71, **400mh**: Nicolai Hartling DEN 50.16, **HJ**: Janick Klausen DEN 2.24, **PV**: Ivan Horvat CRO 5.40, **LJ**: Marko Prigovecki CRO 7.65, **TJ**: Rumen Dimitrov BUL 16.77w, **SP**: Georgi Tsonov BUL 16.36, **DT**: Zoltán Kövágó HUN 64.73, **HT**: Krisztián Pars HUN 77.27, **JT**: Vedran Samac SRB 79.52, **4x100m**: HUN 39.88, **4x400m**: DEN 3:08.01. **Women**: **100m/200m**: Ivet Lalova BUL 11.11/22.90, **400m**: Tamara Salaski SRB 53.29, **800m/1500m**: Amela Terzic SRB 1:59.90/4:16.13, **3000m** : Sonja Stolic SRB 9:19.88, **5000m**: Militsa Mircheva BUL 16:30.14, **3000mSt**: Silvia Danekova BUL 9:43.34, **100mh**: Andrea Ivancevic CRO 13.38, **400mh**: Sara Petersen DEN 55.13, **HJ**: Mirela Demireva BUL 1.91, **PV**: Iben Høgh-Pedersen DEN 4.00, **LJ**: Hafdis Sigurdardóttir ISL 6.45, **TJ**: Gabriela Petrova BUL 14.85w, **SP**: Anita Márton HUN 18.36, **DT**: Dragana Tomasevic SRB 58.16, **HT**: Barbara Spiler SLO 63.80, **JT**: Ásdis Hjálmsdóttir ISL 60.06, **4x100m**: CYP 44.75, **4x400m**: BUL 3:38.78.

Third League *at Baku, Azerbaijan 22-23 June*

1. SVK 458.5, 2. AUT 458, 3. ISR 439, 4. MDA 401, 5. AZE 387, 6. BIH 336, 7. LUX 317, 8. GEO 283, 9. MLT 243.5, 10. MNE 240, 11. AND 161, 12. MKD 142, 13. ALB 115, 14. AAS (Small States) 99.

European Cup Combined Events

Super League At Aubagne, France 4-5 July

1. RUS 41,700, 2. FRA 40,724, 3. EST 39,875, 4. UKR 39,461, 5. BLR 39,414, 6. GBR 38,791, 7. NED 38,753, 8. CZE 36,767. **Men Dec**: 1. Ilya Shkurenyov RUS 8378, 2. Oleksiy Kasyanov UKR 8105, 3. Romain Barras FRA 8007, 4. Florian Geffrouais FRA 7970, 5. Yevgeniy Sarantsev RUS 7851; **Women Hep**: 1. Alina Fyodorova UKR 6278. 2. Grit Sadeiko EST 6196, 3. Anna Blank RUS 6037, 4. Ulyana Aleksandrova RUS 5963, 5. Yana Maksimova BLR 5870

First League *At Inowroclaw. Poland 4-5 July*

1. SUI 39,694, 2. POL 39,229, 3. ESP 39,069, 4. ITA 37,053, 5. SWE 36,710, 6. ROU 33,775. **Men Dec**: 1. Martin Roe NOR 7875, 2. Pau Tonnesen ESP 7841, 3. Pawel Wiesiolek POL 7767; **Women Hep**: 1. Karolina Tyminska POL 6174, 2. Linda Züblin SUI 6047, 3. Valérie Reggel SUI 5894

Second League. *At Inowroclaw. Poland 4-5 July*

1. FIN 36,948, 2. POR 36,311, 3. LAT 36,296, 4. GRE 35,547; **Men Dec**: Joli Koivu FIN 7462; **Women Hep**: Laura Ikauniece-Admidina LAT 6470.

European Cup Race Walking

At Murcia, Spain 17 May

Men 20km: 1. Miguel Ángel López ESP 1:19:52, 2. Matej Tóth SVK 1:20:21, 3. Yohann Diniz FRA 1:20:37, 4. Denis Simanovich BLR 1:21:11, 5. Ihor Hlavan UKR 1:21:24, 6. Andrey Krivov RUS 1:22:05, 7. Christopher Linke GER 1:22:06, 8. Perseus Karlström SWE 1:22:44, 9. Denis Strelkov RUS 1:22:47, 10. Ato Ibáñez SWE 1:22:48; 44 of 49 finished; Team: 1. GER 32, 2. RUS 35, 3. UKR 37, 4. ESP 57, 5. FRA 58, 6. SVK 68, 7. ITA 71, 8. FIN 80. **50km**: 1. Mikhail Ryzhov RUS 3:43:22, 2. Ivan Noskov RUS 3:43:57, 3. Marco De Luca ITA 3:46:21, 4. Ivan Banzeruk UKR 3:49:02, 5. Roman Yevstifeyev RUS 3:51:00, 6. Serhiy Budza UKR 3:51:33, 7. Aléxandros Papamihaíl GRE 3:51:38, 8. Teodorico Caporaso ITA 3:51:44, 9. Grzegorz Sudol POL 3:51:46, 10. Benjamin Sánchez ESP 3:55:55; 22 of 29 finished; Team: 1. RUS 8, 2. ITA 23, 3. UKR 23. **U20 Men 10km**: 1. Diego García ESP 40:38, 2. Jean Blancheteau FRA 41:11, 3. Pablo Oliva ESP 41:19; 38 of 40 finished; Team: 1. ESP 4, 2. FRA 11, 3. GER 17, 4. RUS 20, 5. ITA 27, 6. GBR 27, 7. SVK 32, 8. UKR 40, 9. TUR 45, 10. BLR 46, 11. POR 52, 12. EST 75, **Women 20 km**: 1. Elmira Alembekova RUS 1:26:15, 2. Eleonora Giorgi ITA 1:26:17 rec, 3. Svetlana Vasilyeva RUS 1:26:31, 4. Anezka Drahotová CZE 1:26:53, 5. Marina Pandakova RUS 1:26:58, 6. Vera Sokolova RUS 1:27:08, 7. Lyudmyla Olyanovska UKR 1:27:09, 8. Elisa Rigaudo ITA 1:28:01, 9. Ana Cabecinha POR 1:28:28, 10. Laura García-Caro ESP 1:29:32; 39 of 4558 finished; Team: 1. RUS 9, 2. ITA 30, 3. POR 38, 4. UKR 39, 5. ESP 39, 6. FRA 84, 7. ROU 8, **U20 Women 10km**: 1. Klavdiya Afanasyeva RUS 45:55, 2. Mariya Losinova RUS 46:11, 3. Mária Pérez ESP 47:08; 28 of 32 finished; Team: 1. RUS 3, 2. ESP 9, 3. ITA 12, 4. LTU 16, 5. POL 18, 6. POR 29, 7. BLR 30, 8. UKR 35, 9. GER 39.

European Cup 10,000m

At Chia, Italy 6 June

Men: 1. Polat Kemboi Arikan TUR 28:09.47, 2. Juan Pérez ESP 28:25.66, 3. Jamel Chatbi ITA 28:39.01; Team: 1. ITA 1:26:23.97, 2. ESP 1:27:09.28, 3. TUR 1:27:51.98. **Women**: 1. Trihas Gebre ESP 32:14.94, 2. Valeria Straneo ITA 32:32.41, 3. Lily Partridge GBR 33:02.03; Team: 1. GBR 1:39:23.86, 2. ESP 1:39:44.91, 3. ITA 1:39:58.66.

10th European U23 Championships

At Tallinn, Estonia 9-12 July

100m	1. Giovanni Galbieri ITA 10.33
(0.0)	2. Denis Dimitrov BUL 10.34
	3. Guy-Elphège Anouman FRA 10.39
200m	1. Karol Zalewski POL 20.49
(1.1)	2. Leon Reid GBR 20.63
	3. Jan Jirka CZE 20.82
400m	1. Thomas Jordier FRA 45.50
	2. Pavel Ivashko RUS 45.73
	3. Luka Janezic SLO 45.73
800m	1. Artur Kuciapski POL 1:48.11
	2. Saul Ordóñez ESP 1:48.23
	3. Zan Rudolf SLO 1:48.47
1500m	1. Marc Alcalá ESP 3:44.54
	2. Mohad Sheikh Ali ITA 3:44.91
	3. Neil Gourley GBR 3:45.04
5000m	1. Ali Kaya TUR 13:20.16*
	2. Isaac Kimeli BEL 13:54.33
	3. Carlos Mayo ESP 13:55.19
10,000m	1. Ali Kaya TUR 27:53.38*
	2. Mikhail Strelkov RUS 28:53.94
	3. Yassine Rachik ITA 28:53.99
3000mSt	1. Mitko Tsenov BUL 8:37.79
	2. Viktor Bakharev RUS 8:40.75
	3. Osama Zoghlami ITA 8:42.00
110mh	1. David Omoregie GBR 13.63
(1.5)	2. Javier Colomo ESP 13.73
	3. Lorenzo Perini ITA 13.86
400mh	1. Patryk Dobek POL 48.84
	2. Jussi Kanervo FIN 49.66
	3. Nicolai Hartling DEN 50.02
HJ	1. Ilya Ivanyuk RUS 2.30
	2. Dmitriy Kroyter ISR 2.24
	3= Eugenio Meloni ITA 2.21
	3= Chris Kandu GBR 2.21
PV	1. Robert Renner SLO 5.55
	2. Leonid Kobelev RUS 5.55
	3. Adrián Valles ESP 5.50
LJ	1. Fabian Heinle GER 8.14/-0.4
	2. Radek Juska CZE 8.00/1.1
	3. Bachana Khorava GEO 7.97/1.0
TJ	1. Dmitriy Chizhikov RUS 17.05/-0.7
	2. Georgi Tsonov BUL 16.77/-0.2
	3. Ilya Potaptsev RUS 16.46/0.9
SP	1. Filip Mihaljevic CRO 19.35
	2. Bob Bertemes LUX 19.29
	3. Andrzej Regin POL 19.08
DT	1. Alin Firfirica ROU 60.64
	2. Wojciech Praczyk POL 58.96
	3. Róbert Szikszai HUN 58.82
HT	1. Nick Miller GBR 74.46

2. Valeriy Pronkin RUS 74.29
3. Bence Pásztor HUN 74.06

JT 1. Kacper Oleszczuk POL 82.29
2. Maksym Bohdan UKR 81.08
3. Bernhard Seifert GER 80.57

Dec 1. Pieter Braun NED 8195
2. Jorge Ureña ESP 7983
3. Janek Oiglane EST 7945

20kW 1. Nikolay Markov RUS 1:23:49
2. Álvaro Martín ESP 1:24:51
3. Pavel Parshin RUS 1:25:26

4x100m 1. FRA (Anouman, Zeze, Romain, Dutamby) 39.36
2. CZE 39.38
3. RUS 39.45

4x400m 1. FRA 3:04.92 (Vaillant 46.9, Divet 47.3, Courbiere 45.64, Jordier 45.02)
2. POL 3:05.35
3. GER 3:05.97

Women

100m (0.2) 1. Rebekka Haase GER 11.47
2. Alexandra Burghardt GER 11.54
3. Stella Akakpo FRA 11.55

200m (0.6) 1. Rebekka Haase GER 23.16
2. Anna-Lena Freese GER 23.22
3. Brigitte Ntiamoah FRA 23.49

400m 1. Bianca Razor ROU 51.31
2. Yekaterina Renzhina RUS 51.51
3. Patrycja Wyciszkiewicz POL 51.63

800m 1. Renelle Lamote FRA 2:00.19
2. Anastasiya Tkachuk UKR 2:00.43
3. Christina Hering GER 2:00.88

1500m 1. Amela Terzic SRB 4:04.77
2. Sofia Ennaoui POL 4:04.90
3. Nataliya Pryshchepa UKR 4:06.29

5000m 1. Liv Westphal FRA 15:30.61
2. Louise Carton BEL 15:32.75
3. Viktoriya Kalyuzhna UKR 15:38.38

10,000m 1. Jip Vastenburg NED 32:18.69
2. Rhona Auckland GBR 32:22.79
3. Alice Wright GBR 32:46.57

3000mSt 1. Tugba Güvenc TUR 9:36.14*
2. Maeva Danois FRA 9:40.89
3. Emma Oudiou FRA 9:44.74

100mh (-0.2) 1. Noemi Zbären SUI 12.71
2. Karolina Koleczek POL 12.92
3. Nadine Visser NED 13.01

400mh 1. Elise Malmberg SWE 55.88
2. Stina Troest DEN 56.01
3. Aurélie Chaboudez FRA 56.04

HJ 1. Alessia Trost ITA 1.90
2. Nafissatou Thiam BEL 1.87
3. Iryna Herashchenko UKR 1.87

PV 1. Angelica Bengtsson SWE 4.55
2. Michaela Meijer SWE 4.50
3. Natalya Demidenko RUS 4.35

LJ 1. Malaika Mihambo GER 6.73/1.6
2. Jazmin Sawyers GBR 6.71/0.6
3. Alina Rotaru ROU 6.69/0.1

TJ 1. Dovilé Dzindzaletaité LTU 14.23/1.9
2. Elena Panturoiu ROU 14.13/1.8
3. Tetyana Ptashkina UKR 14.05/1.0

SP 1. Viktoriya Kolb BLR 17.47
2. Shanice Craft GER 17.29
3. Sara Gambetta GER 16.99

DT 1. Shanice Craft GER 63.83
2. Anna Rüh GER 61.27
3. Kristin Pudenz GER 59.94

HT 1. Alexandra Tavernier FRA 72.50 (72.98*q)
2. Alena Soboleva BLR 71.20
3. Malwina Kopron POL 68.57

JT 1. Christin Hussong GER 65.60*
2. Kateryna Derun UKR 58.60
3. Liveta Jasiunaité LTU 55.77

Hep 1. Xénia Krizsán HUN 6303
2. Lyubov Tkach RUS 6055
3. Ivona Dadic AUT 6033

20kW 1. Mariya Ponomaryova RUS 1:27:17*
2. Anezka Drahotová CZE 1:27:25
3. Lyudmyla Olyanovska UKR 1:28:41

4x100m 1. GER (Lederer, Burghardt, Haase, Freese) 43.47
2. ITA 44.06
3. SUI 44.24

4x400m 1. GBR (Bundy-Davies 52.1, Clark 52.7, V Ohuruogu 53.18, McAslan 51.99) 3:30.07
2. POL 3:30.24
3. RUS 3:30.78

Medal and points table

Nation	*G*	*S*	*B*	*Points*
GER	7	4	5	176
RUS	4	7	5	158
POL	4	5	3	126
GBR	3	3	3	112.5
FRA	6	1	5	109
ITA	2	2	4	108.5
UKR	-	3	5	75.5
ESP	1	4	2	73.5
NED	2	-	1	56
ROU	2	1	1	49
SWE	2	1	-	48
CZE	-	3	1	40
HUN	1	-	2	37
FIN	-	1	-	36
SUI	1	-	1	35
BLR	1	1	-	34
TUR	3	-	-	29
BEL	-	3	-	28
BUL	1	2	-	25
NOR	-	-	-	25
SLO	1	-	2	24
DEN	-	1	1	22

CRO (1G) 17, AUT (1B) 16, EST (AB) 15, LTU (1G, 1B) 14, ISR (1S) 11; GEO (1B), GRE 11; SRB (1G), IRL 10; LUX (1S), SVK 7; POR 6, BIH, LAT 5; CYP 1.5; ARM 1. Note: sharing points for ties unlike official table.

23rd European U20 Championships

At Eskilstuna, Sweden 16-19 July

100m (-1.0) 1. Ojie Edoburun GBR 10.36
2. Joseph Dewar GBR 10.46
3. Emil von Barth SWE 10.64

200m (4.1) 1. Tommy Ramdhan GBR 20.57w
2. Elliott Powell GBR 20.72
3. Even Meinseth NOR 20.94

400m 1. Benjamin Lobo Vedel DEN 46.48
2. Karsten Warholm NOR 46.50
3. Batuhan Altintas TUR 46.95

800m 1. Kyle Langford GBR 1:48.99
2. Konstantin Tolokonnikov RUS 1:49.00

3. Mateusz Borkowski POL 1:49.21

1500m 1. Josh Kerr GBR 3:49.62
2. Baptiste Mischler FRA 3:49.88
3. Andriy Aliksiychuk UKR 3:50.22

5000m 1. Alex George GBR 14:34.42
2. Simon Debognies BEL 14:34.67
3. Yemaneberhan Crippa ITA 14:35.39

10,000m 1. Pietro Riva ITA 30:20.45
2. Fabian Gering GER 30:20.69
3. Dieter Kersten BEL 30:21.85

3000mSt 1. Yohannes Chiappinelli ITA 8:47.58
2. Patrick Karl GER 8:54.10
3. Balázs Juhász HUN 8:58.11

110mh (3.4) 99cm 1. Kamil Salimullin RUS 13.60w
2. Florian Lickteig GER 13.64
3. Henrik Hannemann GER 13.67

400mh 1. Victor Coroller FRA 50.53
2. Joshua Abuaku GER 51.46
3. Dominik Hufnagl AUT 51.74

HJ 1. Jonas Kløjgaard Jensen DEN 2.23
2. Dawid Wawrzyniak POL 2.23
3. Oleksandr Barannikov UKR 2.19

PV 1. Adam Hague GBR 5.50
2. Niko Koskinen FIN 5.35
3. Alioune Sène FRA 5.30

LJ 1. Anatoliy Ryapolov RUS 7.96/0.0
2. Jacob Fincham-Dukes GBR 7.75/0.0
3. Filippo Randazzo ITA 7.74/0.9

TJ 1. Nazim Babayev AZE 17.04*/1.5
2. Tobia Bocchi ITA 16.51w/2.1
3. Pavlo Beznits UKR 16.10w/3.0

SP 6kg 1. Konrad Bukowiecki POL 22.62*
2. Andrei Toader ROU 20.78
3. Sebastiano Bianchetti ITA 20.71

DT 1.75kg 1. Bartlomiej Stoj POL 68.02*
2. Martin Markovic CRO 67.11
3. Henning Prüfer GER 64.18

HT 6kg 1. Bence Halász HUN 79.60*
2. Miguel Alberto Blanco ESP 79.05
3. Matija Greguric CRO 77.35

JT 1. Matija Muhar SLO 79.20
2. Simon Litzell SWE 78.34
3. Edis Matusevicius LTU 77.48

Dec jnr 1. Jan Dolezal CZE 7929
2. Karsten Warholm NOR 7764
3. Maksim Andraloits BLR 7717

10,000W 1. Diego García ESP 40:05.21
2. Vladislav Saraykin RUS 40:59.28
3. Pablo Oliva ESP 41:00.73

4x100m 1. SWE (Emil von Barth, Austin Hamilton, Thobias Nilsson Montier, Gustav Kjell) 39.73
2. POL 40.00
3. FRA 40.02

4x400m 1. RUS (Andrey Yefremov, Andrey Kukharenko, Konstantin Tololonnikov, Ilya Krasnov) 3:08.35
2. ITA 3:10.04
3. GER 3:10.12

Women

100m (-1.2) 1. Ewa Swoboda POL 11.52
2. Lisa Mayer GER 11.64
3. Kristina Sivkova RUS 11.68

200m (2.6) 1. Gina Lückenkemper GER 22.41w
2. Shannon Hylton GBR 22.73
3. Maroussia Pare FRA 23.05

400m 1. Laviai Nielsen GBR 52.58
2. Cheriece Hylton GBR 53.16
3. Anastasiya Bednova RUS 53.27

800m 1. Renée Eykens BEL 2:02.83
2. Sarah Schmidt GER 2:04.55
3. Aníta Hinriksdóttir ISL 2:05.04

1500m 1. Bobby Clay GBR 4:17.91
2. Amy Griffiths GBR 4:20.41
3. Konstanze Klosterhalfen GER 4:20.84

3000m 1. Alina Reh GER 9:12.29
2. Célia Antón ESP 9:16.36
3. Anna Emilie Møller DEN 9:17.36

5000m 1. Alina Reh GER 16:02.01
2. Anna Emilie Møller DEN 16:07.43
3. Carmela Cardama ESP 16:23.81

3000mSt 1. Sümeyye Erol TUR 10:19.15
2. Carolina Johnson SWE 10:28.31
3. Alisa Vainio FIN 10:30.83

100mh (2.6) 1. Elvira Herman BLR 13.15w
2. Luca Kozák HUN 13.20
3. Laura Valette FRA 13.21

400mh 1. Nenah De Coninck BEL 57.85
2. Inge Drost NED 57.88
3. Ayomide Folorunso ITA 58.44

HJ 1. Morgan Lake GBR 1.91
2. Nawal Meniker FRA 1.86
3. Ellen Ekholm SWE 1.83

PV 1. Angelica Moser SUI 4.35
2. Alyona Lutkovskaya RUS 4.20
3. Kamila Przybyla POL 4.20

LJ 1. Florentina Marincu ROU 6.78w/3.8
2. Anna Bühler GER 6.55w/3.0
3. Fatima Diame ESP 6.55w/4.0

TJ 1. Valentina Kosolapova RUS 13.27/0.3
2. Kristina Malaya RUS 13.25/-0.7
3. Florentina Marincu ROU 13.08/-1.0

SP 1. Emel Dereli TUR 18.40
2. Claudine Vita GER 17.13
3. Alyona Bugakova RUS 16.81

DT 1. Claudine Vita GER 57.47
2. Veronika Domjan SLO 56.63
3. Anastasiya Vityugova RUS 54.21

HT 1. Audrey Ciofani FRA 67.20
2. Beatrice Nedberge Llano NOR 64.76
3. Katarzyna Furmanek POL 63.80

JT 1. Maria Andrejczyk POL 59.73
2. Anete Kocina LAT 58.88
3. Aleksandra Ostrowska POL 56.24

Hep 1. Caroline Agnou SUI 6123
2. Hanne Maudens BEL 5720
3. Louisa Grauvogel GER 5704

10,000W 1. Klavdiya Afanasyeva RUS 43:36.88
2. Olga Shargina RUS 44:01.08
3. Mariya Losinova RUS 44:07.44

4x100m 1. GBR (Shannon Malone, Shannon Hylton, Charlotte McLennaghan, Imani Lansiquot) 44.18
2. POL 45.28
3. FRA 45.35

4x400m 1. GBR (Cheriece Hylton, Lina Nielsen, Lily Beckford, Laviai Nielsen) 3:34.36
2. ITA 3:37.45
3. RUS 3:37.57

Medal and Points Table

Nation	1	2	3	Points
GBR	11	6	-	192.5
GER	4	8	5	186.5
RUS	5	5	6	165
ITA	2	3	4	112.5
POL	4	3	4	110
FRA	2	2	5	96
SWE	1	2	2	76
ESP	1	2	3	73
BEL	2	2	1	60.5
FIN	-	1	1	59
NOR	-	3	1	49
TUR	2	-	1	40
HUN	1	1	1	40
DEN	1	1	1	39
UKR	-	-	3	31
BLR	1	-	1	27.5
SUI	2	-	-	27.5
ROU	1	1	1	26
SLO	1	1	-	23
NED	-	1	-	23
CRO	-	1	1	18
IRL	-	-	-	17

GRE 15, AUT (1B) 11, AZE (1G) 8, LAT (1S) 7, ISL (1B) 6, BUL, CYP 4; SVK 3, EST 2. 18 countries won at least one gold medal; 33 at least one medal and 33 scored at least 1 point.

Games of the Small States of Europe

At Reykjavik, Iceland 2-6 June

Men: **100m**: Panayiotis Ioannou CYP 10.64w, **200m/400m**: Kevin Moore MLT 21.54/47.86, **800m/1500m**: Amine Khadiri CYP 1:56.72/3:51.97, **5000m**: Hlynur Andrésson ISL 14:45.94, **10,000m**: Marcos Sanza AND 30:59.42, **3000mSt**: Arnar Pétursson 9:22.16, **110mh**: Milan Trajkovic CYP 13.86, **400mh**: Ívar Kristinn Jasonarson 53.21, **HJ**: Vasilios Constantinou CYP 2.18, **PV**: Nikandros Stylianou CYP 5.15, **LJ**: Kristinn Torfason ISL 7.24, **TJ**: Panayiotis Volou CYP 15.53, **SP**: Bob Bertemes LUX 19.11, **DT**: Gudni Valur Gudnason ISL 56.40, **JT**: Gudmundur Sverrisson ISL 74.38, **4x100m**: CYP 41.94, **4x400m**: ISL 3:17.06. **Women**: **100m/200m**: Charlotte Wingfield 11.71w/24.19w, **400m**: Thórdis Eva Steinsdóttir ISL 55.72, **800m**: Charline Mathias LUX 2:08.61, **1500m**: Aníta Hinriksdóttir ISL 4:26.37, **5000m/10,000m**: Sladana Perunovic MNE 16:53.78/36:58.48, **100mh**: Kim Reuland LUX 14.02, **400mh**: Arna Stefania Gudmundsdóttir ISL 60.77, **HJ**: Marija Vukovic MNE 1.80, **PV**: Gina Reuland LUX 4.30, **LJ/TJ**: Hafdís Sigurdardóttir ISL 6.50w/12.49, **SP**: Stéphanie Krumlovsky LUX 13.68, **DT**: Androniki Lada CYP 53.73, **HT**: Catherine Beatty CYP 60.09, **JT**: Asdis Hjálmsdóttir ISL 58.85, **4x100m/4x400m**: ISL 46.62/3:44.31. **Medals**: ISL 15G-15S-10B, CYP 10-11-5, LUX 5-4-10, MLT 4-3-1, MNE 3-0-1, AND 1-1-2, MON 0-2-5, SMR 0-2-1.

15th Gulf Countries Championships

At Qatif, Saudi Arabia 9-11 April

Men: **100m**: Meshaal Al-Mutairi KUW 10.46, **200m**: Barakat Al-Harthi OMA 21.18, **400m**: Mazen Al-Yassin KSA 46.98, **800m**: Ali Al-Daran KSA 1:47.85, **1500m**: Mohamed Ayoub BRN 3:52.92, **5000m/10,000m**: Zouhair Aouad BRN 14:42.70/29:19.64, **3000mSt**: Linus Kiplagat BRN 8:53.07, **110mh**: Abdulaziz Al-Mandeel KUW 13.61, **400mh**: Abdullah Al-Melihi KSA 51.81, **HJ**: Muamar Essa Barshim QAT 2.23, **LJ**: Ahmed Al-Dosari KSA 8.11, **TJ**: Rasheed Al-Mannai QAT 16.14, **SP**: Ahmad Gholoum KUW 18.35, **DT**: Essa Al-Zankawi KUW 62.35, **HT**: Ashraf Amjad El-Seifi QAT 75.33, **JT**: Mohamed Khaida QAT 66.10, **10,000mW**: Mabrouk Saleh Nasser QAT 47:27.50, **4x100m/4x400m**: OMA 39.89/3:07.86. **Medal table**: KSA 5-11-7, QAT 5-5-4, KUW 4-3-4, BRN 4-0-2, OMA 3-2-1, UAE 0-0-2.

NACAC Open Championships

At San José, Costa Rica (1122m altitude) 7-9 August

The North American, Central American and Caribbean senior area championships.

Men: **100m**: Remontay McClain USA 10.09, **200m**: Rasheed Dwyer JAM 20.12, **400m**: Lalonde Gordon TTO 44.89, **800m**: Ryan Martin USA 1:45.79, **1500m**: Andrew Wheating USA 3:45.08, **5000m**: Lopez Lomong USA 13:37.53, **3000mSt**: Andy Bayer USA 8:44.88, **110mh**: Mikel Thomas TTO 13.23, **400mh**: Javier Culson PUR 48.70, **HJ**: JaCorian Duffield USA 2.25, **PV**: Natan Rivera ESA 4.70, **LJ**: Cameron Burrell USA 8.06, **TJ**: Yordanis Durañona DMA 16.98, **SP**: Jonathan Jones USA 20.54, **DT**: Russ Winger USA 60.68, **HT**: Roberto Janet CUB 70.72, **JT**: Riley Dolezal USA 79.30, **4x100m**: Jamaica 38.07, **4x400m**: USA 3:00.07. **Women**: **100m**: Barbara Pierre USA 11.12, **200m**: Kyra Jefferson USA 22.50, **400m**: Courtney Okolo USA 51.57, **800m**: Chanelle Price USA 2:00.48, **1500m**: Rachel Schneider USA 4:14.78, **5000m**: Kellyn Taylor USA 16:24.86, **3000mSt**: Ashley Higginson USA 9:56.75, **100mh**: Lolo Jones USA 12.63w, **400mh**: Tiffany Williams USA 54.35, **HJ**: Levern Spencer LCA 1.91, **PV**: Kristen Hixson USA 4.50, **LJ**: Quanesha Burks USA 6.93, **TJ**: Shanieka Thomas JAM 14.23, **SP**: Jill Camarena-Williams USA 18.62, **DT**: Summer Pierson USA 56.64, **HT**: Amber Campbell USA 72.41, **JT**: Kara Winger USA 60.34, **4x100m/4x400m**: USA 42.24/3:25.39.

Oceania Championships

At Cairns, Australia 8-10 May

Men: **100m**: Ratu Banuve Tabakaucoro FIJ 10.22, **200m**: Jeremy Dodson SAM 20.57, **400m**: Batinasavu Uluiyata FIJ 48.22, **800m/1500m**: Sam Russell AUS 1:54.02/4:05.76, **5000m**: Joshua Torley AUS 15:34.31, **10000m**: Matthew Dryden AUS 34:18.41, **110mh**: Jack Conway AUS 14.40, **400mh**: Mike Cochrane NZL 50.69, **HJ**: John Dodds AUS 2.15, **PV**: Triston Vincent AUS 4.10, **LJ**: Waisale Dausoko FIJ 7.51w. **TJ**: Tim McGuire AUS 14.97w, **SP/DT**: Alex Rose SAM 16.89/60.95, **HT**: Warren Button NZL 58.14, **JT**: John Crandell AUS 64.35, **Dec**: Brent Newdick NZL 7140, **5000mW/10000mW**: Jared Free NZL 24:18.39/46:17.0, **4x100m**: FIJ 40.98, **4x400m**: AUS 3:15.55; **Women**: **100m/200m**: Toea Wisli PNG 11.41w/23.71, **400m/400mh**: Betty Burua PNG 54.32/59.10, **800m**: Donna Koniel PNG 2:09.58, **1500m**: Coreena Cleland AUS 4:27.36, **5000m**: Sharon Firisua SOL 18:35.51, **10000m**: Mary Kua PNG 40:39.52, **3000mSt**: Rama Kumilgo PNG 11:10.48, **100mh**: Fiona Morrison NZL 13.57, **HJ**: Ashleigh Reid AUS 1.80, **LJ**: Catherine Hannell AUS 5.82w, **TJ/SP**: Milika Tuivanuavou FIJ 12.29w/14.35, **DT**: Siositina Hakeai NZL 56.06, **HT**: Kaysanne Hockey AUS 54.01, **JT**: Laura Overton NZL 45.87, **Hep**: Sarah Wood AUS 5052, **5000mW/10000mW**: Zoe Hunt 25:28.75/50:21.0, **4x100m/4x400m**: PNG 46.31/3:52.66.

At Gold Coast 5 July: **Men**: **HMar**: Liam Adams 63:29, **Mar**: Jonathan Peters AUS 2:21:14; **Women: HMar**: Eloise Wellings AUS 70:10, **Mar**: Victoria Beck NZL 2:45:48

WALKS *At Adelaide, Australia 22 February.* **Men**: 20kW: Jared Tallent AUS 1:24:05; **Women**: 20kW: Tanya Holliday AUS 1:34:05

Pacific Games

At Port Moresby, Papua New Guinea 13-18 July

Men: **100m/200m**: Ratu Banuve Tabakaucoro FIJ 10.55/20.53*, **400m**: Nelson Stone PNG 47.56, **800m**: Kaminiel Matlaun PNG 1:53.85, **1500m**: Adrien Kela NC 4:19.00, **5000m**: Nordine Benfodda NC 15:54.55, **10000m**: Rosefelo Siosi SOL 33:06.03, **HMar**: Kupsy Bisamo PNG 1:14:11, **3000mSt**: Sapolai Yao PNG 9:38.89, **110mh**: Wala Gime PNG 14.80, **400mh**: Mowen Boino PNG 52.51, **HJ**: Rajendra Prased FIJ 2.03, **PV**: Eric Reuillard NC 4.60, **LJ**: Raihau Maiau PYF 8.14w, **TJ**: Eugene Vollmer FIJ 15.27, **SP**: Tumatai Dauphin PYF 19.14*, **DT**: Alex Rose SAM 56.40, **HT**: Erwan Cassier NC 61.52, **JT**: Leslie Copeland FIJ 70.31, **Dec**: Robson Yinambe PNG 6288, **4x100m/4x400m**: PNG 40.62/3:13.86; **Women**: **100m/200m/400m**: Toea Wisli PNG 11.86/24.05/54.17, **800m/400mh**: Donna Koniel PNG 2:12.78/58.28, **1500m**: Miriam Goiye 4:45.44, **5000m/10000m/HMar**: Sharon Kikini Firisua SOL 18:20.09*/38:33.04/1:29:26, **3000mSt**: Rama Kumilgo PNG 11:26.51, **100mh**: Shjaron Kwarula PNG 14.40, **HJ/LJ/TJ**: Rellie Kaputin PNG 1.77/5.97/12.65, **PV**: Pascale Gacon NC 3.70*, **SP**: Milika Tuivanuavou FIJ 14.59, **DT**: Treapii Tapoki COK 48.70, **HT**: Elise Takosi NC 52.51, **JT**: Linda Selui NC 47.72, **Hep**: Adrine Monagi PNG 5019, **4x100m**: FIJ 46.17, **4x400m**: PNG 3:45.13. **Most medals:** PNG 23G-21S-18B; New Caledonia 10-12-10, FIJ 7-6-7, SOL 4-2-1, NC = New Caledonia.

Pan-American Games

At Toronto, Canada 18-26 July

Men

100m (1.1)
1. Andre De Grasse CAN 10.05 (9.97w ht)
2. Ramon Gittens BAR 10.07
3. Antoine Adams SKN 10.09

200m (0.3)
1. Andre De Grasse CAN 19.88
2. Rasheed Dwyer JAM 19.90 (19.80* ht)
3. Alonso Edward PAN 19.90

400m
1. Luguelín Santos DOM 44.56
2. Machel Cedenio TTO 44.70
3. Kyle Clemons USA 44.84

800m
1. Clayton Murphy USA 1:47.19
2. Rafith Rodríguez COL 1:47.23
3. Ryan Martin USA 1:47.73

1500m
1. Andrew Wheating USA 3:41.41
2. Nate Brannen CAN 3:41.66
3. Charles Philibert-Thiboutot CAN 3:41.79

5000m
1. Juan Luis Barrios MEX 13:46.47
2. David Torrence USA 13:46.60
3. Víctor Aravena CHI 13:46.94

10,000m
1. Mohammed Ahmed CAN 28:49.96
2. Aron Rono USA 28:50.83
3. Juan Luis Barrios MEX 28:51.57

Mar
1. Richer Pérez CUB 2:17:04
2. Raúl Pacheco PER 2:17:13
3. Mariano Mastromarino ARG 2:17:45

3000mSt
1. Matt Hughes CAN 8:32.18
2. Alexandre Genest CAN 8:33.83
3. Cory Leslie USA 8:36.83

110mh (0.8)
1. David Oliver USA 13.07*
2. Mikel Thomas TTO 13.17
3. Shane Brathwaite BAR 13.21

400mh
1. Jeffery Gibson BAH 48.51
2. Javier Culson PUR 48.67
3. Roxroy Cato JAM 48.72

HJ
1. Derek Drouin CAN 2.37
2. Mike Mason CAN 2.31
3. Donald Thomas BAH 2.28

PV
1. Shawn Barber CAN 5.80*
2. Germán Chiaraviglio ARG 5.75
3= Mark Hollis USA 5.40
3= Jake Blankenship USA 5.40

LJ
1. Jeffrey Henderson USA 8.54w/4.1
2. Marquise Goodwin USA 8.27w/4.5
3. Emiliano Lasa URU 8.17w/3.1

TJ
1. Pedro Pablo Pichardo CUB 17.54w/2.1
2. Leevan Sands BAH 16.99/1.7
3. Ernesto Revé CUB 16.94/0.9

SP
1. O'Dayne Richards JAM 21.69*
2. Tim Nedow CAN 20.53
3. Germán Lauro ARG 20.24

DT
1. Fedrick Dacres JAM 64.80
2. Ronald Julião BRA 64.65
3. Russ Winger USA 62.64

HT
1. Kibwe Johnson USA 75.46
2. Roberto Janet CUB 74.78
3. Conor McCullough USA 73.74

JT
1. Keshorn Walcott TTO 83.27
2. Riley Dolezal USA 81.62
3. Júlio César de Oliveira BRA 80.94

Dec
1. Damian Warner CAN 8659*
2. Kurt Felix GRN 8269(w)
3. Luiz Alberto de Araújo BRA 8179(w)

20kW
1. Evan Dunfee CAN 1:23:06
2. Inaki Gómez CAN 1:24:25
3. Caio Bonfim BRA 1:24:43

50kW
1. Andrés Chocho ECU 3:50:13
2. Erick Barrondo GUA 3:55:57
3. Horacio Nava MEX 3:57:28

4x100m
1. USA (Lee, Spearmon, K Williams, McClain) 38.27
2. BRA (G dos Santos, V dos Santos, de Barros, A G da Silva) 38.68
3. TTO (Sorrillo, Bledman, Callender, Telesford) 38.69
dnf. ANT (Walsh, Bailey, Greene, Francis) (38.14* ht)

4x400m
1. TTO (Quow, Solomon, Mayers, Cedenio) 2:59.60
2. CUB (Collazo, Chacón, Pellicier, Lescay) 2:59.84

3. USA (Clemons, J Harris, Chambers, Clement) 3:00.2

Women

100m (0.9) 1. Sherone Simpson JAM 10.95
2. Angela Tenerio ECU 10.99
3. Barbara Pierre USA 11.01 (10.92* ht)

200m (1.1) 1. Kaylin Whitney USA-Y 22.65
2. Kyra Jefferson USA 22.72
3. Simone Facey JAM 22.74

400m 1. Kendall Baisden USA 51.27
2. Shakima Wimbley USA 51.36
3. Kineke Alexander VIN 51.50

800m 1. Melissa Bishop CAN 1:59.62
2. Alysia Montaño USA 1:59.76
3. Flávia de Lima BRA 2:00.40

1500m 1. Muriel Coneo COL 4:09.05
2. Nicole Sifuentes CAN 4:09.13
3. Sasha Gollish CAN 4:10.11

5000m 1. Juliana Paula dos Santos BRA 15:45.97
2. Brenda Flores MEX 15:47.19
3. Kellyn Taylor USA 15:52.78

10,000m 1. Brenda Flores MEX 32:41.33*
2. Desiree Linden USA 32:43.99
3. Lanni Marchant CAN 32:46.03

Mar 1. Adriana da Silva BRA 2:35:40*
2. Lindsey Flanagan USA 2:36:30
3. Rachel Hannah CAN 2:41:06
drugs dq. (1) Gladys Tejeda PER 2:33:03(*)

3000mSt 1. Ashley Higginson USA 9:48.12*
2. Shalaya Kipp USA 9:49.96
3. Genevieve Lalonde CAN 9:53.03

100mh (1.4) 1. Queen Harrison USA 12.52*
2. Tenaya Jones USA 12.84
3. Nikkita Holder CAN 12.85

400mh 1. Shamier Little USA 55.50
2. Sarah Wells CAN 56.17
3. Déborah Rodríguez URU 56.41

HJ 1. Laverne Spencer LCA 1.94
2. Priscilla Frederick ANT 1.91
3. Akela Jones BAR 1.91

PV 1. Yarisley Silva CUB 4.85*
2. Fabiana Murer BRA 4.80
3. Jenn Suhr USA 4.60

LJ 1. Christabel Nettey CAN 6.90/1.1
2. Bianca Stuart BAH 6.69/0.5
3. Sha'Keela Saunders USA 6.66/1.1

TJ 1. Caterine Ibargüen COL 15.08w/2.3
2. Keila Costa BRA 14.50w/2.9
3. Yosiri Urrutia COL 14.38w/3.3

SP 1. Cleopatra Borel TTO 18.67
2. Jill Camarena-Williams USA 18.65
3. Natalia Ducó CHI 18.01

DT 1. Denia Caballero CUB 65.39
2. Yaimi Pérez CUB 64.99
3. Gia Lewis-Smallwood USA 61.26

HT 1. Rosa Rodríguez VEN 71.61
2. Amber Campbell USA 71.22
3. Sultana Frizell CAN 69.51

JT 1. Liz Gleadle CAN 62.83
2. Kara Winger USA 61.44
3. Jucilene de Lima BRA 60.42

Hep 1. Yorgelis Rodríguez CUB 6332*
2. Heather Miller Koch USA 6178
3. Vanessa Spínola BRA 6035

20kW 1. María Guadelupe González MEX 1:29:24*
2. Érica de Sena BRA 1:30:03
3. Paola Pérez ECU 1:31:53

4x100m 1. USA (Pierre, Lawson, Akinosun, Whitney) 42.58*
2. JAM (Henry-Robinson, Stewart, Calvert, Facey) 42.68
3. CAN (Emmanuel, Hyacinthe, Westney, Bingham) 43.00

4x400m 1. USA (Little, Jefferson, Wimbley, Baisden) 3:25.68
2. JAM (Le-Roy, Chambers, Gordon, Wilkins-Gooden) 3:27.27
3. CAN (Theisen-Eaton, Sharpe, Watson, Wells) 3:27.74

Medal table

Nation	*G*	*S*	*B*
USA	13	15	13
CAN	11	7	9
CUB	5	3	1
JAM	3	3	2
TRI	3	2	1
MEX	3	1	2
BRA	2	5	6
COL	2	1	1
BAH	1	2	1
ECU	1	1	1

25 nations won medals (and 13 won gold).

Pan-American Junior Championships

At Medellín, Colombia (A) 23-25 August

100m: Reynier Mena CUB 10.17, **200m**: Noah Lyles 20.27, **400m**: Jamal Walton CAY 46.09, **800m**: Carlton Orange USA 1:48.06, **1500m**: Blake Haney USA 3:56.49, **5000m**: Matthew Maton USA 14:20.58, **10000m**: Connor Hendrickson USA 30:46.66, **3000mSt**: Bailey Roth USA 9:02.45, Jnr **110mh**: Misana Viltz USA 13.30, **400mh**: Norman Grimes USA 50.10, **HJ**: Randall Cunningham USA 2.16, **PV**: Paulo Benavides USA 5.40, **LJ**: Juan Miguel Echevarría CUB 7.76, **TJ**: Leslie Caesa CUB 16.83w, 6kg **SP**: John Maurins USA 19.49, 1.75kg **DT**: Payton Otterdahl 57.96, 6kg **HT**: Humberto Mansilla CHI 80.21*, **JT**: Christopher Mirabelli USA 72.63, Jnr **Dec**: Harrison Williams USA 8037*, **4x100m**: JAM 40.15, **4x400m**: USA 3:07.07, **10,000mW**: César Rodríguez 42:12.81, **Women: 100m**: Khalifa St. Fort TTO 11.31, **200m**: Deanna Hill USA 23.18, **400m**: Kendra Clarke CAN 52.55, **800m**: Raevyn Rogers USA 2:04.62, **1500m**: Kate Murphy USA 4:21.36, **3000m**: Erin Dietz USA 9:37.51, **5000m**: Rachel Reddy USA 16:23.35, **3000mSt**: Charlotte Prouse CAN 10:12.44, **100mh**: Dior Hall USA 13.20, **400mh**: Anna Cockrell USA 57.10, **HJ**: Vashti Cunningham USA 1.96*, **PV**: Robeilys Peinado VEN 4.10, **LJ**: Samiyah Samuels USA 6.23, **TJ**: Núbia Soares BRA 14.16w, **SP**: Raven Saunders USA 18.27*, **DT**: Josie Natrasevschi USA 52.60, **HT**: Haley Showalter USA 58.45, **JT**: Yulenmis Aguilar CUB 63.86*, **Hep**: Ashtin Zamzow USA 5462, **10000mW**: Stefany Coronado BOL 47:05.11*, **4x100m/4x400m**: USA 43.79/3:31.49.

Pan-American Race Walking Cup

At Arica, Chile 9-10 May

Men: **20kmW**: 1. Erick Barrondo GUA 1:21:25, 2. Caio Bonfim BRA 1:21:26, 3, Iván Garrido COL 1:21:39, 4. Evan Dunfee CAN 1:21:54, 5. Eder Sánchez MEX 1:21:58; **50kmW**: 1. Horacio Nava MEX 3:45:41, 2, Cristian Berdeja MEX 3:50:19, 3. James Rendón COL 3:50:47, 4, José Leyver Ojeda MEX 3:55:04, 5. Luis Bustamante MEX 3:57:27; **Women 20kmW**: 1. María Guadalupe González MEX 1:29:21, 2. Kimberly García PER 1:31:13; 3. Mirna Ortíz GUA 1:31:31, 4. Alejandra Ortega MEX 1:31:38, 5. Maria Michta-Coffey USA 1:34:06.

South American Championships

At Lima, Peru 12-14 June

Men

100m (-1.1)
1. Diego Palomeque COL10.40
2. Alex Quiñónez ECU 10.43
3. Ifrish Alberg SUR 10.57

200m (0.0)
1. Alex Quiñónez ECU 20.76
2. Diego Palomeque COL 21.15
3. Arturo Deliser PAN 21.25

400m
1. Alberth Bravo VEN 45.26
2. Hederson Estefani BRA 45.57
3. Freddy Mezones VBEN 45.67

800m
1. Rafith Rodríguez COL 1:46.48
2. Lucirio Garrido VEN 1:47.83
3. Jhon Sinisterra COL 1:48.50

1500m
1. Carlos Díaz CHI 3:40.79
2. Federico Bruno ARG 3:42.21
3. Gerard Giraldo COL 3:42.38

5000m
1. Víctor Aravena CHI 14:06.14
2. Federico Bruno ARG 14:06.25
3. Bayron Piedra ECU 14:08.84

10000m
1. Bayron Piedra ECU 28:30.80
2. Mauricio González COL 28:33.53
3. José Luis Ostos PER 28:43.10

3000mSt
1. Gerard Giraldo COL 8:29.53*
2. Mauricio Valdivia CHI 8:40.28
3. Enzo Yáñez CHI 8:43.28

110mh (-1.2)
1. João Vitor de Oliveira BRA 13.96
2. Jorge McFarlane PER 13.99
3. Javier McFarlane PER 14.00

400mh
1. Hederson Estefani BRA 49.54
2. Víctor Solarte VEN 50.83
3. Yeison Rivas COL 50.88

drugs dq. Andrés Silva URU 49.43

HJ
1. Fernando Ferreira BRA 2.22
2. Talles Silva BRA 2.22
3. Alexander Bowen PAN 2.19

PV
1. Germán Chiaraviglio ARG 5.70
2. Daniel Zupeuc CHN 5.00
3. Josué Gutierrez PER 4.70

LJ
1. Emiliano Lasa URU 8.09/1.9
2. Diego Hernández VEN 7.91w/2.2
3. Mauro Vinícius da Silva BRA 7.81/2.0

TJ
1. Jhon Freddy Murillo COL 16.55/1.6
2. Jefferson Sabino BRA 16.34/1.7
3. Divie Murillo COL 16.34/0.0

SP
1. Germán Lauro ARG 20.77
2. Darlan Romani BRA 20.32
3. Nelson Fernandes BRA 18.28

DT
1. Mauricio Ortega COL 61.36
2. Ronald Julião BRA 59.80
3. Juan José Caicedo ECU 54.88

HT
1. Wágner Domingos BRA 71.47
2. Allan Wolski BRA 69.82
3. Juan Ignacio Cerra ARG 67.70

JT
1. Júlio César de Oliveira BRA 81.22*
2. Braian Toledo ARG 79.34
3. Arley Ibargüen COL 75.47

Dec
1. Luiz Alberto de Araújo BRA 7799
2. Geormis Jaramillo VEN 7454
3. Oscar Campos VEN 68.57

4x100m
1. ECU (Quintero, Valencia, Nazareno, Quiñónez) 39.94
2. VEN 40.19
3. COL 40.80

4x400m
1. VEN (Bravo, Meléndez, Aguilar, Mezones) 3:04.96
2. CHI 3:10.32
3. PER 3:14.64

20000mW
1. Pavel Chihuán PER 1:23:34.0
2. Juan Manuel Cano ARG 1:23:56.0
3. Mauricio Arteaga ECU 1:24:18.0

Women

100m (-1.0)
1. Nedian Vargas VEN 11.45
2. Isidora Jiménez CHI 11.51
3. Vanusa dos Santos BRA 11.60

200m (-0.9)
1. Nercely Soto VEN 23.15
2. Isidora Jiménez CHI 23.38
3. Nedian Vargas VEN 23.60

400m
1. Geisa Coutinho BRA 53.07
2. Nercely Soto VEN 54.38
3. Liliane Fernandes BRA 54.53

800m
1. Déborah Rodríguez URU 2:01.46
2. Flávia de Lima BRA 2:02.05
3. Ydanis Navas VEN 2:07.92

1500m
1. Muriel Coneo COL 4:10.14*
2. Flávia de Lima BRA 4:13.58
3. María Pía Fernández URU 4:19.37

5000m
1. María Balvina Pastuña ECU 15:49.33
2. Tatiele de Carvalho BRA 15:50.62
3. Carolina Tabares COL 15:59.28

10000m
1. Inés Melchor PER 32:28.87
2. María Balvina Pastuña ECU 32:51.33
3. Wilma Arizapana PER 33:01.15

3000mSt
1. Muriel Coneo COL 9:53.1
2. Tatiane da Silva BRA 9:56.8
3. Belén Casetta ARG 9:57.1

100mh (-2.2)
1. Yvette Lewis PAN 13.31
2. Briggit Merlano COL 13.43
3. Adelly Santos BRA 13.53

400mh
1. Déborah Rodríguez URU 56.33*
2. Magdalena Mendoza VEN 56.65
3. Liliane Fernandes BRA 58.44

HJ
1. Ana Paula de Oliveira BRA 1.82
2. Candy Toche PER 1.76
3. Betsabé Páez ARG 1.76

PV
1. Robeilys Peinado VEN 4.35
2. Valeria Chiaraviglio ARG 4.10
3. Karla da Silva BRA 4.10

LJ
1. Paola Mautino PER 6.52w/3.2
2. Tânia da Silva BRA 6.37w/2.9

	3. Yuliana Angulo ECU 6.25/1.9
TJ	1. Yulimar Rojas VEN 14.14w/2.8
	2. Tânia da Silva BRA 13.60/1.9
	3. Giselly Landázuri COL 13.35/1.3
SP	1. Geisa Arcanjo BRA 17.76
	2. Natalia Ducó CHI 17.56
	3. Ahymara Espinoza VEN 17.25
DT	1. Andressa de Morais BRA 61.15*
	2. Fernanda Borges BRA 58.22
	3. Rocío Comba ARG 57.15
HT	1. Rosa Rodríguez VEN 71.66
	2. Eli Johana Moreno COL 66.05
	3. Jennifer Dahlgren ARG 64.76
JT	1. Jucilene de Lima BRA 60.16*
	2. Flor Denis Ruiz COL 59.86
	3. María Paz Ríos CHI 51.12
Hep	1. Evelis Aguilar COL 5902*
	2. Guillercy González VEN 5444
	3. Giovana Cavaleti BRA 5426
4x100m	1. VEN (Hidalgo, Mendoza, Vargas, Soto) 44.28
	2. BRA 44.43
	3. CHI 44.83
4x400m	1. BRA (V dos Santos, Fernandes, J Sousa, J de Lima) 3:34.51
	2. VEN 3:37.05
	3. CHI 3:40.56
20000mW	1. Lorena Arenas COL 1:31:02.25*
	2. Ingrid Hernández COL 1:36:42.08
	3. Ángela Castro BOL 1:41:38.29

41st South American Junior Championships

At Cuenca, Ecuador (A), 29-31 May

Men: **100m**: Vitor Hugo dos Santos BRA 10.29, **200m**: Arturo Deliser PAN 21.00, **400m**: Maykon do Nascimento BRA 46.73, **800m**: Pedro de Palma BRA 1:51.76, **1500m**: Rodrigo Silva BRA 4:05.83; **5000m/10,000m**: Bryan Revelo ECU 15:34.45/32:35.46, **3000mSt**: Gerson Montes de Oca ECU 9:53.00, **110mh**-J: Diego Delmónaco CHI 13.74*, **400mh**: Mikael de Jesús BRA 50.96*, **HJ**: Javier Moreno VEN 2.13, **PV**: José Rodolfo Pacho ECU 5.15, **LJ**: Samory Fraga BRA 7.62, **TJ**: Ulisses Costa BRA 16.23, 6k **SP**: Eduardo Espin ECU 18.68, 1.75k **DT**: Cleverson Oliveira BRA 57.02, 6k **HT**: Joaquín Gómez ARG 80.59*, **JT**: Francisco Muse CHI 70.18, Jnr **Dec**: Hellerson da Costa BRA 7211, **10,000mW**: César Rodríguez PER 43:04.18 **4x100m/4x400m**: BRA 39.90/3:08.86. **Women**: **100m/200m**: Ángela Tenorio ECU 11.09*/22.84*, **400m**: Tabata de Carvalho BRA 54.52, **800m**: Pietra da Silva BRA 2:17.41, **1500m/3000mSt**: Katherine Tisalema ECU 4:41.50/11:03.52, **3000m/5000m**: Zaida Meneses PER 10:08.12/17:43.21, **100mh**: Clara Marín CHI 13.48*, **400mh**: Virginia Villalba ECU 61.13, **HJ**: Ana de Oliveira BRA 1,86*, **PV**: Robeilys Peinado VEN 4.35*, **LJ**: Letícia Melo BRA 6.17, **TJ**: Adriana Chalá ECU 12.97, **SP**: Grace Conley BOL 14.88, **DT**: Catalina Bravo CHI 47.66, **HT**: Jenny Mina ECU 55.45, **JT**: Noelia Paredes PAR 51.44*, **Hep**: Fiorella Chiappe ARG 52.42, **10,000mW**: Karla Jaramillo ECU 48:43.94, **4x100m/4x400m**: BRA 44.67/3:47.04. **Medal table leaders**: BRA 17G-14S-8B, ECU 13-8-10, CHI 4-4-7, PER 3-8-11, ARG 2-4-0, VEN 2-2-5.

28th South East Asia Games

At Singapore 6-12 June

Men: **100m/400mh**: Eric Cray PHI 10.25/49.40*, **200m**: Le Trong Hinh VIE 20.89, **400m**: Kunanon Sukkaew THA 46.00*, **800m/1500m**: Duong Van Thai VIE 1:51.43/3:47.04, **5000m**: Nguyen Van Lai VIE 14:04.82*, **10,000m**: Agus Prayogo INA 29:41.56, **Mar**: Soh Rui Yong SIN 2:34:56, **3000mSt**: Christopher Ulboc PHI 8:59.07, **110mh**: Jumrus Rittidet THA 13.69*, **HJ**: Nauraj Singh Randhawa MAS 2.13, **PV**: Porranot Poorahong THA 5.30*, **LJ**: Suphanara Ayudhaya THA 7.75, **TJ**: Muhammad Ismail MAS 16.75*, **SP**: Promrob Janthima THA 17.47, **DT**: Muhd Irfan Shamsuddin MAS 56.62, **HT**: Caleb Stuart PHI 65.63*, **JT**: Peerachet Janthra THA 75.18, **Dec**: Nguyen Van Hue VIE 7232, **4x100m/4x400m**: THA 38.99/3:06.81, **20kmW**: Hendro INA 1:34:23. **Women**: **100m**: Kayla Richardson PHI 11.76, **200m**: Veronica Pereira SIN 23.60, **400m/400mh**: Nguyen Thi Huyen VIE 52.00/56.15*, **800m/1500m**: Do Thi Thao VIE 2:05.22/4:28.39, **5000m/10,000m**: Triyaningsih INA 16:18.06/33:44.53, **Mar**: Natthaya Thanaronnawath THA 3:03:25, **3000mSt**: Rina Budiarti INA 10:20.40, **100mh**: Wallapa Punsoongneun THA 13.56, **HJ**: Wanida Boonwan THA 1.85, **PV**: Sukanya Chomchuendee THA 4.10, **LJ/TJ**: Maria Natalia Londa INA 6.70/13.75, **SP**: Zhang Guirong SIN 14.60, **DT**: Subenrat Insaeng THA 59.56*, **HT**: Mingkamon Koomphon THA 56.57*, **JT**: Natta Nachan THA 54.38, **Hep**: Sunisa Khotseemueang THA 5396, **4x100m**: THA 44.27/3:36.58, **4x400m**: VIE 3:31.46*,**20kmW**: Nguyen Thi Thanh Phuc VIE 1:45:20. **Medals**: THA 17G-13S-9B, VIE 11-15-8, INA 7-4-4, PHI 5-7-9, SIN 3-3-3, MAS 3-2-9, MYA 0-2-4.

6th World Military Games (CISM)

At Mungyeong, Korea 4-8 October, Marathons 11 October

Men: **100m**: Barakat Al-Harthi OMA 10.16, **200m**: Eseosa Desalu ITA 20.64, **400m**: Youssef Al-Masrahi KSA 45.18*, **800m**: Ali Saad Al-Daran KSA 1:45.50, **1500m**: Fouad El Kaam MAR 3:44.79, **5000m**: Albert Rop BRN 13:23.70, **10,000m**: El Hassan El-Abbassi BRN 27:41.76*; **Mar**: Alemu Bekele BRN 2:15:07, **3000mSt**: Amor Benyahia TUN 8:24.68, **110mh**: Sergey Shubenkov RUS 13.43, **400mh**: Abdelmalik Lahoulou ALG 49.43, **HJ**: Majid Eldein Ghazal SYR 2.31*, **PV**: Jin Min-sub KOR 5.40, **LJ**: Pavel Shalin RUS 7.66 **TJ**: Dmitriy Sorokin RUS 17.01, **SP**: Darlan Romani BRA 20.08, **DT**: Zoltán Kövágó HUN 66.01, **HT**: Kirill Ikonnikov RUS 75.88, **JT**: Ari Mannio FIN 79.78, **4x100m**: POL 39.35, **4x400m**: RUS 3:03.01. **Women**: **100m**: Rosângela Santos BRA 11.17*, **200m**: Ofinime Odiong BRN 23.18w, **400m**: Salwa Eid Nasser BRN-Y 51.39, **800m**: Nataliya Lupu UKR 1:59.99*, **1500m**: Selah Busienei KEN 4:07.58, **5000m**: Pauline Korikwiang KEN 15:23.85, **Mar**: Iwona Lewandowska POL 2:31:25, **3000mSt**: Ruth

Chebet BRN 9:30.24*, **100mh**: Yekaterina Galitskaya RUS 13.06, **400mh**: Kemi Adekoya BRN 55.50*, **HJ**: Mariya Kuchina RUS 1.95, **LJ/TJ**: Yekaterina Koneva RUS 6.39/14.28, **SP**: Gao Yang CHN 18.14, **DT:** Feng Bin CHN 62.07, **HT**: Zhang Wenxiu CHN 74.87*, **JT**: Zhang Li CHN 62.95*, **4x100m**: BRA 43.87, **4x400m**: RUS 3:28.75*.

** Championships record throughout this section*

IAU 50Km World Championships

At Doha, Qatar 4 December.

Men: 1. Tony Migliozzi USA 2:52:09; 2. Arnold Kiptoi KEN 2:55:35, 3. Samuel Ongeki KEN 2:56:16; Team: Kenya 8:49:09. **Women** – 1. Camille Herron USA 3:20:59, 2. Marija Vrajic CRO 3:28:16, 3. Catrin Jones CAN 3:28:30; Team: Croatia 10:50:08.

IAU 100Km World Championships

At Winschoten, Netherlands 12 September. Incorporating European Championships.

Men: 1. Jonas Buud SWE 6:22:44, 2. Asier Cuevas ESP 6:35:49, 3. Giorgio Calcaterra ITA 6:36:49, 4. Vasiliy Larkin RUS 6:38:48, 5. Wouter Decock BEL 6:41:27, 6. Fritjof Fagerlund SWE 6:42:51, 7. Vsevolod Chudykov RUS 6:43:13, 8. Jérôme Bellanca FRA 6:43:41, Team: 1. SWE 19:59:40, 2. ITA 20:32:29, 3. FRA 20:37:43, 4. USA 21:01.26, 5. RUS 21:19:31. 21 teams scored. **Women** – 1. Camille Herron USA 7:08:35, 2. Kajsa Berg SWE (1 Eur) 7:20:48, 3. Marija Vrajic CRO (2 Eur) 7:27:11, 4. Sarah Bard USA 7:29:01, 5. Joasia Zakrzewski GBR (3 Eur) 7:31:33, 6. Marina Zhalybina RUS 7:34:09, 7. Stina Svensson SWE 7:38:15, 8. Kirstin Bull AUS 7:39:28, Team: 1. USA 22:39.35, 2. SWE (1 Eur) 22:51:06, 3. RUS (2 E) 23:30:05, 4. CRO (3 E) 23:37:13, 5. FRA 24:20:00. 10 teams scored.

27th IAU World 24 Hours Championships

At Torino, Italy 11-12 April. Incorporating European Championships.

Men: 1. Florian Reus GER 263.899k, 2. Pawel Szynal POL 261.181, 3. Robbie Britton GBR 261.140, 4. Ivan Macaj SLO 258.333, 5. Kim Hansen DEN 257.753, 6. David Proctor CAN 257.093, 7. Patrick Robbins GBR 256.801, 8. Richard Riopel USA 256,743. Team: 1. GBR 770,777k, 2. AUS 752,665, 3. GER 745,075, 4. USA 740,452, 5. FRA 736,237, 6. POL 727,222, 34 scored. **Women** – 1. Katalin Nagy USA 244,495k, 2. Traci Falbu USA 239,740, 3. Maria Jansson SWE (1 EC) 238,964 rec, 4. Maggie Guterl USA 235,811, 5. Patrycja Bereznowska POL (2 EC) 233,395, 6. Jodie Oborne AUS 230,244, 7. Annika Nilrud SWE (3 EC) 230,054, 8. Isobel Wykes GBR 227,090. Team: 1. USA 720,046k, 2. SWE 694,981, 3. POL 678,468, 4. GBR 668,305, 5. GER 660,618, 6. RUS 610,572, 28 scored

IAAF World Half Marathon Championships 2016

At Cardiff, GBR 26 March

Men

1. Geoffrey Kamworor KEN	59:10
2. Bidan Karoki KEN	59:36
3. Mohamed Farah GBR	59:59
4. Abayneh Ayele ETH	59:59
5. Tamirat Tola ETH	60:06
6. Simon Cheprot KEN	60:12
7. Abrar Osman ERI	60:58
8. Samsom Gebreyohannes ERI	60:13
9. Mule Wasihun ETH	61:11
10. Stephen Mokoka RSA	61:27
11. Teshome Mekonen ETH	61:39
12. Edwin Kipyego KEN	61:52
13. Nguse Amsolom ERI	61:54
14. Paul Pollock IRL	62:46
15. Callum Hawkins GBR	62:51

85 of 88 finished

Teams: 1. KEN 2:58:58, 2. ETH 3:01:16, 3, ERI 3:06:18, 4. GBR 3:07:00, 5, JPN 3:12:11, 6. USA 3:12:28, 7. RSA 3:13:13, 8. IRL 3:13:29, 9. PER 3:15:27, 10. FRA 3:16:20. 14 teams scored.

Women

1. Peres Jepchirchir KEN	67:31
2. Cynthis Limo KEN	67:34
3. Mary Wacera Ngugi KEN	67:54
4. Netsanet Gudeta ETH	68:01
5. Genet Yalew ETH	68:15
6. Gladys Chesire KEN	68:46
7. Pascalia Kipkoech KEN	69:44
8. Deninninet Demswe ETH	70:13
9. Gladys Tejeda PER	70:14
10. Yuka Ando JPN	70:34
11. Janet Cherobon-Bawcom USA	70:46
12. Eloise Wellings AUS	70:47
13. Milly Clark AUS	70:48
14. Miho Simizu JPN	70:51
15. Sara Hall USA	70:58

80 of 83 finished

Teams: 1. KEN 3:22:59, 2. ETH 3:26:29, 3. JPN 3:32:35, 4. AUS 3:32:48, 5. USA 3:34:26, 6. CAN 3:36:54, 7. ITA 2:38:44, 8. MEX 3:39:07, 9. COL 3:39:23, 10. PER 3:39:46. 15 teams scored.

IAAF DIAMOND LEAGUE 2015

The IAAF's successor to the Golden League, the expanded and more globally widespread Diamond League, was launched in 2010 with 14 meetings spread across Asia, Europe, the Middle East and the USA. The total prize money was increased from $6.63 million (with a $50,000 bonus for any new world record) in 2010 to $8 million from 2011. Winners of each Race receive a Diamond Trophy (4 carats of diamonds) and a $40,000 cash prize.

DIAMOND LEAGUE – winners

D Doha May 15, **Sh** Shanghai May 17, **E** Eugene May 31, **R** Rome Jun 4, **Bi** Birmingham Jun 7, **O** Oslo Jun 11, **NY** New York Jun 13, **P** Paris Saint-Denis Jul 4,

L Lausanne Jul 9, **M** Monaco Jul 17, **Lo** London Jul 24-25, **St** Stockholm Jul 30; Finals with double points at: **Z** Zürich Sep 3, **Br** Brussels Sep 11

Men:

100m: Justin Gatlin D- 9.74, R- 9.75, M- 9.78, Br- 9.98; Marvin Bracy Bi- 9.93; Tyson Gay NY- 10.12, Asafa Powell P- 9.81

200m: Alonso Edward Sh- 20.33, St- 20.04, Z- 20.03; Zharnel Hughes L- 20.13, Lo- 20.05; Justin Gatlin E- 19.68; Christophe Lemaitre O- 20.21

400m: Wayde van Niekerk P- 43.96, Lo- 44.63; Kirani James Sh- 44.66, E- 43.95; Machel Cedenio St- 44.97, Steven Gardiner O- 44.64; LaShawn Merritt Z- 44.18

800m: Nijel Amos Bi- 1:46.77, L- 1:43.27; Mohammed Aman R- 1:43.56; Ayanleh Souleiman D- 1:43.78; David Rudisha NY- 1:43.58; Amel Tuka M- 1:42.51; Adam Ksczot Br- 1:45.12

1500m/1M: Asbel Kiprop O- 3:51.45M, Lo- 3:54.87M, Z- 3:35.79; Ayanleh Souleiman E- 3:51.10M, St- 3:33.33; Silas Kiplagat Sh- 3:35.29, P- 3:30.12

3000m: Hagos Gebrhiwet D- 7:38.08; Caleb Ndiku M- 7:35.13

5000m: Yomif Kejelcha R- 12:58.39, Br- 12:53.98; Tom Longosiwa Bi- 13:07.26; Ben True NY- 13:29.48, Mo Farah L- 13:11.77

3000mSt: Joseph Birech Sh- 8:05.36, O- 8:05.63, P- 7:58.83; Ezekiel Kemboi E- 8:01.71; Conseslus Kipruto Lo- 8:09.47; Hicham Sigueni MAR St- 8:16.54, Paul K Koech Z- 8:10.24

110mh: Orlando Ortega P- 12.94, St- 13.18; David Oliver Sh- 13.17, NY- 13.19; Pascal Martinot-Lagarde E- 13.06, Jason Richardson Lo- 13.19; Sergey Shubenkov Z- 13.84

400mh: Bershawn Jackson D- 48.09, L- 48.71, M- 48.23; Johnny Dutch E- 48.20, R- 48.13; Javier Culson NY- 48.48; Jeffery Gibson Br- 48.72

HJ: Mutaz Essa Barshim Sh- 2.38, E- 2.41, Z- 2.32; JaCorian Duffield St- 2.32, Marco Fassinotti Lo- 2.31, Daniyil Tsyplakov P- 2.31, Zhang Guowei O- 2.36

PV: Renaud Lavillenie E- 6.05*, R- 5.91, M- 5.92; Br- 5.95; Konstadínos Filppídis D- 5.75, P- 5.91; Pawel Wojciechowski L- 5.84

LJ: Greg Rutherford Bi- 8.35, O- 8.25, St- 8.34, Z- 8.32; Aleksandr Menkov Sh- 8.27; Marquis Dendy Lo- 8.38, Michael Hartfield P- 8.19

TJ: Christian Taylor Bi- 17.40, L- 18.06*, M- 17.75; Br- 17.59; Pedro Paulo Pichardo D- 18.06*, R- 17.96, NY- 17.56

SP: Joe Kovacs E- 22.12, NY- 21.67, M- 22.56*; David Storl D- 21.51, R- 21.46, L- 22.20; Tom Walsh Br- 21.39

DT: Piotr Malachowski Sh- 64.65, E- 65.59, P- 65.57, St- 65.95; Robert Urbanek O- 63.85, Z- 65.78, Philip Milanov Lo- 65.14

JT: Tero Pitkämäki D- 88.62, M- 88.97, Br- 87.37; Vitezslav Vesely R- 88.14, NY- 83.62; Julius Yego Bi- 91.39*; Keshorn Walcott L- 90.16

Women

100m: Shelly-Ann Fraser-Pryce E- 10.81, P- 10.74, St- 10.93, Z- 10.93; Blessing Okagbare Sh- 10.98; Murielle Ahouré O- 11.03; Dafne Schippers Lo- 10.92

200m: Jenba Tarmoh R- 22.77, Bi- 22.29; Allyson Felix D- 21.98*. L- 22.09; Candyce McGrone M- 22.08; Tori Bowie NY- 22.23; Dafne Schippers Br- 22.12

400m: Francena McCorory D- 50.21, R- 50.36, NY- 49.86, M- 49.83; Shaunae Miller L- 49.92, Br- 50.48; Stephenie Ann McPherson Bi- 52.14

800m: Eunice Sum Sh- 2:00.28, E- 1:57.82, P- 1:56.99, Lo- 1:58.44, Z- 1:59.14; Rénelle Lamote St- 1:59.91; Ajee' Wilson NY- 1:58.83

1500m: Sifan Hassan Bi- 4:00.30, L- 4:02.36; Genzebe Dibaba M- 3:50.07*; Jennifer Simpson R- 3:59.31; Dawit Seyaum D- 4:00.96; Faith Kipyegon Br- 4:16.71M; Laura Muir O- 4:00.39

3000m: Almaz Ayana Z- 8:22.34; Katie Mackey St- 8:52.99

5000m: Genzebe Dibaba E- 14:19.76, O- 14:21.29, P- 14:15.41; Almaz Ayana Sh- 14:14.32*; Mercy Cherono NY- Lo- 14:54.81

3000mSt: Virginia Nyambura D- 9:21.51, Bi- 9:24.01, L- 9:16.99; Habiba Ghribi M- 9:11.28, Br- 9:05.36; Hyvin Jepkemoi R- 9:15.08; Hiwot Ayalew NY- 9:25.26

100mh: Dawn Harper-Nelson Bi- 12.58, L- 12.55, Br- 12.63; Sharika Nelvis R- 12.52, M- 12.46; Jasmin Stowers D- 12.35*, O- 12.84

400mh: Zuzana Hejnová P- 53.76, Lo- 53.99, St- 54.37, Z- 54.47; Kaliese Spencer Sh- 54.71, Bi- 54.45, O- 54.15

HJ: Ruth Beitia R- 2.00, NY- 1.97; Mariya Kuchina M- 2.00, Br- 2.01; Kamila Licwinko Bi- 1.97; Airine Palsyte D- 1.94; Anna Chicherova L- 2.03

PV: Nikoléta Kiriakopoúlou Sh- 4.73, P- 4.83*, Lo- 4.79, Z- 4.77; Fabiana Murer Bi- 4.72, NY- 4.80; Yarisley Silva St- 4.81

LJ: Tianna Bartoletta D- 6.99, E- 7.11w, L- 6.86; Ivana Spanovic M- 6.87, Z- 7.02; Darya Klishina R- 6.89; Christabel Nettey NY- 6.92

TJ: Caterine Ibargüen Sh- 14.85, E- 15.18w, O- 14.68, P- 14.87, St- 14.69, Br- 14.60; Olga Rypakova Lo- 14.33

SP: Christina Schwanitz Bi- 19.68, O- 20.14, P- 20.31, St, Z- 19.91; Gong Lijiao SH- 20.23; Michelle Carter Lo- 19.74

DT: Sandra Perkovic D- 68.10, R- 67.92, Bi- 69.23, NY- 68.44, M- 66.80, Br- 67.50; Yaimí Pérez DT L- 67.13

JT: Barbora Spotáková P- 64.42, St- 65.66, Z- 64.31; Christian Obergföll E- 63.07; Lu Huihui Sh- 64.08; Marharyta Dorozhon O- 64.56; Madara Palmeika Lo- 65.01

FINAL PLACINGS

Diamond Race final placings: Men – 100: 1. Gatlin 20, 2. Vicaut 7, 3. Rodgers 5; **200**: 1. Edward 16, 2. Jobodwana 11, 3. Dwyer 4; **400**: 1. James 14, 2. Merritt 11, 3. van Niekerk 10; **800**: 1. Amos 16, 2. Kszczot 10, 3. Tuka 6; **1500**: 1. Kiprop 17, 2. Kiplagat 10, 3. Manangoi 4; **5000**: 1. Kejelcha 14, 2. Gebrhiwet 9, 3. Longosiwa 5; **3000SC**: 1. Birech 20, 2. Koech 12, 3. C Kipruto 9; **110H**: 1. Oliver 16, 2. Ortega 12, 3. Shubenkov 11; **400H**: 1. Jackson 18; 2= Dutch. Gibson 9; **HJ**: 1. Barshim 20, 2. Zhang 9, 3. Bondarenko 6; **PV**: 1. Lavillenie 21, 2. Filippídis 12; 3= Barber. Kendricks. Wojciechowski 4; **LJ**: 1. Rutherford 21, 2. Dendy 10, 3. Hartfield 8; **TJ**: 1. Taylor 22, 2. Pichardo 20, 3. Craddock 3; **SP**: 1. Kovacs 16, 2. Storl 14,

3. Walsh 9; **DT**: 1. Malachowski 21, 2. Urbanek 19, 3. Milanov 6; **JT**: 1. Pitkämäki 17, 2. Vesely 15, 3. Walcott 8; **Women – 100**: 1. Fraser-Pryce 20, 2. Okagbare 12, 3. Bowie 7; **200**: 1. Felix 14, 2. Schippers 12, 3. Tarmoh 9; **400**: 1. McCorory 20, 2. Miller 14, 3. McPherson 12; **800**: 1. Sum 24, 2. Sharp 7, 3. Lamote 4; **1500**: 1. Hassan 18, 2. Kipyegon 12, 3. Seyaum 6; **5000**: 1. G Dibaba 16, 2. Ayana 14; 3= Cherono & Teferi 5; **3000SC**: 1. Nyambura 15, 2. Jepkemoi 13, 3. Ghribi 12; **100H**: 1. Harper Nelson 18, 2. Nelvis 14, 3. Stowers 12; **400H**: 1. Hejnová 22, 2. Spencer 12, 3. Petersen 8; **HJ**: 1. Beitia 14, 2. Kuchina 13, 3. Chicherova 10; **PV**: 1. Kiriakopoúlou 24, 2. Murer 14, 3. Silva 11; **LJ**: 1. Bartoletta 20, 2. Spanovic 12, 3. Proctor 9; **TJ**: 1. Ibargüen 28, 2. Rypakova 7, 3. Koneva 6; **SP**: 1. Schwanitz 26, 2. Carter 13, 3. Márton 3; **DT**: 1. Perkovic 30, 2. Pérez 7, 3. Caballero 5; **JT**: 1. Spotáková 19, 2. Viljoen 7, 3. Palameika 5.

MIssed in ATHLETICS 2015

IAAF Continental Cup 2014

At Marrakech, Morocco, September 13-14

Prize Money: Individual: 1st $30,000; 2nd $15,000, 3rd $10,000, 4th $7000, 5th $5000, 6th $3000, 7th $2000, 8th $1000; Relay (for team): 1st $30,000; 2nd $20,000, 3rd $10,000, 4th $8000.

TEAM: 1. Europe 447.5, 2. Americas 390, 3. Africa 339, 4. Asia Pacific 257.5

100 Metres (a) (-0.1)
1. James Dasaolu GBR/EUR 10.03
2. Mike Rodgers USA/AM 10.04
3. Femi Ogunode QAT/AP 10.04
4. Mark Jelks NGR/AFR 10.12
5. Christoph Lemaitre FRA/EUR 10.13
6. Zhang Peimeng CHN/AP 10.18
7. Wilfried Koffi CIV/AFR 10.22
8. Richard Thompson TTO/AM 10.24

200 Metres (b) (0.2)
1. Alonso Edward PAN/AM 19.98
2. Rasheed Dwyer JAM/AM 19.98
3. Femi Ogunode QAT/AP 20.17
4. Christoph Lemaitre FRA/EUR 20.28
5. Serhiy Smelyk UKR/EUR 20.37
6. Isaac Makwala BOT/AFR 20.49
7. Wilfried Koffi CIV/AFR 20.62
8. Masafumi Naoki JPN/AP 21.12

400 Metres (a)
1. LaShawn Merritt USA/AM 44.60
2. Isaac Makwala BOT/AFR 44.84
3. Youssef Al-Masrahi KSA/AP 45.03
4. Wayde van Niekerk RSA/AFR 45.27
5. Luguelín Santos DOM/AM 45.34
6. Donald Sanford ISR/EUR 45.40
7. Martyn Rooney GBR/EUR 45.93
8. Yuzo Kanemaru JPN/AP 48.08

800 Metres (b)
1. Nijel Amos BOT/AFR 1:44.88
2. Mohamed Aman ETH/AFR 1:45.34
3. Adam Kszczot POL/EUR 1:45.72
4. Mark English IRL/EUR 1:45.74
5. Jeff Riseley AUS/AP 1:46.20
6. Duane Solomon USA/AM 1:46.21
7. Abdulrahman Musaeb Balla QAT/AP 1:48.50
8. Wesley Vásquez PUR/AM 1:49.32

1500 Metres (a)
1. Ayanleh Souleiman DJI/AFR 3:48.91
2. Asbel Kiprop KEN/AFR 3:49.10
3. Mahiedine Mekhissi-Benabbad FRA/EUR 3:49.53
4. Henrik Ingebrigtsen NOR/EUR 3:49.76
5. Benson Seurei BRN/AP 3:49.91
6. Nick Willis NZL/AP 3:50.00
7. Leonel Manzano USA/AM 3:50.35
8. Charles Philibert-Thiboutot CAN/AM 3:51.97

3000 Metres (b)
1. Caleb Ndiku KEN/AFR 7:52.64
2. Hayle Ibrahimov AZE/EUR 7:53.14
3. Bernard Lagat USA/AM 7:53.95
4. Nick Willis NZL/AP 7:55.50
5. Aweke Ayalew BRN/AP 7:56.58
6. Abrar Osman ERI/AFR 8:01.20
7. Richard Ringer GER/EUR 8:02.87
8. Carlos dos Santos BRA/AM 8:08.50

5000 Metres (a)
1. Isiah Koech KEN/AFR 13:26.86
2. Zane Robertson NZL/AP 13:29.27
3. Nguse Tesfaldet ERI/AFR 13:31.31
4. Albert Rop BRN/AP 13:36.62
5. Ali Kaya TUR/EUR 13:42.45
6. Boabdellah Tahri FRA/EUR 13:43.95
7. Andrew Bumbalough USA/AM 14:51.36
dnf. Iván López CHI/AM

3000m Steeplechase (b)
1. Jairus Birech KEN/AFR 8:13.18
2. Evan Jager USA/AM 8:14.08
3. Ali Abubaker Kamal QAT/AP 8:17.27
4. Chala Beyo ETH/AFR 8:25.45
5. John Koech BRN/AP-J 8:28.96
6. Ivan Lukyanov RUS/EUR 8:29.91
7. Matt Hughes CAN/AM 8:40.10
8. Krystian Zalewski POL/EUR 8:47.68

110 Metres Hurdles (b) (0.1)
1. Sergey Shubenkov RUS/EUR 13.23
2. Ronnie Ash USA/AM 13.25
3. William Sharman GBR/EUR 13.25
4. Xie Wenjun CHN/AP 13.44
5. Ty Akins NGR/AFR 13.48
6. Abdulaziz Al-Mandeel KUW/AP 13.49
7. Yordan O'Farrill CUB/AM 13.67
8. Ruan de Vries RSA/AFR 14.31

400 Metres Hurdles (a)
1. Cornel Fredericks RSA/AFR 48.34
2. Kariem Hussein SUI/EUR 48.47
3. Javier Culson PUR/AM 48.88
4. Rasmus Mägi EST/EUR 49.23
5. Amechi Morton NGR/AFR 49.65
6. Takyuki Kishimoto JPN/AP 49.78
7. Michael Tinsley USA/AM 52.25
8. Mike Cochrane NZL/AP 52.93

High Jump (a)
1. Bohdan Bondarenko UKR/EUR 2.37
2. Ivan Ukhov RUS/EUR 2.34
3. Mutaz Essa Barshim QAT/AP 2.34
4. Derek Drouin CAN/AM 2.31
5. Erik Kynard USA/AM 2.31
6. Zhang Guowei CHN/AP 2.27
7. Fernand Djouméssi CMR/AFR 2.23
8. Kabelo Kgosiemang BOT/AFR 2.18

Pole Vault (b)
1. Renaud Lavillenie FRA/EUR 5.80

2. Xue Changrui CHN/AP 5.65
3. Mark Hollis USA/AM 5.55
4. Augusto Dutra de Oliveira BRA/AM 5.40
5. Pawel Wojciechowski POL/EUR 5.40
6. Cheyne Rahme RSA/AFR 5.20
7. Joel Pocklington AUS/AP 5.20
8. Mohamed Amine Romdhana TUN/AFR 5.00

Long Jump (a)
1. Ignisious Gaisah NED/EUR 8.11/-0.7
2. Will Claye USA/AM 7.98/0.3
3. Zarck Visser RSA/AFR 7.96/0.8
4. Henry Frayne AUS/AP 7.95/0/5
5. Li Jinzhe CHN/AP 7.82/0.0
6. Robert Martey GHA/AFR 7.76/0.4
7. Luis Rivera MEX/AM 7.75/0.3
8. Kafétien Gomis FRA/EUR 7.67/1.5

Triple Jump (b)
1. Benjamin Compaoré FRA/EUR 17.48/-0.1
2. Khotso Mokoena RSA/AFR 17.35/0.2
3. Will Claye USA/AM 17.21/0.5
4. Tosin Oke NGR/AFR 16.89/0.3
5. Cao Shuo CHN/AP 16.83/0.3
6. Lyukman Adams RUS/EUR 16.82/0.3
7. Jonathan Silva BRA/AM 16.04/-0.4
8. Renjith Maheswary IND/AP 15.91/-0.9

Shot (a)
1. David Storl GER/EUR 21.55
2. O'DayneRichards JAM/AM 21.10
3. Joe Kovacs USA/AM 20.87
4. Tomas Walsh NZL/AP 20.70
5. Tomasz Majewski POL/EUR 20.35
6. Orazio Cremona RSA/AFR 19.96
7. Frank Elemba CGO/AFR 19.72 rec
8. Sultan Al-Hebshi KSA/AP 19.09

Discus (b)
1. Gerd Kanter EST/EUR 64.46
2. Jorge Fernández CUB/AM 62.97
3. Jason Morgan JAM/AM 62.70
4. Victor Hogan RSA/AFR 62.69
5. Benn Harradine AUS/AP 61.97
6. Robert Urbanek POL/EUR 60.27
7. Stephen Mozia NGR/AFR 57.31
8. Sultan Al-Dawoodi KSA/AP 56.73

Hammer (a)
1. Krisztián Pars HUN/EUR 78.99
2. Mostafa Al-Gamal EGY/AFR 78.89
3. Pawel Fajdek POL/EUR 78.05
4. Dilshod Nazarov TJK/AP 77.06
5. Mohamed Ali Al-Zankawi KUW/AP 72.24
6. Roberto Janet CUB/AM 71.98
7. Chris Harmse RSA/AFR 71.71
8. Kibwé Johnson USA/AM 71.36

JT (b)
1. Ihab Abdelrahman EGY/AFR 85.44
2. Vitezslav Vesely CZE/EUR 83.77
3. Keshorn Walcott TTO/AM 83.52
4. Julius Yego KEN/AFR 83.06
5. Tim Glover USA/AM 79.67
6. Joshua Robinson AUS/AP 78.58
7. Ivan Zaytsev UZB/AP 78.37
8. Antti Ruuskanen FIN/EUR 77.78

4x100 Metres (a)
1. Americas (K Collins, Rodgers, Carter, Thompson) 37.97
2. Europe/GBR (Ellington, Aikines-Aryeetey, Kilty, Lemaitre FRA) 38.62
3. Africa/NGR (Jelks, Edwards, Metu, Ogho-Oghene) 39.10
4. Asia-Pacific JPN (Oseto, Taniguchi, Naoki, Onabuta) 39.50

4x400 Metres (b)
1. Africa 3:00.02 (Tumuti 46.0e, Makwala 43.9e, Kombe 45.56, van Niekerk 44.74)
2. Europe 3:00.10 (C Williams 45.7e, Krzewina 45.3e, Sanford 44.33, Rooney 44.82)
3. Americas 3:02.78 (Culson 45.7e, C Brown 44.6e, K Collins 47.22, Merritt 45.25)
4. Asia-Pacific/JPN 3:03.77 (Tamura 46.2e, Kitagawa 45.3e, Yui 45.90, Walsh 46.43).

Women

100 Metres (a) (-1.5)
1. Veronica Campbell-Brown JAM/AM 11.08
2. Michelle-Lee Ahye TTO/AM 11.25
3. Dafne Schippers NED/EUR 11.26
4. Marie Josée Ta Lou CIV/AFR 11.28
5. Myriam Soumaré FRA/EUR 11.36
6. Gloria Asumnu NGR/AFR 11.37
7. Olga Safronova KAZ/AP 11.60
8. Melissa Breen AUS/AP 11.75

200 Metres (0.3)
1. Dafne Schippers NED/EUR 22.28
2. Joanna Atkins USA/AM 22.53
3. Myriam Soumaré FRA/EUR 22.58
4. Anthonique Strachan BAH/AM 22.73
5. Marie Josée Ta Lou CIV/AFR 22.78
6. Olga Safronova KAZ/AP 22.99
7. Dominique Duncan NGR/AFR 23.63
8. Melissa Breen AUS/AP 23.81

400 Metres (a)
1. Francena McCorory USA/AM 49.94
2. Novlene Williams-Mills JAM/AM 50.08
3. Libania Grenot ITA/EUR 50.60
4. Kabange Mupopo ZAM/AFR 50.87
5. Olha Zemlyak UKR/EUR 51.00
6. Sade Abugan NGR/AFR 51.78
7. Anneliese Rubie AUS/AP 54.33
8. Louise Jones NZL/AP 55.07

800 Metres (a)
1. Eunice Sum KEN/AFR 1:58.21
2. Ajee' Wilson USA/AM 2:00.07
3. Marina Arzamasova BLR/EUR 2:00.31
4. Tigist Assefa ETH/AFR-J 2:00.57
5. Lynsey Sharp GBR/EUR 2:00.80
6. Sahily Diago CUB/AM-J 2:00.96
7. Angie Smit NZL/AP 2:02.37
8. Tintu Luka IND/AP 2:03.13

1500 Metres (b)
1. Sifan Hassan NED/EUR 4:05.99
2. Shannon Rowbury USA/AM 4:07.21
3. Dawit Seyaum ETH/AFR-J 4:07.61
4. Hellen Obiri KEN/AFR 4:08.15
5. Renata Plis POL/EUR 4:08.68
6. Mimi Belete BRN/AP 4:09.14
7. Nicole Sifuentes CAN/AM 4:11.18
8. Selma Kajan AUS/AP 4:19.61

3000 Metres (a)
1. Genzebe Dibaba ETH/AFR 8:57.53
2. Meraf Bahta SWE/EUR 8:58.48
3. Susan Kuijken NED/EUR 9:01.41
4. Janet Kisa KEN/AFR 9:01.72
5. Mimi Belete BRN/AP 9:04.11
6. Gabrielle Grunewald USA/AM 9:05.58

7. Jessica O'Connell CAN/AM 9:11.04
8. Yuiki Mori JPN/AP 9:31.10

5000 Metres (b)
1. Almaz Ayana ETH/AFR 15:33.32
2. Joyce Chepkirui KEN/AFR 15:58.31
3. Jo Pavey GBR/EUR 15:58.67
4. Eloise Wellings AUS/AP 16:00.14
5. Clémence Calvin FRA/EUR 16:03.31
6. Brenda Flores MEX/AM 16:19.07
7. Tejitu Daba BRN/AP 16:37.62
8. Katie Mackey USA/AM 17:06.25

3000m Steeplechase (b)
1. Emma Coburn USA/AM 9:50.67
2. Hiwot Ayalew ETH/AFR 9:51.59
3. Ruth Chebet BRN/AP-J 9:55.24
4. Svetlana Kudzelich BLR/EUR 9:56.31
5. Vharlotta Fougberg SWE/EUR 10:07.62
6. Salima Alami El Ouali MAR/AFR 10:08.35
7. Jessica Furlan CAN/AM 10:16.51
8. Stella Radford AUS/AP-J 11:07.02

100 Metres Hurdles: (0.7)
1. Dawn Harper-Nelson USA/AM 12.47*
2. Tiffany Porter GBR/EUR 12.51 rec
3. Cindy Roleder GER/EUR 13.02
4. Lavonne Idlette DOM/AM 13.06
5. Rikenette Steenkamp RSA/AFR 13.16
6. Ayako Kimura JPN/AP 13.17
7. Amaka Ogoegbunam NGR/AFR 13.59
8. Sarah Cowley NZL/AP 15.30

400 Metres Hurdles (a)
1. Kaliese Spencer JAM/AM 53.81
2. Eilidh Child GBR/EUR 54.42
3. Kemi Adekoya BRN/AP 54.70
4. Anna Titimets UKR/EUR 55.20
5. Wenda Nel RSA/AFR 55.80
6. Amaka Ogoegbunam NGR/AFR 55.83
7. Kori Carter USA/AM 56.80
8. Lauren Wells AUS/AP 57.09

High Jump (b)
1. Mariya Kuchina RUS/EUR 1.99
2. Chaunté Lowe USA/AM 1.97
3. Ana Simic CRO/EUR 1.95
4. Svetlana Radzivil UZB/AP 1.93
5. Levern Spencer LCA/AM 1.87
6. Ghizliane Siba MAR/AFR-J 1.79
7. Sarah Cowley NZL/AP 1.79
8. Besnet Moussad Mohamed EGY/AFR 1.69

Pole Vault (a)
1. Li Ling CHN/AP 4.55
2. Angelina Zhuk-Krasnova RUS/EUR 4.45
3= Lisa Ryzih GER/EUR 4.30
3= Alana Boyd AUS/AP 4.30
5. Becky Holliday USA/AM 4.30
6. Nisrine Dinar MAR/AFR 3.95
7. Sirine Ebondo TUN/AFR 3.95
nh, Fabiana Murer BRA/AM

Long Jump (b)
1. Éloyse Lesueur FRA/EUR 6.66/-0.4
2. Ivana Spanovic SRB/EUR 6.56/-0.1
3. Tianna Bartoletta USA/AM 6.45/0.0
4. Christabel Nettey CAN/AM 6.35/0.2
5. Ese Brume NGR/AFR-J 6.34/0.2
6. Joëlle Mbumi Nkouindjin CMR/AFR 6.23/-0.1
7. Lu Minjia CHN/AP 6.14/0.2
8. Margaret Gayen AUS/AP 5.92/0.3

Triple Jump (a)
1. Caterine Ibargüen COL/AM 14.52/-0.5
2. Yekaterina Koneva RUS/EUR 14.27/-0.2
3. Olha Saladukha UKR/EUR 14.26/0.3
4. Kimberly Williams JAM/AM 13.93/0.1
5. Li Yanmei CHN/AP 13.37/0.0
6. Joëlle Mbumi Nkouindjin CMR/AFR 13.34/-0.4
7. Nadia Eke GHA/AFR 13.28/0.1
8. Linda Leverton AUS/AP 13.10/-0.1

Shot (b)
1. Christina Schwanitz GER/EUR 20.02
2. Michelle Carter USA/AM 19.84
3. Gong Lijao CHN/AP 19.23
4. Yevgeniya Kolodko RUS/EUR 18.80
5. Cleopatra Borel TTO/AM 18.68
6. Chinwe Okoro NGR/AFR 16.35
7. Auriole Dongmo CMR/AFR 15.77
dns, Valerie Adams NZL/AP

Discus (a)
1. Gia Lewis-Smallwood USA/AM 64.55
2. Dani Samuels AUS/AP 64.39
3. Sandra Perkovic CRO/EUR 62.08
4. Mélina Robert-Michon FRA/EUR 61.89
5. Yaimí Pérez CUB/AM 59.38
6. Yang Yanbo CHN/AP 55.98
7. Chinwe Okoro NGR/AFR 52.30
8. Amina Moudden MAR/AFR 49.07

Hammer (b)
1. Anita Wlodarczyk POL/EUR 75.21
2. Amanda Bingson USA/AM 72.38
3. Martina Hrasnová SVK/EUR 70.47
4. Wang Zheng CHN/AP 70.15
5. Sultana Frizell CAN/AM 70.06
6. Amy Sène SEN/AFR 59.18
7. Laëtitia Bambara BUR/AFR 58.22
8. Natalie Debeljuh AUS/AP 53.73

Javelin (a)
1. Barbora Spotakova CZE/EUR 65.52
2. Sunette Viljoen RSA/AFR 63.76
3. Liz Gleadle CAN/AM 61.38
4. Kimberley Mickle AUS/AP 61.33
5. Linda Stahl GER/EUR 60.14
6. Zhang Li CHN/AP 59.27
7. Kara Patterson USA/AM 52.22
8. Mary Zuta Nartey GHA/AFR 49.84

4x100 Metres (a)
1. Americas (Bartoletta, Ahye, Henry-Robinson, Campbell-Brown) 42.44
2. Europe/GBR (Philip, Nelson, Onuora, Henry J) 42.98
3. Asia-Pacific JPN (Miyazawa, Nakamura, Tsuchihashi, Jimbo) 45.40
dq (baton outside zone) Africa (Asumnu, Ta Lou, Duncan, Palframan)

4x400 Metres (b)
1. Americas 3:20.93 (Day 51.3e, McCorory 50.01e, McPherson 49.72, Williams-Mills 49.86)
2. Europe 3:24.12 (Terrero 52.4e, Holub 50.1e, Zemlyak 50.24, Grenot 51.40)
3. Africa 3:25.51 (P George 51.7e, Abugan 50.5e, Benjamin 52.47, Mpopo 50.84)
4. Asia-Pacific/AUS 3:36.89 (Thornton 54.9e, Rubie 53.1e, Wells 53.60, Pekin 55.31)

MAJOR MEETINGS 2015-2016

Diamond League, World Challenge and European Athletics Premium Meetings

DL – Diamond League, WC – World Challenge, EAP European Premium Meeting

2015 date		Meeting	2016 date	
21 Mar	WC	Melbourne World Challenge, AUS	5 Mar	WC
9 May	WC	Jamaica International, KIngston JAM	7 May	WC
15 May	DL	Qatar Super Grand Prix, Doha, QAT	6 May	DL
10 May	WC	Golden Grand Prix, Kawasaki, JPN	8 May	WC
17 May	DL	Shanghai Golden Grand Prix, CHN	14 May	DL
20 May	WC	Beijing, CHN	18 May	WC
23 May	WC	Ponce Grand Prix, PUR	–	
23 May	WC	Dakar, Sénégal	25 May	WC
26 May	WC	Golden Spike, Ostrava, CZE	20 May	WC
30 May	DL	Prefontaine Classic, Eugene, Oregon, USA	28 May	DL
4 Jun	DL	Golden Gala, Rome, ITA	2 Jun	DL
7 Jun	DL	British Grand Prix, Birmingham, GBR	5 Jun	DL
8 Jun	WC	Fanny Blankers-Koen Games, Hengelo, NED	22 May	WC
8 Jun	EAP	Josef Odlozil Memorial, Prague, CZE	6 Jun	EAP
11 Jun	DL	ExxonMobil Bislett Games, Oslo, NOR	9 Jun	DL
13 Jun	DL	adidas Grand Prix, New York (RI), USA	18 Jun	Street
14 Jun	WC	Mohammed VI d'Athlétisme, Rabat 2015, MAR	22 May	DL
25 Jun	EAP	Paavo Nurmi Games, Turku, Finland	29 Jun	EAP
4 Jul	DL	Meeting AREVA Paris Saint-Denis, FRA	27 Aug	DL
9 Jul	DL	Athletissima, Lausanne, SUI	25 Aug	DL
11 Jul	WC	Atletismo Madrid, ESP	23 Jun	WC
17 Jul	DL	Herculis, Monaco, MON	15 Jul	DL
24/25 Jul	DL	Anniversary Games, London (OS) 2015	22-23 Jul	DL
30 Jul	DL	Bauhaus, Stockholm, SWE	16 Jun	DL
Not held		GP Brasil de Atletismo, São Bernardo do Campo, BRA	26 Jun	
3 Sep	DL	Weltklasse, Zürich, SUI	1 Sep	DL
6 Sep	WC	ISTAF, Berlin, GER	3 Sep	WC
8 Sep	WC	Zagreb, CRO	6 Sep	WC
8 Sep	EAP	Palio Citta della Quercia, Rovereto, ITA	6 Sep	EAP
11 Sep	DL	Memorial Van Damme, Brussels, BEL	9 Sep	DL
13 Sep	WC	Rieti, ITA	11 Sep	WC

INDOORS

IAAF and EAA – respective indoor permit meetings; US USATF series in USA.

2015 date		Meeting	2016 date	
24 Jan	EAA	Sainsbury's International, Glasgow, GBR	20 Feb	IAAF
29 Jan	EAA	International PSD Bank, Düsseldorf, GER	3 Feb	EAA
30-31		Armory Track Invitational, New York, USA	31 Jan	US
31 Jan	IAAF	BW-Bank Meeting, Karlsruhe, GER	6 Feb	IAAF
1 Feb	IAAF	Russian Winter, Moscow, RUS	–	
19 Feb	IAAF	Globen Galan, Stockholm, SWE	17 Feb	IAAF
6 Feb		Flanders Indoor, Gent, BEL	13 Feb	EAA
7 Feb	US	New Balance Indoor GP, Boston (Roxbury), USA	14 Feb	IAAF/US
14 Feb		Millrose Games, New York (Armory), USA	14 Feb	US
17 Feb	EAA	Pedro's Cup, Bydgoszcz 2014, Lódz 2015, POL	5 Feb	EAA
21 Feb	IAAF	British Indoor Grand Prix, Birmingham, GBR	—	
27 Feb-1 Mar	US	USA Indoor Champs. Boston (R)/ Portland	28 Feb-1 Mar	US

IAAF WORLD COMBINED EVENTS CHALLENGE 2015 & 2016

2015	Meeting	2016
	Oceania Combined Events Champs, Sydney, AUD	31 Mar-3 Apr
	Afru8can Cimbined Events Champs, Réduit, MRI	2-3 Apr
15/16 May	Multistars, Firenze, ITA	29/30 Apr
30/31 May	Hypo-Mehrkampf Meeting, Götzis, AUT	28/29 May
12/13 Jun	TNT Express Meeting, Kladno, CZE	10/11 Jun
19/20 Jun	Pan-American CE Cup Ottawa, CAN	17/18 Jun
27/28 Jun	Erdgas DLV Mehrkampf, Ratingen, GER	25/26 Jun
19/20 Sep	Decastars, Talence, FRA	17/18 Sep

Plus International Games and Championships

European Athletics Combined Events Permit: Arona, ESP 6-7/4-5 Jun

IAAF WORLD RACE WALKING CHALLENGE 2015 & 2016

22 Feb	Adelaide, AUS	21 Feb
7 Mar	2015 Chihuahua, 2016 Ciudad Juárez MEX	6 Mar
15 Mar	Asian Champs, Nomi, JPN	20 Mar
21 Mar	Dudince, SVK	19 Mar
18 Apr	Rio Maior, POR	9 Apr
1-2 May	Taicang, CHN (RW Cup in 2014)	23 Apr
6 Jun	Gran Premio Cantones de La Coruña, ESP	28 May

Plus International Championships

European Athletics Race Walking Permit Meetings 2015

Lugano, SUI 15 Mar/-, Podebrady, CZE 11/9 Apr, Alytus, LTU 12/10 Jun, Dublin IRL -/18 Jun, Voronovo RUS 12-13/10 Sep

IAAF HAMMER THROW CHALLENGE 2016

At the following meetings (above): Melbourne AUS, Kingston JAM, Beijing CHN, Ostrava CZE, Hengelo NED, Dakar SEN, Szczecin POL, São Bernardo do Campo BRA, Turku FIN, Székesfehérvár HUN, Zagreb CRO, Rieti ITA & Olympic Games.

MARATHON MAJORS 2016

Tokyo 28 Feb, Boston 18 Apr, London 24 Apr, Berlin 25 Sep, Chicago 9 Oct, New York 6 Nov.

EUROPEAN AA CLASSIC MEETINGS 2016 *(with 2015 dates of these meetings first)*

Huelva ESP (Iberoamerican) 10/3 Jun, Zhukovskiy RUS (Znamenskiy Memorial) 18-19 Jul/4-5 Jun, Bydgoszcz POL (European Athletics Festival) 14/5 Jun, Montreuil-sous-Bois FRA 9/7 Jun, Luzern SUI (Spitzen) 14 Jul/14 Jun, Tomblaine FRA 1 Jul/14 Jun, Velenje SLO 1 Jul/14 Jun, Szczecin POL (Janusz Kusocinski Memorial) 9 Aug/18 Jun, Sollentuna SWE 25 Jun, Göteborg SWE Sep 5/Jul 15, Heusden-Zolder, BEL 18/16 Jul, Andújar ESP -/16 Jul, Padova ITA 6 Sep/17 Jul, Székesfehérvár HUN (István Gyulai Memorial) 7/18 Jul, Sotteville-lès-Rouen FRA 6/18 Jul, Karlstad SWE 22/27 Jul.

A further 12 meetings in eight countries have been designated as **European Athletics outdoor area permit meetings**

NORTH AMERICA NACAC MEETINGS 2016 (selection)

Des Moines (Drake Relays) USA 24-25/29-30 Apr, Philadelphia (Penn Relays) USA 23-24/230 Apr, Baie Mahault, Guadeloupe 2/14 May, George Town CAY 16/14 May, Halifax (Alison Meagher International Classic) CAN 14/2 Jun, Vancouver (Harry Jerome Track Classic) CAN 8/17 Jun, Victoria CAN 10/19 Jun, Edmonton CAN 12/16 Jull

MAJOR INTERNATIONAL EVENTS 2016–2021

2016

World University Cross Country Championships – Monte Cassino, Italy (11-13 March)
European Throwing Cup, Arad, Romania (12-13 Mar)
IAAF World Indoor Championships – Portland, Oregon, USA (17-20 March)
IAAF World Half Marathon Championships – Cardiff, GBR (26 March)
IAAF Race Walking Team Championships – Rome, Italy (7-8 May)
European 10,000m Cup, Mersin, Turkey – (5 Jun)
African Championships – xx, South Africa (22-26 Jun)
NACAC U20 Championships – Hamilton, Bermuda (1-3 July)
European Championships – Amsterdam, Netherlands (6-10 July)
European Youth Championships ¬ Tbilisi, Georgia (14-17 July)
NACAC U23 Championships – Mayagüez, Puerto Rico (15-17 July)
IAAF World Junior Championships – Bydgoszcz, Poland (19-24 July))
Olympic Games – Rio de Janeiro, Brazil (12-31 Aug)
European Cross Country Championships – Chia, Italy (11 Dec)

2017

European Indoor Championships – Belgrade, Serbia (3-5 March)
IAAF World Cross Country Championships – Kampala, Uganda (26 March)
IAAF World Relays – Nassau, Bahamas (22-23 April)
European Race Walking Cup, Podébrady, Czech Republic (21 May)
European Team Championships Super League – Lille, France (24-25 June)
European U23 Championships – Bydgoszcz, Poland (13-16 Jul)
Commonwealth Youth Games – Nassau, Bahamas (19-23 Jul)
European U20 Championships – Grosseto, Italy (20-23 Jul)
IAAF World Youth Championships – Nairobi, Kenya (12-16 Jul)
IAAF World Championships – London, GBR (5-13 August)
World University Games – Taipeh, Taiwan (20-25 Aug)
European Cross Country Championships – Samorin, Slovakia (10 Dec)

2018

Asian Indoor Championships – Ranchi, India (February)
IAAF World Indoor Championships – Birmingham, GBR (2-4 March)
Commonwealth Games – Gold Coast, Australia (4-15 April)
IAAF World Half Marathon Championships – Valencia, Spain
IAAF World Junior Championships – Tampere, Finland
IAAF World Race Walking Cup – Cheboksary, Russia
African Championships – Lagos, Nigeria
Central American & Caribbean Games – Barranquilla, Colombia (19 Jul – 3 Aug)
European Championships – Berlin, Germany (7-12 Aug)
Asian Games – Jakarta, Indonesia
IAAF Continental Cup – Ostrava, Czech Republic (7-8 Sep)
Youth Olympic Games – Buenos Aires, Argentina (11-23 Sep)

2019

Pan-American Games – Lima, Peru (16 Jul - 11 Aug)
World University Games – Brasilia, Brazil
IAAF World Championships – Doha, Qatar (28 Sep – 6 Oct)
Asian Games – Hanoi, Vietnam

2020

Olympic Games – Tokyo, Japan (31 July – 9 August)

2021

IAAF World Championships – Eugene, USA

The **IAAF Competition Rules 2016-2017**, which came into force on 1 Nov 2015, included some notable changes. The IAAF World Cross Country Champs distances have been standardised at approximately 10k for both men and women (previously 12k for men and 8k for women); the distance medley relay (1200m, 400m, 800m, 1600m) and women's 50,000m track walk and 50k road walk have become official world record events (the initial walk records will be recognised on December 31); and "Junior" and "Youth" are now designated as "U20" and "U18".

European Team Championship: The next edition will be held in 2017 and there is a good chance that it will involve eight, rather than 12, teams. The new European Athletics President, Svein Arne Hansen stated: "Cheboksary 2015 was an excellent championships with a lot of great performances but for me it is clear that the Super League should go back to eight teams like the old European Cup from the current 12 teams. The 12-team format with two heats is just not as engaging for the fans. If we could change back, which I will ask our Event & Competition Commission to look at, I think it will make for a shorter, more exciting, easier-to-follow programme."

A potentially worrying development is that the Internaional Olympic Committee has released recommendations that **transgender athletes** should be allowed to compete in the Olympics and other international events without undergoing sex reassignment surgery. Apparently they would need only to declare themselves female and keep their testosterone levels below 10 nmol/L for a year before competing. Tsetosterone levels for heathy men range between 75 and 25 nmol/L, but the potential unfairness is shown by the fact that normal levels in women range from 0.20 to 3 nmol/L So the male-to-female trans athlete could be alowed more than three times the upper range of this performance-enhancing hormone There many not be many athletes in such a category but any incidence of them competing in women's events, and there could be a big incentive for them to do so, could result in gross unfairness.

WORLD INDOOR CHAMPIONSHIPS 2016

Portland, Oregon, USA 17–20 March

ALTHOUGH NUMBERS OF competitors were down, all too many citing Olympic prepation for staying away, the 16th edition of the IAAF World Indoor Championships, staged with capacity crowds of over 7000 in the Convention Centre in Portland was a great success – well organised with true championships action. Some great athletes dominated, while in other events there were close races and field contests. Enhanced presentation included introductions of the athletes as they entered the arena one by one for each final and the medal ceremonies being staged downtown with free access for the general public.

The top performances were the three championship records. Renaud Lavillenie soared over 6.02 in the pole vault at the conclusion of the novel, and very well supported, venture of having the men's and women's vaults in parallel as the only events of the first evening of the meeting. This was after Jenn Suhr had won gold in her event at 4.90. On the next day Brittany Reese came back to top form in the women's long jump as she moved from second to the gold medal in the final round with a terrific 7.22, just 3cm short of her all-time best

The United States had a wonderful championship, with the highest medal tally in the history of the event, their 13 gold medals exceeding the previous record of ten they achieved in Istanbul in 2012. While not quite matching his top form, local hero Ashton Eaton duly won the heptathlon with 6470 by a margin of 288 points and followed his wife Brianne, who had studied at the University of Oregon, and who won the heptathlon with a Canadian record 4881 to make them the first husband and wife gold medallists. Theisen-Eaton's win was particularly notable as she had to beat Anatasasyia Mokhnyuk by at least 11 seconds in the 800m and succeeded. There was similar domination to that by Ashton Eaton by Genzebe Dibaba, who, after her 3000m had started very slowly, ran the last 200m in 5:31.70, and by Tom Walsh, who had five throws in the shot over 50cm beyond the next man's best, including Oceania records at 21.60, 21.64 and 21.78.

Excessively high qualifying standards for the field events (unfair discrimination against athletes for whom the indoor season is most important) meant that the numbers of competitors were small in those events and no qualifying rounds were needed.

MEN

60 Metres (b-b-b)

1. Trayvon Bromell USA	6.47
2. Asafa Powell JAM	6.50
3. Ramon Gittens BAR	6.51
4. Xie Zhenye CHN	6.53
5. Su Bingtian CHN	6.54
6. Mike Rodgers USA	6.54
7. Marvin Bracy USA	6.56
8. Kim Collins SKN	6.56

400 Metres (b-b-c)

1. Pavel Maslák CZE	45.44
2. Abdelilah Haroun QAT-J	45.59
3. Deon Lendore TTO	46.17
4. Bralon Taplin GRN	46.56
5. Boniface Mweresa KEN	46.86
6. Lalonde Gordon TTO	47.62

800 Metres (b-c)

1. Boris Berian USA	1:45.83
2. Antoine Gakeme BDI	1:46.65
3. Erik Sowinski USA	1:47.22
4. Mohammed Aman ETH	1:47.97
5. Abdulrahman Musaeb Balla QAT	1:48.31
6. Mostafa Smaili MAR-J	1:52.32

1500 Metres (a-b)

1. Matthew Centrowitz USA	3:44.22
2. Jakub Holusa CZE	3:44.30
3. Nick Willis NZL	3:44.37
4. Robby Andrews USA	3:44.77
5. Dawit Wolde ETH	3:44.81
6. Aman Wote ETH	3:44.86
7. Vincent Kibet KEN	3:45.17
8. Chris O'Hare GBR	3:46.50
9. Ayanleh Souleiman DJI	3:53.69

3000 Metres (b-d)

1. Yomif Kejelcha ETH-J	7:57.21
2. Ryan Hill USA	7:57.39
3. Augustine Choge KEN	7:57.43
4. Abdelaati Iguider MAR	7:58.04
5. Caleb Ndiku KEN	7:58.81
6. Lee Emanuel GBR	8:00.70
7. Paul Chelimo USA	8:00.76
8. Isiah Koech KEN	8:01.70

60 Metres Hurdles (c-d-d)

1. Omar McLeod JAM	7.41
2. Pascal Martinot-Lagarde FRA	7.46
3. Dimitri Bascou FRA	7.48
4. Jarret Eaton USA	7.50
5. Spencer Adams USA	7.64
6. Balázs Baji HUN	7.65
7. Eddie Lovett ISV	7.75
8. Shane Brathwaite BAR	7.88

High Jump (c)

1. Gianmarco Tamberi ITA	2.36
2. Robbie Grabarz GBR	2.33
3. Erik Kynard USA	2.33
4. Mutaz Essa Barshim QAT	2.29
5. Konstadínos Baniótis GRE	2.29
6. Zhang Guowei CHN	2.29
7. Andriy Protsenko UKR	2.29
8. Chris Baker GBR	2.29

Pole Vault (a)

1. Renaud Lavillenie FRA	6.02*
2. Sam Kendricks USA	5.80
3. Piotr Lisek POL	5.75
4= Shawn Barber CAN	5.75
4= Jan Kudlicka CZE	5.75
6. Robert Sobera POL	5.65
7. Konstadínos Filippídis GRE	5.65
8. Mike Arnold USA	5.65

Long Jump (d)

1. Marquis Dendy USA	8.26
2. Fabrice Lapierre AUS	8.25
3. Huang Changzhou CHN	8.21
4. Jeff Henderson USA	8.19
5. Rushwal Samaai RSA	8.18
6. Dan Bramble GBR	8.14
7. Emiliano Lasa URU	7.94
8. Wang Jianan CHN	7.93

Triple Jump (c)

1. Dong Bin CHN	17.33
2. Max Hess GER	17.14
3. Benjamin Compaoré FRA	17.09
4. Nelson Évora POR	16.89
5. Omar Craddock USA	16.87
6. Tosin Oke NGR	16.73
7. Pablo Torrijos ESP	16.67
8. Nazim Babayev AZE-J	16.43

Shot (b)

1. Tomas Walsh NZL	21.78
2. Andrei Gag ROU	20.89
3. Filip Mihaljevic CRO	20.87
4. Konrad Bukowiecki POL-J	20.53
5. Jonathan Jones USA	20.31
6. Germán Lauro ARG	20.24
7. Tim Nedow CAN	20.23
8. Tobias Dahm GER	20.22

Heptathlon (b/c)

1. Ashton Eaton USA	6470
2. Oleksiy Kasyanov UKR	6182
3. Mathias Brugger GER	6126
4. Curtis Beach USA	6118

5. Adam Sebastian Helcelet CZE 6003
6. Kurt Felix GRN 5986
7. Tim Nowak GER 5832
8. Jérémy Lelièvre FRA 5769
9. Samuel Remédios POR 5733
10. Petter Olsson SWE 5697

4 x 400 Metres (c-d)
1. USA 3:02.45
K Clemons 46.6, C Smith 45.6, C Giesting 45.3. V Norwood 44.9
2. BAH 3:04.75
M Mathieu 46.8, A Russell 45.6, S Hart 46.6, C Brown 45.8
3. TTO 3:05.51
J Solomon 47.4, L Gordon 45.1, A Alleyne-Forte 46.8, D Lendore 46.2
4. JAM 3:06.02
5. NGR 3:08.55
6. BEL 3:09.71

WOMEN

60 Metres (c-c-c)
1. Barbara Pierre USA 7.02
2. Dafne Schippers NED 7.04
3. Elaine Thompson JAM 7.06
4. Michelle Lee Ahye TTO 7.11
5. Asha Philip GBR 7.14
6. Tori Bowie USA 7.14
7. Marie Josée Ta Lou CIV 7.29
dns. Dina Asher-Smith GBR –

400 Metres (b-b-c)
1. Kemi Adekoya BRN 51.45
2. Ashley Spencer USA 51.72
3. Quanera Hayes USA 51.76
4. Stephenie Ann McPherson JAM 52.20
5. Justyna Swiety POL 52.46
6. Iveta Putalová SVK 54.39

800 Metres (c-d)
1. Francine Niyonsaba BDI 2:00.01
2. Ajeé Wilson USA 2:00.27
3. Margaret Wambui KEN 2:00.44
4. Laura Roseler USA 2:00.80
5. Anita Hinriksdóttir ISL 2:02.58
6. Habitam Alemu ETH-J 2:04.61

1500 Metres (b-c)
1. Sifan Hassan NED 4:04.96
2. Dawit Seyaum ETH 4:05.30
3. Gudaf Tsegay ETH-J 4:05.71
4. Axumawit Embaye ETH 4:09.37
5. Brenda Martinez USA 4:09.57
6. Melissa Duncan AUS 4:09.69
7. Renata Plis POL 4:10.14
8. Violah Lagat KEN 4:10.45
9. Danuta Urbanik POL 4:12.59

3000 Metres (d)
1. Genzebe Dibaba ETH 8:47.43
2. Meseret Defar ETH 8:54.26
3. Shannon Rowbury USA 8:55.55
4. Maureen Koster NED 8:56.44
5. Abbey D'Agostino USA 8:58.40
6. Stephanie Twell GBR 9:00.38
7. Betsy Saina KEN 9:01.86
8. Betlhem Desalegn UAE 9:03.30

60 Metres Hurdles (b-b)
1. Nia Ali USA 7.81
2. Brianna Rollins USA 7.82
3. Tiffany Porter GBR 7.90
4. Andrea Ivancevic CRO 7.95
5. Angela Whyte CAN 7.99
6. Alina Talay BLR 8.00
7. Serita Solomon GBR 8.29
8. Kendra Harrison USA 8.87

High Jump (d)
1. Vashti Cunningham USA-J 1.96
2. Ruth Beitia ESP 1.96
3. Kamila Licwinko POL 1.96
4. Airine Palsyté LTU 1.96
5= Levern Spencer LCA 1.93
5= Sofie Skoog SWE 1.93
7. Alessia Trost ITA 1.93
8. Erika Kinsey SWE 1.93

Pole Vault (a)
1. Jennifer Suhr USA 4.90*
2. Sandi Morris USA 4.85
3. Ekateríni Stefanídi GRE 4.80
4. Nicole Büchler SUI 4.80
5. Eliza McCartney NZL 4.70
6= Fabiana Murer BRA 4.60
6= Nikoléta Kiriakapoúlou GRE 4.60
8. Romana Malácová CZE 4.50

Long Jump (b
1. Brittney Reese USA 7.22*
2. Ivana Spanovic SRB 7.07
3. Lorraine Ugen GBR 6.93
4. Janay DeLoach USA 6.89
5. Brooke Stratton AUS 6.75
6. Alexandra Wester GER 6.67
7. Ksenija Balta EST 6.60
8. Shara Proctor GBR 6.57

Triple Jump (c)
1. Yulimar Rojas VEN 14.41
2. Kristin Gierisch GER 14.30
3. Paraskevi Papahrístou GRE 14.15
4. Keturah Orji USA 14.14
5. Elena Panturoiu ROU 14.11
6. Kristiina Mäkelä FIN 14.07
7. Jeanine Assani Issouf FRA 14.07
8. Shanieka Thomas JAM 13.95

Shot (c)
1. Michelle Carter USA 20.21
2. Anita Márton HUN 19.33
3. Valerie Adams NZL 19.25
4. Cleopatra Borel TTO 18.38
5. Jill Camerena-Williams USA 18.17
6. Radoslava Mavrodieva BUL 18.00
7. Lena Urbaniak GER 17.91
8. Gao Yang CHN 17.67

Pentathlon (b)
1. Brianne Theisen-Eaton CAN 4881
2. Anastasiya Mokhnyuk UKR 4847
3. Alla Fyodorova UKR 4770
4. Barbara Nwaba USA 4661
5. Gyula Zsivoczky-Farkas HUN 4656
6. Kendell Williams USA 4586
7. Morgan Lake GBR 4499
8. Katerina Cachová CZE 4403
9. Makeba Alcide LCA 4368
10. Georgia Ellenwood CAN 4324

4 x 400 Metres (d)
1. USA 3:26.38
N Hastings 51.89, Q Hayes 51.02, C Okolo 50.71, A Spencer 52.76
2. POL 3:31.15
E Ptak 54.6, M Holub 51.9, M Gorkowska 53.0, J Swiety 51.7
3. ROU 3:31.51
A Pastor 54.1, M Lavric 53.1, A Miklos 52.7, B Razor 51.6
4. NGR 3:34.03
5. UKR 3:40.42
dnf. JAM –

Leading Nations – Medals & Points

Nation	G	S	B	Points
USA	13	6	4	249
ETH	2	2	1	56
GBR	-	1	2	39
POL	-	1	2	33
JAM	1	1	1	32
FRA	1	1	2	30
GER	-	2	1	28
CHN	1	-	1	28
UKR	-	2	1	26
KEN	-	-	2	26
CZE	1	1	-	25.5
TTO	-	-	2	25
NZL	1	-	2	24
GRE	-	-	2	20.5
NED	1	1	-	20
CAN	1	-	-	18.5
ROU	-	1	1	17
QAT	-	1	-	16
BDI	1	1	-	15

13 nations won gold, 29 medals and 53 placed athletes in top 8.

ASIAN INDOOR CHAMPIONSHIPS 2016

February 19-21, Doha

Men: 60m: Hassan Taftian IRI 6.56*, 400m: Abdelilah Haroun QAT-J 45.88*, 800m: Abdelrahman Musaeb Balla QAT 1:46.92*, 1500m/3000m: Mohamed Al-Garni QAT 3:36.35*/ 7:39.23*, 60mh: Abdulaziz Al-Mandeel KUW 7.60* HJ: Mutaz Essa Barshim QAT 2.35, PV: Huang Bokai CHN 5.75*, LJ: Zhang Yaoguang CHN 7.99, TJ: Roman Valiyev KAZ 16.69, SP: Liu Yang CHJN 19.30, Hep: Akihiko Nakamura JPN 5831, 4x400m: QAT 3:08.20*. **Women**: 60m: Viktorita Zyabkina KAZ 7.27, 400m: Kemi Adekoya BRN 51.67*, 800m: Marta Hirpato BRN 2:04.59, 1500m/3000m: Betlhem Desalegn UAE 4:21.65/8:44.59, 60mh: Anastasiya Soprunova KAZ 8.17, HJ: Svetlana Radzivil UZB 1.92, PV: Li Ling CHN 4.70*, LJ: Mayookha Johny IND 6.35, TJ: Olga Rypakova 14.32*, SP: Geng Shuang CHN 18.06, Pen: Yekaterina Voronina KAZ 4224, 4x400m: BRN (Naser, Y Jamal, Essa, Adekoya) 3:35.07*. **Medal table**: QAT 6-1-3 (all men), CHN 5-5-2, KAZ 4-2-4, BRN 3-5-1, UZB 2-1-2, UAE 2-0-1, IRI 1-4-1, IND 1-3-3, JPN 1-1-3, KUW 1-1-0, 7 other nations won silver or bronze medals.

** Championship records*

OLYMPIC GAMES

THE FIRST Olympic Games of the modern era were staged in Athens, Greece from the 6th to 15th April 1896. Those in Rio de Janeiro, the Games of the XXXI Olympiad, will be the 28th to be staged, including the intercalated Games of 1906.

Just 59 athletes from ten nations contested the athletics events in 1896. In 2016 more than 10,500 sportsmen and women from the 206 National Olympic Committees (including Kosovo and South Sudan for the first time) are expected to compete at the 28 sport on the programme.

Olympic Games Records after 2012

Men

100m	9.63	Usain Bolt JAM 2012
200m	19.30	Usain Bolt JAM 2008
400m	43.49	Michael Johnson USA 1996
800m	1:40.91	David Rudisha KEN 2012
1500m	3:32.07	Noah Ngeny KEN 2000
5000m	12:57.82	Kenenisa Bekele ETH 2008
10000m	27:01.17	Kenenisa Bekele ETH 2008
Mar	2:06:32	Sammy Wanjiru KEN 2008
3000mSt	8:05.51	Julius Kariuki KEN 1988
110mh	12.91	Liu Xiang CHN 2004
400mh	46.78	Kevin Young USA 1992
HJ	2.39	Charles Austin USA 1996
PV	5.97	Renaud Lavillenie FRA 2012
LJ	8.90A	Bob Beamon USA 1968
TJ	18.17w	Mike Conley USA 1992
	18.09	Kenny Harrison USA 1996
SP	22.47	Ulf Timmermann GDR 1988
DT	69.89	Virgilijus Alekna LTU 2004
HT	84.80	Sergey Litvinov URS 1988
JT	90.57	Andreas Thorkildsen NOR 2008
old	94.58	Miklós Németh HUN 1976
Dec	8893	Román Sebrle CZE 2004
4x100m	36.84	Jamaica 2012
4x400m	2:55.39	USA 2008
20kmW	1:18:46	Chen Ding CHN 2012
50kmW	3:35:59	Sergey Kirdyapkin RUS 2012

Women

100m	10.62	Florence Griffith-Joyner USA 1988
	10.54w	Florence Griffith-Joyner USA 1988
200m	21.34	Florence Griffith-Joyner USA 1988
400m	48.25	Marie-José Pérec FRA 1996
800m	1:53.43	Nadezhda Olizarenko URS 1980
1500m	3:53.96	Paula Ivan ROU 1988
3000m	8:26.53	Tatyana Samolenko URS 1988
5000m	14:40.79	Gabriela Szabo ROU 2000
10000m	29:54.66	Tirunesh Dibaba ETH 2008
Mar	2:23:07	Tiki Gelana ETH 2012
3000mSt	8:58.81	Gulnara Galkina RUS 2008
100mh	12.35	Sally Pearson AUS 2012
400mh	52.64	Melaine Walker JAM 2008
HJ	2.06	Yelena Slesarenko RUS 2004
PV	5.05	Yelena Isinbayeva RUS 2008
LJ	7.40	Jackie Joyner-Kersee USA 1988
TJ	15.39	Françoise Mbango CMR 2008
SP	22.41	Ilona Slupianek GDR 1980
DT	72.30	Martina Hellmann GDR 1988
HT	78.18	Tatyana Lysenko RUS 2012
JT	71.53	Osleidys Menéndez CUB 2004
old	74.68	Petra Felke GDR 1988
Hep	7291	Jackie Joyner-Kersee USA 1988
4x100m	40.82	USA 2012
4x400m	3:15.17	USSR 1988
20kmW	1:25:02	Yelena Lashmanova RUS 2012

Most gold medals – all events

Men

10 Raymond Ewry USA StHJ and StLJ 1900-04-06-08, StTJ 1900-04

9 Paavo Nurmi FIN 1500m 1924, 5000m 1924, 10000m 1920-28, 3000mSt 1924, CC 1920-24, CC team 1920-24

9 Carl Lewis USA 100m, 200m, LJ & 4x100mR 1984; 100m, LJ 1988; LJ, 4x100mR 1992; LJ 1996

6 Usain Bolt JAM 100m, 200m & 4x100m 2008 & 2012

5 Martin Sheridan USA DT 1904-06-08, SP 1906, DT Greek style 1908

5 Ville Ritola FIN 10000m, 3000mSt, CC team & 3000m team 1924, 5000m 1928

5 Michael Johnson USA 200m 1996, 400m 1996-2000, 4x400m 1992-2000

4 thirteen men

Women

4 Fanny Blankers-Koen NED 100m, 200m, 80mh & 4x100mR 1948

4 Betty Cuthbert AUS 100m, 200m, 4x100mR 1956, 400m 1964

4 Bärbel Eckert/Wöckel GDR 200m & 4x100mR 1976-80

4 Evelyn Ashford USA 100m 1984, 4x100mR 1984-88-92

4 Allyson Felix USA 4x400m 2008, 200m, 4x100m & 4x400m 2012

Most medals – all events

G gold, S silver, B bronze

Men

12 Paavo Nurmi FIN 9G as above; 3S 5000m 1920-28, 3000mSt 1928

10 Raymond Ewry USA 10G as above

10 Carl Lewis USA 9G as above; 1S 200m 1988

9 Martin Sheridan USA 5G as above; 3S StHJ, StLJ & Stone 1906; 1B StLJ 1908

8 Ville Ritola FIN 5G as above; 3S 5000m & CC 1924, 10000m 1928

7 Eric Lemming SWE 4G JT 1906-08-12 freestyle 1908, 3B SP, Pen, Tug of War 1906

Women

9 Merlene Ottey JAM 3S 100m, 200m 1996; 4x100mR 1980; 6B 1996; 100m 1984, 2000; 200m 1980, 1984, 1992

7 Shirley Strickland/de la Hunty AUS 3G 80mh 1952-56, 4x100mR 1956; 1S 4x100mR 1948; 3B 100m 1948-52, 80mh 1948 (later evidence showed that she should also have been awarded the 1948 200m bronze)
7 Irena Kirszenstein/Szewinska POL 3G 200m 1968, 400m 1976, 4x100mR 1964; 2S 200m & LJ 1964, 2B 100m 1968, 200m 1972

Most gold medals at one Games: Men: 5 Paavo Nurmi FIN 1924; Women: 4 Fanny Blankers-Koen NED *as above*

Most medals at one Games: Men: 6 – 4 gold, 2 silver – Ville Ritola FIN 1924; Women: 4 – 4 gold Fanny Blankers-Koen NED *as above*, 4 – 3 gold, 1 silver – Florence Griffith-Joyner USA 1988.

Note 5 – 3 gold, 2 bronze – Marion Jones 2000 lost through subsequent drugs disqualification.

Most Games contested

7 Merlene Ottey JAM/SLO 1980-2004 at women's 100m/200m/4x100m
6 seven athletes

Most finals or first eight at the same event

6 Lia Manoliu ROU W DT 1952-72: 6-9-3-3-1-9
5 Vladimir Golubnichiy URS 20kmW 1960-76: 1-3-1-2-7
5 Jan Zelezny CZE JT 1988-2004: 2-1-1-1-9
5 Maria Mutola MOZ W 800m: 1992-2008 5-3-1-4-5

Medal table of leading nations 1896-2012

including 1906 Games

Nat	*G*	*S*	*B*	*Mdls*
USA	331	255	202	788
USSR/CIS	71	66	77	214
United Kingdom	56	84	63	203
Germany *	32	57	63	152
Finland	49	35	32	116
GDR	38	36	35	109
Sweden	1	25	46	92
Kenya	24	31	24	79
Russia	26	26	26	78
Australia	20	26	27	73
Jamaica	17	30	19	66
France	14	23	25	62
Italy	19	15	26	60
Canada	14	15	26	55
Poland	23	18	13	54
Ethiopia	21	7	17	45
Hungary	11	15	18	44
Cuba	10	14	16	40
Romania	11	14	10	35
Greece	7	14	14	35
Czechoslovakia	11	8	5	24
South Africa	6	12	6	24
Japan	7	7	9	23
China	6	4	11	21
New Zealand	10	2	8	20
Norway	7	5	8	20
Morocco	6	5	8	19
Belarus	4	6	9	19
Bulgaria	5	7	6	18
Ukraine	3	3	12	18
Netherlands	6	3	6	15
Brazil	4	3	7	14
Trinidad & Tobago	2	4	8	14
Nigeria	2	3	8	13
Belgium	3	7	2	12
Spain	2	4	5	11
Portugal	4	2	4	10
Mexico	3	5	2	10

Subject to changes with possible pending drugs disqualifcations

In all 94 nations have won medals at track and field events

* Germany 1896-1952 and from 1992, Federal Republic of Germany 1956-88. Medals won by the combined German teams of 1956, 1960 and 1964 have been allocated to FRG or GDR according to the athlete's origin.

Jamaica also one bronze for British West Indies Federation

Oldests – Men

Winner	42y 23d	Pat McDonald USA 56lb Wt 1920
Medallist	48y 195d	Matt McGrath USA 1924
Competitor	52y 199d	Percy Wyer CAN Mar 1936

Oldests – Women

Winner	39y 315d	Ellina Zvereva BLR DT 2000
Medallist	40y 143d	Merlene Ottey JAM 4x100mR 2000
Competitor	48y 234d	Lourdes Klitzkie GUM 63rd Mar 1988

Youngests – Men

Winner	17y 263d	Bob Mathias USA Dec 1948
Medallist	17y 169d	Frank Castleman USA 2nd 200mh 1904
	17y 206d	Pál Simon HUN 3rd Medley relay 1908
	born 1891, but exact date unknown, 17-206 is oldest possible	
Ind. medal	17y 263d	Bob Mathias as above

Youngests – Women

Winner	15y 123d	Barbara Pearl Jones USA 4x100mR 1952
Ind.winner	16y 123d	Ulrike Meyfarth FRG HJ 1972
Medallist	15y 123d	Barbara Pearl Jones as above
Ind. medal	16y 115d	Dorothy Odam GBR 2nd HJ 1936

y – years, d – days

OLYMPIC QUALIFYING STANDARDS 2016

Event	Men	Women
100m	10.16	11.32
200m	20.50	23.20
400m	45.40	52.20
800m	1:46.00	2:01.50
1500m	3:36.20	4:07.00
5000m	13:25.00	15:24.00
10,000m	28:00.00	32:15.00
Mar	2:19:00	2:45:00
3000mSt	8:30.00	9:45:00
110/100mh	13.00	13.47
400mh	49.40	56.20
HJ	2.29	1.93
PV	5.70	4.50
LJ	8.15	6.70
TJ	16.85	14.15
SP	20.50	17.75
DT	65.00	61.00
HT	77.00	71.00
JT	83.00	62.00
Dec/Hep	8100	6200
20kmW	1:24:00	1:36:00
50kmW	4:06:00	–

Relays: top 8 at 2015 World Relays + 8 from top lists

Qualification period for 10,000m, marathon, walks & combined events is 1 Jan 2015 to 11 Jul 2016; for all other events it is 1 May 2015 to 11 Jul 2016.

OLYMPIC TIMETABLE 2016

Dates are given in final columns for days in August for each round (p preliminary round, h heats, s semi-finals, F final Q qualifying)

Event	*Men*	*Women*
100 Metres	p, h 13; s, F 14	p, h 12; s, F 13
200 Metres	h 16, s 17, F 18	h 15, s 16
400 Metres	h 12, s 13, F 14	h 13, s 14, F 15
800 Metres	h 12, s 13, F 15	h 17, s 18, F 20
1500 Metres	h 16, s 18, F 20	h 12, s 14, F 16
5000 Metres	h 17, F 20	h 16, F 19
10,000 Metres	13	F 12
Marathon	21	14
3000m Steeple	h 15, F 17	h 13, F 15
110/100m Hurdles	h 15, s, F 16	h 16. s, F 17
400m Hurdles	h 15, s 16, F 18	h 15, s 16, F 18
High Jump	Q 14, F 16	Q 18, F 20
Pole Vault	Q 13, F 15	Q 16, F 19
Long Jump	Q 12, F 13	Q 16, F 17
Triple Jump	Q 15, F 16	Q 13, F 14
Shot	Q, F 18	Q, F 12
Discus	Q 12, F 13	Q 15, F 16
Hammer	Q 17, F 19	Q 12, F 15
Javelin	Q 17	Q 16, F 18
Decathlon/Heptathlon	17/18	12/13
20 Km Walk	12	19
50 Km Walk	19	
4x100m Relay	h 18, F 19	h 18, F 19
4x400m Relay	h 19, F 20	h 19, F 20

World Junior Championships

THE 16th IAAF World Junior Championships will be staged at Bydgoszcz, Poland on 19-24 July 2016. They were first held in Athens, Greece in 1986 and have been held every two years since then.

Championship bests after 2014

Men

100m	10.05	Adam Gemili GBR	2012
200m	20.28	Andrew Howe ITA	2004
	20.04w	Trentavis Friday USA	2014
400m	44.66	Hamdam Al-Bishi KSA	2000
800m	1:43.79	Nijel Amos BOT	2012
1500m	3:35.53	Abdelati Iguider MAR	2004
5000m	13:08.57	Abreham Cherkos ETH	2008
10000m	27:30.85	Josphat Bett KEN	2008
3000mSt	8:06.10	Conseslus Kiprono KEN	2012
110mh (3'3")	12.99	Wilhem Belocian FRA	2015
400mh	48.51	Kerron Clement USA	2004
HJ	2.37	Dragutin Topic YUG	1990
	2.37	Steve Smith GBR	1992
PV	5.71	Germán Chiaraviglio ARG	2006
LJ	8.20	James Stallworth USA q	1990
TJ	17.13	Lázaro Martínez CUB	2014
	17.31w	Teddy Tamgho FRA	2008
SP 6kg	22.20	Jacko Gill NZL	2012
DT 1.75kg	67.32	Margus Hunt EST	2006
HT 6kg	85.97	Ashraf Amjad El-Seify QAT	2012
JT	83.07	Robert Oosthuizen RSA	2006
Dec jnr	8135	Jirí Sykora CZE	2014
10kmW	39:35.01	Stanislav Yemelyanov URS	2008
4x100mR	38.66	USA	2004
		(Trell Kimmons, Demi Omole, Ivory Williams, LaShawn Merritt)	
4x400mR	3:01.09	USA	2004
		(Brandon Johnson, LaShawn Merritt, Jason Craig, Kerron Clement)	

Women

100m	11.12	Veronica Campbell JAM	2000
200m	22.53	Anthonique Strachan BAH	2012
400m	50.50	Ashley Spencer USA	2012
800m	2:00.06	Elena Mirela Lavric ROU	2008
1500m	4:04.96	Faith Kipyegon KEN	2012
3000m	8:46.86	Zhang Linli CHN	1992
5000m	15:08.06	Genzebe Dibaba ETH	2010
3000mSt	9:31.35	Christien Muyanga KEN	2008
100mh	12.89	Kendell Williams USA	2014
	12.81w	Anay Tejeda CUB	2002
400mh	54.70	Lashinda Demus USA	2002
HJ	2.00	Galina Astafei ROU	1988
PV	4.50	Angelica Bengtsson SWE	2012
	4.50	Alyona Lutkovskaya RUS	2014
LJ	6.82 &		
	6.88w	Fiona May GBR	1988
TJ	14.62	Tereza Marinova BUL	1996
SP	18.76	Cheng Xiaoyan CHN	1994
DT	68.24	Ilke Wyludda GDR	1988
HT	70.62	Alexandra Tavernier FRA	2012
JT (new)	63.01	Vira Rebryk UKR	2008
Hep	6470	Carolina Klüft SWE	2002
10kmW	42:47.25	Anezka Drahotová CZE	2014
4x100mR	43.40	Jamaica	2002
	(Sherone Simpson, Kerron Stewart, Annesisha McLaughlin, Simone Facey)		
4x400mR	3:27.60	USA	2004
	(Alexandria Anderson, Stephanie Smith, Ashlee Kidd, Natasha Hastings)		

Events no longer contested

Most gold medals

Men: 4 Chris Nelloms USA 4x400mR 1988, 400m, 4x100mR & 4x400mR 1990

Women: 4 Gillian Russell JAM 100mh & 4x100mR 1990 & 1992

Most medals: 5 Katrin Krabbe GDR 3rd 200m, 2nd 4x100mR 1986; 1st 200m & 4x100mR, 2nd 100m 1988

Youngest champions

Men	15y 183d	Jacko Gill NZL SP 2010
	15y 332d	Usain Bolt JAM 200m 2002
Women	15y 102d	Wang Yan CHN 5kmW 1986
	15y 169d	Ann Mwangi KEN 3000m 1988
	15y 196d	Susana Feitor POR 5kmW 1990
	15y 245d	Diane Smith GBR 200m 1990

Youngest medalists

Men	15y 169d	Ismael Kirui KEN 2nd 10,000m 1990
	15y 183d	Jacko Gill NZL 1st SP 2010
Women	14y 182d	Sally Barsosio KEN 3rd 10,000m 1992
	14y 279d	Jackline Maranga KEN 2nd 1500m 1992

Miscellany

Who is the **oldest ever Olympic athletics medallist**? It had long been thought to be Britain's Tebbs Lloyd-Johnson, who was third in the 1948 50k walk at the age of 48 years and 120 days. However, research by Tom Hunt discovered from the relevant birth certificate that Irish-born Matt McGrath (USA) was born on 28 Dec 1875 rather than the previously quoted 18 Dec 1877 or 1878. The Dictionary of Irish Biography confirms he was born in 1875. So he replaces Lloyd-Johnson as the oldest medallist, being 48 years and 195 days when placing second in the hammer at the 1924 Games.

The **greatest dominance** by individuals in 2015 were by the Polish hammer throwers. Anita Wlodarczyk had the top eight women's performances of the year and, including all in a series had the best 21 throws of the year plus another four in the irregular competition at Wroclaw (ahead of the next best, 76.33 by Zhang Wenxiu). She put six marks into the all-time top 30 performances so that she now has 15 of these, and with ancillary marks now has 30 of the 46 throws over 77.50 (including the top four). Pawel Fajdek had the top 13 performances from 80.06 to 83.93 and the best 24 throws (23 over 80m ahead of the next best Krisztían Pars 79.91). He had less impact on the all-time list, however, as his Polish record 83.93 made him tenth.

Renaud Lavillenie matched Wlodarczyk in having the top eight pole vault performances of the year(5.95 to 6.05). Next on the list of athletes who dominated in 2015 world lists were: Men: Justin Gatlin five at 100m, Women: Christina Schwanitz four at shot.

Shawn Barber became, on 15 January 2016, the 16th man to pole vault 6 metres. The most seasons at 6m plus: 13 Sergey Bubka 1985-97, 6 Renaud Lavillenie 2009, 2011, 2013-16; 4 Jeff Hartwig 1998-2000, 2002; 3 Rodion Gataullin 1989, 1993-4; Steve Hooker 2008-10; 2 Maksim Tarasov & Tim Lobinger 1997, 1999; Dmitriy Markov 1998, 2001; Brad Walker 2006-08.

Father/daughter pole vault record**. Demi Payne 4.90i in 2016, her father, Bill Payne** 5.86 in 1991 for a combined height of 10.61m. Previous best 10.32 by Aleksandr (5.82) and Liz (4.50) Parnov. Then 10.23 by Jan (5.50) and Chesea (4.73) Johnson.

Junior and Master over-40 world records. In 2015 Susana Feitor (Portugal) set women's over-40 world records at 10,000m and 20km walk. The super longevity of her career is shown by the fact that she had set a world junior best for 50000m (21:01.8 in 1993). This matched the achievement of Dragutin Topic (Serbia) at high jump, with a world junior record 2.37 in 1990 and six world over-40 records 2011 to 2.28 in 2012.

OBITUARY 2015

See ATHLETICS 2015 for obituaries from early 2015: Margaret ARNOLD, Dmitriy BAGRYANOV, Daundre BARNABY, Gordon DICKSON, Shane DONNELLY, Jim DUNAWAY, Evelyn FURTSCH, Benny GARCIA, Harry GORDON, Jack HEYWOOD, Jim HOGAN, Patrick JOURNOUD, Jaroslav KOVÁR, Vänoö KUISMA, Esko LIPSONEN, Franjo MIHALIC, Oleg SAKIRKIN, Gustav SCHWENK, Eino SIMELIUS, Lang STANLEY, Charlie THOMAS, Dan TUNSTALL PEDOE, Markku TUOKKO, Klaus ULONSKA, Gerda VAN DER KADE-KOUDIJS.

James Dudley **'Jim' ACHURCH** (Australia) (b. 21 Jan 1928) on 5 November in Nambour, Queensland. A javelin thrower, he won the 1954 Empire Games title, was Australian champion in 1953-4, and competed (dnq 21) at the 1956 Olympic Games. He set four AUS records from 62.51 (1953) to 68.93 (1956).

Frank BAILEY (GBR) (b. 14 Apr 1928) in November. His one walks international was when he was 6th at 50k walk at the 1954 European Championships. RWA 50k champion 1953. Polytechnic Harriers. Pb 4:39:51 (1954).

Theodosios 'Sakli' BALAFAS (Greece) (b. 27 Aug 1923 Kardista) on 6 April in West Kendall, Florida, USA. He competed at pole vault at the Olympic Games of 1948 (dnq 14=) and 1952 (17th); pb 4.10 (1952). He was a notable tennis coach in Miami, where he lived from 1965.

Yuliya Vladimirova **BALYKINA** (Ukraine/ Belarus) (b. 12 Apr 1984 Bulgan, Mongolia) was murdered in Minsk on 28 October. Having switched from Ukraine to Belarus on 2 Jan 2008, she competed at 100m and 4x100m at the 2012 Olympics and that year set her pbs of 60m 7.24i, 100m 11.38/11.32w and 200m 23.64. At the European Champs she was a finalist at 4x100m in 2010 and 2012 and a semi-finalist at 100m in 2012. BLR champion 100m 2011-12 and 200m 2011. She failed a drugs test on 11 June 2013 and served a 2-year ban to 24 July 2015.

Cameron BEAN (USA) (b. 17 Dec 1986) after being struck by a car while out running on September 19 in Chattanooga. 3000m steeplechase pb 8:32.57 (2013).

Betty BEAZLEY (née Judge) (Australia) (b. 21 Mar 1921) on 13 September. She set Australian 880y records at 2:24.7 in 1940 and 2:24.2 in 1947 and was Australian champion (and 2nd at 440y) in 1940. Pb 440y 60.1 (1940). She later coached and was president 1948-52 of the Australian Women's Amateur Athletic Union. Her husband Kim Beazley was minister of education in Australia and their son was the country's deputy prime minister in 1995-6 and later Australia's ambassador to the USA.

Sven **Gösta BERGKVIST** (Sweden) (b. 29 Mar 1920 Sågmyra, Bjursås) on 5 October in Gävle. At 1500m he was 5th at the 1948 Olympic Games and 3rd on the world list in 1947-8. He ran for Sweden 'B' in 1939 and competed for the Nordic countries combined team in 1947 and 1949. At Swedish Championships he was 3rd at 1500m in 1947 and 1949 and won the 4k cross-country in 1947-8. Pbs: 400m 49.5 (1941), 800m 1:52.2 (1946), 1000m 2:24.1 (1949), 1500m 3:46.6 (1947), 1M 4:05.8 (1949), 2000m 5:16.0 (1947). He ran on his club team Gefle IF that set world records for 4x1500m 1947 and 1949 and 4x1M 1949 and two Swedish records at 4x800m.

Patrick BOURBEILLON (France) (b. 24 Mar 1943 Angers) on 13 July in Leon. He ran on French 4x100m teams that won the 1969 European 4x100m and was 7th at the 1972 Olympics. 16 internationals 1967-72. Pbs: 50m 5.84i (1972), 60m 6.6i (1970), 100m 10.45 (1969), 10.2 (1971), 200m 21.0/21.50 (1971), 20.9w (1972). National sprint coach.

Esther Cornelia **BRAND** (South Africa) (b. 29 Sep 1924 Springbok, Northern Cape; née van Heerden) on 20 June in Bloemfontein. She won the Olympic gold medal at high jump in 1952 (and dnq 20 discus). She had set four national records from 1.61 in 1939 to topping the year lists with 1.65 in 1940 and 1.66 in 1941 (later recognized as a world record) and improved that to 1.67 when she won in Helsinki. She also set a South African discus record with 38.74 in 1950 and was RSA champion at high jump in 1938-40, 1946-9 and 1951-2 and discus 1946 and 1949.

Annual progression at HJ: 1938- 1.57, 1939- 1.61, 1940- 1.65, 1941- 1.66, 1945- 1.50, 1946- 1.54, 1947- 1.53, 1948- 1.55, 1949- 1.53, 1951- 1.635, 1952- 1.67. Pbs: SP 12.03 (1952), DT 40.30 (1952).

Sharon Marie **CALLAHAN** (later McKNIFF) (USA) (b. 25 Mar 1952 Whittier, California) on 30 April. Having won the 1968 US Olympic Trials at high jump while still at high school with a pb of 1.71 and 3rd at the US Champs, she did not qualify for the Olympic final. She married basketball player John McKniff.

Henry William **CARR** (USA) (b. 27 Nov 1942 Montgomery, Alabama) on 29 May in Griffin, Georgia. The powerful, smooth-running Carr was Olympic champion at 200m, winning by two clear metres, and at 4 x 400m relay in 1964. He set world records at 220 yards, 20.4 and 20.3 in 1963, improving to 20.2 in 1964, when his time to win the Olympic title was 20.36, a record on automatic timing. He showed that he could have been one of the greatest 400m athletes of all-time, running the anchor leg of the US team's world record of 3:00.5 in Tokyo 1964 in 44.5, and the previous year he had helped the Arizona State University team set a world record at 4 x 440 yards. However, he ran the individual event only rarely, with a best time of 45.4 in 1963, as didn't need to stretch himself when he was supreme at half a lap, at which he was AAU champion in 1963 (when he tied with Paul Drayton) and 1964, and NCAA champion in 1963. He played American football with limited success 1965-7 with the New York Giants and Detroit Lions.

Annual progression at 100y/100m, 200m/220ySt, 400m: 1959- 9.7, 21.0ySt; 1960- 9.6, 20.6ySt; 48.0*; 1961- 9.5/9.4w, 20.6/20.0wySt, 47.5*; 1962- 9.4, 10.3, 20.1ySt; 1963- 9.3, 10.3/10.0w, 20.2*t, 45.4; 1964- 9.3/10.2, 20.1*, 45.6.

Ronald William **CLARKE** (Australia) (b. 21 Feb 1937 Melbourne) on 17 June in Gold Coast. The hero of a generation of distance runners, Clarke didn't just break records but took them into entirely new territory. When he won the 1965 AAA 3 miles he took his own record from 13:00.4 to 12:52.4 and in Oslo four days later he smashed his month-old time for 10,000m of 28:14.0 with 27:39.4. In a dazzling month and a half in June and July of that glorious summer of 1965 he set eight world records (of 19 in his complete career, 17 of which were ratified), as in company with Michel Jazy (mile, 3000m, 2M) and Kip Keino (3000m) distance running records were comprehensively revised. Sadly however Clarke didn't win a major championship gold medal, though he did own one, as, in one of the most heart-warming stories in the world of sport, the great Emil Zátopek gave him one of his.

Clarke set a world junior 1 mile record with 4:06.8 in 1956 and at the end of that year carried the Olympic torch into the stadium in Melbourne, but slipped into obscurity before returning in 1961 and setting his first world records in 1963. He was Australian champion at 3 miles/5000m 1965-9, 6 miles 1966, 10,000m 1969-70 and cross-country 1963. In part Clarke's finishing kick let him down, but he was also cruelly deprived at his peak of Olympic glory due to the 1968 Games being held at the high altitude of Mexico City. It seems inconceivable that he would not have run away from his rivals at sea-level (as he had shown with 27:49.4 at Crystal Palace, London in August, 15 seconds faster than anyone else that year), but he ran himself into collapse with 6th at 10,000m and 5th at 5000m. A big man at 1.83m/72kg, he had won the Olympic bronze at 10,000m in

Ron Clarke's annual progression

	1500m	1M	3000m	2M	3M	5000m	6M	10000m
1953		4:31.1						
1954		4:27.2						
1955	3:55.6	4:19.4	8:54.5	9:17.8				
1956	3:48.2	4:06.8	8:58.8	8:56.2				
1957	3:49.6	4:07.2			14:01.6			
1958		4:08.1						
1960					14:22.6			
1961		4:14.0				14:23.0		30:36.0
1962		4:13.4		8:50.2	13:31.4	14:11.6	28:11.6	29:53.0
1963		4:03.4	8:00.0	8:35.2	13:27.5	13:51.6	27:17.6	28:15.6
1964	3:50.6	4:07.1	8:02.6		13:07.6	13:39.0	27:27.0	28:25.8
1965 (.89)		4:04.2	7:51.0	8:24.9	12:52.4	13:25.8	26:47.0	27:39.4
1966	3:47.9	4:02.0	7:51.8		12:50.4	13:16.6	26:52.0	27:54.0
1967	3:45.8	4:03.1	7:47.2	8:19.8	12:54.8	13:18.8	27:21.0	
1968	3:44.1	4:00.2	7:48.2	8:19.6	13:01.6	13:27.8	26:57.2	27:49.4
1969		4:04.0	7:53.8	8:30.0	13:08.0	13:33.8	27:09.6	28:03.6
1970		4:12.0	8:02.8	8:38.8	13:19.2	13:32.4	27:20.0	28:13.45

1964, when also 9th at 5000m and marathon, and won Commonwealth silvers at 3 miles in 1962 (dnf 6 miles), both 3 and 6 miles 1966, and 10,000m 1970 (5th 5000m). He later had serious heart surgery, which he always felt was attributable to excess strain at high altitude. He was a successful businessman and served as Mayor of the Gold Coast 2004-12, which will be the venue for the 2018 Commonwealth Games. It was there that he helped develop the idyllic Runaway Bay Training Centre. He was appointed MBE in 1966 for services to athletics and in 2013 was made an Officer of the Order of Australia for his distinguished service to the community.

Clarke's bests at his world record distances: 2 miles 8:19.6 (1968), 3 miles 12:50.4 (1966), 5000m 13:16.6 (1966), 6 miles 26:47.0 (1965), 10,000m 27:39.4 (1965), 10 miles 47:12.8 (1965), 20km 59:22.8 (1965), 1 hour 20,232m (1965). Other bests: 1500m 3:44.1 (1968), 1M 4:00.2 (1968), 3000m 7:47.2 (1967), 15km 44:13.0 (1965), 30km 1:34:35.0 (1966), Marathon 2:20:27 (1964).

His elder brother Jack was a top Australian Rules footballer.

Imre DEÁK NAGY (Hungary) (b. 1 Nov 1955, Hódmezövásárhely), on 30 July in Gödöllö. He took part at the World University Games in 1977 (800m and 1500m heats), was Hungarian champion at 1500m in 1981 and had 7 internationals 1974-82. Pbs: 400m 49.3 (1973), 800m 1:48.4 (1978), 1000m 2:22.0 (1978), 1500m 3:38.66 (1981), 1M 4:00.84 (1981), 2000m 5:07.3 (1979), 3000m 8:07.6 (1979), 5000m 14:53.1 (1980). His son Marcell Deák Nagy is the HUN 400m record holder (45.42), EJ and WUG champion in 2011, 2nd EC 2012.

Eddy DE LEEUW (Belgium) (b. 16 Jun 1956 Bambrugge) on 26 November in Asse. He competed at 400m and 4x100m at the 1980 Olympics (qf) and 1978 Europeans (sf) and was Belgian 400m champion in 1980. Pbs: 100m 10.6 (1978), 200m 21.42/21.2 (1979), 400m 46.10 (1981), 400mh 55.9 (1978).

Jacques DEGATS (France) (b. 20 Sep 1930 Vendrest) on 20 March in St-Pierre-les-Nemours. At 4x400m he was European champion in 1954 and 6th at the 1956 Olympics. At 400m: qf 1952 and 1956 Olympics, dq final of 1954 Europeans; French champion 1951, 1954 and 1957 and 34 internationals. He set French records with 47.5 (1952) and 47.3 (1955). Other pbs: 100m 10.9 (1959), 10.6w (1957); 200m 21.8 (1955).

Ronald DESRUELLLES (Belgium) (b. 14 Feb 1955 Louvain) on 1 November; he committed suicide at his apartment at Patong in Thailand. He won the World Indoor long jump bronze in 1985 and five medals at the European Indoor Championships: 60m: gold in 1986, silver in 1988 and bronze in 1984-5; long jump: silver in 1978. However, after winning the 1980 European Indoor LJ he was disqualified on a positive drugs test, and he also a failed a drugs test for amphetamines at the 1991 Belgian indoors. He competed at the long jump without qualifying for the final at the 1976 Olympics and 1978 and 1982 Europeans, and at 100m was a quarter-finalist at the 1984 Olympics and 1987 Worlds, and at the European 100m 1978-heat, 1986- sf. He set Belgian records outdoors at 100m 10.25 (1984) plus 10.02 with a doubtful wind reading in 1985 and a hand-timed 9.9 in 1978, 200m 20.66 (1984) plus 20.5w (1985), LJ (7 records) from 7.79 (1976) to 8.08 (1979). Other pbs: 400m 49.0 (1984), HJ 2.02 (1982), PV 4.10 (1974), LJ 8.08 (1979), Dec 7217 (1984). Indoor record 60m to 6.56 (1988).

His brother Patrick set 13 Belgian pole vault records from 5.00 (1977) to 5.60 (1981).

Marianne DICKERSON (USA) (b. 4 Nov 1960 St. Joseph, Illinois) on 14 October. A graduate of the University of Illinois and later of the Harvard Business School, in her third marathon she won the silver medal at marathon at the 1983 Worlds in a personal best time of 2:31:09, but did not break 2:40 again after that year. Other pbs: 1500m 4:38.4i (1980), 1M 4:51.3i (1981), 3000m 10:07.18 (1981), 2M 10:23.7i (1982), 3M 15:43.26i (1983), 5000m 16:17.22i (1983), 10,000m 34:39.0 (1982).

Erich DRECHSLER (GDR/Germany) (b. 30 Jun 1934 Achtern) on 1 October. A former German long jump coach, he was the father-in-law of Heike Drechsler. Pb DT 38.67 (1957).

Patricia De Glas, née **DUGGAN** (Australia) (b. 10 Dec 1937 Rockhampton, Queensland) on 29 June. She reached the quarter-final of the 100m, 4th in her heat of the 200m and was a member of the 4x100m relay that was disqualified in the heats at the 1960 Olympics, but that year ranked 3rd in the world at 200m with her pb 23.4 for 220y, set pbs of 10.6 for 100y and 11.5/11.4w for 100m and was Australian champion at 100y.

Valentin DZHONEV (Bulgaria) (b. 20 Jun 1952 Kyustendil) on 12 September. At the javelin (old) he set four Bulgarian records from 81.50 (1974) to 84.00 (1976), was 15th in the 1976 Olympics and 3rd at the 1977 World University Games. He was Balkan champion in 1975 and 1977 and Bulgarian in 1974, 1976, 1978 and 1980.

Norman EDWARDS (Jamaica) (b. 24 Sep 1962 Jamaica) on 13 July in Washington DC. A semi-finalist at 100m, he ran in the heats for the Jamaican team that went on to win the silver medal at 4x100m at the 1984 Olympic Games. He had dual citizenship with the USA and had pbs: 100m 10.21 (1984), 10.16w (1985); 200m

20.90/20.76w (1986). He ran for the University of Georgia and later worked in the financial industry.

Ayo FALOLA (GBR) (b. 29 Jul 1968) in December. He was a highly popular, respected and most successful coach, notably of top women including Donna Fraser, Jo Fenn, Montell Douglas and most recently Shalayna Oskan-Clarke as well as paralympian Danny Crates. A sprinter with Woodford Green he set pbs of 60m 6.82i (1995), 100m 10.50 and 10.3w (1995), 200m 21.15 (1991), 20.93w (1995), 110mh 14.80 (1997), 400mh 53.94 (1998).

Ralph James **FESSENDEN** (USA) (b. Oct 1932) on 4 October in Missoula, Montana. In 1954 he was 4th in the US 440y in 47.4 while at the University of Illinois and improved to 47.3 in 1955. He taught chemistry at the University of Montana.

Olga FOMENKOVÁ- KREJCI (Czech Republic) (b. 17 Nov 1936 Prague) on 16 December in Horw, Switzerland. She set a Czechoslovak record for 400m of 57.2 (1960) and was champion at long jump 1961 and pentathlon 1959-63. Ten internationals 1958-66 with 11th European Champs pentathlon in 1966. She emigrated with husband Josef to Switzerland in August 1968.

Ljubica **'Gabre' GABRIC- CALVESI** (Italy) (b. 14 Oct 1917 Imotski, Croatia) on 16 December in Brescia. Born in what was then Austria-Hungary, she lived in Chicago in the USA for several years before returning to Zadar, now Croatia, but then Italy, for whom she competed at discus at the Olympic Games of 1936 (10th) and 1948 (17th). She was 6th in 1938 and 7th in 1950 at the Europeans, was Italian champion 1937, 1939-40 and 1942, and set nine Italian records from 37.57 (1936) to 43.35 (1939); 22 internationals 1936-52. Pb SP 12.40 (1942). She won many World and European Masters titles at throwing events up to being a world record-setter in the W95 age group. She married hurdler Sandro Calvesi, and their daughter Lyana married Eddy Ottoz.

Régis GHESQUIÈRE (Belgium) (b. 15 Jul 1949 Mouscron) on 21 April in Mouscron. At decathlon he was 11th in 1972 and dnf 1976 at the Olympics and 20th in 1971 and 10th in 1974 at the Europeans; he was Belgian champion 1972, 1974-5 and 1979. Pb 7905/7765 (1984 tables) (1973).

Michiko **'Miki' GORMAN** (USA) (née Suwa, b. 9 Aug 1935 China to Japanese parents) on 19 September in Bellingham, Washington. A pioneer of women's marathon running, she set a world best with 2:46:36 at Culver City on 2 Dec 1973, improving her best to 2:39:11 to win in New York City in 1976, then the second fastest-ever time, when the race went through the city's five boroughs for the first time. She was also first woman at Boston in 1974 and 1977, Culver City in 1975 and New York again in 1977. She had moved to the USA in 1963 at the age of 28 and married businessman Michael Gorman. Taking up running, she was coached by László Tábori in Los Angeles.

Stevan GROMILOVIC (Serbia) (b. 29 Apr 1942 Sombor) on 11 January in Sombor. Hammer thrower with 12 internationals for Yugoslavia and nine times national championship runner-up. Pb 66.26 (1972).

George James **GUIDA** (USA) (b. 29 Aug 1922 Philadelphia) on 7 September in San Francisco. Despite having missed most of the season through injury, he was a surprise third placer in the US Olympic Trials 400m in 1948 and was 6th at the Games. He served in the Navy in WW II and studied at Villanova University, winning the AAU indoor 600y, IC4A 440y and 4th in the NCAA 220y in 1947, and at AAU Championships was 3rd at 200m straight in 1943 (in 20.7w), 200m turn in 1945 and at 400m in 1947. Pbs: 100y 9.8 (1945), 200mSt 20.9 (1943), 220yt 21.4 (1949), 440y 47.2 (1949).

GUO Jie (China) (b. 16 Jan 1912 Dalian) in Xi'an on 15 November at the age of 103, making him, it is thought, the longest lived of all athletics Olympians. In 1936 he set a Chinese discus record of 41.13 and competed at the Olympic Games.

Linda HAGLUND (Sweden) (b. 15 Jun 1956 Enskede) in Stockholm on 21 November. Competing for Hanvikens SK throughout her career, she set seven Swedish records at 100m from a hand-timed 11.4 in 1975 to 11.16 with which she was 4th at the 1980 Olympic Games in Moscow, and seven at 200m from 23.47 in 1974 to 22.82 in 1979 as well as indoor bests of 6.17 for 50m and 7.13 for 60m in 1978 and 1981. All these are still standing as national records. She made her Olympic debut in 1972 at the age of 16 at 100m and 4x100m and also competed at 100m in 1976. At the European Indoor Champs at 60m she won in 1976, was 2nd in 1978 and 1980 and 5th in 1979 with a third silver medal at 50m in 1981. After being a 100m semi-finalist in 1974 she won the silver medal at 100m and was 7th at 200m in 1978 at the Europeans and helped the European team to win the 4x100m at the 1979 World Cup. Swedish champion 100m 1974-9 and 1981, 200m 1975-9, and 60m indoors 1972-4, 1976, 1978-9, 1981. She retired in 1984 but made a one-meet comeback in 1989, including LJ pb 5.60. She received an 18-month ban from a positive drugs test at the Swedish Championships on 9 Aug 1981 and was disqualified from the 200m that she had won. She thus also 'lost' the 11.06w for 100m that she ran later that month (having posted a 11.08w earlier that year). She married Houston McTear (qv). Her autobiography *Linda's Journey* was published in 2013.

Annual progression at 100m, 200m: 1970- 12.2, 25.5; 1971- 11.8, 25.0; 1972- 11.7, 24.2; 1973- 11.9, 24.2; 1974- 11.5/11.57, 23.47; 1975- 11.35, 23.4/23.51; 1976- 11.1/11.33, 23.1/23.48; 1977- 11.3/11.41, 23.15; 1978- 11.18, 22.90; 1979- 11.2/11.37/11.30w, 22.82; 1980- 11.16, 22.90; 1981- 11.24/11.06w, 22.90; 1983- 11.70, 23.8w; 1984- 11.73/11.62w, 24.31. 33 international matches.

Norman HARRIS (New Zealand) (b. 24 Jan 1940 Te Kohai near Hamilton) on 20 November in Richmond, London. He wrote several books on New Zealand athletics including *Lap of Honour, The Lonely Breed* and *The Legend of Lovelock* before emigrating to Britain where he worked as a journalist on a wide range of sports for several newspapers. In the 1980s he ran the very successful *Sunday Times* Fun Run that annually attracted runners of all ages to Hyde Park in London. His most recent books were *Scottie*, the story of the maverick distance runner Neville Scott, for SportsBooks, and *At Last He Comes* (2013; about the 1908 Olympic Marathon).

Anthony Francis **HIGNELL** (GBR) (b. 7 Jul 1928) in Bodmin, Cornwall on 23 October. He was 4th in the Empire Games for England in 1950 and competed twice for Britain at javelin 1949-51, with a best of 60.66 (1950). A Cambridge University graduate, he joined the RAF, trained as a doctor and became Deputy Director of Medical Planning for the service. He was awarded the OBE. Before his retirement he was director of public health in Bodmin.

His son Alastair (b. 4 Sep 1955) won 14 caps for England at rugby union at full back and played first-class cricket for Gloucestershire before working for the BBC as a sports commentator.Diagnosed with multiple sclerosis in 1999, he was awarded the CBE in 2009

Johannes Ernst **'Hans' HUNEKE** (b. 12 Jan Schwalenberg) (FRG/Germany) on 14 August in Drenbach. In his best year of 1958 he ranked fourth in the world, won the European bronze medal and ran a FRG records of 8:37.4 for 3000m steeplechase and 8:03.6 for 3000m flat. He was FRG steeplechase champion in 1959. Pbs: 1500m 3:49.1 (1958), 5000m 14:06.0 (1958), 10000m 30:14.4 (1961). 14 internationals 1956-65, dnf ht 1960 Olympic Games.

Mohamed ISSANGAR (Morocco) (b. 12 Dec 1964) was one of 31 people killed in a bus crash near Tan-Tan in Morocco on 10 April, when he, as their coach, was accompanying a team of young athletes returning from School Games. At 5000m he was 9th at the 1992 Olympic Games and 3rd at the African Championships in 1988 and 1990, winning the Arab title in 1995. He burst onto the Grand Prix scene in 1989, 3rd at the Bislett Games in 13:19.54 and in 1990 he showed further improvement by winning at Lausanne, Oslo (pb 7:39.40) and London (third fastest in the world that year 13:08.51 a time that remained his pb). Other pbs: 1500m 3:39.51 (1991), 1M 3:57.03 (1990).

Kenneth Edward **JOHNSON** (GBR) (b. 14 Oct 1928 Leicester) on 12 December in Oadby, Leicestershire. As a steeplechaser he had four internationals for Britain, including heats at the 1952 Olympics and 1954 Europeans. He set his steeple pbs at AAA Championships: 2 miles 10:03.6 for 2nd in 1953 and 3000m 9:00.8 to win in 1954. He worked as an electrical engineer.

Milovan JOVANCIC (Yugoslavia) (b. 9 Jun 1929 Roge, near Uzice) on 18 June in Karlstad, Sweden, having lived in Sweden from 1968. He won the Yugoslav 100m in 1954 and 200m in 1953, Balkan Games 100m 1953-4, and was 2nd at 100m and 200m at the 1953 World University Games. He competed at 100m and 4x100m at the 1954 Europeans, in 16 internationals, and set Yugoslav records for 100m 10.5 (1953) and 200m 22.1 (1949) and 21.7 (1953).

Neeltje Jannetje **'Nel' KARELSE** (Netherlands) (b. 25 Jan 1926 Kortgene, Zeeland) on 20 October in Breda. She was fifth in the long jump and a semi-finalist at 200m at the 1948 Olympic Games and Dutch champion at 200m in 1949. Pbs: 100m 12.4, 200m 25.2, LJ 5.715 (all 1948).

Árpád KISS (Hungary) (b. 26 Aug 1956 Budapest) at the beginning of July. He was the first Hungarian to score over 8000 points (old scoring table) in the decathlon, the third of his national records: 7908h (1978), 7741 & 8005/7968 (new tables) (1979). He was 6th at the 1977 World University Games and 21st at the 1978 Europeans; HUN champion 1976-9 and 1981, and 6 internationals 1978-82. Pbs: 100m 10.94 (1979), 400m 49.30 (1977), 1500m 4:40.2 (1979), 60mh 7.9hi (1979), 8.23i (1982); 110mh 14.58 (1979), HJ 2.04 (1974), PV 4.80i (1980), 4.80 (1982); LJ 7.47 (1982), SP 16.65i (1982), 16.64 (1986); DT 48.30 (1981), JT 59.36 (1979).

Svetlana KITOVA (Russia) (b. 25 Jun 1960 Dushanbe) in November in the USA. She was European Indoor champion at 800m in 1983 and 1500m in 1986 (2nd 1987 and 3rd 1989) and was 3rd in 1987 and 2nd in 1989 at the World Indoors. Outdoors at 1500m she was 6th at the 1986 Europeans, 9th 1987 Worlds and 1st in

1985 and 2nd in 1987 at the World University Games.

Progress at 800m, 1500m: 1978- 2:07.1; 1979- 2:06.5; 1980- 2:01.3; 1981- 2:02.1; 1982- 1:59.51; 1983- 1:58.82; 1984- *1:58.08*; 1985- 1:59.6, 4:05.77; 1986- 2:01.43i, 4:01.83; 1987- 2:00.0, 4:03.03; 1988- 1:58.1, *4:01.02*; 1989- 2:01.69, 4:02.08; 1990- 2:00.91, 4:04.13; 1991- 4:33.05Mi, 1992- 4:08.40. Other pbs: 1000m 2:37.93i (1985), 1M 4:22.52 (1989), 2000m 5:41.11 (1990).

Grover KLEMMER (USA) (b. 16 Mar 1921 San Francisco) on 30 August in Oakland, California. Representing San Francisco Olympic Club he won AAU 400m titles in 1940, when he ranked joint third in the world at 46.7 (47.0 for 440y), and in 1941. The latter, in Philadelphia on June 29, was the greatest race in depth to that time. Klemmer's 46.0 tied the world record set by Rudolf Harbig in 1939) as he won from his great Californian rival Hubie Kerns 46.1 and Cliff Bourland 46.1. On May 24 in Los Angeles he had run on the University of California team that set a world record for 4x880y and on May 31 at Berkeley, in beating Kerns, he had tied the world 440y record of 46.4 set by Ben Eastman in 1932. Then at the Pacific Coast Championships on June 17 he ran a 46.1 anchor leg for the U.CaI team that set a world record of 3:09.4 for 4x440y. Kerns won the NCAA 440y title on June 21 in 46.6 with Klemmer third in 46.8. The War, during which he played American football at the Naval Academy in Chicago, virtually ended his brief but brilliant career. He was a football coach and administrator at City College of San Francisco for 39 years and an NFL referee 1955-86.

Annual progression at 400m (* 440y less 0.3): 1939- 49.2*, 1940- 46.7*, 1941- 46.0, 1942- 48.3*, 1945- 48.9*. Pbs: 220y St 21.2 (1940), 880y 1:51.7 (1941).

MIROSLAV KODEJS (Czech Republic) (b. 7 Jul 1950 Prague) on 9 August in Prague. He set seven Czechoslovak records for 400m hurdles from 50.0 in 1973 to 49.1 (49.34 on auto timing) in 1974 and a European record of 49.4 440 yards hurdles in 1974. TCH champion at 400mh in 1970, 1973-4, 1978-9 and 1981; 25 internationals 1970-82. Silver medallist at the 1973 World University Games, he competed at the European Champs in 1974 (sf) and 1978 (h).

Tauno KONTIO (Finland) (b. 14 Sep 1929 Alatornio) on 12 December. He won two Finnish 800m silver medals and two 400m bronzes (all in 1954 & 1956), ran at the 1954 Europeans (heat 800m) and in 13 international matches 1953-8 with three wins. Pbs: 400m 49.0 (1954), 800m 1:49.5 (1956), 1000m 2:25.2 (1954), 400mh 54.3 (1957).

Elzbieta KRZESINSKA (née Dunska) (Poland) (b. 11 Nov 1934 Warsaw) on 29 December in Warsaw. She was twice a long jump medallist at the Olympics (1st 1956 and 2nd 1960) and Europeans (2nd 1962 and 3rd 1954). She set four Polish long jump records, at 6.12 in 1954 and after 6.22, two world records at 6.35 in 1956, the last when winning the Olympic title. She emerged internationally in 1952 when she was 12th in the Olympics and won the first of eight Polish long jump titles (the last in 1963). She was also Polish champion at 80m hurdles in 1957. With her husband Andrzej (pole vault 12 OG 1960) she became a notable coach.

Annual progression at LJ (position on world list): 1949- 4.75, 1950- 5.30, 1951- 5.39 (99=), 1952- 5.83 (14), 1953- 5.79 (17), 1954- 6.12 (3), 1955- 6.05 (5=), 1956- 6.35 (1), 1957- 6.27 (2), 1959- 6.12 (13), 1960- 6.32 (4)/6.33w, 1961- 6.14 (17), 1962- 6.30 (4=), 1963- 6.13 (20=), 1964- 5.94, 1965- 5.81. Pbs: 60mh 11.1 (1960), Pen 4567 (1954 tables) (1960).

Sven KUUS (Germany) (b. 10 Oct 1936 Reval, Estonia) on 11 April in Rastede. He was a leading German statistician for many years, compiling annual German top 100 lists from 1990 to 2014.

John Noel **'Sean' KYLE** (Northern Ireland) (b. 28 Dec 1926 Ballymena) on 10 November in Ballymena. He built a great reputation as a leading coach (Northern Ireland National Coach for 20 years) and athletics enthusiast, and was married to Maeve (née Shankey), one of Ireland's greatest ever woman athletes (and hockey player). Together they founded Ballymena and Antrim Athletics Club in 1955.

Sven LAINE (Finland) (b. 23 Apr 1927 Porvoo) on 28 November. A steeplechase specialist with fine technique, his first sub-9 mins time came against FRG at Helsinki in August 1955. Beaten by teammate and WR holder Pentti Karvonen by just 0.2 sec, his 8:48.0 took him to sixth on the world all-time list. He never improved that time but went on to seven consecutive national championship medals 1953-9 (five silvers, two bronzes), 13 internationals 1952-9 and 9:26.6 at age 40 in 1967. Other pbs: 3000m 8:26.8 (1955), 5000m 14:39.6 (1958), 10000m 30:53.4 (1957).

Joseph **'Joe' LANCASTER** (GBR) (b. 4 Dec 1926) on 14 December. On 22 October 1955 at Walton-on-Thames he set world track bests of 1:47:53.0 for 20 miles and 22 miles 418 yards (35,788m) for 2 hours, with a British record 1:40:53.0 en route at 30,000m. He set his marathon best of 2:26:29 for 4th in the AAA race in 1957, but hopes of international success were dashed when he fell ill with TB. He became a sports reporter specialising in football and athletics and achieved his greatest fame locally when he was the fitness trainer for Manchester City when they won the Football League in 1967/8 and FA Cup in 1969. He later took on the same role with Manchester United when George Best was coming to the end of his days at the club. As a running coach his greatest success was Trevor Wright, 2nd 1971 European marathon.

Ernst Willy **LARSEN** (Norway) (b. 18 Jul 1926 Trondheim) on 2 December in Trondheim. He was the bronze medallist at 3000m steeplechase at the 1954 Europeans and at the 1956 Olympics, when Chris Brasher was originally disqualified for obstructing him, but reinstated when both parties concluded that this was unintentional. He was Norwegian champion at 3000mSt 1951, 1955-7 and 1959, 5000m 1955 and 1958, and 3/4km cross-country 1954 and 1957-8 and set national records at 3000m 8:09.4 (1956), 5000m three from 1955 to 14:03.8 (1957) and 3000mSt eleven from 1951 to 8:42.4 (1956).

Annual progression at 3000mSt: 1949- 9:29.6, 1950- 9:17.8, 1951- 9:11.4, 1953- 9:12.2, 1954- 8:53.2, 1955- 8:46.8, 1956- 8:42.4, 1957- 8:44.4, 1958- 8:49.4, 1959- 8:56.4. Other pbs: 1500m 3:52.8 (1956), 2000m 5:26.0 (1956), 10,000m 30:04.0 (1958).

Pierre-Yvon LENOIR (France) (b. 8 Aug 1936 Belle-Isle-en-Terre) on 24 November at Pléneuf-Val-André. He set French records for 800m 1:48.0 and 1000m 2:20.1 in 1959, was French champion at 800m 1959-60 and won the Mediterranean Games 800m in 1959. Pb 1500m 3:48.7 (1959), 13 internationals 1957-60. He was a vice-president of the FFA 1997-2004, a director of IBM France and marketing director for adidas.

Carl Haines **McBAIN** (USA) (b. 3 Mar 1918) in Los Angeles on 22 September. After third place in 1939, he won the AAU 400m hurdles title in 1940 in 51.6 to top the world list that year and for equal second all-time. A graduate of UCLA, his company McBain Instruments (now McBain Systems) that he founded in 1965 became one of the USA's largest microscope distributors in the 1970s. He was also a major philanthropist, establishing several scholarship programs at UCLA.

Gerard MACH (Poland) (b. 16 Sep 1926 Gdansk/Danzig) on 22 September in Ottawa, Canada. He competed at the Olympic Games in 1952 at 200m (qf) and 400m (ht) and at 400m at the Europeans in 1954 (ht) and 1958 (sf). He set a Polish 400m record of 48.0 in 1954 with pbs of 200m 21.4 (1957) and 400m 47.5 (1958), and was Polish champion at 200m in 1952 and 1956, and 400m 1948-9, 1951-4 and 1958. Renowned as a coach, his most notable Polish protégé was Irena Szewinska, and he moved to Canada in 1973 to be the national head coach for sprints and hurdles.

Ernest John **'Ernie' McCULLOUGH** (Canada) (b. 8 Dec 1925 Calgary) on 21 July in Calgary. He went to the University of Notre Dame and ran at the 1948 Olympic Games (heats 400m and 4x400m) and was Canadian champion at 440y in 1946. Pb 400m 49.4 (1948). After graduate studies at the University of Toronto, he was made Professor Emeritus at St. Mary's University in Calgary and played a major role in bringing the Winter Olympics to Calgary in 1988.

Joseph **'Joe' McGHEE** (GBR) (b 9 Jul 1929) on 17 April in Edinburgh. He will ever be remembered as the man who won the 1954 Empire Games marathon for Scotland in 2:39:36, finishing in the stadium in Vancouver long after Jim Peters had been carried off after collapsing just prior to the finish due to the heat and humidity. He was Scottish champion 1954-6, including his personal best 2:25:50 in 1955. An RAF flight lieutenant he went to Glasgow University and ran for Shettleston Harriers, becoming an English teacher.

Houston McTEAR (USA) (b. 12 Feb 1957 Okaloosa County, Florida) on 1 November in Stockholm. At the age of 18 he set a world record for 100y at 9.0 at the Florida High School Championship at Winter Park on 9 May 1975, but this was 9.30 on automatic timing. In 1976 he was 2nd at 100m at the US Olympic Trials but had to withdraw from the Olympic team through injury. His best year at 100m was 1977, when he set his legal pb of 10.13 and *Track and Field News* ranked him second in the world. In January-February 1978 he ran world bests of 6.54 for 60m and 6.11 and 6.05 for 60y indoors. The last came in winning the AAU title and his one outdoor AAU placing at 100m was 3rd in 1980. Other pbs: 100m 10.0 (1975), 9.9w (1978), 200m 20.9 (1975), 20.3w (1976). He was married to the Swedish sprinter Linda Haglund (qv).

Yrjö MÄKELÄ (Finland) (b. 2 Dec 1926 Loppi) on 23 May in Espoo. He was 13th in the 1948 Olympic decathlon and won the Finnish title in 1950 with silver in 1948. After a working career as a chief of a sawmill, and later living in Tenerife, he returned to athletics after a hiatus of 50 years, winning World and European Masters titles in throws pentathlon and javelin in 2007-8 in the M80 age group. Decathlon pb 6148 in 1950 (1985 tables).

Raymond Andrew **MALOTT** (USA) (b. 3 Mar 1917 Bakersfield, California) on 3 August in Palo Alto, California. He was AAU 400m champion in 1937 and 1938 and, for Stanford University, won the NCAA 440y title in 1938 after 2nd in 1937. In 1938 he ran the four best times in the world at 400m/440y topped by 46.6 for 440y and captained the AAU team that toured Europe. His series of wins included beating Rudolf Harbig in Berlin. Having graduated with a petroleum engineering degree, he worked for Shell Oil for 43 years, becoming chief of drilling operations. Pbs: 220y St 21.2 (1938), 880y 1:54.0 (1938).

Andreu MARTÍNEZ (Spain) (b. 10 Jul 1978 Valencia) on 25 July in Valencia. He was a bronze medallist at 4x400m at the 1998 Europeans. Pbs: 100m 10.50 (1999), 100m hand 10.1, 200m 20.95 and 400m 46.85 (all 2000).

Turo MERILÄINEN (Finland) (b. 4 Apr 1968 Noormarkku) on 27 February in Helsinki. In 1990 he won the Finnish 100m title and against Sweden in his only international match; in the European Champs in Split he ran in the heats. Pbs: 100m 10.58 (1990) & 10.37w (1990), 60m 6.69i (1990, Finnish champion 1990-1).

Sven Osvald **'Ossi' MILDH** (Finland) (b. 12 May 1930 Helsinki) on 16 September in Helsinki. An ice hockey player with four internationals and a member of the Finnish championship handball team in 1951, he found his vocation at 400m, heat at the 1952 Olympics. Moving to hurdles, he went to the 1954 Europeans in Bern with a pb of 52.6 and improved the Finnish record to 51.8 in the semis and to 51.5 in the final for a most surprising bronze medal. Another bronze came in the 4x400m. His time in Bern remained his career best although he ran 52.2 or faster 13 times, including in the 1956 Olympic heats and 1958 European semis. In 1953-60 he ran the 400mh in 23 international matches with 14 wins and 4 second places. Finnish champion at 400m 1953, 110mh 1957 and 400mh 1953-4 and 1957-8. He was SUL hurdles head coach 1960-8. Other pbs: 200m 22.3 (1954), 400m 48.6 (1954), 110mh 14.7 (1957), 200mh 25.3 (1955)

Irving 'Moon' MONDSCHEIN (USA) (7 Feb 1924 Brooklyn, New York) on 5 June in Hershey, Pennsylvania. He was AAU decathlon champion in 1944, 1946 and 1947 before placing 8th in the 1948 Olympic Games. His best score was 6711 (on the 1985 tables, then 7191 on 1934 tables) for 3rd in the USA v Nordic Countries match in 1949. He also won the NCAA high jump in 1947 and tied for first in 1948 with a tie for second in 1949 for New York University. At the AAUs he was also 2nd in the decathlon in 1948-9, at HJ was 2nd 1947 and 3rd 1949 and at TJ 5th in 1944 and 1947. He was merit ranked third in the world in 1947 and 1949 at high jump. Pbs: HJ 2.03 (1949), LJ 7.35 (1949). He later became a coach of track, basketball, and football at Lincoln University and was also an advisor to the Israeli Ministry of Education, helping to prepare Israel's athletes for the 1952 Olympics. His sons Brian had a decathlon best of 7650 (1980) and Mark was a pole vaulter, as was his son Brian, pb 5.63i (2008), 5.60 (2009).

Charles James **MORRIS** (Australia) (b. 7 Jun 1926) on 4 June in Melbourne. He was the Australian hammer champion in 1957-8, was 6th in 1958 and 4th in 1962 at the Commonwealth Games, and dnq 19th at the 1956 Olympic Games. Pb 59.89 (1962).

Robert NEMETH (Austria) (b. 5 Jun 1958 Hofors, Sweden) on 15 December at Mauerbach. At 1500m he was a semi-finalist at the 1980 Olympics and 1983 Worlds, and, after going out in his heat in 1978, came 4th at the 1982 Europeans both indoors and out. 8th at the 1977 European Juniors, Austrian champion at 800m 1978 and 1981-2, 1500m 1981-5, and 10000m 1986-7. Austrian records: 1000m (3) to 2:18.20 '82, 1500m (4) from 3:38.14 '80 to 3:35.8 '84, 1M (4) to 3:42.42 '81, 2000m (3) to 4:59.46 '84. Other pbs: 800m 1:48.65 '83, 3000m 7:44.08 '84, 5000m 13:35.90 '84, 10,000m 29:01.2 '82, 3000mSt 8:42.98 '81.

Hildegard Hansen **NISSEN** (Denmark) (b. 6 May 1921 Frankfurt am Main, Germany) on 4 November in Copenhagen. She ran on the Danish team that came 5th at 4x100m at the 1948 Olympics and in the heats of the 100m and 200m at the 1946 Europeans. Danish records in 1946: 12.6 for 100m and four times 26.7-26.6 at 200m, Danish champion 100m 1946 and 200m 1945-6. Pbs 100m 12.3, 200m 26.0 (both 1948).

Gordon Alexander **NOBLE** (Australia) (b. 28 Dec 1936) on 30 July in Melbourne. He ran at 1 mile at the 1962 Commonwealth Games (heat) and had pbs: 1M 4:03.9 (1963), 2M 8:41.8, 3M 13:32.0, 5000m 13:58.2 and 6M 28:56.45 (all 1966). He was the brother-in-law of Derek Clayton.

Brian Thomas **OLIVER** (Australia) (b. 26 Sep 1929) in Perth on 20 October. He was the triple jump champion at the Empire Games in 1950 with his pb of 15.60 for fourth on the world list that year, and 3rd in 1954, also winning bronze medals at 4x110y and 4x440y relays. He competed at the 1956 Olympic Games (dnq 23) and was Australian champion at long jump 1953 and 1956 and triple jump 1953-4 and 1956. Pbs: 100y 10.0 (1950), LJ 7.32 (1954).

Niall O'SHAUGHNESSY (Ireland) (b. 23 Nov 1955) on 17 September at Alpharetta, Georgia. In 1975 at age 19 he set an Irish record for 800m with 1:46.79 and was the youngest member of the Irish athletics team at the 1976 Olympics (heats 800m and 1500m). In 1977 he set a European Indoor mile record with 3:55.4, then the second fastest ever indoors. He attended St. Munchin's College in Limerick and won the 800m at the Catholic Student Games (FISEC) in 1973. He went to the University of Arkansas and was twice runner-up in the NCAA indoor mile and third in the outdoor 1500m in 1977. He graduated in 1978 with Bachelor's of Science degree in civil engineering and completed a Master's in environmental engineering. He qualified for the 1980 Olympics but declined his position on the team in sympathy with the US-led boycott, retiring from athletics later that summer. Other pbs: 1500m 3:39.59 (1980), 1M outdoor 3:56.96 (1976).

Nina OTKALENKO (USSR/Russia) (b. 23 May 1928 Kursk, née Pletnyova) on 13 May. She ran seven world records for 800 metres, of which five were ratified, from 2:12.0 in 1951, one each year, to 2:05.0 in 1955, but that distance did not return to the Olympics until 1960; she also ran a world record 2:06.6 for 880y in 1956. She was European champion in 1954 and won four Soviet titles, 1951-4, followed by four second places and a third up to 1960. She also ran world bests for 400m of 55.5 in 1954 (improving to a pb 55.0 in 1955) and for 1500m of 4:37.0 in 1955, and ran on five world record teams at 4 x 800m relay.

Annual progression at 800m (progression on world list): 1951- 2:12.0 (1), 1952- 2:08.5 (1), 1953- 2:07.3 (1), 1954- 2:06.6 (1), 1955- 2:05.0 (1), 1956- 2:05.8 (2), 1957- 2:05.8 (2), 1958- 2:05.8 (1), 1959- 2:08.8 (17=), 1960- 2:06.7 (11=), 1961- 2:08.6 (17=).

Her husband Vladimir was a leading statistician and ATFS executive committee member.

William Oliver **'Whitey' OVERTON** (USA) (b. 10 Oct 1928 Montgomery, Alabama) on 1 July in Lancaster, Ohio. He ran at 3000m steeplechase (heats) at the 1948 Olympics after 2nd at the NCAAs (in a pb 9:26.0 for Alabama Polytechnic, now Auburn University) and 3rd in the US Trials. Pb 2M 9:21.5 (1949).

Jean-Pierre PAUMEN (Belgium) (b. 16 Dec 1956 Bree) on 15 June in Neeroeteren. Belgian champion at 1500m in 1980 and 10,000m in 1988, he had pbs of 1500m 3:39.87 (1981), 1M 3:59.6 (1980), 3000m 7:53.0 (1986), 5000m 13:43.36 (1981), 10,000m 28:44.69 (1984), HMar 63:57 (1986), Mar 2:12:15 (1987).

Patrick PETERSEN (USA) (b. 3 Dec 1959 New York) on 31 May. He set a US marathon record of 2:10:04, a time that put him joint 14th on the world list that year, when 7th in London in 1989, having been 6th in 1985 (2:11:23) and 4th in 1986 (2:12:56). He also finished in the top five in the New York Marathon three times in the 1980s (4th 1984 in 2:16:35, 3rd 1985 in 2:12:59, 4th 1987 in 2:12:03), after 12th in 2:12:06 on his marathon debut in 1983, but had to drop out of the 1988 Olympic Trials race due to stomach problems. He went to Manhattan College in New York and worked as a financial analyst. Track pbs: 3000m 7:52.92i (1987), 5000m 13:42.49i (1986), 10,000m 28:19.3 (1984).

Anacleto PINTO (Portugal) (b. 25 Feb 1948) on 21 March. He was 22nd in 1976 and 16th in 1980 in the Olympic marathon. He set Portuguese records at marathon with 2:14:37 (1976), and at 10,000m 30:05.8 (1967) and 29:57.6 in (1968) but later set his pb of 28:34.9 (1977). Pb 5000m 13:56.4 (1974). Portuguese champion at 5000m 1966 and 1976-7, marathon 1976 and 1978, and cross-country 1966.

Peter James **PIRIE** (GBR) (b. 4 Jun 1929 Leeds) on 4 April in Simcoe, Ontario, Canada. An elder brother of the late Gordon Pirie, he had pbs of 3M 13:50.2 (1955), 5000m 14:27.2 (1954), 6M 29:23.5 (1954) and won the National Youth cross-country in 1947.

Borislav PISIC (Serbia) (b. 31 Jan 1949 Rodjevici village near Zvornik) on 21 April in Belgrade. At 110m hurdles he set five national records from 13.8 in 1976 to 13.6 in 1976 plus three auto-timed 14.04 (1975) to 13.85 (1979) and had a wind-aided 13.79w (1979); also 200mh 23.2 (1973) and 23.1 (1975); pb 100m 10.81 (1973). He competed at Olympic Games 1980 (ht), European Champs 1978 (sf) and European Indoors 1978-9 (ht) and was YUG champion in 1972-6, 1978-81 and 1983 (and at 100m 1972 and 1974-6), Balkan Games winner in 1975 and 1978-9 and at Mediterranean Games 1975 and 1979; also 3rd World University Games 1975. 47 internationals for Yugoslavia. His daughter Maja was Serbian 100m hurdles champion 2006.

Adolph PLUMMER (USA) (b. 3 Jan 1938 Brooklyn, New York) on 30 November in Denver. He set a world record for 440 yards at the Western Athletic Conference meeting in Tempe on 25 May 1963. Running for the University of New Mexico, his 44.9 (also equalling the 400m WR) was well ahead of his great rival Ulis Williams 45.6. That year, he was ranked second in the world, his third year in the top ten. He was NCAA 440y champion in 1961 and at AAU Champs at 440y/400m he was successively 3rd, 5th, 2nd and 4th 1961-4, and then at 220y was champion in 1965 (when he was ranked as world number one) and 2nd in 1966. Pbs: 100y 9.6; 200m turn 20.5 (1960), 220y turn 20.5w (1966); auto 220y 20.65w (1966); 220y St 20.3/20.0w (1962).

Hans Georg **RING** (Sweden) (b. 19 Jun 1928) on 9 April in Bromma. At 800m he was 9th at the 1952 Olympics, heat 1954 Europeans and Swedish champion 1954 and 1956 (2nd 1952);

pbs: 400m 49.4 (1956), 800m 1:50.4 (1952), 1000m 2:27.5 (1957).

Aarno RISTIMÄKI (Finland) (b. 3 Apr 1945 Punkalaidun) on 18 August in Turku. His finest run was 2nd in Pekka Päivärinta's 25,000m world record track race in Oulu on 15 May 1975; his 1:14:51.0 also bettering Seppo Nikkari's WR from 1973. At the marathon he was Finnish silver medallist in 1978 and 1982, and 24th in the 1978 Europeans; six international matches. Pbs: 3000m 8:05.6i, 5000m 13:39.27, 10,000m 28:32.33 (all 1973), marathon 2:15:12 (1982), 1 hour 20,092m (1975).

Bert ROSENTHAL (USA) (b. 10 Jun 1936 New York) in Scottsdale, Arizona on 15 November. A notable sports journalist, he worked for Associated Press from 1957 to 2001, covered seven Olympic Games from 1976 to 2000 and was president of the Track & Field Writers of America for two years.

Jindrich ROUDNY (Czech Republic) (b. 14 Feb 1924 Fukov) on 10 May in Prague. He won the European 3000m steeplechase title in 1950 in a national record 9:05.4, after placing 7th in 1946 and ran at the 1952 Olympics (5th heat). Czechoslovak champion 3000mSt 1946-8, 1950 and 1953, 5000m 1949. Other pbs 1500m 3:55.2 (1948), 3000m 8:36.8 (1953), 5000m 14:47.8 (1953); 10 internationals 1947-53.

Jakop RYPDAL (Norway) (b. 19 Feb 1926) on 6 December. An international 1950-8, he was Norwegian triple jump champion in 1953-5 and 1957 and competed at the 1958 Europeans (dnq). Pbs: LJ 6.86, TJ 15.06 (both 1960).

Theodorus Antoon **'Theo' SAAT** (Netherlands) (b. 13 May 1928 Arnhem) on 2 June in Noordwijk. He was a semi-finalist at 100m and quarter-finalist at 200m at the 1952 Olympics, and at the 1954 Europeans he was 6th at 100m and semi-finalist at 200m. Dutch champion at 100m 1951-2 and 1954-7 and 200m 1951-2, with pbs 100m 10.6 (1952) and 200m 21.4 (1954).

Joel Warren **SHANKLE** (USA) (b. 2 Mar 1933 Fines Creek, North Carolina) on 8 April in Culpepper, Virginia. He was third behind Lee Calhoun and Jack Davis in both the US Final Trials and Olympic Games at 110m hurdles in 1956, when he was also 2nd at the AAUs in 13.80 behind Calhoun and ahead of Davis, and ran his pb of 13.7 for 120 yards hurdles (then 6th equal all-time). He was also 3rd in the AAU decathlon in 1955 (4th 1953, 5th 1954) and won the NCAA long jump for Duke University in 1955 (with 3rd at 120yh). Pbs 100y 9.7 (1954), HJ 1.93 (1955), PV 4.19 (1956), LJ 7.52 (1955), Dec 6445 on 1952 tables (6532 on current tables (1955). He was a naval aviator in the US Navy 1959-65 and was a captain for American Airlines for 28 years.

Muhammad SHARIF Butt (Pakistan) (b. 1 Jan 1926) on 8 June in Rawalpindi. A rare Pakistani international athlete, he competed at 100m and 200m at three Olympic Games 1948, 1952 and 1956. At the Asian Games he won the 200m and was 4th at 100m in 1954 and 4th at 200m in 1958, and at the Commonwealth Games was a semi-finalist at 100y and 220y in 1954, again competing at both events in 1958. Pbs 100m 10.5, 200m 21.5 PAK record (both 1954).

John SHORT (South Africa) (b. 28 Apr 1929 Breyton, Mpumalanga) in Pretoria in September. He set a national shot record of 15.76 in 1956 and was South African champion in 1953 and 1956. He became a most successful coach, particularly of sprinters and hurdlers and most notably Paul Nash. His wife Eugene (née Brasler) was a Springbok 100m hurdler.

Annarita SIDOTI (Italy) (b. 25 Jul 1969 Gioiosa Marea, Messina, Sicily) on 21 May in Gioiosa Marea, Messina. At 1.50m tall, she became the smallest ever major champion when she won the 1990 European 10km walk and, after 2nd in 1994, she won this title again in 1998. She also took the 1997 World title after coming in as a last-minute replacement for Rossella Giordano, having been 9th 1991 and 1993 and 12th 1995. At Olympic Games she was 7th in 1992 and 11th in 1996. She won in 1995 and was 3rd in 1991 and 1997 at the World University Games, with consistent performances in the World Cup: 1989- 8th, 1991- 9th, 1993- 7th, 1995- 8th, 1997- 6th, and winning at the European Cup in 1996. After 7th 1987 European Juniors and 4th 1988 World Juniors at 5000m, at 3000m indoors she was European champion in 1994 (3rd 1990 and 4th 1992), and was 6th at the 1993 World Indoors. With the event for women moving to 20km, she did not finish at the 2000 Olympics, and at the Worlds was dnf 1999 and 8th 2001, 8th at the 2002 Europeans and 5th 2000 European Cup. Italian champion 5000mW 1995, 10kmW 1991, 20kmW 1992, 1995, 2000, 2002. She set a European walks record with 20:21.69 for 5000m in 1995 and had other pbs: 1M 6:46.53 (1990), 3000m 11:54.32 (1994), 12:09.3 (1995); 10000m 42:55.49 (1997); road: 10k 41:46 (1994), 20k 1:28:38 (2000). 47 internationals.

Raimo SIUKOLA (Finland) (b. 28 Jul 1932 Heinola) on 13 April. At 110m hurdles he won four Finnish titles (1954-5, 1958-9) with two silvers. In 1954-60 he ran in 25 international matches, six of those versus Hungary every one of which he won. Pb 14.6 (several times in 1956, 1958, 1960). At 200m hurdles he ran 24.5

in Lahti on 31 Oct 1954, still the latest date for a Finnish record in any event on home soil.

William Alfred '**Bill**' **SKINNER** (USA) (b. 27 Dec 1939) on 5 October in Georgetown, Kentucky. At the javelin he was AAU champion in 1970-1, 2nd at the Pan-American Games in 1971 and NCAA champion for the University of Tennessee in 1970 after 2nd in 1969. Pb (old javelin) 88.94 when 1st for USA v FRG in 1970.

Lonnie Vernon '**Lon**' **SPURRIER** (USA) (b. 27 May 1932 Cass Township, Missouri) on 23 June in San Pablo, California. A member of the San Francisco Olympic Club, in 1955 he was 2nd in the Pan-American Games 800m and won gold at 4x400m, and two weeks later set a world record for 880y with 1:47.5 in a virtually solo effort (2nd was 1:52.9) at Berkeley on 26 March. In April he ran a world best 2:08.5 for 1000 yards and went on to 5th in the AAUs. Then in a consistent year in 1956 he was 4th in the AAUs, 3rd in the US Final Olympic Trials and 6th at the Olympic Games, also running on US teams that set world records for 4x440y (3:07.3 in Los Angeles) and 4x880y (7:23.0 in the post-Olympic British Empire v USA match in Sydney). He was 5th in the NCAA 880y for California in 1953 and 1954. Other pbs: 440y 47.2, 1M 4:08.4 (both 1955). He became a jet pilot in the Air Force before a career in financial management.

Draga STAMEJCIC – POKOVEC (Yugoslavia /Slovenia) (b. 27 Feb 1937 Ljubljana) on 16 August in Bokalce, Ljubljana. She tied the world record for 80m hurdles with 10.5 on 5 Sep 1964 at Celje after four previous Yugoslav records from 10.9 in 1959, 11 Yugoslav pentathlon records from 3937 (1956) to 4790 (1964) and six YUG long jump records from 5.68 (1955) to 6.19 (1964). She competed at the Olympic Games in 1960 (hts 80mh) and 1964 (7th 80mh, 5th pentathlon). At the Europeans she was 10th pentathlon 1958, 6th Pen, 4th 4x100m and sf 80mh in 1962. Balkan champion 80mh 1959 and 1964, Pen 1957-9 and 1961-4; Yugoslav 80mh 1959-60, 1962, 1964; LJ 1956-9, 1964; Pen 1957-8 and 1962-3. 30 YUG internationals. Other pbs: 60m 7.76 (1960), 100m 12.0 (1964), 200m 24.8 (1964), 80mh auto 10.73 (1984), HJ 1.57 (1964), SP 13.23 (1962), JT 39.17 (1960).

Hilde STAVIK (Norway) (b. 6 Sep 1962) on 8 April. A regular in the Norwegian team, she competed at the 1979 European Juniors (800m), 1981 World Cross, 1992 & 1994 World Half Marathon, 1994 European (1500m & 3000m) and 1994 Worlds (5000m), She was NOR champion at 1500m 1982 and 1992-5 and 3000m 1992-5. Pbs: 400m 56.8 (1979), 800 2:04.7 (1982), 1500m 4:10.51 (1992), 1M 4:34.59 (1994), 2000m 5:52.62 (1993), 3000m 8:47.47 (1994), 5000m 15:22.77 (1996), HMar 70:21 (1994), Mar 2:59:55 (1990), 400mh 64.0 (1979).

Josef '**Sepp**' **STEGER** (Switzerland) (b. 24 Mar 1925) on 22 August. He set Swiss records at 400m, 47.9 in 1951, and 800m, 1:49.8 in 1955, and ran at the 1952 Olympics (ht 400m) and 1954 Europeans (ht 800m). Swiss champion 400m 1951, 800m 1954.

Larry Raymond **STUART** (USA) (b. 19 Oct 1937) on 6 June in Irvine, California. He won the US javelin title in 1963 while at the University of Southern California and was 2nd in 1965. He had previously been at Santa Ana Junior College. His pb (old javelin) was 84.56 in 1970 (15th on the world list that year). He set an M45 record with the new javelin when it was first introduced, 73.02 in 1986, and set unrecognised age records at M50 65.76, M55 65.74 and M60 64.74 before a ratified M65 57.83 (600g) in 2003.

Robert Edwin '**Bob**' **THOMAS** (b. 20 Mar 1939) (New Zealand) on 26 January in Waipu. Having started as a high jumper. he turned to long jump and set NZ records at 7.86 in 1967 and 8.05, his country's first 8m jump, at Whangeri on 20 Jan 1968. Sadly the NZ selectors only chose one man, Dave Norris, for the ensuing Olympics. NZ champion HJ 1959-60, LJ 1965, 1967, 1969. Pbs: HJ 1.94 (1959), TJ 15.19 (1960).

Jacques VERNIER (France) (b. 21 Jul 1923 Grand Charmont) on 14 April in Avignon. He became the first Frenchman to beat Jean Bouin's 14:36.8 at the 1912 Olympics with 14:35.8 in 1948 and improved that French record to 14:20.6 in 1949. French 5000m champion 1948 and 16 internationals, he ran at the 1948 Olympics (ht) and 1950 Europeans (dnf). Other pbs: 1500m 3:52.8 (1950), 1M 4:11.8 (1950), 3000m 8:22.8 (1950), 10,000m 30:56.4 (1949). His twin brother Jean (French records 2000m 5:17.4 in 1950 and 3000m 8:19.6 in 1949) died in 2006.

Carlo VITTORI (Italy) (b. 10 Mar 1931 Ascoli Piceno) on 23 December at Ascoli Piceno. Eight times an Italian international 1951-4 and champion at 100m 1952-3, he competed at 100m and 4x100m at the 1952 Olympics; pbs: 10.6 (1952), 200m 21.6 (1953). He coached many top Italians including Pietro Mennea and Marcello Fiasconaro.

Henk VISSER (Netherlands) (b. 23 Mar 1932 Willemstad, Curaçao) in Arnhem on 13 November. A top long jumper, he was ranked in the world top ten five times between 1951 and 1960. At the Olympic Games he had no jumps in the final in 1952 but was 7th in 1960, having missed 1956 when in his prime as the

Netherlands boycotted the Games due to the Hungarian rebellion. He was Dutch champion in 1952-6 and 1958 as well as 100m in 1958 and HJ 1951 and 1953-4, and won the AAU title in 1960 while at the University of California Santa Barbara. He set five Dutch LJ records from 7.48 (1951) to a European record 7.98 (1956); other pbs: 100y 9.6 (1960), 100m 10.5 (1958), 220y 21.3 (1959), 110mh 14.7 (1959).

Zygfryd WEINBERG (Poland) (b. 3 Feb 1930 Bydgoszcz) on 8 August. A triple jumper, who set Polish records at 15.22, 15.29 and 15.30 in 1954, he was 10th at the 1952 Olympics, 4th at the 1954 Europeans and Polish champion in 1950-1 and 1953-5.

Jan Ivar WESTLUND (Sweden) (b. 1 Nov 1953 Rätan) on 17 April. After three race walking internationals (youth and juniors in 1971-2) he concentrated on running with three internationals, including 50th marathon at the 1983 Worlds. Pbs: 10,000m 29:12.78 (1981), 20km 1:04:47 (1985), 25km 1:16:47 (1982), Marathon 2:14:56 (1983).

Sven Olof WESTLUND (Sweden) (b. 12 Feb 1932 Hofors) on 4 August. Ran on Swedish 4x100 m team at European Championships 1954 (6th) and 1958 (dnf, also 100 m sf). 23 internationals 1954-60, Swedish champion 200 m 1959. Pbs: 100m 10.6 (1957), 10.4 dt & 10.5w (1959); 200m 21.5 (1959).

Malvin Groston **WHITFIELD** (b. 11 Oct 1924 Bay City, Texas) on 19 November in Washington, DC. He was the world's best two-lap runner,when from June 1948 to the end of the 1954 season he lost only three of 69 races at 800m or 880y. He was Olympic champion at both 800m and 4 x 400m in 1948 and at 800m in 1952, with bronze at 400m in 1948 and silver at the relay in 1952, when he was sixth at 400m. He won the Pan-American treble at 400m, 800m and relay in 1951 and after 2nd at 800m in 1946-7 and 400m in 1948, he won eight AAU titles: 400m 1952, 800m/880y 1949-51, 1953-4; and indoor 600y 1953 and 1000y 1954. He won the US Olympic Trials at 400m and 800m in 1948 and 1952. Although he never approached the world record for 800m that Rudolf Harbig had set at 1:46.6 in 1939, Whitfield set two world records at 880y, 1:49.2 in 1950 and 1:48.6 in 1953, and one at 1000m, 2:20.8 at Eskilstuna in 1953 (that was followed just one hour later by American records of 45.9 for 400m and 46.2 for 440 yards), as well as records at 4 x 440y and at 4 x 880y (both in 1952). He set US 800m records at 1:48.6 in 1982 and 1:47.9 in 1953. He also set world bests for 500m 1:01.0 (1948) and at 660y 1:17.3 (1952) and indoors at 500y 56.6, 500m 1:02.9 (twice) and 600y 1:10.2 and 1:09.5. Pb 1 mile 4:12.6 (1954).

After 2nd at 880y in 1946, he was NCAA two-lap champion in 1948 (also 4th at 400m) and 1949 for Ohio State University, and was in the US Air Force when he won his first Olympic gold medal. He was the Sullivan Award winner in 1954 (the first black man ever so honoured) and retired after placing 3rd at the AAU and 5th at 800m in the US Olympic Trials in 1956. He was then appointed a Sports Goodwill Ambassador for the US Department of State, travelling throughout the world (visiting 132 countries!), coaching extensively in Africa for 47 years and setting up The Whitfield Foundation that has distributed 5000 athletic scholarships.

Annual progression at 400m (* 440y less 0.3), 800m (* 880y less 0.7) (position on world list): 1946- 1:52.1* (16=), 1947- 47.4 (11=), 1:51.0 (15=); 1948- 46.6/46.77 (3), 1:49.2 (2); 1949- 46.2 (1=), 1:49.6* (1); 1950- 46.7 (5), 1:48.5* (1); 1951- 46.7 (3), 1:51.2* (19); 1952- 46.4 (4=), 1:48.0 (1); 1953- 45.9 (1), 1:47.9 (12); 1954- 1:49.1* (7), 1955- 46.9* (11), 1:48.3 (13); 1956- 47.2 (13=), 1:48.2 (13=).

Alexandre YANKOFF (France) (b. 27 Jun 1931) on 2 November at Condrieu. At 400mh he was French champion in 1958 and ran in the heats at the 1956 Olympics. 8 internationals 1956-63. Pbs: 110mh 15.3 (1955), 400mh 52.6 (1963).

Died in 2016

Iolanda BALAS (Romania) (b. 12 Dec 1936 Timosoara) on 11 March in Bucharest. 1.85m tall, she achieved the greatest domination of an event ever seen in the history of athletics. She set 14 world records for the women's high jump, from 1.75m on 14 Jul 1956 in Bucharest to 1.91m at Sofia on 16 Jul 1961, to set a record for any event (since surpassed by Sergey Bubka). By the end of 1963 she had jumped 1.80m or higher in 72 competitions, yet it was not until 27 Sep 1964 that another woman, Michele Brown (Australia), jumped as high. By the end of her career Balas had jumped 1.80m or higher in 94 competitions while the rest of the world had a count of five between them.

From her fifth place at the Olympic Games on 1 Dec 1956 she won 150 consecutive competitions until she lost to Dagmar Melzer (GDR) on 11 Jun 1967. She was Olympic champion in 1960 and 1964, European champion in 1958 and 1962 (and silver medallist in 1954), won the first European Indoor Games title in 1966 and a record eight World Student titles between 1954 and 1961. She was Romania's first European and Olympic medallist in athletics, won 16 successive national titles from 1951, at the age of 14, to 1966, and set 36 national records from 1.49m in 1951. Her style was described as a cross between a scissors and the Eastern cut-off. At the end of 1967 she married her coach Ian Söter, who, from 1.87m in 1947 to 2.055m in 1956, set 15 Romanian men's high jump records.

She became a leading international sports official, president of the Romanian Athletic Federation 1988-2005 and vice president of the executive committee of the Romanian Olympic Committee.

Annual progression (and position in world list): 1948- 1.28, 1949- 1.35, 1950- 1.40, 1951- 1.51 (89), 1952- 1.53 (49), 1953- 1.60 (10), 1954- 1.65 (7), 1955- 1.70 (2), 1956- 1.75 (2), 1957- 1.76 (2), 1958- 1.83 (1), 1959- 1.84 (1), 1960- 1.86 (1), 1961- 1.91 (1), 1962- 1.87 (1), 1963- 1.88 (1), 1964- 1.90 (1), 1965- 1.86 (1), 1966- 1.84 (1), 1967- 1.68 (56).

Richard L 'Dick **BROWN** (USA) on 27 February. The renowned coach and physiologist was the director of the Athletics West programme in the 1980s, having previously coached in high school and at the US Naval Academy and coached many world-class athletes in Eugene.

Lawrence James '**Lawrie CROXSON** (New Zealand) (b. 1938) at Waikato on 15 January. He was NZ long jump champion in 1959, when he jumped 25'2"/7.67 for the first New Zealander to exceed 25 feet but it was wind assisted, and again in 1962. Pb 7.40 (1964). He became the New Zealand Dental Association Executive Director and was made an Officer of the New Zealand Order of Merit for services to dental health in the 2001 Queen's Birthday honours.

Henri DELERUE (b. 14 Nov 1939 Beuvry) on 9 January at Loué. French walks champion: 20k 1959-59, 50k 1967-69. 37 internationals 1960-72, Olympics: 1960-- 12th 20k; 1964- 13th 20k, 15th 50k; 1968- 21st 50k; Europeans: 1962- 12th 20k, 19066- 8th 20k, 6th 50k; 1969- 9th 1969. French walk records: track 1 hour (3) to 13,485m (1965), 20,000m 1:33:39.8 (1959), 20k road (3) to 1:28:42 (1965). Other walks pbs: 20,000mt 1:30:01.2 (1966), 2 Hr 25,225m (1962), 50,000mt 4:16:26.4 (1966).

John Ivor **DISLEY** (b. 20 Nov 1928 Corris, Caernarfonshire and Merionethshire) on 8 February. Coached by Geoff Dyson, he was a world-class steeplechaser who set four British records at 2 miles, from 10:12.6 in 1950 to 9:44.0 in 1952, and five at 3000m from 9:18.4 in 1950 to 8:44.2 in 1955. At the 1952 Olympics he improved from 9:11.8 to 8:59.59 in the heats and to 8:51.94 for the bronze medal in the final. Four years later he entered the Games as Britain's No.1, and nearly matched his best with 8:44.6, but with that he was sixth in the final won by his teammate Chris Brasher. His numerous Welsh records on the flat included bests of 1500m 3:53.4 (1956), 1 mile 4:05.4 (1958), 2000m 5:10.9 (1955), 3000m 8:09.6 (1957), 2 miles 8:43.8 (1957), 5000m 14:13.2 (1957).

After studying at Loughborough College he was AAA champion in 1952, 1955 and 1957 and won the Welsh 1 mile in 1949, 1951, 1954 and 1958. He ran for London AC and was a schoolmaster before becoming the first chief instructor at the CCPR's flagship mountaineering and outdoor pursuits centre, Plas y Brenin in Snowdonia. He helped Brasher to promote orienteering in Britain from the mid-1960s, and succeeded him as chairman of the British Orienteering Federation 1970-2 and was a member of the International Orienteering Federation 1972-8. He was awarded the CBE in 1979 for his work in outdoor education, and was vice-chairman of the Sports Council 1974-82. He was also chairman of British Olympians 1996-2002.

With Brasher he helped set up the London Marathon, first run in 1981, from their visit to the New York Marathon in 1979. He was a director of the organisation and then chairman of the London Marathon Trust from 2006, remaining an active member of the London marathon family throughout its 35 years.

In 1958 he married **Sylvia Cheeseman** (b. 19 May 1929), who set British records at 100y 11.0 (1951) and 220y 24.5 (1949), won silver and bronze medals in relay races at the 1950 Empire Games and relay bronze at the 1952 Olympics, and was WAAA champion at 100m 1949 and 200m/220y 1946-9 and 1951-2.

Yuriy Eduardovich **DUMCHEV** (USSR/ Russia) (b. 5 Aug 1958 Rossosh, Voronezh) on 10 February in Adler. A big man (2.00m and 128kg), at discus he set a world record of 71.86 in Moscow on 29 May 1983, having been European Junior champion in 1977, and at the Olympic Games was 5th in 1980 and 4th in 1988, and dnq 17 at the Worlds in 1983. He was USSR champion in 1980, 1981 and 1988, and had also set USSR records at 68.16 (1980), 69.16 (1982) and 69.44 (1983).

Progress at DT: 1976- 53.57, 1977- 58.32, 1978- 59.28, 1979- 61.64, 1980- 68.16, 1981- 66.42, 1982- 69.16, 1983- 71.86, 1984- 67.42, 1985- 66.18, 1986- 63.14, 1987- 64.42, 1988- 70.30, 1989- 62.48, 1990- 62.48, 1991- 59.24, 1992- 60.94, 1993- 57.68, 1994- 45.82, 1995- 57.24, 1996- 56.82, 1997- 52.96. pb SP 18.40 (1982).

Bennie GREYLING (South Africa) (b. 1 Feb 1965) in January. He broke 4 minutes for the mile with 3:59.7 just 22 days after his 17th birthday in 1982. Pbs: 800m 1:48.02 (1988), 1000m 2:18.03 (1988), 1500m 3:40.33 (1988), 1M 3:54.59 (1987), 2000m 5:04.00 (1988), 3000m 7:55.90 (1988).

Martin JENSEN (Norway) (b. 3 Jan 1942) on 12 February. He set three Norwegian triple jump records to 16.27 (1965) and competed at the European Championship (dnq 19) and European Indoor Games (dnq 7) in 1966. Norwegian champion 1961, 1964-6 and 1969. Other pbs: 100m 10.9 (1964), 110mh 15.0 (1962), 400mh 54.2 (1964), LJ 6.82 (1964), Dec 5359 (1961).

Arthur Patrick **KEILY** (GBR) (b. 18 Mar 1921 Derby) on 2 March in Alvaston, Derby. At the marathon he was 12th in the 1958 Empire Games and 25th in the 1960 Olympic Games after leading early on and 5th at 25k. He won the Poly Marathon in 1960 in his pb of 2:19:06, after 3rd in1956 and 2nd in 1957 and 1959. His first marathon win was in the All-Ireland race in 1954 and that year he also won the Doncaster to Sheffield race (that he was to win twice more) and had the first of three successive wins in the Liverpool City Marathon. He was 3rd in the AAAs in 1957 and in all he won 11 of his 25 marathons. He ran for Derby & County. Other pbs: 6M 29:43.0 '57, 30M/50k 2:50:49.4/2:57:29.4 '56, 4:05:55 '57. He set a world age-70 best of 3:24:22 in the 1991 London Marathon. Published in 2013 was "Arthur: The story of a Marathon Legend" by George Edwards (Email george.edwards4@ ntlworld.com).

James 'Jim' **McNAMARA** (Ireland) (b. 17 Apr 1939) on 9 March. A member of Donore Harriers, he was 39th in the marathon at the 1976 Olympic Games and did not finish at the 1966 Europeans. He was Irish champion at 3 miles 1964-5 and 1967, 10,000m in 1966 and marathon 1965-6, and also ran four times in the International Cross-country Championships. He ran his marathon best of 2:14:44 when 2nd in the Irish Champs in 1974. He went on to win many medals at World (from 1982) and European (from 1982) Masters Championships and was still competing until last year. In 1984 he ran a world age M45 record of 14:47.8 for 5000m.

Edmund PIATKOWSKI (Poland) (b. 31 Jan 1936 Konstantynow, Lódz province) died in Warsaw on March 28 at the age of 80. He ranked in the world top ten at discus of 12 successive years 1957-68. He won the European title in 1958, going on to 4th in 1962 and 1966 and 12th in 1969, and at the Olympic Games was 5th in 1960 and 7th in 1964 and 1968. He won at the European Cuyp in 1967 and was Polish champion 1955, 1957-66 and 1968-9 (2nd 1954 and 1967, 3rd 1956). He set 13 Polish records from 50.93 in 1955 to 61.12 in 1967 and the tenth of these was world record of 59.91 in Warsaw on 14 June 1959. Pb shot 18.05 (1964).

Annual progression (and position in world list): 1952- 38.35, 1953- 42.37, 1954- 47.21, 1955- 50.93 (33), 1956- 51.03 (49), 1957- 54.67 (9), 1958- 56.78 (4), 1959- 59.91 (1), 1960- 57.01 91), 1961- 60.47 (2), 1962- 59.52 (7), 1963- 58.66 (9), 1964- 60.12 (6), 1965- 60.32 (9), 1966- 61.06 (6), 1967- 61.12 (15), 1968 – 60.54 (21), 1969- 60.40 (22).

Dr David William **'Dave' SIME** (USA) (b. 25 Jul 1936 Paterson, New Jersey) on 13 January in Miami Beach, Florida. A multi-sport talent in high school, he passed up football and baseball offers to concentrate on sprinting and later medical school at Duke University. A great sprinter, and powerful at 1.89m/81kg, he broke through to world prominence in 1956, starting with an American indoor record of 9.5 in January and then being unbeaten from April to the first half of June, setting five world records: 220y hurdles straight in 22.2 at Durham on May 5, 100y at 9.3 in Raleigh May 18 and Sangar Jun 9, and 220y straight 20.1 at Durham on May 11 and 20.0 in Sangar on June 9. This brilliant series came to an end at the NCAAs, when he was well beaten by Bobby Morrow in the 100m and after a 21.1 heat in his first ever race around a turn, pulled up with a left thigh pull in the 200m aggravating an injury sustained horseback riding. Two weeks later he tried to compete at the US Olympic Trials, but lasted only four yards in his 100m heat. Thus ended the Olympic hopes of the "Blue Devil of Duke". He returned in 1957 with another 9.3 tied world record at Raleigh on May 18 and was 2nd in the AAU Champs at 100y, also winning all five 200m/220y races. Although he ran 9.4 for 100y in 1958 and 1959 in limited competition, he had rather faded from sight before another attempt at Olympic honours in 1960. He started moderately and was 5th at 100m and 6th at 200m at the AAUs, then scraped into the US team with 3rd at 100m at the Olympic Trials. In Rome at the Games he had a poor start but took the silver medal as he almost caught Armin Hary (10.32 to 10.35 on auto times). Then he finished his career with a great anchor leg for the USA in the 4x100m to make up a two-metre deficit on the West Germans. He broke the tape in a world record time (39.4) only for the USA to be disqualified for a faulty first changeover.

He worked as an eye surgeon in the Miami area for 42 years, including many sport stars and US President Richard Nixon amongst his patients.

Annual progression at 100y (100m), 220ySt (200mt): 1955- 9.6, 21,1; 1956- 9.3 (10.2), 20.0 (21.1); 1957- 9.3 (10.3), 20.4 (21.0); 1958- 9.4, 20.6; 1959- 9.4, 21.0w; 1960- 9.5 (10.1), (20.8). Other pbs: LJ 7.16 (1956), DT 41.16 (1956), JT 64.87 (1958).

Thyge THØGERSON (Denmark) (b, 4 Nov 1926 Vodder) on 18 February in Copenhagen. The 'running postman' won 34 Danish titles (8 at 5000m, 12 at 10,000m, 4 CC, 7 20k road, 3 marathon) between 1951 and 1968, and at international championships: Olympics 1952- 24 10,000m, 1956- 8 5000m, 15 10,000m; 1960- 6 marathon; Europeans: 1954- 15 10,000m, 1958- 10 10,000m, 1962- 7 marathon, 1966- dnf marathon. His 22 Danish records included: 5000m (4) 14:24.8 (1955) to 14:09.4 (1956), 10,000m (5) 30:20.6 (1954) to 29:45.0 (1957), marathon 2:21:03.4 (1960), with other bests of 1Hr 19,463m and 20,000m 1:01:35.4 in 1962.

Yeóryios TSAKANÍKAS (b. 10 Nov 1934) in Athens on 1 March. The first Greek shot putter over the 16m, 17m and 18m, he set 15 consecutive national records, from 15.58 (equal) in 1954 to 18.21 in 1964, his lifetime pb. He competed in three Olympic Games: 1956 (8th), 1960 (dnq 18th) and 1964 (13th shot and dnq 22nd discus) and won the gold medal in the 1959 Mediterranean Games and in five Balkan Games 1955, 1957, 1959-61. He was also third in the 1959 World University Games, competed in three European Championships (1958, 1962 & 1966) and was ten times Greek champion at shot 1955-67 and twice at discus 1962 & 1964). Discus pb 55.17 (1964).

Mirko VUJACIC (Yugoslavia/ Montenegro) (1 Sep 1924 Golubovci, Montenegro) on 2 January in Podgorica. At javelin he was 7th at the 1948 Olympics, 4th in 1950 and 11th in 1954 at the Europeans, Balkan champion in 1956-7 and Yugoslav champion in 1947-8, 1950, 1953, 1956 and 1959. He set five Yugoslav records from 66.22 in 1947 to 72.86 in 1957 and set his pb of 74.54 in 1960.

Add to Died in 2014

Jean-Claude ERNWEIN (France) (b. 18 May 1937 Pfaffenhofen) on 31 August in Pfaffenhofen. Dnq 17th shot at 1962 Europeans; 20 internationals 1960-6. Pbs SP 17.24 (1965), DT 44.64 (1962).

Roger FRINOT (France) (b. 9 Apr 1915 Vierzon) on 14 June in Strasbourg. French javelin champion 1937-8 and national record 62.08 (1939) with exhibition 63.30 (1939); 11 internationals 1936-46.

Alan Duncan **GORDON** (GBR) (b. 21 Aug 1932). While at Oxford University he was 4th in Roger Banister epic first four-minute mile. Pbs: 1000m 2:22.1 (1956), 1500m 3:45.4 (1957), 1M 4:03.7 (1957), 2000m 5:13.1 (1958), 2M 8:48.4 (1958).

Werner KUPPER (Germany/GDR) (b. 27 Aug 1926 Lebus) on 20 December in Leipzig. GDR discus champion 1954-6, 8 internationals 1954-60. Pbs: SP 14.55 (1956), DT 51.88 (1956).

Jean-Pierre LASSAU (France) (b. 23 Sep 1934 Paris) on 2 December in Villejuif. French shot records: 16.00 (1955) and 16.55 (1957); 3rd World University Games 1957; 19 internationals 1955-60. Pb DT 46.86 (1960).

Thomas Hilt **NILSSON** (Sweden) (b. 9 Apr 1926 Ljungby, Falkenberg) on 18 November in Kalmar. He set a Swedish marathon record of 2:22:05.4 to win at Kosice in 1956 and went on to 9th in the Olympic Games and 12th at the 1958 Europeans. 9th European Champs 10,000m 1954. Swedish champion at 10,000m 1953, 25km 1955, 8km cross 1956, and marathon 1956 (2nd 1955, 1957-8). Pbs: 3000m 8:18.6 (1955), 5000m 14:28.0 (1955), 10,000m 30:09.6 (1954), 1 hour 18727m (1954), 20,000m 1:04:06.4 (1954), 25,000m 1:20:50.0 (1954, NR). 8 track internationals.

His son Toralf Nilsson became an EA Council member.

Evelyne PINARD-OSTERHOLD (France) (b. 15 Aug 1923 Strasbourg, née Osterhold) on 4 September in Strasbourg. French champion at javelin 1947-53, 1955-7 and pentathlon 1945. Three French javelin records: 38.36 (1948), 40.61 (1950), 42.38 (1955); 24 internationals 1947-57.

Died in 2013

Jacques LÉVÊQUE (France) (b. 1 Oct 1917 Paris) on 15 November at Lalheue near Sennecey. French record 500m 1:03.5 (1937). At 800m: 2nd Europeans 1938 and World University Games 1939, French champion 1938; 8 internationals 1937-9. Pbs: 400m 48.6e (1937), 800m 1:51.8 (1938).

Died in 2009

René BIENÈS (b. 2 Aug 1923 Toulouse) in September in Bordeaux. Best known as a rugby player, who played 29 times as a flanker for France 1950-6 (two as captain), he also had six internationals for France at the javelin 1945-50, pb 58.10 (1949).

DRUGS BANS 2015

Drugs bans in 2015

As announced by IAAF or national governing bodies. Suspension: L - life ban, y = years, m = months, W = warning and disqualification, P = pending hearing

Leading athletes

Men Name	*Date*	*Ban*
Anis Ananenko BLR		4y
Dushane Farrier CAN	3 Jul	4y
Anastásios Galazoúlas GRE	29 May	W
Samson Idiata NGR	17 Sep	P
Robert Kajuga RWA	May 15	4y
Pavel Krivitskiy BLR	11 May	4y
Ahmed Mainy MAR	25 Feb	4y
Brian Mariano NED	6 Feb 16	P
Mohamed Marhoum ESP	15 Mar?	2y
Dzmitriy Marshin AZE	29 May	4y
Curtis Moss CAN	8 Jun	2m
Bertrand Moulinet FRA	30 Mar	4y
Angel Mullera ESP	15	P
Cyrus Njui KEN	30 Aug	8m
Ivan Noskov RUS	Jun	P
Mikhail Ryzhov RUS	Jun	P
Bohdan Semenovych UKR	11 Oct	2y
Andrés Silva URU	2 Jun	6m
Denis Strelkov RUS	Jun	P
Yuriy Vasilchenko BLR	24 May	4y
Aleksandr Yargunkin RUS		
Women		
Tatyana Akulinuyrkina RUS	20 Feb	4y
Elmira Alembekova RUS	Jun	P
Chinazor Amadi NGR	16 Sep	4y
Fanny Appes Ekanga CMR	24 Jan	2y
Mariya Bespalova RUS	6 Sep	4y
Emily Chebet KEN	4 Jun	4y
Agnes Cheserek KEN	19 Apr	4y
Agnes Jepkosgei KEN	4 Jul	4y
Agatha Kimaswai KEN	14 Apr	4y
Nabil Kirame MAR	1 Aug	4y
Francisca Koki KEN	20 Aug	4y
Lilian Moraa Mariita KEN	4 Jul	8y
Mariya Nikolayeva * RUS	18 Feb	4y
Deborah Odeyemi NGR	30 Jul	4y
Josephine Onyia ESP	1 Aug	L
María Pastuña ECU	21 Jul	4y
Sueli Pereira BRA		4y
Khaija Sammah MAR	25 Jan	4y
Vera Sokolova RUS	Jun	P
Gladys Tejeda PER	17 Jul	6m
Joy Zakari KEN	21 Aug	4y

8y: Rashed Al-Meqbali RSA (31 May); **5y**: Migiuel Ángel Gamonal ESP (29 Sep); **4y**: Chaltu Beji AZE (21 Jun), Denis Borisov BLR (22 Jun), Vladislav Bredikhin RUS (2 Jul), Alejandra Cardénas MEX (14 May), Binuaquito Chandrasekaran IND (28 May), Violetta Demidovich RUS (25 Apr), Daouda Diagne SEN (7 Jul), Achala Dias SRI (9 May), Khadija Ghazal MAR (25 Apr), Subhra Ghosh IND (29 May), Kristina Ilyushova RUS (26 Feb), Dmitriy Khasanov RUS (7 May), Fulan Khatun IND (28 May), Judy Jesire Kimuge KEN, Yaroslav Kholopov RUS (24 Feb), Andriy Kozyr UKR (20 Feb), Anastasiya Kurhina RUS (8 May), Smritikana Manna IND (29 May), Betzabel Menendez MEX (29 Mar), Brahim Merzaq MAR (25 Apr), Diego Moreno MEX (25 Apr), Bernard Mwendia KEN, Yelena Nikulina RUS (1 Jul), Hiago Pereira BRA (1 Jul), K.M. Rachna IND (10 Feb), Hristina Risteska MKD (4 May), Oleksandr Shelest UKR (8 Jun), Nikolai Vedehin EST (5 Feb), Yuliya Zaytseva RUS (1 Jul), Abdelghani Zghali MAR (9 May); **3y 8m**: Danel Novia CAN (5 Jul); **2y 3m**: Corrado Cultrera ITA (6 Jul); **2y**: Thozana April RSA (21 Sep), Imelda Bac GUA (23 Aug), Brian Cooshay USA (25 Jul), Larbi Es Raidi FRA (14 Jun), Georgi Georgiev BUL (14 Feb), Momhed Khalifa BRN (15 Apr), Nemenja Kojic SRB (25 Jul), Andriy Kozyr UKR (20 Feb), Mohamed Marhoum Jaghloul ESP (10 May), Tetyana Markova UKR (21 Feb), Analia de Oliveira POR (7 Mar), Jamil Santos BRA (3 Jun), Vincent Van Den Bosch BEL (1 Aug), Christelle Vallotton SUI (13 May), Mehmet Yarimay TUR (22 Apr); **18m**: Andrej Bician SVK (9 May), Marcin Blazinski GER (11 Feb), Ivanildo dos Anjos BRA (3 Jun), Mustapha Habbani FRA (10 May); **1y**: Tetyana Vernyhor UKR; **9m**: Sabine Petitjean FRA (21 Dec); 6m: Marilyn Bouche FRA (14 Dec), Yevgeniy Nushtayev RUS (12 Jun); 2m: Frédéric Gilbert FRA (10 May); **W**: Robert Arello USA (29 Aug), Maude Mathys SUI (6 Mar), María Pastuña ECU (Jul)

Add to Drugs Bans 2014

Men		
Adil Bouafif SWE	13 Aug	2y
Steven Colvert IRL	20 May	2y
Mohamed El Hachimi MAR	19 Jan	6y
Nelson Fernandes BRA	7 May	3m
Andreas Gustafsson SWE	14 Dec	2y
Antonio D. Jiménez	11 Mar	3y
Simon Magakwe RSA	22 Dec	2y
Women		
Martyna Bielawska POL	13 Dec	W
Vanda Gomes BRA	25 Sep	2y
Josephine Jepkoech KEN	31 Dec	2y
Natalya Kholodilina RUS	13 Sep	2y
Joyce Jemutai Kiplimo KEN	20 Apr	2y
Lilian Mariita KEN	14 Dec	4y
Eliane Pereira BRA	24 Aug	2y
Leila Traby FRA	7 Nov	3y

4y: Lahlal El Hassan MAR (28 Dec), Ivan Palamarchuk UKR (Nov), Hristina Risteska MDA (4 May), Victor Salazar ESP (11 Mar), **3y**: Ginevra Benedetti ITA (26 Oct), Joseph Mutinda KEN (16 Feb); **2y**: Mohsen Ali Nourozi SWE (20 Feb), Elias Bastos BRA (6 Apr), Youssef Bouissane MAR (28 Dec), Hanna Dunkan UKR/RUS (16 Dec), Sofia Hedman SWE (2 Jun), Iván Hierro ESP (11 Mar), Cristinel Irimia ROU (15 Nov), Atalech Ketema USA (18 May), Harish Singh Kopranga KEN (26 Nov), Kulwant Singh IND (30 Nov), Sathish Kumar IND (30 Nov), Simon Larsson SWE (7 Oct), Sekeke Lesole LES (6 Dec), Loh Chooi Fern MAS (12 Oct), Elias Mabane RSA (5 Oct), Umberto Macale ITA (9 Aug), Asaf Malka ISR (23 Nov), Tamo Matheleli LES (16 Dec), Francis Merry IND (29 Nov), Ramolefi Motsieloa LES (2 Nov), Joseph Mphuti RSA (12 Apr), Niklas Nilsson SWE (20 Oct), Genesis Olivera VEN (27 Sep), Andreas Olofsson SWE (13 Nov), Parmvir Singh IND (29 Nov), Veronica Pennavaria ITA (6 Jul), Silvano Pinto BRA (24 Aug), Kishore Saha IND (16 Dec), Getnet Selomie ETH (16 Nov), Hari Shankar Sharma IND (28 Nov), Assefa Tesfaye ETH (31 Oct), Mamorallo Tjoka LES (12 Oct); **18m**: Guza Silva BRA (24 Aug); **1y**: Lourenco de Carvalho BRA (7 Jul); 8m: Massimo Leonardi ITA (26 Oct); **6m**: Chiedza Chukore ZIM (28 Sep), Siyabonga RSA (16 Dec); **W**: M.Laura Bazallo Novella URU (6 Dec).

2013

Men		
Konstadínos Baniótis GRE	28 Nov	W
Angel Mullera ESP	28 Jul	2y
Umit Tan TUR	1 May	2y
Women		
Alicia Brown CAN	26 Nov	2y
Aleksandra Duliba * BLR	11 Oct	2y
Adrienne Herzog NED	13 Nov	2y
Lu Huihui CHN	27 Apr	1y

2y: Christos Chatziangelidis CYP (28 May), Álvaro Lozano ESP (Jun), Bernard Muthini KEN (6 Oct), Ilja Nicolajev EST (16 Apr)

2012 Women

Svetlana Kireyeva * RUS 26 Jun 2y
Irina Maracheva * RUS 26 Jun 2y
Anna Mishchenko * UKR 28 Jun 2y
Meliz Redif TUR 26 Jun 3y
Yuliya Ruban UKR 8 Mar 2y
Svitlana Shmidt UKR 8 Mar 4y
loses all marks from 8 Mar 2012, ban ends 17 Mar 2019
Alena Kudashkina RUS 9 Jun 2.5y
loses marks 9.6.12-9.8.12, 17.8.13-17.8.13, 9.6.14-9.8.14

2011 Men

Abderamdane Bouramdane * MAR 14 Apr 2y
Hafid Chani * MAR 19 Mar 4y
Women
Bahar Dogan TUR 3 Jun 2.5y
Rkia El Moukim * MAR 19 Mar 2y

Tetyana Gamera-Shmyrko * UKR 26 Aug 4y to 29 Sep 2019 results annulled from 26 Aug 2011
2.5y: Ummu Kiraz TUR & Semiha Mutlu-Ozdemir TUR (3 Jun)

2010 Women

Asli Cakir Alptekin TUR 29 Jul 8y to 9 Jan 2021 – results annulled from 29 Jul 2010
Anna Lukyanova * RUS 19 Jul 2y

2005-09 Women

Marta Dominguez ESP * 5 Aug 09 3y to 7 Jul 2016 Results annulled from 5 Aug 2009
Mariya Konovalova * RUS 14 Aug 09 2y to 26 Oct 2017 – results annulled from 14 Aug 2009
Liliya Shobukhova RUS 9 Oct 09 3y 2m (to March 2016) reduced to 2y 7m.
Elvan Abeylegesse TUR 07
Tatyana Andrianova RUS 9 Aug 05 2y from 22 Sep 2015. Results annulled 9 Aug 2005 to 8 Aug 2007

* Athlete Biological Passport case

Some Recent Marriages

Female	*Male*	
Elmira Alembekova RUS	Aleksandr Ivanov RUS	29.8.15
Zudikey Rodríguez MEX	Eder Sánchez MEX	.12.15
Shannon Rowbury USA	Pablo Solares MEX	11.4.15

Further recent women's name changes

Original	*Married name*
Xenia Achkinadze GER	Stolz
Gulfiya Agafonova RUS	Khanafeyeva
Lindsey Bergevin CAN	Mix
Anastasiya Bessoltseva RUS	Podolskaya
Lina Bikulova RUS	Kalutskaya
Fionnuala Britton IRL	McCormack
Christie Chamberlain AUS	Baker
Eilidh Child GBR	Doyle
Marrion Flack FRA	Sidea
Viktoriya Dolgacheva RUS	Prokopenko
Christie Gordon CAN	Moerman
Kaitlin Gregg USA	Goodman
Lina Grincikaite LTU	Samuole
Patricia Hall JAM	Pritchett
Madeline Heiner AUS	Hills
Jess Herauf USA	Lehman
Yelena (Alena) Kopets BLR	Abramchuk
Tatyana Lysenko RUS	Beloborodov
Anneisha McLaughlin JAM	Whilby
Veronika Mosina RUS	Semashko
Alena Novogrodskaya BLR	Soboleva
Mary Saxer USA	Sibears
Anastasita Shatybelko BLR	Kolomoyets
Kseniya Ustalova RUS	Aksyonova
Erika Wiklund SWE	Kinsey
Anna Yermakova UKR	Lunyova
Liliya Zubkova RUS	Molchanova
Men	
Solomon Ijah USA	Simmons

Change of name and nationality

Men
Winston Barnes JAM to Emre Zafer Barnes TUR .15
Mike Kigen KEN to Kaan Kigen Özbilen TUR 18.10.15
Oleksiy Sokyrskyy UKR to Aleksey Sokirskiy RUS 8.7.15
Women: Misiker Mekonnin ETH to Misiker Demissie USA 16.10.15 (also ran as Teyba Naser BRN in 2007-10)
Aminat Odeyemi NGR to Amina Youssef BRN

Retired: Julia Mächtig GER, Lisa Urech SUI

Transfer of Nationality/Allegiance

Name	*From*	*To*	*Noted*	*Eligible*
Ahmed Ali	USA	SUD	15.7.15	
Zouhair Aouad	MAR	BRN	31.12.14	
Worku Beyi	ETH	USA	27.2.15	7.7.15
Sam Chelanga	KEN	USA	14.8.15	
Paul Chelimo	KEN	USA	23.7.14	15.6.15
Yidiel Contreras	CUB	ESP	24.4.15	15.6.15
Rustem Dremdzhy	UKR	RUS	5.5.14	8.7.15
Peter Emelieze	NGR	GER	.1.16	
Ezekiel Ewolu	GBR	NGR	5.5.15	
Ilias Fifa	MAR	ESP	6.6.15	30.7.15
Mamadou Kasse Hann	SEN	FRA	22.8.14	11.6.15
Alvin Harrison	DOM	USA	5.6.15	
Zharnel Hughes	AIA	GBR	19.6.12	19.6.15
Shadrack Kipchirchir	KEN	USA	12.1.15	10.6.15
Tosin Ogunode	NGR	QAT	29.1.15	2.4.15
Orlando Ortega	CUB	ESP	9.9.15	
Yassine Rachik	MAR	ITA	10.6.15	3.7.15
Sean Safo-Antwi	GBR	GHA	.3.16	
Nick Scarvelis/Skarvélis	USA	GRE	10.6.15	
David Smith	USA	PUR	1.4.15	
Sergey Timshin	UZB	RUS	22.5.13	25.6.15
Mohammed Ayoub Tiouali	MAR	BRN	31.3.15	
Lukas Verzbicas	LTU	USA	25.1.16	
Women				
Kelsie Ahbe	USA	CAN	13.1.15	
Stephanie Bendrat	GER	AUT		
Anastasiya Bondar	UKR	RUS	11.6.14	8.7.15
Yelena Chebanu	UKR	AZE	11.4.14	5.5.15
Elizeba Cherono	KEN	NED	.1.16	
Victoria Dronsfield	SWE	GBR	24.11.14	15.6.15
Tigist Gashaw	ETH	BRN	9.10.14	9.10.15
Yvana Hepburn-Bailey	USA	BAH	28.6.14	
Sarah Howard	USA	CAN	7.7.15	
Amalie Ieul	DEN	NOR	26.6.15	7.7.15
Yekaterina Kuntsevich	RUS	AUT	.12.15	
Cindy Ofili	USA	GBR	31.12.13	
Reina-Flor Okori	FRA	GEQ	3.7.15	
Elaine O'Neill	GBR	IRL	31.7.15	
Alexi-Maria Pappas	USA	GRE	22.12.15	
Aisha Praught	USA	JAM		
Vira Rebryk	UKR	RUS	11.4.14	1.7.15
Claudia Saunders	USA	FRA		
Kseniya Savina	UKR	RUS	20.6.14	31.7.15
Stamatia Scarvelis	USA	GRE	10.6.15	
Hanna Skydan	UKR	AZE	15.1.15	1.6.15
Montenae Speight	USA	GBR		
Vashti Thomas	USA	PAN	1.11.14	
Jaleesa Williams	USA	TTO		

STYLISH OR STURDY

By Bob Phillips

THAT VENERABLE BUT still vibrant British publication *Athletics Weekly* celebrated its 70th anniversary in December of last year, and one of the most apt feature articles in the special commemorative issue was an interview with Eric Shirley at the age of 86. He was an Olympic steeplechase finalist in 1956, but more appropriately in this instance he could also span almost the entire history of 'AW', having first had his name printed in its columns for winning the Middlesex county youths' cross-country title early in 1946 … and still, seven decades later, getting a mention every now and then for his successes in over-85 age-group races. The editor of 'AW', Jason Henderson, caught up with the evergreen Shirley after one of his regular training sessions – six laps of the track, 8-to-12 x 100 metres strides, and a two-lap warm-down!

The steeplechase at the Melbourne Games of 1956 was unexpectedly won by another Briton, Chris Brasher, and there could scarcely have been a greater contrast in their upbringing. Brasher, educated at one of Britain's most renowned public schools, Rugby, and at Cambridge University; Shirley, born to a single mother in a back-street London hostel for the destitute, taken away to be fostered, and brought up in poverty. Close followers of athletics over the last 60 years would likely say that they always thought that Shirley had the greater potential than Brasher as a steeplechaser. Certainly, Shirley was a faster miler and a better stylist over the barriers. He was 1.80m in height but very slim, and he looked taller and aesthetically most appealing on the track, especially in comparison with the stocky build of Brasher and the Welshman, John Disley, who had been the bronze-medallist at the 1952 Games.

But, come the Olympic final, Brasher had his day of days in winning the gold, leaving Disley to salvage 6th place and Shirley 8th. There seemed to be some sort of hidden agenda about this unforeseen success because Jack Crump, the British Amateur Athletic Board team manager, who was customarily the soul of discretion, was to remark in his autobiography published shortly before his death in 1966, that 'For their lack of generosity I had to remonstrate with several of our team who had hoped that one of our other two finalists would win.' Maybe the moral of the story is that abrasiveness, and not necessarily popularity, wins races. There was other disquiet, too, among the British competitors in Melbourne, volubly expressed later by Shirley: 'We received a daily allowance of five shillings, and we knew that perhaps there was some "creative accounting" going on.' This mistreatment came close to rousing team-members to open mutiny, and two years later Brasher, Disley and Shirley were all instrumental in the formation of a British international athletes' club to promote their cause against intransigent management. Shirley is the last survivor of that illustrious trio – Brasher having died in 2003 and Disley earlier this year at the age of 87.

In 1955 all three had ranked in the top ten steeplechasers in the world. In Moscow in September Disley had famously beaten his Soviet opponents in a British record 8:44.2, thus ranking 2nd only to Jerzy Chromik, of Poland, in the world all-time list. In October Shirley had set a domestic British record of 8:47.6. Quaintly pedestrian as these times might seem in 2016, they were regarded all those years ago as sensational by us youthful enthusiasts. In the early months of 1956 the major domestic cross-country races brought together, as always, the great majority of the leading British distance-runners, and particularly those with Olympic ambitions, culminating in the National championship over its customary nine-mile course. However, none of the three steeplechasers were habitual cross-country runners, and Shirley's only noteworthy appearance had been in the Middlesex county race in January, in which he was 7th.

Though indoor athletics scarcely existed in Europe, and even less so in Britain, Disley and Brasher went off to a couple of embryonic meetings in Germany in February in which they ran at a moderate pace 1000 and 3000 metres on the flat – or, to be more precise, round the steeply-banked circuits of Dortmund and Kiel. Jack Crump, in charge as always, even if university graduates like Brasher and Disley were perfectly capable of looking after themselves, declared himself envious of the German facilities, and in his wily fashion he soon had his eye open for a rather more exotic venture. In March both he and the other doyen of British athletics, Harold Abrahams (and their wives), accompanied a team of six, including Eric Shirley, to Trinidad, where the hospitality was lavish but three of the athletes suffered injuries in unaccustomed strenuous early-season competition and Shirley developed painful blisters in a 5000 metres on an unforgiving track.

There were other more Spartan international opportunities available, but on a somewhat arbitrary basis. England's best cross-country runners were welcome guests at continental races most weekends throughout the winter, similar in many respects to the current IAAF 'permit' events, followed by the International Championship, which had been in existence since 1903, but that involved only the various countries in Britain against France, Belgium and Ireland. Other separate ruling bodies around Britain dealt with English, Scottish, Welsh and Northern Irish cross-country, as they did for track and field events.

Shirley took advantage of another annual institution by signing on for some of the numerous spring-time road-relays, safely held in what was then largely traffic-free circumstances. Making a valuable contribution to his club, Finchley Harriers, in the classic London-to-Brighton event on 14 April, he ran the fastest time on the second stage, moving through from 11th place to 3rd. Around the same time 'AW' published a survey of athletics facilities in Britain which revealed that 17 English counties – including Cambridgeshire and Oxfordshire, whose most famous universities had produced so many British internationals, including Brasher – did not possess a single public cinder track; let alone any all-weather surfaces, which were still a dozen years in the future.

Regardless of the Olympic Games not starting until November, the outdoor track season began in earnest as usual in May on the unpredictable cinders of the White City track, in West London, with the two-day 'British Games' and Inter-Counties' Championships, which attracted 62,000 spectators. Not the least curious aspect of this meeting was that none of the counties had yet held their own meetings, and so selections were perforce based on what had happened the year before. Thanks to sponsorship from the garish but benevolent Sunday newspaper. the *News of the World*, various foreign athletes were invited – for expenses only, of course – and Ken Wood won a speedy 1500 metres in 3:43.4 from the Hungarians, Rózsavölgyi and Tábori, with Gordon Pirie 4th and an East German, Richtzenhain, 5th. Only the most observant of track 'nuts' would have noticed Eric Shirley's performance because he finished unremarked in 6th position in 3:47.0, which was significantly better than Disley and Brasher – or, for that matter, any steeplechaser of whatever nationality – had ever done.

In their first tentative steeplechases of the year against modest local opposition Disley ran 9:09.6 in May and Shirley 9:06.8 in June, and those Inter-Counties' events had led on to the district championships (North, Midlands, South), which were also held in high esteem, though only Brasher took part, winning the Southern title in 9:14.6 but reported as being exhausted at the finish. That was the sum of the current familiarity with their event of Britain's steeplechasing trio on the eve of the AAA Championships in July that would decide the composition of the Olympic team (even though the Games were still more than four months hence). Nevertheless, Jimmy Green, the founder-editor of 'AW', remarked sagely, 'Win or lose this weekend, I consider Eric our best prospect for a Melbourne title so far as our men are concerned.' Shirley duly won the AAA race in a Championship record 8:51.6 from Disley and Brasher.

Shirley had to ask his employers for time off to race on Saturdays. He worked in retail sales, on his feet from 8 am to 5.30 pm, then going straight to training for 1½ hours and home to eat and sleep. Even so, Jimmy Green was to observe once more of steeplechase prospects later in the year, with the Olympics now only two months off, that 'Disley has had only three proper races this season and Shirley only one.' Though both had suffered from health problems, it was undoubtedly the age-old formalised structure of the British athletics calendar that was to blame.

So far as international competition was concerned, there were occasional excursions into Europe sanctioned by Jack Crump and the BAAB for small groups of athletes or even by lone adventurers such as Gordon Pirie, who beat the Hungarians and the world record for 3000 metres on one such jaunt. Yet the key dates of the season in the BAAB's estimation were the regular two-a-side international matches, as had been the case for the previous 35 years or so, and in 1956 the series of such fixtures had a very odd look about it, indeed. The full Great Britain team took on Hungary and Czechoslovakia, but other teams labelled 'London' and 'Prague' and 'London' and 'Budapest', involving very much the same athletes, also met. In addition, there should have been an historic GB-v-USSR match at the White City, but this was cancelled for banal reasons which had nothing to do with athletics and are far too complex to go into here. In July Disley had won in 8:49.2 against Prague and a fortnight later did so again in 8:46.6 against the same two Czech opponents now elevated to full international status. Shirley's view in hindsight is that these fixtures were mainly arranged for political reasons and any benefit to the athletes was of much less consideration, but he always believed it was his patriotic duty to put on the GB vest and represent his country.

Unfortunately suffering from fibrositis, which made hurdling painful, Shirley mainly occupied himself by running in various minor local races on the flat: 3rd in the Middlesex 880 yards; 3rd again in a ¾-mile on the Paddington track where Jack Lovelock was alleged to have run a 3:52.8 mile in training a decade before; a very close 2nd at a mile to Chris Chataway; and a winning 4:10.4 mile for the Amateur Athletic Association against Kent which was said to be 'worth several seconds less on a faster track in better conditions'. Most bizarre of all, at the Ibrox Park football ground in Glasgow in September, Shirley won a two-man inter-club four-mile relay, averaging 4:08 or so per mile, with his Finchley clubmate, Frank Salvat. There were rather more meaningful successes in international races at that same meeting for Ian Boyd over the Olympic champion, Josy Barthel, at 1500 metres and for the unpronounceable Pole, Zdzislaw Krzyszkowiak, over Derek Ibbotson at 3000 metres.

Disley and Shirley then made a long and tiring journey to Budapest with their GB colleagues for the match against Hungary at the end of September. Disley still won in 8:47.6, but Shirley was a fair way back, 3rd in 8:56.2, and 'AW' reported mournfully that 'his lack of competition was apparent here.' Hungary beat GB 108–104 in the men's match, but the British women won 70–43, and such victories or defeats were thought to be of great importance in those long ago days. Whether or not it was proved that one country's standard of athletics was superior to another's, who could say, but there was soon a further chance to make such comparisons when ten days later the 'Budapest' visitors to the White City lost to 'London' 98–90 (men) and 35–48 (women). Disley won yet again, in 8:57.2, but Shirley hit a barrier, fell, severely bruised a knee and retired from the race. 'His immediate prospects seemed dimmed,' remarked 'AW' with masterly understatement. Brasher also took a tumble, and rather embarrassingly it was headlong into the water. No mention was made of his Olympic chances for a simple reason – nobody, except possibly Brasher himself, thought he had any.

For the Hungarians there were about to be rather more pressing considerations, with the populace's valiant uprising against the USSR's troops beginning less than a fortnight later. Among other repercussions, this put paid to the Olympic hopes of such as Rózsavölgyi, though their European steeplechase champion, Sándor Rosznyói, who had missed the international matches against the Britons, astonishingly was to get the silver behind Brasher. In the Olympic preview issue of their highly-regarded monthly magazine *Athletics World* Norris and Ross McWhirter invited various respected experts to make their predictions, and Roberto Quercetani, Don Potts, Cordner Nelson and the McWhirter twins between them named nine different steeplechasers as likely medallists, Rosznyói was the general favourite. Disley was the only other one to get four nominations; Shirley was listed twice. Brasher was not chosen by anyone. Nor were any Africans – there weren't any in the steeplechase.

Returning to normal duty after the Olympics, Eric Shirley began 1957 as he had 1956 by running in the Middlesex cross-country championships, though this time rather further down the field in 22nd place. This was truly the era of amateur athletics. Derek Ibbotson's only tangible rewards for taking the bronze medal in the Olympic 5000 metres were being elected to life membership of his Yorkshire club, Longwood Harriers, and starting on New Year's Day a new job as a trainee junior sales representative with the W.T.Healey cable-manufacturing company. There were, though, tangible advantages to be gained from a prominent athletics career if you were in the know: Chris Brasher, who had been an oil-company executive fitting his track training into his lunchtime break, had promptly retired from competition in a golden afterglow and was appointed sports editor of the Sunday newspaper *The Observer*. He and John Disley, a schoolteacher by profession, were later to devise the London Marathon.

Bemoaning the lack of support for aspiring young athletes in Britain, the astute AAA chief coach, Geoff Dyson, wrote in a prophetic article for 'AW' later that January of 1957 that 'our whole social structure stands in marked contrast to the USA, certain European and Scandinavian countries, the USSR and other communist countries. All, by various means, give their youth more encouragement than we do in Britain. How I hate it when I hear people saying of the American and Russian athletes, "Oh, well, of course, they are professionals". It is my belief that the pampered circumstances of the foreign athlete are greatly magnified in Britain. Much rubbish is talked and written about these things, largely by way of excuse. We have much to do. Let's get on with it.'

After another four years of trying to 'get on with it', Dyson became discouraged beyond measure by the antagonism of certain leading British athletics officials and resigned his post to emigrate to Canada, where his expertise was welcomed with open arms. Eric Shirley – self-made man in life at large as much as on the track, and equally as forceful a character as was Dyson, having continued to contribute to the sport as an industrious administrator – nowadays views the age of professional athletics with a sceptical eye. He told the 'AW' editor in that 70th anniversary interview that in his opinion there 'were better ways for the government to spend its money than giving out lottery funding so that athletes can train for an hour or so and then sit around all day.'

WORLD LIST TRENDS - MEN

This table shows the 10th and 100th bests in the year lists for the last eight years, with previous bests.

10th Bests	To 2007	2008	2009	2010	2011	2012	2013	2014	2015
100m	9.98- 97	9.95	9.97	9.95	**9.89**	9.94	9.96	9.96	9.91
200m	20.03- 00	20.17	20.17	20.11	20.16	20.10	20.10	20.08	**19.97**
400m	44.51- 96	44.70	44.81	44.81	44.78	44.77	44.82	44.71	**44.36**
800m	**1:43.66- 96**	1:44.10	1:43.82	1:43.89	1:44.07	1:43.71	1:43.87	1:43.71	1:43.72
1500m	3:31.10- 04	3:32.16	3:31.90	3:32.20	3:31.84	3:31.61	3:31.94	3:30.98	**3:30.29**
5000m	**12:54.99- 03**	13:03.04	12:58.16	12:55.95	12:59.15	12:55.99	13:01.64	13:03.85	13:05.30
10000m	**27:00.30- 07**	27:08.06	27:15.94	27:17.61	26:52.84	27:03.49	27:21.50	27:28.27	27:18.86
Half Mar	59:32- 07	59:37	59:30	59:40	59:39	**59:15**	59:54	59:21	59:28
Marathon	2:06:48- 03	2:06:25	2:06:14	2:05:52	2:05:45!	**2:04:54**	2:05:16	2:05:13	2:06:00
3000mSt	**8:08.14- 02**	8:12.72	8:10.63	8:09.87	8:08.43	8:10.20	8:08.83	8:11.86	8:13.37
110mh	13.19- 07	13.24	13.21	13.28	13.23	**13.13**	13.18	13.19	**13.13**
400mh	**48.25- 02**	48.52	48.30	48.47	48.47	48.41	48.46	48.69	48.44
HJ	**2.36- 88**	2.34	2.33	2.32	2.33	2.32	2.34	2.34	2.33
PV	**5.90- 98**	5.81	5.80	5.80	5.80	5.73	5.80	5.76	5.82
LJ	**8.35- 97**	8.25	8.30	8.25	8.27	8.26	8.29	8.28	8.29
TJ	**17.48- 85**	17.43	17.41	17.29	17.35	17.31	17.26	17.27	17.24
SP	**21.63- 84**	21.19	20.99	21.29	21.16	21.14	21.09	21.37	21.14
DT	**68.20- 82**	67.91	66.19	66.90	67.21	67.50	65.98	66.11	66.40
HT	**81.88- 88**	80.58	79.48	78.73	79.27	79.56	79.16	78.27	78.22
JT	**87.12- 96/97**	85.05	84.24	85.12	84.81	84.72	84.61	85.92	86.21
Decathlon	**8526- 98**	8372	8406	8253	8288	8322	8390	8311	8398
20kmW	**1:18:30- 05**	1:19:15	1:19:55	1:20:36	1:19:57	1:19:20	1:19:36	1:19:43	1:19:14
50kmW	3:41:30- 05	3:45:21	3:41:55	3:47:54	3:44:03	**3:41:24**	3:43:38	3:43:02	3:44:17

Peak years shown in bold

Men 100th Bests		2008	2009	2010	2011	2012	2013	2014	2015
100m	10.24- 00	10.23	10.22	10.26	10.21	10.20	10.21	10.18	**10.16**
200m	20.66- 99/00/07	20.67	20.68	20.71	20.63	20.57	20.60	**20.51**	**20.51**
400m	45.78- 00	45.89	45.86	45.92	45.91	45.79	45.87	45.69	**45.61**
800m	1:46.54- 99	1:46.70	1:46.88	1:46.76	1:46.50	1:46.56	**1:46.44**	1:46.60	1:46.51
1500m	3:38.42- 97	3:38.57	3:38.60	3:38.47	3:37.77	**3:36.84**	3:37.77	3:38.47	3:38.13
5000m	13:25.68- 05	13:25.05	13:26.90	13:25.88	13:26.29	**13:23.58**	13:27.29	13:28.60	13:27.10
10000m	28:10.73- 07	**28:04.47**	28:18.00	28:21.00	28:15.79	28:06.74	28:18.68	28:20.77	28:08.4
Half Mar	61:54- 07	61:50	61:28	61:38	61:31	61:19	61:25	61:17	**60:58**
Marathon	2:10:38- 03	2:10:22	2:09:53	2:09:31	2:09:19!	**2:08:32**	2:09:06	2:08:58	2:09:14
3000mSt	**8:31.06- 04**	8:32.12	8:35.21	8:35.29	8:35.45	8:31.2	8:34.42	8:35.05	8:33.69
110mh	13.72- 96/07	13.67	13.71	13.68	13.67	13.66	13.67	13.67	**13.62**
400mh	**50.06- 00**	50.33	50.35	50.41	50.28	50.15	50.16	50.21	**50.06**
HJ	**2.24- 84/88/89/92/96**	2.23	2.23	2.23	**2.24**	**2.24**	**2.24**	**2.24**	**2.24**
PV	**5.55- 00**	5.50	5.46	5.42	5.45	5.50	5.50	5.50	5.50
LJ	**7.96- 04**	7.93	7.94	7.91	7.94	7.93	7.92	7.89	7.90
TJ	**16.60- 88**	16.53	16.46	16.46	16.53	16.49	16.40	16.38	16.44
SP	19.48- 84	19.21	19.15	19.08	19.18	19.51	19.41	19.47	**19.55**
DT	**60.96- 84**	60.77	60.00	59.77	59.98	60.95	60.21	60.64	60.36
HT	**73.06- 84**	70.89	70.66	70.78	70.44	71.22	70.49	70.48	70.73
JT	77.14- 91	76.28	77.03	76.71	77.38	**77.78**	77.10	77.16	77.51
Decathlon	**7702- 88**	7594	7623	7526	7678	7648	7586	7559	7594
20kmW	**1:22:48- 05**	1:23:32	1:23:57	1:24:24	1:23:40	1:23:10	1:22:56	1:23:07	1:23:24
50kmW	4:03:49- 99	4:05:05	4:09:24	4:08:08	4:06:15	4:03:04	4:08:33	4:06:22	**4:02:26**

! From 2011 main marathon lists no longer include Boston or other such excessively downhill races

Number of athletes achieving base level standards for world lists:

Men		2010	2011	2012	2013	2014	2015			2010	2011	2012	2013	2014	2015
100m	10.29	133	166	198	187	228	220	HJ	2.20	194	192	216	197	211	216
200m	20.69	90	122	165	140	187	194	PV	5.40	138	139	177	179	178	168
400m	46.19	154	151	184	177	202	216	LJ	7.80	173	186	183	180	182	182
800m	1:47.59	169	198	220	190	202	208	TJ	16.30	139	142	144	120	124	126
1500m	3:39.99	152	170	201	185	173	171	SP	18.60	168	153	191	164	193	199
5000m	13:37.0	177	193	203	180	169	204	DT	58.00	156	155	177	166	173	171
10000m	28:35.0	157	172	199	168	155	225	HT	68.00	158	149	158	146	149	156
HMar	61:59	145	147	199	171	199	182	JT	74.00	168	173	199	190	187	199
Mar	2:10:59	175	215	233	212	207	191	Dec	7400	136	165	173	143	150	157
3000St	8:39.9	135	147	184	141	138	144	20kmW	1:25:00	124	154	175	175	151	163
110mh	13.89	196	194	214	199	208	215	50kmW	4:10:00	103	110	132	106	113	133
400mh	50.79	155	171	186	177	191	200	TOTAL		3476	3764	4311	3923	4069	4243

The 2015 numbers compared to those of 2014: for 10th best 13-10, 100th best 17-3 (3 tie), base level 16-6 (1 tie)

WORLD LIST TRENDS - WOMEN

This table shows the 10th and 100th bests in the year lists for the last eight years, with previous bests.

10th Bests	To 2007	2008	2009	2010	2011	2012	2013	2014	2015
100m	**10.92- 88**	10.95	11.04	11.08	11.01	10.99	10.93	11.01	**10.92**
200m	22.24- 88	22.43	22.45	22.49	22.55	22.37	22.40	22.46	**22.23**
400m	**49.74- 84**	50.11	50.27	50.43	50.67	50.06	50.19	50.74	50.32
800m	**1:56.91- 88**	1:57.9	1:58.80	1:58.67	1:58.21	1:57.77	1:58.92	1:58.84	1:58.34
1500m	**3:58.07- 97**	4:02.44	4:00.86	4:00.25	4:01.73	3:59.71	4:01.48	4:00.17	4:01.26
5000m	14:43.87- 05	14:43.89	14:41.62	**14:38.64**	14:39.44	14:50.80	14:47.12	14:52.67	14:47.75
10000m	30:55.67- 05	**30:39.96**	30:51.92	31:29:03	31:10.02	30:59.19	31:04.85	31:48.6	31:13.29
Half Mar	68:23- 00	68:51	68:14	67:52	68:07	67:42	**67:39**	68:13	68:18
Marathon	2:23:22- 06	2:24:14	2:25:06	2:23:44	2:22:43!	**2:20:57**	2:23:00	2:22:30	2:22:51
3000mSt	9:26.63- 07	9:21.76	**9:18.54**	9:24.84	9:25.96	9:23.52	9:27.49	9:23.43	9:20.64
100mh	12.60- 04	**12.58**	12.67	12.65	12.73	12.62	12.81	12.71	12.59
400mh	**53.99- 04**	54.45	54.49	54.58	54.69	54.21	54.38	54.74	54.37
HJ	**2.01- 03**	1.98	1.98	1.97	1.96	1.96	1.97	1.97	1.97
PV	4.70- 07	4.70	4.65	4.66	4.71	4.70	4.71	4.71	**4.72**
LJ	**7.07- 88**	6.89	6.87	6.89	6.88	6.97	6.91	6.90	6.93
TJ	14.78- 04	**14.84**	14.62	14.48	14.57	14.60	14.50	14.10	14.32
SP	**20.85-** 87	19.29	19.38	19.47	19.26	19.60	18.81	19.03	18.89
DT	**70.34- 88**	64.10	63.89	64.04	63.91	64.45	64.46	65.51	64.79
HT	74.31- 06	74.40	73.07	73.40	72.65	**75.59**	75.02	74.20	73.66
JT	64.89- 00	63.24	63.89	63.36	63.50	64.91	63.55	64.50	**65.01**
Heptathlon	**6540- 88**	6465	6323	6204	6338	6466	6345	6395	6458
20kmW	1:27:52- 04	1:27:18	1:28:50	1:29:20	1:28:41	**1:27:08**	1:27:53	1:27:54	1:27:09

Peak years shown in bold

Women 100th Bests	To 2007	2008	2009	2010	2011	2012	2013	2014	2015
100m	11.36- 00	11.36	11.41	11.40	11.36	11.34	11.35	11.32	**11.31**
200m	23.21- 00	23.17	23.26	23.27	23.21	23.10	23.19	23.17	**23.08**
400m	52.14- 04/07	**52.08**	52.44	52.52	52.33	52.16	52.25	52.36	52.25
800m	2:01.50- 84	2:02.50	2:02.13	2:02.14	2:01.86	**2:01.48**	2:02.05	2:02.05	2:02.06
1500m	4:10.22- 84	4:11.64	4:11.06	4:10.50	4:09.88	**4:09.06**	4:09.98	4:10.09	4:10.24
5000m	**15:27.20- 0**4	15:27.50	15:37.31	15:37.45	15:31.67	15:32.88	15:35.74	15:33.42	15:32.67
10000m	32:32.47- 00	32:30.10	32:54.64	32:57.59	32:53.44	32:38.95	32:48.60	32:43.90	**32:29.06**
Half Mar	71:15- 07	71:19	70:57	70:59	71:06	70:48	**70:44**	70:45	70:46
Marathon	2:31:05- 01	2:29:53	2:30:08	2:29:36	2:28:32	**2:28:01**	2:29:10	2:29:17	2:28:24
3000mSt	10:03.2- 07	9:56.48	10:02.94	10:03.50	9:59.44	9:53.79	9:56.50	9:53.19	**9:52.62**
100mh	13.22- 00	13.22	13.28	13.23	13.16	**13.11**	13.19	13.14	13.17
400mh	57.21- 07	57.46	57.45	57.22	57.26	57.14	57.40	57.34	**57.08**
HJ	**1.88- 86/87/88/92/93**	1.86	1.86	1.87	1.86	1.87	1.87	1.86	1.86
PV	4.22- 07	4.25	4.21	4.25	4.30	4.31	4.30	4.30	**4.32**
LJ	6.53- 88	6.52	6.49	6.51	6.50	**6.55**	6.49	6.45	6.49
TJ	13.70- 04	**13.75**	13.65	13.67	13.70	13.71	13.69	13.60	13.62
SP	**17.19- 87**	16.49	16.43	16.46	16.60	16.82	16.65	16.60	16.84
DT	**58.50- 92**	55.43	56.06	55.05	56.12	56.94	55.70	56.27	56.26
HT	64.34- 07	64.81	63.77	64.12	64.79	**65.78**	64.65	64.79	65.67
JT	55.55- 00	54.81	55.16	54.98	55.34	**55.97**	55.10	55.78	55.95
Heptathlon	**5741- 88**	5687	5586	5568	5591	5702	5560	5668	5715
20kmW	1:34:11- 05	1:34:30	1:35:54	1:36:32	1:34:52	**1:33:43**	1:33:48	1:35:20	1:34:16

All-time record levels indicated in bold.

! From 2011 main marathon lists no longer include Boston or other such excessively downhill races.

Number of athletes achieving base level standards for world lists:

Women		2010	2011	2012	2013	2014	2015
100m	11.50	171	195	217	208	227	228
200m	23.39	135	146	185	187	175	215
400m	52.99	167	187	210	196	190	213
800m	2:03.50	153	176	196	166	184	191
1500m	4:13.5	152	161	197	167	169	164
5000m	15:45.0	139	163	201	167	172	191
10000m	33:15.0	133	146	200	153	175	212
HMar	72:00	156	174	199	204	193	200
Mar	2:32:00	152	165	212	170	171	195
3000mSt	10:12.0	144	177	200	191	203	208
100mh	13.39	154	177	198	175	195	191

		2010	2011	2012	2013	2014	2015
400mh	58.44	169	181	228	193	194	232
HJ	1.85	142	172	164	155	148	142
PV	4.15	156	176	189	181	203	234
LJ	6.35	180	185	212	171	168	186
TJ	13.30	182	191	199	184	171	169
SP	15.85	159	163	180	177	189	194
DT	53.65	144	153	172	159	152	165
HT	61.00	167	181	205	190	193	205
JT	53.00	151	160	177	159	172	176
Hep	5450	126	146	157	140	156	155
20kmW	1:38:00	123	167	173	191	148	176
TOTAL		3355	3742	4270	3884	3948	4242

The 2015 numbers compared to those of 2014: for 10th best 14-7 (1 tie), 100th best 16-5 (1 tie), base level 17-5

AMENDMENTS TO ATHLETICS 2015

p.5 Primo Nebiolo died in 1999
p.20 Aug 29-31. Finland v Sweden was in Helsinki.
p.39 Hammer: Zhang Wenxiu's drugs ban was overturned, so she ranks 4th in the world rankings, the rest moving down a place, and reinstated as Asian Games champion (p.75).
p.48 Add 1 Nov Algiers: Milton Rotich KEN 2:09:40, Mestawat Tadesse ETH 2:37:10
p.78 European Team: W DT: Mélina Robert-Michon FRA 65.51. 2nd League: PV: Arents, W HT: Hrasnová 71.30
p.81 Diamond League 2014: Brussels on Sep 5
p.96 Buhl 3000mSt 8:34.0 1960. Bullard 30 Jul 1937
p.106 Journoud French record in 1987 not 1967
p.118 Das war die DDR-Leichtathletik 1945-1990
p.123 World List Trends Women: Heading should be same as for men on previous page: so To 2004, and 2007 to 2014
p.144+ National champions 2014: Belgium (p.144): 20kW: Dirk Bogaert (age 57) 1:52:11, delete W HT: Vanessa Sterckendries 59.09; Croatia (p.151): delete TJ: Andro Duzevic 15.21; Netherlands (p.204): delete 200m Spillekom
p.275 Records in 2014: W35 200H St 22.61 Félix SÁNCHEZ DOM Manchester 17 May 14
W35 20,000m track walk 1:19:42.1 Yohann DINIZ FRA Bogny-sur-Meuse 25 May 14

2014 World Lists

Men

100m: 10.11 Hart 6.9.92 (& 200m 20.35), 10.27/10.20w Haynes 11.3.92, 10.28 1.9 Adetoye Durotoye NGR 9.5.86 2 Jul; 10.21w 3.1 Idrissa Adam CMR 28.12.84 17 May; Jnrs: 10.30 1.1 Divine Oduduru NGR 14.5.96 2h4 NC Calabar 19 Jun

200m: 20.49A Brenes, best at la: 20.70 -1.9 24 May, 20.61w 2.7 14 Jun, 20.25w Divine Oduduru

400m: 44.53 Santos 12.11.72 (and amend for previous years and in Jnr AT lists, best 44.71A in 2011), 45.66 Bilderback 27.8.93 (& 200m 20.61w), 45.95 Williams Collazo, 45.98i Braddy 18.10.91

600m: Indoors: delete 1:16.11 Sowinski (has 1:15.79)

800m: 1:47.1A Jackson Kivuva KEN 11.8.88 15 May, 1:47.2A Patrick Ryan KEN-J .96 1 Nakuru 25 May

1500m: 3:38.06 Chala Regassa ETH-Y .97, 3:38.7A Vincent Letting KEN 16.6.93 26 Apr, 3:39.5A Geoffrey Rono KEN 21.4.87 26 Apr; Jnrs: 3:41.0A Yenew Tebekew ETH 14.3.94 4 Addis Ababa 15 Jun, 3:41.4A Hosea Cheromei 2h3 Nairobi 24 May (from 3:42.4), 3:42.0A John Koech KEN .95 5h2 NC Nairobi 5 Jun

3000m: 7:46.55i Blankenship 15.12.89 (& 1500m 3:39.33); Jnrs: 7:59.51 Kibrab, Indoors: 7:53.94 Debeli Gezmu ETH 14.4.86 4 Praha 25 Feb

5000m: 13:16.06 Mwangi b. 23.3.94 (13:44.2A- 13), 13:37.64 McGorty 8.3.95, 13:37.8A John Chepkwony KEN .88 15 May

10,000m: 27:23.66 Mwangi b. 23.3.94 (-0-), 28:23.05A Isaac Kibet KEN-J 5.5.96 1 Kampala 19 Apr, 28:23.2A Charles Kwemoi UGA 12 Jul, 28:32.4 Joseph Tiofil Panga TAN-J 26.6.95 2 NC Dar-es-Salaam 13 Jul, 28:32.47A Ben Somikwo UGA 4.10.96 1 Kampala 15 Apr, 28:34.5A Moses Kurong UGA 7.7.94 12 Jul; Jnrs: 28:42.1A Abdellah Mande UGA 20.5.95 1 Kampala 21 Jun

HMar: 60:08 Wasihun 20.10.93, 61:09 Mwangi 12.10.89, 61:13 Kiptoo 14.8.93, 61:25 Josphat Kiptis KEN 16.11.93 1 Nov, 61:26 John Lottang KEN 25 May, 61:31 Mark Kangogo .89 1 Nov, 61:40 Isaac Korir BRN, 61:45+ Kitur 10.1.90

Mar: 2:09:40 Milton Rotich 1 Nov (from 2:10:48), 2:10:16 Lawrence Cherono KEN 1 Nov, 2:10:44 Mike Mutai KEN .83 22 Mar

2000mSt: 5:37.63 Hicham Chemlal 2 Afr-Y Gaborone 29 May

3000mSt: 8:25.45 Beyo ETH-J 18.1.96 (add to juniors), 8:30.54 Rotich 20.10.90

110mh: 13.65 Trajkovic 17.3.92, Siddhanth Thingalaya 3.1.91; delete repeated 13.27 Porter

HJ: 2.20i Abdoulaye Diarra MLI 27.5.88 19 Dec

PV: 5.48 Drew Volz 20.11.92 9 Aug

LJ: 7.83 Abderrahim Zahouani MAR 21.6.91 26 Apr

TJ: 10th best was Laine at 17.27. wa: 16.36w 2.1 Kongmil; Jnr: 15.90 Liu Mingxian 16.5.97

SP: 18.87 to drugs dq Fernandes BRA #, 18.75i Josh Uchtmann USA 18.12.88 1 Feb

DT: 59.80 Yunio Lastre

HT: 71.24 Vasilchenko 3 Novopolotsk 28 Nov (from 69.51), 70.69 Alaa El-Din Mohamed El-Ashry EGY 6.1.91 1 Nairobi 13 Jul; 100th 70.50, 70.17 Noleysis Vicet, 68.35 Collin Post USA 13.2.82 31 May. Unconfirmed: 74.36 Jacob Freeman 1 Riverdale 22 May (from 71.43); Jnrs: 66.19 Mansilla. 6kg Jnrs: 77.34 Mitskov 1 NC-j Brest 25 Jun (from 74.82), 76.06 Roman Zhloludyev BLR 8.1.96 2 NC-j Brest 25 Jun

JT: 76.71A Holtzhausen, 75.38 Muhar J 22.7.96

Dec: 8599w Hardee, Jnrs: 7021(w) Nuytinck

4x100m: 39.88 IRL (one athlete drugs dq)

10,000mW: 40:19.53 Noda 24.1.96

20kmW: 1:22:19 Amezua 1.5.92

35kmW: 2:30:00 Yevstifeyev

Women

200m: 23.31w Mitchell 25.11.95; hand timed: 23.1w 2.7 Bukola Abogunloko NGR 18.8.94 30 Oct

400m: 51.73 Daysiurami Bonne, 52.77 Yaimeisi Borlot

800m: 2:01.97 Yusneisis Santisuti

1500m: 4:07.59 Sado 12.1.96; Juniors: 4:16.7A Sintayehu Lewetegn ETH .96 4 NC Addis Ababa 14 Jun

3000m: delete 8:57.31 Oljira (see 8:44.2), 9:01.30i Shmidt to drugs dq

10,000m: 32:24.38 Reina Iwade, 33:06.48 Trengove, 33:09.39 Trihas Gebre ETH 29.4.90 3 May; 32:49.24 Kudashkina to drugs dq

HMar: 69:12 Chepchirchir 27.9.93 (& 10k 31:34), 70:43 Chebet 6.6.92, 71:36 Pauline Muchiri KEN .89 20 Apr

Mar: 2:27:57 Winny Jepkorir 10.6.90, 2:30:43 Chaltu Waka ETH .85 22 Mar; drugs dq: 2:23:43 Konovalova, 2:24:37 Hamera-Shmyrko (& 25/30k), also loses London 7th, so move up from 2:26:46 Félix to 7.

2000mSt: 6:27.98A Tefera 27.2.97

100mh: 13.27 Rujaine Coto

400mh: 55.46 Ogoegbunam, hand timed 57.0 Ghofrane Al-Mohamed SYR 6.6.89 1 Damascus 12 Aug (57.42- 06)

PV: 4.20 Lucas 20.2.93, Best out: delete 4.20 Galiart

TJ: 14.01 Yargeris Savigne, 13.39 0.8 Yevdokimova 23 Jun (from 13.38).

DT: 66.03 Yaimé Pérez

HT: 77.33 Zhang Wenxiu at Asian Games (not drugs dq) as reinstated (74.14, 72.56, 74.27, 75.96, 76.20, 77.33); Jnr: 59.98 Elianne Despaigne

JT: 63.80A Ruíz 29.1.91, 60.23 Sudarushkina 1 Sankt-Peterburg 23 May, 53.89 Schol 28 Sep

4x100m: 45.09 SLO 21 Jun; 45.12 CUB is best at low altitude

4x1500m: 17:05.72A 3 Nengampi

50kW: 4:34:46.5t Erin Taylor-Talcott 1 Banks 9 Mar (world track best)

Index changes are reflected in this year's Annual.

Amendments to World Indoor Lists 2015

60m: 6.50 Bailey 13 Feb, 6.51A Haynes 11.3.92, 6.60 Yang Yang 26.6.91; **200m**: 20.57 Hart 6.9.92; **400m**: 45.98 Bilderback 27.8.93; **600m**: 1:16.22A Dennison 13.8.94; **1500m**: 3:35.26 Ngetich 15.9.95; **1500m/1M/3000m/2M**: Blankenship 15.12.89; **Hep**: 6070 Wieland 7.2.94, 5948 Sarantsev 5.2.88, 5941 Abdullah 6.10.93; **W 200m**: 22.96 Mitchell 25.11.95; **300m**: 37.13 Mamina 30.5.90; **600m**: 1:26.73 Chambers 11.9.90; 1500m: 4:06.44 Cichocka; **1M**: 4:31.34 Nicole Tully USA 30.10.86 14 Feb; **3000m**: 8:37.20+ Dibaba 19 Feb; 5000m: 14:18.86 Genzebe Dibaba ETH 8.2.91 1 XLG Stockholm 19 Feb; **PV**: 4.53 Gergel 24.4.89, 4.47 Ahbe CAN, 4.35 Sadovnikova 22.6.95

Amendments to Previous World Lists

2014 Indoors: W TJ: 14.25 Irina Gumenyuk 1, 14.09 Irina Kosko 2 Sankt-Peterburg 26 Jan

2013: 2000mSt: 6:19.55 Kettunen 10.2.94; PV: 5.38 Christian Sanderfer USA 25.3.93 4 Jul; JT: 65.62 Lu Huihui ¶ drugs dq so not Asian record, best is her 64.48 on 18 Mar; 56.83 Sui 3, 59.21 Song Xiaodan 3, 57.74 Song Dan 4; Hep 6135 Profit, 6000 Carrier-Eades.

2012: 4x100: to drugs dq: 37.04 USA (Gay ¶); 20kW: drugs dq 1:17:47 Ruzavin 18 Feb (rest move up a place, Krivov 1, Trofimov 2 etc.) replace by 1:20:37 5 WCp Saransk 12 May; 3000mSt: 9:37.02 Zhudina 1, 9:42.72 Danekova 5h1, 9:43.08 Koubaa 6h1. 9:44.91 Shatalova 2, 9:47.45 Mara 2; 100mh: drugs dq 12.58/12.58.12.61 Yanit, best earlier 13.05 1 Ankara 5 Jun

2010: Mar: 2:22:19 Abitova ¶, adjust placings of the rest

Marks annulled due to drugs disqualifications (adjust placings of the rest):

Liliya Shobukhova results from 9 Oct 2009 annulled (her 2-year ban from that date was listed in ATHLETICS 2015): 2009- Mar 2:25:5; 2010- HMar 70:00, 2 marks in 25k/30k list, Mar 2:20:25 & 2:22:00; 2011- HMar 69:25, Mar 2:18:20 & 2:20:15; 2012- Mar 2:22:59;. Loses her marathon 'wins' in London 2010 (& 2nd 2011), Chicago 2009-11 and the World Marathon Majors Series titles of 2009/10 and 2010/11. The revised 1-2-3 of those five marathons are: 2009 Chicago: 1, Mikitenko GER 2:26:31; 2, Grigoryeva RUS 2:26:47; 3, Erkesso ETH 2:26:56; 2010 London: 1, Mergia ETH 2:22:38; 2, Bekele ETH 2:23:17; 3, Tafa ETH 2:24:39; 2010 Chicago: 1, Bayisa ETH 2:23:40; 2, Davila USA 2:26:20, 3. Mikitenko GER 2:26:40; 2011 London: 1, Keitany KEN 2:19:19; 2, E Kiplagat KEN 2:20:46; 3, Bekele 2:23:42; 2011 Chicago: 1, E Dibaba ETH 2:22:09; 2, Fukushi JPN 2:24:38; 3, Gebre ETH 2:26:17.

Marta Domínguez results from 5 Aug 2009 annulled. 2009- 3kSt 9:07.32 (replace by 9:09.39), 2010- 1500m 4:04.27, 3kSt 9:17.07; 2011- 10kRd dh 32:49; 2012- 10kRd 31:37, 3kSt 9:24.26

Asli Çakir results from 29 Jul 2010 annulled. 1500m: 2010- 4:02.17 (replace by 4:04.8 1 NC Izmir 29 Jun); 2011- 4:05.53, 2012- 3:56.62

Abderrahime Bouramdane: 2011- 2:08:42, 2012- 2:10:13

Hafid Chani: 2009- 10k Rd 28:18, 2013- 2:09:11.

Aleksandra Duliba: 2013- HMar 71:30+, Mar 2:23:44 (replace by 2:26:08dh 1 Los Angeles 17 Mar); 2014- HMar 71:46+, Mar 2:24:43 & 2:21:29dh

Rkia El Moukim: 2011- 3000m 8:59.20. 5000m 15:34.75, 10k 32:13, HMar 70:38; 2012- 1500m 4:09.36, 5000m 15:21.88; 2013- 10k 32:34, HMar 70:53; 2014- 10k 32:07, HMar 70:03.

Svetlana Kireyeva: 2012- 1500m 4:08.30; 2013- 1000m 2:39.72i, 2000m 5:44.08i, 3000m 8:48.27i, 5000m 15:40.03; 2014- 1500m 4:12.23, 5000m 15:43.77

Mariya Konovalova: 2010- 2000m 5:38.98i, 5000m 14:49.68, HMar 70:39, Mar 2:23:50; 2011- 70:30/2:25:18; 2012- W 5000m 15:27.54, HMar 69:56, Mar 2:25:38; 2013- W 5000m 15:27.16, HMar 69:20, Mar 2:22:46.

Anna Lukyanova: results annulled from 19 Jul 2010. 2010- 10000mW best track 44:17.96; 2011: 10kW 43:27 & 20kW 1:27:49; 2012- 10k 44:29, 20kW 1:27:08

Irina Maracheva: results annulled from 26 Jun 2012. 2012- 1500m 4:10.37; 2013 Indoor: 800m 2:02.22; 2013- 800m 2:00.82; 2014- 800m 2:02.2

Anna Mishchenko: results annulled from 28 Jun 2012. 2012- 1500m 4:01.16 (replace by 4:03.33 3 Bisl Oslo 7 Jun), 2014: 1500m- 4:05.54, 2015- 4:01.95.

Tetyana Hamera-Shmyrko: 2012- 10,000m 32:50.13, Mar 2:24:32; 2013- HMar 71:40, Mar 2:23:58.

Svitlana Shmidt: 3000mSt: 2012- 9:31.16, 2013- 9:37.33

Championships Changes. Drugs dqs – move rest up accordingly

2013 World Juniors: W 5000m: (6) Kudashkina

2011 World University Games: W 3kSt: (1) Zaripova

2013 South East Asia Games: W 20kW: Saw dq, winner: Nguyen Thi Thanh Phuc VIE 1:37:08.

2012 Olympics: 4x100m: USA lost 2nd place due to Tyson Gay drugs dq. 2. TTO, 3, FRA etc; 50kW: (1) Kirdyapkin, (6) Bakulin; W 1500m: (1) Çakir; Mar: (5) Hamera-Shmyrko, 3000mSt (12) Domínguez, 100mh: (5) Yanit, so rest move up; 20k: (2) Kaniskina,

2012 Europeans: W 800m: (2) Maracheva, so 2. Marina Arzamasova BLR, 3. Liliya Lobanova UKR; 1500m: (3) Mishchenko, so 3. Nuria Fernández ESP (originally 5th); 3000mSt: (2) Shmidt, so 2. Möldner-Schmidt, 3. Krause etc; 100mh: (1) Yanit, so 1. Talay, 2, Poplavskaya, 3. Schrott etc.

2012 European Juniors: W 5000m: (3) Kudshakina, so 3. Rebecca Weston GBR 16:09.90

2012 Balkan Champs: W 100mh: Olivía Petsoúdi GRE 13.55 (dq Nevin Yanit TUR 12.61)

2012: **World Race Walking Cup**: 20k: (3) Kanaykin, (10) Borchin; 50k: (3) Kanaykin, (10) Borchin; W 20k: (2) Kaniskina

2012 World Indoors: W 1500m (3) Çakir

2011 Worlds: Mar (4) Bouramdane, World Marathon Cup: dq 3 MAR, so 3. ESP...; 20kW: (1) Borchin, (2) Kanaykin; 50kW: (1) Bakulin; W 3kSt: (1) Zaripova, 20kW: (1) Kaniskina

2011 World University Games: W 1500m: (1) Cakir, 1. Mishchenko, 2. Krebs (originally 5th!), add 3. Liu Fang CHN 4:07.90

2011 European Race Walking Cup: 20k: (5) Kanaykin

2010 World Juniors: W 10,000mW: (2) Anna Lukyanova RUS, so 2. Kumiko Okada JPN, 3. He Qin CHN.

2010 Europeans: W 1500m: (5) Cakir. add 7. Oksana Zbrozhek RUS 4:04.91, 8. Hannah England GBR 4:05.07; W 5000m: (5) Konovalova (also RUS Champ goes to Olga Golovkina 15:16.95); 3000mSt: (2) Domínguez; 20kW: (1) Kanisjina.

2010 Continental Cup: W 1500m: (5) Çakir

2009 Worlds: 20kW: (1) Borchin; 50kW: (1) Kirdyapkin; W 10000m: (11) Konovalova, 3000mSt: (1) Domínguez, 20kw: (1) Kaniskina.

These include CAS confirmation in March 2016 of bans and results annulled for these top Russian athletes: **Sergey Bakulin** 25 Feb 11-24 Dec 12; **Valeriy Borchin** 14 Aug 09-15 Oct 12, **Vladimir Kanaykin** (8-year ban) 25 Feb 11-17 Dec 12, **Olga Kaniskina** 15 Aug 09-15 Oct 12, **Sergey Kirdyapkin** 20 Aug 09-15 Oct 12; **Yuliya Zaripova** 2 Jul 11-25 Jul 13.

Correction to ATHLETICS 2014

p.26 Merit rankings for 110mh should be: 1. Oliver, 2. Wilson, 3. Shubenkov, 4. Richardson, 5. Merritt, 6. Riley, 7. Brathwaite, 8. Robles, 9. Sharman, 10. P Martinot-Lagarde

REFERENCE BOOKS 2015-16

World's Greatest in Athletics by Jonas Hedman, Richard Hymans and Peter Matthews. 832 pages, 240 x 170mm, 315 pictures. Contents are: a never-before-published top-10 world all-time ranking of athletes at all standard events with career details, best performances and annual progressions for the top selections (228 pages), 500 deep all-time lists (510 pages) to the end of 2014 and top-10 decade lists 1900-2010 (96 pages). Copies ordered via www.worldsgreatestinathletics.com or email jonas.hedman@textograf.com.

Pre-payment by Paypal from the website: $US 49 plus postage.

Running Through The Ages Second Edition by Edward S. Sears. 254x177mm, 332 pages. The author has completely revised and updated this superb book, acclaimed when it was first published in 2001. It tells of the story of running from the time when running was necessary for survival to the running for fun of today as well as the feats of the greatest athletes of all-time. Published in the USA by McFarland & Company Inc. www.mcfarlandpub.com

World Women's Athletics 100 Best Performers Year Lists 1911-1962 by John Brant and Janusz Wasko. 488 pp. The fourth edition of the author's most important work has been expanded to include year lists from 1911 to 1925, a decade in which there was a very gradual expansion of female athletics – the first time that such lists have ever been published. The deep research of the authors and their helpers has resulted in over 2000 changes and additions being made to the lists that go up to 100 deep for the main events from 1926 to 1962. Details of price from john@apshipping.co.uk or rwasko@onet.eu.

Women High Jump – All Time Best Performances and Performers by Enzo Rivis. A5, 96 pages. This includes all performances (outdoor and indoor) over 1.95m (3307 performances) and all performers over 1.87m (950 performers) to the end of 2014, with best outdoor marks for athletes with indoor best performance. Date of birth, height and weight details are given for all athletes. Also listed are best Juniors (over 1.92m) and Youths (over 1.90m) and best performances by age. There are also summaries of the most prolific women over 1.95m and 2m, best longevity over 1.86m and 2m, top tens by countries and best height differentials. enzo.rivis@libero.it for cost and payment details.

Progression of IAAF World Records 2015 edition. A5 634 pages. Edited by Richard Hymans and Imre Matrahazi, this most important work has been updated and is the 8th edition from the first, that was principally the work of Ekkehard zur Megede, in 1987. Full details are given of every ratified and unratified record, going back into the middle of the 19th century, including track and road, at current events and previously recognised events and distances as well, with a comprehensive index of world-record setting athletes. In particular much additional information on early women's marks has been added through the great work of John Brant and Janusz Wasko in their World Women's Athletics 100 Best Performers Lists 1921-62 to which John Brant has added a wealth of detail from 1870 to 1905. There are also appendices with the most prolific record holders, youngest and oldest and cities and stadia with the most records. This can be downloaded at: http://iaaf-ebooks.s3.amazonaws.com/2015/Progression-of-IAAF-World-Records-2015/index.htm

British Athletics 1953 (A4 120 pages) and **British Athletics 1954** (A4 140 pages) by Michael Sheridan. Published by the author, 27 Yew Tree Park, Congresbury, Somerset BS49 5ER, UK. Price including postage £15 each or £28 if purchased together. Customers in other countries should e-mail mesheridan1@talktalk.net for details of cost. The author has continued his invaluable work with these books that contain deep British year lists (men and women) for each year with indexes of all athletes listed. Back in those days the only lists published were 10 (perhaps up to 20 in a few men's events) deep, so Mike has done (and continues to do) a huge amount of work in gathering the information in his series of books that now cover from 1946 to 1954.

Thanks And No Thanks Mr Hitler: The Dorothy Odam-Tyler Story by Mike Fleet. Obtainable from Amazon, £10.95 post free in UK or email the author at mike@mafleet.co.uk. The career story of the remarkable athlete who won Olympic high jump silver medals in 1936 and 1948 and set four UK records to 1.68 in 1948 including a world record at 1.66 in 1939.

Men's Marathon & 3000 Metres Steeplechase by Ari Törmä. A4 126 pages. This is the 11th volume in the series of "The Greatest Athletes of the Modern Era. Statistics from the Early Years to the Present." There are 75 deep all-time lists at four-yearly intervals for marathon (including distances from c.38k plus) from 1900 and for steeplechase from 1924 with annual top tens and results of each Olympic final plus yearly progressions for the top three men on Törmä's scoring system of points for yearly world rankings. Enquiries to athletics@aritorma.net or mikko.nieminen@dlc.fi.

Polska Lekkoatletyka 1945-60 [2 volumes] – 456 pages each inc. 24 pages of photos in volume 1. National Championships and annual top 50 lists.

Historia Memorialu Janusza Kusocinskiego – 272 pages, inc. 29 pages of photographs. The athlete Janusz Kusocinski and full results of the meeting in this name,

Historia Polskiej lkekkoatletyki halowj 1922-2014 – 488 pages, inc. 32 pages of photographs. Polish indoor athletics.

For the above detailed Polish statistical productions contact janusz.rozum@gmail.com

Intriguing Facts & Figures From Athletics History 1860-2014 by Roberto L Quercetani. Obtainable from the publishers, Roberto Vallardi Editore www.editvallardi.com; email: segreteria@editvallardi.com. Price (including postage): Italy 30 euros; rest of Europe 35 euros; Americas & Far East 40 euros; Australia & NZ 47 euros.

ANNUALS

L'athlétisme Africain/African Athletics 2015. A5, 152 pages. By Yves Pinaud. Published by Éditions Polymédias with support from the IAAF, the 34th edition in this splendid series has 100 deep men's and women's lists for Africa for 2014, with all-time lists, national championships and major meetings results. 20 euro, £18 or US $30 including postage from La Mémoire du Sport, 166 rue de Decize, 03000 Moulins, France. (Also available: booklist with very extensive list of athletics books and magazines for sale).

2015 Combined Events Annual by Hans van Kuijen. A5, 200pp. The latest edition of this annual contain outdoor and indoor all-time lists, 2015 ranking lists, national records, 50 bests' biographies etc. 35 EUR or 35 GBP or 50 USD. From Hans van Kuijen, de Bergen 66, 5706 RZ Helmond, Netherlands. email: j.kuijen4@upcmail.nl. No cheques, but payments can be made to BIC-code: ABNANL2A, IBAN-code: NL79ABNA0523127898.

Copies still available: each year 2005-14 and Hans' books on decathlon history and Götzis special.

Sadly, Hans writes that this, the 23rd edition, will be the last in printed form due to declining sales and increase in costs of printing and postage. One hopes that he succeeds in finding other ways to publish his valuable collection of data.

British Athletics 2015. A5 432 pages. The 56th NUTS Annual, edited by Rob Whittingham, Tony Miller and Peter Matthews. Deep UK ranking lists for all age groups in 2014, top 12 merit rankings, all-time lists, results etc. Also further investigation into participation trends in British athletics by Rob Whittingham. £20 UK, £24 Europe, £26 outside Europe from Rob Whittingham, 7 Birch Green, Croft Manor, Glossop, Derbyshire SK13 8PR, UK. Cash or sterling cheques. Overseas orders may be made using PayPal – see the NUTS web site for details, at www.nuts.org.uk

Asian Athletics 2014 Rankings. A5 97 pages. Heinrich Hubbeling continues his magnificent annual job as this booklet contains top 30 lists for 2014 for athletes from Asian nations, with continuation lists for countries other than China and Japan (up to 4 best per country), with new national records, and full lists of Asian records. Euro 20/US $30 in cash or by International Money Order from the author, Haaksbergener Str 25, 48691 Vreden, Germany. email hhubbeling@t-online.de. Copies also available for 1998, 2005-09, 2011-13 and Asian all-time rankings as at 31.12.2000 at €15/US $22 each.

Athlérama 2014. A5 720pp. The 52nd edition of the French Annual, edited by Patricia Doilin with a strong team of compilers, is again a superb reference book accompanied by a CD containing a pdf of the contents. Worldwide only the Spanish group of statisticians can begin to match this magnificent work. Packed with information on French athletics – records, profiles of 95 top athletes, results, deep year lists for 2014 for all age groups plus all-time lists and indexes. There is a special survey by Patrice Bertignon of the career of their "Champion of Champions" Renaud Lavillenie. Maintaining the sequence, there are French top ten lists and reviews for 1914 and 1964. 28 euros from the FFA, 33 avenue Pierre de Coubertin, 7540 Paris Cedex 13, France. email Patricia.Doilin@athle.org

Friidrott 2015. 170 x 240 mm 488 pp, hardback. Edited by Jonas Hedman, text in Swedish. This high quality production reviews world and Nordic athletics, including detailed championships and major events results with narrative (in Swedish), world outdoor top 50 year and all-time-lists, top 25 Nordic and Swedish year and all-time lists plus indoor top tens and record lists for World, Europe, Nordic nations and Sweden. 495 kronor from TextoGraf Förlag, Jonas Hedman, Springarvägen 14, 142 61 Trångsund, Sweden. See www.textograf.com. Email jonas.hedman@textograf.com

Israeli Athletics Annual 2015/16. 240 x 170mm, 56pp, illustrated. By David Eiger. Records, championship results, 2015 top 20s and all-time lists, with profiles of leading Israeli athletes. 8 euro or US $9 from David Eiger, 10

Ezra Hozsofer Str, Herzliya 46 371, Israel. Past editions from 1986 onwards are also available.

including chronology of the year, records, results, 50 athlete profiles and year and all-time lists, compiled by Andris Stagis. From the Latvian Athletic Association, Augsiela 1, Riga LV-1009, Latvia. email: lvs@lat-athletics.lv

Latvijas Vieglatletikas Gadagramata 2016. A5 280 pp. Comprehensive coverage of Latvian athletics for 2015, including chronology of the year, records, results, 50 athlete profiles and year and all-time lists, compiled by Andris Stagis. From the Latvian Athletic Association, Augsiela 1, Riga LV-1009, Latvia. email: lvs@lat-athletics.lv

Annuaire FLA 2015. A4 272p. The Luxembourg Annual, edited by Georges Klepper, is again a magnificent and extraordinarily comprehensive volume, with reviews, results, 2015 and all-time lists, plus many colour photographs. 15 euros locally, by post €18 in Luxembourg, €27 elsewhere to account no. LU32 1111 0200 0321 0000. See www.fla.lu.

Southeast Asia Athletics Annual 2014/15. A5, 170 pages. By ATFS member Jad Adrian Washif. South East Asia rankings, records and national championship results with statistical profiles for leading athletes. Price EUR 15 (outside SEA) or US$20 inc. shipping and handling fees. Email: info@adriansprints.com

Anuario Athlético Español 2014/2015. 1350 pp. This massive publication with results, 2015 year and all-time lists, with all-time Spanish champions, current biographies and much more is available for downloading in sections – see publications and available DVDs at www.rfea.es.

Statistisch Jaarboek 2014. The Dutch Annual is available to download at http://www.atletiekunie.nl/index.php?page=949 . Records, results and ranking lists for all age groups for 2014.

Ukraine Statistics 2015 by Ivan Kachkivskiy. A5, 136 pages. Ukrainian lists for 2015 in roman script. Attractively produced. The initial 2014 publication was 256 page with 16 pages of colour photographs and in Cyrillic script. Contact <ikachkivskyi@flau.org.ua> for details.

2015 USA Track & Field Fast Annual. General editor Tom Casacky. A5 606pp. The 37th FAST Annual, contains records, 50-deep US lists for 2014 and all-time, with 15-deep junior and college all-time lists. The final index section includes annual progressions and championships details for top American athletes. $25 post paid in the USA or $42 or 38 Euros airmail from Tom Casacky, PO Box 4288, Napa, CA 94558, USA. Payment is easiest by PayPal (to tom@interis.com).

Yleisurheilu 2015. A5 672pp. The Finnish Yearbook, published by Suomen Urheilulitto (Finnish Athletics) and compiled by Juhani and Mirko Jalava, contains every conceivable statistic for Finnish athletics (with results and deep year lists) in 2015 and also world indoor, outdoor and junior lists for the year as known at November. 19 euros plus 10 euros for postage and packaging. Orders by e-mail to juhani@tilastopaja.fi.

Statistical Bulletins

TRACK STATS. The NUTS quarterly journal. **May 2015** had a strong Czech flavour with a detailed review of Dana Zátopková's career by Bob Phillips, who also wrote about his pilgrimage to the Stará Boleslav track on which Emil Zátopek set so many records. Tom Hurst compiled a list of Helena Fibingerová's shot competitions and there was a profile of Denmark's 400/800m runner Niels Holst Sørensen.

August 2015 included career records of Ron Clarke and Ingrid Kristiansen, a lengthy profile of Bob Tisdall and career reminiscences by John Parlett.

December 2015 included Ron Clarke's 15 races in Britain, a 50-deep list of national records for 4x800m relay and a tribute to *Athletics Weekly* on the occasion of the magazine's 70th birthday.

Subscription details from Liz Sissons at lizsissons9@gmail.com

The **Spanish group, the AEEA** continues to produce magnificent publications. Membership (four bulletins per year) is 55 euros per year (€61 outside Europe) from AEEA secretary Ignacio Mansilla, C/Encinar del Rey, 18 - 28450 Collado Mediano, Madrid, Spain. email: comunicacion@rfea.es

Their **Bulletin No.95** was a massive 562 pages. Of these, pages 17 to 414 provided Historia del Atletismo en Madrid 2nd part (1946-65). Then followed Spanish top 100 performer lists for 2014 plus top 20 performances for all events (actually for the year from 1 Nov 2013).

Bulletin 96 December 2015, 444 pages, of which 206 covered Spanish all-time list for under 23s, c. 50 performances and 60+ performers; 26p Spanish records for age groups 13-22 set in 2013-15; 165p Spanish lists for 2015: top 20 performances and 100 performers per event; 28p Ibero-American all-time lists as at 31.12.53; 24p analysis of finalists by continent at global outdoor championships 1983-2015.

The **DGLD** – the **German** statistical group, Deutsche Gesellschaft für Leichtathletik-Dokumentation celebrated its silver jubilee, having been founded on 21 October 1990.

It produces annual national ranking lists

(**Deutsche Bestenliste 2014**, 192 pages) for Germany and impressive bulletins of up to 292 pages, packed with historical articles and statistical compilations. Each issue (three per year) includes statistical profiles of athletes born 70, 75, 80, 85, 90 years ago etc. Membership, with free Deutsche Bestenliste – euro 55 per year. Contact Hans Waynberg, Liebigstrasse 9, 41464 Neuss, Germany; hans.waynberg@t-online.de. Website: www.ladgld.de

Latvijas Vieglatletikas Gadagramata 2016. A5 280 pp. Comprehensive coverage of Latvian athletics for 2015,

The latest in the series of books published by the DGLD dealing with the history of 100 years of athletics in Germany, event-by-event – **100 Jahre Leichtathletik in Deutschland** is **Diskuswurf – Frauen** (women's discus). Detailed German championship results 1922-2015, younger age-group championships, best performances, international match and championships results, illustrations and more in 400 pages. 25 euros from Hans Waynberg (as above). No cheques from outside Germany.

Their Bulletin **No. 73** was dated 1 November 2015. The majority of the 290 pages had results of all finals of German Championships 2000-15.

Hammer Throw Stats History and News Bulletin No. 15. By Zdenek Procházka. pdf of 78 pages. The latest in this series features deep men's hammer lists for 2014 for seniors, juniors and youths, performers, performances, analysis and index, plus national records. Four bulletins (usually of between 54 -200 pages). Contact Zdenek at atlet2003@volny.cs

IAAF Handbooks

The statistics handbook for the **IAAF World Youth Champs** (Cali, July 15-19). 190pp, by Ottavio Castellini and Félix Capilla, is available as an ebook from the IAAF website (www.iaaf.org). It features the leading results from the previous championships, world youth all-time lists etc.

The **IAAF World Championships Beijing 2015 Statistics Handbook**. A5 828pp. Edited by Mark Butler, this was once again a masterpiece in the style of previous editions. It is available to download from the IAAF website (www.iaaf.org).

More Downloads

Statistics Handbook European Cup Race Walking Murcia 2015 by Francisco Javier Ascorbe, György Csiki, José Luis Hernández, Thomas Hurst and Miguel Villeseñor for the RFEA is available on-line as a pdf file (174 pages) with event's details at the European Athletics website www.european-athletics.org. Or from the Spanish Federation website

http://www.rfea.es/competi/2015_ECRW_Murcia/PDF/statistics_handbook.pdf.

Complete results of all previous editions of the Cup meeting from 1996 with analysis, athletes' index and European all-time lists and records.

European Athletics produced **Statistics Handbooks** for both the **U23 Championships** in Tallinn and the **U20 Championships** in Eskilstuna. Both gave complete results for previous championships, analysis and lists of medallists by country, European records, all-time lists for the age group and national records. Whereas the former was a nicely produced 286 pages, the latter came out at 684 pages because the font was too big for the layout, so that lines in the lists overflowed totally unnecessarily and thus the pagination was about twice as large as it need have been. Still the statistics provided by Mirko Jalava with help from Tomas Magnusson were great!

http://tallinn2015.org/assets/Statistics%20HandbookTallinn%202015.pdf

https://www.dropbox.com/s/xx70veh0jymczay/Eskilstuna%202015.pdf?dl=0

TRACKINSUN Results Contact: car.baronet@gmail.com

Pdf files sent out weekly for:

European Athletics (indoor and outdoor season 2016) 60 euros/year. Very deep results from athletics competitions in all European countries (senior, u23, junior and youth categories u18 and u16) and results of European athletes in USA.

South West Europe (France-Italy-Spain-Portugal) indoor and outdoor season 2016) 25 euros/year.

USA Results (University-College-High School) (indoor and outdoor season 2016) 60 euros/year.

Central-America and Caribbean Results (outdoor season 2016) 20 euros/year. Every other week.

Mixed pack TRACKINSUN RESULTS (USA, Central America and Caribbean and Europe) 95 euros/year.

Asian Athletics Digest Four editions published so far by Ram. Murali Krishnan. For instance No. 4 was a special for the 2016 Asian Indoor Championships. It contained Asian all-time indoor top tens and national indoor records for all Asian nations for all standard men's and women's indoor events. Contact him at sportsmurali@yahoo.com.

HALL OF FAME 2015

WE STARTED a Hall of Fame in ATHLETICS 2001. Five athletes are added each year – a mix of past and current stars. Prior to this year 96 athletes have been included (there was a bumper selection in ATHLETICS 2003 following a survey of the best athletes for each event).

Current stars can be included if they have had at least ten years in international competition and this year we include Valerie Adams

Valerie ADAMS (New Zealand) (b. 6 Oct 1984 Rotorua). At 1.93m/123kg the hugely imposing Adams has dominated shot putting for a decade, ranking world number one each year 2005-14 (except when Nadezhda Ostapchuk took first in 2005 and 2010 before being discredited by drugs disqualifications). Adams matched her age with metres from 14 to 18 and won the Olympic gold medal in 2008 and 2012, the World title 2007, 2009, 2011 and 2013, World Indoors 2008 and 2012, Commonwealth Games 2006, 2010 & 2014 (2nd 2002), World Cup 2006, World Athletics Final 2008-09 and the Diamond League crown each year 2011-14. She has set nine Oceania & Commonwealth records from 19.87 in 2005 to 21.24 in 2011 (22 New Zealand records 2002-11). She had 28 successive shot wins from September 2007 to World Indoor silver in March 2010. The winner there, Ostapchuk beat Adams six more times that year before Adams had a comfortable win over the Belarussian at the Continental Cup. In 2011 Adams won all her 13 competitions and beat Ostapchuk by a massive 1.19m at the Worlds. In 2012 Ostapchuk found extra distance (up to 21.58m) and beat Adams 21.36 to 20.70 at the Olympics. However, only a few days later came news that Ostapchuk was disqualified with a failed drugs test, so Adams retained her title. She had further unbeaten seasons with 12 wins in 2013 and 14 in 2014 to take her win streak to 56.

Her father came from England and her mother from Tonga. She won the World Youth title in 2001 and World Junior 2002, was 5th in 2003 and 2nd in 2005 at her first Worlds and 7th at the 2004 Olympics. She has won 14 New Zealand shot titles (2001-11 and 2013-14) as well as the hammer in 2003 and discus in 2004.
After surgery to her right elbow and left shoulder, she had just four competitions in July 2015 but decided that she could not compete as she would like at the Worlds. In November 2004 she married New Caledonia thrower Bertrand Vili, but they separated. and she is now engaged to Gabriel Price from Tonga.

Sally Jane Janet **GUNNELL** (Great Britain) (b. 29 Jul 1966 Chigwell, Essex). There have been other athletes in the 400m hurdles with better basic speed, but none with her crisp efficient hurdling that she combined with tremendous competitive fire, and she has the greatest record at the event. Olympic champion in 1992, she added the World title in 1993, when she ran a world record (and her eighth British record) time of 52.74. Gunnell also won bronze medals for 4 x 400m with the British team at both these events. She added the European 400m hurdles title in 1994 as well as Commonwealth golds at 400m hurdles and 4 x 400m and thus became the first woman to hold the big four major titles for British athletes.

Her first national titles were at long jump: WAAA junior 1980, intermediate 1981. After UK age records, 15-17 at heptathlon and 16-17 at 100m hurdles, under the guidance of Bruce Longden she won the English Schools 100mh in 1983-4 (after the junior long jump in 1980) and the Commonwealth gold for 100mh in 1986. After one race (in 59.9) in 1987, she moved to the 400m hurdles in 1988, improving very rapidly to set four British records from 55.40 to 54.03 when 5th at the Olympics. She also ran a British record of 12.82 for 100m hurdles. In 1989 she won the European Indoor 400m and in 1990 won Commonwealth gold medals at 400m hurdles and 4 x 400m relay and silver at 100m hurdles. In 1991 she improved her British 400mh record to 53.78 and 53.62 and took the World silver in a Commonwealth record 53.16. She also won the European Cup in 1993 and 1994 and World Cup in 1994, but was hindered thereafter by foot injuries. Her national titles: UK 100mh 1986, WAAA 100mh 1986-9 and 1991-3, 400mh 1988, indoor 200m 1987, 400m 1988. Sports Writers Association British Sportswoman of the Year each year 1992-4.

Awarded the MBE in 1993 and OBE in 1998, she married 800m runner Jon Bigg in 1992.

Other bests: 100m 11.83 (1990), 11.8 (1987), 11.79w (1986); 200m 23.30 (1993), 300m 36.44 (1993), 400m 51.04 (1994), 800m 2:08.36i (1991), 60mh 8.27i (1990), high jump 1.67 (1983), long jump 6.08 (1983), shot 11.18 (1984), heptathlon 5493 (1984)

Bobby Joe MORROW (USA) (b. 15 Oct 1935 Harlingen, Texas). At the age of just 21 Morrow was a most impressive Olympic triple gold medallist at 100m, 200m and relay in 1956. His time at 200m was a world record 20.6 (20.75 on automatic timing), having run 20.6 twice earlier in 1956, to win the NCAA and US Olympic Trials, but neither was ratified. At 100m he tied the world record of 10.2 three times in 1956 and continued his brilliant form in 1957, when at 100 yards he lost just once and equalled the world record with 9.3 in his heat at the NCAAs, and won all six finals at 220y. He also set six relay world records, two on US teams and four for Abilene Christian College, for whom he completed the NCAA sprint double in 1956 and 1957. He was AAU champion at 100y/100m in 1955, 1956 and 1958 and at 220y in 1958. He was *Sports Illustrated* Sportsman of the Year for 1956 and was long recognised as the best ever white sprinter.

He progressed at 100y from 9.9 in 1952, 9.7 in 1953 and 9.6w in 1954 to break into world class in his freshman year in 1955 when he was undefeated at 100y including winning the NAIA title in 9.1 with a 7 mph wind (after a legal 9.4 in his heat). He also won all his 220y races, including the world's fastest time of 1955, 20.6 around a turn (but wind assisted) in his NAIA heat before completing a double at that meeting, until he was 4th at the AAUs. He was ranked 2nd at 100 and 4th at 200 in the annual *Track & Field News* world rankings in 1955, 1st at both events in 1956 and 1957 and 1st at 100 and 2nd at 200 in 1958. After a brief retirement he was back at 6th and 9th in 1959, but was then injured. Nonetheless he came close to making the US Olympic team in 1960 with 4th in AAU and Olympic Trials at 200m. Best times at 220y straight: 20.4 (1958), 20.0w (1957); 440y 48.0 (1959).

Ana Fidelia QUIROT Moret (Cuba) (b. 23 Mar 1963 Palma Soriano, Santiago de Cuba). Quirot made a wonderful recovery from a life-threatening accident to win two World titles at 800 metres. She started with silver at 4x400m at the 1979 Pan-American Games, in all winning eight medals at these Games, including the 400m and 800m double in 1987 and 1991. She was 4th in the World 800m in 1987 and won 39 successive 800m finals from the 1987 Grand Prix final to third at Zürich in 1990. She was unable to take part in the 1988 Olympics, but won the 800m bronze in 1992 after a triple win at 400m, 800m (in her pb 1:54.44) and 4x400m at the 1989 World Cup. She matched this triple at the Central American Games of 1986 and 1990, and won 400m and 800m at the 1989 World Student Games and 1990 Goodwill Games. She was the Grand Prix series winner at 800m 1987, 1989, 1991 and 1997, and 400m 1988 and 1990; and took World 800m silver in 1991.

She suffered severe burns in a household accident in January 1993, after which she give birth prematurely to a daughter, Javiana, who died a few days later. Formerly married to Raúl Cascaret, world freestyle wrestling champion at 74kg 1985-6, but divorced in 1991; he helped her recuperate. She made a brave return and took the Central American and Caribbean Games silver at 800m in November 1993 but then missed the 1994 season. Few could have anticipated her further success, but it came with the World title at 800m in 1995 and 1997 and the Olympic silver in 1996. Her 1:54.82 in Köln 1997 was her fastest time since 1989.

Other bests: 200m 23.07 (1988) and 22.9 (1984), 400m 49.61 (1991), 49.2 (1989); 600m 1:22.63 (1997, world best), 1000m 2:33.12 (1989), 1500m 4:13.08 (1997). She finally retired after the 1998 season and now works for the Cuban Parliament and is a member of its Medical and Health Commission.

James Ronal**d 'Jim' RYUN** (USA) (b. 29 Apr Wichita, Kansas). Plenty of athletes have won more medals and titles than Ryun, but very few have so excited the public as Ryun did. A prodigy, he set an age-16 mile record of 4:07.8 in 1963, and in 1964 ran 3:39.0 for 1500m and 3:59.0 for 1 mile, when at 17 he became by far the youngest four-minute miler. While a teenager he was the world's supreme middle-distance runner, with his first world records, 1:44.9 for 880 yards and 3:51.3 for the mile, at 19 in 1966, when he also set a US record for 2 miles at 8:25.2. and was the Sullivan Award winner.

Coached by Bob Timmons at Kansas State University, for whom he won the 1967 NCAA mile title, he won his third successive AAU mile in 1967 in 3:51.1 at Bakersfield having led from the gun, finishing with a devastating last lap in 52.5. Two weeks later at the Los Angeles Coliseum he took an amazing 2.5 seconds off the world record for 1500m that Herb Elliott had set at the 1960 Olympics, as with 3:33.1 (last 880y in 1:51.3) Ryun left Kip Keino well beaten on 3:37.2.

Ryun had the world at his feet, but there were more world records or titles after the 1968 NCAA indoor 2 miles. He was second to Keino in the 1968 Olympic 1500m, beaten mentally by the high altitude in Mexico City and the way that Keino blazed away. Ryun had the desperate misfortune to fall in the heats of the 1972 Olympic 1500m. He ran for a while with the ITA pro group and later as a veteran but suffered from allergies and never again approached the brilliant style of his glory days.

He served as a Republican in the US House of Representatives for Kansas 1996-2006.

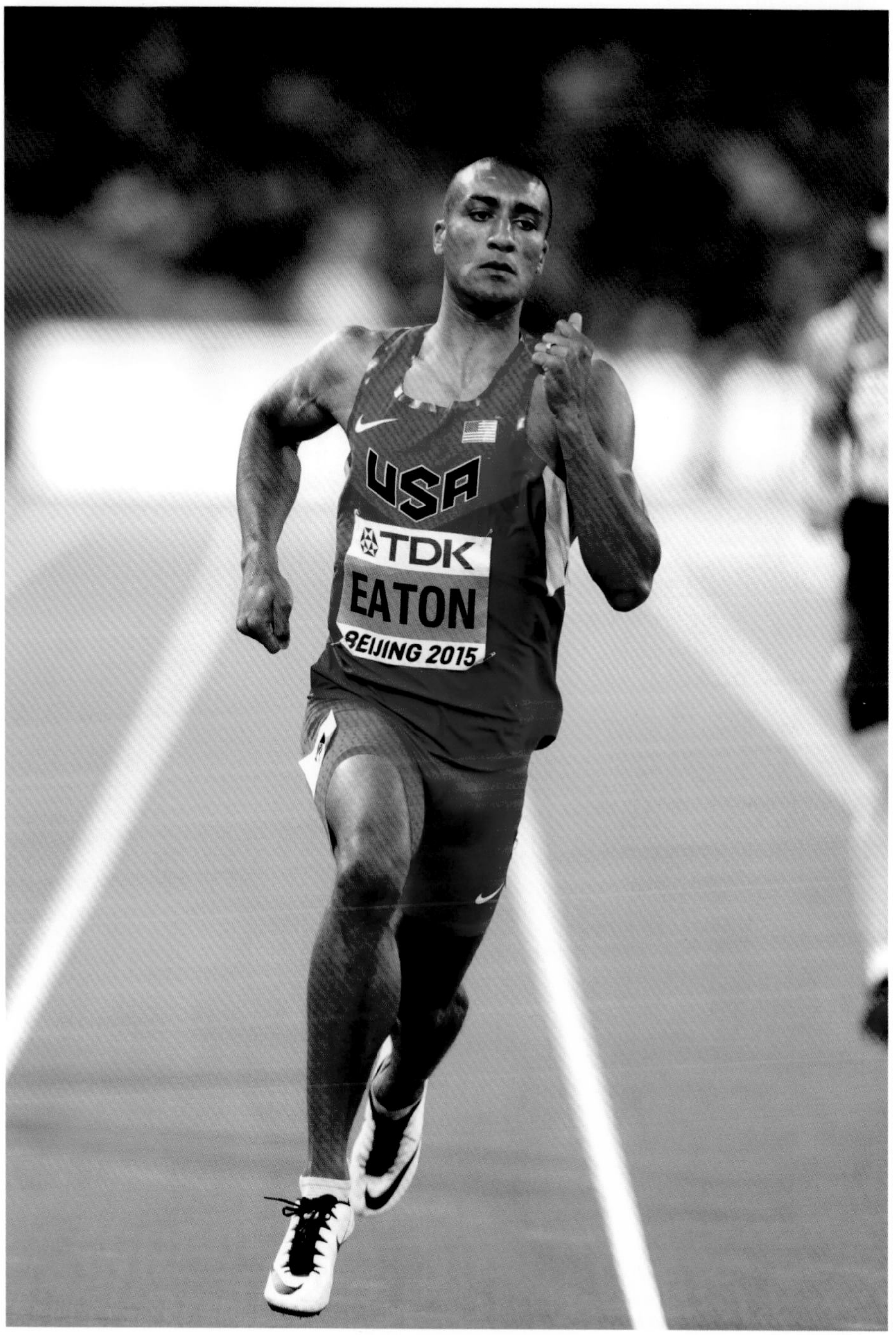

Ashton Eaton was the top man at the World Championships with 9045 points world record for the decathlon including an amazing 45.00 for 400m.

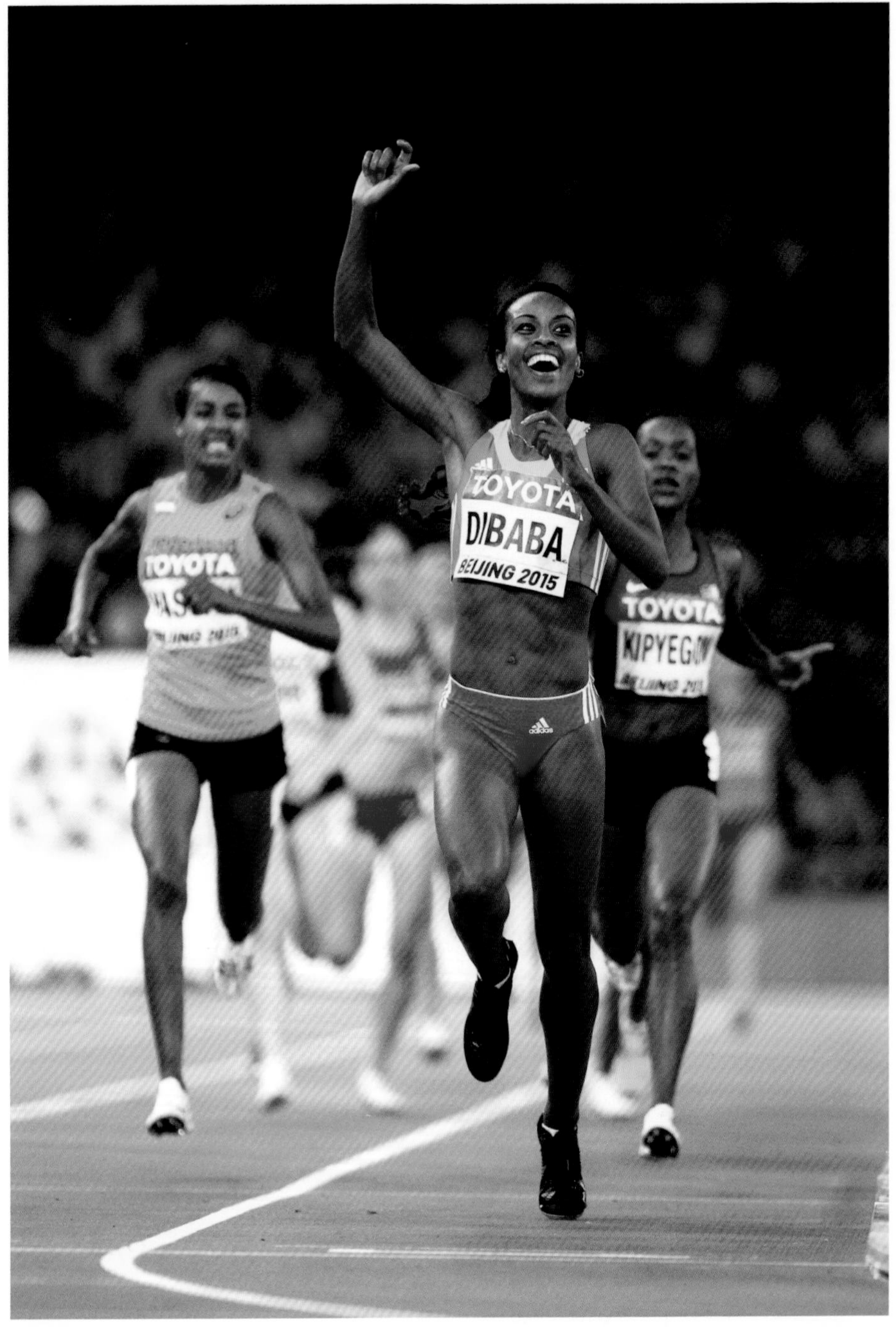

Genzebe Dibaba, seen here after taking the world 1500m title in Beijing, broke the 22-year-old world record with 3:50.07 for 1500m at Monaco after an earlier indoor 5000m world record.

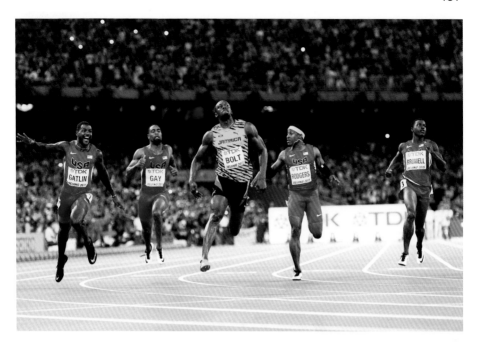

The most keenly awaited clash at the 2015 World Championships was at 100m, where Usain Bolt held off the challenge of Justin Gatlin to win by 13 hundredths of a second.

Anita Wlodarczyk produced the first three 80m throws in the history of women's hammer throwing, two of them in the World final.

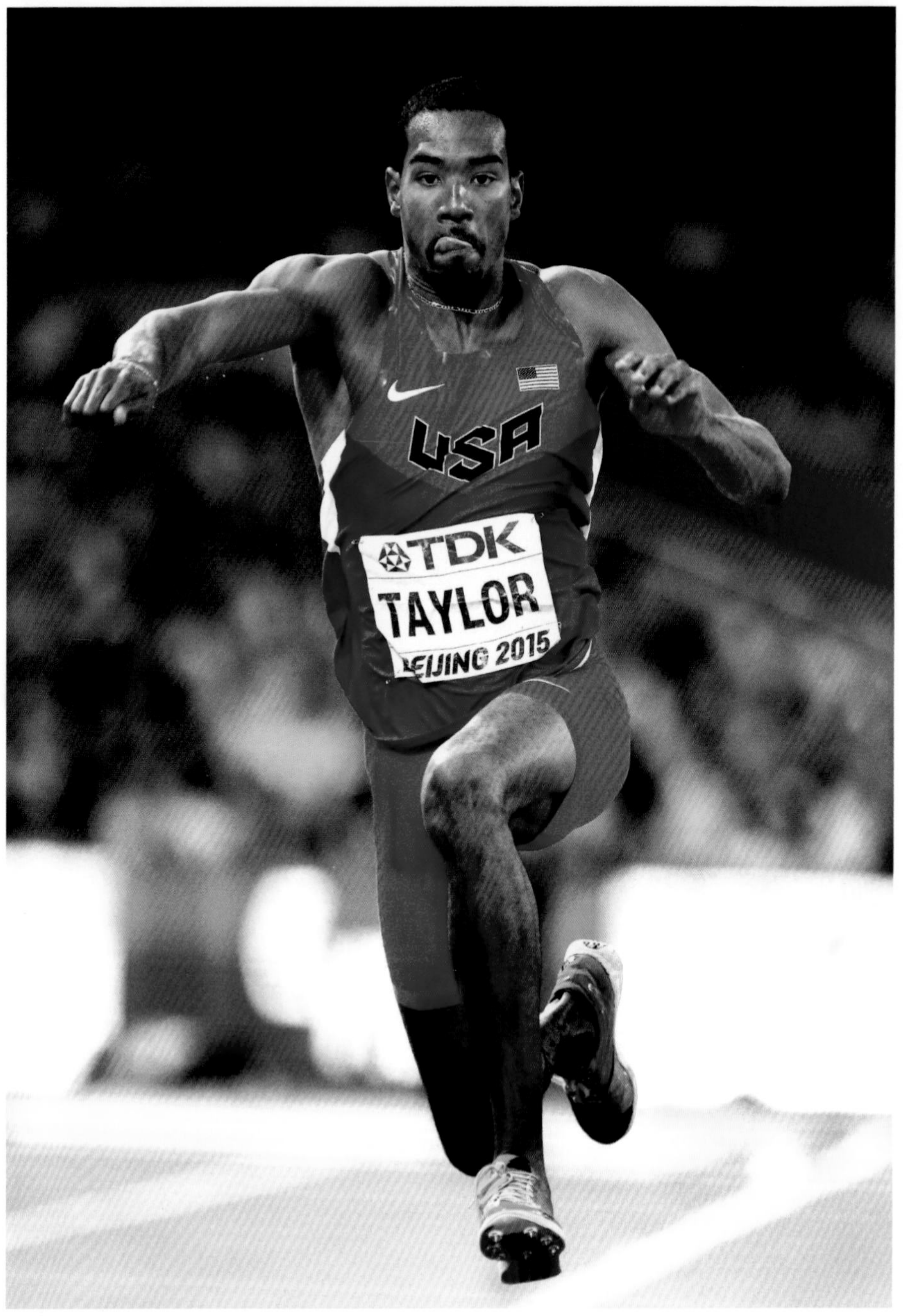

Christian Taylor and Pedro Paulo Pichardo had a series of epic battles in the triple jump in 2015 and Taylor jumped to the world's second longest ever legal jump with 18.21 at the Worlds.

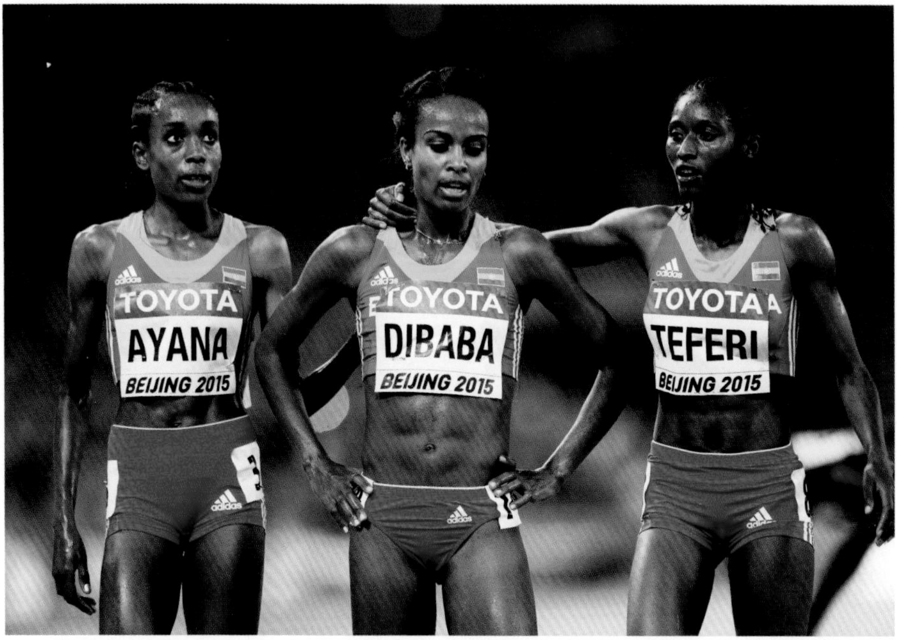

Almaz Ayana had a great year, capped by her win over Genzabe Dibaba (3rd) in the World 5000m. Ethiopian compatriot Senbere Teferi was runner-up.

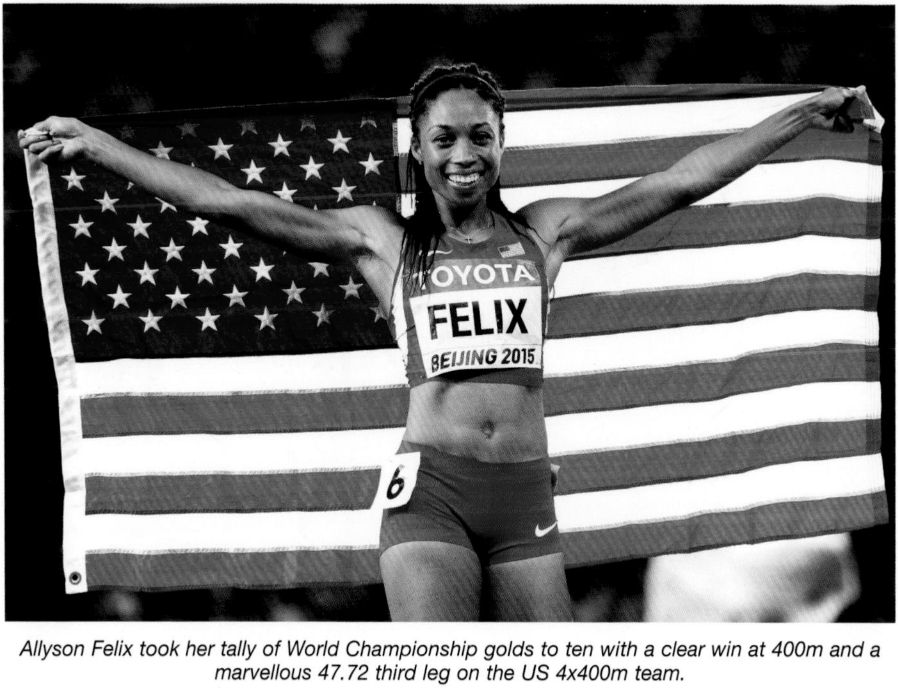

Allyson Felix took her tally of World Championship golds to ten with a clear win at 400m and a marvellous 47.72 third leg on the US 4x400m team.

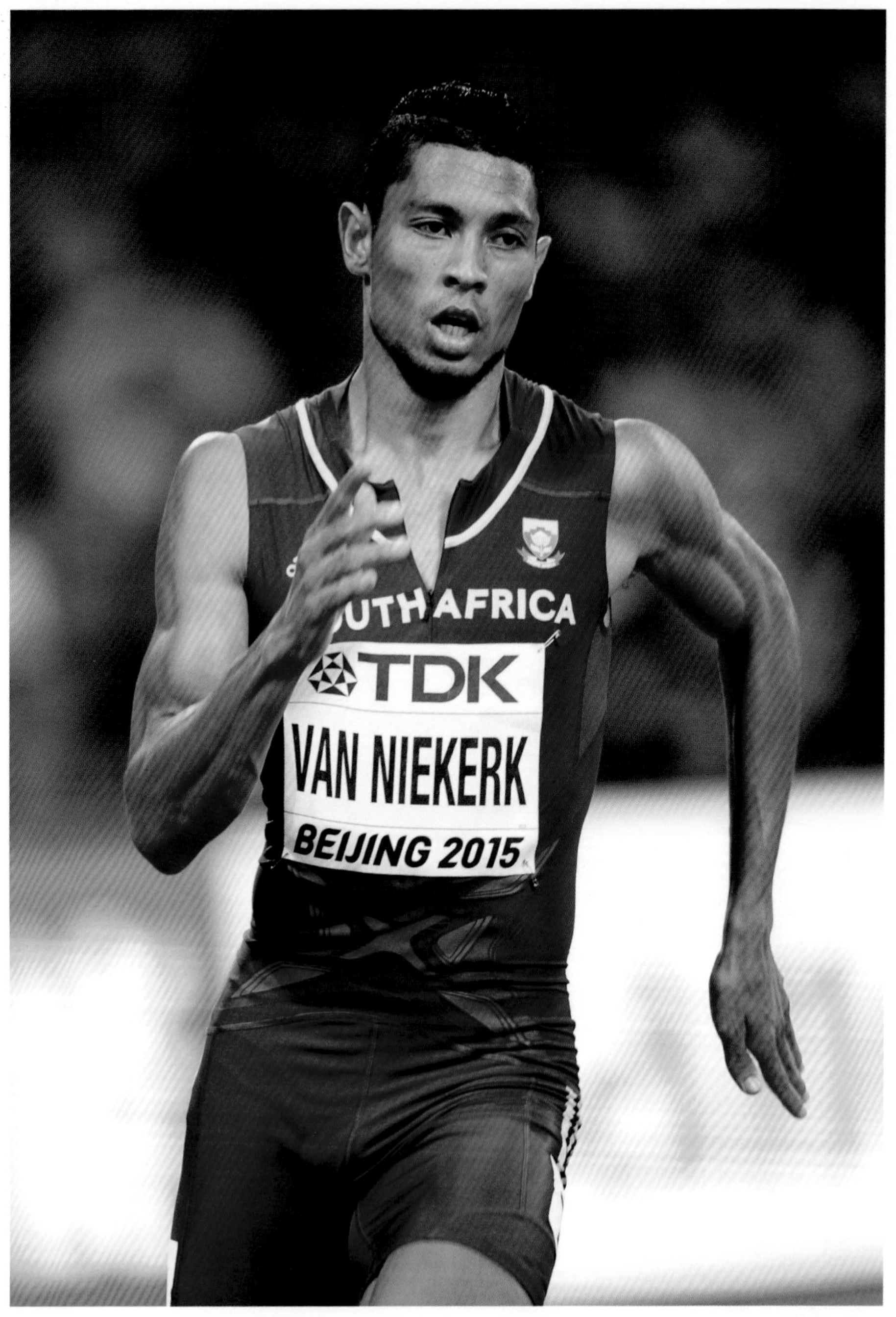

Wayde van Niekerk smashed the African record for 400m with 43.48 to win the World title.

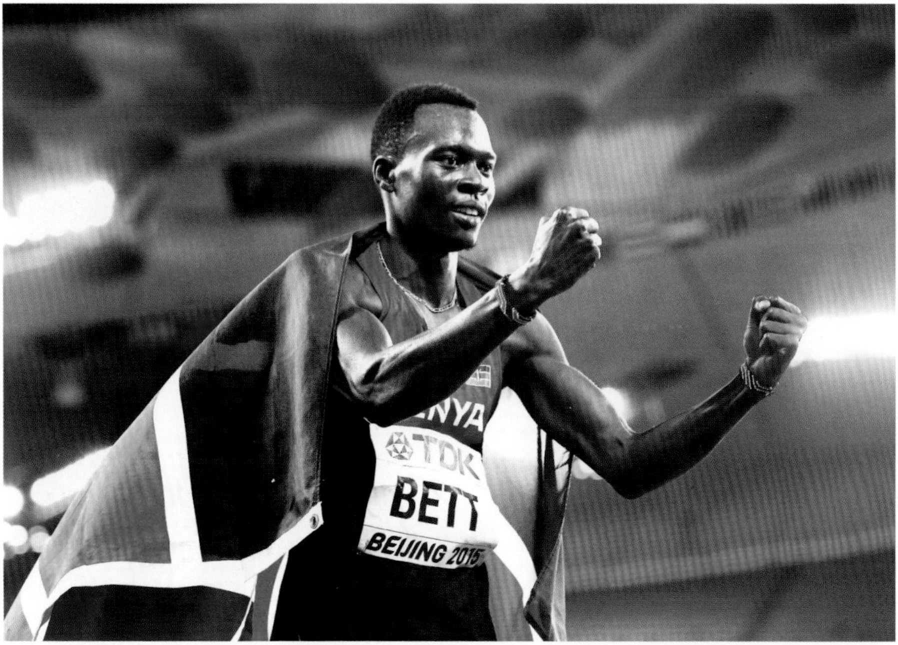

Nicholas Bett improved during the year from 49.03 to his startling gold medal-winning 47.79 for 400m hurdles in the outside lane at the World Championships.

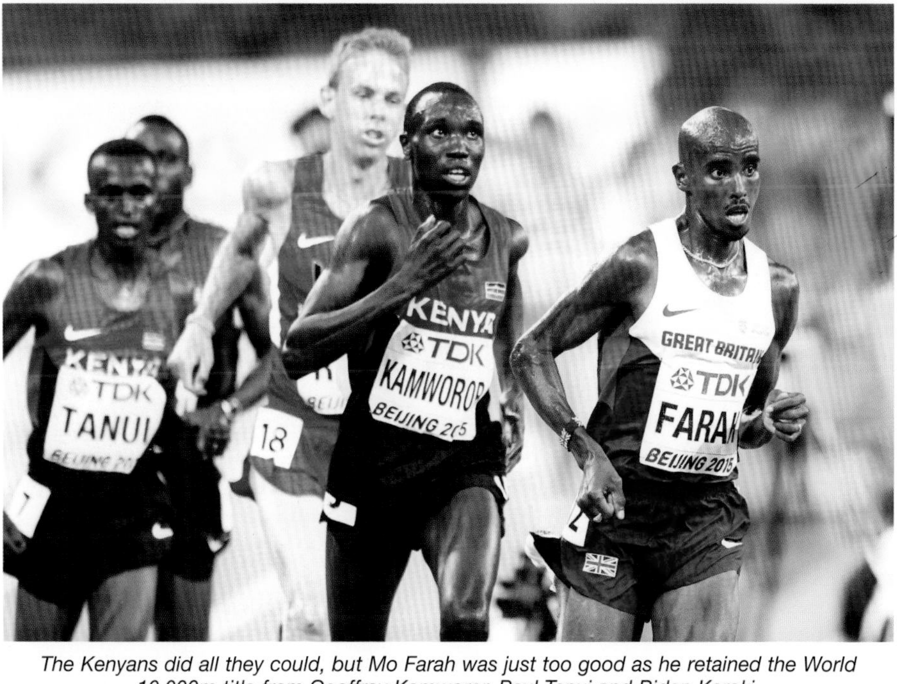

The Kenyans did all they could, but Mo Farah was just too good as he retained the World 10,000m title from Geoffrey Kamworor, Paul Tanui and Bidan Karoki.

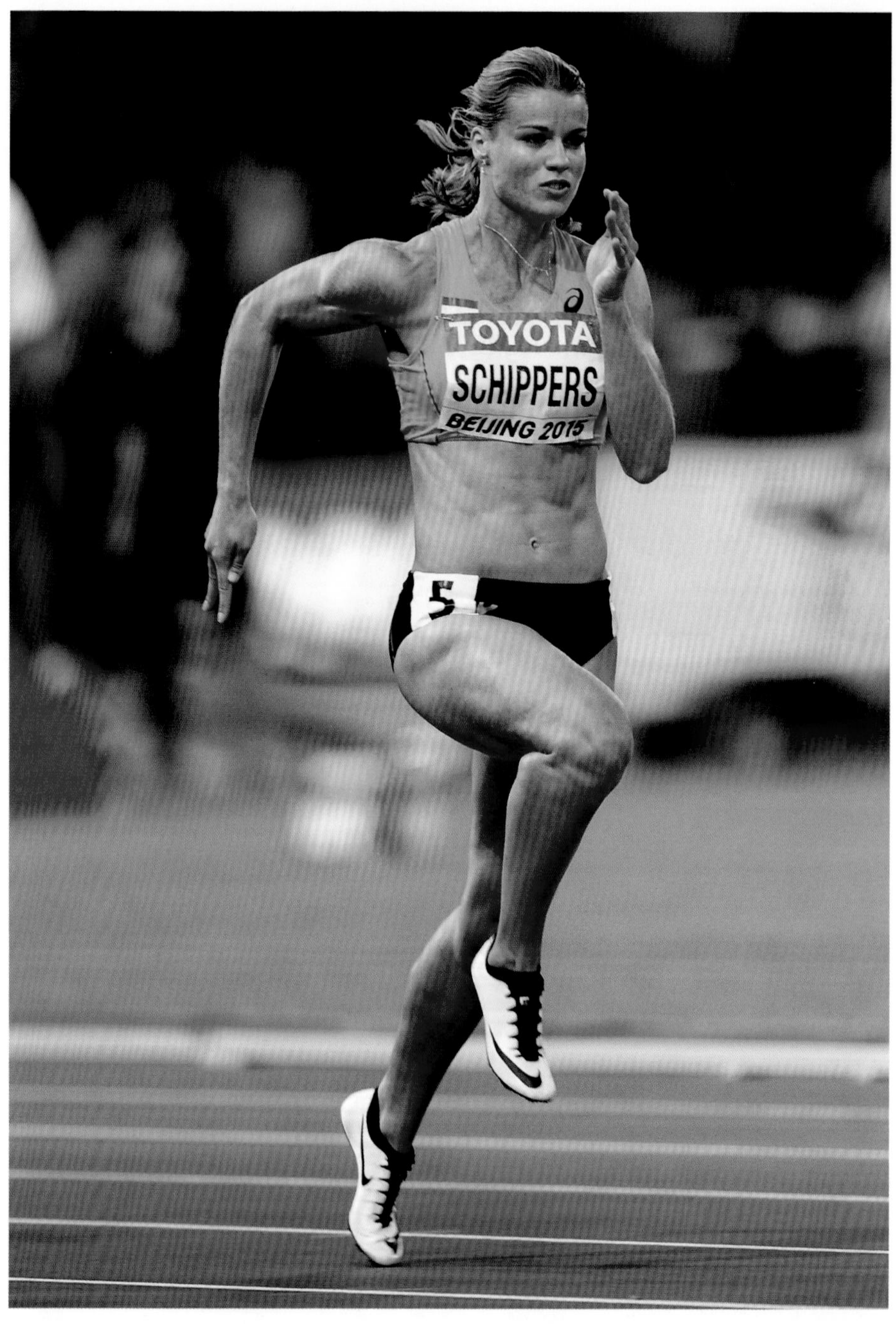

Dafne Schippers was on the shortlist for female athlete of the year after her stellar sprints season, including her narrow win in the World 200m.

NATIONAL CHAMPIONS 2015 and BIOGRAPHIES OF LEADING ATHLETES

By Peter Matthews

THIS SECTION incorporates biographical profiles of 791 of the world's top athletes this year - 414 men and 377 women, listed by nation. Also listed are national champions at standard events in 2015 for the leading countries prominent in athletics (for which I have such details).

The athletes profiled have, as usual, changed quite considerably from the previous year. Most notably the number of Russians included is down from 71 to 47. All entries have been updated, but also many newcomers have been included to replace those who have retired or faded a little from the spotlight. The choice of who to include is always invidious, but I have concentrated on those who are currently in the world's top 10-15 per event, those who have the best championship records and some up-and-coming athletes who I consider may make notable impact during the coming year.

Since this section was introduced in the 1985 Annual, biographies have been given for a total of 4695 different athletes (2650 men and 2045 women).

The ever continuing high turnover in our sport is reflected in the fact that there are a very large number of newcomers to this section (170 in all, 89 men, 81 women), as well as 9 athletes (5 men, 4 women) reinstated from previous Annuals. The athlete to have had the longest continuous stretch herein is Jesús Ángel García at 22 years, Athletes who have retired or whi have been given drugs bans have generally been omitted, although a few have been retained as they had significant achievements in 2015.

No doubt some of those dropped from this compilation will also again make their presence felt; the keen reader can look up their credentials in previous Annuals, and, of course, basic details may be in the athletes' index at the end of this book.

Athletes included in these biographies are identified in the index at the end of this Annual by * for those profiled in this section and by ^ for those who were included in previous Annuals.

The biographical information includes:

a) Name, date and place of birth, height (in metres), weight (in kilograms).
b) Previous name(s) for married women; club or university; occupation.
c) Major championships record – all placings in such events as the Olympic Games, World Championships, European Championships, Commonwealth Games, World Cup and Continental Cup; leading placings in finals of the World Indoor Championships, European or World Junior Championships, European Under-23 Championships and other Continental Championships; and first three to six in European Indoors or World University Games. European Cup/Team Champs and IAAF Grand Prix first three at each event or overall. World Athletics Final (WAF) and Diamond League series (DL) winners
d) National (outdoor) titles won or successes in other major events.
e) Records set: world, continental and national; indoor world records/bests (WIR/WIB).
f) Progression of best marks over the years at each athlete's main event(s).
g) Personal best performances at other events.
h) Other comments.

See Introduction to this Annual for lists of abbreviations used for events and championships.

Information given is as known at 1 April 2016 (to include performances at the World Indoor Championships and World Half Marathon Championships as well as some other early indoor and outdoor events of 2016).

I am most grateful to various ATFS members who have helped check these details. Additional information or corrections would be welcomed for next year's Annual.

Peter Matthews

ALGERIA

Governing body: Fédération Algerienne d'Athlétisme, BP n°61, Dely-Ibrahim 160410, Alger. Founded 1963.

National Champions 2015: **Men**: 100m: Djamil Skandar Athmani 10.56, 200m/400m: Soufiane Bouhada 21.20/46.76, 800m: Mohamed Belbachir 1:51.20, 1500m: Salim Keddar 3:43.97, 5000m: Abdelghani Bensaadi 14:16.12, 3000mSt: Miloud Madoui 8:52.46, 110mh: Lyès Mokdal 13.54, 400mh: Admelmalik Lahoulou 49.11, HJ: Mohamed Amine Fodil 2.10, PV: Hichem Cherabi 5.20, LJ: Yasser Triki 7.67, TJ: Issam Nima 16.57, SP: Mohamed Benzaaza 14.68, HT: Abdelwahab Maamar 59.45, JT: Lardi Bouradaa 64.00, 20kW: Hicham Medjber 1:32:35; **Women**. 100m/200m: Souheir Bouali 11.97/24.20, 400m: Meriem Boulahsa 56.33, 800m: Zahra Bouras 2:09.58, 1500m: Amina Betiche 4:22.58, 5000m/10000m: Souad Aït Salem 16:10.35/32:50.62, 3000mSt: Nawal Yahi 10:20.74, 100mh/400mh: Samira Messaad 13.96/58.78, HJ: Yousra Arrar 1.64, LJ: Romaissa Belbiod 6.06, TJ: Kaoutar Selmi 12.19, SP/HT: Zouina Bouzebra 13.32/58.10, DT: Dalila Makheloufi 42.50, 20kW: Nedjema Larbi Pacha 1:55:54.

Larbi BOURAADA b. 10 May 1988 1.87m 84kg.
At Dec (/PV): WCh: '09- 13, '11- 10, '15- 5; AfG: '07- 3, '11- dnf/1; AfCh: '08- 1/2, '10- 1/2, '14- 1. Three African decathlon records 2009-15, ALG record 2014
Progress at Dec: 2007- 7349, 2008- 7697, 2009- 8171, 2010- 8148A, 2011- 8302, 2012- 8332dq, 2014- 8311, 2015- 8461. pbs: 60m 6.89i '10, 100m 10.67 '10, 10.61w '11, 10.58dq '12; 400m 46.69 '09, 1000m 2:39.86i '10, 1500m 4:12.15 '09, 60mh 8.05i '10, 110mh 14.00 '15, HJ 2.10 '09, PV 5.00 '11, LJ 7.69 '09, 7.94w '11; SP 14.00i '10, 13.73 '15; DT 41.53 '15, JT 65.53A '10, 67.68dq '12; Hep 5911i '10. Two-years drugs ban from positive test 15 Jun 2012.

Taoufik MAKHLOUFI b. 29 Apr 1988 Souk Ahras 1.81m 66kg.
At (800m)/1500m: OG: '12- 1; WCh: '09/11- sf, '15- 4; AfG: '11- 1/3; AfCh: '10- h, '12- (1), '14- (3). Algerian 1000m record 2015.
Progress at 800m, 1500m: 2008- 3:43.4, 2009- 1:49.40, 3:34.34; 2010- 1:48.39, 3:32.94; 2011- 1:46.32, 3:34.4; 2012- 1:43.71, 3:30.80; 2013- 3:36.30, 2014- 1:43.53, 3:30.40; 2015- 1:44.24, 3:28.75. pbs: 1000m 2:13.08 '15, 1M 3:52.16 '14.

ARGENTINA

Governing body: Confederación Argentina de Atletismo (CADA), 21 de Noviembre No. 207. 3260 Concepción del Uruguay, Entre Ríos. Founded 1954 (original governing body founded 1919). **National Championships** first held in 1920 (men), 1939 (women). **2015 Champions**: **Men**: 100m/200m: Matías Robledo 10.75/22.04, 400m: Gonzalo Rodríguez 48.51, 800m: Mateo Rosetto 1:51.89, 1500m/5000m/Mar: Joaquín Arbe 3:49.59/14:29.49/2:20:10, 10000m: Mariano Mastromarino 29:34.57, 3000mSt: Marcelo Fabricius 9:17.93, 110mh: Agustín Carrera 14.20, 400mh: Jaime Rodríguez 53.80, HJ: Carlos Layoy 2.11, PV: Germán Chiaraviglio 5.00, LJ: Dafne Ibardorde 7.65w, TJ: Federico Guerrero 15.21, SP: Germán Lauro 19.18, DT: Juan Ignacio Solito 49.34, HT: Joaquín Gómez 63.58, JT: Braian Toledo 79.19, Dec: Román Gastaldi 7882w, 10,000mW: Juan Manuel Cano 40:44.59. **Women**: 100m: Vanesa Wohlgemuth 11.93, 200m/400m: Juliana Menéndez 24.50/56.01, 800m/1500m: Carolina Lozano 2:08.37/4:27.38, 5000m: María Angélica Ovejero 16:45.50, 10000m: Liliana Godoy 33:17.47, Mar: Paola Griffa 3:15:11, 3000mSt: Karen Cejas 11:37.99, 100mh/Hep: Martina Corrá 14.11/5055, 400mh: Valeria Barón 62.72, HJ: Mariana Rojas 1.74, PV: Valeria Chiaraviglio 4.00, LJ: Andrea Ubiedo 5.65, TJ: Paula Pitzinger 11.93w, SP: Ailén Armada 13.29, DT: Maia Varela 47.38, HT: Jennifer Dahlgren 62.39, JT: Bárbara López 48.50

Germán LAURO b. 2 Apr 1984 Trenque Lauquen, Buenos Aires 1.85m 127kg. Ferro Carril Oeste.
At SP/(DT): OG: '08- dnq 31, '12- 6/dnq 37; WCh: '07-09-11: dnq 23/nt/20; 13- 7, '15- 9; WI: '12-14-16: 6/6/6; PAm: '07- 5/4, '11- 3, '15- 3; SAG: '14- 1/3; SACh: '05-06-07-09-11-13-15: 4/1/1&1/1&1/1&2/1&1/1. Won S.AmG 2014, IbAm SP & DT 2012, 2014; ARG SP 2005-13, 2015; DT 2007-13. Shot Records: 6 South American indoor 2012-14; 13 Argentinian 2006-13.
Progress at SP: 2001- 15.24, 2002- 15.14, 2003- 16.87, 2004- 17.79, 2005- 18.17, 2006- 19.78, 2007- 19.67, 2008- 19.88, 2009- 19.20, 2010- 20.43, 2011- 20.42, 2012- 20.84, 2013- 21.26, 2014- 21.04i/20.70, 2015- 20.77. pb DT 63.55 '12.
6th in 2012 was best Argentinian placing at Olympics for 56 years.

AUSTRALIA

Governing body: Athletics Australia, Suite 22, Fawkner Towers, 431 St.Kilda Rd, Melbourne, Victoria 3004. Founded 1897.

National Championships first held in 1893 (men) (Australasian until 1927), 1930 (women). **2015 Champions**: **Men**: 100m: Josh Clarke 10.19, 200m: Alex Hartmann 20.67, 400m: Craig Burns 45.94, 800m/1500m: Jeff Riseley 1:47.13/3:43.8, 3000m: Brenton Rowe 8:07.52, 5000m: Brett Robinson 13:32.54, 10000m: Dave McNeill 28:03.69, Mar: Rob Pope GBR 2:30:00, 3000mSt: Craig Appleby 8:54.81, 110mh: Nicholas Hough 13.42, 400mh: Tristan Thomas 50.31, HJ: Brandon Starc 2.28, PV: Angus Armstrong 5.35, LJ: Robert Crowther 8.05, TJ: Alwyn Jones 15.98, SP: Damien Birkenhead 19.04, DT: Julian Wruck 62.03, HT: Matthew Denny 69.15, JT: Matt

Outzen 80.00, Dec: David Brock 7733, 10000mW: Dane Bird-Smith 39:53.89, 20kW: Jared Tallent 1:24:05/Ian Rayson 1:25:46, 50kW: Chris Erickson 3:54.10. **Women**: 100m: Melissa Breen 11.26, 200m: Ella Nelson 23.04, 400m: Anneliese Rubie 52.77, 800m: Brittany McGowan 2:03.49, 1500m: Heidi See 4:09.60, 3000m: Bridey Delaney 9:23.98, 5000m: Madeline Heiner 15:21.09, 10000m: Eloise Wellings 32:02.61, Mar: Kelly-Ann Varey 2:48:03, 3000mSt: Genevieve LaCaze 9:52.87, 100mh: Sally Pearson 12.59, 400mh: Lauren Wells 56.51, HJ: Eleanor Patterson 1.91, PV: Alana Boyd 4.60, LJ: Chelsea Jaensch 6.74w, TJ: Ellen Pettitt 13.46w, SP: Chelsea Lenarduzzi 15.27, DT: Dani Samuels 64.44, HT: Lara Nielsen 66.37, JT: Kimberley Mickle 61.02, Hep: Ashleigh Hamilton 5295, 10000mW/20kW: Tanya Holliday 44:56.44/1:34:05, 20kW: Regan Lambie 1:32:51.

Dane BIRD-SMITH b. 15 Jul 1992 Brisbane 1.78m 66kg. Racewalking Queensland.
At 20kW: WCh: '13- 11, '15- 8; WCp: '14- 14; WUG: '15- 1. At 10000mW: WJ: '10- 5; WY: '09- 8. OCE Champion 2016, AUS 5000mW 2013, 10000mW 2014-15, 20kW 2013-14.
Oceania 5000m walk record 2016.
Progress at 20kW: 2011- 1:26:38, 2012- 1:23:15, 2013- 1:22:03, 2014- 1:20:27, 2015- 1:20:05, 2016- 1:20:04. pbs: 3000mW 10:56.23 '14, 5000mW 18:38.97 '16, 10000mW 38:57.16 '14.

Benn HARRADINE b. 14 Oct 1982 Newcastle, NSW 1.98m 115kg. Ringwood. Personal trainer.
At DT: OG: '08- dnq 31, '12- 9; WCh: '09-11-13-15: dnq 15/5/dnq 20/10; CG: '06-10-14: 8/1/4; CCp: '10- 2, '14- 5. AUS champion 2007-08, 2010-12, 2014. Discus records: Two Commonwealth 2012-3, five Oceania 2008-13.
Progress at DT: 2000- 51.50, 2001- 54.76, 2002- 57.78, 2003- 55.25, 2004- 57.68, 2005- 63.65, 2006- 60.70, 2007- 62.99, 2008- 66.37, 2009- 64.97, 2010- 66.45, 2011- 66.07, 2012- 67.53, 2013- 68.20, 2014- 65.94, 2015- 66.75. pb SP 15.17 '05.

Fabrice LAPIERRE b. 17 Oct 1983 Réduit, Mauritius 1.79m 66kg. Westfields. Science graduate of Texas A&M University, USA.
At LJ: OG: '08- dnq 16; WCh: '09-11-13-15: 4/dnq 21/dnq/2; CG: '06- 3, '10- 1, '14- 4; WJ: '02- 2 (qf 100m); WI: '10- 1; WCp: '06- 8, '10- 7. Won WAF 2008-09, NCAA 2005, AUS 2006, 2009-10, 2013.
Oceania indoor long jump records 2010 & 2016.
Progress at LJ: 2000- 7.39, 2001- 7.31, 2002- 7.74, 2003- 7.66i/7.57/7.85w, 2004- 7.61i/7.52/7.94Aw, 2005- 7.90i/7.83/8.15w, 2006- 8.19, 2007- 7.98, 2008- 8.15, 2009- 8.35/8.57w, 2010- 8.40/8.78w, 2011- 8.02, 2012- 8.10/8.14w, 2013- 8.25, 2014- 8.00, 2015- 8.29, 2016- 8.25i. pbs: 60m 6.89i '06, 100m 10.56/10.48w '02, 200m 21.40 '00, TJ 15.24 '04. Former football player.

Jared TALLENT b. 17 Oct 1984 Ballarat 1.78m 60kg. Ballarat YCW. Graduate of University of Canberra.
At 20kW(/50kW): OG: '08- 3/2, '12- 7/1; WCh: '05- 18, '07- dq, '09- 6/7, '11- 23/2, 13- (3), '15- 26/2; CG: '06- 3, '10- 1; WCp: '06-08-10-12-14: 14/10/(3)/(1)/(3). At 10000mW: WJ: '02- 19; WY: '01- 7. Won AUS 5000mW 2012, 20kW 2008-13; 30kW 2004, 50kW 2007, 2009, 2011.
Commonwealth 5000m walk record 2009.
Progress at 20kW, 50kW: 2002- 1:40:21, 2003- 1:31:24, 2004- 1:27:02, 2005- 1:22:53, 2006- 1:21:36, 3:55:08; 2007- 1:21:25, 3:44:45, 2008- 1:19:41, 3:39:27; 2009- 1:19:42, 3:38:56; 2010- 1:19:15, 3:54:55; 2011- 1:19:57, 3:43:36; 2012- 1:20:02, 3:36:53; 2013- 1:20:41, 3:40:03; 2014- 1:20:55, 3:42:48; 2015- 1:24:05, 3:42.17. pbs: 3000mW 11:15.07 '09, 5000mW 18:41.83 '09, 10000mW 40:41.5 '06, 10kW 38:29 '10, 30kW 2:10:52 '13, 35kW 2:32:37 '12.
Won IAAF Walks Challenge 2008 and 2013. Married Claire Woods on 30 Aug 2008, she has 20kW pb 1:28:53 '12, 2 CG '10. Younger sister Rachel Tallent (b. 20 Feb 1993) has 20kW pb 1:31:33 to win OCE title 2016, 34 WCh '15.

Women

Alana BOYD b. 10 May 1984 Melbourne 1.71m 61kg. Maroochy AC.
At PV: OG: '08- dnq 16=, '21- 11; WCh: '11- dnq 13=, '15- 11; CG: '10- 1, '14: 1; CCp: '10- 6, '14- 3=; WI: '12- 9. AUS champion 2008-9, 2013, 2015.
Three Oceania pole vault records 2012-16.
Progress at PV: 2002- 3.15, 2003- 3.85, 2004- 3.65, 2005- 4.30, 2006- 4.40, 2007- 4.55, 2008- 4.56, 2009- 4.35, 2010- 1.73, 2011- 1.82, 2012- 4.76, 2013- 4.50, 2014- 4.65, 2015- 4.65, 2016- 4.77.
Here father and mother were both Olympians. Ray won 12 AUS pole vault titles and after 4th in 1970 and 1974 won at the Commonwealth Games in 1982, Denise (née Robertson) was 7th in the Olympic 200m in 1976 and 1980 and won 8 Commonwealth Games medals (100m/200m/4x100m/4x400m: '74- 3/2/1/-, '78- 3/1/3/2, '82- -/4/4/2). Alana's sister Jacinta (LJ pb 6.64 '06) and brother Matthew (PV 5.35 '08) competed at World Youths and Juniors.

Kimberley MICKLE b. 28 Dec 1984 Perth 1.69m 69kg. Mandurah/Rockingham.
At JT: OG: '12- dnq 17; WCh: '09-11-13-15: dnq 15/6/2/dnq 22; CG: '06-10-14: 4/2/1; WJ: '02- 9; WY: '01- 1; WCp: '06-10-14: 5/3/4. AUS champion 2005-07, 2009-15.
Oceania javelin record 2014.
Progress at JT: 1999- 45.13, 2000- 45.76, 2001- 51.83, 2002- 52.77, 2003- 48.03, 2004- 50.38, 2005- 58.16, 2006- 58.56, 2007- 59.36, 2008- 57.64, 2009- 63.49, 2010- 61.36, 2011- 63.82, 2012- 64.12, 2013- 66.60, 2014- 66.83, 2015- 66.57.

Kathryn MITCHELL b. 10 Jul 1982 Hamilton, Victoria 1.68m 75kg. Eureka AC.
At JT: OG: '12- 9; WCh: '13- 5, '15- dnq 17; CG: '06-10-14: 6/5/4; AUS champion 2008.
Progress at JT: 1999- 43.17, 2000- 51.44, 2001-

54.98, 2002- 54.72, 2003- 57.11, 2004- 48.10, 2005- 54.87, 2006- 58.81, 2007- 58.61, 2008- 58.77, 2010- 59.68, 2011- 59.47, 2012- 64.34, 2013- 63.77, 2014- 66.10, 2015- 63.70, 2016- 64.37.

Eleanor PATTERSON b. 22 May 1996 Leongatha, Victoria 1.82m 62kg. South Coast Athletics.
At HJ: WCh: '15- 8; CG: '14: 1; WY: '13- 1. Won AUS 2014-15.
World youth & Oceania junior HJ record 2013.
Progress at HJ: 2010- 1.73, 2011- 1.82, 2012- 1.87, 2013- 1.96, 2014- 1.94, 2015- 1.96.

Sally PEARSON b. 19 Sep 1986 Sydney 1.66m 60kg. née McLellan. Gold Coast Victory. Griffith University.
At (100m)/100mh: OG: '08- 2, '12- 1; WCh: '03- hR, '07- sf/sf, '09-11-13: 5/1/2; CG: '06- 7/fell/3R, '10- dq/1, '14- 1; WJ: '04- 3/4; WY: '03- 1; WCp: '06- 8/4, '10- 1. At 60mh: WI: '12- 1, '14- 2. At 200m: WY: '03- 5; AUS champion 100m & 100mh 2005-7, 2009, 2011, 2014-15; 200m 2011.
Records: Oceania 100mh (8) 2007-11, 60m 2009 & 60mh indoors (3) 2009-12; Commonwealth 100mh (2) 2011.
Progress at 100mh: 2003- 14.01, 2004- 13.30, 2005- 13.01, 2006- 12.95, 2007- 12.71, 2008- 12.53, 2009- 12.50, 2010- 12.57, 2011- 12.28, 2012- 12.35, 2013- 12.50, 2014- 12.5, 2015- 12.59. pbs: 60m 7.16 '11, 100m 11.14 '07, 150m 16.86 '10, 200m 23.02/ 22.66w '09, 300m 38.34 '09, 400m 53.86mx '11, 200mh 27.54 '06, 60mh 7.73i '12, 200mh 26.96 '09, 400mh 62.98 '07.
Married Kieran Pearson on 3 April 2010. IAAF female Athlete of the Year 2011.

Dani SAMUELS b. 26 May 1988 Fairfield, Sydney 1.82m 82kg. Westfields, University of Western Sydney.
At DT/(SP): OG: '08- 9, '12- 11; WCh: '07-09-11-13-15: dnq 13/1/10/10/6; CG: '06- 3/12, '14- 1; WJ: '06- 1/7; WY: '05- 1/3; WCp: '06- 6; WUG: '07- 2, '09- 1; CCp: '10- 4, '14- 2. AUS champion SP 2006-07, 2009, 2012; DT 2005-12, 2014-15.
Progress at DT: 2001- 39.17, 2002- 45.52, 2003- 47.29, 2004- 52.21, 2005- 58.52, 2006- 60.63, 2007- 60.47, 2008- 62.95, 2009- 65.44, 2010- 65.84, 2011- 62.33, 2012- 63.97, 2013- 64.46, 2014- 67.99, 2015- 66.21, 2016- 66.41. pbs: SP 17.05 '14, HT 45.39 '05.
Sisters Jamie and Casey played basketball for Australia.

Brooke STRATTON b. 12 Jul 1993 Box Hill, Melbourne 1.68m 58kg. Nunawading. Was at Deakin University, Melbourne.
At LJ: WCh: '15- dnq 14; WJ: '10- 6, '12- 7; WY: '09- 10; WI: '16- 5. AUS champion 2014.
Oceania long jump record 2016.
Progress at LJ: 2004- 5.38, 2005- 5.40, 2006- 5.52, 2007- 5.90, 2008- 6.06, 2009- 6.13, 2010- 6.30, 2011- 6.60, 2012- 6.56, 2013- 6.53, 2014- 6.70, 2015- 6.73, 2016- 7.05. Pbs: 100m 11.98 '13, 200m 24.79 '16, 100mh 14.18 '10, TJ 13.34 '12.

AUSTRIA

Governing body: Österreichischer Leichtathletik Verband OLV), 1040 Vienna, Prinz Eugenstrasse 12. Founded 1902.
National Championships first held in 1911 (men), 1918 (women). **2015 Champions**: **Men**: 100m: Markus Fuchs 10.67, 200m: Christoph Haslauer 21.69, 400m: Mario Gebhardt 47.76, 800m: Günther Matzinger 1:58.42, 1500m: Nikolaus Franzmair 3:50.22, 5000m/3000mSt: Christian Steinhammer 15:08.94/9:04.74, 10000m: Christoph Sander 31:48.99, HMar: Simon Lechleitner 68:28, Mar: Edwin Kemboi KEN 2:21:05, 110mh: Dominik Siedlaczek 14.33, 400mh: Dominik Hufnagl 51.69, HJ: Josip Kopic 2.05, PV: Matthias Freinberger 5.15, LJ: Martin Schwingenschuh 7.30, TJ: Roman Schmied 15.78, SP/DT: Lukas Weisshaidinger 18.03/63.08, HT: Benjamin Siart 55.77, JT: Matthias Kaserer 68.54, Dec: Felix Schmid-Schutti 7072, 20kW: Dietmar Hirschmugl 1:53:47, 50kW: Roman Brzezowsky 5:21:35. **Women**: 100m: Viola Kleiser 11.90, 200m: Carina Pölzi 24.03, 400m: Julia Schwarzinger 56.12, 800m/400mh: Verena Menapace 2:06.87/59.35, 1500m/10000m: Jennifer Werth 4:25.39/33:54.61, 5000m: Anita Baierl 16:58.32, HMar/Mar: Karin Freitag 78:59/2:42:32, 3000mSt: Julia Millonig 10:57.23, 100mh: Beate Schrott 13.27, HJ: Monika Gollner 1.86, PV: Agnes Hodi 3.90, LJ: Sarah Lagger 6.31, TJ: Michaele Egger 12.54, SP/DT: Veronika Watzek 13.91/52.81, HT: Julia Siart 51.30, JT: Andrea Lindenthaler 53.34, Hep: Verena Preiner 5598, 20kW: Andrea Kovacs HUN 1:48:33.

AZERBAIJAN

Hayle IBRAHIMOV b. 18 Jan 1990 Mek'ele, Tigray, Ethiopia 1.68m 58kg. Baku.
At 5000m: OG: '12- 9; WCh: '14- h; EC: '10- 3, '12- 6, '14- 2; EJ: '09- 1 (1 10000m); WUG: '13- 1, '15- 1. At 3000m: CCp: '14- 2; WI: '14- 6; EI: '11- 2, '13- 1. Eur U23 CC: '12- 8.
AZE records: 3000m (2) 2012-13, 5000m (5) 2010-14.
Progress at 5000m: 2009- 13:53.60, 2010- 13:32.98, 2011- 13:34.54, 2012- 13:11.54, 2013- 13:23.59, 2014- 13:09.17, 2015- 13:22.11. pbs: 1500m 3:44.76 '10, 3000m 7:34.57 '13, 10000m 30:03.57 '11.
Formerly Haile Desta Hagos of Ethiopia, switched to AZE 1 Feb 2009.

BAHAMAS

Governing body: Bahamas Association of Athletics Associations, P.O.Box SS 5517, Nassau. Founded 1952.
National Champions 2015: **Men**: 100m/200m: Shavez Hart 10.26/20.45, 400m: Steven Gardiner 44.27, 800m: Lesley Taylor 1:54.25, 1500m:, 5000m: Benjamin Najman 15:14.53, 110mh: Tasman Evans 14.92, 400mh: Jeffrey Gibson 49.83, HJ: Ryan Ingraham 2.28, LJ: Raymond

Higgs 7.78, TJ: Latario Collie-Minns SP: Perry Adderley 14.97, DT: Drexel Maycock 46.30, JT: Denzel Pratt 61.64. **Women**: 100m: Sheniqua Ferguson 11.41, 200m: Anthonique Strachan 22.84, 400m: Shaunae Miller 50.69, 100mh: Adanaca Brown 13.00, 400mh: Katrina Seymour 57.73, HJ: Kenya Culmer 1.68, LJ: Bianca Stuart 6.83, TJ: Tamara Myers 13.12, SP: Serena Brown 12.95, DT: Brashe Wood 47.07.

Christopher BROWN b. 15 Oct 1978 Nassau 1.78m 68kg. Was at Norfolk State University.
At 400m/4x400mR: OG: '00- qf/3R, '04- sf, '08- 4/2R, '12- 4/1R; WCh: '01-03-05-07-09-11-13-15: h&1R/sf&3R/4&2R/4&2R/5/sf/sf/sf; CG: '02- 7/3R, '06- 4, '14- dns/2R; PAm: '07- 1/1R. '11- 7; PAm-J: '97- 2R; CAG: '98- 3R, '99- 1R, '03- 2/1R; CCp: '14- 3R; WI: '06-08-10-12-14: 3/3/1/3/2, '16- 2R; BAH champion 2002, 2004, 2007-09. At 800m: CG: '98- h.
Bahamas records 300m 2015, 400m 2007 & 2008, 800m 1998. CAC & Commonwealth 4x400m record 2012. World M35 records 400m 2014 & 2015, 300m 2015.
Progress at 400m: 1997- 47.46, 1998- 46.44, 1999- 45.96, 2000- 45.08, 2001- 45.45, 2002- 45.11, 2003- 44.94A/45.16, 2004- 45.09, 2005- 44.48, 2006- 44.80, 2007- 44.45, 2008- 44.40, 2009- 44.81, 2010- 45.05, 2011- 44.79, 2012- 44.67, 2013- 45.18, 2014- 44.59, 2015- 44.54. pbs: 100m 10.26+ '14, 150mSt 15.10 '14, 200m 20.58 '15, 20.56w '06; 300m 31.99 '15, 800m 1:49.54 '98.
Fourth at four global championships outdoors. Had fastest split (43.42 anchor leg) in 2005 World 4x400m. Men's record six WI medals.

Steven GARDINER b. 12 Sep 1995 Moore's Island 1.88m 75kg.
At 400m: WCh: '15- sf; WJ: '14- 6R (sf 200m); BAH champion 2015.
Bahamas 400m record 2015.
Progress at 400m: 2013- 47.78, 2015- 44.27. pbs: 200m 20.66 '14, 20.51w '15; 300m 32.64 '16.

Jeffery GIBSON b. 15 Aug 1990 Freeport 1.86m 79kg. Was at Oral Roberts University, USA.
At 400mh: WCh: '13- sf. '15- 3; CG: '14- 3; PAm: '15- 1/3R. BAH champion 2011, 2013-15; NACAC 2012. Seven BAH 400mh records 2013-5.
At 400mh: 2008- 52.45, 2010- 51.80, 2011- 50.82, 2012- 50.27A/50.69, 2013- 49,39, 2014- 48.78, 2015- 48.17. pbs: 100m 10.56w '12, 200m 21.39w '12, 400m 46.30A '12, 46.62 '11.

Donald THOMAS b. 1 Jul 1984 Freeport 1.90m 75kg. Lindenwood University, USA.
At HJ: OG: '08/12- dnq 21=/30=; WCh: '07-09-11-13-15: 1/dnq 15/11/6/6; CG: '06-10-14: 4/1/9=; PAm: '07-11-15; 2/1/3; CAG: '06- 4=, '10- 1; CCp: '10- 2. Won WAF & NCAA indoors 2007, BAH 2007, 2010-11.
Progress at HJ: 2006- 2.24, 2007- 2.35, 2008- 2.28i/2.26, 2009- 2.30, 2010- 2.32, 2011- 2.32, 2012- 2.27, 2013- 2.32, 2014- 2.33i/2.25, 2015- 2.34, 2016- 2.33i.
A basketball player, he made a sensational start by clearing 2.22 indoors in January 2006 with no high jump training since he had jumped at school five years earlier. 19 months later he was world champion.

Women

Shaunae MILLER b. 15 Apr 1994 Nassau 1.85m 69kg. University of Georgia, USA.
At (200m)/400m: OG: '12- ht; WCh: '13- (4), '15- 2; CG: '14- 6; WJ: '10- 1, '12- 4; WY: '11- 1; WI: '14- 3. Won BAH 400m 2010-11, 2014-15; NCAA indoor 400m 2013.
BAH 200m record 2015. CAC junior records 200m 2013, 400m 2013.
Progress at 200m, 400m: 2009- 55.52, 2010- 24.09, 52.45; 2011- 23.70, 51.84; 2012- 22.70, 51.25; 2013- 22.45/22.41w, 50.70; 2014- 22.87, 51.63i/51.86; 2015- 22.14, 49.67. Pbs: 60m 7.59i '13, 100m 11.40 '14, 300m 36.10i '14.
Great-uncle Leslie Miller set BAH 400m record of 46.99 at 1968 Olympics.

Anthonique STRACHAN b. 22 Aug 1993 Nassau 1.68m 57kg. Going to Auburn University, USA.
At (100m)/200m: OG: '12- sf; WCh: '11/13- sf; WJ: '10- sf, '12- 1/1; PAm: '15- dnf; CCp: '14- 4; PAm-J: '11- 1. Won BAH 100m 2014, 200m 2013, 2015.
Two CAC junior 200m records 2011-12.
Progress at 200m: 2009- 23.95, 2010- 23.66, 2011- 22.70, 2012- 22.53, 2013- 22.32, 2014- 22.50, 2015- 22.69. Pbs: 100m 11.20 '12, 400m 53.61 '15.
Won IAAF Female Rising Star Award 2012.

BAHRAIN

Governing body: Bahrain Athletics Association, PO Box 29269, Isa Twon-Manama. Founded 1974.

El Hassan EL ABBASSI b. 15 Jul 1979 1.76m 55kg.
At 10000m: WCh: '15- 12; AsiG: '14- 1; Arab, Gulf & WMilG champion 2015. World CC: '15- 15.
Progress at 5000m, 10000m: 2010- 13:57.9, 2012- 28:12.40, 2014- 13:33.95, 27:32.96; 2015- 27:25.02. Pbs: 1500m 3:49.2 '09, HMar 61:09'13.
Switched from Morocco to Bahrain from 12 Aug 2013.

Albert Kibichii **ROP** b. 17 Jul 1992 Kapsabet, Kenya 1.76m 55kg.
At 5000m: WCh: '15- 11; AsiG: '14- 3; AsiC: '15- 2; CCp: '14- 4; Arab champion 2013, WMilG & Gulf 2015. World CC: '15- 11. Asian CC champion 2016.
Records: 1 Asian, 2 Bahrain 5000m and Bahrain 3000m 2013; 2 Asian indoor 3000m 2014 (if eligible).
Progress at 5000m: 2010- 14:15.81A, 2011- 13:03.70, 2012- 13:01.91, 2013- 12:51.96, 2014- 13:06.12, 2015- 13:06.74. Pbs: 1500m 3:45.7A '13, 3000m 7:35.53 '13.

Bahrain citizen from 2 Apr 2013, international eligibility 1 Apr 2014.

Women

Oluwa**kemi ADEKOYA** b. 16 Jan 1993 Nigeria 1.68m 57kg. Accountancy graduate of University of Lagos.
At 400mh: WCh: '15- h (dq); AsiG: '14- 1 (1 400m); AsiC: '15- 1; CCp: '14- 3. At 400m: WI: '16- 1; Won Arab 400m & W.MilG 400mh 2015.
4 Asian indoor 400m records to 51.45 in 2016.
Progress at 400mh: 2012- 57.16, 2013- 55.30, 2014- 54.59. 2015- 54.12. pbs: 100m 11.55 '14, 400m 50.86 '15.
Bahrain 400m (3) & 400mh (3) records 2014-5.
Switched nationality from Nigeria to Bahrain from 11 Sep 2013, with international eligibility from 10 Sep 2014.

Mimi BELETE b. 9 Jun 1988 Ethiopia 1.64m 62kg.
At 1500m/(5000m): OG: '12- sf; WCh: '09-11-13-15: sf/7/sf/(11); AsiG: '10- 3/1, '14- 2/2; AsiC: '09- 6, '13- 2; CCp: '10- 4, '14- 6 (5 3000m); won W.Asian 2010, Arab 5000m 2015.
Asian 2M record 2014.
Progress at 1500m, 5000m: 2007- 4:13.55, 2008- 4:06.84, 15:44.20; 2009- 4:04.36, 2010- 4:00.25, 15:15.59; 2011- 4:03.13, 2012- 4:01.72, 2013- 4:03.63, 2014- 4:00.08, 15:00.87; 2015- 4:05.37, 14:54.71 pbs: 800m 2:04.63 '10, 2000m 5:38.0+ '14, 3000m 8:30.00 '14, 2M 9:13.85 '14.
From Ethiopia, has lived in Belgium from 2005; BRN from 2009. Younger sister Almensch Belete BEL pbs 1500m 4:06.87 '10, 5000m 15:03.63 '11; 5 EI 3000m 2013.

Ruth CHEBET (JEBET) b. 17 Nov 1996 Kenya 1.65m 49kg.
At 3000mSt: WCh: '15- 11; WJ: '14- 1; AsiG: '14- 1; AsiC: '13- 1 but ineligible; CCp: '14- 3. Won WMilG 2015, Arab 2015, Arab-J 3000m 2014 World CC: '15- 9J.
Asian 3000m steeplechase record 2014.
Progress at 3000mSt: 2013- 9:40.84, 2014- 9:20.55, 2015- 9:21.40. pbs: 3000m 9:09.8A '13, 5000m 16:16.1A '13, road 10k 32:18 '14, 2000mSt 6:17.33 '13.
Switched nationality from Kenya to Bahrain from 19 May 2013, with international eligibility from 19 May 2014.

Maryam Yusuf **JAMAL** b. 16 Sep 1984 Alkesa, Arsi Province, Ethiopia 1.70m 54kg. Stade Lausanne, Switzerland.
At (800m)/1500m: OG: '08- 5, '12- 2; WCh: '05-07-09-11: 5/1/1/11; WI: '06- 3, '08- 2; AsiG: '06- 1/1, '10- 6/1, '14- 1 (1 5000m); WCp: '06- 1. At 3000m: WI: '14- 3. World CC: '09- 9, '11- 23; Won WAF 2005-08, Swiss CC 2003, P.Arab 800m, 1500m & 5000m 2005, Arab 4k CC 2006, Asian indoor 1500m & 3000m 2014, CC 2007, 2009.
Records: Two Asian 1M 2007, 2000m 2009, Bahrain 800m (3), 1500m (3), 2000m, 3000m (3), 5000m 2005-09. Asian indoor 1500m 2006 & 2008, 1M (4:24.71) 2010.
Progress at 800m, 1500m, 5000m: 2003- 4:18.12, 2004- 2:02.18, 4:07.78, 15:19.45mx; 2005- 1:59.69, 3:56.79, 14:51.68; 2006- 1:59.04, 3:56.18, 2007- 3:58.75, 15:20.28; 2008- 1:57.80, 3:59.79i/3:59.84; 2009- 1:59.98, 3:56.55; 2010- 1:59.89, 3:58.93; 2011- 4:00.33, 2012- 2:00.44, 4:01.19; 2013- 4:07.31, 2014- 4:04.10, 14:59.69; 2015- 4:09.63. pbs: 1M 4:17.75 '07, 2000m 5:31.88 '09, 3000m 8:28.87 '05, 2M 9:33.47 '14, HMar 71:43 '04.
Has a record 16 sub-4 min 1500m times. Formerly Ethiopian Zenebech Kotu Tola, based in Switzerland, ran series of fast times after converting to Jamal of Bahrain in 2005. First Olympic medallist for Bahrain at any sport. Married to Mnashu Taye (now Tareq Yaqoob BRN).

Eunice JEPKIRUI Kirwa b. 20 May 1984 1.65m 52kg.
At Mar: WCh: '15- 3; AsiG: '14- 1. At 1500m: WY: '99/01- h.
Bahrain records: marathon (2) 2014-1, half marathon 2016.
Progress at Mar: 2012- 2:21:41, 2013- 2:23:34, 2014- 2:25:37, 2015- 2:22:08, 2016- 2:22:40. Pbs: 1500m 4:27.62 '99, 2000mSt 6:33.0A '03, 3000mSt 10:18.3A '05, Road: 10k 31:57 '12, HMar 68:06 '16.
Won marathons in Asunción 2012, Lanzhou and Danzhou 2014, Nagoya 2015-16. Transferred from Kenya 11 Dec 2013 with eligibility to compete for Bahrain from 15 Jul 2014. Married to Joshua Kiprugut Kemei (pb HMar 62:53 '11) with one son.

BARBADOS

Governing body: Amateur Athletic Association of Barbados, P.O.Box 46, Bridgetown. Founded 1947.
National Champions 2015: **Men**: 100m: Levi Cadogan 10.06, 200m: Buckheart Ellis 20.68, 400m: Brandon Valentine-Parris VIN 46.78; 800m: Antonio Mascoll 1:50.90, 1500m: Raheem Skinner 4:01.57, 110mh: Shane Brathwaite 13.26, 400mh: Kion Joseph 51.19, HJ: Thorrold Murray 2.10, LJ: Shamar Rock 7.65, TJ: Barry Batson 15.42, SP: Tristan Whitehall 15.57, DT: Romario Antoine 51.31. JT: Lamar Clarke 48.07. **Women**: 100m: Ashley Marshall 11.37, 200m: Jade Bailey 23.57, 400m: Kineke Alexander VIN 52.27, 800m: Alena Brooks TTO 2:08.09, 1500m/3000m: Elizabeth Williams 4:42.81/10:36.13, 100mh: Kierre Beckles 13.12, 400m: Tia Adana Belle 57.45, HJ/TJ: Ashantia Phillips 1.65/11.83, LJ/SP: Akela Jones 6.43/13.62, DT: Ashley Williams 35.33, JT: Jenila Atherley 44.52.

Shane BRATHWAITE b. 8 Feb 1990 Bridgetown 1.82m 75kg. Was at Texas Tech University, USA.
At 110mh: OG: '12- h; WCh: '15- sf; CG: '14- 3; PAm: '15- 3; won CAC 2013, BAR 2014-15. At Oct: WY: '07- 1. At 60mh: WI: '16- 8. At 400mh: WJ: '08- sf.

Progress at 110mh: 2008- 14.54, 2009- 13.83, 2010- 13.71A/13.80w, 2011- 13.58, 2012- 13.31A/ 13.46/13.43w, 2013- 13.44/13.43w, 2014- 13.24, 2015- 13.21. pbs: 100m 10.43 '09, 200m 20.97 '14, 400m 46.97 '11, 1000m 2:48.01 '07, 55mh 7.15i '13, 60mh 7.64i '16, 400mh 50.90 '12, HJ 1.86 '07, LJ 7.02/7.13w '08. No relation to Ryan Brathwaite (1 WCh 110mh 2009).

Ramon GITTENS b. 20 Jul 1987 Bridgetown 1.80m 77kg. Saint Augustine's College, USA.
At 100m: OG: '12- h; WCh: '09/11- h, '13/15- sf; CG: '14- 8; PAm: '11- sf, '15- 2. At 200m: WCh: '09- h; WJ: '06- 5, PAm: '07- sf. At 60m: WI: '16- 3.
Progress at 110mh: 2008- 14.54, 2009- 13.83, 2010- 13.71A/13.80w, 2011- 13.58, 2012- 13.31A/ 13.46/13.43w, 2013- 13.44/13.43w, 2014- 13.24, 2015- 13.21. pbs: 50m 6.51i '16, 200m 20.44 '14.

Women

Akela JONES b. 21 Apr 1995 Saint Michael 1.86m 77kg. Student at Kansas State University.
At LJ: WJ: '12- dnq 18; '14- 1; WY: '11- 6; PAm: '15- 6 (h 100mh).
CAC Indoor pentathlon record 2016
Progress at HJ, LJ, Hep: 2008- 1.71, 2009- 1.81, 5.85w; 2010- 1.85, 2011- 1.75, 6.16; 2012- 1.81, 6.36; 2013- 1.85i/1.80, 6.26i/6.35w; 2014- 1.87i/1.85, 6.55; 2015- 1.91, 6.60. 6371; 2016- 1.98i, 6.80i. pbs: 60m 7.47i '15, 100m 11.64 '15, 11.59w '13; 200m 23.72/23.45w '15, 800m 2:21.62 '15, 60mh 8.00i '16, 100mh 13.10/13.08Aw '15, SP 14.85 '15, JT 38.13 '15, Pen 4643i '16.

BELARUS

Governing body: Belarus Athletic Federation, Kalinovskogo Street 111A, Minsk 220119. Founded 1991.

National Champions 2015: **Men**: 100m/200m: Ilya Sirotyuk 10.59/21.65, 400m: Aleksandr Krasovskiy 48.00, 800m: Pyotr Khodasevich 1:48.98, 1500m/5000m: Artyom Logish 3:49.72/ 14:12.37, 10000m: Ilya Slavenskiy 30:12.34, 3000mSt: Sergey Litovchik 8:47.22, 110mh: Maksim Lynsha 13.59, 400mh: Nikita Yakovlev 51.57, HJ: Andrey Skobeiko 2.21, PV: Dmitriy Gashuk 5.10, LJ: Konstantin Borichevskiy 8.22w, TJ: Artyom Bondarenko 16.26, SP: Pavel Lyzhin 19.80, DT: Sergey Roganov 57.09, HT: Pavel Boreysha 76.06, JT: Vladimir Kozlov 76.05, Dec: Yuriy Yeremich 7632, 20kW: Aleksandr Lyakhovich 1:21:49. **Women**: 100m: Yeketerina Gonchar 11.52, 200m/100mh: Alina Talay 23.78/12.74, 400m: Ilona Usovich 52.89, 800m: Marina Arzamasova 2:03.56, 1500m: Dariya Borisevich 4:15.42, 5000m/10000m: Nina Savina 16:00.12/33:19.98, 3000mSt: Anastasiya Puzakova 10:23.65, 400mh: Yekaterina Artyukh 57.65, HJ: Anna Gorodskaya 1.83, PV: Irina Yakoltsevich 4.20, LJ: Anastasiya Mironchik-Ivanova 6.82, TJ: Kseniya Detsuk 13.97, SP: Alyona Dubitskaya 18.88, DT: Yelena Abramchuk 55.16, HT: Yelena Soboleva 69.26, JT: Tatyana Kholodovich 61.07, Hep: Yekaterina Netsvetayeva 5962, 20kW: Dariya Bolkunets 1:34:04.

Andrey KRAVCHENKO b. 4 Jan 1986 Petrikov, Gomel region 1.87m 84kg.
At Dec: OG: '08- 2; WCh: '07- dq 100m, '09- 10, 13- 12; EC: '10- 3, '14- 1; WJ: '04- 1; EU23: '07- 1; EJ: 05- 1; ECp: '08-09: 1/1. At Oct: WY: '03- 2. At Hep: WI: '08-10-12-14: 2/4/6/2; EI: '07- 3, '11- 1.
World youth record for octathlon (6415) 2003.
Progress at Dec: 2005- 7833, 2006- 8013, 2007- 8617, 2008- 8585, 2009- 8336, 2010- 8370, 2011- 8023, 2013- 8390, 2014- 8616. pbs: 60m 7.03i '08, 100m 10.86 '07, 400m 47.17 '07, 1000m 2:39.80i '11, 1500m 4:24.44 '06, 60mh 7.90i '10, 110mh 13.93 '07, HJ 2.22 '14, PV 5.30i/5.20 '08, LJ 7.90 '07, SP 15.42i/15.19 '14, DT 47.46 '14, JT 68.11 '14, Hep 6303i '13. Added 604 points to pb to win with European U23 record at Götzis 2007. Won IAAF Combined Events Challenge 2008 and 2013.

Women

Marina ARZAMASOVA b. 17 Dec 1987 Minsk 1.73m 57kg. née Kotovich. Minsk.
At 800m: OG: '12- h; WCh: '11/13- sf, '15- 1; EC: '12- 2, '14- 1; WJ: '06- h; CCp: '14- 3; WI: '14- 3; EI: '13- 3. Won W.MilG 2011, BLR 800m 2008, 2013, 2015; 1500m 2013.
Progress at 800m: 2004- 2:09.37, 2005- 2:07.24, 2006- 2:06.39, 2007- 2:04.33, 2008- 2:02.67, 2009- 2:05.53i, 2011- 1:59.30, 2012- 1:59.63, 2013- 1:59.60, 2014- 1:58.15, 2015- 1:57.54. pbs: 400m 52.81 '12, 600m 1:27.28i '13, 1000m 2:37.93 '11, 1500m 4:15.99 '12.
Married to Ilya, with daughter Sashenka born 2010. Parents were Aleksandr Kotovich UKR (HJ 2.35i '85, 2.33 '84; 2 EI 85) and Ravilya Agletdinova BLR (800m 1:56.1 '82, 1500m 3:58.40 '85, 1 EC 86, 4 WCh 83).

Alyona DUBITSKAYA b. 25 Jan 1990 1.82m 77k. née Hryshko. Grodnenskaya.
At SP: WCh: '13- dnq 27, '15- 6; EC: '14- 7; WJ: '08- 4; WY: '07- 1; EJ: '09- 1; ET: '15- 3. BLR champion 2009, 2014-15.
Progress at SP: 2007- 15.91, 2008- 16.55, 2009- 17.95, 2010- 18.12i/17.75, 2012- 16.63, 2013- 17.88, 2014- 19.03, 2015- 18.88. pb DT 46.30 '14.
6-month drugs ban 2014-15.

Yuliya LEONTYUK b. 31 Jan 1984 1.85m 80kg. Brest.
At SP: WCh: '13- dnq 16, '15- 7; EC: '14- 4; WJ: '02- 7; WY: '01- 3; EU23: '05- 4; EJ: '03- 2; WUG: '07- 2; ECp: '08- dq (1); WI: '14- 7; EI: '07- 4, '15- 2.
Progress at SP: 2001- 15.16, 2002- 16.47, 2003- 17.44, 2004- 16.37, 2005- 17.91, 2006- 18.86, 2007- 18.86, 2008- 19.79, 2013- 18.47, 2014- 18.87, 2015- 19.00i/18.86. pb DT 48.72 '14.
Two-year drugs ban 2008-10.

Oksana MENKOVA b. 28 Mar 1982 Krichev, Mogilev region 1.83m 91kg.
At HT: OG: '08- 1, '12- 7; WCh: '03-07-09-13: dnq

23/nt/13/22; EC: '02/06/14: dnq 27/23/13; EU23: 03- 2; EJ: '01- 5; WUG: '05- 5; ECp: '07- 2, '08- 1. Five Belarus hammer records 2006-12.
Progress at HT: 1999- 47.87, 2000- 56.50, 2001- 59.24, 2002- 66.42, 2003- 67.58, 2004- 70.23, 2005- 70.15, 2006- 76.86, 2007- 73.94, 2008- 77.32, 2009- 76.32, 2010- 67.27, 2011- 67.78, 2012- 78.69, 2013- 75.45, 2014- 71.56, 2015- 73.26.
Had a terrible record at major events and only 11th in qualifying, but took gold with Olympic record 76.34 in 2008. Daughter Anna born on 25 Sep 2010.

Anastasiya MIRONCHIK-IVANOVA b. 13 Apr 1989 Slutsk 1.71m 54kg. Minsk.
At LJ: OG: '12- 7; WCh: '09- 11, '11- 4, '15- 9; EC: '10- 6; WJ: '08- 2; WY: '05- 8; EU23: '09- 2, '11- 6; WI: '12- 5; EI: '11- 6. BLR champion 2007, 2010-12, 2015.
Progress at LJ: 2004- 5.90, 2005- 6.10/6.13w, 2007- 6.03i/5.89, 2008- 6.71, 2009- 6.65/6.76w, 2010- 6.84, 2011- 6.85/6.92w, 2012- 7.08/7.22w, 2013- 6.60, 2015- 6.82, 2016- 6.84i. pb TJ 14.29 '11.
Son born June 2014.

Yelena SOBOLEVA b. 11 Mar 1993 1.80m 96kg. Grodnenskaya.
At HT: WCh: '15- 10; WJ: '12- 3; WY: '09- 11, EU23: 03- 2; EJ: '13- 6, '15- 2; EJ: '11- 4, Yth OG: '10- 2. BLR champion 2014-15.
Progress at HT: 2008- 53.49, 2009- 56.90, 2010- 60.42, 2011- 62.24, 2012- 67.13, 2013- 66.10, 2014- 68.96, 2015- 72.86.

Olga SUDAREVA b. 22 Feb 1984 Gomel 1.76m 63kg. née Serygeyenko. Gomel.
At LJ: OG: '08/12- dnq 32/13; WCh: '13- 4, '15- dnq 13; EC: '12- 2, '14- 11; ET: '15- 2; BLR champion 2008, 2011, 2013-14.
Progress at LJ: 2005- 6.01i/6.00, 2006- 6.33, 2007- 6.46, 2008- 6.72, 2011- 6.40, 2012- 6.85, 2013- 6.82, 2014- 6.67, 2015- 6.86. pbs: 60m 7.86i '08, 200m 24.86 '08.

Alina TALAY b. 14 May 1989 Orsha, Vitebsk 1.64m 54kg.
At 100mh: OG: '12- sf; WCh: '13- sf, '15- 3; EC: '10-12-14: sf/1/5; WJ: '08- 4; EU23: '09- 3, '11- 1; WUG: '13- 2; ET: '11- 2, '15- 1; won W.MilG 2011, BLR 2009-10, 2013-15 (200m 2015). At 60mh: WI: '12- 3, '16- 6; EI: '11-13-15: 5/1/1.
BLR 100m hurdles record 2015.
Progress at 100mh: 2007- 14.38/14.01w, 2008- 13.31, 2009- 13.07, 2010- 12.87, 2011- 12.91, 2012- 12.71, 2013- 12.78, 2014- 12.89, 2015- 12.66. pbs: 60m 7.31i '15, 100m 11.48 '11, 200m 23.59 '11, 50mh 6.89i '11, 60mh 7.85i '15.

BELGIUM

Governing bodies: Ligue Royale Belge d'Athlétisme, Stade Roi Baudouin, avenue du Marathon 199B, 1020 Bruxelles (KBAB/LRBA). Vlaamse Atletiekliga (VAL); Ligue Belge Francophone d'Athlétisme (LBFA). Original governing body founded 1889.

National Championships first held in 1889 (women 1921). **2015 Champions**: **Men**: 100m: Yannick Meyer 10.63, 200m: Arnout Matthys 21.05, 400m: Jonathan Borlée 45.27, 800m: Aurèle Vandeputte 1:48.65, 1500m: Jérôme Kahia 3:50.65, 5000m: Koen Naert 14:16.55, 10000m/HMar/Mar: Abdelhadi El Hakimi 29:03.33/ 66:03/2:15:12, 3000mSt: Steven Casteele 8:55.27, 110mh: Dario De Borger 13.87, 400mh: Michaël Bultheel 49.04, HJ: Fabiano Kalandula 2.13, PV: Arnaud Art 5.30, LJ: Cedric Nolf 7.73, TJ: Solomon Commey 15.29, SP: Jurgen Verbrugghe 17.08; DT: Philip Milanov 56.92, HT: Tim De Coster 60.76, JT: Timothy Herman 71.07, Dec: Bertrand Namurois 7024, 20000mW: Dirk Bogaert 1:54:37, 50kW: Daniel Lhoest 5:21:01. **Women**: 100m/ 100mh: Anne Zagré 11.49/12.87, 200m: Olivia Borlée 23.36; 400m: Laetitia Libert 53.20, 800m: Lotte Scheldeman 2:12.96, 1500m/3000mSt: Sofie Van Accom 4:22.12/10:24.97 (first hurdle missing), 5000m: Veerle Van Linden 16:30.98, 10000m: Ferahiwat Gamachu 36:30.45, HMar/Mar: Els Rens 77:00/2:38:13, 400mh: Axelle Dauwens 55.93, HJ: Claire Orcel 1.82, PV: Chloé Henry 4.10, LJ: Nafissatou Thiam 6.40, TJ: Sietske Lenchant 12.98, SP/HT: Jolien Boumkwo 15.11/60.54, DT: Annelies Peetroons 53.93, HT: Vanessa Sterckendries 63.29, JT: Melissa Dupré 54.30, Hep: Elien Hooyberghs 4858, 10000mW: Myriam Nicolas 57:38.13, 20kW: Annelies Sarrazin 1:59:54.

Jonathan BORLÉE b. 22 Feb 1988 Woluwe-Saint Lambert 1.80m 70kg. Racing Club of Brussels. Was at Florida State University.
At 400m: OG: '08- sf/5R, '12- 6; WCh: '11- 5, '13- 4, '15- sf; EC: '10- 7/3R, '12- 1R, '14- dns; WJ: '06- 4; WY: '05- 5; EJ: '07- h; WI: '10- 2R; EI: '11- 3R, '15- 1R. Won NCAA 2009. At 200m: EC: '12- 4. Won BEL 200m 2012-13, 400m 2006, 2011, 2015.
Four Belgian 400m records 2009-12, 300m 2012.
Progress at 400m: 2005- 47.50, 2006- 46.06, 2007- 47.85, 2008- 45.11, 2009- 44.78, 2010- 44.71, 2011- 44.78, 2012- 44.43, 2013- 44.54, 2014- 45.37, 2015- 44.67. pbs: 60m 6.81i '07, 100m 10.78 '07, 200m 20.31 '12, 300m 31.87 '12, 500m 1:00.76i '15, 600m 1:18.60i '11.
Twin brother of Kevin Borlée, their sister Olivia (b. 10 Apr 1986) has pbs 100m 11.39 '07, 200m 22.98 '06, 3 WCh '07, 2 OG '08 at 4x100mR. Younger brother **Dylan** (b. 20 Sep 1992) pb 45.57 '15 and 2 EI '15 (the three brothers ran on BEL 4x400m team 5th WCh 2013. 1st EI 2015). Their father Jacques was an international 400m runner (45.4 '79), mother Edith Demartelaere had pbs 200m 23.89 and 400m 54.09 in 1984.

Kévin BORLÉE b. 22 Feb 1988 Woluwe-Saint Lambert 1.80m 71kg. Racing Club of Brussels. Was at Florida State University.
At 400m: OG: '08- sf/5R, '12- 5; WCh: '09- sf/4R,

'11- 3, '13-15: sf; EC: '10- 1/3R, '12- 1R, '14- sf; WJ: '06- sf; WI: '10- 2R; EI: '11- 3R, '15- 1R; CCp: '10- 4/2R. At 200m: WY: '05- sf. Won DL 2012, BEL 200m 2009, 2011; 400m 2007, 2013.
Belgian 400m records 2008 and 2012.
Progress at 400m: 2005- 47.86, 2006- 46.63, 2007- 46.38, 2008- 44.88, 2009- 45.28, 2010- 45.01, 2011- 44.74, 2012- 44.56, 2013- 44.73, 2014- 45.28, 2015- 44.74. pbs: 60m 6.85i '13, 100m 10.62 '07, 200m 20.72 '11, 300m 32.72i '13, 32.76 '08; 600m 1:15.65i '11.

Philip MILANOV b. 6 Jul 1991 Bruges 1.91m 118kg. Vilvoorde AC, Lille Metropole, FRA.
At DT: WCh: '15- 2; EC: '14- dnq 20; EU23: '13- 5; WUG: '15- 1. Belgian champion 2011-15.
Five Belgian discus records 2014-15.
Progress at DT: 2011- 56.00, 2012- 57.66, 2013- 61.81, 2014- 66.02, 2015- 66.90. pb SP 17.91 '15.
His father Emil Milanov had DT pb 58.28 '82, moved from Bulgaria to Belgium in 1989.

Women

Nafissatou THIAM b. 19 Aug 1994 Namur 1.84m 69kg. RFCL. Student of geographical science at University of Liège.
At Hep: WCh: '13- 14, '15- 11; EC: '14- 3; WJ: '12- 14; WY: '11- 4; EJ: '13- 1. At Pen: EI: '13- 6, '15- 2. At HJ: EU23: '15- 2; WI: '14- 8=. Won BEL Hep 2012, LJ 2015.
Two Belgian heptathlon records 2013-14. World junior heptathlon best 2013.
Progress at HJ, Hep: 2010- 1.74, 2011- 1.81, 2012- 1.88, 5916; 2013- 1.92, 6298, 2014- 1.97, 6508; 2015- 6412. pbs: 60m 7.81i '13, 200m 24.78 '14, 800m 2:20.79 '14, 60mh 8.42i '15, 100mh 13.79 '15, LJ 6.51i '16, 6.43 '13; TJ: 12.82 '14, SP 15.24 '15, JT 52.03 '15, Pen 4696i '15.
Tied world best in a heptathlon with 1.97 high jump at EC 2014.

BOSNIA & HERZEGOVINA

Amel TUKA b. 9 Jan 1991 Kakanj 1.87m 77kg. AK Zenica. Mechanical engineering graduate.
At 800m: WCh: '15- 3; EC: '12- sf, '14- 6; EU23: '13- 3.
BIH records: 400m (3) 2012-13, 800m (5) 2013-15.
Progress at 800m: 2010- 1:51.04, 2011- 1:51.09, 2012- 1:48.31, 2013- 1:46.29, 2014- 1:46.12, 2015- 1:42.51. pb 400m 47.19 '13.

BOTSWANA

Governing body: Botswana Athletics Association, PO Box 2399, Gaborone. Fd 1972.

Nijel AMOS b. 15 Mar 1994 Marobela 1.79m 60kg.
At 800m: OG: '12- 2; WCh: '15- sf; CG: '14- 1; WJ: '12- 1, WY: '11- 5; AfG: '15- 1.2R; AfCh: 14- 1/1R; CG: '14- 1; WUG: '13- 1. Won DL 2014-15.
World junior 800m and two Botswana 800m records 2012.
Progress at 800m: 2011- 1:47.28, 2012- 1:41.73, 2013- 1:44.71, 2014- 1:42.45, 2015- 1:42.66. pbs: 200m 21.34 '15, 400m 45.56 '14, 600m 1:15.0+ 12.

Isaac MAKWALA b. 29 Sep 1986 Tutume 1.83m 79kg.
At (200m)/400m: OG: '12- h; WCh: '09- h, '13- (h), '15- 5; CG: '10- sf, '14- sf; AfG: '07- sf/1R, '11- 7, '15- 1/2R; AfCh: '08-10-12-14: 2/sf/1/1 & (2)/1R; CCp: '14- 6/2/1R.
Records: Commonwealth 400m 2015, African 400m (2) 2014-15, Botswana 100m (2) 2013-14, 200m 2013-14, 400m (4) 2014-15.
Progress at 200m, 400m: 2007- 46.48, 2008- 21.20, 45.64A; 2009- 20.73, 45.56; 2010- 21.33, 46.07; 2011- 21.17, 46.27; 2012- 20.87, 45.25; 2013- 20.21, 45.86; 2014- 19.96/19.7A, 44.01; 2015- 20.44A/20.77, 43.72. Pb 100m 10.20A/10.14wA '14.

BRAZIL

Governing body: Confederação Brasileira de Atletismo (CBAt), Rua Jorge Chammas, 310, Vila Mariana, São Paulo, SP- CEP: 04.106-07. Founded 1914 (Confederação 1977).
National Championships first held in 1925.
2015 Champions: **Men**: 100m: Vitor Hugo dos Santos 10.22, 200m: Aldemir G da Silva 20.44, 400m: Hugo de Sousa 45.44, 800m/1500m: Thiago André 1:47.74/3:42.07, 5000m: Altobelli da Silva 14:05.19, 10000m: Giovani dos Santos 28:39.54, 3000mSt: Jean Carlos Machado 8:54.17, 110mh: João Vitor de Oliveira 13.70, 400mh: Hederson Estefani 49.40, HJ: Fernando Ferreira 2.25, PV: Thiago Braz da Silva 5.65, LJ: Mauro da Silva 8.03, TJ: Jefferson Sabino 16.36, SP: Darlan Romani 20.10, DT: Ronald Julião 58.93, HT: Wágner Domingos 73.66, JT: Julio de Oliveira 75.67, Dec: Luiz Alberto de Araújo 8034, 20kW: Caio Bonfim 1:24:53, 50kW: Jonathan Reickmann 4:18:56. **Women:** 100m: Rosângela Santos 11.08, 200m: Ana Cláudia Silva 23.08, 400m: Geisa Coutinho 51.43, 800m/1500m: Flávia de Lima 2:02.03/4:13.29, 5000m/10000m: Tatiele de Carvalho 16:02.41/33:43.93, 3000mSt: Tatiana da Silva 9:57.52, 100mh: Adelly Santos 13.06, 400mh: Jaílma de Lima 58.14, HJ: Ana Paula de Oliveira 1.82, PV: Fabiana Murer 4.65, LJ/TJ: Keila Costa 6.70/14.03, SP: Geisa Arcanjo 17.35, DT: Andressa de Morais 64.15, HT: Carla Michel 60.25, JT: Jucilene de Lima 60.54, Hep: Vanessa Spinola 5915, 20000mW: Érica de Sena 1:37:10.

Caio BONFIM b. 19 Mar 1991 Brasilia 1.70m 58kg. CASO.
At 20kW: OG: '12- 39; WCh: '11- 18, '13- dq, '15- 6; WCp: '12-14- 15/16; PAm: 15- 3, SACh: '13- 1; BRA champion 2012-15. At 10000mW: WJ: '08- 6, '10- 4; WY: '07- 12.
Progress at 20kW: 2009- 1:30:17.9t, 2010- 1:27:21.3t, 2011- 1:20:58.5t, 2012- 1:21:26, 2013- 1:22:14, 2014- 1:20:28, 2015- 1:20:44. Pbs: 5000mW 19:47.99 '11, 10000mW 40:40.0 '09.
His mother, Gianetti de Sena Bonfim (b. 13.3.65), won the 1996 Ibero-American 10,000m

walk, and had pbs 5000m: 23:28.9 '96, 10000m: 47:42.0 '96, 20k: 1:41:07 '04.

Augusto Dutra de OLIVEIRA b. 16 Jul 1990 Marília, São Paulo 1.80m 70kg. BM&F Bovespa.
At PV: WCh: '13- 11, '15- 9=; WI: '14- 7; SAG: '14- 1; SACh: '11- 4; CCp: '14- 4; won SAm-J '2009.
Two South American pole vault records and two indoors 2013.
Progress at PV: 2008- 4.60, 2009- 5.00, 2010- 5.40, 2011- 5.32, 2012- 5.45, 2013- 5.82, 2014- 5.70, 2015- 5.81.

Mauro Vinícius da SILVA b. 26 Dec 1986 Presidente Prudente 1.83m 69kg. BM&F Bovespa.
At LJ: OG: '08- dnq 26, '12- 7; WCh: '13- 5; WI: '12- 1, '14- 1; SAG: '14- 3; SACh: '13- 1, '15- 3. BRA champion 2010, 2012-13, 2015.
Progress at LJ: 2005- 7.35/7.73w, 2006- 7.61, 2007- 7.66, 2008- 8.10/8.20w?, 2009- 8.04i/7.94, 2010- 8.12, 2011- 8.27, 2012- 8.28i/8.11, 2013- 8.31, 2014- 8.28i/7.88/8.08w, 2015- 8.03. pbs: 60m 6.76i '09, 100m 10.40 '07, 200m 21.02 '07.
Won World Indoor title with 8.23 but took off behind the board with 24cm to spare. Knee surgery at end of 2015 season.

Thiago Braz da SILVA b. 16 Dec 1993 Marília 1.93m 84kg. Orcampi/Unimed.
At PV: WCh: '13-15: dnq 14=/19; WJ: '12- 1; WI: '14- 4; PAm: '15-f nh; SACh: '13- 1; Yth Oly: '10- 2, won BRA 2015, PAm-J 2011.
Four South American pole vault records 2013-15, indoors (5) 2014-16.
Progress at PV: 2009- 4.60, 2010- 5.10, 2011- 5.31, 2012- 5.55, 2013- 5.83, 2014- 5.76i/5.73, 2015- 5.92, 2016- 5.93i.
Married Ana Paula de Oliveira (HJ 1.82 '14) on 13 Dec 2014.

Women

Keila da Silva **COSTA** b. 6 Feb 1983 Recife 1.70m 62kg. BM&F Bovespa.
At LJ/(TJ): OG: '04- dnq 30, '08- 11, '12- (dnq 20); WCh: '07- 7/9, '09- nj, '11- dnq 24/12,'13- (dnq 13).'15= dnq 26/12; PAm: 07- 2/2, 11- 5/4, '15- 9/2; SACh: '01- (1), '03- 1/1, '05- 2/2, '07- 2/1, '09- 1, '13- 2/1; SAG: '14- 1/1; WJ: '00- (11), '02- dnq 18/3; PAm-J: '01- 3/2; WI: '08- 7, '10- 3. Won IbAm LJ 2006, SAm-J TJ 2000, BRA LJ 2003-05, 2007, 2009-10, 2015; TJ 2003-05, 2007, 2010-13, 2015.
South American TJ record 2007, indoor record (14.11) 2006, S.Am junior records TJ 2001, LJ 2002. BRA TJ 2007 & 2013.
Progress at LJ, TJ: 1998- 11.74/11.91w, 1999- 5.83, 12.62; 2000- 6.05A/5.88, 13.23/13.65w, 2001- 6.20/ 6.24w, 14.00/14.15w; 2002- 6.46, 13.78/13.80w; 2003- 6.52, 13.68/13.69w; 2004- 6.61, 13.80/ 13.82w; 2005- 6.63, 13.95; 2006- 6.59, 14.17; 2007- 6.88, 14.57/15.10w; 2008- 6.79, 2009- 6.79, 13.35i; 2010- 6.68, 13.79/14.03w; 2011- 6.67, 14.24; 2012- 6.68, 14.31; 2013- 6.56, 14.58; 2014- 6.63, 14.13; 2015- 6.70, 14.17/14.50w.

Fabiana de Almeida **MURER** b. 16 Mar 1981 Campinas, São Paulo 1.72m 64kg. BM&F Bovespa. Degree in physiotherapy.
At PV: OG: '08- 10=, '12- dnq 14; WCh: '05-07-09-11-13-15: dnq 15/6=/5/1/5=/2; WJ: '98- dnq 14=, '00- 10; PAm: '99-07-11-15: 9/1/2/2; WI: '08-10-14-16: 3=/1/4/6=; SAG: '14- 1; SACh: '99-01-05-06-07-09-11: 3/6/2/1/1/1/1; WCp: '06-10-14: 2/3/ nh. Won DL 2010, 2014; IbAm 2006, 2010; SAmG 2014; SAm-J 1998-2000, BRA 2005-07, 2010, 2013, 2015.
14 South American pole vault records, 16 indoors 2006-15, 30 BRA records 1998-2015.
Progress at PV: 1998- 3.66, 1999- 3.81, 2000- 3.90, 2001- 3.91, 2002- 3.70, 2003- 4.06, 2004- 4.25, 2005- 4.40, 2006- 4.66, 2007- 4.66i/4.65, 2008- 4.80, 2009- 4.82, 2010- 4.85, 2011- 4.85, 2012- 4.77, 2013- 4.75, 2014- 4.80, 2015- 4.85.
Married to coach Élson de Souza (pb 5.02 '89).

Érica de SENA b. 3 May 1985 Camaragibe, Pernambuco 1.68m 55kg. Orcampi Unimed.
At 20kW: WCh: '15- 6; PAm: 15- 2; BRA champion 2011-15.
Four S.American 20k walk records 2014-16; BRA records: 10000mW 2014, 20kW (4) 2012-16.
Progress at 20kW: 2006- 1:51:45.5t, 2007- 1:44:52.96t, 2008- 1:44:14.6t, 2009- 1:44:27, 2010- 1:38:59, 2011- 1:35:29.6t, 2012- 1:31:53, 2013- 1:32:59, 2014- 1:30:43, 2015- 1:29:37, 2016- 1:28:22. Pbs: 5000mW 23:10.59 '11, 10000mW 43:31.30 '14.
Married to and coached by Ecuadorian Andrés Chocho (qv). Lives in Cuenca, Ecuador.

BULGARIA

Governing body: Bulgarian Athletics Federation, 75 bl. Vassil Levski, Sofia 1000. Founded 1924.

National Championships first held in 1926 (men), 1938 (women). **2015 Champions: Men:** 100m: Denis Dimitrov 10.18w, 200m: Borislav Tonev 21.55, 400m: Krasimir Braykov 47.87, 800m: Nikolai Parvanov 1:54.94, 1500m: Mitko Tsenov 3:44.17, 5000m/10000m/HMar/3000mSt: Yolo Nikolov 14:26.93/30:21.74/69:14/8:59.01, Mar: Ismail Senangi UGA 2:18:48, 110mh: Tsvetomir Kirov 14.47w, 400mh: Milen Valkanov 54.32, HJ: Tikhomir Ivanov 2.19, PV: Plamen Piskov, LJ: Denis Eradiri 8.01, TJ: Momchil Karailiev 16.57, SP: Georgi Ivanov 20.00, DT: Rosen Karamfilov 50.34, HT: Aykhan Apti 68.90, JT: Mark Salvov 65.34, Dec: Kiril Zagorski 5798, 20kW: Bozhidar Vasilev 1:47:15. **Women**: 100m/200m: Inna Eftimova 11.51/ 23.35, 400m/800m: Katia Khristova 54.40/2:05.78, 1500m/5000m/10000m: Silvia Danekova 4:19.09/16:19.08/34:13.13, 10000m: Dobrinka Shalamanova 36:25.81, HMar/Mar: Militsa Mircheva 1:25:33/2:53:00, 100mh: Elena Miteva 14.04, 400mh: Vania Stambolova 58.99, HJ: Galina Nikolova 1.70, PV: Temenuga Atanasova 3.00, LJ: Milena Mitkova 6.32w, TJ: Andriana

Bânova 14.06w, SP: Radoslava Mavrodieva 17.78, DT: Renata Petkova 48.95, HT: Antonia Shtereva 41.70, JT: Rumyana Karapetrova 46.94, Hep: Aleksandra Rubarova 3381, 20kW: Radosveta Simeonova 1:49:13.

Women

Ivet LALOVA-COLLIO b. 18 May 1984 Sofia 1.68m 56kg. née Lalova.

At 100m/(200m): OG: '04- 4/5, '08- sf/qf, '12- sf/sf; WCh: '07- qf, '09- qf/h, '11- 7/sf, '13- sf/sf, '15- sf/7; EC: '10- h, '12- 1/sf, '14- 5/sf; WJ: '02- sf; WY: '01- h/sf; EJ: '03: 1/1; EI: '05- (1). At 60m: WI: '12- 8; EI: '13- 3. Won BUL 100m 2004-05, 200m 2004; Balkan 100m 2011, 2013.

Bulgarian 100m record 2004.

Progress at 100m, 200m: 1998- 13.0, 27.2; 1999- 12.71, 2000- 12.14, 25.24; 2001- 11.72, 24.03; 2002- 11.59, 24.4; 2003- 11.14, 22.87; 2004- 10.77, 22.51/22.36w; 2005- 11.03, 22.76; 2007- 11.26/11.15w, 23.00; 2008- 11.31/11.28w, 23.13; 2009- 11.48/11.24w, 23.60; 2010- 11.43, 23.71; 2011- 10.96, 22.66; 2012- 11.06/11.01w, 22.98; 2013- 11.04, 22.78; 2014- 11.10, 23.17/22.92w; 2015- 11.09, 22.32. pbs: 50m 6.23i+ '12, 60m 7.12i '13.

Broke her leg in a warm-up collision with two athletes on 14 Jun 2005. Married Simone Collio (Italy, 60m 6.55 ITA record 2008, 100m 10.06 in 2009) on 20 Sep 2013. Her father Miroslav Lalov had 100m best of 10.4 and was BUL 200m champion in 1966, mother Liliya was a pentathlete.

Gabriela PETROVA b. 29 Jun 1992 Haskovo 1.67m 61kg.

At SP: WCh: '15- 4; EC: '14- 4; WJ: '10- dnq 17; WY: '09- dnq 18; EU23: '13- 1; EJ: '11- 5, BUL champion 2010, 2013.

Progress at LJ: 2007- 12.43, 2008- 12.72i, 2009- 12.64, 2010- 13.35, 2011- 13.27/13.44w, 2012- 13.45, 2013- 14.14i/13.92/13.96w, 2014- 14.13, 2015- 14.66/14.85w. pb LJ 6.46 '15.

BURUNDI

Francine NIYONSABA b. 5 May 1993 Nkanda Bweru, Ruyiqi 1.61m 56kg.

At 800m: OG: '12- 6; AfCh: '12- 1; WI: '16- 1.

Five Burundi 800m records 2012.

Progress at 800m: 2012- 1:56.59, 2013- 1:56.72, 2015- 1:57.62 pbs: 400m 54.3 '13, 600m 1:27.6 '12.

Won World title on her indoor debut in 2016.

CANADA

Governing body: Athletics Canada, Suite B1-110, 2445 S-Laurent Drive, Ottawa, Ontario K1G 6C3. Formed as Canadian AAU in 1884.

National Championships first held in 1884 (men), 1925 (women). **2015 Champions: Men**: 100m: André De Grasse 9.95, 200m: Aaron Brown 20.11w, 400m: Philip Osei 46.59, 800m: Cameron Provevait 1:52.73, 1500m: Thomas Riva 4:06.16, 5000m: Cam Levins 13:51.34, 10000m: Kelly Wiebe 28:58.90. HMar: Kip Kangogo 66:39, Mar: Eric Gillis 2:11:31, 3000mSt: Matt Hughes 8:31.95, 110mh: Damian Warner 13.27, 400mh: Gabriel Slythe Léveillé 51.67, HJ: Derek Drouin 2.34, PV: Shawnacy Barber 5.60, LJ: Jared Kerr 7.85, TJ: Aaron Hernandez 14.98w, SP/DT: Tim Nedow 20.53/60.09, HT: James Steacy 71.15, JT: Caleb Jones 74.45, Dec: Patrick Arbour 7147, 10,000mW: Evan Dunfee 40:29.04. **Women**: 100m: Khamica Bingham 11.19, 200m: Kimberley Hyacinthe 22.56w, 400m: Carline Muir 51.84, 800m: Fiona Benson 2:08.52, 1500m/5000m: Nicole Sifuentes 4:20.29/16:17.32, 10000m: Laura Batterink 33:58.77, HMar/Mar: Lanni Marchant 72:17/2.:28:09, 3000mSt: Erin Teschuk 9:54.18, 100mh: Brianne Theisen-Eaton 13.06, 400mh: Sarah Wells 56.03, HJ: Alyx Treasure 1.86, PV: Kelsie Ahbe 4.30, LJ: Christabel Nettey 6.76w, TJ: Julia Wallace 13.18w, SP: Taryn Suttie 16.88, DT: Quinn Erickson 48.49, HT: Sultana Frizell 70.97, JT: Liz Gleadle 59.93, Hep: Maddie Buttinger 5643, 10,000mW: Rachel Seaman 44:16.98.

Shawnacy BARBER b. 27 May 1994 Las Cruces, New Mexico, USA 1.90m 82kg. Student at Akron University, USA.

At PV: WCh: '13- dnq 27, '15- 1; CG: '14- 3; WJ: '12- 3; PAm: '15- 1; PAm-J: 13- 1; WI: '16- 4=; Canadian champion 2013-14, NCAA 2015.

Pole vault records: Four Canadian 2013-15, indoors (7) 2014-16, N.American indoor 2016.

Progress at PV: 2010- 4.42, 2011- 5.03, 2012- 5.57, 2013- 5.71, 2014- 5.75Ai/5.65, 2015- 5.93, 2016- 6.00Ai.

His father George vaulted 5.29 in 1985 and in 1983 competed for Canada at the Worlds (nh) and was Canadian champion.

Andre DE GRASSE b. 10 Nov 1994 Scarborough, Ontario 1.80m 73kg. University of Southern California.

At (100m)/200m: WCh: '15- (3=)/3R; CG: '14- sf; PAm: '15- 1/1; PAm-J: '13- 2/3. Won NCAA 100m & 200m 2015, CAN 100m 2015.

Three Canadian 200m records 2015.

Progress at 100m, 200m: 2012- 10.59, 2013- 10.25/9.96w, 20.74A/20.57w; 2014- 10.15/10.03w, 20.38; 2015- 9.75w, 19.88/19.58w. pbs: 55m 6.21i '13, 60m 6.60i '15, 400m 47.93 '14.

Father came from Barbados and mother from Trinidad.

Derek DROUIN b. 6 Mar 1990 Sarnia, Ontario 1.95m 80kg. Student of exercise science at Indiana University.

At HJ: OG: '12- 3=; WCh: '13- 3, '15- 1; CG: '14- 1; WY: '07- 10; PAm: '15- 1; CCp: '14- 4. Won PAmJ 2009, CAN 2012-15, NCAA 2013, Franc G 2013.

Commonwealth high jump record 2014, four Canadian high jump records 2013-14.

Progress at HJ: 2007- 2.07, 2008- 2.11, 2009- 2.27, 2010- 2.28i/2.26, 2011- 2.33i/2.23, 2012- 2.31, 2013- 2.38, 2014- 2.40, 2015- 2.37. pbs: 60mh 7.98i

'12, 1000m 2:45.06i '13, 110mh 14.04 '13, PV 4.15i '13. 3.65 '11; LJ 7.20i '13, 6.85 '11; Hep 5817i '13. His sister Jillian (b. 30 Sep 1986) set a heptahlon pb of 5972w to win the Pan-Am Cup in 2014; 6th CG 2010.

Evan DUNFEE b. 28 Sep 1990 Richmond, BC 1.86m 68kg.
At 50kW: WCh: '13- 36, '15- 12 (12 20kW). At 20kW: WCp: '14- 11; CG: '10- 6; PAm: '15- 1, won NACAC 2012. At 10000mW: WJ: '08- 10; WY: '07- 23. CAN champion 10000mW 2012, 2015, 20kW 2010-11, 2014. Notth American records: 20k & 20,000m 2014, 50kW 2015.
Progress at 50kW: 2013- 3:59:28, 2014- 3:58:34, 2015- 3:43:45. pbs: 5000mW 18:53.06 '14, 10000mW 39:55.52 '12, 20kW 1:20:13 '14, 30kW 2:11:54 '14.

Matthew HUGHES b. 3 Aug 1989 Oshawa, Ontario 1.80m 64kg. Was at University of Louisville, USA.
At 3000mSt: WCh: '11- h, '13- 6, '15- 8; CG: '14- 4; WJ: '08- h; PAm: '15- 1; CCp: '14- 7; CAN champion 2013-15.
Canadian 3000m steeplechase record 2013.
Progress at 3000mSt: 2007- 9:20.61, 2008- 8:59.83, 2009- 8:47.36, 2010- 8:34.18, 2011- 8:24.87, 2012- 8:31.77, 2013- 8:11.64, 2014- 8:12.81, 2015- 8:18.63. pbs: 1500m 3:41.49 '15, 3000m 7:51.87i '15, 8:11.64 '13; 5000m 13:19.56 '15.

Tim NEDOW b. 16 Oct 1990 Brockville 1.98m 125kg. Ottawa Lions. Was at University of Tulsa and DePaul University, USA.
At SP: WCh: '13/15- dnq 24/20; CG: '14- 3; WI: '16- 7; PAm: '15- 2 (6 DT); PAm-J: '09- 3. Won CAN SP 2013-15, DT 2012-15
Progress at SP: 2010- 17.90, 2011- 19.18i/18.84, 2012- 20.51i/20.21, 2013- 20.74, 2014- 20.98, 2015- 20.78, 2016- 21.33i. pb DT 61.49 '15.

Benjamin THORNE b. 19 Mar 1993 Kitimat 1.80m 57kg. Racewalk West. University of British Columbia.
At 20kW: WCh: '13- 20, '15- 3; WCp: '14- 13; WUG: 15- 2; At 10000mW: WJ: '12- dq. Won CAN 10kW 2011, 20kW 2012
North American 20k walk record 2015.
Progress at 20kW: 2012- 1:31:26, 2013- 1:24:26, 2014- 1:20:19, 2015- 1:19:57, 2016- 1:20:08. Pbs 5000mW 19:00.92 '14, 10000mW 40:26.0A '12.

Damian WARNER b. 4 Nov 1989 London, Ontario 1.85m 83kg. LWTF.
At Dec: OG: '12- 5; WCh: '11- 18, '13- 3, '15- 2; CG: '14- 1; PAm: '15- 1. Won Canadian 110mh 2014-15, Dec 2011-13. At Hep: WI: '14- 7.
Two Canadian decathlon records 2015.
Progress at Dec: 2010- 7449, 2011- 8102A/7832, 2012- 8442, 2013- 8512, 2014- 8282, 2015- 8695. pbs: 60m 6.74i '10, 100m 10.28 '15, 200m 20.96 '13, 400m 46.36i/47.04 '15, 1000m 2:37.98i '14, 1500m 4:24.73 '15, 60mh 7.63i '16, 110mh 13.27 '15, HJ 2.09 '13, PV 4.80A '12, LJ 7.65/7.68w '15, TJ 14.75w '08, SP 14.44 '15, DT 50.26 '16, JT 64.67 '13, Hep: 6129 14.
Made 340 points improvement on pb when 5th at 2012 Olympics, setting six pbs, and 70 more at 2013 Worlds, with three pbs. Won Götzis & Talence 2013. Ran fastest ever 110mh in decathlon 13.44 '15.

Women

Melissa BISHOP b. 5 Aug 1988 Eganville, Ontario 1.73m 57kg. University of Windsor.
At 800m: OG: '12- h; WCh: '13- h, '15- 2; CG: '14- 8; PAm: '15- 1; CAN champion 2013-14. At 400m: WY: '05- h.
Canadian 800m record 2015.
Progress at 800m: 2007- 2:10.51 2008- 2:10.12, 2009- 2:06.77, 2010- 2:04.12, 2011- 2:02.69, 2012- 1:59.82, 2013- 1:59.76, 2014- 1:59.70, 2015- 1:57.52. pbs: 400m 56.27 '10, 600m 1:27.95i '13, 1:28.14 '14, 1000m 2:38.75 '14, 1500m 4:17.91i '16.

Sultana FRIZELL b. 24 Oct 1984 Perth, Ontario 1.83m 110kg. Was at University of Georgia.
At HT: OG: '08/12- dnq 33/25; WCh: '09- 10, '1/15- dnq 16/13; CG: '10- 1, '14- 1; PAm: '07-11-15: 7/2/3; PAm-J: '03- 4; CCp: '14- 5; Canadian champion 2007-08, 2010, 2013-15.
Five Commonwealth hammer records 2009-14, N.American 2012 & 2014, 8 Canadian 2008-14.
Progress at HT: 2002- 54.75, 2003- 57.95, 2004- 63.36, 2005- 66.42, 2006- 63.39, 2007- 67.92, 2008- 70.94, 2009- 72.07, 2010- 72.24, 2011- 71.46, 2012- 75.04, 2013- 71.57, 2014- 75.73, 2015- 73.66. pbs: SP 15.82 '06, Wt 20.37i '05, JT 46.58 '04.

Liz GLEADLE b. 5 Dec 1988 Vancouver 1.83m 95kg. Chinooks.
At JT: OG: '12- 12; WCh: '15- 11; CG: '14- 5; PAm: '15- 1; WJ: '06- 12; WY: '05- 5; CCp: '14- 3. Canadian champion 2008-09, 2012, 2014-15.
Five Canadian javelin records 2009-15.
Progress at JT: 2005- 50.53, 2006- 50.86, 2007- 52.36, 2008- 54.13, 2009- 58.21, 2010- 57.84, 2011- 58.40, 2012- 61.15, 2013- 54.13, 2014- 64.50, 2015- 64.83.

Christabel NETTEY b. 2 Jun 1991 Brampton, Ontario 1.62m 59kg. Was at Arizona State University (justice studies).
At LJ: WCh: '13- dnq 20, '15- 4; CG: '14- 3; WY: '07- dnq 14 (8 100mh); PAm: '15- 1; PAm-J: '09- 2; CCp: '14- 4. At 100mh: WY: '07- 8 (3 MedR). Won CAN LJ 2013-15, NACAC 2012
Three Canadian long jump records 2015, four indoor 2014-15.
Progress at LJ: 2006- 6.12, 2007- 6.14, 2008- 6.21, 2009- 6.05/6.10w, 2010- 6.42i/6.28, 2011- 6.49/6.55i, 2012- 6.58, 2013- 6.75, 2014- 6.73, 2015- 6.99. pbs: 100m 12.14 '06, 60mh 8.25i '13, 100mh 13.42 '13, HJ 1.66 '11, TJ 12.80 '12, 12.90w '07; SP 12.16 '11, Hep 5068 '11.
Older sister Sabrina has LJ pbs 6.32i '14, 6.26 '12.

Brianne THEISEN-EATON b. 18 Dec 1988 Humboldt 1.80m 64kg. Sasketchewan. Student

at University of Oregon, USA.
At Hep: OG: '12- 10; WCh: '09- 14, '13- 2, '15- 2; CG: '14- 1; WJ: '06- 17. Won CAN 2013 (100mh 2015), PAm-J 2007, NCAA 2009-10, 2012. At Pen: WI: '14- 2, '16- 1. At LJ: PAm: '15- 4 (3 1600mR).
Records: Two Canadian heptathlon 2014-15, North American indoor pentathlon 2016.
Progress at Hep: 2005- 5181, 2006- 5240, 2007- 5413, 2008- 5738, 2010- 6094, 2012- 6440, 2013- 6530, 2014- 6641, 2015- 6808. pbs: 200m 23.34 '15, 300m 37.47i '16, 400m 52.33 '15, 800m 2:09.03 '13, 60mh 8.04i '16, 100mh 12.98 '15, HJ 1.89 '15, LJ 6.72 '15, SP 13.92 '14, JT 46.47 '12, Pen 4881i '16.
Won Götzis heptathlon 2013 and 2015. Married Ashton Eaton on 15 July 2013, unique husband and wife Double win at 2016 World Indoors.

Jessica ZELINKA b. 3 Sep 1981 London, Ontario 1.72m 62kg. Calgary AB.
At Hep(/100mh): OG: '08- 5, '12- 6/6; WCh: '05- 11, '11- 9, '13- (sf); CG: '06-10-14: 4/2/2; PAm: '07- 1, '15- dnf; WJ: '00- 5/h. Won CAN Hep 2001, 2004-06, 2008, 2010, 2012; 100mh 2012.
Six Canadian heptathlon records 2006-12.
Progress at 100mh. Hep: 1996- 4700, 1997- 4586, 1998- 14.18/14.13w, 4859; 1999- 14.18, 5059; 2000- 13.81, 5583; 2001- 13.67, 5702; 2002- 5962, 2003- 13.52, 6031; 2004- 13.26/13.10w, 6296; 2005- 13.42/13.15w, 6137; 2006- 13.08, 6314; 2007- 13.25, 6343; 2008- 12.97, 6490; 2010- 13.19, 6204; 2011- 13.01, 6353; 2012- 12.65, 6599A/6480; 2013- 12.86/ 12.66w, 2014- 12.83, 6270. pbs: 50m 6.56i '02, 60m 7.53i '04, 100m 11.63 '14, 11.36w '13; 200m 23.32 '12, 800m 2:07.95 '08, 60mh 8.19i '06, HJ 1.79 '07, LJ 6.19/6.23w '06, SP 14.97 '07, JT 46.60A '12, Pen 4386i '07.

CHILE

Governing body: Federación Atlética de Chile, Calle Santo Toribio No 660, Ñuñoa, Santiago de Chile. Founded 1914.
National Champions 2015: **Men**: 100m: Ignacio Rojas 10.60, 200m/400m: Sergio Germain 21.47/ 46.99, 800m: Mauro Zuñiga 1:49.70, 1500m: Carlos Díaz 3:50.42, 5000m: Matías Silva 14:32.57, 10000m: Leslie Encina 31:07.81, Mar: Eugenio Galaz 2:21:58, 3000mSt: Enzo Yáñez 8:49.14, 110mh: Víctor Arancibia 14.29, 400mh: Alfredo Sepúlveda 51.23, HJ:, PV: Daniel Zupeuc 4.80, LJ/TJ: Ignacio Cortez 7.13/15.68, SP: Matías López 17.53, DT: Maximiliano Alonso 50.02, HT: Roberto Sáez 65.83, JT: Ignacio Guerra 68.70, 10000mW: Yerko Araya 41:13.32. Women: 100m: Isidora Jiménez 11.55, 200m/400m: Paula Goñi 24.58/54.11, 800m: Valentina Barrientos 2:14.33, 1500m: Verónica Angel 4:39.43, 5000m/ 3000mSt: Margarita Masías 17:30.67/11:23.25, 10000m: Jennifer González 36:32.90, Mar: Erika Olivera 2:44:04, 100mh: María Ignacia Eguiguren 14.23, 400mh: Javiera Errázuriz 62.80, HJ: Marta Herrera 1.65, PV: Victoria Fernández 3.85, LJ: Macarena Reyes 6.07, TJ:, SP: Ivanna Gallardo 15.57, DT: Karen Gallardo 58.33, HT: Marcela Solano 57.48, JT: María Paz Rios 53.00, Hep: Javiera Brahm 4918, 10000mW: Veronica Colindres 48:02.50.

CHINA

Governing body: Athletic Association of the People's Republic of China, 2 Tiyuguan Road, Beijing 100763.
National Championships first held in 1910 (men), 1959 (women). **2015 Champions**: **Men**: 100m: Zhang Peimeng 10.27, 200m: Xie Zhenye 20.60, 400m: Guo Zhongze 46.47, 800m: Ma Junyi 1:53.18, 1500m: Ying Jun 4:00.38, 5000m: Qi Zhenfei 13:53.13, 10000m: Dong Guojian 29:24.46, Mar: Muhan Hasi 2:14:26, 3000mSt: Xu Pengcheng 9:01.94, 110mh: Xie Wenjun 13.52, 400mh: Cheng Wen 49.85, HJ: Wang Yu 2.24, PV: Yao Jie & Xia Xiang 5.50, LJ: Gao Xinglong 8.06, TJ: Dong Bin 16.84, SP: Liu Yang 19.28, DT: Tan Shen 58.40, HT: Wan Yong 70.24, JT: Ma Qun 77.34, Dec: Hu Yufei 7488, 20kW: Wang Zhen 1:19:29, 50kW: Luo Yadong 3:54:42. **Women**: 100m/200m: Wei Yongli 11.41/23.39, 400m: Yang Huizhen 53.03, 800m/1500m: Zhao Jing 2:05.20/ 4:17.29, 5000m/10000m: Ding Changqin 15:52.38/33:01.84, HMar: He Yinli 71:48, Mar: Ding Changqin 2:26:54, 3000mSt: Sun Ran 10:07.09, 100mh: Wu Shuijiao 13.13, 400mh: Wang Huan 57.30, HJ: Wang Yang 1.88, PV: Li Ling 4.40, LJ: Xu Xiaoling 6.45, TJ: Wang Wupin 14.02, SP: Bian Ka 18.71, DT: Feng Bin 61.04, HT: Zhang Wenxiu 74.08, JT: Li Lingwei 60.77, Hep: Wang Qingling 5417, 20kW: Qieyang Shenjie 1:28:27.

CAI Zelin b. 11 Apr 1991 Dali, Yunnan 1.72m 55kg.
At 20kW: OG: '12- 4; WCh: '13- 26, '15- 5; AsiG: '14- 4; WCp: '14- 2. At 10000mW: WJ: '10- 2; WCp: '10- 2J. CHN 20kW champion 2012.
Progress at 20kW: 2010- 1:22:28, 2011- 1:21:07, 2012- 1:18:47, 2013- 1:18:55, 2014- 1:18:52, 2015- 1:19:45, 2016- 1:19:48. Pbs: 5000mW 19:35.00 '14, 10,000mW 38:59.98 '12, 30kW 2:45:13 '09.

CHEN Ding b. 5 Aug 1992 Dali, Yunnan 1.80m 62kg. Guangdong.
At 20kW: OG: '12- 1; WCh: '13- 2, '15- 9; WCp: '10- 5, '12- 8. At 10000mW: WJ: '08- 2; WCp: '08- 2J.
World youth 10,000m walk record 2008.
Progress at 20kW: 2008- 1:20:16, 2009- 1:21:21, 2010- 1:21:59, 2011- 1:18:52, 2012- 1:17:40, 2013- 1:21:09, 2014- 1:20:48, 2015- 1:18:44, 2016- 1:19:32.
Pbs: 10kW 38:23 '10, 39:47.20t '08; 30kW 2:12:16 '10.

DONG Bin b. 22 Nov 1988 Changshan. 1.79m 67kg.
At TJ: OG: '12- 10; WCh: '13- 9, '15- dnq 18; WJ: '06- dnq 14; AsiG: '14- 2; AsiC: '11- 5, '15- 4; WI: '12- 8, '16- 1. Won Asian indoors 2010, 2012
Asian indoor triple jump record 2016.
Progress at TJ: 2006- 16.22, 2007- 16.25, 2008- 16.54, 2009- 16.89i/16.675, 2010- 16.86, 2011-

17.01i/16.86, 2012- 17.38, 2013- 17.16i/16.98, 2014- 16.95, 2015- 17.12/17.21w, 2016- 17.41i. pb LJ 7.09 '07, 7.32w '06.

GAO Xinglong b. 12 Mar 1994 Heilongjiang Prov 1.81m 65kg.
At LJ: WCh: '15- 4; AsiG: '14- 3; AsiC: '15- 1. Won CHN 2014-15.
Progress at LJ: 2012- 7.27, 2013- 8.02i/7.98, 2014- 8.18/8.21w, 2015- 8.34.

HUANG Changzhou b. 12 Mar 1994 Sichuan Prov 1.83m 64kg.
At LJ: AsiC: '15- dnq; WI: '16- 3
Progress at LJ: 2012- 7.79, 2013- 7.97, 2014- 8.12, 2015- 8.17, 2016- 8.21i.

LI Jinzhe b. 1 Sep 1989 Beijing 1.88m 64kg.
At LJ: OG: '12- dnq 20; WCh: '09- dnq 13, '13- 12, '15- 5; WI: '14- 2; AsiG: '14- 1; AsiC: '07-09-11: 6/1/5; CCp: '10- 4, '14- 4; won E.Asian 2009, Asian indoors 2012, CHN 2009, CHN NG 2013. Chinese long jump record 2014.
Progress at LJ: 2006- 7.19i, 2007- 7.85, 2008- 7.79, 2009- 8.18, 2010- 8.12/8.29w, 2011- 8.02, 2012- 8.25, 2013- 8.34, 2014- 8.47, 2015- 8.26.

SU Bingtian b. 29 Aug 1989 Zhongshan, Guangdong Prov. 1.85m 65kg. Guandong.
At 100m: OG: '12- sf; WCh: '13- h, '15- 9/2R; AsiG: '14- 2/1R; WUG: '11- 3. Won Chinese 100m 2009, 2011-13, E.Asian G 2013. At 60m: WI: '14- 4, '16- 5.
Records: Asian indoor 60m 2016, Chinese 100m (3) 2011-15 and 200m 2013.
Progress at 100m: 2006- 10.59, 2007- 10.45, 2008- 10.41, 2009- 10.28, 2010- 10.32, 2011- 10.16, 2012- 10.19/10.04w, 2013- 10.06, 2014- 10.10, 2015- 9.99. pbs: 60m 6.50i '16, 200m 21.23 '08.

WANG Jianan b. 27 Aug 1996 Jiangsu Prov. 1.78m 61kg.
At LJ: WCh: '13- dnq 23, '15- 3; WJ: '14- 1; AsiC: '13- 1.
Asian junior long jump record 2015.
Progress at LJ: 2012- 8.04, 2013- 7.95, 2014- 8.10, 2015- 8.25, 2016- 8.18i. pbs: 60m 6.89i '12, 100m 10.88 '12, 60mh 8.46i '12, HJ 1.94 '12, PV 5.00 '12, Dec 7063 '12.

WANG Zhen b. 24 Aug 1991 Changzhou 1.80m 62kg. Heilongjiang.
At 20kW: OG: '12- 3; WCh: 11- 2, '13- dq, '15- 2; AsiG: '14- 1; WCp: '12- 1, 14- 6; CHN champion 2011, 2015; NG 2013. Won World Race Walking Challenge Final 10k 2010, 2012 (2nd 2011).
Walks records: World junior 10k 2010, Asian 20k 2012, 10,000m track 2012 & 2015.
Progress at 20kW: 2008- 1:28:01, 2009- 1:22:10, 2010- 1:20:42, 2011- 1:18:30, 2012- 1:17:36, 2013- 1:19:08, 2014- 1:19:40. 2015- 1:18:00, 2016- 1:19:12. Pbs: 3000mW 11:23.2 14, 5000mW 18:49.10 '14, 10kW 37:44 '10, 38:23.73 '15; 30kW 2:08:46 '08, 50kW 3:53:00 '09.
At 18 in 2015 he became the youngest ever male World Champs medallist at a field event.

WANG Zhendong b. 11 Jan 1991 1.80m 55kg.
At 50kW: AsiG: '14- 3.
Progress at 50kW: 2011- 4:16:44, 2012- 3:57:47, 2013- 4:09:17, 2014- 3:47:18, 2016- 3:41:02. Pbs: 5000mW 20:06.65 '14, 20kW 1:21:55 '13, 30kW 2:12:36 '10.

XIE Wenjun b. 11 Jul 1990 Shanghai 1.88m 77kg, Shanghai
At 110mh: OG: '12- sf; WCh: '13- h, '15- sf AsiG: '14- 1; AsiC: '15- 1; CCp: '14- 4; Won CHN 2012, 2015; NG 2013.
Progress at 110mh: 2007- 14.09, 2008- 13.47, 2009- 13.53, 2010- 13.47, 2011- 13.45, 2012- 13.34, 2013- 13.28, 2014- 13.23, 2015- 13.36. pbs: 100m 11.04 '06, 60mh 7.60i '13.

XUE Changrui b. 31 May 1991 Shandong prov. 1.83m 60kg
At PV: WCh: '13- 12; WI: '14- 5, AsiG: '14- 1; AsiC: '13- 1; CCp: '14- 2; Won CHN NG 2013.
Chinese pole vault record 2014.
Progress at PV: 2011- 5.30, 2012- 5.60, 2013- 5.75i/5.65, 2014- 5.80, 2015- 5.40, 2016- 5.81i. pb LJ 7.15 '08

YU Wei b. 11 Sep 1987 1.80m 60kg. ShaTALLENT ndong.
At 50kW: WCh: '15- 7. At 20kW: AsiC: '09- 2.
Progress at 50kW: 2008- 4:03:54, 2009- 3:58:00, 2010- 3:58:23, 2011- 3:51:46, 2014- 4:00:57, 2015- 3:45:21, 2016- 3:42:54. Pbs: 10,000mW 40:30.50 '12, 20kW 1:19:07 '13.

ZHANG Guowei b. 4 Jun 1991 Binzhon, Shandong prov. 2.00m 77kg.
At HJ: OG: '12- dnq 21=; WCh: '11- 10, '13- 9, '15- 2=; WI: '12-14-16: 4=/7/6, AsiG: '14- 2; AsiC: '11- 8; CCp: '14- 6. CHN champion 2011.
Progress at HJ: 2010- 2.23, 2011- 2.31, 2012- 2.31, 2013- 2.32i/2.29, 2014- 2.34, 2015- 2.38.

ZHANG Lin b. 11 Nov 1993 1.75m 55kg.
At 50kW: WCh: '15- 6; AsiG: '14- 6; WCp: '14- 7.
Progress at 50kW: 2013- 4:07:28, 2014- 3:48:49, 2015- 3:44:39. Pbs: 10,000mW 40:36.84 '15, 20kW 1:28:39 '12, 30kW 2:14:24 '15, 35kW 2:36:18 '15.

ZHAO Qinggang b. 24 Jul 1985 Dalian 1.84m 93kg.
At JT: WCh: '13/15- dnq 22/17; AsiG: '14- 1. CHN champion 2012-14, NG 2013, E.Asian 2013 Asian and three Chinese javelin records 2014.
Progress at JT: 2006- 68.07, 2007- 72.57, 2008- 77.20, 2009- 79.62, 2010- 79.80, 2011- 78.40, 2012- 81.74, 2013- 83.14, 2014- 89.15, 2015- 79.47.
At 2014 Asian Games improved pb from 83.14 to NRs 85.29 and 86.50 and Asian record 89.15.

Women

GAO Yang b. 1 Mar 1993. 1.78m 110kg. Army.
At SP: WCh: '15- 5; WJ: '10- 2; AsiC: '13- 3, '15- 2; WI: '16- 8. Won W.MilG 2015.
Progress at SP: 2012- 17.07, 2013- 17.76, 2014- 17.52, 2015- 19.04.

GONG Lijiao b. 24 Jan 1989 Luquan, Hebei Prov. 1.74m 110kg. Hebei.
At SP: OG: '08- 5, '12- 3; WCh: '07-09-11-13-15: 7/3/4/3/2; WI: '10- 8, '14- 3; AsiG: '10- 2, '14- 1; AsiC: '09- 1; CCp: '10- 3, '14- 3. Chinese champion 2007-12, 2014; NG 2009, 2013; Asian indoor 2008.
Progress at SP: 2005- 15.41i, 2006- 17.92, 2007- 19.13, 2008- 19.46, 2009- 20.35, 2010- 20.13, 2011- 20.11, 2012- 20.22, 2013- 20.12, 2014- 19.65, 2015- 20.34. pb JT 53.94 '07.

LI Ling b. 6 Jul 1989 Zhubo, Henan Province 1.80m 65kg. Zhejiang
At PV: OG: '08/12- dnq 27=/30; WCh: '09-11-13-15: dnq 18/dnq 29/11/9; WJ: '06- nh; AsiG: '10- 2, '14- 1; AsiC: '11-13-15: 2/1/1; CCp: '14- 1; WUG: '15- 1. Won CHN 2008-09, 2011-13, 2015; NG 2013, Asian Indoors 2009, 2012, 2016.
Asian PV records: 2013 & 2015, indoor (4) 2015-16, junior 2008.
Progress at PV: 2005- 3.90i/3.70, 2006- 4.15, 2007- 4.30, 2008- 4.45, 2009- 4.40, 2010- 4.45i/4.40, 2011- 4.40, 2012- 4.50i/4.40, 2013- 4.65, 2014- 4.61, 2015- 4.66, 2016- 4.70.

LI Lingwei b. 26 Jan 1989 Yantai 1.72m 75kg.
At JT: OG: '12- dnq 30; WCh: '15- 5; WJ: '06- 8, '08- 2; AsiG: '10- 3, '14- 2; won CHN 2013, 2015; NG 2013. Asian javelin record 2012.
Progress at JT: 2002- 49.60, 2003- 55.38, 2004- 51.19, 2005- 58.87, 2006- 58.87, 2007- 57.88, 2008- 59.25, 2009- 57.82, 2010- 60.60, 2011- 57.39, 2012- 65.11, 2013- 63.06, 2014- 62.56, 2015- 65.07.

LIU Hong b. 12 May 1987 Anfu, Jiangxi Prov. 1.61m 48kg. Guangdong.
At 20kW: OG: '08- 4, '12- 4; WCh: '07-09-11-13-15: 19/2/1/3/1; WCp: '06- 6, 14- 2; AsiG: '06- 1, '10- 1; won CHN 2010-11, NG 2009. At 10000mW: WJ: '06- 1; won IAAF Race Walking Challenge 10k 2012, 2014 (2nd 2011).
Walk records: World 20k 2015, Asian 5000m & 20k 2012.
Progress at 20kW: 2004- 1:35:04, 2005- 1:29:39, 2006- 1:28:26, 2007- 1:29:41, 2008- 1:27:17, 2009- 1:28:11, 2010- 1:30:06, 2011- 1:27:17, 2012- 1:25:46, 2013- 1:27:06, 2014- 1:26:58, 2015- 1:24:38, 2016- 1:25:56. pbs: 3000mW 12:18.18 '05, 5000mW 20:34.76 '12, 10kW 42:30R '10, 43:16.68t '12. Running: Mar 2:51:23 '15. Won IAAF Race Walking Challenge 2012 and 2015.

LU Huihui b. 26 Jun 1989 Huwan, Henan 1.71m 68kg.
At JT: OG: '12- 5; WCh: '15- 2.
Asian javelin records 2012 & 2015.
Progress at JT: 2005- 49.62, 2006- 49.96, 2010- 55.35, 2011- 58.72, 2012- 64.95, 2013- 64.48/65.62dq, 2015- 66.13. One-year drugs ban for positive test 27 Apr 2013.

LU Xiuzhi b. 26 Oct 1993 Chuzhou 1.67m 52kg.
At 20kW: OG: '12- 6; WCh: '15- 2; AsiG: '14- 1; WCp: '12- 3, 14- 6; 3rd RWC 2012, won CHN 2014, NG 2013.
Asian 20k walk record 2015, junior 2012.
Progress at 20kW: 2011- 1:29:50, 2012- 1:27:01, 2013- 1:27:53, 2014- 1:27:15, 2015- 1:25:12, 2016- 1:28:07. pb 10kW 43:16 '12.

QIEYANG Shenjie b. 11 Nov 1990 Haiyan, Qinghai Prov. 1.60m 50kg.
At 20kW: OG: '12- 3; WCh: '11- 4, '13- 15; WCp: '12- 14. CHN champion 2015.
Asian 20k walk record 2012.
Progress at 20kW: 2009- 1:35:54, 2010- 1:30:33, 2011- 1:28:04, 2012- 1:25:16, 2013- 1:28:05, 2015- 1:27:44, 2016- 1:28:16. pbs: 5000mW 20:42.67 '12, 10kW 43:16 '12.
First athlete from Tibet to win an Olympic medal.

SU Xinyue b. 4 8 Nov 1991 1.79m 70kg. Hebei
At DT: WCh: '13- dnq 19, '15- 8; AsiC: '13- 1, '15- 1; WJ: '10- dnq 13.
Progress at DT: 2007- 48.29, 2009- 52.51, 2010- 56.11, 2011- 57.57, 2012- 60.32, 2013- 61.67, 2014- 61.31, 2015- 64.27.

WANG Zheng b. 14 Dec 1987 Xian, Shanxi Province 1.74m 108kg.
At HT: OG: '08- dnq 32; WCh: '13- 4, '15- 5; WJ: '06- 9; AsiG: '10- 2, '14- 2; AsiC: '13- 1; CCp: '14- 5; won Asi-J 2006, E.Asian 2009, CHN 2014.
Asian hammer record 2014.
Progress at HT: 2000- 60.30, 2001- 66.30, 2002- 67.13, 2003- 70.60, 2004- 72.42, 2005- 73.24, 2006- 74.15, 2007- 74.86, 2008- 74.32, 2009- 74.25, 2010- 73.83, 2011- 75.65, 2012- 75.72, 2012- 76.99, 2013- 75.58, 2014- 77.68, 2015- 73.83.

ZHANG Wenxiu b. 22 Mar 1986 Dalian 1.82m 108kg. Army.
At HT: OG: '04- 7, '08- 3, '12- 4; WCh: '01-03-05-07-09-11-13-15: 11/dnq 14/4/3/5/3/3/2; WJ: '02- dnq 20; AsiG: '06-10-14: 1/1/1; AsiC: '05- 1, '09- 1; WCp: '06- 4, '10- 2. Won Asi-J 2002, W.Mil 2003, 2007, 2011, 2015; CHN 2004, 2006-10, 2012, 2015; NG 2003, 2009, 2013.
Nine Asian hammer records 2001-12, world youth 2003, two world junior 2004-05.
Progress at HT: 2000- 60.30, 2001- 66.30, 2002- 67.13, 2003- 70.60, 2004- 72.42, 2005- 73.24, 2006- 74.15, 2007- 74.86, 2008- 74.32, 2009- 74.25, 2010- 73.83, 2011- 75.65, 2012- 76.99, 2013- 75.58, 2014- 77.33, 2015- 76.33.
World age bests at 15-16-18. Originally lost third Asian Games title with a positive drugs test in 2014, but she was reinstated in May 2015 when it was ruled that her positive test was due to contaminated food.

COLOMBIA

Governing body: Federación Colombiana de Atletismo, Calle 27° No. 25-18, Apartado Aéreo 6024, Santafé de Bogotá. Founded 1937.

National Games Champions 2015: Men: 100m: Diego Palomeque 10.11w, 200m: Bernardo

Baloyes 20.38, 400m: Jhon Alejandro Perlaza 46.17, 800m/1500m: Rafith Rodríguez 1:45.63/ 3:46.07, 5000m/10000m: José Mauricio González 14:20.65/29:45.01, Mar: Juan Carlos Cardona 2:26:23, 3000mSt: Andrés Camargo 8:51.77, 110mh: Paulo César Villar 13.62, 400mh: Yeison Rivas 49.90, HJ: Wanner Miller 2.20, PV: Walter Viáfara 5.25, LJ: Jefferson Valencia 7.42, TJ: Jhon Murillo 15.86, SP: Levin Moreno 17.52, DT: Mauricio Ortega 61.48, HT: Elías Mauricio Díaz 62.50, JT: Arley Ibargüen 80.67, Dec: José Gregorio Lemus 6990, 20kW: Iván Garrido 1:27:42, 50kW: James Rendón 4:02:07. **Women:** 100m/200m: Evelin Rivera 11.47w/23.26, 400m: Yenifer Padilla 52.77, 800m/1500m: Muriel Coneo 2:03.67/4:16.81, 5000m: Carolina Tabares 16:37.47, 10000m/Mar: Erika Abril 34:23.54/2:53:18, 100mh: Lina Florez 13.00, 400mh: Evelis Aguilar 58.26, HJ/LJ: Caterine Ibargüen 1.78/6.66w, PV: Giseth Montaño 4.05, DT: Johana Martínez 56.43, HT: Johana Moreno 62.92, Hep: Sandra Denis 4838, 20000mW: Lorena Arenas 1:34:51.

Eider ARÉVALO b. 9 Mar 1993 Bogotá 1.65m 58kg.
At 20kW: OG: '12- 20; WCh: '15- 7; PAm: 15- 5, SACh: '13- 2; COL champion 2012-13. At 10000mW: WJ: '12- 1; SAmJ: '11- 1.
Colombian 20k walk record 2013.
Progress at 20kW: 2012- 1:21:49, 2013- 1:19:45, 2014- 1:21:28, 2015- 1:20:41. Pb 10000mW 39:56.01A '11.

Women

Caterine IBARGÜEN b. 12 Feb 1984 Apartadó, Antioquia 1.81m 65kg. Studying nursing.
At TJ/(LJ): OG: '12- 2; WCh: '11- 3, '13- 1, '15- 1; WJ: '02: dnq 17; PAm: '11- 1/3; '15- 1; SACh: '03- 3/2, '05- 3/3, '06- 2/2, '07- (3), '09- 1, '11- 1/3; CAG: '02-06-10-14: 2/(2)/2/1; CCp: '14- 1. At HJ: OG: '04- dnq 28=; WCh: '09- dnq 28=; PAm: '07- 4; SACh: '99-05-06-07-09: 3/1/1/1/1; CAG: '02- 2, '06- 2. Won DL 2013-15, COL HJ 1999, 2001-03, 2005-12, 2015; LJ 2003-04, 2006-08, 2011-12, 2015; TJ 2002-05, 2007-12, 2014.
Records: South American triple jump (7) 2011-14, junior HJ 2003. Colombia HJ (7) 2002-05, LJ (7) 2004-11, TJ (15) 2004-14.
Progress at TJ: 2001- 12.90, 2002- 13.38A, 2003- 13.23A, 2004- 13.64A, 2005- 13.66A, 2006- 13.91A/13.98Aw, 2007- 12.66A, 2008- 13.79A, 2009- 13.96A/13.93, 2010- 14.29, 2011- 14.99A/ 14.84, 2012- 14.95A/14.85, 2013- 14.85/14.93w, 2014- 15.31, 2015- 14.90/15.18w. pbs: 200m 25.34 '08, 100mh 14.09 '11, HJ 1.93A '05, LJ 6.73A/ 6.87Aw/6.63/6.66w '12, SP 13.79 '10, JT 44.81 '09, Hep 5742 '09.
Formely a high jumper, concentrating fully on TJ from 2010. First Colombian woman to win a medal in world champs. Unbeaten in 9 competitions in 2013, 11 in 2014 and 9 in 2015, taking her to 30 in succession 2012-15. She lives in Puerto Rico.

Yosiri URRUTIA b. 26 Jun 1986 Chigorodó Antioquia 1.75m 61kg. Graduated from nursing school at Universidad Metropolitana, Puerto Rico.
At (LJ/)TJ: WCh: '15- 10; PAm: '15- 3; SACh: 13- 5/2; CAG: '14- 3. Won Ib Am 2014, BolG 2013, COL LJ 2010, 2013.
Progress at TJ: 2005- 12.00, 2007- 12.43A, 2010- 12.94, 2013- 14.08, 2014- 14.58, 2015- 14.22/14.36w. pbs: 100mh 14.40 '10, LJ 6.53A/6.42 '10.
Previously a long jumper, she focused fully on the triple jump from 2013,

CROATIA

Governing body: Hrvatski Atletski Savez, Trg kralja Petra Svacica 17, 10000 Zagreb. Fd 1912.
National Champions 2015 Men: 100m: Zvonimir Ivaskovic 10.48, 200m/400m: Zeljko Vincek 21.67/46.92, 800m: Jurej Pavlek 1:53.40, 1500m/5000m/10000m: Dino Bosnjak 3:52.97/ 14:45.28.29:31.0, HMar: Danijel Fak 69:32, Mar: Robert Radojkovic 2:41:27, 3000mSt: Ivan Malic 9:35.84, 110mh: Marin Jurjevic 14.52, 400mh: Filip Pestic 52.20, HJ: Alen Melon 2.05, PV: Ivan Horvat 5.65, LJ: Dino Pervan 7.53, TJ: Sanjin Simic 15.03, SP: Stipe Zunic 20.38, DT: Filip Mihaljevic 62.42, HT: Andras Haklits 68.58, JT: Sasa Milosevic 65.15, Dec: Marin Jurjevic 6027, 20kW: Bruno Erent 1:52:36. **Women**: 100m: Andrea Ivancevic 11.30, 200m: Lucija Pokos 24.10, 400m: Kristina Dudek 53.75, 800m: Nikolina Hrelec 2:15.45, 1500m: Ana Varesko 4:50.01, 3000m/5000m: Matea Parlov 9:45.01/17:23.72, 10000m: Nikolina Stepan 37:05.0, HMar: Matea Matosevic 77:38, Mar: Nikolina Sustic 2:54:49. 3000mSt: Kristina Bozic 11:05.96, 100mh: Ivana Loncarek 13.51, 400mh: Marina Banovic 60.13, HJ: Lucija Zupcic 1.78, PV: Elija Valentic 3.60, LJ/TJ: Paola Borvic 5.98/12.65, SP/DT: Ivana Muzaric 12.85/47.07, HT: Anamari Kozul 59.49, JT: Katarina Gasparovic 50.35, Hep: Karla Petkovic 4554, 10kW: Ivana Renic 59:14.

Filip MIHALJEVIC b. 31 Jul 1994 Livno, Bosnia & Herzegovina 2.01m 113kg. University of Virginia, USA.
At SP/(DT): EU23: '15- 1/4; EJ: '13- 2/11; WI: '16- 2. Won CRO SP 2013, DT 2015.
Shot records: three Oceania 2015, four NZL 2013-15 and five Oceania indoor 2014-16.
Progress at SP: 2012- 16.52, 2013- 17.54, 2014- 19.65, 2015- 20.16, 2016- 20.78i. pb DT 63.11 '15.
Father Mirko Yugoslav CC champion 1987-8.

Stipe ZUNIC b. 13 Dec 1990 1.88m 115kg. ASK Split. Sociology student at University of Florida, USA.
At SP: EC: '14- 4; WY: '07- dnq 29; EI: '15- 7; NCAA indoor champion 2015. At JT: WJ: '08- dnq 18; WY: '07- 7; EJ: '09-9 (11 DT); EU23: '11- 11; Croatian champion SP 2015, JT 2009-10.
Progress at SP: 2007- 15.36, 2008- 15.87, 2009- 16.83, 2011- 17.39i/16.60, 2012- 17.30i, 2014- 20.68,

2015- 21.11i/20.38. pbs: DT 59.09 '15, JT 77.89 '12 Huge improvement at shot in 2014-15 after switching from javelin. Formerly world junior champion at kick-boxing.

Women

Sandra PERKOVIC b. 21 Jun 1990 Zagreb 1.83m 80kg. Zagreb.
At DT(/SP): OG: '12- 1; WCh: '09- 9, '13- 1, '15- 2; EC: '10-12-14: 1/1/1; WJ: '06- dnq 21, '08- 3/dnq 13; WY: '07- 2/dnq 13; EJ: '07- 2, '09- 1/5; CCp: '10- 2, '14- 3. Won DL 2012-15, Med G 2013; CRO SP 2008-10, DT 2010, 2012.
9 Croatian DT records 2009-14, 2 SP 2010-11.
Progress at DT: 2006- 50.11, 2007- 55.42, 2008- 55.89, 2009- 62.79, 2010- 66.93, 2011- 67.96/69.99dq, 2012- 69.11, 2013- 68.96, 2014- 71.08, 2015- 70.08. pb SP 16.99i/16.40 '11.
First woman to win European and Olympic gold for Croatia. Won 42 of 48 competitions 2012-15. Her 70.51 and 71.08 to win her third European title in 2014 were the women's world's best discus throws since 1992. Six months drugs ban 2011.

Ana SIMIC b. 5 May 1990 Gradacac, Bosnia 1.77m 58kg. Zagreb.
At HJ: OG: '12- dnq 29=WCh: '13- dnq 19, '15- 9=; EC: '10-12: dnq 22=/20, '14- 3; WJ: '08- dnq 14=; WY: '07- dnq 21=; EU23: '11- 7; EJ: '09- dnq 18; CCp: '14- 3; CRO champion 2006-09, 2011.
Progress at HJ: 2006- 1.78, 2007- 1.73, 2008- 1.82, 2009- 1.87, 2010- 1.92, 2011- 1.92, 2012- 1.91i/1.88, 2013- 1.96, 2014- 1.99, 2015- 1.95i/1.94.

Blanka VLASIC b. 8 Nov 1983 Split 1.92m 75kg. ASK Split.
At HJ: OG: '00- dnq 17, '04- 11, '08- 2; WCh: '01-03-05-07-09-11-15: 6/7/dnq 19=/1/1/2/2; EC: '02- 5=, '06- 4, 10- 1; WJ: '00- 1, '02- 1; WY: '99- 8; EU23: '03- 1; EJ: '01- 7; WI: '03-04-06-08-10-14: 4/3/2/1/1/6; EI: '07- 4, '09- 5=; CCp: '10- 1. Won WAF 2007-09, DL 2010-11, MedG 2001, CRO 2001-02, 2005.
Ten Croatian high jump records 2003-09.
Progress at HJ: 1998- 1.68, 1999- 1.80, 2000- 1.93, 2001- 1.95, 2002- 1.96, 2003- 2.01, 2004- 2.03, 2005- 1.95, 2006- 2.05i/2.03, 2007- 2.07, 2008- 2.06, 2009- 2.08, 2010- 2.06i/2.05, 2011- 2.03, 2013- 2.00, 2014- 2.00, 2015- 2.01.
IAAF Woman Athlete of the Year 2010. Won 5/6 Golden League HJs in both 2007 and 2008. She has had 106 competitions at 2m or higher to the end of 2015 (and 174 jumps over 2m), including 42 successive Jul 2007- Feb 2009, but in 2008 lost on count-back both at Olympic Games (when she won first ever athletics medal for Croatia) and in the final Golden League meeting, thus losing her share of the Jackpot. She had 60 attempts at the world record 2007-10. Her father Josko set the Croatian decathlon record with 7659 (1983) and named Blanka after Casablanca, where he won a Mediterranean Games title.

CUBA

Governing body: Federación Cubana de Atletismo, Calle 13 y C, Vedado 601, Zona Postal 4, La Habana 10400. Founded 1922.

National Champions 2015: Men: 100m: Robert Skyers 10.17, 200m: Yancarlos Martínez 20.43, 400m: Raidel Acea 45.18, 800m: Jorge Félix Liranzo 1:49.84, 1500m: Andy González 3:50.64, 5000m: Francisco Estévez 15:06.60, 10000m: Richer Pérez 30:25.2, 110mh: Yohany Portilla 13.57, 400mh: José Luís Gaspar 51.20, HJ: Sergio Mestre 2.10, PV: Lázaro Borges 5.20, LJ: Juan Echeverría 7.96, TJ: Pedro Pablo Pichardo 18.08, SP: Yosnier Ortíz 17.31, DT: Jorge Fernández 62.35, HT: Roberto Janet 78.02, JT: Osmani Laffita 77.18, Dec: Leonel Suárez 8027. **Women**: 100m: Arialis Gandulla 11.54w, 200m: Dulaimi Odelín 23.73w, 400m: Lisneidy Veitía 52.63, 800m/1500m: Rose Mary Almanza 2:08.05/4:21.98, 5000m/10000m: Yanisleidis Castillo 16:52.1/35:10.35, 3000mSt: Milena Pérez 10:33.05, 100mh: Belkis Milanés 13.48, 400mh: Zurian Hechavarría 57.26, HJ: Isis Guerra 1.70, PV: Yarisley Silva 4.50, LJ: Irisdaymi Herrera 6.53, TJ: Dailenis Alcántara 14.03, SP: Sally Viart 17.29, DT: Denia Caballero 69.51, HT: Yirisleydi Ford 72.40, JT: Yulenmos Aguilar 59.18, Hep: Jersy Díaz 5161.

Alexis COPELLO b. 12 Aug 1985 Santiago de Cuba 1.85m 80kg.
At TJ: OG: '08- dnq 13, '12- 8; WCh: '09- 3, '11- 4; WI: '12- 7; PAmG: '11- 1; CAG: '06- 2; CCp: '10- 2. Won IbAm 2010, CAC 2009, Cuban 2009, 2011.
Progress at TJ: 2002- 15.38, 2003- 16.34, 2004- 16.90, 2005- 16.95/17.09w, 2006- 17.38, 2007- 16.87/17.15w, 2008- 17.50, 2009- 17.65/17.69w, 2010- 17.55, 2011- 17.68A/17.47, 2012- 17.17, 2014- 17.05, 2015- 17.15/17.24w. pb LJ 7.35 '04.
Elder brother Alexander (b. 19 Feb 1978) decathlon pb 7359 '02.

Jorge FERNÁNDEZ b. 2 Dec 1987 Matanzas 1.90m 100kg.
At DT: OG: '08- dnq 27, '12- 11; WCh: '11- 8, '13- 10; PAmG: '11- 1, '15- 5; CAG: '14- 1; WJ: '06- 5; CCp: '14- 2. Won CAC 2008-09, Cuban 2009-16 (& SP 2014).
Progress at DT: 2005- 53.69, 2006- 54.77, 2007- 57.57, 2008- 63.31, 2009- 63.92, 2010- 66.00, 2011- 65.89, 2012- 66.05, 2013- 65.09, 2014- 66.50, 2015- 62.35. pb SP 16.94 '14.

Roberto JANET b. 29 Aug 1986 Santiago de Cuba 1.87m 106kg.
At DT: OG: '12- dnq 19; WCh: '13- dnq 23, '15- 12; PAm: '11- 5, '15- 2; CCp: '10- 5, '14- 6. Won CAC 2009, 2011, Cuban 2009-12, 2014-16.
CAC hammer record 2015.
Progress at HT: 2005- 61.30, 2006- 68.43, 2007- 70.89, 2008- 71.92, 2009- 74.95, 2010- 76.50, 2011- 76.40, 2012- 77.08, 2013- 76.75, 2014- 75.99, 2015- 78.02.

Lázaro MARTÍNEZ b. 3 Nov 1997 Guantánamo 1.92m 83kg.
At TJ: WJ: '14- 1; WY: '13- 1; CAG: '14- 2; PAm-J: '13- 1. Cuban champion 2016.
World youth triple jump record 2014.
Progress at TJ: 2011- 14.62, 2012- 15.38, 2013- 16.63, 2014- 17.24, 2015- 17.02.

Yordan O'FARRILL b. 9 Feb 1993 Santa Cruz del Sur 1.85m 77kg.
At 110mh: WCh: '15- h; WJ: '12- 1; PAm: '15- 6; CCp: '14- 7. Won CAC-J 2012, CUB 2014.
Progress at 110mh: 2012- 13.91, 2013- 13.44, 2014- 13.19/12.9, 2015- 13.23. Pbs: 100m 10.44 '14, 60mh 7.65i '13.

Pedro Pablo PICHARDO b. 30 Jun 1993 Santiago de Cuba 1.85m 71kg.
At TJ: WCh: '13- 2, '15- 2; WJ: '12- 1; PAm: '15- 1; WI: '14- 3. Won CAC-J 2012, CUB 2014-15.
Three CAC triple jump records 2015.
Progress at TJ: 2009- 14.55, 2010- 15.35/15.45w, 2011- 16.09, 2012- 16.79, 2013- 17.69, 2014- 17.76, 2015- 18.08. pb LJ 7.81 '15.
Father Jorge was a 2.10 high jumper.

Ernesto REVÉ b. 26 Feb 1992 Guantánamo 1.81m 70kg.
At TJ: WJ: '10- 2; PAm: '15- 3; CAG: '14- 1; WI: '14- 2. Cuban champion 2012-13.
CAC junior triple jump record (=) 2011.
Progress at TJ: 2006- 14.97, 2007- 15.22, 2008- 16.32, 2009- 16.56, 2010- 16.73, 2011- 17.40, 2012- 17.13, 2013- 17.46, 2014- 17.58, 2015- 17.02. pb LJ 7.00 '13.

Dayron ROBLES b. 19 Nov 1986 Guantánamo 1.91m 91kg.
At 110mh: OG: '08- 1, '12- dq; WCh: '05-07-09-11: sf/4/sf/dq(1); WJ: '04- 2, WY: '03- 6; CAG: '06- 1; PAm: '07- 1, '11- 1; WCp: '06- 3; won PAm-J 2005, WAF 2007, CAC 2009, Cuban 2006-07, DL 2011. At 60mh: WI: '06- 2, '10- 1.
World 110mh record 2008, three Cuban & CAC 2006-08, CAC junior record 2005. Two CAC 60mh indoor records 2008.
Progress at 110mh: 2002- 15.01, 2003- 14.30, 2004- 13.75, 2005- 13.46/13.2/13.41w, 2006- 13.00, 2007- 12.92, 2008- 12.87, 2009- 13.04, 2010- 13.01, 2011- 13.00, 2012- 13.10, 2013- 13.18, 2014- 13.29, 2015- 13.32. pbs: 100m 10.70 '06, 200m 21.85 '06, 50mh 6.39i '08, 60mh 7.33i '08.
Disqualified for obstructing Liu Xiang after finishing first at 2011 Worlds. Pulled muscle in 2012 Olympic final. Left home in 2013 in agreement with Cuban authorities; competed in Europe representing AS Monaco. Returned in 2015 and rejoined the national team.

Leonel SUÁREZ b. 1 Sep 1987 Holguín 1.81m 76kg.
At Dec: OG: '08- 3, '12- 3; WCh: '09- 2, '11- 3, '13- 10; PAm: '07-11-15: 4/1/dnf. CAC champion 2009, Cuban 2009, 2015. At Hep: WI: '10- 7.
Decathlon records, four records 2008-09, CAC 2009.
Progress at Dec: 2005- 7267, 2006- 7357, 2007- 8156, 2008- 8527, 2009- 8654, 2010- 8328, 2011- 8501, 2012- 8523, 2013- 8317, 2015- 8027, 2016- 8347. pbs: 60m 7.11i '09, 100m 10.90 '08, 10.6w '06; 400m 47.65 '09, 1000m 2:36.12i '10, 1500m 4:16.70 '08, 60mh 7.90i '10, 110mh 14.12 '08, HJ 2.17 '08, PV 5.00 '09, LJ 7.52 '11, SP 15.20 '09, DT 47.32 '11, JT 78.29 '16, Hep 5964i '10.
Won at Talence 2010. Won IAAF Combined Events Challenge 2011.

Women

Rose Mary ALMANZA b. 13 Jul 1992 Camagüey 1.66m 53kg.
At 800m: OG: '12- sf; WCh: '13- sf; WJ: '10- 4; WY: '09- 4; PAm: '11- 4, '15- 4; CAG: '14- 1. Won Cuban 800m 2010-11, 2014-15; 1500m 2013, 2015.
Two CAC junior 800m records 2010-11.
Progress at 800m: 2008- 2:11.1, 2009- 2:03.61, 2010- 2:02.04, 2011- 2:00.56, 2012- 1:59.55, 2013- 1:59.4, 2014- 1:59.48, 2015- 1:57.70. pbs: 400m 54.64 '12, 600m 1:26.33mx '14, 1:26.9 '13; 1000m 2:38.1 '14, 1500m 4:14.53 '14.

Denia CABALLERO b. 13 Jan 1990 Caibarién, Villa Clara 1.75m 73kg. VCL.
At DT: OG: '12- dnq 26; WCh: '11-9, '13- 8, '15- 1; PAm: '11- 3, '15- 1; CAG: '14- 1. Won CAC 2011, Cuban 2015.
Progress at DT: 2006- 43.77, 2007- 46.08, 2008- 52.10, 2009- 57.21, 2010- 59.92, 2011- 62.94, 2012- 65.60, 2013- 63.47, 2014- 64.89, 2015- 70.65.

Yaimé PÉREZ b. 29 May 1991 Santiago de Cuba 1.74m 78kg.
At DT: OG: '12- dnq 29; WCh: '13- 11, '15- 4; WJ: '10- 1; PAm: '15- 2; CAG: '14- 2. Cuban champion 2013-14, 2016.
Progress at DT: 2007- 46.29, 2008- 51.80, 2009- 55.23, 2010- 59.30, 2011- 59.26, 2012- 62.50, 2013- 66.01, 2014- 66.03, 2015- 67.13, 2016- 68.86. pbs SP 13.88 '08.

Yarisley SILVA b. 1 Jun 1987 Pinar del Rio 1.69m 68kg.
At PV: OG: '08- dnq 27=, '12- 2; WCh: '11- 5, '13- 3, '15- 1; WI: '12- 7, '14- 1; WJ: '06- dnq; PAm: '07-11-15: 3/1/1; CAG: '14- 1; Won CAC 2009, Cuban 2004, 2006-07, 2009, 2012-13, 2015.
Pole vault records: 19 Cuban & CAC 2007-15 (9 in 2011), 8 CAC indoor 2012 & 2013 (to 4.82).
Progress at PV: 2001- 2.50, 2002- 3.10, 2003- 3.70, 2004- 4.00, 2005- 4.10, 2006- 4.20, 2007- 4.30, 2008- 4.50, 2009- 4.50, 2010- 4.40, 2011- 4.75A/4.70, 2012- 4.75, 2013- 4.90, 2014- 4.70, 2015- 4.91.

CYPRUS

Governing body: Amateur Athletic Association of Cyprus, Olympic House, 2025 Strovolos, Nicosia. Founded 1983. **National Championships** first held in 1896, 1952 (women). **2015 Champions**: **Men**: 100m: Panayiotis Ioannou 10.68, 200m/110mh: Milan

Trajkovic 21.56/13.84, 400m/ 800m: Christos Demetriou 48.01/1:49.01, 1500m: Theofanis Michaelas 3:52.99, 5000m/3000mSt: Nikolas Fraggou 15:10.42/9:00.13, 10000m: Marius-Marian Busca 31:53.5, HMar/Mar: Kassahum Ahmed Jebel ETH 73:57/2:46:05, 400mh: Tasos Vasiliou 53.84, HJ: Dimitrios Hondrkoukis 2.26, PV: Nikandros Stylianou 5.35, LJ: Mattheos Volou 7.48, TJ: Zacharias Arnos 16.05, SP: Georgios Arestis 17.09, DT: Apostolos Parellis 63.09, HT: Constantinos Stathelakos 73.24, JT: Michail Kakotas 65.71, Dec: Andreas Christodoulou 6524. **Women**: 100m/200m: Ramona Papaioannou 11.60/23.34, 400m: Christiana Katsari 54.47, 800m/1500m: Natalia Evangelidou 2:09.43/ 4:31.05, 5000m: Meropi Panayiotou 17:21.17, 10000m/ HMar: Marilena Sofocleous 37:56.5/ 1:24:41, Mar: Ioulia Kannava 3:38:58 3000mSt: Elpida Christodoulidou 10:51.00, Mar:, 100mh: Natalia Christofi 14.11, 400mh: Kalypso Stavrou 62.32, HJ: Maria Christodoulou 1.72, PV: Maria Aristotelous 3.92, LJ: Nektaria Panayi 6.43, TJ: Eleftheria Christofi 12.77, SP: Gavriella Fella 13.36, DT: Androniki Lada 53.78, HT: Paraskevi Theodorou 60.03, JT/Hep: Rafailia Ioannou 44.30/4539.

Apostolos PARELLIS b. 24 Jul 1985 Limassol 1.86m 110kg.

At DT: OG: '12- dnq 13; WCh: '13- dnq 19, '15- 6; CG: '10- 4, '14- 2; EC: '10-12-14: dnq 17/13/16; EU23: '07- 3. CYP champion 2007-15.

16 CYP discus records 2007-12.

Progress at DT: 2004- 48.40, 2005- 50.88, 2006- 53.77, 2007- 58.16, 2008- 56.41, 2009- 61.07, 2010- 61.92, 201161.44, 2012- 65.36, 2013- 62.48, 2014- 63.89, 2015- 65.04.

CZECH REPUBLIC

Governing body: Cesky atleticky svaz, Diskarská 100, 16900 Praha 6 -Strahov, PO Box 40. AAU of Bohemia founded in 1897.

National Championships first held in 1907 (Bohemia), 1919 (Czechoslovakia), 1993 CZE.

2015 Champions: **Men**: 100m: Jan Jirka 10.67, 200m: Pavel Maslák 20.58, 400m: Jan Tesar 46.35, 800m: Matej Pavlícek 1:51.22, 1500m/ 5000m: Petr Vitner 3:47.96/14:40.36, 10000m: Lukás Olejnicek 30:10.58, HMar/Mar: Vit Pavlista 65:58/2:17:51, 3000mSt: Lukás Olejnícek 8:59.85, 110mh: Petr Svoboda 13.54, 400mh: Michal Broz 50.29, HJ: Martin Heindl 2.22, PV: Jan Kudlicka 5.73, LJ: Radek Juska 7.67, TJ: Martin Vachata 15.64w, SP: Martin Novák 19.70, DT: Marek Bárta 56.07, HT: Lukás Melich 71.10, JT: Jakub Vadlejch 81.91, Dec: Tomás Vojtek 6595, 20kW: Pavel Schrom 1:30:11, 50kW: Lukás Gdula 3:59:03. **Women**: 100m: Barbora Procházková 11.81, 200m: Nikola Bendová 23.76, 400m: Helena Jiranová 55.15, 800m: Diana Mezuliánová 2:07.74, 1500m/5000m: Kristiina Mäki 4:25.48/16:11.78, 10000m: Moira Stewartová 36:04.54, HMar: Ivana Sekyrová 78:37, Mar: Sárka Machácková 2:51:01, 3000mSt: Michaela Drábková 10:15.41, 100mh: Katerina Cachová 13.35, 400mh: Denisa Rosolová 55.26, HJ: Oldriska Maresová 1.89, PV: Jirina Ptácníková 4.63, LJ: Jana Koresová 6.19, TJ: Lucie Májková 13.69, SP: Markéta Cervenková 16.04, DT: Eliska Stanková 58.66, HT: Tereza Králová 66.67, JT: Barbora Spotáková 61.00, Hep: Michaela Broumová 5295, 20kW: Anezka Drahotová 1:33:30.

Jaroslav BÁBA b. 2 Sep 1984 Karviná 1.96m 82kg. Dukla Praha.

At HJ: OG: '04- 3, '08- 6, '12- dnq 21=; WCh: '03-05-07-09-11-13-15: 11/5=/8/5=/4/dnq 14=/7; EC: '10-12-14: 5/8=/4; WJ: '02- 8; WY: '01- 10=; EU23: '05- 1; EJ: '03- 1; WI: '03-04-08: 9/3=/9; EI: '05-11-13-15: 4/2/3/5; ET: '09-11-14: 2/3=/3. Won CZE 2003, 2005, 2009-14.

Czech high jump record 2005.

Progress at HJ: 1997- 1.72i, 1998- 1.81i/1.75, 1999- 1.93i/1.92, 2000- 1.95, 2001- 2.16i/2.15, 2002- 2.27/2.28et, 2003- 2.32i/2.30, 2004- 2.34, 2005- 2.37i/2.36, 2006- 2.28i/2.05, 2007- 2.29, 2008- 2.30i/ 2.29, 2009- 2.33, 2010- 2.28, 2011- 2.34i/ 2.32, 2012- 2.31i/2.28, 2013- 2.31i/2.27, 2014- 2.31, 2015- 2.31. pb TJ 15.43 '03.

Jakub HOLUSA b. 29 Apr 1988 Opava 1.83m 72kg. Dukla Praha.

At 800m: OG: '08/12- h; EC: '10- 5, '12- 5; EU23: '09- h; WI: '10- 5, '12- 2. At 1500m: WCh: '15- h EC: '14- h; EU23: '09- 3; WI: '14- 5, '16- 2; EI: '11- 5, '15- 1; ET: '14- 1 (2 3000m). At 2000mSt: WY: '05- 7. At 3000mSt: EJ: '07- 1, Won CZE 800m 2008, 5000m 2014.

Czech 1500m record 2015.

Progress at 1500m: 2006- 3:56.23, 2007- 3:46.93, 2008- 3:41.48i/3:43.02, 2009- 3:42.15, 2010- 3:38.47, 2011- 3:38.10, 2012- 3:42.44i/3:42.79, 2013- 3:38.71, 2014- 3:35.26, 2015- 3:34.25. pbs: 400m 47.29 '10, 800m 1:45.12 '12, 1000m 2:16.79 '14, 1M 3:53.46 '14, 3000m 7:51.43 '14, 5000m 14:06.32 '14, 2000mSt 5:43.39 '05, 3000mSt 8:50.30 '07, 400mh 54.46 '07. Has used devastating sprint finish to good effect in major championships.

Jan KUDLICKA b. 29 Apr 1988 Opava 1.84m 76kg. Dukla Praha.

At PV: OG: '08- 10, '12- 8; WCh: '09-11-13-15: dnq 23=/9/7/13=; EC: '10- 12-14: 10/6/3=; WJ: '06- 5=; WY: '05- 6; EU23: '09- 8=; WI: '14- 3, '16- 4=; EI: '13- 5, '15- 7=; ET: '14- 2=; Won CZE 2008, 2010-15.

Progress at PV: 2002- 3.65, 2003- 4.21, 2004- 4.80, 2005- 5.09, 2006- 5.30, 2007- 5.61/5.62ex, 2008- 5.70, 2009- 5.62, 2010- 5.65, 2011- 5.81ex/5.65, 2012- 5.73, 2013- 5.83ex/5.77i/5.76, 2014- 5.80i/ 5.72/5.76ex, 2015- 5.75, 2016- 5.77i. pbs: 60m 7.11i '07, HJ 2.05i/2.03 '07, LJ 7.55 '07, TJ 14.41 '07.

Pavel MASLÁK b. 21 Feb 1991 Havírov 1.76m 67kg. Dukla Praha.

At 400m: OG: '12- sf (h 200m); WCh: '13- 5, '15-

h; EC: '12- 1; WY: '07- h; WI: '12-14-16: 5/1/1; EI: '13- 1/3R, '15- 1/3R. At 200m: WCh: '11- sf; WJ: '10- 7; EU23: '11- 3, '13- 3; EJ: '09- 5/2R. At 100m: WJ: '08- h. Won CZE 200m 2012-13, 2015; 400m 2011.
European indoor 300m & 500m bests 2014. CZE records: 200m (4) 2012-13, 400m (5) 2012-14.
Progress at 400m: 2006- 50.41, 2007- 48.30, 2008- 47.60, 2009- 47.44, 2010- 46.89, 2011- 47.05i/47.43, 2012- 44.91, 2013- 44.84, 2014- 44.79, 2015- 45.09. pbs: 60m 6.65i '14, 100m 10.36 '13, 200m 20.49 '13, 300m 32.15i '14, 32.34 '13; 500m 1:00.35 '13.
European Athletics Rising Star Award 2012. Master of indoor running.

Tomás STANEK b. 13 Jun 1991 1.90m 127kg. Dukla Praha.
At SP: WCh: '15- dnq 19; EC: '14: dnq 14; EU23: '13- 5.
Progress at SP: 2011- 17.16, 2012- 18.52, 2013- 19.50, 2014- 20.93, 2015- 20.94i/20.64, 2016- 21.30i.

Jakub VADLEJCH b. 10 Oct 1990 Praha 1.90m 93kg. Dukla Praha.
At JT: OG: '12- dnq 25; WCh: '11/15- dnq 16/20; EC: '10/14- dnq 16/20; WJ: '08- 10; EJ: '09- 8. Czech champion 2014.
Progress at JT: 2007- 66.12, 2008- 76.59, 2009- 81.95, 2010- 84.47, 2011- 84.08, 2012- 80.40A, 2013- 75.85, 2014- 82.97, 2015- 86.21.

Vitezslav VESELY b. 27 Feb 1983 Hodonin 1.86m 94kg. Dukla Praha.
At JT: OG: '08- 12, '12- 4; WCh: '09-11-13-15: dnq 28/4/1/8; EC: '10-12-14: 9/1/2; WJ: '02- 9; CCp: '14- 2. Won DL 2012-13, CZE 2008, 2010-12.
Progress at JT: 2001- 66.18, 2002- 73.22, 2003- 66.95, 2004- 72.32, 2006- 75.98, 2007- 79.45, 2008- 81.20, 2009- 80.35, 2010- 86.45, 2011- 84.11, 2012- 88.34, 2013- 87.68, 2014- 87.38, 2015- 88.18.

Women

Anezka DRAHOTOVÁ b. 22 Jul 1995 Rumburk 1.83m 63kg. USK Praha.
At 20kW: WCh: '13- 7, '15- 8; EC: '14- 3; EU23: '15- 2. At 10000mW: WJ: '12- 6, '14- 1; EJ: '11- 13, '13- 1 (9 3000mSt); WCp: '14- 3J; ECp: '13- 2J, '15- 4. At 5000mW: WY: '11- 6. World Mountain Running: '12- 7J. Won CZE 20kW 2014-15.
World junior 10000m walk record 2014. Czech records 3000mW 2015, 10000mW 2013, 20kW (4) 2013-15.
Progress at 20kW: 2013- 1:29:05, 2014- 1:28:08. 2015- 1:26:53. pbs: 1500m 4:24.46i '14, 4:24.89 '13; 3000m 9:26.28 '13, 5000m 16:03.18 '15, 3000mSt 10:10.45 '13, 10kmRd 33:59 '13, 3000mW 11:52.38 '15, 5000mW 21:21.15 '14, 10000mW 42:47.25 '14, HMar 74:25 '14.
19th junior women's world road race at cycling in 2013. Twin Eliska 4/3 EJ 10000mW 2011/2013, pb 20kW 1:37:39 '14.

Zuzana HEJNOVÁ b. 19 Dec 1986 Liberec 1.70m 54kg. Dukla Praha.
At 400mh/4x400mR: OG: '08- 7, '12- 3; WCh: '05-07-09- sf, '11- 7, '13- 1, '15- 1; EC: '06- sf, '10- 4, 12- 4/3R; EU23: '07- 3; WJ: '02- 5, '04- 2; EJ: '03- 3; '05- 1; WY: '03- 1; WI: '10- 3R; ET: '09- 3, '11- 1. Won DL 2013, 2015. At 400m: EI: '13- 4/3R. At Pen: EI: '11- 7. Won CZE 400m 2006, 2009.
12 Czech 400mh records 2005-13. 3 world bests 300mh 2011 (38.91) and 2013 (38.75 & 38.16).
Progress at 400mh: 2002- 58.42, 2003- 57.54, 2004- 57.44, 2005- 55.89, 2006- 55.83, 2007- 55.04, 2008- 54.96, 2009- 54.90, 2010- 54.13, 2011- 53.29, 2012- 53.38, 2013- 52.83, 2014- 55.86, 2015- 53.50. pbs: 150m 17.66 '13, 200m 23.65 '13, 300m 37.49A/37.80 '13, 400m 51.90/51.27i '13, 600m 1:28.04i '15, 800m 2:03.60i '15, 60mh 8.25i '11, 100mh 13.36 '11, 13.18w '10; 300mh 38.16 '13, HJ 1.80i '11, 1.74 '04; LJ 5.96i '11, 5.76 '07, SP 12.11i '11, JT 36.11 '10, Pen 4453i '11.
Unbeaten season at hurdles in 2013. Sister of Michaela Hejnová (b. 10 Apr 1980) pb Hep 6174w/6065 '04; OG: '04- 26; EC '02- 7; EU23: '01- 5; WJ: '98- 5; EJ: '97- 6/'99- 6 (100mh); WUG: '01- 5, '03- 3.

Eliska KLUCINOVÁ b. 14 Apr 1988 Prague 1.77m 69kg. USK Praha.
At Hep: OG: '12- 17; WCh: '09- 22, '13- 7, '15- 13; EC: '10-12-14: 6/7/dnf; WJ: '06- 8; WY: '05- 8; EU23: '09- 4, EJ: '07- 2; WUG: '13- 4. At Pen: EI: '15- 3. Won CZE LJ 2012, 2014; Hep 2008-09.
Four CZE heptathlon records 2010-14.
Progress at Hep: 2004- 5006, 2005- 5074, 2006- 5468, 2007- 5844, 2008- 5728, 2009- 6015, 2010- 6268, 2012- 6283, 2013- 6332, 2014- 6460, 2015- 6349. pbs: 200m 24.56 '12, 800m 2:12.50 '13, 60mh 8.53i '15, 100mh 13.81 '14, HJ 1.90 '14, LJ 6.43 '14, SP 15.07i/14.69 '15, JT 51.09 '15, Pen 4687i '15 (CZE rec).

Jirina PTÁCNÍKOVÁ b. 20 May 1986 Plzen 1.75m 69kg. Was Svobodová. USK Praha.
At PV: OG: '12- 6=; WCh: '09-11-13-15: dnq 16=/7/8=/dnq; EC: '06-10-12-14: dnq 27/5/1/6; WJ: '02/04- nh; EJ: '03- 6, '05- 4; WY: '03- 5; WUG: '09- 1; WI: '10-12-14: 5/6/2=; EI: '11- 4=, '13- 4; ET: '09-11-14: 5/3/2. CZE champion 2009-11, 2013, 2015.
Czech pole vault record 2013.
Progress at PV: 2001- 3.20, 2002- 4.00, 2003- 4.02, 2004- 4.11i/3.90, 2005- 4.15, 2006- 4.27, 2007- 4.22i/4.00, 2008- 4.28, 2009- 4.55, 2010- 4.66, 2011- 4.65, 2012- 4.72, 2013- 4.76, 2014- 4.71i/4.60, 2015- 4.72. pb LJ 5.85 '10, 5.95i '11.
Father Frantisek Ptacník was Czech indoor record holder at 60m (6.59 '87, 3= EI 1987), pb 100m 10.25 '85. She married Petr Svoboda (1 EI 60mh 2011, CZE 110mh record 13.27 '10) on 19 Sep 2012, but marriage ended two years later.

Denisa ROSOLOVÁ b. 21 Aug 1986 Karvina 1.75m 63kg. née Scerbová. USK Praha.
At 400m/4x400mR: WCh: '11- sf; EC: '10- 5; WI: '10- 3R, '12- 6; EI: '11- 1, '13- 5/3R, '15- 6; ET: '11- 2. At 400mh: OG: '12- 7; WCh: '13/15- sf; EC: '12- 2/3R, '14- 4. At LJ: OG: '04/08- dnq 24/20;

WCh: '07- dnq 13; WJ: '04- 1; WY: '01- 10, '03- 2; EU23: '07- 2; EJ: '03- 4, '05- 1; EI: '07- 3. At Hep: OG: '08- dnf; EC: '06- dnf. Won CZE LJ 2004, 2007-08; 200m 2008, 2010-11, 2013; 400mh 2012, 2014-15.

Progress at 400m, 400mh: 2001- 57.26, 2002- 55.55, 2004- 60.09H, 2007- 54.05i, 2008- 53.61i, 2009- 55.63i, 2010- 50.85, 2011- 50.84, 2012- 52.07, 54.24; 2013- 52.12i, 54.38; 2014- 52.37i, 54.54; 2015- 52.30, 55.15. pbs: 60m 7.44i '11, 100m 11.61/11.32w '10, 200m 23.03 '10, 300m 36.58 '14, 800m 2:11.70 '08, 60mh 8.20i '08, 100mh 13.32 '08, 200mhSt 25.86 '14, 300mh 38.99 '15, HJ 1.80i/1.77 '06, LJ 6.68 '04, TJ 13.10 '05, SP 12.48 '08, JT 35.12 '07, Pen 4632i '06, Hep 6104 '08.

Divorced from husband tennis player Lukas Rosol, who achieved top fame in 2012 by beating Rafael Nadal at Wimbledon.

Barbora SPOTÁKOVÁ b. 30 Jun 1981 Jablonec nad Nisou 1.82m 80kg. Dukla Praha.

At JT: OG: '04- dnq 23, '08- 1, '12- 1; WCh: '05-07-09-11-15: dnq 13/1/2/2/9; EC: '02-06-10-14: dnq 17/2/3/1; EU23: '03- 6; WUG: '03- 4, '05- 1; CCp: '14- 1; ET: '09-11-14: 2/3/1; won DL 2010, 2012, 2014-15; WAF 2006-08, Czech 2003, 2005-12, 2015. At Hep: WJ: '00- 4.

World javelin record 2008, two European records 2008, 11 Czech records 2006-08. World heptathlon javelin best (60.90) in 2012.

Progress at JT: 1996- 31.32, 1997- 37.28, 1998- 44.56, new: 1999- 41.69, 2000- 54.15, 2001- 51.97, 2002- 56.76, 2003- 56.65, 2004- 60.95, 2005- 65.74, 2006- 66.21, 2007- 67.12, 2008- 72.28, 2009- 68.23, 2010- 68.66, 2011- 71.58, 2012- 69.55, 2013- 62.33, 2014- 67.99, 2015- 65.66. pbs: 200m 25.33/25.11w '00, 800m 2:18.29 '00, 60mh 8.68i '07, 100mh 13.99 '00, 400mh 62.68 '98, HJ 1.78 '00, LJ 5.65 '00, SP 14.53 '07, DT 36.80 '02, Hep 5880 '12, Dec 6749 '04. Son Janek born 24 May 2013.

DENMARK

Governing body: Dansk Athletik Forbund, Idraettens Hus, Brøndby Stadion 20, DK-2605 Brøndby. Founded 1907.

National Championships first held in 1894. **2015 Champions**: **Men**: 100m: Morten Dalgaard Madsen 10.64, 200m/400m: Nick Ekelund-Arenander 21.07/46.78, 800m: Andreas Bube 1:50.38, 1500m: Nick Jensen 13:51.32, 5000m/10000m/HMar: Abdi Hakim Ulad 14:15.91/28:58.89/62:48, Mar: Jesper Faurschou 2:17:42, 3000mSt: Ole Hesselbjerg 8:56.94, 110mh: Andreas Martinsen 13.68w, 400mh: Nicolai Hartling 50.72, HJ: Jonas Kløjgaard Jensen 2.13, PV: Rasmus Jørgensen 5.25, LJ: Morten Jensen 7.76w, TJ: Massin Ait Bouziad 14.59, SP: Kenneth Mertz 17.73, DT: Emil Mikkelsen 53.70, HT: Taj Murmann 63.67, JT: Lukas Björnvad 64.65, Dec: Christian Laugesen 6722, 5000mW/10000mW/30kW: Andreas W. Nielsen 22:11.20/47:51.7/2:47:42. **Women**: 100m: Mathilde U. Kramer 12.04, 200m/100mh: Mette Graversgaard 24.76/13.85, 400m: Anne Sofie Kirkegaard 54.70, 800m: Mia Helene Mørck 2:09.73, 1500m/5000m: Anna Emilie Møller 4:32.84/16:14.72, 10000m/HMar: Anna Holm Baumeister 33:56.55/73:34, Mar: Louise Lamgelund Batting 2:38:57, 3000mSt: Simone Glad 10:23.07, 400mh: Sara Petersen 55.56, HJ: Sofie Albrechtsen 1.75, PV: Iben Høgh-Pedersen 4.05, LJ: Martha Traoré 6.11, TJ: Janne Nielsen 12.97, SP: Trine Mulbjerg 15.66, DT: Kathrine Bebe 50.33, HT: Celina Julin 60.31, JT: Fawzie Otour 44.83, Hep: Tine Bach Ejlersen 5360, 5000mW: Birgit Klaproth 36:52.1.

Sara Slott **PETERSEN** b. 9 Apr 1987 Nykøbing Falster, Sjælland 1.71m 57kg. Århus 1900 AM.

At 400mh: OG: 12- sf; WCh: 09/11- sf, '15- 4; EC: '10- h, 12- sf; WJ: '94- h; EU23: '07- 6, 09- 6; EJ: '05- 4; WUG: '09- 3. Won Danish 400mh 2002-09, 2011-12, 2014-15, 100m 2007, 2009, 200m 2009, 2012.; 400m 2008-09.

11 Danish 400m records 2007-15.

Progress at 400mh: 2002- 60.67, 2003- 59.42, 2004- 60.60, 2005- 58.21, 2006- 57.65, 2007- 57.01, 2008- 57.06, 2009- 56.40, 2010- 57.28, 2011- 55.97, 2012- 55.68, 2014- 56.44, 2015- 53.99. pbs: 60m 7.62i '15, 100m 12.07 '07, 11.93w '09; 200m 24.33 '14, 24.18w '12; 400m 52.83i '15, 54.31 '08; 60mh 18.58i '07, 1500m 4:27.96 '11.

Son Tobias born 8 Oct 2013.

DJIBOUTI

Hassan **Ayanleh SOULEIMAN** b. 3 Dec 1992 Djibouti City 1.72m 60kg.

At (800m)/1500m: WCh: '13- 3/sf, '15- h; WI: '12- 5; AfG: '11- 6; AfCh: '12- 2, '14- 1; CCp: '14- 1; WI: '14- 1, '16- 9; won DL 2013, Arab G 2011, Franc G 2013. At 3000m: WY: '09- h. Won Arab 5000m 2015.

World indoor 1000m record 2016. DJI records: 800m (5) 2012-15, 1000m 2013, 1500m (3) 2011-14, 1M (3) 2012-14, 3000m 2012.

Progress at 800m, 1500m: 2011- 1:51.78A, 3:34.32; 2012- 1:47.45, 3:30.31; 2013- 1:43.63, 3:31.64; 2014- 1:43.69, 3:29.58; 2015- 1:42.97, 3:30.17. pbs: 1000m 2:14.20i '16, 2:15.77 '13; 1M 3:47.32 '14, 3000m 7:39.81i '13, 7:42.22 '12, 5000m 13:17.97 '15.

In 2013 became Djibouti's first ever world champion and 2016 set first official WR by a DJI athlete.

DOMINICAN REPUBLIC

Governing body: Federación Dominicana de Asociaciones de Atletismo. Avenida J.F. Kennedy, Centro Olímpico "Juan Pablo Duarte". Santo Domingo. Founded 1953.

Luguelín SANTOS b. 12 Nov 1992 Bayaguana 1.73m 61kg. Universidad Interamericana de San Germán, Puerto Rico.

At 400m: OG: '12- 2; WCh: '13- 3 (h 200m), '15- 4; WJ: '10- 6, '12- 1; PAm: '11- 2/2R, '15- 1; CCp: '14- 5; YthOG: '10- 1; WUG: '15- 1.

DOM records 200m 2013, 400m (5) 2011-15. CAC indoor 600m best 2015.
Progress at 400m: 2009- 47.88, 2010- 46.19, 2011- 44.71A, 2012- 44.45, 2013- 44.52, 2014- 44.53, 2015- 44.11. pbs: 200m 20.55A '13, 20.73 '12; 300m 32.4+/32.56 '12, 500m 1:00.41 '16, 600m 1:15.15 '15, 800m 1:49.18 '14.
Younger brother Juander (b. 7 May 1995) has pbs 400m 45.93A '14, 400mh 50.27 '15.

ECUADOR

Governing body: Federación Ecuatoriana de Atletismo, Casilla 01-01-736, Cuenca. F'd 1925.

Andrés CHOCHO b. 4 Nov 1983 Cuenca 1.67m 67kg.
At 20kW: OG: '08- 38; WCh: '09- 39; SACh: '11- 1, '13- 3; WUG: '11- 3. At 50kW: WCh: '11- 10, '15- 8; PAm: '15- 1; won BolG 2013. Won SA-J 10,000W 2001. Four S.American 50k records 2011-16.
Progress at 50kW: 2010- 3:54:42, 2011- 3:49:32, 2012- 3:49:26, 2013- 3:58:50, 2014- 3:57:00, 2015- 3:46:00, 2016- 3:42:57. pbs: 10kW 41:15 '15, 41:55.50tA '15, 20kW 1:20:40 '15, 30kW 2:16:46 '14, 35kW 2:36:56 '15.
Married to Érica de Sena (Brazil) (qv).

EGYPT

Governing body: Egyptian Amateur Athletic Federation, Sport Federation Building, El Estad El Bahary, Nasr City – Cairo. Founded 1910.

Ihab ABDELRAHMAN El-Sayed b. 1 May 1989 Al-Sharqiyah 1.94m 96kg.
At JT: OG: '12- dnq 29; WCh: '11- dnq 35, '13- 7, '15- 2; AfG: '11- 5; AfCh: '10-12-14: 1/5/2; WJ: '08- 2; Af-J: '07- 3; CCp: '14- 1; Arab champion 2009, 2011, 2013, 2015.
African JT record 2014, six Egyptian 2010-14.
Progress at JT: 2007- 71.15, 2008- 76.20, 2009- 78.44, 2010- 81.84, 2011- 78.83, 2012- 82.25, 2013- 83.62, 2014- 89.21, 2015- 88.99.
Egypt's first ever World Champs medal 2015.

Mostafa Hicham AL-GAMAL b. 1 Oct 1988 Giza 1.91m 105kg.
At HT: OG: '12- dnq 29; WCh: '11- dnq 30, '15- 7; AfG: '11- 1, '15- 1; AfCh: '08-10-12-14: 2/3/3/1; CCp: '14- 2; Won Med G 2013, Arab Ch 2015.
African hammer record 2014.
Progress at HT: 2006- 61.44, 2007- 66.26, 2008- 71.15, 2009- 71.88, 2010- 73.27, 2011- 74.76, 2012- 77.14, 2013- 77.73, 2014- 81.27, 2015- 79.90.

ERITREA

Governing body: Eritrean National Athletics Federation, PO Box 1117, Asmara. F'd 1992.

Ghirmay GHEBRESLASSIE b. 14 Nov 1995 Kisadeka.
At Mar: WCh: '15- 1. W HMar: '14- 7; CC: '13- 7J.
Progress at Mar: 2014- 2:09:08, 2015- 2:07:47. pbs: 5000m 13:40.17 '12, 10000m 28:33.37 '12; Road: 10M 46:29 '12, HMar 60:09 '13, 30k 1:28:46 '14.
Youngest ever world marathon champion at 19 in 2015 after 2nd in Hamburg Marathon.

Teklemariam MEDHIN Weldeselassie b. 24 Jun 1989 Hazega 1.78m 57kg.
At (5000m/)10000m: OG: '08- 32,'12- 7; WCh: '09- 15/12, '13- dnf, '15- 19; WJ: '06- (12). World CC: 2006-07-08-09-10-11-13-15: 13J/14J/23/9/2/14/3/17. African CC: '12- 2.
Progress at 5000m, 10000m: 2006- 14:13.9, 2008- 13:48.18, 27:46.50; 2009- 13:11.01, 27:58.89; 2010- 13:04.55, 28:50.63A; 2011- 13:16.53, 27:37.21; 2012- 13:17.25, 27:16.69; 2013- 13:32.86, 27:19.97; 2014- 27:38.83, 2015- 28:39.26. pbs: 3000m 7:48.6+ '11, Road 10M 47:11 '09, HMar 61:47 '14.

Abrar OSMAN Adem b. 24 Jun 1989 Adi Shumakele, Debub 1.73m 55kg.
At 10000m: WCh: '15- 6 (h 5000m). At 5000m: OG: '12- h; WJ: '12- 2; AfG: '15- 4; AfCh: '14- 3. At 3000m: WY: '11- 3; CCp: '14- 6; Yth Oly: '10- 1. World CC: '13- 18, '15- 13; HMar: '16- 7.
Progress at 5000m, 10000m: 2011- 13:43.02, 2012- 13:17.32, 2013- 13:20.79, 2014- 13:16.45, 2015- 13:14.00, 27:41.69. pbs: 3000m 7:39.70 '13, HMar 60:39 '15.

Zersenay TADESE b. 8 Feb 1982 Adi Bana 1.60m 56kg. C.A. Adidas. Madrid, Spain.
At (5000m)/10000m: OG: '04- 7/3, '08- 5, '12- 6; WCh: '03- (8), '05- 14/6, '07- 4, '09- 2, '11- 4; AfCh: '02- 6, AfG: '07- 1, '15 (1 HMar). World CC: 2002-03-04-05-06-07-08-09: 30/9/6/2/4/1/3/3; 20k: '06- 1; HMar: '02-03-07-08-09-10-12-14: 21/7/1/1/1/2/1/4.
Records: World 20km and half marathon 2010. Eritrean 3000m (2), 2M, 5000m (4), 10000m (5) HMar (3) 2003-10.
Progress at 5000m, 10000m, HMar: 2002- 13:48.79, 28:47.29, 63:05; 2003- 13:05.57, 28:42.79, 61:26; 2004- 13:13.74, 27:22.57; 2005- 13:12.23, 27:04.70, 59:05; 2006- 12:59.27, 26:37.25, 59:16; 2007- 27:00.30, 58:59; 2008- 27:05.11, 59:56; 2009- 13:07.02, 26:50.12, 59:35; 2010- 58:23, 2011- 12:59.32, 26:51.09, 58:30; 2012- 27:33.51, 59:34; 2013- 60:10, 2014- 59.38, 2015- 28:05.34, 59:24. pbs: 3000m 7:39.93 '05, 2M 8:19.34 '07, Road: 15k 41:27 '05, 10M 45:52 '07, 20k 55:21+ '10, Mar 2:10:41 '12.
Won Eritrea's first medal at Olympics in 2004 and World CC in 2005 and first gold in 2006 World 20k before four more at half marathon. 15 wins in 18 half marathons 2002-13; ran 59:05 for the fastest ever to win the Great North Run (slightly downhill overall) in 2005 and won Lisbon 2010-11 in two fastest ever times. Won a national road cycling title in 2001 before taking up athletics. His younger brother **Kidane** (b. 31 Aug 1987) has pbs 5000m 13:11.85 '10, 10,000m 27:06.16 '08; at 5000m/(10000m): OG: '08- 10/12, WCh: '09- h/9; World CC: '12- 6.

ESTONIA

Governing body: Eesti Kergejôustikuliit, Maakri 23, Tallinn 10145. Founded 1920.

National Championships first held in 1917. **2015: Men**: 100m: Kaspar Mesila 10.66w, 200m: Markus Ellisaar 21.49, 400m: Marek Niit 46.40, 800m/1500m: Andi Noot 1:52.22/3:59.80, 5000m: Tiidrek Nurme 14:23.50, 10000m: Priit Aus 30:14.11, HMar: Roman Fosti 69:01, Mar: Sergei Tserepannikov 2:23:48, 3000mSt: Priit Aus 9:04.70, 110mh: Andres Raja 14.51w, 400mh: Rasmus Mägi 48.65, HJ: Karl Lumi 2.10, PV: Anri Mulin 5.00, LJ: Henrik Kutberg 7.64w, TJ: Igor Syunin 15.65, SP: Kristo Galeta 18.12, DT: Gerd Kanter 63.75, HT: Martin Lehemets 64.14, JT: Magnus Kirt 81.32, Dec: Taavi Tsernjavski 7568, 20000mW: Lauri Lelumees 1:38:40.14, 50kW: Margus Luik 4:36:21. **Women**: 100m: Maarja Kalev 11.84, 200m/400m/400mh: Maris Mägi 23.60/53.66/57.73, 800m/1500m: Kelly Nevolihhin 2:16.13/4:46.49, 5000m/3000mSt: Jekaterina Patjuk 16:13.73/10:18.90, 10000m: Annika Rihma 36:16.30, HMar: Lily Luik 1:20:27, Mar: Kaisa Kukk 2:52:40, 100mh: Grit Sadeiko 13.34, HJ: Eleriin Haas 1.84, PV: Reena Koll 3.90, LJ: Ksenija Balta 6.66, TJ: Tähti Alver 12.77, SP: Anu Teesaar 16.00, DT: Kätlin Töllasson 51.01, HT: Kati Ojaloo 65.30, JT: Helina Karvak 48.11, Hep: Mari Klaup 6023, 20kW: Anna Kukankova 1:58:03.

Gerd KANTER b. 6 May 1979 Tallinn 1.96m 125kg. Tallinna SS Kalev. Business management graduate.
At DT: OG: '04- dnq 19, '08- 1, '12- 3; WCh: '03-05-07-09-11-13-15: dnq 25/2/1/3/2/3/4; EC: '02-06-10-12-14: 12/2/4/2/2; EU23: '01- 5; CCp: '14- 1; WUG: '05- 1. Won WAF 2007-08, DL 2012-13, Estonian 2004-09, 2011-15.
Five Estonian discus records 2004-06.
Progress at DT: 1998- 47.37, 1999- 49.65, 2000- 57.68, 2001- 60.47, 2002- 66.31, 2003- 67.13, 2004- 68.50, 2005- 70.10, 2006- 73.38, 2007- 72.02, 2008- 71.88, 2009- 71.64, 2010- 71.45, 2011- 67.99, 2012- 68.03, 2013- 67.59, 2014- 66.28, 2015- 66.02. pb SP 17.31i '04, 16.11 '00.
Threw over 70m in four rounds at Helsingborg on 4 Sep 2006; a feat matched only by Virgilijus Alekna. Six successive seasons over 70m.

Rasmus MÄGI b. 4 May 1992 Tartu 1.88m 74kg. Tartu University ASK.
At 400mh: OG: '12- h; WCh: '13 & 15- sf; EC: '12- 5, '14- 2; WJ: '10- h; EU23: '13- 3; EJ: '11- 4; CCp: '14- 4. Won EST 400m 2012, 400mh 2009, 2014-15. Six Estonian 400mh records 2012-14
Progress at 400mh: 2010- 52.79, 2011- 50.14, 2012- 49.54, 2013- 49.19, 2014- 48.54, 2015- 48.65. pbs: 200m 21.90 '11, 400m 46.40 '13, 200mh 24.01 '11, LJ 7.73 '12.
His sister Maris has won 22 Estonian titles in sprints and hurdles, pbs: 400m 52.21 '11, 400mh 56.56 '13 (EST record).

Maicel UIBO b. 27 Dec 1992 Pölva 1.88m 86kg. Pölva.
At Dec: WCh: '13- 19, '15- 10; NCAA champion 2014-15. At HJ: EU23: '13- dnq 21. At HJ: WY: :09- dnq 19.
Progress at Dec: 2012- 7548, 2013- 8223, 2014- 8182, 2015- 8356. pbs: 60m 7.16Ai '14, 7.18 '15; 100m 10.99 '13, 400m 50.24 '15, 1000m 2:39.72i '13, 1500m 4:25.53 '15, 60mh 8.25Ai '14, 8.28i '13; 110mh 14.78/14.67w '13, HJ 2.18 '15; PV 5.25i/5.20 '15, LJ 7.82 '13, SP 14.46i/14.45 '15; DT 49.14 '15, JT 64.51 '15, Hep 6044Ai '14.

ETHIOPIA

Governing body: Ethiopian Athletic Federation, Addis Ababa Stadium, PO Box 3241, Addis Ababa. Founded 1961. **2015 National Champions**: **Men**: 800m: Yobsen Girma 1:47.1, 1500m: Mulgeta Assefa 3:46.8, 5000m: Getaneh Mola 13:54.9, 1000m: Mule Wasihun 29:25.3; 3000SC: Tafese Seboka 8:42.8, **Women**: 800: Chaltu Shume 2:03.4, 1500m: Kokeb Tesfaye 4:16.8, 5000m: Habtamnesh Tesfaye 16:21.9, 10000: Yebrqual Melese 32:40.3,3000mSt: Tigist Getnet 10:03.4.

Ayele ABSHERO Biza b. 28 Dec 1990 Yeboda 1.67m 52kg.
At 5000m: Af-J: '09- 4. At Mar: OG: '12- dnf. World CC: '08- 2J, '09- 1J.
Progress at 10000m, Mar: 2009- 27:54.29, 2011- 27:48.94, 2012- 2:04:23, 2013- 2:06:57, 2014- 2:06:31, 2015- 2:08:53. pbs: 3000m 7:40.08 '10, 5000m 13:11.38 '09; Road: 15k 42:02 '10, 10M 45:33 '10, HMar 59:42 '11.
Second fastest ever debut marathon to win at Dubai in 2012, 3rd London 2013. Elder brother Tessema has marathon pb 2:08:26 '08.

Yenew ALAMIREW b. 27 May 1990 Tilili 1.75m 57kg.
At 5000m: OG: '12- 12; WCh: '13- 9; AfG: '11- 2; AfCh: '14- 5; won DL 2013. At 3000m: WI: '12- 9, '16- 12.
Progress at 5000m: 2010- 13:16.53, 2011- 13:00.46, 2012- 12:48.77, 2013- 12:54.95, 2014- 13:00.21, 2015- 13:05.53. pbs: 1500m 3:35.09+ '11, 1M 3:50.43 '11, 3000m 7:27.26 '11, Road: 10k 28:22 '15, 15k 42:30 '14, 10M 46:04 '15.

Mohammed AMAN Geleto b. 10 Jan 1994 Asella 1.69m 55kg.
At 800m: OG: '12- 6; WCh: '11- 8, '13- 1, '15- dq sf; WY: '11- 2; WI: '12-14-16: 1/1/4; AfCh: '14- 2; CCp: '14- 2; won DL 2012-13, Afr-J 2011, Yth OG 1000m 2010.
Records: Ethiopian 800m (6) 2011-13, 1000m 2014, world youth 800m indoors and out 2011, world junior 600m indoor 2013 (1:15.60), African indoor 800m 2014.
Progress at 800m: 2008- 1:50.29, 2009- 1:46.34, 2010- 1:48.5A, 2011- 1:43.37, 2012- 1:42.53, 2013- 1:42.37, 2014- 1:42.83, 2015- 1:43.56. pbs: 600m

1:15.0+ '12, 1000m 2:15.75 '14, 1500m 3:43.52 '11, 1M 3:57.14 '11.
Was disqualified from taking the African Junior 800m gold in 2009 for being under-age (at 15). Youngest ever World Indoor champion at 18 years 60 days in 2012. Beat David Rudishsa in the latter's last races in both 2011 and 2012.

Kenenisa BEKELE b. 13 Jun 1982 near Bekoji, Arsi Province 1.62m 54kg.
At 5000m(/10000m): OG: '04- 2/1, '08- 1/1, '12- (4); WCh: '03- 3/1, '05- (1), '07- (1), '09- 1/1; WJ: '00- 2; AfG: '03- 1; AfCh: '06- 1, '08- 1. At 3000m: WY: '99- 2; WI: '06- 1; WCp: '06- 2. World CC: '99- 9J, 4k: '01- 1J/2 4k, '02-03-04-05-06: all 1/1, '08- 1. Won WAF 3000m 2003, 2009; 5000m 2006. World records: 5000m 2004, 10000m 2004 & 2005, indoor 5000m (12:49.60) 2004, 2000m 2007, 2M 2008; World junior record 3000m 2001.
Progress at 5000m, 10000m, Mar: 2000- 13:20.57, 2001- 13:13.33, 2002- 13:26.58, 2003- 12:52.26, 26:49.57; 2004- 12:37.35, 26:20.31; 2005- 12:40.18, 26:17.53; 2006- 12:48.09, 2007- 12:49.53, 26:46.19; 2008- 12:50.18, 26:25.97; 2009- 12:52.32, 26:46.31; 2011- 13:27e+, 26:43.16; 2012- 12:55.79, 27:02.59; 2013- 13:07.88, 27:12.08; 2014- 2:05:04. pbs: 1000m 2:21.9+ '07, 1500m 3:32.35 '07, 1M 3:56.2+ '07, 2000m 4:49.99i '07, 4:58.40 '09, 3000m 7:25.79 '07, 2M 8:04.35i '08, 8:13.51 '07; Road: 15k 42:42 '01, 10M 46:06 '13, 20k 57:19 '13, HMar 60:09 '13, 25k 1:13:42 '14, 30k 1:28:40 '14.
At cross-country has a record 16 (12 individual, 4 team) world gold medals. Unbeaten in 27 races from Dec 2001 to March 2007 when he did not finish in the Worlds. After winning all his 12 10,000m track races including five major gold medals, from 2003 until he dropped out of World 10,000 in 2011 before running the year's fastest time to win at Brussels. 17 successive wins at 5000m 2006-09. Shared Golden League jackpot in 2009. Won Great North Run on half marathon debut 2013. Won in Paris on marathon debut 2014, then 4th Chicago. IAAF Athlete of the Year 2004-05. He married film actress Danawit Gebregziabher on 18 Nov 2007.

Tariku BEKELE b. 21 Jan 1987 near Bekoji 1.68m 52kg.
At 5000m: OG: '08- 6; WCh: '05- 7, '07- 5; WJ: '04- 3, '06- 1; AfG: '07- 3; AfCh: '08- 4, '10- 6. At 10000m: OG: '12- 3. At 3000m: WY: '03- 2; WI: '06-08-10: 6/1/4; CCp: '10- 4; won WAF 3000m 2006. World CC: '05- 6J, '06- 3J.
World junior indoor 2M best 2006.
Progress at 5000m, 10000m: 2004- 13:11.97, 2005- 12:59.03, 2006- 12:53.81, 2007- 13:01.60, 2008- 12:52.45, 2010- 12:53.97, 2011- 12:59.25, 2012- 12:54.13, 27:03.24; 2013- 13:13.61, 27:38.15; 2014- 13:28.41. pbs: 1500m 3:37.26 '08, 2000m 5:00.1 '06, 3000m 7:28.70 '10, 2M 8:04.83 '07, Road: 15k 43:35 '11, 10M 46:33 '10, HMar 61:39dh '14.
Younger brother of Kenenisa Bekele.

Lelisa DESISA Benti b. 14 Jan 1990 Shewa 1.70m 52kg.
At 10000m: Af-J: '09- 1. At: HMar: WCh: '10- 7, AfG: '11- 1. At Mar: WCh: '13- 2, '15- 7.
Progress at 10000m, HMar, Mar: 2009- 28:46.74, 2010- 59:39; 2011- 59:30, 2012- 27:11.98, 62:50; 2013- 2:04:45, 2014- 59:36, 2:11:06; 2015- 2:05:52. pbs: 5000m 13:22.91 '12, Road: 15k 42:25 '10, 10M 45:36 '11.
Brilliant marathon debut to win Dubai 2013 and then won Boston and 2nd Worlds. 2nd New York 2014 (3rd 2015), Dubai 2015. Won Boston again in 2015.

Muktar EDRIS Awel b. 14 Jan 1994 Adio 1.72m 57kg.
At 5000m: WCh: '13- 7; WJ: '12- 1. At 10000m: WCh: '15- 10; Af-J: '11- 4. World CC: '11-13-15: 7J/3J/3; AfCC: 12- 1J.
Progress at 5000m, 10000m: 2011- 28:44.95A, 2012- 13:04.34, 2013- 13:03.69, 2014- 12:54.83, 2015- 13:00.30, 27:17.18. pbs: 3000m 7:46.0 '14, , 10k Rd 28:11 '13.

Mekonnen GEBREMEDHIN Woldegiorgis b. 11 Oct 1988 Addis Ababa 1.80m 64kg.
At 1500m: OG: '12- 6; WCh: '07-09-11-13-15: sf/h/7/7/sf; WI: '08-10-12: 6/4/3; AfG: '15- 1; AfCh: '10- 3, '14- 4; CCp: '10- 2. At 800m: WJ: '06- sf.
Progress at 1500m: 2004- 3:47.1A, 2006- 3:41.00, 2007- 3:36.04, 2008- 3:35.68, 2009- 3:34.49, 2010- 3:31.57, 2011- 3:31.90, 2012- 3:31.45, 2013- 3:32.43, 2014- 3:32.79, 2015- 3:35.67. pbs: 800m 1:46.63 '12, 1M 3:49.70 '11, 3000m 7:41.42 '11, 3000mSt 8:59.06 '12.

Dejen GEBREMESKEL b. 24 Nov 1989 Adiqrat, Tigray region 1.78m 53kg.
At 5000m: OG: '12- 2; WCh: '11- 3; WJ: '08- 3; Af-J: '07- 2. At 10000m: WCh: '13- 16. At 3000m: WI: '10- 12-14: 10/5/3. World CC: '08- 18J.
Progress at 5000m, 10000m: 2007- 13:21.05, 2008- 13:08.96, 2009- 13:03.13, 2010- 12:53.56, 2011- 12:55.89, 2012- 12:46.81, 2013- 13:31.02, 26:51.02; 2014- 13:09.73, 2015- 13:00.49. pbs: 3000m 7:34.14i '12, 7:45.9+ '10, HMar 62:36 '14.
Fastest ever debut 10,000m at Sollentuna 2013.

Hagos GEBRHIWET Berhe b. 11 May 1994 Tsaedaenba, Tigray region 1.67m 55kg. Mesfen Engineering
At 5000m: OG: '12- 11; WCh: '13- 2, '15- 3; AfCh: '14- dnf. At 3000m: WY: '11- 5; WI: '14- 5. World CC: '13- 1J, '15- 4, AfCC: '12- 4J.
World junior records 5000m 2012, indoor 3000m 2013.
Progress at 5000m: 2011- 14:10.0A, 2012- 12:47.53, 2013- 12:55.73, 2014- 13:06.88, 2015- 12:54.70. pbs: 3000m 7:30.36 '13, 10k Rd 27:57dh '11.

Markos GENETI b. 30 May 1984 Walega 1.75m 55kg.
At 5000m: WJ: '02- 2; AfG: '03- 4. At 3000m: WY: '01- 1; WI: '04- 3. At 1500m: WCh: '05- sf. World CC: '07- 15.

Progress at 5000m: 2001- 13:50.14, 2002- 13:28.83, 2003- 13:11.87, 2004- 13:17.57, 2005- 13:00.25, 2006- 13:13.98, 2007- 13:07.65, 2008- 13:08.22, 2009- 13:31.71i, 2010- 13:18.64i/13:21.99. At Mar: 2011- 2:06:35, 2012- 2:04:54, 2013- 2:12:44, 2014- 2:05:13, 2015- 2:07:25. pbs: 1500m 3:33.83 '05, 1M 4:08.8 '10, 3000m 7:32.69i '07, 7:38.11 '05; 2M 8:08.39i '04, 8:19.61 '06, Road: 10k 29:38 '11, HMar 61:38 '14, 30k 1:28:15 '14.
Won in Los Angeles 2011 in sixth fastest ever debut marathon time. 3/2 Dubai 2012/2014.

Mosinet GEREMEW b. 12 Feb 1992 1.74m 57kg.
At 10000m: WCh: '15- 11.
Progress at 10000m, HMar: 2013- 62:57, 2014- 59:11, 2015- 59:21, 27:18.86. pbs: 5000m 13:17.41 '12.

Tsegaye KEBEDE Wordofa b. 15 Jan 1987 Gerar Ber 1.58m 50kg.
At Mar: OG: '08- 3; WCh: '09- 3, '13- 4.
Progress at Mar: 2007- 2:08:16, 2008- 2:06:10, 2009- 2:05:18, 2010- 2:05:19, 2011- 2:07:48, 2012- 2:04:38, 2013- 2:06:04, 2014- 2:06:30, 2015- 2:07:58. pbs: Road: 10k 28:10 '08, HMar 59:35 '08.
Marathon wins: Addis Ababa 2007, Paris 2008, Fukuoka 2008-09, London 2010 & 2013 (2nd 2009, 3rd 2012, 2014), Chicago 2012 (2nd 2010); 2nd New York 2013 (3rd 2011). World Marathon Majors winner 2012/13. Has record 12 sub-2:08 and 14 sub-2:09 times. Won Great Ethiopian Run 2007, Great North Run 2008.

Yomif KEJELCHA Atomsa b. 1 Aug 1997 1.86m 58kg.
At 5000m: WCh: '15- 4; WJ: '14- 1; Af-J: '15- 1; won DL 2015. At 3000m: WY: '13- 1; Yth OG: '12- 1; WI: '16- 1.
Progress at 5000m: 2014- 13:25.19, 2015- 12:53.98. pbs: 2000m 4:57.74i '14, 3000m 7:36.28 '14, 10k Rd 28:13 '13.

Abera KUMA Lema b. 31 Aug 1990 Ambo 1.60m 50kg.
At 5000m: WCh: '11- 5; Af-J: '09- 1. At 10000m: WCh: '13- 5. At 3000m: WY: '07- 5.
Tied world 30km record 2014.
Progress at 5000m, 10000m, Mar: 2009- 13:29.40, 2010- 13:07.83, 2011- 13:00.15, 27:22.54; 2012- 13:09.32, 27:18.39; 2013- 26:52.85, 2014- 2:05:56, 2015- 2:06:47. pbs: 1500m 3:48.73 '09, 3000m 7:39.09i/7:40.85 '12, Road: 15k 42:01 '10, 10M 45:28 '11, HMar 60:19 '12, 25k 1:13:08 '14, 30k 1:27:38 '14.
3rd Berlin Marathon 2014, won Rotterdam 2015.

Hayle LEMI b. 13 Sep 1994 Hasasa, 1.72m 56kg.
At Mar: WCh: '15- 15.
Progress at Mar: 2014- 2:10:40, 2015- 2:05:28, 2016- 2:04:33. pb HMar 61:37 '15.
Marathon wins: Zürich & Taiyuan 2014, Dubai 2015 (2nd 2016) & Warsaw 2015.

Sisay LEMMA Kasaye b. 12 Dec 1990.
At Mar: WCh: '15- 15.
Progress at Mar: 2012- 2:11:58, 2013- 2:09:02, 2015- 2:06:26, 2016- 2:05:16. pb HMar 62:06 '15, 30k 1:29:33 '15. Marathon wins: Carpi 2012 (debut), Warsaw 2013, Vienna & Frankfurt 2015.

Feyisa LILESA b. 1 Feb 1990 Tullu Bultuma 1.58m 50kg.
At Mar: WCh: '11- 3, '13- dnf, World CC: 2008-09-10-11-13: 14J/12/25/17/9. Won ETH CC 2013.
Progress at Mar: 2009- 2:09:12, 2010- 2:05:23, 2011- 2:10:32, 2012- 2:04:52, 2013- 2:07:46, 2014- 2:08:26, 2015- 2:06:35, 2016- 2:06:56. pbs: 5000m 13:34.80 '08, 10000m 27:46.97 '08; Road: 15k 42:15+ '13, 20k 56:19+ '12, HMar 59:22 '12, 25k 1:13:22 '13, 30k 1:28:05 '13.
Marathons won: Dublin 2009, Xiamen 2010, Tokyo 2016. 3rd/2nd Chicago 2010/2012, 4th Rotterdam 2010 in then fastest ever by 20 year-old, 4th London 2013.

Tsegaye MEKONNEN Asefa b. 15 Jun 1995 1.74m 56kg.
At 5000m: WJ: '12- 5.
World junior marathon record 2014.
Progress at Mar: 2014- 2:04:32, 2015- dnf, 2016- 2:04:46. pbs: 5000m 13:44.43 '14; Road: 10k 28:36 '12, HMar 61:05 '15.
Marathons: 1st Dubai 2014 (3rd 2016), 5th London 2014.

Imane MERGA Jida b. 15 Oct 1988 Tulu Bolo, Oromia region 1.74m 61kg. Defence.
At 5000m/(10000m): WCh: '09- (4), '11- dq/3, '13- (12), '15- 13/dnf; AfCh: '10- 5, '14- (5); Af-J: '07- (3); CCp: '10- 5; won DL 2010-11, WAF 2009. World CC: '07-11-13: 7J/1/2.
Progress at 5000m, 10000m: 2007- 13:33.52, 30:12.03; 2008- 13:08.20, 27:33.53, 2009- 12:55.66, 27:15.94; 2010- 12:53.58; 2011- 12:54.21, 26:48.35; 2012- 12:59.77, 27:14.02; 2013- 13:09.17, 26:57.33; 2014- 13:11.94, 28:17.75; 2015- 12:59.04, 27:17.63. pbs: 3000m 7:39.96 '15, HMar 59:56 '12.
Disqualified for running inside the kerb after finishing 3rd in World 5000m 2011.

Adugna TEKELE Bikila b. 26 Feb 1989 1.70m 55kg.
At 10000m: AfG: '15- 3; AfCh: '14- 4. At HMar: WCh: '14- 9.
Progress at 10000m: 2013- 29:13.1A, 2014- 28:12.28, 2015- 27:19.34. pbs: HMar 60:15 '14, Mar 2:08:31 '14.

Tadesse TOLA Woldegeberal b. 31 Oct 1987 Addis Ababa 1.78m 60kg.
At Mar: '13- 3. At 10000m: WCh: '07- 13; AfCh: '06- 5; AfG: '07- 2. World 20k: '06- 7; World CC: '06- 10J, '07- 7, '09- 17.
Progress at 10000m, Mar: 2006- 28:15.16, 2007- 27:04.89, 2008- 27:15.17, 2009- 28:51.4A, 2:15:48; 2010- 2:06:31, 2011- 2:07:13, 2012- 2:05:10, 2013- 2:04:49, 2014- 2:05:57, 2015- 2:10:30. pbs: 3000m 7:43.70 '07, 5000m 13:18.82 '07, 10000m 27:04.89 '07; Road: 15k 43:49 '08, 20k 57:27 '06, HMar 59:49 '10. Won Paris Marathon 2010 (2nd 2013), Beijing 2013, Warsaw 2014; 2nd Frankfurt 2010 & Tokyo 2014. Pb when 3rd at Dubai 2013.

Yemane TSEGAY Adhane b. 8 Apr 1985.
At Mar: WCh: '09- 4, '13- 8, '15- 2.
Progress at Mar: 2008- 2:13:29, 2009- 2:06:30, 2010- 2:07:11, 2011- 2:10:24, 2012- 2:04:48, 2013- 2:09:11, 2014- 2:06:51, 2015- 2:09:48dh. pbs: HMar 61:37 '10, 30k 1:27:40 '12.
Marathon wins: Macau 2008, Gongju 2009, Lake Biwa 2010, Taipei 2011, Rotterdam 2012, Eindhoven 2013, Daegu 2014; 2nd Boston 2015.

Aman WOTE Fete b. 18 Apr 1984 Kabete 1.81m 64kg.
At 1500m: OG: '12- ht; WCh: 13- sf, '15- dnf; AfG: '11- 5; AfCh: '10- 7; WI: '12-14-16: 4/2/6. Won ETH 1500m 2014.
Ethiopian records 1500m (2) & 1M 2014.
Progress at 1500m: 2010- 3:38.89A 2011- 3:35.61, 2012- 3:35:38, 2013- 3:32.65, 2014- 3:29.91, 2015- 3:30.29. pbs: 800m 1:44.99 '13, 1M 3:48.60 '14, 3000m 7:43.99i '13.

Tabalu ZEWEDE b. 2 Nov 1987 1.84m 65kg.
At 10000m: AfG: '15- 1; AfCh: '12- 4.
Progress at 10000m, Mar: 2012- 28:03.16, 2014- 2:07:10, 2015- 27:20.54, 2:08:46. pb HMar 60:33 '13. Won Joongang marathon in Seoul 2015.

__Women__

Sofia ASSEFA Abebe b. 14 Nov 1987 Tenta District, S.Wello 1.71m 58kg. Ethiopian Bank.
At 3000mSt: OG: '08- h, '12- 2; WCh: '09-11-13-15: 12/6/3/4; AfG: '15- 1; AfCh: '08-10-14: 4/2/2; CCp: '10- 3.
Ethiopian 3000mSt records 2011 and 2012.
Progress at 3000mSt: 2006- 10:17.48, 2007- 9:48.46, 2008- 9:31.58, 2009- 9:19.91, 2010- 9:20.72, 2011- 9:15.04, 2012- 9:09.00, 2013- 9:12.84, 2014- 9:11.39, 2015- 9:12.63. pbs: 1000m 2:49.79 '07, 5000m 15:59.74 '07, 2000mSt 6:33.49 '07.

Hiwot AYALEW Yemer b. 6 Mar 1990 Gojam, Amhara 1.73m 51kg. Commercial Bank.
At 3000mSt: OG: '12- 4; WCh: '13- 4, '15- 6; AfG: '11- 2, 15- 2; AfCh: '14- 1; CCp: '14- 2; won DL 2014. At 3000m: WI: '14-11. World CC: '11- 11, '13- 2.
Progress at 3000mSt: 2011- 9:23.88, 2012- 9:09.61, 2013- 9:15.25, 2014- 9:10.64, 2015- 9:14.73. pbs: 3000m 8:43.29i '14, 2M: 9:21.59i '14, 5000m 14:49.36 '12, 10k Rd 31:47 '14.

Wude AYALEW Yimer b. 4 Jul 1987 Sekela, Amhara region 1.50m 44kg.
At 10000m: WCh: '09- 3; AfG: '11- 2, '15- 4; AfCh: '08- 3, '10- 4. At 5000m: WJ: '06- 5. World CC: '06-07-09-11: 5/10/5/6. Won ETH CC 2009.
Progress at 5000m, 10000m: 2006- 14:57.23, 33:57.0; 2008- 15:07.65, 31:06.84; 2009- 14:38.44, 30:11.87; 2010- 15:02.47, 32:29.92A; 2011- 14:59.71, 31:24.09; 2013- 31:16.68, 2015- 30:58.03. pbs: 1500m 4:14.85 '07, 3000m 8:30.93 '09; Road: 15k 48:15 '14, 20k 65:28 '14, HMar 67:58 '09.
Won Great Ethiopian Run 2008. Older sister of Hiyot Ayalew.

Almaz AYANA Eba b. 21 Nov 1991 Benshangul 1.65m 50kg.
At 5000m: WCh: '13- 3, '15- 1; AfCh: '14- 1; CCp: '14- 1. At 3000mSt: WJ: '10- 5; won ETH 5000m 2014, 3000mSt 2013.
World junior 3000m steeplechase record 2010.
Progress at 5000m, 3000mSt: 2009- 10:03.75, 2010- 9:22.51, 2011- 15:12.24, 9:30.23; 2012- 14:57.97, 9:38.62; 2013- 14:25.84, 9:27.49; 2014- 14:29.19, 2015- 14:14.32. pbs: 2000m 5:35.10+ '15, 3000m 8:22.22 '15, 10k rd 32:19 '10.
Married to Soresa Fida (1500m 3:34.72 '11, 3 AfChh '11).

Gelete BURKA Bati b. 15 Feb 1986 Kofele 1.65m 45kg.
At 1500m: OG: '08- h; WCh: '05- 8, '09- 10 (fell), '11- sf, '13- h; WI: '08- 1, '10- 3; AfG: '07- 1; AfCh: '08- 1, '10- 2; CCp: '10- 6. At 3000m: WI: '12- 3. At 5000m: OG: '12- 5; WCh: '07- 10. At 10000m: WCh: '15- 2; AfG: '15- 3. World CC: '03-05-06-07-08-09: 3J/1J/1 4k/4/6/8. Won ETH 800m 2011, 1500m 2004-05, 2007; 5000m 2005, 4k CC 2006.
African records: 1M 2008, 200m 2009, indoor 1500m 2008, junior 1500m 2005. World youth 1M best (4:30.81) 2003.
Progress at 1500m, 5000m, 10000m, Mar: 2003- 4:10.82, 16:23.8A, 2004- 4:06.10, 2005- 3:59.60, 14:51.47; 2006- 4:02.68, 14:40.92; 2007- 4:00.48, 14:31.20; 2008- 3:59.75i/4:00.44, 14:45.84; 2009- 3:58.79, 2010- 3:59.28, 2011- 4:03.28, 2012- 14:41.43, 2013- 4:04.36, 14:42.07, 2:30:40; 2014- 2:26:03, 2015- 14:40.50, 30:49.68. pbs: 800m 2:02.89 '10, 1M 4:18.23 '08, 2000m 5:30.19 '09, 3000m 8:25.92 '06; Rd: 15k 49:26 '12, HMar 71:10+ 13, 25k 1:25:39 '14, 30k 1:43:03 '14.
Married Taddele Gebrmehden in 2007.

Firehiwot DADO Tufa b. 9 Jan 1984 Assefa, Arsi prov. 1.65m.
Progress at Mar: 2008- 2:37:34, 2009- 2:27:08, 2010- 2:25:28, 2011- 2:23:15, 2012- 2:34:56dh, 2014- 2:23:34. pbs: Road: 10k 31:49 '13, 15k 48:32+ '12, 20k 65:06+ '12, HMar 68:35 '12, 30k 1:40:45 '11.
Marathon wins: New York 2011, Rome 2009-11, Florence 2010, Prague 2014. 3rd Dubai 2014.

Mamitu DASKA Molisa b. 16 Oct 1983 Liteshoa 1.64m 45kg.
At HMar: AfG: '11- 2, '15- 1. World CC: '09-10-15: 12/8/8. ETH half marathon record 2015.
Progress at 10,000m, Mar: 20008- 32:45.46, 2009- 31:36.88, 2:26:38; 2010- 2:24:19, 2011- 2:21:59, 2012- 32:54.9A, 2:23:52; 2013- 2:23:23, 2014- 2:29:35, 2015- 30:55.56, 2016- 2:28:53. pbs: Road: 5k 14:52 '15, 10M 51:54 '14, HMar 66:28 '15, 30k 1:39:46 '11.
Marathon wins: Dubai 2010, Houston and Frankfurt 2011.

Buzunesh DEBA Dejene b. 8 Sep 1987 Arsi 1.62m 45kg.
Progress at Mar: 2009- 2:32:17, 2010- 2:27:24, 2011- 2:23:19, 2013- 2:24:26, 2014- 2:19:59dh/

2:31:40, 2015- 2:25:09dh. pbs: 5000m 15:52.33 '04, Road: 10k 32:10 '10, 15k 49:05 '14, HM 68:59 '14. Married Worku Bayi in 2005, lives in Bronx, New York. Marathon wins: Sacramento 2009, Jacksonville, Duluth, St.Paul & Sacramento 2010, Los Angeles & San Diego 2011. 2nd New York 2011 & 2013, Houston 2013, Boston 2014 (3rd 2015).

Meseret DEFAR b. 19 Nov 1983 Addis Ababa 1.55m 42kg.
At 5000m(/10000m): OG: '04- 1, '08- 3, '12- 1; WCh: '03- h, '05- 2, '07- 1, '09- 3/5, '11- 3/dnf, '13- 1; WJ: '00- 2, '02- 1; AfG: '03- 1, '07- 1; AfCh: '00-06-08-10: 2/1/2/2; WCp: '06- 1. At 3000m: WJ: '02- 1; WY: '99- 2; WI: '03-04-06-08-10-12-16: 3/1/1/1/1/2/2; CCp: '10- 1. Won WAF 3000m 2004-09, 5000m 2005, 2008-09; DL 5000m 2013. World CC: '02- 13J.
Records: World 5000m 2006 & 2007, 2M 2007 (2); indoor 3000m 2007, 2M 2008 (9:10.50) & 2009 (9:06.26), 5000m 2009; African 5000m 2005, Ethiopian 3000m (2) 2006-07. World 5k road best 14:46 Carlsbad 2006.
Progress at 3000m, 5000m, 10000m: 1999- 9:02.08, 33:54.9A; 2000- 8:59.90, 15:08.36; 2001- 8:52.47, 15:08.65; 2002- 8:40.28, 15:26.45; 2003- 8:38.31, 14:40.34; 2004- 8:33.44i/8:36.46, 14:44.81; 2005- 8:30.05i/8:33.57, 14:28.98; 2006- 8:24.66, 14:24.53; 2007- 8:23.72i/8:24.51, 14:16.63; 2008- 8:27.93i/8:34.53, 14:12.88; 2009- 8:26.99i/8:30.15, 14:24.37i/14:36.38, 29:59.20; 2010- 8:24.46i/8:36.09, 14:24.79i/14:38.87; 2011- 8:36.91i/8:50.36+, 14:29.52, 31:05.05; 2012- 8:31.56i/8:46.49, 14:35.85; 2013- 8:30.29, 14:26.90, 30:08.06. pbs: 1500m 4:02.00 '10, 1M: 4:28.5ei '06, 4:33.07+ '07; 2000m 5:34.74i/5:38.0 '06, 2M 8:58.58 '07, road 15k 47:30 '13, HMar 66:09 '13.
Married to Teodros Hailu. IAAF woman athlete of the year 2007. Record nine WAF wins. Reclrd 45 times under 15 mins for 5000m. Daughter Gabriella born on 23 June 2014.

Shure DEMISE Ware b. 12 Jan 1996 Bore 1.59m 45kg.
World junior marathon record 2015 (4th on debut at Dubai).
Progress at Mar: 2015- 2:20:59, 2016- 2:25:04. pbs: 10000m: 32:54.1A '15, 15k 49:22 '14, HMar 68:53 '14. Won Toronto marathon 2015.

Birhane DIBABA b. 11 Sep 1993 Moyagajo 1.59m 44kg.
Progress at Mar: 2012- 2:29:22, 2013- 2:23:01, 2014- 2:22:30, 2015- 2:23:15, 2016- 2:23:16. pbs: HMar 71:13 '13, 69:34dh '14.
Won Valencia marathon 2012, Tokyo 2015; 2nd São Paulo 2012, Nagoya 2013, Tokyo 2014; 3rd Frankfurt 2013, Chicago 2014-15.

Genzebe DIBABA b. 8 Feb 1991 Bekoji. Muger Cement. 1.68m 52kg.
At 1500m: OG: '12- h; WCh: '13- 8, '15- 1; WI: '12- 1. At 3000m: CCp: '14- 1; WI: '14- 1, '16- 1. At 5000m: WCh: '09 -8, '11- 8, '15- 3; AfCh: '14- 2; WJ: '08- 2, '10- 1; Af-J: '09- 1. World CC: '07-08-09-10-11: 5J/1J/1J/11J/9. Won DL 5000m 2015, ETH 1500m 2010.
Records: World 1500m 2015, indoor 1500m, 3000m & 2M 2014, 5000m 2015, 1M 2016. Two African 1500m 2015. Ethiopian 1500m (3) 2012-15, 2000m 2014.
Progress at 1500m, 5000m: 2007- 15:53.46, 2008- 15:02.41, 2009- 14:55.52, 2010- 4:04.80i/4:06.10, 15:08.06; 2011- 4:05.90, 14:37.56; 2012- 3:57.77, 2013- 3:57.54, 14:37.68; 2014- 3:55.17i/4:01.00, 14:28.88; 2015- 3:50.07, 14:15.41. pbs: 1000m 2:35.6+ '15, 1M 4:13.31i '16, 4:22.2e '14; 2000m 5:27.50 '14, 3000m 8:16.60i/8:26.21 '14, 2M 9:00.48i/9:14.28 '14.
Laureus World Sportswomen of the Year 2014. Younger sister of Ejegayehu (2 OG 10000m 2004, 3 WCh 5000 & 10000m 2005) and Tirunesh Dibaba.

Mare DIBABA Hurssa b. 20 Oct 1989 Sululta 1.52m 40kg.
At Mar: WCh: '15- 1; OG: '12- 22. At HMar: AfG: '11- 1. Won AZE 3000m and 5000m 2009.
AZE records (as Mare Ibrahimova) at 3000m and 5000m 2009.
Progress at HMar, Mar: 2008- 70:28, 2009- 68:45, 2010- 67:13, 2:25:27, 2011- 68:39, 2:23:25; 2012- 67:44, 2:19:52; 2014- 68:56, 2:21:36/2:20:35dh; 2015- 2:19:52. pbs: 3000m 9:16.94 '09, 5000m 15:42.83 '09, Road: 10k 31:55+ '10, 15k 48:04+ '10, 10M 51:29+ '10, 20k 63:47+ '10, 30k 1:39:19 '14.
She switched to Azerbaijan in December 2008 but back to Ethiopia as of 1 Feb 2010. Major marathons: won at Xiamen 2014 and 2015, 2nd Chicago 2014, 3rd Dubal 2012, Boston 2014.

Tirunesh DIBABA Kenene b. 1 Oct 1985 Chefa near Bekoji, Arsi region 1.60m 47kg.
At 5000m(/10000m): OG: '04- 3, '08- 1/1, '12- 3/1; WCh: '03- 1, '05- 1/1, '07- (1), '13- (1); WJ: '02- 2; AfG: '03- 4; AfCh: '06- 2, '08- (1), '10- (1). At 3000m: WCp: '06- 1. World CC: '01-02-03-05-06-07-08-10: 5J/2J/1J/1/1/2/1/4; 4k: '03-04-05: 7/2/1. Won WAF 5000m 2006, ETH 4k CC & 5000m 2003. 8k CC 2005.
World records: 5000m 2008, indoor 5000m 2005 (14:32.93) & 2007, junior 5000m 2003-04, indoor 3000m & 5000m 2004, world road 5k best 14:51 2005, 15k 2009. African 10000m record 2008.
Progress at 5000m, 10000m, Mar: 2002- 14:49.90, 2003- 14:39.94, 2004- 14:30.88, 2005- 14:32.42, 30:15.67; 2006- 14:30.40, 2007- 14:27.42i/14:35.67, 31:55.41; 2008- 14:11.15, 29:54.66; 2009- 14:33.65, 2010- 14:34.07, 31:51.39A; 2012- 14:50.80, 30:20.75; 2013- 14:23.68, 30:26.67; 2014- 2:20:35. pbs: 2000m 5:42.7 '05, 3000m 8:29.55 '06, 2M 9:12.23i '10, road 15k 46:28 '09, HMar 66:56 '13, 30k 1:39:14 '14.
In 2003 she became, at 17 years 333 days, the youngest ever world champion at an individual event and in 2005 the first woman to win the 5000m/10000m double (with last laps of 58.19

and 58.4) at a global event after earlier in the year winning both World CC titles. Now has women's record 21 World CC medals. Married Sileshi Sihine on 26 Oct 2008; son Natan Seleshi born 26 Mar 2015. Retained the Olympic 10,000m title and won the Great North Run on half marathon debut in 2012. Third in London on marathon debut 2014. She has run eleven 10,000m track races – and won them all.

Buze DIRIBA Kejela b. 9 Feb 1994 Arsi 1.60m 43kg.
At 5000m: WCh: '13- 5; WJ: '12- 1. World CC: '11- 10J, '13- 9J
Progress at 5000m, 10000m: 2012- 14:53.06, 2013- 14:50.02, 2014- 15:16.83, 2015- 31:33.27. pbs: 1500m 4:10.96 '12, 3000m 8:39.65 '12, 2M 9:29.03i '15, 9:40.01 '14; 10M Rd 52:55 '15, HMar 72:56 '15.

Etenesh DIRO Neda b. 10 May 1991 Jeidu, Oromiya 1.69m 47kg.
At 3000mSt: OG: '12- 5; WCh: '13- 5, '15- h; AfG: '15- 6; AfCh: '14- 4.
Progress at 3000mSt: 2011- 9:49.18, 2012- 9:14.07, 2013- 9:16.97, 2014- 9:19.71, 2015- 9:29.10. pbs: 3000m 9:00.39 '11, 5000m 15:19.77 '12, Road: 10k 33:32A '11, 15k 51:21 '09, HMar 71:35 '10.

Axumawit EMBAYE Abraya b. 18 Oct 1994 1.60m 50kg.
At 1500m: WJ: '12- 7; AfCh: '14- 4; WI: '14- 2, '16- 4.
Progress at 1500m: 2012- 4:12.92, 2013- 4:05.16, 2014- 4:02.35, 2015- 4:02.92i/4:03.00. pbs: 800m 2:03.27i '15, 1000m 2:37.43 '15, 1M 4:23.50i/4:26.84 '15, 3000m 8:51.82 '15.

Erba **Tiki GELANA** b. 22 Oct 1987 Bekoji, Oromiya 1.65m 48kg.
At Mar: OG: '12- 1; WCh: '13- dnf.
Ethiopian marathon record 2012.
Progress at Mar: 2009- 2:33:49, 2010- 2:28:28, 2011- 2:22:08, 2012- 2:18:58, 2013- 2:36:55, 2014- 2:26:58, 2015- 2:24:26. pbs: 3000m 8:55.88 '08, 5000m 15:17.74 '08, 10000m 31:27.80 '08; Road: 15k 48:09 '12, 20k 65:06+ '12, HMar 67:48 '12, 30k 1:40:45 '11. Won Amsterdam Marathon 2011, Rotterdam 2012; 3rd Tokyo 2015.

Amane GOBENA Gemeda b. 1 Sep 1982.
World 4k CC: '02- 8, '04- 11.
Progress at Mar: 2009- 2:26:53, 2010- 2:24:13, 2011- 2:31:49, 2012- 2:28:38, 2013- 2:23:50, 2014- 2:27:05, 2015- 2:23:30, 2016- 2:21:51 pbs: 1500m 4:11.04 '04, 1M 4:41.57 '03, 3000m 9:01.46 '02, 5000m 15:19.50 '04, Road: 10km 31:44 '14, 15km 47:55 '10, HMar 68:16 '09, 30k 1:43:24 '09.
Won Toronto Marathon 2009, Osaka and Seoul 2010, Xiamen 2011, Santa Monica 2014; 2nd Paris 2015, Tokyo 2016.

Meseret HAILU b. 12 Sep 1990 Oromia region 1.68m 54kg.
At Mar: WCh: '13- dnf. World HMar: '12- 1.
Progress at Mar: 2009- 2:43:29, 2010- 2:30:42, 2011- 2:34:38, 2012- 2:21:09, 2013- 2:26:58, 2014- 2:26:20, 2015- 2:24:33. pbs: 10k 31:18 '13, HMar 66:56 '13, 30k 1:41:06 '12.
Won Amsterdam Marathon 2012, Hamburg 2015; 2nd Boston 2013, 3rd Berlin 2015.

Alemitu HAROYE Banata b. 9 May 1995 1.60m 44kg.
At 10000m: WCh: '15- 7; At 5000m: WJ: '14- 1; AfCh: '12- 4, Af-J: '13- 3. At 3000m: WY: '11- 5. World CC: '13- 3J, '15- 4; Af CC: '12- 5J, '14- 2J.
Progress at 5000m, 10000m: 2011- 16:14.3A, 2012- 15:55.36, 2013- 15:05.08, 2014- 14:52.67, 2015- 14:43.28, 30:50.83. pbs: 3000m 8:36.87 '14, 2M 9:20.81 '14.

Aberu KEBEDE Shewaye b. 12 Sep 1989 Shewa 1.63m 50kg.
At Mar: WCh: '11- 12, '13- 13. World HMar: '09- 3; CC: '07- 16J. Won ETH 10000m 2009.
Progress at 10000m, Mar: 2009- 30:48.26, 2010- 32:17.74, 2:23:58; 2011- 2:24:34, 2012- 31:09.28, 2:20:30; 2013- 2:23:28, 2014- 2:22:21, 2015- 2:20:48, 2016- 2:23:01. pbs: 5km Rd 15:13 '09, HMar 67:39 '09, 30k 1:39:50 '14.
Won Rotterdam and Berlin marathons 2010 after 2nd Dubai on debut, won Berlin again in 2012 and Tokyo and Shanghai 2013, Frankfurt 2014, 2nd Berlin 2015.

Yebrqual MELESE b. 18 Apr 1990 1.64m 55kg.
Won ETH 10000m 2015.
Progress at Mar: 2014- 2:26:21, 2015- 2:23:23. pbs: 10000m: 32:40.3A '15, 10k 31:40 '13, HM 68:21 '15.
Marathon wins: Hangzhou 2014, Houston & Prague 2015, 2nd Paris 2014, Chicago 2015.

Meselech MELKAMU b. 27 Apr 1985 Debre Markos, Amhara region 1.58m 47kg.
At 5000m(/10000m): OG: '08- 8; WCh: '05- 4, '07- 6, '09- 5/2, '11- (5); AfG: '07- 2, '11- (dnf); AfCh: '06- 6, '08- 1, '10- (2); WJ: '04- 1. At Mar: WCh: '13- dnf. At 3000m: WI: '08- 2. World CC: '03-04-05-06-07-08-09-10-11: 4J/1J/4 & 6/3 & 3/3/9/3/3/4 (17 medals). Won ETH 5000m 2004, 4k CC 2005, CC 2006-07.
African 10000m record 2009.
Progress at 5000m, 10000m, Mar: 2003- 15:27.93, 2004- 15:00.02, 2005- 14:38.97, 2006- 14:37.44, 2007- 14:33.83, 2008- 14:38.78, 31:04.93; 2009- 14:34.17, 29:53.80; 2010- 14:31.91, 31:04.52; 2011- 14:39.44, 30:56.55m 2012- 2:21:01, 2013- 2:25:46, 2014- 2:25:23, 2:21:28dh; 2015- 2:26:45, 2016- 2:22:29. pbs: 1500m 4:07.52 '07, 1M 4:33.94 '03, 2000m 5:39.2i+, 5:46.3+ '07; 3000m 8:23.74i '07, 8:34.73 '05, Road: HMar 68:05 '13, 25k 1:23:23 '12, 1:22:27dh '14; 30k 1:39:58 '12, 1:39:21dh '14.
Third fastest ever marathon debut to win at Frankfurt 2012. 2nd Dubai 2014 (3rd 2016), won Daegu 2015.

Aselefech MERGIA b. 23 Jan 1985 Woliso 1.68m 51kg.
At Mar: OG: '12- 42; WCh: '09- 3, '11- dnf. HMar: WCh: '08- 2. World CC: '08- 16.
Ethiopian marathon record 2012.

Progress at HMar, Mar: 2006- 74:13, 2007- 74:50, 2008- 68:17, 2009- 67:48, 2:25:02; 2010- 67:22, 2:22:38; 2011- 67:21, 2:22:45; 2012- 69:42+, 2:19:31; 2014- 73:49, 2015- 71:42, 2:20:02. pbs: 1500m 4:14.85 '07, 3000m 8:54.42 '08; Road: 10k 31:25+ '08, 15k 47:53 '09, 20k 63:41 '09, 30k 1:41:52 '09.
2nd Paris Marathon 2009 on debut, won London 2010 and Dubai 2011-12 and 2015; 2nd New York 2015. Daughter Sena born July 2013.

Belaynesh OLJIRA Jemane b. 26 Jun 1990 Welek'a, Amhara 1.65m 49kg.
At 10000m: OG: '12- 5; WCh: '13- 3, '15- 9; AfCh: '14- 3. World CC: '11-13-15: 10/3/9; AfCC: '12- 5. Won ETH 10000m 2011.
Ethiopian 1500m record 2012.
Progress at 10000m, Mar: 2011- 31:17.80, 2012- 30:26.70, 2013- 30:31.44, 2:25:01; 2014- 32:49.39, 2:24:21dh; 2015- 30:53.69. pbs: 1500m 4:33.14 '12, 3000m 8:40.73 '10, 2M 9:23.32 '14, 5000m 14:58.16 '10, Road: 15k 49:08 '14, 10M 52:40 '14, HMar 67:27 '11, 30k 1:39:33dh '14.

Mulu SEBOKA Seyfu b. 13 Jan 1984 1.58m 45kg.
World 20k: '06- 25.
Progress at Mar: 2003- 2:43:30, 2004- 2:37:29, 2005- 2:30:54, 2006- 2:30:41, 2007- 2:33:27, 2008- 2:29:06, 2009- 2:29:38, 2010- 2:30:47, 2011- 2:35:14, 2012- 2:25:45, 2013- 2:23:43, 2014- 2:23:15, 2015- 2:21:56, 2016- 2:24:24. pbs: 15k 48:38 '12, HMar 69:11 '15, 30k 1:41:13 '14.
Marathon wins: Mumabi 2005-06, Toronto 2008, Melbourne 2010, Guangzhou 2012, Jakarta 2013, Dubai, Daegu & Toronto 2014.

Dawit SEYAUM Biratu b. 27 Jul 1996 Tumano 1.58m 45kg.
At 1500m: WCh: '15- 4; WJ: '14- 1; WY: '13- 2; AfG: '15- 1; AfCh: '14- 2; Af-J: '13/15- 1; CCp: '14- 3.; WI: '16- 2.
Progress at 1500m: 2013- 4:09.00, 2014- 3:59.53, 2015- 3:59.76, 2016- 4:00.48i. pbs: 1M 4:32.13i '15, 2000m 5:35.46i '15.

Feysa TADESE Boru b. 19 Nov 1988 Shirka 1.67m 53kg.
At Mar: WCh: '13- dnf. World HMar: '10- 4, '12- 2; CC: '10- 7.
Progress at Mar: 2009- 2:36:57, 2011- 2:25:20, 2012- 2:23:07, 2013- 2:21:06, 2014- 2:20:27. pbs: 10000m 32:29.07 '10, Road: 10k 32:21 '13, 15k 48:51 '12, 20k 65:41 '12, HMar 68:35 '13, 30k 1:39:18 '14.
Four wins in nine marathons: Seoul and Shanghai 2012, Paris 2013; 2nd Berlin 2014.

Senbere TEFERI Sora b. 3 May 1995 1.59m 45kg. Oromiya.
At 1500m: WCh: '13- h; WJ: '12- 3; WY: '11- 2; At 5000m: WCh: '15- 2; World CC: '15- 2.
Progress at 1500m, 5000m: 2011- 16:09.0A, 2012- 15:36.74, 2013- 4:04.55, 16:21.0A, 2014- 4:08.49, 2015- 4:01.86, 14:38.57. pbs: 2000m 5:34.27 '14, 3000m 8:34.32 '15.

Gudaf TSEGAY Desta b. 23 Jan 1997 1.59m 45kg.
At 1500m: WJ: '14- 2; WI: '16- 3.
World junior indoor 1500m record 2016.
Progress at 1500m: 2013- 4:07.27, 2014- 4:02.83, 2015- 4:03.09, 2016- 4:01.81i. pbs: 1M 4:24.984i '16, 15k Rd 15:37 '15.

Tirfi TSEGAYE Beyene b. 25 Nov 1984 Bokoji 1.65m 54kg.
At Mar: WCh: '15- 8. World HMar: '09- 6.
Progress at Mar: 2008- 2:35:32, 2009- 2:28:16, 2010- 2:22:44, 2011- 2:24:12, 2012- 2:21:19, 2013- 2:23:23, 2014- 2:20:18, 2015- 2:23:41, 2016- 2:19:41. pbs: 15k 49:48 '14, HMar 67:42 '12, 30k 1:39:17 '14.
Marathon wins: Porto 2008, Shanghai 2010, Paris 2012, Dubai 2013 & 2016, Tokyo & Berlin 2014. 3rd London 2015.

Tigist TUFA Demisse b. 26 Jan 1987 1.55m 40kg.
At Mar: WCh: '15- 6.
Progress at Mar: 2011- 2:41:50, 2013- 2:29:24, 2014- 2:21:52, 2015- 2:23:22. pbs: 15k 51:05 '14, HMar 70:03 '08.
Marathon wins: Ottawa & Shanghai 2014, London 2015; 3rd New York 2015.

FINLAND

Governing body: Suomen Urheiluliitto, Radiokatu 20, SF-00240 Helsinki. Founded 1906.

National Championships first held in 1907 (men), 1913 (women). **2015 Champions**: **Men**: 100m:V ille Myllymäki 10.39, 200m: Samuli Samuelsson 21.29, 400m: Jani Koskela 47.85, 800m: Ville Lampinen 1:55.29, 1500m: Ilari Piipponen 3:56.44, 5000m: Jarkko Järvenpää 14:35.16, 10000m: Arttu Vattulainen 29:46.46, HMar: Jussi Utriainen 67:59; Mar: Jaakko Nieminen 2:26:29, 3000mSt: Janne Ukonmaanaho 8:59.17, 110mh: Elmo Lakka 13.99, 400mh: Oskari Mörö 50.85, HJ: Jussi Viita 2.20, PV: Eemeli Salomäki 5.30, LJ: Eero Haapala 7.83, TJ: Simo Lipsanen 16.17, SP: Arttu Kangas 19.73, DT: Pyry Niskala 61.10, HT: David Söderberg 74.68, JT: Antti Ruuskanen 88.98, Dec: Elmo Savola 7616, 20kW: Aleksi Ojala 1:26:27. **Women**: 100m/200m: Hanna-Maari Latvala 11.70/24.03, 400m: Hilla Uusimäki 55.07, 800m: Karin Storbacka 2:07.27, 1500m/5000m: Kristiina Mäki 4:23.71/16:08.24, 10000m: Alisa Vainio 32:58.17, HMar: Oona Kettunen 75:15, Mar: Laura Markovaara 2:47:27, 3000mSt: Sandra Eriksson 9:36.90, 100mh: Nooralotta Neziri 13.08, 400mh: Venla Paunonen 57.78, HJ: Sini Lällä 1.82, PV: Minna Nikkanen 4.56, LJ: Sanna Nygård 6.28, TJ: Kristiina Mäkelä 13.84, SP/DT: Sanna Kämäräinen 15.70/57.87, HT: Inga Linna 67.29, JT: Oona Sormunen 58.11, Hep: Jutta Heikkinen 5618, 10kW: Taika Nummi 46:16, 20kW: Mikaela Löfbacka 1:43:53.

Ari MANNIO b. 23 Jul 1987 Lehtimäki 1.85m 104kg. Lehtimäen Jyske.

At JT: OG: '12- 11; WCh: '11/15- dnq 14/dnq 14; EC: '12- 3; WJ: '04- 6, '06- 2; EU23: '07- 4, '09- 1; EJ: '05- 3; ET: '10- 3. Finnish champion 2011, W.Military 2011, 2015.
Progress at JT: 2004- 70.83, 2005- 76.40, 2006- 79.68, 2007- 80.31, 2008- 81.54, 2009- 85.70, 2010- 85.12, 2011- 85.12, 2012- 84.62, 2013- 84.65, 2014- 83.70, 2015- 86.82.

Tero PITKÄMÄKI b. 19 Dec 1982 Ilmajoki 1.95m 92kg. Nurmon Urheilijat. Electrical engineer.
At JT: OG: '04- 8, '08- 3, '12- 5; WCh: '05-07-09-11-13-15: 4/1/5/dnq 17/2/3; EC: '06-10-12-14: 2/3/11/3; EU23: '03- 3; EJ: '01- 6; ECp: '06- 1, '15- 1. Won WAF 2005, 2007; DL 2015, Finnish 2004-07, 2013.
Progress at JT: 1999- 66.83, 2000- 73.75, 2001- 74.89, 2002- 77.24, 2003- 80.45, 2004- 84.64, 2005- 91.53, 2006- 91.11, 2007- 91.23, 2008- 87.70, 2009- 87.79, 2010- 86.92, 2011- 85.33, 2012- 86.98, 2013- 89.03, 2014- 86.63, 2015- 89.09.
Partner is Niina Kelo (b. 26 Mar 1980) pb Hep 5956 (15 EC 2006).

Antti RUUSKANEN b. 21 Feb 1984 Kokkola 1.89m 86kg. Pielaveden Sampo.
At JT: OG: '12- 3; WCh: '09-11-13-15: 6/9/5/5; EC: '14- 1; EU23: '05- 2; EJ: '03- 3; CCp: '14- 8. Finnish champion 2012, 2014-15.
Progress at JT: 2002- 66.08, 2003- 72.87, 2004- 75.84, 2005- 79.75, 2006- 84.10, 2007- 82.71/87.88dh, 2008- 87.33, 2009- 85.39, 2010- 83.45, 2011- 82.29, 2012- 87.79, 2013- 85.70, 2014- 88.01, 2015- 88.98.

David SÖDERBERG b. 11 Aug 1979 Vörå 1.85m 100kg. IF VOM Vöyri.
At HT: OG: '04-12: dnq 21/26; WCh: '07-09- dnq 20/18, '15- 6; EC: '02-06-10: dnq 18/16/13, '14- 8; EU23: '01- nt; WUG: '03- 3. Finnish 2013-15.
Progress at HT: 1997- 58.20, 1998- 61.02, 1999- 64.23, 2000- 68.53, 2001- 72.25, 2002- 76.51, 2003- 78.83, 2004- 75.56, 2005- 76.89, 2006- 75.58, 2007- 77.18, 2008- 75.82, 2009- 75.44, 2010- 76.05, 2011- 77.34, 2012- 77.53, 2013- 75.67, 2014- 77.57, 2015- 76.92.

FRANCE

Governing body: Fédération Française d'Athlétisme, 33 avenue Pierre de Coubertin, 75640 Paris cedex 13. Founded 1920.

National Championships first held in 1888 (men), 1918 (women). **2015 Champions: Men**: 100m: Jimmy Vicaut 9.92, 200m: Christophe Lemaitre 20.28, 400m: Teddy Venel 45.72, 800m: Pierre-Ambroise Bosse 1:46.69, 1500m: Mourad Amdouni 3:48.59, 5000m: Benjamin Choquert 14:10.41, 10000m: Riad Guerfi 29:09.69, HMar: Yosi Goasdoue 69:34, Mar: Michael Gras 2:18:32, 3000mSt: Yoann Kowal 8:37.41, 110mh: Garfield Darien 13.17, 400mh: Mickaël François 50.29, HJ: Mickaël Hanany 2.24, PV: Renaud Lavillenie 5.85, LJ: Kafétien Gomis 7.78, TJ: Harold Correa 16.78, SP: Gaëtan Bucki 19.72, DT: Lolassonn Djouhan 59.54, HT: Jérôme Bortoluzzi 73.65, JT: Jérôme Haeffler 70.40, Dec: Gaël Quérin 7738, 10000mW: Kevin Campion 41:11.73, 20kW: Yohann Diniz 1:17:02, 50kW: Hugo Andrieu 4:16:44. **Women**: 100m: Véronique Mang 11.23, 200m: Lénora Guion-Firmin 23.64, 400m: Floria Guei 51.06, 800m: Lisa Blameble 2:05.00, 1500m: Élodie Normand 4:19.23, 5000m: Clémence Calvin 16:16.73, 10000m: Carmen Oliveras 34:40.15, HMar/Mar: Aline Camboulives 1:20:12/2:37:02 , 3000mSt: Ophélie Claude-Boxberger 9:59.86, 100mh: Cindy Billaud 12.89, 400mh: Maeva Contion 56.03, HJ: Sandrine Champion 1.85, PV: Marion Lotout 4.40, LJ: Haoua Kessely 6.30, TJ: Teresa Nzola Meso Ba 13.69, SP: Jessica Cérival 17.29, DT: Mélina Robert-Michon 62.57, HT: Jessika Guehaseim 66.30, JT: Mathilde Andraud 59.05, Hep: Gaëlle Le Foll 5848, 10000mW: Émilie Menuet 45:06.18, 20kW: Ines Pastorino 1:36:04.

Dimitri BASCOU b. 20 Jul 1987 Schoelcher, Martinique 1.82m 79kg. Racing Club de France.
At 110mh: OG: '12- sf; WCh: '09/11- sf, '15- 5; EC: '10- 4, 14- dq; EU23: '07- h, '09- 4; EJ: '05- h; won FRA 2009-11. At 60mh: WI: '16- 3; EI: '11- 6, '15- 2.
Progress at 110mh: 2004- 14.61w, 2005- 14.35, 2006- 14.24, 2007- 13.76, 2008- 13.61/13.39w, 2009- 13.49, 2010- 13.41, 2011- 13.37/13.26w, 2012- 13.34, 2013- 13.51, 2014- 13.25, 2015- 13.16. pbs: 60m 6.88i '14, 100m 10.72 '07, 200m 21.62 '09, 50mh 6.57i '12, 60mh 7.41i '16.
Disqualified for obstruction after finishing 3rd at the 2014 Europeans.

Wilhem BELOCIAN b. 22 Jun 1995 les Abymes, Guadeloupe 1.78m 78kg. Stade Lamertin.
At 110mh: WJ: '12- 3, '14- 1; WY: '11- 3 (3 Med R); EJ: '13- 1; At 60mh: EI: '15- 3.
World junior record 99cm 110mh 12.99 in 2014, three European JR 2014-14.
Progress at 110mh: 2014- 13.54, 2015- 13.28. pbs: 60m 6.82i '12, 100m 10.61 '16, 60mh 7.52i '15.

Pierre-Ambroise BOSSE b. 11 May 1992 Nantes 1.85m 68kg. UA Gujan Mestras.
At 800m: OG: '12- sf; WCh: '13- 7, '15- 5; EC: '12- 3, '14- 8; WJ: '10- 8; EU23: '13- 1; EJ: '11- 1; ET: 15- 2; French champion 2012, 2014-15.
FRA 800m & European U23 1000m records 2014.
Progress at 800m: 2007- 2:02.81, 2008- 1:56.05, 2010- 1:48.38, 2011- 1:46.18, 2012- 1:44.97, 2013- 1:43.76, 2014- 1:42.53, 2015- 1:43.88. pbs: 400m 48.54 '11, 600m 1:15.63i '13, 1000m 2:15.31 '14, 1500m 3:54.81 '09.

Benjamin COMPAORÉ b. 5 Aug 1987 Bar-le-Duc 1.89m 86kg. Strasbourg AA.
At TJ: OG: '12- 6; WCh: '11- 8, '15- 12; EC: '10- 5, '14- 1; WJ: '06- 1; EJ: '05- 5; CCp: '14- 1; WI: '12- 6, '16- 3. FRA champion 2014.
Progress at TJ: 2003- 14.50, 2004- 15.48, 2005-

16.00/16.12w, 2006- 16.61, 2007- 16.62, 2008- 17.05, 2009- 16.98, 2010- 17.21/17.28w, 2011- 17.31, 2012- 17.17, 2013- 17.07, 2014- 17.48, 2015- 17.01. pbs: 60m 7.13i '08, 100m 10.76 '13, 400m 48.69 '12, 1500m 4:44.43 '12, 110mh 15.72 '12, HJ 1.98 '12, LJ 7.88 '08, Dec 6704 '12.
Father came from Burkina Faso.

Garfield DARIEN b. 22 Dec 1987 Lyon 1.87m 76kg. EA Chambéry.
At 110mh: OG: '12- sf; WCh: '09- sf, '15- 8; EC: '10- 2, '12- 2; WJ: '04- 7; EJ: '05- 1; CCp: '10- 4; ET: '11- 2; French champion 2012, 2015. At 60mh: WI: '14- 3; EI: '09- 6, '11- 2.
Progress at 110mh: 2004- 14.03/13.98w, 2005- 13.73, 2006- 13.94/13.92w, 2008- 13.50/13.43w, 2009- 13.36, 2010- 13.34, 2011- 13.37, 2012- 13.15, 2013- 14.47, 2014- 14.01, 2015- 13.17. pbs: 200m 22.05 '06, 60mh 7.47i '14, HJ 1.83 '04.
Father Daniel Darien had 110mh pb 13.76 '87.

Yohann DINIZ b. 1 Jan 1978 Epernay 1.85m 69kg. EFS Reims Athlétisme.
At 20kW: ECp: '07- 1; At 50kW: OG: '08- dnf, '12- dq; WCh: '05-07-09-11-13: dq/2/12/dq/10; EC: '06-10-14: 1/1/1; ECp: '05-13-15: 4/1/3. Won French 10000mW 2010, 2012, 2014; 20kW 2007-09, 2015; 50kW 2005.
World walks records: track 50,000m 2011, road 50k 2014, 20k 2015. French records 5000mW (3) 2006-08, 10000mW 2014, 20000mW 2014, 20kW (4) 2005-15, 50kW 2006 & 2009, 1 Hr 2010.
Progress at 20kW, 50kW: 2001- 1:35:05.0t, 2002- 1:30:40, 2003- 1:26:54.99t, 2004- 1:24:25, 3:52:11.0t; 2005- 1:20:20, 3:45:17; 2006- 1:23:19, 3:41:39; 2007- 1:18:58, 3:44:22; 2008- 1:22:31, 2009- 1:22:50, 3:38:45; 2010- 1:20:23, 3:40:37; 2011- 3:35:27.2t, 2012- 1:17:43, 2013- 1:23:17, 3:41:07; 2014- 1:19:42.1t, 3:32:33; 2015- 1:17:02, 2016- 3:37:48. pbs: 3000mW 10:52.44 '08, 5000mW 18:16.76i '14, 18:18.01 '08; 10000mW 38:08.13 '14, 20000mW 1:19:42.1 '14, 1HrW 15,395m '10, 35kW 2:32:24 '12.

Kafétien GOMIS b. 23 Mar 1980 Saint Quentin 1.83m 67kg. Lille Metropole Athlétisme.
At LJ: OG: '04- dnq 14; WCh: '09- dnq 21, '15- 7; EC: '06-10-12-14: 5/2/9/3; EI: '07-09-11: 4/4/2; CCp: '10- 2, '14- 8; ET: '10- 2, '15- 2. French champion 2007, 2015.
Progress at LJ: 2000- 7.35w, 2001- 7.56i/7.53, 2002- 7.77, 2003- 7.85, 2004- 8.21, 2005- 7.98, 2006- 8.03, 2007- 8.09i/7.91, 2008- 8.08, 2009- 8.15, 2010- 8.24, 2011- 8.12/8.22w, 2012- 8.05/8.13w, 2013- 8.02, 2014- 8.19, 2015- 8.26, 2016- 8.23i. pbs: 60m 6.91i '06, 100m 10.76 '03, HJ 2.07 '00.

Renaud LAVILLENIE b. 18 Sep 1986 Barbezieux-Saint-Hilaire 1.77m 69kg. Clermont Athl. Auvergne.
At PV: OG: '12- 1; WCh: '09-11-13-15: 3/3/2/3=; WI: '12- 1, '16- 1; EC: '10-12-14: 1/1/1; EU23: '07- 10; EI: '09-11-13-15: 1/1/1/1; CCp: '10- 2, '14- 1; ET: '09-10-13-14-15: 1/1/1/1/1. Won DL 2010-15, French 2010, 2012-15.
World indoor pole vault record 2014.
French record (indoors) 2011 and outdoors 2013.
Progress at PV: 2002- 3.40, 2003- 4.30, 2004- 4.60, 2005- 4.81i/4.70, 2006- 5.25i/5.22, 2007- 5.58i/5.45, 2008- 5.81i/5.65, 2009- 6.01, 2010- 5.94, 2011- 6.03i/5.90, 2012- 5.97, 2013- 6.02, 2014- 6.16i/5.93, 2015- 6.05, 2016- 6.03i. pbs: 60m 7.23i '08, 100m 11.04 '11, 60mh 8.41i '08, 100m 11.04 '11, 110mh 14.51 '10, HJ 1.89i '08, 1.87 '07; LJ 7.31 '10, Hep 5363i '08.
Broke Sergey Bubka's 21 year-old absolute world pole vault record indoors in 2014. 23 successive wins 31 Aug 2013 to EC 2014, only man to win all six Diamond League titles from 2010. IAAF Male Athlete of the Year 2014.
His brother **Valentin** (b. 16 Jul 1991) has PV pb 5.80i '15, 5.65 '13; 3rd EU23 and nh WCh in 2013; 6 EI '15.

Christophe LEMAITRE b. 11 Jun 1990 Annecy 1.89m 74kg. AS Aix-les-Bains.
At 100m/(200m): OG: '12- (6)/3R; WCh: '09- qf, '11- 4/3/2R, '13- 7, '15- sf/sf; EC: '10- 1/1/1R, '12- 1/3R, '14- 2/2/3R; WJ: '08- (1); WY: '07- 4/5; EJ: '09- 1; CCp: '10- 1, '14- 5/4/2R; ET: '10- 2, '11- 1/1, '13- (1), '15- 1/2R. At 60m: EI: '11- 3. Won French 100m 2010-12, 2014; 200m 2010-15.
Records: European 4x200m 2014; French 100m (7) 2010-11, 200m (2) 2010-11, European junior 100m 2009. U23 100m 2010-11, 200m 2011.
Progress at 100m, 200m: 2005- 11.46, 2006- 10.96, 2007- 10.53, 21.08; 2008- 10.26, 20.83; 2009- 10.04/10.03w, 20.68; 2010- 9.97, 20.16; 2011- 9.92, 19.80; 2012- 10.04/9.94w, 19.91; 2013- 10.00/9.98w, 20.07; 2014- 10.10, 20.08; 2015- 10.07, 20.21. pbs: 60m 6.55i '10, 150m St 14.90 '13.
First Caucasian sub-10.00 100m runner and first to win sprint treble at European Champs; now has men's record eight EC medals.

Pascal MARTINOT-LAGARDE b. 22 Sep 1991 St Maur-des-Fossés 1.90m 80kg. Neuilly Plaisance Sport.
At 110mh: WCh: '13- h, '15- 4; EC: '14- 3; WJ: '10- 1; EU23: '11- h; EJ: '09- 4; ET: '13-14-15: 2/3/2; won DL 2014, FRA 2014. At 60mh: WI: '12-14-16: 3/2/2; EI: '13- 3, '15- 1.
French 110m hurdles record 2014.
Progress at 110mh: 2008- 15.03, 2009- 14.13, 2010- 13.74, 2011- 13.94, 2012- 13.41/13.30w, 2013- 13.12, 2014- 12.95, 2015- 13.06. pbs: 60m 7.07i '10, 100m 10.94 '13, 60mh 7.45i '14.
His brother **Thomas** (b. 7 Feb 1988) has 110mh pb 13.26, 7 WCh and French champion in 2013.

Kevin MAYER b. 10 Feb 1992 Argenteuil 1.86m 77kg. EA Tain-Tournon.
At Dec: OG: '12- 15; WCh: '13- 4; EC: '12- dnf, '14- 2; WJ: '10- 1; EJ: '11- 1; ECp: '13- 1. At Oct: WY: '09- 1. At Hep: EI: '13- 2.
Progress at Dec: 2011- 7992, 2012- 8447w/8415, 2013- 8446, 2014- 8521, 2015- 8469. pbs: 60m 7.10i '13, 100m 11.04 '13, 400m 48.66 '11, 1000m

2:37.30i '13, 1500m 4:18.04 '12, 60mh 8.01i '13, 110mh 14.21 '12, HJ 2.10i '10, 2.09 '12; PV 5.35 '15, LJ 7.65 '14, SP 15.55i '16, 15.33 '15; DT 45.83 '15, JT 66.09 '13, Hep 6297i '13.

Mahiédine MEKHISSI-BENABBAD b. 15 Mar 1985 Reims 1.90m 75kg. EFS Reims.
At 3000mSt: OG: '08- 2, '12- 2; WCh: '07/09- h, '11- 3, '13- 3; EC: '10- 1, '12- 1, '14- dq (1 1500m); WJ: '04- h; EU23: '05- h, '07- 1; CCp: '10- 3; ECp: '07- 2, '08- 1. At 1500m: WI: '10- 8; EI: '13- 1; WCp: '06- 7, '14- 3. Won FRA 1500m 2014, 3000mSt 2008, 2012-13.
Records: World best 2000m steeplechase 2010. European 3000mSt 2013, French 1M 2014.
Progress at 3000mSt: 2003- 9:52.07, 2004- 9:01.01, 2005- 8:34.45, 2006- 8:28.25, 2007- 8:14.22, 2008- 8:08.95, 2009- 8:06.98, 2010- 8:02.52, 2011- 8:02.09, 2012- 8:10.90, 2013- 8:00.09, 2014- 8:03.23. pbs: 800m 1:53.61 '04, 1000m 2:17.14 '09, 1500m 3:33.12 '13, 1M 3:51.55 '14, 2000m 4:56.85 '13, 3000m 7:43.72i '13, 7:44.98 '10; 5000m 14:32.9 '05, 2000mSt 5:10.68 '10.
Disqualified after he took his vest off in the finishing straight when finishing well clear in 2014 EC steeplechase.

Kévin MENALDO b. 12 Jul 1992 Bordeaux 1.76m 66kg. E. Franconville Cesame Val d'Oise.
At PV: WCh: '15- 6; EC: '14- 3=; EU23: '13- dnq 15; EJ: '11- 2.
Progress at PV: 2007- 4.15i/4.00, 2008- 4.71, 2009- 5.05, 2010- 5.10i/5.05, 2011- 5.50, 2012- 5.43i/5.40, 2013- 5.65i/5.60, 2014- 5.75i/5.72, 2015- 5.81.

Teddy TAMGHO b. 15 Jun 1989 Paris 1.87m 82kg. CA Montreuil.
At TJ: WCh: '09- 11, '13- 1; EC: '10- 3; WI: '10- 1; WJ: '08- 1; EJ: '07- 4; EI: '11- 1 (4 LJ); ET: '10- 3, '13- 2. Won DL 2010, French 2009-10, 2013.
Four World indoor triple jump records 2010 (17.90) & 2011, four absolute French records 2009-13; three Eur U23 records 2010.
Progress at TJ: 2004- 12.56, 2005- 14.89, 2006- 15.58, 2007- 16.53i/16.35/16.42w, 2008- 17.19/17.33w, 2009- 17.58i/17.11, 2010- 17.98, 2011- 17.92i/ 17.91, 2013- 18.04, 2015- 17.24. pbs: 60m 6.92i '06, 100m 10.60 '09, LJ 8.01i '11, 7.81 '13.
2011 season ended when broke ankle in warm-up for European U23s and also missed all of 2012. His 18.04 to win 2013 World title was third best ever and world's best for 17 years. Fractured his shin in November 2013 and missed all the 2014 season.

Jimmy VICAUT b. 27 Feb 1992 Bondy 1.88m 83kg. Paris Avenir Athletic.
At 100m/(200m)/4x100mR: OG: '12- sf/3R; WCh: '11- 6/2R, '13- sf/sf, '15- 8; EC: '10- 1R, '12- 2/3R (res), '14- sf; WJ: '10- 3; WY: '09- 7; EJ: '11- 1/1R; ET: '13- 1, '14- 1. At 60m: EI: '13- 1. Won French 100m 2013, 2015.
Equalled European 100m record 2015.
Progress at 100m: 2005- 13.0, 2006- 12.50, 2007- 11.0, 2008- 10.75/10.69w, 2009- 10.56, 2010- 10.16, 2011- 10.07, 2012- 10.02, 2013- 9.95, 2014- 9.95/9.89w, 2015- 9.86. pbs: 60m 6.48i '13, 200m 20.30 '13.
His brother Willi was French U17 shot champion in 2012 and has senior pb of 17.33 '14.

Women

Cindy BILLAUD b. 11 Mar 1986 Coulommiers 1.65m 59kg. Athlé Sud 77.
At 100mh: WCh: '09-11-13-15: sf/h/7/h; EC: '14- 2; WJ: '04- sf; EU23: '07- sf; EJ: '05- 3; ET: '14- 1; FRA champion 2013-15. At 60mh: WI: '14- 4; EI: '09- 7. French 100mh record 2014.
Progress at 100mh: 2004- 13.48, 2005- 13.57, 2006- 13.49/13.46w, 2007- 13.25, 2008- 12.99/ 12.97w, 2009- 12.97, 2010- 13.11, 2011- 12.93, 2012- 12.97, 2013- 12.59, 2014- 12.56, 2015- 12.83. pbs: 60m 7.64i '08, 100m 12.00 '05, 200m 24.68 '08, 50mh 7.14+i '12, 60mh 7.87i '14.

Rénelle LAMOTE b. 26 Dec 1993 Annecy 1.68m 57kg. Annecy Haute Savoie.
At 800m: WCh: '15- 8; EC: '14- sf; WJ: '12- sf; EU23: '13- h, 15- 1; ET: '14- 2, '15- 1. French champion 2014.
Progress at 80m: 2009- 2:18.24, 2010- 2:14.53, 2011- 2:08.39, 2012- 2:05.23, 2013- 2:02.40, 2014- 2:00.06, 2015- 1:58.86. Pbs: 400m 54.05 '15, 1500m 4:35.93 '13, 10kRd 37:13 '14.

Éloyse LESUEUR b. 15 Jul 1988 Créteil 1.79m 65kg. SCO Saint Marguerite, Marseille.
At LJ: OG: '12- 8; WCh: '09- 11-13: dnq 18/26/22; EC: '14- 1; WI: '08- 4, '14- 1; WY: '05- 2 (7 100m); EC: '12- 1; EU23: '09- 3; EJ: '07- 2; EI: '11-13-15: 4/2/5; CCp: '14- 1; ET: '10-11-13-14: 1/3/1/2. Won FRA 2006, 2010-14. At Hep: WJ: '06- dnf.
Progress at LJ: 2002- 5.72, 2003- 5.50, 2004- 5.68, 2005- 6.40, 2006- 6.30/6.47w, 2007- 6.47, 2008- 6.84i/6.50, 2009- 6.64/6.72w, 2010- 6.78, 2011- 6.91, 2012- 6.81/7.04w, 2013- 6.90i/6.78, 2014- 6.92/ 6.94w. pbs: 60m 7.34i '12, 100m 11.54, 11.52w '14, 200m 24.11 '06, 800m 2:21.67 '06, 100mh 13.89 '06, HJ 1.75 '06, Hep 5370w/5320 '06.

Antoinette NANA DJIMOU Ida b. 2 Aug 1985 Douala, Cameroon 1.74m 69kg. CA Montreuil.
At Hep: OG: '08- 18, '12- 5; WCh: '07-09-11-13: dnf/7/7/8; EC: '06-10-12-14: 21/dnf/1/1; WJ: '04- 4; EU23: '05- 5, '07- 7; ECp: '08- 2, '14- 2. At Pen: WI: '10- 4; EI: '09-11-13-15: 3/1/1/5. Won French LJ 2008, Hep 2006-07.
CMR heptathlon record 2003, French indoor pentathlon record 2011.
Progress at Hep: 2003- 5360, 2004- 5649, 2005- 6089w/5792, 2006- 5981, 2007- 5982, 2008- 6204, 2009- 6323, 2010- 5994, 2011- 6409, 2012- 6576, 2013- 6326, 2014- 6551. pbs: 60m 7.51i '11, 100m 11.78 '08, 200m 24.36 '11, 800m 2:15.22 '14, 60mh 8.11i '10, 100mh 12.96 '12, HJ 1.84i '10, 1.83 '11; LJ 6.44i '09, 6.42 '12, 6.61w '08; SP 15.41i/14.84 '13, JT 57.27 '12, Pen 4723i '11.

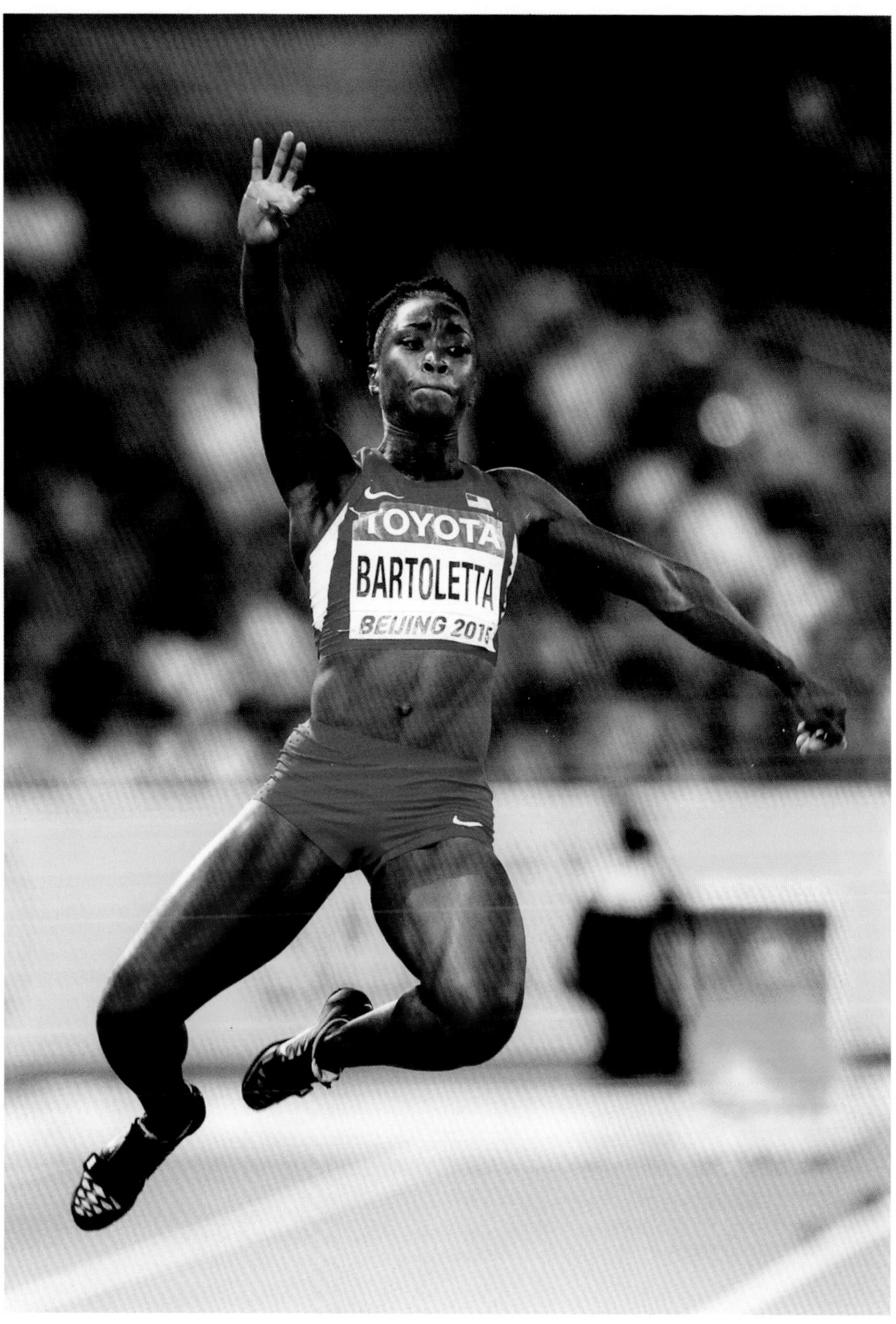

Ten years after winning the World long jump in 2005, Tianna Bartoletta regained that title, with a last round 7.14 in Beijing.

Yarisley Silva came through strongly for the top two women's vault marks of the year, 4.91 at Beckum and 4.90 to win the World title.

Julius Yego smashed the African javelin record with 91.39 in Birmingham and 92.72 at the Worlds. At the Worlds with runner up Ihab Abdelrahman El Sayed (right) and Tero Pitkämäki

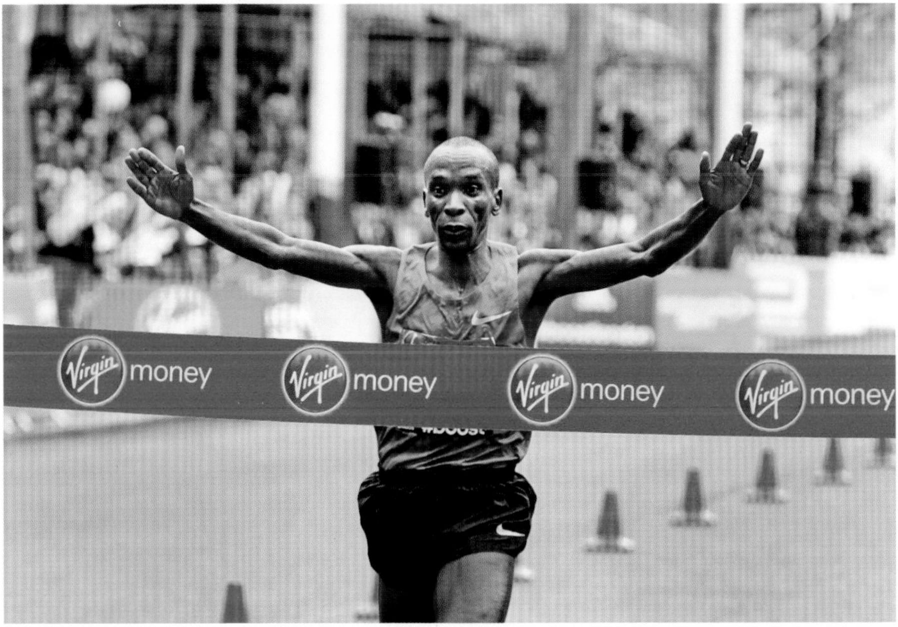

Eliud Kipchoge showed that he is the world's top marathoner with wins in London (above) and Berlin.

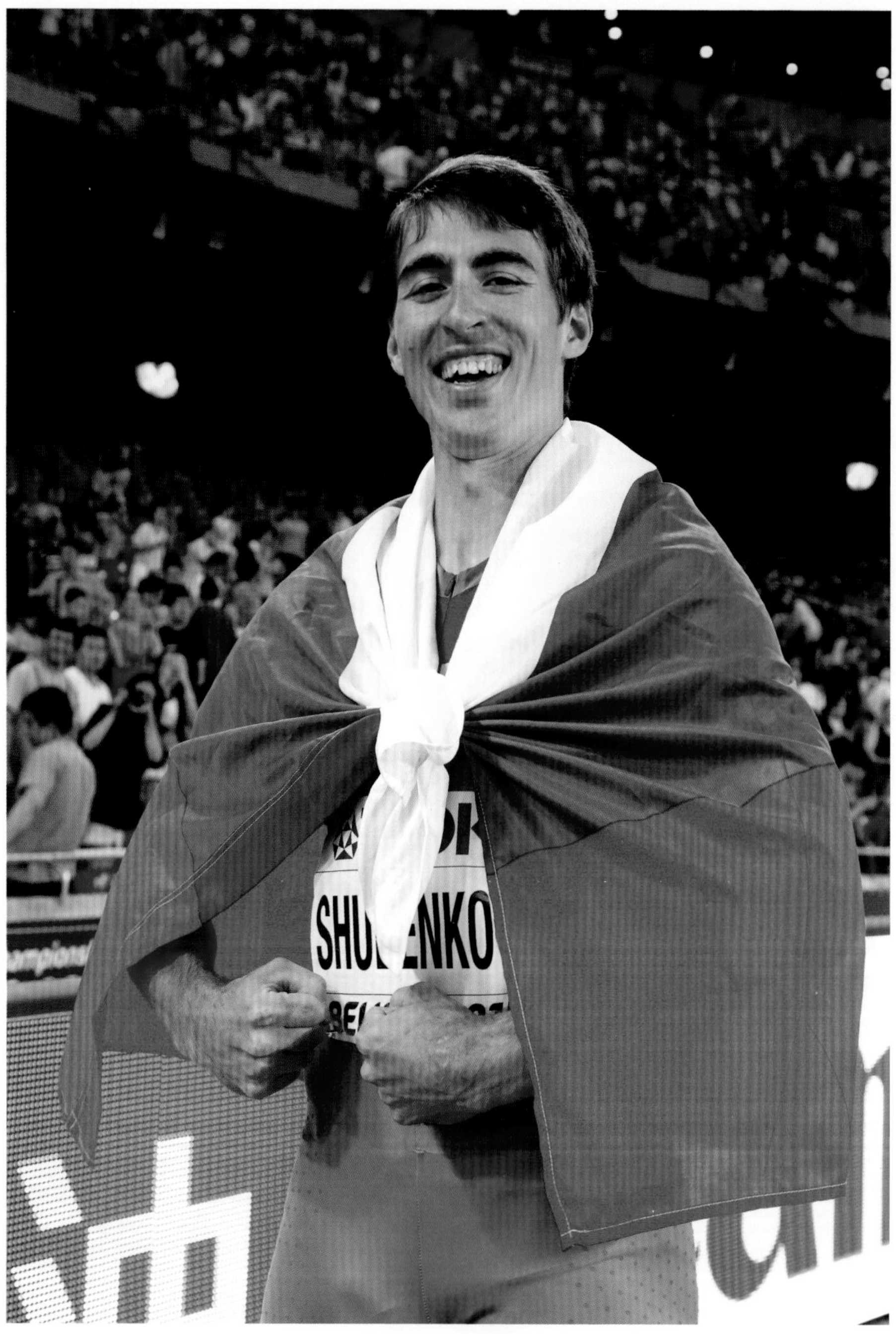

Sergey Shubenkov surprised the Americans with a fluent 110m hurdles win in a Russian record 12.98 at the Worlds.

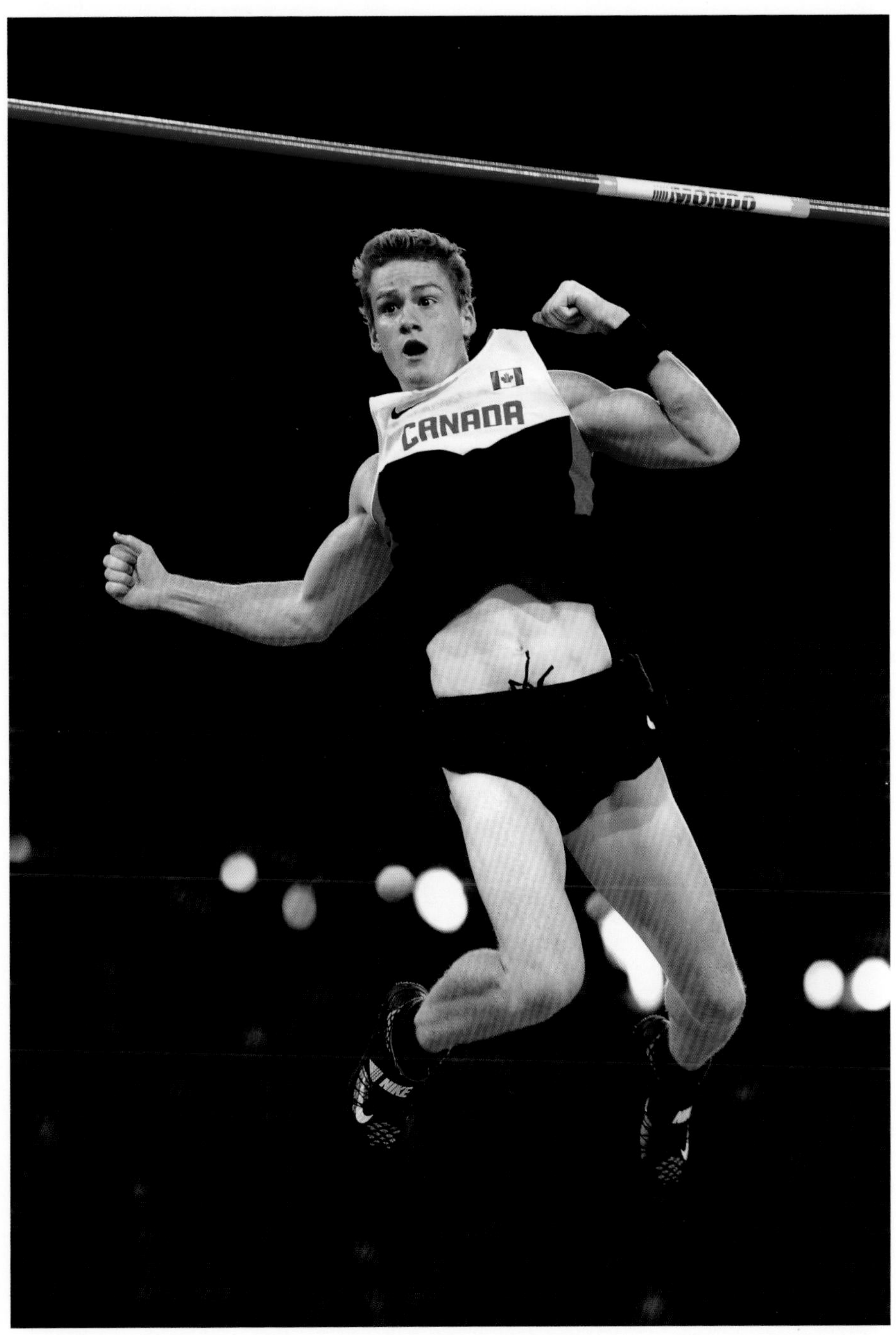

Shawn Barber set five Canadian records indoors and three outdoors in 2015, before becoming a 6m vaulter in January 2016.

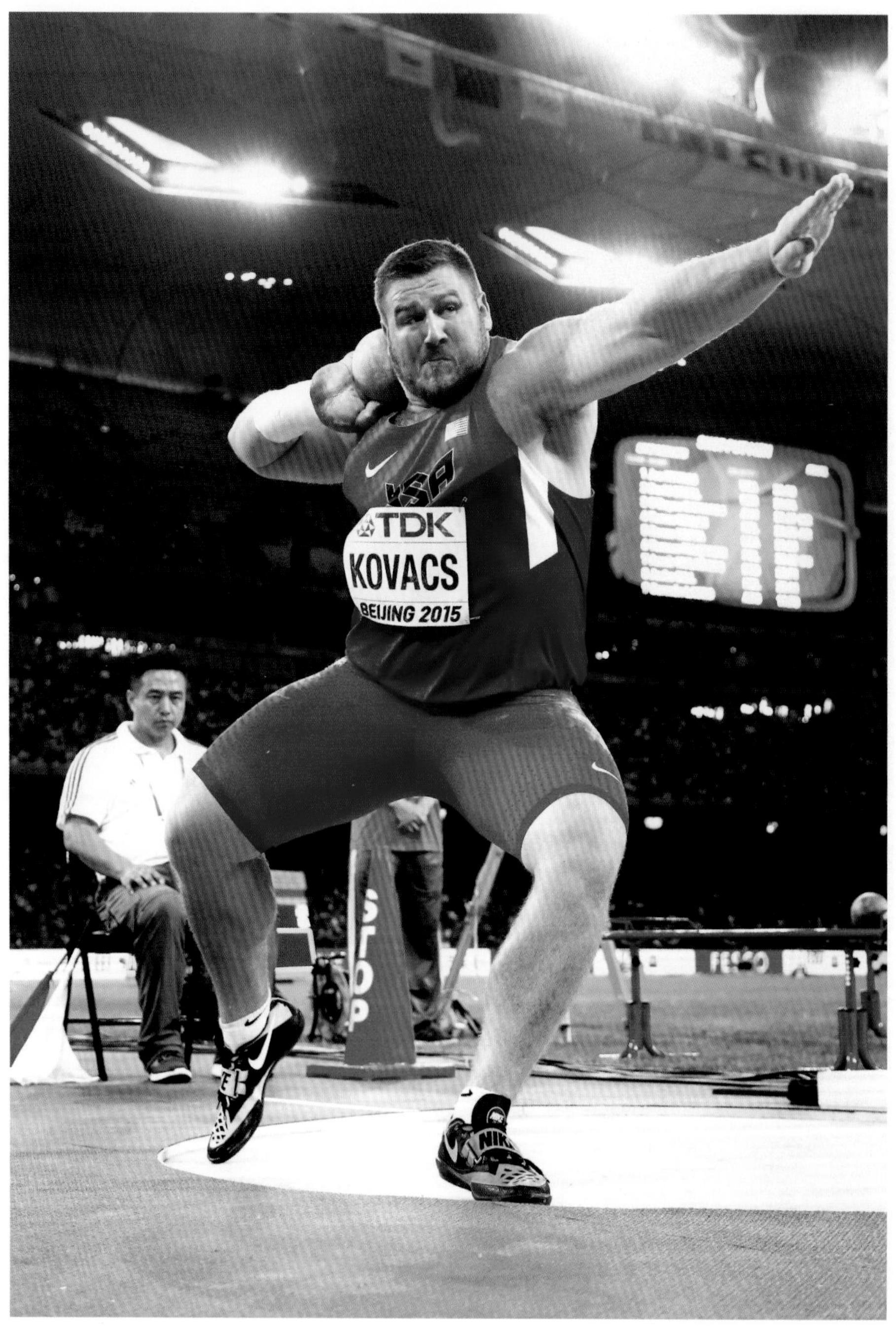

Joe Kovacs was the world top shot putter and his 22.56 was the world's best since 2003.

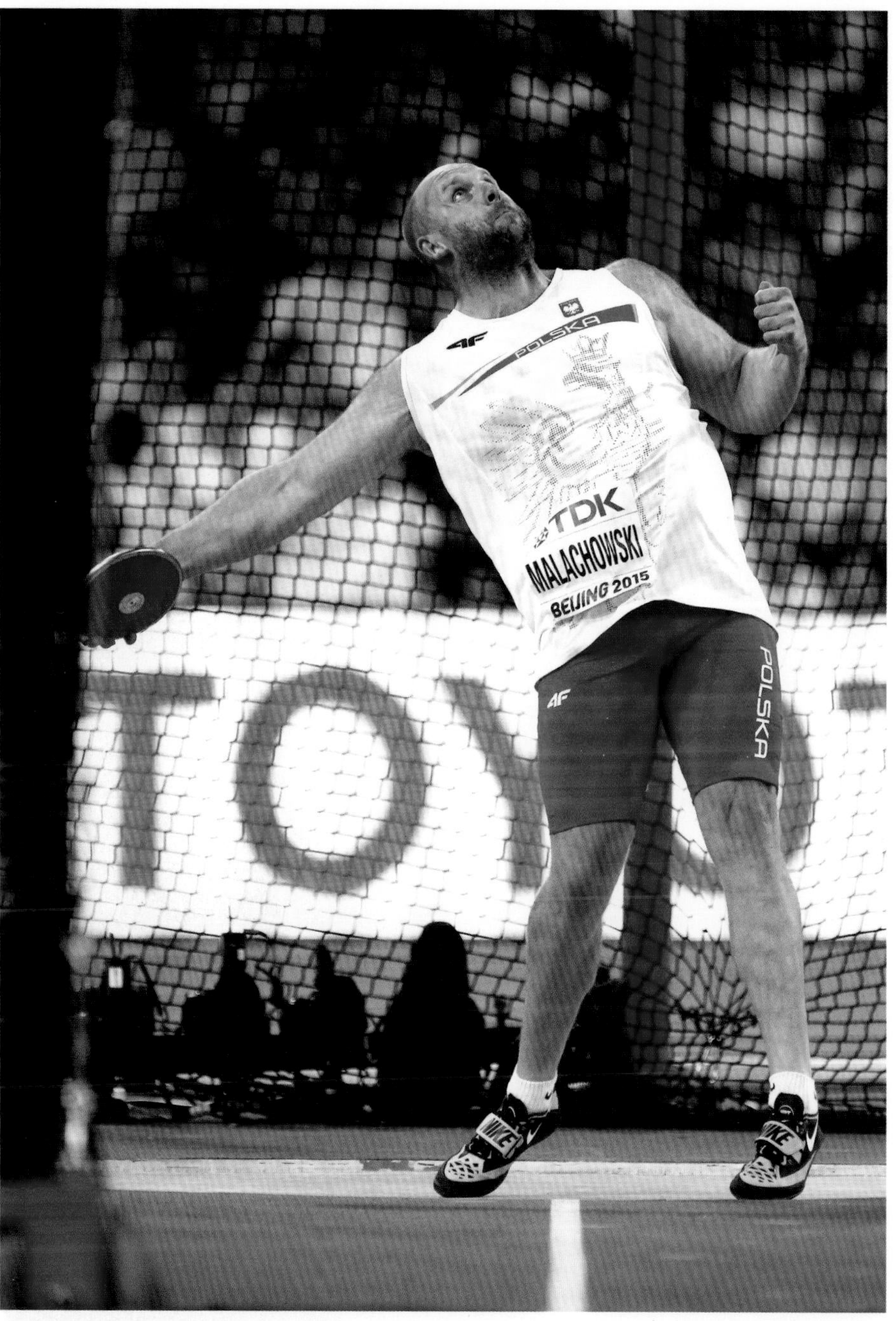

After nine years in the world top ten (three at second) Piotr Malachowski finally hit the top and took the World title.

The greatest Chinese success at the Worlds in Beijing came in the women's 20k walk in which Liu Hong beat Lu Xiuzhi by a stride.

Came to France at age 14, naturalised French citizen in 2004. Three pbs when winning European gold in 2012.

Mélina ROBERT-MICHON b. 18 Jul 1979 Voiron 1.80m 85kg. Lyon Athlétisme

At DT: OG: '00/04- dnq 29/30, '08- 8, '12- 5; WCh: '01-03-07-09-13-15: dnq 20/11/11/8/2/10; EC: '98-02-06-12-14: dnq 29/12/dnq 16/6/2; WJ: '98- 2; EU23: '99-12, '01- 1; WUG: '01- 3; CCp: '14- 4; ECp: '00-01-02-03-04-06-07-08-09-13-14-15: 5/6/8/2/4/7/5/4/2/1/1/1. French champion 2000-09, 2011-15; MedG 2009.

Five French discus records 2000-13.

Progress at DT: 1997- 49.10, 1998- 59.27, 1999- 60.17, 2000- 63.19/63.61dh, 2001- 63.87, 2002- 65.78, 2003- 64.27, 2004- 64.54, 2005- 58.01, 2006- 59.89, 2007- 63.48, 2008- 62.21, 2009- 63.04, 2010- 56.52, 2011- 61.07, 2012- 63.98, 2013- 66.28, 2014- 65.51, 2015- 65.04. pbs: SP 15.23 '07, HT 47.92 '02.

Daughter Elyssa born in 2010. Broke her 11 year-old French record in winning 2013 World silver.

Alexandra TAVERNIER b. 13 Dec 1993 Annecy 1.70m 82kg. Annecy Haute Savoie.

At HT: WCh: '15- 3; EC: '14- 6; WJ: '12- 1; EU23: '15- 1; EJ: '11- 6; ET: '15- 3. FRA champion 2014.

Progress at HT: 2009- 44.96, 2010- 58.44, 2011- 62.13, 2012- 70.62, 2013- 70.79, 2014- 71.17, 2015- 74.39. Pbs: SP 11.81 '14, DT 41.58 '10.

GERMANY

Governing body: Deutscher Leichtathletik Verband (DLV), Alsfelder Str. 27, 64289 Darmstadt. Founded 1898.

National Championships first held in 1891. **2015 Champions**: **Men**: 100m/200m: Julian Reus 10.12/20.42, 400m: Eric Krüger 46.05, 800m: Dennis Krüger 1:48.93, 1500m: Florian Orth 3:44.61, 5000m: Richard Ringer 14:04.05, 10000m: Jannik Arbogast 29:23.13, HMar: Philipp Pflieger 64:13, Mar: Arne Gabius 2:08:33, 3000mSt: Martin Grau 8:41.50, 110mh: Gregor Traber 13.32, 400mh: Jonas Hanßen 49.97, HJ: David Nopper 2.25, PV: Raphael Holzdeppe 5.94, LJ: Fabian Heinle 8.03, TJ: Raul Spanl 16.29, SP: David Storl 21.47, DT: Christoph Harting 64.06, HT: Alexander Ziegler 73.91, JT: Thomas Röhler 84.73, Dec: *not held*, 10000W: Christopher Linke 39:04.82; 20kW: Nils Brembach 1:21:21, 50kW: Carl Dohmann 3:50:12. **Women**: 100m: Verena Sailer 11.20, 200m: Rebekka Haase 22.95, 400m: Ruth Sophia Spelmeyer 52.41, 800m: Fabienne Kohlmann 1:59.28, 1500m: Maren Kock 4:09.25, 5000m: Alina Reh 15:51.48, 10000m: Isabell Teegen 34:22.73, HMar: Simret Restle-Apel 74:37, Mar: Lisa Hahner 2:28:39, 3000mSt: Gesa-Felicitas Krause 9:32.20, 100mh: Cindy Roleder 13.05, 400mh: Jackie Baumann 57.18, HJ: Marie-Laurence Jungfleisch 1.95, PV: Lisa Ryzih 4.60, LJ: Lena Malkus 6.74, TJ: Kristin Gierisch 14.38, SP: Christina Schwanitz 20.00, DT: Julia Fischer 65.98, HT: Betty Heidler 75.34, JT: Katharina Molitor 65.40, Hep: *not held*, 5000W: Lea Dederichs 23:45.38, 20kW: Lea Dederichs 1:41:40.

Arthur ABELE b. 30 Jul 1986 Mutlangen, Baden-Württemberg 1.84m 80kg. SSV Ulm 1846.

At Dec: OG: '08- dnf; WCh: '07- 9; EC: '14- 5; WJ: '04- 7; EJ: '05- 2; ECp: '04- 4. German champion 2013. At Hep: '15- 2.

Progress at Dec: 2006- 8012, 2007- 8269, 2008- 8372, 2013- 8251, 2014- 8477. pbs: 60m 6.93i '15, 100m 10.67 '14, 200m 22.41 '14, 400m 47.98 '08, 1000m 2:35.64i '15, 1500m 4:15.35 '08, 60mh 7.67i '15, 110mh 13.55 '14, 400mh 51.71 '04, HJ 2.04 '07, PV 5.01 '14, LJ 7.56i '15, 7.55 '14; SP 15.54i '15, 15.39 '14; DT 44.69 '14, JT 69.53 '13, Hep 6279i '15.

Five individual event absolute bests in 2015 European Indoor heptathlon, but Achilles injury cost him the summer season.

Pascal BEHRENBRUCH b. 19 Jan 1985 Offenbach 1.96m 94kg. LG Eintracht Frankfurt.

At Dec: OG: '12- 10; WCh: '09- 6, '11- 7, '13- 11; EC: '06- 5, '12- 1; EJ: '03- 10; EU23: '07- 2. At Hep: WI: '14- 8.

Progress at Dec: 2005- 7842, 2006- 8209, 2007- 8239, 2008- 8242, 2009- 8439, 2010- 8202, 2011- 8232, 2012- 8558, 2013- 8514, 2014- 8055, 2015- 7826. pbs: 60m 7.08i '10, 100m 10.84 '07, 10.73w '13; 400m 48.40 '13, 1000m 2:53.39i '06, 1500m 4:24.16 '06, 60mh 8.10i '10, 110mh 14.02 '09, HJ 2.03 '08, PV 5.00 '12, LJ 7.21 '11, 7.32w '07, SP 16.89 '12, DT 51.31 '09, JT 71.40 '11, Hep 5604i '06.

Rico FREIMUTH b. 14 Mar 1988 Potsdam 1.96m 92kg. SV Halle.

At Dec: OG: '12- 6; WCh: '11- dnf, '13- 7; EC: '14- 7; EU23: 09- 10; EJ: '07- 3.

Progress at Dec: 2009- 7689, 2010- 7826, , '15- 32011- 8287, 2012- 8322, 2013- 8488w/8382, 2014- 8356, 2015- 8561. pbs: 60m 6.98i '12, 100m 10.40 '14, 10.36w '13; 200m 21.39 '12, 400m 47.51 '12, 1000m 2:48.22i '12, 1500m 4:34.60 '13, 60mh 7.83i '14, 110mh 13.63 '14, HJ 1.99 '13, PV 4.90 '12, LJ 7.55 '13, SP 15.62 '15, DT 50.37 '14, JT 65.04 '11, Hep 5715i '12.

Won IAAF Combined Events Challenge 2014. His father Uwe had decathlon best of 8794 (1984), and was 4th at 1983 Worlds and 1986 Europeans and twice winner at Götzis. Uwe and Rico are the highest scoring father-son combination. His uncle Jörg won the high jump bronze medal at the 1980 Olympic Games in a pb of 2.31.

Christoph HARTING b. 4 Oct 1990 Cottbus 2.05m 117kg. SCC Berlin. Police officer.

At DT: WCh: '13- dnq 13, '15- 8; EU23: '11- 5. German champion 2015.

Progress at DT: 2008- 52.00, 2009- 50.19, 2010- 61.19, 2011- 62.12, 2012- 61.22, 2013- 64.99, 2014- 63.78, 2015- 67.93. pb SP 17.75 '12.

Robert HARTING b. 18 Oct 1984 Cottbus 2.01m 126kg. SCC Berlin.
At DT: OG: 08- 4, '12- 1; WCh: '07-09-11-13: 2/1/1/1; ECh: '06-10-12-14: dnq 13/2/1/1; CCp: '10- 1; ECp: '07-08-09-10-11-13-14: 2/2/2/1/1/1/1; WJ: '02- dnq 13; WY: '01- 2; EU23: '05- 1. German champion 2007-14.
Progress at DT: 2002- 54.25, 2003- 59.54, 2004- 64.05, 2005- 66.02, 2006- 65.22, 2007- 66.93, 2008- 68.65, 2009- 69.43, 2010- 69.69, 2011- 68.99, 2012- 70.66, 2013- 69.91, 2014- 68.47. pb SP 18.63 '07.
35 successive wins 2011-13. Brother of Christoph (qv). His father Gert had pbs SP 16.05, DT 42.80 '88, and mother Bettina SP 15.04 and DT 43.06 '80.

Max HESS b. 13 Jul 1996 1.85m 77kg. LAC Erdgas Chemnitz.
At TJ: WJ: '14- 2; WY: '13- 8; WI: '16- 2.
Progress at TJ: 2012- 14.58, 2013- 15.52, 2014- 16.55, 2015- 16.34i/16.07, 2016- 17.14i. pbs: 60m 6.98i '16, LJ 8.03i '16.

Andreas HOFMANN b. 16 Dec 1991 Heidelberg 1.95m 108kg. MTG Mannheim. Sports student.
At JT: WCh: '15- 6; EC: '14- 19; EJ: '09- 1; ET: '11- 1.
Progress at JT: 2008- 65.03, 2009- 77.84, 2010- 66.75, 2011- 73.98, 2012- 80.81, 2013- 75.56, 2014- 86.13, 2015- 86.14. pb SP 17.21i '15.

Raphael HOLZDEPPE b. 28 Sep 1989 Kaiserslautern 1.81m 78kg. LAZ Zweibrücken.
At PV: OG: 08- 8, '12- 3; WCh: '11- dnq 20, '13- 1, '15- 2; EC '10- 9, '12- 3; WJ: '06- 5, '08- 1; EU23: '09- 1; EJ: '07- dnq; ET: '15- 2; EI: '13- 8. GER champion 2015.
World junior pole vault record (=) 2008 (and indoors 5.68).
Progress at PV: 2002- 3.45, 2003- 4.25, 2004- 4.50, 2005- 5.00, 2006- 5.42, 2007- 5.50, 2008- 5.80, 2009- 5.65, 2010- 5.80, 2011- 5.72, 2012- 5.91, 2013- 5.91, 2014- 5.53, 2015- 5.94.

Kai KAZMIREK b. 28 Jan 1991 Torgau 1.89m 91kg. LG Rhein-Wied.
At Dec: WCh: '15- 6; EC: '14- 6; WJ: '10- 6; EU23: '11- 6, '13- 1; EJ: '09- 3. German champion 2012. At Hep: WI: '14- 6.
Progress at Dec: 2011- 7802, 2012- 8130, 2013- 8366, 2014- 8471, 2015- 8462. pbs: 60m 7.01i '15, 100m 10.75 '14, 10.61w '13; 200m 21.40 '12, 400m 46.75 '11, 1000m 2:39.51i '14, 1500m 4:33.78 '14, 60mh 8.00i '14, 110mh 14.05 '14, HJ 2.15 '14, PV 5.20 '13, LJ 7.68 '14, SP 14.53i '16, 14.34 '14; DT 45.83 '15, JT 64.45 '15, Hep 6173i '13.
Won Götzis decathlon 2015.

Jan Felix KNOBEL b. 16 Jan 1989 Bad Homburg 1.92m 91kg. LG Eintracht Frankfurt. Architecture student.
At Dec: OG: '12- dnf; WCh: '11- 8; WJ: '06- 1; EU23: '11- 19. German champion 2009. At Oct: WY: 05- 5.
Progress at Dec: 2009- 7758, 2010- dnf, 2011- 8288, 2012- 8228, 2013- 8396w, 2015- 8045. pbs: 60m 7.18i '10, 100m 11.04 '12, 10.85w '13; 400m 48.89 '12, 1000m 2:49.22i '10, 1500m 4:43.12 '11, 60mh 8.20i '14, 110mh 14.59 '13, HJ 2.01 '11, PV 5.06 '15, LJ 7.37 '15, SP 16.42i '15, 16.06 '11; DT 50.87 '13, JT 76.36 '13, Hep 5778i '10.

Malte MOHR b. 24 Jul 1986 Bochum 1.92m 84kg. TV Wattenscheid.
At PV: OG: '12- 9=; WCh: '09- 14, '11- 5, '13- 5; EC: '10- dnq 17=, '12- 4; WI: '10-12-14: 2/4/2; EI: '11- 3, 13- 3; ET: '09- 2, '11- 2. Won GER 2010-12.
Progress at PV: 2003- 4.81, 2004- 5.11i, 2005- 5.30, 2006- 5.71, 2007- 5.31, 2008- 5.76, 2009- 5.80, 2010- 5.90, 2011- 5.86i/5.85, 2012- 5.91, 2013- 5.86, 2014- 5.90i/5.70.
His father (and coach) Wolfgang Mohr had a best of 5.41 in 1976 and his mother Gisela Derksen was a good junior multi-eventer.

Thomas RÖHLER b. 30 Sep 1991 Jena 1.95m 83kg. LC Jena. Sports student.
At JT: WCh: '13- dnq 29, '15- 4; EC: '12- dnq 13, '14- 12; WJ: '10- 9; EU23: '11- 7, '13- 3; ET: '13- 2. Won DL 2014, German champion 2012-15.
Progress at JT: 2009- 61.26, 2010- 76.37, 2011- 78.20, 2012- 80.79, 2013- 83.95, 2014- 87.63, 2015- 89.27.

Tobias SCHERBARTH b. 17 Aug 1985 Leipzig 1.95m 84kg. TSV Bayer 04 Leverkusen.
At PV: WCh: '15- 7=; EC: '14- dnq; EU23: '05- dnq, '07- 5. German champion 2014.
Progress at PV: 2002- 4.20, 2003- 4.60, 2004- 4.80, 2005- 5.42, 2006- 5.55, 2007- 5.60, 2008- 5.75i/5.61, 2009- 5.76i/5.70, 2010- 5.71, 2011- 5.30, 2012- 5.61, 2013- 5.75i/5.70, 2014- 5.73, 2015- 5.70.

Michael SCHRADER b. 1 Jul 1987 Duisberg-Homburg 1.86m 84kg. SC Hessen Dreieich.
At Dec: OG: '08- 10; WCh: '13- 2, '15- 7; EU23: '07- 6. German champion 2010.
Progress at Dec: 2007- 7947, 2008- 8248, 2009- 8522, 2010- 8003, 2013- 8670, 2015- 8419. pbs: 100m 10.52 '13, 200m 21.70 '09, 400m 47.12 '15, 1500m 4:19.32 '08, 110mh 14.02 '13, HJ 2.00 '12, PV 5.10 '13, LJ 8.05 '09, SP 14.88 '15, DT 47.19 '15, JT 65.67 '13.
Won Götzis decathlon with seven pbs 2009, set three pbs when adding 148 points to pb for World silver 2013.

David STORL b. 21 Jul 1990 Rochlitz 1.99m 122kg. Leipzig SC DHfK. Federal police officer.
At SP: OG: '12- 2; WCh: '09- dnq 27, '11- 1, '13- 1, '15- 2; EC: '10-12-14: 4/1/1; WJ: '08- 1; WY: '07- 1; EU23: '11- 1; EJ: '09- 1; WI: '10-13-14: 6/2/2; EI: '11- 2, '15- 1; WCp: '14- 1; ET: '11-13-14-15: 1/1/1/1. German champion 2011-12, 2014-15.
World junior shot record and three with 6kg (to 22.73) 2009.
Progress at SP: 2008- 18.46, 2009- 20.43, 2010- 20.77, 2011- 21.78, 2012- 21.88i/21.86, 2013- 21.73, 2014- 21.97, 2015- 22.20.
9 major international titles plus 5 second places.

Homiyu TESFAYE Heyi b. 23 Jun 1993 Debre Zeyit, Ethiopia 1.83m 66kg. LG Eintracht Frankfurt.
At 1500m: WCh: '13- 5; EC: '14- 5; WI: '14- 7; EI: '15- 4; ET: '14- 2.
European U23 1500m record 2014.
Progress at 1500m: 2011- 3:46.02, 2012- 3:38.56, 2013- 3:34.18, 2014- 3:31.98, 2015- 3:34.13i. pbs: 800m 1:46.40 '13, 1000m 2:17.56 '14, 1M 3:49.86 '14, 3000m 7:58.09i '14, 8:03.95 '12; 5000m 13:58.73 '13, 10000m 29:08.44 '13, Rd 10k 27:54 '15. Claimed asylum in Germany in 2010, and German citizen from 27 Jun 2013.

Johannes VETTER b. 26 Mar 1993 Dresden 1.88m 105kg. LG Offenburg.
At JT: WCh: '15- 7; EU23: '15- 4; EJ: '11- 12.
Progress at JT: 2010- 63.60, 2011- 71.60, 2012- 60.19, 2013- 76.58, 2014- 79.75, 2015- 85.40.

Martin WIERIG b. 10 Jun 1987 Neindorf 2.02m 108kg. SC Magdeburg. Federal police officer.
At DT: OG: '12- 6; WCh: '11- dnq 18, '13- 4, '15- dnq 19; EC: '10- 12-14: 7/dnq 14/11; WJ: '04- 8, '06- 3; EU23: '07- 1, '09- 3; EJ: '05- 3 (dnq SP); ET: '15- 2.
Progress at DT: 2005- 57.44, 2006- 57.37, 2007- 61.10, 2008- 63.09, 2009- 63.90, 2010- 64.93, 2011- 67.21, 2012- 68.33, 2013- 67.46, 2014- 66.59, 2015- 65.94. pb SP 17.30 '11.

Women

Shanice CRAFT b. 15 May 1993 Mannheim 1.85m 89kg. MTG Mannheim. Police officer.
At (SP)/DT: WCh: '15- 7; EC: '14- 3; WJ: '12- 1/2; WY: '09- 3; EU23: '13- 2/2, '15- 2/1; EJ: '11- 1; ET: '14- 2. Won GER 2014, Yth Oly 2010,
Progress at DT: 2007- 44.86, 2008- 48.14, 2009- 50.57, 2010- 55.49, 2011- 58.65, 2012- 62.92, 2013- 60.77, 2014- 65.88, 2015- 64.79. Pb SP 17.75 '14.

Julia FISCHER b. 1 Apr 1990 Berlin 1.92m 95kg. SCC Berlin. Police officer.
At DT: OG: '12- dnq 20; WCh: '13- dnq 13, '15- 5; EC: '12- 5, '14- 5; WJ: '08- 2; WY: '07- 1; EU23: '11- 1; EJ: '09- 2; ET: '13- 2. GER champion 2015.
Progress at DT: 2005- 45.69, 2006- 50.23, 2007- 51.39, 2008- 55.92, 2009- 56.74, 2010- 57.49, 2011- 59.60, 2012- 64.22, 2013- 66.04, 2014- 66.46, 2015- 65.98.

Kristin GIERISCH b. 20 Aug 1990 Zwickau 1.78m 59kg. LAC Erdgas Chemnitz. Police.
At TJ: WCh: '15- 8; EC: '14- 9; WY: '07- 6; EU23: '11- dns; EJ: '09- 5; EI: '15- 4; ET: '15- 2; WI: '14- 2. German champion 2014-15.
Progress at TJ: 2006- 12.09, 2007- 13.00, 2008- 12.22, 2009- 14.02, 2010- 13.84, 2011- 14.10i/13.47, 2012- 14.19i/13.94, 2013- 13.91i/13.67, 2014- 14.31/14.34w, 2015- 14.46i/14.38/14.46w, 2016- 14.30i. pbs: 60m 7.59i '12, LJ 6.46i '15, 6.21 '14.

Betty HEIDLER b. 14 Oct 1983 Berlin 1.75m 80kg. LG Eintracht Frankfurt. Federal police officer.
At HT: OG: '04- 4, '08- 9, '12- 3; WCh: '03-05-07-09-11-13-15: 11/dnq 29/1/2/2/dnq 18/7; EC: '06-10-12-14: 5/1/dnq 16/5; EU23: '03- 4, '05- 2; WJ: '00/02- dnq 19/17; EJ: '01- 9, WUG: '09- 1; CCp: '10- 4; ECp: '04-07-09-10-11-13-14-15: 3/1/2/1/1/1/1/2. Won WAF 2006, 2009; IAAF HT challenge 2010-12, German 2005-13, 2015.
World hammer record 2011, seven German records 2004-11.
Progress at HT: 1999- 42.07, 2000- 56.02, 2001- 60.54, 2002- 63.38, 2003- 70.42, 2004- 72.73, 2005- 72.19, 2006- 76.55, 2007- 75.77, 2008- 74.11, 2009- 77.12, 2010- 76.38, 2011- 79.42, 2012- 78.07, 2013- 76.48, 2014- 78.00, 2015- 75.73.

Christin HUSSONG b. 17 Apr 1994 Zweibrücken 1.87m 82kg. LAZ Zweibrücken. Sports student
At JT: WCh: '6; EC: '14- 7; WJ: '12- 7; WY: '11- 1; EU23: '13- 2, '15- 1; EJ: '13- 2, YthOG: '10- 4.
Progress at JT: 2009- 49.93, 2010- 55.35, 2011- 59.74, 2012- 55.74, 2013- 58.55, 2014- 63.34, 2015- 65.92. Pbs: SP 15.02i '14, 14.02 '11.

Marie-Laurence JUNGFLEISCH b. 7 Oct 1990 Paris, France 1.81m 68kg. VfB Stuttgart. Soldier.
At HJ: WCh: '13- nh, '15- 6; EC: '14- 5; EU23: '11- 8; ET: '15- 3; EJ: '09- 6. Won GER 2013-15.
Progress at HJ: 2006- 1.70, 2007- 1.75, 2008- 1.78, 2009- 1.86, 2010- 1.90, 2011- 1.93, 2012- 1.95, 2013- 1.95, 2014- 1.97, 2015- 1.99.

Kathrin KLAAS b. 6 Feb 1984 Haiger 1.68m 72kg. LG Eintracht Frankfurt. Police inspector.
At HT: OG: '08- dnq 24, '12- 5; WCh: '05-07-13: dnq -/ 27/20, '09-11-15: 4/7/6; EC: '06-10-12-14: 6/ dnq 15/4/4; EJ: '03-8, EU23: '05- 4; WUG: '09- 3. German champion 2014.
Progress at HT: 2000- 44.24, 2001- 50.10, 2002- 57.74, 2003- 63.72, 2004- 68.01, 2005- 70.91, 2006- 71.67, 2007- 73.45, 2008- 70.39, 2009- 74.23, 2010- 74.53, 2011- 75.48, 2012- 76.05, 2013- 72.57, 2014- 74.62, 2015- 73.18.

Fabienne KOHLMANN b. 6 Nov1989 Würzburg 1.70m 57kg. LG Karlstadt/Gambach/Lohr. Psychology student..
At 800m: WCh: '15- sf; WUG: '15- 3. At 400m: OG: '12- hR; WJ: '08- 9. At 400mh: EC: '10- sf; EU23: '09- sf; EJ: '07- 1; won GER 800m 2013, 2015; 400mh 2010.
Progress at 800m: 2005- 2:10.07, 2007- 2:05.32, 2010- 2:00.72, 2011- 2:10.14, 2012- 2:06.28, 2013- 2:03.61, 2014- 2:01.70, 2015- 1:58.34. pbs: 100m 12.17 '05, 200m 24.61 '07, 400m 52.30 '10, 600m 1:26.10 '14 400mh 55.49 '10.
Sister Corinne pb 400m 54.55 '13, 3R EJ 4x400m 2013.

Gesa Felicitas KRAUSE b. 3 Aug 1992 Ehringshausen 1.67m 55kg. LG Eintracht Frankfurt. Student.
At 3000mSt: OG: '12- 7; WCh: '11- 6, '13- 9, '15- 3; EC: '12- 3, '14- 5; WJ: '10- 4; EU23: '13- 1; EJ: '11- 1; ET: 15- 1; GER champion 2015. At 2000mSt: WY:

'09- 7. At 1500m: EI: '15- 5.
European junior 3000mSt record 2011, two German 2000m Steeple 2015.
Progress at 3000mSt: 2010- 9:47.78, 2011- 9:32.74, 2012- 9:23.52, 2013- 9:37.11, 2014- 9:35.46, 2015- 9:19.25. pbs: 800m 2:05.25 '11, 1000m 2:44.68 '10, 1500m 4:08.91i '16, 4:11.03 '15; 3000m 8:49.43i '16, 9:02.04 '15; 5k Rd 16:15 '11, 10k Rd 33:26 '15, 2000mSt 6:04.20 '15.

Lena MALKUS b. 6 Aug 1993 Bremen 1.80m 72kg. SC Preußen Münster. Psychology student.
At LJ: WCh: '13/15- dnq 17/22; WJ: '12- 2; EU23: '13- 1; EJ: '11- 1; Yth Oly: '10- 1. German champion 2015.
Progress at LJ: 2008- 6.01, 2009- 6.33, 2010- 6.44, 2011- 6.70, 2012- 6.72/6.80w, 2013- 6.76, 2014- 6.88, 2015- 6.94. pbs: 60m 7.66i '09, 100m 11.88 '09, 200m 23.65 '15.
Mother Ruth Holzhausen played on 1984 German Olympic volleyball team.

Malaika MIHAMBO b. 3 Feb 1994 Heidelberg 1.70m 52kg. LG Kurpfalz. Political science student at Mannheim University.
At LJ: WCh: '13- dnq 14, '15- 6; EC: '14- 4; WJ: '12- dnq 14; WY: '11- 9; EU23: '15- 1; EJ: '13- 1; ET: '14- 1.
Progress at LJ: 2008- 5.55, 2009- 5.81, 2010- 5.96, 2011- 6.40, 2012- 6.45i/6.32/6.50w, 2013- 6.70/6.80w, 2014- 6.90, 2015- 6.84. pbs: 200m 23.96 '15, HJ 1.78i/1.75 '10.Tanzanian father, German mother.

Sosthene Taroum **MOGUENARA** b. 17 Oct 1989 Sarh, Moyen-Chari, Chad 1.82m 68kg. LG LAZ Saar 05 Saarbrücken.
At LJ: OG: '12- dnq 20; WCh: '11- dnq 31, '13- 12, '15- dnq 27; EC: '12- 4, '14- 9; EU23: '09- 4, '11- 3; ET: '15- 3; EI: '15- 2. German champion 2013.
Progress at LJ: 2007- 6.22, 2008- 6.37, 2009- 6.61/6.69w, 2010- 6.65, 2011- 6.83, 2012- 6.88, 2013- 7.04, 2014- 6.82, 2015- 6.94. pbs: 60m 7.66i '08, 100m 11.94 '10, 200m 24.85 '07.
Has lived in Germany from the age of nine.

Katharina MOLITOR b. 8 Nov 1983 Bedurg, Erft 1.82m 76kg. TSV Bayer 04 Leverkusen.
At JT: OG: '08- 8, 12- 6; WCh: '11- 5, '13- dnq 13, '15- 1; EC: '10-12-14: 4/5/9; EU23: '05- 2; WUG: '07- 6, '09- 4. German champion 2010, 2015.
Progress at JT: 2000- 42.94, 2001- 48.53, 2002- 49.01, 2003- 48.03, 2004- 50.04, 2005- 57.01, 2006- 57.58, 2007- 58.87, 2008- 61.74, 2009- 62.69, 2010- 64.53, 2011- 64.67, 2012- 63.20, 2013- 63.55, 2014- 63.40, 2015- 67.69.
Played volleyball in the Bundesliga.

Nadine MÜLLER b. 21 Nov 1985 Leipzig 1.93m 90kg. Hallesche LA-Freunde. Federal police officer.
At DT: OG: '12- 4; WCh: '07-09-11-13-15: dnq 23/6/2/4/3; EC: '10- 8, '12- 2; WJ: '04- 3; EU23: '05- 10, '07- 8; EJ: '03- 2; ET: '10- 1. German champion 2010-13.
Progress at DT: 2000- 36.10, 2001- 46.27, 2002- 48.90, 2003- 53.44, 2004- 57.85, 2005- 59.35, 2006- 58.46, 2007- 62.93, 2008- 61.36, 2009- 63.46, 2010- 67.78, 2011- 66.99, 2012- 68.89, 2013- 66.89, 2014- 67.30, 2015- 65.72.

Christina OBERGFÖLL b. 22 Aug 1981 Lahr (Baden) 1.75m 79kg. LG Offenburg.
At JT: OG: '04- dnq 15, '08- 3, '12- 2; WCh: '05-07-09-11-13-15: 2/2/5/4/1/4; EC: '06-10-12: 4/2/2; EU23: '01- 9, '03- 8; WJ: '00- 8; ECp: '07-09-10-11-13-15: 1/1/1/1/1/1. Won DL 2011, 2013; German 2007-08, 2011-12.
European javelin records 2005 & 2007.
Progress at JT: 1997- 49.20, 1998- 48.52, new: 1999- 50.57, 2000- 54.50, 2001- 56.83, 2002- 60.61, 2003- 57.40, 2004- 63.34, 2005- 70.03, 2006- 66.91, 2007- 70.20, 2008- 69.81, 2009- 68.59, 2010- 68.63, 2011- 69.57, 2012- 67.04, 2013- 69.05, 2015- 64.61.
Made a great breakthrough at the 2005 World Champs to take her pb from 64.59 to a European record 70.03 and the silver medal. Married her coach Boris Henry (JT: 90.44 '97; 3rd Worlds 1995 & 2003, Europeans 2002) on 14 Sep 2013; son Marlon born in June 2014.

Jennifer OESER b. 29 Nov 1983 Brunsbüttel 1.76m 65kg. TSV Bayer 04 Leverkusen. Federal police officer.
At Hep: OG: '08- 11, '12- 29 (dnf 800m); WCh: '07-09-11-15: 7/2/3/10; EC: '06- 4, '10- 3; WJ: '02- 8; EU23: '03- 1. German champion 2006.
Progress at Hep: 2000- 5167, 2001- 5531, 2002- 5595, 2003- 5901, 2004- 5936, 2005- 5637, 2006- 6376, 2007- 6378, 2008- 6436, 2009- 6493, 2010- 6683, 2011- 6663, 2012- 6345, 2015- 6308. pbs: 200m 23.95 '11, 800m 2:10.39 '11, 60mh 8.56i '09, 100mh 13.14 '11, HJ 1.86 '06, LJ 6.68 '10, 6.70w '11; SP 14.29 '09, JT 51.30 '11, Pen 4423i '09.
Four pbs in EC Heptathlon bronze 2010. Son Jakob born on 6 Oct 2014.

Claudia RATH b. 25 Apr 1986 Hadamar, Hessen 1.75m 65kg. LG Eintracht Frankfurt.
At Hep: WCh: '11- 4, '15- 5; EC: '10-12-14: 10/6/8. German champion 2010-11. At WI: '14- 5.
Progress at Hep: 2003- 5231, 2004- 5353, 2005- 5323, 2007- 5274, 2008- 5697, 2009- 5941, 2010- 6107, 2011- 6098, 2012- 6210, 2013- 6462, 2014- 6314, 2015- 6458. pbs: 200m 23.77 '14, 800m 2:06.43 '13, 60mh 8.43i '14, 100mh 13.44 '15, HJ 1.83 '13, LJ 6.84w '15, 6.73 '14; SP 13.78 '14, JT 43.45 '14, Pen 4681i '14.

Cindy ROLEDER b. 21 Aug 1989 Chemnitz 1.78m 68kg. LAZ Leipzig. Police officer.
At 100mh: OG: '12- sf, WCh: '11- sf, '15- 2; EC: '10- h, '12- 6, '14- 3; WJ: '08- sf; EU23: '09- sf, '11- 3; EJ: '07- 4; CCp: '14- 3; ET: '15- 3; GER champion 2011, 2015. At 60mh: WI: '14- 6; EI: '15- 4.
Progress at 100mh: 2007- 13.49, 2008- 13.72, 2009- 13.38, 2010- 12.97, 2011- 12.91, 2012- 12.91, 2013- 13.03/12.93w, 2014- 12.80, 2015- 12.59. pbs: 60m 7.34i '15, 100m 11.72 '13, 150m 17.40 '15, 200m 23.35 '15, 800m 2:15.49 '15, 50mh 7.14+i '10,

60mh 7.93i '15, HJ 1.66 '15, LJ 6.32i '14, 6.17 '13, 6.18w '15; SP 13.25 '15, JT 36.33 '15, Pen 4187i '14, Hep 6055 '15.

Anna RÜH b. 17 Jun 1993 Greifswald 1.86m 78kg. SC Neubrandenburg.
At DT: '12- 9; EC: '12- 4, '14- 4; WJ: '10- dnq 21, '12- 1; EU23: '13- 1, '15- 2; EJ: '11- 2 (3 SP).
Progress at DT: 2009- 44.43, 2010- 51.67, 2011- 59.97, 2012- 63.38, 2013- 64.33, 2014- 64.17, 2015- 66.14. pb SP 17.09i '16, 16.01 '11.

Elisaveta **'Lisa' RYZIH** b. 27 Sep 1988 Omsk, Russia 1.79m 59kg. Formerly Ryshich. ABC Ludwigshafen. Psychology student.
At PV: OG: '12- 6=; WCh: '13- 8=, '15- 12; EC: '10-12-14: 3/7/4; WJ: '04- 1, '06- nh; WY: '03- 1; EU23: '09- 1; EJ: '07- 4; EI: '11- 7; CCp: '10- 2, '14- 3. German champion 2014-15.
Progress at PV: 2002- 3.92, 2003- 4.10, 2004- 4.30, 2005- 4.15, 2006- 4.35, 2007- 4.35, 2008- 4.52i/4.50, 2009- 4.50, 2010- 4.65, 2011- 4.65i, 2012- 4.65, 2013- 4.55, 2014- 4.71, 2015- 4.72i/4.70. pb LJ 5.38w '06.
Set world age bests at 13 in 2002 and 15 in 2004. Her sister 'Nastja' was World Indoor champion in 1999 and set four world junior and five European junior PV records in 1996 to 4.15, and three German records in 1999 to 4.50i/4.44 and had a pb of 4.63 in 2006. Their family left Omsk in Siberia in 1992 to live in Ulm; mother Yekaterina Ryzhikh (née Yefimova b. 20 Jan 1959) had HJ pb 1.91i '85 and 1.89 '81, and father Vladimir is a pole vault coach.

Carolin SCHÄFER b. 5 Dec 1991 Bad Wildungen 1.78m 64kg. TV Friedrichstein.
At Hep: WCh: '15- dnf; EC: '12- 10, '14- 4; WJ: '08- 1; EU23: '11- 5, '13- 6; EJ: '09- 1. German champion 2013.
Progress at Hep: 2007- 5545, 2008- 5833, 2009- 5697, 2010- 5333, 2011- 5941, 2012- 6072, 2013- 5972, 2014- 6395, 2015- 6547. pbs: 60m 7.86i '07, 200m 23.53 '15, 800m 2:14.10 '15, 60mh 8.45i '16, 100mh 13.20 '14, HJ 1.84 '14, LJ 6.30 '14, SP 14.32 '15, JT 49.50 '12, Pen 4098i '09.

Christina SCHWANITZ b. 24 Dec 1985 Dresden 1.80m 103kg. LV 90 Erzebirge. Soldier.
At SP: OG: '08- 11, '12- 10; WCh: '05-09-11-13-15: 7/12/12/2/1; EC: '12- 5, '14- 1; WJ: '04- 3; EU23: '05- 2; WI: '08- 6, '14- 2; EI: '11- 2, '13- 1; CCp: '14- 1; ET: '08-13-14-15: 1/1/1/1. Won DL 2015, German 2011, 2013-15.
Progress at SP: 2001- 13.57, 2002- 14.26, 2003- 15.25, 2004- 16.98, 2005- 18.84, 2007- 17.06, 2008- 19.68i/19.31, 2009- 19.06, 2010- 18.28, 2011- 19.20, 2012- 19.15i/19.05, 2013- 20.41, 2014- 20.22, 2015- 20.77. pb DT 47.27 '03.

Lilli SCHWARZKOPF b. 28 Aug 1983 Novo Pokrovka, Kyrgyzhstan 1.74m 65kg. SSV Ulm 1846. Student.
At Hep: OG: '08- 8, '12- 2; WCh: '05-07-09-11: 13/5/dnf/6; EC: '06- 3, '14- 5; WJ: '02- 5; EU23: '05- 2. German champion 2004.
Progress at Hep: 2001- 5079, 2002- 5597, 2003- 5735, 2004- 6161, 2005- 6146, 2006- 6420, 2007- 6439, 2008- 6536, 2009- 6355, 2010- 6386, 2011- 6370, 2012- 6649, 2014- 6426, 2015- dnf. pbs: 100m 12.22 '10, 200m 24.72 '11, 800m 2:09.63 '06, 60mh 8.46i '10, 100mh 13.26 '12, HJ 1.85 '14, LJ 6.35i/6.34 '07, SP 15.06 '15, JT 55.25 '09, Pen 4641i '08. Has lived in Germany from age 7.

Silke SPIEGELBURG b. 17 Mar 1986 Georgsmarienhütte 1.73m 64kg. TSV Bayer 04 Leverkusen. Economics student.
At PV: OG: '04- 13, '08- 7, '12- 4; WCh: '07-09-11-13-15: nh/4/9/4/dnq 17=; EC: '06-10-12: 6/2/4=; WJ: '02- 8; WY: '01- 1; EU23: '07- 4; EJ: '03- 1, '05- 1; WI: '06-12-14: 8/4/7; EI: '07-09-11: 5/2/2; ECp: '08-09-10-11-13-15: 3/3/2/2/1/1; Won WAF 2008, DL 2012-13, German 2005-10, 2012.
PV records: World junior 2005, German 2012.
Progress at PV: 1998- 2.75, 1999- 3.30, 2000- 3.75, 2001- 4.00, 2002- 4.20, 2003- 4.20i/4.15, 2004- 4.40, 2005- 4.48i/4.42, 2006- 4.56, 2007- 4.60, 2008- 4.70, 2009- 4.75i/4.70, 2010- 4.71, 2011- 4.76i/4.75, 2012- 4.82, 2013- 4.79, 2014- 4.72i/4.50, 2015- 4.75.
Brothers: Henrik PV pb 4.80, Christian (b. 15 Apr 1976) 5.51 '98; **Richard** (b. 12 Aug 1977) 5.85 '01; 6= WCh 01, 1 WUG 99.

Linda STAHL b. 2 Oct 1985 Steinheim 1.74m 72kg. TSV Bayer 04 Leverkusen. Doctor.
At JT: OG: '12- 3; WCh: '07-09-11-13-15: 8/6/dns/4/10; EC: '10-12-14: 1/3/3; EU23: '07- 1; CCp: '10- 4, '14- 5; ET: '14- 3. Won GER 2013-14.
Progress at JT: 2000- 42.94, 2001- 43.96, 2002- 47.23, 2003- 47.32, 2004- 50.11, 2005- 53.94, 2006- 57.17, 2007- 62.80, 2008- 66.06, 2009- 63.86, 2010- 66.81, 2011- 60.78, 2012- 64.91, 2013- 65.76, 2014- 67.32, 2015- 64.65. pb SP 13.91i '06.

Martina STRUTZ b. 4 Nov 1981 Schwerin 1.60m 57kg. SC Neubrandenburg. Police officer.
At PV: OG: '12- 5; WCh: '11- 2, '15- 8; EC: '06- 5, '12- 2; WJ: '00- 5; EU23: '01- 4, '03- 9=; WCp: '06- 4. German champion 2011, 2013.
Two German pole vault records 2011.
Progress at PV: 1996- 3.30, 1997- 3.60i/3.50, 1998- 3.80, 1999- 4.10, 2000- 4.20, 2001- 4.42, 2002- 4.30, 2003- 4.20, 2004- 4.31, 2005- 4.40i/4.35, 2006- 4.50, 2007- 4.45, 2008- 4.52, 2009- 4.40, 2010- 4.30, 2011- 4.80, 2012- 4.60, 2013- 4.65, 2014- 4.46i/4.41, 2015- 4.65.

Alexandra WESTER b. 21 Mar 1994 The Gambia 1.73m 59kg. ASV Köln.
At LJ: WI: '16- 6.
Progress at LJ: 2009- 6.19, 2010- 5.97i/5.86, 2011- 5.83, 2012- 5.82, 2013- 6.29, 2014- 6.13, 2015- 6.59, 2016- 6.95i. pbs: 60m 7.53i '15, 100m 12.00 '09, 200m 25.27i '10, 60mh 8.47i '15, HJ 1.68 '09, SP 11.51i '14, 11.42 '11; Hep 5523 '14.
German father, Ghanian mother.

GREECE

Governing body: Hellenic Amateur Athletic Association (SEGAS), 137 Siggroú Avenue, 171 21 Nea Smirni, Athens. Founded 1897.

National Championships first held in 1896 (men), 1930 (women). **2015 Champions**: 100m/200m: Likoúrgos-Stéfanos Tsákonas 10.27/20.71, 400m: Mihaíl Dardaneliótis 47.59, 800m: Andréas Dimitrákis 1:50.91, 1500m: Konstadínos Nakópoulos 3:48.73, 5000m/ 10000m: Dímos Maggínas 14:59.24/30:34.86, HMar: Mihaíl Parmákis 72:00, Mar: Hristófouros Meroúsis 2:21:22, 3000mSt: Ilías Kássos 9:19.41, 110mh: Konstadínos Douvalídis 13.50, 400mh: Periklís Iakovákis 51.69, HJ: Konstadínos Baniótis 2.24, PV: Konstadínos Filippídis 5.82, LJ: Loúis Tsátoumas 8.09, TJ: Dimítrios Baltadoúros 16.14, SP: Panayiótis Bouziánis 17.40, DT: Yeóryios Trémos 57.96, HT: Mihaíl Anastasákis 73.23, JT: Paraskevás Batzávalis 81.04, Dec: Panayiótis Mántis 7147w, 20kW: Aléxandros Papamihaíl 1:25:48, 50kW: Konstadínos-Aléxandros Dedópoulos 4:27:22. **Women**: 100m/200m: María Belibasáki 11.47/ 23.12, 400m: Iríni Vasilíou 53.78, 800m: Eléni Filándra 2:07.83, 1500m: Anastasía-Panayióta Marinákou 4:24.75, 5000m: Anastasía Karakatsáni 17:08.97, 10000m/Mar: Ouranía Reboúli 34:57.38/2:54:32, HMar: Sofía Ríga 1:21:58, 3000mSt: María Pardaloú 10:39.74, 100mh: Elisávet Pesirídou 13.37, 400mh: Effrosíni Theodórou 59.20, HJ: Tatiána Goúsin 1.79, PV: Ekateríni Stefanídi 4.65, LJ: Háido Alexoúli 6.41, TJ: Paraskevi Papahrístou 13.89, SP: Evaggelía Sofáni 16.20, DT: Hrisoúla Anagnostopoúlou 60.66, HT: Iliána Korosídou 66.47, JT/ Hep: Sofía Ifantídou 56.54/6113, 20kW: Adigóni Drisbióti 1:33:56.

Konstadínos FILIPÍDDIS b. 26 Nov 1986 Athens 1.88m 73kg. Panellínios YS Athens. Postgraduate student at Athens University of Economics and Business.
At PV: OG: '12- 7; WCh: '05-09-11-13-15: dnq 14=/dnq 17/6/10/dnq 25=; EC: '06-10: dnq 26/21=, '12-14: 5/7; WJ: '04- 4; WY: '03- 4; EJ: '05- 2; WI: '10-12-14-16: 4=/7/1/7; EI: '11-13-15: 5/4/5; WUG: '05- 2; ET: '09/10- 4; Won MedG 2005; Greek champion 2005, 2009-15.
Ten Greek pole vault records 2005-15.
Progress at PV: 2001- 3.70, 2002- 4.80, 2003- 5.22, 2004- 5.50, 2005- 5.75, 2006- 5.55, 2007- 5.35i/5.30/5.40dq, 2009- 5.65, 2010- 5.70i/5.55, 2011- 5.75, 2012- 5.80, 2013- 5.83i/5.82, 2014- 5.80i/5.70, 2015- 5.91.
Two-year drugs ban (reduced to 18 months) from positive test on 16 June 2007.

Loúis TSÁTOUMAS b. 12 Feb 1982 Messíni 1.87m 76kg. Messiniakós YS (Kalamáta).
At LJ: OG: '04-08-12: dnq 22/nj/dnq 29; WCh: '03-09-11-13: 12/11/dnq 14/10; EC: '06-10-14: 8/6/2; WJ: '00- dnq 21; WY: '99- 4; EU23: '03- 1; EJ: '01- 1; WI: '06-12-14: 4/6/4; EI: '07-13-15: 2/5/4; WCp: '06- nj; ECp: '03-07-08-09-13: 1/1/1/3/2; Greek champion 2003-08, 2010-11. 2013-15 (& 8 indoors); MedG 2013, Balkan 2015.
Greek long jump record 2007.
Progress at LJ: 1996- 6.56, 1997- 7.07, 1998- 7.41/7.43w, 1999- 7.64, 2000- 7.52, 2001- 7.93/7.98w, 2002- 8.17, 2003- 8.34, 2004- 8.19/8.37w, 2005- 8.15i/8.14, 2006- 8.30, 2007- 8.66, 2008- 8.44, 2009- 8.21, 2010- 8.09/8.17w, 2011- 8.26, 2012- 8.05i/7.98, 2013- 8.23/8.24w, 2014- 8.25, 2015- 8.09. pb 200m 22.3 '98.
8.66 is best outdoors by European at sea-level.

Women

Nikoléta KIRIAKOPOÚLOU b. 21 Mar 1986 Athens 1.67m 54kg. AYES Kámiros Rhodes.
At PV: OG: '08/12- dnq 27=/19=; WCh: '09-11-13-15: dnq 19/8/dnq 13=/3; EC: '10-12-14: dnq 13/3/7=; WJ: '04- 6; EJ: '05- 7; WI: '16- 6=; EI: '11- 9, '15- 5=. Won DL 2015, Balkan 2008, Med G 2009, Greek 2009, 2011-14.
Nine Greek pole vault records 2010-15.
Progress at PV: 2001- 2.90, 2002- 3.10, 2003- 3.70, 2004- 4.00, 2005- 4.10, 2006- 3.60, 2007- 4.00i/3.90, 2008- 4.45, 2009- 4.50, 2010- 4.55, 2011- 4.71, 2012- 4.60, 2013- 4.65, 2014- 4.72i/4.67, 2015- 4.83, 2016- 4.81i.

Paraskeví 'Voula' PAPAHRÍSTOU b. 17 Apr 1989 Athens 1.70m 53kg. AEK (Athens).
At TJ: WCh: '09/11- dnq 29/16; EC: '12- 11; WJ: '08- 3; EU23: '09/11- 1/1; WI: '16- 3. Won Greek LJ 2011-12, TJ 2009, 2011, 2015.
Progress at TJ: 2005- 12.75, 2006- 12.81/13.13w, 2007- 12.98i/12.92, 2008- 13.86i/13.79/13.94w, 2009- 14.47i/14.35, 2010- 13.94i/13.85, 2011- 14.72, 2012- 14.58/14.77w, 2013- 14.21, 2015- 13.99/14.20w, 2016- 14.21i. pb LJ 6.60 '12.

Ekateríni STEFANÍDI b. 4 Feb 1990 Athens 1.72m 63kg. Was at Stanford University, USA and then as a graduate student in cognitive psychology at Arizona State University.
At PV: OG: '12- dnq 24; WCh: '15- dnq 15; EC: '12- nh, '14- 2; WJ: '08- 3; WY: '05- 1, '07- 2; EU23: '11- 2; WI: '16- 3; EI: '15- 2; WUG: '11- 3. Greek champion 2015, NCAA 2012.
World youth pole vault best 2005.
Progress at PV: 2002- 3.40, 2003- 3.90, 2004- 4.14, 2005- 4.37i/4.30, 2006- 4.10, 2007- 4.25, 2008- 4.25, 2009- 4.13, 2010- 4.30, 2011- 4.45, 2012- 4.51, 2013- 4.45Ai/4.40, 2014- 4.71, 2015- 4.77Ai/4.71, 2016- 4.90i.

GRENADA

Governing body: Grenada Athletic Assocation, PO Box 419, St George's. Founded 1924.

Kirani JAMES b. 1 Sep 1992 St George's 1.85m 74kg. Student at University of Alabama, USA
At (200m)/400m: OG: '12- 1; WCh: '11- 1, '13- 7, '15- 3; CG: '14- 1; WJ: '08- 2, '10- 1; WY: '07- 2,

'09- 1/1; WI: '12- 6. Won DL 2011, PAm-J 400m 2009, 200m 2011; NCAA 2010-11.
Records: CAC & Commonwealth 400m 2012 & 2014, GRN 200m 2011, 400m (2) 2011-12; Indoor 400m: CAC & Commonwealth 2010 (45.24) &. 2011, World Junior (44.80) 2011.
Progress at 400m: 2007- 46.96, 2008- 45.70, 2009- 45.24, 2010- 45.01, 2011- 44.36, 2012- 43.94, 2013- 43.96, 2014- 43.74, 2015- 43.78. pbs: 200m 20.41A/20.53w '11, 20.76 '10; 300m: 32.0+ '12.
He set world age bests at 14 and 15. In 2011 he became the youngest ever World or Olympic champion at 400m and in 2012 the first Olympic medallist for Grenada at any sport. In January 2012 the 'Kirani James Boulevard' was opened in the Grenadan capital St. George. IAAF Rising Star award 2011.

GUATEMALA

Governing body: Federación Nacional de Atletismo, Palacio de los Deportes, 26 Calle 9-31, Zona 5, Ciudad de Guatemala. Fd 1896.

Erick BARRONDO b. 14 Jun 1991 San Cristóbal Verapaz 1.72m 60kg.
At 20kW(/50kW): OG: '12- 2/dq; WCh: '11- 7, '13- dq, '15- (dq); PAm: '11- 1, '15- dq; CAG: '14- (1). Won PAmCp 20k 2015, Bol G 20kW 2013, GUA 50kW 2012.
50k walk records: CAC 2013, GUA 2012-13.
Progress at 20kW, 50kW: 2010- 1:23:16A, 2011- 1:20:58, 2012- 1:18:25, 3:44:59; 2013- 1:20:25, 3:41:09; 2014- 1:21:14, 3:49:40A; 2015- 1:21:25, 3:55:57. pb 10000mW 40:10.73A '13, 40:04R '15.
Won Guatemala's first Olympic medal at any sport in 2012. His cousin José Alejandro Barrondo has 10000mW pb 42:00.98 '13.

HUNGARY

Governing body: Magyar Atlétikai Szövetség, 1146 Budapest, Istvánmezei út 1-3. Fd 1897.

National Championships first held in 1896 (men), 1932 (women). **2015 Champions. Men**: 100m: Dániel Szabó 10.65, 200m: Bálint Móricz 21.63, 400m: Zoltán Kovács 47.45, 800m: Tamás Kazi 1:48.72, 1500m/5000m/10000m: László Gregor 3:47.17/14:13.68/29:51.52, HMar: Gábor Józsa 66:41, Mar: Daniel Soós 2:25:21, 3000mSt: Balázs Juhász 8:53.06, 110mh: Balázs Baji 13.51, 400mh: Máté Koroknai 50.72, HJ: Péter Bakosi 2.22, PV: Tamás Kéri 5.20, LJ/TJ/Dec: Tibor Galambos 7.57w/15.97w/6786(w), SP: Tibor Rakovszky 17.50, DT: Zoltán Kövágó 62.71, HT: Krisztián Pars 78.35, JT: Norbert Rivasz-Tóth 72.18, 20kW: Máté Helebrandt 1:23:04, 50kW: Miklós Domonkos Srp 4:01:44. **Women**: 100m/200m: Éva Kaptur 11.87/24.65, 400m/800m: Bianka Kéri 54.74/2:06.94, 1500m: Zsanett Kenesei 4:25.50, 5000m/10000m/HMar/3000mSt: Zita Kácser 16:55.70/34:13.04/76:51/10:38.59, Mar: Timea Merényi 2:45:11, 100mh: Xénia Krizsán 13.70, 400mh/Hep: Noémi Szücs 59.33/4798(w), HJ: Barbara Szabó 1.92, PV: Fanni Juhász 4.00, LJ: Györgyi Zsivoczky-Farkas 6.26, TJ: Eszter Bajnok 12.92, SP/DT: Anita Márton 18.36/58.29, HT: Éva Orbán 69.67, JT: Réka Szilágyi 54.92, 20kW:Viktória Madarász 1:31:31.

Zoltán KÖVÁGÓ b. 10 Apr 1979 Szolnok 2.04m 127kg. Szolnoki Honvéd SE. Army lieutenant.
At DT: OG: '00- dnq, '04- 2, '08- dnq 21; WCh: '01-03-05-07-09-11-15: dnq 20/dnq 19/10/9/6/ dnq 15/dnq 18; EC: '02-10-12-14: 7/dnq 21/dq (3)/ dnq 14; WJ: '96- 4, '98- 1; EJ: '97- 3; EU23: '99- 6, '01- 1. HUN champion 2001, 2004-05, 2008-11, 2014-15; W.MilG 2015.
Progress at DT: 1995- 49.78, 1996- 59.70, 1997- 62.16, 1998- 60.27, 1999- 63.23, 2000- 66.76, 2001- 66.93, 2002- 65.98, 2003- 66.03, 2004- 68.93, 2005- 66.00, 2006- 69.95, 2007- 66.42, 2008- 68.17, 2009- 67.64, 2010- 69.69, 2011- 69.50, 2012- 68.21dq, 2014- 65.82, 2015- 67.39. pb SP 15.93 '01.
2-year drugs ban 2011-13.

Krisztián PARS b. 18 Feb 1982 Körmend 1.88m 113kg. Dobó SE.
At HT: OG: '04- 5, '08- 4, '12- 1; WCh: '05-07-09-11-13-15: 6/5/4/2/2/4; EC: '06-10-12-14: 5/3/1/1; WY: '99- 1; EJ: '01- 1; EU23: '03- 1; CCp: '14- 1. Won HUN 2005-15; World HT challenge 2011-12, 2014.
World junior records with 6kg hammer: 80.64 & 81.34 in 2001.
Progress at HT: 1998- 54.00, 1999- 61.92, 2000- 66.80, 2001- 73.09, 2002- 74.18, 2003- 78.81, 2004- 80.90, 2005- 80.03, 2006- 82.45, 2007- 81.40, 2008- 81.96, 2009- 81.43, 2010- 79.64, 2011- 81.89, 2012- 82.28, 2013- 82.40, 2014- 82.69, 2015- 79.91. pbs: SP 15.60 '05, DT 53.80 '06.

Women

Anita MÁRTON b. 15 Jan 1989 Szeged 1.71m 84kg. Békéscsabai AC.
At SP: OG: '12- dnq 23; WCh: '09-11-13: dnq 24/22/20, '15- 4; EC: '10-12-14: 11/7/3; WJ: '06- dnq 15, '08- 7; WY: '05- 11; EU23: '09- 5, '11- 5; EJ: '07- 7; WUG: '13- 4; WI: '14- 6, '16- 2; EI: '11-5, '15- 1; won HUN SP 2006-15, DT 2008-15.
Two Hungarian shot records 2014-15.
Progress at SP: 2004- 13.88, 2005- 14.12i/13.90, 2006- 15.57, 2007- 15.68, 2008- 16.90, 2009- 17.27, 2010- 18.20, 2011- 18.15, 2012- 18.48, 2013- 18.18, 2014- 19.04, 2015- 19.48, 2016- 19.33i. pbs: DT 59.27 '14, HT 48.87 '08.
Improved pb from 18.48/18.63i to 19.04 to take EC bronze 2014, indoor best to 19.23i for EI gold and outdoor pb to 19.48 for World 4th 2015; HUN indoor record 19.33 for 2nd WI 2016.

Györgyi ZSIVOCZKY-FARKAS b. 13 Feb 1985 Budapest 1.70m 58kg. Honved SE.
At Hep: OG: '08- 28, '12- 21; WCh: '11- 23, '13- 15, '15- 6; EC: '12- 13, '14- 10; WJ: '02- 10, '04- 7; EU23: '05- 16. At Pen: WI: '16- 5;EI: '15- 6. Won HUN LJ 2010, Hep 2008, 2010-11.
Progress at Hep: 2002- 5339, 2004- 5550, 2005-

5342, 2006- 5033, 2008- 5842, 2009- dnf, 2010- 5874, 2011- 6068, 2012- 6030, 2013- 6269, 2014- 6180, 2015- 6389. pbs: 200m 25.21 '15, 800m 2:11.88 '15, 60mh 8.44i '15, 100mh 13.85 '15, HJ 1.86 '15, LJ 6.32 '13, SP 14.62 '15, DT 42.06 '07, JT 50.73 '14, Pen 4691i '15.
Married to Attila Zsivoczky (Dec 8554 '00, 4/3 WCh 01/05, 8/6 OG 00/04. 2 EC 06).

ICELAND

Governing body: Frjálsíthróttasamband Islands, Engjavegur 6, IS-104 Reykjavik. Founded 1947.

National Championships first held in 1927. **2015 champions: Men:** 100m/200m: Kolbeinn Hödur Gunnarsson 10.89/21.76, 400m: Kormákur Ari Haflidason 48.84, 800m: Kristin Thór Kristinsson 1:53.03, 1500m: Sigurbjörn Árni Arngrimsson 4:10.36, 5000m: Arnar Pétursson 15:58.19, 3000mSt: Sæmundur Ólafsson 10:03.42, 110mh: Gudmundur Gudmundsson 15.27, 400mh: Ivar Kristinn Jasonarson 54.50, HJ: Stefán Thór Jósefsson 1.82, PV: Ingi Rúnar Kristinsson 4.30, LJ/TJ: Thorsteinn Ingvarsson 7.39/13.80, SP: Ódinn Björn Thorsteinsson 18.28, DT: Gudni Valur Gudnason 55.90, HT: Hilmar Örn Jónsson 69.79, JT: Gudmundur Sverisson 74.19. **Women:** 100m/200m/LJ: Hafdís Sigurdardóttir 12.02/24.43/6.39, 400m/100mh/400mh: Arna Stefanía Gudmundsdóttir 54.54/14.14/59.62, 800m: Anita Hinriksdóttir 2:05.38, 1500m: Rebekka Fugle 4:39.62, 3000m: Marna Leila Egholm 10:09.38, HJ: Thóranna Ósk Sigurjónsdóttir 1.63, Hulda Thorsteinsdóttir 4.22, TJ: Thelma Lind Kristjánsdóttir 11.63, SP/DT/JT: Ásdis Hjálmsdóttir 14.74/49.31/55.38, HT: Vigdis Jónsdóttir 55.07.

INDIA

Governing body: Athletics Federation of India, WZ-72, Todapur Main Road, Dev Prakash Shastri Marg, New Delhi - 110012. Fd 1946.

National Championships first held as Indian Games in 1924. **2015 Champions: Men**: 100m: Murugiah M Raj 10.70, 200m Manikanda Arumugam 21.35, 400m: Arokia Rajiv 45.70, 800m/1500m: Ajay Kumar Saroj 1:54.87/3:47.33, 5000m: Govindan Lakshmanan 14:00.77, 10000m: T. Gopi 30:07.70, 3000mSt: Naveen Kumar 8:42.79, 110mh: Thingalaya Siddhanth 13.96, 400m: Duresh Kumar Pal 50.40, HJ: Jagdeep Singh 2.16, PV: Anuj Singh 5.02, LJ: Kumaravel Premjumar 7.74, TJ: Arpinder Singh 16.36, SP: Inderjeet Singh 19.82, DT: Dharam Raj Yadav 56.12, HT: Neeraj Kumar 67.73, JT: Neeraj Chopra 77.67, Dec: Gurjar Daya Ram 6927, 20kW: Babu Bhai Panocha 1:33:44, 50kW:. **Women**: 100m/200m: Dutee Chand 11.68/23.69, 400m: M.R.Poovamma 53.55, 800m: Tintu Luka 2:00.56, 1500m: Sugandha Kumari 4:24.45, 5000m: Orchatteri P. Jaisha 15:31.73, 10000m: Suriya Loganathan 33:44.84, 3000mSt: Lalita Babar 9:39.83, 100mh: Govindaraj Gayathry 14.16, 400mh: Anu Raghavan 58.73, HJ: Sahana Kumari 1.80, PV: Mariya Jaison 3.70, LJ: Shraddha Bhaskar Ghule 6.38, TJ: Mayookha M. Johny 13.78, SP: Manpreet Kaur 17.96, DT: Navjeet Kaur 51.17, HT: Sarita Prakash Singh 58.97, JT: Annu Rani 58.85, Hep: Swapna Burman 5350, 20kW: Khushbir Kaur 1:49:09.

Vikas GOWDA b. 5 Jul 1983 Mysore, Karnataka 1.96m 115kg. Studied statistics at University of North Carolina, USA.
At DT: OG: '04/08- dnq 14/22, '12- 8; WCh: '05/07- dnq 14/17, '11-13-15: 7/7/9; CG: '06-10-14: 6/2/1; WJ: '02- 12; AsiG: '06-10-14: 6/3/2; AsiC: 05-11-13-15: 2/2/1/1. Won NCAA 2006.
Three Indian discus records 2005-12
Progress at DT: 2002- 55.28, 2003- 59.32, 2004- 64.35, 2005- 64.69, 2006- 61.76, 2007- 64.96, 2008- 64.83, 2010- 63.69, 2011- 64.91, 2012- 66.28, 2013- 65.82. 2014- 65.62, 2015- 65.75. pb SP 19.62 '06.
Moved to USA at age 6.

IRAN

Governing body: Amateur Athletic Federation of Islamic Republic of Iran, Shahid Keshvari Sports Complex, Razaneh Junibi St Mirdamad Ave, Tehran. Founded 1936.

Ehsan HADADI b. 21 Jan 1985 Ahvaz 1.93m 125kg.
At DT: OG: '08- dnq 17, '12- 2; WCh: '07- 7, '11- 3, '15- dnq 24; WJ: '04- 1; AsiG: '06-10-14: 1/1/1; AsiC: '03-05-07-09-11: 8/1/1/1/1; AsiJ: '04- 1; WCp: '06- 2, '10- 3. W.Asian champion 2005.
Eight Asian discus records 2005-08.
Progress at DT: 2002- 53.66, 2003- 54.40, 2004- 54.96, 2005- 65.25, 2006- 63.79, 2007- 67.95, 2008- 69.32, 2009- 66.19, 2010- 68.45, 2011- 66.08, 2012- 68.20, 2013- 66.98, 2014- 65.24, 2015- 65.22. pb SP 17.82i '08, 16.00 '06.
First Iranian athlete to win an Olympic medal.

IRELAND

Governing Body: The Athletic Association of Ireland (AAI), Unit 19, Northwood Court, Northwood Business Campus, Santry, Dublin 9. Founded in 1999. Original Irish federation (Irish Champions AC) founded in 1873.

National Championships first held in 1873. **2015 Champions**: **Men**: 100m/200m: Marcus Lawler 10.68/21.17, 400m: Brian Gregan 46.20, 800m: Mark English 1:50.94, 1500m: Eoin Everard 3:55.01, 5000: Kevin Batt 14:20.97, 10000m: Mark Christie 29:52.84, HMar: Paul Pollock 65:10, Mar: Sean Hehir 2:19:47, 3000mSt: Tomás Cotter 8:47.52, 110mh: Ben Reynolds 13.84, 400mh: Thomas Barr 49.68, HJ: Barry Pender 2.15, PV: Ian Rogers 4.50, LJ: Adam McMullen 7.89w, TJ: Denis Finnegan 15.19w, SP: Sean Breathnach 17.63, DT: Colin Quirke 54.09,

HT: Padraig White 60.13, JT: Sean McBride 63.21, Dec: Kourosh Foroughi 6227, 10000mW: Alex Wright 40:04.29, 20kW: Cian McMenamon 1:32:26t. **Women**: 100m/200m: Kelly Proper 11.75/23.81, 400m: Sinead Denny 53.98, 800m: Ciara Mageean 2:02.98, 1500m/3000mSt: Sara Treacy 4:18.62/9:58.92, 5000m: Mary Cullen 16:07.40, HMar: Lizzie Lee 73:28, Mar: Pauline Curley 2:49:32, 100mh: Sarah Connolly 15.40, 400mh: Christine McMahon 59.19, HJ: Cathriona Farrell 1.80, PV: Tori Pena 4.20, LJ/TJ: Mary McLoone 6.01/12.71w, SP/DT: Clare Fitzgerald 14.83/52.52, HT: Alice Akers 55.05, JT: Anita Fitzgibbon 51.56, Hep: Karen Dunne 3913, 5000mW: Veronica Burke 25:18.96.

Robert HEFFERNAN b. 20 Feb 1978 Cork City 1.73m 55kg. Togher AC.
At 20kW/(50kW): OG: '00- 28, '04- dq, '08- 8, '12- 9/3; WCh: '01-05-07-09-13-15: 14/dq/6/15/(1)/(5); EC: '02- 8, '10- 3/4, '14- (dnf); WCp: '08- 9, '12- 9; ECp: '07-09-11-13: 5/4/8/9. At 10000mW: EJ: '97- 14; EU23: '99- 13. Won Irish 10000mW 2001-02, 2004-5, 2007-11; 20kW 2000-02, 2004, 2009; 30kW 2008.
Irish records: 3000mW 2013, 20kW (4) 2001-08, 50kW (3) 2010-12. World M35 3000mW 2013.
Progress at 20kW, 50kW: 1999- 1:26:45, 2000- 1:22:43, 2001- 1:21:11, 2002- 1:20:25, 2003- 1:23:03, 2004- 1:20:55, 2005- 1:24:20, 2006- 1:22:24, 2007- 1:20:15, 2008- 1:19:22, 2009- 1:22:09, 2010- 1:20:45, 3:45:30; 2011- 1:20:54, 3:49:28; 2012- 1:20:18, 3:37.54; 2013- 1:21:59, 3:37:56; 2014- 1:20:57, 2015- 3:44:17. pbs: 1MW 5:39.75i '14, 3000mW 11:09.08 14, 5000mW 18:51.46i '08, 18:59.37 '07; 10000mW 38:27.57 '08, 30kW 2:07:48 '11, 35kW 2:31:19 '00.
Married to Marian Andrews (b. 16 Apr 1982, Irish 400m champion 2008-09, pb 53.10 '11).

ISRAEL

Governing body: Israeli Athletic Association, PO Box 24190, Tel Aviv 61241. Founded as Federation for Amateur Sport in Palestine 1931.
National Championships first held in 1935. **2015 Champions**: **Men**: 100m/200m: Imri Pressiado 10.47/21.25, 400m: Donald Blair-Sanford 45.52, 800m: Dustin Emrani 1:50.45, 1500m: Omer Almog 3:51.22, 5000m: Aimeru Almeya 14:24.59, 10000m/HMar: Girmaw Amare 28:10.32/67:36, Mar: Zohar Zimro 2:18:08, 3000mSt: Noam Ne'eman 8:57.64, 110mh: Tomer Almogi 14.29, 400mh: Maor Szeged 52.08, HJ: Dmitriy Kroyter 2.21, PV: Eduard Plotnikov 5.05, LJ: Rohi Elyakim 7.33, TJ: Yochai Halevi 16.25, SP: Itamar Levi 18.20, DT: Mark Alterman 53.04, HT: Viktor Zaginaiko 61.80, JT: Alan Ferber 66.48, Dec: Konstantin Krinitzkiy 7025. **Women**: 100m/200m: Olga Lenskiy 11.57/23.45, 400m: Dariya Lukshin 56.38, 800m: Shanie Landen 2:09.26, 1500m: Maor Tiyouri 4:28.07, 5000m/100000m/HMar: Azawant Taka 17:31.12/36:25.00/1:21:40, Mar: Riki Salem 2:54:02, 3000mSt: Danna Levinn 11:03.38, 100mh: Maya Aviezer 14.25, 400mh: Alexandra Lokshin 61.10, HJ: Maayan Shahaf 1.85, PV/Hep: Olga Bronstein 3.65/3885 (30th national title), LJ: Yiff'at Zelikovitz 5.89w, TJ: Hanna Minenko 14.37, SP: Inbal Cohen 12.74, DT: Estelle Valleanu 39.81, HT: Yevgeniya Zabolotniy (12th successive title) 57.64, JT: Margaryta Dorozhon 61.78.

Marharyta DOROZHON b. 4 Sep 1987 Dnepropetrovsk, Ukraine 1.80m 75kg. Hapoel Emek Hefer
At JT: OG: '12- dnq 28; WCh: '13-15: dnq 19/16; WJ: '04- dnq 14, '06- 3; EU23: '07- dnq 22; EJ: '05- 7. UKR champion 2013, ISR 2015.
Three Israeli javelin records 2015.
Progress at JT: 2003- 49.35. 2004- 53.90, 2005- 55.32, 2006- 57.68, 2007- 55.88, 2008- 57.45, 2009- 60.60, 2010- 49.56, 2011- 54.40, 2012- 61.84, 2013- 62.01, 2014- 61.34, 2015- 64.56.
Emigarted from Ukraine to Israel in 2014 and married coach Alex Bogoslavskiy.

Hanna MINENKO b. 25 Sep 1989 Periaslav-Khmelnytskyi 1.78m 61kg. née Knyazyeva. Maccabi Tel Aviv.
At TJ: OG: '12- 4; WCh: '13- 6, '15- 2; WJ: '08- 4; EJ: '07- 2; EU23: '11- 5; EI: '14- 3. Won UKR TJ 2012, ISR LJ 2013-14; TJ 2014-15.
Eight Israeli triple jump records 2013-15 and one long jump 2014.
Progress at TJ: 2005- 12.87, 2006- 13.28, 2007- 13.85, 2009- 13.61, 2010- 13.65, 2011- 14.20, 2012- 14.71, 2013- 14.58, 2014- 14.29, 2015- 14.78. pb LJ 6.52 '14.
Married Anatoliy Minenko (Dec 7046 '10) in November 2012 and switched from Ukraine to Israel on 12 May 2013.

ITALY

Governing Body: Federazione Italiana di Atletica Leggera (FIDAL), Via Flaminia Nuova 830, 00191 Roma. Constituted 1926. First governing body formed 1896.
National Championships first held in 1897 (one event)/1906 (men), 1927 (women). **2015 Champions**: **Men**: 100m: Fabio Cerutti 10.31, 200m: Davide Mamneti 21.00, 400m: Matteo Galvan 46.11, 800m: Giordano Benedetti 1:47.38, 1500m: Mohad Abdikadar Sheikh Ali 3:42.79, 5000m: Marouan Razine 13:50.87, 10000m: Said El Otmani 29:22.46, HMar: Andrea Lalli 62:54, Mar: Dario Santoro 2:24:25, 3000mSt: Jamal Chatbi 8:30.35, 110mh: Hassane Fofana 13.59, 400mh: Leonardo Capotosti 49.95, HJ: Marco Fassinotti 2.30, PV: Claudio Michel Stecchi 5.50, LJ: Filippo Randazzo 7.76, TJ: Fabrizio Donato 16.91, SP: Daniele Secci 19.18, DT: Hannes Kirchler 60.25, HT: Marco Bortolato 70.85, JT: Roberto Bertolini 79.32, Dec: Simone Cairoli 7482, 10kW/50kW: Federico Tontodonati 40:36/3:55:09, 20kW: Massimo Stano 1:22:16. **Women**:

100m/200m: Gloria Hooper 11.47/23.48, 400m: Libania Grenot 51.47, 800m: Marta Zenoni 2:04.18, 1500m: Margherita Magnani 4:19.29, 5000m: Solvia Weissteiner 16:03.55, 10000m: Claudia Pinna 34:04.71, HMar: Laila Soufyane 73:10, Mar: Catherine Bertone 2:39:19, 3000mSt: Valeria Roffino 10:07.23, 100mh: Giulia Tessaro 13.14, 400mh: Yadisleidy Pedroso 55.96, HJ: Desirée Rossit 1.86, PV: Sonia Malavisi 4.30, LJ: Martina Lorenzetto 6.49, TJ: Ottavia Cestonaro 13.76, SP: Chiara Rosa 17.33, DT: Natalina Capoferri 52.36, HT: Sara Fantini 57.81, JT: Ilaria Casarotto 47.59, Hep: Federica Palumbo 5385, 10kW: Elisa Rigaudo 43:08, 20kW: Valentina Trapletti 1:31:48.

Marco DE LUCA b. 12 May 1981 Rome 1.89m 72kg. Fiamme Gialle.
At 50kW: OG: '08- 19, '12- 14; WCh: 05-07-09-11-13-15: 13/dnf/8/11/15/16; EC: '06-10-14: 7/6/7; WCp: 06-08-10-12: 9/8/14/6; ECp: '07-09-11-15: 8/8/2/3. Won Italian 20kW 2011, 50kW 2006, 2009.
Progress at 50kW: 2002- 4:07:06, 2003- 4:13:24, 2004- 4:05:01, 2005- 3:55:30, 2006- 3:48:08, 2007-3:47:04, 2008- 3:49:21, 2009- 3:46:31, 2010- 3:48:36, 2011- 3:49:40, 2012- 3:47:19, 2013- 3:48:05, 2014-3:45:25, 2015- 3:46:21. pbs: 3000mW 12:03.79 '09, 5000mW 19:29.54i '15, 20:03.6 '05, 10000mW 40:48.0 '09, 20kW 1:22:38 '10, 30kW 2:09:37 '04, 35kW 2:28:53 '10.

Fabrizio DONATO b. 14 Aug 1976 Latina 1.89m 82kg. Fiamme Gialle.
At TJ: OG: '00/04/08: dnq 25/21/21, '12- 3; WCh: '03/07-09-13: dnq 13/32/41/15, '11- 10; EC: '02-06-10-12-14: 4/dnq 16/9/1/7; EJ: '95- 5; WI: '01-08-10-12: 6/4/5/4; EI: '00-02-09-11: 6/4/1/2; ECp: '00-02-03-04-06-14-15: 2/2/1/6/1/2/1. Won MedG 2001, Italian 2000, 2004, 2006-08, 2010-11, 2015. Italian triple jump record 2000.
Progress at TJ: 1992- 12.88, 1993- 14.36, 1994-15.27, 1995- 15.81, 1996- 16.35, 1997- 16.40A, 1998-16.73, 1999- 16.66i/16.53w, 2000- 17.60, 2001-17.05, 2002- 17.17, 2003- 17.16, 2004- 16.90, 2005-16.65/16.68w, 2006- 17.33i/17.24, 2007- 16.97/17.06w, 2008- 17.27i/16.91/17.29w, 2009- 17.59i/15.81, 2010- 17.39i/17.08, 2011- 17.73i/17.17, 2012-17.53/17.63w, 2013- 16.86, 2014- 16.89/17.24w, 2015- 16.91/17.11w. pb LJ 8.03i '11, 8.00 '06.
Italian indoor record to win 2009 European Indoor title. Married Patrizia Spuri (400m 51.74 '98, 8 EC 98, 800m 1:59.96 '98) on 27 Sep 2003.

Marco FASSINOTTI b. 29 Apr 1989 Turin 1.90m 71kg. Aeronautica Militare.
At HJ: EC: '10- 9, '14- 7; WJ: '08- 7; EU23: '09- 6, '11- 5; WI: '14- 6; EI: '11- 6; ET: '15- 2; Italian champion 2013, 2015.
Italian HJ record 2015, indoors (3) 2014-16.
Progress at HJ: 2005- 1.70, 2006- 1.90, 2007- 2.08, 2008- 2.17, 2009- 2.22, 2010- 2.28, 2011- 2.29i/2.25, 2012- 2.26i/2.24, 2013- 2.27, 2014- 2.34i/2.30, 2015- 2.34i/2.33, 2016- 2.35i.

Giorgio RUBINO b. 15 Apr 1986 Roma 1.74m 56kg. Fiamme Gialle.
At 20kW: OG: '08- 18, '12- 42; WCh: '07-09-11-13-15: 5/4/dq/28; EC: '06-10-14: 8/4/8/20; EU23: '07- dq; ECp: '09- 1, '11- 4. At 10000mW: WJ: '04-10; WY: '03- 4; EJ: '05- 3; ECp: '05- 2J. Won Italian 10kW 2012, 2014; 20kW 2005, 2014.
Progress at 20kW: 2005- 1:23:58, 2006- 1:22:05, 2007- 1:21:17, 2008- 1:22:11, 2009- 1:19:37, 2010-1:22:12, 2011- 1:20:44, 2012- 1:20:10, 2013- 1:21:07, 2014- 1:20:44, 2015- 1:21:38. pbs: 5000mW 19:14.33i '08, 19:38.5 '06; 10000mW 39:43.20 '11, 38:00R '10; 35kW 2:36:50 '09.

Gianmarco TAMBERI b. 1 Jun 1992 Civitanove Marche 1.92m 77kg. Fiamme Gialle.
At HJ: WCh: '15- 8=; EC: '12- 5, '14- 7=; WY: '09-dnq 18; EU23: '13- dnq 13=; EJ: '11- 3; WI: '16- 1; EI: '13- 5, '15- 7; Italian champion 2012, 2014.
Two Italian high jump records 2015 (3 indoor 2016).
Progress at HJ: 1005- 1.52, 2006- 1.62i, 2007- 1.80, 2008- 2.01, 2009- 2.07, 2010- 2.14, 2011-2.25, 2012-2.31, 2013- 2.30i/2.25, 2014- 2.29, 2015- 2.37, 2016-2.38i. His father Marco had pb 2.28i/2.27 '83, elder brother Gianluca 4th EJ JT 2009.

Women

Eleonora GIORGI b. 14 Sep 1989 Cuneo 1.63m 52kg. Fiamme Azzurre. Graduated in social-economic law from University "Bocconi" of Milan.
At 20kW: OG: '12- 13; WCh: '13- 10, '15- dq; EC: '14- 5; EU23: '09- 11, '11- 4; WCp: '12- 13, '14- 5; ECp: '13- 6, '15- 2; won MedG 2013. At 10000mW: WJ: '08- 18.
Walk records: World best 5000m 2014, 25k & 30k 2016; Italian 20k (3) 2014-15.
Progress at 20kW: 2009- 1:34:27, 2010- 1:34:00, 2011- 1:33:46, 2012- 1:29:48, 2013- 1:30:01, 2014-1:27:05, 2015- 1:26:17, 2016- 1:28:05. pbs: 3000mW 11:50.08i/12:05.83 '13, 5000mW 20:01.80 '14, 10kW 44:33.56t '13, 44:14R '14; 25kW 1:56:12 '16, 30kW 2:19:43 '16.

Libania GRENOT b. 12 Jul 1983 Santiago de Cuba 1.75m 61kg. Fiamme Galle.
At 400m: OG: '08/12- sf; WCh: '01- hR, '05- h, '09/13/15- sf; EC: '10-12-14: 4/6/1; WY: '99- 5; PAm: '03- 4; CCp: '10- 6/2R, '14- 3/2R; ET: '09- 1, 15- 3. Won MedG 2009, CUB 2003-05, ITA 400m 2009-10, 2014-15; 200m 2012.
Four Italian 400m records 2008-09.
Progress at 400m: 1997- 56.2, 1998- 54.9, 1999-53.87, 2000- 53.79, 2001- 52.91, 2002- 53.34A, 2003- 52.20, 2004- 51.68, 2005- 51.51, 2007- 54.21, 2008- 50.83, 2009- 50.30, 2010- 50.43, 2011- 52.17, 2012- 50.55, 2013- 50.47, 2014- 50.55, 2015- 51.07. pbs: 200m 22.85, 22.45w '12, 300m 36.82 '14. 500m 1:08.26 '09.
Switched from Cuba to Italy after she married Silvio Scaffetti in 2006 and gained Italian citizenship on 18 Mar 2008.

Antonella PALMISANO b. 6 Aug 1991 Mottola, Taranto 1.66m 49kg. Fiamme Galle.
At 20kW: WCh: '13- 13, '15- 5; EC: '14- 7; EU23: '11- 2, '13- 3; WCp: '14- 9. At 10000mW: WJ: '08- 9, '10- 4; EJ: '09- 2; WCp: '10- 1J; ECp: '09- 3J. At 5000mW: WY: '07- 5.
Progress at 20kW: 2009- 1:38:47, 2010- 1:36:21, 2011- 1:34:31, 2012- 1:34:27, 2013- 1:30:50, 2014- 1:27:51, 2015- 1:28:40. pbs: 3000mW 12:05.68i '15, 10kW 44:45.78t '13, 42:50R '14.

Elisa RIGAUDO b. 17 Jun 1980 Cuneo 1.68m 56kg. Fiamme Gialle.
At 20kW: OG: '04- 6, '08- 3, '12- 6; WCh: '03-05-07-09-11-13-15: 10/7/dnf/8/3/5/dq; EC: '06- 3; EU23: '01- 1; WCp: '02-04-06-12: 16/5/10/6; ECp: '05-07-11-15: 3/4/3/8. At 5000mW: WJ: '98- 7; EJ: '99-6. Won MedG 20kW 2005, Italian 5000mW 2004, 2007; 10000mW 2013, 2015; 20kW 2004-05, 2008.
Progress at 20kW: 1999- 1:42:40. 2000- 1:32:50, 2001- 1:29:54, 2002- 1:30:42, 2003- 1:30:34, 2004- 1:27:49, 2005- 1:29:26, 2006- 1:28:37, 2007- 1:29:15, 2008- 1:27:12, 2009- 1:29:04, 2011- 1:30:44, 2012- 1:27:36, 2013- 1:28:41, 2015- 1:28:01. pbs: 3000mW 11:57.00i '04, 12:28.92 '02; 5000mW 20:56.29 '02, 10kW 42:29.06t '13.
Won IAAF Walks Challenge 2004. Daughters Elena born in September 2010 and Simone on 8 Sep 2014.

Alessia TROST b. 8 Mar 1993 Pordenone 1.88m 68kg. Fiamme Gialle.
At HJ: WCh: '13- 7=; EC: '14- 9=; WJ: '12- 1; WY: '09- 1; EU23: '13- 1, '15- 1; EJ: '11- 4; WI: '16- 6; EI: '13- 4=, '15- 2; ET: '13- 2; YthOly: '10- 2. Italian champion 2013-14.
Progress at HJ: 2003- 1.37, 2004- 1.55, 2005- 1.62, 2006- 1.68, 2008- 1.81, 2009- 1.89, 2010- 1.90, 2011- 1.87, 2012- 1.92, 2013- 2.00i/1.98, 2014- 1.96i/1.91, 2015- 1.97i/1.94, 2016- 1.95i. pbs: 100mh 15.5 '11, LJ 6.01 '14, SP 10.76i '14, Pen 4035i '14.

IVORY COAST

Governing Body: Fédération Ivoirienne d'Athlétisme, Abidjan. Founded 1960.

Murielle AHOURÉ b. 23 Aug 1987 Abidjan 1.67m 57kg. Graduated in criminal law from the University of Miami, USA.
At 100m/200m: OG: '12- 7/6; WCh: '13- 2/2, '15- sf/-; AfCh: '14- 2/1. At 60m: WI: '12- 2, 14- 2. Won NCAA Indoor 200m 2009.
Two African 60m indoor records 2013. CIV records 100m (7) 2009-15, 200m (3) 2012-13.
Progress at 100m: 2005- 11.96, 2006- 11.42, 23.33; 2007- 11.41/11.28w, 23.34; 2008- 11.45, 23.50; 2009- 11.09, 22.78; 2010- 11.41, 2011- 11.06/10.86w, 2012- 10.99, 22.42; 2013- 10.91, 22.24; 2014- 10.97, 22.36; 2015- 10.81, 22.29. pbs: 60m 6.99i '13, 300m 38.09i '07, 400m 54.77 '08.
Lived in Paris from age 2, then USA from age 12. Won first medals for Ivory Coast at World Championships.

Marie Josée TA LOU Gonerie b. 18 Nov 1988 1.59m 57kg.
At 100m/200m: WCh:'15- sf/sf; AfG: '11- 7/6, 15- 1/1/3R; AfCh: '10- sf/-, '12- 4/3/3R, '14- 3/2/2R; CCp; '14- 4/5. At 60m: WI: '16- 7.
Progress at 100m: 2010- 12.10/11.6, 24.3; 2011- 11.56, 24.12; 2012- 11.53, 23.26; 2013- 11.58, 23.63; 2014- 11.20, 22.78; 2015- 11.02/10.95w, 22.56. pb 60m 7.06i '16.

JAMAICA

Governing body: Jamaica Athletics Administrative Association, PO Box 272, Kingston 5. Founded 1932.
2015 Champions: **Men** 100m: Asafa Powell 9.84, 200m: Nickel Ashmeade 20.36, 400m: Javon Francis 44.70, 800m: Ricardo Cunningham 1:47.15, 1500m: Oriane Wint 3:54.90, 5000m: Kemoy Campbell 13:51.34, 110mh: Omar McLeod 12.97, 400mh: Annsert Whyte 48.90, HJ/TJ: Clayton Bryan 2.15/16.17, LJ: Damar Forbes 7.98, SP: O'Dayne Richards 20.13, DT: Fedrick Dacres 63.23, JT: Orlando Thomas 70.12. **Women**: 100m: Shelly-Ann Fraser-Pryce 10.79, 200m: Elaine Thompson 22.51, 400m: Christine Day 50.16, 800m: Natoya Goule 1:59.63, 1500m: Aisha Praught 4:15.92, 100mh: Danielle Williams 12.71, 400mh: Janeive Russell 55.10, HJ: Kimberly Williamson 1.81, LJ: Chanice Porter 6.39, TJ: Kimberly Williams 14.34, SP/DT: Danniel Thomas 16.98/57.67, HT: Daina Levy 63.03, JT: Olivia McKoy 46.45.

Nickel ASHMEADE b. 7 Apr 1990 Ocho Rios, Saint-Ann 1.84m 87kg.
At 200m/4x100mR (100m): WCh: '11- 5, '13- 4/1R (5), '15- 8/1R (sf); CG: 14- 3/1R; WJ: '08- 2/2R (2 4x400m); WY: '07- 3 (2, 3 MedR); PAm-J: '09- 1; won DL 2012, JAM 2015, CAC 2009.
World 4x200m record 2014.
Progress at 100m, 200m: 2006- 10.60, 21.30; 2007- 10.39, 20.76; 2008- 10.34, 20.80/20.16w; 2009- 10.37/10.21w, 20.40; 2010- 10.39, 20.63; 2011- 9.96, 19.91; 2012- 9.93, 19.85; 2013- 9.90, 19.93; 2014- 9.97/9.95w, 19.95; 2015- 9.91, 20.18. pbs: 60m 6.62i '14, 400m 47.19 '12.

Kemar BAILEY-COLE b. 10 Jan 1992 St. Catherine 1.95m 83kg. Racers TC.
At 100m/4x100mR (200m): OG: '12- res (1)R; WCh: '13- 4/1R; CG: '14- 1/1R; WY: '09- sf/sf.
Progress at 100m: 2008- 10.85, 2009- 10.41/10.38w, 2010- 10.53, 2011- 10.28, 2012- 9.97, 2013- 9.93, 2014- 9.96/9.95w, 2015- 9.92. pbs: 150mSt 15.00 '14, 200m 20.66 '15, 400m 47.36 '14.

Yohan BLAKE b. 26 Dec 1989 St. James 1.81m 79kg. Racers TC.
At 100m/4x100mR: OG: '12- 2/2/1R; WCh: '11- 1/1R; WJ: '06- 3/1R, '08- 4/2R; WY: '05- 7; PAm-J: '07- 2 (3 4x400m); won CAC-J 100m & 200m 2006; JAM 100m & 200m 2012.
World record 4x100m 2012, 4x200m 2014.

Progress at 100m, 200m: 2005- 10.56, 22.10; 2006- 10.33, 20.92; 2007- 10.11, 20.62; 2008- 10.27/10.20w, 21.06; 2009- 10.07/9.93dq, 20.60; 2010- 9.89, 19.78; 2011- 9.82/9.80w, 19.26; 2012- 9.69, 19.44; 2013- 20.72, 2014- 10.02, 20.48; 2015- 10.12, 21.57. pbs: 60m 6.75i '08, 150mSt 14.71 '14, 400m 46.32 '13.

3-month drugs ban from positive test at Jamaican Champs 25 Jun 2009. Cut 200m pb from 20.60 to 19.78 in Monaco 2010 and then to 19.26 in Brussels 2011. Youngest ever World 100m champion at 21 in 2011.

Usain BOLT b. 21 Aug 1986 Sherwood Content, Trelawny 1.96m 88kg. Racers TC.

At (100m)/200m/4x100mR: OG: '04- h, '08 & '12- 1/1/1R; WCh: '05- 8, '07- 2/2R, '09- 1/1/1R, '11- dq/1/1R, '13- 1/1/1R, '15- 1/1/1R; CG: '14- 1R; WJ: 02- 1/2R/2R; WY: '01- sf, '03- 1; PAm-J: '03- 1/2R; WCp: '06- 2; won WAF 200m 2009, DL 100m 2012, CAC 200m 2005, JAM 100m 2008-09, 2013; 200m 2005, 2007-09.

World records: 100m (3), 200m (2), 4x100m (4) 2008-12, best low altitude 300m 2010, CAC records 100m (4) 2008-09, 200m (3) 2007-09, WJR 200m 2003 & 2004, World U18 200m record 2003.

Progress at 100m, 200m, 400m: 2000- 51.7; 2001- 21.73, 48.28; 2002- 20.58, 47.12; 2003- 20.13, 45.35; 2004- 19.93, 2005- 19.99, 2006- 19.88, 2007- 10.03, 19.75, 45.28; 2008- 9.69, 19.30, 46.94; 2009- 9.58, 19.19, 45.54; 2010- 9.82, 19.56, 45.87; 2011- 9.76, 19.40; 2012- 9.63, 19.32; 2013- 9.77, 19.66, 46.44; 2014- 9.98, 2015- 9.79, 19.55, 46.38. pbs: 60m 6.31+ '09, 100y 9.14+ '11, 150m 14.35 straight & 14.44+ turn '09 (world bests), 300m 30.97 '10 (world low altitude best).

Bolt was the sensational superstar of the 2008 Olympics when he won triple gold – all in world records. In 2009 he smashed both the 100m and 200m WRs at the World Champs and after two more golds at the 2011 Worlds (dq for false start at 100m) he repeated his Olympic treble in 2012 and won further World trebles in 2013 and 2015, so that his 13 World Champs medals and 11 golds are records. In 2002, after running 20.61 to win the CAC U17 200m title, he became the youngest ever male world junior champion at 15y 332d and set a world age best with 20.58, with further age records for 16 and 17 in 2003-04. Won IAAF 'Rising Star' award for men in 2002 and 2003 and male Athlete of the Year award 2008-09, 2011-12. He has won 42 of his 46 100m finals 2007-15. He was appointed an Ambassador-at-Large for Jamaica.

Nesta CARTER b. 11 Oct 1985 Banana Ground 1.78m 70kg. MVP TC.

At 100m/4x100mR: OG: '08/12- 1R; WCh: '07- sf/2R, '11- 7/1R, '13- 3/1R, '15- 1R; CCp: '14- 1R. At 200m: WJ: '04- sf/res (2)R. At 60m: WI: '10-12-14: 7/2/7.

Three world 4x100m records 2008-12.

Progress at 100m: 2004- 10.0/10.56/10.52w, 2005- 10.59, 2006- 10.20, 2007- 10.11, 2008- 9.98, 2009- 9.91, 2010- 9.78, 2011- 9.89, 2012- 9.95, 2013- 9.87, 2014- 9.96/9.89w, 2015- 9.98. pbs: 50m 5.67i '12, 60m 6.49i '12, 200m 20.25 '11, 400m 47.46 '15.

Fedrick DACRES b. 28 Feb 1994 Kingston 1.91m 77kg.

At DT: WCh: '15- 7; PAm: '15- 1; WJ: '12- 1; WY '11- 1; won CAC-J 2012; JAM 2015.

Progress at DT: 2011- 53.05, 2012- 55.45, 2013- 59.30, 2014- 66.75, 2015- 66.40. pb SP 18.99 '14.

Rasheed DWYER b. 29 Jan 1989 St. Mary 1.88m 80kg. G.C.Foster College.

At 200m/4x100mR: WCh: '15- res 1R; CG : '10- sf/2R, '14- 1; WJ: '08- res2R; PAm: '15- 2; WUG: '11- 1, '13- 2; CCp: '14- 2.

CAC 4x200m record 2014.

Progress at 200m: 2006- 21.67, 2007- 21.81, 2008- 21.84, 2009- 21.12/20.82w, 2010- 20.49, 2011- 20.20, 2012- 20.59, 2013- 20.15, 2014- 19.98, 2015- 19.80. pbs: 100m 10.16 '15, 400m 46.76 '16.

Javon FRANCIS b. 14 Dec 1994 1.83m 73kg. Akan TC.

At 400m/4x400mR: WCh: '13- sf/2R, '15- sf; WJ: '12- 9. JAM champion 20.15.

Progress at 400m: 2012- 46.06, 2013- 45.24, 2014- 45.00, 2015- 44.50. Pbs: 200m 20.58 '14.

Brilliant anchor relay legs at Worlds: 2013- 44.05 to move JAM from 5th to 2nd, and 43.52 in 2015, when pipped for 3rd place.

Jason LIVERMORE b. 25 Apr 1988 Kingston 1.78m 77kg. Akan TC.

At (100m)/200m/4x100mR: WCh: '13- sf; CG: '14- 6/3/1R; PAm: '07-(h), '11- sf, '15- 7/h.

CAC 4x200m record 2014.

Progress at 100m, 200m: 2007- 10.64, 22.02; 2008- 10.61, 2009- 10.66, 2010- 10.43, 21.61; 2011- 10.31, 20.73A; 2012- 10.31, 21.00; 2013- 10.07, 20.13; 2014- 10.05, 20.25; 2015- 10.06/10.10w, 20.54. pbs: 200m 20.83 '12, 400m 47.36 '14.

Rusheen McDONALD b. 17 Aug 1992 Mandeville, Manchester 1.75m 73kg. Utech.

At 400m/4x400mR: OG: '12- h; WCh: '13- 2R, '15- sf; CG: '14- sf.

Jamaican 400m record 2015.

Progress at 400m: 2011- 47.32, 2012- 45.10, 2013- 45.28, 2014- 45.25, 2015- 43.93. Pbs: 200m 20.57 '15, 300m 31.94 '15.

Omar McLEOD b. 25 Apr 1994 1.80m 73kg. Studied business management at University of Arkansas, USA.

At 110mh: WCh: '15- 6; WY: '11- 4 (8 400mh). At 60mh: WI: '16- 1.At 4x400m: WJ: '12-1. Won JAM 2015, NCAA 110mh 2015 (& 60mh indoors 2014-15).

Progress at 110mh: 2014- 13.44, 2015- 12.97. Pbs: 60m 6.71i '15, 200m 21.09i '14, 400m 47.41i '15, 60mh 7.41i '16, 400mh 49.98 '13.

Hansle PARCHMENT b. 17 Jun 1990 Saint Thomas 1.96m 90kg. Student of psychology at University of the West Indies.
At 110mh: OG: '12- 3; WCh: '13- sf, '15- 2; CG: '10- 5; WY: '07- sf; WUG: '11- 1. Won JAM 2012. Three Jamaican 110mh records 2012-13.
Progress at 110mh: 2010- 13.71, 2011- 13.24, 2012- 13.12, 2013- 13.05, 2014- 12.94, 2015- 13.03. Pb 400mh 53.74 '08.

Asafa POWELL b. 23 Nov 1982 St Catherine 1.90m 88kg. MVP. Studied sports medicine at Kingston University of Technology.
At 100m/4x100mR: OG: '04- 5 (dns 200), '08- 5/1R, '12- 7; WCh: '03- qf, '07- 3/2R, '09- 3/1R, '15- 7/1R; CG: '02- sf/2R, '06- 1/1R; PAm-J: '01- 2R. At 60m: WI: '16- 2. Won JAM 100m 2003-05, 2007, 2011, 2015; 200m 2006, 2010; WAF 100m 2004, 2006-08; 200m 2004; DL 100m 2011, GL 2006.
Four world 100m records, five CAC & Commonwealth 2005-07, seven JAM 2004-7; WR 4x100m 2008. Two world bests 100y 2010. Two CAC 60m indoor records 2016.
Progress at 100m, 200m: 2001- 10.50, 2002- 10.12, 20.48; 2003- 10.02/9.9, 2004- 9.87, 20.06; 2005- 9.77, 2006- 9.77, 19.90; 2007- 9.74, 20.00; 2008- 9.72, 2009- 9.82, 2010- 9.82/9.72w, 19.97; 2011- 9.78, 20.55; 2012- 9.85, 2013- 9.88, 2014- 9.87, 2015- 9.81. pbs: 50m 5.64i '12, 60m 6.42+ '09, 6.44i '16; 100y 9.07+ '10, 400m 45.94 '09.
Disqualified for false start in World quarters 2003 after fastest time (10.05) in heats. In 2004 he tied the record of nine sub-10 second times in a season and in 2005 he took the world record for 100m at Athens, tying that at Gateshead and Zürich in 2006, when he ran a record 12 sub-10 times and was world athlete of the year. Took record to 9.74 in Rieti 2007 and ran 15 sub-10 times in 2008, including seven sub-9.90 in succession after 5th place at Olympics. Now has record 93 sub-10 times (plus 7w and 1 while banned). Withdrew from 2011 Worlds through injury. IAAF Athlete of the Year 2006. He tested positive for a banned stimulant on 21 Jun 2013; an original 18-month ban was reduced to 6 months by the CAS. Elder brother Donovan (b. 31 Oct 1971): at 60m: 6.51i '96 (won US indoors '96, 6 WI '99); 100m 10.07/9.7 '95.

O'Dayne RICHARDS b. 14 Dec 1988 St. Andrew 1.78m 117kg. MVP TC. Data communications graduate.
At SP: WCh: '13- dnq 20, '15- 3; CG: '14- 1; PAm: '15- 1; WUG: '11- 1; CCp: '14- 2; won CAC 2011, 2013; JAM 2013-15.
Three CAC shot records 2014-15.
Progress at SP: 2008- 16.76, 2009- 18.05, 2010- 18.74, 2011- 19.93, 2012- 20.31, 2013- 20.97, 2014- 21.61, 2015- 21.69. pb DT 58.31 '12.

Andrew RILEY b. 6 Sep 1988 Saint Thomas 1.88m 80kg. Economics graduate of University of Illinois.
At 110mh: OG: '12- h; WCh: '11- sf, '13- 8, '15- sf; CG: 14- 1. Jamaican champion 2011, 2013-14; won NCAA 100m 2012, 110mh 2010 & 2012. At 60mh: WI: '14 dns final.
Progress at 110mh: 2009- 13.74/13.61w, 2010- 13.45, 2011- 13.32, 2012- 13.19, 2013- 13.14, 2014- 13.19, 2015- 13.28. Pbs: 60m 6.57i '12, 100m 10.02 '12, 200m 21.25w '12, 60mh 7.53i '12, HJ 2.10 '08.
First to win NCAA 100m and 110mh double 2012.

Warren WEIR b. 31 Oct 1989 Trelawny 1.78m 75kg. Racers TC.
At 200m/4x100mR: OG: '12- 3; WCh: '13- 2/res 1R, '15- sf; CG: '14- 2; won DL 2013, JAM 2013. At 110mh: WJ: '08- sf.
World 4x200m record 2014.
Progress at 200m: 2008- 22.26, 2009- 21.46w, 2010- 21.52, 2011- 20.43, 2012- 19.84, 2013- 19.79, 2014- 19.82, 2015- 20.24. pbs: 100m 10.02 '13, 400m 46.23 '13, 110mh 13.65 '07, 13.45w '08; 400mh 53.28 '09.

Women

Veronica CAMPBELL-BROWN b. 15 May 1982 Clarks Town, Trelawny 1.63m 61kg. Adidas. Was at University of Arkansas, USA.
At (100m)/200m/4x100mR: OG: '00- 2R, '04- 3/1/1R, '08- 1, '12- 3/4/2R; WCh: '05- 2/4/2R, '07- 1/2/2R, '09- 4/2, '11- 2/1/2R, '15- 4/3/1R; CG: '02- (2)/2R, '06- 2, 14- (2)/1R; WJ: '98- (qf), '00- 1/1/2R; WY: '99- (1)/1R; PAm-J: '99- 2R; CCp: '14- (1)/1R. At 60m: WI: '10-12-14: 1/1/5. Won WAF 100m 2004-05, 200m 2004; DL 100m 2014; CAC-J 100m 2000, JAM 100m 2002, 2004-05, 2007, 2011, 2014; 200m 2004-05, 2007-09, 2011.
Four CAC & Commonwealth 4x100m records 2004-15. CAC junior 100m record 2000.
Progress at 100m, 200m: 1999- 11.49, 23.73; 2000- 11.12/11.1, 22.87; 2001- 11.13/22.92; 2002- 11.00, 22.39; 2004- 10.91, 22.05; 2005- 10.85, 22.35/22.29w; 2006- 10.99, 22.51; 2007- 10.89, 22.34; 2008- 10.87/10.85w, 21.74; 2009- 10.89/ 10.81w, 22.29; 2010- 10.78, 21.98; 2011- 10.76, 22.22; 2012- 10.81, 22.32; 2013- 11.01/10.78w, 22.53/ 22.18w; 2014- 10.86, 22.94/22.30w, 2015- 10.89, 21.97. pbs: 50m 6.08i '12, 60m 7.00i '10, 100y 9.91+ '11 (world best), 400m 52.24i '05, 52.25 '11.
In 2000 became the first woman to become World Junior champion at both 100m and 200m. Unbeaten at 200m in 28 finals (42 races in all) from 11 March 2000 to 22 July 2005 (lost to Allyson Felix). Married Omar Brown (1 CG 200m 2006) on 3 Nov 2007. She received a public warning for a positive test for a banned diuretic on 4 May 2013 and was suspended for the season, but the Court of Arbitration for Sport upheld her appeal against the suspension in February 2014.

Christine DAY b. 12 Aug 1986 St. Mary 1.68m 51kg. Cameron Blazers TC.
At 400m/4x400mR: OG: '12- sf/3R; WCh: '09- sf,

'15- 4/1R; CG: 14- 3/1R; CCp: '14- 1R. JAM champion 2015.
Progress at 400m: 2006- 55.33, 2007- 53.91, 2008- 53.10, 2009- 51.54, 2010- 52.43, 2011- 52.08, 2012- 50.85, 2013- 50.91, 2014- 50.16, 2015- 50.14. pb 200m 23.73 '13.

Shelly-Ann FRASER-PRYCE b. 27 Dec 1986 Kingston 1.60m 52kg. MVP. Graduate of the University of Technology. née Fraser. Married Jason Pryce on 7 Jan 2011.
At 100m/(200m)/4x100mR: OG: '08- 1, '12- 1/2/2R; WCh: '07- res (2)R, '09- 1/1R, '11- 4/2R, '13- 1/1/1R, '15- 1/1R; CG: '14- 1R. At 60m: WI: '14- 1. Won WAF 2008, DL 100m 2012-13, 2015; 200m 2013; JAM 100m 2009, 2012, 2015; 200m 2012-13.
CAC and Commonwealth records 100m 2009 & 2012, 4x100m (4) 2011-15; CAC 4x100m 4x200m 2014.
Progress at 100m, 200m: 2002- 11.8, 2003- 11.57, 2004- 11.72, 24.08; 2005- 11.72; 2006- 11.74, 24.8; 2007- 11.31/11.21w, 23.5; 2008- 10.78, 22.15; 2009- 10.73, 22.58; 2010- 10.82dq, 22.47dq; 2011- 10.95, 22.59/22.10w; 2012- 10.70, 22.09; 2013- 10.71, 22.13; 2014- 11.01, 22.53; 2015- 10.74, 22.37. pb 60m 6.98i '14, 400m 55.67 '15.
Double World and Olympic champion with eight global gold medals (and four silver). Huge improvement in 2008 and moved to joint third on world all-time list for 100m when winning 2009 world 100m title. 6-month ban for positive test for a non-performance enhancing drug on 23 May 2010. IAAF Athlete of the Year 2013.

Shericka JACKSON b. 15 Jul 1994 1.74m 59kg. UTech.
At 400m/4x400mR: WCh: '15- 3/1R. At 200m: WJ: '12- 8/2R; WY: '11- 3/1 MedR; Yth OG: '10- 4.
Progress at 400m: 2008- 54.27, 2009- 53.13, 2010- 53.71, 2011- 52.94, 2012- 53.34, 2013- 51.60, 2014- 51.32, 2015- 49.99. pb 200m 22.84 '13.

Stephenie Ann McPHERSON b. 25 Nov 1988 1.68m 55kg. MVP. Was at Kingston University of Technology.
At 400m/4x400mR: WCh: '13- 4, '15- 5/1R; CG: 14- 1/1R; CCp: '14- 1R; WI: 14- 2R, '16- 4.
Progress at 400m: 2006- 56.42, 2007- 55.77, 2008- 52.80, 2009- 51.95, 2010- 51.64, 2012- 52.98, 2013- 49.92, 2014- 50.12, 2015- 50.32. pbs: 100m 11.44 '10, 200m 22.93 '14, 800m 2:15.24 '12, 400mh 57.46 '12.

Natasha MORRISON b. 17 Nov 1992 1.70m 57kg. GGOF.
At 100m/4x100mR: WCh: '15- 7/1R.
CAC and Commonwealth 4x100m record 2015.
Progress at 100m: 2007- 12.06, 2008- 12.00, 2010- 11.98/11.47w, 2011- 11.42, 2013- 11.17/11.12w, 2014- 11.06, 2015- 10.96. pb 200m 23.08 '13.

Janeive RUSSELL b. 14 Nov 1993 Manchester 1.75m 63kg. UTech.
At 400mh/4x400mR: WCh: '15- 5; CG: '14- 3; WJ: '12- 1/2R. At 400m: WJ: '10- sf/3R. At WY: '09- 9. Won JAM Hep 2011, 400mh 2015.
Progress at 400mh: 2011- 57.71, 2012- 56.62, 2013- 56.30, 2014- 54.75, 2015- 54.64. pbs: 200m 24.10 '11, 400m 51.88 '15, 800m 2:11.5 '15, 100mh 13.80 '12, HJ 1.80 '09, LJ 6.20 '10, 6.26w '11; SP 10.86 '11, JT 26.53 '11, Hep 5361 '11.

Sherone SIMPSON b. 12 Aug 1984 Manchester, Jamaica 1.75m 59kg. MVP. Graduate of Kingston University of Technology.
At 100m/(200m)/4x100mR: OG: '04- 6/1R, '08- 2=/6, '12- (sf)/2R; WCh: '05- 6/2R, '11- (8)/2R, '15- sf/8/res 1R; CG: '06- (1)/1R; WJ: '02- 1R; PAm: '15- 1; PAm-J: '03- 2/2R; WCp: '06- 1/1R. Won WAF 100m 2006, JAM 100m 2006, 2010; 200m 2006.
Three CAC& Commonwealth 4x100m records 2004-12.
Progress at 100m, 200m: 2000- 12.54, 2001- 12.17, 25.01; 2002- 11.60, 24.21; 2003- 11.37/11.1, 23.60; 2004- 11.01, 22.70; 2005- 10.97, 22.54; 2006- 10.82, 22.00; 2007- 11.43, 22.76; 2008- 10.87, 22.11; 2009- 11.15/11.04w; 2010- 11.02, 22.65/22.64w; 2011- 11.00, 22.73; 2012- 11.01, 22.37; 2013- 11.27/11.03dq, 22.83/22.73w/22.55dq; 2014- 11.34, 23.38; 2015- 10.95, 22.50. pbs: 400m 51.25 '08, 100mh 14.10 '02.
18-month drugs ban for positive test at 2013 Jamaican Champs, but reduced to 6 months by the CAS.

Kaliese SPENCER b. 6 May 1987 Westmoreland 1.73m 59kg. Cameron Blazers TC. Was at University of Texas.
At 400mh/4x400mR: OG: '12- 4; WCh: '07-09-11-13-15: sf/4&res 2R/4/dq h/8; CG: 14- 1; WJ: '06- 1/3R; CCp: '14- 1; Won DL 2010-12, 2014; JAM 2011, 2014. At 400m: WI: '14- 2/2R.
Progress at 400mh: 2006- 55.11, 2007- 55.62, 2009- 53.56, 2010- 53.33, 2011- 52.79, 2012- 53.49, 2013- 54.22, 2014- 53.41, 2015- 54.15. pbs: 200m 23.11 '13, 400m 50.19 '13, 800m 2:03.01 '11.

Kerron STEWART b. 16 Apr 1984 Kingston 1.75m 61kg. Adult education student at Auburn University, USA.
At 100m/(200m)/4x100mR: OG: '08- 2=/3, '12- sf/2R; WCh: '07- 7/2R, '09- 2/1R, '11- 6/5/2R, '13- 5/1R; CG: '14- 3/1R; PAm: '15- (5)/2R; WJ: '02- 4/1R; WY: '01- 2/2R. Won NCAA 200m 2007, indoor 60m & 200m 2007; JAM 100m 2008, 2013.
Three CAC & Commonwealth 4x100m records 2011-13.
Progress at 100m, 200m: 2000- 11.89, 24.09w; 2001- 11.70, 23.90; 2002- 11.46, 24.21; 2003- 11.34, 23.50; 2004- 11.40, 23.63i/23.66; 2005- 11.63, 23.77i/24.22/23.46w; 2006- 11.03, 22.65; 2007- 11.03, 22.41; 2008- 10.80, 21.99; 2009- 10.75, 22.42; 2010- 10.96, 22.57/22.34w; 2011- 10.87, 22.63; 2012- 10.92, 22.70; 2013- 10.96, 22.71; 2014- 11.02, 23.64; 2015- 11.17, 22.72. pbs: 55m 6.71i '06, 60m 7.14i '07, 400m 51.83 '13.

Elaine THOMPSON b. 28 Jun 1992 Manchester 1.69m 57kg. MVP. Kingston University of Technology.
At 200m/4x100mR: WCh: '15- 2/1R; CG: '14- res 1R. JAM champion 2015. At 60m: WI: '16- 3.
CAC and Commonwealth 4x100m record 2015.
Progress at 100m, 200m: 2008- 12.16, 25.56; 2009- 12.01, 24.35; 2010- 11.94w, 2012- 23.89, 2013- 11.41, 23.73; 2014- 11.17, 23.23; 2015- 10.84, 21.66. pbs: 60m 7.04i '16, 150mSt 15.00 '14, 200m 20.83 '12, 400m 47.36 '14.

Danielle WILLIAMS b. 14 Sep 1992 St.Andrew 1.68m 59kg. Johnson C.Smith University, USA.
At 100mh: WCh: '13- sf, '15- 1; CG: '14- 4; WJ: '10- 4; WUG: '13- 3, '15- 1; PAm-J: '10- 2. JAM champion 2013, 2015.
CAC and Commonwealth 4x100m record 2015.
Progress at 100mh: 2010- 13.46/13.41w, 2011- 13.32/13.13w, 2012- 14.02, 2013- 12.69, 2014- 12.99, 2015- 12.57. pbs: 60m 7.32i '14, 100m 11.24A/ 11.41/11.34w '13, 200m 22.62A/23.43i '13, 23.48 '14; 60mh 8.02i '15.
Her sister **Shermaine** (b. 4 Feb 1990) at 100mh: OG: '12- sf; WCh: '13- sf, '15- 7; WJ: '08- 2; WY: '05- 6, '07- 2; pb 12.78/12.65w '12.

Kimberly WILLIAMS b. 3 Nov 1988 Saint Thomas 1.69m 66kg. Florida State University, USA.
At TJ: OG: '12- 6; WCh: '09/11 dnq 15/14, '13- 4, '15- 5; CG: '14- 1; WJ: '06- dnq 15; WY: '05- dnq; CAG: '10- 1; PAm-J: '07- 2; CCp: '14- 4; WI: '12- 5, '14- 3. Won NCAA LJ & TJ 2009, JAM TJ 2010, 2012-15.
Progress at TJ: 2004- 12.53/12.65w, 2005- 12.63/13.09w, 2006- 13.18, 2007- 13.52, 2008- 13.82i/13.69/13.83w, 2009- 14.08/14.38w, 2010- 14.23, 2011- 14.25, 2012- 14.53, 2013- 14.62/14.78w, 2014- 14.59, 2015- 14.45. pbs: 100m 11.76 '12, 200m 24.55 '11, LJ 6.55i 11, 6.42/6.66w '09.

Novlene WILLIAMS-MILLS b. 26 Apr 1982 Saint Ann 1.70m 57kg. Studied recreation at University of Florida, USA.
At 400m/4x400mR: OG: '04- sf/3R, '08- sf/3R, '12- 5/3R; WCh: '05- 2R, '07- 3/2R, '09- 4/2R, '11- 8/2R, '13- 8, '15- 6/1R; CG: '06- 3, '14- 2/1R; PAm: '03- 6/2R; WI: '06- 5; WCp: '06- 3/1R, '14- 2/1R. Won DL 2014, JAM 400m 2006-07, 2009-14.
Progress at 400m: 1999- 55.62, 2000- 53.90, 2001- 54.99, 2002- 52.05, 2003- 51.93, 2004- 50.59, 2005- 51.09, 2006- 49.63, 2007- 49.66, 2008- 50.11, 2009- 49.77, 2010- 50.04, 2011- 50.05, 2012- 49.78, 2013- 50.01, 2014- 50.05, 2015- 50.47. pbs: 200m 23.25 '10, 500m 1:11.83i '03.
Married 2007. Younger sister **Clora Williams** (b. 26.11.83) joined her on JAM's 3rd place 4x400m team at 2010 WI; she has 400m pb 51.06 and won NCAA 2006.

JAPAN

Governing body: Nippon Rikujo-Kyogi Renmei, 1-1-1 Jinnan, Shibuya-Ku, Tokyo 150-8050. Founded 1911.
National Championships first held in 1914 (men), 1925 (women). **2015 Champions**: **Men**: 100m: Kei Takase 10.28, 200m: Kenji Fujimitsu 20.32, 400m: Yuzo Kanemaru 46.10, 800m: Sho Kawamoto 1:49.02, 1500m: Nanami Arai 3:43.47, 5000m: Kota Murayama 13:37.22, 10000m: Tetsuya Yoroizaka 28:18.53, Mar: Sataru Sasaki 2:08:56, 3000mSt: Hironori Tsuetaki 8:32.89, 110mh: Shun-ya Takayama 13.81, 400mh: Yuki Matsushita 49.76, HJ: Naoto Tobe 2.26, PV: Hiroki Ogita 5.50, LJ: Yohei Sugai 7.88, TJ: Kazuyoshi Ishikawa 16.30, SP: Satoshi Hatase 18.78, DT: Yuji Tsutsumi 57.15, HT: Horoshi Noguchi 71.98, JT: Ryohei Arai 84.13, Dec: Keisuke Ushiro 8058, 20kW: Eiki Takahashi 1:18:03, 50kW: Hirooki Arai 3:40:20. **Women**: 100m/200m: Chisato Fukushima 11.50/23.23, 400m: Sayaka Aoki 53.05, 800m: Hana Yamada 2:08.20, 1500m: Chihiro Sunaga 4:15.69, 5000m: Misaki Onishi 15:18.77, 10000m: Kasumi Nishihara 32:06.48, Mar: Risa Shigetomo 2:26:39, 3000mSt: Anju Takamizawa 9:55.79, 100mh: Hitomi Shimura 13.27, 400mh: Manami Kira 57.92, HJ: Yuki Watanabe 1.81, PV: Kanae Tatsuta 4.15, LJ: Saeko Okayama 6.21, TJ: Arisa Nakao 13.09, SP: Aya Ota 15.65, DT: Ayumi Sakaguchi 53.58, HT: Masumi Aya 66.05, JT: Yuki Ebihara 59.11, Hep: Megu Hemphill 5622, 20kW: Kumiko Okada 1:31:57

Ryohei ARAI b23 Jun 1991 Saitama pref. 1.82m 93kg.
At JT: WCh: '14- 9; AsiG: '14- 2. JPN champion 2014-15.
Progress at JT: 2011- 78.21, 2012- 78.00, 2013- 78.19, 2014- 86.83, 2015- 84.66.

Yusuke SUZUKI b. 1 Feb 1988 Yokohama 1.71m 58kg. Fujitsu.
At 20kW: OG: '12- 36; WCh: '09-11-13-15: 42/5/12;/dnf WCp: '14- 4; AsiG: '10- 5, '14- 2; WUG: '14- 4; Asian champion 2013, 2015; JPN 2011, 2013. At 10000mW: WJ: 04- 17, '06- 3; WY: '05- 3.
Walk records: World 20k 2015, Asian 5000m 2015, 10000m (2) 2014-15, Japanese 10k & 10000mW 2015, 20k (3) 2013-15.
Progress at 20kW: 2007- 1:24:40, 2008- 1:22:34, 2009- 1:22:05, 2010- 1:20:06, 2011- 1:21:13, 2012- 1:22:30, 2013- 1:18:34, 2014- 1:18:17, 2015- 1:16:36. pbs: 5000mW 18:37.22 '15, 10kW 38:05 '15, track 38:10.23 '15.

Eiki TAKAHASHI b. 19 Nov 1992 1.75m 56kg.
At 20kW: WCh: '15- 47; WCp: '14- 9; AsiG: '14- 7. JPN champion 2015-16.
Walk records: Asian 5000m & 10000m 2015, Japanese 20k 2015.
Progress at 20kW: 2011- 1:26:16, 2012- 1:22:33, 2013- 1:20:25, 2014- 1:18:41, 2015- 1:18:03, 2016-

1:18:26. pbs: 5000mW 18:51.93 '15, 10000mW 38:01.49 '15.

Takayuki TANII b. 14 Feb 1983 Namerikawa, Toyama 1.67m 57kg. Sagawa, was at Nihon University.
At (20kW)/50kW: OG: '04- (15), '08- 29, '12- dnf; WCh: '05-07-09-11-13-15: (23)/(21)/dq/8/9/3; AsiG: '14- 1; At 10000mW: WJ: '02- 7; WY: '99- 3. Won Asian 20kW 2007, JPN 20kW 2004-05, 50kW 2013-14.
Japanese 50k walk record 2003.
Progress at 50kW: 2003- 3:47:54, 2006- 3:47:23, 2007- 3:50:08, 2008- 3:49:33, 2009- 3:52:22, 2010- 3:53:27, 2011- 3:48:03, 2012- 3:43:56, 2013- 3:44:25, 2014- 3:40:19, 2015- 3:42:01. pbs: 5000mW 19:36.78 '13, 10000mW 40:03.42 '03, 20kW 1:20:39 '04, 30kW 2:11:34 '14, 35kW 2:33:37 '14.

Yuki YAMAZAKI b. 16 Jan 1984 Toyama 1.79m 65kg. Was at Juntendo University.
At (20kW)/50kW: OG: '04- 16, '08- 11/7, '12- dq; WCh: '05-07-09-15: 8/dnf/dq/34; WCp: '10- 6; AsiG: '02- dq/dq, '06- (4), '14- dq; AsiC: '03- (2), '07- 2. At 10000mW: WJ: '00- 20, '02- 5; WY: '01- 4. Won JPN 20kW 2002, 50kW 2004-10, 2012.
Four Japanese 50k walk records 2006-09. World youth 5000m walk best 2001.
Progress at 50kW: 2004- 3:55:20, 2005- 3:50:40, 2006- 3:43:38, 2007- 3:47:40, 2008- 3:41:29, 2009- 3:40:12, 2010- 3:46:46, 2011- 3:44:03, 2012- 3:41:47, 2014- 3:44:23, 2015- 3:43:40. pbs: 5000mW 19:35.79 '01, 10000mW 39:29.00 '08, 20kW 1:20:38 '03, 30kW 2:11:31 '12, 35kW 2:33:06 '12.

Women

Kayoko FUKUSHI b. 25 Mar 1982 Itayanagi, Aiomori pref. 1.60m 45kg. Wacoal.
At Mar: WCh: '13- 3. At 5000m/(10000m): OG: '04- (26), '08- h/11, '12- h/10; WCh: '03- h/11, '05- 12/11, '07- 14/10, '09- (9); WJ: '00- 4; AsiG: '02- 2/2, '06- (1), '10- 5/4; WCp: '06- 3 (5 3000m). World 20km: '06- 6; CC: '02- 15, '06- 6. Won JPN 5000m 2002, 2004-07, 2010; 10000m 2002-07, 2010.
World 15km record & Asian 20km & HMar records 2006, Japanese records: 3000m 2002, 5000m (4) 2002-05.
Progress at 5000m, 10,000m, Mar: 1998- 16:56.35, 1999- 16:38.69, 35:37.54; 2000- 15:29.70, 2001- 15:10.23, 31:42.05; 2002- 14:55.19, 30:51.81; 2003- 15:09.02, 31:10.57; 2004- 14:57.73, 31:05.68; 2005- 14:53.22, 31:03.75; 2006- 15:03.17, 30:57.90; 2007- 15:05.73, 32:13.58; 2008- 15:12.7, 31:01.14, 2:40:54; 2009- 15:23.44mx, 31:23.49; 2010- 15:17.86, 31:29.03; 2011- 30:54.29, 2:24:38; 2012- 15:09.31, 31:10.35; 2013- 32:42.56, 2:24:21; 2014- 32:48.87, 2:26:25; 2015- 2:24:25, 2016- 2:22:17. pbs: 3000m 8:44.40 '02, 15k 46:55 '06, 20k 63:41 '06, HMar 67:26 '06, 30k 1:41:25 '08.
Set Japanese junior records at 3000m, 5000m and 10000m in 2001. Won Osaka marathon 2013 & 2016.

KAZAKHSTAN

Governing body: Athletic Federation of the Republic of Kazakhstan, Abai Street 48, 480072 Almaty. Founded 1959.

2015 National Champions: **Men**: 100m: Vitaliy Zems 10.46, 200m: Vladislav Leshin 21.74, 400m: Mikhail Litvin 46.30, 800m: Sergey Zaykov 1:52.77, 1500m: Artem Kosinov 4:05.74, 5000m: Andrey Leymenov 14:50.17, 10000m: Mikhail Krasilov 31:25.89, 3000mSt: Dmitriy Ivanchukov 9:14.92, 110mh: Denis Semenov 14.21, 400mh: Dmitriy Koblov 50.76, HJ: Vitaliy Tsykunov 2.20, PV: Nikita Filippov 5.55, LJ: Konstantin Safronov 7.54, TJ: Roman Valiyev 16.37, SP: Ivan Ivanov 19.03, DT: Yevgeniy Labutov 53.02, HT: Aleksandr Enchu 55.95, JT: Anton Bodnar 56.97, Dec: Aleksandr Martirosov 5991, 20000mW: Georgiy Sheyko 1:25:35.53; **Women**: 100m/200m: Viktoriya Zyabkina 11.20/23.11, 400m: Yuliya Rakhmanova 52.61, 800m: Yevgeniya Fandyushina 2:08.12, 1500m: Tatyana Neroznak 4:26.92, 5000m/10000m: Gulzhanat Zhanatbek 16:03.30/34:02.61, 3000mSt: Tatyana Palkina 11:12.47, 100mh: Anastasiya Soprunova 13.51, 400mh: Mergen Ishanguliyeva 58.30, HJ: Marina Aitova 1.84, PV: Olga Lapina 4.00, LJ/TJ: Olga Rypakova 6.19/14.00, SP: Olga Khizhnyakova 12.68, DT: Mariya Telushkina 52.22, HT: Diana Nusupbekova 54.61, JT: Asiya Rabayeva 48.49, Hep: Nadezhda Kirnos 4815, 20kW: Regina Rypakova 1:40:30.

Women

Olga RYPAKOVA b. 30 Nov 1984 Kamenogorsk 1.83m 62kg. née Alekseyeva.
At TJ/(LJ): OG: '08- 4 (dnq 29), '12- 1; WCh: '07-09-11-15: 11/10/2/3; WJ: '00- (dnq 23); AsiG: '06- (3), '10- 1/2, '14- 1; AsiC: '07- 1/1, '09- 1; WI: '08-10-12: 4/1/2; WUG: '07- (1); WCp: '06- (8), '10: 1/3; won DL TJ 2012, Asian Indoor LJ 2008-09, TJ 2009, 2016; Pen 2005-06. At Hep: WJ: '02- 2; WY: '01- 4; AsiG: '06- 1; won C.Asian 2003. Won KAZ LJ 2005, 2008, 2011, 2015; TJ 2008, 2011, 2015; Hep 2006.
Four Asian TJ records 2008-10, five indoors 2008-10, seven KAZ records 2007-10.
Progress at LJ, TJ: 2000- 6.23, 2001- 6.00, 2002- 6.26, 2003- 6.34i/6.14, 2004- 6.53i, 2005- 6.60, 2006- 6.63, 2007- 6.85, 14.69; 2008- 6.52/6.58w, 15.11; 2009- 6.58i/6.42, 14.53/14.69w; 2010- 6.60, 15.25; 2011- 6.56, 14.96; 2012- 14.98, 2014- 14.37, 2015- 14.77. pbs: 200m 24.83 '02, 800m 2:20.12 '02, 60mh 8.67i '06, 100mh 14.02 '06, HJ 1.92 '06, SP 13.04 '06, JT 41.60 '03, Hep 6122 '06, Pen 4582i '06 (Asian rec).
Former heptathlete, concentrated on long jump after birth of daughter. Four KAZ and three Asian TJ records with successive jumps in Olympic final 2008, three Asian indoor records when won World Indoor gold in 2010. Son born June 2013.

KENYA

Governing body: Kenya Amateur Athletic Association, PO Box 46722, 00100 Nairobi. Founded 1951.

2015 National Champions: **Men**: 100m/200m: Mike Mokamba 10.23/20.50, 400m: Alphas Kishoyan 44.75, 800m: Alphas Kishoyan 44.75, 800: Asbel Kiptop 1:45.4, 1500m: Elijah Mwanangoi 3:38.91, 5000m: Geoffrey Kamworor 13:14.7, 10000m: Vincent Yator 27:51.0, 3000mSt: Joash Kiplimo 8:24.26, 110mh: William Mbevi 14.33, 400mh: Boniface Mucheru 48.92, HJ: Mathew Sawe 2.24, PV: Kennedy Magut 4.05, LJ/TJ: Elijah Kimitei 7.78/16.36, SP: Manaseh Onyango 16.26, DT: David Limo 49.49, HT: Dominic Abuda 57.53, JT: Alex Kiprotich 72.89, Dec: Elijah Chesoen 6306, 20kW: Samuel Gathimba 1:23:30. **Women**: 200m/400m: Joyce Zakari 22.4/51.14, 800m: Annette Mwanzi 2:04.9, 1500m: Vivian Cheruiyot 4:09.88, 5000m: Janet Kisa 15:28.1, 10000m: Joyce Chepkirui 32:07.0, 3000mSt: Purity Kirui 9:33.40, 100mh/Hep: Priscilla Tabunda 14.08/5074, 400mh: Francisca Koki 55.82, HJ/LJ: Lissa Labiche SEY 1.85/6.25, TJ: Caroline Cherotich 3.20, SP: Getrude Chepchirchir 13.16, SP: Priscilla Isiaho 13.49, DT: Betty Chebet 43.83, HT: Rebecca Kerubo 47.77, JT: Lucy Aber 49.84, 20kW: Grace Thoiothi 1:42:35.

Leonard Kiplimo **BARSOTON** b. 21 Oct 1994 1.66m 56kg.
At 10000m: AfG: '15- 2. World CC: '13- 2J, '15- 5; AfCC: '14- 1.
Progress at 10000m: 2013- 27:33.13, 2014- 27:20.74, 2015- 27:27.55. pb 5000m 13:16.25 '15.

Emmanuel Kipkemei **BETT** b. 30 Mar 1983 1.70m 55kg.
Progress at 10000m: 2011- 26:51.95, 2012- 26:51.16, 2013- 27:28.71, 2014- 27:21.61, 2015- 27:22.34. pbs: 3000m 7:48.8 '14, 2M 8:25.55 '14, 5000m 13:08.35 '12, 15k 43:00+ '11, HMar 60:08 '15.

Josphat Kipkoech **BETT** b. 12 Jun 1990 Kericho 1.73m 60kg.
At 10000m: CG: '14- 2; AfCh: '14- 3; WJ: '10- 1. Kenyan champion 2014.
Progress at 5000m, 10000m: 2008- 13:44.51, 27:30.85; 2009- 12:57.43, 28:21.51; 2010- 13:11.60, 28:05.46A; 2011- 13:11.29, 26:48.99; 2012- 13:32.20i, 27:39.65; 2013- 13:19.46, 27:44.26A; 2014- 13:48.5A, 27:56.14; 2015- 13:54.5A, 27:40.20. pbs: 3000m 7:42.38 '09, 10M 46:22 '14, HMar 61:01 '12.

Nicholas Kiptanui **BETT** b. 14 Jun 1992 1.86m 77kg. Kenya Police.
At 400mh/4x400mR: WCh: '15- 1; CG: '14- 1; AfCh: '14- 3/3R.
Keyan 400mh record 2015.
Progress at 400mh: 2010- 53.11A, 2011- 50.35A, 2012- 53.2A, 2013- 49.70A, 2014- 49.03, 2015- 47.79. pb 800m 1:49.34 '15.

Jairus Kipchoge **BIRECH** b. 14 Dec 1992 Uasin Gishu 1.67m 56kg.
At 3000mSt: WCh: '15- 4; CG: '14- 2; AfG: '11- 4; AfCh: '14- 1; Af-J: '11- 2; CCp: '14- 1. Won DL 2014-15, Kenyan 2014.
Progress at 3000mSt: 2010- 8:50.0A, 2011- 8:11.31, 2012- 8:03.43, 2013- 8:08.72, 2014- 7:58.41, 2015- 7:58.83. pbs: 2000m 4:58.76 '11, 3000m 7:41.83 '13, 5000m 13:48.0A '14, 10000m 28:55.9A '16.

Bethwel Kiprotich **BIRGEN** b. 6 Aug 1988 Eldoret 1.78m 64kg.
At 1500m: WCh: '13- sf; WI: '14- 8.
Progress at 1500m: 2010- 3:35.60, 2011- 3:34.59, 2012- 3:31.00, 2013- 3:30.77, 2014- 3:31.22, 2015- 3:34.62i. pbs: 800m 1:48.32 '11, 1M 3:50.42 '13, 3000m 7:37.15 '13, 5000m 14:01.0A '12.

Robert Kiptoo **BIWOTT** b. 28 Jan 1996 1.80m 68kg.
At 1500m: WY: '13- 1; Af-J: '13-1 (1 800m).
Progress at 800m, 1500m: 2013- 1:46.98, 3:36.77; 2014- 1:44.69, 3:43.91A; 2015- 1:43.56, 3:30.10. pbs: 600m 1:15.91 '15.

Stanley Kipleting **BIWOTT** b. 21 Apr 1986 1.76m 60kg.
Progress HMar, Mar: 2006- 2:14:25, 2007- 61:20, 2010- 2:09:41, 2011- 60:23, 2:07:03; 2012- 59:44, 2:05:12; 2013- 58:56, 2014- 59:18, 2:04:55; 2015- 59:20, 2:06:41. Road pbs: 10k 28:00 '12, 15k 42:13 '13, 20k 56:02 '13, 30k 1:28:06 '12.
Marathon wins: São Paulo 2010, Chunchon 2011, Paris 2012, New York 2015; 2nd London 2014. His brother Norris Biwott was a marathon best of 2:11:29 for the marathon in 2013.

Collins CHEBOI Kiprotich b. 25 Sep 1987 1.75m 64kg.
At 1500m: AfG: '11- 2.
World 4x1500m record 2014.
Progress at 1500m: 2007- 3:49.0A, 2009- 3:36.24, 2010- 3:34.17, 2011- 3:32.45, 2012- 3:32.08, 2013- 3:31.53, 2014- 3:32.00, 2015- 3:30.34. pbs: 1M 3:49.56 '14, 2000m 5:00.30+ '12, 3000m 7:51.41 '10, 5000m 13:51.3A '13.

Abraham CHEROBEN b. 10 Nov 1992 1.76m 60kg.
Progress HMar: 2012- 63:53, 2013- 60:38 2014- 58:48, 2015- 59:10. Road pbs: 10k 27:35 '15, 15k 41:55 '14, 20k 55:50 '14, 25k 1:11:47 '14.

Ferguson Rotich CHERUIYOT b. 30 Nov 1989 1.83m 73kg.
At 800m: WCh: '13- sf, '15- 4; CG: '14- 4; AfCh: '14- 4. Kenyan champion 2014.
Progress at 800m: 2013- 1:43.22, 2014- 1:42.84, 2015- 1:43.60A. pb 1000m 2:16.88 '14, 1500m 3:49.0A '14
Changed first name from Simon to Ferguson in honour of Manchester United manager Alex Ferguson.

Timothy CHERUIYOT b. 20 Nov 1995 1.78m 64kg.

At 1500m: WCh: '15- 7.
Progress at 1500m: 2015- 3:34.86A. pbs: 800m 1:45.92A '14, 1M 3:55.80 '15.

Augustine Kiprono **CHOGE** b. 21 Jan 1987 Kipsigat, Nandi 1.62m 53kg.
At 5000m: CG: '06- 1; WJ: '04- 1. At 3000m: WY: '03- 1; WI: '10-12-14-16: 11/2/9/3. At 1500m: OG: '08- 9; WCh: '05- h, '09- 5. World CC: '03-05-06-08: 4J/1J/7 (4k)/12. Won KEN 1500m 2013, E.African Youth 800m/1500m/3000m 2003, Junior 1500m 2004.
Records: World 4x1500m 2009, world youth 5000m 2004, world junior 3000m 2005.
Progress at 1500m, 5000m: 2003- 3:37.48, 13:20.08; 2004- 3:36.64, 12:57.01; 2005- 3:33.99, 12:53.66; 2006- 3:32.48, 12:56.41; 2007- 3:31.73, 2008- 3:31.57, 13:09.75; 2009- 3:29.47, 2010- 3:30.22, 13:04.64; 2011- 3:31.14, 13:21.24; 2012- 3:37.47, 13:15.50; 2013- 3:33.21, 13:05.31; 2014- 3:35.5A, 13:06.12. pbs: 800m 1:44.86 '09, 1000m 2:17.79i '09, 1M 3:50.01 '13, 2000m 4:56.30i '07, 3000m 7:28.00i/7:28.76 '11, 10000m 29:06.5A '02.
At 17 in 2004 he become youngest to break 13 minutes for 5000m.

Dickson Kiptolo **CHUMBA** b. 27 Oct 1986 1.67m 50kg. Nandi.
Progress at Mar: 2010- 2:09:20dh, 2011- 2:07:23, 2012- 2:05:46, 2013- 2:10:15, 2014- 2:04:32, 2015- 2:06:34, 2016- 2:07:34. pbs: 1500m 3:44.33 '10, 5000m 13:41.34 '10, road: 10k 28:09 '13, HMar 61:34 '12, 60:39dh '14; 30k 1:28:36 '12.
Marathon wins: Rome 2011, Eindhoven 2012, Tokyo 2014 (3rd 2015-16), Chicago 2015 (3rd 2014).

Geoffrey Kipsang KAMWOROR b. 28 Nov 1992 1.68m 54kg.
At 10000m: WCh: '15- 2. World CC: '11- 1J, '15- 1; HMar: '14- 1, '16- 1. Won KEN 5000m 2015, CC 2016.
Tied world 30km record 2014.
Progress at 10000m, HMar, Mar: 2011- 27:06.35, 59:31; 2012- 59:26, 2:06:12; 2013- 28:17.0A, 58:54, 2:06:26; 2014- 59:08, 2:06:39; 2015- 26:52.65, 2:10:48. pbs: 1500m 3:40.7A '15, 3000m 7:54.15 '10. 5000m 13:12:23 '11; Road: 15k 41:41 '16, 20k 56:02 '13, 30k 1:27:37 '14.
3rd in Berlin Marathon 2012 (on debut) and 2013 (4th 2014), 2nd New York 2015. Won RAK half marathon 2013.

Bidan KAROKI Muchiri b. 21 Aug 1990 Nyandarua 1.69m 53kg. S&B Foods, Japan.
At 10000m: OG: 12- 5; WCh: '13- 6, '15- 4; AfG: '11- 2. World CC: '15- 2; HMar: '16- 2 Won Kenyan CC 2012.
Progress at 10000m: 2010- 27:23.62, 2011- 27:13.67, 2012- 27:05.50; 2013- 27:13.12, 2014- 26:52.36, 2015- 27:04.77 pbs: 1500m 3:50.91 '08, 3000m 7:37.68 '13, 5000m 13:15.25 '14, 15k 41:41 '16, 10M 45:02 '14, HMar 59:14 '15.
Went to Japan in 2007.

Clement KEMBOI b. 1 Feb 1992 1.80m 65kg.
At 3000mSt: AfG: '15- 1.
Progress at 3000mSt: 2010- 9:03.4A, 2011- 8:28.13, 2012- 8:25.67, 2013- 8:17.18, 2014- 8:16.96, 2015- 8:12.68. pbs: 1M 4:02.19 '14, 3000m 7:56.28 '13, 10kRd 28:44 '14.

Ezekiel KEMBOI Cheboi b. 25 May 1982 Matira, near Kapsowar, Marakwet District 1.75m 62kg.
At 3000mSt: OG: '04- 1, '08- 7, '12- 1; WCh: '03-05-07-09-11-13-15: 2/2/2/1/1/1/1; CG: '02-06-10-14: 2/1/2/3; AfG: '03- 1, '07- 2; AfCh: '02-06-10-14: 4/dq/2/3; Af-J: '01- 1. Won WAF 2009, Kenyan 2003, 2006-07.
Progress at 3000mSt: 2001- 8:23.66, 2002- 8:06.65, 2003- 8:02.49, 2004- 8:02.98, 2005- 8:09.04, 2006- 8:09.29, 2007- 8:05.50, 2008- 8:09.25, 2009- 7:58.85, 2010- 8:01.74, 2011- 7:55.76, 2012- 8:10.55, 2013- 7:59.03, 2014- 8:04.12, 2015- 8:01.71. pbs: 1500m 3:40.8A '04, 3000m 7:44.24 '12, 5000m 13:50.61 '11, 10k Rd 28:38 '11.
Five gold and three silver medals from global 3000m steeplechase races.

Stephen Kipkosgei **KIBET** b. 9 Nov 1986 1.72m 55kg.
At HMar: WCh: '12- 5.
Progress at HMar: 2009- 60:34, 2010- 60:09, 2011- 60:20, 2012- 58:54, 2013- 59:59, 2014- 59:21, 2015- 59:58. pbs: 5000m 13:38.47 '15; road: 10k 27:44 '14, 15k 42:01+ '12, 20k 55:55+ '12, Mar 2:08:05 '12. Six successive half marathon wins 2009-12.

Vincent KIBET b. 6 May 1991 Uasin Gishu 1.70m 57kg.
At 1500m: WI: '16- 7.
Progress at 1500m: 2010- 3:46.7A, 2011- 3:42.7A, 2012- 3:40.51A, 2013- 3:35.62, 2014- 3:31.96, 2015- 3:34.91i/3:36.80. pbs: 800m 1:46.71 '14, 1000m 2:19.93i '15, 1M 3:52.15 '14, 3000m 7:44.87i '16, :58.9 '14.

Dennis Kipruto **KIMETTO** b. 22 Jan 1984 near Kapngetuny 1.72m 57kg.
At Mar: WCh: '15- dnf.
World records 25km road 2012, marathon 2014.
Progress at Mar: 2012- 2:04:16, 2013- 2:03:45, 2014- 2:02:57, 2015- 2:05:50. Road pbs: 10k 28:21 '12, 15k 42:46 '11, HMar 59:14 '12, 25k 1:11:18 '12, 30k 1:27:38 '14.
Second Berlin 2012 in fastest ever marathon debut after earlier major road wins at half marathon and 25k in Berlin in 2012. Won Tokyo and Chicago marathons 2013. Dnf Boston before WR in Berlin marathon 2014. 3rd London 2015.

Eliud KIPCHOGE b. 5 Nov 1984 Kapsisiywa, Nandi 1.67m 52kg.
At 5000m: OG: '04- 3, '08- 2; WCh: '03-05-07-09-11: 1/4/2/5/7; CG: '10- 2. At 3000m: WI: '06- 3. World CC: '02-03-04-05: 5J/1J/4/5; HMar: '12- 6. Won WAF 5000m 2003, 3000m 2004, Kenyan CC 2005.

World junior 5000m record 2003. World road best 4M 17:10 '05.
Progress at 1500m, 5000m, 10000m: 2002- 13:13.03, 2003- 3:36.17, 12:52.61; 2004- 3:33.20, 12:46.53; 2005- 3:33.80, 12:50.22; 2006- 3:36.25i, 12:54.94; 2007- 3:39.98, 12:50.38, 26:49.02; 2008- 13:02.06, 26:54.32; 2009- 12:56.46, 2010- 3:38.36, 12:51.21; 2011- 12:55.72i/12:59.01, 26:53.27; 2012- 12:55.34, 27:11.93. At HMar, Mar: 2012: 59:25, 2013- 60:04, 2:04:05, 2014- 60:52, 2:04:11; 2015- 60:50, 2:04:00. pbs: 1M 3:50.40 '04, 2000m 4:59.?+ '04, 3000m 7:27.66 '11, 2M 8:07.39i '12, 8:07.68 '05; Road: 10k 26:55dh '06, 27:34 '05; 25k 1:13:42 '14, 30k 1:28:46 '14.
Kenyan Junior CC champion 2002-03, followed World Junior CC win by winning the World 5000m title, becoming at 18 years 298 days the second youngest world champion. Age 19 bests for 3000m & 5000m 2004. Ran 26:49.02 in 10,000m debut at Hengelo in 2007. All his six marathons have been in 2:05:30 or better; he won at Hamburg on debut then 2nd Berlin in 2013, 1st Rotterdam & Chicago 2014, London & Berlin 2015. Won World Marathon Majors 2015/16.

Alfred KIPKETER b. 26 Dec 1996 1.69m 61kg.
At 800m: WCh: '15- 8; WJ: '14- 1; WY: '13- 1.
Progress at 800m: 2013- 1:46.2A, 2014- 1:43.95, 2015- 1:44.07A. pb 600m 1:15.60 '15.

Silas KIPLAGAT b. 20 Aug 1989 Siboh village, Marakwet 1.70m 57kg.
At 1500m: OG: '12- 7; WCh: '11-13-15: 2/6/5; CG: '10- 1; AfCh: '10- 4; WI: '12- 6. Won DL 2012, 2014; Kenyan 2011.
World 4x1500m record 2014.
Progress at 1500m: 2009- 3:39.1A, 2010- 3:29.27, 2011- 3:30.47, 2012- 3:29.63, 2013- 3:30.13, 2014- 3:27.64, 2015- 3:30.12. pbs: 800m 1:44.8A '12, 1M 3:47.88 '14, 3000m 7:39.94 '10, 5000m 13:55.0A '13, 10k Rd 28:00 '09.

Asbel Kipruto **KIPROP** b. 30 Jun 1989 Uasin Gishu, Eldoret. North Rift 1.86m 70kg.
At (800m)/1500m: OG: '08- 1, '12- 12; WCh: '07- 4, '09- sf/4, '11-13-15: 1/1/1; AfG: '07- 1; AfCh: '10- 1, '14- 2; CCp: '10- 6, '14- 2; Won DL 2010, 2015. At 800m: AfCh: '08- 3. World CC: '07- 1J. Won Kenyan 800m 2015, 1500m 2007, 2010.
World 4x1500m record 2014.
Progress at 800m, 1500m: 2007- 3:35.24, 2008- 1:44.71, 3:31.64; 2009- 1:43.17, 3:31.20; 2010- 1:43.45, 3:31.78; 2011- 1:43.15, 3:30.46; 2012- 1:45.91, 3:28.88; 2013- 1:44.8A, 3:27.72; 2014- 1:43.34, 3:28.45; 2015- 1:44.4A, 3:26.69. pbs: 1000m 2:17.38 '15, 1M 3:48.50 '09, 3000m 7:42.32 '07, 5000m 13:48.43A '10.
Father David Kebenei was a 1500m runner.

Brimin KIPRUTO b. 31 Jul 1985 Korkitony, Marakwet District 1.76m 54kg.
At 3000mSt: OG: '04- 2, '08- 1 '12- 5; WCh: '05-07-09-11-13: 3/1/7/2/3; CG: '10- 3; Af-J: '03- 2; KEN champion 2011. At 1500m: WJ: '04- 3. At 2000St: WY: '01- 2. World 4k CC: '06- 18.
Commonwealth & African 3000mSt record 2011.
Progress at 3000mSt: 2002- 8:33.0A, 2003- 8:34.5A, 2004- 8:05.52, 2005- 8:04.22, 2006- 8:08.32, 2007- 8:02.89, 2008- 8:10.26, 2009- 8:03.17, 2010- 8:00.90, 2011- 7:53.64, 2012- 8:01.73, 2013- 8:06.86, 2014- 8:04.64, 2015- 8:10:09. pbs: 1500m 3:35.23 '06, 2000m 4:58.76i '07, 3000m 7:39.07i '12, 7:47.33 '06; 5000m 13:58.82 '04, 2000mSt 5:36.81 '01.
First name is actually Firmin, but he stayed with the clerical error of Brimin, written when he applied for a birth certificate in 2001.

Conseslus KIPRUTO b. 8 Dec 1994 Eldoret 1.71m 55kg.
At 3000mSt: WCh: '13- 2, '15- 2; WJ: '12- 1; won DL 2013. At 2000St: WY: '11- 1. World CC: 2013- 5J.
Progress at 3000mSt: 2011- 8:27.30, 2012- 8:03.49, 2013- 8:01.16, 2014- 8:09.81, 2015- 8:05.20. pbs: 800m 1:49.0A '15, 1000m 2:19.85 '12, 1500m 3:39.57 '13, 3000m 7:44.09 '12, 2000mSt 5:28.65 '11.

Wilson KIPSANG Kiprotich b. 15 Mar 1982 Keiyo district 1.78m 59kg.
At Mar: OG: '12- 3; WCh: '15- dnf; HMar: WCh: '09- 4.
World marathon record 2013.
Progress at HMar, Mar: 2008- 59:16, 2009- 58:59, 2010- 60:04, 2:04:57; 2011- 60:49, 2:03:42; 2012- 59:06, 2:04:44; 2013- 61:02, 2:03:23; 2014- 60:25, 2:04:29; 2015- 61:23, 2:04:47. pbs: 5000m 13:55.7A '09, 10000m 28:37.0A '07; Road: 10k 27:42 '09, 15k 41:51+ '11, 10M 44:59+ '11, 20k 56:10+ '12, 25k 1:12:58 '13, 30k 1:28:02 '13.
Eight wins from 14 marathons: third in Paris in 2:07:13 on debut, won Frankfurt in 2010 and 2011, Lake Biwa 2011, London 2012 and 2014 (2nd 2015), Honolulu 2012, Berlin 2013 and New York 2014. Won World Marathon Majors 2013/14. Has record five marathons inside 2:05. Won Great North Run 2012.

Eliud KIPTANUI b. 6 Jun 1989 Kaplelach, Uasin Gishu 1.69m 55kg.
At Mar: WCh: '11- 5.
Progress at Mar: 2009- 2:12:17, 2010- 2:05:39, 2011- 2:09:08, 2012- 2:06:44, 2013- 2:15:10, 2014- 2:07:28, 2015- 2:05:21. pbs: 3000m 8:04.57 '09, Road: 25k 1:13:38 '14, 30k 1:29:18 '14; HMar 61:24 '11.
Won Safaricom Marathon in Kisimu in December 2009, then made a stunning improvement to win Prague Marathon in 2010; 3rd Seoul & 2nd Beijing 2012, 2nd Berlin 2015.

Mark Kosgei **KIPTOO** b. 21 Jun 1976 Lugafri 1.75m 64kg. Kenyan Air Force.
At 5000m: CG: '10- 3; AfG: '07- 9; AfCh: '10- 3, '12- 1 (2 10000m). World CC: '08- 14, '09- 7. Won W.MilG 5000m & 2nd 10000m 2007, KEN 5000m 2008.

Progress at 5000m, 10000m, Mar: 2007- 13:12.60, 28:22.62; 2008- 13:06.60, 27:14.67; 2009- 12:57.62, 2010- 12:53.46, 28:37.4A; 2011- 12:59.91, 26:54.64; 2012- 13:06.23, 27:18.22; 2013- 13:20.51, 28:24.04A, 2:06:16; 2014- 2:06:49, 2015- 2:06:00. pbs: 1500m 3:48.0A '05, 3000m 7:32.97 '09, 2M 8:29.96 '12, HMar 60:29 '11

Won Frankfurt Marathon 2014 (2nd 2013 on debut); 2nd Rotterdam 2015.

Bernard KIPYEGO Kiprop b. 16 Jul 1986 Kapkitony, Keiyo district 1.60m 50kg.

At 10000m: WCh: '09- 5; Af-J: '03- 3. At Mar: WCh: '13- 12. World CC: '05-07-08: 2J/3/10; HMar: '09- 2.

Progress at 10000m, Mar: 2003- 29:29.09, 2004- 28:18.94, 2005- 27:04.45, 2006- 27:19.45, 2007- 26:59.51, 2008- 27:08.06, 2009- 27:18.47, 2010- 2:07:01, 2011- 2:06:29, 2012- 2:06:40, 2013- 28:36.5A, 2:07:19, 2014- 2:06:22, 2015- 2:06:19, 2016- 2:07:33. pbs: 3000m 7:54.91 '05, 5000m 13:09.96 '05, Road: 15k 42:34 '11, 10M 45:44 '11, HMar 59:10 '09, 30k 1:29:51 '14.

Won in Berlin on half marathon debut in 59:34 in 2009, 5th Rotterdam on marathon debut 2010, won Amsterdam 2014-15, 2nd Paris 2011, Beijing 2013, Tokyo 2016; 3rd Chicago 2011, Boston 2012, Tokyo 2013 and Rotterdam 2014.

Michael Kipkorir **KIPYEGO** b. 2 Oct 1983 Kemeloi, Marakwet 1.68m 59kg.

At 3000mSt: WCh: '03- h; WJ: '02- 1; AfCh: '08- 2. At 3000m: WY: '99- 8; Af-J: '01- 2. At Mar: WCh: '13- 25. World CC: '02-03-07: 12J/4 4k/6.

Progress at 3000mSt: 2001- 8:41.26, 2002- 8:22.90, 2003- 8:13.02, 2004- 8:23.14, 2005- 8:10.66, 2006- 8:14.99, 2007- 8:11.62, 2008- 8:09.05, 2009- 8:08.48, 2010- 8:16.46. At Mar: 2011- 2:06:48, 2012- 2:07:37, 2013- 2:06:58, 2014- 2:06:58. pbs: 1500m 3:39.93 '05, 3000m 7:50.03 '09.

Won Tokyo Marathon 2012, 2nd 2013, 4th 2014. Brother of Sally Kipyego.

Abel KIRUI b. 4 Jun 1982 Bornet, Rift Valley 1.77m 62kg. Police.

At Mar: OG: '12- 2; WCh: '09- 1, '11- 1.

Progress at Mar: 2006- 2:15:22, 2007- 2:06:51, 2008- 2:07:38, 2009- 2:05:04, 2010- 2:08:04, 2011- 2:07:38, 2012- 2:07:56, 2014- 2:09:04, 2015- 2:10:55, 2016- 2:089:06. pbs: 1500m 3:46.10 '05, 3000m 7:55.90 '06, 5000m 13:52.71 '05, 10000m 28:16.86A '08; Road: 10k 27:59 '09, 15k 42:22 '07, 10M 46:40 '11, HMar 60:11 '07, 25k: 1:13:41 '08, 30k 1:28:25 '08.

Brilliantly retained World marathon title with halves of 65:07 and 62:31 and a fastest 5k split of 14:18. Won Vienna Marathon 2008, 2nd Berlin 2007, 3rd Rotterdam 2009. Uncle Mike Rotich has marathon pb 2:06:33 '03.

Timothy KITUM b. 20 Nov 1994 Marakwet 1.72m 60kg.

At 800m: OG: '12- 3; WJ: '12- 2; WY: '11- 3; AfG: '15- 4.

Progress at 800m: 2011- 1:44.98, 2012- 1:42.53, 2013- 1:44.45, 2014- 1:43.65, 2015- 1:45.0A. pbs: 600m 1:14.4A '12, 1000m 2:17.62 '15.

Sammy Kiprop **KITWARA** b. 26 Nov 1986 Sagat village, Marakwet district 1.77m 54kg.

At 10000m: Kenyan champion 2009. World HMar: '09- 10, '10- 3.

Progress at 10,000m, HMar, Mar: 2007- 28:11.6A, 2008- 28:12.26A, 60:54; 2009- 27:44.46A, 58:58; 2010- 28:32.77A, 59:34; 2011- 58:47, 2012- 2:05:54, 2013- 61:53, 2:05:16; 2014- 60:24, 2:04:28; 2015- 60:25, 2:07:43. pbs: 5000m 13:34.0A '08, Road: 10k 27:11 '10, 15k 41:54 '09, 10M 45:17 '08, 20k 57:42 '08, 25k 1:13:42 '14, 30k 1:28:46 '14.

2nd Chicago marathon 2014-15 (3rd 2013, 4th 2012), 3rd Rotterdam 2013, Tokyo 2014

Isiah Kiplangat **KOECH** b. 19 Dec 1993 Kericho 1.78m 60kg.

At 5000m: OG: '12- 5; WCh: '11- 4, '13- 3, '15- 8; CG: '14- 2; AfCh: '14- 2; CCp: '14- 1; won DL 5000m 2012, Kenyan 2011, 2013. At 3000m: WY: '09- 1; WI: '16- 8. World CC: '10- 4J, '11- 10J.

World junior records indoors: 5000m 2011, 3000m 2011 & 2012.

Progress at 5000m, 10000m: 2010- 13:07.70, 2011- 12:53.29i/12:54.18, 2012- 12:48.64, 27:17.03; 2013- 12:56.08, 2014- 13:07.55, 2015- 13:07.33. pbs: 1500m 3:38.7A '12, 3000m 7:30.43 '12, 2M 8:14.16 '11.

Paul Kipsiele **KOECH** b. 10 Nov 1981 Cheplanget, Buret District 1.68m 57kg.

At 3000mSt: OG: '04- 3; WCh: '05- 7, '09- 4, '13- 4; AfG: '03- 2; AfCh: '06- 1; WCp: '06- 2; won DL 2010-12, WAF 2005-08. At 3000m: WI: 08- 2.

Progress at 3000mSt: 2001- 8:15.92, 2002- 8:05.44, 2003- 7:57.42, 2004- 7:59.65, 2005- 7:56.37, 2006- 7:59.94, 2007- 7:58.80, 2008- 8:00.57, 2009- 8:01.26, 2010- 8:02.07, 2011- 7:57.32, 2012- 7:54.31, 2013- 8:02.63, 2014- 8:05.47, 2015- 8:10.24. pbs: 1500m 3:37.92 '07, 2000m 5:00.9+i '08, 5:01.84 '14; 3000m 7:32.78i '10, 7:33.93 '05; 2M 8:06.48i/8:13.31 '08, 5000m 13:02.69i 12, 13:05.18 '10.

Younger brother John Koech (b. 23 Aug 1995) transferred to Bahrain in 2013; 3000mSt: 8:14.75 '15; WCh: '15- 5, AsiC: '15- 1, CCP: '14- 5.

Leonard Patrick **KOMON** b. 10 Jan 1988 Korungotuny Village, Mt. Eldon District 1.75m 52kg.

World CC: '06-07-08-09-10: 2J/4J/2/4/4.

World road records 10km and 15km 2010.

Progress at 5000m, 10000m: 2006- 13:04.12, 2007- 13:04.79, 2008- 13:17.48, 26:57.08; 2009- 12:58.24, 28:02.24A; 2010- 12:59.15, 2011- 26:55.29, 2012- 27:01.58. pbs: 2000m 5:04.0+ '07, 3000m 7:33.27 '09, 2M 8:22.56 '07, road 10k 26:44 '10, 15k 41:13 '10, 10M 44:27 '11, HMar 59:14 '14.

Ran fastest ever debut half marathon, 59:14 to win at Berlin in 2014.

Ronald KWEMOI b. 19 Sep 1995 Mt. Elgon 1.80m 68kg.

At 1500m: CG: '14- 2; AfG: '15- 4; AfCh: '14- 3; Kenyan champion 2014. World CC: '13- 9J.
World junior 1500m record 2014.
Progress at 1500m: 2013- 3:45.39, 2014- 3:28.81, 2015- 3:30.43. pbs: 1M 3:52.57 '15, 5000m 13:16.14 '15.

Thomas Pkemei **LONGOSIWA** b. 14 Jan 1982 West Pokot 1.75m 57kg. North Rift.
At 5000m: OG: '08- 12, '12- 3; WCh: '11- 6, '13- 4; AfG: '07- 6. World CC: '06- 13J (but dq after birthdate found to be 1982). Won Kenyan 5000m 2007.
Progress at 5000m: 2006- 13:35.3A, 2007- 12:51.95, 2008- 13:14.36, 2009- 13:03.43, 2010- 13:05.60, 2011- 12:56.08, 2012- 12:49.04, 2013- 12:59.81, 2014- 12:56.16, 2015- 12:59.72. pbs: 1500m 3:41.92 '13, 2000m 5:01.6+ '10, 3000m 7:30.09 '09, 10000m 28:11.3A '06.

Wilson Erupe **LOYANAE** b. 20 Nov 1988 Lodwar, Turkana.
At Mar: WCh: '13- dnf.
Progress at Mar: 2010- ?. 2011- 2:09:23, 2012- 2:05:37, 2015- 2:06:11, 2016- 2:05:13. pb HMar 61:46 '12.
Marathon wins: Mombasa and Gyongju 2011-12, Seoul 2012, 2015-16. Two-year drugs ban for EPO 2013-15.

James Kiplagat **MAGUT** b. 20 Jul 1990 Nandi 1.80m 64kg.
At 1500m: CG: '10- 2, '14- 1; WJ: '08- 2, AfCh: '12- 3, '14- 5; Af-J: '09- 1.
World 4x1500m record 2014.
Progress at 1500m: 2008- 3:42.3A, 2009- 3:36.8A, 2010- 3:40.47, 2012- 3:33.31, 2013- 3:35.2A, 2014- 3:30.61, 2015- 3:31.76. pbs: 800m 1:48.0A '15, 1000m 2:19.72 '13, 1M 3:49.43 '14.

Patrick MAKAU Musyoki b. 2 Mar 1985 Manyanzwani, Tala Kangundo district 1.73m 57kg.
World HMar: '07- 2, '08- 2.
World 30km and marathon records 2011.
Progress at HMar, Mar: 2005- 62:00, 2006- 62:42, 2007- 58:56, 2008- 59:29, 2009- 58:52, 2:06:14; 2010- 59:51, 2:04:48; 2011- 2:03:38, 2012- 2:06:08, 2013- 2:14:10, 2014- 2:08:22. pbs: 3000m 7:54.50 '07, 5000m 13:42.84 '06. Road: 10k 27:27 '07, 15k 41:30 '09, 10M 45:41 '12, 20k 55:53 '07, 30k 1:27:38 '11.
Second fastest ever debut marathon when 4th Rotterdam 2009 and won there a year later in 2:04:48 for fourth world all-time. Won Berlin 2010 and 2011, Frankfurt 2012, Fukuoka 2014-15.

Elijah Motonei **MANANGOI** b. 5 Jan 1993 1.81m 65kg.
At 1500m: WCh: '15- 2; CG: '14- 12. Kenyan champion 2015
Progress at 1500m: 2014- 3:35.0A, 2015- 3:29.67. pbs: 400m 47.33A '13, 800m 1:47.40 '15, 1000m 2:17.09i '16.

Moses Cheruiyot **MOSOP** b. 17 Jul 1985 Kamasia, Marakwet 1.72m 57kg. Police officer.
At 10000m: OG: '04- 7; WCh: '05- 3. World CC: '02-03-05-07-09: 10J/7J/18/2/11; HMar: '10- 10. Won KEN 10000m 2006, CC 2009.
World records 25,000m and 30,000m 2011.
Progress at 5000m, 10000m: 2002- 29:38.6A, 2003- 13:11.75, 27:13.66; 2004- 13:09.68, 27:30.66; 2005- 13:06.83, 27:08.96; 2006- 12:54.46, 27:17.00; 2007- 13:07.89, 26:49.55. At Mar: 2011- 2:05:37/2:03:06wdh, 2012- 2:05:03, 2013- 2:11:19, 2014- 2:20:37, 2015- 2:06:19. pbs: 3000m 7:36.88 '06, 15k Rd 42:25+ '10, HMar 59:20 '10, 20000m 58:02.2 '11, 25000m 1:12:25.4 '11, 30000m 1:26:47.4 '11.
Second with fastest ever marathon debut at Boston and won at Chicago 2011 and Xiamen 2015. 3rd Rotterdam 2012. Formerly married to Florence Kiplagat.

Boniface MUCHERU Tumuti b. 2 May 1992 Laikipia District 1.85m 75kg. Central.
At 400mh/4x400mR (400m): OG: '12- 6; WCh: '15- 5; CG: '14- 6; AfCh: '10- 6, '12- 3/3R, 14- (3)/3R; WJ: '10- 8 (h). Kenyan champion 2012, 2015.
Kenyan 400mh record 2015.
Progress at 400mh: 2008- 52.79A, 2010- 51.04A, 2011- 50.35A, 2012- 49.45, 2013- 49.59A, 2014- 49.25A/49.67, 2015- 48.29. pbs: 200m 22.23 '15, 400m 45.07 '14, 800m 1:49.34 '15.

Abel Kiprop **MUTAI** b. 2 Oct 1988 Nandi 1.72m 73kg.
At 3000mSt: OG: '12- 3; WCh: '13- 7; AfCh: '12- 1; Af-J: '07- 1; Kenyan champion 2012. At 2000mSt: WY: '05- 1.
Progress at 3000mSt: 2006- 8:35.38, 2007- 8:29.76, 2009- 8:11.40, 2011- 8:21.02, 2012- 8:01.67, 2013- 8:08.83, 2014- 8:15.83, 2015- 8:20.38. pbs: 3000m 8:05.16 '06, 5000m 14:07.80 '06, 2000mSt 5:24.69 '05.

Emmanuel Kipchirchir **MUTAI** b. 12 Oct 1984 Tulwet, Rift Valley 1.68m 54kg.
At Mar: OG: '12- 17; WCh: '09- 2.
World 30k record in Berlin Marathon 2014.
Progress at Mar: 2007- 2:06:29, 2008- 2:06:15, 2009- 2:06:53, 2010- 2:06:23, 2011- 2:04:40, 2012- 2:08:01, 2013- 2:03:52, 2014- 2:03.13, 2015- 2:07:46. pbs: 10000m 28:21.14 '06, Road: 10k 27:51 '06, 15k 42:11 '10, 20k 56:44 '10, HMar 59:52 '11, 25k 1:13:08 '14, 30k 1:27:37 '14.
Made marathon debut with 7th in Rotterdam in 2:13:06 in 2007, then won in Amsterdam. London: 4th 2008 & 2009, 2nd 2010 & 2013, 1st 2011. 2nd New York 2010-11, Chicago 2013, Berlin 2014 (4th 2015). World Marathon Majors winner 2010/11.

Caleb Mwangangi **NDIKU** b. 9 Oct 1992 Machakos 1.83m 68kg.
At 1500m: WJ: '10- 1; WY: '09- 2; AfG: '11- 1; AfCh: '12- 1; Kenyan champion 2012. At 3000m: CCp: '14- 1; WI: '14- 1, '16- 5. At 5000m: WCh: '15- 2; CG: '14- 1; AfCh: '14- 1; won DL 2014 World CC: '10- 1J.

Progress at 1500m, 5000m: 2009- 3:38.2A, 2010- 3:37.30, 2011- 3:32.02, 2012- 3:32.39, 2013- 3:29.50, 13:03.80; 2014- 3:35.8A, 12:59.17; 2015- 3:38.13, 13:05.30. pbs: 800m 1:52.6A '07, 1M 3:49.77 '11, 3000m 7:30.99 '12, 10000m 28:28.4A '14.

His father David was a javelin thrower.

Jonathan Muia **NDIKU** b. 18 Sep 1991 1.73m 60kg. Team Hitachi Cable, Japan.

At 3000mSt: CG: '14- 1; AfCh: '14- 2; WJ: '08- 1, '10- 1; Af-J: '09- 1. At 2000mSt: WY: '07- 4.

Progress at 3000mSt: 2008- 8:17.28, 2009- 8:28.1A, 2010- 8:19.25A. 2011- 8:07.75, 2012- 8:17.88, 2013- 8:18.78, 2014- 8:10.44, 2015- 8:11.64. pbs: 1500m 3:39.27 '10, 3000m 7:39.63 '14, 5000m 13:11.99 '09, 10000m 27:37.72 '09, 2000mSt 5:37.30 '07.

Lucas Kimeli **ROTICH** b. 16 Apr 1990 1.71m 57kg.

At 3000mSt: WY: '07- 2. World CC: '08- 3J, '10- 18.

Progress at 5000m, 10000m, Mar: 2007- 29:12.5A, 2008- 13:15.54, 2009- 12:58.70, 28:15.0A; 2010- 12:55.06, 27:33.59; 2011- 13:00.02, 26:43.98; 2012- 13:09.58, 27:09.38; 2014- 2:07:18, 2015- 28:21.0A, 2:07:17. pbs: 1500m 3:43.64 '08, 3000m 7:35.57 '11, HMar 59:44 '11.

Won Hamburg marathon 2015, 2nd Amsterdam 2014.

David Lekuta **RUDISHA** b. 17 Dec 1988 Kilgoris 1.89m 73kg. Masai.

At 800m: OG: '12- 1; WCh: '09- sf, '11- 1, '15- 1; CG: '14- 2; WJ: '06- 1/4R; AfCh: '08- 1, '10- 1; Af-J: '07- 1; CCp: '10- 1. Won DL 2010-11, WAF 2009, Kenyan 2009-11.

Three world 800m records 2010-12, four African records 2009-10.

Progress at 800m: 2006- 1:46.3A, 2007- 1:44.15, 2008- 1:43.72, 2009- 1:42.01, 2010- 1:41.01, 2011- 1:41.33, 2012- 1:40.91, 2013- 1:43.87, 2014- 1:42.98, 2015- 1:43.58. pbs: 400m 45.50 '10, 45.2A '13; 600m 1:13.71 '14.

IAAF Male Athlete of the Year 2010, won 26 successive 800m finals 2009-11. His father Daniel won 4x400m silver medal at 1968 Olympics with 440y pb 45.5A '67.

Stephen Kiptoo **SAMBU** b. 3 Jul 1988 Eldoret 1.69m 55kg. Was at University of Arizona.

Progress at 10000m: 2009- 28:37.96, 2010- 29:01.34, 2011- 27:28.64, 2012- 28:06.16, 2014- 26:54.61. pbs: 1500m 3:43.56 '12, 3000m 7:51.59i/8:13.69 '12, 5000m 13:13.74i '12, 13:25.13 '15; 10M Rd 43:20 '15, HMar 60:41 '13.

Edwin Cheruiyot **SOI** b. 3 Mar 1986 Kericho 1.72m 55kg.

At 5000m: OG: '08- 3, '12- h; WCh: '13- 5, '15- 10; AfCh: '10- 1; CCp: '10- 4. At 3000m: WI: '08- 4, '12- 3; won WAF 3000m 2007, 5000m 2007-08. World CC: '06- 8 4k, '07- 9.

Progress at 5000m, 10000m: 2002- 29:06.5A, 2004- 13:22.57, 2005- 13:10.78, 2006- 12:52.40, 27:14.83; 2007- 13:10.21, 2008- 13:06.22, 2009- 12:55.03, 2010- 12:58.91, 2011- 12:59.15, 2012- 12:55.99, 2013- 12:51.34, 26:49.41; 2014- 12:59.82, 2015- 13:11.97. pbs: 1500m 3:40.52 '13, 2000m 5:01.4+ '10, 3000m 7:27.55 '11, 2M 8:14.10 '11, 10k Rd 28:13 '08.

Paul Kipngetich **TANUI** b. 22 Dec 1990 Chesubeno village, Moio district 1.72m 54kg. Kyudenko Corporation, Japan.

At 10000m: WCh: '11- 9, '13- 3, '15- 3. World CC: '09-10-11: 4J/8/2. Won Kenyan CC 2010.

Progress at 5000m, 10000m: 2008- 13:59.2A, 2009- 13:37.15, 27:25.24; 2010- 13:14.87, 27:17.61; 2011- 13:04.65, 26:50.63; 2012- 13:19.18, 27:27.56; 2013- 13:16.57, 27:21.50, 2014- 13:00.53, 26:49.41; 2015- 12:58.69, 26:51.86. pbs: 1500m 3:43.97 '10, 3000m 7:46.83+ '15, HMar 62:48 '14.

Hillary Kipsang **YEGO** b. 2 Apr 1992 1.78m 60kg.

At 2000mSt: WY: '09- 1.

Progress at 3000mSt: 2009- 8:46.8A, 2010- 8:19.50, 2011- 8:07.71, 2012- 8:11.83. 2013- 8:03:57, 2014- 8:09.07, 2015- 8:13.10. pbs: 1500m 3:43.3 '10, 3000m 7:53.18 '10, 2000mSt 5:25.33 '09, 10k Rd 29:10 '11, Mar 2:16:51 '13.

Won 2013 Athens Classic Marathon on debut at the distance.

Julius Kiplagat **YEGO** b. 4 Jan 1989 Cheptonon, Nandi district1.75m 90kg.

At JT: OG: '12- 12; WCh: '13- 4, '15- 1; CG: '10- 7, '14- 1; AfG: '11- 1; AfCh: '10-12-14: 3/1/1; CCp: '14- 4. Kenyan champion 2008-14.

Javelin records: Commonwealth & two African 2015, nine Kenyan 2011-15.

Progress at JT: 2008- 72.18A, 2009- 74.00A, 2010- 75.44, 2011- 78.34A, 2012- 81.81; 2013- 85.40, 2014- 84.72, 2015- 92.72.

His winning throw at the 2015 Worlds was the world's best javelin throw since 2001.

Women

Alice APROT Nawowuna b. 11 Mar 1994 1.74m 55kg.

At (5000m)/10000m: WJ: '10- 3; AfG: '15- 5/1. World CC: '10- 9J; AfCC: 14- 3. Won Kenyan CC 2016.

Progress at 5000m, 10000m: 2010- 15:16.74, 2011- 16:36.8A, 2014- 16:22.8A, 2015- 15:31.82, 31:24.18. pbs: 1500m 4:23.92 '14, 3000m 8:53.55 '14, 10k Rd 31:02 '15.

Elder brother Joseph Ebuya won World CC in 2010, pb 5000m 12:51.00 '07.

Milcah CHEMOS Cheywa b. 24 Feb 1986 Bugaa Village, Mt. Elgon district 1.63m 48kg. Police.

At 3000mSt: OG: '12- 3; WCh: '09- 2, '11- 2, '13- 1; CG: '10- 1, '14- 2; AfCh: '10- 1; CCp: '10- 2. Won DL 2010-13, KEN 2010-11.

Commonwealth & African 3000mSt record 2012.

Progress at 3000mSt: 2009- 9:08.57, 2010- 9:11.71, 2011- 9:12.89, 2012- 9:07.14, 2013- 9:11.65, 2014- 9:21.91. pbs: 800m 2:04.35A '11, 1500m 4:12.3A

'09, 2000m 5:41.64 '09, 3000m 8:43.92 '09, 2000mSt 6:16.95 '13.
Married to Alex Sang (pb 800m 1:46.84 '08). Started athletics seriously after birth of daughter Lavine Jemutai and in first season, 2008, was 4th in Kenyan 800m. Rapid progress from first steeplechase in April 2009.

Joyce CHEPKIRUI b. 20 Aug 1988 Bureti 1.52m 48kg.
At 10000m: OG: '12- dnf; CG: '14- 1; AfCh: '14- 1. At 5000m: CCp: '14- 2. At 1500m: AfG: '11- 2; Af-J: '07- 5. At HMar: WCh: '10- 5. AfCC: '12- 1. Won Kenyan CC 2012, 10000m 2015.
Progress at 10000m, HMar, Mar: 2007- 75:11, 2009- 71:47, 2010- 69:25, 2011- 31:26.10, 69:04; 2012- 32:34.71A, 67:03; 2013- 68:15, 2:35:54; 2014- 32:09.35, 66:19, 2:30:23; 2015- 32:08.00A, 68:42, 2:24:11; 2016- 67:41. pbs: 1500m 4:08.80A '11, 5000m 15:58.31 '14, 3000mSt 10:26.7A '08; Road: 10k 30:37 '11, 15k 46:49 '14, 10M 51:30 '15, 20k 62:55 '14.
Won Honolulu Marathon 2014-15, Amsterdam 2015. Married Erick Kibet, pb HMar 61:10 '10, in 2009.

Lydia Tum **CHEPKURUI** b. 23 Aug 1984 1.70m 52kg.
At 3000mSt: WCh: '13- 2; AfG: '11- 4, Kenyan champion 2013.
Progress at 3000mSt: 2011- 9:30.73, 2012- 9:14.98, 2013- 9:12.55, 2014- 9:24.07, 2015- 9:20.44. pbs: 1500m 4:14.97 '12, 3000m 8:55.21i '14, 2M 9:45.97i '14.

Irene Chebet **CHEPTAI** b. 4 Feb 1992 1.60m 45kg.
At 5000m: WCh: '15- 7. At 3000m: WY: '07- 7. World CC: '08- 2Jm '13- 10, '15- 7.
Progress at 5000m: 2012- 16:02.0A, 2013- 14:50.99, 2014- 15:17.76, 2015- 14:53.32. pbs: 1500m 4:13.75 '14, 3000m 8:48.03 '15, 10k rd 31:45A '14.

Gladys Kiprono **CHERONO** b. 12 May 1983 Kericho 1.66m 50kg.
At 10000m: WCh: '13- 2; AfCh: '12- 1 (1 5000m). World HMar: '14- 1. Won Kenyan 5000m 2012.
Progress at 5000m, 10000m, Mar: 2005- 16:16.8A, 2007- 16:03.8A, 2008- 15:56.0A, 2012- 15:39.5A, 32:41.40; 2013- 14:47.12, 30:29.23; 2014- 16:49.8A, 34:13.0A; 2015- 15:50.3A, 32:24.10A, 2:19:25. pbs: 1500m 4:25.13 '04, 3000m 8:34.05 '13, Road: 15k 47:43 '13, 20k 63:26 '13, HMar 66:07 '16.
Second Dubai Marathon (2:20:03, third fastest ever debut) and won Berlin in 2015. Married to Joseph Bwambok (62:25 HMar 2010).

Mercy CHERONO b. 7 May 1991 Kericho 1.68m 54kg.
At (3000m)/5000m: WCh: '11- 5, '13- 2, '15- 5; CG: '14- 1; AfCh: '14- 5; WJ: '08- (1), '10- 1/2; WY: '07- (1); Af-J: '09- 1/2; won DL 2014, KEN 5000m 23014. World CC: '07-09-10: 23J/2J/1J. Won Afr CC 2011.
Two world 4x1500m records 2014. Commonwealth 2M best 2014.
Progress at 1500m, 5000m: 2007- 16:49.13A, 2009- 4:13.70, 15:46.74A; 2010- 14:47.13, 2011- 4:02.31, 14:35.13; 2012- 4:06.42, 14:47.18; 2013- 4:05.82, 14:40.33; 2014- 4:08.57, 14:43.11; 2015- 4:01.26, 14:34.10. pbs: 800m 2:05.7A '13, 1M 4:22.67 '15, 2000m 5:35.65 '10, 3000m 8:21.14 '14, 2M 9:11.49 '14, 10000m 34:33.4A '06, 3000mSt 10:41.4A '13.

Sharon Jemutai **CHEROP** b. 16 Mar 1984 Marakwet district 1.57m 45kg.
At Mar: WCh: '11- 3. At 10000m: AfG: '99- 5. At 5000m: WJ: '00- 3. World CC: '02- 10J.
Progress at Mar: 2007- 2:38:45, 2008- 2:39:52, 2009- 2:33:53, 2010- 2:22:43, 2011- 2:22:42wdh/ 2:29:14, 2012- 2:22:39, 2013- 2:22:28, 2014- 2:23:44, 2015- 2:24:16. pbs: 3000m 9:09.23 '04, 5000m 15:40.7A '00, 10000m 32:03.0A '11, HMar 67:08 '11, 30k 1:39:21dh/1:40:04 '14.
Marathon wins: Toronto and Hamburg 2010, Boston and Turin 2012, Singapore 2013; 2nd Berlin 2013, Frankfurt 2014, Toronto 2015; 3rd Boston 2011, 2013.

Vivian CHERUIYOT b. 11 Sep 1983 Keiyo 1.55m 38kg.
At 5000m (/10000m): OG: '00- 14, '08- 5, '12- 2/3; WCh: '07- 2, '09- 1, '11- 1/1, '15- (1); CG: '10- 1; WJ: '02- 3; AfG '99- 3; AfCh: '10- 1; Af-J: '10- 1; CCp: '10- 1; won DL 2010-12. At 3000m: WY: '99- 3; WI: '10- 2. World CC: '98-9-00-01-02-04-06-07-11: 5J/2J/1J/4J/3J/8 4k/8 4k/8/1. Won KEN 1500m 2009, 5000m 2010-11, 10000m 2011-12.
African 2000m record 2009, Commonwealth 5000m 2009 & 2011, indoor 3000m (8:30.53) 2009; Kenyan 5000m 2007 & 2011.
Progress at 5000m, 10000m: 1999- 15:42.79A, 2000- 15:11.11, 2001- 15:59.4A, 2002- 15:49.7A, 2003- 15:44.8A, 2004- 15:13.26, 2006- 14:47.43, 2007- 14:22.51, 2008- 14:25.43, 2009- 14:37.01, 2010- 14:27.41, 2011- 14:20.87, 30:48.98; 2012- 14:35.62, 30:30.44; 2015- 14:46.69, 31:13.29. pbs: 1500m 4:06.6A '12, 4:06.65 '07; 2000m 5:31.52 '09, 3000m 8:28.66 '07, 2M 9:12.35i '10, 10M Rd 51:17 '15.
Laureus Sportswomen of the Year for 2011. Married Moses Kirui on 14 Apr 2012; son Allan born 19 Oct 2013.

Flomena Daniel **CHEYECH** b. 5 Jul 1982 West Pokot 1.68m 49kg.
At Mar: CG: '14- 1.
Progress at Mar: 2006- 2:42:15A, 2012- 2:34:13, 2013- 2:24:34, 2014- 2:22:44, 2015- 2:24:38. pbs: 3000m 9:16.21 '07, 5000m 15:19.47 '09, 10000m 31:58.50 '08, road: 15k 48:26 '13, HMar 67:39 '13, 30k 1:40:33 '14.
Marathon wins: Porto Alegre 2012, Vienna & Toronto 2013, Paris 2014; 2nd Amsterdam 2015.

Irene JELAGAT b. 10 Dec 1988 Samutet, Nyanza 1.62m 45kg.
At 1500m: OG: '08- h; WCh: '09- h; CG: '10- 6; AfG: '11- 1; AfCh: '08- 5, '10- 4; WJ: '06- 1; WY: '05- dns; WI: '10- 5. At 3000m: WI: 13- 4.
Two world 4x1500m records 2014.
Progress at 1500m: 2005- 4:21.3A, 2006- 4:08.88, 2007- 4:10.27, 2008- 4:04.59, 2009- 4:03.62, 2010- 4:03.76, 2011- 4:02.59, 2014- 4:04.07, 2015- 4:07.75. pb 800m 2:02.99 '06, 2000m 5:46.4 '14, 3000m 8:28.51 '14, 2M 9:12.90 '14, 5000m 14:55.49 '15.

Jemima Sumgong JELAGAT b. 21 Dec 1984 Eldoret 1.61m 47kg.
At Mar: WCh: '15- 4.
Progress at Mar: 2006- 2:35:22, 2007- 2:29:41, 2008- 2:30:18, 2010- 2:32:34, 2011- 2:28:32, 2012- 2:31:52, 2013- 2:20:48, 2014- 2:20:41dh/2:25:10, 2015- 2:24:23. pbs: 1500m 4:26.95 '15, 5000m 16:51.0A '13, 10000m 33:08.0A '13, Road: 10k 31:15 '06, 15k 47:14 '13, 10M 50:38 '13, 20k 62:32 '13, HMar 66:39 '16, 30k 1:39:20dh '14.
Marathon wins: Las Vegas 2006, Castellón 2011, Rotterdam 2013; 2nd Boston 2012, Chicago 2013 & New York 2014. Married Noah Talam in 2009, daughter born in 2011. Originally given a 2-year ban in 2012, but later cleared by the IAAF.

Peres JEPCHIRCHIR b. 27 Sep 1993 Usain Gishu 1.53m 40kg.
World HMar: '16- 1.
Progress at HMar: 2014- 69:12, 2015- 67:17, 2016- 66:39. pbs: Road: 10k 30:55 '15, 15k 48:14 '16, Mar 2:47:33A '13.

Hyvin Kiyeng **JEPKEMOI** b. 13 Jan 1992 1.56m 45kg.
At 3000mSt: WCh: '13- 6, '15- 1; AfG: '11- 1 (4 5000m); AfCh: '12- 3. Kenyan champion 2015.
Progress at 3000mSt: 2011- 10:00.50, 2012- 9:23.53, 2013- 9:22.05, 2014- 9:22.58, 2015- 9:10.15. pbs: 1500m 4:19.44 '11, 3000m 9:07.51 '11, 5000m 15:42.64 '11, 10000m 35:14.0A '14.

Janeth JEPKOSGEI Busienei b. 13 Dec 1983 Kabirirsang, near Kapsabet 1.67m 47kg. North Rift.
At 800m: OG: '08- 2, '12- 7; WCh: '07-09-11-15: 1/2/3/h; CG: '06- 1, '14- sf; AfCh: '06-10-14: 1/2/2 (& 2R); WJ: '02- 1; WY: '99- h; WCp: '06- 2, '10- 1; won DL 2010, WAF 2007, KEN 2011.
Five Kenyan 800m records 2005-07, Commonwealth & African 4x800m 2014.
Progress at 800m, 1500m: 1999- 2:11.0A, 2001- 2:06.21, 2002- 2:00.80, 2003- 2:03.05, 2004- 2:00.52, 4:11.91; 2005- 1:57.82, 4:15.77; 2006- 1:56.66, 4:15.43; 2007- 1:56.04, 4:14.70; 2008- 1:56.07, 4:08.48; 2009- 1:57.90, 4:13.87; 2010- 1:57.84, 4:04.17; 2011- 1:57.42, 4:02.32; 2012- 1:57.79, 4:07.34; 2013- 1:58.71, 4:12.61; 2014- 1:58.70, 2015- 1:59.37. pbs: 400m 54.06A '10, 600m 1:25.0+ '08, 1000m 2:37.98 '02, 1M 4:28.72 '08.
Brilliant front-running victory at 2007 Worlds.

Priscah JEPTOO Chepsisor b. 26 Jun 1984 Chemnoet Village, Nandi 1.65m 49kg.
At Mar: OG: '12- 2; WCh: '11- 2. At 10000m: AfG: '99- 5. At 5000m: WJ: '00- 3. Won KEN CC 2014.
Progress at Mar: 2009- 2:30:40, 2010- 2:27:02, 2011- 2:22:55, 2012- 2:20:14, 2013- 2:20:15, 2015- 2:25:01. pbs: 3000m 9:05.7 '13, road: 10k 31:18 '13, 15k 46:59 '14, 10M 50:38 '13, 20k 62:32 '13, HMar 65:45 '13.
Marathon wins: Porto 2009, Turin 2010, Paris 2011, London 2013 (3rd 2012), New York 2013. World Marathon Majors winner 2012/13. Won Great North Run 2013. Married to Douglas Chepsiro, son born 20 Feb 2009.

Lucy Wangui KABUU b. 24 Mar 1984 Ichamara, Nyeri region 1.55m 41kg. Suzuki, Japan.
At (5000m)/10000m: OG: '04- 9, '08- 7; CG: '06- 3/1; AfCh: '08- 4. At Mar: WCh: '13- 24. World 4k CC: '05- 5; HMar: '14- 4. Won KEN 10000m 2013.
Progress at 5000m, 10000m, HMar, Mar: 2001- 15:45.04, 2002- 15:33.03, 32:54.70; 2003- 15:10.23, 31:06.20; 2004- 14:47.09, 31:05.90, 69:47; 2005- 15:00.20, 31:22.37; 2006- 14:56.09, 31:29.66; 2007- 14:57.55, 31:32.52; 2008- 14:33.49, 30:39.96; 2009- 16:50.3A, 2011- 67:04, 2012- 2:19:34, 2013- 32:44.1A, 66:09, 2:24:06; 2014- 32:50.37A, 68:37, 2:24:16; 2015- 68:51, 2:20:21. pbs: 1500m 4:08.6A '12, 3000m 8:46.15 '08. Road 15k 47:13+ 13, 20k 62:48 '13, 25k 1:21:37 '13.
At the marathon set the pace in Osaka 2007, but at her first proper try was 2nd in 2:19:34 at Dubai 2012. 3rd Chicago 2012, Tokyo 2014, Dubai 2015. Won Great North Run 2011, RAK half marathon 2013.

Mary Jepkosgei **KEITANY** b. 18 Jan 1982 Kisok, Kabarnet 1.58m 45kg.
At Mar: OG: '12- 4. World HMar: '07- 2, '09- 1.
Records: World 25km 2010, 10M, 20km, half marathon 2011. African and two Kenyan half marathon 2009. Kenyan marathon 2012.
Progress at HMar, Mar: 2000- 72:53, 2002- 73:01, 2003- 73:25, 2004- 71:32, 2005- 70:18, 2006- 69:06, 2007- 66:48, 2009- 66:36, 2010- 67:14, 2:29:01; 2011- 65:50, 2:19:19; 2012- 66:49, 2:18:37; 2014- 65:39, 2:25:07; 2015- 66:02, 2:23:40. pbs: 1500m 4:24.33 '99, 10000m 32:18.07 '07; Road: 5k 15:25 '11, 10k 30:45 '11, 15k 46:40 '11, 10M 50:05 '11, 20k 62:36 '11, 25k 1:19:53 '10.
14 wins in 15 half marathons 2006-15 (12 successive wins from 2009) inc. Great North Run 2014-15, RAK 2011-12, 2015. Marathons: won London 2011-12 (2nd 2015), New York 2014-15 (3rd 2010-11). Won World Marathon Majors 2015/16. Married to Charles Koech (pbs 10k 27:56 & HMar 61:27 '07), son Jared born in June 2008 and daughter Samantha on 5 Apr 2013.

Sylvia Chibiwott **KIBET** b. 28 Mar 1984 Kapchorwa, Keiyo district 1.57m 44kg. Kenya Police.
At 5000m: OG: '08- 4; WCh: '07- 4, '09- 2, '11- 2;

CG: '10- 2; AfG: '07- 3; AfCh: '06- 3. At 3000m: WI: '08-10-12: 4/4/4, won Afr-Y 1998. At 1500m: WY: '99- 2. World CC: '11- 13. Won KEN 5000m 2011.
Progress at 5000m, 10000m: 2006- 15:02.54, 31:39.34; 2007- 14:57.37, 2008- 15:00.03, 2009- 14:37.77, 30:47.20; 2010- 14:31.91, 2011- 14:35.43, 2012- 14:46.73, 2013- 14:58.26. pbs: 1500m 4:05.33i/4:07.87 '10, 3000m 8:37.47 '13, 2M 9:16.62 '07, Road: 15k 48:24 '12, 10M 51:42 '12, HMar 69:32 '15, Mar 2:26:16 '15.
Did not compete in 2001-02. Married Erastus Limo in 2003, daughter Britney Jepkosgei born in 2004. 2nd in Hamburg on marathon debut in 2015. Older sister is Hilda Kibet NED and cousin of Lornah Kiplagat NED.

Viola Jelagat **KIBIWOT** b. 22 Dec 1983 Keiyo 1.57m 45kg.
At 1500m: OG: '08- h; WCh: '07- 5, '09/11- sf; CG: '06- 7, '10- 7; WJ: '02- 1. At 5000m: OG: '12- 6; WCh: '13- 4, '15- 4. World CC: '00-01-02-13: 3J/1J/1J/7; AfCC: '11-2.
Progress at 1500m, 5000m: 2003- 15:32.87, 2004- 4:06.64, 2006- 4:08.74, 2007- 4:02.10, 2008- 4:04.17, 14:51.59; 2009- 4:02.70, 2010- 4:03.39, 14:48.57; 2011- 4:05.51, 14:34.86; 2012- 3:59.25, 14:39.53; 2013- 4:00.76, 14:33.48; 2014- 4:00.46, 14:33.73; 2015- 4:01.41, 14:34.22. pbs: 800m 2:04.7A '12, 1M 4:24.31 '15, 2000m 5:38.2+ '14, 3000m 8:24.41 '14, 2M 9:12.59 '14, 10k Rd 32:49 '14, HMar 72:18 '14.

Edna Ngeringwony **KIPLAGAT** b. 15 Nov 1979 Eldoret 1.71m 54kg. Corporal in Kenyan Police.
At Mar: OG: '12- 19; WCh: '11- 1, '13- 1, '15- 5. At 3000m: WJ: '96- 2, '98- 3. World CC: '96-97-06: 5J/4J/13.
African record 30km 2008.
Progress at Mar: 2005- 2:50:20, 2010- 2:25:38, 2011- 2:20:46, 2012- 2:19:50, 2013- 2:21:32, 2014- 2:20:21, 2015- 2:27:16, 2016- 2:22:36. pbs: 3000m 8:53.06 '96, 5000m 15:57.3A '06, 10000m 33:27.0A '07; Road: 5k 15:20 '10, 10k 31:18 '10, 15k 47:57 '10, 10M 54:56 '09, HMar 67:41 '12, 30k 1:39:11 '14.
Won Los Angeles and New York Marathons 2010, London 2014 (2nd 2011-13); 3rd Tokyo 2016. Won World Marathon Majors 2013/14. Married to Gilbert Koech (10000m 27:55.30 '01, 10k 27:32 '01, Mar 2:13:45 dh '05, 2:14:39 '09); two children.

Florence Jebet **KIPLAGAT** b. 27 Feb 1987 Kapkitony, Keiyo district 1.55m 42kg.
At 5000m: WJ: '06- 2. At 10000m: WCh: '09- 11; CG: '14- 2. World CC: '07- 5, '09- 1; HMar: '10- 1. Won Kenyan 1500m 2007, 10000m 2014, CC 2007 & 2009.
World records 20k and half marathon 2014 & 2015, 15k 2015.. Kenyan 10000m record 2009.
Progress at 5000m, 10000m, HMar, Mar: 2006- 15:32.34, 2007- 14:40.74, 31:06.20; 2009- 14:40.14, 30:11.53; 2010- 14:52.64, 32:46.99A, 67:40; 2011- 68:02, 2:19:44; 2012- 30:24.85, 66:38, 2:20:57; 2013- 67:13, 2:21:13; 2014- 31:48.6A, 65:12, 2:20:24; 2015- 65:09, 2:23:33. pbs: 1500m 4:09.0A '07, 3000m 8:40.72 '10, Road: 15k 46:14 '15, 20k 61:54 '15, 30k 1:39:11 '14.
Won half marathon debut in Lille in 2010, followed a month later by World title. Did not finish in Boston on marathon debut in 2011; won Berlin 2011 and 2013; Chicago 2015 (2nd 2014), 2nd London 2014. Formerly married to Moses Mosop, daughter Aisha Chelagat born April 2008. Niece of William Kiplagat (Mar 2:06:50 '99, 8 WCh '07).

Helah KIPROP Jelagat b. 7 Apr 1985 Keiyo district 1.64m 48kg.
At Mar: WCh: '15- 2.
Progress at Mar: 2013- 2:28:02, 2014- 2:27:14, 2015- 2:24:03, 2016- 2:21:27. Pbs: 1500m 4:19.14 '07, 3000m 9:21.02 '06, 5000m 15:33.90 '07, 10000m 33:03.8A '09, 3000mSt 10:25.6A '09, Road: 10k 31:44 '12, 15k 47:32 '13, 20k 64:10 '13, HMar 67:39 '13.
Won Seoul marathon 2014, Tokyo 2016 (2nd 2015). Baby born 2008.

Sally Jepkosgei **KIPYEGO** b. 19 Dec 1985 Kapsowar, Marakwet district 1.68m 52kg. Was at Texas Tech University, USA.
At (5000m)/10000m: OG: '12- 4/2; WCh: '11- 2, '15- 5. World CC: '01- 8J. Won record equalling nine NCAA titles 5000m 2008, 10000m 2007, CC 2006-08, indoor 3000m 2007, 5000m 2007-09.
Progress at 5000m, 10000m: 2005- 16:34.90, 2006- 16:13.39, 2007- 15:19.72, 31:56.72; 2008- 15:11.88, 31:25.48; 2009- 15:09.03, 33:44.7A; 2010- 14:38.64, 2011- 14:30.42, 30:38.35; 2012- 14:43.11, 30:26.37; 2014- 14:37.18, 30:42.26; 2015- 14:47.75, 31:44.42. pbs: 800m 2:08.26 '08, 1500m 4:06.23 '11, 1M 4:27.19i/4:29.64 '09, 2000m 5:35.20 '09, 3000m 8:34.18 '14, 2M 9:21.04i, 9:22.10 '14, Road: 15k 48:51 '14, 20k 64:54 '14, HMar 68:31 '14.
Married to Kevin Chelimo (5000m 13:14.57 '12). One of her eight brothers is Mike Kipyego (3000mSt 8:08.48).

Faith Chepngetich **KIPYEGON** b. 10 Jan 1994 Bornet 1.57m 42kg.
At 1500m: OG: '12- h; WCh: '13- 5, '15- 2; CG: '14- 1; AfCh: '14- 5; WJ: '12- 1; WY: '11- 1. World CC: '10-11-13: 4J/1J/1J; AfCC: '12- 1J, '14- 1.
Records: World 4x1500m 2014, Commonwealth, African junior & Kenyan 1500m 2013, African & Commonwealth 1M 2015.
Progress at 1500m, 5000m: 2010- 4:17.1A, 2011- 4:09.48, 2012- 4:03.82, 2013- 3:56.98, 2014- 3:58.01, 2015- 3:59.32, 14:31.95. pbs: 800m 1:58.02 '15, 1M 4:16.71 '15, 2000m 5:37.8+ '14, 3000m 8:23.55 '14.
Older sister Beatrice Mutai (b. 19 Apr 1987) 11 World CC 2013, HMar 69:30 '14.

Purity Cherotich **KIRUI** b. 13 Aug 1991 Kericho 1.62m 47kg.
At 3000mSt: CG: '14- 1; AfG: '15- 3; AfCh: '14- 6; WJ: '10- 1; Kenyan champion 2014.
Progress at 3000mSt: 2008- 10:27.19A, 2009-

10:05.1A, 2010- 9:36.34, 2011- 9:37.85, 2012- 9:35.61, 2013- 9:19.42, 2014- 9:23.43, 2015- 9:17.74. pbs: 800m 2:07.6A '14, 1500m 4:31.83 '08, 5000m 16:13.42 '11.

Janet KISA b. 5 Mar 1992 1.60m 48kg.
At 3000m: CCp: '14- 4. At 5000m: WCh: '15- 6; CG: '14- 2; AfCh: '14- 3; Af-J: '11- 2. World CC: '11-13-15: 5J/6/12; AfCC: '14- 2.
Progress at 5000m: 2010- 16:02.2A, 2011- 15:24.75, 2012- 14:57.68, 2013- 15:05.89, 2014- 14:52.59, 2015- 15:02.68. pbs: 1500m 4:14.77 '11, 2000m 5:45.9 '14, 3000m 8:32.66 '14, 10k Rd 33:55 '13, HMar 71:01 '14.

Cynthia LIMO b. 18 Dec 1989 1.55m 45kg.
World HMar: '16- 2.
Progress at HMar: 2010- 73:19, 2011- 70:39, 2012- 70:06, 2013- 69:59, 2014- 68:24, 2015- 67:02, 2016- 66:04. pbs: Road: 10k 31:07 '15, 15k 47:11 '15, 20k 62:48 '16.
Won RAK Half marathon 2016.

Linet Chepkwemoi **MASAI** b. 5 Dec 1989 Kapsokwony, Mount Elgon district 1.70m 55kg.
At (5000m)/10000m: OG: '08- 4; WCh: '09- 1, '11- 6/3; AfCh: '10- 3. World CC: '07-08-09-10-11: 1J/3/2/2/2. Won KEN 10000m 2010, CC 2010-11.
World junior record and Kenyan record at 10000m 2008, World 10 miles road record 2009.
Progress at 5000m, 10000m: 2007- 14:55.50, 2008- 14:47.14, 30:26.50; 2009- 14:34.36, 30:51.24; 2010- 14:31.14, 31:59.36A; 2011- 14:32.95, 30:53.59; 2012- 14:53.93, 2013- 15:02.98, 31:02.89. pbs: 1500m 4:12.26 '09, 2000m 5:33.43 '09, 3000m 8:38.97 '07. Road: 15k 47:21 '09, 10M 50:39 '09, HMar 71:45 '14.
Younger sister of Moses (qv) and Dennis Masai. Younger sister Magdalene (b. 4 Apr 1993) has pbs: 5000m 14:58.54 '15, HMar 67:31 '16, 3000mSt 9:29.16 '15.

Virginia NYAMBURA b. 20 Jul 1993 1.65m 48kg.
At 3000mSt: WCh: '15- 7; won DL 2015. 2000mSt: Yth OG: '10- 1.
World best 2000m steeplechase 2015.
Progress at 3000mSt: 2008- 10:27.46A, 2009- 10:13.6A, 2010- 10:28.19A, 2013- 9:58.08, 2014- 10:02.18, 2015- 9:13.85. pbs: 1500m 4:10.0A '15, 2000m 6:05.45 '13, 5000m 16:38.6A '13, 2000mSt 6:02.16 '15.
Took 36.57 secs off pb at Doha 2015 after being the pacemaker and continuing to win.

Hellen Onsando **OBIRI** b. 13 Dec 1989 Nyangusu, Kisii 1.55m 45kg.
At 1500m: OG: '12- 9; WCh: '11- 10 (fell), '13- 3; CG: '14- 6; AfCh: '14- 1; CCp: '14- 4. At 3000m: WI: '12- 1, '14- 2. Won Kenyan 1500m 2011-14.
Two world 4x1500m records 2014. African & Commonwealth 3000m record 2014.
Progress at 1500m: 2011- 4:02.42, 2012- 3:59.68, 2013- 3:58.58, 2014- 3:57.05. pbs: 800m 2:00.54 '11, 1000m 2:46.00i '12, 2000m 5:37.7+ '14, 3000m 8:20.68 '14, 5000m 15:49.7A '13.
Daughter born in May 2015.

Betsy SAINA b. 30 Jun 1988 Sokosik, Nandi 1.63m 48kg. Bowerman TC, USA. Graduate of Iowa State University, USA
At 10000m: WCh: '15- 8; AfCh: '12- 3. At 3000m: WI: '16- 7. Won NCAA indoor 5000m & CC 2012.
Progress at 5000m, 10000m: 2009- 16:15.74, 36:34.94; 2010- 16:10.69, 33:13.13; 2011- 15:50.74i/16:06.05, 33:13.87; 2012- 15:36.09i, 31:15.97; 2013- 15:12.05, 31:37.22; 2014- 14:39.49, 30:57.30; 2015- 15:00.48, 31:51.35; 2016- 14:57.18i. pbs: 1M 4:40.98i '13, 2000m 5:45.7 '14, 3000m 8:38.01 '14, 2M 9:16.95 '14, Rd 10k 30:46 '14, 10M 51:55 '14, HMar 69:27 '14.

Eunice Jepkoech **SUM** b. 2 Sep 1988 Burnt Forest, Uasin Gishu 1.72m 53kg. Police.
At 800m: WCh: '11- sf, '13- 1, '15- 3; CG: '14- 1; AfCh: '10- h,'12- 2, '14- 1; CCp: '14- 1; won DL 2013-15. At 1500m: OG: '12- h, Won Kenyan 800m 2012, 2014.
World 4x1500m record 2014, Commonwealth & African 4x800m 2014..
Progress at 800m, 1500m: 2009- 2:07.4A, 2010- 2:00.28, 2011- 1:59.66A, 4:12.41; 2012- 1:59.13, 4:04.26; 2013- 1:57.38, 4:02.05; 2014- 1:57.92, 4:01.54; 2015- 1:56.99, 4:09.7A. pb 3000m 8:53.12 '12. Daughter Diana Cheruto born in 2008.

Agnes Jebet **TIROP** b. 23 Oct 1995 1.59m 44kg.
At 5000m: WJ: '12- 3, '14- 3; World CC: '13-15: 2J/1; AfCC: '12- 2J, '14- 1J.
Progress at 5000m: 2011- 16:09.0A, 2012- 15:36.74, 2013- 14:50.36, 2014- 15:00.19. pbs: 1500m 4:12.68 '13, 2000m 5:48.65 '13, 3000m 8:39.13 '13, 10000m 32:55.41 '15, 3000mSt 10:27.4A '12.

Mercy WACERA Ngugi b. 17 Dec 1988 1.55m.
World HMar: '14- 2, '16- 3. At 5000m: WJ: '06- 3; Af-J: 07- 1.
Progress at HMar: 2012- 70:54, 2013- 70:32, 2014- 67:44, 2015- 70:21, 2016- 66:29. pbs: 1500m 4:24.4A '08, 3000m 8:55.89 '09, 5000m 15:20.30 '09, Road: 10k 31:28 '12, 15k 48:49 '15.
Widow of Samuel Wanjiru (2008 Olympic marathon champion). Daughter born 2010.

KOREA

Governing body: Korea Athletics Federation, 10 Chamshil Dong, Songpa-Gu, Seoul. Founded 1945. **National Champions 2015**: **Men:** 100m: Kim Kuk-young 10.36, 200m: Lim Chan-ho 21.23, 400m: Park Bong-ko 46.57, 800m: Hong In-ki 1:50.76, 1500m: Ryu Ji-san 3:51.25, 5000m: Son Myung-jun 14:30.28, 10000m: Kim Min 30:10.19, 3000mSt: Choi Dong-il 9:18.83, 110mh: Lee Jung-joon 13.84, 400mh: Kim Dae-hong 51.03, HJ: Woo Sang-hyuk 2.22, PV: Jin Min-sub 5.50, LJ: Kim Duk-hyun 7.89w, TJ: Kim Dong-han 15.99, SP: Jung Il-woo 18.95, DT: Lee Hoon 54.10, HT: Lee Yun-chul 69.44, JT: Jung Sang-jin

75.36, Dec: Kim Kun-woo 7062, 20kW: Park Chil-sung 1:29:38. Women: 100m/200m: Kim Min-ji 11.93/24.13, 400m: Lee Ah-young 55.31, 800m: Oh Ji-young 2:17.81, 1500m: Lee Se-jung 4:31.58, 5000m: Oh Dal-nim 16:57.63, 10000m: Yeum Ko-eun 35:10.30, 3000mSt: Shon You-na 10:55.86, 100mh: Jung Hye-lim 13.55, 400mh: Kim Kyong-hwa 59.49, HJ: Han Da-rye 1.73, PV: Choi Yea-eun 4.20, LJ: Kim Min-ji 6.23, TJ: Bae Chan-mi 13.54, SP: Lee Su-jung 15.25, DT: Cho Hye-lim 50.43, HT: Kang Na-ru 61.82, JT: Kim Kyong-ae 56.84, Hep: Jung Yeon-jin 4889, 20kW:.

KIM Hyun-sub b. 31 May 1985 Sokcho 1.75m 53kg.
At 20kW: OG: '08- 23, '12- 17; WCh: '07-09-11-13-15: 20/34/3/10/10; AsiG: '06-10-14: 2/3/3; WUG: '05-07-09: 2/6/5. Asian champion 2011, 2014 (2nd 2015); KOR 2005-06, 2008-13. At 10000m/10kW: WJ: '04- 3; WCp: '04- 8.
Five Korean 20km road walk records 2008-15.
Progress at 20kW: 2004- 1:24:58, 2005- 1:22:15, 2006- 1:21:45, 2007- 1:20:54, 2008- 1:19:41, 2009- 1:22:00, 2010- 1:19:36, 2011- 1:19:31, 2012- 1:21:36, 2013- 1:21:22, 2014- 1:19:24, 2015- 1:19:13. Pb 10000mW 39:30.56 '09, 38:13R '10.

LATVIA

Governing body: Latvian Athletic Association, 1 Augsiela Str, Riga LV-1009. Founded 1921.
National Championships first held in 1920 (men), 1922 (women). **2015 Champions**: **Men:** 100m/200m: Janis Mezitis 10.68/21.63, 400m: Austris Karpinskis 48.52, 800m/1500m: Pauls Arents 1:50.91/3:49.50, 3000m: Alberts Blajs 8:23.80, 5000m/HMar: Janis Viskers 14:41.26/ 67:13, Mar: Kristaps Berzins 2:29:49, 3000mSt: Dmitrijs Serjogins 9:20.57, 110mh: Kristaps Sietins 14.33, 400mh: Janis Baltuss 52.81, HJ: Sendijs Ziemelis 2.07, PV: Mareks Arents 5.40, LJ: Elvijs Misans 7.68, TJ: Ilmars Klanins 14.74, SP/DT: Maris Urtans 19.44/54.50, HT: Igors Sokolovs 74.28, JT: Ainars Kovals 76.76, Dec: Ingus Zarins 6585, 20kW/50kW: Arnis Rumbenieks 4:03:44. **Women**: 100m: Sindija Buksa 11.85, 200m/400m: Gunta Latiseva-Cudare 24.00/53.94, 800m/1500m: Jejena Abele 2:11.10/4:24.52, 3000m/5000m/10k: Karina Helmane-Sorocenková 10:14.83/17:33.94/38:14, HMar: Ilona Marhele 1:19:00, Mar: Kitija Valtere 2:57:04, 3000mSt: Lina Sulgina 11:27.91, 100mh: Ilona Dramaconoka 14.40, 400mh: Liga Velvere 56.77, HJ: Madara Onuzane 1.80, PV: Ilze Bortascenoka 3.50, LJ: Mara Griva 6.35, TJ: Madara Apine 13.04, SP: Linda Ozola 13.26, DT: Dace Steinerte 48.94, HT: Karina Orlova 51.18, JT: Madara Palameika 63.06, Hep: Jolanta Kaupe 5056.

Women

Laura IKAUNIECE-ADMIDINA b. 31 May 1992 Jürmala 1.79m 60kg. Jürmalas SS.
At Hep: OG: '12- 8; WCh: '13- 11, '15- 3; EC: '12- 2, '14- 6; WJ: '10- 6; WY: '09- 2; EJ: '11- 3; WUG: '13- 2. Won LAT 100m 2012-13, 200m 2009, 2013; 100mh & HJ 2010.
Four Latvian heptathlon records 2012-15.
Progress at Hep: 2010- 5618, 2011- 6063, 2012- 6414, 2013- 6321, 2014- 6320, 2015- 6516. Pbs: 60m 7.58i '16, 100m 11.96 '14, 11.91w '13; 200m 23.95 '15, 800m 2:11.83 '14, 60mh 8.38i '14, 100mh 13.21 '15, HJ 1.85i '12, 1.84 '14; LJ 6.49i '16, 6.32 '15; SP 13.22 '15, JT 53.73 '12, Pen 4496i '14.
Her mother Vineta Ikauniece set Latvian records at 100m 11.34A '87, 200m 22.49A '87 and 400m 50.71 '88, and her father Aivars Ikaunieks had 110mh bests of 13.71A '87 and 13.4 '84.

Madara PALAMEIKA b. 18 Jun 1987 Valdemarpils 1.85m 76kg. Ventspils.
At JT: OG: '12- 8; WCh: '09-13-15: dnq 27/27/13, '11- 11; EC: '10-12-14: 8/8/4; WJ: '06- dnq 16; EU23: '07- 3, '09- 1; EJ: '05- dnq 17. Won LAT 2009-11, 2014-15.
Latvian javelin records 2009 & 2014.
Progress at JT: 2002- 42.31, 2003- 49.11, 2004- 51.50, 2005- 51.75, 2006- 54.19, 2007- 57.98, 2008- 53.45, 2009- 64.51, 2010- 62.02, 2011- 63.46, 2012- 62.74, 2013- 62.72, 2014- 66.15, 2015- 65.01.

LITHUANIA

Governing body: Athletic Federation of Lithuania, Kareiviu 6, LT-09117 Vilnius. Founded 1921.
National Championships first held in 1921 (women 1922). **2015 Champions: Men:** 100m/200m: Rytis Sakalauskas 10.54/21.09, 400m: Rokas Pacevicius 47.63, 800m: Mindaugas Striokas 1:51.43, 1500m: Petras Gliebus 3:50.22, 5000m: Simas Bertasius 14:44.59, 10000m: Tomas Venckunas 31:53.99, HMar: Valdas Dopolskas 67:09, Mar: Andrej Jegorov 2:31:20, 3000mSt: Justinas Berzanskis 9:05.36, 110mh/400mh: Rapolas Saulius 14.49/54.61, HJ: Raivydas Stanys 2.13, PV: Osvaldas Gedrimas 4.60 LJ: Mantas Silkauskas 7.56, TJ: Darius Aucyna 15.35, SP: Sarunas Banevicius 19.18, DT: Aleksas Abromavicius 62.25, HT: Martynas Sedys 61.83, JT: Edis Matusevicius 74.31, 20kW: Marius Ziukas 1:24:46 **Women**: 100m: Lina Grincikaite Samuole 11.61, 200m: Eva Misiunaite 24.35, 400m: Modesta Morauskaite 53.96, 800m: Monika Elenska 2:09.49, 1500m: Rasa Drazdauskaite 4:26.06, 5000m: Lina Grisiute 18:08.78, 10000m: Gintare Juknyteb 45:27.26, HMar: Zivile Balciunaite 1:21:45, Mar: Loreta Bliujiene 3:06:08, 3000mSt: Evelina Usevaite 10:45.57, 100mh: Sonata Tamosaityte 13.71, 400mh: Egle Staisiunaite 58.01, HJ: Airine Palsyte 1.95, PV: Migle Juodeskaite 3.50, LJ: Asta Dauksaite 5.92, TJ: Dovile Dzindzaletaite 13.96, SP: Giedre Kupstyte 15.95, DT: Zinaida Sendriute 58.36, HT: Aiste Ziginskaite 48.27, JT: Indre Jakubaityte 55.75, 10kW: Brigita Virbalyte 43:26, 20kW: Neringa Aidietyte 1:30:02.

Women

Airine PALSYTE b. 13 Jul 1992 Vilnius 1.86m 62kg. COSMA. Vilnius University.
At HJ: OG: '12- 11; WCh: '13- 12, '15- dnq 14=; WJ: '08- dnq 23, '10- 2; WY: '09- 4; EC: '10- dnq 18, '14- 13; EJ: '11- 2; EU23: '13- 2; WUG: '11- 2, '15- 1; WI: '16- 4; EI: '15- 4; Lithuanian champion 2010, 2012-15.
Three LTU high jump records 2011-14
Progress at HJ: 2003- 1.45, 2004- 1.40i, 2005- 1.60, 2006- 1.71, 2007- 1.70i/1.55, 2008- 1.80, 2009- 1.86i/1.83, 2010- 1.92, 2011- 1.96, 2012- 1.95, 2013- 1.95, 2014- 1.98, 2015- 1.98i/1.95, 2016- 1.97i. pb 200m 24.78 '12, TJ 12.70i '12.

Zinaida SENDRIUTE b. 20 Dec 1984 Klaisiai, Skuodas 1.88m 89kg. COSMA.
At DT: OG: '08- dnq 33, '12- 8; WCh: '09-11-13-15: dnq 31/12/9/dnq 13; EC: '06-10-12-14: dnq 17/5/ dnq 17/6; EJ: '03- 7; EU23: '05- 6; WUG: '11- 2; Lithuanian champion 2003, 2005-08, 2010-15.
Progress at DT: 2000- 33.37, 2001- 40.55, 2002- 48.66, 2003- 50.62, 2004- 51.38, 2005- 55.25, 2006- 57.26, 2007- 56.74, 2008- 59.42, 2009- 60.21, 2010- 60.70, 2011- 62.49, 2012- 64.03, 2013- 65.97, 2014- 65.83, 2015- 61.37. pbs: SP 14.15 '10, HT 33.19 '04.

LUXEMBOURG

Governing body: Fédération Luxembourgeoise d'Athlétisme, 3 Route d'Arlon, L-8009 Strassen, Luxembourg. Founded 1928.

2015 National Champions: **Men**: 100m/LJ: Yoann Bebon 11.01/6.49, 200m: Pol Bidaine 22.50, 400m: Tom Scholler 49.74, 800m: Christophe Bestgen 1:58.74, 1500m: Charles Grethen 3:52.78, 5000m/10000m: Pol Mellina 14:50.98/30:54.64, HMar: Yannick Leiners 71:19, Mar: Pierre Weimerskirch 2:35:07, 3000mSt: Luc Scheller 10:01.44, 110mh: Claude Godart 14.51w, 400mh: Jacques Frisch 53.88, HJ: Kevin Rutare 2.05, PV: Roy Michel 3.90, TJ: Ben Kiffer 13.35, SP: Bob Bertemes 18.92, DT: Sven Forster 49.34, HT: Ken Hoffmann 43.44, JT: Jéremy Kirsch 52.91, Dec: Wesley Charlet 5541. **Women**: 100m/ 200m: Laurence Jones 11.94/24.92, 400m/400mh: Kim Reuland 57.74/62.24, 800m/1500m: Jenny Gloden 2:19.08/4:57.48, 3000m: Martine Mellina 9:58.64, 10000m: Pascale Schmoetten 37:54.51, HMar: Annetet Jaffke 1:22:23, Mar: Karin Schank 2:57:26, 3000mSt: Liz Weiler 11:29.76, 100m: Cathy Schmit 17.11, HJ: Nadine Lanners 1.69, PV: Lara Buekens 3.50, LJ/Hep: Lara Merx 5.70, TJ: Nita Bokomba 11.74, SP: Stéphanie Krumlovsky 13.42, DT/HT: Isabeau Pleimling 34.84/44.43, JT: Véronique Michel 42.97.

MEXICO

Governing body: Federación Mexicana de Atletismo, Anillo Periférico y Av. del Conscripto, 11200 México D.F. Founded 1933.

National Champions 2015: Men: 100m: Héctor Ruíz 10.24w, 200m: César Ramirez 20.55, 400m: Gilberto Guzmán 47.09, 800m: Jesús López 1:48.68, 1500m/5000m: José Esparza 3:46.15/ 14:23.69, 10000m: Juan Luis Barrios 30:29.66, 3000mSt: Luis Ibarra 9:18.48, 110mh: Pedro Bustamante 14.00, 400mh: Sergio Rios 51.92, HJ: Edgar Rivera 2.23, PV: Guillermo Silva 5.10, LJ: Luis Rivera 7.85, TJ: Alberto Álvarez 16.25, SP: Stephen Sáenz 19.03, DT: Mario Cota 59.16, HT: Diego del Real 70.62, JT: Josué Menedez 72.42, Dec: Roman Garibay 7382. **Women:** 100m: Cecilia Tamayo 11.75, 200m: Iza Daniela Flores 23.97, 400m/800m: Gabriela Medina 52.83/2:04.23, 1500m: Sandra López 4:31.50, 5000m: Brenda Flores 16:32.40, 10000m: Marisol Romero 35:07.22, 3000mSt: Ana Narvaez 10:38.24, 100mh: Gabriela Santos 13.84, 400mh: Zudikey Rodríguez 58.47, HJ: Fabiola Elizabeth Ayala 1.76, PV: Carmelita Correa 4.13, LJ/Hep: Jessamyn Sauceda 6.31/ 5212, TJ: Ivonne Rangel 13.33, SP: Cecilia Dzul 15.26, DT: Ana González 50.42, HT: Michelle Hernández 56.00, JT:Abigail Gómez 59.26:.

Jorge **Horacio NAVA** b. 20 Jan 1982 Chihuahua 1.75m 62kg.
At 50kW: OG: '08- 6, '12- 13; WCh: '05-07-09-13: 9/9/19/32; PAm: '07-11-15: 2/1/3; CAG: '10- 1; WCp: '06-08-10-12: 7/5/2/9. At 20kW: WCh: '11- 16, '15- 28; CAG: '14- 1. At 10000mW: WY: '99- 5; PAm-J: '01- 2. Won MEX 20000mW 2013, 20kW 2014; PAmCp 50k 2015.
Progress at 50kW: 2005- 3:53:57, 2006- 3:48:22, 2007- 3:52:35, 2008- 3:45:21, 2009- 3:56:26, 2010- 3:54:16, 2011- 3:45:29, 2012- 3:46:59, 2013- 3:58:00, 2014- 3:42:51, 2015- 3:45:41. pbs: 5000m 18:40.11 '09, 10000mW 40:33.52 '04, 20kW 1:22:04 '12.

Luis RIVERA Morales b. 21 Jun 1987 Agua Prieta, Sonora 1.83m 79kg. Degree in engineering from University of Arizona.
At LJ: OG: '12- dnq 32; WCh: '13- 3; PAm: '15- 9; WI: '14- 7; CCp: '14- 6; WUG: '13- 1. Won IbAm LJ 2014, Mexican LJ 2006-07, 2009-10, 2012-13, 2015; TJ 2005-07.
Two Mexican long jump records 2013.
Progress at LJ: 2006- 7.31/7.47w, 2007- 7.60, 2008- 7.84i/7.61, 2009- 7.99i/7.95, 2010- 7.93, 2011- 7.77Ai/7.32, 2012- 8.22, 2013- 8.46, 2014- 8.24, 2015- 7.87. pbs: 110mh 15.02 '07, TJ 15.97 '09.
Brother Edgar (b. 13 Feb 1991) has HJ pb 2.28 '11 (5 WY 07, 6 WJ 10).

MOLDOVA

Governing Body: Federatia de Atletism din Republica Moldova. Founded 1991.

Zalina MARGHIEVA b. 5 Feb 1988 Vladikavkaz, North Osetia, Russia 1.74m 90kg. AS-CSPLN.
At HT: OG: '08- dnq 37, '12- dq8; WCh: '09- dq dnq 26, '11- dq8, '15- 8; EC: '10- dq5, '12- dq8; WJ: '06- 4; WY: '05- 7; EU23: '09- 1; EJ: '07- 5; WUG: '11- dq1, '13- dq3. Won Balkan 2015.

Nine Moldovan hammer records 2005-16 (and 3 disqualified).
Progress at HT: 2005- 61.80, 2006- 65.50, 2007- 65.40, 2008- 70.22, 2009- 71.56, 2015- 73.97, 2016- 74.31; DQ: 2010- 71.50, 2011- 72.93, 2012- 74.47, 2013- 74.28.
Drugs ban announced in 2013 with all results annulled from 2009 Worlds to 2013. Sister **Marina** (now **Nikisenko**) (b. 28 Jun 1986) HT: 72.53 '09, seven MDA records 2007-09, WCh: '11/15- dnq 17/25; EC: '10- 5, received a 3-year drugs ban from 24 July 2012. Brother **Serghei** (b. 6 Nov 1992) four MDA HT recs to 78.72 '15, 2 EJ '11.

MOROCCO

Governing Body: Fédération Royale Marocaine d'Athlétisme, Complex Sportif Prince Moulay Abdellah, PO Box 1778 R/P, Rabat. Fd. 1957.
2015 National Champions: Men: 100m: Aziz Ouhadi 10.47, 200m: Abdelhafid Haddadi 21.51, 400m: Mustapha Gheziane 48.10, 800m: Amine El Manaoui 1:45.76, 1500m: Youness Essalhi 3:44.28, 5000m: Soufiyan Bouqantar 13:49.35, 10000m: Hassan Ouazzine 29:05.38, 3000mSt: Brahim Taleb 8:30.87, 110mh: Abdallah Sadofi 14.95, 400mh: Soufiyane Masaoudi 51.30, HJ: Zakaria Mejhour 2.05, PV: Mouhcine Cheaouri 5.20, LJ: Hicham Douiri 7.36, TJ: Adil Goundou 15.44, SP/DT: Mohamed Gharrous 18.16/54.74, HT: Abdellah Hassar 59.33, JT: Abdullah Charii 66.29. **Women**: 100m/200m: Assia Raziki 12.13/24.05, 400m: Khadija Ouardi 56.59, 800m: Sanae El Otmani 2:07.33, 1500m/3000mSt: Fadwa Sidi Madane 4:25.35/9:43.63, 5000m: Kaltoum Bouaasayriya 15:32.44, 10000m: Fouzia Majdoubi 33:46.62, 100mh: Lamiae Lhabze 14.35, 400mh: Hayat Lambarki 56.67, HJ: Fatima Zahra El Alaoui 1.65, PV: Dinar Nasrine 3.20, LJ/TJ: Jamaa Chnaïk 6.10/13.06, SP: Sara Chebbawi 11.61, DT: Amina Moudden 48.38, HT: Soukana Zakkour 56.57. JT: Nezha Marzak 40.01.

Abdelaati IGUIDER b. 25 Mar 1987 Errachidia 1.70m 52kg.
At 1500m(/5000m): OG: '08- 5, '12- 3/6; WCh: '07-09-11-13-15: h/11/5/sf/3; WJ: '04- 1, '06- 2; WI: '10-12-14: 2/1/3. At 3000m: WI: '16- 4.
Progress at 1500m, 5000m: 2004- 3:35.53, 2005- 3:35.63, 2006- 3:32.68, 2007- 3:32.75, 2008- 3:31.88, 2009- 3:31.47, 2010- 3:34:25, 2011- 3:31.60, 2012- 3:33.99, 13:09.17; 2013- 3:33.29, 2014- 3:29.83, 2015- 3:28.79, 12:59.25. pbs: 800m 1:46.67 '15, 1000m 2:19.14 '07, 1M 3:49.09 '14, 3000m 7:34.92i '13, 7:34.99 '14.

Brahim TALEB b. 16 Feb 1985 Rabat 1.82m 70kg.
At 3000mSt: OG: '08- h, '12- 11; WCh: '07- h, '15- 7; AfCh: '06- 4; MAR champion 2013, 2015. At 2000mSt: WY: '01- 5.
Progress at 3000mSt: 2004- 8:37.99, 2005- 8:27.17, 2006- 8:14.75, 2007- 8:07.02, 2008- 8:14.32, 2010- 8:17.71, 2011- 8:51.03, 2012- 8:10.20, 2013- 8:30.05, 2014- 8:15.48, 2015- 8:16.56. pbs: 800m 1:54.45 '06, 1500m 3:42.04 '07, 3000m 7:49.13 '15, 5000m 13:54.81 '13, 10k Rd 28:54 '08, 2000mSt 5:27.66 '06.

Women

Malika AKKAOUI b. 25 Dec 1987 Zaida, Meknès-Tafilalet 1.60m 46kg.
At 800m/(1500m): OG: '12- sf; WCh: '11- (h), '13- sf, '15- sf/12; AfCh: '10-12-14: 3/3/6; WJ: '06- h. Won MAR 400m 2014, 800m 2007-08, MedG 800m 2013, Arab 800m 2015.
Progress at 800m: 2004- 2:09.2, 2005- 2:08.1, 2006- 2:06.29, 2007- 2:05.04, 2008- 2:04.25, 2009- 2:02.10, 2010- 2:00.6, 2011- 1:59.75, 2012- 1:59.01i/ 1:59.54, 2013- 1:57.64, 2014- 2:00.58, 2015- 1:59.03. pbs: 400m 53.19 '13, 1000m 2:39.86 '13, 1500m 4:04.49 '15.

Salima Alami **EL OUALI** b. 29 Dec 1983 Karia Ba Mohamed 1.67m 53kg.
At 3000mSt: OG: '12- h; WCh: '11- h, '13- 15, '15- 10; AfCh: '14- 3; CCp: '14- 6.
Two Moroccan 3000mSt records 2014-15.
Progress at 3000mSt: 2010- 10:21.66, 2011- 9:42.51, 2012- 9:31.03, 2013- 9:35.88, 2014- 9:21.24, 2015- 9:20.64. pbs: 1500m 4:08.53 '15, 3000m 8:50.12 '15, 5000m 16:10.29 '09.

Rabab ARRAFI b. 12 Jan 1991 1.67m 54kg. ASOAK.
At (800m)/1500m: WCh: '13- sf, '15- 4/9; AfCh: 12- 1, '14- 3; WI: '14- dq after finishing 3rd. At 3000m: WY: '07- 12. Won FrancG 2013.
Progress at 800m, 1500m: 2006- 24:21.59, 2011- 2:09.24, 2012- 2:04.60, 4:05.80; 2013- 2:00.58, 4:05.22; 2014- 2:03.18i, 4:02.71; 2015- 1:58.55, 4:02.94. pbs: 1M 4:23.50 '15, 3000m 8:58.32i '13, 9:34.78 '07.

NETHERLANDS

Governing body: Koninklijke Nederlandse Atletiek Unie (KNAU), Postbus 60100, NL-6800 JC Arnhem. Founded 1901.
National Championships first held in 1910 (men), 1921 (women). **2015 Champions: Men**: 100m: Churandy Martina 10.08, 200m/400m: Lee-Marvin Bonevacia 20.62/46.72, 800m: Thijmen Kupers 1:45.28, 1500m: Jurjen Polderman 4:03.00, 5000m: Dennis Licht 14:12.94, 10000m: Roy Hoornweg 29:16.70, HMar: Bart van Nynen 64:35, Mar: Abdi Nageeye 2:12:33, 3000mSt: Nils Pennekamp 9:09.60, 110mh: Gregory Sedoc 13.77, 400mh: Jesper Arts 51.48, HJ: Jan Peter Larsen 2.16, PV: Menno Vloon 5.20, LJ: Ronald Hertog 7.47, TJ: Fabian Florant 16.65, SP/HT: Denzel Comenentia 19.28/64.60, DT: Rutger Smith 60.67, JT: Daan Meijer 75.53, 20kW/50kW: Rob Tersteeg 1:42:16/4:22:27. **Women**: 100m: Dafne Schippers 11.02, 200m: Jamile Samuel 23.00,

400m: Nicky van Leuveren 52.70, 800m: Lisanne de Witte 2:05.89, 1500m: Maureen Koster 4:26.01, 5000m: Jamie van Lieshout 16:23.95, HMar: Stefanie Bouma 78:11, Mar: Miranda Boonstra 2:32:13, 3000mSt: Kristel van den Berg 10:50.34, 100mh: Nadine Visser 13.04, 400mh: Bianca Baak 58.92, HJ: Sietska Noorman 1.81, PV: Femke Pluim 4.55, LJ: Nadine Broersen 6.24w, TJ: Nora Ritzen 13.09, SP: Melissa Boekelman 17.34, DT: Corinne Nugter 52.33, HT: Wendy Koolhaas 62.91, JT: Lisanne Schol 52.66, Hep: Maureen Rots 5452, 10kW: Anne van Andel 56:33.

Churandy MARTINA b. 3 Jul 1984 Willemstad, Curaçao 1.78m 75kg. Rotterdam Atletiek. Studied civil engineering at University of Texas at El Paso, USA.
At 100m/(200m): OG: '04- qf, '08- 4/dq, '12- 5/5; WCh: '03- h, '05- qf, '07- 5/5, '09- qf, '11/15- sf/sf, '13- sf/7; EC: '14- sf/4; WJ: '00- h/h, '02- qf; WY: '99- sf; EC: '12- (1)/1R; PAm: '03- sf, '07- 1; CAG: '06- 1/1R, '10- 1/1/3R; CCp: '10- (2)/1R. Won PAm-J 2003; NED 100m 2011-15; 200m 2011, 2014.
Records: AHO 100m (8) 2004-08, 200m (6) 2005-10, 400m 2007; NED 100m (2) 2011-12, 200m (2) 2012.
Progress at 100m, 200m: 2000- 10.73, 21.73; 2001- 10.64A, 21.55; 2002- 10.30, 20.81; 2003- 10.29/10.26w, 20.71; 2004- 10.13, 20.75; 2005- 10.13/9.93Aw, 20.32/20.31w; 2006- 10.04A/10.06/9.76Aw/9.99w, 20.27A; 2007- 10.06, 20.20; 2008- 9.93, 20.11; 2009- 9.97, 20.76; 2010- 10.03A/10.07/ 9.92w, 20.08; 2011- 10.10, 20.38; 2012- 9.91, 19.85; 2013- 10.03, 20.01; 2014- 10.13, 20.25; 2015- 10.06, 20.20. pbs: 60m 6.58i '10, 400m 46.13A '07.
At 2008 Olympics set three national records at 100m and one at 200m before crossing line in second place in final in 19.82 only to be disqualified for running out of his lane. Competed for Netherlands Antilles until 2010.

Eelco SINTNICOLAAS b. 7 Apr 1987 Dordrecht 1.86m 81kg. AV '34 (Apeldoorn). Economics student.
At Dec: OG: '12- 11; WCh: '09-11-13-15: dnf/5/5. dnf; EC: '10- 2, '14- 4; WJ: '06- 8; EU23: '09- 1; EJ: '05- 14; ECp: '14- 1. At Hep: WI: '14- 4; EI: '11-13-15: 4/1/3.
Dutch decathlon record 2012.
Progress at Dec: 2007- 7466, 2008- 7507w, 2009- 8112, 2010- 8436, 2011- 8304, 2012- 8506, 2013- 8391, 2014- 8478, 2015- 8298. pbs: 60m 6.88i '13, 100m 10.62 '15, 200m 21.62 '10, 400m 47.88 '10, 1000m 2:37.42i '06, 1500m 4:22.29 '11, 60mh 7.88i '13, 110mh 13.92/13.89w '13, 400mh 51.59 '10, HJ 2.08i/2.02 '13, PV 5.52i '11, 5.45 '10; LJ 7.65i, 7.76w '09, 7.65 '12; SP 14.67 '15, DT 43.38 '14, JT 63.59 '12, Hep 6372i '13.
Set six pbs in improving pb by 277 points for European silver 2010.

Women

Nadine BROERSEN b. 29 Apr 1990 Hoorn 1.71m 62kg. AV Sprint Breda.
At Hep: OG: '12- 12; WCh: '13- 10, '15- 4; EC: '14- 2; EU23: '11- 9; EJ: '09- 5; ECp: '14- 1. At Pen: WI: '14- 1. Won NED HJ 2010-11, 2014; LJ 2015; JT 2013.
Four Dutch high jump records 2013-14 and indoors 2014.
Progress at Hep: 2009- 5507, 2010- 5967, 2011- 5932(w)/5854, 2012- 6319, 2013- 6345, 2014- 6539, 2015- 6531. pbs: 200m 24.57 '14, 800m 2:11.11 '14, 60mh 8.32i '13, 100mh 13.39 '14, HJ 1.94 '14, LJ 6.39 '14, SP 14.93i '14, 14.82 '15; JT 54.97 '12, Pen 4830i '14.
Lost c.200 points in stumbling at last hurdle in first event of 2013 World heptathlon. Won IAAF Combined Events Challenge 2014.

Sifan HASSAN b. '1 Jan' 1993 Adama, Ethiopia 1.70m 49kg. Eindhoven Atletiek.
At 1500m/(5000m): WCh: '15- 3 (sf 800m); EC: '14- 1/2; CCp: '14- 1; WI: '15- 1; EI: 15- 1; won DL 2015. At 3000m: WI: '14- 5; ET: '14- 1. Eur CC: '13- 1 U23, '15- 1.
Records: European U23 1500m (3) 2014-15, Dutch 1500m (4), 1M, 3000m & 5000m 2014-15.
Progress at 800m, 1500m, 5000m: 2011- 4:20.13, 2012- 4:08.74, 2013- 2:00.86, 4:03.73. 2014- 1:59.95, 3:57.00, 14:59.23; 2015- 1:58.50, 3:56.05; 2016- 4:01.40i. pbs: 1000m 2:34.68 '15, 1M 4:18.20 '15, 2000m 5:46.1 '14, 3000m 8:29.38 '14, 10kRd 34:28 '12, HMar 77:10 '11.
Came to the Netherlands as a refugee at age 15. Dutch eligibility from 29 Nov 2013.

Maureen KOSTER b. 3 Jul 1992 Gouda 1.75m 56kg. Phanos.
At 1500m: WCh: '13/15- sf; EC: '14- h; WJ: '10- h. At 3000m: WI: '16- 4; EI: '15- 3. Eur CC: '14- 5 U23, '15- 9. Won NED 1500m 2012-13, 2015.
Progress at 1500m: 2007- 4:37.38, 2008- 4:28.11, 2009- 4:24.32, 2010- 4:19.28, 2011- 4:17.64, 2012- 4:13.48; 2013- 4:06.50, 2014- 4:04.92, 2015- 3:59.79. pbs: 800m 2:02.15 '14, 1000m 2:40.09 '14, 3000m 8:49.18i '16, 9:23.20 '11; 5000m 15:07.73 '15, 10kRd: 134:27 '14.

Dafne SCHIPPERS b. 15 Jun 1992 Utrecht 1.79m 68kg. Hellas.
At Hep: OG: '12- 11; WCh: '13- 3; WJ: '10- 1; EJ: '09- 4, '11- 1. At 100m/LJ: EU23: '13- 1/3. At (100m)/200m/4x100mR: WCh: '11- sf, '15- 2/1; EC: 12- 5/2R, '14- 1/1; WJ: '10- 3R; EU23: '13- (1) (3 LJ); CCp: '14- 3/1; ET: '14- 1. At 60m: WI: '16- 2; EI: '13- 4, 15- 1. Won NED 100m 2011-12, 2014-15; LJ 2012, 2014.
European 200m record 2015, Dutch records: 100m (5) 2014-15, 200m (5) 2011-15, LJ 2014, Hep 2013 & 2014.
Progress at 100m, 200m, Hep: 2007- 12.09/12.08w, 2008- 12.26/12.01w, 2009- 11.79, 24.21, 5507; 2010- 11.56, 23.70/23.41w, 5967; 2011- 11.19/

11.13w, 22.69, 6172; 2012- 11.36, 22.70, 6360; 2013- 11.09, 22.84, 6477; 2014- 11.03, 22.03, 6545; 2015- 10.81, 21.63. pbs: 60m 7.00i '16, 150m 16.93 '13, 800m 2:08.59 '14, 60mh 8.18i '12, 100mh 13.13 '14, HJ 1.80 '12, LJ 6.78 '14, SP 14.66 '15, JT 42.22 '15. Added 117 points to pb and reduced 800m best from 2:15.52 to 2:08.62 in taking 2013 World heptathlon bronze. First Dutch woman to win a medal in World Championships and emulated Fanny Blankers-Koen (1950) by winning EC sprint double 2014. European Athlete of the Year 2014-15.

Anouk VETTER b. 4 Feb 1993 Amsterdam 1.77m 62kg. Sprint.
At Hep: WCh: '15- 12; EC: '14- 7; WJ: '12- dnf; EJ: '11- dnf. At Pen: EI: '15- 8.
Progress at Hep: 2011- 5549, 2012- 5764, 2013- 5872, 2014- 6316, 2015- 6458. pbs: 60m 7.46i '16, 100m 11.63 '15, 200m 23.82 '15, 800m 2:20.38 '15, 60mh 8.33i '15, 100mh 13.48 '15, HJ 1.81 '13, LJ 6.34 '15, SP 15.50 '15, JT 53.10 '13, Pen 4548i '15.

Nadine VISSER b. 9 Feb 1995 Hoorn 1.75m 63kg. SAV.
At Hep (100mh): WCh: '15- 8; EC: '14 (h); WJ: '12- 11, 14- 3 (3); EU23: '15- (3, 11 LJ); EJ: '13- 4. Won NED 100mh 2015.
Progress at Hep: 2011- 5171, 2012- 5475, 2013- 5774, 2014- 6110, 2015- 6467. pbs: 100m 11.60 '14, 150m 17.69 '15, 200m 23.62 '15, 800m 2:13.08 '15, 60mh 8.08i '15, 100mh 12.81 '15, HJ 1.80 '14, LJ 6.48 '15, SP 13.20 '15, JT 44.01 '15, Pen 4268i '14.

NEW ZEALAND

Governing body: Athletics New Zealand, PO Box 305 504, Triton Plaza, Auckland.
National Championships first held in 1887 (men), 1926 (women). **2015 Champions: Men**: 100m: Kodi Harman 10.47, 200m: James Mortimer 21.47, 400m: Tama Toki 47.47, 800m: Brad Mathas 1:49.89, 1500m: Nick Willis 3:50.90, 3000m: Hamish Carson 7:56.19, 5000m: Jake Robertson 14:03.71, 10000m/Mar: Aaron Pulford 29:33.62/2:27:01, HMar: Callan Moody 65:13, 3000mSt: Daniel Balchin 9:07.56, 110mh: Joshua Hawkins 14.41w, 400mh: Cameron French 50.28, HJ: Hamish Kerr 2.13, PV: Nick Southgate 4.95, LJ: Jordan Peters 7.18, TJ: Phillip Wyatt 15.40, SP: Tom Walsh 20.73, DT: Marshall Hall 57.43, HT: Matt Bloxham 63.50, JT: Stuart Farquhar 78.17, Dec: Brent Newdick 7034, 3000mW: Mike Parker 14:43.95, 20kW: Graeme Jones 1:45:51. **Women**: 100m: Kelsey Berryman 11.88, 200m/100mh/LJ: Portia Bing 23.89/13.74w/6.23w, 400m: Louise Jones 55.28, 800m: Angie Petty 2:03.90, 1500m: Nikki Hamblin 4:12.02, 5000m: Camille Buscomb 16:20.02, 3000m/3000mSt: Rosa Flanagan 9:07.85/9:54.18, 10000m/HMar: Lydia O'Donnell 35:06.80/74:40, Mar: Kate Kemp 2:42:35, 400mh: MacKenzie Keenan 61.53, HJ: Keeley O'Hagen 1.84, PV: Eliza McCartney 3.70, TJ: Nneka Okpala 13.31, SP: Te Rina Keenan 15.03, DT: Siositina Hakeai 57.27, HT: Nicole Bradley 52.48, JT: Tori Peeters 53.25, Hep: Veronica Torr 5435, 3000mW: Courtney Ruske 13:45.72, 20kW: Courtney Ruske 1:45:27/Corrine Smith 1:56:09.

Jacko GILL b. 20 Dec 1994 Auckland 1.90m 118kg. Takapuna.
At SP: WCh: '15- 8; CG: '14- 11; WJ: '10- 1, '12- 1; WY: '11- 1, YthOG: '10- 2. Oceania champion 2014.
Five World youth shot records 5kg 23.86 '10, 24.35 and 24.45 '11; 6kg (4) 21.34 to 22.31, 7.26kg (3) in 2011. World junior 6kg record 23.00 '13. Three NZL records 2011.
Progress at SP: 2010- 18.57, 2011- 20.38, 2012- 20.05, 2014- 20.70, 2015- 20.75, 2016- 20.83.
First name actually Jackson. World age 15 and 16 bests for 5kg, 6kg and 7.26kg shot. His father Walter was NZ champion at SP 1987 & 1989, DT 1975, pbs 16.57 '86 & 53.78 (1975); his mother Nerida (née Morris) had discus best of 51.32 and was NZ champion in 1990. His sister Ayla was 6th in WJ hammer 2010.

Zane ROBERTSON b. 14 Nov 1989 Hamilton 1.80m 65kg. Hamilton City Hawks.
At 5000m: WCh: '13- 14; CG: 14- 3 (h 1500m); CCp: '14- 2.
Oceania 15k, 20k and half marathon records 2015.
Progress at 5000m: 2011- 13:58.37, 2013- 13:13.83, 2014- 13:14.69, 2015- 13:25.41. pbs: 1500m 3:34.19 '14, 1M 3:53.72 '14, 3000m 7:41.37 '14, 2M 8:22.82 '14, 10000m 27:46.82 '15, road: 15k 42:17 '15, 20k 56:40 '15, HMar 59:47 '15.
Twin brother **Jake** pbs 5000m 13:15.54 '13, 10000m 27:45.46 '13. CG '14: 7 10000m, 9 5000m.

Tomas WALSH b. 1 Mar 1992 Timaru 1.86m 123kg. South Canterbury.
At SP: CG: '14- 2; WJ: '10- dnq 16; WY: '09- 6 (dnq 31 DT), CCp: '14- 4; WI: '14- 3. NZ champion SP 2010-16, DT 2013.
Shot records: three Oceania 2015, four NZL 2013-15 and five Oceania indoor 2014-16.
Progress at SP: 2010- 17.57, 2011- 18.83, 2012- 19.33, 2013- 20.61, 2014- 21.26i/21.16, 2015- 21.62, 2016- 21.78i. pb DT 53.58 '14.
At World Indoors: set four NZ indoor records in 2014 and three Oceania records in 2016.

Nick WILLIS b. 25 Apr 1983 Lower Hutt 1.83m 68kg. Economics graduate of University of Michigan, USA.
At 1500m: OG: '04- sf, '08- 2, '12- 9; WCh: '05-07-11-13-15: sf/10/12/sf/6; CG: '06-1, '10- 3, '14-3 (10 5000m); WJ: '02- 4; WI: '08/14- dq, '16- 3; WCp: '06- 3, '14- 6 (4 3000m). Won NCAA indoor 2005, NZ 1500m 2006, 2015; 3000m 2013, 2016; 5000m 2011-12.
Records: NZ 1500m (6) 2005-15, 3000m 2014. Oceania 1500m (3) 2012-15 and indoors 1500m (3:35.80) 2010, 1M 2015 & 2016 (3:50.63).
Progress at 1500m: 2001- 3:43.54, 2002- 3:42.69,

2003- 3:36.58, 2004- 3:32.64, 2005- 3:32.38, 2006- 3:32.17, 2007- 3:35.85, 2008- 3:33.51, 2009- 3:38.85i, 2010- 3:35.17, 2011- 3:31.79, 2012- 3:30.35, 2013- 3:32.57, 2014- 3:29.91, 2015- 3:29.66. pbs: 800m 1:45.54 '04, 1000m 2:16.58 '12, 1M 3:49.83 '14, 3000m 7:36.91 '14, 5000m 13:20.33 '14, HMar 67:06 '14.

His brother Steve (b. 25 Apr 1975) had pbs: 1500m 3:40.29 '99, 1M 3:59.04 '00.

Women

Valerie ADAMS b. 6 Oct 1984 Rotorua 1.93m 123kg. Auckland City.

At SP: OG: '04- 7, '08- 1, '12- 1; WCh: '03-05-07-09-11-13: 5/2/1/1/1/1; CG: '02-06-10-14: 2/1/1/1; WJ: '02- 1; WY: '99- 10, '01- 1; WI: '04-08-10-12-14-16: dnq 10/1/2/1/1/3; WCp: '02- 6, '06- 1, '10- 1. Won WAF 2005, 2008-09, DL 2011-14, NZL SP 2001-11, 2013-14; DT 2004, HT 2003.

Nine Oceania & Commonwealth shot records 2005-11, 22 NZ 2002-11, 10 OCE indoor 2004-13.

Progress at SP: 1999- 14.83, 2000- 15.72, 2001- 17.08, 2002- 18.40, 2003- 18.93, 2004- 19.29, 2005- 19.87, 2006- 20.20, 2007- 20.54, 2008- 20.56, 2009- 21.07, 2010- 20.86, 2011- 21.24, 2012- 21.11, 2013- 20.98i/20.90, 2014- 20.67i/20.59, 2015- 18.73. pbs: DT 58.12 '04, HT 58.75 '02.

Nine senior global shot titles. IAAF Female Athlete of the Year 2014. Matched her age with metres at the shot from 14 to 18 and missed that at 19 by only two months. 28 successive shot wins from September 2007 to World Indoor silver in March 2010, and another 56 from August 2010 to July 2015. Her father came from England and her mother from Tonga. Married New Caledonia thrower Bertrand Vili (SP 17.81 '02, DT 63.66 '09, 4 ECp '07 for France) in November 2004 (divorced in 2010).

Eliza McCARTNEY b. 11 Dec 1996 Auckland 1.79m 65kg. North Harbour Bays.

At PV: WJ: '14- 3; WY: '13- 4; WUG: '15- 2; WI: '16- 5. NZ champion 2016.

Pole vault records: World junior 2015, Oceania & Commonwealth 2016, six NZ 2014-16.

Progress at PV: 2012- 3.85, 2013- 4.11, 2014- 4.45, 2015- 4.64, 2016- 4.80.

NIGERIA

Governing body: The Athletic Federation of Nigeria, P.O.Box 18793, Garki, Abuja. F'd 1944.

2015 National Champions: **Men**: 100m: Seye Ogunlewe 10.19, 200m: Odele Tega 20.47, 400m: Chide Okezie 46.15, 800m/1500m: Hamajan Soudi 1:50.04/3:50.73, 5000m/3000mSt: Ismail Sadjo 14:25.81/9:12.96, 10000m: Emmanuel Gwom Gyang 30:13.07, 110mh: Ty Akins 13.68, 400mh: Miles Ukaoma 48.84, HJ: Tadius Okpara 2.10, LJ: Samson Idiata 7.89, TJ: Tosin Oke 16.98, SP: Onwuka Kalu Eke 17.16, DT: Ifeanyi Augustina Nwoye 51.21, JT: Friday Osayande 68.33, 20kW: Kaseem Adeyemi 1:37:02. **Women**: 100m: Gloria Asumnu 11.42, 200m: Praise Idamadudu 23.48, 400m: Patience George 51.31, 800m/1500m: Abike Egbeniyi 2:07.50/4:33.31, 5000m/10000m: Deborah Pam 17:24.27/36:27.04, 100mh: Lindsay Lindley 13.40, 400mh: Amaka Ogoegbunam 55.78, HJ: Doreen Amata 1.85, LJ: Chinazor Amadi 6.24, TJ: Blessing Ibrahim 13.32, SP/DT: Claire Uke 16.56/50.91, HT: Becky Famurewa 58.96, JT: Kelechi Nwanga 47.32, Hep: Uhunoma Osazuwa 6106, 20kW: Faustina Oguh 1:45:18.

Tosin OKE b. 1 Oct 1980 London, UK 1.78m 77kg. Woodford Green, UK. Chemistry graduate of Manchester University.

At TJ: OG: '12- 7; WCh: '09/11- dnq 16/16, '15- 8; EC: '02- nj; CG: '02-10-14: 5/1/2; AfG: '11- 1, '15- 1; AfCh: '10-12-14: 1/1/2; EJ: '99- 1; CCp: '10- 6; '14- 4; ECp: '03- 4; WI: '16- 6. Won UK 2007, NGR 2009-10, 2012-13, 2015.

Progress at TJ: 1997- 14.07, 1998- 15.16/15.62w, 1999- 16.57, 2000- 16.04/16.37w, 2001- 16.08i/15.72, 2002- 16.65, 2003- 16.61i/16.59, 2004- 16.49/16.75w, 2005- 16.12/16.30w, 2006- 16.33/16.50w, 2007- 16.86, 2008- 16.47/16.63w, 2009- 16.87, 2010- 17.22A/17.16, 2011- 17.21, 2012- 17.23, 2013- 16.87i/16.64, 2014- 16.97/17.21w, 2015- 17.00. pb LJ 7.31 '05.

Switched allegiance from Britain to Nigeria (grandfather) from 10 Feb 2009.

Women

Blessing OKAGBARE b. 9 Oct 1988 Sapele 1.80m 68kg. Married name Ighoteguonor. Was at University of Texas at El Paso, USA.

At LJ/(100m): OG: '08- 3, '12- dnq 17/8; WCh: '11- dnq 18/5, '13- 2/6 (3 200m), '15- (8); CG: 1 100m & 200m/2R; AfG: '07- 2 (4 TJ), '11- 1/2; AfCh: '10- 1/1/1R, '12- 1/2, '14- (1)/1R; WJ: '06- 16 (dnq 17 TJ); CCp: '10- 6/3/3R; Won Nigerian 100m 2009-14, 200m 2013-14, LJ 2008-09, 2011-13; TJ 2008; NCAA 100m & LJ 2010.

Two African 100m records 2013, 4x200m 2015, Nigerian & African junior TJ record 2007.

Progress at 100m, 200m, LJ: 2004- 5.85 irreg, 2006- 6.16, 2007- 6.51, 2008- 23.76A, 6.91; 2009- 11.16, 6.73/6.90w; 2010- 11.00/10.98w/10.7Aw, 22.71, 6.88; 2011- 11.08/11.01w, 22.94, 6.78/6.84w; 2012- 10.92, 22.63, 6.97; 2013- 10.79/10.75w, 22.31, 7.00/7.14w; 2014- 10.85, 22.23, 6.86; 2015- 10.80, 22.67, 6.66. pbs: 60m 7.18i '10, 300m 37.04 '13, 400m 53.34 '15, TJ 14.13 '07.

Majestic winner of Commonwealth Games sprint double in 2014. Married football international Jude Igho Otegheri on 7 Nov 2014.

NORWAY

Governing body: Norges Friidrettsforbund, Serviceboks 1, Ullevaal Stadium, 0840 Oslo. Founded 1896.

National Championships first held in 1896 (men), 1947 (women, walks 1937). **2015**

Champions: **Men**: 100m: Jaysuma Saidy Ndure 10.82, 200m: Jonathan Quarcoo 21.08, 400m/400mh: Karsten Warholm 47.39/51.09, 800m: Andreas Roth 1:56.04, 1500m: Snorre Holtan Løken 3:49.98, 5000m: Henrik Ingebrigtsen 14:22.17. 10000m/HMar: Sondre Nordstad Moen 30:25.78/64:55, Mar: Ebrahim Abdulaziz ERI 2:25:49, 3000mSt: Bjørnar Kristensen 9:03.18, 110mh: Vladimir Vukicevic 13.85, HJ: Ivan Kristoffer Nilsen 2.08, PV: Eirik Greibokkk Dolve 4.60, LJ: Jonas Mögenburg 7.59w, TJ: Sindre Almsengen 15.36, SP/DT: Sven Martin Skagestad 17.57/58.68, HT: Eivind Henriksen 70.65, JT: Håkon Kveseth 71.80, Dec: Martin Roe 7585, 5000mW/10kW/20kW: Erik Tysse 19:19.07/40:23/1:21:24. **Women**: 100m: Ezinne Okparaebo 11.71, 200m: Elisabeth Slettum 23.88, 400m: Tara Marie Norum 53.38, 800m: Ida Fillingsnes 2:10.67, 1500m: Karoline Bjerkeli Grøvdal 4:16.48, 5000m/10000m: Silje Fjørtoft 16:44.39/34:33.10, HMar: Heidi Pharo 76:43, Mar: Marthe Katrine Myhre 2:49:04, 3000mSt: Karoline E. Skatteboe 10:45.95, 100mh: Isabelle Pedersen 12.88, 400mh: Marlen Aakre 60.6, HJ: Katarina Mögenburg 1.75, PV: Lene Retzius 4.00, LJ: Nadia Akpana Assa 6.31w, TJ: Chiamaka Okparaebo 13.02, SP: Kristin Sundsteigen 13.39, DT: Grete Etholm 50.34, HT: Beatrice Nedberge Llano 67.05, JT: Marie-Therese Obst 53.85, Hep: Anne Engen Andersen 5090, W 3000mW/10kW: Merete Heigheim 13:45.31/49:03; 5kW: Vilde Lundin 26:51.

Henrik INGEBRIGTSEN b. 24 Feb 1991 Stavanger 1.80m 69kg. Sandnes IL
At 1500m: OG: '12- 5; WCh: '13- 8, '15- h; EC: '10-12-14: h/1/2; WJ: '10- h; EU23: '11- h; EJ: '09- h; CCp: '14- 4; EI: '15- 6 (3 3000m). At 5000m: EU23: '13- 1. Won NOR 800m 2013, 1500m 2010, 2012, 2014; 5000m 2015. Eur U23 CC: '12- 1.
Norwegian records: 1500m (4) 2012-14, 1M (3) 2012-14.
Progress at 1500m: 2004- 4:30.63, 2005- 4:22.48, 2006- 4:04.15, 2007- 3:54.08, 2008- 3:50.63, 2009- 3:44.53, 2010- 3:38.61, 2011- 3:39.50, 2012- 3:35.43, 2013- 3:33.95, 2014- 3:31.46, 2015- 3:32.85. pbs: 800m 1:48.09 '14, 1M 3:50.72 '14, 3000m 7:42.19 '13, 5000m 13:27.10 '15, 2000mSt 5:41.03 '09, 3000mSt 8:52.56 '09.
Younger brothers: Filip (b. 20 Apr 1993) 1500m pb 3:38.76 '13 (10 WJ '12, 6 EU23 '13); Jakub (b. 19 Sep 00) European age 14 1500m bests to 3:48.37 '15.

Andreas THORKILDSEN b. 1 Apr 1982 Kristiansand 1.88m 90kg. Kristiansands IF.
At JT: OG: '04- 1, '08- 1, '12- 6; WCh: '01-03-05-07-09-11-13: dnq 26/11/2/2/1/2/6; EC: '02-06-10-12: dnq 15/1/1/4; WJ: '00- 2; EU23: '03- 4; EJ: '99- 7, '01- 2; EY: '97- 1; WCp: '06- 1; CCp: '10- 1; ET: '10- 2. Won DL 2010, WAF 2006, 2009; NOR 2001-06, 2009-11, 2013.
World junior javelin record 2001, seven Norwegian records 2005-06.
Progress at JT: 1996- 53.82, 1998- 61.57, 1999- 72.11, 2000- 77.48, 2001- 83.87, 2002- 83.43, 2003- 85.72, 2004- 86.50, 2005- 89.60, 2006- 91.59, 2007- 89.51, 2008- 90.57, 2009- 91.28, 2010- 90.37, 2011- 90.61, 2012- 84.72, 2013- 84.64, 2014- 80.79. pbs: SP 9.96 '01, DT 38.02 '01.
His mother Bente Amundsen was a Norwegian champion at 100mh (pb 14.6), father Tomm was a junior international with bests of 100m 10.9 and javelin 71.64.

PANAMA

Governing body: Federación Panameña de Atletismo, Apartado 0860-00684, Villa Lucre, Ciudad de Panamá. Founded 1945.

Alonso EDWARD b. 8 Dec 1989 Ciudad de Panamá 1.83m 73kg. Was at Barton County CC.
At (100m)/200m: OG: '12- h; WCh: '09-11-13-15: 2/dnf/sf/4; WJ: '08-; PAm: '15- 3; SAG: '14- (1); SACh: '09- 1/1, SAm-J: '07- (1), SAm-Y: '06- 1/1; CCp: '14- 1. Won DL 2014-15, C. American 2012, C.AmG 100m 2010, 200m 2013; SAmG 100m 2014.
Records: S.American 200m 2009, Panama 100m (2) 2009-14, 200m (5) 2007-09; South American Junior 100m 2007.
Progress at 100m, 200m: 2006- 10.60, 21.18; 2007- 10.28/10.25w, 20.62; 2008- 10.63, 20.96; 2009- 10.09/9.97w, 19.81; 2010- 10.24/10.08w, 2011- 20.28, 2012- 21.23A, 2013- 10.13, 20.37/20.32w; 2014- 10.02, 19.84; 2015- 10.29, 19.87. pb 400m 47.40i '10.
World age-19 best 19.81 in World final 2009. Injured in April 2010; did not compete for the rest of the season, and then suffered a 10cm career-threatening hamstring tear in the 2011 World 200m final. Younger brother Mateo (b. 1 May 1993): 60m 6.73i PAN record, 100m 10.29, and 200m 21.48 in 2014.

POLAND

Governing body: Polski Zwiazek Lekkiej Atletyki (PZLA), ul. Myslowicka 4, 01-612 Warszawa. Founded 1919.

National Championships first held in 1920 (men), 1922 (women). **2015 Champions**: **Men**: 100m: Przemyslaw Slowikowski 10.39, 200m: Karol Zalewski 20.47, 400m: Lukasz Krawczuk 46.21, 800m: Adam Kszczot 1:46.70, 1500m: Grzegorz Kalinowski 3:45.51, 5000m: Krzysztof Zebrowski 14:21.97, 10000m: Marek Skorupa 29:36.08, HMar: Artur Kozlowski 64:36, Mar: Henryk Szost 2:10:11, 3000mSt: Krystian Zalewski 8:35.48, 110mh: Artur Noga 13.39, 400mh: Patryk Dobek 50.80, HJ: Sylwester Bednarek 2.25, PV: Pawel Wojciechowski 5.70, LJ: Tomasz Jaszczuk 7.87, TJ: Adrian Swiderski 16.63, SP: Tomasz Majewski 20.80, DT: Piotr Malachowski 65.60, HT: Pawel Fajdek 79.74, JT: Marcin Krukowski 80.76, Dec: Pawel Wiesiolek

7657, 20kW: Grzegorz Sudol 1:25:41, 50kW: Rafal Augustyn 3:43:55. **Women**: 100m: Marika Popowicz 11.44, 200m: Anna Kielbasinska 22.94, 400m: Patrycja Wyciszkiewicz 51.95, 800m: Joanna Józwik 2:02.99, 1500m: Sofia Ennaoui 4:12.12, 5000m: Renata Plis 15:36.18, 10000m: Paulina Kaczynska 33:26.59, HMar/ 3000mSt: Katarzyna Kowalska 72:39/9:55.39, Mar: Monika Stefanowicz 2:29:28, 100mh: Karolina Koleczek 12.92, 400mh: Joanna Linkiewicz 56.38, HJ: Kamila Licwinko 1.98, PV: Justyna Smietanka 4.20, LJ: Teresa Dobija 6.43, TJ: Malgorzata Trybanska-Stronska 13.46, SP: Paulina Guba 17.63, DT: Zaneta Glanc 59.30, HT: Anna Wlodarczyk 78.24, JT: Marcelina Witek 56.80, Hep: Izabela Mikolajczyk 5823, 20kW: Monika Kapera 1:35:26.

Konrad BUKOWIECKI b. 17 Mar 1997 Olsztyn 1.91m 129kg. PKS Gwardia Szczytno.
At SP: WCh: '15- dnq; WJ: '14- 1; WY: '13- 5; EJ: '15- 1 (dnq 13 DT); Yth OG: '14- 1; WI: '16- 4; EI: '15- 6.
Shot records: Two world junior 7.26kg 2015, indoor 6kg 22.38i '15 & 22.48i '16, World youth 5kg 2 out to 22.24 & 5 indoor to 24.24 in 2014; European junior (5) 2015, indoor (3) 2016.
Progress at SP: 2014- 17.29i, 2015- 20.78, 2016- 20.61i.

Patryk DOBEK b. 13 Feb 1994 Koscierzyna 1.83m 75kg. SKLA Sopot.
At 400mh: WCh: '15- 7; EC: '14- sf; EU23: '15- 1/2R; Polish champion 2014-15. At 400m: WJ: '12- sf/2R; WY: '11- 3; EJ: '13- 2/2R.
Progress at 400mh: 2012- 52.00, 2013- 50.67, 2014- 49.13, 2015- 48.40. pbs: 200m 21.38 '15, 300m 33.34 '13, 400m 46.15 '13, 600m 1:15.78 '14.

Pawel FAJDEK b. 4 Jun 1989 Swiebodzice 1.86m 118kg. KS Agros Zamosc.
At HT: OG: '12- dnq; WCh: '11- 11, '13- 1, '15- 1; EC: 14- 2; WJ: '08- 4; EU23: '09- 8, '11- 1; WUG: '11-13-15: 1/1/1; CCp: '14- 3; ET: '11-13-14-15: 2/1/2/1. Won POL 2012, 2014-15; Franc G 2013, World HT challenge 2013, 2015.
Two Polish hammer records 2014-15.
Progress at HT: 2008- 64.58, 2009- 72.36, 2010- 76.07, 2011- 78.54, 2012- 81.39, 2013- 82.27, 2014- 83.48, 2015- 83.93. pb Wt 23.22i '14.
Won 16 of 17 competitions in 2015 and had the top 12 performances of the year at hammer.

Adam KSZCZOT b. 2 Sep 1989 Opoczno 1.78m 64kg. RKS Lódz. Studied organisation and management.
At 800m: OG: '12- sf; WCh: '09/13- sf, '11- 6, '15- 2; EC: '10- 3, '14- 1; WJ: '08- 4; EU23: '09/11- 1; EJ: '07- 3; WI: '10-12-14: 3/4/2; EI: '09-11-13: 4/1/1; CCp: '14- 3; ET: '11-13-14-15: 1/1/2/3. Polish champion 2009-10, 2012, 2014-15.
Polish 1000m record 2011 and 2014.
Progress at 800m: 2005- 1:59.57, 2006- 1:51.09, 2007- 1:48.10, 2008- 1:47.16, 2009- 1:45.72, 2010- 1:45.07, 2011- 1:43.30, 2012- 1:43.83, 2013- 1:44.76, 2014- 1:44.02, 2015- 1:43.45. pbs: 400m 46.51 '11, 600m 1:14.55 '10, 1000m 2:15.72 '14, 1500m 3:46.53 '10.

Marcin LEWANDOWSKI b. 13 Jun 1987 Szczecin 1.80m 64kg. SL WKS Zawisza Bydgoszcz. PE student.
At 800m: OG: '08/12- sf; WCh: '09-11-13-15: 8/4/4/sf; EC: '10- 1, '14- 5; WJ: '06- 4; EU23: '07- 1, '09- 2; WI: '14- dq; EI: '09-11-15: 6/2/1; CCp: '10- 2; ECp: '08- 2, '10- 3; won W.MilG 2011. At 1500m: EJ: '05- 7; EI: '13- 4; ET: '13-14-15: 3/3/2. Won Polish 800m 2011, 1500m 2008, 2010, 2014.
Polish 1000m record 2011.
Progress at 800m: 2002- 1:57.86, 2003- 1:53.31, 2004- 1:51.73, 2005- 1:48.86, 2006- 1:46.69, 2007- 1:45.52, 2008- 1:45.84, 2009- 1:43.84, 2010- 1:44.10, 2011- 1:44.53, 2012- 1:44.34, 2013- 1:43.79, 2014- 1:44.03, 2015- 1:43.72. pbs: 400m 47.76 '09, 600m 1:15.17 '14, 1000m 2:15.76 '11, 1500m 3:37.37i, 3:38.19 '14.
Coached by brother Tomasz (1:51.00 '03).

Piotr LISEK b. 16 Aug 1992 Duszniki, Poznan 1.88m 85kg. OSOT Szczecin.
At PV: WCh: '15- 3=; EC: '14- 6; EU23: '13- dnq 17; ET: '15- 3; WI: 16- 3; EI: '15- 3.
Polish indoor pole vault record 2015.
Progress at PV: 2006- 3.20, 2007- 3.30, 2008- 4.10, 2009- 4.42, 2010- 4.70, 2011- 5.10i/5.00, 2012- 5.20, 2013- 5.60, 2014- 5.82, 2015- 5.87i/5.82, 2016- 5.77i.
6-months drugs ban in 2012.

Tomasz MAJEWSKI b. 30 Aug 1981 Nasielsk 2.04m 140kg. AZS-AWF Warszawa. Graduated in political science from Cardinal Wyszynski University.
At SP: OG: '04- dnq 17, '08- 1, '12- 1; WCh: '05-07-09-11-13-15: 7/4/2/8/6/6; EC: '06-10-14: 6/1/3; EU23: '03- 4; WI: '04-06-08-10-12-14: 4/6/3/4/3/4; EI: '09- 1; WUG: '03- 5, '05- 1; CCp: '10- 2, '14- 5; ECp: '07-08-09-10-11-13-14-15: 3/2/1/1/2/2/2/2. Won WAF 2008, Polish 2002-05, 2007-15; Franc G 2013.
Polish shot record 2009.
Progress at SP: 1998- 12.91, 1999- 15.77, 2000- 17.77, 2001- 18.34, 2002- 19.33, 2003- 20.09, 2004- 20.83i/20.52, 2005- 20.64, 2006- 20.66, 2007- 20.87, 2008- 21.51, 2009- 21.95, 2010- 21.44, 2011- 21.60, 2012- 21.89, 2013- 20.98, 2014- 21.04, 2015- 20.82. pb DT 51.79 '07.
Improved pb every year of his career to 2009. Went from 20.97 to 21.04 in qualifying and 21.21 and 21.51 in final to win Olympic gold in 2008.

Piotr MALACHOWSKI b. 7 Jun 1983 Zuromin 1.94m 135kg. WKS Slask Wroclaw. Army corporal.
At DT: OG: '08- 2, '12- 5; WCh: '07-09-11-13-15: 12/2/9/2/1; EC: '06-10-14: 6/1/4; WJ: '02- 6; EU23: '03- 9, '05- 2; EJ: '01- 5; CCp: '10- 4; ECp: '06-07-08-09-10-11-14: 1/1/3/1/2/3/2. Won DL 2010, 2014-15; POL 2005-10, 2012-15.

Nine Polish discus records 2006-13.
Progress at DT: 1999- 39.48, 2000- 52.04, 2001- 54.19, 2002- 56.84, 2003- 57.83, 2004- 62.04, 2005- 64.74, 2006- 66.21, 2007- 66.61, 2008- 68.65, 2009- 69.15, 2010- 69.83, 2011- 68.49, 2012- 68.94, 2013- 71.84, 2014- 69.28, 2015- 68.29.

Lukasz NOWAK b. 18 Dec 1988 Poznan 1.94m 77kg. AZS Poznan.
At 50kW: OG: '12- 6; WCh: '13- 8, '15- dq; EC: '10- 8, 14- dnf. At 20kW: EU23: '09- 13. Won POL 20kW 2014, 50kW 2012.
Progress at 50kW: 2009- 3:58:57, 2010- 3:50:30, 2011- 3:46:40, 2012- 3:42:47, 2013- 3:43:38, 2015- 3:44:53. pbs: 3000mW 11:41.30 '11; 5000mW 19:13.08i '14, 19:24.57 '11; 10kW 40:30 '13; 20kW 1:20:48 '13; 30kW 2:13:07 '13; 35kW 2:35:17 '13.

Wojciech NOWICKI b. 22 Feb 1989 Bialystok 1.96m 112kg. KS Podlasie Bialystok.
At HT: WCh: '15- 3; EU23: '11- 5.
Progress at HT: 2008- 55.71, 2009- 64.41, 2010- 69.59, 2011- 72.72, 2012- 73.52, 2013- 75.87, 2014- 76.14, 2015- 78.71. pb Wt 22.72i '14.

Robert SOBERA b. 19 Jan 1991 Wroclaw 1.90m 77kg. KS AZS AWF Wroclaw.
At PV: WCh: '13- dnq, '15- 15; EC: '14- nh; WJ: '10- 4; EU23: '11- 11, '13- 2; EJ: '09- nh; WUG: '15- 3; WI: '14- 6, '16- 6; EI: '13- 6=, '15- 4. Polish champion 2014.
Progress at PV: 2005- 2.80, 2006- 4.12, 2007- 4.60, 2008- 5.00, 2009- 5.30, 2010- 5.30, 2011- 5.40, 2012- 5.42, 2013- 5.71i/5.61, 2014- 5.75i/5.70/5.80exh, 2015- 5.81i/5.70, 2016- 5.77i.

Robert URBANEK b. 29 Apr 1987 Leczyca 2.00m 120kg. MKS Aleksandrów Lódzki.
At DT: OG: '12- dnq 32; WCh: '13- 6, '15- 3; EC: '12- 6, '14- 3; EU23: '09- 7; CCp: '14- 6; ET: '15- 1.
Progress at PV: 2004- 47.09, 2005- 47.83, 2006- 50.84, 2007- 56.18, 2008- 62.22, 2009- 60.54, 2010- 60.74, 2011- 64.37, 2012- 66.93, 2013- 65.30, 2014- 65.75, 2015- 66.31. pb SP 16.21 '07.

Pawel WOJCIECHOWSKI b. 6 Jun 1989 Bydgoszcz 1.90m 81kg. SL WKS Zawisza Bydgoszcz. PE student.
At PV: OG: '12- dnq; WCh: '11- 1, '15- 3=; EC: '14- 2; WJ: '08- 2; EU23: '11- 1; EJ: '07- dnq 16; EI: '11- 4; CCp: '14- 5. Won W.MilG 2011, POL 2015.
Polish pole vault record 2011.
Progress at PV: 2001- 2.50, 2002- 2.70, 2003- 3.10, 2004- 3.50, 2005- 4.10, 2006- 4.70, 2007- 5.00, 2008- 5.51, 2009- 5.40i/5.22, 2010- 5.60, 2011- 5.91, 2012- 5.62, 2014- 5.80, 2015- 5.84, 2016- 5.84i.

Women

Joanna FIODOROW b. 4 Mar 1989 Augustów 1.69m 89kg. OS AZS Poznan.
At HT: OG: '12- 9; WCh: '11-15: dnq 21/17; EC: '14- 3; WJ: '08- dnq 19; EU23: '09- 4, '11- 2; ET: '14- 2; WUG: '15- 2.
Progress at HT: 2005- 40.96, 2006- 50.18, 2007- 55.93, 2008- 61.22, 2009- 62.80, 2010- 64.66, 2011- 70.06, 2012- 74.18, 2013- 68.92, 2014- 74.39, 2015- 72.67. pbs: SP 12.87 '10, JT 35.56 '09.

Joanna JÓZWIK b. 30 Jan 1991 Walbrzych 1.68m 53kg. AZS-AWF Warszawa.
At HJ: WCh: '15- 7; EC: '14- 3; WJ: '10- sf; EU23: '11- h, '13- 8; ET: '15- 2; EI: '15- 4. Polish champion 2014-15.
Progress at 800m: 2007- 2:12.90, 2008- 2:11.55, 2009- 2:07.31, 2010- 2:05.09, 2011- 2:03.15, 2012- 2:05.87, 2013- 2:02.39, 2014- 1:59.63, 2015- 1:58.35. pbs: 200m 24.16 '14, 300m 39.83 '11, 400m 53.08 '14, 600m 1:25.04 '15, 1000m 2:35.57 '15.

Justyna KASPRZYCKA b. 20 Aug 1987 Glubczyce 1.83m 62kg. AZS-AWF Wroclaw
At HJ: WCh: '13- 6; EC: '14- 4; EU23: '07- 9=, '09- 9; WI: '12- 4; EI: '15- 6; Polish champion 2013-14.
Polish high jump record 2014
Progress at HJ: 2001- 1.58, 2002- 1.67, 2003- 1.77, 2004- 1.76i/1.72, 2005- 1.74, 2006- 1.78, 2007- 1.86, 2008- 1.79i/1.74, 2009- 1.87, 2010- 1.88, 2011- 1.84i, 2012- 1.84, 2013- 1.97, 2014- 1.99, 2015- 1.94.

Kamila LICWINKO b. 22 Mar 1986 Bielsk Podlaski 1.83m 66kg. née Stepaniuk. KS Podlasie Bialystok.
At HJ: WCh: '09- dnq 16, '13- 7=, '15- 4; EC: '14- 9=; EU23: '07- 4; EJ: '05- 7; WI: '14- 1=,'16- 3; EI: '09- 8, '15- 3; ET: '13-14-15: 2/2=/3; WUG: '13- 1. Won POL 2007-09, 2015.
Polish high jump records 2013 & 2014, three indoor 2015.
Progress at HJ: 1999- 1.46, 2000- 1.61, 2001- 1.66, 2002- 1.75, 2003- 1.75, 2004- 1.84, 2005- 1.86, 2006- 1.85i/1.84, 2007- 1.90, 2008- 1.91, 2009- 1.93, 2010- 1.92i/1.89, 2011- 1.88i, 2012- 1.89, 2013- 1.99, 2014- 2.00i/1.97, 2015- 2.02i/1.99.
Married her trainer Michal Licwinko in 2013.

Karolina TYMINSKA b. 4 Oct 1984 Swiebodzin 1.75m 69kg. SKLA Sopot.
At Hep: OG: '08- 7, '12- dnf; WCh: '07-09-11-13-15: 15/dnf/4/9/20; EC: '06- dnf (dnq LJ), '10- 4, '14- 11; EU23: '05- dnf (LJ dnq 17); ECp: '06-09-13: 2/3/1. At Pen: WI: '08-10-12-14: 6/5/4/8; EI: '05-07-09-11: 8/7/5/4. Won POL 100mh 2011, Hep 2006-07, 2011.
Progress at Hep: 2002- 5147, 2004- 5787, 2005- 6026, 2006- 6402, 2007- 6200, 2008- 6428, 2009- 6191, 2010- 6230, 2011- 6544, 2012- dnf, 2013- 6360, 2014- 6266, 2015- 6174. pbs: 60m 7.55i '14, 100m 11.88 '14, 200m 23.32 '06, 400m 55.11 '14, 800m 2:05.21 '11, 60mh 8.34i '10, 100mh 13.12 '11, HJ 1.78 '11, LJ 6.63 '08, SP 15.11i/14.82 '08, JT 42.40 '13, Pen 4769i '08.

Anita WLODARCZYK b. 8 Aug 1985 Rawicz 1.78m 95kg. RKS Skra Warszawa. PE student.
At HT: OG: '08- 6, '12- 2; WCh: '09-11-13-15: 1/5/2/1; EC: '10- 3, '12- 1, '14- 1; EU23: '07- 9; CCp: '14- 1; ET: '09- 1, '13- 2. Won POL 2009, 2011-12, 2014-15; Franc G 2013, IAAF HT challenge 2013-15.
Four world hammer records 2009-15, six Polish records 2009-14.

Progress at HT: 2002- 33.83, 2003- 43.24, 2004- 54.74, 2005- 60.51, 2006- 65.53, 2007- 69.07, 2008- 72.80, 2009- 77.96, 2010- 78.30, 2011- 75.33, 2012- 77.60, 2013- 78.46, 2014- 79.58, 2015- 81.08. pbs: SP 13.25 '06, DT 52.26 '08, Wt 20.09i '14.

Won all 11 hammer competitions in 2015 and had the eight best throws of the year, including when she became first woman to throw hammer over 80m with 81.08 at Cetniewo on 1 Aug 2015, and two 80m throws (80.27 and 80.85) later that month at the World Champs.

PORTUGAL

Governing body: Federação Portuguesa de Atletismo, Largo da Lagoa, 1799-538 Linda-a-Velha. Founded in 1921.

National Championships first held in 1910 (men), 1937 (women). **2015 Champions**: **Men**: 100m: Yazaldes Nascimento 10.32, 200m/400m: Ricardo dos Santos 21.04/47.05, 800m: Sandy Martins 1:51.58, 1500m: Paulo Rosário 3:56.25, 5000m: Rui Pinto 14:17.80, 10000m: Samuel Barata 29:26.96, Mar: Carlos Freitas 2:35:56, 3000mSt: Miguel Borges 9:06.06, 110mh: Rasul Dabó 14.26, 400mh: Diogo Mestre 52.11, HJ: Paulo Conceição 2.16, PV: Ruben Miranda 5.35, LJ: Marcos Chuva 7.37, TJ: Nelson Évora 16.39, SP: Tsanko Arnaudov 19.79, DT: Jorge A. Grave 58.22, HT: Dário Manso 69.09, JT: Tiago Aperta 66.65, Dec: Samuel Remédios 6924, 10,000mW: João Vieira 41:20.75, 20kW: Sergio Vieira 1:23:24, 50kW: Pedro Martins 4:34:03. **Women**: 100m: Olimpia Barbosa 11.99, 200m: Rivinilda Mentai 23.89, 400m: Cátia Azevedo 53.80, 800m: Salomé Afonso 2:07.62, 1500m: Joana Costa 4:32.59, 5000m: Sara Moreira 16:01.07, 10000m: Sara Moreira 31:12.93, Mar: Rosa Madureira 2:51:59, 3000mSt: Joana Soares 10:21.47, 100mh: Eva Vital 13.82, 400mh: Andreia Crespo 58.96, HJ: Anabela Neto 1.80, PV: Marta Onofre 4.25, LJ: Shaina Anthony Mags 6.10, TJ: Patricia Mamona 13.68, SP: Ophélie Oliveira 12.89, DT: Irina Rodrigues 56.30, HT: Vânia Silva 61.53, JT: Sílvia Cruz 45.49, Hep: Lecabela Quaresma 5321, 10000mW/20kW: Ana Cabecinha 43:19.12/ 1:29:27.

Nelson ÉVORA b. 20 Apr 1984 Abidjan, Côte d'Ivoire 1.81m 64kg. Sport Lisboa e Benfica.

At (LJ/)TJ: OG: '04- dnq 40, '08- 1; WCh: '05-07-09-11-15: dnq 14/1/2/5/3; EC: '06- 6/4, '14- 6; WJ: '02- dnq 18/6; EU23: '05- 3; EJ: '03- 1/1; WUG: '09- 1, '11- 1; WI: '06-08-16: 6/3/4; EI: '07- 5, '15- 1; ECp: '09- 2/1; Won WAF TJ 2008, POR LJ 2006-07, TJ 2003-04, 2006-07, 2009-11, 2013-15.

Six Portuguese triple jump records 2006-07, Cape Verde LJ & TJ records 2001-02.

Progress at TJ: 1999- 14.35, 2000- 14.93i, 2001- 16.15, 2002- 15.87, 2003- 16.43, 2004- 16.85i/16.04, 2005- 16.89, 2006- 17.23, 2007- 17.74, 2008- 17.67, 2009- 17.66/17.82w, 2010- 16.36, 2011- 17.35, 2013- 16.68, 2014- 16.97, 2015- 17.52. pbs: HJ 2.07i '05, 1.98 '99; LJ 8.10 '07.

Portugal's first male world champion in 2007. He suffered a serious injury in right tibia (in same place where he had an operation in February 2010) in January 2012 and missed season. Father from Cape Verde, mother from Côte d'Ivoire, relocating to Portugal when he was five. Switched nationality in 2002. Sister Dorothé (b. 28 May 1991) 400m pb 55.11 '13.

Women

Jéssica AUGUSTO b. 8 Nov 1981 Paris, France 1.65m 46kg. Sporting CP.

At Mar: OG: '12- 6; EC: '14- 3. At 3000mSt: OG: '08- h (h 5000); WCh: '09- 10. At 5000m/ (10000m): WCh: '05- h, '07- 15, '11- (10); EC: '10- 3/2; EU23: '03- dnf; WUG: '07- 1; CCp: '10- 7; ECp: '14- (2). At 3000m (1500m): WJ: '00- 8; EU23: '01- (10); EJ: '99- 6 (12); WI: '08- 8, '10- 7; EI: '09- 10. World CC: '07- 12, '10- 21; Eur CC: '98-99-00-02-04-05-06-07-08-09-10: 12J/8J/1J/16/18/ 30/9/11/2/4/1. Won POR 1500m 2007, 2011; 5000m 2006, 10000m 2014; IbAm 3000m 2004, 2006, 2010.

Two Portuguese 3000m steeplechase records 2008-10, European indoor 2M best 2010.

Progress at 5000m, 10000m, Mar, 3000mSt: 2003- 15:51.63, 2004- 15:15.76, 2005- 15:20.45, 2006- 15:37.55, 2007- 14:56.39, 2008- 15:19.67, 9:22.50; 2009- 9:25.25, 2010- 14:37.07, 31:19.15, 9:18.54; 2011- 15:19.60, 32:06.68, 2:24:33; 2012- 2:24:59, 2013- 15:38.73, 2:29:11; 2014- 31:55.56, 2:24:25. pbs: 800m 2:07.97i '02, 1500m 4:07.89i/ 4:08.32 '10, 1M 4:32.58i '09, 4:42.15 '99, 2000m 5:45.6i '09, 3000m 8:41.53 '07, 2M 9:19.39i '10, 9:22.89 '07; road 15k 48:40 '08, 10M 53:15 '08, HMar 69:08 '09, 30k 1:41:37 '11.

Won Great North Run 2009. Daughter Leonor born 15 Jun 2015 (father is football goalkeeper Eduardo Carvalho).

Ana CABECINHA b. 29 Apr 1984 Beja 1.68m 52kg. CO Pechão.

At 20kW: OG: '08- 8, '12- 8; WCh: '11-13-15: 6/8/4; EC: '10- 7, '14- 6; EU23: '05- 4; WCp '08-10-12-14: 11/8/8/8; ECp: '13- 5, '15- 9. At 5000mW: WY: '01- 10. At 10000mW: WJ: '02- 12; EJ: '03- 3; won IbAm 2006, 2010; 2nd RWC 2012; POR 10000mW 2005, 2008, 2010, 2012, 2014-15; 20kW 2012-15.

POR records 10,000m and 20km walk 2008.

Progress at 20kW: 2004- 1:37:39, 2005- 1:34:13, 2006- 1:31:02, 2007- 1:32:46, 2008- 1:27:46, 2009- 1:33:05, 2010- 1:31:14, 2011- 1:31:08, 2012- 1:28:03, 2013- 1:29:17, 2014- 1:27:49, 2015- 1:28:28, 2016- 1:29:11. pbs: 3000mW 12:17.50 '14, 5000mW 21:22.23 '15, 21:21R '12; 10000mW 43:08.17 '08; running 1500m 4:31.73 '07, 3000m 9:46.08 '13, 5000m 17:57.34 '12.

Patrícia MAMONA b. 21 Nov 1988 Lisbon 1.68m 53kg. Sporting CP. Was at Clemson University, USA.

At TJ: OG: '12- dnq 13; WCh: '11-15: dnq 27/16; WJ: '06- 4; WY: '05- 7; EC: '10-12-14: 8/2/dnq 13; EU23: '09- 5; EJ: '07- dnq 15; WI: '14- 4; EI: '13- 8, '15- 5; WUG: '11- 2. POR champion 2008-15, NCAA 2010-11.
Seven Portuguese triple jump records 2009-12.
Progress at TJ: 2004- 12.71, 2005- 12.87, 2006- 13.37/13.38w, 2007- 13.24, 2008- 13.51, 2009- 13.83, 2010- 14.12, 2011- 14.42, 2012- 14.52, 2013- 14.02/14.07w, 2014- 14.36/14.49w, 2015- 14.32i/ 14.19. pbs: 200m 24.42 '10, 800m 2:19.70i '09, 60mh 8.41i '09, 100mh 13.53/13.49w '10, HJ 1.69i '09, 1.69 '11; LJ 6.21i '09, 6.16 '05; Pen 4081i '09, Hep 5293 '11.

Sara MOREIRA b. 17 Oct 1985 Santo Tirso 1.68m 51kg. Sporting CP.
At (5000m)/3000mSt: OG: '08- h; WCh: '07- 13, '09- 10/h, '11- dq; EC: '10- (2), '12- (3), '14- (6); EU23: '07- 3; WUG: '07- 4, '09- 1/1, '11- (2); ET: '11- 2. At 3000m: WI: '10- 5; EI: '09- 2, '13- 1; CCp: '10- 6. At 1500m: EI: '11- 7. At 10000m: OG: '12- 14; WCh: '15- 12; EC: '14- 5; ECp: '10-11-12: 3/1/1. Eur CC: '09-10-12: 10/9/12. Won POR 1500m 2010, 2012; 5000m 2014-15, 10000m 2015, 3000mSt 2007-09, 2011.
POR 3000mSt record 2008.
Progress at 5000m, 10000m, Mar, 3000mSt: 2005- 10:27.72, 2007- 9:42.47, 2008- 9:34.30; 2009- 14:58.11, 9:28.64; 2010- 14:54.71, 31:26.55; 2011- 15:11.97, 31:39.11, 9:35.11; 2012- 15:08.33, 31:16.44; 2014- 15:20.01, 32:01.42, 2:26:00; 2015- 15:50.09, 31:12.93, 2:24:49. pbs: 1500m 4:07.11 '10, 3000m 8:42.69 '10, 2M 9:47.99i '10, 15kRd 48:48 '13, HMar 70:08 '10.
Third in New York on marathon debut 2014, 2nd Prague 2015. 6-months drugs ban 2011-12.

PUERTO RICO

Governing body: Federación de Atletismo Amateur de Puerto Rico, 90, Ave. Río Hondo, Bayamón, PR 00961-3113. Founded 1947.
National Champions 2015: Men: 100m: Marquis Holston 10.52, 200m: Carlos Rodríguez 21.20, 400m: Jonathan Batista 47.87, 800m: Kenneth Rivera 1:52.67, 1500m: Alfredo Santana 3:59.45, 5000m: Misael Carreras 14:35.09, 3000mSt: Richard Estremera 9:01.10, 110mh: Enrique Llanos 14.24, 400mh: Anthony Monroig 52.96, HJ: Nomar Galarza 2.06, PV: Emanuel Rivera 4.60, LJ: Jeffrey Burgos 7.50, TJ: Manuel Montano 14.94, SP: David Lopez 13.60, DT: Alfredo Romero 50.32, HT: Alexis Figueroa 64.11, JT: Hector Cruz 59.86. **Women**: 100m/ 200m: Genoiska Cancel 11.63/24.07, 400m: Krystal Magarinos 57.86, 800m: Priscilla Morales 2:09.56, 1500m: Angelin Figueroa 4:48.14, 5000m: Priscilla Muñoz 20:28.78, 3000mSt: Melinda Martínez 10:18.79, 100mh: Natshalie Isaac 14.03, 400mh: Kathyenid Rivera 60.56, HJ: Jeschika Guzmán 1.60, PV: Yaritza Diaz 3.50, LJ: Maria Hodge 5.96, TJ: Noelys Morales 11.37, DT: Brenda Oyola 45.03, HT: Keishla Luna 56.46, JT: Coralys Ortiz 53.10, Hep: Kayth Agosto 4292.

Javier CULSON b. 25 Jul 1984 Ponce 1.98m 79kg.
At 400mh: OG: '08- sf, '12- 3; WCh: '07-09-11-13-15: sf/2/2/6/sf; PAm: '07- 6; CAG: '06- 5, '10- 2; PAm-J: '03- 3; WUG: '07- 3; CCp: '10- 2, '14- 3/3R; won DL 2012-13, IbAm 2006, CAC 2009.
Seven Puerto Rican 400mh records 2007-10.
Progress at 400mh: 2002- 54.47, 2003- 51.10, 2004- 50.77, 2005- 50.62, 2006- 49.48, 2007- 49.07, 2008- 48.87, 2009- 48.09, 2010- 47.72. 2011- 48.32, 2012- 47.78, 2013- 48.14, 2014- 48.03, 2015- 48.48. pbs: 200m 21.64w '07, 400m 45.99 '12, 800m 1:49.83 '14, 110mh 13.84 '07.

QATAR

Governing body: Qatar Association of Athletics Federation, PO Box 8139, Doha. Founded 1963.

Abdulrahman Musaeb BALLA b. 19 Mar 1989 Khartoum, Sudan 1.75m 60kg.
At 800m: OG: '12- h; WCh: '13- 1sf, '15- 6; AsiG: '10- 3; AsiC: '13- 1, '15 1/1R; CCp: '14- 7; WI: '16- 5; won Asian Indoor 2014, 2016; Franc 2013.
Qatar 800m records 2013 & 2015.
Progress at 800m: 2007- 1:52.45, 2008- 1:51.33, 2010- 1:46.19, 2011- 1:45.92, 2012- 1:45.19, 2013- 1:43.93, 2014- 1:44.03, 2015- 1:43.82. pbs: 400m 46.44 '13, 600m 1:15.83i '14, 1:15.99 '13; 1000m 2:21.71i '11, 1500m 3:40.69 '15.

Mutaz Essa BARSHIM b. 24 Jun 1991 Doha 1.92m 70kg. Team Aspire.
At HJ: OG: '12- 3=; WCh: '11- 7, '13- 2, '15- 4; WJ: '10- 1; AsiG: '10- 1, '14- 1; AsiC: '11- 1; WI: '12-14-16: 9=/1/4; CCp: '14- 3; won DL 2014-15, Asian indoors 2010, 2012, 2014, 2016; Asi-J 2010, W.Mil G 2011, Arab 2011, 2013, 2015; Gulf 2013.
Five Asian high jump records 2012-14 and indoors (3) 2013-15, 14 Qatar records 2010-13.
Progress at HJ: 2008- 2.07, 2009- 2.14, 2010- 2.31, 2011- 2.35, 2012- 2.39, 2013- 2.40, 2014- 2.43, 2015- 2.41.
His 2.43 at Brussels in 2014 was the world's best since 1993, second only to Javier Sotomayor. Qatari father (who was a race walker), Sudanese mother. Younger brother Muamer Aissa Barshim (b. 3 Jan 1994) has HJ pb 2.28 '14 and was 3rd 2014 Asian Games.

Ashraf Amjad EL-SEIFY (Al-Saifi) b. 20 Feb 1995 Egypt 1.83m 93kg.
At HT: WCh: '15- 9; WJ: '12- 1, '14- 1.
Records: world youth 5kg 85.26 '11, world junior 6kg 85.57 '12, Asian junior 7.36k 2013, Two Qatar 2013-15.
Progress at HT: 2013- 76.37, 2014- 71.81, 2015- 78.04.
Former Egyptian.

Abdelilah HAROUN b. 1 Jan 1997 Sudan 1.83m 93kg.

At 400m: AsiC: '15- 1/1R; WI: '16- 2. Asian indoor champion 2016, Arab 2015.
Asian 400m records indoors and out 2015. World best 500m indoors 2016.
Progress at 400m: 2014- 45.74, 2015- 44.27. Pb 500m 59.83i '16.
Qatar citizen from 2 Feb 2015, having lived there from 2013.

Femi Seun **OGUNODE** b. 15 May 1991 Nigeria 1.83m 79kg.
At (100m)/200m: WCh: '11- sf (8 400m), '15- sf/7; AsiG: '10- 1 (1 400m), 14- 1/1; AsiC: '11- 1; CCp: '14- 3/3; Won Arab 100m 2011, 100m/200m 2015; W.Asian 100m/200m 2010, W.MilG 100m/200m 2011. At 60m: WI: '14- 3.
Asian records 100m (2) 2014-15, 200m 2015, four Qatar 200m 2011-15.
Progress at 100m, 200m: 2010- 10.25, 20.43; 2011- 10.07, 20.30; 2014- 9.93, 20.06; 2015- 9.91, 19.97. pbs: 60m 6.51Ai/6.52i '14, 400m 45.12 '10.
Two-year drugs ban 2012-14. Switched allegiance from Nigeria to Qatar from 31 Oct 2009. Younger brother Tosin suddenly emerged with 6.50i for 60m in 2014 and has pb 100m 10.35 '14.

ROMANIA

Governing body: Federatia Romana de Atletism, 2 Primo Nebiolo Str, 011349 Bucuresti. Founded 1912.
National Championships first held in 1914 (men), 1925 (women). **2015 Champions**: **Men**: 100m: Ioan Melnicescu 10.54, 200m: Alexandru Terpezan 21.29, 400m: Adrian Dragan 47.81, 800m: Cristian Vorovenci 1:49.56, 1500m: Ioan Zaizan 3:43.36, 5000m/3000mSt: Andrei Stefana 14:28.90/8:48.98, 10000m: Nicolae Soare 31:05.18, Mar: Sorin Mineran 2:35:36, 110mh: Cosmin Dumitrache 14.33, 400mh: Attila Nagy 51.99, HJ: Mihai Donisan 2.27, PV: Andrei Deliu 5.00, LJ: Adrian Vasile 7.88, TJ: Marian Oprea 16.89, SP: Andrei Gag 20.49, DT: Alin Firfirica 59.93, HT: Cosmin Sorescu 65.53, JT: Levente Bartha 75.12, Dec: Ionel Cojan 7441; 20kW: Adrian Dragomir 1:30:11/Marius Cocioran 1:27:51, 50kW: Florin Stirbu 4:39:48. **Women**: 100m: Andreea Ograzeanu 11.50, 200m/400m: Bianca Razor 23.35/51.49, 800m: Mihaela Nunu 2:05.10, 1500m: Florina Pierdevara 4:15.93, 5000m: Ancuta Bobocel 16:13.31, 10000m: Monica Florea 34:44.62, Mar: Paula Todoran 2:52:45, 3000mSt: Elena Panaet 9:52.14, 100mh: Anamaria Ionita 13.47, 400mh: Angela Morosanu 56.53, HJ: Daniela Stanciu 1.85, PV: Gabriela Bulov 4.00, LJ: Alina Rotaru 6.75, TJ: Cristina Bujin 14.11w, SP: Lenuta Burueana 15.97, DT: Elena Asmarandei 50.16, HT: Bianca Lazar 64.64, JT: Nicoleta Anghelescu 53.15, Hep: Georgiana Muscalu 5096, 20kW: Andrea Arsine 1:36:29/1:34:53.

Andrei GAG b. 27 Apr 1991 1.95m 118kg. CSM Arad, University of Suceava.
At SP: WCh: '15- dnq 17; EC: '14- dnq 20, WUG: '15- 2; WI: '16- 2; At DT: WJ: '08- dnq 30, '10- 2; EU23: '11/13- dnq 19/11; EJ: '09- 10. Won ROU SP 2014-15, DT 2014; Balkan SP 2015.
Romanian shot record 2015.
Progress at SP: 2008- 14.71i, 2009- 15.91, 2010- 16.00i/15.92, 2011- 16.95, 2012- 17.73, 2013- 18.41, 2014- 20.17i/19.64, 2015- 20.96, 2016- 20.89i. pb DT 61.27 '14.

Marian OPREA b. 6 Jun 1982 Pitesti 1.90m 80kg. Rapid Bucuresti & Dinamo Bucuresti. Sports teacher.
At TJ: OG: '04- 2, '08- 5; WCh: '01-03-11: dnq 13/17/15, '05-13-15: 3/6/6; EC: '02-06-10-12-14: dnq 14/3/2/dnq 21/5; WJ: '00- 1; WY: '99- 4; EU23: '03- 2; EJ: '99- 3, '01- 1; WI: '03-04-06-14: 8/5/4/4; EI: '02-11-15: 2/3/3; WUG: '01- 2; WCp: '06- 3, '10- 1. Won Balkan LJ 2014, TJ 2001-03, 2013-14; ROU LJ 2014, TJ 2001, 2003-08, 2013, 2015.
Romanian TJ records 2003 and 2005.
Progress at TJ: 1997- 14.37, 1998- 14.78, 1999- 15.98, 2000- 16.49, 2001- 17.11/17.13w, 2002- 17.29i/17.11/17.39w, 2003- 17.63, 2004- 17.55, 2005- 17.81, 2006- 17.74i/17.56, 2007- 17.32, 2008- 17.28, 2010- 17.51, 2011- 17.62i/17.19, 2012- 16.97i/16.56/16.68w, 2013- 17.24/17.32w, 2014- 17.30i/16.94, 2015- 17.07. pb LJ 7.78 '14, 8.06w '11.
Silver medal in 2004 was best ever Olympic placing by a Romanian male. Major surgery on his left knee in October 2008 meant that he did not compete in 2009.

Women

Florentina MARINCU b. 8 Apr 1996 Deva 1.78m 60kg. CN Sp.Cetate Deva.
At LJ(/TJ)): WCh: '15- dnq; WY: '13- 1/1; EJ: '13- dnq 15/4; EI: '15- 3.
Progress at LJ: 2011- 6.07, 2013- 6.54, 2014- 6.71/6.73w, 2015- 6.79i/6.66/6.78w. pbs: 60m 7.40i '14, 100m 11.85 '14, TJ 13.81 '13.

Alina ROTARU b. 5 Jun 1993 Bucharest 1.75m 54kg. CSA Steaua Bucharest.
At LJ: WCh: '15- dnq 15; EC: '12- dnq 20, '14- 7; WJ: '10- dnq 19, '12- 5; WY: '09- 2 (4 HJ); Yth OG: '10- 2; EU23: '13- 5, '15- 3; EJ: '11- 2; EI: '15- 4. ROU champion 2014-15.
Progress at LJ: 2008- 6.08i/5.99, 2009- 6.26, 2010- 6.40, 2011- 6.46, 2012- 6.57/6.58w, 2013- 6.63, 2014- 6.74, 2015- 6.75. pbs: 60m 7.63i '15, 60mh 8.86i '14, HJ 1.85i '12, 1.82 '09; TJ 13.24i/13.21 '12, Pen 4111i '12.

RUSSIA

Governing body: All-Russia Athletic Federation, Luzhnetskaya Nab. 8, Moscow 119992. Founded 1911.
National Championships first held 1908, USSR women from 1922. **2015 Champions**: **Men**: 100m: Konstantin Petryashov 10.43, 200m: Artur Reysbikh 20.92, 400m: Maksim Dyldin

46.04, 800m: Konstantin Tolokonnikov 1:45.76, 1500m: Valentin Smirnov 3:48.18, 5000m: Aleksey Popov 13:39.26, 10000m/HMar: Anatoliy Rybakov 28:22.01/63:36, Mar: Yuriy Chechun 2:14:10, 3000mSt: Ildar Minshin 8:34.36, 110mh: Konstantin Shabanov 13.61, 400mh: Denis Kudryavtsev 49.07, HJ: Daniyil Tsyplakov 2.31, PV: Aleksandr Gripich 5.65, LJ: Pavel Shalin 8.05w, TJ: Lyukman Adams 17.34, SP: Maksim Sidorov 20.58, DT: Gleb Sidorchenko 61.34, HT: Sergey Litvinov 76.01, JT: Dmitriy Tarvin 84.70, Dec: Sergey Timshin 7984, 20kW: Denis Strelkov 1:20:04, 50kW: Aleksandr Yargunkin 3:45:41. **Women**: 100m/200m: Anna Kukashkina 11.36/23.19, 400m: Kseniya Aksyonova 51.44, 800m: Anastasiya Bazdyreva 2:01.42, 1500m: Tatyana Tomashova 4:04.48, 5000m: Yelena Korobkina 15:57.59, 10000m: Natalya Popkova 32:25.22, HMar: Gulnara Vygovskaya 74:31 (dq Mariya Konovalova 71:49), Mar: Sardana Trofimova 2:29:29, 3000mSt: Natalya Aristarkhova 9:35.07, 100mh: Nina Morozova 12.88, 400mh: Darya Korableva 55.69, HJ: Anna Chicherova 2.00, PV: Anzhelika Sidorova 4.50, LJ: Yuliya Pidluzhnaya 6.87, TJ: Yekaterina Koneva 14.27, SP: Irina Tarasova 18.01, DT: Yeena Panova 63.22, HT: Oksana Kondratyeva 68.60, JT: Vera Rebryk 64.93, Hep: Lyubov Tkach 6151, 20kW: Vera Sokolova 1:26:17.

Lyukman ADAMS b. 24 Sep 1988 St. Petersburg 1.94m 87kg.
At TJ: OG: '12- 9; WCh: '15- 5; EC: '10- 6, '14- 2; EJ: '07- 1; CCp: '14- 6; WI: '12- 3, '14- 1. Russian champion 2012, 2015.
Progress at TJ: 2005- 15.97, 2006- 15.16, 2007- 16.75, 2008- 16.86i/16.78, 2009- 16.22i/16.20, 2010- 17.17/17.21w, 2011- 17.32i/15.60, 2012- 17.53, 2013- 16.82, 2014- 17.37i/17.29, 2015- 17.34, 2016- 17.12i. pb LJ 8.01 '15.
Married Yevgeniya Polyakova (60m 7.09 '08, 1 EI '09; 100m 11.09 '07; 4x100m 1 OG '08) on 5 Apr 2014.

Viktor BUTENKO b. 10 Mar 1993 Stavropol 1.96m 116kg. Stavropolskiy.
At DT: WCh: '13- 8; EC: '14- 5; WJ: '12- 4; EU23: '13- 2; EJ: '11- 6; ET: '14- 3.
Progress at DT: 2011- 51.89, 2012- 57.32, 2013- 65.97, 2014- 65.89, 2015- 65.44.

Dmitriy CHIZHIKOV b. 6 Dec 1993.
At TJ: EU23: '15- 1; EJ: '11- 4.
Progress at TJ: 2011- 15.75/15.95w, 2012- 15.82i/15.72/15.80w, 2013- 16.16, 2014- 16.51, 2015- 17.20. pb LJ 7.60 '15.

Aleksey DMITRIK b. 12 Apr 1984 Slantsy. Leningrad reg, 1.91m 69kg. St Petersburg YR.
At HJ: WCh: '11- 2, '13- dnq 25=; EC: '10- 7, '14- dnq 23; WJ: '02- 14; WY: '01- 1; EJ: '03- 2; EU23: '05- 6; EI: '09- 2=, '13- 2; ECp: '05- 1, '11- 2. Russian champion 2011.
Progress at HJ: 2000- 2.08, 2001- 2.23, 2002- 2.26, 2003- 2.28, 2004- 2.30, 2005- 2.34i/2.30, 2006- 2.28, 2007- 2.30, 2008- 2.33i/2.27, 2009- 2.33, 2010- 2.32i/2.31, 2011- 2.36, 2012- 2.35i/2.33, 2013- 2.36i/2.30, 2014- 2.40i/2.30, 2015- 2.32.
Mother Yelana was a 1.75m high jumper.

Aleksey FYODOROV b. 25 May 1991 Smolensk 1.84m 73kg. Mosoovskaya Smolenskaya.
At TJ: WCh: '11- dnq 18, 13- 5; EC: '12- 4, '14- 3; WJ: '10- 1; WY: '07- 2; EU23: '11-2, '13- 1; EJ: '09- 1; EI: '13- 3, '15- 4; WUG: '13- 2; ET: '13-14-15: 1/1/2. Russian champion 2011, 2013-14.
Progress at TJ: 2007- 15.59, 2008- 16.08, 2009- 16.62, 2010- 17.12/17.18w, 2011- 17.05i/17.01, 2012- 17.19, 2013- 17.13, 2014- 17.07/17.12w, 2015- 17.42.
Parents Leonid and Tatyana were triple jumpers.

Aleksandr GRIPICH b. 21 Sep 1986 Slavyabsk-n-Kubani 1.90m 80kg. Krasnodar VS. Kuban State University.
At PV: WCh: '09- 5, '13-15: dnq 24=/17; EC: '10- dnq, '14- 5; EI: '15- 2; WUG: '09- 1, '11- 2=; ET: '11- 3, '14- 2=. RUS champion 2015.
Progress at PV: 2003- 4.95, 2004- 5.30, 2005- 5.40, 2006- 5.45i/5.20, 2007- 5.65i/5.50, 2008- 5.55, 2009- 5.75, 2010- 5.70i/5.60, 2011- 5.75, 2012- 5.47i/5.00, 2013- 5.60, 2014- 5.70, 2015- 5.85i/5.71.

Aleksandr IVANOV b. 25 Apr 1994 Nizhny Tagiul, Sverdlovsk reg. 1.82m 68kg. Mordoviya VS.
At 20kW: WCh: '13- 1; EC: '14- 2; EU23: '13- 2; ECp: '13- 4. At 10000mW: WJ: '12- 2; WCp: 'EJ: '11- 6; 12- 2J.
Progress at 20kW: 2013- 1:20:58, 2014- 1:19:45, 2015- 1:20:06. pbs: 5000mW 19:35.0 '12, 10000mW: 40:12.90 '12, 39:29R '13.
At 20 in 2013 he became the youngest ever World walking champion. Married Elmira Alembekova in August 2015.

Andrey KRIVOV b. 14 Nov 1985 Komsomolsky, Mordovia 1.85m 72kg. Mordovia. Sports student.
At 20kW: OG: '12- 37; WCh: '09- 17; EC: '10- 5; EU23: '07- 2; WCp: '08-10-12: 5/3/2; ECp: '11- 6, '15- 6; WUG: '11- 1, '13- 1. Russian champion 2009, 2011.
Progress at 20kW: 2005- 1:22:21, 2007- 1:20:12, 2008- 1:19:06, 2009- 1:19:55, 2010- 1:22:20, 2011- 1:20:16, 2012- 1:18:25, 2013- 1:20:47, 2015- 1:20:43. pbs: 10000mW: 40:35.2 '05, 35kW 2:29:44 '06.

Denis KUDRYAVTSEV b. 13 Apr 1992 Chelyabinsk 1.87m 77kg. Tyumenskaya Chelyabinsk.
At 400mh: WCh: '13- h, '15- 2; EC: '14- 3; EU23: '13- sf; EJ: '11- sf; ET: '14- 1, '15- 1. RUS champion 2013, 2015.
Russian 400mh record 2015.
Progress at 400mh: 2010- 53.18, 2011- 51.45, 2012- 52.68, 2013- 49.40, 2014- 48.95, 2015- 48.05. pbs: 200m 21.44 '14, 400m 45.86 '15.

Aleksandr LESNOY b. 28 Jul 1988 Krasnodar 1.94m 116kg.
At SP: WCh: '13-15: dnq 21/16; EC: '14- 10; WUG: '13- 1; WI: '14- 8; ET: '13-14: 3/3. RUS champion 2014.
Progress at SP: 2008- 16.46, 2009- 16.80, 2010- 19.09, 2011- 19.60, 2012- 20.05, 2013- 20.60, 2014- 21.40, 2015- 20.70i/20.55. pb DT 58.80 '12.

Sergey LITVINOV b. 27 Jan 1986 Rostov-on-Don, Russia 1.85m 105kg.
At HT: WCh: '09-11-13-15: 5/dnq 15/11/5; EC: '14- 3; WJ: '04- 9; EU23: '07- 11; EJ: '05- 9; WUG: '13- 3; ET: '14- 1. German champion 2009, Russian 2013, 2015.
Progress at HT: 2004- 60.00, 2005- 73.98, 2006- 66.46, 2007- 74.80, 2008- 75.35, 2009- 77.88, 2010- 78.98, 2011- 78.90, 2012- 80.98, 2013- 80.89, 2014- 79.35, 2015- 77.24.
Switched from Belarus to Germany 15 Jul 2008 and from 1 Jan 2011 to Russia. His father Sergey Litvinov (USSR) set three world records at hammer 1980-3 with a pb of 86.04 '86; he was Olympic champion 1988 (2nd 1980) and World champion 1983 and 1987. His mother was born in Germany.

Aleksandr MENKOV b. 7 Dec 1990 Minusinsk, Krasnoyarsk reg. 1.78m 74kg. Krasnoyarsk VS. Krasnoyarsk State University.
At LJ: OG: '12- 11; WCh: '09-11-13-15: dnq 32/6/1/6; EC: '14- dnq 13; WI: '12- 3, '14- 5; EU23: '11- 1; EJ: '09- 1; EI: '13- 1; WUG: '13- 2; ET: '11-13-15: 1/1/1. Won DL 2012-13, Russian 2012.
Two Russian records 2013.
Progress at LJ: 2008- 6.98, 2009- 8.16, 2010- 8.10, 2011- 8.28, 2012- 8.29, 2013- 8.56, 2014- 8.30i/8.02, 2015- 8.27. pbs: HJ 2.15 '10, TJ 15.20 '09.

Ivan NOSKOV b. 17 Jul 1988 Perm 1.77m 62kg. Army.
At 50kW: WCh: '13- 7; EC: '14- 3WCp: '14- 2; ECp: '13- 3, '15- 2.
Progress at 50kW: 2012- 3:55:16, 2013- 3:41:36, 2014- 3:37:41, 2015- 3:43:57. pbs: 20kW: 1:23:49 '11, 30kW 2:05:56 '12, 35kW 2:26:33 '12. Suspended in 2015.

Mikhail RYZHOV b. 17 Dec 1991 1.80m 65kg. Mordoviya.
At 50kW: WCh: '13- 2; EC: '14- 4; WCp: '14- 1; ECp: '13- 2, '15- 1; At 20kW: WUG: '11- 2.
Progress at 50kW: 2012- 3:53:49, 2013- 3:38:58, 2014- 3:39.05, 2015- 3:43:32. pbs: 5000mW 19:09.86i '14, 10kW 39:11 '12, 20kW: 1:21:49 '11, 30kW 2:05:39 '12, 35kW 2:25:54 '15. Suspended in 2015.

Ilya SHKURENYOV b. 11 Jan 1991 Linevo, Volgograd reg. 1.91m 82kg. Volgograd Dyn.
At Dec: OG: '12- 16; WCh: '13- 8, '15- 4; EC: '12- 3, '14- 3; WJ: '10- 2; EU23: '11- 5, '13- 2; ECp: '15- 1. Russian champion 2013. At Hep: WI: '12- 4; EI: '13- 5, '15- 1.
Progress at Dec: 2011- 7894, 2012- 8219, 2013- 8370, 2014- 8498, 2015- 8538. pbs: 60m 6.98i '15, 100m 10.91 '13, 400m 47.88 '15, 1000m 2:41.65i '13, 1500m 4:24.98 '15, 60mh 7.86i '15, 110mh 14.02 '15, HJ 2.11i '15, 2.10 '14; PV 5.40 '13, LJ 7.78i/7.55 '15, SP 14.84i '11, 14.24 '15; DT 46.04 '14, JT 63.58 '14, Hep 6353i '15.

Sergey SHUBENKOV b. 4 Oct 1990 Barnaul, Altay Kray 1.90m 75kg. Tyumen State University.
At 110mh: OG: '12- sf; WCh: '11- h, '13- 3, '15- 1; EC: '12- 1, '14- 1; EU23: '11- 1; EJ: '09- 2, WUG: '13- 3; CCp: '14- 1; ET: '13-14-15: 1/1. Won WMilG 2015, Russian 2013. At 60mh: EI: '13- 1. Six Russian 110mh records 2012-15.
Progress at 110mh: 2010- 13.54, 2011- 13.46, 2012- 13.09, 2013- 13.16/13.10w, 2014- 13.13, 2015- 12.98. pb 60mh 7.49i '13.
Mother Natalya Shubenkova had heptathlon pb 6859 '04; 4th 1988 OG and 3rd 1986 EC.

Aleksandr SHUSTOV b. 29 Jun 1984 Karaganda, Kazakhstan 1.99m 85kg. Moskva VS.
At HJ: OG: '12- dnq 15; WCh: '11- 8, '13- 7; EC: '10- 1; EU23: '05- 12; WUG: '07- 1; EI: '09-11-15: 4=/3/4; ET: '09-10: 3/1. Russian champion 2010.
Progress at HJ: 2002- 2.10, 2003- 2.11, 2004- 2.15, 2005- 2.23, 2006- 2.28, 2007- 2.31, 2008- 2.30, 2009- 2.32i, 2010- 2.33, 2011- 2.36, 2012- 2.35, 2013- 2.32, 2014- 2.26i/2.25, 2015- 2.30. pbs: LJ 7.18i '12, Hep 4564i '12.
Married to Yekaterina Kondratyeva (200m 22.64 '04, 2 WUG '03, 6 EC '06).

Dmitriy SOROKIN b. 27 Sep 1992 1.76m 73kg. Siberian Sate University of Physical Culture. Omsk.
At TJ: WCh: '15- 7; WY: 09- dnq 13; WUG: '15- 1; EI: '15- 6. Won WMilG 2015.
Progress at TJ: 2009- 15.62, 2010- 16.28/16.41w, 2011- 16.38dq, 2013- 15.30, 2014- 16.96, 2015- 17.29. pb LJ 7.63i '15, 7.55 '10.
2-year drugs ban 2011-13.

Dmitriy TARABIN b. 29 Oct 1991 Berlin, Germany 1.76m 85kg. Student at Russian State University of Physical Education, Moscow
At JT: WCh: '11- 10, '13- 3, '15- dnq 25; EC: '14- 5; WJ: '10- 3; WY: '07- dnq 23; EU23: '11- 3; EJ: '09- dnq 13; WUG: '13- 1; ET: '13- 1, '14- 2. Won RUS 2013, 2015.
Progress at JT: 2007- 55.18, 2008- 67.39, 2009- 69.63, 2010- 77.65, 2011- 85.10, 2012- 82.75; 2013- 88.84, 2014- 85.92, 2015- 84.70.
Switched from Moldova to Russia 9 June 2010. Married Mariya Abakumova on 12 Oct 2012.

Daniyil TSYPLAKOV b. 29 Jul 1992 Khabarovsk reg. 1.78m 70kg. Khabarovskiy.
At HJ: WCh: '15- 5; EC: '14- 5; WY: '09- 3; EU23: '13- 2; EJ: '11- 4; ET: '15- 1; WUG: '15- 1; WI: '14- 5; EI: '15- 1. RUS champion 2014-15.
Progress at HJ: 2008- 2.11, 2009- 2.21, 2010- 2.21, 2011- 2.26, 2012- 2.31, 2013- 2.30, 2014- 2.34i/2.33, 2015- 2.33.

Ivan UKHOV b. 29 Mar 1986 Chelyabinsk 1.92m 83kg. Sverdlovsk TU.
At HJ: OG: '12- 1; WCh: '09-11-13-15: 10/5=/4/dnq 24; EC: '06-10-14: 12=/2/3; WJ: '04- dnq 13; EJ: '05- 1; CCp: '14- 2; WUG: '05- 4; WI: '10-12-14: 1/3/2; EI: '09- 1, '11- 1. Won DL 2010, Russian 2009, 2012-13.
Russian high jump record 2014 (& 2 indoors).
Progress at HJ: 2004- 2.15, 2005- 2.30, 2006- 2.37i/2.33, 2007- 2.39i/2.20, 2008- 2.36i/2.30, 2009- 2.40i/2.35, 2010- 2.38i/2.36, 2011- 2.38i/2.34, 2012- 2.39, 2013- 2.35, 2014- 2.42i/2.41, 2015- 2.32.
Former discus thrower.

Women

Mariya ABAKUMOVA b. 15 Jan 1986 Stavropol 1.78m 85kg. Krasnodar VS.
At JT: OG: '08- 2, '12- 10; WCh: '07- 09-11-13-15: 7/3/1/3/dnq 30; EC: '10- 5; WJ: '04- dnq 25; WY: '03- 4; EU23: '07- 6; EJ: '05- 1; WUG: '13- 1; CCp: '10- 1; ECp: '08-09-10: 2/3/3. Won WAF 2009, Russian 2008, 2011-13.
European javelin record 2008, four Russian 2008-11.
Progress at JT: 2002- 51.81, 2003- 51.41, 2004- 58.26, 2005- 59.53, 2006- 60.12, 2007- 64.28, 2008- 70.78, 2009- 68.92, 2010- 68.89, 2011- 71.99, 2012- 66.86, 2013- 70.53, 2015- 61.27.
Married Dmitriy Tarabin on 12 Oct 2012, twin daughters Kira and Milana born 17 Jun 2014.

Elmira ALEMBEKOVA b. 30 Jun 1990 Saransk. Mordoviya.
At 20kW: EC: '14- 1; WCp: '14- 3; ECp: '15- 1. At 10000m/10kW: WJ: '08- 2; EJ: '09- 1; WCp: '08- 3J, At 5000mW: WY: '05- 2.
World best for 20k walk 2015.
Progress at 20kW: 2010- 1:35:53, 2011- 1:27:35, 2012- 1:25:27, 2014- 1:27:02, 2015- 1:24:47. pbs: 10000mW: 43:45.26 '08.
Suspended in 2015. Married Aleksandr Ivanov in August 2015.

Tatyana BELOBORODOVA b. 9 Oct 1983 Bataisk, Rostov region 1.86m 81kg. née Lysenko. Bataisk VS.
At HT: OG: '04- dnq 19, '12- 1; WCh: '05-09-11-13: 2/6/1/1; EC: '06- 1, '10- 2; EU23: '03- 5; WUG: '03- 5; WCp: '06- 2, '10- 1; ECp: '06-07-10-11: 1/dq1/2/2. Won RUS 2005, 2009-13.
Three world hammer records, nine Russian records 2005-13.
Progress at HT: 2000- 49.08, 2001- 55.73, 2002- 61.85, 2003- 67.19, 2004- 71.54, 2005- 77.06, 2006- 77.80, 2007- 77.30/78.61dq, 2009- 76.41, 2010- 76.03, 2011- 77.13, 2012- 78.51, 2013- 78.80, 2014- 70.62, 2015- 63.81.
Two-year drugs ban after positive test on 9 May 2007. Son Makariy born 14 Feb 2015.

Anna BULGAKOVA b. 17 Jan 1988 Stavropol 1.73m 90kg. Stavropol VS.
At HT: OG: '08- dnq 20; WCh: '13- 5; EC: '12- 3, '14- nt; WJ: '04- 4, '06- 2; WY: '05- 2; EJ: '07- 4; ET: '14- 3. RUS champion 2014.
Progress at HT: 2003- 57.24, 2004- 63.83, 2005- 64.43, 2006- 67.79, 2007- 68.49, 2008- 73.79, 2010- 66.29, 2011- 69.10, 2012- 74.02, 2013- 76.17, 2014- 74.16, 2015- 72.15. pb DT 44.19 '06.

Anna CHICHEROVA b. 22 Jul 1982 Yerevan, Armenia 1.80m 57kg. Moskva VS. Physical culture graduate.
At HJ: OG: '04- 6, '08- 3, '12- 1; WCh: '03-05-07-09-11-13-15: 6/4/2=/2/1/3=/3; EC: '06- 7=; WJ: '00- 4; WY: '99- 1; EJ: '01- 2; WUG: '05- 1; WI: '03-04-12: 3/2/2=; EI: '05- 1, '07- 5=; ECp: '06- 3. Russian champion 2004, 2007-09, 2011-12, 2015.
Progress at HJ: 1998- 1.80, 1999- 1.89, 2000- 1.90, 2001- 1.92, 2002- 2.00i/1.89, 2003- 2.04i/2.00, 2004- 2.04i/1.98, 2005- 2.01i/1.99, 2006- 1.96i/1.95, 2007- 2.03, 2008- 2.04, 2009- 2.02, 2011- 2.07, 2012- 2.06i/2.05, 2013- 2.02, 2014- 2.01, 2015- 2.01.
Moved with family to Russia at the beginning of the 1990s. Married to Gennadiy Chernoval KAZ, pbs 100m 10.18, 200m 20.44 (both 2002), 2 WUG 100m & 200m 2001, 2 AsiG 2002 2002; their daughter Nika born on 7 Sep 2010.

Irina DAVYDOVA b. 27 May 1988 Alexandrov, Vladimir reg. 1.70m 65kg. Moskva SC.
At 400mh: OG: '12- sf; WCh: '13- sf; EC: '12- 1, '14- 3; EU23: '09- 5; WUG: '11- 2, '13- 3; ET: '14- 3. Russian champion 2013-14.
Progress at 400mh: 2006- 60.27, 2007- 58.55, 2008- 58.62, 2009- 56.14, 2010- 55.74, 2011- 55.48, 2012- 53.77, 2013- 54.79, 2014- 54.60. pbs: 200m 24.53i '11, 400m 51.94i '12, 53.12 '11; 500m 1:10.54i '12.

Irina GORDEYEVA b. 9 Oct 1986 Leningrad 1.85m 55kg. Yunost Rossii.
At HJ: OG: '12- 10; WCh: '13- 9=; EC: '10- dnq 13=, '12- 3=; WJ: '04- 9; WY: '03- 7=; EJ: '05- 4; EI: '09- 5=.
Progress at HJ: 2001- 1.75, 2002- 1.82, 2003- 1.84, 2004- 1.88, 2005- 1.88, 2006- 1.88, 2007- 1.87i/1.83, 2008- 1.95, 2009- 2.02, 2010- 1.97, 2011- 1.94, 2012- 2.04, 2013- 1.99, 2014- 1.95, 2015- 1.96i/1.94.

Anisya KIRDYAPKINA b. 23 Oct 1989 Saransk, Mordoviya 1.65m 51kg. née Kornikova. Mordovia TU.
At 20kW: OG: '12- 4; WCh: '09- 3, '11- 2, '13- 2; EC: '10- 1; WCp: '10-12-14: 6/5/1; ECp: '09-11-13: 2/2/1; WUG: '13- 1, '15- 1; RUS champion 2010, 2012. At 10000mW: EJ: '07- 1; ECp: '07- 1J.
World junior 20km walk best 2008.
Progress at 20kW: 2007- 1:28:00, 2008- 1:25:30, 2009- 1:25:26, 2010- 1:25:11, 2011- 1:25:09, 2012- 1:26:26. 2013- 1:25:59, 2014- 1:26:31, 2015- 1:26:44. pbs: 3000mW 11:44.10i '12, 5000mW 21:06.3 '06, 10000mW 43:27.30 '07, 42:04R '11.
Married to Sergey Kirdyapkin (50kW: 1 OG 08, 1dq 12., 1 WCh 05, 1dq09, pb 3:35:59 '12).

Darya KLISHINA b. 15 Jan 1991 Tver 1.80m 57kg. Moskva. Model.

At LJ: WCh: '11- 7, '13- 7, '15- 10; EC: '14- 3; WY: '07- 1; EU23: '11- 1; EJ: '09- 1; WI: '10-12-14: 5/4/7; EI: '11- 1, '13- 1, WUG: '13- 1; ET: '11- 1, '13- 2. RUS champion 2014.
Progress at LJ: 2005- 5.83, 2006- 6.33/6.47w, 2007- 6.49, 2008- 6.52i/6.20, 2009- 6.80, 2010- 7.03, 2011- 7.05, 2012- 6.93, 2013- 7.01i/6.90/6.98w, 2014- 6.90, 2015- 6.95.

Anna KLYASHTORNAYA b. 3 Feb 1986 Sankt-Petersburg 1.72m 58kg. née Nazarova.
At LJ: OG: '12- 5; EC: '12- 10; WJ: '04- dnq; EJ: '05- 3; EU23: '07- 1; WUG: '11- 1; WI: '10- 6.
Progress at LJ: 2003- 6.00/6.12w, 2004- 6.48, 2005- 6.50i/6.31, 2006- 6.66, 2007- 6.81, 2008- 6.71/6.75w, 2009- 6.60, 2010- 6.75i/6.54, 2011- 6.89i/6.88, 2012- 7.11, 2014- 6.93, 2015- 6.34i. pb TJ 13.80i '07, 13.39 '10.
Daughter born April 2013.

Yevgeniya KOLODKO b. 2 Jul 1990 Neryungi, Yakutia 1.88m 85kg. Luch Moskva.
At SP: OG: '12- 2; WCh: '11- 5, '13- 5; EC: '14- 2; WI: '12- 7, '14- 4; EU23: '11- 1; EJ: '09- 9; CCp: '14- 4; EI: '13- 2. Russian champion 2012-14.
Progress at SP: 2007- 14.26, 2008- 15.04i/14.87, 2009- 15.38, 2010- 16.73, 2011- 19.78, 2012- 20.48, 2013- 19.97i/19.86, 2014- 19.52.

Oksana KONDRATYEVA b. 22 Nov 1985 Moskva 1.80m 80kg. Moscow State University of PE.
At HT: WCh: '13- 7; WUG: '13- 2. Won US 2015.
Progress at HT: 2004- 57.36, 2005- 62.24, 2006- 61.81, 2007- 64.09, 2008- 66.08, 2009- 67.84, 2010- 71.90, 2011- 69.87, 2012- 73.31, 2013- 77.13, 2014- 72.17, 2015- 72.01.
Mother Lydmila Kondratyeva (1980 Olympic 100m champion) and father Yuriy Sedykh (hammer world record holder).

Yekaterina KONEVA b. 25 Sep 1988 Khabarovsk 1.69m 55kg. Khabarovskiy.
At TJ: WCh: '13- 2, '15- 7; EC: '14- 2; WI: '14- 1; WUG: '11-13-15: 1/1/1; CCp: '14- 2; EI: '15- 1; ET: '13-14-15: 2/1/1. RUS champion 2014-15, WMilG LJ & TJ 2015.
Progress at TJ: 2010- 13.93/14.00w, 2011- 14.46, 2012- 14.60i/14.36, 2013- 14.82, 2014- 14.89, 2015- 15.04. pbs: 60m 7.39i '07, 100m 11.76 '09, 200m 23.89 '09, LJ 6.82i '15, 6.70/6.80w '11.
Two-year drugs ban 2007-09.

Angelina KRASNOVA b. 7 Feb 1991 Moskva 1.68m 55kg. née Zhuk. Irkutskaya.
At PV: WCh: '13- 7; EC: '14- 3; EU23: '13- 1; CCp: '14- 2; EI: '13- 5, '15- 4.
Progress at PV: 2007- 3.60i, 2008- 3.80, 2010- 4.10, 2011- 4.30i/4.25, 2012- 4.40, 2013- 4.70, 2014- 4.65, 2015- 4.67i/4.60, 2016- 4.66i.

Olga KUCHERENKO b. 5 Nov 1985 Sidory, Volgograd region 1.72m 59kg. Lokomotiv Penza.
At LJ: WCh: '09- 5, '11- 2, '13- 5; EC: '10- 3; EU23: '07- 12; EI: '09-3, '13- 6; ET: '09-10: 2/2.
Progress at LJ: 2002- 6.08, 2004- 6.30, 2005- 6.34, 2006- 6.72/6.80w, 2007- 6.41/6.70w, 2008- 6.87i/6.70, 2009- 6.91, 2010- 7.13, 2011- 6.86, 2012- 7.03, 2013- 7.00i/6.81, 2014- 6.70, 2015- 6.78.

Mariya KUCHINA b. 14 Jan 1993 Prokhladny, Kabardino-Balkar 1.82m 60kg. Moskovskaya.
At HJ: WCh: '15- 1; EC: '14- 2; WJ: '12- 3; WY: '09- 2=; EU23: '15- 12; EJ: '11- 1; WI: '14- 1=; EI: '15- 1; WUG: '13- 2; CCp: '14- 1; ET: '13-14-15: 1/1/1. Won DL 2014, Yth Oly 2010, RUS champion 2014, W.MilG 2015.
World junior indoor high jump record 2011.
Progress at HJ: 2009- 1.87, 2010- 1.91, 2011- 1.97i/1.95, 2012- 1.96i/1.89, 2013- 1.98i/1.96, 2014- 2.01i/2.00, 2015- 2.01.

Alyona LUTKOVSKAYA b. 15 Mar 1996 Irkutsk 1.64m 55kg. Irkutsk.
At PV: EC: '14- 7=; WJ: '14- 1; WY: '13- 2; EJ: '13- 1, '15- 2.
World junior outdoor PV best 2015.
Progress at PV: 2012- 4.20, 2013- 4.30, 2014- 4.50, 2015- 4.61.

Marina PANDAKOVA 1 Mar 1989. Churvashkaya Reg.
At 20kW: WCp: '14- 10. ECp: '13- 3, '15- 5; WUG: '15- 2.
Progress at 20kW: 2008- 1:38:19, 2011- 1:33:00, 2012- 1:28:29, 2013- 1:27:39, 2014- 1:27:54, 2015- 1:25:03. pbs: 3000mW: 11:57.89i '14, 5000mW 21:40.41i '13, 10kW 43:29 '12.

Vira REBRYK b. 25 Feb 1989 Yalta 1.76m 65kg.
At JT: OG: '08/12- dnq 16/19; WCh: '09- 11-13-15: 9/dnq 16/11.dnq 24; EC: '10- dnq 17, '12- 1; WJ: '06- 2, '08- 1; WY: '05- 2; EU23: '09- 2, '11- 2; EJ: '07- 1; WUG: '09- 2, '11- 4; ET: '13- 3. Won UKR 2010-12, RUS 2015.
World junior javelin record 2008; three UKR records 2012.
Progress at JT: 2003- 44.94, 2004- 52.47, 2005- 57.48, 2006- 59.64, 2007- 58.48, 2008- 63.01, 2009- 62.26, 2010- 63.36, 2011- 61.60, 2012- 66.86, 2013- 64.30, 2014- 61.57, 2015- 64.93.
Crimean athlete, transferred to Russia in 2015.

Anastasiya SAVCHENKO b. 15 Nov 1989 Omsk 1.75m 65kg. Luch Moskva.
At PV: OG: '12- dnq 26-; WCh: '13- 5=; EC: '12- 4; EU23: '09- 8, '11- 6; WUG: '13- 1; WI: '14- 11; EI: '13- 5=.
Progress at PV: 2005- 3.80, 2006- 3.80i/3.70, 2007- 3.90, 2008- 4.20i/4.10, 2009- 4.30i/4.20, 2010- 4.30, 2011- 4.40, 2012- 4.60, 2013- 4.73, 2014- 4.50, 2015- 4.60i/4.20.

Svetlana SHKOLINA b. 9 Mar 1986 Yartsevo, Smolensk reg. 1.87m 66kg. Luch Moskva.
At HJ: OG: '08- 14, '12- 3; WCh: '09- 6, '11- 5, 13- 1; EC: '10- 4; WJ: '04- 2; WY: '03- 2=; EU23: '07- 1; EJ: '05- 1; WI: '10- 4; EI: '09- 4=, '11- 4=; WUG: '05-4, '07- 4; ECp: '10: 2. Won DL 2013, Russian 2010, 2013.
Progress at HJ: 2001- 1.75, 2002- 1.84, 2003- 1.88,

2004- 1.91, 2005- 1.92, 2006- 1.92, 2007- 1.96, 2008- 1.98, 2009- 1.98, 2010- 2.00i/1.98, 2011- 2.00i/1.99, 2012- 2.03, 2013- 2.03, 2015- 1.95i/1.94. Missed 2014 season due to a take-off foot injury.

Anzhelika SIDOROVA b. 28 Jun 1991 Moskva 1.70m 52kg. Moskva Youth.
At PV: WCh: '15- nh; EC: '14- 1; WJ: '10- 4; EU23: '13- 2; WI: '14- 2=; EI: '13- 3, '15- 1; ET: '13-14-15:- 2/1/2. RUS champion 2014-15.
Progress at PV: 2007- 3.80, 2008- 4.00, 2009- 4.10i/4.00, 2010- 4.30, 2011- 4.40i/4.30, 2012- 4.50, 2013- 4.62i/4.60, 2014- 4.72i/4.70, 2015- 4.80i/4.79, 2016- 4.75i.

Vera SOKOLOVA b. 8 Jun 1987 Solianoy, Chuvashiya 1.51m 51kg. Mordovia VS.
At 20kW: WCh: '09- 13, '11- 10, '13- dq; EC: '10- 2, '14- 4; WCp: '10- 4, '14- 4; ECp: '09-11-13-15: 10/1/2/6; Russian champion 2009, 2014-15. At 10000mW: WJ: '02-04-06: 9/3/4; EJ: '05- 1; WCp: '04/06- 1J; ECp: '03- 2J, '05- 1J. At 5000mW: WY: '03- 1.
Walks records: World 20km 2011, world junior 10,000m and 5000m indoors 2005.
Progress at 20kW: 2006- 1:40:03, 2007- 1:32:56, 2008- 1:30:11, 2009- 1:25:26, 2010- 1:25:35, 2011- 1:25:08, 2012- 1:28:06. 2013- 1:26:00, 2014- 1:27:03, 2015- 1:25:38. pbs: 3000m 11:58.44i '14, 12:51.96 '04, 5000mW 20:10.3i '10, 10kW 42:04+ '11, 43:11.34t '05. Suspended in 2015.

Yelena SOKOLOVA b. 23 Jul 1986 Staryi Oskol, Belgorod reg. 1.70m 61kg. née Kremneva. Krasnodarsk krai.
At LJ: OG: '12- 2; WCh: '09- dnq 13, '13- 9, '15- dnq 23; EU23: '07- 3; EI: '07- 5, '09- 2; WUG: '07- 2, '13- 2. Won DL 2012, Russian 2009, 2012, 2015.
Progress at LJ: 2002- 6.33, 2003- 6.39i?/6.31, 2006- 6.53, 2007- 6.71, 2008- 6.74, 2009- 6.92, 2010- 6.72/6.90w, 2011- 6.76, 2012- 7.07, 2013- 6.91, 2015- 6.70. pbs: 60m 7.34i '12, 100m 11.61 '12, TJ 13.15i/12.93 '03.
Son born on 23 Aug 2014.

Irina TARASOVA b. 15 Apr 1987 Kovrov 1.83m 110kg. Army.
At SP: OG: '12- 8; WCh: '13- 7; ECh: '12- 2, '14- 6; WI: '12- 8; WJ: '04- 5, '06- 3; WY: '03- 5; EU23: '07- 1; EJ: '05- 2; EI: '13- 5; WUG: '07-11-13: 1/1/1; ET: '14- 2, '15- 2. RUS champion 2015.
Progress at SP: 2002- 14.01, 2003- 15.04, 2004- 16.16, 2005- 16.79i/16.53, 2006- 17.11, 2007- 18.27, 2008- 18.45, 2009- 18.21, 2010- 18.18, 2011- 18.72, 2012- 19.35, 2013- 19.20, 2014- 18.38, 2015- 18.53.

Svetlana VASILYEVA b. 24 Jul 1992. Mordovia VS.
At 20kW: EU23: '13- 1; ECp: '15: 3. At 10000mW: EJ: '11- 2; WCp: '10- 5J; ECp: '11- 1J. At 5000mW: WY: '09- 3.
Progress at 20kW: 2012- 1:28:30. 2013- 1:29:56, 2014- 1:28:49, 2015- 1:25:04. pbs: 3000m 11:57.71i '14, 10kW 42:43.0t '11.

SAINT KITTS & NEVIS

Governing body: Saint Kitts Amateur Athletic Association, PO Box 932, Basseterre, St Kitts. Founded 1961.

Kim COLLINS. b. 5 Apr 1976 Ogees, Saint-Peter 1.75m 64kg. Studied sociology at Texas Christian University, USA.
At 100m (/200m): OG: '96- qf, 00- 7/sf, '04- 6, '08- sf/6; WCh: '95- hR, '97- h, 99- h/h, '01- 5/3=, '03- 1, '05- 3, '07- sf, '09- qf/qf, '11- 3/sf/3R, '15- h; CG: '02- 1; PAm: '07- 5, '11- 2; PAm-J: '95- 2; CAC: '99- 2, '01- 1/1, '03- 1; WCp: '02- 2/2R, '14- 1R/3 4x400mR. At 60m: WI: '03-08-16: 2/2=/8. Won NCAA indoor 60m & 200m 2001.
SKN records: 100m from 1996 to 2014, 200m from 1998, 400m 2000. CAC indoor 60m 2015. M35 world records: 100m 2013 & 2014, indoor 60m (4) 2014-15.
Progress at 100m, 200m: 1995- 10.63, 21.85; 1996- 10.27, 21.06; 1998- 10.18/10.16w, 20.88/20.78w; 1999- 10.21, 20.43, 2000- 10.13A/10.15/10.02w, 20.31A/20.18w; 2001- 10.04A/10.00?/9.99w, 20.20/20.08w; 2002- 9.98, 20.49; 2003- 9.99/9.92w, 20.40w; 2004- 10.00, 20.98; 2005- 10.00, 2006- 10.33, 21.53; 2007- 10.14, 2008- 10.05, 20.25; 2009- 10.15/10.08w, 20.45; 2010- 10.20, 21.35/20.76w; 2011- 10.00A/10.01, 20.52; 2012- 10.01/9.96w, 2013- 9.97, 21.37i, 2014- 9.96, 2015- 9.98/9.94w. pbs: 60m 6.47i '15, 400m 46.93 '00.
The first athlete from his country to make Olympic and World finals and in 2003 the first to win a World Indoor medal and a World title; won a further medal in 2011 and has now competed in ten World Champs. Oldest man to have broken 10 secs for 100m. There is a 'Kim Collins Highway' in St Kitts.

ST LUCIA

Governing body: Saint Lucia Athletics Association, Olympic House, Barnard Hill P.O.GM 697 Gable Woods Mall, Castries.

Levern SPENCER b. 23 Jun 1984 Cacao Babonneau 1.80m 54kg. Was at University of Georgia.
At HJ: OG: '08/12- dnq 27/19; WCh: '05-07-09-11-13-15: dnq 22/15=/dnq 24=/dnq 13/11/12=; CG: '02-06-10-14: 12=/5/3/3; WJ: '02- 8; WY: '01- 3; PAm: '03- 5, '07- 3, '15- 1; CAG: '06-10-14: 3/1/1; WI: '14- 7, '16- 5=; CCp: '10- 3=, '14- 5. CAC champion 2001, 2005, 2008-09, 2011, 2013.
Nine St. Lucia high jump records 2004-10.
Progress at HJ: 2000- 1.80, 2001- 1.81, 2002- 1.83, 2003- 1.86, 2004- 1.88, 2005- 1.94, 2006- 1.90, 2007- 1.94, 2008- 1.93, 2009- 1.95, 2010- 1.98, 2011- 1.94, 2012- 1.91, 2013- 1.95A, 2014- 1.96, 2015- 1.94, 2016- 1.95i. pbs: 200m 24.22 '05, LJ 6.08 '14.

SAUDI ARABIA

Governing body: Saudi Arabian Athletics Federation, PO Box 5802, Riyadh 11432. Fd 1963.

Youssef Ahmed **AL-MASRAHI** b. 31 Dec 1987 Njaran 1.76m 76kg.
At 400m: OG: 12- sf; WCh: '09- h, '13- 6, '15- 8; AsiG: '10- 3/1R, '14- 1; AsiC: '11- 1, '13- 1/1R, '15- 2/2R; CCp: '14- 3; Gulf champion 2009, Arab 2011, 2013- 1, WMilG 2015.
400m records: Asian (2) 2014-15, KSA (3) 2013-15,
Progress at 400m/4x400mR: 2007- 48.89, 2008- 46.45, 2009- 45.84, 2010- 45.48, 2011- 45.44, 2012- 45.43, 2013- 44.61, 2014- 44.43, 2015- 43.93. pbs: 200m 20.96 '15, 800m 1:54.14 '07.
Lived in the USA from 2011.

SERBIA

Governing body: Athletic Federation of Serbia, Strahinjica Bana 73a, 11000 Beograd. Founded in 1921 (as Yugoslav Athletic Federation).
National Championships (Yugoslav) first held in 1920 (men) and 1923 (women). **2015 Champions**: **Men**: 100m: Goran Podunavac 10.89, 200m: Nemanja Bozic 21.89, 400m: Stefan Vukadinovic 47.71, 800m: Milan Todorovic 1:52.50, 1500m: Nenad Radanovic 3:57.74, 3000m: Marko Nisic 8:33.47, 5000m/10000m: Muamer Hasanovic 14:51.85/31:08.08, HMar: Sasa Stolic 69:26, Mar: Ivan Miskeljin 2:35:17, 3000mSt: Milos Mitrovic 9:27.06, 110mh: Milan Ristic 13.99, 400mh: Nikola Trifunovic 53.41, HJ: Milos Todosijevic 2.10, PV: Milos Savic 4.80, LJ/TJ: Lazar Anic 7.50/15.24, SP: Asmir Kolasinac 20.48, DT: Darko Radakovic 49.33, HT: Zoran Lancar 53.91, JT: Vedran Samac 80.58, Dec: Nemanja Maksic 5167, 10kW: Vladimir Savanovic 42:20. **Women**: 100m: Milana Tirnanic 11.79, 200m: Maja Ciric 24.28, 400m/800m: Tamara Salaski 53.45/2:11.36, 1500m/3000mSt: Biljana Cvijanovic 4:34.51/10:39.02, 3000m/ 10000m: Sonja Stolic 10:19.31/33:31.72, 5000m: Elvedina Zornic 18:10.99, HMar: Olivera Jevtic 75:20, Mar: Mariana Cegar 3:16:59, 100mh: Ivana Petkovic 14.38, 400mh: Jelena Grujic 62.08, HJ: Dunja Spajic 1.67, PV: Jelena Damnjanovic 3.70, LJ: Marija Milutinovic 5.89, TJ: Biljana Topic 13.36, SP: Dijana Sefcic 14.19, DT: Dragana Tomasevic 60.11, HT: Sara Savatovic 57.00, JT: Marija Vucenovic 51.49, Hep: Kristina Radivojevic 3688, 5kW: Milica Stojanovic 26:09.

Asmir KOLASINAC b. 15 Oct 1984 Skopje, Macedonia 1.86m 137kg. AC Partizan, Belgrade.
At SP: OG: '08- dnq 32, '12- 7; WCh: '09-11-13-15: dnq 21/10/10/7; EC: '10-12-14: 8/3/5; EU23: '05- dnq; EI: '13- 1, '15- 2; Won Balkan 2011; SRB 2008, 2010-15.
Progress at SP: 2004- 15.50, 2005- 17.88, 2006- 17.85, 2007- 19.30, 2008- 19.99, 2009- 20.41, 2010- 20.52i/20.38, 2011- 20.50, 2012- 20.85, 2013- 20.80, 2014- 20.79, 2015- 21.58.

Women

Ivana SPANOVIC b. 10 May 1990 Zrenjanin 1.76m 65kg. AC Vojvodina, Novi Sad.
At LJ: OG: '08- dnq 30, '12- 11; WCh: '13- 3, '15- 3; EC: '10- 8, '12- dnq 14, '14- 2; WJ: '06- 7, '08- 1; WY: '05- dnq, '07- 2; EU23: '11- 2; EJ: '07- 5, '09- 2; WUG: '09- 1; CCp: '14- 2; WI: '14- 3, '16- 2; EI: '13- 5, '15- 1. Serbian champion 2006, 2008, 2011-13, Balkan 2011, 2013.
Nine Serbian long jump records 2009-15 (five indoor 2007-16).
Progress at LJ: 2003- 5.36, 2004- 5.91, 2005- 6.43, 2006- 6.48i/6.38, 2007- 6.53i/6.41, 2008- 6.65, 2009- 6.71, 2010- 6.78, 2011- 6.71/6.74w, 2012- 6.64, 2013- 6.82, 2014- 6.92i/6.88, 2015- 7.02, 2016- 7.07i. pbs: 60m 7.31i '15, 100m 11.90 '13, 60mh 8.49i '13, HJ 1.78i '13, 1.65 '05; TJ 13.78 '14, SP 12.40i '13, Pen 4240i '13.
Won first medal for Serbia at World Champs.

SLOVAKIA

Governing body: Slovak Athletic Federation, Junácka 6, 832 80 Bratislava. Founded 1939.
National Championships first held in 1939. **2015 Champions**: **Men**: 100m/200m: Ján Volko 10.64/21.30, 400m: Denis Danac 47.55, 800m: Jozef Repcík 1:51.41, 1500m: Jozef Pelikán 3:47.54, 5000m/10000m/HMar: Jozef Urban 15:16.22/30:16.54/67:50, Mar: Juraj Vitko 2:25:01, 3000mSt: Michal Talán 9:19.09, 110mh: Marco Adrien Drozda 15.62, 400mh: Martin Kucera 52.52, HJ: Matús Bubeník 2.29, PV: Ján Zmoray 5.22, LJ: Peter Horák 6.80, TJ: Daniel Turcsányi 14.32, SP: Matús Olej 18.24, DT: Michal Holica 53.48, HT: Marcel Lomnicky 77.20, JT: Martin Benák 76.15, Dec: Stefan Sedlák 4499, 20kW/ 50kW: Matej Tóth 1:20:51/3:34:38. **Women**: 100m: Lenka Krsáková 11.67, 200m/400m: Iveta Putalová 23.71/53.41, 800m/1500m: Lucia Klocová 2:06.21/4:26.18, 5000m/10000m: Katarína Beresová 16:56.39/34:31.36, HMar: Jana Martinská 1:25:14, Mar: Silvia Sebestian 3:01:12, 3000mSt: Katarína Pokorná 11:00.60, 100mh: Lucia Mokrásová 134.18, 400mh: Michaela Pesková 58.02, HJ: Katarína Kustárová 1.73, PV: Sona Krajnáková 3.40, LJ: Jana Veldáková 6.63, TJ: Dana Veldáková 14.27, SP/ DT: Ivana Kristofícová 13.64/41.26, HT: Martina Hrasnová 68.28, JT: Miroslava Vargová 45.33, Hep: Katarina Kustarová 5124, 20kW: Mária Gálíková 1:31:42.

Marcel LOMNICKY b. 6 Jul 1987 Nitra 1.77m 106kg. TJ Stavbár Nitra. Was at Virginia Tech University, USA.
At HT: OG: '12- dnq 15; WCh: '11- dnq 21, '13- 8, '15- 8; WJ: '04- dnq 17, '06- 3; EC: '10-12-14: dnq 24/11/7; EU23: '07- 3, '09- 6; EJ: '05- 8; WUG: '11- 2, '13- 2. SVK champion 2012-15, won NCAA HT 2009, indoor Wt 2012.
Progress at HT: 2005- 64.27, 2006- 69.53, 2007- 72.17, 2008- 72.66, 2009- 71.78, 2010- 74.83, 2011- 75.84, 2012- 77.43, 2013- 78.73, 2014- 79.16, 2015- 77.63. pbs: SP 15.73 '07, DT 43.82 '08, Wt 23.05i '12.

Sister Nikola Lomnická (b. 16 Sep 1988) has hammer best 71.58 '14, won NCAA 2010 and was 8th EC 2014.

Matej TÓTH b. 10 Feb 1983 Nitra 1.85m 73kg. Dukla Banská Bystrica.
At 20kW/(50kW): OG: '04- 32, '08- 26, '12- (5); WCh: '05- 21, 07- 14, '09- 9/10, '11- 10/dnf, '13- (5), '15- (1); EC: '06- 6, '10- 6, '14- (2); EU23: '03- 6; WCp: '10- (1); ECp: '09-11-13-15: 9/1/3/2. At 10000mW: WJ: '02- 16, WY: '99- 8; EJ: '01- 6. Won SVK 20kW 2005-08, 2010-12, 2015; 50kW 2011.
Four SVK 50k walk records 2009-15.
Progress at 20kW, 50kW: 1999- 1:34:29, 2000- 1:30:28, 2001- 1:29:33, 2003- 1:13:17, 2004- 1:23:18, 2005- 1:21:38, 2006- 1:21:39, 2007- 1:25:10, 2008- 1:21:24, 2009- 1:20:53, 3:41:32; 2010- 1:22:04, 3:53:30; 2011- 1:20:16, 3:39:46; 2012- 1:20:25, 3:41:24; 2013- 1:20:14, 3:41:07; 2014- 1:19:48, 3:36:21; 2015- 1:20:21, 3:34:38. pbs: 3000mW 10:57.32i '11, 11:05.95 '12; 5000mW 18:34.56i '12, 18:54.39 '11; 10000W 39:45.03 '06, 39:07R '10; 30kW 2:12:44 '13, 35kW 2:34:23 '13.
First ever World gold medallist for Slovakia. Won IAAF Race Walking Challenge 2015.

Women

Martina HRASNOVÁ b. 21 Mar 1983 Bratislava 1.77m 88kg. née Danisová. Dukla Banská Bystrica.
At HT: OG: '08- 8, '12- dnq 19; WCh: '01-07-13-15: dnq 23/12/21/16, '09- 3; EC: '02 & '06- dnq 26, '12- 2, '14- 2; WJ: '00- 5, '02- 2; EJ: '99- 4, '01- 2; CCp: '14- 3; WUG: '07- 5, '09- 2. Won SVK SP 2003, 2006; HT 2000-01, 2006, 2008-09, 2011-15.
14 Slovakian hammer records 2001-09.
Progress at HT: 1999- 58.61, 2000- 61.62, 2001- 68.50, 2002- 68.22, 2003- 66.36, 2005- 69.24, 2006- 73.84, 2007- 69.22, 2008- 76.82, 2009- 76.90, 2011- 72.47, 2012- 73.34, 2013- 72.41, 2014- 75.27, 2015- 74.27. pbs: 60m 7.96i '12, SP 15.60i '15, 15.02 '06; DT 43.15 '06, Wt 21.74i '11.
Two-year drugs ban (nandrolone) from July 2003. Daughter Rebeka born on 4 July 2010. Brother of Branislav Danis (HT 69.20 '06).

Dana VELDÁKOVÁ b. 3 Jun 1981 Roznava 1.79m 60kg. Dukla Banská Bystrica.
At (LJ/)TJ: OG: '08- dnq, '12- 12; WCh: '05-07-09-11-13-15: dnq 17/12/8/11/11.dnq 15; EC: '02/06- dnq 15/24, '10-12-14: 7/5/6; WJ: '98- 6, '00- 4/3; EU23: '01- 5, '03- 4; EJ: '99- 8; WI: '06-10-12-14: 8/6/8/8; EI: '07-09-11: 6/3/3; WUG: '03- 5, '07- 2. Won SVK 100mh 2003, TJ 2002-05, 2007-15, Hep 2001, 2004.
Two SVK triple jump records 2007-08.
Progress at TJ: 1998- 13.12, 1999- 13.13/13.19w, 2000- 13.92, 2001- 13.73, 2002- 13.99, 2003- 14.02, 2004- 13.96A, 2005- 14.16, 2006- 14.19, 2007- 14.41, 2008- 14.51, 2009- 14.43, 2010- 14.32/14.59w, 2011- 14.48, 2012- 14.36, 2013- 14.31, 2014- 14.10i/13.91, 2015- 14.27. pbs: 60m 7.73i '06, 100m 11.99 '14, 60mh 8.82i '03, 100mh 14.38 '01, HJ 1.75 '01, LJ 6.56 '08, SP 11.56i '04, Hep 5191 '01, Pen 3746i '03.
Twin **Jana** LJ 6.72 '08, 6.88w '10; TJ 13.40 '04; 19 Slovak LJ titles.

SLOVENIA

Governing body: Atletska Zveza Slovenije, Letaliska cesta 33c, 1122 Ljubljana. Current organisation founded 1948.

2015 National Champions: Men: 100m/200m: Luka Janezic 10.50/20.88, 400m: Jernej Jeras 48.42, 800m: Zan Rudolf 1:55.29, 1500m: Jan Petrac 3:52.68, 3000m: Mitja Krevs 8:33.89, 5000m: Rok Puhar 15:11.28, 10000m: Domen Hafner 33:11.81, HMar: Robert Kotnik 70:31, Mar: Mitja Kosovelj 2:20:53, 3000mSt: Blaz Grad 9:26.31, 110mh: Gregor Kokalovic 14.85, 400mh: Peter Hribarsek 53.19, HJ: Uros Veselic 2.01, PV: Robert Renner 5.45, LJ: Urban Cehovin 7.16, TJ: Andrej Batagelj 15.39, SP: Blaz Zupancic 18.13, DT: Tadej Hribar 52.63, HT: Nejc Plesko 71.78, JT: Blaz Marn 73.14, Dec: Simon Blatnik 5215. **Women**: 100m: Maja Mihalinec 1144, 200m: Sabina Veit 23.27, 400m: Maja Pogorevc 54.92, 800m: Mateja Pokrivac 2:11.91, 1500m/3000m: Marusa Mismas 4:25.70/9:47.95, 5000m: Neja Krsinar 17:47.65, 10000m: Alenka Radej 31:13.62, HMar: Lea Einfalt 1:25:25, Mar: Neza Mravlje 2:49:33, 3000mSt: *not held*, 100mh: Joni Tomicic Prezelj 13.88, 400mh: Anita Horvat 63.97, HJMarusa Cernjul 1.73, PV: Tina Sutej 4.15, LJ: Nina Kolaric 6.06, TJ: Sasa Babsek 13.25, SP/DT: Veronika Domjan 14.40/53.41, HT: Barbara Spiler 63.25, JT: Bernarda Letnar 48.12, Hep: Stasa Trajkovic 4797.

Women

Martina RATEJ b. 2 Nov 1981 Celje 1.78m 69kg. AD Kladivar Celje.
At JT: OG: '08- dnq 37, '12- 7; WCh: '09-11-13-15: 11/7/dnq 20/dnq 23; EC: '06-10-12-14: dnq 21/7/dnq 21/6; WJ: '00- dnq 15. SLO champion 2005-14, MedG 2013, Balkan 2015.
Five SLO javelin records 2008-10.
Progress at JT: 1999- 48.74, 2000- 46.83, 2005- 50.86, 2006- 57.49, 2007- 58.49, 2008- 63.44, 2009- 63.42, 2010- 67.16, 2011- 65.89, 2012- 65.24, 2013- 62.60, 2014- 66.13, 2015- 65.75.

SOUTH AFRICA

Governing body: Athletics South Africa, PO Box 2712, Houghton 2041. Original body founded 1894.

National Championships first held in 1894 (men), 1929 (women). **2015 Champions**: **Men**: 100m: Akani Simbine 10.25, 200m: Anaso Jobodwana 20.35, 400m: Wade van Niekerk 44.91, 800m: André Olivier 1:46.02, 1500m: Johan Cronje 3:37.93, 5000m/10000m: Stephen Mokoka 13:11.44/28:15.56, HMar: Lucky Mohale 62:06, Mar: Coolboy Ngamole 2:17:26, 3000mSt: Dikotsi Lekopa 8:32.17, 110mh: Antonio Alkana

13.54, 400mh: L.J.van Zyl 49.29, HJ: Mpho Links 2.23, PV: Cheyne Rahme 5.20, LJ: Rushwal Samaai 8.38, TJ: Khotso Mokoena 16.63, SP: Orazio Cremona 20.49, DT: Victor Hogan 62.86, HT: Chris Harmse 71.98 (20th successive title), JT: Rocco van Rooyen 77.96, Dec: Gert Swanepoel 6818, 20kW: Lebogang Shange 1:23:00. **Women**: 100m: Carina Horn 11.40, 200m/400m: Justine Palframan 23.26/52.49, 800m: Caster Semenya 2:05.05, 1500m/5000m: Dinah Lebo Phalula 4:14.43/16:19.72, 10000m: Nolena Conrad 34:26.63, HMar: Lebo Phalula 71:54, Mar: Makhosazana Mhlongo 2:48:16, 3000mSt: Thembi Baloyi 10:28.33, 100mh: Claudia Heunis 13.36, 400mh: Wenda Nel 55.27, HJ: Julia du Plessis 1.80, PV: Marileze Vos 3.60, LJ: Lynique Prinsloo 6.55, TJ: Patience Ntshingila 13.32, SP: Ischke Senekal 15.51, DT: Geraldine Duvenage 53.00, HT: Charne Coetzee 52.64, JT: Sunette Viljoen 64.14, Hep: June Roelofse 4809, 20kW: Anél Oosthuizen 1:38:03.

Willem COERTZEN b. 30 Dec 1982 Nigel, Gauteng 1.86m 80kg. Shaftesbury Barnet H, GBR.
At Dec: OG: '12- 9; WCh: '09-11-13-15: 14/dnf/9/dnf; CG: '14- dnf; AfCh: '08- 2; RSA champion 2008, 2011-12, 2014.
Three African decathlon records 2009-15, five RSA records 2009-15.
Progress at Dec: 2007- 7245, 2008- 7721, 2009- 8146, 2012- 8244, 2013- 8343, 2014- 8199A, 2015- 8398. pbs: 100m 10.88 '14, 10.74w '13; 400m 48.32 '13, 1500m 4:22.22 '15, 110mh 14.06 '15, HJ 2.08 '13, PV 4.63 '12, LJ 7.58 '09, 7.64w '11; SP 14.50 '15, DT 44.84 '15, JT 69.40A '14.

Johan CRONJE b. 13 Apr 1982 Bloemfontein 1.82m 69kg.
At 1500m: OG: '04- sf; WCh: '05-09-13-15: sf/h/3/sf; CG: '14- 4; WJ: '00- 5; WY: '99- 5; AfCh: '04-06-10-12-14: 5/6/9/5/7; RSA champion 2002, 2004, 2008-09, 2012-13, 2015.
South African records 1500m (2) 2013, 1M 2014.
Progress at 1500m: 1998- 3:53.5A, 1999- 3:46.45, 2000- 3:41.21, 2001- 3:40.29, 2002- 3:37.28, 2003- 3:43.85, 2004- 3:37.83, 2005- 3:35.58, 2006- 3:36.73, 2007- 3:37.67, 2008- 3:38.37, 2009- 3:33.63, 2010- 3:35.24, 2012- 3:35.23, 2013- 3:31.93, 2014- 3:33.31, 2015- 3:36.34. pbs: 800m 1:45.64 '13, 1000m 2:18.48i '08, 2:18.56 '10; 1M 3:50.70 '14, 3000m 7:52.33i '15, 8:02.14 '04; 5000m 13:59.52 '09.
Mother Sarina had pbs 1500m 4:08.6 and 1M 4:28.4 (1980), 3000m 8:49.3 (1981), father Danie 1500m 3:44.8 (1979), 1M 4:00.5 (1980).

Cornel FREDERICKS b. 3 Mar 1990 Caledon 1.78m 70kg.
At 400mh/4x400mR: OG: '12- h; WCh: '11- 5, '13- sf; CG: '14- 1; WJ: '08- 4; WY: '07- 5; AfCh: '10- 2, '14- 1; CCp: '14- 1; WUG: '09- 4; Won RSA 2010, 2012-14; Af-J 110mh & 400mh 2009.
Progress at 400mh: 2008- 50.39, 2009- 49.92, 2010- 48.79A/48.99, 2011- 48.14, 2012- 48.91, 2013- 48.78, 2014- 48.25, 2015- 49.50. pbs: 400m 46.90 '10, 300mh 35.15 '10.

Victor HOGAN b. 25 Jul 1989 Vredenburg, Western Cape 1.98m 108kg.
At DT: WCh: '13- 5, '15- dnq 13; CG: '14-10; WJ: '08- 4; AfG: '11- 2; AfCh: '10-12-14: 3/1/1; CCp: '10- 8, '14- 4; Af-J: '07- 1; RSA champion 2010-15.
Progress at DT: 2008- 59.21, 2009- 57.67A, 2010- 58.30, 2011- 62.60, 2012- 62.76, 2013- 65.33, 2014- 64.16, 2015- 64.56.

Anaso JOBODWANA b. 30 Jul 1992 Aberdeen, Eastern Cape 1.87m 71kg. Was at Jacksonville State University, USA.
At (100m)/200m: OG: '12- 8; WCh: '13- sf/6, '15- 5/3; WUG: '13- 1/1. Won RSA 200m 2015.
South African 200m record 2015.
Progress at 100m, 200m: 2009- 21.68A, 2010- 20.95A, 2012- 10.34/10.24w, 20.27; 2013- 10.10, 20.13/20.00w; 2015- 10.13, 19.87. pb 60m 6.60Ai '15, 6.66i '13.

Godfrey Khotso MOKOENA b. 6 Mar 1985 Heidelberg, Gauteng 1.90m 73kg. Tuks AC, Pretoria.
At LJ/(TJ): OG: '04- (dnq 29), '08- 2, '12- 8; WCh: '05-07-09-11-13-15: 7/5/2/dnq 15=/7/dnq 13 & 9; CG: '06- 4/2, '14- (1); WJ: '02- 12, '04- 2/1; AfG: '03- 3/2, '07- 3; AfCh: '06- 2/2, '10- 1, '14- 2/1; CCp: '14- (2); WI: '06-08-10: 5/1/2. At HJ: WY: '01- 5. Won DL LJ 2014, RSA LJ 2005-07, 2009-11; TJ 2004-06, 2014--15.
Records: African LJ (3) 2009, RSA LJ (5) 2005-09, TJ (3) 2004-14, African junior TJ 2004.
Progress at LJ, TJ: 2001- 7.17A, 2002- 7.82A, 16.03A; 2003- 7.84A/7.83, 16.28; 2004- 8.09, 16.96A/16.77; 2005- 8.37A/8.22, 17.25; 2006- 8.39/8.45w, 16.95; 2007- 8.34A/8.28/8.32w, 16.75; 2008- 8.25/8.35w, 2009- 8.50, 2010- 8.23A/8.15/8.22w, 2011- 8.25/8.31w, 2012- 8.29A/8.24, 2013- 8.30, 15.68i; 2014- 8.19, 17.35; 2015- 8.16, 16.85. pbs: 100m 10.7A '09, HJ 2.10 '01.
Returned to triple jumping in 2014.

André OLIVIER b. 29 Dec 1989 Pietermaritzburg 1.92m 72kg.
At 800m: OG: '12- sf; CG: '14- 3; WJ: '08- 3; WI: '14- 4; AfCh: '12- 3; Af-J: '07- 4; RSA champion 2013-15. At 1500m: WY: '05- 11. At 4x400m: WUG: '11- 3.
RSA 600m best 2014.
Progress at 800m: 2004- 1:57.7A, 2005- 1:52.2A, 2006- 1:49.58A, 2007- 1:47.92, 2008- 1:46.85, 2009- 1:45.41, 2011- 1:46.84, 2012- 1:44.29, 2013- 1:44.37, 2014- 1:44.42, 2015- 1:45.73. pbs: 400m 46.81A '14, 600m 1:15.03 '14, 1000m 2:18.11 '14, 1500m 3:39.40 '09.

Wayde van NIEKERK b. 15 Jul 1992 Cape Town 1.83m 73kg. University of the Free State, Bloemfontein.
At (200m)/400m: WCh: '13- h, '15- 1; CG: '14- sf/2; AfCh: '14- 2; WJ: '10- (4); CCp: '14- 4/1R. Won RSA 200m 2011, 400m 2013-15.
Records: Commonwealth 400m 2015, African

300m & 400m (2) 2015, RSA 200m & 400m (2) 2015.
Progress at 200m, 400m: 2010- 21.02, 2011- 20.57, 2012- 20.91, 46.43; 2013- 20.84A, 45.09; 2014- 20.19, 44.38; 2015- 19.94, 43.48. pbs: 100m 9.98A '16, 10.51 '10; 300m 31.63 '15.
His 9.98A for 100m in March 2016 made hin the fifth best ever combination 100-200-400 man.

Rushwal SAMAAI b. 25 Sep 1991 Paarl 1.78m 73kg.
At LJ: WCh: '15- dnq 20; CG: '14- 3; AfCh: '14- 3; WI: '16- 5; RSA champion 2015.
Progress at LJ: 2009- 6.93A, 2010- 7.41, 2011- 7.75/7.80w, 2012- 7.94A/7.61w, 2013- 7.96A/7.74, 2014- 8.13A/8.08, 2015- 8.38. pb TJ 16.10A '14.

Louis J. van ZYL b. 20 Jul 1985 Bloemfontein 1.86m 75kg. Tuks AC, Pretoria.
At 400mh/4x400mR: OG: '08- 5, '12- h; WCh: '05-07-09-11-13-15: 6/h/sf/3&2R/h/sf; CG: '06- 1/2R, '10- 2, '14- h; AfG: '07- 1; AfCh: '06-08-10-14: 1/1&1R/1/4; WJ: '02- 1, '04- 4/2R; WY: '01- 3; WCp: '06- 2, '10- 5; RSA champion 2003, 2005-06, 2008, 2011, 2015.
Two RSA 400m hurdles records 2011. Tied world best for 200m hurdles straight 2015.
Progress at 400mh: 2001- 51.14A, 2002- 48.89, 2003- 49.22, 2004- 49.06, 2005- 48.11, 2006- 48.05, 2007- 48.24, 2008- 48.22, 2009- 47.94, 2010- 48.51A/48.63, 2011- 47.66, 2012- 49,42A, 2013- 49.11, 2014- 48.96A/48.97, 2015- 48.78. pbs: 100m 10.62 '07, 10.3Aw '03, 10.5A '01; 200m 20.71A '15, 300m 32.32 '09, 400m 44.86A '11, 46.02 '08; 200mhSt 22.10 '15, 300mh 35.76 '04.
Ran world U18 record of 48.89 to win World Junior title in 2002 after world age record at 15 in 2001. Commonwealth Games record to win 400mh gold and ran brilliant final leg in 4x400m to take RSA from fifth to second in 2006. Married Irvette van Blerk (pbs HMar 70:56 '11, Mar 2:31:26 '13) on 29 Sep 2012.

Zarck VISSER b. 15 Sep 1989 Welkom 1.78m 70kg.
At LJ: WCh: '13/15- dnq 13/19; CG: '14- 2; AfCh: '12- 2, '14- 1; CCp: '14- 3; RSA champion 2012-14.
Progress at LJ: 2007- 7.21A, 2008- 7.62A, 2009- 7.77, 2010- 7.76A/7.79Aw, 2011- 7.85, 2012- 8.15A/8.07/8.21w, 2013- 8.32, 2014- 8.31A/8.18, 2015- 8.41. pb TJ 15.66A '08.

Women

Wenda NEL b. 27 May 1988 Worcester, Western Cape 1.69m 52kg. née Theron. TUKS.
At 400mh: WCh: '11- sf, '15- 7; CG: '14- h; AfG: '11- 2; AfCh: '10-12-14:- 7/5/1; CCp: '14- 5. RSA champion 2011-2, 2014-15. At 100m/200m: WJ: '06- h/h; WY: '05: h/-.
Progress at 400mh: 2008- 60.23A, 2009- 56.45, 2010- 56.97, 2011- 56.13, 2012- 55.36A/55.79, 2013- 55.80, 2014- 54.82, 2015- 54.37. pbs: 100m 11.88A '06, 200m 24.05A '11, 400m 52.53A '14, 600: 1:28.05A 15, 100mh 14.23 '07.

Caster SEMENYA b. 7 Jan 1991 Polokwane, Limpopo Province 1.70m 64kg. Tuks AC, Pretoria. Student of sports science at University of Pretoria.
At 800m (1500m): OG: '12- 2; WCh: ' 09- 1, '11- 2; AfG: '15- 1 (8); WJ: '08- h; Afr-J: '09- 1 (1), won RSA 800m 2011-12, 2014-15; 1500m 2011, Southern Africa 800m 2009.
Two RSA 800m records 2009, 600m 2012.
Progress at 800m: 2007- 2:09.35, 2008- 2:04.23, 2009- 1:55.45, 2010- 1:58.16, 2011- 1:56.35, 2012- 1:57.23, 2013- 1:58.92, 2014- 2:02.66, 2015- 1:59.59. pbs: 400m 51.47A '16, 53.16 '11; 600m 1:25.56 '12, 1500m 4:08.01 '09, 3000m 9:49.85 '15.
Questions over her gender arose at the African Junior and World Champs in 2009, and she was barred from competing by Athletics South Africa until the IAAF determined whether she was free to compete again. They did so in July 2010 but saying that the medical details of her case remained confidential.

Sunette VILJOEN b. 6 Oct 1983 Johannesburg 1.70m 70kg. University of North West, Potchefstroom.
At JT: OG: '04/08- dnq 35/33, '12- 4; WCh: '03/09- dnq 16/18, '11-13-15: 3/6/3; CG: '06-10-14: 1/1/2; AfG: '03- 3, '07- 3; AfCh: '04-06-08-10-14: 1/2/1/1/1; WUG: '07- 5, '09- 1, '11- 1; CCp: '10- 2, '14- 2. Won Afro-Asian Games 2003, RSA 2003-04, 2006, 2009-15.
Four African javelin records 2009-12, two Commonwealth 2011-12.
Progress at JT: 1999- 43.89A, 2000- 45.50A, 2001- 50.70A, 2002- 58.33A, 2003- 61.59, 2004- 61.15A, 2005- 57.31, 2006- 60.72, 2007- 58.39, 2008- 62.24A, 2009- 65.43, 2010- 66.38, 2011- 68.38, 2012- 69.35, 2013- 64.51, 2014- 65.32, 2015- 66.62.
Son Hervé born in 2005.

SPAIN

Governing body: Real Federación Española de Atletismo (RFEA), Avda. Valladolid, 81 - 1°, 28008 Madrid, Spain. Founded 1918.
National Championships first held in 1917 (men), 1931 (women). **2015 Champions**: **Men**: 100m: Ángel David Rodríguez 10.37, 200m: Bruno Hortelano 20.85, 400m: Lucas Bua 45.98, 800m: Kevin López 1:47.56, 1500m/5000m: Adel Mechaal 3:45.09/14:10.59, 10000m: Antonio Abadía 28:19.38, HMar: Carles Castillejo 66:02, Mar: Pedro Nimo 2:15:57, 3000mSt: Sebastián Martos 8:27.30, 110mh: Yidiel Contreras 13.39, 400mh: Sergio Fernández 50.18, HJ: Miguel Ángel Sancho 2.20, PV: Igor Bychkov 5.50, LJ: Eusebio Cáceres 7.90, TJ: Pablo Torrijos 16.61, SP: Borja Vivas 20.28, DT: Frank Casañas 61.48, HT: Javier Cienfuegos 73.29, JT: Jordi Sánchez 71.75, Dec: Jorge Ureña 7853, 10000mW/20kW/35kW: Miguel Ángel López 39:15.61/1:19:52/2:32:56. **Women**: 100m:Cristina Lara 11.65, 200m: Nana Jacob 23.71, 400m: Aauri Lorena

Bokesa 52.94, 800m: Esther Guerrero 2:05.69, 1500m: Solange Andreia Pereira 4:17.21, 5000m/10000m: Lidia Rodríguez 16:18.25/ 32:41.44, HMar: Paula González 76:35, Mar: Verónica Pérez 2:34:45, 3000mSt: Irene Sánchez-Escribano 9:53.65, 100mh: Caridad Jerez 13.03, 400mh: Laura Natali Sotomayor 58.50, HJ: Ruth Beitia 1.98, PV: Naroa Agirre 4.30, LJ: María del Mar Jover 6.42, TJ: Ana Peleteiro 13.95, SP: Úrsula Ruiz 16.58, DT: Sabina Asenjo 61.36, HT: Laura Redondo 66.51, JT: Lidia Parada 59.03, Hep: Estefania Estrella Fortes 5520, 10000mW: Julia Takacs 44:00.36, 20kW: Raquel González 1:31:13.

Eusebio CÁCERES b. 10 Sep 1991 Onil, Alicante 1.76m 69kg. CD Nike Running.
At LJ: OG: '12- dnq 14; WCh: '11- dnq 19, '13- 4; EC: '10-12-14: 8/5/4; WJ: '08- '3, '10- 2; EJ: '09- 6; EU23: '11- 8, '13- 1; ET: '09- 1, '14- 3. Spanish champion 2012, 2014-15.
European junior long jump record 2010. World junior indoor heptathlon best 5984 '10.
Progress at LJ: 2002- 4.39, 2003- 4.93, 2004- 5.57/ 5.60w, 2005- 6.77, 2006- 7.36, 2007- 7.57, 2008- 7.86, 2009- 8.00/8.17w, 2010- 8.27, 2011- 8.23, 2012- 8.06/8.31w, 2013- 8.37, 2014- 8.11/8.16w, 2015- 8.16i/8.06. pbs: 60m 6.77i '12, 100m 10.43 '11, 10.34w '09; 200m 21.43 '13, 60mh 8.29i '11, 110mh 14.93w '11, HJ 1.96i '10, 1.93 '09; PV 4.60i '10, 4.30 '09; JT 53.32 '11, Hep 5667i '11, Dec 7273w '11.

Jesús Ángel GARCÍA b. 17 Oct 1969 Madrid 1.72m 64kg. CA Laietania.
At 50kW: OG: '92-96-00-04-08-12: 10/ dnf/12/5/4/17; WCh: '93-5-7-9-01-03-05-07-09-11-13-15: 1/5/2/dnf/2/6/dq/dq/3/dq/12/9; EC: '94-98-02-06-10-14: 4/dq/3/2/5/8; WCp: '93-5-7-9-02-04-06-08-10-12-14: 2/2/1/4/dq/6/6/14/5/4/ 20; ECp: '96-8-00-01-09: 1/2/1/1/2. At 20kW: WUG: '91- 5. Won Spanish 50kW 1997, 2000, 2007, 2012.
World M40 50km walk record 2010.
Progress at 50kW: 1991- 4:05:10, 1992- 3:48:24, 1993- 3:41:41, 1994- 3:41:28, 1995- 3:41:54, 1996- 3:46:59, 1997- 3:39.54, 1998- 3:43:17, 1999- 3:40:40, 2000- 3:42:51, 2001- 3:43:07, 2002- 3:44:33, 2003- 3:43:56, 2004- 3:44:42, 2005- 3:48:19, 2006- 3:42:48, 2007- 3:46:08, 2008- 3:44:08, 2009- 3:41:37, 2010- 3:47:56, 2011- 3:48:11, 2012- 3:48.15, 2013- 3:46:44, 2014- 3:45:41, 2015- 3:46:43. pbs: 5000mW 19:33.3 '01, 10000mW 40:38.86 '09, road: 5kW 20:07 '04, 10kW 40:25 '99, 20kW 1:23:00 '09, 30kW 2:08:47 '01, 35km 2:31:06 '94; running Mar 2:47:43 '09.
Competed in all major champs 1992-2015, inc. tying men's record of six Olympic Games and six European Champs and setting men's record of 12 World Champs; has 58 races under 4 hours and 43 sub 3:50 for 50km and 24 years walking sub 3:50. In 1997 he married Carmen Acedo, who won a rhythmic gymnastics world title in 1993.

Miguel Ángel LÓPEZ b. 3 Jul 1988 Murcia 1.81m 70kg. CA Llano de Brujas-Murcia.
At 20kW: OG: '12- 5; WCh: '11- 13, '13- 3, '15- 1; EC: '10- 13, '14- 1; EU23: '09- 1; WCp: '10- 12, '14- 5; ECp: '11- 5, '13- 2, '15- 1. At 10kW: WJ: '06- 14; WY: '05- 6; EJ: '05- 9, '07- 8; WCp: '06- 2J; ECp: '07- 2J. Won Spanish 10000mW 2010, 2012-15; 20kW 2010, 2012, 2015; 50kW 2016.
Progress at 20kW: 2008- 1:23:44, 2009- 1:22:23, 2010- 1:23:08, 2011- 1:21:41, 2012- 1:19:49, 2013- 1:21:21, 2014- 1:19:21, 2015- 1:19:14. pbs: 3000mW 11:39.92 '13, 5000mW 19:20.50 '13, 10000mW 38:53.42 '15, 35kW 2:32:56 '15, 50kW 3:53:52 "16..

Orlando ORTEGA b. 29 Jul 1991 La Habana, Cuba 1.85m 70kg. Club d'Atletisme de la Vall d'Albaida.
At 110mh: OG: '12- 6; WCh: '13- h; WJ: '10- h; PAm: '11- 3. Cuban champion 2011.
Progress at 110mh: 2009- 14.11, 2010- 13.99, 2011- 13.29/13.1w, 2012- 13.09, 2013- 13.08, 2014- 13.01, 2015- 12.94. pbs: 60m 6.71i '16, 100m 10.62 '11, 400m 47.84 '09, 50mh 6.66+i '12, 60mh 7.45i '15.
Left Cuba in 2013, becoming ineligible to represent the country internationally. Now living in Madrid, Spain and given Spanish citizenship on 9 Sep 2015 with eligibility to compete for them if agreed by the Cuban federation.

Women

Ruth BEITIA b. 1 Apr 1979 Santander 1.92m 71kg. Piélagos Inelecma. Graduate of physical therapy at University of Santander.
At HJ: OG: '04- dnq 16=, '08- 7=, '12- 4; WCh: '03-05-07-09-11-13-15: 11=/dnq 19=/6/5/dnq 16/3=/5; EC: '02-06-10-12-14: 11/9/6=/1/1; WJ: '96- dnq, '98- 8, EU23: '01- 1; EJ: '97- 9; WI: '01-03-06-08-10-12-14-16: 7/5=/3/4/2/6/3/2; EI: '05-07-09-11-13-15: 2/3/2/2/1/5; WCp: '02- 6=; ECp: '03-06-07-09-11-14-15: 2/2/2/2/3/3/2; Won DL 2015, IbAm 2010, Med G 2005, Spanish 2003, 2006-15 (and 15 indoors 2002-16).
Nine Spanish HJ records 1998-2007 (and eight indoors 2001-07). Equal world W35 record 2014.
Progress at HJ: 1989- 1.29, 1990- 1.39, 1991- 1.50, 1992- 1.55, 1993- 1.66, 1994- 1.74, 1995- 1.80, 1996- 1.85, 1997- 1.87i/1.86, 1998- 1.89, 1999- 1.83, 2000- 1.86i/1.85, 2001- 1.94i/1.91, 2002- 1.94, 2003- 2.00, 2004- 2.00i/1.96, 2005- 1.99i/1.97, 2006- 1.98i/1.97; 2007- 2.02, 2008- 2.01, 2009- 2.01, 2010- 2.00, 2011- 1.96i/1.95, 2012- 2.00, 2013- 1.99i/1.97, 2014- 2.01, 2015- 2.00. pbs: 200m 25.26 '02, 100mh 14.95 '97, 14.93w '00; LJ 6.04 '03, TJ 12.43/12.73w '11.
Has competed at a record nine World Indoor Champs. She is a deputy of the Parliament of Cantabria, her autonomous community. Her sister Inmaculada (b. 8 Sep 1975) had TJ pb 13.43 '00.

Beatriz PASCUAL b. 9 May 1982 Barcelona 1.63m 64kg. Valencia Terra i Mar.
At 20kW: OG: '08- 6, '12- 7; WCh: '07-09-11-13:

13/5/8/6; EC: '02-06-10-14: 12/20/4/8; EU23: '03-4; WCp: '10- 11, '12- 5; ECp: '09- 6, '13- 9. At 10kW: WJ: '00- 6; EJ: '01- 3. Won Spanish 10000mW 2008, 2010, 2012; 20kW 2006, 2008-09, 2011, 2016.
Spanish walk records 5000m (3) 2008-12, 10000m 2010.
Progress at 20kW: 2002- 1:32:38, 2003- 1:31:31, 2004- 1:30:22, 2005- 1:32:49, 2006- 1:33:55, 2007-1:30:37, 2008- 1:27:44, 2009- 1:29:54, 2010- 1:28:05, 2011- 1:28:51, 2012- 1:27:56, 2013- 1:29:00, 2014-1:29:02, 2015- 1:31:51, 2016- 1:29:27. pbs: 3000mW 13:06.48 '04, 5000mW 20:45:11 '12, 10000mW 42:40.33 '10; HMar (run) 82:43 '08.

SRI LANKA

Governing body: Athletic Association of Sri Lanka, n°33 Torrington Avenue, Colombo 7. Founded 1922.

National Champions 2015: **Men**: 100m/200m: W.K. Himasha Eashan 10.49/21.41, 400m: W.A.Dilhan Aloka 47.10, 800m: Indunil Madushan Herath 1:49.93, 1500m: R.K.S. Somawardana 3:51.27, 5000m/10000m: D.Lionel Samarajeewa 14:46.13/30:51.85, 3000mSt: R.M.S.Pushpakumara 8:57.91, 110mh: K.P.Hasitha Nirmal 14.66, 400mh: S.M.Aravinda Chathuranga 51.57, HJ: Manjula Kumara Wijesekara 2.22, PV: M.H.Ishara Sandaruwan 4.75, LJ: Janaka Prasad Wimalasiri 7.80, TJ: I.D.Sanjaya Jayasinghe 16.00, SP: Joy Danuskha Perera 14.68, DT: Gayan Upendra Jayawardana 51.65, HT: L.A.D.Elansan 44.97, JT: R.M.Sumedha Ranasinghe 76.51, Dec: W.K.D.S. Perera 6275, 20kW: T.G.S.N.Appuhami 1:41:50. **Women**: 100m: N.C.D.Priyadharshani 12.30, 200m: A.G.Thakshila Karunathilake 25.01, 400m: Chandrika Subashini Rasnayake 53.79, 800m: W.K.L.A. Nimali 2:09.73, 1500m: Eranga Rasika Dulakshi 4:22.78, 5000m/10000m: Niluka Geethani Rajasekara 16:24.12/34:50.39, 3000mSt: U.K.Nilani Rathnayake 10:09.49, 100mh: R.A.Ireshani Rajasinghe 14.86, 400mh: Eranga Rasika Dulakshi 59.37, HJ: D.K. Ranasinghe 1.68; PV: Anoma Karunawansa 3.33, LJ/TJ: H.D.Vidusha Lakshani 5.96/13.30, SP: Tharika Kumudumali Fernando 14.14, DT: Amanthi Silva 39.46, HT: Shanika A. Amarasinghe 42.22, JT: Nadeeka Lakmali 57.47, Hep: W.V.L. Sugandhi 4404, 20kW: P.B.G. Gayani 1:58:27.

SUDAN

Governing body: Sudan Athletic Association, PO Box 13274, 11 111 Khartoum. Founded 1959.

Abubaker KAKI Khamis b. 21 Jun 1989 Elmuglad 1.76m 63kg.
At 800m: OG: '08- sf, '12- 7; WCh: '07- h, '09- sf, '11- 2; WJ: '06- 6, '08- 1; WI: '08- 1, '10- 1; AfG: '07- 1. At 1500m: WY: '05- 3. At 4x400m: AfCh: '08- 2R. Won Pan Arab G 800m & 1500m 2007.
World junior records 800m & 1000m (& indoor 1000m) 2008. SUD records 800m (3), 1000m (2) 2008-10, 1500m 2011.
Progress at 800m, 1500m: 2005- 1:48.43, 3:45.06; 2006- 1:45.78, 3:47.58; 2007- 1:43.90, 3:47.92; 2008-1:42.69, 3:39.71; 2009- 1:43.09, 3:39.89; 2010-1:42.23, 2011- 1:43.13, 3:31.76; 2012- 1:43.32, 3:34.34; 2013- 1:46.57i, 2014- 1:44.09. pbs: 1000m 2:13.62 '10, 10k Rd 30:18 '07.
Ran world's fastest 800m (WJR) for five years at Oslo 2008.

SWEDEN

Governing body: Svenska Friidrottsförbundet, Heliosgatan 3, 120 30 Stockholm. Founded 1895.

National Championships first held in 1896 (men), 1928 (women). **2015 Champions**: **Men**: 100m/200m: Tom Kling-Baptiste 10.41/20.55w, 400m: Felix Francois 47.26, 800m: Andreas Almgren 1:48.06, 1500m: Kalle Berglund 3:49.93, 5000m/10000m/HMar: Abraham Adhanom ERI 14:08.44/29:43.58/64:38, Mar: Fredrik Johansson 2:23:05, 3000mSt: Daniel Lundgren 8:41.73, 110mh: Alexander Brorsson 13.91, 400mh: Joel Groth 50.79, HJ: Fredrik Löfgren 2.14, PV: David Kappelin 5.22, LJ: Michel Tornéus 8.07w, TJ: Mathias Ström 15.79, SP: Daniel Ståhl 18.58. DT: Benn Harradine AUS 63.54, HT: Elias Håkansson 71.31, JT: Kim Amb 82.40, Dec: Fredrik Samuelsson 7352, 10000mW/20000mW: Perseus Karlström 39:19.5/1:25:41.4, 50kW: Christer Svensson 4:48:50. **Women**: 100m/200m: Daniella Busk 11.62/23.63, 400m: Lisa Duffy 54.30, 800m/1500m: Anna Silvander 2:04.86/4:15.37, 5000m/3000mSt: Charlotta Fougberg 16:24.37/9:51.86, 10000m/HMar/Mar: Isabellah Andersson 34:54.59/71:56/2:34:14, 100mh: Malin Eriksson 14.13, 400mh: Elise Malmberg 57.91, HJ: Sofie Skoog 1.92, PV: Angelica Bengtsson 4.61, LJ: Khaddi Sagnia 6.78, TJ: Madeleine Nilsson 12.92, SP: Fanny Roos 16.83, DT: Sofia Larsson 58.05, HT: Tracey Andersson 68.73, JT: Anna Wessman 56.12, Hep: Lovisa Östervall 5548, 5000mW/10000mW: Monica Svensson 23:54.1/49:54.8, 20kW: Ellinor Hogrell 2:18:25.

Kim AMB b. 31 Jul 1990 Solna 1.80m 85kg. F Bålsta IK.
At JT: OG: '12- dnq 18; WCh: '13- 10, '15- 11; EC: '12- 7, '14- dnq; WJ: '08- dnq 13; EU23: '11- 4. Swedish champion 2011-13, 2015.
Progress at JT: 2007- 55.01, 2008- 69.34, 2009-66.06, 2010- 77.81, 2011- 80.09, 2012- 81.84, 2013-84.61, 2014- 84.14, 2015- 82.40. Pb PV 3.45 '06.
His father Björn had a best with the old javelin of 62.60 '79 and sister Emilia has JT best of 49.34 '12.

Daniel STÅHL b. 27 Aug 1992 2.00m 145kg. Spårvägens FK.
At (SP)/DT: WCh: '15- 5; EC: '14- dnq 24; EU23: '13- 4; WJ: '10- (dnq 27); WY: '09- dnq 16/dnq 16; EJ: '11- (dnq 20). Won SWE SP 2015, DT 2014.

Progress at DT: 2008- 40.36, 2009- 44.34, 2010- 50.32, 2011- 55.60, 2012- 62.16, 2013- 61.29, 2014- 66.89, 2015- 64.73. pbs: SP 19.17 '14, HT 45.50 '14, JT 43.78 '13.

Father Jan had pbs SP 16.80 & HT 59.14 '80, mother Gaina DT 51.90 '88, sister Annell HT 59.74 '13.

Michel TORNÉUS b. 26 May 1986 Botkyrka 1.84m 70kg. Hammarby IF.

At LJ: OG: '12- 4; WCh: '09-11-13-15: dnq 28/27/19.dnq; EC: '10-12-14: 9/3/5; EU23: '07- 10; EJ: '05- 4; WI: '14- 3; EI: '11-13-15: 7/2/1; ET: '11- 2. Won Swedish LJ 2005, 2007-10, 2012-15; TJ 2012.

Swedish long jump record 2012.

Progress at LJ: 2001- 6.48, 2002- 6.74/6.86w, 2003- 7.07, 2004- 7.41, 2005- 7.94, 2006- 7.68, 2007- 7.85, 2008- 7.86, 2009- 8.11, 2010- 8.12/8.21w, 2011- 8.19, 2012- 8.22, 2013- 8.29i/8.00/8.12w, 2014- 8.21i/8.09/8.10w, 2015- 8.30i/7.83/8.07w. pbs: 60m 6.93i '12, 100m 10.71/10.63w '11, 400mh 55.48 '04, HJ 1.99i '05, 1.92 '04; TJ 15.90 '12, Dec 6115 '04.

Father came from DR of Congo.

Women

Abeba AREGAWI Gebretsadik b. 5 Jul 1990 Adigrat, Tigray 1.69m 48kg. Hammarby IF.

At 1500m: OG: '12- 4; WCh: '13- 1, '15- 6; EC: '14- 2; WI: 14- 1; EI: '13- 1; ET: '14- 1; won DL 2012-13. At 800m: Af-J: '09- 3. Won ETH 800m 2009.

Records: Swedish 800m 2013, 1M 2015; 1500m: Ethiopian 2012, Swedish 2013, European indoor 2014.

Progress at 1500m: 2010- 4:01.96, 2011- 4:01.47i/4:10.30, 2012- 3:56.54, 2013- 3:56.60, 2014- 3:57.57, 2015- 4:01.97. pbs: 800m 1:59.20 '13, 1M 4:23.07 '15.

Lived in Stockholm from 2009; granted Swedish citizenship on 28 Jun 2012 and accepted by the IAAF to compete for Sweden from 10 Dec 2012 but from then has lived in Ethiopia and divorced from her husband and coach Henok Weldegebriel. Unbeaten at 1500m in 2013. Reported in February 2016 to have failed an out-of-competition drugs test.

Meraf BAHTA Ogbagaber b. 24 Jun 1989 Dekishahay, Eritrea 1.77m 51kg. Hälle IF.

At 5000m: EC: '14- 1; ET: '14- 1. At 3000m: CCp: '14- 2. At 1500m: WJ: '06- 5. World CC: '06- 12J, '07- 6J; Eur CC: '14-3. Won SWE 5000m 2011, 4k & 8k CC 2013-14.

Swedish 5000m record 2014.

Progress at 1500m, 5000m: 2006- 4:16.01, 2007- 4:15.12, 15:56.30; 2008- 4:12.52, 15:58.31; 2009- 4:28.93, 2010- 4:22.86, 16:28.77; 2011- 4:19.82, 16:29.08; 2012- 4:14.09, 2013- 4:05.11, 2014- 4:01.34, 14:59.49; 2015- 4:06.42i, 15:46.97. pbs: 800m 2:07.19 '08, 3000m 8:57.06 '14, 10k road 32:40 '14.

Came from Eritrea to Sweden as a refugee in 2009; received Swedish citizenship on 23 Dec 2013.

Angelica BENGTSSON b. 8 July 1993 Väckelsång 1.64m 51kg. Hässelby SK.

At PV: OG: '12- dnq 19=, WCh: '13- dnq 16, '15- 4=; EC: '12- 10, '14- 5; WJ: '10- 1, '12- 1; WY: '09- 1; EU23: '13- 3, '15- 1; EJ: '11- 1; YthOG: '10- 1; EI: '15- 3. SWE champion 2012, 2014-15.

Pole vault records: Two world youth 2010; four world junior indoors 2011, two world junior outdoor bests, six Swedish 2011-15.

Progress at PV: 2005- 3.10, 2006- 3.40, 2007- 3.90, 2008- 4.12, 2009- 4.37, 2010- 4.47, 2011- 4.63i/4.57, 2012- 4.58, 2013- 4.55, 2014- 4.62i/4.50, 2015- 4.70. pbs: LJ 5.22i '13, JT 34.67 '14.

Rising Star Awards: IAAF 2010, European Athletics 2012. Her father Glenn had JT pb 67.08 '82, sister Victoria PV 4.00 '09.

Erica JARDER b. 2 Apr 1986 Stockholm 1.73m 59 kg. Spårvägens FK. Law student.

At LJ: WCh: '13- 10, '15- 12; EC: '14- 8; EU23: '07- dnq 18; WI: '14- 8; EI: '13- 3. SWE champion 2007, 2012-14.

Progress at LJ: 2000- 5.12i, 2005- 5.52/5.59w, 2006- 6.04, 2007- 6.18, 2008- 6.26, 2009- 6.21i/6.15, 2010- 6.33, 2011- 6.42/6.43w, 2012- 6.48, 2013- 6.71i/6.66, 2014- 6.68/6.84w, 2015- 6.70. pbs: 60m 7.46i '14, 100m 11.75 '11, 200m 25.20/25.19w '07, HJ 1.78i '07, 1.76 '06; TJ 12.90 '14.

Erika KINSEY b. 10 Mar 1988 Nälden 1.85m 68kg. née Wiklund. Trångsvikens IF. Was at University of Central Missouri.

At HJ: WCh: '15- dnq 18; WJ: '06- 8; WY: '05- 5; EU23: '09- 8, EJ: '07- 1; WI: '16- 8.

Progress at HJ: 2002- 1.58, 2003- 1.65, 2004- 1.86, 2005- 1.84, 2006- 1.84, 2007- 1.85/1.87i, 2008- 1.91, 2009- 1.88, 2011- 1.84, 2013- 1.75, 2014- 1.88, 2015- 1.97. Pbs: LJ 6.28/6.46w '15, TJ 13.11 '15, Pen 3935 '09.

Lives in Warrensburg, MO, USA. Married Daniel Kinsey USA (b. 25 Jul 1986, Dec: 7563 '09) in July 2014. At age 16 improved by 21 cm in one year in 2004 to 1.86. Won EJ in 2007 but lost motivation for HJ in 2012-13 and played icehockey in Norway. Came back to athletics in 2014 and had a big breakthrough in '15, improving her seven year old pb by 6 cm to 1.97.

Khaddijatou **'Khaddi' SAGNIA** b. 20 Apr 1994 Helsingborg 1.73cm 63kg. Ullevi FK.

At LJ: WCh: '15- 7; WY: '11- 11; EU23: '15- 4. At TJ: WY: '11- 9; YthOG: '10- 1. Won SWE TJ 2011, LJ 2015.

Progress at LJ: 2007- 5.18i, 2008- 5.56, 2009- 6.03i/5.89/6.00w, 2010- 6.26, 2011- 6.32, 2014- 6.55, 2015- 6.78. Pbs: 60m 7.40i '15, 100m 12.05w '14, 200m 25.14 '14, 100mh 13.93 '15, 13.62w '14; HJ 1.78 '11, TJ 13.65/13.86w '11, JT 41.47 '14, Hep 5287 '11.

SWITZERLAND

Governing body: Schweizerischer Leichtathletikverband (SLV), Haus des Sports, Postfach 606, 3000 Bern 22. Formed 1905 as Athletischer Ausschuss des Schweizerischen Fussball-Verbandes.

National Championships first held in 1906 (men), 1934 (women). **2015 Champions**: **Men**: 100m/200m: Alex Wilson 10.18/20.58, 400m: Silvan Lutz 47.81, 800m: Hugo Santacruz 1:51.20, 1500m/5000m: Jan Hochstrasser 3:50.71/14:27.82, 10000m: Adrian Lehmann 30:24.58, HMar: Tadesse Abraham 64:42, Mar: Fabian Kuery 2:26:18, 3000mSt: Jari Piller 9:21.30, 110mh: Tobias Furer 14.10, 400mh: Kariem Hussein 48.45, HJ: Loïc Gasch 2.15, PV: Marquis Richards 5.30, LJ: Benjamin Gföhler 7.72, TJ: Andreas Graber 15.74, SP: Romain Gotteland 17.45, DT: Lukas Jost 53.79, HT: Robin Santoli 53.25, JT: Lukas Wieland 66.55, Dec: Jonas Fringeli 7541, 20kW:. **Women**: 100m/200m: Mujinga Kambundji 11.19/22.80, 400m: Pascale Gränicher 54.81, 800m: Stefanie Barmet 2:12.69, 1500m: Delia Sclabas 4:25.15, 5000m: Valérie Lehmann 16:41.26, 10000m: Leanie Schweickhardt 35:11.13, HMar: Patricia Morceli 75:30, Mar: Conny Berchtold 2:45:20, 3000mSt: Cléa Formaz 10:44.28, 100mh: Noemi Zbären 13.00, 400mh: Petra Fontanive 56.36, HJ: Salome Lang 1.80, PV: Nicole Büchler 4.71, LJ: Linda Züblin 6.27, TJ: Barbara Leuthard 13.32, SP: Jasmin Lukas 14.49, DT: Angela Peter 42.79, HT: Nicole Zihlmann 58.69, JT/Hep: Elodie Jakob 50.90/5803, 10000mW/20kW: Laura Polli 48:28.53/1:43:38.

Kariem HUSSEIN b. 1 Apr 1989 Münsterlingen 1.90m 77kg. TV Amriswil
At 400mh: WCh: '15- sf; EC: '12- sf, '14- 1; EU23: '11- sf; CCp: '14- 2; Swiss champion 2011-15.
Swiss 300mh record 2014.
Progress at 400mh: 2009- 52.33, 2010- 51.64, 2011- 51.09, 2012- 49.61, 2013- 49.78, 2014- 48.47, 2015- 48.45. pbs: 60mh 8.14i '11, 110mh 14.51 '11, 300mh 35.54 '15.
Successive pbs at end of 2014 from 49.08 to 48.96 EC, 48.70 WK, 48.47 CCp. Father Ehab came from Egypt to Switzerland in the early 1980s.

Women

Selina BÜCHEL b. 26 Jul 1991 Mosnang 1.68m 55kg. KTV Bütschwil
At 800m: WCh: '15- sf; EC: '14- sf; WJ: '10- sf; EU23: '11- 5, 13- 2; EJ: '09- 7; WI: '14- 4; EI: '15- 1. Swiss champion 2011, 2013.
Swiss 800m record 2015.
Progress at 800m: 2008- 2:11.68, 2009- 2:06.20, 2010- 2:05.95, 2011- 2:04.25, 2012- 2:04.02, 2013- 2:01.64i/2:01.66, 2014- 2:00.93i/2:01.42, 2015- 1:57.95. pbs: 400m 54.76 '15, 600m 1:25.45 '15, 1500m 4:08.95i '16, 4:18.57 '15.

Nicole BÜCHLER b. 17 Dec 1983 Biel 1.62m 55kg. LC Zürich.
At PV: OG: '08/12- dnq 22/25 WCh: '09/11/13/15- dnq 14/16/15/17=; EC: '14- dnq 17; EU23: '05- 12; WUG: '07- 3, '09- 2; WI: '12- 8, '16- 4. Swiss champion 2009, 2012-13, 2015.
11 Swiss pole vault records (and 14 indoors).
Progress at PV: 2004- 3.80, 2005- 4.15, 2006- 4.10, 2007- 4.35, 2008- 4.40, 2009- 4.50, 2010- 4.47i/4.00, 2011- 4.50, 2012- 4.60, 2013- 4.61, 2014- 4.67, 2015- 4.71, 2016- 4.80i. pbs: 60mh 8.65i '09, 100mh 14.01 '09, LJ 5.65 '07.
She competed for Switzerland at two World and four European championships at rhythmic gymnastics, taking up pole vaulting at the age of 20. Married US pole vaulter Mitch Greeley (5.56sq '08, 5.55i '09) in 2010.

Noemi ZBÄREN b. 12 Mar 1994 Langnau im Emmenthal 1.77m 65kg. SK Langnau.
At 100mh: OG: '12- h; WCh: '13- h, '15- 6; EC: '14: sf; WJ: '12- 2; WY: '11- 2; EU23: '15- 1/3R; EJ: '13- 1; Yth OG: '10- 3. Swiss champion 2013-15.
Progress at 100mh: 2011- 13.61, 2012- 13.15, 2013- 13.04, 2014- 12.92, 2015- 12.71. pbs: 60m 7.59i '13, 100m 11.50 '15, 200m 24.88i '15, 24.91 '12; 800m 2:28.39 '14, 60mh 8.11i '15, 200mh 25.79 '14, HJ 1.83i/1.78 '12, LJ 6.04 '11, SP 11.33 '12, JT 33.79 '12, Hep 5627 '14.

TADJIKISTAN

Governing body: Athletics Federation of Tadjikistan, Rudski Avenue 62, Dushanbe 734025. Founded 1932.

Dilshod NAZAROV b. 6 May 1982 Dushanbe 1.87m 115kg.
At HT: OG: '08- 11, '12- 10; WCh: '05-07-09-11-13-15: dnq 15/dnq 21/11/10/5/2; WJ: '98- dnq 15, '00- 5, AsiG: '98-02-06-10-14: 7/9/1/1/1; AsiC: '03-05-07-09-13-15: 3/2/2/1/1/1; CCp: '10- 2, '14- 4. Won Asi-J 1999, 2001, C.Asian 2003.
Progress at HT: 1998- 63.91, 1999- 63,56, 2000- 66.50, 2001- 68.08, 2002- 69.86, 2003- 75.56, 2004- 76.58, 2005- 77.63, 2006- 74.43, 2007- 78.89, 2008- 79.05, 2009- 79.28, 2010- 80.11, 2011- 80.30, 2012- 77.70, 2013- 80.71, 2014- 80.62, 2015- 79.36.
President of national federation.

TRINIDAD & TOBAGO

Governing body: National Association of Athletics Administrations of Trinidad & Tobago, PO Box 605, Port of Spain, Trinidad. Founded 1945, reformed 1971.

National Championships girst held in 1946 (men) and 1947 (women). **2015 Champions**: **Men**: 100m: Keston Bleedman 9.86, 200m: Kyle Greaux 20.42, 400m: Renny Quow 44.90, 800m: Jamaal James 1:49.36, 1500m: Nicholas Landeau 4:01.11, 5000m: Jules La Rode 16:17.15. 10000m: Jameel Cupidore 38:05.59, 3000mSt: George Smith 10:40.23, 110mh: Mikel Thomas 13.47w; 400m: Jehue Gordon 50.06, HJ: Omari Benoit 1.90, PV: Ian West 3.00, LJ: Dwaine Herbert

7.45w, TJ: Elton Walcott 16.40w, SP: Hezekiel Romeo 17.04, DT: Quincy Wilson 57.78, HT: Emmanuel Stewart 52.49, JT: Keshorn Walcott 84.84, Dec: Victor Isaac 5872. **Women**: 100m: Kelly-Ann Baptiste 10.84, 200m: Reyare Thomas 22.97w, 400m: Janeil Bellille 53.39, 800m: Alena Brooks 2:06.71, 1500m: Dawnel Collymore 4:42.64, 5000m: April Francis 20:50.43, 100mh: Deborah John 13.37w, 400mh: Josanne Lucas 56.76, HJ: Deandra Daniel 1.70, LJ: Josanne Joseph 5.76w, TJ: Ayanna Alexander 13.60, SP: Cleopatra Borel 18.46, DT: Jaleesa Williams 55.19, HT: Tamara Lewis 32.09, JT: Geraldine George 42.72, Hep: Marsha Mark 4793.

Keston BLEDMAN b. 8 Mar 1988 San Fernando 1.83m 75kg. Simplex.
At 100m/4x100mR: OG: '08- 2R, '12- sf/2R; WCh: '07- qf, '09- res(2)R, '11/13- sf, '15- h; CG: '14- sf/3R; WJ: '06- 7 (h 200m); WY: '05- 3; PAm: '07- sf, '15- 4/3R; CAG: '10- 7/1R. Won PAm-J 2007, CAC 2011, TTO 2012-13, 2015.
Progress at 100m: 2005- 10.48, 2006- 10.32, 2007- 10.14/10.05w, 2008- 10.18, 2009- 10.10/10.0, 2010- 10.01/9.93w, 2011- 9.93, 2012- 9.86/9.85w, 2013- 10.02/9.86w, 2014- 10.00, 2015- 9.86. pbs: 60m 6.62i '12, 200m 20.73 '08.

Machel CEDENIO b. 6 Sep 1995 San Fernando 1.83m 70kg. Simplex.
At 400m/4x400mR: WCh: '15- 7/2R; WJ: '12- 5/3R, '14- 1; WY: '11- 6 MedR; PAm: '15- 2/1R; WI: '16- res 3R. Won CAC-J 2014.
Progress at 400m: 2010- 48.12, 2011- 46.89, 2012- 46.02, 2013- 45.93, 2014- 45.13, 2015- 44.36. Pb 200m 21.15 '13.

Jehue GORDON b. 15 Dec 1991 Port of Spain 1.90m 80kg. adidas. Sports management student at University of West Indies, Trinidad.
At 400mh: OG: '12- 6; WCh: '09- 4, '11- sf, '13- 1, 15- h; CG: '14- 2/res 3R; WJ: '08- sf, '10- 1; PAn: '15- res 1R; PAm-J: '09- 2. TTO champion 2008-11, 2013, 2015.
Three TTO 400mh records 2009-13.
Progress at 400mh: 2008- 51.39, 2009- 48.26, 2010- 48.47, 2011- 48.66, 2012- 47.96, 2013- 47.69, 2014- 48.75, 2015- 49.22. pbs: 200m 21.26 '14, 400m 46.43 '10, 600m 1:20.65 '14, 800m 1:53.32 '10, 110mh 13.82 '12, 200mhSt 23.00 '12.

Lalonde GORDON b. 25 Nov 1988 Lowlands, Tobago 1.88m 83kg. Tigers. Studied at Mohawk Valley CC.
At 400m/4x400mR: OG: '12- 3/3R; WCh: '15- sf/2R; CG: '10- sf, '14- 3/3R; CAG: '10- 3R; WI: '12- 3R, '14- 5, '16- 6/3R. At 200m: WCh: '13- sf. Won NACAC 2015, TTO 200m 2013-14, 400m 2012.
Progress at 400m: 2009- 49.47, 2010- 46.33, 2011- 45.51, 2012- 44.52, 2013- 45.67, 2014- 44.78, 2015- 44.64A/44.70. pbs: 100m 10.45 '12, 200m 20.26 '13, 300m 32.47i '14 (CAC record), 32.5+ '12.
Moved with his family to New York at the age of seven, and still lives there.

Deon LENDORE b. 28 Oct 1992 Arima 1.79m 75kg. Was at Texas A&M University, USA.
At 400m/4x400mR: OG: '12- h/3R; WCh: '13- sf, '15- h/2R; WJ: '10- sf; WY: '09- sf; WI: '16- 3/3R. TTO champion 2013, NCAA 2014.
Progress at 400m: 2009- 47.61, 2010- 46.59, 2011- 46.50, 2012- 45.13, 2013- 44.94, 2014- 44.36, 2015- 44.41. pb 200m 20.68i '14, 21.20 '11.

Renny QUOW b. 25 Aug 1987 Morvant 1.70m 66kg. Zenith. Was at Florida State University and South Plains College (Texas).
At 400m/4x400mR: OG: '08- 7; WCh: '05-07-09-11-13-15: hR/h/3/sf/6R/sf & 2R; CG: '14- dnf/3R; WJ: '04- sf, '06- 1; PAm: '07- sf, '15- 1R; CAG: '06- sf/2R; WI: '12- 3R. Won CAC 2008, 2011; CAC-J 2004, 2006; TTO 2007-09, 2011, 2014-15.
Progress at 400m: 2004- 46.60, 2005- 45.82, 2006- 45.74, 2007- 45.35, 2008- 44.82, 2009- 44.53, 2010- 45.10, 2011- 44.84, 2012- 45.48, 2013- 45.65, 2014- 45.08, 2015- 44.54. pbs: 200m 20.39 '14, 300m 32.36 '14, 500m 1:01.90i '14, 600y 1:08.04i '14.
One of triplets with Ronald and Ryan.

Richard THOMPSON b. 7 Jun 1985 Cascade 1.87m 79kg. Memphis. Was at Louisiana State University.
At 100m: OG: '08- 2/2R, '12- 6/2R; WCh: '07- qf, '09- 5/2R, '11/13- sf; CG: '14- sf/3R; PAm: '07- h; CCp: '14- 8/1R. Won TTO 100m 2009-11, 2014; 200m 2010; NACAC 100m 2007, NCAA 100m & 60m indoor 2008.
Progress at 100m, 200m: 2004- 10.65, 2005- 10.47, 21.73; 2006- 10.27/10.26w, 21.24; 2007- 10.09/9.95w, 20.90; 2008- 9.89, 20.18; 2009- 9.93, 20.65; 2010- 10.01/9.89w, 20.37; 2011- 9.85, 20.85; 2012- 9.96, 20.80; 2013- 10.14/9.91w, 21.06; 2014- 9.82/9.74w, 20.81/20.63w; 2015- 10.04, 20.81w. pbs: 60m 6.45+ '09, 6.51i '08.

Keshorn WALCOTT b. 2 Apr 1993 Toco 1.88m 90kg. Toco tafac.
At JT: OG: '12- 1; WCh: '13/15- dnq 19/26; CG: '14- 2; WJ: '10- dnq, '12- 1; WY: '09- dnq 13; PAm: '11- 7, '15- 1; CCp: '14- 3. Won CAC-J 2010, 2012; TTO 2012, 2015.
Javelin records: CAC 2015, nine TTO 2012-15, eight CAC junior 2011-12.
Progress at JT: 2009- 60.02, 2010- 67.01, 2011- 75.77A, 2012- 84.58, 2013- 84.39, 2014- 85.77, 2015- 90.16. pb TJ 14.28 '10.
First Caribbean Olympic champion and youngest ever Olympic champion in throwing events. Won IAAF Rising Star Award 2012. Elder brother Elton TJ pb 16.43/16.51w '11 & 4 WY '09, aunt Anna Lee Walcott Hep pb 5224 '00.

Women

Michelle-Lee AHYE b. 10 Apr 1992 Port of Spain 1.68m 59kg.
At 100m/(200m): OG: '12- sf; WCh: '11- sf, '13- sf, '15- 5/3R; CG: '14- sf; WY: '07- qf; CCp: '14- 2/1R;

PAm-J: '11- 1. At 60m: WI: '14- 6, '16- 4. TTO champion 100m & 200m 2014.
Progress at 100m, 200m: 2006- 11.94, 24.60; 2007- 11.76/11.63w, 24.30/24.23w; 2008- 11.48, 23.80; 2009- 11.69, 2010- 11.32, 24.14/13.71w; 2011- 11.20/11.15w, 22.92w; 2012- 11.19, 23.13; 2013- 11.06, 22.98; 2014- 10.85, 22.77; 2015- 10.97/10.87w, 23.19i, 22.01w. pbs: 50m 6.33i '13, 60m 7.09i '16.
Unbeaten Outdoors in 2014 up to an injury in Luzern in July.

Kelly-Ann BAPTISTE b. 14 Oct 1986 Plymouth, Tobago 1.60m 54kg. Zenith. Studied psychology at Louisiana State University.
At 100m/(200m): OG: '08- qf, '12- 6; WCh: '05- qf, '09: sf/sf, '11- 3, '15- 6/3R; WJ: '02- sf, '04- (4); WY: '03- 3; PAm: '03- h, '15- 5; CCp: '10- 1/1R. Won NCAA 100m & indoor 60m 2008, TTO 100m 2005-06, 2008-10, 2012-13, 2015; 200m 2005, 2013.
TTO records: 100m (6) 2005-14, 200m (5) 2005-13.
Progress at 100m, 200m: 2002- 11.71, 24.03; 2003- 11.48, 23.22; 2004- 11.40, 23.41/22.99w; 2005- 11.17/11.04w, 22.93; 2006- 11.08, 22.73; 2007- 11.22, 22.90i/22.95; 2008- 11.06/10.97w, 22.67; 2009- 10.94/10.91w, 22.60; 2010- 10.84, 22.78/22.58w; 2011- 10.90, 2012- 10.86, 22.33w; 2013- 10.83, 22.36; 2015- 10.84, 22.91w. pbs: 55m 6.73i '06, 60m 7.13i '08.
She was withdrawn from 2013 World Champs team after failing a drugs test and was given a 2-year ban by the IAAF, but that was withdrawn by her governing body in August 2014 and after the IAAF appealed this to the CAS the suspension was lifted.

Cleopatra BOREL b. 3 Oct 1979 Port of Spain 1.68m 93kg. Was at University of Maryland; assistant coach at Virginia Tech University.
At SP: OG: '04- 9, '08- dnq 17, '12- 12; WCh: '05-07-09-13-15: dnq 17/18/13/14, '11/15- 13/12; CG: '02-06-10-14: 4/3/2/2; PAm: '03-07-11-15: 6/3/2/1; CAG: '06-10-14: 3/1/1; CCp: '14- 5; WI: '04-06-08-16: dnq 11/7/7/4. Won CAC 2008, 2011; TTO 2002, 2004, 2006-10, 2012, 2014-15.
Eight TTO records at shot 2004-11.
Progress at SP: 2000- 14.64i, 2001- 16.44, 2002- 17.50i/16.90, 2003- 17.95i/17.79, 2004- 19.48i/18.90, 2005- 18.44, 2006- 18.81, 2007- 18.91, 2008- 18.87, 2009- 18.52, 2010- 19.30, 2011- 19.42, 2012- 18.82, 2013- 17.84, 2014- 19.13, 2015- 19.26. pb HT 51.28 '01. Formerly competed under married name Borel-Brown.

TUNISIA

Governing body: Fédération Tunisienne d'Athlétisme, B.P. 264, Cité Mahrajane 1082, Tunis. Founded 1957.

Women

Habiba GHRIBI b. 9 Apr 1984 Kairouan 1.70m 57kg. Entente Franconville Cesame Va, FRA.
At 3000mSt: OG: '08- 13, '12- 1; WCh: '05-09-11-15: h/5/2/2; AfCh: '06- 2, '14- 5 (6 1500m). At 5000m: AfCh: '02- 11. Won FRA 1500m 2014
African 3000mSt record 2015, Tunisian: 1500m 2014, 3000m (3) 2008-13, 3000mSt (10) 2005-15.
Progress at 3000mSt: 2005- 9:51.49, 2006- 10:14.36, 2007- 9:50.04, 2008- 9:25.50, 2009- 9:12.52, 2011- 9:11.97, 2012- 9:08.37, 2014- 9:15.23, 2015- 9:05.36. pbs: 1500m 4:06.38 '14, 3000m 8:46.61i '15, 8:49.5+ '13; 5000m 16:12.9 '03, 10000m 35:03.83 '05, 10kRd 33:30 '04.
Missed 2010 season after toe surgery. Won first Olympic medal for a woman from Tunisia.

TURKEY

Governing body: Türkiye Atletizm Federasyonu, 19 Mayis Spor Kompleksi, Ulus-Ankara. Founded 1922.

National Champions 2015: **Men**: 100m: Yigitcan Hekimoglu 10.69, 200m: Izzet Safer 21.33, 400m: Mehmet Güzel 47.53, 800m: Levent Ates 1:50.23, 1500m: Süleyman Bekmezci 3:42.56, 5000m: Cihat Ulus 14:03.41, 10000m: Ali Kaya 27:24.09, 3000mSt: Yusuf Alici 9:02.96, 110mh: Mustafa Günes 14.29, 400mh: Yasmani Copello 51.05, HJ: Metin Dogu 2.00, PV: Mustafa Tilki 5.10, LJ: Alper Kulaksiz 7.42, TJ: Musa Tüzen 16.03, SP: Murat Gündüz 17.85, DT: Ercument Olgundeniz 56.10, HT: Mahmut Sami Duru 55.78, JT: Yalcin Kaba 59.66, Dec: Ramazan Can 6067w, 5000mW: Salih Korkmaz 21:46.98, 10kW: Sahin Senoduncu 41:08. **Women**: 100m: Nimet Karakus 12.00, 200m: Zeynep Bas 24.88, 400m: Meryem Kasap 54.61, 800m/1500m: Asli Arik 2:06.43/4:32.87, 5000m: Tugba Koyuncu 16:42.84, 10000m: Emine Hatun Tuna 33:33.41, 3000mSt: Tugba Güvenc 9:51.02, 100mh: Serpil Koçak 14.12, 400mh: Emel Sanli 59.68, HJ: Burcu Yüksel 1.86, PV: Demet Parlak 4.00, LJ: Büsra Mutay 5.86, TJ: Beyza Tilki 12.72, SP: Emel Dereli 17.85, DT: Zehra Uzunbilek 50.61, HT: Zeliha Uzunbilek 50.61, JT: Eda Tugusz 53.59, Hep: Sevim Serbest-Sinmez 4349, 5000mW: Derya Karakurt 25:23.60, 20kW: Nergis Adas 1:55:50.

Tasmani COPELLO Escobar. b. 15 Apr 1987 1.96m 86kg. Fenerbahçe.
At 400mh: WCh: '15- 6; Balkan champion 2015, Cuban NG 2010.
Four Turkish 400mh records 2015.
Progress at 400mh: 2006- 52.30, 2007- 49.99, 2008- 50.08, 2009- 49.56, 2010- 51.23, 2011- 49.76, 2012- 50.28, 2013- 49.89, 2014- 50.62, 2015- 48.46. pbs: 200m 21.44 '09, 400m 46.77 '09, 110mh 14.35A '08.
Former Cuban, has lived in Turkey from 2012, acquired citizenship 21 Oct 2013, cleared to compete for them from 30 Apr 2014.

Ramil GULIYEV b. 29 May 1990 Baku 1.87m 73kg. Baku
At (100m)/200m: OG: '08- qf; WCh: '09- 7, '15- 6; EC: '14- h/6; WJ: '06- (h), '08- 5; WY: '07- 2; EJ:

'09- 2/1; WUG: '09- 1, '15- 3/3; ET: '14- 3/2. At 60m: EI: '09- 7. Won Balkan 100m 2014, 200m 2014-15, TUR 100m 2012.
Records: European Junior 200m 2009; AZE 100m (2) 2009, 200m (4) 2007-09; TUR 100m (2) & 200m (4) 2011-15.
Progress at 200m: 2006- 21.74, 2007- 20.72, 2008- 20.66, 2009- 20.04, 2010- 20.73, 2011- 20.32, 2012- 20.53, 2013- 20.46, 2014- 20.38, 2015- 19.88. pbs: 60m 6.58i '12, 100m 10.08 '09, 300m 33.62i '09.
Switched from Azerbaijan to Turkey on 26 Apr 2011, but not eligible to compete for Turkey until 1 Mar 2014.

Ali KAYA b. 20 Apr 1994 Eldoret, Kenya. Ex Stanley Kiprotich KEN. Fenerbahçe.
At 5000m/(10000m): WCh: '15- 9/7; EC: '14- 9/3; EU23: '15- 1/1; ECp: '14- 3/2; EJ: '13- 1/1; CCp: '14- 5. At 3000m: EI: '15- 1. Eur CC: '13-1J, '14- 2, '15- 1.
Records: European U23 & Turkish 5000m & 10,000m 2015; TUR 3000m & half marathon 2015.
Progress at 5000m, 10000m: 2013- 13:31.39, 28:31.16; 2014- 13:34.83, 28:08.72; 2015- 13:00.31, 27:24.09. pbs: 3000m 7:38.42i/7:38.65 '15, HMar 61:21 '15.
Moved to Turkey in 2010 and became a Turkish citizen on 6 Jun 2013.

Ilham Tanui ÖZBILEN (formerly William Biwott Tanui KEN) b. 5 Mar 1990 Kocholwo, Keiyo, Kenya 1.77m 61kg. ENKA.
At 1500m: OG: '12- 8; WCh: '13/15- sf; EC: '12- 6, '14- h; WI: '12- 2, '14- 4; EI: '13- 2, '15- 2; ET: '13- 1 (2 800m); won WAF 2009, MedG 2013 (& 800m).
Records: World 4x1500m & world junior 1M 2009; Turkish 800m (6), 1000m, 1500m (2), 1M (2) 2011-14.
Progress at 800m, 1500m: 2008- 3:42.5A, 2009- 3:31.70, 2010- 3:33.67, 2011- 1:44.25, 3:31.37; 2012- 3:33.32, 2013- 1:44.00, 3:31.30; 2014- 1:47.38, 3:32.09; 2015- 1:46.14, 3:32.68. pbs: 1000m 2:15.08 '14, 1M 3:49.29 '09, 3000m 7:50.61i '12.
Became a Turkish citizen on 9 Jun 2011.

Kaan Kigen ÖZBILEN (Mike Kipruto **KIGEN)** b. 15 Jan 1986 Keiyo district, Kenya 1.70m 54kg.
At 5000m/(10000m): AfCh: '06- 2/2; WCp: '06- 2. World CC: '06- 5. Won Kenyan 5000m 2006.
Progress at 5000m, 10000m, Mar: 2005- 13:22.48, 2006- 12:58.58, 28:03.70; 2008- 13:09.84, 2009- 13:04.38, 2011- 13:11.65, 27:30.53; 2012- 13:21.55A, 27:03.49; 2013- 13:36.51, 2:08:24; 2014- 13:26.6, 2:06:59; 2015- 2:07:42, 2016- 2:06:10. pbs: 3000m 7:35.87 '06, 2M 8:20.09 '05, Road: 10M 45:34 '14, HMar 59:58 '11, 25k 1:14:17 '14, 30k 1:29:15 '14.
2nd Frankfurt marathon 2014, 3rd Amsterdam 2015. Acquired Turkish citizenship as Kaan Kigen Özbilen on 27 Sep 2015. 3rd Seoul Marathon 2016, but his 2:06:10 may not be eligible for European record.

UGANDA

Governing body: Uganda Athletics Federation, PO Box 22726, Kampala. Founded 1925.

Joshua Kiprui **CHEPTEGEI** b. 12 Sep 1996 1.67m 52kg.
At 10000m: WCh: '15- 9; WJ: '14- 1 (4 5000m); won Afr-J 2015. UGA champion 5000m 2014-15.
Progress at 10000m: 2013- 28:53.52A, 2014- 27:56.26, 2015- 27:27.57. pbs: 5000m 13:28.50A '15, 3000mSt 8:43.21A '13.

Stephen KIPROTICH b. 27 Feb 1989 Kapchorwa 1.72m 56kg.
At Mar: OG: '12- 1; WCh: '11- 8, '13- 1, '15- 6. At 5000m: WCh: '07- h. At 10000m: WJ: '08- 5, AfCh: '10- 6, World CC: '08- 12J, '11- 6; AfChC: '11- 2.
Ugandan marathon records 2011 & 2015.
Progress at Mar: 2011- 2:07:20, 2012- 2:07:50, 2013- 2:08:05, 2014- 2:11:37, 2015- 2:06:33, 2016- 2:07:46. Pbs: 3000m 7:48.06 '07, 5000m 13:23.70 '08, 10000m 27:58.03 '1, HMar 61:15 '13, 3000mSt 8:26.66 '10.
Won Enschede marathon on debut 2011. Became the second man ever to win Olympic and World titles at marathon. 2nd Tokyo 2015.

Moses KIPSIRO b. 2 Sep 1986 Chesimat 1.74m 59kg.
At 5000m(/10000m): OG: '08- 4, '12- 15/10; WCh: '05- h, '07- 3, '09- 4, '13- (13); CG: '06- 7, '10- 1/1, '14- 8/1; AfG: '07- 1, '11- 1; Af Ch: '06- 3/1, '10- 4/2; CCp: '10- 2 (2 3000m). At 3000m: WI: '12- 7. World CC: '03-05-08-09-10-11-13: 17J/20J/13/2/3/11/4.
Ugandan records: 3000m (4) 2005-09, 5000m 2007.
Progress at 5000m: 2005- 13:13.81, 2006- 13:01.88, 28:03.46; 2007- 12:50.72, 2008- 12:54.70, 2009- 12:59.27, 2010- 13:00.15, 27:33.37A; 2011- 13:09.17, 2012- 13:00.68, 27:04.48; 2013- 13:11.56, 27:44.53; 2014- 13:28.23, 27:56.11; 2015- 13:31.37, 30:05.01A. pbs: 1500m 3:37.6 '08, 2000m 5:00.66+ '11, 3000m 7:30.95 '09, 2M 8:08.16i '12, Road: 10M 47:01 '15, HMar 60:41 '15.
Sealed brilliant 5k/10k double at 2010 CG with last laps of 53.01 and 53.96.

UKRAINE

Governing body: Ukrainian Athletic Federation, P.O. Box 607, Kiev 01019. Founded 1991. **National Champions 2015**: **Men**: 100m/200m: Vitaliy Korzh 10.37/20.87, 400m: Vitaliy Butrym 45.77, 800m: Roman Yarko 1:51.27, 1500m/5000m: Stanislav Maslov 3:42.47/ 13:53.99, 10000m: Dmytro Lashyn 29:08.48, HMar: Roman Romanenko 66:04, Mar: Ihor Olefirenko 2:12:04, 3000mSt: Illya Sukharyev 8:35.21, 110mh: Artem Shamatryn 13.81, 400mh: Stanislav Melnikov 49.62, HJ: Dmytro Yakovenko 2.25, PV: Oleksandr Korchmid 5.45, LJ: Taras Neledva 7.70, TJ: Viktor Yastrebov

16.22w, SP: Viktor Samolyuk 18.90, DT: Mykyta Nesterenko 62.50, HT: Yevgen Vynogradov 74.45, JT: Dmytro Kosynskyy 79.00, Dec: Vasyl Ivanytskyy 7414, 20kW: Ivan Losev 1:22:37, 50kW: Andriy Hrechkovskyy 3:53:53. **Women**: 100m/200m: Nataliya Pogrebnyak 11.09/22.75, 400m: Nataliya Pyhyda 51.85, 800m: Nataliya Lupu 2:00.11, 1500m: Tamara Tverdostup 4:12.45, 5000m: Valentyna Zhudina 15:37.86, 10000m: Olha Skrypak 33:06.81, HMar: Viktoriya Poteryuk 76:45, Mar: Olha Kotovska 2:35:35, 3000mSt: Mariya Shatalova 9:42.34, 100mh: Anna Plotitsyna 13.07w, 400mh: Viktoria Tkachuk 56.35, HJ: Oksana Okunyeva 1.92, PV: Maryna Kylypko 4.00, LJ: Maryna Bekh 6.60, TJ: Tetyana Ptashkina 13.70, SP: Halyna Obleshchuk 17.46, DT: Natalya Semenova 59.82, HT: Alyona Shamotina 68.17, JT: Kateryna Derun 61.90, Hep: Inna Synytsya 5404, 20kW: Nadiya Borovska 1:33:10.

Bohdan BONDARENKO b. 30 Aug 1989 Kharkiv 1.97m 80kg.
At HJ: OG: '12- 7; WCh: '11- dnq 15=, '13- 1, '15- 2=; EC: '12- 11, '14- 1; WJ: '06- 3, '08- 1; EU23: '11- 1; EJ: '07- 9; WUG: '11- 1, CCp: '14- 1; ET: '13- 1. Won DL 2013.
Two UKR high jump records 2013-14.
Progress at HJ: 2005- 2.15, 2006- 2.26, 2007- 2.25i/2.19, 2008- 2.26, 2009- 2.27/2.15, 2010- 2.10, 2011- 2.30, 2012- 2.31, 2013- 2.41, 2014- 2.42, 2015- 2.37.
His father Viktor had decathlon pb of 7480 '87.

Ruslan DMYTRENKO b. 22 Mar 1986 Kirove, Kyiv region 1.80m 62kg. Donetsk.
At 20kW: OG: '12- 30; WCh: '09-11-13-15: 33/4/7/21; EC: '10- 11, '14- 4; WCp: '12- 3, '14- 1; EU23: '07- 6; ECp: '13- 5; WUG: '13- 2; Won IAAF Race Walking Challenge 2014; UKR champion 2009, 2011. At 10000m/10kW: EJ: '05- 11; ECp: '05- 6J.
UKR 20k walk record 2014 (and unofficial 10,000mW).
Progress at 20kW: 2006- 1:27:16, 2007- 1:23:31, 2008- 1:25:26, 2009- 1:21:21, 2010- 1:21:54, 2011- 1:21:31, 2012- 1:20:17, 2013- 1:20:38, 2014- 1:18:37, 2015- 1:21:25. pbs: 5000mW 18:21.76i '14, 10000mW 39:26.90i '12, 39:33.91 '10, 38:50R '14.

Igor HLAVAN b. 25 Sep 1990 Nazarivka, Kirovohrad 1.72m 62kg.
At (20kW)/50kW: OG: '12- 16; WCh: '13- 4, '15- 4/dq; EC: '14- 6; WCp: '12- 10, '14- (7); ECp: '13- 4, '15- (5). Won UKR 35kW 2013.
UKR 50km walk record 2013.
Progress at 20kW, 50kW: 2010- 1:30:31, 4:08:08; 2011- 1:25:58, 4:03:18; 2012- 3:48:07, 2013- 1:22:32, 3:40:39; 2014- 1:19:59, 3:45:08; 2015- 1:20:29. pbs: 5000mW 19:11.87 '14, 10000mW 39:15.1 '14, 35k 2:31:15 '13.

Oleksiy KASYANOV b. 26 Aug 1985 Stakhanov, Lugansk 1.91m 87kg. Spartak Zaporozhye.
At Dec: OG: '08- 7, '12- 7; WCh: '09-11-13-15: 4/12/dnf/9; EC: '10-12-14: dnf/2/8; EU23: '07- 4; WUG: '07- 4; ECp: '09- 3, '15- 2. UKR champion 2008. At Hep: WI: '10-12-14-16: 6/2/5/2; EI: '09- 2.
Progress at Dec: 2006- 7599, 2007- 7964, 2008- 8238, 2009- 8479, 2010- 8381, 2011- 8251, 2012- 8312, 2014- 8231, 2015- 8262. pbs: 60m 6.83i '09, 100m 10.50 '11, 200m 21.54 '15, 400m 47.46 '08, 1000m 2:39.44i '14, 1500m 4:22.27 '08, 60mh 7.85i '13, 110mh 13.92 '15, HJ 2.08i 14, 2.05 '09; PV 4.82 '09, LJ 8.04i/7.97 '10, SP 15.72 '09, DT 51.95 '10, JT 55.84 '07, Hep 6254i '10.
Won Talence decathlon 2009. Married Hanna Melnychenko (qv) on 18 Oct 2014.

Andriy PROTSENKO b. 20 May 1988 Kherson 1.94m 65kg. Khersonskaya. Biotechnology graduate.
At HJ: OG: '12- 9; WCh: '09-11-13-15: dnq 25/27/23=/17; EC: '10-12: dnq 17/13=, '14- 2; EU23: '09- 3; EJ: '07- 2; WI: '14- 3, '16- 7; EI: '15- 6; WUG: '13- 2; ET: '10- 3, '14- 1. UKR champion 2012.
Progress at HJ: 2005- 2.10, 2006- 2.18i/2.10, 2007- 2.21, 2008- 2.30, 2009- 2.25, 2010- 2.25, 2011- 2.31, 2012- 2.31, 2013- 2.32, 2014- 2.40, 2015- 2.33i/2.32.

Women

Alina FYODOROVA b. 31 Jul 1989 Kniazhychi, Kyiv region 1.75m 70kg.
At Hep: WCh: '11- 20, '15- 17; WJ: '08- 18; EU23: '11- 6; ECp: 11- 5, '15- 1; won UKR 2013. At Pen: WI: '14- 3, '16- 3; EI: '13- 8, '15- 7.
Progress at Hep: 2006- 5193, 2007- 5437, 2008- 5475, 2009- 5742, 2010- 5760, 2011- 6008, 2012- 6126, 2013- 5792, 2014- 6090, 2015- 6278. pbs: 200m 24.70 '15, 800m 2:14.77 '15, 60mh 8.27i '16, 100mh 13.80 '15, HJ 1.90i '13, 1.85 '16; LJ 6.35i '15, 6.33 '12; SP 15.97i '16, 15.01 '15; JT 40.60 '11, Pen 4770i '16.

Hanna KASYANOVA b. 24 Apr 1983 Tbilisi, Georgia 1.78m 67kg. née Melnychenko.
At Hep: OG: '08- 14, '12- 9; WCh: '07- dnf, '09- 6, '13- 1; EC: '06- 16, '10- dnf; EU23: '05- 13; WUG: '07- 3; ECp: '07-08-09-10-13: 3/1/1/1/2. UKR champion 2003, 2012. At Pen: WI: '14- 7; EI: '13- 3.
Progress at Hep: 2001- 4907, 2002- 5083, 2003- 5523, 2004- 5720, 2005- 5809, 2006- 6055w, 2007- 6143, 2008- 6306/6349u, 2009- 6445, 2010- 6098, 2012- 6407, 2013- 6586, 2014- 5937, 2015- 6277. pbs: 200m 23.85 '13, 800m 2:09.85 '13, 60mh 8.18i '14, 100mh 13.26 '13, HJ 1.86 '07, LJ 6.74 '12, TJ 13.21/13.40w '03, SP 14.19i '14, 14.09 '13, JT 45.11 '09, Pen 4748i '12.
Won IAAF Combined Events Challenge 2013. Formerly married to William Frullani ITA (Dec 7984 '02, Hep 5972 rec 6th EI '09), married Oleksiy Kasyanov (qv) on 18 Oct 2014.

Anastasiya MOKHNYUK b. 1 Jan 1991 1.75m 67kg. Kyivskiya.
At Hep: WCh: '15- 7; EC: '14- 14; EU23: '13- 3; WJ: '10- 11. At Pen: WI: '16- 2. At LJ: EI: '13- 8.

Won UKR LJ 2013.
Progress at Hep: 2009- 4970, 2010- 5496, 2011- 5497, 2012- 5830, 2013- 5941, 2014- 6220, 2015- 6359. pbs: 200m 24.30 '15, 800m 2:15.52 '14, 60mh 8.11i '16, 100mh 13.00 '15, HJ 1.85i '16, 1.83 '15; LJ 6.66i '16, 6.57 '13; SP 15.01i '16, 14.96 '15; JT 39.76 '15, Pen 4745i '16.

Oksana OKUNEVA b. 14 Mar 1990 Mykolaiv 1.75m 61kg. Mykolaivska.
At HJ: WCh: '11-13-15: dnq 19/15/14=; EC: '14- 6; WY: '07- 6; EU23: '11- 2; EJ: '09- 6; EI: '11- 7; ET: '14- 2. UKR champion 2011, 2013-14.
Progress at HJ: 2005- 1.60, 2006- 1.75, 2007- 1.78, 2008- 1.80, 2009- 1.90, 2010- 1.92, 2011- 1.94, 2012- 1.93i/1.87, 2013- 1.92, 2014- 1.98, 2015- 1.92.

Lyudmyla OLYANOVSKA b. 20 Feb 1993 Solobkivtsi, Khmelnitskya 1.72m 57kg. Khmelnitskya.
At 20kW: WCh: '13- 12, '15- 3; EC: '14- 2; WCp: '14- 7; EU23: '13- 2, '15- 3; ECp: '13- 7, '15- 7. At 10000m/10kW: WJ: '12- 4; EJ: '11- 7; WCp: '12- 5J.
Two UKR 20k road walk records 2014-15 (and unofficial 5000m & 10,000m (2)).
Progress at 20kW: 2013- 1:30:26, 2014- 1:27:27, 2015- 1:27:09. pbs: 3000mW 12:38.43i '13, 5000mW 20:15.71 '14, 10000mW 41:42.5 '14.

Anna RYZHYKOVA b. 24 Nov 1989 Dnipropetrovsk 1.76m 67kg. née Yaroshchuk.
At 400mh/4x400mR: OG: '12- sf; WCh: '11- sf, '13- 6, '15- sf; EC: '10- sf, '12- 3, '14- h/2R; WJ: '08- 6/2R; EU23: '09- 8, '11- 1/2R; WUG: '11- 1, '13- 2; ET: '13- 2, '14- 1. UKR champion 2009, 2015. At 200m: EJ: '07- h/2 4x100m.
Progress at 400mh: 2006- 57.52, 2007- 56.46, 2008- 56.09, 2009- 57.23, 2010- 55.60, 2011- 54.77, 2012- 54.35, 2013- 54.77, 2014- 55.00, 2015- 55.16. pbs: 60m 7.74i '06, 200m 23.49 '10, 400m 52.11 '14, LJ 6.05 '13.

Olga SALADUKHA b. 4 Jun 1983 Donetsk 1.75m 55kg.
At TJ: OG: '08- 9, '12- 3; WCh: '07-11-13-15: 7/1/3/6; EC: '06-10-12-14: 4/1/1/1; WJ: '02- 5; EU23: '05- 4; EJ: '01- 9; WI: '08- 6, '14- 2; EI: '13- 1; WUG: '05- 2, '07- 1; WCp: '06-10-14: 6/2/3; ECp: '06-08-10-11-13-14: 1/1/1/1/1/2. Won DL 2011, UKR 2007-08.
Progress at TJ: 1998- 13.32, 1999- 12.86, 2000- 13.26, 2001- 13.48, 2002- 13.66i/13.63, 2003- 13.26i/13.03, 2004- 13.22, 2005- 14.04, 2006- 14.41/14.50w, 2007- 14.79, 2008- 14.84, 2010- 14.81, 2011- 14.98/15.06w, 2012- 14.99, 2013- 14.88i/14.85, 2014- 14.73, 2015- 14.62. pb LJ 6.37 '06.
Married to professional road cyclist Denys Kostyuk with a daughter Diana.

Hanna TITIMETS b. 5 Mar 1989 Pavlograd, Dnipropetrovsk 1.73m 62kg. Dnipropetrovsk.
At 400mh: OG: '12- sf; WCh: '09- h, '11- sf, '13- 4; EC: '10/12- sf, '14- 2; WJ: '08- 4; EU23: '09- 4, '11- 2; EJ: '07- 8 (2 4x100m); CCp: '14- 4; ET: '15- 2; WUG: '11- 1 4x100m, '13- 1. UKR champion 2010, 2012-14.
Progress at 400mh: 2006- 59.79, 2007- 58.35, 2008- 57.22, 2009- 55.95, 2010- 55.58, 2011- 54.69, 2012- 54.98, 2013- 54.63, 2014- 54.56, 2015- 54.75. pbs: 60m 7.46i '11, 200m 23.60 '09, 400m 52.73 '11, 60mh 8.50i '13.

UNITED KINGDOM

Governing body: British Athletics, Alexander Stadium, Walsall, Perry Barr, Birmingham B42 2BE. Founded 1999 (replacing British Athletics, founded 1991, which succeeded BAAB, founded 1932). The Amateur Athletic Association was founded in 1880 and the Women's Amateur Athletic Association in 1922.
National Championships (first were English Championships 1866-79, then AAA 1880-2006, WAAA from 1922). **2015 UK Champions**: **Men**: 100m: Chijindu Ujah 10.10, 200m: Zharnel Hughes 20.42, 400m: Rabah Yousif 45.01, 800m: Kyle Langford 1:49.70, 1500m: Charlie Grice 3:50.66, 5000m: Tom Farrell 13:42.20, 10000m: Jonathan Mellor 28:46.80, HMar: Ryan McLeod 74:17, Mar: Scott Overll 2:13:13, 3000mSt: Rob Mullett 8:38.95, 110mh: Lawrence Clarke 13.55, 400mh: Niall Flannery 50.16, HJ: Robbie Grabarz 2.28, PV: Steven Lewis 5.35, LJ: Greg Rutherford 8.11, TJ: Julian Reid 16.95, SP: Scott Lincoln 18.54, DT: Brett Morse, 58.83, HT: Nick Miller 75.88, JT: Bonne Buwembo 70.34, Dec: Jack Andrew 6932, 5000mW/Tom Bosworth 19:00.73/1:28:16, 50kW: Adrian Edwards 5:39:26.
Women: 100m: Dina Asher-Smith 11.08, 200m: Margaret Adeoye 23.51, 400m: Anyika Onuora 51.87, 800m: Lynsey Sharp 2:02.40, 1500m: Laura Muir 4:10.37, 5000m: Stephanie Twell 15:38.01, 10000m: Rhona Auckland 32:28.32, HMar: Jessica Coulson 71:34, Mar: Sonia Samuels 2:31:46, 3000mSt: Lennie Waite 10:15.04, 100mh: Tiffany Porter 12.83, 400mh: Eilidh Child 55.58, HJ: Isobel Pooley 1.97, PV: Holly Bradshaw 4.50, LJ: Shara Proctor 6.86, TJ: Sineade Gutzmore 13.35, SP: Rachel Wallader 17.42, DT: Jade Lally 57.37, HT: Sophie Hitchon 71.10, JT: Izzy Jeffs 53.50, Hep: Elise Lovell 5197, 5000mW: Johanna Atkinson 22:03.55, 20kW: Heather Lewis 1:43:36.

Lawrence CLARKE b. 13 Jan 1990 London 1.86m 75kg. Windsor, Slough, Eton & Hounslow. Graduate of Bristol University.
At 110mh: OG: '12- 4; WCh: '11- h; EC: '14- dns; CG: '10- 3, '14- 8; E23: '11- 3; EJ: '09- 1; ET: '15- 3. UK champion 2011, 2015. At 60mh: EI: '15- 5.
Progress at 110mh: 2008- 15.3, 2009- 13.91/13.82w, 2010- 13.69/13.51w, 2011- 13.58, 2012- 13.31/13.14w, 2013- 13.81, 2014- 13.41, 2015- 13.39. Pbs: 100m 10.64 '12, 60mh 7.59i '15.

Mohamed FARAH b. 23 March 1983 Mogadishu, Somalia 1.71m 65kg. Newham & Essex Beagles.
At 5000m (/10000m): OG: '08- h, '12- 1/1; WCh:

'07- 6, '09- 7, '11- 1/2, '13- 1/1, '15- 1/1; EC: '06- 2, '10- 1/1, '12- 1, '14- 1/1; CG: '06- 9; WJ: '00- 10; EJ: '01- 1; EU23: '03 & '05- 2; ECp: '08-09-10-13: 1/1/1 &(1)/1. At 3000m: WY: '99- 6; WI: '08- 6, '12- 4; EI: '05-07-09-11: 6/5/1/1; ECp: '05-06: 2/2. World CC: '07- 11, '10- 20; HMar: '16- 3; Eur CC: '99-00-01-04-05-06-08-09: 5J/7J/2J/15/21/1/2/2. Won UK 5000m 2007, 2011; Mar 2014.

Records: World indoor 2M 2015, European 10000m & indoor 5000m 2011, 1500m 2013; indoor 2M 2012, 20k and half marathon 2015, 15k 2016; UK 2M 2014, 5000m 2010 & 2011, half marathon (3) 2011-15.

Progress at 1500m, 5000m, 10000m: 1996- 4:43.9, 1997- 4:06.41, 1998- 3:57.67, 1999- 3:55.78, 2000- 3:49.60, 14:05.72; 2001- 3:46.1, 13:56.31; 2002- 3:47.78, 14:00.5; 2003-3:43.17, 13:38.41; 2004- 3:43.4, c.14:25; 2005- 3:38.62, 13:30.53; 2006- 3:38.02, 13:09.40; 2007- 3:45.2i+, 3:46.50, 13:07.00; 2008- 3:39.66, 13:08.11, 27:44.54; 2009- 3:33.98, 13:09.14; 2010- 12:57.94, 27:28.86; 2011- 12:53.11, 26:46.57; 2012- 3:34.66, 12:56.98, 27:30.42; 2013- 3:28.81, 13:05.88, 27:21.71; 2014- 13:23.42, 28:08.11; 2015- 3:28.93, 13:11.77, 26:50.97. pbs: 800m 1:48.69 '03, 1M 3:56.49 '05, 2000m 5:02.9i '15, 5:06.34 '06; 3000m 7:34.47i '09, 7:34.66 '15; 2M 8:03.40i '15, 8:07.85 '14. 2000mSt 5:55.72 '00; road 15k 42:04+ '16, 10M 45:32+ '15, 20k 56:27 '15. HMar 59:22dh/59:32 '15, Mar 2:08:21 '14.

Joined his father in England in 1993. Sixth man ever to win Olympic 5000m/10,000m double at same Games; first British athlete to win either title. In 2013 became third man to win World 5000m/10000m double and he repeated that in 2015; now has record six global distance running titles. Won in New York on half marathon debut 2011 and won Great North Run 2014-15.

Adam GEMILI b. 6 Oct 1993 London 1.78m 73kg. Blackheath & Bromley.

At 100m/(200m)/4x100mR: OG: '12- sf; WCh: '13- (5); EC: (1)/1R; CG: '14- 2; WJ: '12- 1; EU23: '13- 1/4/1R; EJ: '11- 2/2R; ET: '13- 1R.

Progress at 100m, 200m: 2009- 11.2, 2010- 10.80/10.72w, 21.87w; 2011- 10.35/10.23w, 20.98; 2012- 10.05, 20.38; 2013- 10.06, 19.98; 2014- 10.04, 19.98; 2015- 9.97. Pb 60m 6.59i '16.

Sixth equal all-time junior list 10.05 to win World Junior 100m in 2012, improved 200m best from 20.30 to 20.17 and 19.98 at 2013 Worlds before 5th in final in 20.08. As a footballer he was a member of the youth academy at Chelsea before playing for Dagenham & Redbridge and then making a huge impact as a sprinter from 2011. Won European Athletics Rising Star award 2014.

Robbie GRABARZ b. 3 Oct 1987 Enfield 1.92m 87kg. Newham & Essex Beagles.

At HJ: OG: '12- 3=; WCh: '13- 8; EC: '12- 1; WJ: '06- 12; EU23: '09- 11; WI: '12- 6=, '16- 2; EI: '13- 6; won DL 2012, UK 2012-13, 2015.

UK high jump record 2012.

Progress at HJ: 2002- 1.75, 2004- 2.00, 2005- 2.22, 2006- 2.20i/2.14, 2007- 2.21, 2008- 2.27, 2009- 2.23i/2.22, 2010- 2.28, 2011- 2.28, 2012- 2.37, 2013- 2.31, 2014- 2.27i, 2015- 2.28, 2016- 2.33i. pb TJ 14.40 '09.

David 'Dai' GREENE b. 11 Apr 1986 Llanelli 1.83m 75kg. Swansea Harriers.

At 400mh: OG: '12- 4; WCh: '09- 7 (res (2)R), '11- 1, '13- sf; EC: '06- h, '10- 1; CG: '10- 1, '14- h; EU23: '07- 1; EJ: '05- 2; CCp: '10- 1; ET: '09-10-11-13: 1/1/1/2. Won DL 2011, UK 2009-10, 2012-13; won DL 2011.

Progress at 400mh: 2003- 55.0/55.06, 2004- 53.42, 2005- 51.14, 2006- 49.91, 2007- 49.58, 2008- 49.53, 2009- 48.27, 2010- 47.88, 2011- 48.20, 2012- 47.84, 2013- 48.66, 2014- 49.89, 2015- 49.85. pbs: 100m 11.1 '06, 200m 22.1 '05, 21.73w '08; 400m 45.82 '11, 600m 1:16.22i '13.

Matthew HUDSON-SMITH b. 26 Oct 1994 Wolverhampton 1.96m. Birchfield H.

At 400m/4x400mR: EC: 2014- 2/1R; CG: '14- 1R. At 200m: EJ: '13- 3/3R.

Progress at 400m: 2009- 52.09, 2011- 50.61, 2013- 48.76i, 2014- 44.75, 2015- 45.09. pbs: 60m 6.96i '12, 100m 10.9 '13, 10.8w '12; 200m 20.88 '13.

Zharnell HUGHES b. 13 Jul 1995 Sandy Ground, Anguilla 1.90m 79kg. Racers TC, Jamaica.

At (100m)/200m: WCh: '15- 5; WJ: '12- sf/h, '14- 5. Won CAC-J 2014, UK 2015, PAm-J 100m 2013.

Records: Anguilla: 100m (4), 200m (6) 2012-14.

Progress at 200m: 2012- 20.90, 2013- 20.79/20.77w, 2014- 20.32, 2015- 20.02. pbs: 100m 10.12 '14, 400m 46.95 '16.

Switched from Anguilla and cleared to compete for Britain from 19 June 2015.

Richard KILTY b. 2 Sep 1989 Middlesbrough 1.84m 80kg. Gateshead H.

At 200m/4x100mR: EC: '14- 1R; CG: '14- sf/2R; EU23: '09- 7, '11- 2R; WJ: '08- sf; CCp: '14- 2R. At 100m: WCh: '13- hR, '15- sf; ET: '15- 2/1R. At 60m: WI: '14- 1; EI: 15- 1.

Progress at 100m, 200m: 2004- 11.43/11.3w, 2005- 10.96/10.90w, 22.60; 2006- 10.76/10.75w, 21.96; 2007- 10.61, 21.37; 2008- 10.60/10.5/10.51w, 21.19; 2009- 10.43, 20.80; 2010- 10.44, 21.41i; 2011- 10.32, 20.53; 2012- 10.23/10.15w, 20.50; 2013- 10.10, 20.34; 2014- 10.12, 20.73; 2015- 10.05, 20.54. pbs: 60m 6.49i '14, 400m 48.58 '13.

Nick MILLER b. 1 May 1993 Carlisle 1.88m 112kg. Border H, Oklahoma State University, USA.

At HT: WCh: '15: 11; CG: '14- 2; WJ: '12- dnq 25; EU23: '13- 9, '15- 1; ET: '15- 2. UK champion 2014-15.

UK hammer record 2015.

Progress at HT: 2010- 49.86, 2011- 57.74, 2012- 67.56, 2013- 71.60, 2014- 74.38, 2015- 77.55. Pbs: DT 45.37 '13, Wt 22.46i '15.

Martyn ROONEY b. 3 Apr 1987 Croydon 1.98m 78kg. Croydon H. Was at Loughborough University.
At 400m/4x400mR: OG: '08- 6, '12- sf; WCh: '07- h, '09- sf/2R, '11- sf, '13- 4R, '15- sf/3R; EC: '10- 3/2R, '14- 1/1R; CG: '06- 5, '14- 4; WJ: '06- 3/3R; EJ: '05- 2/1R; CCp: '10- 2R,'14- 7/2R; ECp: '07-08-10: 3/1&2R/1. Won UK 2008, 2010-12, 2014.
Progress at 400m: 2003- 49.4, 2004- 47.46, 2005- 46.44, 2006- 45.35, 2007- 45.47, 2008- 44.60, 2009- 45.35, 2010- 44.99, 2011- 45.30, 2012- 44.92, 2013- 45.05, 2014- 44.71, 2015- 44.45. pbs: 60m 7.12i '09, 200m 21.08 '13, 20.87w '11; 600m 1:16.9 '05, 800m 1:50.55 '05.
Ran anchor leg in 43.73 on 4x400m at 2008 Olympics. Married Kate Dennison (six UK PV records to 4.60 '09, 3= CG 2010) on 19 Sep 2014.

Greg RUTHERFORD b. 17 Nov 1986 Milton Keynes 1.88m 84kg. Marshall Milton Keynes.
At LJ: OG: '08- 10, '12- 1; WCh: '09- 5, '15- 1, '07-11-13- dnq 21/15=/14; EC: '06- 2, '14- 1; CG: '06-10-14: 8/2/1; EJ: '05- 1; EI: '09- 6; ET: '13- 3, '14- 2. Won DL 2015, AAA 2005-06, UK 2008, 2012, 2015.
Three UK Long jump records 2009-14.
Progress at LJ: 1999- 5.04, 2001- 6.16, 2003- 7.04, 2004- 7.28, 2005- 8.14, 2006- 8.26, 2007- 7.96, 2008- 8.20, 2009- 8.30, 2010- 8.22, 2011- 8.27/8.32w, 2012- 8.35, 2013- 8.22, 2014- 8.51, 2015- 8.41. pbs: 60m 6.68i '09, 100m 10.26 '10.
European Athlete of the Year 2015. Great-grandfather Jock Rutherford played 11 internationals for England at football 1904-08.

William SHARMAN b. 12 Sep 1984 Lagos, Nigeria 1.88m 82kg. Belgrave Harriers. Economics graduate of University of Leicester.
At 110mh: WCh: '09- 4, '11- 5=, '13- 5; EC: '06-10-12-14: h/sf/sf/2; CG: '10- 2, '14- 2; EU23: '05- 4; EJ: '03- 5; CCp: '14- 3; ET: '14- 2. Won UK 2010, 2013-14. At 60mh: WI: '14- 7.
Progress at 110mh: 2003- 14.31, 2004- 13.94/13.86w, 2005- 13.88/13.72w, 2006- 13.49/13.45w, 2007- 13.68, 2008- 13.67/13.6/13.59w, 2009- 13.30, 2010- 13.39/13.35w/12.9w, 2011- 13.47, 2012- 13.50, 2013- 13.26, 2014- 13.16, 2015- 13.53. pbs: 60m 6.89i '07, 100m 10.86 '05, 10.66w '13; 200m 21.59 '06, 400m 48.53 '05, 1500m 4:45.25 '05, 60mh 7.53i '14, HJ 2.08 '05, PV 4.00 '05, LJ 7.14 '04, 7.15w '05; SP 12.99 '05, DT 33.99 '03, JT 43.45 '05, Dec 7384 '05, Hep 5278i '05.
National junior decathlon champion 2003. Improved pb from 13.44 to 13.38 and 13.30 at 2009 Worlds.

Chijindu UJAH b. 5 Mar 1994 Enfield 1.80m 75kg. Enfield & Haringey..
At 100m: WCh: '15- sf; WJ: '12- 6; WY: '11- 8; EJ: '13- 1; UK champion 2015.
Progress at 2009- 11.61, 2010- 10.83, 2011- 10.58/10.49w, 2012- 10.26, 2013- 10.32, 2014- 9.96, 2015- 9.96. pbs: 60m 6.53i '15, 200m 20.47 '15.

Rabah YOUSIF Bkheit b. 11 Dec 1986 Khartoum, Sudan 1.83m 73kg. Newham & Essex Beagles.
At 400m/4x400mR: OG: '12- sf; WCh: '09- sf, '11- sf, '15- 6/3R; EC: '14- res 1R; AfG: '11- 1; AfCh: '08- sf/2R, '10- 2/4R; CCp: '10- 5/3R; Won UK 2015, Arab 2009, 2011.
Progress at 400m: 2004- 46.36, 2005- 46.33, 2006- 46.89, 2007- 45.72, 2008- 47,13, 2009- 45.15, 2010- 45.18A/45.38, 2011- 45.13, 2012- 45.13, 2013- 46.06, 2014- 45.41, 2015- 44.54. pbs: 60m 6.88i '07, 100m 10.79 '07, 200m 21.06 '12, 20.85w '07; 300m 32.31 '14, HJ 2.05i '04, LJ 7.61 '07.
Came to Britain in 2002, granted British nationality 23 Jan 2013, eligible to compete from 13 Jun 2013, previously Sudan.

Women

Dina ASHER-SMITH b. 4 Dec 1995 Farnborough 1.65m 55kg. Blackheath & Bromley. Student at King's College, London.
At 200m/4x100mR (100m): WCh: '13- 3R, '15- 5; EC: '14- dnf; WJ: '12- 7, '14- (1); EJ: '13- 1/1R. At 60m: WI: '16- dns; EI: '15- 2. Won UK 100m 2015.
UK records 100m (2) & 200m 2015.
Progress at 100m, 200m: 2009- 12.10, 24.83; 2010- 12.00/24.50; 2011- 11.96, 24.16/24.11w; 2012- 11.54, 23.49; 2013- 11.38/11.30w, 23.14; 2014- 11.14/11.93w, 22.61; 2015- 10.99, 22.07. pbs: 60m 7.08i '15, 150mSt 16.82 '15, 400m 53.49 '14.

Kate AVERY b. 1 Jul 1991 Bishop Auckland 1.75m 50kg. Shiledon R & Gateshead. Was at Iona College, USA.
At 10000m: CG: '14- 4. At 5000m: WJ: '10- 11. At 3000m: EJ: '09- 2. Eur CC: '09-10-13-14-15: 3J/12J/4 U23/2/2. Won NCAA CC 2014.
Progress at 10000m: 2013- 33:27.44, 2014- 32:33.35, 2015- 31:41.44. pbs: 800m 2:12.27mx/2:12.7 '09, 1500m 4:15.97 '12, 1M 4:38.16i '14, 3000m 8:53.12i '15, 8:56.24 14; 5000m 15:25.63 '14.

Holly BRADSHAW b. 2 Nov 1991 Preston 1.75m 68kg. née Bleasdale. Blackburn Harriers.
At PV: OG: '12- 6=; WCh: '11- dnq, '15- 7; WI: '12- 3, '14- 9; WJ: '10- 3; EU23: '11- 1; EI: '13- 1. UK champion 2011-12, 2015.
Three UK pole vault records 2011-12, five indoors 2011-12.
Progress at PV: 2007- 2.30, 2008- 3.10i, 2009- 4.05, 2010- 4.35, 2011- 4.71i/4.70, 2012- 4.87i/4.71, 2013- 4.77i/4.60, 2014- 4.73i, 2015- 4.70. pbs: SP 11.32 '11, JT 37.60 '11.
World age-19 best 2011, age-20 best 2012. Married 800m runner Paul Bradshaw (1:47.37 '09) on 25 Oct 2014.

Eilidh CHILD/DOYLE b. 20 Feb 1987 Perth 1.72m 59kg. Pitreavie. PE degree from Edinburgh University.
At 400mh/4x400mR: OG: '12- sf; WCh: '09/11-sf, '13- 5/3R; EC: '10- 8, '12- 4R, '14- 1/3R; CG: '10- 2; EU23: '07- 5, '09- 2; CCp: '14- 2; ET: '09-10-13-14: 3R/2/1&1R/2; UK champion 2014-15. At

400m: WI: '14- 3R; EI: '13- 2/1R.
Progress at 400mh: 2003- 59.8mx, 2004- 59.53, 2005- 59.78, 2006- 59.7/60.05, 2007- 57.11, 2008- 56.84, 2009- 55.32, 2010- 55.16, 2011- 55.67, 2012- 54.96, 2013- 54.22, 2014- 54.39, 2015- 54.46. pbs: 200m 24.51i '13, 24.56 '08; 300m 37.1i '13, 400m 51.45i/51.83 '13, 800m 2:24.2 '04, 60mh 8.89i '06, 100mh 14.51 '04, 14.38w '07, 200mhSt 25.84 '14.
Married Brian Doyle (400m 47.12 '06) in October 2015.

Jessica ENNIS-HILL b. 28 Jan 1986 Sheffield 1.64m 57kg. Sheffield. Studied psychology at University of Sheffield.
At Hep: OG: '12- 1; WCh: '07-09-11-15: 4/1/2/1; EC: '06- 8, '10- 1; CG: '06- 3; WJ: '04- 8; WY: '03- 5; EJ: '05- 1; WUG: '05- 3; ECp: '07- 1. At Pen: WI: '10- 1, '12- 2; EI: '07- 6. At 100mh: EU23: '07- 3. Won UK 100mh 2007, 2009, 2012; HJ 2007, 2009, 2011-12.
Records: Commonwealth heptathlon (2) 2012, indoor pentathlon 2010 & 2012, UK high jump 2007, 100mh 2012, indoor 60mh 2010.
Progress at Hep: 2001- 4801, 2002- 5194, 2003- 5116, 2004- 5542, 2005- 5910, 2006- 6287, 2007- 6469, 2009- 6731, 2010- 6823, 2011- 6790, 2012- 6955, 2015- 6669. pbs: 60m 7.36i '10, 100m 11.39+ '10, 150mStr 16.99 '10, 200m 22.83 '12, 800m 2:07.81 '11, 60mh 7.87i '12, 100mh 12.54 '12, HJ 1.95 '07, LJ 6.51 '10, 6.54w '07; SP 14.79i '12, 14.67 '11; JT 48.33 '13, Pen 4965i '12.
Set four pbs in adding 359 points to best score for third at 2006 Commonwealth Games. Stress fracture ended 2008 season in May. Set SP pb when winning 2009 World title and three indoor bests when winning 2010 World Indoor gold. Three pbs en route to Olympic gold 2012. Won Götzis heptathlon 2010-12. Laureus World Sportswoman of the Year 2013. Married Andy Hill on 18 May 2013. Son Reggie born 17 July 2014.

Sophie HITCHON b. 11 Jul 1991 Burnley 1.70m 74kg. Blackburn H.
At HT: OG: '12- 11; WCh: '11- dnq 25, '13- dnq 19,'15- 4; EC: '12- 10, '14- dnq 19; CG: '14- 4; WJ: '08- 7, '10- 1; WY: '07- dnq 17; EU23: '11- 3, '13- 1; EJ: '09- 3; ET: '13- 3; won Comm-Y 2008, UK 2011-12, 2014-15.
12 UK hammer records 2011-15.
Progress at HT: 2006- 40.98, 2007- 54.56, 2008- 60.73, 2009- 63.18, 2010- 66.01, 2011- 69.59, 2012- 71.98, 2013- 72.97, 2014- 71.53, 2015- 73.86. pbs: 100m 12.2/12.40 '09, 200m 25.2 '08, 25.51 '09; SP 10.75 '08.

Katarina JOHNSON-THOMPSON b. 9 Jan 1993 Liverpool 1.83m 70kg. Liverpool H.
At Hep: OG: '12- 14; WCh: '13- 5, '15- 28 (11); WY: '09- 1; EU23: '13- 1; EJ: '09- 8, '11- 6. At LJ: WJ: '12- 1 (sf 100mh); WI: '14- 2. At Hep: EI: '15- 1. Won UK LJ 2014.
UK indoor records: high jump (2) 2014-15, long jump & pentathlon 2015.
Progress at LJ, Hep: 2006- 5.11, 2007- 5.77i/5.65, 2008- 6.11i/5.90/6.07w, 5343; 2009- 6.31, 5481; 2010- 6.25i/5.58, 2011- 6.44, 5787; 2012- 6.51/ 6.81w, 6267; 2013- 6449, 6.56; 2014- 6.92, 6682; 2015- 6.93i/6.79, 5039. pbs: 60m 7.50i '14, 100m 12.35 '08, 12.2 '09, 11.30w '14; 200m 22.89 '14, 300m 38.56i '08, 400m 53.7 '14, 800m 2:07.64 '13, 60mh 8.18i '15, 100mh 13.37 '15, 200mhSt 25.31 '15, 400mh 58.3 '14, HJ 1.97i '15, 1.90 '14; TJ 12.83, 13.35w '14; SP 12.49i '14, 12.47 '15; JT 42.01 '15, Pen 5000i '12.
Set pbs in the each of the last four events when adding 182 points to her pb for 5th at the 2013 Worlds and 474 points to pentathlon best to win 2015 European Indoors, including a 6.89 long jump, the best ever in a pentathlon. Three no-jumps (last by 1 cm) in 2015 WCh Hep LJ. Has all all-time record 27 English age-group titles U15 to U23.

Morgan LAKE b. 12 May 1997 Milton Keynes 1.78m 64kg. Windsor, Slough, Eton & Honslow.
At Hep/(HJ): WCh: '15- (dnq 14=); EC: '14- (dnq 17=); WJ: '14- 1/1; WY: '13- dnf; EJ: '15- (1). At Pen: WI: '16- 7; EI: '15- 9.
World youth indoor pentathlon record 2014.
Progress at HJ, Hep: 2007- 1.28, 2008- 1.50, 2009- 1.57, 2010- 1.70, 2011- 1.76, 2012- 1.80, 2013- 1.90, 2014- 1.94, 6148; 2015- 1.94, 5082. pbs: 60m 7.98i '13, 200m 24.59 '14, 800m 2:18.53i '16, 2:21.06 '14; 60mh 8.63i '16, 100mh 14.25 '14, LJ 6.32 '14, TJ 12.35, 12.45w '13; SP 14.85 '14, JT 41.66 '14, Pen 4527i '15.
27 English age-group titles 2010-15 (12 indoors, 15 out). Father Eldon had a TJ pb of 15.43 (1989).

Laura MUIR b. 9 May 1993 Milnathort, Kinross 1.62m 54kg. Dundee Hawkhill H. Was at Glasgow University.
At 1500m: WCh: '15- 5; EC: '14- h; CG: '14- 11; EU23: '13- 3. At 800m: WCh: '13- sf, At 3000m: WJ: '11- 16; EI: '15- 4. Won UK 2015. Eur CC: '15- 4 U23.
Progress at 1500m: 2005- 5:33.16, 2006- 5:12.39, 2007- 4:48.97, 2008- 4:47.92, 2009- 4:58.77, 2010- 4:50.91. 2011- 4:38.90, 2012- 4:14.52mx/4:17.81, 2013- 4:07.76, 2014- 4:00.07, 2015- 3:58.66. pbs: 400m 55.36i mx '16, 55.71i '14, 56.78 '12; 800m 2:00.42 '15, 3000m 8:38.47 '15, 10k Rd 38:23 '11.

Christine OHURUOGU b. 17 May 1984 Forest Gate, London 1.75m 70kg. Newham & Essex Beagles. Studied linguistics at University College, London.
At 400m/4x400mR: OG: '04- sf/4R, '08- 1, '12- 2; WCh: '05- sf/3R, '07- 1/3R, '09- 5, '11- h, '13- 1/3R; EC: '14- 4; CG: '06- 1, '14- 3R; EU23: '05- 2/2R; EJ: '03- 3/3R; WI: '12- 1R, '14- 3R; EI: '13- 1R; ET: '13- 1R. At 200m: ECp: '08- 2, '09- 3. Won AAA 400m 2004, UK 2009, 2012-13.
UK 400m record 2013.
Progress at 400m: 2000- 59.0, 2001- 55.29, 2003- 54.21, 2004- 50.50, 2005- 50.73, 2006- 50.28, 2007-

49.61, 2008- 49.62, 2009- 50.21, 2010- 50.88, 2011- 50.85, 2012- 49.70, 2013- 49.41, 2014- 51.38. pbs: 60m 7.39i '06, 100m 11.35 '08, 150mStr 16.94 '09, 200m 22.85 '09, 300m 36.76+ '09.
Played for England U17 and U19 at netball. Withdrawn from GB European Champs team in 2006 after missing three drugs tests, receiving a one-year ban. Younger sister Victoria (b. 28 Feb 1993) 400m pb 52.62 '13; res 3R WI '14.

Asha PHILLIP b. 25 Oct 1990 Leytonstone, London 1.63m 54kg. Newham & Essex Beagles. Studied drama at Kingston University.
At 100m/4x100mR: WCh: '13/15- sf; EC: '14- sf/1R; CG: '14- 4/2R; WJ: '06- 4/6R; WY: '07- 1; EJ: '07- 1R; ET: '15- 1. At 60m: WI: '14- 4, 16- 5; EI: '13- 5. Won UK 100m 2013-14.
UK records 100m (2) & 200m 2015.
Progress at 100m: 2004- 12.14/12.04w, 2005- 11.83, 2006- 11.45, 2007- 11.37, 2010- 12.0, 2011- 11.47, 2012- 11.53, 2013- 11.20, 2014- 11.18/11.11w, 2015- 11.10. pbs: 60m 7.09i '14, 150mSt 16.69 '14, 200m 23.45/23.07w '13.
World U17 double-mini trampoline champion in 2006, but ruptured her knee in 2007 and unable to compete until 2010.

Isobel POOLEY b. 21 Dec 1992 London 1.91m 70kg. Aldershot, Farnham & District. Was at Nottingham University.
At HJ: WCh: '15- dnq 19=; EC: '12- dnq 21; CG: '14- 2; WJ: '10- dnq 14=; EU23: '13- 4, EJ: '11- dnq 14. Won UK 2014-15.
Two UK high jump records 2014-15.
Progress at HJ: 2007- 1.55, 2008- 1.71i/1.70, 2009- 1.79i/1.77, 2010- 1.83, 2011- 1.86i/1.80, 2012- 1.90, 2013- 1.91, 2014- 1.96, 2015- 1.97.
Uncle Guy Pooley rowed in the 1992 and 1996 Olympic Games and for Cambridge in four University Boat Races.

Tiffany PORTER b. 13 Nov 1987 Ypsilanti, USA 1.72m 62kg. née Ofili. Doctorate in pharmacy from University of Michigan.
At 100mh: OG: '12- sf; WCh: '11- 4, '13- 3, '15- 5; EC: '14- 1; CG: '14- 2; WJ: '06- 3 (for USA); CCp: '14- 2; ET: '13- 1. At 60mh: WI: '12-14-16: 2/3/3; EI: '11- 2. Won UK 100mh 2011, 2013-15; NCAA 100mh & 60mh indoors 2009.
Four British 100mh records 2011-14, world best 4x100mh 2014 & 2015.
Progress at 100mh: 2005- 14.19, 2006- 13.37/13.15w, 2007- 12.80, 2008- 12.73, 2009- 12.77/12.57w, 2010- 12.85, 2011- 12.56, 2012- 12.65/12.47w, 2013- 12.55, 2014- 12.51, 2015- 12.56. pbs: 60m 7.41i '11, 100m 11.70 '09, 11.63w '08; 200m 23.90 '08, 400mh 61.96 '06, LJ 6.48 '09; UK records: 50mh 6.83i '12, 55mh 7.38i '12, 60mh 7.80i '11.
Opted for British nationality in September 2010 through her mother being born in London (father born in Nigeria). Married US hurdler Jeff Porter (qv) in May 2011. Sister **Cindy Ofili** (b. 5 Aug 1994) won NCAA indoor 60mh in pb 7.89 '16, pb 100mh 12.93 '14.

Shara PROCTOR b. 16 Sep 1988 The Valley, Anguilla 1.74m 56kg. Birchfield H. Was at University of Florida, USA.
At LJ: OG: '12- 9; WCh: '07-09-11-13-15: dnq 29/6/dnq 20/6/2; WI: '12-14-16: 3/4/8; CG: '06- dnq 13, '14- nj; WJ: '06- dnq 16; WY: '05- 6; EI: '13- 4; ET: '13- 3. Won DL 2013, CAC 2009, UK 2011-13.
Records: Anguilla: LJ 2005-09, TJ 2007-09; UK LJ (4) 2012-15.
Progress at LJ: 2003- 5.64, 2004- 5.99A. 2005- 6.24, 2006- 6.17, 2007- 6.17, 2008- 6.54A/6.52/6.61w, 2009- 6.71, 2010- 6.69, 2011- 6.81, 2012- 6.95, 2013- 6.92, 2014- 6.82, 2015- 7.07. pbs: 60m 7.36i '16, 100m 12.27 '08, 12.10w '10; TJ 13.88i '10, 13.74 '09.
Switched from Anguilla (a British Dependent Territory without a National Olympic Committee) to Britain from 16 Nov 2010. Younger sister Shinelle (b. 27 Jun 91) set Anguillan high jump records at 1.70 in 2009 and 2010 and 1.72i in 2014.

Lynsey SHARP b. 11 Jul 1990 Dumfries 1.75m 60kg. Edinburgh AC. Law graduate of Edinburgh Napier University.
At 800m: OG: '12- sf; WCh: '15- sf; EC: '12- 1, '14- 2; CG: '14- 2; WJ: '08- sf; WY: '07- sf; EU23: '11- 2; CCp: '14- 5. Won UK 2012, 2014-15.
Progress at 800m: 2000- 2:38.2, 2002- 2:25.97, 2003- 2:16.57, 2004- 2:09.98, 2005- 2:10.44, 2006- 2:10.91i, 2007- 2:06.92, 2008- 2:04.44, 2011- 2:00.65, 2012- 2:00.52, 2013- 2:02.63, 2014- 1:58.80, 2015- 1:57.71. pbs: 400m 54.74 '14, 600m 1:27.51 '14, 1500m 4:36.27 '11.
Father Cameron (1982: 4th 100m, 2nd 200m EC; 3rd 100m, 200m, 4x100m CG; pbs: 100m 10.20 '83, 200m 20.47 '82); mother Carol Lightfoot (800m 2:02.91 '82).

Lorraine UGEN b. 22 Sep 1991 London 1.78m 64kg. Blackheath & Bromley. Was at Texas Christian University, USA.
At LJ: WCh: '13- dnq, '15- 5; CG: '14- 5; WJ: '10- dnq 17; EU23: '13- dns F; EJ: '09- dnq 21; WI: '16- 3; won NCAA 2013.
Progress at LJ: 2007- 5.55, 2008- 5.79, 2009- 6.29, 2010- 6.35/6.42w, 2011- 6.54, 2012- 6.74/6.83w, 2013- 6.77, 2014- 6.73Ai/6.59i/6.39/6.40w, 2015- 6.92/6.96w, 2016- 6.93i. pbs: 60m 7.50Ai '12, 7.51i '14; 100m 11.42 '15, 11.34w '12; 200m 23.81/23.71w '15, 100mh 15.2/15.42 '08, HJ 1.56 '08, Hep 4307 '08.

Laura WEIGHTMAN b. 1 Jul 1991 Alnwick 1.72m 58kg. Morpeth H. Leeds Met University.
At 1500m: OG: '12- 8; WCh: '13- h, '15- sf; EC: '14- 3; CG: '14- 2; WJ: '10- 6. Won UK 2012, 2014.
At 3000m: ET: '13- 2. Eur U23 CC: '13- 8.
Progress at 1500m: 2004- 4:50.5, 2005- 4:44.0, 2006- 4:37.20, 2007- 4:26.02, 2008- 4:22.20, 2009- 4:14.9mx/4:19.9, 2010- 4:09.60mx/4:12.82, 2011- 4:07.94mx/4:15.51, 2012- 4:02.99, 2013- 4:05.36,

2014- 4:00.17, 2015- 4:04.70. pbs: 400m 58.43 '09, 800m 2:02.52 '12, 1000m 2:38.49 '13, 1M 4:52.7 '09, 2000m 5:44.22 '13, 3000m 8:43.46mx '13, 9:02.62 '12; 5k Rd 16:43 '12.

Jodie WILLIAMS b. 28 Sep 1993 Welwyn Garden City 1.74m 65kg. Herts Phoenix.
At (100m)/200m/4x100mR: WCh: '13- sf; EC: '14- 2/1R; CG: '14- 2/2R; WJ: '10- 1/2; WY: '09- 1/1; EU23: '13- 2/1/2R; EJ: '11- 1/1/3R. At 60m: WI: '11- 4. Won UK 200m 2014.
Progress at 100m, 200m: 2005- 13.1, 27.22/27.07w; 2006- 13.05/12.8, 26.88; 2007- 12.01/11.85w, 24.77/24.57w; 2008- 11.56, 24.14; 2009- 11.39, 23.08; 2010- 11.24, 22.79; 2011- 11.18, 22.94, 2012- 11.66, 2013- 11.32/11.23w, 22.92; 2014- 11.20/ 11.13w, 22.46; 2015- 11.50, 22.88. pbs: 60m 7.21i '11, 300m 38.00 '11. 400m 52.55 '14, LJ 5.33 '07.
Unbeaten in 151 races to 2nd in World Juniors 200m 2010. He sister Hannah was 6th WY 400m, pb 53.24A in 2015

USA

Governing body: USA Track and Field, One RCA Dome, Suite #140, Indianapolis, IN 46225. Founded 1979 as The Athletics Congress, when it replaced the AAU (founded 1888) as the governing body.
National Championships first held in 1876 (men), 1923 (women). **2015 Champions**: **Men**: 100m: Tyson Gay 9.87, 200m: Justin Gatlin 19.57, 400m: David Verburg 44.63, 800m: Nick Symmonds 1:44.53, 1500m: Matthew Centrowitz 3:37.25, 5000m: Ryan Hill 13:50.69, 10000m: Galen Rupp 28:11.61, HMar Diego Estrada 60:51, Mar: Jason Ward 2:12:56, 3000mSt: Evan Jager 8:12.29, 110mh: David Oliver 13.04, 400mh: Bershawn Jackson 48.20, HJ: Erik Kynard 2.37, PV: Sam Kendricks 5.75, LJ: Marquis Dendy 8.68w, TJ: Omar Craddock 17.53, SP: Joe Kovacs 21.84, DT: Jared Schuurmans 64.64, HT: Kibwe Johnson 76.96, JT: Sean Furey 83.08, Dec: Trey Hardee 8725, 20000mW/50kW: John Nunn 1:28:39.48/4:03:40. **Women**: 100m: Tori Bowie 10.81, 200m: Jenna Prabndini 22.20, 400m: Alyson Felix 50.19, 800m: Alysia Montaño 1:59.65, 1500m: Jenny Simpson 4:14.86, 5000m: Nicole Tully 15:06.44, 10000m: Molly Huddle 31:39.20, HMar: Kim Conley 69:44, Mar: Blake Russell 2:34:57, 3000mSt: Emma Coburn 9:15.59, 100mh: Dawn Harper Nelson 12.55, 400mh: Shamier Little 53.83, HJ: Chaunté Lowe 1.91, PV: Jenn Suhr 4.82, LJ: Tianna Bartoletta 7.12, TJ: Christine Epps 14.09, SP: Michelle Carter 20.02, DT: Gia Lewis-Smallwood 63.09, HT: Amber Campbell 72.36, JT: Kara Ringer 64.94, Hep: Barbara Nwaba 6500, 20000mW: Miranda Melville 1:36:33.99.
NCAA Championships first held in 1921 (men), 1982 (women). **2015 Champions**: **Men**: 100m/200m: Andre de Grasse CAN 9.75w/19.58w, 400m: Vernon Norwood 45.10, 800m: Edward Kemboi KEN 1:49.26, 1500m: Chad Noelle 3:54.96, 5000m/10000m: Edward Cheserek KEN 13:48.67/28:58.92, 3000mSt: Anthony Rotich KEN 8:33.90, 110mh: Omar McLeod JAM 13.01w, 400mh: Michael Stigler 48.84, HJ: JaCorian Duffield 2.28, PV: Shawn Barber CAN 5.60, LJ/TJ: Marquis Dendy 8.43w/17.71w, SP: Jonathan Jones 20.78, DT: Sam Mattis 62.48, HT: Conor McCullough 76.91, JT: Sam Crouser 79.19, Dec: Maicel Uibo EST 8356. **Women**: 100m: Jenna Prandini 10.96w, 200m: Dezerea Bryant 22.18, 400m: Kala Funderburk 51.67, 800m: Raevyn Rogers 1:59.71, 1500m: Rhianwedd Price GBR 4:09.56, 5000m: Emily Sisson 15:34.10, 10000m: Molly Seidel 33:18.37, 3000mSt: Colleen Quigley 9:29.32, 100mh: Kendra Harrison 12.55, 400mh: Shamier Little 53.74, HJ: Jeanelle Scheper LCA 1.90, PV: Demi Payne 4.70, LJ: Quanesha Burks 6.91w, TJ: Keturah Orji 14.15, SP: Raven Saunders 18.35, DT: Shelbi Vaughan 61.39, HT: DeAnna Price 71.49, JT: Irena Sedivá CZE 58.76, Hep: Akela Jones BAR 6371.

Devon ALLEN b. 12 Dec 1994 Phoenix, Arizona 1.90m 86kg. Student at University of Oregon.
At 110mh: Won US & NCAA 2014.
Progress at 110mh: 2014- 13.16. pbs: 60m 6.85Ai '14, 100m 10.36 '16, 200m 20.75 '12, 60mh 7.56i '16, 400mh 51.19 '14.
On a football scholarship, wide receiver. Suffered a knee injury on the opening kickoff of the Rose Bowl at the end of 2014 and missed 2015 track season.

Robby ANDREWS b. 29 Mar 1991 Mamalapan Township, New Jersey 1.77m 68kg. adidas. Was at University of Virginia.
At 800m: WJ: '10- 3. At 1500m: WCh: '15- 11; WI: '16- 4. Won US 1500m (& indoor 1000m) 2015; NCAA 800m 2011.
Progress at 800m, 1500m: 2008- 4:12.48Mi/4:12.82M, 2009- 1:48.66, 4:03.49M; 2010- 1:45.54, 3:14.09; 2011- 1:44.71, 3:40.77; 2012- 1:45.06, 3:34.78; 2013- 1:47.13Ai/1:48.18, 3:43.52; 2014- 1:46.28, 3:42.54; 2015- 1:45.98, 3:35.52. pbs: 1000m 2:17.90i '13, 1M 3:53.16i '16, 3:57.15 '15.

Ronnie ASH b. 2 Jul 1988 Raleigh NC 1.88m 86kg. Nike. Was at University of Oklahoma.
At 110mh: WCh: '15- h; CCp: '14- 2; won NACAC 2010, NCAA 2009.
Progress at 110mh: 2008- 13.44, 2009- 13.27, 2010- 13.19/12.98w, 2011- 13.25/13.24w, 2012- 13.20/13.10w, 2014- 12.99, 2015- 13.13. pbs: 200m 22.08 '08, 60mh 7.55i '10.

Ryan BAILEY b. 13 Apr 1989 Portland, Oregon 1.93m 98kg. Nike.
At 100m/4x100mR: OG: '12- 4/dq2R. At 4x400m: WJ: '08- res (1)R.
N.American 4x100m record 2012 & 2015.
Progress at 100m, 200m: 2006- 22.48i, 2007- 10.48/10.45w, 21.13/21.11w; 2008- 10.28, 20.69;

2009- 10.05, 20.45; 2010- 9.88, 20.10; 2012- 9.88, 20.43; 2013- 10.10/10.00w, 2014- 10.12/10.03w, 20.37; 2015- 9.93/9.89w, 20.85. pbs: 55m 6.20i '09, 60m 6.50i '15, 300m 33.50 '07, 400m 47.05 '08, 60mh 7.97i '08, 110mh 14.13 '08.
His nephew Eric Bailey 400mh pb 50.04 '11.

Boris BERIAN b. 19 Dec 1992 Colorado Springs 1.80m 73kg. Adans State University.
At 800m: WI: '16- 1.
Progress at 800m: 2011- 1:52.18A, 2012- 1:48.93, 2013- 1:48.89, 2015- 1:43.34. pbs: 400m 47.34A '12, 600m 1:15.51i '16, 1:16.14 '15.

Marvin BRACY b. 15 Dec 1993 Orlando, Florida 1.75m 74kg. adidas. Was at Florida State University.
At 100m/4x100mR: WJ: '10- res 1R; PAm-J: 11-1. At 60m: WI: '14- 2, '16- 7.; won US indoor 2014-16.
Progress at 100m: 2010- 10.42/10.19w, 2011- 10.28/10.05w, 2012- 10.25/10.06w, 2013- 10.09, 2014- 10.08, 2015- 9.93. pbs: 55m 6.08i '12, 60m 6.48Ai/6.51i '14, 200m 20.55 '14.
Wide receiver at American Football at University.

Trayvon BROMELL b 10 Jul 1995 St. Petersburg, Florida 1.75m 71kg. New Balance. Baylor University.
At 100m/4x100mR: WCh: '15- 3=; WJ: '14- 2/1R; PAm-J: 13- 3/1R. At 60m: WI: '16- 1.
Two world junior 100m records 2014.
Progress at 100m, 200m: 2012- 10.40, 21.01; 2013- 10.27/9.99Aw, 20.91/20.86w; 2014- 9.97/9.77w, 20.59/20.23w; 2015- 9.84/9.76w, 20.03/19.86w. pb 60m 6.47i '16.
Fastest ever teenager with 9.84 for 100m in 2015.

Christian CANTWELL b. 30 Sep 1980 Jefferson City, Missouri 1.93m 154kg. Nike. Studied hotel and restaurant management at University of Missouri.
At SP: OG: '08- 2, '12- 4; WCh: '05-09-11-15: 4/1/3/dns; WI: '04-08-10: 1/1/1; CCp: '10- 1; won DL 2010, WAF 2003, 2009; US 2005, 2009-10. At DT: PAm-J: '99- 2.
Progress at SP: 1999- 15.85, 2000- 19.67, 2001- 19.71, 2002- 21.45, 2003- 21.62, 2004- 22.54, 2005- 21.67, 2006- 22.45, 2007- 21.96, 2008- 22.18i/21.76, 2009- 22.16, 2010- 22.41, 2011- 22.07, 2012- 22.31, 2013- 20.13i/19.86, 2014- 21.85, 2015- 21.64. pbs: DT 59.32 '01, HT 57.18 '01, Wt 22.04i '03.
Three competitions over 22m in 2004, then 4th in US Olympic Trials. Married Teri Steer (b. 3 Oct 1975, SP pb 19.21 '01, 3 WI 1999) 29 Oct 2005.

Matthew CENTROWITZ b. 18 Nov 1989 Beltsville, Maryland 1.76m 61kg. Nike Oregon Project. Studied sociology at the University of Oregon.
At 1500m: OG: '12- 4; WCh: '11-13-15: 3/2/8; WI: '12- 7, '16- 1. At 5000m WJ: '08- 11. Won US 2011, 2013, 2015; NCAA 2011, PAm-J 2007.
Progress at 1500m: 2007- 3:49.54, 2008- 3:44.98, 2009- 3:36.92, 2010- 3:40.14, 2011- 3:34.46, 2012- 3:31.96, 2013- 3:33.58, 2014- 3:31.09, 2015- 3:30.40. pbs: 800m 1:45.86 '13, 1000m 2:17.00i '15, 1M 3:50.53 '14, 3000m 7:40.74i '16, 2M 8:40.55 '07, 5000m 13:20.06 '14.
Father Matt pbs: 1500m 3:36.60 '76, 3:54.94 '82, 5000m US record 13:12.91 '82, 10000m 28:32.7 '83; h OG 1500m 1976; 1 PAm 5000m 1979. Sister Lauren (b. 25 Sep 1986) 1500m pb 4:10.23 '09.

Jordan CLARKE b. 10 Jul 1990 Anchorage, Alaska 1.93m 125kg. Was at Arizona State University.
At SP: WCh: '15- dnq 13; PAm-J: '09- 2. Won NCAA 2011-12.
Progress at SP: 2009- 19.49, 2010- 19.21, 2011- 19.75, 2012- 20.86i/20.40, 2013- 20.59i/20.28, 2014- 21.37, 2015- 21.49. pbs: DT 61.16 '09, HT 66.18 '13, Wt 19.96i '13.

Will CLAYE b. 13 Jun 1991 Phoenix 1.80m 68kg. Nike. Was at University of Oklahoma, then Florida.
At (LJ)/TJ: OG: '12- 3/2; WCh: '11- 9/3, '13- 3, '15- dnq 19; WI: '12- 4/1; CCp: '14- 2/3; won US 2014, PAm-J and NCAA 2009.
Progress at LJ, TJ: 2007- 14.91/15.19w, 2008- 7.39/7.48w, 15.97; 2009- 7.89/8.00w, 17.19/17.24w; 2010- 7.30w, 16.30; 2011- 8.29, 17.50/17.62w; 2012- 8.25, 17.70i/17.62; 2013- 8.10, 17.52; 2014- 8.19/ 8.29w, 17.75; 2015- 8.07/8.11w, 17.48/17.50w. pb 100m 10.64/10.53w '12.
Possibly youngest ever NCAA champion – he won 2009 title on his 18th birthday with 17.24w (and US junior record 17.19). First athlete to win Olympic medals at both LJ and TJ since 1936.

Kerron CLEMENT b. 31 Oct 1985 Port of Spain, Trinidad 1.88m 84kg. Was at University of Florida.
At 400mh/4x400mR: OG: '08- 2/res1R, '12- 8; WCh: '05- 4, '07- 1/res 1R, '09- 1/1R, '11-13-15: sf/8/4; WJ: '04- 1/1R; PAm: '15- 4/2R; WI: '10- res 1R; WCp: '06- 1. Won WAF 2008-09, US 2005-06, NCAA 2004-05.
World junior 4x400m record 2004, world indoor records: 400m 2005, 4x400m 2006.
Progress at 400mh: 2002- 49.77, 2003- 50.13, 2004- 48.51; 2005- 47.24; 2006- 47.39; 2007- 47.61; 2008- 47.79; 2009- 47.91; 2010- 47.86; 2011- 48.74; 2012- 48.12; 2013- 48.06; 2015- 48.18. pbs: 60m 6.89i '10, 100m 10.23 '07, 200m 20.40i '05, 20.49 '07; 300m 31.94i '06, 400m 44.48 '07, 55mh 7.28i '05, 60mh 7.80i '04, 110mh 13.78 '04.
Born in Trinidad, moved to Texas in 1998, US citizenship confirmed in 2005. Ran 47.24, the world's fastest time since 1998, to win 2005 US 400mh title.

Omar CRADDOCK b. 26 Apr 1991 Killeen, Texas 1.78m 79kg. Jump Corps. Was at University of Florida.
At TJ: WCh: '13- dnq 13, '15- 4; WJ: '10- 3; WI: '16- 5. Won US 2015, NCAA 2012-13.
Progress at TJ: 2006- 14.67, 2007- 15.16A, 2008-

15.53, 2009- 14.87i, 2010- 16.56, 2011- 16.57i/16.46, 2012- 16.75i/16.71/16.92w, 2013- 16.92/17.15w, 2014- 16.98/17.26w, 2015- 17.53. pb LJ 7.63i '13, 7.60 '15, 7.70w '12.

Ryan CROUSER b. 18 Dec 1992 Portland 2.01m 127kg. University of Texas.
At SP/DT: WY: '09- 1/2. Won NCAA shot 2013-14, indoors 2014.
Progress at SP: 2011- 19.48i, 2012- 20.29i/19.32, 2013- 21.09, 2014- 21.39, 2015- 21.14i/21.11, 2016-21.73i. pbs: DT 63.90 '14, JT 61.16 '09.
Set High School 1.62kg DT record 72.40 '11. His father Mitch SP 20.04i '83, 19.94 '82, DT 67.22 '85; uncle Dean SP 21.07 '82, DT 65.88 '83, won NCAA SP 1982 & DT 1982-3; uncle Brian JT 83.00 '87, old JT 95.10 '85, won NCAA 1982 & 1985, dnq OG 1988 & 1992; Dean's children: Sam SP 17.62 '13, JT 83.30 '15, US junior & HS record '10, won NCAA 2014-15; Haley US junior JT record 55.22 '12, 4 WY '11.

Marquis DENDY b. 17 Nov 1992 Middleton, Delaware 1.92m 75kg. Nike. Was at University of Florida.
At LJ/(TJ): WCh: '13- dnq 27, '15- dnq 21/dnq 13; WI: '16- 1. At TJ: WJ: '10- 8; won US LJ 2015; NACAC LJ 2012, NCAA LJ 2015, TJ 2014-15, indoor LJ 2013, 2015-16; TJ 2015.
Progress at LJ, TJ: 2009- 7.20, 15.40; 2010- 7.45, 16.03; 2011- 7.47/7.56w, 15.62; 2012- 8.06i/7.81, 15.55; 2013- 8.28i/8.10/8.29w, 16.25i/16.03; 2014-8.00, 16.52/17.05w; 2015- 8.39/8.68w, 17.50/17.71w; 2016- 8.41i. pbs: 60m 6.88i '14, 100m 10.31 '15.

Dedric DUKES b. 4 Feb 1992 Miami 1.80m 70kg. Was at University of Florida.
At 200m: WY: '09- 4/1 MedR. Won NCAA 2014.
Progress at 200m: 2007- 21.88/21.79w, 2008-21.19/21.12w, 2009- 20.94, 2011- 20.88w, 2012-20.47, 2013- 20.45/20.34w, 2014- 19.97/19.91w, 2015- 19.99/19.86w. pbs: 60m 6.77i '14, 100m 10.18/10.17w '15, 400m 45.66 '14.
Football wide receiver in high school.

Johnny DUTCH b. 20 Jan 1989 Clayton NC 1.80m 82kg. Studied media arts at University of South Carolina.
At 400mh: WCh: '09/15- sf; WJ: '08- 2; PAm-J: '07- 1/2R. Won US 2014, NCAA 2010.
Progress at 400mh: 2005- 52.06, 2006- 51.72, 2007- 50.07, 2008- 48.52, 2009- 48.18, 2010- 47.63, 2011- 48.47, 2012- 48.90, 2013- 48.02, 2014- 48.93, 2015- 48.13. pbs: 400m 46.75 '13, 500m 1:03.25i '15, 55mh 7.31i '10, 60mh 7.71i '09, 110mh 13.50/13.30w '10.

Ashton EATON b. 21 Jan 1988 Portland, Oregon 1.86m 86kg. Oregon TC Elite. Graduate of University of Oregon.
At Dec: OG: '12- 1; WCh: '09- 18, '11- 2, '13- 1; won US 2012-13, NCAA 2008-10. At Hep: WI: '12-14-16: 1/1/1.
Records: World decathlon 2012 & 2015, indoor heptathlon 2010 (6499), 2011 (6568) and 2012.
Progress at Dec: 2007- 7123, 2008- 8122, 2009-8241w/8091, 2010- 8457, 2011- 8729, 2012- 9039, 2013- 8809, 2015- 9045. At 400mh: 2014- 48.69. pbs: 60m 6.66i '11, 100m 10.21 '12, 10.19w '10; 200m 20.76 '13, 400m 45.00 '15, 800m 1:55.90i '10, 1000m 2:32.67i '10, 1500m 4:14.48 '12, 60mh 7.51i '15, 110mh 13.35 '11, 13.34w '12; HJ 2.11i '10, 2.11 '12; PV 5.40 '15, LJ 8.23 '12, SP 15.40 '13, DT 47.36 '11, JT 66.64 '13, Hep 6645i '12.
Set best ever marks in decathlons with 100m 10.21 and LJ 8.23 in WR in Eugene 22/23 June 2012 and with 45.00 for 400m in Beijing 28 Aug 2015. Married Brianne Theisen CAN on 15 July 2013.

Justin GATLIN b. 10 Feb 1982 Brooklyn, NY 1.85m 79kg. XTEP. Was at University of Tennessee.
At 100m/(200m)/4x100mR: OG: '04- 1/3/2R, '12- 3/dq2R; WCh: '05- 1/1, '11- sf, '13- 2/2R, '15-2/2. At 60m: WI: '03- 1, '12- 1. Won DL 100m 2013-15, US 100m 2005-06, 2012; 200m 2005, 2015; (indoor 60m 2003), NCAA 100m & 200m 2001-02 (& indoor 60m/200m 2002).
N.American 4x100m record 2012 & 2015.
Progress at 100m, 200m: 2000- 10.36, 2001- 10.08, 20.29/19.86w; 2002: under international suspension 10.05/10.00w, 19.86; 2003- 9.97, 20.04; 2004- 9.85, 20.01; 2005- 9.88/9.84w, 20.00; 2006-9.77dq, 2010- 10.09, 20.63; 2011- 9.95, 20.20; 2012-9.79, 20.11; 2013- 9.85, 20.21; 2014- 9.77/9.76w, 19.68; 2015- 9.74, 19.57. pbs: 60m 6.45i '03, 100y 9.10 '14, 55mh 7.39i '02, 60mh 7.86i '01, 110mh 13.41dq '02, 13.78/13.74w '01; LJ 7.34i '01, 7.21 '00.
Top hurdler in high school (110mh 13.66 and 300mh 36.74 on junior hurdles). Retained NCAA sprint titles while ineligible for international competition in 2002 after failing a drugs test in 2001 (when he won 100m, 200m and 110mh at the US Juniors) for a prescribed medication to treat Attention Deficit Disorder. Reinstated by IAAF in July 2002. Won 2005 World 100m title by biggest ever winning margin of 0.17. Won all five 100m competitions in 2006, including tying the world record with 9.77 in Doha and taking the US title, but had tested positive for testosterone before these performances. He received a four-year drugs ban but returned to competition in August 2010. In 2014 he was unbeaten at 100m and 200m (the first man to do so since Usain Bolt in 2009) and in Brussels on 5 Sep recorded the best-ever one-day sprint double with 9.77 and 19.71. His run of successive wins (26 finals and 7 prelims) in 2014-15 ended by Usain Bolt in World 100m in 2015.

Tyson GAY b. 9 Aug 1982 Lexington 1.83m 73kg. adidas. Studied marketing at University of Arkansas.
At 100m/(200m)/4x100mR: OG: '08- sf, '12-dq(4/2R); WCh: '05- (4), '07- 1/1/1R, '09- 2, 15- 6; WCp: '06- 1/1R, '10- 1R. Won DL 2010, WAF

100m 2009, 200m 2005-06, US 100m 2007-08, 2013, 2015; 200m 2007, 2013; NCAA 100m 2004. Five N.American 100m records 2008-12, 4x100m 2015.
Progress at 100m, 200m: 1999- 10.81, 22.29i; 2000- 10.56, 21.27; 2001- 10.46/10.28w, 21.23; 2002- 10.27/10.08w, 20.88/20.21w; 2003- 10.01Aw/10.14w, 21.15/20.31w; 2004- 10.06/10.10w, 20.07; 2005- 10.08, 19.93; 2006- 9.84, 19.68; 2007- 9.84/9.76w, 19.62; 2008- 9.77/9.68w, 20.00; 2009- 9.69, 19.58; 2010- 9.78, 19.76; 2011- 9.79, 2012- 9.86/9.80dq, 20.21dq; 2013- 9.75dq, 19.74dq; 2014- 9.93, 20.22; 2015- 9.87/9.79w. pbs: 60m 6.39+ '09, 6.55i '05; 150mSt 14.51 '11, 200m/220ySt 19.41/19.54 '10, 400m 44.89 '10.
Ran four 200m races in under 19.85 in 2006. Then greatest ever sprint double (9.84 and 19.62) at 2007 US Champs and ran fastest ever 100m 9.68w/+4.1 (after US record in qf) to win US Olympic Trials in 2008 but pulled hamstring in 200m qf and unable to compete again until Olympics, where he was not back to top form. IAAF Athlete of the Year 2007. He tested positive for a banned substance (later reported as a steroid) in May 2013 and withdrew from the World Championships; case resolved with a 1-year ban and annulment of results from 15 Jul 2012, thus including his Olympic 2012 results.

Marquise GOODWIN b. 19 Nov 1990 Austin, Texas 1.78m 82kg. Studied kinesiology at University of Texas.
At LJ: OG: '12- 10; WCh: '11- dnq 13; WJ: '10- 1/1R; PAm: '15- 2; WUG: '11- 2; won NCAA 2010, 2012; US 2011-12.
Progress at LJ: 2007- 7.62, 2008- 7.74/7.96w, 2009- 8.18, 2010- 8.15, 2011- 8.17/8.33w, 2012- 8.33, 2015- 8.13/8.37w. pbs: 60m 6.68i '16, 100m 10.35 '12, 10.24w '09; 200m 21.57/21.24w '09, TJ 15.20/15.38w '09.
A wide receiver at American football. Returned to athletics in 2015.

James Edward '**Trey**' **HARDEE** b. 7 Feb 1984 Birmingham, Alabama 1.96m 95kg. Nike. Was at Mississippi State University and University of Texas.
At Dec: OG: '08- dnf, '12- 2; WCh: '09-11-13-15: 1/1/dnf/dnf; won NCAA 2005, US 2009, 2014-15. At Hep: WI: '10- 2.
Progress at Dec: 2003- 7544, 2004- 8041(w), 2005- 7881, 2006- 8465, 2008- 8534, 2009- 8790, 2011- 8689, 2012- 8671, 2013- dnf, 2014- 8599w/8518, 2015- 8725. pbs: 55m 6.30i '06, 60m 6.71i '06, 100m 10.39 '10, 10.28w '06; 200m 20.98 '06, 300m 33.69 '14, 400m 47.51 '06, 1000m 2:45.67i '12, 1500m 4:40.94 '12, 60mh 7.70i '10, 110mh 13.54 '12; HJ 2.06i '10, 2.05 '08; PV 5.35 '15, LJ 7.88 '11, SP 15.94i '09, 15.72 '12; DT 52.68 '08, JT 68.99 '11, Hep 6208Ai '06.
Won IAAF Combined Events Challenge 2009 and in Götzis 2014. Married Chelsea Johnson (PV 4.73 '08, 2= WCh 2009) in 2014; her father Jan Johnson set a world indoor PV best 5.36 '70, won at the 1971 Pan-Ams and was the 1972 Olympic bronze medallist.

Aleec HARRIS b. 31 Oct 1990 Lawrenceville, Georgia 1.85m 77kg. adidas. Studied sociology at University of Southern California.
At 110mh: WCh: '15- sf. Won US indoor 60mh 2015. World 4x110mh best 2015.
Progress at 110mh: 2010- 14.15/13.88w, 2011- 13.65/13.55w, 2013- 13.69/13.55w, 2014- 13.14, 2015- 13.11. pbs: 55mh 7.18i '11, 60mh 7.50i '15.

Mike HARTFIELD b. 29 Mar 1990 Manchester, Connecticut 1.90m 77kg. adidas. Was at Ohio State University.
At LJ: WCh: '15- nj.
Progress at LJ: 2007- 7.19w, 2008- 7.42/7.52w, 2009- 7.57, 2010- 7.61i, 2011- 7.91/7.95w, 2012- 7.96, 2013- 8.15, 2014- 8.15/8.17w, 2015- 8.27/8.42w. pb TJ 15.84 '13.
Broke 77 year-old Ohio State University record set by Jesse Owens.

Jeffery HENDERSON b. 16 Feb 1989 Sherwood, Arkansas 1.78m 82kg. Was at Florida Memorial University and Stillman College.
At LJ: WCh: '15- 9; PAm: '15- 1; WI: '16- 4; US champion 2014, indoors 2012.
Progress at LJ: 2006- 7.14i, 2007- 7.51i/7.41, 2008- 7.74/7.77w, 2009- 8.15u/7.88/8.19w, 2010- 7.94Ai/7.90i, 2011- 7.78, 2012- 7.91w, 2013- 8.22, 2014- 8.43/8.52w, 2015- 8.52/8.54w. pbs: 55m 6.31i '09, 60m 6.58i '16, 100m 10.18A '13, 10.25 '11, 10.19w '15; 200m 20.65A '13, TJ 14.90i '08.

Ryan HILL b. 31 Jan 1990 Hickory, North Carolina 1.76m 60kg. Bowerman TC. Was at North Carolina State University.
At 5000m: WCh: '13- 10, '15- 7. At 3000m: WI: '16- 2. Won US 5000m 2015.
Progress at 5000m: 2009- 14:09.63, 2010- 13:44.36, 2011- 13:31.67, 2012- 13:26.34, 2013- 13:14.22, 2014- 13:14.31, 2015- 13:05.69. pbs: 800m 1:50.22iA '14, 1000m 2:20.26 '13, 1500m 3:37.10 '14, 1M 3:54.89i '14, 3:56.78 '12; 3000m 7:34.87i/7:38.64 14, 2M 8:26.72i '15, 10000m 29:32.28 '10.

Reese HOFFA b. 8 Oct 1977 Evans, Georgia 1.81m 133kg. New York AC. Was at University of Georgia.
At SP: OG: '04- dnq 21, '08- 6, '12- 3; WCh: '03-07-09-11-13-15: dnq/1/4/4/4/5; PAm: '03- 1; WI: '04-06-08-12: 2/1/2/4; WUG: '01- 9; WCp: '06- 2; won WAF 2006-07, DL 2012, 2014; USA 2007-08, 2012.
Progress at SP: 1998- 19.08, 1999- 19.35, 2000- 19.79, 2001- 20.22, 2002- 20.47, 2003- 20.95, 2004- 21.67, 2005- 21.74i/21.29, 2006- 22.11i/21.96, 2007- 22.43, 2008- 22.10, 2009- 21.89, 2010- 22.16, 2011- 22.09, 2012- 22.00, 2013- 21.71, 2014- 21.88, 2015- 21.30. pb HT 60.05 '02.
Added 37cm to his best to win World Indoor gold 2006. Married Renata Foerst (HT 55.49 '04) in 2005.

Daniel HULING b. 16 Jul 1983 Denver 1.85m 70kg. Nike. Was at Miami University (Ohio).
At 3000mSt: WCh: '09/11/13- h, '15- 5; CCp: '10- 8; US champion 2010.
Progress at 3000mSt: 2004- 8:58.88, 2005- 8:43.59, 2006- 8:27.41, 2008- 8:20.84, 2009- 8:14.69, 2010- 8:13.29, 2011- 8:25.95, 2012- 8:20.81, 2013- 8:21.92, 2014- 8:15.61, 2015- 8:14.11. pbs: 1500m 3:37.53 '12, 1M 3:58.24i '12, 2000m 5:02.41i '14, 3000m 7:44.42 '13, 5000m 13:18.42 '13, 10000m 30:37.25 '06.

Bershawn JACKSON b. 8 May 1983 Miami 1.73m 69kg. Nike. Studied accountancy at St Augustine's University, Florida.
At 400mh/4x400mR: OG: '08- 3; WCh: '03- h (dq), '05- 1, '07- sf/res 1R, '09- 3/res 1R, '11- 6/1R, '13- sf, '15- h; WJ: '02- 3/1R; CCp: '10- 3/1R; won DL 2010, 2015; WAF 2004-05, US 2003, 2008-10, 2015. At 400m: WI: '10- 5/1R; won US indoor 2005, 2010.
Progress at 400mh: 1999- 54.53, 2000- 52.17, 2001- 50.86, 2002- 50.00, 2003- 48.23, 2004- 47.86, 2005- 47.30, 2006- 47.48, 2007- 48.13, 2008- 48.02, 2009- 47.98, 2010- 47.32, 2011- 47.93, 2012- 48.20, 2013- 48.09, 2014- 48.76, 2015- 48.09. pbs: 200m 21.03/20.46w '04, 400m 45.06 '07, 500m 1:00.70i '15, 600m 1:18.65i '06, 800m 1:53.40 '11, 200mhSt 22.26 '11.

Evan JAGER b. 8 Mar 1989 Algonquin, Illinois 1.86m 66kg. Bowerman TC. Was at University of Wisconsin.
At 3000mSt: OG: '12- 6; WCh: '13- 5, '15- 6; CCp: '14- 2; US champion 2012-15. At 1500m: WJ: '08- 8. At 5000m: WCh: '09- h.
Three N.American 3000m steeplechase records 2012-15.
Progress at 5000m, 3000mSt: 2009- 13:22.18, 2012- 8:06.81, 2013- 13:02.40, 8:08.60; 2014- 13:08.63, 8:04.71; 2015- 8:00.45. pbs: 800m 1:50.10i '10, 1:51.04 '08; 1000m 2:20.29i '15, 1500m 3:32.97 '15, 1M 3:53.33 '14, 2000m 4:57.56 '14, 3000m 7:35.16 '12, 2M 8:14.95i '13.
Set US record in only his fifth steeplechase race, improving pb by 10.59 secs. In 2009 he had come 3rd in the US Champs in only his second race at 5000m.

Sam KENDRICKS b. 7 Sep 1992 Oxford, Mississippi 1.89m 79kg. Nike. Was at University of Mississippi.
At PV: WCh: '15- 9=; WUG: '13- 1; WI: '16- 2; US champion 2014-15, NCAA 2013-4.
Progress at PV: 2010- 4.68, 2011- 5.18, 2012- 5.50, 2013- 5.81, 2014- 5.75, 2015- 5.86Ai/5.82, 2016- 5.90i.

Joe KOVACS b. 28 Jun 1989 Bethlehem, Pennsylvania 1.85m 114kg. Nike. Was at Penn State University.
At SP: WCh: '15- 1; CCp: '14- 3; Won DL 2015, US 2014-15.
Progress at SP: 2007- 16.49, 2008- 16.86i, 2009- 18.53, 2010- 19.36i/18.73, 2011- 19.84i/19.15, 2012- 21.08, 2013- 20.82, 2014- 22.03. 2015- 22.56. pbs: DT 56.08 '11, HT 61.50 '11, Wt 19.07i '11.

Erik KYNARD b. 3 Feb 1991 Toledo, Ohio 1.93m 86kg. Nike Jordan. Was at Kansas State University.
At HJ: OG: '12- 2; WCh: '11- dnq 14, '13- 5, '15- 8=; WJ: '08- dnq 19=; CCp: '14- 5; WI: '14- 4, '16- 3; Won US 2013-14, NCAA 2011-12.
Progress at HJ: 2007- 2.13i/2.05, 2008- 2.23i/2.15, 2009- 2.24i/2.22, 2010- 2.25, 2011- 2.33i/2.31, 2012- 2.34, 2013- 2.37, 2014- 2.37, 2015- 2.37. pb LJ 7.15i '09.

Bernard LAGAT b. 12 Dec 1974 Kapsabet, Kenya 1.75m 61kg. Nike. Studied business management at Washington State University, USA.
At 1500m (/5000m): OG: '00- 3, '04- 2, '08- sf/9, '12- (4); WCh: '01- 2, '05- sf, '07- 1/1, '09- 3/2, '11- (2), '13- (6); WI: '03- 2; AfCh: '02- 1; WUG: '99- 1; WCp: '02- 1; 2nd GP 1999-2000-02, WAF 2005-06. At 3000m: WI: '01-04-10-12-14: 6/1/1/1/2; CCp: '10- 1/(1), '14- 3. Won WAF 3000m 2005, 2008; KEN 1500m 2002, US 1500m 2006, 2008; 5000m 2006-08, 2010-11, 2013-14; NCAA 5000m 1999 (and indoor 1M/3000m).
Records: Commonwealth and KEN 1500m 2001, N.American 1500m 2005, 3000m 2010, 5000m 2010 & 2011, indoor 2000m 2014, 3000m 2007, 2M 2011 & 2013, 5000m 2010, 2012. World M35 3000m & 5000m 2010, 1M and 5000m 2011, 2000m 2014; M40 1500m, 1M, 3000m (2), 5000m, 10k Rd; indoor 1500m, 1M, 3000m (3), 2M 2015.
Progress at 1500m, 5000m: 1996- 3:37.7A, 1997- 3:41.19, 13:50.33; 1998- 3:34.48, 13:42.73; 1999- 3:30.56, 13:36.12; 2000- 3:28.51, 13:23.46; 2001- 3:26.34, 13:30.54; 2002- 3:27.91, 13:19.14; 2003- 3:30.55, 2004- 3:27.40, 2005- 3:29.30, 12:59.29; 2006- 3:29.68, 12:59.22; 2007- 3:33.85, 13:30.73; 2008- 3:32.75, 13:16.29; 2009- 3:32.56, 13:03.06; 2010- 3:32.51, 12:54.12; 2011- 3:33.11, 12:53.60; 2012- 3:34.63, 12:59.92; 2013- 3:36.36, 12:58.99; 2014- 13:06.68, 2015- 3:40.20i/3:41.87, 13:14.97. pbs: 800m 1:46.00 '03, 1000m 2:16.18 '08, 1M 3:47.28 '01, 2000m 4:54.74i '14, 4:55.49 '99; 3000m 7:29.00 '10, 2M 8:09.49i '13, 8:12.45 '08, 10k 27:48 '15, HMar 62:33 '13.
Gave up his final year of scholastic eligibility (as under NCAA rules no payments can be received) at his university in order to compete (for money) in the 1999 GP Final, in which he was 2nd. He was 2nd to Hicham El Guerrouj six times in 2001, including his 3:26.34 at Brussels for 2nd on the world all-time list, and six times in 2002. Withdrew from 2003 Worlds after testing positive for EPO, but this was later repudiated. Lives in Tucson, Arizona, gained US citizenship 2005. First man ever to win 1500m/5000m double at the US Champs in 2006 and at World Champs in 2007. Oldest ever male World Indoor champion at 37y 89d in 2012 and medallist at 39y 87d in 2014.

A sister **Mary Chepkemboi** competed at the 1982 Commonwealth Games and won African 3000m in 1984, and another **Evelyne Jerotich Langat** has 71:35 half marathon pb. Of his brothers **William Cheseret** has a marathon pb of 2:12:09 '04 and **Robert Cheseret** won NCAA 5000m in 2004 and 10000m in 2005, pbs 5000m 13:13.23 & 10000m 28:20.11 '05.

Jarrion LAWSON b. 6 May 1994 1.88m 75kg. University of Arkansas.
At LJ: WJ: '12- 3 (dnq 22 TJ).
Progress at LJ: 2011- 7.26/7.46w, 2012- 7.82/7.89w, 2013- 7.93, 2014- 8.39Ai/7.92/8.13w, 2015- 8.34/8.36w. pbs: 60m 6.60i '16, 100m 10.04/9.90w '15, 200m 20.86 '15, TJ 15.80 '12.

Tony McQUAY b. 16 Apr 1990 West Palm Beach, Florida 1.80m 70kg. adidas. Was at University of Florida.
At 400m: OG: '12- sf/2R; WCh: '11- h, '13- 2/1R, '15- 1R; US champion 2011, NCAA 2012.
Progress at 400m: 2008- 48.09, 2009- 46.84, 2010- 45.37, 2011- 44.68, 2012- 44.49, 2013- 44.40, 2014- 44.92, 2015- 44.81. pbs: 100m 10.22 '13, 10.13w '14; 200m 20.60 '12, 300m 32.40 '13.

Leonel MANZANO b. 12 Sep 1984 Dolores Hidalgo, Guanajuato, Mexico 1.65m 57kg. Hoka One One. Was at the University of Texas.
At 1500m: OG: '08- sf,'12- 2; WCh: '07-09-11-13-15: h/12/sf/sf/10; CCp: '10- 3, '14- 7. Won US 2012, 2014; NCAA 2005, 2008.
N.American 4x1500m record 2014.
Progress at 1500m: 2003- 4:07.83M, 2005- 3:37.13, 2006- 3:39.49, 2007- 3:35.29, 2008- 3:36.67, 2009- 3:33.33, 2010- 3:32.37, 2011- 3:33.66, 2012- 3:34.08, 2013- 3:33.14, 2014- 3:30.98, 2015- 3:36.16. pbs: 800m 1:44.56 '10, 1000m 2:19.73 '09, 1M 3:50.64 '10, 3000m 8:14.59i '06.
Has lived in the USA from the age of 4.

Cory MARTIN b. 22 May 1985 Bloomington, Indiana 1.96m 125kg. Nike. Was at Auburn University.
At SP: WCh: '13- 9; WJ: '04- 11 (dnq 15 HT); Won NCAA SP & HT 2008.
Progress at SP: 2004- 17.95i/17.60, 2005- 18.85, 2006- 18.42i, 2007- 19.63, 2008- 20.35, 2009- 20.43, 2010- 22.10, 2011- 20.72, 2012- 21.31, 2013- 20.67, 2014- 20.73, 2015- 20.74. pbs: DT 58.59 '08, HT 75.06 '09, 35lbWt 24.38i '10.

Aries MERRITT b. 24 Jul 1985 Marietta, Georgia 1.83m 74kg. Nike. Studied sports management at University of Tennessee.
At 110mh: OG: '12- 1; WCh: '09-11-13-15: h/5=/6/3; WJ: '04- 1. At 60mh: WI: '12-1, Won DL 110mh 2012, NCAA 60mh indoors & 110mh 2006, US indoor 60mh & 110mh 2012.
World 110mh record 2012.
Progress at 110mh: 2004- 13.47, 2005- 13.38/13.34w, 2006- 13.12, 2007- 13.09, 2008- 13.24, 2009- 13.15, 2010- 13.61, 2011- 13.12, 2012- 12.80, 2013- 13.09, 2014- 13.27, 2015- 13.04. pbs: 55m 6.43i '05, 60m 6.90i '10, 200m 21.31 '05, 50mh 6.54i '12, 55mh 7.02+i '12, 60mh 7.43Ai/7.44i '12, 400mh 51.94 '04.
Record 8 (and 2w) sub-13 second times in 2012. Revealed in 2015 that he had been suffering for two years from a kidney disorder and remarkably won World bronze medal just before undergoing a kidney transplant.

LaShawn MERRITT b. 27 Jun 1986 Portsmouth, Virginia 1.88m 82kg. Nike. Studied sports management at Old Dominion University, Norfolk, Virginia.
At 400m/4x400mR: OG: '08- 1/1R, '12- dnf ht; WCh: '05- res(1)R, '07- 2/1R, '09- 1/1R, '11- 2/1R. '13- 1/1R, '15- 2/1R; WJ: '04- 1/1R (1 at 4x100); WI: '06- 1R; WCp: '06- 1/1R, '14- 1/3R; won WAF 2007-09, DL 2013-14; US 2008-09, 2012-13.
World junior records 4x100m and 4x400m 2004, World indoor 400m junior best (44.93) 2005. World 4x110mh best 2015,
Progress at 200m, 400m: 2002- 21.46, 2003- 21.33, 47.69, 2004- 20.72/20.69w, 45.25; 2005- 20.38, 44.66; 2006- 20.10, 44.14; 2007- 19.98, 43.96; 2008- 20.08/19.80w, 43.75; 2009- 20.07, 44.06; 2011- 20.13, 44.63; 2012- 20.16, 44.12; 2013- 20.26, 43.74; 2014- 20.42, 43.92; 2015- 43.65. pbs: 55m 6.33i '04, 60m 6.68i '06, 100m 10.47/10.38w '04, 300m 31.30 '09, 500m 1:01.39i '12.
World age-18 400m record with 44.66 in 2005 and world low-altitude 300m best 2006 and 2009. Spent a year at East Carolina University before signing for Nike and returning home to Portsmouth. Two-year drugs ban for three positive tests from October 2009, reduced by three months after US arbitration panel declared that he had taken the steroid accidentally in buying a product intended for sexual enhancement; successfully challenged IOC rule preventing anyone serving 6 months or more from a drugs offence from competing in the next Games. Injured, he had to pull up in 2012 Olympic heat. Has won six successive World 4x400m gold medals.

Curtis MITCHELL b. 11 Mar 1989 Daytona Beach 1.88m 79kg. adidas. Was at Texas A&M University.
At 200m: WCh: '13- 3; WJ: '08- 4; Won US 2014, NCAA indoors 2010, NACC 2010.
Progress at 200m: 2007- 21.62, 2008- 20.74, 2009- 20.58, 2010- 19.99, 2011- 20.98, 2012- 20.89/20.24w, 2013- 19.97, 2014- 20.13/19.99w, 2015- 20.36. pbs: 60m 6.85i '10, 100m 10.25 '10, 10.23w '08.

Bryshon NELLUM b. 1 May 1989 Los Angeles 1.83m 79kg. Was at University of Southern California.
At 400m/4x400mR: OG: '12- sf/2R; WCh: '15- sf/1R; WJ: '06- 1R; WY: '05- 3; PAm-J: '07- 1. Won NCAA 2013.
Progress at 400m: 2004- 47.27, 2005- 46.81, 2006- 46.20, 2007- 45.38, 2010- 45.94, 2011- 45.56, 2012- 44.80, 2013- 44.73, 2014- 48.19, 2015- 44.65. pbs:

200m 20.23/19.99w '13, 300m 32.07 '15.
Career seriously threatened when he was shot three times in the leg by gang in 2009.

Vernon NORWOOD b. 10 Apr 1992 1.87m 77kg. New Balance. Was at Louisiana State University.
At 400m/4x400mR: WCh: '15- sf/res1R; WI: '16- 1R. Won NCAA indoors and out 2015.
Progress at 400m: 2011- 47.47, 2012- 45.72A/45.98, 2013- 45.56A/45.67, 2014- 45.02, 2015- 44.44. pbs: 200m 20.77 '15, 300m 32.07 '15, 600y 1:08.80i '13, 600m 1:18.57Ai '15.

David OLIVER b. 24 Apr 1982 Orlando 1.88m 93kg. Nike. Marketing graduate of Howard University.
At 110mh: OG: '08- 3; WCh: '07-11-13-15: sf/4/1/7; PAm: '15- 1; CCp: '10- 1. Won DL 2010, 2013, 2015; WAF 2008, US 2008, 2010-11, 2015. At 60mh: WI: '10- 3.
Two North American 110mh records 2010, world 4x110mh best 2015.
Progress at 110mh: 2001- 14.04, 2002- 13.92/13.88w, 2003- 13.60, 2004- 13.55, 2005- 13.29/13.23w, 2006- 13.20, 2007- 13.14, 2008- 12.95/12.89w, 2009- 13.09, 2010- 12.89, 2011- 12.94, 2012- 13.07, 2013- 13.00, 2014- 13.21, 2015- 12.98. pbs: 60m 6.88i '04, 50mh 6.50i '12, 55mh 7.01+i '12, 60mh 7.37i '11.
Mother, Brenda Chambers, 400mh pb 58.54 '80.

Omoghan OSAGHAE b. 18 May 1988 Lubbock 1.84m 75kg. adidas. Was at Texas Tech University.
At 60mh: WI: '14- 1; US indoor champion 2011, 2013-14.
Progress at 110mh: 2007- 13.99, 2008- 13.65, 2009- 13.51/13.42w, 2011- 13.23/13.18w, 2012- 13.24, 2013- 13.35/13.31w, 2014- 13.41/13.40w, 2015- 13.56/13.34w. pbs: 50m 6.36i '15, 60m 6.90Ai '14, 100m 10.62 '11, 60m 7.01i '08, 100m 10.64 '11, 200m 21.13 '09, 50mh 6.52i '12, 55mh 7.05i '14. 60mh 7.45i '14.
His father played soccer for Nigeria.

Jeff PORTER b. 27 Nov 1985 Summit, New Jersey 1.83m 84kg. Sports management degree from University of Michigan.
At 110mh: OG: '12- sf; PAm: '11- 4. Won NCAA indoor 60mh 2007.
Progress at 110mh: 2004- 14.08, 2005- 14.12, 2006- 13.93/13.92w, 2007- 13.57, 2008- 13.47, 2009- 13.37, 2010- 13.45, 2011- 13.26, 2012- 13.08, 2013- 13.35, 2014- 13.27/13.12w, 2015- 13.25. pbs: 60m 6.77i '14, 100m 10.56 '11, 50mh 6.50i '12, 60mh 7.46i '14.
Married to Tiffany Porter (see UK). His twin brother Joe played in the NFL.

Jason RICHARDSON b. 4 Apr 1986 Houston 1.86m 73kg. Nike. Was at University of South Carolina.
At 110mh: OG: '12- 2; WCh: '11- 1, '13- 4; WY: '03- 1 (1 400mh); won NCAA 2008.
World 4x110mh best 2015.
Progress at 110mh: 2004- 13.76, 2005- 13.50, 2006- 13.43/13.36w, 2008- 13.21, 2009- 13.29, 2010- 13.34, 2011- 13.04, 2012- 12.98, 2013- 13.20/13.17w, 2014- 13.29/13.27w, 2015- 13.12. pbs: 100m 10.90 '03, 200m 21.13 '03, 400m 46.96 '12, 60mh 7.53i '08, 400mh 49.79 '04.

Gil ROBERTS b. 15 Mar 1989 Oklahoma City 1.88m 81kg. Nike. Was at Texas Tech University.
At 400m/4x400mR: WCh: '09- h; WI: '12- 1R; US champion 2014, indoors 2012.
Progress at 400m: 2005- 47.47, 2006- 47.72A, 2007- 46.16, 2008- 46.14, 2009- 44.86, 2011- 45.22, 2012- 44.84, 2013- 45.73, 2014- 44.53, 2015- 45.29. pbs: 55m 6.26i '12, 100m 10.12/9.92w '14, 200m 20.22 '14, 300m 32.8+ '14.

Kurt ROBERTS b. 20 Feb 1988 Lancaster, Ohio 1.91m 127kg. Nike, Was at Ashland University. Won NACAC 2010, US indoor SP 2016.
Progress at SP: 2007- 16.39, 2008- 17.81, 2009- 18.78, 2010- 19.80i/18.76, 2011- 19.55, 2012- 21.14, 2013- 20.98, 2014- 21.50i/21.47, 2015- 19.79, 2016- 21.57i.

Michael RODGERS b. 24 Apr 1985 Brenham, Texas 1.78m 73kg. Nike. Studied kinesiology at Oklahoma Baptist University.
At 100m/4x100mR: WCh: '09- sf, '13- 6/2R, '15- 5; CCp: '14- 2/1R. At 60m: WI: '08-10-16: 4/2/6. Won US 100m 2009, 2014; indoor 60m 2008.
N.American 4x100m record 2015.
Progress at 100m: 2004- 10.55/10.31w, 2005- 10.30/10.25w, 2006- 10.29/10.18w, 2007- 10.10, 10.07w, 2008- 10.06/10.01w, 2009- 9.94/9.9/9.85w, 2010- 10.00/9.99w, 2011- 9.85, 2012- 9.94, 2013- 9.90, 2014- 9.91/9.80w, 2015- 9.86. pbs: 60m 6.48Ai/ 6.50i '11, 150mSt 15.33 '14, 200m 20.24 '09.
Dropped out of US World Champs team after positive test for stimulant on 19 July 2011, for which he subsequently received a 9-month suspension. Younger sister Alishea Usery won US junior 400m 2009, pb 53.27 '09.

Galen RUPP b. 8 May 1986 Portland 1.80m 62kg. Nike Oregon Project. Studied business at University of Oregon.
At (5000/)10000m: OG: '08- 13, '12- 7/2; WCh: '07- 11, '09- 8, '11- 9/7, '13- 8/4, '15- 5/5. At 5000m: WJ: '04- 9; PAm-J: '03- 1. At 3000m: WI: '10- 5, '14- 4; WY: '03- 7. Won US 5000m 2012, 10000m 2009-15, NCAA 5000m & 10000m (& indoor 3000m & 5000m) 2009, CC 2008.
N.American records: 10000m 2011 & 2014, junior 5000m 2004, 10000m 2005; indoor 5000m (13:11.44) 2011 & 2014, 3000m 2013, 2M 2012, 2014.
Progress at 5000m, 10000m: 2002- 14:34.05, 2003- 14:20.29, 2004- 13:37.91, 29:09.56; 2005- 13:44.72. 28:15.52; 2006- 13:47.04, 30:42.10; 2007- 13:30.49, 27:33.48; 2008- 13:49.8+, 27:36.99; 2009- 13:18.12i/13:42.59+, 27:37.99; 2010- 13:07.35, 27:10.74; 2011- 13:06.86, 26:48.00; 2012- 12:58.90, 27:25.33;

2013- 13:01.37, 27:24.39; 2014- 13:00.99, 26:44.36; 2015- 13:08.38, 27:08.91. pbs: 800m 1:49.87i/1:50.00 '09, 1500m 3:34.15 '14, 1M 3:50.92i/3:52.11 '13, 3000m 7:30.16i '13, 7:43.24 '10, 2M 8:07.41i '14, HMar 60:30 '11, Mar 2:11:12 '16.
Won US Olympic Trials on marathon debut 2016.

Duane SOLOMON b. 28 Dec 1984 Lompoc, California 1.91m 77kg. Saucony. Sociology graduate of University of Southern California.
At 800m: OG: '12- 4; WCh: '07- h, '13- 6; PAm: '07- h; CCp: '14- 6. Won US 2013-14, US indoor 2011.
World indoor 4x800m record 2014.
Progress at 800m: 2002- 1:51.76, 2003- 1:49.79, 2005- 1:47.84, 2006- 1:47.45, 2007- 1:45.69, 2008- 1:45.71, 2009- 1:46.82, 2010- 1:45.23, 2011- 1:45.86, 2012- 1:42.82, 2013- 1:43.27, 2014- 1:43.88, 2015- 1:45.56. pbs: 400m 45.98 '12, 600m 1:13.28 '13, 1000m 2:17.84 '10, 1500m 3:48.29 '08, 1M 4:03.26 '10.

Wallace SPEARMON b. 24 Dec 1984 Chicago 1.90m 80kg. Was at University of Arkansas.
At 200m/4x100mR: OG: '08- dq, '12- 4; WCh: '05-07-09-13: 2/3&1R/3/sf; PAm: '15- 5/1R; WCp: '06- 1/1R, '10- 1/1R. Won DL 2010, US 2006, 2010, 2012; NCAA 2004-05. At 4x400m: WI: '06- 1R.
WIR 4x400m and world indoor best 300m 2006. Two US indoor 200m records 2005.
Progress at 100m, 200m: 2003- 21.05, 2004- 10.38, 20.25/20.12w; 2005- 10.35/10.21w, 19.89; 2006- 10.11, 19.65; 2007- 9.96, 19.82; 2008- 10.07, 19.90; 2009- 10.18, 19.85; 2010- 10.15, 19.79/19.77w; 2011- 20.18; 2012- 10.26/10.06w, 19.90/19.82w; 2013- 10.29/9.92w, 20.10; 2014- 20.19, 2015- 20.03. pbs: 60m 6.66i '12, 100m 9.96 '07, 150mSt 14.87 '12, 300m 31.88i '06, 32.14 '09; 400m 45.22 '06.
Disqualified for running out of his lane after crossing the line in 3rd place at the 2008 Olympics. 3-month doping ban for use of a stimulant on 6 Jul 2014. His father (also Wallace, b. 3 Sep 1962) had pbs: of 100m 10.19 '87, 10.05w '86, 10.0w '81; 200m 20.27/20.20w '87; 1 WUG 200/4x100m, 3 PAm 200m 1987.

Nick SYMMONDS b. 30 Dec 1983 Blytheville, Arkansas 1.78m 73kg. Brooks Beasts TC. Biochemistry graduate of Willamette University.
At 800m: OG: '08- sf, '12- 5; WCh: '07-09-11-13: sf/6/5/2; WI: '08- 6; CCp: '10- 5. US champion 2008-12, 2015.
Progress at 800m: 2003- 1:49.51, 2004- 1:50.87, 2005- 1:48.82, 2006- 1:45.83, 2007- 1:44.54, 2008- 1:44.10, 2009- 1:43.83, 2010- 1:43.76, 2011- 1:43.83, 2012- 1:42.95, 2013- 1:43.03, 2014- 1:47.29i/1:51.20, 2015- 1:44.53. pbs: 400m 48.84 '04, 600m 1:14.47 '08, 1000m 2:16.35 '10, 1500m 3:34.55 '13, 1M 3:56.72i '07, 4:00.21 '13.

Christian TAYLOR b. 18 Jun 1990 Fayetteville 1.90m 75kg. Li Ning. Studied at the University of Florida.
At (LJ/)TJ: OG: '12- 1; WCh: '11- 1, '13- 4, '15- 1; WI: '12- 2; WJ: '08- 7/8 (res 1 4x400m); WY: '07- 3/1. Won DL 2012-15, NACAC 2010-11, US 2011-12, NCAA indoor 2009-10.
North American triple jump record 2015.
Progress at LJ, TJ: 2007- 7.29, 15.98; 2008- 7.79i/7.68/7.77w, 16.05; 2009- 8.02i/7.72, 16.98i/16.65/16.91w; 2010- 8.19, 17.18i/17.02/17.09w; 2011- 8.00/8.07w/17.96; 2012- 8.12, 17.81; 2013- 8.01/8.07w, 17.66; 2014- 8.09, 17.51; 2015- 8.18, 18.21. pbs: 60m 6.79i '11, 200m 20.70 '13, 400m 45.17 '14.
His 18.21 in the final round of the 2015 World Champs was the second longest ever legal TJ mark; it was 18.32 from take-off to landing. Both parents came from Barbados.

Michael TINSLEY b. 21 Apr 1984 Little Rock, Arkansas 1.85m 74kg. adidas. Studied criminal justice at Jackson State University.
At 400mh: OG: '12- 2; WCh: '13- 2, '15- 8; CCp: '14- 7; won DL 2014, NCAA 2008, US 2012-13.
Progress at 400mh: 2002- 52.5, 2004- 50.87, 2005- 48.55, 2006- 48.25, 2007- 48.02, 2008- 48.84, 2009- 48.53, 2010- 48.46, 2011- 48.45, 2012- 47.91, 2013- 47.70, 2014- 48.25, 2015- 48.34. pbs: 60m 6.92i '05, 200m 20.66 '09, 20.34w '13; 400m 46.02i '06, 46.05 '07; 55mh 7.39i '04, 60mh 7.84i '06, 110mh 13.86 '04.

Ben TRUE b. 29 Dec 1985 North Yarmouth. Maine 1.83m 70kg. Saucony. Studied art history and architecture at Dartmouth College.
At 5000m: WCh: '15- 6. World CC: '13- 6.
Progress at 5000m: 2006- 14:18.61, 2007- 13:14.85, 2010- 13:43.98, 2011- 13:24.11, 2012- 13:20.53, 2013- 13:11.59, 2014- 13:02.74, 2015- 13:05.54. pbs: 800m 1:50.07 '07, 1500m 3:40.07 '13, 1M 4:02.61 '07, 3000m 7:36.59 '13, 10000m 27:41.17 '12, road: 10M 46:48 '11, 15k 43:04 '14.
Married to Sarah Groff, 4th at 2012 Olympics in triathlon.

David VERBURG b. 14 May 1991 Oklahoma 1.68m 64kg. adidas. Was at George Mason University.
At 400m/4x400mR: WCh: '13- 1R, '15- sf/1R; WJ: 10- 1R; WI: '14- 4/1R. US champion 2015.
Progress at 400m: 2009- 47.15, 2010- 46.27, 2011- 46.09, 2012- 45.06, 2013- 44.75, 2014- 45.03, 2015- 44.41. pbs: 200m 20.63 '15, 300m 32.17 '15, 500m 1:01.29i '13, 600m 1:18.06i '12.

Ryan WHITING b. 24 Nov 1986 Harrisburg, Pennsylvania 1.91m 134kg. Nike. Studied civil engineering at Arizona State University.
At SP: OG: '12- 9; WCh: '11- 6, '13- 2; WI: '12- 1, '14- 1; PAm-J: '05- 1 (1 DT); Won DL 2013, US 2013, NACAC 2009, NCAA 2009-10, indoor 2008-10, DT 2010.
Progress at SP: 2006- 19.75, 2007- 20.35, 2008-

21.73i/20.60, 2009- 20.99, 2010- 21.97, 2011- 21.76, 2012- 22.00i/21.66, 2013- 22.28, 2014- 22.23i/21.31, 2015- 21.80i/21.37. pb DT 61.11 '08, Wt 18.94i '10.

Jesse WILLIAMS b. 27 Dec 1983 Modesto 1.84m 75kg. Oregon TC Elite. Graduate of University of Southern California, formerly at North Carolina State.
At HJ: OG: '08- dnq 19=, '12- 9=; WCh: '05/07- dnq 15/26, '11- 1, '13/15- dnq 23=/22=; WJ: '02- 4=; PAm: '15- 4=; WI: '08-10-12: 6=/5/6=; Won US 2008, 2010-11; NCAA indoors and out 2005-06; DL 2011.
Progress at HJ: 2001- 2.16, 2002- 2.21, 2003- 2.24, 2004- 2.24, 2005- 2.30, 2006- 2.32, 2007- 2.33, 2008- 2.32i/2.30, 2009- 2.36i/2.34, 2010- 2.34Ai/ 2.30, 2011- 2.37, 2012- 2.36, 2013- 2.31, 2014- 2.29, 2015- 2.31. pb LJ 7.53 '06.
Also a wrestler in high school.

Isiah YOUNG b. 5 Jan 1990 Manhattan, Kansas 1.83m 75kg. Was at University of Mississippi.
At 200m: OG: '12- sf; WCh: '13- sf, '15- h.
Progress at 100m, 200m: 2008- 10.96; 2009- 10.44, 21.22; 2010- 10.32, 20.98; 2011- 10.31, 20.81; 2012- 10.09/10.08w, 20.33/20.16w; 2013- 9.99/9.93w, 19.86; 2014- 10.23, 20.58/20.55w; 2015- 10.00/9.82w, 19.93/19.75w. pb 60m 6.61i '12.

Women

Nia ALI b. 23 Oct 1988 Philadelphia 1.70m 64kg. Nike. Was at University of Southern California.
At 100mh: WCh: '13- sf; WUG: '11- 1. Won NCAA 2011. At 60mh: WI: '14- 1, '16- 1; won US indoor 2013-14.
Progress at 100mh: 2005- 14.20, 2006- 13.63/13.55w, 2007- 13.25, 2008- 13.14, 2009- 13.17, 2011- 12.73/12.63w, 2012- 12.78, 2013- 12.48, 2014- 12.75. pbs: 60m 7.43i '14, 200m 23.90 '09, 800m 2:24.55 '07, 60mh 7.80i '14, HJ 1.86 '11, LJ 5.89 '09, SP 13.61 '09, JT 39.24 '09, Hep 5824 '09.
Son Titus born to her and Michael Tinsley in May 2015.

Kendall BAISDEN b. 5 Mar 1995 Ann Arbor, Michigan 1.80m 61kg. Student at University of Texas.
At 400m/4x400mR: WJ: '12- 1R, 14- 1/1R; WY: 11- 6 (2 Med R); PAm: '15- 1/1R; PAm-J: '13- 2/1R. Won NACAC 2015, NCAA 2014.
Progress at 400m: 2007- 57.68, 2008- 54.72, 2009- 53.05, 2010- 52.59, 2011- 52.87, 2012- 52.60, 2013- 52.03, 2014- 50.46, 2015- 50.50. pbs: 60m 7.39i '15, 100m 11.63/11.12w '15, 200m 22.60 '15.

Brigetta BARRETT b. 24 Dec 1990 Valhalla, New York 1.83m 64kg. Was at University of Arizona.
At HJ: OG: '12- 2; WCh: '11- 10, '13- 2; WUG: '11- 1. Won US 2011, 2013; NCAA 2011-13.
Progress at HJ: 2007- 1.72, 2008- 1.83A, 2009- 1.83, 2010- 1.91, 2011- 1.96, 2012- 2.03, 2013- 2.04, 2014- 1.95. pb 400m 55.04 '13.
Missed 2015 season due to a hip injury.

Tianna BARTOLETTA b. 30 Aug 1985 Elyria, Ohio 1.68m 60kg. née Madison. Nike. Studied biology at University of Central Florida, formerly at University of Tennessee.
At 100m/4x100mR: OG: '12- 4/1R; won US 2014. At LJ: WCh: '05- 1, '07- 9, '15- 1; CCp: '14- 3/1R; WI: '06- 1; PAm-J: '03- 4, won DL 2014-15, US 2015, NCAA indoors and out 2005. At 60m: WI: '12- 3, '14- 3; won US indoor 2012.
Progress at 100m, LJ: 2000- 5.73, 2001- 6.07, 2002- 11.98/11.91w, 6.20; 2003- 11.68, 6.28; 2004- 11.50/11.35w, 6.60; 2005- 11.41, 6.89/6.92w; 2006- 11.52/11.50w, 6.80i/6.60; 2007- 6.60/6.61w; 2008- 11.54, 6.53/6.58w; 2009- 11.05, 6.48; 2010- 11.20, 6.44; 2011- 11.29, 6.21/6.58w; 2012- 10.85, 6.48; 2013- 11.41; 2014- 10.92, 7.02; 2015- 10.94/10.90w, 7.14. pbs: 55m 6.69i '09, 60m 7.02i '12, 200m 22.37/22.33w '12.
Set long jump pbs in qualifying and final of 2005 Worlds. Competed on the US bobsled team in 2012/13. Married John Bartoletta in 2012.

Jessica BEARD b. 8 Jan 1989 Euclid, Ohio 1.68m 57kg. adidas. Studied psychology at Texas A&M University.
At 400m/4x400mR: WCh: '09- sf/res (1)R, '11- sf/1R, '13- 2R, 15- res 2R; WJ: '06- 5/1R, '08- 2/1R; PAm-J: '07- 3; won NCAA 2011.
Progress at 400m: 2004- 55.22, 2005- 52.39, 2006- 51.89, 2007- 51.63, 2008- 51.09A/51.47, 2009- 50.56, 2010- 51.02, 2011- 51.06, 2012- 51.19, 2013- 51.05, 2014- 50.81, 2015- 50.68. pbs: 60m 7.52i '11, 100m 11.86 '09, 11.49w '11; 200m 22.81 '13, 300m 36.65i '15.

Amanda BINGSON b. 20 Feb 1990 Victorville, California 1.70m 89kg. New York AC. Sports psychology graduate of University of Nevada, Las Vegas.
At HT: OG: '12- dnq 27; WCh: '13- 10, '15- 9; CCp: '14- 2; US champion 2013-14, NACAC 2012. North American hammer record 2013.
Progress at HT: 2009- 55.19, 2010- 64.07, 2011- 69.79, 2012- 71.78, 2013- 75.73, 2014- 75.12, 2015- 72.35. Pbs: DT 46.08A '11, Wt 22.42i '14.
Former gymnast.

Brittany BORMAN b. 1 Jul 1989 Festus, Missouri 1.80m 77kg. Nike. Was at University of Oklahoma.
At JT: OG: 12- dnq 15; WCh: '13- dnq 22, '15- 12. US champion 2013, NCAA 2010-12 (& DT 2010).
Progress at JT: 2006- 42.49, 2007- 47.28A, 2008- 43.20, 2009- 45.87, 2010- 53.00, 2011- 54.32, 2012- 61.51, 2013- 60.91, 2014- 62.05, 2015- 64.75. Pbs: SP 15.60i '11, 14.99 '10; DT 56.72 '10.

Tori BOWIE b. 27 Aug 1990 Sandhill, Mississippi 1.75m 61kg. adidas. Studied psychology at University of Southern Mississippi.
At 100m: WCh: '15- 3; US champion 2015. At 60m: WI: '16- 6. At LJ: won NCAA 2011.

Progress at 100m, 200m, LJ: 2008- 12.21w, 6.03w; 2009- 11.82, 23.99, 6.30/6.60w; 2010- 11.76/11.72w, 24.55/23.98w, 6.43/6.50w; 2011- 6.64, 2012- 11.28, 24.06, 6.78; 2013- 11.14/11.04w, 6.91, 2014- 10.80, 22.18, 6.95i/6.82; 2015- 10.81/10.75w, 22.23. pbs: 60m 7.11i '16, TJ 13.09i/12.65 '14.
First name actually Frentorish.

Tia BROOKS b. 2 Aug 1990 Saginaw, Michigan 1.83m 109kg. Nike. Was at University of Oklahoma.
At SP: OG: '12- dnq 19, WCh: '13- 8, '15- dnq 13. NCAA champion indoors and out 2012-13.
Progress at SP: 2008- 14.64, 2009- 14.13i/14.09, 2010- 17.37, 2011- 18.00, 2012- 19.00i/18.47, 2013- 19.22i/18.96, 2014- 18.83, 2015- 19.00. pb DT 46.64 '08.

Dezerea BRYANT b. 27 Apr 1993 Milwaukee 1.57m 50kg. University of Kentucky.
At 100m/200m: WJ: '10- 1R, '12-sf/3/1R; Won NCAA 200m 2015.
Progress at 100m, 200m: 2007- 25.33, 2009- 11.86/11.76w, 24.02; 2010- 11.59, 23.51; 2012- 11.29, 22.97; 2013- 11.20, 22.87/22.54w; 2014- 11.24/10.96w, 22.68; 2015- 11.00/10.99w, 22.18. pbs: 60m 7.12Ai '14, 7.15i '15; 300m 36.70i '15, 400m 54.46 '13.

Quanesha BURKS b. 15 Mar 1995 Ozark, Alabama 1.60m 55kg. University.of Alabama
At LJ: WJ: 14- 5; PAm: '15- 8; Won NCAA, NACAC 2015.
Progress at LJ: 2012- 6.13, 2013- 5.84w, 2014- 6,38, 2015- 6.93A/6.84/6.91w, 2016- 6.80i. pbs: 60m 7.33i '16, 100m 11.52 '14.

Mary CAIN b. 3 May 1996 New York 1.70m 50kg. Nike Oregon Project. Student at Fordham University (formerly Portland).
At 1500m: WCh: '13- 10; WJ: '12- 6. At 3000m: WJ: '14- 1.
Two world junior indoor 1000m records 2014; North American junior records: 800m, 1500m, indoor 1500m 2013-14, 1M 2014.
Progress at 1500m: 2011- 4:23.59, 2012- 4:11.01, 2013- 4:04.62, 2014- 4:06.34, 2015- 4:09.08. pbs: 500m 1:21.43i '14, 800m 1:59.51 '13, 1000m 2:35.80i '14, 2:38.57 '15; 1M 4:24.11i '14, 4:39.28 '12; 3000m 8:58.48 '14, 2M 9:38.68i '13, 5000m 15:45.46 '13.

Jillian CAMARENA-WILLIAMS b. 2 Aug 1982 Woodland, CA 1.80m 91kg. New York AC. Was at Stanford University.
At SP: OG: '08- 12, '12- dnq 15; WCh: '07/09: dnq 21/23, '11- 3; PAm: '07- 4, '15- 2; WI: '06-10-12-16: 6/6/4/5; WCp: '06- 6, '10- 5. Won PAm-J 2001, USA 2006, 2012 (indoor 2005-12).
North American shot record 2011, indoors 2012.
Progress at SP: 1999- 15.53, 2000- 15.23, 2001- 16.38, 2002- 16.82i/16.79, 2003- 17.49, 2004- 18.15, 2005- 17.94, 2006- 19.26i/19.02, 2007- 18.92, 2008- 18.51, 2009- 18.59i/18.08, 2010- 19.50, 2011- 20.18, 2012- 19.89i/19.82, 2015- 18.71. pb DT 52.52 '03.
Six-month doping ban from 1 Jul 2013. Married physiotherapist Dustin Williams on 5 Sep 2009. Daughter Miley born 24 June 2014.

Amber CAMPBELL b. 5 Jun 1981 Indianapolis 1.70m 91kg. Mjolnar. Was at Coastal Carolina University.
At HT: OG: '08/12- dnq 21/12; WCh: '05-11-13: dnq 18/13/13, '09- 11, '15- nt; PAm: '11- 3, '15- 2. Won US HT 2012, 2015; indoor Wt 2007-11.
Progress at HT: 2000- 49.16, 2001- 62.08, 2002- 63.76, 2003- 64.58, 2004- 67.23, 2005- 69.52, 2006- 67.52, 2007- 70.33, 2008- 70.19, 2009- 70.61, 2010- 71.94, 2011- 72.59, 2012- 71.80, 2013- 73.03, 2014- 73.61, 2015- 72.81. pbs: SP 14.81i '02, 14.42 '04; 20lb Wt 24.70i '10.

Kori CARTER b. 6 Mar 1992 Pasadena, California 1.65m 57kg. Nike. Human biology student at Stanford University.
At 400mh: WCh: '15- sf; WJ: '08- h; CCp: '14- 7; Won US 2014, NCAA 2013. At 100mh: WY: '09- 2.
Progress at 400mh: 2007- 62.21, 2008- 60.22, 2009- 59.89, 2010- 60.47, 2011- 57.10, 2012- 57.60, 2013- 53.21, 2014- 53.84, 2015- 54.41. pbs: 100m 11.57 '11, 200m 23.67 '12, 60mh 8.17Ai '13, 100mh 12.76 '13.

Michelle CARTER b. 12 Oct 1985 San Jose 1.75m 110kg. Nike. Liberal arts graduate from University of Texas.
At SP: OG: '08- 15, '12- 5; WCh: '09-11-13-15: 6/9/4/3; WI: '12-14-16: 3/5/1; WJ: '04- 1; WY: '01- 2; PAm: '11- 3; PAm-J: '03- 1; CCp: '14- 2. Won US 2008-09, 2011, 2013-15; NCAA indoor 2006.
North American shot record 2013 and indoors 2016.
Progress at SP: 2000- 14.76, 2001- 15.23, 2002- 16.25, 2003- 16.73, 2004- 17.55, 2005- 18.26, 2006- 17.98, 2007- 17.57, 2008- 18.85, 2009- 19.13, 2010- 18.80, 2011- 19.86, 2012- 19.60, 2013- 20.24, 2014- 19.84, 2015- 20.02, 2016- 20.21i. pbs: DT 54.06 '07.
Her father Mike set a world junior shot record in 1979 and won the Olympic silver in 1984, seven NCAA titles (4 in, 3 out) (for a unique father-daughter double) and WUG gold in 1981 and 1983, pb 21.76 '84. Her younger sister D'Andra (b. 17 Jun 1987) won the NCAA discus in 2009, pb 57.73 '08.

Kristi CASTLIN b. 7 Jul 1988 Douglasville, Georgia 1.70m 79kg. adidas. Political science graduate of Virginia Tech University.
At 100mh: Won PAm-J 2007. At 60mh: WI: '12- dq/false start ht; won US indoors 2012.
World best 4x100mh 2014 & 2015.
Progress at 100mh: 2005- 13.85, 2006- 13.73, 2007- 12.91/12.82w, 2008- 12.81, 2009- 12.89, 2010- 12.83/12.59w, 2011- 12.83/12.68w, 2012- 12.56/12.48w, 2013- 12.61, 2014- 12.58, 2015- 12.71. pbs: 55m 7.04i '08, 60m 7.47i '08, 100m 11.60 '12, 11.49w '11; 200m 23.46 '12, 50mh 6.81+i '12, 55mh 7.37i '12, 60mh 7.84Ai/7.91i '12. 400mh 60.44 '07.

Emma COBURN b. 19 Oct 1990 Boulder 1.73m 55kg. New Balance. Marketing graduate of University of Colorado.
At 3000mSt: OG: '12- 8; WCh: '11- 9, '15- 5; CCp: '14- 1; US champion 2011-12, 2014-15; NCAA 2011, 2013.
North American 3000m steeple record 2014 (unratified as no doping test).
Progress at 3000mSt: 2009- 10:06.21, 2010- 9:51.86, 2011- 9:37.16, 2012- 9:23.54, 2013- 9:28.26, 2014- 9:11.42, 2015- 9:15.59. pbs: 800m 2:09.81 '10, 1500m 4:05.29 '14, 1M 4:29.86i '13, 4:33.24 '12; 2000m 5:41.11i '15, 3000m 8:59.76 '15.

Vashti CUNNINGHAM b. 18 Jan 1998 1.85m 66kg. Nike. High school in Las Vegas, Nevada.
At HJ: WI: '16- 1; PAm-J: 15- 1; won US indoor 2016.
High jump records: World youth (=) 2015, World junior indoor 2016.
Progress at HJ: 2012- 1.76, 2013- 1.83, 2014- 1.90, 2015- 1.96, 2016- 1.99i. Pb LJ 5.85w '15.
Father Randall Cunningham was a quarterback in the NFL. Her brother Randall (b. 4 Jan 1996) has HJ pbs 2.26i 16, 2.24 '15.

Sharon DAY-MONROE b. 9 Jun 1985 Brooklyn, New York 1.75m 70kg. née Day. Asics. Was at Cal Poly San Luis Obispo.
At Hep: OG: '12- 15; WCh: '09-11-13-15: 9/17/6/14. US champion 2011, 2013-14. At Hep: WI: '14- 4. At HJ: OG: '08- dnq 24=; WCh: '09- dnq 17=; WJ: '04- 3; PAm: '07- 6; won PAm-J 2003, USA 2014, NCAA 2005.
US indoor heptathlon record 2014.
Progress at Hep: 2007- 5244, 2008- 5642, 2009- 6177, 2010- 6006(w), 2011- 6058, 2012- 6343, 2013- 6550, 2014- 6470, 2015- 6458. pbs: 200m 24.02 '13, 400m 56.54 '07, 800m 2:08.94 '13, 55mh 7.98i '12, 60mh 8.43i '14, 100mh 13.31 '15, HJ 1.95 '08, LJ 6.15 '12, 6.16w '13; SP 15.62 '15, JT 47.38 '13, Pen 4805Ai '14.
Married Dan Monroe on 1 Sep 2014.

Cynthia **'Janay' DeLOACH** b. 12 Oct 1985 Panama City, Florida 1.65m 59kg. Nike. Psychology graduate of Colorado State University.
At LJ: OG: '12- 3; WCh: '11- 6, '13- 11, '15- 8; WI: '12- 2, '16- 4; PAm: '07- 10. Won US 2013, US indoor 2011-13. At 60mh: WI: '14- 5.
Progress at LJ: 2004- 6.14Ai/6.05/6.14w, 2005- 6.27A/6.43w, 2006- 6.21Ai, 2007- 6.42Ai/6.41/6.45w, 2008- 6.48/6.51w, 2009- 6.33i/6.04, 2010- 6.61, 2011- 6.99Ai/6.97, 2012- 7.03/7.15w, 2013- 6.99/7.08w, 2014- 6.53Ai/6.41, 2015- 6.95, 2016- 6.89i. pb 55m 6.85Ai '05, 60m 7.31Ai '06, 100m 11.45 '08, 200m 24.60 '07, 24.26Aw '08; 60mh 7.82Ai '14, 7.85i '16; 100mh 12.84 '15, HJ 1.73i '11, SP 13.44i '14, Pen 4289i '11.
Married Patrick Soukup in September 2012.

Lashinda DEMUS b. 10 Mar 1983 Palmdale, California 1.70m 62kg. Nike. Was at University of South Carolina.
At 400mh/4x400mR: OG: '04- sf, '12- 2; WCh: '05-09-11-13: 2/2&1R/1/3; WJ: '02- 1/1R; WCp: '06- 2/2R. Won WAF 2005-06, PAm-J 1999, US 2005-06, 2009, 2011; NCAA 2002.
Two world junior records 400mh 2002.
Progress at 400mh: 1998- 64.61, 1999- 57.04, 2001- 55.76, 2002- 54.70, 2003- 55.65, 2004- 53.43, 2005- 53.27, 2006- 53.02, 2008- 53.99, 2009- 52.63, 2010- 52.82, 2011- 52.47, 2012- 52.77, 2013- 54.22, 2014- 55.17, 2015- 54.44. pbs: 50m 6.64i '01, 60m 7.73i '01, 100m 11.5 '01, 200m 23.35 '08. 400m 51.09 '10, 500y 1:05.8i '01, 800m 2:07.49 '12, 55mh 7.65i '04, 60mh 8.11i '04, 100mh 12.96 '11, 12.93w '05.
Twin sons Duane and Donte born 5 Jun 2007. Her mother, Yolanda Rich, had a 400m best of 52.19 in 1980.

Kimberlyn DUNCAN b. 2 Aug 1991 Katy, Texas 1.73m 59kg. Nike. Was at Louisiana State University.
At 200m: WCh: '13- sf; won US 2013, NCAA 2011-13 (and indoors).
Progress at 100m, 200m: 2007- 24.54, 2008- 24.33, 2009- 23.46, 2010- 11.84, 23.08/22.96w; 2011- 11.09/11.02w, 22.24/22.18w, 2012- 10.96/10.94w, 22.19; 2013- 11.08/11.02w, 22.35/21.80w; 2014- 11.20, 22.53/22.10w; 2015- 11.13/11.08w, 22.83. pb 60m 7.16i '13.

Allyson FELIX b. 18 Nov 1985 Los Angeles 1.68m 57kg. Nike. Elementary education graduate of University of Southern California.
At 200m/4x400mR: OG: '04- 2, '08- 2/1R, '12- 1/1R (1 4x100mR); WCh: '03- qf, '05- 1, '07- 1/1 4x100mR/1R, '09- 1/1R, '11- 3/1R (2 400m, 1 4x100m), '13- dnf, '15- 1 400m (2 4x100m & 4x400m); WJ: '02- 5; PAm: '03- 3; WI: '10- 1R. At 100m: OG: '12- 5; WY: '01- 1 (1 Medley R). Won DL 200m 2010, 2014-15; 400m 2010, WAF 200m 2005-06, 2009; US 100m 2010, 200m 2004-05, 2007-09, 2012; 400m 2011, 2015.
World junior record 200m 2004 after unratified (no doping test) at age 17 in 2003.
Progress at 100m, 200m, 400m: 2000- 12.19/ 11.99w, 23.90; 2001- 11.53, 23.31/23.27w; 2002- 11.40, 22.83/22.69w, 55.01; 2003- 11.29/11.12w, 22.11A/22.51, 52.26; 2004- 11.16, 22.18, 51.83A; 2005- 11.05, 22.13, 51.12; 2006- 11.04, 22.11; 2007- 11.01, 21.81, 49.70; 2008- 10.93, 21.93/21.82w, 49.83; 2009- 11.08, 21.88, 49.83; 2010- 11.27, 22.03, 50.15; 2011- 11.26+, 22.32, 49.59; 2012- 10.89, 21.69; 2013- 11.06+, 22.30, 50.19; 2014- 11.01, 22.02, 50.81; 2015- 11.09, 21.98, 49.26. pbs: 50m 6.43i '02, 60m 7.10i '12, 150mSt 16.36 '13 (world best), 300m 36.33i '07.
First teenager to won a World sprint title. Unbeaten in ten 200m competitions 2005 and in five 2007. Has women's record nine World gold medals including three in 2007 when she had a record 0.53 winning margin at 200m and ran a 48.0 400m relay leg, and four Olympic gold medals. Ran 47.72 relay leg at the 2015 Worlds.

IAAF female Athlete of the Year 2012. Older brother Wes Felix won World Junior bronze at 200m and gold in WJR at 4x100m in 2002, pbs: 100m 10.23 '05, 200m 20.43 '04.

Shalane FLANAGAN b. 8 Jul 1981 Boulder 1.65m 50kg. Bowerman TC. Was at University of North Carolina.
At 5000m/(10000m): OG: '04- h, '08- 10/3; WCh: '05- h, '07- 8, '09- (13), '11- (7), '13- (8), '15- (6). At Mar: OG: '12- 9. World CC: '10- 12, '11-3; 4k: '04-14, 05- 20. Won US 5000m 2005, 10000m 2008, 2011, 2013; HMar 2010, Mar 2012, CC 2008, 2010-11, 2013; 4km CC 2004-05, indoor 3000m 2007, NCAA CC 2002-03, indoor 3000m 2003.
North American records: 5000m and indoor 3000m 2007, 10000m (2) 2008, 15km & 25km road 2014.
Progress at 5000m, 10000m, Mar: 2001- 16:29.68, 2003- 15:20.54, 2004- 15:05.08, 2005- 15:10.96, 2007- 14:44.80, 2008- 14:59.69, 30:22.22; 2009-14:47.62i/15:10.86, 31:23.43; 2010- 14:49.08, 2:28:40; 2011- 14:45.20, 30:39.57; 2012- 31:59.69, 2:25:38; 2013- 31:04.85, 2:27:08; 2014- 2:21:14, 2015- 15:10.02, 31:09.02, 2:27:47dh. pbs: 800m 2:09.28 '02, 1500m 4:05.86 '07, 1M 4:33.81i '11, 4:48.47 '00; 3000m 8:33.25i/8:35.34 '07, Road: 15k 47:03 '14, 10M 51:45 '10, HMar 68:31 '13, 25k 1:22:36 '14, 30k 1:39:15 '14.
2nd New York 2010 on marathon debut and won Olympic Trials 2012. Married to Steve Edwards. Mother, Cheryl Bridges, set marathon world best with 2:49:40 in 1971 and was 4th in 1969 International CC, father Steve ran in World Cross 1976-7, 1979.

Phyllis FRANCIS b. 4 May 1992 New York 1.78m 61kg. Nike. Was at University of Oregon.
At 400m/4x400mR: WCh: '15- 7/res2R; PAm-J: '11- 3/1R. Won NCAA indoors 2014.
Progress at 400m: 2010- 55.82i, 2011- 52.93, 2012-51.22, 2013- 50.86, 2014- 50.46Ai/50.59, 2015-50.50. pbs: 60m 7.41i '14, 200m 22.77 '13, 600m 1:27.38i '11, 800m 2:04.83 '08.
Younger sister Claudia pbs 400m 52.51 '15, 800m 2:02.92 '15

Octavious FREEMAN b. 20 Apr 1992 Lake Wales, Florida 1.69m 57kg. adidas. Was at University of Central Florida.
At 100m/4x100mR: WCh: '13- 8/2R.
Progress at 100m, 200m: 2008- 11.64/11.59w, 23.95/23.71w; 2009- 11.48/11.20Aw, 23.20; 2010-11.18/11.11Aw, 23.24/23.19Aw; 2011- 11.21, 22.96; 2012- 11.09, 22.74; 2013- 10.87, 22.55; 2014- 11.35; 2015- 11.79. pbs: 60m 7.15i '12, LJ 6.05 '12.

Stephanie GARCIA b. 19 Oct 1990 1.68m 52kg. New Balance. Was at University of Virginia.
At 3000mSt: WCh: '11- h, '15- 9.
North American 3000m steeple record 2014 (unratified as no doping test).
Progress at 3000mSt: 2007- 10:15.83, 2008-10:17.38, 2009- 10:08.48, 2010- 10:05.05, 2011-9:41.12, 2012- 9:47.76, 2013- 9:45.78, 2014- 9:24.28, 2015- 9:23.48. pbs: 1500m 4:05.39 '15, 1M 4:28.84 '15, 2000m 5:48.25i '14, 3000m 8:58.09 '14, 2M 10:04.14i '15, 5000m 15:19.50 '15.

English GARDNER b. 22 Apr 1992 Philadelphia 1.62m 50kg. Nike. Was at University of Oregon.
At 100m/4x100mR: WCh: '13- 4/2R, '15- sf/2R; Won NCAA 100m 2013, indoor 60m 2012.
Progress at 100m, 200m: 2005- 11.99, 24.53; 2007-11.61, 24.01; 2008- 11.82/11.49w, 24.27/24.19w; 2011- 11.03, 23.02; 2012- 11.10/11.00w, 22.82; 2013- 10.85, 22.62; 2014- 11.01, 22.81; 2015- 10.79, 22.74. pbs: 60m 7.12i '12, 400m 53.73 '12.

Dawn HARPER NELSON b. 13 May 1984 Norman, Oklahoma 1.68m 61kg. Nike. Studied psychology at UCLA.
At 100mh: OG: '08- 1, '12- 2; WCh: '09-11-13-15: 7/3/4/sf; CCp: '14- 1; won DL 2012-15, PAm-J 2003, US 2009, 2014-5.
World best 4x100mh 2015.
Progress at 100mh: 2002- 13.63, 2003- 13.33/13.21w, 2004- 13.16/12.91w, 2005- 12.91, 2006-12.80A/12.86, 2007- 12.67, 2008- 12.54, 2009-12.48/12.36w, 2010- 12.77w, 2011- 12.47, 2012-12.37, 2013- 12.48, 2014- 12.44, 2015- 12.48. pbs: 60m 7.70i '05, 100m 11.66 '07, 200m 23.97 '06, 50mh 6.96i '12, 60mh 7.98i '06.
Married Craig Everhart (b. 13 Sep 1983, 400m 44.89 '04) in October 2007, and then Alonzo Nelson on 27 March 2013.

Kendra HARRISON b. 18 Sep 1992 Clayton, North Carolina 1.63m 52kg. University of Kentucky.
At 100mh: WC: '15- sf. At 60mh: WI: '16- 8. Won NCAA 100mh & 60mh indoors 2015.
Progress at 100mh, 400mh: 2010- 13.79, 59.19; 2011- 13.49, 59.13; 2012- 13.03/13.02w, 56.72; 2013-12.88/12.87w, 55.75; 2014- 12.71/12.68w, 54.76; 2015- 12.50/12.46w, 54.09. pbs: 60m 7.31i '14, 100m 11.64 '15, 200m 23.47i '14, 23.69 '15; 300m 37.84i '15, 400m 53.82i '13, 60mh 7.77i '16.

Queen HARRISON b. 10 Sep 1988 Loch Sheldrake, New York 1.70m 60kg. Studied of business marketing at Virginia Tech.
At 100mh: WCh: '13- 5; PAm: '15- 1. At 400mh: OG: '08- sf; WCh: '11- sf; PAm-J: '07- 1 (2 100mh); won NCAA 100mh, 400mh & 60mh indoors 2010.
World best 4x100mh 2014 & 2015.
Progress at 100mh, 400mh: 2007- 12.98, 55.81; 2008- 12.70, 54.60; 2009- 13.14/12.98w, 56.03; 2010- 12.61/12.44w, 54.55; 2011- 12.88, 54.78; 2012- 12.62, 55.32; 2013- 12.43, 2014- 12.46, 2015-12.52/12.50w. pbs: 400m 52.88 '08, 60mh 7.83i '16, LJ 5.82i '06.

Natasha HASTINGS b. 23 Jul 1986 Brooklyn, New York 1.73m 63kg. Under Armour. Studied exercise science at University of South Carolina.
At 400m/4x400m: OG: '08- res 1R; WCh: '07- sf/res 1R, '09/11- res 1R, '13- 5/2R, '15- sf/2R; WJ:

'04- 1/1R; WY: '03- 1; WI: '10/14/16- 1R, '12- 3/2R; PAm-J: '03- 1R, '05- 1/1R. Won US 2013, NCAA indoors and out 2007.
World junior 500m indoor best 2005, North American indoor 4x400m record 2014.
Progress at 400m: 2000- 54.21, 2001- 55.06, 2002- 53.42, 2003- 52.09, 2004- 52.04, 2005- 51.34, 2006- 51.45, 2007- 49.84, 2008- 50.80, 2009- 50.89, 2010- 50.53, 2011- 50.83Ai/50.97, 2012- 50.72, 2013- 49.94, 2014- 50.53, 2015- 50.24. pbs: 55m 7.08i '02, 60m 7.26i '13, 100m 11.24 '13, 11.08w '14; 200m 22.61 '07, 22.55w '14; 300m 35.9+ '07, 500m 1:10.05i '05.
Father from Jamaica, mother Joanne Gardner was British (ran 11.89 to win WAAA U15 100m at 14 in 1977).

Candace HILL b. 11 Feb 1999 Conyers, Georgia. 1.75m 59kg.
At 100/200m: WY: '15- 1/1.
World youth records 100m & 200m 2015
Progress at 100m, 200m: 2013- 11.81, 23.85; 2014- 11.44/11.34w, 23.14; 2015- 10.98, 22.43A/23.05.

Molly HUDDLE b. 31 Aug 1984 Elmira, New York 1.63m 48kg. Saucony. Was at University of Notre Dame.
At 5000m: OG: '12- 11; WCh: '11- h, '13- 6; CCp: '10- 3. At 10000m: WCh: '15- 4. Won US 5000m 2011, 2014; 10000m 2015. World CC: '10- 19, '11- 17.
Two North American 5000m records 2010-14.
Progress at 5000m, 10000m: 2003- 15:36.95, 2004- 15:32.55, 2005- 16:12.17i, 2006- 15:40.41, 32:37.87; 2007- 15:17.13, 33:09.27; 2008- 15:25.47, 31:27.12; 2009- 15:53.91, 32:42.11; 2010- 14:44.76, 31:27.12; 2011- 15:10.01, 31:28.66; 2012- 15:01.32, 2013- 14:58.15, 2014- 14:42.64, 30:47.59; 2015- 14:57.23, 31:39.20. pbs: 1500m 4:08.09 '13, 1M 4:26.84 '14, 3000m 8:42.99 '13, Rd: 15k 48:52 '14, 10M 51:44 '15, 20k 64:06 '16, HMar 67:41 '16.
Married Kurt Benninger CAN (pbs 1500m 3:38.03 '08, 1M 3:56.99 '08, 5000m 13:30.27 '09) in 2009. Won US road running titles in 2014 at a women's record four distances.

Emily INFELD b. 21 Mar 1990 University Heights, Ohio 1.63m 48kg. Saucony. Was at Georgetown University.
At 10000m: WCh: '15- 3. World CC: '13-21. Won NCAA indoor 3000m 2012.
Progress at 10000m: 2015- 31:38.71. pbs: 800m 2:06.05 '09, 1000m 2:44.56i '09, 1500m 4:07.77 '12, 1M 4:31.50i '13, 4:38.01 '10; 3000m 8:41.43 '13, 5000m 15:00.91i '16, 15:07.18 '15.
Older sister Maggie (b.10 Apr 1986) has pb 1500m 4:08.31 '12.

Kyra JEFFERSON b. 234 Sep 1994 Detroit 1.65m 57kg. Student at University of Florida.
At 200m/4x400mR: PAm: '15- 2/1R. Won NACAC 2015.
Progress at 200m: 2009- 24.27, 2010- 24.24/24.07w, 2011- 23.53, 2012- 24.11i/24.27, 2013- 23.43i, 2014- 22.78, 2015- 22.24. pbs: 60m 7.34i '14, 100m 11.73 '12, 11.66w '10; 400m 51.50 '15.

Carmelita JETER b. 24 Nov 1979 Los Angeles 1.63m 63kg. Nike. Was at California State University, Dominguez Hills.
At 100m/(200m)/4x100mR: OG: '12- 2/3/1R; WCh: '07- 3/res 1R, '09- 3, '11- 1/2/1R, '13- 3; won DL 100m 2010-11, 200m 2011; WAF 100m 2007, 2009; US 100m 2009, 2011-12. At 60m: WI: '10- 2.
Progress at 100m, 200m: 1998- 11.88, 2000- 11.69, 23.65/23.99w; 2001- 11.82, 24.20; 2002- 11.77/ 11.46w, 24.10; 2003- 11.61/11.43w, 23.67; 2004- 11.56, 23.98; 2005- 12.00/11.72w, 2006- 11.48, 23.54; 2007- 11.02, 22.82; 2008- 10.97, 22.47/22.35w; 2009- 10.64, 22.59; 2010- 10.82, 22.54; 2011- 10.70, 22.20; 2012- 10.78, 22.11; 2013- 10.93, 22.77; 2014- 11.24, 2015- 11.01/10.76w, 22.88/22.84w. pbs: 60m 7.02Ai/7.05i '10, 300m 37.52 '13, 400m 53.08 '09.
Second fastest woman of all-time at 100m.

Oluwafunmilayo **'Funmi' JIMOH** b. 29 May 1984 Seattle 1.73m 64kg. Nike. Was at Rice University.
At LJ: OG: '08- 12; WCh: '09/11/13- dnq 21/nj/ dnq 13; won US 2008-09, NCAA 2008.
Progress at LJ: 2004- 6.14, 2005- 6.31, 2006- 6.44, 2007- 6.46/6.62w, 2008- 6.91, 2009- 6.96, 2010- 6.81/6.87w, 2011- 6.88, 2012- 6.82, 2013- 6.92, 2014- 6.81, 2015- 6.74i/6.72. pbs: 60m 7.67i '04, 100m 12.03 '08, 11.65w '11; 200m 23.91A '11, 24.28 '08, 23.65w '06; 400m 59.57i '09, 60mh 8.32i '07, 100mh 13.51 '05, 13.39w '07; HJ 1.75i '05, 1.66 '07; SP 10.68i '06, Pen 3937i '06, Hep 5335 '07.

Lori **'Lolo' JONES** b. 5 Aug 1982 Des Moines 1.75m 60kg. Asics. Spanish & economics graduate of Louisiana State University.
At 100mh: OG: '08- 7, '12- 4; WCh: '07- 6; CCp: '10- 2; Won US 2008, 2010; NACAC 2004. At 60mh: WI: '08- 1, '10- 1; won NCAA indoor 2003, US indoor 2007-09.
North American indoor 60m hurdles record 2010.
Progress at 100mh: 2000- 14.04, 2001- 13.31/13.17w/12.7w, 2002- 12.84, 2003- 12.90, 2004- 12.77, 2005- 12.76, 2006- 12.56, 2007- 12.57, 2008- 12.43/12.29w, 2009- 12.47, 2010- 12.55, 2011- 12.67, 2012- 12.58, 2013- 12.50/12.44w, 2014- 12.55, 2015- 12.65/12.62w. pbs: 55m 6.87i '03, 60m 7.27i '03, 100m 11.24 '06, 200m 23.76 '04, 23.50w '03; 50mh 6.78i '12, 55mh 7.57i '03, 60mh 7.72i '10, 400mh 59.95 '00.
Crashed into 9th hurdle when leading Olympic final after pb 12.43 in semi in 2008. Won gold in the 2-man bobsled as brakeman on the US team at the 2013 World Championships and was 11th at the 2014 Winter Olympics.

Gia LEWIS-SMALLWOOD b. 1 Apr 1979 Urbana, Illinois 1.83m 93kg. Nike. Was at University of Illinois.

At DT: OG: '12- dnq 15; WCh: '11- dnq 15, '13- 5, '15- 11; PAm: '11- 4, '15- 3; CCp: '14- 1. US champion 2013-15.
North American discus record 2014.
Progress at DT: 2000- 53.52, 2001- 57.76, 2002- 52.28, 2003- 54.95, 2004- 57.88, 2005- 50.85, 2006- 49.95, 2007- 52.02, 2008- 59.96, 2009- 60.32, 2010- 65.58, 2011- 62.26, 2012- 63.97, 2013- 66.29, 2014- 69.17, 2015- 64.01. pb Wt 18.91i '02.

Shamier LITTLE b. 20 Mar 1995 Louisville, Kentucky 1.63m 52kg. Texas A&M University.
At 400mh: WCh: '15- 2; WJ: '12- dnf, '14- 1/1R; PAm: '15- 1/1R; won US 2015, NCAA 2014-15.
Progress at 400mh: 2011- 57.83, 2012- 57.44, 2013- 58.80, 2014- 55.07, 2015- 53.74. pbs: 200m 23.41 '14, 400m 51.06 '14, 60mh 8.43i '14, 100mh 13.77 '14.
Mother Tiffany Mayfield had HJ pb 1.73.

Chaunté LOWE b. 12 Jan 1984 Templeton, California 1.75m 59kg. née Howard. Nike. Economics graduate of Georgia Tech University.
At HJ: OG: '04- dnq 26=, '08- 6, '12- 6; WCh: '05- 2, '09- 7=, '15- dnq; PAm-J: '03- 3; CCp: '14- 2; WI: '06-10-12: 8/3/1; Won DL 2012, US 2006, 2008-10, 2012, 2014-15; NCAA 2004, indoors 2004-05.
3 North American HJ records 2010, indoors 2012.
Progress at HJ: 2000- 1.75, 2001- 1.84, 2002- 1.87, 2003- 1.89, 2004- 1.98A, 2005- 2.00, 2006- 2.01, 2008- 2.00, 2009- 1.98, 2010- 2.05, 2011- 1.78, 2012- 2.02Ai/2.01, 2014- 1.97, 2015- 1.91. pbs: 100m 11.83 '05, 100mh 13.78 '04, LJ 6.90 '10, TJ 12.93 '04, 12.98w '05.
Married Mario Lowe (b. 20 Apr 1980, TJ pb 16.15 '02) in 2005, daughters Jasmine born 30 Jul 2007 and Aurora in 4 Apr 2011 and son Mario Josiah in August 2013.

Molly LUDLOW b. 4 Aug 1987 Worthington, Ohio 1.73m 59kg. née Beckwith. Saucony. Was at University of Indiana.
At 800m: WCh: '15- sf.
North American 4x800m record 2015.
Progress at 800m: 2007- 2:13.99i/2:14.17, 2008- 2:06.46, 2009- 2:02.51, 2010- 1:59.83, 2011- 1:59.12, 2012- 1:59.18, 2014- 1:59.30, 2015- 1:58.68. pbs: 400m 54.13 '09, 600m 1:27.22i '10, 1000m 2:37.19i '14, 1500m 4:07.88 '14, 1M 4:34.44i '14.
Went to university on a soccer scholarship. Married Reed Ludlow in 2013.

Francena McCORORY b. 20 Oct 1988 Hampton, Virginia 1.70m 60kg. adidas. Psychology graduate of Hampton University.
At 400m/4x400mR: OG: '12- 7/1R; WCh: '11- 4/1R, '13- 6/2R, '15- 2R; CCp: '14- 1/1R; WI: '14- 1/1R; won DL 2015, US 2014, NCAA indoors 2009-10, out 2010.
World junior indoor 300m best 2007, North American indoor 4x400m record 2014.
Progress at 400m: 2004- 54.54, 2005- 55.26i, 2006- 51.93i, 2008- 51.54, 2009- 50.58, 2010- 50.52, 2011- 50.24, 2012- 50.06, 2013- 49.86, 2014- 49.48, 2015- 49.83. pbs: 55m 6.86i '06, 60m 7.43i '07, 100m 11.55 '16, 200m 22.92 '10, 300m 35.7+ '13, 500m 1:09.01i '12, 600m 1:29.07i '13, 800m 2:20.25i '07.

Candyce McGRONE b. 29 Mar 1989 Indianapolis 1.68m 59kg. adidas. Was at University of Oklahoma, formerly Florida State.
At 200m: WCh: '15- 4; won NCAA 100m 2011.
Progress at 100m, 200m: 2007- 11.54/11.29w, 23.82/23.24w; 2008- 11.50/11.37w, 23.47; 2009- 11.44, 23.30/23.17w; 2010- 22.84; 2011- 11.08/11.07w, 22.81; 2012- 11.38, 23.49; 2013- 11.19, 22.85; 2014- 11.26/11.20w, 23.43; 2015- 11.00/10.91w, 22.08. pbs: 60m 7.21Ai/7.27i '12, 400m 55.34 '11.

Brenda MARTINEZ b. 8 Sep 1987 Upland, California 1.63m 52kg. New Balance. Studied sociology and law at University of California - Riverside.
At 800m: WCh: '13- 3, '15- sf. At 1500m: WI: '16- 5.
N.American 4x800m & 4x1500m records 2014.
Progress at 800m, 1500m: 2007- 2:04.22, 4:21.18; 2008- 2:02.34, 4:17.09; 2009- 2:00.85, 4;09.52; 2010- 2:04.76, 4:18.17; 2011- 2:01.07, 4:10.77; 2012- 1:59.14, 4:06.96; 2013- 1:57.91, 4:00.94; 2014- 1:58.84, 4:01.36; 2015- 1:59.06; 2016- 4:04.58i. pbs: 1000m 2:38.48 '12, 1M 4:26.76 '12, 3000m 9:07.99+i '13, 2M 9:51.91i '13, 5000m 15:30.89mx '13, 15:41.50 '14; 5km Rd 15:24 '14.
Married Carlos Handler in October 2012.

Georganne MOLINE b. 6 Mar 1990 Phoenix, Arizona 1.78m 59kg. Nike Psychology and communications student at University of Arizona.
At 400mh: OG: '12- 5; WCh: '13- h.
Progress at 400mh: 2010- 57.88, 2011- 57.41, 2012- 53.92, 2013- 53.72, 2014- 54.00, 2015- 54.24. pbs: 200m 23.37 '13, 400m 52.08 '15, 500m 1:08.84i '15, 600m 1:26.70i '16, 800m 2:08.67i '13. 2:09.58 '14.
53.92 in Olympic final was seventh 400mh pb of her 2012 season.

Alysia MONTAÑO b. 26 Apr 1986 Queens, New York 1.70m 61kg. née Johnson. Nike. Was at University of California.
At 800m: OG: '12- 5; WCh: '07-11-13-15: h/4/4/h; PAm: '07- 6, '15- 2/res 1R; WI: '10- 3; CCp: '10- 8; won US 2007, 2010-13, 2015; NCAA 2007.
North American records: 4x800m 2015, indoor 600m 2013.
Progress at 800m: 2004- 2:08.97, 2005- 2:05.49, 2006- 2:01.80, 2007- 1:59.29, 2008- 2:00.57, 2009- 2:01.09, 2010- 1:57.34, 2011- 1:57.48, 2012- 1:57.37, 2013- 1:57.75, 2015- 1:59.15. pbs: 200m 24.41iA '13, 400m 52.09 '10, 600m 1:23.59i '13, 1:26.7+ '12; 1500m 4:28.43 '09.
Always runs with a flower in her hair. Married Louis Montaño on 19 Mar 2011, daughter Linnea Dori born 15 Aug 2014.

Sandi MORRIS b. 8 Jul 1992 Downers Grove, Illinois 1.63m 54kg. Student at University of Arkansas, formerly North Carolina.
At PV: WCh: '15- 4=; WI: '16- 2; PAm-J: 11- 2. Won NACAC 2014.
Progress at PV: 2009- 3.81, 2010- 4.05, 2011- 4.30, 2012- 4.23i/4.15, 2013- 4.43i/4.02, 2014- 4.55, 2015- 4.76, 2016- 4.95i.

Sharika NELVIS b. 10 May 1990 Memphis 1.78m 64kg. adidas. Sociology student at Arkansas State University.
At 100mh: WCh: '15- 8. Won NCAA 100mh & indoor 60mh 2014.
World best 4x100mh 2015.
Progress at 100mh: 2008- 14.23, 2009- 14.03, 2011- 13.45, 2012- 13.22/12.99w, 2013- 12.84, 2014- 12.71/12.52w, 2015- 12.34. pbs: 60m 7.28i '14, 100m 11.27/11.17w '14, 200m 23.19 '15, 22.70w '14; 400m 54.62 '13, 60mh 7.83i '15, LJ 6.32i '13, 6.27 '14.

Barbara NWABA b. 18 Jan 1989 Los Angeles 1.75m 64kg. Santa Barbara TC .Was at UC Santa Barbara.
At Hep: WCh: '15- 27 (dnf 100mh). US champion 2015.
Progress at Hep: 2009- 5039, 2010- 5552, 2011- 5733, 2012- 5986, 2014- 6307, 2015-- 6500. pbs: 200m 23.76 '15, 800m 2:07.13 '15, 60mh 8.40i '15, 100mh 13.38 '15, 400mh 60.51 '10, HJ 1.88 '16, LJ 6.23 '15, SP 15.00i '16, 14.64 '15; JT 46.60 '11, Pen 4661i '16.

Courtney OKOLO b. 15 Mar 1994 Carrolltown, Texas 1.68m 54kg. Student at University of Texas.
At 400m/4x400mR: WI: '16- 1R; PAm-J: '13- 1/1R. Won NACAC 2015, NCAA 2014.
Progress at 400m: 2009- 56.50, 2010- 54.34, 2011- 53.03, 2012- 52.40, 2013- 51.04, 2014- 50.03, 2015- 50.82A/50.99, 2016- 50.69i. pbs: 60m 7.52i '14, 100m 11.53 '16, 200m 22.93 '15, 600y 1:18.24i '15.

Demi PAYNE b. 30 Sep 1991 New Braunfels, Texas 1.82m 65kg. Student at Stephen F.Austin University, formerly University of Kansas.
At PV: WCh: '15- dnq 19; PAm: '15- 4; Won NCAA 2015.
Progress at PV: 2008- 3.81, 2009- 3.94, 2010- 3.92i/3.86, 2011- 4.06, 2012- 4.22i/4.20, 2013- 4.25i, 2014- 4.29irr/4.21, 2015- 4.75i/4.71, 2016- 4.90i.
Big improvement to three US collegiate records indoors in January 2015. Daughter Carlee born October 2013. Her father Bill Payne (b. 21 Dec 1967) in 1991 had pb best of 5.86 (US collegiate best) and was 2nd WUG.

Barbara PIERRE b. 28 Apr 1987 Port-au-Prince, Haiti 1.75m 60kg. Nike. Was at St. Augustine's College.
At 100m/4x100mR: OG: '08- qf; PAm: '11- 2/2R, '15- 3/1R. At 60m: WI: '12- 4, "16- 1.
Haiti records at 100m 2009, 200m 2008-09.
Progress at 100m: 2003- 11.98, 2005- 11.78, 2006- 11.66, 2007- 11.30, 2008- 11.40A, 2009- 11.18, 2010- 11.35, 2011- 11.14, 2012- 11.34, 2013- 10.85, 2014- 11.05, 2015- 10.92. pbs: 50m 6.22+i '12, 55m 6.89i '07, 60m 7.00i '16, 100y 10.38y '11, 200m 23.23 '10, 400m 57.04 '08.
With dual citizenship, she switched from US to Haiti 31 Dec 2007, and back to US 24 Mar 2010.

Jenna PRANDINI b. 20 Nov 1992 Clovis, California 1.72m 59kg. Student of psychology at University of Oregon.
At 200/4x100mR: WCh: '15- sf/2R. Won NCAA 100m 2015, LJ 2014; US 200m 2015.
Progress at 100m, 200m, LJ: 2008- 12.18/11.74w, 5.86; 2009- 11.81, 24.48/24.02w; 2010- 11.34, 24.61, 6.15/6.29w; 2011- 11.51/11.44w, 23.75/23.51w, 6.20; 2012- 24.07, 2013- 11.31/11.14w, 23.15, 6.15; 2014- 11.11, 22.60, 6.55; 2015- 10.92, 22.20, 6.80. pbs: 60m 7.15i '15, TJ 12.73/12.98w '10.

Chanelle PRICE b. 22 Aug 1990 Livingston, NJ 1.66m 53kg. Nike. Studied journalism at University of Tennessee.
At 800m: WY: '07- 6; WI: '14- 1; won US indoor 2013-14.
Two North American 4x800m records 2014-15.
Progress at 800m: 2004- 2:13.54, 2005- 2:08.72, 2006- 2:06.23, 2007- 2:02.38, 2008- 2:01.61, 2009- 2:03.30, 2010- 2:03.12i, 2011- 2:02.84, 2012- 2:00.15, 2013- 2:00.88, 2014- 1:59.75, 2015- 1:59.10. pbs: 400m 54.26 '13, 500m 1:10.30i 08, 1000m 2:36.63i '14, 1500m 4:16.52 '14, 1M 4:31.68 '14.

Brittney REESE b. 9 Sep 1986 Gulfport, Mississippi 1.73m 64kg. Nike. English graduate of University of Mississippi.
At LJ: OG: '08- 5, '12- 1; WCh: '07-09-11-13-15: 8/1/1/1/dnq 24; WI: '10-12-16: 1/1/1; won DL 2010-11, WAF 2009, US 2008-12, 2014; NCAA 2007-08.
North American indoor long jump record 2012.
Progress at LJ: 2004- 6.31, 2006- 5.94, 2007- 6.83, 2008- 6.95, 2009- 7.10, 2010- 6.94/7.05w, 2011- 7.19, 2012- 7.23i/7.15, 2013- 7.25, 2014- 6.92, 2015- 6.97, 2016- 7.22i. pbs: 50m 6.23i '12, 60m 7.24i '11, 100m 11.63 '09, 11.20w '11; HJ 1.88i/1.84 '08, TJ 13.16 '08.
Concentrated on basketball at Gulf Coast Community College in 2005-06. Has won six successive global titles

Sanya RICHARDS-ROSS b. 26 Feb 1985 Kingston, Jamaica 1.73m 61kg. Nike. University of Texas.
At (200m)/400m/4x400m: OG: '04- 6/1R, '08- 3/1R, '12- 5/1/1R; WCh: '03- sf/1R, '05- 2, '07- (5)/1R, '09- 1/1R, '11- 7/1R, '15- 2R; WJ: '02- 3/2; WCp: '06- 1/1; WI: '12- 1/2R. Won WAF 200m 2008, 400m 2005-09, US 2003, 2005-06, 2008-09, 2012; NCAA 2003.
WR distance medley 2015, US & North American 400m record 2006, world junior indoor bests 200m, 400m (2) 2004.

Progress at 200m, 400m: 1999- 23.84, 2000- 23.57, 54.34; 2001- 23.09, 53.49; 2002- 23.01, 50.69; 2003- 22.80i/22.86, 50.58; 2004- 22.49i/22.73, 49.89; 2005- 22.53, 48.92; 2006- 22.17, 48.70; 2007- 22.31, 49.27; 2008- 22.49, 49.74; 2009- 22.29, 48.83; 2010- 51.82; 2011- 22.63, 49.66; 2012- 22.09, 49.28; 2013- 51.43, 2014- 49.66, 2015- 22.87, 49.95. pbs: 60m 7.21i '04, 100m 10.97 '07, 10.89w '12; 300m 35.6 '05, 800m 2:10.74 '10, LJ 6.08 '01.

Left Jamaica at the age of 12 and gained US citizenship on 20 May 2002. Her 48.92 at Zürich in 2005 and then 48.70 at the World Cup in 2006 (to beat 22 year-old US record) were the world's fastest 400m times since 1996. Unbeaten in 13 finals outdoors at 400m in 2006 and after WAF win scored 200m/400m double at World Cup. Record 49 times sub-50 secs for 400m. Shared Golden League jackpot 2006, 2007 and 2009. IAAF female Athlete of the Year 2006 & 2009. Married US pro football cornerback Aaron Ross on 26 Feb 2010.

Brianna ROLLINS b. 18 Aug 1991 Miami 1.64m 55kg. Nike. Was at Clemson University.

At 100mh: WCh: '13- 1, '15- 4; Won US 2013, NACAC 2012. At 60mh: WI: '16- 2; won US indoor 60mh 2016, NCAA 100mh 2013, indoor 60mh 2011 & 2013.

North American 100m hurdles record 2013, world best 4x100mh 2014 & 2015.

Progress at 100mh: 2007- 14.48, 2008- 13.93, 2009- 13.83, 2011- 12.99/12.88w, 2012- 12.70/12.60Aw, 2013- 12.26, 2014- 12.53, 2015- 12.56. pbs: 60m 7.29i '16, 200m 23.04/23.02w '13, 300m 37.90i '10, 400m 53.93 '13, 60mh 7.76i '16, 400mh 60.58 '09.

Undefeated in 2013: inc. heats 200m- 7, 400m- 1, 60mh- 8, 100mh- 18.

Shannon ROWBURY b. 19 Sep 1984 San Francisco 1.65m 52kg. Nike Oregon Project. Was at Duke University.

At 1500m: OG: '08- 7, '12- 5; WCh: '09- 3, '11- sf, '15- 7; CCp: '14- 2; Won US 2008-09, NCAA indoor mile 2007. At 3000m: WI: '14- 8, '16- 3; CCp: '10- 2. At 5000m: WCh: '13- 7.

WR distance medley 2015, North American records: 2M 2014, 1500m 2015.

Progress at 1500m, 5000m: 2004- 4:17.41, 2005- 4:14.81, 2006- 4:12.31, 15:38.42; 2007- 16:59.97i, 2008- 4:00.33, 2009- 4:00.81, 15:12.95; 2010- 4:01.30, 15:00.51; 2011- 4:05.73, 2012- 4:03.15, 2013- 4:01.28, 15:06.10, 2014- 3:59.49, 14:48.68; 2015- 3:56.29. pbs: 800m 2:00.03 '15, 1000m 2:40.25i '15, 1M 4:20.34 '08, 2000m 5:46.2 '14, 3000m 8:29.93 '14, 2M 9:20.25 '14, 3000mSt 9:59.4 '06.

Former ballet and Irish dancer. Married Pablo Solares (Mexican 1500m record 3:36.67 '09) on 11 April 2015.

Raven SAUNDERS b. 15 May 1996 Charleston, SC 1.65m 89kg. Student at Southern Illinois University.

At SP: WJ: 14- 2.

Progress at SP: 2014- 17.82, 2015- 18.62i/18.35, 2016- 19.23i/18.75. pbs: DT 56.85 '16, HT 56.91 '16, Wt 20.78i '16.

Four indoor and four outdoor US junior records 2015.

Mary SAXER SIBEARS b. 21 Jun 1987 Buffalo, NY 1.69m 57kg. Nike. Marketing graduate of University of Notre Dame.

At PV: WI: '12- 4, 14- 8.

Progress at PV: 2004- 4.09i/3.81, 2005- 4.32i/4.19, 2006- 4.05i/3.90, 2007- 3.86i/3.80, 2008- 4.06, 2009- 4.30, 2010- 4.50, 2011- 4.60, 2012- 4.62Ai/4.53, 2013- 4.70, 2014- 4.71Ai/4.58, 2015- 4.62, 2016- 4.71Ai.

Married Justin Sibears on 9 Nov 2013.

Jennifer SIMPSON b. 23 Aug 1986 Webster City, Iowa 1.65m 50kg. née Barringer. New Balance. Studied political science at University of Colorado.

At 1500m: OG: '12- sf; WCh: '11- 1, '13- 2, '15- 11; won DL 2014. At 3000mSt: OG: '08- 9; WCh: '07- h, '09- 4; won NCAA 2006, 2008-09. Won US 1500m 2014-15, 5000m 2013, 3000mSt 2009.

North American records: 3000m steeplechase (3) 2008-09, indoor 2 miles 2015.

Progress at 1500m, 5000m, 3000mSt: 2006- 16:15.23, 9:53.04, 2007- 4:21.53, 15:48.24, 9:33.95; 2008- 4:11.36, 9:22.26; 2009- 3:59.90, 15:01.70i/15:05.25, 9:12.50; 2010- 4:03.63, 15:33.33; 2011- 4:03.54, 15:11.49; 2012- 4:04.07, 2013- 4:00.48, 14:56.26; 2014- 3:57.22, 2015- 3:57.30. pbs: 800m 2:00.45 '13, 1M 4:22.18 '15, 2000m 5:45.7 '14, 3000m 8:29.58 '14, 2M 9:18.35i '15.

Married Jason Simpson on 8 Oct 2010. Won 5th Avenue Mile 2011.

Brittany SMITH b. 25 Mar 1991 1.78m 89kg. Was at Illinois State University.

At SP: WJ: 10- 6. Won NACAC 2012.

Progress at SP: 2008- 13.52, 2009- 13.88, 2010- 15.98, 2011- 17.19i/15.83, 2012- 17.92, 2013- 17.85, 2014- 18.57, 2015- 19.01i/18.96. pbs: DT 55.15 '15, HT 70.27 '14, Wt 21.51i '13.

Shalonda SOLOMON b. 19 Dec 1985 Inglewood, California 1.69m 56kg. Reebok. Was at University of South Carolina.

At (100m)/200m/4x100m: WCh: '11- 4/res (1)R; WJ: '04- 1/1R; PAm-J: '03- 1/1/1R; CCp: '10- (2)/1R. Won NCAA 200m 2006, NCAAC 100m & 200m 2006.

Progress at 100m, 200m: 2001- 11.57/11.37w, 23.65/23.22w; 2002- 11.51/11.46w, 23.31; 2003- 11.35/11.25w, 22.93; 2004- 11.41/11.32w, 22.82; 2005- 11.29, 22.74/22.72w; 2006- 11.09/11.07w, 22.36/22.30w; 2007- 11.33, 22.77; 2008- 11.16, 22.48/22.36w; 2009- 11.04/11.00w, 22.41; 2010- 10.90, 22.47; 2011- 11.08/10.90w, 22.15; 2012- 11.26, 22.82; 2013- 11.04/10.97w, 22.41/22.33w; 2014- 11.12, 22.64/22.54w; 2015- 11.06/10.97w, 22.56. pbs: 55m 6.72i '09, 60m 7.15Ai '11, 7.21i '06; 300m 36.45i '09, 400m 52.83 '16.

Ashley SPENCER b. 8 Jun 1993 Indianapolis 1.68m 54kg. Student at University of Texas, formerly Illinois.
At 400m/4x400mR: WCh: '13- sf/2R; WJ: '12- 1/1R; WI: '16- 2/1R. Won NCAA 2012-13.
Progress at 400m: 2012- 50.50, 2013- 50.28, 2014- 51.38, 2015- 51.72, 2016- 51.29i. pbs: 60m 7.42i '13, 100m 11.34/11.27w '14, 200m 22.92/22.69w '14, 100mh 14.40/14.28w '11, 400mh 56.32 '13.

Jeneva STEVENS b. 28 Oct 1989 Dolton, Illinois 1.78m 102kg. née McCall. Was at Southern Illinois University.
At HT: WCh: '11- dnq 14, '13- 9; WUG: '13- 1. At SP: WCh: '15- 10; PAm: '15- 6; WI: '14- 8. Won NCAA DT 2010, HT 2012.
Progress at HT: 2009- 55.83, 2010- 64.17, 2011- 69.55, 2012- 69.38, 2013- 74.77, 2014- 70.78, 2015- 72.69. Pbs: SP 19.10i '12, 18.47 '13, DT 59.45 '12, Wt 23.94i '13.
Daughter of 1994-5 WBC world heavyweight boxing champion Oliver McCall.

Jasmin STOWERS b. 23 Sep 1991 Pendleton, SC 1.75m 64kg. Degree in nutrition from Louisiana State University.
At 100mh: WY: '07- 4; won NCAA indoor 60mh 2013, US 2015.
World best 4x100mh 2015.
Progress at 100mh: 2005- 14.27w, 2006- 14.05/13.82Aw, 2007- 13.69/13.68w, 2008- 13.66/13.46w, 2009- 13.59/13.32Aw, 2010- 14.47, 2011- 12.88/12.86w, 2012- 12.92, 2013- 13.00/ 12.88w, 2014- 12.71/12.54w, 2015- 12.35. pbs: 60m 7.51i '12, 100m 11.82 '11, 60mh 7.84i '15, 400mh 61.17 '08.

Jennifer SUHR b. 6 Feb 1982 Fredonia, New York 1.80m 64kg. adidas. née Stuczynski. Graduate of Roberts Wesleyan University, now studying child psychology.
At PV: OG: '08- 2, '12- 1; WCh: '07-11-13-15: 10/4/2/4=; PAm: '15- 3; WI: '08-14-16: 2/5=/1; WCp: '06- nh; US champion 2006-10, 2012-15; indoors 2005, 2007-09, 2011-13.
Records: world indoors 2013 & 2016, four North American pole vault records 2007-08, four indoors 2009-13.
Progress at PV: 2002- 2.75, 2004- 3.49, 2005- 4.57i/4.26, 2006- 4.68i/4.66, 2007- 4.88, 2008- 4.92, 2009- 4.83i/4.81, 2010- 4.89, 2011- 4.91, 2012- 4.88i/4.81, 2013- 5.02Ai/4.91, 2014- 4.73i/4.71, 2015- 4.82, 2016- 5.03i. pbs: 55mh 8.07i '05, JT 46.82 '05.
All-time top scorer at basketball at her university, then very rapid progress at vaulting.

Jeneba TARMOH b. 27 Sep 1989 San Jose CA 1.67m 59kg. Nike. Was at Texas A&M University.
At (100m)/200m/4x100m: OG: '12- res (1)R; WCh: '11- h, '13- 5/2R, '15- 6; WJ: '06- 7/1R, '08- (1)/1R. Won NCAAC 100m 2010.
Progress at 100m, 200m: 2004- 12.07w, 2005- 11.81/11.61w, 24.04/23.56w; 2006- 11.24, 23.14; 2007- 11.27, 23.34/23.20w; 2008- 11.21, 22.94; 2009- 11.31, 23.31i/23.43/23.16w; 2010- 11.19/ 11.00w, 22.65; 2011- 11.23/10.94w, 22.28; 2012- 11.07, 22.35/22.30w; 2013- 10.93, 22.70/22.15w; 2014- 11.11, 22.41/22.06w; 2015- 10.93, 22.23. pbs: 50m 6.14+i '12. 55m 6.86Ai '06, 60m 7.22i '12.
Her parents came from Sierra Leone.

Cassandra TATE b. 11 Sep 1990 Hammond, Louisiana 1.74m 64kg. Management graduate of Louisiana State University.
At 400m/4x400m: WCh: '15- 3; WI: '14- 1R; won NCAA & NACAC 2012.
Progress at 400mh: 2010- 56.87, 2011- 55.99, 2012- 55.22, 2013- 55.45, 2014- 54.70, 2015- 54.01. pbs: 60m 7.49i '11, 100m 11.79 '08, 11.47w '10; 200m 23.37i '10, 23.68 '09; 400m 52.40Ai '14, 52.51 '15; 60mh 8.61i '09, 100mh 14.21 '08, 14.08w '07.

Jasmine TODD b. 23 Dec 1993 San Diego 1.65m 55kg. Student of psychology at University of Oregon.
At 100m/LJ/4x100m: '15- sf/dq 19, 2R.
Progress at 100m, LJ: 2010- 11.99/11.64Aw, 6.08i/6.07; 2011- 11.80/11.73w, 6.01; 2012- 11.76, 6.13; 2013- 12.02/12.00w, 5.95; 2014- 11.25, 6.50Ai/6.06; 2015- 10.92/10.86w, 6.84. pbs: 60m 7.15i '15, 200m 22.89 '15, TJ 13.10 '15.

Kaylin WHITNEY b. 9 Mar 1998 Kissimmee, Florida 1.67m 57kg. Nike.
At (100m)/200m: WJ: '14- 3/1/1R; PAm: '15- 1/1R.
World youth records 100m 2014, 200m (3) 2014-15
Progress at 100m, 200m: 2012- 11.91, 2013- 11.54/11.47Aw, 23.40/23.28Aw; 2014- 11.10, 22.49; 2015- 11.37/11.01w, 22.47.

Charonda WILLIAMS b. 27 Mar 1987 Richmond, California 1.67m 55kg. adidas. Was at Arizona State University.
At 200m: WCh: '09- sf, '13- 6. Won DL 2012.
Progress at 200m: 2006- 24.19/24.08w, 2007- 23.53, 2008- 23.09, 2009- 22.55/22.39w, 2010- 22.97, 2011- 22.85/22.78w, 2012- 22.52, 2013- 22.71, 2014- 23.41, 2015- 22.32. pbs: 55m 6.99Ai '08, 60m 7.29Ai '09, 7.36i '11; 100m 11.07 '13, 10.95w '12; 300m 37.04i '11, 400m 52.71 '11, LJ 5.91 '07, 6.03w '00.

Kendell WILLIAMS b. 14 Jun 1995 1.73m 64kg. Student at University of Georgia.
At Hep: WJ: '12- 8; WY: '11- 11. At Pen: WI: '16- 6. At 100mh: WJ: '14- 1; WY: '11- 3.
Progress at Hep: 2011- 5169, 2012- 5578, 2014- 5572A, 2014- 6018, 2015- 6223. pbs: 200m 24.26/23.67w '15, 800m 2:17.30i '15, 2:18.86 '14; 60mh 8.09i '16, 100mh 12.87 '14, 400mh 58.63 '10, HJ 1.88Ai/1.83 '14, LJ 6.54i/6.46 '15, SP 13.55i '16, 12.59 '14; JT 38,74 '15, Pen 4703i '16.

Tiffany WILLIAMS b. 5 Feb 1983 Miami 1.58m 57kg. née Ross. Reebok. Retail management graduate of University of Southern Carolina.
At 400mh: OG: '08- 8; WCh: '07- 7, '09- 5; WJ:

'02- 4/1R; WI: '06- 2R. Won NACAC 2015, US 2007-08.
Progress at 400mh: 2000- 58.50, 2001- 57.91, 2002- 55.22, 2003- 55.89, 2005- 54.56, 2006- 53.79, 2007- 53.28, 2008- 53.54, 2009- 53.83, 2011- 55.77, 2012- 55.01, 2013- 55.04, 2014- 54.74, 2015- 54.27. pbs: 200m 24.40 '08, 24.35i '06; 300m 37.36 '12, 400m 52.43i '05, 52.45 '06; 55mh 7.63i '03, 60mh 8.29i '05, 100mh 12.99 '05, 12.8 '08; TJ 12.49.
Married to Steven Williams, they have a daughter, Samya, born in 2004.

Ajee' WILSON b. 8 May 1994 Neptune, New Jersey 1.69m 55kg. adidas. Student of kinesiology at Temple University, Philadelphia.
At 800m: WCh: '13- 6; WJ: '10- 5, '12- 1; WY: 11- 1; CCp: '14- 2; WI: '16- 2; won US 2014, indoor 2013-14, 2016.
Records: WR distance medley 2015, North American 4x800m 2014, world junior 600m & North American junior 800m 2013.
Progress at 800m: 2008- 2:11.43, 2009- 2:07.08, 2010- 2:04.18, 2011- 2:02.64, 2012- 2:00.91, 2013- 1:58.21, 2014- 1:57.67, 2015- 1:57.87. pbs: 400m 53.63 '14, 500m 1:10.27i '15, 600m 1:26.45 '13, 1000m 2:48.88i '14, 1500m 4:12.10 '14, 1M 4:50.22i '16, 3000m 10:13.41 '07.
Elder sister Jade has 400mh pb 59.90 '12.

Kara WINGER b. 10 Apr 1986 Seattle 1.83m 84kg. née Patterson. Studied interior design at Purdue University.
At JT: OG: '08/12- dnq 41/31; WCh: '09/11- dnq 29/21; PAm: '15- 2; PAm-J: '05- 2; CCp: '10- 6, '14- 7. US Champion 2008-11, 2014-15.
North American javelin record 2010.
Progress at JT: 2003- 44.75, 2004- 48.51. 2005- 52.09, 2006- 567.19, 2008- 61.56, 2009- 63.95, 2010- 66.67, 2011- 62.76, 2012- 60.49, 2013- 57.12, 2014- 62.90, 2015- 66.47. Pb DT 35.17 '11.
Married Russ Winger (pbs SP 21.29i '08, 21.25 '10; DT 66.04 '11, dnq 26 WCh 15) on 28 Sep 2014.

UZBEKISTAN

Governing body: Athletic Federation of Uzbekistan, Navoi str. 30, 100129 Tashkent.

Svetlana RADZIVIL b. 17 Jan 1987 Tashkent 1.84m 61kg
At HJ: OG: '08- dnq 18, '12- 7; WCh: '09- dnq 21=, '11- 8=, '15- 9=; AsiG: '06-10-14: 7/1/1; AsiC: '09-11-13-15: 3/2/2/1; WJ: '02- dnq, '04- 13, '06- 1; WY: '03- dnq; CCp: '14- 4; WI: '12- 8. Won Asi-J 2006, Asian indoor 2014, 2016.
Progress at HJ: 2002- 1.84, 2003- 1.78, 2004- 1.88, 2005- 1.85, 2006- 1.91, 2007- 1.91, 2008- 1.93, 2009- 1.91, 2010- 1.95, 2011- 1.95, 2012- 1.97, 2013- 1.94, 2014- 1.96, 2015- 1.94.

VENEZUELA

Governing body: Federación Venezolana de Atletismo, Apartado Postal 29059, Caracas. Founded 1948.

National Champions 2015: **Men** 100m: Yeiker Mendoza 10.49, 200m: Alvaro Cassiani 20.95, 400m: Freddy Mezones 45.53, 800m/1500m: Lucirio Garrido 1:48.78/3:52.14, 10000m: Walter Suárez 30:57.82, 3000mSt: John Alfonso 9:15.78, 110mh: Javier González 14.73, 400mh: Victor Solarte 51.92, HJ: Albert Bravo 2.11, PV: José Milanesse & Aniels Vargas 4.20, LJ: Diego Hernández 7.82, TJ: Roy Martínez 15.88, SP: Yosner Ortiz 17.50, DT: Jesús Parejo 56.35, HT: Prinston Quailey 61.25, JT: Manuel Cruz 64.20, Dec: Oscar Campos 7138, 20kW/20000mW: Yerenman Salazar 1:29:49/1:33:20.3. **Women**: 100m: ?, 200m: Nercely Soto 23.38, 400m/400mh: Magdalena Mendoza 54.14/ 58.65, 800m: Ydanis Navas 2:10.01, 1500m: María Garrido 4:40.51, 10000m: Zuleima Amaya 36:40.49, 100mh: Génesis Romero 13.48, HJ: Arianna Gutiérrez 1.75, PV: Robeilys Peinado 4.35, LJ/TJ: Yulimar Rojas 6.57/14.17, SP: Ahymará Espinoza 16.87, DT: Elizabeth Álvarez 49.95, HT: Diurkina Freytes 53.33, JT: Estefany Chacón 49.16, Hep: Daryelis Key 4232, 20kW/20000mW: Nayibet Rosales 1:51:10/1:50:49.7.

Rosa RODRÍGUEZ b. 2 Jul 1986 Acarigua, Portuguesa 1.80m 85kg. Zheus.
At HT: OG: '12: dnq 26; WCh: '07-09-13: dnq 34/29/15, '15- 11; WJ: '04- dnq; WY: '03- 13; PAm: '11- 8, '15- 1; SACh: '05-09-11-13-15: 3/4/3/1/1; Won SAm-U23 2008; VEN 2005, 2007-08, 2010-11.
Six Venezuelan hammer records 2006-13.
Progress at HT: 2002- 53.75, 2003- 56.23, 2004- 59.24, 2005- 62.85, 2006- 64.22, 2007- 66.96, 2008- 65.96, 2009- 69.46, 2010- 69.10, 2011- 67.90, 2012- 72.83, 2013- 73.64, 2014- 72.20, 2015- 73.06. pb SP 15.07 '11.

Yulimar ROJAS b. 21 Oct 1995 Caracas 1.89m 75kg.
At TJ (LJ): WJ: '14- dnq 17 (11); PAm: '15- 4 (11); SACh: '15- 1; WI: '16- 1. Won SAu23 LJ & TJ 2014, SAmJ HJ 2011.
Venezuelan records: LJ & TJ (2) 2015. Three South American indoor TJ records 2016.
Progress at TJ: 2014- 13.65, 2015- 14.20, 2016- 14.69i. Pbs: 100m 11.94 '13, HJ 1.87 '13, LJ 6.57 '15.
Lives in Madrid and coached by Iván Pedroso.

ZAMBIA

Kabange MUPUPO b. 21 Sep 1992 1.70m 57kg.
At 400m: WCh: '15- sf; CG: '14- sf; AfG: '15- 1; AfCh: '14- 2; CCp: '14- 4/3R.
Zambian records 100m & 200m 2014, 400m (4) 2014-15.
Progress at 400m: 2014- 50.87, 2015- 50.22. pb: 100m 11.69A '14, 200m 23.35A '14.
Before turning to athletics in the spring of 2014, Mupopo captained the Zambian football team.

INTRODUCTION TO WORLD LISTS AND INDEX

Records

World, World U20 and U18, Olympic, Area and Continental records are listed for standard events. In running events up to and including 400 metres, only fully automatic times are shown. Marks listed are those which are considered statistically acceptable by the ATFS, and thus may differ from official records. These are followed by 'odd events', road bests and bests by over 35/40 masters.

World All-time and Year Lists

Lists are presented in the following format: Mark, Wind reading (where appropriate), Name, Nationality (abbreviated), Date of birth, Position in competition, Meeting name (if significant), Venue, Date of performance.

In standard events the best 30 or so performances are listed followed by the best marks for other athletes. Position, meet and venue details have been omitted beyond 100th in year lists.

In the all-time lists performances which have been world records (or world bests, thus including some unratified marks) are shown with WR against them (or WIR for world indoor records).

Juniors (U20) are shown with-J after date of birth, and Youths (U18) with -Y.

Indexes

These contain the names of all athletes ranked with full details in the world year lists for standard events (and others such as half marathon). The format of the index is as follows:

Family name, First name, Nationality, Birthdate, Height (cm) and Weight (kg), 2015 best mark, Lifetime best (with year) as at the end of 2014.

* indicates an athlete who is profiled in the Biographies section, and ^ one who has been profiled in previous editions.

General Notes

Altitude aid

Marks set at an altitude of 1000m or higher have been suffixed by the letter "A" in events where altitude may be of significance.

Although there are no separate world records for altitude assisted events, it is understood by experts that in all events up to 400m in length (with the possible exclusion of the 110m hurdles), and in the horizontal jumps, altitude gives a material benefit to performances. For events beyond 800m, however, the thinner air of high altitude has a detrimental effect.

Supplementary lists are included in relevant events for athletes with seasonal bests at altitude who have low altitude marks qualifying for the main list.

Some leading venues over 1000m

Addis Ababa ETH	2365m
Air Force Academy USA	2194
Albuquerque USA	1555
Antananarivo MAD	1350
Ávila ESP	1128
Bloemfontein RSA	1392
Bogotá COL	2644
Boulder USA	1655
Bozeman USA	1467
Calgary CAN	1045
Cali COL	1046
Ciudad de Guatemala GUA	1402
Ciudad de México MEX	2247
Cochabamba BOL	2558
Colorado Springs USA	1823
Cuenca ECU	2561
Denver USA	1609
El Paso USA	1187
Flagstaff USA	2107
Fort Collins USA	1521
Gabarone BOT	1006
Germiston RSA	1661
Guadalajara MEX	1567
Harare ZIM	1473
Johannesburg RSA	1748
Kampala UGA	1189
Krugersdorp RSA	1740
La Paz BOL	3630
Levelland USA	1069
Logan USA	1372
Medellín COL	1541
Monachil ESP	2302
Nairobi KEN	1675
Orem USA	1455
Pietersburg RSA	1230
Pocatello USA	1361
Potchefstroom RSA	1351
Pretoria RSA	1400
Provo USA	1380
Pueblo USA	1487
Reno USA	1369
Roodepoort RSA	1623
Rustenburg RSA	1215
Salt Lake City USA	1321
San José CRC	1200
Sasolberg RSA	1488
Secunda RSA	1628
Sestriere ITA	2050
Soría ESP	1056
South Lake Tahoe USA	1909
Sucre BOL	2750
Toluca MEX	2680
Windhoek NAM	1725
Xalapa MEX	1356
Some others over 500m	
Albertville FRA	550
Almaty KZK	847
Ankara TUR	902
Bangalore, IND	949
Bern SUI	555
Blacksburg USA	634

Boise USA	818
Canberra AUS	581
La Chaux de Fonds SUI	997
Caracas VEN	922
Edmonton CAN	652
Jablonec CZE	598
Las Vegas USA	619
Lausanne SUI	597
Lubbock USA	981
Madrid ESP	640
Magglingen SUI	751
Malles ITA	980
Moscow, Idaho USA	787
München GER	520
Nampa, Idaho USA	760
Salamanca ESP	806
Santiago de Chile CHI	520
São Paulo BRA	725
Sofia BUL	564
Spokane USA	576
Trípoli GRE	655
Tucson USA	728
Uberlândia BRA	852
350m-500m	
Banská Bystrica SVK	362
Fayetteville USA	407
Genève SUI	385
Götzis AUS	448
Johnson City USA	499
Rieti ITA	402
Sindelfingen GER	440
Stuttgart GER	415
Tashkent UZB	477
Zürich SUI	410

Automatic timing

In the main lists for sprints and hurdles, only times recorded by fully automatic timing devices are included.

Hand timing

In the sprints and hurdles supplementary lists are included for races which are hand timed. Athletes with a hand timed best 0.01 seconds or more better than his or her automatically timed best has been included, but hand timed lists have been terminated close to the differential levels considered by the IAAF to be equivalent to automatic times, i.e. 0.24 sec. for 100m, 200m, 100mh, 110mh, and 0.14 sec. for 400m and 400mh. It should be noted that this effectively recognises bad hand timekeeping, for there should be no material difference between hand and auto times, but badly trained timekeepers anticipate the finish, having reacted to the flash at the start.

In events beyond 400m, auto times are integrated with hand timed marks, the latter identifiable by times being shown to tenths. All-time lists also include some auto times in tenths of a second, identified with '.

Indoor marks

Indoor marks are included in the main lists for field events and straightway track events, but not for other track events as track sizes vary in circumference (200m is the international standard) and banking, while outdoor tracks are standardised at 400m. Outdoor marks for athletes with indoor bests are shown in a supplemental list.

Mixed races

For record purposes athletes may not, except in road races, compete in mixed sex races. Statistically there would not appear to be any particular logic in this, and women's marks set in such races are shown in our lists – annotated with mx. In such cases the athlete's best mark in single sex competition is appended.

Field event series

Field event series are given (where known) for marks in the top 30 performances lists.

Tracks and Courses

As well as climatic conditions, the type and composition of tracks and runways will affect standards of performance, as will the variations in road race courses.

Wind assistance

Anemometer readings have been shown for sprints and horizontal jumps in metres per second to one decimal place. If the figure was given to two decimal places, it has been rounded to the next tenth upwards, e.g. a wind reading of +2.01m/s, beyond the IAAF legal limit of 2.0, is rounded to +2.1; or -1.22m/s is rounded up to -1.2.

For multi-events a wind-assisted mark is one in which the average of the three wind-measured events is > 2m/s.

Drugs bans

The IAAF Council may decertify an athlete's records, titles and results if he or she is found to have used a banned substance before those performances. Performances at or after such a positive finding are shown in footnotes. Such athletes are shown with ¶ after their name in year lists, and in all-time lists if at any stage of their career they have served a drugs suspension of a year or more (thus not including athletes receiving public warnings or 3 month bans for stimulants etc., which for that year only are indicated with a #). This should not be taken as implying that the athlete was using drugs at that time. Nor have those athletes who have subsequently unofficially admitted to using banned substances been indicated; the ¶ is used only for those who have been caught.

Venues

Place names occasionally change. Our policy is to use names in force at the time that the performance was set. Thus Leningrad prior to 1991, Sankt-Peterburg from its re-naming.

Amendments

Keen observers may spot errors in the lists. They are invited to send corrections as well as news and results for 2016.

Peter Matthews
Email p.matthews121@btinternet.com

WORLD & CONTINENTAL RECORDS

As at 1 April 2015. **Key**: W = World, Afr = Africa, Asi = Asia, CAC = Central America & Caribbean, Eur = Europe, NAm = North America, Oce = Oceania, SAm = South America, Com = Commonwealth, W20 = World Junior (U20), W18 = World Youth (U18, not officially ratified by IAAF). h hand timed.
Successive columns show: World or Continent, performance, name, nationality, venue, date.
A altitude over 1000m, + timing by photo-electric-cell, # awaiting ratification, § not officially ratified

100 METRES

W,CAC,Com	9.58	Usain BOLT	JAM	Berlin	16 Aug 2009
NAm	9.69	Tyson GAY	USA	Shanghai	20 Sep 2009
Afr	9.85	Olusoji FASUBA	NGR	Doha	12 May 2006
Eur	9.86	Francis OBIKWELU	POR	Athína	22 Aug 2004
	9.86	Jimmy VICAUT	FRA	Saint-Denis	4 Jul 2015
Asi	9.91	Femi Seun OGUNODE	QAT	Wuhan	4 Jun 2015
Oce	9.93	Patrick JOHNSON	AUS	Mito	5 May 2003
SAm	10.00A	Róbson da SILVA	BRA	Ciudad de México	22 Jul 1988
W20	9.97	Trayvon BROMELL	USA	Eugene	13 Jun 2014
W18	10.19	Yoshihide KIRYU	JPN	Fukuroi	3 Nov 2012

200 METRES

W,CAC,Com	19.19	Usain BOLT	JAM	Berlin	20 Aug 2009
NAm	19.32	Michael JOHNSON	USA	Atlanta	1 Aug 1996
Afr	19.68	Frank FREDERICKS	NAM	Atlanta	1 Aug 1996
Eur	19.72A	Pietro MENNEA	ITA	Ciudad de México	12 Sep 1979
SAm	19.81	Alonso EDWARD	PAN	Berlin	20 Aug 2009
Asi	19.97	Femi Seun OGUNODE	QAT	Bruxelles	11 Sep 2015
Oce	20.06A	Peter NORMAN	AUS	Ciudad de México	16 Oct 1968
W20	19.93	Usain BOLT	JAM	Hamilton, BER	11 Apr 2004
W18	20.13	Usain BOLT	JAM	Bridgetown	20 Jul 2003

400 METRES

W, NAm	43.18	Michael JOHNSON	USA	Sevilla	26 Aug 1999
Afr, Com	43.48	Wayde van NIEKERK	RSA	Beijing	26 Aug 2015
CAC	43.74	Kirani JAMES	GRN	Lausanne	3 Jul 2014
Asi	43.93	Yousef Ahmed AL-MASRAHI	KSA	Beijing	23 Aug 2015
SAm	44.29	Sanderlei PARRELA	BRA	Sevilla	26 Aug 1999
Eur	44.33	Thomas SCHÖNLEBE	GER	Roma	3 Sep 1987
Oce	44.38	Darren CLARK	AUS	Seoul	26 Sep 1988
W20	43.87	Steve LEWIS	USA	Seoul	28 Sep 1988
W18	45.14	Obea MOORE	USA	Santiago de Chile	2 Sep 1995

800 METRES

W, Afr, Com	1:40.91	David RUDISHA	KEN	London (OS)	9 Aug 2012
Eur	1:41.11	Wilson KIPKETER	DEN	Köln	24 Aug 1997
SAm	1:41.77	Joaquim CRUZ	BRA	Köln	26 Aug 1984
NAm	1:42.60	Johnny GRAY	USA	Koblenz	28 Aug 1985
Asi	1:42.79	Youssef Saad KAMEL	BRN	Monaco	29 Jul 2008
CAC	1:42.85	Norberto TELLEZ	CUB	Atlanta	31 Jul 1996
Oce	1:44.3+ h	Peter SNELL	NZL	Christchurch	3 Feb 1962
W20	1:41.73	Nijel AMOS	BOT	London (OS)	9 Aug 2012
W18	1:43.37	Mohamed AMAN	ETH	Rieti	10 Sep 2011

1000 METRES

W, Afr, Com	2:11.96	Noah NGENY	KEN	Rieti	5 Sep 1999
Eur	2:12.18	Sebastian COE	GBR	Oslo	11 Jul 1981
NAm	2:13.9	Rick WOHLHUTER	USA	Oslo	30 Jul 1974
SAm	2:14.09	Joaquim CRUZ	BRA	Nice	20 Aug 1984
Asi	2:14.72	Youssef Saad KAMEL	BRN	Stockholm	22 Jul 2008
Oce	2:16.09	Jeff RISELEY	AUS	Ostrava	17 Jun 2014
CAC	2:17.0	Byron DYCE	JAM	København	15 Aug 1973
W20	2:13.93 §	Abubaker KAKI	SUD	Stockholm	22 Jul 2008
W18	2:17.44	Hamza DRIOUCH	QAT	Sollentuna	9 Aug 2011

1500 METRES

W, Afr	3:26.00	Hicham EL GUERROUJ	MAR	Roma	14 Jul 1998
Com	3:26.34	Bernard LAGAT	KEN	Bruxelles	24 Aug 2001
Eur	3:28.81	Mo FARAH	GBR	Monaco	19 Jul 2013
Asi	3:29.14	Rashid RAMZI	BRN	Roma	14 Jul 2006
NAm	3:29.30	Bernard LAGAT	USA	Rieti	28 Aug 2005

Oce	3:29.26	Nick WILLIS	NZL	Monaco	17 Jul 2015
SAm	3:33.25	Hudson Santos de SOUZA	BRA	Rieti	28 Aug 2005
CAC	3:35.03	Maurys CASTILLO	CUB	Huelva	7 Jun 2012
W20	3:28.81	Ronald KWEMOI	KEN	Monaco	18 Jul 2014
W18	3:33.72	Nicholas KEMBOI	KEN	Zürich	18 Aug 2006

1 MILE

W, Afr	3:43.13	Hicham El GUERROUJ	MAR	Roma	7 Jul 1999
Com	3:43.40	Noah NGENY	KEN	Roma	7 Jul 1999
Eur	3:46.32	Steve CRAM	GBR	Oslo	27 Jul 1985
NAm	3:46.91	Alan WEBB	USA	Brasschaat	21 Jul 2007
Asi	3:47.97	Daham Najim BASHIR	QAT	Oslo	29 Jul 2005
Oce	3:48.98	Craig MOTTRAM	AUS	Oslo	29 Jul 2005
SAm	3:51.05	Hudson de SOUZA	BRA	Oslo	29 Jul 2005
CAC	3:57.34	Byron DYCE	JAM	Stockholm	1 Jul 1974
	3:57.34	Juan Luis BARRIOS	MEX	Dublin	17 Jul 2013
W20	3:49.29	William BIWOTT TANUI	KEN	Oslo	3 Jul 2009
W18	3:54.56	Isaac SONGOK	KEN	Linz	20 Aug 2001

2000 METRES

W, Afr	4:44.79	Hicham EL GUERROUJ	MAR	Berlin	7 Sep 1999
Com	4:48.74	John KIBOWEN	KEN	Hechtel	1 Aug 1998
Oce	4:50.76	Craig MOTTRAM	AUS	Melbourne	9 Mar 2006
Eur	4:51.39	Steve CRAM	GBR	Budapest	4 Aug 1985
NAm	4:52.44	Jim SPIVEY	USA	Lausanne	15 Sep 1987
Asi	4:55.57	Mohammed SULEIMAN	QAT	Roma	8 Jun 1995
SAm	5:03.34	Hudson Santos de SOUZA	BRA	Manaus	6 Apr 2002
CAC	5:03.4	Arturo BARRIOS	MEX	Nice	10 Jul 1989
W20	4:56.25	Tesfaye CHERU	ETH	Reims	5 Jul 2011
W18	4:56.86	Isaac SONGOK	KEN	Berlin	31 Aug 2001

3000 METRES

W, Afr, Com	7:20.67	Daniel KOMEN	KEN	Rieti	1 Sep 1996
Eur	7:26.62	Mohammed MOURHIT	BEL	Monaco	18 Aug 2000
NAm	7:29.00	Bernard LAGAT	USA	Rieti	29 Aug 2010
Asi	7:30.76	Jamal Bilal SALEM	QAT	Doha	13 May 2005
Oce	7:32.19	Craig MOTTRAM	AUS	Athína	17 Sep 2006
CAC	7:35.71	Arturo BARRIOS	MEX	Nice	10 Jul 1989
SAm	7:39.70	Hudson Santos de SOUZA	BRA	Lausanne	2 Jul 2002
W20	7:28.78	Augustine CHOGE	KEN	Doha	13 May 2005
W18	7:32.37	Abreham CHERKOS Feleke	ETH	Lausanne	11 Jul 2006

5000 METRES

W, Afr	12:37.35	Kenenisa BEKELE	ETH	Hengelo	31 May 2004
Com	12:39.74	Daniel KOMEN	KEN	Bruxelles	22 Aug 1997
Eur	12:49.71	Mohammed MOURHIT	BEL	Bruxelles	25 Aug 2000
Asi	12:51.96	Albert ROP	BRN	Monaco	19 Jul 2013
NAm	12:53.60	Bernard LAGAT	USA	Monaco	22 Jul 2011
Oce	12:55.76	Craig MOTTRAM	AUS	London	30 Jul 2004
CAC	13:07.79	Arturo BARRIOS	MEX	London (CP)	14 Jul 1989
SAm	13:19.43	Marilson dos SANTOS	BRA	Kassel	8 Jun 2006
W20	12:47.53	Hagos GEBRHIWET	ETH	Saint-Denis	6 Jul 2012
W18	12:54.19	Abreham CHERKOS Feleke	ETH	Roma	14 Jul 2006

10,000 METRES

W, Afr	26:17.53	Kenenisa BEKELE	ETH	Bruxelles	26 Aug 2005
Com	26:27.85	Paul TERGAT	KEN	Bruxelles	22 Aug 1997
Asi	26:38.76	Abdullah Ahmad HASSAN	QAT	Bruxelles	5 Sep 2003
NAm	26:44.36	Galen RUPP	USA	Eugene	30 May 2014
Eur	26:46.57	Mohamed FARAH	GBR	Eugene	3 Jun 2011
CAC	27:08.23	Arturo BARRIOS	MEX	Berlin	18 Aug 1989
Oce	27:24.95	Ben ST LAWRENCE	AUS	Stanford	1 May 2011
SAm	27:28.12	Marilson dos SANTOS	BRA	Neerpelt	2 Jun 2007
W20	26:41.75	Samuel WANJIRU	KEN	Bruxelles	26 Aug 2005
W18	27:02.81	Ibrahim JAYLAN Gashu	ETH	Bruxelles	25 Aug 2006

HALF MARATHON

W, Afr	58:23	Zersenay TADESE	ERI	Lisboa	21 Mar 2010
Com	58:33	Samuel WANJIRU	KEN	Den Haag	17 Mar 2007
Eur	59:32	Mohamed FARAH	GBR	Lisboa	21 Mar 2015
SAm	59:33	Marilson dos SANTOS	BRA	Udine	14 Oct 2007

NAm	59:43	Ryan HALL	USA	Houston	14 Jan 2007
Oce	59:47	Zane ROBERTSON	NZL	Marugame	1 Feb 2015
CAC	60:14	Armando QUINTANILLA	MEX	Tokyo	21 Jan 1996
Asi	60:25	Atsushi SATO	JPN	Udine	14 Oct 2007
W20	59:16	Samuel WANJIRU	KEN	Rotterdam	11 Sep 2005
W18	60:38	Faustin BAHA Sulle	TAN	Lille	4 Sep 1999

MARATHON

W, Afr, Com	2:02:57	Dennis KIMETTO	KEN	Berlin	28 Sep 2014
NAm	2:05:38	Khalid KHANNOUCHI (ex MAR)	USA	London	14 Apr 2002
SAm	2:06:05	Ronaldo da COSTA	BRA	Berlin	20 Sep 1998
Asi	2:06:16	Toshinari TAKAOKA	JPN	Chicago	13 Oct 2002
Eur	2:06:36 §	António PINTO	POR	London	16 Apr 2000
	2:06:36	Benoît ZWIERZCHIEWSKI	FRA	Paris	6 Apr 2003
Oce	2:08:16	Steve MONEGHETTI	AUS	Berlin	30 Sep 1990
CAC	2:08:30	Dionicio CERÓN	MEX	London	2 Apr 1995
W20	2:04:32	Tsegaye MEKONNEN	ETH	Dubai	24 Jan 2014
W18	2:11:43	LI He	CHN	Beijing	14 Oct 2001

3000 METRES STEEPLECHASE

W, Asi	7:53.63	Saïf Saaeed SHAHEEN	QAT	Bruxelles	3 Sep 2004
Afr, Com	7:53.64	Brimin KIPRUTO	KEN	Monaco	22 Jul 2011
Eur	8:00.09	Mahiedine MEKHISSI-BENABBAD	FRA	Saint-Denis	6 Jul 2013
NAm	8:00.45	Evan JAGER	USA	Saimt-Denis	4 Jul 2015
Oce	8:14.05	Peter RENNER	NZL	Koblenz	29 Aug 1984
SAm	8:14.41	Wander MOURA	BRA	Mar del Plata	22 Mar 1995
CAC	8:25.69	Salvador MIRANDA	MEX	Barakaldo	9 Jul 2000
W20	7:58.66	Stephen CHERONO (now Shaheen)	KEN	Bruxelles	24 Aug 2001
W18	8:17.28 §	Jonathan NDIKU	KEN	Bydgoszcz	13 Jul 2008

110 METRES HURDLES

W, NAm	12.80	Aries MERRITT	USA	Bruxelles	7 Sep 2012
CAC	12.87	Dayron ROBLES	CUB	Ostrava	12 Jun 2008
Asi	12.88	LIU Xiang	CHN	Lausanne	11 Jul 2006
Eur, Com	12.91	Colin JACKSON	GBR/Wal	Stuttgart	20 Aug 1993
Afr	13.24	Lehann FOURIE	RSA	Bruxelles	7 Sep 2012
SAm	13.27A	Paulo César VILLAR	COL	Guadalajara	28 Oct 2011
Oce	13.29	Kyle VANDER-KUYP	AUS	Göteborg	11 Aug 1995
W20	13.12	LIU Xiang (with 3'6" hurdles)	CHN	Lausanne	2 Jul 2002
W20 99cm h	12.99	Wilhem BELOCIAN	FRA	Eugene	24 Jul 2014
W18	13.43	SHI Dongpeng	CHN	Shanghai	6 May 2001
W18 91cm h	12.96	Jaheel HYDE	JAM	Nanjing	23 Aug 2014

400 METRES HURDLES

W, NAm	46.78	Kevin YOUNG	USA	Barcelona	6 Aug 1992
Afr, Com	47.10	Samuel MATETE	ZAM	Zürich	7 Aug 1991
CAC	47.25	Felix SÁNCHEZ	DOM	Saint-Denis	29 Aug 2003
Eur	47.37	Stéphane DIAGANA	FRA	Lausanne	5 Jul 1995
Asi	47.53	Hadi Soua'an AL-SOMAILY	KSA	Sydney	27 Sep 2000
SAm	47.84	Bayano KAMANI	PAN	Helsinki	7 Aug 2005
Oce	48.28	Rohan ROBINSON	AUS	Atlanta	31 Jul 1996
W20	48.02	Danny HARRIS	USA	Los Angeles	17 Jun 1984
W18	48.89	L.J. VAN ZYL	RSA	Kingston	19 Jul 2002

HIGH JUMP

W, CAC	2.45	Javier SOTOMAYOR	CUB	Salamanca	27 Jul 1993
Asi	2.43	Mutaz Essa BARSHIM	QAT	Bruxelles	5 Sep 2014
Eur	2.42	Patrik SJÖBERG	SWE	Stockholm	30 Jun 1987
	2.42 i§	Carlo THRÄNHARDT	FRG	Berlin	26 Feb 1988
	2.42i	Ivan UKHOV	RUS	Praha	25 Feb 2014
	2.42	Bogdan BONDARENKO	UKR	New York	14 Jun 2014
NAm	2.40 i§	Hollis CONWAY	USA	Sevilla	10 Mar 1991
	2.40	Charles AUSTIN	USA	Zürich	7 Aug 1991
NAm=, Com	2.40	Derek DROUIN	CAN	Des Moines	25 Apr 2014
Afr	2.38	Jacques FREITAG	RSA	Oudtshoorn	5 Mar 2005
Oce	2.36	Tim FORSYTH	AUS	Melbourne	2 Mar 1997
SAm	2.33	Gilmar MAYO	COL	Pereira	17 Oct 1994
W20	2.37	Dragutin TOPIC	YUG	Plovdiv	12 Aug 1990
		Steve SMITH	GBR	Seoul	20 Sep 1992
W18	2.33	Javier SOTOMAYOR	CUB	La Habana	19 May 1984

POLE VAULT

W, Eur	6.16 i	Renaud LAVILLENIE	FRA	Donetsk	15 Feb 2014
	6.14 A	Sergey BUBKA (best outdoor mark)	UKR	Sestriere	31 Jul 1994
Oce, Com	6.05	Dmitriy MARKOV	AUS	Edmonton	9 Aug 2001
NAm	6.04	Brad WALKER	USA	Eugene	8 Jun 2008
Afr	6.03	Okkert BRITS	RSA	Köln	18 Aug 1995
Asi	5.92i	Igor POTAPOVICH	KAZ	Stockholm	19 Feb 1998
	5.90	Grigoriy YEGOROV	KAZ	Stuttgart	19 Aug 1993
	5.90	Grigoriy YEGOROV	KAZ	London (CP)	10 Sep 1993
	5.90	Igor POTAPOVICH	KAZ	Nice	10 Jul 1996
SAm	5.93i	Thiago BRAZ da SILVA	BRA	Berlin	13 Feb 2016
	5.92	Thiago BRAZ da SILVA	BRA	Baku	24 Jun 2015
CAC	5.90	Lázaro BORGES	CUB	Daegu	29 Aug 2011
W20	5.80	Maksim TARASOV	RUS	Bryansk	14 Jul 1989
	5.80	Raphael HOLZDEPPE	GER	Biberach	28 Jun 2008
W18	5.51	Germán CHIARAVIGLIO	ARG	Pôrto Alegre	1 May 2004

LONG JUMP

W, NAm	8.95	Mike POWELL	USA	Tokyo	30 Aug 1991
Eur	8.86 A	Robert EMMIYAN	ARM	Tsakhkadzor	22 May 1987
SAm	8.73	Irving SALADINO	PAN	Hengelo	24 May 2008
CAC	8.71	Iván PEDROSO	CUB	Salamanca	18 Jul 1995
Com	8.62	James BECKFORD	JAM	Orlando	5 Apr 1997
Oce	8.54	Mitchell WATT	AUS	Stockholm	29 Jul 2011
Afr	8.50	Khotso MOKOENA	RSA	Madrid	4 Jul 2009
Asi	8.48	Mohamed Salim AL-KHUWALIDI	KSA	Sotteville	2 Jul 2006
W20	8.35	Sergey MORGUNOV	RUS	Cheboksary	20 Jun 2012
W18	8.25	Luis Alberto BUENO	CUB	La Habana	28 Sep 1986

TRIPLE JUMP

W, Eur, Com	18.29	Jonathan EDWARDS	GBR/Eng	Göteborg	7 Aug 1995
NAm	18.21	Christian TAYLOR	USA	Beijing	27 Aug 2015
CAC	18.08	Pedro Pablo PICHARDO	CUB	La Habana	28 May 2015
SAm	17.90	Jadel GREGÓRIO	BRA	Belém	20 May 2007
Asi	17.59	LI Yanxi	CHN	Jinan	26 Oct 2009
Oce	17.46	Ken LORRAWAY	AUS	London (CP)	7 Aug 1982
Afr	17.37	Tareq BOUGTAÏB	MAR	Khémisset	14 Jul 2007
W20	17.50	Volker MAI	GDR	Erfurt	23 Jun 1985
W18	17.24	Lazaro MARTÍNEZ	CUB	La Habana	1 Feb 2014

SHOT

W, NAm	23.12	Randy BARNES	USA	Westwood	20 May 1990
Eur	23.06	Ulf TIMMERMANN	GER	Haniá	22 May 1988
Com	22.21	Dylan ARMSTRONG	CAN	Calgary	25 Jun 2011
Afr	21.97	Janus ROBBERTS	RSA	Eugene	2 Jun 2001
CAC	21.69	O'Dayne RICHARDS	JAM	Beijing	23 Aug 2015
Oce	21.78i	Tomas WALSH	NZL	Portland	18 Mar 2016
	21.62	Tomas WALSH	NZL	Zagreb	7 Sep 2015
SAm	21.26	Germán LAURO	ARG	Doha	10 May 2013
Asi	21.13	Sultan Abdulmajeed AL-HEBSHI	KSA	Doha	8 May 2009
W20	21.05 i§	Terry ALBRITTON	USA	New York	22 Feb 1974
	20.78	Konrad BUKOWIECKI	POL	Zagreb	7 Sep 2015
W18	20.38	Jacko GILL	NZL	Auckland (North Shore)	5 Dec 2011
W20 6kg	23.00	Jacko GILL	NZL	Auckland (North Shore)	18 Aug 2013
W18 5kg	24.45	Jacko GILL	NZL	Auckland (North Shore)	19 Dec 2011

DISCUS

W, Eur	74.08	Jürgen SCHULT	GDR	Neubrandenburg	6 Jun 1986
NAm	72.34 ¶	Ben PLUCKNETT	USA	Stockholm	7 Jul 1981
	71.32 §	Ben PLUCKNETT	USA	Eugene	4 Jun 1983
CAC	71.06	Luis DELIS	CUB	La Habana	21 May 1983
Afr, Com	70.32	Frantz KRUGER	RSA	Salon-de-Provence	26 May 2002
Asi	69.32	Ehsan HADADI	IRI	Tallinn	3 Jun 2008
Oce	68.20	Benn HARRADINE	AUS	Townsville	10 May 2013
SAm	66.32	Jorge BALLIENGO	ARG	Rosario	15 Apr 2006
W20	65.62 §	Werner REITERER	AUS	Melbourne	15 Dec 1987
W18/20	65.31	Mykyta NESTERENKO	UKR	Tallinn	3 Jun 2008
W20 1.75kg	70.13	Mykyta NESTERENKO	UKR	Halle	24 May 2008
W18 1.5kg	77.50	Mykyta NESTERNKO	UKR	Koncha Zaspa	19 May 2008

¶ Disallowed by the IAAF following retrospective disqualification for drug abuse, but ratified by the AAU/TAC

HAMMER

W, Eur	86.74	Yuriy SEDYKH	UKR/RUS	Stuttgart	30 Aug 1986
Asi	84.86	Koji MUROFUSHI	JPN	Praha	29 Jun 2003
NAm	82.52	Lance DEAL	USA	Milano	7 Sep 1996
Afr	81.27	Mostafa Hicham AL-GAMAL	EGY	Al-Qâhira	21 Mar 2014
Com	80.63	Chris HARMSE	RSA	Durban	15 Apr 2005
Oce	79.29	Stuart RENDELL	AUS	Varazdin	6 Jul 2002
CAC	78.02	Roberto JANET	CUB	La Habana	28 May 2015
SAm	76.42	Juan CERRA	ARG	Trieste	25 Jul 2001
W20	78.33	Olli-Pekka KARJALAINEN	FIN	Seinäjoki	5 Aug 1999
W18	73.66	Vladislav PISKUNOV	UKR	Kyiv	11 Jun 1994
W20 6kg	85.57	Ashraf Amgad EL-SEIFY	QAT	Barcelona	14 Jul 2012
W18 5kg	87.16	Bence HALÁSZ	HUN	Baku	31 May 2014

JAVELIN

W, Eur	98.48	Jan ZELEZNY	CZE	Jena	25 May 1996
Afr, Com	92.72	Julius YEGO	KEN	Beijing	26 Aug 2015
NAm	91.29	Breaux GREER	USA	Indianapolis	21 Jun 2007
CAC	90.16	Keshorn WALCOTT	TTO	Lausanne	9 Jul 2015
Asi	89.15	ZHAO Qinggang	CHN	Incheon	2 Oct 2014
Oce	89.02	Jarrod BANNISTER	AUS	Brisbane	29 Feb 2008
SAm	84.70	Edgar BAUMANN	PAR	San Marcos	17 Oct 1999
W20	84.69	Zigismunds SIRMAIS	LAT	Bauska	22 Jun 2011
W18 700g	89.34	Braian Ezequiel TOLEDO	ARG	Mar del Plata	6 Mar 2010

DECATHLON

W, NAm	9045	Ashton EATON	USA	Beijing	29 Aug 2015
Eur	9026	Roman SEBRLE	CZE	Götzis	27 May 2001
Com	8847	Daley THOMPSON	GBR/Eng	Los Angeles	9 Aug 1984
Asi	8725	Dmitriy KARPOV	KAZ	Athína	24 Aug 2004
CAC	8654	Leonel SUÁREZ	CUB	La Habana	4 Jul 2009
Oce	8490	Jagan HAMES	AUS	Kuala Lumpur	18 Sep 1998
Afr	8461	Larbi BOURAADA	ALG	Beijing	29 Aug 2015
SAm	8393	Carlos Eduardo CHININ	BRA	São Paulo	8 Jun 2013
W20	8397	Torsten VOSS (with 3'6" hurdles)	GDR	Erfurt	7 Jul 1982
W18	8104h	Valter KÜLVET	EST	Viimsi	23 Aug 1981
	7829	Valter KÜLVET	EST	Stockholm	13 Sep 1981

4 X 100 METRES RELAY

W, CAC, Com	36.84	JAM (Carter, M Frater, Blake, Bolt)	London (OS)	11 Aug 2012
NAm	37.38	USA (Demps, Patton, Kimmons, Gatlin)	London (OS)	10 Aug 2012
	37.38	USA (Rodgers, Gatlin, Gay, Bailey)	Nassau	2 May 2015
Eur	37.73	GBR (Gardener, Campbell, Devonish, Chambers)	Sevilla	29 Aug 1999
SAm	37.90	BRA (V Lima, Ribeiro, A da Silva, Cl da Silva)	Sydney	30 Sep 2000
Asi	37.92	CHN (CMo Y, Xie Z,, Su Bingtian, Zhang Peimeng)	Beijing	29 Aug 2015
Afr	37.94	NGR (O Ezinwa, Adeniken, Obikwelu, D Ezinwa)	Athína	9 Aug 1997
Oce	38.17	AUS (Henderson, Jackson, Brimacombe, Marsh)	Göteborg	12 Aug 1995
W20	38.66	USA (Kimmons, Omole, Williams, Merritt)	Grosseto	18 Jul 2004
W18	40.03	JAM (W Smith, M Frater, Spence, O Brown)	Bydgoszcz	18 Jul 1999

4 X 400 METRES RELAY

W, NAm	2:54.29	USA (Valmon, Watts, Reynolds, Johnson)	Stuttgart	22 Aug1993
Eur	2:56.60	GBR (Thomas, Baulch, Richardson, Black)	Atlanta	3 Aug 1996
CAC, Com	2:56.72	BAH (Brown, Pinder, Mathieu, Miller)	London (OS)	10 Aug 2012
SAm	2:58.56	BRA (C da Silva, A J dosSantos, de Araújo, Parrela)	Winnipeg	30 Jul 1999
Afr	2:58.68	NGR (Chukwu, Monye, Nada, Udo-Obong)	Sydney	30 Sep 2000
Oce	2:59.70	AUS (Frayne, Clark, Minihan, Mitchell)	Los Angeles	11 Aug 1984
Asi	3:00.76	JPN (Karube, K Ito, Osakada, Omori)	Atlanta	3 Aug 1996
W20	3:01.09	USA (Johnson, Merritt, Craig, Clement)	Grosseto	18 Jul 2004
W18	3:12.05	POL (Zrada, Kedzia, Grzegorczyk, Kowalski)	Kaunas	5 Aug 2001

20 KILOMETRES WALK

W, Asi	1:16:36	Yusuke SUZUKI	JPN	Nomi	15 Mar 2015
Eur	1:17:02	Yohann DINIZ	FRA	Arles	8 Mar 2015
	1:16:43 §	Sergey MOROZOV	RUS	Saransk	8 Jun 2008
SAm	1:17:21	Jefferson PÉREZ	ECU	Saint-Denis	23 Aug 2003
CAC	1:17:25.6 t	Bernardo SEGURA	MEX	Bergen (Fana)	7 May 1994
Oce, Com	1:17:33	Nathan DEAKES	AUS	Cixi	23 Apr 2005
Afr	1:19:02	Hatem GHOULA	TUN	Eisenhüttenstadt	10 May 1997
NAm	1:19:20	Inaki Gómez	CAN	Nomi	20 Mar 2016

W20	1:18:06 §	Viktor BURAYEV	RUS	Adler	4 Mar 2001
W18	1:18:07	LI Gaobo	CHN	Cixi	23 Apr 2005

20,000 METRES TRACK WALK

W, CAC	1:17:25.6	Bernardo SEGURA	MEX	Bergen (Fana)	7 May 1994
Asi	1:18:03.3	BU Lingtang	CHN	Beijing	7 Apr 1994
Eur	1:18:35.2	Stefan JOHANSSON	SWE	Bergen (Fana)	15 May 1992
Oce, Com	1:19:48.1	Nathan DEAKES	AUS	Brisbane	4 Sep 2001
SAm	1:20:23.8	Andrés CHOCHO	ECU	Buenos Aires	5 Jun 2011
NAm	1:21:57.0	Evan DUNFEE	CAN	Moncton	27 Jun 2014
Afr	1:22:51.84	Hatem GHOULA	TUN	Leutkirch	8 Sep 1994
W20	1:20:11.72	LI Gaobo	CHN	Wuhan	2 Nov 2007
W18	1:24:28.3	ZHU Hongjun	CHN	Xian	15 Sep 1999

50 KILOMETRES WALK

W, Eur	3:32:33	Yohann DINIZ	FRA	Zürich	15 Aug 2014
Oce, Com	3:35:47	Nathan DEAKES	AUS	Geelong	2 Dec 2006
Asi	3:36:06	YU Chaohong	CHN	Nanjing	22 Oct 2005
CAC	3:41:09	Erick BARRONDO	GUA	Dudince	23 Mar 2013
SAm	3:42:57	Andrés CHOCHO	ECU	Ciudad Juárez	6 Mar 2016
NAm	3:43:45	Evan DUNFEE	CAN	Melbourne	13 Dec 2015
Afr	3:54:12	Marc MUNDELL	RSA	Melbourne	13 Dec 2015
W20	3:41:10	ZHAO Jianguo	CHN	Wajima	16 Apr 2006
W18	3:45:46	YU Guoping	CHN	Guangzhou	23 Nov 2001

50,000 METRES TRACK WALK

W, Eur	3:35:27.2	Yoahnn DINIZ	FRA	Reims	12 Mar 2011
CAC	3:41:38.4	Raúl GONZÁLEZ	MEX	Bergen (Fana)	25 May 1979
Oce, Com	3:43:50.0	Simon BAKER	AUS	Melbourne	9 Sep 1990
Asi	3:48:13.7	ZHAO Yongshen	CHN	Bergen (Fana)	7 May 1994
NAm	3:56:13.0	Tim BERRETT	CAN	Saskatoon	21 Jul 1991
SAm	3:57:58.0	Claudio dos SANTOS	BRA	Blumenau	20 Sep 2008
Afr	4:21:44.5	Abdelwahab FERGUÈNE	ALG	Toulouse	25 Mar 1984

World Records at other men's events recognised by the IAAF

20,000m	56:25.98+	Haile GEBRSELASSIE	ETH	Ostrava	27 Jun 2007
1 Hour	21,285 m	Haile GEBRSELASSIE	ETH	Ostrava	27 Jun 2007
25,000m	1:12:25.4	Moses MOSOP	KEN	Eugene	3 Jun 2011
30,000m	1:26:47.4	Moses MOSOP	KEN	Eugene	3 Jun 2011
U18 Octathlon	6491	Jake STEIN	AUS	Villeneuve d'Ascq	7 Jul 2011
4 x 200m	1:18.63	National team	JAM	Nassau	24 May 2014
		(Nickel Ashmeade, Warren Weir, Jermaine Brown, Yohan Blake)			
4 x 800m	7:02.43	National Team	KEN	Bruxelles	25 Aug 2006
		(Joseph Mutua, William Yiampoy, Ismael Kombich, Wilfred Bungei)			
4 x 1500m	14:22.22	C Cheboi, A Kiplagat, Magut, A Kiprop	KEN	Nassau	25 May 2014
Distance Medley	9:15.50	Merber,Spratting,Johnson,Blankenship	USA	Nassau	3 May 2015

Walking

2 Hours track	29,572m+	Maurizio DAMILANO	ITA	Cuneo	3 Oct 1992
30km track	2:01:44.1	Maurizio DAMILANO	ITA	Cuneo	3 Oct 1992
U20 10,000m track	38:46.4	Viktor BURAYEV	RUS	Moskva	20 May 2000
U20 10km road	37:44	WANG Zhen	CHN	Beijing	18 Sep 2010
W18 10km road	38:57	LI Tianlei	CHN	Beijing	18 Sep 2010

WOMEN

100 METRES

W, NAm	10.49	Florence GRIFFITH JOYNER	USA	Indianapolis	16 Jul 1988
CAC, Com	10.70	Shelly-Ann FRASER	JAM	Kingstobn	29 Jun 2012
Eur	10.73	Christine ARRON	FRA	Budapest	19 Aug 1998
Asi	10.79	LI Xuemei	CHN	Shanghai	18 Oct 1997
Afr	10.79	Blessing OKAGBARE	NGR	London (OS)	27 Jul 2013
SAm	10.99	Angela TENORIO	ECU	Toronto	22 Jul 2015
Oce	11.11	Melissa BREEN	AUS	Canberra	9 Feb 2014
W20	10.88	Marlies OELSNER/GÖHR	GDR	Dresden	1 Jul 1977
W18	10.98	Candace HILL	USA	Shoreline	20 Jun 2015

200 METRES

W, NAm	21.34	Florence GRIFFITH JOYNER	USA	Seoul	29 Sep 1988
CAC, Com	21.64	Merlene OTTEY	JAM	Bruxelles	13 Sep 1991
Eur	21.63	Dafne SCHIPPERS	NED	Beijing	28 Aug 2015
Asi	22.01	LI Xuemei	CHN	Shanghai	22 Oct 1997
Afr	22.06 A§	Evette DE KLERK	RSA	Pietersburg	8 Apr 1989

	22.07	Mary ONYALI	NGR	Zürich	14 Aug 1996
Oce	22.23	Melinda GAINSFORD-TAYLOR	AUS	Stuttgart	13 Jul 1997
SAm	22.48	Ana Cláudia da SILVA	BRA	São Paulo	6 Aug 2011
W20	22.18	Allyson FELIX	USA	Athína	25 Aug 2004
	22.11A §	Allyson FELIX (no doping control)	USA	Ciudad de México	3 May 2003
W18	22.43A	Candace HILL	USA	Cali	19 Jul 2015

400 METRES

W, Eur	47.60	Marita KOCH	GDR	Canberra	6 Oct 1985
Oce, Com	48.63	Cathy FREEMAN	AUS	Atlanta	29 Jul 1996
NAm	48.70	Sanya RICHARDS	USA	Athína	16 Sep 2006
CAC	48.89	Ana GUEVARA	MEX	Saint-Denis	27 Aug 2003
Afr	49.10	Falilat OGUNKOYA	NGR	Atlanta	29 Jul 1996
SAm	49.64	Ximena RESTREPO	COL	Barcelona	5 Aug 1992
Asi	49.81	MA Yuqin	CHN	Beijing	11 Sep 1993
W20	49.42	Grit BREUER	GER	Tokyo	27 Aug 1991
W18	50.01	LI Jing	CHN	Shanghai	18 Oct 1997

800 METRES

W, Eur	1:53.28	Jarmila KRATOCHVÍLOVÁ	CZE	München	26 Jul 1983
Afr,W20,Com	1:54.01	Pamela JELIMO	KEN	Zürich	29 Aug 2008
CAC	1:54.44	Ana Fidelia QUIROT	CUB	Barcelona	9 Sep 1989
Asi	1:55.54	LIU Dong	CHN	Beijing	9 Sep 1993
NAm	1:56.40	Jearl MILES CLARK	USA	Zürich	11 Aug 1999
SAm	1:56.68	Letitia VRIESDE	SUR	Göteborg	13 Aug 1995
Oce	1:58.25	Toni HODGKINSON	NZL	Atlanta	27 Jul 1996
W18	1:57.18	WANG Yuan	CHN	Beijing	8 Sep 1993

1000 METRES

W, Eur	2:28.98	Svetlana MASTERKOVA	RUS	Bruxelles	23 Aug 1996
Afr	2:29.34	Maria Lurdes MUTOLA	MOZ	Bruxelles	25 Aug 1995
Com	2:29.66	Maria Lurdes MUTOLA	MOZ	Bruxelles	23 Aug 1996
NAm	2:31.80	Regina JACOBS	USA	Brunswick	3 Jul 1999
SAm	2:32.25	Letitia VRIESDE	SUR	Berlin	10 Sep 1991
CAC	2:33.21	Ana Fidelia QUIROT	CUB	Jerez de la Frontera	13 Sep 1989
Asi	2:33.6 §	Svetlana ULMASOVA	UZB	Podolsk	5 Aug 1979
	2:40.53	ZHAO Jing	CHN	Changbaishan	2 Sep 2014
Oce	2:37.28	Angie PETTY	NZL	Chiba	15 Aug 2015
W20	2:35.4a	Irina NIKITINA	RUS	Podolsk	5 Aug 1979
	2:35.4	Katrin WÜHN	GDR	Potsdam	12 Jul 1984
W18	2:38.58	Jo WHITE	GBR	London (CP)	9 Sep 1977

1500 METRES

W,Afr	3:50.07	Genzebe DIBABA	ETH	Monaco	17 Jul 15
As i	3:50.46	QU Yunxia	CHN	Beijing	11 Sep 1993
Eur	3:52.47	Tatyana KAZANKINA	RUS	Zürich	13 Aug 1980
NAm	3:56.29	Shannon ROWBURY	USA	Monaco	17 Jul 2015
Com	3:56.98	Faith KIPYEGON	KEN	Doha	10 May 2013
Oce	4:00.93	Sarah JAMIESON	AUS	Stockholm	25 Jul 2006
CAC	4:01.84	Yvonne GRAHAM	JAM	Monaco	25 Jul 1995
SAm	4:05.67	Letitia VRIESDE	SUR	Tokyo	31 Aug 1991
W20	3:51.34	LANG Yinglai	CHN	Shanghai	18 Oct 1997
W18	3:54.52	ZHANG Ling	CHN	Shanghai	18 Oct 1997

1 MILE

W, Eur	4:12.56	Svetlana MASTERKOVA	RUS	Zürich	14 Aug 1996
NAm	4:16.71	Mary SLANEY	USA	Zürich	21 Aug 1985
Afr, Com	4:16.71	Faith KIPYEGON	KEN	Bruxelles	11 Sep 2015
Asi	4:17.75	Maryam Yusuf JAMAL	BRN	Bruxelles	14 Sep 2007
Oce	4:22.66	Lisa CORRIGAN	AUS	Melbourne	2 Mar 2007
CAC	4:24.64	Yvonne GRAHAM	JAM	Zürich	17 Aug 1994
SAm	4:30.05	Soraya TELLES	BRA	Praha	9 Jun 1988
W20	4:17.57	Zola BUDD	GBR	Zürich	21 Aug 1985
W18	4:30.81	Gelete BURKA	ETH	Heusden	2 Aug 2003

2000 METRES

W, Eur	5:25.36	Sonia O'SULLIVAN	IRL	Edinburgh	8 Jul 1994
Com	5:26.93	Yvonne MURRAY	GBR/Sco	Edinburgh	8 Jul 1994
Afr	5:27.50	Genzebe DIBABA	ETH	Ostrava	17 Jun 2014
Asi	5:29.43+§	WANG Junxia	CHN	Beijing	12 Sep 1993
	5:31.88	Maryam Yusuf JAMAL	BRN	Eugene	7 Jun 2009

NAm	5:32.7	Mary SLANEY	USA	Eugene	3 Aug 1984
Oce	5:37.71	Benita JOHNSON	AUS	Ostrava	12 Jun 2003
W20	5:33.15	Zola BUDD	GBR	London (CP)	13 Jul 1984
W18	5:46.5+	Sally BARSOSIO	KEN	Zürich	16 Aug 1995

3000 METRES

W, Asi	8:06.11	WANG Junxia	CHN	Beijing	13 Sep 1993
Afr, Com	8:20.68	Hellen OBIRI	KEN	Doha	9 May 2014
Eur	8:21.42	Gabriela SZABO	ROU	Monaco	19 Jul 2002
NAm	8:25.83	Mary SLANEY	USA	Roma	7 Sep 1985
Oce	8:35.31	Kimberley SMITH	NZL	Monaco	25 Jul 2007
CAC	8:37.07	Yvonne GRAHAM	JAM	Zürich	16 Aug 1995
SAm	9:02.37	Delirde BERNARDI	BRA	Linz	4 Jul 1994
W20	8:28.83	Zola BUDD	GBR	Roma	7 Sep 1985
W18	8:36.45	MA Ningning	CHN	Jinan	6 Jun 1993

5000 METRES

W, Afr	14:11.15	Tirunesh DIBABA	ETH	Oslo	6 Jun 2008
Com	14:20.87	Vivian CHERUIYOT	KEN	Stockho;lm	29 Jul 2011
Eur	14:23.75	Liliya SHOBUKHOVA	RUS	Kazan	19 Jul 2008
Asi	14:28.09	JIANG Bo	CHN	Shanghai	23 Oct 1997
NAm	14:42.64	Molly HUDDLE	USA	Monaco	18 Jul 2014
Oce	14:45.93	Kimberley SMITH	NZL	Roma	11 Jul 2008
CAC	15:04.32	Adriana FERNÁNDEZ	MEX	Gresham	17 May 2003
SAm	15:18.85	Simone Alves da SILVA	BRA	São Paulo	20 May 2011
W20	14:30.88	Tirunesh DIBABA	ETH	Bergen (Fana)	11 Jun 2004
W18	14:45.71	SONG Liqing	CHN	Shanghai	21 Oct 1997

10,000 METRES

W, Asi	29:31.78	WANG Junxia	CHN	Beijing	8 Sep 1993
Afr	29:53.80	Meselech MELKAMU	ETH	Utrecht	14 Jun 2009
Eur	29:56.34	Elvan ABEYLEGESSE	TUR	Beijing	15 Aug 2008
Com	30:01.09	Paula RADCLIFFE	GBR/Eng	München	6 Aug 2002
NAm	30:22.22	Shalane FLANAGAN	USA	Beijing	15 Aug 2008
Oce	30:35.54	Kimberley SMITH	NZL	Stanford	4 May 2008
CAC	31:10.12	Adriana FERNANDEZ	MEX	Brunswick	1 Jul 2000
SAm	31:47.76	Carmen de OLIVEIRA	BRA	Stuttgart	21 Aug 1993
W20	30:26.50	Linet MASAI	KEN	Beijing	15 Aug 2008
W18	31:11.26	SONG Liqing	CHN	Shanghai	19 Oct 1997

HALF MARATHON

W, Afr, Com	65:09	Florence KIPLAGAT	KEN	Barcelona	15 Feb 2015
Eur	66:25	Lornah KIPLAGAT	NED	Udine	14 Oct 2007
Oce	67:11	Kimberley SMITH	NZL	Philadelphia	18 Sep 2011
Asi	67:26	Kayoko FUKUSHI	JPN	Marugame	5 Feb 2006
NAm	67:34	Deena KASTOR	USA	Berlin	2 Apr 2006
CAC	68:34 dh	Olga APPELL	MEX	Tokyo	24 Jan 1993
	69:28	Adrian FERNÁNDEZ	MEX	Kyoto	9 Mar 2003
SAm	70:14	Gladys TEJEDA	PER	Cardiff	26 Mar 2016
W20	67:57	Abebu GELAN	ETH	Ra's Al Khaymah	20 Feb 2009
W18	72:31	LIU Zhuang	CHN	Yangzhou	24 Apr 2011

MARATHON

W, Eur, Com	2:15:25	Paula RADCLIFFE	GBR/Eng	London	13 Apr 2003
Afr	2:18:37	Mary KEITANY	KEN	London	22 Apr 2012
Asi	2:19:12	Mizuki NOGUCHI	JPN	Berlin	25 Sep 2005
NAm	2:19:36	Deena KASTOR	USA	London	23 Apr 2006
Oce	2:22:36	Benita JOHNSON	AUS	Chicago	22 Oct 2006
CAC	2:22:59	Madai PÉREZ	MEX	Chicago	22 Oct 2006
SAm	2:26:48	Inés MELCHOR	PER	Berlin	28 Sep 2014
W20	2:20:59	Shure DEMISE	ETH	Dubai	23 Jan 2015

3000 METRES STEEPLECHASE

W, Eur	8:58.81	Gulnara GALKINA	RUS	Beijing	17 Aug 2008
Afr	9:05.36	Habiba GHRIBI	TUN	Bruxelles	11 Sep 2015
Com	9:07.14	Milcah CHEMOS Cheywa	KEN	Oslo	7 Jun 2012
NAm	9:11.42	Emma COBURN	USA	Glasgow	12 Jul 2014
Oce	9:18.35	Donna MacFARLANE	AUS	Oslo	6 Jun 2008
Asi	9:20.55	Ruth CHEBET	BRN	Zürich	28 Aug 2014
CAC	9:27.21	Mardrea HYMAN	JAM	Monaco	9 Sep 2005
SAm	9:41.22	Sabine HEITLING	BRA	London	25 Jul 2009

W20	9:20.37	Birtukan ADAMU	ETH	Roma	26 May 2011
W18	9:28.36	Tigist MEKONEN	ETH	Glasgow	12 Jul 2014

100 METRES HURDLES

W, Eur	12.21	Yordanka DONKOVA	BUL	Stara Zagora	20 Aug 1988
NAm	12.26	Brianna ROLLINS	USA	Des Moines	22 Jun 2013
Oce, Com	12.28	Sally PEARSON	AUS	Daegu	3 Sep 2011
Asi	12.44	Olga SHISHIGINA	KAZ	Luzern	27 Jun 1995
Afr	12.44	Glory ALOZIE	NGR	Monaco	8 Aug 1998
	12.44	Glory ALOZIE	NGR	Bruxelles	28 Aug 1998
	12.44	Glory ALOZIE	NGR	Sevilla	28 Aug 1999
CAC	12.45	Brigitte FOSTER	JAM	Eugene	24 May 2003
SAm	12.67	Yvette LEWIS	PAN	Lahti	17 Jul 2013
W20	12.74	Dior HALL	USA	Eugene	13 Jun 2015
W18	12.95	Candy YOUNG	USA	Walnut	16 Jun 1979

400 METRES HURDLES

Eur, W	52.34	Yuliya PECHONKINA	RUS	Tula	8 Aug 2003
CAC, Com	52.42	Melaine WALKER	JAM	Berlin	20 Aug 2009
NAm	52.47	Lashinda DEMUS	USA	Daegu	1 Sep 2011
Afr	52.90	Nezha BIDOUANE	MAR	Sevilla	25 Aug 1999
Oce	53.17	Debbie FLINTOFF-KING	AUS	Seoul	28 Sep 1988
Asi	53.96	HAN Qing	CHN	Beijing	9 Sep 1993
	53.96	SONG Yinglan	CHN	Guangzhou	22 Nov 2001
SAm	55.84	Lucimar TEODORO	BRA	Belém	24 May 2009
W20	54.40	WANG Xing	CHN	Nanjing	21 Oct 2005
W18	55.20	Leslie MAXIE	USA	San Jose	9 Jun 1984

HIGH JUMP

W, Eur	2.09	Stefka KOSTADINOVA	BUL	Roma	30 Aug 1987
Afr, Com	2.06	Hestrie CLOETE	RSA	Saint-Denis	31 Aug 2003
NAm	2.05	Chaunté HOWARD-LOWE	USA	Des Moines	26 Jun 2010
CAC	2.04	Silvia COSTA	CUB	Barcelona	9 Sep 1989
Asi	1.99	Marina AITOVA	KAZ	Athína	13 Jul 2009
Oce	1 98	Vanessa WARD	AUS	Perth	12 Feb 1989
	1.98	Alison INVERARITY	AUS	Ingolstadt	17 Jul 1994
SAm	1.96	Solange WITTEVEEN	ARG	Oristano	8 Sep 1997
W20	2.01	Olga TURCHAK	KAZ	Moskva	7 Jul 1986
	2.01	Heike BALCK	GDR	Chemnitz	18 Jun 1989
W18	1.96A	Charmaine GALE	RSA	Bloemfontein	4 Apr 1981
	1.96	Olga TURCHAK	UKR	Donetsk	7 Sep 1984
	1.96	Eleanor PATTERSON	AUS	Townsville	7 Dec 2013
	1.96	Vashti CUNNINGHAM	USA	Edmonton	1 Aug 2015

POLE VAULT

W, Eur	5.06	Yelena ISINBAYEVA	RUS	Zürich	28 Aug 2009
NAm	5.031	Jennifer SUHR	USA	Brockport	30 Jan 2016
	4.92	Jennifer STUCZYNSKI/SUHR	USA	Eugene	6 Jul 2008
CAC	4.91	Yarisley SILVA	CUB	Beckum	2 Aug 2015
Com	4.87i	Holly BLEASDALE	GBR	Villeurbanne	21 Jan 2012
SAm	4.85	Fabiana MURER	BRA	San Fernando	4 Jun 2010
	4.85	Fabiana MURER	BRA	Daegu	30 Aug 2011
	4.85	Fabiana MURER	BRA	Beijing	26 Aug 2015
Oce	4.80	Eliza McCARTNEY	NZL	Dunedin	5 Mar 2016
Asi	4.70i	LI Ling	CHN	Doha	19 Feb 2016
	4.66	LI Ling	CHN	Wuhan	6 Jun 2015
Afr	4.42	Elmarie GERRYTS	RSA	Wesel	12 Jun 2000
W20	4.64	Eliza McCARTNEY	NZL	Auckland	19 Dec 2015
W18	4.47	Angelica BENGTSSON	SWE	Moskva	22 May 2010

LONG JUMP

W, Eur	7.52	Galina CHISTYAKOVA	RUS	Sankt-Peterburg	11 Jun 1988
NAm	7.49	Jackie JOYNER-KERSEE	USA	New York	22 May 1994
	7.49A §	Jackie JOYNER-KERSEE	USA	Sestriere	31 Jul 1994
SAm	7.26A	Maurren MAGGI	BRA	Bogotá	26 Jun 1999
CAC, Com	7.16A	Elva GOULBOURNE	JAM	Ciudad de México	22 May 2004
Afr	7.12	Chioma AJUNWA	NGR	Atlanta	1 Aug 1996
Asi	7.01	YAO Weili	CHN	Jinan	5 Jun 1993
Oce	7.05	Brooke STRATTON	AUS	Perth	12 Mar 2016
W20	7.14	Heike DAUTE/Drechsler	GDR	Bratislava	4 Jun 1983
W18	6.91	Heike DAUTE/Drechsler	GDR	Jena	9 Aug 1981

TRIPLE JUMP

W, Eur	15.50	Inessa KRAVETS	UKR	Göteborg	10 Aug 1995
Afr, Com	15.39	Françoise MBANGO Etone	CMR	Beijing	17 Aug 2008
SAm	15.31	Caterine IBARGÜEN	COL	Monaco	18 Jul 2014
CAC	15.29	Yamilé ALDAMA	CUB	Roma	11 Jul 2003
Asi	15.25	Olga RYPAKOVA	KAZ	Split	4 Sep 2010
NAm	14.45	Tiombé HURD	USA	Sacramento	11 Jul 2004
Oce	14.04	Nicole MLADENIS	AUS	Hobart	9 Mar 2002
	14.04	Nicole MLADENIS	AUS	Perth	7 Dec 2003
W20	14.62	Tereza MARINOVA	BUL	Sydney	25 Aug 1996
W18	14.57	HUANG Qiuyan	CHN	Shanghai	19 Oct 1997

SHOT

W, Eur	22.63	Natalya LISOVSKAYA	RUS	Moskva	7 Jun 1987
Asi	21.76	LI Meisu	CHN	Shijiazhuang	23 Apr 1988
Oce, Com	21.24	Valerie ADAMS	NZL	Daegu	29 Aug 2011
CAC	20.96	Belsy LAZA	CUB	Ciudad de México	2 May 1992
NAm	20.24	Michelle CARTER	USA	Des Moines	22 Jun 2013
SAm	19.30	Elisângela ADRIANO	BRA	Tunja	14 Jul 2001
Afr	18.43	Vivian CHUKWUEMEKA	NGR	Walnut	19 Apr 2003
W20	20.54	Astrid KUMBERNUSS	GDR	Orimattila	1 Jul 1989
W18	19.08	Ilke WYLUDDA	GDR	Karl-Marx-Stadt	9 Aug 1986

DISCUS

W, Eur	76.80	Gabriele REINSCH	GDR	Neubrandenburg	9 Jul 1988
Asi	71.68	XIAO Yanling	CHN	Beijing	14 Mar 1992
CAC	70.88	Hilda RAMOS	CUB	La Habana	8 May 1992
NAm	69.17	Gia LEWIS-SMALWOOD	USA	Angers	30 Aug 2014
Oce, Com	68.72	Daniela COSTIAN	AUS	Auckland	22 Jan 1994
Afr	64.87	Elizna NAUDE	RSA	Stellenbosch	2 Mar 2007
SAm	64.21	Andressa de MORAIS	BRA	Barquisimeto	10 Jun 2012
W20	74.40	Ilke WYLUDDA	GDR	Berlin	13 Sep 1988
W18	65.86	Ilke WYLUDDA	GDR	Neubrandenburg	1 Aug 1986

HAMMER

W, Eur	81.08	Anita WLODARCZYK	POL	Cetniewo	1 Aug 2015
Asi	77.68	WANG Zheng	CHN	Chengdu	29 Mar 2014
CAC	76.62	Yipsi MORENO	CUB	Zagreb	9 Sep 2008
NAm, Com	75.73	Sultana FRIZELL	CAN	Tucson	22 May 2014
SAm	73.74	Jennifer DAHLGREN	ARG	Buenos Aires	10 Apr 2010
Oce	71.12	Bronwyn EAGLES	AUS	Adelaide	6 Feb 2003
Afr	69.70	Amy SÈNE	SEN	Forbach	25 May 2014
W20	73.24	ZHANG Wenxiu	CHN	Changsha	24 Jun 2005
W18	70.60	ZHANG Wenxiu	CHN	Nanning	5 Apr 2003
W18 3kg	76.04	Réka GYURÁTZ	HUN	Zalaegerszeg	23 Jun 2013

JAVELIN

W, Eur	72.28	Barbora SPOTÁKOVÁ	CZE	Stuttgart	13 Sep 2008
CAC	71.70	Osleidys MENÉNDEZ	CUB	Helsinki	14 Aug 2005
Afr, Com	69.35	Sunette VILJOEN	RSA	New York	9 Jun 2012
Oce	66.83	Kimberley MICKLE	AUS	Melbourne	22 Mar 2014
NAm	66.67	Kara PATTERSON	USA	Des Moines	25 Jun 2010
Asi	66.13	LU Huihui	CHN	Beijing	30 Aug 2015
SAm	63.80A	Flor Dennis RUIZ	COL	Xalapa	27 Nov 2014
W20	63.86	Yulenmis AGUILAR	CUB	Edmonton	2 Aug 2015
W18	62.93	XUE Juan	CHN	Changsha	27 Oct 2003

HEPTATHLON

W, NAm	7291	Jackie JOYNER-KERSEE	USA	Seoul	24 Sep 1988
Eur	7032	Carolina KLÜFT	RUS	Osaka	26 Aug 2007
Com	6955	Jessica ENNIS	GBR/Eng	London (OS)	4 Aug 2012
Asi	6942	Ghada SHOUAA	SYR	Götzis	26 May 1996
Oce	6695	Jane FLEMMING	AUS	Auckland	28 Jan 1990
CAC	6527	Diane GUTHRIE-GRESHAM	JAM	Knoxville	3 Jun 1995
Afr	6423	Margaret SIMPSON	GHA	Götzis	29 May 2005
SAm	6160	Lucimara DA SILVA	BRA	Barquisimeto	10 Jun 2012
W20	6542	Carolina KLÜFT	SWE	München	10 Aug 2002
W18	6185	SHEN Shengfei	CHN	Shanghai	18 Oct 1997

DECATHLON

W, Eur	8358	Austra SKUJYTE	LTU	Columbia, MO	15 Apr 2005
Asi	7798 §	Irina NAUMENKO	KAZ	Talence	26 Sep 2004
NAm	7577 §	Tiffany LOTT-HOGAN	USA	Lage	10 Sep 2000
CAC	7245 §	Magalys GARCÍA	CUB	Wien	29 Jun 2002
Afr, Com	6915	Margaret SIMPSON	GHA	Réduit	19 Apr 2007
SAm	6570	Andrea BORDALEJO	ARG	Rosario	28 Nov 2004
Oce	5740	Preya CAREY	AUS	Brisbane	6 Sep 2001

4 X 100 METRES RELAY

W, NAm	40.82	USA (Madison, Felix, Knight, Jeter)	London (OS)	10 Aug 2012
CAC, Com	41.07	JAM (Campbell-Brown, Morrison, Thompson, Fraser-Pryce)	Beijing	29 Aug 2015
Eur	41.37	GDR (Gladisch, Rieger, Auerswald, Göhr)	Canberra	6 Oct 1985
Asi	42.23	Sichuan CHN (Xiao Lin, Li Yali, Liu Xiaomei, Li Xuemei)	Shanghai	23 Oct 1997
SAm	42.29	BRA (E dos Santos, Silva, Krasucki, R Santos)	Moskva	18 Aug 2013
Afr	42.39	NGR (Utondu, Idehen, Opara-Thompson, Onyali)	Barcelona	7 Aug 1992
Oce	42.99A	AUS (Massey, Broadrick, Lambert, Gainsford-Taylor)	Pietersburg	18 Mar 2000
W20	43.29	USA (Knight, Tarmoh, Olear, Mayo)	Eugene	8 Aug 2006
W18	44.05	GDR (Koppetsch, Oelsner, Sinzel, Brehmer)	Athína	24 Aug 1975

4 X 400 METRES RELAY

W, Eur	3:15.17	URS (Ledovskaya, Nazarova, Pinigina, Bryzgina)	Seoul	1 Oct 1988
NAm	3:15.51	USA (D.Howard, Dixon, Brisco, Griffith Joyner)	Seoul	1 Oct 1988
CAC, Com	3:18.71	JAM (Whyte, Prendergast, N Williams-Mills, S Williams)	Daegu	3 Sep 2011
Afr	3:21.04	NGR (Bisi Afolabi, Yusuf, Opara, Ogunkoya)	Atlanta	3 Aug 1996
Oce	3:23.81	AUS (Peris, Lewis, Gainsford-Taylor, Freeman)	Sydney	30 Sep 2000
Asi	3:24.28	Hebei CHN (An X, Bai X, Cao C, Ma Y)	Beijing	13 Sep 1993
SAm	3:26.68	BRA (Coutinho, de Oliveira, Souza, de Lima)	São Paulo	7 Aug 2011
W20	3:27.60	USA (Anderson, Kidd, Smith, Hastings)	Grosseto	18 Jul 2004
W18	3:36.98	GBR (Ravenscroft, E McMeekin, Kennedy, Pettett)	Duisburg	26 Aug 1973

10 KILOMETRES WALK

W, Eur	41:04	Yelena NIKOLAYEVA	RUS	Sochi	20 Apr 1996
Asi	41:16	WANG Yan	CHN	Eisenhüttenstadt	8 May 1999
Oce, Com	41:30	Kerry SAXBY-JUNNA	AUS	Canberra	27 Aug 1988
CAC	42:42	Graciela MENDOZA	MEX	Naumburg	25 May 1997
NAm	44:17	Michelle ROHL	USA	Göteborg	7 Aug 1995
SAm	44:22+	Erica de SEÑA	BRA	Dudince	21 Mar 2015
Afr	45:06A	Susan VERMEULEN	RSA	Bloemfontein	17 Apr 1999
W20	41:52 §	Tatyana MINEYEVA	RUS	Penza	5 Sep 2009
	41:57 §	GAO Hongmiao	CHN	Beijing	8 Sep 1993
W18	43:28	Aleksandra KUDRYASHOVA	RUS	Adler	19 Feb 2006

10,000 METRES TRACK WALK

W, Asi	41:37.9 §	GAO Hongmiao	CHN	Beijing	7 Apr 1994
W, Eur	41:56.23	Nadyezhda RYASHKINA	RUS	Seattle	24 Jul 1990
Oce, Com	41:57.22	Kerry SAXBY-JUNNA	AUS	Seattle	24 Jul 1990
SAm	43:41.30	Erica de SEÑA	BRA	São Paulo	1 Aug 2014
NAm	44:30.1 m	Alison BAKER	CAN	Bergen (Fana)	15 May 1992
	44:06 no kerb	Michelle ROHL	USA	Kenosha	2 Jun 1996
CAC	44:16.21	Cristina LÓPEZ	ESA	San Salvador	13 Jul 2007
Afr	46:34.68 mx	Chahinez NASRI	TUN	Balma	15 Nov 2015
	47:30.28	Chahinez AL-NASRI	TUN	Amman	16 May 2012
W20	42:47.25	Anezka DRAHOTOVÁ	CZE	Eugene	23 Jul 2014
W18	42:56.09	GAO Hongmiao	CHN	Tangshan	27 Sep 1991

20,000 METRES TRACK WALK

W, Eur	1:26:52.3	Olimpiada IVANOVA	RUS	Brisbane	6 Sep 2001
Asi, W20	1:29:32.4 §	SONG Hongjuan	CHN	Changsha	24 Oct 2003
SAm	1:31:02.25	Sandra Lorena ARENAS	COL	Lima	13 Jun 2015
CAC	1:31:53.8A	Mirna ORTIZ	GUA	Ciudad de Guatemala	9 Aug 2014
NAm, Com	1:32:54.0	Rachel SEAMAN	CAN	Moncton	27 Jun 2014
Oce	1:33:40.2	Kerry SAXBY-JUNNA	AUS	Brisbane	6 Sep 2001
Afr	1:36:43.43A	Nicolene CRONJE	RSA	Germiston	20 Mar 2004
W18	1:34:21.56	WANG Xue	CHN	Wuhan	1 Nov 2007

20 KILOMETRES WALK

W,Asi	1:24:38	LIU Hong	CHN	La Coruna	6 Jun 2015
Eur	1:24:47 §	Elmira ALEMBEKOVA	RUS	Sochi	27 Feb 2015
	1:25:02	Yeoena LASHMANOVA	RUS	London	11 Aug 2012
Oce, Com	1:27:44	Jane SAVILLE	AUS	Naumburg	2 May 2004

SAm	1:28:22	Erica de SEÑA	BRA	Dudince	19 Mar 20165
CAC	1:28:31	Mima ORTIZ	GUA	Rio Maior	6 Apr 2013
NAm	1:29:54	Rachel SEAMAN	CAN	Nomi	15 Mar 2015
Afr	1:34:19 §	Grace WANJIRU NJUE	KEN	Nairobi	1 Aug 2010
W20	1:25:30	Anisya KIRDYAPKINA	RUS	Adler	23 Feb 2008
W18	1:30:28	ZHOU Tongmei	CHN	Cixi	23 Apr 2005

World Records at other track & field events recognised by the IAAF

1 Hour	18,517 m	Dire TUNE	ETH	Ostrava	12 Jun 2008
20,000m	1:05:26.6	Tegla LOROUPE	KEN	Borgholzhausen	3 Sep 2000
25,000m	1:27:05.84	Tegla LOROUPE	KEN	Mengerskirchen	21 Sep 2002
30,000m	1:45:50.0	Tegla LOROUPE	KEN	Warstein	6 Jun 2003
4x200m	1:27.46	L Jenkins, L Colander, N Perry, M Jones	USA	Philadelphia	29 Apr 2000
4x800m	7:50.17	Olizarenko, Gurina, Borisova, Podyalovskaya	USSR	Moskva	5 Aug 1984
4x1500m	16:33.58	M Cherono, Kipyegon, I Jelagat, Obiri	KEN	Nassau	24 May 2014

WORLD BESTS AT NON-STANDARD EVENTS

Men

50m	5.47+e	Usain Bolt	JAM	Berlin (in 100m)	16 Aug 2009
60m	6.31+	Usain Bolt	JAM	Berlin (in 100m)	16 Aug 2009
100 yards	9.07	Asafa Powell	JAM	Ostrava	27 May 2010
150m turn	14.44+	Usain Bolt	JAM	Berlin (in 200m)	20 Aug 2009
150m straight	14.35	Usain Bolt	JAM	Manchester	17 May 2009
300m	30.85A	Michael Johnson	USA	Pretoria	24 Mar 2000
	30.97	Usain Bolt	JAM	Ostrava	27 May 2010
500m	59.32	Orestes Rodríguez	CUB	La Habana	15 Feb 2013
600m	1:12.81	Johnny Gray	USA	Santa Monica	24 May 1986
2 miles	7:58.61	Daniel Komen	KEN	Hechtel	19 Jul 1997
2000m Steeple	5:10.68	Mahiedine Mekhissi	FRA	Reims	30 Jun 2010
200mh	22.55	Laurent Ottoz	ITA	Milano	31 May 1995
(hand time)	22.5	Martin Lauer	FRG	Zürich	7 Jul 1959
200mh straight	22.10	Andrew Turner	GBR	Manchester	15 May 2011
	22.10	L.J. van Zyl	RSA	Manchester	9 May 2015
220yh straight	21.9	Don Styron	USA	Baton Rouge	2 Apr 1960
300mh	34.48	Chris Rawlinson	GBR	Sheffield	30 Jun 2002
35lb weight	25.41	Lance Deal	USA	Azusa	20 Feb 1993
Pentathlon	4282 points	Bill Toomey	USA	London (CP)	16 Aug 1969
(1985 tables)		(7.58, 66.18, 21.3, 44.52, 4:20.3)			
Double decathlon	14,571	Joe Detmer	USA	Lynchburg	24/25 Sep 2010
	10.93w, 7.30, 200mh 24.25w, 12.27, 5k 18:25.32, 2:02.23, 1.98, 400m 50.43, HT 31.82, 3kSt 11:22.47				
	15.01, DT 40.73, 200m 22.58, 4.85, 3k 10:25.99, 400mh 53.83, 51.95, 4:26.66, TJ 13.67, 10k 40:27.26				
4x110mh	52.94	USA Richardson, Harris, Merritt, Oliver		Des Moines	25 Apr 2015
3000m track walk	10:47.11	Giovanni De Benedictis	ITA	San Giovanni Valdarno	19 May 1990
5000m track walk	18:05.49	Hatem Ghoula	TUN	Tunis	1 May 1997
10,000m track walk	37:53.09	Francisco Javier Fernández	ESP	Santa Cruz de Tenerife	27 Jul 2008
10 km road walk	37:11	Roman Rasskazov	RUS	Saransk	28 May 2000
30 km road walk	2:01:13+	Vladimir Kanaykin	RUS	Adler	19 Feb 2006
35 km road walk	2:21:31	Vladimir Kanaykin	RUS	Adler	19 Feb 2006
100 km road walk	8:38:07	Viktor Ginko	BLR	Scanzorosciate	27 Oct 2002

Women

50m	5.93+	Marion Jones	USA	Sevilla (in 100m)	22 Aug 1999
60m	6.85+	Marion Jones	USA	Sevilla (in 100m)	22 Aug 1999
100 yards	9.91	Veronica-Campbell-Brown	JAM	Ostrava	31 May 2011
150m	16.10+	Florence Griffith-Joyner	USA	Seoul (in 200m)	29 Sep 1988
300m	34.1+	Marita Koch	GDR	Canberra (in 400m)	6 Oct 1985
500m	1:05.9	Tatána Kocembová	CZE	Ostrava	2 Aug 1984
600m	1:22.63	Ana Fidelia Quirot	CUB	Guadalajara, ESP	25 Jul 1997
2 miles	8:58.58	Meseret Defar	ETH	Bruxelles	14 Sep 2007
2000m Steeple	6:03.38	Wioletta Janowska	POL	Gdansk	15 Jul 2006
200mh	24.8	Yadisleidis Pedroso	ITA	Caserta	6 Apr 2013
	25.79	Noemi Zbären	SUI	Basel	17 May 2014
300mh	38.16	Zuzana Hejnová	CZE	Cheb	2 Aug 2013
Double heptathlon	10,798	Milla Kelo	FIN	Turku	7/8 Sep 2002
	100mh 14.89, HJ 1.51, 1500m 5:03.74, 400mh 62.18, SP 12.73, 200m 25.16, 100m 12.59				
	LJ 5.73w, 400m 56.10, JT 32.69, 800m 2:23.94, 200mh 28.72, DT 47.86, 3000m 11:48.68				
4x100mh	50.50	USA Castlin, Q Harrison, Harper-Nelson, Rollins		Des Moines	24 Apr 2015
3000m track walk	11:48.24	Ileana Salvador	ITA	Padova	29 Aug 1993
5000m track walk	20:01.80	Eleonora Giorgi	ITA	Misterbianco	17 May 2014
30 km road walk	2:19:43	Eleonora Giorgi	ITA	Catania	31 Jul 2016
50 km road walk	4:10:59	Monica Svensson	SWE	Scanzorosciate	21 Oct 2007
100 km road walk	10:04:50	Jolanta Dukure	LAT	Scanzorosciate	21 Oct 2007

LONG DISTANCE WORLD BESTS – MEN TRACK

	hr:min:sec	*Name*	*Nat*	*Venue*	*Date*
15,000m	0:42:18.7+	Haile Gebrselassie	ETH	Ostrava	27 Jun 2007
10 miles	0:45:23.8+	Haile Gebrselassie	ETH	Ostrava	27 Jun 2007
15 miles	1:11:43.1	Bill Rodgers	USA	Saratoga, Cal.	21 Feb 1979
20 miles	1:39:14.4	Jack Foster	NZL	Hamilton, NZ	15 Aug 1971
30 miles	2:42:00+	Jeff Norman	GBR	Timperley, Cheshire	7 Jun 1980
50 km	2:48:06	Jeff Norman	GBR	Timperley, Cheshire	7 Jun 1980
40 miles	3:48:35	Don Ritchie	GBR	London (Hendon)	16 Oct 1982
50 miles	4:51:49	Don Ritchie	GBR	London (Hendon)	12 Mar 1983
100 km	6:10:20	Don Ritchie	GBR	London (CP)	28 Oct 1978
150 km	10:34:30	Denis Zhalybin	RUS	London (CP)	20 Oct 2002
100 miles	11:28:03	Oleg Kharitonov	RUS	London (CP)	20 Oct 2002
200 km	15:10:27+	Yiannis Kouros	AUS	Adelaide	4-5 Oct 1997
200 miles	27:48:35	Yiannis Kouros	GRE	Montauban	15-16 Mar 1985
500 km	60:23.00+ ??	Yiannis Kouros	GRE	Colac, Aus	26-29 Nov 1984
500 miles	105:42:09+	Yiannis Kouros	GRE	Colac, Aus	26-30 Nov 1984
1000 km	136:17:00	Yiannis Kouros	GRE	Colac, Aus	26-31 Nov 1984
1500 km	10d 17:28:26	Petrus Silkinas	LTU	Nanango, Qld	11-21 Mar 1998
1000 mile	11d 13:54:58+	Petrus Silkinas	LTU	Nanango, Qld	11-22 Mar 1998
2 hrs	37.994 km	Jim Alder	GBR	Walton-on-Thames	17 Oct 1964
12 hrs	162.400 km +	Yiannis Kouros	GRE	Montauban	15 Mar 1985
24 hrs	303.506 km	Yiannis Kouros	AUS	Adelaide	4-5 Oct 1997
48 hrs	473.797 km	Yiannis Kouros	AUS	Surgères	3-5 May 1996
6 days	1036.8 km	Yiannis Kouros	GRE	Colac, Aus	20-26 Nov 2005

LONG DISTANCE ROAD RECORDS & BESTS – MEN

Where superior to track bests (over 10km) and run on properly measured road courses. (I) IAAF recognition.

10 km (I)	0:26:44	Leonard Patrick Komon	KEN	Utrecht	26 Sep 2010
15 km (I)	0:41:13	Leonard Patrick Komon	KEN	Nijmegen	21 Nov 2010
10 miles	0:44:24 §	Haile Gebrselassie	ETH	Tilburg	4 Sep 2005
	0:44:45	Paul Koech	KEN	Amsterdam-Zaandam	21 Sep 1997
20 km (I)	0:55:21+	Zersenay Tadese	ERI	Lisboa	21 Mar 2010
25 km (I)	1:11:18	Dennis Kimetto	KEN	Berlin	6 May 2012
30 km (I)	1:27:37	Emmanuel Mutai KEN, Geoffrey Kamworor KEN §		Berlin	28 Sep 2014
	1:27:36+ §	Wilfred KIRWA	KEN	Berlin (dnf)	28 Sep 2014
20 miles	1:35:22+	Steve Jones	GBR	Chicago	10 Oct 1985
30 miles	2:37:31+	Thompson Magawana	RSA	Claremont-Kirstenbosch	2 Apr 1988
50km	2:43:38+	Thompson Magawana	RSA	Claremont-Kirstenbosch	2 Apr 1988
40 miles	3:45:39	Andy Jones	CAN	Houston	23 Feb 1991
50 miles	4:50:21	Bruce Fordyce	RSA	London-Brighton	25 Sep 1983
100 km (I)	6:13:33	Takahiro Sunada	JPN	Yubetsu	21 Jun 1998
1000 miles	10d:10:30:35	Yiannis Kouros	GRE	New York	21-30 May 1988
12 hrs	162.543 km	Yiannis Kouros	GRE	Queen's, New York	7 Nov 1984

LONG DISTANCE WORLD BESTS – WOMEN TRACK

15 km	0:48:54.91+	Dire Tune	ETH	Ostrava	12 Jun 2008
10 miles	0:54:21.8	Lorraine Moller	NZL	Auckland	9 Jan 1993
20 miles	1:59:09 !	Chantal Langlacé	FRA	Amiens	3 Sep 1983
30 miles	3:12:25+	Carolyn Hunter-Rowe	GBR	Barry, Wales	3 Mar 1996
50 km	3:18:52+	Carolyn Hunter-Rowe	GBR	Barry, Wales	3 Mar 1996
40 miles	4:26:43	Carolyn Hunter-Rowe	GBR	Barry, Wales	7 Mar 1993
50 miles	5:48:12.0+	Norimi Sakurai	JPN	San Giovanni Lupatoto	27 Sep 2003
100 km	7:14:05.8	Norimi Sakurai	JPN	San Giovanni Lupatoto	27 Sep 2003
150 km	13:45:54	Hilary Walker	GBR	Blackpool	5-6 Nov 1988
100 miles	13:52.02+	Mami Kudo	JPN	Soochow	10-11 Dec 2011
200 km	17:52.18+	Mami Kudo	JPN	Soochow	10-11 Dec 2011
200 miles	39:09:03	Hilary Walker	GBR	Blackpool	5-7 Nov 1988
500 km	77:53:46	Eleanor Adams	GBR	Colac, Aus.	13-16 Nov 1989
500 miles	130:59:58+	Sandra Barwick	NZL	Campbelltown, AUS	18-23 Nov 1990
1000 km	8d 00:27:06+	Eleanor Robinson	GBR	Nanango, Qld	11-19 Mar 1998
1500 km	12d 06:52:12+	Eleanor Robinson	GBR	Nanango, Qld	11-23 Mar 1998
1000 miles	13d 02:16:49	Eleanor Robinson	GBR	Nanango, Qld	11-24 Mar 1998
2 hrs	32.652 km	Chantal Langlacé	FRA	Amiens	3 Sep 1983
12 hrs	147.600 km	Ann Trason	USA	Hayward, Cal	3-4 Aug 1991
24 hours	255.303 km	Mami Kudo	JPN	Soochow	10-11 Dec 2011
48 hrs	385.130 km	Mami Kudo	JPN	Surgères	22-24 May 2010
6 days	883.631 km	Sandra Barwick	NZL	Campbelltown, AUS	18-24 Nov 1990

! Timed on one running watch only

LONG DISTANCE ROAD RECORDS & BESTS - WOMEN

	hr:min:sec	Name	Nat	Venue	Date
10 km (l)	0:30:21	Paula Radcliffe	GBR	San Juan	23 Feb 2003
15 km (l)	46:14+	Florence Kiplaget	KEN	Barcelona	15 Feb 2015
10 miles	0:50:05+	Mary Keitany	KEN	Ra's Al-Khaymah	18 Feb 2011
	0:50:01+ dh	Paula Radcliffe	GBR	Newcastle	21 Sep 2003
20 km (l)	1:01:54+	Florence Kiplaget	KEN	Barcelona	15 Feb 2015
25 km (l)	1:19:53	Mary Keitany	KEN	Berlin	9 May 2010
30 km (l)	1:38:23+ §	Liliya Shobukhova	RUS	Chicago	9 Oct 2011
	1:36:36+ dh	Paula Radcliffe	GBR	London	13 Apr 2003
20 miles	1:43:33+	Paula Radcliffe	GBR	London	13 Apr 2003
30 miles	3:01:16+	Frith van der Merwe	RSA	Claremont-Kirstenbosch	25 Mar 1989
50 km	3:08:39	Frith van der Merwe	RSA	Claremont-Kirstenbosch	25 Mar 1989
40 miles	4:26:13+	Ann Trason	USA	Houston	23 Feb 1991
50 miles	5:40:18	Ann Trason	USA	Houston	23 Feb 1991
100 km (l)	6:33:11	Tomoe Abe	JPN	Yubetsu	25 Jun 2000
100 miles	13:47:41	Ann Trason	USA	Queen's, New York	4 May 1991
200 km	18:45:51	Mami Kudo	JPN	Steenbergen	11-12 May 2013
1000 km	7d 01:11:00+	Sandra Barwick	NZL	New York	16-23 Sep 1991
1000 miles	12d 14:38:40	Sandra Barwick	NZL	New York	16-29 Sep 1991
Ekiden (6 stages)	2:11:22	(l)	ETH	Chiba	24 Nov 2003
Berhane Adere, Tirunesh Dibaba, Eyerusalem Kuma, Ejegayou Dibaba, Meseret Defar, Werknesh Kidane					
12 hours	144.840 km	Ann Trason	USA	Queen's, New York	4 May 1991
24 hours	252.205 km	Mami Kudo	JPN	Steenbergen	12 May 2013

100 KILOMETRES CONTINENTAL RECORDS

Men

W, Asi	6:13:33	Takahiro SUNADA	JPN	Yubetsu	21 Jun 1998
Eur	6:16:41	Jean-Paul PRAET	BEL	Torhout	24 Jun 1989
SAm	6:18:09	Valmir NUNES	BRA	Winschoten	16 Sep 1995
Afr	6:25:07	Bruce FORDYCE	RSA	Stellenbosch	4 Feb 1989
NAm	6:27:43	Maxwell KING	USA	Doha	21 Nov 2014
Oce	6:29:23	Tim SLOAN	AUS	Ross-Richmond	23 Apr 1995

Women

W, Asi	6:33:11	Tomoe ABE	JPN	Yubetsu	25 Jun 2000
NAm	7:00:48	Ann TRASON	USA	Winschoten	16 Sep 1995
Eur	7:10:32	Tatyana ZHYRKOVA	RUS	Winschoten	11 Sep 2004
SAm	7:20:22	Maria VENÂNCIO	BRA	Cubatão	8 Aug 1998
Afr	7:31:47	Helena JOUBERT	RSA	Winschoten	16 Sep 1995
Oce	7:39:28	Kirstin Bull	AUS	Winschoten	12 Sep 2015

WORLD INDOOR RECORDS

Men — to March 2015

50 metres	5.56A	Donovan Bailey	CAN	Reno	9 Feb 1996
60 metres	6.39	Maurice Greene	USA	Madrid	3 Feb 1998
	6.39	Maurice Greene	USA	Atlanta	3 Mar 2001
100 metres	9.98	Usain Bolt	JAM	Warszawa	23 Aug 2014
200 metres	19.92	Frank Fredericks	NAM	Liévin	18 Feb 1996
400 metres	44.57	Kerron Clement	USA	Fayetteville	12 Mar 2005
800 metres	1:42.67	Wilson Kipketer	KEN	Paris (Bercy)	9 Mar 1997
1000 metres	2:14.20	Ayanleh Souleiman	DJI	Stockholm	17 Feb 2016
1500 metres	3:31.18	Hicham El Guerrouj	MAR	Stuttgart	2 Feb 1997
1 mile	3:48.45	Hicham El Guerrouj	MAR	Gent	12 Feb 1997
2000 metres #	4:49.99	Kenenisa Bekele	ETH	Birmingham	17 Feb 2007
3000 metres	7:24.90	Daniel Komen	KEN	Budapest	6 Feb 1998
2 miles #	8:04.35	Kenenisa Bekele	ETH	Birmingham	16 Feb 2008
5000 metres	12:49.60	Kenenisa Bekele	ETH	Birmingham	20 Feb 2004
10000 metres #	27:50.29	Mark Bett	KEN	Gent	10 Feb 2002
50 m hurdles	6.25	Mark McKoy	CAN	Kobe	5 Mar 1986
60 m hurdles	7.30	Colin Jackson	GBR	Sindelfingen	6 Mar 1994
110 m hurdles	13.03	Orlando Ortega	CUB	Warszawa	23 Aug 2014
High jump	2.43	Javier Sotomayor	CUB	Budapest	4 Mar 1989
Pole vault	6.16	Renaud Lavillenie	FRA	Donetsk	15 Feb 2014
Long jump	8.79	Carl Lewis	USA	New York	27 Jan 1984
Triple jump	17.92	Teddy Tamgho	FRA	Paris (Bercy)	6 Mar 2011
Shot	22.66	Randy Barnes	USA	Los Angeles	20 Jan 1989
Javelin #	85.78	Matti Närhi	FIN	Kajaani	3 Mar 1996
35 lb weight #	25.86	Lance Deal	USA	Atlanta	4 Mar 1995
3000m walk #	10:31.42	Andreas Erm	GER	Halle	4 Feb 2001

5000m walk	18:07.08	Mikhail Shchennikov	RUS	Moskva	14 Feb 1995
10000m walk #	38:31.4	Werner Heyer	GDR	Berlin	12 Jan 1980
4 x 200m	1:22.11	United Kingdom		Glasgow	3 Mar 1991
		(Linford Christie, Darren Braithwaite, Ade Mafe, John Regis)			
4 x 400m	3:02.13	USA		Sopot	9 Mar 2014
		(Kyle Clemons, David Verburg, Kind Butler, Calvin Smith)			
	3:01.96 §	USA (not ratified – no EPO analysis)		Fayetteville	11 Feb 2006
		(Kerron Clement, Wallace Spearmon, Darold Williamson, Jeremy Wariner)			
4 x 800m	7:13.11	USA All-Stars		Boston (Roxbury)	8 Feb 2014
		(Richard Jones, David Torrence, Duane Solomon, Erik Sowinski)			
Distance Med	9:19.93	USA		New York (Armory)	31 Jan 2015
		(Matthew Centrowitz, Mike Berry, Erik Sowinski, Pat Casey)			
Heptathlon	6645 points	Ashton Eaton	USA	Istanbul	9/10 Mar 2012
		(6.79 60m, 8.16 LJ, 14.56 SP, 2.03 HJ, 7.68 60mh, 5.20 PV, 2:32.77 1000m)			
Women					
50 metres	5.96+	Irina Privalova	RUS	Madrid	9 Feb 1995
60 metres	6.92	Irina Privalova	RUS	Madrid	11 Feb 1993 & 9 Feb 1995
200 metres	21.87	Merlene Ottey	JAM	Liévin	13 Feb 1993
400 metres	49.59	Jarmila Kratochvílová	CZE	Milano	7 Mar 1982
800 metres	1:55.82	Jolanda Ceplak	SLO	Wien	3 Mar 2002
1000 metres	2:30.94	Maria Lurdes Mutola	MOZ	Stockholm	25 Feb 1999
1500 metres	3:55.17	Genzebe Dibaba	ETH	Karlsruhe	1 Feb 2014
1 mile	4:13.31	Genzebe Dibaba	ETH	Stockholm	17 Feb 2016
2000 metres #	5:30.53	Gabriela Szabo	ROU	Sindelfingen	8 Mar 1998
3000 metres	8:16.60	Genzebe Dibaba	ETH	Stockholm	6 Feb 2014
2 miles #	9:00.48	Genzebe Dibaba	ETH	Birmingham	15 Feb 2014
5000 metres	14:18.86	Genzebe Dibaba	ETH	Stockholm	19 Feb 2015
50 m hurdles	6.58	Cornelia Oschkenat	GDR	Berlin	20 Feb 1988
60 m hurdles	7.68	Susanna Kallur	SWE	Karlsruhe	10 Feb 2008
100 m hurdles	12.64	Ludmila Engquist	SWE	Tampere	10 Feb 1997
High jump	2.08	Kajsa Bergqvist	SWE	Arnstadt	4 Feb 2006
Pole vault	5.03	Jenn Suhr	USA	Brockport	30 Jan 2016
Long jump	7.37	Heike Drechsler	GDR	Wien	13 Feb 1988
Triple jump	15.36	Tatyana Lebedeva	RUS	Budapest	5 Mar 2004
Shot	22.50	Helena Fibingerová	CZE	Jablonec	19 Feb 1977
Javelin #	61.29	Taina Uppa/Kolkkala	FIN	Mustasaari	28 Feb 1999
20 lb weight #	25.56	Brittany Riley	USA	Fayetteville	10 Mar 2007
3000m walk	11:35.34 un	Gillian O'Sullivan	IRL	Belfast	15 Feb 2003
	11:40.33	Claudia Iovan/Stef	ROU	Bucuresti	30 Jan 1999
5000m walk #	20:37.77	Margarita Turova	BLR	Minsk	13 Feb 2005
10000m walk	43:54.63	Yelena Ginko	BLR	Mogilyov	22 Feb 2008
4 x 200m	1:32.41	Russia		Glasgow	29 Jan 2005
		(Yekaterina Kondratyeva, Irina Khabarova, Yuliya Pechonkina, Yuliya Gushchina)			
4 x 400m	3:23.37	Russia		Glasgow	28 Jan 2006
		(Yuliya Gushchina, Olga Kotlyarova, Olga Zaytseva, Olesya Krasnomovets)			
4 x 800m	8:06.24	Moskva	RUS	Moskva	18 Feb 2011
		(Aleksandra Bulanova, Yekaterina Martynova, Yelena Kofanova , Anna Balakshina)			
Distance Med	10:42.57	Newa Balance TC	USA	Boston (Roxbury)	7 Feb 2015
		(Sarah Brown, Mahogany Jones, Megan Krumpoch, Brenda Martinez)			
Pentathlon	5013 points	Nataliya Dobrynska	UKR	Istanbul	9 Mar 2012
		(8.38 60mh, 1.84 HJ, 16.51 SP, 6.57 LJ, 2:11.15 800m)			

events not officially recognised by the IAAF

WORLD INDOOR JUNIOR (U20) RECORDS

First approved by IAAF Council in 2011. **Men**

60 metres	6.51	Mark Lewis-Francis	GBR	Lisboa	11 Mar 2001
200 metres	20.37	Walter Dix	USA	Fayetteville	11 Mar 2005
400 metres	44.80	Kirani James	GRN	Fayetteville	27 Feb 2011
800 metres	1:44.35	Yuriy Borzakovskiy	RUS	Dortmund	30 Jan 2000
1000 metres	2:15.77	Abubaker Kaki	SUD	Stockholm	21 Feb 2008
1500 metres	3:36.28	Belal Mansoor Ali (overage!)	BRN	Stockholm	20 Feb 2007
One mile	3:55.02	German Fernandez	USA	College Station	28 Feb 2009
3000 metres	7:32.87	Hagos Gebrhiwet	ETH	Boston (Roxbury)	2 Feb 2013
5000 metres	12:53.29	Isiah Koech	KEN	Düsseldorf	11 Feb 2011
60mh (99cm)	7.48 §	Wilhem Belocian	FRA	Val-de-Reuil	9 Mar 2014
	7.50	Konstadínos Douvalidís	GRE	Athína	11 Feb 2006
	7.50 #	David Omoregie	GBR	Cardiff	9 Mar 2014
High jump	2.35	Volodymyr Yashchenko	URS	Milano	12 Mar 1978
Pole vault	5.68	Raphael Holzdeppe	GER	Halle	1 Mar 2008
Long jump	8.22	Viktor Kuznetsov	UKR	Brovary	22 Jan 2005

Triple jump	17.14	Volker Mai	GDR	Piréas	2 Mar 1985
Shot (6kg)	22.48	Konrad Bukowiecki	POL	Torun	8 Jan 2016
Heptathlon (jnr imps)	6022	Gunnar Nixon (7.10, 7.53, 13.97, 2.15, 8.21, 4.50, 2:40.15)	USA	Fayetteville	27/28 Jan 2012
Women					
60 metres	7.07	Ewa Swoboda	POL	Torun	12 Feb 2016
200 metres	22.40	Bianca Knight	USA	Fayetteville	14 Mar 2008
400 metres	50.82	Sanya Richards	USA	Fayetteville	13 Mar 2004
800 metres	2:01.03	Meskerem Legesse	ETH	Fayetteville	14 Feb 2004
1000 metres	2:35.80	Mary Cain	USA	Boston (Roxbury)	8 Feb 2014
1500 metres	4:01.81	Gudaf Tsegay	ETH	Glasgow	20 Feb 2016
One mile	4:24.10	Kalkidan Gezahegne	ETH	Birmingham	20 Feb 2010
3000 metres	8:33.56	Tirunesh Dibaba	ETH	Birmingham	20 Feb 2004
5000 metres	14:53.99	Tirunesh Dibaba	ETH	Boston	31 Jan 2004
60m hurdles	8.01	Dior Hall	USA	Fayetteville	13 Mar 2015
High jump	1.99	Vashti Cunningham	USA	Portland	12 Mar 2016
Pole vault	4.71	Wilma Murto	FIN	Zweibrücken	31 Jan 2016
Long jump	6.88	Heike Daute	GDR	Berlin	1 Feb 1983
Triple jump	14.37	Ren Ruiping	CHN	Barcelona	11 Mar 1995
Shot	20.51	Heidi Krieger	GDR	Budapest	8 Feb 1984
Pentathlon	4635A	Kendell Williams (8.21, 1.88, 12.05, 6.32, 2:17.31)	USA	Albuquerque	15 Mar 2014

WORLD VETERANS/MASTERS RECORDS

MEN – aged 35 or over

100 metres	9.96	Kim Collins (5.4.76)	SKN	London (HG)	20 Jul 2014
200 metres	20.11	Linford Christie (2.4.60)	GBR	Villeneuve d'Ascq	25 Jun 1995
400 metres	44.54	Chris Brown (15.10.78)	BAH	Eugene	30 May 2015
800 metres	1:43.36	Johnny Gray (19.6.60)	USA	Zürich	16 Aug 1995
1000 metres	2:18.8+	William Tanui (22.2.64)	KEN	Rome	7 Jul 1999
1500 metres	3:32.45	William Tanui (22.2.64)	KEN	Athína	16 Jun 1999
1 mile	3:51.38	Bernard Lagat (12.12.74)	USA	London (CP)	6 Aug 2011
2000 metres	4:58.3+ e	William Tanui (22.2.64	KEN	Monaco	4 Aug 1999
	4:54.74i	Bernard Lagat (12.12.74)	USA	New York	15 Feb 2014
3000 metres	7:29.00	Bernard Lagat (12.12.74)	USA	Rieti	29 Aug 2010
5000 metres	12:53.60	Bernard Lagat (12.12.74)	USA	Monaco	22 Jul 2011
10000 metres	26:51.20	Haile Gebrselassie (18.4.73)	ETH	Hengelo	24 May 2008
20000 metres	57:44.4+	Gaston Roelants (5.2.37)	BEL	Bruxelles	20 Sep 1972
1 Hour	20,822m	Haile Gebrselassie (18.4.73)	ETH	Hengelo	1 Jun 2009
Half Marathon	59:10 dh	Paul Tergat (17.6.69)	KEN	Lisboa	13 Mar 2005
	59:50	Haile Gebrselassie (18.4.73)	ETH	Den Haag	14 Mar 2009
Marathon	2:03:59	Haile Gebrselassie (18.4.73)	ETH	Berlin	28 Sep 2008
3000m steeple	8:04.95	Simon Vroemen (11.5.69)	NED	Bruxelles	26 Aug 2005
110m hurdles	12.96	Allen Johnson (1.3.71)	USA	Athína	17 Sep 2006
400m hurdles	48.10	Felix Sánchez (30.8.77)	DOM	Moskva	13 Aug 2013
High jump	2.31	Dragutin Topic (12.3.71)	SRB	Kragujevac	28 Jul 2009
	2.31	Jamie Nieto (2.11.76)	USA	New York	9 Jun 2012
Pole vault	5.90i	Björn Otto (16.10.77)	GER	Cottbus	30 Jan 2013
	5.90i	Björn Otto		Düsseldorf	8 Feb 2013
	5.90	Björn Otto		Eugene	1 Jun 2013
Long jump	8.50	Larry Myricks (10.3.56)	USA	New York	15 Jun 1991
	8.50	Carl Lewis (1.7.61)	USA	Atlanta	29 Jul 1996
Triple jump	17.92	Jonathan Edwards (10.5.66)	GBR	Edmonton	6 Aug 2001
Shot	22.67	Kevin Toth ¶ (29.12.67)	USA	Lawrence	19 Apr 2003
Discus	71.56	Virgilijus Alekna (13.2.72)	LTU	Kaunas	25 Jul 2007
Hammer	83.62	Igor Astapkovich (4.1.63)	BLR	Staiki	20 Jun 1998
Javelin	92.80	Jan Zelezny (16.6.66)	CZE	Edmonton	12 Aug 2001
Decathlon	8241	Kip Janvrin (8.7.65) (10.98, 7.01, 14.21, 1.89, 48.41, 14.72, 45.59, 5.20, 60.41, 4:14.96)	USA	Eugene	22 Jun 2001
20 km walk	1:17:02	Yohann Diniz (1.1.78)	FRA	Arles	8 Mar 2015
20000m t walk	1:19:42.1	Yohann Diniz (1.1.78)	FRA	Bogny-sur-Meuse	25 May 2014
50 km walk	3:32:33	Yohann Diniz (1.1.78)	FRA	Zürich	15 Aug 2014
50000m t walk	3:49:29.7	Alain Lemercier (11.1.57)	FRA	Franconville	3 Apr 1994

MEN – aged 40 or over

100 metres	10.29	Troy Douglas (30.11.62)	NED	Leiden	7 Jun 2003
200 metres	20.64	Troy Douglas (30.11.62)	NED	Utrecht	9 Aug 2003
400 metres	47.82	Enrico Saraceni (19.5.64)	ITA	Århus	25 Jul 2004
	47.5u	Lee Evans (25.2.47)	USA		Apr 1989
800 metres	1:48.05	Anthony Whiteman (13.11.71)	GBR	Manchester (Stretford)	12 Jul 2014
1000 metres	2:24.93i	Vyacheslav Shabunin (27.9.69)	RUS	Moskva	10 Jan 2010

1500 metres	3:40.20i+	Bernard Lagat (12.12.74)	USA	New York (Armory)	14 Feb 2015
	3:41.87	Bernard Lagat		Birmingham	7 Jun 2015
1 mile	3:54.91i+	Bernard Lagat		New York (Armory)	14 Feb 2015
	3:57.91	Bernard Lagat		London (OS)	25 Jul 2015
3000 metres	7:37.92i+	Bernard Lagat (12.12.74)	USA	Metz	25 Feb 2015
	7:42.75	Bernard Lagat		Luzern1	14 Jul 2015
5000 metres	13:14.97	Bernard Lagat		Eugene	29 May 2015
10000 metres	28:30.88	Martti Vainio (30.12.50)	FIN	Hengelo	25 Jun 1991
10 km road	27:48	Bernard Lagat (12.12.74)	USA	Manchester	10 May 2015
1 Hour	19.710k	Steve Moneghetti (26.9.62)	AUS	Geelong	17 Dec 2005
Half marathon	60:41 dh	Haile Gebrselassie (18.4.73)	ETH	South Shields	15 Sep 2013
	61:09	Haile Gebrselassie		Glasgow	6 Oct 2013
Marathon	2:08:42	Kenneth Mungara (7.9.73)	KEN	Gold Coast	5 Jul 2015
3000m steeple	8:38.40	Angelo Carosi (20.1.64)	ITA	Firenze	11 Jul 2004
110m hurdles	13.97	David Ashford (24.1.63)	USA	Indianapolis	3 Jul 2004
	13.79 ?	Roger Kingdom (26.8.62)	USA	Slippery Rock	23 Jun 2004
400m hurdles	49.69	Danny McFarlane (14.2.72)	JAM	Kingston	29 Jun 2012
High jump	2.28	Dragutin Topic (12.3.71)	SRB	Beograd	20 May 2012
Pole vault	5.71i	Jeff Hartwig (25.9.67)	USA	Jonesboro	31 May 2008
	5.70	Jeff Hartwig		Eugene	29 Jun 2008
Long jump	7.68A	Aaron Sampson (20.9.61)	USA	Cedar City, UT	21 Jun 2002
	7.59i	Mattias Sunneborn (27.9.70)	SWE	Sätra	3 Feb 2013
	7.57	Hans Schicker (3.10.47)	FRG	Kitzingen	16 Jul 1989
Triple jump	16.58	Ray Kimble (19.4.53)	USA	Edinburgh	2 Jul 1993
Shot	21.41	Brian Oldfield USA (1.6.45)	USA	Innsbruck	22 Aug 1985
Discus	70.28	Virgilijus Alekna (13.2.72)	LTU	Klaipeda	23 Jun 2012
Hammer	82.23	Igor Astapkovich (4.1.63)	BLR	Minsk	10 Jul 2004
Javelin	85.92	Jan Zelezny (16.6.66)	CZE	Göteborg	9 Aug 2006
Pentathlon	3510	Werner Schallau (8.9.38)	FRG	Gelsenkirchen	24 Sep 1978
		6.74, 59.20, 23.0, 43.76, 5:05.7			
Decathlon	7525	Kip Janvrin (8.7.65)	USA	San Sebastián	24 Aug 2005
		11.56, 6.78, 14.01, 1.80, 49.46, 15.40, 42.70, 4.70, 58.43, 4:25.87			
20 km walk	1:20:20	Andriy Kovenko (25.11.73)	UKR	Alushta	28 Feb 2014
20000m t walk	1:24:58.8	Marcel Jobin (3.1.42)	CAN	Sept Isles	12 May 1984
50 km walk	3:40:46	Yuriy Andronov (6.11.71)	RUS	Moskva	11 Jun 2012
50000m t walk	3:51:54.5	José Marín (21.1.50)	ESP	Manresa	7 Apr 1990
4x100m	42.20	SpeedWest TC	USA	Irvine	2 May 2004
		(Frank Strong, Cornell Stephenson, Kettrell Berry, Willie Gault)			
4x400m	3:20.83	S Allah, K Morning, E Gonera, R Blackwell	USA	Philadelphia	27 Apr 2001

WOMEN – aged 35 or over

100 metres	10.74	Merlene Ottey (10.5.60)	JAM	Milano	7 Sep 1996
200 metres	21.93	Merlene Ottey (10.5.60)	JAM	Bruxelles	25 Aug 1995
400 metres	50.27	Jearl Miles Clark (4.9.66)	USA	Madrid	20 Sep 2002
800 metres	1:56.53	Lyubov Gurina (6.8.57)	RUS	Hechtel	30 Jul 1994
1000 metres	2:31.5	Maricica Puica (29.7.50)	ROU	Poiana Brasov	1 Jun 1986
1500 metres	3:57.73	Maricica Puica (29.7.50)	ROU	Bruxelles	30 Aug 1985
1 mile	4:17.33	Maricica Puica (29.7.50)	ROU	Zürich	21 Aug 1985
2000 metres	5:28.69	Maricica Puica (29.7.50)	ROU	London (CP)	11 Jul 1986
3000 metres	8:23.23	Edith Masai (4.4.67)	KEN	Monaco	19 Jul 2002
5000 metres	14:33.84	Edith Masai (4.4.67)	KEN	Oslo	2 Jun 2006
10000 metres	30:30.26	Edith Masai (4.4.67)	KEN	Helsinki	6 Aug 2005
Half Marathon	67:16	Edith Masai (4.4.67)	KEN	Berlin	2 Apr 2006
Marathon	2:19:19	Irina Mikitenko (23.8.72)	GER	Berlin	28 Sep 2008
3000m steeple	9:24.26	Marta Domínguez (3.11.75)	ESP	Huelva	7 Jun 2012
100m hurdles	12.40	Gail Devers (19.11.66)	USA	Lausanne	2 Jul 2002
400m hurdles	52.94	Marina Styepanova (1.5.50)	RUS	Tashkent	17 Sep 1986
High jump	2.01	Inga Babakova (27.6.67)	UKR	Oslo	27 Jun 2003
	2.01	Ruth Beitia (1.4.79)	ESP	Zürich	17 Aug 2014
Pole vault	4.70	Stacy Dragila (25.3.71)	USA	Chula Vista	22 Jun 2008
Long jump	6.99	Heike Drechsler (16.12.64)	GER	Sydney	29 Sep 2000
Triple jump	14.68	Tatyana Lebedeva (21.7.76)	RUS	Cheboksary	3 Jul 2012
	14.82i	Yamilé Aldama (14.8.72)	GBR	Istanbul	10 Mar 2012
Shot	21.46	Larisa Peleshenko (29.2.64)	RUS	Moskva	26 Aug 2000
	21.47i	Helena Fibingerová (13.7.49)	CZE	Jablonec	9 Feb 1985
Discus	69.60	Faina Melnik (9.7.45)	RUS	Donetsk	9 Sep 1980
Hammer	72.42	Iryna Sekyachova (21.7.76)	UKR	Yalta	4 Jun 2012
Javelin	68.34	Steffi Nerius (1.7.72)	GER	Berlin (Elstal)	31 Aug 2008
Heptathlon	6533	Jane Frederick (7.4.52)	USA	Talence	27 Sep 1987
		13.60, 1.82, 15.50, 24.73; 6.29, 49.70, 2:14.88			
5000m walk	20:12.41	Elisabetta Perrone (9.7.68)	ITA	Rieti	2 Aug 2003

10km walk	41:41	Kjersti Tysse Plätzer (18.1.72)	NOR	Kraków	30 May 2009
10000m t walk	43:26.5	Elisabetta Perrone (9.7.68)	ITA	Saluzzo	4 Aug 2004
20km walk	1:25:59	Tamara Kovalenko (5.6.64)	RUS	Moskva	19 May 2000
20000m t walk	1:27:49.3	Yelena Nikolayeva (1.2.66)	RUS	Brisbane	6 Sep 2001
4x100m	48.63	Desmier, Sulter, Andreas, Apavou	FRA	Eugene	8 Jun 1989
4x400m	3:50.80	Mitchell, Mathews, Beadnall, Gabriel	GBR	Gateshead	8 Aug 1999

WOMEN – aged 40 or over

100 metres	10.99	Merlene Ottey (10.5.60)	JAM	Thessaloniki	30 Aug 2000
200 metres	22.72	Merlene Ottey (10.5.60)	SLO	Athína	23 Aug 2004
400 metres	53.05A	María Figueirêdo (11.11.63)	BRA	Bogotá	10 Jul 2004
	53.14	María Figueirêdo (11.11.63)	BRA	San Carlos, VEN	19 Jun 2004
800 metres	1:59.25	Yekaterina Podkopayeva (11.6.52)	RUS	Luxembourg	30 Jun 1994
1000 metres	2:36.16	Yekaterina Podkopayeva (11.6.52)	RUS	Nancy	14 Sep 1994
	2:36.08i	Yekaterina Podkopayeva	RUS	Liévin	13 Feb 1993
1500 metres	3:59.78	Yekaterina Podkopayeva (11.6.52)	RUS	Nice	18 Jul 1994
1 mile	4:23.78	Yekaterina Podkopayeva (11.6.52)	RUS	Roma	9 Jun 1993
3000 metres	9:01.1+	Jo Pavey (20.9.73)	GBR	Roma	5 Jun 2014
5000 metres	15:04.87	Jo Pavey (20.9.73)	GBR	Roma	5 Jun 2014
10000 metres	31:31.18	Edith Masai (4.4.67)	KEN	Alger	21 Jul 2007
1 hour	16.056k	Jackie Fairweather (10.11.67)	AUS	Canberra	24 Jan 2008
Half Marathon	69:37	Deena Kastor (14.2.73)	USA	Philadelphia	21 Sep 2014
Marathon	2:24:54	Irina Mikitenko (23.8.72)	GER	Berlin	29 Sep 2013
3000m steeple	10:00.75	Minori Hayakari (29.11.72)	JPN	Kumagaya	22 Sep 2013
100 m hurdles	13.20	Patricia Girard (8.4.68)	FRA	Paris	14 Jul 2008
400 m hurdles	58.35	Barbara Gähling (20.3.65)	GER	Erfurt	21 Jul 2007
	58.3 h	Gowry Retchakan (21.6.60)	GBR	Hoo	3 Sep 2000
High jump	1.94i	Venelina Veneva-Mateeva (13.6.74)	BUL	Dobrich 15 Feb & Praha	6 Mar 2015
	1.90	Venelina Veneva-Mateeva	BUL	Plovdiv 12 Jul & Pitesti	27 Jul 2014
Pole vault	4.10	Doris Auer (10.5.71)	AUT	Innsbruck	6 Aug 2011
	4.11 §	Doris Auer	AUT	Wien	5 Jul 2011
Long jump	6.64	Tatyana Ter-Mesrobian (12.5.68)	RUS	Sankt-Peterburg	31 May 2008
	6.64i	Tatyana Ter-Mesrobian	RUS	Sankt-Peterburg	5 Jan 2010
Triple jump	14.06	Yamilé Aldama (14.8.72)	GBR	Eugene	1 Jun 2013
Shot	19.05	Antonina Ivanova (25.12.32)	RUS	Oryol	28 Aug 1973
	19.16i	Antonina Ivanova	RUS	Moskva	24 Feb 1974
Discus	67.89	Iryna Yatchenko (31.10.65)	BLR	Staiki	29 Jun 2008
Hammer	59.29	Oneithea Lewis (11.6.60)	USA	Princeton	10 May 2003
Javelin	61.96	Laverne Eve (16.6.65)	BAH	Monaco	9 Sep 2005
Heptathlon	5449	Tatyana Alisevich (22.1.69)	BLR	Staiki	3 Jun 2010
		14.80, 1.62, 13.92, 26.18, 5.55, 45.44, 2:24.39			
5000m walk	21:46.68	Kelly Ruddick (19.4.73)	AUS	Brisbane	29 Mar 2014
10000m t walk	44:50.19	Susana Feitor (28.1.75)	POR	Leiria	25 Jul 2015
20km walk	1:31:58	Susana Feitor		Rio Maior	18 Apr 2015
	1:31:58	Susana Feitor		Murcia	17 May 2015
20000m t walk	1:33:28.15t	Teresa Vaill (20.11.62)	USA	Carson	25 Jun 2005
4x100m	48.22	Cadinot, Barilly, Valouvin, Lapierre	FRA	Le Touquet	24 Jun 2006
4x400m	3:57.28	Loizou, Kay, Smithe, Cearns	AUS	Brisbane	14 Jul 2001

WORLD AND CONTINENTAL RECORDS SET IN 2015

OUTDOORS – MEN

§ Not ratified

100	Asi	9.91	Femi Seun OGUNODE	QAT	Wuhan	4 Jun 15
	Eur=	9.86	Jimmy VICAUT	FRA	Saint-Denis	4 Jul 15
200	Asi	19.97	Femi Seun OGUNODE	QAT	Bruxelles	11 Sep 15
300	Asi	32.21	Kenji FUJIMITSU	JPN	Hamayama	12 Apr 15
	Afr	31.63	Wayde van NIEKERK	RSA	Birmingham	7 Jun 15
	W35	31.99	Chris BROWN	BAH	Birmingham	7 Jun 15
400	W35	44.54	Chris BROWN	BAH	Eugene	30 May 15
	Afr	43.96	Wayde van NIEKERK	RSA	Saint-Denis	4 Jul 15
	Afr, Com	43.72	Isaac MAKWALA	BOT	La Chaux-de-Fonds	5 Jul 15
	Asi	44.27	Abdalelah HAROUN	QAT	La Chaux-de-Fonds	5 Jul 15
	Asi	43.93	Youssef AL-MASRAHI	KSA	Beijing	23 Aug 15
	Afr, Com	43.48	Wayde van NIEKERK	RSA	Beijing	26 Aug 15
	Dec/W	45.00	Ashton EATON	USA	Beijing	28 Aug 15
1500	W40	3:41.87	Bernard LAGAT	USA	Birmingham	7 Jun 15
	Oce	3:29.66	Nick WILLIS	NZL	Monaco	17 Jul 15
1M	W40	3:57.91	Bernard LAGAT	USA	London (OS)	25 Jul 15
3000	W40	8:00.23+	Bernard LAGAT	USA	Eugene	29 May 15
	W40	7:42.75	Bernard LAGAT	USA	Luzern	14 Jul 15
5000	W40	13:14.97	Bernard LAGAT	USA	Eugene	29 May 15
10k	W40	27:48	Bernard LAGAT	USA	Manchester	10 May 15

Event	Record	Mark	Athlete	Nat	Venue	Date
15k	Oce	42:17+	Zane ROBERTSON	NZL	Marugame	1 Feb 15
20k	Oce	56:40+	Zane ROBERTSON	NZL	Marugame	1 Feb 15
	Eur	56:27+	Mo FARAH	GBR	Lisboa	22 Mar 15
	Asi=	57:24+	Masato KIKUCHI	JPN	Yamaguchi	15 Feb 15
HMar	Oce	59:47	Zane ROBERTSON	NZL	Marugame	1 Feb 15
	Eur	59:32	Mo FARAH	GBR	Lisboa	22 Mar 15
	Eur	59:22 dh	Mo FARAH	GBR	South Shields	13 Sep 15
Mar	W40	2:08:44	Kenneth MUNGARA	KEN	Milano	12 Apr 15
	W40	2:08:42	Kenneth MUNGARA	KEN	Gold Coast	5 Jul 15
3000SC	NAm	8:00.45	Evan JAGER	USA	Saint-Denis	4 Jul 15
110H	Dec/W	13.44	Damian WARNER	CAN	Toronto	23 Jul 15
200H (St)	W=	22.10	L.J. van ZYL	RSA	Manchester	9 May 15
PV	SAm	5.86	Thiago Braz DA SILVA	BRA	Roma	4 Jun 15
	SAm	5.87 & 5.92	Thiago Braz DA SILVA	BRA	Baku	24 Jun 15
TJ	CAC	17.94	Pedro Pablo PICHARDO	CUB	La Habana	8 May 15
	CAC	18.06	Pedro Pablo PICHARDO	CUB	Doha	15 May 15
	CAC	18.08	Pedro Pablo PICHARDO	CUB	La Habana	28 May 15
	NAm	18.21	Christian TAYLOR	USA	Beijing	27 Aug 15
SP	Oce	21.37	Tom WALSH	NZL	Melbourne	21 Mar 15
	CAC	21.69	O'Dayne RICHARDS	JAM	Toronto	21 Jul 15
	Oce	21.50	Tom WALSH	NZL	Mutterstadt	25 Jul 15
	CAC=	21.69	O'Dayne RICHARDS	JAM	Beijing	23 Aug 15
	Oce	21.58	Tom WALSH	NZL	Beijing	23 Aug 15
	Oce	21.62	Tom WALSH	NZL	Zagreb	7 Sep 15
	W20	20.75 & 20.78	Konrad BUKOWIECKI	POL	Zagreb	7 Sep 15
HT	CAC	78.02	Roberto JANET	CUB	La Habana	28 May 15
JT	Afr	91.39	Julius YEGO	KEN	Birmingham	7 Jun 15
	CAC	90.16	Keshorn WALCOTT	TTO	Lausanne	9 Jul 15
	Afr, Com	92.72	Julius YEGO	KEN	Beijing	26 Aug 15
Dec (U18)	W18	8002A	Niklas KAUL	GER	Cali	16 Jul 15
		(11.59, 6.76, 16.08, 2.05, 51.20 / 15.44, 44.09, 4.70, 78.20, 4:42.29)				
Dec	Afr	8398	Willem COERTZEN	RSA	Götzis	31 May 15
		(10.99, 7.46, 14.14, 2.03, 48.73 / 14.17, 44.84, 4.60, 68.43, 4:22.22)				
	W, NAm	9045	Ashton EATON	USA	Beijing	29 Aug 15
		(10.23, 7.88, 14.52, 2.01, 45.00 / 13.69, 43.34, 5.20, 63.63, 4:17.52)				
	Afr	8461	Larbi BOURAADA	ALG	Beijing	29 Aug 15
		(10.83, 7.51, 13.73, 2.07, 47.60 / 14.26, 41.53, 4.80, 63.82, 4:16.61)				
4x100 R	NAm=	37.38	Rodgers, Gatlin, Gay, Bailey	USA	Nassau	2 May 15
	Asi	37.92	Mo Youxue, Xie Zhenye, Su Bingtian, Zhang Peimen	CHN	Beijing	29 Aug 15
4x200 R	SAm	1:24.42	Harris, George, Bascom, James	GUY	Philadelphia	25 Apr 15
Dist.Med.R	W, NAm	9:15.50	Merber, Spratting, Johnson, Blankenship	USA	Nassau	3 May 15
4x110H	W	52.94	Richardson, Harris, Merritt, Oliver	USA	Des Moines	25 Apr 15
5000W	Asi	18:51.93	Eiki TAKAHASHI	JPN	Kumagaya	16 May 15
	Asi	18:37.22	Yusuke SUZUKI	JPN	Kitami	12 Jul 15
10000W	Asi	38:23.73	WANG Zhen	CHN	Genova	8 Feb 15
	Asi	38:10.23	Yusuke SUZUKI	JPN	Abashiri	16 Jul 15
	Asi	38:01.49	Eiki TAKAHASHI	JPN	Isahaya	13 Dec 15
20kW	W,W35,Eur	1:17:02	Yohann DINIZ	FRA	Arles	8 Mar 15
	W, Asi	1:16:36	Yusuke SUZUKI	JPN	Nomi	15 Mar 15
	NAm	1:19:57	Benjamin THORNE	CAN	Beijing	23 Aug 15
50kW	SAm	3:46:00	Andrés CHOCHO	ECU	Beijing	29 Aug 15
	NAm	3:43:45	Evan DUNFEE	CAN	Melbourne	13 Dec 15
	Afr	3:54:12	Marc MUNDELL	RSA	Melbourne	13 Dec 15

OUTDOORS – WOMEN

Event	Record	Mark	Athlete	Nat	Venue	Date
100	SAm	11.01	Ana Cláudia SILVA	BRA	Walnut	18 Apr 15
	W18	10.98	Candace HILL	USA	Shoreline	20 Jun 15
	SAm	10.99	Angela TENORIO	ECU	Toronto	22 Jul 15
200	W18	22.49= & 22.47	Kaylin WHITNEY	USA	Eugene	28 Jun 15
	W18	22.43A	Candace HILL	USA	Cali	19 Jul 15
	Eur	21.63	Dafne SCHIPPERS	NED	Beijing	28 Aug 15
1000	Oce	2:37.28	Angie PETTY	NZL	Chiba	15 Aug 15
1500	Afr	3:54.11	Genzebe DIBABA	ETH	Barcelona	8 Jul 15
	W, Afr	3:50.07	Genzebe DIBABA	ETH	Monaco	17 Jul 15
	NAm	3:56.29	Shannon ROWBURY	USA	Monaco	17 Jul 15
1M	Afr, Com	4:16.71	Faith KIPYEGON	KEN	Bruxelles	11 Sep 15
15k	W,Afr,Com	46:14+	Florence KIPLAGAT	KEN	Barcelona	15 Feb 15
10M	W40	52:44	Jo PAVEY	GBR	Portsmouth	25 Oct 15
20k	W,Afr,Com	61:54+	Florence KIPLAGAT	KEN	Barcelona	15 Feb 15
25k	W40	1:24:16+ dq	Mariya KONOVALOVA	RUS	Nagoya	8 Mar 15

Event	Record	Mark	Athlete	Nat	Venue	Date
	SAm	1:25:57+	Gladys TEJEDA	PER	Rotterdam	12 Apr 15
30k	W20	1:38:47+	Shure DEMISE	ETH	Dubai	23 Jan 15
	W40	1:41:10+ dq	Mariya KONOVALOVA	RUS	Nagoya	8 Mar 15
HMar	W,Afr,Com	65:09	Florence KIPLAGAT	KEN	Barcelona	15 Feb 15
Mar	W20	2:20:59	Shure DEMISE	ETH	Dubai	23 Jan 15
	W40	2:22:27 dq	Mariya KONOVALOVA	RUS	Nagoya	8 Mar 15
100k	Oce	7:39:28	Kirstin BULL	AUS	Winschoten	12 Sep 15
2000SC	W,Afr,Com	6:02.16	Virginia NYAMBURA	KEN	Berlin	6 Sep 15
	Oce	6:16.86	Genevieve LACAZE	AUS	Berlin	6 Sep 15
	Asi	6:14.34	Tigist MEKONEN	BRN	Berlin	6 Sep 15
3000SC	Afr	9:05.36	Habiba GHRIBI	TUN	Bruxelles	11 Sep 15
100H	W20	12.74	Dior HALL	USA	Eugene	13 Jun 15
HJ	W40=	1.90	Venelina VENEVA-MATEEVA	BUL	Sofia	11 Jul 15
	W18=	1.96	Vashti CUNNINGHAM	USA	Edmonton	1 Aug 15
PV	W20	4.59 out	Nina KENNEDY	AUS	Perth	14 Feb 15
	W20	4.61 out	Alena LUTKOVSKAYA	RUS	Irkutsk	21 May 15
	Asi	4.66	LI Ling	CHN	Wuhan	6 Jun 15
	CAC	4.91	Yarisley SILVA	CUB	Beckum	2 Aug 15
	SAm=	4.85	Fabiana de Almeida MURER	BRA	Beijing	26 Aug 15
	W20	4.64	Eliza McCARTNEY	NZL	Auckland	19 Dec 15
HT	W, Eur	79.83 exh	Anita WLODARCZYK	POL	Wroclaw	27 Jun 15
	W, Eur	81.08	Anita WLODARCZYK	POL	Cetniewo	1 Aug 15
JT	W20	63.86	Yulenmis AGUILAR	CUB	Edmonton	2 Aug 15
	Asi	66.13	LU Huihui	CHN	Beijing	30 Aug 15
4x100 R	CAC, Com	41.07	Campbell-Brown, Morrison, Thompson, Fraser-Pryce	JAM	Beijing	29 Aug 15
4x200 R	Afr	1:30.52	Okagbare, George, Duncan, Udoh	NGR	Nassau	2 May 15
	Asi	1:34.89	Yuan Qiqi, Kong Lingwei, Liang Xiaojing, Lin Huijun	CHN	Nassau	2 May 15
4x800 R	NAm	8:00.62	Price,Vessey,Beckwith-Ludlow,Montana	USA	Nassau	3 May 15
	CAC	8:15.84	Almanza, Thaureaux, Casanova, Diago	CUB	Nassau	3 May 15
Dist.Med.R	W, NAm	10:36.50	Moser,Richards-Ross,Wilson,Rowbury	USA	Nassau	2 May 15
	Afr, Com	10:43.55	Busienei,Zakari,Chesebe,Nyambura	KEN	Nassau	2 May 15
	Eur	10:45.32	Broniatowska, Szczesina, Cichocka, Ennaoui	POL	Nassau	2 May 15
	Oce	10:46.94	Duncan, Lind, McGowan, See	AUS	Nassau	2 May 15
4x100H R	W	50.50	Castlin, Q Harrison, Harper-Nelson, Rollins	USA	Des Moines	24 Apr 15
10000W	W40	44:50.19	Susana FEITOR	POR	Leiria	25 Jul 15
	Afr	46:34.68 mx	Chahinez NASRI	TUN	Balma	15 Nov 15
20000W	SAm	1:31:02.25	Sandra Lorena ARENAS	COL	Lima	13 Jun 15
20kW	W, Eur	1:24:47 §	Elmira ALEMBEKOVA	RUS	Sochi	27 Feb 15
	NAm	1:29:54	Rachel SEAMAN	CAN	Nomi	15 Mar 15
	Asi	1:25:12	LU Xiuzhi	CHN	Beijing	20 Mar 15
	SAm	1:29:37	Erica DE SENA	BRA	Dudince	21 Mar 15
	W40	1:31:58	Susana FEITOR	POR	Rio Maior	18 Apr 15
	W40=	1:31:58	Susana FEITOR	POR	Murcia	17 May 15
	W, Asi	1:24:38	LIU Hong	CHN	La Coruna	6 Jun 15

See ATHLETICS 2015 for Indoor Records set in January - March 2015 – and add

INDOORS – MEN

Event	Record	Mark	Athletes	Nat	Venue	Date
4x200 R	W35	1:29.74	Ossai, Collins, Bolan-Ashworth, Beardsell	GBR	Torun	28 Mar 15

WORLD AND CONTINENTAL RECORDS SET IN JAN-MAR 2016

INDOORS – MEN # on oversized track

Event	Record	Mark	Athlete	Nat	Venue	Date
60	CAC	6.44 (twice)	Asafa POWELL	JAM	Portland	18 Mar 16
	Asi	6.50	SU Bingtian	CHN	Portland	18 Mar 16
500	W,W20,Asi	59.83	Abdelilah HAROUN	QAT	Stockholm	17 Feb 16
800	CAC	1:46.20	Andrés ARROYO	PUR	Fayetteville	27 Feb 16
1000	W, Afr	2:14.20	Ayanleh SOULEIMAN	DJI	Stockholm	17 Feb 16
1M	Oce, Com	3:51.06	Nick WILLIS	NZL	New York	20 Feb 16
3000	CAC	7:40.79	Kemoy CAMPBELL	JAM	New York	20 Feb 16
PV	NAm	6.00A	Shawn BARBER	CAN	Reno	15 Jan 16
	W18	5.49	Armand DUPLANTIS	SWE	Baton Rouge	6 Feb 16
	W18	5.53	Emmanouil KARÁLIS	GRE	Pireás	13 Feb 16
	SAm	5.77, 5.85 & 5.93	Thiago Braz DA SILVA	BRA	Berlin	13 Feb 16
	W18	5.54	Emmanouil KARÁLIS	GRE	Jablonec	5 Mar 16
LJ	W35	8.23	Kafetien GOMIS	FRA	Aubiére	28 Feb 16
	Oce	8.25	Fabrice LAPIERRE	AUS	Portland	20 Mar 16
TJ	W18	16.34	Martin LAMOU	FRA	Padova	27 Feb 16
	Asi	17.41	DONG Bin	CHN	Nanjing	29 Feb 16

SP/6kg	W20	22.48	Konrad BUKOWIECKI	POL	Torun	8 Jan 16
SP	Asi	20.51 §	Ivan IVANOV	KAZ	Ust-Kamenogorsk	30 Jan 16
	Oce, Com	21.60, 21.64 & 21.78	Tom WALSH	NZL	Portland	18 Mar 16
Hep (U20)	W18	5510	Sam TALBOT	GBR	Sheffield	10 Jan 16
		(7.00, 7.51, 12.62, 1.87 / 8.05, 3.82, 2:44.60)				
4x200 R	W18?	1:28.59	Harris, Hill, Blackley, Byrd	USA	New York	13 Mar 16
5000W	W20	18:51.9 §	MIZINOV Vasiliy	RUS	Chelyabinsk	6 Jan 16

INDOORS – WOMEN

60	SAm=	7.19	Rosângela SANTOS	BRA	Karlsruhe	6 Feb 16
	W20	7.07	Ewa SWOBODA	POL	Torun	12 Feb 16
	SAm	7.17	Rosângela SANTOS	BRA	Berlin	13 Feb 16
400	Asi	51.68	Kemi ADEKOYA	BRN	Doha	19 Feb 16
	Asi	51.67	Kemi ADEKOYA	BRN	Doha	20 Feb 16
	W18	51.84	Sydney McLAUGHLIN	USA	New York	13 Mar 16
	Asi	51.47	Kemi ADEKOYA	BRN	Portland	18 Mar 16
	Asi	51.45	Kemi ADEKOYA	BRN	Portland	19 Mar 16
1500	Oce	4:06.93	Melissa Duncan	AUS	Boston (R)	14 Feb 16
	W20	4:01.81	Gudaf TSEGAY	ETH	Glasgow	20 Feb 16
1M	W, Afr	4:13.31	Genzebe DIBABA	ETH	Stockholm	17 Feb 16
HJ	W35	1.98	Ruth BEITIA	ESP	Madrid	6 Mar 16
	W20	1.99	Vashti CUNNINGHAM	USA	Portland	12 Mar 16
PV	W, NAm	5.03	Jenn SUHR	USA	Brockport	30 Jan 16
	W20	4.65 & 4.71	Wilma MURTO	FIN	Zweibrücken	31 Jan 16
	W18	4.47	Lisa GUNNARSSON	SWE	Eaubonne	9 Feb 16
	W18	4.49	Lisa GUNNARSSON	SWE	Stockholm	17 Feb 16
	Asi	4.60 & 4.70	LI Ling	CHN	Doha	19 Feb 16
TJ	SAm	14.09, 14.25 & 14.69	Yulimar ROJAS	VEN	Madrid	23 Jan 16
SP	NAm	20.21	Michelle CARTER	USA	Portland	19 Mar 16
Wt	Afr	21.27	Precious OGUNLEYE	NGR	New York	6 Feb 16
Pen	CAC	4643	Akela JONES	BAR	Manhattan, KS	22 Jan 16
			(8.25, 1.85, 12.99, 6.64, 2:25.63)			
	W18	4354	Alina SHUKH	UKR	Zaporizhzhya	27 Jan 16
			(9.08, 1.82, 13.45, 5.94, 2:16.63)			
	SAm	4292	Vanessa SPINOLA	BRA	Tallinn	14 Feb 16
			(8.81, 1.75, 13.62, 5.87, 2:18.25)			
	NAm	4881	Brianne THEISEN-EATON	CAN	Portland	18 Mar 16
			(8.04, 1.85, 13.70, 6.42, 2:09.99)			
4x400 R	Asi	3:35.07	Nasser, Jamal, Essa, Adekoya	BRN	Doha	21 Feb 16

OUTDOORS – MEN

15k	Eur	42:04	Mohamed FARAH	GBR	Cardiff	26 Mar 16
30k	W, Afr	1:27:20+	Sisay LEMMA	ETH	Dubai	22 Jan 16
5000W	Oce	18:38.97	Dane BIRD-SMITH	AUS	Melbourne	5 Mar 16
20kW	NAm	1:19:20	Inaki GÓMEZ	CAN	Nomi	20 Mar 16
50kW	SAm	3:42:57	Andres CHOCHO	ECU	Ciudad Juárez	6 Mar 16

OUTDOORS – WOMEN

HMar	SAm	70:14	Gladys TEJEDA	PER	Cardiff	26 Mar 16
PV	Oce	4.77	Alana BOYD (& outdoor Com)	AUS	Sippy Downs	28 Jan 16
	Oce	4.80	Eliza McCARTNEY (" Com)	NZL	Dunedin	5 Mar 16
LJ	Oce	7.05	Brooke STRATTON	AUS	Perth	12 Mar 16
10000W	Afr	44:41.8A	Grace WANJIRU	KEN	Thika	5 Mar 16
20kW	Afr	1:34:35	Chahinez NASRI	TUN	Saint-Sebastien-sur-Loire	13 Mar 16
	SAm	1:28:22	Erica de SENA	BRA	Dudince	19 Mar 16
25kW	W, Eur	1:56:12+	Eleonora GIORGI	ITA	Catania	31 Jan 16
30kW	W, Eur	2:19:43	Eleonora GIORGI	ITA	Catania	31 Jan 16
50kW	Asi	4:34:01	ZHOU Kang	CHN	Huangshan	6 Mar 16

Most World Records: Sergey Bubka USR/UKR set a total of 35 at pole vault: 17 outdoors from 5.85 (1984) to 6.14 (1994) and 18 indoors (9 ratified by IAAF) from 5.81 (1844) to 6.15 (1993). Paavi Nurmi FIN set 22 official and 13 unofficial world records at distances from 1500m to 20,000m between 1921 and 1931.
The most world records by a woman at one event is 28 at pole vault (15 outdoors, 13 indoors) by Yelena Isinbayeva RUS 2003-09.

Oldest: 41y 238d Yekaterina Podkopayeva RUS women's 4x800m indoor 8:18.71 Moskva 4 Feb 1994.

Youngest: 14y 334d Wang Yan CHN 5000m walk 21:33.8 Jian 9 Mar 1986 (unratified).

Youngest male: 17y 198d Thomas Ray PV 3.42m Ulverston 19 Sep 1879 (prior to IAAF jurisdiction (from 1913).

Most world records set in one day: 6 Jesse Owens USA at Ann Arbor 25 May 1935: 100y 9.4, LJ 8.13m, 220y straight (& 200m) 20.3, 220y hurdles straight (& 220yh) 22.6.

Record span of setting world records: Men: 15 years Haile Gebrselassie ETH 1994-2009

WORLD MEN'S ALL-TIME LISTS

100 METRES

Mark	Wind	Name		Nat	Born	Pos	Meet	Venue	Date
9.58 WR	0.9	Usain	Bolt	JAM	21.8.86	1	WCh	Berlin	16 Aug 09
9.63	1.5		Bolt			1	OG	London (OS)	5 Aug 12
9.69 WR	0.0		Bolt			1	OG	Beijing	16 Aug 08
9.69	2.0	Tyson	Gay ¶	USA	9.8.82	1		Shanghai	20 Sep 09
9.69	-0.1	Yohan	Blake	JAM	26.12.89	1	Athl	Lausanne	23 Aug 12
9.71	0.9		Gay			2	WCh	Berlin	16 Aug 09
9.72 WR	1.7		Bolt			1	Reebok	New York (RI)	31 May 08
9.72	0.2	Asafa	Powell	JAM	23.11.82	1rA	Athl	Lausanne	2 Sep 08
9.74 WR	1.7		Powell			1h2	GP	Rieti	9 Sep 07
9.74	0.9	Justin	Gatlin ¶	USA	10.2.82	1	DL	Doha	15 May 15
9.75	1.1		Blake			1	NC	Kingston	29 Jun 12
9.75	1.5		Blake			2	OG	London (OS)	5 Aug 12
9.75	0.9		Gatlin			1	GGala	Roma	4 Jun 15
9.75	1.4		Gatlin			1	Athl	Lausanne	9 Jul 15
9.76	1.8		Bolt			1		Kingston	3 May 08
9.76	1.3		Bolt			1	VD	Bruxelles	16 Sep 11
9.76	-0.1		Bolt			1	GGala	Roma	31 May 12
9.76	1.4		Blake			1	WK	Zürich	30 Aug 12
9.77 WR	1.6		Powell			1	Tsik	Athína	14 Jun 05
9.77 WR	1.5		Powell			1	BrGP	Gateshead	11 Jun 06
9.77 WR	1.0		Powell			1rA	WK	Zürich	18 Aug 06
9.77	1.6		Gay			1q1	NC/OT	Eugene	28 Jun 08
9.77	-1.3		Bolt			1	VD	Bruxelles	5 Sep 08
9.77	0.9		Powell			1h1	GP	Rieti	7 Sep 08
9.77	0.4		Gay			1	GGala	Roma	10 Jul 09
9.77	-0.3		Bolt			1	WCh	Moskva	11 Aug 13
9.77	0.6		Gatlin			1	VD	Bruxelles	5 Sep 14
9.77	0.9		Gatlin			1s2	WCh	Beijing	23 Aug 15
9.78	0.0		Powell			1	GP	Rieti	9 Sep 07
9.78	-0.4		Gay			1	LGP	London (CP)	13 Aug 10
9.78	0.9	Nesta	Carter	JAM	10.11.85	1		Rieti	29 Aug 10
9.78	1.0		Powell			1	Athl	Lausanne	30 Jun 11
9.78	-0.3		Gatlin			1	Herc	Monaco	17 Jul 15
		(34 performances by 6 athletes)							
9.79 WR	0.1	Maurice	Greene	USA	23.7.74	1rA	Tsik	Athína	16 Jun 99
9.80	0.4	Steve	Mullings ¶	JAM	29.11.82	1	Pre	Eugene	4 Jun 11
9.82	1.7	Richard	Thompson	TTO	7.6.85	1	NC	Port of Spain	21 Jun 14
9.84 WR	0.7	Donovan	Bailey	CAN	16.12.67	1	OG	Atlanta	27 Jul 96
		(10)							
9.84	0.2	Bruny	Surin	CAN	12.7.67	2	WCh	Sevilla	22 Aug 99
9.85 WR	1.2	Leroy	Burrell	USA	21.2.67	1rA	Athl	Lausanne	6 Jul 94
9.85	1.7	Olusoji	Fasuba	NGR	9.7.84	2	SGP	Doha	12 May 06
9.85	1.3	Michael	Rodgers	USA	24.4.85	2	Pre	Eugene	4 Jun 11
9.86 WR	1.2	Carl	Lewis	USA	1.7.61	1	WCh	Tokyo	25 Aug 91
9.86	-0.4	Frank	Fredericks	NAM	2.10.67	1rA	Athl	Lausanne	3 Jul 96
9.86	1.8	Ato	Boldon	TTO	30.12.73	1rA	MSR	Walnut	19 Apr 98
9.86	1.4	Keston	Bledman	TTO	8.3.88	1	NC	Port-of-Spain	23 Jun 12
9.86	0.6	Francis	Obikwelu	NGR/POR	22.11.78	2	OG	Athína	22 Aug 04
9.86	1.3	Jimmy	Vicaut	FRA	27.2.92	2	DL	Saint-Denis	4 Jul 15
		(20)							
9.87	0.3	Linford	Christie ¶	GBR	2.4.60	1	WCh	Stuttgart	15 Aug 93
9.87A	-0.2	Obadele	Thompson	BAR	30.3.76	1	WCp	Johannesburg	11 Sep 98
9.88	1.8	Shawn	Crawford ¶	USA	14.1.78	1	Pre	Eugene	19 Jun 04
9.88	0.6	Walter	Dix	USA	31.1.86	2		Nottwil	8 Aug 10
9.88	0.9	Ryan	Bailey	USA	13.4.89	2		Rieti	29 Aug 10
9.88	1.0	Michael	Frater	JAM	6.10.82	2	Athl	Lausanne	30 Jun 11
9.89	1.6	Travis	Padgett	USA	13.12.86	1q2	NC/OT	Eugene	28 Jun 08
9.89	1.6	Darvis	Patton	USA	4.12.77	1q3	NC/OT	Eugene	28 Jun 08
9.89	1.3	Ngonidzashe	Makusha	ZIM	11.3.87	1	NCAA	Des Moines	10 Jun 11
9.90	0.4	Nickel	Ashmeade	JAM	7.4.90	1s2	WCh	Moskva	11 Aug 13
		(30)							
9.91	1.2	Dennis	Mitchell ¶	USA	20.2.66	3	WCh	Tokyo	25 Aug 91
9.91	0.9	Leonard	Scott	USA	19.1.80	2	WAF	Stuttgart	9 Sep 06
9.91	-0.5	Derrick	Atkins	BAH	5.1.84	2	WCh	Osaka	26 Aug 07
9.91	-0.2	Daniel	Bailey	ANT	9.9.86	2	GL	Saint-Denis	17 Jul 09
9.91	0.7	Churandy	Martina	NED	3.7.84	2s1	OG	London (OS)	5 Aug 12

Mark	Wind	Name		Nat	Born	Pos	Meet	Venue	Date
9.91	1.1	James	Dasaolu	GBR	5.9.87	1s2	NC	Birmingham	13 Jul 13
9.91	1.8	Femi Seun	Ogunode ¶	QAT	15.5.91	1	AsiC	Wuhan	4 Jun 15
9.92	0.3	Andre	Cason	USA	20.1.69	2	WCh	Stuttgart	15 Aug 93
9.92	0.8	Jon	Drummond	USA	9.9.68	1h3	NC	Indianapolis	12 Jun 97
9.92	0.2	Tim	Montgomery ¶	USA	28.1.75	2	NC	Indianapolis	13 Jun 97
		(40)							
9.92A	-0.2	Seun	Ogunkoya	NGR	28.12.77	2	WCp	Johannesburg	11 Sep 98
9.92	1.0	Tim	Harden	USA	27.1.74	1	Spitzen	Luzern	5 Jul 99
9.92	2.0	Christophe	Lemaitre	FRA	11.6.90	1	NC	Albi	29 Jul 11
9.92	-0.8	Kemar	Bailey-Cole	JAM	10.1.92	3	DL	London (OS)	24 Jul 15
9.92	-0.5	Andre	De Grasse	CAN	10.11.94	3=	WCh	Beijing	23 Aug 15
9.93A	WR 1.4	Calvin	Smith	USA	8.1.61	1	USOF	USAF Academy	3 Jul 83
9.93	-0.6	Michael	Marsh	USA	4.8.67	1	MSR	Walnut	18 Apr 92
9.93	1.8	Patrick	Johnson	AUS	26.9.72	1		Mito	5 May 03
9.93	1.1	Ivory	Williams #	USA	2.5.85	1rA		Réthimno	20 Jul 09
9.93	1.8	Kemarley	Brown	JAM	20.7.92	1		Walnut	17 May 14
9.93	1.7	Clayton	Vaughn	USA	15.5.92	1		Mobile	10 May 15
9.93	2.0	Marvin	Bracy	USA	15.12.93	1	DL	Bimingham	7 Jun 15
		(52)	100th man 9.99, 200th 10.06, 300th 10.11, 400th 10.14, 500th 10.17						
Doubtful wind reading									
9.91	-2.3	Davidson	Ezinwa ¶	NGR	22.11.71	1		Azusa	11 Apr 92
Wind-assisted – performances to 9.76, performers listed to 9.89									
9.68	4.1	Tyson	Gay ¶	USA	9.8.82	1	NC/OT	Eugene	29 Jun 08
9.69A	5+	Obadele	Thompson	BAR	30.3.76	1		El Paso	13 Apr 96
9.72	2.1		Powell			1	Bisl	Oslo	4 Jun 10
9.74	w	Richard	Thompson	TTO	7.6.85	1		Clermont	31 May 14
9.75	3.4		Gay			1h1	NC	Eugene	25 Jun 09
9.75	2.6		Powell			1h2	DL	Doha	14 May 10
9.75	4.3	Darvis	Patton	USA	4.12.77	1rA	TexR	Austin	30 Mar 13
9.75	2.7	Andre	De Grasse	CAN	10.11.94	1	NCAA	Eugene	12 Jun 15
9.76A	6.1	Churandy	Martina	AHO	3.7.84	1		El Paso	13 May 06
9.76	2.2		Gay			1	GP	New York	2 Jun 07
9.76	2.7		Gatlin			1	Pre	Eugene	31 May 14
9.76	3.7	Trayvon	Bromell	USA	10.7.95	1s1	NC	Eugene	26 Jun 15
9.78	5.2	Carl	Lewis	USA	1.7.61	1	NC/OT	Indianapolis	16 Jul 88
9.78	3.7	Maurice	Greene	USA	23.7.74	1	GP II	Stanford	31 May 04
9.79	5.3	Andre	Cason	USA	20.1.69	1h4	NC	Eugene	16 Jun 93
9.80	4.1	Walter	Dix	USA	31.1.86	2	NC/OT	Eugene	29 Jun 08
9.80	2.7	Michael	Rodgers	USA	24.4.85	2	Pre	Eugene	31 May 14
9.82	3.0	Isiah	Young	USA	5.1.90	1		Clermont	16 May 15
9.82	4.9	Remontay	McClain	USA	21.9.92	1h3	NC	Eugene	25 Jun 15
9.83	7.1	Leonard	Scott	USA	19.1.80	1r1	Sea Ray	Knoxville	9 Apr 99
9.83	2.2	Derrick	Atkins	BAH	5.1.84	2	GP	New York	2 Jun 07
9.84	5.4	Francis	Obikwelu	NGR/POR	22.11.78	1		Zaragoza	3 Jun 06
9.85	4.8	Dennis	Mitchell ¶	USA	20.2.66	2	NC	Eugene	17 Jun 93
9.85A	3.0	Frank	Fredericks	NAM	2.10.67	1		Nairobi	18 May 02
9.85	4.1	Travis	Padgett	USA	13.12.86	4	NC/OT	Eugene	29 Jun 08
9.85	3.6	Keston	Bledman	TTO	8.3.88	1rA		Clermont	2 Jun 12
9.85	3.2	Charles	Silmon	USA	4.7.91	1s1	NC	Des Moines	21 Jun 13
9.85A	3.0	Kemar	Hyman	CAY	11.10.89	1s2	NACAC	San José, CRC	7 Aug 15
9.86	2.6	Shawn	Crawford ¶	USA	14.1.78	1	GP	Doha	14 May 04
9.86	3.6	Michael	Frater	JAM	6.10.82	2h4	NC	Kingston	23 Jun 11
9.86	3.2	Rakieem "Mookie"	Salaam	USA	5.4.90	2s1	NC	Des Moines	21 Jun 13
9.86	3.7	Diondre	Batson	USA	13.7.92	2s1	NC	Eugene	26 Jun 15
9.87	11.2	William	Snoddy	USA	6.12.57	1		Dallas	1 Apr 78
9.87	4.9	Calvin	Smith	USA	8.1.61	1s2	NC/OT	Indianapolis	16 Jul 88
9.87	2.4	Michael	Marsh	USA	4.8.67	1rA	MSR	Walnut	20 Apr 97
9.87	3.3	Yoshihide	Kiryu	JPN	15.12.95	1r1	TexR	Austin	28 Mar 15
9.87	2.1	Tevin	Hester	USA	10.1.94	1	ACC	Tallahassee	16 May 15
9.88	2.3	James	Sanford	USA	27.12.57	1		Los Angeles (Ww)	3 May 80
9.88	5.2	Albert	Robinson	USA	28.11.64	4	NC/OT	Indianapolis	16 Jul 88
9.88	4.9	Tim	Harden	USA	27.1.74	1	NC	New Orleans	20 Jun 98
9.88	4.5	Coby	Miller	USA	19.10.76	1		Auburn	1 Apr 00
9.88	3.6	Patrick	Johnson	AUS	26.9.72	1		Perth	8 Feb 03
9.88	3.0	Darrel	Brown	TTO	11.10.84	1	NC	Port of Spain	23 Jun 07
9.88	3.7	Ivory	Williams #	USA	2.5.85	1	TexR	Austin	3 Apr 10
9.89	4.2	Ray	Stewart	JAM	18.3.65	1s1	PAm	Indianapolis	9 Aug 87
Rolling start: 9.89w	3.7	Patrick	Jarrett ¶	JAM	2.10.77	1	Pre	Eugene	27 May 01
Hand timing and three men at 9.7w									
9.7	1.9	Donovan	Powell ¶	JAM	31.10.71	1rA		Houston	19 May 95

Mark	Wind	Name		Nat	Born	Pos	Meet	Venue	Date
9.7	1.9	Carl	Lewis	USA	1.7.61	2rA		Houston	19 May 95
9.7	1.9	Olapade	Adeniken	NGR	19.8.69	3rA		Houston	19 May 95

Drugs disqualification

Mark	Wind	Name		Nat	Born	Pos	Meet	Venue	Date
9.75	1.1		Gay ¶			(1)	NC	Des Moines	21 Jun 13
9.77	1.7		Gatlin ¶	USA	10.2.82	(1)	SGP	Doha	12 May 06
9.78	2.0	Tim	Montgomery ¶	USA	28.1.75	(1)	GPF	Paris (C)	14 Sep 02
9.79	1.1	Ben	Johnson ¶	CAN	30.12.61	(1)	OG	Seoul	24 Sep 88
9.87	2.0	Dwain	Chambers ¶	GBR	5.4.78	(2)	GPF	Paris (C)	14 Sep 02
9.7w ht	3.5		Johnson	CAN	30.12.61	(1)		Perth	24 Jan 87
9.75w	2.4		Gay			(1s2)	NC	Des Moines	21 Jun 13

200 METRES

Mark	Wind	Name		Nat	Born	Pos	Meet	Venue	Date
19.19	WR -0.3	Usain	Bolt	JAM	21.8.86	1	WCh	Berlin	20 Aug 09
19.26	0.7	Yohan	Blake	JAM	26.12.89	1	VD	Bruxelles	16 Sep 11
19.30	WR -0.9		Bolt			1	OG	Beijing	20 Aug 08
19.32	WR 0.4	Michael	Johnson	USA	13.9.67	1	OG	Atlanta	1 Aug 96
19.32	0.4		Bolt			1	OG	London (OS)	9 Aug 12
19.40	0.8		Bolt			1	WCh	Daegu	3 Sep 11
19.44	0.4		Blake			2	OG	London (OS)	9 Aug 12
19.53	0.7	Walter	Dix	USA	31.1.86	2	VD	Bruxelles	16 Sep 11
19.54	0.0		Blake			1	VD	Bruxelles	7 Sep 12
19.55	-0.1		Bolt			1	WCh	Beijing	27 Aug 15
19.56	-0.8		Bolt			1		Kingston	1 May 10
19.57	0.0		Bolt			1	VD	Bruxelles	4 Sep 09
19.57	0.4	Justin	Gatlin ¶	USA	10.2.82	1	NC	Eugene	28 Jun 15
19.58	1.3	Tyson	Gay ¶	USA	9.8.82	1	Reebok	New York	30 May 09
19.58	1.4		Bolt			1	Athl	Lausanne	23 Aug 12
19.59	-0.9		Bolt			1	Athl	Lausanne	7 Jul 09
19.62	-0.3		Gay			1	NC	Indianapolis	24 Jun 07
19.63	0.4	Xavier	Carter	USA	8.12.85	1	Athl	Lausanne	11 Jul 06
19.63	-0.9		Bolt			1	Athl	Lausanne	2 Sep 08
19.65	0.0	Wallace	Spearmon	USA	24.12.84	1		Daegu	28 Sep 06
19.66	WR 1.7		M Johnson			1	NC	Atlanta	23 Jun 96
19.66	0.0		Bolt			1	WK	Zürich	30 Aug 12
19.66	0.0		Bolt			1	WCh	Moskva	17 Aug 13
19.67	-0.5		Bolt			1	GP	Athína	13 Jul 08
19.68	0.4	Frank	Fredericks	NAM	2.10.67	2	OG	Atlanta	1 Aug 96
19.68	-0.1		Gay			1	WAF	Stuttgart	10 Sep 06
19.68	-0.1		Bolt			1	WAF	Thessaloníki	13 Sep 09
19.68	-0.5		Gatlin			1	Herc	Monaco	18 Jul 14
19.68	0.9		Gatlin			1	Pre	Eugene	30 May 15
19.69	0.9		Dix			1	NCAA-r	Gainesville	26 May 07
		(30/9)							
19.72A	WR 1.8	Pietro	Mennea (10)	ITA	28.6.52	1	WUG	Ciudad de México	12 Sep 79
19.73	-0.2	Michael	Marsh	USA	4.8.67	1s1	OG	Barcelona	5 Aug 92
19.75	1.5	Carl	Lewis	USA	1.7.61	1	NC	Indianapolis	19 Jun 83
19.75	1.7	Joe	DeLoach	USA	5.6.67	1	OG	Seoul	28 Sep 88
19.77	0.7	Ato	Boldon	TTO	30.12.73	1rA		Stuttgart	13 Jul 97
19.79	1.2	Shawn	Crawford ¶	USA	14.1.78	1	OG	Athína	26 Aug 04
19.79	0.9	Warren	Weir	JAM	31.10.89	1	NC	Kingston	23 Jun 13
19.80	0.8	Christophe	Lemaitre	FRA	11.6.90	3	WCh	Daegu	3 Sep 11
19.80	2.0	Rasheed	Dwyer	JAM	29.1.89	1s1	PAm	Toronto	23 Jul 15
19.81	-0.3	Alonso	Edward	PAN	8.12.89	2	WCh	Berlin	20 Aug 09
19.83A	WR 0.9	Tommie	Smith	USA	6.6.44	1	OG	Ciudad de México	16 Oct 68
		(20)							
19.84	1.7	Francis	Obikwelu	NGR/POR	22.11.78	1s2	WCh	Sevilla	25 Aug 99
19.85	-0.3	John	Capel ¶	USA	27.10.78	1	NC	Sacramento	23 Jul 00
19.85	-0.5	Konstadínos	Kedéris ¶	GRE	11.7.73	1	EC	München	9 Aug 02
19.85	1.4	Churandy	Martina	NED	3.7.84	2	Athl	Lausanne	23 Aug 12
19.85	0.0	Nickel	Ashmeade	JAM	4.7.90	2	WK	Zürich	30 Aug 12
19.86A	1.0	Don	Quarrie	JAM	25.2.51	1	PAm	Cali	3 Aug 71
19.86	1.6	Maurice	Greene	USA	23.7.74	2rA	DNG	Stockholm	7 Jul 97
19.86	1.5	Jason	Young	JAM	21.3.91	1	Spitzen	Luzern	17 Jul 12
19.86	1.6	Isiah	Young	USA	5.1.90	1	NC	Des Moines	23 Jun 13
19.87	0.8	Lorenzo	Daniel	USA	23.3.66	1	NCAA	Eugene	3 Jun 88
		(30)							
19.87A	1.8	John	Regis	GBR	13.10.66	1		Sestriere	31 Jul 94
19.87	1.2	Jeff	Williams	USA	31.12.65	1		Fresno	13 Apr 96
19.87	-0.1	Anaso	Jobodwana	RSA	30.7.92	3	WCh	Beijing	27 Aug 15
19.88	-0.3	Floyd	Heard	USA	24.3.66	2	NC	Sacramento	23 Jul 00

Mark	Wind	Name		Nat	Born	Pos	Meet	Venue	Date
19.88	0.1	Joshua 'J.J'	Johnson	USA	10.5.76	1	VD	Bruxelles	24 Aug 01
19.88	0.3	Andre	De Grasse	CAN	10.11.94	1	PAm	Toronto	24 Jul 15
19.88	-0.4	Ramil	Guliyev	AZE/TUR	29.5.90	1		Zagreb	8 Sep 15
19.89	-0.8	Claudinei	da Silva	BRA	19.11.70	1	GPF	München	11 Sep 99
19.89	1.3	Jaysuma	Saidy Ndure	NOR	1.1.84	1	WAF	Stuttgart	23 Sep 07
19.90	1.3	Asafa	Powell	JAM	23.11.82	1	NC	Kingston	25 Jun 06
		(40)							
19.92A	WR1.9	John	Carlos	USA	5.6.45	1	FOT	Echo Summit	12 Sep 68
19.94	0.6	Wayde	van Niekerk	RSA	15.7.92	1rB		Luzern	14 Jul 15
19.96	-0.9	Kirk	Baptiste	USA	20.6.63	2	OG	Los Angeles	8 Aug 84
19.96	0.4	Robson	da Silva	BRA	4.9.64	1	VD	Bruxelles	25 Aug 89
19.96	-0.3	Coby	Miller	USA	19.10.76	3	NC	Sacramento	23 Jul 00
19.96	-0.4	Isaac	Makwala	BOT	29.9.86	1		La Chaux-de-Fonds	6 Jul 14
19.97	-0.9	Obadele	Thompson	BAR	30.3.76	1	Super	Yokohama	9 Sep 00
19.97	0.0	Curtis	Mitchell	USA	11.3.89	1s1	WCh	Moskva	16 Aug 13
19.97	-0.6	Dedric	Dukes	USA	2.4.92	1	FlaR	Gainesville	4 Apr 14
19.97	-0.4	Femi Seun	Ogunode ¶	QAT	15.5.91	1	VD	Bruxelles	11 Sep 15
		(50)	100th man 20.11, 200th 20.23, 300th 20.32, 400th 20.38, 500th 20.43						

Wind-assisted 2 performances to 19.69, performers listed to 19.93

Mark	Wind	Name		Nat	Born	Pos	Meet	Venue	Date
19.58	2.4	Andre	De Grasse	CAN	10.11.94	1	NCAA	Eugene	12 Jun 15
19.61	>4.0	Leroy	Burrell	USA	21.2.67	1	SWC	College Station	19 May 90
19.73	3.3	Shawn	Crawford ¶	USA	14.1.78	1	NC	Eugene	28 Jun 09
19.75	4.1	Isiah	Young	USA	5.1.90	1rA		Clermont	16 May 15
19.80	3.2	LaShawn	Merritt ¶	USA	27.6.86	1		Greensboro	19 Apr 08
19.83	9.2	Bobby	Cruse	USA	20.3.78	1r2	Sea Ray	Knoxville	9 Apr 99
19.86	4.6	Roy	Martin	USA	25.12.66	1	SWC	Houston	18 May 86
19.86	2.4	Dedric	Dukes	USA	2.4.92	2	NCAA	Eugene	12 Jun 15
19.86	2.4	Trayvon	Bromell	USA	10.7.95	3	NCAA	Eugene	12 Jun 15
19.90	3.8	Steve	Mullings ¶	JAM	29.11.82	1		Fort Worth	17 Apr 04
19.91		James	Jett	USA	28.12.70	1		Morgantown	18 Apr 92
19.93	2.4	Sebastián	Keitel	CHI	14.2.73	1		São Leopoldo	26 Apr 98

Low altitude mark for athletes with lifetime bests at high altitude

19.94 0.3 Regis 2 WCh Stuttgart 20 Aug 93 19.96 0.0 Mennea 1 Barletta 17 Aug 80

Hand timing

Mark	Wind	Name		Nat	Born	Pos	Meet	Venue	Date
19.7A		James	Sanford	USA	27.12.57	1		El Paso	19 Apr 80
19.7A	0.2	Robson C.	da Silva	BRA	4.9.64	1	AmCp	Bogotá	13 Aug 89

300 METRES

In 300m races only, not including intermediate times in 400m races

Mark	Name		Nat	Born	Pos	Meet	Venue	Date
30.85A	Michael	Johnson	USA	13.9.67	1		Pretoria	24 Mar 00
30.97	Usain	Bolt	JAM	21.8.86	1	GS	Ostrava	27 May 10
31.30	LaShawn	Merritt	USA	27.6.86	1	Pre	Eugene	7 Jun 09
31.31		Merritt			1		Eugene	8 Aug 06
31.48	Danny	Everett	USA	1.11.66	1		Jerez de la Frontera	3 Sep 90
31.48	Roberto	Hernández	CUB	6.3.67	2		Jerez de la Frontera	3 Sep 90
31.56	Doug	Walker ¶	GBR	28.7.73	1		Gateshead	19 Jul 98
31.61	Anthuan	Maybank	USA	30.12.69	1		Durham	13 Jul 96
31.63	Wayde	van Niekerk	RSA	15.7.92	1		Birmingham	7 Jun 15
31.67	John	Regis	GBR	13.10.66	1	Vaux	Gateshead	17 Jul 92
31.70	Kirk	Baptiste (10)	USA	20.6.63	1	Nike	London (CP)	18 Aug 84
31.72	Jeremy	Wariner	USA	31.1.84	1	GS	Ostrava	12 Jun 08
31.73	Thomas	Jefferson	USA	8.6.62	1	DCG	London (CP)	22 Aug 87
31.74	Gabriel	Tiacoh	CIV	10.9.63	1		La Coruña	6 Aug 86

400 METRES

Mark	Name		Nat	Born	Pos	Meet	Venue	Date
43.18 WR	Michael	Johnson	USA	13.9.67	1	WCh	Sevilla	26 Aug 99
43.29 WR	Butch	Reynolds ¶	USA	8.6.64	1	WK	Zürich	17 Aug 88
43.39		Johnson			1	WCh	Göteborg	9 Aug 95
43.44		Johnson			1	NC	Atlanta	19 Jun 96
43.45	Jeremy	Wariner	USA	31.1.84	1	WCh	Osaka	31 Aug 07
43.49		Johnson			1	OG	Atlanta	29 Jul 96
43.48	Wayde	van Niekerk	RSA	15.7.92	1	WCh	Beijing	26 Aug 15
43.50	Quincy	Watts	USA	19.6.70	1	OG	Barcelona	5 Aug 92
43.50		Wariner			1	DNG	Stockholm	7 Aug 07
43.62		Wariner			1rA	GGala	Roma	14 Jul 06
43.65		Johnson			1	WCh	Stuttgart	17 Aug 93
43.65	LaShawn	Merritt ¶	USA	27.6.86	2	WCh	Beijing	26 Aug 15
43.66		Johnson			1	NC	Sacramento	16 Jun 95
43.66		Johnson			1rA	Athl	Lausanne	3 Jul 96
43.68		Johnson			1	WK	Zürich	12 Aug 98
43.68		Johnson			1	NC	Sacramento	16 Jul 00
43.71		Watts			1s2	OG	Barcelona	3 Aug 92

Mark	Wind	Name		Nat	Born	Pos	Meet	Venue	Date
43.72		Isaac	Makwala	BOT	29.9.86	1		La Chaux-de-Fonds	5 Jul 15
43.74			Johnson			1	NC	Eugene	19 Jun 93
43.74			Merritt			1	WCh	Moskva	13 Aug 13
43.74		Kirani	James	GRN	1.9.92	1	Athl	Lausanne	3 Jul 14
43.75			Johnson			1		Waco	19 Apr 97
43.75			Merritt			1	OG	Beijing	21 Aug 08
43.76			Johnson			1	GWG	Uniondale, NY	22 Jul 98
43.78			James			3	WCh	Beijing	26 Aug 15
43.81		Danny	Everett	USA	1.11.66	1	NC/OT	New Orleans	26 Jun 92
43.82			Wariner			1	WK	Zürich	29 Aug 08
43.83			Watts			1	WK	Zürich	19 Aug 92
43.84			Johnson			1	OG	Sydney	25 Sep 00
43.86A	WR	Lee	Evans	USA	25.2.47	1	OG	Ciudad de México	18 Oct 68
43.86			Johnson			1	Bisl	Oslo	21 Jul 95
43.86			Wariner			1	Gaz	Saint-Denis	18 Jul 08
		(32/10)							
43.87		Steve	Lewis	USA	16.5.69	1	OG	Seoul	28 Sep 88
43.93		Youssef	Al-Masrahi	KSA	31.12.87	1h2	WCh	Beijing	23 Aug 15
43.93		Rusheen	McDonald	JAM	17.8.92	2h2	WCh	Beijing	23 Aug 15
43.97A		Larry	James	USA	6.11.47	2	OG	Ciudad de México	18 Oct 68
44.05		Angelo	Taylor	USA	29.12.78	1	NC	Indianapolis	23 Jun 07
44.09		Alvin	Harrison ¶	USA/DOM	20.1.74	3	NC	Atlanta	19 Jun 96
44.09		Jerome	Young ¶	USA	14.8.76	1	NC	New Orleans	21 Jun 98
44.10		Gary	Kikaya	COD	4.2.78	2	WAF	Stuttgart	9 Sep 06
44.11		Luguelín	Santos	DOM	12.11.92	4	WCh	Beijing	26 Aug 15
44.13		Derek	Mills	USA	9.7.72	1	Pre	Eugene	4 Jun 95
		(20)							
44.14		Roberto	Hernández	CUB	6.3.67	2		Sevilla	30 May 90
44.15		Anthuan	Maybank	USA	30.12.69	1rB	Athl	Lausanne	3 Jul 96
44.16		Otis	Harris	USA	30.6.82	2	OG	Athína	23 Aug 04
44.17		Innocent	Egbunike	NGR	30.11.61	1rA	WK	Zürich	19 Aug 87
44.18		Samson	Kitur	KEN	25.2.66	2s2	OG	Barcelona	3 Aug 92
44.20A		Charles	Gitonga	KEN	5.10.71	1	NC	Nairobi	29 Jun 96
44.21		Ian	Morris	TTO	30.11.61	3s2	OG	Barcelona	3 Aug 92
44.26		Alberto	Juantorena	CUB	21.11.50	1	OG	Montreal	29 Jul 76
44.27		Alonzo	Babers	USA	31.10.61	1	OG	Los Angeles	8 Aug 84
44.27		Antonio	Pettigrew ¶	USA	3.11.67	1	NC	Houston	17 Jun 89
		(30)							
44.27		Darold	Williamson	USA	19.2.83	1s1	NCAA	Sacramento	10 Jun 05
44.27		Steven	Gardiner	BAH	12.9.95	1	NC	Nassau	27 Jun 15
44.27		Abdelilah	Haroun	QAT	1.1.97	2		La Chaux-de-Fonds	5 Jul 15
44.28		Andrew	Valmon	USA	1.1.65	4	NC	Eugene	19 Jun 93
44.28		Tyree	Washington	USA	28.8.76	1		Los Angeles (ER)	12 May 01
44.29		Derrick	Brew	USA	28.12.77	1	SEC	Athens, GA	16 May 99
44.29		Sanderlei	Parrela	BRA	7.10.74	2	WCh	Sevilla	26 Aug 99
44.30		Gabriel	Tiacoh	CIV	10.9.63	1	NCAA	Indianapolis	7 Jun 86
44.30		Lamont	Smith	USA	11.12.72	4	NC	Atlanta	19 Jun 96
44.31		Alejandro	Cárdenas	MEX	4.10.74	3	WCh	Sevilla	26 Aug 99
		(40)							
44.33		Thomas	Schönlebe	GDR	6.8.65	1	WCh	Roma	3 Sep 87
44.34		Darnell	Hall	USA	26.9.71	1	Athl	Lausanne	5 Jul 95
44.35		Andrew	Rock	USA	23.1.82	2	WCh	Helsinki	12 Aug 05
44.36		Iwan	Thomas	GBR	5.1.74	1	NC	Birmingham	13 Jul 97
44.36		Deon	Lendore	TTO	28.10.92	1	SEC	Lexington	18 May 14
44.36		Machel	Cedenio	TTO	6.9.95	1		George Town	16 May 15
44.37		Roger	Black	GBR	31.3.66	2rA	Athl	Lausanne	3 Jul 96
44.37		Davis	Kamoga	UGA	17.7.68	2	WCh	Athína	5 Aug 97
44.37		Mark	Richardson	GBR	26.7.72	1	Bisl	Oslo	9 Jul 98
44.38		Darren	Clark	AUS	6.9.65	3s1	OG	Seoul	26 Sep 88
		(50)	100th man 44.60, 200th 44.85, 300th 45.05, 400th 45.23, 500th 45.35						
Drugs disqualification									
44.21		Antonio	Pettigrew ¶	USA	3.11.67	1		Nassau	26 May 99
Hand timing			** 440 yards time less 0.3 secs*						
44.1		Wayne	Collett	USA	20.10.49	1	OT	Eugene	9 Jul 72
44.2*		John	Smith	USA	5.8.50	1	AAU	Eugene	26 Jun 71
44.2		Fred	Newhouse	USA	8.11.48	1s1	OT	Eugene	7 Jul 72

600 METRES

Mark	Wind	Name		Nat	Born	Pos	Meet	Venue	Date
1:12.81		Johnny	Gray	USA	19.6.60	1		Santa Monica	24 May 86
1:13.2 + ?		John	Kipkurgat	KEN	16.3.44	1		Pointe-à-Pierre	23 Mar 74

Mark Wind	Name		Nat	Born	Pos	Meet	Venue	Date
1:13.28	Duane	Solomon	USA	28.12.84	1		Burnaby	1 Jul 13
1:13.49	Joseph	Mutua	KEN	10.12.78	1		Liège (NX)	27 Aug 02
1:13.71	David	Rudisha	KEN	17.12.88	1	DL	Birmingham	24 Aug 14
1:13.80	Earl	Jones	USA	17.7.64	2		Santa Monica	24 May 86
1:13.9	Raidel	Acea	CUB	31.10.90	1		La Habana	20 Apr 13

800 METRES

Mark Wind	Name		Nat	Born	Pos	Meet	Venue	Date
1:40.91 WR	David	Rudisha	KEN	17.12.88	1	OG	London (OS)	9 Aug 12
1:41.01 WR		Rudisha			1rA		Rieti	29 Aug 10
1:41.09 WR		Rudisha			1	ISTAF	Berlin	22 Aug 10
1:41.11 WR	Wilson	Kipketer	DEN	12.12.70	1	ASV	Köln	24 Aug 97
1:41.24 WR		Kipketer			1rA	WK	Zürich	13 Aug 97
1:41.33		Rudisha			1		Rieti	10 Sep 11
1:41.51		Rudisha			1	NA	Heusden-Zolder	10 Jul 10
1:41.54		Rudisha			1	DL	Saint-Denis	6 Jul 12
1:41.73! WR	Sebastian	Coe	GBR	29.9.56	1		Firenze	10 Jun 81
1:41.73 WR		Kipketer			1rA	DNG	Stockholm	7 Jul 97
1:41.73	Nijel	Amos	BOT	15.3.94	2	OG	London (OS)	9 Aug 12
1:41.74		Rudisha			1	adidas	New York	9 Jun 12
1:41.77	Joaquim	Cruz	BRA	12.3.63	1	ASV	Köln	26 Aug 84
1:41.83		Kipketer			1	GP II	Rieti	1 Sep 96
1:42.01		Rudisha			1	GP	Rieti	6 Sep 09
1:42.04		Rudisha			1	Bisl	Oslo	4 Jun 10
1:42.12A		Rudisha			1	OT	Nairobi	23 Jun 12
1:42.17		Kipketer			1	TOTO	Tokyo	16 Sep 96
1:42.20		Kipketer			1	VD	Bruxelles	22 Aug 97
1:42.23	Abubaker	Kaki	SUD	21.6.89	2	Bisl	Oslo	4 Jun 10
1:42.27		Kipketer			1	VD	Bruxelles	3 Sep 99
1:42.28	Sammy	Koskei	KEN	14.5.61	2	ASV	Köln	26 Aug 84
1:42.32		Kipketer			1	GP II	Rieti	8 Sep 02
1:42.33 WR		Coe			1	Bisl	Oslo	5 Jul 79
1:42.34		Cruz			1r1	WK	Zürich	22 Aug 84
1:42.34	Wilfred	Bungei	KEN	24.7.80	2	GP II	Rieti	8 Sep 02
1:42.37	Mohammed	Aman	ETH	10.1.94	1	VD	Bruxelles	6 Sep 13
1:42.41		Cruz			1	VD	Bruxelles	24 Aug 84
1:42.45		Amos			1	Herc	Monaco	18 Jul 14
1:42.47	Yuriy	Borzakovskiy	RUS	12.4.81	1	VD	Bruxelles	24 Aug 01
	(30/10)		*! photo-electric cell time*					
1:42.51	Amel	Tuka	BIH	9.1.91	1	Herc	Monaco	17 Jul 15
1:42.53	Timothy	Kitum	KEN	20.11.94	3	OG	London (OS)	9 Aug 12
1:42.53	Pierre-Ambroise	Bosse	FRA	11.5.92	2	Herc	Monaco	18 Jul 14
1:42.55	André	Bucher	SUI	19.10.76	1rA	WK	Zürich	17 Aug 01
1:42.58	Vebjørn	Rodal	NOR	16.9.72	1	OG	Atlanta	31 Jul 96
1:42.60	Johnny	Gray	USA	19.6.60	2r1		Koblenz	28 Aug 85
1:42.62	Patrick	Ndururi	KEN	12.1.69	2rA	WK	Zürich	13 Aug 97
1:42.67	Alfred	Kirwa Yego	KEN	28.11.86	2	GP	Rieti	6 Sep 09
1:42.69	Hezekiél	Sepeng ¶	RSA	30.6.74	2	VD	Bruxelles	3 Sep 99
1:42.69	Japheth	Kimutai	KEN	20.12.78	3	VD	Bruxelles	3 Sep 99
	(20)							
1:42.79	Fred	Onyancha	KEN	25.12.69	3	OG	Atlanta	31 Jul 96
1:42.79	Youssef Saad	Kamel	KEN/BRN	29.3.83	2	Herc	Monaco	29 Jul 08
1:42.81	Jean-Patrick	Nduwimana	BDI	9.5.78	2rA	WK	Zürich	17 Aug 01
1:42.82	Duane	Solomon	USA	28.12.84	4	OG	London (OS)	9 Aug 12
1:42.84	Ferguson	Cheruiyot	KEN	30.11.89	4	Herc	Monaco	18 Jul 14
1:42.85	Norberto	Téllez	CUB	22.1.72	4	OG	Atlanta	31 Jul 96
1:42.86	Mbulaeni	Mulaudzi	RSA	8.9.80	3	GP	Rieti	6 Sep 09
1:42.88	Steve	Cram	GBR	14.10.60	1rA	WK	Zürich	21 Aug 85
1:42.91	William	Yiampoy	KEN	17.5.74	3	GP II	Rieti	8 Sep 02
1:42.95	Boaz	Lalang	KEN	8.2.89	2rA		Rieti	29 Aug 10
	(30)							
1:42.95	Nick	Symmonds	USA	30.12.83	5	OG	London (OS)	9 Aug 12
1:42.97	Peter	Elliott	GBR	9.10.62	1		Sevilla	30 May 90
1:42.97	Ayanleh	Souleiman	DJI	3.12.92	3	Herc	Monaco	17 Jul 15
1:42.98	Patrick	Konchellah	KEN	20.4.68	2	ASV	Köln	24 Aug 97
1:43.03	Kennedy/Kenneth	Kimwetich	KEN	1.1.73	2		Stuttgart	19 Jul 98
1:43.06	Billy	Konchellah	KEN	20.10.62	1	WCh	Roma	1 Sep 87
1:43.07	Yeimer	López	CUB	20.8.82	1		Jerez de la Frontera	24 Jun 08
1:43.08	José Luiz	Barbosa	BRA	27.5.61	1		Rieti	6 Sep 91
1:43.09	Djabir	Saïd-Guerni	ALG	29.3.77	5	VD	Bruxelles	3 Sep 99
1:43.13	Abraham Kipchirchir	Rotich	KEN	26.6.93	1	Herc	Monaco	20 Jul 12
	(40)							

Mark Wind	Name		Nat	Born	Pos	Meet	Venue	Date
1:43.15	Mehdi	Baala	FRA	17.8.78	5	GP II	Rieti	8 Sep 02
1:43.15	Asbel	Kiprop	KEN	30.6.89	2	Herc	Monaco	22 Jul 11
1:43.16	Paul	Ereng	KEN	22.8.67	1	WK	Zürich	16 Aug 89
1:43.17	Benson	Koech	KEN	10.11.74	1		Rieti	28 Aug 94
1:43.20	Mark	Everett	USA	2.9.68	1rA	Gugl	Linz	9 Jul 97
1:43.22	Pawel	Czapiewski	POL	30.3.78	5rA	WK	Zürich	17 Aug 01
1:43.25	Amine	Laâlou ¶	MAR	13.5.82	1	GGala	Roma	14 Jul 06
1:43.26	Sammy	Langat (Kibet)	KEN	24.1.70	1rB	WK	Zürich	14 Aug 96
1:43.30	William	Tanui	KEN	22.2.64	2		Rieti	6 Sep 91
1:43.30	Adam	Kszczot	POL	2.9.89	2		Rieti	10 Sep 11
	(50)	100th man 1:43.84, 200th 1:44.59, 300th 1:45.03, 400th 1:45.38, 500th 1:45.67						

1000 METRES

Mark Wind	Name		Nat	Born	Pos	Meet	Venue	Date
2:11.96 WR	Noah	Ngeny	KEN	2.11.78	1	GP II	Rieti	5 Sep 99
2:12.18 WR	Sebastian	Coe	GBR	29.9.56	1	OsloG	Oslo	11 Jul 81
2:12.66		Ngeny			1	Nik	Nice	17 Jul 99
2:12.88	Steve	Cram	GBR	14.10.60	1		Gateshead	9 Aug 85
2:13.08	Taoufik	Makhloufi	ALG	29.4.88	1		Tomblaine	1 Jul 15
2:13.40 WR		Coe			1	Bisl	Oslo	1 Jul 80
2:13.56	Kennedy/Kenneth	Kimwetich	KEN	1.1.73	2	Nik	Nice	17 Jul 99
2:13.62	Abubaker	Kaki	SUD	21.6.89	1	Pre	Eugene	3 Jul 10
2:13.73	Noureddine	Morceli	ALG	28.2.70	1	BNP	Villeneuve d'Ascq	2 Jul 93
2:13.9 WR	Rick	Wohlhuter	USA	23.12.48	1	King	Oslo	30 Jul 74
2:13.96	Mehdi	Baala	FRA	17.8.78	1		Strasbourg	26 Jun 03
2:14.09	Joaquim	Cruz	BRA	12.3.63	1	Nik	Nice	20 Aug 84
2:14.28	Japheth	Kimutai	KEN	20.12.78	1	DNG	Stockholm	1 Aug 00
	(11)	50th man 2:15.81, 100th 2:16.6, 200th 2:17.56						

1500 METRES

Mark Wind	Name		Nat	Born	Pos	Meet	Venue	Date
3:26.00 WR	Hicham	El Guerrouj	MAR	14.9.74	1	GGala	Roma	14 Jul 98
3:26.12		El Guerrouj			1	VD	Bruxelles	24 Aug 01
3:26.34	Bernard	Lagat	KEN/USA	12.12.74	2	VD	Bruxelles	24 Aug 01
3:26.45		El Guerrouj			1 rA	WK	Zürich	12 Aug 98
3:26.69	Asbel	Kiprop	KEN	30.6.89	1	Herc	Monaco	17 Jul 15
3:26.89		El Guerrouj			1	WK	Zürich	16 Aug 02
3:26.96		El Guerrouj			1	GP II	Rieti	8 Sep 02
3:27.21		El Guerrouj			1	WK	Zürich	11 Aug 00
3:27.34		El Guerrouj			1	Herc	Monaco	19 Jul 02
3:27.37 WR	Noureddine	Morceli	ALG	28.2.70	1	Nik	Nice	12 Jul 95
3:27.40		Lagat			1rA	WK	Zürich	6 Aug 04
3.27.52		Morceli			1	Herc	Monaco	25 Jul 95
3:27.64		El Guerrouj			2rA	WK	Zürich	6 Aug 04
3:27.64	Silas	Kiplagat	KEN	20.8.89	1	Herc	Monaco	18 Jul 14
3:27.65		El Guerrouj			1	WCh	Sevilla	24 Aug 99
3:27.72		Kiprop			1	Herc	Monaco	19 Jul 13
3:27.91		Lagat			2	Herc	Monaco	19 Jul 02
3:28.12	Noah	Ngeny	KEN	2.11.78	2	WK	Zürich	11 Aug 00
3:28.21+		El Guerrouj			1	in 1M	Roma	7 Jul 99
3.28.37		Morceli			1	GPF	Monaco	9 Sep 95
3:28.37		El Guerrouj			1	Herc	Monaco	8 Aug 98
3:28.38		El Guerrouj			1	GP	Saint-Denis	6 Jul 01
3:28.40		El Guerrouj			1	VD	Bruxelles	5 Sep 03
3:28.45		Kiprop			2	Herc	Monaco	18 Jul 14
3:28.51		Lagat			3	WK	Zürich	11 Aug 00
3:28.57		El Guerrouj			1rA	WK	Zürich	11 Aug 99
3:28.6+		Ngeny			2	in 1M	Roma	7 Jul 99
3:28.73		Ngeny			2	WCh	Sevilla	24 Aug 99
3:28.75	Taoufik	Makhloufi	ALG	29.4.88	2	Herc	Monaco	17 Jul 15
3:28.79	Abdelaati	Iguider	MAR	25.3.87	3	Herc	Monaco	17 Jul 15
	(30/8)							
3:28.81	Mohamed	Farah	GBR	23.3.83	2	Herc	Monaco	19 Jul 13
3:28.81	Ronald	Kwemoi (10)	KEN	19.9.95	3	Herc	Monaco	18 Jul 14
3:28.95	Fermín	Cacho	ESP	16.2.69	2rA	WK	Zürich	13 Aug 97
3:28.98	Mehdi	Baala	FRA	17.8.78	2	VD	Bruxelles	5 Sep 03
3:29.02	Daniel Kipchirchir	Komen	KEN	27.11.84	1	GGala	Roma	14 Jul 06
3:29.14	Rashid	Ramzi ¶	MAR/BRN	17.7.80	2	GGala	Roma	14 Jul 06
3:29.18	Vénuste	Niyongabo	BDI	9.12.73	2	VD	Bruxelles	22 Aug 97
3:29.29	William	Chirchir	KEN	6.2.79	3	VD	Bruxelles	24 Aug 01
3:29.46 WR	Saïd	Aouita	MAR	2.11.59	1	ISTAF	Berlin	23 Aug 85
3:29.46	Daniel	Komen	KEN	17.5.76	1	Herc	Monaco	16 Aug 97

Mark Wind	Name		Nat	Born	Pos	Meet	Venue	Date
3:29.47	Augustine	Choge	KEN	21.1.87	1	ISTAF	Berlin	14 Jun 09
3:29.50	Caleb	Ndiku	KEN	9.10.92	3	Herc	Monaco	19 Jul 13
	(20)							
3:29.51	Ali	Saïdi-Sief ¶	ALG	15.3.78	1	Athl	Lausanne	4 Jul 01
3:29.53	Amine	Laâlou	MAR	13.5.82	2	Herc	Monaco	22 Jul 10
3:29.58	Ayanleh	Souleiman	DJI	3.12.92	4	Herc	Monaco	18 Jul 14
3:29.66	Nick	Willis	NZL	25.4.83	5	Herc	Monaco	17 Jul 15
3:29.67 WR	Steve	Cram	GBR	14.10.60	1	Nik	Nice	16 Jul 85
3:29.67	Elijah	Manangoi	KEN	5.1.93	6	Herc	Monaco	17 Jul 15
3:29.77	Sydney	Maree	USA	9.9.56	1	ASV	Köln	25 Aug 85
3:29.77	Sebastian	Coe	GBR	29.9.56	1		Rieti	7 Sep 86
3:29.77	Nixon	Chepseba	KEN	12.12.90	2	Herc	Monaco	20 Jul 12
3:29.91	Laban	Rotich	KEN	20.1.69	2rA	WK	Zürich	12 Aug 98
	(30)							
3:29.91	Aman	Wote	ETH	18.4.84	6	Herc	Monaco	14 Jul 14
3:30.04	Timothy	Kiptanui	KEN	5.1.80	2	GP	Saint-Denis	23 Jul 04
3:30.07	Rui	Silva	POR	3.8.77	3	Herc	Monaco	19 Jul 02
3:30.10	Robert	Biwott	KEN	28.1.96	7	Herc	Monaco	17 Jul 15
3:30.18	John	Kibowen	KEN	21.4.69	3rA	WK	Zürich	12 Aug 98
3:30.20	Haron	Keitany	KEN	17.12.83	2	ISTAF	Berlin	14 Jun 09
3:30.24	Cornelius	Chirchir	KEN	5.6.83	4	Herc	Monaco	19 Jul 02
3:30.33	Ivan	Heshko	UKR	19.8.79	2	VD	Bruxelles	3 Sep 04
3:30.34	Collins	Cheboi	KEN	25.9.87	9	Herc	Monaco	17 Jul 15
3:30.40	Matthew	Centrowitz	USA	18.10.89	10	Herc	Monaco	17 Jul 15
	(40)							
3:30.46	Alex	Kipchirchir	KEN	26.11.84	3	VD	Bruxelles	3 Sep 04
3:30.54	Alan	Webb	USA	13.1.83	1	Gaz	Saint-Denis	6 Jul 07
3:30.55	Abdi	Bile	SOM	28.12.62	1		Rieti	3 Sep 89
3:30.57	Reyes	Estévez	ESP	2.8.76	3	WCh	Sevilla	24 Aug 99
3:30.58	William	Tanui	KEN	22.2.64	3	Herc	Monaco	16 Aug 97
3:30.61	James	Magut	KEN	20.7.90	5	DL	Doha	9 May 14
3:30.67	Benjamin	Kipkurui	KEN	28.12.80	2	Herc	Monaco	20 Jul 01
3:30.72	Paul	Korir	KEN	15.7.77	3	VD	Bruxelles	5 Sep 03
3:30.77 WR	Steve	Ovett	GBR	9.10.55	1		Rieti	4 Sep 83
3:30.77	Bethwel	Birgen	KEN	6.8.88	4	Herc	Monaco	19 Jul 13
	(50)	100th man 3:31.96, 200th 3:33.83, 300th 3:34.85, 400th 3:35.69, 500th 3:36.30						
Drugs disqualification: 3:30.77		Adil Kaouch ¶	MAR	1.1.79	1	GGala	Roma	13 Jul 07

1 MILE

Mark Wind	Name		Nat	Born	Pos	Meet	Venue	Date
3:43.13 WR	Hicham	El Guerrouj	MAR	14.9.74	1	GGala	Roma	7 Jul 99
3:43.40	Noah	Ngeny	KEN	2.11.78	2	GGala	Roma	7 Jul 99
3:44.39 WR	Noureddine	Morceli	ALG	28.2.70	1		Rieti	5 Sep 93
3:44.60		El Guerrouj			1	Nik	Nice	16 Jul 98
3:44.90		El Guerrouj			1	Bisl	Oslo	4 Jul 97
3:44.95		El Guerrouj			1	GGala	Roma	29 Jun 01
3:45.19		Morceli			1	WK	Zürich	16 Aug 95
3:45.64		El Guerrouj			1	ISTAF	Berlin	26 Aug 97
3:45.96		El Guerrouj			1	BrGP	London (CP)	5 Aug 00
3:46.24		El Guerrouj			1	Bisl	Oslo	28 Jul 00
3:46.32 WR	Steve	Cram	GBR	14.10.60	1	Bisl	Oslo	27 Jul 85
3:46.38	Daniel	Komen	KEN	17.5.76	2	ISTAF	Berlin	26 Aug 97
3:46.70	Vénuste	Niyongabo	BDI	9.12.73	3	ISTAF	Berlin	26 Aug 97
3:46.76	Saïd	Aouita	MAR	2.11.59	1	WG	Helsinki	2 Jul 87
3:46.78		Morceli			1	ISTAF	Berlin	27 Aug 93
3:46.91	Alan	Webb	USA	13.1.83	1		Brasschaat	21 Jul 07
3:46.92		Aouita			1	WK	Zürich	21 Aug 85
3:47.10		El Guerrouj			1	BrGP	London (CP)	7 Aug 99
3:47.28	Bernard	Lagat	KEN/USA	12.12.74	2	GGala	Roma	29 Jun 01
3:47.30		Morceli			1	VD	Bruxelles	3 Sep 93
3:47.32	Ayanleh	Souleiman (10)	DJI	3.12.92	1	Pre	Eugene	31 May 14
3:47.33 WR	Sebastian	Coe	GBR	29.9.56	1	VD	Bruxelles	28 Aug 81
	(22/11)							
3:47.65	Laban	Rotich	KEN	20.1.69	2	Bisl	Oslo	4 Jul 97
3:47.69	Steve	Scott	USA	5.5.56	1	OsloG	Oslo	7 Jul 82
3:47.79	José Luis	González	ESP	8.12.57	2	Bisl	Oslo	27 Jul 85
3:47.88	John	Kibowen	KEN	21.4.69	3	Bisl	Oslo	4 Jul 97
3:47.88	Silas	Kiplagat	KEN	20.8.89	2	Pre	Eugene	31 May 14
3:47.94	William	Chirchir	KEN	6.2.79	2	Bisl	Oslo	28 Jul 00
3:47.97	Daham Najim	Bashir	KEN/QAT	8.11.78	1	Bisl	Oslo	29 Jul 05
3:48.17	Paul	Korir	KEN	15.7.77	1	GP	London (CP)	8 Aug 03

Mark Wind	Name		Nat	Born	Pos	Meet	Venue	Date
3:48.23	Ali	Saïdi-Sief ¶	ALG	15.3.78	1	Bisl	Oslo	13 Jul 01
	(20)							
3:48.28	Daniel Kipchirchir	Komen	KEN	27.11.84	1	Pre	Eugene	10 Jun 07
3:48.38	Andrés Manuel	Díaz	ESP	12.7.69	3	GGala	Roma	29 Jun 01
3:48.40 WR	Steve	Ovett	GBR	9.10.55	1	R-W	Koblenz	26 Aug 81
3:48.50	Asbel	Kiprop	KEN	30.6.89	1	Pre	Eugene	7 Jun 09
3:48.60	Aman	Wote	ETH	18.4.84	3	Pre	Eugene	31 May 14
3:48.78	Haron	Keitany	KEN	17.12.83	2	Pre	Eugene	7 Jun 09
3:48.80	William	Kemei	KEN	22.2.69	1	ISTAF	Berlin	21 Aug 92
3:48.83	Sydney	Maree	USA	9.9.56	1		Rieti	9 Sep 81
3:48.95	Deresse	Mekonnen	ETH	20.10.87	1	Bisl	Oslo	3 Jul 09
3:48.98	Craig	Mottram	AUS	18.6.80	5	Bisl	Oslo	29 Jul 05
	(30)							
3:49.08	John	Walker	NZL	12.1.52	2	OsloG	Oslo	7 Jul 82
3:49.09	Abdelaati	Iguider	MAR	25.3.87	4	Pre	Eugene	31 May 14
3:49.20	Peter	Elliott	GBR	9.10.62	2	Bisl	Oslo	2 Jul 88
3:49.22	Jens-Peter	Herold	GDR	2.6.65	3	Bisl	Oslo	2 Jul 88
3:49.29	William	Biwott/Özbilen	KEN/TUR	5.3.90	2	Bisl	Oslo	3 Jul 09
3:49.31	Joe	Falcon	USA	23.6.66	1	Bisl	Oslo	14 Jul 90
3:49.34	David	Moorcroft	GBR	10.4.53	3	Bisl	Oslo	26 Jun 82
3:49.34	Benjamin	Kipkurui	KEN	28.12.80	3	VD	Bruxelles	25 Aug 00
3:49.38	Andrew	Baddeley	GBR	20.6.82	1	Bisl	Oslo	6 Jun 08
3:49.40	Abdi	Bile	SOM	28.12.62	4	Bisl	Oslo	2 Jul 88
	(40)							
3:49.43	James	Magut	KEN	20.7.90	5	Pre	Eugene	31 May 14
3:49.45	Mike	Boit	KEN	6.1.49	2	VD	Bruxelles	28 Aug 81
3:49.50	Rui	Silva	POR	3.8.77	3	GGala	Roma	12 Jul 02
3:49.56	Fermín	Cacho	ESP	16.2.69	2	Bisl	Oslo	5 Jul 96
3:49.56	Collins	Cheboi	KEN	25.9.87	6	Pre	Eugene	31 May 14
3:49.60	José Antonio	Redolat	ESP	17.2.76	4	GGala	Roma	29 Jun 01
3:49.70	Mekonnen	Gebremedhin	ETH	11.10.88	4	Pre	Eugene	4 Jun 11
3:49.75	Leonard	Mucheru	KEN/BRN	13.6.78	5	GGala	Roma	29 Jun 01
3:49.77	Ray	Flynn	IRL	22.1.57	3	OsloG	Oslo	7 Jul 82
3:49.77	Wilfred	Kirochi	KEN	12.12.69	2	Bisl	Oslo	6 Jul 91
3:49.77	Caleb	Ndiku	KEN	9.10.92	5	Pre	Eugene	4 Jun 11
	(51)	100th 3:51.05, 200th 3:53.24, 300th 3:54.81						

2000 METRES

Mark Wind	Name		Nat	Born	Pos	Meet	Venue	Date
4:44.79 WR	Hicham	El Guerrouj	MAR	14.9.74	1	ISTAF	Berlin	7 Sep 99
4:46.88	Ali	Saïdi-Sief ¶	ALG	15.3.78	1		Strasbourg	19 Jun 01
4:47.88 WR	Noureddine	Morceli	ALG	28.2.70	1		Paris (JB)	3 Jul 95
4:48.36		El Guerrouj			1		Gateshead	19 Jul 98
4:48.69	Vénuste	Niyongabo	BDI	9.12.73	1	Nik	Nice	12 Jul 95
4:48.74	John	Kibowen	KEN	21.4.69	1		Hechtel	1 Aug 98
4:49.00		Niyongabo			1		Rieti	3 Sep 97
4:49.55		Morceli			1	Nik	Nice	10 Jul 96
4:50.08	Noah	Ngeny	KEN	2.11.78	1	DNG	Stockholm	30 Jul 99
4:50.76	Craig	Mottram	AUS	18.6.80	1		Melbourne (OP)	9 Mar 06
4:50.81 WR	Saïd	Aouita	MAR	2.11.59	1	BNP	Paris (JB)	16 Jul 87
4:51.30	Daniel	Komen	KEN	17.5.76	1		Milano	5 Jun 98
4:51.39 WR	Steve	Cram (10)	GBR	14.10.60	1	BGP	Budapest	4 Aug 85
Indoors								
4:49.99	Kenenisa	Bekele	ETH	13.6.82	1		Birmingham	17 Feb 07

3000 METRES

Mark Wind	Name		Nat	Born	Pos	Meet	Venue	Date
7:20.67 WR	Daniel	Komen	KEN	17.5.76	1		Rieti	1 Sep 96
7:23.09	Hicham	El Guerrouj	MAR	14.9.74	1	VD	Bruxelles	3 Sep 99
7:25.02	Ali	Saïdi-Sief ¶	ALG	15.3.78	1	Herc	Monaco	18 Aug 00
7:25.09	Haile	Gebrselassie	ETH	18.4.73	1	VD	Bruxelles	28 Aug 98
7:25.11 WR	Noureddine	Morceli	ALG	28.2.70	1	Herc	Monaco	2 Aug 94
7:25.16		Komen			1	Herc	Monaco	10 Aug 96
7:25.54		Gebrselassie			1	Herc	Monaco	8 Aug 98
7:25.79	Kenenisa	Bekele	ETH	13.6.82	1	DNG	Stockholm	7 Aug 07
7:25.87		Komen			1	VD	Bruxelles	23 Aug 96
7:26.02		Gebrselassie			1	VD	Bruxelles	22 Aug 97
7:26.03		Gebrselassie			1	GP II	Helsinki	10 Jun 99
7:26.5 e		Komen			1	in 2M	Sydney	28 Feb 98
7:26.62	Mohammed	Mourhit ¶	BEL	10.10.70	2	Herc	Monaco	18 Aug 00
7:26.69		K Bekele			1	BrGP	Sheffield	15 Jul 07
7:27.18	Moses	Kiptanui	KEN	1.10.70	1	Herc	Monaco	25 Jul 95

Mark	Wind	Name		Nat	Born	Pos	Meet	Venue	Date
7:27.26		Yenew	Alamirew	ETH	27.5.90	1	DL	Doha	6 May 11
7:27.3+			Komen			1	in 2M	Hechtel	19 Jul 97
7:27.42			Gebrselassie			1	Bisl	Oslo	9 Jul 98
7:27.50			Morceli			1	VD	Bruxelles	25 Aug 95
7:27.55		Edwin	Soi (10)	KEN	3.3.86	2	DL	Doha	6 May 11
7:27.59		Luke	Kipkosgei	KEN	27.11.75	2	Herc	Monaco	8 Aug 98
7:27.66		Eliud	Kipchoge	KEN	5.11.84	3	DL	Doha	6 May 11
7:27.67			Saïdi-Sief			1	Gaz	Saint-Denis	23 Jun 00
7:27.72			Kipchoge			1	VD	Bruxelles	3 Sep 04
7:27.75		Thomas	Nyariki	KEN	27.9.71	2	Herc	Monaco	10 Aug 96
7.28.04			Kiptanui			1	ASV	Köln	18 Aug 95
7:28.28			Kipkosgei			2	Bisl	Oslo	9 Jul 98
7:28.28		James	Kwalia	KEN/QAT	12.6.84	2	VD	Bruxelles	3 Sep 04
7:28.37			Kipchoge			1	SGP	Doha	8 May 09
7:28.41		Paul	Bitok	KEN	26.6.70	3	Herc	Monaco	10 Aug 96
		(30/15)							
7:28.45		Assefa	Mezegebu	ETH	19.6.78	3	Herc	Monaco	8 Aug 98
7:28.67		Benjamin	Limo	KEN	23.8.74	1	Herc	Monaco	4 Aug 99
7:28.70		Paul	Tergat	KEN	17.6.69	4	Herc	Monaco	10 Aug 96
7:28.70		Tariku	Bekele	ETH	21.1.87	1		Rieti	29 Aug 10
7:28.72		Isaac K.	Songok	KEN	25.4.84	1	GP	Rieti	27 Aug 06
		(20)							
7:28.76		Augustine	Choge	KEN	21.1.87	4	DL	Doha	6 May 11
7:28.93		Salah	Hissou	MAR	16.1.72	2	Herc	Monaco	4 Aug 99
7:28.94		Brahim	Lahlafi	FRA/MAR	15.4.68	3	Herc	Monaco	4 Aug 99
7:29.00		Bernard	Lagat	USA	12.12.74	2		Rieti	29 Aug 10
7:29.09		John	Kibowen	KEN	21.4.69	3	Bisl	Oslo	9 Jul 98
7:29.34		Isaac	Viciosa	ESP	26.12.69	4	Bisl	Oslo	9 Jul 98
7:29.45	WR	Saïd	Aouita	MAR	2.11.59	1	ASV	Köln	20 Aug 89
7:29.92		Sileshi	Sihine	ETH	29.1.83	1	GP	Rieti	28 Aug 05
7:30.09		Ismaïl	Sghyr	MAR/FRA	16.3.72	2	Herc	Monaco	25 Jul 95
7:30.09		Thomas	Longosiwa	KEN	14.1.82	2	SGP	Doha	8 May 09
		(30)							
7:30.15		Vincent	Chepkok	KEN	5.7.88	5	DL	Doha	6 May 11
7:30.36		Mark	Carroll	IRL	15.1.72	5	Herc	Monaco	4 Aug 99
7:30.36		Hagos	Gebrhiwet	ETH	11.5.94	1	DL	Doha	10 May 13
7:30.43		Isiah	Koech	KEN	19.12.93	1	DNG	Stockholm	17 Aug 12
7:30.50		Dieter	Baumann ¶	GER	9.2.65	6	Herc	Monaco	8 Aug 98
7:30.53		El Hassan	Lahssini	MAR/FRA	1.1.75	6	Herc	Monaco	10 Aug 96
7:30.53		Hailu	Mekonnen	ETH	4.4.80	1	VD	Bruxelles	24 Aug 01
7:30.62		Boniface	Songok	KEN	25.12.80	3	VD	Bruxelles	3 Sep 04
7:30.76		Jamal Bilal	Salem	KEN/QAT	12.9.78	4	SGP	Doha	13 May 05
7:30.78		Mustapha	Essaïd	FRA	20.1.70	7	Herc	Monaco	8 Aug 98
		(40)							
7:30.84		Bob	Kennedy	USA	18.8.70	8	Herc	Monaco	8 Aug 98
7:30.95		Moses	Kipsiro	UGA	2.9.86	1	Herc	Monaco	28 Jul 09
7:30.99		Khalid	Boulami	MAR	7.8.69	1	Nik	Nice	16 Jul 97
7:30.99		Caleb	Ndiku	KEN	9.10.92	2	DNG	Stockholm	17 Aug 12
7:31.13		Julius	Gitahi	KEN	29.4.78	6	Bisl	Oslo	9 Jul 98
7:31.14		William	Kalya	KEN	4.8.74	3	Herc	Monaco	16 Aug 97
7:31.20		Joseph	Kiplimo	KEN	20.7.88	1	GP	Rieti	6 Sep 09
7:31.41		Sammy Alex	Mutahi	KEN	1.6.89	2	GP	Rieti	6 Sep 09
7:31.41		Daniel Kipchirchir	Komen	KEN	27.11.84	6	DL	Doha	6 May 11
7:31.59		Manuel	Pancorbo	ESP	7.7.66	7	Bisl	Oslo	9 Jul 98
		(50)	100th man 7:35.08, 200th man 7:39.30, 300th 7:41.82, 400th 7:43.66, 500th 7:4534						
Indoors									
7:24.90			Komen			1		Budapest	6 Feb 98
7:26.15			Gebrselassie			1		Karlsruhe	25 Jan 98
7:26.80			Gebrselassie			1		Karlsruhe	24 Jan 99
7:27.80			Alamirew			1	Spark	Stuttgart	5 Feb 11
7:27.93			Komen			1	Spark	Stuttgart	1 Feb 98
7:28.00		Augustine	Choge	KEN	21.1.87	2	Spark	Stuttgart	5 Feb 11
7:30.16		Galen	Rupp	USA	8.5.86	1		Stockholm	21 Feb 13

2 MILES

Mark	Wind	Name		Nat	Born	Pos	Meet	Venue	Date
7:58.61	WR	Daniel	Komen	KEN	17.5.76	1		Hechtel	19 Jul 97
7:58.91			Komen			1		Sydney	28 Feb 98
8:01.08	WR	Haile	Gebrselassie	ETH	18.4.73	1	APM	Hengelo	31 May 97
8:01.72			Gebrselassie			1	BrGP	London (CP)	7 Aug 99

Mark	Wind	Name		Nat	Born	Pos	Meet	Venue	Date
8:01.86			Gebrselassie			1	APM	Hengelo	30 May 99
8:03.50		Craig	Mottram	AUS	18.6.80	1	Pre	Eugene	10 Jun 07
8:03.54	WR		Komen			1		Lappeenranta	14 Jul 96
8:04.83		Tariku	Bekele	ETH	21.1.87	2	Pre	Eugene	10 Jun 07
Indoors									
8:03.40		Mohamed	Farah	GBR	23.3.83	1	GP	Birmingham	21 Feb 15
8:04.35		Kenenisa	Bekele	ETH	13.6.82	1	GP	Birmingham	16 Feb 08
8:04.69			Gebrselassie			1	GP	Birmingham	21 Feb 03
8:06.48		Paul Kipsiele	Koech	KEN	10.11.81	2	GP	Birmingham	16 Feb 08
8:06.61		Hicham	El Guerrouj	MAR	14.9.74	1		Liévin	23 Feb 03

5000 METRES

Mark	Wind	Name		Nat	Born	Pos	Meet	Venue	Date
12:37.35	WR	Kenenisa	Bekele	ETH	13.6.82	1	FBK	Hengelo	31 May 04
12:39.36	WR	Haile	Gebrselassie	ETH	18.4.73	1	GP II	Helsinki	13 Jun 98
12:39.74	WR	Daniel	Komen	KEN	17.5.76	1	VD	Bruxelles	22 Aug 97
12:40.18			K Bekele			1	Gaz	Saint-Denis	1 Jul 05
12:41.86	WR		Gebrselassie			1	WK	Zürich	13 Aug 97
12:44.39	WR		Gebrselassie			1	WK	Zürich	16 Aug 95
12:44.90			Komen			2	WK	Zürich	13 Aug 97
12:45.09			Komen			1	WK	Zürich	14 Aug 96
12:46.53		Eliud	Kipchoge	KEN	5.11.84	1	GGala	Roma	2 Jul 04
12:46.81		Dejen	Gebremeskel	ETH	24.11.89	1	DL	Saint-Denis	6 Jul 12
12:47.04		Sileshi	Sihine	ETH	29.9.83	2	GGala	Roma	2 Jul 04
12:47.53		Hagos	Gebrhiwet	ETH	11.5.94	2	DL	Saint-Denis	6 Jul 12
12:48.09			K Bekele			1	VD	Bruxelles	25 Aug 06
12:48.25			K Bekele			1	WK	Zürich	18 Aug 06
12:48.64		Isiah	Koech	KEN	19.12.93	3	DL	Saint-Denis	6 Jul 12
12:48.66		Isaac K.	Songok	KEN	25.4.84	2	WK	Zürich	18 Aug 06
12:48.77		Yenew	Alamirew (10)	ETH	27.5.90	4	DL	Saint-Denis	6 Jul 12
12:48.81		Stephen	Cherono/Shaheen	KEN/QAT	15.10.82	1	GS	Ostrava	12 Jun 03
12:48.98			Komen			1	GGala	Roma	5 Jun 97
12:49.04		Thomas	Longosiwa	KEN	14.1.82	5	DL	Saint-Denis	6 Jul 12
12:49.28		Brahim	Lahlafi	MAR	15.4.68	1	VD	Bruxelles	25 Aug 00
12:49.50		John	Kipkoech	KEN	29.12.91	6	DL	Saint-Denis	6 Jul 12
12:49.53			K Bekele			1	Aragón	Zaragoza	28 Jul 07
12:49.64			Gebrselassie			1	WK	Zürich	11 Aug 99
12:49.71		Mohammed	Mourhit ¶	BEL	10.10.70	2	VD	Bruxelles	25 Aug 00
12:49.87		Paul	Tergat	KEN	17.6.69	3	WK	Zürich	13 Aug 97
12:50.16			Sihine			1	VD	Bruxelles	14 Sep 07
12:50.18			K Bekele			1	WK	Zürich	29 Aug 08
12:50.22			Kipchoge			1	VD	Bruxelles	26 Aug 05
12:50.24		Hicham (30/17)	El Guerrouj	MAR	14.9.74	2	GS	Ostrava	12 Jun 03
12:50.25		Abderrahim	Goumri ¶	MAR	21.5.76	2	VD	Bruxelles	26 Aug 05
12:50.55		Moses	Masai	KEN	1.6.86	1	ISTAF	Berlin	1 Jun 08
12:50.72		Moses (20)	Kipsiro	UGA	2.9.86	3	VD	Bruxelles	14 Sep 07
12:50.80		Salah	Hissou	MAR	16.1.72	1	GGala	Roma	5 Jun 96
12:50.86		Ali	Saïdi-Sief ¶	ALG	15.3.78	1	GGala	Roma	30 Jun 00
12:51.00		Joseph	Ebuya	KEN	20.6.87	4	VD	Bruxelles	14 Sep 07
12:51.34		Edwin	Soi	KEN	3.3.86	1	Herc	Monaco	19 Jul 13
12:51.45		Vincent	Chepkok	KEN	5.7.88	2	DL	Doha	14 May 10
12:51.96		Albert	Rop	KEN/BRN	17.7.92	2	Herc	Monaco	19 Jul 13
12:52.33		Sammy	Kipketer	KEN	29.9.81	2	Bisl	Oslo	27 Jun 03
12:52.45		Tariku	Bekele	ETH	21.1.87	2	ISTAF	Berlin	1 Jun 08
12:52.80		Gebre-egziabher	Gebremariam	ETH	10.9.84	3	GGala	Roma	8 Jul 05
12:52.99		Abraham (30)	Chebii	KEN	23.12.79	4	Bisl	Oslo	27 Jun 03
12:53.11		Mohamed	Farah	GBR	23.3.83	1	Herc	Monaco	22 Jul 11
12:53.41		Khalid	Boulami	MAR	7.8.69	4	WK	Zürich	13 Aug 97
12:53.46		Mark	Kiptoo	KEN	21.6.76	1	DNG	Stockholm	6 Aug 10
12:53.58		Imane	Merga	ETH	15.10.88	3	DNG	Stockholm	6 Aug 10
12:53.60		Bernard	Lagat	USA	12.12.74	2	Herc	Monaco	22 Jul 11
12:53.66		Augustine	Choge	KEN	21.1.87	4	GGala	Roma	8 Jul 05
12:53.72		Philip	Mosima	KEN	2.1.77	2	GGala	Roma	5 Jun 96
12:53.84		Assefa	Mezegebu	ETH	19.6.78	1	VD	Bruxelles	28 Aug 98
12:53.98		Yomif	Kejelcha	ETH	1.8.97	1	VD	Bruxelles	11 Sep 15
12:54.07		John (40)	Kibowen	KEN	21.4.69	4	WCh	Saint-Denis	31 Aug 03
12:54.15		Dejene	Berhanu	ETH	12.12.80	3	GGala	Roma	2 Jul 04

Mark	Wind	Name		Nat	Born	Pos	Meet	Venue	Date
12:54.19		Abreham	Cherkos	ETH	23.9.89	5	GGala	Roma	14 Jul 06
12:54.46		Moses	Mosop	KEN	17.7.85	3	Gaz	Saint-Denis	8 Jul 06
12:54.58		James	Kwalia	KEN/QAT	12.6.84	5	Bisl	Oslo	27 Jun 03
12:54.70		Dieter	Baumann ¶	GER	9.2.65	5	WK	Zürich	13 Aug 97
12:54.83		Muktar	Edris	ETH	14.1.94	1	DNG	Stockholm	21 Aug 14
12:54.85		Moses	Kiptanui	KEN	1.10.70	3	GGala	Roma	5 Jun 96
12:54.99		Benjamin	Limo	KEN	23.8.74	3	Gaz	Saint-Denis	4 Jul 03
12:55.06		Lucas	Rotich	KEN	16.4.90	4	Bisl	Oslo	4 Jun 10
12:55.52		Hicham	Bellani	MAR	15.9.79	7	GGala	Roma	14 Jul 06
		(50)	100th man 13:00.95, 200th 13:08.55, 300th 13:12.40, 400th 13:16.11, 500th 13:18.67						
Indoors: 12:49.60			K Bekele			1		Birmingham	20 Feb 04

10,000 METRES

Mark	Wind	Name		Nat	Born	Pos	Meet	Venue	Date
26:17.53	WR	Kenenisa	Bekele	ETH	13.6.82	1	VD	Bruxelles	26 Aug 05
26:20.31	WR		K Bekele			1	GS	Ostrava	8 Jun 04
26:22.75	WR	Haile	Gebrselassie	ETH	18.4.73	1	APM	Hengelo	1 Jun 98
26:25.97			K Bekele			1	Pre	Eugene	8 Jun 08
26:27.85	WR	Paul	Tergat	KEN	17.6.69	1	VD	Bruxelles	22 Aug 97
26:28.72			K Bekele			1	FBK	Hengelo	29 May 05
26:29.22			Gebrselassie			1	VD	Bruxelles	5 Sep 03
26:30.03		Nicholas	Kemboi	KEN/QAT	25.11.83	2	VD	Bruxelles	5 Sep 03
26:30.74		Abebe	Dinkesa	ETH	6.3.84	2	FBK	Hengelo	29 May 05
26:31.32	WR		Gebrselassie			1	Bisl	Oslo	4 Jul 97
26:35.63		Micah	Kogo	KEN	3.6.86	1	VD	Bruxelles	25 Aug 06
26:36.26		Paul	Koech	KEN	25.6.69	2	VD	Bruxelles	22 Aug 97
26:37.25		Zersenay	Tadese	ERI	8.2.82	2	VD	Bruxelles	25 Aug 06
26:38.08	WR	Salah	Hissou	MAR	16.1.72	1	VD	Bruxelles	23 Aug 96
26:38.76		Abdullah Ahmad	Hassan (10)	QAT	4.4.81	3	VD	Bruxelles	5 Sep 03
		(Formerly Albert Chepkurui KEN)							
26:39.69		Sileshi	Sihine	ETH	29.9.83	1	FBK	Hengelo	31 May 04
26:39.77		Boniface	Kiprop	UGA	12.10.85	2	VD	Bruxelles	26 Aug 05
26:41.58			Gebrselassie			2	FBK	Hengelo	31 May 04
26:41.75		Samuel	Wanjiru	KEN	10.11.86	3	VD	Bruxelles	26 Aug 05
26:41.95			Kiprop			3	VD	Bruxelles	25 Aug 06
26:43.16			K Bekele			1	VD	Bruxelles	16 Sep 11
26:43.53	WR		Gebrselassie			1	APM	Hengelo	5 Jun 95
26:43.98		Lucas	Rotich	KEN	16.4.90	2	VD	Bruxelles	16 Sep 11
26:44.36		Galen	Rupp	USA	8.5.86	1	Pre	Eugene	30 May 14
26:46.19			K Bekele			1	VD	Bruxelles	14 Sep 07
26:46.31			K Bekele			1	WCh	Berlin	17 Aug 09
26:46.44			Tergat			1	VD	Bruxelles	28 Aug 98
26:46.57		Mohamed	Farah	GBR	23.3.83	1	Pre	Eugene	3 Jun 11
26:47.89			Koech			2	VD	Bruxelles	28 Aug 98
26:48.00			Rupp			3	VD	Bruxelles	16 Sep 11
		(30/16)							
26:48.35		Imane	Merga	ETH	15.10.88	2	Pre	Eugene	3 Jun 11
26:48.99		Josphat	Bett	KEN	12.6.90	3	Pre	Eugene	3 Jun 11
26:49.02		Eliud	Kipchoge	KEN	5.11.84	2	FBK	Hengelo	26 May 07
26:49.20		Moses	Masai	KEN	1.6.86	2	VD	Bruxelles	14 Sep 07
		(20)							
26:49.38		Sammy	Kipketer	KEN	29.9.81	1	VD	Bruxelles	30 Aug 02
26:49.41		Paul	Tanui	KEN	22.12.90	2	Pre	Eugene	30 May 14
26:49.55		Moses	Mosop	KEN	17.7.85	3	FBK	Hengelo	26 May 07
26:49.90		Assefa	Mezegebu	ETH	19.6.78	2	VD	Bruxelles	30 Aug 02
26:50.20		Richard	Limo	KEN	18.11.80	3	VD	Bruxelles	30 Aug 02
26:51.02		Dejen	Gebremeskel	ETH	24.11.89	1		Sollentuna	27 Jun 13
26:51.16		Emmanuel	Bett	KEN	30.3.83	1	VD	Bruxelles	7 Sep 12
26:51.49		Charles	Kamathi	KEN	18.5.78	1	VD	Bruxelles	3 Sep 99
26:51.68		Vincent	Chepkok	KEN	5.7.88	2	VD	Bruxelles	7 Sep 12
26:52.23	WR	William	Sigei	KEN	14.10.69	1	Bisl	Oslo	22 Jul 94
		(30)							
26:52.30		Mohammed	Mourhit ¶	BEL	10.10.70	2	VD	Bruxelles	3 Sep 99
26:52.33		Gebre-egziabher	Gebremariam	ETH	10.9.84	4	FBK	Hengelo	26 May 07
26:52.36		Bidan	Karoki	KEN	21.8.90	3	Pre	Eugene	30 May 14
26:52.65		Kenneth	Kipkemoi	KEN	2.8.84	3	VD	Bruxelles	7 Sep 12
26:52.65		Geoffrey	Kamworor	KEN	28.11.92	3	Pre	Eugene	29 May 15
26:52.85		Abera	Kuma	ETH	31.8.90	2		Sollentuna	27 Jun 13
26:52.87		John Cheruiyot	Korir	KEN	13.12.81	5	VD	Bruxelles	30 Aug 02
26:52.93		Mark	Bett	KEN	22.12.76	6	VD	Bruxelles	26 Aug 05
26:54.25		Mathew	Kisorio ¶	KEN	16.5.89	7	Pre	Eugene	3 Jun 11

Mark	Wind	Name		Nat	Born	Pos	Meet	Venue	Date
26:54.61		Stephen	Sambu	KEN	7.7.88	4	Pre	Eugene	30 May 14
		(40)							
26:54.64		Mark	Kiptoo	KEN	21.6.76	8	Pre	Eugene	3 Jun 11
26:55.29		Leonard Patrick	Komon	KEN	10.1.88	9	Pre	Eugene	3 Jun 11
26:55.73		Geoffrey	Kirui	KEN	16.2.93	6	VD	Bruxelles	16 Sep 11
26:56.74		Josphat	Menjo	KEN	20.8.79	1		Turku	29 Aug 10
26:57.36		Josphat	Muchiri Ndambiri	KEN	12.2.85	1		Fukuroi	3 May 09
26:57.56		Yigrem	Demelash	ETH	28.1.94	4	VD	Bruxelles	7 Sep 12
26:58.38	WR	Yobes	Ondieki	KEN	21.2.61	1	Bisl	Oslo	10 Jul 93
26:59.51		Bernard	Kipyego	KEN	16.7.86	4	VD	Bruxelles	14 Sep 07
26:59.60		Chris	Solinsky	USA	5.12.84	1		Stanford	1 May 10
26:59.81		Titus	Mbishei	KEN	28.10.90	7	VD	Bruxelles	16 Sep 11
		(50)	100th man 27:14.84, 200th 27:29.74, 300th 27:39.55, 400th 27:43.93, 500th 27:49.73						

20,000 METRES & 1 HOUR

Mark	Distance	Name		Nat	Born	Pos	Meet	Venue	Date
56:25.98+	21 285m	Haile	Gebrselassie	ETH	18.4.73	1	GS	Ostrava	27 Jun 07
56:55.6+	21 101	Arturo	Barrios	MEX	12.12.63	1		La Flèche	30 Mar 91
57:24.19+	20 944	Jos	Hermens	NED	8.1.50	1		Papendal	1 May 76
57:18.4+	20 943	Dionísio	Castro	POR	22.11.63	1		La Flèche	31 Mar 90

HALF MARATHON

Included are the slightly downhill courses: Newcastle to South Shields 30.5m, Tokyo 33m, Lisboa (Spring to 2008) 69m

Mark	Wind	Name		Nat	Born	Pos	Meet	Venue	Date
58:23	WR	Zersenay	Tadese	ERI	8.2.82	1		Lisboa	21 Mar 10
58:30			Z Tadese			1		Lisboa	20 Mar 11
58:33	WR	Samuel	Wanjiru	KEN	10.11.86	1		Den Haag	17 Mar 07
58:46		Mathew	Kisorio ¶	KEN	16.5.89	1		Philadelphia	18 Sep 11
58:47		Atsedu	Tsegay	ETH	17.12.91	1		Praha	31 Mar 12
58:48		Sammy	Kitwara	KEN	26.11.86	2		Philadelphia	18 Sep 11
58:48		Abreham	Cheroben	KEN	10.11.92	1		Valencia	19 Oct 14
58:52		Patrick	Makau	KEN	2.3.85	1		Ra's Al Khaymah	20 Feb 09
58:53	WR		Wanjiru			1		Ra's Al Khaymah	9 Feb 07
58:54		Stephen	Kibet	KEN	9.11.86	1		Den Haag	11 Mar 12
58:54		Geoffrey	Kamworor	KEN	28.11.92	1		Ra's Al-Khaymah	15 Feb 13
58:55	WR	Haile	Gebrselassie (10)	ETH	18.4.73	1		Tempe	15 Jan 06
58:56			Makau			1		Berlin	1 Apr 07
58:56	dh	Martin	Mathathi	KEN	25.12.85	1	GNR	South Shields	18 Sep 11
58:56		Stanley	Biwott	KEN	21.4.86	2		Ra's Al-Khaymah	15 Feb 13
58:58			Kitwara			1		Rotterdam	13 Sep 09
58:58		Geoffrey	Mutai	KEN	7.10.81	3		Ra's Al-Khaymah	15 Feb 13
58:59			Z Tadese			1	WCh	Udine	14 Oct 07
58:59		Wilson	Kipsang	KEN	15.3.82	2		Ra's Al Khaymah	20 Feb 09
59:01		Kenneth	Kipkemoi	KEN	2.8.84	2		Valencia	19 Oct 14
59:02			Makau			2	WCh	Udine	14 Oct 07
59:02		Jonathan	Maiyo	KEN	5.5.88	2		Den Haag	11 Mar 12
59:05	dh		Tadese			1	GNR	South Shields	18 Sep 05
59:05		Evans	Cheruiyot	KEN	10.5.82	3	WCh	Udine	14 Oct 07
59:05		Ezekiel	Chebii	KEN	3.1.91	1		Lille	1 Sep 12
59:06	dh	Paul	Tergat	KEN	17.6.69	1		Lisboa	26 Mar 00
59:06	dh		Kipsang			1	GNR	South Shields	16 Sep 12
59:06			G Mutai			1		Udine	22 Sep 13
59:06		Guye	Adola (20)	ETH	20.10.90	1		New Delhi	23 Nov 14
59:07		Paul	Kosgei	KEN	22.4.78	1		Berlin	2 Apr 06
59:07	dh	Micah	Kogo	KEN	3.6.86	2	GNR	South Shields	16 Sep 12
59:07			Kamworor			2		New Delhi	23 Nov 14
(32/22)									
59:09		James Kipsang	Kwambai	KEN	28.2.83	3		Rotterdam	13 Sep 09
59:10		Bernard	Kipyego	KEN	16.7.86	4		Rotterdam	13 Sep 09
59:10		Bernard	Koech	KEN	31.1.88	2		Lille	1 Sep 12
59:11		Mosinet	Geremew	ETH	12.2.92	3		New Delhi	23 Nov 14
59:12		Cyprian	Kotut	KEN	.92	4		New Delhi	23 Nov 14
59:14		Dennis	Kimetto	KEN	22.1.84	1		Berlin	1 Apr 12
59:14		Leonard Patrick	Komon	KEN	10.1.88	1		Berlin	30 Mar 14
59:14		Bidan	Karoki	KEN	21.8.90	1		København	13 Sep 15
		(30)							
59:15		Deriba	Merga	ETH	26.10.80	1		New Delhi	9 Nov 08
59:15		Wilson	Chebet	KEN	12.7.85	5		Rotterdam	13 Sep 09
59:15		Wilson	Kiprop	KEN	14.4.87	2		Berlin	1 Apr 12
59:19		Tilahun	Regassa	ETH	18.1.90	1		Abu Dhabi	7 Jan 10
59:19		Robert	Chemosin	KEN	1.2.89	2		Ostia	3 Mar 13
59:20	dh	Hendrick	Ramaala	RSA	2.2.72	2		Lisboa	26 Mar 00

Mark	Wind	Name		Nat	Born	Pos	Meet	Venue	Date
59:20		Moses	Mosop	KEN	17.7.85	1	Stra	Milano	21 Mar 10
59:20		Simon	Cheprot	KEN	2.7.93	3		Ostia	3 Mar 13
59:20		Berhanu	Legesse	ETH	11.9.94	1		New Delhi	29 Nov 15
59:21	dh	Robert Kipkoech	Cheruiyot	KEN	26.9.78	2		Lisboa	13 Mar 05
		(40)							
59:21		Samuel	Tsegay	ERI	24.2.88	2	WCh	København	29 Mar 14
59:22		Feyisa	Lilesa	ETH	1.2.90	1		Houston	15 Jan 12
59:22		Peter Cheruiyot	Kirui	KEN	2.1.88	1		Praha	5 Apr 14
59:22dh		Mohamed	Farah	GBR	23.3.83	1	GNR	South Shields	13 Sep 15
59:23		John Kiprotich	Chemisto	KEN	5.6.83	6		Rotterdam	13 Sep 09
59:25		Pius	Kirop	KEN	8.1.90	4		Berlin	1 Apr 12
59:25		Eliud	Kipchoge	KEN	5.11.84	3		Lille	1 Sep 12
59:25		Aziz	Lahbabi	MAR	3.2.91	1		Ostia	2 Mar 14
59:26		Francis	Kibiwott	KEN	15.9.78	2		Berlin	1 Apr 07
59:26		Edwin Kiprop	Kiptoo	KEN	14.8.93	4		New Delhi	29 Nov 15
	(50)	100th man 59:51, 200th man 60:19, 300th 60:41, 400th 60:57, 500th 61:08							
Short course:		58:51 Paul	Tergat	KEN	17.6.69	1	Stra	Milano 49m sh	30 Mar 96
Excessively downhill:		58:42 Bernard	Koech	KEN	31.1.88	1		San Diego (dh 86m)	2 Jun 13

MARATHON

In second column: P = point-to-point or start/finish more than 30% apart, D = point-to-point and downhill over 1/1000

Mark	Wind	Name		Nat	Born	Pos	Meet	Venue	Date
2:02:57	WR	Dennis	Kimetto	KEN	22.1.84	1		Berlin	28 Sep 14
2:03:13		Emmanuel	Mutai	KEN	12.10.84	2		Berlin	28 Sep 14
2:03:23	WR	Wilson	Kipsang	KEN	15.3.82	1		Berlin	29 Sep 13
2:03:38	WR	Patrick	Makau	KEN	2.3.85	1		Berlin	25 Sep 11
2:03:42			W Kipsang			1		Frankfurt	30 Oct 11
2:03:45			Kimetto			1		Chicago	13 Oct 13
2:03:52			Mutai			2		Chicago	13 Oct 13
2:03:59	WR	Haile	Gebrselassie	ETH	18.4.73	1		Berlin	28 Sep 08
2:04:00		Eliud	Kipchoge	KEN	5.11.84	1		Berlin	27 Sep 15
2:04:05			Kipchoge			2		Berlin	29 Sep 13
2:04:11			Kipchoge			1		Chicago	12 Oct 14
2:04:15		Geoffrey	Mutai	KEN	7.10.81	1		Berlin	30 Sep 12
2:04:16			Kimetto			2		Berlin	30 Sep 12
2:04:23		Ayele	Abshero	ETH	28.12.90	1		Dubai	27 Jan 12
2:04:26	WR		Gebrselassie			1		Berlin	30 Sep 07
2:04:27		Duncan	Kibet	KEN	25.4.78	1		Rotterdam	5 Apr 09
2:04:27		James Kipsang	Kwambai (10)	KEN	28.2.83	2		Rotterdam	5 Apr 09
2:04:28		Sammy	Kitwara	KEN	26.11.86	2		Chicago	12 Oct 14
2:04:29			Kipsang			1		London	13 Apr 14
2:04:32		Tsegaye	Mekonnen	ETH	15.6.95	1		Dubai	24 Jan 14
2:04:32		Dickson	Chumba	KEN	27.10.86	3		Chicago	12 Oct 14
2:04:38		Tsegaye	Kebede	ETH	15.1.87	1		Chicago	7 Oct 12
2:04:40			E Mutai			1		London	17 Apr 11
2:04:42			Kipchoge			1		London	26 Apr 15
2:04:44			W Kipsang			1		London	22 Apr 12
2:04:45		Lelisa	Desisa	ETH	14.1.90	1		Dubai	25 Jan 13
2:04:47			W Kipsang			2		London	26 Apr 15
2:04:48			Makau			1		Rotterdam	11 Apr 10
2:04:48		Yemane	Tsegay	ETH	8.4.85	1		Rotterdam	15 Apr 12
2:04:48		Berhanu	Shiferaw	ETH	31.5.93	2		Dubai	25 Jan 13
2:04:49		Tadesse	Tola	ETH	31.10.87	3		Dubai	25 Jan 13
2:04:50		Dino	Sefir	ETH	28.5.88	2		Dubai	27 Jan 12
2:04:50		Getu	Feleke	ETH	28.11.86	2		Rotterdam	15 Apr 12
		(33/20)							
2:04:52		Feyisa	Lilesa	ETH	1.2.90	2		Chicago	7 Oct 12
2:04:52		Endeshaw	Negesse	ETH	13.3.88	4		Dubai	25 Jan 13
2:04:53		Bernard	Koech	KEN	31.1.88	5		Dubai	25 Jan 13
2:04:54		Markos	Geneti	ETH	30.5.84	3		Dubai	27 Jan 12
2:04:55	WR	Paul	Tergat	KEN	17.6.69	1		Berlin	28 Sep 03
2:04:55		Stanley	Biwott	KEN	21.4.86	2		London	13 Apr 14
2:04:56		Sammy	Korir	KEN	12.12.71	2		Berlin	28 Sep 03
2:04:56		Jonathan	Maiyo	KEN	5.5.88	4		Dubai	27 Jan 12
2:05:03		Moses	Mosop	KEN	17.7.85	3		Rotterdam	15 Apr 12
2:05:04		Abel	Kirui	KEN	4.6.82	3		Rotterdam	5 Apr 09
		(30)							
2:05:04		Kenenisa	Bekele	ETH	13.6.82	1		Paris	6 Apr 14
2:05:10		Samuel	Wanjiru	KEN	10.11.86	1		London	26 Apr 09
2:05:13		Vincent	Kipruto	KEN	13.9.87	3		Rotterdam	11 Apr 10
2:05:15		Martin	Lel	KEN	29.10.78	1		London	13 Apr 08

Mark	Wind	Name		Nat	Born	Pos	Meet	Venue	Date
2:05:16		Levi	Matebo Omari	KEN	3.11.89	2		Frankfurt	30 Oct 11
2:05:21		Eliud	Kiptanui	KEN	6.6.89	2		Berlin	27 Sep 15
2:05:25		Bazu	Worku	ETH	15.9.90	3		Berlin	26 Sep 10
2:05:25		Albert	Matebor	KEN	20.12.80	3		Frankfurt	30 Oct 11
2:05:27		Jaouad	Gharib	MAR	22.5.72	3		London	26 Apr 09
2:05:27		Wilson	Chebet	KEN	12.7.85	1		Rotterdam	10 Apr 11
		(40)							
2:05:27		Tilahun	Regassa	ETH	18.1.90	3		Chicago	7 Oct 12
2:05:28		Hayle	Lemi	ETH	13.9.94	1		Dubai	23 Jan 15
2:05:30		Abderrahim	Goumri ¶	MAR	21.5.76	3		London	13 Apr 08
2:05:37	P	Wilson	Loyanae ¶	KEN	20.11.88	1		Seoul	18 Mar 12
2:05:38	WR	Khalid	Khannouchi	MAR/USA	22.12.71	1		London	14 Apr 02
2:05:38		Peter	Some	KEN	5.6.90	1		Paris	7 Apr 13
2:05:41		Yami	Dadi	ETH	.82	6		Dubai	27 Jan 12
2:05:42		Abdullah Dawit	Shami	ETH	16.7.84	7		Dubai	27 Jan 12
2:05:42		Deresse	Chimsa	ETH	21.11.76	8		Dubai	27 Jan 12
2:05:48		Jafred	Kipchumba	KEN	8.8.83	1		Eindhoven	9 Oct 11
		(50)	100th man 2:06:34, 200th 2:07:27, 300th 2:08:01, 400th 2:08:33, 500th 2:08:56						

Downhill point-to-point course – Boston marathon is downhill overall (139m) and sometimes strongly wind-aided.

Mark	Wind	Name		Nat	Born	Pos	Meet	Venue	Date
2:03:02		Geoffrey	Mutai	KEN	7.10.81	1		Boston	18 Apr 11
2:03:06		Moses	Mosop	KEN	17.7.85	2		Boston	18 Apr 11
2:04:53		Gebre-egziabher	Gebremariam	ETH	10.9.84	3		Boston	18 Apr 11
2:04:58		Ryan	Hall	USA	14.10.82	4		Boston	18 Apr 11

2000 METRES STEEPLECHASE

Mark	Wind	Name		Nat	Born	Pos	Meet	Venue	Date
5:10.68		Mahiedine	Mekhissi-Benabbad	FRA	15.3.85	1		Reims	30 Jun 10
5:13.47		Bouabdellah	Tahri	FRA	20.12.78	1		Tomblaine	25 Jun 10
5:14.43		Julius	Kariuki	KEN	12.6.61	1		Rovereto	21 Aug 90
5:14.53		Saïf Saaeed	Shaheen	QAT	15.10.82	1	SGP	Doha	13 May 05
5:16.22		Phillip	Barkutwo	KEN	6.10.66	2		Rovereto	21 Aug 90
5:16.46		Wesley	Kiprotich	KEN	31.7.79	2	SGP	Doha	13 May 05
5:16.85		Eliud	Barngetuny	KEN	20.5.73	1		Parma	13 Jun 95

3000 METRES STEEPLECHASE

Mark	Wind	Name		Nat	Born	Pos	Meet	Venue	Date
7:53.63	WR	Saïf Saaeed	Shaheen	KEN/QAT	15.10.82	1	VD	Bruxelles	3 Sep 04
7:53.64		Brimin	Kipruto	KEN	31.7.85	1	Herc	Monaco	22 Jul 11
7:54.31		Paul Kipsiele	Koech	KEN	10.11.81	1	GGala	Roma	31 May 12
7:55.28	WR	Brahim	Boulami ¶	MAR	20.4.72	1	VD	Bruxelles	24 Aug 01
7:55.51			Shaheen			1	VD	Bruxelles	26 Aug 05
7:55.72	WR	Bernard	Barmasai	KEN	6.5.74	1	ASV	Köln	24 Aug 97
7:55.76		Ezekiel	Kemboi	KEN	25.5.82	2	Herc	Monaco	22 Jul 11
7:56.16		Moses	Kiptanui	KEN	1.10.70	2	ASV	Köln	24 Aug 97
7:56.32			Shaheen			1	Tsik	Athína	3 Jul 06
7:56.34			Shaheen			1	GGala	Roma	8 Jul 05
7:56.37			P K Koech			2	GGala	Roma	8 Jul 05
7:56.54			Shaheen			1	WK	Zürich	18 Aug 06
7:56.58			P K Koech			1	DL	Doha	11 May 12
7:56.81		Richard	Mateelong	KEN	14.10.83	2	DL	Doha	11 May 12
7:56.94			Shaheen			1	WAF	Monaco	19 Sep 04
7:57.28			Shaheen			1	Tsik	Athína	14 Jun 05
7:57.29		Reuben	Kosgei	KEN	2.8.79	2	VD	Bruxelles	24 Aug 01
7:57.32			P K Koech			3	Herc	Monaco	22 Jul 11
7:57.38			Shaheen			1	WAF	Monaco	14 Sep 03
7:57.42			P K Koech			2	WAF	Monaco	14 Sep 03
7:58.09			Boulami			1	Herc	Monaco	19 Jul 02
7:58.10			S Cherono			2	Herc	Monaco	19 Jul 02
7:58.41		Jairus	Birech (10)	KEN	14.12.92	1	VD	Bruxelles	5 Sep 14
7:58.50			Boulami			1	WK	Zürich	17 Aug 01
7:58.66			S Cherono			3	VD	Bruxelles	24 Aug 01
7:58.80			P K Koech			1	VD	Bruxelles	14 Sep 07
7:58.83			Birech			1	DL	Saint-Denis	4 Jul 15
7:58.85			Kemboi			1	SGP	Doha	8 May 09
7:58.98			Barmasai			1	Herc	Monaco	4 Aug 99
7:59.03			Kemboi			1	DL	Saint-Denis	6 Jul 13
		(30/10)							
7:59.08	WR	Wilson	Boit Kipketer	KEN	6.10.73	1	WK	Zürich	13 Aug 97
8:00.09		Mahiedine	Mekhissi-Benabbad	FRA	15.3.85	2	DL	Saint-Denis	6 Jul 13
8:00.45		Evan	Jager	USA	8.3.89	2	DL	Saint-Denis	4 Jul 15
8:01.16		Conseslus	Kipruto	KEN	8.12.94	1	DL	Shanghai	18 May 13
8:01.18		Bouabdellah	Tahri	FRA	20.12.78	3	WCh	Berlin	18 Aug 09

Mark	Wind	Name		Nat	Born	Pos	Meet	Venue	Date
8:01.67		Abel	Mutai	KEN	2.10.88	2	GGala	Roma	31 May 12
8:01.69		Kipkirui	Misoi	KEN	23.12.78	4	VD	Bruxelles	24 Aug 01
8:03.41		Patrick	Sang	KEN	11.4.64	3	ASV	Köln	24 Aug 97
8:03.57		Ali	Ezzine	MAR	3.9.78	1	Gaz	Saint-Denis	23 Jun 00
8:03.57		Hillary	Yego	KEN	2.4.92	3	DL	Shanghai	18 May 13
8:03.74		Raymond	Yator	KEN	7.4.81	3	Herc	Monaco	18 Aug 00
		(20)							
8:03.81		Benjamin	Kiplagat	UGA	4.3.89	2	Athl	Lausanne	8 Jul 10
8:03.89		John	Kosgei	KEN	13.7.73	3	Herc	Monaco	16 Aug 97
8:04.95		Simon	Vroemen ¶	NED	11.5.69	2	VD	Bruxelles	26 Aug 05
8:05.01		Eliud	Barngetuny	KEN	20.5.73	1	Herc	Monaco	25 Jul 95
8:05.35 WR		Peter	Koech	KEN	18.2.58	1	DNG	Stockholm	3 Jul 89
8:05.37		Philip	Barkutwo	KEN	6.10.66	2		Rieti	6 Sep 92
8:05.4 WR		Henry	Rono	KEN	12.2.52	1		Seattle	13 May 78
8:05.43		Christopher	Kosgei	KEN	14.8.74	2	WK	Zürich	11 Aug 99
8:05.51		Julius	Kariuki	KEN	12.6.61	1	OG	Seoul	30 Sep 88
		(30)							
8:05.68		Wesley	Kiprotich	KEN	1.8.79	4	VD	Bruxelles	3 Sep 04
8:05.75		Mustafa	Mohamed	SWE	1.3.79	1	NA	Heusden-Zolder	28 Jul 07
8:05.88		Bernard	Mbugua Nganga	KEN	17.1.85	2	ISTAF	Berlin	11 Sep 11
8:05.99		Joseph	Keter	KEN	13.6.69	1	Herc	Monaco	10 Aug 96
8:06.13		Tareq Mubarak	Taher	BRN	24.3.84	3	Tsik	Athína	13 Jul 09
8:06.16		Roba	Gari	ETH	12.4.82	3	DL	Doha	11 May 12
8:06.77		Gideon	Chirchir	KEN	24.2.66	2	WK	Zürich	16 Aug 95
8:06.88		Richard	Kosgei	KEN	29.12.70	2	GPF	Monaco	9 Sep 95
8:06.96		Gilbert	Kirui	KEN	22.1.94	2	DL	London (OS)	27 Jul 13
8:07.02		Brahim	Taleb	MAR	16.2.85	2	NA	Heusden-Zolder	28 Jul 07
		(40)							
8:07.13		Paul	Kosgei	KEN	22.4.78	2	GP II	Saint-Denis	3 Jul 99
8:07.18		Obaid Moussa	Amer ¶	KEN/QAT	18.4.85	4	OG	Athína	24 Aug 04
8:07.44		Luis Miguel	Martín	ESP	11.1.72	2	VD	Bruxelles	30 Aug 02
8:07.59		Julius	Nyamu	KEN	1.12.77	5	VD	Bruxelles	24 Aug 01
8:07.62		Joseph	Mahmoud	FRA	13.12.55	1	VD	Bruxelles	24 Aug 84
8:07.75		Jonathan	Ndiku Muia	KEN	18.9.91	6	Herc	Monaco	22 Jul 11
8:07.96		Mark	Rowland	GBR	7.3.63	3	OG	Seoul	30 Sep 88
8:08.02 WR		Anders	Gärderud	SWE	28.8.46	1	OG	Montreal	28 Jul 76
8:08.12		Matthew	Birir	KEN	5.7.72	3	GGala	Roma	8 Jun 95
8:08.14		Sa'ad Shaddad	Al-Asmari	KSA	24.9.68	4	DNG	Stockholm	16 Jul 02
		(50)	100th man 8:12.25, 200th 8:18.02, 300th 8:21.41, 400th 8:23.80, 500th 8:25.94						

7:53.63 Shaheen formerly Stephen Cherono KEN

Drugs disqualification: 7:53.17	Brahim Boulami ¶	MAR	20.4.72	1	WK	Zürich	16 Aug 02

110 METRES HURDLES

Mark	Wind	Name		Nat	Born	Pos	Meet	Venue	Date
12.80 WR	0.3	Aries	Merritt	USA	24.7.85	1	VD	Bruxelles	7 Sep 12
12.87 WR	0.9	Dayron	Robles	CUB	19.11.86	1	GS	Ostrava	12 Jun 08
12.88 WR	1.1		Liu Xiang	CHN	13.7.83	1rA	Athl	Lausanne	11 Jul 06
12.88	0.5		Robles			1	Gaz	Saint-Denis	18 Jul 08
12.89	0.5	David	Oliver	USA	24.4.82	1	DL	Saint-Denis	16 Jul 10
12.90	1.1	Dominique	Arnold	USA	14.9.73	2rA	Athl	Lausanne	11 Jul 06
12.90	1.6		Oliver			1	Pre	Eugene	3 Jul 10
12.91 WR	0.5	Colin	Jackson	GBR	18.2.67	1	WCh	Stuttgart	20 Aug 93
12.91 WR	0.3		Liu Xiang			1	OG	Athína	27 Aug 04
12.91	0.2		Robles			1	DNG	Stockholm	22 Jul 08
12.92 WR	-0.1	Roger	Kingdom	USA	26.8.62	1	WK	Zürich	16 Aug 89
12.92	0.9	Allen	Johnson	USA	1.3.71	1	NC	Atlanta	23 Jun 96
12.92	0.2		Johnson			1	VD	Bruxelles	23 Aug 96
12.92	1.5		Liu Xiang			1	GP	New York	2 Jun 07
12.92	0.0		Robles			1	WAF	Stuttgart	23 Sep 07
12.92	-0.3		Merritt			1	OG	London (OS)	8 Aug 12
12.93 WR	-0.2	Renaldo	Nehemiah	USA	24.3.59	1	WK	Zürich	19 Aug 81
12.93	0.0		Johnson			1	WCh	Athína	7 Aug 97
12.93	-0.6		Liu Xiang			1	WAF	Stuttgart	9 Sep 06
12.93	0.1		Robles			1	OG	Beijing	21 Aug 08
12.93	1.7		Oliver			1	NC	Des Moines	27 Jun 10
12.93	-0.3		Oliver			1	WK	Zürich	19 Aug 10
12.93	1.2		Merritt			1	NC/OT	Eugene	30 Jun 12
12.93	0.6		Merritt			1	LGP	London (CP)	13 Jul 12
12.93	0.0		Merritt			1	Herc	Monaco	20 Jul 12
12.94	1.6	Jack	Pierce (10)	USA	23.9.62	1s2	NC	Atlanta	22 Jun 96
12.94	1.8		Oliver			1	Pre	Eugene	4 Jun 11

Mark	Wind	Name		Nat	Born	Pos	Meet	Venue	Date
12.94	0.1		Merritt			1s2	OG	London (OS)	8 Aug 12
12.94	0.8	Hansle	Parchment	JAM	17.6.90	1	DL	Saint-Denis	5 Jul 14
12.94	0.5	Orlando	Ortega	CUB/ESP	29.7.91	1	DL	Saint-Denis	4 Jul 15
		(30/12)							
12.95	1.5	Terrence	Trammell	USA	23.11.78	2	GP	New York	2 Jun 07
12.95	0.2	Pascal	Martinot-Lagarde	FRA	22.9.91	1	Herc	Monaco	18 Jul 14
12.97	1.0	Ladji	Doucouré	FRA	28.3.83	1	NC	Angers	15 Jul 05
12.97	1.0	Omar	McLeod	JAM	25.4.94	1	NC	Kingston	27 Jun 15
12.98	0.6	Mark	Crear	USA	2.10.68	1		Zagreb	5 Jul 99
12.98	1.5	Jason	Richardson	USA	4.4.86	1s3	NC/OT	Eugene	30 Jun 12
12.98	0.2	Sergey	Shubenkov	RUS	4.10.90	1	WCh	Beijing	28 Aug 15
12.99	1.2	Ronnie	Ash	USA	2.7.88	1s1	NC	Sacramento	29 Jun 14
		(20)							
13.00	0.5	Anthony	Jarrett	GBR	13.8.68	2	WCh	Stuttgart	20 Aug 93
13.00	0.6	Anier	García	CUB	9.3.76	1	OG	Sydney	25 Sep 00
13.01	0.3	Larry	Wade ¶	USA	22.11.74	1rA	Athl	Lausanne	2 Jul 99
13.02	1.5	Ryan	Wilson	USA	19.12.80	3	GP	New York	2 Jun 07
13.02	1.7	David	Payne	USA	24.7.82	3	WCh	Osaka	31 Aug 07
13.03	-0.2	Greg	Foster	USA	4.8.58	2	WK	Zürich	19 Aug 81
13.03	1.0	Reggie	Torian	USA	22.4.75	1	NC	New Orleans	21 Jun 98
13.05	1.4	Tony	Dees ¶	USA	6.8.63	1		Vigo	23 Jul 91
13.05	-0.8	Florian	Schwarthoff	GER	7.5.68	1	NC	Bremen	2 Jul 95
13.08	1.2	Mark	McKoy	CAN	10.12.61	1	BNP	Villeneuve-d'Ascq	2 Jul 93
		(30)							
13.08	0.0	Stanislav	Olijar	LAT	22.3.79	2	Athl	Lausanne	1 Jul 03
13.08	1.2	Jeff	Porter	USA	27.11.85	3	NC/OT	Eugene	30 Jun 12
13.09	2.0	Antwon	Hicks	USA	12.3.83	2s2	NC/OT	Eugene	6 Jul 08
13.11	0.5	Aleec	Harris	USA	31.10.90	4	DL	Saint-Denis	4 Jul 15
13.12	1.5	Falk	Balzer ¶	GER	14.12.73	2	EC	Budapest	22 Aug 98
13.12	1.0	Duane	Ross ¶	USA	5.12.72	3	WCh	Sevilla	25 Aug 99
13.12	1.9	Anwar	Moore	USA	5.3.79	1	ModR	Modesto	5 May 07
13.13	1.6	Igor	Kovác	SVK	12.5.69	1	DNG	Stockholm	7 Jul 97
13.13	2.0	Dexter	Faulk	USA	14.4.84	2	GS	Ostrava	17 Jun 09
13.14	0.1	Ryan	Brathwaite	BAR	6.6.88	1	WCh	Berlin	20 Aug 09
		(40)							
13.14	0.0	Andrew	Riley	JAM	6.9.88	4	DL	Saint-Denis	6 Jul 13
13.15	0.3	Robin	Korving	NED	29.7.74	5rA	Athl	Lausanne	2 Jul 99
13.15	0.1	Dwight	Thomas	JAM	23.9.80	2	Bisl	Oslo	9 Jun 11
13.15	-0.3	Garfield	Darien	FRA	22.12.87	1s3	EC	Helsinki	1 Jul 12
13.16	1.3	Devon	Allen	USA	12.12.94	1	NCAA	Eugene	14 Jun 14
13.16	0.4	William	Sharman	GBR	12.9.84	1s1	EC	Zürich	14 Aug 14
13.16	-0.1	Dimitri	Bascou	FRA	20.7.87	1s3	WCh	Beijing	27 Aug 15
13.17	-0.4	Sam	Turner	USA	17.6.57	2	Pepsi	Los Angeles (Ww)	15 May 83
13.17	0.0	Tonie	Campbell	USA	14.6.60	3	WK	Zürich	17 Aug 88
13.17	0.5	Courtney	Hawkins	USA	11.7.67	1		Ingolstadt	26 Jul 98
13.17	0.4	Mike	Fenner	GER	24.4.71	1		Leverkusen	9 Aug 98
13.17	-0.1	Maurice	Wignall	JAM	17.4.76	1s1	OG	Athína	26 Aug 04
13.17	0.8	Mikel	Thomas	TTO	23.11.87	2	PAm	Toronto	24 Jul 15
		(53)	100th man 13.27, 200th 13.41, 300th 13.49, 400th 13.55, 500th 13.60						

Rolling start but accepted by race officials

Mark	Wind	Name		Nat	Born	Pos	Meet	Venue	Date
13.10A	2.0	Falk	Balzer ¶	GER	14.12.73	1	WCp	Johannesburg	13 Sep 98

Doubtful timing: Scheessel 4 Jun 95 +1.3 1. Mike Fenner GER 24.4.71 13.06, 2. Eric Kaiser ¶ GER 7.3.71 13.08

Wind-assisted marks *Performances to 12.94, performers to 13.17*

Mark	Wind	Name		Nat	Born	Pos	Meet	Venue	Date
12.87	2.6	Roger	Kingdom	USA	26.8.62	1	WCp	Barcelona	10 Sep 89
12.87	2.4		Liu Xiang	CHN	13.7.83	1	Pre	Eugene	2 Jun 12
12.89	3.2	David	Oliver	USA	24.4.82	1s1	NC/OT	Eugene	6 Jul 08
12.91	3.5	Renaldo	Nehemiah	USA	24.3.59	1	NCAA	Champaign	1 Jun 79
12.94A	2.8		Jackson			1rA		Sestriere	31 Jul 94
12.98	3.1	Ronnie	Ash	USA	2.7.88	1	NACAC	Miramar	9 Jul 10
13.00	2.6	Anwar	Moore	USA	5.3.79	1	DrakeR	Des Moines	28 Apr 07
13.05	3.6	Ryan	Brathwaite	BAR	6.6.88	1		Austin	2 May 09
13.06	2.1	Mark	McKoy	CAN	10.12.61	1	Gugl	Linz	13 Aug 92
13.12	2.4	Dexter	Faulk	USA	14.4.84	4	Pre	Eugene	2 Jun 12
13.14	2.9	Igor	Kazanov	LAT	24.9.63	1r1	Znam	Leningrad	8 Jun 86
13.14	4.7	Lawrence	Clarke	GBR	12.3.90	1h1		Madrid	7 Jul 12
13.14	3.8	Wayne	Davis	TTO	22.8.91	1	NCAA	Eugene	8 Jun 13
13.15	2.1	Courtney	Hawkins	USA	11.7.67	1		Salamanca	10 Jul 98

Hand timing

Mark	Wind	Name		Nat	Born	Pos	Meet	Venue	Date
12.8	1.0	Renaldo	Nehemiah	USA	24.3.59	1		Kingston	11 May 79
12.9	0.0	Yordan	O'Farrill	CUB	9.2.93	1	Barr	La Habana	23 May 14

Mark	Wind	Name		Nat	Born	Pos	Meet	Venue	Date
Wind-assisted									
12.8	2.4	Colin	Jackson	GBR	18.2.67	1		Sydney	10 Jan 90
12.9	4.1	Mark	Crear	USA	2.10.68	1rA	S&W	Modesto	8 May 93
12.9	3.1	William	Sharman	GBR	12.9.84	1r2		Madrid	2 Jul 10

400 METRES HURDLES

Mark		Name		Nat	Born	Pos	Meet	Venue	Date
46.78	WR	Kevin	Young	USA	16.9.66	1	OG	Barcelona	6 Aug 92
47.02	WR	Edwin	Moses	USA	31.8.55	1		Koblenz	31 Aug 83
47.03		Bryan	Bronson ¶	USA	9.9.72	1	NC	New Orleans	21 Jun 98
47.10		Samuel	Matete	ZAM	27.7.68	1rA	WK	Zürich	7 Aug 91
47.13	WR		Moses			1		Milano	3 Jul 80
47.14			Moses			1	Athl	Lausanne	14 Jul 81
47.17			Moses			1	ISTAF	Berlin	8 Aug 80
47.18			Young			1	WCh	Stuttgart	19 Aug 93
47.19		Andre	Phillips	USA	5.9.59	1	OG	Seoul	25 Sep 88
47.23		Amadou	Dia Bâ	SEN	22.9.58	2	OG	Seoul	25 Sep 88
47.24		Kerron	Clement	USA	31.10.85	1	NC	Carson	26 Jun 05
47.25		Félix	Sánchez	DOM	30.8.77	1	WCh	Saint-Denis	29 Aug 03
47.25		Angelo	Taylor	USA	29.12.78	1	OG	Beijing	18 Aug 08
47.27			Moses			1	ISTAF	Berlin	21 Aug 81
47.30		Bershawn	Jackson (10)	USA	8.5.83	1	WCh	Helsinki	9 Aug 05
47.32			Moses			1		Koblenz	29 Aug 84
47.32			Jackson			1	NC	Des Moines	26 Jun 10
47.35			Sánchez			1rA	WK	Zürich	16 Aug 02
47.37			Moses			1	WCp	Roma	4 Sep 81
47.37			Moses			1	WK	Zürich	24 Aug 83
47.37			Moses			1	NC/OT	Indianapolis	17 Jul 88
47.37			Young			1	Athl	Lausanne	7 Jul 93
47.37		Stéphane	Diagana	FRA	23.7.69	1	Athl	Lausanne	5 Jul 95
47.38			Moses			1	Athl	Lausanne	2 Sep 86
47.38		Danny	Harris ¶	USA	7.9.65	1	Athl	Lausanne	10 Jul 91
47.38			Sánchez			1rA	WK	Zürich	17 Aug 01
47.39			Clement			1	NC	Indianapolis	24 Jun 06
47.40			Young			1	WK	Zürich	19 Aug 92
47.42			Young			1	ASV	Köln	16 Aug 92
47.43			Moses			1	ASV	Köln	28 Aug 83
47.43		James	Carter	USA	7.5.78	2	WCh	Helsinki	9 Aug 05
		(31/13)							
47.48		Harald	Schmid	FRG	29.9.57	1	EC	Athína	8 Sep 82
47.53		Hadi Soua'an	Al-Somaily	KSA	21.8.76	2	OG	Sydney	27 Sep 00
47.54		Derrick	Adkins	USA	2.7.70	2	Athl	Lausanne	5 Jul 95
47.54		Fabrizio	Mori	ITA	28.6.69	2	WCh	Edmonton	10 Aug 01
47.60		Winthrop	Graham	JAM	17.11.65	1	WK	Zürich	4 Aug 93
47.63		Johnny	Dutch	USA	20.1.89	2	NC	Des Moines	26 Jun 10
47.66A		L.J. 'Louis'	van Zyl	RSA	20.7.85	1		Pretoria	25 Feb 11
		(20)							
47.67		Bennie	Brazell	USA	2.6.82	2	NCAA	Sacramento	11 Jun 05
47.69		Jehue	Gordon	TTO	15.12.91	1	WCh	Moskva	15 Aug 13
47.70		Michael	Tinsley	USA	21.4.84	2	WCh	Moskva	15 Aug 13
47.72		Javier	Culson	PUR	25.7.84	1		Ponce	8 May 10
47.75		David	Patrick	USA	12.6.60	4	NC/OT	Indianapolis	17 Jul 88
47.79		Nicholas	Bett	KEN	14.6.92	1	WCh	Beijing	25 Aug 15
47.81		Llewellyn	Herbert	RSA	21.7.77	3	OG	Sydney	27 Sep 00
47.82	WR	John	Akii-Bua	UGA	3.12.49	1	OG	München	2 Sep 72
47.82		Kriss	Akabusi	GBR	28.11.58	3	OG	Barcelona	6 Aug 92
47.82		Periklis	Iakovákis	GRE	24.3.79	2	GP	Osaka	6 May 06
		(30)							
47.84		Bayano	Kamani	PAN	17.4.80	2s1	WCh	Helsinki	7 Aug 05
47.84		David	Greene	GBR	11.4.86	2	DL	Saint-Denis	6 Jul 12
47.89		Dai	Tamesue	JPN	3.5.78	3	WCh	Edmonton	10 Aug 01
47.91		Calvin	Davis	USA	2.4.72	1s2	OG	Atlanta	31 Jul 96
47.92		Aleksandr	Vasilyev	BLR	26.7.61	2	ECp	Moskva	17 Aug 85
47.93		Kenji	Narisako	JPN	25.7.84	3	GP	Osaka	6 May 06
47.93		Jeshua	Anderson	USA	22.6.89	1	NC	Eugene	26 Jun 11
47.93		Omar	Cisneros	CUB	19.11.89	1s3	WCh	Moskva	13 Aug 13
47.94		Eric	Thomas	USA	1.12.73	1	GGala	Roma	30 Jun 00
47.97		Maurice	Mitchell	USA	14.5.71	2rA	WK	Zürich	14 Aug 96
		(40)							
47.97		Joey	Woody	USA	22.5.73	3	NC	New Orleans	21 Jun 98
47.98		Sven	Nylander	SWE	1.1.62	4	OG	Atlanta	1 Aug 96

Mark	Wind	Name		Nat	Born	Pos	Meet	Venue	Date
48.00		Danny	McFarlane	JAM	14.2.72	1s2	OG	Athína	24 Aug 04
48.02A		Ockert	Cilliers	RSA	21.4.81	1		Pretoria	20 Feb 04
48.04		Eronilde	de Araújo	BRA	31.12.70	2	Nik	Nice	12 Jul 95
48.05		Ken	Harnden	ZIM	31.3.73	1	GP	Paris (C)	29 Jul 98
48.05		Kemel	Thompson	JAM	25.9.74	1	GP	London (CP)	8 Aug 03
48.05		Isa	Phillips	JAM	22.4.84	1	NC	Kingston	27 Jun 09
48.05		Emir	Bekric	SRB	14.3.91	3	WCh	Moskva	15 Aug 13
48.05		Denis	Kudryavtsev	RUS	13.4.92	2	WCh	Beijing	25 Aug 15
		(50)	100th man 48.47, 200th man 48.98, 300th man 49.25, 400th 49.43, 500th 49.61						
Best at low altitude:		47.66	van Zyl	1	GS	Ostrava	31 May 11		
Drugs disqualification		47.15	Bronson ¶	1	GWG	Uniondale, NY	19 Jul 98		

HIGH JUMP

Mark	Wind	Name		Nat	Born	Pos	Meet	Venue	Date
2.45	WR	Javier	Sotomayor ¶	CUB	13.10.67	1		Salamanca	27 Jul 93
2.44	WR		Sotomayor			1	CAC	San Juan	29 Jul 89
2.43	WR		Sotomayor			1		Salamanca	8 Sep 88
2.43i			Sotomayor			1	WI	Budapest	4 Mar 89
2.43		Mutaz Essa	Barshim	QAT	24.6.91	1	VD	Bruxelles	5 Sep 14
2.42	WR	Patrik	Sjöberg	SWE	5.1.65	1	DNG	Stockholm	30 Jun 87
2.42i	WR	Carlo	Thränhardt	FRG	5.7.57	1		Berlin	26 Feb 88
2.42			Sotomayor			1		Sevilla	5 Jun 94
2.42i		Ivan	Ukhov	RUS	29.3.86	1		Praha	25 Feb 14
2.42		Bohdan	Bondarenko	UKR	30.8.89	1	adidas	New York	14 Jun 14
2.42			Barshim			2	adidas	New York	14 Jun 14
2.41	WR	Igor	Paklin	KGZ	15.6.63	1	WUG	Kobe	4 Sep 85
2.41i			Sjöberg			1		Pireás	1 Feb 87
2.41i			Sotomayor			1	WI	Toronto	14 Mar 93
2.41			Sotomayor			1	NC	La Habana	25 Jun 94
2.41			Sotomayor			1	TSB	London (CP)	15 Jul 94
2.41			Bondarenko			1	Athl	Lausanne	4 Jul 13
2.41			Bondarenko			1	WCh	Moskva	15 Aug 13
2.41i			Ukhov			1		Chelyabinsk	16 Jan 14
2.41			Ukhov			1	DL	Doha	9 May 14
2.41			Barshim			1	GGala	Roma	5 Jun 14
2.41			Barshim			1		Eberstadt	22 Aug 14
2.41i			Barshim			1		Athlone	18 Feb 15
2.41		(24/7)	Barshim			1	Pre	Eugene	30 May 15
2.40	WR	Rudolf	Povarnitsyn	UKR	13.6.62	1		Donetsk	11 Aug 85
2.40		Sorin	Matei	ROU	6.7.63	1	PTS	Bratislava	20 Jun 90
2.40i		Hollis	Conway (10)	USA	8.1.67	1	WI	Sevilla	10 Mar 91
2.40		Charles	Austin	USA	19.12.67	1	WK	Zürich	7 Aug 91
2.40		Vyacheslav	Voronin	RUS	5.4.74	1	BrGP	London (CP)	5 Aug 00
2.40i		Stefan	Holm	SWE	25.5.76	1	EI	Madrid	6 Mar 05
2.40i		Aleksey	Dmitrik	RUS	12.4.84	1		Arnstadt	8 Feb 14
2.40		Derek	Drouin	CAN	6.3.90	1	DrakeR	Des Moines	25 Apr 14
2.40		Andriy	Protsenko	UKR	20.5.88	2	Athl	Lausanne	3 Jul 14
2.40	24 more performances: Sotomayor 13, Bondarenko 4, Sjöberg, Ukhov, Barshim 2, Thränhardt1 for (57/16)								
2.39	WR		Zhu Jianhua	CHN	29.5.63	1		Eberstadt	10 Jun 84
2.39i		Dietmar	Mögenburg	FRG	15.8.61	1		Köln	24 Feb 85
2.39i		Ralf	Sonn	GER	17.1.67	1		Berlin	1 Mar 91
2.38i		Gennadiy	Avdeyenko	UKR	4.11.63	2	WI	Indianapolis	7 Mar 87
		(20)							
2.38		Sergey	Malchenko	RUS	2.11.63	1		Banská Bystrica	4 Sep 88
2.38		Dragutin	Topic ¶	YUG	12.3.71	1		Beograd	1 Aug 93
2.38i		Steve	Smith	GBR	29.3.73	2		Wuppertal	4 Feb 94
2.38i		Wolf-Hendrik	Beyer	GER	14.2.72	1		Weinheim	18 Mar 94
2.38		Troy	Kemp	BAH	18.6.66	1	Nik	Nice	12 Jul 95
2.38		Artur	Partyka	POL	25.7.69	1		Eberstadt	18 Aug 96
2.38i		Matt	Hemingway	USA	24.10.72	1	NC	Atlanta	4 Mar 00
2.38i		Yaroslav	Rybakov	RUS	22.11.80	1		Stockholm	15 Feb 05
2.38		Jacques	Freitag	RSA	11.6.82	1		Oudtshoorn	5 Mar 05
2.38		Andriy	Sokolovskyy	UKR	16.7.78	1	GGala	Roma	8 Jul 05
		(30)							
2.38i		Linus	Thörnblad	SWE	6.3.85	2	NC	Göteborg	25 Feb 07
2.38		Andrey	Silnov	RUS	9.9.84	1	LGP	London (CP)	25 Jul 08
2.38			Zhang Guowei	CHN	4.6.91	2	Pre	Eugene	30 May 15
2.37		Valeriy	Sereda	RUS	30.6.59	1		Rieti	2 Sep 84
2.37		Tom	McCants	USA	27.11.62	1	Owens	Columbus	8 May 88
2.37		Jerome	Carter	USA	25.3.63	2	Owens	Columbus	8 May 88
2.37		Sergey	Dymchenko	UKR	23.8.67	1		Kyiv	16 Sep 90

Mark Wind	Name		Nat	Born	Pos	Meet	Venue	Date
2.37i	Dalton	Grant	GBR	8.4.66	1	EI	Paris	13 Mar 94
2.37i	Jaroslav	Bába	CZE	2.9.84	2		Arnstadt	5 Feb 05
2.37	Jesse	Williams	USA	27.12.83	1	NC	Eugene	26 Jun 11
	(40)							
2.37	Robbie	Grabarz	GBR	3.10.87	3	Athl	Lausanne	23 Aug 12
2.37	Eric	Kynard	USA	3.2.91	2	Athl	Lausanne	4 Jul 13
2.37	Gianmarco	Tamberi	ITA	1.6.92	2		Eberstadt	2 Aug 15
2.36 WR	Gerd	Wessig	GDR	16.7.59	1	OG	Moskva	1 Aug 80
2.36	Sergey	Zasimovich	KZK	6.9.62	1		Tashkent	5 May 84
2.36	Eddy	Annys	BEL	15.12.58	1		Gent	26 May 85
2.36i	Jim	Howard	USA	11.9.59	1		Albuquerque	25 Jan 86
2.36i	Jan	Zvara	CZE	12.2.63	1	vGDR	Jablonec	14 Feb 87
2.36i	Gerd	Nagel	FRG	22.10.57	1		Sulingen	17 Mar 89
2.36	Nick	Saunders	BER	14.9.63	1	CG	Auckland	1 Feb 90
	(50)							
2.36	Doug	Nordquist	USA	20.12.58	2	NC	Norwalk	15 Jun 90
2.36	Georgi	Dakov	BUL	21.10.67	2	VD	Bruxelles	10 Aug 90
2.36	Lábros	Papakóstas	GRE	20.10.69	1	NC	Athína	21 Jun 92
2.36i	Steinar	Hoen	NOR	8.2.71	1		Balingen	12 Feb 94
2.36	Tim	Forsyth	AUS	17.8.73	1	NC	Melbourne	2 Mar 97
2.36	Sergey	Klyugin	RUS	24.3.74	1	WK	Zürich	12 Aug 98
2.36	Konstantin	Matusevich	ISR	25.2.71	1		Perth	5 Feb 00
2.36	Martin	Buss	GER	7.4.76	1	WCh	Edmonton	8 Aug 01
2.36	Aleksander	Walerianczyk	POL	1.9.82	1	EU23	Bydgoszcz	20 Jul 03
2.36	Michal	Bieniek	POL	17.5.84	1		Biala Podlaska	28 May 05
2.36i	Andrey	Tereshin	RUS	15.12.82	1	NC	Moskva	17 Feb 06
2.36A	Dusty	Jonas	USA	19.4.86	1	Big 12	Boulder	18 May 08
2.36	Aleksandr	Shustov	RUS	29.6.84	2	NC	Cheboksary	23 Jul 11
	(63)	100th man 2.34, 200th 2.31, 300th 2.30, 400th 2.28, 500th 2.27						

Best outdoor marks for athletes with indoor bests

Mark	Name	Pos	Meet	Venue	Date
2.41	Ukhov	1	DL	Doha	9 May 14
2.39	Conway	1	USOF	Norman	30 Jul 89
2.39	Ukhov	1	NC	Cheboksary	5 Jul 12
2.38	Avdeyenko	2=	WCh	Roma	6 Sep 87
2.37	Thränhardt	2		Rieti	2 Sep 84
2.37	Smith	1	WJ	Seoul	20 Sep 92
2.37	Holm	1		Athína	13 Jul 08
2.36	Mögenburg	3		Eberstadt	10 Jun 84
2.36	Howard	1		Rehlingen	8 Jun 87
2.36	Zvara	1		Praha	23 Aug 87
2.36	Grant	4	WCh	Tokyo	1 Sep 91
2.36	Hoen	1		Oslo	1 Jul 97
2.36	Bába	2=	GGala	Roma	8 Jul 05
2.36	Dmitrik	1	NC	Chelyabinsk	23 Jul 11

Ancillary jumps – en route to final marks

Mark	Name	Date
2.40	Sotomayor	8 Sep 88
2.30	Bondarenko	14 Jun 14
2.40	Sotomayor	29 Jul 89
2.40	Barshim	14 Jun 14
2.40	Sotomayor	5 Jun 94
2.40	Barshim	5 Sep 14

POLE VAULT

Mark Wind	Name		Nat	Born	Pos	Meet	Venue	Date
6.16i WR	Renaud	Lavillenie	FRA	18.9.86	1		Donetsk	15 Feb 14
6.15i WR	Sergey	Bubka	UKR	4.12.63	1		Donetsk	21 Feb 93
6.14i WIR		Bubka			1		Liévin	13 Feb 93
6.14A WIR		Bubka			1		Sestriere	31 Jul 94
6.13i WIR		Bubka			1		Berlin	21 Feb 92
6.13 WR		Bubka			1	TOTO	Tokyo	19 Sep 92
6.12i WIR		Bubka			1	Mast	Grenoble	23 Mar 91
6.12 WR		Bubka			1		Padova	30 Aug 92
6.11i WIR		Bubka			1		Donetsk	19 Mar 91
6.11 WR		Bubka			1		Dijon	13 Jun 92
6.10i WIR		Bubka			1		San Sebastián	15 Mar 91
6.10 WR		Bubka			1	MAI	Malmö	5 Aug 91
6.09 WR		Bubka			1		Formia	8 Jul 91
6.08i WIR		Bubka			1	NC	Volgograd	9 Feb 91
6.08 WR		Bubka			1	Znam	Moskva	9 Jun 91
6.08i		Lavillenie			1		Bydgoszcz	31 Jan 14
6.07 WR		Bubka			1	Super	Shizuoka	6 May 91
6.06 WR		Bubka			1	Nik	Nice	10 Jul 88
6.06i	Steve	Hooker	AUS	16.7.82	1		Boston (R)	7 Feb 09
6.05 WR		Bubka			1	PTS	Bratislava	9 Jun 88
6.05i		Bubka			1		Donetsk	17 Mar 90
6.05i		Bubka			1		Berlin	5 Mar 93
6.05		Bubka			1	GPF	London (CP)	10 Sep 93
6.05i		Bubka			1	Mast	Grenoble	6 Feb 94
6.05		Bubka			1	ISTAF	Berlin	30 Aug 94
6.05		Bubka			1	GPF	Fukuoka	13 Sep 97
6.05	Maksim	Tarasov	RUS	2.12.70	1	GP II	Athína	16 Jun 99
6.05	Dmitriy	Markov	BLR/AUS	14.3.75	1	WCh	Edmonton	9 Aug 01
6.05		Lavillenie			1	Pre	Eugene	30 May 15

MEN All-time

Mark	Wind	Name		Nat	Born	Pos	Meet	Venue	Date
6.04		Brad	Walker	USA	21.6.81	1	Pre	Eugene	8 Jun 08
6.04i			Lavillenie			1		Rouen	25 Jan 14
6.04i		(32/6)	Lavillenie			1	EI	Praha (O2)	7 Mar 15
6.03		Okkert	Brits	RSA	22.8.73	1	ASV	Köln	18 Aug 95
6.03		Jeff	Hartwig	USA	25.9.67	1		Jonesboro	14 Jun 00
6.02i		Rodion	Gataullin	RUS	23.11.65	1	NC	Gomel	4 Feb 89
6.01		Igor	Trandenkov	RUS	17.8.66	1	NC	Sankt Peterburg	4 Jul 96
		Hit bar hard, but kept it on with his hand illegally. Next best 5.95				1		Dijon	26 May 96
		(10)							
6.01		Tim	Mack	USA	15.9.72	1	WAF	Monaco	18 Sep 04
6.01		Yevgeniy	Lukyanenko	RUS	23.1.85	1	EAF	Bydgoszcz	1 Jul 08
6.01	sq	Björn	Otto	GER	16.10.77	1		Aachen	5 Sep 12
6.00		Tim	Lobinger	GER	3.9.72	1	ASV	Köln	24 Aug 97
6.00i		Jean	Galfione	FRA	9.6.71	1	WI	Maebashi	6 Mar 99
6.00i		Danny	Ecker	GER	21.7.77	1		Dortmund	11 Feb 01
6.00		Toby	Stevenson	USA	19.11.76	1eA	CalR	Modesto	8 May 04
6.00		Paul	Burgess	AUS	14.8.79	1		Perth	25 Feb 05
5.98		Lawrence	Johnson	USA	7.5.74	1		Knoxville	25 May 96
5.97		Scott	Huffman	USA	30.11.64	1	NC	Knoxville	18 Jun 94
		(20)							
5.96		Joe	Dial	USA	26.10.62	1		Norman	18 Jun 87
5.95		Andrei	Tivontchik	GER	13.7.70	1	ASV	Köln	16 Aug 96
5.95		Michael	Stolle	GER	17.12.74	1	Herc	Monaco	18 Aug 00
5.95		Romain	Mesnil	FRA	13.6.77	1		Castres	6 Aug 03
5.94i		Philippe	Collet	FRA	13.12.63	1	Mast	Grenoble	10 Mar 90
5.94		Raphael	Holzdeppe	GER	28.9.89	1	NC	Nürnberg	26 Jul 15
5.93i	WIR	Billy	Olson	USA	19.7.58	1		East Rutherford	8 Feb 86
5.93i		Tye	Harvey	USA	25.9.74	2	NC	Atlanta	3 Mar 01
5.93		Alex	Averbukh	ISR	1.10.74	1	GP	Madrid (C)	19 Jul 03
5.93		Shawnacy	Barber	CAN	27.5.94	2	DL	London (OS)	25 Jul 15
		(30)							
5.92		István	Bagyula	HUN	2.1.69	1	Gugl	Linz	5 Jul 91
5.92		Igor	Potapovich	KAZ	6.9.67	2		Dijon	13 Jun 92
5.92		Dean	Starkey	USA	27.3.67	1	Banes	São Paulo	21 May 94
5.92		Thiago	Braz da Silva	BRA	16.12.93	2		Baku	24 Jun 15
5.91	WR	Thierry	Vigneron	FRA	9.3.60	2	GGala	Roma	31 Aug 84
5.91i		Viktor	Ryzhenkov	UZB	25.8.66	2		San Sebastián	15 Mar 91
5.91A		Riaan	Botha	RSA	8.11.70	1		Pretoria	2 Apr 97
5.91		Pawel	Wojciechowski	POL	6.6.89	1		Szczecin	15 Aug 11
5.91		Malte	Mohr	GER	24.7.86	1		Ingolstadt	22 Jun 12
5.91		Konstadinos	Filippídis ¶	GRE	26.11.86	1	DL	Saint-Denis	4 Jul 15
		(40)							
5.90		Pierre	Quinon	FRA	20.2.62	2	Nik	Nice	16 Jul 85
5.90i		Ferenc	Salbert	HUN/FRA	5.8.60	1	Mast	Grenoble	14 Mar 87
5.90		Miroslaw	Chmara	POL	9.5.64	1	BNP	Villeneuve d'Ascq	27 Jun 88
5.90i		Grigoriy	Yegorov	KAZ	12.1.67	1		Yokohama	11 Mar 90
5.90		Denis	Petushinskiy ¶	RUS	28.6.67	1	Znam	Moskva	13 Jun 93
5.90i		Pyotr	Bochkaryov	RUS	3.11.67	1	EI	Paris (B)	12 Mar 94
5.90		Jacob	Davis	USA	29.4.78	1	TexR	Austin	4 Apr 98
5.90		Viktor	Chistyakov	RUS/AUS	9.2.75	1		Salamanca	15 Jul 99
5.90		Pavel	Gerasimov	RUS	29.5.79	1		Rüdlingen	12 Aug 00
5.90		Nick	Hysong (50)	USA	9.12.71	1	OG	Sydney	29 Sep 00
5.90		Giuseppe	Gibilisco	ITA	5.1.79	1	WCh	Saint-Denis	28 Aug 03
5.90i		Igor	Pavlov	RUS	18.7.79	1	EI	Madrid	5 Mar 05
5.90		Lázaro	Borges	CUB	19.6.86	2	WCh	Daegu	29 Aug 11
5.90i		Dmitriy	Starodubtsev	RUS	3.1.86	1		Chelyabinsk	18 Dec 11
5.90i		Piotr	Lisek	POL	16.8.92	1		Bad Oeynhausen	28 Feb 15
		(55)	100th man 5.81, 200th 5.72, 300th 5.65, 400th 5.60, 500th 5.55						

Best outdoor marks for athletes with lifetime bests indoors

6.00	Gataullin	1	Tokyo	16 Sep 89	5.93	Ecker	1	Ingolstadt	26 Jul 98
6.00	Hooker	1	Perth	27 Jan 08	5.90	Yegorov	2 WCh	Stuttgart	19 Aug 93
5.98	Galfione	1	Amiens	23 Jul 99	**Ancillary jump:**	6.05i	Bubka	13 Feb 93	

Exhibition or Market Square competitions

Mark	Name		Nat	Born	Pos	Venue	Date
6.00	Jean	Galfione	FRA	9.6.71	1	Besançon	23 May 97
5.95	Viktor	Chistiakov	RUS/AUS	9.2.75	1	Chiari	8 Sep 99
5.90	Pyotr	Bochkaryov	RUS	3.11.67	1	Karlskrona	28 Jun 96

LONG JUMP

Mark	Wind	Name		Nat	Born	Pos	Meet	Venue	Date
8.95 WR	0.3	Mike	Powell	USA	10.11.63	1	WCh	Tokyo	30 Aug 91
8.90A WR	2.0	Bob	Beamon	USA	29.8.46	1	OG	Ciudad de México	18 Oct 68
8.87	-0.2	Carl	Lewis	USA	1.7.61	*	WCh	Tokyo	30 Aug 91

Mark	Wind	Name		Nat	Born	Pos	Meet	Venue	Date
8.86A	1.9	Robert	Emmiyan	ARM	16.2.65	1		Tsakhkadzor	22 May 87
8.79	1.9		Lewis			1	TAC	Indianapolis	19 Jun 83
8.79i	-		Lewis			1		New York	27 Jan 84
8.76	1.0		Lewis			1	USOF	Indianapolis	24 Jul 82
8.76	0.8		Lewis			1	NC/OT	Indianapolis	18 Jul 88
8.75	1.7		Lewis			1	PAm	Indianapolis	16 Aug 87
8.74	1.4	Larry	Myricks ¶	USA	10.3.56	2	NC/OT	Indianapolis	18 Jul 88
8.74A	2.0	Erick	Walder	USA	5.11.71	1		El Paso	2 Apr 94
8.74	1.2	Dwight	Phillips	USA	1.10.77	1	Pre	Eugene	7 Jun 09
8.73	1.2	Irving	Saladino	PAN	23.1.83	1	FBK	Hengelo	24 May 08
8.72	-0.2		Lewis			1	OG	Seoul	26 Sep 88
8.71	-0.4		Lewis			1	Pepsi	Los Angeles (Ww)	13 May 84
8.71	0.1		Lewis			1	OT	Los Angeles	19 Jun 84
8.71	1.9	Iván	Pedroso	CUB	17.12.72	1		Salamanca	18 Jul 95
8.71i		Sebastian	Bayer (10)	GER	11.6.86	1	EI	Torino	8 Mar 09
8.70	0.8		Myricks			1	NC	Houston	17 Jun 89
8.70	0.7		Powell			1		Salamanca	27 Jul 93
8.70	1.6		Pedroso			1	WCh	Göteborg	12 Aug 95
8.68	1.0		Lewis			Q	OG	Barcelona	5 Aug 92
8.68	1.6		Pedroso			1		Lisboa	17 Jun 95
8.67	0.4		Lewis			1	WCh	Roma	5 Sep 87
8.67	-0.7		Lewis			1	OG	Barcelona	6 Aug 92
8.66	0.8		Lewis			*	MSR	Walnut	26 Apr 87
8.66	1.0		Myricks			1		Tokyo	23 Sep 87
8.66	0.9		Powell			1	BNP	Villeneuve d'Ascq	29 Jun 90
8.66A	1.4		Lewis			*		Sestriere	31 Jul 94
8.66	0.3		Pedroso			1		Linz	22 Aug 95
8.66	1.6	Loúis	Tsátoumas	GRE	12.2.82	1		Kalamáta	2 Jun 07
		(31/11)							
8.63	0.5	Kareem	Streete-Thompson	CAY/USA	30.3.73	1	GP II	Linz	4 Jul 94
8.62	0.7	James	Beckford	JAM	9.1.75	1		Orlando	5 Apr 97
8.59i		Miguel	Pate	USA	13.6.79	1	NC	New York	1 Mar 02
8.56i	-	Yago	Lamela	ESP	24.7.77	2	WI	Maebashi	7 Mar 99
8.56	0.2	Aleksandr	Menkov	RUS	7.12.90	1	WCh	Moskva	16 Aug 13
8.54	0.9	Lutz	Dombrowski	GDR	25.6.59	1	OG	Moskva	28 Jul 80
8.54	1.7	Mitchell	Watt	AUS	25.3.88	1	DNG	Stockholm	29 Jul 11
8.53	1.2	Jaime	Jefferson	CUB	17.1.62	1	Barr	La Habana	12 May 90
8.52	0.7	Savanté	Stringfellow	USA	6.11.78	1	NC	Stanford	21 Jun 02
		(20)							
8.52	1.8	Jeff	Henderson	USA	19.2.89	*	PAm	Toronto	22 Jul 15
8.51	1.7	Roland	McGhee	USA	15.10.71	2		São Paulo	14 May 95
8.51	1.7	Greg	Rutherford	GBR	17.11.86	1		Chula Vista	24 Apr 14
8.50	0.2	Llewellyn	Starks	USA	10.2.67	2		Rhede	7 Jul 91
8.50	1.3	Godfrey Khotso	Mokoena	RSA	6.3.85	2	GP	Madrid	4 Jul 09
8.49	2.0	Melvin	Lister	USA	29.8.77	1	SEC	Baton Rouge	13 May 00
8.49	0.6	Jai	Taurima	AUS	26.6.72	2	OG	Sydney	28 Sep 00
8.49	0.7	Christian	Reif	GER	24.10.84	1		Weinheim	31 May 14
8.48	0.8	Joe	Greene	USA	17.2.67	3		São Paulo	14 May 95
8.48	0.6	Mohamed Salim	Al-Khuwalidi	KSA	19.6.81	1		Sotteville-lès-Rouen	2 Jul 06
		(30)							
8.47	1.9	Kevin	Dilworth	USA	14.2.74	1		Abilene	9 May 96
8.47	0.9	John	Moffitt	USA	12.12.80	2	OG	Athína	26 Aug 04
8.47	-0.2	Andrew	Howe	ITA	12.5.85	2	WCh	Osaka	30 Aug 07
8.47	0.0		Li Jinzhe	CHN	1.9.89	1		Bad Langensalza	28 Jun 14
8.46	1.2	Leonid	Voloshin	RUS	30.3.66	1	NC	Tallinn	5 Jul 88
8.46	1.6	Mike	Conley	USA	5.10.62	2		Springfield	4 May 96
8.46	1.8	Cheikh Tidiane	Touré	SEN/FRA	25.1.70	1		Bad Langensalza	15 Jun 97
8.46	0.3	Ibrahin	Camejo	CUB	28.6.82	1		Bilbao	21 Jun 08
8.46	1.3	Luis	Rivera	MEX	21.6.87	1	WUG	Kazan	12 Jul 13
8.45	2.0	Nenad	Stekic	YUG	7.3.51	1	PO	Montreal	25 Jul 75
		(40)							
8.44	1.7	Eric	Metcalf	USA	23.1.68	1	NC	Tampa	17 Jun 88
8.43	0.8	Jason	Grimes	USA	10.9.59	*	NC	Indianapolis	16 Jun 85
8.43	1.8	Giovanni	Evangelisti	ITA	11.9.61	1		San Giovanni Valdarno	16 May 87
8.43i	-	Stanislav	Tarasenko	RUS	23.7.66	1		Moskva	26 Jan 94
8.43	0.1	Luis Felipe	Méliz	CUB/ESP	11.8.79	2	OD	Jena	3 Jun 00
8.43	-0.2	Ignisious	Gaisah	GHA/NED	20.6.83	2	GGala	Roma	14 Jul 06
8.42	0.4	Salim	Sdiri	FRA	26.10.78	1		Pierre-Bénite	12 Jun 09
8.41	1.5	Craig	Hepburn	BAH	10.12.69	1	NC	Nassau	17 Jun 93
8.41i	-	Kirill	Sosunov	RUS	1.11.75	2	WI	Paris (B)	8 Mar 97

Mark	Wind	Name		Nat	Born	Pos	Meet	Venue	Date
8.41	0.9	Zarck	Visser	RSA	15.9.89	1		Bad Langensalza	4 Jul 15
		(50)	100th man 8.33, 200th 8.23, 300th 8.17, 400th 8.13, 500th 8.09						

Best at low altitude: 8.61 1.3 Emmiyan 1 GWG Moskva 6 Jul 86 8.58 1.8 Walder 1 Springfield 4 May 86

Wind-assisted marks performances to 8.70, performers to 8.43

Mark	Wind	Name		Nat	Born	Pos	Meet	Venue	Date
8.99A	4.4	Mike	Powell	USA	10.11.63	1		Sestriere	21 Jul 92
8.96A	1.2+	Iván	Pedroso	CUB	17.12.72	1		Sestriere	29 Jul 95
8.95A	3.9		Powell			1		Sestriere	31 Jul 94
8.91	2.9	Carl	Lewis	USA	1.7.61	2	WCh	Tokyo	30 Aug 91
8.90	3.7		Powell			1	S&W	Modesto	16 May 92
8.79	3.0		Pedroso			1	Barr	La Habana	21 May 92
8.78	3.1	Fabrice	Lapierre	AUS	17.10.83	1	NC	Perth	18 Apr 10
8.77	3.9		Lewis			1	Pepsi	Los Angeles (Ww)	18 May 85
8.77	3.4		Lewis			1	MSR	Walnut	26 Apr 87
8.73	4.6		Lewis			Q	NC	Sacramento	19 Jun 81
8.73	3.2		Lewis			Q	NC	Indianapolis	17 Jun 83
8.73A	2.6		Powell			1		Sestriere	31 Jul 91
8.73	4.8		Pedroso			1		Madrid	20 Jun 95
8.72	2.2		Lewis			1	NYG	New York	24 May 92
8.72A	3.9		Lewis			2		Sestriere	31 Jul 94
8.70	2.5		Pedroso			1		Padova	16 Jul 95
8.68	4.9	James	Beckford	JAM	9.1.75	1	JUCO	Odessa, Tx	19 May 95
8.68	3.7	Marquis	Dendy	USA	17.11.92	1	NC	Eugene	25 Jun 15
8.66A	4.0	Joe	Greene	USA	17.2.67	2		Sestriere	21 Jul 92
8.64	3.5	Kareem	Streete-Thompson	CAY/USA	30.3.73	2	NC	Knoxville	18 Jun 94
8.63	3.9	Mike	Conley	USA	5.10.62	2	NC	Eugene	20 Jun 86
8.57	5.2	Jason	Grimes	USA	10.9.59	1	vFRG,AFR	Durham	27 Jun 82
8.54	4.1	Jeff	Henderson	USA	19.2.89	1	PAm	Toronto	22 Jul 15
8.53	4.9	Kevin	Dilworth	USA	14.2.74	1		Fort-de-France	27 Apr 02
8.51	3.7	Ignisious	Gaisah	GHA	20.6.83	1	AfCh	Bambous	9 Aug 06
8.49	2.6	Ralph	Boston	USA	9.5.39	1	OT	Los Angeles	12 Sep 64
8.49	4.5	Stanislav	Tarasenko	RUS	23.7.66	2		Madrid	20 Jun 95
8.48	2.8	Kirill	Sosunov	RUS	1.11.75	1		Oristano	18 Sep 95
8.48	3.4	Peter	Burge	AUS	3.7.74	1		Gold Coast (RB)	10 Sep 00
8.48	2.1	Brian	Johnson	USA	25.3.80	1	Conseil	Fort-de-France	8 May 08
8.46	3.4	Randy	Williams	USA	23.8.53	1		Eugene	18 May 73
8.46		Vernon	George	USA	6.10.64	1		Houston	21 May 89
8.44		Keith	Talley	USA	28.1.64	Q		Odessa, Tx	16 May 85
Exhibition: 8.46		Yuriy	Naumkin	RUS	4.11.68	1		Iglesias	6 Sep 96

Best outdoors

8.56 1.3 Lamela 1 Torino 24 Jun 99 8.49 1.6 Bayer 1 NC Ulm 4 Jul 09

8.46A 0.0 Pate 1 Cd. de México 3 May 03 and 8.45 1.5 2 NC Stanford 21 Jun 02, 8.48w 5.6 1 Fort Worth 21 Apr 01

Ancillary marks – other marks during series (to 8.67/8.70w)

8.84	1.7	Lewis	30 Aug 91	8.89Aw	2.4	Pedroso	29 Jul 95	8.75w	2.1	Lewis	16 Aug 87
8.71	0.6	Lewis	19 Jun 83	8.84Aw	3.8	Powell	21 Jul 92	8.75Aw	3.4	Powell	21 Jul 92
8.68	0.3	Lewis	18 Jul 88	8.83w	2.3	Lewis	30 Aug 91	8.73w	2.4	Lewis	18 May 85
8.68	0.0	Lewis	30 Aug 91	8.80Aw	4.0	Powell	21 Jul 92	8.73w		Powell	16 May 92
8.67	-0.2	Lewis	5 Sep 87	8.78Aw		Powell	21 Jul 92	8.71Aw		Powell	31 Jul 91

TRIPLE JUMP

Mark	Wind	Name		Nat	Born	Pos	Meet	Venue	Date
18.29 WR	1.3	Jonathan	Edwards	GBR	10.5.66	1	WCh	Göteborg	7 Aug 95
18.21	0.2	Christian	Taylor	USA	18.6.90	1	WCh	Beijing	27 Aug 15
18.09	-0.4	Kenny	Harrison	USA	13.2.65	1	OG	Atlanta	27 Jul 96
18.08	0.0	Pedro Pablo	Pichardo	CUB	30.6.93	1	Barr	La Habana	28 May 15
18.06	0.8		Pichardo			1	DL	Doha	15 May 15
18.06	1.1		Taylor			1	Athl	Lausanne	9 Jul 15
18.04	0.3	Teddy	Tamgho	FRA	15.6.89	1	WCh	Moskva	18 Aug 13
18.04	0.8		Taylor			2	DL	Doha	15 May 15
18.01	0.4		Edwards			1	Bisl	Oslo	9 Jul 98
18.00	1.3		Edwards			1	McD	London (CP)	27 Aug 95
17.99	0.5		Edwards			1	EC	Budapest	23 Aug 98
17.99	1.8		Pichardo			2	Athl	Lausanne	9 Jul 15
17.98 WR	1.8		Edwards			1		Salamanca	18 Jul 95
17.98	1.2		Tamgho			1	DL	New York	12 Jun 10
17.97 WR	1.5	Willie	Banks	USA	11.3.56	1	TAC	Indianapolis	16 Jun 85
17.96	0.1		Taylor			1	WCh	Daegu	4 Sep 11
17.96	-0.4		Pichardo			1	GGala	Roma	4 Jun 15
17.94	0.0		Pichardo			1		La Habana	8 May 15
17.93	1.6		Harrison			1	DNG	Stockholm	2 Jul 90
17.92	1.6	Khristo	Markov	BUL	27.1.65	1	WCh	Roma	31 Aug 87

Mark	Wind	Name		Nat	Born	Pos	Meet	Venue	Date
17.92	1.9	James	Beckford	JAM	9.1.75	1	JUCO	Odessa, TX	20 May 95
17.92i	WIR -		Tamgho			1	EI	Paris (Bercy)	6 Mar 11
17.92	0.7		Edwards			1	WCh	Edmonton	6 Aug 01
17.91i	WIR -		Tamgho			1	NC	Aubière	20 Feb 11
17.91	1.4		Tamgho			1	Athl	Lausanne	30 Jun 11
17.90	1.0	Vladimir	Inozemtsev	UKR	25.5.64	1	PTS	Bratislava	20 Jun 90
17.90	0.4	Jadel	Gregório (10)	BRA	16.9.80	1	GP	Belém	20 May 07
17.90i			Tamgho			1	WI	Doha	14 Mar 10
17.89A	WR 0.0	João Carlos	de Oliveira	BRA	28.5.54	1	PAm	Ciudad de México	15 Oct 75
17.88	0.9		Edwards			2	OG	Atlanta	27 Jul 96
		(30/11)							
17.87	1.7	Mike	Conley	USA	5.10.62	1	NC	San José	27 Jun 87
17.86	1.3	Charles	Simpkins	USA	19.10.63	1	WUG	Kobe	2 Sep 85
17.85	0.9	Yoelbi	Quesada	CUB	4.8.73	1	WCh	Athína	8 Aug 97
17.83i	WIR -	Aliecer	Urrutia	CUB	22.9.74	1		Sindelfingen	1 Mar 97
17.83i	WIR -	Christian	Olsson	SWE	25.1.80	1	WI	Budapest	7 Mar 04
17.81	1.0	Marian	Oprea	ROU	6.6.82	1	Athl	Lausanne	5 Jul 05
17.81	0.1	Phillips	Idowu	GBR	30.12.78	1	EC	Barcelona	29 Jul 10
17.78	1.0	Nikolay	Musiyenko	UKR	16.12.59	1	Znam	Leningrad	7 Jun 86
17.78	0.6	Lázaro	Betancourt ¶	CUB	18.3.63	1	Barr	La Habana	15 Jun 86
		(20)							
17.78	0.8	Melvin	Lister	USA	29.8.77	1	NC/OT	Sacramento	17 Jul 04
17.77	1.0	Aleksandr	Kovalenko	RUS	8.5.63	1	NC	Bryansk	18 Jul 87
17.77i	-	Leonid	Voloshin	RUS	30.3.66	1		Grenoble	6 Feb 94
17.75	0.3	Oleg	Protsenko	RUS	11.8.63	1	Znam	Moskva	10 Jun 90
17.75	0.8	Will	Claye	USA	13.6.91	1	NC	Sacramento	27 Jun 14
17.74	1.4	Nelson	Évora	POR	20.4.84	1	WCh	Osaka	27 Aug 07
17.73i		Walter	Davis	USA	2.7.79	1	WI	Moskva	12 Mar 06
17.73i	-	Fabrizio	Donato	ITA	14.8.76	2	EI	Paris (Bercy)	6 Mar 11
17.72i		Brian	Wellman	BER	8.9.67	1	WI	Barcelona	12 Mar 95
17.72	1.3	Sheryf	El-Sheryf	UKR	2.1.89	1	EU23	Ostrava	17 Jul 11
		(30)	El-Sheryf now Seref Osmanoglou TUR						
17.70i		Daniele	Greco	ITA	1.3.89	1	EI	Göteborg	2 Mar 13
17.69	1.5	Igor	Lapshin	BLR	8.8.63	1		Stayki	31 Jul 88
17.69i		Yoandri	Betanzos	CUB	15.2.82	2	WI	Doha	14 Mar 10
17.68	0.4	Danil	Burkenya	RUS	20.7.78	1	NC	Tula	31 Jul 04
17.68A	1.6	Alexis	Copello	CUB	12.8.85	1		Ávila	17 Jul 11
17.66	1.7	Ralf	Jaros	GER	13.12.65	1	ECp	Frankfurt-am-Main	30 Jun 91
17.65	1.0	Aleksandr	Yakovlev	UKR	8.9.57	1	Znam	Moskva	6 Jun 87
17.65	0.8	Denis	Kapustin	RUS	5.10.70	2	Bisl	Oslo	9 Jul 98
17.64	1.4	Nathan	Douglas	GBR	4.12.82	1	NC	Manchester (SC)	10 Jul 05
17.63	0.9	Kenta	Bell	USA	16.3.77	1c2	MSR	Walnut	21 Apr 02
		(40)							
17.62i	-	Yoel	García	CUB	25.11.73	2		Sindelfingen	1 Mar 97
17.62	-0.2	Arne David	Girat	CUB	26.8.84	3	ALBA	La Habana	25 Apr 09
17.60	0.6	Vladimir	Plekhanov	RUS	11.4.58	2	NC	Leningrad	4 Aug 85
17.59i	-	Pierre	Camara	FRA	10.9.65	1	WI	Toronto	13 Mar 93
17.59	0.3	Vasiliy	Sokov	RUS	7.4.68	1	NC	Moskva	19 Jun 93
17.59	0.8	Charles	Friedek	GER	26.8.71	1		Hamburg	23 Jul 97
17.59	0.9	Leevan	Sands	BAH	16.8.81	3	OG	Beijing	21 Aug 08
17.59	0.0		Li Yanxi	CHN	26.6.84	1	NG	Jinan	26 Oct 09
17.58	1.5	Oleg	Sakirkin	KZK	23.1.66	2	NC	Gorkiy	23 Jul 89
17.58	1.6	Aarik	Wilson	USA	25.10.82	1	LGP	London (CP)	3 Aug 07
17.58	-1.7	Ernesto	Revé	CUB	26.2.92	2		La Habana	7 Feb 14
		(51)	100th man 17.38, 200th 17.19, 300th 17.02, 400th 16.89, 500th 16.79						

Wind-assisted marks – performances to 17.91, performers to 17.59

Mark	Wind	Name		Nat	Born	Pos	Meet	Venue	Date
18.43	2.4	Jonathan	Edwards	GBR	10.5.66	1	ECp	Villeneuve d'Ascq	25 Jun 95
18.20	5.2	Willie	Banks	USA	11.3.56	1	NC/OT	Indianapolis	16 Jul 88
18.17	2.1	Mike	Conley	USA	5.10.62	1	OG	Barcelona	3 Aug 92
18.08	2.5		Edwards			1	BrGP	Sheffield	23 Jul 95
18.03	2.9		Edwards			1	GhG	Gateshead	2 Jul 95
18.01	3.7		Harrison			1	NC	Atlanta	15 Jun 96
17.97	7.5	Yoelbi	Quesada	CUB	4.8.73	1		Madrid	20 Jun 95
17.93	5.2	Charles	Simpkins	USA	19.10.63	2	NC/OT	Indianapolis	16 Jul 88
17.92	3.4	Christian	Olsson	SWE	25.1.80	1	GP	Gateshead	13 Jul 03
17.91	3.2		Simpkins			1	NC	Eugene	21 Jun 86
17.82	2.5	Nelson	Évora	POR	20.4.84	1	NC	Seixal	26 Jul 09
17.81	4.6	Keith	Connor	GBR	16.9.57	1	CG	Brisbane	9 Oct 82
17.76A	2.2	Kenta	Bell	USA	16.3.77	1		El Paso	10 Apr 04
17.75		Gennadiy	Valyukevich	BLR	1.6.58	1		Uzhgorod	27 Apr 86
17.75	7.1	Brian	Wellman	BER	8.9.67	2		Madrid	20 Jun 95

Mark	Wind	Name		Nat	Born	Pos	Meet	Venue	Date
17.73	4.1	Vasiliy	Sokov	RUS	7.4.68	1		Riga	3 Jun 89
17.71	2.4	Marquis	Dendy	USA	17.11.92	1	NCAA	Eugene	12 Jun 15
17.69	3.9	Alexis	Copello	CUB	12.8.85	1	ALBA	La Habana	25 Apr 09
17.63	4.3	Robert	Cannon	USA	9.7.58	3	NC/OT	Indianapolis	16 Jul 88
17.59	2.1	Jerome	Romain	DMA/FRA	12.6.71	3	WCh	Göteborg	7 Aug 95

Best outdoor marks for athletes with indoor bests

Mark	Wind	Name	Pos	Meet	Venue	Date
17.79	1.4	Olsson	1	OG	Athína	22 Aug 04
17.75	1.0	Voloshin	2	WCh	Tokyo	26 Aug 91
17.71	-0.7	Davis	1	NC	Indianapolis	25 Jun 06
17.70	1.7	Urrutia	1	GP II	Sevilla	6 Jun 96
17.67w	3.4	Greco	1	NC	Bressanone	8 Jul 12
17.65	1.4	Betanzos	2	ALBA	La Habana	25 Apr 09
17.67w	5.4		1		Bilbao	1 Jul 06
17.62A	0.1	Wellman	1		El Paso	15 Apr 95
17.60	1.9	Donato	1		Milano	7 Jun 00
17.63w	2.8		1	EC	Helsinki	30 Jun 12

Low altitude best: 17.65 0.1 Copello 1 Barr La Habana 30 May 09

Ancillary marks – other marks during series (to 17.90)

Mark	Wind	Name	Date
18.16 WR	1.3	Edwards	7 Aug 95
18.02	0.8	Taylor	9 Jul 15
17.99	0.1	Harrison	27 Jul 96
17.93	0.2	Pichardo	28 May 15
17.92i		Tamgho	6 Mar 11
18.39w	3.7	Edwards	25 Jun 95
18.06w	4.9	Banks	16 Jul 88
17.90w	2.5	Edwards	25 Jun 95

SHOT

Mark	Name		Nat	Born	Pos	Meet	Venue	Date
23.12 WR	Randy	Barnes ¶	USA	16.6.66	1		Los Angeles (Ww)	20 May 90
23.10		Barnes			1	Jenner	San José	26 May 90
23.06 WR	Ulf	Timmermann	GDR	1.11.62	1	Veniz	Haniá	22 May 88
22.91 WR	Alessandro	Andrei	ITA	3.1.59	1		Viareggio	12 Aug 87
22.86	Brian	Oldfield	USA	1.6.45	1	ITA	El Paso	10 May 75
22.75	Werner	Günthör	SUI	1.6.61	1		Bern	23 Aug 88
22.67	Kevin	Toth ¶	USA	29.12.67	1	KansR	Lawrence	19 Apr 03
22.66i		Barnes			1	Sunkist	Los Angeles	20 Jan 89
22.64 WR	Udo	Beyer	GDR	9.8.55	1		Berlin	20 Aug 86
22.62 WR		Timmermann			1		Berlin	22 Sep 85
22.61		Timmermann			1		Potsdam	8 Sep 88
22.60		Timmermann			1	vURS	Tallinn	21 Jun 86
22.56		Timmermann			1		Berlin	13 Sep 88
22.56	Joe	Kovacs	USA	28.6.89	1	Herc	Monaco	17 Jul 15
22.55i		Timmermann			1	NC	Senftenberg	11 Feb 89
22.54	Christian	Cantwell	USA	30.9.80	1	GP II	Gresham	5 Jun 04
22.52	John	Brenner (10)	USA	4.1.61	1	MSR	Walnut	26 Apr 87
22.51		Timmermann			1		Erfurt	1 Jun 86
22.51	Adam	Nelson	USA	7.7.75	1		Gresham	18 May 02
22.47		Timmermann			1		Dresden	17 Aug 86
22.47		Günthör			1	WG	Helsinki	2 Jul 87
22.47		Timmermann			1	OG	Seoul	23 Sep 88
22.45		Oldfield			1	ITA	El Paso	22 May 76
22.45		Cantwell			1	GP	Gateshead	11 Jun 06
22.43		Günthör			1	v3-N	Lüdenscheid	18 Jun 87
22.43	Reese	Hoffa	USA	8.10.77	1	LGP	London (CP)	3 Aug 07
22.42		Barnes			1	WK	Zürich	17 Aug 88
22.41		Cantwell			1	Pre	Eugene	3 Jul 10
22.40		Barnes			1		Rüdlingen	13 Jul 96
22.40i		Nelson			1		Fayetteville	15 Feb 08
22.39		Barnes			2	OG	Seoul	23 Sep 88
	(30/11)							
22.28	Ryan	Whiting	USA	24.11.86	1	DL	Doha	10 May 13
22.24	Sergey	Smirnov	RUS	17.9.60	2	vGDR	Tallinn	21 Jun 86
22.21	Dylan	Armstrong	CAN	15.1.81	1	NC	Calgary	25 Jun 11
22.20	John	Godina	USA	31.5.72	1		Carson	22 May 05
22.20	David	Storl	GER	27.7.90	1	Athl	Lausanne	9 Jul 15
22.10	Sergey	Gavryushin	RUS	27.6.59	1		Tbilisi	31 Aug 86
22.10	Cory	Martin	USA	22.5.85	1		Tucson	22 May 10
22.09	Sergey	Kasnauskas	BLR	20.4.61	1		Stayki	23 Aug 84
	(20)							
22.09i	Mika	Halvari	FIN	13.2.70	1		Tampere	7 Feb 00
22.02i	George	Woods	USA	11.2.43	1	LAT	Inglewood	8 Feb 74
22.02	Dave	Laut	USA	21.12.56	1		Koblenz	25 Aug 82
22.00 WR	Aleksandr	Baryshnikov	RUS	11.11.48	1	vFRA	Colombes	10 Jul 76
21.98	Gregg	Tafralis ¶	USA	9.4.58	1		Los Gatos	13 Jun 92
21.97	Janus	Robberts	RSA	10.3.79	1	NCAA	Eugene	2 Jun 01
21.96	Mikhail	Kostin	RUS	10.5.59	1		Vitebsk	20 Jul 86
21.95	Tomasz	Majewski	POL	30.8.81	1	DNG	Stockholm	30 Jul 09
21.93	Remigius	Machura ¶	CZE	3.7.60	1		Praha	23 Aug 87
21.92	Carl	Myerscough ¶	GBR	21.10.79	1	NCAA	Sacramento	13 Jun 03
	(30)							

Mark	Wind	Name		Nat	Born	Pos	Meet	Venue	Date
21.87		C.J.	Hunter ¶	USA	14.12.68	2	NC	Sacramento	15 Jul 00
21.85	WR	Terry	Albritton	USA	14.1.55	1		Honolulu	21 Feb 76
21.83i		Aleksandr	Bagach ¶	UKR	21.11.66	1		Brovary	21 Feb 99
21.82	WR	Al	Feuerbach	USA	14.1.48	1		San José	5 May 73
21.82		Andy	Bloom	USA	11.8.73	1	GPF	Doha	5 Oct 00
21.81		Yuriy	Bilonog ¶	UKR	9.3.74	1	NC	Kiev	3 Jul 03
21.78	WR	Randy	Matson	USA	5.3.45	1		College Station	22 Apr 67
21.78		Dan	Taylor	USA	12.5.82	1		Tucson	23 May 09
21.77i		Mike	Stulce ¶	USA	21.7.69	1	v GBR	Birmingham	13 Feb 93
21.77		Dragan	Peric	YUG	8.5.64	1		Bar	25 Apr 98
		(40)							
21.76		Michael	Carter	USA	29.10.60	2	NCAA	Eugene	2 Jun 84
21.74		Janis	Bojars	LAT	12.5.56	1		Riga	14 Jul 84
21.73		Augie	Wolf ¶	USA	3.9.61	1		Leverkusen	12 Apr 84
21.69		Reijo	Ståhlberg	FIN	21.9.52	1	WCR	Fresno	5 May 79
21.69		Andrey	Mikhnevich ¶	BLR	12.7.76	1	WCh	Saint-Denis	23 Aug 03
21.69		O'Dayne	Richards			1	PAm	Toronto	21 Jul 15
21.68		Geoff	Capes	GBR	23.8.49	1	4-N	Cwmbrân	18 May 80
21.68		Edward	Sarul	POL	16.11.58	1		Sopot	31 Jul 83
21.67		Hartmut	Briesenick	GDR	17.3.49	1		Potsdam	1 Sep 73
21.63i		Joachim	Olsen	DEN	31.5.77	1		Tallinn	25 Feb 04
21.63		Maris	Urtans	LAT	9.2.81	1	ET-2	Beograd	19 Jun 10
		(51)	100th man 21.19, 200th 20.75, 300th 20.40, 400th 20.12, 500th 19.92						

Not recognised by GDR authorities: 22.11 Rolf Oesterreich GDR 24.8.49 1 Zschopau 12 Sep 76

Drugs disqualification

Mark	Wind	Name		Nat	Born	Pos	Meet	Venue	Date
22.84			Barnes			1		Malmö	7 Aug 90
22.10		Andrey	Mikhnevich ¶	BLR	12.7.76	1		Minsk	11 Aug 11
21.82		Mike	Stulce ¶	USA	21.7.69	1		Brenham	9 May 90

Best outdoor marks for athletes with indoor bests

21.70 Stulce ¶ 1 OG Barcelona 31 Jul 92 | 21.63 Woods 2 CalR Modesto 22 May 76

Ancillary marks – other marks during series (to 22.45)

22.84 WR	Andrei	12 Aug 87	22.72 WR	Andrei	12 Aug 87	22.55	Barnes	20 May 90
22.76	Barnes	20 May 90	22.70	Günthör	23 Aug 88	22.49	Nelson	18 May 02
22.74	Andrei	12 Aug 87	22.58	Beyer	20 Aug 86	22.45	Timmermann	22 May 88

DISCUS

Mark	Wind	Name		Nat	Born	Pos	Meet	Venue	Date
74.08	WR	Jürgen	Schult	GDR	11.5.60	1		Neubrandenburg	6 Jun 86
73.88		Virgilijus	Alekna	LTU	13.2.72	1	NC	Kaunas	3 Aug 00
73.38		Gerd	Kanter	EST	6.5.79	1		Helsingborg	4 Sep 06
72.02			Kanter			1eA		Salinas	3 May 07
71.88			Kanter			1eA		Salinas	8 May 08
71.86	WR	Yuriy	Dumchev	RUS	5.8.58	1		Moskva	29 May 83
71.84		Piotr	Malachowski	POL	7.6.83	1	FBK	Hengelo	8 Jun 13
71.70		Róbert	Fazekas ¶	HUN	18.8.75	1		Szombathely	14 Jul 02
71.64			Kanter			1		Kohila	25 Jun 09
71.56			Alekna			1		Kaunas	25 Jul 07
71.50		Lars	Riedel	GER	28.6.67	1		Wiesbaden	3 May 97
71.45			Kanter			1		Chula Vista	29 Apr 10
71.32		Ben	Plucknett ¶	USA	13.4.54	1	Pre	Eugene	4 Jun 83
71.26		John	Powell	USA	25.6.47	1	NC	San José	9 Jun 84
71.26		Rickard	Bruch	SWE	2.7.46	1		Malmö	15 Nov 84
71.26		Imrich	Bugár (10)	CZE	14.4.55	1	Jenner	San José	25 May 85
71.25			Fazekas			1	WCp	Madrid (C)	21 Sep 02
71.25			Alekna			1	Danek	Turnov	20 May 08
71.18		Art	Burns	USA	19.7.54	1		San José	19 Jul 83
71.16	WR	Wolfgang	Schmidt	GDR	16.1.54	1		Berlin	9 Aug 78
71.14			Plucknett			1		Berkeley	12 Jun 83
71.14		Anthony	Washington	USA	16.1.66	1eA		Salinas	22 May 96
71.12			Alekna			1	WK	Zürich	11 Aug 00
71.08			Alekna			1		Réthimno	21 Jul 06
71.06		Luis Mariano	Delís ¶	CUB	12.12.57	1	Barr	La Habana	21 May 83
71.06			Riedel			1	WK	Zürich	14 Aug 96
71.00			Bruch			1		Malmö	14 Oct 84
70.99			Alekna			1		Stellenbosch	30 Mar 01
70.98		Mac	Wilkins	USA	15.11.50	1	WG	Helsinki	9 Jul 80
70.98			Burns			1	Pre	Eugene	21 Jul 84
		(30/16)							
70.82		Aleksander	Tammert	EST	2.2.73	1		Denton	15 Apr 06
70.66		Robert	Harting	GER	18.10.84	1	Danek	Turnov	22 May 12
70.54		Dmitriy	Shevchenko ¶	RUS	13.5.68	1		Krasnodar	7 May 02

Mark	Wind	Name		Nat	Born	Pos	Meet	Venue	Date
70.38	WRu	Jay	Silvester	USA	27.8.37	1		Lancaster	16 May 71
		(20)							
70.32		Frantz	Kruger	RSA/FIN	22.5.75	1		Salon-de-Provence	26 May 02
70.06		Romas	Ubartas ¶	LTU	26.5.60	1		Smalininkay	8 May 88
70.00		Juan	Martínez ¶	CUB	17.5.58	2	Barr	La Habana	21 May 83
69.95		Zoltán	Kövágó	HUN	10.4.79	1		Salon-de-Provence	25 May 06
69.91		John	Godina	USA	31.5.72	1		Salinas	19 May 98
69.90		Jason	Young	USA	27.5.81	1		Lubbock	26 Mar 10
69.70		Géjza	Valent	CZE	3.10.53	2		Nitra	26 Aug 84
69.62		Knut	Hjeltnes ¶	NOR	8.12.51	2	Jen	San José	25 May 85
69.62		Timo	Tompuri	FIN	9.6.69	1		Helsingborg	8 Jul 01
69.50		Mario	Pestano	ESP	8.4.78	1	NC	Santa Cruz de Tenerife	27 Jul 08
		(30)							
69.46		Al	Oerter	USA	19.9.36	1	TFA	Wichita	31 May 80
69.44		Georgiy	Kolnootchenko	BLR	7.5.59	1	vUSA	Indianapolis	3 Jul 82
69.40		Art	Swarts ¶	USA	14.2.45	1		Scotch Plains	8 Dec 79
69.36		Mike	Buncic	USA	25.7.62	1		Fresno	6 Apr 91
69.32		Ehsan	Hadadi	IRI	21.1.85	1		Tallinn	3 Jun 08
69.28		Vladimir	Dubrovshchik	BLR	7.1.72	1	NC	Staiki	3 Jun 00
69.26		Ken	Stadel	USA	19.2.52	2	AAU	Walnut	16 Jun 79
68.94		Adam	Setliff	USA	15.12.69	1		Atascadero	25 Jul 01
68.91		Ian	Waltz	USA	15.4.77	1		Salinas	24 May 06
68.90		Jean-Claude	Retel	FRA	11.2.68	1		Salon-de-Provence	17 Jul 02
		(40)							
68.88		Vladimir	Zinchenko	UKR	25.7.59	1		Dnepropetrovsk	16 Jul 88
68.76		Jarred	Rome	USA	21.12.76	2cA		Chula Vista	6 Aug 11
68.64		Dmitriy	Kovtsun ¶	UKR	29.9.55	1		Riga	6 Jul 84
68.58		Attila	Horváth	HUN	28.7.67	1		Budapest	24 Jun 94
68.52		Igor	Duginyets	UKR	20.5.56	1	NC	Kyiv	21 Aug 82
68.50		Armin	Lemme	GDR	28.10.55	1	vUSA	Karl-Marx-Stadt	10 Jul 82
68.49A		Casey	Malone	USA	6.4.77	1		Fort Collins	20 Jun 09
68.48	WR	John	van Reenen	RSA	26.3.47	1		Stellenbosch	14 Mar 75
68.44		Vaclovas	Kidykas	LTU	17.10.61	1		Sochi	1 Jun 88
68.33		Martin	Wierig	GER	10.6.87	1		Schönebeck	26 Jul 12
		(50)	100th man 67.13, 200th 65.36, 300th 64.36, 400th 63.20, 500th 62.16						
Subsequent to or at drugs disqualification				! recognised as US record					
72.34!		Ben	Plucknett ¶	USA	13.4.54	(1)	DNG	Stockholm	7 Jul 81
71.20			Plucknett			(1)	CalR	Modesto	16 May 81
70.84		Kamy	Keshmiri ¶	USA	23.1.69	(1)		Salinas	27 May 92
Sloping ground									
72.08		John	Powell	USA	25.6.47	1		Klagshamn	11 Sep 87
69.80		Stefan	Fernholm	SWE	2.7.59	1		Klagshamn	13 Aug 87
69.44		Adam	Setliff	USA	15.12.69	1		La Jolla	21 Jul 01
68.46		Andy	Bloom	USA	11.8.73	2cA		La Jolla	25 Mar 00

Ancillary marks – other marks during series (to 70.98)

72.35 Alekna 3 Aug 00 72.30 Kanter 4 Sep 06 71.08 Plucknett 4 Jun 83

HAMMER

Mark	Wind	Name		Nat	Born	Pos	Meet	Venue	Date
86.74	WR	Yuriy	Sedykh	RUS	11.6.55	1	EC	Stuttgart	30 Aug 86
86.66	WR		Sedykh			1	vGDR	Tallinn	22 Jun 86
86.34	WR		Sedykh			1		Cork	3 Jul 84
86.04		Sergey	Litvinov	RUS	23.1.58	1	OD	Dresden	3 Jul 86
85.74			Litvinov			2	EC	Stuttgart	30 Aug 86
85.68			Sedykh			1	BGP	Budapest	11 Aug 86
85.60			Sedykh			1	PTG	London (CP)	13 Jul 84
85.60			Sedykh			1	Drz	Moskva	17 Aug 84
85.20			Litvinov			2		Cork	3 Jul 84
85.14			Litvinov			1	PTG	London	11 Jul 86
85.14			Sedykh			1	Kuts	Moskva	4 Sep 88
85.02			Sedykh			1	BGP	Budapest	20 Aug 84
84.92			Sedykh			2	OD	Dresden	3 Jul 86
84.90		Vadim	Devyatovskiy ¶	BLR	20.3.77	1		Staiki	21 Jul 05
84.88			Litvinov			1	GP-GG	Roma	10 Sep 86
84.86		Koji	Murofushi	JPN	8.10.74	1	Odlozil	Praha	29 Jun 03
84.80			Litvinov			1	OG	Seoul	26 Sep 88
84.72			Sedykh			1	GWG	Moskva	9 Jul 86
84.64			Litvinov			2	GWG	Moskva	9 Jul 86
84.62		Igor	Astapkovich	BLR	4.1.63	1	Expo	Sevilla	6 Jun 92
84.60			Sedykh			1	8-N	Tokyo	14 Sep 84
84.58			Sedykh			1	Znam	Leningrad	8 Jun 86

Mark	Wind	Name		Nat	Born	Pos	Meet	Venue	Date
84.51		Ivan	Tikhon ¶	BLR	24.7.76	1	NC	Grodno	9 Jul 08
84.48		Igor	Nikulin	RUS	14.8.60	1	Athl	Lausanne	12 Jul 90
84.46			Sedykh			1		Vladivostok	14 Sep 88
84.46			Tikhon			1		Minsk	7 May 04
84.40		Jüri	Tamm	EST	5.2.57	1		Banská Bystrica	9 Sep 84
84.36			Litvinov			2	vGDR	Tallinn	22 Jun 86
84.32			Tikhon			1		Staiki	8 Aug 03
84.26			Sedykh			1	Nik	Nice	15 Jul 86
		(30/8)							
84.19		Adrián	Annus ¶	HUN	28.6.73	1		Szombathely	10 Aug 03
83.93		Pawel	Fajdek	POL	4.6.89	1	Kuso	Szczecin	9 Aug 15
		(10)							
83.68		Tibor	Gécsek ¶	HUN	22.9.64	1		Zalaegerszeg	19 Sep 98
83.46		Andrey	Abduvaliyev	TJK/UZB	30.6.66	1		Adler	26 May 90
83.43		Aleksey	Zagornyi	RUS	31.5.78	1		Adler	10 Feb 02
83.40	@	Ralf	Haber	GDR	18.8.62	1		Athína	16 May 88
		82.54				1		Potsdam	9 Sep 88
83.38		Szymon	Ziólkowski	POL	1.7.76	1	WCh	Edmonton	5 Aug 01
83.30		Olli-Pekka	Karjalainen	FIN	7.3.80	1		Lahti	14 Jul 04
83.04		Heinz	Weis	GER	14.7.63	1	NC	Frankfurt	29 Jun 97
83.00		Balázs	Kiss	HUN	21.3.72	1	GP II	Saint-Denis	4 Jun 98
82.78		Karsten	Kobs	GER	16.9.71	1		Dortmund	26 Jun 99
82.69		Krisztián	Pars	HUN	18.2.82	1	EC	Zürich	16 Aug 14
		(20)		*@ competitive meeting but unsanctioned by GDR federation*					
82.64		Günther	Rodehau	GDR	6.7.59	1		Dresden	3 Aug 85
82.62		Sergey	Kirmasov ¶	RUS	25.3.70	1		Bryansk	30 May 98
82.62		Andrey	Skvaruk	UKR	9.3.67	1		Koncha-Zaspa	27 Apr 02
82.58		Primoz	Kozmus	SLO	30.9.79	1		Celje	2 Sep 09
82.54		Vasiliy	Sidorenko	RUS	1.5.61	1		Krasnodar	13 May 92
82.52		Lance	Deal	USA	21.8.61	1	GPF	Milano	7 Sep 96
82.40		Plamen	Minev	BUL	28.4.65	1	NM	Plovdiv	1 Jun 91
82.38		Gilles	Dupray	FRA	2.1.70	1		Chelles	21 Jun 00
82.28		Ilya	Konovalov ¶	RUS	4.3.71	1	NC	Tula	10 Aug 03
82.24		Benjaminas	Viluckis	LIT	20.3.61	1		Klaipeda	24 Aug 86
		(30)							
82.24		Vyacheslav	Korovin	RUS	8.9.62	1		Chelyabinsk	20 Jun 87
82.23		Vladislav	Piskunov ¶	UKR	7.6.78	2		Koncha-Zaspa	27 Apr 02
82.22		Holger	Klose	GER	5.12.72	1		Dortmund	2 May 98
82.16		Vitaliy	Alisevich	BLR	15.6.67	1		Parnu	13 Jul 88
82.08		Ivan	Tanev	BUL	1.5.57	1	NC	Sofia	3 Sep 88
82.00		Sergey	Alay ¶	BLR	11.6.65	1		Stayki	12 May 92
81.88		Jud	Logan ¶	USA	19.7.59	1		State College	22 Apr 88
81.81		Libor	Charfreitag	SVK	11.9.77	3	Odlozil	Praha	29 Jun 03
81.79		Christophe	Épalle	FRA	23.1.69	1		Clermont-Ferrand	30 Jun 00
81.78		Christoph	Sahner	FRG	23.9.63	1		Wemmetsweiler	11 Sep 88
		(40)							
81.70		Aleksandr	Seleznyov	RUS	25.1.63	2		Sochi	22 May 93
81.66		Aleksandr	Krykun	UKR	1.3.68	1		Kiev	29 May 04
81.64		Enrico	Sgrulletti	ITA	24.4.65	1		Ostia	9 Mar 97
81.56		Sergey	Gavrilov	RUS	22.5.70	1	Army	Rostov	16 Jun 96
81.56		Zsolt	Németh	HUN	9.11.71	1		Veszprém	14 Aug 99
81.52		Juha	Tiainen	FIN	5.12.55	1		Tampere	11 Jun 84
81.49		Valeriy	Svyatokho	BLR	20.7.81	1	NCp	Brest	27 May 06
81.45		Esref	Apak ¶	TUR	3.1.82	1	Cezmi	Istanbul	4 Jun 05
81.44		Yuriy	Tarasyuk	BLR	11.4.57	1		Minsk	10 Aug 84
81.35		Wojciech	Kondratowicz	POL	18.4.80	1		Bydgoszcz	13 Jul 03
		(50)	100th man 80.08, 200th 77.60, 300th 75.77, 400th 74.48, 500th 7321						

Drugs disqualification

Mark	Wind	Name		Nat	Born	Pos	Meet	Venue	Date
86.73		Ivan	Tikhon ¶	BLR	24.7.76	1	NC	Brest	3 Jul 05

Ancillary marks – other marks during series (to 84.85)

86.68	Sedykh	30 Aug 86	85.82	Sedykh	22 Jun 86	85.42	Sedykh	11 Aug 86	85.20	Sedykh	3 Jul 84
86.62	Sedykh	30 Aug 86	85.52	Sedykh	13 Jul 84	85.28	Sedykh	30 Aug 86	85.04	Sedykh	13 Jul 84
86.00	Sedykh	3 Jul 84	85.46	Sedykh	30 Aug 86	85.26	Sedykh	11 Aug 86	84.98	Sedykh	4 Sep 88
86.00	Sedykh	22 Jun 86	85.42	Litvinov	3 Jul 86	85.24	Sedykh	11 Aug 86	84.92	Litvinov	3 Jul 86

JAVELIN

Mark	Wind	Name		Nat	Born	Pos	Meet	Venue	Date
98.48	WR	Jan	Zelezny	CZE	16.6.66	1		Jena	25 May 96
95.66	WR		Zelezny			1	McD	Sheffield	29 Aug 93
95.54A	WR		Zelezny			1		Pietersburg	6 Apr 93
94.64			Zelezny			1	GS	Ostrava	31 May 96
94.02			Zelezny			1		Stellenbosch	26 Mar 97

Mark	Wind	Name		Nat	Born	Pos	Meet	Venue	Date
93.09		Aki	Parviainen	FIN	26.10.74	1		Kuortane	26 Jun 99
92.80			Zelezny			1	WCh	Edmonton	12 Aug 01
92.72		Julius	Yego	KEN	4.1.89	1	WCh	Beijing	26 Aug 15
92.61		Sergey	Makarov	RUS	19.3.73	1		Sheffield	30 Jun 02
92.60		Raymond	Hecht	GER	11.11.68	1	Bisl	Oslo	21 Jul 95
92.42			Zelezny			1	GS	Ostrava	28 May 97
92.41			Parviainen			1	ECp-1A	Vaasa	24 Jun 01
92.28			Zelezny			1	GPF	Monaco	9 Sep 95
92.28			Hecht			1	WK	Zürich	14 Aug 96
92.12			Zelezny			1	McD	London (CP)	27 Aug 95
92.12			Zelezny			1	TOTO	Tokyo	15 Sep 95
91.82			Zelezny			1	McD	Sheffield	4 Sep 94
91.69		Kostadínos	Gatsioúdis	GRE	17.12.73	1		Kuortane	24 Jun 00
91.68			Zelezny			1	GP	Gateshead	1 Jul 94
91.59		Andreas	Thorkildsen	NOR	1.4.82	1	Bisl	Oslo	2 Jun 06
91.53		Tero	Pitkämäki	FIN	19.12.82	1		Kuortane	26 Jun 05
91.50			Zelezny			1	Kuso	Lublin	4 Jun 94
91.50A			Zelezny			1		Pretoria	8 Apr 96
91.50			Hecht			1		Gengenbach	1 Sep 96
91.46	WR	Steve	Backley	GBR	12.2.69	1		Auckland (NS)	25 Jan 92
91.40			Zelezny			1	BNP	Villeneuve d'Ascq	2 Jul 93
91.39			Yego			1	DL	Birmingham	7 Jun 15
91.34			Zelezny			1		Cape Town	8 Apr 97
91.33			Pitkämäki			1	WAF	Monaco	10 Sep 05
91.31			Parviainen			2	WCh	Edmonton	12 Aug 01
91.30			Zelezny			1	ISTAF	Berlin	1 Sep 95
91.29		Breaux	Greer	USA	19.10.76	1	NC	Indianapolis	21 Jun 07
		(32/10) 79 over 90m (most: Zelezny 34, Parviainen 8, Thorkildsen 8, Hecht & Pitkämäki 6, Makarov 5)							
90.73		Vadims	Vasilevskis	LAT	5.1.82	1		Tallinn	22 Jul 07
90.60		Seppo	Räty	FIN	27.4.62	1		Nurmijärvi	20 Jul 92
90.44		Boris	Henry	GER	14.12.73	1	Gugl	Linz	9 Jul 97
90.16		Keshorn	Walcott	TTO	2.4.93	1	Athl	Lausanne	9 Jul 15
89.27		Thomas	Röhler	GER	30.9.91	1		Kuortane	8 Aug 15
89.21		Ihab	Abdelrahman	EGY	1.5.89	1	DL	Shanghai	18 May 14
89.16A		Tom	Petranoff	USA	8.4.58	1		Potchefstroom	1 Mar 91
89.15			Zhao Qinggang	CHN	24.7.85	1	AsiG	Incheon	2 Oct 14
89.10	WR	Patrik	Bodén	SWE	30.6.67	1		Austin	24 Mar 90
89.02		Jarrod	Bannister ¶	AUS	3.10.84	1	NC	Brisbane	29 Feb 08
		(20)							
88.98		Antti	Ruuskanen	FIN	21.2.84	1	NC	Pori	2 Aug 15
88.90		Aleksandr	Ivanov	RUS	25.5.82	1	Znam	Tula	7 Jun 03
88.84		Dmitriy	Tarabin	RUS	29.10.91	1	NC	Moskva	24 Jul 13
88.75		Marius	Corbett	RSA	26.9.75	1	CG	Kuala Lumpur	21 Sep 98
88.70		Peter	Blank	GER	10.4.62	1	NC	Stuttgart	30 Jun 01
88.36		Matthias	de Zordo	GER	21.2.88	1	VD	Bruxelles	16 Sep 11
88.34		Vitezslav	Vesely	CZE	27.2.83	Q	OG	London (OS)	8 Aug 12
88.24		Matti	Närhi	FIN	17.8.75	1		Soini	27 Jul 97
88.23		Petr	Frydrych	CZE	13.1.88	1	GS	Ostrava	27 May 10
88.22		Juha	Laukkanen	FIN	6.1.69	1		Kuortane	20 Jun 92
		(30)							
88.20		Gavin	Lovegrove	NZL	21.10.67	1	Bisl	Oslo	5 Jul 96
88.00		Vladimir	Ovchinnikov	RUS	2.8.70	1		Tolyatti	14 May 95
87.83		Andrus	Värnik	EST	27.9.77	1		Valga	19 Aug 03
87.82		Harri	Hakkarainen	FIN	16.10.69	1		Kuortane	24 Jun 95
87.60		Kazuhiro	Mizoguchi	JPN	18.3.62	1	Jenner	San José	27 May 89
87.40		Vladimir	Sasimovich ¶	BLR	14.9.68	2		Kuortane	24 Jun 95
87.34		Andrey	Moruyev	RUS	6.5.70	1	ECp	Birmingham	25 Jun 94
87.23		Teemu	Wirkkala	FIN	14.1.84	1		Joensuu	22 Jul 09
87.20		Viktor	Zaytsev	UZB	6.6.66	1	OT	Moskva	23 Jun 92
87.20		Peter	Esenwein	GER	7.12.67	1		Rehlingen	31 May 04
		(40)							
87.20A		Guillermo	Martínez	CUB	28.6.81	1	PAm	Guadalajara	28 Oct 11
87.17		Dariusz	Trafas	POL	16.5.72	1		Gold Coast (RB)	17 Sep 00
87.12		Tom	Pukstys	USA	28.5.68	2	OD	Jena	25 May 97
87.12		Emeterio	González	CUB	11.4.73	1	OD	Jena	3 Jun 00
86.98		Yuriy	Rybin	RUS	5.3.63	1		Nitra	26 Aug 95
86.94		Mick	Hill	GBR	22.10.64	1	NC	London (CP)	13 Jun 93
86.83		Ryohei	Arai	JPN	23.6.91	1		Isahaya	21 Oct 14
86.82		Ari	Mannio	FIN	23.7.87	1		Raasepori	7 Jun 15
86.80		Einar	Vihljálmsson	ISL	1.6.60	1		Reykjavik	29 Aug 92

Mark	Wind	Name		Nat	Born	Pos	Meet	Venue	Date
86.80		Robert	Oosthuizen	RSA	23.1.87	1		Oudtshoorn	1 Mar 08

(50) 100th man 84.61, 200th 82.20, 300th 80.40, 400th 79.23 new javelin introduced in 1986

Ancillary marks – other marks during series (to 91.40)

95.34	Zelezny	29 Aug 93	92.26	Zelezny	26 Mar 97	91.44	Zelezny	25 May 96
92.88	Zelezny	25 May 96	91.88	Zelezny	27 Aug 95	91.44	Zelezny	26 Mar 97
92.30	Zelezny	26 Mar 97	91.48	Zelezny	15 Sep 95			

Javelins with roughened tails, now banned by the IAAF

Mark	Wind	Name		Nat	Born	Pos	Meet	Venue	Date
96.96	WR	Seppo	Räty	FIN	27.4.62	1		Punkalaidun	2 Jun 91
94.74	Irreg		Zelezny			1	Bisl	Oslo	4 Jul 92
91.98	WR		Räty			1	Super	Shizuoka	6 May 91
90.82		Kimmo	Kinnunen	FIN	31.3.68	1	WCh	Tokyo	26 Aug 91
87.00		Peter	Borglund	SWE	29.1.64	1	vFIN	Stockholm	13 Aug 91

DECATHLON

Mark	Wind	Name		Nat	Born	Pos	Meet	Venue	Date
9045	WR	Ashton	Eaton	USA	21.1.88	1	WCh	Beijing	29 Aug 15
10.23/-0.4	7.88/0.0	14.52	2.01	45.00	13.69/-0.2	43.34	5.20	63.63	4:17.52
9039	WR		Eaton			1	NC/OT	Eugene	23 Jun 12
10.21/0.4	8.23/0.8	14.20	2.05	46.70	13.70/-0.8	42.81	5.30	58.87	4:14.48
9026	WR	Roman	Sebrle	CZE	26.11.74	1		Götzis	27 May 01
10.64/0.0	8.11/1.9	15.33	2.12	47.79	13.92/-0.2	47.92	4.80	70.16	4:21.98
8994	WR	Tomás	Dvorák	CZE	11.5.72	1	ECp	Praha	4 Jul 99
10.54/-0.1	7.90/1.1	16.78	2.04	48.08	13.73/0.0	48.33	4.90	72.32	4:37.20
8902			Dvorák			1	WCh	Edmonton	7 Aug 01
10.62/1.5	8.07/0.9	16.57	2.00	47.74	13.80/-0.4	45.51	5.00	68.53	4:35.13
8900			Dvorák			1		Götzis	4 Jun 00
10.54/1.3	8.03/0.0	16.68	2.09	48.36	13.89/-1.0	47.89	4.85	67.21	4:42.33
8893			Sebrle			1	OG	Athína	24 Aug 04
10.85/1.5	7.84/0.3	16.36	2.12	48.36	14.05/1.5	48.72	5.00	70.52	4:40.01
8891	WR	Dan	O'Brien	USA	18.7.66	1		Talence	5 Sep 92
10.43w/2.1	8.08/1.8	16.69	2.07	48.51	13.98/-0.5	48.56	5.00	62.58	4:42.10
8869			Eaton			1	OG	London (OS)	9 Aug 12
10.35/0.4	8.03/0.8	14.66	2.05	46.90	13.56/0.1	42.53	5.20	61.96	4:33.59
8847	WR	Daley	Thompson	GBR	30.7.58	1	OG	Los Angeles	9 Aug 84
10.44/-1.0	8.01/0.4	15.72	2.03	46.97	14.33/-1.1	46.56	5.00	65.24	4:35.00
8844w			O'Brien			1	TAC	New York	13 Jun 91
10.23	7.96	16.06	2.08	47.70	13.95W/4.2	48.08	5.10	57.40	4:45.54
8842			Sebrle			1		Götzis	30 May 04
10.92/0.5	7.86w/3.3	16.22	2.09	48.59	14.15/0.3	47.44	5.00	71.10	4:34.09
8837			Dvorák			1	WCh	Athína	6 Aug 97
10.60/0.8	7.64/-0.7	16.32	2.00	47.56	13.61/0.8	45.16	5.00	70.34	4:35.40
8832	WR	Jürgen	Hingsen	FRG	25.1.58	1	OT	Mannheim	9 Jun 84
10.70w/2.9	7.76/-1.6	16.42	2.07	48.05	14.07/0.2	49.36	4.90	59.86	4:19.75
8832		Bryan	Clay	USA	3.1.80	1	NC/OT	Eugene	30 Jun 08
10.39/-0.4	7.39/-1.6	15.17	2.08	48.41	13.75/1.9	52.74	5.00	70.55	4:50.97
8825	WR		Hingsen			1		Bernhausen	5 Jun 83
10.92/0.0	7.74	15.94	2.15	47.89	14.10	46.80	4.70	67.26	4:19.74
8824			O'Brien			1	OG	Atlanta	1 Aug 96
10.50/0.7	7.57/1.4	15.66	2.07	46.82	13.87/0.3	48.78	5.00	66.90	4:45.89
8820			Clay			2	OG	Athína	24 Aug 04
10.44w/2.2	7.96/0.2	15.23	2.06	49.19	14.13/1.5	50.11	4.90	69.71	4:41.65
8817			O'Brien			1	WCh	Stuttgart	20 Aug 93
10.57/0.9	7.99/0.4	15.41	2.03	47.46	14.08/0.0	47.92	5.20	62.56	4:40.08
8815		Erki	Nool	EST	25.6.70	2	WCh	Edmonton	7 Aug 01
10.60/1.5	7.63/2.0	14.90	2.03	46.23	14.40/0.0	43.40	5.40	67.01	4:29.58
8812			O'Brien			1	WCh	Tokyo	30 Aug 91
10.41/-1.6	7.90/0.8	16.24	1.91	46.53	13.94/-1.2	47.20	5.20	60.66	4:37.50
8811			Thompson			1	EC	Stuttgart	28 Aug 86
10.26/2.0	7.72/1.0	15.73	2.00	47.02	14.04/-0.3	43.38	5.10	62.78	4:26.16
8809			Eaton			1	WCh	Moskva	11 Aug 13
10.35/-0.5	7.73/0.3	14.39	1.93	46.02	13.72/0.4	45.00	5.20	64.83	4:29.80
8807			Sebrle			1		Götzis	1 Jun 03
10.78/-0.2	7.86/1.2	15.41	2.12	47.83	13.96/0.0	43.42	4.90	69.22	4:28.63
8800			Sebrle			1		Götzis	2 Jun 02
10.95/0.5	7.79/1.8	15.50	2.12	48.35	13.89/1.6	48.02	5.00	68.97	4:38.16
8800			Sebrle			1	EC	München	8 Aug 02
10.83/1.3	7.92/0.8	15.41	2.12	48.48	14.04/0.0	46.88	5.10	68.51	4:42.94
8792		Uwe	Freimuth	GDR	10.9.61	1	OD	Potsdam	21 Jul 84
11.06/0.4	7.79/1.2	16.30	2.03	48.43	14.66/1.9	46.58	5.15	72.42	4:25.19
8791			Clay			1	OG	Beijing	22 Aug 08
10.44/0.3	7.78/0.0	16.27	1.99	48.92	13.93/-0.5	53.79	5.00	70.97	5:06.59

Mark Wind	Name		Nat	Born	Pos	Meet	Venue			Date
8790	Trey	Hardee (10)	USA	7.2.84	1	WCh	Berlin			20 Aug 09
	10.45/0.2	7.83/1.9	15.33	1.99	48.13	13.86/0.3	48.08	5.20	68.00	4:48.91
8784	Tom	Pappas	USA	6.9.76	1	NC	Stanford			22 Jun 03
	10.78/0.2	7.96/1.4	16.28	2.17	48.22	14.13/1.7	45.84	5.20	60.77	4:48.12
	(30/11)									
8762	Siegfried	Wentz	FRG	7.3.60	2		Bernhausen			5 Jun 83
	10.89	7.49/	15.35	2.09	47.38	14.00	46.90	4.80	70.68	4:24.90
8735	Eduard	Hämäläinen	FIN/BLR	21.1.69	1		Götzis			29 May 94
	10.50w/2.1	7.26/1.0	16.05	2.11	47.63	13.82/-3.0	49.70	4.90	60.32	4:35.09
8727	Dave	Johnson	USA	7.4.63	1		Azusa			24 Apr 92
	10.96/0.4	7.52w/4.5	14.61	2.04	48.19	14.17/0.3	49.88	5.28	66.96	4:29.38
8725	Dmitriy	Karpov	KAZ	23.7.81	3	OG	Athína			24 Aug 04
	10.50w/2.2	7.81/-0.9	15.93	2.09	46.81	13.97/1.5	51.65	4.60	55.54	4:38.11
8709	Aleksandr	Apaychev	UKR	6.5.61	1	vGDR	Neubrandenburg			3 Jun 84
	10.96/	7.57/	16.00	1.97	48.72	13.93/	48.00	4.90	72.24	4:26.51
8706	Frank	Busemann	GER	26.2.75	2	OG	Atlanta			1 Aug 96
	10.60/0.7	8.07/0.8	13.60	2.04	48.34	13.47/0.3	45.04	4.80	66.86	4:31.41
8698	Grigoriy	Degtyaryov	RUS	16.8.58	1	NC	Kiyev			22 Jun 84
	10.87/0.7	7.42/0.1	16.03	2.10	49.75	14.53/0.3	51.20	4.90	67.08	4:23.09
8695	Damian	Warner	CAN	4.11.89	2	WCh	Beijing			29 Aug 15
	10.31/-0.4	7.65/0.2	14.44	2.04	47.30	13.63/-0.2	44.99	4.80	63.50	4:31.51
8694	Chris	Huffins	USA	15.4.70	1	NC	New Orleans			20 Jun 98
	10.31w/3.5	7.76w/2.5	15.43	2.18	49.02	14.02/1.0	53.22	4.60	61.59	4:59.43
	(20)									
8680	Torsten	Voss	GDR	24.3.63	1	WCh	Roma			4 Sep 87
	10.69/-0.3	7.88/1.2	14.98	2.10	47.96	14.13/0.1	43.96	5.10	58.02	4:25.93
8670	Michael	Schrader	GER	1.7.87	2	WCh	Moskva			11 Aug 13
	10.73/-0.5	7.85/0.2	14.56	1.99	47.66	14.29/0.4	46.44	5.00	65.67	4:25.38
8667 WR	Guido	Kratschmer	FRG	10.1.53	1		Bernhausen			14 Jun 80
	10.58w/2.4	7.80/	15.47	2.00	48.04	13.92/	45.52	4.60	66.50	4:24.15
8654	Leonel	Suárez	CUB	1.9.87	1	CAC	La Habana			4 Jul 09
	11.07/0.7	7.42/0.8	14.39	2.09	47.65	14.15/-0.6	46.07	4.70	77.47	4:27.29
8644	Steve	Fritz	USA	1.11.67	4	OG	Atlanta			1 Aug 96
	10.90/0.8	7.77/0.9	15.31	2.04	50.13	13.97/0.3	49.84	5.10	65.70	4:38.26
8644	Maurice	Smith	JAM	28.9.80	2	WCh	Osaka			1 Sep 07
	10.62/0.7	7.50/0.0	17.32	1.97	47.48	13.91/-0.2	52.36	4.80	53.61	4:33.52
8634 WR	Bruce	Jenner	USA	28.10.49	1	OG	Montreal			30 Jul 76
	10.94/0.0	7.22/0.0	15.35	2.03	47.51	14.84/0.0	50.04	4.80	68.52	4:12.61
8627	Robert	Zmelík	CZE	18.4.69	1		Götzis			31 May 92
	10.62w/2.1	8.02/0.2	13.93	2.05	48.73	13.84/1.2	44.44	4.90	61.26	4:24.83
8626	Michael	Smith	CAN	16.9.67	1		Götzis			26 May 96
	11.23/-0.6	7.72/0.6	16.94	1.97	48.69	14.77/-2.4	52.90	4.90	71.22	4:41.95
8617	Andrey	Kravchenko	BLR	4.1.86	1		Götzis			27 May 07
	10.86/0.2	7.90/0.9	13.89	2.15	47.46	14.05/-0.1	39.63	5.00	64.35	4:29.10
	(30)									
8603	Dean	Macey	GBR	12.12.77	3	WCh	Edmonton			7 Aug 01
	10.72/-0.7	7.59/0.4	15.41	2.15	46.21	14.34/0.0	46.96	4.70	54.61	4:29.05
8583w	Jón Arnar	Magnússon	ISL	28.7.69	1	ECp-2	Reykjavik			5 Jul 98
	10.68/2.0	7.63/2.0	15.57	2.07	47.78	14.33W/5.2	44.53	5.00	64.16	4:41.60
	8573				3		Götzis			31 May 98
	10.74/0.5	7.60/-0.2	16.03	2.03	47.66	14.24/0.7	47.82	5.10	59.77	4:46.43
8574	Christian	Plaziat	FRA	28.10.63	1	EC	Split			29 Aug 90
	10.72/-0.6	7.77/1.1	14.19	2.10	47.10	13.98/0.7	44.36	5.00	54.72	4:27.83
8574	Aleksandr	Yurkov	UKR	21.7.75	4		Götzis			4 Jun 00
	10.69/0.9	7.93/1.8	15.26	2.03	49.74	14.56/-0.9	47.85	5.15	58.92	4:32.49
8571	Lev	Lobodin	RUS	1.4.69	3	EC	Budapest			20 Aug 98
	10.66w/2.2	7.42/0.2	15.67	2.03	48.65	13.97/0.9	46.55	5.20	56.55	4:30.27
8566	Sebastian	Chmara	POL	21.11.71	1		Alhama de Murcia			17 May 98
	10.97w/2.9	7.56/1.2	16.03	2.10	48.27	14.32/1.8	44.39	5.20	57.25	4:29.66
8561	Rico	Freimuth	GER	14.3.88	3	WCh	Beijing			29 Aug 15
	10.51/-0.4	7.51/0.5	15.50	1.95	47.82	13.91/-0.2	50.17	4.80	60.61	4:37.05
8558	Pascal	Behrenbruch	GER	19.1.85	1	EC	Helsinki			28 Jun 12
	10.93/0.8	7.15/-0.8	16.89	1.97	48.54	14.16/0.2	48.24	5.00	67.45	4:34.02
8554	Attila	Zsivoczky	HUN	29.4.77	5		Götzis			4 Jun 00
	10.64w/2.1	7.24/-1.0	15.72	2.18	48.13	14.87/-0.9	45.64	4.65	63.57	4:23.13
8548	Paul	Meier	GER	27.7.71	3	WCh	Stuttgart			20 Aug 93
	10.57/0.9	7.57/1.1	15.45	2.15	47.73	14.63/0.0	45.72	4.60	61.22	4:32.05
	(40)	Peñalver below (7.19w/4.0)								
8547	Igor	Sobolevskiy	UKR	4.5.62	2	NC	Kiyev			22 Jun 84
	10.64/0.7	7.71/0.2	15.93	2.01	48.24	14.82/0.3	50.54	4.40	67.40	4:32.84

Mark Wind	Name		Nat	Born	Pos	Meet	Venue	Date
8538	Ilya	Shkurenyov	RUS	11.1.91	4	WCh	Beijing	29 Sep 15
	11.01/-0.7 7.50/0.5 14.09 2.10 47.88 14.27/-0.2 44.53 5.20 60.99 4:24.98							
8534	Siegfried	Stark	GDR	12.6.55	1	OT	Halle	4 May 80
	11.10w 7.64 15.81 2.03 49.53 14.86w 47.20 5.00 68.70 4:27.7							
8534w/8478	Antonio	Peñalver	ESP	1.12.68	1		Alhama de Murcia	24 May 92
	10.76w/3.9 7.42W/6.2 16.50 2.12 49.50 14.32/0.8 47.38 5.00 59.32 4:39.94							
8528	Aleksandr	Pogorelov	RUS	10.1.80	3	WCh	Berlin	20 Aug 09
	10.95/-0.3 7.49/-0.4 16.65 2.08 50.27 14.19/0.3 48.46 5.10 63.95 4:48.70							
8526	Francisco Javier	Benet	ESP	25.3.68	2		Alhama de Murcia	17 May 98
	10.72w/2.9 7.45/-1.2 14.57 1.92 48.10 13.83/1.8 46.12 5.00 65.37 4:26.81							
8526	Kristjan	Rahnu	EST	29.8.79	1		Arles	5 Jun 05
	10.52w/2.2 7.58/1.6 15.51 1.99 48.60 14.04w/3.1 50.81 4.95 60.71 4:52.18							
8524	Sébastien	Levicq	FRA	25.6.71	4	WCh	Sevilla	25 Aug 99
	11.05/0.2 7.52/-0.4 14.22 2.00 50.13 14.48/0.6 44.65 5.50 69.01 4:26.81							
8521	Kevin	Mayer	FRA	10.2.92	2	EC	Zürich	13 Aug 14
	11.10/-0.9 7.65/0.2 15.14 2.01 49.23 14.28/0.5 44.53 5.20 64.03 4:24.16							
8519	Yuriy	Kutsenko	RUS	5.3.52	3	NC	Kiyev	22 Jun 84
	11.07/0.5 7.54/-0.1 15.11 2.13 49.07 14.94/0.3 50.38 4.60 61.70 4:12.68							
8519	Hans	Van Alphen	BEL	12.1.82	1		Götzis	27 May 12
	10.96/1.0 7.62/1.1 15.23 2.06 49.54 14.55/0.4 45.45 4.96 64.15 4:20.87							
	(51)	100th man 8334, 200th 8181, 300th 8071, 400th 7983, 500th 7907						

4 x 100 METRES RELAY

Mark		Nat	Team	Pos	Meet	Venue	Date
36.84	WR	JAM	N Carter 10.1, Frater 8.9, Blake 9.0, Bolt 8.8	1	OG	London (OS)	11 Aug 12
37.04	WR	JAM	N Carter, Frater, Blake, Bolt	1	WCh	Daegu	4 Sep 11
37.10	WR	JAM	N Carter, Frater, Bolt, Powell	1	OG	Beijing	22 Aug 08
37.31		JAM	Mullings, Frater, Bolt, Powell	1	WCh	Berlin	22 Aug 09
37.36		JAM	Carter, Bailey Cole, Ashmeade, Bolt	1	WCh	Moskva	18 Aug 13
37.36		JAM	Carter, Powell, Ashmeade, Bolt	1	WCh	Beijing	29 Aug 15
37.38		USA	Demps, Patton, Kimmons, Gatlin	1h2	OG	London (OS)	10 Aug 12
37.38		USA	Rodgers, Gatlin, Gay, R.Bailey	1	W.Rly	Nassau	2 May 15
37.39		JAM	Carter, Frater, Blake, Bailey-Cole	1h1	OG	London (OS)	10 Aug 12
37.40	WR	USA	Marsh, Burrell, Mitchell, C Lewis	1	OG	Barcelona	8 Aug 92
37.40	WR	USA	Drummond, Cason, D Mitchell, L Burrell	1s1	WCh	Stuttgart	21 Aug 93
37.41		JAM	Carter, Powell, Dwyer, Ashmeade	1h2	WCh	Beijing	29 Aug 15
37.45		USA	Kimmons, Spearmon, Gay, Rodgers	1	WK	Zürich	19 Aug 10
37.48		USA	Drummond, Cason, D Mitchell, L Burrell	1	WCh	Stuttgart	22 Aug 93
37.50	WR	USA	Cason, Burrell, Mitchell, C Lewis	1	WCh	Tokyo	1 Sep 91
37.58		USA	'Red' Silmon, Rodgers, Salaam, Gatlin	1	Herc	Monaco	19 Jul 13
37.58		JAM	Livermore, Bailey-Cole, Ashmeade, Bolt	1	CG	Glasgow	2 Aug 14
37.59		USA	Drummond, Montgomery, B Lewis, Greene	1	WCh	Sevilla	29 Aug 99
37.59		USA	Conwright, Spearmon, Gay, Smoots	1	WCp	Athína	16 Sep 06
37.61		USA	Drummond, Williams, B Lewis, Greene	1	OG	Sydney	30 Sep 00
37.61		USA	Kimmons, Gatlin, Gay, Bailey	1	Herc	Monaco	20 Jul 12
37.62		TTO	Brown, Burns, Callander, Thompson	2	WCh	Berlin	22 Aug 09
37.65		USA	Drummond, Williams, C Johnson, Greene	1	ISTAF	Berlin	1 Sep 00
37.66		USA	Silmon, Rodgers, Salaam, Gatlin	2	WCh	Moskva	18 Aug 13
37.67	WR	USA	Marsh, Burrell, Mitchell, C Lewis	1	WK	Zürich	7 Aug 91
37.68		JAM	Carter, Bailey Cole, Ashmeade, Bolt	2	W.Rly	Nassau	2 May 15
37.69		CAN	Esmie 10.47, Gilbert 9.02, Surin 9.25, Bailey 8.95	1	OG	Atlanta	3 Aug 96
37.70		JAM	Clarke, Frater, Mullins, Bolt	1	WK	Zürich	28 Aug 09
37.71		JAM	Carter, Bailey-Cole, Forte, Fisher	1h2	WRly	Nassau	25 May 14
37.73		GBR	Gardener, Campbell, Devonish, Chambers	2	WCh	Sevilla	29 Aug 99
37.73		USA	Trammell, Rodgers, Patton, Spearmon	2	WK	Zürich	28 Aug 09
			(31 performances by teams from 5 nations) Further bests by nations:				
37.79	WR	FRA	Morinière, Sangouma 8.90, Trouabal, Marie-Rose	1	EC	Split	1 Sep 90
37.90		BRA	de Lima, Ribeiro, A da Silva, Cl da Silva	2	OG	Sydney	30 Sep 00
37.92		CHN	Mo Youxue, Xie Zhenye, Su Bingtian, Zhang Peimeng	3h2	WCh	Beijing	29 Aug 15
37.94		NGR	O Ezinwa, Adeniken, Obikwelu, D Ezinwa	1s2	WCh	Athína	9 Aug 97
38.00		CUB	Simón, Lamela, Isasi, Aguilera	3	OG	Barcelona	8 Aug 92
		(10)					
38.01		ANT	Walsh, D.Bailey, Jarvis, Francis	4h2	WCh	Beijing	29 Aug 15
38.02		URS	Yevgenyev, Bryzgin, Muravyov, Krylov	2	WCh	Roma	6 Sep 87
38.02		GER	Reus, Unger, Kosenkow, Jakubczyk	1		Weinheim	27 Jul 12
38.03		JPN	Tsukahara, Suetsugu 9.08, Takahira, Asahara	5	WCh	Osaka	1 Sep 07
38.12		GHA	Duah, Nkansah, Zakari, Tuffour	1s1	WCh	Athína	9 Aug 97
38.17		AUS	Henderson, Jackson, Brimacombe, Marsh	1s2	WCh	Göteborg	12 Aug 95
38.17		ITA	Donati, Collio, Di Gregorio, Checcucci	2	EC	Barcelona	1 Aug 10
38.29		NED	Mariano, Martina, Codrington, van Luijk	3h1	OG	London (OS)	10 Aug 12
38.31		POL	Masztak, Kuc, Kubaczyk, Krynski	6h2	OG	London (OS)	10 Aug 12

Mark	Wind	Name	Pos	Meet	Venue	Date
38.35	RSA	Bruintjies, Magakwe, Titi, Simbine	4	CG	Glasgow	2 Aug 14
	(20)					
38.41	SKN	Lestrod, Rogers, Adams, Lawrence	6h1	OG	London (OS)	10 Aug 12
38.45	AHO	Goeloe, Raffaela, Duzant, Martina	6	WCh	Helsinki	13 Aug 05
38.46	URS/RUS	Zharov, Krylov, Fatun, Goremykin	4	EC	Split	1 Sep 90
38.46	ESP	Viles, Ruiz, Hortelano, Rodríguez	4h1	WCh	Moskva	18 Aug 13
38.47	HKG	Tang Yik Chun, Lai Chun Ho, Ng Ka Fung, Tsui Chi Ho	1		Taipei	26 May 12
38.52	BAH	Griffith, Fraser, Hart, T.Smith	3h1	CG	Glasgow	1 Aug 14
38.53	UKR	Rurak, Osovich, Kramarenko, Dologodin	1	ECp	Madrid	1 Jun 96
38.54	SUI	Mancini, Schenkel, Somasundaran, Wilson	2h1	EC	Zürich	18 Aug 14
38.55A	BAR	Cadogan, Gittens, Deshong, Ellis	3	NACAC	San José, CRC	9 Aug 15
38.60	CIV	Meité, Douhou, Sonan, N'Dri (30)	3s1	WCh	Edmonton	12 Aug 01
Multi-nation team						
37.46	Racers TC	Bailey/ANT, Blake JAM, Forsythe JAM, Bolt JAM	1	LGP	London (CP)	25 Jul 09
One man disqualified for drugs						
37.04	USA	Kimmons 10.1, Gatlin 8.9, Gay ¶ 9.0, Bailey 9.0	(2)	OG	London (OS)	11 Aug 12
37.91	NGR	Asonze ¶, Obikwelu, Effiong, Aliu	(3)	WCh	Sevilla	29 Aug 99

4 x 200 METRES RELAY

Mark	Team	Name	Pos	Meet	Venue	Date
1:18.63	JAM	Ashmeade 20.5, Weir 19.2, J Brown 19.6, Y Blake 19.4	1	WRly	Nassau	24 May 14
1:18.68 WR	USA - Santa Monica Track Cluc	Marsh 20.0, Burrell 19.6, Heard 19.7, C Lewis 19.4	1	MSR	Walnut	17 Apr 94
1:19.10	World All-Stars	Drummond USA 20.4, Mitchell USA 19.3, Bridgewater USA 20.3, Regis GBR 19.1	2	MSR	Walnut	17 Apr 94
1:19.11 WR	Santa Monica TC/USA	M.Marsh, L Burrell, Heard, C Lewis	1	Penn	Philadelphia	25 Apr 92
1:19.16	USA Red Team	Crawford, Clay, Patton, Gatlin	1	PennR	Philadelphia	26 Apr 03
1:19.38 WR	Santa Monica TC/USA	Everett, Burrell, Heard, C Lewis	1	R-W	Koblenz	23 Aug 89
1:19.39	USA Blue	Drummond, Crawford, B Williams, Greene	1	PennR	Philadelphia	28 Apr 01
1:19.45	Santa Monica TC/USA	DeLoach, Burrell, C.Lewis, Heard	1	Penn	Philadelphia	27 Apr 91
1:19.47	Nike Int./USA	Brokenburr, A Harrison, Greene, M Johnson	1	Penn	Philadelphia	24 Apr 99
Best non-US nations						
1:20.51	SKN	A Adams, L Roland, BJ Lawrence, A Clarke	2	WRly	Nassau	24 May 14
1:20.66	FRA	Lemaitre, Fonsat, Bassaw, Romain	3	WRly	Nassau	25 May 14
1:21.10	ITA	Tilli, Simionato, Bongiorno, Mennea	1		Cagliari	29 Sep 83
1:21.22	POL	Tulin, Balcerzak, Pilarczyk, Urbas	2		Gdansk	14 Jul 01
1:21.29	GBR	Adam, Mafe, Christie, Regis	1	vURS	Birmingham	23 Jun 89

4 x 400 METRES RELAY

Mark	Team	Name	Pos	Meet	Venue	Date
2:54.29 WR	USA	Valmon 44.5, Watts 43.6, Reynolds 43.23, Johnson 42.94	1	WCh	Stuttgart	22 Aug 93
2:55.39	USA	Merritt 44.4, Taylor 43.7, Neville 44.16, Wariner 43.18	1	OG	Beijing	23 Aug 08
2:55.56	USA	Merritt 44.4, Taylor 43.7, Williamson 44.32, Wariner 43.10	1	WCh	Osaka	2 Sep 07
2:55.74 WR	USA	Valmon 44.6, Watts 43.00, M Johnson 44.73, S Lewis 43.41	1	OG	Barcelona	8 Aug 92
2:55.91	USA	O Harris 44.5, Brew 43.6, Wariner 43.98, Williamson 43.83	1	OG	Athína	28 Aug 04
2:55.99	USA	L Smith 44.62, A Harrison 43.84, Mills 43.66, Maybank 43.87	1	OG	Atlanta	3 Aug 96
2:56.16A WR	USA	Matthews 45.0, Freeman 43.2, James 43.9, Evans 44.1	1	OG	Ciud. México	20 Oct 68
2:56.16 WR	USA	Everett 43.79, S Lewis 43.69, Robinzine 44.74, Reynolds 43.94	1	OG	Seoul	1 Oct 88
2:56.60	GBR	I Thomas 44.92, Baulch 44.19, Richardson 43.62, Black 43.87	2	OG	Atlanta	3 Aug 96
2:56.65	GBR	Thomas 44.8, Black 44.2, Baulch 44.08, Richardson 43.57	2	WCh	Athína	10 Aug 97
2:56.72	BAH	Brown 44.9, Pinder 43.5, Mathieu 44.25, Miller 44.01	1	OG	London (OS)	10 Aug 12
2:56.75	JAM	McDonald 44.5, Haughton 44.4, McFarlane 44.37, Clarke 43.51	3	WCh	Athína	10 Aug 97
2:56.91	USA	Rock 44.7, Brew 44.3, Williamson 44.40, Wariner 43.49	1	WCh	Helsinki	14 Aug 05
2:57.05	USA	Nellum 45.2, Mance 43.5, McQuay 43.41, Taylor 44.85	2	OG	London (OS)	10 Aug 12
2:57.25	USA	Verburg 44.8, McQuay 44.1, C Taylor 44.6, L Merritt 43.8	1	WRly	Nassau	25 May 14
2:57.29	USA	Everett 45.1, Haley 44.0, McKay 44.20, Reynolds 44.00	1	WCh	Roma	6 Sep 87
2:57.32	USA	Ramsey 44.9, Mills 44.6, Reynolds 43.74, Johnson 44.11	1	WCh	Göteborg	13 Aug 95
2:57.32	BAH	McKinney 44.9, Moncur 44.6, A Williams 44.43, Brown 43.42	2	WCh	Helsinki	14 Aug 05
2:57.53	GBR	Black 44.7, Redmond 44.0, Regis 44.22, Akabusi 44.59	1	WCh	Tokyo	1 Sep 91
2:57.57	USA	Valmon 44.9, Watts 43.4, D.Everett 44.31, Pettigrew 44.93	2	WCh	Tokyo	1 Sep 91
2:57.59	BAH	L Williams 45.0, Pinder 43.8, C Brown 44.2, Mathieu 44.6	2	WRly	Nassau	25 May 14
2:57.82	USA	Verburg 45.0, McQuay 44.3, Nellum 44.38, Merritt 44.18	1	WCh	Beijing	30 Aug 15
2:57.86	USA	Taylor 45.4, Wariner 43.6, Clement 44.72, Merritt 44.16	1	WCh	Berlin	23 Aug 09
2:57.87	USA	L Smith 44.59, Rouser 44.33, Mills 44.32, Maybank 44.63	1s2	OG	Atlanta	2 Aug 96
2:57.91	USA	Nix 45.59, Armstead 43.97, Babers 43.75, McKay 44.60	1	OG	Los Angeles	11 Aug 84
2:57.97	JAM	McDonald, Haughton McFarlane, D Clarke	1	PAm	Winnipeg	30 Jul 99
2:58.00	POL	Rysiukiewicz 45.6, Czubak 44.2, Haczek 44.0, Mackowiak 44.2	2	GWG	Uniondale, NY	22 Jul 98
2:58.03	BAH	Bain 45.9, Mathieu 44.1, A Williams 44.02, Brown 44.05	2	OG	Beijing	23 Aug 08
2:58.06	RUS	Dyldin 45.5, Frolov 44.6, Kokorin 44.34, Alekseyev 43.56	3	OG	Beijing	23 Aug 08
2:58.07	JAM	Ayre 44.9, Simpson 44.9, Spence 44.48, Clarke 43.81	3	WCh	Helsinki	14 Aug 05
	(30/6)	plus six times for teams that contained an athlete who was subsequently banned for drugs abuse				
2:58.20	TTO	Quow 44.8, L Gordon 44.1, Lendore 44.85, Cedenio 44.47	2	WCh	Beijing	30 Aug 15

Mark Wind	Nat	Name	Pos	Meet	Venue	Date
2:58.56	BRA	Cl. da Silva 44.6, A dos Santos 45.1, de Araújo 45.0, Parrela 43.9	2	PAm	Winnipeg	30 Jul 99
2:58.68	NGR	Chukwu 45.18, Monye 44.49, Bada 44.70, Udo-Obong 44.31	1	OG	Sydney	30 Sep 00
2:58.96	FRA	Djhone 45.4, Keita 44.7, Diagana 44.69, Raquil 44.15	2	WCh	Saint-Denis	31 Aug 03
	(10)					
2:59.13	CUB	Martínez 45.6, Herrera 44.38, Tellez 44.81, Hernández 44.34	1h2	OG	Barcelona	7 Aug 92
2:59.21	RSA	Pistorius 45.58, Mogawane 43.97, de Beer 44.46, Victor 45.20	3h1	WCh	Daegu	1 Sep 11
2:59.28	BEL	D.Borlée 45.8, J.Borlée 44.2, Gillet 45.48, K.Borlée 43.78	2h1	WCh	Beijing	29 Aug 15
2:59.63	KEN	D Kitur 45.4, S Kitur 45.13, Kipkemboi 44.76, Kemboi 44.34	3h2	OG	Barcelona	7 Aug 92
2:59.70	AUS	Frayne 45.38, Clark 43.86, Minihan 45.07, Mitchell 45.39	4	OG	Los Angeles	11 Aug 84
2:59.86	GDR	Möller 45.8, Schersing 44.8, Carlowitz 45.3, Schönlebe 44.1	1	vURS	Erfurt	23 Jun 85
2:59.95	YUG	Jovkovic, Djurovic, Macev, Brankovic 44.3	2h3	WCh	Tokyo	31 Aug 91
2:59.95	BOT	Nkobolo 45.2, Amos 44.1, Maotoanong 46.05, Makwala 44.63	5h2	WCh	Beijing	29 Aug 15
2:59.96	FRG	Dobeleit 45.7, Henrich 44.3, Itt 45.12, Schmid 44.93	4	WCh	Roma	6 Sep 87
3:00.15	DOM	Cuesta 45.4, Soriano 43.8, J.Santos 46.58, L.Santos 44.36	6h2	WCh	Beijing	29 Aug 15
	(20)					
3:00.64	SEN	Diarra 46.53, Dia 44.94, Ndiaye 44.70, Faye 44.47	4	OG	Atlanta	3 Aug 96
3:00.76	JPN	Karube 45.88, Ito 44.86, Osakada 45.08, Omori 44.94	5	OG	Atlanta	3 Aug 96
3:00.79	ZIM	Chiwira 46.2, Mukomana 44.6, Ngidhi 45.79, Harnden 44.20	2h3	WCh	Athína	9 Aug 97
3:00.82A	VEN	A Ramírez 45.7, Aguilar 45.3, Acevedo 44.7, Longart 45.2	3	PAm	Guadalajara	28 Oct 11
3:01.44		Ramirez 46.0, Bravo 45.0, Meléndez 45.6, Mezones 44.8	6	W.Rly	Nassau	25 May 14
3:01.12	FIN	Lönnqvist 46.7, Salin 45.1, Karttunen 44.8, Kukkoaho 44.5	6	OG	München	10 Sep 72
3:01.26	IRL	Gregan 46.1, Murphy 45.2, Barr 45.05, English 44.96	8h2	WCh	Beijing	29 Aug 15
3:01.37	ITA	Bongiorni 46.2, Zuliani 45.0, Petrella 45.3, Ribaud 44.9	4	EC	Stuttgart	31 Aug 86
3:01.42	ESP	I Rodríguez 46.0, Canal 44.1, Andrés 45.88, Reina 45.48	4h1	WCh	Edmonton	11 Aug 01
3:01.60	BAR	Louis 46.67, Peltier 44.97, Edwards 45.04, Forde 44.92	6	OG	Los Angeles	11 Aug 84
3:01.61	BUL	Georgiev 45.9, Stankulov 46.0, Raykov 45.07, Ivanov 44.66	2h1	WCh	Stuttgart	21 Aug 93
	(30)					

Including subsequently banned athlete

Mark	Nat	Name	Pos	Meet	Venue	Date
2:54.20(WR)	USA	Young 44.3, Pettigrew ¶ 43.2, Washington 43.5, Johnson 43.2	(1)	GWG	Uniondale, NY	22 Jul 98
2:56.35	USA	A Harrison 44.36, Pettigrew 44.17, C Harrison 43.53, Johnson 44.29	(1)	OG	Sydney	30 Sep 00
2:56.45	USA	J Davis 45.2, Pettigrew 43.9, Taylor 43.92, M Johnson 43.49	(1)	WCh	Sevilla	29 Aug 99
2:56.47	USA	Young 44.6, Pettigrew 43.1, Jones 44.80, Washington 44.80	(1)	WCh	Athína	10 Aug 97
2:56.60	USA Red	Taylor 45.0, Pettigrew 44.2, Washington 43.7, Johnson 43.7	(1)	PennR	Philadelphia	29 Apr 00
2:57.54	USA	Byrd 45.9, Pettigrew 43.9, Brew 44.03, Taylor 43.71	1	WCh	Edmonton	12 Aug 01

4 x 800 METRES RELAY

Mark	Nat	Name	Pos	Meet	Venue	Date
7:02.43	KEN	Mutua 1:46.73, Yiampoy 1:44.38, Kombich 1:45.92, Bungei 1:45.40	1	VD	Bruxelles	25 Aug 06
7:02.82	USA	J Harris 1:47.05, Robinson 1:44.03, Burley 1:46.05, Krummenacker 1:45.69	2	VD	Bruxelles	25 Aug 06
7:03.89 WR	GBR	Elliott 1:49.14, Cook 1:46.20, Cram 1:44.54, Coe 1:44.01	1		London (CP)	30 Aug 82
7:04.70	RSA	van Oudtshoorn 1:46.9, Sepeng 1:45.2, Kotze 1:48.3, J Botha 1:44.3	1		Stuttgart	6 Jun 99
7:06.66	QAT	Sultan 1:45.81, Al-Badri 1:46.71, Suleiman 1:45.89, Ali Kamal 1:48.25	4	VD	Bruxelles	25 Aug 06
7:07.40	URS	Masunov, Kostetskiy, Matvetev, Kalinkin	1		Moskva	5 Aug 84
7:08.5 WR	FRG	Kinder 1:46.9, Adams 1:47.5, Bogatzki 1:47.9, Kemper 1:46.2	1		Wiesbaden	13 Aug 66
7:08.89	POL	Konieczny 1:48.9, Krawczyk 1:49.1, Lewandowski 1:45.9, Kszczot 1:44.8	2	WRly	Nassau	24 May 14

4 x 1500 METRES RELAY

Mark	Nat	Name	Pos	Meet	Venue	Date
14:22.22 WR	KEN	C Cheboi 3:38.5, S Kiplagat 3:32.4, Magut 3:39.0, A Kiprop 3:32.3	1	WRly	Nassau	25 May 14
14:36.23 WR	KEN	W Biwott 3:38.5, Gathimba 3:39.5, G Rono 3:41.4, Choge 3:36.9	1	VD	Bruxelles	4 Sep 09
14:38.8 WR	FRG	Wessinghage 3:38.8, Hudak 3:39.1, Lederer 3:44.6, Fleschen 3:36.3	1		Köln	16 Aug 77
14:40.4 WR	NZL	Polhill 3:42.9, Walker 3:40.4, Dixon 3:41.2, Quax 3:35.9	1		Oslo	22 Aug 73
14:40.80	USA	Casey 3:38.2, Torrence 3:36.6, Leer 3:39.3, Manzano 3:46.7	2	WRly	Nassau	25 May 14
14:41.22	ETH	Gebremedhin 3:39.9, Fida 3:37.5, Z Alemayehu 3:46.5, Wote 3:37.3	3	WRly	Nassau	25 May 14
14:45.63	URS	Kalutskiy, Yakovlev, Legeda, Lotarev	1		Leningrad	4 Aug 85
14:46.04	AUS	Gregson 3:39.1, McEntee 3:44.9, Birmingham 3:38.3, Williamsz 3:43.7	4	WRly	Nassau	25 May 14
14:46.16	Larios, ESP	Jiménez 3:40.9, Pancorbo 3:41.2, A García 3:43.9, Viciosa 3:40.2	1		Madrid	5 Sep 97
14:48.2	FRA	Bégouin 3:44.5, Lequement 3:44.3, Philippe 3:42.2, Dien 3:37.2	2		Bourges	23 Jun 79
Mixed Team: 14:44.31		Ali BRN, Birgen KEN, N Kemboi KEN, Campbell IRL	2	VD	Bruxelles	4 Sep 09

4 x 1 MILE RELAY

Mark	Nat	Name	Pos	Meet	Venue	Date
15:49.08	IRL	Coghlan 4:00.2, O'Sullivan 3:55.3, O'Mara 3:56.6, Flynn 3:56.98	1		Dublin	17 Aug 85
15:59.57	NZL	Rogers 3:57.2, Bowden 4:02.5, Gilchrist 4:02.8, Walker 3:57.07	1		Auckland	2 Mar 83

4 x 110m/120y HURDLES

Mark	Nat	Name	Pos	Meet	Venue	Date
52.94	USA Blue	Richardson, Harris, Merritt, Oliver	1	DrakeR	Des Moines	25 Apr 15
53.08	All Stars	Riley JAM, R Brathwaite BAR, Parchment JAM, Swift BAR	2	DrakeR	Des Moines	25 Apr 15
53.31y	USA Red	Oliver, Herring, Brown, Merritt	1	PennR	Philadelphia	25 Apr 08
53.36	USA	Bramlett, Moore, Payne, Merritt	1	DNG	Stockholm	7 Aug 07
53.62	USA	(ACC All-Stars) A Johnson, Reese, Brown, Ross	1		Clemson	16 May 98
53.83	JAM	Riley, D Carter, Parchment, Fennell)	2	DrakeR	Des Moines	26 Apr 14

3000 METRES TRACK WALK

Mark Wind	Name		Nat	Born	Pos	Meet	Venue	Date
10:47.11	Giovanni	De Benedictis	ITA	8.1.68	1		S.Giovanni Valdarno	19 May 90
10:52.44+	Yohann	Diniz	FRA	1.1.78	1	in 5k	Villeneuve d'Ascq	27 Jun 08
10:56.22	Andrew	Jachno	AUS	13.4.62	1		Melbourne	7 Feb 91
10:56.23	Dane	Bird-Smith	AUS	15.7.92	1		Cork	8 Jul 14
10:56.34+	Roman	Mrázek	SVK	21.1.62	1	in 5k	Bratislava	14 Jun 89
10:58.16	Kevin	Campion	FRA	23.5.88	2		Cork	8 Jul 14
10:58.47	Alex	Wright	IRL	19.12.90	3		Cork	8 Jul 14
10:59.04	Luke	Adams	AUS	22.10.76	1		Cork	3 Jul 10
11:00.2+	Jozef	Pribilinec	SVK	6.7.60	1	in 10k	Banská Bystrica	30 Aug 85
11:00.50+	Francisco Javier	Fernández ¶	ESP	6.3.77	1	in 5k	Villeneuve d'Ascq	8 Jun 07
Indoors								
10:31.42	Andreas	Erm	GER	12.3.76	1		Halle	4 Feb 01
10:50.0	Denis	Nizhegorodov	RUS	26.7.80	1		Saransk	4 Dec 06
10:53+	Mikhail	Shchennikov	RUS	24.12.67	1	in 5k	Moskva	14 Feb 95
10:53.3	Igor	Yerokhin	RUS	4.9.85	2		Saransk	4 Dec 06
10:54.61	Carlo	Mattioli	ITA	23.10.54	1		Milano	6 Feb 80
10:56.77+	Ivano	Brugnetti	ITA	1.9.76	1	in 5k	Torino	21 Feb 09
10:56.88	Reima	Salonen	FIN	19.11.55	1		Turku	5 Feb 84
10:57.32	Matej	Tóth	SVK	10.2.83	1		Wien	12 Feb 11

5000 METRES TRACK WALK

Mark Wind	Name		Nat	Born	Pos	Meet	Venue	Date
18:05.49	Hatem	Ghoula	TUN	7.6.73	1		Tunis	1 May 97
18:17.22	Robert	Korzeniowski	POL	30.7.68	1		Reims	3 Jul 92
18:18.01	Yohann	Diniz	FRA	1.1.78	1		Villeneuve d'Ascq	27 Jun 08
18:27.34	Francisco Javier	Fernández ¶	ESP	6.3.77	1		Villeneuve d'Ascq	8 Jun 07
18:28.80	Roman	Mrázek	SVK	21.1.62	1	PTS	Bratislava	14 Jun 89
18:30.43	Maurizio	Damilano	ITA	6.4.57	1		Caserta	11 Jun 92
Indoors								
18:07.08	Mikhail	Shchennikov	RUS	24.12.67	1		Moskva	14 Feb 95
18:08.86	Ivano	Brugnetti	ITA	1.9.76	1	NC	Ancona	17 Feb 07
18:11.41	Ronald	Weigel	GDR	8.8.59	1mx		Wien	13 Feb 88
18:11.8	Valeriy	Borchin ¶	RUS	11.9.86	1		Saransk	30 Dec 10
18:15.25	Grigoriy	Kornev	RUS	14.3.61	1		Moskva	7 Feb 92
18:15.54	Andrey	Ruzavin	RUS	28.3.86	1		Samara	30 Jan 14
18:16.54 ?	Frants	Kostyukevich	BLR	4.4.63	2	NC	Gomel	4 Feb 89
18:16.76	Yohann	Diniz	FRA	1.1.78	1		Reims	7 Dec 14
18:19.97	Giovanni	De Benedictis	ITA	8.1.68	1	EI	Genova	28 Feb 92
18:21.76	Ruslan	Dmytrenko	UKR	22.3.86	2		Samara	30 Jan 14
18:22.25	Andreas	Erm	GER	12.3.76	1	NC	Dortmund	25 Feb 01
18:23.18	Rishat	Shafikov	RUS	23.1.70	1		Samara	1 Mar 97
18:24.13	Francisco Javier	Fernández ¶	ESP	6.3.77	1		Belfast	17 Feb 07
18:27.15	Alessandro	Gandellini	ITA	30.4.73	1	NC	Genova	12 Feb 00
18:27.80	Jozef	Pribilinec	SVK	6.7.60	2	WI	Indianapolis	7 Mar 87
18:27.95	Stefan	Johansson	SWE	11.4.67	3	EI	Genova	28 Feb 92
18:28.54	Igor	Yerokhin	RUS	4.9.85	1		Samara	31 Jan 13
Drugs dq: 18:17.13	Vladimir	Kanaykin ¶	RUS	21.3.85	(2)	Winter	Moskva	5 Feb 12
18:26.82	Sergey	Bakulin ¶	RUS	13.11.86	(3)	Winter	Moskva	5 Feb 12

10,000 METRES TRACK WALK

Mark Wind	Name		Nat	Born	Pos	Meet	Venue	Date
37:53.09	Francisco Javier	Fernández ¶	ESP	6.3.77	1	NC	Santa Cruz de Tenerife	27 Jul 08
37:58.6	Ivano	Brugnetti	ITA	1.9.76	1		Sesto San Gioavnni	23 Jul 05
38:01.49	Eiki	Takahashi	JPN	19.11.92	1		Isahaya	13 Dec 15
38:02.60	Jozef	Pribilinec	SVK	6.7.60	1		Banská Bystrica	30 Aug 85
38:06.6	David	Smith	AUS	24.7.55	1		Sydney	25 Sep 86
38:08.13	Yohann	Diniz	FRA	1.1.78	1	NC	Reims	12 Jul 14
38:10.23	Yusuke	Suzuki	JPN	2.1.88	1		Abashiri	16 Jul 15
38:12.13	Ronald	Weigel	GDR	8.8.59	1		Potsdam	10 May 86
38:18.0+	Valdas	Kazlauskas	LTU	23.2.58	1		Moskva	18 Sep 83
38:20.0	Moacir (10)	Zimmermann	BRA	30.12.83	1		Blumenau	7 Jun 08
38:23.73		Wang Zhen	CHN	24.8.91	1		Genova	8 Feb 15
38:24 0+	Bernardo	Segura	MEX	11.2.70	1	SGP	Fana	7 May 94
38:24.31	Hatem	Ghoula	TUN	7.6.73	1		Tunis	30 May 98
38:26.4	Daniel	García	MEX	28.10.71	1		Sdr Omme	17 May 97
38:26.53	Robert	Korzeniowski	POL	30.7.68	1		Riga	31 May 02
38:27.57	Robert	Heffernan	IRL	20.2.78	1	NC	Dublin	20 Jul 08
38:32.0	Erik	Tysse	NOR	4.12.80	1	NC	Bergen (Fana)	13 Jun 08
38:37.02	Kevin	Campion	FRA	23.5.88	1	NC	Paris (C)	13 Jul 13
38:37.6+	Jefferson	Pérez	ECU	1.7.74	1	in 20k	Fana	9 May 98
Indoors								
38:31.4	Werner	Heyer	GDR	14.11.56	1		Berlin	12 Jan 80

20 KILOMETRES WALK

Mark	Wind	Name		Nat	Born	Pos	Meet	Venue	Date
1:16:36	WR	Yusuke	Suzuki	JPN	2.1.88	1	AsiC	Nomi	15 Mar 15
1:16:43		Sergey	Morozov ¶	RUS	21.3.88	1	NC	Saransk	8 Jun 08
1:17:02		Yohann	Diniz	FRA	1.1.78	1	NC	Arles	8 Mar 15
1:17:16	WR	Vladimir	Kanaykin ¶	RUS	21.3.85	1	RWC	Saransk	29 Sep 07
1:17:21	WR	Jefferson	Pérez	ECU	1.7.74	1	WCh	Saint-Denis	23 Aug 03
1:17:22	WR	Francisco Javier	Fernández ¶	ESP	6.3.77	1		Turku	28 Apr 02
1:17:23		Vladimir	Stankin	RUS	2.1.74	1	NC-w	Adler	8 Feb 04
1:17:24			Diniz			1		Lugano	15 Mar 15
1:17:25.6t		Bernardo	Segura	MEX	11.2.70	1	SGP	Bergen (Fana)	7 May 94
1:17:30		Alex	Schwazer ¶	ITA	26.12.84	1		Lugano	18 Mar 12
1:17:33		Nathan	Deakes (10)	AUS	17.8.77	1		Cixi	23 Apr 05
1:17:36			Kanaykin			1	NC	Cheboksary	17 Jun 07
1:17:36			Wang Zhen	CHN	24.8.91	1		Taicang	30 Mar 12
1:17:38		Valeriy	Borchin ¶	RUS	11.9.86	1	NC-w	Adler	28 Feb 09
1:17:40			Chen Ding	CHN	5.8.92	2		Taicang	30 Mar 12
1:17:41			Zhu Hongjun	CHN	18.8.83	2		Cixi	23 Apr 05
1:17:43			Diniz			2		Lugano	18 Mar 12
1:17:46		Julio	Martínez	GUA	27.9.73	1		Eisenhüttenstadt	8 May 99
1:17:46		Roman	Rasskazov	RUS	28.4.79	1	NC	Moskva	19 May 00
1:17:52			Fernández			1		La Coruña	4 Jun 05
1:17:53			Cui Zhide	CHN	11.1.83	3		Cixi	23 Apr 05
1:17:55			Borchin			1	NC-w	Adler	23 Feb 08
1:17:56		Alejandro	López	MEX	9.2.75	2		Eisenhüttenstadt	8 May 99
1:18:00			Fernández			2	WCh	Saint-Denis	23 Aug 03
1:18:00			Wang Zhen			1		La Coruña	6 Jun 15
1:18:03		Eiki	Takahashi	JPN	19.11.92	1	NC	Kobe	15 Feb 15
1:18:03.3t	WR		Bo Lingtang (20)	CHN	12.8.70	1	NC	Beijing	7 Apr 94
1:18:05		Dmitriy	Yesipchuk	RUS	17.11.74	1	NC-w	Adler	4 Mar 01
1:18:06		Viktor	Burayev ¶	RUS	23.8.82	2	NC-w	Adler	4 Mar 01
1:18:06		Vladimir	Parvatkin	RUS	10.10.84	1	NC-w	Adler	12 Mar 05
		(30/23)							
1:18:07			Li Gaobo	CHN	4.5.89	4		Cixi	23 Apr 05
1:18:12		Artur	Meleshkevich	BLR	11.4.75	1		Brest	10 Mar 01
1:18:13	WR	Pavol	Blazek	SVK	9.7.58	1		Hildesheim	16 Sep 90
1:18:13			Wang Hao	CHN	16.8.89	1	NG	Jinan	22 Oct 09
1:18:14		Mikhail	Khmelnitskiy	BLR	24.7.69	1	NC	Soligorsk	13 May 00
1:18:14		Noé	Hernández	MEX	15.3.78	4	WCh	Saint-Denis	23 Aug 03
1:18:16		Vladimir	Andreyev	RUS	7.9.66	2	NC	Moskva	19 May 00
		(30)							
1:18:17		Ilya	Markov	RUS	19.6.72	2	NC-w	Adler	12 Mar 05
1:18:18		Yevgeniy	Misyulya	BLR	13.3.64	1		Eisenhüttenstadt	11 May 96
1:18:18		Sergey	Bakulin ¶	RUS	13.11.86	2	NC-w	Adler	23 Feb 08
1:18:20	WR	Andrey	Perlov	RUS	12.12.61	1	NC	Moskva	26 May 90
1:18:20		Denis	Nizhegorodov	RUS	26.7.80	3	NC-w	Adler	4 Mar 01
1:18:22		Robert	Korzeniowski	POL	30.7.68	1		Hildesheim	9 Jul 00
1:18:23		Andrey	Makarov	BLR	2.1.71	2	NC	Soligorsk	13 May 00
1:18:25		Andrey	Krivov	RUS	14.11.85	3	NC-w	Sochi	18 Feb 12
1:18:25		Erick	Barrondo	GUA	14.6.91	3		Lugano	18 Mar 12
1:18:27		Daniel	García	MEX	28.10.71	2	WCp	Podebrady	19 Apr 97
		(40)							
1:18:27			Xing Shucai	CHN	4.8.84	5		Cixi	23 Apr 05
1:18:28		Pyotr	Trofimov	RUS	28.11.83	1	NC-w	Sochi	23 Feb 13
1:18:30			Yu Chaohong	CHN	12.12.76	6		Cixi	23 Apr 05
1:18:31			Han Yucheng	CHN	16.12.78	7		Cixi	23 Apr 05
1:18:32			Li Zewen	CHN	5.12.73	4	WCp	Podebrady	19 Apr 97
1:18:33			Liu Yunfeng ¶	CHN	3.8.79	8		Cixi	23 Apr 05
1:18:34		Eder	Sánchez	MEX	21.5.86	3	WCp	Cheboksary	10 May 08
1:18:35.2t		Stefan	Johansson	SWE	11.4.67	1	SGP	Bergen (Fana)	15 May 92
1:18:36		Mikhail	Shchennikov	RUS	24.12.67	1	NC	Sochi	20 Apr 96
1:18:37		Aleksandr	Pershin	RUS	4.9.68	2	NC	Moskva	26 May 90
1:18:37		Ruslan	Shafikov	RUS	27.6.75	1	NC-w23	Adler	11 Feb 95
1:18:37		Ruslan	Dmytrenko	UKR	22.3.86	1	WCp	Taicang	4 May 14
		(52)	100th man 1:19:25, 200th 1:20:28, 300th 1:21:14, 400th 1:21:49, 500th 1:22:14						
Probable short course									
1:18:33		Mikhail	Shchennikov	RUS	24.12.67	1	4-N	Livorno	10 Jul 93
Drugs disqualification									
1:16:53		Vladimir	Kanaykin ¶	RUS	21.3.85	(2)	NC	Saransk	8 Jun 08
1:17:47		Andrey	Ruzavin ¶	RUS	28.3.86	(1)	NC-w	Sochi	18 Feb 12
1:17:52			Morozov ¶			(2)	NC-w	Sochi	18 Feb 12

Mark	Wind	Name		Nat	Born	Pos	Meet	Venue	Date
1:18:29		Stanislav	Yemelyanov ¶	RUS	23.10.90	(4)	NC-w	Sochi	18 Feb 12

Note that the full effects of recently announced bans on some Russian walkers have yet to be fully determined.

30 KILOMETRES WALK

Mark	Name		Nat	Born	Pos	Meet	Venue	Date
2:01:13+	Vladimir	Kanaykin ¶	RUS	21.3.85	1	in 35k	Adler	19 Feb 06
2:01:44.1t	Maurizio	Damilano	ITA	6.4.57	1		Cuneo	3 Oct 92
2:01:47+		Kanaykin			1	in 35k	Adler	13 Mar 05
2:02:27+		Kanaykin			1	in 35k	Adler	8 Feb 04
2:02:41	Andrey	Perlov	RUS	12.12.61	1	NC-w	Sochi	19 Feb 89
2:02:45	Yevgeniy	Misyulya	BLR	13.3.64	1		Mogilyov	28 Apr 91
2:03:06	Daniel	Bautista	MEX	4.8.52	1		Cherkassy	27 Apr 80
2:03:50+	Vladimir	Parvatkin	RUS	10.10.84	2	in 35k	Adler	19 Feb 06
2:03:56.5t	Thierry	Toutain	FRA	14.2.62	1		Héricourt	24 Mar 91
2:04:00	Aleksandr	Potashov	BLR	12.3.62	1		Adler	14 Feb 93
2:04:24	Valeriy	Spitsyn	RUS	5.12.65	1	NC-w	Sochi	22 Feb 92
2:04:30	Vitaliy	Matsko (10)	RUS	8.6.60	2	NC-w	Sochi	19 Feb 89
2:04:49+	Semyon	Lovkin	RUS	14.7.77	1=	in 35k	Adler	1 Mar 03
2:04:49+	Stepan	Yudin	RUS	3.4.80	1=	in 35k	Adler	1 Mar 03
2:04:50+	Sergey	Kirdyapkin ¶	RUS	16.1.80	2	in 35k	Adler	13 Mar 05
2:04:55.5t	Guillaume	Leblanc	CAN	14.4.62	1		Sept-Iles	16 Jun 90
2:05:01	Sergey	Katureyev	RUS	29.9.67	2	NC-w	Sochi	22 Feb 92
2:05:05	Pyotr	Pochenchuk	UKR	26.7.54	2		Cherkassy	27 Apr 80
2:05:06	Nathan	Deakes	AUS	17.8.77	1	NC	Hobart	27 Aug 06
2:05:08+	Denis	Nizhegorodov	RUS	26.7.80	3	in 35k	Adler	19 Feb 06
2:05:09	Mikhail	Shchennikov	RUS	24.12.67	1	NC-w	Adler	11 Feb 96
2:05:12	Valeriy	Suntsov (20)	RUS	10.7.55	3		Cherkassy	27 Apr 80

35 KILOMETRES WALK

Mark	Name		Nat	Born	Pos	Meet	Venue	Date
2:21:31	Vladimir	Kanaykin ¶	RUS	21.3.85	1	NC-w	Adler	19 Feb 06
2:23:17		Kanaykin			1	NC-w	Adler	8 Feb 04
2:23:17		Kanaykin			1	NC-w	Adler	13 Mar 05
2:24:25	Semyon	Lovkin	RUS	14.7.77	1	NC-w	Adler	1 Mar 03
2:24:25	Sergey	Bakulin ¶	RUS	13.11.86	1	NC-w	Adler	1 Mar 09
2:24:50	Denis	Nizhegorodov	RUS	26.7.80	2	NC-w	Adler	19 Feb 06
2:24:56		Nizhegorodov			2	NC-w	Adler	1 Mar 09
2:25:19	Andrey	Ruzavin ¶	RUS	28.3.86	3	NC-w	Adler	1 Mar 09
2:25:38	Stepan	Yudin	RUS	3.4.80	2	NC-w	Adler	1 Mar 03
2:25:54	Mikhail	Ryzhov	RUS	17.12.91	1	NC-w	Sochi	27 Feb 15
2:25:57		Kirdyapkin			2	NC-w	Adler	13 Mar 05
2:25:58	German	Skurygin ¶	RUS	15.9.63	1	NC-w	Adler	20 Feb 98
2:25:59		Kanaykin ¶			1	NC-w	Adler	23 Feb 08
2:25:59		Ryzhov			1	NC-w	Sochi	18 Feb 12
	(15/9)							
2:26:16	Alex	Schwazer ¶ (10)	ITA	26.12.84	1		Montalto Di Castro	24 Jan 10
2:26:25	Aleksey	Voyevodin ¶	RUS	9.8.70	2	NC-w	Adler	8 Feb 04
2:26:29	Yuriy	Andronov	RUS	6.11.71	4	NC-w	Adler	1 Mar 09
2:26:33	Ivan	Noskov	RUS	16.7.88	2	NC-w	Sochi	18 Feb 12
2:26:36	Igor	Yerokhin ¶	RUS	4.9.85	1	NC-w	Sochi	26 Feb 11
2:26:46	Oleg	Ishutkin	RUS	22.7.75	1	NC-w	Adler	9 Feb 97
2:27:02	Yevgeniy	Shmalyuk	RUS	14.1.76	1	NC-w	Adler	20 Feb 00
2:27:07	Dmitriy	Dolnikov	RUS	19.11.72	2	NC-w	Adler	20 Feb 98
2:27:21	Pavel	Nikolayev	RUS	18.12.77	3	NC-w	Adler	20 Feb 98
2:27:29	Nikolay	Matyukhin	RUS	13.12.68	2	NC-w	Adler	9 Feb 97
2:27:42	Aleksey	Bartsaykin (20)	RUS	22.3.89	2	NC-w	Sochi	23 Feb 13
DQ: 2:25:42	Sergey	Kirdyapkin ¶	RUS	18.6.80	(1)	NC-w	Sochi	18 Feb 12

50 KILOMETRES WALK

Mark	Name		Nat	Born	Pos	Meet	Venue	Date
3:32:33 WR	Yohann	Diniz	FRA	1.1.78	1	EC	Zürich	15 Aug 14
3:34:14 WR	Denis	Nizhegorodov	RUS	26.7.80	1	WCp	Cheboksary	11 May 08
3:34:38	Matej	Tóth	SVK	10.2.83	1		Dudince	21 Mar 15
3:35:27.2t WR		Diniz			1		Reims	12 Mar 11
3:35:29		Nizhegorodov			1	NC	Cheboksary	13 Jun 04
3:35:47	Nathan	Deakes	AUS	17.8.77	1	NC	Geelong	2 Dec 06
3:36:03 WR	Robert	Korzeniowski	POL	30.7.68	1	WCh	Saint-Denis	27 Aug 03
3:36:04	Alex	Schwazer ¶	ITA	26.12.84	1	NC	Rosignano Solvay	11 Feb 07
3:36:06		Yu Chaohong	CHN	12.12.76	1	NG	Nanjing	22 Oct 05
3:36:13		Zhao Chengliang	CHN	1.6.84	2	NG	Nanjing	22 Oct 05
3:36:20		Han Yucheng	CHN	16.12.78	1	NC	Nanning	27 Feb 05
3:36:21		Tóth			2	EC	Zürich	15 Aug 14
3:36:39 WR		Korzeniowski			1	EC	München	8 Aug 02

Mark	Wind	Name		Nat	Born	Pos	Meet	Venue	Date
3:36:42		German	Skurygin ¶ (10)	RUS	15.9.63	2	WCh	Saint-Denis	27 Aug 03
3:36:53		Jared	Tallent	AUS	17.10.84	1	OG	London	11 Aug 12
3:37:04			Schwazer			2	WCp	Cheboksary	11 May 08
3:37:09			Schwazer			1	OG	Beijing	22 Aug 08
3:37:16			Si Tianfeng	CHN	17.6.84	2	OG	London	11 Aug 12
3:37:26	WR	Valeriy	Spitsyn	RUS	5.12.65	1	NC	Moskva	21 May 00
3:37:41	WR	Andrey	Perlov	RUS	12.12.61	1	NC	Leningrad	5 Aug 89
3:37:41		Ivan	Noskov	RUS	16.7.88	3	EC	Zürich	15 Aug 14
3:37:46		Andreas	Erm	GER	12.3.76	3	WCh	Saint-Denis	27 Aug 03
3:37:54		Robert	Heffernan	IRL	20.2.78	3	OG	London	11 Aug 12
3:37:56			Heffernan			1	WCh	Moskva	14 Aug 13
3:37:58			Xing Shucai	CHN	4.8.84	2	NC	Nanning	27 Feb 05
3:38:01		Aleksey	Voyevodin ¶	RUS	9.8.70	4	WCh	Saint-Denis	27 Aug 03
3:38:02			Nizhegorodov			1	WCp	La Coruña	14 May 06
3:38:08		Sergey	Kirdyapkin ¶ (20)	RUS	16.1.80	1	WCh	Helsinki	12 Aug 05
3:38:08		Igor	Yerokhin ¶	RUS	4.9.85	1	NC	Saransk	8 Jun 08
3:38:08			Kirdyapkin			1	WCp	Saransk	13 May 12
		(30/21)							
3:38:17	WR	Ronald	Weigel	GDR	8.8.59	1	IM	Potsdam	25 May 86
3:38:29		Vyacheslav	Ivanenko	RUS	3.3.61	1	OG	Seoul	30 Sep 88
3:38:43		Valentí	Massana	ESP	5.7.70	1	NC	Orense	20 Mar 94
3:38:58		Mikhail	Ryzhov ¶	RUS	17.12.91	2	WCh	Moskva	14 Aug 13
3:39:01			Li Jianbo	CHN	14.11.86	4	OG	London	11 Aug 12
3:39:17			Dong Jimin	CHN	10.10.83	4	NC	Nanning	27 Feb 05
3:39:21		Vladimir	Potemin	RUS	15.1.80	2	NC	Moskva	21 May 00
3:39:22		Sergey	Korepanov	KAZ	9.5.64	1	WCp	Mézidon-Canon	2 May 99
3:39:34		Valentin	Kononen	FIN	7.3.69	1		Dudince	25 Mar 00
		(30)							
3:39:45		Hartwig	Gauder	GDR	10.11.54	3	OG	Seoul	30 Sep 88
3:39:54		Jesús Angel	García	ESP	17.10.69	1	WCp	Podebrady	20 Apr 97
3:40:02		Aleksandr	Potashov	BLR	12.3.62	1	NC	Moskva	27 May 90
3:40:07		Andrey	Plotnikov	RUS	12.8.67	2	NC	Moskva	27 May 90
3:40:08		Tomasz	Lipiec ¶	POL	10.5.71	2	WCp	Mézidon-Canon	2 May 99
3:40:12		Oleg	Ishutkin	RUS	22.7.75	2	WCp	Podebrady	20 Apr 97
3:40:12		Yuki	Yamazaki	JPN	16.1.84	1		Wajima	12 Apr 09
3:40:13		Nikolay	Matyukhin	RUS	13.12.68	3	WCp	Mézidon-Canon	2 May 99
3:40:19		Takayuki	Tanii	JPN	14.2.83	2	AsiG	Incheon	1 Oct 14
3:40:20		Hiroki	Arai	JPN	18.5.88	1	NC	Wajima	19 Apr 15
		(40)							
3:40:23			Gadasu Alatan	CHN	27.1.84	3	NG	Nanjing	22 Oct 05
3:40:39		Igor	Hlavan	UKR	25.9.90	4	WCh	Moskva	14 Aug 13
3:40:40		Vladimir	Kanaykin ¶	RUS	21.3.85	1	NC	Saransk	12 Jun 05
3:40:46	WR	José	Marín	ESP	21.1.50	1	NC	Valencia	13 Mar 83
3:40:46		Yuriy	Andronov ¶	RUS	6.11.71	1		Moskva	11 Jun 12
3:40:57.9t		Thierry	Toutain	FRA	14.2.62	1		Héricourt	29 Sep 96
3:41:02		Francisco Javier	Fernández ¶	ESP	6.3.77	1	NC	San Pedro del Pinatar	1 Mar 09
3:41:09		Érick	Barrondo	GUA	14.6.91	1		Dudince	23 Mar 13
3:41:10			Zhao Jianguo	CHN	19.1.88	1	AsiC	Wajima	16 Apr 06
3:41:16		Trond	Nymark	NOR	28.12.76	2	WCh	Berlin	21 Aug 09
		(50)	100th man 3:44:36, 200th 3:49:11, 300th 3:51:47, 400th 3:54:20, 500th 3:56:53						
Drugs disqualification			Russians – Noskov, Ryzhov, Strelkov and Yargunkin suspended pending investigation						
3:35:59		Sergey	Kirdyapkin ¶	RUS	16.1.80	(1)	OG	London	11 Aug 12
3:36:55		Vladimir	Kanaykin ¶	RUS	21.3.85	(2)	WCp	Cheboksary	11 May 08
3:37:54		Igor	Yerokhin ¶	RUS	4.9.85	(5)	OG	London	11 Aug 12
3:38:46		Sergey	Bakulin ¶	RUS	13.11.86	(1)	NC	Saransk	12 Jun 11

100 KILOMETRES WALK

Mark	Wind	Name		Nat	Born	Pos	Meet	Venue	Date
8:38.07		Viktor	Ginko	BLR	7.12.65	1		Scanzorosciate	27 Oct 02
8:43:30			Ginko			1		Scanzorosciate	29 Oct 00
8:44:28			Ginko			1		Scanzorosciate	19 Oct 03
8:48:28		Modris	Liepins	LAT	30.8.66	1		Scanzorosciate	28 Oct 01
8:54:35		Aleksey	Rodionov	RUS	5.3.57	1		Scanzorosciate	15 Nov 98
8:55:12		Pascal	Kieffer	FRA	6.5.61	1		Besançon	18 Oct 92
8:55:40		Vitaliy	Popovich	UKR	22.10.62	1		Scanzorosciate	31 Oct 99
8:58:12		Gérard	Lelièvre	FRA	13.11.49	1		Laval	7 Oct 84
8:58:47		Zóltan	Czukor	HUN	18.12.62	2		Scanzorosciate	27 Oct 02

Oldest mark in top 50 World Lists: Men: in wind assisted sections: LJ 8.49w Ralph Boston USA 2 Sep 1964, 100m 9.91w Bob Hayes USA 15 Oct 1964; in main lists: SP: 37= 21.78 Randy Matson USA 22 Apr 1967.
Women: by an individual – just outside: 100mh 52= 12.59 Anneliese Ehrhardt GDR 8 Sep 1972.

WOMEN'S ALL-TIME WORLD LISTS

100 METRES

Mark	Wind	Name		Nat	Born	Pos	Meet	Venue	Date
10.49WR	0.0	Florence	Griffith Joyner	USA	21.12.59	1q1	NC/OT	Indianapolis	16 Jul 88
		@ Probably strongly wind-assisted, but recognised as a US and world record							
10.61	1.2		Griffith Joyner			1	NC/OT	Indianapolis	17 Jul 88
10.62	1.0		Griffith Joyner			1q3	OG	Seoul	24 Sep 88
10.64	1.2	Carmelita	Jeter	USA	24.11.79	1		Shanghai	20 Sep 09
10.65A	1.1	Marion	Jones ¶	USA	12.10.75	1	WCp	Johannesburg	12 Sep 98
10.67	-0.1		Jeter			1	WAF	Thessaloníki	13 Sep 09
10.70 (WR)	1.6		Griffith Joyner			1s1	NC/OT	Indianapolis	17 Jul 88
10.70	-0.1		Jones			1	WCh	Sevilla	22 Aug 99
10.70	2.0		Jeter			1	Pre	Eugene	4 Jun 11
10.70	0.6	Shelly-Ann	Fraser-Pryce	JAM	27.12.86	1	NC	Kingston	29 Jun 12
10.71	0.1		Jones			1		Chengdu	12 May 98
10.71	2.0		Jones			1s2	NC	New Orleans	19 Jun 98
10.71	-0.3		Fraser-Pryce			1	WCh	Moskva	12 Aug 13
10.72	2.0		Jones			1	NC	New Orleans	20 Jun 98
10.72	0.0		Jones			1	Herc	Monaco	8 Aug 98
10.72	0.0		Jones			1	Athl	Lausanne	25 Aug 98
10.72	-0.3		Fraser-Pryce			1	VD	Bruxelles	6 Sep 13
10.73	2.0	Christine	Arron	FRA	13.9.73	1	EC	Budapest	19 Aug 98
10.73	0.1		Fraser-Pryce			1	WCh	Berlin	17 Aug 09
10.74	1.3	Merlene	Ottey	JAM/SLO	10.5.60	1	GPF	Milano	7 Sep 96
10.74	0.2		Fraser-Pryce			1	DL	Saint-Denis	4 Jul 15
10.75	0.6		Jones			1	GGala	Roma	14 Jul 98
10.75	0.4	Kerron	Stewart	JAM	16.4.84	1	GGala	Roma	10 Jul 09
10.75	0.1		Stewart			2	WCh	Berlin	17 Aug 09
10.75	1.5		Fraser-Pryce			1	OG	London (OS)	4 Aug 12
10.76 WR	1.7	Evelyn	Ashford	USA	15.4.57	1	WK	Zürich	22 Aug 84
10.76	0.9		Jones			1	VD	Bruxelles	22 Aug 97
10.76	0.3		Jones			1q4	WCh	Sevilla	21 Aug 99
10.76	1.1	Veronica	Campbell-Brown	JAM	15.5.82	1	GS	Ostrava	31 May 11
10.76	-0.3		Fraser-Pryce			1	WCh	Beijing	24 Aug 15
		(30 performances by 9 athletes)							
10.77	0.9	Irina	Privalova (10)	RUS	22.11.68	1rA	Athl	Lausanne	6 Jul 94
10.77	0.7	Ivet	Lalova	BUL	18.5.84	1	ECp-1A	Plovdiv	19 Jun 04
10.78A	1.0	Dawn	Sowell	USA	27.3.66	1	NCAA	Provo	3 Jun 89
10.78	1.8	Torri	Edwards ¶	USA	31.1.77	1s2	OT	Eugene	28 Jun 08
10.79	0.0		Li Xuemei	CHN	5.1.77	1	NG	Shanghai	18 Oct 97
10.79	-0.1	Inger	Miller	USA	12.6.72	2	WCh	Sevilla	22 Aug 99
10.79	1.1	Blessing	Okagbare	NGR	9.10.88	1	DL	London (OS)	27 Jul 13
10.79	1.5	English	Gardner	USA	22.4.92	1s1	NC	Eugene	26 Jun 15
10.80	0.8	Tori	Bowie	USA	27.8.90	21	Herc	Monaco	18 Jul 14
10.81 WR	1.7	Marlies	Göhr'	GDR	21.3.58	1	OD	Berlin	8 Jun 83
10.81	1.7	Murielle	Ahouré	CIV	23.8.87	2	Pre	Eugene	30 May 15
		(20)							
10.81	-0.3	Dafne	Schippers	NED	15.6.92	2	WCh	Beijing	24 Aug 15
10.82	-1.0	Gail	Devers	USA	19.11.66	1	OG	Barcelona	1 Aug 92
10.82	0.4	Gwen	Torrence	USA	12.6.65	2	GPF	Paris	3 Sep 94
10.82	-0.3	Zhanna	Pintusevich-Block ¶	UKR	6.7.72	1	WCh	Edmonton	6 Aug 01
10.82	-0.7	Sherone	Simpson	JAM	12.8.84	1	NC	Kingston	24 Jun 06
10.83	1.7	Marita	Koch	GDR	18.2.57	2	OD	Berlin	8 Jun 83
10.83	-1.0	Juliet	Cuthbert	JAM	9.4.64	2	OG	Barcelona	1 Aug 92
10.83	0.1	Ekateríni	Thánou ¶	GRE	1.2.75	2s1	WCh	Sevilla	22 Aug 99
10.83	1.6	Kelly-Ann	Baptiste	TTO	14.10.86	1	NC	Port of Spain	22 Jun 13
10.84	1.3	Chioma	Ajunwa ¶	NGR	25.12.70	1		Lagos	11 Apr 92
		(30)							
10.84	1.9	Chandra	Sturrup	BAH	12.9.71	1	Athl	Lausanne	5 Jul 05
10.84	1.5	Elaine	Thompson	JAM	28.6.92	2rB	Pre	Eugene	30 May 15
10.85	2.0	Anelia	Nuneva	BUL	30.6.62	1h1	NC	Sofia	2 Sep 88
10.85	1.0	Muna	Lee	USA	30.10.81	1	OT	Eugene	28 Jun 08
10.85	1.5	Tianna	Bartoletta'	USA	30.8.85	4	OG	London (OS)	4 Aug 12
10.85	2.0	Barbara	Pierre	HAI/USA	28.4.87	1s1	NC	Des Moines	21 Jun 13
10.85	1.6	Michelle-Lee	Ahye	TTO	10.4.92	1	NC	Port of Spain	21 Jun 14
10.86	0.6	Silke	Gladisch'	GDR	20.6.64	1	NC	Potsdam	20 Aug 87
10.86	1.2	Chryste	Gaines ¶	USA	14.9.70	1	WAF	Monaco	14 Sep 03
10.86	2.0	Marshevet	Hooker/Myers	USA	25.9.84	2	Pre	Eugene	4 Jun 11
		(40)							
10.87	1.8	Octavious	Freeman	USA	20.4.92	2	NC	Des Moines	21 Jun 13

Mark	Wind	Name		Nat	Born	Pos	Meet	Venue	Date
10.88	0.4	Lauryn	Williams	USA	11.9.83	2	WK	Zürich	19 Aug 05
10.89	1.8	Katrin	Krabbe ¶	GDR	22.11.69	1		Berlin	20 Jul 88
10.89	0.0		Liu Xiaomei	CHN	11.1.72	2	NG	Shanghai	18 Oct 97
10.89	1.5	Allyson	Felix	USA	18.11.85	5	OG	London (OS)	4 Aug 12
10.90	1.4	Glory	Alozie	NGR/ESP	30.12.77	1		La Laguna	5 Jun 99
10.90	1.8	Shalonda	Solomon	USA	19.12.85	2		Clermont	5 Jun 10
10.91	0.2	Heike	Drechsler'	GDR/GER	16.12.64	2	GWG	Moskva	6 Jul 86
10.91	1.1	Savatheda	Fynes	BAH	17.10.74	2	Athl	Lausanne	2 Jul 99
10.91	1.5	Debbie	Ferguson McKenzie	BAH	16.1.76	1	CG	Manchester	27 Jul 02
10.91	1.7	Alexandria	Anderson	USA	28.1.87	3s2	NC	Des Moines	21 Jun 13
		(51)	100th women 11.02, 200th 11.12, 300th 11.18, 400th 11.23, 500th 11.27						
Doubtful wind reading									
10.83	0.0	Sheila	Echols	USA	2.10.64	1q2	NC/OT	Indianapolis	16 Jul 88
10.86	0.0	Diane	Williams	USA	14.12.60	2q1	NC/OT	Indianapolis	16 Jul 88
Probably semi-automatic timing									
10.87	1.9	Lyudmila	Kondratyeva	RUS	11.4.58	1		Leningrad	3 Jun 80
Low altitude best: 10.91	1.6		Sowell			1	NC	Houston	16 Jun 89
Wind-assisted performances to 10.75 and performers to 10.89									
10.54	3.0		Griffith Joyner			1	OG	Seoul	25 Sep 88
10.60	3.2		Griffith Joyner			1h1	NC/OT	Indianapolis	16 Jul 88
10.68	2.2		Jones			1	DNG	Stockholm	1 Aug 00
10.70	2.6		Griffith Joyner			1s2	OG	Seoul	25 Sep 88
10.71	2.2		Fraser-Pryce			1	Pre	Eugene	1 Jun 13
10.72	3.0		Jeter			1s1	NC	Eugene	26 Jun 09
10.72	3.2	Tori	Bowie	USA	27.8.90	1s2	NC	Eugene	26 Jun 15
10.74	2.7		Jeter			1	NC	Eugene	24 Jun 11
10.75	4.1		Jones			1h3	NC	New Orleans	19 Jun 98
10.75	2.2	Blessing	Okagbare	NGR	9.10.88	2	Pre	Eugene	1 Jun 13
10.76	3.4	Marshevet	Hooker/Myers	USA	25.9.84	1q1	NC/OT	Eugene	27 Jun 08
10.76	5.4	English	Gardner	USA	22.4.92	1	Athl	Lausanne	9 Jul 15
10.77	2.3	Gail	Devers	USA	19.11.66	1	Jen	San José	28 May 94
10.77	2.3	Ekateríni	Thánou ¶	GRE	1.2.75	1		Rethymno	28 May 99
10.78	5.0	Gwen	Torrence	USA	12.6.65	1q3	NC/OT	Indianapolis	16 Jul 88
10.78	3.3	Muna	Lee	USA	30.10.81	2	NC	Eugene	26 Jun 09
10.79	3.3	Marlies	Göhr'	GDR	21.3.58	1	NC	Cottbus	16 Jul 80
10.80	2.9	Pam	Marshall	USA	16.8.60	1	NC	Eugene	20 Jun 86
10.80	2.8	Heike	Drechsler'	GDR	16.12.64	1	Bisl	Oslo	5 Jul 86
10.82	2.2	Silke	Gladisch/Möller	GDR	20.6.64	1s1	WCh	Roma	30 Aug 87
10.83	3.9	Sheila	Echols	USA	2.10.84	1h2	NC/OT	Indianapolis	16 Jul 88
10.84	2.9	Alice	Brown	USA	20.9.60	2	NC	Eugene	20 Jun 86
10.86	3.4	Lauryn	Williams	USA	11.9.83	2q1	NC/OT	Eugene	27 Jun 08
10.86	3.2	Jasmine	Todd	USA	23.12.93	3s2	NC	Eugene	26 Jun 15
10.87	3.0	Me'Lisa	Barber	USA	4.10.80	1s1	NC	Carson	25 Jun 05
10.88	5.9	Alexandria	Anderson	USA	28.1.87	1		Austin	14 Apr 12
10.89	3.1	Kerstin	Behrendt	GDR	2.9.67	2		Berlin	13 Sep 88
10.89	2.9	Sanya	Richards-Ross	USA	26.2.85	1	TexR	Austin	31 Mar 12
Hand timing									
10.6	0.1	Zhanna	Pintusevich ¶	UKR	6.7.72	1		Kiev	12 Jun 97
Drugs disqualification									
10.75	-0.4		Jones			(1)	OG	Sydney	23 Sep 00
10.78	0.1		Jones			(1)	ISTAF	Berlin	1 Sep 00
10.85	0.9	Kelli	White ¶	USA	1.4.77	(1)	WCh	Saint-Denis	24 Aug 03
10.79w	2.3	Kelli	White ¶	USA	1.4.77	(1)		Carson	1 Jun 03
10.89w	4.6	Tahesia	Harrigan-Scott	IVB	15.2.82	(1h1)		Clernont	4 Jun 11

200 METRES

Mark	Wind	Name		Nat	Born	Pos	Meet	Venue	Date
21.34WR	1.3	Florence	Griffith Joyner	USA	21.12.59	1	OG	Seoul	29 Sep 88
21.56WR	1.7		Griffith Joyner			1s1	OG	Seoul	29 Sep 88
21.62A	-0.6	Marion	Jones ¶	USA	12.10.75	1	WCp	Johannesburg	11 Sep 98
21.63	0.2	Dafne	Schippers	NED	15.6.92	1	WCh	Beijing	28 Aug 15
21.64	0.8	Merlene	Ottey	JAM	10.5.60	1	VD	Bruxelles	13 Sep 91
21.66	-1.0		Ottey			1	WK	Zürich	15 Aug 90
21.66	0.2	Elaine	Thompson	JAM	28.6.92	2	WCh	Beijing	28 Aug 15
21.69	1.0	Allyson	Felix	USA	18.11.85	1	NC/OT	Eugene	30 Jun 12
21.71WR	0.7	Marita	Koch	GDR	18.2.57	1	v CAN	Karl-Marx-Stadt	10 Jun 79
21.71WR	0.3		Koch			1	OD	Potsdam	21 Jul 84
21.71WR	1.2	Heike	Drechsler'	GDR	16.12.64	1	NC	Jena	29 Jun 86
21.71WR	-0.8		Drechsler			1	EC	Stuttgart	29 Aug 86
21.72	1.3	Grace	Jackson	JAM	14.6.61	2	OG	Seoul	29 Sep 88
21.72	-0.1	Gwen	Torrence (10)	USA	12.6.65	1s2	OG	Barcelona	5 Aug 92
21.74	0.4	Marlies	Göhr'	GDR	21.3.58	1	NC	Erfurt	3 Jun 84

Mark	Wind	Name		Nat	Born	Pos	Meet	Venue	Date
21.74	1.2	Silke	Gladisch'	GDR	20.6.64	1	WCh	Roma	3 Sep 87
21.74	0.6	Veronica	Campbell-Brown	JAM	15.5.82	1	OG	Beijing	21 Aug 08
21.75	-0.1	Juliet	Cuthbert	JAM	9.4.64	2s2	OG	Barcelona	5 Aug 92
21.76	0.3		Koch			1	NC	Dresden	3 Jul 82
21.76	0.7		Griffith Joyner			1q1	OG	Seoul	28 Sep 88
21.76	-0.8		Jones			1	WK	Zürich	13 Aug 97
21.77	-0.1		Griffith Joyner			1q2	NC/OT	Indianapolis	22 Jul 88
21.77	1.0		Ottey			1	Herc	Monaco	7 Aug 93
21.77	-0.3		Torrence			1	ASV	Köln	18 Aug 95
21.77	0.6	Inger	Miller	USA	12.6.72	1	WCh	Sevilla	27 Aug 99
21.78	-1.3		Koch			1	NC	Leipzig	11 Aug 85
21.79	1.7		Gladisch			1	NC	Potsdam	22 Aug 87
21.80	-1.1		Ottey			1	Nik	Nice	10 Jul 90
21.80	0.4		Jones			1	GWG	Uniondale, NY	20 Jul 98
21.81	-0.1	Valerie	Brisco	USA	6.7.60	1	OG	Los Angeles	9 Aug 84
21.81	0.4		Ottey			1	ASV	Köln	19 Aug 90
21.81	-0.6		Torrence			1	OG	Barcelona	6 Aug 92
21.81	0.0		Torrence			1	Herc	Monaco	25 Jul 95
21.81	1.6		Jones			1	Pre	Eugene	30 May 99
21.81	1.7		Felix			1	WCh	Osaka	31 Aug 07
		(35/15)							
21.83	-0.2	Evelyn	Ashford	USA	15.4.57	1	WCp	Montreal	24 Aug 79
21.85	0.3	Bärbel	Wöckel'	GDR	21.3.55	2	OD	Potsdam	21 Jul 84
21.87	0.0	Irina	Privalova	RUS	22.11.68	2	Herc	Monaco	25 Jul 95
21.93	1.3	Pam	Marshall	USA	16.8.60	2	NC/OT	Indianapolis	23 Jul 88
		(20)							
21.95	0.3	Katrin	Krabbe ¶	GDR	22.11.69	1	EC	Split	30 Aug 90
21.97	1.9	Jarmila	Kratochvílová	CZE	26.1.51	1	PTS	Bratislava	6 Jun 81
21.99	0.9	Chandra	Cheeseborough	USA	10.1.59	2	NC	Indianapolis	19 Jun 83
21.99	1.1	Marie-José	Pérec	FRA	9.5.68	1	BNP	Villeneuve d'Ascq	2 Jul 93
21.99	1.1	Kerron	Stewart	JAM	16.4.84	2	NC	Kingston	29 Jun 08
22.00	1.3	Sherone	Simpson	JAM	12.8.84	1	NC	Kingston	25 Jun 06
22.01	-0.5	Anelia	Nuneva'	BUL	30.6.62	1	NC	Sofia	16 Aug 87
22.01	0.0		Li Xuemei	CHN	5.1.77	1	NG	Shanghai	22 Oct 97
22.01	0.6	Muna	Lee	USA	30.10.81	4	OG	Beijing	21 Aug 08
22.01	0.2	Candyce	McGrone	USA	24.3.89	4	WCh	Beijing	28 Aug 15
		(30)							
22.04A	0.7	Dawn	Sowell	USA	27.3.66	1	NCAA	Provo	2 Jun 89
22.06A	0.7	Evette	de Klerk'	RSA	21.8.65	1		Pietersburg	8 Apr 89
22.07	-0.1	Mary	Onyali	NGR	3.2.68	1	WK	Zürich	14 Aug 96
22.07	0.2	Dina	Asher-Smith	GBR	4.12.95	5	WCh	Beijing	28 Aug 15
22.09	-0.3	Sanya	Richards-Ross	USA	26.2.85	1	DL	New York	9 Jun 12
22.09	-0.2	Shelly-Ann	Fraser-Pryce	JAM	27.12.86	2	OG	London (OS)	8 Aug 12
22.10	-0.1	Kathy	Cook'	GBR	3.5.60	4	OG	Los Angeles	9 Aug 84
22.11	1.0	Carmelita	Jeter	USA	24.11.79	2	NC/OT	Eugene	30 Jun 12
22.11	0.1	Myriam	Soumaré	FRA	29.10.86	2	VD	Bruxelles	5 Sep 14
22.13	1.2	Ewa	Kasprzyk	POL	7.9.57	2	GWG	Moskva	8 Jul 86
		(40)							
22.14	-0.6	Carlette	Guidry	USA	4.9.68	1	NC	Atlanta	23 Jun 96
22.14	0.2	Shaunae	Miller	BAH	15.4.94	1		Kingston	9 May 15
22.15	1.0	Shalonda	Solomon	USA	19.12.85	1	NC	Eugene	26 Jun 11
22.17A	-2.3	Zhanna	Pintusevich-Block ¶	UKR	6.7.72	1		Monachil	9 Jul 97
22.18	-0.6	Dannette	Young-Stone	USA	6.10.64	2	NC	Atlanta	23 Jun 96
22.18	0.9	Galina	Malchugina	RUS	17.12.62	1s2	NC	Sankt Peterburg	4 Jul 96
22.18	0.5	Merlene	Frazer	JAM	27.12.73	1s2	WCh	Sevilla	25 Aug 99
22.18	1.5	Tori	Bowie	USA	27.8.90	1	Pre	Eugene	31 May 14
22.18	1.9	Dezerea	Bryant	USA	27.4.93	1	NCAA	Eugene	13 Jun 15
22.19	1.5	Natalya	Bochina	RUS	4.1.62	2	OG	Moskva	30 Jul 80
22.19	0.0	Debbie	Ferguson McKenzie	BAH	16.1.76	1	GP II	Saint-Denis	3 Jul 99
22.19	1.9	Kimberlyn	Duncan	USA	2.8.91	1s2	NCAA	Des Moines	7 Jun 12
22.19	1.0	Aleksandra	Fedoriva	RUS	13.9.88	1	NC	Cheboksary	6 Jul 12
		(53)	100th woman 22.34, 200th 22.59, 300th 22.74, 400th 22.84, 500th 22.91						
Wind-assisted			*Performers listed to 22.16*						
21.80	3.2	Kimberlyn	Duncan	USA	2.8.91	1	NC	Des Moines	23 Jun 13
21.82	3.1	Irina	Privalova	RUS	22.11.68	1	Athl	Lausanne	6 Jul 94
21.91	2.8	Muna	Lee	USA	30.10.81	1		Fort-de-France	10 May 08
22.01	2.9	Michelle-Lee	Ahye	TTO	10.4.92	1		San Marcos	25 Apr 15
22.06	3.8	Jeneba	Tarmoh	USA	27.9.89	1	NC	Sacramento	29 Jun 14
22.16	3.1	Dannette	Young-Stone	USA	6.10.64	2	Athl	Lausanne	6 Jul 94
22.16	3.2	Nanceen	Perry	USA	19.4.77	1		Austin	6 May 00

Mark	Wind	Name		Nat	Born	Pos	Meet	Venue	Date
22.16	3.2	Kamaria	Brown	USA	21.12.92	4	NC	Des Moines	23 Jun 13
Hand timing									
21.9	-0.1	Svetlana	Goncharenko	RUS	28.5.71	1		Rostov-na-Donu	31 May 98
21.6w	2.5	Pam	Marshall	USA	16.8.60	1	NC	San José	26 Jun 87
Drugs disqualification									
22.05	-0.3	Kelli	White ¶	USA	1.4.77	1	WCh	Saint-Denis	28 Aug 03
22.18i		Michelle	Collins ¶	USA	12.2.71	1	WI	Birmingham	15 Mar 03

300 METRES

Times in 300m races only

Mark		Name		Nat	Born	Pos	Meet	Venue	Date
35.30A		Ana Gabriela	Guevara	MEX	4.3.77	1		Ciudad de México	3 May 03
35.46		Kathy	Cook'	GBR	3.5.60	1	Nike	London (CP)	18 Aug 84
35.46		Chandra	Cheeseborough	USA	10.1.59	2	Nike	London (CP)	18 Aug 84
Indoors									
35.45		Irina	Privalova	RUS	22.11.68	1		Moskva	17 Jan 93
35.48	#	Svetlana	Goncharenko	RUS	28.5.71	1		Tampere	4 Feb 98

400 METRES

Mark		Name		Nat	Born	Pos	Meet	Venue	Date
47.60	WR	Marita	Koch	GDR	18.2.57	1	WCp	Canberra	6 Oct 85
47.99	WR	Jarmila	Kratochvílová	CZE	26.1.51	1	WCh	Helsinki	10 Aug 83
48.16	WR		Koch			1	EC	Athína	8 Sep 82
48.16			Koch			1	Drz	Praha	16 Aug 84
48.22			Koch			1	EC	Stuttgart	28 Aug 86
48.25		Marie-José	Pérec	FRA	9.5.68	1	OG	Atlanta	29 Jul 96
48.26			Koch			1	GO	Dresden	27 Jul 84
48.27		Olga	Vladykina'	UKR	30.6.63	2	WCp	Canberra	6 Oct 85
48.45			Kratochvílová			1	NC	Praha	23 Jul 83
48.59		Tatána	Kocembová'	CZE	2.5.62	2	WCh	Helsinki	10 Aug 83
48.60	WR		Koch			1	ECp	Torino	4 Aug 79
48.60			Vladykina			1	ECp	Moskva	17 Aug 85
48.61			Kratochvílová			1	WCp	Roma	6 Sep 81
48.63		Cathy	Freeman	AUS	16.2.73	2	OG	Atlanta	29 Jul 96
48.65			Bryzgina'			1	OG	Seoul	26 Sep 88
48.70		Sanya	Richards	USA	26.2.85	1	WCp	Athína	16 Sep 06
48.73			Kocembová			2	Drz	Praha	16 Aug 84
48.77			Koch			1	v USA	Karl-Marx-Stadt	9 Jul 82
48.82			Kratochvílová			1	Ros	Praha	23 Jun 83
48.83		Valerie	Brisco	USA	6.7.60	1	OG	Los Angeles	6 Aug 84
48.83			Pérec			1	OG	Barcelona	5 Aug 92
48.83			Richards			1	VD	Bruxelles	4 Sep 09
48.85			Kratochvílová			2	EC	Athína	8 Sep 82
48.86			Kratochvílová			1	WK	Zürich	18 Aug 82
48.86			Koch			1	NC	Erfurt	2 Jun 84
48.87			Koch			1	VD	Bruxelles	27 Aug 82
48.88			Koch			1	OG	Moskva	28 Jul 80
48.89	WR		Koch			1		Potsdam	29 Jul 79
48.89			Koch			1		Berlin	15 Jul 84
48.89		Ana Gabriela	Guevara	MEX	4.3.77	1	WCh	Saint-Denis	27 Aug 03
		(30/9)							
49.05		Chandra (10)	Cheeseborough	USA	10.1.59	2	OG	Los Angeles	6 Aug 84
49.07		Tonique	Williams-Darling	BAH	17.1.76	1	ISTAF	Berlin	12 Sep 04
49.10		Falilat	Ogunkoya	NGR	12.5.68	3	OG	Atlanta	29 Jul 96
49.11		Olga	Nazarova ¶	RUS	1.6.65	1s1	OG	Seoul	25 Sep 88
49.16		Antonina	Krivoshapka	RUS	21.7.87	1	NC	Cheboksary	5 Jul 12
49.19		Mariya	Pinigina'	UKR	9.2.58	3	WCh	Helsinki	10 Aug 83
49.24		Sabine	Busch	GDR	21.11.62	2	NC	Erfurt	2 Jun 84
49.26		Allyson	Felix	USA	18.11.85	1	WCh	Beijing	27 Aug 15
49.28	WR	Irena	Szewinska'	POL	24.5.46	1	OG	Montreal	29 Jul 76
49.28		Pauline	Davis-Thompson	BAH	9.7.66	4	OG	Atlanta	29 Jul 96
49.28		Yuliya	Gushchina	RUS	4.3.83	2	NC	Cheboksary	5 Jul 12
		(20)							
49.29		Charity	Opara ¶	NGR	20.5.72	1	GGala	Roma	14 Jul 98
49.30		Petra	Müller'	GDR	18.7.65	1		Jena	3 Jun 88
49.30		Lorraine	Fenton'	JAM	8.9.73	2	Herc	Monaco	19 Jul 02
49.32		Shericka	Williams	JAM	17.9.85	2	WCh	Berlin	18 Aug 09
49.33		Amantle	Montsho ¶	BOT	4.7.83	1	Herc	Monaco	19 Jul 13
49.35		Anastasiya	Kapachinskaya ¶	RUS	21.11.79	1	NC	Cheboksary	22 Jul 11
49.40		Jearl	Miles-Clark	USA	4.9.66	1	NC	Indianapolis	14 Jun 97
49.41		Christine	Ohuruogu	GBR	17.5.84	1	WCh	Moskva	12 Aug 13
49.42		Grit	Breuer ¶	GER	16.2.72	2	WCh	Tokyo	27 Aug 91
49.43		Kathy	Cook'	GBR	3.5.60	3	OG	Los Angeles	6 Aug 84
		(30)							

Mark Wind	Name		Nat	Born	Pos	Meet	Venue	Date
49.43A	Fatima	Yusuf	NGR	2.5.71	1	AfG	Harare	15 Sep 95
49.47	Aelita	Yurchenko	UKR	1.1.65	2	Kuts	Moskva	4 Sep 88
49.48	Francena	McCorory	USA	20.10.88	1	NC	Sacramento	28 Jun 14
49.49	Olga	Zaytseva	RUS	10.11.84	1	NCp	Tula	16 Jul 06
49.53	Vanya	Stambolova ¶	BUL	28.11.83	1	GP	Rieti	27 Aug 06
49.56	Bärbel	Wöckel'	GDR	21.3.55	1		Erfurt	30 May 82
49.56	Monique	Hennagan	USA	26.5.76	1	NC/OT	Sacramento	17 Jul 04
49.57	Grace	Jackson	JAM	14.6.61	1	Nik	Nice	10 Jul 88
49.58	Dagmar	Rübsam'	GDR	3.6.62	3	NC	Erfurt	2 Jun 84
49.59	Marion	Jones ¶	USA	12.10.75	1r6	MSR	Walnut	16 Apr 00
	(40)							
49.59	Katharine	Merry	GBR	21.9.74	1	GP	Athína	11 Jun 01
49.61	Ana Fidelia	Quirot	CUB	23.3.63	1	PAm	La Habana	5 Aug 91
49.63	Novlene	Williams-Mills	JAM	26.4.82	1		Shanghai	23 Sep 06
49.64	Gwen	Torrence	USA	12.6.65	2	Nik	Nice	15 Jul 92
49.64	Ximena	Restrepo	COL	10.3.69	3	OG	Barcelona	5 Aug 92
49.64	Deedee	Trotter	USA	8.12.82	1	NC	Indianapolis	23 Jun 07
49.64	Debbie	Dunn ¶	USA	26.3.78	1	NC	Des Moines	26 Jun 10
49.65	Natalya	Nazarova	RUS	26.5.79	1	NC	Tula	31 Jul 04
49.65	Nicola	Sanders	GBR	23.6.82	2	WCh	Osaka	29 Aug 07
49.66	Christina	Brehmer/Lathan	GDR	28.2.58	3	OG	Moskva	28 Jul 80
49.66	Lillie	Leatherwood	USA	6.7.64	1	NC	New York	15 Jun 91
	(51)	100th woman 50.19, 200th 50.82, 300th 51.14, 400th 51.39, 500th 51.61						
Hand timing								
48.9	Olga	Nazarova ¶	RUS	1.6.65	1	NP	Vladivostok	13 Sep 88
49.2A	Ana Fidelia	Quirot	CUB	23.3.63	1	AmCp	Bogotá	13 Aug 89

600 METRES

Mark	Name		Nat	Born	Pos	Meet	Venue	Date
1:22.63	Ana Fidelia	Quirot	CUB	23.3.63	1		Guadalajara, ESP	25 Jul 97
1:22.87	Maria Lurdes	Mutola	MOZ	27.10.72	1		Liège (NX)	27 Aug 02
1:23.35	Pamela	Jelimo	KEN	5.12.89	1		Liège (NX)	5 Jul 12
1:23.5A	Doina	Melinte	ROU	27.12.56	1		Poiana Brasov	27 Jul 86

800 METRES

Mark	Name		Nat	Born	Pos	Meet	Venue	Date
1:53.28 WR	Jarmila	Kratochvílová	CZE	26.1.51	1		München	26 Jul 83
1:53.43 WR	Nadezhda	Olizarenko'	UKR	28.11.53	1	OG	Moskva	27 Jul 80
1:54.01	Pamela	Jelimo	KEN	5.12.89	1	WK	Zürich	29 Aug 08
1:54.44	Ana Fidelia	Quirot	CUB	23.3.63	1	WCp	Barcelona	9 Sep 89
1:54.68		Kratochvílová			1	WCh	Helsinki	9 Aug 83
1:54.81	Olga	Mineyeva	RUS	1.9.52	2	OG	Moskva	27 Jul 80
1:54.82		Quirot			1	ASV	Köln	24 Aug 97
1:54.85 WR		Olizarenko			1	Prav	Moskva	12 Jun 80
1:54.87		Jelimo			1	OG	Beijing	18 Aug 08
1:54.94 WR	Tatyana	Kazankina ¶	RUS	17.12.51	1	OG	Montreal	26 Jul 76
1:54.97		Jelimo			1	Gaz	Saint-Denis	18 Jul 08
1:54.99		Jelimo			1	ISTAF	Berlin	1 Jun 08
1:55.04		Kratochvílová			1	OsloG	Oslo	23 Aug 83
1:55.05	Doina	Melinte	ROU	27.12.56	1	NC	Bucuresti	1 Aug 82
1:55.1 '		Mineyeva			1	Znam	Moskva	6 Jul 80
1:55.16		Jelimo			1	VD	Bruxelles	5 Sep 08
1:55.19	Maria Lurdes	Mutola	MOZ	27.10.72	1	WK	Zürich	17 Aug 94
1:55.19	Jolanda	Ceplak ¶	SLO	12.9.76	1rA	NA	Heusden	20 Jul 02
1:55.26	Sigrun	Wodars/Grau (10)	GDR	7.11.65	1	WCh	Roma	31 Aug 87
1:55.29		Mutola			2	ASV	Köln	24 Aug 97
1:55.32	Christine	Wachtel	GDR	6.1.65	2	WCh	Roma	31 Aug 87
1:55.41		Mineyeva			1	EC	Athína	8 Sep 82
1:55.41		Jelimo			1	Bisl	Oslo	6 Jun 08
1:55.42	Nikolina	Shtereva	BUL	25.1.55	2	OG	Montreal	26 Jul 76
1:55.43		Mutola			1	WCh	Stuttgart	17 Aug 93
1:55.45	Caster	Semenya	RSA	7.1.91	1	WCh	Berlin	19 Aug 09
1:55.46	Tatyana	Providokhina	RUS	26.3.53	3	OG	Moskva	27 Jul 80
1:55.5		Mineyeva			1	Kuts	Podolsk	21 Aug 82
1:55.54	Ellen	van Langen	NED	9.2.66	1	OG	Barcelona	3 Aug 92
1:55.54		Liu Dong	CHN	24.12.73	1	NG	Beijing	9 Sep 93
	(30/16)							
1:55.56	Lyubov	Gurina	RUS	6.8.57	3	WCh	Roma	31 Aug 87
1:55.60	Elfi	Zinn	GDR	24.8.53	3	OG	Montreal	26 Jul 76
1:55.68	Ella	Kovacs	ROU	11.12.64	1	RomIC	Bucuresti	2 Jun 85
1:55.69	Irina	Podyalovskaya	RUS	19.10.59	1	Izv	Kyiv	22 Jun 84
	(20)							

Mark	Wind	Name		Nat	Born	Pos	Meet	Venue	Date
1:55.74		Anita	Weiss'	GDR	16.7.55	4	OG	Montreal	26 Jul 76
1:55.87		Svetlana	Masterkova	RUS	17.1.68	1	Kuts	Moskva	18 Jun 99
1:55.87		Mariya	Savinova	RUS	13.8.85	1	WCh	Daegu	4 Sep 11
1:55.96		Lyudmila	Veselkova	RUS	25.10.50	2	EC	Athína	8 Sep 82
1:55.96		Yekaterina	Podkopayeva'	RUS	11.6.52	1		Leningrad	27 Jul 83
1:55.99		Liliya	Nurutdinova ¶	RUS	15.12.63	2	OG	Barcelona	3 Aug 92
1:56.00		Tatyana	Andrianova	RUS	10.12.79	1	NC	Kazan	18 Jul 08
1:56.0	WR	Valentina	Gerasimova	KAZ	15.5.48	1	NC	Kyiv	12 Jun 76
1:56.0		Inna	Yevseyeva	UKR	14.8.64	1		Kyiv	25 Jun 88
1:56.04		Janeth	Jepkosgei	KEN	13.12.83	1	WCh	Osaka	28 Aug 07
		(30)							
1:56.09		Zulia	Calatayud	CUB	9.11.79	1	Herc	Monaco	19 Jul 02
1:56.1		Ravilya	Agletdinova'	BLR	10.2.60	2	Kuts	Podolsk	21 Aug 82
1:56.2 '		Totka	Petrova ¶	BUL	17.12.56	1		Paris (C)	6 Jul 79
1:56.2		Tatyana	Mishkel	UKR	10.6.52	3	Kuts	Podolsk	21 Aug 82
1:56.21		Martina	Kämpfert'	GDR	11.11.59	4	OG	Moskva	27 Jul 80
1:56.21		Zamira	Zaytseva	UZB	16.2.53	2		Leningrad	27 Jul 83
1:56.21		Kelly	Holmes	GBR	19.4.70	2	GPF	Monaco	9 Sep 95
1:56.24			Qu Yunxia	CHN	8.12.72	2	NG	Beijing	9 Sep 93
1:56.40		Jearl	Miles-Clark	USA	4.9.66	3	WK	Zürich	11 Aug 99
1:56.42		Paula	Ivan	ROU	20.7.63	1	Balk	Ankara	16 Jul 88
		(40)							
1:56.43		Hasna	Benhassi	MAR	1.6.78	2	OG	Athína	23 Aug 04
1:56.44		Svetlana	Styrkina	RUS	1.1.49	5	OG	Montreal	26 Jul 76
1:56.51		Slobodanka	Colovic	YUG	10.1.65	1		Beograd	17 Jun 87
1:56.53		Patricia	Djaté	FRA	3.1.71	3	GPF	Monaco	9 Sep 95
1:56.56		Ludmila	Formanová	CZE	2.1.74	4	WK	Zürich	11 Aug 99
1:56.57		Zoya	Rigel	RUS	15.10.52	3	EC	Praha	31 Aug 78
1:56.59		Natalya	Khrushchelyova	RUS	30.5.73	2	NC	Tula	31 Jul 04
1:56.59		Francine	Niyonsaba	BDI	5.5.93	1	VD	Bruxelles	7 Sep 12
1:56.60		Natalya	Tsyganova	RUS	7.2.71	1	NC	Tula	25 Jul 00
1:56.6		Tamara	Sorokina'	RUS	15.8.50	5	Kuts	Podolsk	21 Aug 82
		(50)	100th woman 1:57.5, 200th 1:58.53, 300th 1:59.27, 400th 1:59.72, 500th 2:00.19						
Indoors: 1:55.85		Stephanie	Graf	AUT	26.4.73	2	EI	Wien	3 Mar 02
Drugs disqualification									
1:54.85		Yelena	Soboleva ¶	RUS	3.10.82	(1)	NC	Kazan	18 Jul 08

1000 METRES

Mark	Wind	Name		Nat	Born	Pos	Meet	Venue	Date
2:28.98	WR	Svetlana	Masterkova	RUS	17.1.68	1	VD	Bruxelles	23 Aug 96
2:29.34	WR	Maria Lurdes	Mutola	MOZ	27.10.72	1	VD	Bruxelles	25 Aug 95
2:30.6	WR	Tatyana	Providokhina	RUS	26.3.53	1		Podolsk	20 Aug 78
2:30.67	WR	Christine	Wachtel	GDR	6.1.65	1	ISTAF	Berlin	17 Aug 90
2:30.85		Martina	Kämpfert'	GDR	11.11.59	1		Berlin	9 Jul 80
2:31.50		Natalya	Artyomova ¶	RUS	5.1.63	1	ISTAF	Berlin	10 Sep 91
2:31.5 A		Maricica	Puica	ROU	29.7.50	1		Poiana Brasov	1 Jun 86
2:31.51		Sandra	Gasser ¶	SUI	27.7.62	1		Jerez de la Frontera	13 Sep 89

1500 METRES

Mark	Wind	Name		Nat	Born	Pos	Meet	Venue	Date
3:50.07	WR	Genzebe	Dibaba	ETH	8.2.91	1	Herc	Monaco	17 Jul 15
3:50.46	WR		Qu Yunxia	CHN	8.12.72	1	NG	Beijing	11 Sep 93
3:50.98			Jiang Bo	CHN	13.3.77	1	NG	Shanghai	18 Oct 97
3:51.34			Lang Yinglai	CHN	22.8.79	2	NG	Shanghai	18 Oct 97
3:51.92			Wang Junxia	CHN	9.1.73	2	NG	Beijing	11 Sep 93
3:52.47	WR	Tatyana	Kazankina ¶	RUS	17.12.51	1	WK	Zürich	13 Aug 80
3:53.91			Yin Lili ¶	CHN	11.11.79	3	NG	Shanghai	18 Oct 97
3:53.96		Paula	Ivan'	ROU	20.7.63	1	OG	Seoul	1 Oct 88
3:53.97			Lan Lixin	CHN	14.2.79	4	NG	Shanghai	18 Oct 97
3:54.11			Dibaba			1		Barcelona	8 Jul 15
3:54.23		Olga	Dvirna (10)	RUS	11.2.53	1	NC	Kyiv	27 Jul 82
3:54.52			Zhang Ling	CHN	13.4.80	5	NG	Shanghai	18 Oct 97
3:55.0 '	WR		Kazankina ¶			1	Znam	Moskva	6 Jul 80
3:55.01			Lan Lixin			1h2	NG	Shanghai	17 Oct 97
3:55.07			Dong Yanmei	CHN	16.2.77	6	NG	Shanghai	18 Oct 97
3:55.30		Hassiba	Boulmerka	ALG	10.7.68	1	OG	Barcelona	8 Aug 92
3:55.33		Süreyya	Ayhan ¶	TUR	6.9.78	1	VD	Bruxelles	5 Sep 03
3:55.38			Qu Yunxia			2h2	NG	Shanghai	17 Oct 97
3:55.47			Zhang Ling			3h2	NG	Shanghai	17 Oct 97
3:55.60			Ayhan			1	WK	Zürich	15 Aug 03
3:55.68		Yuliya	Chizhenko ¶	RUS	30.8.79	1	Gaz	Saint-Denis	8 Jul 06
3:55.82			Dong Yanmei			4h2	NG	Shanghai	17 Oct 97
3:56.0	WR		Kazankina ¶			1		Podolsk	28 Jun 76

WOMEN All-time

Mark Wind		Name	Nat	Born	Pos	Meet	Venue	Date
3:56.05	Sifan	Hassan	ETH/NED	.93	2	Herc	Monaco	17 Jul 15
3:56.14	Zamira	Zaytseva	UZB	16.2.53	2	NC	Kyiv	27 Jul 82
3:56.18	Maryam	Jamal	BRN	16.9.84	1	GP	Rieti	27 Aug 06
3:56.22		Ivan			1	WK	Zürich	17 Aug 88
3:56.29	Shannon	Rowbury	USA	19.9.84	3	Herc	Monaco	17 Jul 15
3:56.31		Liu Dong	CHN	24.12.73	5h2	NG	Shanghai	17 Oct 97
3:56.33mx		Hassan			1		Langenthal	12 Aug 15
	(30/20)							
3:56.43	Yelena	Soboleva ¶	RUS	3.10.82	2	Gaz	Saint-Denis	8 Jul 06
3:56.50	Tatyana	Pozdnyakova	RUS	4.3.56	3	NC	Kyiv	27 Jul 82
3:56.54	Abeba	Aregawi	ETH/SWE	5.7.90	1	GGala	Roma	31 May 12
3:56.63	Nadezhda	Ralldugina	UKR	15.11.57	1	Drz	Praha	18 Aug 84
3:56.65	Yekaterina	Podkopayeva'	RUS	11.6.52	1		Rieti	2 Sep 84
3:56.7 '	Lyubov	Smolka	UKR	29.11.52	2	Znam	Moskva	6 Jul 80
3:56.7	Doina	Melinte	ROU	27.12.56	1		Bucuresti	12 Jul 86
3:56.77+	Svetlana	Masterkova	RUS	17.1.68	1	WK	Zürich	14 Aug 96
3:56.8 '	Nadezhda	Olizarenko'	UKR	28.11.53	3	Znam	Moskva	6 Jul 80
3:56.91	Lyudmila	Rogachova	RUS	30.10.66	2	OG	Barcelona	8 Aug 92
	(30)							
3:56.91	Tatyana	Tomashova ¶	RUS	1.7.75	1	EC	Göteborg	13 Aug 06
3:56.97	Gabriela	Szabo	ROU	14.11.75	1	Herc	Monaco	8 Aug 98
3:56.98	Faith	Kipyegon	KEN	10.1.94	2	DL	Doha	10 May 13
3:57.03		Liu Jing	CHN	3.2.71	6h2	NG	Shanghai	17 Oct 97
3:57.05	Svetlana	Guskova	MDA	19.8.59	4	NC	Kyiv	27 Jul 82
3:57.05	Hellen	Obiri	KEN	13.12.89	1	Pre	Eugene	31 May 14
3:57.12	Mary	Decker/Slaney	USA	4.8.58	1	vNord	Stockholm	26 Jul 83
3:57.22	Maricica	Puica	ROU	29.7.50	1		Bucuresti	1 Jul 84
3:57.22	Jennifer	Simpson	USA	23.8.86	2	DL	Saint-Denis	5 Jul 14
3:57.40	Suzy	Favor Hamilton	USA	8.8.68	1	Bisl	Oslo	28 Jul 00
	(40)							
3:57.4 '	Totka	Petrova ¶	BUL	17.12.56	1	Balk	Athína	11 Aug 79
3:57.41	Jackline	Maranga	KEN	16.12.77	3	Herc	Monaco	8 Aug 98
3:57.46		Zhang Linli	CHN	6.3.73	3	NG	Beijing	11 Sep 93
3:57.71	Christiane	Wartenberg'	GDR	27.10.56	2	OG	Moskva	1 Aug 80
3:57.71	Carla	Sacramento	POR	10.12.71	4	Herc	Monaco	8 Aug 98
3:57.72	Galina	Zakharova	RUS	7.9.56	1	NP	Baku	14 Sep 84
3:57.73	Natalya	Yevdokimova	RUS	17.3.78	2	GP	Rieti	28 Aug 05
3:57.90	Kelly	Holmes	GBR	19.4.70	1	OG	Athína	28 Aug 04
3:57.92	Tatyana	Samolenko/Dorovskikh ¶	UKR	12.8.61	4	OG	Barcelona	8 Aug 92
3:58.12	Naomi	Mugo	KEN	2.1.77	5	Herc	Monaco	8 Aug 98
	(50)	100th woman 3:59.9, 200th 4:02.30, 300th 4:04.25, 400th 4:05.73, 500th 4:06.71						
Indoors: 3:55.17 WIR		G Dibaba			1		Karlsruhe	1 Feb 14
Drugs disqualification: 3:56.15		Mariem Alaoui Selsouli ¶	MAR	8.4.84	(1)	DL	Saint-Denis	6 Jul 12
3:56.62	Asli	Çakir Alptekin ¶	TUR	20.8.85	(2)	DL	Saint-Denis	6 Jul 12
3:57.65	Anna	Alminova ¶	RUS	17.1.85	(1)	DL	Saint-Denis	16 Jul 10

1 MILE

Mark		Name	Nat	Born	Pos	Meet	Venue	Date
4:12.56 WR	Svetlana	Masterkova	RUS	17.1.68	1	WK	Zürich	14 Aug 96
4:15.61 WR	Paula	Ivan'	ROU	20.7.63	1	Nik	Nice	10 Jul 89
4:15.8	Natalya	Artyomova ¶	RUS	5.1.63	1		Leningrad	5 Aug 84
4:16.71 WR	Mary	Slaney (Decker)	USA	4.8.58	1	WK	Zürich	21 Aug 85
4:16.71	Faith	Kipyegon	KEN	10.1.94	1	VD	Bruxelles	11 Sep 15
4:17.25	Sonia	O'Sullivan	IRL	28.11.69	1	Bisl	Oslo	22 Jul 94
4:17.33	Maricica	Puica	ROU	29.7.50	2	WK	Zürich	21 Aug 85
4:17.57	Zola	Budd'	GBR	26.5.66	3	WK	Zürich	21 Aug 85
4:17.14 **indoor**	Doina	Melinte	ROU	27.12.56	1		East Rutherford	9 Feb 90
Drugs dq: 4:15.63	Yelena	Soboleva ¶	RUS	3.10.82	1		Moskva	29 Jun 07

2000 METRES

Mark		Name	Nat	Born	Pos	Meet	Venue	Date
5:25.36 WR	Sonia	O'Sullivan	IRL	28.11.69	1	TSB	Edinburgh	8 Jul 94
5:26.93	Yvonne	Murray	GBR	4.10.64	2	TSB	Edinburgh	8 Jul 94
5:27.50	Genzebe	Dibaba	ETH	8.2.91	1	GS	Ostrava	17 Jun 14
5:28.69 WR	Maricica	Puica	ROU	29.7.50	1	PTG	London (CP)	11 Jul 86
5:28.72 WR	Tatyana	Kazankina ¶	RUS	17.12.51	1		Moskva	4 Aug 84
5:29.43+		Wang Junxia	CHN	9.1.73	1h2	NG	Beijing	12 Sep 93
5:29.64	Tatyana	Pozdnyakova	UKR	4.3.56	2		Moskva	4 Aug 84
5:30.19	Zola	Budd'	GBR	26.5.66	3	PTG	London (CP)	11 Jul 86
5:30.19	Gelete	Burka	ETH	15.2.86	1	VD	Bruxelles	4 Sep 09
5:30.92	Galina	Zakharova	RUS	7.9.56	3		Moskva	4 Aug 84
5:31.03	Gulnara	Samitova/Galkina	RUS	9.7.78	1		Sochi	27 May 07
Indoors: 5:30.53	Gabriela	Szabo	ROU	14.11.75	1		Sindelfingen	8 Mar 98

3000 METRES

Mark	Wind	Name		Nat	Born	Pos	Meet	Venue	Date
8:06.11 WR			Wang Junxia	CHN	9.1.73	1	NG	Beijing	13 Sep 93
8:12.18			Qu Yunxia	CHN	8.12.72	2	NG	Beijing	13 Sep 93
8:12.19 WR			Wang Junxia			1h2	NG	Beijing	12 Sep 93
8:12.27			Qu Yunxia			2h2	NG	Beijing	12 Sep 93
8:16.50			Zhang Linli	CHN	6.3.73	3	NG	Beijing	13 Sep 93
8:19.78			Ma Liyan	CHN	6.9.68	3h2	NG	Beijing	12 Sep 93
8:20.68		Hellen	Obiri	KEN	13.12.89	1	DL	Doha	9 May 14
8:21.14		Mercy	Cherono	KEN	7.5.91	2	DL	Doha	9 May 14
8:21.26			Ma Liyan			4	NG	Beijing	13 Sep 93
8:21.42		Gabriela	Szabo	ROU	14.11.75	1	Herc	Monaco	19 Jul 02
8:21.64		Sonia	O'Sullivan	IRL	28.11.69	1	TSB	London (CP)	15 Jul 94
8:21.84			Zhang Lirong	CHN	3.3.73	5	NG	Beijing	13 Sep 93
8:22.06 WR			Zhang Linli			1h1	NG	Beijing	12 Sep 93
8:22.20		Paula	Radcliffe (10)	GBR	17.12.73	2	Herc	Monaco	19 Jul 02
8:22.22		Almaz	Ayana	ETH	21.11.91	1		Rabat	14 Jun 15
8:22.34			Ayana			1	WK	Zürich	3 Sep 15
8:22.44			Zhang Lirong			2h1	NG	Beijing	12 Sep 93
8:22.62 WR		Tatyana	Kazankina ¶	RUS	17.12.51	1		Leningrad	26 Aug 84
8:23.23		Edith	Masai	KEN	4.4.67	3	Herc	Monaco	19 Jul 02
8:23.26		Olga	Yegorova ¶	RUS	28.3.72	1	WK	Zürich	17 Aug 01
8:23.55		Faith	Kipyegon	KEN	10.1.94	3	DL	Doha	9 May 14
8:23.75			Yegorova			1	GP	Saint-Denis	6 Jul 01
8:23.96			Yegorova			1	GGala	Roma	29 Jun 01
8:24.19			Szabo			2	WK	Zürich	17 Aug 01
8:24.31			Szabo			1	GP	Paris (C)	29 Jul 98
8:24.41		Viola	Kibiwot	KEN	22.12.83	4	DL	Doha	9 May 14
8:24.51+		Meseret	Defar	ETH	19.11.83	1	in 2M	Bruxelles	14 Sep 07
8:24.58			Ayana			5	DL	Doha	9 May 14
8:24.66			Defar			1	DNG	Stockholm	25 Jul 06
8:25.03			Szabo			1	WK	Zürich	11 Aug 99
		(30/17)							
8:25.40		Yelena	Zadorozhnaya	RUS	3.12.77	2	GGala	Roma	29 Jun 01
8:25.56		Tatyana	Tomashova ¶	RUS	1.7.75	3	GGala	Roma	29 Jun 01
8:25.62		Berhane	Adere (20)	ETH	21.7.73	3	WK	Zürich	17 Aug 01
8:25.83		Mary	Slaney	USA	4.8.58	1	GGala	Roma	7 Sep 85
8:25.92		Gelete	Burka	ETH	15.2.86	2	DNG	Stockholm	25 Jul 06
8:26.21		Genzebe	Dibaba	ETH	8.2.91	6	DL	Doha	9 May 14
8:26.48		Zahra	Ouaziz	MAR	20.12.69	2	WK	Zürich	11 Aug 99
8:26.53		Tatyana	Samolenko' ¶	UKR	12.8.61	1	OG	Seoul	25 Sep 88
8:26.78 WR		Svetlana	Ulmasova	UZB	4.2.53	1	NC	Kyiv	25 Jul 82
8:27.12 WR		Lyudmila	Bragina	RUS	24.7.43	1	v USA	College Park	7 Aug 76
8:27.15		Paula	Ivan'	ROU	20.7.63	2	OG	Seoul	25 Sep 88
8:27.62		Getenesh	Wami	ETH	11.12.74	4	WK	Zürich	17 Aug 01
8:27.83		Maricica	Puica	ROU	29.7.50	2	GGala	Roma	7 Sep 85
		(30)							
8:28.41		Sentayehu	Ejigu	ETH	21.6.85	1	Herc	Monaco	22 Jul 10
8:28.51		Irene	Jelagat	KEN	10.12.88	7	DL	Doha	9 May 14
8:28.66		Vivian	Cheruiyot	KEN	11.9.83	2	WAF	Stuttgart	23 Sep 07
8:28.80		Marta	Domínguez	ESP	3.11.75	3	WK	Zürich	11 Aug 00
8:28.83		Zola	Budd'	GBR	26.5.66	3	GGala	Roma	7 Sep 85
8:28.87		Maryam	Jamal	BRN	16.9.84	1	Bisl	Oslo	29 Jul 05
8:29.02		Yvonne	Murray	GBR	4.10.64	3	OG	Seoul	25 Sep 88
8:29.06		Priscah	Cherono	KEN	27.6.80	3	WAF	Stuttgart	23 Sep 07
8:29.14		Lydia	Cheromei ¶	KEN	11.5.77	5	WK	Zürich	11 Aug 00
8:29.36		Svetlana	Guskova	MDA	19.8.59	2	NC	Kyiv	25 Jul 82
		(40)							
8:29.38		Sifan	Hassan	NED	.93	2	VD	Bruxelles	5 Sep 14
8:29.52		Mariem Alaoui	Selsouli ¶	MAR	8.4.84	1	Herc	Monaco	25 Jul 07
8:29.55		Tirunesh	Dibaba	ETH	1.10.85	1	LGP	London (CP)	28 Jul 06
8:29.58		Jennifer	Simpson'	USA	23.8.86	4	VD	Bruxelles	5 Sep 14
8:29.93		Shannon	Rowbury	USA	19.9.84	5	VD	Bruxelles	5 Sep 14
8:30.00		Mimi	Belete	BRN	9.6.88	8	DL	Doha	9 May 14
8:30.18		Mariya	Pantyukhova	RUS	14.8.74	4	WK	Zürich	11 Aug 99
8:30.22		Carla	Sacramento	POR	10.12.71	2	Herc	Monaco	4 Aug 99
8:30.39		Irina	Mikitenko	GER	23.8.72	6	WK	Zürich	11 Aug 00
8:30.45		Yelena	Romanova	RUS	20.3.63	4	OG	Seoul	25 Sep 88
		(50)	100th woman 8:35.89, 200th 8:42.99, 300th 8:47.4						

Indoors:

Mark	Wind	Name		Nat	Born	Pos	Meet	Venue	Date
8:16.60 WIR		Genzebe	Dibaba	ETH	8.2.91	1		Stockholm	6 Feb 14

Mark	Wind	Name		Nat	Born	Pos	Meet	Venue	Date
8:23.72	WIR	Meseret	Defar	ETH	19.11.83	1	Spark	Stuttgart	3 Feb 07
8:23.74		Meselech	Melkamu	ETH	27.4.85	2	Spark	Stuttgart	3 Feb 07
8:25.27		Sentayehu	Ejigu	ETH	21.6.85	2	Spark	Stuttgart	6 Feb 10
8:27.86	WIR	Liliya	Shobukhova ¶	RUS	13.11.77	1	NC	Moskva	17 Feb 06
8:28.49		Anna	Alminova ¶	RUS	17.1.85	2	Spark	Stuttgart	7 Feb 09
8:29.00		Olesya	Syreva ¶	RUS	25.11.83	2	NC	Moskva	17 Feb 06

5000 METRES

Mark	Wind	Name		Nat	Born	Pos	Meet	Venue	Date
14:11.15	WR	Tirunesh	Dibaba	ETH	1.10.85	1	Bisl	Oslo	6 Jun 08
14:12.88		Meseret	Defar	ETH	19.11.83	1	DNG	Stockholm	22 Jul 08
14:14.32		Almaz	Ayana	ETH	21.11.91	1	DL	Shanghai	17 May 15
14:15.41		Genzebe	Dibaba	ETH	8.2.91	1	DL	Saint-Denis	4 Jul 15
14:16.63	WR		Defar			1	Bisl	Oslo	15 Jun 07
14:19.76			G Dibaba			1	Pre	Eugene	30 May 15
14:20.87		Vivian	Cheruiyot	KEN	11.9.83	1	DNG	Stockholm	29 Jul 11
14:21.29			G Dibaba			1	Bisl	Oslo	11 Jun 15
14:21.97			Ayana			2	DL	Saint-Denis	4 Jul 15
14:22.51			Cheruiyot			2	Bisl	Oslo	15 Jun 07
14:23.46			T Dibaba			1	GP	Rieti	7 Sep 08
14:23.68			T Dibaba			1	DL	Saint-Denis	6 Jul 13
14:23.75		Liliya	Shobukhova ¶	RUS	13.11.77	1	NC	Kazan	19 Jul 08
14:24.53	WR		Defar			1		New York (RI)	3 Jun 06
14:24.68	WR	Elvan	Abeylegesse	TUR	11.9.82	1	Bisl	Bergen (Fana)	11 Jun 04
14:25.43			Cheruiyot			1	VD	Bruxelles	5 Sep 08
14:25.52			Defar			2	VD	Bruxelles	5 Sep 08
14:25.84			Ayana			2	DL	Saint-Denis	6 Jul 13
14:26.83			Ayana			1	WCh	Beijing	30 Aug 15
14:26.90			Defar			1	Bisl	Oslo	13 Jun 13
14:27.41			Cheruiyot			1	DL	Saint-Denis	16 Jul 10
14:28.09	WR		Jiang Bo	CHN	13.3.77	1	NG	Shanghai	23 Oct 97
14:28.39		Sentayehu	Ejigu	ETH	21.6.85	2	DL	Saint-Denis	16 Jul 10
14:28.88			G Dibaba			1	Herc	Monaco	18 Jul 14
14:28.98			Defar			1	VD	Bruxelles	26 Aug 05
14:29.11		Paula	Radcliffe (10)	GBR	17.12.73	1	ECpS	Bydgoszcz	20 Jun 04
14:29.19			Ayana			2	Herc	Monaco	18 Jul 14
14:29.32		Olga	Yegorova	RUS	28.3.72	1	ISTAF	Berlin	31 Aug 01
14:29.32		Berhane	Adere	ETH	21.7.73	1	Bisl	Oslo	27 Jun 03
14:29.52			Defar			1	DL	Saint-Denis	8 Jul 11
14:29.82			Dong Yanmei	CHN	16.2.77	2	NG	Shanghai	23 Oct 97
		(31/13)							
14:30.42		Sally	Kipyego	KEN	19.12.85	2	WK	Zürich	8 Sep 11
14:30.88		Getenesh	Wami	ETH	11.12.74	1	NA	Heusden-Zolder	5 Aug 00
14:31.14		Linet	Masai	KEN	5.12.89	2	DL	Shanghai	23 May 10
14:31.20		Gelete	Burka	ETH	15.2.86	2	GS	Ostrava	27 Jun 07
14:31.48		Gabriela	Szabo	ROU	14.11.75	1	ISTAF	Berlin	1 Sep 98
14:31.91		Meselech	Melkamu	ETH	27.4.85	3	DL	Shanghai	23 May 10
14:31.91		Sylvia	Kibet	KEN	28.3.84	4	DL	Shanghai	23 May 10
		(20)							
14:31.95		Faith	Kipyegon	KEN	10.1.94	2	Pre	Eugene	30 May 15
14:32.08		Zahra	Ouaziz	MAR	20.12.69	2	ISTAF	Berlin	1 Sep 98
14:32.33			Liu Shixiang ¶	CHN	13.1.71	3h1	NG	Shanghai	21 Oct 97
14:32.74		Ejagayehu	Dibaba	ETH	25.6.82	3	Bisl	Bergen (Fana)	11 Jun 04
14:33.04		Werknesh	Kidane	ETH	21.11.81	2	Bisl	Oslo	27 Jun 03
14:33.13		Gulnara	Galkina'	RUS	9.7.78	2	NC	Kazan	19 Jul 08
14:33.48		Viola	Kibiwot	KEN	22.12.83	2	Bisl	Oslo	13 Jun 13
14:33.49		Lucy Wangui	Kabuu	KEN	24.3.84	2	Bisl	Oslo	6 Jun 08
14:33.84		Edith	Masai	KEN	4.4.67	3	Bisl	Oslo	2 Jun 06
14:34.10		Mercy	Cherono	KEN	7.5.91	3	DL	Saint-Denis	4 Jul 15
		(30)							
14:35.30		Priscah	Jepleting/Cherono	KEN	27.6.80	4	Bisl	Oslo	2 Jun 06
14:36.44		Senbere	Teferi	ETH	3.5.95	5	DL	Saint-Denis	4 Jul 15
14:36.45	WR	Fernanda	Ribeiro	POR	23.6.69	1		Hechtel	22 Jul 95
14:36.52		Mariem Alaoui	Selsouli ¶	MAR	8.4.84	1	G Gala	Roma	13 Jul 07
14:37.07		Jéssica	Augusto	POR	8.11.81	5	DL	Saint-Denis	16 Jul 10
14:37.33	WR	Ingrid	Kristiansen'	NOR	21.3.56	1		Stockholm	5 Aug 86
14:38.09		Mariya	Konovalova ¶	RUS	14.8.74	3	NC	Kazan	19 Jul 08
14:38.21		Isabella	Ochichi	KEN	28.10.79	4	VD	Bruxelles	26 Aug 05
14:38.44		Wude	Ayalew	ETH	4.7.87	5	Bisl	Oslo	3 Jul 09
14:39.19		Ines	Chenonge	KEN	1.2.82	6	DL	Saint-Denis	16 Jul 10
		(40)							

Mark Wind		Name	Nat	Born	Pos	Meet	Venue	Date
14:39.22	Tatyana	Tomashova ¶	RUS	1.7.75	4	ISTAF	Berlin	31 Aug 01
14:39.49	Betsy	Saina	KEN	30.6.88	5	Herc	Monaco	18 Jul 14
14:39.83	Leah	Malot	KEN	7.6.72	1	ISTAF	Berlin	1 Sep 00
14:39.96		Yin Lili ¶	CHN	11.11.79	4	NG	Shanghai	23 Oct 97
14:39.96	Jo	Pavey	GBR	20.9.73	3	VD	Bruxelles	25 Aug 06
14:40.14	Florence	Kiplagat	KEN	27.2.87	6	Bisl	Oslo	3 Jul 09
14:40.41		Sun Yingjie ¶	CHN	3.10.77	1	AsiG	Busan	12 Oct 02
14:40.47	Yelena	Zadorozhnaya	RUS	3.12.77	1	ECp-S	Bremen	24 Jun 01
14:40.48	Margaret	Muriuki	KEN	21.3.86	4	Bisl	Oslo	13 Jun 13
14:41.02	Sonia	O'Sullivan	IRL	28.11.69	2	OG	Sydney	25 Sep 00
	(50)	100th woman 14:50.15, 200th 15:04.98, 300th 15:11.01, 400th 15:16.83, 500th 15:20.93						
Indoors: 14:18.86		G Dibaba			1	XL-G	Stockholm	19 Feb 15
14:24.37 WIR		Defar			1		Stockholm	18 Feb 09
14:24.79		Defar			1	GE Galan	Stockholm	10 Feb 10
14:27.42 WIR		T Dibaba			1	BIG	Boston (R)	27 Jan 07
14:39.89	Kimberley	Smith	NZL	19.11.73	1		New York (Armory)	27 Feb 09
Drugs disqualification: 14:36.79	Alemitu	Bekele ¶	TUR	17.9.77	4	VD	Bruxelles	27 Aug 10

10,000 METRES

Mark Wind		Name	Nat	Born	Pos	Meet	Venue	Date
29:31.78 WR		Wang Junxia	CHN	9.1.73	1	NG	Beijing	8 Sep 93
29:53.80	Meselech	Melkamu	ETH	27.4.85	1		Utrecht	14 Jun 09
29:54.66	Tirunesh	Dibaba	ETH	1.10.85	1	OG	Beijing	15 Aug 08
29:56.34	Elvan	Abeylegesse	TUR	11.9.82	2	OG	Beijing	15 Aug 08
29:59.20	Meseret	Defar	ETH	19.11.83	1	NC	Birmingham	11 Jul 09
30:01.09	Paula	Radcliffe	GBR	17.12.73	1	EC	München	6 Aug 02
30:04.18	Berhane	Adere	ETH	21.7.73	1	WCh	Saint-Denis	23 Aug 03
30:07.15	Werknesh	Kidane	ETH	21.11.81	2	WCh	Saint-Denis	23 Aug 03
30:07.20		Sun Yingjie ¶	CHN	3.10.77	3	WCh	Saint-Denis	23 Aug 03
30:08.06		Defar			1		Sollentuna	27 Jun 13
30:11.53	Florence	Kiplagat (10)	KEN	27.2.87	2		Utrecht	14 Jun 09
30:11.87	Wude	Ayalew	ETH	4.7.87	3		Utrecht	14 Jun 09
30:12.53	Lornah	Kiplagat (KEN)	NED	1.5.74	4	WCh	Saint-Denis	23 Aug 03
30:13.37		Zhong Huandi	CHN	28.6.67	2	NG	Beijing	8 Sep 93
30:13.74 WR	Ingrid	Kristiansen'	NOR	21.3.56	1	Bisl	Oslo	5 Jul 86
30:15.67		T Dibaba			1		Sollentuna	28 Jun 05
30:17.15		Radcliffe			1	GP	Gateshead	27 Jun 04
30:17.49	Derartu	Tulu	ETH	21.3.72	1	OG	Sydney	30 Sep 00
30:18.39	Ejegayehu	Dibaba	ETH	25.6.82	2		Sollentuna	28 Jun 05
30:19.39		Kidane			1	GP II	Stanford	29 May 05
30:20.75		T Dibaba			1	OG	London (OS)	3 Aug 12
30:21.67		Abeylegesse			1	ECp	Antalya	15 Apr 06
30:22.22	Shalane	Flanagan	USA	8.7.81	3	OG	Beijing	15 Aug 08
30:22.48	Getenesh	Wami	ETH	11.12.74	2	OG	Sydney	30 Sep 00
30:22.88	Fernanda	Ribeiro	POR	23.6.69	3	OG	Sydney	30 Sep 00
30:23.07	Alla	Zhilyayeva (20)	RUS	5.2.69	5	WCh	Saint-Denis	23 Aug 03
30:23.25		Kristiansen			1	EC	Stuttgart	30 Aug 86
30:24.02		T Dibaba			1	WCh	Helsinki	6 Aug 05
30:24.36		Xing Huina	CHN	25.2.84	1	OG	Athína	27 Aug 04
30:24.39		T Dibaba			1	Pre	Eugene	1 Jun 12
	(30/21)							
30:26.20	Galina	Bogomolova	RUS	15.10.77	6	WCh	Saint-Denis	23 Aug 03
30:26.37	Sally	Kipyego	KEN	19.12.85	2	OG	London (OS)	3 Aug 12
30:26.50	Linet	Masai	KEN	5.12.89	4	OG	Beijing	15 Aug 08
30:26.70	Belaynesh	Oljira	ETH	26.6.90	3	Pre	Eugene	1 Jun 12
30:29.21mx	Philes	Ongori	KEN	19.7.86	1mx		Yokohama	23 Nov 08
30:29.23	Gladys	Cherono	KEN	12.5.83	2	GS	Ostrava	27 Jun 13
30:29.36	Liliya	Shobukhova ¶	RUS	13.11.77	1	NC	Cheboksary	23 Jul 09
30:30.26	Edith	Masai	KEN	4.4.67	5	WCh	Helsinki	6 Aug 05
30:30.44	Vivian	Cheruiyot	KEN	11.9.83	3	OG	London (OS)	3 Aug 12
	(30)							
30:31.03	Mariya	Konovalova ¶	RUS	14.8.74	2	NC	Cheboksary	23 Jul 09
30:31.42	Inga	Abitova ¶	RUS	6.3.82	1	EC	Göteborg	7 Aug 06
30:32.03	Tegla	Loroupe	KEN	9.5.73	3	WCh	Sevilla	26 Aug 99
30:32.36	Susanne	Wigene	NOR	12.2.78	2	EC	Göteborg	7 Aug 06
30:32.72	Lidiya	Grigoryeva	RUS	21.1.74	3	EC	Göteborg	7 Aug 06
30:35.54	Kimberley	Smith	NZL	19.11.81	2		Stanford	4 May 08
30:35.91	Birhane	Ababel	ETH	10.6.90	4	GS	Ostrava	27 Jun 13
30:37.68	Benita	Johnson	AUS	6.5.79	8	WCh	Saint-Denis	23 Aug 03
30:38.09		Dong Yanmei	CHN	16.2.77	1	NG	Shanghai	19 Oct 97
30:38.33	Mestawat	Tufa	ETH	14.9.83	1		Nijmegen	25 Jun 08
	(40)							

Mark	Wind	Name		Nat	Born	Pos	Meet	Venue	Date
30:38.78		Jelena	Prokopcuka	LAT	21.9.76	6	EC	Göteborg	7 Aug 06
30:39.41			Lan Lixin	CHN	14.2.79	2	NG	Shanghai	19 Oct 97
30:39.96		Lucy Wangui	Kabuu	KEN	24.3.84	7	OG	Beijing	15 Aug 08
30:39.98			Yin Lili ¶	CHN	11.11.79	3	NG	Shanghai	19 Oct 97
30:47.02		Emily	Chebet	KEN	18.2.86	4	WCh	Moskva	11 Aug 13
30:47.20		Sylvia	Kibet	KEN	28.3.84	4		Utrecht	14 Jun 09
30:47.22			Dong Zhaoxia	CHN	13.11.74	4	NG	Shanghai	19 Oct 97
30:47.25		Shitaye	Eshete	BRN	21.5.90	6	OG	London (OS)	3 Aug 12
30:47.59		Sonia	O'Sullivan	IRL	28.11.69	2	EC	München	6 Aug 02
30:47.59		Molly	Huddle	USA	31.8.84	2	Jordan	Stanford	4 May 14
		(50)	100th woman 31:10.12, 200th 31:34.01, 300th 31:47.23, 400th 32:00.11, 500th 32:07.66						

HALF MARATHON

Slightly downhill courses included: Newcastle-South Shields 30.5m, Tokyo 33m (to 1998), Lisboa (Spring to 2008) 69m

Mark	Wind	Name		Nat	Born	Pos	Meet	Venue	Date
65:09	WR	Florence	Kiplagat	KEN	27.2.87	1		Barcelona	15 Feb 15
65:12	WR		F Kiplagat			1		Barcelona	16 Feb 14
65:39	dh	Mary	Keitany	KEN	18.1.82	1	GNR	South Shields	7 Sep 14
65:40	dh	Paula	Radcliffe	GBR	17.12.73	1	GNR	South Shields	21 Sep 03
65:44	dh	Susan	Chepkemei	KEN	25.6.75	1		Lisboa	1 Apr 01
65:45	dh	Priscah	Jeptoo	KEN	26.6.84	1	GNR	South Shields	15 Sep 13
65:50	WR		Keitany			1		Ra's Al Khaymah	18 Feb 11
66:02			Keitany			1		Ra's Al-Khaymah	13 Feb 15
66:09		Lucy Wangui	Kabuu	KEN	24.3.84	1		Ra's Al-Khaymah	15 Feb 13
66:09	dh	Meseret	Defar	ETH	19.11.83	2	GNR	South Shields	15 Sep 13
66:11			P Jeptoo			2		Ra's Al-Khaymah	15 Feb 13
66:19		Joyce	Chepkirui	KEN	20.8.88	1		Praha	5 Apr 14
66:25		Lornah	Kiplagat	NED	1.5.74	1	WCh	Udine	14 Oct 07
66:27		Rita	Jeptoo ¶ (10)	KEN	15.2.81	3		Ra's Al-Khaymah	15 Feb 13
66:28		Mamitu	Daska	ETH	16.10.83	2		Ra's Al-Khaymah	13 Feb 15
66:34	dh		Kiplagat			2		Lisboa	1 Apr 01
66:36			Keitany			1	WCh	Birmingham	11 Oct 09
66:38			F Kiplagat			1		Ostia	26 Feb 12
66:38		Gladys	Cherono	KEN	12.5.83	1		Istanbul	26 Apr 15
66:38			Keitany			1		Olomouc	20 Jun 15
66:40*		Ingrid	Kristiansen	NOR	21.3.56	1	NC	Sandnes	5 Apr 87
66:43	dh	Masako	Chiba	JPN	18.7.76	1		Tokyo	19 Jan 97
66:44		Elana	Meyer	RSA	10.10.66	1		Tokyo	15 Jan 99
66:47			Radcliffe			1	WCh	Bristol	7 Oct 01
66:48			Keitany			2	WCh	Udine	14 Oct 07
66:48			G Cherono			1		Praha	6 Apr 13
66:49		Esther	Wanjiru	KEN	27.3.77	2		Tokyo	15 Jan 99
66:49			Keitany			1		Ra's Al-Khaymah	17 Feb 12
66:54			Keitany			1		New Delhi	1 Nov 09
66:56			L Kiplagat			1	City-Pier	Den Haag	25 Mar 00
66:56		Meseret	Hailu	ETH	12.9.90	4		Ra's Al-Khaymah	15 Feb 13
66:56	dh	Tirunesh	Dibaba	ETH	1.10.85	3	GNR	South Shields	15 Sep 13
		(32/18)	* uncertain course measurement						
66:57	dh	Kara	Goucher	USA	9.7.78	1	GNR	South Shields	30 Sep 07
67:02		Cynthia	Limo	KEN	18.12.89	3		Ra's Al-Khaymah	13 Feb 15
		(20)							
67:03	dh	Derartu	Tulu	ETH	21.3.72	3		Lisboa	1 Apr 01
67:07		Elvan	Abeylegesse	TUR	11.9.82	1		Ra's Al Khaymah	19 Feb 10
67:08		Sharon	Cherop	KEN	16.3.84	2		New Delhi	21 Nov 11
67:11	dh	Liz	McColgan	GBR	24.5.64	1		Tokyo	26 Jan 92
67:11		Kimberley	Smith	NZL	19.11.81	1		Philadelphia	18 Sep 11
67:12	dh	Tegla	Loroupe	KEN	9.5.73	1		Lisboa	10 Mar 96
67:13		Mare	Dibaba	ETH	20.10.89	2		Ra's Al Khaymah	19 Feb 10
67:14		Worknesh	Degefa	ETH	28.10.90	1		Praha	28 Mar 15
67:16		Edith	Masai	KEN	4.4.67	1		Berlin	2 Apr 06
67:17		Pasalia	Kipkoech	KEN	22.12.88	1		Rio de Janeiro	19 Aug 12
		(30)							
67:17		Peris	Jepchirchir	KEN	.93	1		Ústí nad Labem	12 Sep 15
67:18		Dire	Tune	ETH	19.6.85	1		R'as Al Khaymah	20 Feb 09
67:19	dh	Sonia	O'Sullivan	IRL	28.11.69	1	GNR	South Shields	6 Oct 02
67:21		Aselefech	Mergia	ETH	23.1.85	3		New Delhi	21 Nov 11
67:22		Agnes	Kiprop	KEN	12.12.79	2		Ostia	26 Feb 12
67:23		Margaret	Okayo	KEN	30.5.76	1		Udine	28 Sep 03
67:26		Kayoko	Fukushi	JPN	25.3.82	1		Marugame	5 Feb 06
67:26		Lydia	Cheromei ¶	KEN	11.5.77	2		Praha	31 Mar 12
67:27		Belaynesh	Oljira	ETH	26.6.90	4		New Delhi	27 Nov 11

Mark	Wind	Name		Nat	Born	Pos	Meet	Venue	Date
67:28		Worknesh	Kidane	ETH	21.11.81	2		Philadelphia	18 Sep 11
		(40)							
67:31		Netsanet	Gudeta	ETH	12.2.91	1		Valencia	18 Oct 15
67:32	dh	Berhane	Adere	ETH	21.7.73	2	GNR	South Shields	21 Sep 03
67:34		Deena	Kastor	USA	14.2.73	2		Berlin	2 Apr 06
67:34		Atsede	Baysa	ETH	16.4.87	1		Barcelona	17 Feb 13
67:38		Philes	Ongori	KEN	19.7.86	2	WCh	Birmingham	11 Oct 09
67:39		Aberu	Kebede	ETH	12.9.89	3	WCh	Birmingham	11 Oct 09
67:39		Helah	Kiprop	KEN	7.4.85	6		Ra's Al-Khaymah	15 Feb 13
67:39		Filomena	Cheyech	KEN	5.7.82	1		Ostia	3 Mar 13
67:41		Teyiba	Erkesso	ETH	30.10.82	4		Ra's Al Khaymah	19 Feb 10
67:41dh		Edna	Kiplagat	KEN	15.9.79	2	GNR	South Shields	16 Sep 12
		(50)	100th woman 68:31, 200th 69:12, 300th 69:41, 400th 70:08, 500th 70:28						

MARATHON

L = loop course or start and finish within 30%, P = point-to-point or start and finish more than 30% apart, D + point-to-point and downhil over 1/1000. 2nd column: M mixed marathon (men and women), W women only race

Mark	Wind	Name		Nat	Born	Pos	Meet	Venue	Date
2:15:25	LM	Paula	Radcliffe	GBR	17.12.73	1		London	13 Apr 03
2:17:18	LM		Radcliffe			1		Chicago	13 Oct 02
2:17:42	LW		Radcliffe			1		London	17 Apr 05
2:18:37	LW	Mary	Keitany	KEN	18.1.82	1		London	22 Apr 12
2:18:47	LM	Catherine	Ndereba	KEN	21.7.72	1		Chicago	7 Oct 01
2:18:56	LW		Radcliffe			1		London	14 Apr 02
2:18:58	LW	Tiki	Gelana	ETH	22.10.87	1		Rotterdam	15 Apr 12
2:19:12	LM	Mizuki	Noguchi	JPN	3.7.78	1		Berlin	25 Sep 05
2:19:19	LM	Irina	Mikitenko	GER	23.8.72	1		Berlin	28 Sep 08
2:19:19	LW		Keitany			1		London	17 Apr 11
2:19:25		Gladys	Cherono	KEN	12.5.83	1		Berlin	27 Sep 15
2:19:26	LM		Ndereba			2		Chicago	13 Oct 02
2:19:31	LM	Aselefech	Mergia	ETH	23.1.85	1		Dubai	27 Jan 12
2:19:34	LM	Lucy Wangui	Kabuu	KEN	24.3.84	2		Dubai	27 Jan 12
2:19:36	LW	Deena	Kastor (10)	USA	14.2.73	1		London	23 Apr 06
2:19:39	LM		Sun Yingjie ¶	CHN	3.10.77	1		Beijing	19 Oct 03
2:19:41	LM	Yoko	Shibui	JPN	14.3.79	1		Berlin	26 Sep 04
2:19:44	LM	Florence	Kiplagat	KEN	27.2.87	1		Berlin	25 Sep 11
2:19:46	LM	Naoko	Takahashi	JPN	6.5.72	1		Berlin	30 Sep 01
2:19:50	LW	Edna	Kiplagat	KEN	15.11.79	2		London	22 Apr 12
2:19:51	PM		Zhou Chunxiu	CHN	15.11.78	1	Dong-A	Seoul	12 Mar 06
2:19:52	LM	Mare	Dibaba	ETH	20.10.89	3		Dubai	27 Jan 12
2:19:52			M Dibaba			1		Xiamen	3 Jan 15
2:19:55	LM		Ndereba			2		London	13 Apr 03
2:19:57	L	Rita	Jeptoo ¶	KEN	15.2.81	1		Chicago	13 Oct 13
2:20:02			Mergia			1		Dubai	23 Jan 15
2:20:03			Cherono			2		Dubai	23 Jan 15
2:20:14	LW	Priscah	Jeptoo	KEN	26.6.84	3		London	22 Apr 12
2:20:15	LW		P Jeptoo			1		London	21 Apr 13
2:20:18	LM	Tirfi	Tsegaye	ETH	25.11.84	2		Berlin	28 Sep 14
		(30/20)							
2:20:27	LM	Feyse	Tadesse	ETH	19.11.88	2		Berlin	28 Sep 14
2:20:30	LM	Bezunesh	Bekele	ETH	29.1.83	4		Dubai	27 Jan 12
2:20:30	LM	Aberu	Kebede	ETH	12.9.89	1		Berlin	30 Sep 12
2:20:35	LW	Tirunesh	Dibaba	ETH	1.10.85	3		London	13 Apr 14
2:20:42	LM	Berhane	Adere	ETH	21.7.73	1		Chicago	22 Oct 06
2:20:43	LM	Tegla	Loroupe	KEN	9.5.73	1		Berlin	26 Sep 99
2:20:47	LM	Galina	Bogomolova	RUS	15.10.77	2		Chicago	22 Oct 06
2:20:48	L	Jemima	Jelagat	KEN	21.12.84	2		Chicago	13 Oct 13
2:20:59		Shure	Demise	ETH	21.1.96	4		Dubai	23 Jan 15
2:21:01	LM	Meselech	Melkamu	ETH	27.4.85	1		Frankfurt	28 Oct 12
		(30)							
2:21:06	LM	Ingrid	Kristiansen	NOR	21.3.56	1		London	21 Apr 85
2:21:09	LM	Meseret	Hailu	ETH	12.9.90	1		Amsterdam	21 Oct 12
2:21:14	LM	Shalane	Flanagan	USA	8.7.81	3		Berlin	28 Sep 14
2:21:21	LM	Joan	Benoit'	USA	16.5.57	1		Chicago	20 Oct 85
2:21:29	LW	Lyudmila	Petrova	RUS	7.10.68	2		London	23 Apr 06
2:21:30	LM	Constantina	Dita	ROU	23.1.70	2		Chicago	9 Oct 05
2:21:30	LM	Lydia	Cheromei ¶	KEN	11.5.77	6		Dubai	27 Jan 12
2:21:31	LM	Svetlana	Zakharova	RUS	15.9.70	4		Chicago	13 Oct 02
2:21:31	LM	Askale	Tafa	ETH	27.9.84	2		Berlin	28 Sep 08
2:21:34	LM	Getenesh	Wami	ETH	11.12.74	1		Berlin	25 Sep 06
		(40)							

Mark	Wind	Name		Nat	Born	Pos	Meet	Venue	Date
2:21:39	LM	Georgina	Rono	KEN	19.5.84	2		Frankfurt	28 Oct 12
2:21:41	LM	Eunice	Jepkirui Kirwa	KEN	20.5.84	2		Amsterdam	21 Oct 12
2:21:45	LW	Masako	Chiba	JPN	18.7.76	2		Osaka	26 Jan 03
2:21:46	LW	Susan	Chepkemei ¶	KEN	25.6.75	3		London	23 Apr 06
2:21:51	LW	Naoko	Sakamoto	JPN	14.11.80	3		Osaka	26 Jan 03
2:21:52	LM	Tigist	Tufa	ETH	26.1.87	1		Shanghai	2 Nov 14
2:21:56		Mulu	Seboka	ETH	24.9.84	6		Dubai	23 Jan 15
2:21:59	LM	Mamitu	Daska	ETH	16.10.83	1		Frankfurt	30 Oct 11
2:22:03		Atsede	Baysa	ETH	16.4.87	1		Chicago	7 Oct 12
2:22:09	LM	Ejegayehu	Dibaba	ETH	25.6.82	2		Chicago	9 Oct 11
		(50)	100th woman 2:23:33, 200th 2:25:34, 300th 2:26:38, 400th 2:27:38, 500th 2:28:28						
Drugs disqualification									
2:18:20	LM	Liliya	Shobukhova	RUS	13.11.77	1		Chicago	9 Oct 11
2:20:15	LW		Shobukhova			2		London	17 Apr 11
2:20:23	LM		Wei Yanan ¶	CHN	6.12.81	1		Beijing	20 Oct 02
2:20:25	LM		Shobukhova			1		Chicago	10 Oct 10
Downhill point-to-point course – Boston marathon is downhill overall (139m) and sometimes strongly wind-aided.									
2:18:57	DM	Rita	Jeptoo ¶	KEN	15.2.81	1		Boston	21 Apr 14
2:19:59	DM	Buzunesh	Deba	ETH	8.9.87	2		Boston	21 Apr 14
2:20:41	DM	Jemima	Jelagat	KEN	21.12.84	4		Boston	21 Apr 14
2:20:43	DM	Margaret	Okayo	KEN	30.5.76	1		Boston	15 Apr 02
2:21:29	DM	Aleksandra	Duliba	BLR	9.1.88	6		Boston	21 Apr 14
2:21:45	DM	Uta	Pippig ¶	GER	7.9.65	1		Boston	18 Apr 94

2000 METRES STEEPLECHASE

Mark	Name		Nat	Born	Pos	Meet	Venue	Date
6:02.16	Virginia	Nyambura	KEN	20.7.93	1	ISTAF	Berlin	6 Sep 15
6:02.47	Beatrice	Chepkoech	KEN	6.7.91	2	ISTAF	Berlin	6 Sep 15
6:03.38	Wioletta	Janowska	POL	9.6.77	1		Gdansk	15 Jul 06
6:04.20	Gesa-Felicitas	Krause	GER	3.8.92	3	ISTAF	Berlin	6 Sep 15
6:04.46	Dorcus	Inzikuru	UGA	2.2.82	1	GP II	Milano	1 Jun 05
6:10.82	Magdalene	Masai	KEN	4.4.93	4	ISTAF	Berlin	6 Sep 15

3000 METRES STEEPLECHASE

Mark	Name		Nat	Born	Pos	Meet	Venue	Date
8:58.81 WR	Gulnara	Samitova/Galkina	RUS	9.7.78	1	OG	Beijing	17 Aug 08
9:01.59 WR		Samitova/Galkina			1		Iráklio	4 Jul 04
9:05.36	Habiba	Ghribi	TUN	9.4.84	1	VD	Bruxelles	11 Sep 15
9:06.57	Yekaterina	Volkova	RUS	16.2.78	1	WCh	Osaka	27 Aug 07
9:07.14	Milcah	Chemos Cheywa	KEN	24.2.86	1	Bisl	Oslo	7 Jun 12
9:07.41	Eunice	Jepkorir	KEN	17.2.82	2	OG	Beijing	17 Aug 08
9:07.64		Volkova			3	OG	Beijing	17 Aug 08
9:08.21		Galkina			1	NC	Kazan	18 Jul 08
9:08.33 WR		Samitova			1	NC	Tula	10 Aug 03
9:08.37		Ghribi			2	OG	London (OS)	6 Aug 12
9:08.39	Yuliya	Zaripova' ¶	RUS	26.4.86	2	WCh	Berlin	17 Aug 09
9:08.57		Chemos			3	WCh	Berlin	17 Aug 09
9:09.00	Sofia	Assefa	ETH	14.11.87	2	Bisl	Oslo	7 Jun 12
9:09.19	Tatyana	Petrova	RUS	8.4.83	2	WCh	Osaka	27 Aug 07
9:09.39	Marta	Dominguez ¶	ESP	3.11.75	1		Barcelona	25 Jul 09
9:09.61	Hiwot	Ayalew (10)	ETH	6.3.90	3	Bisl	Oslo	7 Jun 12
9:09.84		Samitova			1		Réthimno	23 Jun 04
9:09.84		Assefa			3	OG	London (OS)	6 Aug 12
9:09.88		Chemos			4	OG	London (OS)	6 Aug 12
9:10.15	Hyvin	Jepkemoi	KEN	13.1.92	2	VD	Bruxelles	11 Sep 15
9:10.36		Ghribi			2	DNG	Stockholm	17 Aug 12
9:10.64		Ayalew			1	DL	Glasgow	12 Jul 14
9:11.09		Galkina			4	WCh	Berlin	17 Aug 09
9:11.18		Jepkorir			1		Huelva	13 Jun 08
9:11.28		Ghribi			1	Herc	Monaco	17 Jul 15
9:11.39		Assefa			1	Pre	Eugene	31 May 14
9:11.42	Emma	Coburn	USA	19.10.90	2	DL	Glasgow	12 Jul 14
9:11.58		Galkina			1	GGala	Roma	10 Jul 09
	(29/12)							
9:12.50	Jennifer	Simpson'	USA	23.8.86	5	WCh	Berlin	17 Aug 09
9:12.55	Lydia	Chepkurui	KEN	23.8.84	2	WCh	Moskva	13 Aug 13
9:13.16	Ruth	Bisibori	KEN	2.1.88	7	WCh	Berlin	17 Aug 09
9:13.22	Gladys	Kipkemboi	KEN	15.10.86	2	GGala	Roma	10 Jun 10
9:13.53	Gülcan	Mingir	TUR	21.5.89	1	Pavlov	Sofia	9 Jun 12
9:13.85	Virginia	Nyambura	KEN	20.7.93	3	Herc	Monaco	17 Jul 15
9:14.07	Etenesh	Diro	ETH	10.5.91	3	DNG	Stockholm	17 Aug 12
9:15.04	Dorcus	Inzikuru	UGA	2.2.82	1	SGP	Athína	14 Jun 05
	(20)							

Mark	Wind	Name		Nat	Born	Pos	Meet	Venue	Date
9:16.51	WR	Alesya	Turova	BLR	6.12.79	1		Gdansk	27 Jul 02
9:16.85		Cristina	Casandra	ROU	21.10.77	5	OG	Beijing	17 Aug 08
9:16.94		Mercy	Njoroge	KEN	10.6.86	2	DL	Doha	6 May 11
9:17.15		Wioletta	Frankiewicz/Janowska	POL	9.6.77	1	SGP	Athína	3 Jul 06
9:17.74		Purity	Kirui	KEN	13.8.91	5	VD	Bruxelles	11 Sep 15
9:17.85		Zemzem	Ahmed	ETH	27.12.84	7	OG	Beijing	17 Aug 08
9:18.03		Lydia	Rotich	KEN	8.8.88	3	Bisl	Oslo	4 Jun 10
9:18.35		Donna	MacFarlane	AUS	18.6.77	3	Bisl	Oslo	6 Jun 08
9:18.54		Antje	Möldner-Schmidt	GER	13.6.84	9	WCh	Berlin	17 Aug 09
9:18.54		Jéssica	Augusto	POR	8.11.81	1		Huelva	9 Jun 10
		(30)							
9:19.25		Gesa-Felicitas	Krause	GER	3.8.92	3	WCh	Beijing	26 Aug 15
9:20.23		Mekdes	Bekele	ETH	20.1.87	2		Huelva	13 Jun 08
9:20.37		Birtukan	Adamu	ETH	29.4.92	4	GGala	Roma	26 May 11
9:20.55		Ruth	Chebet	KEN/BRN	17.11.96	4	WK	Zürich	28 Aug 14
9:20.64		Salima	El Ouali	MAR	29.12.83	7	Herc	Monaco	17 Jul 15
9:20.65		Tigist	Mekonen	BRN	7.7.97	8	Herc	Monaco	17 Jul 15
9:21.56		Madeline	Heiner/Hills	AUS	5.3.88	5	GGala	Roma	4 Jun 15
9:21.94		Lyubov	Ivanova' ¶	RUS	2.3.81	2	Tsik	Athína	3 Jul 06
9:22.12		Hanane	Ouhaddou	MAR	.82	1	NA	Heusden-Zolder	18 Jul 09
9:22.15		Yelena	Sidorchenkova	RUS	30.5.80	2	NC	Cheboksary	23 Jul 09
		(40)							
9:22.29	WR	Justyna	Bak	POL	1.8.74	1		Milano	5 Jun 02
9:22.51		Almaz	Ayana	ETH	21.11.91	3	VD	Bruxelles	27 Aug 10
9:22.76		Anna	Willard/Pierce	USA	31.3.84	2	NA	Heusden-Zolder	20 Jul 08
9:23.48		Stephanie	Garcia	USA	3.5.88	2	NC	Eugene	27 Jun 15
9:23.35		Jeruto	Kiptum	KEN	12.12.81	2	GP	Rieti	27 Aug 06
9:23.96		Charlotta	Fougberg	SWE	19.6.85	4	DL	Glasgow	12 Jul 14
9:24.24		Barbara	Parker	GBR	8.11.82	4	Pre	Eugene	2 Jun 12
9:24.29		Melissa	Rollison	AUS	13.4.83	2	CG	Melbourne	22 Mar 06
9:24.59		Nicole	Bush	USA	4.4.86	1	NA	Heusden-Zolder	19 Jul 14
9:24.70		Sandra	Eriksson	FIN	4.5.89	6	DL	Glasgow	12 Jul 14
		(50)	100th woman 9:31.36, 200th 9:43.00, 300th 9:51.64, 400th 9:57.12						
Drugs disqualification									
9:05.02		Yuliya	Zaripova	RUS	26.4.86	(1)	DNG	Stockholm	17 Aug 12
9:06.72			Zaripova			(1)	OG	London (OS)	6 Aug 12
9:07.03			Zaripova	RUS	26.4.86	(1)	WCh	Daegu	30 Aug 11
9:07.32		Marta	Dominguez ¶	ESP	3.11.75	(1)	WCh	Berlin	17 Aug 09
9:09.99			Zaripova			(1)	NC	Cheboksary	3 Jul 12
9:24.06		Binnaz	Uslu ¶	TUR	12.3.85	(1h1)	WCh	Daegu	27 Aug 11
100 METRES HURDLES									
12.21	WR 0.7	Yordanka	Donkova	BUL	28.9.61	1		Stara Zagora	20 Aug 88
12.24	0.9		Donkova			1h		Stara Zagora	28 Aug 88
12.25	WR 1.4	Ginka	Zagorcheva	BUL	12.4.58	1	v TCH,GRE	Drama	8 Aug 87
12.26	WR 1.5		Donkova			1	Balk	Ljubljana	7 Sep 86
12.26	1.7	Lyudmila	Narozhilenko ¶	RUS	21.4.64	1rB		Sevilla	6 Jun 92
		(later Ludmila Engquist SWE)							
12.26	1.2	Brianna	Rollins	USA	18.8.91	1	NC	Des Moines	22 Jun 13
12.27	-1.2		Donkova			1		Stara Zagora	28 Aug 88
12.28	1.8		Narozhilenko			1	NC	Kyiv	11 Jul 91
12.28	0.9		Narozhilenko			1rA		Sevilla	6 Jun 92
12.28	1.1	Sally	Pearson'	AUS	19.9.86	1	WCh	Daegu	3 Sep 11
12.29	WR-0.4		Donkova			1	ASV	Köln	17 Aug 86
12.32	1.6		Narozhilenko			1		Saint-Denis	4 Jun 92
12.33	1.4		Donkova			1		Fürth	14 Jun 87
12.33	-0.3	Gail	Devers	USA	19.11.66	1	NC	Sacramento	23 Jul 00
12.34	-0.5		Zagorcheva			1	WCh	Roma	4 Sep 87
12.34	1.9	Sharika	Nelvis	USA	10.5.90	1h3	NC	Eugene	26 Jun 15
12.35	WR 0.1		Donkova			1h2	ASV	Köln	17 Aug 86
12.35	-0.2		Pearson			1	OG	London (OS)	7 Aug 12
12.35	0.9	Jasmin	Stowers	USA	23.9.91	1	DL	Doha	15 May 15
12.36	WR 1.9	Grazyna	Rabsztyn	POL	20.9.52	1	Kuso	Warszawa	13 Jun 80
12.36	WR-0.6		Donkova			1	NC	Sofia	13 Aug 86
12.36	1.1		Donkova			1		Schwechat	15 Jun 88
12.36	0.3		Pearson			1s2	WCh	Daegu	3 Sep 11
12.37	1.4		Donkova			1	ISTAF	Berlin	15 Aug 86
12.37	0.7		Devers			1	WCh	Sevilla	28 Aug 99
12.37	1.5	Joanna	Hayes (10)	USA	23.12.76	1	OG	Athína	24 Aug 04
12.37	-0.2	Dawn	Harper Nelson	USA	13.5.84	2	OG	London (OS)	7 Aug 12

Mark	Wind	Name		Nat	Born	Pos	Meet	Venue	Date
12.37	2.0		Nelvis			1s1	NC	Eugene	27 Jun 15
12.38	0.0		Donkova			1	BGP	Budapest	11 Aug 86
12.38	-0.7		Donkova			1	EC	Stuttgart	29 Aug 86
12.38	0.2		Donkova			1	OG	Seoul	30 Sep 88
		(31/11)							
12.39	1.5	Vera	Komisova'	RUS	11.6.53	1	GGala	Roma	5 Aug 80
12.39	1.8	Natalya	Grigoryeva ¶	UKR	3.12.62	2	NC	Kyiv	11 Jul 91
12.42	1.8	Bettine	Jahn	GDR	3.8.58	1	OD	Berlin	8 Jun 83
12.42	2.0	Anjanette	Kirkland	USA	24.2.74	1	WCh	Edmonton	11 Aug 01
12.43	-0.9	Lucyna	Kalek (Langer)	POL	9.1.56	1		Hannover	19 Aug 84
12.43	-0.3	Michelle	Perry	USA	1.5.79	1s1	NC	Carson	26 Jun 05
12.43	0.2	Lolo	Jones	USA	5.8.82	1s1	OG	Beijing	18 Aug 08
12.43	1.2	Queen	Harrison	USA	10.9.88	2	NC	Des Moines	22 Jun 13
12.44	-0.5	Gloria	Uibel (-Siebert)	GDR	13.1.64	2	WCh	Roma	4 Sep 87
		(20)							
12.44	-0.8	Olga	Shishigina ¶	KAZ	23.12.68	1	Spitzen	Luzern	27 Jun 95
12.44	0.4	Glory	Alozie	NGR/ESP	30.12.77	1	Herc	Monaco	8 Aug 98
12.44	0.6	Damu	Cherry ¶	USA	29.11.77	2rA	Athl	Lausanne	11 Jul 06
12.45	1.3	Cornelia	Oschkenat'	GDR	29.10.61	1		Neubrandenburg	11 Jun 87
12.45	1.4	Brigitte	Foster-Hylton	JAM	7.11.74	1	Pre	Eugene	24 May 03
12.45	1.5	Olena	Krasovska	UKR	17.8.76	2	OG	Athína	24 Aug 04
12.45	1.4	Virginia	Powell/Crawford	USA	7.9.83	1	GP	New York	2 Jun 07
12.46	0.7	Perdita	Felicien	CAN	29.8.80	1	Pre	Eugene	19 Jun 04
12.47	1.1	Marina	Azyabina	RUS	15.6.63	1s2	NC	Moskva	19 Jun 93
12.47	1.1	Danielle	Carruthers	USA	22.12.79	2	WCh	Daegu	3 Sep 11
		(30)							
12.48	-0.2	Kellie	Wells	USA	16.7.82	3	OG	London (OS)	7 Aug 12
12.48	1.2	Nia	Ali	USA	23.10.88	3	NC	Des Moines	22 Jun 13
12.49	0.9	Susanna	Kallur	SWE	16.2.81	1	ISTAF	Berlin	16 Sep 07
12.49	1.0	Priscilla	Lopes-Schliep	CAN	26.8.82	2	VD	Bruxelles	4 Sep 09
12.50	0.0	Vera	Akimova'	RUS	5.6.59	1		Sochi	19 May 84
12.50	-0.1	Delloreen	Ennis-London	JAM	5.3.75	3	WCh	Osaka	29 Aug 07
12.50	0.8	Josephine	Onyia ¶	NGR/ESP	15.7.86	1	ISTAF	Berlin	1 Jun 08
12.50	1.8	Kendra	Harrison	USA	18.9.92	1	SEC	Starkville	16 May 15
12.51	1.4	Miesha	McKelvy	USA	26.7.76	2	Pre	Eugene	24 May 03
12.51	0.7	Tiffany	Porter'	USA/GBR	13.11.87	2	C.Cup	Marrakech	14 Sep 14
		(40)							
12.52	-0.4	Michelle	Freeman	JAM	5.5.69	1s1	WCh	Athína	10 Aug 97
12.53	0.2	Tatyana	Reshetnikova	RUS	14.10.66	1rA	GP II	Linz	4 Jul 94
12.53	-0.4	Svetla	Dimitrova ¶	BUL	27.1.70	1	Herc	Stara Zagora	16 Jul 94
12.53	1.0	Melissa	Morrison	USA	9.7.71	1	DNG	Stockholm	5 Aug 98
12.54	0.4	Kerstin	Knabe	GDR	7.7.59	3	EC	Athína	9 Sep 82
12.54	0.9	Sabine	Paetz/John'	GDR	16.10.57	1		Berlin	15 Jul 84
12.54	1.7	Nichole	Denby	USA	10.10.82	2s2	OT	Eugene	6 Jul 08
12.54	1.3	Jessica	Ennis	GBR	28.1.86	1H5	OG	London (OS)	3 Aug 12
12.56	1.2	Johanna	Klier'	GDR	13.9.52	1r2		Cottbus	17 Jul 80
12.56	1.2	Monique	Ewanjé-Epée	FRA	11.7.67	1	BNP	Villeneuve d'Ascq	29 Jun 90
12.56	0.7	Kristi	Castlin	USA	7.7.88	2	Bisl	Oslo	7 Jun 12
12.56	1.2	Cindy	Billaud	FRA	11.3.86	1h1	NC	Reims	12 Jul 14
		(52)	100th woman 12.68, 200th 12.83, 300th 12.93, 400th 13.02, 500th 13.10						

Wind assisted performances to 12.37, performers to 12.53

Mark	Wind	Name		Nat	Born	Pos	Meet	Venue	Date
12.28	2.7	Cornelia	Oschkenat'	GDR	29.10.61	1		Berlin	25 Aug 87
12.29	3.5		Donkova			1	Athl	Lausanne	24 Jun 88
12.29	2.7	Gail	Devers	USA	19.11.66	1	Pre	Eugene	26 May 02
12.29	3.8	Lolo	Jones	USA	5.8.82	1	NC/OT	Eugene	6 Jul 08
12.30	2.8		Rollins			1s1	NC	Des Moines	22 Jun 13
12.33	2.3		Rollins			1h3	NC	Des Moines	21 Jun 13
12.35	2.4	Bettine	Jahn	GDR	3.8.58	1	WCh	Helsinki	13 Aug 83
12.35	3.7	Kellie	Wells	USA	16.7.82	1		Gainesville	16 Apr 11
12.36	2.2	Dawn	Harper Nelson	USA	13.5.84	1	NC	Eugene	28 Jun 09
12.37	2.7	Gloria	Uibel/Siebert'	GDR	13.1.64	2		Berlin	25 Aug 87
12.37	3.4	Danielle	Carruthers	USA	22.12.79	1s1	NC	Eugene	26 Jun 11
12.40	2.1	Michelle	Freeman	JAM	5.5.69	1	GPF	Fukuoka	13 Sep 97
12.41	2.2	Olga	Shishigina ¶	KAZ	23.12.68	1rA	Athl	Lausanne	5 Jul 95
12.42	2.4	Kerstin	Knabe	GDR	7.7.59	2	WCh	Helsinki	13 Aug 83
12.43	2.7	Yvette	Lewis	USA/PAN	16.3.85	1	MSR	Walnut	20 Apr 13
12.44	2.6	Melissa	Morrison	USA	9.7.71	1		Carson	22 May 04
12.45	2.1	Perdita	Felicien	CAN	29.8.80	1	NC	Victoria	10 Jul 04
12.46	2.3	Kendra	Harrison	USA	18.9.92	1h1	NC	Eugene	26 Jun 15
12.47	3.0	Tiffany	Porter	USA/GBR	13.11.87	1		Gainesville	21 Apr 12
12.48	3.8	Kristi	Castlin	USA	7.7.88	1		Clermont	2 Jun 12

Mark	Wind	Name		Nat	Born	Pos	Meet	Venue	Date
12.50	2.7	Svetla	Dimitrova ¶	BUL	27.1.70	1		Saint-Denis	10 Jun 94
12.51	3.2	Johanna	Klier'	GDR	13.9.52	1	NC	Cottbus	17 Jul 80
12.51	3.6	Sabine	Paetz/John'	GDR	16.10.57	1		Dresden	27 Jul 84
12.51A	3.3	Yuliya	Graudyn	RUS	13.11.70	1		Sestriere	31 Jul 94
12.52	3.1	Angela	Whyte	CAN	22.5.80	2		Edmonton	29 Jun 13
12.52	2.8	Sharika	Nelvis	USA	10.5.90	1	NCAA	Eugene	14 Jun 14
12.53	2.2	Mihaela	Pogacian	ROU	27.1.58	1	IAC	Edinburgh	6 Jul 90

Probably hand timed Officially 12.36, but subsequent investigations showed this unlikely to have been auto-timed

Mark	Wind	Name		Nat	Born	Pos	Meet	Venue	Date
12.4	0.7	Svetla	Dimitrova ¶	BUL	27.1.70	1		Stara Zagora	9 Jul 97

Hand timed

Mark	Wind	Name		Nat	Born	Pos	Meet	Venue	Date
12.3 WR	1.5	Anneliese	Ehrhardt	GDR	18.6.50	1	NC	Dresden	22 Jul 73
12.3		Marina	Azyabina	RUS	15.6.63	1		Yekaterinburg	30 May 93
12.0w	2.1	Yordanka	Donkova	BUL	28.9.61	1		Sofia	3 Aug 86
12.1w	2.1	Ginka	Zagorcheva	BUL	12.4.58	2		Sofia	3 Aug 86

400 METRES HURDLES

Mark	Wind	Name		Nat	Born	Pos	Meet	Venue	Date
52.34 WR		Yuliya	Nosova-Pechonkina'	RUS	21.4.78	1	NC	Tula	8 Aug 03
52.42		Melaine	Walker	JAM	1.1.83	1	WCh	Berlin	20 Aug 09
52.47		Lashinda	Demus	USA	10.3.83	1	WCh	Daegu	1 Sep 11
52.61 WR		Kim	Batten	USA	29.3.69	1	WCh	Göteborg	11 Aug 95
52.62		Tonja	Buford-Bailey	USA	13.12.70	2	WCh	Göteborg	11 Aug 95
52.63			Demus			1	Herc	Monaco	28 Jul 09
52.64			Walker			1	OG	Beijing	20 Aug 08
52.70		Natalya	Antyukh	RUS	26.6.81	1	OG	London (OS)	8 Aug 12
52.73			Walker			2	WCh	Daegu	1 Sep 11
52.74 WR		Sally	Gunnell	GBR	29.7.66	1	WCh	Stuttgart	19 Aug 93
52.74			Batten			1	Herc	Monaco	8 Aug 98
52.77		Faní	Halkiá	GRE	2.2.79	1s2	OG	Athína	22 Aug 04
52.77			Demus			2	OG	London (OS)	8 Aug 12
52.79		Sandra	Farmer-Patrick	USA	18.8.62	2	WCh	Stuttgart	19 Aug 93
52.79		Kaliese	Spencer (10)	JAM	6.5.87	1	LGP	London (CP)	5 Aug 11
52.82		Deon	Hemmings	JAM	9.10.68	1	OG	Atlanta	31 Jul 96
52.82			Halkiá			1	OG	Athína	25 Aug 04
52.82			Demus			1	GGala	Roma	10 Jun 10
52.83		Zuzana	Hejnová	CZE	19.12.86	1	WCh	Moskva	15 Aug 13
52.84			Batten			1	WK	Zürich	12 Aug 98
52.89		Daimí	Pernía	CUB	27.12.76	1	WCh	Sevilla	25 Aug 99
52.90			Buford			1	WK	Zürich	16 Aug 95
52.90		Nezha	Bidouane	MAR	18.9.69	2	WCh	Sevilla	25 Aug 99
52.90			Pechonkina			1	WCh	Helsinki	13 Aug 05
52.92			Antyukh			1	EC	Barcelona	30 Jul 10
52.94 WR		Marina	Styepanova'	RUS	1.5.50	1s	Spart	Tashkent	17 Sep 86
52.95		Sheena	Johnson/Tosta	USA	1.10.82	1	NC/OT	Sacramento	11 Jul 04
52.96A			Bidouane			1	WCp	Johannesburg	11 Sep 98
52.96			Demus			2	WCh	Berlin	20 Aug 09
52.97			Batten			1	NC	Indianapolis	14 Jun 97
52.97		(31/16)	Bidouane			1	WCh	Athína	8 Aug 97
53.02		Irina	Privalova	RUS	22.11.68	1	OG	Sydney	27 Sep 00
53.11		Tatyana	Ledovskaya	BLR	21.5.66	1	WCh	Tokyo	29 Aug 91
53.17		Debbie	Flintoff-King	AUS	20.4.60	1	OG	Seoul	28 Sep 88
53.20		Josanne	Lucas	TTO	14.5.84	3	WCh	Berlin	20 Aug 09
		(20)							
53.21		Marie-José	Pérec	FRA	9.5.68	2	WK	Zürich	16 Aug 95
53.21		Kori	Carter	USA	6.3.92	1	NCAA	Eugene	7 Jun 13
53.22		Jana	Pittman/Rawlinson	AUS	9.11.82	1	WCh	Saint-Denis	28 Aug 03
53.24		Sabine	Busch	GDR	21.11.62	1	NC	Potsdam	21 Aug 87
53.25		Ionela	Târlea-Manolache	ROU	9.2.76	2	GGala	Roma	7 Jul 99
53.28		Tiffany	Ross-Williams	USA	5.2.83	1	NC	Indianapolis	24 Jun 07
53.32		Sandra	Glover	USA	30.12.68	3	WCh	Helsinki	13 Aug 05
53.36		Andrea	Blackett	BAR	24.1.76	4	WCh	Sevilla	25 Aug 99
53.36		Brenda	Taylor	USA	9.2.79	2	NC/OT	Sacramento	11 Jul 04
53.37		Tetyana	Tereshchuk	UKR	11.10.69	3s2	OG	Athína	22 Aug 04
		(30)							
53.47		Janeene	Vickers	USA	3.10.68	3	WCh	Tokyo	29 Aug 91
53.48		Margarita	Ponomaryova'	RUS	19.6.63	3	WCh	Stuttgart	19 Aug 93
53.58		Cornelia	Ullrich'	GDR	26.4.63	2	NC	Potsdam	21 Aug 87
53.63		Ellen	Fiedler'	GDR	26.11.58	3	OG	Seoul	28 Sep 88
53.65A	mx	Myrtle	Bothma'	RSA	18.2.64	mx		Pretoria	12 Mar 90
		53.74A				1		Johannesburg	18 Apr 86
53.67		Perri	Shakes-Drayton	GBR	21.12.88	2	DL	London (OS)	26 Jul 13

Mark Wind	Name		Nat	Born	Pos	Meet	Venue	Date
53.68	Vania	Stambolova ¶	BUL	28.11.83	1		Rabat	5 Jun 11
53.72	Yekaterina	Bikert	RUS	13.5.80	2	NC	Tula	30 Jul 04
53.72	Georgeanne	Moline	USA	6.3.90	2	NCAA	Eugene	7 Jun 13
53.74	Shamier	Little	USA	20.3.95	1	NCAA	Eugene	13 Jun 15
	(40)							
53.77	Irina	Davydova	RUS	27.5.88	1	EC	Helsinki	29 Jun 12
53.83	Dalilah	Muhammad	USA	7.2.90	1	NC	Des Moines	23 Jun 13
53.84	Natasha	Danvers	GBR	19.9.77	3	OG	Beijing	20 Aug 08
53.85	Angela	Morosanu	ROU	26.7.86	2	DL	Shanghai	18 May 13
53.86	Anna	Jesien	POL	10.12.78	1s3	WCh	Osaka	28 Aug 07
53.88	Debbie-Ann	Parris	JAM	24.3.73	3s1	WCh	Edmonton	6 Aug 01
53.93	Yevgeniya	Isakova	RUS	27.11.78	1	EC	Göteborg	9 Aug 06
53.96		Han Qing ¶	CHN	4.3.70	1	NG	Beijing	9 Sep 93
53.96		Song Yinglan	CHN	14.9.75	1	NG	Guangzhou	22 Nov 01
53.96	Anastasiya	Rabchenyuk	UKR	14.9.83	4	OG	Beijing	20 Aug 08
	(50)	100th woman 54.54, 200th 55.42, 300th 55.82, 400th 56.18, 500th 56.49						
Drugs disqualification: 53.38		Jiang Limei ¶	CHN	.3.70	(1)	89	Shanghai	22 Oct 97

HIGH JUMP

Mark Wind	Name		Nat	Born	Pos	Meet	Venue	Date
2.09 WR	Stefka	Kostadinova	BUL	25.3.65	1	WCh	Roma	30 Aug 87
2.08 WR		Kostadinova			1	NM	Sofia	31 May 86
2.08i	Kajsa	Bergqvist	SWE	12.10.76	1		Arnstadt	4 Feb 06
2.08	Blanka	Vlasic	CRO	8.11.83	1	Hanz	Zagreb	31 Aug 09
2.07 WR	Lyudmila	Andonova ¶	BUL	6.5.60	1	OD	Berlin	20 Jul 84
2.07 WR		Kostadinova			1		Sofia	25 May 86
2.07		Kostadinova			1		Cagliari	16 Sep 87
2.07		Kostadinova			1	NC	Sofia	3 Sep 88
2.07i	Heike	Henkel'	GER	5.5.64	1	NC	Karlsruhe	8 Feb 92
2.07		Vlasic			1	DNG	Stockholm	7 Aug 07
2.07	Anna	Chicherova	RUS	22.7.82	1	NC	Cheboksary	22 Jul 11
2.06		Kostadinova			1	ECp	Moskva	18 Aug 85
2.06		Kostadinova			1		Fürth	15 Jun 86
2.06		Kostadinova			1		Cagliari	14 Sep 86
2.06		Kostadinova			1		Wörrstadt	6 Jun 87
2.06		Kostadinova			1		Rieti	8 Sep 87
2.06i		Kostadinova			1		Pireás	20 Feb 88
2.06		Bergqvist			1		Eberstadt	26 Jul 03
2.06	Hestrie	Cloete	RSA	26.8.78	1	WCh	Saint-Denis	31 Aug 03
2.06	Yelena	Slesarenko	RUS	28.2.82	1	OG	Athína	28 Aug 04
2.06		Vlasic			1		Thessaloníki	30 Jul 07
2.06		Vlasic			1	ECp-1B	Istanbul	22 Jun 08
2.06		Vlasic			1	GP	Madrid	5 Jul 08
2.06	Ariane	Friedrich	GER	10.1.84	1	ISTAF	Berlin	14 Jun 09
2.06i		Vlasic			1		Arnstadt	6 Feb 10
2.06i		Chicherova			1		Arnstadt	4 Feb 12
2.05 WR	Tamara	Bykova (10)	RUS	21.12.58	1	Izv	Kyiv	22 Jun 84
2.05	Inga	Babakova	UKR	27.6.67	1		Tokyo	15 Sep 95
2.05i	Tia	Hellebaut	BEL	16.2.78	1	EI	Birmingham	3 Mar 07
2.05	Chaunté	Lowe'	USA	12.1.84	1	NC	Des Moines	26 Jun 10
Further 2.05 performances: Kostadinova 10, Vlasic 10, Bergqvist, Chicherova 2, Hellebaut, Henkel, Cloete, Friedrich 1								
	(58/13)							
2.04	Silvia	Costa	CUB	4.5.64	1	WCp	Barcelona	9 Sep 89
2.04i	Alina	Astafei	GER	7.6.69	1		Berlin	3 Mar 95
2.04	Venelina	Veneva ¶	BUL	13.6.74	1		Kalamáta	2 Jun 01
2.04i	Antonietta	Di Martino	ITA	1.6.78	1		Banská Bystrica	9 Feb 11
2.04	Irina	Gordeyeva	RUS	9.10.86	1		Eberstadt	19 Aug 12
2.04	Brigetta	Barrett	USA	24.12.90	1	NC	Des Moines	22 Jun 13
2.03 WR	Ulrike	Meyfarth	FRG	4.5.56	1	ECp	London (CP)	21 Aug 83
	(20)							
2.03	Louise	Ritter	USA	18.2.58	1		Austin	8 Jul 88
2.03	Tatyana	Motkova	RUS	23.11.68	2		Bratislava	30 May 95
2.03	Níki	Bakoyiánni	GRE	9.6.68	2	OG	Atlanta	3 Aug 96
2.03i	Monica	Iagar/Dinescu	ROU	2.4.73	1		Bucuresti	23 Jan 99
2.03i	Marina	Kuptsova	RUS	22.12.81	1	EI	Wien	2 Mar 02
2.03	Svetlana	Shkolina	RUS	9.3.86	3	OG	London (OS)	11 Aug 12
2.02i	Susanne	Beyer'	GDR	24.6.61	2	WI	Indianapolis	8 Mar 87
2.02	Yelena	Yelesina	RUS	4.4.70	1	GWG	Seattle	23 Jul 90
2.02	Viktoriya	Styopina	UKR	21.2.76	3	OG	Athína	28 Aug 04
2.02	Ruth	Beitia	ESP	1.4.79	1	NC	San Sebastián	4 Aug 07
	(30)							

Mark Wind		Name	Nat	Born	Pos	Meet	Venue	Date
2.02i	Kamila	Licwinko'	POL	22.3.86	1	NC	Torun	21 Feb 15
2.01 WR	Sara	Simeoni	ITA	19.4.53	1	v Pol	Brescia	4 Aug 78
2.01	Olga	Turchak	UKR	5.3.67	2	GWG	Moskva	7 Jul 86
2.01A	Desiré	du Plessis	RSA	20.5.65	1		Johannesburg	16 Sep 86
2.01i	Gabriele	Günz	GDR	8.9.61	2		Stuttgart	31 Jan 88
2.01	Heike	Balck	GDR	19.8.70	1	vUSSR-j	Karl-Marx-Stadt	18 Jun 89
2.01i	Ioamnet	Quintero	CUB	8.9.72	1		Berlin	5 Mar 93
2.01	Hanne	Haugland	NOR	14.12.67	1	WK	Zürich	13 Aug 97
2.01i	Tisha	Waller	USA	1.12.70	1	NC	Atlanta	28 Feb 98
2.01	Yelena	Gulyayeva	RUS	14.8.67	2		Kalamáta	23 May 98
	(40)							
2.01	Vita	Palamar	UKR	12.10.77	2=	WK	Zürich	15 Aug 03
2.01	Amy	Acuff	USA	14.7.75	4	WK	Zürich	15 Aug 03
2.01	Iryna	Myhalchenko	UKR	20.1.72	1		Eberstadt	18 Jul 04
2.01	Emma	Green Tregaro	SWE	8.12.84	2	EC	Barcelona	1 Aug 10
2.01i	Mariya	Kuchina	RUS	14.1.93	1		Stockholm	6 Feb 14
2.00 WR	Rosemarie	Ackermann'	GDR	4.4.52	1	ISTAF	Berlin	26 Aug 77

2.00 by 21 others (67) 100th woman 1.98, 200th 1.95, 300th 1.93, 400th 1.95, 500th 1.90

Best outdoor marks

Mark	Name	Pos	Meet	Venue	Date
2.05	Henkel	1	WCh	Tokyo	31 Aug 91
2.05	Hellebaut	1	OG	Beijing	23 Aug 08
2.03	Di Martino	1	ECp-1B	Milano	24 Jun 07
2.02	Iagar/Dinescu	1		Budapest	6 Jun 98
2.02	Kuptsova	1	FBK	Hengelo	1 Jun 03
2.01	Astafei	2		Wörrstadt	27 May 95
2.01	Kuchina	1	WCh	Beijing	29 Aug 15
2.00	five women				

Ancillary jumps: 2.06 Kostadinova 30 Aug 87, 2.05i Henkel 8 Feb 92, 2.05i Bergqvist 4 Feb 06, 2.05 Vlasic 31 Aug 09

POLE VAULT

Mark Wind		Name	Nat	Born	Pos	Meet	Venue	Date
5.06 WR	Yelena	Isinbayeva	RUS	3.6.82	1	WK	Zürich	28 Aug 09
5.05 WR		Isinbayeva			1	OG	Beijing	18 Aug 08
5.04 WR		Isinbayeva			1	Herc	Monaco	29 Jul 08
5.03 WR		Isinbayeva			1	GGala	Roma	11 Jul 08
5.02Ai WIR	Jennifer	Suhr	USA	5.2.82	1	NC	Albuquerque	2 Mar 13
5.01 WR		Isinbayeva		2	1	WCh	Helsinki	12 Aug 05
5.01i WIR		Isinbayeva			1	XL Galan	Stockholm	23 Feb 12
5.00 WR		Isinbayeva			1	LGP	London (CP)	22 Jul 05
5.00i		Isinbayeva			1		Donetsk	15 Feb 09
4.95 WR		Isinbayeva			1	GP	Madrid	16 Jul 05
4.95i		Isinbayeva			1		Donetsk	16 Feb 08
4.93 WR		Isinbayeva			1	Athl	Lausanne	5 Jul 05
4.93		Isinbayeva			1	VD	Bruxelles	26 Aug 05
4.93i		Isinbayeva			1		Donetsk	10 Feb 07
4.93		Isinbayeva			1	LGP	London (CP)	25 Jul 08
4.92 WR		Isinbayeva			1	VD	Bruxelles	3 Sep 04
4.92		Stuczynski/Suhr			1	NC/OT	Eugene	6 Jul 08
4.91 WR		Isinbayeva (this jump on 25 Aug)			1	OG	Athína	25 Aug 04
4.91i		Isinbayeva			1		Donetsk	12 Feb 06
4.91		Isinbayeva			1	LGP	London (CP)	28 Jul 06
4.91		Isinbayeva			1	Gaz	Saint-Denis	6 Jul 07
4.91		Suhr			1		Rochester, NY	26 Jul 11
4.91		Suhr			1		Lyndonville	14 Jun 13
4.91	Yarisley	Silva	CUB	1.6.87	1		Beckum	2 Aug 15
4.90 WR		Isinbayeva			1	GP	London (CP)	30 Jul 04
4.90i		Isinbayeva			1	EI	Madrid	6 Mar 05
4.90		Isinbayeva			1	Athl	Lausanne	11 Jul 06
4.90		Isinbayeva			1	GGala	Roma	13 Jul 07
4.90		Stuczynski			1	adidas	Carson	18 May 08
4.90i		Isinbayeva			1		Praha (O2)	26 Feb 09
4.90		Silva			1	FBK	Hengelo	8 Jun 13
4.90		Silva			1	WCh	Beijing	26 Aug 15
	(32/3)							
4.88 WR	Svetlana	Feofanova	RUS	16.7.80	1		Iráklio	4 Jul 04
4.87i	Holly	Bleasdale/Bradshaw	GBR	2.11.91	1		Villeurbanne	20 Jan 12
4.85	Fabiana	Murer	BRA	16.3.81	1	IbAm	San Fernando	4 Jun 10
4.85i	Anna	Rogowska	POL	21.5.81	1	EI	Paris (Bercy)	6 Mar 11
4.83	Stacy	Dragila	USA	25.3.71	1	GS	Ostrava	8 Jun 04
4.83	Nikoléta	Kiriakopoúlou	GRE	21.3.86	1	DL	Saint-Denis	4 Jul 15
4.82	Monika	Pyrek	POL	11.8.80	2	WAF	Stuttgart	22 Sep 07
	(10)							
4.82	Silke	Spiegelburg	GER	17.3.86	1	Herc	Monaco	20 Jul 12
4.80	Martina	Strutz	GER	4.11.81	2	WCh	Daegu	30 Aug 11
4.80i	Anzhelika	Sidorova	RUS	28.6.91	1	EI	Praha (O2)	8 Mar 15

Mark	Wind	Name		Nat	Born	Pos	Meet	Venue	Date
4.78		Tatyana	Polnova	RUS	20.4.79	2	WAF	Monaco	19 Sep 04
4.77		Annika	Becker	GER	12.11.81	1	NC	Wattenscheid	7 Jul 02
4.77Ai		Ekateríni	Stefanídi	GRE	4.2.90	1		Flagstaff	20 Feb 15
4.76		Alana	Boyd	AUS	10.5.84	1		Perth	24 Feb 12
4.76		Jirina	Ptácníková'	CZE	20.5.86	1		Plzen	4 Sep 13
4.76		Sandi	Morris	USA	8.7.92	2	NA	Heusden-Zolder	18 Jul 15
4.75		Katerina	Badurová	CZE	18.12.82	2	WCh	Osaka	28 Aug 07
		(20)							
4.75i		Yuliya	Golubchikova	RUS	27.3.83	1		Athína (P)	13 Feb 08
4.75Ai		Kylie	Hutson	USA	27.11.87	2	NC	Albuquerque	2 Mar 13
4.75Ai		Demi	Payne	USA	30.9.91	1		Albuquerque	24 Jan 15
4.73		Chelsea	Johnson	USA	20.12.83	1		Los Gatos	26 Jun 08
4.73		Anastasiya	Savchenko	RUS	15.11.89	1	NCp	Yerino	15 Jun 13
4.72i		Kym	Howe	AUS	12.6.80	2		Donetsk	10 Feb 07
4.72i		Jillian	Schwartz	USA/ISR	19.9.79	1		Jonesboro	15 Jun 08
4.72		Carolin	Hingst	GER	18.9.80	1		Biberach	9 Jul 10
4.72i		Elizaveta 'Lisa'	Ryzih	GER	27.9.88	1		Metz	25 Feb 15
4.71i		Tina	Sutej	SLO	7.11.88	1		Moskva	2 Feb 14
		(30)							
4.71Ai		Mary	Saxer	USA	21.6.87	1	NC	Albuquerque	23 Feb 14
4.71i		Marion	Fiack	FRA	13.10.92	1		Aubière	10 Jan 15
4.71		Nicole	Büchler	SUI	17.12.83	1	NC	Zug	8 Aug 15
4.70		Yvonne	Buschbaum	GER	14.7.80	1	NC	Ulm	29 Jun 03
4.70		Vanessa	Boslak	FRA	11.6.82	2	ECp-S	Málaga	28 Jun 06
4.70		Angelina	Zhuk/Krasnova	RUS	7.2.91	1	EU23	Tampere	13 Jul 13
4.70i		Angelica	Bengtsson	SWE	8.7.93	3	EI	Praha (O2)	8 Mar 15
4.68		Anna	Battke	GER	3.1.85	5	ISTAF	Berlin	14 Jun 09
4.67i		Kellie	Suttle	USA	9.5.73	1		Jonesboro	16 Jun 04
4.66i		Christine	Adams	GER	28.2.74	1	IHS	Sindelfingen	10 Mar 02
		(40)							
4.66i		Lacy	Janson	USA	20.2.83	1		Fayetteville	12 Feb 10
4.66i		Kristina	Gadschiew	GER	3.7.84	1		Potsdam	18 Feb 11
4.66			Li Ling	CHN	6.7.89	1	AsiC	Wuhan	6 Jun 15
4.65		Mary	Sauer/Vincent	USA	31.10.75	2		Madrid (C)	3 Jul 02
4.65		Anastasiya	Ivanova/Shvedova	RUS/BLR	3.5.79	1	Odlozil	Praha	13 Jun 07
4.65		Aleksandra	Kiryashova	RUS	21.8.85	1	NCp	Tula	1 Aug 09
4.65i		Becky	Holliday	USA	12.3.80	1		Jonesboro	16 Apr 15
4.65		Katharina	Bauer	GER	12.6.90	3		Beckum	2 Aug 15
4.64i		Pavla	Hamácková/Rybová	CZE	20.5.78	4		Bydgoszcz	14 Feb 07
4.64			Gao Shuying	CHN	28.10.79	2	GP	New York	2 Jun 07
4.64		Eliza	McCartney	NZL	11.12.96	1		Auckland	19 Dec 15
		(51)	100th woman 4.51, 200th 4.40, 300th 4.30, 400th 4.25, 500th 4.20						

Outdoor best

Mark	Name	Pos	Meet	Venue	Date
4.79	Sidorova	2	DL	London (OS)	25 Jul 15
4.75	Golubchikova	4	OG	Beijing	18 Aug 08
4.71	Bleasdale	1	NC	Birmingham	24 Jun 12
4.71	L Ryzih	1	adidas	New York	14 Jun 14
4.71	E Stefanídi	3	Herc	Monaco	18 Jul 14
4.71	Payne	1		Hammond	8 May 15
4.70	Hutson	1		Terre Haute	15 Jun 13
4.70	Saxer	1		Chula Vista	6 Jun 13
4.70	Bengtsson	4=	WCh	Beijing	26 Aug 15
4.65	Howe	1		Saulheim	30 Jun 07

Ancillary jumps: Isinbayeva: 4.97 15 Feb 09, 4.96 WR 22 Jul 05, 4.95 18 Aug 08, 4.93 29 Jul 08, 4.92i 23 Feb 12

Exhibition: 4.72 Anastasiya Shvedova RUS 3.5.79 1 Aosta 5 Jul 08

LONG JUMP

Mark	Wind	Name		Nat	Born	Pos	Meet	Venue	Date
7.52 WR	1.4	Galina	Chistyakova	RUS	26.7.62	1	Znam	Leningrad	11 Jun 88
7.49	1.3	Jackie	Joyner-Kersee	USA	3.3.62	1	NYG	New York	22 May 94
7.49A	1.7		Joyner-Kersee			1		Sestriere	31 Jul 94
7.48	1.2	Heike	Drechsler	GER	16.12.64	1	v ITA	Neubrandenburg	9 Jul 88
7.48	0.4		Drechsler			1	Athl	Lausanne	8 Jul 92
7.45 WR	0.9		Drechsler'			1	v USSR	Tallinn	21 Jun 86
7.45 WR	1.1		Drechsler			1	OD	Dresden	3 Jul 86
7.45 WR	0.6		Joyner-Kersee			1	PAm	Indianapolis	13 Aug 87
7.45	1.6		Chistyakova			1	BGP	Budapest	12 Aug 88
7.44 WR	2.0		Drechsler			1		Berlin	22 Sep 85
7.43 WR	1.4	Anisoara	Cusmir/Stanciu	ROU	28.6.62	1	RomIC	Bucuresti	4 Jun 83
7.42	2.0	Tatyana	Kotova ¶	RUS	11.12.76	1	ECp-S	Annecy	23 Jun 02
7.40	1.8		Daute' (Drechsler)			1		Dresden	26 Jul 84
7.40	0.7		Drechsler			1	NC	Potsdam	21 Aug 87
7.40	0.9		Joyner-Kersee			1	OG	Seoul	29 Sep 88
7.39	0.3		Drechsler			1	WK	Zürich	21 Aug 85
7.39	0.5	Yelena	Byelevskaya'	BLR	11.10.63	1	NC	Bryansk	18 Jul 87
7.39			Joyner-Kersee			1		San Diego	25 Jun 88
7.37i	-		Drechsler			1	v2N	Wien	13 Feb 88
7.37A	1.8		Drechsler			1		Sestriere	31 Jul 91

Mark	Wind		Name	Nat	Born	Pos	Meet	Venue	Date
7.37		Inessa	Kravets ¶	UKR	5.10.66	1		Kyiv	13 Jun 92
7.36	0.4		Joyner			1	WCh	Roma	4 Sep 87
7.36	1.8		Byelevskaya			2	Znam	Leningrad	11 Jun 88
7.36	1.8		Drechsler			1		Jena	28 May 92
7.35	1.9		Chistyakova			1	GPB	Bratislava	20 Jun 90
7.34	1.6		Daute'			1		Dresden	19 May 84
7.34	1.4		Chistyakova			2	v GDR	Tallinn	21 Jun 86
7.34			Byelevskaya			1		Sukhumi	17 May 87
7.34	0.7		Drechsler			1	v USSR	Karl-Marx-Stadt	20 Jun 87
7.33	0.4		Drechsler			1	v USSR	Erfurt	22 Jun 85
7.33	2.0		Drechsler			1		Dresden	2 Aug 85
7.33	-0.3		Drechsler			1	Herc	Monaco	11 Aug 92
7.33	0.4	Tatyana	Lebedeva	RUS	21.7.76	1	NC	Tula	31 Jul 04
		(33/8)							
7.31	1.5	Yelena	Kokonova'	UKR	4.8.63	1	NP	Alma-Ata	12 Sep 85
7.31	1.9	Marion	Jones ¶	USA	12.10.75	1	Pre	Eugene	31 May 98
		(10)							
7.27	-0.4	Irina	Simagina/Meleshina	RUS	25.5.82	2	NC	Tula	31 Jul 04
7.26A	1.8	Maurren	Maggi ¶	BRA	25.6.76	1	SACh	Bogotá	26 Jun 99
7.25	1.6	Brittney	Reese	USA	9.9.86	1	DL	Doha	10 May 13
7.24	1.0	Larisa	Berezhnaya	UKR	28.2.61	1		Granada	25 May 91
7.21	1.6	Helga	Radtke	GDR	16.5.62	2		Dresden	26 Jul 84
7.21	1.9	Lyudmila	Kolchanova	RUS	1.10.79	1		Sochi	27 May 07
7.20 WR	-0.5	Valy	Ionescu	ROU	31.8.60	1	NC	Bucuresti	1 Aug 82
7.20	2.0	Irena	Ozhenko'	LTU	13.11.62	1		Budapest	12 Sep 86
7.20	0.8	Yelena	Sinchukova'	RUS	23.1.61	1	BGP	Budapest	20 Jun 91
7.20	0.7	Irina	Mushayilova	RUS	6.1.67	1	NC	Sankt-Peterburg	14 Jul 94
		(20)							
7.17	1.8	Irina	Valyukevich	BLR	19.11.59	2	NC	Bryansk	18 Jul 87
7.16		Iolanda	Chen	RUS	26.7.61	1		Moskva	30 Jul 88
7.16A	-0.1	Elva	Goulbourne	JAM	21.1.80	1		Ciudad de México	22 May 04
7.14	1.8	Nijole	Medvedeva ¶	LTU	20.10.60	1		Riga	4 Jun 88
7.14	1.2	Mirela	Dulgheru	ROU	5.10.66	1	Balk G	Sofia	5 Jul 92
7.13	2.0	Olga	Kucherenko	RUS	5.11.85	1		Sochi	27 May 10
7.12	1.6	Sabine	Paetz/John'	GDR	16.10.57	2		Dresden	19 May 84
7.12	0.9	Chioma	Ajunwa ¶	NGR	25.12.70	1	OG	Atlanta	2 Aug 96
7.12	1.3	Naide	Gomes	CPV/POR	10.11.79	1	Herc	Monaco	29 Jul 08
7.14	1.2	Tianna	Bartoletta'	USA	30.8.85	1	WCh	Beijing	28 Aug 15
		(30)							
7.11	0.8	Fiona	May	GBR/ITA	12.12.69	2	EC	Budapest	22 Aug 98
7.11	1.3	Anna	Nazarova	RUS	3.2.86	1	Mosc Ch	Moskva	20 Jun 12
7.10	1.6	Chelsea	Hayes	USA	9.2.88	2	NC/OT	Eugene	1 Jul 12
7.09 WR	0.0	Vilhelmina	Bardauskiené	LTU	15.6.53	Q	EC	Praha	29 Aug 78
7.09	1.5	Ljudmila	Ninova	AUT	25.6.60	1	GP II	Sevilla	5 Jun 94
7.08	0.5	Marieta	Ilcu ¶	ROU	16.10.62	1	RumIC	Pitesti	25 Jun 89
7.08	1.9	Anastasiya	Mironchik-Ivanova	BLR	13.4.89	1		Minsk	12 Jun 12
7.07	0.0	Svetlana	Zorina	RUS	2.2.60	1		Krasnodar	15 Aug 87
7.07	0.5	Yelena	Sokolova	RUS	23.7.86	2	OG	London (OS)	8 Aug 12
7.07	0.4	Shara	Proctor	AIA/GBR	16.9.88	2	WCh	Beijing	28 Aug 15
		(40)							
7.06	0.4	Tatyana	Kolpakova	KGZ	18.10.59	1	OG	Moskva	31 Jul 80
7.06	-0.1	Niurka	Montalvo	CUB/ESP	4.6.68	1	WCh	Sevilla	23 Aug 99
7.06		Tatyana	Ter-Mesrobyan	RUS	12.5.68	1		Sankt Peterburg	22 May 02
7.05	0.6	Lyudmila	Galkina	RUS	20.1.72	1	WCh	Athína	9 Aug 97
7.05	-0.4	Eunice	Barber	FRA	17.11.74	1	WAF	Monaco	14 Sep 03
7.05	1.1	Darya	Klishina	RUS	15.1.91	1	EU23	Ostrava	17 Jul 11
7.04	0.5	Brigitte	Wujak'	GDR	6.3.55	2	OG	Moskva	31 Jul 80
7.04	0.9	Tatyana	Proskuryakova'	RUS	13.1.56	1		Kyiv	25 Aug 83
7.04	2.0	Yelena	Yatsuk	UKR	16.3.61	1	Znam	Moskva	8 Jun 85
7.04	0.3	Carol	Lewis	USA	8.8.63	5	WK	Zürich	21 Aug 85
7.04	1.5	Sosthene	Moguenara	GER	17.10.89	1		Weinheim	2 Aug 13
		(51)	100th woman 6.93, 200th 6.81, 300th 6.76, 400th 6.70, 500th 6.65						
Wind assisted			*Performances to 7.35, performers to 7.05*						
7.63A	2.1	Heike	Drechsler	GER	16.12.64	1		Sestriere	21 Jul 92
7.45	2.6		Joyner-Kersee			1	NC/OT	Indianapolis	23 Jul 88
7.39	2.6		Drechsler			1		Padova	15 Sep 91
7.39	2.9		Drechsler			1	Expo	Sevilla	6 Jun 92
7.39A	3.3		Drechsler			2		Sestriere	31 Jul 94
7.36	2.2		Chistyakova			1	Znam	Volgograd	11 Jun 89
7.35	3.4		Drechsler			1	NC	Jena	29 Jun 86
7.23A	4.3	Fiona	May	ITA	12.12.69	1		Sestriere	29 Jul 95

Mark	Wind	Name		Nat	Born	Pos	Meet	Venue	Date
7.22	4.3	Anastasiya	Mironchik-Ivanova	BLR	13.4.89	1	NC	Grodno	6 Jul 12
7.19A	3.7	Susen	Tiedtke ¶	GER	23.1.69	1		Sestriere	28 Jul 93
7.17	3.6	Eva	Murková	SVK	29.5.62	1		Nitra	26 Aug 84
7.15	2.8	Janay	DeLoach-Soukup	USA	12.10.85	Q	NC/OT	Eugene	29 Jun 12
7.14A	4.5	Marieke	Veltman	USA	18.9.71	2		Sestriere	29 Jul 95
7.14	2.2	Blessing	Okagbare	NGR	9.10.88	2	DL	Doha	10 May 13
7.12A	5.8	Níki	Xánthou	GRE	11.10.73	3		Sestriere	29 Jul 95
7.12A	4.3	Nicole	Boegman	AUS	5.3.67	4		Sestriere	29 Jul 95
7.09	2.9	Renata	Nielsen	DEN	18.5.66	2		Sevilla	5 Jun 94
7.08	2.2	Lyudmila	Galkina	RUS	20.1.72	1		Thessaloniki	23 Jun 99
7.07A	5.6	Valentina	Uccheddu	ITA	26.10.66	5		Sestriere	29 Jul 95
7.07A	2.7	Sharon	Couch	USA	13.9.67	1		El Paso	12 Apr 97
7.07A	w	Erica	Johansson	SWE	5.2.74	1		Vygieskraal	15 Jan 00
7.06	3.4		Ma Miaolan	CHN	18.1.70	1	NG	Beijing	10 Sep 93

Best at low altitude:

7.06 0.8 Maggi ¶ 1 Milano 3 Jun 03 | 7.12w 3.4 May 1 NC Bologna 25 May 96
7.17w 2.6 1 São Paulo 13 Apr 02

Ancillary marks – other marks during series (to 7.34/7.36w)

7.45 1.0 Chistyakova 11 Jun 88 | 7.47Aw 3.1 Drechsler 21 Jul 92 | 7.38w 2.2 Chistyakova 11 Jun 88
7.37 Drechsler 9 Jul 88 | 7.39Aw 3.1 Drechsler 21 Jul 92 | 7.36w Joyner-Kersee 31 Jul 94

TRIPLE JUMP

Mark	Wind	Name		Nat	Born	Pos	Meet	Venue	Date
15.50 WR	0.9	Inessa	Kravets ¶	UKR	5.10.66	1	WCh	Göteborg	10 Aug 95
15.39	0.5	Françoise	Mbango	CMR	14.4.76	1	OG	Beijing	17 Aug 08
15.36i		Tatyana	Lebedeva	RUS	21.7.76	1	WI	Budapest	6 Mar 04
15.34	-0.5		Lebedeva			1		Iráklio	4 Jul 04
15.33	-0.1		Kravets			1	OG	Atlanta	31 Jul 96
15.33	1.2		Lebedeva			1	Athl	Lausanne	6 Jul 04
15.32	0.5		Lebedeva			1	Super	Yokohama	9 Sep 00
15.32	0.9	Hrisopiyi	Devetzí ¶	GRE	2.1.76	Q	OG	Athína	21 Aug 04
15.32	0.5		Lebedeva			2	OG	Beijing	17 Aug 08
15.31	0.0	Caterine	Ibargüen	COL	12.2.84	1	Herc	Monaco	18 Jul 14
15.30	0.6		Mbango			1	OG	Athína	23 Aug 04
15.29	0.3	Yamilé	Aldama	CUB/SUD/GBR	14.8.72	1	GGala	Roma	11 Jul 03
15.28	0.3		Aldama			1	GP	Linz	2 Aug 04
15.28	0.9	Yargelis	Savigne	CUB	13.11.84	1	WCh	Osaka	31 Aug 07
15.27	1.3		Aldama			1	GP	London (CP)	8 Aug 03
15.25	-0.8		Lebedeva			1	WCh	Edmonton	10 Aug 01
15.25	-0.1		Devetzí			2	OG	Athína	23 Aug 04
15.25	1.7	Olga	Rypakova	KAZ	30.11.84	1	C.Cup	Split	4 Sep 10
15.23	0.8		Lebedeva			1		Réthimno	23 Jun 04
15.23	0.6		Lebedeva			1	Tsik	Athína	3 Jul 06
15.23	1.6		Devetzí			3	OG	Beijing	17 Aug 08
15.22	1.5		Devetzí			1		Thessaloníki	9 Jul 08
15.21	1.2		Aldama			2		Réthimno	23 Jun 04
15.20	0.0	Sarka	Kaspárková	CZE	20.5.71	1	WCh	Athína	4 Aug 97
15.20	-0.3	Tereza	Marinova (10)	BUL	5.9.77	1	OG	Sydney	24 Sep 00
15.20	1.3		Savigne			1	Vard	Réthimno	14 Jul 08
15.19	0.5		Lebedeva			1	Athl	Lausanne	11 Jul 06
15.18	0.3	Iva	Prandzheva ¶	BUL	15.2.72	2	WCh	Göteborg	10 Aug 95
15.18	-0.2		Lebedeva			1	WCh	Saint-Denis	26 Aug 03
15.16	0.1	Rodica	Mateescu ¶	ROU	13.3.71	2	WCh	Athína	4 Aug 97
15.16i WIR	-	Ashia	Hansen	GBR	5.12.71	1	EI	Valencia	28 Feb 98
15.16	0.7	Trecia	Smith	JAM	5.11.75	2	GP	Linz	2 Aug 04
		(32/14)							
15.14	1.9	Nadezhda	Alekhina	RUS	22.9.78	1	NC	Cheboksary	26 Jul 09
15.09 WR	0.5	Anna	Biryukova	RUS	27.9.67	1	WCh	Stuttgart	21 Aug 93
15.09	-0.5	Inna	Lasovskaya	RUS	17.12.69	1	ECCp-A	Valencia	31 May 97
15.08i		Marija	Sestak	SLO	17.4.79	1		Athína (P)	13 Feb 08
15.07	-0.6	Paraskeví	Tsiamíta	GRE	10.3.72	Q	WCh	Sevilla	22 Aug 99
15.04	1.7	Yekaterina	Koneva	RUS	25.9.88	2	Pre	Eugene	30 May 15
		(20)							
15.03i		Iolanda	Chen	RUS	26.7.61	1	WI	Barcelona	11 Mar 95
15.03	1.9	Magdelin	Martinez	ITA	10.2.76	1		Roma	26 Jun 04
15.02	0.9	Anna	Pyatykh	RUS	4.4.81	3	EC	Göteborg	8 Sep 06
15.00	1.2	Kène	Ndoye	SEN	20.11.78	2		Iráklio	4 Jul 04
14.99	0.2	Olha	Saladukha	UKR	4.6.83	1	EC	Helsinki	29 Jun 12
14.98	1.8	Sofia	Bozhanova ¶	BUL	4.10.67	1		Stara Zagora	16 Jul 94
14.98	0.2	Baya	Rahouli	ALG	27.7.79	1	MedG	Almeria	1 Jul 05
14.96	0.7	Yelena	Hovorova	UKR	18.9.73	4	OG	Sydney	24 Sep 00

Mark	Wind		Name	Nat	Born	Pos	Meet	Venue	Date
14.94i	–	Cristina	Nicolau	ROU	9.8.77	1	NC	Bucuresti	5 Feb 00
14.94i		Oksana	Udmurtova	RUS	1.2.82	1		Tartu	20 Feb 08
		(30)							
14.90	1.0		Xie Limei	CHN	27.6.86	1		Urumqi	20 Sep 07
14.89	0.6	Yekaterina	Koneva	RUS	25.9.88	2	Herc	Monaco	18 Jul 14
14.85	1.2	Viktoriya	Gurova	RUS	22.5.82	3	NC	Kazan	19 Jul 08
14.83i	-	Yelena	Lebedenko	RUS	16.1.71	1		Samara	1 Feb 01
14.83	0.5	Yelena	Oleynikova	RUS	9.12.76	1	Odlozil	Praha	17 Jun 02
14.79	1.7	Irina	Mushayilova	RUS	6.1.67	1	DNG	Stockholm	5 Jul 93
14.78i		Adelina	Gavrila	ROU	26.11.78	1		Bucuresti	3 Feb 08
14.78	-0.1	Hanna	Minenko	UKR/ISR	25.9.89	2	WCh	Beijing	24 Aug 15
14.76	0.9	Galina	Chistyakova	RUS	26.7.62	1	Spitzen	Luzern	27 Jun 95
14.76	1.1	Gundega	Sproge ¶	LAT	12.12.72	3		Sheffield	29 Jun 97
		(40)							
14.76	0.4	Kseniya	Detsuk	BLR	23.4.86	*	NCp	Brest	26 May 12
14.72	1.8		Huang Qiuyan	CHN	25.1.80	1	NG	Guangzhou	22 Nov 01
14.72		Paraskeví	Papahrístou	GRE	17.4.89	1	Veniz	Haniá	11 Jun 11
14.71	1.4	Athanasía	Pérra	GRE	2.2.83	1	NC	Athína	16 Jun 12
14.70i		Oksana	Rogova	RUS	7.10.78	1		Volgograd	6 Feb 02
14.69	1.2	Anja	Valant	SLO	8.9.77	3		Kalamáta	4 Jun 00
14.69	1.2	Simona	La Mantia	ITA	14.4.83	1		Palermo	22 May 05
14.69	2.0	Teresa	N'zola Meso	ANG/FRA	30.11.83	1	ECp-S	München	23 Jun 07
14.68i		Anastasiya	Taranova-Potapova	RUS	6.9.85	1	EI	Torino	8 Mar 09
14.67	1.2	Ólga	Vasdéki	GRE	26.9.73	1	Veniz	Haniá	28 Jul 99
14.67	1.5	Natalya	Kutyakova	RUS	28.11.86	1		Huelva	2 Jun 11
14.67	0.4	Mabel	Gay	CUB	5.5.83	4	WCh	Daegu	1 Sep 11
		(52)	100th woman 14.44, 200th 14.15, 300th 13.98, 400th 13.79, 500th 13.67						

Wind assisted *Performances to 15.14, performers to 14.75*

Mark	Wind		Name	Nat	Born	Pos	Meet	Venue	Date
15.24A	4.2	Magdelin	Martinez	ITA	10.2.76	1		Sestriere	1 Aug 04
15.18w	2.1	Caterine	Ibargüen	COL	12.2.84	1	Pre	Eugene	30 May 15
15.17	2.4	Anna	Pyatykh	RUS	4.4.81	2	SGP	Athína	3 Jul 06
15.10	2.7	Keila	Costa	BRA	6.2.83	1		Uberlandia	6 May 07
15.06	2.6	Olga	Saladukha	UKR	4.6.83	1	DNG	Stockholm	29 Jul 11
14.99	6.8	Yelena	Hovorova	UKR	18.9.73	1	WUG	Palma de Mallorca	11 Jul 99
14.85	2.5	Gabriela	Petrova	BUL	29.6.92	1	ET-2	Stara Zagora	20 Jun 15
14.84	4.1	Galina	Chistyakova	RUS	26.7.62	1		Innsbruck	28 Jun 95
14.83	8.3		Ren Ruiping	CHN	1.2.76	1	NC	Taiyuan	21 May 95
14.83	2.2	Heli	Koivula-Kruger	FIN	27.6.75	2	EC	München	10 Aug 02
14.81	2.4	Kseniya	Detsuk	BLR	23.4.86	1	NCp	Brest	26 May 12
14.78	2.7	Kimberly	Williams	JAM	3.11.88	3	Pre	Eugene	1 Jun 13
14.77	2.3	Paraskeví	Papahrístou	GRE	17.4.89	1		Ankara	5 Jun 12
14.75	4.2	Jelena	Blazevica	LAT	11.5.70	1	v2N	Kaunas	23 Aug 97

Best outdoor mark for athlete with all-time best indoors

Mark	Wind	Name	Pos	Meet	Venue	Date
15.15	1.7	Hansen	1	GPF	Fukuoka	13 Sep 97
15.03	1.1	Sestak	6	OG	Beijing	17 Aug 08
14.97WR	0.9	Chen	1	NC	Moskva	18 Jun 93
14.85	1.4	Udmurtova	1		Padova	31 Aug 08
14.75	1.1	Gavrila	3	GP II	Rieti	7 Sep 03
14.70	1.3	Nicolau	1	EU23	Göteborg	1 Aug 99

Ancillary marks – other marks during series (to 15.19)

Mark	Wind	Name	Date
15.30	0.5	Mbango	23 Aug 04
15.21	-0.2	Mbango	23 Aug 04
15.28	-0.3	Ledebeva	4 Jul 04
15.19	1.0	Lebedeva	3 Jul 06
15.25i		Ledebeva	6 Mar 04
15.19	1.3	Mbango	17 Aug 08

SHOT

Mark		Name	Nat	Born	Pos	Meet	Venue	Date
22.63 WR	Natalya	Lisovskaya	RUS	16.7.62	1	Znam	Moskva	7 Jun 87
22.55		Lisovskaya			1	NC	Tallinn	5 Jul 88
22.53 WR		Lisovskaya			1		Sochi	27 May 84
22.53		Lisovskaya			1		Kyiv	14 Aug 88
22.50i	Helena	Fibingerová	CZE	13.7.49	1		Jablonec	19 Feb 77
22.45 WR	Ilona	Slupianek' ¶	GDR	24.9.56	1		Potsdam	11 May 80
22.41		Slupianek			1	OG	Moskva	24 Jul 80
22.40		Slupianek			1		Berlin	3 Jun 83
22.38		Slupianek			1		Karl-Marx-Stadt	25 May 80
22.36 WR		Slupianek			1		Celje	2 May 80
22.34		Slupianek			1		Berlin	7 May 80
22.34		Slupianek			1	NC	Cottbus	18 Jul 80
22.32 WR		Fibingerová			1		Nitra	20 Aug 77
22.24		Lisovskaya			1	OG	Seoul	1 Oct 88
22.22		Slupianek			1		Potsdam	13 Jul 80
22.19	Claudia	Losch	FRG	10.1.60	1		Hainfeld	23 Aug 87
22.14i		Lisovskaya			1	NC	Penza	7 Feb 87
22.13		Slupianek			1		Split	29 Apr 80
22.06		Slupianek			1		Berlin	15 Aug 78
22.06		Lisovskaya			1		Moskva	6 Aug 88

Mark	Wind	Name		Nat	Born	Pos	Meet	Venue	Date
22.05			Slupianek			1	OD	Berlin	28 May 80
22.05			Slupianek			1		Potsdam	31 May 80
22.04			Slupianek			1		Potsdam	4 Jul 79
22.04			Slupianek			1		Potsdam	29 Jul 79
21.99	WR		Fibingerová			1		Opava	26 Sep 76
21.98			Slupianek			1		Berlin	17 Jul 79
21.96			Fibingerová			1	GS	Ostrava	8 Jun 77
21.96			Lisovskaya			1	Drz	Praha	16 Aug 84
21.96			Lisovskaya			1		Vilnius	28 Aug 88
21.95		(30/4)	Lisovskaya			1	IAC	Edinburgh	29 Jul 88
21.89	WR	Ivanka	Khristova	BUL	19.11.41	1		Belmeken	4 Jul 76
21.86		Marianne	Adam	GDR	19.9.51	1	v URS	Leipzig	23 Jun 79
21.76			Li Meisu	CHN	17.4.59	1		Shijiazhuang	23 Apr 88
21.73		Natalya	Akhrimenko	RUS	12.5.55	1		Leselidze	21 May 88
21.70i		Nadezhda	Ostapchuk ¶	BLR	12.10.80	1	NC	Mogilyov	12 Feb 10
21.69		Viktoriya	Pavlysh ¶	UKR	15.1.69	1	EC	Budapest	20 Aug 98
		(10)							
21.66			Sui Xinmei ¶	CHN	29.1.65	1		Beijing	9 Jun 90
21.61		Verzhinia	Veselinova	BUL	18.11.57	1		Sofia	21 Aug 82
21.60i		Valentina	Fedyushina	UKR	18.2.65	1		Simferopol	28 Dec 91
21.58		Margitta	Droese/Pufe	GDR	10.9.52	1		Erfurt	28 May 78
21.57	@	Ines	Müller'	GDR	2.1.59	1		Athína	16 May 88
		21.45				1		Schwerin	4 Jun 86
21.53		Nunu	Abashidze ¶	UKR	27.3.55	2	Izv	Kyiv	20 Jun 84
21.52			Huang Zhihong	CHN	7.5.65	1	NC	Beijing	27 Jun 90
21.46		Larisa	Peleshenko ¶	RUS	29.2.64	1	Kuts	Moskva	26 Aug 00
21.45	WR	Nadezhda	Chizhova	RUS	29.9.45	1		Varna	29 Sep 73
21.43		Eva	Wilms	FRG	28.7.52	2	HB	München	17 Jun 77
		(20)	*@ competitive meeting, but unsanctioned by GDR federation*						
21.42		Svetlana	Krachevskaya'	RUS	23.11.44	2	OG	Moskva	24 Jul 80
21.31	@	Heike	Hartwig'	GDR	30.12.62	2		Athína	16 May 88
		21.27				1		Haniá	22 May 88
21.27		Liane	Schmuhl	GDR	29.6.61	1		Cottbus	26 Jun 82
21.24		Valerie	Adams	NZL	6.10.84	1	WCh	Daegu	29 Aug 11
21.22		Astrid	Kumbernuss	GDR/GER	5.2.70	1	WCh	Göteborg	5 Aug 95
21.21		Kathrin	Neimke	GDR	18.7.66	2	WCh	Roma	5 Sep 87
21.19		Helma	Knorscheidt	GDR	31.12.56	1		Berlin	24 May 84
21.15i		Irina	Korzhanenko ¶	RUS	16.5.74	1	NC	Moskva	18 Feb 99
21.10		Heidi	Krieger	GDR	20.7.65	1	EC	Stuttgart	26 Aug 86
21.06		Svetlana	Krivelyova ¶	RUS	13.6.69	1	OG	Barcelona	7 Aug 92
		(30)							
21.05		Zdenka	Silhavá' ¶	CZE	15.6.54	2	NC	Praha	23 Jul 83
21.01		Ivanka	Petrova-Stoycheva	BUL	3.2.51	1	NC	Sofia	28 Jul 79
21.00		Mihaela	Loghin	ROU	1.6.52	1		Formia	30 Jun 84
21.00		Cordula	Schulze	GDR	11.9.59	4	OD	Potsdam	21 Jul 84
20.96		Belsy	Laza	CUB	5.6.67	1		Ciudad de México	2 May 92
20.95		Elena	Stoyanova ¶	BUL	23.1.52	2	Balk	Sofia	14 Jun 86
20.91		Svetla	Mitkova	BUL	17.6.64	1		Sofia	24 May 87
20.80		Sona	Vasícková	CZE	14.3.62	1		Praha	2 Jun 88
20.77		Christina	Schwanitz	GER	24.12.85	1		Beijing	20 May 15
20.72		Grit	Haupt/Hammer	GDR	4.6.66	3		Neubrandenburg	11 Jun 87
		(40)							
20.70		Natalya	Mikhnevich' ¶	BLR	25.5.82	2	NC	Grodno	8 Jul 08
20.61		María Elena	Sarría	CUB	14.9.54	1		La Habana	22 Jul 82
20.61		Yanina	Korolchik' ¶	BLR	26.12.76	1	WCh	Edmonton	5 Aug 01
20.60		Marina	Antonyuk	RUS	12.5.62	1		Chelyabinsk	10 Aug 86
20.54			Zhang Liuhong	CHN	16.1.69	1	NC	Beijing	5 Jun 94
20.53		Iris	Plotzitzka	FRG	7.1.66	1	ASV	Köln	21 Aug 88
20.50i		Christa	Wiese	GDR	25.12.67	2	NC	Senftenberg	12 Feb 89
20.48		Yevgeniya	Kolodko	RUS	2.7.90	2	OG	London (OS)	6 Aug 12
20.47		Nina	Isayeva	RUS	6.7.50	1		Bryansk	28 Aug 82
20.47			Cong Yuzhen	CHN	22.1.63	2	IntC	Tianjin	3 Sep 88
		(50)	100th woman 19.69, 200th 18.86, 300th 18.18, 400th 17.77, 500th 17.48						

Best outdoor marks

21.58	Ostapchuk ¶	1	Minsk	18 Jul 12
21.08	Fedyushina	1	Leselidze	15 May 88
20.82	Korzhanenko ¶	1	Rostov na Donu	30 May 94
	21.06 drugs dq	(1) OG	Athína	18 Aug 04

Ancillary marks – other marks during series (to 22.09)

22.60	Lisovskaya (WR)	7 Jun 87
22.40	Lisovskaya	14 Aug 88
22.34	Slupianek	11 May 80
22.33	Slupianek	2 May 80
22.20	Slupianek	13 Jul 80
22.19	Lisovskaya	5 Jul 88
22.14	Slupianek	25 May 80
22.14	Slupianek	13 Jul 80
22.12	Slupianek	13 Jul 80
22.11	Slupianek	7 May 80
22.10	Slupianek	25 May 80
22.09	Slupianek	7 May 80

DISCUS

Mark	Wind	Name		Nat	Born	Pos	Meet	Venue	Date
76.80	WR	Gabriele	Reinsch	GDR	23.9.63	1	v ITA	Neubrandenburg	9 Jul 88
74.56	WR	Zdenka	Silhavá' ¶	CZE	15.6.54	1		Nitra	26 Aug 84
74.56		Ilke	Wyludda	GDR	28.3.69	1	NC	Neubrandenburg	23 Jul 89
74.44			Reinsch			1		Berlin	13 Sep 88
74.40			Wyludda			2		Berlin	13 Sep 88
74.08		Diana	Gansky'	GDR	14.12.63	1	v USSR	Karl-Marx-Stadt	20 Jun 87
73.90			Gansky			1	ECp	Praha	27 Jun 87
73.84		Daniela	Costian ¶	ROU	30.4.65	1		Bucuresti	30 Apr 88
73.78			Costian			1		Bucuresti	24 Apr 88
73.42			Reinsch			1		Karl-Marx-Stadt	12 Jun 88
73.36	WR	Irina	Meszynski	GDR	24.3.62	1	Drz	Praha	17 Aug 84
73.32			Gansky			1		Neubrandenburg	11 Jun 87
73.28		Galina	Savinkova'	RUS	15.7.53	1	NC	Donetsk	8 Sep 84
73.26	WR		Savinkova			1		Leselidze	21 May 83
73.26			Sachse/Gansky			1		Neubrandenburg	6 Jun 86
73.24			Gansky			1		Leipzig	29 May 87
73.22		Tsvetanka	Khristova ¶	BUL	14.3.62	1		Kazanlak	19 Apr 87
73.10		Gisela	Beyer	GDR	16.7.60	1	OD	Berlin	20 Jul 84
73.04			Gansky			1		Potsdam	6 Jun 87
73.04			Wyludda			1	ECp	Gateshead	5 Aug 89
72.96			Savinkova			1	v GDR	Erfurt	23 Jun 85
72.94			Gansky			2	v ITA	Neubrandenburg	9 Jul 88
72.92		Martina	Opitz/Hellmann	GDR	12.12.60	1	NC	Potsdam	20 Aug 87
72.90			Costian			1		Bucuresti	14 May 88
72.78			Hellmann			2		Neubrandenburg	11 Jun 87
72.78			Reinsch			1	OD	Berlin	29 Jun 88
72.72			Wyludda			1		Neubrandenburg	23 Jun 89
72.70			Wyludda			1	NC-j	Karl-Marx-Stadt	15 Jul 88
72.54			Gansky			1	NC	Rostock	25 Jun 88
72.52			Hellmann			1		Frohburg	15 Jun 86
72.52		(31/10)	Khristova			1	BGP	Budapest	11 Aug 86
72.14		Galina	Murashova	LTU	22.12.55	2	Drz	Praha	17 Aug 84
71.80	WR	Maria	Vergova/Petkova	BUL	3.11.50	1	NC	Sofia	13 Jul 80
71.68			Xiao Yanling ¶	CHN	27.3.68	1		Beijing	14 Mar 92
71.58		Ellina	Zvereva' ¶	BLR	16.11.60	1	Znam	Leningrad	12 Jun 88
71.50	WR	Evelin	Schlaak/Jahl	GDR	28.3.56	1		Potsdam	10 May 80
71.30		Larisa	Korotkevich	RUS	3.1.67	1	RusCp	Sochi	29 May 92
71.22		Ria	Stalman	NED	11.12.51	1		Walnut	15 Jul 84
71.08		Sandra	Perkovic	CRO	21.6.90	1	EC	Zürich	16 Aug 14
70.88		Hilda Elia	Ramos ¶	CUB	1.9.64	1		La Habana	8 May 92
70.80		Larisa	Mikhalchenko	UKR	16.5.63	1		Kharkov	18 Jun 88
		(20)							
70.68		Maritza	Martén	CUB	16.8.63	1	Ib Am	Sevilla	18 Jul 92
70.65		Denia	Caballero	CUB	13.1.90	1		Bilbao	20 Jun 15
70.50	WR	Faina	Melnik	RUS	9.6.45	1	Znam	Sochi	24 Apr 76
70.34	@	Silvia	Madetzky	GDR	24.6.62	3		Athína	16 May 88
		69.34				1		Halle	26 Jun 87
70.02		Natalya	Sadova ¶	RUS	15.7.72	1		Thessaloniki	23 Jun 99
69.86		Valentina	Kharchenko	RUS	.49	1		Feodosiya	16 May 81
69.72		Svetla	Mitkova	BUL	17.6.64	2	NC	Sofia	15 Aug 87
69.68		Mette	Bergmann	NOR	9.11.62	1		Florø	27 May 95
69.51		Franka	Dietzsch	GER	22.1.68	1		Wiesbaden	8 May 99
69.50		Florenta	Craciunescu'	ROU	7.5.55	1	Balk	Stara Zagora	2 Aug 85
		(30)							
69.17		Gia	Lewis-Smallwood	USA	1.4.79	1	Déca	Angers	30 Aug 14
69.14		Irina	Yatchenko ¶	BLR	31.10.65	1		Staiki	31 Jul 04
69.08		Carmen	Romero	CUB	6.10.50	1	NC	La Habana	17 Apr 76
69.08		Mariana	Ionescu/Lengyel	ROU	14.4.53	1		Constanta	19 Apr 86
68.92		Sabine	Engel	GDR	21.4.54	1	v URS,POL	Karl-Marx-Stadt	25 Jun 77
68.89		Nadine	Müller	GER	21.11.85	1	ECp-w	Bar	18 Mar 12
68.80A		Nicoleta	Grasu	ROU	11.9.71	1		Poiana Brasov	7 Aug 99
68.64		Margitta	Pufe'	GDR	10.9.52	1	ISTAF	Berlin	17 Aug 79
68.62			Yu Hourun	CHN	9.7.64	1		Beijing	6 May 88
68.62			Hou Xuemei	CHN	27.2.62	1	IntC	Tianjin	4 Sep 88
		(40)							
68.60		Nadezhda	Kugayevskikh	RUS	19.4.60	1		Oryol	30 Aug 83
68.58		Lyubov	Zverkova	RUS	14.6.55	1	Izv	Kyiv	22 Jun 84
68.52		Beatrice	Faumuiná	NZL	23.10.74	1	Bisl	Oslo	4 Jul 97

Mark	Wind	Name		Nat	Born	Pos	Meet	Venue	Date
68.38		Olga	Burova'	RUS	17.9.63	2	RusCp	Sochi	29 May 92
68.18		Tatyana	Lesovaya	KAZ	24.4.56	1		Alma-Ata	23 Sep 82
68.18		Irina	Khval	RUS	17.5.62	1		Moskva	8 Jul 88
68.18		Barbara	Hechevarría	CUB	6.8.66	2		La Habana	17 Feb 89
68.03		Yarelis	Barrios	CUB	12.7.83	1	NC	La Habana	22 Mar 12
67.99		Dani	Samuels	AUS	26.5.88	1	Werfer	Wiesbaden	10 May 14
67.98			Li Yanfeng	CHN	15.5.79	1		Schönebeck	5 Jun 11

(50) 100th woman 65.96, 200th 63.73, 300th 61.88, 400th 60.10, 500th 59.04

Unofficial meeting: Berlin 6 Sep 88: 1. Martina Hellmann 78.14, 2. Ilke Wyludda 75.36

Downhill: 69.44 Suzy Powell USA 3.9.76 1 La Jolla 27 Apr 02

Drugs disqualification:

Mark	Wind	Name		Nat	Born	Pos	Meet	Venue	Date
70.69		Darya	Pishchalnikova ¶	RUS	19.7.85	(1)	NC	Cheboksary	5 Jul 12

Ancillary marks – other marks during series (to 72.92)

Mark	Name	Date
73.32	Reinsch	13 Sep 88
73.28	Gansky	11 Jun 87
73.28	Gansky	27 Jun 87
73.16	Wyludda	13 Sep 88
73.10	Reinsch	9 Jul 88
73.06	Gansky	27 Jun 87
72.92	Hellmann	20 Aug 87

HAMMER

Mark	Wind	Name		Nat	Born	Pos	Meet	Venue	Date
81.08	WR	Anita	Wlodarczyk	POL	8.8.85	1	Skol	Cetniewo	1 Aug 15
80.85			Wlodarczyk			1	WCh	Beijing	27 Aug 15
79.58	WR		Wlodarczyk			1	ISTAF	Berlin	31 Aug 14
79.42	WR	Betty	Heidler	GER	14.10.83	1		Halle	21 May 11
78.80		Tatyana	Lysenko ¶	RUS	9.10.83	1	WCh	Moskva	16 Aug 13
78.76			Wlodarczyk			1	EC	Zürich	15 Aug 14
78.69		Oksana	Menkova	BLR	28.3.82	1		Minsk	18 Jul 12
78.51			Lysenko			1	NC	Cheboksary	5 Jul 12
78.46			Wlodarczyk			2	WCh	Moskva	16 Aug 13
78.30	WR		Wlodarczyk			1	EAF	Bydgoszcz	6 Jun 10
78.28			Wlodarczyk			1	ET	Cheboksary	21 Jun 15
78.24			Wlodarczyk			1	NC	Kraków	21 Jul 15
78.22			Wlodarczyk			1		Dubnica nad Vahom	21 Aug 13
78.19			Menkova			1		Brest	28 Apr 12
78.19			Menkova			1		Minsk	12 Jun 12
78.18			Lysenko			1	OG	London (OS)	10 Aug 12
78.17			Wlodarczyk			1		Cetniewo	26 Jul 14
78.16			Wlodarczyk			1	Skol	Warszawa	13 Sep 15
78.15			Lysenko			1	NC	Moskva	24 Jul 13
78.07			Heidler			1	GS	Ostrava	24 May 12
78.00			Heidler			1	GS	Ostrava	16 Jun 14
77.96	WR		Wlodarczyk			1	WCh	Berlin	22 Aug 09
77.80	WR		Lysenko			1		Tallinn	15 Aug 06
77.73			Wlodarczyk			1		Beijing	20 May 15
77.68			Wang Zheng	CHN	14.12.87	1		Chengdu	29 Mar 14
77.66			Wlodarczyk			1		Warszawa	23 Aug 14
77.60			Wlodarczyk			2	OG	London (OS)	10 Aug 12
77.53			Heidler			1		Fränkisch-Crumbach	12 Jun 11
77.53			Heidler			1		Elstal	9 Sep 11
77.41	WR	(30/5)	Lysenko			1	Znam	Zhukovskiy	24 Jun 06
77.33			Zhang Wenxiu ¶	CHN	22.3.86	(1)	AsiG	Incheon	28 Sep 14
77.26	WR	Gulfiya	Khanafeyeva ¶	RUS	4.6.82	1	NC	Tula	12 Jun 06
77.13		Oksana	Kondratyeva	RUS	22.11.85	1	Znam	Zhukovskiy	30 Jun 13
76.90		Martina	Hrasnová' ¶	SVK	21.3.83	1		Trnava	16 May 09
76.83		Kamila	Skolimowska	POL	4.11.82	1	SGP	Doha	11 May 07
		(10)							
76.72		Mariya	Bespalova	RUS	21.5.86	2		Zhukovskiy	23 Jun 12
76.66		Olga	Tsander	BLR	18.5.76	1		Staiki	21 Jul 05
76.63		Yekaterina	Khoroshikh ¶	RUS	21.1.83	2	Znam	Moskva	24 Jun 06
76.62		Yipsi	Moreno	CUB	19.11.80	1	GP	Zagreb	9 Sep 08
76.56		Alena	Matoshko	BLR	23.6.82	2		Minsk	12 Jun 12
76.33		Darya	Pchelnik	BLR	20.12.81	2		Staiki	29 Jun 08
76.21		Yelena	Konevtsova	RUS	11.3.81	3		Sochi	26 May 07
76.17		Anna	Bulgakova	RUS	17.1.88	2	NC	Moskva	24 Jul 13
76.07	WR	Mihaela	Melinte ¶	ROU	27.3.75	1		Rüdlingen	29 Aug 99
76.05		Kathrin	Klaas	GER	6.2.84	5	OG	London (OS)	10 Aug 12
		(20)							
75.73		Amanda	Bingson	USA	20.2.90	1	NC	Des Moines	22 Jun 13
75.73		Sultana	Frizell	CAN	24.10.84	1		Tucson	22 May 14
75.68		Olga	Kuzenkova ¶	RUS	4.10.70	1	NCp	Tula	4 Jun 00
75.09		Yelena	Rigert'	RUS	2.12.83	1	Kuts	Moskva	15 Jul 13
75.08		Ivana	Brkljacic	CRO	25.1.83	2	Kuso	Waszawa	17 Jun 07
74.77		Jeneva	McCall/Stevens	USA	28.10.89	2		Dubnica nad Vahom	21 Aug 13

Mark	Wind	Name		Nat	Born	Pos	Meet	Venue	Date
74.66		Manuèla	Montebrun	FRA	13.11.79	1	GP II	Zagreb	11 Jul 05
74.65		Mariya	Smolyachkova	BLR	10.2.85	2		Staiki	19 Jul 08
74.52		Iryna	Sekachyova	UKR	21.7.76	1	NC	Kyiv	2 Jul 08
74.39		Joanna	Fiodorow	POL	4.3.89	2	Werfer	Halle	17 May 14
		(30)							
74.39		Alexandra	Tavernier	FRA	13.12.93	Q	WCh	Beijing	26 Aug 15
74.21		Hanna	Skydan	UKR/AZE	14.5.92	1	NC	Yalta	14 Jun 12
74.20		Jessica	Cosby Toruga	USA	31.5.82	3		Tucson	22 May 14
74.17		Tugçe	Sahutoglu ¶	TUR	1.5.88	1		Izmir	19 May 12
74.10		Iryna	Novozhylova	UKR	7.1.86	1		Kyiv	19 May 12
73.97		Zalina	Marghieva ¶	MDA	5.2.88	1	BalkC	Pitesti	2 Aug 15
73.90		Arasay	Thondike	CUB	28.5.86	1		La Habana	18 Jun 09
73.87		Erin	Gilreath	USA	11.10.80	1	NC	Carson	25 Jun 05
73.86		Sophie	Hitchon	GBR	11.7.91	4	WCh	Beijing	27 Aug 15
73.81		Gwen	Berry	USA	29.6.89	1		Lisle	8 Jun 13
		(40)							
73.74		Jennifer	Dahlgren	ARG	21.4.84	1		Buenos Aires	10 Apr 10
73.64		Rosa	Rodríguez	VEN	2.7.86	1		Barquisimeto	16 May 13
73.61		Amber	Campbell	USA	5.6.81	1		Edmonton	6 Jul 14
73.59		Ester	Balassini	ITA	20.10.77	1	NC	Bressanone	25 Jun 05
73.52		Bianca	Perie	ROU	1.6.90	1	NC	Bucuresti	16 Jul 10
73.44		Éva	Orbán	HUN	29.11.84	2	Werfer	Halle	25 May 13
73.40		Stéphanie	Falzon	FRA	7.1.83	1	NC	Albi	26 Jul 08
73.21		Eileen	O'Keeffe	IRL	31.5.81	1	NC	Dublin	21 Jul 07
73.16		Yunaika	Crawford	CUB	2.11.82	3	OG	Athína	25 Aug 04
73.06			Liu Tingting	CHN	29.10.90	4	Werfer	Halle	17 May 14
		(50)	100th woman 70.28, 200th 67.14, 300th 64.69, 400th 63.34, 500th 62.28						
Downhill: 75.20		Manuéla	Montebrun	FRA	13.11.79	1		Vineuil	18 May 03

Ancillary marks – other marks during series to 77.94

80.27	Wlodarczyk	27 Aug 15	79.04	Wlodarczyk	31 Aug 14	78.52	Wlodarczyk	27 Aug 15
79.31	Wlodarczyk	27 Aug 15	78.64	Wlodarczyk	31 Aug 14	78.46	Wlodarczyk	31 Aug 14
79.07	Wlodarczyk	1 Aug 15	78.53	Wlodarczyk	1 Aug 15	77.94	Wlodarczyk	31 Aug 14

Drugs disqualification

78.61		Lysenko			(1)		Sochi	26 May 07
77.71		Lysenko			(1)	GS	Ostrava	27 Jun 07
77.36	Gulfiya	Khanafeyeva ¶	RUS	4.6.82	(2)		Sochi	26 May 07
74.47	Zalina	Marghieva ¶	MDA	5.2.88	1	Univ Ch	Chisinau	7 May 12

JAVELIN

Mark	Wind	Name		Nat	Born	Pos	Meet	Venue	Date
72.28	WR	Barbora	Spotáková	CZE	30.6.81	1	WAF	Stuttgart	13 Sep 08
71.99		Mariya	Abakumova	RUS	15.1.86	1	WCh	Daegu	2 Sep 11
71.70	WR	Osleidys	Menéndez	CUB	14.11.79	1	WCh	Helsinki	14 Aug 05
71.58			Spotáková			2	WCh	Daegu	2 Sep 11
71.54	WR		Menéndez			1		Réthimno	1 Jul 01
71.53			Menéndez			1	OG	Athína	27 Aug 04
71.42			Spotáková			1	OG	Beijing	21 Aug 08
70.78			Abakumova			2	OG	Beijing	21 Aug 08
70.53			Abakumova			1	ISTAF	Berlin	1 Sep 13
70.20		Christina	Obergföll	GER	22.8.81	1	ECp-S	München	23 Jun 07
70.03			Obergföll			2	WCh	Helsinki	14 Aug 05
69.82			Menéndez			1	WUG	Beijing	29 Aug 01
69.81			Obergföll			1		Berlin (Elstal)	31 Aug 08
69.75			Abakumova			1		Berlin (Elstal)	25 Aug 13
69.57			Obergföll			1	WK	Zürich	8 Sep 11
69.55			Spotáková			1	OG	London (OS)	9 Aug 12
69.53			Menéndez			1	WCh	Edmonton	7 Aug 01
69.48	WR	Trine	Hattestad	NOR	18.4.66	1	Bisl	Oslo	28 Jul 00
69.45			Spotáková			1	Herc	Monaco	22 Jul 11
69.35		Sunette	Viljoen	RSA	6.1.83	1	DL	New York	9 Jun 12
69.34			Abakumova			1	ECp-w	Castellón	16 Mar 13
69.15			Spotáková			1		Zaragoza	31 May 08
69.09			Abakumova			Q	WCh	Moskva	16 Aug 13
69.05			Obergföll			1	WCh	Moskva	18 Aug 13
68.94			Abakumova			1	WK	Zürich	29 Aug 13
68.92			Abakumova			Q	WCh	Berlin	16 Aug 09
68.91			Hattestad			1	OG	Sydney	30 Sep 00
68.89			Abakumova			1	DL	Doha	14 May 10
68.86			Obergföll			1	NC	Kassel	24 Jul 11
68.81			Spotáková			1	Odlozil	Praha	16 Jun 08
		(30/6)							

Mark	Wind	Name		Nat	Born	Pos	Meet	Venue	Date
68.34		Steffi	Nerius	GER	1.7.72	2		Berlin (Elstal)	31 Aug 08
67.69		Katharina	Molitor	GER	8.11.83	1	WCh	Beijing	30 Aug 15
67.67		Sonia	Bisset	CUB	1.4.71	1		Salamanca	6 Jul 05
67.51		Miréla	Manjani/Tzelíli	GRE	21.12.76	2	OG	Sydney	30 Sep 00
		(10)							
67.32		Linda	Stahl	GER	2.10.85	1	adidas	New York	14 Jun 14
67.29		Hanna	Hatsko-Fedusova	UKR	3.10.90	1	NC	Kirovohrad	26 Jul 14
67.20		Tatyana	Shikolenko	RUS	10.5.68	1	Herc	Monaco	18 Aug 00
67.16		Martina	Ratej	SLO	2.11.81	3	DL	Doha	14 May 10
66.91		Tanja	Damaske	GER	16.11.71	1	NC	Erfurt	4 Jul 99
66.86		Vira	Rebryk	UKR	25.2.89	1	EC	Helsinki	29 Jun 12
66.83		Kimberley	Mickle	AUS	28.12.84	1		Melbourne	22 Mar 14
66.80		Louise	McPaul/Currey	AUS	24.1.69	1		Gold Coast (RB)	5 Aug 00
66.67		Kara	Patterson/Winger	USA	10.4.86	1	NC	Des Moines	25 Jun 10
66.17		Goldie	Sayers	GBR	16.7.82	1	LGP	London (CP)	14 Jul 12
		(20)							
66.15		Madara	Palameika	LAT	18.6.87	1		Jelgava	26 Jun 14
66.13			Lu Huihui ¶	CHN	26.6.89	2	WCh	Beijing	30 Aug 15
66.10		Kathryn	Mitchell	AUS	10.7.82	2		Adelaide	15 Feb 14
65.92		Christin	Hussong	GER	17.4.94	Q	WCh	Beijing	28 Aug 15
65.91		Nikola	Brejchová'	CZE	25.6.74	1	GP	Linz	2 Aug 04
65.47			Zhang Li	CHN	17.1.89	1	AsiG	Incheon	1 Oct 14
65.30		Claudia	Coslovich	ITA	26.4.72	1		Ljubljana	10 Jun 00
65.29		Xiomara	Rivero	CUB	22.11.68	1		Santiago de Cuba	17 Mar 01
65.17		Karen	Forkel	GER	24.9.70	2	NC	Erfurt	4 Jul 99
65.11			Li Lingwei	CHN	26.1.89	1		Fuzhou	23 Jun 12
		(30)							
65.08		Ana Mirela	Termure ¶	ROU	13.1.75	1	NC	Bucuresti	10 Jun 01
64.90		Paula	Huhtaniemi'	FIN	17.2.73	1	NC	Helsinki	10 Aug 03
64.89		Yekaterina	Ivakina	RUS	4.12.64	4	Bisl	Oslo	28 Jul 00
64.87		Kelly	Morgan	GBR	17.6.80	1	NC	Birmingham	14 Jul 02
64.83		Christina	Scherwin	DEN	11.7.76	3	WAF	Stuttgart	9 Sep 06
64.83		Liz	Gleadle	CAN	5.12.88	1		Kawasaki	10 May 15
64.75		Brittany	Borman	USA	1.7.89	2		Kawasaki	10 May 15
64.62		Joanna	Stone	AUS	4.10.72	2		Gold Coast (RB)	5 Aug 00
64.62		Nikolett	Szabó	HUN	3.3.80	1		Pátra	22 Jul 01
64.61		Oksana	Makarova	RUS	21.7.71	2	ECp	Paris (C)	19 Jun 99
		(40)							
64.56		Margaryta	Dorozhon	UKR/ISR	4.9.87	1	Bisl	Oslo	11 Jun 15
64.51		Monica	Stoian	ROU	25.8.82	4	WCh	Berlin	18 Aug 09
64.49		Valeriya	Zabruskova	RUS	29.7.75	1	Znam	Tula	7 Jun 03
64.46		Dörthe	Friedrich	GER	21.6.73	1	NC	Wattenscheid	7 Jul 02
64.38		Sinta	Ozolina-Kovale	LAT	26.2.88	1		Riga	30 May 13
64.21		Tatjana	Jelaca	SRB	10.8.90	2	EC	Zürich	14 Aug 14
64.19		Kim	Kreiner	USA	26.7.77	1		Fortaleza	16 May 07
64.08		Barbara	Madejczyk	POL	30.9.76	1	ECp-S	Málaga	28 Jun 06
64.07		Mercedes	Chilla	ESP	19.1.80	1		Valencia	12 Jun 10
64.06		Taina	Uppa/Kolkkala	FIN	24.10.76	1		Pihtipudas	23 Jul 00
		(50)	100th woman 61.89, 200th 58.77, 300th 56.89						

Ancillary marks – other marks during series (to 68.80)

Mark	Name	Date	Mark	Name	Date	Mark	Name	Date
71.25	Abakumova	2 Sep 11						
69.42	Menéndez	7 Aug 01	69.22	Spotáková	21 Aug 08	68.82	Abakumova	1 Sep 13
69.35	Abakumova	25 Aug 13	69.08	Abakumova	21 Aug 08			
69.32	Abakumova	21 Aug 08	68.95	Obergföll	8 Sep 11			

Specification changed from 1 May 1999. See ATHLETICS 2000 for Old specification all-time list.

Mark	Wind	Name		Nat	Born	Pos	Meet	Venue	Date
80.00 WR		Petra	Felke	GDR	30.7.59	1		Potsdam	9 Sep 88

HEPTATHLON

Mark	Name		Nat	Born	Pos	Meet	Venue	Date
7291 WR	Jackie	Joyner-Kersee	USA	3.3.62	1	OG	Seoul	24 Sep 88
	12.69/0.5	1.86	15.80	22.56/1.6	7.27/0.7	45.66	2:08.51	
7215 WR		Joyner-Kersee			1	NC/OT	Indianapolis	16 Jul 88
	12.71/-0.9	1.93	15.65	22.30/ 0.0	7.00/-1.3	50.08	2:20.70	
7158 WR		Joyner-Kersee			1	USOF	Houston	2 Aug 86
	13.18/-0.5	1.88	15.20	22.85/1.2	7.03w/2.9	50.12	2:09.69	
7148 WR		Joyner-Kersee			1	GWG	Moskva	7 Jul 86
	12.85/0.2	1.88	14.76	23.00/0.3	7.01/-0.5	49.86	2:10.02	
7128		Joyner-Kersee			1	WCh	Roma	1 Sep 87
	12.91/0.2	1.90	16.00	22.95/1.2	7.14/0.9	45.68	2:16.29	
7044		Joyner-Kersee			1	OG	Barcelona	2 Aug 92
	12.85/-0.9	1.91	14.13	23.12/0.7	7.10/1.3	44.98	2:11.78	

Mark Wind		Name	Nat	Born	Pos	Meet	Venue	Date
7032	Carolina	Klüft	SWE	2.2.83	1	WCh	Osaka	26 Aug 07
	13.15/0.1	1.95	14.81	23.38/0.3	6.85/1.0	47.98	2:12.56	
7007	Larisa	Nikitina ¶	RUS	29.4.65	1	NC	Bryansk	11 Jun 89
	13.40/1.4	1.89	16.45	23.97/1.1	6.73w/4.0	53.94	2:15.31	
7001		Klüft			1	WCh	Saint-Denis	24 Aug 03
	13.18/-0.4	1.94	14.19	22.98/1.1	6.68/1.0	49.90	2:12.12	
6985	Sabine	Braun	GER	19.6.65	1		Götzis	31 May 92
	13.11/-0.4	1.93	14.84	23.65/2.0	6.63w/2.9	51.62	2:12.67	
6979		Joyner-Kersee			1	NC	San José	24 Jun 87
	12.90/2.0	1.85	15.17	23.02/0.4	7.25/2.3	40.24	2:13.07	
6955	Jessica	Ennis-Hill	GBR	28.1.86	1	OG	London (OS)	4 Aug 12
	12.54/1.3	1.86	14.28	22.83/-0.3	6.48/-0.6	47.49	2:08.65	
6952		Klüft			1	OG	Athína	21 Aug 04
	13.21/0.2	1.91	14.77	23.27/-0.1	6.78/0.4	48.89	2:14.15	
6946 WR	Sabine	Paetz'	GDR	16.10.57	1	NC	Potsdam	6 May 84
	12.64/0.3	1.80	15.37	23.37/0.7	6.86/-0.2	44.62	2:08.93	
6942	Ghada	Shouaa	SYR	10.9.72	1		Götzis	26 May 96
	13.78/0.3	1.87	15.64	23.78/0.6	6.77/0.6	54.74	2:13.61	
6935 WR	Ramona	Neubert	GDR	26.7.58	1	v USSR	Moskva	19 Jun 83
	13.42/1.7	1.82	15.25	23.49/0.5	6.79/0.7	49.94	2:07.51	
6910		Joyner			1	MSR	Walnut	25 Apr 86
	12.9/0.0	1.86	14.75	23.24w/2.8	6.85/2.1	48.30	2:14.11	
6906		Ennis			1		Götzis	27 May 12
	12.81/0.0	1.85	14.51	22.88/1.9	6.51/0.8	47.11	2:09.00	
6897		John'			2	wOG	Seoul	24 Sep 88
	12.85/0.5	1.80	16.23	23.65/1.6	6.71/ 0.0	42.56	2:06.14	
6889	Eunice	Barber	FRA	17.11.74	1		Arles	5 Jun 05
	12.62w/2.9	1.91	12.61	24.12/1.2	6.78w/3.4	53.07	2:14.66	
6887		Klüft			1	WCh	Helsinki	7 Aug 05
	13.19/-0.4	1.82	15.02	23.70/-2.5	6.87/0.2	47.20	2:08.89	
6880	Tatyana	Chernova ¶ (10)	RUS	29.1.88	1	WCh	Daegu	30 Aug 11
	13.32/0.9	1.83	14.17	23.50/-1.5	6.61/-0.7	52.95	2:08.04	
6878		Joyner-Kersee			1	NC	New York	13 Jun 91
	12.77	1.89	15.62	23.42	6.97/0.4	43.28	2:22.12	
6875		Nikitina			1	ECp-A	Helmond	16 Jul 89
	13.55/-2.1	1.84	15.99	24.29/-2.1	6.75/-2.5	56.78	2:18.67	
6861		Barber			1	WCh	Sevilla	22 Aug 99
	12.89/-0.5	1.93	12.37	23.57/0.5	6.86/-0.3	49.88	2:15.65	
6859	Natalya	Shubenkova	RUS	25.9.57	1	NC	Kyiv	21 Jun 84
	12.93/1.0	1.83	13.66	23.57/-0.3	6.73/0.4	46.26	2:04.60	
6858	Anke	Vater/Behmer	GDR	5.6.61	3	OG	Seoul	24 Sep 88
	13.20/0.5	1.83	14.20	23.10/1.6	6.68/0.1	44.54	2:04.20	
6847		Nikitina			1	WUG	Duisburg	29 Aug 89
	13.47	1.81	16.12	24.12	6.66	59.28	2:22.07	
6845 WR		Neubert			1	v URS	Halle	20 Jun 82
	13.58/1.8	1.83	15.10	23.14/1.4	6.84w/2.3	42.54	2:06.16	
6845	Irina	Belova ¶	RUS	27.3.68	2	OG	Barcelona	2 Aug 92
	13.25/-0.1	1.88	13.77	23.34/0.2	6.82/0.0	41.90	2:05.08	
	(30/13)							
6832	Lyudmila	Blonska ¶	UKR	9.11.77	2	WCh	Osaka	26 Aug 07
	13.25/0.1	1.92	14.44	24.09/0.3	6.88/1.0	47.77	2:16.68	
6831	Denise	Lewis	GBR	27.8.72	1		Talence	30 Jul 00
	13.13/1.0	1.84	15.07	24.01w/3.6	6.69/-0.4	49.42	2:12.20	
6808	Brianne	Theisen-Eaton	CAN	18.12.88	1	Hypo	Götzis	31 May 15
	13.05/-0.2	1.89	13.73	23.34/1.4	6.72/0.9	42.96	2:09.37	
6803	Jane	Frederick	USA	7.4.52	1		Talence	16 Sep 84
	13.27/1.2	1.87	15.49	24.15/1.6	6.43/0.2	51.74	2:13.55	
6778	Nataliya	Dobrynska	UKR	29.5.82	2	EC	Barcelona	31 Jul 10
	13.59/-1.6	1.86	15.88	24.23/-0.2	6.56/0.3	49.25	2:12.06	
6765	Yelena	Prokhorova	RUS	16.4.78	1	NC	Tula	23 Jul 00
	13.54/-2.8	1.82	14.30	23.37/-0.2	6.72/1.0	43.40	2:04.27	
6750		Ma Miaolan	CHN	18.1.70	1	NG	Beijing	12 Sep 93
	13.28/1.5	1.89	14.98	23.86/	6.64/	45.82	2:15.33	
	(20)							
6741	Heike	Drechsler	GER	16.12.64	1		Talence	11 Sep 94
	13.34/-0.3	1.84	13.58	22.84/-1.1	6.95/1.0	40.64	2:11.53	
6735(w)	Hyleas	Fountain	USA	14.1.81	1	NC	Des Moines	26 Jun 10
	12.93w/2.6	1.90	13.73	23.28w/3.3	6.79w/2.7	42.26	2:17.80	

Mark	Wind	Name		Nat	Born	Pos	Meet	Venue	Date
6703		Tatyana	Blokhina	RUS	12.3.70	1		Talence	11 Sep 93
		13.69/-0.6 1.91 14.94		23.95/-0.4		5.99/-0.3		52.16 2:09.65	
6702		Chantal	Beaugeant ¶	FRA	16.2.61	2		Götzis	19 Jun 88
		13.10/1.6 1.78 13.74		23.96w/3.5		6.45/0.2		50.96 2:07.09	
6695		Jane	Flemming	AUS	14.4.65	1	CG	Auckland	28 Jan 90
		13.21/1.4 1.82 13.76		23.62w/2.4		6.57/1.6		49.28 2:12.53	
6683		Jennifer	Oeser	GER	29.11.83	3	EC	Barcelona	31 Jul 10
		13.37/-1.0 1.83 13.82		24.07/-0.3		6.68/-0.3		49.17 2:12.28	
6682		Katarina	Johnson-Thompson	GBR	9.1.93	1		Götzis	1 Jun 14
		13.47/-1.2 1.90 12.17		22.89/1.5		6.70/-0.1		41.44 2:08.16	
6681		Kristina	Savitskaya	RUS	10.6.91	1	NC	Cheboksary	3 Jun 12
		13.52/0.0 1.88 15.27		24.61/0.0		6.65/0.0		46.83 2:14.73	
6660		Ines	Schulz	GDR	10.7.65	3		Götzis	19 Jun 88
		13.56/0.4 1.84 13.95		23.93w/2.8		6.70/0.7		42.82 2:06.31	
6658		Svetla	Dimitrova ¶	BUL	27.1.70	2		Götzis	31 May 92
		13.41/-0.7 1.75 14.72		23.06w/2.4		6.64/1.9		43.84 2:09.60	
		(30)							
6649		Lilli	Schwarzkopf	GER	28.8.83	2	OG	London (OS)	4 Aug 12
		13.26/0.9 1.83 14.77		24.77/0.9		6.30/-0.7		51.73 2:10.50	
6646		Natalya	Grachova	UKR	21.2.52	1	NC	Moskva	2 Aug 82
		13.80 1.80 16.18		23.86		6.65w/3.5		39.42 2:06.59	
66635		Sibylle	Thiele	GDR	6.3.65	2	GWG	Moskva	7 Jul 86
		13.14/0.6 1.76 16.00		24.18		6.62/1.0		45.74 2:15.30	
6635		Svetlana	Buraga	BLR	4.9.65	3	WCh	Stuttgart	17 Aug 93
		12.95/0.1 1.84 14.55		23.69/0.0		6.58/-0.2		41.04 2:13.65	
6633		Natalya	Roshchupkina	RUS	13.1.78	2	NC	Tula	23 Jul 00
		14.05/-2.8 1.88 14.28		23.47/-0.2		6.45/0.4		44.34 2:07.93	
6623		Judy	Simpson'	GBR	14.11.60	3	EC	Stuttgart	30 Aug 86
		13.05/0.8 1.92 14.73		25.09/0.0		6.56w/2.5		40.92 2:11.70	
6619		Liliana	Nastase	ROU	1.8.62	4	OG	Barcelona	2 Aug 92
		12.86/-0.9 1.82 14.34		23.70/0.2		6.49/-0.3		41.30 2:11.22	
6616		Malgorzata	Nowak'	POL	9.2.59	1	WUG	Kobe	31 Aug 85
		13.27w/4.0 1.95 15.35		24.20/0.0		6.37w/3.9		43.36 2:20.39	
6604		Remigija	Nazaroviene'	LTU	2.6.67	2	URSCh	Bryansk	11 Jun 89
		13.26/1.4 1.86 14.27		24.12/0.7		6.58/0.9		40.94 2:09.98	
6604		Irina	Tyukhay	RUS	14.1.67	3		Götzis	28 May 95
		13.20/-0.7 1.84 14.97		24.33/1.7		6.71/0.5		43.84 2:17.64	
		(40)							
6599A		Jessica	Zelinka	CAN	3.9.81	1	NC	Calgary	28 Jun 12
		12.76/-0.6 1.77 14.74		23.42w/2.1		5.98w/2.9		46.60 2:08.95	
6599		Austra	Skujyté	LTU	12.8.79	5	OG	London (OS)	4 Aug 12
		14.00/0.7 1.92 17.31		25.43/0.9		6.25/-0.6		51.13 2:20.59	
6598		Svetlana	Moskalets	RUS	22.1.69	1	NC	Vladimir	17 Jun 94
		13.20/0.8 1.82 13.78		23.56/0.1		6.74/0.8		42.48 2:14.54	
6591		Svetlana	Sokolova	RUS	9.1.81	1	NC	Tula	23 Jun 04
		13.56/1.1 1.82 15.09		24.02/0.6		6.26/0.3		45.07 2:07.23	
6586		Anna	Melnychenko	UKR	24.4.83	1	WCh	Moskva	13 Aug 13
		13.29/-0.6 1.86 13.85		23.87/0.0		6.49/0.2		41.87 2:09.85	
6577		DeDee	Nathan	USA	20.4.68	1		Götzis	30 May 99
		13.28/-0.1 1.76 14.74		24.23/0.2		6.59/1.6		50.08 2:16.92	
6576		Antoinette	Nana Djimou	FRA	2.8.85	5	OG	London (OS)	4 Aug 12
		12.96/1.3 1.80 14.26		24.72/0.3		6.13/-0.2		55.87 2:15.94	
6573		Rita	Ináncsi	HUN	6.1.71	3		Götzis	29 May 94
		13.66/2.0 1.84 13.94		24.20w/2.5		6.78/1.4		46.28 2:16.02	
6572		Heike	Tischler	GDR	4.2.64	2	EC	Split	31 Aug 90
		14.08/-0.9 1.82 13.73		24.29/0.9		6.22/-0.7		53.24 2:05.50	
6563		Natalya	Sazanovich	BLR	15.8.73	2	OG	Atlanta	28 Jul 96
		13.56/-1.6 1.80 14.52		23.72/-0.3		6.70/1.1		46.00 2:17.92	
		(50) 100th woman 6404, 200th 6211, 300th 6096, 400th 6003, 500th 5914							

Drugs disqualification

Mark	Wind	Name		Nat	Born	Pos	Meet	Venue	Date
6618		Lyudmyla	Yosypenko ¶	UKR	24.9.84	4	OG	London (OS)	4 Aug 12
		13.25/0.9 1.83 13.90		23.68/0.6		6.31/-0.6		49.63 2:13.28	

DECATHLON

Mark	Wind	Name		Nat	Born	Pos	Meet	Venue	Date
8358	WR	Austra	Skujyte	LTU	12.8.79	1		Columbia, MO	15 Apr 05
		12.49/1.6 46.19 3.10 48.78 57.19				14.22w/2.4		6.12/1.6 16.42 1.78	5:15.86
8150		Marie	Collonvillé	FRA	23.11.73	1		Talence	26 Sep 04
		12.48/0.4 34.69 3.50 47.19 56.15				13.96/0.4		6.18/1.0 11.90 1.80	5:06.09
7885		Mona	Steigauf	GER	17.1.70	1		Ahlen	21 Sep 97
		12.15/1.2 5.93 12.49 1.73 55.34				13.75/0.2		34.68 3.10 42.24	5:07.95

IAAF approved order: 100m, DT, PV, JT, 400m / 100mh, LJ, SP, HJ, 1500m. 1997 above was men's order

Mark Wind Name Nat Born Pos Meet Venue Date

4 x 100 METRES RELAY

Mark	Nat	Team	Pos	Meet	Venue	Date
40.82 WR	USA	Madison (-Bartoletta), Felix, Knight, Jeter	1	OG	London (OS)	10 Aug 12
41.07	JAM	Campbell-Brown, Morrison, Thompson, Fraser-Pryce	1	WCh	Beijing	29 Aug 15
41.29	JAM	Russell, Stewart, Calvert, Fraser-Pryce	1	WCh	Moskva	18 Aug 13
41.37 WR	GDR	Gladisch, Rieger, Auerswald, Göhr	1	WCp	Canberra	6 Oct 85
41.41	JAM	Fraser-Pryce, Simpson, Campbell-Brown, Stewart	2	OG	London (OS)	10 Aug 12
41.47	USA	Gaines, Jones, Miller, Devers	1	WCh	Athína	9 Aug 97
41.49	RUS	Bogoslovskaya, Malchugina, Voronova, Privalova	1	WCh	Stuttgart	22 Aug 93
41.49	USA	Finn, Torrence, Vereen, Devers	2	WCh	Stuttgart	22 Aug 93
41.52	USA	Gaines, Jones, Miller, Devers	1h1	WCh	Athína	8 Aug 97
41.53 WR	GDR	Gladisch, Koch, Auerswald, Göhr	1		Berlin	31 Jul 83
41.55	USA	Brown, Williams, Griffith, Marshall	1	ISTAF	Berlin	21 Aug 87
41.56	USA	B Knight, Felix, Myers, Jeter	1	WCh	Daegu	4 Sep 11
41.58	USA	Brown, Williams, Griffith, Marshall	1	WCh	Roma	6 Sep 87
41.58	USA	L.Williams, Felix, Lee, Jeter	1		Cottbus	8 Aug 09
41.60 WR	GDR	Müller, Wöckel, Auerswald, Göhr	1	OG	Moskva	1 Aug 80
41.60	JAM	Simpson, Morrison, Thompson, Fraser-Pryce	1	WK	Zürich	3 Sep 15
41.61A	USA	Brown, Williams, Cheeseborough, Ashford	1	USOF	USAF Academy	3 Jul 83
41.63	USA	Brown, Williams, Cheeseborough, Ashford	1	v GDR	Los Angeles	25 Jun 83
41.64	USA	Madison, Tarmoh, Knight, L Williams	1h1	OG	London (OS)	9 Aug 12
41.65	USA	Brown, Bolden, Cheeseborough, Ashford	1	OG	Los Angeles	11 Aug 84
41.65	GDR	Gladisch, Koch, Auerswald, Göhr	1	ECp	Moskva	17 Aug 85
		(21 performances by 4 nations) from here just best by nation				
41.78	FRA	Girard, Hurtis, Félix, Arron	1	WCh	Saint-Denis	30 Aug 03
41.92	BAH	Fynes, Sturrup, Davis-Thompson, Ferguson	1	WCh	Sevilla	29 Aug 99
42.03	TTO	Baptiste, Ahye, Thomas, Hackett	3	WCh	Beijing	29 Aug 15
42.04	UKR	Povh, Stuy, Ryemyen, Bryzgina	3	OG	London (OS)	10 Aug 12
42.08mx	BUL	Pavlova, Nuneva, Georgieva, Ivanova	mx		Sofia	8 Aug 84
		42.29 Pencheva, Nuneva, Georgieva, Donkova	1		Sofia	26 Jun 88
42.21	GBR	Philip, Nelson, Onuora, Henry (10)	1	WK	Zürich	28 Aug 14
42.23	CHN	(Sichuan) Xiao Lin, Li Yali, Liu Xiaomei, Li Xuemei	1	NG	Shanghai	23 Oct 97
42.29	BRA	E dos Santos, Silva, Krasucki, R Santos	2h3	WCh	Moskva	18 Aug 13
42.32	NED	Visser, Schippers, Sedney, Samuel	3h2	WCh	Beijing	29 Aug 15
42.39	NGR	Utondu, Idehen, Opara-Thompson, Onyali	2h2	OG	Barcelona	7 Aug 92
42.54	BEL	Borlée, Mariën, Ouédraogo, Gevaert	2	OG	Beijing	22 Aug 08
42.56	BLR	Nesterenko, Sologub, Nevmerzhitskaya, Dragun	3	WCh	Helsinki	13 Aug 05
42.59	FRG	Possekel, Helten, Richter, Kroniger	2	OG	Montreal	31 Jul 76
42.60	CAN	Emmanuel, Hyacinthe, Fofanah, Bingham	3h1	WCh	Beijing	29 Aug 15
42.68	POL	Popowicz, Korczynska, Jeschke, Wedler	3	EC	Barcelona	1 Aug 10
42.89	CUB	Ferrer, López, Duporty, Allen	6	WCh	Stuttgart	22 Aug 93
	(20)					
42.94	SUI	Kambundji, Lavanchy, E.Sprunger, L.Sprunger	3	Athl	Lausanne	3 Jul 14
42.98	CZE/TCH	Sokolová, Soborová, Kocembová, Kratochvílová	1	WK	Zürich	18 Aug 82
42.99A	AUS	Massey, Broadrick, Lambert, Gainsford-Taylor	1		Pietersburg	18 Mar 00
43.03A	COL	M.Murillo, Palacios, Obregón, D Murillo	2	SAm-r	Bogotá	10 Jul 04
43.04	ITA	Pistone, Calí, Arcioni, Alloh	3	ECp-S	Annecy	21 Jun 08
43.07	GRE	Tsóni, Kóffa, Vasarmídou, Thánou	2	MedG	Bari	18 Jun 97
43.19	GHA	Akoto, Twum, Anim, Nsiah	5s1	OG	Sydney	29 Sep 00
43.25A	RSA	Hartman, Moropane, Holtshausen, Seyerling	2		Pietersburg	18 Mar 00
43.28	DOM	M Sánchez, Chala, Mejía, Manzueta	5h1	WCh	Moskva	18 Aug 13
43.30	KAZ	Ivanchukova, Zyabkina, Rakhmanova, Safronova	1	Kosanov	Almaty	25 Jul 15

Best at low altitude

Mark	Nat	Team	Pos	Meet	Venue	Date
43.03	COL	M.Murillo, Palacios, Obregón, N.González	3h2	WCh	Helsinki	12 Aug 05
43.18	AUS	Wilson, Wells, Robertson, Boyle	5	OG	Montreal	31 Jul 76

One or more athlete susbsequently drugs dq

Mark	Nat	Team	Pos	Meet	Venue	Date
41.67	USA	A Williams, Jones ¶, L Williams, Colander	(1)	3-N	München	8 Aug 04
41.67	USA	A Williams, Jones ¶, L Williams, Colander	(1h1)	OG	Athína	26 Aug 04

4 x 200 METRES RELAY

Mark	Nat	Team	Pos	Meet	Venue	Date
1:27.46 WR	USA Blue	Jenkins, Colander-Richardson, Perry, M Jones	1	PennR	Philadelphia	29 Apr 00
1:28.15 WR	GDR	Göhr, R.Müller, Wöckel, Koch	1		Jena	9 Aug 80
1:29.42	Texas A & M (USA)	Tarmoh, Mayo, Beard, Lucas	1	Penn R	Philadelphia	24 Apr 10
1:29.45	USA	Solomon, Meadows, Knight, K Duncan	1	WRly	Nassau	25 May 14
1:29.61	GBR	Henry, A Onuora, B Williams, A Philip	2	WRly	Nassau	25 May 14
Drugs dq: 1:29.40	USA Red	Colander, Gaines, Miller, M Jones ¶	1	Penn	Philadelphia	24 Apr 04

4 x 400 METRES RELAY

Mark	Nat	Team	Pos	Meet	Venue	Date
3:15.17 WR	URS		1	OG	Seoul	1 Oct 88
		Ledovskaya 50.12, O.Nazarova 47.82, Pinigina 49.43, Bryzgina 47.80				
3:15.51	USA		2	OG	Seoul	1 Oct 88
		D.Howard 49.82, Dixon 49.17, Brisco 48.44, Griffith Joyner 48.08				

Mark	Wind	Nat	Name	Pos	Meet	Venue	Date
3:15.92	WR	GDR	G.Walther 49.8, Busch 48.9, Rübsam 49.4, Koch 47.8	1	NC	Erfurt	3 Jun 84
3:16.71		USA	Torrence 49.0, Malone 49.4, Kaiser-Brown 49.48, Miles 48.78	1	WCh	Stuttgart	22 Aug 93
3:16.87		GDR	Emmelmann 50.9, Busch 48.8, Müller 48.9, Koch 48.21	1	EC	Stuttgart	31 Aug 86
3:16.87		USA	Trotter 50.3, Felix 48.1, McCorory 49.39, Richards-Ross 49.10	1	OG	London (OS)	11 Aug 12
3:17.83		USA	Dunn 50.5, Felix 48.8, Demus 50.14, Richards 48.44	1	WCh	Berlin	23 Aug 09
3:18.09		USA	Richards-Ross 49.3, Felix 49.4, Beard 49.84, McCorory 49.52	1	WCh	Daegu	3 Sep 11
3:18.29		USA		1	OG	Los Angeles	11 Aug 84
			Leatherwood 50.50, S.Howard 48.83, Brisco-Hooks 49.23, Cheeseborough 49.73				
3:18.29		GDR	Neubauer 50.58, Emmelmann 49.89, Busch 48.81, Müller 48.99	3	OG	Seoul	1 Oct 88
3:18.38		RUS		2	WCh	Stuttgart	22 Aug 93
			Ruzina 50.8, Alekseyeva 49.3, Ponomaryova 49.78, Privalova 48.47				
3:18.43		URS	Ledovskaya 51.7, Dzhigalova 49.2, Nazarova 48.87, Bryzgina 48.67	1	WCh	Tokyo	1 Sep 91
3:18.54		USA	Wineberg 51.0, Felix 48.6, Henderson 50.06, Richards 48.93	1	OG	Beijing	23 Aug 08
3:18.55		USA	Trotter 51.2, Felix 48.0, Wineberg 50.24, Richards 49.07	1	WCh	Osaka	2 Sep 07
3:18.58		URS	I.Nazarova, Olizarenko, Pinigina, Vladykina	1	ECp	Moskva	18 Aug 85
3:18.63		GDR	Neubauer 51.4, Emmelmann 49.1, Müller 48.64, Busch 49.48	1	WCh	Roma	6 Sep 87
3:18.71		JAM	Whyte 50.0, Prendergast 49.6, Williams-Mills 49.84, Williams 49.22	2	WCh	Daegu	3 Sep 11
3:18.82		RUS	Gushchina 50.6, Litvinova 49.2, Firova 49.20, Kapachinskaya 49.82	2	OG	Beijing	23 Aug 08
3:19.01		USA	Trotter 49.8, Henderson 49.7, Richards 49.81, Hennagan 49.73	(1)	OG	Athína	28 Aug 04
			Note team was disqualified as Crystal Cox (subject of retrospective drugs ban) ran for them in the heat				
3:19.04	WR	GDR	Siemon' 51.0, Busch 50.0, Rübsam 50.2, Koch 47.9	1	EC	Athína	11 Sep 82
3:19.12		URS	Baskakova, I.Nazarova, Pinigina, Vladykina	1	Drz	Praha	18 Aug 84
3:19.23	WR	GDR	Maletzki 50.05, Rohde 49.00, Streidt 49.51, Brehmer 49.79	1	OG	Montreal	31 Jul 76
3:19.36		RUS		3	WCh	Daegu	3 Sep 11
			Krivoshapka 50.3, Antyukh 50.0, Litvinova 49.96, Kapachinskaya 49.22				
3:19.49		GDR	Emmelmann, Busch, Neubauer, Koch 47.9	1	WCp	Canberra	4 Oct 85
3:19.50		URS	Yurchenko 51.2, O.Nazarova 50.2, Pinigina 49.09, Bryzgina 49.03	2	WCh	Roma	6 Sep 87
3:19.60		USA	Leatherwood 50.7 , S.Howard 50.0, Brisco-Hooks 48.7, Cheeseborough 50.2	1	Walnut		25 Jul 84
3:19.62		GDR	Kotte, Brehmer, Köhn, Koch 48.3	1	ECp	Torino	5 Aug 79
			(27/5 with USSR and Russia counted separately)				
3:20.04		GBR	Ohuruogu 50.6, Okoro 50.9, McConnell 49.79, Sanders 48.76	3	WCh	Osaka	2 Sep 07
3:20.32		CZE/TCH		2	WCh	Helsinki	14 Aug 83
			Kocembová 48.93, Matejkovicová 52.13, Moravcíková 51.51, Kratochvílová 47.75				
3:21.04		NGR	Afolabi 51.13, Yusuf 49.72, Opara 51.29, Ogunkoya 48.90	2	OG	Atlanta	3 Aug 96
3:21.21		CAN	Crooks 50.30, Richardson 50.22, Killingbeck ¶ 50.62, Payne 50.07	2	OG	Los Angeles	11 Aug 84
3:21.85		BLR	Kozak 52.0, Khlyustova 50.3, I Usovich 49.85, S Usovich 49.69	4	OG	Beijing	23 Aug 08
		(10)					
3:21.94		UKR	Dzhigalova, Olizarenko, Pinigina, Vladykina	1	URS Ch	Kyiv	17 Jul 86
3:22.34		FRA	Landre 51.3, Dorsile 51.1, Elien 50.54, Pérec 49.36	1	EC	Helsinki	14 Aug 94
3:22.49		FRG	Thimm 50.81, Arendt 49.95, Thomas 51.50, Abt 50.23	4	OG	Seoul	1 Oct 88
3:23.21		CUB	Díaz 51.1, Calatayud 51.2, Clement 50.47, Terrero 50.46	6	OG	Beijing	23 Aug 08
3:23.81		AUS	Peris-K 51.71, Lewis 51.69, Gainsford-T 51.06, Freeman 49.35	4	OG	Sydney	30 Sep 00
3:24.28		CHN	(Hebei) An X, Bai X, Cao C, Ma Y	1	NG	Beijing	13 Sep 93
3:24.49		POL	Guzowska 52.2, Bejnar 50.2, Prokopek 50.47, Jesien 51.59	4	WCh	Helsinki	14 Aug 05
3:25.68		ROU	Ruicu 52.69, Rîpanu 51.09, Barbu 52.64, Tîrlea 49.26	2	ECp	Paris (C)	20 Jun 99
3:25.7a		FIN	Eklund 53.6, Pursiainen 50.6, Wilmi 51.6, Salin 49.9	2	EC	Roma	8 Sep 74
3:25.71		ITA	Bazzoni 53.7, Milani 50.8, Spacca 51.64, Grenot 49.61	4	EC	Barcelona	1 Aug 10
		(20)					
3:25.81		BUL	Ilieva, Stamenova, Penkova, Damyanova	1	v Hun,Pol	Sofia	24 Jul 83
3:26.33		GRE	Kaidantzi 53.2, Goudenoúdi 51.6, Boudá 51.76, Halkiá 49.75	3	ECpS	Bydgoszcz	20 Jun 04
3:26.68		BRA	(Bovespa) Coutinho, de Oliveira, Sousa, de Lima	1	NC	São Paulo	7 Aug 11
3:26.89		IND	R Kaur 53.1, Beenamol 51.4, Soman 52.51, M Kaur 49.85	3h2	OG	Athína	27 Aug 04
3:27.08		CMR	Nguimgo 51.7, Kaboud 52.1, Atangana 51.98, Béwouda 51.35	7	WCh	Saint-Denis	31 Aug 03
3:27.14		MEX	Rodríguez 53.3, Medina 51.2, Vela 52.94, Guevara 49.70	4h2	WCh	Osaka	1 Sep 07
3:27.48		IRL	Andrews 53.4, Cuddihy 49.9, Bergin 52.60, Carey 51.54	4h3	WCh	Daegu	2 Sep 11
3:27.54		LTU	Navickaite, Valiuliene, Mendzoryte, Ambraziene	3	SPART	Moskva	22 Jun 83
3:27.57		ESP	Merino 52.2, Lacambra 52.0, Myers 50.85, Ferrer 52.56	7	WCh	Tokyo	1 Sep 91
3:27.86		HUN	Orosz, Forgács, Tóth, Pál (30)	5	OG	Moskva	1 Aug 80

4 x 800 METRES RELAY

Mark	Wind	Nat	Name	Pos	Meet	Venue	Date
7:50.17	WR	USSR	Olizarenko, Gurina, Borisova, Podyalovskaya	1		Moskva	5 Aug 84
7:54.10	WR	GDR	Zinn, Hoffmeister, Weiss, Klapezynski	1	NC	Karl-Marx-Stadt	6 Aug 76
8:00.62		USA	Price 2:01.30, Vessey 2:00.92, Ludlow 1:59.50, Montaño 1:58.90	1	WRly	Nassau	3 May 15

4 x 1500 METRES RELAY

Mark	Wind	Nat	Name	Pos	Meet	Venue	Date
16:33.58	WR	KEN	M Cherono 4:07.5, Kipyegon 4:08.5, Jelagat 4:10.5, Obiri 4:07.1	1	WRly	Nassau	24 May 14
16:55.33		USA	Kampf 4:09.2, Mackey, Grace, Martinez 4:10.2	2	WRly	Nassau	24 May 14
17:08.65		AUS	Buckman 4:08.1, Delaney 4:15.5, McGowan, Duncan 4:16.0	3	WRly	Nassau	25 May 14

5000 METRES WALK (TRACK)

Mark	Wind	Name		Nat	Born	Pos	Meet	Venue	Date
20:01.80	WR	Eleonora	Giorgi	ITA	14.9.89	1		Misterbianco	18 May 14
20:02.60	WR	Gillian	O'Sullivan	IRL	21.8.76	1	NC	Dublin (S)	13 Jul 02
20:03.0	WR	Kerry	Saxby-Junna	AUS	2.6.61	1		Sydney	11 Feb 96
20:07.52	WR	Beate	Anders/Gummelt	GDR	4.2.68	1	vURS	Rostock	23 Jun 90
20:11.45		Sabine	Zimmer/Krantz	GER	6.2.81	1	NC	Wattenscheid	2 Jul 05
20:12.41		Elisabetta	Perrone	ITA	9.7.68	1	NC	Rieti	2 Aug 03
20:15.71		Lyudmyla	Olyanovska	UKR	20.2.93	1		Kyiv	4 Jun 14
20:18.87		Melanie	Seeger	GER	8.1.77	1	NC	Braunschweig	10 Jul 04
20:21.69		Annarita	Sidoti	ITA	25.7.69	1	NC	Cesenatico	1 Jul 95
20:27.59	WR	Ileana	Salvador	ITA	16.1.62	1		Trento	3 Jun 89

10 KILOMETRES WALK

Mark	Wind	Name		Nat	Born	Pos	Meet	Venue	Date
41:04	WR	Yelena	Nikolayeva	RUS	1.2.66	1	NC	Sochi	20 Apr 96
41:16			Wang Yan	CHN	3.5.71	1		Eisenhüttenstadt	8 May 99
41:16		Kjersti	Plätzer (Tysse)	NOR	18.1.72	1	NC	Os	11 May 02
41:17		Irina	Stankina	RUS	25.3.77	1	NC-w	Adler	9 Feb 97
41:24		Olimpiada	Ivanova ¶	RUS	26.8.70	2	NC-w	Adler	9 Feb 97
41:29	WR	Larisa	Ramazanova	RUS	23.9.71	1	NC	Izhevsk	4 Jun 95
41:30	WR	Kerry	Saxby-Junna	AUS	2.6.61	1	NC	Canberra	27 Aug 88
41:30			O Ivanova			2	NC	Izhevsk	4 Jun 95
41:31		Yelena	Gruzinova	RUS	24.12.67	2	NC	Sochi	20 Apr 96
41:37.9t			Gao Hongmiao	CHN	17.3.74	1	NC	Beijing	7 Apr 94
41:38		Rossella	Giordano (10)	ITA	1.12.72	1		Naumburg	25 May 97
41:41			Nikolayeva			2		Naumburg	25 May 97
41:41			Tysse Plätzer			1		Kraków	30 May 09
41:42		Olga	Kaniskina ¶	RUS	19.1.85	2		Kraków	30 May 09
41:42.5t		Lyudmyla	Olyanovska	UKR	20.2.93	1		Mukachevo	1 Nov 14
41:45			Liu Hongyu	CHN	11.1.75	2		Eisenhüttenstadt	8 May 99
41:46		Annarita	Sidoti	ITA	25.7.69	1		Livorno	12 Jun 94
41:46			O Ivanova			1	NC/w	Adler	11 Feb 96
41:47			Saxby-Junna			1		Eisenhüttenstadt	11 May 96
41:48		(20/15)	Li Chunxiu	CHN	13.8.69	1	NG	Beijing	8 Sep 93
41:50		Yelena	Arshintseva	RUS	5.4.71	1	NC-w	Adler	11 Feb 95
41:51		Beate	Anders/Gummelt	GER	4.2.68	2		Eisenhüttenstadt	11 May 96
41:52		Tatyana	Mineyeva ¶	RUS	10.8.90	1	NCp-j	Penza	5 Sep 09
41:52		Tatyana	Korotkova	RUS	24.4.80	1		Buy	19 Sep 10
41:53		Tatyana	Sibileva	RUS	17.5.80	1	RWC-F	Beijing	18 Sep 10
		(20)							
41:56		Yelena	Sayko	RUS	24.12.67	2	NC/w	Adler	11 Feb 96
41:56.23t		Nadezhda	Ryashkina	RUS	22.1.67	1	GWG	Seattle	24 Jul 90
42:01		Tamara	Kovalenko	RUS	5.6.64	3	NC-w	Adler	11 Feb 95
42:01		Olga	Panfyorova	RUS	21.8.77	1	NC-23	Izhevsk	16 May 98
42:03		Lina	Bikulova	RUS	1.10.88	1		Bui	13 Sep 14
42:04+		Vera	Sokolova	RUS	8.6.87	1=	in 20k	Sochi	26 Feb 11
42:04+		Anisya	Kirdyapkina	RUS	23.10.89	1=	in 20k	Sochi	26 Feb 11
42:04+		Tatyana	Shemyakina	RUS	3.9.87	1=	in 20k	Sochi	26 Feb 11
42:05+		Margarita	Turova	BLR	28.12.80	1+	in 20k	Adler	12 Mar 05
42:06		Valentina	Tsybulskaya	BLR	19.2.68	4		Eisenhüttenstadt	8 May 99
		(30)							
42:07		Ileana	Salvador	ITA	16.1.62	1		Sesto San Giovanni	1 May 92
42:09		Elisabetta	Perrone	ITA	9.7.68	4		Eisenhüttenstadt	11 May 96
42:11		Nina	Alyushenko	RUS	29.5.68	3	NC	Izhevsk	4 Jun 95
42:12+		Elmira	Alembekova	RUS	30.6.90	1	in 20k	Sochi	27 Feb 15
42:12+		Marina	Pandakova	RUS	1.3.89	2	in 20k	Sochi	27 Feb 15
42:12+		Svetlana	Vasilyeva	RUS	24.7.92	3	in 20k	Sochi	27 Feb 15
42:13		Natalya	Misyulya	BLR	16.4.66	5		Eisenhüttenstadt	8 May 99
42:13.7t		Madelein	Svensson	SWE	20.7.69	2	SGP	Fana	15 May 92
42:15			Gu Yan	CHN	17.3.74	3	WCp	Podebrady	19 Apr 97
42:15		Erica	Alfridi	ITA	22.2.68	5		Naumburg	25 May 97
42:15		Jane	Saville	AUS	5.11.74	6		Eisenhüttenstadt	8 May 99
		(40)	50th woman 42:30, 100th 43:10, 200th 43:58, 300th 44:38						

Best track times

Mark	Wind	Name		Nat	Born	Pos	Meet	Venue	Date
41:57.22		Kerry	Saxby-Junna	AUS	2.6.61	2	GWG	Seattle	24 Jul 90
42:11.5		Beate	Anders/Gummelt	GER	4.2.68	1	SGP	Fana	15 May 92

20 KILOMETRES WALK

Mark	Wind	Name		Nat	Born	Pos	Meet	Venue	Date
1:24:38	WR		Liu Hong	CHN	12.5.87	1		La Coruña	6 Jun 15
1:24:47		Elmira	Alembekova	RUS	30.6.90	1	NC-w	Sochi	27 Feb 15
1:24:50		Olimpiada	Ivanova ¶	RUS	26.8.70	1	NC-w	Adler	4 Mar 01

Mark Wind	Name		Nat	Born	Pos	Meet	Venue	Date
1:24:56	Olga	Kaniskina ¶	RUS	19.1.85	1	NC-w	Adler	28 Feb 09
1:25:02 WR	Yelena	Lashmanova ¶	RUS	9.4.92	1	OG	London	11 Aug 12
1:25:03	Marina	Pandakova	RUS	1.3.89	2	NC-w	Sochi	27 Feb 15
1:25:04	Svetlana	Vasilyeva	RUS	24.7.92	3	NC-w	Sochi	27 Feb 15
1:25:08 WR	Vera	Sokolova	RUS	8.6.87	1	NC-w	Sochi	26 Feb 11
1:25:09	Anisya	Kirdyapkina	RUS	23.10.89	2	NC-w	Sochi	26 Feb 11
1:25:11		Kaniskina			1	NC-w	Adler	23 Feb 08
1:25:11		Kirdyapkina			1	NC-w	Sochi	20 Feb 10
1:25:12		Lu Xiuzhi (10)	CHN	26.10.93	1	WCT	Beijing	20 Mar 15
1:25:16		Qieyang Shenjie	CHN	11.11.90	2	OG	London	11 Aug 12
1:25:18	Tatyana	Gudkova	RUS	23.1.78	1	NC	Moskva	19 May 00
1:25:20	Olga	Polyakova	RUS	23.9.80	2	NC	Moskva	19 May 00
1:25:26		Sokolova			2	NC-w	Adler	28 Feb 09
1:25:26		Kirdyapkina			3	NC-w	Adler	28 Feb 09
1:25:27		Alembekova			1	NC-w	Sochi	18 Feb 12
1:25:29	Irina	Stankina	RUS	25.3.77	3	NC	Moskva	19 May 00
1:25:30		Kirdyapkina			2	NC-w	Adler	23 Feb 08
1:25:32	Yelena	Shumkina	RUS	24.1.88	4	NC-w	Adler	28 Feb 09
1:25:35		Sokolova			2	NC-w	Sochi	20 Feb 10
1:25:38		Sokolova			4	NC-w	Sochi	27 Feb 15
1:25:41 WR		Ivanova			1	WCh	Helsinki	7 Aug 05
1:25:42		Kaniskina			1	WCp	Cheboksary	11 May 08
1:25:46	Tatyana	Shemyakina	RUS	3.9.87	3	NC-w	Adler	23 Feb 08
1:25:46		Liu Hong			1		Taicang	30 Mar 12
1:25:49		Lashmanova			1	NC-w	Sochi	23 Feb 13
1:25:52	Larisa	Yemelyanova	RUS	6.1.80	5	NC-w	Adler	28 Feb 09
1:25:52	Tatyana	Sibileva	RUS	17.5.80	3	NC-w	Sochi	20 Feb 10
	(30/18)							
1:25:59	Tamara	Kovalenko	RUS	5.6.64	4	NC	Moskva	19 May 00
1:26:11	Margarita	Turova (20)	BLR	28.12.80	1	NC	Nesvizh	15 Apr 06
1:26:14	Irina	Petrova	RUS	26.5.85	2	NC-w	Adler	19 Feb 06
1:26:16	Lyudmila	Arkhipova	RUS	25.11.78	5	NC-w	Adler	23 Feb 08
1:26:17	Eleonora	Giorgi	ITA	14.9.89	2	ECp	Murcia	17 May 15
1:26:22 WR		Wang Yan	CHN	3.5.71	1	NG	Guangzhou	19 Nov 01
1:26:22 WR	Yelena	Nikolayeva	RUS	1.2.66	1	ECp	Cheboksary	18 May 03
1:26:23		Wang Liping	CHN	8.7.76	2	NG	Guangzhou	19 Nov 01
1:26:28	Iraida	Pudovkina	RUS	2.11.80	1	NC-w	Adler	12 Mar 05
1:26:34	Tatyana	Kalmykova	RUS	10.1.90	1	NC	Saransk	8 Jun 08
1:26:35		Liu Hongyu	CHN	11.1.75	3	NG	Guangzhou	19 Nov 01
1:26:46		Song Hongjuan	CHN	4.7.84	1	NC	Guangzhou	20 Mar 04
	(30)							
1:26:47	Irina	Yumanova ¶	RUS	6.11.90	3	NC-w	Sochi	18 Feb 12
1:26:50	Natalya	Fedoskina	RUS	25.6.80	2	ECp	Dudince	19 May 01
1:26:53	Anezka	Drahotová	CZE	22.7.95	4	ECp	Murcia	17 May 15
1:26:57	Lyudmila	Yefimkina	RUS	22.8.81	3	NC-w	Adler	19 Feb 06
1:27:07	Kjersti	Tysse Plätzer	NOR	18.1.72	2	OG	Beijing	21 Aug 08
1:27:09	Elisabetta	Perrone	ITA	9.7.68	3	ECp	Dudince	19 May 01
1:27:09	Lyudmyla	Olyanovska	UKR	20.2.93	7	ECp	Murcia	17 May 15
1:27:12	Elisa	Rigaudo	ITA	17.6.80	3	OG	Beijing	21 Aug 08
1:27:14	Antonina	Petrova	RUS	1.5.77	1	NC-w	Adler	1 Mar 03
1:27:17	Mariya	Ponomaryova	RUS	18.6.95	1	EU23	Tallinn	10 Jul 15
	(40)							
1:27:18	Alena	Nartova	RUS	1.1.82	6	NC-w	Adler	23 Feb 08
1:27:19		Jiang Jing	CHN	23.10.85	1	NC	Nanning	25 Feb 05
1:27:22	Gillian	O'Sullivan	IRL	21.8.76	1		Sesto San Giovanni	1 May 03
1:27:25	María	Vasco	ESP	26.12.75	5	OG	Beijing	21 Aug 08
1:27:27	Vira	Zozulya	UKR	31.8.70	1	NC	Sumy	7 Jun 08
1:27:29	Erica	Alfridi	ITA	22.2.68	4	ECp	Dudince	19 May 01
1:27:30 WB	Nadezhda	Ryashkina	RUS	22.1.67	1	NC-w	Adler	7 Feb 99
1:27:30	Tatyana	Kozlova	RUS	2.9.83	2	NC-w	Adler	12 Mar 05
1:27:35	Tatyana	Korotkova	RUS	24.4.80	2	NC	Cheboksary	12 Jun 04
1:27:36		Sun Huanhuan	CHN	15.3.90	1	NC	Taicang	1 Mar 13
	(50)	100th best woman 1:28:52, 200th 1:30:44, 300th 1:32:12, 400th 1:33:56						
Drugs dq: 1:25:09		Kaniskina			(2)	OG	London	11 Aug 12
1:27:08	Anna	Lukyanova ¶	RUS	23.4.91	(5)	NC-w	Sochi	18 Feb 12

50 KILOMETRES WALK

Mark	Name		Nat	Born	Pos	Meet	Venue	Date
4:10:59	Monica	Svensson	SWE	26.12.78	1		Scanzorosciate	21 Oct 07
4:12:16	Yelena	Ginko	BLR	30.7.76	1		Scanzorosciate	17 Oct 04
4:16:27	Jolanta	Dukure	LAT	20.9.79	1		Paralepa	9 Sep 06

JUNIOR MEN'S ALL-TIME LISTS

100 METRES

Mark	Wind	Name		Nat	Born	Pos	Meet	Venue	Date
9.97	1.8	Trayvon	Bromell	USA	10.7.95	1	NCAA	Eugene	13 Jun 14
10.00	1.6	Trentavis	Friday	USA	5.6.95	1h1	NC-j	Eugene	5 Jul 14
10.01	0.0	Darrel	Brown	TTO	11.10.84	1q3	WCh	Saint-Denis	24 Aug 03
10.01	1.6	Jeffery	Demps	USA	8.1.90	2q1	NC/OT	Eugene	28 Jun 08
10.01	0.9	Yoshihide	Kiryu	JPN	15.12.95	1h3	Oda	Hiroshima	29 Apr 13
10.03	0.7	Marcus	Rowland	USA	11.3.90	1	PAm-J	Port of Spain	31 Jul 09
10.04	1.7	DeAngelo	Cherry	USA	1.8.90	1h4	NCAA	Fayetteville	10 Jun 09
10.04	0.2	Christoph	Lemaitre	FRA	11.6.90	1	EJ	Novi Sad	24 Jul 09
10.05		Davidson	Ezinwa	NGR	22.11.71	1		Bauchi	4 Jan 90
10.05	0.1	Adam	Gemili	GBR	6.10.93	1	WJ	Barcelona	11 Jul 12
Wind assisted to 10.03									
9.77	4.2	Trayvon	Bromell	USA	10.7.95	1	Big 12	Lubbock	18 May 14
9.83	7.1	Leonard	Scott	USA	19.1.80	1		Knoxville	9 Apr 99
9.96	4.5	Walter	Dix	USA	31.1.86	1rA	TexR	Austin	9 Apr 05
9.97	??	Mark	Lewis-Francis	GBR	4.9.82	1q3	WCh	Edmonton	4 Aug 01
9.96	5.0	André	De Grasse	CAN	10.11.94	1	JUCO	Hutchinson, KS	18 May 13
9.98	5.0	Tyreek	Hill	USA	1.3.94	2	JUCO	Hutchinson, KS	18 May 13
10.02	2.8	DeAngelo	Cherry	USA	1.8.90	1h2	NC-j	Eugene	26 Jun 09
10.02	2.4	Marcus	Rowland	USA	11.3.90	1	NC-j	Eugene	26 Jun 09
10.03	4.9	Christoph	Lemaitre	FRA-	11.6.90	1		Forbach	31 May 09

200 METRES

Mark	Wind	Name		Nat	Born	Pos	Meet	Venue	Date
19.93	1.4	Usain	Bolt	JAM	21.8.86	1		Hamilton, BER	11 Apr 04
20.04	0.1	Ramil	Guliyev	AZE	29.5.90	1	WUG	Beograd	10 Jul 09
20.07	1.5	Lorenzo	Daniel	USA	23.3.66	1	SEC	Starkville	18 May 85
20.13	1.7	Roy	Martin	USA	25.12.66	1		Austin	11 May 85
20.14	1.8	Tyreek	Hill	USA	1.3.94	1		Orlando	26 May 12
20.16A	-0.2	Riaan	Dempers	RSA	4.3.77	1	NC-j	Germiston	7 Apr 95
20.18	1.0	Walter	Dix	USA	31.1.86	1s2	NCAA	Sacramento	9 Jun 05
20.18	1.8	Noah	Lyles	USA	18.7.97	1	NC-j	Eugene	27 Jun 15
20.22	1.7	Dwayne	Evans	USA	13.10.58	2	OT	Eugene	22 Jun 76
20.23	0.5	Michael	Timpson	USA	6.6.67	1		State College	16 May 86
Wind assisted									
19.86	4.0	Justin	Gatlin	USA	10.2.82	1h2	NCAA	Eugene	30 May 01
20.01	2.5	Derald	Harris	USA	5.4.58	1		San José	9 Apr 77
20.03	2.9	Trentavis	Friday	USA	5.6.95	1	NC-j	Eugene	6 Jul 14
20.08	9.2	Leonard	Scott	USA	19.1.80	2r2		Knoxville	9 Apr 99
20.10	4.6	Stanley	Kerr	USA	19.6.67	2r2	SWC	Houston	18 May 86
20.16	5.2	Nickel	Ashmeade	JAM	4.7.90	1	Carifta	Basseterre	24 Mar 08
Hand timing: 19.9		Davidson	Ezinwa	NGR	22.11.71	1		Bauchi	18 Mar 89

400 METRES

Mark	Wind	Name		Nat	Born	Pos	Meet	Venue	Date
43.87		Steve	Lewis	USA	16.5.69	1	OG	Seoul	28 Sep 88
44.27		Abdelilah	Haroun	QAT	1.1.97	2		La Chaux-de-Fonds	5 Jul 15
44.36		Kirani	James	GRN	1.9.92	1	WK	Zürich	8 Sep 11
44.66		Hamdam Odha	Al-Bishi	KSA	5.5.81	1	WJ	Santiago de Chile	20 Oct 00
44.66		LaShawn	Merritt	USA	27.6.86	1		Kingston	7 May 05
44.69		Darrell	Robinson	USA	23.12.63	2	USOF	Indianapolis	24 Jul 82
44.71A		Luguelín	Santos	DOM	12.11.93	2	PAm	Guadalajara	26 Oct 11
44.73A		James	Rolle	USA	2.2.64	1	USOF	USAF Academy	2 Jul 83
44.75		Darren	Clark	AUS	6.9.65	4	OG	Los Angeles	8 Aug 84
44.75		Deon	Minor	USA	22.1.73	1s1	NCAA	Austin	5 Jun 92
44.82		Arman	Hall	USA	14.2.94	4s1	NC	Des Moines	21 Jun 13
44.93		Nagmeldin	El Abubakr	SUD	22.2.86	1	Is.Sol	Makkah	14 Apr 05
44.93		Akeem	Bloomfield	JAM	10.11.97	1		Kingston	28 Mar 15

800 METRES

Mark	Wind	Name		Nat	Born	Pos	Meet	Venue	Date
1:41.73		Nijel	Amos	BOT	15.3.94	2	OG	London (OS)	9 Aug 12
1:42.37		Mohammed	Aman	ETH	10.1.94	1	VD	Bruxelles	6 Sep 13
1:42.53		Timothy	Kitum	KEN	20.11.94	3	OG	London (OS)	9 Aug 12
1:42.69		Abubaker	Kaki	SUD	21.6.89	1	Bisl	Oslo	6 Jun 08
1:43.13		Abraham Kipchirchir	Rotich	KEN	26.6.93	1	Herc	Monaco	20 Jul 12
1:43.40		Leonard	Kosencha	KEN	21.8.94	2	Herc	Monaco	20 Jul 12
1:43.56		Robert	Biwott	KEN	28.1.96	2		Barcelona	8 Jul 15
1:43.64		Japheth	Kimutai	KEN	20.12.78	3rB	WK	Zürich	13 Aug 97
1:43.81		Edwin	Melly	KEN	24.3.94	2		Rieti	9 Sep 12
1:43.95		Alfred	Kipketer	KEN	26.12.96	1	WJ	Eugene	27 Jul 14
1:43.99		David	Mutua	KEN	20.4.92	4	Herc	Monaco	22 Jul 11

Jnr MEN All-time

1000 METRES

Mark	Wind	Name		Nat	Born	Pos	Meet	Venue	Date
2:13.93		Abubaker	Kaki	SUD	21.6.89	1	DNG	Stockholm	22 Jul 08
2:15.00		Benjamin	Kipkurui	KEN	28.12.80	5	Nik	Nice	17 Jul 99

1500 METRES

Mark	Wind	Name		Nat	Born	Pos	Meet	Venue	Date
3:28.81		Ronald	Kwemoi	KEN	19.9.95	3	Herc	Monaco	18 Jul 14
3:30.10		Robert	Biwott	KEN	28.1.96	7	Herc	Monaco	17 JUl 15
3:30.24		Cornelius	Chirchir	KEN	5.6.83	4	Herc	Monaco	19 Jul 02
3:31.13		Mulugueta	Wondimu	ETH	28.2.85	2rA	NA	Heusden	31 Jul 04
3:31.42		Alex	Kipchirchir	KEN	26.11.84	5	VD	Bruxelles	5 Sep 03
3:31.54		Isaac	Songok	KEN	25.4.84	1	NA	Heusden	2 Aug 03
3:31.64		Asbel	Kiprop	KEN	30.6.89	1	GGala	Roma	11 Jul 08
3:31.70		William	Biwott	KEN	5.3.90	3	GGala	Roma	10 Jul 09
3:32.02		Caleb	Ndiku	KEN	9.10.92	4	FBK	Hengelo	29 May 11
3:32.48		Augustine	Choge	KEN	21.1.87	1	ISTAF	Berlin	3 Sep 06
3:32.68		Abdelaati	Iguider	MAR	25.3.87	5	VD	Bruxelles	25 Aug 06

1 MILE

Mark	Wind	Name		Nat	Born	Pos	Meet	Venue	Date
3:49.29		William	Biwott	KEN	5.3.90	2	Bisl	Oslo	3 Jul 09
3:49.77		Caleb	Ndiku	KEN	9.10.92	5	Pre	Eugene	4 Jun 11
3:50.25		Alex	Kipchirchir	KEN	26.11.84	2	GP II	Rieti	7 Sep 03
3:50.39		James	Kwalia	KEN	12.6.84	1	FBK	Hengelo	1 Jun 03
3:50.41		Noah	Ngeny	KEN	2.11.78	2	Nik	Nice	16 Jul 97
3:50.69		Cornelius	Chirchir	KEN	5.6.83	5	GGala	Roma	12 Jul 02
3:50.83		Nicholas	Kemboi	KEN	18.12.89	6	Bisl	Oslo	6 Jun 08

2000 METRES

Mark	Wind	Name		Nat	Born	Pos	Meet	Venue	Date
4:56.25		Tesfaye	Cheru	ETH	2.3.93	1		Reims	5 Jul 11
4:56.86		Isaac	Songok	KEN	25.4.84	6	ISTAF	Berlin	31 Aug 01
4:58.18		Soresa	Fida	ETH	27.5.93	4		Reims	5 Jul 11
4:58.76		Jairus	Kipchoge	KEN	15.12.92	7		Reims	5 Jul 11

3000 METRES

Mark	Wind	Name		Nat	Born	Pos	Meet	Venue	Date
7:28.78		Augustine	Choge	KEN	21.1.87	2	SGP	Doha	13 May 05
7:29.11		Tariku	Bekele	ETH	21.1.87	2	GP	Rieti	27 Aug 06
7:30.36		Hagos	Gebrhiwet	ETH	11.5.94	1	DL	Doha	10 May 13
7:30.43		Isiah	Koech	KEN	19.12.93	1	DNG	Stockholm	17 Aug 12
7:30.67		Kenenisa	Bekele	ETH	13.6.82	2	VD	Bruxelles	24 Aug 01
7:30.91		Eliud	Kipchoge	KEN	5.11.84	2	VD	Bruxelles	5 Sep 03
7:32.37		Abreham	Cherkos	ETH	23.9.89	2	Athl	Lausanne	11 Jul 06
7:32.72		John	Kipkoech	KEN	29.12.91	4		Rieti	29 Aug 10
7:33.00		Hailu	Mekonnen	ETH	4.4.80	2		Stuttgart	6 Jun 99
7:33.01		Levy	Matebo	KEN	3.11.89	2	GP	Rieti	7 Sep 08
7:34.32		Richard	Limo	KEN	18.11.80	4	VD	Bruxelles	3 Sep 99

5000 METRES

Mark	Wind	Name		Nat	Born	Pos	Meet	Venue	Date
12:47.53		Hagos	Gebrhiwet	ETH	11.5.94	2	DL	Saint-Denis	6 Jul 12
12:48.64		Isiah	Koech	KEN	19.12.93	3	DL	Saint-Denis	6 Jul 12
12:52.61		Eliud	Kipchoge	KEN	5.11.84	3	Bisl	Oslo	27 Jun 03
12:53.66		Augustine	Choge	KEN	21.1.87	4	GGala	Roma	8 Jul 05
12:53.72		Philip	Mosima	KEN	2.1.77	2	GGala	Roma	5 Jun 96
12:53.81		Tariku	Bekele	ETH	21.1.87	4	GGala	Roma	14 Jul 06
12:53.98		Yomif	Kejelcha	ETH	1.8.97	1	VD	Bruxelles	11 Sep 15
12:54.07		Sammy	Kipketer	KEN	29.9.81	2	GGala	Roma	30 Jun 00
12:54.19		Abreham	Cherkos	ETH	23.9.89	5	GGala	Roma	14 Jul 06
12:54.58		James	Kwalia	KEN	12.6.84	5	Bisl	Oslo	27 Jun 03
12:56.15		Daniel	Komen	KEN	17.5.76	2	GG	Roma	8 Jun 95

10,000 METRES

Mark	Wind	Name		Nat	Born	Pos	Meet	Venue	Date
26:41.75		Samuel	Wanjiru	KEN	10.11.86	3	VD	Bruxelles	26 Aug 05
26:55.73		Geoffrey	Kirui	KEN	16.2.93	6	VD	Bruxelles	16 Sep 11
26:57.56		Yigrem	Demelash	ETH	28.1.94	4	VD	Bruxelles	7 Sep 12
27:02.81		Ibrahim	Jeylan	ETH	12.6.89	4	VD	Bruxelles	25 Aug 06
27:04.00		Boniface	Kiprop	UGA	12.10.85	5	VD	Bruxelles	3 Sep 04
27:04.45		Bernard	Kipyego	KEN	16.7.86	4	FBK	Hengelo	29 May 05
27:06.35		Geoffrey	Kipsang	KEN	28.11.92	10	Pre	Eugene	3 Jun 11
27:06.47		Habtanu	Fikadu	ETH	13.3.88	8	FBK	Hengelo	26 May 07
27:07.29		Moses	Masai	KEN	1.6.86	7	VD	Bruxelles	3 Sep 04
27:11.18		Richard	Chelimo	KEN	21.4.72	1	APM	Hengelo	25 Jun 91
27:12.42		Sammy Alex	Mutahi	KEN	1.6.89	1		Tokamchi	29 Sep 07
27:13.66		Moses	Mosop	KEN	17.7.85	7	VD	Bruxelles	5 Sep 03

Mark	Wind	Name		Nat	Born	Pos	Meet	Venue	Date

3000 METRES STEEPLECHASE

Mark	Wind	Name		Nat	Born	Pos	Meet	Venue	Date
7:58.66		Stephen	Cherono	KEN	15.10.82	3	VD	Bruxelles	24 Aug 01
8:01.16		Conseslus	Kipruto	KEN	8.12.94	1	DL	Shanghai	18 May 13
8:03.74		Raymond	Yator	KEN	7.4.81	3	Herc	Monaco	18 Aug 00
8:05.52		Brimin	Kipruto	KEN	31.7.85	1	FBK	Hengelo	31 May 04
8:06.96		Gilbert	Kirui	KEN	22.1.94	2	DL	London (OS)	27 Jul 13
8:07.18		Moussa	Omar Obaid	QAT	18.4.85	4	OG	Athína	24 Aug 04
8:07.69		Paul	Kosgei	KEN	22.4.78	5	DNG	Stockholm	7 Jul 97
8:07.71		Hillary	Yego	KEN	2.4.92	3	DL	Shanghai	15 May 11
8:09.37		Abel	Cheruiyot/Yugut	KEN	26.12.84	2	NA	Heusden	2 Aug 03
8:11.31		Jairus	Birech	KEN	15.12.92	5	DL	Saint Denis	8 Jul 11
8:12.91		Thomas	Kiplitan	KEN	15.6.83	7	GP	Doha	15 May 02

110 METRES HURDLES (106cm)

Mark	Wind	Name		Nat	Born	Pos	Meet	Venue	Date
13.12	1.6		Liu Xiang	CHN	13.7.83	1rB	Athl	Lausanne	2 Jul 02
13.23	0.0	Renaldo	Nehemiah	USA	24.3.59	1r2	WK	Zürich	16 Aug 78
13.40	-1.0		Shi Dongpeng	CHN	6.1.84	1	NC	Shanghai	14 Sep 03
13.44	-0.8	Colin	Jackson	GBR	18.2.67	1	WJ	Athína	19 Jul 86
13.46	1.8	Jon	Ridgeon	GBR	14.2.67	1	EJ	Cottbus	23 Aug 85
13.46	-1.6	Dayron	Robles	CUB	19.11.86	1	PAm-J	Windsor	29 Jul 05
13.47	1.9	Holger	Pohland	GDR	5.4.63	2	vUSA	Karl-Marx-Stadt	10 Jul 82
13.47	1.2	Aries	Merritt	USA	24.7.85	4	NCAA	Austin	12 Jun 04
13.47	0.2		Xie Wenjun	CHN	11.7.90	2	GP	Shanghai	20 Sep 08
13.49	0.6	Stanislav	Olijar	LAT	22.3.79	1		Valmiera	11 Jul 98
13.49	1.2	Booker	Nunley	USA	2.7.90	2	SEC	Gainesville	17 May 09
Wind assisted									
13.41	2.6	Dayron	Robles	CUB	19.11.86	2	CAC	Nassau	10 Jul 05
13.42	4.5	Colin	Jackson	GBR	18.2.67	2	CG	Edinburgh	27 Jul 86
13.42	2.6	Antwon	Hicks	USA	12.3.83	1	WJ	Kingston	21 Jul 02
13.47	2.1	Frank	Busemann	GER	26.2.75	1	WJ	Lisboa	22 Jul 94

99 cm Hurdles

Mark	Wind	Name		Nat	Born	Pos	Meet	Venue	Date
12.99	0.5	Wilhem	Belocian	FRA	22.6.95	1	WJ	Eugene	24 Jul 14
13.06	0.5	Tyler	Mason	JAM	15.1.95	2	WJ	Eugene	24 Jul 14
13.08	2.0	Wayne	Davis	USA	2.7.90	1	PAm-J	Port of Spain	31 Jul 09
13.14	1.6	Eddie	Lovett	USA	25.6.92	1	PAm-J	Miramar	23 Jul 11
13.17	-0.7	David	Omoregie	GBR	1.11.95	1	NC-j	Bedford	22 Jun 14
13.18	1.0	Yordan	O'Farrill	CUB	9.2.93	1	WJ	Barcelona	12 Jul 12
13.21	1.5	Misana	Viltz	USA	21.2.96	1	NC-j	Eugene	25 Jun 15
13.22	0.1	Jaheel	Hyde	JAM	2.2.97	1		Kingston	7 Mar 15
Wind assisted to 13.20									
13.03	2.9	Eddie	Lovett	USA	25.6.92	1h1	PAm-J	Miramar	23 Jul 11
13.15	2.7	Brendan	Ames	USA	6.10.88	1	NC-j	Indianapolis	21 Jun 07
13.18		Arthur	Blake	USA	19.8.66	1	GWest	Sacramento	9 Jun 84
13.19	3.8	Chad	Zallow	USA	25.4.97	1		Greensboro	20 Jun 15
Hand timed: 12.9y		Renaldo	Nehemiah	USA	24.3.59	1		Jamaica, NY	30 May 77

400 METRES HURDLES

Mark	Wind	Name		Nat	Born	Pos	Meet	Venue	Date
48.02		Danny	Harris	USA	7.9.65	2s1	OT	Los Angeles	17 Jun 84
48.26		Jehue	Gordon	TTO	15.12.91	4	WCh	Berlin	18 Aug 09
48.51		Kerron	Clement	USA	31.10.85	1	WJ	Grosseto	16 Jul 04
48.52		Johnny	Dutch	USA	20.1.89	5	NC/OT	Eugene	29 Jun 08
48.62		Brandon	Johnson	USA	6.3.85	2	WJ	Grosseto	16 Jul 04
48.68		Bayano	Kamani	USA	17.4.80	1	NCAA	Boise	4 Jun 99
48.68		Jeshua	Anderson	USA	22.6.89	1	WJ	Bydgoszcz	11 Jul 08
48.72		Angelo	Taylor	USA	29.12.78	2	NCAA	Bloomington	6 Jun 97
48.74		Vladimir	Budko	BLR	4.2.65	2	DRZ	Moskva	18 Aug 84
48.76A		Llewellyn	Herbert	RSA	21.7.77	1		Pretoria	7 Apr 96
48.79		Kenneth	Ferguson	USA	22.3.84	1	SEC	Knoxville	18 May 03

HIGH JUMP

Mark	Wind	Name		Nat	Born	Pos	Meet	Venue	Date
2.37		Dragutin	Topic	YUG	12.3.71	1	WJ	Plovdiv	12 Aug 90
2.37		Steve	Smith	GBR	29.3.73	1	WJ	Seoul	20 Sep 92
2.36		Javier	Sotomayor	CUB	13.10.67	1		Santiago de Cuba	23 Feb 86
2.35i		Vladimir	Yashchenko	UKR	12.1.59	1	EI	Milano	12 Mar 78
		2.34				1	Prv	Tbilisi	16 Jun 78
2.35		Dietmar	Mögenburg	FRG	15.8.61	1		Rehlingen	26 May 80
2.34		Tim	Forsyth	AUS	17.8.73	1	Bisl	Oslo	4 Jul 92
2.33			Zhu Jianhua	CHN	29.5.63	1	AsiG	New Delhi	1 Dec 82
2.33		Patrik	Sjöberg	SWE	5.1.65	1	OsloG	Oslo	9 Jul 83
2.32i		Jaroslav	Bába	CZE	2.9.84	3		Arnstadt	8 Feb 03
2.32			Huang Haiqiang	CHN	8.2.88	1	WJ	Beijing	17 Aug 06

Mark	Wind	Name		Nat	Born	Pos	Meet	Venue	Date

POLE VAULT

Mark	Wind	Name		Nat	Born	Pos	Meet	Venue	Date
5.80		Maksim	Tarasov	RUS	2.12.70	1	vGDR-j	Bryansk	14 Jul 89
5.80		Raphael	Holzdeppe	GER	28.9.89	2		Biberach	28 Jun 08
5.75		Konstadínos	Filippídis	GRE	26.11.86	2	WUG	Izmir	18 Aug 05
5.72		Andrew	Irwin	USA	23.1.93	1	SEC	Baton Rouge	13 May 12
5.71		Lawrence	Johnson	USA	7.5.74	1		Knoxville	12 Jun 93
5.71		Germán	Chiaraviglio	ARG	16.4.87	1	WJ	Beijing	19 Aug 06
5.71		Shawn	Barber	CAN	27.5.94	2	TexR	Austin	29 Mar 13
5.70		Viktor	Chistyakov	RUS	9.2.75	1		Leppävirta	7 Jun 94
5.70		Artyom	Kuptsov	RUS	22.4.84	1	Znam	Tula	7 Jun 03
5.67i		Leonid	Kivalov	RUS	1.4.88	1	NC-j	Penza	1 Feb 07

LONG JUMP

Mark	Wind	Name		Nat	Born	Pos	Meet	Venue	Date
8.35	1.1	Sergey	Morgunov	RUS	9.2.93	1	NC-j	Cheboksary	19 Jun 12
8.34	0.0	Randy	Williams	USA	23.8.53	Q	OG	München	8 Sep 72
8.28	0.8	Luis Alberto	Bueno	CUB	22.5.69	1		La Habana	16 Jul 88
8.27	1.7	Eusebio	Cáceres	ESP	10.9.91	Q	EC	Barcelona	30 Jul 10
8.25	0.9		Wang Jianan	CHN	27.8.96	3	DL	Shanghai	17 May 15
8.24	0.2	Eric	Metcalf	USA	23.1.68	1	NCAA	Indianapolis	6 Jun 86
8.24	1.8	Vladimir	Ochkan	UKR	13.1.68	1	vGDR-j	Leningrad	21 Jun 87
8.22		Larry	Doubley	USA	15.3.58	1	NCAA	Champaign	3 Jun 77
8.22		Iván	Pedroso	CUB	17.12.72	1		Santiago de Cuba	3 May 91
8.22i		Viktor	Kuznetsov	UKR	14.7.86	1		Brovary	22 Jan 05
8.21A	2.0	Vance	Johnson	USA	13.3.63	1	NCAA	Provo	4 Jun 82
Wind assisted to 8.23									
8.40	3.2	Kareem	Streete-Thompson	CAY	30.3.73	1		Houston	5 May 91
8.35	2.2	Carl	Lewis	USA	1.7.61	1	NCAA	Austin	6 Jun 80
8.29	2.3	James	Beckford	JAM	9.1.75	1		Tempe	2 Apr 94
8.23	4.4	Peller	Phillips	USA	23.6.70	1		Sacramento	11 Jun 88

TRIPLE JUMP

Mark	Wind	Name		Nat	Born	Pos	Meet	Venue	Date
17.50	0.4	Volker	Mai	GDR	3.5.66	1	vURS	Erfurt	23 Jun 85
17.42	1.3	Khristo	Markov	BUL	27.1.65	1	Nar	Sofiya	19 May 84
17.40A	0.4	Pedro	Pérez	CUB	23.2.52	1	PAm	Cali	5 Aug 71
17.40	0.8	Ernesto	Revé	CUB	26.2.92	1		La Habana	10 Jun 11
17.31	-0.2	David	Girat Jr.	CUB	26.8.84	Q	WCh	Saint-Denis	23 Aug 03
17.29	1.3	James	Beckford	JAM	9.1.75	1		Tempe	2 Apr 94
17.27		Aliecer	Urrutia	CUB	22.9.74	1		Artemisa	23 Apr 93
17.24	0.7	Lázaro	Martínez	CUB	3.11.97	2		La Habana	1 Feb 14
17.23	0.2	Yoelbi	Quesada	CUB	4.8.73	1	NC	La Habana	13 May 92
17.19	-0.4	Teddy	Tamgho	FRA	15.6.89	4	Herc	Monaco	29 Jul 08
17.19	2.0	Will	Claye	USA	13.6.91	*	NCAA	Fayetteville	13 Jun 09
Wind assisted									
17.33	2.1	Teddy	Tamgho	FRA	15.6.89	1	WJ	Bydgoszcz	11 Jul 08
17.24	2.5	Will	Claye	USA	13.6.91	1	NCAA	Fayetteville	13 Jun 09

SHOT

Mark	Wind	Name		Nat	Born	Pos	Meet	Venue	Date
21.05i		Terry	Albritton	USA	14.1.55	1	AAU	New York	22 Feb 74
		20.38				2	MSR	Walnut	27 Apr 74
20.78		Konrad	Bukowiecki	POL	17.3.97	3		Zagreb	7 Sep 15
20.65		Mike	Carter	USA	29.10.60	1	vSU-j	Boston	4 Jul 79
20.43		David	Storl	GER	27.7.90	2		Gerlingen	6 Jul 09
20.39		Janus	Robberts	RSA	10.3.79	1	NC	Germiston	7 Mar 98
20.38		Jacko	Gill	NZL	10.12.94	1		Auckland (NS)	5 Dec 11
20.20		Randy	Matson	USA	5.3.45	2	OG	Tokyo	17 Oct 64
20.20		Udo	Beyer	GDR	9.8.55	2	NC	Leipzig	6 Jul 74
20.13		Jeff	Chakouian	USA	20.4.82	2		Atlanta	18 May 01
19.99		Karl	Salb	USA	19.5.49	4	OT	Echo Summit	10 Sep 68
6 kg Shot									
23.00		Jacko	Gill	NZL	10.12.94	1		Auckland	18 Aug 13
22.73		David	Storl	GER	27.7.90	1		Osterode	14 Jul 09
22.62		Konrad	Bukowiecki	POL	17.3.97	1	EJ	Eskilstuna	16 Sep 15
21.96		Edis	Elkasevic	CRO	18.2.83	1	NC-j	Zagreb	29 Jun 02
21.90		John	Maurins	USA	3.8.96	1	NC-j	Eugene	25 Jun 15
21.79		Mustafa Amer	Ahmed	EGY	16.12.95	1	Arab	Cairo	23 Feb 14
21.78		Krzysztof	Brzozowski	POL	15.7.93	2	WJ	Barcelona	11 Jul 12
21.68		Marin	Premeru	CRO	29.8.90	1		Rijeka	19 May 09

DISCUS

Mark	Wind	Name		Nat	Born	Pos	Meet	Venue	Date
65.62		Werner	Reiterer	AUS	27.1.68	1		Melbourne	15 Dec 87
65.31		Mykyta	Nesterenko	UKR	15.4.91	3		Tallinn	3 Jun 08

Mark	Wind	Name		Nat	Born	Pos	Meet	Venue	Date
63.64		Werner	Hartmann	FRG	20.4.59	1	vFRA	Strasbourg	25 Jun 78
63.26		Sergey	Pachin	UKR	24.5.68	2		Moskva	25 Jul 87
63.22		Brian	Milne	USA	7.1.73	1		State College	28 Mar 92
62.58		Matthew	Denny	AUS	2.6.96	2	WUG	Gwangju	11 Jul 15
62.52		John	Nichols	USA	23.8.69	1		Baton Rouge	23 Apr 88
62.43		Martin	Markovic	CRO	13.1.96	1	NC-w	Split	8 Mar 15
62.36		Tulake	Nuermaimaiti	CHN	8.3.82	2	NG	Guangzhou	21 Nov 01
62.16		Zoltán	Kövágó	HUN	10.4.79	1		Budapest	9 May 97

1.75kg Discus

Mark	Wind	Name		Nat	Born	Pos	Meet	Venue	Date
70.13		Mykyta	Nesterenko	UKR	15.4.91	1		Halle	24 May 08
68.48		Martin	Markovic	CRO	13.1.96	1	NC-j	Varazdin	28 Jun 15
68.02		Bartlomiej	Stój	POL	15.5.96	1	EJ	Eskilstuna	19 Jul 15
67.32		Margus	Hunt	EST	14.7.87	1	WJ	Beijing	16 Aug 06
66.88		Traves	Smikle	JAM	7.5.92	1		Kingston	31 Mar 11
66.81		Matthew	Denny	AUS	2.6.96	1		Brisbane	23 Nov 14
66.45		Gordon	Wolf	GER	17.1.90	1		Halle	23 May 09
65.88		Omar	El-Ghazaly	EGY	9.2.84	1		Cairo	7 Nov 03
65.71		Marin	Premeru	CRO	29.8.90	1		Split	31 May 09
65.66		Sven Martin	Skagestad	NOR	13.1.95	1		Oslo	12 Jun 14

HAMMER

Mark	Wind	Name		Nat	Born	Pos	Meet	Venue	Date
78.33		Olli-Pekka	Karjalainen	FIN	7.3.80	1	NC	Seinäjoki	5 Aug 99
78.14		Roland	Steuk	GDR	5.3.59	1	NC	Leipzig	30 Jun 78
78.00		Sergey	Dorozhon	UKR	17.2.64	1		Moskva	7 Aug 83
76.54		Valeriy	Gubkin	BLR	3.9.67	2		Minsk	27 Jun 86
76.42		Ruslan	Dikiy	TJK	18.1.72	1		Togliatti	7 Sep 91
76.37		Ashraf Amjad	El-Seify	QAT	20.2.95	1		Doha	10 Apr 13
75.52		Sergey	Kirmasov	RUS	25.3.70	1		Kharkov	4 Jun 89
75.42		Szymon	Ziolkowski	POL	1.7.76	1	EJ	Nyíregyhazá	30 Jul 95
75.24		Christoph	Sahner	FRG	23.9.63	1	vPOL-j	Göttingen	26 Jun 82

6kg Hammer

Mark	Wind	Name		Nat	Born	Pos	Meet	Venue	Date
85.57		Ashraf Amjad	El-Seify	QAT-Y	20.2.95	1	WJ	Barcelona	14 Jul 12
82.97		Javier	Cienfuegos	ESP	15.7.90	1		Madrid	17 Jun 09
82.84		Quentin	Bigot	FRA	1.12.92	1		Bondoufle	16 Oct 11
82.62		Yevgeniy	Aydamirov	RUS	11.5.87	1	NC-j	Tula	22 Jul 06
81.34		Krisztián	Pars	HUN	18.2.82	1		Szombathely	2 Sep 01
81.16		Özkan	Baltaci	TUR	13.2.94	1		Ankara	31 Jul 13
81.15		Ákos	Hudi	HUN	10.8.91	1		Veszprém	7 Jul 10
81.04		Werner	Smit	RSA	14.9.84	1		Bellville	29 Mar 03

JAVELIN

Mark	Wind	Name		Nat	Born	Pos	Meet	Venue	Date
84.69		Zigismunds	Sirmais	LAT	6.5.92	2		Bauska	22 Jun 11
84.58		Keshorn	Walcott	TTO	2.4.93	1	OG	London (OS)	11 Aug 12
83.87		Andreas	Thorkildsen	NOR	1.4.82	1		Fana	7 Jun 01
83.55		Aleksandr	Ivanov	RUS	25.5.82	2	NC	Tula	14 Jul 01
83.07		Robert	Oosthuizen	RSA	23.1.87	1	WJ	Beijing	19 Aug 06
82.52		Harri	Haatainen	FIN	5.1.78	4		Leppävirta	25 May 96
82.52		Till	Wöschler	GER	9.6.91	1	WJ	Moncton	23 Jul 10
81.95		Jakub	Vadlejch	CZE	10.10.90	1		Domazlice	26 Sep 09
81.80		Sergey	Voynov	UZB	26.2.77	1		Tashkent	6 Jun 96
81.04		Neeraj	Chopra	IND	24.12.97	Q	Univs Ch	Patiala	31 Dec 15

DECATHLON

Mark	Name		Nat	Born	Pos	Meet	Venue	Date
8397	Torsten	Voss	GDR	24.3.63	1	NC	Erfurt	7 Jul 82
	10.76 7.66 14.41		2.09 48.37			14.37	41.76 4.80 62.90	4:34.04
8257	Yordani	García	CUB	21.11.88	8	WCh	Osaka	1 Sep 07
	10.73/0.7 7.15/0.2 14.94		2.09 49.25			14.08/-0.2	42.91 4.70 68.74	4:55.42
8114	Michael	Kohnle	FRG	3.5.70	1	EJ	Varazdin	26 Aug 89
	10.95 7.09/0.1 15.27		2.02 49.91			14.40	45.82 4.90 60.82	4:49.43
8104	Valter	Külvet	EST	19.2.64	1		Viimsi	23 Aug 81
	10.7 7.26 13.86		2.09 48.5			14.8	47.92 4.50 60.34	4:37.8
8082	Daley	Thompson	GBR	30.7.58	1	ECp/s	Sittard	31 Jul 77
	10.70/0.8 7.54/0.7 13.84		2.01 47.31			15.26/2.0	41.70 4.70 54.48	4:30.4
8041		Qi Haifeng	CHN	7.8.83	1	AsiG	Busan	10 Oct 02
	11.09/0.2 7.22/0.0 13.05		2.06 49.09			14.54/0.0	43.16 4.80 61.04	4:35.17
8036	Christian	Schenk	GDR	9.2.65	5		Potsdam	21 Jul 84
	11.54 7.18 14.26		2.16 49.23			15.06	44.74 4.20 65.98	4:24.11
7992	Kevin	Mayer	FRA	10.2.92	8		Kladno	16 Jun 11
	11.23/0.1 7.34/0.2 12.44		2.01 48.66			14.74/-2.0	38.64 4.90 60.96	4:19.79
7938	Frank	Busemann	GER	26.2.75	1		Zeven	2 Oct 94
	10.68/1.6 7.37/1.1 13.08		2.03 50.41			14.34/-1.1	39.84 4.40 63.00	4:37.31

Mark	Wind	Name	Nat	Born	Pos	Meet	Venue	Date
7927		Jiri Sykora	CZE	20.1.95	2	ECp-1	Ribeira Brava	6 Jul 14
		10.85w/3.8 7.34/0.1 13.87 2.01 48.80 15.08/-1.3 44.84 4.60 59.91 4:52.61						

IAAF Junior specification with 99cm 110mh, 6kg shot, 1.75kg Discus

Mark	Wind	Name	Nat	Born	Pos	Meet	Venue	Date
8135		Jiri Sykora	CZE	20.1.95	1	WJ	Eugene	23 Jul 14
		10.92/0.5 7.35/2.0 15.50 1.94 49.00 14.23/-0.1 48.55 4.40 60.56 4:42.10						
8131		Arkadiy Vasilyev	RUS	19.1.87	1		Sochi	27 May 06
		11.28/-0.8 7.70/2.0 14.59 2.00 49.17 14.67/0.6 46.30 4.70 56.96 4:32.10						
8126		Andrey Kravchenko	BLR	4.1.86	1	WJ	Grosseto	15 Jul 04
		11.09/-0.5 7.46-0.2 14.51 2.16 48.98 14.55*/0.4 43.41 4.50 52.84 4:28.46						
8124		Kévin Mayer	FRA	10.2.92	1	EJ	Tallin	24 Jul 11
		11.40/-1.7 7.52/1.5 14.65 2.04 49.41 14.09/0.7 41.00 4.80 56.60 4:25.23						

10,000 METRES WALK

Mark	Name	Nat	Born	Pos	Meet	Venue	Date
38:46.4	Viktor Burayev	RUS	23.8.82	1	NC-j	Moskva	20 May 00
38:54.75	Ralf Kowalsky	GDR	22.3.62	1		Cottbus	24 Jun 81
39:08.23	Daisuke Matsunaga	JPN	24.3.95	1		Tama	14 Dec 13
39:28.63	Toshizaku Yamanishi	JPN	15.2.96	2		Osaka	13 Sep 15
39:28.45	Andrey Ruzavin	RUS	28.3.86	1	EJ	Kaunas	23 Jul 05
39:30.15	Yuga Yamashita	JPN	6.2.96	1		Tama	12 Dec 15
39:35.01	Stanislav Yemelyanov	RUS	23.10.90	1	WJ	Bydgoszcz	11 Jul 08
39:39.49	Ryosuke Kawagishi	JPN	15.6.96	2		Tama	12 Dec 15

20 KILOMETRES WALK

Mark	Name	Nat	Born	Pos	Meet	Venue	Date
1:18:06	Viktor Burayev	RUS	23.8.82	2	NC-w	Adler	4 Mar 01
1:18:07	Li Gaobo	CHN	23.7.89	4		Cixi	23 Apr 05
1:18:44	Chu Yafei	CHN	5.9.88	5		Yangzhou	22 Apr 06
1:18:52	Chen Ding	CHN	5.8.92	3		Taicang	22 Apr 11
1:18:57	Bai Xuejin	CHN	6.6.87	7		Yangzhou	22 Apr 06
1:19:02	Éder Sánchez	MEX	21.5.86	11		Cixi	23 Apr 05
1:19:14	Xu Xingde	CHN	12.6.84	3	NC	Yangzhou	12 Apr 03
1:19:34	Li Jianbo	CHN	14.11.86	16		Cixi	23 Apr 05

4 x 100 METRES RELAY

Mark	Nat	Team	Pos	Meet	Venue	Date
38.66	USA	Kimmons, Omole, I Williams, L Merritt	1	WJ	Grosseto	18 Jun 04
38.97	JAM	Tracey, Skeen, Minzie, Murphy	2	WJ	Barcelona	14 Jul 12
39.01	JPN	Oseto, Hashimoto, Cambridge, Kanamori	1h1	WJ	Barcelona	13 Jul 12
39.05	GBR	Edgar, Grant, Benjamin, Lewis-Francis	1	WJ	Santiago de Chile	22 Oct 00
39.17	TTO	Simpson, Burns, Holder, Brown	3	WJ	Kingston	21 Jul 02
39.25	FRG	Dobeleit, Klameth, Evers, Lübke	1	EJ	Schwechat	28 Aug 83
39.29	BRA	de Araújo, Monteiro, R dos Santos Jnr, Rocha	2h1	WJ	Barcelona	13 Jul 12
39.31	POL	Bijowski, Slowikowski, Zalewski, Jabłonski	3h1	WJ	Barcelona	13 Jul 12

4 x 400 METRES RELAY

Mark	Nat	Team	Pos	Meet	Venue	Date
3:01.09	USA	B Johnson, L Merritt, Craig, Clement	1	WJ	Grosseto	18 Jul 04
3:03.80	GBR	Grindley, Patrick, Winrow, Richardson	2	WJ	Plovdiv	12 Aug 90
3:04.06	JAM	S Clarke, Bolt, Myers, Gonzales	2	WJ	Kingston	21 Jul 02
3:04.11	JPN	Walsh, Yui, Kitagawa, Kato	2	WJ	Eugene	27 Jul 14
3:04.22	CUB	Cadogan, Mordoche, González, Hernández	2	WJ	Athína	20 Jul 86
3:04.50	RSA	le Roux, Gebhardt, Julius, van Zyl	2	WJ	Grosseto	18 Jul 04
3:04.58	GDR	Preusche, Löper, Trylus, Carlowitz	1	EJ	Utrecht	23 Aug 81
3:04.74	AUS	McFarlane, Batman, Thom, Vincent	1	WJ	Annecy	2 Aug 98

JUNIOR WOMEN'S ALL-TIME LISTS

100 METRES

Mark	Wind	Name	Nat	Born	Pos	Meet	Venue	Date
10.88	2.0	Marlies Oelsner	GDR	21.3.58	1	NC	Dresden	1 Jul 77
10.89	1.8	Katrin Krabbe	GDR	22.11.69	1rB		Berlin	20 Jul 88
10.98	2.0	Candace Hill	USA	11.2.99	1		Shoreline	20 Jun 15
10.99	0.9	Angela Tenorio	ECU	27.1.96	2	PAm	Toronto	22 Jul 15
11.03	1.7	Silke Gladisch	GDR	20.6.64	3	OD	Berlin	8 Jun 83
11.03	0.6	English Gardner	USA	22.4.92	1	Pac10	Tucson	14 May 11
11.04	1.4	Angela Williams	USA	30.1.80	1	NCAA	Boise	5 Jun 99
11.07	0.7	Bianca Knight	USA	2.1.89	4q2	NC/OT	Eugene	27 Jun 08
11.08	2.0	Brenda Morehead	USA	5.10.57	1	OT	Eugene	21 Jun 76
11.10	0.9	Kaylin Whitney	USA	9.3.98	1	NC-j	Eugene	5 Jul 14

Uncertain timing: 10.99 1.9 Natalya Bochina RUS 4.1.62 2 Leningrad 3 Jun 80

Wind assisted to 11.08

Mark	Wind	Name	Nat	Born	Pos	Meet	Venue	Date
10.96	3.7	Angela Williams	USA	30.1.80	1		Las Vegas	3 Apr 99
10.97	3.3	Gesine Walther	GDR	6.10.62	4	NC	Cottbus	16 Jul 80
11.01	5.4	Kaylin Whitney	USA	9.3.98	3	Athl	Lausanne	9 Jul 15
11.02	2.1	Nikole Mitchell	JAM	5.6.74	1	Mutual	Kingston	1 May 93

Mark	Wind	Name		Nat	Born	Pos	Meet	Venue	Date
11.03	2.2	Dina	Asher-Smith	GBR	4.12.95	1		Mannheim	5 Jul 14
11.04	5.6	Kelly-Ann	Baptiste	TTO	14.10.86	1rB	TexR	Austin	9 Apr 05
11.04	3.1	Desiree	Henry	GBR	26.8.95	1		Clermont	26 Apr 14
11.06	2.2	Brenda	Morehead	USA	5.10.57	1s2	OT	Eugene	21 Jun 76

200 METRES

Mark	Wind	Name		Nat	Born	Pos	Meet	Venue	Date
22.11A	-0.5	Allyson	Felix	USA	18.11.85	1		Ciudad de México	3 May 03
		22.18	0.8			2	OG	Athína	25 Aug 04
22.19	1.5	Natalya	Bochina	RUS	4.1.62	2	OG	Moskva	30 Jul 80
22.37	1.3	Sabine	Rieger	GDR	6.11.63	2	vURS	Cottbus	26 Jun 82
22.42	0.4	Gesine	Walther	GDR	6.10.62	1		Potsdam	29 Aug 81
22.43	0.8	Bianca	Knight	USA	2.1.89	1	Reebok	New York (RI)	31 May 08
22.43A	-0.7	Candace	Hill	USA	11.2.99	1	WY	Calí	19 Jul 15
22.45	0.5	Grit	Breuer	GER	16.2.72	2	ASV	Köln	8 Sep 91
22.45	0.9	Shaunae	Miller	BAH	15.4.94	2	NC	Freeport	22 Jun 13
22.47	0.4	Kaylin	Whitney	USA	9.3.98	4	NC	Eugene	28 Jun 15
22.51	2.0	Katrin	Krabbe	GDR	22.11.69	3		Berlin	13 Sep 88
22.52	1.2	Mary	Onyali	NGR	3.2.68	6	WCh	Roma	3 Sep 87
Indoors									
22.40		Bianca	Knight	USA	2.1.89	1r2	NCAA	Fayetteville	15 Mar 08
22.49		Sanya	Richards	USA	26.2.85	2rA	NCAA	Fayetteville	12 Mar 04
Wind assisted									
22.25	5.6	Bianca	Knight	USA	2.1.89	5	NC/OT	Eugene	6 Jul 08
22.34	2.3	Katrin	Krabbe	GDR	22.11.69	1	WJ	Sudbury	30 Jul 88
22.41	3.1	Shaunae	Miller	BAH	15.4.94	1		Athens, GA	13 Apr 13
22.41	2.6	Gina	Lückenkemper	GER	21.11.96	1	EJ	Eskilstuna	18 Jul 15
22.49	2.3	Brenda	Morehead	USA	5.10.57	1	OT	Eugene	24 Jun 76

400 METRES

Mark	Wind	Name		Nat	Born	Pos	Meet	Venue	Date
49.42		Grit	Breuer	GER	16.2.72	2	WCh	Tokyo	27 Aug 91
49.77		Christina	Brehmer	GDR	28.2.58	1		Dresden	9 May 76
49.89		Sanya	Richards	USA	26.2.85	2	NC/OT	Sacramento	17 Jul 04
50.01			Li Jing	CHN	14.2.80	1	NG	Shanghai	18 Oct 97
50.19		Marita	Koch	GDR	18.2.57	3	OD	Berlin	10 Jul 76
50.46		Kendall	Baisden	USA	5.3.95	2	Big 12	Lubbock	18 May 14
50.50		Ashley	Spencer	USA	8.6.93	1	WJ	Barcelona	13 Jul 12
50.59		Fatima	Yusuf	NGR	2.5.71	1	HGP	Budapest	5 Aug 90
50.70		Shaunae	Miller	BAH	15.4.94	2	NCAA	Eugene	7 Jun 13
50.74		Monique	Henderson	USA	18.2.83	1		Norwalk	3 Jun 00
50.78		Danijela	Grgic	CRO	28.9.88	1	WJ	Beijing	17 Aug 06

800 METRES

Mark	Wind	Name		Nat	Born	Pos	Meet	Venue	Date
1:54.01		Pamela	Jelimo	KEN	5.12.89	1	WK	Zürich	29 Aug 08
1:55.45		Caster	Semenya	RSA	7.1.91	1	WCh	Berlin	19 Aug 09
1:56.59		Francine	Niyonsaba	BDI	5.5.93	1	VD	Bruxelles	7 Sep 12
1:57.18			Wang Yuan	CHN	8.4.76	2h2	NG	Beijing	8 Sep 93
1:57.45		Hildegard	Ullrich	GDR	20.12.59	5	EC	Praha	31 Aug 78
1:57.62			Lang Yinglai	CHN	22.8.79	1	NG	Shanghai	22 Oct 97
1:57.63		Maria	Mutola	MOZ	27.10.72	4	WCh	Tokyo	26 Aug 91
1:57.74		Sahily	Diago	CUB	26.8.95	1	Barr	La Habana	25 Jul 14
1:57.77			Lu Yi	CHN	10.4.74	4	NG	Beijing	9 Sep 93
1:57.86		Katrin	Wühn	GDR	19.11.65	1		Celje	5 May 84
1:58.16			Lin Nuo	CHN	18.1.80	3	NG	Shanghai	22 Oct 97

1000 METRES

Mark	Wind	Name		Nat	Born	Pos	Meet	Venue	Date
2:35.4		Irina	Nikitina	RUS	16.6.61	5	Kuts	Podolsk	5 Aug 79
2:35.4		Katrin	Wühn	GDR	19.11.65	3		Potsdam	12 Jul 84

1500 METRES

Mark	Wind	Name		Nat	Born	Pos	Meet	Venue	Date
3:51.34			Lang Yinglai	CHN	22.8.79	2	NG	Shanghai	18 Oct 97
3:53.91			Yin Lili	CHN	11.11.79	3	NG	Shanghai	18 Oct 97
3:53.97			Lan Lixin	CHN	14.2.79	4	NG	Shanghai	18 Oct 97
3:54.52			Zhang Ling	CHN	13.4.80	5	NG	Shanghai	18 Oct 97
3:56.98		Faith	Kipyegon	KEN	10.1.94	2	DL	Doha	10 May 13
3:59.53		Dawit	Seyaum	ETH	27.7.96	1		Marrakech	8 Jun 14
3:59.60		Gelete	Burka	ETH	15.2.86	5	GP	Rieti	28 Aug 05
3:59.81			Wang Yuan	CHN	8.4.76	7	NG	Beijing	11 Sep 93
3:59.96		Zola	Budd	GBR	26.5.66	3	VD	Bruxelles	30 Aug 85
4:00.05			Lu Yi	CHN	10.4.74	8	NG	Beijing	11 Sep 93
4:00.65		Besu	Sado	ETH	12.1.96	7	Herc	Monaco	17 Jul 15
1 MILE:	4:17.57	Zola	Budd	GBR	26.5.66	3	WK	Zürich	21 Aug 85

Mark	Wind	Name		Nat	Born	Pos	Meet	Venue	Date

3000 METRES

Mark	Wind	Name		Nat	Born	Pos	Meet	Venue	Date
8:28.83		Zola	Budd	GBR	26.5.66	3	GG	Roma	7 Sep 85
8:35.89		Sally	Barsosio	KEN	21.3.78	2	Herc	Monaco	16 Aug 97
8:36.45			Ma Ningning	CHN	1.6.76	4	NC	Jinan	6 Jun 93
8:36.87		Alemitu	Haroye	ETH	9.5.95	14	VD	Bruxelles	5 Sep 14
8:38.61		Kalkedan	Gezahegn	ETH	8.5.91	5	WAF	Thessaloníki	13 Sep 09
8:38.97		Linet	Masai	KEN	5.12.89	5	GP	Rieti	9 Sep 07
8:39.13		Agnes	Tirop	KEN	23.10.95	3		Rieti	8 Sep 13
8:39.65		Buze	Diriba	ETH	9.2.94	3	Herc	Monaco	20 Jul 12
8:39.90		Gelete	Burka	ETH	15.2.86	3	SGP	Doha	13 May 05
8:40.08		Gabriela	Szabo	ROU	14.11.75	3	EC	Helsinki	10 Aug 94
8:40.28		Meseret	Defar	ETH	19.11.83	10	VD	Bruxelles	30 Aug 02

5000 METRES

Mark	Wind	Name		Nat	Born	Pos	Meet	Venue	Date
14:30.88		Tirunesh	Dibaba	ETH	1.10.85	2	Bisl	Bergen (Fana)	11 Jun 04
14:35.18		Sentayehu	Ejigu	ETH	21.6.85	4	Bisl	Bergen (Fana)	11 Jun 04
14:39.96			Yin Lili	CHN	11.11.79	4	NG	Shanghai	23 Oct 97
14:43.29		Emebet	Anteneh	ETH	13.1.92	5	Bisl	Oslo	9 Jun 11
14:45.33			Lan Lixin	CHN	14.2.79	2h2	NG	Shanghai	21 Oct 97
14:45.71			Song Liqing	CHN	20.1.80	3h2	NG	Shanghai	21 Oct 97
14:45.90			Jiang Bo	CHN	13.3.77	1		Nanjing	24 Oct 95
14:45.98		Pauline	Korikwiang	KEN	1.3.88	7	Bisl	Oslo	2 Jun 06
14:46.71		Sally	Barsosio	KEN	21.3.78	3	VD	Bruxelles	22 Aug 97
14:47.13		Mercy	Cherono	KEN	7.5.91	7	DL	Shanghai	23 May 10
14:47.14		Linet	Masai	KEN	5.12.89	4	FBK	Hengelo	24 May 08

10,000 METRES

Mark	Wind	Name		Nat	Born	Pos	Meet	Venue	Date
30:26.50		Linet	Masai	KEN	5.12.89	4	OG	Beijing	15 Aug 08
30:31.55			Xing Huina	CHN	25.2.84	7	WCh	Saint-Denis	23 Aug 03
30:39.41			Lan Lixin	CHN	14.2.79	2	NG	Shanghai	19 Oct 97
30:39.98			Yin Lili	CHN	11.11.79	3	NG	Shanghai	19 Oct 97
30:59.92		Merima	Hashim	ETH	.81	3	NA	Heusden-Zolder	5 Aug 00
31:06.20		Lucy	Wangui	KEN	24.3.84	1rA		Okayama	27 Sep 03
31:11.26			Song Liqing	CHN	20.1.80	7	NG	Shanghai	19 Oct 97
31:15.38		Sally	Barsosio	KEN	21.3.78	3	WCh	Stuttgart	21 Aug 93
31:16.50		Evelyne	Kimwei	KEN	25.8.87	1		Kobe	21 Oct 06
31:17.30			Zhang Yingying	CHN	4.1.90	1		Wuhan	2 Nov 07
31:20.38		Tigist	Kiros	ETH	8.6.92	4	GS	Ostrava	31 May 11

MARATHON

Mark	Wind	Name		Nat	Born	Pos	Meet	Venue	Date
2:20:59		Shure	Demise	ETH	21.1.96	4		Dubai	23 Jan 15
2:22:38			Zhang Yingying	CHN	4.1.90	1	NC	Xiamen	5 Jan 08
2:23:06		Merima	Mohamed	ETH	10.6.92	3		Toronto	26 Sep 10
2:23:37			Liu Min	CHN	29.11.83	1		Beijing	14 Oct 01
2:23:57			Zhu Xiaolin	CHN	20.4.84	4		Beijing	20 Oct 02
2:25:48			Jin Li	CHN	29.5.83	6		Beijing	14 Oct 01
2:26:34			Wei Yanan	CHN	6.12.81	1		Beijing	15 Oct 00
2:27:05			Chen Rong	CHN	18.5.88	1		Beijing	21 Oct 07

3000 METRES STEEPLECHASE

Mark	Wind	Name		Nat	Born	Pos	Meet	Venue	Date
9:20.37		Birtukan	Adamu	ETH	29.4.92	4	GGala	Roma	26 May 11
9:20.55		Ruth	Chebet	KEN/BRN	17.11.96	4	WK	Zürich	28 Aug 14
9:20.65		Tigist Getnet	Mekonen	BRN	7.7.97	8	Herc	Monaco	17 Jul 15
9:22.51		Almaz	Ayana	ETH	21.11.91	3	VD	Bruxelles	27 Aug 10
9:24.51		Ruth	Bisibori	KEN	2.1.88	1		Daegu	3 Oct 07
9:25.91		Rosefline	Chepngetich	KEN	17.6.97	3h2	WCh	Beijing	24 Aug 15
9:26.25			Liu Nian	CHN	26.4.88	1		Wuhan	2 Nov 07
9:29.52		Korahubish	Itaa	ETH	28.2.92	1		Huelva	10 Jun 09
9:30.70		Melissa	Rollison	AUS	13.4.83	1	GWG	Brisbane	4 Sep 01
9:31.35		Christine	Muyanga	KEN	21.3.91	1	WJ	Bydgoszcz	10 Jul 08

100 METRES HURDLES

Mark	Wind	Name		Nat	Born	Pos	Meet	Venue	Date
12.74	1.7	Dior	Hall	USA	2.1.96	3	NCAA	Eugene	13 Jun 15
12.84	1.5	Aliuska	López	CUB	29.8.69	2	WUG	Zagreb	16 Jul 87
12.87	2.0	Kendell	Williams	USA	14.6.95	1	NC-j	Eugene	6 Jul 14
12.88	1.5	Yelena	Ovcharova	UKR	17.6.76	2	ECp	Villeneuve d'Ascq	25 Jun 95
12.89	1.3	Anay	Tejeda	CUB	3.4.83	1		Padova	1 Sep 02
12.91	1.8	Kristina	Castlin	USA	7.7.88	1	NCAA-r	Gainesville	26 May 07
12.92	0.0		Sun Hongwei	CHN	24.11.79	6	NG	Shanghai	18 Oct 97
12.95	1.5	Candy	Young	USA	21.5.62	2	AAU	Walnut	16 Jun 79
12.95A	1.5	Cinnamon	Sheffield	USA	8.3.70	2	NCAA	Provo	3 Jun 89

Mark	Wind	Name		Nat	Born	Pos	Meet	Venue	Date
12.97	-1.1	Daeshon	Gordon	JAM	8.11.96	4	NC	Kingston	28 Jun 15
12.98	1.8	Queen	Harrison	USA	10.9.88	5	NCAA	Sacramento	8 Jun 07
Wind assisted									
12.81	3.4	Anay	Tejeda	CUB	3.4.83	1	WJ	Kingston	21 Jul 02
12.82	2.1	Kristina	Castlin	USA	7.7.88	1		College Park	21 Apr 07
12.90	3.0	Adrianna	Lamalle	FRA	27.9.82	1		Fort-de-France	28 Apr 01
12.95	2.4	Shermaine	Williams	JAM	4.2.90	1	NCAA II	San Angelo	23 May 09

400 METRES HURDLES

Mark	Wind	Name		Nat	Born	Pos	Meet	Venue	Date
54.40			Wang Xing	CHN	30.11.86	2	NG	Nanjing	21 Oct 05
54.58		Ristananna	Tracey	JAM	5.9.92	2	NC	Kingston	24 Jun 11
54.70		Lashinda	Demus	USA	10.3.83	1	WJ	Kingston	19 Jul 02
54.93			Li Rui	CHN	22.11.79	1	NG	Shanghai	22 Oct 97
55.07		Shamier	Little	USA	20.3.95	1	NCAA	Eugene	13 Jun 14
55.11		Kaliese	Spencer	JAM	6.4.87	1	WJ	Beijing	17 Aug 06
55.15			Huang Xiaoxiao	CHN	3.3.83	2	NG	Guangzhou	22 Nov 01
55.20		Lesley	Maxie	USA	4.1.67	2	TAC	San Jose	9 Jun 84
55.20A		Jana	Pittman	AUS	9.11.82	1		Pietersburg	18 Mar 00
55.22		Tiffany	Ross	USA	5.2.83	2	NCAA	Baton Rouge	31 May 02
55.26		Ionela	Tîrlea	ROU	9.2.76	1	Nik	Nice	12 Jul 95
Drugs disqualification:	54.54		Peng Yinghua ¶	CHN	21.2.79	(2)	NG	Shanghai	22 Oct 97

HIGH JUMP

Mark	Wind	Name		Nat	Born	Pos	Meet	Venue	Date
2.01		Olga	Turchak	UKR	5.3.67	2	GWG	Moskva	7 Jul 86
2.01		Heike	Balck	GDR	19.8.70	1	vURS-j	Karl-Marx-Stadt	18 Jun 89
2.00		Stefka	Kostadinova	BUL	25.3.65	1		Sofia	25 Aug 84
2.00		Alina	Astafei	ROU	7.6.69	1	WJ	Sudbury	29 Jul 88
1.98		Silvia	Costa	CUB	4.5.64	2	WUG	Edmonton	11 Jul 83
1.98		Yelena	Yelesina	RUS	5.4.70	1	Druzh	Nyiregyháza	13 Aug 88
1.97		Svetlana	Isaeva	BUL	18.3.67	2		Sofia	25 May 86
1.97i		Mariya	Kuchina	RUS	14.1.93	1		Trinec	26 Jan 11
1.96A		Charmaine	Gale	RSA	27.2.64	1	NC-j	Bloemfontein	4 Apr 81
1.96i		Desislava	Aleksandrova	BUL	27.10.75	2	EI	Paris (B)	12 Mar 94
1.96		Marina	Kuptsova	RUS	22.12.81	1	NC	Tula	26 Jul 00
1.96		Blanka	Vlasic	CRO	8.11.83	1	WJ	Kingston	20 Jul 02
1.96		Airine	Palsyte	LTU	13.7.92	2	WUG	Shenzhen	21 Aug 11
1.96		Eleanor	Patterson	AUS	22.5.96	1	N.Sch	Townsville	7 Dec 13
1.96		Vashti	Cunningham	USA	18.1.98	1	PAm-J	Edmonton	1 Aug 15

POLE VAULT

Mark	Wind	Name		Nat	Born	Pos	Meet	Venue	Date
4.64		Eliza	McCartney	NZL	11.12.96	1		Auckland	19 Dec 15
4.63i		Angelica	Bengtsson	SWE	8.7.93	2		Stockholm	22 Feb 11
		4.58				1		Sollentuna	5 Jul 12
4.61		Alyona	Lutkovskaya	RUS	15.3.96	1		Irkutsk	21 May 15
4.60i		Hanna	Shelekh	UKR	14.7.93	3		Donetsk	11 Feb 12
4.60i		Roberta	Bruni	ITA	8.3.94	1	NC	Ancona	17 Feb 13
4.60		Robeilys	Peinado	VEN	26.11.97	1		Barquisimeto	20 May 15
4.59		Nina	Kennedy	AUS	5.4.97	1		Perth	14 Feb 15
4.52i		Katie	Byres	GBR	11.9.93	2		Nevers	18 Feb 12
4.50		Valeriya	Volik	RUS	11.5.89	1		Krasnodar	4 Jun 08
4.50		Liz	Parnov	AUS	9.5.94	1		Perth	17 Feb 12
4.48i		Silke	Spiegelburg	GER	17.3.86	2		Münster	25 Aug 05

LONG JUMP

Mark	Wind	Name		Nat	Born	Pos	Meet	Venue	Date
7.14	1.1	Heike	Daute	GDR	16.12.64	1	PTS	Bratislava	4 Jun 83
7.03	1.3	Darya	Klishina	RUS	15.1.91	1	Znam	Zhukovskiy	26 Jun 10
7.00	-0.2	Birgit	Grosshennig	GDR	21.2.65	2		Berlin	9 Jun 84
6.94	-0.5	Magdalena	Khristova	BUL	25.2.77	2		Kalamáta	22 Jun 96
6.91	0.0	Anisoara	Cusmir	ROU	28.6.62	1		Bucuresti	23 May 81
6.90	1.4	Beverly	Kinch	GBR	14.1.64	*	WCh	Helsinki	14 Aug 83
6.88	0.6	Natalya	Shevchenko	RUS	28.12.66	2		Sochi	26 May 84
6.84		Larisa	Baluta	UKR	13.8.65	2		Krasnodar	6 Aug 83
6.83	1.7	Kate	Hall	USA	12.1.97	1		Greensboro NC	21 Jun 15
6.82	1.8	Fiona	May	GBR	12.12.69	*	WJ	Sudbury	30 Jul 88
6.81	1.6	Carol	Lewis	USA	8.8.63	1	TAC	Knoxville	20 Jun 82
6.81	1.4	Yelena	Davydova	KZK	16.11.67	1	NC-j	Krasnodar	17 Jul 85
Wind assisted to 6.82									
7.27	2.2	Heike	Daute	GDR	16.12.64	1	WCh	Helsinki	14 Aug 83
6.93	4.6	Beverly	Kinch	GBR	14.1.64	5	WCh	Helsinki	14 Aug 83
6.88	2.1	Fiona	May	GBR	12.12.69	1	WJ	Sudbury	30 Jul 88
6.84	2.8	Anu	Kaljurand	EST	16.4.69	2		Riga	4 Jun 88

TRIPLE JUMP

Mark	Wind	Name		Nat	Born	Pos	Meet	Venue	Date
14.62	1.0	Tereza	Marinova	BUL	5.9.77	1	WC	Sydney	25 Aug 96
14.57	0.2		Huang Qiuyan	CHN	25.1.80	1	NG	Shanghai	19 Oct 97
14.52	0.6	Anastasiya	Ilyina	RUS	16.1.82	q	WJ	Santiago de Chile	20 Oct 00
14.46	1.0		Peng Fengmei	CHN	2.7.79	1		Chengdu	18 Apr 98
14.43	0.6	Kaire	Leibak	EST	21.5.88	1	WJ	Beijing	17 Aug 06
14.38	-0.7		Xie Limei	CHN	27.6.86	1	AsiC	Inchon	1 Sep 05
14.37i	-		Ren Ruiping	CHN	1.2.76	3	WI	Barcelona	11 Mar 95
		14.36	0.0			1	NC	Beijing	1 Jun 94
14.36	0.0	Dailenys	Alcántara	CUB	10.8.91	3	Barr/NC	La Habana	29 May 09
14.35		Yana	Borodina	RUS	21.4.92	1J	Mosc Ch	Moskva	15 Jun 11
14.32	-0.1	Yelena	Lysak ¶	RUS	19.10.75	1		Voronezh	18 Jun 94
Wind assisted									
14.83	8.3		Ren Ruiping	CHN	1.2.76	1	NC	Taiyuan	21 May 95
14.55	3.7	Dailenis	Alcántara	CUB	10.8.91	1	Barr/NC	La Habana	21 Mar 10
14.43	2.7	Yelena	Lysak ¶	RUS	19.10.75	1	WJ	Lisboa	21 Jul 94

SHOT

Mark	Wind	Name		Nat	Born	Pos	Meet	Venue	Date
20.54		Astrid	Kumbernuss	GDR	5.2.70	1	vFIN-j	Orimattila	1 Jul 89
20.51i		Heidi	Krieger	GDR	20.7.65	2		Budapest	8 Feb 84
		20.24				5		Split	30 Apr 84
20.23		Ilke	Wyludda	GDR	28.3.69	1	NC-j	Karl-Marx-Stadt	16 Jul 88
20.12		Ilona	Schoknecht	GDR	24.9.56	2	NC	Erfurt	23 Aug 75
20.02			Cheng Xiaoyan	CHN	30.11.75	3	NC	Beijing	5 Jun 94
19.90		Stephanie	Storp	FRG	28.11.68	1		Hamburg	16 Aug 87
19.63			Wang Yawen	CHN	23.8.73	1		Shijiazhuang	25 Apr 92
19.57		Grit	Haupt	GDR	4.6.66	1		Gera	7 Jul 84
19.48		Ines	Wittich	GDR	14.11.69	5		Leipzig	29 Jul 87
19.46			Gong Lijiao	CHN	24.1.89	Q	OG	Beijing	16 Aug 08
19.42		Simone	Michel	GDR	18.12.60	3	vSU	Leipzig	23 Jun 79

DISCUS

Mark	Wind	Name		Nat	Born	Pos	Meet	Venue	Date
74.40		Ilke	Wyludda	GDR	28.3.69	2		Berlin	13 Sep 88
		75.36 unofficial meeting				2		Berlin	6 Sep 88
67.38		Irina	Meszynski	GDR	24.3.62	1		Berlin	14 Aug 81
67.00		Jana	Günther	GDR	7.1.68	6	NC	Potsdam	20 Aug 87
66.80		Svetla	Mitkova	BUL	17.6.64	1		Sofia	2 Aug 83
66.60		Astrid	Kumbernuss	GDR	5.2.70	1		Berlin	20 Jul 88
66.34		Franka	Dietzsch	GDR	22.1.68	2		Saint-Denis	11 Jun 87
66.30		Jana	Lauren	GDR	28.6.70	1	vURS-j	Karl-Marx-Stadt	18 Jun 89
66.08			Cao Qi	CHN	15.1.74	1	NG	Beijing	12 Sep 93
65.96		Grit	Haupt	GDR	4.6.66	3		Leipzig	13 Jul 84
65.22		Daniela	Costian	ROU	30.4.65	3		Nitra	26 Aug 84

HAMMER

Mark	Wind	Name		Nat	Born	Pos	Meet	Venue	Date
73.24			Zhang Wenxiu	CHN	22.3.86	1	NC	Changsha	24 Jun 05
71.71		Kamila	Skolimowska	POL	4.11.82	1	GPF	Melbourne	9 Sep 01
70.62		Alexandra	Tavernier	FRA	13.12.93	1	WJ	Barcelona	14 Jul 12
70.39		Mariya	Smolyachkova	BLR	10.2.85	1		Staiki	26 Jun 04
70.39		Réka	Gyurátz	HUN	31.5.96	1		Budapest	23 May 15
69.73		Natalya	Zolotukhina	UKR	4.1.85	1		Kyiv	24 Jul 04
69.63		Bianca	Perie	ROU	1.6.90	1	NC-j	Bucuresti	14 Aug 09
69.25		Audrey	Ciofani	FRA	13.3.96	1		Gagny	10 May 15
68.74		Arasay	Thondike	CUB	28.5.86	2	Barr	La Habana	2 May 05
68.50		Martina	Danisová	SVK	21.3.83	1		Kladno	16 Jun 01
68.49		Anna	Bulgakova	RUS	17.1.88	6		Sochi	26 May 07

JAVELIN

Mark	Wind	Name		Nat	Born	Pos	Meet	Venue	Date
63.86		Yulenmis	Aguilar	CUB	3.8.96	1	PAm-J	Edmonton	2 Aug 15
63.01		Vira	Rebryk	UKR	25.2.89	1	WJ	Bydgoszcz	10 Jul 08
62.93			Xue Juan	CHN	10.2.86	1	NG	Changsha	27 Oct 03
62.11		Maria	Andrejczyk	POL	9.3.96	1	Skol	Cetniewo	1 Aug 15
62.09			Zhang Li	CHN	17.1.89	1		Beijing	25 May 08
61.99			Wang Yaning	CHN	4.1.80	1	NC	Huizhou	14 Oct 99
61.96		Sofi	Flink	SWE	8.7.95	Q	WCh	Moskva	16 Aug 13
61.79		Nikolett	Szabó	HUN	3.3.80	1		Schwechat	23 May 99
61.61			Chang Chunfeng	CHN	4.5.88	1	NC-j	Chengdu	4 Jun 07
61.49			Liang Lili	CHN	16.11.83	1	NC	Benxi	1 Jun 02
Pre 1999 specification									
71.88		Antoaneta	Todorova	BUL	8.6.63	1	ECp	Zagreb	15 Aug 81
71.82		Ivonne	Leal	CUB	27.2.66	1	WUG	Kobe	30 Aug 85

Mark	Wind	Name		Nat	Born	Pos	Meet	Venue		Date
70.12		Karen	Forkel	GDR	24.9.70	1	EJ	Varazdin		26 Aug 89
68.94		Trine	Solberg	NOR	18.4.66	1	vURS	Oslo		16 Jul 85

HEPTATHLON

Mark		Name		Nat	Born	Pos	Meet	Venue		Date
6768w		Tatyana	Chernova	RUS	29.1.88	1		Arles		3 Jun 07
	13.04w/6.1	1.82	13.57	23.59w/5.2		6.61/1.2		53.43	2:15.05	
		6227				1	WJ	Beijing		19 Aug 06
	13.70/1.6	1.80	12.18	24.05/0.3		6.35/-0.4		50.51	2:25.49	
6542		Carolina	Klüft	SWE	2.2.83	1	EC	München		10 Aug 02
	13.33/-0.3	1.89	13.16	23.71/-0.3		6.36/1.1		47.61	2:17.99	
6465		Sibylle	Thiele	GDR	6.3.65	1	EJ	Schwechat		28 Aug 83
	13.49	1.90	14.63	24.07		6.65		36.22	2:18.36	
6436		Sabine	Braun	FRG	19.6.65	1	vBUL	Mannheim		9 Jun 84
	13.68	1.78	13.09	23.88		6.03		52.14	2:09.41	
6428		Svetla	Dimitrova ¶	BUL	27.1.70	1	NC	Sofia		18 Jun 89
	13.49/-0.7	1.77	13.98	23.59/-0.2		6.49/0.7		40.10	2:11.10	
6403		Emilia	Dimitrova	BUL	13.11.67	6	GWG	Moskva		7 Jul 86
	13.73	1.76	13.46	23.17		6.29		43.30	2:09.85	
6298		Nafissatou	Thiam	BEL	19.8.94	1	EJ	Rieti		19 Jul 13
	13.87/1.2	1.89	14.26	25.15/-0.6		6.37/0.1		46.94	2:24.89	
6276		Larisa	Nikitina	RUS	29.4.65	8	URS Ch	Kiyev		21 Jun 84
	13.87/1.6	1.86	14.04	25.26/-0.7		6.31/0.1		48.62	2:22.76	
6267		Katarina	Johnson-Thompson	GBR	9.1.93	15	OG	London (OS)		4 Aug 12
	13.48/0.9	1.89	11.32	23.73/-0.3		6.19/-0.4		38.37	2:10.76	
6231		Yorgelis	Rodríguez	CUB	25.1.95	1		La Habana		22 Feb 14
	14.01/0.0	1.84	14.21	24.93/0.0		6.03/0.0		47.58	2:17.93	
Drugs disqualification: 6534		Svetla	Dimitrova	BUL	27.1.70	(3)	ECp	Helmond		16 Jul 89
	13.30/1.0	1.84	14.35	23.33/-2.2		6.47/-1.4		39.20	2:13.56	

10 KILOMETRES WALK

Mark	Wind	Name		Nat	Born	Pos	Meet	Venue	Date
41:52		Tatyana	Mineyeva	RUS	10.8.90	1	NCp-j	Penza	5 Sep 09
41:55		Irina	Stankina	RUS	25.3.77	1	NC-wj	Adler	11 Feb 95
41:57			Gao Hongmiao	CHN	17.3.74	2	NG	Beijing	8 Sep 93
42:15+		Anisya	Kirdyapkina	RUS	23.10.89	1=	in 20k	Adler	23 Feb 08
42:29		Tatyana	Kalmykova	RUS	10.1.90	1	NC-wj	Adler	23 Feb 08
42:31		Irina	Yumanova	RUS	17.6.90	2	NC-wj	Adler	23 Feb 08
42:43.0	t	Svetlana	Vasilyeva	RUS	24.7.92	1	NC-wj	Sochi	27 Feb 11
42:44			Long Yuwen	CHN	1.8.75	3	NC	Shenzen	18 Feb 93
42:45			Li Yuxin	CHN	4.12.74	4		Shenzhen	18 Feb 93
42:45		Kseniya	Trifonova	RUS	7.5.90	2	NC-wj	Adler	28 Feb 09

20 KILOMETRES WALK

Mark	Name		Nat	Born	Pos	Meet	Venue	Date
1:25:30	Anisya	Kirdyapkina	RUS	23.10.89	2	NC-w	Adler	23 Feb 08
1:26:36	Tatyana	Kalmykova	RUS	10.1.90	1	NC	Saransk	8 Jun 08
1:27:01		Lu Xiuzhi	CHN	26.10.93	2		Taicang	30 Mar 12
1:27:16		Song Hongjuan	CHN	4.7.84	1	NC	Yangzhou	14 Apr 03
1:27:34		Jiang Jing	CHN	23.10.85	2	WCp	Naumburg	2 May 04
1:27:35	Natalya	Fedoskina	RUS	25.6.80	2	WCp	Mézidon-Canon	2 May 99
1:28:08	Anezka	Drahotová	CZE	22.7.95	3	EC	Zürich	14 Aug 14

4 X 100 METRES RELAY

Mark	Nat	Team	Pos	Meet	Venue	Date
43.29	USA (Blue)	Knight, Tarmoh, Olear, Mayo	1		Eugene	8 Aug 06
43.40	JAM	Simpson, Stewart, McLaughlin, Facey	1	WJ	Kingston	20 Jul 02
43.42	GER	Burghardt, Grompe, Pinto, Frese	1	EJ	Tallinn	24 Jul 11
43.44A	NGR	Utondu, Iheagwam, Onyali, Ogunkoya	1	AfrG	Nairobi	9 Aug 87
43.68	FRA	Vouaux, Jacques-Sebastien, Kamga, Banco	3	WJ	Grosseto	18 Jul 04
43.81	GBR	Miller, Asher-Smith, S Wilson, Henry	1	EJ	Rieti	21 Jul 13
43.87	URS	Lapshina, Doronina, Bulatova, Kovalyova	1	vGDR-j	Leningrad	20 Jun 87
43.98	BRA	Silva, Leoncio, Krasucki, Santos	2	PAm-J	São Paulo	7 Jul 07
44.04	CUB	Riquelme, Allen, López, Valdivia	2	WJ	Sudbury	31 Jul 88

4 X 400 METRES RELAY

Mark	Nat	Team	Pos	Meet	Venue	Date
3:27.60	USA	Anderson, Kidd, Smith, Hastings	1	WJ	Grosseto	18 Jul 04
3:28.39	GDR	Derr, Fabert, Wöhlk, Breuer	1	WJ	Sudbury	31 Jul 88
3:29.66	JAM	Stewart, Morgan, Walker, Hall	1	PennR	Philadelphia	28 Apr 01
3:30.03	RUS	Talko, Shapayeva, Soldatova, Kostetskaya	2	WJ	Grosseto	18 Jul 04
3:30.38	AUS	Scamps, R Poetschka, Hanigan, Andrews	1	WJ	Plovdiv	12 Aug 90
3:30.46	GBR	Wall, Spencer, James, Miller	2	WJ	Kingston	21 Jul 02
3:30.72	BUL	Kireva, Angelova, Rashova, Dimitrova	3	v2N	Sofia	24 Jul 83
3:30.84	NGR	Abugan, Odumosu, Eze, Adesanya	2	WJ	Beijing	20 Aug 06
3:31.57	ROU	Petrea, Florea, Tîrlea, Nedelcu	1	WJ	Seoul	20 Sep 92

MEN'S WORLD LISTS 2015

60 METRES INDOORS

Mark	Name		Nat	Born	Pos	Meet	Venue	Date
6.47	Kim	Collins	SKN	5.4.76	1	Pedros	Lódz	17 Feb
6.48		Collins			1	Winter	Moskva	1 Feb
6.48		Collins			1		Torun	3 Feb
6.50	Ryan	Bailey	USA	13.4.89	1h5		Seattle	13 Feb
6.50		Collins			1	ISTAF	Berlin	14 Feb
6.50		Collins			1	GP	Birmingham	21 Feb
6.51A	Akeem	Haynes	CAN	11.3.92	1		Flagstaff	31 Jan
6.51	Trell	Kimmons	USA	13.7.85	1	NB GP	Boston (Roxbury)	7 Feb
6.51	Richard	Kilty	GBR	2.9.89	1	EI	Praha (O2)	8 Mar
	(9/5)							
6.52	James	Dasaolu	GBR	5.9.87	2		Düsseldorf	29 Jan
6.52	Michael	Rodgers	USA	24.4.85	1h1	NB GP	Boston (Roxbury)	7 Feb
6.52	Asafa	Powell	JAM	23.11.82	2	NB GP	Boston (Roxbury)	7 Feb
6.52	John	Teeters	USA	19.5.93	1h3	Tyson	Fayetteville	13 Feb
6.52	Ronnie	Baker	USA	15.10.93	1	NCAA	Fayetteville	14 Mar
	(10)							
6.53	Joe	Morris	USA	4.10.89	1		Seattle	31 Jan
6.53	Chijindu	Ujah	GBR	5.3.94	1A2		London (LV)	1 Feb
6.53	Marvin	Bracy	USA	15.12.93	1	Mill	New York (Armory)	14 Feb
6.54	Clayton	Vaughn	USA	15.5.92	1		Houston	16 Jan
6.54	Trayvon	Bromell	USA	10.7.95	1		Lexington	24 Jan
6.54	Jalen	Miller	USA	17.6.95	1h2	NCAA	Fayetteville	13 Mar
6.55	Yunier	Pérez	CUB/TUR	16.2.85	4	Pedros	Lódz	17 Feb
6.56	Christian	Blum	GER	10.3.87	1rA		Chemnitz	7 Feb
6.56	Kendal	Williams	USA	23.9.95	1	ACC	Blacksburg	28 Feb
6.56	Tevin	Hester	USA	10.1.94	2	ACC	Blacksburg	28 Feb
	(20)							
6.56A	Odean	Skeen	JAM	28.8.94	1	JUCO	Albuquerque	7 Mar
6.57	Rondell	Sorrillo	TTO	21.1.86	2		Lexington	24 Jan
6.57	Christophe	Lemaitre	FRA	11.6.90	1		Lyon	31 Jan
6.57A	Eric	Cray	PHI	6.11.88	1h1		Albuquerque	14 Feb
6.57	Daniel	Bailey	ANT	9.9.86	2h1	ISTAF	Berlin	14 Feb
6.57	Justyn	Warner	CAN	28.6.87	4	GP	Birmingham	21 Feb
6.57	Senoj-Jay	Givans	JAM	30.12.93	2h2	NCAA	Fayetteville	13 Mar
6.58	Christian	Coleman	USA-J	6.3.96	1		Blacksburg	6 Feb
6.58	Sean	McLean	USA	23.3.92	7	NB GP	Boston (Roxbury)	7 Feb
6.58	Lucas	Jakubczyk	GER	28.4.85	2	NC	Karlsruhe	21 Feb
	(30)							
6.58	Adam	Harris	GUY	21.7.87	1		Metz	25 Feb
6.58	Marquesh	Woodson	USA	6.9.93	2	SEC	Lexington	28 Feb
6.59	Bryce	Robinson	USA	13.11.93	1h4	Tyson	Fayetteville	13 Feb
6.59	Antoine	Adams	SKN	31.8.88	5		Malmö	25 Feb
6.60A	Cameron	Burrell	USA	11.9.94	1		Albuquerque	24 Jan
6.60	Trentavis	Friday	USA	5.6.95	3		Lexington	24 Jan
6.60	Darrell	Wesh	USA	21.1.92	2		Blacksburg	6 Feb
6.60	Julian	Reus	GER	29.4.88	3		Chemnitz	7 Feb
6.60	Andre	De Grasse	CAN	10.11.94	1		Lincoln	7 Feb
6.60A	Anaso	Jobodwana	RSA	30.7.92	2r2		Albuquerque	14 Feb
	(40)							
6.60	Winston	Barnes	JAM	7.11.88	1		Athlone	18 Feb
6.60	Hugh	Graham	JAM	10.10.92	1h1	SEC	Lexington	27 Feb
6.60A	Ridge	Jones	USA	25.3.94	1	MWC	Albuquerque	28 Feb
6.60		Yang Yang	CHN	26.6.91	1rA		Shanghai	1 Mar
6.60	Desmond	Lawrence	USA	19.12.91	3h2	NC	Boston (Roxbury)	1 Mar
6.60		Xie Zhenye	CHN	17.8.93	1r1		Xianlin	8 Mar
6.60	Pascal	Mancini	SUI	18.4.89	2s2	EI	Praha (O2)	8 Mar
6.60		Zhang Peimeng	CHN	13.3.87	2		Beijing	15 Mar
6.61A	Cameron	Hudson	USA	5.3.94	2		Albuquerque	31 Jan
6.61	Keith	Ricks	USA	9.10.90	3=		Torun	3 Feb
	(50)							
6.61	Sean	Safo-Antwi	GBR	31.10.90	3=		Torun	3 Feb
6.61	Jaysuma	Saidy Ndure	NOR	1.1.84	1h1	Flanders	Gent	7 Feb
6.61	DionDre	Batson	USA	13.7.92	1	Tyson	Fayetteville	13 Feb
6.61	Catalin	Cîmpeanu	ROU	10.3.85	1h1	NC	Bucuresti	14 Feb
6.61		Su Bingtian	CHN	29.8.89	3	Mill	New York (Armory)	14 Feb
6.61	Beejay	Lee	USA	5.3.93	1r2		Seattle	28 Feb
6.61A	Chris	Lewis	USA	6.8.95	2	JUCO	Albuquerque	7 Mar

Mark	Wind	Name		Nat	Born	Pos	Meet	Venue	Date
6.61		Emmanuel	Biron	FRA	29.7.88	2s1	EI	Praha (O2)	8 Mar
6.61		Michael	Tumi	ITA	12.2.90	4	EI	Praha (O2)	8 Mar
6.62		Harry	Adams	USA	27.11.89	4		Düsseldorf	29 Jan
		(60)							
6.62		Daveon	Collins	USA	3.10.92	3		Seattle	31 Jan
6.62A		Kendrick	Smith	USA	19.5.92	3	JUCO	Albuquerque	7 Mar

Best at low altitude: 6.56 Haynes 5 NB GP Boston (Roxbury) 7 Feb

Outdoors: Jan 31, Kingston: 1. Nesta Carter JAM 6.53, 2. Jermaine Brown 6.58, 3. Julian Forte 6.59

100 METRES

Mark	Wind	Name		Nat	Born	Pos	Meet	Venue	Date
9.74	0.9	Justin	Gatlin	USA	10.2.82	1	DL	Doha	15 May
9.75	0.9		Gatlin			1	GGala	Roma	4 Jun
9.75	1.4		Gatlin			1	Athl	Lausanne	9 Jul
9.77	0.9		Gatlin			1s2	WCh	Beijing	23 Aug
9.78	-0.3		Gatlin			1	Herc	Monaco	17 Jul
9.79	-0.5	Usain	Bolt	JAM	21.8.86	1	WCh	Beijing	23 Aug
9.80	-0.5		Gatlin			2	WCh	Beijing	23 Aug
9.81	1.3	Asafa	Powell	JAM	23.11.82	1	DL	Saint-Denis	4 Jul
9.84	1.8		Powell			1		Kingston	9 May
9.84	1.3	Trayvon	Bromell	USA	10.7.95	1h4	NC	Eugene	25 Jun
9.84	0.9		Powell			1	NC	Kingston	26 Jun
9.86	1.1	Keston	Bledman	TTO	8.3.88	1	NC	Port of Spain	27 Jun
9.86	1.3	Jimmy	Vicaut	FRA	27.2.92	2	DL	Saint-Denis	4 Jul
9.86	0.9	Michael	Rodgers	USA	24.4.85	2s2	WCh	Beijing	23 Aug
9.87	0.0	Tyson	Gay	USA	9.8.82	1	NC	Eugene	26 Jun
9.87	0.0		Powell			1		Luzern	14 Jul
9.87	0.0		Powell			1		Bellinzona	21 Jul
9.87	-0.8		Bolt			1	DL	London (OS)	24 Jul
9.87	-1.2		Bolt			1h2	DL	London (OS)	24 Jul
9.88	1.5		Gay			1	Pre	Eugene	30 May
9.88	1.4		Rodgers			1		Madrid	11 Jul
9.90	1.5		Rodgers			2	Pre	Eugene	30 May
9.90	1.7		Bromell			1s1	NCAA	Eugene	10 Jun
9.90	-0.8		Rodgers			2	DL	London (OS)	24 Jul
9.91	1.8	Femi Seun	Ogunode	QAT	15.5.91	1	AsiC	Wuhan	4 Jun
9.91	0.9	Nickel	Ashmeade (10)	JAM	7.4.90	2	NC	Kingston	26 Jun
9.91	0.5		Bromell			1h4	WCh	Beijing	22 Aug
9.92	1.7		Rodgers			1h2	NC	Eugene	25 Jun
9.92	1.4		Powell			2	Athl	Lausanne	9 Jul
9.92	1.4		Gay			3	Athl	Lausanne	9 Jul
9.92	0.7		Vicaut			1	NC	Villeneuve d'Ascq	11 Jul
9.92	-1.2		Rodgers			2h2	DL	London (OS)	24 Jul
9.92	-0.8	Kemar	Bailey-Cole	JAM	10.1.92	3	DL	London (OS)	24 Jul
9.92	0.3		Vicaut			1h5	WCh	Beijing	22 Aug
9.92	-0.5		Bromell			3=	WCh	Beijing	23 Aug
9.92	-0.5	Andre	De Grasse	CAN	10.11.94	3=	WCh	Beijing	23 Aug
		(36/12)							
9.93	1.8	Ryan	Bailey	USA	13.4.89	2		Kingston	9 May
9.93	1.7	Clayton	Vaughn	USA	15.5.92	1		Mobile	10 May
9.93	2.0	Marvin	Bracy	USA	15.12.93	1	DL	Bimingham	7 Jun
9.94	1.7	Diondre	Batson	USA	13.7.92	2h2	NC	Eugene	25 Jun
9.94	1.4	Andrew	Fisher	JAM	15.12.91	2		Madrid	11 Jul
9.96	1.3	Quentin	Butler	USA	18.9.92	2h4	NC	Eugene	25 Jun
9.96	-0.8	Chijindu	Ujah	GBR	5.3.94	4	DL	London (OS)	24 Jul
9.97	2.0	Adam	Gemili	GBR	6.10.93	2	DL	Birmingham	7 Jun
		(20)							
9.97	0.8	Henricho	Bruintjies	RSA	16.7.93	1h1		La Chaux-de-Fonds	5 Jul
9.97	0.0	Akani	Simbine	RSA	21.9.93	1	WUG	Gwangju	9 Jul
9.98	1.8	Nesta	Carter	JAM	10.11.85	3		Kingston	9 May
9.98	1.8	Kim	Collins	SKN	5.4.76	1	NC	Basseterre	13 Jun
9.99	1.6	Bryce	Robinson	USA	13.11.93	1		Storrs, CT	17 May
9.99	1.5		Su Bingtian	CHN	29.8.89	3	Pre	Eugene	30 May
9.99	1.7	Beejay	Lee	USA	5.3.93	3h2	NC	Eugene	25 Jun
10.00	0.0	Isiah	Young	USA	5.1.90	4	NC	Eugene	26 Jun
10.01	1.7	Sean	McLean	USA	23.3.92	4h2	NC	Eugene	25 Jun
10.01	-0.2	Jak Ali	Harvey	TUR	5.4.89	1		Ankara	4 Sep
		(30)							
10.02	1.7	Charles	Silmon	USA	4.7.91	5h2	NC	Eugene	25 Jun
10.02	-0.3	Ramon	Gittens	BAR	20.7.87	2h3	WCh	Beijing	22 Aug

MEN 2015

Mark	Wind	Name		Nat	Born	Pos	Meet	Venue	Date
10.03	0.9	Senoj-Jay	Givans	JAM	30.12.93	1s2	NCAA	Eugene	10 Jun
10.03	1.8	Antoine	Adams	SKN	31.8.88	2	NC	Basseterre	13 Jun
10.04	1.0	Richard	Thompson	TTO	7.6.85	1		Baton Rouge	18 Apr
10.04	1.5	Calesio	Newman	USA	20.8.86	1		Greensboro, NC	17 May
10.04	1.7	Jarrion	Lawson	USA	6.5.94	3s1	NCAA	Eugene	10 Jun
10.04	1.4	Kolby	Listenbee	USA	25.1.94	1s3	NCAA	Eugene	10 Jun
10.04	1.4	Ameer	Webb	USA	19.3.91	3		Madrid	11 Jul
10.04	-2.1	?Ben Youssef	Meité	CIV	11.11.86	1	AfG	Brazzaville	14 Sep
		(40)							
10.05	1.8	Ronnie	Baker	USA	15.10.93	1h1	Big 12	Ames	16 May
10.05	1.8	Tevin	Hester	USA	10.1.94	1h5	NCAA-E	Jacksonville	28 May
10.05	2.0	Richard	Kilty	GBR	2.9.89	5	DL	Birmingham	7 Jun
10.06	1.9	Julian	Forte	JAM	1.7.93	3h1	DL	Birmingham	7 Jun
10.06	1.6	Levi	Cadogan	BAR	8.11.95	1	NC	Bridgetown	20 Jun
10.06	1.0	Jason	Livermore	JAM	25.4.88	3h3	NC	Kingston	25 Jun
10.06	-0.2	Churandy	Martina	NED	3.7.84	3h7	WCh	Beijing	22 Aug
10.06	0.3	Egweru	Ogho-Oghene	NGR	26.11.88	1s2	AfG	Brazzaville	13 Sep
10.07	1.9	John	Teeters	USA	19.5.93	2h2	Big 12	Ames	16 May
10.07	1.4	Kendal	Williams	USA	23.9.95	2s3	NCAA	Eugene	10 Jun
		(50)							
10.07	0.0	Remontay	McClain	USA	21.9.92	5	NC	Eugene	26 Jun
10.07	1.4	Kemar	Hyman	CAY	11.10.89	4		Madrid	11 Jul
10.07	0.7	Christophe	Lemaitre	FRA	11.6.90	2	NC	Villeneuve d'Ascq	11 Jul
10.07	-0.8	Trell	Kimmons	USA	13.7.85	6	DL	London (OS)	24 Jul
10.07A	1.9	Sheldon	Mitchell	JAM	19.7.90	1h2	NACAC	San José, CRC	7 Aug
10.08	0.7	Harry	Adams	USA	27.11.89	1		Coral Gables	11 Apr
10.09	-0.1	Hua Wilfried	Koffi	CIV	24.9.89	1		Kawasaki	10 May
10.09	-0.1	Kei	Takase	JPN	25.11.88	2		Kawasaki	10 May
10.09	1.1	Gavin	Smellie	CAN	26.6.86	1h1	NC	Edmonton	3 Jul
10.09	1.8	Julian	Reus	GER	29.4.88	1h1	NC	Nürnberg	25 Jul
		(60)							
10.09	0.3	Yoshihide	Kiryu	JPN	15.12.95	1		Tottori	18 Oct
10.10	0.7	Shavez	Hart	BAH	6.9.92	2		Waco	18 Apr
10.10	1.7	Jaylen	Bacon	USA-J	5.8.96	2		Mobile	10 May
10.10	1.4	Aaron	Brown	CAN	27.5.92	1h3	NC	Edmonton	3 Jul
10.10	0.4	Hasan	Taftian	IRI	4.5.93	1		Almaty	25 Jul
10.11	0.3	Kemarley	Brown	JAM	20.7.92	1		Kingston	11 Apr
10.11	1.4	Mosito	Lehata	LES	8.4.89	1		Réduit	12 Apr
10.11	1.8	Daniel	Bailey	ANT	9.9.86	6		Kingston	9 May
10.11	1.5	Maurice	Eaddy	USA	1.6.95	2		Greensboro, NC	17 May
10.11	0.8	Jacques	Riparelli	ITA	27.3.83	3h1		La Chaux-de-Fonds	5 Jul
		(70)							
10.12	1.0	Justin	Walker	USA	30.11.90	2		Baton Rouge	18 Apr
10.12	1.9	Ramil	Guliyev	TUR	29.5.90	1		Isparta	9 May
10.12	0.4	Jalen	Miller	USA	17.6.95	2	SEC	Starkville	16 May
10.12	1.4	Aaron	Ernest	USA	8.11.93	4s3	NCAA	Eugene	10 Jun
10.12	1.4	Yohan	Blake	JAM	26.12.89	1		Dublin (S)	24 Ju
10.12	-1.2	James	Dasaolu	GBR	5.9.87	5h2	DL	London (OS)	24 Ju
10.12	0.4	Reza	Ghasemi	IRI	24.7.87	2		Almaty	25 Ju
10.13	1.5	Taffawee	Johnson	JAM	10.3.88	3		Greensboro, NC	17 May
10.13	1.9	Sven	Knipphals	GER	20.9.85	1h4		Regensburg	6 Jun
10.13	1.5	Anaso	Jobodwana	RSA	30.7.92	2	Odlozil	Praha	8 Jun
		(80)							
10.13	-0.3		Zhang Peimeng	CHN	13.3.87	5h3	WCh	Beijing	22 Aug
10.14	0.8	Tyquendo	Tracey	JAM	10.6.93	3h2	NC	Kingston	25 Jun
10.14	1.0	Michael	Frater	JAM	6.10.82	4h3	NC	Kingston	25 Jun
10.14	2.0	Noah	Lyles	USA-J	18.7.97	1	NC-j	Eugene	26 Jun
10.14	1.9	Yancarlos	Martínez	DOM	8.7.92	4h1	PAm	Toronto	21 Ju
10.15	1.9	Jamol	James	TTO	16.7.92	1		Tempe	2 May
10.15	1.5	Keith	Ricks	USA	9.10.90	4		Greensboro, NC	17 May
10.15	1.6	Zharnel	Hughes	AIA/GBR	13.7.95	1		Kingston	30 May
10.15	1.8	Brijesh "BJ"	Lawrence	SKN	27.12.89	3	NC	Basseterre	13 Jun
10.15	1.1	Marcus	Duncan	TTO	4.12.86	2	NC	Port of Spain	27 Jun
		(90)							
10.15	1.1	Akeem	Haynes	CAN	3.11.92	2h1	NC	Edmonton	3 Ju
10.16	1.5	Darrell	Wesh	HAI	21.1.92	5		Greensboro, NC	17 May
10.16	1.7	Tremayne	Acy	USA	21.1.95	4s1	NCAA	Eugene	10 Jun
10.16	1.1	Rondell	Sorrillo	TTO	21.1.86	3	NC	Port of Spain	27 Jun
10.16	1.5	Justyn	Warner	CAN	28.6.87	3	NC	Edmonton	3 Ju
10.16	0.8	Aziz	Ouhadi	MAR	24.7.84	4h1		La Chaux-de-Fonds	5 Ju
10.16	1.8		Kim Kuk-young	KOR	19.4.91	2s1	WUG	Gwangju	9 Ju

Mark	Wind	Name		Nat	Born	Pos	Meet	Venue	Date
10.16	1.4	Yazaldes	Nascimento	POR	17.4.86	6		Madrid	11 Jul
10.16	1.6	Harry	Aikines-Aryeetey	GBR	29.8.88	1A1		Loughborough	18 Jul
10.16	1.6	Sean (100)	Safo-Antwi	GBR	31.10.90	2A1		Loughborough	18 Jul
10.16	1.4	Rasheed	Dwyer	JAM	29.1.89	4		Rieti	13 Sep
10.16	1.7	Barakat	Al-Harthi	OMA	15.6.88	1	WMilG	Mungyeong	6 Oct

Mark	Wind	Name		Nat	Born	Date
10.17	0.7	Marc	Burns	TTO	7.1.83	18 Apr
10.17	1.5	Gerald	Phiri	ZAM	6.10.88	24 Apr
10.17	1.3	Walter	Dix	USA	31.1.86	24 Apr
10.17	1.0	Roberto	Skyers	CUB	12.11.91	26 May
10.17	1.8	Jason	Rogers	SKN	31.8.91	13 Jun
10.17	0.8	Alex	Wilson	SUI	19.9.90	5 Jul
10.17	-0.3	Emmanuel	Biron	FRA	29.7.88	17 Jul
10.17	0.4	Reynier	Mena	CUB-J	21.11.96	31 Jul
10.18	0.7	Michael	Mathieu	BAH	24.6.83	11 Apr
10.18A	1.6	Stanly	del Carmen	DOM	20.9.95	9 May
10.18	0.4	Dedric	Dukes	USA	2.4.92	16 May
10.18	0.9	Markesh	Woodson	USA	6.9.93	10 Jun
10.18	1.1	Ryan	Clark	USA-J	14.9.96	13 Jun
10.18	0.2	Jevaughn	Minzie	JAM	20.7.95	25 Jun
10.18	0.2	Dexter	Lee	JAM	18.1.91	13 Jun
10.18	2.0	Christian	Coleman	USA-J	6.3.96	26 Jun
10.18A	1.9	Sydney	Siame	ZAM-J	7.10.97	27 Jun
10.19	1.1	Joshua	Clarke	AUS	19.5.95	28 Mar
10.19	0.4	Takuya	Nagata	JPN	14.6.94	14 Jun
10.19	1.6	Seye	Ogunlewe	NGR	30.8.91	18 Jul
10.19	1.5	Joe	Morris	USA	4.10.89	23 Jul
10.19	-0.4	James	Ellington	GBR	6.9.85	1 Aug
10.20	1.0	Hanoj	Carter	USA	26.6.94	18 Apr
10.20A	1.6	Yoandry	Andujar	DOM	5.7.90	9 May
10.20	1.7	Jaysuma	Saidy Ndure	NOR	1.7.84	11 Jul
10.20	1.5	Tlotliso Gift	Leotlela	RSA-Y	12.5.98	7 Sep
10.21A	-0.5	Odean	Skeen	JAM	28.8.94	21 Mar
10.21	1.5	Mario	Burke	BAR-J	18.3.97	4 Apr
10.21	2.0	Aleksandr	Brednev	RUS	4.2.88	6 Jun
10.21	1.1	Emmanuel	Callender	TTO	10.5.84	27 Jun
10.22A		Diego	Palomeque	COL	5.12.93	9 May
10.22	-0.1	Ratu	Tabakaucoro	FIJ	4.9.92	10 May
10.22	-0.1	Vitor Hugo	dos Santos	BRA-J	1.2.96	14 May
10.22	0.0	Winston	Barnes	JAM	7.11.88	16 May
10.22	1.8	Chevaughn	Walsh	ANT	29.12.87	6 Jun
10.22	1.2	Sulayman	Bah	SWE	21.1.86	6 Jun
10.22	1.4	Carl	Horsley	USA	17.6.92	10 Jun
10.22	0.3	Andrew	Robertson	GBR	17.12.90	19 Jun
10.22	1.4	Dontae	Richards-Kwok	CAN	1.3.89	3 Jul
10.23	0.5	Michael	O'Hara	JAM-J	29.9.96	14 Mar
10.23	1.8	Jonathan	Nmaju	NGR	9.1.93	9 May
10.23	1.3	Kyree	King	USA	9.7.94	15 May
10.23	-0.3	Nicholas	Imhoaperamhe	NGR	18.4.92	11 Jun
10.23	1.0	Bernardo	Brady	JAM	14.6.91	25 Jun
10.23	1.5	Benjamin	Williams	CAN	15.5.92	3 Jul
10.23A	0.8	Mike	Nyangau	KEN	28.8.94	11 Jul
10.23	0.5	Yuniel	Pérez	CUB	16.2.85	1 Aug
10.23A	1.9	Julius	Morris	MNT	14.4.94	7 Aug
10.23	-0.4	Ashton	Eaton	USA	21.1.88	28 Aug
10.24	0.4	Albert	Huntley	USA	3.1.90	11 Apr
10.24	1.7	Brandon	Carnes	USA	-.3.95	2 May
10.24A	0.5	Roscoe	Engel	RSA	6.3.89	8 May
10.24	1.4	Justin	Jenkins	USA	18.2.93	10 May
10.24		John	Lundy	USA	15.3.92	17 May
10.24	1.3	Marvin	René	FRA	11.4.95	20 Jun
10.24	1.1	Mikel	Thomas	TTO	23.11.87	27 Jun
10.24	1.8		Yang Yang	CHN	26.6.91	9 Jul
10.24	-0.1	Kenji	Fujimitsu	JPN	1.5.86	21 Jul
10.24	1.9	Ojie	Edoburun	GBR-J	2.6.96	8 Aug
10.25	-1.6	Demek	Kemp	USA-J	26.4.96	1 Apr
10.25	1.0	Cejhae	Greene	ANT	6.10.95	2 May
10.25	0.2	José Carlos	Moreira	BRA	28.9.83	14 May
10.25	1.5	Blake	Smith	USA	28.5.93	15 May
10.25	1.8		Xie Zhenye	CHN	17.8.93	4 Jun
10.25	0.0	Eric	Cray	PHI	6.11.88	9 Jun
10.25	0.2	Oshane	Bailey	JAM	9.8.89	13 Jun
10.26	1.5	Adolphus	Nevers	JAM	19.3.90	14 Mar
10.26	1.0	Trevorvano	Mackey	BAH	5.1.92	30 Apr
10.26	0.9	Mario	Forsythe	JAM	30.10.85	16 May
10.26	1.0	James	Harrington	USA	3.7.93	16 May
10.26	1.0	Yaniel	Carrero	CUB	17.8.95	26 May
10.26	0.6	Peter	Emelieze	NGR	19.4.88	8 Aug
10.27	1.6	Kieran	Showler-Davis	GBR	14.11.91	18 Apr
10.27	0.9	Gideon	Trotter	RSA	3.3.92	8 May
10.27	1.4	Bruno	de Barros	BRA	7.1.87	14 May
10.27	1.8	Devin	Duvernay	USA-J	.97	16 May
10.27	-0.9	Likoúrgos-Stéfanos	Tsákonas	GRE	8.3.90	29 May
10.27	1.8	Meshal Khalifa	Al-Mutairi	KUW-J	16.3.97	4 Jun
10.27	0.9	Denis	Dimitrov	BUL	10.2.94	10 Jun
10.27	1.0	Catalin	Câmpeanu	ROU	10.3.85	13 Jun
10.27	1.1	Andrew	Ford-Azonwanna	CAN	29.11.95	3 Jul
10.27	1.0		Jung Jin-su	AUS	16.11.93	9 Jul
10.27	0.8	Maurice	Mitchell	USA	22.12.89	14 Jul
10.27	1.8	Robert	Hering	GER	14.6.90	25 Jul
10.27A	1.7	Alistar	Clarke	SKN	3.3.90	7 Aug
10.27	1.2	Shuhei	Tada	JPN-J	24.6.96	29 Aug
10.27	-1.0	Aaron	Stubbs	AUS	13.7.90	28 Nov
10.28	1.7	Justin	Scruggs	USA	18.5.94	10 Apr
10.28	1.0	Kendrick	Smith	USA	8.8.95	18 Apr
10.28	1.0	Aldrich	Bailey	USA	6.2.94	2 May
10.28	0.6	Jeff	Henderson	USA	19.2.89	2 May
10.28	0.9	Brendon	Rodney	CAN	9.4.92	3 May
10.28	0.5	Jeffrey	Vanan	SUR	21.12.92	16 May
10.28	0.1	Miguel	Francis	ANT	28.2.95	30 May
10.28	1.2	Obinna	Metu	NGR	12.7.88	7 Jun
10.28	0.3	Tom	Gamble	AUS	25.11.91	9 Jul
10.28A	-0.4	Abdul Hakim	Sani Brown	JPN-Y	6.3.99	15 Jul
10.28	1.4	Damian	Warner (200)	CAN	4.11.89	22 Jul
10.28	1.3	Kazuma	Oseto	JPN	5.8.94	26 Jul
10.28	0.6	Hensley	Paulina	NED	26.6.93	8 Aug
10.28	2.0	Wataru	Inuzuka	JPN-J	8.7.97	2 Oct

Wind assisted

Mark	Wind	Name		Nat	Born	Pos	Meet	Venue	Date
9.75	2.7	Andre	De Grasse	CAN	10.11.94	1	NCAA	Eugene	12 Jun
9.76	3.7	Trayvon	Bromell	USA	10.7.95	1s1	NC	Eugene	26 Jun
9.79	3.0	Tyson	Gay	USA	9.8.82	1s2	NC	Eugene	26 Jun
9.82	3.0	Isiah	Young	USA	5.1.90	1		Clermont	16 May
9.82	4.9	Remontay	McClain	USA	21.9.92	1h3	NC	Eugene	25 Jun
9.83	2.1		Gatlin			1h6	WCh	Beijing	22 Aug
9.85	2.1		Young			1h1	NC	Eugene	25 Jun
9.85	4.9		Gay			2h3	NC	Eugene	25 Jun
9.85A	3.0	Kemar	Hyman	CAY	11.10.89	1s2	NACAC	San José, CRC	7 Aug
9.86	3.7	Diondre	Batson	USA	13.7.92	2s1	NC	Eugene	26 Jun
9.86	3.0		Rodgers			2s2	NC	Eugene	26 Jun
9.87	3.3	Yoshihide	Kiryu	JPN	15.12.95	1r1	TexR	Austin	28 Mar
9.87	4.0		De Grasse			1	MSR	Walnut	18 Apr
9.87	2.1	Tevin	Hester	USA	10.1.94	1	ACC	Tallahassee	16 May
9.88	2.7		Bromell			2	NCAA	Eugene	12 Jun
9.89	3.3	Ryan (16/11)	Bailey	USA	13.4.89	2r1	TexR	Austin	28 Mar
9.90	2.7	Jarrion	Lawson	USA	6.5.94	3	NCAA	Eugene	12 Jun
9.91	3.3	Charles	Silmon	USA	4.7.91	3r1	TexR	Austin	28 Mar

Mark	Wind	Name		Nat	Born	Pos	Meet	Venue	Date
9.94	3.4	Kim	Collins	SKN	5.4.76	1h1	NC	Basseterre	13 Jun
9.94	2.1	Ronnie	Baker	USA	15.10.93	3h1	NC	Eugene	25 Jun
9.94	3.7	Beejay	Lee	USA	5.3.93	4s1	NC	Eugene	26 Jun
9.95	2.6	John	Teeters	USA	19.5.93	1h4	NCAA-W	Austin	28 May
9.96	3.3	Mark	Jelks	NGR	10.4.84	4r1	TexR	Austin	28 Mar
9.96	3.7	Bryce	Robinson	USA	13.11.93	1		Lubbock	30 Apr
9.97	2.7	Senoj-Jay	Givans	JAM	30.12.93	4	NCAA	Eugene	12 Jun
9.98	2.1	Kendal	Williams	USA	23.9.95	2	ACC	Tallahassee	16 May
9.98	2.9	Joe	Morris	USA	4.10.89	1		Joensuu	23 Jul
9.98A	2.7	Jason	Rogers	SKN	31.8.91	2s2	NACAC	San José, CRC	7 Aug
9.99	3.7	Adam	Harris	GUY	21.7.87	1		Miramar	14 Jun
10.00	3.4	Gerald	Phiri	ZAM	6.10.88	2r1		Clermont	18 Apr
10.01	3.0	Trell	Kimmons	USA	13.7.85	5s2	NC	Eugene	26 Jun
10.01A	2.7	Ramon	Gittens	BAR	20.7.87	1s1	NACAC	San José, CRC	7 Aug
10.01A	2.7	Jason	Livermore	JAM	25.4.88	4=s2	NACAC	San José, CRC	7 Aug
10.01A	3.0	Levi	Cadogan	BAR	8.11.95	4=s2	NACAC	San José, CRC	7 Aug
10.03	2.6	Carl	Horsley	USA	17.6.92	2h4	NCAA-W	Austin	28 May
10.03	2.7	Kolby	Listenbee	USA	25.1.94	7	NCAA	Eugene	12 Jun
10.03	2.1	Aaron	Brown	CAN	27.5.92	2h6	WCh	Beijing	22 Aug
10.05	4.1	Barakat	Al-Harthi	OMA	15.6.88	2	Arab C	Manama	25 Apr
10.05	3.9	Christian	Blum	GER	10.3.87	1A		Clermont	16 May
10.05	3.0	Gavin	Smellie	CAN	26.6.86	2		Clermont	16 May
10.06		Meshal Khalifa	Al-Mutairi	KUW-J	16.3.97	1h1	Arab C	Manama	25 Apr
10.06	3.0	Akeem	Haynes	CAN	3.11.92	3		Clermont	16 May
10.06	3.0	Justin	Walker	USA	30.11.90	4		Clermont	16 May
10.06A	3.0	Julius	Morris	MNT	14.4.94	6s2	NACAC	San José, CRC	7 Aug
10.07	3.4	Sven	Knipphals	GER	20.9.85	4r1		Clermont	18 Apr
10.07		Aziz	Ouhadi	MAR	24.7.84	2h1	Arab C	Manama	25 Apr
10.07	2.4	Julian	Reus	GER	29.4.88	1h1		Zeulenroda	10 Jul
10.07	4.3	Noah	Lyles	USA-J	18.7.97	1h2	PAm-J	Edmonton	31 Jul
10.08	3.3	Justyn	Warner	CAN	28.6.87	1r2		Clermont	18 Apr
10.08	4.8	Reynier	Mena	CUB-J	21.11.96	1h1	PAm-J	Edmonton	31 Jul
10.09	3.4	Lucas	Jakubczyk	GER	28.4.85	5r1		Clermont	18 Apr
10.09	2.3	Aaron	Ernest	USA	8.11.93	1h3	SEC	Starkville	15 May
10.10	2.3	James	Ellington	GBR	6.9.85	1h1		Clermont	18 Apr
10.10	3.0	Brandon	Carnes	USA	-.3.95	1		Normal	17 May
10.11	2.6	Blake	Smith	USA	28.5.93	4h4	NCAA-W	Austin	28 May
10.11	4.9	Kyree	King	USA	9.7.94	3h3	NC	Eugene	25 Jun
10.11A	2.6	Diego	Palomeque	COL	5.12.93	1	NG	Cali	16 Nov
10.12	3.3	Tremayne	Acy	USA	21.1.95	3r2	TexR	Austin	28 Mar
10.12	4.3	Ivory	Williams	USA	2.5.85	1		Wichita	11 Apr
10.12	4.9	Thurgood	Dennis	USA	30.9.92	1		La Crosse	2 May
10.12	5.1	Roscoe	Engel	RSA	6.3.89	2		Dakar	23 May

Mark	Wind	Name		Nat	Born	Date
10.13	3.2	Walter	Dix	USA	31.1.86	13 Jun
10.13	2.3	Roberto	Skyers	CUB	12.11.91	25 Jun
10.13	4.9	Keith	Ricks	USA	9.10.90	25 Jun
10.13	3.6	Tom	Kling-Baptiste	SWE	29.8.90	29 Aug
10.14	2.4	Markesh	Woodson	USA	6.9.93	28 May
10.14	4.9	Mookie	Salaam	USA	5.4.90	25 Jun
10.14	3.2	Kenji	Fujimitsu	JPN	1.5.86	18 Jul
10.15	3.3	Ryota	Yamagata	JPN	10.6.92	28 Mar
10.15	4.3	Eli	Minor	USA-J	.96	11 Apr
10.15	4.9	Emeilo	Ferguson	JAM	16.4.93	15 May
10.15	2.4	Robert	Hering	GER	14.6.90	10 Jul
10.16	4.7	Kameron	Cowan	USA	17.1.91	26 Apr
10.16	3.9	Martin	Keller	GER	26.9.86	16 May
10.16	3.3	Christian	Coleman	USA-J	6.3.96	31 Jul
10.16A	2.6	Isidro	Montoya	COL	3.11.90	16 Nov
10.17	2.3	Cameron	Hudson	USA	5.3.94	15 May
10.17	2.5	Dedric	Dukes	USA	2.4.92	15 May
10.17	2.1	Trentavis	Friday	USA	5.6.95	16 May
10.17	3.7	Justin	Jenkins	USA	18.2.93	28 May
10.18	5.1	Sydney	Siame	ZAM-J	7.10.97	23 May
10.18	2.6	Denis	Dimitrov	BUL	10.2.94	10 Jun
10.18	4.8	Vitor Hugo	dos Santos	BRA-J	1.2.96	31 Jul
10.19	2.9	Aldrich	Bailey	USA	6.2.94	28 Mar
10.19	4.1	Albert	Huntley	USA	3.1.90	4 Apr
10.19	3.3	Giovanni	Codrington	NED	17.7.88	18 Apr
10.19A	5.4	Kabroderan	Handsborough	USA	.93	18 Apr
10.19	4.0	Jeff	Henderson	USA	19.2.89	18 Apr
10.19	3.3	Emmanuel	Matadi	USA	15.4.91	8 May
10.19	5.4	Jonathan	Nmaju	NGR	9.1.93	23 May
10.19	3.7	Andrew	Robertson	GBR	17.12.90	31 May
10.19	3.6	Sulayman	Bah	SWE	21.1.86	29 Aug
10.20	7.5	Soshi	Watanabe	JPN	7.1.95	18 Apr
10.20	2.6	Tarrick "TJ"	Brock	USA-Y	3.2.98	18 Apr
10.20	3.7	Justin	Scruggs	USA	18.5.94	30 Apr
10.20	3.6	Ashton	Eaton	USA	21.1.88	8 May
10.20	3.9	Alexander	Kosenkow	GER	14.3.77	16 May
10.20	5.1	Adama	Jammeh	GAM	10.6.93	23 May
10.20	2.5	Ojie	Edoburun	GBR-J	2.6.96	27 May
10.20	2.2	Vitaliy	Korzh	UKR	5.10.87	4 Jun
10.20	2.3	Giovanni	Galbieri	ITA	8.1.93	9 Jul
10.20		Joseph	Dewar	GBR-J	27.1.96	19 Aug
10.20	3.6	Odain	Rose	SWE	19.7.92	29 Aug
10.21	4.4	Rubin	Williams	USA	9.7.83	17 Apr
10.21	3.4	Chevaugn	Walsh	ANT	29.12.87	13 Jun
10.21	3.0	Benjamin	Williams	CAN	15.5.92	26 Jul
10.22	4.1	Marvin	René	FRA	11.4.95	11 Apr
10.22	4.4	Alexander	Donigian	USA	20.10.93	17 Apr
10.22	3.4	Roy	Ejiakuekwu	GBR	2.2.95	18 Apr
10.22	3.1	Kenneth	Turner	USA	28.8.91	16 May
10.22A		Edward	Clarke	JAM	9.9.95	6 Jun
10.22	3.7	J-Mee	Samuels	USA	20.5.87	14 Jun
10.22	7.1	Geoffrey	Thomas	FRA	31.7.94	25 Jul
10.23	2.6	Jeff	Fraley	USA	30.7.93	3 May
10.23	2.5	Lamar	Hargrove	USA	21.4.94	21 May
10.23	3.0	Seyi	Smith	CAN	21.2.87	24 May
10.23	2.5	Leon	Powell	USA-J	1.9.96	29 May

Low altitude bests 10.13 0.8 S Mitchell 2h2 NC Kingston 25 Jun 10.26 1.9 Siame 6 Jun

Hand timing

Mark	Wind	Name		Nat	Born	Pos	Meet	Venue	Date
9.9A		Mike	Nyangau	KEN	28.8.94	1	WCT	Nairobi	1 Aug
9.9		Winston	George	GUY	19.5.87	1		Georgetown	15 Oct

Drugs disqualification: 10.27 1.4 Dushane Farrier ¶ CAN 16.1.90 3 Jul

JUNIORS

See main list for top 2 juniors. 9 performances by 6 men to 10.19. Additional marks and further juniors:

Mark	Wind	Name		Nat	Born	Pos	Meet	Venue	Date
Bacon		10.19 1.6 1h1 Mobile 9 May				10.13w 3.7 2h1	NCAAw	Austin	28 May
Lyles		10.18 0.4 2 PAm-J Edmonton 31 Jul							
10.17	0.4	Reynier	Mena	CUB	21.11.96	1	PAm-J	Edmonton	31 Jul
10.18	1.1	Ryan	Clark	USA	14.9.96	1	vCUB-J	La Habana	13 Jun
10.18	2.0	Christian	Coleman	USA	6.3.96	2	NC-j	Eugene	26 Jun
		10.19 1.7 5s1 NCAA Eugene 10 Jun							
10.18A	1.9	Sydney	Siame	ZAM	7.10.97	1h1		Lusaka	27 Jun
10.20	1.5	Tlotliso Gift	Leotlela	RSA-Y	12.5.98	1		Apia	7 Sep
10.21	1.5	Mario	Burke	BAR	18.3.97	1		Basseterre	4 Apr
10.22	-0.1	Vitor Hugo	dos Santos	BRA	1.2.96	1	NC	São Bernardo do Campo	14 May
10.23	0.5	Michael	O'Hara (10)	JAM	29.9.96	1		Kingston	14 Mar
10.24	1.9	Ojie	Edoburun	GBR	2.6.96	2		Kuortane	8 Aug
10.25	-1.6	Demek	Kemp	USA	26.4.96	1		Savannah	1 Apr
10.27	1.8	Devin	Duvernay	USA	.97	1		Austin	16 May
10.27	1.8	Meshal Khalifa	Al-Mutairi	KUW	16.3.97	6	AsiC	Wuhan	4 Jun
10.27	1.2	Shuhei	Tada	JPN	24.6.96	1		Nara	29 Aug
10.28A	-0.4	Abdul Hakim	Sani Brown	JPN-Y	6.3.99	1	WY	Cali	15 Jul
10.28	2.0	Wataru	Inuzuka	JPN	8.7.97	1s2		Wakayama	2 Oct
10.29	-0.8	Kenta	Oshima	JPN	3.9.97	1		Wakayama	30 Jul
10.29	0.3	Brian	Kasinda	ZAM	31.12.97	1s3	AfG	Brazzaville	13 Sep
10.29	0.3	(20)	Yang Chun-Han	TPE	1.1.97	1		Kaohsiung	19 Oct
10.29	2.0	Badrul Hisham Abdel Manap		MAS	1.1.97	1	AS SchG	Tutong	23 Nov

Wind assisted

See main list for top 3 juniors. 7 performances by 5 men to 10.16. Additional mark and juniors to 10.26w:

Mark	Wind	Name		Nat	Born	Pos	Meet	Venue	Date
Al-Mutairi		10.09 4.1 4 ArabC Manama 25 Apr							
10.15	4.3	Eli	Minor	USA	.96	2		Wichita	11 Apr
10.16	3.3	Christian	Coleman	USA	6.3.96	1h3	PAm-J	Edmonton	31 Jul
10.18	5.1	Sydney	Siame	ZAM	7.10.97	4		Dakar	23 May
10.18	4.8	Vitor Hugo	dos Santos	BRA	1.2.96	2h1	PAm-J	Edmonton	31 Jul
10.20	2.6	Tarrick "TJ"	Brock	USA-Y	3.2.98	1	MSR	Walnut	18 Apr
10.20	2.5	Ojie	Edoburun	GBR	2.6.96	1		London (LV)	27 May
10.20		Joseph	Dewar	GBR	27.1.96	2A1		London (LV)	19 Aug
10.23	2.5	Leon	Powell	USA	1.9.96	5q2	NCAA-W	Austin	29 May
10.24A	3.7	Darryl	Haraway	USA	20.3.97	2		Albuquerque	6 Jun
10.25	2.5	Brian	Kasinda	ZAM	31.12.97	1h3		La Chaux-de-Fonds	5 Jul
10.26	4.8	Shivnarine	Smalling	JAM	28.9.96	3h1	PAm-J	Edmonton	31 Jul

150 METRES STRAIGHT

Gateshead 12 Sep: (3.6) 1. Nickel Ashmeade JAM 14.63w, 2. Richard Kilty GBR 14.64, 3. Danny Talbot GBR 14.79w

200 METRES

Mark	Wind	Name		Nat	Born	Pos	Meet	Venue	Date
19.55	-0.1	Usain	Bolt	JAM	21.8.86	1	WCh	Beijing	27 Aug
19.57	0.4	Justin	Gatlin	USA	10.2.82	1	NC	Eugene	28 Jun
19.68	0.9		Gatlin			1	Pre	Eugene	30 May
19.74	-0.1		Gatlin			2	WCh	Beijing	27 Aug
19.80	2.0	Rasheed	Dwyer	JAM	29.1.89	1s1	PAm	Toronto	23 Jul
19.87	-0.2		Gatlin			1s2	WCh	Beijing	26 Aug
19.87	-0.1	Anaso	Jobodwana	RSA	30.7.92	3	WCh	Beijing	27 Aug
19.87	-0.1	Alonso	Edward	PAN	8.12.89	4	WCh	Beijing	27 Aug
19.88	0.3	Andre	De Grasse	CAN	10.11.94	1	PAm	Toronto	24 Jul
19.88	-0.4	Ramil	Guliyev	TUR	29.5.90	1		Zagreb	8 Sep
19.90	1.1		Gatlin			1s2	NC	Eugene	28 Jun
19.90	0.3		Dwyer			2	PAm	Toronto	24 Jul
19.90	0.3		Edward			3	PAm	Toronto	24 Jul
19.92	1.7		Gatlin			1h2	NC	Eugene	27 Jun
19.93	0.4	Isiah	Young	USA	5.1.90	2	NC	Eugene	28 Jun
19.94	0.6	Wayde	van Niekerk	RSA	15.7.92	1rB		Luzern	14 Jul
19.95	0.8		Bolt			1s3	WCh	Beijing	26 Aug
19.97	-0.4	Femi Seun	Ogunode (10)	QAT	15.5.91	1	VD	Bruxelles	11 Sep
19.99	0.6	Dedric	Dukes	USA	2.4.92	1	SEC	Starkville	16 May
19.99	1.7		Young			2h2	NC	Eugene	27 Jun
20.01	-0.3		Guliyev			1h1	WCh	Beijing	25 Aug
20.01	0.8		Jobodwana			2s3	WCh	Beijing	26 Aug
20.02	1.5	Ameer	Webb	USA	19.3.91	1		Norwalk	6 Jun
20.02	0.3	Roberto	Skyers	CUB	12.11.91	4	PAm	Toronto	24 Jul
20.02	-0.2		Edward			2s2	WCh	Beijing	26 Aug
20.02	-0.1	Zharnel	Hughes	AIA/GBR	13.7.95	5	WCh	Beijing	27 Aug

Mark	Wind	Name		Nat	Born	Pos	Meet	Venue	Date
20.03	-0.3		De Grasse			1h1	Pac-12	Los Angeles (Ww)	16 May
20.03	1.8		Dukes			1s2	NCAA	Eugene	10 Jun
20.03	2.0	Trayvon	Bromell	USA	10.7.95	1s3	NCAA	Eugene	10 Jun
20.03	0.6		Edward			2rB		Luzern	14 Jul
20.03	0.4	Wallace	Spearmon	USA	24.12.84	2s1	PAm	Toronto	23 Jul
20.03	0.4		Edward			1	WK	Zürich	3 Sep
		(32/16)							
20.04	1.1	Julian	Forte	JAM	1.7.93	1s2	NC	Kingston	27 Jun
20.05	2.0	Miguel	Francis	ANT	28.2.95	3s1	PAm	Toronto	23 Jul
20.09	0.8	Likoúrgos-Stéfanos	Tsákonas	GRE	8.3.90	1	GGala	Roma	4 Jun
20.11	0.4	Beejay	Lee	USA	5.3.93	4	NC	Eugene	28 Jun
		(20)							
20.12	1.5	Remontay	McClain	USA	21.9.92	2		Norwalk	6 Jun
20.13	0.6	Kenji	Fujimitsu	JPN	1.5.86	3rB		Luzern	14 Jul
20.14	1.9	Carvin	Nkanata	KEN	6.5.91	1		Clermont	18 Apr
20.14	1.0	Kei	Takase	JPN	25.11.88	1		Kumagaya	17 May
20.14	2.0	Tevin	Hester	USA	10.1.94	2s3	NCAA	Eugene	10 Jun
20.16	1.8	Terrel	Cotton	USA	19.7.88	2h5	NC	Eugene	27 Jun
20.17A		Pako	Seribe	BOT	7.4.91	1		Molepolole	22 Feb
20.17	1.8	Tremayne	Acy	USA	21.1.95	2s2	NCAA	Eugene	10 Jun
20.18	0.9	Nickel	Ashmeade	JAM	7.4.90	3	Pre	Eugene	30 May
20.18	1.8	Noah	Lyles	USA-J	18.7.97	1	NC-j	Eugene	27 Jun
		(30)							
20.18	-0.4	Brendon	Rodney	CAN	9.4.92	3h5	WCh	Beijing	25 Aug
20.20	0.4	Churandy	Martina	NED	3.7.84	3s1	WCh	Beijing	26 Aug
20.21	-1.2	Christophe	Lemaitre	FRA	11.6.90	1	Bisl	Oslo	11 Jun
20.22	1.3	Aaron	Ernest	USA	8.11.93	1q3	NCAA-E	Jacksonville	30 May
20.22	1.0	Yancarlos	Martínez	DOM	8.7.92	4s2	PAm	Toronto	23 Jul
20.23	0.6	Shavez	Hart	BAH	6.9.92	2	SEC	Starkville	16 May
20.23	-0.4	Akani	Simbine	RSA	21.9.93	4h5	WCh	Beijing	25 Aug
20.24	1.8	Michael	Norman	USA-J	3.12.97	2	NC-j	Eugene	27 Jun
20.24	-0.1	Warren	Weir	JAM	31.10.89	2h6	WCh	Beijing	25 Aug
20.25	1.8	Harry	Adams	USA	27.11.89	3h5	NC	Eugene	27 Jun
		(40)							
20.26	1.8	Kendal	Williams	USA	23.9.95	2	ACC	Tallahassee	16 May
20.27	0.8	Danny	Talbot	GBR	1.5.91	6s3	WCh	Beijing	26 Aug
20.29	-0.1	Justin	Walker	USA	30.11.90	1r2		Montverde	6 Jun
20.29	1.8	Khalil	Henderson	USA	18.11.94	3s2	NCAA	Eugene	10 Jun
20.30	1.8	Bryce	Robinson	USA	13.11.93	1		Lubbock	30 Apr
20.30	1.8	Aldrich	Bailey	USA	6.2.94	2		Austin	2 May
20.30	0.7	Aaron	Brown	CAN	27.5.92	3		Kingston	9 May
20.31	-0.4	Jeremy	Dodson	SAM	30.8.87	5h5	WCh	Beijing	25 Aug
20.32	2.0	Reynier	Mena	CUB-J	21.11.96	5s1	PAm	Toronto	23 Jul
20.33A	0.0	José Carlos	Herrera	MEX	5.2.86	1		Ciudad de México	29 Mar
		(50)							
20.34	1.4	Tim	Faust	USA	11.8.92	1	Big 10	East Lansing	17 May
20.34	2.0	Teray	Smith	BAH	28.9.94	5s3	NCAA	Eugene	10 Jun
20.34A	-0.4	Abdul Hakim	Sani Brown	JPN-Y	6.3.99	1	WY	Cali	19 Jul
20.36	1.0	Curtis	Mitchell	USA	11.3.89	1h4	NC	Eugene	27 Jun
20.37A	-1.9	Bernardo	Baloyes	COL	6.1.94	2		Medellin	9 May
20.37	1.4	D.J.	Zahn	USA	31.1.93	2	Big 10	East Lansing	17 May
20.37	1.8	Sean	McLean	USA	23.3.92	4h5	NC	Eugene	27 Jun
20.38	-0.4	Jeffrey	John	FRA	6.6.92	1		Paris (C)	5 Jul
20.38	-1.1	Jak Ali	Harvey	TUR	5.4.89	1		Ankara	5 Sep
20.39	0.6	Cameron	Echols-Luper	USA	9.4.95	1h1	Big 12	Ames	16 May
		(60)							
20.39	1.5	Bryshon	Nellum	USA	1.5.89	3		Norwalk	6 Jun
20.39	1.6	Tyquendo	Tracey	JAM	10.6.93	2s1	NC	Kingston	27 Jun
20.39	-0.3	Hua Wilfried	Koffi	CIV	24.9.89	4h1	WCh	Beijing	25 Aug
20.40	0.3	Michael	Mathieu	BAH	24.6.83	1		Coral Gables	11 Apr
20.40	0.0	Delano	Williams	GBR	23.12.93	4		George Town	16 May
20.41	1.6	Bruno	de Barros	BRA	7.1.87	2h2	PAm	Toronto	23 Jul
20.42	-0.2	Jimmy	Vicaut	FRA	27.2.92	1		Rabat	14 Jun
20.42	1.4	Shota	Iizuka	JPN	25.6.91	1h3	NC	Niigata	26 Jun
20.42	1.7	Kyle	Greaux	TTO	26.4.88	1	NC	Port of Spain	28 Jun
20.42	0.2	Mosito	Lehata	LES	8.4.89	2		Tomblaine	1 Jul
		(70)							
20.42	1.0	Julian	Reus	GER	29.4.88	1	NC	Nürnberg	26 Jul
20.43	0.6	Joe	Morris	USA	4.10.89	2		Tempe	11 Apr
20.44A		Isaac	Makwala	BOT	29.9.86	1		Molopolole	22 Feb
20.44	0.3	Aldemir	da Silva	BRA	8.6.92	1	NC	São Bernardo do Campo	17 May

Mark	Wind	Name		Nat	Born	Pos	Meet	Venue	Date
20.45	0.9	Karol	Zalewski	POL	7.8.93	1		Gdansk	6 Jun
20.45	-0.9	Sergiy	Smelyk	UKR	19.4.87	1rB	ET	Cheboksary	21 Jun
20.45	0.7	Jonathan	Borlée	BEL	22.2.88	1	NA	Heusden-Zolder	18 Jul
20.45A	0.8	Julius	Morris	MNT	14.4.94	2s2	NACAC	San José, CRC	7 Aug
20.45	0.8	Odele	Tega	NGR	12.6.95	1h6	AfG	Brazzaville	16 Sep
20.45	-1.2	Divine	Oduduru	NGR-J	7.10.96	2	AfG	Brazzaville	17 Sep
		(80)							
20.46	-0.1	Rondell	Sorrillo	TTO	21.1.86	1r4	FlaR	Gainesville	3 Apr
20.46	-0.1	Just'n	Thymes	USA	24.1.94	2r4	FlaR	Gainesville	3 Apr
20.46	1.6	Ahmed	Ali	USA/SUD	15.11.93	1		Norman	18 Apr
20.46A	0.2	Tatenda	Tsumba	ZIM	12.11.91	1s5		Provo	25 Apr
20.46	1.8	Ryan	Clark	USA-J	14.9.96	3	NC-j	Eugene	27 Jun
20.46	1.0	Maurice	Mitchell	USA	22.12.89	2h4	NC	Eugene	27 Jun
20.47	0.8	Chijindu	Ujah	GBR	5.3.94	4	GGala	Roma	4 Jun
20.47	2.0	Senoj-Jay	Givans	JAM	30.12.93	6s3	NCAA	Eugene	10 Jun
20.47	0.4	Mohamed Hussein	Abaraghi	IRI	5.1.95	1		Almaty	26 Jul
20.47A	1.8	Antoine	Adams	SKN	31.8.88	3	NACAC	San José, CRC	9 Aug
		(90)							
20.48A	1.9	Mike	Nyangau	KEN	28.8.94	1	WCT	Nairobi	1 Aug
20.49	1.9	James	Ellington	GBR	6.9.85	3		Clermont	18 Apr
20.49	1.6	Robin	Erewa	GER	24.6.91	1r2		Clermont	16 May
20.49	0.6	Kevin	Harris	USA	4.12.95	2h1	Big 12	Ames	16 May
20.50	1.7	James	Harrington	USA	3.7.93	1h2	Big 10	East Lansing	16 May
20.50A	1.9	Diego	Palomeque	COL	5.12.93	2	NG	Cali	21 Nov
20.51	0.3	Jermaine	Brown	JAM	4.7.91	2	MSR	Walnut	18 Apr
20.51A	-0.3	Roscoe	Engel	RSA	6.3.89	1		Potchefstroom	9 May
20.51	0.6	Terrell	Smith	USA	10.10.94	3h1	Big 12	Ames	16 May
20.51	1.5	Kyree	King	USA	9.7.94	4		Norwalk	6 Jun
		(100)							

Mark	Wind	Name		Nat	Born	Date
20.52	1.5	Parker	Bluth	USA	.92	16 May
20.52	0.1		Liang Jinsheng	CHN-J	12.1.96	29 May
20.53	1.1	Lalonde	Gordon	TTO	25.11.88	9 May
20.53	0.3	Antônio Cesar	Rodrigues	BRA	12.1.93	17 May
20.53	1.7	Dan-Neil	Telesford	TTO	9.9.90	28 Jun
20.53	-1.5	Ratu	Tabakaucoro	FIJ	4.9.92	16 Jul
20.53A	-1.0	Sydney	Siame	ZAM-J	7.10.97	1 Aug
20.53	-0.3		Yang Chun-Han	TPE-J	1.1.97	21 Oct
20.54	0.0	Jason	Livermore	JAM	25.4.88	16 May
20.54	0.0	Emmanuel	Matadi	USA	15.4.91	23 May
20.54	-1.2	Richard	Kilty	GBR	2.9.89	11 Jun
20.54	0.5	Edino	Steele	JAM	6.1.87	14 Jul
20.54	0.2	Chris	Clarke	GBR	25.1.90	23 Aug
20.55	2.0	Ben	Bassaw	FRA	9.7.89	14 Jun
20.55A	-0.1	César	Ramirez	MEX	21.1.94	14 Jun
20.55	-0.7	Enrico	Demonte	ITA	25.9.88	5 Jul
20.55	-0.9	Ben Youssef	Meité	CIV	11.11.86	22 Jul
20.55	0.0	Obinna	Metu	NGR	12.7.88	16 Sep
20.56	0.4	Lamar	Hargrove	USA	21.4.94	11 Apr
20.56	1.9	Yoshihide	Kiryu	JPN	15.12.95	18 Apr
20.56A		Baboloki	Thebe	BOT-J	18.3.96	31 May
20.57	1.2	Rusheen	McDonald	JAM	17.8.92	23 May
20.57A	-0.4	Kyle	Appel	RSA-Y	10.5.98	19 Jul
20.57	-0.6	Takuya	Nagata	JPN	14.6.94	13 Sep
20.58A		Gaone	Maotoanong	BOT	7.5.91	22 Feb
20.58	0.0	Chris	Brown	BAH	15.10.78	27 Jun
20.58	1.3	Pavel	Maslák	CZE	21.2.91	28 Jun
20.58	0.5	Alex	Wilson	SUI	19.9.90	8 Aug
20.58	1.0	Fahad	Al-Subaie	KSA	4.2.94	25 Oct
20.59	1.8	Alex	Hartmann	AUS	7.3.93	7 Feb
20.59	-1.8	Michael	O'Hara	JAM-J	29.9.96	28 Mar
20.59	0.3	Marvin	René	FRA	11.4.95	25 Apr
20.59	1.5	Rubin	Williams	USA	9.7.83	6 Jun
20.59	1.9	Walter	Dix	USA	31.1.86	5 Sep
20.60	-0.2	Nesta	Carter	JAM	10.11.85	11 Apr
20.60	1.2	Kolby	Listenbee	USA	25.1.94	16 May
20.60	1.9	Tristan	Walker	JAM	24.10.87	28 Jun
20.60		Egweru	Ogho-Oghene	NGR	26.11.88	31 Jul
20.60	-0.2		Xie Zhenye	CHN	17.8.93	24 Sep
20.61A	1.4	Emmanuel	Dasor	GHA	14.9.95	17 May
20.61	1.3	Christian	Coleman	USA-J	6.3.96	30 May
20.61	0.9	Pierre-Alexis	Pessonneaux	FRA	25.11.87	6 Jun
20.61	1.0	Mario	Forsythe	JAM	30.10.85	27 Jun
20.61	1.1	Sheldon	Mitchell	JAM	19.7.90	27 Jun
20.61	-1.2	Stirley	Jones	USA	13.12.84	11 Jul
20.62	1.1	Trey	Hadnot	USA	7.3.92	9 May
20.62	0.9	Leon	Reid	GBR	26.7.94	6 Jun
20.62	-1.6	Winston	George	GUY	19.5.87	6 Jun
20.62	0.4	Henricho	Bruintjies	RSA	16.7.93	14 Jun
20.62	-0.4	Liemarvin	Bonevacia	NED	5.4.89	4 Aug
20.63A	0.2	Tlotliso Gift	Leotlela	RSA-Y	12.5.98	20 Mar
20.63		Michael	Rodgers	USA	24.4.85	3 Apr
20.63	-0.1	David	Verburg	USA	14.5.91	3 Apr
20.63	1.6	Corneil	Lionel	LCA	28.10.91	18 Apr
20.63	0.8	Trentavis	Friday	USA	5.6.95	15 May
20.63	0.8	Ceolamar	Ways	USA	22.11.94	15 May
20.63	2.0	Arthur	Delaney	USA	23.6.93	29 May
20.63	0.7	Robert	Hering	GER	14.6.90	10 Jul
20.64	1.3	Kind	Butler	USA	8.4.89	16 Apr
20.64	1.1	Sven	Knipphals	GER	20.9.85	16 May
20.64	-0.1	Davide	Manenti	ITA	16.4.89	17 May
20.64A	-1.0	Chidamba	Hazemba	ZAM-J	.97	1 Aug
20.64	1.7	Eseosa	Desalu	ITA	19.2.94	8 Oct
20.65	1.2	Michael	Bryan	USA	9.6.91	9 May
20.65A	0.4	Oluwasegun	Makinde	CAN	6.7.91	14 May
20.65	1.3	Brandon	Stryganek	USA	7.1.93	29 May
20.65	1.4	Shota	Hara	JPN	18.7.92	26 Jun
20.65A	0.8	Nicholas	Deshong	BAR	24.4.92	7 Aug
20.66	0.0	Kemar	Bailey-Cole	JAM	10.1.92	14 Mar
20.66	2.0	Jeff	Fraley	USA	30.7.93	3 May
20.66A	-1.9	Yoandry	Andujar	DOM	5.7.90	9 May
20.66	1.6	Hanoj	Carter	USA	26.6.94	10 May
20.66	1.0	Dharambir	Singh	IND	10.12.90	7 Jun
20.66	?	Rosen	Daniel	LCA	23.3.93	28 Jun
20.66A	1.2	Brijesh "BJ"	Lawrence	SKN	27.12.89	7 Aug
20.67	-0.4	Winston	Barnes	JAM	7.11.88	23 May
20.67	0.2	Dontae	Richards-Kwok	CAN	1.3.89	30 May
20.67	0.8	John	Lundy	USA	15.3.92	12 Jul
20.68	1.6	Johnathan	Farquharson	BAH	3.2.93	18 Apr
20.68	0.6	Jorge Henrique	Vides	BRA	24.11.92	16 May
20.68	0.6	Sam	Watts	GBR	14.2.92	16 May
20.68	0.5	Burkheart	Ellis	BAR	18.9.92	21 Jun
20.68	0.9	Elliott	Powell	GBR-J	5.3.96	28 Jun
20.68	-2.5	Ncincihli	Titi	RSA	15.12.93	10 Jul
20.68	-1.2	Paul	Dedewo	USA	4.6.91	11 Jul
20.68	0.4	Reza	Ghasemi	IRI	24.7.87	26 Jul
20.69	0.0	Tony	McQuay	USA	16.4.90	3 Apr
20.69	-0.1	Steven	Gardiner	BAH	12.9.95	3 Apr
20.69	1.1	Clayton	Parros	USA	11.12.90	16 May
20.69	1.2	Charles	Anumnu	USA	24.6.95	16 May
20.69	1.6	Kotaro	Taniguchi	JPN	3.11.94	17 May
20.69	0.2	Gavin	Smellie	CAN	26.6.86	30 May
20.69	0.3	Aleixo Platini	Menga	GER	29.9.87	6 Jun
20.69	0.6	Aziz	Ouhadi	MAR	24.7.84	12 Jul

Mark	Wind	Name		Nat	Born	Date
20.70	1.8	Trevorvano	Mackey	BAH	5.1.92	30 Apr
20.70	0.4	Jefferey	Pendergrass	USA	25.3.89	2 May
20.70	1.9	Denis	Ogarkov	RUS	3.7.93	29 May
20.70	0.4	Carl	Horsley	USA	17.6.92	29 May
20.70	1.1	Vitaliy	Korzh	UKR	5.10.87	4 Jun
20.70	0.8	Reece	Prescod	GBR-J	29.2.96	6 Jun

Wind assisted (200)

Mark	Wind	Name		Nat	Born	Pos	Meet	Venue	Date
19.58	2.4	Andre	De Grasse	CAN	10.11.94	1	NCAA	Eugene	12 Jun
19.75	4.1	Isiah	Young	USA	5.1.90	1rA		Clermont	16 May
19.86	2.4	Dedric	Dukes	USA	2.4.92	2	NCAA	Eugene	12 Jun
19.86	2.4	Trayvon	Bromell	USA	10.7.95	3	NCAA	Eugene	12 Jun
19.87	4.5	(5/5)	Jobodwana			1	TexR	Austin	28 Mar
20.04	2.4	Tremayne	Acy	USA	21.1.95	4	NCAA	Eugene	12 Jun
20.09	4.5	Kei	Takase	JPN	25.11.88	2	TexR	Austin	28 Mar
20.11	2.4	Aaron	Ernest	USA	8.11.93	5	NCAA	Eugene	12 Jun
20.11	2.1	Aaron	Brown	CAN	27.5.92	1	NC	Edmonton	5 Jul
20.16	4.5	Aldrich	Bailey	USA	6.2.94	3	TexR	Austin	28 Mar
20.16	2.7	Gavin	Smellie	CAN	26.6.86	1rB		Clermont	16 May
20.24	2.3	Antoine	Adams	SKN	31.8.88	1	NC	Basseterre	14 Jun
20.29	2.1	Bryce	Robinson	USA	13.11.93	1h6	NCAA-W	Austin	29 May
20.31	3.8	Brandon	Carnes	USA	-.3.95	1		Normal	17 May
20.36	2.7	Aldemir	da Silva	BRA	8.6.92	1rC		Clermont	18 Apr
20.37	2.3	Calesio	Newman	USA	20.8.86	1		Greensboro, NC	17 May
20.40	4.6	Antwon	Smith	USA	18.6.95	1h4	JUCO	Hutchinson, KS	15 May
20.41	w?	Walter	Dix	USA	31.1.86	1		Daytona Beach	21 Feb
20.42	4.5	Maurice	Mitchell	USA	22.12.89	4	TexR	Austin	28 Mar
20.43	2.4	Akiyuki	Hashimoto	JPN	18.11.94	1h3	Oda	Hiroshima	18 Apr
20.46	3.0	Renard	Howell	USA	3.3.95	1h2	JUCO	Hutchinson, KS	15 May
20.46A	2.6	Michael	O'Hara	JAM-J	29.9.96	1		Albuquerque	6 Jun
20.48	2.3	Tim	Price	USA	26.12.87	1		San Marcos	25 Apr
20.49	4.5	Shota	Hara	JPN	18.7.92	6	TexR	Austin	28 Mar

Mark	Wind	Name		Nat	Born	Date
20.51	2.6	Steven	Gardiner	BAH	12.9.95	11 Jul
20.54	2.5	Ben Youssef	Meité	CIV	11.11.86	29 Jul
20.55A	2.6	Maxwell	Willis	USA-Y	2.9.98	6 Jun
20.55	2.5	Tom	Kling-Baptiste	SWE	29.8.90	9 Aug
20.56	2.3	Dionte	Robinson	USA-J	15.3.96	4 Apr
20.56	2.6	Tlotliso Gift	Leotlela	RSA-Y	12.5.98	9 Sep
20.56	2.6	Toby	Harries	GBR-Y	30.9.98	9 Sep
20.57	4.1	Tommy	Ramdhan	GBR-J	28.11.96	18 Jul
20.59	2.2	Alex	Quiñónez	ECU	11.8.89	23 Jul
20.59A	3.5	Dontae	Richards-Kwok	CAN	1.3.89	7 Aug
20.60	2.3	Norvel	Mohammed	USA	5.12.94	4 Apr
20.61	7.2	Thurgood	Dennis	USA	30.9.92	2 May
20.64	4.3	Ronnie	Baker	USA	15.10.93	11 Apr
20.64	3.8	Anderson	Devonish	BAR	12.3.94	17 May
20.65A	2.3	Lebogang	Moeng	RSA	10.10.89	28 Feb
20.65	3.7	Rodrigo	do Nascimento	BRA	26.9.94	16 May
20.65	2.3	Ncincihli	Titi	RSA	15.12.93	17 May
20.66	2.5	Barakat	Al-Harthi	OMA	15.6.88	27 Apr
20.66	2.3	Brijesh "BJ"	Lawrence	SKN	27.12.89	14 Jun
20.67	5.1	Deviyon	Pendergrass	USA	25.3.89	28 Mar
20.67	2.2	Elroy	McBride	BAH	23.12.93	30 Apr
20.67A	3.3	Ventavius	Sears	USA	14.5.95	17 May
20.67	2.1	Luka	Janezic	SLO	14.11.95	14 Jun

Doubtful performance: 19.76 -1.1 Miguel Francis ANT 28.2.95 1 NC St.John's 28 Jun

Hand timing

Mark	Wind	Name		Nat	Born	Pos	Meet	Venue	Date
20.2A		Mike	Nyangau	KEN	28.8.94	1h1	NC	Nairobi	10 Jul
20.4		Winston	George	GUY	19.5.87	1		Georgetown	5 Oct

Low altitude bests

20.35 0.0 Sani Brown 2h4 WCh Beijing 25 Aug
20.51 -0.3 Nyangau 5h1 WCh Beijing 25 Aug
20.56 0.1 Julius Morris 25 Aug
20.60 1.6 Ramírez 26 Apr
20.63 1.9 A Adams 25 Apr
20.67 1.3 Dasor 30May

Irregular: San Marcos 6 Jun: (0.9) 1. Tre Houston BER 12.1.87 20.42, 2. Courtney Williams VIN 31.1.91 20.59

JUNIORS

See main list for top 6 juniors. 14 performances by 6 men to 20.46. Additional marks and further juniors:

Name	Mark	Wind	Pos	Meet	Venue	Date	Mark	Wind	Pos	Meet	Venue	Date
Lyles	20.27	1.3	1	PAm-J	Edmonton	1 Aug						
Norman	20.30	0.7	1		Clovis	6 Jun	20.46	-0.9	1		Norwalk	29 May
Mena	20.34	1.3	2	PAm-J	Edmonton	1 Aug	20.45	-1.7	1		La Habana	13 Jun
	20.37	-0.3	3h1	WCh	Beijing	25 Aug	20.45	1.9	4h3	PAm	Toronto	23 Jul

Mark	Wind	Name		Nat	Born	Pos	Meet	Venue	Date
20.52	0.1		Liang Jinsheng	CHN	12.1.96	1	NC-j	Fuzhou	29 May
20.53A	-1.0	Sydney	Siame	ZAM	7.10.97	1		Lusaka	1 Aug
20.53	-0.3		Yang Chun-Han	TPE	1.1.97	1		Kaohsiung	21 Oct
20.56A		Baboloki	Thebe (10)	BOT	18.3.96	1		Gaborone	31 May
20.57A	-0.4	Kyle	Appel	RSA-Y	10.5.98	2	WY	Cali	19 Jul
20.59	-1.8	Michael	O'Hara	JAM	29.9.96	1		Kingston	28 Mar
20.61	1.3	Christian	Coleman	USA	6.3.96	4q3	NCAA-E	Jacksonville	30 May
20.63A	0.2	Tlotliso Gift	Leotlela	RSA-Y	12.5.98	1		Pretoria	20 Mar
20.64A	-1.0	Chidamba	Hazemba	ZAM	.97	2		Lusaka	1 Aug
20.68	0.9	Elliott	Powell	GBR	5.3.96	1		Mannheim	28 Jun
20.70	0.8	Reece	Prescod	GBR	29.2.96	1rB		Genève	6 Jun
20.71	1.6	Jaylen	Bacon	USA	5.8.96	2		Mobile	10 May
20.71	1.0	Mohamed	Yacoub Salem	BRN	1.3.96	2	Gulf G	Qatif	25 Oct
20.74A	-0.4	Josephus	Lyles (20)	USA-Y	22.7.98	3	WY	Cali	19 Jul

Wind assisted. See main list for top 1 junior. 7 performances by 6 men to 20.48. Additional marks and further juniors:

Mark	Wind	Name		Nat	Born	Pos	Meet	Venue	Date
Norman		20.39	3.4			1		Norwalk	23 May
20.55A	2.6	Maxwell	Willis	USA-Y	2.9.98	2		Albuquerque	6 Jun
20.56	2.3	Dionte	Robinson	USA	15.3.96	1		San Antonio	4 Apr

Mark	Wind	Name		Nat	Born	Pos	Meet	Venue	Date
20.56	2.6	Tlotliso Gift	Leotlela	RSA-Y	12.5.98	1	Comm-Y	Apia	9 Sep
20.56	2.6	Toby	Harries	GBR-Y	30.9.98	2	Comm-Y	Apia	9 Sep
20.57	4.1	Tommy	Ramdhan	GBR	28.11.96	1	EJ	Eskilstuna	18 Jul

300 METRES

Mark	Name		Nat	Born	Pos	Meet	Venue	Date
31.53	LaShawn	Merritt	USA	27.6.86	1		Atlanta	1 Aug
31.63	Wayde	van Niekerk	RSA	15.7.92	1		Birmingham	7 Jun
31.94	Rusheen	McDonald	JAM	17.8.92	1		Rieti	13 Sep
31.99	Chris	Brown	BAH	15.10.78	2		Birmingham	7 Jun
32.07	Bryshon	Nellum	USA	1.5.89	2		Atlanta	1 Aug
32.14	Delano	Williams	GBR	23.12.93	3		Birmingham	7 Jun
32.17	David	Verburg	USA	14.5.91	4		Birmingham	7 Jun
32.21	Kenji	Fujimitsu	JPN	1.5.86	1		Izumo	12 Apr
32.21	Lalonde	Gordon	TTO	25.11.88	1		Liège (NX)	15 Jul
32.25	Karol	Zalewski	POL	7.8.93	1	GS	Ostrava	26 May
32.29	Chris	Clarke	GBR	25.1.90	2		Rieti	13 Sep
32.35	Pavel	Maslák	CZE	21.2.91	2	GS	Ostrava	26 May
32.36	Terrel	Cotton	USA	19.7.88				13 Sep
32.43	Jonathan	Borlée	BEL	22.2.88				15 Jul
32.55	Alldrich	Bailey	USA	6.2.94				1 Aug
32.58	Rafal	Omelko	POL	16.1.89				26 May

400 METRES

Mark	Name		Nat	Born	Pos	Meet	Venue	Date
43.48	Wayde	van Niekerk	RSA	15.7.92	1	WCh	Beijing	26 Aug
43.65	LaShawn	Merritt	USA	27.6.86	2	WCh	Beijing	26 Aug
43.72	Isaac	Makwala	BOT	29.9.86	1		La Chaux-de-Fonds	5 Jul
43.78	Kirani	James	GRN	1.9.92	3	WCh	Beijing	26 Aug
43.93	Youssef	Al-Masrahi	KSA	31.12.87	1h2	WCh	Beijing	23 Aug
43.93	Rusheen	McDonald	JAM	17.8.92	2h2	WCh	Beijing	23 Aug
43.95		James			1	Pre	Eugene	30 May
43.96		van Niekerk			1	DL	Saint-Denis	4 Jul
44.11		Makwala			1s2	WCh	Beijing	24 Aug
44.11	Luguelín	Santos	DOM	12.11.92	4	WCh	Beijing	26 Aug
44.16		James			1s1	WCh	Beijing	24 Aug
44.17		James			2	DL	Saint-Denis	4 Jul
44.18		Merritt			1	WK	Zürich	3 Sep
44.19		Makwala			3h2	WCh	Beijing	23 Aug
44.22		James			1	DrakeR	Des Moines	24 Apr
44.24		van Niekerk			1	adidas	New York	13 Jun
44.26		Santos			2s1	WCh	Beijing	24 Aug
44.27	Steven	Gardiner	BAH	12.9.95	1	NC	Nassau	27 Jun
44.27	Abdelilah	Haroun	QAT-J	1.1.97	2		La Chaux-de-Fonds	5 Jul
44.28		James			2	WK	Zürich	3 Sep
44.30		Gardiner			1	Gyulai	Székesfehérvár	7 Jul
44.31		James			1		Tempe	11 Apr
44.31		van Niekerk			1s3	WCh	Beijing	24 Aug
44.34		Merritt			2s3	WCh	Beijing	24 Aug
44.35		van Niekerk			3	WK	Zürich	3 Sep
44.35		Makwala			1	AfG	Brazzaville	15 Sep
44.36	Machel	Cedenio (10)	TTO	6.9.95	1		George Town	16 May
44.36		Merritt			1		Edmonton	12 Jul
44.40		Al-Masrahi			2s2	WCh	Beijing	24 Aug
44.41	Deon	Lendore	TTO	28.10.92	1	SEC	Starkville	16 May
44.41	David	Verburg	USA	14.5.91	1s1	NC	Eugene	26 Jun
	(31/12)							
44.44	Vernon	Norwood	USA	10.4.92	1		Baton Rouge	18 Apr
44.45	Martyn	Rooney	GBR	3.4.87	4h2	WCh	Beijing	23 Aug
44.50	Javon	Francis	JAM	14.12.94	1rA		Kingston	13 Jun
44.54	Chris	Brown	BAH	15.10.78	3	Pre	Eugene	30 May
44.54	Renny	Quow	TTO	25.8.87	2h6	WCh	Beijing	23 Aug
44.54	Rabah	Yousif	GBR	11.12.86	3s2	WCh	Beijing	24 Aug
44.64A	Lalonde	Gordon	TTO	25.11.88	1h3	NACAC	San José, CRC	7 Aug
44.65	Bryshon	Nellum	USA	1.5.89	3h6	WCh	Beijing	23 Aug
	(20)							
44.67	Jonathan	Borlée	BEL	22.2.88	3h1	WCh	Beijing	23 Aug
44.69	Peter	Matthews	JAM	13.11.89	4h1	WCh	Beijing	23 Aug
44.72	Liemarvin	Bonevacia	NED	5.4.89	5h2	WCh	Beijing	23 Aug
44.74	Kévin	Borlée	BEL	22.2.88	4s1	WCh	Beijing	24 Aug
44.75A	Alphas	Kishoyan	KEN	12.10.94	1	NC	Nairobi	11 Jul
44.79	Najee	Glass	USA	12.6.94	1		Gainesville	24 Apr
44.80A	Nery	Brenes	CRC	25.9.85	1h1	NACAC	San José, CRC	7 Aug

Mark	Name		Nat	Born	Pos	Meet	Venue	Date
44.81	Tony	McQuay	USA	16.4.90	6	Pre	Eugene	30 May
44.84	Kyle	Clemons	USA	27.8.90	3	PAm	Toronto	23 Ju
44.89	Bralon	Taplin	GRN	8.5.92	2		Tempe	11 Ap
	(30)							
44.93	Akeem	Bloomfield	JAM-J	10.11.97	1		Kingston	28 Ma
44.93A	Ricardo	Chambers	JAM	7.10.84	2h1	NACAC	San José, CRC	7 Aug
44.95	Marcus	Chambers	USA	3.11.94	4s1	NC	Eugene	26 Jur
44.95	Orukpe	Erayokan	NGR	20.12.93	1s2	AfG	Brazzaville	14 Sep
45.00	Michael	Mathieu	BAH	24.6.83	2	NC	Nassau	27 Jur
45.00	Ashton	Eaton	USA	21.1.88	1D	WCh	Beijing	28 Aug
45.01	Vitaliy	Butrym	UKR	10.1.91	1		Almaty	25 Ju
45.01	Boniface	Mweresa	KEN	13.11.93	2	AfG	Brazzaville	15 Sep
45.04	Donald	Blair-Sanford	ISR	5.2.87	1	Znam	Zhukovskiy	19 Ju
45.06	Conrad	Williams	GBR	20.3.82	1		Genève	6 Jur
	(40)							
45.09	Matthew	Hudson-Smith	GBR	26.10.94	2	Bisl	Oslo	11 Jur
45.09	Jarryd	Dunn	GBR	30.1.92	1	ET	Cheboksary	20 Jur
45.09	Pavel	Maslák	CZE	21.2.91	1		Velenje	1 Ju
45.09A	Gustavo	Cuesta	DOM	14.11.88	2h3	NACAC	San José, CRC	7 Aug
45.10	Onkabetse	Nkobolo	BOT	22.7.93	2s2	AfG	Brazzaville	14 Sep
45.13	Michael	Berry	USA	10.12.91	3h2	NC	Eugene	25 Jur
45.13A	Yoandys	Lescay	CUB	5.1.94	3h3	NACAC	San José, CRC	7 Aug
45.15	Jarrin	Solomon	TTO	11.1.86	1rB		La Chaux-de-Fonds	5 Ju
45.15	Abbas	Abubaker	BRN-J	17.5.96	1		Plovdiv	25 Ju
45.18	Raidel	Acea	CUB	31.10.90	1	Barr	La Habana	26 May
	(50)							
45.19	Michael	Norman	USA-J	3.12.97	1		Clovis	6 Jur
45.19	Edino	Steele	JAM	6.1.87	1s1	NC	Kingston	27 Jur
45.22	Yuzo	Kanemaru	JPN	18.9.87	1h1	NC	Niigata	27 Jur
45.22A	Alex	Sampao	KEN-J	31.12.96	2	NC	Nairobi	11 Ju
45.23A	Philip	Osei	CAN	30.10.90	4h3	NACAC	San José, CRC	7 Aug
45.24A	James	Harris	USA	18.9.91	3h1	NACAC	San José, CRC	7 Aug
45.25	Clayton	Parros	USA	11.12.90	5s1	NC	Eugene	26 Jur
45.25	Pavel	Ivashko	RUS	16.11.94	5h1	WCh	Beijing	23 Aug
45.25	Winston	George	GUY	19.5.87	5h6	WCh	Beijing	23 Aug
45.26	Alberth	Bravo	VEN	29.8.87	3	SACh	Lima	12 Jur
	(60)							
45.26	Mame-Ibra	Anne	FRA	7.11.89	2	ET	Cheboksary	20 Jur
45.27A	Christopher	Taylor	JAM-Y	29.9.99	1	WY	Cali	17 Ju
45.28	Luka	Janezic	SLO	14.11.95	6h1	WCh	Beijing	23 Aug
45.29	Gil	Roberts	USA	15.3.89	6	DrakeR	Des Moines	24 Ap
45.30	Nathon	Allen	JAM	28.10.95	2		Kingston	28 Ma
45.30	LaToy	Williams	BAH	28.5.88	3	NC	Nassau	27 Jur
45.36	Ramon	Miller	BAH	17.2.87	4	NC	Nassau	27 Jur
45.36	Hederson	Estefani	BRA	11.9.91	5h4	WCh	Beijing	23 Aug
45.38	Aldrich	Bailey	USA	6.2.94	3		Edmonton	12 Ju
45.39A	Raymond	Kibet	KEN-J	4.2.96	3	NC	Nairobi	11 Ju
	(70)							
45.41	Calvin	Smith	USA	10.12.87	1		Charlotte, NC	19 Jur
45.41	Paul	Dedewo	USA	5.6.91	1		New York	11 Ju
45.41	Sadam	Koumi	SUD	6.4.94	2s3	AfG	Brazzaville	14 Sep
45.42A	Barend	Koekemoer	RSA	12.6.95	1		Potchefstroom	9 May
45.42	Delano	Williams	GBR	23.12.93	1rB		Kingston	9 May
45.42	Jeremy	Wariner	USA	31.1.84	4		Edmonton	12 Ju
45.42	Hugo	Souza	BRA	5.3.87	6h6	WCh	Beijing	23 Aug
45.43	Michael	Cherry	USA	23.3.95	1	ACC	Tallahassee	16 May
45.43	Aleksandr	Linnik	BLR	28.1.91	3	ET	Cheboksary	20 Jur
45.46	Brycen	Spratling	USA	10.3.92	1	Jerome	Burnaby	8 Jur
	(80)							
45.46A	Josephus	Lyles	USA-Y	22.7.98	2	WY	Cali	17 Ju
45.49	Darrell	Bush	USA	13.5.93	1		Tucson	11 Ap
45.49	Ceolamar	Ways	USA	22.11.94	2s1	NCAA	Eugene	10 Jur
45.50	Thomas	Jordier	FRA	12.8.94	1	EU23	Tallinn	11 Ju
45.51	Patrick	Feeney	USA	29.12.91	1		Baie Mahault	2 May
45.51A	Ofentse	Mogawane	RSA	20.2.82	2		Potchefstroom	9 May
45.51	D.J.	Zahn	USA	31.1.93	1h2	Big 10	East Lansing	16 May
45.52	Takamasa	Kitagawa	JPN-J	5.9.96	2h1	NC	Niigata	27 Jur
45.53	Freddy	Mezones	VEN	24.9.87	1	NC	Barinas	17 Ap
45.53	Zack	Bilderback	USA	27.8.93	3s1	NCAA	Eugene	10 Jur
	(90)							
45.56	Javere	Bell	JAM	20.9.92	1rB		Kingston	9 May

Mark	Name		Nat	Born	Pos	Meet	Venue	Date
45.56	Mamadou-Elimane	Hanne	FRA	6.3.88	1		Nogent-sur-Marne	28 Jun
45.56	Maksim	Dyldin	RUS	19.5.87	5	Gyulai	Székesfehérvár	7 Jul
45.57	Dylan	Borlée	BEL	20.9.92	2		Oordegem	23 May
45.57	Saviour	Kombe	ZAM	3.8.91	3s3	AfG	Brazzaville	14 Sep
45.57	Arokia	Rajiv	IND	22.5.91	2	WMilG	Mungyeong	6 Oct
45.58	Kentaro	Sato	JPN	16.11.94	3h1	NC	Niigata	27 Jun
45.61	Joseph	Richards	USA	14.10.93	1		Abilene	11 Apr
45.61	Anas	Beshr	EGY	19.7.93	2	Arab C	Manama	25 Apr
45.61A	Emmanuel (100)	Dasor	GHA	14.9.95	1		El Paso	17 May

Mark	Name		Nat	Born	Date
45.62	Dane	Hyatt	JAM	22.1.84	27 Jun
45.63	Michael	Bingham	GBR	13.4.86	19 Jun
45.63	Jonia	McDonald	JAM	16.12.89	27 Jun
45.63	Gaone	Maotoanong	BOT	7.5.91	10 Jul
45.64	Kind	Butler	USA	8.4.89	6 Jun
45.65A	Alonzo	Russell	BAH	8.2.92	7 Aug
45.65	Yavuz	Can	TUR	23.2.87	4 Sep
45.66	Chris	Giesting	USA	10.12.92	29 May
45.66		Guo Zhongze	CHN-J	7.8.96	28 Jun
45.66A	Yon	Soriano	DOM	2.1.87	7 Aug
45.67	Steven	Gayle	JAM	19.3.94	16 May
45.67A	Christopher	Hall	USA	1.1.93	17 May
45.67	Lamar	Bruton	USA	26.5.95	29 May
45.68	Pedro	de Oliveira	BRA	17.2.92	18 Apr
45.70	Quincy	Downing	USA	16.1.93	2 May
45.72	Teddy	Venel	FRA	16.3.85	12 Jul
45.73	Demetrius	Pinder	BAH	13.2.89	16 May
45.73	Jan	Tesar	CZE	26.3.90	10 Jul
45.74	Nijel	Amos	BOT	15.3.94	27 Jun
45.75	Keshun	Reed	USA-Y	17.3.98	16 May
45.75	Stephan	James	GUY	23.6.93	14 Jun
45.76	Nathan	Strother	USA	6.9.95	29 May
45.78	Omar	Johnson	JAM	25.11.88	18 Apr
45.78	Fitzroy	Dunkley	JAM	20.5.93	16 May
45.79	Jonathan	da Silva	BRA	17.8.90	28 Mar
45.80	Samson	Oghenewegba	NGR-J	30.8.97	14 Sep
45.81	Brian	Gregan	IRL	31.12.89	8 Aug
45.82	Jeff	Green	USA	18.8.95	16 May
45.82	Jermaine	Griffith	USA	28.5.95	29 May
45.82	Terrence	Agard	NED	16.4.90	5 Jul
45.82	Manteo	Mitchell	USA	6.7.87	7 Jul
45.83	Dedric	Dukes	USA	2.4.92	24 Apr
45.83	Zacharia	Kamberuka	BOT	28.12.87	10 Jul
45.83	Karabo	Sibanda	BOT-Y	2.7.98	8 Sep
45.84	Nigel	Levine	GBR	30.4.89	2 Aug
45.85	Jon	Seeliger	RSA	27.4.95	18 Apr
45.85	Kosuke	Horii	JPN	27.4.94	26 Jun
45.85A	Joseph	Loshangar	KEN	2.7.90	11 Jul
45.85	Josh	Mance	USA	21.3.92	11 Jul
45.86	Toumany	Coulibaly	FRA	6.1.88	6 Jun
45.86	Denis	Kudryavtsev	RUS	13.4.92	19 Jul
45.88	Payton	Hazzard	GRN	6.9.93	16 May
45.88	Jakub	Krzewina	POL	10.10.89	5 Jul
45.88	Ali Khamis	Abbas	BRN	30.6.95	18 Jul
45.90	Nicholas	Maitland	JAM	27.11.89	16 May
45.90	George	Caddick	GBR	29.7.94	17 May
45.90	Andrew	Steele	GBR	19.9.84	26 Jul
45.91	Jereem	Richards	TTO	13.1.94	30 Apr
45.91A	Thapelo	Phora	RSA	21.11.91	9 May
45.91	Adrián	Chacón	CUB	10.12.88	15 May
45.91	Naoki	Kobayashi	JPN	20.12.90	27 Jun
45.91	Alex	Beck	AUS	7.2.92	10 Jul
45.91	Pavel	Trenikhin	RUS	24.3.86	19 Jul
45.92	Steven	Champlin	USA-J	16.2.96	11 Apr
45.92	Osmaidel	Pellicier	CUB	30.3.92	15 May
45.92	Dontavius	Wright	USA	3.1.94	23 May
45.92	Alfred	Larry	USA	9.4.93	29 May
45.92	Yevhen	Hutsol	UKR	13.5.90	25 Jul
45.92	Julian	Walsh	JPN-J	18.9.96	26 Jul
45.93	Twayne	Crooks	JAM	25.9.95	14 Mar
45.94	Craig	Burns	AUS	7.10.88	28 Mar
45.94	Arman	Hall	USA	12.2.94	28 May
45.94	Hideyuki	Hirose	JPN	20.7.89	27 Jun
45.95	William	Collazo	CUB	31.8.86	26 May
45.95	Matteo	Galvan	ITA	24.8.88	5 Jul
45.96	Wilbert	London	USA-J	17.8.97	23 May
45.96	Alexander	Gladitz	GER	19.12.94	14 Jun
45.96	Kazushi	Kimura	JPN	17.1.93	27 Jun
45.96	William	Shell	USA	12.6.91	11 Jul
45.98	Sajad	Hashemi	IRI	22.8.91	25 Jun
45.98	Lucas	Bua	ESP	12.1.94	2 Aug
45.99	Marqueze	Washington	USA	.94	1 May
45.99	Marcus	Boyd	USA	3.3.89	6 Jun
45.99	Richard	Buck	GBR	14.11.86	6 Jun
45.99		Quach Cong Lich	VIE	27.8.93	29 Jun
45.99A	Jamal	Walton	CAY-Y	25.11.98	17 Jul
46.00A	Shaquille	Walker	USA	24.6.93	25 Apr
46.00	Kunanon	Sukkaew	THA	30.9.94	12 Jun
46.00	Pako	Seribe	BOT	7.4.91	1 Jul
46.01	Benjamin	Lobo Vedel	DEN-J	23.9.97	27 Jun
46.01	Nick	Ekelund-Arenander	DEN	23.1.89	9 Jul
46.02	Michael	Courtney	USA	12.6.86	6 Jun
46.02	Soufiane	Bouhada	ALG	8.6.90	1 Jul
46.03A	Shaun	de Jager	RSA	28.6.91	9 May
46.03	Kazuya	Watanabe	JPN	20.7.88	27 Jun
46.03	Ludvy	Vaillant	FRA	15.3.95	9 Jul
46.04	Wágner	Cardoso	BRA	20.3.89	18 Apr
46.04	Daniel	Awde	GBR	22.6.88	24 Apr
46.04	Mehdi	Zamani	IRI	20.12.89	25 Jul
46.04	Rodwell	Ndlovu	ZIM	4.3.91	14 Sep
46.05	Lennox	Williams	JAM	23.10.94	6 Jun
46.05	Eric	Krüger	GER	21.3.88	26 Jul
46.07	Chidi	Okezie	USA	8.8.93	29 May
46.07		Zhu Chenbin	CHN	17.3.90	25 Jun
46.07	Tomoya	Tamura	JPN	20.8.92	27 Jun
46.08	Mikhail	Litvin	KAZ-J	5.1.96	12 May
46.09	Chance	Tanner	USA	7.4.93	10 May
46.10	Marek	Niit	EST	9.8.87	1 May
46.10A	Elbert	Rogers	USA	.94	17 May
46.10	Cole	Lambourne	USA	.94	29 May
46.10	Robin (201)	Vanderbemden	BEL	10.2.94	9 Jul

Indoors

Mark	Name		Nat	Born	Date
45.91	Cody	Rush	USA	11.11.93	28 Feb
45.98	Hugh	Graham	JAM	10.10.92	31 Jan

Low altitude bests

Mark	Name	Pos	Meet	Venue	Date
44.70	L Gordon	4s2	WCh	Beijing	24 Aug
44.85	Brenes	4	PAm	Toronto	23 Jul
45.31	Sampao	1s3	AfG	Brazzaville	14 Sep
45.33	Cuesta	1		Ponce	18 Apr
45.53	Harris	2		Baie Mahault	2 May
45.55	C Taylor	3		Kingston	13 Jun
45.56	R Chambers	2s2	NC	Kingston	27 Jun

Mark	Name	Date
45.63	Mogawane	1 Jul
45.66	Kibet	14 Sep
45.71	Russell	27 Jun
45.77	J Lyles	1 Jul
45.80	Osei	16 May
45.81	Kishoyan	23 May
45.84	Lescay	15 May

JUNIORS

See main list for top 3 juniors. 10 performances by 6 men to 45.27. Additional marks and further juniors:

	Mark	Pos	Meet	Venue	Date	Mark	Pos	Meet	Venue	Date
Haroun	44.63	1		Madrid	11 Jul	44.68	1	AsiC	Wuhan	4 Jun
	44.68A	1		Sasolburg	19 Mar	44.80	5	Pre	Eugene	30 May
	44.68	1	ArabC	Manama	25 Apr	44.85	1	DL	Doha	15 May

Mark	Name		Nat	Born	Pos	Meet	Venue	Date
45.66		Guo Zhongze	CHN	7.8.96	1		Beijing	28 Jun
45.75	Keshun	Reed (10)	USA-Y	17.3.98	1		Austin	16 May
45.80	Samson	Oghenewegba	NGR	30.8.97	4s1	AfG	Brazzaville	14 Sep

Mark	Name		Nat	Born	Pos	Meet	Venue	Date
45.83	Karabo	Sibanda	BOT-Y	2.7.98	1	Comm-Y	Apia	8 Se
45.92	Steven	Champlin	USA	16.2.96	2		Abilene	11 Ap
45.92	Julian	Walsh	JPN	18.9.96	1		Tokyo	26 Ju
45.96	Wilbert	London	USA	17.8.97	1		Waco	23 Ma
45.99A	Jamal	Walton	CAY-Y	25.11.98	4	WY	Cali	17 Ju
46.01	Benjamin Lobo	Vedel	DEN	23.9.97	1		Mannheim	27 Ju
46.08	Mikhail	Litvin	KAZ	5.1.96	1		Almaty	12 Ma
46.18	Ilya	Krasnov	RUS	17.5.96	1	NC-j	Cheboksary	26 Ju
46.19	Rai	Benjamin (20)	ANT	27.7.97	2	Carifta	Basseterre	4 Ap

500 METRES

Mark	Name		Nat	Born	Pos	Meet	Venue	Date
1:00.41	Pavel	Maslák	CZE	21.2.91	1	Danek	Turnov	19 Ma
Indoors								
1:00.06	Brycen	Spratling	USA	10.3.92	1	Mill	New York (Armory)	14 Fe

Mark	Name		Nat	Born	Date	Mark	Name		Nat	Born	Date
1:00.43	Michael	Berry	USA	10.12.91	14 Feb	1:00.70	Bershawn	Jackson	USA	8.5.83	14 Feb
1:00.68	Jakub	Krzewina	POL	10.10.89	1 Feb	1:00.76	Jonathan	Borlée	BEL	22.2.88	14 Feb

600 METRES

Mark	Name		Nat	Born	Pos	Meet	Venue	Date
1:14.33	Charles	Jock	USA	23.11.89	1		Portland	14 Ju
1:15.07	Harun	Abda	USA	1.1.90	2		Portland	14 Ju
1:15.44	Duane	Solomon	USA	28.12.84	1	MSR	Walnut	18 Ap
1:15.58A	Reinhardt	van Rensburg	RSA	23.3.92	1		Pretoria	30 Ja
1:15.60	Alfred	Kipketer	KEN-J	26.12.96	1	Flame	Amsterdam	5 Se
1:15.63+	Nijel	Amos	BOT	15.3.94	1	in 800	Berlin	6 Se

Mark	Name		Nat	Born	Date	Mark	Name		Nat	Born	Date
1:15.71	Mark	English	IRL	18.3.93	5 Sep	1:16.02	Adam	Kszczot	POL	2.9.89	26 May
1:15.81	Mark	Wieczorek	USA	25.12.84	14 Jun	1:16.11A	Ranti	Dikgale	RSA	12.7.87	30 Jan
1:15.87	Nicholas	Kipkoech	KEN	22.10.92	5 Sep	1:16.13	Nick	Symmonds	USA	30.12.83	14 Jun
1:15.91	Robert	Biwott	KEN-J	28.1.96	5 Sep	1:16.14	Boris	Berian	USA	19.12.92	18 Apr
1:15.97+	Pierre-Ambroise	Bosse	FRA	11.5.92	17 Jul	1:16.35+	David	Rudisha	KEN	17.12.88	9 Jul

Indoors

Mark	Name		Nat	Born	Pos	Meet	Venue	Date
1:15.33i	Casimir	Loxsom	USA	17.3.91	1	NC	Boston (R)	1 Ma

Mark	Name		Nat	Born	Date	Mark	Name		Nat	Born	Date
1:15.99i	Abdulrahman	Musaeb Balla	QAT	19.3.89	1 Feb	1:16.01i	Luguelín	Santos	DOM	12.11.92	21 Feb

800 METRES

Mark	Name		Nat	Born	Pos	Meet	Venue	Date
1:42.51	Amel	Tuka	BIH	9.1.91	1	Herc	Monaco	17 Ju
1:42.66	Nijel	Amos	BOT	15.3.94	2	Herc	Monaco	17 Ju
1:42.97	Ayanleh	Souleiman	DJI	3.12.92	3	Herc	Monaco	17 Ju
1:43.08		Souleiman			1		Barcelona	8 Ju
1:43.27		Amos			1	Athl	Lausanne	9 Ju
1:43.28		Amos			1	ISTAF	Berlin	6 Se
1:43.34	Boris	Berian	USA	19.12.92	4	Herc	Monaco	17 Ju
1:43.45	Adam	Kszczot	POL	2.9.89	5	Herc	Monaco	17 Ju
1:43.56	Mohammed	Aman	ETH	10.1.94	1	GGala	Roma	4 Ju
1:43.56	Robert	Biwott	KEN-J	28.1.96	2		Barcelona	8 Ju
1:43.58	David	Rudisha	KEN	17.12.88	1	adidas	New York	13 Ju
1:43.60A	Ferguson	Cheruiyot	KEN	30.11.89	1	WCT	Nairobi	1 Au
1:43.72	Marcin	Lewandowski (10)	POL	13.6.87	6	Herc	Monaco	17 Ju
1:43.76		Rudisha			2	Athl	Lausanne	9 Ju
1:43.78		Souleiman			1	DL	Doha	15 Ma
1:43.80		Amos			2	GGala	Roma	4 Ju
1:43.82	Abdulrahman Musaeb Balla		QAT	19.3.89	3		Barcelona	8 Ju
1:43.84		Berian			2	adidas	New York	13 Ju
1:43.84		Tuka			1		Madrid	11 Ju
1:43.88	Pierre-Ambroise	Bosse	FRA	11.5.92	3	adidas	New York	13 Ju
1:43.89A		Rudisha			2	WCT	Nairobi	1 Au
1:43.92	Job	Kinyor	KEN	2.9.90	3	GGala	Roma	4 Ju
1:43.92		Cheruiyot			7	Herc	Monaco	17 Ju
1:43.94		Kszczot			4	GGala	Roma	4 Ju
1:44.00		Cheruiyot			5	GGala	Roma	4 Ju
1:44.07A	Alfred	Kipketer	KEN-J	26.12.96	3	WCT	Nairobi	1 Au
1:44.09	Antoine	Gakémé	BDI	24.12.91	2		Madrid	11 Ju
1:44.09		Kinyor			3		Madrid	11 Ju
1:44.09		Aman			8	Herc	Monaco	17 Ju
1:44.19		Tuka			1		Velenje	1 Ju
	(30/15)							
1:44.24	Taoufik	Makhloufi	ALG	29.4.88	4	ISTAF	Berlin	6 Se
1:44.4A	Asbel	Kiprop	KEN	30.6.89	1		Nairobi	21 Ma
1:44.50	Edwin	Melly	KEN	23.4.94	4		Barcelona	8 Ju
1:44.51A	Willy	Tarbei	KEN-Y	30.5.98	1		Nairobi	17 Ju
1:44.53	Nick	Symmonds	USA	30.12.83	1	NC	Eugene	28 Ju
	(20)							

Mark	Name		Nat	Born	Pos	Meet	Venue	Date
1:44.55A	Kipyegon	Bett	KEN-Y	2.1.98	2		Nairobi	17 Jun
1:44.56A	Jackson	Kivuva	KEN	11.8.88	4	WCT	Nairobi	1 Aug
1:44.62	Matthew	Centrowitz	USA	18.10.89	4	adidas	New York	13 Jun
1:44.64	Nader	Belhanbel	MAR	1.7.94	5		Barcelona	8 Jul
1:44.84	Erik	Sowinski	USA	21.12.89	2	NC	Eugene	28 Jun
1:44.9A	Nicholas	Kipkoech	KEN	22.10.92	1h2		Nairobi	10 Jun
1:44.92	Casimir	Loxsom	USA	17.3.91	1s1	NC	Eugene	26 Jun
1:44.99	Jeff	Riseley	AUS	11.11.86	1		Lignano Sabbiadoro	7 Jul
1:45.0A	Jonathan	Kitilit	KEN	24.4.94	2h2		Nairobi	10 Jun
1:45.0A	Timothy	Kitum	KEN	20.11.94	3h2	WCT	Nairobi	31 Jul
	(30)							
1:45.07	Giordano	Benedetti	ITA	22.5.89	8	GGala	Roma	4 Jun
1:45.20	Amine	El Manaoui	MAR	20.11.91	3rA		Rieti	13 Sep
1:45.2A	Fredrick	Korir	KEN	17.4.87	3h2		Nairobi	10 Jun
1:45.2A	Patrick Kiprotich	Rono	KEN-J	9.4.96	4h2	WCT	Nairobi	31 Jul
1:45.21	Artur	Kuciapski	POL	26.12.93	9	GGala	Roma	4 Jun
1:45.24	Leonel	Manzano	USA	12.9.84	5	adidas	New York	13 Jun
1:45.25	Kevin	López	ESP	12.6.90	4		Madrid	11 Jul
1:45.28	Thijmen	Kupers	NED	4.10.91	1	NC	Amsterdam	2 Aug
1:45.33	Abraham	Rotich	BRN	26.6.93	2		Sotteville-lès-Rouen	6 Jul
1:45.38	Alex	Rowe	AUS	8.7.92	1		Canberra	7 Feb
	(40)							
1:45.40	Charles	Jock	USA	23.11.89	1		Ponce	23 May
1:45.40	Rynhardt	van Rensburg	RSA	23.3.92	2		Velenje	1 Jul
1:45.40	Jozef	Repcík	SVK	3.8.86	2		Lignano Sabbiadoro	7 Jul
1:45.4A	Edwin	Kemboi	KEN	22.8.86	4h2		Nairobi	10 Jun
1:45.47	Michael	Rutt	USA	28.10.87	3s1	NC	Eugene	26 Jun
1:45.48	Robin	Schembera	GER	1.10.88	2	FBK	Hengelo	24 May
1:45.49	Mark	English	IRL	18.3.93	4	DL	London (OS)	25 Jul
1:45.50	Jeremiah	Mutai	KEN	27.12.92	7	DL	Doha	15 May
1:45.50	Ali Saad	Al-Daran	KSA	17.4.90	1	WMilG	Mungyeong	6 Oct
1:45.5A	Sammy	Kirongo	KEN	4.2.94	1s2	NC	Nairobi	9 Jul
	(50)							
1:45.53	Rafith	Rodríguez	COL	1.6.89	2		Ponce	23 May
1:45.56	Duane	Solomon	USA	28.12.84	4s1	NC	Eugene	26 Jun
1:45.58	Brannon	Kidder	USA	18.11.93	2	Jordan	Stanford	2 May
1:45.58	Edward	Kemboi	KEN	12.12.91	1s1	NCAA	Eugene	10 Jun
1:45.58	Shaquille	Walker	USA	24.6.93	1s2	NC	Eugene	26 Jun
1:45.59	Andreas	Almgren	SWE	12.6.95	1		Sollentuna	25 Jun
1:45.59	Clayton	Murphy	USA	26.2.95	4	NC	Eugene	28 Jun
1:45.6A	Boniface	Mutisya	KEN		2s2	NC	Nairobi	10 Jul
1:45.62	Samir	Dahmani	FRA	3.4.91	4		Lignano Sabbiadoro	7 Jul
1:45.67	Michael	Rimmer	GBR	3.2.86	5	DL	London (OS)	25 Jul
	(60)							
1:45.68	Bernard	Kipyegon	KEN	.94	5		Madrid	11 Jul
1:45.73	André	Olivier	RSA	29.12.89	3	FBK	Hengelo	24 May
1:45.76	Jesse	Jorgensen	USA	1.9.91	5s1	NC	Eugene	26 Jun
1:45.76	Konstantin	Tolokonnikov	RUS-J	26.2.96	1	NC	Cheboksary	4 Aug
1:45.78	Abdellatif	El Guers	MAR	27.2.93	2	NC	Rabat	6 Jun
1:45.78	Kyle	Langford	GBR-J	2.2.96	7	DL	London (OS)	25 Jul
1:45.78	Andreas	Bube	DEN	13.7.87	2	DL	Stockholm	30 Jul
1:45.79	Yassine	Hathat	ALG	30.7.91	1		Alger	9 Jul
1:45.79	Joshua	Ralph	AUS	27.10.91	1		Ninove	1 Aug
1:45.79A	Ryan	Martin	USA	23.3.89	1	NACAC	San José, CRC	9 Aug
	(70)							
1:45.81	Jakub	Holusa	CZE	20.2.88	1		Tábor	28 Jul
1:45.87	Brandon	McBride	CAN	15.6.94	1h2	SEC	Starkville	14 May
1:45.89	Mark	Wieczorek	USA	25.12.84	3	Jordan	Stanford	2 May
1:45.91	Alex	Amankwah	USA/GHA	2.3.92	1	FlaR	Gainesville	3 Apr
1:45.92	Amine	Laâlou ¶	MAR	13.5.82	3	NC	Rabat	6 Jun
1:45.97	Sofiane	Selmouni	FRA	22.9.89	1		Oordegem	30 May
1:45.98	Robby	Andrews	USA	29.3.91	6	adidas	New York	13 Jun
1:46.00	Zan	Rudolf	SLO	9.5.93	3		Velenje	1 Jul
1:46.0A	Jena	Umar	ETH	24.12.95	1		Assela	12 Jul
	1:46.07				1		Montbéliard	5 Jun
1:46.0A	Yobsen	Girma	ETH		2		Assela	12 Jul
	(80)							
1:46.04	Maurys Surel	Castillo	CUB	19.10.84	7		Madrid	11 Jul
1:46.06	Khaled	Benmahdi	ALG	22.10.88	2		Oordegem	30 May
1:46.13	Craig	Engels	USA	1.5.94	2		Baton Rouge	2 May
1:46.13	Yeimer	López	CUB	20.8.82	1	Bisl	Oslo	11 Jun

Mark	Name		Nat	Born	Pos	Meet	Venue	Date
1:46.14	Ilham Tanui	Özbilen	TUR	5.3.90	2	ECCp	Mersin	31 May
1:46.16	Jamal	Al-Hayrani	QAT	26.5.93	2		Kessel-Lo	8 Aug
1:46.17	Julian	Parker	USA	20.7.91	1	SEC	Starkville	16 May
1:46.2A	Kumari	Taki	KEN-Y	6.5.99	2		Eldoret	23 May
1:46.27	Antonio Manuel	Reina	ESP	13.6.81	1		Valencia	6 Aug
1:46.28	Andy	González	CUB	17.10.87	3		Ponce	23 May
	(90)							
1:46.3A	Mike	Kemboi	KEN	.89	4		Nairobi	12 Jun
1:46.33	Harun	Abda	USA	1.1.90	4		Ponce	23 May
1:46.36	Thiago	André	BRA	4.8.95	1		São Paulo	3 May
1:46.43	Theo	Blundell	GBR	30.11.95	4		Kessel-Lo	8 Aug
1:46.45	Mouhcine	El Amine	MAR	8.1.82	4	NC	Rabat	6 Jun
1:46.46	Mohamed Amine	Belferrar	ALG	6.2.91	5	WMilG	Mungyeong	6 Oct
1:46.49	Andrés	Arroyo	PUR	7.6.95	3	SEC	Starkville	16 May
1:46.5A	Moses	Kibet	KEN	20.11.94	3		Eldoret	23 May
1:46.5A	Felix	Konchellah	KEN	15.11.90	1s1		Nairobi	10 Jun
1:46.5	Alberto	Mamba	MOZ	9.10.94	1		Maputo	3 Oct
	(100)							

Mark	Name		Nat	Born	Date
1:46.51	Peter	Bol	AUS	22.2.94	7 Feb
1:46.52	Sho	Kawamoto	JPN	1.3.93	30 May
1:46.52	Luis Alberto	Marco	ESP	20.8.86	26 Jun
1:46.54	Masato	Yokota	JPN	19.11.87	30 May
1:46.57	Mostafa	Smaïli	MAR-J	9.1.97	17 Jun
1:46.58	Anthony	Romaniw	CAN	15.9.91	14 May
1:46.65	Guy	Learmonth	GBR	24.4.92	21 Jul
1:46.65	Dennis	Krüger	GER	24.4.93	9 Aug
1:46.67	Brice	Leroy	FRA	26.6.89	10 May
1:46.67	Abdelaati	Iguider	MAR	25.3.87	6 Sep
1:46.68	Hugo	Santacruz	SUI	6.5.88	21 Jul
1:46.70	Ivan	Nesterov	RUS	10.2.85	4 Aug
1:46.74	Ronald	Musagala	UGA	16.12.92	10 May
1:46.74	Jan	Van Den Broeck	BEL	11.3.89	8 Aug
1:46.75A	Silas	Kiplagat	KEN	20.8.89	20 Jun
1:46.77	Kléberson	Davide	BRA	20.7.85	27 Sep
1:46.79	Jacopo	Lahbi	ITA	1.6.93	14 May
1:46.8A	Jonah	Koech	KEN-J	12.12.96	18 Feb
1:46.80	Boitumelo	Masilo	BOT	.95	15 Sep
1:46.83	Jesús	Gómez	ESP	24.4.91	11 Jul
1:46.85	Stanislav	Maslov	UKR	19.1.89	21 Jun
1:46.85	Kalle	Berglund	SWE-J	11.3.96	21 Jun
1:46.86	Samir	Jamaa	MAR	9.2.90	17 May
1:46.86	Bob	van der Ham	NED	6.7.90	23 May
1:46.87	Collins	Kibet	KEN	.88	28 Mar
1:46.87	Mohamed Ahmed	Hamada	EGY	22.10.92	13 Sep
1:46.89	Ryan	Schnulle	USA	8.9.93	3 Apr
1:46.89	Daniel	Andújar	ESP	14.5.94	22 Jul
1:46.90	Jared	West	AUS	14.7.88	7 Feb
1:46.90	Brandon	Johnson	USA	6.3.85	18 Apr
1:46.9	Hocine	Khelif	ALG	3.11.94	16 Jun
1:46.91A	Jacob	Rozani	RSA	24.1.88	9 May
1:46.91	David	Palacio	ESP	8.6.88	6 Aug
1:46.92	Lukas	Rifesser	ITA	17.7.86	28 Aug
1:46.93	Jordan	Williamsz	AUS	21.8.92	7 Jul
1:47.03	Jesse	Garn	USA	4.6.93	17 Apr
1:47.03	Blair	Henderson	USA	4.10.94	2 May
1:47.03	Thomas	Roth	NOR	11.2.91	9 Aug
1:47.03	Karol	Konieczny	POL	5.5.93	9 Aug
1:47.06	Abubaker Haydar	Abdallah	QAT-J	28.8.96	8 Aug
1:47.07A	Jamaal	James	TTO	4.9.88	9 Aug
1:47.08	Salah	Echchibani	MAR	1.7.91	5 Jun
1:47.11	Mohammed Ayoub	Tiouali	BRN	26.5.91	1 Aug
1:47.13	Saul	Ordóñez	ESP	10.4.94	24 Jun
1:47.14	Badr	El Jalaoui	MAR	28.1.93	6 Jun
1:47.14A	Ricardo	Cunningham	JAM	3.10.80	9 Aug
1:47.15	Mohamed	Belbachir	ALG	11.1.94	5 Jun
1:47.15	Linus	Kiplagat	BRN	23.12.94	6 Oct
1:47.18A	Bryan Antonio	Martinez	MEX	1.8.94	29 Mar
1:47.20	Dylan	Capwell	USA	1.7.95	29 May
1:47.20	Henco	Uys	RSA	4.6.92	15 Jul
1:47.20	Mourad	Amdouni	FRA	21.1.88	6 Sep
1:47.20	Emad Yahya	Al Jizani	KSA	.94	13 Sep
1:47.2A	Bacha	Morka	ETH-Y	6.6.98	12 Jul
1:47.21	Chris	Low	USA	29.8.92	14 Jun
1:47.22	Nikolay	Verbitskiy	RUS	16.12.95	4 Aug
1:47.22	Amine	Khadiri	CYP	20.11.88	8 Aug
1:47.23	Kyle	Merber	USA	19.11.90	17 Apr
1:47.23	Manuel	Olmedo	ESP	17.5.83	1 Jul
1:47.24	Evans	Kipkorir	KEN	4.4.94	25 May
1:47.27	Ayoub	Sniba	MAR-J	5.4.97	17 Jun
1:47.27	Sean	Obinwa	NGR	4.1.91	12 Jul
1:47.28	Brandon	Hazouri	USA	21.10.93	29 May
1:47.28	Richard	Charles	GBR	31.5.94	30 May
1:47.28	Alejandro	Rodríguez	ESP	1.5.89	30 May
1:47.28	Declan	Murray	IRL	4.6.91	4 Jun
1:47.28	Mor	Seck	SEN	24.9.85	13 Sep
1:47.30	Charel	Grethen	LUX	22.6.92	29 May
1:47.3A	Mengistu	Alemu	ETH		14 Jun
1:47.31	Ayoub	Labser	MAR	7.4.93	6 Jun
1:47.32	Goaner	Deng	USA	30.6.93	10 Jun
1:47.33	Jamie	Webb	GBR	1.6.94	23 May
1:47.34	Kamil	Gurdak	POL	17.10.90	30 May
1:47.36	Nicky	Coemans	BEL	18.5.90	30 May
1:47.36	Benedikt	Huber	GER	13.10.89	15 Jul
1:47.36	Jake	Wightman	GBR	11.7.94	22 Aug
1:47.37	Aaron	Evans	BER	31.1.90	4 Jun
1:47.38	Brandon	Lasater	USA	9.10.92	3 Apr
1:47.38	Keffri	Neal	CAN	26.10.93	14 May
1:47.39	Brad	Mathas	NZL	24.6.93	14 Mar
1:47.39	Karl	Griffin	IRL	5.6.95	23 May
1:47.39	Sebastian	Keiner	GER	22.8.89	19 Jun
1:47.40	Joseph	White	USA	16.11.95	29 May
1:47.40	Rory	Graham-Watson	GBR	3.6.90	5 Sep
1:47.40	Elijah	Manangoi	KEN	5.1.93	11 Sep
1:47.43	Mathew	Kiptanui	KEN	20.10.94	1 Jul
1:47.45	Timas	Harik	AUS	1.1.94	7 Feb
1:47.45	Aaron	Botterman	BEL	1.5.94	23 May
1:47.45	Konstantin	Kholmogorov	RUS-J	7.2.96	26 Jun
1:47.46	Anthony	Chemut	KEN	17.12.92	10 May
1:47.47	Holland	Sherrer	USA	17.8.93	14 May
1:47.47	Moussa	El Haiba	MAR	17.2.89	6 Jun
1:47.49	James	Bowness	GBR	26.11.91	30 May
1:47.49	Álvaro	de Arriba	ESP	2.6.94	20 Jun
	(194)				

Drugs disqualification

Mark	Name		Nat	Born	Date
1:47.42	Ahmed	Mainy ¶	MAR	20.8.86	28 Mar

Indoors

Mark	Name		Nat	Born	Date
1:46.70	Dylan	Capwell	USA	1.7.95	14 Mar
1:46.98	Jesse	Garn	USA	4.6.93	14 Feb
1:47.34	Ryan	Manahan	USA	14.7.94	21 Feb
1:47.38	Joe	McAsey	USA	1.6.93	14 Feb

JUNIORS

See main list for top 8 juniors. 11 performances by 5 men to 1:45.2. Additional marks and further juniors:

	Mark	Pos	Meet	Venue	Date	Mark	Pos	Meet	Venue	Date
Kipketer	1:44.33	9	Herc	Monaco	17 Jul	1:45.0A	2		Nairobi	21 Mar
	1:44.59	3	DL	Doha	15 May	1:45.14	4	Athl	Lausanne	9 Jul
	1:44.99	2s1	WCh	Beijing	23 Aug	1:45.2A	3h1	WCT	Nairobi	31 Jul

Mark	Name		Nat	Born	Pos	Meet	Venue	Date
1:46.57	Mostafa	Smaïli	MAR	9.1.97	1	NC-j	Meknès	17 Jun
1:46.8A	Jonah	Koech (10)	KEN	12.12.96	2		Nairobi	18 Feb

Mark	Name		Nat	Born	Pos	Meet	Venue	Date
1:46.85	Kalle	Berglund	SWE	11.3.96	6	ET	Cheboksary	21 Jun
1:47.06	Abubaker Haydar	Abdallah	QAT	28.8.96	1		Granollers	8 Aug
1:47.2A	Bacha	Morka	ETH-Y	6.6.98	3		Assela	12 Jul
1:47.27	Ayoub	Sniba	MAR	5.4.97	2	NC-j	Meknès	17 Jun
1:47.45	Konstantin	Kholmogorov	RUS	7.2.96	1	NC-j	Cheboksary	26 Jun
1:47.53	Abdi Waiss	Mouhyadin	DJI	3.7.96	3		Mataró	18 Jul
1:47.55	Donavan	Brazier	USA	15.4.97	1		Shoreline	20 Jun
1:47.6A	Isaac	Kipkosgei	KEN	.96	3h1		Eldoret	22 May
1:47.67	Carlton	Orange	USA	11.3.97	1	NC-j	Eugene	27 Jun
1:47.73	Mateusz	Borkowski (20)	POL	2.4.97	2rB		Oordegem	23 May

1000 METRES

Mark	Name		Nat	Born	Pos	Meet	Venue	Date
2:13.08	Taoufik	Makhloufi	ALG	29.4.88	1		Tomblaine	1 Jul
2:15.78	Jonathan	Kitilit	KEN	24.4.94	2		Tomblaine	1 Jul
2:17.25	Marcin	Lewandowski	POL	13.6.87	1	GS	Ostrava	26 May
2:17.38	Asbel	Kiprop	KEN	30.6.89	2	GS	Ostrava	26 May
2:17.51	Edwin	Melly	KEN	23.4.94	3		Tomblaine	1 Jul
2:17.62	Timothy	Kitum	KEN	20.11.94	3	GS	Ostrava	26 May
2:17.92	Abderrahmane	Anou	ALG	29.1.91	1			Jul
2:18.42	Jakub	Holusa	CZE	20.2.88				26 May

Indoors

Mark	Name		Nat	Born	Pos	Meet	Venue	Date
2:17.00i	Matthew	Centrowitz	USA	18.10.89	1		Boston (R)	7 Feb
2:18.30i	Patrick	Casey	USA	23.5.90	2		Boston (R)	7 Feb

Best junior: 2:20.28 Abdi Waiss Mouhyadin DJI 3.7.96 2 Göteborg 5 Sep

1500 METRES

Mark	Name		Nat	Born	Pos	Meet	Venue	Date
3:26.69	Asbel	Kiprop	KEN	30.6.89	1	Herc	Monaco	17 Jul
3:28.75	Taoufik	Makhloufi	ALG	29.4.88	2	Herc	Monaco	17 Jul
3:28.79	Abdelaati	Iguider	MAR	25.3.87	3	Herc	Monaco	17 Jul
3:28.93	Mohamed	Farah	GBR	23.3.83	4	Herc	Monaco	17 Jul
3:29.66	Nick	Willis	NZL	25.4.83	5	Herc	Monaco	17 Jul
3:29.67	Elijah	Manangoi	KEN	5.1.93	6	Herc	Monaco	17 Jul
3:30.10	Robert	Biwott	KEN-J	28.1.96	7	Herc	Monaco	17 Jul
3:30.12	Silas	Kiplagat	KEN	20.8.89	1	DL	Saint-Denis	4 Jul
3:30.17	Ayanleh	Souleiman	DJI	3.12.92	2	DL	Saint-Denis	4 Jul
3:30.29	Aman	Wote (10)	ETH	18.4.84	8	Herc	Monaco	17 Jul
3:30.34	Collins	Cheboi	KEN	25.9.87	9	Herc	Monaco	17 Jul
3:30.40	Matthew	Centrowitz	USA	18.10.89	10	Herc	Monaco	17 Jul
3:30.43	Ronald	Kwemoi	KEN	19.9.95	3	DL	Saint-Denis	4 Jul
3:30.50		Makhloufi			4	DL	Saint-Denis	4 Jul
3:31.39		Biwott			5	DL	Saint-Denis	4 Jul
3:31.51		Iguider			6	DL	Saint-Denis	4 Jul
3:31.76	James	Magut	KEN	20.7.90	7	DL	Saint-Denis	4 Jul
3:31.88		Cheboi			8	DL	Saint-Denis	4 Jul
3:32.03		Wote			9	DL	Saint-Denis	4 Jul
3:32.68	Ilham Tanui	Özbilen	TUR	5.3.90	10	DL	Saint-Denis	4 Jul
3:32.85	Henrik	Ingebrigtsen	NOR	24.2.91	11	DL	Saint-Denis	4 Jul
3:32.97	Evan	Jager	USA	8.3.89	1		Portland	14 Jun
3:33.33		Souleiman			1	DL	Stockholm	30 Jul
3:33.45	Sadik	Mikhou	MAR	25.7.90	1		Kessel-Lo	8 Aug
3:33.64		Biwott			1	FBK	Hengelo	24 May
3:34.03A		Kiprop			1	WCT	Nairobi	1 Aug
3:34.05	Mourad	Amdouni	FRA	21.1.88	11	Herc	Monaco	17 Jul
3:34.13	Garrett	Heath (20)	USA	3.11.85	2		Portland	14 Jun
3:34.23	Charles	Philibert-Thiboutot	CAN	31.12.90	12	Herc	Monaco	17 Jul
3:34.26	Jakub	Holusa	CZE	20.2.88	2	DL	Stockholm	30 Jul
	(30/22)							
3:34.29	Yassine	Bensghir	MAR	3.1.83	1		Rabat	14 Jun
3:34.53	Fouad	El Kaam	MAR	27.5.88	1rA	NA	Heusden-Zolder	18 Jul
3:34.54	Kyle	Merber	USA	19.11.90	1		Greenville, SC	30 May
3:34.83	Chris	O'Hare	GBR	23.11.90	1rB	NA	Heusden-Zolder	18 Jul
3:34.86A	Timothy	Cheruiyot	KEN	20.11.95	5	WCT	Nairobi	1 Aug
3:35.02	Ronald	Musagala	UGA	16.12.94	2	FBK	Hengelo	24 May
3:35.14	Benson	Seurei	BRN	27.3.84	12	DL	Saint-Denis	4 Jul
3:35.20	Hillary	Maiyo	KEN	2.10.93	1		Barcelona	8 Jul
	(30)							
3:35.29	Charlie	Grice	GBR	7.11.93	2rA	NA	Heusden-Zolder	18 Jul
3:35.33	Anthony	Kiptoo	KEN-J	19.8.97	3	FBK	Hengelo	24 May
3:35.36	Cory	Leslie	USA	24.10.89	2		Greenville, SC	30 May
3:35.40	Hillary	Ngetich	KEN	15.9.95	2	DL	Shanghai	17 May

Mark	Name		Nat	Born	Pos	Meet	Venue	Date
3:35.42	Nathan	Brannen	CAN	8.9.82	3rA	NA	Heusden-Zolder	18 Jul
3:35.48	Ben	Blankenship	USA	15.12.89	4	DL	Shanghai	17 May
3:35.52	Robby	Andrews	USA	29.3.91	5	DL	Stockholm	30 Jul
3:35.67	Mekonnen	Gebremedhin	ETH	11.10.88	4rA	NA	Heusden-Zolder	18 Jul
3:35.69	Enoch	Omwamba	KEN	4.4.93	1		Yokohama	15 May
3:35.71	Amine	Laâlou ¶	MAR	13.5.82	3		Tomblaine	1 Jul
	(40)							
3:35.78	Mohamed	Al-Garni	QAT	2.7.92	2		Sollentuna	25 Jun
3:35.82	Younès	Essalhi	MAR	20.2.93	6	DL	Stockholm	30 Jul
3:35.84	Elijah	Kiptoo	KEN	9.6.86	4		Tomblaine	1 Jul
3:35.86A	Charles	Simotwo	KEN	6.5.95	8	WCT	Nairobi	1 Aug
3:35.87	Dawit	Wolde	ETH	19.5.91	5rA	NA	Heusden-Zolder	18 Jul
3:35.90	Thiago	André	BRA	4.8.95	5	FBK	Hengelo	24 May
3:35.92	Salim	Keddar	ALG	23.11.93	1		Alger	8 Aug
3:35.95	Pieter Jan	Hannes	BEL	30.10.92	6	FBK	Hengelo	24 May
3:35.97	David	Bustos	ESP	25.8.90	6rA	NA	Heusden-Zolder	18 Jul
3:36.05	Florian	Orth	GER	24.7.89	7rA	NA	Heusden-Zolder	18 Jul
	(50)							
3:36.09	Abdi Waiss	Mouhyadin	DJI-J	3.7.96	3		Sollentuna	25 Jun
3:36.16	Leonel	Manzano	USA	12.9.84	13	Herc	Monaco	17 Jul
3:36.21	Othmane	El Goumri	MAR	28.5.92	5		Rabat	14 Jun
3:36.34	Johan	Cronje	RSA	13.4.82	7	FBK	Hengelo	24 May
3:36.35	Lee	Emanuel	GBR	24.1.85	8rA	NA	Heusden-Zolder	18 Jul
3:36.36	Dumisani	Hlaselo	RSA	8.6.89	6		Tomblaine	1 Jul
3:36.37	Nixon	Chepseba	KEN	12.12.90	9	DL	Shanghai	17 May
3:36.38A	Kumari	Taki	KEN-Y	6.5.99	1	WY	Cali	17 Jul
3:36.46	Sebastian	Keiner	GER	22.8.89	2rB	NA	Heusden-Zolder	18 Jul
3:36.49	Riley	Masters	USA	5.4.90	2		Portland	2 Jul
	(60)							
3:36.51	Ryan	Gregson	AUS	26.4.90	1		Sydney	14 Mar
3:36.54	Yassine	Hathat	ALG	30.7.91	2		Alger	8 Aug
3:36.55	Adel	Mechaal	ESP	5.12.90	2		Barcelona (S)	8 Jul
3:36.56	Colby	Alexander	USA	13.6.91	3		Portland	2 Jul
3:36.70	Jeff	See	USA	6.6.86	3		Greenville, SC	30 May
3:36.73	Aman	Kedi	ETH	16.9.94	1		Bruay-la-Buissière	1 Jul
3:36.77	Andrew	Bayer	USA	3.2.90	4rB	NA	Heusden-Zolder	18 Jul
3:36.80	Vincent	Kibet	KEN	6.5.91	11	DL	Shanghai	17 May
3:36.84	Bryan	Cantero	FRA	28.4.91	11rA	NA	Heusden-Zolder	18 Jul
3:36.85	Jeremy	Rae	CAN	19.5.91	5rB	NA	Heusden-Zolder	18 Jul
	(70)							
3:36.86	Ismael	Kombich	KEN	16.10.85	7		Tomblaine	1 Jul
3:36.87	Jeff	Riseley	AUS	11.11.86	2		Sydney	14 Mar
3:36.93	Frezer	Legesse	USA	4.6.90	4		Greenville, SC	30 May
3:36.96	Youssouf Hiss	Bachir	DJI	.87	1		Ninove	1 Aug
3:36.98	Ford	Palmer	USA	6.10.90	6rB	NA	Heusden-Zolder	18 Jul
3:37.05	Samir	Dahmani	FRA	3.4.91	14	DL	Saint-Denis	4 Jul
3:37.06	Isaac	Presson	USA	7.2.92	5		Greenville, SC	30 May
3:37.08	Edward	Cheserek	KEN	2.2.94	4		Portland	2 Jul
3:37.08	Mohamed Ismail	Ibrahim	DJI-J	.97	1		Mataró	18 Jul
3:37.20	Jordan	McNamara	USA	7.3.87	7rB	NA	Heusden-Zolder	18 Jul
	(80)							
3:37.24	Regasa	Chala	ETH-J	.97	2		Ninove	1 Aug
3:37.30	Álvaro	Rodríguez	ESP	25.5.87	6		Barcelona (S)	8 Jul
3:37.34	Thomas	Riva	CAN	31.1.92	8rB	NA	Heusden-Zolder	18 Jul
3:37.37	Julian	Matthews	NZL	21.7.88	9rB	NA	Heusden-Zolder	18 Jul
3:37.4A	Abednego	Chesebe	KEN	20.6.82	1		Nairobi	6 Jun
3:37.56	Daniel	Winn	USA	30.7.91	5		Portland	2 Jul
3:37.59	Rashid	Ramzi	BRN	17.7.80	3		Ninove	1 Aug
3:37.70	Víctor José	Corrales	ESP	12.3.89	3		Mataró	18 Jul
3:37.75	Hélio	Gomes	POR	27.12.84	4		Mataró	18 Jul
3:37.76	Zakaria	Maazouzi	MAR	15.6.85	1		Fez	2 May
	(90)							
3:37.76	Ross	Murray	GBR	8.10.90	1		Watford	27 Jun
3:37.81	Martin	Sperlich	GER	28.8.91	10rB	NA	Heusden-Zolder	18 Jul
3:37.86	Carlos	Díaz	CHI	9.7.93	7		Barcelona	8 Jul
3:37.88	Peter	Callahan	USA	1.6.91	1		Oordegem	4 Aug
3:37.89	Abdelhadi	Labali	MAR	26.4.93	7		Rabat	14 Jun
3:37.91	Mathew	Kiptanui	KEN	.94	1		Ponzano Veneto	3 Jul
3:37.97	Elroy	Gelant	RSA	25.8.86	8	FBK	Hengelo	24 May
3:38.02	Stanislav	Maslov	UKR	19.1.89	2	Sidlo	Sopot	27 Jun
3:38.02	Tom	Lancashire	GBR	2.7.85	4	VD	Bruxelles	11 Sep

Mark	Name		Nat	Born	Pos	Meet	Venue	Date
3:38.13	Caleb (100)	Ndiku	KEN	9.10.92	7	WK	Zürich	3 Sep
3:38.17	Ryan	Hill	USA	31.1.90				14 Jun
3:38.20	Jeroen	D'Hoedt	BEL	10.1.90				24 May
3:38.23	Grzegorz	Kalinowski	POL	22.9.90				27 Jun
3:38.24	Dan	Huling	USA	16.7.83				14 Jun
3:38.30	Dorian	Ulrey	USA	11.7.87				30 May
3:38.35	Chad	Noelle	USA	12.4.93				2 May
3:38.35	Federico	Bruno	ARG	18.6.93				8 Jul
3:38.42	Marc	Alcalá	ESP	7.11.94				18 Jul
3:38.44	Sami	Lafi	ALG	25.4.90				1 Jul
3:38.49	Graham	Crawford	USA	29.12.92				2 Jul
3:38.51	Jonathan	Sawe	KEN	22.5.95				9 Jun
3:38.52	John	Bolas	USA	1.11.87				2 Jul
3:38.53	Mohad	Abdikadar	ITA	12.6.93				3 Jul
3:38.56	Yoann	Kowal	FRA	28.5.87				5 Jun
3:38.57	Thomas	Farrell	GBR	23.3.91				27 Jun
3:38.58A	Mark	Bett	KEN	.94				20 Jun
3:38.58	Carlos	Alonso	ESP	15.9.89				11 Sep
3:38.62	Vincent	Mutai	KEN	3.11.94				1 Jul
3:38.64	Llorenc	Sales	ESP	14.7.88				18 Jul
3:38.65	Dale	Clutterbuck	GBR	1.1.92				18 Jul
3:38.7A	Bernard	Muia	KEN	26.5.95				21 Mar
3:38.75	Andrew	Wheating	USA	21.11.87				14 Mar
3:38.80	Patrick	Casey	USA	23.5.90				18 Jul
3:38.94	Andreas	Bueno	DEN	7.7.88				1 Aug
3:38.97	Abderrahmane	Anou	ALG	29.1.91				20 Jun
3:38.98	Eric	Jenkins	USA	24.11.91				11 Jul
3:38.99	Youssef Saad	Kamel	BRN	29.3.83				17 Jul
3:39.02	Robby	Creese	USA	30.8.93				2 May
3:39.02	Edward	Kemboi	KEN	12.12.91				3 Jul
3:39.05	Josh	Wright	AUS	3.5.91				14 Mar
3:39.05	Kirubel	Erassa	USA	17.6.93				2 May
3:39.10	Jerry	Motsau	RSA	12.3.90				27 Jun
3:39.13	Aleksey	Kharitonov	RUS	4.7.91				10 Jul
3:39.15	Cameron	Boyek	GBR	9.10.93				22 Aug
3:39.16	Ross	Proudfoot	CAN	4.7.92				10 Jun
3:39.16	Dmitrijs	Jurkevics	LAT	7.1.87				27 Jun
3:39.18	Mohammed Ayoub	Tiouali	BRN	26.5.91				29 Jul
3:39.20	Abdelali	Razyn	MAR	1.1.91				10 Jul
3:39.22	Teshome	Dirirsa	ETH	25.4.94				8 Aug
3:39.25	Awet Nftalem	Kibrab	ERI-J	9.5.97				29 Aug
3:39.32	Collis	Birmingham	AUS	27.12.84				11 Sep
3:39.37	Tesfaye	Cheru	ETH	2.3.93				21 Jun
3:39.38	Duncan	Phillips	USA	7.6.89				10 Jun
3:39.4A	Abraham	Kiplagat	KEN	8.9.84				6 Jun
3:39.42	Imad	Touil	ALG	11.2.89				8 Jul
3:39.43	Thomas	Joyce	USA	20.7.93				11 Apr
3:39.47	Salah	Echchibani	MAR	1.7.91				8 Aug
3:39.50	David	Njugana	KEN	6.9.89				26 Sep
3:39.51	David	Torrence	USA	26.11.85				1 Aug
3:39.53	Jordan	Williamsz	AUS	21.8.92				17 Apr
3:39.61	Diego	Ruiz	ESP	5.2.82				18 Jul
3:39.62	Abdullah Obaid	Al-Salhi	KSA	.94				8 Aug
3:39.66	Justyn	Knight	CAN-J	19.7.96				18 Apr
3:39.66	Daniel	Herrera	USA	29.11.92				2 Jul
3:39.68	Cristian	Soratos	USA	26.9.92				2 May
3:39.68	Hicham	Oueladha	MAR	.95				2 May
3:39.68	Staffan	Ek	SWE	13.11.91				10 Jul
3:39.71	Richard	Douma	NED	17.4.93				27 May
3:39.71A	Vincent	Letting	KEN	16.6.93				11 Jul
3:39.73A	Bernard	Koros	KEN	7.5.94				20 Jun
3:39.73	Isaac	Kimeli	BEL	9.3.94				1 Aug
3:39.78	Soufiane	El Kabbouri	ITA	5.3.93				13 Sep
3:39.81	Jonathan	Kitilit	KEN	24.4.94				25 Jun
3:39.82A	Cornelius	Kiplangat	KEN	21.12.92				11 Jul
3:39.84	Valentin	Smirnov	RUS	13.2.86				5 Jun
3:39.86	Amine	Khadiri	CYP	20.11.88				27 May
3:39.87	Artur	Ostrowski	POL	10.7.88				25 Jun
3:39.88	André	Olivier	RSA	29.12.89				25 Apr
3:39.88	Marco	Pettenazzo	ITA	28.10.92				3 Jul
3:39.91	Bekele	Gutema	ETH	.94				7 Jul
3:39.94	Dennis	Licht	NED	30.5.84				24 May
3:40.01	Lawi	Lalang	KEN	15.6.91				2 May
3:40.01	Taylor	Milne	CAN	14.9.81				30 May
3:40.01	Sofiane	Selmouni	FRA	22.9.89				5 Jul
3:40.04	James	Mwangi	KEN	23.3.94				4 Apr
3:40.04	Mac	Fleet	USA	17.10.90				14 May
3:40.05	Zebene	Alemayehu	ETH	4.9.92				21 Jun
3:40.05	Will	Geoghegan	USA	15.7.92				27 Jun
3:40.05	Jake	Wightman	GBR	11.7.94				17 Jul
3:40.06	Marcel	Fehr	GER	20.6.92				5 Jun
3:40.06	Yegor	Nikolayev	RUS	28.4.88				10 Jul
3:40.09	Ross	Millington	GBR	19.9.89				27 Jun
3:40.10	Abiyot	Abinet	ETH	10.5.89				5 Jul
3:40.14	Brahim	Kaazouzi	MAR	15.6.90				27 Jun
3:40.18	Mohammed	Ahmed	CAN	5.1.91				14 Jun
3:40.20	Michael	Atchoo	USA	16.8.91				2 May
3:40.20	Eoin	Everard	IRL	23.4.86				1 Aug
3:40.21	Oli	Aitchison (188)	GBR	13.3.92				2 May

Disqualified – obstruction

Mark	Name		Nat	Born	Date
3:39.77	Levent	Ates	TUR	20.3.91	10 Jul

Short – 1493m at Marseille 6 Jun:
1. Iguider 3:32.88, 2. Fouad El Kaam MAR 27.5.88 3:33.27, 4. Elijah Kiptoo KEN 9.6.86 3:33.98, 5. Benson Seurei BRN 27.3.84 3:34.32, 6, Jonathan Sawe KEN 22.5.95 3:34.68, 8. Bekele Gutema ETH .94 3:34.90 , 9. Gilbert Kwemboi KEN-J 3.10.97 3:35.68, 10, Vincent Mutai KEN 3.11.94 3:35.81, 13, Imad Touil ALG 11.2.89 3:37.12

Indoors

Mark	Name		Nat	Born	Pos	Venue	Date
3:34.13	Homiyu	Tesfaye	GER	23.6.93	1	Stockholm	19 Feb
3:34.62	Bethwel	Birgen	KEN	6.8.88	2	Stockholm	19 Feb
3:34.91	Vincent	Kibet	KEN	6.5.91	1	Birmingham	21 Feb
3:35.26	Hillary	Ngetich	KEN	15.9.95	3	Birmingham	21 Feb
3:35.28	Ben	Blankenship	USA	15.12.89	4=	Birmingham	21 Feb
3:35.28	Nixon	Chepseba	KEN	12.12.90	3	Birmingham	21 Feb
3:35.66	Lee	Emanuel	GBR	24.1.85	6	Birmingham	21 Feb
3:38.28+	Patrick	Casey	USA	23.5.90			14 Feb
3:38.68	Marcin	Lewandowski	POL	13.6.87			31 Jan
3:38.74	Valentin	Smirnov	RUS	13.2.86			1 Feb
3:38.86	Teshome	Dirirsa	ETH	25.4.94			21 Feb
3:39.75+	Cameron	Levins	CAN	28.3.89			31 Jan
3:40.03	Johan	Rogestedt	SWE	27.1.93			19 Feb
3:40.20+	Bernard	Lagat	USA	12.12.74			14 Feb

JUNIORS

See main list for top 6 juniors. 11 performances by 6 men to 3:37.5. Additional marks and further juniors:

	Mark	Pos	Meet	Venue	Date
Biwott 3+	3:34.71A	3	WCT	Nairobi	1 Aug
	3:35.75	5	DL	Shanghai	17 May
	3:36.04	3	WK	Zürich	3 Sep

Mark	Name		Nat	Born	Pos	Meet	Venue	Date
3:39.25	Awet Nftalem	Kibrab	ERI	9.5.97	2		Oslo	29 Aug
3:39.66	Justyn	Knight	CAN	19.7.96	1		Charlottesville	18 Apr
3:40.47	Gilbert	Kwemboi	KEN	3.10.97	3		Rehlingen	25 May
3:40.61	Ibrahim Hassan	Bouh (10)	DJI	.96	11		Mataró	18 Jul
3:40.77	Lawi	Kosgei	KEN-Y	14.1.99	2	Comm-Y	Apia	7 Sep
3:40.81	Blake	Haney	USA	29.3.96	2s2	NCAA	Eugene	10 Jun
3:41.03	Tesfu	Tewelde	ERI	21.7.97	6		Nijmegen	27 May
3:41.10A	Mulugeta	Asefa	ETH-Y	12.3.98	2	WY	Cali	17 Jul
3:41.13	Patrick	Mathenge	KEN	.96	2		Yokohama	15 May

Mark	Name		Nat	Born	Pos	Meet	Venue	Date
3:41.64	Nabil	Oussama	MAR	18.2.96	6		Amiens	27 Jun
3:41.66	Jordi	Torrents	ESP	25.9.97	16		Barcelona	8 Jul
3:41.74A	Welde	Tufa	ETH-Y	23.9.99	4	WY	Cali	17 Jul
3:41.85A	Brimin	Kiprotich	KEN-Y	20.8.99	3	NC-j	Nairobi	16 Jun
3:41.92	Kalle	Berglund (20)	SWE	11.3.96	3		Göteborg	14 Aug

1 MILE

Mark	Name		Nat	Born	Pos	Meet	Venue	Date
3:51.10	Ayanleh	Souleiman	DJI	3.12.92	1	Pre	Eugene	30 May
3:51.20	Matthew	Centrowitz	USA	18.10.89	2	Pre	Eugene	30 May
3:51.25	Asbel	Kiprop	KEN	30.6.89	3	Pre	Eugene	30 May
3:51.45		Kiprop			1	Bisl	Oslo	11 Jun
3:51.72	Silas	Kiplagat	KEN	20.8.89	2	Bisl	Oslo	11 Jun
3:51.84	Pieter Jan	Hannes	BEL	30.10.92	3	Bisl	Oslo	11 Jun
3:52.33	James	Magut	KEN	20.7.90	5	Pre	Eugene	30 May
3:52.57	Ronald	Kwemoi	KEN	19.9.95	6	Pre	Eugene	30 May
3:52.63	Collins	Cheboi	KEN	25.9.87	7	Pre	Eugene	30 May
3:53.02	Johan	Cronje	RSA	13.4.82	8	Pre	Eugene	30 May
3:53.21	Abdelaati	Iguider (10)	MAR	25.3.87	9	Pre	Eugene	30 May
3:53.43	Henrik	Ingebrigtsen	NOR	24.2.91	10	Pre	Eugene	30 May
3:53.46	Jakub	Holusa	CZE	20.2.88	6	Bisl	Oslo	11 Jun
3:53.55	Leonel	Manzano	USA	12.9.84	11	Pre	Eugene	30 May
3:53.91 *	David	Torrence	USA	26.11.85	1		Huntington Station	9 Sep
3:54.51 *	Garrett	Heath	USA	3.11.85	2		Huntington Station	9 Sep
	3:56.53				5r2	Pre	Eugene	30 May
3:54.52	Charles	Philibert-Thiboutot	CAN	31.12.90	8	Bisl	Oslo	11 Jun
3:54.88	Ryan	Gregson	AUS	26.4.90	9	Bisl	Oslo	11 Jun
3:55.27	Charlie	Grice	GBR	7.11.93	4	DL	London (OS)	25 Jul
3:55.48	Ben	Blankenship	USA	15.12.89	5	DL	London (OS)	25 Jul

Mark	Name		Nat	Born	Date
3:55.65	Vincent	Kibet (20)	KEN	6.5.91	30 May
3:55.71	Ross	Murray	GBR	8.10.90	25 Jul
3:55.76	Jonathan	Sawe	KEN	22.5.95	30 May
3:55.80	Timothy	Cheruiyot	KEN	20.11.95	30 May
3:56.35	Chris	O'Hare	GBR	23.11.90	25 Jul
3:56.87	Tom	Lancashire	GBR	2.7.85	25 Jul
3:57.09	Eric	Jenkins	USA	24.11.91	8 May
3:57.09	Jeff	Riseley	AUS	11.11.86	24 Jul
3:57.15	Robby	Andrews	USA	29.3.91	4 Jun
3:57.28	Patrick	Casey	USA	23.5.90	30 May
3:57.34	Aman	Wote)(30)	ETH	18.4.84	30 May
3:57.48	Riley	Mastes	USA	5.4.90	24 Jul
3:57.53	Will	Geoghegan	USA	15.7.92	8 May
3:57.60	Duncan	Phillips	USA	7.6.89	24 Jul
3:57.80	Jake	Wightman	GBR	11.7.94	25 Jul
3:57.91	Bernard	Lagat	USA	12.12.74	25 Jul
3:57.94	Julian	Matthews	NZL	21.7.88	24 Jul
3:57.97	Abdi Waiss	Mouhyadin	DJI-J	3.7.96	30 May
3:57.97	Kyle	Merber	USA	19.11.90	7 Aug

* no curb at Huntington Station; cones were placed improperly

Indoors

Mark	Name		Nat	Born	Pos	Meet	Venue	Date
3:51.46	Nick	Willis	NZL	25.4.83	2	Mill	New York (Arm)	14 Feb
3:53.13	Ben	Blankenship	USA	15.12.89	2		Boston (R)	7 Feb
3:54.36	Patrick	Casey	USA	23.5.90	3	Mill	New York (Arm)	14 Feb
3:54.74	Cameron	Levins	CAN	28.3.89	1		New York (Arm)	31 Jan
3:54.91	Bernard	Lagat	USA	12.12.74	4	Mill	New York (Arm)	14 Feb
3:55.25	Evan	Jager	USA	8.3.89	5	Mill	New York (Arm)	14 Feb
3:55.27	Cristian	Soratos	USA	26.9.92	1		Seattle	14 Feb
3:55.35	Chris	O'Hare	GBR	23.11.90	6	Mill	New York (Arm)	14 Feb

Mark	Name		Nat	Born	Date
3:56.15	Riley	Masters	USA	5.4.90	7 Feb
3:56.43	Edward	Cheserek	KEN	2.2.94	14 Feb
3:56.79	Ford	Palmer	USA	6.10.90	14 Feb
3:56.84	Ryan	Hill	USA	31.1.90	31 Jan
3:56.86	Pablo	Solares	MEX	22.12.84	15 Jan
3:56.99	Cory	Leslie	USA	24.10.89	31 Jan
3:57.13	Brannon	Kidder	USA	18.11.93	14 Feb
3:57.15	Lawi	Lalang	KEN	15.6.91	14 Feb
3:57.22	Julian	Oakley	NZL	23.6.93	14 Feb
3:57.28	Michael	Rutt	USA	28.10.87	14 Feb
3:57.36	Matthew	Elliott	USA	8.9.85	14 Feb
3:57.42	Andrew	Wheating	USA	21.11.87	31 Jan
3:57.47	John	Gregorek	USA	7.12.91	14 Feb
3:57.54	Will	Leer	USA	15.4.85	31 Jan
3:57.58	Michael	Atchoo	USA	16.8.91	14 Feb
3:57.62	Daniel	Winn	USA	30.7.91	14 Feb
3:57.78	Chad	Noelle	USA	12.4.93	14 Feb
3:57.81	Izaic	Yorks	USA	17.4.94	28 Feb
3:57.86	Robert	Creese	USA	30.8.93	7 Feb

JUNIORS

Mark	Name		Nat	Born	Pos	Meet	Venue	Date
3:57.97	Abdi Waiss	Mouhyadin	DJI	3.7.96	9r2	Pre	Eugene	30 May
3:59.38	Matthew	Maton	USA	28.3.96	3		Eugene	8 May
3:59.38	Grant	Fisher	USA	22.4.97	3		St. Louis	4 Ju
3:59.51i	Justyn	Knight	CAN	19.7.96	3		University Park	31 Jan

2000 METRES

Mark	Name		Nat	Born	Pos	Meet	Venue	Date
5:02.9i+	Mohamed	Farah	GBR	23.3.83	1	in 2M	Birmingham	21 Feb

3000 METRES

Mark	Name		Nat	Born	Pos	Meet	Venue	Date
7:34.66	Mohamed	Farah	GBR	23.3.83	1	DL	London (OS)	24 Jul
7:35.13	Caleb	Ndiku	KEN	9.10.92	1	Herc	Monaco	17 Jul
7:36.39	Yenew	Alamirew	ETH	27.5.90	2	Herc	Monaco	17 Jul

Mark	Name		Nat	Born	Pos	Meet	Venue	Date
7:36.71	Othmane	El Goumri	MAR	28.5.92	2	DL	London (OS)	24 Jul
7:37.05	Emmanuel	Kipsang	KEN	13.6.91	3	DL	London (OS)	24 Jul
7:37.16	Isiah	Koech	KEN	19.12.93	3	Herc	Monaco	17 Jul
7:37.85	Edwin	Soi	KEN	3.3.86	4	Herc	Monaco	17 Jul
7:37.97	Garrett	Heath	USA	3.11.85	5	Herc	Monaco	17 Jul
7:38.08	Hagos	Gebrhiwet	ETH	11.5.94	1	DL	Doha	15 May
7:38.08	Ben	Blankenship (10)	USA	15.12.89	6	Herc	Monaco	17 Jul
7:38.22		Farah			2	DL	Doha	15 May
7:38.47		Alamirew			4	DL	London (OS)	24 Jul
7:38.65	Ali	Kaya	TUR	20.4.94	7	Herc	Monaco	17 Jul
7:39.22	Thomas	Longosiwa	KEN	14.1.82	3	DL	Doha	15 May
7:39.70	Hillary	Maiyo	KEN	2.10.93	8	Herc	Monaco	17 Jul
7:39.85	Collis	Birmingham	AUS	27.12.84	5	DL	London (OS)	24 Jul
7:39.96	Imane	Merga	ETH	15.10.88	4	DL	Doha	15 May
7:39.99	Yomif	Kejelcha	ETH-Y	1.8.97	5	DL	Doha	15 May
	(18/16)							
7:40.44	Bashir	Abdi	BEL	10.2.89	6	DL	London (OS)	24 Jul
7:41.74	Yasin	Haji	ETH-J	22.1.96	9	Herc	Monaco	17 Jul
7:41.79	Eric	Jenkins	USA	24.11.91	1		Lignano Sabbiadoro	7 Jul
7:42.03	Benson	Seurei	BRN	27.3.84	8	DL	Doha	15 May
	(20)							
7:42.19	Lopez	Lomong	USA	1.1.85	1		Luzern	14 Jul
7:42.75	Bernard	Lagat	USA	12.12.74	2		Luzern	14 Jul
7:43.26	Vincent	Rono	KEN	11.11.90	3		Luzern	14 Jul
7:43.77	Chris	Derrick	USA	17.10.90	8	DL	London (OS)	24 Jul
7:43.94	Dejene	Debela	ETH	.94	2		Sotteville-lès-Rouen	6 Jul
7:44.59	Abrar	Osman	ERI	1.1.94	9	DL	Doha	15 May
7:45.97	Brett	Robinson	AUS	8.5.91	5		Luzern	14 Jul
7:45.99	Aman	Kedi	ETH	16.9.94	3		Sotteville-lès-Rouen	6 Jul
7:46.14	Suguru	Osako	JPN	23.5.91	10	DL	London (OS)	24 Jul
7:46.36	Albert	Rop	BRN	17.7.92	11	DL	Doha	15 May
	(30)							
7:46.53	Jesús	España	ESP	21.8.78	10	Herc	Monaco	17 Jul
7:46.59	Henrik	Ingebrigtsen	NOR	24.2.91	13	DL	Doha	15 May
7:46.80	Fredrick	Kipkosgei	KEN-J	13.11.96	13	DL	Doha	15 May
7:46.83+	Paul	Tanui	KEN	22.12.90	1	in 5000m	Roma	4 Jun
7:47.21	Cornelius	Kangogo	KEN	31.12.93	1		Bellinzona	21 Jul
7:47.22	Stanislav	Maslov	UKR	19.1.89	4		Sotteville-lès-Rouen	6 Jul
7:47.35	Elroy	Gelant	RSA	25.8.86	11	DL	London (OS)	24 Jul
7:47.48	Moses	Koech	KEN-J	5.4.97	3		Rieti	13 Sep
7:47+	Muktar	Edris	ETH	14.1.94		in 5000m	Roma	4 Jun
7:47+	Illias	Fifa	MAR/ESP	16.5.89		in 5000m	Roma	4 Jun
	(40)							
7:47+	Dejen	Gebremeskel	ETH	24.11.89		in 5000m	Roma	4 Jun

Mark	Name		Nat	Born	Date	Mark	Name		Nat	Born	Date
7:48.21	Sami	Lafi	ALG	25.4.90	6 Jul	7:49.64	Ross	Proudfoot	CAN	4.7.92	24 Jul
7:48.35	Sam	McEntee	AUS	3.2.92	24 Jul	7:49.73	Brahim	Kaazouzi	MAR	15.6.90	6 Jul
7:48.50	Awet Nftalem	Kibrab	ERI-J	9.5.97	5 Sep	7:49.88	Soufiane	El Bakkali	MAR-J	7.1.96	6 Jul
7:48.59	Andrew	Bayer	USA	3.2.90	14 Jul	7:50.24	Saïd	El Otmani	ITA	14.10.91	13 Sep
7:48.7A	Clement	Langat	KEN	.91	23 May	7:50.72	Sindre	Buraas	NOR	8.5.89	13 Sep
7:48.79	Will	Geoghegan	USA	15.7.92	24 Jul	7:51.13	Andrew	Vernon	GBR	7.1.86	24 Jul
7:48.81	Soufiyan	Bouqantar	MAR	30.8.93	21 Jul	7:51.30	Lee	Emanuel	GBR	24.1.85	24 Jul
7:48.82	Roberto	Alaiz	ESP	20.7.90	16 May	7:51.64	Ryan	Gregson	AUS	26.4.90	8 Aug
7:49.13	Brahim	Taleb	MAR	16.2.85	21 Jul	7:51.7A	Edward	Rono	KEN-Y	6.8.98	16 Jun
7:49.35	Tom	Lancashire	GBR	2.7.85	5 Sep	7:51.76	Jeff	See	USA	6.6.86	7 Jul
7:49.61	Carlos	Alonso	ESP	15.9.89	13 Sep		(62)				

Indoors

Mark	Name		Nat	Born	Pos	Meet	Venue	Date
7:33.1+	Mohamed	Farah	GBR	23.3.83	1		Birmingham	21 Feb
7:37.92	Bernard	Lagat	USA	12.12.74	1		Metz	25 Feb
7:38.42	Ali	Kaya	TUR	20.4.94	1	EI	Praha (O2)	7 Mar
7:39.68	Paul Kipsiele	Koech	KEN	10.11.81	2		Metz	25 Feb
7:42.65	Nixon	Chepseba	KEN	12.12.90	3		Metz	25 Feb
7:43.77	Bethwel	Birgen	KEN	6.8.88	4		Metz	25 Feb
7:44.48	Lee	Emanuel	GBR	24.1.85	2	EI	Praha (O2)	7 Mar
7:44.97+	Galen	Rupp	USA	8.5.86	1	in 2M	New York (Arm)	31 Jan
7:45.21+	Cameron	Levins	CAN	28.3.89	2	in 2M	New York (Arm)	31 Jan
7:45.54	Henrik	Ingebrigtsen	NOR	24.2.91	3	EI	Praha (O2)	7 Mar
7:45.62+	Suguru	Osako	JPN	23.5.91	4	in 2M	New York (Arm)	31 Jan
7:45.71	Will	Geoghegan	USA	15.7.92	2	Mill	New York (Arm)	14 Feb
7:46.18	Richard	Ringer	GER	27.2.89	2		Karlsruhe	31 Jan
7:46.92	Adel	Mechaal	ESP	5.12.90	2h2	EI	Praha (O2)	6 Mar
7:47.55	Pieter Jan	Hannes	BEL	30.10.92	3h2	EI	Praha (O2)	6 Mar

Mark	Name		Nat	Born	Date	Mark	Name		Nat	Born	Date
7:48.13	Kemoy	Campbell	JAM	14.1.91	14 Feb	7:48.19	Dejen	Gebremeskel	ETH	24.11.89	7 Feb

MEN 2015

Mark	Name		Nat	Born	Date
7:48.36	Yegor	Nikolayev	RUS	12.2.88	31 Jan
7:48.48	Jeramy	Elkaim	USA	25.12.92	28 Feb
7:48.59	Florian	Carvalho	FRA	9.3.89	6 Mar
7:48.72	Hassan	Mead	USA	28.8.89	7 Feb
7:48.80	Will	Leer	USA	15.4.85	7 Feb
7:49.25	Colby	Gilbert	USA	17.3.95	14 Feb
7:49.48	Florian	Orth	GER	24.7.89	31 Jan
7:49.49	Halil	Akkas	TUR	1.7.83	7 Feb
7:49.51	Aleksey	Popov	RUS	17.6.87	17 Feb
7:49.56	Edward	Cheserek	KEN	2.2.94	24 Jan
7:49.74	Stanley	Kebenei	USA	6.11.89	14 Feb
7:50.11	Lukasz	Parszczynski	POL	4.5.85	7 Mar
7:50.36	Robert	Creese	USA	30.8.93	14 Feb
7:50.49	Fabian	Clarkson	GER	13.12.90	14 Feb
7:50.60	Isaac	Presson	USA	7.2.92	14 Feb
7:50.92	Andrew "AJ"	Acosta	USA	13.4.88	14 Feb
7:51.1+	Philip	Hurst	GBR	3.10.90	21 Feb
7:51.26	Andrew	Bumbalough	USA	14.3.87	31 Jan
7:51.26	Erik	Olson	USA	15.3.92	28 Feb
7:51.3+	Thomas	Farrell	GBR	23.3.91	21 Feb
7:51.62+	Reed	Connor	USA	25.9.90	31 Jan
7:51.87	Kevin	Batt	IRL	28.2.91	14 Feb
7:51.87	Matt	Hughes	CAN	3.8.89	14 Feb
7:51.93	Morgan	Pearson	USA	22.9.93	28 Feb

JUNIORS

See main list for top 5 juniors. 6 performances by 6 men to 7:50.0, Further juniors:

Mark	Name		Nat	Born	Pos	Meet	Venue	Date
7:49.88	Soufiane	El Bakkali	MAR	7.1.96	7		Sotteville-lès-Rouen	6 Jul
7:51.7A	Edward	Rono	KEN-Y	6.8.98	1h2	NC-j	Nairobi	16 Jun
7:52.04	Abdiwak	Tura	ETH	.97	1		Madrid	11 Jul
7:52.27	Geoffrey	Korir	KEN	2.5.96	4		Bellinzona	21 Jul
7:53.3A	Richard	Yator	KEN-Y	6.4.98	1	NC-j	Nairobi	16 Jun
7:53.6A	Davis	Kiplangat (10)	KEN-Y	10.7.98	1		Nairobi	1 Apr
7:53.7A	Richard	Kimunyan	KEN-Y	.98	2		Nairobi	1 Apr
7:54.63	Paul	Kamais	KEN	24.10.96	1		Unnan	16 Ma
7:55.04A	Tefera	Mosisa	ETH-Y	10.3.99	3	WY	Cali	19 Jul
7:56.66	Merhawi	Ghebreselasie	ERI-Y	.98	1		Pliezhausen	17 Ma
7:56.93	Vedic	Kipkoech	KEN	.96	3		Bilbao	20 Jun
7:57.2A	Victor	Kibet	KEN-Y	.98	3		Nairobi	1 Apr
7:58.83	Berhane	Emanuel	ERI	.96	7		Madrid	11 Jul
7:59.2A	Peter	Langat	KEN-Y	20.10.98	4	NC-j	Nairobi	16 Jun
7:59.67	Chala	Beyo (20)	ETH	18.1.96	9		Sotteville-lès-Rouen	6 Jul
Best European: 8:02.75	Alex	George	GBR	6.2.96	15		Dublin (S)	24 Jul
Indoors								
7:55.20	Morgan	McDonald	AUS	23.4.96	1		Ames	14 Feb

2 MILES INDOORS

Mark	Name		Nat	Born	Pos	Meet	Venue	Date
8:03.40	Mohamed	Farah	GBR	23.3.83	1	GP	Birmingham	21 Feb
8:13.46	Paul Kipsiele	Koech	KEN	10.11.81	2	GP	Birmingham	21 Feb
8:15.38	Cameron	Levins	CAN	28.3.89	1		New York (Armory)	31 Jan
8:16.47	Suguru	Osako	JPN	23.5.91	2		New York (Armory)	31 Jan
8:16.53	Ben	Blankenship	USA	15.12.89	3		New York (Armory)	31 Jan
8:17.05	Bernard	Lagat	USA	12.12.74	4	GP	Birmingham	21 Feb
8:17.24	Galen	Rupp	USA	8.5.86	4		New York (Armory)	31 Jan
8:21.24	Lee	Emanuel	GBR	24.1.85	5		New York (Arm)	31 Jan

Mark	Name		Nat	Born	Date
8:26.01	Thomas	Farrell	GBR	23.3.91	21 Feb
8:26.56	Philip	Hurst	GBR	3.10.90	21 Feb
8:26.72	Ryan	Hill	USA	31.1.90	28 Feb

5000 METRES

Mark	Name		Nat	Born	Pos	Meet	Venue	Date
12:53.98	Yomif	Kejelcha	ETH-J	1.8.97	1	VD	Bruxelles	11 Sep
12:54.70	Hagos	Gebrhiwet	ETH	11.5.94	2	VD	Bruxelles	11 Sep
12:58.39		Kejelcha			1	GGala	Roma	4 Jun
12:58.69	Paul	Tanui	KEN	22.12.90	2	GGala	Roma	4 Jun
12:58.69		Gebrhiwet			3	GGala	Roma	4 Jun
12:59.04	Imane	Merga	ETH	15.10.88	4	GGala	Roma	4 Jun
12:59.25	Abdelaati	Iguider	MAR	25.3.87	3	VD	Bruxelles	11 Sep
12:59.72	Thomas	Longosiwa	KEN	14.1.82	4	VD	Bruxelles	11 Sep
12:59.78		Longosiwa			5	GGala	Roma	4 Jun
13:00.30	Muktar	Edris	ETH	14.1.94	6	GGala	Roma	4 Jun
13:00.31	Ali	Kaya	TUR	20.4.94	7	GGala	Roma	4 Jun
13:00.49	Dejen	Gebremeskel	ETH	24.11.89	8	GGala	Roma	4 Jun
13:05.30	Caleb	Ndiku (10)	KEN	9.10.92	5	VD	Bruxelles	11 Sep
13:05.38		Gebremeskel			1	NA	Heusden-Zolder	18 Jul
13:05.53	Yenew	Alamirew	ETH	27.5.90	6	VD	Bruxelles	11 Sep
13:05.54	Ben	True	USA	29.12.85	7	VD	Bruxelles	11 Sep
13:05.61	Illias	Fifa	MAR/ESP	16.5.89	9	GGala	Roma	4 Jun
13:05.69	Ryan	Hill	USA	31.1.90	8	VD	Bruxelles	11 Sep
13:06.10	Bashir	Abdi	BEL	10.2.89	2rA	NA	Heusden-Zolder	18 Jul
13:06.15		True			3rA	NA	Heusden-Zolder	18 Jul
13:06.74	Albert	Rop	BRN	17.7.92	4	NA	Heusden-Zolder	18 Jul
13:07.26		Longosiwa			1	DL	Birmingham	7 Jun
13:07.33	Isiah	Koech	KEN	19.12.92	10	GGala	Roma	4 Jun
13:07.33	Eric	Jenkins	USA	24.11.91	5	NA	Heusden-Zolder	18 Jul
13:07.74	Paul Kipsiele	Koech	KEN	10.11.81	9	VD	Bruxelles	11 Sep

Mark	Name		Nat	Born	Pos	Meet	Venue	Date
13:08.38	Galen	Rupp (20)	USA	8.5.86	10	VD	Bruxelles	11 Sep
13:08.40	Suguru	Osako	JPN	23.5.91	6	NA	Heusden-Zolder	18 Jul
13:08.55	Emmanuel	Kipsang	KEN	13.6.91	11	VD	Bruxelles	11 Sep
13:08.86		P Koech			1	ISTAF	Berlin	6 Sep
13:08.94		I Koech			1	PNG	Turku	25 Jun
	(30/22)							
13:10.00	Mohammed	Ahmed	CAN	5.1.91	12	VD	Bruxelles	11 Sep
13:10.38	Hassan	Mead	USA	28.8.89	2	ISTAF	Berlin	6 Sep
13:10.48	Thomas	Farrell	GBR	23.3.91	7	NA	Heusden-Zolder	18 Jul
13:10.67	Yasin	Haji	ETH-J	22.1.96	13	VD	Bruxelles	11 Sep
13:10.69	Phillip	Kipyeko	UGA	10.1.95	8	NA	Heusden-Zolder	18 Jul
13:10.83	Bernard	Kimani	KEN	10.9.93	9	NA	Heusden-Zolder	18 Jul
13:10.94	Richard	Ringer	GER	27.2.89	10	NA	Heusden-Zolder	18 Jul
13:11.44	Stephen	Mokoka	RSA	31.1.85	1	NC	Stellenbosch	18 Apr
	(30)							
13:11.77	Mohamed	Farah	GBR	23.3.83	1	Athl	Lausanne	9 Jul
13:11.96	Sindre	Buraas	NOR	8.5.89	11	NA	Heusden-Zolder	18 Jul
13:11.97	Edwin	Soi	KEN	3.3.86	2	Pre	Eugene	29 May
13:12.63	Tetsuya	Yoroizaka	JPN	20.3.90	12	NA	Heusden-Zolder	18 Jul
13:13.16	Jonathan	Ndiku	KEN	18.9.91	1		Tokyo	3 Oct
13:13.17	Abadi	Embaye	ETH-Y	99?	13	NA	Heusden-Zolder	18 Jul
13:13.28A	Geoffrey	Kamworor	KEN	28.11.92	1h2	NC	Nairobi	10 Jul
13:13.66	Hiram	Ngatia	KEN-J	1.1.96	1		Kumamoto	4 Apr
13:13.90	Othmane	El Goumri	MAR	28.5.92	1		Huelva	10 Jun
13:14.00	Abrar	Osman	ERI	1.1.94	1		Bottrop	21 Jun
	(40)							
13:14.97	Bernard	Lagat	USA	12.12.74	4	Pre	Eugene	29 May
13:15.07	Leul	Gebrselassie	ETH	20.9.93	1		Barcelona	8 Jul
13:15.56	Moses	Koech	KEN-J	5.4.97	2		Barcelona	8 Jul
13:15.71	Juan Luis	Barrios	MEX	24.6.83	1	Jordan	Stanford	2 May
13:16.11	Lawi	Lalang	KEN	15.6.91	7	Pre	Eugene	29 May
13:16.14	Ronald	Kwemoi	KEN	19.9.95	1		Nobeoka	9 May
13:16.25	Leonard	Barsoton	KEN	21.10.94	1	Oda	Hiroshima	18 Apr
13:16.31	Garrett	Heath	USA	4.2.89	2	Jordan	Stanford	2 May
13:16.98	Alemayehu	Bezabeh	ESP	22.9.86	14	NA	Heusden-Zolder	18 Jul
13:17.30	Diego	Estrada	USA	12.12.89	3	Jordan	Stanford	2 May
	(50)							
13:17.49	Collis	Birmingham	AUS	27.12.84	8	Pre	Eugene	29 May
13:17.62	Aron	Kifle	ERI-Y	20.2.98	3		Barcelona	8 Jul
13:17.85	Will	Geoghegan	USA	15.7.92	15	NA	Heusden-Zolder	18 Jul
13:17.97	Ayanleh	Souleiman	DJI	3.12.92	1	Arab C	Manama	27 Apr
13:17.97	Riley	Masters	USA	5.4.90	5	Jordan	Stanford	2 May
13:18.95	Younès	Essalhi	MAR	20.2.93	16	NA	Heusden-Zolder	18 Jul
13:19.14	Birhan	Nebebew	ETH	14.8.94	9	Pre	Eugene	29 May
13:19.56	Matt	Hughes	CAN	3.8.89	6	Jordan	Stanford	2 May
13:19.56	Chris	Derrick	USA	17.10.90	17	NA	Heusden-Zolder	18 Jul
13:19.62	Kota	Murayama	JPN	23.2.93	2		Nobeoka	9 May
	(60)							
13:19.80	Aweke	Ayalew	BRN	23.2.93	11	GGala	Roma	4 Jun
13:20.21	Ibrahim	Jeylan	ETH	12.6.89	10	Pre	Eugene	29 May
13:20.34	Victor	Chumo	KEN	1.1.87	3		Huelva	10 Jun
13:20.34	Andrew	Vernon	GBR	7.1.86	1		Ninove	1 Aug
13:20.39	Kemoy	Campbell	JAM	14.1.91	7	Jordan	Stanford	2 May
13:20.68	Cameron	Levins	CAN	28.3.89	1		Portland	14 Jun
13:21.16	Jeff	See	USA	6.6.86	8	Jordan	Stanford	2 May
13:21.23	Brett	Robinson	AUS	8.5.91	5	DL	Birmingham	7 Jun
13:21.26	Bidan	Karoki	KEN	21.8.90	6	Athl	Lausanne	9 Jul
13:21.32	Lopez	Lomong	USA	1.1.85	9	Jordan	Stanford	2 May
	(70)							
13:21.52	Paul	Kamais	KEN-J	24.10.96	1rB	Oda	Hiroshima	18 Apr
13:21.6+	Geoffrey	Kirui	KEN	16.2.93	3	Pre	Eugene	29 May
13:21.88	Getaneh	Tamire	ETH	.94	1	AfG	Brazzaville	17 Sep
13:22.0+	Emmanuel	Bett	KEN	30.3.83	5	Pre	Eugene	29 May
13:22.04	Alfred	Ngeno	KEN-J	2.5.97	2		Bottrop	21 Jun
13:22.11	Nick	Willis	NZL	25.4.83	1		Waitakere	26 Feb
13:22.11	Hayle	Ibrahimov	AZE	18.1.90	2		Ninove	1 Aug
13:22.36	William	Malel Sitonik	KEN	1.3.94	1		Yokohama	15 Nov
13:22.42	Abiyot	Abinet	ETH	10.5.89	1		Konosu	24 Oct
13:22.92	Jesús	España	ESP	21.8.78	13	GGala	Roma	4 Jun
	(80)							
13:23.00	Dennis	Licht	NED	30.5.84	10	Jordan	Stanford	2 May

Mark	Name		Nat	Born	Pos	Meet	Venue	Date
13:23.26	Berhanu	Legesse	ETH	11.9.94	3		Bottrop	21 Jun
13:23.66	Fredrick	Kipkosgei	KEN-J	13.11.96	1		Oordegem	23 May
13:23.80	Ambrose	Bore	KEN	8.8.95	2		Oordegem	23 May
13:23.91	Amos	Kibitok	KEN	4.4.94	1	RUS Ch	Cheboksary	3 Aug
13:24.21	John	Maina	KEN	14.7.93	7		Nobeoka	9 May
13:24.41	Ronald	Musagala	UGA	16.12.94	1		Nijmegen	27 May
13:24.50	James	Mwangi	KEN	23.6.84	1		Fukuroi	27 Jun
13:24.69	David	Njuguna	KEN	6.9.89	8		Nobeoka	9 May
13:24.87	Kassa (90)	Mekashaw	ETH	19.3.84	2		Konosu	24 Oct
13:25.00	Cyrus	Rutto	KEN	21.4.92	2		Nijmegen	27 May
13:25.00	Tariq	Al-Amri	KSA	23.12.90	1		Kessel-Lo	8 Aug
13:25.13	Stephen	Sambu	KEN	7.7.88	6	DL	Birmingham	7 Jun
13:25.24	Johana	Maina	KEN	25.12.90	2		Yokohama	7 Jun
13:25.41	Zane	Robertson	NZL	14.11.89	2		Waitakere	26 Feb
13:25.70	Dejene	Debela	ETH	.94	1		Carquefou	19 Jun
13:26.19	Zouhaïr	Aouad	BRN	7.4.89	2	WMilG	Mungyeong	8 Oct
13:26.25	Joseph	Chacha	KEN	4.9.92	2		Tokyo	3 Oct
13:26.98	Antonio	Abadía	ESP	2.7.90	1		Mataró	18 Jul
13:27.10	Henrik (100)	Ingebrigtsen	NOR	24.2.91	11	Jordan	Stanford	2 May

Mark	Name		Nat	Born	Date
13:27.25	Soufiyan	Bouqantar	MAR	30.8.93	19 Jun
13:27.38	Thierry	Ndikumwenayo	BDI-J	26.3.97	17 Sep
13:27.44	Daniel	Kipkemoi	KEN-J	5.7.96	26 Apr
13:27.66	Samuel	Mwangi	KEN-J	19.9.97	3 Oct
13:27.70	Sefu	Tura	ETH	.95	8 Jul
13:28.07A	Geoffrey	Koech	KEN	28.8.93	10 Jul
13:28.18	Paul	Kuira	KEN	25.1.90	26 Apr
13:28.26	David	McNeill	AUS	6.10.86	23 Jul
13:28.39	Berhane	Afewerki	ERI-J	6.5.96	19 Jun
13:28.41	Enoch	Omwamba	KEN	4.4.93	4 Apr
13:28.50	Nuguse	Hirsuato	ETH	13.2.82	6 Jun
13:28.50A	Joshua	Cheptegei	UGA-J	12.9.96	18 Jul
13:28.56	Teklit	Teweldebrhan	ERI	1.10.93	19 Jun
13:28.61	Shuho	Dairokuno	JPN	23.12.92	18 Jul
13:28.62	Ronald	Kwemoi Chumo	KEN-J	3.3.97	12 Jul
13:28.67	Hassan	Chani	BRN	8.10.91	19 Jun
13:28.69	Elroy	Gelant	RSA	25.8.86	26 May
13:29.01	Japheth	Korir	KEN	30.6.93	26 May
13:29.32	Ross	Proudfoot	CAN	4.7.92	18 Jul
13:29.49	Andrew	Butchart	GBR	14.10.91	1 Aug
13:29.54	Martin	Sperlich	GER	28.8.91	1 Aug
13:29.63	Florian	Orth	GER	24.7.89	23 May
13:29.77	Marouan	Razine	ITA	9.4.91	8 Sep
13:29.79	Lucas	Bruchet	CAN	23.2.91	1 Aug
13:30.09	Brian	Shrader	USA	22.7.91	18 Jul
13:30.11	Youssouf Hiss	Bachir	DJI	.87	27 May
13:30.20	Nixon	Chepseba	KEN	12.12.90	8 Jul
13:30.22	Nguse	Tesfaldet	ERI	10.11.86	13 Jun
13:30.35	David	Torrence	USA	26.11.85	14 Jun
13:30.50	Samuel	Stabler	GBR	17.5.92	3 Apr
13:30.60	Olivier	Irabaruta	BDI	25.8.90	1 Aug
13:30.76	Polat Kemboi	Arikan	TUR	12.12.90	30 May
13:30.76	Alexander	Mutiso	KEN-J	10.9.96	15 Nov
13:30.81	José Juan	Esparza	MEX	26.8.90	3 Apr
13:30.83	Stefano	La Rosa	ITA	22.9.85	23 May
13:30.94	Mulaku	Abera	ETH	20.4.94	18 Apr
13:30.95	Haron	Lagat	KEN	15.8.83	6 Sep
13:30.98	Abraham	Habte	ERI-J	14.7.96	23 Jul
13:31.00	Patrick	Mwaka	KEN	2.11.92	4 Apr
13:31.02	Said	El Otmani	ITA	14.10.91	8 Sep
13:31.14	Tsegay	Tuemay	ERI	20.12.95	23 Jul
13:31.23A	Cornelius	Kangogo	KEN	31.12.93	20 Jun
13:31.33	Tariq	Haddadi	MAR	.95	1 Aug
13:31.37	Moses	Kipsiro	UGA	2.9.86	13 Jun
13:31.41	Roy	Hoornweg	NED	8.5.89	18 Jul
13:31.59	Anthony	Rotich	KEN	.92	3 Apr
13:31.88	Geoffrey	Korir	KEN-J	2.5.96	26 May
13:32.06	Tyler	Pennel	USA	21.12.87	14 Jun
13:32.16	Edwin	Mokua	KEN	31.12.93	26 Apr
13:32.21	Joe	Stilin	USA	5.12.89	1 Aug
13:32.23	Reed	Connor	USA	25.9.90	18 Jul
13:32.39	Mohamed Ali	Mohamed	SOM	11.11.89	1 Aug
13:32.68	Arne	Gabius	GER	22.3.81	13 Jun
13:32.71	Dawit	Wolde	ETH	19.5.91	26 May
13:32.72	Naohiro	Domoto	JPN	23.7.89	18 Apr
13:32.80A	Willy	Kwemoi	KEN-J	8.10.97	10 Jul
13:32.91	Ibrahim Hassan	Bouh	DJI-J	.96	1 Aug
13:33.08	Aitor	Fernández	ESP	13.8.91	18 Jul
13:33.14	Merhawi	Ghebreselasie	ERI-Y	.98	23 May
13:33.16	Ben	St. Lawrence	AUS	7.11.81	21 Mar
13:33.16	George	Alex	USA	20.1.90	18 Jul
13:33.17	Jonathan	Peterson	USA	6.1.89	18 Jul
13:33.24	Yemane	Halleselassie	ERI-Y	21.2.98	18 Jul
13:33.29	Thomas	Awad	USA	27.5.94	3 Apr
13:33.56A	Joseph	Kiplimo	KEN	20.7.88	10 Jul
13:33.58	Teressa	Nyakora	ETH	26.2.95	7 Jun
13:33.64	Charles	Ndirangu	KEN	8.2.93	18 Apr
13:33.73A	Bernard	Kipkemoi	KEN	.94	10 Jul
13:33.90A	Mang'ata	Ndiwa	KEN	12.12.87	10 Jul
13:34.00	Aaron	Braun	USA	28.5.87	14 Jun
13:34.02	Yuichiro	Ueno	JPN	29.7.85	18 Apr
13:34.16	Vedic	Cheruiyot	KEN-J	5.3.96	26 May
13:34.21A	Leonard	Oloitiptip	KEN	.90	9 Jul
13:34.21	Craig	Forys	USA	13.7.89	18 Jul
13:34.42	Thomas	Joyce	USA	20.7.93	2 May
13:34.47	Mohamed	Al-Garni	QAT	2.7.92	4 Jun
13:34.63	Alemu	Bekele	BRN	23.3.90	26 May
13:34.68	Yuta	Shitara	JPN	18.12.91	18 Apr
13:34.76	Debele	Gezmu	ETH-J	14.4.96	26 May
13:34.85	Josephat	Onsarigo	KEN	.93	16 Jul
13:34.86	Justyn	Knight	CAN-J	19.7.96	2 May
13:34.96	Jason	Witt	USA	9.12.89	17 Apr
13:35.17A	Stephen	Arita	KEN	26.6.88	12 Jun
13:35.32A	Edward	Rono	KEN-Y	6.8.98	9 Jul
13:35.43	Anatoliy	Rybakov	RUS	27.2.85	28 May
13:35.54	Andrew "AJ"	Acosta	USA	13.4.88	3 Apr
13:35.67	Ben	Bruce	USA	10.9.82	3 Apr
13:35.70	Martin	Hehir	USA	19.12.92	2 May
13:35.75	Rinas	Akhmadiyev	RUS	6.3.89	28 May
13:35.77	Zouhair	Talbi	MAR	8.4.95	19 Jun
13:35.91	Tasama	Dame	ETH	12.10.87	23 May
13:35.99	Andrew	Springer	USA	10.3.91	4 Jun
13:36.09	Takashi	Ichida	JPN	16.6.92	9 May
13:36.20	Jim	Spisak	USA	18.11.90	4 Jun
13:36.22	Morgan	Pearson	USA	22.9.93	17 Apr
13:36.42	Masaki	Toda	JPN	21.6.93	16 Jul
13:36.62	Govindan	Lakshmanan	IND	5.6.90	4 Jun
13:36.66	Joseph	Mumo	KEN-J	25.11.97	3 Oct
13:36.69	Christopher	Landry	USA	29.4.86	17 Apr
13:36.7A	James (200)	Kibet	KEN	.88	11 Jul

Indoors

Mark	Name		Nat	Born	Pos	Meet	Venue	Date
13:27.53	Arne	Gabius	GER	22.3.81	1		Düsseldorf	29 Jan
13:28.64	Andrew	Bumbalough	USA	14.3.87	5	Mill	New York (Arm)	14 Feb
13:28.64	Donn	Cabral	USA	12.12.89	4	Mill	New York (Arm)	14 Feb

+ intermediate time in longer race, A made at an altitude of 1000m or higher, D made in a decathlon, h made in a heat, qf quarter-final, sf semi-final, i indoors, Q qualifying round, r race number, -J juniors, -Y youths (b. 1998 or later)

JUNIORS

See main list for top 9 juniors. 12 performances by 9 men to 13:20.0. Additional marks and further juniors:

Kejelcha 2+ 13:10.54 1 Pre Eugene 29 May 13:19.38 1h2 WCh Beijing 26 Aug
13:12.59 2 Athl Lausanne 9 Jul
Haji 13:18.18 4 Athl Lausanne 9 Jul
Ngatia 13:17.16 2 Oda Hiroshima 18 Apr

Mark	Name		Nat	Born	Pos	Meet	Venue	Date
13:27.38	Thierry	Ndikumwenayo (10)	BDI-	26.3.97	9	AfG	Brazzaville	17 Sep
13:27.44	Daniel	Kipkemoi	KEN	5.7.96	1		Yokohama	26 Apr
13:27.66	Samuel	Mwangi	KEN	19.9.97	3		Tokyo	3 Oct
13:28.39	Berhane	Afewerki	ERI	6.5.96	3		Carquefou	19 Jun
13:28.50A	Joshua	Cheptegei	UGA	12.9.96	1	NC	Kampala	18 Jul
13:28.62	Ronald	Kwemoi Chumo	KEN	3.3.97	2		Kitami	12 Jul
13:30.76	Alexander	Mutiso	KEN	10.9.96	3		Yokohama	15 Nov
13:30.98	Abraham	Habte	ERI	14.7.96	2		Joensuu	23 Jul
13:31.88	Geoffrey	Korir	KEN	2.5.96	6	GS	Ostrava	26 May
13:32.80A	Willy	Kwemoi	KEN	8.10.97	3h1	NC	Nairobi	10 Jul
13:32.91	Ibrahim Hassan	Bouh (20)	DJI	.96	10		Ninove	1 Aug
Best European: 13:48.21	Julian	Wanders	SUI	18.3.96	4rB		Oordegem	23 May

10,000 METRES

Mark	Name		Nat	Born	Pos	Meet	Venue	Date
26:50.97	Mohamed	Farah	GBR	23.3.83	1	Pre	Eugene	29 May
26:51.86	Paul	Tanui	KEN	22.12.90	2	Pre	Eugene	29 May
26:52.65	Geoffrey	Kamworor	KEN	28.11.92	3	Pre	Eugene	29 May
27:01.13		Farah			1	WCh	Beijing	22 Aug
27:01.76		Kamworor			2	WCh	Beijing	22 Aug
27:02.83		Tanui			3	WCT	Beijing	22 Aug
27:04.77	Bidan	Karoki	KEN	21.8.90	4	WCh	Beijing	22 Aug
27:07.51	Cameron	Levins	CAN	28.3.89	4	Pre	Eugene	29 May
27:08.21		Tanui			1		Kitakyushu	16 May
27:08.91	Galen	Rupp	USA	8.5.86	5	WCh	Beijing	22 Aug
27:11.89A		Kamworor			1	WCT	Nairobi	1 Aug
27:15.33A		Karoki			2	WCT	Nairobi	1 Aug
27:17.18	Muktar	Edris	ETH	14.1.94	1	NC	Hengelo	17 Jun
27:17.63	Imane	Merga	ETH	15.10.88	2	NC	Hengelo	17 Jun
27:17.91	Geoffrey	Kirui	KEN	16.2.93	5	Pre	Eugene	29 May
27:18.45A		Tanui			3	WCT	Nairobi	1 Aug
27:18.86	Mosinet	Geremew (10)	ETH	12.2.92	3	NC	Hengelo	17 Jun
27:19.34	Adugna	Tekele	ETH	26.2.89	4	NC	Hengelo	17 Jun
27:20.54	Tebalu	Zawude	ETH	2.11.87	5	NC	Hengelo	17 Jun
27:22.12	William	Malel Sitonik	KEN	1.3.94	1		Machida	28 Nov
27:22.34	Emmanuel	Bett	KEN	30.3.83	6	Pre	Eugene	29 May
27:22.64	Tamirat	Tola	ETH	11.8.91	6	NC	Hengelo	17 Jun
27:22.89	Leul	Gebrselassie	ETH	20.9.93	7	NC	Hengelo	17 Jun
27:24.09	Ali	Kaya	TUR	20.4.94	1	NC	Mersin	2 May
27:25.02	El Hassan	El Abbassi	BRN	15.7.79	7	Pre	Eugene	29 May
27:26.92	Johana	Maina	KEN	24.12.90	2		Machida	28 Nov
27:27.19		Zawude			1	AfG	Brazzaville	14 Sep
27:27.55	Leonard	Barsoton (20)	KEN	21.10.94	2	AfG	Brazzaville	14 Sep
27:27.57	Joshua	Cheptegei	UGA-J	12.9.96	8	Pre	Eugene	29 May
27:28.40		Tekele			3	AfG	Brazzaville	14 Sep
27:29.69	Kota	Murayama	JPN	23.2.93	3		Machida	28 Nov
27:29.74	Tetsuya	Yoroizaka	JPN	20.3.90	4		Machida	28 Nov
27:30.53	Diego	Estrada	USA	12.12.89	9	Pre	Eugene	29 May
27:31.48	Titus (34/25)	Mbishei	KEN	28.10.90	10	Pre	Eugene	29 May
27:33.04	Hassan	Mead	USA	28.8.89	11	Pre	Eugene	29 May
27:33.45A	Vincent	Yator	KEN	11.7.89	4	WCT	Nairobi	1 Aug
27:33.82	Azmeraw	Mengistu	ETH	15.9.92	8	NC	Hengelo	17 Jun
27:35.54	John	Maina	KEN	3.8.94	5		Machida	28 Nov
27:38.93	Teressa (30)	Nyakora	ETH	26.2.95	6		Machida	28 Nov
27:39.71	Timothy	Toroitich	UGA	10.10.91	12	Pre	Eugene	29 May
27:39.76	Bernard	Kimani	KEN	10.9.93	7		Machida	28 Nov
27:39.95	Kenta	Murayama	JPN	23.2.93	1		Nobeoka	9 May
27:40.20	Josphat	Bett	KEN	12.6.90	13	Pre	Eugene	29 May
27:40.64	Jonathan	Ndiku	KEN	18.9.91	1		Hiratsuka	27 Sep
27:40.78	Nuguse	Hirsuato	ETH	31.2.82	1		Fukagawa	9 Jul
27:41.69	Abrar	Osman	ERI	1.1.94	1		Leiden	13 Jun
27:41.74	Hiram	Ngatia	KEN-J	1.1.96	2		Fukagawa	9 Jul

Mark	Name		Nat	Born	Pos	Meet	Venue	Date
27:42.09	Ronald	Kwemoi Chumo	KEN-J	3.3.97	2		Hiratsuka	27 Sep
27:42.62	Andrew	Vernon	GBR	7.1.86	1	Jordan	Stanford	2 May
	(40)							
27:42.71	Yuta	Shitara	JPN	18.12.91	2		Nobeoka	9 May
27:43.25	James	Mwangi	KEN	23.3.94	2		Gifu	25 Sep
27:43.59	Karemi Jeremiah	Thuku	KEN	7.7.94	3		Fukagawa	9 Jul
27:43.73	Stephen	Mokoka	RSA	31.1.85	14	Pre	Eugene	29 May
27:43.79	Ben	True	USA	29.12.85	2	Jordan	Stanford	2 May
27:43.93	Arne	Gabius	GER	22.3.81	15	Pre	Eugene	29 May
27:44.24	Ben	St. Lawrence	AUS	7.11.81	3	Jordan	Stanford	2 May
27:45.01	David	McNeill	AUS	6.10.86	4	Jordan	Stanford	2 May
27:45.24	Suguru	Osako	JPN	23.5.91	16	Pre	Eugene	29 May
27:45.92	Kassa	Mekashaw	ETH	19.3.84	5		Fukagawa	9 Jul
	(50)							
27:46.21	Agato	Yashin Hasen	ETH	19.1.86	8		Machida	28 Nov
27:46.34	Othmane	El Goumri	MAR	28.5.92	17	Pre	Eugene	29 May
27:46.55	Shuho	Dairokuno	JPN	23.12.92	9		Machida	28 Nov
27:46.82	Zane	Robertson	NZL	14.11.89	18	Pre	Eugene	29 May
27:46.90	Mohammed	Ahmed	CAN	5.1.91	5	Jordan	Stanford	2 May
27:47.55	Bashir	Abdi	BEL	10.2.89	6	Jordan	Stanford	2 May
27:48.53	Amos	Kibitok	KEN	4.4.94	2	TUR Ch	Mersin	2 May
27:49.46	Joseph	Kamathi	KEN-J	23.11.96	6		Fukagawa	9 Jul
27:50.09A	James	Rungaru	KEN	14.1.93	7	WCT	Nairobi	1 Aug
27:50.14	Nguse	Tesfaldet	ERI	10.11.86	1		San Sebastián	24 Jul
	(60)							
27:50.70	Yitayal	Atnafu	ETH	20.1.93	9	NC	Hengelo	17 Jun
27:50.81	Paul	Kuira	KEN	25.1.90	11		Machida	28 Nov
27:50.93	Samuel	Mwangi	KEN-J	19.9.97	12		Machida	28 Nov
27:53.19	Daniel	Kipkemoi	KEN-J	5.7.96	3		Gifu	12 Oct
27:54.25	Jason	Witt	USA	9.12.89	9	Jordan	Stanford	2 May
27:54.6A	Charles	Yosei	KEN-J	.96	2	NC	Nairobi	11 Jul
27:54.98	Parker	Stinson	USA	3.3.92	10	Jordan	Stanford	2 May
27:54.98	Patrick Wambui	Mathenge	KEN-J	2.11.96	1		Abashiri	16 Jul
27:55.02	Tsuyoshi	Ugachi	JPN	27.4.87	15		Machida	28 Nov
27:55.17A	Stephen	Arita	KEN	26.6.88	9	WCT	Nairobi	1 Aug
	(70)							
27:55.19	Christopher	Landry	USA	29.4.86	11	Jordan	Stanford	2 May
27:55.19	Melaku	Abera	ETH	20.4.94	4		Gifu	25 Sep
27:55.40	Hiroyuki	Yamamoto	JPN	30.4.86	16		Machida	28 Nov
27:56.59	Bobby	Curtis	USA	28.11.84	12	Jordan	Stanford	2 May
27:56.87	Alexander	Mutiso	KEN-J	10.9.96	3		Yokohama (M)	27 Sep
27:56.9	Gladwin	Mzazi	RSA	28.8.88	2		Stellenbosch	25 Apr
27:57.13	Yuki	Sato	JPN	26.11.86	13	Jordan	Stanford	2 May
27:57.85	Hiroyuki	Ono	JPN	10.3.86	2		Abashiri	16 Jul
27:58.40	Ken	Yokote	JPN	27.4.93	3		Abashiri	16 Jul
27:58.58	Patrick	Mwaka	KEN	2.11.92	17		Machida	28 Nov
	(80)							
27:59.37	Jake	Riley	USA	11.2.88	14	Jordan	Stanford	2 May
27:59.88	Jonathan	Grey	USA	13.2.88	15	Jordan	Stanford	2 May
28:00.41	Enoch	Omwamba	KEN	4.4.93	4		Abashiri	16 Jul
28:01.87	Joseph	Ndirangu	KEN	9.9.94	5		Tajimi	12 Oct
28:02.70	Kensuke	Takezawa	JPN	11.10.86	18		Machida	28 Nov
28:03.27	Brendan	Gregg	USA	15.5.89	17	Jordan	Stanford	2 May
28:03.86	Emmanuel	Kipsang	KEN	13.6.91	2	WMilG	Mungyeong	5 Oct
28:04.07	Berhane	Afewerki	ERI	6.5.96	2		San Sebastián	24 Jul
28:04.57	Tsegay	Tadese	ETH-J	30.11.96	1		Tel Aviv	18 Jan
28:04.60	Ryan	Vail	USA	19.3.86	18	Jordan	Stanford	2 May
	(90)							
28:04.65	Minato	Oishi	JPN	19.5.88	5		Abashiri	16 Jul
28:05.28	Keita	Shitara	JPN	18.12.91	6		Abashiri	16 Jul
28:05.34	Zersenay	Tadese	ERI	8.2.82	3		San Sebastián	24 Jul
28:05.64	Polat Kemboi	Arikan	TUR	12.12.90	4		San Sebastián	24 Jul
28:06.10	Tsubasa	Hayakawa	JPN	2.7.90	20		Machida	28 Nov
28:06.44	Shinobu	Kubota	JPN	12.12.91	21		Machida	28 Nov
28:06.5A	Joseph	Kiptum	KEN	25.9.87	1		Nairobi	5 Jun
28:06.8A	Geoffrey	Korir	KEN-J	2.5.96	2		Nairobi	5 Jun
28:07.4A	David	Bett	KEN	18.10.92	5	NC	Nairobi	11 Jul
28:08.4A	Emmanuel	Ngatuny	KEN	10.10.92	6	NC	Nairobi	11 Jul
	(100)							

28:09.02	Yuma	Hattori	JPN	13.11.93	16 Jul
28:09.42	Aimeru	Almeya	ISR	8.6.90	18 Jan
28:09.86	Shogo	Nakamura	JPN	16.9.92	16 Jul
28:10.05	Charles	Ndungu	KEN-J	20.2.96	16 Jul

Mark	Name		Nat	Born	Date
28:10.32	Girmaw	Amare	ISR	26.10.87	28 Apr
28:10.5A	David	Tarus	KEN	.81/78?	19 Jun
28:10.66	Charles	Ndirangu	KEN	8.2.93	28 Nov
28:11.28	Goitom	Kifle	ERI	3.12.93	24 Jul
28:11.46	Hassan	Chani	BRN	8.10.91	5 Oct
28:11.49	Dominic	Nyairo	KEN-J	22.8.97	16 Jul
28:12.72	Abdallah	Mande	UGA	10.5.95	13 Jun
28:12.91	Juan Luis	Barrios	MEX	24.6.83	3 Apr
28:12.95	Yuichiro	Ueno	JPN	29.7.85	25 Sep
28:12.96	Hiroto	Inoue	JPN	6.1.93	16 May
28:13.0A	Wilson	Kiprop	KEN	14.4.87	19 Jun
28:13.42	Aritaka	Kajiwara	JPN	16.6.88	14 Nov
28:13.81	Cyrus	Kingori	KEN-Y	5.1.97	14 Nov
28:13.85	Alemu	Bekele	BRN	23.3.90	13 Jun
28:14.24	Martin	Mathathi	KEN	25.12.85	25 Apr
28:16.30	Shadrack	Kipchirchir	USA	22.2.89	22 Aug
28:16.5A	Leonard	Langat	KEN	7.8.90	11 Jul
28:16.61	Tsegay	Tuemay	ERI	20.12.95	2 May
28:17.09	Takashi	Ichida	JPN	16.6.92	16 May
28:17.16	Alex	Mwangi	KEN	14.6.90	25 Apr
28:17.56	Keisuke	Nakatani	JPN	12.1.95	14 Nov
28:17.7A	Philemon	Cheboi	KEN	8.11.93	11 Jul
28:18.03	Yigrem	Demelash	ETH	28.1.94	17 Jun
28:18.2A	Norbert	Kigen	KEN	24.1.93	11 Jul
28:18.44	Aron	Kifle	ERI-Y	20.2.98	24 Jul
28:18.54	Shuhei	Yamamoto	JPN	24.5.91	9 Jul
28:18.81	Naohiro	Domoto	JPN	23.7.89	28 Nov
28:19.3	Daniel	da Silva	BRA	10.7.88	1 May
28:19.38	Antonio	Abadía	ESP	2.7.90	11 Apr
28:19.46	Chiharu	Nakagawa	JPN	8.4.86	28 Nov
28:19.5A	Daniel	Salel	KEN	11.12.90	5 Jun
28:20.65	Jim	Spisak	USA	18.11.90	2 May
28:20.77	Kazuya	Deguchi	JPN	14.8.88	16 May
28:20.9	Giovani	dos Santos	BRA	1.7.8	11 May
28:20.97	Edwin	Mokua	KEN	31.12.93	23 May
28:21.0A	Lucas	Rotich	KEN	16.4.90	5 Jun
28:21.26	Josephat	Onsarigo	KEN	.93	14 Nov
28:21.28	Keita	Baba	JPN	28.4.86	28 Nov
28:21.35	Akinobu	Murasawa	JPN	28.3.91	28 Nov
28:21.84	Amos	Kirui	KEN-Y	9.2.98	28 Nov
28:21.89	Keigo	Yano	JPN	3.12.91	28 Nov
28:22.01	Anatoliy	Rybakov	RUS	27.2.85	19 Jul
28:22.59	Shintaro	Miwa	JPN	4.1.92	5 Dec
28:22.86	Akihiko	Tsumurai	JPN	10.7.84	25 Apr
28:22.89	Ryo	Kiname	JPN	22.1.91	9 Jul
28:22.90	Tyler	Pennel	USA	21.12.87	2 May
28:23.0A	Solomon	Yego	KEN	.87	11 Jul
28:23.22	Ezekiel	Chebotibon	JPN	10.7.92	28 Jun
28:23.71	Dmitriy	Safronov	RUS	9.10.81	19 Jul
28:23.75	Sota	Hoshi	JPN	6.1.88	25 Apr
28:23.85	Naoki	Kudo	JPN	5.9.95	14 Nov
28:23.87	Mule	Wasihun	ETH	20.10.93	14 Sep
28:24.01	Masato	Kikuchi	JPN	18.9.90	28 Nov
28:24.35	Yudai	Okamoto	JPN	29.12.91	16 Jul
28:24.42	Stefano	La Rosa	ITA	22.9.85	2 May
28:24.49	Brett	Robinson	AUS	8.5.91	5 Dec
28:24.50	Kazuma	Kubota	JPN	24.9.93	21 Nov
28:24.73	Aron	Rono	USA	1.11.82	25 Jun
28:24.89	Hisanori	Kitajima	JPN	16.10.84	9 Jul
28:25.23	Sondre	Norstad Moen	NOR	12.1.91	2 May
28:25.31	Gideon	Kipketer	KEN	10.11.92	13 Jun
28:25.66	Juan Antonio	Pérez	ESP	6.11.88	6 Jun
28:25.86	Kenta	Matsumoto	JPN	1.6.91	16 Jul
28:25.97	Yuki	Matsuoka	JPN	14.1.86	25 Apr
28:26.08	Erik	Peterson	USA	15.6.94	2 May
28:26.27	Masaru	Aoki	JPN	16.5.90	25 Apr
28:26.30	Omar	Oughif	MAR	25.8.85	11 Apr
28:26.35	Kenji	Yamamoto	JPN	17.11.89	28 Nov
28:26.5A	Evans	Biwott	KEN	.88	5 Jun
28:26.56	Mitsunori	Asaoka	JPN	11.1.93	28 Nov
28:26.61	Keijiro	Mogi	JPN	21.10.95	17 Oct
28:26.77	Tim	Ritchie	USA	7.8.87	2 May
28:26.88	Shota	Hattori	JPN	28.10.91	28 Nov
28:26.96	Naoki	Aiba	JPN	24.1.91	28 Nov
28:26.98	John	Crain	USA	30.12.85	2 May
28:27.01	Benjamin	Gandu	KEN	21.5.91	16 May
28:27.14	Takuya	Fujikawa	JPN	17.12.92	28 Nov
28:27.42	Hideyuki	Tanaka	JPN	9.10.90	28 Nov
28:27.70	Martin	Hehir	USA	19.12.92	3 Apr
28:27.89	Takuya	Noguchi	JPN	2.7.88	28 Nov
28:28.22	Naohiro	Yamada	JPN	18.12.84	28 Nov
28:28.27	Masaki	Toda	JPN	21.6.93	28 Nov
28:28.56	Brian	Shrader	USA	22.7.91	2 May
28:28.64	Daniel	Kitonyi	KEN	12.1.94	2 Jun
28:29.06	Shota	Shinjo	JPN	11.10.92	28 Nov
28:29.53	Seref	Dirli	TUR	1.1.92	2 May
28:29.61	Luke	Caldwell	GBR	2.8.91	2 May
28:29.62	Shota	Kai	JPN	10.5.91	28 Nov
28:29.64	Yuki	Takamiya	JPN	2.12.87	28 Nov
28:29.78	Takayuki	Matsumiya	JPN	21.2.80	16 Jul
28:30.0A	Justus	Kangogo	KEN	.95	5 Jun
28:30.13	Trevor	Dunbar	USA	29.4.91	3 Apr
28:30.33	Marc	Scott	GBR	21.12.93	3 Apr
28:30.76	Yuki	Hirota	JPN	28.5.94	21 Nov
28:30.80	Bayron	Piedra	ECU	19.8.82	14 Jun
28:31.14	Marvin (200)	Blanco	VEN	16.5.88	6 Dec

JUNIORS

See main list for top 11 juniors. 14 performances by 9 men to 27:58.0. Additional marks and further juniors:

Ngatia	27:45.36	1		Tajimi	12 Oct				
Chumo	27:45.22	1		Gifu	12 Oct	27:49.70	10	Machida	28 Nov
Cheptegei	27:48.89	9	WCh	Beijing	22 Aug				
Kamathi	27:53.79	13		Machida	28 Nov				

28:10.05	Charles	Ndungu	KEN	20.2.96	9	Abashiri	16 Jul
28:11.49	Dominic	Nyairo	KEN	22.8.97	10	Abashiri	16 Jul
28:13.81	Cyrus	Kingori	KEN-Y	5.1.97	2	Yokohama	14 Nov
28:18.44	Aron	Kifle	ERI-Y	20.2.98	6	San Sebastián	24 Jul
28:21.84	Amos	Kirui	KEN-Y	9.2.98	1rB	Machida	28 Nov
28:32.47A	Benjamin	Somikwo	UGA	.96	1	Kampala	15 Apr
28:32.85	Kazuya	Shiojiri	JPN	8.11.96	3	Yokohama	21 Nov
28:33.77	Yuta	Shimoda	JPN	31.3.96	4	Yokohama	21 Nov
28:36.12	Julius	Tanki (20)	KEN	15.7.97	16	Fukagawa	9 Jul

Best European: 29:37.23 Dieter Kersten BEL 25.10.96 7rB Huelva 11 Apr

The road lists that follow are very hard to compile. Some statisticians ignore intemediate times, but that is surely lazy and inappropriate. I like to include what athletes actually achive, but such information will be incomplete and perhaps not always completely accurate. We also have problems with varying names for Kenyan, and sometimes other East African, runners. There is also the problem with times, that should be gun times for listing purposes, but are often reported at net times.

10 KILOMETRES ROAD

27:30	Stephen	Sambu	KEN	7.2.88	1	Manchester	10 May
27:35	Abreham	Cheroben	KEN	10.11.92	1	Utrecht	27 Sep
27:38	Stephen	Mokoka	RSA	1.4.85	2	Manchester	10 May
27:42	Daniel	Chebii	KEN	28.5.85	1	Praha	5 Sep

Mark	Name		Nat	Born	Pos	Meet	Venue	Date
27:43	Zersenay	Tadese	ERI	8.2.82	1		Koutobia	17 May
27:45	Aziz	Lahbabi	MAR	3.2.91	2		Koutobia	17 May
27:45	Gilbert	Masai	KEN	20.5.81	2		Praha	5 Sep
27:46	Barselius	Kipyego	KEN	.93	3		Praha	5 Sep
27:47	Japheth	Korir	KEN	30.6.93	1		Würzburg	26 Apr
27:48	Bernard	Lagat	USA	12.12.74	3		Manchester	10 May
27:48	Jaouad	Laaris	MAR	6.12.83	3		Koutobia	17 May
27:49	Salah Eddine	Bounasser	MAR	27.9.90	4		Koutobia	17 May
27:50	Teshome	Mekonen	ETH	15.6.95	5		Praha	5 Sep
27:52	Bernard	Bett	KEN	4.1.93	6		Praha	5 Sep
27:53	Wilson	Kipsang	KEN	15.3.82	4		Manchester	10 May
27:54	Homiyu	Tesfaye	GER	23.6.93	1		Paderborn	4 Apr
27:54+	Edwin	Kiptoo	KEN	14.8.93	1	in 10M	Zaandam	20 Sep
27:55	Hicham	Bellani	MAR	15.9.79	5		Koutobia	17 May
27:55	Nicholas	Bor	KEN	27.4.88	1		Ottawa	23 May
27:56	Evans	Kurui	KEN	8.1.93	7		Praha	5 Sep
27:57	Simon	Cheprot	KEN	2.2.93	2		Ottawa	23 May
27:58	Amos	Mitei	KEN	24.6.94	2		Paderborn	4 Apr
27:58	John	Langat	KEN	31.12.96	1		Appingedam	27 Jun
28:01	Mark	Kangogo	KEN	.89	6		Koutobia	17 May
28:04	Dawit	Fikadu	ETH	.95	1		Laredo	21 Mar
28:05	Julius	Kogo	KEN	12.8.85	1		Edinburg	7 Feb
28:05	Philemon	Cheboi	KEN	8.11.93	2		Berlin	11 Oct
28:05	Abayneh	Degu	ETH		3		Berlin	11 Oct
28:06	Ahmed	Tamri	MAR	8.2.85	2		Taroudant	8 Mar
28:08	Moussaab	Hadout	MAR	11.3.88	7		Koutobia	17 May

Mark	Name		Nat	Born	Date
28:09	Daniel	Salel	KEN	11.12.90	21 Jun
28:09	Geoffrey	Ronoh	KEN	29.11.82	5 Sep
28:10	Cornelius	Kangogo	KEN	31.12.93	27 Dec
28:11	Haymanot	Alewe	ETH-J	11.11.97	27 Dec
28:12	Leul	Gebrselassie	ETH	20.9.93	11 Oct
28:13	Merhawi	Kesete	ERI	.86	27 Jun
28:14	Isaac	Langat	KEN	18.12.94	19 Apr
28:15	Geoffrey	Kenisi	KEN	.87	7 Feb
28:15	Serhiy	Lebid	UKR	15.2.75	20 Sep
28:16	David	Kogei	KEN	.85	23 May
28:17	Joseph	Kiplimo	KEN	20.2.88	21 Mar
28:17	Dominic	Kiptarus	KEN	3.8.96	26 Apr
28:18	Jesper	van der Wielen	NED	2.8.91	4 Apr
28:18	Fikadu	Seboka	ETH	.95	17 May
28:18	Abdelilah	Cherkaoui	MAR	27.2.84	17 May
28:19	Fredrick	Ngeny	KEN	.88	4 Apr
28:20	Agunafr	Bekele	ETH		21 Mar
28:20	Victor	Chumo	KEN	1.1.87	6 Apr
28:20	Edwin	Rotich	KEN	.88	17 May
28:20	Geoffrey	Mutai	KEN	7.10.81	30 May
28:21	Birhan	Nebebew	ETH	14.8.94	11 Apr
28:21	Samir	Jouhar	MAR	29.4.85	7 Jun
28:21	Mohamed	Zouak Ziani	MAR	.93	7 Jun
28:22	Mustapha	El Aziz	MAR	.85	7 Jun
28:22	Richard	Mengich	KEN	3.4.89	27 Jun
28:23	Cleophas	Ngetich	KEN	.90	7 Feb
28:23	Tesfaalem	Mehari	ETH	.93	10 May
28:23	Hassan	Ouazzin	MAR	.90	17 May
28:23	Kenneth	Keter	KEN	.96	5 Sep
28:23	Demoz	Hailu	ETH		11 Oct
28:24	Charles	Cheruiyot	KEN	4.8.88	27 Jun
28:24	Alfonce	Kigen	KEN		11 Oct
28:25	Shadrack	Kimaiyo	KEN	.92	4 Apr
28:25	Fredrick	Moranga	KEN	.95	17 May
28:25	Paul Kipsiele	Koech	KEN	10.11.81	11 Oct
28:26	Leonard	Korir	KEN	10.12.86	21 Jun
28:27	Zakaria	Boudad	MAR	2.10.93	8 Mar
28:27	Nicodemus	Kipkurui	KEN	.94	12 Jun
28:28	Kennedy	Kimutai	KEN	18.6.90	4 Apr
28:28	Abdellah	Tagharrafet	MAR	1.1.85	7 Jun
28:29	Nicodemus	Lagat	KEN		29 Mar
28:29	Micah	Kogo	KEN	3.6.86	17 May
28:29	Stephen	Kibet	KEN	9.11.86	1 Aug
28:29	Geoffrey	Koech	KEN	28.8.93	6 Sep
28:30	Cosmas Jairus	Kipchoge	KEN	14.12.92	26 Apr
28:30	Lawi	Lalang	KEN	15.6.91	27 Sep

Also many intermediate times in longer races (to 28:20):
København 30 Sep: 27:57 Emmanuel Bett KEN, Nicholas Kamakya KEN, Joel Kimurer KEN, Edwin Kipyego KEN, Alex Oleitiptip KEN, Phillip Langat KEN, Paul Lonyangata KEN, Richard Kiprotich Sigei KEN; 27:58 Mogos Shumay KEN, 28:00 Berhanu Legesse ETH
Ostia 1 Mar: 28:06 William Kibor KEN, Geoffrey Kusuro UGA, Peter Kwemoi KEN, Eric Leon Ndiema KEN, 28:07 John Kiprotich KEN
Valencia 18 Oct: 28:05 Mathew Kisorio KEN, 28:06 Hayle Lemi ETH, Emmanuel Bor KEN, Hiskel Tewelde ERI, Dawit Weldesilasie ERI; 28:07 John Kipsang Loitang KEN; 28:15 Kenneth Kipkemoi KEN
Marugame 1 Feb (point-to-point): 28:09 Juan Luis Barrios MEX, Bernard Koech; 28:10 Masato Kikuchi JPN, Benjamin Gandu KEN, Jacon Wanjuki KEN; 28:15 Daichi Kamino JPN
Praha 28 Mar: 28:09 Vincent Rono KEN; 28:11 Peter Kirui KEN, Leonard Komon KEN, Amanuel Mesel ERI, Adugna Tekele ETH, Danile Wanjiru KEN; 28:12 Samson Gebreyohanes ERI, Felix Kandie KEN, Berhanu Tsegay ERI; 28:13 Joe Kimutai; 28:19 Atalay Yirsaw ETH
Den Haag 8 Mar: 28:10 Stanley Biwott KEN, Eliud Tarus KEN, Mark Kiptoo KEN, Cyprian Kotut KEN
Adana 4 Jan: 28:17 Amos Kipruto KEN, 28:18 Mike Kigen KEN, Youssef Adana MAR
Verbania 19 Apr: 28:19 Cosmas Kipchoge KEN, Festus Talam KEN, Solomon Yego KEN
Olomouc 20 Jun: 28:20 Josphat Kiptis KEN, Jonathan Maiyo KEN

15/20 KILOMETRES ROAD

See also Half Marathon lists

20k	15k	Name		Nat	Born	Pos	Meet	Venue	Date
	42:20+	Hiskel	Tewelde	ERI	15.9.86	1	in HMar	Valencia	18 Oct
	42:24+	Eric Leon	Ndiema	KEN	1.1.90		in HMar	Ostia	1 Mar
	42:36+	Jonathan	Maiyo	KEN	5.5.88		in HMar	Olomouc	20 Jun
	42:38+	Jairus	Birech	KEN	14.12.92		in HMar	Olomouc	20 Jun

ark		Name		Nat	Born	Pos	Meet	Venue	Date
	42:39	Joshua	Cheptegei	UGA-J	12.9.96	1		Nijmegen	15 Nov
	42:40+	Emmanuel	Bor	KEN	14.4.88		in HMar	Valencia	18 Oct
7:38	42:45+	Azmeraw	Mengistu	ETH	15.9.92		in HMar	Den Haag	8 Mar
7:44	42:46+	Emmanuel	Bett	KEN	30.3.83	7	in HMar	København	13 Sep
	42:48+	Masato	Kikuchi	JPN	18.9.90		in HMar	Marugame	1 Feb
	42:52+	Titus	Mbishei	KEN	28.10.90		in HMar	Valencia	18 Oct
	42:55	Geoffrey	Yegon	KEN		2		's-Heerenberg	6 Dec
	43:04+	Keita	Shitara	JPN	18.12.91		in HMar	Marugame	1 Feb
	43:05+	Samson	Gebreyohanes	ERI	7.2.92		in HMar	Valencia	18 Oct
	43:08	Fredrick	Kipkosgei	KEN-J	13.11.96	3		's-Heerenberg	6 Dec
	43:09+	Elijah	Tirop	KEN	1.1.92		in HMar	Karlovy Vary	23 May
7:12+	43:11	Mike	Kigen	KEN	15.1.86		in HMar	Ra's Al-Khaymah	13 Feb
7:12+		Jonathan	Maiyo	KEN	5.5.88		in HMar	Ra's Al-Khaymah	13 Feb

10 MILES ROAD

	15k			Nat	Born	Pos	Meet	Venue	Date
5:19	42:15	Edwin	Kiptoo	KEN	14.8.93	1		Zaandam	20 Sep
5:19		Jeremiah	Thuku	KEN	7.7.94	1		Kosa	29 Nov
5:21		Bernard	Koech	KEN	31.1.88	1		Tilburg	6 Sep
5:32+		Mohamed	Farah	GBR	23.3.83	1	in HMar	South Shields	13 Sep
5:32+		Stanley	Biwott	KEN	21.4.86	2	in HMar	South Shields	13 Sep
5:37	42:33	John	Langat	KEN	31.12.96	2		Tilburg	6 Sep
5:37	42:32	Yohanes	Gebregergish	ERI		3		Tilburg	6 Sep
5:40	42:33	Gilbert	Kirwa	KEN	20.12.85	4		Tilburg	6 Sep
5:50	42:39	Vincent	Chepkok	KEN	5.7.88	5		Tilburg	6 Sep
5:58	42:48	John	Mwangangi	KEN	1.11.90	2		Zaandam	20 Sep
6:00	42:48	Moses	Kipsiro	UGA	2.9.86	1		Portsmouth	25 Oct
6:04	42:50	Yenew	Alamirew	ETH	27.5.90	3		Zaandam	20 Sep
6:07		Charles	Ndungu	KEN-J	20.2.96	2		Kosa	29 Nov
6:08		Emmanuel	Kipsang	KEN	13.6.91	2		Portsmouth	25 Oct
6:08		Keijiro	Mogi	JPN	21.10.95	3		Kosa	29 Nov
6:08		Kenta	Murayama	JPN	23.2.93	4		Kosa	29 Nov

6:11	Emmanuel	Bett	KEN	30.3.83	25 Oct
6:14	Evans	Kurui	KEN	8.1.93	25 Oct
6:16	Martin	Mathathi	KEN	25.12.85	25 Oct
6:16	Japheth	Korir	KEN	30.6.93	25 Oct
6:27	Kenneth	Kipkemoi	KEN	2.8.84	6 Sep
6:30	Bonsa	Dida	ETH	21.1.95	20 Sep
6:35	Merhawi	Kesete	ERI	.86	20 Sep
6:36	Wilson	Too	KEN	.91	6 Sep
46:36	Masato	Imai	JPN	2.4.84	29 Nov
46:37	Yuki	Oshikawa	JPN	2.6.90	29 Nov
46:38	Ryuji	Waranabe	JPN	2.11.88	29 Nov
46:39	Kaoru	Hirosue	JPN	8.11.93	29 Nov
46:40	Charles	Cheruiyot	KEN	4.8.88	15 Aug
46:40	Abdi	Nageeye	NED	2.3.89	6 Sep
46:40	Khalid	Choukoud	MED	23.3.86	6 Sep
46:40	Bashir	Abdi	BEL	10.2.89	20 Sep

HALF MARATHON

Slighly downhill race: 30.5m South Shields

	20k	15k			Nat	Born	Pos	Meet	Venue	Date
9:10	56:07	42:01	Abreham	Cheroben	KEN	10.11.92	1		Valencia	18 Oct
9:14	56:10	42:05	Bidan	Karoki	KEN	21.8.90	1		København	13 Sep
9:20	56:16	42:13	Stanley	Biwott	KEN	21.4.86	1		Den Haag	8 Mar
9:20			Berhanu	Legesse	ETH	11.9.94	1		New Delhi	29 Nov
9:21			Mosinet	Geremew	ETH	12.2.92	2		New Delhi	29 Nov
9:22dh	56:40	42:29	Mohamed	Farah	GBR	23.3.83	1	GNR	South Shields	13 Sep
9:24dh		42:28		Biwott			2	GNR	South Shields	13 Sep
9:24			Zersenay	Tadese	ERI	8.2.82	3		New Delhi	29 Nov
9:26			Edwin Kiprop	Kiptoo	KEN	14.8.93	4		New Delhi	29 Nov
9:26			Jonathan	Maiyo	KEN	5.5.88	5		New Delhi	29 Nov
9:28	56:27	42:15	Cyprian	Kotut (10)	KEN	.92	2		Den Haag	8 Mar
9:28	56:25	42:07	Alex	Oleitiptip	KEN	22.9.82	2		København	13 Sep
9:30	56:25	42:07	Edwin	Kipyego	KEN	16.11.90	3		København	13 Sep
9:32	56:27			Farah			1		Lisboa	22 Mar
9:32	56:26	42:07	Simon	Cheprot	KEN	2.7.93	4		København	13 Sep
9:33	56:27		Micah	Kogo	KEN	3.6.86	2		Lisboa	22 Mar
9:35	56:27	42:14		Edwin K Kiptoo			3		Den Haag	8 Mar
9:37		42:11	Robert	Chemosin	KEN	1.2.89	1		Ostia	1 Mar
9:38			Geoffrey	Kirui	KEN	16.2.93	6		New Delhi	29 Nov
9:39		42:11		Cheprot			2		Ostia	1 Mar
9:43		42:11	Geoffrey	Kusuro	UGA	12.2.89	3		Ostia	1 Mar
9:45		42:41		Legesse			1		Berlin	29 Mar
9:46		42:41	David	Kogei	KEN	5.5.85	2		Berlin	29 Mar
9:47	56:40	42:18	Paul	Kuira	KEN	25.1.90	1		Marugame	1 Feb
9:47	56:40	42:17	Zane	Robertson (20)	NZL	14.11.89	2		Marugame	1 Feb
9:49		42:41		Cheroben			3		Berlin	29 Mar
9:51	56:45	42:47	Daniel	Wanjiru	KEN	25.5.92	1		Praha	28 Mar
9:52	56:52	42:43		Geremew			1		Yangzhou	19 Apr
9:52	56:35	42:01	Mathew	Kisorio	KEN	16.5.89	2		Valencia	18 Oct

Mark			Name		Nat	Born	Pos	Meet	Venue	Date
59:54			Edwin	Koech	KEN	.87	1		Sarnen	6 Sep
59:55	56:52	42:42		G Kirui			2		Yangzhou	19 Apr
59:55	56:52	42:42	Nguse	Tesfaldet	ERI	10.11.86	3		Yangzhou	19 Apr
59:55	56:52	42:42	Vincent	Yator	KEN	11.7.89	4		Yangzhou	19 Apr
59:57	56:46	42:46	Wilfred	Murgor	KEN	12.12.88	2		Praha	28 Mar
59:57	56:51	42:47	Leonard Patrick	Komon	KEN	10.1.88	3		Praha	28 Mar
59:58	56:35		Stephen	Kibet	KEN	9.11.86	3		Lisboa	22 Mar
59:59		42:41	Richard	Mengich	KEN	.89	4		Berlin	29 Mar
			(37/29)							
60:01	56:54	42:08	Paul	Lonyangata	KEN	12.12.92	5		København	13 Sep
60:03		42:41	Abraham	Kipyatich	KEN	.93	5		Berlin	29 Mar
60:04	56:50	42:14	Eliud	Tarus	KEN	3.3.93	4		Den Haag	8 Mar
60:04	56:54	42:13	Philip	Langat	KEN	23.4.90	6		København	13 Sep
60:04			Solomon	Yego	KEN	.87	1		Udine	20 Sep
60:05	56:58	42:17	Bernard	Kimani	KEN	10.9.93	5		Den Haag	8 Mar
60:06		42:11	Leonard	Langat	KEN	7.8.90	3		Ostia	1 Mar
60:08			Emmanuel	Bett	KEN	30.3.83	1		Azpeitia	28 Mar
60:08	56:58	42:44	Tamirat	Tola	ETH	11.8.91	5		Yangzhou	19 Apr
60:09	56:54	42:17	Ber)nard	Koech	KEN	31.1.88	3		Marugame	1 Feb
60:09	56:55	42:46	Nicholas	Bor	KEN	27.4.88	4		Praha	28 Mar
			(40)							
60:10		42:41	Fentahun	Hunegnaw	ETH		6		Berlin	29 Mar
60:10dh			Mike	Kigen	KEN	15.1.86	3	GNR	South Shields	13 Sep
60:11	57:13		Edwin Kibet	Kiptoo	KEN	28.12.87	4		Ra's Al-Khaymah	13 Feb
60:12	56:58	42:17	James	Rungaru	KEN	14.1.93	1		Nice	26 Apr
60:13		42:22	John	Kiprotich	KEN	30.3.89	5		Ostia	1 Mar
60:13			Evans	Kiplagat	KEN	5.3.88	1		Istanbul	26 Apr
60:17		42:42	Kenneth	Kipkemoi	KEN	2.8.84	7		Berlin	29 Mar
60:17			Joseph	Kiptum	KEN	25.9.87	3		Istanbul	26 Apr
60:18	57:07	42:58	Charles	Ndirangu	KEN	8.2.93	1		Yamaguchi	15 Feb
60:18			Titus	Mbishei	KEN	28.10.90	4		Istanbul	26 Apr
			(50)							
60:19	57:14	43:05	Stephen	Chebogut	KEN	9.1.85	1		Lille	5 Sep
60:19	57:14	43:05	Bonse	Dida	ETH	21.1.95	2		Lille	5 Sep
60:19	57:14	43:04	Vincent	Kipruto	KEN	13.9.87	3		Lille	5 Sep
60:20	57:04	42:18	Benjamin	Gandu	KEN	21.5.90	4		Marugame	1 Feb
60:21		42:37	Josphat	Kiptis	KEN	16.11.93	1		Olomouc	20 Jun
60:23	57:14		Cosmas	Kipchoge	KEN	21.3.86	4		Lille	5 Sep
60:25			Abraham	Kasongor	KEN	.93	6		Istanbul	26 Apr
60:25			Sammy	Kitwara	KEN	26.11.86	1		Luanda	6 Sep
60:26	57:10	42:47	Adugna	Tekele	ETH	26.2.89	5		Praha	28 Mar
60:26	57:10	42:47	Amanuel	Mesel	ERI	29.12.90	6		Praha	28 Mar
			(60)							
60:26	57:22	42:28	Dawit	Weldesilasie	ERI	10.12.94	3		Valencia	18 Oct
60:27	57:10	42:46	Teshome	Mekonen	ETH	5.8.95	7		Praha	28 Mar
60:28	57:15	42:46	Geoffrey	Ronoh	KEN	29.11.82	8		Praha	28 Mar
60:29	57:20	42:42	Hiskel	Tewelde	ERI	15.9.86	6		Yangzhou	19 Apr
60:30	57:23	42:58	Joseph	Ndirangu	KEN	9.9.94	2		Yamaguchi	15 Feb
60:32	57:24	42:58	Masato	Kikuchi	JPN	18.9.90	3		Yamaguchi	15 Feb
60:33	57:26	42:51	Alfers	Lagat	KEN	7.8.86	1		Venlo	22 Mar
60:33		42:55	Thomas	Lokomwa	KEN	.87	1	Stra	Milano	29 Mar
60:34	57:25	42:44	Leul	Gebrselassie	ETH	20.9.93	7		Yangzhou	19 Apr
60:35	57:15	43:05	Norbert	Kigen	KEN	24.1.93	5		Lille	5 Sep
			(70)							
60:36	57:27	42:51	Ezra	Sang	KEN	8.6.94	2		Venlo	22 Mar
60:37			Asbel	Kipsang	KEN	10.9.93	2		Sarnen	6 Sep
60:39		42:55	Kennedy	Kipyeko	KEN	.91	2	Stra	Milano	29 Mar
60:39			Abrar	Osman	ERI	24.6.89	7		New Delhi	29 Nov
60:40dh			Stephen	Mokoka	RSA	31.1.85	4	GNR	South Shields	13 Sep
60:41			Moses	Kipsiro	UGA	2.9.86	8		New Delhi	29 Nov
60:42	57:43		Tadesse	Abraham	SUI	12.8.82	1		Barcelona	15 Feb
60:42	57:26	42:47	Felix	Kandie	KEN	10.4.87	9		Praha	28 Mar
60:42	57:18	42:44	Mule	Wasihun	ETH	20.10.93	8		Yangzhou	19 Apr
60:43	57:27	42:47	Bernard	Bett	KEN	4.1.93	10		Praha	28 Mar
			(80)							
60:45	57:42		Getu	Feleke	ETH	28.11.86	2		Barcelona	15 Feb
60:45			Eric Leon	Ndiema	KEN	1.1.90	6		Ostia	1 Mar
60:45	57:20		Guye	Adola	ETH	20.10.90	4		Lisboa	22 Mar
60:46	57:34	42:37	Juan Luis	Barrios	MEX	24.6.83	5		Marugame	1 Feb
60:48	57:35	42:38	Jacob	Wanjuki	KEN	16.1.86	6		Marugame	1 Feb
60:48			Azmeraw	Mengistu	ETH	15.9.92	3		Barcelona	15 Feb

Mark			Name		Nat	Born	Pos	Meet	Venue	Date
60:48			Mark	Korir	KEN	10.1.85	2		Paris	8 Mar
60:50	57:39		Eliud	Kipchoge	KEN	5.11.84	6		Ra's Al-Khaymah	13 Feb
60:51			Barselius	Kipyego	KEN	.93	1		Adana	4 Jan
60:51	57:45	43:14	Diego	Estrada	USA	12.12.89	1	NC	Houston	18 Jan
60:52	57:39	42:47	Vincent	Rono	KEN	22.12.90	6		Den Haag	8 Mar
60:52			Stephen	Arita	KEN	26.6.88	2		Azpeitia	28 Mar
60:52		42:58	Daniel Kiprop	Limo	KEN	1.1.93	1		Warszawa	29 Mar
60:52			Merhawi	Kesete	ERI	.86	1		Hamburg	21 Jun
60:55		42:39	William	Kibor	KEN	10.1.85	7		Ostia	1 Mar
60:55			Elijah	Tirop	KEN	1.1.92	2		Nice	26 Apr
60:56			Festus	Talam	KEN	20.10.94	2		Verbania	19 Apr
60:56			Daniel	Salel	KEN	11.12.90	1		Boston	11 Oct
60:58			Emmanuel	Ngatuny	KEN	10.10.92	8		Berlin	29 Mar
60:58	57:43	42:46	Joel	Kimurer	KEN	21.1.88	7		København	13 Sep
		(100)								

Mark		Name		Nat	Born	Date
61:01		Edwin	Rotich	KEN	.88	28 Mar
61:02		Amos	Choge	KEN	.77	4 Jan
61:04	42:53	John Kipsang Loitang		KEN	.91	18 Oct
61:05		Tsegaye	Mekonnen	ETH	15.6.95	13 Feb
61:05		Mustapha	El Aziz	MAR	.85	18 Oct
61:06		Abrha	Milaw	ETH	3.1.88	8 Mar
61:06		Leonard	Korir	KEN	10.12.86	16 Mar
61:06		Abraham	Yano	KEN	.87	4 Apr
61:06		Emmanuel	Bor	KEN	14.4.88	20 Sep
61:06		Kidane	Tadese	ERI	31.8.87	18 Oct
61:07		Abera	Kuma	ETH	31.8.90	13 Feb
61:07		Stephen	Sambu	KEN	7.7.88	16 Mar
61:08		Temesgen	Ejersa	ETH	.93	4 Apr
61:08	42:57	Richard	Kiprotich Sigei	KEN	11.5.84	13 Sep
61:09	42:57	Moges	Shuway	ERI-J	.97	13 Sep
61:10		Seboka	Bira	ETH	.94	11 Oct
61:12		Keita	Shitara	JPN	18.12.91	15 Feb
61:12		Thomas	Ayeko	UGA	10.2.92	28 Mar
61:13	43:09	Nicholas	Kipkemboi	KEN	5.7.86	23 May
61:13		Benjamin	Somikwo	UGA-J	.96	11 Oct
61:16		Yitayal	Atnafu	ETH	20.1.93	15 Feb
61:17	42:47	Peter	Kirui	KEN	2.1.88	28 Mar
61:17		Justus	Kangogo	KEN	.95	11 Oct
61:18	43:21	Justus	Kanda	KEN-J	26.6.97	22 Mar
61:20		Samson	Gebreyohanes	ERI	7.2.92	28 Mar
61:20		Galen	Rupp	USA	8.5.86	13 Dec
61:21		Ali	Kaya	TUR	20.4.94	4 Jan
61:21	43:04	Daichi	Jinno (Kamino)	JPN	13.9.93	1 Feb
61:21		Lusapho	April	RSA	24.5.82	16 Mar
61:21	42:53	Berhanu	Tsegay	ERI	.83	28 Mar
61:22		Abel	Kirui	KEN	4.6.82	15 Feb
61:23		Wilson Kipsang Kiprotich		KEN	15.3.82	13 Jun
61:23		Timothy	Ritchie	USA	7.8.87	31 Oct
61:25	43:26	Shota	Hattori	JPN	28.10.91	15 Feb
61:26	43:22	Bernard	Kitur	KEN	10.1.90	22 Mar
61:29	43:20	Johana	Maina	KEN	24.12.90	15 Feb
61:31	43:26	Taku	Fujimoto	JPN	11.9.89	15 Feb
61:32		Youssef	Nasir	MAR	15.2.90	4 Jan
61:32		Morris Munene Gachaga		KEN	7.4.95	13 Sep
61:33		Bethwel	Chemweno	KEN	6.8.88	4 Apr
61:36		Demise	Tsegay	ETH	13.3.88	13 Feb
61:37	43:05	Ken	Yokote	JPN	27.4.93	1 Feb
61:37		Titus	Komen	KEN	.91	19 Apr
61:37	42:53	Hayle	Lemi	ETH	13.9.94	18 Oct
61:38	42:53	Peter	Kwemoi	KEN		1 Mar
61:39		Ghirmay	Ghebrselassie	ERI	14.11.95	7 Feb
61:39		Hassan	Chahdi	FRA	7.5.89	8 Mar
61:39		Tujuba	Megersa	ETH	15.10.87	26 Apr
61:39		Tsegay	Tuemay	ERI	20.12.95	4 Oct
61:40	43:26	Yuji	Osuda	JPN	18.11.90	15 Feb
61:40		Philip Sanga Koech		KEN	6.2.87	11 Oct
61:41		Timothy	Kiptoo	KEN	2.8.84	8 Mar
61:41		Eliud Macharia Mwangi		KEN	12.10.89	29 Mar
61:42		Jared	Ward	USA	9.9.88	18 Jan
61:42		Yohanes	Gebregergish	ERI		7 Feb
61:42		Christiopher	Cheruiyot	KEN	25.11.91	13 Sep
61:43		Simon	Tesfai	ERI	15.3.85	29 Mar
61:44		Geoffrey	Koech	KEN	.93	19 Apr
61:44		Elisha	Barno	KEN	.85	25 Apr
61:46		Pius	Nyantika	KEN	.87	25 Apr
61:46		Henry	Kiplagat	KEN	16.12.82	23 May
61:46		Samuel	Tsegay	ERI	24.10.88	6 Sep
61:51		Joel	Kimutai	KEN	5.10.88	28 Mar
61.51A		Mike	Mutai	KEN	.87	4 Oct
61:52		Daniel	Yator	KEN	.88	21 Jun
61:53		Silas	Limo	KEN	.92	25 Apr
61.53		Laban	Korir	KEN	30.12.85	23 Aug
61.53+		Eliud	Kiptanui	KEN	6.6.89	27 Sep
61.53+		Geoffrey	Mutai	KEN	7.10.81	27 Sep
61.53+		Emmanuel	Mutai	KEN	12.10.84	27 Sep
61.53+		Feyisa	Lilesa	ETH	1.2.90	27 Sep
61:55		Kenta	Matsumoto	JPN	1.6.91	15 Feb
61:55		Paul	Sugut	KEN	12.10.86	11 Oct
61:56		Kevin	Kochei	KEN	2.12.89	22 Mar
61:56		Frederick	Ngeny	KEN	.88	29 Mar
61.56A		Hosea	Macharinyang	KEN	12.6.85	4 Oct
61:56		Rodgers	Maiyo	KEN	3.9.95	11 Oct
61:57		Charles	Cheruiyot	KEN	4.8.88	21 Jun
61.58		Isaac	Kiplagat	KEN	6.2.87	4 Oct
61:59		Hosea	Kisorio	KEN	22.11.90	3 May
61:59		Fabiano	Sulle	TAN	1.10.94	4 Oct
		(181)				

Uncertain distance: Mar 8, Nairobi KEN (A): 1. Moses Kosgei 61:28, 2. Andrew Kimutai 61:35, 4. Alfred Kimeli

JUNIORS

Mark		Name		Nat	Born	Pos	Venue	Date
61:09	42:57	Moges	Shuway	ERI	.97	10	København	13 Sep
61:13		Benjamin	Somikwo	UGA	.96	2	Reims	11 Oct
61:18	43:21	Justus	Kanda	KEN	26.6.97	4	Venlo	22 Mar
62:17		Abraham	Habte	ERI	14.7.96	12	København	13 Sep
62:22		Yuta	Shimoda	JPN	31.3.96	9	Tachikawa	1 Mar
62:29		Kenneth	Keter	KEN	.96	6	Ústí nad Labem	12 Sep
62:48		Jameson	Wangechi	KEN	.96	4	Casablanca	24 May
62:54		Haruki	Minatoya	JPN	25.4.96	3	Ageo	15 Nov
63:27		Solomon	Mogos	ERI	.97	8	Massawa	7 Feb
63:27		Yihunilign	Adane	ETH	29.2.96	2	Montbéliard	27 Sep
63:28		Moses	Wamaitha	KEN-Y	.98	6	Krems	13 Sep

25 – 30 KILOMETRES ROAD

25k 30k In addition to those shown in Marathon listing

25k	30k	Name		Nat	Born	Pos	Meet	Venue	Date
1:12:31		Abreham	Cheroben	KEN	10.11.92	1	BIG	Berlin	10 May
1:13:28		Temesgen	Ejersse	ETH	.93	2	BIG	Berlin	10 May
1:13:29	1:28:49+	Tamirat	Tola	ETH	11.8.91		in Mar	Berlin	27 Sep

MEN 2015

Mark		Name		Nat	Born	Pos	Meet	Venue	Date
1:13:48	1:28:53+	Abayneh	Ayele	ETH	4.11.87		in Mar	Rotterdam	12 Apr
1:13:48	1:28:54+	Tebalu	Zawude	ETH	2.11.87		in Mar	Rotterdam	12 Apr
1:13:54+		Megersa	Bacha	ETH	18.1.85		in Mar	Rotterdam	12 Apr
1:14:04	1:29:05+	Stephen	Chemlany	KEN	9.8.82		in Mar	Eindhoven	11 Oct
	1:29:34+	Wilfred Kirwa	Kigen	KEN	21.1.86		in Mar	Frankfurt	25 Oct
	1:29:50+	Richard	Mengich	KEN	.89		in Mar	Tokyo	22 Feb
	1:29:54+	Tsegaye	Mekonnen	ETH	15.6.95		in Mar	London	26 Apr
1:14:11	1:29:57+	Vincent	Chepkok	KEN	5.7.88		in Mar	Eindhoven	11 Oct
	1:29:57+	Norbert	Kigen	KEN	24.1.93		in Mar	Frankfurt	25 Oct
	1:29:58+	Sentayehu	Merga	ETH	18.3.85				
1:14:18		Kenneth	Kipkemoi	KEN	2.8.84	3	BIG	Berlin	10 May

MARATHON

Mark	25k	30k	Name		Nat	Born	Pos	Venue	Date
2:04:00	1:13:25	1:28:10	Eliud	Kipchoge	KEN	5.11.84	1	Berlin	27 Sep
2:04:42	1:14:03	1:28:56		Kipchoge			1	London	26 Apr
2:04:47	1:14:04	1:28:56	Wilson	Kipsang	KEN	15.3.82	2	London	26 Apr
2:05:21	1:13:25	1:28:11	Eliud	Kiptanui	KEN	6.6.89	2	Berlin	27 Sep
2:05:28			Hayle	Lemi	ETH	13.9.94	1	Dubai	23 Jan
2:05:49			Mark	Korir	KEN	10.1.85	1	Paris	12 Apr
2:05:50	1:14:04	1:28:56	Dennis	Kimetto	KEN	22.1.84	3	London	26 Apr
2:05:52			Lelisa	Desisa	ETH	14.1.90	2	Dubai	23 Jan
2:05:52	1:14:03	1:28:52	Stephen	Chebogut	KEN	9.1.85	1	Eindhoven	11 Oct
2:05:58	1:14:03	1:28:52	Deribe	Robi	ETH	26.9.84	2	Eindhoven	11 Oct
2:06:00	1:14:45	1:29:50	Endeshaw	Negesse (10)	ETH	13.3.88	1	Tokyo	22 Feb
2:06:00	1:14:03	1:28:52	Mark	Kiptoo	KEN	21.6.76	3	Eindhoven	11 Oct
2:06:06				Robi			3	Dubai	23 Jan
2:06:11			Wilson	Loyanae	KEN	20.11.88	1	Seoul	15 Mar
2:06:13	1:14:56	1:30:00	John	Mwangangi	KEN	1.11.90	1	Valencia	15 Nov
2:06:19			Moses	Mosop	KEN	17.7.85	1	Xiamen	3 Jan
2:06:19	1:15:08	1:30:05	Bernard	Kipyego	KEN	16.7.86	1	Amsterdam	18 Oct
2:06:26		1:29:33	Sisay	Lemma	ETH	12.12.90	1	Frankfurt	25 Oct
2:06:33	1:14:45	1:29:50	Stephen	Kiprotich	UGA	18.4.89	2	Tokyo	22 Feb
2:06:33	1:14:55	1:29:59	Mathew	Kisorio	KEN	16.5.89	2	Valencia	15 Nov
2:06:34	1:14:45	1:29:51	Dickson	Chumba	KEN	27.10.86	3	Tokyo	22 Feb
2:06:34		1:29:57	Lani	Rutto (20)	KEN	29.3.89	2	Frankfurt	25 Oct
2:06:35			Feyisa	Lilesa	ETH	1.2.90	4	Dubai	23 Jan
2:06:41	1:14:04	1:28:56	Stanley	Biwott	KEN	21.4.86	4	London	26 Apr
2:06:47	1:13:48	1:28:54	Abera	Kuma	ETH	31.8.90	1	Rotterdam	12 Apr
2:06:48		1:29:57	Alfers	Lagat	KEN	7.8.86	3	Frankfurt	25 Oct
2:06:54			Tilahun	Regassa	ETH	18.1.90	2	Xiamen	3 Jan
2:06:57	1:13:25	1:28:10		Lilesa			3	Berlin	27 Sep
2:06:59			Felix	Kiprotich	KEN	.88	2	Seoul	15 Mar
2:07:01				Loyanae			1	Gyeongju	11 Oct
2:07:06				Lemma			5	Dubai	23 Jan
2:07:07			Samuel Kiplimo	Kosgei	KEN	20.1.86	1	Kosice	4 Oct
2:07:07	1:14:55	1:29:59	Felix	Kandie	KEN	10.4.87	3	Valencia	15 Nov
2:07:09			Bazu	Worku	ETH	15.9.90	6	Dubai	23 Jan
2:07:14			Paul	Lonyangata (30)	KEN	12.12.92	1	Shanghai	8 Nov
2:07:16	1:14:04	1:28:56		Regassa			5	London	26 Apr
2:07:16	1:14:04	1:28:53	Abayneh	Ayele	ETH	4.11.87	4	Eindhoven	11 Oct
2:07:17			Lucas	Rotich	KEN	16.4.90	1	Hamburg	26 Apr
2:07:18		1:30:05	Ezekiel	Chebii	KEN	3.1.91	2	Amsterdam	18 Oct
2:07:20	1:14:45	1:29:50	Shumi	Dechasa	BRN	28.5.89	4	Tokyo	22 Feb
2:07:20			Luka	Kanda	KEN	.87	2	Paris	12 Apr
2:07:21	1:13:48	1:28:53		Kiptoo			2	Rotterdam	12 Apr
			(42/35)						
2:07:22	1:14:45	1:29:51	Peter	Some	KEN	5.6.90	5	Tokyo	22 Feb
2:07:25	1:14:44	1:29:50	Markos	Geneti	ETH	30.5.84	6	Tokyo	22 Feb
2:07:26		1:29:55	Birhanu	Gebru	ETH	22.11.86	1	Daegu	5 Apr
2:07:33			Seboka	Dibaba Tola	ETH	10.11.87	3	Paris	12 Apr
2:07:39	1:14:45	1:29:50	Masato	Imai	JPN	2.4.84	7	Tokyo	22 Feb
			(40)						
2:07:40			Stephen	Mokoka	RSA	31.1.85	2	Shanghai	8 Nov
2:07:42			Mike	Kigen	KEN	15.1.86	4	Paris	12 Apr
2:07:43	1:14:04	1:28:56	Sammy	Kitwara	KEN	26.11.86	6	London	26 Apr
2:07:44			Gilbert	Kirwa	KEN	20.12.85	5	Paris	12 Apr
2:07:46	1:13:25	1:28:10	Emmanuel	Mutai	KEN	12.10.84	4	Berlin	27 Sep
2:07:47			Jacob	Kendagor	KEN	24.8.84	3	Seoul	15 Mar

Mark			Name		Nat	Born	Pos Meet	Venue	Date
2:07:47			Ghirmay	Ghebreslassie	ERI	14.11.95	2	Hamburg	26 Apr
2:07:54			Laban	Korir	KEN	30.12.85	6	Paris	12 Apr
2:07:56			Deressa	Chimsa	ETH	21.11.86	7	Paris	12 Apr
2:07:57			Ernest	Ngeno	KEN	20.5.95	1	Hengshui	26 Sep
			(50)						
2:07:58	1:14:44	1:29:50	Tsegaye	Kebede	ETH	15.1.87	8	Tokyo	22 Feb
2:08:02	1:13:48	1:28:53	Bernard	Koech	KEN	31.1.88	3	Rotterdam	12 Apr
2:08:03			Berhanu	Gedefa	ETH	.94	1	Houston	18 Jan
2:08:05			Dadi	Yami	ETH	.82	4	Seoul	15 Mar
2:08:05			Robert	Chemosin	KEN	1.2.89	2	Warszawa	26 Apr
2:08:08			Collins	Tanui	KEN	.92	2	Kosice	4 Oct
2:08:09			Abrha	Milaw	ETH	3.1.88	3	Xiamen	3 Jan
2:08:11			Chala	Dechase	ETH	13.6.84	7	Dubai	23 Jan
2:08:11			Joel	Kimurer	KEN	21.1.88	2	Gyeongju	11 Oct
2:08:12			Gebo	Burka	ETH	27.9.87	2	Houston	18 Jan
			(60)						
2:08:14			Abreham	Cherkos	ETH	23.9.89	5	Seoul	15 Mar
2:08:16			Philip	Kangogo	KEN		1	Barcelona	15 Mar
2:08:17	1:14:03	1:28:52	Edwin	Kibet	KEN-J	7.7.96	5	Eindhoven	11 Oct
2:08:18			Robert	Kwambai	KEN	22.11.85	4	Xiamen	3 Jan
2:08:18			Amanuel	Mesel	ERI	29.12.90	4	Warszawa	26 Apr
2:08:18			Philemon	Rono	KEN	8.2.91	4	Hamburg	26 Apr
2:08:18			Patrick	Makau	KEN	2.3.85	1	Fukuoka	6 Dec
2:08:19			Limenih	Getachew	ETH	30.4.90	1	Ljubljana	25 Oct
2:08:21		1:29:55	Stephen	Chemlany	KEN	9.8.82	2	Daegu	5 Apr
2:08:28			Richard	Kiprotich Sigei	KEN	11.5.84	5	Warszawa	26 Apr
			(70)						
2:08:29			Elijah	Kemboi	KEN	10.9.84	6	Warszawa	26 Apr
2:08:31			Getu	Feleke	ETH	28.11.86	2	Fukuoka	6 Dec
2:08:33		1:30:35	Arne	Gabius	GER	22.3.81	4	Frankfurt	25 Oct
2:08:37			Mulugeta	Wami	ETH	12.7.82	2	Ljubljana	25 Oct
2:08:38	1:14:56	1:30:00	Gebretsadik	Adhana	ETH	16.7.92	4	Valencia	15 Nov
2:08:42			Kenneth	Mungara	KEN	7.9.73	1	Gold Coast	5 Jul
2:08:45		1;29:55	Benjamin	Mutai	KEN	13.7.82	3	Daegu	5 Apr
2:08:45		1:30:06	Wilson	Chebet	KEN	12.7.85	5	Amsterdam	18 Oct
2:08:46			Tebalu	Zawude	ETH	2.11.87	1	Seoul	1 Nov
2:08:49		1:29:57	Suleiman	Simotwo	KEN	21.4.80	5	Frankfurt	25 Oct
			(80)						
2:08:50			Evans Kiplagat	Chebet	KEN	5.3.88	2	Praha	3 May
2:08:51			Workneh	Tiruneh	ETH	.84	1	Marrakech	25 Jan
2:08:53			Ayele	Abshero	ETH	28.12.90	3	Gyeongju	11 Oct
2:08:53			Tola	Shura	ETH-J	.96	3	Shanghai	8 Nov
2:08:54			Silah	Limo	KEN	1.2.92	2	Gold Coast	5 Jul
2:08:55			Cyprian	Kotut	KEN	.92	2	Milano	12 Apr
2:08:55			Evans	Ruto	KEN	14.1.84	3	Gold Coast	5 Jul
2:08:56			Samuel	Mwaniki	KEN	.84	2	Marrakech	25 Jan
2:08:56		1:30:02	John Kemboi	Cheruiyot	KEN	5.7.90	6	Frankfurt	25 Oct
2:08:56			Satoru	Sasaki	JPN	16.10.85	3	Fukuoka	6 Dec
			(90)						
2:08:59			Samuel	Rutto	KEN	.95	3	Ljubljana	25 Oct
2:09:00			Ishmael	Busendich	KEN	7.7.91	1	Toronto	18 Oct
2:09:01			Gideon	Kipketer	KEN	10.11.92	2	Seoul	1 Nov
2:09:05			Felix	Keny	KEN	25.12.85	1	Gunsan	12 Apr
2:09:07			Debebe	Tolossa	ETH	7.7.91	3	Houston	18 Jan
2:09:08			Samuel	Ndungu	KEN	4.4.88	1	Otsu	1 Mar
2:09:08			Philemon	Baaru	KEN	20.5.81	3	Milano	12 Apr
2:09:11			Oleksandr	Sitkovskiy	UKR	9.6.78	3	Marrakech	25 Jan
2:09:12	1:14:45	1:29:50	Hiroaki	Sano	JPN	28.2.88	9	Tokyo	22 Feb
2:09:14		1:30:06	Siboke	Nigusse	ETH	.84	6	Amsterdam	18 Oct
			(100)						
2:09:14			Marius	Kimutai	KEN	.89	1	Rennes (64.5m dh)	25 Oct
2:09:16		1:30:05	Tewelde	Estifanos	ERI	2.10.87	7	Frankfurt	25 Oct
2:09:18	1:14:45	1:29:51	Benjamin	Gandu	KEN	21.5.90	10	Tokyo	22 Feb
2:09:19			Ezequiel	Omullo	KEN		1	Warszawa	27 Sep
2:09:21			Koji	Gokaya	JPN	22.2.88	11	Tokyo	22 Feb
2:09:21	23?		Marius	Kipserem	KEN	.88	1	Hefei	25 Oct
2:09:23			James	Kwambai	KEN	28.2.83	4	Seoul	1 Nov
2:09:25			Norbert	Kigen	KEN	24.1.93	1	La Rochelle	29 Nov
2:09:26			Asbel	Kipsang	KEN	10.9.93	1	Lisboa	18 Oct
2:09:29	1:13:25	1:28:15	Geoffrey	Mutai	KEN	7.10.81	5	Berlin	27 Sep
2:09:32			Jacob Chesari	Kirui	KEN	6.4.84	1	Hannover	19 Apr

Mark	Name		Nat	Born	Date
2:09:32	Robert	Kiplimo	KEN	.88	19 Apr
2:09:33	Javier	Guerra	ESP	10.11.83	26 Apr
2:09:33 dh	Kipkemei	Mutai	KEN	25.7.86	25 Oct
2:09:36	Kibrom	Ghebrezgiabhier	ERI	1.2.87	26 Apr
2:09:37	Wilfred	Murgor	KEN	12.12.88	1 Nov
2:09:38	Yakob	Jarso	ETH	5.2.88	15 Mar
2:09:39	Adugna	Tekele	ETH	26.2.89	23 Jan
2:09:39	Lawrence	Cherono	KEN		22 Feb
2:09:39	Anthony	Maritim	KEN	.86	19 Apr
2:09:40	Dominic	Ondoro	KEN	.88	18 Jan
2:09:40	Evans	Cheruiyot	KEN	10.5.82	19 Apr
2:09:41	Yared	Asmeron	ETH	3.2.79	22 Feb
2:09:41	Bekana	Daba	ETH	29.7.88	15 Mar
2:09:42	Bekele	Adugna	ETH	.89	19 Apr
2:09:43	Peter	Kiplagat	KEN	4.2.84	25 Oct
2:09:44	Kaleab	Keshebo	ETH	13.1.93	19 Apr
2:09:46	Tesfaye	Abera	ETH	31.3.92	18 Jan
2:09:47	Edwin	Kimaiyo	KEN	.86	19 Apr
2:09:48	Benteyehu	Assefa	ETH		1 Nov
2:09:49	Gilbert	Masai	KEN	20.5.81	29 Nov
2:09:50	Martin	Kosgei	KEN	.89	19 Apr
2:09:54	Levi	Matebo	KEN	3.11.89	25 Oct
2:09:54	Tujuba	Megersa	ETH	15.10.87	29 Nov
2:09:55	Laban	Mutai	KEN	.85	15 Nov
2:09:57	Sentayehu	Merga	ETH	18.3.85	6 Dec
2:09:58	Willy	Kotile Kibor	KEN	10.1.85	12 Apr
2:09:58	Pius	Kirop	KEN	8.1.90	12 Apr
2:09:59	Andualem	Belay	ETH	5.4.92	23 Jan
2:10:01	Fikre	Assefa	ETH	18.1.89	3 Ma
2:10:01	Nixson	Kurgat	KEN	7.11.87	25 Oct
2:10:01	Abdellah	Tagharrafet	MAR	.85	6 Dec
2:10:02	Belachew	Alemayehu	ETH	.85	1 Nov
2:10:04	Dawit	Wolde	ETH	19.5.91	25 Jan
2:10:04	Abdisa	Sori	ETH	.80	26 Apr
2:10:06	Raymond	Chemungor	KEN	.88	25 Oct
2:10:09	Sammy	Kigen	KEN	29.9.85	15 Nov
2:10:09	Geoffrey	Ronoh	KEN	29.11.82	15 Nov
2:10:10	Aleksey	Reunkov	RUS	28.1.84	26 Apr
2:10:11	Henryk	Szost	POL	20.1.82	26 Apr
2:10:11	William Kiprono	Yegon	KEN	10.1.83	25 Oct
2:10:13	Hassane	Ahouchar	MAR	.75	15 Nov
2:10:15	Duncan	Maiyo	KEN	5.8.90	12 Apr
2:10:15	Ser-Od	Bat-Ochir	MGL	7.10.81	26 Apr
2:10:15	Nixon	Machichin	KEN	.83	4 Oct
2:10:17	Herpasa	Negassa	ETH	.93	4 Oct
2:10:18	Rachid	Kisri	MAR	1.3.75	24 Ma
2:10:21	Serhiy	Lebid	UKR	15.7.75	26 Apr
2:10:22	Henry	Chirchir	KEN	14.5.85	25 Oct
2:10:23	Peter	Kirui	KEN	2.1.88	24 Ma
2:10:24	Luke	Puskedra	USA	8.2.90	11 Oct
2:10:24	Abdi	Nageeye	ETH	2.3.89	18 Oct
2:10:24	Micah	Kogo	KEN	3.6.86	25 Oct
2:10:26	Jared	Kipchumba	KEN	8.8.83	22 Feb
2:10:27	Samson	Bungei	KEN	.82	12 Apr
2:10:28	Reid	Coolsaet	CAN	29.7.79	27 Sep
2:10:30	Tadesse	Tola	ETH	31.10.87	3 Jan
2:10:31	Dereje	Debele	ETH	26.7.86	18 Jan
2:10:31	Koen	Naert	BEL	3.9.89	27 Sep
2:10:32	Belay	Asefa	ETH	17.6.92	18 Oct
2:10:33	Gilbert	Maina	KEN	.91	12 Apr
2:10:35	Abdelmajid	El Hissouf	MAR	23.9.92	1 Nov
2:10:38	Elisha	Barno	KEN	.85	20 Jun
2:10:39	Wesley	Korir	KEN	15.11.82	11 Oct
2:10:41	Abraraw	Misganaw	ETH	.88	25 Jan
2:10:42	Solomon	Mutai	KEN	22.10.92	19 Apr
2:10:42	Jonathan	Kiptoo	KEN	76	25 Oct
2:10:43	Barnabas	Kiptum	KEN	8.10.86	8 Nov
2:10:45	Augustine	Rono	KEN	.81	19 Apr
2:10:45	Victor	Kipchirchir	KEN	5.12.87	27 Sep
2:10:45	Eliud	Tarus	KEN	3.3.93	18 Oct
2:10:46	Hiroki	Kadota	JPN	1.5.85	1 Feb
2:10:46	Jamin	Ngaukon	KEN		11 Oct
2:10:47	Yared	Shegumo	POL	11.1.83	27 Sep
2:10:48	Geoffrey	Kamworor	KEN	28.11.92	1 Nov
2:10:55	Abel	Kirui	KEN	4.6.82	18 Oct
2:10:55	Chiharu	Takada	JPN	9.7.81	6 Dec
2:10:57	Luke	Kibet	KEN	12.4.83	18 Jan
2:10:57	Mule	Wasihun	ETH	20.10.93	23 Jan
2:10:58	Johnstone	Maiyo	KEN	6.10.88	27 Sep
2:11:00	Marílson	dos Santos	BRA	6.8.77	26 Apr
2:11:00	Mariko (192)	Kipchumba	KEN	10.1.82	20 Sep

Downhill

Mark	Name		Nat	Born	Pos	Venue	Date
2:09:48	Yemane	Tsegay Adhane	ETH	8.4.85	2	Boston (136m dh)	20 Apr
2:10:36	Daniel Kiprop	Limo	KEN	1.1.93			15 Mar
2:10:52	Frankline	Chepkwony	KEN	15.6.84			20 Apr

JUNIORS

See main list for top 2 juniors. Further junior:

Mark	Name		Nat	Born	Pos	Venue	Date
2:16:32	Teferi	Regasa	ETH	3.3.97	6	Alger	27 Nov

100 KILOMETRES

Mark	Name		Nat	Born	Pos	Meet	Venue	Date
6:22:44	Jonas	Buud	SWE	28.3.74	1	WCh	Winschoten	12 Sep
6:35:49	Yoshikazu	Hara	JPN	13.8.72	2		Yubetsu	28 Jun
6:35:49	Asier	Cuevas	ESP	16.1.73	2	WCh	Winschoten	12 Sep
6:36:39	Tsutomu	Nagata	JPN	20.2.84	2		Yubetsu	28 Jun
6:36:49	Giorgio	Calcaterra	ITA	11.2.72	3	WCh	Winschoten	12 Sep
6:38:48	Vasily	Larkin	RUS	19.8.91	4	WCh	Winschoten	12 Sep
6:40:33	Tatsuya	Itagaki	JPN	4.1.88	3		Yubetsu	28 Jun
6:41:27	Wouter	De Cock	BEL	23.9.83	5	WCh	Winschoten	12 Sep
6:42:04	Yoshiki	Takada	JPN	18.7.83	4		Yubetsu	28 Jun
6:42:51	Fritjof	Fagerlund (10)	SWE	27.6.74	6	WCh	Winschoten	12 Sep
6:43:13	Vsevolod	Khudyakov	RUS	8.2.89	7	WCh	Winschoten	12 Sep
6:43:35	Ross	Houston	GBR	5.12.79	1		Redwick	2 May
6:43:41	Jérôme	Bellanca	FRA	25.9.77	8	WCh	Winschoten	12 Sep
6:44:09	Yoshifumi	Kiyomoto	JPN	27.11.78	5		Yubetsu	28 Jun
6:46:44	Takaaki	Sakamoto	JPN	.91	6		Yubetsu	28 Jun
6:47:51	Kaoru	Higashida	JPN	2.6.87	7		Yubetsu	28 Jun
6:47:53	Ibon	Esparza	ESP	12.2.77	1		Seregno	22 Mar
6:49:13	Florian	Neuschwander	GER	1.6.81	9	WCh	Winschoten	12 Sep

Mark	Name		Nat	Born	Date
6:50:34	Aleksandr	Sorokin	LTU	30.9.81	12 Sep
6:52:45	Yoshihiko	Ishikawa (20)	JPN	25.4.88	28 Jun
6:53:32	Craig	Holgate	GBR	21.9.76	12 Sep
6:53:57	Tomasz	Walerowicz	POL	16.1.81	7 Nov
6:54:05	Henrik	Jannborg	SWE	10.6.80	12 Sep
6:54:14	Yosuke	Maeda	JPN	16.6.85	28 Jun
6:54:30	Koji	Hayasaka	JPN	5.12.83	28 Jun
6:54:50	Hermann	Achmüller	ITA	17.2.71	12 Sep
6:54:51	Takeshi	Ozaki	JPN	.78	28 Jun

24 HOURS

Mark	Name		Nat	Born	Pos	Meet	Venue	Date
263.899km	Florian	Reus	GER	2.3.84	1	WCh	Torino	12 Apr

Mark	Name		Nat	Born	Pos	Meet	Venue	Date
263.418t	Pete	Kostelnick	USA	12.9.87	1		Phoenix	20 Dec
261.181	Pawel	Szynal	POL	20.11.73	2	WCh	Torino	12 Apr
261.140	Robert	Britton	GBR	15.12.86	3	WCh	Torino	12 Apr
258.333	Ivan	Macaj	SVK	13.2.70	4	WCh	Torino	12 Apr
257.753	Kim	Hansen	DEN	31.5.75	5	WCh	Torino	12 Apr
257.093	David	Proctor	CAN	20.11.80	6	WCh	Torino	12 Apr
256.801	Patrick	Robbins	GBR	12.3.72	7	WCh	Torino	12 Apr
256.743	Richard	Riopel	USA	16.10.73	8	WCh	Torino	12 Apr
256.531t	Marco	Consani (10)	GBR	15.11.74	1		Barcelona	20 Dec
255.470	Harvey	Lewis	USA	13.4.76	9	WCh	Torino	12 Apr
255.033	Matthew	Eckford	AUS	15.7.80	10	WCh	Torino	12 Apr
252.836	Steve	Holyoak	GBR	8.9.64	11	WCh	Torino	12 Apr
252.469	Tetsuo	Kiso	JPN	1.5.68	12	WCh	Torino	12 Apr
252.030	Takayoshi	Shigemi	JPN	8.6.82	1		Tokyo	20 Dec
250.731t	Ivan	Cudin	ITA	15.2.75	1		Soochow	22 Nov
250.006	Stéphane	Ruel	FRA	21.1.66	13	WCh	Torino	12 Apr

Mark	Name		Nat	Born	Date	Mark	Name		Nat	Born	Date
249.716	Ewan	Horsburgh	AUS	22.10.77	12 Apr	246.793	Kim	Klitgaard Sørensen	DEN	6.7.84	31 May
248.276	Ludovic	Dilmi	FRA	11.4.65	12 Apr	246.606	Olivier	Leblond	USA	30.4.72	20 Sep
247.916	Michael	Thwaites (20)	AUS	23.3.74	12 Apr	246.555t	Paris	Canals	ESP	7.3.72	20 Dec
247.026	Mohamed	Saoute	MAR	1.1.71	29 Mar						

Indoors

Mark	Name		Nat	Born	Pos	Meet	Venue	Date
257.606	Bjørn Tore	Taranger	NOR	23.4.79	1	NC	Oslo (B)	21 Nov

2000 METRES STEEPLECHASE

Mark	Name		Nat	Born	Pos	Meet	Venue	Date
5:25.12	Mitko	Tsenov	BUL	13.6.93	1		Sofia	20 May
5:27.17A	Vincent	Kipyegon	KEN-Y	31.12.98	1	NC-y	Nairobi	17 Jun
5:29.41A	Wogene	Sebisibe	ETH-Y	23.6.98	2	WY	Cali	19 Jul
5:30.0A	Nickson	Kiplagat	KEN-Y	11.5.98	2	NC-y	Nairobi	17 Jun
5:30.16A	Geoffrey	Rotich	KEN-Y	28.10.98	3	WY	Cali	19 Jul

JUNIORS

4 performances by 3 men to 5:30.0. Additional marks and further juniors:

Kipyegon 5:27.58A 1 WY Cali 19 Jul 5:29.1A 1h1 NC-j Nairobi 17 Jun
5:28.2A 1 Nairobi 1 Apr

Mark	Name		Nat	Born	Pos	Meet	Venue	Date
5:33.2A	Kevin	Sang	KEN-Y	11.5.98	2h1	NC-j	Nairobi	17 Jun
5:34.9A	Tegenu	Mengistu	ETH-Y	29.4.98			Assela	15 May
5:35.5A	Justine	Moseti	KEN-Y	7.6.99	2h2	NC-j	Nairobi	17 Jun
5:37.0A	Robert	Mwei	KEN-Y	11.4.98	4h1	NC-j	Nairobi	17 Jun

3000 METRES STEEPLECHASE

Mark	Name		Nat	Born	Pos	Meet	Venue	Date
7:58.83	Jairus	Birech	KEN	14.12.92	1	DL	Saint-Denis	4 Jul
8:00.45	Evan	Jager	USA	8.3.89	2	DL	Saint-Denis	4 Jul
8:01.71	Ezekiel	Kemboi	KEN	25.5.82	1	Pre	Eugene	30 May
8:01.83		Birech			2	Pre	Eugene	30 May
8:05.20	Conseslus	Kipruto	KEN	8.12.94	3	Pre	Eugene	30 May
8:05.28		Jager			4	Pre	Eugene	30 May
8:05.36		Birech			1	DL	Shanghai	17 May
8:05.63		Birech			1	Bisl	Oslo	11 Jun
8:09.47		C Kipruto			1	DL	London (OS)	25 Jul
8:09.81		Birech			2	DL	London (OS)	25 Jul
8:09.90		C Kipruto			3	DL	Saint-Denis	4 Jul
8:10.09	Brimin	Kipruto	KEN	31.7.85	4	DL	Saint-Denis	4 Jul
8:10.24	Paul Kipsiele	Koech	KEN	10.11.81	1	WK	Zürich	3 Sep
8:11.28		E Kemboi			1	WCh	Beijing	24 Aug
8:11.39		Koech			2	DL	Shanghai	17 May
8:11.42		Birech			1		Rabat	14 Jun
8:11.64	Jonathan	Ndiku	KEN	18.9.91	1		Beijing	20 May
8:11.92		C Kipruto			2	Bisl	Oslo	11 Jun
8:12.13		Koech			3	DL	London (OS)	25 Jul
8:12.20		Koech			3	Bisl	Oslo	11 Jun
8:12.29		Jager			1	NC	Eugene	28 Jun
8:12.38		C Kipruto			2	WCh	Beijing	24 Aug
8:12.54		B Kipruto			3	WCh	Beijing	24 Aug
8:12.62		Birech			4	WCh	Beijing	24 Aug
8:12.68	Clement	Kemboi	KEN	1.2.92	5	DL	Saint-Denis	4 Jul
8:12.98		C Kemboi			2		Beijing	20 May
8:13.10	Hillary	Yego	KEN	2.4.92	4	DL	London (OS)	25 Jul
8:13.37	Donn	Cabral (10)	USA	12.12.89	2	NC	Eugene	28 Jun
8:13.95		Koech			5	Pre	Eugene	30 May
8:14.11	Dan	Huling	USA	16.7.83	3	NC	Eugene	28 Jun
	(30/11)							

Mark	Name		Nat	Born	Pos	Meet	Venue	Date
8:14.75	John	Koech	BRN	23.8.95	3		Beijing	20 May
8:15.66	Bernard Mbugua	Nganga	KEN	17.1.85	4		Beijing	20 May
8:16.54	Hicham	Sigueni	MAR	30.1.93	1	DL	Stockholm	30 Jul
8:16.56	Brahim	Taleb	MAR	16.2.85	2	DL	Stockholm	30 Jul
8:18.08	Andrew	Bayer	USA	3.2.90	6	DL	London (OS)	25 Jul
8:18.38	Yoann	Kowal	FRA	28.5.87	6		Rabat	14 Jun
8:18.49	Ilgizar	Safiulin	RUS	9.12.92	10	DL	Saint-Denis	4 Jul
8:18.51	Lawrence	Kemboi	KEN	15.6.93	5		Beijing	20 May
8:18.63	Matt	Hughes	CAN	3.8.89	8	WCh	Beijing	24 Aug
	(20)							
8:18.78	Hamid	Ezzine	MAR	5.10.83	6		Beijing	20 May
8:19.26	Nicholas	Bett	KEN-J	20.12.96	1	NA	Heusden-Zolder	18 Jul
8:19.30	Amor	Benyahia	TUN	1.7.85	7		Beijing	20 May
8:19.85	Roberto	Alaiz	ESP	20.7.90	9	Pre	Eugene	30 May
8:19.90	Taylor	Milne	CAN	14.6.81	2	NA	Heusden-Zolder	18 Jul
8:20.38	Abel	Mutai	KEN	2.10.88	8	DL	Shanghai	17 May
8:21.15	Bilal	Tabti	ALG	7.6.93	1		Amiens	27 Jun
8:21.22	Krystian	Zalewski	POL	11.4.89	9	WCh	Beijing	24 Aug
8:21.59	Tarik Langat	Akdag	TUR	16.6.88	1	ECCp	Mersin	31 May
8:21.78	Fernando	Carro	ESP	1.4.92	3	NA	Heusden-Zolder	18 Jul
	(30)							
8:21.89	Mitko	Tsenov	BUL	13.6.93	5	DL	Stockholm	30 Jul
8:21.93	Barnabas	Kipyego	KEN	12.6.95	11	Pre	Eugene	30 May
8:22.10	Abraham	Kibiwot	KEN-J	4.6.96	8	DL	London (OS)	25 Jul
8:22.38	Sebastián	Martos	ESP	20.6.89	13	DL	Saint-Denis	4 Jul
8:22.46	Víctor	García	ESP	13.3.85	9	DL	London (OS)	25 Jul
8:22.49	Halil	Akkas	TUR	1.7.83	4	NA	Heusden-Zolder	18 Jul
8:22.9	Tolossa	Nurgi	ETH	29.3.90	1		Montbéliard	5 Jun
8:22.96	Hillary	Kemboi	KEN	.86	2	AfG	Brazzaville	13 Sep
8:23.0	Nikolay	Chavkin	RUS	24.4.84	2		Montbéliard	5 Jun
8:23.93	Stanley	Kebenei	USA	6.11.89	1	Jordan	Stanford	2 May
	(40)							
8:24.19	Hailemariyam	Amare	ETH-J	22.2.97	3	AfG	Brazzaville	13 Sep
8:24.26A	Joash	Kiplimo	KEN	.91	1	NC	Nairobi	11 Jul
8:24.58	Mohamed Ismail	Ibrahim	DJI-J	.97	7	DL	Stockholm	30 Jul
8:24.65	Hichem	Bouchicha	ALG	19.5.89	2		Amiens	27 Jun
8:24.81A	Geoffrey	Ngeno	KEN	11.1.94	3	NC	Nairobi	11 Jul
8:24.84	Alexandre	Genest	CAN	30.6.86	3	Jordan	Stanford	2 May
8:25.04	Haron	Lagat	KEN	15.8.83	5	NA	Heusden-Zolder	18 Jul
8:25.54	Patrick	Churkor	KEN	17.2.91	2	WMilG	Mungyeong	8 Oct
8:25.56	Tafese	Soboka	ETH	29.9.93	1		Hérouville	18 Jun
8:25.74	Cory	Leslie	USA	24.10.89	4	Odlozil	Praha	8 Jun
	(50)							
8:25.82	Chala	Beyo	ETH-J	18.1.96	4		Kawasaki	10 May
8:25.99A	Wilson	Maraba	KEN	2.12.86	4	NC	Nairobi	11 Jul
8:26.24	Festus	Kiprono	KEN	29.12.95	12	DL	Shanghai	17 May
8:26.34	Abdelaziz	Merzougui	ESP	30.8.91	9		Rabat	14 Jun
8:26.37	Justus	Lagat	KEN-J	20.5.96	2		Sollentuna	25 Jun
8:26.55	Chris	Winter	CAN	22.7.86	11	DL	London (OS)	25 Jul
8:26.62	Wogene	Sebisibe	ETH-Y	23.6.98	4	AfG	Brazzaville	13 Sep
8:26.81	Tabor	Stevens	USA	21.6.91	5	Jordan	Stanford	2 May
8:27.08	Travis	Mahoney	USA	25.7.90	3		Los Angeles (ER)	14 May
8:27.43	Ibrahim	Ezzaydouny	MAR	28.4.91	2	ESP Ch	Castellón	2 Aug
	(60)							
8:27.7	Birhan	Getahun	ETH	5.9.91	5		Montbéliard	5 Jun
8:27.79	Soufiane	El Bakkali	MAR-J	7.1.96	3		Amiens	27 Jun
8:27.86	Donnie	Cowart	USA	24.10.85	2	Jerome	Burnaby	8 Jun
8:27.93	Festus	Rono	KEN	28.12.93	3		Sollentuna	25 Jun
8:27.95	Ángel	Mullera	ESP	20.4.84	9	Bisl	Oslo	11 Jun
8:27.99A	Philip	Yego	KEN	.79	5	NC	Nairobi	11 Jul
8:28.41	Alex	Kibet	KEN	20.10.90	1		Doha	30 Apr
8:28.78	Hicham	Chemlal	MAR-J	2.12.97	10		Rabat	14 Jun
8:29.5	Montacer	Zaghou	MAR	1.1.89	1		Rabat	9 May
8:29.53	Gerald	Giraldo	COL	21.3.89	1	SAmC	Lima	14 Jun
	(70)							
8:29.7	Younès	Kniya	MAR	15.8.95	2		Rabat	9 May
8:29.83	Benjamin	Kiplagat	UGA	4.3.89	13	DL	Shanghai	17 May
8:30.0	Mustapha	Houdadi	MAR	5.8.86	3		Rabat	9 May
8:30.03	Jeroen	D'Hoedt	BEL	10.1.90	6	NA	Heusden-Zolder	18 Jul
8:30.35	Jamal	Chatbi	ITA	30.4.84	1	NC	Torino	26 Jul
8:31.04	Gilbert	Kirui	KEN	22.1.94	5		Kawasaki	10 May

Mark	Name		Nat	Born	Pos	Meet	Venue	Date
8:31.08	Abdelhamid	Zerrifi	ALG	20.6.86	4		Amiens	27 Jun
8:31.10	Jaouad	Chemlal	MAR	11.4.94	3		Huelva	10 Jun
8:31.32	Rob	Mullett	GBR	31.7.87	12	DL	London (OS)	25 Jul
8:31.35	Nelson (80)	Kipkosgei	BRN	9.3.93	4	Arab C	Manama	25 Apr
8:31.47	José Gregorio	Peña	VEN	12.1.87	6	Jordan	Stanford	2 May
8:31.55	Martin	Grau	GER	26.3.92	1	WUG	Gwangju	11 Jul
8:31.8A	Willy	Komen	KEN	22.12.87	5h1	NC	Nairobi	10 Jul
8:31.82	Mateusz	Demczyszak	POL	18.1.86	15	DL	Saint-Denis	4 Jul
8:32.05	Yemane	Halleselassie	ERI-Y	21.2.98	6	AfG	Brazzaville	13 Sep
8:32.17	Dikotsi	Lekopa	RSA	7.7.88	1r2	NC	Stellenbosch	18 Apr
8:32.23	Kaur	Kivistik	EST	29.4.91	2	WUG	Gwangju	11 Jul
8:32.45	Viktor	Bakharev	RUS	5.5.94	2		Sochi	28 May
8:32.48A	Isaac	Yego	KEN	.89	8	NC	Nairobi	11 Jul
8:32.54	Sisay (90)	Korme	ETH	9.1.85	12	Bisl	Oslo	11 Jun
8:32.89	Hironori	Tsuetaki	JPN	8.5.93	1	NC	Niigata	26 Jun
8:33.02	Tumisang	Monnatlala	RSA	31.1.95	1r1	NC	Stellenbosch	18 Apr
8:33.09	Yuriy	Kloptsov	RUS	22.12.89	3	WUG	Gwangju	11 Jul
8:33.22	Ole	Hesselbjerg	DEN	23.4.90	7	Jordan	Stanford	2 May
8:33.25	Mohamed Hashim	Salah	QAT	15.4.94	5		Sollentuna	25 Jun
8:33.37	Yuri	Floriani	ITA	25.12.81	6		Huelva	10 Jun
8:33.40	Dominic	Kiptarus	KEN-J	3.8.96	2		Dessau	29 May
8:33.51	Daniel	Lundgren	SWE	4.7.85	1		Oordegem	23 May
8:33.52	Evans	Chematot	BRN-J	19.3.96	4	WMilG	Mungyeong	8 Oct
8:33.69	Aoi (100)	Matsumoto	JPN	7.9.87	7		Kawasaki	10 May

Mark	Name		Nat	Born	Date
8:33.76	Chris	Dulhanty	CAN	6.4.92	19 Jul
8:33.78	Edwin	Kibichy	KEN	2.4.92	15 May
8:33.90	Anthony	Rotich	KEN	.93	12 Jun
8:33.96	Yousif Abdalla	Timbo	SUD-J	28.9.96	13 Sep
8:34.36	Ildar	Minshin	RUS	5.2.85	13 Sep
8:34.40	Craig	Forys	USA	13.7.89	28 Jun
8:34.75	Maksim	Yakushev	RUS	15.3.92	28 May
8:34.81	James	Nipperess	AUS	21.5.90	5 Aug
8:34.84	Zak	Seddon	GBR	28.6.94	29 May
8:35.10	Andrey	Farnosov	RUS	9.7.80	28 May
8:35.21	Ilya	Suharyev	UKR	17.6.86	31 Jul
8:35.25	Darren	Fahy	USA	14.5.94	28 Jun
8:35.41	Jun	Shinoto	JPN	2.4.85	19 Jul
8:35.45	Mason	Ferlic	USA	5.8.93	29 May
8:35.67	Matt	Cleaver	USA	7.11.89	28 Jun
8:35.72A	Silas	Kitum	KEN	25.5.90	11 Jul
8:35.8A	Peter	Lagat	KEN	26.5.92	10 Jul
8:36.16	Mathieu	Bazin	FRA	17.2.90	18 Jun
8:36.3A	Edwin	Kibet	KEN-J	7.7.96	10 Jul
8:36.32	Edwin	Melly	KEN-J	10.8.96	2 Jun
8:36.61	Minato	Yamashita	JPN	15.11.88	26 Jun
8:36.68	Hosea	Kisorio	KEN	22.11.90	26 Sep
8:36.88	Jackson	Neff	USA	9.7.92	29 May
8:36.98	Emil	Blomberg	SWE	9.4.92	17 Apr
8:37.11	Ala	Zoghlami	ITA	19.6.94	12 Jun
8:37.2A	Felix	Kirong	KEN		23 May
8:37.3A	Kipkemoi	Chirchir	KEN		10 Jul
8:37.33	Tumelo	Motlagale	RSA	26.11.86	18 Apr
8:37.43	Ivan	Lukyanov	RUS	31.1.81	5 Aug
8:37.51	Ikageng	Gaorekwe	RSA-J	17.9.97	18 Apr
8:37.62	Giuseppe	Gerratana	ITA	8.11.92	3 Jul
8:37.64	Mark	Parrish	USA	2.12.91	29 May
8:37.7A	Justine	Moseti	KEN-Y	7.6.99	9 Jul
8:37.75	Ryan	Brockerville	CAN	29.7.89	14 May
8:38.09	Andrés	Camargo	COL	30.6.86	17 Apr
8:38.3	Romain	Collenot-Spriet	FRA	9.1.92	5 Jun
8:38.35	Brandon	Doughty	USA	14.5.93	12 Jun
8:38.63	Abdellah	Dacha	MAR	26.1.92	18 Jul
8:38.7A	Hillary	Kipruto	KEN		9 Jul
8:38.76	Youssef	Jaadi	MAR	18.2.91	11 Jul
8:38.77	Austin	Bussing	USA	17.4.90	28 Jun
8:38.91	Patrick	Nasti	ITA	30.8.89	19 Jul
8:38.98	Najibe Marco	Salami	ITA	7.7.85	29 May
8:39.12	Yohannes	Chiappinelli	ITA-J	18.8.97	12 Jun
8:39.72	Kyle (145)	King	USA	4.4.93	29 May

JUNIORS

See main list for top 12 juniors. 10 performances by 5 men to 8:26.0. Additional marks and further juniors:

Bett	8:20.21	2	Gyulai Székesfehérvár	7 Jul	8:23.93	11 DL	Shanghai	17 May
	8:21.56	9	Beijing	20 May				
Amare	8:25.1	3	Montbéliard	5 Jun	8:25.36	6h3 WCh	Beijing	22 Aug

Mark	Name		Nat	Born	Pos	Meet	Venue	Date
8:33.96	Yousif Abdalla	Timbo	SUD	28.9.96	7	AfG	Brazzaville	13 Sep
8:36.3A	Edwin	Kibet	KEN	7.7.96	4h2	NC	Nairobi	10 Jul
8:36.32	Edwin	Melly	KEN	10.8.96	1		Orvieto	2 Jun
8:37.51	Ikageng	Gaorekwe	RSA	17.9.97	3r1	NC	Stellenbosch	18 Apr
8:37.7A	Justine	Moseti	KEN-Y	7.6.99	6h2	NC	Nairobi	9 Jul
8:39.12	Yohannes	Chiappinelli	ITA-	18.8.97	1	NC-j	Rieti	12 Jun
8:41.7A	Vincent	Kipyegon	KEN-Y	31.12.98	2		Nairobi	18 Feb
8:42.49	Abraham	Habte (20)	ERI	14.7.96	6		Lapinlahti	19 Jul

60 METRES HURDLES INDOORS

Mark	Name		Nat	Born	Pos	Meet	Venue	Date
7.45	Orlando	Ortega	ex-CUB	29.7.91	1	Pedros	Lódz	17 Feb
7.45	Omar	McLeod	JAM	25.4.94	1	NCAA	Fayetteville	14 Mar
7.46	Dimitri	Bascou	FRA	20.7.87	1s2	EI	Praha (O2)	6 Mar
7.48		Bascou			1	NC	Aubière	21 Feb
7.49		McLeod			1	SEC	Lexington	28 Feb
7.49	Pascal	Martinot-Lagarde	FRA	22.9.91	1	EI	Praha (O2)	6 Mar
7.50	Aleec	Harris	USA	31.10.90	1	Mill	New York (Armory)	14 Feb
7.50		Bascou			2	EI	Praha (O2)	6 Mar

Mark		Name	Nat	Born	Pos	Meet	Venue	Date
7.51		Bascou			1		Mondeville	7 Feb
7.51		Ortega			1	ISTAF	Berlin	14 Feb
7.51	David	Oliver	USA	24.4.82	2	Mill	New York (Armory)	14 Feb
7.51	Ashton	Eaton	USA	21.1.88	3	Mill	New York (Armory)	14 Feb
(12/7)								
7.52	Aries	Merritt	USA	24.7.85	2		Malmö	25 Feb
7.52	Wilhem	Belocian	FRA	22.6.95	3	EI	Praha (O2)	6 Mar
7.53	Dayron	Robles	CUB	19.11.86	2	ISTAF	Berlin	14 Feb
7.54	Greggmar	Swift	BAR	16.2.91	4	Mill	New York (Armory)	14 Feb
7.58	Kevin	Craddock	USA	25.6.87	1	GP	Birmingham	21 Feb
7.59	Lawrence	Clarke	GBR	12.3.90	2		Mondeville	7 Feb
7.59	Jarret	Eaton	USA	24.6.89	2	NC	Boston (Roxbury)	1 Mar
7.59	Erik	Balnuweit	GER	21.9.88	3s2	EI	Praha (O2)	6 Mar
7.60	Jeff	Porter	USA	27.11.85	5	Mill	New York (Armory)	14 Feb
7.61	Konstantin	Shabanov	RUS	17.11.89	1h4	EI	Praha (O2)	6 Mar
7.61	Petr	Svoboda	CZE	10.10.84	2s1	EI	Praha (O2)	6 Mar
7.62	Jason	Richardson	USA	4.4.86	2		Winston-Salem	31 Jan
7.62		Xie Wenjun	CHN	11.7.90	2		Karlsruhe	31 Jan
7.62	Balázs	Baji	HUN	9.6.89	1r2		Budapest (SH)	22 Feb
7.62	Konstadínos	Douvalídis	GRE	10.3.87	3s1	EI	Praha (O2)	6 Mar
7.63	Dominik	Bochenek	POL	14.5.87	1	NC	Torun	22 Feb
7.64	Myles	Hunter	USA	16.8.95	1		Brookings	13 Feb
7.64	Chris	Caldwell	USA	6.4.94	2h2	NCAA	Fayetteville	13 Mar
7.65	Spencer	Adams	USA	10.9.89	1		Clemson	10 Jan
7.65	Gregory	Sedoc	NED	16.10.81	5s2	EI	Praha (O2)	6 Mar
7.66	Damian	Warner	CAN	4.11.89	1h3		Geneva	14 Feb
7.66	João	Almeida	POR	5.4.88	2h2	EI	Praha (O2)	6 Mar
7.67	Omo	Osaghae	USA	18.5.88	7	Mill	New York (Armory)	14 Feb
7.67	Milan	Trajkovic	CYP	17.9.92	2	GRE Ch	Athína (Pireás)	15 Feb
7.67	Damian	Czykier	POL	10.8.92	2	NC	Torun	22 Feb
7.67	Wayne	Davis	TTO	22.8.91	4		Malmö	25 Feb
7.67	Arthur	Abele	GER	30.7.86	1H	EI	Praha (O2)	8 Mar
7.68	Damien	Broothaerts	BEL	13.3.83	1	NC	Gent	21 Feb
7.69	Ray	Stewart	USA	5.4.89	5		Düsseldorf	29 Jan
7.69	Simon	Krauss	FRA	12.2.92	3	NC	Aubière	21 Feb
7.70	Mikel	Thomas	TTO	23.11.87	6	GP	Birmingham	21 Feb
7.71	David	Omoregie	GBR	1.11.95	1h3	NC	Sheffield	14 Feb
7.71	David	King	GBR	13.6.94	2		Metz	25 Feb
7.72	Isaac	Williams	USA	30.11.93	1		Houston	9 Jan
7.72	Dondre	Echols	USA	6.7.93	1s1		New York (Armory)	30 Jan
7.72	Sebastian	Barth	GER	1.12.93	1		Cedar Falls	31 Jan
7.72	Alexander	John	GER	3.5.86	3		Chemnitz	7 Feb
7.72	Yevgeniy	Borisov	RUS	7.3.84	2	NC	Moskva	18 Feb
7.72	Maksim	Lynsha	BLR	6.4.85	1	NC	Mogilyov	21 Feb
7.72	Oladapo	Akinmoladun	USA	28.2.94	1r1	Big Ten	Geneva	28 Feb
7.72	Trey	Holloway	USA	7.7.94	3	NCAA	Fayetteville	14 Mar
7.73	Keith	Hayes	USA	16.2.90	1		Columbus	9 Jan
7.73	Gerard	O'Donnell	IRL	6.5.88	1	Flanders	Gent	7 Feb
7.73	Josh	Thompson	USA	16.1.93	1	Tyson	Fayetteville	13 Feb
7.73A	Vanier	Joseph	USA	9.9.91	1		Flagstaff	20 Feb
7.73	William	Taylor	USA	9.11.93	1		Seattle	28 Feb
7.73	Andreas	Martinsen	DEN	17.7.90	6s2=	EI	Praha (O2)	6 Mar
7.75A	Trevor	Brown	USA	24.3.92	1h		Golden	13 Dec
7.75	Yidiel	Contreras	CUB	27.11.91	2		Nantes	24 Jan
7.75	Ronald	Forbes	CAY	5.4.85	5h4	EI	Praha (O2)	6 Mar
7.75A	Angelo	Goss	USA	.94	1	JUCO	Albuquerque	7 Mar

110 METRES HURDLES

Mark	Wind		Name	Nat	Born	Pos	Meet	Venue	Date
12.94	0.5	Orlando	Ortega	CUB/ESP	29.7.91	1	DL	Saint-Denis	4 Jul
12.97	1.0	Omar	McLeod	JAM	25.4.94	1	NC	Kingston	27 Jun
12.98	0.5	David	Oliver	USA	24.4.82	2	DL	Saint-Denis	4 Jul
12.98	0.2	Sergey	Shubenkov	RUS	4.10.90	1	WCh	Beijing	28 Aug
13.03	0.2	Hansle	Parchment	JAM	17.6.90	2	WCh	Beijing	28 Aug
13.04	0.4		Oliver			1	NC	Eugene	28 Jun
13.04	0.2	Aries	Merritt	USA	24.7.85	3	WCh	Beijing	28 Aug
13.06	1.5	Pascal	Martinot Lagarde	FRA	22.9.91	1	Pre	Eugene	30 May
13.06	0.5		Shubenkov			3	DL	Saint-Denis	4 Jul
13.07	0.8		Oliver			1	PAm	Toronto	24 Jul
13.08	1.0		Parchment			2	NC	Kingston	27 Jun
13.08	0.7		Oliver			1s1	NC	Eugene	28 Jun

Mark	Wind	Name		Nat	Born	Pos	Meet	Venue	Date
13.08	-0.2		Merritt			1s2	WCh	Beijing	27 Aug
13.09	0.0		Shubenkov			1s1	WCh	Beijing	27 Aug
13.11	0.5	Aleec	Harris	USA	31.10.90	4	DL	Saint-Denis	4 Jul
13.11	0.5		Shubenkov			1		Zagreb	8 Sep
13.12	1.5		Merritt			2	Pre	Eugene	30 May
13.12	2.0	Jason	Richardson	USA	4.4.86	1s2	NC	Eugene	28 Jun
13.13	0.4	Ronnie	Ash (10)	USA	2.7.88	2	NC	Eugene	28 Jun
13.13	0.3		Ash			1B		Bellinzona	21 Jul
13.14	1.5		Oliver			3	Pre	Eugene	30 May
13.14	1.5		Ortega			4	Pre	Eugene	30 May
13.14	-0.2		McLeod			2s2	WCh	Beijing	27 Aug
13.14	0.4		Shubenkov			1	WK	Zürich	3 Sep
13.15	0.6		Oliver			1		Beijing	20 May
13.15	-0.1		Oliver			1h3	PAm	Toronto	24 Jul
13.15	-1.0		Oliver			1h3	WCh	Beijing	26 Aug
13.16	-0.6		Harris			1	DrakeR	Des Moines	24 Apr
13.16	1.0		Harris			1		Kingston	9 May
13.16	-0.1	Dimitri	Bascou	FRA	20.7.87	1s3	WCh	Beijing	27 Aug
13.16	0.0		Parchment			2s1	WCh	Beijing	27 Aug
		(31/11)							
13.17	0.7	Garfield	Darien	FRA	22.12.87	1	NC	Villeneuve d'Ascq	12 Jul
13.17	0.8	Mikel	Thomas	TTO	23.11.87	2	PAm	Toronto	24 Jul
13.21	0.8	Shane	Brathwaite	BAR	8.2.90	3	PAm	Toronto	24 Jul
13.23	-0.2	Yordan	O'Farrill	CUB	9.2.93	1		Tomblaine	1 Jul
13.25	0.4	Jeff	Porter	USA	27.11.85	5	NC	Eugene	28 Jun
13.27	1.9	Damian	Warner	CAN	4.11.89	1	NC	Edmonton	4 Jul
13.28	1.5	Andrew	Riley	JAM	6.9.88	6	Pre	Eugene	30 May
13.28	1.5	Wilhem	Belocian	FRA	22.6.95	3		Montreuil-sous-Bois	9 Jun
13.28	0.8	Greggmar	Swift	BAR	16.2.91	4	PAm	Toronto	24 Jul
		(20)							
13.30	0.8	Jhoanis	Portilla	CUB	24.7.90	5	PAm	Toronto	24 Jul
13.31A	1.5	Eddie	Lovett	ISV	25.6.92	3	NACAC	San José, CRC	8 Aug
13.32	-0.3	Dayron	Robles	CUB	19.11.86	2	PNG	Turku	25 Jun
13.32	0.4	Gregor	Traber	GER	2.12.92	1	NC	Nürnberg	25 Jul
13.32A	1.5	Tyler	Mason	JAM	15.1.95	4	NACAC	San José, CRC	8 Aug
13.32	0.5	Antonio	Alkana	RSA	12.4.90	1	AfG	Brazzaville	14 Sep
13.33	-1.2	Konstadínos	Douvalídis	GRE	10.3.87	1rB	Gyulai	Székesfehérvár	7 Jul
13.34	0.4	Ray	Stewart	USA	5.4.89	7	NC	Eugene	28 Jun
13.34	-0.1	Matthias	Bühler	GER	2.9.86	3s3	WCh	Beijing	27 Aug
13.35	-1.0	Yidiel	Contreras	ESP	27.11.92	1		La Roche-sur-Yon	22 Jul
		(30)							
13.36	0.4		Xie Wenjun	CHN	11.7.90	6	DL	Shanghai	17 May
13.37	1.9	Johnathan	Cabral	CAN	31.12.92	2	NC	Edmonton	4 Jul
13.37	-0.1	Artur	Noga	POL	2.5.88	4s3	WCh	Beijing	27 Aug
13.38	-0.2	Ashton	Eaton	USA	21.1.88	1		Edmonton	12 Jul
13.39	1.1	Lawrence	Clarke	GBR	12.3.90	3rA		Luzern	14 Jul
13.41	1.2	Jarret	Eaton	USA	24.6.89	2		Clermont	16 May
13.42	1.5	Nick	Hough	AUS	20.10.93	1	NC	Brisbane	29 Mar
13.42	0.6	Dwight	Thomas	JAM	23.9.80	4	FlaR	Gainesville	3 Apr
13.43	1.9	Sekou	Kaba	CAN	25.8.90	3	NC	Edmonton	4 Jul
13.44	0.4	Petr	Svoboda	CZE	10.10.84	3		Sotteville-lès-Rouen	6 Jul
		(40)							
13.44	-0.4	Balázs	Baji	HUN	9.6.89	1h1		Linz	1 Aug
13.45	0.0	João Vitor	de Oliveira	BRA	15.5.92	6s1	WCh	Beijing	27 Aug
13.46	1.9	Dondre	Echols	USA	6.7.93	2	SEC	Starkville	16 May
13.46	1.4	Éder Antônio	de Souza	BRA	15.10.86	1h2	NC	São Bernardo do Campo	16 May
13.46	0.4	Alexander	John	GER	3.5.86	1		Mannheim	15 Jul
13.47	1.9	Jordan	Moore	USA	13.12.93	3	SEC	Starkville	16 May
13.47	1.3	Ronald	Forbes	CAY	5.4.85	1		La Chaux-de-Fonds	5 Jul
13.48	0.2	Spencer	Adams	USA	10.9.89	1		Charlotte, NC	11 Apr
13.48	0.0	Kevin	Craddock	USA	25.6.87	3		Bellinzona	21 Jul
13.48	0.1	Ben	Reynolds	IRL	26.9.90	1	CAU	Bedford	1 Aug
		(50)							
13.49	-0.2	Thomas	Martinot Lagarde	FRA	7.2.88	3=		Tomblaine	1 Jul
13.49A	1.0	Deuce	Carter	JAM	28.9.90	3h2	NACAC	San José, CRC	7 Aug
13.49	0.5	Lyès	Mokdel	ALG	20.6.90	1	AfG	Brazzaville	14 Sep
13.50	1.2	Milan	Ristic	SRB	8.8.91	3		Clermont	16 May
13.50	-1.4	David	Omoregie	GBR	1.11.95	3h2	DL	London (OS)	24 Jul
13.51	1.5	Angelo	Goss	USA	.94	1	JUCO	Hutchinson, KS	16 May
13.52	1.1	Justin	Johnson	USA	25.10.92	1s2	NCAA	Eugene	10 Jun

Mark	Wind	Name		Nat	Born	Pos	Meet	Venue	Date
13.53	0.9		Kim Byung-jun	KOR	15.8.91	1		Gainesville	24 Apr
13.53	1.1		Zhang Honglin	CHN	12.1.94	1		Shanghai	15 Jul
13.53	0.8	William	Sharman	GBR	12.9.84	2		Bedford	1 Aug
		(60)							
13.54	1.5	Sam	Baines	AUS	8.2.91	2	NC	Brisbane	29 Mar
13.54	0.0	Ryan	Wilson	USA	19.12.80	4		Baie Mahault	2 May
13.54	-0.2	Jonatha	Mendes	BRA	14.4.90	1		São Paulo	2 May
13.54	0.5	Tyrone	Akins	NGR	6.1.86	3	AfG	Brazzaville	14 Sep
13.54	0.2	Hideki	Omuro	JPN	25.7.90	1		Kitakyushu	3 Nov
13.55	1.9	Josh	Thompson	USA	16.1.93	4	SEC	Starkville	16 May
13.55	1.1	Andreas	Martinsen	DEN	17.7.90	1h1		Göteborg	5 Jul
13.56	1.6	Chris	Caldwell	USA	5.4.94	1	TexR	Austin	28 Mar
13.56	0.6	Omo	Osaghae	USA	18.5.88	6	FlaR	Gainesville	3 Apr
13.56	1.6	Will	Barnes	USA	17.3.94	1		Auburn	18 Apr
		(70)							
13.56	1.8	Isaac	Williams	USA	30.11.93	4	MSR	Walnut	18 Apr
13.56	0.0	Logan	Taylor	USA	3.4.86	1		Norwalk	6 Jun
13.56	0.9	Gregory	Sedoc	NED	16.10.81	1		Zeulenroda	10 Jul
13.56	0.7	Erik	Balnuweit	GER	21.9.88	1rB		Mannheim	15 Jul
13.56	-0.7	Dario	De Borger	BEL	20.3.92	1	VD	Bruxelles	11 Sep
13.57	0.6	Trey	Holloway	USA	7.7.94	1		Greensboro, NC	2 May
13.57A	0.4	Tshepo	Lefete	RSA	2.2.92	2		Germiston	16 May
13.57	0.0	Ronald	Brookins	USA	5.7.89	3		Norwalk	6 Jun
13.57	0.7	Konstantin	Shabanov	RUS	17.11.89	2	WUG	Gwangju	11 Jul
13.58		Yacoub	Al-Yoha	KUW	31.1.93	1		Doha	31 Mar
		(80)							
13.58	1.7	Adarius	Washington	USA	19.10.92	2	DrakeR	Des Moines	25 Apr
13.58	0.3	Spencer	Dunkerley-Offor	USA	6.1.95	1s3	NCAA	Eugene	10 Jun
13.59	1.3	Wayne	Davis	TTO	22.8.91	3		Greensboro, NC	11 Apr
13.59	1.1	Don	Pollitt	USA	1.10.91	1		Ithaca	2 May
13.59	0.8	Aaron	Mallett	USA	26.9.94	4h2	NC	Eugene	27 Jun
13.59	1.6	Maksim	Lynsha	BLR	6.4.85	1	NC	Grodno	24 Jul
13.59	1.8	Hassane	Fofana	ITA	28.4.92	1	NC	Torino	25 Jul
13.59	0.5	Simon	Krauss	FRA	12.2.92	2h1	NC	Castres	29 Jul
13.60A	0.3	Ruan	de Vries	RSA	1.2.86	2		Potchefstroom	9 May
13.60	1.9	Nick	Anderson	USA	28.4.95	5	SEC	Starkville	16 May
		(90)							
13.60	0.5	Koen	Smet	NED	9.8.92	2	FBK	Hengelo	24 May
13.60	0.7	Lloyd	Sicard	USA	31.5.95	1q2	NCAA-W	Austin	30 May
13.61	-0.8	Abdulaziz	Al-Mandeel	KUW	22.5.89	1	Gulf C	Qatif	9 Apr
13.61	0.6	Cameron	Hall	USA	12.5.93	2		Greensboro	2 May
13.61	0.8		Jiang Fan	CHN	16.9.89	1		Beijing	29 Jun
13.62	0.6	Tremayne	Banks	USA	29.7.92	3		Greensboro	2 May
13.62	2.0	Freddie	Crittenden	USA	3.8.94	6s2	NC	Eugene	28 Jun
13.62	0.4	Bano	Traoré	MLI	25.4.85	8rB	DL	Saint-Denis	4 Jul
13.62	1.2	Francisco Javier	López	ESP	29.12.89	2	NC	Castellón	2 Aug
13.62	-0.1	Andrew	Pozzi	GBR	15.5.92	1h1		Göteborg	14 Aug
		(100)							
13.62A	1.2	Paulo César	Villar	COL	28.7.78	1	NG	Cali	16 Nov

Mark	Wind	Name		Nat	Born	Date
13.63	1.9	Ronald	Levy	JAM	30.10.92	11 Apr
13.63	0.5	Dominik	Bochenek	POL	14.5.87	26 Jul
13.64	1.8	Kirk	Thornton	USA	13.7.86	2 May
13.64	1.0	Genta	Masuno	JPN	24.5.93	15 May
13.64	0.1	Ramón	Sosa	DOM	11.1.86	30 May
13.64	1.1	Cameron	Viney	USA	6.9.93	10 Jun
13.65A	1.2	Ingvar	Moseley	CAN	24.11.91	7 Aug
13.67	1.1	David	Kendziera	USA	9.9.94	10 Jun
13.67A	1.2	Jeffrey	Julmis	HAI	6.1.87	7 Aug
13.68	0.9	Sean	Wells	USA	16.4.94	23 May
13.68	0.5	Yanick	Hart	JAM	10.1.93	29 May
13.68	-0.1		Chen Kuei-Ju	TPE	22.9.93	19 Oct
13.69	1.5	Joshua	Hawkins	NZL	9.2.94	29 Mar
13.69	-0.1	Fábio	dos Santos	BRA	10.8.83	2 May
13.69	1.6	David	King	GBR	13.6.94	17 May
13.69	0.9	Lorenzo	Johnson	USA	26.5.93	23 May
13.69	0.7	Matthew	Viverette	USA	.92	30 May
13.69	0.2	Jamras	Rittidet	THA	1.2.89	11 Jun
13.69	1.0	Sancho	Barrett	USA/JAM	18.1.93	27 Jun
13.70	1.8	Bryce	Grace	USA	18.7.94	18 Apr
13.70	-0.1	Artie	Burns	USA	1.5.95	16 May
13.70	0.8	Alex	Al-Ameen	NGR	2.3.89	14 Jun
13.70	0.7	Ladji	Doucouré	FRA	28.3.83	21 Jun
13.70	0.6	Maximilian	Bayer	GER	5.12.90	15 Jul
13.71	1.0	Caleb	Cross	USA	31.5.91	8 May
13.71	1.3	Trey	Hardee	USA	7.2.84	26 Jun
13.72	1.7	Isaiah	Moore	USA-J	12.6.96	29 May
13.72	-0.5	João	Almeida	POR	5.4.88	31 May
13.72	1.9	Malcolm	Anderson	USA	18.9.89	14 Jun
13.72	0.7	Damian	Czykier	POL	10.8.92	11 Jul
13.72	0.3	Damien	Broothaerts	BEL	12.11.84	15 Jul
13.73	1.9	Robert	Semien	USA	15.4.93	16 May
13.73	1.9	Jermaine	Collier	USA	5.7.93	16 May
13.73	-1.5	Javier	Colomo	ESP	26.3.94	11 Jul
13.73	1.1		Zhu Haibao	CHN	6.1.90	15 Jul
13.73	-0.4	Jorge	McFarlane	PER	20.2.88	24 Jul
13.73A	1.2	Yeison	Rivas	COL	24.9.87	1 Aug
13.73	1.2	Arnau	Erta	ESP	5.4.92	2 Aug
13.73	0.6	Vladimir	Vukicevic	NOR	6.5.91	13 Sep
13.74	1.0	Yuta	Notoya	JPN	8.7.89	10 May
13.74	1.6	Paul	Lyons	USA	18.2.93	29 May
13.74	2.0	Julian	Marquart	GER	2.4.91	10 Jul
13.75	-0.2	Gabriel	Constantino	BRA	9.2.95	2 May
13.75	1.0	Kemar	Clarke	JAM	20.5.88	8 May
13.75	0.3	Michael	Prejean	USA	.93	30 May
13.75	1.4	Tatsuya	Wado	JPN	4.10.90	5 Oct
13.76	1.0	Othman	Hadj Lazib	ALG	10.5.83	11 Apr
13.76	-0.3	Shun-ya	Takayama	JPN	3.9.94	27 Jun
13.77	0.1	Justin	Merlino	AUS	10.12.86	7 Feb
13.77	1.3	Ro'Derick	Spears	USA	14.8.94	11 Apr

Mark	Wind	Name		Nat	Born	Date
13.77	1.8	Chris	Thomas	USA	9.2.81	18 Apr
13.77	0.9	Marquis	Morris	USA-J	6.2.96	30 May
13.77	0.7	Cameron	Taylor	USA	9.11.93	30 May
13.77	1.3	Khai	Riley-La Borde	GBR	8.11.95	14 Jun
13.77	1.8	Lorenzo	Perini	ITA	22.7.94	25 Jul
13.77	-2.9	Aleksandr	Yevgenyev	RUS	5.7.92	4 Aug
13.78	0.7	Milan	Trajkovic	CYP	17.3.92	11 Jul
13.78	1.0	Tjendo	Samuel	NED	19.12.89	18 Jul
13.78	0.5		Yang Wei-Ting	TPE	22.9.94	18 Oct
13.79	1.5	Wataru	Yazawa	JPN	2.7.91	29 Mar
13.79	0.4	Takumu	Furuya	JPN-J	12.3.97	27 Jun
13.79	0.2		Ji Wei	CHN	5.2.84	28 Jun
13.80	1.9	Christian	Lupica	USA	17.5.93	3 Apr
13.80	1.3	Vincent	Wyatt	USA	18.10.92	8 May
13.80A	-2.5	Javier	McFarlane	PER	21.10.91	9 May
13.80	1.3	Desmond	Wallace	USA	4.7.93	16 May
13.80	0.3	Christian	Cook	USA	.93	29 May
13.80	1.1	Eduardo	de Deus	BRA	8.10.95	30 May
13.80	0.6	Denis	Hanjoul	BEL	17.1.91	30 May
13.80	1.2	Sebastian	Barth	GER	1.2.93	14 Jun
13.81	0.8		Lu Yang	CHN-J	9.1.96	30 Apr
13.81	1.0	Hiroki	Fudaba	JPN	4.2.94	15 May
13.81	0.9	Tobias	Furer	SUI	13.8.87	27 Jun
13.81	0.0	Elmo	Lakka	FIN	10.4.93	28 Jun
13.81	1.4	Artem	Shamatryn	UKR	15.6.91	30 Jul
13.82	1.7	Jonathas	Brito	BRA	30.11.92	4 Apr
13.82	0.9	Calvin	Arsenault	CAN	29.9.93	11 Apr
13.82	0.0	Ruebin	Walters	TTO	2.4.95	11 Apr
13.82	0.6		Ma Lei	CHN	29.6.89	30 Apr
13.82	0.0	Siddhanth	Thingalaya	IND	3.1.91	4 May
13.82	0.9	Elijha	Owens	USA	16.2.93	23 May
13.82	0.3	Antoine	Lloyd	USA-J	10.6.96	30 May
13.83	-0.1	Felipe	dos Santos	BRA	30.7.94	2 May
13.83	1.0	Hiroyuki	Sato	JPN	6.8.90	10 May
13.83	1.8	Edirin	Okoro	GBR	4.4.89	31 May
13.83	1.4	Masanori	Nishizawa	JPN	16.7.87	5 Oct
13.84	1.1		Lee Jung-joon	KOR	26.3.84	14 Mar
13.84	0.7	Nicolas	Borome	FRA	7.10.93	25 Jul
13.84	1.4	Joseph	Hylton	GBR	17.11.89	5 Aug
13.85	1.6	Vernon	Jamison	USA	24.6.93	30 May
13.85	0.7	Chris	Williams	USA	5.3.94	30 May
13.85	1.4	Nao	Kanai	JPN-J	4.6.97	2 Aug
13.86	1.4	Gianni	Frankis	GBR	16.4.88	17 May
13.86	-0.7	Yutaro	Furukawa	JPN	3.6.85	27 Sep
13.87	0.6	Adrien	Deghelt	BEL	10.5.85	30 May
13.87	0.2	Gerard	O'Donnell (197)	IRL	6.5.88	21 Jul

13.88 eight men, 13.89 nine men

Wind assisted

Mark	Wind	Name		Nat	Born	Pos	Meet	Venue	Date
13.01	3.9		McLeod			1	NCAA	Eugene	12 Jun
13.08	2.6		McLeod			1s1	NCAA	Eugene	10 Jun
13.22	3.9	Johnathan	Cabral	CAN	31.12.92	2	NCAA	Eugene	12 Jun
13.31	3.9	Isaac	Williams	USA	30.11.93	3	NCAA	Eugene	12 Jun
13.32	3.7	Abdulaziz	Al-Mandeel	KUW	22.5.89	1		Doha	29 Apr
13.34	3.1	Omo	Osaghae	USA	18.5.88	1		Lubbock	30 Apr
13.34	3.9	Josh	Thompson	USA	16.1.93	4	NCAA	Eugene	12 Jun
13.37	7.3	Yacoub	Al-Yoha	KUW	31.1.93	2	Arab C	Manama	25 Apr
13.40	3.8	Jarret	Eaton	USA	24.6.89	1h2		Clermont	16 May
13.40	3.9	Aaron	Mallett	USA	26.9.94	5	NCAA	Eugene	12 Jun
13.42	2.3	Alexander	John	GER	3.5.86	1h1		Mannheim	15 Jul
13.45	2.7	Ro'Derick	Spears	USA	14.8.94	1h1	JUCO	Hutchinson, KS	15 May
13.45	3.9	Spencer	Dunkerley-Offor	USA	6.1.95	6	NCAA	Eugene	12 Jun
13.49	2.1		Kim Byung-jun	KOR	15.8.91	3		Clermont	18 Apr
13.52	2.9	Cameron	Viney	USA	6.9.93	2	Big 10	East Lansing	17 May
13.52	2.5	Simon	Krauss	FRA	12.2.92	2		Castres	29 Jul
13.53	2.7	Ruebin	Walters	TTO	2.4.95	2h1	JUCO	Hutchinson, KS	15 May
13.54	2.2	Bano	Traoré	MLI	25.4.85	2		Nivelles	27 Jun
13.55	3.1	Erik	Balnuweit	GER	21.9.88	3	Odlozil	Praha	8 Jun
13.56	2.7	David	Kendziera	USA	9.9.94	1h3	NCAA-W	Austin	29 May
13.57A	2.8	Ruan	de Vries	RSA	1.2.86	1		Pretoria	21 Mar
13.57	3.4	Tremayne	Banks	USA	29.7.92	1		Miramar	27 Apr
13.59	2.2	Ladji	Doucouré	FRA	28.3.83	2		Nivelles	27 Jun
13.60	7.3	Othman	Hadj Lazib	ALG	10.5.83	2	Arab C	Manama	25 Apr
13.60	2.2	Hassane	Fofana	ITA	28.4.92	3		Genève	6 Jun
13.61	3.0	David	King	GBR	13.6.94	1		London (LV)	19 Aug

Mark	Wind	Name		Nat	Born	Date
13.62	2.9	Donovan	Robertson	USA	8.11.93	17 May
13.63	2.3	Michael	Prejean	USA	.93	26 Apr
13.63	4.9	Luke	Campbell	USA	22.11.94	23 May
13.65	3.0	Alex	Al-Ameen	NGR	2.3.89	19 Aug
13.69	2.9	Antoine	Lloyd	USA-J	10.6.96	17 May
13.71	2.5	Norihiro	Kiriyama	JPN	29.10.92	20 Sep
13.72	2.1	Malcolm	Anderson	USA	18.9.89	18 Apr
13.72	2.4	Elijha	Owens	USA	16.2.93	22 May
13.72	2.3	Vladimir	Vukicevic	NOR	6.5.91	29 Aug
13.74	7.3	Ali Hussein	Al-Zaki	KSA	11.5.85	25 Apr
13.74	2.9	Sean	Pille	USA	28.6.93	17 May
13.76	3.1	Tramaine	Maloney	BAR	1.6.94	30 Apr
13.77	2.4	Gianni	Frankis	GBR	16.4.88	18 Apr
13.77	2.8	Nicolas	Borome	FRA	7.10.93	26 Jul
13.78	2.2	Michael	Stigler	USA	5.4.92	11 Apr
13.78	2.8	Edirin	Okoro	GBR	4.4.89	31 May
13.78	2.6	Christian	Cook	USA	.93	10 Jun
13.78	2.8	Jake	Porter	GBR	13.11.93	21 Jun
13.78	2.5	Akihiro	Ogata	JPN	8.6.93	5 Oct
13.79	2.6	Ashtyn	Davis	USA-J	10.10.96	29 May
13.80	2.5	N'Aithan	Scott	USA	18.10.88	18 Apr
13.80	3.8	Myles	Hunter	USA	16.8.95	9 May
13.81	5.7	Reggie	Rucker	USA	7.10.83	18 Apr
13.81	2.7	Chris	Williams	USA	5.3.94	29 May
13.81	3.5	Shin-ya	Tanaka	JPN	23.6.93	18 Jul
13.84	3.5	Dale "D.J."	Morgan	USA	3.1.92	3 May
13.84	3.5	Keyunta	Hayes	USA	15.2.92	17 May

Low altitude bests

Mark	Wind	Name	Pos	Meet	Venue	Date
13.39	1.0	Mason	4	NC	Kingston	27 Jun
13.41	0.4	Lovett	3h1	NC	Bridgetown	20 Jun
13.53	1.0	Carter	6	NC	Kingston	27 Jun
13.67	1.9	Moseley				4 Jul
13.71	0.3	Julmis				27 Jun
13.72	0.8	de Vries				14 Jun
13.81	0.4	Villar				26 Sep
13.88	0.6	Javier McFarlane				11 Apr

Hand timed: 13.2 Matheus Rocha BRA 19.12.94 1 Jundoaí 8 Jul

JUNIORS

Mark	Wind	Name		Nat	Born	Pos	Meet	Venue	Date
13.72	1.7	Isaiah	Moore	USA-J	12.6.96	1h3	NCAA-E	Jacksonville	29 May
		13.76 1.9 8 SEC Starkville 16 May							
13.77	0.9	Marquis	Morris	USA-J	6.2.96	4q1	NCAA-W	Austin	30 May
		13.79 1.9 3h5 NCAAw Austin 29 May							
13.79	0.4	Takumu	Furuya	JPN-J	12.3.97	1h2	NC	Niigata	27 Jun

Five performances to 3 mern to 13.79

Mark	Wind	Name		Nat	Born	Pos	Meet	Venue	Date
13.81	0.8		Lu Yang	CHN-J	9.1.96	1h1		Jinan	30 Apr
13.82	0.3	Antoine	Lloyd	USA-J	10.6.96	5q3	NCAA-W	Austin	30 May
13.85	1.4	Nao	Kanai	JPN-J	4.6.97	1		Wakayama	2 Aug
13.89	0.9	Ashtyn	Davis	USA-J	10.10.96	6q1	NCAA-W	Austin	30 May
13.92	1.7	Davon	Anderson	USA	24.8.96	4h3	NCAA-E	Jacksonville	29 May
14.00	0.7	Rohan	Cole	JAM	28.10.97	1		Kingston	30 May
14.01	0.3	Misana	Viltz	USA	21.2.96	6q3	NCAA-W	Austin	30 May
14.03	0.3	Dylan	Caty	FRA	11.1.97	3	NC	Bruzelles	26 Jul
14.04	0.2		Li Jiming	CHN	14.3.96	3h1	NC	Suzhou	23 Sep
Wind assisted									
13.69	2.9	Antoine	Lloyd	USA	10.6.96	4	Big 10	East Lansing	17 May
13.79	2.6	Ashtyn	Davis	USA	10.10.96	2h1	NCAA-W	Austin	30 May
13.86	2.8	Misana	Viltz	USA	21.2.96	4h6	NCAA-W	Austin	30 May

110 Metres Hurdles – 99 cm hurdles

Mark	Wind	Name		Nat	Born	Pos	Meet	Venue	Date
13.21	1.5	Misana	Viltz	USA	21.2.96	1	NC-j	Eugene	26 Jun
		13.30 1.1 1	PAm-J Edmonton	1 Aug		11 performances by 10 men to 13.48			
13.22	0.1	Jaheel	Hyde	JAM-Y	2.2.97	1		Kingston	7 Mar
13.29	1.5	Marquis	Morris	USA-J	6.2.96	1h2	NC-j	Eugene	25 Jun
13.32	1.2	Roger	Iribarne	CUB	2.1.96	2	PAm-J	Edmonton	1 Aug
13.36	-0.1		Lu Yang	CHN	9.1.96	1	NC-j	Fuzhou	29 May
13.42	0.1	Seanie	Selvin	JAM	6.9.96	2		Kingston	7 Mar
13.42	1.4	Kendall	Sheffield	USA	30.5.96	1		Austin	15 May
13.45	1.7	Isaiah	Moore	USA	12.6.96	1h2	NC-j	Eugene	26 Jun
13.48	1.7	Chad	Zallow	USA	25.4.97	2h2	NC-j	Eugene	26 Jun
13.48	1.0	Karsten	Warholm (10)	NOR	28.2.96	1		Mannheim	27 Jun
13.49	-3.8	Michael	O'Hara	JAM	29.9.96	1	N.Sch	Kingston	28 Mar
13.49	1.5	Ashtyn	Davis	USA	10.10.96	3	NC-j	Eugene	26 Jun
13.49	1.2	Ricardo	Torres	PUR	13.2.96	3	PAm-J	Edmonton	1 Aug
13.50	1.2	Florian	Lickteig	GER	24.3.96	1	NC-j	Jena	1 Aug
13.51	1.2	Roje Jackson	Chin	JAM	5.1.97	4	PAm-J	Edmonton	1 Aug
13.57	1.6	Henrik	Hannemann	GER	19.7.97	1h4		Mannheim	27 Jun
13.59	0.3	Michael	Nicholls	BAR	6.4.97	1		Bridgetown	20 Mar
13.59	1.0	Gerard	Porras	GER	14.4.96	2		Mannheim	27 Jun
13.59	1.6	Patrick	Elger	GER	25.1.96	2h4		Mannheim	27 Jun
13.61A	-1.8	Ifeanyichukwu	Atuma (20)	NGR	2.10.96	1h1	Af-J	Addis Ababa	7 Mar
Wind assisted									
13.19	3.8	Chad	Zallow	USA	25.4.97	1		Greensboro	20 Jun
Hyde		13.36 3.3 1	Carifta Basseterre	6 Apr					
Morris		13.40 2.5 1h1	NC-j Eugene	26 Jun		7 performances by 7 men to 13.40			
13.37	5.1	Marcus	McWilliams	USA	20.2.97	1		Austin	16 May
13.37	5.1	Isaiah	Lucas	USA-Y	21.5.98	2		Austin	16 May
13.40	5.1	Chevis	Armstead	USA	14.7.97	3		Austin	16 May
13.40	3.8	Daniel	Roberts	USA-Y	13.4.98	2		Greensboro	20 Jun
13.42	2.5	Ashtyn	Davis	USA	10.10.96	2h1	NC-j	Eugene	26 Jun
13.51	3.3	Xavier	Coakley	BAH	1.10.96	2	Carifta	Basseterre	6 Apr
13.53	3.3	Charles	Graham	USA	3.1.97	1		Harrisonburg	6 Jun
13.55	3.7	Jack	Hatton	GBR	14.2.96	1	NC-j	Bedford	21 Jun

200 METRES HURDLES STRAIGHT

Mark	Wind	Name		Nat	Born	Pos	Meet	Venue	Date
22.1	1.8	Louis 'LJ'	van Zyl	RSA	20.7.85	1		Manchester	8 May

400 METRES HURDLES

Mark	Name		Nat	Born	Pos	Meet	Venue	Date
47.79	Nicholas	Bett	KEN	14.6.92	1	WCh	Beijing	25 Aug
48.05	Denis	Kudryavtsev	RUS	13.4.92	2	WCh	Beijing	25 Aug
48.09	Bershawn	Jackson	USA	8.5.83	1	DL	Doha	15 May
48.13	Johnny	Dutch	USA	20.1.89	1	GGala	Roma	4 Jun
48.17	Jeffery	Gibson	BAH	15.8.90	3	WCh	Beijing	25 Aug
48.18	Kerron	Clement	USA	31.10.85	4	WCh	Beijing	25 Aug
48.20		Dutch			1	Pre	Eugene	30 May
48.22		Jackson			2	Pre	Eugene	30 May
48.23		Jackson			1	Herc	Monaco	17 Jul
48.23		Kudryavtsev			1s2	WCh	Beijing	23 Aug
48.29		Jackson			1	NC	Eugene	27 Jun
48.29A		Bett			1	WCT	Nairobi	1 Aug
48.29	Boniface	Mucheru	KEN	2.5.92	1s1	WCh	Beijing	23 Aug
48.33		Mucheru			5	WCh	Beijing	25 Aug
48.34	Michael	Tinsley	USA	21.4.84	2	GGala	Roma	4 Jun
48.37		Bett			1h1	WCh	Beijing	22 Aug
48.37		Gibson			2s2	WCh	Beijing	23 Aug

Mark	Wind	Name		Nat	Born	Pos	Meet	Venue	Date
48.38			Dutch			1		Greensboro, NC	17 May
48.40		Patryk	Dobek	POL	13.2.94	3s2	WCh	Beijing	23 Aug
48.43			Dutch			2	NC	Eugene	27 Jun
48.44		Michael	Stigler (10)	USA	5.4.92	1	TexR	Austin	27 Mar
48.44			Clement			3	NC	Eugene	27 Jun
48.45		Kariem	Hussein	SUI	1.4.89	1	NC	Zug	8 Aug
48.46		Yasmani	Copello	TUR	15.4.87	4s2	WCh	Beijing	23 Aug
48.47			Jackson			1		Kingston	9 May
48.47			Tinsley			1s3	WCh	Beijing	23 Aug
48.48		Javier	Culson	PUR	25.7.84	1	adidas	New York	13 Jun
48.50			Clement			2s1	WCh	Beijing	23 Aug
48.51			Gibson			1	PAm	Toronto	23 Jul
48.51			Kudryavtsev			1h5	WCh	Beijing	22 Aug
		(30/13)							
48.65		Thomas	Barr	IRL	24.7.92	4	GGala	Roma	4 Jun
48.65		Rasmus	Mägi	EST	4.5.92	1		Tallinn	9 Aug
48.67		Abdelmalik	Lahoulou	ALG	7.5.92	1	AfG	Brazzaville	16 Sep
48.69		Timofey	Chalyy	RUS	7.4.94	3s1	WCh	Beijing	23 Aug
48.72		Roxroy	Cato	JAM	1.5.88	3	PAm	Toronto	23 Jul
48.78		Louis 'L.J'	van Zyl	RSA	20.7.85	2	adidas	New York	13 Jun
48.84		Miles	Ukaoma	NGR	21.7.92	1	NC	Warri	31 Jul
		(20)							
48.90		Annsert	Whyte	JAM	10.4.87	1	NC	Kingston	26 Jun
48.90		Niall	Flannery	GBR	26.4.91	2h3	WCh	Beijing	22 Aug
48.95		Jeshua	Anderson	USA	22.6.89	5	PAm	Toronto	23 Jul
49.01		Jaheel	Hyde	JAM-J	2.2.97	1		Kingston	27 Mar
49.04		Ivan	Shablyuyev	RUS	17.4.88	3	WUG	Gwangju	10 Jul
49.04		Michaël	Bultheel	BEL	30.6.86	1	NC	Bruxelles	26 Jul
49.05			Chen Chieh	TPE	8.5.92	1		Kaohsiung	21 Oct
49.08		Keisuke	Nozawa	JPN	7.6.91	1h1		Gifu	26 Sep
49.12		Eric	Cray	PHI	6.11.88	1		George Town	16 May
49.14		Yuki	Matsushita	JPN	9.9.91	1		Chiba	15 Aug
		(30)							
49.15		Kurt	Couto	MOZ	14.5.85	4h1	WCh	Beijing	22 Aug
49.17		Takayuki	Kishimoto	JPN	6.5.90	1		Tokyo	26 Jul
49.20		Adam	Durham	USA	30.8.85	2		Greensboro, NC	17 May
49.22		Leford	Green	JAM	14.11.86	2		Kingston	9 May
49.22		Jehue	Gordon	TTO	15.12.91	7	GGala	Roma	4 Jun
49.22		Mohamed	Sghaier	TUN	18.7.88	1		La Chaux-de-Fonds	5 Jul
49.23		Eric	Alejandro	PUR	15.4.86	2	FlaR	Gainesville	3 Apr
49.24		Jordin	Andrade	USA	5.5.92	2	NCAA	Eugene	12 Jun
49.24		Miloud	Rahmouni	ALG	13.12.83	2	NC	Alger	2 Aug
49.26		Omar	Cisneros	CUB	19.11.89	2		Padova	6 Sep
		(40)							
49.31		Jack	Green	GBR	6.10.91	4	DL	Doha	15 May
49.36		Tom	Burton	GBR	29.10.88	1		Genève	6 Jun
49.37		Jaak-Heinrich	Jagor	EST	11.5.90	2	NC	Tallinn	9 Aug
49.38		Haron	Koech	KEN	27.1.90	5h5	WCh	Beijing	22 Aug
49.39		Scottie	Hearn	USA	3.1.94	1	SEC	Starkville	16 May
49.40		Hederson	Estefani	BRA	11.9.91	1	NC	São Bernardo do Campo	17 May
49.41		Desmond	Palmer	USA	30.7.95	1	ACC	Tallahassee	16 May
49.43		Saber	Boukamouche	ALG	20.4.92	3	NC	Alger	2 Aug
49.43		William	Mutunga	KEN	17.9.93	4	AfG	Brazzaville	16 Sep
49.45		Eric	Futch	USA	25.4.93	2		Gainesville	24 Apr
		(50)							
49.48		Keyunta	Hayes	USA	15.2.92	2	TexR	Austin	27 Mar
49.50		Cornel	Fredericks	RSA	3.3.90	4		Madrid	11 Jul
49.53		Drew	Branch	USA	13.5.93	2	SEC	Starkville	16 May
49.56		David	Kendziera	USA	9.9.94	3	NCAA	Eugene	12 Jun
49.56			Cheng Wen	CHN	18.3.92	4h4	WCh	Beijing	22 Aug
49.58		Yuta	Konishi	JPN	31.7.90	1	AsiC	Wuhan	6 Jun
49.58		Mickaël	François	FRA	12.3.88	2	BEL Ch	Bruxelles	26 Jul
49.58		Justin	Gaymon	USA	13.12.86	3		Atlanta	1 Aug
49.58		Michael	Cochrane	NZL	13.8.91	7h1	WCh	Beijing	22 Aug
49.59		Mahau	Suguimati	BRA	13.11.84	1h1		Kumagaya	17 May
		(60)							
49.60		Kenny	Selmon	USA-J	27.8.96	2	ACC	Tallahassee	16 May
49.62		Stanislav	Melnykov	UKR	26.2.87	1h1	NC	Kirovohrad	31 Jul
49.63		Patrick	Bodie	BAH	27.3.92	2rB	FlaR	Gainesville	3 Apr
49.63		Quincy	Downing	USA	16.1.93	4	SEC	Starkville	16 May

Mark	Name		Nat	Born	Pos	Meet	Venue	Date
49.65	Javonte	Lipsey	USA	17.10.92	3	ACC	Tallahassee	16 May
49.66	Jussi	Kanervo	FIN	1.2.93	2	EU23	Tallinn	12 Ju
49.67A	Trevor	Brown	USA	24.3.92	1		Laramie	1 May
49.67A	José Luis	Gaspar	CUB	25.8.95	2	NACAC	San José	9 Aug
49.68	Josef	Robertson	JAM	14.5.87	4	NC	Kingston	26 Jun
49.70	Greg	Coleman	USA	24.7.93	3s3	NCAA	Eugene	10 Jun
	(70)							
49.72	Cameron	French	NZL	17.5.92	1		Sydney	14 Mar
49.73	Artur	Langowski	BRA	8.5.91	4	WUG	Gwangju	10 Ju
49.80	Emanuel	Mayers	TTO	9.3.89	1		New York	11 Ju
49.84	Sebastian	Rodger	GBR	29.6.91	1		Leixlip	13 Jun
49.84A	Kiprono	Kosgei	KEN		4	WCT	Nairobi	1 Aug
49.85	David 'Dai'	Greene	GBR	11.4.86	5	DL	London (OS)	25 Ju
49.87A	Wouter	le Roux	RSA	17.1.86	2		Pretoria	7 Mar
49.87	Andre	Clarke	JAM	6.6.92	3h1	NC	Kingston	25 Jun
49.87	Jonas	Hanßen	GER	15.7.95	1		Mannheim	28 Jun
49.89	Takaoki	Hashimoto	JPN	18.7.92	1		Osaka	13 Sep
	(80)							
49.90	Marvin	Williams	JAM-J	13.6.96	1h3	NC	Kingston	25 Jun
49.90A	Yeison	Rivas	COL	24.9.87	1	NG	Cali	19 Nov
49.92	Cam	Viney	USA	6.9.93	1		Tucson	11 Apr
49.92	Yasuhiro	Fueki	JPN	20.12.85	4		Gifu	26 Sep
49.93	Leonardo	Capotosti	ITA	24.7.88	3	ET	Cheboksary	20 Jun
49.94	Javan	Gallimore	JAM	7.8.93	1h2	NC	Kingston	25 Jun
49.95	Kazuaki	Yoshida	JPN	31.8.87	3	AsiC	Wuhan	6 Jun
49.96	Khallifah	Rosser	USA	13.7.95	3h2	NC	Eugene	25 Jun
49.97	Rai	Benjamin	ANT-J	27.7.97	1		Greensboro, NC	21 Jun
49.97	Yoshihiro	Watanabe	JPN-J	7.1.97	1	NC-j	Mizuho	18 Oct
	(90)							
50.00	Lindsay	Hanekom	RSA	15.5.93	1		Stellenbosch	25 Apr
50.00A	Sergio	Fernández	ESP	1.4.93	1		Monachil	8 Aug
50.01	Henry	Okorie	NGR	11.4.87	7	AfG	Brazzaville	16 Sep
50.02	Rilwan	Alowonle	NGR	12.12.93	4	ACC	Tallahassee	16 May
50.02	Nicolai	Hartling	DEN	17.1.94	3	EU23	Tallinn	12 Jul
50.03	Joshua	Taylor	USA	19.6.92	1		Hammond, LA	10 May
50.04		Yu Chia-Hsuan	TPE	22.1.95	2		Kaohsiung	21 Oct
50.05	Martin	Carrere	FRA	31.10.90	3h1	NC	Villeneuve d'Ascq	11 Jul
50.06	Silvio	Schirrmeister	GER	7.12.88	4		Gainesville	24 Apr
50.06	Naoto	Noguchi	JPN	27.5.94	4		Chiba	15 Aug
	(100)							

Mark	Name		Nat	Born	Date
50.07	Oleg	Mironov	RUS	5.3.93	12 Jul
50.08	Le Roux	Hamman	RSA	6.1.92	25 Apr
50.09	Aleksandr	Skorobogatko	RUS	7.8.94	12 Jul
50.10	Ali Khamis	Abbas	BRN	30.6.95	27 Apr
50.10	Norman	Grimes	USA-Y	6.1.98	1 Aug
50.13	Victor	Coroller	FRA-J	21.9.97	12 Jun
50.14A	Hardus	Maritz	NAM	10.5.90	9 May
50.14	Jovan	Davis	USA	20.11.91	16 May
50.14	Shotaro	Tanabe	JPN	23.4.94	27 Jun
50.15A	Mark	Ujakpor	ESP	18.1.87	8 Aug
50.16	Amadou	Ndiaye	SEN	6.12.92	28 Jun
50.16	Kyron	McMaster	IVB-J	3.1.97	1 Aug
50.16	Masaki	Toyota	JPN-Y	17.1.98	18 Oct
50.17	Piet "PC"	Beneke	RSA	18.7.90	18 Apr
50.17A	Vincent	Kosgei	KEN	11.11.85	10 Jul
50.18	Masayuki	Obayashi	JPN-J	6.2.96	18 Oct
50.20	Taylor	McLaughlin	USA-J	2.8.97	21 Jun
50.20	Mario	Lambrughi	ITA	5.2.92	26 Jul
50.21	Eusebio	Haliti	ITA	1.1.91	26 Jul
50.22	Diego	Cabello	ESP	14.1.88	20 Jun
50.23A	Félix	Sánchez	DOM	30.8.77	9 Aug
50.25	Andrés	Silva #	URU	27.3.86	23 May
50.26	Michal	Broz	CZE	16.6.92	1 Aug
50.27	Juander	Santos	DOM	7.5.95	9 Jul
50.27	Isshu	Takada	JPN-J	27.11.97	31 Jul
50.27	Jack	Houghton	GBR	3.9.93	8 Aug
50.29	Durgesh	Kumar Pal	IND	20.4.94	2 May
50.29		Quach Cong Lich	VIE	27.8.93	10 Jun
50.30	Denys	Nechyporenko	UKR	7.1.90	1 Aug
50.31	Tristan	Thomas	AUS	23.5.86	29 Mar
50.31	Wesley Diego	Martins	BRA	23.3.93	17 May
50.31	Christian	Heimann	GER	15.11.91	6 Jun
50.31	Georg	Fleischhauer	GER	21.10.88	20 Jun
50.31	LaRon	Bennett	USA	25.11.82	26 Jun
50.32	Ben	Thiel	USA	6.12.93	17 May
50.32	Mica-Jonathan	Petit-Homme	USA	9.4.94	29 May
50.33	Stéphane	Yato	FRA	11.9.92	12 Jul
50.34	Maurice	Jones	USA	17.12.91	23 May
50.34	Tim	Rummens	BEL	16.12.87	6 Jun
50.35	M.	Ramachandran	IND	29.12.91	2 May
50.35	Antonio	Blanks	USA	17.10.92	29 May
50.35	Rafal	Omelko	POL	16.1.89	14 Jun
50.38	Jacob	Paul	GBR	6.2.95	6 Jun
50.39	Thiago	Sales	BRA	12.8.86	17 May
50.40A	Geoffrey	Cheruiyot	KEN-J	4.6.96	1 Aug
50.41	Atsushi	Yamada	JPN	3.7.91	27 Jun
50.42	Byron	Robinson	USA	16.2.95	27 Mar
50.44	Máté	Koroknai	HUN	13.1.93	12 Jul
50.46	Jurmarcus	Shelvin	USA	4.4.94	27 Mar
50.47	Isa	Phillips	JAM	22.4.84	25 Jun
50.47	Nikita	Andriyanov	RUS	7.2.90	9 Jul
50.49	Drew	Wiseman	USA	24.8.94	29 May
50.50	Akihiko	Nakamura	JPN	23.10.90	3 May
50.50	Danylo	Danylenko	UKR	10.10.94	8 Jun
50.50	Amaechi	Morton	NGR	30.10.89	18 Jul
50.51	Elijah	Owens	USA	16.2.93	23 May
50.52	Leandro	Zamora	CUB-J	11.3.96	1 Aug
50.53	Ludvy	Vaillant	FRA	15.3.95	26 Jul
50.53A	Gerald	Drummond	CRC	5.9.94	7 Aug
50.55	Eric	Lund	USA	1.4.88	27 Mar
50.55	Alfredo	Sepúlveda	CHI	3.8.93	31 May
50.55	Aramis	Díaz	ITA	22.11.74	6 Jun
50.55	Jithin	Paul	IND	13.3.90	11 Jul
50.55	Naoya	Nakano	JPN	3.7.94	13 Sep
50.57	Takahiro	Matsumoto	JPN	19.9.94	17 May
50.57	Luke	Campbell	USA	22.11.94	23 May
50.59	Derick	Díaz	PUR-J	24.7.96	18 Apr
50.60	Austin	Hollimon	USA	12.1.90	1 Aug
50.61	Márcio	Teles	BRA	27.1.94	8 Aug
50.61	Esau	Somda	BUR	13.9.95	15 Sep

Mark		Name	Nat	Born	Date
50.61		Cai Junqi	CHN-J	11.3.96	23 Oct
50.62	Yuriy	Ledenev	URS	10.6.94	16 Jun
50.63	Dennis	Pugh	USA	.93	2 May
50.63	Tibor	Koroknai	HUN	24.1.90	9 Jul
50.64	Tait	Nyusten	CAN	29.5.91	7 Feb
50.64	Demar	Murray	JAM	31.8.91	16 May
50.64	Pavel	Agafonov	RUS	28.8.95	16 Jun
50.64	Kakeru	Inoue	JPN-J	19.3.96	11 Jul
50.66	Shawn	Rowe	JAM	7.12.92	8 May
50.66	Richard	Yates	GBR	26.1.86	15 Jul
50.68	Martin	Kucera	SVK	10.5.90	16 May
50.68	Vishnu	Sabu	IND	19.1.93	21 Jul
50.68		Xun Zhizhun	CHN	12.4.92	24 Sep
50.69	Kotaro	Miyao	JPN	12.7.91	10 May
50.70	Yudai	Nakayama	JPN	16.10.91	11 Jul
50.72	Paul	Byrne	IRL	18.4.90	4 Jul
50.72	Seiya	Kato	JPN	22.11.92	11 Jul
50.73	J.W.	Smith	USA	1.1.95	27 Mar
50.74	Mattia	Contini	ITA	27.10.94	26 Jul
50.74	Anatoliy	Sinyanskyy	UKR	4.2.91	1 Aug
50.74		Wang Yang	CHN-J	20.9.96	23 Oct
50.75	Maxime	Martin	FRA	10.8.93	1 Jul
50.76	Dmitriy	Koblov	KAZ	30.11.92	15 Jun
50.77	Raymond	Smith	AUS	16.12.92	7 Feb
50.77	Mark	Carlson	USA	.92	29 May
50.78	Mickael	Bertil	FRA	2.1.94	26 Jul
50.79A	Bernard	Pretorius	RSA	6.1.93	9 May
50.79	Yoan	Décimus	FRA	30.11.87	6 Jun
50.79	Mizuki	Endo	JPN	27.5.92	5 Jul
50.79	Joel	Groth	SWE	14.5.91	9 Aug
	(200)				

Hand timing

Mark		Name	Nat	Born	Date
50.4A	Christopher	Ngetich	KEN	25.12.92	6 Jun
50.7	Mamadou Kassé	Hann	SEN	10.10.86	10 May

Low altitude bests

49.79 T Brown 1 Port of Spain 28 Mar
50.12 Gaspar 12 Jun 50.18 Fernández 2 Aug 50.88 Rivas 3 Jun

Drugs disqualification

49.43 Andrés Silva # URU 27.3.86 (1) SAmC Lima 13 Jun

JUNIORS

See main list for top 5 juniors. 12 performances by 6 men to 50.10. Additional marks and further juniors:

Hyde 49.78 1 Kingston 7 Mar 49.87 1 Kingston 6 Jun
49.83 2h1 NC Kingston 25 Jun
Williams 49.90 5 NC Kingston 26 Jun
Selmon 50.04 2q3 NCAAe Jacksonville 29 May

Mark		Name	Nat	Born	Pos	Meet	Venue	Date
50.10	Norman	Grimes	USA-Y	6.1.98	1	PAm-J	Edmonton	1 Aug
50.13	Victor	Coroller	FRA	21.9.97	2		Colmar	12 Jun
50.16	Kyron	McMaster	IVB	3.1.97	1h1	PAm-J	Edmonton	1 Aug
50.16	Masaki	Toyota	JPN-Y	17.1.98	2	NC-j	Mizuho	18 Oct
50.18	Masayuki	Obayashi (10)	JPN	6.2.96	3	NC-j	Nagoya	18 Oct
50.20	Taylor	McLaughlin	USA	2.8.97	2		Greensboro, NC	21 Jun
50.27	Isshu	Takada	JPN	27.11.97	1		Wakayama	31 Jul
50.40A	Geoffrey	Cheruiyot	KEN	4.6.96	6	WCT	Nairobi	1 Aug
50.52	Leandro	Zamora	CUB	11.3.96	4	PAm-J	Edmonton	1 Aug
50.59	Derick	Díaz	PUR	24.7.96	2		Ponce	18 Apr
50.61		Cai Junqi	CHN	11.3.96	1		Fuzhou	23 Oct
50.64	Kakeru	Inoue	JPN	19.3.96	1		Osaka	11 Jul
50.74		Wang Yang	CHN	20.9.96	2		Fuzhou	23 Oct
50.84	Shinosuka	Hase	JPN	.96	4	NC-j	Nagoya	18 Oct
50.90	Deron	Gordon (20)	JAM	8.11.96	1		Norman	18 Apr

MEN 2015

HIGH JUMP

2.41i Mutaz Essa Barshim QAT 24.6.91 1 Athlone 18 Feb
2.20/1 2.25/1 2.33/1 2.37/1 2.41/1 2.44/xxx
2.41 1 Pre Eugene 30 May 2.24/1 2.28/1 2.35/1 2.41/1
2.40i 1 Banská Bystrica 4 Feb 2.25/1 2.31/2 2.33/1 2.35/2 2.40/1 2.44/x
2.38 1 DL Shanghai 17 May 2.25/1 2.29/2 2.32/1 2.35/1 2.38/1
2.36 1 Gyulai Székesfehérvár 7 Jul 2.20/2 2.24/1 2.30/1 2.32/1 2.34xx 2.36/1 2.40/xxx
2.34i 1 Malmö 25 Feb 2.21/1 2.26/1 2.30/2 2.34/2 2.38/xxx

2.38 Zhang Guowei CHN 4.6.91 2 Pre Eugene 30 May
2.20/1 2.24/1 2.28/1 2.32/2 2.35/2 2.38/2
2.36 1 Bisl Oslo 11 Jun 2.20/1 2.25/1 2.29/1 2.33/2 2.36/3 2.40/xxx
2.35 1 MSR Walnut 18 Apr 2.13/1 2.18/1 2.23/1 2.28/3 2.33/1 2.35/3
2.34 1 Beijing 20 May 2.15/1 2.20/1 2.28/1 2.31/1 2.34/3 2.40/xxx

2.37 Bogdan Bondarenko UKR 30.8.89 1 Kawasaki 10 May
2.20/1 2.31/1 2.37/2 2.41/xxx
2.36 1 Rabat 14 Jun 2.24/1 2.31/1 2.36/1 2.40/xxx

2.37 Eric Kynard USA 3.2.91 1 NC Eugene 26 Jun
2.15/1 2.20/1 2.25/1 2.28/1 2.31/1 2.34/2 2.37/2 2.41/xxx
2.35 3 Pre Eugene 30 May 2.20/1 2.24/1 2.28/2 2.32/2 2.25/2 2.38/xx 2.41/x
2.34i 1 NC Boston (R) 28 Feb 2.15/1 2.20/1 2.25/1 2.28/1 2.31/2 2.34/1 2.41/xxx

2.37 Derek Drouin CAN 6.3.90 1 PAm Toronto 25 Jul
2.15/1 2.20/1 2.25/1 2.28/2 2.31/1 2.34/3 2.37/2 2.41/xxx
2.37 1 Eberstadt 2 Aug 2.20/1 2.24/2 2.30/1 2.33/1 2.35/1 2.37/1 2.39/xx 2.41/x
2.34 1 NC Edmonton 4 Jul 2.16/1 2.22/1 2.25/1 2.28/1 2.31/1 2.34/2 2.37/xxx
2.34 1 WCh Beijing 30 Aug 2.20/1 2.25/1 2.28/1 2.29/1 2.33/1 2.36/xxxx 2.34/1

2.37 Gianmarco Tamberi ITA 1.6.92 2 Eberstadt 2 Aug
2.20/1 2.27/1 2.30/3 2.33/1 2.35/3 2.37/1 2.39/xxx
2.34 1 Köln 1 Jul 2.16/1 2.20/1 2.24/2 2.28/1 2.30/1 2.32/1 2.34/1 2.36/xxx

Mark	Name		Nat	Born	Pos	Meet	Venue	Date
2.34i	Marco	Fassinotti	ITA	29.4.89	1		Hustopece	24 Jan
			2.22/1 2.25/1 2.28/1 2.30/3 2.32/3 2.34/3 2.36/xxx					
2.34	Jacorian	Duffield	USA	2.9.92	2	NC	Eugene	26 Jun
			2.15/1 2.20/2 2.25/1 2.28/1 2.31/1 2.34/2 2.37/xx 2.40/x					
2.34	Donald	Thomas	BAH	1.7.84	2	Gyulai	Székesfehérvár	7 Jul
			2.15/1 2.20/2 2.24/1 2.27/1 2.30/1 2.32/x 2.34/2 2.36/xxx					
	(24/9)	plus 15 performances at 2.33: also Barshim, Bondarenko, Mason, Thomas, Zhang 2; Kynard 1						
2.33i	Andriy	Protsenko (10)	UKR	20.5.88	2		Banská Bystrica	4 Feb
2.33	Daniyil	Tsyplakov	RUS	29.7.92	1	ET	Cheboksary	20 Jun
2.33	Michael	Mason	CAN	30.9.86	2		Edmonton	12 Jul
2.32i	Dimitrios	Hondrokoukis	CYP	26.1.88	1	NC	Pireás	14 Feb
2.32	Ivan	Ukhov	RUS	29.3.86	4	Pre	Eugene	30 May
2.32	Eike	Onnen	GER	3.8.82	1		Bühl	28 Jun
2.32	Aleksey	Dmitrik	RUS	12.4.84	3	Gyulai	Székesfehérvár	7 Jul
2.32		Yoon Seung-hyun	KOR	1.6.94	1		Yeosu	1 Sep
2.31i	Dmitriy	Semyonov	RUS	2.8.92	2		Moskva	1 Feb
2.31i	Matús	Bubeník	SVK	14.11.89	6		Banská Bystrica	4 Feb
2.31i	Jesse	Williams	USA	27.12.83	1	Mill	New York (Arm)	14 Feb
	(20)							
2.31i	Ricky	Robertson	USA	19.9.90	2	NC	Boston (R)	28 Feb
2.31i	Silvano	Chesani	ITA	17.7.88	2=	EI	Praha (O2)	8 Mar
2.31i	Adónios	Mástoras	GRE	6.1.91	2=	EI	Praha (O2)	8 Mar
2.31	Jeron	Robinson	USA	30.4.91	1		San Angelo	9 May
2.31		Wang Yu	CHN	18.8.91	2		Beijing	20 May
2.31	Brandon	Starc	AUS	24.11.93	Q	WCh	Beijing	28 Aug
2.31	Konstadínos	Baniótis	GRE	6.11.86	Q	WCh	Beijing	28 Aug
2.31	Jaroslav	Bába	CZE	2.9.84	Q	WCh	Beijing	28 Aug
2.31	Majed El Dein	Ghazal	SYR	21.4.87	1	WMilG	Mungyeong	5 Oct
2.30	Bryan	McBride	USA	10.12.91	1		Tempe	2 May
	(30)							
2.30	Mateusz	Przybylko	GER	9.3.92	1		Weinheim	30 May
2.30	Dmytro	Yakovenko	UKR	17.9.92	1		Kirovohrad	9 Jun
2.30	Aleksandr	Shustov	RUS	29.6.84	2		Baku	25 Jun
2.30	Ilya	Ivanyuk	RUS	9.3.93	1	EU23	Tallinn	11 Jul
2.30	Sylwester	Bednarek	POL	28.4.89	1		Tábor	28 Jul
2.29Ai	Nick	Ross	USA	8.8.91	1		Albuquerque	24 Jan
2.29i	Allan	Smith	GBR	6.11.92	1	NC	Sheffield	15 Feb
2.29i	Bradley	Adkins	USA	30.12.93	2	NCAA	Fayetteville	14 Mar
2.29	Naoto	Tobe	JPN	31.3.92	4	DL	Shanghai	17 May
2.29	Kyriakos	Ioannou	CYP	26.7.84	1		Haniá	6 Jun
	(40)							
2.29	Mihai	Donisan	ROU	24.7.88	1		Pitesti	6 Jun
2.29	Dmitriy	Kroyter	ISR	18.2.93	1		Schifflange	2 Aug
2.29	Trevor	Barry	BAH	14.6.83	Q	WCh	Beijing	28 Aug
2.29		Hsiang Chun-Hsien	TPE	4.9.93	1	NG	Kaohsiung	21 Oct
2.29i	Mikhail	Veryovkin	RUS	28.6.91	1		Kineshma	6 Dec
2.28i	Wally	Ellenson	USA	4.5.94	1		Madison	17 Jan
2.28i	Raivydas	Stanys	LTU	3.2.87	1		Vilnius	31 Jan
2.28i	Christoffe	Bryan	JAM-J	26.4.96	1		Fayetteville	14 Feb
2.28i	Andriy	Kovalyov	UKR	11.6.92	1	NC	Sumy	14 Feb
2.28	Marcus	Jackson	USA	8.7.91	1	FlaR	Gainesville	4 Apr
	(50)							
2.28	Talles	Silva	BRA	20.8.91	1		São Bernardo do Campo	18 Apr
2.28	Takashi	Eto	JPN	5.2.91	1		Fukuroi	3 May
2.28	Hiromi	Takahari	JPN	13.11.87	4		Kawasaki	10 May
2.28	Yuji	Hiramatsu	JPN-J	11.1.97	1		Yokohama	16 May
2.28	Ali Mohamed	Younes Idris	SUD	15.9.89	1		Namur	27 May
2.28	Mikhail	Tsvetkov	RUS	4.5.80	1		Sochi	29 May
2.28	Dusty	Jonas	USA	19.4.86	5	NC	Eugene	26 Jun
2.28	Yuriy	Krymarenko	UKR	11.8.83	1		Berdychiv	27 Jun
2.28	Ryan	Ingraham	BAH	2.11.93	1	NC	Nassau	27 Jun
2.28	Robbie	Grabarz	GBR	3.10.87	1	NC	Birmingham	5 Jul
	(60)							
2.27	Eugenio	Rossi	SMR	6.3.92	1		Camprino Veronese	28 Jun
2.26i	Lev	Missirov	RUS	4.8.90	2		Kherson	17 Jan
2.26i	Andrea	Lemmi	ITA	12.5.84	1		Lucca	24 Jan
2.26i	Andrey	Churyla	BLR	19.5.93	1		Gomel	7 Feb
2.26i	Chris	Kandu	GBR	10.9.95	3		Birmingham	21 Feb
2.26i	David	Smith	GBR	14.7.91	5		Birmingham	21 Feb
2.26	Fernando	Ferreira	BRA	13.12.94	1		São Paulo	2 May
2.26	Wojciech	Theiner	POL	25.6.86	1		Opole	31 May

Mark	Name		Nat	Born	Pos	Meet	Venue	Date
2.26	Yevgeniy	Korshunov	RUS	11.4.86	2		Smolensk	5 Jun
2.26	Vadim	Vrublevskiy	RUS	18.3.93	1	NC-23	Saransk	17 Jun
	(70)							
2.26	Keyvan	Ghanbarzadeh	IRI	26.5.90	1		Bangkok	22 Jun
2.26	Vasilios	Konstantinou	CYP	13.9.92	3		Limasol	27 Jun
2.26	Joel	Baden	AUS-J	1.2.96	21q	WCh	Beijing	28 Aug
2.25i	Tihomir	Ivanov	BUL	11.7.94	6		Hustopece	24 Jan
2.25i	Lukás	Beer	SVK	23.8.89	10		Banská Bystrica	4 Feb
2.25i	Muamer Aissa	Barshim	QAT	3.1.94	2		Athlone	18 Feb
2.25	Eure	Yáñez	VEN	20.5.93	1		Barquisimeto	27 Feb
2.25	Maalik	Reynolds	USA	26.4.92	1		Philadelphia	21 Mar
2.25	Mickaël	Hanany	FRA	25.3.83	2		Baie Mahault	2 May
2.25	Edgar	Rivera	MEX	13.2.91	1		Colmar	10 May
	(80)							
2.25	Fernand	Djoumessi	CMR	5.9.89	2		Colmar	10 May
2.25	Martin	Günther	GER	8.10.86	1		Eppingen	16 May
2.25	Abdoulaye	Diarra	MLI	27.5.88	2		Tourcoing	24 May
2.25	Artyom	Zaytsev	BLR	7.12.84	1		Brest	26 May
2.25	Szymon	Kiecana	POL	26.3.89	1		Biala Podlaska	30 May
2.25	Artyom	Naumovich	BLR	19.2.91	1		Minsk	6 Jun
2.25	Dmitriy	Nabokov	BLR-J	20.1.96	2		Minsk	6 Jun
2.25	Avion	Jones	USA	31.1.94	3	NCAA	Eugene	12 Jun
2.25	David	Nopper	GER	25.1.95	1	NC-23	Wetzlar	13 Jun
2.25	Matthew	Roberts	GBR	22.12.84	4		Bühl	28 Jun
	(90)							
2.25	Kabelo Mmono	Kgosiemang	BOT	7.1.86	5		Bühl	28 Jun
2.25	Miguel Ángel	Sancho	ESP	24.4.90	1		Barcelona (S)	15 Jul
2.25	Mike	Edwards	GBR	11.7.90	1		Birmingham	19 Jul
2.25	Batyrkhan	Baymukhambetov	KAZ	7.9.92	1		Almaty	25 Jul
2.25		Yu Shisuo	CHN	20.2.90	2		Beijing	25 Jul
2.25A	Matthew	Sawe	KEN	2.7.88	1	WCT	Nairobi	1 Aug
2.25	Sergey	Mudrov	RUS	8.9.90	3	NC	Cheboksary	4 Aug
2.25	Ryoichi	Akamatsu	JPN	2.5.95	1		Osaka	13 Sep
2.24i	Mikhail	Akimenko	RUS	6.12.95	5=		Volgograd	24 Jan
2.24i	Deante	Kemper	USA	27.3.93	1		Ames	14 Feb
	(100)							

Mark	Name		Nat	Born	Date
2.24	Randall	Cunningham	USA-J	4.1.96	4 Apr
2.24	Douwe	Amels	NED	16.9.91	9 May
2.24	Andrei	Miticov	MDA	15.11.86	21 Jun
2.24	Janick	Klausen	DEN	3.4.93	20 Jun
2.24	Andrey	Skobeyko	BLR	11.6.95	21 Jun
2.24	Ilya	Spitsyn	RUS-J	28.7.96	27 Jun
2.24		Guo Jinqi	CHN	21.9.92	29 Jun
2.24		Woo Sang-hyuk	KOR-J	23.4.96	10 Jul
2.24	Jussi	Viita	FIN	26.9.85	22 Aug
2.24	Mohammad	Reza Vazifehdoost	IRI	13.10.93	5 Oct
2.24		Chen Ji	CHN	27.1.90	5 Oct
2.23	Mpho	Links	RSA-J	20.6.96	18 Apr
2.23	Natron	Gipson	USA	30.4.95	2 May
2.23		Wang Chen	CHN	27.2.90	22 Jun
2.23	Manjula Kumara	Wijesekara	SRI	30.1.84	29 Jun
2.23	Jonas Kløjgaard	Jensen	DEN-J	29.2.96	18 Jul
2.23	Dawid	Wawrzyniak	POL-J	20.5.96	18 Jul
2.22i	James	Harris	USA	18.9.91	22 Jan
2.22	Nauraj Singh	Randhawa	MAS	27.1.92	7 Feb
2.22i	David	Smith	USA/PUR	2.5.92	27 Feb
2.22i	James	White	USA	22.1.92	28 Feb
2.22	Trey	McRae	USA	12.7.93	21 Mar
2.22	Donte	Nall	USA	27.1.88	9 May
2.22	Taira	Omata	JPN	12.9.89	17 May
2.22	Danyil	Lysenko	RUS-J	19.5.97	29 May
2.22	Jamal	Wilson	BAH	1.9.88	27 Jun
2.22	Luis Joel	Castro	PUR	28.1.91	28 Jun
2.22	Torsten	Sanders	GER	8.9.94	28 Jun
2.22	Martin	Heindl	CZE	2.6.92	28 Jun
2.22		Pai Long	CHN	8.10.89	25 Jul
2.22	Tobias	Potye	GER	16.3.95	31 Jul
2.22	Péter	Bakosi	HUN	23.6.93	8 Aug
2.22	Ryo	Sato	JPN	21.7.94	13 Sep
2.22	Chris	Moleya	RSA-J	27.1.97	17 Sep
2.21i	Kyle	Landon	USA	16.10.94	31 Jan
2.21i	Ivan	Ilyichev	RUS	14.10.86	8 Feb
2.21Ai	Django	Lovett	CAN	6.7.92	13 Feb
2.21i	Cameron	Ostrowski	USA	15.6.92	14 Feb
2.21i	Justin	Fondren	USA	2.2.94	14 Feb
2.21i	Nick	Giancana	USA	18.10.91	14 Feb
2.21i	Isaac	Jean-Paul	USA	4.2.93	13 Mar
2.21i	Robert	Valdez	USA	18.4.94	13 Mar
2.21A	Arturo Joaquin	Abascal	MEX	19.6.95	11 Apr
2.21	Geoff	Davis	USA	8.8.90	24 Apr
2.21	Lath	Kisling	USA-J		2 May
2.21	Alexander	Bowen	PAN	3.4.93	8 May
2.21	Anton	Bodnar	KAZ	12.4.92	12 May
2.21	Tiago	Pereira	POR	19.9.93	16 May
2.21	Kazuhiro	Ota	JPN	11.6.95	17 May
2.21	Oleksandr	Barannikov	UKR-J	23.1.97	24 May
2.21	Kirill	Rudov	RUS	23.10.92	7 Jun
2.21	Simón	Siverio	ESP	2.8.88	24 Jun
2.21	Hiroshi	Kunimoto	JPN	20.4.87	20 Jul
2.21	Eugenio	Meloni	ITA	28.8.94	11 Jul
2.21	Aleksandr	Asanov	RUS-J	30.3.96	15 Jul
2.21	Andy	Gilmore	USA	16.8.80	25 Jul
2.21	Bram	Ghuys	BEL	14.2.93	1 Aug
2.21	Ken	Ishibashi	JPN	27.2.94	3 Oct
2.20i	Ihor	Hryhoyev	UKR	16.4.92	10 Jan
2.20i	Tom	Parsons	GBR	5.5.84	11 Jan
2.20i	Viktor	Shapoval	UKR	17.10.79	11 Jan
2.20i	Jonathan	Wells	USA-J	18.4.96	17 Jan
2.20i	Dmytro	Demyanyuk	UKR	30.6.83	17 Jan
2.20i	Vitaliy	Samoylenko	UKR	22.5.84	17 Jan
2.20	Sreenith	Mohan	IND	24.3.95	17 Jan
2.20i	Alen	Melon	CRO	25.10.91	24 Jan
2.20i	Justin	Frick	USA	3.8.88	24 Jan
2.20i	Azer	Akhmedov	AZE	28.2.89	24 Jan
2.20i	Sergey	Kurbatov	RUS	13.4.94	24 Jan
2.20i	Ivan	Toporkov	RUS	13.2.93	28 Jan
2.20i	Serhiy	Spilnak	UKR	4.6.95	28 Jan
2.20i	Ferrante	Graselli	ITA	4.4.91	31 Jan
2.20i	Ray	Bobrownicki	GBR	3.3.84	1 Feb
2.20i	Joris	Chapon	FRA	13.12.94	1 Feb
2.20i	Manny	Durden	USA-J	2.3.96	12 Feb
2.20i	Tori	Brooks	USA	14.6.91	13 Feb
2.20i	Norbert	Kobielski	POL-J	28.1.97	15 Feb
2.20i	Andrey	Rybakov	BLR-J	14.12.96	20 Feb
2.20i	David	Bolado	ESP	10.9.92	21 Feb
2.20i	Barry	Pender	IRL	2.4.90	22 Feb

Mark	Name		Nat	Born	Pos	Meet	Venue	Date
2.20i	Kris	Kornegay-Gober	USA	6.10.91				28 Feb
2.20i	Montez	Blair	USA	23.10.90				28 Feb
2.20i	Hoova	Taylor	USA	11.6.87				28 Feb
2.20i		Sun Zhao	CHN	8.2.90				8 Mar
2.20	Zack	Blackham	USA	10.8.92				27 Mar
2.20	Liam	Zamel-Paez	IRL	4.8.88				28 Mar
2.20	Briar	Ploude	USA	9.3.91				28 Mar
2.20	Nawaf Ahmed	Al-Yami	KSA	21.7.91				11 Apr
2.20	Dakarai	Hightower	USA	15.7.94				17 Apr
2.20		Zhu Gezhen	CHN	14.4.93				29 Apr
2.20	Keyth	Fightmaster	USA	24.11.95				2 May
2.20		Bi Xiaoliang	CHN	26.12.92				8 May
2.20	Kei-Jian	Buckley	USA	27.4.94				8 May
2.20	Stefano	Sottile	ITA-Y	26.1.98				10 May
2.20		Sun Zhao	CHN	8.2.90				12 May
2.20		Sun Bin	CHN	10.12.94				12 May
2.20	Viktor	Lonskyy	UKR	27.10.95				13 May
2.20	Giulio	Ciotti	ITA	5.10.76				16 May
2.20	Ken	LeGassey	USA	20.5.94				28 May
2.20	(200)	Zhang Tianhao	CHN-J	25.5.97				30 May
2.20A	Abobe	Tshwanelo	BOT	31.1.95				31 May
2.20A	Gobe	Takobana	BOT	7.9.91				31 May
2.20	Pavel	Kipra	BLR	3.7.94				6 Jun
2.20	Chris	Baker	GBR	2.2.91				6 Jun
2.20	Victor	Korst	POR-J	21.10.96				7 Jun
2.20	Shuichi	Matsumoto	JPN-J	14.11.96				13 Jun
2.20	Clayton	Brown	JAM-J	8.12.96				13 Jun
2.20	Vitaliy	Tsykunov	KAZ	22.1.87				15 Jun
2.20	Andreas	Carlsson	SWE	5.4.95				28 Jun
2.20	Artur	Kolesnyk	UKR	6.7.95				21 Jul
2.20	Dan	Lazarica	ROU	11.5.92				25 Jul
2.20	Hamdi Mahamat	Alamine	QAT-J	15.4.97				14 Aug
2.20	Carlos	Layoy	ARG	26.2.91				14 Nov
2.20A	Wanner	Miller	COL	22.7.87				21 Nov
2.20	Japheth	Cato	USA	25.12.90				5 Dec
2.20i	ümit	Tan	TUR	16.7.90				26 Dec

Best outdoor marks

Mark	Name	Pos	Meet	Venue	Date
2.33	Fassinotti	2	Bisl	Oslo	11 Jun
2.32	Protsenko	4	Gyulai	Székesfehérvár	7 Jul
2.31	Williams	3	NC	Eugene	26 Jun
2.31	Hondrokoukis	Q	WCh	Beijing	28 Aug
2.30	Mástoras	6	Gyulai	Székesfehérvár	7 Jul
2.29	Bubeník	1	NC	Banská Bystrica	2 Aug
2.26	Ross	1D		Tucson	9 Apr
2.26	Lemmi	1		Campi Bisenzio	10 May
2.26	Semyonov	1		Smolensk	5 Jun
2.25	Adkins	2	NCAA	Eugene	12 Jun
2.25	Robertson	7	NC	Eugene	26 Jun
2.25	Kovalyov	3		Berdychiv	27 Jun
2.25	T Ivanov	1		Kragujevac	8 Aug

Mark	Name	Date
2.24	Bryan	16 Apr
2.24	Akimenko	17 Jun
2.24	Stanys	20 Jun
2.24	D.Smith	11 Jul
2.24	A.Smith	11 Jul
2.23	Muamer Barshim	1 Apr
2.21	Giancana	16 May
2.21	Ostrowski	16 May
2.21	Missirov	18 Jun
2.21	Kandu	11 Jul
2.20	Landon	11 Apr
2.20	Sun Zhao	12 May
2.20	H Taylor	17 May
2.20	Sawe	24 May
2.20	Ellenson	28 May
2.20	White	28 May
2.20	Kornegay-Gober	6 Jun
2.20	Churyla	12 Jun
2.20	Shapoval	27 Jun
2.20	D J Smith	27 Jun
2.20	Beer	10 Jul
2.20	Frick	11 Jul
2.20	Veryovkin	8 Aug

JUNIORS

See main list for top 4 juniors. 11 performances (inc. 2 indoors) by 7 men to 2.24. Additional marks and further juniors:

	Mark	Pos	Meet	Venue	Date
Bryan	2.25i	1		Manhattan KS	17 Jan
Bryan	2.24	3	Big12	Ames	16 May
Baden	2.26	1		Gold Coast	30 Sep

Mark	Name		Nat	Born	Pos	Meet	Venue	Date
2.24	Randall	Cunningham	USA	4.1.96	2	FlaR	Gainesville	4 Apr
2.24	Ilya	Spitsyn	RUS	28.7.96	1	NC-j	Cheboksary	27 Jun
2.24		Woo Sang-hyuk	KOR	23.4.96	5	WUG	Gwangju	10 Jul
2.23	Mpho	Links	RSA	20.6.96	1	NC	Stellenbosch	18 Apr
2.23	Jonas Kløjgaard	Jensen	DEN	29.2.96	1	EJ	Eskilstuna	18 Jul
2.23	Dawid	Wawrzyniak	POL	20.5.96	2	EJ	Eskilstuna	18 Jul
2.22	Danyil	Lysenko (10)	RUS	19.5.97	4		Sochi	29 May
2.22	Chris	Moleya	RSA	27.1.97	2	AfG	Brazzaville	17 Sep
2.21	Lath	Kisling	USA		1		Pierce City	2 May
2.21	Oleksandr	Barannikov	UKR	23.1.97	1		Kirovohrad	24 May
2.21	Oleksandr	Barannikov	UKR	23.1.97	1		Kirovohrad	24 May
2.21	Aleksandr	Asanov	RUS	30.3.96	3	Kuts	Moskva	15 Jul
2.20i	Jonathan	Wells	USA	18.4.96	1		Champaign	17 Jan
2.20i	Manny	Durden	USA	2.3.96	1		Seward	12 Feb
2.20i	Norbert	Kobielski	POL	28.1.97	1	NC-j	Torun	15 Feb
2.20i	Andrey	Rybakov	BLR	14.12.96	2	NC	Mogilev	20 Feb
2.20	Stefano	Sottile (20)	ITA-Y	26.1.98	1		Torino	10 May
2.20		Zhang Tianhao	CHN	25.5.97	1	NC-j	Fuzhou	30 May
2.20	Victor	Korst	POR	21.10.96	1		Lisboa	7 Jun
2.20	Shuichi	Matsumoto	JPN	14.11.96	3		Hiratsuka	13 Jun
2.20	Clayton	Brown	JAM	8.12.96	1		Kingston	13 Jun
2.20	Hamdi Mahamat	Alamine	QAT	15.4.97	1		Göteborg	14 Aug

POLE VAULT

6.05 Renaud Lavillenie FRA 18.9.86 1 Pre Eugene 30 May
5.70/3 5.86/2 5.96/1 6.05/1 6.16/xxx

Mark	Pos	Meet	Venue	Date	Series
6.04i	1	EI	Praha (O2)	7 Mar	5.75/1 5.90/1 6.04/2 6.17/xxx
6.03	1	DL	London (OS)	25 Jul	5.73/1 5.87/1 5.93/1 6.03/1 6.10/xxx
6.02i	1	ISTAF	Berlin	14 Feb	5.73/1 5.93/1 6.02/1 6.17/xxx
6.01i	1		Nevers	7 Feb	5.70/1 5.87/1 6.01/3 6.17/xxx
6.01i	1	NC	Aubière	22 Feb	5.72/2 5.94/1 6.01/2 6.18/xxx
6.00i	1		Rouen	24 Jan	5.70/1 5.86/1 6.00/3 6.10/xxx
5.95	1	VD	Bruxelles	11 Sep	5.65/1 5.80/x 5.85/1 5.90/2 5.95/2 6.00/xxx
5.93	1		Salzburg	4 Sep	5.40/2 5.50/1 5.60/1 5.70/1 5.80/3 5.93/1 6.01/xxx
5.92Ai	1		Reno	16 Jan	5.65/1 5.80/1 5.86/x 5.92/1 6.00/xxx
5.92i	1		Malmö	25 Feb	5.78/1 5.92/2 6.03/xxx
5.92	1	Herc	Monaco	17 Jul	5.82/1 5.92/1 6.02/xxx

Mark	Name		Nat	Born	Pos	Meet	Venue	Date
	5.91 1 GGala Roma 4 Jun 5.71/2 5.86/x 5.91/1 6.01/xxx							
	5.86i 1 Karlsruhe 31 Jan 5.73/2 5.86/1 6.01/xxx							
5.94	Raphael	Holzdeppe	GER	28.9.89	1	NC	Nürnberg	26 Jul
	5.60/1 5.70/1 5.94/1 6.02/xxx							
	5.92 1 Baku 24 Jun 5.62/2 5.72/1 5.82/3 5.87/1 5.92/1 6.02/xxx							
	5.90 2 WCh Beijing 24 Aug 5.65/1 5.80/2 5.90/3 6.00/xxx							
5.93	Shawnacy	Barber	CAN	27.5.94	2	DL	London (OS)	25 Jul
	5.30/1 5.50/1 5.65/1 5.81/1 5.93/3 6.03/xxx							
	5.92i 1 WK Zürich 2 Sep 5.42/1- 5.57/2 5.67/1 5.77/1 5.92/2 6.01/xxx							
	5.91i 1 NCAA Fayetteville 13 Mar 5.30/1 5.45/1 5.55/1 5.65/1 5.75/1 5.80/1 5.91/3 6.00/xxx							
	5.91 1 Austin 2 May 5.35/1 5.50/1 5.70/2 5.80/1 5.90/x 5.91/1 6.00/xxx							
	5.90i 1 Fayetteville 14 Feb 5.25/1 5.40/1 5.55/1 5.65/1 5.75/1 5.80/1 5.91/3 6.00/xxx							
	5.90 1 TexR Austin 28 Mar 5.45/1 5.60/1 5.80/2 5.90/2 6.00/xxx							
	5.90 1 WCh Beijing 24 Aug 5.50/1 5.65/1 5.80/1 5.90/1 6.00/xxx							
	5.88i 1 Akron 7 Feb 5.35/1 5.50/1 5.65/1 5.80/1 5.88/1 6.00/xxx							
	5.87i 1 Belton 3 Jan 5.25/1 5.41/2 5.56/2 5.63/1 5.71/2 5.79/2 5.87/1							
5.92	Thiago	Braz da Silva	BRA	16.12.93	2		Baku	24 Jun
	5.52/2 5.72/3 5.82/3 5.92/1 6.02/xxx							
	5.86 2 GGala Roma 4 Jun 5.56/2 5.71/1 5.81/3 5.86/1 5.91/xxx							
	5.86 2 DL Saint-Denis 4 Jul 5.56/3 5.71/3 5.81/1 5.86/3 6.01/xxx							
5.91	Konstadinos	Filippídis	GRE	26.11.86	1	DL	Saint-Denis	4 Jul
	5.56/1 5.71/1 5.81/2 5.91/2 6.01/xxx							
5.90i	Piotr	Lisek	POL	16.8.92	1		Bad Oeynhausen	28 Feb
	5.40/1 5.50/1 5.60/1 5.72/1 5.85/x 5.90/1							
	5.87i 1 Dessau 11 Feb 5.36/1 5.51/1 5.61/2 5.71/1 5.81/3 5.87/3							
5.86Ai	Sam	Kendricks	USA	7.9.92	2		Reno	16 Jan
	(33/7) 5.35/1 5.45/1 5.55/1 5.65/2 5.80/2 5.86/1 5.92/xxx							
5.85i	Aleksandr	Gripich	RUS	21.9.86	2	EI	Praha (O2)	7 Mar
5.84	Pawel	Wojciechowski	POL	6.6.89	1	Athl	Lausanne	9 Jul
5.82	Michal	Balner	CZE	12.9.82	4		Baku	24 Jun
	(10)							
5.81i	Robert	Sobera	POL	19.1.91	2	ISTAF	Berlin	14 Feb
5.81	Kévin	Menaldo	FRA	12.7.92	4	DL	Saint-Denis	4 Jul
5.81	Augusto	Dutra de Oliveira	BRA	16.7.90	3	DL	London (OS)	25 Jul
5.80i	Valentin	Lavillenie	FRA	16.7.91	2		Nevers	7 Feb
5.80i	Jacob	Blankenship	USA	15.3.94	2	NCAA	Fayetteville	13 Mar
5.80	Carlo	Paech	GER	18.12.92	1		Zweibrücken	14 Jun
5.78i	Ilya	Mudrov	RUS	17.11.91	3		Malmö	25 Feb
5.75i	Andrew	Irwin	USA	23.1.93	2		Fayetteville	14 Feb
5.75	Jan	Kudlicka	CZE	29.4.88	2	ET-1	Iráklio	21 Jun
5.75	Germán	Chiaraviglio	ARG	16.4.87	2	PAm	Toronto	21 Jul
	(20)							
5.72	Brad	Walker	USA	21.6.81	5	Herc	Monaco	17 Jul
5.72A	Mike	Arnold	USA	13.8.90	1		Pueblo	5 Sep
5.71Ai	Steve	Lewis	GBR	20.5.86	1		Albuquerque	6 Feb
5.70i	Anton	Ivakin	RUS	3.2.91	2		Volgograd	24 Jan
5.70i	Tobias	Scherbarth	GER	17.8.85	1	NC	Karlsruhe	22 Feb
5.70A	Jack	Whitt	USA	12.4.90	1		Ciudad de México	2 Aug
5.70	Robert	Renner	SLO	8.3.94	Q	WCh	Beijing	22 Aug
5.70	Ivan	Gertleyn	RUS	25.9.87	Q	WCh	Beijing	22 Aug
5.70	Ivan	Horvat	CRO	17.8.93	Q	WCh	Beijing	22 Aug
5.70	Seito	Yamamoto	JPN	11.3.92	1		Gifu	27 Sep
	(30)							
5.68i	Jeff	Coover	USA	1.12.87	1		Cedar Falls	20 Feb
5.66Ai	Victor	Weirich	USA	25.10.87	2		Albuquerque	6 Feb
5.65i	Hiroki	Ogita	JPN	30.12.87	1eB		Orléans	17 Jan
5.65	Jax	Thoirs	GBR	7.4.93	1	Pac-12	Los Angeles (Ww)	16 May
5.65	Adrián	Vallés	ESP	16.3.95	1		Storrs	16 May
5.65	Arnaud	Art	BEL	28.1.93	3	ET-1	Iráklio	21 Jun
5.65		Zhang Wei	CHN	22.3.94	1		Beijing	27 Jun
5.65		Yao Jie	CHN	21.9.90	2		Beijing	27 Jun
5.65	Mareks	Arents	LAT	6.8.86	3		Praha	1 Jul
5.65	Artem	Burya	RUS	11.4.86	2		Madrid	11 Jul
	(40)							
5.65	Nikita	Filippov	KAZ	7.10.91	1		Almaty	18 Jul
5.65	Vladislav	Revenko	UKR	15.11.84	1		Kyiv	21 Jul
5.65	Georgiy	Gorokhov	RUS	20.4.93	3	NC	Cheboksary	4 Aug
5.65	Scott	Houston	USA	11.6.90	1		Rock Hill	15 Aug
5.64	Peter	Geraghty	USA	11.6.91	1		La Crosse	4 Jul
5.61i	Jérôme	Clavier	FRA	3.5.83	1		Aulnay-sous-Bois	18 Dec
5.60i	Damiel	Dossévi	FRA	3.2.83	3		Orléans	17 Jan

Mark	Name		Nat	Born	Pos	Meet	Venue	Date
5.60i	Edi	Maia	POR	10.11.87	5		Orléans	17 Jan
5.60i	Luke	Cutts	GBR	13.2.88	1		Manchester	1 Feb
5.60i	Nicolas	Homo	FRA	24.11.88	4		Nevers	7 Feb
	(50)							
5.60i	Diogo	Ferreira	POR	30.7.90	4		Potsdam	7 Feb
5.60i	Chris	Pillow	USA	8.7.93	2	NC	Boston (R)	28 Feb
5.60i	Dídac	Salas	ESP	19.5.93	10q	EI	Praha (O2)	6 Mar
5.60	Adam	Hague	GBR-J	29.8.97	6	TexR	Austin	28 Mar
5.60	Reese	Watson	USA	8.10.93	3		Austin	2 May
5.60	Karsten	Dilla	GER	17.7.89	4		Zweibrücken	14 Jun
5.60A	Jordan	Scott	USA	22.2.88	2		Ciudad de México	2 Aug
5.60	Mark	Hollis	USA	1.12.84	1		Veracruz	8 Aug
5.60Ai	Cale	Simmons	USA	5.2.91	1		Air Force Academy	11 Dec
5.56	Nick	Mossberg	USA	5.4.86	1		Phoenix	8 May
	(60)							
5.56	Leonid	Kivalov	RUS	1.4.88	4		Plock	17 Jun
5.56	Przemyslaw	Czerwinski	POL	28.7.83	5		Plock	17 Jun
5.55i	Daniel	Clemens	GER	28.4.92	1		Ludwigshafen	17 Jan
5.55Ai	Joseph	Uhle	USA	14.11.92	3		Air Force Academy	24 Jan
5.55Ai	Sam	Pierson	USA	7.4.88	1		Air Force Academy	1 Feb
5.55Ai	Mike	Woepse	USA	29.5.91	1		Albuquerque	13 Feb
5.55i	Oleksandr	Korchmid	UKR	22.1.82	5		Lódz	17 Feb
5.55	Menno	Vloon	NED	11.5.94	1		Rotterdam	7 Jun
5.55	Pauls	Pujats	LAT	6.8.91	2	NCAA	Eugene	10 Jun
5.55	Hendrik	Gruber	GER	28.9.86	5		Landau	25 Jun
	(70)							
5.55	Igor	Bychkov	ESP	7.3.87	5		Madrid	11 Jul
5.55	Leonid	Kobelev	RUS	24.6.95	2	EU23	Tallinn	11 Jul
5.55	Stanley	Joseph	FRA	24.10.91	3	NC	Villeneuve d'Ascq	12 Jul
5.55	Claudio Michel	Stecchi	ITA	23.11.91	3		Liège (NX)	15 Jul
5.55	Axel	Chapelle	FRA	24.4.95	1	NC-23	Tomblaine	25 Jul
5.55	Alexandre	Feger	FRA	22.1.90	1		Castres	29 Jul
5.53	Dylan	Duvio	USA	6.4.95	1		Austin	2 May
5.53	Rasmus	Jørgensen	DEN	23.1.89	5		Leverkusen	7 Aug
5.53	Marvin	Caspari	GER	9.8.91	6		Leverkusen	7 Aug
5.53	Florian	Gaul	GER	21.9.91	7		Leverkusen	7 Aug
	(80)							
5.53		Jin Min-sub	KOR	2.9.92	8		Leverkusen	7 Aug
5.52i	Chris	Uhle	USA	14.11.92	2		Blacksburg	24 Jan
5.51	Oleg	Zernikel	GER	16.4.95	1		Kaiserslautern	5 Jul
5.51	Hiroki	Sasase	JPN	17.8.89	1		Shizuoka	12 Jul
5.51		Han Do-hyun	KOR	28.7.94	1	NSF	Gangneung	18 Oct
5.51i	Noël	Ost	FRA	15.11.89	5		Aulnay-sous-Bois	18 Dec
5.50i	Max	Eaves	GBR	31.5.88	1		Loughborough	10 Jan
5.50i	Josh	Dangel	USA	21.1.91	4		Akron	10 Jan
5.50i	Mikhail	Gelmanov	RUS	18.3.90	1		Chelyabinsk	16 Jan
5.50i		Huang Bokai	CHN-J	26.9.96	3		Düsseldorf	29 Jan
	(90)							
5.50i	Baptiste	Boirie	FRA	26.12.92	6		Nevers	7 Feb
5.50Ai	Derick	Hinch	USA	2.2.91	2		Albuquerque	13 Feb
5.50Ai	Zachary	Siegmeier	USA	8.1.91	2		Flagstaff	20 Feb
5.50i	Chase	Wolfle	USA	9.10.92	3	SEC	Lexington	28 Feb
5.50i		Xia Xiang	CHN	28.3.91	1		Shanghai	1 Mar
5.50	Seth	Arnold	USA	29.7.92	1	TexR	Austin	28 Mar
5.50	Cody	Doerflein	USA	11.6.90	1		Jonesboro	25 Apr
5.50	Aaron	Unterberger	USA	12.7.89	1		Athens, GA	9 May
5.50	Nils	Mulder	NED	25.6.87	1		Vught	6 Jun
5.50	Audie	Wyatt	USA-J	30.4.96	4	NCAA	Eugene	10 Jun
	(100)							
5.50	Mitch	Greeley	USA	5.5.86	6		Zweibrücken	14 Jun
5.50	Hicham	Cherabi	ALG	30.3.93	8		Zweibrücken	14 Jun
5.50	Danyil	Kotov	RUS	14.11.95	2	NC-23	Saransk	17 Jun
5.50	Eirik Greibrokk	Dolve	NOR	5.5.95	1		Göteborg	3 Jul
5.50	Timur	Morgunov	RUS-J	12.10.96	1		Chelyabinsk	24 Jul
5.50	Sergey	Grigoryev	KAZ	24.6.92	1		Almaty	25 Jul
5.50	Michael	Frauen	GER	19.1.86	2		Salzburg	4 Sep

Mark			Nat	Born	Date
5.48i	Casey	Bowen	USA	11.1.93	27 Feb
5.47i	Levi	Marcus	USA	18.9.94	14 Feb
5.47i	Grant	Sisserson	USA	4.2.95	21 Feb
5.47i	Nikita	Kirillov	USA	5.6.93	28 Feb
5.47i	Deakin	Volz	USA-J	12.1.97	14 Mar
5.46i	Steven	Cahoy	USA	30.7.94	7 Feb
5.46Ai	Paulo	Benavides	USA-J	27.7.97	7 Feb
5.45Ai	Logan	Cunningham	USA	30.5.91	16 Jan
5.45Ai	Dylan	Bell	USA	21.7.93	24 Jan
5.45Ai	Colton	Ross	USA	4.6.92	24 Jan
5.45i	Jason	Colwick	USA	25.1.88	31 Jan
5.45i	Max	Babits	USA	30.5.92	6 Feb

Mark	Name		Nat	Born	Pos	Meet	Venue	Date

Mark	Name		Nat	Born	Date
5.45i	Ruben	Miranda	POR	10.6.93	14 Feb
5.45i	Andrew	Sutcliffe	GBR	10.7.91	15 Feb
5.45i	Darren	Niedermeyer	USA	2.4.82	21 Feb
5.45i	Per Magne	Florvaag	NOR	21.2.93	6 Mar
5.45	Ethan	Sandusky	USA	26.6.92	10 May
5.45	Luke	Winder	USA	2.8.95	15 May
5.45	Zachary	Ziemek	USA	23.2.93	26 Jun
5.45	Sean	Collins	USA-J	29.8.97	27 Jun
5.45	Eemeli	Salomäki	FIN	11.10.87	11 Jul
5.45	Ernest John	Obiena	PHI	17.11.95	27 Sep
5.43	Akira	Onodera	JPN	2.4.80	16 Aug
5.43	Angus	Armstrong	AUS-J	17.3.97	12 Dec
5.43i	Adam	Bragg	USA	18.4.93	11 Dec
5.42	Kurtis	Marschall	AUS-J	25.4.97	15 Jan
5.42	João Gabriel	Sousa	BRA	6.11.84	14 Feb
5.42	Tomoki	Yamamoto	JPN	25.8.92	17 May
5.42	Harry	Coppell	GBR-J	11.7.96	6 Jun
5.42	Dimítrios	Patsoukákis	GRE	18.3.87	25 Jul
5.41	Ryo	Tanaka	JPN	11.12.91	11 Apr
5.41	Drew	Volz	USA	20.11.92	22 Apr
5.41	Michael	Montgomery	USA	.94	16 May
5.41	Tomas	Wecksten	FIN-J	2.11.96	5 Aug
5.40i	Thibault	Boisseau	FRA	10.10.93	10 Jan
5.40i	Dmitry	Zhelyabin	RUS	20.5.90	27 Jan
5.40Ai	John	Prader	USA	10.2.91	31 Jan
5.40i	Maksym	Mazuryk	UKR	2.4.83	8 Feb
5.40i	Dmitriy	Lyubushkin	RUS	23.3.94	19 Feb
5.40i	Ivan	Yeryomin	UKR	30.5.89	20 Feb
5.40i	Marco	Boni	ITA	21.5.84	21 Feb
5.40i		Yang Yancheng	CHN	5.1.88	25 Feb
5.40i	Adam	Pasiak	CZE	18.7.90	25 Feb
5.40	Tyler	Porter	USA	14.12.91	26 Mar
5.40	Nick	Maestretti	USA	24.7.93	26 Mar
5.40	Kyle	Wait	USA	20.2.92	16 Apr
5.40	Fábio Gomes da Silva		BRA	4.8.83	18 Apr
5.40	Nariharu	Matsuzawa	JPN	6.1.92	18 Apr
5.40		Xue Changrui	CHN	31.5.91	29 Apr
5.40	Vincent	Favretto	FRA	5.4.84	10 May
5.40	Karol	Pawlik	POL	17.3.94	7 Jun
5.40	Logan	Pflibsen	USA	11.11.91	10 Jun
5.40	Craig	Hunter	USA	18.11.94	10 Jun
5.40A	Ethan	Ostrom	USA	1.1.90	14 Jun
5.40	Dmitriy	Sokolov	RUS	16.1.93	17 Jun
5.40	Denis	Berdnikov	RUS	2.6.93	17 Jun
5.40	Shota	Doi	JPN	10.4.90	27 Jun
5.40	Jason	Wurster	CAN	23.9.84	7 Jun
5.40	Lázaro	Borges	CUB	19.6.86	21 Jul
5.40	Kota	Suzuki	JPN	18.12.95	1 Aug
5.40	Ashton	Eaton	USA	21.1.88	8 Aug
5.38i	Justin	Estala	USA	.94	7 Feb
5.38	Gonzalo	Barroilhet	CHI	19.8.86	2 May
5.38	Jesse	Johnson	USA		8 May
5.37i	Tim	Ehrhardt	USA	16.3.95	27 Feb
5.37	Sam	Bell	USA	15.5.91	25 Apr
5.37	Cole	Phillips	USA		2 May
5.36i	Mikkel M.	Nielsen	DEN	13.9.88	17 Jan
5.36	Devin	King	USA	12.3.96	18 Apr
5.36	Jordan	Yamoah	GHA	30.9.93	8 May
5.36	Terry	Batemon	USA	8.9.94	17 May
5.36 x	Alex	Bishop	USA	17.5.91	6 Jun
5.36	Masaki	Ejima	JPN	6.3.99	24 Oct
	(180)				

Exhibition

Mark	Name		Nat	Born	Date
5.38	Jordan	Yamoah	GHA	30.9.93	1 Apr

Best outdoor marks

Mark	Name	Pos	Meet	Venue	Date
5.82	Kendricks	3	Herc	Monaco	17 Jul
5.82	Lisek	3		Baku	24 Jun
5.80	Blankenship	3	TexR	Austin	28 Mar
5.71	Gripich	3	GGala	Roma	4 Jun
5.70	V Lavillenie	4	Pre	Eugene	30 May
5.70	Sobera	3	Slus	Zary	7 Jun
5.70	Scherbarth	1		Madrid	11 Jul
5.65	Irwin	1		Fayetteville	11 Apr
5.65	Ogita	1		Fukuroi	3 May
5.60	Cutts	5	TexR	Austin	28 Mar
5.55	Maia	1		Pombal	7 Jun
5.55	Ferreira	1		Avila	19 Jul
5.52	Ivakin	6		Baku	24 Jun
5.52	Clemens	1		Püttlingen	19 Jul
5.51	Mudrov	2		Rovereto	8 Sep
5.50	Huang Bokai	3		Jinan	29 Apr
5.50	Lewis	4		Austin	2 May
5.50	Coover	1		Chula Vista	23 May
5.50	Hinch	2		Chula Vista	23 May
5.50	Siegmeier	4		Chula Vista	23 May
5.50	Boirie	2		Tourcoing	24 May
5.50	Xia Xiang	3		Beijing	27 Jun
5.50	Weirich	8	NC	Eugene	27 Jun
5.50	Clavier	2		Bron	2 Jul
5.50	Ost	1		La Roche-sur-Yon	22 Jul

Mark	Name	Date
5.46	Woepse	8 May
5.45	Colwick	28 Mar
5.45	Benavides	27 Jun
5.45	Sutcliffe	28 Jun
5.45	Niedermeyer	7 Aug
5.45	Korchmid	30 Jul
5.42	Bragg	2 May
5.42	Dangel	6 Jun
5.41	Babits	11 Apr
5.41	C Uhle	11 Apr
5.41A	Pillow	17 May
5.40	Wolfle	26 Mar
5.40	Cahoy	28 Mar
5.40	Eaves	10 May
5.40	Miranda	16 May
5.40	Salas	23 May
5.40	Pasiak	14 Jun
5.40	Pierson	27 Jun
5.40	Yeryomin	21 Jul
5.40	Gelmanov	24 Jul
5.38	Volz	20 Apr
5.38	Cunningham	5 Jun
5.36	Dossévi	5 Jul

JUNIORS

See main list for top 4 juniors. 13 performances by 4 men to 5.50. Additional marks and further juniors:

Name	Mark	Pos	Meet	Venue	Date	Mark	Pos	Meet	Venue	Date
Hague	5.55i	1		Wien	31 Jan	5.50	1	EJ	Eskilstuna	19 Jul
	5.51i	1		Sheffield	17 Jan					
Huang 2+	5.50	3	AsiC	Wuhan	4 Jun	5.50	1		Beijing	8 Aug
	5.50	1		Bron	2 Jul	5.50	1	NYG	Fuzhou	22 Oct
Wyatt	5.50	1	NC-j	Eugene	27 Jun					

Mark	Name		Nat	Born	Pos	Meet	Venue	Date
5.47i	Deakin	Volz	USA	12.1.97	1		New York (Arm)	14 Mar
	5.38				1		Bloomington	20 Apr
5.46Ai	Paulo	Benavides	USA	27.7.97	1		Albuquerque	7 Feb
	5.45				2	NC-j	Eugene	27 Jun
5.45	Sean	Collins	USA	29.8.97	3	NC-j	Eugene	27 Jun
5.43	Angus	Armstrong	AUS	17.3.97	1		Sydney (Bankstown)	12 Dec
5.42	Kurtis	Marschall	AUS	25.4.97	1		Melbourne	15 Jan
5.42	Harry	Coppell (10)	GBR	11.7.96	1		Bebington	6 Jun
5.41	Tomas	Wecksten	FIN	2.11.96	1		Orimattila	5 Aug
5.36	Devin	King	USA	12.3.96	1		Baton Rouge	18 Apr
5.36	Brandon	Bray	USA	24.4.97	1		Waco	22 Apr
5.36	Masaki	Ejima	JPN-Y	6.3.99	1		Maebashi	24 Oct
5.35	Niko	Koskinen	FIN	14.7.96	2	EJ	Eskilstuna	19 Jul
5.35	José Rodolfo	Pacho	ECU	30.1.96	3	PAm-J	Edmonton	31 Jul
5.32	Luigi Robert	Colella	ITA	2.4.96	1	NC-j	Rieti	13 Jun
5.30i	Tim	Jaeger	GER	23.2.96	1	v2N-j	Lyon	28 Feb

Mark	Wind	Name		Nat	Born	Pos	Meet	Venue	Date
5.30		Aleix	Pi	ESP	27.1.96	1		Zaragoza	23 May
5.30		Alioune	Sène (20)	FRA	3.2.96	2		Valence	24 May
5.30		Koki	Kuruma	JPN	25.3.96	2		Sagamihara	18 Jul
5.30		Armand	Duplantis	SWE-Y	10.11.99	1	WY	Cali	19 Jul
5.30		Vladyslav	Malykin	UKR-Y	15.1.98	2	WY	Cali	19 Jul
5.30		Charlie	Myers	GBR	12.6.97	1	Scot Ch	Aberdeen	16 Aug

LONG JUMP

Mark	Wind	Name		Nat	Born	Pos	Meet	Venue	Date
8.52	1.8	Jeff	Henderson	USA	19.2.89	*	PAm	Toronto	22 Jul
					8.54w/4.1 x 8.21w p x 8.52				
	8.50 1.8	1 MSR	Walnut	18 Apr	8.50 p p p p p				
	8.44 -0.3	2 NC	Eugene	25 Jun	8.44 8.24w 3 8.24w 8.16w 8.40w/2.3				
	8.36 0.7	Q WCh	Beijing	24 Aug	8.36				
	8.26 0.1	2 DL	Shanghai	17 May	8.26 7.93 p p 8.01 8.08				
8.41	0.9	Zarck	Visser	RSA	15.9.89	1		Bad Langensalza	4 Jul
					7.83 8.40/1.8 8.41 x p 7.93				
8.41	0.3	Greg	Rutherford	GBR	17.11.86	1	WCh	Beijing	25 Aug
					x 8.29/-1.0 x 8.41 p p				
	8.35 1.7	1 DL	Birmingham	7 Jun	8.35 8.24 p p p				
	8.34 0.9	1 DL	Stockholm	30 Jul	8.34 8.32/0.1 8.13 p p				
	8.32 0.9	1 WK	Zürich	3 Sep	8.27/-0.3 8.21 x 8.32 p				
	8.25 0.0	1 Bisl	Oslo	11 Jun	8.16 8.25 p p p				
	8.25 0.3	Q WCh	Beijing	24 Aug	x 8.25				
8.39	1.3	Marquis	Dendy	USA	17.11.92	*	NC	Eugene	25 Jun
					8.68w 8.03w 8.54w/3.7 7.73w p 8.39				
	8.38 -0.2	1 DL	London (OS)	25 Jul	x 7.96 8.09 8.16 x 8.38				
	8.34 1.4	* NCAA	Eugene	10 Jun	8.00w x 8.43w 8.27/1.4 8.34 x				
	8.32 0.4	2 WK	Zürich	3 Sep	7.91 x 8.02 8.32 7.84 8.11				
	8.31	1	Berlin	5 Sep	7.66 7.77 7.65 8.31				
	8.28i	1 NCAA	Fayetteville	13 Mar	x 8.28 x x- x 8.27				
8.38	1.4	Rushwal	Samaai	RSA	25.9.91	1	NC	Stellenbosch	17 Apr
					8.38 x x p p p				
8.34	0.2	Jarrion	Lawson	USA	6.5.94	2	NCAA	Eugene	10 Jun
					7.88 8.24w p x 8.20w 8.34				
	8.27i	2 NCAA	Fayetteville	13 Mar	7.44 7.93 7.44 7.72 5.39 8.27				
8.34	1.5		Gao Xinglong	CHN	12.3.94	1		Beijing	7 Aug
					x 8.13 8.34 8.00 x x				
8.30i		Michel	Tornéus	SWE	26.5.86	1	EI	Praha (O2)	6 Mar
					x 8.30 8.03 p p p				
8.30	0.0?	Jeremy	Hicks ¶	USA	19.9.86	1		Houston	11 Jun
8.29	0.0	Fabrice	Lapierre (10)	AUS	17.10.83	1		Zagreb	8 Sep
					7.70 x 8.13 x 8.29 p				
	8.27 -0.1	3 WK	Zürich	3 Sep	7.68 7.51 7.97 7.97 7.91 8.27				
8.27	0.4	Aleksandr	Menkov	RUS	7.12.90	1	DL	Shanghai	17 May
					7.92 8.10 8.16 8.03 8.27 p				
	8.26 2.0	1 ET	Cheboksary	20 Jun	8.14 x 8.26 x				
8.27	0.7	Mike	Hartfield	USA	29.3.90	1		Beijing	20 May
					x x 7.98 8.27 p p				
8.26	1.3		Li Jinzhe	CHN	1.9.89	1		Beijing	8 May
8.26	0.4	Kafétien	Gomis	FRA	23.3.80	2	ET	Cheboksary	20 Jun
					x 7.86 7.91 8.26				
8.25	0.9		Wang Jianan	CHN-J	27.8.96	3	DL	Shanghai	17 May
					x x 7.96 8.25 6.72 x				
8.25	1.9	Fabian (33/16)	Heinle	GER	14.5.94	1		Oberteuringen	6 Jun
8.22	0.4	Alyn	Camara	GER	31.3.89	1		Leverkusen	5 Jun
8.21	1.8	Daniel	Bramble	GBR	14.10.90	1		Clermont	18 Apr
8.20	0.8	Tyrone	Smith	BER	7.8.86	1		Rabat	14 Jun
8.20	1.3	Sergey (20)	Polyanskiy	RUS	29.10.89	1		Yerino	9 Jul
8.19	1.9	Ignisious	Gaisah	NED	20.6.83	2		Clermont	18 Apr
8.18	1.8	Christian	Taylor	USA	18.6.90	3		Clermont	18 Apr
8.18	1.3	Yohei	Sugai	JPN	30.8.85	2	MSR	Walnut	18 Apr
8.17	1.5	Damar	Forbes	JAM	18.9.90	1		Baie Mahault	2 May
8.17	1.8		Tang Gongchen	CHN	24.4.89	1		Chanthaburi	29 Jun
8.17	1.6	Konstantin	Borichevskiy	BLR	29.5.90	1	Znam	Zhukovskiy	19 Jul
8.17	-0.5		Huang Changzhou	CHN	20.8.94	2		Beijing	8 Aug
8.16i		Eusebio	Cáceres	ESP	10.9.91	1		Karlsruhe	31 Jan
8.16	1.0	Khotso	Mokoena	RSA	6.3.85	2		Rabat	14 Jun
8.15	0.4	Radek (30)	Juska	CZE	8.3.93	1		Innsbruck	30 May

Mark	Wind	Name		Nat	Born	Pos	Meet	Venue	Date
.13	0.5	Marquise	Goodwin	USA	19.11.90	*	PAm	Toronto	22 Jul
.12i		Jarvis	Gotch	USA	25.3.92	1		Nashville	24 Jan
.12	1.7	Aleksandro	Melo	BRA	26.9.95	1		São Paulo	4 Apr
.12	0.0	Maykel	Massó	CUB-Y	8.5.99	1		La Habana	9 May
.11	1.3	Ahmad Fayez	Al-Dosari	KSA	6.9.79	1	Gulf C	Qatif	9 Apr
.11	1.6	Shin-ichiro	Shimono	JPN	10.10.90	1		Fukuoka	2 Aug
.09	1.9	Emiliano	Lasa	URU	25.1.90	1	SAmC	Lima	13 Jun
.09	0.3	Loúis	Tsátoumas	GRE	12.2.82	1	NC	Athína	26 Jul
.08	0.1	Ted	Hooper (Hou Yubo)	TPE	31.1.91	1		Irvine	1 May
.07	-0.5	Will	Claye	USA	13.6.91	*		Baie Mahault	2 May
		(40)							
.07	0.6	Julian	Reid	GBR	23.9.88	1	LI	Loughborough	17 May
.07	0.0	Higor	Alves	BRA	23.2.94	1		São Bernardo do Campo	11 Jul
.06i		Andreas	Otterling	SWE	25.5.86	3	EI	Praha (O2)	6 Mar
.06A	-0.4	Cameron	Burrell	USA	11.9.94	1	NACAC	San José, CRC	8 Aug
.05	0.5	Robert	Crowther	AUS	2.8.87	1	NC	Brisbane	29 Mar
.05		Juan Miguel	Echevarría	CUB-Y	11.8.98	1		La Habana	15 May
.05	1.2	Tomasz	Jaszczuk	POL	9.3.92	2	FBK	Hengelo	24 May
.04i		Julian	Howard	GER	3.4.89	2		Karlsruhe	31 Jan
.04	1.3	Ankit	Sharma	IND	20.7.92	1		Trivandrum	10 Feb
.04	1.3	Kumaravel	Premkumar	IND	6.2.93	3	MSR	Walnut	18 Apr
		(50)							
.04	0.0	Wilfredo	Martínez	ex-CUB	9.1.85	1		Plasencia	24 Jun
.04A	0.4	Jean Marie	Okutu	ESP	4.8.88	1		Monachil	8 Aug
.03i		Max	Hess	GER-J	13.7.96	1		Chemnitz	17 Jan
.03i		Lamont Marcell	Jacobs	ITA	26.9.94	Q		Padova	22 Feb
.03	0.2	Will	Williams	USA	31.1.95	1		Lexington	2 May
.03	1.9	Tomoya	Takamasa	JPN	13.6.93	1		Yokohama	15 May
.03	1.5	Mauro Vinícius	da Silva	BRA	26.12.86	1	NC	São Bernardo do Campo	17 May
.03	-0.7	Ashton	Eaton	USA	21.1.88	3	FBK	Hengelo	24 May
.02i		Keandre	Bates	USA-J	24.5.96	3	NCAA	Fayetteville	13 Mar
.02	1.4	Damarcus	Simpson	USA	14.7.93	1	NCAA-2	Allendale	21 May
		(60)							
.01	1.8	Bachana	Khorava	GEO	15.3.93	1	AZE Ch	Baku	5 Jun
.01	1.6	Roelf	Pienaar	RSA	23.12.93	3	NCAA	Eugene	10 Jun
.01	0.4	Pavel	Shalin	RUS	15.3.87	1		Moskva	10 Jun
.01	0.8	Lyukman	Adams	RUS	24.9.88	2		Moskva	10 Jun
.01	1.4	Denis	Eradiri	BUL	24.10.83	1	NC	Sofia	11 Jun
.01A	0.5	Darcy	Roper	AUS-Y	31.3.98	2	WY	Cali	16 Jul
.01	0.8	Aleksandr	Petrov	RUS	9.8.86	3	NC	Cheboksary	4 Aug
.00i		Vasiliy	Kopeykin	RUS	9.3.88	1	NC	Moskva	19 Feb
.00		Ndiss Kaba	Badji	SEN	21.9.83	1	NC	Saint-Louis	2 Aug
.99	0.8	Valentin	Toboc	ROU	17.3.92	1		Pitesti	7 Jun
		(70)							
.99i		Raihau	Maiau	PYF	1.8.92	1		Bompas	19 Dec
.98i		Kirill	Sukharev	RUS	24.5.92	1		Moskva	8 Feb
.98	0.5		Zhang Yaoguang	CHN	21.6.93	2	NC	Suzhou	23 Sep
.97i		Elvijs	Misans	LAT	8.4.89	1		Kuldiga	17 Jan
.97i		Adrian	Strzalkowski	POL	28.3.90	2		Torun	3 Feb
.97i		Jalen	Ramsey	USA	24.10.94	4	NCAA	Fayetteville	13 Mar
.97A	1.7	Daniel	Pineda	CHI	19.9.85	1		Monachil	11 Jul
.96	0.2	Tyron	Stewart	USA	8.7.89	3		Baie Mahault	2 May
.96	1.4	Anatoliy	Ryapolov	RUS-J	31.1.97	1		Krasnodar	23 May
.96	1.5	Chris	Tomlinson	GBR	15.9.81	7	DL	Birmingham	7 Jun
		(80)							
.95	1.7	Nick	Gordon	JAM	17.9.88	*		Kingston	28 Feb
.95	1.7	Eero	Haapala	FIN	10.7.89	1		Jämsä	27 Jun
.95	2.0	Pavel	Karavayev	RUS	27.8.88	5	NC	Cheboksary	4 Aug
.94	0.0	Junior	Díaz	CUB	28.4.87	2		La Habana	9 May
.94	1.0	Aubrey	Smith	CAN	30.6.88	1		Clermont	16 May
.93	1.8	Leon	Hunt	ISV	17.5.87	2		Clermont	16 May
.93	1.3	Henri	Väyrynen	FIN	16.10.91	2		Jämsä	27 Jun
.93	0.5	Benjamin	Gföhler	SUI	27.1.94	5	EU23	Tallinn	10 Jul
.92i			Li Zhipeng	CHN	1.5.95	4		Xianlin	8 Mar
.92	0.1		Kim Duk-hyung	KOR	8.12.85	1		Yecheon	23 Apr
		(90)							
.92	1.2	Marko	Prugovecki	CRO	1.1.87	1		Zagreb	9 Jun
.91i		Cedric	Nolf	BEL	18.6.89	1	NC	Gent	21 Feb
.91i		Cameron	Echols-Luper	USA	9.4.95	5	NCAA	Fayetteville	13 Mar
.91	0.0	Yuhi	Oiwa	JPN	17.2.91	*		Fukuoka	4 Apr
.91	0.9	Tiago	da Silva	BRA	23.10.93	2		São Paulo	4 Apr

Mark	Wind	Name		Nat	Born	Pos	Meet	Venue	Date
7.91	0.0		Fang Yaoqing	CHN-J	20.4.96	Q		Fuzhou	28 May
7.91	1.9	Adoreé	Jackson	USA	18.9.95	5	NCAA	Eugene	10 Jun
7.91	1.4	Salim	Sdiri	FRA	26.10.78	1		Artashat	5 Sep
7.90	0.9	Saleh Abdelaziz	Al-Haddad	KUW	7.4.86	2	Gulff C	Qatif	9 Ap
7.90	1.2	Dino (100)	Pervan	CRO	12.1.91	2		Zagreb	9 Jun
7.90	0.1	Tadius	Okpara	NGR-J	7.7.96	1		Warri	24 Ju

Mark	Wind	Name		Nat	Born	Date
7.89	2.0	Hussein Taher	Al-Sabee	KSA	14.11.79	18 Apr
7.89	1.5	Artyom	Bondarenko	BLR	14.1.91	26 May
7.89	0.9		Chan Ming Tai	HKG	30.1.95	12 Jul
7.89	0.1	Samson	Idiata	NGR	28.2.82	31 Jul
7.88i		Sergiu	Caciuriac	ROU	22.4.93	15 Feb
7.88i			Zhang Yu	CHN	17.7.92	8 Mar
7.88	1.4	Henry	Frayne	AUS	14.4.90	29 Mar
7.88	1.7	Mohamed	Al-Absi	KSA	9.2.93	18 Apr
7.88	0.5	Hiroyuki	Fukasawa	JPN	10.12.92	15 May
7.88A		Sobhan	Taherkhani	IRI	21.9.92	20 May
7.88	2.0	Kota	Minemura	JPN	22.12.92	19 Jul
7.88	0.0	Adrian	Vasile	ROU	9.4.86	26 Jul
7.88A	2.0	Kamal	Fuller	JAM	20.1.91	8 Aug
7.87i		Kevin	Ojiaku	ITA	20.4.89	1 Feb
7.87i		Rain	Kask	EST	11.6.91	22 Feb
7.87i		Aaron	George	USA	2.8.95	23 Feb
7.87	0.0	Angus	Gould	AUS	8.1.94	21 Mar
7.87	0.0	Lutalo	Boyce	USA	11.8.91	21 May
7.87	0.3	Luis	Rivera	MEX	21.6.87	24 May
7.87	0.8	Jonathan	Addison	USA	27.2.95	28 May
7.87	1.4	Ifeanyi	Otuonye	TKS	27.6.94	29 May
7.87	1.8	Dmitriy	Plotnikov	RUS	30.1.87	6 Jun
7.87	1.0	Daiki	Oda	JPN-J	15.1.96	7 Jun
7.87	2.0	Vladyslav	Mazur	UKR-J	21.11.96	15 Jun
7.87	1.3		Kim Duk-hyung	KOR	8.12.85	27 Jun
7.87	0.8	Maksim	Kolesnikov	RUS	28.2.91	9 Aug
7.86i		Keneil	Grant	JAM	13.9.93	21 Feb
7.86	1.1	Mikese	Morse	USA	30.10.87	22 May
7.86		Mamadou	Guèye	SEN	1.4.86	2 Aug
7.86A		Mohammad	Arzandeh	IRI	30.10.87	2 Sep
7.85	0.4	David	Registe	DMA	2.5.88	17 Apr
7.85	0.3	Yan	Chaginov	RUS	13.6.90	3 Jul
7.85	1.1	Jared	Kerr	CAN	25.6.95	5 Jul
7.85	1.3	Fyodor	Kiselkov	RUS	3.6.95	9 Jul
7.85	1.2	Ezekiel	Ewulo	NGR	29.1.86	31 Jul
7.85	-0.9		Lin Hung-Min	TPE	7.9.90	18 Oct
7.84i		Stefano	Tremigliozzi	ITA	7.5.85	1 Feb
7.84i		Cameron	Hudson	USA	5.3.94	13 Feb
7.84	1.3	Curtis	Beach	USA	22.7.90	22 May
7.84	1.0	Ventavius	Sears	USA	14.5.95	28 May
7.84	1.2	Grant	Holloway	USA-J	19.11.97	6 Jun
7.84	1.3	Krzysztof	Tomasiak	POL	3.4.90	13 Jun
7.84	0.8	Semen	Popov	RUS	26.5.94	16 Jun
7.84	1.2		Kim Jang-jun	KOR	10.5.87	27 Jun
7.84	1.2	Norris	Frederick	USA	17.2.86	4 Ju
7.83i		Dmitriy	Bobkov	RUS	20.3.88	19 Feb
7.83	0.5		Lin Qing	CHN	5.4.95	30 Ap
7.82i		Braxton	Drummond	USA	1.7.94	17 Jan
7.82i		Trey	McRae	USA	12.7.93	24 Jan
7.82i			Jie Lei	CHN	8.5.89	15 Ma
7.82	2.0	Rikiya	Saruyama	JPN	15.2.84	4 Ap
7.82	0.9	Diego	Hernández	VEN	21.2.95	17 Ap
7.82	1.5	Eric	Sloan	USA	20.6.94	17 Ap
7.82	1.5	Blake	Smith	USA	28.5.93	15 May
7.82	0.3	Anastásios	Galazoúlas #	GRE	2.10.92	14 Jun
7.82	0.2	Corentin	Campener	BEL	5.10.90	27 Jun
7.82	1.6		Li Chengbin	CHN	22.2.90	29 Jun
7.82A	-0.1	Caio	dos Santos	BRA	24.3.93	5 Ju
7.82	0.7	Sho	Matsubara	JPN	19.4.93	5 Aug
7.82	1.5	Kodai	Sakuma	JPN-J	29.4.96	18 Oc
7.81i		Nelson	Évora	POR	20.4.84	14 Feb
7.81	0.9	Jordan	Latimer	USA	4.3.94	28 May
7.81	0.6	Natsuki	Yamakawa	JPN	24.7.95	7 Jun
7.81	0.1	Pedro Pablo	Pichardo	CUB	30.6.93	20 Jun
7.81	0.6	Michael	Schrader	GER	1.7.87	27 Jun
7.81	0.8	Fredrik	Samuelsson	SWE	16.2.95	11 Ju
7.81	1.8	Guillaume	Victorin	FRA	26.5.90	29 Ju
7.81	1.6	Toyin	Oladimeji	NGR	5.6.93	31 Ju
7.80i		Sergey	Mikhailovskiy	RUS	11.5.87	24 Jan
7.80i		Adam	McMullen	IRL	5.7.90	22 Feb
7.80i		Ja'Mari	Ward	USA-Y	21.7.98	14 Ma
7.80	0.3	Olivier	Huet	FRA	11.2.89	18 Ap
7.80	2.0	Ramone	Bailey	JAM	31.10.91	2 May
7.80	0.0	Kristian	Pulli	FIN	2.9.94	3 Jun
7.80	0.0	Taras	Neledva	UKR	7.6.92	8 Jun
7.80	-1.2	Andrey	Ovcharenko	RUS	21.4.94	16 Jun
7.80	1.9	Jonathan	Drack	MRI	6.11.88	27 Ju
7.80	1.6		Ju Eun-jae	KOR	12.6.93	27 Ju
7.80	0.4	Sergey	Morgunov	RUS	9.2.93	9 Ju
7.80	1.2	Jean-Pierre	Bertrand	FRA	5.11.92	13 Ju
7.80		Janaka Prasad	Wimalasiri	SRI	8.9.92	26 Ju
		(182)				

Wind assisted

Mark	Wind	Name		Nat	Born	Pos	Meet	Venue	Date
8.68	3.7	Marquis	Dendy	USA	17.11.92	1	NC	Eugene	25 Jun
8.54	4.1	Jeff	Henderson	USA	19.2.89	1	PAm	Toronto	22 Ju
8.43	2.3		Dendy	(see main list)		1	NCAA	Eugene	10 Jun
8.42	2.5	Mike	Hartfield	USA	29.3.90	3	NC	Eugene	25 Jun
					8.15w	x	x	8.26w/2.5 6.42w	8.42w
8.37	3.6	Marquise	Goodwin	USA	19.11.90	4	NC	Eugene	25 Jun
					8.01w	8.09w	8.02w	8.37w 8.04	8.28w/3.2
	8.27	4.5	2 PAm	Toronto 22	Jul	8.13	x	8.27w x	8.06w
x									
8.36	2.4	Jarrion	Lawson	USA	6.5.94	5	NC	Eugene	25 Jun
					8.11w	8.33w/2.4	8.08	x 8.35w/3.0	8.36w
8.29	2.3	David	Registe	DMA	2.5.88	1		Azusa	17 Ap
					7.85	7.67	7.85	8.29w	
8.29	6.5	Pavel	Shalin	RUS	15.3.87	1	WUG	Gwangju	12 Ju
		(9/7)			7.75	7.95	8.29w	7.76 7.79	x
8.22	3.0	Konstantin	Borichevskiy	BLR	29.5.90	1	NC	Grodno	25 Ju
8.17	3.5	Cameron	Burrell	USA	11.9.94	6	NC	Eugene	25 Jun
8.17	3.1	Emiliano	Lasa	URU	25.1.90	3	PAm	Toronto	22 Ju
8.14	4.1	Laderrick	Ward	USA	28.12.92	1	NCAA-W	Austin	28 May
8.14	4.5	Raihau	Maiau	PYF	1.8.92	1		Port Moresby	17 Ju
8.13	3.1	Roelf	Pienaar	RSA	23.12.93	1		Jonesboro	24 Ap
8.13	4.4	Vasiliy	Kopeykin	RUS	9.3.88	2	WUG	Gwangju	12 Ju
8.13	2.5	Andreas	Otterling	SWE	25.5.86	1		Karlstad	22 Ju
8.12	2.5	Mamadou	Guèye	SEN	1.4.86	1		Dakar	23 May
8.11	2.4	Will	Claye	USA	13.6.91	2		Baie Mahault	2 May
8.08	2.1	Kota	Minemura	JPN	22.12.92	1		Kobe	26 Ap

Mark	Wind	Name		Nat	Born	Pos	Meet	Venue	Date
.08	2.5	Tomasz	Jaszczuk	POL	9.3.92	1		Biala Podlaska	30 May
.08	2.4	Julian	Reid	GBR	23.9.88	2		Marseille	6 Jun
.08	2.5	Ronald	Brookins	USA	5.7.89	1		Chula Vista	13 Jun
.04	4.0	Olabanji	Asekun	USA	15.7.92	1	TexR	Austin	28 Mar
.04	3.2	Samson	Idiata	NGR	28.2.82	1		Huelva	10 Jun
.03	2.4	Damarcus	Simpson	USA	14.7.93	7	NC	Eugene	25 Jun
.02	2.7	Biliaminu	Lawal	USA	12.3.85	1		Norwalk	6 Jun
.02	2.9	Mikese	Morse	USA	30.10.87	9	NC	Eugene	25 Jun
.01	w?	Mikese	Morse	USA	30.10.87	4		Clermont	18 Apr
.01	3.7	Hiroyuki	Fukasawa	JPN	10.12.92	2		Yokohama	15 May
.01	2.8		Zhang Yaoguang	CHN	21.6.93	1		Shanghai	15 Jul
.99	2.3	Jonathan	Addison	USA	27.2.95	4	NCAA	Eugene	10 Jun
.99	2.4	Diego	Hernández	VEN	21.2.95	5	PAm	Toronto	22 Jul
.98	2.3	Yuhi	Oiwa	JPN	17.2.91	1		Fukuoka	4 Apr
.98	1.4	Ifeanyi	Otuonye	TKS	27.6.94	1		Lawrence	2 May
.98A	5.7	Ventavius	Sears	USA	14.5.95	1		El Paso	17 May
.96	5.8	Cameron	Echols-Luper	USA	9.4.95	3	TexR	Austin	28 Mar
.96	2.8	Saleh Abdelaziz	Al-Haddad	KUW	7.4.86	1	Arab C	Manama	27 Apr
.95	4.3	Paulo Sérgio	Oliveira	BRA	1.6.93	2		Huelva	10 Jun
.95	3.0	Maksim	Kolesnikov	RUS	28.2.91	1	Kuso	Szczecin	9 Aug
.94	3.0	Ronald	Taylor	USA	13.8.90	2		Chula Vista	13 Jun

Mark	Wind	Name		Nat	Born	Date
.91	2.1		Kim Jang-jun	KOR	10.5.87	18 Jun
.90A	4.8	Donovant	Arriola	PHI	16.1.92	18 Apr
.90	2.9	Ezekiel	Ewulo	NGR	29.1.86	21 Jun
.90A	2.4	Kamal	Fuller	JAM	20.1.91	8 Aug
.88	2.7	Eric	Sloan	USA	20.6.94	17 Apr
.88	2.5	Manuel	Ziegler	GER	28.7.90	18 Apr
.88	2.5	Tenju	Togawa	JPN-J	8.1.97	13 Jun
.87	2.7	Shontaro	Shiroyama	JPN	6.3.95	26 Apr
.86	2.2	Latario	Collie-Minns	BAH	10.3.94	4 Apr
.86	3.6	Yasuhiro	Moro	JPN	21.12.94	26 Apr
.86		Andreas	Trajkovski	DEN	18.3.93	1 May
.86	4.0	(7.92i)	Li Zhipeng	CHN	1.5.95	8 May
.86	3.9	Lavon	Allen	USA	26.11.90	17 May
.86	3.0	Melvin	Echard	USA	29.8.89	25 Jun
7.85	2.2	Ngonidzashe	Makusha	ZIM	11.3.87	8 May
7.84	2.1	Yves	Zellweger	SUI	27.3.87	23 May
7.84	2.3	Jonathan	Drack	MRI	6.11.88	27 Jun
7.83	6.4	Rogério	Bispo	BRA	16.11.85	28 Feb
7.83	4.2	Trevor	Ferguson	USA	4.6.91	28 May
7.83	2.3	Takuma	Ito	JPN	2.8.94	1 Aug
7.82	3.3	Bruno	Costa	POR	3.5.92	9 May
7.81	2.1	Danylo	Martins	BRA	21.11.92	28 Feb
7.81	2.2	Yann	Randrianasolo	FRA	3.2.94	18 Apr
7.80	4.6	Duwayne	Boer	RSA	6.1.95	17 Apr
7.80	2.1	Bryan	McBride	USA	10.12.91	28 May
7.80	3.2	Walter	Jones	USA	6.7.95	28 May
7.80	2.8	Benjamin	Gabrielsen	DEN	13.6.95	13 Jun
7.80	2.9	Jorge	McFarlane	PER	20.2.88	21 Jul

Best outdoor marks

Mark	Wind	Name	Pos	Meet	Venue	Date
.06	1.5	Otterling	3		Bad Langensalza	4 Jul
.06	0.3	Cáceres	4	DL	Saint-Denis	4 Jul
.98	1.7	Maiau	3		Marseille	6 Jun
.97	0.9	Howard	1		Mannheim	15 Jul
7.96	0.0	Ramsey	1	ACC	Tallahassee	14 May
7.96	0.2	Sukharev	4	Znam	Zhukovskiy	19 Jul
7.96	1.5	Kopeykin	2		Karlstad	22 Jul

Mark	Wind	Name	Date
.88	1.6	Strzalkowski	9 Aug
.88	1.6	Misans	16 Aug
7.88i		Addison	7 Feb
7.83	-0.2	Tornéus	28 Jul
7.80	-2.1	Cacuriac	27 Jun
7.83w	6.1	Nolf	12 Jul

Mark	Wind	Name	Pos	Meet	Venue	Date
.07w	3.2	Tornéus	1	NC	Söderhamn	8 Aug
7.97w	3.0	Bates	3	SEC	Starkville	15 May

Low altitude bests

Mark	Wind	Name	Pos	Meet	Venue	Date
.96i	1.0	Okutu	1		Antequera	21 Feb
7.90	1.0		1		Zaragoza	13 Jun
7.99	2.1		1		Orense	18 Jul
7.92	0.1	Pineda	1		Santiago de Chile	11 Apr
7.91	1.6	Roper	3	NC	Brisbane	29 Mar
7.82	0.1	Burrell	2		Houston	11 Jun

With prosthetic legs

Mark	Wind	Name		Nat	Born	Pos	Meet	Venue	Date
.40	1.8	Markus	Rehm	GER	22.8.88	1	IPC	Doha	23 Oct

x 7.97w 8.40 8.03w x x

Drugs disqualification

Mark	Wind	Name		Nat	Born	Pos	Meet	Venue	Date
.91	1.2	Anastásios	Galazoulas #	GRE	2.10.92	(1)		Kalamáta	29 May

JUNIORS

See main list for top 9 juniors. 11 performances (inc. 2 indoors) by 6 men to 7.98. Additional marks and further juniors:

Name	Mark	Wind	Pos	Meet	Venue	Date	Mark	Wind	Pos	Venue	Date
Wang	8.18	0.0	3	WCh	Beijing	25 Aug	8.09	0.5	2	Beijing	8 May
	8.12	0.4	Q	WCh	Beijing	24 Aug	8.09	0.0	5	Beijing	20 May
Massó	8.05A	0.5	1	WY	Cali	16 Jul					

Mark	Wind	Name		Nat	Born	Pos	Meet	Venue	Date
.87	1.0	Daiki	Oda (10)	JPN	15.1.96	1		Tokyo	7 Jun
.87	2.0	Vladyslav	Mazur	UKR	21.11.96	1		Kharkiv	15 Jun
.84	1.2	Grant	Holloway	USA	19.11.97	1		Newport News	6 Jun
.82	1.5	Kodai	Sakuma	JPN	29.4.96	1	NC-j	Mizuho	18 Oct
.80i		Ja'Mari	Ward	USA-Y	21.7.98	1		New York	14 Mar
		7.78	1.8			1		Belleville	28 Apr
.78	0.3	Serhiy	Honcharenko	UKR	17.3.96	2	NC-j	Kharkiv	15 Jun
.77	0.0	Samory	Fraga	BRA	29.11.96	1		Porto Alegre	20 Jun
.76A	0.1	Eberson	Silva	BRA-Y	25.7.99	3	WY	Cali	16 Jul
.76	-1.1	Filippo	Randazzo	ITA	27.4.96	1	NC	Torino	25 Jul
.75	0.0	Jacob	Fincham-Dukes	GBR	12.1.97	2	EJ	Eskilstuna	17 Jul
.74i			Lu Tianjie	CHN	15.3.96	4		Shanghai	1 Mar
.74	0.9	Kirii	Matsuzoe	JPN	22.9.96	3		Yokohama	15 May
.74	0.6	Kazuma	Adachi	JPN	16.10.97	1		Wakayama	31 Jul

Mark Wind Name Nat Born Pos Meet Venue Date

Wind assisted

7.88 2.5 Tenju Togawa JPN 8.1.97 1 Hiratsuka 13 Ju
7.79 4.2 Nate Moore USA 28.5.96 11q NCAA-W Austin 28 Ma
7.76 2.9 Saahir Bethea USA 11.9.96 1 Shippensburg 23 Ma

TRIPLE JUMP

18.21 0.2 Christian Taylor USA 18.6.90 1 WCh Beijing 27 Au
16.85 17.49/0.2 17.60/0.2 17.68/0.1 17.22/0.1 18.21
18.06 1.1 1 Athl Lausanne 9 Jul 17.33/1.0 17.76/1.1 17.24/1.2 x 18.02/0.8 18.06
18.04 0.8 2 DL Doha 15 May 17.01 17.46/2.0 16.97 17.05 x 18.04
17.75 -0.8 1 Herc Monaco 17 Jul 17.33/0.0 17.75 17.33/-0.3 17.43/-0.7 17.74/0/3 17.64/-0.
17.59 0.1 1 VD Bruxelles 11 Sep 17.06 17.46/0.2 16.89 p 17.59 17.48/0.
17.52 -0.8 1 GS Ostrava 26 May 16.84 16.99 17.52 p x 16.83
17.40 0.7 1 DL Birmingham 7 Jun 17.14w 17.37/0.4 17.40 17.37/0.9 17.26/1.0 x
17.28 0.3 Q WCh Beijing 26 Aug 16.77 17.28
18.08 0.0 Pedro Pablo Pichardo CUB 30.6.93 1 Barr La Habana 28 Ma
17.93/0.2 18.08 p p p p
18.06 0.8 1 DL Doha 15 May 17.33/0.5 x 18.06 p p 17.79/1.
17.99 1.8 2 Athl Lausanne 9 Jul 17.85/1.4 17.28/1.4 17.99 16.74 x 15.33
17.96 -0.4 1 GGala Roma 4 Jun 17.58/-0.5 17.96 x p p x
17.94 0.0 1 La Habana 8 May 17.34/0.0 17.52/-1.7 17.94 p p p
17.73 1.0 2 Herc Monaco 17 Jul 15.10 17.66/-0.2 16.86 17.73 x x
17.73 0.2 2 WCh Beijing 27 Aug 17.52/-0.6 17.44/0.2 17.60/0.2 17.33/-0.1 17.52/-1.4 17.7
17.56 -2.5 1 adidas New York 13 Jun 17.54/-0.2 17.56 p p p p
17.46 1.5 * PAm Toronto 24 Jul 17.29/-1.1 x 17.46 17.54w/2.1 p 17.34/-0.7
17.43 0.4 Q WCh Beijing 26 Aug 16.94 x 17.43
17.53 1.0 Omar Craddock USA 26.4.91 1 NC Eugene 28 Ju
16.85 x 16.79 17.53 17.40/0.7 16.32
17.37 0.2 4 WCh Beijing 27 Aug 17.14 17.08 x 17.14 17.37 16.50
17.35 0.8 3 Herc Monaco 17 Jul 17.05 17.35 17.08 17.16 17.14 17.28/-0.6
17.52 0.3 Nelson Évora POR 20.4.84 3 WCh Beijing 27 Au
17.28/0.3 x 17.29/-0.6 x x 17.52
17.50 1.2 Marquis Dendy USA 17.11.92 * NCAA Eugene 12 Ju
17.50 16.53 17.15 17.54w/3.6 16.91w 17.71w
17.37i 1 NCAA Fayetteville 14 Mar x 16.46 16.58 17.07 x 17.37
17.48 0.5 Will Claye USA 13.6.91 2 NC Eugene 28 Ju
17.07 17.16 x 17.44/1.4 17.43/1.2 17.48
17.38 1.5 * Chula Vista 22 May 17.38w/3.7 17.22w/2.4 17.50w 17.34w/3.5 x 17.38
17.42 1.9 Aleksey Fyodorov RUS 25.5.91 1 Sochi 29 Ma
16.45w 17.42 p x x x
17.34 1.7 Lyukman Adams RUS 24.9.88 1 NC Cheboksary 5 Au
17.34 14.26 x 16.90 17.07w p
17.28 0.3 5 WCh Beijing 27 Aug x 17.12 17.28 x 17.21/0.0 17.23/0.
17.29 0.2 Dmitriy Sorokin RUS 27.9.92 1 WUG Gwangju 9 Ju
(30/9) x 16.92 17.29 x p x
17.24 0.7 Teddy Tamgho (10) FRA 15.6.89 3 DL Doha 15 Ma
17.20 1.7 Dmitriy Chizhikov RUS 6.12.93 1 NC-23 Saransk 17 Ju
17.18 1.9 Latario Collie-Minns BAH 10.3.94 * SEC Starkville 16 Ma
17.15 -0.4 Alexis Copello ex-CUB 12.8.85 2 GGala Roma 4 Ju
17.12 1.5 Dong Bin CHN 22.11.88 * Sapporo 12 Ju
17.07 1.5 Marian Oprea ROU 6.6.82 Q WCh Beijing 26 Au
17.04i Pablo Torrijos ESP 12.5.92 2 EI Praha (O2) 7 Ma
17.04 1.5 Nazim Babayev AZE-J 8.10.97 1 EJ Eskilstuna 19 Ju
17.03 0.5 Georgi Tsonov BUL 2.5.93 1 Stara Zagora 18 Ju
17.02 Lázaro Martínez CUB-J 3.11.97 1 La Habana 15 Ma
17.02 0.9 Ernesto Revé CUB 26.2.92 2 Barr La Habana 28 Ma
(20)
17.01 2.0 Benjamin Compaoré FRA 5.8.87 2 DL Birmingham 7 Ju
17.00i Roman Valiyev KAZ 27.3.84 1 NC Ust-Kamenogorsk 15 Fe
17.00 1.8 Kim Duk-hyung KOR 8.12.85 * Sapporo 12 Ju
17.00 0.5 Tosin Oke NGR 1.10.80 1 AfG Brazzaville 14 Se
16.99 1.7 Leevan Sands BAH 16.8.81 1 PAm Toronto 24 Ju
16.98A 1.4 Yordanys Durañona DMA 16.6.88 1 NACAC San José, CRC 7 Au
16.98 0.9 Olu Olamigoke NGR 19.9.90 2 AfG Brazzaville 14 Se
16.96 1.5 Jonathan Drack MRI 6.11.88 1 Castres 29 Ju
16.95 1.0 Chris Benard USA 4.4.90 4 NC Eugene 28 Ju
16.95 0.0 Julian Reid GBR 23.9.88 1 NC Birmingham 4 Ju
(30)
16.94 0.8 Nathan Douglas GBR 4.12.82 2 NC Birmingham 4 Ju
16.93 0.4 Xu Xiaolong CHN 20.12.92 1 Taiyuan 13 Ma

Mark	Wind	Name		Nat	Born	Pos	Meet	Venue	Date
16.91	0.5	Fabrizio	Donato	ITA	14.8.76	1	NC	Torino	26 Jul
16.90	2.0	Ilya	Potaptsev	RUS	19.4.93	1	NC-23	Saransk	17 Jun
16.89	0.9	Alphonso	Jordan	USA	1.11.87	5	NC	Eugene	28 Jun
16.87	1.7	Rumen	Dimitrov	BUL	19.9.86	2		Stara Zagora	18 Jul
16.86	1.4	Fabrizio	Schembri	ITA	27.1.81	*		Savona	11 Jul
16.85	0.5	Khotso	Mokoena	RSA	6.3.85	1		Kuortane	8 Aug
16.84i		Donald	Scott	USA	23.2.92	2	NCAA	Fayetteville	14 Mar
16.83	0.3		Wu Ruiting	CHN	29.11.95	2	NC	Suzhou	25 Sep
		(40)							
16.81i		Aleksandr	Yurchenko	RUS	30.7.92	1		Orenburg	26 Feb
16.81		Andy	Diaz	CUB	25.12.95	2		La Habana	15 May
16.81	0.5	Adrian	Swiderski	POL	26.9.86	1		Biala Podlaska	30 May
16.81	1.5	Jean Marc	Pontvianne	FRA	6.8.94	1	NC-23	Tomblaine	26 Jul
16.81	1.5	Harold	Corréa	FRA	26.6.88	*		Castres	29 Jul
16.80	1.3	Jean	Rosa	BRA	1.2.90	1		São Bernardo do Campo	15 Mar
16.79	1.2		Fu Haitao	CHN	1.11.93	2		Taiyuan	13 May
16.79	1.1	Josh	Honeycutt	USA	7.3.89	1		Phoenix	12 Jun
16.78	0.0		Li Jialei	CHN	14.9.94	3		Taiyuan	13 May
16.78	1.5	José Ernesto	Martínez	CUB	1.1.91	3	Barr	La Habana	28 May
		(50)							
16.77i		Aleksey	Tsapik	BLR	4.8.88	1		Mogilev	27 Feb
16.77	-0.1		Cao Shuo	CHN	8.10.91	2	AsiC	Wuhan	6 Jun
16.76	-0.2	Muhammad Hakimi	Ismail	MAS	8.4.91	1	SEAG	Singapore	9 Jun
16.76	1.9	Louhab	Kafia	ALG	24.2.87	1		Alger	17 Jun
16.76	0.4	Fabrice	Zango	BUR	25.6.93	2	WUG	Gwangju	9 Jul
16.75	1.8	Brandon	Roulhac	USA	13.12.83	1		Clermont	18 Apr
16.74	-0.1	Seref	Osmanoglu	TUR	2.1.89	2	ECCp	Mersin	31 May
16.74	1.4	Ben	Williams	GBR	25.1.92	4	NCAA	Eugene	12 Jun
16.71i		Chris	Carter	USA	11.3.89	1		Houston	31 Jan
16.68A	-0.3	Sergio	Solanas	ESP	28.4.87	1		Monachil	11 Jul
		(60)							
16.67i		Jorge	Gimeno	ESP	16.2.90	2	NC	Antequera	22 Feb
16.66i		Maksim	Nesterenko	BLR	1.9.92	1		Minsk	16 Jan
16.66	1.5	Renjith	Maheswary	IND	30.1.86	1		Trivandrum	12 Feb
16.65i		Dmitriy	Plotnitskiy	BLR	26.8.88	1	NC	Mogilev	20 Feb
16.65	1.2	Nathan	Fox	GBR	21.10.90	1		Warri	24 Jul
16.65	1.6	Fabian	Florant	NED	1.2.83	1	NC	Amsterdam	2 Aug
16.63	1.5	Kevin	Luron	FRA	8.11.91	1		Montgeron	17 May
16.63	1.0	Vladislav	Poluboyarov	RUS	17.4.94	3	NC-23	Saransk	17 Jun
16.63A		Elijah	Kimitei	KEN	25.12.86	1	WCT	Nairobi	1 Aug
16.62	0.6	Jefferson	Sabino	BRA	4.11.82	1		São Bernardo do Campo	19 Apr
		(70)							
16.61i		Manuel	Ziegler	GER	28.7.90	1		Blacksburg	28 Jan
16.61	1.6	Louis-Grégory	Occin	FRA	2.6.89	*		Saint-Denis	26 Jun
16.60	1.4	Dimítrios	Baltadoúros	GRE	1.10.89	2	Balk C	Pitesti	2 Aug
16.59i		Zlatozar	Atanasov	BUL	12.12.89	1	NC	Dobrich	14 Feb
16.58	1.6	Lasha	Torgvaidze	GEO	26.5.93	1		Baku	6 Jun
16.58	1.9	Momchil	Karailiev	BUL	21.5.82	2		Ruen	7 Jun
16.58	0.8	Issam	Nima	ALG	8.4.79	1		Alger	8 Aug
16.55	0.5		Fang Yaoqing	CHN-J	20.4.96	4		Taiyuan	13 May
16.55	1.7	Adil	Gandou	FRA	18.8.93	2		Montgeron	17 May
16.55	1.6	Jhon Freddy	Murillo	COL	13.6.84	1	SAmC	Lima	14 Jun
		(80)							
16.55	0.6	Stefano	Magnini	ITA	17.11.88	2	NC	Torino	26 Jul
16.55	0.6	Vladimir	Letnicov	MDA	7.10.81	4	Balk C	Pitesti	2 Aug
16.55	0.3	Mamadou Cherif	Dia	MLI	13.3.85	3	AfG	Brazzaville	14 Sep
16.54	-0.4	Tobia	Bocchi	ITA-J	7.4.97	3	NC	Torino	26 Jul
16.52	0.1	Alvaro	Cortéz	CHI	27.10.95	1		Santiago de Chile	11 Apr
16.50	2.0	Fyodor	Kiselkov	RUS	3.6.95	4	NC-23	Saransk	17 Jun
16.50		Mamadou	Guèye	SEN	1.4.86	1	NC	St-Louis de Sénégal	31 Jul
16.49	1.6	Andrea	Chiari	ITA	12.2.91	4	NC	Torino	26 Jul
16.49	-0.5	Daigo	Hasegawa	JPN	27.2.90	1		Gifu	27 Sep
16.48		Leslie	Caesa	CUB-J	14.1.97	3		La Habana	15 May
		(90)							
16.47	-1.0	Michael	Wamer	USA	21.12.94	3	FlaR	Gainesville	4 Apr
16.47	0.8	Rashid Ahmed	Al-Mannai	QAT	18.6.88	*		Stara Zagora	18 Jul
16.46	-0.9	Mateus	de Sá	BRA	21.11.95	2		São Bernardo do Campo	15 Mar
16.46	-0.9	Mark	Jackson	USA	12.10.91	1		San Marcos	25 Apr
16.45i		Dimítrios	Tsiámis	GRE	12.1.82	1		Athina (E)	24 Jan
16.45i		Jonathan	Gardner	USA	10.12.91	3		Blacksburg	28 Feb
16.45		Cristian	Nápoles	CUB-Y	27.11.98	4		La Habana	15 May

Mark	Wind	Name		Nat	Born	Pos	Meet	Venue	Date
16.45	-0.1		Lu Zhiwei	CHN-J	4.4.96	4	NC	Suzhou	25 Sep
16.44i		Matthew	O'Neal	USA	10.6.94	6	NCAA	Fayetteville	14 Ma
16.44	0.8	Igor	Spasovkhodskiy	RUS	1.8.79	4	NC	Cheboksary	5 Au
		(100)							

Mark	Wind	Name		Nat	Born	Date
16.43	1.4	Jonathan	Silva	BRA	21.7.91	18 Apr
16.43	0.8	Samyr	Laine	HAI	17.7.84	24 Jul
16.42i		Artyom	Primak	RUS	14.1.93	17 Jan
16.42i		Keandre	Bates	USA-J	24.5.96	14 Mar
16.42	0.7	Bruno	de Souza	BRA	29.9.95	19 Apr
16.42	0.2		Kim Dong-han	KOR	5.6.89	21 Oct
16.41	0.9	Arpinder	Singh	IND	30.12.92	12 Feb
16.41	1.4	Yuma	Okabe	JPN	13.7.90	2 Aug
16.40	-0.8	Roger	Haitengi	NAM	12.9.83	14 Sep
16.39i		Ulrick	Bolosier	FRA	12.5.91	21 Feb
16.39	0.1	Yevgeniy	Chettykbayev	KAZ	29.3.88	25 Jul
16.37	0.0	Miguel	van Assen	SUR-J	30.7.97	16 May
16.37	1.5	Viktor	Yastrebov	UKR	13.1.82	9 Jun
16.36	-0.1	Carlos	Veiga	POR	22.2.89	6 Jun
16.35Ai		Milad	Darisavi	IRI	7.4.92	13 Feb
16.35	0.6	Kazuyoshi	Ishikawa	JPN	6.11.82	27 Sep
16.34i		Max	Hess	GER-J	13.7.96	25 Jan
16.34	0.0	Divie	Murillo	COL	3.6.93	14 Jun
16.33A	0.0	Yoann	Rapinier	FRA	29.9.89	21 Mar
16.32	1.7	Elton	Walcott	TTO	23.2.92	28 Jun
16.31i		Alexandru	Baciu	ROM	25.2.91	14 Feb
16.31	-0.8	Tomas	Veszelka	SVK	9.7.95	12 Jul
16.30	1.6	Alwyn	Jones	AUS	28.2.85	26 Mar
16.30	0.6	Ulisses	Costa	BRA-J	11.2.96	26 Apr
16.30	1.8	Vladimir	Kozlov	RUS	15.3.94	17 Jun
16.30A		Tera	Langat	KEN	26.12.85	1 Aug
16.29	1.5	K.V.Rakesh	Babu	IND	20.3.90	12 Feb
16.29	-0.1	Daniel	Cavazzani	ITA	4.12.92	23 May
16.29	1.2	Karol	Hoffmann	POL	1.6.89	19 Ju
16.29	0.1	Raul	Spank	GER	13.7.88	25 Ju
16.29	0.0	Jayakumar	Surendhar	IND	11.4.91	19 Sep
16.28	-0.9	Aleksandro	Melo	BRA	26.9.95	15 May
16.28A		Levon	Aghasyan	ARM	19.1.95	6 Aug
16.27i		Yevgeniy	Ognev	RUS	25.2.94	17 Jan
16.27i		Phillip	Young	USA	9.10.92	14 Mar
16.26	-1.1		Bi Shiqing	CHN	28.7.94	13 May
16.26	1.0	Zacharias	Arnos	CYP	24.11.86	6 Jun
16.26	0.2	Artyom	Bondarenko	BLR	19.6.91	24 Jul
16.25i		Adrian	Daianu	ROU	27.11.87	14 Feb
16.25	1.1	Tom	Ya'acobov	ISR	30.6.92	16 May
16.25	1.7	Yochai	Halevi	ISR	10.5.82	1 Jul
		(141)				

No wind information: 16.74 Artyom Bondarenko BLR 19.6.91 1 Minsk 2 Ju

Wind assisted

Mark	Wind	Name		Nat	Born	Pos	Meet	Venue	Date
17.71	2.4	Marquis	Dendy	USA	17.11.92	1	NCAA	Eugene	12 Jun
17.35	2.6	SEC	Starkville	16 May	16.96w 16.98 17.21w 17.21w 17.35w x				
17.54	2.1		Pichardo			1	PAm	Toronto	24 Ju
17.50	3.1	Will	Claye	USA	13.6.91	1		Chula Vista	22 May
17.30	2.1		Craddock			3	Athl	Lausanne	9 Ju
				17.11 x 17.30w 15.58 16.48 17.14					
17.25	3.2	Latario	Collie-Minns	BAH	10.3.94	2	SEC	Starkville	16 May
17.24	3.3	Alexis	Copello	ex-CUB	12.8.85	1		Kawasaki	10 May
17.21	2.8		Dong Bin	CHN	22.11.88	1		Sapporo	12 Ju
17.11	4.3	Georgi	Tsonov	BUL	2.5.93	1		Ruen	7 Jun
17.11	3.3	Fabrizio	Donato	ITA	14.8.76	1	ET	Cheboksary	21 Jun
17.07	2.5		Kim Duk-hyung	KOR	8.12.85	2		Sapporo	12 Ju
17.05	3.6	Jonathan	Drack	MRI	6.11.88	1		Saint-Paul, Réunion	1 Aug
16.98	3.0		Cao Shuo	CHN	8.10.91	3		Sapporo	12 Ju
16.94	2.5	Fabrizio	Schembri	ITA	27.1.81	1		Savona	11 Ju
16.87	2.1	Harold	Corréa	FRA	26.6.88	2		Castres	29 Ju
16.83	4.4	Kevin	Luron	FRA	8.11.91	1		Forbach	31 May
16.83	2.1	Leslie	Caesa	CUB-J	14.1.97	1	PAm-J	Edmonton	1 Aug
16.78	4.5	Issam	Nima	ALG	8.4.79	1	Arab C	Manama	26 Apr
16.63	2.1	Louis-Grégory	Occin	FRA	2.6.89	1		Saint-Denis	26 Jun
16.62	2.3	Simo	Lipsanen	FIN	13.9.95	3	ET	Cheboksary	21 Jun
16.60	4.9	Julio César	Carbonell	CUB-Y	16.5.99	2		Las Tunas	9 Ju
16.58	2.4	Rashid Ahmed	Al-Mannai	QAT	18.6.88	1	Gulf G	Qatif	24 Oct
16.56	2.7	Marcel	Kornhardt	GER	3.8.93	6	ET	Cheboksary	21 Jun
16.52	2.2	Jonathan	Reid	JAM	9.5.92	5	NCAA	Eugene	12 Jun
16.50	4.2	Jeremiah	Green	USA	9.2.94	6	NCAA	Eugene	12 Jun
16.49	2.2	Viktor	Yastrebov	UKR	13.1.82	1		Kirovohrad	9 Jun
16.46	2.8	Jonathan	Silva	BRA	21.7.91	1	MSR	Walnut	18 Apr
16.45	3.0	Zacharias	Arnos	CYP	24.11.86	1		Haniá	6 Jun

Mark	Wind	Name		Nat	Born	Date
16.44	2.8	Samyr	Laine	HAI	17.7.84	22 May
16.44	4.2	Karol	Hoffmann	POL	1.6.89	31 May
16.42	2.1	Alexandru	Baciu	ROM	25.2.91	2 Aug
16.40	3.9	Elton	Walcott	TTO	23.2.92	28 Jun
16.39	3.1	Bheesham	Singh	IND	22.1.93	20 Jul
16.34	2.8	Damon	McLean	JAM	21.11.90	22 May
16.31	0.9	Hikaru	Ikehata	JPN	31.8.94	18 Ju
16.31	2.3	Pavlo	Beznits	UKR-J	17.6.97	16 Jun
16.27		Ronald	Woodley	USA	31.5.90	31 May
16.27	4.2	Clive	Pullen	JAM	18.10.94	12 Jun
16.27	2.6	Troy	Doris	USA	12.4.89	13 Jun
16.26	3.4	Steve	Waithe	TTO	7.1.93	12 Jun

Best outdoor marks

Mark	Wind	Name	Pos	Meet	Venue	Date
16.74	0.1	Valiyev	1	Kosanov	Almaty	25 Jul
16.71	1.9	Scott	*	NCAA	Eugene	12 Jun
16.83w	2.5		3	NCAA	Eugene	12 Jun
16.70		Carter	6	NC	Eugene	28 Jun
16.38A	1.5	Gimeno				11 Jul
16.37	0.8	O'Neal				27 Mar
16.28	1.0	Tsiámis				6 Jun
16.61	0.0	Torrijos	1	NC	Castellón	1 Aug
16.59	1.8	Nesterenko	4	ET	Cheboksary	21 Jun
16.57	1.0	Yurchenko	1		Yerino	6 Jun
16.46	1.0	Atanasov	3		Sofia	10 Jun

Low altitude bests

Mark	Wind	Name	Pos	Venue	Date
16.73	0.0	Durañona	1	Ponce	23 May
16.52	-1.9	Solanas	2	La Chaux-de-Fonds	5 Jul

Symbols/Abbreviations

+ intermediate time in longer race, A made at an altitude of 1000m or higher, D made in a decathlon, h made in a heat, qf quarter-final, sf semi-final, i indoors, Q qualifying round, r race number, -J juniors, -Y youths (b. 1998 or later)

Mark Wind Name Nat Born Pos Meet Venue Date

JUNIORS

See main list for top 7 juniors. 12 performances by 7 men to 16.45 plus 5 by 4 men under 16.50w. Additional marks and further juniors:

Babayev 16.61 1.8 1 Baku 23 May 16.54 1.7 2 NC Baku 6 Jun
Martínez 16.73 -0.6 2 La Habana 8 May 16.65 0.0 5 Barr La Habana 28 May
16.91w 4.7 1 NC-j Las Tunas 9 Jul 16.52w 2.4 2 PAm-J Edmonton 1 Aug

Mark	Wind	Name		Nat	Born	Pos	Meet	Venue	Date
16.42i		Keandre	Bates	USA	24.5.96	7	NCAA	Fayetteville	14 Mar
16.37	0.0	Miguel	van Assen	SUR	30.7.97	1		George Town	16 May
16.34i		Max	Hess (10)	GER	13.7.96	1		Chemnitz	25 Jan
		16.08	0.0			4		Forbach	31 May
16.30	0.6	Ulisses	Costa	BRA	11.2.96	1		São Bernardo do Campo	26 Apr
16.24	0.9	Simone	Forte	ITA	20.1.96	5	NC	Torino	26 Jul
16.21	1.3		Sung Jin-slok	KOR	2.1.97	1		Yecheon	19 Apr
16.21	0.0	Julio César	Carbonell	CUB-Y	16.5.99	*	NC-j	Las Tunas	9 Jul
16.18			Liu Mingxuan	CHN	16.5.97	5		Jinan	1 May
16.17	1.0	Clayton	Brown	JAM	8.12.96	1	NC	Kingston	25 Jun
16.17	0.9	O'Brien	Wasome	JAM	24.1.97	3	PAm-J	Edmonton	1 Aug
16.15	1.1	Pavel	Markin	RUS	23.1.96	1	NC-j	Cheboksary	27 Jun
16.13	0.2		Liu Ruihai	CHN	23.12.96	7		Taiyuan	13 May
16.06i		Martin	Lamou (20)	FRA-Y	13.5.99	1	v2N-j	Lyon	28 Feb
16.06	0.5	Vitaliy	Pavlov	RUS	12.1.97	2	NC-j	Cheboksary	27 Jun
16.06	0.3	Yugo	Takahashi	JPN	8.2.96	1	NC-j	Nagoya	17 Oct

Wind assisted

Bocchi 16.51w 2.1 2 EJ Eskilstuna 19 Jul

Mark	Wind	Name		Nat	Born	Pos	Meet	Venue	Date
16.31	2.3	Pavlo	Beznits	UKR	17.6.97	1	NC-j	Kharkiv	16 Jun
16.24	2.9	O'Brien	Wasome	JAM	24.1.97	1	N.Sch	Kingston	27 Mar

SHOT

22.56 Joe Kovacs USA 28.6.89 1 Herc Monaco 17 Jul
21.53 22.56 x 21.16 21.12 21.91
22.35 1 Los Angeles (Ww) 11 Apr 21.06 21.32 22.35 x 21.77 x
22.12 1 Pre Eugene 29 May 21.69 21.72 21.95 21.32 21.92 22.12
22.06 1 La Jolla 25 Apr 21.53 x 21.82 20.76 22.06 21.47
21.93 1 WCh Beijing 23 Aug 21.23 20.48 x 21.67 21.93 21.66
21.84 1 NC Eugene 28 Jun 20.65 x 20.18 21.84 20.79 21.61
21.71 2 Athl Lausanne 9 Jul 20.31 21.71 21.03 21.49 21.26 x
21.67 1 adidas New York 13 Jun 21.24 21.67 21.26 x 21.40 20.80
22.20 David Storl GER 27.7.90 1 Athl Lausanne 9 Jul
21.64 x x 22.20 21.56 x
21.94 1 Schönebeck 26 Jun x 21.76 21.94 x x 21.43
21.92 2 Pre Eugene 29 May 21.25 21.80 21.88 21.85 x 21.92
21.84 1 Biberach 13 Jul 21.55 x 21.57 x x 21.84
21.74 2 WCh Beijing 23 Aug x 21.46 x 20.44 21.74 21.28
21.72 1 Halle 16 May 21.43 -21.25 21.57 x 21.72 21.66
21.68 1 Gotha 19 Jul x 21.52 x 21.49 21.68 x
21.51 1 DL Doha 15 May 19.95 21.51 x p x x
21.47 1 NC Nürnberg 26 Jul 21.01 21.15 21.28 21.00 21.47 20.98
21.46 1 GGala Roma 4 Jun 20.93 21.09 21.46 21.41 x x
21.80i Ryan Whiting USA 24.11.86 1 Pedros Lódz 17 Feb
x 20.84 20.62 21.45 20.95 21.80
21.43i 1 Boston 7 Feb 20.66 20.83 x 21.43 21.18 x
21.69 O'Dayne Richards JAM 14.12.88 1 PAm Toronto 21 Jul
20.36 21.69 20.50 20.07 20.23 x
21.69 3 WCh Beijing 23 Aug x 20.79 21.69 x 20.54 x
21.64 Christian Cantwell USA 30.9.80 2 NC Eugene 28 Jun
20.40 21.17 21.45 x x 21.64
21.50 1 Kans R Lawrence (downtown) 17 Apr 21.49 & 21.50 only measured throws
21.62 Tom Walsh NZL 1.3.92 1 Zagreb 7 Sep
20.60 20.60 21.00 20.74 20.65 21.62
21.58 4 WCh Beijing 23 Aug 20.05 x 20.64 21.58 21.01 x
21.50 1 Mutterstadt 25 Jul 21.50 20.90 20.34 20.59 x x
21.47 1 ISTAF Berlin 6 Sep 20.71 20.49 21.47 20.74 x 20.84
21.58 Asmir Kolasinac SRB 15.10.84 1 Beograd 27 Jun
21.58 21.15 x 21.06 20.92 21.24
21.49 Jordan (30/8) Clarke USA 10.7.90 3 NC Eugene 28 Jun
20.49 20.41 21.11 20.93 21.12 21.49

Mark	Name		Nat	Born	Pos	Meet	Venue	Date
21.30	Reese	Hoffa	USA	8.10.77	2	DL	Doha	15 May
21.14i	Ryan	Crouser (10)	USA	18.12.92	1	Big 12	Ames	28 Feb
21.11i	Stipe	Zunic	CRO	13.12.90	1	NCAA	Fayetteville	14 Mar
21.06	Tsanko	Arnaudov	POR	14.3.92	1		Lisboa	17 May
20.98i	Tim	Nedow	CAN	16.10.90	1		Provo	12 Nov

MEN 2015

Mark	Name		Nat	Born	Pos	Meet	Venue	Date
20.96	Andrei	Gag	ROU	27.4.91	1	Balk C	Pitesti	2 Aug
20.94i	Tomás	Stanek	CZE	13.6.91	2	Pedros	Lódz	17 Feb
20.92	Jonathan	Jones	USA	23.4.91	5	NC	Eugene	28 Jun
20.90	Darlan	Romani	BRA	9.4.91	1		São Paulo	4 Apr
20.86	Darrell	Hill	USA	17.8.93	1		University Park	8 May
20.82	Tomasz	Majewski	POL	30.8.81	6	WCh	Beijing	23 Aug
20.78	Konrad	Bukowiecki	POL-J	17.3.97	3		Zagreb	7 Sep
	(20)							
20.77	Germán	Lauro	ARG	2.4.84	1	SAmC	Lima	13 Jun
20.75	Jacko	Gill	NZL	20.12.94	1	Aus Ch	Brisbane	29 Mar
20.74	Cory	Martin	USA	22.5.85	2		Kingston	9 May
20.71i	Jan	Marcell	CZE	4.6.85	1	NC	Praha	22 Feb
20.70i	Aleksandr	Lesnoy	RUS	28.7.88	1		Krasnodar	8 Feb
20.67	Hamza	Alic	BIH	20.1.79	2		Slovenska Bistrica	30 May
20.66i	Borja	Vivas	ESP	26.5.84	1	NC	Antequera	21 Feb
20.66i	Ladislav	Prásil	CZE	17.5.90	3	EI	Praha (O2)	6 Mar
20.65	Inderjeet	Singh	IND	19.4.88	1		Mangalore	2 May
20.58	Maksim	Sidorov	RUS	13.5.86	1	NC	Cheboksary	4 Aug
	(30)							
20.58	Marin	Premeru	CRO	29.8.90	1		Kragujevac	8 Aug
20.57	Mustafa Amer	Ahmed Hassan	EGY	16.12.95	1		Cairo	12 Mar
20.57	Konstantin	Lyadusov	RUS	2.3.88	1		Yerino	25 Jul
20.56i	Bob	Bertemes	LUX	24.5.93	Q	EI	Praha (O2)	5 Mar
20.55i	Jakub	Szyszkowski	POL	21.8.91	1	NC	Torun	21 Feb
20.54	Georgi	Ivanov	BUL	13.3.85	1		Gabrovo	1 May
20.51	Bobby	Grace	USA	10.10.90	8	NC	Eugene	28 Jun
20.49	Orazio	Cremona	RSA	1.7.89	1	NC	Stellenbosch	17 Apr
20.49	Kemal	Mesic	BIH	4.8.85	3		Slovenska Bistrica	30 May
20.45	Jaco	Engelbrecht	RSA	8.3.87	2	NC	Stellenbosch	17 Apr
	(40)							
20.45	Kurt	Roberts	USA	20.2.88	1		Ashland	5 Jun
20.40	Damien	Birkinhead	AUS	8.4.93	1		Leiden	13 Jun
20.37i	Maris	Urtans	LAT	9.2.81	1		Vilnius	31 Jan
20.31i	Ashinia	Miller	JAM	6.6.93	1		Lexington	24 Jan
20.25i	Ivan	Emilianov	MDA	19.2.77	1		Bucuresti	15 Feb
20.25	Frank	Elemba	CGO	21.7.90	1	AfG	Brazzaville	14 Sep
20.25	Nedzad	Mulabegovic	CRO	4.2.81	1		Novo Mesto	18 Sep
20.23	Yoiser	Toledo	ESP	24.4.83	2	NC	Castellón	2 Aug
20.21	Leif	Arrhenius	SWE	15.7.86	1		Provo	14 May
20.19	Pavel	Lyzhyn	BLR	24.3.81	1		Brest	30 Apr
	(50)							
20.18	Stephen	Mozia	NGR	16.8.93	1		Ithaca	18 Apr
20.18	Gaëtan	Bucki	FRA	9.5.80	1		Forbach	31 May
20.16	Filip	Mihaljevic	CRO	31.7.94	1		Charlottesville	18 Apr
20.16	JC	Murasky	USA	6.2.93	2	Big 10	East Lansing	17 May
20.15	Josh	Freeman	USA	22.8.94	4	NCAA	Eugene	10 Jun
20.13	Willy	Irwin	USA	2.6.92	1		Redlands	15 May
20.13	Eric	Werskey	USA	17.7.87	2		Tucson	23 May
20.13	Carlos	Tobalina	ESP	2.8.85	1		Gijon	25 Jul
20.10i	Michael	Haratyk	POL	10.4.92	1		Torun	3 Feb
20.10i	Tumatai	Dauphin	FRA/PYF	12.1.88	1	NC	Aubière	21 Feb
	(60)							
20.10	Christian	Jagusch	GER	13.7.92	1		Neubrandenburg	30 Ma
20.09i	Arttu	Kangas	FIN	13.7.93	1	NC	Tampere	22 Feb
20.07i	Rafal	Kownatke	POL	24.3.85	2	NC	Torun	21 Feb
20.06	Mateusz	Mikos	POL	10.4.87	1		Warszawa	26 Ju
20.06	Maksim	Afonin	RUS	6.1.92	3	NC	Cheboksary	4 Aug
20.00	Eldred	Henry	IVB	18.9.94	1		Glendale	21 Feb
19.99i	Justin	Rodhe	CAN	17.10.84	3		Boston	7 Feb
19.99i	Nick	Vena	USA	16.4.93	2		Blacksburg	7 Feb
19.99	Aleksandr	Bulanov	RUS	26.12.89	1		Yerino	6 Jun
19.99	Mesud	Pezer	BIH	27.8.94	3	NC	Zenica	13 Jun
	(70)							
19.97i	Tobias	Dahm	GER	23.5.87	Q	EI	Praha (O2)	5 Ma
19.96i	Matt	Babicz	USA	.92	1		Notre Dame	21 Feb
19.87	Dillon	Simon	DMA	5.3.92	2		Charlottesville	18 Ap
19.87	Frédéric	Dagée	FRA	11.12.92	4		Sotteville-lès-Rouen	6 Ju
19.83	David W.	Pless	USA	19.11.90	1		Gresham	2 M
19.82	Nicholas	Skarvélis	USA/GRE	2.2.93	1		Los Angeles (Ww)	4 Ap
19.80	Jordan	Young	CAN	21.6.93	3		Charlottesville	18 Ap
19.79	Mikhail	Abramchuk	BLR	15.11.92	2		Amiens	27 Ju

Mark	Name		Nat	Born	Pos	Meet	Venue	Date
19.78	Mohamed	Hamza	EGY-J	30.8.96	2	AfG	Brazzavile	14 Sep
19.75	Marco	Fortes	POR	26.9.82	2	NC	Leiria	25 Jul
	(80)							
19.74i	Vladislav	Tulácek	CZE	9.7.88	2		Jablonec nad Nisou	28 Jan
19.74	Matt	DeChant	USA	31.5.89	2		Ashland	4 Jun
19.70	Martin	Novák	CZE	5.10.92	1	NC	Plzen	28 Jun
19.69		Liu Yang	CHN	29.10.86	1		Beijing	29 Jun
19.68i	Brad	Szypka	USA	13.2.93	4		Lexington	24 Jan
19.67i	Anton	Tikhomirov	RUS	29.4.88	2		Sankt-Peterburg	10 Feb
19.67	Stephen	Sáenz	MEX	23.8.90	3		Ashland	5 Jun
19.65	Richard	Garrett	USA	21.12.90	3		Tucson	23 Ma
19.63i	Sarunas	Banevicius	LTU	23.1.91	1		Klaipeda	23 Jan
19.61i	Richard	Chavez	USA	30.7.92	1		Jonesboro	31 Jan
	(90)							
19.61	Braheme	Days	USA	18.1.95	2		Los Angeles	3 Ma
19.61		Tian Zhizhong	CHN	15.12.92	1		Sapporo	12 Jul
19.60	Nélson	Fernandes	BRA	9.7.94	2	NC	São Bernardo do Campo	15 May
19.57	Krzysztof	Brzozowski	POL	15.7.93	3		Katowice	24 Jun
19.56i	Daniele	Secci	ITA	9.3.92	1	NC	Padova	22 Feb
19.56		Chang Ming-Huang	TPE	7.8.82	2	AsiC	Wuhan	3 Jun
19.55	Hayden	Baillio	USA	22.7.91	1		San Antonio	4 Apr
19.55		Wang Guangfu	CHN	15.11.87	2		Chanthaburi	29 Jun
19.55i	Garrett	Appier	USA	15.10.92	1		Pittsburg KS	5 Dec
19.53i	Darian	Brown	USA	30.7.93	1		Houston	13 Feb
	(100)							
19.53	Patrick	Cronie	NED	5.11.89	1		Hoorn	16 Ma
19.53	Nick	Ponzio	USA	5.1.95	8	NCAA	Eugene	10 Jun

Mark	Name		Nat	Born	Date
19.52	Soslan	Tsirikhov	RUS	24.11.84	4 Aug
19.50i	Derek	Sievers	USA	18.10.92	17 Jan
19.49	Nate	Hunter	USA	4.10.86	26 Apr
19.49	Raymond	Brown	JAM	15.1.88	13 Jun
19.49		Jung Il-woo	KOR	28.3.86	12 Jul
19.46	Chukwuebuka	Enekwechi	USA	28.1.93	11 Apr
19.45	Anatoliy	Garmashov	RUS	5.7.88	10 Feb
19.45	Coy	Blair	USA	10.6.94	25 Apr
19.41	Chase	Sammons	USA	9.12.92	11 Apr
19.39	Cody	Riffle	USA	14.4.91	17 May
19.39	Dominik	Witczak	POL	10.3.92	27 Jun
19.38	Luke	Pinkelman	USA	5.5.88	9 May
19.37	Sergey	Dementyev	UZB	1.6.90	25 Jul
19.36i	Kole	Weldon	USA	25.3.92	14 Feb
19.35	Timothy	Hendry-Gallagher	CAN	3.2.90	8 Aug
19.35	Sultan	Al-Hebshi	KSA	23.2.83	29 Aug
19.33	Denzel	Comenentia	NED	25.11.95	31 Jul
19.31	Jan Josef	Jeuschede	GER	23.4.93	29 May
19.29i	Nick	Baatz	USA	4.1.90	4 Dec
19.26	Darien	Moore	USA	10.6.91	2 May
19.26		Guo Yanxiang	CHN	29.1.87	25 Jun
19.26	Michal	Rozporski	POL	20.12.88	21 Jul
19.24	Dennis	Lewke	GER	23.7.93	6 Jun
19.24	Tejinder Pal	Singh	IND	13.11.94	8 Jul
19.21	Bodo	Göder	GER	27.6.93	13 Jun
19.20i	Kyle	McKelvey	USA	15.7.92	27 Feb
19.18	Ivan	Ivanov	KAZ	3.1.92	25 Jul
19.17i	Aaron	Castle	USA	7.10.93	28 Feb
19.17	Mark	Jennings	USA	22.4.92	17 May
19.17	Valeriy	Kokoyev	RUS	25.7.88	3 Aug
19.16i	Kristo	Galeta	EST	9.4.83	14 Feb
19.16	Denis	Ananiyev	RUS	13.2.79	29 May
19.11i	Tavis	Bailey	USA	1.6.92	24 Jan
19.11	Andrei	Toader	ROU-J	26.5.97	7 Jun
19.10	Curtis	Jensen	USA	1.11.90	23 May
19.09		Han Zibin	CHN	5.4.87	12 May
19.09	Hendrik	Müller	GER	28.8.90	26 Jun
19.09	Kristo	Galeta	EST	9.4.83	19 Jul
19.08	Aleksey	Nichipor	BLR	10.4.93	15 May
19.08	Andrzej	Regin	POL	21.2.94	12 Jul
19.05i	Ben	Bonhurst	USA-J	2.6.96	7 Feb
19.05	Tomas	Söderlund	FIN	14.5.89	7 Jun
19.01	Rimantas	Martisauskas	LTU	18.9.86	20 Jun
18.99	Patrick	Müller	GER-J	4.2.96	17 May
18.98i	Derrick	Vicars	USA	8.5.89	21 Feb
18.98	Jacek	Wisniewski	POL	29.1.91	26 May
18.97i	Tom	Anderson	USA	26.7.93	14 Feb
18.97	Ayomidotun	Ogundeji	USA-J	24.2.96	9 May

Mark	Name		Nat	Born	Date
18.96	Curtis	Wideman	USA	26.4.93	17 Apr
18.96	Jaromír	Mazgal	CZE	20.1.93	18 Sep
18.95i	Antonio	James	USA	7.4.92	7 Feb
18.95	Maksim	Zakharenko	BLR	15.10.91	26 May
18.93	Austin	Droogsma	USA	4.3.95	11 Apr
18.90	Viktor	Samolyuk	UKR	5.9.86	1 Aug
18.90i	Mitchell	Pope	USA	21.1.84	5 Dec
18.89i	Albert	Fournette	USA	21.10.91	14 Feb
18.89	Anton	Lyuboslavskiy	RUS	26.6.84	4 Jun
18.89	Niklas	Arrhenius	SWE	10.9.82	13 Sep
18.88	Isaiah	Simmons	USA	3.12.92	28 Mar
18.87i	Chris	Reed	USA	22.7.92	7 Feb
18.87i	Kyle	Felpel	USA	26.7.93	28 Feb
18.86i	Robert	Dippl	GER	21.10.83	11 Jan
18.85i	Chris	Cook	USA	17.5.95	1 Mar
18.85	Abdolla	Jamshidi	IRI		15 Sep
18.84	Andriy	Semenov	UKR	4.7.84	22 May
18.83	Will	Lohman	USA	31.3.91	28 Mar
18.81i	Roger	Steen	USA	.93	14 Mar
18.79	Willian	Venâncio	BRA	6.1.94	27 Sep
18.78	Satoshi	Hatase	JPN	18.12.82	28 Jun
18.77i	Sebastiano	Bianchetti	ITA-J	20.1.96	5 Dec
18.76	Taylor	Miller	USA	23.8.91	11 Apr
18.76	Justin	Baker	USA	7.7.89	29 May
18.75	Tomás	Kozák	CZE	1.5.90	16 Aug
18.74	Tomas	Djurovic	MNE	14.2.94	7 Mar
18.74	Andy	Dittmar	GER	5.7.74	27 Jun
18.73	John	Maurins	USA-J	3.8.96	16 May
18.72	Matt	Hoty	USA	21.10.91	15 May
18.70	Luke	Johnson	USA	10.7.92	29 May
18.70	Daniel	Ståhl	SWE	27.8.92	25 Jun
18.68i	Ali	Samari	IRI	7.1.93	13 Feb
18.68	Artur	Hoppe	GER	3.5.88	25 Apr
18.67	Alex	Renner	USA		14 May
18.67	Aleksey	Kulayev	RUS	7.5.94	29 May
18.67	Mario	Cota	MEX	11.9.90	13 Jun
18.65i	Cameron	Cornelius	USA	.95	9 Jan
18.65i	Cody	Snyder	USA	27.4.92	20 Feb
18.65	Kyle	Lillie	USA	.92	16 May
18.64	Gustavo	de Mendonça	BRA	10.4.84	1 May
18.64	Zack	Stetler	USA	28.11.91	14 May
18.63	Mohamed	Gharous	MAR	2.2.87	25 Apr
18.62	Artyom	Podolskiy	RUS	21.7.93	10 Jul
18.61	Ethan	Cochran	USA	9.1.94	11 Apr
18.60i	Grigoriy	Kamulya ¶	UZB	31.1.89	22 Jan
18.60	Ahmed Hassan	Gholoum	KUW	31.5.80	29 Apr
18.60	Dmytro	Savytskyy	UKR	14.12.90	12 May
	(200)				

MEN 2015

Mark	Name		Nat	Born	Pos	Meet	Venue	Date

Best outdoor marks

Mark	Name	Pos	Meet	Venue	Date
21.37	Whiting	3	Pre	Eugene	29 May
21.11	Crouser	1	TexR	Austin	28 Mar
20.78	Nedow	1		Stockholm	28 Jul
20.64	Stanek	3	GGala	Roma	4 Jun
20.55	Lesnoy	1		Sochi	29 May
20.55	Szyszkowski	5	GGala	Roma	4 Jun
20.38	Zunic	1	Jones	Gainesville	24 Apr
20.32	Marcell	Q	WCh	Beijing	23 Aug
20.28	Vivas	1	NC	Castellón	2 Aug
20.23	Urtans	1		Maidla	25 Jul
19.95	Haratyk	2	NC	Kraków	21 Jul
19.93	Dahm	2		Schifflange	2 Aug
19.92	Emilianov	1	NC	Chisinau	31 May
19.91	Kownatke	3		Cetniewo	1 Aug
19.87	Bertemes	14q	WCh	Beijing	23 Aug
19.84	Miller	2	TexR	Austin	28 Mar
19.82	Dauphin	1		Grenoble	10 Jun
19.80	Vena	6	NCAA	Eugene	10 Jun
19.79	Kangas	1		Raasepori	7 Jun
19.73	Rodhe	7	KansR	Lawrence	17 Apr

Mark	Name	Date	Mark	Name	Date
19.52	Babicz	29 May	19.18	Banevicius	7 Aug
19.49	Szypka	2 May	19.10	Tikhomirov	24 Apr
19.37	Chavez	10 Apr	19.10	Weldon	16 May
19.18	Secci	25 Jul	19.10	Tikhomirov	24 Apr
19.09	Galeta	19 Jul	18.81	Bailey	30 May
19.05	Brown	18 Apr	18.73	Steen	23 May
18.97	Castle	11 Apr	18.64	Sievers	24 Apr
18.83	Pope	19 Jun	18.63	Bianchetti	27 Sep
18.82	James	18 Apr	18.60	Anderson	23 May

Unknown irregularity

Mark	Name		Nat	Born	Pos	Meet	Venue	Date
21.35	Thomas	Schmitt	GER	23.1.89	1		Übach-Palenberg	21 Mar

JUNIORS

Mark	Name		Nat	Born	Pos	Meet	Venue	Date
20.78	Konrad	Bukowiecki	POL-J	17.3.97	3		Zagreb	7 Sep

Mark	Pos	Meet	Venue	Date	Mark	Pos	Meet	Venue	Date
20.46i	Q	EI	Praha	5 Mar	19.89	4		Cietniewo	1 Aug
20.46i	6	EI	Praha	6 Mar	19.84	1		Lomza	2 Jun
20.42	3		Llock	17 Jun	19.80	4	Kuso	Szzcecin	9 Aug
20.38	1		Katowice	24 Jun	19.75	3	NC	Kraków	21 Jul
20.17	1		Bialystok	20 Jun	19.68	1		Lódz	7 Jun
20.02i	3	NC	Torun	21 Feb	19.61	5	Skol	Warszawa	13 Sep
19.96i	1		Spala	7 Feb	15 performances by 2 men over 19.60				

Mark	Name		Nat	Born	Pos	Meet	Venue	Date
19.78	Mohamed	Hamza	EGY	30.8.96	2	AfG	Brazzavile	14 Sep
19.11	Andrei	Toader	ROU	26.5.97	2		Pitesti	7 Jun
19.05i	Ben	Bonhurst	USA	2.6.96	5		Blacksburg	7 Feb
	18.49				2		Coral Gables	11 Apr
18.99	Patrick	Müller	GER	4.2.96	2		Halle	17 May
18.97	Ayomidotun	Ogundeji	USA	24.2.96	4		Los Angeles (ER)	9 May
18.77i	Sebastiano	Bianchetti	ITA-J	20.1.96	2		Schio	5 Dec
18.73	John	Maurins	USA-J	3.8.96	2		Tallahassee	16 May
	18.63				1		Jesolo	27 Sep
18.42		Sun Shuai	CHN	20.1.96	1	Univ Ch	Guilin	24 Jul
18.17	Nick	Demaline	USA	1.3.76	17q	NCAA-E	Jacksonville	30 May
18.15	Devon	Patterson	USA	27.4.96	2		Muncie	15 May
18.11	Payton	Otterdahl	USA	2.4.96	7	DrakeR	Des Moines	25 Apr

6 KG SHOT

Mark	Name		Nat	Born	Pos	Meet	Venue	Date
22.62	Konrad	Bukowiecki	POL-Y	17.3.97	1	EJ	Eskilstuna	16 Jul

Mark	Pos	Meet	Venue	Date	Mark	Pos	Meet	Venue	Date
22.38i	1		Torun	24 Jan	21.82i	1	NC-j	Torun	15 Feb
22.21	Q	NC-j	Biala Podlaska	28 Jun	21.42	1	Werfer	Halle	16 May
22.12	1	NC-j	Biala Podlaska	28 Jun	21.20	1		Bojanowo	2 May

Mark	Name		Nat	Born	Pos	Meet	Venue	Date
21.90	John	Maurins	USA	3.8.96	1	NC-j	Eugene	25 Jun
21.23	Sebastiano	Bianchetti	ITA	20.1.96	1		Caorle	3 Oct
21.04	Mohamed	Hamza	EGY	30.8.96	1		Cairo	11 Nov
20.99	Andrei	Toader	ROU	26.5.97	1	Balk-j	Pitesti	5 Jul
	20.78				2	EJ	Eskilstuna	16 Jul
	13 performances by 6 men to 20.72							
20.72i	Patrick	Müller	GER	4.2.96	1		Rochlitz	1 Feb
	20.69				2	Werfer	Halle	16 May
20.67	Dotun	Ogundeji	USA	24.2.96	2	NC-j	Eugene	25 Jun
20.65	Willie	Morrison	USA	23.11.96	3	NC-j	Eugene	25 Jun
20.39		Sun Shuai	CHN	20.1.96	1	NYG	Fuzhou	22 Oct
20.37i	Henning	Prüfer	GER	7.3.96	2		Rochlitz	1 Feb
20.11	Matt	Katnik	USA	10.10.96	4	NC-j	Eugene	25 Jun
20.03	Jamal	Whitaker	USA	19.7.96	5	NC-j	Eugene	25 Jun
19.76	Payton	Otterdahl	USA	2.4.96	6	NC-j	Eugene	25 Jun
19.71	Martin	Markovic	CRO	13.1.96	5	EJ	Eskilstuna	16 Jul
19.69	Matthew	Denny	AUS	2.1.96	1	NC-j	Sydney	13 Mar
19.65	Bartlomiej	Stój	POL	15.5.96	1		Rzeszów	17 May
19.55	Clemens	Prüfer	GER	13.8.97	2	NC-j	Jena	2 Aug
19.52	Gemar	Gayle	JAM	30.3.96	1	N.Sch	Kingston	28 Mar
19.50	Sergey	Panchekhin	RUS	11.5.97	1		Adler	24 Apr
19.46	Ben	Bonhurst	USA	2.6.96	7	NC-j	Eugene	25 Jun
19.43	Frántsi	Latifllári	GRE	8.8.96	1	NC-j	Sérres	27 Jun

12 lb (5.44kg) Shot

Mark	Name		Nat	Born	Pos	Meet	Venue	Date
22.02	Matt	Katnik	USA	10.10.96	1		R.Santa Margarita	8 May
21.40	Willie	Morrison	USA	23.11.96	1		Greensboro	20 Jun
21.05	Jordan	Geist	USA-Y	21.7.98	1		Pittsburgh	1 May

DISCUS

Mark	Name		Nat	Born	Pos	Meet	Venue		Date
68.29	Piotr	Malachowski	POL	7.6.83	1		Cetniewo		1 Aug
				68.29	x	66.95	x	67.33	x
67.49	1 Kuso	Szczecin	9 Aug	66.82	66.78	66.02	67.49	x	65.78
67.40	1 WCh	Beijing	29 Aug	65.09	67.40	62.04	64.40	64.59	64.84
66.13	1 ISTAF	Berlin	6 Sep	64.31	65.24	64.83	65.20	65.03	66.13
65.95	1 DL	Stockholm	30 Jul	56.18	61.46	x	63.26	63.40	65.95
68.19	Jason	Morgan	JAM	6.10.82	1		Pearl		6 Jun
				61e	63e	62e	62e	68.19	63e
67.93	Christophe	Harting	GER	4.10.90	1		Halle		16 May
				x	66.41	x	67.93	x	66.43
67.53	1	Wiesbaden	10 May	67.53	x	x	64.57	p	65.42
67.39	Zoltán	Kövágó	HUN	10.4.79	1		Szombathely		17 Jun
					only best throw measured				
66.01	1 WMilG	Mungyeong	8 Oct	61.54	66.01	x	x	65.47	x
65.64	1	Szentes	25 Apr		only best throw measured				
67.24	Lukas	Weißhaidinger	AUT	20.2.92	1		Schwechat		1 Aug
				60.60	60.72-	63.12	64.62	x	67.24
67.20	Gerhard	Mayer	AUT	20.5.80			Schwechat		5 May
				64.30	64.44	x	63.88	67.20	x
66.90	Philip	Milanov	BEL	6.7.91	2	WCh	Beijing		29 Aug
				60.06	64.38	66.90	x	62.32	65.67
66.66	1	Kessel-Lo	8 Aug	63.03	x	x	66.66	x	65.94
66.43	1	Kessel-Lo	25 Apr	62.59	65.27	66.43	p	p	p
66.75	Benn	Harradine	AUS	14.10.82	2		Wiesbaden		10 May
				60.51	64.08	62.40	63.96	66.75	64.70
66.67	Martin	Kupper	EST	31.5.89	1	ECp-w	Leiria		14 Mar
				62.60	66.67	61.65	60.10	x	62.69
66.40	Fedrick	Dacres (10)	JAM	28.2.94	1		Mona		21 Mar
66.30	1	Kingston	24 Jan						
65.77	Q WCh	Beijing	27 Aug	65.77					
66.31	Robert	Urbanek	POL	29.4.87	2	Kuso	Szczecin		9 Aug
				66.31	x	64.08	64.12	62.84	64.68
65.78	1 WK	Zürich	3 Sep	61.60	x	x- 63.03	65.78	63.24	
66.10	Jared	Schuurmans	USA	20.8.87	1		Claremont		7 Jun
				62.34	x	63.60	62.75	64.88	66.10
66.02	Gerd	Kanter	EST	6.5.79	1		Kohila		24 Jul
				66.02	62.75	x	x	x	62.59
65.94	Martin	Wierig	GER	10.6.87	1		Schönebeck		26 Jun
			2	65.64	x	x	65.94	65.67	65.34
65.93	Daniel	Jasinski	GER	5.8.89	1		Leiria		8 Aug
				61.85	65.93	61.78	x	x	x
65.75	Vikas	Gowda	IND	5.7.83	1		La Jolla		25 Apr
	(32/16)								
65.51	Andrius	Gudzius	LTU	14.2.91	2	ECp-w	Leiria		14 Mar
65.44	Viktor	Butenko	RUS	10.3.93	3	ECp-w	Leiria		14 Mar
65.42	Chase	Madison	USA	13.9.85	1		Rock Island		18 Apr
65.30	Lois Maikel	Martínez	CUB/ESP	3.6.81	1		Málaga		10 Jun
	(20)								
65.22	Ehsan	Hadadi	IRI	21.1.85	1		Grevenmacher		19 Jul
65.04	Apostolos	Parellis	CYP	24.7.85	4	ECp-w	Leiria		14 Mar
65.04	Rodney	Brown	USA	21.5.93	1	PennR	Philadelphia		25 Apr
65.03	Chad	Wright	JAM	25.3.91	2		La Jolla		25 Apr
64.80A	Mason	Finley	USA	7.10.90	1		Monument		25 Jul
64.73	Daniel	Ståhl	SWE	27.8.92	5	WCh	Beijing		29 Aug
64.72	Axel	Härstedt	SWE	28.2.87	1		Bottaryd		27 Jun
64.65	Ronald	Julião	BRA	16.6.85	2	PAm	Toronto		23 Jul
64.57	Erik	Cadée	NED	15.2.84	1		Leiden		13 Jun
64.56	Victor	Hogan	RSA	25.7.89	2		Leiria		9 Aug
	(30)								
64.47A	Mauricio	Ortega	COL	4.8.94	1		Medellin		9 May
64.34	Russ	Winger	USA	2.8.84	2	NC	Eugene		25 Jun
64.30	Markus	Münch	GER	13.6.86	2		Schönebeck		26 Jun
63.91	Andrew	Evans	USA	25.1.91	2		Claremont		7 Jun
63.90	Rutger	Smith	NED	9.7.81	3		Claremont		7 Jun
63.88	Julian	Wruck	AUS	6.7.91	1		Brisbane		7 Feb
63.85A	Niklas	Arrhenius	SWE	10.9.82	1		Provo		26 Sep
63.50	Gudni Valur	Gudnason	ISL	11.10.95	1		Hafnarfjördur		10 Sep
63.42	Brett	Morse	GBR	11.2.89	1	LI	Loughborough		17 May
63.34	Mykyta	Nesterenko	UKR	15.4.91	1		Uman		3 Jul
	(40)								

Mark	Name		Nat	Born	Pos	Meet	Venue	Date
63.33	Danijel	Furtula	MNE	31.7.92	1		Sremska Mitrovica	13 Sep
63.22	Essa Mohamed	Al-Zankawi	KUW	17.10.92	1	Arab C	Manama	27 Apr
63.21	Eligijus	Ruskys	LTU	1.12.90	1		Kaunas	21 Jul
63.17	Jacob	Armbrust	USA	22.2.94	1		Rock Island	18 Apr
63.11	Filip	Mihaljevic	CRO	31.7.94	2	PennR	Philadelphia	25 Apr
63.08A	Mahmoud	Samimi	IRI	18.9.88	1		Tehran	1 May
63.07	Ercüment	Olgundeniz	TUR	7.7.76	6	ECp-w	Leiria	14 Mar
63.01	Ahmed Mohamed	Dheeb	QAT	29.9.85	2	Arab C	Manama	27 Apr
63.01	Roland	Varga	CRO	22.10.77	1		Zagreb	9 Jun
62.79	Nikolay	Sedyuk	RUS	29.4.88	1		Adler	12 Feb
	(50)							
62.75	Aleksas	Abromavicius	LTU	6.12.84	1		Klaipeda	20 Jun
62.74	Russel	Tucker	RSA	4.11.90	1		Stellenbosch	25 Apr
62.70	Przemyslaw	Czajkowski	POL	26.10.88	5	Danek	Turnov	19 May
62.66	David	Wrobel	GER	13.2.91	6		Halle	16 May
62.58	Matthew	Denny	AUS-J	2.6.96	2	WUG	Gwangju	11 Jul
62.56	Hannes	Kirchler	ITA	22.12.78	1		Castiglione della Pescaia	1 Jun
62.50	Giovanni	Faloci	ITA	13.10.85	1		Tarquinia	21 May
62.48	Sam	Mattis	USA	19.3.94	1	NCAA	Eugene	12 Jun
62.43	Martin	Markovic	CRO-J	13.1.96	1	NC-w	Split	8 Mar
62.35	Oleksiy	Semenov	UKR	27.6.82	1		Kyiv	22 Ma
	(60)							
62.35	Jorge	Fernández	CUB	2.10.87	1	Barr	La Habana	27 May
62.27	Jordan	Young	CAN	21.6.93	1Q	NCAA-E	Jacksonville	29 May
62.20	Tavis	Bailey	USA	6.1.92	1		Knoxville	2 May
62.19	Märt	Israel	EST	23.9.83	2		Helsingborg	28 Jun
61.96	Casey	Malone	USA	6.4.77	5		Claremont	7 Jun
61.78	Federico	Apolloni	ITA	14.3.87	2		Savona	30 Ma
61.74	Jason	Harrell	USA	10.1.91	1		Chula Vista	23 Apr
61.70	Mario	Pestano	ESP	8.4.78	1		Cartagena	30 Apr
61.54	Mike	Torie	USA	12.3.86	1c2		Claremont	7 Jun
61.53	Sven Martin	Skagestad	NOR	13.1.95	1		Helsingborg	3 Aug
	(70)							
61.52	Lolassonn	Djouhan	FRA	18.5.91	1		Montgeron	17 May
61.49	Frank	Casañas	ESP	18.10.78	1	NC	Barcelona (S)	8 Jul
61.49	Tim	Nedow	CAN	16.10.90	6	PAm	Toronto	23 Jul
61.46	Pawel	Pasinski	POL	6.3.93	5	Kuso	Szczecin	9 Aug
61.41	Macklin	Tudor	USA	13.6.94	1		Louisville	8 May
61.35	Alex	Rose	SAM	7.11.91	2e2		Claremont	7 Jun
61.34	Stephen	Mozia	NGR	16.8.93	1	IC4A	Princeton	16 May
61.34	Gleb	Sidorchenko	RUS	15.5.86	1	NC	Cheboksary	4 Aug
61.31	Robert	Szikszai	HUN	30.9.94	1		Abbeville	16 May
61.30	János	Huszák	HUN	5.2.92	1	NC-w	Budapest	21 Feb
	(80)							
61.28	Mikhail	Dvornikov	RUS	15.8.89	2		Adler	12 Feb
61.25	Aleksey	Khudyakov	RUS	31.3.95	1		Yerino	10 Jul
61.23	Ivan	Panasyuk	UKR	8.10.91	1		Pacov	1 Aug
61.17	Pyry	Niskala	FIN	6.11.90	1		Kauhajoki	22 Aug
61.04	Alin Alexandru	Firfirica	ROU	3.11.95	1		Pitesti	6 Jun
61.00A	Lance	Brooks	USA	1.1.84	1		Boulder	11 Apr
61.00	Reggie	Jagers	USA	13.8.94	1		Akron	9 May
60.99	Antonio	James	USA	7.4.92	4	NCAA	Eugene	12 Jun
60.93	Aleksander	Tammert	EST	2.2.73	1		Tallinn	1 Oct
60.73	Tomás	Vonavka	CZE	4.6.90	1		Domazlice	18 Sep
	(80)							
60.70	Hayden	Reed	USA	4.4.94	1		Norman	18 Apr
60.70	Marin	Premeru	CRO	29.8.90	4	NC	Varazdin	26 Ju
60.60	Mustapha Katem	Dagher	IRQ	29.11.95	3	Arab C	Manama	27 Apr
60.59	Pedro José	Cuesta	ESP	22.8.83	6		Leiria	8 Aug
60.45	Jan	Marcell	CZE	4.6.85	1		Ostrava	16 May
60.43	Sultan M.	Al-Dawoodi	KSA	16.6.77	1		Radom	27 Jun
60.42A	Mohammed	Samimi	IRI	29.3.87	2		Shiraz	3 Sep
60.39	Henning	Prüfer	GER-J	7.3.96	1	NC-23	Wetzlar	14 Jun
60.36	András	Seres	HUN	31.1.89	2		Abbeville	16 May
60.36	Leif	Arrhenius	SWE	15.7.86	1eB	ECp-w	Leiria	14 Mar

(100)

Mark	Name		Nat	Born	Date	Mark	Name		Nat	Born	Date
60.25	Simon	Pettersson	SWE	3.1.94	23 May	60.11	Carl	Myerscough	GBR	21.10.79	6 Jun
60.18	Ryan	Crouser	USA	18.12.92	12 Jun	60.08	Jason	Tunks	CAN	7.5.75	21 Feb
60.15	Marek	Bárta	CZE	8.12.92	16 May	60.03	Tautvydas	Kieras	LTU	17.10.91	25 Apr
60.13	Dillon	Simon	DMA	5.3.92	21 Mar	59.97	Ola Stunes	Isene	NOR	29.1.95	30 Jun
60.13	Virgilijus	Alekna	LTU	13.2.72	23 Apr	59.89		Wu Jian	CHN	25.5.86	1 May

Mark	Name		Nat	Born	Date
59.89	Mario	Cota	MEX	11.9.90	23 Jul
59.87	Marshall	Hall	NZL	7.10.88	8 May
59.84	Kord	Ferguson	USA	19.6.95	28 Mar
59.82	Valeriy	Golubkovich	BLR	21.1.95	30 Apr
59.82	Mike	Guidry	USA	29.10.79	9 May
59.78	Kole	Weldon	USA	25.3.92	28 May
59.76	Felipe	Lorenzon	BRA	11.11.93	16 May
59.76	Caniggia	Raynor	JAM	3.11.90	22 May
59.76	Bartlomiej	Stój	POL-J	15.5.96	1 Aug
59.72	Jan-Louw	Kotze	RSA	18.3.94	10 May
59.67	Nick	Jones	USA	22.6.89	11 Apr
59.65	Wojciech	Praczyk	POL	10.1.93	17 May
59.60	Aleksandr	Kirya	RUS	23.3.92	23 Feb
59.37	Roman	Ryzhyy	UKR	17.1.85	22 May
59.35	Yeóryios	Trémos	GRE	21.3.89	2 May
59.34	Gerhard	de Beer	RSA	5.7.94	1 May
59.28	Cody	Snyder	USA	27.4.92	26 Mar
59.23	Sebastian	Scheffel	GER	17.11.93	26 Jun
59.20	Grant	Havard	USA	20.4.92	15 May
59.16	Matthew	Kosecki	USA	1.7.91	2 May
59.09	Benedikt	Stienen	GER	12.1.92	10 May
59.09	Stipe	Zunic	CRO	13.12.90	16 May
59.09	James	Plummer	USA	19.8.90	11 Jul
59.08	Aleksandr	Dobrenshkiy	RUS	11.3.94	10 Jul
59.08	Zane	Duquemin	GBR	23.9.91	29 Aug
59.05	Magomed	Magomedov	RUS	26.7.91	6 Jun
58.97	Jouni	Waldén	FIN	9.1.82	21 Jul
58.96	János	Káplar	HUN	8.2.94	21 Feb
58.96	Traves	Smikle	JAM	7.5.92	25 Apr
58.96	Stefano	Petrei	ITA	27.12.93	22 May
58.90	Maksim	Gigashvili	RUS	22.4.92	6 Jun
58.88	Pave;l	Derkach	RUS	2.10.93	4 Jul
58.86	Péter	Savanyú	HUN	26.6.87	7 Jun
58.84	Dan	Block	USA	8.1.91	25 Apr
58.80	Priidu	Niit	EST	27.1.90	8 Aug
58.79	Nazzareno	Di Marco	ITA	30.4.85	18 Jul
58.78	James	Plummer	USA	5.1.95	21 Mar
58.73	Sergey	Roganov	BLR	17.4.86	10 Jul
58.71	Ivan	Kukulicic	MNE	9.10.86	3 Jun
58.64	Maarten	Persoon	NED	15.3.87	16 May
58.63	Igor	Gondor	CZE	10.3.79	13 Jul
58.61	Jorge	Grave	POR	5.9.82	16 May
58.55	Bryan	Powlen	USA	3.12.87	25 Jun
58.54	Nick	Percy	GBR	5.12.94	29 Jul
58.51	Arjun Kumar	Singh	IND	1.7.93	4 May
58.49	Michael	Ohakwe	USA	.92	12 Jun
58.47	Stephan	Dekker	NED	17.2.87	9 May
58.46	Fredrik	Amundgård	NOR	12.1.89	2 Jul
58.41	Dharam Raj	Yadav	IND	26.1.91	4 May
58.40		Tan Shen	CHN	9.3.91	22 Sep
58.38	Clint	Harris	USA	1.1.92	25 Apr
58.35	Austin	Gamble	USA	27.9.90	8 May
58.32	Domantas	Poska	LTU-J	10.1.96	5 Jun
58.31	Josh	Awotunde	USA	12.6.95	24 Apr
58.26	Joe	Williams	USA	21.8.94	28 Mar
58.19	Mitch	Cooper	AUS	2.6.95	12 Jun
58.13	Luke	Vaughn	USA	24.8.94	15 May
58.12	Vladimir	Tocari	MDA	16.1.84	30 May
58.06	Nicolai	Ceban	MDA	4.2.95	2 May
58.04	Mohd Irfan	Shamsuddin	MAS	16.8.95	28 Mar
58.03	Tony	Zeuke	GER-J	14.8.96	14 Jun
	(171)				

JUNIORS

See main list for top 3 juniors. 10 performances by 3 men over 59.00. Additional marks and further juniors:

Mark	Name		Nat	Born	Pos	Meet	Venue	Date
Denny	62.37 1 St. Pölten 4 Jun	59.76 1 Huizingen 6 Jun						
	61.55 2 Brisbane 7 Mar	59.30 2 Perth 14 Feb						
Markovic	61.91 2 NC Varazdin 26 Jul	59.10 3 Zagreb 9 Jun						
59.76	Bartlomiej	Stój	POL	15.5.96	4		Cetniewo	1 Aug
58.32	Domantas	Poska	LTU	10.1.96	4		Kaunas	5 Jun
58.03	Tony	Zeuke	GER	14.8.96	3	NC-23	Wetzlar	14 Jun
56.68	Viktor	Trus	BLR	11.11.96	1		Brest	21 Jun
56.62	Matthew	Zajac	USA	23.1.96	14q	NCAA-E	Jacksonville	29 May
55.71	Reno	Tuufuli	USA	15.2.96	3		Iowa City	2 May
55.24	Clemens	Prüfer (10)	GER	13.8.97	1cB	Werfer	Halle	17 May
55.15		Cheng Yulong	CHN	1.2.97	5		Jinan	1 May
55.00	Johan	Scholtz	RSA	4.3.96	6	NC	Stellenbosch	18 Apr
54.82	Amir Ali	Patterson	USA	30.1.96	7		Chula Vista	13 Jun

1.75 KG DISCUS

Mark	Name		Nat	Born	Pos	Meet	Venue	Date
68.48	Martin	Markovic	CRO	13.1.96	1	NC-j	Varazdin	28 Jun
	67.47 1 Zagreb 2 May	64.58 1 NCp Zagreb 24 May						
	67.11 2 EJ Eskilstuna 19 Jul	12 performances by 5 men to 64.20						
68.02	Bartlomiej	Stój	POL	15.5.96	1	EJ	Eskilstuna	19 Jul
66.66	Matthew	Denny	AUS	2.6.96	1	Werfer	Halle	16 May
	66.48 1 Brisbane 21 Nov	64.26 1 Hobart 12 Dec						
65.03	Henning	Prüfer	GER	7.3.96	1		Wiesbaden	10 May
	64.44 1 Potsdam 28 Jan	64.36 1 Leipzig 6 Jun						
64.98	Domantas	Poska	LTU	10.1.96	1		Kaunas	12 May
63.29	Clemens	Prüfer	GER	13.8.97	1		Neubrandenburg	30 May
62.11	Giulio	Anesa	ITA	7.7.96	5	EJ	Eskilstuna	19 Jul
61.30	Viktor	Trus	BLR	11.11.96	6	EJ	Eskilstuna	19 Jul
61.21	Tony	Zeuke	GER	14.8.96	1	NC-j	Jena	1 Aug
61.09	Sebastiano	Bianchetti (10)	ITA	20.1.96	1		Tarquinia	21 May
60.73	Oskari	Perälampi	FIN	24.7.96	7	EJ	Eskilstuna	19 Jul
60.47	Konrad	Bukowiecki	POL	17.3.97	1	ECCp-J	Istanbul	19 Sep
60.45	Maximilian	Klaus	GER-Y	7.2.98	1		Leipzig	21 Jun
59.98	Payton	Otterdahl	USA	2.4.96	1	NC-j	Eugene	27 Jun
59.93	Bence	Halász	HUN	4.8.97	1		Szombathely	23 Sep
59.86	Lukas	Koller	GER	.96	2	NC-j	Jena	1 Aug
59.06	Reno	Tuufuli	USA	15.2.96	2	NC-j	Eugene	27 Jun
58.72	George	Armstrong	GBR	8.12.97	1		Darlington	18 Apr
57.62	Stefan=	Mura	MDA	2.6.97	9	EJ	Eskilstuna	19 Jul
57.60A	Johan	Scholtz (20	RSA	4.3.96	1	NC-j	Bloemfontein	10 Apr

1.62 KG DISCUS

Mark	Name		Nat	Born	Pos	Meet	Venue	Date
65.34	Carlos	Davis	USA	22.8.96	1		Blue Springs	25 Apr

HAMMER

Mark	Name		Nat	Born	Pos	Meet	Venue		Date
83.93	Pawel	Fajdek	POL	4.6.89	1	Kuso	Szczecin		9 Aug
				83.83	83.93	81.44	x	p	p
	83.12 1 Gyulai	Székesfehérvár	7 Jul	79.05	81.16	80.08	x	81.99	83.12
	82.76 1	Halle	16 May	77.49	80.79	77.78	77.71	x	82.76
	82.07 1	Cetniewo	1 Aug	78.46	80.47	x	x	77.87	82.07
	81.99 1 Skol	Warszawa	13 Sep	x	77.60	81.99	77.89	80.64	x
	81.64 1 ET	Cheboksary	20 Jun	79.96	81.64	x	80.73		
	80.96 1	Rieti	12 Sep	x	80.49	x	80.96	78.46	79.66
	80.88 1 WCh	Beijing	23 Aug	76.40	x	80.64	80.88	79.34	78.29
	80.75 1 GS	Ostrava	25 May	x	80.75	x	x	80.16	79.88
	80.71 1 PNG	Turku	25 Jun	x	77.07	78.19	80.71	x	77.48
	80.13 1	Buenos Aires	27 Mar	80.13	78.57	79.42	79.00		
	80.05 1 WUG	Gwangju	8 Jul	x	x	77.31	76.40	x	80.05
	79.90 1	Rabat	14 Jun	77.99	79.24	76.79	x	77.62	79.90
	79.79 1	Buenos Aires	11 Apr	x	x	78.25	x	79.26	79.79
	79.74 1 NC	Kraków	20 Jul	78.62	79.74	x	x	77.40	78.04
	78.99 1	Buenos Aires	29 Mar	74.90	78.53	78.44	78.99		
	78.67 1	Biala Podaska	30 May	78.02	x	x	78.67	x	x
79.91	Krisztián	Pars	HUN	18.2.82	2		Cetniewo		1 Aug
				78.68	79.91	78.33	78.07	78.51	77.30
	79.24 1 ECp-w	Leiria	14 Mar	77.55	77.31	75.92	79.24	x	78.64
	79.23 2 Gyulai	Székesfehérvár	7 Jul	77.44	77.55	77.12	x	77.74	79.23
	78.73 2 Skol	Warszawa	13 Sep	76.73	78.73	x	77.14	76.96	76.56
79.90	Mostafa	Al-Gamal	EGY	1.10.88	1		Cairo		25 Jul
79.36	Dilshod	Nazarov	TJK	6.5.82	2	GS	Ostrava		25 May
				x	78.99	78.86	78.22	79.29	79.36
	78.55 2 WCh	Beijing	23 Aug	76.83	77.61	76.17	78.06	78.55	76.60
79.25	Yevgen	Vynogradov	UKR	30.4.84	1		Uman		3 Jul
				74.27	76.57	79.25	x		
78.72	Serghei	Marghiev	MDA	6.11.92	1	NC	Chisinau		30 May
				77.92	78.68	x	78.72	78.22	76.28
78.71	Wojciech	Nowicki	POL	22.2.89	1		Bialystok		3 May
				76.07	76.64	78.71	p	p	p
	78.58 1	Kielce	9 May	x	77.28	x	77.29	78.03	78.58
	78.55 3 WCh	Beijing	23 Aug	76.14	76.73	77.20	x	75.80	78.55
78.52	Dmitriy	Marshin	AZE	24.2.72	1		Brest		15 May
	(30/8)								
78.29	Marco	Lingua	ITA	4.6.78	1	LEAP	Loughborough		18 Jul
78.22	Sukhrob	Khodjayev (10)	UZB	21.5.93	1		Almaty		25 Jul
78.04	Ashraf Amjad	El-Seify	QAT	20.2.95	1		Rhede		4 Jul
78.02	Roberto	Janet	CUB	29.8.86	1	Barr	La Habana		28 May
77.63	Marcel	Lomnicky	SVK	6.7.87	1		Trnava		10 May
77.55	Nick	Miller	GBR	1.5.93	2		Karlstad		22 Jul
77.46	Ivan	Tikhon ¶	BLR	24.7.76	1		Yerino		24 Jul
77.43	Sergey	Kolomoyets	BLR	11.8.89	1		Minsk		26 Jun
77.24	Sergey	Litvinov	RUS	27.1.86	5	WCh	Beijing		23 Aug
77.15	Kirill	Ikonnikov	RUS	5.3.84	2		Yerino		24 Jul
77.03	Pavel	Boreysha	BLR	16.2.91	1		Jablonec		29 Apr
76.95	Kibwé	Johnson	USA	17.7.81	1	NC	Eugene		25 Jun
	(20)								
76.93	Mark	Dry	GBR	11.10.87	1	LI	Loughborough		17 May
76.92	David	Söderberg	FIN	11.8.79	6	WCh	Beijing		23 Aug
76.91	Conor	McCullough	IRL/USA	31.1.91	1	NCAA	Eugene		10 Jun
76.87	A.G.	Kruger	USA	18.2.79	1		Ashland		4 Jun
76.85	Yuriy	Shayunov	BLR	22.10.87	3		Minsk		10 Apr
76.82	Esref	Apak	TUR	3.1.82	1	Balk C	Pitesti		2 Aug
76.80	Valeriy	Pronkin	RUS	15.6.94	4		Yerino		24 Jul
76.67	Oleg	Dubitskiy	BLR	14.10.90	1		Brest		27 May
76.42	Aleksey	Korolyov	RUS	5.4.82	5		Yerino		24 Jul
76.38	Anatoliy	Pozdnyakov	RUS	1.2.87	1		Adler		11 Feb
	(30)								
76.37	Roberto	Sawyers	CRC	17.10.86	1		Jablonec		10 Jun
76.21	Lukás	Melich	CZE	16.9.80	2	Odlozil	Praha		8 Jun
76.18	Igors	Sokolovs	LAT	17.8.74	1		Riga		9 May
75.74	Bence	Pásztor	HUN	5.2.95	1		Veszprém		7 Jun
75.41	Alaa El-Din M.	El-Ashry	EGY	6.1.91	1		Cairo		29 Oct
75.32	Constantinos	Stathelakos	CYP	30.12.87	1		Trípoli		16 May
75.29	Michael	Lihrman	USA	6.12.91	1		Madison		8 May
75.29	Aleksey	Sokirskiy	RUS	16.3.85	6	Znam	Zhukovskiy		18 Jul

Mark	Name		Nat	Born	Pos	Meet	Venue	Date
74.80	Pavel	Krivitskiy ¶	BLR	17.4.84	2		Jablonec	29 Apr
74.76	Javier	Cienfuegos	ESP	15.7.90	1	NC-w	Montijo	7 Mar
	(40)							
74.74		Wan Yong	CHN	22.7.87	3	BLR Ch	Grodno	24 Jul
74.74	Tuomas	Seppänen	FIN	16.5.86	Q	WCh	Beijing	22 Aug
74.73	Alexander	Ziegler	GER	7.7.87	2		Ashland	4 Jun
74.66	Chris	Bennett	GBR	17.12.89	3	LI	Loughborough	17 May
74.61		Wang Shizhu	CHN	20.2.89	1		Chengdu	31 Mar
74.53	Ákos	Hudi	HUN	10.8.91	1		Nikíti	18 Jul
74.31	Jake	Freeman	USA	5.11.80	1		Mount Vernon	22 May
74.30	Kaveh	Mousavi	IRI	27.5.85	1		Shiraz	2 Sep
74.28	Zakhar	Makhrosenko	BLR	10.10.91	6		Brest	27 May
74.20	Wágner	Domingos	BRA	23.6.83	1		Slovenska Bistrica	30 May
	(50)							
74.06	Markus	Esser	GER	3.2.80	1		Erfurt	19 Jul
74.01	Jérôme	Bortoluzzi	FRA	20.5.82	1		Anzin	3 Jul
74.00	Chris	Harmse	RSA	31.5.73	1		Potchefstroom	10 Mar
73.94	Denis	Lukyanov	RUS	11.7.89	2	NC-w	Adler	24 Feb
73.82	Libor	Charfreitag	SVK	11.9.77	2		Trnava	10 May
73.72	Igor	Vinichenko	RUS	11.4.84	6	NC	Cheboksary	5 Aug
73.63	Nejc	Plesko	SLO	9.10.92	1		Celje	4 Jul
73.56	Colin	Dunbar	USA	27.6.88	3		Tucson	23 May
73.52	Allan	Wolski	BRA	18.1.90	1		São Bernardo do Campo	30 May
73.29	Simone	Falloni	ITA	26.9.91	1		Fidenza	22 May
	(60)							
73.23	Mihaíl	Anastasákis	GRE	3.12.94	1	NC	Athína	25 Jul
73.21	Yuriy	Vasilchenko ¶	BLR	4.1.94	2		Minsk	10 Apr
73.18	Reinier	Mejias	CUB	22.9.90	2	Barr	La Habana	28 May
73.15	Szymon	Ziólkowski	POL	1.7.76	7	Odlozil	Praha	8 Jun
73.10	Arkadiusz	Rogowski	POL	30.3.93	1		Warszawa	23 May
73.08	Reza	Moghaddam	IRI	17.11.88	1		Tehran	20 May
73.08	Frédéric	Pouzy	FRA	18.2.83	1		Sherbrooke	13 Jun
73.07	Peyman	Ghalenouei	IRI	29.1.92	2		Tehran	20 May
72.99	Garland	Porter	USA	10.2.82	3		Fränkisch-Crumbach	24 May
72.86	Kamalpreet	Singh	IND	3.11.87	3		Tucson	21 May
	(70)							
72.84	Valeriy	Svyatokho	BLR	20.7.81	6	NC	Grodno	24 Jul
72.77	Chukwuewuka	Enekwechi	USA	28.1.93	1	Big 10	East Lansing	15 May
72.66	Alan Diego	del Real	MEX	6.3.94	2	MSR	Walnut	18 Apr
72.49	James "JC"	Lambert	USA	12.4.90	4	NC	Eugene	25 Jun
72.31	Jesse	Lehto	FIN	12.2.93	1		Krunuupyy	13 Sep
72.20	Oscar	Vestlund	SWE	27.4.93	1		Arvika	26 Jul
72.04	Mikalay	Bashan	RUS	18.11.92	5		Adler	11 Feb
72.04	Andriy	Martynyuk	UKR	25.9.90	1		Kyiv	23 May
71.98	Hiroshi	Noguchi	JPN	3.5.83	1	NC	Niigata	27 Jun
71.94	Matthias	Tayala	USA	27.4.93	5	NC	Eugene	25 Jun
	(80)							
71.86	Serhiy	Reheda	UKR	6.2.94	1		Kyiv	22 May
71.84	Eivind	Henriksen	NOR	14.9.90	1		Tønsberg	31 May
71.83	Andy	Fryman	USA	3.2.85	1		High Point	4 Apr
71.70	Tomás	Postema	USA	17.7.89	1		Delaware, OH	11 May
71.60	James	Steacy	CAN	29.5.84	1		Lethbridge	17 May
71.57	Juho	Saarikoski	FIN	19.5.93	4		Kaustinen	27 Jun
71.39	Yevgeniy	Korotovskiy	RUS	21.6.92	3		Adler	23 Apr
71.31	Elias	Håkansson	SWE	29.2.92	1	NC	Söderhamn	8 Aug
71.28	Dmitriy	Velikopolskiy	RUS	27.11.84	1		Smolensk	7 Jun
71.25	Greg	Skipper	USA	26.3.93	3	NCAA	Eugene	10 Jun
	(90)							
71.25	Isaac	Vicente	ESP	30.4.87	1		Vila Nova de Cerveira	9 Jul
71.20	Sven	Möhsner	GER	30.1.86	8		Halle	16 May
71.16	Konstadínos	Kostoglídis	GRE	10.8.90	2		Athína (K)	6 Jun
71.08	Mergen	Mamedov	TKM	24.12.90	1	NC	Ashkhabad	21 May
71.07	Joachim	Koivu	FIN	5.9.88	3		Kuortane	8 Aug
71.01	Humberto	Mansilla	CHI-J	22.5.96	1		Los Ángeles, CHI	21 Mar
70.97	Kristóf	Németh	HUN	17.9.87	3		Veszprém	7 Jun
70.85	Marco	Bortolato	ITA	11.2.94	1	NC	Torino	26 Jul
70.74	Özkan	Baltaci	TUR	13.2.94	1		Mersin	23 May
70.73	Jordan	Young	CAN	21.6.93	1Q	NCAA-E	Jacksonville	28 May
	(100)							

Mark	Name		Nat	Born	Date	Mark	Name		Nat	Born	Date
70.65	Amanmurat	Hommadov	TKM	28.1.89	20 Oct	70.52	Matt	Denny	AUS-J	2.6.96	17 May
70.64	Remy	Conatser	USA	20.7.90	6 Jun	70.50	Sebastian	Nowicki	POL	26.8.94	23 May

Mark	Name		Nat	Born	Date
70.46	Yushiro	Hosaka	JPN	16.10.91	29 Apr
70.42	Tristan	Schwandke	GER	23.5.92	4 Aug
70.36	Rudy	Winkler	USA	6.12.94	13 Jun
70.35	Paul	Hützen	GER	7.3.91	24 May
70.32	Nicolas	Figère	FRA	19.5.79	10 Jul
70.21		Lee Yun-chul	KOR	28.3.82	18 Oct
70.18	Chris	Shorthouse	GBR	23.6.88	8 Aug
70.13	Ali Mohamed	Al-Zankawi	KUW	27.2.84	28 Jan
70.11	Arno	Laitinen	FIN	9.3.88	11 Jun
70.10	Ayhan	Apti	BUL	25.4.93	28 Jun
70.08	Alexandros	Poursanides	CYP	23.1.93	3 Apr
70.05	Tommi	Remes	FIN	20.1.94	27 Jun
69.99	Johannes	Bichler	GER	3.7.90	11 Jul
69.94	Justin	Welch	USA	29.9.91	11 Apr
69.80	Bence	Halász	HUN-J	4.8.97	7 Jul
69.79	Hilmar Örn	Jonsson	ISL-J	6.5.96	26 Jul
69.73	Miguel Alberto	Blanco	ESP-J	22.2.96	25 Jul
69.70	Simon	Lang	GER	16.8.95	18 Jul
69.67	Renaldo	Frechou	RSA	4.3.92	8 May
69.65	Gianlorenzo	Ferretti	ITA	18.4.91	15 May
69.62	Andrey	Romanov	RUS	19.9.94	24 Feb
69.55	András	Haklits	CRO	23.9.77	22 Jul
69.50	António	e Silva	POR	23.1.88	18 Jul
69.49	Andrew	Frost	GBR	17.4.81	7 Jul
69.42	Mirko	Micuda	CRO	22.12.89	17 May
69.42	Ivan	Aksyonov	RUS	16.8.95	16 Jun
69.41	Markus	Kokkonen	FIN	17.5.95	13 Jun
69.39	Taylor	Campbell	GBR-J	30.6.96	4 May
69.31	Alexej	Mikhailov	GER-J	12.4.96	13 Jun
69.28	Ryan	Loughney	USA	21.8.89	24 Apr
69.22	Alex	Smith	GBR	6.3.88	17 May
69.21	Igor	Buryi	RUS	8.4.93	12 Feb
69.19	Islam Ahmed	Taha	EGY	23.7.94	29 Oct
69.13	Matija	Greguric	CRO-J	17.9.96	19 Sep
69.10	Tomás	Kruzliak	SVK	9.2.92	10 Jun
69.09	Dário	Manso	POR	1.7.82	26 Jul
68.98	Michael	Bomba	GBR	10.10.86	9 Aug
68.95		Qi Dakai	CHN	23.5.87	4 Apr
68.86	Anton	Krykun	UKR	22.1.90	30 Jul
68.80	Toru	Tanaka	JPN	17.5.86	27 Jun
68.79	Salameh Adel	Salem	EGY	,93	29 Oct
68.66	Caleb	Stuart	USA/PHI	7.9.90	14 Mar
68.65	Noleisis	Bicet	CUB	6.2.81	23 May
68.60	Patrizio	Di Blasio	ITA	27.10.93	21 Feb
68.41	Davis	Fraker	USA	26.2.92	2 May
68.34	Ilmari	Lahtinen	FIN	12.10.93	11 Jun
68.26	Juha	Kauppinen	FIN	16.8.86	17 Jul
68.18	Zdravko	Dimitrov	BUL	31.8.91	20 May
68.13	Nicola	Vizzoni	ITA	4.11.73	14 Mar
68.01	Love	Litzell	SWE	9.12.94	17 Apr
68.01	Kyle	Morse	USA	11.11.85	7 Jun
68.00	Ryota	Kashimura	JPN	13.8.91	8 Aug
	(156)				

Exhibition

Mark	Name	Pos	Venue	Date						
81.91	Fajdek	1	Wroclaw	27 Jun	79.81	79.93	x	81.91	x	x
78.68	Pars	2	Wroclaw	27 Jun	76.61	78.27	75.79	77.17	76.84	78.68

Drugs disqualification

Mark	Name		Nat	Born	Pos	Meet	Venue	Date
76.20	Pavel	Krivitskiy ¶	BLR	17.4.84	2		Brest	27 May

JUNIORS

Mark	Name		Nat	Born	Pos	Meet	Venue	Date
71.01	Humberto	Mansilla	CHI-J	22.5.96	1		Los Ángeles, CHI	21 Ma
70.52	Matt	Denny	AUS-	2.6.96	3		Halle	17 May
	69.70	1 Melbourne		21 Mar		6 performances by 5 men over 69.50		
69.80	Bence	Halász	HUN	4.8.97	9	Gyulai	Székesfehérvár	7 Ju
69.79	Hilmar Örn	Jonsson	ISL	6.5.96	1	NC	Kópavogur	26 Ju
69.73	Miguel Alberto	Blanco	ESP	22.2.96	2		Gijon	25 Ju
69.39	Taylor	Campbell	GBR	30.6.96	1		Bedford	4 May
69.31	Alexej	Mikhailov	GER	12.4.96	2	NC-23	Wetzlar	13 Jun
69.13	Matija	Greguric	CRO	17.9.96	1		Zagreb	19 Sep
67.10	Aleksi	Jaakkola	FIN	17.11.97	2		Forssa	25 Ap
66.89		Gong Shixian	CHN	24.8.96	2		Taiyuan	11 May
66.18		Ding Yuanbo (10)	CHN	26.1.97	4		Chengdu	31 Ma
65.57	Joaquín	Gómez	ARG	14.10.96	1		Buenos Aires	16 May
65.10	Karol	Koncos	SVK	3.6.96	4	NC	Banská Bystrica	1 Au
64.87	Ahmed Amgad	Al-Saifi	QAT	1.10.96	1	Gulf Ch	Qatif	25 Oc
64.76	Matt	Bloxham	NZL	16.11.96	1		Hamilton	29 No

6KG HAMMER

Mark	Name		Nat	Born	Pos	Meet	Venue	Date
80.59	Joaquín	Gómez	ARG	14.10.96	1	SAm-J	Cuenca	30 Ma
80.48	Matthew	Denny	AUS	2.6.96	1		Townsville	25 Se
	79.11	2 Leverkusen		30 May				
80.21	Humberto	Mansilla	CHI	22.5.96	1	PAm-J	Edmonton	2 Au
79.96	Alexej	Mikhailov	GER	12.4.96	1		Leverkusen	30 Ma
	78.96	1 Mannheim		27 Jun				
79.86	Bence	Halász	HUN	4.8.97	1	Werfer	Halle	16 Ma
	79.60	1 EJ Eskilstuna		17 Jul		11 performances by 7 men over 78.90		
79.81	Hilmar Örn	Jónsson	ISL	6.5.96	1		Hafnarfjördur	22 Ju
79.05	Miguel Alberto	Blanco	ESP	22.2.96	2	EJ	Eskilstuna.	17 Ju
78.74	Taylor	Campbell	GBR	30.6.96	1	NC-j	Bedford	20 Ju
77.93	Aleksi	Jaakkola	FIN	17.11.97	1	NC-j	Savonlinna	15 Au
77.90	Matija	Greguric (10)	CRO	17.9.96	1		Zagreb	9 Ju
77.86	Gleb	Dudarev	BLR	17.10.96	1		Novopolotsk	27 No
77.54	Gabriel	Kehr	CHI	3.9.96	3	SAm-J	Cuenca	30 Ma
77.32	Yuriy	Kuziv	RUS	29.5.96	4	EJ	Eskilstuna	17 Ju
76.64	Igor	Yevseyev	RUS	27.3.96	1	NC-jw	Adler	23 Fe
76.64	Vlodomyr	Myslyvchuk	UKR	25.4.96	5	EJ	Eskilstuna	17 Ju
76.42	Roman	Zholudzev	BLR	8.1.96	1		Minsk	10 Ap
75.98		Gong Shixian	CHN	24.8.96	1	NYG	Fuzhou	23 Oc
74.60	Gleb	Volik	RUS	17.12.96	1		Krasnodar	7 Ju
74.46	Tareq Ismael	Ahmed	EGY	18.10.97	1	Af-J	Addis Ababa	6 Ma
74.28	Tshepang	Makhethe (20)	RSA	9.2.96	2	Af-J	Addis Ababa	6 Ma

JAVELIN

Mark	Name	Nat	Born	Pos	Meet	Venue	Date	Series
92.72	Julius Yego	KEN	4.1.89	1	WCh	Beijing	26 Aug	x 82.42 92.72 p p x
91.39				1	DL	Birmingham	7 Jun	85.95 p 86.53 p p 91.39
87.71				2	GGala	Roma	4 Jun	83.06 80.69 84.44 87.71 p p
86.88				1	GS	Ostrava	26 May	x 72.87 86.88 p p p
90.16	Keshorn Walcott	TTO	2.4.93	1	Athl	Lausanne	9 Jul	90.16 p x p p p
86.43				3	DL	Birmingham	7 Jun	80.56 85.21 86.43 85.59 x 84.97
86.20				3	GGala	Roma	4 Jun	79.52 80.59 78.77 76.76 81.62 86.20
89.27	Thomas Röhler	GER	30.9.91	1		Kuortane	8 Aug	x x 83.64 82.54 83.89 89.27
87.41				4	WCh	Beijing	26 Aug	86.68 86.03 86.77 87.18 84.00 87.41
86.56				2	VD	Bruxelles	11 Sep	83.03 86.56 x 85.33 85.97 84.51
86.40				1		Thum	4 Sep	86.08 86.40 x 83.19 x 84.66
89.09	Tero Pitkämaki	FIN	19.12.82	1	PNG	Turku	25 Jun	85.08 82.46 84.48 x 84.44 89.09
88.97				1	Herc	Monaco	17 Jul	84.97 83.91 84.77 88.87 p p
88.62				1	DL	Doha	15 May	75.69 77.60 80.14 80.31 81.98 88.62
87.82				2	NC	Pori	2 Aug	87.82 x 82.34 81.17 p p
87.64				3	WCh	Beijing	26 Aug	83.45 85.03 85.08 87.64 84.49 87.34
87.44				3	Athl	Lausanne	9 Jul	83.09 85.60 84.67 87.44 x x
87.37				1	VD	Bruxelles	11 Sep	84.27 87.37 83.18 x 85.69 87.30
88.99	Ihab Abdelrahman	EGY	1.5.89	2	WCh	Beijing	26 Aug	86.07 88.99 x x x x
88.98	Antti Ruuskanen	FIN	21.2.84	1	NC	Pori	2 Aug	79.05 84.13 x x 85.02 88.98
87.46				2		Kuortane	8 Aug	78.54 80.58 x x 81.55 87.46
87.12				5	WCh	Beijing	26 Aug	76.24 81.29 87.12 80.63 84.30 x
86.61				2	DL	Doha	15 May	x x 81.40 76.23 x 86.61
88.18	Vitezslav Vesely	CZE	27.2.83	2	DL	Birmingham	7 Jun	x x 79.55 73.58 80.30 88.18
88.14				1	GGala	Roma	4 Jun	x 88.14 p p p p
87.97				2	Athl	Lausanne	9 Jul	87.67 x 87.97 x x x
86.82	Ari Mannio	FIN	23.7.87	1		Raasepori	7 Jun	81.41 86.82 x 81.52 p x
86.65	Magnus Kirt	EST	10.4.90	1		Kohila	6 Sep	77.56 x 86.65 p p p
86.21	Jakub Vadlejch (10)	CZE	10.10.90	1		Karlstad	22 Jul	80.64 86.21 79.29 84.85 80.77 81.04
86.14	Andreas Hofmann	GER	16.12.91	Q	WCh	Beijing	24 Aug	86.14
	(30/11)							
85.52	Petr Frydrych	CZE	13.1.88	1		Klatovy	6 May	
85.40	Johannes Vetter	GER	26.3.93	1		Jena	31 May	
85.39	Rocco van Rooyen	RSA	23.12.92	1		Cape Town	23 May	
85.20	Marcin Krukowski	POL	14.6.92	1		Katowice	24 Jun	
84.70	Dmitriy Tarabin	RUS	29.10.91	1	NC	Cheboksary	4 Aug	
84.66	Ryohei Arai	JPN	23.6.91	Q	WCh	Beijing	24 Aug	
84.39	Teemu Wirkkala	FIN	14.1.84	3	PNG	Turku	25 Jun	
84.26	Lars Hamann	GER	4.4.89	1		Rieti	13 Sep	
84.24	Bobur Shokirjanov	UZB	5.12.90	1		Dushanbe	17 Oct	
	(20)							
84.09	Tim Glover	USA	1.11.90	1		Knoxville	11 Apr	
83.82	Tanel Laanmäe	EST	29.9.89	2		Kohila	6 Sep	
83.67	Júlio César de Oliveira	BRA	4.2.86	1		São Bernardo do Campo	11 Jul	
83.37	Rolands Strobinders	LAT	14.4.92	1		Riga	28 May	
83.33	Sam Crouser	USA	31.12.91	1		Portland	1 Aug	
83.32	Braian Toledo	ARG	8.9.93	Q	WCh	Beijing	24 Aug	
83.31	Hamish Peacock	AUS	15.10.90	1		Hobart	3 Jan	
83.08	Sean Furey	USA	31.8.82	1	NC	Eugene	25 Jun	
83.04	R.M.Sumedha Ranasinghe	SRI	10.2.91	1		Diyagama	3 Dec	
83.00	Valeriy Iordan	RUS	14.2.92	1	ECp-w	Leiria	15 Mar	
	(30)							
82.94	John Ampomah	GHA	11.7.90	2	AfG	Brazzaville	17 Sep	
82.75	Stuart Farquhar	NZL	15.3.82	1	Porritt	Hamilton	7 Feb	
82.51	Patrik Zenúch	SVK	30.12.90	1		Kosice	3 May	
82.40	Kim Amb	SWE	31.7.90	1	NC	Söderhamn	9 Aug	
82.29	Kacper Oleszczuk	POL	15.5.94	1	EU23	Tallinn	12 Jul	
82.28	Hubert Chmielak	POL	19.6.89	1		Lódz	17 May	

Mark	Name		Nat	Born	Pos	Meet	Venue	Date
82.23	Rajender	Singh Dalvir	IND	5.4.89	1		Trivandrum	12 Feb
82.06	Risto	Mätas	EST	30.4.84	1		Tallinn	13 Jun
81.83	Maksym	Bohdan	UKR	27.2.94	1		Brest	30 Apr
81.80	Matthew	Outzen	AUS	12.10.87	1		Sydney	14 Mar
	(40)							
81.80	Oleksandr	Nychyporchuk	UKR	14.4.92	2		Riga	28 May
81.78		Cheng Chao-Tsun	TPE	17.10.93	3		Kawasaki	10 May
81.63	Oleksandr	Pyatnytsya	UKR	14.7.85	1		Kyiv	22 May
81.62	Toni	Sirviö	FIN	8.1.92	1		Savonlinna	9 May
81.62	Riley	Dolezal	USA	16.11.85	2	PAm	Toronto	24 Jul
81.48		Huang Shih-Feng	TPE	2.3.92	1		Taipei	17 Mar
81.45	Fatih	Avan	TUR	1.1.89	3	ECp-w	Leiria	15 Mar
81.45	Jaroslav	Jílek	CZE	22.10.89	3		Domazlice	18 Sep
81.15	Julian	Weber	GER	29.8.94	1		Rehlingen	25 May
81.04	Paraskevás	Batzávalis	GRE	25.11.94	1	NC	Athína	26 Jul
	(50)							
81.04	Neeraj	Chopra	IND-J	24.12.97	Q	Univs Ch	Patiala	31 Dec
80.97	Roberto	Bertolini	ITA	9.10.85	1		Genève	6 Jun
80.96	Pavel	Meleshko	BLR	24.11.92	2		Brest	30 Apr
80.90	Vedran	Samac	SRB	22.1.90	1		Kragujevac	7 Jun
80.67A	Arley	Ibargüen	COL	4.12.82	1	NG	Cali	19 Nov
80.57	Bernhard	Seifert	GER	15.2.93	3	EU23	Tallinn	12 Jul
80.49A	Adriaan	Beukes	BOT	14.7.94	1	NC	Gaborone	31 May
80.41	Till	Wöschler	GER	9.6.91	1		Bottrop	21 Jun
80.17A	Dayron	Márquez	COL	19.11.83	1		Bogotá	12 Apr
80.06	Gatis	Cakss	LAT	13.6.95	1	Lusis	Jelgava	14 Jun
	(60)							
79.85	Jiannis	Smaliós	SWE	17.2.87	3		Karlstad	22 Jul
79.65	Devender	Singh	IND	18.12.88	1		Mangalore	2 May
79.60	German	Komarov	RUS	14.12.94	1		Sankt Peterburg	10 Jun
79.55	Sami	Peltomäki	FIN	11.1.91	Q	NC	Pori	1 Aug
79.49	Tim	van Liew	USA	25.5.90	3		Tucson	23 May
79.47		Zhao Qinggang	CHN	24.7.85	17q	WCh	Beijing	24 Aug
79.45	Norbert	Bonvecchio	ITA	14.8.85	8	GGala	Roma	4 Jun
79.39		Ma Qun	CHN	8.2.94	1		Chengdu	31 Mar
79.37	Zigismunds	Sirmais	LAT	6.5.92	3	WUG	Gwangju	10 Jul
79.29	Mykola	Shama	UKR	5.4.91	2		Kirovohrad	8 Jun
	(70)							
79.20	Matija	Muhar	SLO-J	22.7.96	1	EJ	Eskilstuna	18 Jul
79.16	Gabriel	Wallin	SWE	14.10.81	5	vFIN	Stockholm	13 Sep
79.05	Yukifumi	Murakami	JPN	23.12.79	3	AsiC	Wuhan	6 Jun
79.00	Dmytro	Kosynskyy	UKR	31.3.89	1	NC	Kirovohrad	1 Aug
78.90	Ainars	Kovals	LAT	21.11.81	4		Riga	28 May
78.86	Bartosz	Osewski	POL	20.3.91	1		Biala Podlaska	29 Aug
78.84A	Alex	Kiprotich	KEN	10.10.94	1		Eldoret	23 May
78.82	Edis	Matusevicius	LTU-J	30.6.96	3		Valmiera	31 Jul
78.73	Simon	Litzell	SWE-J	11.2.97	1		Bålsta	23 May
78.67	Ben	Woodruff	USA	9.5.89	4		Tucson	23 May
	(80)							
78.41	Ioannis	Kiriazis	GRE-J	19.1.96	1	SEC	Starkville	14 May
78.35	Matija	Kranjc	SLO	12.6.84	4	ECp-w	Leiria	15 Mar
78.32A	Strydom	van der Wath	NAM	25.9.91	2		Potchefstroom	8 May
78.15A	Guillermo	Martínez	CUB	28.6.81	2	NACAC	San José, CRC	9 Aug
78.08	Chris	Carper	USA	19.4.92	3		East Stroudsburg	26 Jul
78.06	Krystian	Bondarenko	POL	22.10.91	2	NC	Kraków	19 Jul
78.05	Dejan	Mileusnic	BIH	16.11.91	1		Sremska Mitrovica	21 Jul
77.97	Ben	Langton-Burnell	NZL	10.7.92	1		Hamilton	9 Dec
77.95	Aleksey	Tovarnov	RUS	21.1.85	3	NC	Cheboksary	4 Aug
77.95	Harri	Haatainen	FIN	5.1.78	1		Urjala	29 Aug
	(90)							
77.88	Ahmed Bader	Magour	QAT-J	3.3.96	1		Düsseldorf	30 Aug
77.85	Craig	Kinsley	USA	19.1.89	2	MSR	Walnut	18 Apr
77.81	Ranno	Koorep	EST	24.1.90	3		Kohila	6 Sep
77.75	Amarender	Singh	IND	15.8.91	1		Hyderabad	23 Jul
77.71A	Albert	Reynolds	STL	28.3.88	3	NACAC	San José, CRC	9 Aug
77.69	Víctor	Fatecha	PAR	10.3.88	2		Buenos Aires	29 Mar
77.68	Mikko	Kankaanpää	FIN	17.4.87	2		Saarijärvi	21 Jun
77.67A	Chad	Herman	RSA	25.5.92	1		Pretoria	30 Jan
77.63	Raymond	Dykstra	CAN	18.6.92	2	SEC	Starkville	14 May
77.51	Genki	Dean	JPN	30.12.91	1		Wakayama	5 Oct
	(100)							

Mark		Name	Nat	Born	Date
77.50	Amit	Kumar	IND	18.9.92	23 Jul
77.48	Dawid	Kosciów	POL	5.6.90	19 Sep
77.47	Macauley	Garton	USA	18.3.93	14 May
77.46	Timothy	Herman	BEL	19.10.90	26 Apr
77.46	Daan	Meyer	NED	17.2.83	31 Oct
77.45	Jani	Kiiskilä	FIN	28.12.89	24 May
77.42	Branko	Paukovic	SRB	28.5.9	11 May
77.40	Taisei	Aibara	JPN	18.8.95	11 Apr
77.39	Waruna Lakshan	Dayarathne	SRI	14.5.88	25 Aug
77.34	Janis	Griva	LAT	23.4.93	14 Jun
77.30	Shakiel	Waithe	TTO	10.6.95	28 Jun
77.27	Mart	ten Berge	NED	27.4.9	19 May
77.18	Osmani	Laffita	CUB	14.8.94	26 May
77.02		Park Won-kil	KOR	24.2.90	22 Apr
76.90	Vladimir	Kozlov	BLR	20.4.85	26 May
76.85	Phil-Mar	van Rensburg	RSA	23.6.89	17 Sep
76.76	Shivpal	Singh	IND	6.7.95	23 Jul
76.73		Li Yingchang	CHN	22.6.91	31 Mar
76.65	Abhishek	Singh	IND	29.4.94	23 Jul
76.61	Marcin	Plener	POL	22.8.90	19 Jul
76.54	Jonas	Bonewit	GER	30.7.95	23 May
76.53	Marian	Spannowsky	GER-J	20.9.96	21 Jun
76.48	Martin	Benák	SVK	27.5.88	20 May
76.47	Rohit	Kumar	IND	15.7.94	17 Sep
76.37	Ben	Baker	AUS	19.1.83	10 Jan
76.28	Oliver	Helander	FIN-J	1.1.97	16 Jul
76.25	Yuya	Koriki	JPN	19.10.89	28 Jun
76.12	Shu	Mori	JPN-J	1.11.96	14 May
76.09	Jarrod	Bannister ¶	AUS	3.10.84	4 Jul
76.09	Blaz	Marn	SLO	26.2.93	11 Jul
76.01	Piotr	Lebioda	POL	28.5.92	17 May
75.89	Raul	Rusu	ROU	20.7.95	3 Mar
75.86	Cody	Danielson	USA	1.12.93	22 Jul
75.83	Atsushi	Kawano	JPN-J	6.1.97	27 Sep
75.80	Yeóryios	Íltsios	GRE	28.11.81	7 Jun
75.77	Yevgeniy	Zoteyev	RUS	24.8.91	19 Jul
75.74	D.G.Sampath	Ranasinghe	SRI		3 Dec
75.72	Cyrus	Hostetler	USA	8.8.86	23 May
75.70A	Ayoub	Arokhi	IRI	23.5.82	3 Sep
75.66A	Luis Carlos	Álvarez	COL	13.2.92	19 Nov
75.65	Emin	Õncel	TUR-J	1.5.97	9 Aug
75.62	Curtis	Thompson	USA-J	8.2.96	14 May
75.60	Adrian	Mardare	MDA	20.6.95	8 Feb
75.59	Aleksandr	Kharitonov	RUS	19.7.90	9 May
75.57	Larson	Diaz	PAR	23.3.94	25 Sep
75.54	Aleksandr	Ashomko	BLR	18.2.84	24 Jul
75.54	Takuma	Nakanishi	JPN	8.4.94	13 Sep
75.46	Miro	Määttänen	FIN-J	17.6.96	18 Jul
75.45	Rhys	Stein	AUS-J	15.5.96	28 Feb
75.36	Kohei	Hasegawa	JPN	1.1.90	19 Apr
75.36		Jung Sang-jin	KOR	16.4.84	29 Jun
75.34	David	Golling	GER	13.3.90	4 Sep
75.29	Takuto	Kominami	JPN	26.7.95	5 Oct
75.28	Nick	Howe	USA	17.11.89	23 May
75.27		Kim Ye-ram	KOR	2.3.94	29 Jun
75.26	David	Ocampo	MEX	14.2.92	26 Apr
75.25	Jan	Kubes	CZE	19.6.94	16 May
75.23	Jarmo	Marttila	FIN	24.10.92	2 Aug
75.18	Vipin	Kasana	IND	4.8.89	12 Feb
75.18	Josue	Menendez	MEX	4.5.90	23 May
75.18	Peerachet	Janthra	THA	9.9.90	11 Jun
75.15	Yegor	Nikolayev	RUS-J	5.6.96	9 May
75.14	Samarjeet	Singh	IND	7.11.88	17 Sep
75.12	Levente	Bartha	ROU	8.3.77	26 Jul
75.09	Evan	Karakolis	CAN	30.3.94	24 Jul
75.07	Devin	Bogert	USA	27.5.93	4 Apr
75.03	Kim-Dominik	Seyfried	GER	23.6.92	21 Jun
75.02	Jurriaan	Wouters	NED	18.4.93	11 Jul
74.99		Deng Sheng	CHN	14.11.92	20 May
74.90	Gudmundur	Sverrisson	ISL	24.5.90	15 Mar
74.85	Ansis	Bruns	LAT	30.3.89	8 Aug
74.84	Ilya	Shapovalov	RUS	16.1.94	24 Feb
74.84	Tomoya	Era	JPN	19.6.93	15 May
74.74	Ken	Arai	JPN	22.12.81	12 Jul
74.74		Xiang Jiabo	CHN-J	15.8.97	23 Oct
74.68A	José Orlando	Escobar	ECU	21.8.91	15 Mar
74.68	Almanio	Romano	ITA	1.1.80	11 Jul
74.63	Tomás	Guerra	CHI	26.11.92	28 Mar
74.60	Ilya	Korotkov	RUS	6.12.83	11 Feb
74.55	Fumitaka	Saito	JPN	10.2.92	27 Sep
74.50	Sampo	Lehtola	FIN	10.5.89	19 Sep
74.47		Sun Jianjun	CHN	9.6.91	4 Apr
74.45	Caleb	Jones	CAN	17.5.91	3 Jul
74.42	Kenji	Ogura	JPN	8.6.95	13 Sep
74.41		Ku Chia-ho	TPE	24.9.94	6 May
74.40	Dmitriy	Mishakov	RUS	15.7.95	24 Feb
74.39	Kosei	Matsutani	JPN	3.5.93	28 Mar
74.35	Nikolay	Klimuk	BLR-J	20.12.96	30 Apr
74.28	Sam	Humphreys	USA	12.9.90	21 Mar
74.26	Cruz	Hogan	AUS	22.2.94	6 Feb
74.25	Nikólaos	Efthaliádis	GRE	23.1.91	26 Jul
74.23	Joni	Karvinen	FIN	7.2.94	29 Jun
74.20	Anderson	Peters	GRN-J	21.10.97	28 Jun
74.11	Yuta	Sakiyama	JPN-J	5.4.96	26 Apr
74.10	Ravinder	Singh Khaira	IND	19.3.86	12 Feb
74.10		Bae You-il	KOR	16.6.94	20 Oct
74.09	Vladislav	Panasenkov	RUS-J	22.5.96	18 Jul
74.07	Juan José	Méndez	MEX	27.4.88	20 May
74.02	Jarne	Duchateau (199)	BEL-J	12.11.96	24 Sep

JUNIORS

See main list for top 6 juniors. 11 performances by 6 men over 77.40. Additional marks and further juniors:

Chopra	77.67	1	NC	Kolkata	19 Sep
Muhar	77.60	1	ECp-w23	Leiria	15 Mar
Matusevicius	77.48	3	EJ	Eskilstuna	18 Jul
Litzell	78.34	2	EJ	Eskilstuna	18 Jul
Kiriazís	77.67	1	NCAAw	Austin	29 May

76.53	Marian	Spannowsky	GER	20.9.96	1		Balingen	21 Jun
76.28	Oliver	Helander	FIN	1.1.97	Q	EJ	Eskilstuna	16 Jul
76.12	Shu	Mori	JPN	1.11.96	1		Yokohama	14 May
75.83	Atsushi	Kawano (10)	JPN	6.1.97	1		Kurume	27 Sep
75.65	Emin	Õncel	TUR	1.5.97	1		Mersin	9 Aug
75.62	Curtis	Thompson	USA	8.2.96	4	SEC	Starkville	14 May
75.46	Miro	Määttänen	FIN	17.6.96	5	EJ	Eskilstuna	18 Jul
75.45	Rhys	Stein	AUS	15.5.96	2		Sydney	28 Feb
75.15	Yegor	Nikolayev	RUS	5.6.96	3		Liepaja	9 May
74.74		Xiang Jiabo	CHN	15.8.97	1	NYG	Fuzhou	23 Oct
74.35	Nikolay	Klimuk	BLR	20.12.96	1		Brest	30 Apr
74.20	Anderson	Peters	GRN	21.10.97	3	TTO Ch	Port of Spain	28 Jun
74.11	Yuta	Sakiyama	JPN	5.4.96	1		Tokyo	26 Apr
74.09	Vladislav	Panasenkov (20)	RUS	22.5.96	8	EJ	Eskilstuna	18 Jul

Mark	Name		Nat	Born	Pos	Meet	Venue		Date

DECATHLON

Mark	Name		Nat	Born	Pos	Meet	Venue		Date
9045	Ashton	Eaton	USA	21.1.88	1	WCh	Beijing		29 Aug
10.23/-0.4	7.88/0.0	14.52	2.01	45.00	13.69/-0.2	43.34	5.20	63.63	4:17.52
8725(w)	Trey	Hardee	USA	7.2.84	1	NC	Eugene		26 Jun
10.48/2.0	7.61w/3.4	14.55	1.97	48.41	13.71/1.3	52.05	5.35	61.92	4:45.77
8695	Damian	Warner	CAN	4.11.89	2	WCh	Beijing		29 Aug
10.31/-0.4	7.65/0.2	14.44	2.04	47.30	13.63/-0.2	44.99	4.80	63.50	4:31.51
8659		Warner			1	PAm	Toronto		23 Jul
10.28/1.4	7.68w/2.4	14.36	1.97	47.66	13.44/2.0	47.56	4.60	61.53	4:24.73
8561	Rico	Freimuth	GER	14.3.88	3	WCh	Beijing		29 Aug
10.51/-0.4	7.51/0.5	15.50	1.95	47.82	13.91/-0.2	50.17	4.80	60.61	4:37.05
8538	Ilya	Shkurenyov	RUS	11.1.91	4	WCh	Beijing		29 Sep
11.01/-0.7	7.50/0.5	14.09	2.10	47.88	14.27/-0.2	44.53	5.20	60.99	4:24.98
8469	Kevin	Mayer	FRA	10.2.92	1		Arona		7 Jun
11.12/1.1	7.42/0.7	15.33	1.98	48.91	14.44/-2.0	45.83	5.35	63.46	4:29.59
8462	Kai	Kazmirek	GER	28.1.91	1	Hypo	Götzis		31 May
10.78/0.8	7.56/-1.3	13.85	2.09	47.30	14.52/-0.7	40.96	5.10	64.45	4:34.61
8461	Larbi	Bouraada	ALG	10.5.88	5	WCh	Beijing		29 Aug
10.83/-0.2	7.51/0.6	13.73	2.07	47.60	14.26/-1.0	41.53	4.80	63.82	4:16.61
8448		Kazmirek			6	WCh	Beijing		29 Aug
10.90/-0.2	7.40/0.2	14.27	2.10	46.83	14.39/0.0	40.08	5.20	62.55	4:35.61
8419	Michael	Schrader	GER	1.7.87	1		Ratingen		28 Jun
10.78/-0.4	7.81/0.6	14.80	1.92	48.19	14.08/1.1	44.97	5.00	56.57	4:27.28
8418		Schrader			7	WCh	Beijing		29 Aug
10.78/-0.4	7.71/0.1	14.32	1.95	47.12	14.19/-0.2	44.58	4.60	62.09	4:22.30
8415		Schrader			2		Götzis		31 May
10.68/0.8	7.66/0.0	14.31	1.94	48.21	14.25/1.5	42.11	5.00	61.44	4:22.87
8398	Willem	Coertzen (10)	RSA	30.12.82	3	Hypo	Götzis		31 May
10.99/0.3	7.46/-1.0	14.14	2.03	48.73	14.17/1.5	44.84	4.60	68.43	4:22.22
8380		Freimuth			4		Götzis		31 May
10.53/-0.1	7.54/0.6	15.47	1.91	48.70	13.99/-0.7	48.07	4.80	60.96	4:46.16
8378		Shkurenyov			1	ECp	Aubagne		5 Jul
11.05/-0.1	7.55/0.0	14.24	2.10	49.40	14.32/-0.8	45.99	5.30	56.93	4:39.51
8356	Maicel	Uibo	EST	27.12.92	1	NCAA	Eugene		11 Jun
11.10w/3.2	7.54/1.4	14.38	2.14	51.65	14.99/1.0	46.45	5.20	62.25	4:28.48
8343		Shkurenyov			5		Götzis		31 May
11.07/0.3	7.47/0.8	13.76	2.00	49.00	14.02/1.5	44.97	5.20	59.49	4:28.69
8326		Uibo			1	SEC	Starkville		15 May
11.19/1.0	7.44w/2.1	14.16	2.18	50.89	15.01/1.4	48.33	5.20	56.92	4:28.57
8341		Coertzen			2		Ratingen		28 Jun
11.08/-0.4	7.48w/3.1	14.50	2.01	48.50	14.06/1.1	43.94	4.50	68.79	4:26.52
8303	Jeremy	Taiwo	USA	15.1.90	6	Hypo	Götzis		31 May
10.95/0.8	7.57/0.0	13.95	2.15	48.29	14.47/1.5	43.16	4.90	49.22	4:19.64
8302	Kurt	Felix	GRN	4.7.88	8	WCh	Beijing		29 Aug
11.02/-0.7	7.66/1.4	15.02	2.10	49.89	14.58/-0.2	45.95	4.50	63.41	4:32.57
8298	Eelco	Sintnicolaas	NED	7.4.87	7	Hypo	Götzis		31 May
10.75/-0.1	7.62/-1.0	14.67	1.91	48.48	14.34/-0.7	37.45	5.20	62.74	4:30.18
8269		Felix			2	PAm	Toronto		23 Jul
10.91/1.4	7.54w/3.8	15.23	2.09	49.67	14.71w/2.4	44.54	4.60	64.10	4:38.39
8264		Taiwo			2	NC	Eugene		26 Jun
10.89/2.0	7.54w/2.2	14.93	2.12	47.83	14.40/1.4	41.15	4.95	48.11	4:29.27
8262	Oleksiy	Kasyanov	UKR	26.8.85	9	WCh	Beijing		29 Aug
10.73/-0.2	7.58/-0.1	14.25	2.01	48.13	13.96/0.0	45.84	4.80	49.35	4:31.80
8247	Pau Gaspar	Tonnesen	ESP	24.10.92	2	NCAA	Eugene		11 Jun
11.11w/3.2	7.49/1.8	15.17	2.08	50.68	14.87/0.7	45.53	5.30	57.52	4:41.77
8245		Uibo			10	WCh	Beijing		29 Sep
11.25/-0.5	7.13/0.1	14.45	2.13	50.24	15.01/-0.2	43.69	5.10	64.51	4:25.53
8234	Adam	Helcelet	CZE	27.10.91	11	WCh	Beijing		29 Aug
11.09/-0.5	7.29/0.6	15.30	2.04	49.66	14.20/0.0	42.90	4.90	63.07	4:37.65
8232	Garrett	Scantling	USA	19.5.93	1		Athens, GA		9 Apr
10.85/0.8	7.25/2.0	15.06	2.06	49.04	14.21/0.1	37.19	4.95	67.34	4:44.31
(30/18)									
8197	Pieter	Braun	NED	21.1.93	8	Hypo	Götzis		31 May
10.97/0.5	7.53/1.3	13.97	2.00	48.49	14.25/0.5	42.80	4.90	55.57	4:28.18
8186	Yordani	García	CUB	21.11.88	9	Hypo	Götzis		31 May
10.77/-0.1	6.88/1.5	14.38	2.03	48.42	14.00/-0.7	41.10	4.70	64.28	4:31.67
(20)									
8179(w)	Luiz Alberto	de Araújo	BRA	27.9.87	3	PAm	Toronto		23 Jul
10.81/1.4	7.53w/2.8	15.16	2.00	49.91	14.29/2.0	46.16	4.70	56.36	4:39.77

Mark	Name		Nat	Born	Pos	Meet	Venue	Date
8147	Bastien	Auzeil	FRA	22.10.89	10	Hypo	Götzis	31 May
	11.02/-0.1 7.28/0.5 15.90 1.97 49.57 14.42/0.5 43.58 4.80 64.41 4:46.19							
8140	Pawel	Wiesiolek	POL	13.8.91	11	Hypo	Götzis	31 May
	10.97/0.3 7.61/0.1 14.55 2.00 49.80 14.78/-0.3 46.20 4.70 59.35 4:35.81							
8107	Zach	Ziemek	USA	23.2.93	3	NC	Eugene	26 Jun
	10.57/2.0 7.71w/2.4 14.77 2.06 51.31 14.78/1.6 37.27 5.45 55.43 4:58.93							
8081	Curtis	Beach	USA	22.7.90	1		Chula Vista	23 May
	10.52/1.9 7.84/1.3 12.64 1.98 47.45 14.51w/2.1 36.64 5.05 35.97 4:06.18							
8059	Yevgeniy	Sarantsev	RUS	5.8.88	1		Adler	12 May
	11.41/1.0 7.18/0.0 15.72 2.00 51.40 15.05/0.2 44.90 5.10 65.94 4:42.26							
8058	Keisuke	Ushiro	JPN	24.7.86	1	NC	Nagano	5 Jul
	11.35/0.3 7.01/1.1 15.65 2.03 50.52 15.00/-0.9 49.33 4.80 61.72 4:38.97							
8049	Niels	Pittomvils	BEL	18.7.92	1	FRA Ch	Villeneuve d'Ascq	11 Jul
	11.35/-1.6 7.22/1.0 14.30 2.04 50.23 14.82/-0.4 43.07 5.30 54.82 4:29.76							
8045	Jan Felix	Knobel	GER	16.1.89	1	vUSA	Bernhausen	9 Aug
	11.07/0.2 7.37/-0.9 15.68 1.99 50.28 14.70/1.4 44.43 5.06 62.32 5:05.93							
8043	Akihiko	Nakamura	JPN	23.10.90	1		Wakayama	26 Apr
	10.52w/2.4 7.48/0.8 11.89 2.02 47.57 14.29/-1.8 34.84 4.80 50.57 4:14.79							
	(30)							
8035	Thomas	Van Der Plaetsen	BEL	24.12.90	14	WCh	Beijing	29 Aug
	11.44/-0.5 7.42/1.2 13.60 2.13 50.28 14.76/-1.0 43.01 5.30 55.23 4:47.38							
8027	Leonel	Suárez	CUB	1.9.87	1	Barr	La Habana	27 May
	11.36/0.0 7.00/1.7 13.79 2.05 51.94 14.58/1.6 44.45 4.90 69.74 4:34.24							
8019	Felipe	dos Santos	BRA	30.7.94	4	PAm	Toronto	23 Jul
	10.37/1.4 7.52w/2.1 14.22 2.03 48.65 14.10/2.0 42.38 4.50 47.88 4:48.14							
8009	Mathias	Brugger	GER	6.8.92	2	vUSA	Bernhausen	9 Aug
	11.02/1.3 7.21/-0.8 14.86 1.96 48.91 14.68/1.4 43.59 4.86 52.93 4:29.49							
8007	Romain	Barras	FRA	1.8.80	3	ECp	Aubagne	5 Jul
	11.25/-0.1 6.90/0.9 15.31 2.04 50.01 14.63/-0.8 42.73 4.90 59.60 4:33.62							
7984	Sergey	Timshin	RUS	25.11.92	1	NC	Cheboksary	9 Jun
	11.04/0.7 7.25w/4.0 13.92 2.12 48.98 14.74/0.8 41.69 4.70 54.57 4:36.45							
7983	Jorge	Ureña	ESP	8.10.93	2	EU23	Tallinn	12 Jul
	10.94/1.9 7.47/1.5 13.43 2.04 49.26 14.13/0.7 36.93 4.60 60.87 4:36.97							
7970	Florian	Geffrouais	FRA	5.12.88	4	ECp	Aubagne	5 Jul
	11.17/0.3 7.09/0.6 14.77 1.92 48.74 14.90/-0.9 44.40 4.70 58.83 4:25.32							
7945	Janek	Oiglane	EST	25.4.94	3	EU23	Tallinn	12 Jul
	11.32/0.3 7.23/0.5 14.88 2.04 51.14 14.67/0.7 40.70 4.50 69.15 4:37.75							
7914	Gaël	Quérin	FRA	26.6.87	4		Talence	19 Sep
	11.29/0.2 7.38/0.2 13.00 1.95 49.08 14.35/-0.1 39.80 5.05 51.05 4:20.44							
	(40)							
7907	René	Stauß	GER	17.9.87	3	vUSA	Bernhausen	9 Aug
	11.09/0.2 7.19/-0.5 14.89 2.08 50.02 15.26/-0.3 44.40 4.86 55.35 4:49.17							
7894	Aleksey	Kravtsov	RUS	8.5.93	2	NC	Cheboksary	9 Jun
	10.80/0.7 7.36w/2.9 13.74 2.00 48.94 14.42/0.8 37.38 4.60 55.00 4:33.33							
7892	Marek	Lukás	CZE	16.7.91	1		Kladno	13 Jun
	11.05/-1.7 7.06/2.0 14.35 1.93 50.00 14.56/-1.7 40.38 4.55 65.83 4:31.84							
7884	Fredrik	Samuelsson	SWE	16.2.95	5	EU23	Tallinn	12 Jul
	10.98/1.9 7.81/0.8 13.48 2.04 50.32 14.65/0.6 37.68 4.70 55.33 4:41.23							
7882w	Román	Gastaldi	ARG	25.9.89	1	NC	Mar del Plata	13 Dec
	10.80w/3.6 7.47w/4.5 14.34 2.01 50.08 15.00 44.24 4.60 55.18 4:49.92							
7876	Hans	Van Alphen	BEL	12.1.82	15	Hypo	Götzis	31 May
	11.27/-0.1 7.24/0.7 14.96 1.94 50.43 15.20/-0.2 44.93 4.70 58.25 4:28.86							
7875	Martin	Roe	NOR	1.4.92	1	ECp-1	Inowroclaw	5 Jul
	10.84/-0.9 7.30/0.5 15.28 1.92 49.00 15.49/0.9 44.24 4.40 58.10 4:35.13							
7869	Yevgeniy	Likhanov	RUS	10.1.95	4	NC	Cheboksary	9 Jun
	11.15/0.7 7.49w/2.3 13.79 2.06 51.08 14.93/0.8 42.73 4.60 57.63 4:36.68							
7863(w)	Dakotah	Keys	USA	27.9.91	3	NCAA	Eugene	11 Jun
	11.07w/3.2 7.34w/3.1 13.78 2.02 50.46 14.90/1.6 37.80 4.50 64.12 4:29.33							
7862	Solomon	Ijah/Simmons	USA	26.9.93	1		Muncie	15 May
	10.60/1.9 6.74/1.5 15.04 1.91 49.14 14.38/-0.1 42.09 4.68 59.98 4:52.55							
	(50)							
7857(w)	Liam	Ramsay	GBR	18.11.92	1		Bedford	19 Jul
	11.01/1.4 7.35w/2.7 12.96 2.05 48.44 14.58w/2.2 36.10 4.75 52.06 4:27.90							
7852	Ingmar	Vos	NED	28.5.86	16	Hypo	Götzis	31 May
	10.93/-0.1 7.42/0.7 13.50 2.03 51.09 14.35/1.5 41.05 4.40 59.23 4:37.84							
7832	Jiri	Sykora	CZE	20.1.95	17	Hypo	Götzis	31 May
	11.06/0.8 7.14/0.1 14.95 1.97 49.75 14.88/-0.2 46.49 4.60 61.47 5:04.01							
7827	Tim	Nowak	GER	13.8.95	2		Ulm	28 May
	11.20/1.2 7.10/1.1 14.13 1.98 49.73 14.79/0.0 41.66 4.70 60.19 4:38.33							
7826	Pascal	Behrenbruch	GER	19.1.85	3		Ratingen	28 Jun
	11.27/-0.4 6.76/0.4 15.52 1.98 51.45 14.35/1.1 44.43 4.80 66.74 5:03.77							

Mark	Name		Nat	Born	Pos	Meet	Venue	Date
7825	Romain	Martin	FRA	12.7.88	3		Kladno	13 Jun
	11.16/-1.7 6.97/0.0 14.22 2.02 49.25 14.81/-1.7 39.26 4.75 59.18 4:37.31							
7817	Yuriy	Yeremich	BLR	24.10.95	1		Brest	5 Jun
	10.62/1.9 7.79/0.7 12.38 2.04 50.14 14.98/-0.8 36.21 4.80 55.44 4:48.49							
7806	Harrison	Williams	USA-J	7.3.96	4	NCAA	Eugene	11 Jun
	10.83/1.2 6.98w/2.3 13.29 1.90 47.16 14.68/1.6 37.98 5.00 49.89 4:30.89							
7805	Gonzalo	Barroilhet	CHI	19.8.86	2		Athens, GA	9 Apr
	11.23/0.8 6.88w/2.3 13.96 2.03 51.16 14.48/0.1 42.59 5.25 54.54 4:50.30							
7801	Maxime	Maugein	FRA	27.9.92	7	ECp	Aubagne	5 Jul
	11.19/0.1 6.96/1.2 13.71 1.95 49.47 14.52/-0.8 41.40 4.90 51.83 4:25.72							
	(60)							
7798	John	Lane	GBR	29.1.89	18	Hypo	Götzis	31 May
	10.79/-0.1 7.07/0.3 13.71 1.97 48.92 14.57/0.5 40.17 4.90 50.19 4:42.18							
7793	Aleksandr	Frolov	RUS	5.3.87	5	NC	Cheboksary	9 Jun
	11.46w/2.2 7.02W/4.4 15.31 2.06 53.19 15.84/-1.6 47.99 4.90 59.17 4:38.83							
7791	Thomas	FitzSimons	USA	8.3.89	1		Santa Barbara	4 Apr
	11.26/-0.7 7.16/1.1 12.67 1.96 49.11 15.16/0.0 40.40 4.60 59.45 4:15.64							
7773(w)	James	Turner	CAN	4.8.93	1	MSR	Azusa	16 Apr
	10.74w/2.9 7.40w/2.1 13.09 1.91 49.34 14.71w/2.7 42.05 4.20 57.59 4:31.15							
7771	José Angel	Mendieta	CUB	16.10.91	2	Barr	La Habana	27 May
	11.04/0.0 7.09w/2.5 15.02 1.93 50.60 14.60/1.6 42.18 4.40 63.74 4:47.57							
7764	Friedrich	Pretorius	RSA	4.8.95	1		Pretoria	21 Mar
	10.99 7.33/1.6 13.14 1.93 49.60 14.39/2.8 42.85 4.40 55.98 4:36.50							
7762	Tommy	Barrineau	FIN	28.8.88	3		Athens, GA	9 Apr
	11.05/0.8 6.59/0.0 14.04 1.97 49.05 14.77/-1.1 40.11 4.75 61.69 4:39.12							
7752	Roman	Kondratyev	RUS	15.5.95	6	NC	Cheboksary	9 Jun
	11.01/0.7 7.54w/3.8 13.31 2.06 49.22 14.18/0.8 37.29 4.50 49.88 4:45.74							
7744	Taavi	Tsernjavski	EST	4.3.95	9	ECp	Aubagne	5 Jul
	11.18/-0.1 7.00/0.9 14.05 1.95 49.27 14.94/-0.8 44.52 4.50 56.22 4:34.43							
7743(w)	Miller	Moss	USA	14.3.88	1		Dallas	31 May
	10.87/1.7 7.18/1.9 13.59 1.94 48.65 14.39/2.7 41.98 4.60 50.48 4:45.41							
	(70)							
7743	Elmo	Savola	FIN	10.3.95	7	EU23	Tallinn	12 Jul
	10.96/0.3 7.27/1.6 13.45 1.98 49.84 14.51/0.6 37.37 4.50 62.96 4:48.17							
7742	Lars Vikan	Rise	NOR	23.11.88	4	ECp-1	Inowroclaw	5 Jul
	11.58/-1.4 7.05/-0.7 15.83 2.04 51.25 15.70/1.6 45.15 4.40 61.09 4:33.87							
7733	David	Brock	AUS	8.6.94	1	NC	Brisbane	27 Mar
	11.08/0.5 7.36/1.9 13.57 2.05 50.67 15.17/1.5 41.65 4.50 53.84 4:33.63							
7728	Artem	Lukyanenko	RUS	30.1.90	2		Adler	10 Sep
	10.97/-1.2 6.78/0.8 14.50 1.94 49.78 14.45/-1.8 38.71 5.00 54.50 4:45.46							
7725	Takumi	Otobe	JPN	22.4.89	3	NC	Nagano	5 Jul
	10.53/1.2 7.43/1.0 12.29 2.03 49.23 14.88/-0.7 38.97 4.40 52.39 4:41.54							
7720	Mihail	Dudas	SRB	1.11.89	1	Balk C	Pitesti	2 Aug
	11.17/-0.8 6.95w/3.5 13.63 2.01 50.16 14.86/0.8 42.93 4.60 58.34 4:40.91							
7697	Tsuyoshi	Shimizu	JPN	21.12.93	1		Osaka	13 Sep
	10.97/-1.2 7.54/0.0 12.08 1.93 48.39 14.94/0.1 36.25 4.50 53.37 4:21.84							
7693	Sergey	Sviridov	RUS	20.10.90	2	BLR Ch	Grodno	25 Jul
	11.18/1.3 7.06/-0.5 14.25 1.88 50.54 15.18/0.5 47.01 4.70 62.13 4:54.92							
7693	Patrick	Scherfose	GER	28.11.91	4	vUSA	Bernhausen	9 Aug
	11.03/0.2 7.22/0.1 14.38 1.90 51.03 14.48/0.5 42.19 4.96 50.59 4:49.37							
7689(w)	Kurtis	Brondyke	USA	24.1.89	2		Dallas	31 May
	11.23/1.7 7.16/1.8 13.64 1.96 50.90 14.83w/2.7 46.57 4.40 61.08 4:48.80							
	(80)							
7679	Kazuya	Kawasaki	JPN	2.9.92	4	NC	Nagano	5 Jul
	10.79/1.2 7.39/-0.2 11.39 2.03 49.30 15.73/-0.7 38.71 4.60 57.19 4:32.45							
7679	Basile	Rolnin	FRA	21.1.94	8	EU23	Tallinn	12 Jul
	11.17/0.3 7.23/1.3 13.52 1.86 50.74 14.68/0.7 42.85 4.90 58.10 4:48.65							
7677	Tim	Ehrhardt	USA	16.3.95	5	NCAA	Eugene	11 Jun
	11.00/1.1 7.45/1.3 11.89 1.87 47.99 15.80/1.0 41.06 5.20 49.72 4:36.96							
7669(w)	Stephen	Soerens	USA	18.6.93	6	NCAA	Eugene	11 Jun
	11.11w/3.2 7.36w/2.3 14.86 1.96 50.16 16.05/0.7 41.76 4.30 61.09 4:37.74							
7668	Kristjan	Rosenberg	EST	16.5.94	1		Rakvere	21 Jun
	11.04/1.3 7.30/0.2 13.57 2.02 50.51 15.18/0.1 41.29 4.40 57.74 4:43.05							
7664		Hu Yufei	CHN	9.11.93	1		Guilin	22 Jul
	10.97 7.00 14.09 2.02 50.18 14.61 40.91 4.60 52.72 4:49.41							
7663	Marcus	Nilsson	SWE	3.5.91	3	Pac-12	Los Angeles (Ww)	10 May
	11.45/-0.3 6.72/1.9 14.03 1.90 51.58 14.81/0.5 41.99 4.83 59.64 4:22.35							
7659	Pavel	Rudnev	RUS	26.10.92	7	NC	Cheboksary	9 Jun
	11.07w/2.2 7.47w/2.2 13.01 1.94 50.78 14.87/-1.6 36.22 4.90 50.75 4:27.93							
7651	David	Hall	GBR	25.4.95	5		Kladno	13 Jun
	10.84/-1.7 6.83/0.3 12.16 1.96 46.98 14.98/-0.8 37.86 4.45 53.43 4:24.79							

Mark	Name		Nat	Born	Pos	Meet	Venue	Date
'650	Wolf	Mahler	USA	26.9.94	7	NCAA	Eugene	11 Jun
	10.89/1.2 6.63w/2.2 12.02 1.87 47.20 14.90/1.0 38.80 4.90 51.26 4:20.80							
	(90)							
'647	Scott	Filip	USA	28.1.95	8	NCAA	Eugene	11 Jun
	10.74/1.2 7.32/0.7 13.06 1.99 48.17 15.59/0.7 37.94 4.80 47.01 4:40.80							
'635	Luca	Wieland	GER	7.12.94	1	Big 10	East Lansing	16 May
	10.78/1.8 7.51w/4.0 14.87 2.05 51.19 14.99/0.0 41.00 4.55 48.21 5:06.59							
'630	Martin	Brockman	GBR	13.11.87	4		Arona	7 Jun
	11.44/1.1 7.23/1.2 14.29 2.01 49.51 15.45/-0.1 44.54 4.55 46.56 4:31.64							
'629	Kyle	Cranston	AUS	3.9.92	2	NC	Brisbane	27 Mar
	11.04w/2.9 7.10/0.7 13.00 1.84 49.71 14.99/1.5 43.31 4.60 56.51 4:32.93							
'621	Juuso	Hassi	FIN	4.4.93	9	EU23	Tallinn	12 Jul
	10.97/0.7 7.08/0.7 13.54 1.89 49.27 14.95/0.6 40.45 4.50 59.35 4:45.03							
'611	Simone	Cairoli	ITA	12.9.90	3		Firenze	16 May
	10.92/0.6 7.40/0.1 12.85 1.98 49.13 15.37/-0.4 36.75 4.15 57.04 4:26.36							
'610	Ruben	Gado	FRA	13.12.93	2		Angoulème	7 Jun
	11.13/1.5 6.93/-0.8 12.41 1.93 50.19 15.47/0.7 42.02 5.07 53.08 4:31.06							
'600	Yevgeniy	Chernov	RUS	9.11.91	4		Adler	12 May
	11.02/0.1 7.42/0.7 13.89 1.97 50.25 15.04/-1.4 37.15 4.40 53.38 4:36.00							
'597	Osman	Muskwe	GBR	24.11.85	1		Amersfoort	30 Aug
	11.31/1.0 6.86/1.0 15.03 1.95 50.65 15.66/-0.1 51.97 4.36 55.03 4:49.21							
'594	Kevin	Lazas	USA	25.1.92	1		Fayetteville	16 Apr
	11.32/0.6 7.14/0.9 14.41 1.96 52.43 15.26/0.6 39.21 5.00 59.64 4:49.62							
	(100)							

Mark	First	Last	Nat	Born	Date
'593	Jérémy	Lelièvre	FRA	8.2.91	9 Jul
'591	Guillaume	Thierry	MRI	15.9.86	15 Sep
'588	Nils	Merten	GER	20.2.91	28 May
'579	Austin	Bahner	USA	7.7.91	16 Apr
'578	Mitch	Modin	USA	12.4.95	17 Apr
'575	Yevgeniy	Teptin	RUS	16.3.90	9 Jun
'574	Ánderson	Venâncio	BRA	6.1.87	16 May
'573	Ben	Gregory	GBR	21.11.90	7 Jun
'568w	Mohammed	Jassem Al-Qaree	KSA	11.5.88	27 Apr
'567	Atsu	Nyamadi	GHA	1.6.94	11 Jun
'557(w)	Evan	Weinstock	USA	30.10.91	26 Mar
'556	Ramo	Kask	EST	13.7.89	16 Aug
'555	Mike	Morgan	USA	19.6.94	26 Jun
'554	Derek	Masterson	USA	30.1.90	13 Jun
'550	Justin	Balczak	USA	11.12.92	16 Apr
'549A	K'Vonte	Scott	USA	17.6.93	15 May
'549	Markus	Leemet	EST	22.8.93	11 Jun
'542(w)	Hendrik	Nungess	GER	3.2.94	9 May
'541	Jonas	Fringeli	SUI	12.1.88	16 Aug
'534		Guo Qi	CHN	28.12.90	30 Apr
'531	Jonay	Jordán	ESP	12.5.91	2 Aug
'521	Steele	Wasik	USA	8.12.95	16 Apr
'520		Chen Xiaohong	CHN-J	9.2.97	30 Apr
'518(w)	Matthias	Clark	USA	31.5.87	23 Apr
'509	Rauno	Liitmäe	EST	24.1.93	7 Jun
'504	Juan Carlos	de la Cruz	DOM	16.5.90	20 Jun
'502(w)	Patrick	Arbour	CAN	17.3.88	23 Jul
'498	Martin	Sisas	EST	11.2.89	7 Jun
'498w	Guillermo	Ruggeri	ARG	26.3.92	13 Dec
'492	Yuta	Notoya	JPN	8.7.89	5 Jul
7491	Keegan	Cooke	ZIM	20.6.88	13 Jun
7480	Sho	Aizawa	JPN	24.9.91	5 Jul
7467A	Kevin	Nielsen	USA	12.1.93	23 Apr
7466	Zach	Taylor	USA	3.8.94	15 May
7466		Kim Kun-woo	KOR	29.2.80	20 Oct
7465	Vasyl	Ivanytskyy	UKR	29.1.91	16 May
7462	Joli	Koivu	FIN	18.7.90	5 Jul
7454	Geormis	Jaramillo	VEN	6.3.89	13 Jun
7453	Kojiro	Tani	JPN	30.4.92	5 Jul
7453(w)	Lindon	Victor	GRN	28.2.93	23 Jul
7452	Stefan	Matula	GER	18.7.90	13 Jun
7448	Kaarel	Jõeväli	EST	8.1.90	7 Jun
7446		Bae Sang-hwa	KOR	21.7.90	4 May
7445	Bas	Markies	NED	24.7.84	5 Jul
7441	Ionel	Cojan	ROU	8.5.94	7 Jun
7440	Danilo	Bastida	CUB	5.4.92	27 May
7426	Aleksey	Cherkasov	RUS	22.10.94	8 Sep
7422	Vladislav	Grinchuk	RUS	28.10.93	9 Jun
7421	Felipe	Ruiz	MEX	20.2.95	25 Apr
7421	Maksim	Korolyov	RUS	6.1.88	8 Sep
7419	Román	Garibay	MEX	30.10.88	23 Jul
7418	Hendrik	Lepik	EST	18.4.90	5 Jul
7416	Dino	Dodig	SRB	25.3.93	10 May
7411	Nico	Beckers	GER	3.3.94	28 Jun
7405(w)	Juhan	Kilumets	EST	15.10.89	16 Aug
7402	Joshua	Mulder	USA	16.3.95	18 Apr
7402	Aron	Schreiner	GER	18.1.93	7 Jun
	(157)				

Best non-wind assisted

Mark	First	Last	Nat	Born	Date
7447	Román	Gastaldi	ARG	25.9.89	6 Sep

JUNIORS

Mark	Name		Nat	Born	Pos	Meet	Venue	Date
'806	Harrison	Williams	USA-J	7.3.96	4	NCAA	Eugene	11 Jun
	10.83/1.2 6.98w/2.3 13.29 1.90 47.16 14.68/1.6 37.98 5.00 49.89 4:30.89							
	7679 2 Pac12 Los Angeles (Ww) 10 May							
'520		Chen Xiaohong	CHN-J	9.2.97	2		Jinan	30 Apr
	10.92/1.4 7.40/-0.1 13.38 1.95 49.49 15.44/0.1 41.89 4.10 60.29 5:00.05							
'332		Vitaliy Zhuk	BLR	10.9.96	20	ECp	Aubagne	5 Jul
	11.49/-0.1 6.54w/2.3 14.08 1.92 49.89 15.06/-0.7 41.48 4.30 53.75 4:36.45							
'281	Tanner	Johnson	USA	18.1.96	1		Tallahassee	16 May
	11.44/0.1 6.92/-0.1 12.30 1.90 51.12 15.79/0.1 38.44 4.67 57.12 4:33.35							
'260	Jan	Dolezal	CZE	6.6.96	25	ECp	Aubagne	5 Jul
	10.94/0.3 7.08/-0.1 12.55 2.01 49.47 15.79/-0.9 43.04 4.30 48.90 5:10.04							
'156	Timothy	Duckworth	GBR	18.6.96	5		Starkville	15 May
	11.13/0.8 7.10/0.6 11.05 2.03 51.51 14.87w/2.1 37.48 4.60 53.15 5:18.95							
'112	Santiago	Ford	CUB	25.8.97	5	Barr	La Habana	27 May
	11.49/0.0 6.50/0.1 13.06 1.99 51.42 15.27/1.6 43.92 3.50 59.05 4:40.57							
'042	Rik	Taam	NED	17.1.97	3	NC	Amsterdam	31 Jul
	11.25/1.1 6.71/1.1 12.18 1.80 50.54 15.45/0.0 40.57 4.40 46.73 4:34.81							

Mark	Name		Nat	Born	Pos	Meet	Venue	Date

IAAF JUNIOR SPECIFICATION – WITH 99CM 110MH, 6KG SP, 1.75KG DT

Mark	Name		Nat	Born	Pos	Meet	Venue	Date
8037	Harrison	Williams	USA	7.3.96	1	PAm-J	Edmonton	1 Aug
	10.67w/2.9 6.98w/3.7 13.71		2.03 48.28		14.41/-1.0	39.68	5.00 51.77	4:29.20
	8001 1 NC-j	Eugene	25 Jun					
	10.78/1.0 7.05/1.6 13.61		1.97 48.56		14.06/1.2	40.61	5.05 51.23	4:32.85
7929(w)	Jan	Doležal	CZE	6.6.96	1	EJ	Eskilstuna	19 Ju
	10.91w/2.8 7.19w/2.3 15.30		1.97 49.91		14.01w/2.8	54.75	4.20 54.70	5:08.39
	7583 1 NC-j	Stará Boleslav	24 May					
7764(w)	Karsten	Warholm	NOR	28.2.96	2	EJ	Eskilstuna	19 Ju
	10.53w/2.8 7.66/1.5 12.19		2.00 48.72		13.84w/2.8	39.30	4.30 45.82	4:44.73
7730		Chen Xiaohong	CHN	9.2.97	1	NYG	Fuzhou	26 Oc
	10.80w/2.2 7.57/0.9 13.93		1.92 48.93		14.89/0.3	43.88	4.00 64.53	5:06.62
7717	Manuel	Eitel	GER	28.1.97	1		Filderstadt	7 Jun
	10.63/0.2 7.08/0.0 15.63		1.90 49.52		14.00/0.0	41.29	4.40 51.37	5:01.02
7717	Maksim	Andraloits	BLR	17.6.97	3	EJ	Eskilstuna	19 Ju
	11.02w/2.8 7.29w/2.6 15.32		2.00 50.44		13.98w/2.3	43.49	4.30 45.74	4:47.90
7706	Sybren	Blok	NED	25.6.96	4	EJ	Eskilstuna	19 Ju
	10.67w/2.9 6.98w/3.7 13.71		2.03 48.28		14.41/-1.0	39.68	5.00 51.77	4:29.20
7614	Feliks	Shestopalov	RUS	11.3.96	5	EJ	Eskilstuna	19 Ju
	11.28/1.7 6.95/0.8 12.76		1.97 49.32		14.55w/2.3	39.11	4.50 56.70	4:30.87
	7600 1 NCp	Adler	13 May		11 performances by 8 men over 7600			
7504	Daniel	Sturma	GER	4.12.96	2		Filderstadt	7 Ju
	10.79/0.2 7.00/0.0 13.39		1.99 49.57		14.28/0.0	38.44	4.50 48.13	4:58.39
7457	Damien	Berthenet (10)	FRA	3.9.96	1	NC-j	Tours	28 Jur
	11.31/1.9 6.77/0.6 13.99		2.00 51.98		14.67/-0.6	40.21	4.72 51.50	4:44.55
7457	Andri	Oberholzer	SUI	24.7.96	1	NC-j	Lausanne	16 Au
	11.25/0.1 7.10/0.0 16.09		1.95 54.39		14.62/0.3	44.19	4.60 47.28	4:54.80
7441	Maxence	Pecatte	FRA	9.1.97	1		Oyonnax	31 Ma
	11.17/-0.7 7.26/0.3 13.41		1.94 48.31		14.41/0.8	37.68	3.97 43.32	4:26.51
7440	Travis	Toliver	USA	15.7.96	2	NC-j	Eugene	25 Ju
	11.20/1.0 6.47/1.9 14.49		1.88 51.02		14.67/1.0	42.36	4.65 59.32	4:57.44
7433	Alessandro	Van De Sande	BEL	3.6.97	7	EJ	Eskilstuna	19 Ju
	11.15w/3.0 6.95/1.5 13.96		1.97 49.62		14.56w/2.1	38.86	4.30 46.55	4:39.10
7430		Qin Guoyuan	CHN	20.1.96	2	NYG	Fuzhou	26 Oc
	10.91/1.1 7.19/1.2 13.48		1.95 49.32		14.35/0.5	36.82	4.50 45.13	4:56.11
7414	Santiago	Ford	CUB	25.8.97	1		La Habana	7 Ma
	11.24/-0.5 6.92/1.1 14.89		2.00 51.93		14.78/-0.1	48.15	3.50 58.53	4:54.64
7407	Marvin	Bollinger	GER	7.10.96	1		Kreuztal	17 Ma
	11.09/0.2 6.75/-0.4 12.16		2.09 52.21		14.68/0.0	41.80	4.60 54.44	5:00.53
7402	Artem	Makarenko	RUS	23.4.97	2	NC-j	Cheboksary	10 Ju
	11.04/1.2 7.12/1.1 14.73		1.88 50.43		14.35/0.9	31.38	4.60 49.85	4:45.58
7401	Rafael	Noguera	CUB	28.2.97	1	Barr	La Habana	27 Ma
	10.95/0.0 6.82w/3.7 13.55		1.81 48.91		14.04/0.4	36.46	3.90 55.95	4:32.83

Wind assisted marks: w against a score shows that as per the IAAF rules up to 2009 the wind velocity in an event exceeded 4m/s and the average of the winds in the three measured events exceeded 2 m/s; (w) as per the current IAAF rules the average of the three events exceeded 2m/s but not necessarily any event over 4m/s.

4 X 100 METRES RELAY

Mark	Nat	Team	Pos	Meet	Venue	Date
37.36	JAM	Carter, Powell, Ashmeade, Bolt	1	WCh	Beijing	29 Au
37.38	USA	Rodgers, Gatlin, Gay, R.Bailey	1	W.Rly	Nassau	2 Ma
37.41	JAM	Carter, Powell, Dwyer, Ashmeade	1h2	WCh	Beijing	29 Au
37.68	JAM	Carter, Bailey Cole, Ashmeade, Bolt	2	W.Rly	Nassau	2 Ma
37.87	USA	Rodgers, Gatlin, Gay, R.Bailey	1h3	W.Rly	Nassau	2 Ma
37.87	USA	Bromell, Gatlin, Gay, Rodgers	1	Herc	Monaco	17 Ju
37.88	FRA	Biron, Lemaitre, Anouman, Vicaut	2h2	WCh	Beijing	29 Au
37.91	USA	Bromell, Gatlin, Gay, Rodgers	1h1	WCh	Beijing	29 Au
37.92	CHN	Mo Youxue, Xie Zhenye, Su Bingtian, Zhang Peimeng	3h2	WCh	Beijing	29 Au
38.01	ANT	Walsh, D.Bailey, Jarvis, Francis	4h2	WCh	Beijing	29 Au
38.01	CHN	Mo, Xie, Su, Zhang	2	WCh	Beijing	29 Au
38.03	CAN	Warner, De Grasse, Rodney, A.Brown	5h2	WCh	Beijing	29 Au
38.07	JAM	Carter, Bailey Cole, Ashmeade, Bolt	1h1	W.Rly	Nassau	2 Ma
38.07A	JAM	Forsythe, Livermore, O.Bailey, S.Mitchell	1	NACAC	San José, CRC	9 Au
38.13	CAN	A.Brown, De Grasse, Rodney, Warner	3	WCh	Beijing	29 Au
38.14	ANT	Walsh, D.Bailey, Greene, Francis	1h1	PAm	Toronto	24 Ju
38.15	GER	Reus, Knipphals, Kosenkow, Menga	4	WCh	Beijing	29 Au
38.18	USA	Silmon, Rodgers, Young, Gatlin	1	FlaR	Gainesville	4 Ap
38.20	JPN	Oseto, Fujimitsu, Kiryu, Taniguchi	3	W.Rly	Nassau	2 Ma
38.20	GBR	Kilty, Aikines-Aryeetey, Ellington, Talbot	2h1	WCh	Beijing	29 Au

[20 performances by teams from 9 nations]

lark	Name	Nat	Born	Pos	Meet	Venue	Date
8.32	Bledman, Burns, Sorrillo, Thompson (10)	TTO		1h2	W.Rly	Nassau	2 May
8.41	Bockarie, van Luijk, Bonevacia, Paulina	NED		6h2	WCh	Beijing	29 Aug
8.55A	Cadogan, Gittens, Deshong, Ellis	BAR		3	NACAC	San José, CRC	9 Aug
8.63	de Barros, V dos Santos, A G da Silva, Vides	BRA		4	W.Rly	Nassau	2 May
8.65	Costa, Obikwelu, Abrantes, Nascimento	POR		1		Rieti	1 Aug
8.67	Del Carmen, Andujar, Montas, Martínez	DOM		3h2	PAm	Toronto	24 Jul
8.68	Rodgers, Lawrence, Roland, Adams	SKN		3h2	W.Rly	Nassau	2 May
8.68	Ferraro, Demonte, Manenti, Obou	ITA		2		Rieti	1 Aug
8.79A	Barnes, Harvey, Safer, Hekimoglu	TUR		1		Erzurum	25 Jul
8.79	Kravtsov, Smelyk, Suprun, Korzh	UKR		5h1	WCh	Beijing	29 Aug
8.84	Pawlowski, Slowikowski, Zalewski, Krynski (20)	POL		1	Kuso	Szczecin	9 Aug
8.85	Carrero, Skyers, Mena, Luis	CUB		6h2	W.Rly	Nassau	2 May
8.93	Naliali, Koffi, Meité, Cisse Gué	CIV		1	AfG	Brazzaville	15 Sep
8.96	Fraser, Hart, McBride, T.Smith	BAH		6h1	WCh	Beijing	29 Aug
8.97	Tega, Metu, Odudoru, Egwero	NGR		1h2	AfG	Brazzaville	14 Sep
8.99	Sowan, Promkaew, Meenapra, Sathoengram	THA		1	SEAG	Singapore	12 Jun
9.11 solo	Debntah, Rane, Kumar, Arumugam	IND		1		Bangalore	27 May
39.60	Debnath, Kumar Rane, Mallick Kumar, Arumugam			3		Pathumthani	25 Jun
9.20	Brorsson, Wissman, Kling-Baptiste, Groth	SWE		2rB	ET	Cheboksary	20 Jun
9.22A	Pitigoi, Campeanu, Neagoe, Budin	ROU		2		Erzurum	25 Jul
9.22	Maritz, Kaarijuka, Gurirab, Urikhob	NAM		2	AfG	Brazzaville	15 Sep
9.24	Li Loong, Foo Ee, Lee Cheng Wei, Jamal (30)	SIN		2	SEAG	Singapore	12 Jun
9.24	Lopin, Brednev, Ogarkov, Yefimov	RUS		5	ET	Cheboksary	20 Jun
9.24	Jung Sin Su, Gamble, Hough, Donovan	AUS		1h3	WUG	Gwangju	11 Jul

9.25	HKG	4 Jun	39.32	INA	12 Jun	39.40	ESP	20 Jun	39.50A	KEN	11 Jul	39.67	BLR	20 Jun
9.26	TPE	16 May	39.38	SRI	4 Jun	39.44	RSA	11 Jul	39.67	PUR	15 May	39.70	OMA	4 Jun
9.31	ZAM	14 Sep	39.38	CZE	12 Jul	39.45	FIN	20 Jun	39.67	MAS	12 Jun	39.71	GHA	15 Sep

est at low altitude

8.65	S Brathwaite, Cadogan, Deshong, Ellis	BAR		2h2	PAm	Toronto	24 Jul
8.90	ENKA: Hekimoglu, Safer, Barnes, Harvey	TUR		1		Ankara	4 Sep

9.67 ROU 2 Aug | 39.71 KEN 14 Sep

JUNIORS

9.08	Calabar HS	JAM		1	N.Sch	Kingston	28 Mar
9.35	(Shenzhen) Luo Wenyi, Liang Jinsheng, Lin Renkeng, Mo Youxue	CHN		1	NYG	Fuzhou	25 Oct
9.68	Dewar, Powell, Arthur, Edoburun	GBR		1		Mannheim	27 Jun
9.73	Barth, Hamilton, Nilsson Montler, Kjell	SWE		1	EJ	Eskilstuna	19 Jul
9.82	Gurski, Köllmann, Netzlaff, Schütz	GER		1		Pliezhausen	17 May
9.86	Hanafi, Mnaap, A Hashim, Jantan	MAS		1		Tutong	25 Nov
9.90A	P de Oliveira, D Silva, A dos Santos, R de Oliveira	BRA		1	SAm-J	Cuenca	31 May
9.99A	Igube, Peka, Olisakwe, Odu	NGR		1	Af-J	Addis Ababa	7 Mar
0.00	Wasilewski, Adamski, Wróbel, Hampel	POL		2	EJ	Eskilstuna	19 Jul
0.02	André, Gardes, Barbier, Golitin	FRA		3	EJ	Eskilstuna	19 Jul

4 X 200 METRES RELAY

:20.19	JAM	Dwyer, Livermore, J.Brown, Weir	1h1	W.Rly	Nassau	3 May
:20.64	USA	Morris, M.Mitchell, Webb, Spearmon	1r1	PennR	Philadelphia	25 Apr
:20.78	USA	Morris, Young, Walker, Spearmon	1h2	W.Rly	Nassau	3 May
:20.97	JAM-	U.Tech Fisher, K.Brown, K.Smith, Forte	1r2	PennR	Philadelphia	25 Apr
:21.00	mixed	Star Athletics inc. F Ogunode QAT, Martina NED	1	FlaR	Gainesville	4 Apr
:20.97	JAM	Ashmeade, Dwyer, Livermore, Weir	1	W.Rly	Nassau	3 May
:21.41	FRA	Vincent, Tinmar, Pessonneaux, Bassaw	2h1	W.Rly	Nassau	3 May
:21.45	JAM	J.Brown, Dwyer, Livermore, Bailey	2r1	PennR	Philadelphia	25 Apr
:21.46	GER	Erewa, Knipphals, Menga, Kosenkov	3h1	W.Rly	Nassau	3 May
:21.49	FRA	Tinmar, Lemaitre, Pessonneaux, Bassaw	2	W.Rly	Nassau	3 May

[9/4]

4 X 400 METRES RELAY

:57.82	USA	Verburg 45.0, McQuay 44.3, Nellum 44.38, Merritt 44.18	1	WCh	Beijing	30 Aug
:58.13	USA	Clemons 45.3, McQuay 44.0, Nellum 44.38, Norwood 44.45	1h2	WCh	Beijing	29 Aug
:58.20	TTO	Quow 44.8, L Gordon 44.1, Lendore 44.85, Cedenio 44.47	2	WCh	Beijing	30 Aug
:58.43	USA	Verburg 44.91, McQuay 44.00, Wariner 44.80, Merritt 44.72	1	W.Rly	Nassau	3 May
:58.51	GBR	Yousif 45.1, D.Williams 44.6, Dunn 44.98, Rooney 43.97	3	WCh	Beijing	30 Aug
:58.51	JAM	Matthews 45.2, Chambers 45.2 , McDonald 44.56, Francis 43.52	4	WCh	Beijing	30 Aug
:58.67	TTO	Quow 45.8, Solomon 44.5, Lendore 44.56, L Gordon 43.82	2h2	WCh	Beijing	29 Aug
:58.69	JAM	Matthews 45.2, Chambers 44.0, Hyatt 44.94, Francis 44.56	3h2	WCh	Beijing	29 Aug
:58.91	BAH	R.Miller 45.66, Mathieu 44.50, Gardiner 44.58, Brown 44.17	2	W.Rly	Nassau	3 May
:59.05	GBR	Yousif 45.2, D.Williams 44.2, Dunn 45.37, Rooney 44.28	1h1	WCh	Beijing	29 Aug

MEN 2015

Mark	Nat	Name	Pos	Meet	Venue	Date
2:59.28	BEL	D.Borlée 45.8, J.Borlée 44.2, Gillet 45.48, K.Borlée 43.78	2h1	WCh	Beijing	29 Au
2:59.33	BEL	D.Borlée 45.57, Watrin 45.36, J.Borlée 44.39, K.Borlée 44.01	3	W.Rly	Nassau	3 Ma
2:59.42	FRA	Anne 45.6 , Venel 44.3, Hanne 45.05, Jordier 44.45	3h1	WCh	Beijing	29 Au
2:59.45	RUS	Denmukhametov 46.0, Trenikin 44.5, Kudryavtsev 44.63, Ivashko 44.29	4h1	WCh	Beijing	29 Au
2:59.60	TTO	Quow 45.4, Solomon 44.6, Mayers 45.4, Cedenio 44.2	1	PAm	Toronto	25 Ju
2:59.80	CUB	Collazo 45.9, Acea 44.4, Chacón 44.99, Lescay 44.56	4h2	WCh	Beijing	29 Au
2:59.84	CUB	Collazo 45.6, Chacon 44.4, Pellicier 44.8, Lescay 45.0	2	PAm	Toronto	25 Ju
2:59.95	BOT	Nkobolo 45.2, Amos 44.1, Maotoanong 46.05, Makwala 44.63	5h2	WCh	Beijing	29 Au
3:00.07 A	USA	Parros, C.Smith, Chambers, J.Harris	1	NACAC	San José, CRC	9 Au
3:00.15	DOM	Cuesta 45.4, Soriano 43.8, J.Santos 46.58, L.Santos 44.36	6h2	WCh	Beijing	29 Au
	[20/11]					
3:00.34	KEN	Kibet 45.5, Sampao 45.6, K.Koskei 45.6, Mweresa 43.8	1	AfG	Brazzaville	17 Se
3:00.72	POL	Krawczuk 45.9, Pietrzak 45.1, Omelko 44.81, Krzewina 44.93	5h1	WCh	Beijing	29 Au
3:00.96	BRA	P de Oliveira 45.55, Cardoso 45.97, Estefani 44.44, H Sousa 45.04	5	W.Rly	Nassau	3 Ma
3:01.26	IRL	Gregan 46.1, Murphy 45.2, Barr 45.05, English 44.96	8h2	WCh	Beijing	29 Au
3:02.50	QAT	F Ogunode, Balla, Mohamed, Haroun	1	AsiC	Wuhan	7 Ju
3:02.62	KSA	Al-Yassin, Al-Salhi, Al-Moualed, Al-Masrahi	2	AsiC	Wuhan	7 Ju
3:02.96	VEN	Bravo 46.2, Meléndez 45.3, Ramírez 45.58, Mezones 45.88	6h1	WCh	Beijing	29 Au
3:02.97	JPN	Tamura 46.3, Kanemaru 44.8, Kobayashi 45.80, Kitagawa 46.12	7h1	WCh	Beijing	29 Au
3:03.07	ALG	Laradt 45.5, Rahmani 46.6, Bouhedda 46.4, Lahoulou 44.6	3	AfG	Brazzaville	17 Se
	(20)					
3:03.52	NGR	Oghenewegba 45.9, Simmons 46.6, Okorie 46.0, Erayokan 45.0	4	AfG	Brazzaville	17 Se
3:03.55	GER	Schneider 45.8, Gaba 46.2, Krüger 45.66, Trefz 45.75	5	ET	Cheboksary	21 Ju
3:03.99	NED	Bonevacia, Blauwhof, Agard, Martis	2	FlaR	Gainesville	4 Ap
3:04.06 A	TUR	Escobar, Kilic, Can, Altintas	1		Erzurum	26 Ju
3:04.52	CZE	Tesar, Desensky, Flaska, Maslák	1	ET-1	Iráklio	21 Ju
3:04.76	GHA	Effah, Gyasi, Acheampong, Dasor	1		Warri	24 Ju
3:04.79	RSA	Conradie, Seeliger, Hanekom, de Jager	1h1	WUG	Gwangju	11 Ju
3:05.11	CRC	Robinson, Brenes, J.Lynch, Drummond	5h2	PAm	Toronto	24 Ju
3:05.13	AUS	Burns 46.44, Douglas 46.15, Stevens 46.40, Baird 46.14	4rB	W.Rly	Nassau	3 Ma
3:05.14	IND	Sajin, Dharun, Roby, Rajiv	4	AsiC	Wuhan	7 Ju
	(30)					

3:05.16 UKR 21 Jun	3:05.96 CHN 13 May	3:06.35 ESP 21 Jun	3:06.60 KOR 11 Jul	3:06.84 PHI 11 Jun
3:05.40 CAN 24 Jul	3:06.07 EST 21 Jun	3:06.48 COL 2 May	3:06.71 ITA 21 Jun	3:07.62 CRO 2 Aug
3:05.79 SRI 7 Jun	3:06.23 BRN 27 Apr	3:06.59 ZIM 24 Jul	3:06.81 THA 11 Jun	3:07.73 SEN 17 Sep
3:05.94 OMA 7 Jun				3:07.86 PUR 21 Mar

JUNIORS

Mark	Nat	Name	Pos	Meet	Venue	Date
3:06.76	JAM	(Calabar HS) Carpenter, A Francis, R Wilson, C Taylor	1	N.Sch	Kingston	28 Ma
3:07.07	USA	Q Poole, Allen, Grimes, Kerley	1	PAm-J	Edmonton	2 Au
3:08.35	RUS	Yefremov, Kukharenko, Tolokonnikov, Krasnov	1	EJ	Eskilstuna	19 Ju
3:08.86A	BRA	G dos Santos, Cerqueira, Vitorino, M do Nascimento	1	SAm-J	Cuenca	31 Ma
3:09.91	CAN	Brady, Bedard, Abdullahi, Leliever	3	PAm-J	Edmonton	2 Au

4 X 800 METRES RELAY

Mark	Nat	Name	Pos	Meet	Venue	Date
7:04.84	USA	Solomon 1:47.60, Sowinski 1:44.75, Loxsom 1:45.59, Andrews 1:46.90	1	W.Rly	Nassau	2 Ma
7:09.1A	KEN	A Kipketer, N Kiplagat, J Mutai, T Kitum	1		Nairobi	10 Ap
7:09.98	POL	Kocieczny 1:48.28, Gurdak 1:48.17, Lewandowski 1:46.80, Kszczot 1:46.73	2	W.Rly	Nassau	2 Ma
7:11.4A	KEN	F Rotich, J Kivuva, J Kitilit, C Kiplangat	2		Nairobi	10 Ap
7:16.30	AUS	West 1:48.50, Ralph 1:49.74, Gregson 1:47.81, Williamsz 1:50.25	3	W.Rly	Nassau	2 Ma

DISTANCE MEDLEY RELAY

Mark	Nat	Name	Pos	Meet	Venue	Date
9:15.50	USA	Merber 2:53.56, Spratling 45.95, B.Johnson 1:44.75, Blankenship 3:51.24	1	W.Rly	Nassau	3 Ma
9:17.20	KEN	Chesebe 2:54.48, Kishoyan 45.48, Cheruiyot 1:44.49, Cheruiyot 3:52.75	2	W.Rly	Nassau	3 Ma
9:21.62	AUS	Gregson 2:53.15, Beck 45.83, Williamsz 1:45.64, Birmingham 3:57.00	3	W.Rly	Nassau	3 Ma
9:24.07	POL	Demczyszak 2:54.85, Krawczyk 46.45, Kszczot 1:46.04, Lewandowski 3:57.08	4	W.Rly	Nassau	3 Ma
9:24.37	GER	Keiner 2:54.50, Plass 46.39, Schembera 1:45.75, Orth 3:57.38	5	W.Rly	Nassau	3 Ma
Indoors						
9:19.93	USA	Centrowitz 2:49.47, Berry 46.40, Sowinski 1:47.60, Casey 3:56.48	1		New York (A)	31 Ja

4 X 110 METRES HURDLES

Mark	Team	Name	Pos	Meet	Venue	Date
52.94	USA Blue	Richardson, Harris, Merritt, Oliver	1	DrakeR	Des Moines	25 Ap
53.08	All Stars	Riley JAM, R Brathwaite BAR, Parchment JAM, Swift BAR	2	DrakeR	Des Moines	25 Ap
53.62	USA Red	Ash, Porter, Wilson, Adams	3	DrakeR	Des Moines	25 Ap
53.65	World Express	Lovett ISV, S Adams USA, J Eaton USA, M Thomas TTO	1	FlaR	Gainesville	4 Ap

3000 METRES WALK

/lark	Name		Nat	Born	Pos	Meet	Venue	Date
1:15.20	Quentin	Rew	NZL	16.7.84	1		Wellington	23 Jan
1:19.80	Dane	Bird-Smith	AUS	15.7.92	1		Brisbane	14 Feb
1:20.39A	Lebogang	Shange	RSA	1.8.90	1		Pretoria	7 Mar
1:23.30	Alex	Wright	IRL	19.12.90	1		Templemore	24 May
1:28.45	Erik	Tysse	NOR	4.12.80	1		Bergen	28 May
1:33.10	Rhydian	Cowley	AUS	4.1.91	2		Brisbane	14 Feb
ndoors								
1:17.33	Erik	Tysse	NOR	4.12.80	1		Bergen	24 Jan
1:19.33	Alex	Wright	IRL	19.12.90	1		Athlone	1 Feb
1:29.8+	Massimo	Stano	ITA	27.2.92	1	in 5k	Padova	21 Feb
1:30.35	Tom	Bosworth	GBR	17.1.90	1	NC	Sheffield	15 Feb

5000 METRES WALK

Mark	Name		Nat	Born	Pos	Meet	Venue	Date
8:22.41	Yohann	Diniz	FRA	1.1.78	1		Tourcoing	10 May
8:37.22	Yusuke	Suzuki	JPN	2.1.88	1		Kitami	12 Jul
8:37.60	Eiki	Takahashi	JPN	19.11.92	2		Kitami	12 Jul
8:39.65	Álvaro	Martín	ESP	18.6.94	1		Gijón	25 Jul
8:50.20	Luis Alberto	Amezcua	ESP	1.5.92	2		Gijón	25 Jul
8:51.93		Takahashi			1		Kumagaya	16 May
8:55.56		Diniz			1		Marseille	6 Jun
8:56.74		Martín			1		Plasencia	24 Jun
8:56.84	Lebogang	Shange	RSA	1.8.90	1		Cork	7 Jul
8:57.06	Evan	Dunfee	CAN	28.9.90	1		Vancouver	29 Mar
8:57.42	Kevin	Campion	FRA	23.5.88	1		Hérouville	18 Jun
8:58.19	Richard	Vargas	VEN	28.12.94	2		Plasencia	24 Jun
8:58.63		Amezcua			2		Cork	7 Jul
9:00.15	Alex	Wright (10)	IRL	19.12.90	3		Cork	7 Jul
9:00.73	Tom	Bosworth	GBR	17.1.90	1	NC	Birmingham	5 Jul
	(15/11)							
9:03.16	Diego	Garcia	ESP-J	19.1.96	3		Plasencia	24 Jun
9:04.52	Iván	Pajuelo	ESP	27.8.93	4		Plasencia	24 Jun
9:14.00	Robert	Heffernan	IRL	20.2.78	4		Cork	7 Jul
9:18.19	Hiroki	Arai	JPN	18.5.88	2		Kumagaya	16 May
9:19.07	Erik	Tysse	NOR	4.12.80	1	NC	Haugesund	31 Jul
9:19.98	Matej	Tóth	SVK	10.2.83	1		Bratislava	9 May
9:20.05	Kai	Kobayashi	JPN	28.2.93	3		Kumagaya	16 May
9:23.72	Chris	Erickson	AUS	1.12.81	1		Melbourne	1 Mar
9:24.91	Marc	Tur	ESP	30.11.94	5		Plasencia	24 Jun

Mark	Name		Nat	Born	Date
9:30.76	Satoshi	Maruo	JPN	28.11.91	12 Jul
9:31.78	Pyotr	Trofimov	RUS	28.11.83	6 Jun
9:34.66	Takumo	Saito	JPN	23.3.93	12 Jul
19:35.09	Veli-Matti	Partanen	FIN	28.10.91	25 Jun
19:38.73	Marius	Savelskis	LTU	30.7.94	16 May

Mark	Name		Nat	Born	Pos	Meet	Venue	Date
ndoors								
8:39.92		Diniz			1		Mondeville	7 Feb
9:11.07	Aléxandros	Papamihaíl	GRE	18.9.88	1	NC	Pireás	14 Feb
9:14.82	Marius	Ziukas	LTU	29.6.85	1	NC	Klaipeda	21 Feb
9:16.34	Leonardo	Dei Tos	ITA	27.4.92	1	NC	Padova	21 Feb
9:22.62	Massimo	Stano	ITA	27.2.92	2	NC	Padova	21 Feb
9:25.35	Dawid	Tomala	POL	27.8.89	1	NC	Torun	22 Feb
9:25.67	Igor	Hlavan	UKR	25.9.90	1		Sumy	19 Dec
9:26.24	Máté	Helebrandt	HUN	12.1.89	1	NC	Budapest (SH)	21 Feb

Mark	Name		Nat	Born	Date
9:26.92	Rafal	Augustyn	POL	14.5.84	22 Feb
9:26.94	Federico	Tontodonati	ITA	30.10.89	21 Feb
9:29.54	Marco	De Luca	ITA	12.5.81	21 Feb
9:29.68	Marius	Savelskis	LTU	30.7.94	21 Feb
9:32.42	Veli-Matti	Partanen	FIN	28.10.91	21 Feb
19:32.42	Nick	Christie	USA	29.9.91	7 Mar
19:34.94	Lukasz	Nowak	POL	18.12.88	22 Feb
19:34.97	Sérgio	Vieira	POR	20.2.76	14 Feb
19:36.5	Perseus	Karlström	SWE	2.5.90	29 Nov
19:38.41	Ivan	Banzeruk	UKR	9.2.90	27 Jan

JUNIORS

Mark	Name		Nat	Born	Pos	Meet	Venue	Date
9:03.16	Diego	Garcia	ESP	19.1.96	3		Plasencia	24 Jun
	19:04.02 3	Gijón	25 Jul					
19:40.48	Toshizaku	Yamanishi	JPN	15.2.96	1		Tokyo	1 Oct
9:51.37	Pablo	Oliva	ESP	15.10.96	7		Plasencia	24 Jun
9:59.22	Tomohiro	Noda	JPN	24.1.96	1		Tokyo	1 Nov

10,000 METRES WALK

Mark	Name		Nat	Born	Pos	Meet	Venue	Date
38:01.49	Eiki	Takahashi	JPN	19.11.92	1		Isahaya	13 Dec
38:10.23	Yusuke	Suzuki	JPN	2.1.88	1		Abashiri	16 Jul
38:23.73		Wang Zhen	CHN	24.8.91	1		Genova	8 Feb
38:53.42	Miguel Ángel	López	ESP	3.7.88	1		Cartagena	29 Apr

MEN 2015

Mark	Name		Nat	Born	Pos	Meet	Venue	Date
38:55.49		Takahashi			2		Abashiri	16 Ju
39:04.82	Christopher	Linke	GER	24.10.88	1	NC	Düsseldorf	13 Ju
39:10.61	Nils	Brembach	GER	23.2.93	2	NC	Düsseldorf	13 Ju
39:11.95		Takahashi			1		Gifu	26 Se
39:15.61		López			1	NC	Castellón	2 Au
39:15.91		Cai Zelin	CHN	11.4.91	2		Genova	8 Fe
	(10/7)							
39:18.04	Daisuke	Matsunaga	JPN	24.3.95	1		Osaka	13 Se
39:19.5	Perseus	Karlström	SWE	2.5.90	1	NC	Göteborg	8 Au
39:28.63	Toshizaku	Yamanishi	JPN-J	15.2.96	2		Osaka	13 Se
39:28.68	Kai	Kobayashi	JPN	28.2.93	3		Abashiri	16 Ju
39:30.15	Yuga	Yamashita	JPN-J	6.2.96	1		Tama	12 De
39:33.30	Satoshi	Maruo	JPN	28.11.91	4		Abashiri	16 Ju
39:39.49	Ryosuke	Kawagishi	JPN-J	15.6.96	2		Tama	12 De
39:45.25	Aleksandr	Lyakhovich	BLR	4.7.89	1		Minsk	10 Ju
39:53.89	Dane	Bird-Smith	AUS	15.7.92	1	NC	Brisbane	27 Ma
40:00.09	Tomohiro	Noda	JPN-J	24.1.96	3		Osaka	13 Se
40:03.35	Benjamin	Sánchez	ESP	10.3.85	2	NC	Castellón	2 Au
40:04.29	Alex	Wright	IRL	19.12.90	1	NC	Dublin	9 Au
40:04.89	Yevgeniy	Zalesski	BLR	18.7.93	2		Minsk	10 Ju
40:05.21	Diego	Garcia	ESP-J	19.1.96	1	EJ	Eskilstuna	18 Ju
40:08.46	Takumi	Saito	JPN	23.3.93	3		Gifu	26 Se
40:08.47A	Jesús Tadeo	Vega	MEX	23.5.94	1		Xalapa	11 Ap
40:10.79	Luis Alberto	Amezcua	ESP	1.5.92	2		Cartagena	29 Ap
40:11.58	Hiroki	Arai	JPN	18.5.88	4		Gifu	26 Se
40:11.73	Fumitaka	Oikawa	JPN	5.4.95	4		Osaka	13 Se
40:13.60	Álvaro	Martín	ESP	18.6.94	3	NC	Castellón	2 Au

Mark	Name		Nat	Born	Date	Mark	Name		Nat	Born	Date
40:16.02	Takumi	Nishito	JPN	.93	16 Jul	40:29.04	Evan	Dunfee	CAN	28.9.90	4 Ju
40:17.01	Hagen	Pohle	GER	5.3.92	13 Jun	40:29.90	Inaki	Gómez	CAN	16.1.88	4 Ju

JUNIORS

See main list for top 5 juniors. 10 performances by 5 men to 40:30.0. Additional marks and further juniors:

Name	Mark	Pos	Meet	Venue	Date	Mark	Pos	Venue	Date
Yamanishi	40:28.82	2		Wakayama	4 Oct				
Yamashita	39:56.78	1		Tokyo	4 Apr	40:27.65	1	Konosu	4 No
	40:22.35	2		Yokohama	16 May				
García	40:20.53	4	NC	Castellón	2 Aug				

Mark	Name		Nat	Born	Pos	Meet	Venue	Date
40:50.00		Jun Xiangqian	CHN	18.3.97	1	NYG	Fuzhou	24 Oc
40:59.28	Vladislav	Saraykin	RUS	3.3.97	2	EJ	Eskilstuna	18 Ju
41:00.73	Pablo	Oliva	ESP	15.10.96	3	EJ	Eskilstuna	18 Ju
41:01.71	César	Rodríguez	PER	26.6.97	1	NC-j	Lima	25 Ap
41:07.02		Zhang Jun (10)	CHN-Y	20.7.98	2	NYG	Fuzhou	24 Oc
41:11.4	Maksim	Krasnov	RUS	10.2.96	1		Chelyabinsk	30 May
41:12.68	Vasiliy	Mizinov	RUS	29.12.97	1	NC-j	Cheboksary	13 Jun
41:14.75	Jean	Blancheteau	FRA	7.1.96	4	EJ	Eskilstuna	18 Ju
41:22.43	Kazuki	Takahashi	JPN	.96	7		Osaka	13 Sep
41:30.35	Kohei	Kowaki	JPN	.96	4		Higashihiroshi	29 Nov
41:31.44	Zaharías	Tsamoudákis	GRE	14.1.96	5	EJ	Eskilstuna	18 Ju
41:33.47	Nathaniel	Seller	GER	6.4.96	6	EJ	Eskilstuna	18 Ju
41:34.63	Callum	Wilkinson	GBR	14.3.97	7	EJ	Eskilstuna	18 Ju
41:34.64	Fukumi	Aoyama	JPN	.97	9		Yokohama	16 May
41:36.98		Zhu Guowen (20)	CHN	20.8.97	3	NYG	Fuzhou	24 Oc

10 KILOMETRES ROAD WALK

Where better than track times above. See also intermediate times in 20k lists below.

Mark	Name		Nat	Born	Pos	Meet	Venue	Date
38:50	Aleksandr	Yargunkin	RUS	6.1.81	1		Mis	9 May
38:55	Pyotr	Trofimov	RUS	28.11.83	1		Voronovo	13 Sep
39:05	Nazar	Kovalenko	UKR	9.2.89	2		Voronovo	13 Sep
39:22	Ivan	Losev	UKR	26.1.86	1	NCp	Lutsk	28 Jun
39:25	Kirill	Frolov	RUS	29.9.93	3		Voronovo	13 Sep
39:33	Andriy	Kovenko	UKR	25.11.73	2	NCp	Lutsk	28 Jun
39:43	Ruslan	Dmytrenko	UKR	22.3.86	1		Ayvalik	28 Ma
39:52+	Aleksandr	Ivanov	RUS	25.4.93		in 20k	Murcia	17 May
39:53	Aleksey	Golovin	RUS	24.12.88	2		Mis	9 May
39:56	Matej	Tóth	SVK	10.2.83	1		Borsky Mikulas	6 Jun
40:01	Ivan	Banzeruk	UKR	9.2.90	3	NCp	Lutsk	28 Jun
40:04	Erick	Barrondo	GUA	14.6.91	1		Katowice	5 Sep
40:07+	Toshikazu	Yamanishi	JPN-J	15.2.96		in 20k	Kobe	15 Feb

Mark	Name		Nat	Born	Date	Mark	Name		Nat	Born	Date
40:08	Álvaro	Martín	ESP	18.6.94	13 Dec	40:22		Turkov	BLR		13 Sep
40:14+	Caio	Bonfim	BRA	19.3.91	6 Jun	40:23	Erik	Tysse	NOR	4.12.80	14 Jun
40:14+	Igor	Hlavan	UKR	25.9.90	6 Jun	40:24+	Hagen	Pohle	GER	5.3.92	23 Aug
40:21+	Eider	Arévalo	COL	9.3.93	23 Aug	40:24		Zhang Rongjin	CHN-J	24.4.96	5 Sep

Mark		Name	Nat	Born	Date	Mark		Name	Nat	Born	Date
40:27+	Takumi	Saito	JPN	23.3.93	15 Feb	40:34	Jakub	Jelonek	POL	7.7.85	13 Sep
40:30		Yang Dedong	CHN-J	23.11.96	5 Sep	40:36	Chris	Erickson	AUS	1.12.81	23 May
40:33		Tong Dongliang	CHN-Y	3.4.97	20 Mar	40:36	Jared	Tallent	AUS	17.10.84	23 Aug

JUNIORS

Mark		Name	Nat	Born	Pos	Meet	Venue	Date
40:07+	Toshikazu	Yamanishi	JPN-J	15.2.96		in 20k	Kobe	15 Feb
40:24		Zhang Rongjin	CHN	24.4.96	1	NC-j	Changbaishan	5 Sep
40:30		Yang Dedong	CHN	23.11.96	2	NC-j	Changbaishan	5 Sep
40:33		Tong Dongliang	CHN-Y	3.4.97	1		Beijing	20 Mar
40:36		Zhu Guowen	CHN	20.8.97	3	NC-j	Changbaishan	5 Sep
40:45		Zhang Wanxin	CHN	25.10.96	5	NC-j	Changbaishan	5 Sep
40:47		Li Liangyong	CHN	28.5.96	1		Taicang	1 May
40:48		Liu Qingdong	CHN	9.12.97	2		Beijing	20 Mar
40:48		Gao Yingchao	CHN-Y	18.1.98	1	NC-y	Changbaishan	5 Sep
40:49	Ivan	Kakauev (10)	RUS	13.8.97	3		Mis	9 May
40:53		Fu Yongqiang	CHN	2.6.97	3		Beijing	20 Mar
40:57		Sun Song	CHN	15.12.96	6	NC-j	Changbaishan	5 Sep
40:58		Lu Ning	CHN-Y	12.2.99	1rB	NC-y	Changbaishan	5 Sep
41:03		Zheng Ke	CHN-U	10.1.98	2	NC-y	Changbaishan	5 Sep
41:08		Mu Linjie	CHN	15.3.97	7	NC-j	Changbaishan	5 Sep
41:11	Jean	Blancheteau	FRA	7.1.96	2	ECp-J	Murcia	17 May
41:16		Guo Shuqi	CHN-Y	26.8.98	3	NC-y	Changbaishan	5 Sep

20 KILOMETRES WALK

20k	10k			Nat	Born	Pos	Meet	Venue	Date
1:16:36	38:06	Yusuke	Suzuki	JPN	2.1.88	1	AsiC	Nomi	15 Mar
1:17:02	38:40	Yohann	Diniz	FRA	1.1.78	1	NC	Arles	8 Mar
1:17:24	38:20		Diniz			1		Lugano	15 Mar
1:18:00	39:02		Wang Zhen	CHN	24.8.91	1		La Coruña	6 Jun
1:18:03	39:43	Eiki	Takahashi	JPN	19.11.92	1	NC	Kobe	15 Feb
1:18:13	39:43		Suzuki			2	NC	Kobe	15 Feb
1:18:44	39:26		Chen Ding	CHN	5.8.92	2		La Coruña	6 Jun
1:19:08	39:25	Isamu	Fujisawa	JPN	12.10.87	2		Nomi	15 Mar
1:19:08	39:25	Daisuke	Matsunaga	JPN	24.3.95	3		Nomi	15 Mar
1:19:12	39:28	Kai	Kobayashi	JPN	28.2.93	4		Nomi	15 Mar
1:19:13	39:28		Kim Hyun-sub	KOR	31.5.85	5	2 AsiC	Nomi	15 Mar
1:19:14	40:21	Miguel Ángel	López (10)	ESP	3.7.88	1	WCh	Beijing	23 Aug
1:19:18		Bertrand	Moulinet ¶	FRA	6.1.87	2	NC	Arles	8 Mar
1:19:29	39:35		Wang Zhen			1	WCT	Beijing	20 Mar
1:19:29	40:21		Wang Zhen			2	WCh	Beijing	23 Aug
1:19:42	39:29	Satoshi	Maruo	JPN	28.11.91	6		Nomi	15 Mar
1:19:45	39:17		Cai Zelin	CHN	11.4.91	3		La Coruña	6 Jun
1:19:49			Wang Kaihua	CHN	16.2.94	1	NC	Changbaishan	6 Sep
1:19:52			López			1	NC	Renteria	22 Mar
1:19:52	39:53		López			1	ECp	Murcia	17 May
1:19:53			Chen Ding			1		Taicang	1 May
1:19:57	40:22	Benjamin	Thorne	CAN	19.3.93	3	WCh	Beijing	23 Aug
1:20:04	39:29		López			4		La Coruña	6 Jun
1:20:04	39:59	Denis	Strelkov ¶	RUS	26.10.90	1	NC	Cheboksary	13 Jun
1:20:05	39:30	Dane	Bird-Smith	AUS	15.7.92	5		La Coruña	6 Jun
1:20:06	39:40	Aleksandr	Ivanov	RUS	25.4.93	1	NC-w	Sochi	27 Feb
1:20:08	39:29	Tomohiro	Noda	JPN-J	24.1.96	7		Nomi	15 Mar
1:20:08			Takahashi			6		La Coruña	6 Jun
1:20:10	39:59	Stanislav	Yemelyanov ¶	RUS	23.10.90	2	NC	Cheboksary	13 Jun
1:20:13			Cai Zelin			2	WCT	Beijing	20 Mar
		(30/20)							
1:20:19		Álvaro	Martín	ESP	18.6.94	2	NC	Renteria	22 Mar
1:20:21	40:14	Matej	Tóth	SVK	10.2.83	2	ECp	Murcia	17 May
1:20:29	40:22	Igor	Hlavan	UKR	25.9.90	4	WCh	Beijing	23 Aug
1:20:35	40:06	Hiroki	Arai	JPN	18.5.88	3	NC	Kobe	15 Feb
1:20:37	40:37	Christopher	Linke	GER	24.10.88	1		Podébrady	11 Apr
1:20:40	40:15	Andrés	Chocho	ECU	4.11.83	7		La Coruña	6 Jun
1:20:41	40:39	Eider	Arévalo	COL	9.3.93	1		Rio Maior	18 Apr
1:20:43	39:40	Andrey	Krivov	RUS	14.11.85	2	NC-w	Sochi	27 Feb
1:20:44	40:25	Caio	Bonfim	BRA	19.3.91	6	WCh	Beijing	23 Aug
1:20:52		Erik	Tysse	NOR	4.12.80	1		Vallensbæk	2 May
		(30)							
1:20:53	40:08	Pyotr	Trofimov	RUS	28.11.83	3	NC-w	Sochi	27 Feb
1:20:57			Li Tianlei	CHN	13.1.95	2	NC	Changbaishan	6 Sep
1:21:11		Kirill	Frolov	RUS	29.9.93	5	NC-w	Sochi	27 Feb

Mark		Name		Nat	Born	Pos	Meet	Venue	Date
1:21:11	40:15	Denis	Simanovich	BLR	20.4.87	4	ECp	Murcia	17 May
1:21:15		Takumi	Saito	JPN	23.3.93	9		La Coruña	6 Jun
1:21:20	40:13	Toshikazu	Yamanishi	JPN-J	15.2.96	8		Nomi	15 Mar
1:21:21		Nils	Brembach	GER	23.2.93	1		Naumburg	19 Apr
1:21:25	40:42	Ruslan	Dmytrenko	UKR	22.3.86	4		Rio Maior	18 Apr
1:21:25		Erick	Barrondo	GUA	14.6.91	1	PAmCp	Arica	9 May
1:21:34		Georgiy	Sheyko	KAZ	24.8.89	6	RUS-w	Sochi	27 Feb
		(40)							
1:21:34		Hagen	Pohle	GER	5.3.92	2		Naumburg	19 Apr
1:21:34	40:29	Kevin	Campion	FRA	23.5.88	10		La Coruña	6 Jun
1:21:36	40:13	Gurmeet	Singh	IND	1.7.85	9		Nomi	15 Mar
1:21:38	40:36	Giorgio	Rubino	ITA	15.4.86	5		Rio Maior	18 Apr
1:21:39		Iván	Garrido	COL	25.1.94	3	PAmCp	Arica	9 May
1:21:43		Julio César	Salazar	MEX	8.7.93	4		Taicang	1 May
1:21:43		Lebogang	Shange	RSA	1.8.90	11	WCh	Beijing	23 Aug
1:21:45		Diego	García	ESP-J	19.1.96	3	NC	Renteria	22 Mar
1:21:48		Evan	Dunfee	CAN	28.9.90	13	WCh	Beijing	23 Aug
1:21:49		Aleksandr	Lyakhovich	BLR	4.7.89	1	NC	Grodno	24 Jul
		(50)							
1:21:51		João	Vieira	POR	20.2.76	12		La Coruña	6 Jun
1:21:51		Sérgio	Vieira	POR	20.2.76	13		La Coruña	6 Jun
1:21:55	40:26	Iñaki	Gómez	CAN	16.1.88	15	WCh	Beijing	23 Aug
1:21:56	40:21	Eder	Sánchez	MEX	21.5.86	16	WCh	Beijing	23 Aug
1:22:03		Luis Alberto	Amezcua	ESP	1.5.92	4	NC	Renteria	22 Mar
1:22:08		Chris	Erickson	AUS	1.12.81	10		Nomi	15 Mar
1:22:08		Ivan	Banzeruk	UKR	9.2.90	15		La Coruña	6 Jun
1:22:08			Xie Sichao	CHN	28.2.93	3	NC	Changbaishan	6 Sep
1:22:09		Alex	Wright	IRL	19.12.90	16		La Coruña	6 Jun
1:22:13		Marco	De Luca	ITA	12.5.81	7		Rio Maior	18 Apr
		(60)							
1:22:16		Massimo	Stano	ITA	27.2.92	1	NC	Cassino	29 Mar
1:22:16		Sandeep	Kumar Sangwan	IND	16.12.86	18		La Coruña	6 Jun
1:22:18		Quentin	Rew	NZL	16.7.84	18	WCh	Beijing	23 Aug
1:22:21	40:15	Kenny	Pérez	COL	19.11.94	19		La Coruña	6 Jun
1:22:21		Roman	Yevstifeyev	RUS	19.9.92	5	NC	Cheboksary	13 Jun
1:22:22			Sun Chenggang	CHN	11.3.91	4	NC	Changbaishan	6 Sep
1:22:24		Richard	Vargas	VEN	28.12.94	8		Rio Maior	18 Apr
1:22:24		Carl	Dohmann	GER	18.5.90	3		Naumburg	19 Apr
1:22:33		Tom	Bosworth	GBR	17.1.90	4		Lugano	15 Mar
1:22:33		Federico	Tontodonati	ITA	30.10.89	2	NC	Cassino	29 Mar
		(70)							
1:22:37		Ivan	Losev	UKR	26.1.86	1	NC	Oleksandriya	13 Jun
1:22:37		Mauricio	Arteaga	ECU	8.8.88	1		Valley Cottage	25 Oct
1:22:38		Pavel	Parshin	RUS	2.1.94	7	NC-w	Sochi	27 Feb
1:22:43	40:27	Koichiro	Morioka	JPN	2.4.85	7	NC	Kobe	15 Feb
1:22:43		Aléxandros	Papamihaíl	GRE	18.9.88	5		Lugano	15 Mar
1:22:44		Perseus	Karlström	SWE	2.5.90	8	ECp	Murcia	17 May
1:22:44		Andriy	Kovenko	UKR	25.11.73	2	NC	Oleksandriya	13 Jun
1:22:45		José Leonardo	Montaña	COL	21.3.92	6	PAmCp	Arica	9 May
1:22:48		Anatole	Ibáñez	SWE	14.11.85	10	ECp	Murcia	17 May
1:22:49		José Maria	Raymundo	GUA	1.9.93	8		Podébrady	11 Apr
		(80)							
1:22:50		Nils Christopher	Gloger	GER	6.8.90	9		Podébrady	11 Apr
1:22:50		Manish	Singh Rawat	IND	5.5.91	9		Rio Maior	18 Apr
1:22:56			Wang Qin	CHN	8.5.94	5	NC	Changbaishan	6 Sep
1:22:58		Baljinder	Singh	IND	18.9.86	12	3 AsiC	Nomi	15 Mar
1:22:58			Su Xianzhen	CHN	26.2.95	13		Nomi	15 Mar
1:22:58		Leonardo	Dei Tos	ITA	27.4.92	3	NC	Cassino	29 Mar
1:23:01	40:26	Fumitaka	Oikawa	JPN	5.4.95	5		Takahata	25 Oct
1:23:03		Nazar	Kovalenko	UKR	9.2.89	3	NC	Oleksandriya	13 Jun
1:23:04		Máté	Helebrandt	HUN	12.1.89	1	NC	Békécsaba	25 Apr
1:23:10		Sergey	Sharipov	RUS	14.4.92	7	NC	Cheboksary	13 Jun
		(90)							
1:23:11A		Isaac	Palma	MEX	26.10.90	3		Chihuahua	7 Mar
1:23:12		Chandan	Singh	IND	8.6.87	15		Nomi	15 Mar
1:23:12A		Samuel	Gathimba	KEN		1	WCT	Nairobi	1 Aug
1:23:14		Hassanine	Sbaï	TUN	21.1.84	1		Casablanca	30 May
1:23:15			Gao Wenkui	CHN	28.7.95	7		Taicang	1 May
1:23:16		Vitaliy	Anichkin	KAZ	11.11.88	9	RUS-w	Sochi	27 Feb
1:23:16.34t		Yuga	Yamashita	JPN-J	6.2.96	1		Konosu	19 Dec

Mark	Name		Nat	Born	Pos	Meet	Venue	Date
:23:18A	Erwin	González	MEX	7.2.94	4		Chihuahua	7 Mar
:23:19	Nikolay	Markov	RUS	1.2.95	8	NC	Cheboksary	13 Jun
:23:24	Antonin (100)	Boyez	FRA	9.11.84	6		Lugano	15 Mar

Mark	Name		Nat	Born	Date
:23:27	Rhydian	Cowley	AUS	4.1.91	6 Jun
:23:29	Takuya	Yoshida	JPN	10.8.90	15 Feb
:23:29		Yu Wei	CHN	11.9.87	18 Apr
:23:30		Chen Zongliang	CHN	9.1.92	20 Mar
:23:30	Juan Manuel	Cano	ARG	21.12.87	18 Apr
:23:31		Byun Young-jun	KOR	20.3.84	15 Mar
:23:33	José Ignacio	Díaz	ESP	22.11.79	18 Apr
:23:34.0t	Pavel	Chihuán	PER	19.1.86	12 Jun
:23:35	Marius	Ziukas	LTU	29.6.85	15 Mar
:23:35		Luo Yadong	CHN	15.1.92	1 May
:23:35	Marco Antonio	Rodríguez	BOL	24.1.94	9 May
:23:35	Brian	Pintado	ECU	29.7.95	25 Oct
:23:36	Tomofumi	Kanno	JPN	25.4.93	15 Feb
:23:38		Park Chil-sung	KOR	8.7.82	15 Mar
:23:39		Han Jijiang	CHN	20.7.93	6 Sep
:23:41.46t	Ryosuke	Kawagishi	JPN-J	15.6.96	19 Dec
:23:42	Wayne	Snyman	RSA	8.3.85	18 Apr
:23:44	Tsuyoshi	Tasaka	JPN	30.7.93	15 Mar
:23:45	Yuki	Ito	JPN	12.4.92	15 Feb
:23:45		Choi Byung-kwang	KOR	7.4.91	15 Mar
:23:45A	Simon	Wachira	KEN		1 Aug
:23:48.3t	Jean	Blancheteau	FRA-J	7.1.96	15 Nov
:23:50	Luis Manuel	Corchete	ESP	14.5.84	22 Mar
:23:50	Ivan	Trotskiy	BLR	27.5.76	3 Oct
:23:51	Rafal	Augustyn	POL	14.5.84	18 Apr
:23:52	Marius	Šavelskis	LTU	30.7.94	15 Mar
:23:55		Ma Haijun	CHN	24.11.92	6 Sep
:23:55		Kim Dae-ho	KOR	30.4.88	20 Oct
:23:58		Dong Guozhu	CHN	2.8.92	6 Sep
:24:00		Wu Qianlong	CHN	30.1.90	6 Jun
:24:01	Takayuki	Tanii	JPN	14.2.83	15 Feb
:24:05	Jared	Tallent	AUS	17.10.84	22 Feb
:24:05	Aleksandr	Nazarov	RUS	9.2.94	13 Jun
1:24:09	Aleksey	Golovin	RUS	24.12.88	27 Feb
1:24:09	Francisco	Arcilla	ESP	14.1.84	22 Mar
1:24:12		Kang Kil-dong	KOR	12.7.92	15 Mar
1:24:14		Liu Jianmin	CHN	9.3.88	20 Mar
1:24:19	Kota	Yamada	JPN	27.4.94	15 Mar
1:24:24A	Yerko	Araya	CHI	14.2.86	7 Mar
1:24:26		Zhao Qi	CHN	14.1.93	6 Jun
1:24:26	Jordy	Jiménez	ECU	11.2.94	25 Oct
1:24:30	Shuto	Goto	JPN	26.2.94	15 Mar
1:24:31		Wang Zhendong	CHN	11.1.91	6 Sep
1:24:33	Recep	Celik	TUR	10.6.83	24 Jan
1:24:34	Ersin	Tacir	TUR	1.4.85	24 Jan
1:24:34	Yuki	Yamazaki	JPN	16.1.84	1 Jan
1:24:36	Grzegorz	Sudol	POL	28.8.78	18 Apr
1:24:39	Seiya	Watanabe	JPN	23.5.88	25 Oct
1:24:40		Yang Liang	CHN	25.4.93	20 Mar
1:24:40	Horacio	Nava	MEX	20.1.82	23 Aug
1:24:41A	David	Kimutai	KEN	18.8.69	1 Aug
1:24:42	Genadij	Kozlovskij	LTU	7.1.91	18 Apr
1:24:43	Dmitriy	Solovyov	RUS	12.4.93	27 Feb
1:24:43A	Jesús Tadeo	Vega	MEX	23.5.94	7 Mar
1:24:44	Francesco	Fortunato	ITA	13.12.94	29 Mar
1:24:45	Hikaru	Fukuoka	JPN	31.10.92	1 Jan
1:24:48	Ippei	Yamaguchi	JPN	12.5.95	1 Jan
1:24:48	Ever	Palma	MEX	18.3.92	25 Apr
1:24:49	Dmitriy	Dyubin	BLR	12.7.90	11 Apr
1:24:51		Zhang Lei	CHN	26.5.93	20 Mar
1:24:52	Yuya	Suganami	JPN	.95	25 Oct
1:24:53	Pedro	Isidro	POR	17.7.85	18 Apr
1:24:54	Rafal	Sikora	POL	17.2.87	18 Apr
1:24:57	Devender	Singh	IND	5.12.83	18 Apr
1:24:59	Takeshi	Okuma	JPN	14.12.83	15 Feb
1:25:00	Hayoto (166)	Katsuki	JPN	28.11.90	15 Feb

Best track times

Mark	Name		Nat	Born	Pos	Meet	Venue	Date
:23:20.86t	Lebogang	Shange	RSA	1.8.90	1		Bedford	21 Jun
:23:56.0t	Juan Manuel	Cano	ARG	21.12.87	2	SAmC	Lima	12 Jun
:24:18.0t	Mauricio	Arteaga	ECU	8.8.88	3	SAmC	Lima	12 Jun
:24:24.7t	Sérgio	Vieira	POR	20.2.76	1		Leiria	1 Mar

JUNIORS

See main list for top 4 juniors. 9 performances by 4 men to 1:24:30. Additional marks and further juniors:

Name	Mark	Pos	Meet	Venue	Date
Noda	1:20:59	5	NC	Kobe	16 Feb
Yamanishi	1:23:54	11	NC	Kobe	16 Feb
García	1:24:52	29	WCh	Beijing	23 Aug

Mark	Name		Nat	Born	Pos	Meet	Venue	Date
:23:41.46t	Ryosuke	Kawagishi	JPN-J	15.6.96	2		Konosu	19 Dec
:23:48.3t	Jean	Blancheteau	FRA-J	7.1.96	1		Balma	15 Nov
:26:16	Pablo	Oliva	ESP	15.10.96	21		Rio Maior	18 Apr
:26:20		Li Liangyong	CHN	28.5.96	4		Wuhai	13 Jun
:26:27.0t	Paulo	Yurivilca	PER	23.4.96	5	SAmCh	Lima	12 Jun
:26:47	Maksim	Krasnov	RUS	10.2.96	1	NCp-J	Cheboksary	6 Sep
:27:08	Kyohei	Dairuku	JPN	.96	11		Takahata	25 Oct
:27:09	Kohei	Kowaki	JPN	.96	12		Takahata	25 Oct

30-35 KILOMETRES WALK

30k	35k	Name		Nat	Born	Pos	Meet	Venue	Date
:05:43	2:25:54	Mikhail	Ryzhov	RUS	17.12.91	1	NC-w	Sochi	27 Feb
:06:20	2:27:20	Ivan	Noskov	RUS	16.7.88	2	NC-w	Sochi	27 Feb
:07:02	2:29:33	Sergey	Sharipov	RUS	14.4.92	3	NC-w	Sochi	27 Feb
:07:02	2:29:54	Roman	Yevstifeyev	RUS	19.9.92	4	NC-w	Sochi	27 Feb
:07:21	–	Konstantin	Maksimov	RUS	17.6.82		in 35k	Sochi	27 Feb
:08:21	2:30:25	Aleksandr	Yargunkin	RUS	6.1.81	5	NC-w	Sochi	27 Feb
:09:20	2:30:35+	Matej	Tóth	SVK	10.2.83	1	in 50k	Dudince	21 Mar
	2:32:56	Miguel Ángel	López	ESP	3.7.88	1	NC	Jumilla	1 Mar
:12:32	2:34:25+	Hiroki	Arai	JPN	18.5.88		in 50k	Wajima	19 Apr
:12:32	2:34:30+	Takuya	Yoshida	JPN	10.8.90		in 50k	Wajima	19 Apr
:12:33	2:34:34+	Takayuki	Tanii	JPN	14.2.83		in 50k	Wajima	19 Apr
:13:50			Cha Jinhong	CHN-J	27.5.97	1		Beijing	21 Mar
:13:58	+	Koichiro	Morioka	JPN	2.4.85		in 50k	Takahata	25 Oct
:14:23	2:36:16+	Jared	Tallent	AUS	17.10.84	2	in 50k	Beijing	29 Aug
:14:23	2:36:18+	Robert	Heffernan	IRL	20.2.78	3=	in 50k	Beijing	29 Aug

MEN 2015

Mark		Name		Nat	Born	Pos	Meet	Venue	Date
2:14:24	2:36:18+		Zhang Lin	CHN	11.11.93	3=	in 50k	Beijing	29 Aug
2:13:21	2:36:34	Vladislav	Muratov	RUS	31.12.93	6	NC-w	Sochi	27 Feb
2:13:59	2:36:50+	Yuki	Ito	JPN	12.4.92		in 50k	Wajima	19 Apr
2:14:43	2:36:55+	Rafal	Augustyn	POL	14.5.84	2=	in 50k	Dudince	21 Mar
2:14:43	2:36:55+	Lukasz	Nowak	POL	18.12.88	2=	in 50k	Dudince	21 Mar
	2:36:56	Andrés	Chocho	ECU	4.11.83	1	NC	Sucua	5 Apr
Drugs disqualification									
2:13:22+	2:35:31	Yuriy	Andronov ¶	RUS	6.11.71	(4)	in 50k	Taicang	3 May

Russians – Noskov, Ryzhov, Strelkov and Yargunkin suspended pending investigation

50 KILOMETRES WALK

Mark		Name	Nat	Born	Pos	Meet	Venue	Date
3:34:38	Matej	Tóth	SVK	10.2.83	1		Dudince	21 Mar
3:40:20	Hiroki	Arai	JPN	18.5.88	1	NC	Wajima	19 Apr
3:40:32		Tóth			1	WCh	Beijing	29 Aug
3:42:01	Takayuki	Tanii	JPN	14.2.83	2	NC	Wajima	19 Apr
3:42:17	Jared	Tallent	AUS	17.10.84	2	WCh	Beijing	29 Aug
3:42:55		Tanii			3	WCh	Beijing	29 Aug
3:43:32	Mikhail	Ryzhov ¶	RUS	17.12.91	1	ECp	Murcia	17 May
3:43:40	Yuki	Yamazaki	JPN	16.1.84	3	NC	Wajima	19 Apr
3:43:44		Arai			4	WCh	Beijing	29 Aug
3:43:45	Evan	Dunfee	CAN	28.9.90	1		Melbourne	13 Dec
3:43:55	Rafal	Augustyn	POL	14.5.84	2		Dudince	21 Mar
3:43:57	Ivan	Noskov ¶	RUS	16.7.88	2	ECp	Murcia	17 May
3:44:17	Robert	Heffernan (10)	IRL	20.2.78	5	WCh	Beijing	29 Aug
3:44:27	Koichiro	Morioka	JPN	2.4.85	1		Takahata	25 Oct
3:44:39		Zhang Lin	CHN	11.11.93	6	WCh	Beijing	29 Aug
3:44:53	Lukasz	Nowak	POL	18.12.88	3		Dudince	21 Mar
3:45:21		Yu Wei	CHN	11.9.87	7	WCh	Beijing	29 Aug
3:45:41	Horacio	Nava	MEX	20.1.82	1	PAmCp	Arica	9 May
3:45:41	Aleksandr	Yargunkin	RUS	6.1.81	1	NC	Cheboksary	12 Jun
3:46:00	Andrés	Chocho	ECU	4.11.83	8	WCh	Beijing	29 Aug
3:46:07	Takuya	Yoshida	JPN	10.8.90	4	NC	Wajima	19 Apr
3:46:21	Marco	De Luca	ITA	12.5.81	3	ECp	Murcia	17 May
3:46:43	Jesús Ángel	García (20)	ESP	17.10.69	9	WCh	Beijing	29 Aug
3:46:57		Yu Wei			1	WCT	Beijing	21 Mar
3:47:11		Zhang Lin			2	WCT	Beijing	21 Mar
3:47:35		Wu Qianlong	CHN	30.1.90	3	WCT	Beijing	21 Mar
3:48:44		Heffernan			4		Dudince	21 Mar
3:48:48		Luo Yadong	CHN	15.1.92	4	WCT	Beijing	21 Mar
3:48:48	Quentin	Rew	NZL	16.7.84	10	WCh	Beijing	29 Aug
3:48:55	Brendan	Boyce	IRL	15.10.86	5		Dudince	21 Mar
3:49:02	Veli-Matti	Partanen	FIN	28.10.91	6		Dudince	21 Mar
3:49:02	Ivan	Banzeruk	UKR	9.2.90	4	ECp	Murcia	17 May
3:49:11	Adrian	Blocki	POL	11.4.90	11	WCh	Beijing	29 Aug
3:49:27	Federico	Tontodonati	ITA	30.10.89	1		Andernach	10 Oct
3:49:30		A Blocki			7		Dudince	21 Mar
3:49:52	Matteo	Giupponi	ITA	8.10.88	8		Dudince	21 Mar
3:49:56		Dunfee			12	WCh	Beijing	29 Aug
3:49:57		Xie Sichao	CHN	28.2.93	5	WCT	Beijing	21 Mar
	(38/30)							
3:50:01		Zhang Hang	CHN	28.10.91	6	WCT	Beijing	21 Mar
3:50:12	Carl	Dohmann	GER	18.5.90	2	NC	Andernach	10 Oct
3:50:14A	José	Leyver	MEX	12.11.85	1		Chihuahua	7 Mar
3:50:19	Cristian	Berdeja	MEX	21.6.81	2	PAmCp	Arica	9 May
3:50:47	James	Rendón	COL	7.7.85	3	PAmCp	Arica	9 May
3:51:00		Niu Wenbin	CHN	20.1.91	7	WCT	Beijing	21 Mar
3:51:00	Roman	Yevstifeyev	RUS	19.9.92	5	ECp	Murcia	17 May
3:51:18	Hagen	Pohle	GER	5.3.92	3	NC	Andernach	10 Oct
3:51:26	Chris	Erickson	AUS	1.12.81	13	WCh	Beijing	29 Aug
3:51:33	Sergiy	Budza	UKR	6.12.84	6	ECp	Murcia	17 May
	(40)							
3:51:38	Aléxandros	Papamihaíl	GRE	18.9.88	7	ECp	Murcia	17 May
3:51:44	Teodorico	Caporaso	ITA	14.9.87	8	ECp	Murcia	17 May
3:51:48	Grzegorz	Sudol	POL	28.8.78	9	ECp	Murcia	17 May
3:52:17A	Luis	Bustamante	MEX	10.6.84	3		Chihuahua	7 Mar
3:52:29		Xu Faguang	CHN	17.5.87	8	WCT	Beijing	21 Mar
3:53:53	Andrey	Hrechkovskyy	UKR	30.8.93	1	NC	Ivano-Frankivsk	18 Oct
3:53:55	Damian	Blocki	POL	28.4.89	4		Andernach	10 Oct

Mark	Name		Nat	Born	Pos	Meet	Venue	Date
3:54:12	Marc	Mundell	RSA	7.7.83	3		Melbourne	13 Dec
3:54:24	Tomofumi	Kanno	JPN	25.4.93	2		Takahata	25 Oct
3:55:02A	Omar	Zepeda	MEX	8.7.77	5		Chihuahua	7 Mar
	(50)							
3:55:03	Brendon	Reading	AUS	26.1.89	4	2 NC	Melbourne	13 Dec
3:55:06	Takeshi	Okuma	JPN	14.12.83	5	NC	Wajima	19 Apr
3:55:17	Ian	Rayson	AUS	4.2.88	5	2 NC	Melbourne	13 Dec
3:55:21A	Jorge	Martínez	MEX	25.10.90	6		Chihuahua	7 Mar
3:55:34	Igor	Saharuk	UKR	3.6.88	2	NC	Ivano-Frankivsk	18 Oct
3:55:36	Mário José	dos Santos	BRA	10.9.79	9		Dudince	21 Mar
3:55:43	Luis Fernando	López	COL	3.6.79	20	WCh	Beijing	29 Aug
3:55:44	Pedro	Isidro	POR	17.7.85	21	WCh	Beijing	29 Aug
3:55:44		Han Yucheng	CHN	16.12.78	3	NC	Changbaishan	7 Sep
3:55:45	Benjamin	Sánchez	ESP	10.3.85	10	ECp	Murcia	17 May
	(60)							
3:55:54	Yuki	Ito	JPN	12.4.92	6	NC	Wajima	19 Apr
3:55:57	Erick	Barrondo	GUA	14.6.91	2	PAm	Toronto	26 Jul
3:55:59	Marius	Cocioran	ROU	10.7.83	11	ECp	Murcia	17 May
3:56:16		Hu Wanli	CHN	27.5.92	2		Taicang	2 May
3:56:25		Liu Jian	CHN	19.5.95	9	WCT	Beijing	21 Mar
3:56:27	Tadas	Suskevicius	LTU	22.5.85	22	WCh	Beijing	29 Aug
3:56:42		Park Chil-sung	KOR	8.7.82	23	WCh	Beijing	29 Aug
3:56:46		Luo Dongpo	CHN	23.6.95	3		Taicang	2 May
3:56:50	Håvard	Haukenes	NOR	22.4.90	24	WCh	Beijing	29 Aug
3:57:03	Sandeep	Kumar Sangwan	IND	16.12.86	26	WCh	Beijing	29 Aug
	(70)							
3:57:11	Manish	Singh Rawat	IND	5.5.91	27	WCh	Beijing	29 Aug
3:57:14	Aleksi	Ojala	FIN	9.12.92	11		Dudince	21 Mar
3:57:18	Maryan	Zakalnytskyy	UKR	19.8.94	3	NC	Ivano-Frankivsk	18 Oct
3:57:40	Sergey	Sharipov	RUS	14.4.92	14	ECp	Murcia	17 May
3:57:41	Jaime	Quiyuch	GUA	24.4.88	29	WCh	Beijing	29 Aug
3:57:53		Zhao Qi	CHN	14.1.93	4		Taicang	2 May
3:57:56	Volodymyr	Hontsovskyy	UKR	23.8.91	4	NC	Ivano-Frankivsk	18 Oct
3:58:20	Xavier	Le Coz	FRA	30.12.79	5		Andernach	10 Oct
3:58:23	Jorge	Ruiz	COL	17.5.89	6	PAmCp	Arica	9 May
3:58:47		Zhang Kuo	CHN	12.12.89	5		Taicang	2 May
	(80)							
3:58:57	Dusan	Majdán	SVK	8.9.87	30	WCh	Beijing	29 Aug
3:59:03	Lukás	Gdula	CZE	6.12.91	12		Dudince	21 Mar
3:59:03	Hayato	Katsuki	JPN	28.11.90	4		Takahata	25 Oct
3:59:11	Vladimir	Savanovic	SRB	12.6.85	6		Andernach	10 Oct
3:59:22	Dominic	King	GBR	30.5.83	7		Andernach	10 Oct
3:59:23	Shuto	Goto	JPN	26.2.94	5		Takahata	25 Oct
3:59:30		Bian Tongda	CHN	1.4.91	10	WCT	Beijing	21 Mar
4:00:26	Predrag	Filipovic	SRB	5.10.78	8		Andernach	10 Oct
4:00:56A	Edward	Araya	CHI	14.2.86	8		Chihuahua	7 Mar
4:00:57	Oleksandr	Venhlovskyy	UKR	5.8.85	5	NC	Ivano-Frankivsk	18 Oct
	(90)							
4:00:58	Jonathan	Cáceres	ECU	20.1.90	4	PAm	Toronto	26 Jul
4:01:14	Rafal	Sikora	POL	17.2.87	13		Dudince	21 Mar
4:01:35	Mathieu	Bilodeau	CAN	27.11.83	31	WCh	Beijing	29 Aug
4:01:44	Miklós	Srp	HUN	6.3.93	14		Dudince	21 Mar
4:01:48	Luis Angel	Sánchez	GUA	15.12.93	9	PAmCp	Arica	9 May
4:02:07	Jarkko	Kinnunen	FIN	19.1.84	32	WCh	Beijing	29 Aug
4:02:14	Claudio Paul	Villanueva	ECU	3.8.88	1		Valley Cottage	25 Oct
4:02:20	Caio	Bonfim	BRA	19.3.91	1		Santee	22 Nov
4:02:23	Aleksandr	Shunikhin	RUS	29.11.92	2	NC	Cheboksary	12 Jun
4:02:26	Martin	Tistan	SVK	12.11.92	15	ECp	Murcia	17 May
	(100)							

Mark	Name		Nat	Born	Date
4:02:29	Luis Manuel	Corchete	ESP	14.5.84	17 May
4:02:33	Oleksiy	Shelest ¶	UKR	27.3.73	18 Oct
4:02:45	Lorenzo	Dessi	ITA	4.5.89	17 May
4:02:46	Fredy	Hernández	COL	24.4.78	9 May
4:02:48A	Oleksiy	Kazanin	UKR	22.5.82	7 Mar
4:03:16		Han Jijiang	CHN	20.7.93	21 Mar
4:03:17A	Luis José	Solis	MEX	23.4.84	7 Mar
4:03:20	Anders	Hansson	SWE	10.3.92	17 May
4:03:40	John	Nunn	USA	3.2.78	22 Nov
4:03:44		Li Chengfa	CHN	2.3.92	21 Mar
4:03:44	Arnis	Rumbenieks	LAT	4.4.88	21 Mar
4:03:45	Sergey	Korepanov	RUS	15.7.84	12 Jun
4:04:06	Michele	Antonelli	ITA	23.5.94	10 Oct
4:04:12	Inaki	Gómez	CAN	16.1.88	13 Dec
4:04:14		He Yongqiang	CHN	27.11.93	2 May
4:04:45	Oleksiy	Bilorus	UKR	11.9.92	18 Oct
4:05:01		Yang Liang	CHN	25.4.93	7 Sep
4:05:03	Sándor	Rácz	HUN	14.9.86	21 Mar
4:05:29		Gou Xiaoxin	CHN	18.1.86	2 May
4:05:29	Ferney	Rojas	COL	30.9.87	9 May
4:06:21		Xiong Denghua	CHN	29.5.95	21 Mar
4:07:05		Li Tengliang	CHN	23.5.94	21 Mar
4:07:07		Li Guodong	CHN	17.12.92	7 Sep
4:07:23	Francisco	Arcilla	ESP	14.1.84	29 Aug
4:07:23		Kim Dong-young	KOR	6.3.80	25 Oct
4:07:41		Cheng Min	CHN	6.7.91	21 Mar

MEN 2015

Mark	Name		Nat	Born	Date	Mark	Name		Nat	Born	Date
4:07:46	Eder	Sánchez	MEX	21.5.86	22 Nov	4:08:39		Wang Hao	CHN	16.8.89	7 Sep
4:08:05	Pavel	Schrom	CZE	17.3.91	17 May	4:08:59	Jonathan	Rieckmann	BRA	20.8.87	9 May
4:08:33	Mario Alfonso	Bran	GUA	17.10.89	9 May	4:09:11	Andrea	Agrusti	ITA	30.8.95	1 Feb
4:08:36	Eemeli	Kiiski	FIN	13.8.91	17 May		(133)				

WOMEN'S WORLD LISTS 2015

60 METRES INDOORS

Mark	Name		Nat	Born	Pos	Meet	Venue	Date
7.05	Murielle	Ahouré	CIV	23.8.87	1	Mill	New York (Arm)	14 Feb
7.05	Dafne	Schippers	NED	15.6.92	1	EI	Praha (O2)	8 Mar
7.07		Schippers			1h3	EI	Praha (O2)	7 Mar
7.08		Ahouré			1		Houston	31 Jan
7.08	Remona	Burchell	JAM	15.9.91	1	SEC	Lexington KY	28 Feb
7.08	Tianna	Bartoletta	USA	30.8.85	1	NC	Boston (R)	1 Mar
7.08	Verena	Sailer	GER	16.10.85	1s3	EI	Praha (O2)	8 Mar
7.08	Dina	Asher-Smith	GBR	4.12.95	2	EI	Praha (O2)	8 Mar
7.09		Schippers			1	ISTAF	Berlin	14 Feb
7.09		Sailer			3	EI	Praha (O2)	8 Mar
	(10/6)							
7.10	Ezinne	Okparaebo	NOR	3.3.88	4	EI	Praha (O2)	8 Mar
7.11	Michelle-Lee	Ahye	TTO	10.4.92	2	Mill	New York (Arm)	14 Feb
7.11	Mujinga	Kambundji	SUI	17.6.92	5	EI	Praha (O2)	8 Mar
7.11	Olesya	Povh	UKR	18.10.87	6	EI	Praha (O2)	8 Mar
	(10)							
7.14	Jessica	Young	USA	6.4.87	2h2	GP	Birmingham	21 Feb
7.15	Jasmine	Todd	USA	23.12.93	1		Seattle	17 Jan
7.15	Dezerea	Bryant	USA	27.4.93	1h2	NCAA	Fayetteville	13 Mar
7.15	Jenna	Prandini	USA	20.11.92	1h1	NCAA	Fayetteville	13 Mar
7.18	Flings	Owusu-Agyapong	GHA	16.10.88	1		New York	16 Jan
7.18	Ky	Westbrook	USA	25.2.96	2		Seattle	17 Jan
7.18A	Muna	Lee	USA	30.10.81	1		Flagstaff	31 Jan
7.19	Kelly-Ann	Baptiste	TTO	14.10.86	1		Baton Rouge	20 Feb
7.19		Wei Yongli	CHN	11.10.91	1	NGP	Shanghai	1 Mar
7.19	Jamile	Samuel	NED	24.4.92	7	EI	Praha (O2)	8 Mar
	(20)							
7.19	Khamica	Bingham	CAN	15.6.94	1		Windsor	12 Mar
7.20A	Morolake	Akinosun	USA	17.5.94	1		Albuquerque	7 Feb
7.20	Carina	Horn	RSA	9.3.89	2	ISTAF	Berlin	14 Feb
7.20	Ewa	Swoboda	POL-J	26.7.97	8	EI	Praha (O2)	8 Mar
7.21	Nataliya	Pohrebnyak	UKR	19.2.88	1		Zaporizhzhya	27 Jan
7.21	Tiffany	Townsend	USA	14.6.89	4	Mill	New York (Arm)	14 Feb
7.21	Shayla	Sanders	USA	6.1.94	1h2	SEC	Lexington KY	27 Feb
7.22A	Cierra	White	USA	29.4.93	2		Albuquerque	7 Feb
7.22	Ivet	Lalova-Collio	BUL	18.5.84	2	Pedro	Lódz	17 Feb
7.22	Mikele	Barber	USA	4.10.80	2h2	NC	Boston (R)	1 Mar
	(30)							
7.23	Tynia	Gaither	BAH	16.3.93	2rB		Seattle	28 Feb
7.23	Alexandra	Burghardt	GER	28.4.94	2h3	EI	Praha (O2)	7 Mar
7.23	Mikiah	Brisco	USA-J	14.7.96	4h1	NCAA	Fayetteville	13 Mar
7.24	Rebekka	Haase	GER	2.1.93	1		Chemnitz	31 Jan
7.24	Crystal	Emmanuel	CAN	27.11.91	1		Toronto	7 Feb
7.24	Rachel	Johncock	GBR	4.10.93	2h1	GP	Birmingham	21 Feb
7.24	Yasmin	Kwadwo	GER	9.11.90	2s2	NC	Karlsruhe	21 Feb
7.24	Céline	Distel-Bonnet	FRA	25.7.87	3h2	EI	Praha (O2)	7 Mar
7.24	Audrey	Alloh	ITA	21.7.87	3s3	EI	Praha (O2)	8 Mar
7.25	Tawanna	Meadows	USA	4.8.86	5	NC	Boston (R)	1 Mar
	(40)							
7.26	Maja	Mihalinec	SLO	17.12.89	1		Wien	31 Jan
7.26	Kseniya	Ryzhova	RUS	19.4.87	1s2	NC	Moskva	17 Feb
7.26	Irene	Ekelund	SWE-J	8.3.97	1	NC	Sätra	21 Feb
7.26	Carmelita	Jeter	USA	24.11.79	7	GP	Birmingham	21 Feb
7.27	Alexis	Faulknor	USA	22.9.94	4		Lexington KY	24 Jan
7.27	Aleen	Bailey	JAM	25.11.80	5		Karlsruhe	31 Jan
7.27	Kristina	Sivkova	RUS-J	28.2.97	1	NC-j	Novocheboksarsk	4 Feb
7.27A	Aleia	Hobbs	USA-J	24.2.96	3		Albuquerque	7 Feb
7.27	Marina	Panteleyeva	RUS	16.5.89	1	Mosc Ch	Moskva	8 Feb
7.28	Viktoriya	Yarushkina	RUS	4.4.91	1		Volgograd	24 Jan
	(50)							
7.28	Myasia	Jacobs	USA	8.1.94	1		New York (Arm)	31 Jan
7.28	Tahesia	Harrigan	IVB	15.2.82	2		Eaubonne	10 Feb

Mark	Wind	Name		Nat	Born	Pos	Meet	Venue	Date
7.28		Ayodelé	Ikuesan	FRA	15.5.85	2h2		Eaubonne	10 Feb
7.28		Aaliyah	Brown	USA	6.1.95	4	Tyson	Fayetteville	13 Feb
7.28A		Hannah	Cunliffe	USA-J	9.1.96	4	Kirby	Albuquerque	14 Feb
7.28		Deanna	Hill	USA	13.4.96	3rB		Seattle	28 Feb
7.28		Inna	Eftimova	BUL	19.6.88	5s2	EI	Praha (O2)	8 Mar
7.28		Javienne	Oliver	UDA	26.12.94	1		Bloomington IN	11 Dec
7.29		Ruddy	Zang Milama	GAB	6.6.87	1		Blacksburg	23 Jan
7.29		Stella	Akakpo	FRA	28.2.94	1		Metz	25 Feb
		(60)							
7.29		Véronique	Mang	FRA	15.12.84	2		Metz	25 Feb
7.29		Andrea	Ivancevic	CRO	21.8.84	1	NC	Rijeka	1 Mar

Best at low altitude

7.21 Akinosun 2 Tyson Fayetteville 13 Feb | 7.25 Lee 6 Mill New York (Arm) 14 Feb

Outdoors

Mark	Wind	Name		Nat	Born	Pos	Meet	Venue	Date
7.13	0.8	Shelly-Ann	Fraser-Pryce	JAM	27.12.86	1		Kingston	31 Jan

100 METRES

Mark	Wind	Name		Nat	Born	Pos	Meet	Venue	Date
10.74	0.2	Shelly-Ann	Fraser-Pryce	JAM	27.12.86	1	DL	Saint-Denis	4 Jul
10.76	-0.3		Fraser-Pryce			1	WCh	Beijing	24 Aug
10.79	1.5	English	Gardner	USA	22.4.92	1s1	NC	Eugene	26 Jun
10.79	0.4		Fraser-Pryce			1	NC	KIngston	26 Jun
10.80	0.2	Blessing	Okagbare	NGR	9.10.88	2	DL	Saint-Denis	4 Jul
10.81	1.7		Fraser-Pryce			1	Pre	Eugene	30 May
10.81	1.7	Murielle	Ahouré	CIV	23.8.87	2	Pre	Eugene	30 May
10.81	1.2	Tori	Bowie	USA	27.8.90	1	NC	Eugene	26 Jun
10.81	-0.3	Dafne	Schippers	NED	15.6.92	2	WCh	Beijing	24 Aug
10.82	1.7		Bowie			3	Pre	Eugene	30 May
10.82	0.5		Fraser-Pryce			1s1	WCh	Beijing	24 Aug
10.83	-0.2		Schippers			1s3	WCh	Beijing	24 Aug
10.84	1.5		Gardner			1rB	Pre	Eugene	30 May
10.84	1.5	Elaine	Thompson	JAM	28.6.92	2rB	Pre	Eugene	30 May
10.84	1.4	Kelly-Ann	Baptiste	TTO	14.10.86	1	NC	Port of Spain	27 Jun
10.86	1.2		Gardner			2	NC	Eugene	26 Jun
10.86	-0.3		Bowie			3	WCh	Beijing	24 Aug
10.87	1.7		Okagbare			4	Pre	Eugene	30 May
10.87	0.9		Bowie			1s2	WCh	Beijing	24 Aug
10.88	0.5		Bowie			1h1	WCh	Beijing	23 Aug
10.89	0.5		Okagbare			2s1	WCh	Beijing	24 Aug
10.89	-0.2	Veronica	Campbell-Brown	JAM	15.5.82	2s3	WCh	Beijing	24 Aug
10.90	1.0		Thompson			1		Madrid	11 Jul
10.90	0.9		Baptiste			2s2	WCh	Beijing	24 Aug
10.91	-0.3		Campbell-Brown			4	WCh	Beijing	24 Aug
10.92	1.0		Thompson			1		Kingston	11 Apr
10.92	1.4	Jenna	Prandini (10)	USA	20.11.92	1	MSR	Walnut	18 Apr
10.92	1.5		Prandini			2s1	NC	Eugene	26 Jun
10.92	1.2	Jasmine	Todd	USA	23.12.93	3	NC	Eugene	26 Jun
10.92	1.6	Barbara	Pierre	USA	28.4.87	1h2	PAm	Toronto	21 Jul
10.92	0.1		Schippers			1	DL	London (OS)	25 Jul
		(31/12)							
10.93	1.2	Jeneba	Tarmoh	USA	27.9.89	4	NC	Eugene	26 Jun
10.94	1.2	Tianna	Bartoletta	USA	30.8.85	5	NC	Eugene	26 Jun
10.95	0.9	Sherone	Simpson	JAM	12.8.84	1	PAm	Toronto	22 Jul
10.96	0.9	Natasha	Morrison	JAM	17.11.92	3s2	WCh	Beijing	24 Aug
10.97	-2.5	Michelle-Lee	Ahye	TTO	10.4.92	1	FlaR	Gainesville	2 Apr
10.98	2.0	Candace	Hill	USA-Y	11.2.99	1		Shoreline	20 Jun
10.99	0.9	Ángela	Tenorio	ECU-J	27.1.96	2	PAm	Toronto	22 Jul
10.99	0.1	Dina	Asher-Smith	GBR	4.12.95	1h1	DL	London (OS)	25 Jul
		(20)							
11.00	1.8	Candyce	McGrone	USA	24.3.89	1h4	NC	Eugene	25 Jun
11.00	1.5	Dezerea	Bryant	USA	27.4.93	4s1	NC	Eugene	26 Jun
11.01	1.4	Ana Cláudia	Silva	BRA	6.11.88	2	MSR	Walnut	18 Apr
11.01	1.2	Carmelita	Jeter	USA	24.11.79	7	NC	Eugene	26 Jun
11.01A	1.4	Samantha	Henry-Robinson	JAM	25.9.88	1h3	NACAC	San José, CRC	7 Aug
11.02	1.4	Muna	Lee	USA	30.10.81	3	MSR	Walnut	18 Apr
11.02	0.6	Marie Josée	Ta Lou Gonerie	CIV	18.11.88	1	AfG	Brazzaville	14 Sep
11.04	-2.5	Remona	Burchell	JAM	15.9.91	2	FlaR	Gainesville	2 Apr
11.04	1.5	Rosângela	Santos	BRA	20.12.90	3	Pre	Eugene	30 May
11.06	0.2	Shalonda	Solomon	USA	19.12.85	2	Jones	Gainesville	24 Apr
		(30)							

Mark	Wind	Name		Nat	Born	Pos	Meet	Venue	Date
11.06	1.8	LeKeisha	Lawson	USA	3.6.87	3h4	NC	Eugene	25 Jun
11.06	1.2	Carina	Horn	RSA	9.3.89	1h2		Madrid	11 Jul
11.07	0.9	Mujinga	Kambundji	SUI	17.6.92	5s2	WCh	Beijing	24 Aug
11.08	1.2	Ruddy	Zang Milama	GAB	6.6.87	1		Greensboro NC	17 May
11.08	1.8	Aaliyah	Brown	USA	6.1.95	1s3	NCAA	Eugene	11 Jun
11.08	1.7	Tiffany	Townsend	USA	14.6.89	2h3		Madrid	11 Jul
11.09	0.2	Allyson	Felix	USA	18.11.85	3		Kingston	9 May
11.09	1.8	Keilah	Tyson	USA	6.11.92	2s3	NCAA	Eugene	11 Jun
11.09	1.1	Nataliya	Pohrebnyak	UKR	19.2.88	1	NC	Kirovohrad	30 Jul
11.09	-1.2	Ivet	Lalova-Collio	BUL	18.5.84	2h3	WCh	Beijing	23 Aug
		(40)							
11.10	1.8	Asha	Philip	GBR	25.10.90	3	FBK	Hengelo	24 May
11.10	0.6	Simone	Facey	JAM	7.5.85	1		Edmonton	12 Jul
11.10	0.0	Verena	Sailer	GER	16.10.85	1r1		Mannheim	8 Aug
11.11	1.7	Christania	Williams	JAM	17.10.94	1		Kingston	30 May
11.11	0.0	Desiree	Henry	GBR	26.8.95	2r1		Mannheim	8 Aug
11.12	-1.2	Ezinne	Okparaebo	NOR	3.3.88	4h3	WCh	Beijing	23 Aug
11.13	1.4	Kimberlyn	Duncan	USA	2.8.91	4	MSR	Walnut	18 Apr
11.13	2.0	Aleia	Hobbs	USA-J	24.2.96	2s1	NCAA	Eugene	11 Jun
11.13	0.9	Khamica	Bingham	CAN	15.6.94	6	PAm	Toronto	22 Jul
11.13	0.5	Semoy	Hackett	TTO	27.11.88	5s1	WCh	Beijing	24 Aug
		(50)							
11.14	2.0	Tahesia	Harrigan	IVB	15.2.82	1		New York	11 Jul
11.14	0.0	Charonda	Williams	USA	27.3.87	1	Spitzen	Luzern	14 Jul
11.16	1.8	Sally	Pearson	AUS	19.9.86	1		Canberra	7 Feb
11.16	1.8	Jennifer	Madu	USA	23.9.94	3s3	NCAA	Eugene	11 Jun
11.16	1.5	Alex	Anderson	USA	28.1.87	6s1	NC	Eugene	26 Jun
11.17	1.4	Mikele	Barber	USA	4.10.80	5	MSR	Walnut	18 Apr
11.17	1.8	Ky	Westbrook	USA-J	25.2.96	4s3	NCAA	Eugene	11 Jun
11.17	0.4	Kerron	Stewart	JAM	16.4.84	5	NC	Kingston	26 Jun
11.19A	0.0	Khalifa	St.Fort	TTO-Y	13.2.98	2	WY	Cali	16 Jul
11.19	0.9	Viktoriya	Zyabkina	KAZ	4.9.92	6s2	WCh	Beijing	24 Aug
		(60)							
11.20	0.0	Jessica	Young	USA	6.4.87	3		Bellinzona	21 Jul
11.20	0.0	Olga	Safronova	KAZ	5.11.91	1h2	Kosanov	Almaty	25 Jul
11.21	1.9	Sheniqua	Ferguson	BAH	24.11.89	1h1		Auburn	18 Apr
11.21	1.3	Rebekka	Haase	GER	2.1.93	1s1	NC-23	Wetzlar	13 Jun
11.22	2.0	Yelizaveta	Demirova	RUS	14.8.87	1		Yerino	6 Jun
11.22	2.0	Tawanna	Meadows	USA	4.8.86	1h1		Montverde	6 Jun
11.22	1.4	Reyare	Thomas	TTO	23.11.87	3	NC	Port of Spain	27 Jun
11.23	0.2	Schillonie	Calvert	JAM	27.7.88	6		Kingston	9 May
11.23	1.5	Tatjana	Pinto	GER	2.7.92	1		Regensburg	6 Jun
11.23	-0.5	Chisato	Fukushima	JPN	27.6.88	3h7	WCh	Beijing	23 Aug
		(70)							
11.24	1.6	Ewa	Swoboda	POL-J	26.7.97	1		St. Pölten	4 Jun
11.24	1.6	Yekaterina	Smirnova	RUS	8.9.88	2		St. Pölten	4 Jun
11.24	0.6	Teahna	Daniels	USA-J	25.3.97	1	NC-j	Eugene	25 Jun
11.25	1.8	Jamile	Samuel	NED	24.4.92	4	FBK	Hengelo	24 May
11.25	0.9	Gina	Lückenkemper	GER-J	21.11.96	1s2	NC-23	Wetzlar	13 Jun
11.26	0.9	Melissa	Breen	AUS	17.9.90	1	NC	Brisbane	28 Mar
11.26	1.5	Tristie	Johnson	USA	20.11.93	1	MEAC	Greensboro NC	2 May
11.26	2.0	Zaria	Francis	USA-Y	22.3.98	2		Shoreline	20 Jun
11.26	1.8	Alexis	Faulknor	USA	22.9.94	6h4	NC	Eugene	25 Jun
11.27	0.7	Peace	Uko	NGR	26.12.95	1rB		Clermont	16 May
		(80)							
11.27	1.1	Tynia	Gaither	BAH	16.3.93	2	Pac 12	Los Angeles (Ww)	17 May
11.27	2.0	Kseniya	Ryzhova	RUS	19.4.87	2		Yerino	6 Jun
11.27	1.5	Crystal	Emmanuel	CAN	27.11.91	2	NC	Edmonton	3 Jul
11.27	0.5		Wei Yongli	CHN	11.10.91	8s1	WCh	Beijing	24 Aug
11.28	1.5	Sabria	Hadley	USA	1.1.95	1	ACC	Tallahassee	16 May
11.28	1.0	Marika	Popowicz	POL	28.4.88	1	EAF	Bydgoszcz	14 Jun
11.28	0.6	Sanya	Richards-Ross	USA	26.2.85	5		Edmonton	12 Jul
11.29	-1.3	Janet	Amponsah	GHA	12.4.93	1		Canyon	25 Apr
11.29	-0.3	Morolake	Akinosun	USA	17.5.94	1h2	Big 12	Ames	16 May
11.29	0.2	Véronique	Mang	FRA	15.12.84	9	DL	Saint-Denis	4 Jul
		(90)							
11.30A		Narcisa	Landázuri	ECU	25.11.92			Quito	28 Feb
11.30	2.0	Shayla	Sanders	USA	6.1.94	3s1	NCAA	Eugene	11 Jun
11.30	0.2	Lolo	Jones	USA	5.8.82	3		Bellinzona	21 Jul
11.30	1.1	Andrea	Ivancevic	CRO	21.8.84	1	NC	Varazdin	25 Jul
11.30	0.1	Anna-Lena	Freese	GER	21.1.94	2h1	NC	Nürnberg	25 Jul

Mark	Wind	Name		Nat	Born	Pos	Meet	Venue	Date
11.30	0.6	Yasmin	Kwadwo	GER	9.11.90	1r2		Mannheim	8 Aug
11.31	1.2	Mikiah	Brisco	USA-J	14.7.96	2h3	SEC	Starkville	15 May
11.31	2.0	Yekaterina	Renzhina	RUS	18.10.94	3		Yerino	6 Jun
11.31	1.5	Lisa	Mayer	GER-J	2.5.96	2	NC-23	Wetzlar	13 Jun
11.31	1.5	Kimberly	Hyacinthe	CAN	28.3.89	3	NC	Edmonton	3 Jul
		(100)							

Mark	Wind	Name		Nat	Born	Date
11.32	1.5	Alexandra	Burghardt	GER	28.4.94	13 Jun
11.32	-0.2	Olesya	Povh	UKR	18.10.87	25 Jul
11.33A	0.3	Diamond	Gause	USA	4.4.94	21 Mar
11.33	1.0	Cierra	White	USA	29.4.93	16 May
11.33	2.0	Alfreda	Steele	USA-J	19.12.97	20 Jun
11.33	0.4	Viktoriya	Yarushkina	RUS	4.4.91	18 Jul
11.33	1.6	Isidora	Jiménez	CHI	10.8.93	21 Jul
11.34	0.1	Jada	Martin	USA	8.6.95	18 Apr
11.34	0.7	Lashauntea	Moore	USA	31.7.83	2 May
11.34	1.8	Naomi	Sedney	NED	17.12.94	24 May
11.34	-0.2	Inna	Eftimova	BUL	19.6.88	2 Jun
11.34	1.0	Anna	Kielbasinska	POL	26.6.90	14 Jun
11.34	0.8	Maja	Mihalinec	SLO	17.12.89	1 Aug
11.35	0.8	Chanice	Bonner	JAM-J	6.7.95	21 Mar
11.36	1.4	Jessica	Davis	USA	31.10.92	18 Apr
11.36	1.5	Mercedes	Jackson	USA	12.11.93	3 May
11.36	1.5	Shaina	Harrison	CAN	11.3.94	16 May
11.36A	2.0	Vitória Cristina	Rosa	BRA-J	12.1.96	29 May
11.36	1.4	Ramona	Papaioannou	CYP	15.6.89	20 Jun
11.36	1.8	Ksenija	Balta	EST	11.1.86	19 Jul
11.36		Anna	Kukushkina	RUS	13.12.92	3 Aug
11.37	1.1	Devynne	Charlton	BAH	26.11.95	17 May
11.37	0.6	Céline	Distel-Bonnet	FRA	25.7.87	30 May
11.37	1.8	Jonielle	Smith	JAM-J	30.1.96	11 Jun
11.37	1.8	Ashley	Marshall	BAR	10.9.93	20 Jun
11.37	2.0	Lauren Rain	Williams	USA-Y	25.7.99	20 Jun
11.37	2.0	Krystal	Sparling	USA-J	.97	20 Jun
11.37	-1.2	Kaylin	Whitney	USA-Y	9.3.98	7 Jul
11.37	-0.3	Stephanie	Kalu	NGR	5.8.93	8 Aug
11.38	1.4	Katie	Wise	USA	15.10.93	29 May
11.38	2.0	Myasia	Jacobs	USA	8.1.94	11 Jun
11.38	0.2	Stella	Akakpo	FRA	28.2.94	27 Jun
11.39A	0.3	Alexis	Browner	USA	3.6.93	21 Mar
11.39	0.7	Chelsea	Hayes	USA	9.2.88	2 May
11.39	0.6	Natalya	Rakacheva	RUS	16.4.88	6 Jun
11.39	2.0	Porscha	Lucas	USA	18.6.88	6 Jun
11.39	2.0	Marina	Panteleyeva	RUS	16.5.89	6 Jun
11.39	1.8	Cindy	Ofili	GBR	5.8.94	11 Jun
11.39	-2.7	Shayla	Mahan	USA	18.1.89	19 Jun
11.39	1.8	Dominique	Booker	USA	10.2.92	25 Jun
11.39A	-0.6	Hannah	Brier	GBR-Y	3.2.98	16 Jul
11.40	0.9	Toea	Wisil	PNG	1.1.88	28 Mar
11.40	1.4	A'Keyla	Mitchell	USA	25.11.95	25 Apr
11.40	1.8	MacKenzie	Flannigan	USA	27.8.92	29 May
11.40	0.4	Daryll	Neita	GBR-J	29.8.96	20 Jun
11.40	1.4	Kamaria	Durant	TTO	24.2.91	27 Jun
11.40	0.6	Vanusa	dos Santos	BRA	22.1.90	8 Aug
11.41	1.9	Shannon	Ray	USA	31.12.95	4 Apr
11.41	1.5	Nataliya	Strohova	UKR	26.12.92	12 May
11.41	0.7	Amy	Foster	IRL	2.10.88	16 May
11.41	-0.2	Jessica	Paoletta	ITA	21.3.88	2 Jun
11.41		Krisztina	Khorosheva	RUS	5.4.93	5 Jun
11.41	0.6	Caitland	Smith	USA-J	24.3.96	26 Jun
11.41	0.6	Deanna	Hill	USA-J	13.4.96	26 Jun
11.41A	0.0	Jayla	Kirkland	USA-Y	13.2.99	16 Jul
11.41	2.0	Lorène	Dorcas Bazolo	CGO	4.5.83	17 Jul
11.42	0.0	Flings	Owusu-Agyapong	GHA	16.10.88	2 May
11.42	0.7	Lorraine	Ugen	GBR	22.8.91	2 May
11.42	0.0	Shimayra	Williams	JAM	2.12.95	16 May
11.42	1.4	Brittany	Brown	USA	18.4.95	16 May
11.42	1.0	Zainab	Sanni	USA	20.1.95	16 May
11.42	0.2	Reneazia	Collins	USA-J	21.2.96	17 May
11.42	1.3	María	Belibasáki	GRE	19.6.91	6 Jun
11.42	-1.1	Gloria	Asumnu	NGR	22.5.85	30 Jul
11.43	1.8	Ashleigh	Whittaker	AUS	12.8.93	28 Mar
11.43	2.0	Destinee	Brown	USA	6.7.94	17 Apr
11.43	1.3	Irene	Siragusa	ITA	23.6.93	24 Apr
11.43	1.5	India	Brown	USA-J	29.1.96	2 May
11.43	-0.6	Chesna	Sykes	USA	28.8.92	28 May
11.43	1.7	Anasztázia	Nguyen	HUN	9.1.93	30 May
11.43	0.5	Bianca	Williams	GBR	18.12.93	5 Jul
11.43	1.6	Yelena	Chernyayeva	RUS	19.9.88	9 Jul
11.43	1.8	Phylicia	George	CAN	16.11.87	11 Jul
11.43	1.0	Louise	Bloor	GBR	21.9.85	18 Jul
11.44	0.9	Felicia	Brown	USA	27.10.93	16 May
11.44	0.2	Erica	Alexander	USA	24.6.90	17 May
11.44	-0.2	Carole	Zahi	CIV	12.6.94	11 Jul
11.44	1.7	Cassondra	Hall	USA-J	23.9.97	11 Jul
11.44	1.6	Dulaini D.	Odelín	CUB	21.8.92	21 Jul
11.45A	1.4	Genoiska	Cancel	PUR	21.11.88	18 Apr
11.45	1.0	Erin	Jones	USA	10.3.78	16 May
11.45	0.7	Alexis	Love	USA	24.4.91	16 May
11.45	-1.0	Nediam	Vargas	VEN	5.9.94	12 Jun
11.45	1.2	Shelbi	White	USA		13 Jun
11.45A	1.4	Celiangely	Morales	PUR	2.11.85	7 Aug
11.46	1.7	Anna	Scott	USA	.93	7 May
11.46	2.0	J'Nea	Bellamy	USA	5.11.94	11 Jun
11.46	1.5	Isatu	Fofanah	CAN	13.4.93	3 Jul
11.46	1.8	Lina	Grincikaité-Samuole	LTU	3.5.87	9 Jul
11.46	-0.2	Gloria	Hooper	ITA	3.3.92	17 Jul
11.46	1.6	Sharolyn	Joseph	CRC	1.10.94	21 Jul
11.46	-2.0	Yevgeniya	Polyakova	RUS	29.5.83	3 Aug
11.47	-0.5	Kedisha	Dallas	JAM	3.11.95	11 Apr
11.47	1.7	Lynna	Irby	USA-Y	6.12.98	23 May
11.47	-0.2	Viktoriya	Kashcheyeva	UKR	7.5.89	8 Jun
11.47	0.2	Sandra	Gomis	FRA	21.11.83	27 Jun
11.47	1.8	Candace	Jackson	USA	13.2.91	11 Jul
11.47	1.7	Kristina	Sivkova	RUS-J	28.2.97	16 Jul
11.47	-0.1	Yeoryía	Koklóni	GRE	7.5.81	25 Jul
11.47	1.7	Kadidiatou	Traoré	BUR	9.1.86	29 Jul
11.47	0.6	Eunice	Kadogo	KEN	4.5.94	14 Sep
		(201)				

Wind assisted

Mark	Wind	Name		Nat	Born	Pos	Meet	Venue	Date
10.72	3.2	Tori	Bowie	USA	27.8.90	1s2	NC	Eugene	26 Jun
10.76	3.2	Carmelita	Jeter	USA	24.11.79	2s2	NC	Eugene	26 Jun
10.76	5.4	English	Gardner	USA	22.4.92	1	Athl	Lausanne	9 Jul
10.86	3.2	Jasmine	Todd	USA	23.12.93	3s2	NC	Eugene	26 Jun
10.87	3.7	Michelle-Lee	Ahye	TTO	10.4.92	1	TexR	Austin	28 Mar
10.87	4.5		Jeter			1		Clermont	16 May
10.87	4.5		Jeter			1h2	NC	Eugene	25 Jun
10.87	4.5		Todd			2h2	NC	Eugene	25 Jun
10.88	3.7		Todd			1q1	NCAA-W	Austin	29 May
10.88	2.3		Fraser-Pryce			1h4	WCh	Beijing	23 Aug
10.89	4.0		Todd			1h4	NCAA-W	Austin	28 May
10.89	4.5	Tianna	Bartoletta	USA	30.8.85	3h2	NC	Eugene	25 Jun
10.90	3.9		Schippers			1		Clermont	18 Apr
10.90	3.0	Jenna	Prandini	USA	20.11.92	1h1	NC	Eugene	25 Jun
10.90	3.2		Bartoletta			4s2	NC	Eugene	26 Jun
10.91	3.2	Candyce	McGrone	USA	24.3.89	5s2	NC	Eugene	26 Jun
10.91	5.4	Verena	Sailer	GER	16.10.85	2	Athl	Lausanne	9 Jul
10.94	5.1	Morolake	Akinosun	USA	17.5.94	1	TexR	Austin	28 Mar

Mark	Wind	Name		Nat	Born	Pos	Meet	Venue	Date
10.95	2.3	Marie Josée	Ta Lou	CIV	18.11.88	2h4	WCh	Beijing	23 Au
10.96	4.0	Ana Cláudia	Silva	BRA	6.11.88	1h3	PAm	Toronto	21 Ju
10.97	3.8	Shalonda	Solomon	USA	19.12.85	1h1		Clermont	18 Ap
10.99	4.5	Samantha	Henry-Robinson	JAM	25.9.88	2		Clermont	16 May
10.99	3.0	Dezerea	Bryant	USA	27.4.93	2s2	NCAA	Eugene	11 Jun
11.00	4.0	Khamica	Bingham	CAN	15.6.94	2h3	PAm	Toronto	21 Ju
11.01	5.4	Kaylin	Whitney	USA-Y	9.3.98	3	Athl	Lausanne	9 Ju
11.01	2.2	Rosângela	Santos	BRA	20.12.90	2s2	PAm	Toronto	22 Ju
11.04	3.9	Simone	Facey	JAM	7.5.85	2		Clermont	18 Ap
11.06	4.5	Charonda	Williams	USA	27.3.87	4h2	NC	Eugene	25 Jun
11.06	3.2	Jessica	Young	USA	6.4.87	7s2	NC	Eugene	26 Jun
11.07	5.1	Cierra	White	USA	29.4.93	2	TexR	Austin	28 Ma
11.07	3.9	Tatjana	Pinto	GER	2.7.92	3		Clermont	18 Ap
11.08	4.5	Kimberlyn	Duncan	USA	2.8.91	5h2	NC	Eugene	25 Jun
11.10	3.0	Alex	Anderson	USA	28.1.87	4h1	NC	Eugene	25 Jun
11.11	3.1	Ky	Westbrook	USA-J	25.2.96	4	NCAA	Eugene	13 Jun
11.12	5.1	Jennifer	Madu	USA	23.9.94	3	TexR	Austin	28 Ma
11.12	5.1	Janet	Amponsah	GHA	12.4.93	4	TexR	Austin	28 Ma
11.12	3.4	Kendall	Baisden	USA	5.3.95	1		Austin	2 May
11.13	5.1	Shayla	Sanders	USA	6.1.94	5	TexR	Austin	28 Ma
11.13	3.0	Shayla	Mahan	USA	18.1.89	1		Miramar	14 Jun
11.14	4.0	Laverne	Jones-Ferrette	ISV	16.9.81	4h3	PAm	Toronto	21 Ju
11.15	2.4	Teahna	Daniels	USA-J	25.3.97	1h3		Clermont	18 Ap
11.15	4.0	Katie	Wise	USA	15.10.93	1		Normal	17 May
11.16	4.5	Flings	Owusu-Agyapong	GHA	16.10.88	4		Clermont	16 May
11.16	5.4	Yasmin	Kwadwo	GER	9.11.90	4	Athl	Lausanne	9 Ju
11.18	5.4	Rochene	Smith	JAM	.95	1		Amarillo	10 Ap
11.18	3.0	Alexis	Faulknor	USA	22.9.94	3s2	NCAA	Eugene	11 Jun
11.19	2.1	Lashauntea	Moore	USA	31.7.83	1		San Marcos	5 Jun
11.21	4.5	Marshevet	Hooker	USA	25.9.84	5		Clermont	16 May
11.21	3.5	Ewa	Swoboda	POL-J	26.7.97	1h1		St. Pölten	4 Jun
11.21	2.2	Yekaterina	Renzhina	RUS	18.10.94	1h1		Yerino	6 Jun
11.22	2.3	Ashley	Marshall	USA	10.9.93	4rB	MSR	Walnut	18 Ap
11.24	4.5	Kimberly	Hyacinthe	CAN	28.3.89	6		Clermont	16 May
11.24	3.8	Zaria	Francis	USA-Y	22.3.98	1		Norwalk	23 May
11.24	3.0	Kseniya	Ryzhova	RUS	19.4.87	1h2		Yerino	6 Jun
11.24	3.0	Mikiah	Brisco	USA-J	14.7.96	4s2	NCAA	Eugene	11 Jun
11.25	3.0	Deanna	Hill	USA-J	13.4.96	5s2	NCAA	Eugene	11 Jun
11.26	4.1	Kortnei	Johnson	USA-J	11.8.97	1		Austin	16 May
11.26	2.5	Crystal	Emmanuel	CAN	27.11.91	5s1	PAm	Toronto	22 Ju
11.27	5.1	Jada	Martin	USA	8.6.95	6	TexR	Austin	28 Ma
11.27		Funlayo	Oluwole	USA-J	19.6.97	1		Newport News	23 May
11.27	5.4	Marika	Popowicz	POL	28.4.88	5	Athl	Lausanne	9 Ju
11.27	5.4	Nataliya	Strohova	UKR	26.12.92	6	Athl	Lausanne	9 Ju

Mark	Wind	Name		Nat	Born	Date
11.28	4.3	Sydney	Conley	USA	11.12.93	2 May
11.28	3.2	Destiny	Carter	USA		15 May
11.29	2.6	Ramona	Papaioannou	CYP	15.6.89	15 May
11.29	3.5	Tiffani	McReynolds	USA	4.12.91	17 May
11.30	2.6	Leslie	Cole	USA	16.2.87	15 May
11.30	2.5	Ashton	Purvis	USA	12.7.92	29 May
11.31	3.9	Felicia	Brown	USA	27.10.93	10 Apr
11.32	2.5	Dominique	Booker	USA	10.2.92	15 May
11.32	2.5	Shannon	Ray	USA	31.12.95	15 May
11.32	3.0	Anna	Kukushkina	RUS	13.12.92	6 Jun
11.33	2.6	Nediam	Vargas	VEN	5.9.94	31 May
11.33	3.6	Maja	Mihalinec	SLO	17.12.89	13 Jun
11.33	3.0	Jayla	Kirkland	USA-Y	13.2.99	20 Jun
11.34	3.7	Dominique	Duncan	NGR	7.5.90	28 Mar
11.34	3.4	Stephanie	Kalu	NGR	5.8.93	2 May
11.34	2.8	Stella	Akakpo	FRA	28.2.94	20 Jun
11.34	3.0	Twanisha	Terry	USA-Y	24.1.99	20 Jun
11.35	3.6	Jasmine	Woods	USA		28 May
11.35	4.0	Carole	Zahi	CIV	12.6.94	25 Jul
11.36	3.0	Toea	Wisil	PNG	1.1.88	28 Mar
11.36	2.2	Arialis	Gandulla	CUB	22.6.95	22 Jul
11.37	3.2	Hannah	Brier	GBR-Y	3.2.98	31 May
11.37	3.0	Kate	Hall	USA-J	12.1.97	20 Ju
11.37	2.8	Inna	Weit	GER	5.8.88	25 Ju
11.38	2.1	Danielle	Williams	USA	7.4.91	21 Ma
11.38	3.9	Alexis	Love	USA	24.4.91	18 Ap
11.38	4.0	Nikki	Larch-Miller	USA	13.8.94	17 Ma
11.38	2.7	Janae	Johnson	USA	.82	23 Ma
11.38	2.4	Lorène Dorcas	Bazolo	CGO	4.5.83	11 Ju
11.39	3.9	Margaret	Adeoye	GBR	27.4.85	18 Ap
11.39	4.3	Amy	Foster	IRL	2.10.88	16 Ma
11.39	3.1	Cambrya	Jones	USA	20.9.90	16 Ma
11.40	2.6	Lake	Kwaza	USA	7.11.93	17 Ap
11.40	2.3	Morgan	Snow	USA	26.7.93	2 Ma
11.40	4.0	Marrisa	Kurtimah	CAN	25.5.94	28 Ma
11.40	2.1	Isatu	Fofanah	CAN	13.4.93	3 Ju
11.40	2.1	Lina	Grincikaité-Samuole	LTU	3.5.87	10 Au
11.41	3.0	Taylor	Bennett	USA-J	15.1.97	16 Ma
11.41	3.8	Zainab	Sanni	USA	20.1.95	28 Ma
11.42	3.6	Daja	Gordon	USA-Y	26.5.99	16 Ma
11.42	5.6	Sierra	Pruitt	USA-J	28.10.97	16 Ma
11.42	4.0	Chidera	Obasih	USA	5.4.93	17 Ma
11.42	2.1	Erica	Alexander	USA	24.6.90	25 Ju
11.43	2.4	Kayelle	Clarke	TTO-J	28.2.96	30 Ap
11.43	4.0	Shenel	Crooke	SKN	12.10.93	21 Ju

Best at low altitude

11.08 0.4 Henry-Robinson 2 adidas New York 13 Jun | 11.31 -0.6 St.Fort 1 PAm-J Edmonton 31 Jul

11.44 1.8 Brier 20 Jun | 11.48 1.5 Landázuri 23 Aug | 11.39w 5.4 Browner 10 Apr

11.33w 6.0 21 Jul | 11.40w 2.4 Gause 39 Apr

Hand timed

Mark	Wind	Name		Nat	Born	Pos	Meet	Venue	Date
11.0	1.0	Ezinne	Okparaebo	NOR	3.3.88	1h2		Florø	6 Ju
11.2A		Eunice	Kadogo	KEN	4.5.94	1	WCT	Nairobi	1 Aug

Doubtful: São Bernardo do Campo 30 May: h1 (0.2) 1. E Santos BRA 11.4.85 11.1, 2. I Jiménez CHI 10.8.93 11.2

JUNIORS

See main list for top 11 juniors (& 8 wa). 12 performances by 4 women to 11.18. Additional marks and further juniors:

C Hill 11.08 0.0 1 Shoreline 20 Jun 11.16A -0.1 1s2 WY Cali 16 Jul
Tenorio 11.09A 0.8 1 Cuenca 14 Mar 11.15A 1.2 1 Medellín 9 May
11.09A 1.5 1 SAm-J Cuenca 29 May 11.17A 1h1 Cuenca 14 Mar
11.10A 1.5 1 NC Quito 17 Apr 11.18A 1h1 SAm-J Cuenca 29 May

Mark	Wind	Name		Nat	Born	Pos	Meet	Venue	Date
11.33	2.0	Alfreda	Steele	USA	19.12.97	3		Shoreline	20 Jun
11.35	0.8	Chanice	Bonner	JAM	6.7.95	1		Mona	21 Mar
11.36A	2.0	Vitória Cristina	Rosa	BRA	12.1.96	1h2	SAm-J	Cuenca	29 May
11.37	1.8	Jonielle	Smith	JAM	30.1.96	6s3	NCAA	Eugene	11 Jun
11.37	2.0	Lauren Rain	Williams	USA-Y	25.7.99	4		Shoreline	20 Jun
11.37	2.0	Krystal	Sparling	USA	.97	5		Shoreline	20 Jun
11.37	-1.2	Kaylin	Whitney	USA-Y	9.3.98	6	Gyulai	Székesfehérvár	7 Jul
11.39A	-0.6	Hannah	Brier	GBR-Y	3.2.98	1h8	WY	Cali	16 Jul
11.40	0.4	Daryll	Neita	GBR	29.8.96	1	NC-j	Bedford	20 Jun

Wind assisted: 7 performances by 6 women to 11.17w.

Tenorio 11.10w 2.5 2s1 PAm Toronto 22 Jul 11.17 3.0 2h1 PAm Toronto 22 Jul
Hill 11.15A 2.9 1 Albuquerque 6 Jun
Hobbs 11.16 3.1 6 NCAA Eugene 13 Jun

Mark	Wind	Name		Nat	Born	Pos	Meet	Venue	Date
11.33	3.0	Jayla	Kirkland	USA-Y	13.2.99	1		Greensboro NC	20 Jun
11.34	3.0	Twanisha	Terry	USA-Y	24.1.99	2		Greensboro NC	20 Jun
11.37	3.2	Hannah	Brier	GBR-Y	3.2.98	2A1	BIG	Bedford	31 May
11.37	3.0	Kate	Hall	USA-J	12.1.97	3		Greensboro NC	20 Jun

150 METRES STRAIGHT

Mark	Wind	Name		Nat	Born	Pos	Meet	Venue	Date
16.82	0.3	Dina	Asher-Smith	GBR	4.12.95	1		Manchester	9 May
16.95	0.3	Dafne	Schippers	NED	15.6.92	2		Manchester	9 May

200 METRES

Mark	Wind	Name		Nat	Born	Pos	Meet	Venue	Date
21.63	0.2	Dafne	Schippers	NED	15.6.92	1	WCh	Beijing	28 Aug
21.66	0.2	Elaine	Thompson	JAM	28.6.92	2	WCh	Beijing	28 Aug
21.97	0.2	Veronica	Campbell-Brown	JAM	15.5.82	3	WCh	Beijing	28 Aug
21.98	1.6	Allyson	Felix	USA	18.11.85	1	DL	Doha	15 May
22.01	0.2	Candyce	McGrone	USA	24.3.89	4	WCh	Beijing	28 Aug
22.07	0.2	Dina	Asher-Smith	GBR	4.12.95	5	WCh	Beijing	28 Aug
22.08	-0.3		McGrone			1	Herc	Monaco	17 Jul
22.09	1.9		Felix			1	Athl	Lausanne	9 Jul
22.09	-0.3		Schippers			2	Herc	Monaco	17 Jul
22.10	-0.3		Thompson			1	DL	London (OS)	25 Jul
22.12	-0.1		Asher-Smith			1s3	WCh	Beijing	27 Aug
22.12	0.0		Schippers			1	VD	Bruxelles	11 Sep
22.13	-0.1		Thompson			1s1	WCh	Beijing	27 Aug
22.14	0.2	Shaunae	Miller	BAH	15.4.94	1		Kingston	9 May
22.18	1.9	Dezerea	Bryant	USA	27.4.93	1	NCAA	Eugene	13 Jun
22.20	0.4	Jenna	Prandini	USA	20.11.92	1	NC	Eugene	28 Jun
22.21	1.9		Prandini			2	NCAA	Eugene	13 Jun
22.22	0.4		Asher-Smith			1h7	WCh	Beijing	26 Aug
22.22	0.0		Felix			2	VD	Bruxelles	11 Sep
22.23	-2.3	Tori	Bowie (10)	USA	27.8.90	1	adidas	New York	13 Jun
22.23	-0.3	Jeneba	Tarmoh	USA	27.9.89	3	Herc	Monaco	17 Jul
22.24	1.9	Kamaria	Brown	USA	21.12.92	3	NCAA	Eugene	13 Jun
22.24	1.9	Kyra	Jefferson	USA	23.9.94	4	NCAA	Eugene	13 Jun
22.26	0.5		Jefferson			1q3	NCAA-E	Jacksonville	30 May
22.26	1.8		Jefferson			1s2	NCAA	Eugene	11 Jun
22.26	-0.1		McGrone			2s1	WCh	Beijing	27 Aug
22.26	0.0		Thompson			3	VD	Bruxelles	11 Sep
22.29	0.2		Bowie			2		Kingston	9 May
22.29	1.6	Murielle	Ahouré	CIV	23.8.87	2	DL	Doha	15 May
22.29	1.7		Tarmoh			1	DL	Birmingham	7 Jun
22.29	1.7		Felix			2	DL	Birmingham	7 Jun
22.29	1.9		Schippers			2	Athl	Lausanne	9 Jul
		(32/14)							
22.32	0.8	Charonda	Williams	USA	27.3.87	1	Spitzen	Luzern	14 Jul
22.32	-0.1	Ivet	Lalova-Collio	BUL	18.5.84	3s1	WCh	Beijing	27 Aug
22.37	0.2	Shelly-Ann	Fraser-Pryce	JAM	27.12.86	3		Kingston	9 May
22.43	0.3	Shakima	Wimbley	USA	23.4.95	1	ACC	Tallahassee	16 May
22.43A	-0.7	Candace	Hill	USA-Y	11.2.99	1	WY	Cali	19 Jul
22.47	0.4	Kaylin	Whitney	USA-Y	9.3.98	4	NC	Eugene	28 Jun
		(20)							

Mark	Wind	Name		Nat	Born	Pos	Meet	Venue	Date
22.50	0.2	Sherone	Simpson	JAM	12.8.84	8	WCh	Beijing	28 Aug
22.51A	1.3	Semoy	Hackett	TTO	27.11.88	2	NACAC	San José, CRC	9 Aug
22.52	1.9	Morolake	Akinosun	USA	17.5.94	5	NCAA	Eugene	13 Jun
22.55	1.4	Simone	Facey	JAM	7.5.85	1		Edmonton	12 Ju
22.56	1.4	Shalonda	Solomon	USA	19.12.85	2		Edmonton	12 Ju
22.56	-0.1	Marie Josée	Ta Lou Gonerie	CIV	18.11.88	3s2	WCh	Beijing	27 Aug
22.60	0.4	Muna	Lee	USA	30.10.81	7	NC	Eugene	28 Jun
22.62	0.8	Tiffany	Townsend	USA	14.6.89	3	Spitzen	Luzern	14 Ju
22.64	-0.1	Mujinga	Kambundji	SUI	17.6.92	4s1	WCh	Beijing	27 Aug
22.67	-2.3	Blessing	Okagbare	NGR	9.10.88	2	adidas	New York	13 Jun
		(30)							
22.68	2.0	Chioma	Agwunobi	USA	.95	1q2	NCAA-E	Jacksonville	30 May
22.69	1.6	Anthonique	Strachan	BAH	22.8.93	3	DL	Doha	15 May
22.70	0.1	Phyllis	Francis	USA	4.5.92	2	MSR	Walnut	18 Apr
22.72	1.6	Kerron	Stewart	JAM	16.4.84	2s1	PAm	Toronto	23 Ju
22.74	0.1	English	Gardner	USA	22.4.92	3	MSR	Walnut	18 Apr
22.74	1.2	Kamaria	Durant	TTO	24.2.91	1h2	PAm	Toronto	23 Ju
22.75	0.1	Nataliya	Pohrebnyak	UKR	19.2.88	1	NC	Kirovohrad	31 Ju
22.76	0.2	Natasha	Hastings	USA	23.7.86	2		Austin	11 Apr
22.76	2.0	Felicia	Brown	USA	27.10.93	2q2	NCAA-E	Jacksonville	30 May
22.76	1.8	Jada	Martin	USA	8.6.95	2s2	NCAA	Eugene	11 Jun
		(40)							
22.76	1.9	Aaliyah	Brown	USA	6.1.95	6	NCAA	Eugene	13 Jun
22.77	1.7	Rosângela	Santos	BRA	20.12.90	4	DL	Birmingham	7 Jun
22.77	-0.8	Viktoriya	Zyabkina	KAZ	4.9.92	1	WUG	Gwangju	10 Ju
22.80	0.2	Kendall	Baisden	USA	5.3.95	1h2	Big 12	Ames	16 May
22.82	0.8	Reyare	Thomas	TTO	23.11.87	1		Port of Spain	11 Ju
22.83	0.1	Kimberlyn	Duncan	USA	2.8.91	4	MSR	Walnut	18 Apr
22.84	0.2	Cierra	White	USA	29.4.93	2h2	Big 12	Ames	16 May
22.84	1.9	Khamica	Bingham	CAN	15.6.94	1h3		Windsor	23 May
22.84A	-0.5	Ángela	Tenorio	ECU-J	27.1.96	1	SAm-J	Cuenca	31 May
22.85	0.2	Bianca	Williams	GBR	18.12.93	2h4	WCh	Beijing	26 Aug
		(50)							
22.86	0.4	Aisha	Cavin	USA	3.12.92	1	Big 10	East Lansing	17 May
22.86	1.4	Kimberly	Hyacinthe	CAN	28.3.89	3		Edmonton	12 Ju
22.87	0.8	Shericka	Jackson	JAM	15.7.94	1rB	Spitzen	Luzern	14 Ju
22.87	-0.3	Sanya	Richards-Ross	USA	26.2.85	6	DL	London (OS)	25 Ju
22.88	1.6	Deanna	Hill	USA-J	13.4.96	1rB	FlaR	Gainesville	3 Apr
22.88	-1.8	Carmelita	Jeter	USA	24.11.79	1	Bush	Norwalk	6 Jun
22.88	0.8	Jodie	Williams	GBR	28.9.93	5	Spitzen	Luzern	14 Ju
22.89	1.9	Jasmine	Todd	USA	23.12.93	1h1	Pac 12	Los Angeles (Ww)	16 May
22.89	0.4	Brittany	Brown	USA	18.4.95	2	Big 10	East Lansing	17 May
22.89	0.7	Porscha	Lucas	USA	18.6.88	3h5	NC	Eugene	27 Jun
		(60)							
22.90A	-0.7	Lauren Rain	Williams	USA-Y	25.7.99	2	WY	Cali	19 Ju
22.92	1.6	Margaret	Adeoye	GBR	27.4.85	3rB		Clermont	18 Apr
22.92	1.4	Crystal	Emmanuel	CAN	27.11.91	4		Edmonton	12 Ju
22.92	-0.1	Gloria	Hooper	ITA	3.3.92	5s3	WCh	Beijing	27 Aug
22.93	1.2	Taylor	Ellis-Watson	USA	6.5.93	1		Fayetteville	11 Apr
22.93	1.3	Courtney	Okolo	USA	15.3.94	1h1	Big 12	Ames	16 May
22.93	0.5	Destinee	Gause	USA	4.4.94	2q3	NCAA-E	Jacksonville	30 May
22.94	2.0	Shannon	Hylton	GBR-J	19.12.96	1	LI	Loughborough	17 May
22.94	0.0	Anna	Kielbasinska	POL	26.6.90	1	NC	Kraków	21 Ju
22.94	0.3	Desiree	Henry	GBR	26.8.95	1		Mannheim	8 Aug
		(70)							
22.95	-0.2	Jamile	Samuel	NED	24.4.92	1	ECCp	Mersin	30 May
22.95	-1.1	Samantha	Henry-Robinson	JAM	25.9.88	1h2	NC	Kingston	27 Jun
22.95	-0.8	A'Keyla	Mitchell	USA	25.11.95	2	WUG	Gwangju	10 Ju
22.95	1.2	Isidora	Jiménez	CHI	10.8.93	4h2	PAm	Toronto	23 Ju
22.95	1.0	Rebekka	Haase	GER	2.1.93	1	NC	Nürnberg	26 Ju
22.96	1.9	Justine	Palframan	RSA	4.11.93	1	Univ Ch	Stellenbosch	25 Apr
22.97	0.8	Sally	Pearson	AUS	19.9.86	1		Canberra	7 Feb
22.97	0.7	Tynia	Gaither	BAH	16.3.93	1	Pac 12	Los Angeles (Ww)	17 May
22.97	0.5	Alexis	Faulknor	USA	22.9.94	3h4	NC	Eugene	27 Jun
22.99	2.0	Leslie	Cole	USA	16.2.87	1		Azusa	17 Apr
		(80)							
22.99	0.8	LeKeisha	Lawson	USA	3.6.87	1		Fresno	25 Apr
22.99	1.2	Nercely	Soto	VEN	23.8.90	5h2	PAm	Toronto	23 Ju
23.02	0.7	Tatjana	Pinto	GER	2.7.92	1		Mannheim	28 Jun
23.03	0.2	Salwa	Eid Nasser	BRN-Y	23.5.98	2		Plovdiv	28 Jun
23.03	1.2	Sheniqua	Ferguson	BAH	24.11.89	6h2	PAm	Toronto	23 Ju

Mark	Wind	Name		Nat	Born	Pos	Meet	Venue	Date
3.03A	1.3	Celiangely	Morales	PUR	2.11.85	5	NACAC	San José, CRC	9 Aug
3.04	1.6	Ella	Nelson	AUS	10.5.94	1	NC	Brisbane	29 Mar
3.04	1.6	Janet	Amponsah	GHA	12.4.93	1		Canyon	25 Apr
3.04	0.3	Sabria	Hadley	USA	1.1.95	2	ACC	Tallahassee	16 May
3.04	1.8	Yekaterina (90)	Smirnova	RUS	8.9.88	1		Sochi	29 May
3.04	0.5	Gina	Lückenkemper	GER-J	21.11.96	1J		Mannheim	28 Jun
3.04	-0.1	Maja	Mihalinec	SLO	17.12.89	8s1	WCh	Beijing	27 Aug
3.05	0.4	Jodean	Williams	JAM	11.11.93	3h3	NC	Kingston	27 Jun
3.06	1.3	J'Nea	Bellamy	USA	5.11.94	1		Storrs	17 May
3.07	0.1	Francena	McCorory	USA	20.10.88	1		Hampton	10 Apr
3.08	-0.3	Jessica	Beard	USA	8.1.89	3	FlaR	Gainesville	2 Apr
3.08	1.7	Ana Cláudia	Silva	BRA	6.11.88	1	NC	São Bernardo do Campo	17 May
3.08	1.6	Arialis	Gandulla	CUB	22.6.95	6s1	PAm	Toronto	23 Jul
3.08	1.0	Anna-Lena	Freese	GER	21.1.94	2	NC	Nürnberg	26 Jul
3.08	0.8	Sabina (100)	Veit	SLO	2.12.85	1h2		Maribor	7 Aug
3.08	0.2	Katarina	Johnson-Thompson	GBR	9.1.93	1H	WCh	Beijing	22 Aug

Mark	Wind	Name		Nat	Born	Date
3.09	1.2	Charlotte	McLennaghan	GBR-J	6.9.97	10 May
3.09	0.9	Zaria	Francis	USA-Y	22.3.98	6 Jun
3.09	2.0	Viktoriya	Kashcheyeva	UKR	7.5.89	25 Jun
3.10	0.7	Libania	Grenot	ITA	12.7.83	9 May
3.10	1.8	Yekaterina	Vukolova	RUS	10.8.87	29 May
3.10	0.5	Keilah	Tyson	USA	6.11.92	30 May
3.11	0.5	Anastasia	Le-Roy	JAM	11.9.87	14 Mar
3.11	0.1	Chisato	Fukushima	JPN	27.6.88	10 May
3.11	1.7	Vitória Cristina	Rosa	BRA-J	12.1.96	17 May
3.11	0.6	Yekaterina	Renzhina	RUS	18.10.94	29 May
3.11	0.0	Cynthia	Bolingo Mbongo	BEL	12.1.93	4 Aug
3.12	0.2	Schillonie	Calvert	JAM	27.7.88	20 May
3.12	-1.2	María	Belibasáki	GRE	19.6.91	26 Jul
3.13	1.7	Cambrya	Jones	USA	20.9.90	16 May
3.14	2.0	Ashley	Spencer	USA	8.6.93	11 Jul
3.15	2.0	Shannon	Ray	USA	31.12.95	30 May
3.15	0.0	Candace	Jackson	USA	13.2.91	11 Jul
3.16	1.1	DeeDee	Trotter	USA	8.12.82	2 Apr
3.16	1.6	Le'Quisha	Parker	USA	26.5.93	30 Apr
3.17	0.1	Nataliya	Strohova	UKR	26.12.92	31 Jul
3.18	0.2	Saqukine	Cameron	JAM-J	21.8.96	7 Mar
3.18	0.0	Deajah	Stevens	USA	19.5.95	11 Apr
3.18	0.4	Kenesha	Stephens	JAM	27.10.93	16 May
3.18		Olga	Lenskiy	ISR	24.12.92	25 Jul
3.19	1.8	Sharika	Nelvis	USA	10.5.90	11 Apr
3.19	1.0	Stephenie Ann	McPherson	JAM	25.11.88	11 Apr
3.19	1.7	Jessica	Young	USA	6.4.87	7 Jun
3.19	1.6	Anyika	Onuora	GBR	28.10.84	30 Jul
3.19	1.1	Anna	Kukushkina	RUS	13.12.92	5 Aug
3.19	0.6	Ramona	Papaioannou	CYP	15.6.89	8 Aug
3.20		Hrystyna	Stuy	UKR	3.2.88	9 Jun
3.21	0.1	Diamond	Spaulding	USA-J	29.9.96	9 May
3.21A	1.8	Carrol	Hardy	USA	.94	17 May
3.21	1.8	Olga	Kharitonova	RUS	23.8.90	29 May
3.21	1.4	Mikele	Barber	USA	4.10.80	12 Jul
3.22	-1.6	Daye Shon	Roberson	USA	3.7.95	18 Apr
3.22	0.6	Ky	Westbrook	USA-J	25.2.96	29 May
3.22	0.5	Regina	George	NGR	17.2.91	6 Jul
3.23	1.3	Shania	Collins	USA-J	14.11.96	16 May
3.23	0.2	Ashton	Purvis	USA	12.7.92	30 May
3.23	0.8	Anna	Scott	USA	.93	6 Jun
3.23	1.1	Anna	Yegorova	RUS	25.2.87	5 Aug
3.24	1.6	Tristie	Johnson	USA	20.11.93	30 Apr
3.24	1.8	Laverne	Jones-Ferrette	ISV	16.9.81	2 May
3.24	0.2	Alicia	Whittle	USA	20.4.92	16 May
3.24	2.0	Kelly	Proper	IRL	1.5.88	25 Jun
3.24	0.0	Lénora	Guion-Firmin	FRA	7.8.91	28 Jun
3.24	-0.8	Kedisha	Dallas	JAM	3.11.95	10 Jul
3.24	0.9	Cassondra	Hall	USA-J	23.9.97	30 Jul
3.24	-1.1	Ngozi	Onwumere	NGR	23.1.92	17 Sep

Mark	Wind	Name		Nat	Born	Date
23.25	-0.3	Kineke	Alexander	VIN	21.2.86	2 Apr
23.25	0.9	Alicia	Evans	USA	27.3.92	16 May
23.26	1.6	Ashleigh	Whittaker	AUS	12.8.93	29 Mar
23.26	1.8	Karene	King	IVB	24.10.87	28 Jun
23.26A	1.7	Evelin	Rivera	COL-J	8.12.97	21 Nov
23.27	1.8	Kiara	Porter	USA	22.10.93	18 Apr
23.27	2.0	Charla	Craddock	USA	31.10.92	30 May
23.27	0.0	Vanusa	dos Santos	BRA	22.1.90	11 Jul
23.27	0.0	Marta	Jeschke	POL	2.6.86	21 Jul
23.27	0.6	Eleni	Artymata	CYP	16.5.86	8 Aug
23.28	1.1	Ada	Udaya	LBR	28.6.92	21 Mar
23.28A	2.0	Chris-Ann	Gordon	JAM	18.9.94	18 Apr
23.28	-1.8	Natasha	Morrison	JAM	17.11.92	6 Jun
23.28	0.4	Olga	Safronova	KAZ	5.11.91	26 Aug
23.29	1.6	Melissa	Breen	AUS	17.9.90	29 Mar
23.29	-0.5	Quanera	Hayes	USA	7.3.92	18 Apr
23.29	1.8	Caitland	Smith	USA-J	24.3.96	2 May
23.29	1.2	Dominique	Booker	USA	10.2.92	29 May
23.29	1.9	Marie	Veale	USA	17.11.94	29 May
23.29	-0.2	Hanne	Claes	BEL	4.8.91	6 Jun
23.29	2.0	Moa	Hjelmer	SWE	19.6.90	25 Jun
23.29	0.9	Maroussia	Pare	FRA-J	18.7.96	28 Jun
23.29	-0.3	Lisa	Mayer	GER-J	2.5.96	1 Aug
23.30	1.3	Ashley	Marshall	USA	10.9.93	28 Mar
23.30	1.7	Geisa	Coutinho	BRA	1.6.80	17 May
23.30	0.3	Giulia	Riva	ITA	31.1.92	6 Jun
23.30	0.7	Anglerne	Annelus	USA-J	10.1.97	30 Jul
23.31	0.4	Aaliyah	Barnes	USA	17.2.95	17 May
23.32A	1.7	Yenifer	Padilla	COL	1.1.90	21 Nov
23.33	0.0	Carmiesha	Cox	BAH	16.5.95	11 Apr
23.33	0.8	Céline	Distel-Bonnet	FRA	25.7.87	10 May
23.33	1.3	Nyanka	Moise-Joseph	USA	8.6.93	17 May
23.33	1.1	Nadezhda	Kotlyarova	RUS	12.6.89	5 Aug
23.34	1.6	Gabriella	Cantrell	USA	30.11.95	2 Apr
23.34	2.0	Raquel	Tjernagel	CAN-J	25.10.97	17 Apr
23.34	0.3	Kala	Funderburk	USA	14.9.92	16 May
23.34	1.4	Brianne	Theisen-Eaton	CAN	18.12.88	30 May
23.34	0.1	Audrea	Segree	JAM	5.10.90	27 Jun
23.34	-1.2	Lorène Dorcas	Bazolo	CGO	4.5.83	2 Aug
23.35	1.6	Dominique	Kimpel	USA	6.2.93	2 Apr
23.35	1.9	Briau'na	Watley	USA	1.4.92	2 May
23.35	1.5	Inna	Eftimova	BUL	19.6.88	11 Jun
23.35	0.9	Bianca	Razor	ROU	8.8.94	26 Jul
23.35	1.0	Cindy	Roleder	GER	21.8.89	26 Jul
23.35	1.0	Inna	Weit	GER	5.8.88	26 Jul
23.35	0.6	Olivia	Borlée	BEL	10.4.86	1 Aug
23.36	0.5	Shericka	Williams	JAM	17.9.85	14 Mar
23.36	1.5	India	Brown	USA-J	29.1.96	2 May
23.36	0.4	Venicha	Baker (200)	JAM	13.7.90	27 Jun
23.36	1.8	Ashley	Kelly	IVB	25.3.91	28 Jun

Running with guide: 23.03 0.1 Omara Durand CUB 26.11.91 1 IPC T13 Doha 25 Oct

Indoors

Mark	Name		Nat	Born	Pos	Meet	Venue	Date
3.07	Ariana	Washington	USA	4.9.96	3rB	NCAA	Fayetteville	14 Mar

Mark	Name		Nat	Born	Date
3.16	Robin	Reynolds	USA	22.2.94	14 Feb
3.19	Michelle-Lee	Ahye	TTO	10.4.92	12 Dec
3.24	Kineke	Alexander	VIN	21.2.86	14 Feb
23.30	Nadine	Gonska	GER	23.1.90	22 Feb
23.36	Kseniya	Ryzhova	RUS	19.4.87	18 Feb
23.38	Allison	Peter	ISV	14.7.92	14 Feb

Hand timed

Mark	Name		Nat	Born	Pos	Meet	Venue	Date
2.4A	Joyce	Zakari ¶	KEN	6.6.86	1	NC	Nairobi	11 Jul
3.0	Ngozi	Onwumere	NGR	23.1.92	1	SKN Ch	Basseterre	13 Jun

Mark	Wind	Name		Nat	Born	Pos	Meet	Venue	Date
Wind assisted									
22.01	2.9	Michelle-Lee	Ahye	TTO	10.4.92	1		San Marcos	25 Ap
22.18	2.8	Jenna	Prandini	USA	20.11.92	1h1	NC	Eugene	27 Ju
22.41	2.6	Gina	Lückenkemper	GER-J	21.11.96	1	EJ	Eskilstuna	18 Ju
22.44	2.1	Shalonda	Solomon	USA	19.12.85	1		Clermont	18 Ap
22.56	2.6	Kimberly	Hyacinthe	CAN	28.3.89	1	NC	Edmonton	5 Ju
22.59	2.6	Ángela	Tenorio	ECU-J	27.1.96	1s2	PAm	Toronto	23 Ju
22.65	2.8	Cierra	White	USA	29.4.93	3s3	NCAA	Eugene	11 Ju
22.66	2.8	Aaliyah	Brown	USA	6.1.95	4s3	NCAA	Eugene	11 Ju
22.68	3.2	Lauren Rain	Williams	USA-Y	25.7.99	1		Norwalk	23 Ma
22.68	4.6	Destinee	Gause	USA	4.4.94	3s1	NCAA	Eugene	11 Ju
22.73	2.6	Shannon	Hylton	GBR-J	19.12.96	2	EJ	Eskilstuna	18 Ju
22.75	4.1	Samantha	Henry-Robinson	JAM	25.9.88	1		Tampa	22 Ma
22.81	3.2	Quanera	Hayes	USA	7.3.92	1	NCAA-II	Allendale	23 Ma
22.83	2.6	Khamica	Bingham	CAN	15.6.94	1		Clermont	16 Ma
22.83	2.6	Crystal	Emmanuel	CAN	27.11.91	2	NC	Edmonton	5 Ju
22.84	2.1	Carmelita	Jeter	USA	24.11.79	1rB		Clermont	16 Ma
22.84	3.1	Ana Cláudia	Silva	BRA	6.11.88	1h1	NC	São Bernardo do Campo	16 Ma
22.84	2.8	A'Keyla	Mitchell	USA	25.11.95	3h1	NC	Eugene	27 Ju
22.88	2.1	Anyika	Onuora	GBR	28.10.84	2		Clermont	18 Ap
22.88	2.9	Ashton	Purvis	USA	12.7.92	1h2	NCAA-W	Austin	29 Ma
22.88	2.3	LeKeisha	Lawson	USA	3.6.87	1		Chula Vista	13 Ju
22.91	2.1	Kelly-Ann	Baptiste	TTO	14.10.86	3		Clermont	18 Ap
22.92	2.1	Justine	Palframan	RSA	4.11.93	1h1	Univ Ch	Stellenbosch	25 Ap
22.98	2.2	Ofonime	Odiong	BRN-J	13.3.97	1	ArabC	Manama	27 Ap
22.98	2.6	Alexis	Love	USA	24.4.91	2		Clermont	16 Ma
22.99	4.6	Kineke	Alexander	VIN	21.2.86	1	TexR	Austin	28 Ma
23.01	3.2	Yanique	Ellington	JAM	3.9.92	2	NCAA-II	Allendale	23 Ma
23.01	4.6	Ky	Westbrook	USA-J	25.2.96	4s1	NCAA	Eugene	11 Ju
23.02	2.7	Sabina	Veit	SLO	2.12.85	1		Maribor	24 Ju
23.03	4.6	Shannon	Ray	USA	31.12.95	5s1	NCAA	Eugene	11 Ju

Mark	Wind	Name		Nat	Born	Date
23.05	2.6	Maroussia	Pare	FRA-J	18.7.96	18 Jul
23.06	2.5	Floria	Guei	FRA	2.5.90	29 Jul
23.08	2.8	Mikele	Barber	USA	4.10.80	27 Jun
23.10	4.1	Kiana	Horton	USA-J	29.1.97	16 May
23.10	3.1	Vitoria Cristina	Rosa	BRA-J	12.1.96	16 May
23.10	3.2	Janae	Johnson	USA	.82	23 May
23.12	4.3	Kayelle	Clarke	TTO-J	28.2.96	6 Apr
23.14	4.9	Zainab	Sanni	USA	20.1.95	16 May
23.15	2.9	Cheriece	Hylton	GBR-J	19.12.96	17 May
23.17	2.4	L'Tsha	Fahie	IVB-Y	8.7.98	13 Jun
23.18	2.8	Ashley	Marshall	USA	10.9.93	17 Apr
23.18	4.9	Caitland	Smith	USA-J	24.3.96	16 May
23.19	3.2	Brigitte	Ntiamoah	FRA	5.3.94	10 Jul
23.21	2.3	Diamond	Gause	USA	4.4.94	30 Ap
23.23	3.5	Nikki	Larch-Miller	USA	13.8.94	15 Ap
23.24	4.1	Amy	Foster	IRL	2.10.88	22 May
23.25		Hannah	Brier	GBR-Y	3.2.98	6 Jur
23.27	3.2	Ada	Udaya	LBR	28.6.92	23 May
23.27	4.4	Marie	Gayot	FRA	18.12.89	24 May
23.28	2.9	Allison	Peter	ISV	14.7.92	25 Ap
23.28	2.1	Aleksandra	Fedoriva-Shpayer	RUS	13.9.88	8 Aug
23.30	2.5	Katie	Wise	USA	15.10.93	17 May
23.30	2.6	Praise Idamadudu	Oghenefejir	NGR-Y	18.12.98	9 Sep
23.31	2.4	MacKenzie	Flannigan	USA		16 May
23.32	3.8	Inna	Weit	GER	5.8.88	18 Ap

Best at low altitude

Mark	Wind	Name	Pos	Meet	Venue	Date
22.75	-1.1	Hackett	4s2	WCh	Beijing	27 Aug
22.86	1.2	Tenorio	2h2	PAm	Toronto	23 Jul
23.05	0.9	C Hill	1		Albany	9 May
23.16	0.9	L R Williams				5 Jun
23.34	-0.9	Morales				26 Aug

JUNIORS

See main list for top 8 juniors (& 8 wa). 13 performances by 4 women to 22.88. Additional marks and further juniors:

Name	Mark	Wind	Pos	Meet	Venue	Date
Whitney	22.49	-0.1	2s1	NC	Eugene	28 Jun
	22.54	-0.3	5	Herc	Monaco	17 Jul
	22.65	1.1	1	PAm	Toronto	24 Jul
	22.68	1.6	1s1	PAm	Toronto	23 Jul
	22.72	0.4	1		Montverde	6 Ju
	22.75	0.6	2h3	NC	Eugene	27 Ju
	22.88	1.2	3h2	PAm	Toronto	23 Ju
Tenorio	22.86	1.2	2h2	PAm	Toronto	23 Jul
	22.75	0.1	1h5	EC	Zürich	14 Aug
	22.88	1.1	4	PAm	Toronto	24 Ju
	23.08	-0.6	1		Norwich	27 Ap

Mark	Wind	Name		Nat	Born	Pos	Meet	Venue	Date
23.09	1.2	Charlotte	McLennaghan	GBR	6.9.97	1		Derby	10 Ma
23.09	0.9	Zaria	Francis (10)	USA-Y	22.3.98	1		Clovis	6 Ju
23.11	1.7	Vitória Cristina	Rosa	BRA	12.1.96	2	NC	São Bernardo do Campo	17 Ma
23.18	0.2	Saqukine	Cameron	JAM	21.8.96	1		Kingston	7 Ma
23.21	0.1	Diamond	Spaulding	USA	29.9.96	1		Jacksonville	9 Ma
23.22	0.6	Ky	Westbrook	USA	25.2.96	3q2	NCAA-W	Austin	29 Ma
23.23	1.3	Shania	Collins	USA	14.11.96	3h1	Big 12	Ames	16 Ma
23.24	0.9	Cassondra	Hall	USA	23.9.97	1s3	JunOly	Jacksonville	30 Ju
23.26A	1.7	Evelin	Rivera	COL	8.12.97	1	NG	Cali	21 No
23.29	1.8	Caitland	Smith	USA	24.3.96	5		Austin	2 Ma
23.29	0.9	Maroussia	Pare	FRA	18.7.96	1B-J		Mannheim	28 Ju
23.29	-0.3	Lisa	Mayer (20)	GER	2.5.96	1	NC-j	Jena	1 Au

Wind assisted: 6 performances to 22.80 by 5 women

Name	Mark	Wind	Pos	Meet	Venue	Date
Hill	22.76A	2.8	1		Albuquerque	6 Jun
S Hylton	22.79	4.2	1s1	EJ	Eskilstuna	18 Jul

Mark	Wind	Name		Nat	Born	Pos	Meet	Venue	Date
23.05	2.6	Maroussia	Pare	FRA	18.7.96	3	EJ	Eskilstuna	18 Ju

Mark	Wind	Name		Nat	Born	Pos	Meet	Venue	Date
23.10	4.1	Kiana	Horton	USA	29.1.97	1		Austin	16 May
23.10	3.1	Vitoria Cristina	Rosa	BRA	12.1.96	2h1	NC	São Bernardo do Campo	16 May
23.12	4.3	Kayelle	Clarke	TTO	28.2.96	1	Carifta	Basseterre	6 Apr
23.15	2.9	Cheriece	Hylton	GBR	19.12.96	1rB	LI	Loughborough	17 May
23.17	2.4	L'Tsha	Fahie	IVB-Y	8.7.98	1	NC-y	Basseterre	13 Jun
23.18	4.9	Caitland	Smith	USA	24.3.96	3h3	Big 12	Ames	16 May
23.25		Hannah	Brier	GBR	3.2.98	2		Edinburgh	6 Jun

300 METRES

Mark	Name		Nat	Born	Pos	Meet	Venue	Date
37.11	Gina	Lückenkemper	GER-J	21.11.96	1		Pliezhausen	17 May
37.21	Friederike	Möhlenkamp	GER	19.11.92	1		Leverkusen	17 May
37.25	Patience	George	NGR	25.11.91				14 Mar
37.38	Jordan	Lavender	USA	23.7.93				8 May

Indoors

Mark	Name		Nat	Born	Pos	Meet	Venue	Date
36.52	Natasha	Hastings	USA	23.7.86	1	NC	Boston (R)	28 Feb
36.65	Jessica	Beard	USA	8.1.89	2	NC	Boston (R)	28 Feb
36.74	Tiffany	Townsend	USA	14.6.89	1		Boston	7 Feb
37.07	Floria	Guei	FRA	2.5.90				25 Feb
37.12	Felicia	Brown	USA	27.10.93				11 Dec
37.13	Alena	Mamina	RUS	30.5.90				7 Jan
37.29	Yekaterina	Renzhina	RUS	18.10.94				7 Jan
37.36	Kineke	Alexander	VIN	21.2.86				9 Jan
37.44	Shapri	Romero	USA	13.11.91				28 Feb

JUNIORS

Mark	Name		Nat	Born	Pos	Meet	Venue	Date
37.55	Ayomide	Folorunso	ITA	17.10.96	1		Rieti	25 Apr
37.49i	Sydney	McLaughlin	USA-Y	7.8.99	1		New York (Arm)	31 Jan

400 METRES

Mark	Name		Nat	Born	Pos	Meet	Venue	Date
49.26	Allyson	Felix	USA	18.11.85	1	WCh	Beijing	27 Aug
49.67	Shaunae	Miller	BAH	15.4.94	2	WCh	Beijing	27 Aug
49.83	Francena	McCorory	USA	20.10.88	1	Herc	Monaco	17 Jul
49.85		McCorory			1s2	NC	Eugene	26 Jun
49.86		McCorory			1	adidas	New York	13 Jun
49.89		Felix			1s3	WCh	Beijing	25 Aug
49.92		Miller			1	Athl	Lausanne	9 Jul
49.95	Sanya	Richards-Ross	USA	26.2.85	1		Kingston	9 May
49.99	Shericka	Jackson	JAM	15.7.94	3	WCh	Beijing	27 Aug
50.03		Jackson			2s3	WCh	Beijing	25 Aug
50.05		Felix			1	Pre	Eugene	30 May
50.12		Miller			1s1	WCh	Beijing	25 Aug
50.13		McCorory			1	DrakeR	Des Moines	25 Apr
50.14	Christine	Day	JAM	23.8.86	4	WCh	Beijing	27 Aug
50.16		Day			1	NC	Kingston	28 Jun
50.16	Christine	Ohuruogu	GBR	17.5.84	1s2	WCh	Beijing	25 Aug
50.17		Miller			1		Gainesville	24 Apr
50.19		Felix			1	NC	Eugene	27 Jun
50.21		McCorory			1	DL	Doha	15 May
50.22	Kabange	Mupopo	ZAM	21.9.92	1	AfG	Brazzaville	15 Sep
50.24	Natasha	Hastings	USA	23.7.86	1	DL	London (OS)	24 Jul
50.25		Hastings			2	NC	Eugene	27 Jun
50.28		Hastings			2s2	NC	Eugene	26 Jun
50.29		Richards-Ross			2	Pre	Eugene	30 May
50.30		McCorory			1	Déca	Paris (C)	13 Sep
50.31		Jackson			2	NC	Kingston	28 Jun
50.32	Stephenie Ann	McPherson (10)	JAM	25.11.88	2s2	WCh	Beijing	25 Aug
50.34		McPherson			1h4	WCh	Beijing	24 Aug
50.36		McCorory			1	GGala	Roma	4 Jun
50.37	Bianca (30/11)	Razor	ROU	8.8.94	1h5	WCh	Beijing	24 Aug
50.47	Novlene	Williams-Mills	JAM	26.4.82	3s3	WCh	Beijing	25 Aug
50.50	Kendall	Baisden	USA	5.3.95	3s2	NC	Eugene	26 Jun
50.50	Phyllis	Francis	USA	4.5.92	3s2	WCh	Beijing	25 Aug
50.62	Nataliya	Pyhyda	UKR	30.1.81	4s3	WCh	Beijing	25 Aug
50.68	Jessica	Beard	USA	8.1.89	4s2	NC	Eugene	26 Jun
50.71	Patience	George	NGR	25.11.91	2	AfG	Brazzaville	15 Sep
50.82A	Courtney	Okolo	USA	15.3.94	1h1	NACAC	San José, CRC	7 Aug
50.84	Shakima	Wimbley	USA	23.4.95	1	ACC	Tallahassee	16 May
50.84	Quanera (20)	Hayes	USA	7.3.92	3s1	NC	Eugene	26 Jun
50.86	Kemi	Adekoya	BRN	16.1.93	2	Spitzen	Luzern	14 Jul
50.87	Anyika	Onuora	GBR	28.10.84	5s3	WCh	Beijing	25 Aug
50.89	Floria	Guei	FRA	2.5.90	2h1	WCh	Beijing	24 Aug
50.97	Marie	Gayot	FRA	18.12.89	5s2	WCh	Beijing	25 Aug

Mark	Name		Nat	Born	Pos	Meet	Venue	Date
51.07	Libania	Grenot	ITA	12.7.83	6	Herc	Monaco	17 Ju
51.09	Kala	Funderburk	USA	14.9.92	1q1	NCAA-E	Jacksonville	29 Ma
51.14	Kaliese	Spencer	JAM	6.5.87	1		Kingston	30 Ma
51.14A	Joyce	Zakari ¶	KEN	6.6.86	1	NC	Nairobi	11 Ju
51.18	Taylor	Ellis-Watson	USA	6.5.93	1	SEC	Starkville	16 Ma
51.24	DeeDee	Trotter	USA	8.12.82	6s2	NC	Eugene	26 Ju
	(30)							
51.24	Tosin	Adeloye	NGR-J	7.2.96	2s2	AfG	Brazzaville	14 Se
51.27	Justine	Palframan	RSA	4.11.93	1	WUG	Gwangju	10 Ju
51.28	Anastasia	Le-Roy	JAM	11.9.87	4	NC	Kingston	28 Ju
51.30	Regina	George	NGR	17.2.91	1		Kawasaki	10 Ma
51.31	Patrycja	Wyciszkiewicz	POL	8.1.94	4h1	WCh	Beijing	24 Au
51.36	Alena	Mamina	RUS	30.5.90	1		Chelyabinsk	30 Ma
51.37	Margaret	Bamgbose	USA	19.10.93	1q3	NCAA-E	Jacksonville	29 Ma
51.37	Daye Shon	Roberson	USA	3.7.95	2q1	NCAA-W	Austin	29 Ma
51.39	Salwa Eid	Naser	BRN-Y	23.5.98	1	WMilG	Mungyeong	7 Oc
51.40	Maureen	Maiyo	KEN	28.5.85	4h2	WCh	Beijing	24 Au
	(40)							
51.42	Kiara	Porter	USA	22.10.93	2q1	NCAA-E	Jacksonville	29 Ma
51.42	Nadezhda	Kotlyarova	RUS	12.6.89	3h4	WCh	Beijing	24 Au
51.43	Geisa	Coutinho	BRA	1.6.80	1	NC	São Bernardo do Campo	15 Ma
51.44	Kseniya	Aksyonova	RUS	14.1.88	1	NC	Cheboksary	4 Au
51.45	Mariya	Mikhailyuk	RUS	29.1.91	1		Moskva	2 Ju
51.48	Aiesha	Goggins	USA	13.9.91	1		Storrs	17 Ma
51.48	Seren	Bundy-Davies	GBR	30.12.94	7	DL	London (OS)	24 Ju
51.49	Kineke	Alexander	VIN	21.2.86	1		Baie Mahault	2 Ma
51.49	Yekaterina	Renzhina	RUS	18.10.94	6s2	WCh	Beijing	25 Au
51.50	Kyra	Jefferson	USA	23.9.94	1	FlaR	Gainesville	2 Ap
	(50)							
51.50	Vanessa	Jones	USA	1.1.93	1	Pac 12	Los Angeles (Ww)	17 Ma
51.51	Tjipekapora	Herunga	NAM	1.1.88	3s2	AfG	Brazzaville	14 Se
51.52	Chris-Ann	Gordon	JAM	18.9.94	5	NC	Kingston	28 Ju
51.53	Sonikqua	Walker	JAM	24.9.94	2q3	NCAA-E	Jacksonville	29 Ma
51.61	Olha	Zemlyak	UKR	16.1.90	5	GGala	Roma	4 Ju
51.66	Brianna	Tate	USA	4.4.95	2	Pac 12	Los Angeles (Ww)	17 Ma
51.67	Maria Benedicta	Chigbolu	ITA	27.7.89	3		La Chaux-de-Fonds	5 Ju
51.69	Anneliese	Rubie	AUS	22.4.92	5h1	WCh	Beijing	24 Au
51.70	Carline	Muir	CAN	1.10.87	5h5	WCh	Beijing	24 Au
51.72	Ashley	Spencer	USA	8.6.93	1s3	NCAA	Eugene	11 Ju
	(60)							
51.74	Malgorzata	Holub	POL	30.10.92	5h4	WCh	Beijing	24 Au
51.76	Kamaria	Brown	USA	21.12.92	4	Johnson	Waco	18 Ap
51.77	Shamier	Little	USA	20.3.95	5	Johnson	Waco	18 Ap
51.78	Kenya	Woodall	USA	17.7.94	2		Storrs	17 Ma
51.79A	Lynna	Irby	USA-Y	6.12.98	2	WY	Cali	17 Ju
51.79A	Bobby-Gaye	Wilkins-Gooden	JAM	10.9.88	1h2	NACAC	San José, CRC	7 Au
51.83	Carly	Muscaro	USA	18.5.95	1		Cambridge, MA	9 Ma
51.85	Kseniya	Zadorina	RUS	2.3.87	1h1	NC	Cheboksary	3 Au
51.86	Lilla	McMillan	USA	31.8.94	3		Storrs	17 Ma
51.88	Janeive	Russell	JAM	14.11.93	1		Kingston	14 Ma
	(70)							
51.93	Shapri	Romero	USA	13.11.91	1		George Town	16 Ma
51.93	Robin	Reynolds	USA	22.2.94	2	SEC	Starkville	16 Ma
51.93	Audrey	Jean-Baptiste	CAN	15.7.91	4		Storrs	17 Ma
51.95	Patricia	Hall-Pritchett	JAM	16.10.82	2		Austin	11 Ap
51.97	Kseniya	Ryzhova	RUS	19.4.87	3		Moskva	2 Ju
51.98		Yang Huizhen	CHN	13.8.92	3	WUG	Gwangju	10 Ju
52.00		Nguyen Thi Huyen	VIE	19.8.93	1	SEAG	Singapore	12 Ju
52.01	Destinee	Gause	USA	4.4.94	1rB	Jones	Gainesville	24 Ap
52.02	Iga	Baumgart	POL	11.4.89	6h6	WCh	Beijing	24 Au
52.04	Nicky	van Leuveren	NED	25.5.90	1	ET-1	Iráklio	20 Ju
	(80)							
52.04	Ruth Sophia	Spelmeyer	GER	19.9.90	4	WUG	Gwangju	10 Ju
52.05	Raena	Rhone	USA	27.9.93	3q1	NCAA-W	Austin	29 Ma
52.07	Margaret	Adeoye	GBR	27.4.85	1rB	ET	Cheboksary	20 Ju
52.08	Georganne	Moline	USA	6.3.90	1rC	FlaR	Gainesville	2 Ap
52.09A	Wenda	Nel	RSA	30.7.88	1h1		Potchefstroom	8 Ma
52.09	Deborah	Sananes	FRA	26.10.95	1		Valence	24 Ma
52.11A	Lisneidy Inés	Veitía	CUB	29.4.94	2h2	NACAC	San José, CRC	7 Au
52.13	Kirsten	McAslan	GBR	1.9.93	4h1	EU23	Tallinn	9 Ju
52.17	Gunta	Latiseva-Cudare	LAT	9.3.95	4h3	WCh	Beijing	24 Au

Mark	Name		Nat	Born	Pos	Meet	Venue	Date
52.18	Iveta (90)	Putalová	SVK	24.3.88	5	WUG	Gwangju	10 Jul
52.19	Elexis	Guster	USA	7.7.94	1	Big 10	East Lansing	17 May
52.20A	Aauri Lorena	Bokesa	ESP	14.12.88	1		Monachil	8 Aug
52.21	Montané	Speight	GBR	5.11.92	1rB	Johnson	Waco	18 Apr
52.22	Daysiurami	Bonne	CUB	9.3.88	1		La Habana	26 Jun
52.22	Tatyana	Veshkurova	RUS	23.9.81	1		Cheboksary	24 Jul
52.23	Alina	Lohvynenko	UKR	18.7.90	1		Kharkiv	21 May
52.23	Agnes	Raharolahy	FRA	7.11.92	1		Genève	6 Jun
52.23	Martyna	Dabrowska	POL	5.4.94	1rB	EAF	Bydgoszcz	14 Jun
52.25	Laviai	Nielsen	GBR-J	13.3.96	1		Namur	27 May
52.25	Estelle (100)	Perrossier	FRA	12.1.90	1		Saint-Etienne	13 Jun
52.25	Sharrika	Barnett	USA-J	16.4.97	1		Greensboro NC	21 Jun
52.25	Nicole	Sassine	CAN	24.11.89	2h1	NC	Edmonton	3 Jul
52.25A	Catherine	Reid	GBR-Y	21.4.98	3	WY	Cali	17 Jul

Mark	Name		Nat	Born	Date
52.29	Anna	Yegorova	RUS	25.2.87	28 May
52.29A	Jacinta	Shikanda	KEN	14.7.86	1 Aug
52.30	Denisa	Rosolová	CZE	21.8.86	20 Jun
52.31	Alex	Gholston	USA	3.1.95	29 May
52.32	Kendall	Ellis	USA-J	8.3.96	27 Jun
52.32A	Christine	Amertil	BAH	18.8.79	7 Aug
52.33	Brianne	Theisen-Eaton	CAN	18.12.88	12 Jul
52.33	Laura	Müller	GER	11.12.95	25 Jul
52.34	Margaret	Etim	NGR	28.11.92	14 Sep
52.36	Shericka	Williams	JAM	17.9.85	27 Jun
52.39	Sada	Williams	BAR-J	1.12.97	20 Jun
52.39	Yuliya	Olishevska	UKR	2.2.89	30 Jul
52.40	Gilda	Casanova	CUB	19.12.95	15 May
52.40	Kendra	White	USA	14.3.93	29 May
52.41A	Florence	Uwakwe	NGR	28.7.94	17 May
52.42	Tovea	Jenkins	JAM	27.10.92	18 Apr
52.42	Elea Mariama	Diarra	FRA	8.3.90	1 Jul
52.43	Laniece	Clarke	BAH	4.11.87	9 May
52.43	Ashante	Horsley	USA		17 May
52.43	Aiyanna	Stiverne	CAN	20.2.95	4 Jul
52.43A	Carol	Rodríguez	PUR	16.12.85	7 Aug
52.44A	T'Shelia	Mungo	USA	21.9.93	17 May
52.44	Justyna	Swiety	POL	3.12.92	10 Jul
52.44A	Kyra	Constantine	CAN-Y	1.8.98	17 Jul
52.45	Liliya	Molchanova	RUS	2.3.90	29 May
52.46		Cheng Chong	CHN	22.9.92	28 Jun
52.47	Ayana	Walker	USA		8 May
52.50	Shana	Cox	GBR	22.1.85	2 Apr
52.50	Jessica	Johnson	USA		16 May
52.51	Cassandra	Tate	USA	11.9.90	18 Apr
52.51	Chiara	Bazzoni	ITA	5.7.84	24 Apr
52.51	Claudia	Francis	USA	14.11.93	2 May
52.51	Rita	Ossai	NGR	21.10.95	11 Jul
52.51	Djénébou	Danté	MLI	7.8.89	14 Sep
52.51	Leni	Shida	UGA	22.5.94	14 Sep
52.52	Raquel	Tjernagel	CAN-J	25.10.97	17 Apr
52.52		Quach Thi Lan	VIE	18.10.95	12 Jun
52.52	Anastasiya	Bondar	RUS	21.5.91	3 Aug
52.53	Lisanne	de Witte	NED	10.9.92	11 Sep
52.54	Verone	Chambers	JAM	16.12.88	7 May
52.55	Kendra	Clarke	CAN-J	16.11.96	31 Jul
52.56	Briana	Nelson	USA	18.7.92	11 Apr
52.56	Santina	Williams	USA		29 May
52.57	Natoya	Goule	JAM	30.3.91	15 May
52.57	Jordan	Lavender	USA	23.7.93	29 May
52.57	Lydia	Jele	BOT	22.6.90	14 Sep
52.58	Yana	Glotova	RUS	8.4.95	16 Jun
52.59	Sydney	McLaughlin	USA-Y	7.8.99	29 May
52.60	Joelma	Sousa	BRA	13.7.84	15 May
52.60	Cynthia	Bolingo Mbongo	BEL	12.1.93	27 May
52.60	Taylor	Sharpe	CAN-J	2.12.96	28 May
52.60	Machettira	Raju Poovamma	IND	5.6.90	29 Jun
52.61	Jaílma	de Lima	BRA	31.12.86	15 May
52.61	Yuliya	Rakhmanova	KAZ	25.10.91	14 Jun
52.63	Lénora	Guion-Firmin	FRA	7.8.91	2 Apr
52.63	Funke	Oladoye	NGR	12.5.93	11 Jul
52.63		Nguyen Thi Oanh	VIE-J	22.2.96	12 Oct
52.65	Yaneisi	Borlot	CUB	18.2.91	15 May
52.65	Kelly	Massey	GBR	11.1.85	14 Jun
52.66	Olha	Bibik	UKR	5.2.90	30 Jul
52.66	Morgan	Mitchell	AUS	3.10.94	15 Nov
52.67	Aaliyah	Barnes	USA	17.2.95	29 May
52.69	Sophia	Smellie	JAM	6.11.79	6 Jun
52.69	Samantha	Watson	USA-Y	10.11.99	12 Jun
52.70	Jenna	Martin-Evans	CAN	31.3.88	4 Jul
52.71	Anilda	Thomas	IND	6.5.93	11 Feb
52.71	Kendra	Chambers	USA	11.9.90	2 May
52.72	Cátia	Azevedo	POR	9.3.94	5 Aug
52.73	Nadia	Cummins	BAR	28.4.91	18 Apr
52.73A	Maureen	Thomas	KEN-J	29.12.97	1 Aug
52.74	Shayla	Luckett	USA	18.2.93	16 May
52.74	Madeline	Kopp	USA	4.4.95	29 May
52.74	Darya	Korableva	RUS	23.5.88	25 Jul
52.75	Tiffany	Harris	USA	28.9.91	22 May
52.76	Kristyn	Williams	USA	27.1.94	16 May
52.76	Marta	Milani	ITA	9.3.87	9 Jul
52.77A	Yenifer	Padilla	COL	1.1.90	16 Nov
52.78	Rosemarie	Whyte-Robinson	JAM	8.9.86	21 Mar
52.78	Dawnalee	Loney	JAM-J	15.5.96	28 Mar
52.79A	Roxana	Gómez	CUB-Y	7.1.99	17 Jul
52.79	Marina	Konovalova	RUS	17.9.90	3 Aug
52.79	Fatoumata	Diop	SEN	10.8.86	14 Sep
52.80	Symone	Mason	USA-Y	31.8.99	1 Jul
52.81	Nyanka	Moise-Joseph	USA	8.6.93	17 May
52.81	Monika	Szczesna	POL	20.12.87	14 Jun
52.81	Mary	Iheke	GBR	19.11.90	5 Jul
52.82	Samantha	Edwards	ANT	14.1.90	28 Jun
52.82	Fabienne	Kohlmann	GER	6.11.89	15 Aug
52.83	Anastasiya	Kudinova	KAZ	27.2.88	12 May
52.83A	Gabriela	Medina	MEX	3.3.85	13 Jun
52.85	Hrystyna	Stuy	UKR	3.2.88	27 Jun
52.86	Titania	Markland	JAM	1.2.94	29 May
52.88	Ebony	Eutsey	USA	3.5.92	24 Apr
52.88	Laetitia	Libert	BEL	12.11.79	5 Jul
52.88	Sanda	Belgyan	ROU	17.12.92	9 Jul
52.89	Ilona (200)	Usovich	BLR	14.11.82	24 Jul

Indoors

Mark	Name		Nat	Born	Pos	Meet	Venue	Date
51.37	Shamier	Little	USA	20.3.95	1r2	SEC	Lexington	28 Feb

Mark	Name		Nat	Born	Date
52.32	Laura	Maddox	GBR	13.5.90	21 Feb
52.42	Madiea	Ghafoor	NED	9.9.92	22 Feb
52.63	Indira	Terrero	ESP	29.11.85	7 Mar
52.67	Sparkle	McKnight	TTO	21.12.91	31 Jan
52.69	Morganne	Phillips	USA	10.11.92	28 Feb
52.72	Kiah	Seymour	USA	11.1.94	28 Feb
52.76	Zuzana	Hejnová	CZE	19.12.86	22 Feb
52.83	Sara	Petersen	DEN	9.4.87	14 Feb
52.86	Madison	Reynolds	USA	14.7.94	14 Feb
52.89	Jaide	Stepter	USA	25.4.94	28 Feb

Best at low altitude

Mark	Name	Pos	Meet	Venue	Date
50.99	Okolo	1	Johnson	Waco	18 Apr
52.08	Wilkins-Gooden	6	NC	Kingston	28 Jun
52.25	Veitía	6h5	WCh	Beijing	24 Aug
52.26	Bokesa	1		Alcalá de Henares	19 Jul
52.60	Rodríguez				18 Apr
52.80	Mungo				29 May

Drugs disqualification

Mark	Name		Nat	Born	Pos	Meet	Venue	Date
50.71	Joyce	Zakari ¶	KEN	6.6.86	(2h3) 1	WCh	Beijing	24 Aug

Mark	Name		Nat	Born	Pos	Meet	Venue	Date

JUNIORS

See main list for top 6 juniors. 11 performances by 6 women to 52.25. Additional marks and further juniors:

Adeloye 51.82 4 AfG Brazzaville 15 Sep | 51.92 2 Warri 24 Jul
51.86 2h1 AfG Brazzaville 14 Sep | 52.01 2h1 NC Warri 30 Jul
Naser 51.50A 1 WY Cali 17 Jul

Mark	Name		Nat	Born	Pos	Meet	Venue	Date
52.32	Kendall	Ellis	USA	8.3.96	1	NC-j	Eugene	27 Jun
52.39	Sada	Williams	BAR	1.12.97	2	NC	Waterford	20 Jun
52.44A	Kyra	Constantine	CAN-Y	1.8.98	4	WY	Cali	17 Jul
52.52	Raquel	Tjernagel (10)	CAN	25.10.97	2		Azusa	17 Apr
52.55	Kendra	Clarke	CAN	16.11.96	1	PAm-J	Edmonton	31 Jul
52.59	Sydney	McLaughlin	USA-Y	7.8.99	1		South Plainfield	29 May
52.60	Taylor	Sharpe	CAN	2.12.96	2h1	NCAA-E	Jacksonville	28 May
52.63		Nguyen Thi Oanh	VIE	22.2.96	1	NC	Ho Chi Minh	12 Oct
52.69	Samantha	Watson	USA-Y	10.11.99	1		Albany	12 Jun
52.73A	Maureen	Thomas	KEN	29.12.97	4	WCT	Nairobi	1 Aug
52.78	Dawnalee	Loney	JAM	15.5.96	1	NSch-y	Kingston	28 Mar
52.79A	Roxana	Gómez	CUB-Y	7.1.99	5	WY	Cali	17 Jul
52.80	Symone	Mason	USA-Y	31.8.99	1	NC-y	Lisle	1 Jul
52.95A	Nicole	Montgomery (20)	USA	21.9.96	1		Denver	16 May

500 METRES INDOORS

Mark	Name		Nat	Born	Pos	Meet	Venue	Date
1:08.84i	Georganne	Moline	USA	6.3.90	1		New York (Arm)	30 Jan

600 METRES

Mark	Name		Nat	Born	Pos	Meet	Venue	Date
1:25.04	Joanna	Józwik	POL	30.1.91	1	Kuso	Szczecin	9 Aug
1:25.45	Selina	Büchel	SUI	26.7.91	1		Pliezhausen	17 May
1:25.73	Christina	Hering	GER	9.10.94	2		Pliezhausen	17 May

1:27.22+ Faith Kipyegon KEN 10.1.94 13 Sep | 1:27.71+ Fabienne Kohlmann GER 6.11.89 3 Sep
1:27.47 Paulina Mikiewicz POL 13.7.92 9 Aug | 1:27.96 Ewa Jacniak POL 27.11.90 9 Aug

Indoors

Mark	Name		Nat	Born	Pos	Meet	Venue	Date
1:26.22	Kirsten	McAslan	GBR	1.9.93	1		Manchester	4 Jan
1:26.56	Ajeé	Wilson	USA	8.5.94	1h3	NC	Boston (R)	28 Feb
1:26.59	Alysia	Montaño	USA	26.4.86	1	NC	Boston (R)	1 Mar
1:26.73	Kendra	Chambers	USA	11.9.90	2h3	NC	Boston (R)	28 Feb

1:27.15A Georganne Moline USA 6.3.90 13 Feb | 1:27.87 Megan Malasarte USA 1.8.92 28 Feb
1:27.81 Phoebe Wright USA 30.8.88 28 Feb | 1:27.90 Lenka Masná CZE 22.4.85 23 Jan

800 METRES

Mark	Name		Nat	Born	Pos	Meet	Venue	Date
1:56.99	Eunice	Sum	KEN	2.9.88	1	DL	Saint-Denis	4 Jul
1:57.52	Melissa	Bishop	CAN	5.8.88	1s3	WCh	Beijing	27 Aug
1:57.54	Marina	Arzamasova	BLR	17.12.87	2s3	WCh	Beijing	27 Aug
1:57.56		Sum			3s3	WCh	Beijing	27 Aug
1:57.62	Francine	Niyonsaba	BDI	5.5.93	1		Rieti	13 Sep
1:57.70	Rose Mary	Almanza	CUB	13.7.92	2	DL	Saint-Denis	4 Jul
1:57.71	Lynsey	Sharp	GBR	11.7.90	1	ISTAF	Berlin	6 Sep
1:57.82		Sum			1	Pre	Eugene	30 May
1:57.87	Ajee'	Wilson	USA	8.5.94	2	Pre	Eugene	30 May
1:57.95	Selina	Büchel	SUI	26.7.91	3	DL	Saint-Denis	4 Jul
1:58.02	Faith	Kipyegon	KEN	10.1.94	2		Rieti	13 Sep
1:58.03		Arzamasova			1	WCh	Beijing	29 Aug
1:58.12		Bishop			2	WCh	Beijing	29 Aug
1:58.18		Sum			3	WCh	Beijing	29 Aug
1:58.34	Fabienne	Kohlmann (10)	GER	6.11.89	2	ISTAF	Berlin	6 Sep
1:58.35	Joanna	Józwik	POL	30.1.91	4s3	WCh	Beijing	27 Aug
1:58.37		Kohlmann			1		Beliinzona	21 Jul
1:58.44		Sum			1	DL	London (OS)	25 Jul
1:58.50	Sifan	Hassan	NED	1.1.93	5s3	WCh	Beijing	27 Aug
1:58.55	Rabab	Arrafi	MAR	12.1.91	1s1	WCh	Beijing	27 Aug
1:58.57	Nataliya	Lupu	UKR	4.11.87	2s1	WCh	Beijing	27 Aug
1:58.63		Büchel			3s1	WCh	Beijing	27 Aug
1:58.64	Olha	Lyakhova	UKR	18.3.92	3		Rieti	13 Sep
1:58.68	Molly	Ludlow	USA	4.8.87	4	DL	Saint-Denis	4 Jul
1:58.69		Arzamasova			1h1	WCh	Beijing	26 Aug
1:58.75	Anastasiya	Bazdyreva	RUS	6.3.92	1		Sochi	29 May
1:58.83		Wilson			1	adidas	New York	13 Jun
1:58.86	Shelayna	Oskan-Clarke	GBR	20.1.90	1s2	WCh	Beijing	27 Aug
1:58.86	Renelle	Lamote	FRA	26.12.93	2s2	WCh	Beijing	27 Aug
1:58.88		Arzamasova			3	ISTAF	Berlin	6 Sep
	(30/19)							
1:59.03	Malika	Akkaoui (20)	MAR	25.12.87	6s3	WCh	Beijing	27 Aug

Mark	Name		Nat	Born	Pos	Meet	Venue	Date
1:59.06	Brenda	Martinez	USA	8.9.87	3	Pre	Eugene	30 May
1:59.06	Angela	Petty	NZL	16.8.91	1	WUG	Gwangju	10 Jul
1:59.10	Chanelle	Price	USA	22.8.90	5	DL	Saint-Denis	4 Jul
1:59.14	Lucia	Klocová	SVK	20.11.83	7s3	WCh	Beijing	27 Aug
1:59.15	Alysia	Montaño	USA	26.4.86	1	NC	Eugene	28 Jun
1:59.26	Simoya	Campbell	JAM	1.3.94	2	WUG	Gwangju	10 Jul
1:59.37	Janeth	Jepkosgei	KEN	13.12.83	2	adidas	New York	13 Jun
1:59.54	Christina	Hering	GER	9.10.94	2	NC	Nürnberg	26 Jul
1:59.55	Angelika	Cichocka	POL	15.3.88	5		Rieti	13 Sep
1:59.59	Caster	Semenya	RSA	7.1.91	3h1	WCh	Beijing	26 Aug
	(30)							
1:59.59	Fiona	Benson	CAN	25.5.92	5s2	WCh	Beijing	27 Aug
1:59.63	Natoya	Goule	JAM	30.3.91	1	NC	Kingston	27 Jun
1:59.71	Raevyn	Rogers	USA-J	7.9.96	1	NCAA	Eugene	13 Jun
1:59.90	Amela	Terzic	SRB	2.1.93	1	ET-2	Stara Zagora	20 Jun
1:59.91	Sahily	Diago	CUB	26.8.95	2		Ponce	23 May
1:59.98	Abeba	Aregawi	SWE	5.7.90	4	Pre	Eugene	30 May
2:00.03	Yekaterina	Poistogova	RUS	1.3.91	6	DL	Saint-Denis	4 Jul
2:00.03	Shannon	Rowbury	USA	19.9.84	5	ISTAF	Berlin	6 Sep
2:00.05	Maggie	Vessey	USA	23.12.81	2s2	NC	Eugene	26 Jun
2:00.11	Sofia	Ennaoui	POL	30.8.95	5s1	WCh	Beijing	27 Aug
	(40)							
2:00.14	Yekaterina	Sharmina	RUS	6.8.86	1		Yerino	25 Jul
2:00.21	Eglé	Balciunaité	LTU	31.10.88	4	WUG	Gwangju	10 Jul
2:00.21	Anastasiya	Tkachuk	UKR	20.4.93	2	NC	Kirovohrad	1 Aug
2:00.40	Flávia	de Lima	BRA	1.7.93	3	PAm	Toronto	22 Jul
2:00.42	Laura	Muir	GBR	9.5.93	2	DL	Birmingham	7 Jun
2:00.42	Treniere	Moser	USA	27.10.81	7	adidas	New York	13 Jun
2:00.48	Lauren	Wallace	USA	19.12.88	5s2	NC	Eugene	26 Jun
2:00.50	Alison	Leonard	GBR	17.3.90	1		Oordegem	23 May
2:00.53	Jennifer	Meadows	GBR	17.4.81	7s1	WCh	Beijing	27 Aug
2:00.56	Tintu	Luka	IND	26.4.89	1	NC	Kolkata	19 Sep
	(50)							
2:00.60	Charlene	Lipsey	USA	16.7.91	9	adidas	New York	13 Jun
2:00.61	Phoebe	Wright	USA	30.8.88	3s1	NC	Eugene	26 Jun
2:00.63	Claudia	Saunders	USA	19.5.94	2	NCAA	Eugene	13 Jun
2:00.76	Dana	Mecke	USA	20.9.87	4s1	NC	Eugene	26 Jun
2:00.79	Jennifer	Simpson	USA	23.8.86	2		Los Angeles (ER)	14 May
2:00.81	McKayla	Fricker	USA	19.4.92	6s2	NC	Eugene	26 Jun
2:00.83	Yevgeniya	Subbotina	RUS	30.10.89	2		Yerino	25 Jul
2:00.91	Florina	Pierdevarâ	ROU	29.3.90	4	WMilG	Mungyeong	5 Oct
2:00.95	LaTavia	Thomas	USA	17.12.88	3		Sotteville-lès-Rouen	6 Jul
2:00.97	Noélie	Yarigo	BEN	26.12.85	10	adidas	New York	13 Jun
	(60)							
2:01.01	Aníta	Hinriksdóttir	ISL-J	13.1.96	5h6	WCh	Beijing	26 Aug
2:01.07	Jessica	Smith	CAN	11.10.89	4		Portland	14 Jun
2:01.10	Adele	Tracey	GBR	27.5.93	1		Ninove	1 Aug
2:01.11	Alexa	Efraimson	USA-J	20.2.97	1		Liège (NX)	15 Jul
2:01.17	Hanna	Green	USA	16.10.94	3	NCAA	Eugene	13 Jun
2:01.20	Katie	Mackey	USA	12.11.87	5		Portland	14 Jun
2:01.21	Ciara	Everard	IRL	10.7.90	2		Oordegem	23 May
2:01.23	Gabe	Grunewald	USA	25.6.86	5		Bellinzona	21 Jul
2:01.27	Habitam	Alemu	ETH-J	9.7.97	5		Tomblaine	1 Jul
2:01.30	Charline	Mathias	LUX	23.5.92	6		Bellinzona	21 Jul
	(70)							
2:01.31	Yuliya	Stepanova	RUS	3.7.86	1		Regensburg	6 Jun
2:01.32	Margaret	Wambui	KEN	15.9.95	3	Pre	Eugene	29 May
2:01.43	Esther	Guerrero	ESP	7.2.90	7		Madrid	11 Jul
2:01.44	Sarah	Schmidt	GER-J	4.10.96	1	NC-j	Jena	2 Aug
2:01.46	Déborah	Rodríguez	URU	2.12.92	1	SAmC	Lima	14 Jun
2:01.46A	Annet	Mwanzi	KEN	21.7.87	3	WCT	Nairobi	1 Aug
2:01.56	Sarah	Brown	USA	15.10.86	3		Victoria	10 Jun
2:01.56	Rachel	Aubry	CAN	18.5.90	3		Ninove	1 Aug
2:01.59	Chaltu	Shume	ETH-J	.96	3	AfG	Brazzaville	14 Sep
2:01.60	Kokebe	Tesfaye	ETH-J	5.5.97	1		Kessel-Lo	8 Aug
	(80)							
2:01.60	Hanna	Klein	GER	6.4.93	1		Waiblingen	8 Aug
2:01.61	Chrishuna	Williams	USA	31.3.93	1	Jordan	Stanford	2 May
2:01.61	Svetlana	Uloga	RUS	23.11.86	1	NCp	Yerino	10 Jul
2:01.61	Tatyana	Markelova	RUS	19.12.88	2h2	NC	Cheboksary	3 Aug
2:01.62	Shannon	Leinert	USA	30.6.87	3		St. Louis	4 Jun

Mark	Name		Nat	Born	Pos	Meet	Venue	Date
2:01.69	Trine	Mjåland	NOR	30.6.90	2		Oordegem	30 Ma
2:01.72	Élian	Périz	ESP	1.4.84	8		Madrid	11 Ju
2:01.77	Katie	Snowden	GBR	9.3.94	1		Manchester	30 Ma
2:01.82	Alexandra	Bell	GBR	4.11.92	3		Dublin (S)	24 Ju
2:01.87	Geena (90)	Lara	USA	18.1.87	2rB		Los Angeles (ER)	14 Ma
2:01.87	Annie	Leblanc	CAN	29.4.92	6		Portland	14 Ju
2:01.92	Shelby	Houlihan	USA	8.2.93	1	SunAngel	Tempe	11 Ap
2:01.93	Kendra	Chambers	USA	11.9.90	1		Austin	11 Ap
2:01.93	Natalija	Piliusina	LTU	22.10.90	3	Jordan	Stanford	2 Ma
2:01.93	Lenka	Masná	CZE	22.4.85	2	ET-1	Iráklio	20 Ju
2:01.97	Winnie	Nanyondo	UGA	23.8.93	3		Kortrijk	11 Ju
2:01.97	Emily	Dudgeon	GBR	3.3.93	4		Dublin (S)	24 Ju
2:02.02	Lauren	Johnson	USA	4.5.87	2		Portland	8 Au
2:02.05	Violah	Lagat	KEN	13.3.89	7		Tomblaine	1 Ju
2:02.06	Anastasiya (100)	Kalina	RUS	16.2.94	1	NC-23	Saransk	16 Ju

2:02.06A	Sylivia	Chesebe	KEN	17.5.87	1 Aug
2:02.07	Anna	Shchagina	RUS	7.12.91	10 Jul
2:02.08	Kimarra	McDonald	JAM	14.8.87	27 Jun
2:02.12	Yusneysi	Santiusti	CUB	24.12.84	23 May
2:02.13	Lovisa	Lindh	SWE	9.7.91	18 Jul
2:02.13A	Gabriela	Medina	MEX	3.3.85	9 Aug
2:02.17	Brittany	McGowan	AUS	24.4.91	14 May
2:02.17	Erin	Donohue	USA	8.5.83	26 May
2:02.24	Natalya	Grigoryeva	RUS	8.12.91	29 May
2:02.25	Rachel	François	CAN	14.11.92	10 Jun
2:02.25	Manal	Bahraoui	BRN	6.1.94	1 Aug
2:02.26	Olicia	Williams	USA	26.2.94	2 May
2:02.32	Annette	Melcher	USA	.92	6 Jun
2:02.33	Katy	Brown	GBR	18.11.93	30 May
2:02.34	Samantha	Murphy	CAN	18.3.92	8 Aug
2:02.35	Marilyn	Okoro	GBR	23.9.84	18 Apr
2:02.35	Natalya	Peryakova	RUS	4.3.83	29 May
2:02.36	Natalia	Evangelidou	CYP	10.3.91	23 May
2:02.36	Luiza	Gega	ALB	5.11.88	21 Jun
2:02.36	Marina	Pospelova	RUS	23.7.90	3 Aug
2:02.38A	Winny	Chebet	KEN	20.12.90	1 Aug
2:02.4 mx	Paulina	Mikiewicz	POL	13.7.92	30 Aug
2:02.41	Victoria	Sauleda	ESP	28.8.92	30 May
2:02.43	Kenyetta	Iyevbele	USA	22.8.92	26 Jun
2:02.44	Svetlana	Rogozina	RUS	26.12.92	6 Jun
2:02.46mx	Jessica	Judd	GBR	7.1.95	15 Jul
2:02.49	Karine	Belleau-Béliveau	CAN	29.12.83	14 May
2:02.49	Yekaterina	Kupina	RUS	2.2.86	29 May
2:02.50	Anastasiya	Komarova	AZE	23.3.93	21 Jun
2:02.52	Selma	Kajan	AUS	30.7.91	14 Jun
2:02.53	Anna	Silvander	SWE	22.6.93	11 Jul
2:02.54	Clarisse	Moh	FRA	6.12.86	1 Jul
2:02.55	Renée	Eykens	BEL-J	8.6.96	28 Jun
2:02.59	Olena	Sidorska	UKR	30.7.94	9 Jun
2:02.63	Kaela	Edwards	USA	8.12.93	2 May
2:02.63	Kerri	Gallagher	USA	31.5.89	11 Jul
2:02.64	Kseniya	Savina	RUS	4.6.89	23 May
2:02.67	Alethia	Marrero	PUR	13.5.95	29 May
2:02.74	Hedda	Hynne	NOR	13.3.90	22 Aug
2:02.75	Tola	Kore	ETH-J	.97	8 Jul
2:02.79	Mantegbosh	Melese	ETH	20.1.88	5 Jun
2:02.79	Liga	Velvere	LAT	10.2.90	14 Jun
2:02.82A	Sheila	Chesang	KEN	.86	1 Aug
2:02.84	Dina	Aleksandrova	RUS	9.8.92	3 Aug
2:02.85	Amina	Bakhit	SUD	14.11.90	14 Sep
2:02.87	Yngvild	Elvemo	NOR	28.5.90	22 Aug
2:02.88	Lindsey	Butterworth	CAN	27.9.92	23 May
2:02.90	Sasha	Gollish	CAN	27.12.81	10 Jun
2:02.92	Claudia	Francis	USA	14.11.93	29 May

2:02.95	Natalya	Danilova	RUS	28.8.91	29 Ma
2:02.96	Susan	Kuijken	NED	8.7.86	27 Ma
2:02.97	Lisa	Blamèble	FRA	15.9.92	1 Au
2:02.98	Ciara	Mageean	IRL	12.3.92	9 Au
2:02.99	Yelena	Arzhakova	RUS	8.9.89	3 Au
2:03.00	Mirela	Lavric	ROU	17.2.91	27 Ju
2:03.00	Anna	Musina	RUS	3.11.84	3 Au
2:03.01	Mihaela	Nunu	ROU	10.5.89	23 Ma
2:03.01	Gilda	Casanova	CUB	19.12.95	30 Ma
2:03.01	Selah	Busienei	KEN	27.12.91	5 Oc
2:03.04	Katarzyna	Broniatowska	POL	22.2.90	27 Ju
2:03.08		Zhao Jing	CHN	9.7.88	26 Au
2:03.09	Anna	Kupayeva	RUS	24.11.90	3 Au
2:03.11	Ilona	Usovich	BLR	14.11.82	23 Ma
2:03.11	Oksana	Spasovkhodskaya	RUS	4.9.84	10 Ju
2:03.12	Morgan	Schuetz	USA	8.1.94	2 Ma
2:03.13	Brooke	Feldmeier	USA-J	26.1.96	29 Ma
2:03.13	Heather	Kampf	USA	19.1.87	7 Ju
2:03.22	Leah	Barrow	GBR	21.1.93	8 Au
2:03.23	Olesya	Didovodyuk	UKR	25.7.90	1 Au
2:03.26	Sara	Souhi	MAR-J	15.5.96	5 Ju
2:03.26A	Dorcus	Ajok	UGA	12.7.94	7 Ju
2:03.27	Olga	Rulevich	BLR	7.5.89	6 Ju
2:03.28	Ellie	Staker	USA	11.5.92	10 Ju
2:03.28	Syntia	Ellward	POL	3.3.93	14 Ju
2:03.30	Inessa	Gusarova	RUS	29.10.95	16 Ju
2:03.32	Molly	Long	GBR-J	15.12.96	30 Ma
2:03.34	Bethany	Praska	USA	10.6.89	10 Ju
2:03.36	Maureen	Koster	NED	3.7.92	20 Ju
2:03.36	Eléni	Filándra	GRE	12.1.84	20 Ju
2:03.36A	Fridah	Mwikali	KEN	.88	1 Au
2:03.37	Dominique	Jackson	USA	10.6.89	14 Ju
2:03.38	Alena	Shukhtuyeva	RUS	7.12.93	16 Ju
2:03.40	Marta	Zenoni	ITA-Y	9.3.99	4 Ju
2:03.40	Yuliya	Korol	BLR	26.6.91	10 J
2:03.43	Heather	Wilson	USA	13.6.90	26 Ma
2:03.44	Malin	Edland	NOR-Y	31.3.99	11 Ju
2:03.45	Karin	Storbacka	FIN	27.4.87	22 Au
2:03.46	Alena	Glazkova	RUS	6.5.88	15 Ju
2:03.47	Stephanie	Brown	USA	29.7.91	11 Ap
2:03.47	Stephanie	Charnigo	USA	25.7.88	26 Ma
2:03.47	Carolin	Walter	GER	29.2.88	26 J
2:03.52	Abbey	de la Motte	AUS	24.2.94	14 Ma
2:03.52	Megan	Malasarte	USA	1.8.92	4 Ju
2:03.53	Isabel	Macías	ESP	11.8.84	11 Ju
2:03.54A	Samantha	Watson	USA-Y	10.11.99	19 Ju
2:03.57	Bekka	Simko	USA	31.8.91	29 Ma
2:03.57	Fantu	Magiso	ETH	9.6.92	10 Ju
2:03.59	Laura (198)	Weightman	GBR	1.7.91	27 Ju

Indoors

1:59.21	Jennifer	Meadows	GBR	17.4.81	1		Wien	31 Ja
2:01.71	Ayvika	Malanova	RUS	28.11.92	1		Moskva	28 Ja

2:02.22	Mariya	Nikolayeva ¶	RUS	14.4.91	17 Feb
2:02.66	Stephanie	Charnigo	USA	25.7.88	31 Jan
2:02.71	Irina	Maracheva	RUS	29.9.84	18 Jan
2:02.75	Mary	Cain	USA-J	3.5.96	31 Jan
2:02.84	Yekaterina	Brodovaya	RUS	28.6.91	17 Feb
2:02.91	Jenna	Westaway	CAN	19.6.94	14 Feb
2:02.93	Stina	Troest	DEN	17.1.94	21 Feb

2:02.94	Syntia	Ellward	POL	3.3.93	22 Fe
2:02.99	Oksana	Spasovkhodskaya	RUS	4.9.84	28 Ja
2:03.12	Renata	Plis	POL	5.2.85	3 Fe
2:03.17	Bethany	Praska	USA	10.6.89	14 Fe
2:03.27	Axumawit	Embaye	ETH	18.10.94	25 Fe
2:03.48	Olesya	Muratova	RUS	25.10.92	18 Ja
2:03.60	Zuzana	Hejnová	CZE	19.12.86	6 Fe

Drugs disqualification

2:03.29	Mariya	Nikolayeva ¶	RUS	14.4.91	(3s1)	WUG	Gwangju	9 J

Mark		Name	Nat	Born	Pos	Meet	Venue	Date

JUNIORS

See main list for top 7 juniors. 10 performances by 5 women to 2:01.55. Additional mark and further juniors:

Hinriksdóttir	2:01.15	2	Ninove	1 Aug	2:01.56i	2h1	EI	Prahe (O2)	6 Mar
	2:01.50	5	Oordegem	23 May					
Efraimson	2:01.13	1	Portland	17 May	2:01.33	2		Kortrijk	11 Jul
Alemu	2:01.51	1	Eindhoven	27 Jun					

Mark		Name	Nat	Born	Pos	Meet	Venue	Date
2:02.55	Renée	Eykens	BEL	8.6.96	1		Mannheim	28 Jun
2:02.75	Tola	Kore	ETH	.97	4		Barcelona	8 Jul
2:03.13	Brooke	Feldmeier (10)	USA	26.1.96	3q3	NCAA-E	Jacksonville	29 May
2:03.67A	Gadese	Ejara	ETH-Y	7.7.98	2	WY	Cali	19 Jul
2:03.26	Sara	Souhi	MAR	15.5.96	6		Montbéliard	5 Jun
2:03.32	Molly	Long	GBR	15.12.96	4		Manchester	30 May
2:03.40	Marta	Zenoni	ITA-Y	9.3.99	1J	GGala	Roma	4 Jun
2:03.44	Malin	Edland	NOR-Y	31.3.99	3	Bisl	Oslo	11 Jun
2:03.54A	Samantha	Watson	USA-Y	10.11.99	1	WY	Cali	19 Jul
2:04.00	Olivia	Baker	USA	12.6.96	3		Los Angeles (Ww)	17 May
2:04.00	Chrsitina	Aragon	USA	17.6.97	1		Shoreline	20 Jun
2:04.23	Hannah	Long	USA	4.4.97	5		St. Louis	4 Jun
2:04.53	Yekaterina	Alekseyeva (20)	RUS-Y	22.5.98	1	NC-j	Cheboksary	25 Jun
2:02.75i	Mary	Cain	USA-J	3.5.96	5		New York (Arm)	31 Jan

1000 METRES

Mark		Name	Nat	Born	Pos	Meet	Venue	Date
2:34.68	Sifan	Hassan	NED	.93	1	FBK	Hengelo	24 May
2:35.57	Joanna	Józwik	POL	30.1.91	2	FBK	Hengelo	24 May
2:35.6+	Genzebe	Dibaba	ETH	8.2.91	1	in 1500m	Monaco	17 Jul
2:36.13	Jennifer	Meadows	GBR	17.4.81	3	FBK	Hengelo	24 May
2:36.50	Angelika	Cichocka	POL	15.3.88	4	FBK	Hengelo	24 May
2:36.63	Aníta	Hinriksdóttir	ISL-J	13.1.96	5	FBK	Hengelo	24 May
2:37.28	Angela	Petty	NZL	16.8.91	1		Chiba	15 Aug
2:37.42	Erin	Donohue	USA	8.5.83	1	adidas	New York	13 Jun
2:37.43	Axumawit	Embaye	ETH	18.10.94	1		Göteborg	5 Sep
2:37.53	Treniere	Moser	USA	27.10.81	2	adidas	New York	13 Jun
2:37.73	Besu	Sado	ETH-J	12.1.96	6	FBK	Hengelo	24 May
2:37.89	Dana	Mecke	USA	20.9.87	3	adidas	New York	13 Jun
2:38.57	Mary	Cain	USA-J	3.5.96	4	adidas	New York	13 Jun

Mark	Name		Nat	Born	Date	Mark	Name		Nat	Born	Date
2:38.82	Susan	Kuijken	NED	8.7.86	24 May	2:39.86	Laura	Crowe	IRL	5.9.87	24 May
2:39.52	Jessica	Judd	GBR	7.1.95	24 May	2:40.00	Svetlana	Uloga	RUS	23.11.86	5 Sep
2:39.69	Florina	Pierdevara	ROU	29.3.90	9 May	2:40.17	Lovisa	Lindh	SWE	9.7.91	5 Sep
						2:40.52	Mihaela	Nunu	ROU	10.5.89	9 May

Indoors

Mark		Name	Nat	Born	Pos	Meet	Venue	Date
2:38.25i	Mary	Cain	USA-J	3.5.96	2		Boston	7 Feb

Mark	Name		Nat	Born	Date	Mark	Name		Nat	Born	Date
2:39.16i	Molly	Ludlow	USA	4.8.87	7 Feb	2:40.25i	Shannon	Rowbury	USA	19.9.84	17 Jan
2:39.64i	Stephanie	Brown	USA	29.7.91	7 Feb	2:40.36i	Chanelle	Price	USA	22.8.90	1 Mar
2:39.66i	Sanne	Verstegen	NED	10.11.85	7 Feb	2:40.42i	Lauren	Wallace	USA	19.12.88	1 Mar
2:39.70i	Sasha	Gollish	CAN	27.12.81	13 Feb	2:40.62i	Yekaterina	Poistogova	RUS	1.3.91	7 Jan
2:39.72i	Yevgeniya	Zinurova	RUS	16.11.82	25 Jan	2:40.79i	Charlene	Lipsey	USA	16.7.91	28 Feb
2:39.99i	Morgan	Uceny	USA	10.3.85	7 Feb	2:40.91i	Anastasiya	Bazdyreva	RUS	6.3.92	7 Jan

1500 METRES

Mark		Name	Nat	Born	Pos	Meet	Venue	Date
3:50.07	Genzebe	Dibaba	ETH	8.2.91	1	Herc	Monaco	17 Jul
3:54.11		Dibaba			1		Barcelona	8 Jul
3:56.05	Sifan	Hassan	NED	.93	2	Herc	Monaco	17 Jul
3:56.29	Shannon	Rowbury	USA	19.9.84	3	Herc	Monaco	17 Jul
3:56.33mx		Hassan			1		Langenthal	12 Aug
3:57.30	Jennifer	Simpson	USA	23.8.86	4	Herc	Monaco	17 Jul
3:58.66	Laura	Muir	GBR	9.5.93	5	Herc	Monaco	17 Jul
3:59.12+		Hassan			1	in 1M	Bruxelles	11 Sep
3:59.31		Simpson			1	GGala	Roma	4 Jun
3:59.32+	Faith	Kipyegon	KEN	10.1.94	2	in 1M	Bruxelles	11 Sep
3:59.68		Hassan			2	GGala	Roma	4 Jun
3:59.76	Dawit	Seyaum	ETH-J	27.7.96	3	GGala	Roma	4 Jun
3:59.79	Maureen	Koster	NED	3.7.92	6	Herc	Monaco	17 Jul
4:00.30		Hassan			1	DL	Birmingham	7 Jun
4:00.39		Muir			1	Bisl	Oslo	11 Jun
4:00.61		Muir			4	GGala	Roma	4 Jun
4:00.65	Besu	Sado	ETH-J	12.1.96	7	Herc	Monaco	17 Jul
4:00.94		Kipyegon			2	Bisl	Oslo	11 Jun
4:00.96		Seyaum			1	DL	Doha	15 May
4:00.98		Simpson			1	Pre	Eugene	30 May
4:01.26	Mercy	Cherono (10)	KEN	7.5.91	2	Pre	Eugene	30 May
4:01.40		Hassan			2	DL	Doha	15 May

Mark	Name		Nat	Born	Pos	Meet	Venue	Date
4:01.41	Viola	Kibiwot	KEN	22.12.83	5	GGala	Roma	4 Jun
4:01.46	Anna	Shchagina	RUS	7.12.91	8	Herc	Monaco	17 Jul
4:01.65		Hassan			3	Pre	Eugene	30 May
4:01.85A		Kipyegon			1	WCT	Nairobi	1 Aug
4:01.86	Senbere	Teferi	ETH	3.5.95	3	DL	Doha	15 May
4:01.97	Abeba	Aregawi	SWE	5.7.90	2	DL	Birmingham	7 Jun
4:02.21A		Cherono			2	WCT	Nairobi	1 Aug
4:02.28		Rowbury			4	Pre	Eugene	1 Aug
	(30/14)							
4:02.63	Luiza	Gega	ALB	5.11.88	4	DL	Doha	15 May
4:02.94	Rabab	Arrafi	MAR	12.1.91	7	GGala	Roma	4 Jun
4:03.00	Axumawit	Embaye	ETH	18.10.94	5	Pre	Eugene	30 May
4:03.06	Angelika	Cichocka	POL	15.3.88	9	GGala	Roma	4 Jun
4:03.09	Gudaf	Tsegay	ETH-J	23.1.97	2		Kawasaki	10 May
4:03.09	Nancy	Chepkwemoi	KEN	8.10.93	1		Watford	27 Jun
	(20)							
4:03.20	Sarah	Brown	USA	15.10.86	6	Pre	Eugene	30 May
4:03.28	Beatrice	Chepkoech	KEN	6.7.91	1	NA	Heusden-Zolder	18 Jul
4:03.39	Alexa	Efraimson	USA-J	20.2.97	7	Pre	Eugene	30 May
4:03.56	Kerri	Gallagher	USA	31.5.89	1	Missoni	Lignano	7 Jul
4:03.81	Katie	Mackey	USA	12.11.87	8	Pre	Eugene	30 May
4:04.10	Violah	Lagat	KEN	13.3.89	2	Missoni	Lignano	7 Jul
4:04.17	Lauren	Johnson	USA	4.5.87	2	NA	Heusden-Zolder	18 Jul
4:04.26	Treniere	Moser	USA	27.10.81	9	Pre	Eugene	30 May
4:04.26	Gabe	Grunewald	USA	25.6.86	5	Bisl	Oslo	11 Jun
4:04.26	Sofia	Ennaoui	POL	30.8.95	9	Herc	Monaco	17 Jul
	(30)							
4:04.48	Tatyana	Tomashova	RUS	1.7.75	1	NC	Cheboksary	5 Aug
4:04.49	Malika	Akkaoui	MAR	25.12.87	3		Beijing	20 May
4:04.50	Heather	Kampf	USA	19.1.87	12	GGala	Roma	4 Jun
4:04.66	Siham	Hilali	MAR	2.5.86	5		Beijing	20 May
4:04.70	Laura	Weightman	GBR	1.7.91	6	Bisl	Oslo	11 Jun
4:04.74	Renata	Plis	POL	5.2.85	7	Bisl	Oslo	11 Jun
4:04.77	Amela	Terzic	SRB	2.1.93	1	EU23	Tallinn	12 Jul
4:05.03	Nikki	Hamblin	NZL	20.5.88	6		Beijing	20 May
4:05.10	Emma	Coburn	USA	19.10.90	11	Pre	Eugene	30 May
4:05.24	Fiona	Benson	CAN	25.5.92	2		Rieti	13 Sep
	(40)							
4:05.31	Caroline	Chepkemoi	KEN	1.3.93	4	NA	Heusden-Zolder	18 Jul
4:05.37	Mimi	Belete	BRN	9.6.88	3		Rieti	13 Sep
4:05.39	Stephanie	Garcia	USA	3.5.88	1		Greenville	30 May
4:05.41	Betlhem	Desalegn	UAE	13.11.91	5	NA	Heusden-Zolder	18 Jul
4:05.52	Aisha	Praught	USA/JAM	14.12.89	2		Kawasaki	10 May
4:05.56	Melissa	Duncan	AUS	30.1.90	9	Bisl	Oslo	11 Jun
4:05.58	Tigist	Gashaw	BRN-J	25.12.96	3	Gyulai	Székesfehérvár	7 Jul
4:05.87	Yekaterina	Sharmina	RUS	6.8.86	2	NC	Cheboksary	5 Aug
4:05.89	Nicole	Tully	USA	30.10.86	6	NA	Heusden-Zolder	18 Jul
4:06.29	Nataliya	Pryshchepa	UKR	11.9.94	3	EU23	Tallinn	12 Jul
	(50)							
4:06.30	Zoe	Buckman	AUS	21.12.88	12	Pre	Eugene	30 May
4:06.36	Ann	Mwangi	KEN	8.12.88	3		Kawasaki	10 May
4:06.37	Susan	Kuijken	NED	8.7.86	7		Beijing	20 May
4:06.44	Nicole	Sifuentes	CAN	30.6.86	1		Atlanta	1 Aug
4:06.49	Ciara	Mageean	IRL	12.3.92	5		Rieti	13 Sep
4:06.55	Yelena	Korobkina	RUS	25.11.90	5	Gyulai	Székesfehérvár	7 Jul
4:06.81	Margherita	Magnani	ITA	26.2.87	7	NA	Heusden-Zolder	18 Jul
4:06.90	Rachel	Schneider	USA	18.7.91	8	NA	Heusden-Zolder	18 Jul
4:06.97	Sheila	Reid	CAN	2.8.89	1	Città	Padova	6 Sep
4:07.08	Sasha	Gollish	CAN	27.12.81	2		London ON	21 Jun
	(60)							
4:07.37	Anastasiya	Kalina	RUS	16.2.94	1		Sochi	28 May
4:07.44	Kokebe	Tesfaye	ETH-J	5.5.97	8		Beijing	20 May
4:07.44	Gabriela	Stafford	CAN	13.9.95	3		London ON	21 Jun
4:07.55	Stephanie	Brown	USA	29.7.91	2		Greenville	30 May
4:07.56	Maren	Kock	GER	22.6.90	9	NA	Heusden-Zolder	18 Jul
4:07.58	Selah	Busienei	KEN	27.12.91	1	WMilG	Mungyeong	8 Oct
4:07.75	Irene	Jelagat	KEN	10.12.88	10	Athl	Lausanne	9 Jul
4:07.95	Florina	Pierdevarâ	ROU	29.3.90	4		Lignano	7 Jul
4:08.04	Abbey	D'Agostino	USA	25.5.92	1		Waltham	13 Jun
4:08.15	Heidi	See	AUS	8.9.89	3		Greenville	30 May
	(70)							

Mark	Name		Nat	Born	Pos	Meet	Venue	Date
4:08.31	Muriel	Coneo	COL	15.3.87	10h1	WCh	Beijing	22 Aug
4:08.47	Kate	Van Buskirk	CAN	9.6.87	3		Liège (NX)	15 Jul
4:08.53	Salima Alami	El Ouali	MAR	29.12.83	5		Kawasaki	10 May
4:08.54	Angela	Petty	NZL	16.8.91	1		Leixlip	13 Jun
4:08.54	Gemeda	Feyne	ETH	28.6.92	7	Gyulai	Székesfehérvár	7 Jul
4:08.65	Dominique	Scott	RSA	24.6.92	6		Lignano	7 Jul
4:08.92	Charlene	Thomas	GBR	6.5.82	1		Oxford	18 Jul
4:08.93	Rebecca	Addison	USA	28.5.91	4		Greenville	30 May
4:09.08	Mary	Cain	USA-J	3.5.96	4		Liège (NX)	15 Jul
4:09.10	Olesya	Muratova	RUS	25.10.92	2		Sochi	28 May
	(80)							
4:09.15	Yekaterina	Sokolova	RUS	16.12.95	3		Sochi	28 May
4:09.28	Elina	Sujew	GER	2.11.90	11	NA	Heusden-Zolder	18 Jul
4:09.31	Morgan	Uceny	USA	10.3.85	8	DL	Birmingham	7 Jun
4:09.49	Melissa	Salerno	USA	22.11.86	5		Greenville	30 May
4:09.56	Rhianwedd	Price	GBR	11.8.94	1	NCAA	Eugene	13 Jun
4:09.56	Jessica	Judd	GBR	7.1.95	2		Watford	27 Jun
4:09.57	Heather	Wilson	USA	13.6.90	6		Greenville	30 May
4:09.58	Konstanze	Klosterhalfen	GER-J	18.2.97	2	NC	Nürnberg	26 Jul
4:09.62	Shelby	Houlihan	USA	8.2.93	7		Liège (NX)	15 Jul
4:09.63	Maryam	Jamal	BRN	16.9.84	1		Pfungstadt	3 Jun
	(90)							
4:09.65	Cory	McGee	USA	29.5.92	6h2	NC	Eugene	26 Jun
4:09.7A	Eunice	Sum	KEN	2.9.88	1		Nakuru	18 Apr
4:09.74	Melissa	Courtney	GBR	30.8.93	3		Watford	27 Jun
4:09.88A	Vivian	Cheruiyot	KEN	11.9.83	1	NC	Nairobi	11 Jul
4:09.91	Hanna	Klein	GER	6.4.93	3	NC	Nürnberg	26 Jul
4:09.99	Isabel	Macías	ESP	11.8.84	12	NA	Heusden-Zolder	18 Jul
4:10.0A	Virginia	Nyambura	KEN	20.7.93	1		Nairobi	21 Mar
4:10.04	Corinna	Harrer	GER	19.1.91	2		Regensburg	6 Jun
4:10.17	Madeleine	Murray	GBR	19.10.93	2		Solihull	22 Aug
4:10.24	Faye	Fullerton	GBR	31.5.84	4		Watford	27 Jun
	(100)							

Mark	Name		Nat	Born	Date
4:10.41	Linden	Hall	AUS	29.6.91	18 Jul
4:10.45	Katarzyna	Broniatowska	POL	22.2.90	6 Jun
4:10.68	Juliana Paula	dos Santos	BRA	12.6.83	6 Jun
4:10.78	Marina	Pospelova	RUS	23.7.90	28 May
4:10.78	Hilary	Stellingwerff	CAN	7.8.81	8 Jun
4:10.83	Trychelle	Kingdom	AUS	13.9.90	28 Mar
4:10.90	Stephanie	Twell	GBR	17.8.89	7 Jun
4:10.98	Marta	Pen Freitas	POR	31.7.93	12 Jul
4:10.98	Louise	Carton	BEL	16.4.94	1 Aug
4:11.00	Hannah	Fields	USA	4.2.93	14 Jun
4:11.03	Gesa-Felicitas	Krause	GER	3.8.92	15 Jul
4:11.04	Leah	O'Connor	USA	30.8.92	1 May
4:11.06	Sara	Sutherland	USA	31.1.92	14 Jun
4:11.18	Karolina	Pólrola	POL	4.4.89	6 Jun
4:11.19	Linn	Nilsson	SWE	15.10.90	18 Jul
4:11.21	Karoline	Bjerkeli Grøvdal	NOR	14.6.90	13 Sep
4:11.23A	Winfredah	Nzisa	KEN-J	30.5.97	1 Aug
4:11.46A	Judy	Kiyeng	KEN	.94	11 Jul
4:11.61	Colleen	Quigley	USA	20.11.92	17 Apr
4:11.61	Sofie	Van Accom	BEL	7.6.89	18 Jul
4:11.62	Phoebe	Wright	USA	30.8.88	14 Jun
4:11.63	Monika	Halasa	POL	5.4.92	6 Jun
4:11.66	Perine	Nengampi	KEN	1.1.89	18 Jul
4:11.71	Rebecca	Tracy	USA	20.2.91	30 May
4:11.74	Tamara	Tverdostup	UKR	17.7.79	25 Jun
4:11.80	Darya	Borisevich	BLR	6.4.90	9 Aug
4:11.83	Anastasiya	Tkachuk	UKR	20.4.93	8 Sep
4:11.95	Sally	Kipyego	KEN	19.12.85	14 May
4:12.03	Diana	Sujew	GER	2.11.90	25 Jun
4:12.08	Hannah	England	GBR	6.3.87	25 Jun
4:12.09	Katelyn	Simpson	AUS	28.1.94	28 Mar
4:12.10	Rosie	Clarke	GBR	17.11.91	18 Apr
4:12.20	Bobby	Clay	GBR-J	19.5.97	30 May
4:12.32	Carise	Thompson	CAN	7.3.92	1 Aug
4:12.38	Lauren	Paquette	USA	27.6.86	10 Jun
4:12.41	Claudia	Bobocea	ROU	11.6.92	3 Jun
4:12.42	Solange Andreia	Pereira	ESP	12.12.89	8 Jul
4:12.49	Jennifer	Wenth	AUT	24.7.91	6 Jun
4:12.49	Julia	Cooke	GBR	9.9.88	27 Jun
4:12.50	Manon	Kruiver	NED	3.1.88	18 Jul
4:12.52	Kristiina	Mäki	CZE	22.9.91	26 May
4:12.54	Brittany	McGowan	AUS	24.4.91	7 Feb
4:12.59	Racheal	Bamford	GBR	4.8.89	22 Aug
4:12.79	Kerry	O'Flaherty	IRL	15.7.81	13 Jun
4:12.91	Danuta	Urbanik	POL	24.12.89	8 Sep
4:12.92A	Bedatu	Hirpa	ETH-Y	28.4.99	18 Jul
4:12.93	Stephanie	Charnigo	USA	25.7.88	2 May
4:12.99	Sarah	Inglis	GBR	28.8.91	8 Jun
4:13.06	Diana	Mezuliáníková	CZE	10.4.92	29 May
4:13.13	Katrina	Coogan	USA	15.11.93	2 May
4:13.16	Lianne	Farber	USA	12.6.92	18 Apr
4:13.23	Alison	Leonard	GBR	17.3.90	17 May
4:13.24	Jenna	Hill	GBR	16.10.85	27 Jun
4:13.26	Stephanie	Schappert	USA	25.4.93	30 May
4:13.29	Flávia	de Lima	BRA	1.7.93	17 May
4:13.30	Madeline	Heiner	AUS	5.3.88	7 Feb
4:13.30	Sandra	Eriksson	FIN	4.6.89	8 Aug
4:13.33	Amanda	Eccleston	USA	18.6.90	26 Jun
4:13.34	Dana	Mecke	USA	20.9.87	14 May
4:13.34	Marta	Pérez	ESP	19.4.93	18 Jul
4:13.35A	Dalilah	Abdelkadir Gosa	BRN-Y	27.6.98	18 Jul
4:13.43	Danielle	Aragon	USA	1.7.94	18 Apr
4:13.47	Lauren	Wallace	USA	19.12.88	14 Jun
4:13.49	Angel	Piccirillo	USA	8.1.94	2 May
4:13.64	Svetlana	Uloga	RUS	23.11.86	5 Aug
4:13.69	Agata	Strausa	LAT	2.12.89	6 Jun
4:13.70	Geena	Lara	USA	18.1.87	8 May
4:13.72A	Nelly	Ngeiywo	KEN	10.1.92	1 Aug
4:13.76	Annie	Lehardy	USA	18.10.92	18 Apr
4:13.78	Amanda	Mergaert	USA	4.9.91	14 Jun
4:13.80	Camille	Buscomb	NZL	11.7.90	8 Mar
4:13.8A	Janeth	Chepngetich	KEN-Y	23.7.98	1 Apr
4:13.83	Stephanie	Aldea	CAN	2.1.90	18 Apr
4:13.84	Kristine Eikrem	Engeset	NOR	15.11.88	22 Aug
4:13.92	Bridey	Delaney	AUS	16.7.89	21 Mar
4:13.99	Yuliya	Vasilyeva	RUS	23.3.87	5 Aug
	(176)				

Short Course: 1493m Marseille 6 Jun: 3. Gemeda Feyne ETH 4:06.62

Indoors

Mark	Name		Nat	Born	Pos	Meet	Venue	Date
4:00.46		Hassan			1	XLG	Stockholm	19 Feb
4:02.92	Axumawit	Embaye	ETH	18.10.94	2		Karlsruhe	31 Jan

WOMEN 2015

Mark	Name		Nat	Born	Pos	Meet	Venue	Date
4:06.42	Meraf	Bahta	SWE	24.6.89	3	XL-Galan	Stockholm	19 Feb
4:07.93+	Jordan	Hasay	USA	21.9.91	2	Mill	New York (Arm)	14 Feb
4:08.87	Federica	Del Buono	ITA	12.12.94	1	NC-23	Ancona	7 Feb
4:09.22	Katarzyna	Broniatowska	POL	22.2.90	2		Spala	7 Feb

Mark	Name		Nat	Born	Date	Mark	Name		Nat	Born	Date
4:10.68+	Stephanie	Charnigo	USA	25.7.88	14 Feb	4:13.20	Giulia	Viola	ITA	24.4.91	21 Feb
4:11.89	Sandra	Eriksson	FIN	4.6.89	19 Feb	4:13.91+	Ashley	Higginson	USA	17.3.89	24 Jan

Drugs disqualification

Mark	Name		Nat	Born	Pos	Meet	Venue	Date
4:01.95	Anna	Mishchenko ¶	UKR	25.8.83	(4)	DL	Doha	15 May

JUNIORS

See main list for top 8 juniors. 11 performances by 5 women to 4:05.6. Additional marks and further juniors:

Name	Mark	Pos	Meet	Venue	Date	Mark	Pos	Meet	Venue	Date
Seyaum 2+	4:02.90	3	Bisl	Oslo	11 Jun					
Tsegay	4:04.16	11	GGala	Roma	4 Jun	4:05.29	5	Athl	Lausanne	9 Jul
	4:05.17	1		Rieti	13 Sep					
Sado	4:05.39	1h1	WCh	Beijing	22 Aug					

Mark	Name		Nat	Born	Pos	Meet	Venue	Date
4:11.23A	Winfredah	Nzisa	KEN	30.5.97	7	WCT	Nairobi	1 Aug
4:12.20	Bobby	Clay (10)	GBR	19.5.97	1		Manchester	30 May
4:12.92A	Bedatu	Hirpa	ETH-Y	28.4.99	1	WY	Cali	18 Jul
4:13.35A	Dalilah Abdelkadir	Gosa	BRN-Y	27.6.98	2	WY	Cali	18 Jul
4:13.8A	Janeth	Chepngetich	KEN-Y	23.7.98	1		Nairobi	1 Apr
4:14.05	Elise	Cranny	USA	8.5.96	4	Pac12	Los Angeles (Ww)	17 May
4:14.19	Rosa	Flanahan	NZL	28.2.96	3	NC	Wellington	8 Mar
4:14.50	Marta	Zenoni	ITA-Y	9.3.99	1	NC-j	Milano	21 Jun
4:14.66	Lina Kalstruip	Schulz	DEN	18.7.96	2		Mannheim	27 Jun
4:14.67	Habitam	Alemu	ETH	9.7.97	1		Montbéliard	5 Jun
4:15.0A	Ivine	Chepkemoi	KEN	20.8.97	1		Nairobi	18 Feb
4:15.02	Sintayehu	Lewetegn (20)	ETH	.96	2		Montbéliard	5 Jun

1 MILE

Mark	Name		Nat	Born	Pos	Meet	Venue	Date
4:16.71	Faith	Kipyegon	KEN	10.1.94	1	VD	Bruxelles	11 Sep
4:18.20	Sifan	Hassan	NED	1.1.93	2	VD	Bruxelles	11 Sep
4:22.10	Shannon	Rowbury	USA	19.9.84	3	VD	Bruxelles	11 Sep
4:22.18	Jennifer	Simpson	USA	23.8.86	4	VD	Bruxelles	11 Sep
4:22.67	Mercy	Cherono	KEN	7.5.91	5	VD	Bruxelles	11 Sep
4:23.07	Abeba	Aregawi	SWE	5.7.90	6	VD	Bruxelles	11 Sep
4:23.50	Rabab	Arrafi	MAR	12.1.91	7	VD	Bruxelles	11 Sep
	(7/7)							
4:24.31	Viola	Kibiwot	KEN	22.12.83	8	VD	Bruxelles	11 Sep
4:25.32	Renata	Plis	POL	5.2.85	9	VD	Bruxelles	11 Sep
4:25.79	Fiona	Benson	CAN	25.5.92	1		Portland	8 Aug
4:26.84	Axumawit	Embaye	ETH	18.10.94	10	VD	Bruxelles	11 Sep
4:27.32	Sofia	Ennaoui	POL	30.8.95	11	VD	Bruxelles	11 Sep
4:28.66	Nancy	Chepkwemoi	KEN	8.10.93	12	VD	Bruxelles	11 Sep
4:28.84	Stephanie	Garcia	USA	3.5.88	1		Raleigh	7 Aug
4:29.06	Amanda	Eccleston	USA	18.6.90	2		Raleigh	7 Aug
4:29.39	Heather	Wilson	USA	13.6.90	3		Raleigh	7 Aug
4:30.43	Gabe	Grunewald	USA	25.6.86	2		Portland	8 Aug
4:30.24	Kerri	Gallagher	USA	31.5.89	2		Huntington Station	9 Sep
4:30.37	Heather	Kampf	USA	19.1.87	3		Huntington Station	9 Sep

Mark	Name		Nat	Born	Date	Mark	Name		Nat	Born	Date
4:30.64	Ciara	Mageean	IRL	12.3.92	24 Jul	4:32.1	Cory	McGee	USA	29.5.92	4 Jun
4:31.04	Rachel	Schneider	USA	18.7.91	13 Aug	4:32.32	Ashley	Higginson	USA	17.3.89	13 Aug
4:31.4	Nicole	Tully	USA	30.10.86	4 Jun	4:32.39	Genevieve	LaCaze	AUS	4.8.89	24 Jul
4:31.4	Hannah	Fields	USA	4.2.93	4 Jun	4:32.4	Emily	Lipari	USA	19.11.92	4 Jun
4:31.79	Shelby	Houlihan	USA	8.2.93	24 Jul	4:32.7	Dana	Mecke	USA	20.9.87	4 Jun
4:31.8	Rachel	Schneider	USA	18.7.91	4 Jun	4:32.8	Gabriela	Stafford	CAN	13.9.95	4 Jun
4:31.93	Kate	Van Buskirk	CAN	9.6.87	24 Jul	4:33.43	Treniere	Moser	USA	27.10.81	9 Sep
						4:34.02	Morgan	Uceny	USA	10.3.85	7 Aug

Indoors

Mark	Name		Nat	Born	Pos	Meet	Venue	Date
4:22.66		Rowbury	USA	19.9.84	1		Winston-Salem	31 Jan
4:23.50	Axumawit	Embaye	ETH	18.10.94	1	GP	Birmingham	21 Feb
4:26.84	Gudaf	Tsegay	ETH-J	23.1.97	3	GP	Birmingham	21 Feb
4:27.18	Leah	O'Connor	USA	30.8.92	1	NCAA	Fayetteville	14 Mar
4:27.49	Treniere	Moser	USA	27.10.81	2	Mill	New York (Arm)	14 Feb
4:28.02	Stephanie	Charnigo	USA	25.7.88	3	Mill	New York (Arm)	14 Feb
4:28.27	Jordan	Hasay	USA	21.9.91	4	Mill	New York (Arm)	14 Feb
4:28.71	Shelby	Houlihan	USA	8.2.93	2	NCAA	Fayetteville	14 Mar
4:29.39	Morgan	Uceny	USA	10.3.85	5	Mill	New York (Arm)	14 Feb
4:29.67	Colleen	Quigley	USA	20.11.92	1		Boston	13 Feb
4:30.07	Heather	Kampf	USA	19.1.87	6	Mill	New York (Arm)	14 Feb

Mark	Name		Nat	Born	Date	Mark	Name		Nat	Born	Date
4:30.62	Rachel	Schneider	USA	18.7.91	13 Feb	4:31.34	Nicole	Tully	USA	30.10.86	14 Feb
4:30.70	Rebecca	Addison	USA	28.5.91	21 Feb	4:31.75	Rosie	Clarke	GBR	17.11.91	14 Ma
4:31.24	Erin	Donohue	USA	8.5.83	19 Dec	4:32.31	Ashley	Higginson	USA	17.3.89	24 Jar
4:31.31	Mary	Cain	USA-J	3.5.96	14 Feb	4:32.35	Erin	Teschuk	CAN	25.10.94	14 Ma

Mark	Name		Nat	Born	Date	Mark	Name		Nat	Born	Date
:32.36	Nicole	Sifuentes	CAN	30.6.86	21 Feb	4:32.86	Aisha	Praught	USA	14.12.89	21 Feb
:32.48	Dominique	Scott	RSA	24.6.92	24 Jan	4:33.74	Anastasiya	Kalina	RUS	16.2.94	10 Feb
:32.74	Rhianwedd	Price	GBR	11.8.94	28 Feb	4:34.28	Angel	Piccirillo	USA	8.1.94	14 Feb

2000 METRES

Mark	Name		Nat	Born	Pos	Meet	Venue	Date
:35.10+	Almaz	Ayana	ETH	21.11.91	1	in 3000	Rabat	14 Jun
:35.36+		Ayana			1	in 3000	Zürich	3 Sep
:35.5+	Genzebe	Dibaba	ETH	8.2.91	2	in 3000	Zürich	3 Sep
:36+e		Dibaba				in 5000	Eugene	30 May
:36+e	Alemitu	Haroye	ETH	9.5.95		in 5000	Eugene	30 May
:45.78	Senbere	Teferi	ETH	3.5.95	1	in 5000	Oslo	11 Jun
ndoors								
:35.46	Dawit	Seyaum	ETH-J	27.7.96	1		Boston	7 Feb
:40.35	Sally	Kipyego	KEN	19.12.85	2		Boston	7 Feb
:41.11	Emma	Coburn	USA	19.10.90	3		Boston	7 Feb
:43.82	Heidi	See	AUS	8.9.89	4		Boston	7 Feb
:43.94+	Katarzyna	Broniatowska	POL	22.2.90	1	in 5000	Stockholm	19 Feb

*lote: there will surely be further 2000m times in 3000/5000m races and 3000m times
5000m races that would qualify for world lists, but that have not been recorded*

3000 METRES

Mark	Name		Nat	Born	Pos	Meet	Venue	Date
:22.22	Almaz	Ayana	ETH	21.11.91	1		Rabat	14 Jun
:22.34		Ayana			1	WK	Zürich	3 Sep
:26.54	Genzebe	Dibaba	ETH	8.2.91	2	WK	Zürich	3 Sep
33.33+		Dibaba			1	in 5000	Eugene	30 May
:34.32	Senbere	Teferi	ETH	3.5.95	3	WK	Zürich	3 Sep
:34.43	Jennifer	Simpson	USA	23.8.86	4	WK	Zürich	3 Sep
:35.48	Mercy	Cherono	KEN	7.5.91	5	WK	Zürich	3 Sep
:36.17+		Ayana			1	in 5000	Saint-Denis	4 Jul
:36.4+		Dibaba			2	in 5000	Saint-Denis	4 Jul
:36.53+		Ayana			1	in 5000	Shanghai	17 May
36.90	Irene	Jelagat	KEN	10.12.88	1	FBK	Hengelo	24 May
	(11/6)							
:37.2+e	Viola	Kibiwot	KEN	22.12.83	2	in 5000	Shanghai	17 May
	8:41.93				8	WK	Zürich	3 Sep
:38.47	Laura	Muir	GBR	9.5.93	2	FBK	Hengelo	24 May
:38.91+	Faith	Kipyegon	KEN	10.1.94	2	Pre	Eugene	30 May
:38.91	Vivian	Cheruiyot (10)	KEN	11.9.83	6	WK	Zürich	3 Sep
39.85+	Alemitu	Haroye	ETH	9.5.95	3	Pre	Eugene	30 May
:39.92	Shannon	Rowbury	USA	19.9.84	7	WK	Zürich	3 Sep
:41.93	Viola	Kibiwot	KEN	22.12.83	8	WK	Zürich	3 Sep
:44.20	Madeline	Heiner	AUS	5.3.88	3	FBK	Hengelo	24 May
:45.93	Renata	Plis	POL	5.2.85	4	FBK	Hengelo	24 May
:46.17	Perine	Nengampi	KEN	1.1.89	5	FBK	Hengelo	24 May
:46.83	Svetlana	Kudzelich	BLR	7.5.87	6	FBK	Hengelo	24 May
47.52	Buze	Diriba	ETH	9.2.94	1	Odlozil	Praha	8 Jun
48.03	Irene	Cheptai	KEN	4.2.92	10	WK	Zürich	3 Sep
48.76	Gemeda	Feyne	ETH	28.6.92	2	Odlozil	Praha	8 Jun
	(20)							
49.04	Caroline	Chepkemoi	KEN	1.3.93	3	Odlozil	Praha	8 Jun
49.50	Jip	Vastenburg	NED	21.3.94	7	FBK	Hengelo	24 May
50.07+	Sally	Kipyego	KEN	19.12.85	7	Pre	Eugene	30 May
50.12	Salima Alami	El Ouali	MAR	29.12.83	4		Rabat	14 Jun
50.70mx	Stephanie	Twell	GBR	17.8.89	1mx		Watford	23 Apr
51.23	Alemitu	Hawi	ETH-J	14.11.96	5		Rabat	14 Jun
51.37	Jessica	O'Connell	CAN	10.2.89	6		Rabat	14 Jun
51.82	Axumawit	Embaye	ETH	18.10.94	1	Hanz	Zagreb	8 Sep
52.02	Emily	Infeld	USA	21.3.90	11	WK	Zürich	3 Sep
52.29	Ann	Mwangi	KEN	8.12.88	1		Fukuroi	14 Nov
	(30)							
52.39	Stella	Chesang	UGA-J	1.12.96	8	FBK	Hengelo	24 May
52.83	Karoline Bjerkeli	Grøvdal	NOR	14.6.90	2	Hanz	Zagreb	8 Sep
52.99	Katie	Mackey	USA	12.11.87	1	DL	Stockholm	30 Jul
53.21mx	Konstanze	Klosterhalfen	GER-J	18.2.97	1mx		Bergisch Gladbach	20 Aug
53.75	Betlhem	Desalegn	UAE	13.11.91	3	DL	Stockholm	30 Jul
53.96	Mimi	Belete	BRN	9.6.88	4	DL	Stockholm	30 Jul
54.15	Selah	Busienei	KEN	27.12.91	3	Hanz	Zagreb	8 Sep
54.27	Yelena	Korobkina	RUS	25.11.90	4	Hanz	Zagreb	8 Sep
55.19	Haftamnesh	Tesfay	ETH	28.4.94	5	DL	Stockholm	30 Jul
55.22	Tsadkan	Tesema	ETH-J	26.9.97	1		Isahara	26 Sep
55.40	Alia Mohamed	Saeed	UAE	18.5.91	2		Sollentuna	25 Jun
	(40)							

Mark	Name		Nat	Born	Pos	Meet	Venue	Date
8:55.93	Bezuayehu	Mohamed	ETH-J	4.1.96	4	Odlozil	Praha	8 Ju
8:56.29	Zoe	Buckman	AUS	21.12.88	1		Adelaide	21 Feb

Mark	Name		Nat	Born	Date
8:57.00	Dera	Dida	ETH-J	26.10.96	8 Jun
8:57.20	Amela	Terzic	SRB	2.1.93	27 May
8:57.69	Rosemary	Wanjiru	KEN	9.12.94	17 May
8:58.39	Abbey	D'Agostino	USA	25.5.92	7 Jul
8:59.12mx	Bobby	Clay	GBR-J	19.5.97	9 Sep
8:59.76	Emma	Coburn	USA	19.10.90	3 Sep
9:01.12A	Shuru	Bulo	ETH-Y	27.6.98	15 Jul
9:01.13mx	Laura	Whittle	GBR	27.6.85	11 Aug
9:01.15	Azusa	Sumi	JPN	12.8.96	17 May
9:01.23	Miho	Shimada	JPN-J	26.8.97	27 Sep
9:01.24	Helen	Ekarare	KEN-Y	3.3.99	14 Nov
9:01.67	Sara	Moreira	POR	17.10.85	20 Jun
9:02.04	Gesa-Felicitas	Krause	GER	3.8.92	24 May
9:02.08	Margherita	Magnani	ITA	26.2.87	30 Jul
9:02.53	Nancy	Chepkwemoi	KEN	8.10.93	8 Sep
9:02.55	Ingvill	Måkestad Bovim	NOR	7.8.81	25 Ju
9:02.91	Marusa	Mismas	SLO	24.10.94	8 Se
9:02.92A	Emily	Kipchumba	KEN-Y	16.2.98	15 Ju
9:02.98	Sintayehu	Lewetegn	ETH-J	9.5.96	27 Ma
9:03.26	Mariam	Waithera	KEN-J	23.12.96	26 Se
9:03.95	Paulina	Kaczynska	POL	24.7.91	5 Se
9:04.22	Eloise	Wellings	AUS	9.11.82	21 Fe
9:04.36	Dominika	Nowakowska	POL	25.1.85	18 Ju
9:04.54A	Sheila	Chelangat	KEN-Y	11.4.98	15 Ju
9:04.55	Monica	Margaret	KEN-Y	.98	6 Oc
9:04.56mx	Lauren	Deadman	GBR	27.3.84	3 Ju
9:04.64A	Letesenbet	Gidey	ETH-Y	20.3.98	15 J
9:04.64	Yuliya	Shmatenko	UKR	10.10.91	21 Ju
9:04.68mx	Maren	Kock	GER	22.6.90	20 Au
9:04.69	Yuka	Mukai	JPN-Y	10.12.98	14 No
9:04.87	Viktoriya	Pohoryelska	UKR	4.8.90	25 Ju

Indoors

Mark	Name		Nat	Born	Pos	Meet	Venue	Date
8:37.20+		Dibaba			1	in 5000	Stockholm	19 Feb
8:41.72	Sally	Kipyego	KEN	19.12.85	1	Mill	New York (Arm)	14 Fe
8:43.19	Betsy	Saina	KEN	30.6.88	2	Mill	New York (Arm)	14 Fe
8:45.05	Goytatom	Gebreselassie	ETH	15.1.95	3	Mill	New York (Arm)	14 Fe
8:46.61	Habiba	Ghribi	TUN	9.4.84	1	GP	Birmingham	21 Fe
8:47.61	Yelena	Korobkina	RUS	25.11.90	1		Karlsruhe	31 Ja
8:50.21	Jordan	Hasay	USA	21.9.91	3	GP	Birmingham	21 Fe
8:51.10	Maureen	Koster	NED	3.7.92	4	GP	Birmingham	21 Feb
8:52.57	Dominique	Scott	RSA	24.6.92	1		Seattle	14 Fe
8:52.60	Emily	Sisson	USA	12.10.91	4	Mill	New York (Arm)	14 Fe
8:53.12	Kate	Avery	GBR	10.10.91	6	Mill	New York (Arm)	14 Fe
8:53.22	Sofia	Ennaoui	POL	30.8.95	3		Karlsruhe	31 Ja
8:54.06	Sandra	Eriksson	FIN	4.6.89	5	EI	Praha (O2)	7 Ma
8:54.77	Brie	Felnagle	USA	9.12.86	2		Seattle	14 Fe
8:55.09	Ciara	Mageean	IRL	12.3.92	7	Mill	New York (Arm)	14 Fe
8:55.20	Heidi	See	AUS	8.9.89	1		Boston	13 Fe
8:56.23	Giulia	Viola	ITA	24.4.91	1	NC	Padova	22 Fe

Mark	Name		Nat	Born	Date
8:56.77mx	Liz	Costello	USA	23.2.88	3 Jan
8:56.83	Sara	Moreira	POR	17.10.85	22 Feb
8:57.86	Ashley	Higginson	USA	17.3.89	14 Feb
8:57.87	Maren	Kock	GER	22.6.90	31 Jan
8:57.96	Marusa	Mismas	SLO	24.10.94	6 Mar
8:58.51	Angela	Bizzarri	USA	15.2.88	14 Feb
8:58.84	Alla	Kulyatina	RUS	9.6.90	17 Feb
8:58.88	Kristiina	Mäki	CZE	22.9.91	31 Jan
8:58.88	Elise	Cranny	USA-J	8.5.96	14 Mar
8:59.84	Jennifer	Wenth	AUT	24.7.91	7 Mar
8:59.88	Marielle	Hall	USA	28.1.92	14 Feb
9:00.25	Gesa-Felicitas	Krause	GER	3.8.92	31 Jan
9:00.83	Yekaterina	Sokolenko	RUS	13.9.92	17 Feb
9:01.16	Katrina	Coogan	USA	15.11.93	14 Mar
9:01.19	Federica	Del Buono	ITA	12.12.94	22 Feb
9:01.25	Rachele	Schulist	USA	26.4.94	28 Feb
9:01.33	Natalya	Gorchakova	RUS	17.4.83	17 Fe
9:01.33	Charlotta	Fougberg	SWE	19.6.85	6 Ma
9:01.84	Jessica	Tonn	USA	15.2.92	14 Ma
9:02.40	Erin	Teschuk	CAN	25.10.94	14 Fe
9:02.49	Nicol	Traynor	USA	6.5.89	14 Fe
9:02.50	Rachel	Johnson	USA	30.4.93	14 Ma
9:02.69	Alexi	Pappas	USA	28.3.90	31 Ja
9:02.98	Katie	Matthews	USA	19.11.90	13 Fe
9:03.27	Aisha	Praught	USA	14.12.89	31 Ja
9:03.42	Claudia	Bobocea	ROU	11.6.92	21 Fe
9:03.71	Shelby	Houlihan	USA	8.2.93	24 Ja
9:03.97	Emelia	Gorecka	GBR	29.1.94	6 Ma
9:04.41	Özlem	Kaya	TUR	20.4.90	21 Fe
9:04.77	Sarah	Inglis	GBR	28.8.91	31 Ja

Best in women only race

Mark	Name		Nat	Born	Date
9:03.55	Stephanie	Twell	GBR	17.8.89	21 Fe

JUNIORS

See main list for top 5 juniors. 6 performances (1 indoors) by 6 women to 8:59.0. Further juniors:

Name	Mark	Pos	Meet	Venue	Date	Mark	Pos	Meet	Venue	Date
Haroye	8:43.2+	6	in 2M	Birmingham	24 Aug	8:45.93	10	DL	Doha	9 Ma
Tirop	8:57.00	8	Athl	Lausanne	3 Jul					
Teferi	8:47.94i	6	XLG	Stockholm	6 Feb	8:57.93i	1		Eaubonne	11 Fe

Mark	Name		Nat	Born	Pos	Meet	Venue	Date
8:57.00	Dera	Dida	ETH	26.10.96	5	Odlozil	Praha	8 Ju
8:59.12mx	Bobby	Clay	GBR	19.5.97	1mx		Watford	9 Se
9:01.12A	Shuru	Bulo	ETH-Y	27.6.98	1	WY	Cali	15 J
9:01.23	Miho	Shimada	JPN	26.8.97	1		Konosu	27 Se
9:01.24	Helen	Ekarare (10)	KEN-Y	3.3.99	1		Yokohama	14 No
9:02.92A	Emily	Kipchumba	KEN-Y	16.2.98	2	WY	Cali	15 J
9:02.98	Sintayehu	Lewetegn	ETH	9.5.96	2		Salzburg	27 Ma
9:03.26	Mariam	Waithera	KEN	23.12.96	1		Gifu	26 Se
9:04.54A	Sheila	Chelangat	KEN-Y	11.4.98	3	WY	Cali	15 J
9:04.55	Monica	Margaret	KEN-Y	.98	2		Wakayama	6 Oc
9:04.64A	Letesenbet	Gidey	ETH-Y	20.3.98	4	WY	Cali	15 J
9:04.69	Yuka	Mukai	JPN-Y	10.12.98	1		Hiroshima	14 No
9:05.68	Mary	Cain	USA	3.5.96	3		Cork	7 J
9:05.80	Shinobu	Koyoshigawa (20)	JPN	19.5.97	1		Hiroshima	14 Nc
8:58.88i	Elise	Cranny	USA	8.5.96	2	NCAA	Fayetteville	14 Ma

2 MILES INDOORS

Mark	Name		Nat	Born	Pos	Meet	Venue	Date
:18.35	Jennifer	Simpson	USA	23.8.86	1		Boston	7 Feb
:27.05	Sentayehu	Ejigu	ETH	21.6.85	2		Boston	7 Feb
:29.03	Buze	Diriba	ETH	9.2.94	3		Boston	7 Feb
:31.41	Goytatom	Gebreselassie	ETH	15.1.95	4		Boston	7 Feb

Mark	Name		Nat	Born	Date	Mark	Name		Nat	Born	Date
:38.28	Jordan	Hasay	USA	21.9.91	31 Jan	9:42.58	Ashley	Higginson	USA	17.3.89	31 Jan
:39.38	Nicole	Tully	USA	30.10.86	31 Jan	9:42.78	Liz	Costello	USA	23.2.88	31 Jan
:39.61	Marielle	Hall	USA	28.1.92	31 Jan	9:43.94	Shannon	Rowbury	USA	19.9.84	1 Mar

5000 METRES

Mark	Name		Nat	Born	Pos	Meet	Venue	Date
4:14.32	Almaz	Ayana	ETH	21.11.91	1	DL	Shanghai	17 May
4:15.41	Genzebe	Dibaba	ETH	8.2.91	1	DL	Saint-Denis	4 Jul
4:19.76		Dibaba			1	Pre	Eugene	30 May
4:21.29		Dibaba			1	Bisl	Oslo	11 Jun
4:21.97		Ayana			2	DL	Saint-Denis	4 Jul
4:26.83		Ayana			1	WCh	Beijing	30 Aug
4:31.95	Faith	Kipyegon	KEN	10.1.94	2	Pre	Eugene	30 May
4:34.10	Mercy	Cherono	KEN	7.5.91	3	DL	Saint-Denis	4 Jul
4:34.22	Viola	Kibiwot	KEN	22.12.83	4	DL	Saint-Denis	4 Jul
4:36.44	Senbere	Teferi	ETH	3.5.95	5	DL	Saint-Denis	4 Jul
4:38.57		Teferi			2	Bisl	Oslo	11 Jun
4:40.32		Kibiwot			2	DL	Shanghai	17 May
4:40.43		Kibiwot			3	Bisl	Oslo	11 Jun
4:40.50	Gelete	Burka	ETH	15.2.86	6	DL	Saint-Denis	4 Jul
4:41.55		Burka			4	Bisl	Oslo	11 Jun
4:41.98		Teferi			3	DL	Shanghai	17 May
4:43.28	Alemitu	Haroye	ETH	9.5.95	4	DL	Shanghai	17 May
4:44.07		Teferi			2	WCh	Beijing	30 Aug
4:44.14		Dibaba			3	WCh	Beijing	30 Aug
4:44.51		Kipyegon			7	DL	Saint-Denis	4 Jul
4:44.95		Haroye			8	DL	Saint-Denis	4 Jul
4:46.16		Kibiwot			4	WCh	Beijing	30 Aug
4:46.69	Vivian	Cheruiyot	KEN	11.9.83	3	Pre	Eugene	30 May
4:47.75	Sally	Kipyego (10)	KEN	19.12.85	4	Pre	Eugene	30 May
4:48.52		Haroye			5	Pre	Eugene	30 May
4:53.32	Irene	Cheptai	KEN	4.2.92	6	Pre	Eugene	30 May
4:54.71	Mimi	Belete	BRN	9.6.88	1	NA	Heusden-Zolder	18 Jul
4:54.81		Cherono			1	DL	London (OS)	25 Jul
4:55.49	Irene	Jelagat	KEN	10.12.88	5	DL	Shanghai	17 May
4:57.23mx	Molly	Huddle	USA	31.8.84	1mx		Waltham	13 Jun
	(30/14)							
4:57.33	Goytatom	Gebreselassie	ETH	15.1.95	2	NA	Heusden-Zolder	18 Jul
4:58.54	Magdalene	Masai	KEN	4.4.93	7	DL	Shanghai	17 May
5:00.48	Betsy	Saina	KEN	30.6.88	2	Jordan	Stanford	2 May
5:02.68	Janet	Kisa	KEN	5.3.92	6	WCh	Beijing	30 Aug
5:03.85	Abbey	D'Agostino	USA	25.5.92	3	NA	Heusden-Zolder	18 Jul
5:05.19	Belaynesh	Oljira	ETH	26.6.90	9	DL	Saint-Denis	4 Jul
	(20)							
5:05.58	Nicole	Tully	USA	30.10.86	3	Jordan	Stanford	2 May
5:06.44	Jessica	O'Connell	CAN	10.2.89	4	Jordan	Stanford	2 May
5:06.45	Marielle	Hall	USA	28.1.92	2	NC	Eugene	28 Jun
5:07.18	Emily	Infeld	USA	21.3.90	4	NC	Eugene	28 Jun
5:07.38	Susan	Kuijken	NED	8.7.86	6	Bisl	Oslo	11 Jun
5:07.73	Maureen	Koster	NED	3.7.92	5	Jordan	Stanford	2 May
5:08.29	Ayuko	Suzuki	JPN	8.10.91	9	WCh	Beijing	30 Aug
5:08.39	Perine	Nengampi	KEN	1.1.89	8	DL	Shanghai	17 May
5:09.62	Eloise	Wellings	AUS	9.11.82	10	WCh	Beijing	30 Aug
5:10.02	Shalane	Flanagan	USA	8.7.81	5	NC	Eugene	28 Jun
	(30)							
5:11.17	Madeline	Heiner	AUS	5.3.88	7	Jordan	Stanford	2 May
5:13.16	Alemitu	Hawi	ETH-J	14.11.96	1		Huelva	10 Jun
5:13.73	Selly	Chepyego	KEN	3.10.85	1		Kitakyushu	29 Nov
5:13.82	Stephanie	Twell	GBR	17.8.89	8	Jordan	Stanford	2 May
5:15.18	Karoline Bjerkeli	Grøvdal	NOR	14.6.90	7	Bisl	Oslo	11 Jun
5:15.42	Rosemary	Wanjiru	KEN	9.12.94	1		Gifu	27 Sep
5:15.77	Azmera	Gebru	ETH	5.5.92	12	DL	Saint-Denis	4 Jul
5:16.12	Jennifer	Wenth	AUT	24.7.91	5	NA	Heusden-Zolder	18 Jul
5:16.43	Yuka	Miyazaki	JPN	21.8.92	2		Kitakyushu	29 Nov
5:16.60	Katie	Mackey	USA	12.11.87	9	Jordan	Stanford	2 May
	(40)							

Mark	Name		Nat	Born	Pos	Meet	Venue	Date
15:16.69	Birtukan	Fente	ETH	18.6.89	10	DL	Shanghai	17 Ma
15:16.82	Misaki	Onishi	JPN	24.2.85	10	Jordan	Stanford	2 Ma
15:17.62	Azusa	Sumi	JPN-J	12.8.96	1		Kitami	12 Ju
15:18.02	Nikki	Hamblin	NZL	20.5.88	11	Jordan	Stanford	2 Ma
15:18.53	Ashley	Higginson	USA	17.3.89	12	Jordan	Stanford	2 Ma
15:18.80	Yelena	Korobkina	RUS	25.11.90	8	Pre	Eugene	30 Ma
15:18.85	Jessica	Tonn	USA	15.2.92	13	Jordan	Stanford	2 Ma
15:18.88	Gulshat	Fazlitdinova	RUS	28.8.92	1		Sochi	28 Ma
15:19.01	Gabe	Grunewald	USA	25.6.86	1		Stanford	3 Ap
15:19.06	Emily	Brichacek	AUS	7.7.90	14	Jordan	Stanford	2 Ma
	(50)							
15:19.15	Nicole	Sifuentes	CAN	30.6.86	2		Stanford	3 Ap
15:19.30	Bezuayehu	Mohamed	ETH-J	4.1.96	2		Huelva	10 Ju
15:19.42	Alisha	Williams	USA	5.2.82	3		Stanford	3 Ap
15:19.50	Stephanie	Garcia	USA	3.5.88	15	Jordan	Stanford	2 Ma
15:19.85	Svetlana	Kireyeva	RUS	12.6.87	2		Sochi	28 Ma
15:20.20	Kasumi	Nishihara	JPN	1.3.89	6	NA	Heusden-Zolder	18 Ju
15:20.21	Yuika	Mori	JPN	25.1.88	16	Jordan	Stanford	2 Ma
15:20.52	Haftamnesh	Tesfay	ETH	28.4.94	5	DL	London (OS)	25 Ju
15:21.10	Veronica	Nyaruai	KEN	29.10.89	1		Carquefou	19 Ju
15:21.40	Miyuki	Uehara	JPN	22.11.95	2		Kitami	12 Ju
	(60)							
15:22.00	Laura	Whittle	GBR	27.6.85	7	NA	Heusden-Zolder	18 Ju
15:23.82	Louise	Carton	BEL	16.4.94	8	NA	Heusden-Zolder	18 Ju
15:23.85	Pauline	Korikwiang	KEN	1.3.88	1	WMilG	Mungyeong	5 Oc
15:24.25	Lidia	Rodríguez	ESP	26.5.86	9	NA	Heusden-Zolder	18 Ju
15:24.58	Yelena	Nagovitsyna	RUS	7.12.82	3		Sochi	28 Ma
15:25.01	Stella	Chesang	UGA-J	1.12.96	12	DL	Shanghai	17 Ma
15:25.15	Betlhem	Desalegn	UAE	13.11.91	1	AsiC	Wuhan	4 Ju
15:25.20	Bezunesh	Getachew	ETH-J	.97	3		Carquefou	19 Ju
15:25.21mx		Ding Changqin	CHN	27.11.91	1		Saluzzo	15 Ju
15:25.34	Neely	Spence Gracey	USA	16.4.90	5		Stanford	3 Ap
	(70)							
15:25.54	Rico	Matsuzaki	JPN	24.12.92	4		Niigata	28 Ju
15:25.63	Kate	Avery	GBR	10.10.91	6		Stanford	3 Ap
15:25.78	Sintayehu	Lewetegn	ETH-J	9.5.96	3		Huelva	10 Ju
15:25.84	Emily	Sisson	USA	12.10.91	11	NA	Heusden-Zolder	18 Ju
15:26.46	Mary	Cullen	IRL	17.8.82	12	NA	Heusden-Zolder	18 Ju
15:27.13	Desiree	Linden	USA	26.7.83	2		Concord MA	4 Ju
15:27.60	Rhona	Auckland	GBR	11.5.93	7	DL	London (OS)	25 Ju
15:27.94	Trihas	Gebre	ESP	29.4.90	4		Huelva	10 Ju
15:28.32	Natsuki	Omori	JPN	22.6.94	6	NC	Niigata	28 Ju
15:28.6A	Margaret	Chelimo	KEN-J	2.8.97	2	NC	Nairobi	11 Ju
	(80)							
15:28.71	Liv	Westphal	FRA	22.12.93	9	DL	London (OS)	25 Ju
15:28.74	Alia Mohamed	Saeed	UAE	18.5.91	2	AsiC	Wuhan	4 Ju
15:28.78	Camille	Buscomb	NZL	11.7.90	1		Auckland (NS)	15 De
15:28.81	Dera	Dida	ETH-J	26.10.96	5		Huelva	10 Ju
15:29.26	Dominika	Nowakowska	POL	25.1.85	1		Watford	27 Ju
15:29.50	Jessica	Coulson	GBR	18.4.90	10	DL	London (OS)	25 Ju
15:30.00	Angela	Bizzarri	USA	15.2.88	17	Jordan	Stanford	2 Ma
15:30.43mx	Amy	Cragg	USA	21.1.84	2mx		Waltham	13 Ju
15:31.25	Netsanet	Gudeta	ETH	12.2.91	13	DL	Saint-Denis	4 Ju
15:31.37	Orchatteri P.	Jaisha	IND	23.5.83	1	NG	Trivandrum	9 Fe
	(90)							
15:31.69	Felista	Wanjugu	KEN	18.2.90	1		Abashiri	16 Ju
15:31.82	Brenda	Flores	MEX	4.9.91	2	MSR	Walnut	17 Ap
15:31.82	Alice Aprot	Nawowuna	KEN	11.3.94	3	AfG	Brazzaville	13 Se
15:31.92	Yuka	Mukai	JPN-Y	10.12.98	1		Oita	17 Oc
15:32.04	Kellyn	Taylor	USA	22.7.86	7	NC	Eugene	28 Ju
15:32.44	Kaltoum	Bouaasayriya	MAR	23.8.82	1		Rabat	7 Ju
15:32.46	Emma	Bates	USA	8.7.92	7		Stanford	3 Ap
15:32.53	Mariam	Waithera	KEN-J	23.12.96	2	Oda	Hiroshima	18 Ap
15:32.55	Dominique	Scott	RSA	24.6.92	18	Jordan	Stanford	2 Ma
15:32.67	Yuka	Ando	JPN	16.3.94	2		Fukuroi	14 No
	(100)							

Mark	Name		Nat	Born	Date
15:32.88	Erin	Finn	USA	19.11.94	2 May
15:32.89	Katie	Matthews	USA	19.11.90	4 Jun
15:33.07	Pauline	Kamulu	KEN	16.4.95	27 Sep
15:33.15	Rachel	Cliff	CAN	1.4.88	3 Apr
15:33.27	Almensch	Belete	BEL	26.7.89	5 Aug
15:33.77	Risa	Yokoe	JPN	12.10.94	16 Jul
15:33.82	Paulina	Kaczynska	POL	24.7.91	30 Ma
15:34.23	Rina	Nabeshima	JPN	16.12.93	2 Oc
15:34.59	Chelsea	Reilly	USA	9.5.89	2 Ma
15:34.59	Hanae	Tanaka	JPN	12.2.90	2 Oc
15:35.17	Emelia	Gorecka	GBR	29.1.94	2 Ma
15:35.21	Olga	Mazurenok	BLR	14.4.89	5 Oc

Mark	Name		Nat	Born	Pos Meet	Venue	Date
5:35.21	Misaki	Kato	JPN	15.6.91			29 Nov
5:35.34	Nao	Yamamoto	JPN-J	20.10.96			9 Oct
5:35.43	Elizeba	Cherono	KEN	6.6.88			12 Jun
5:35.53	Miho	Shimizu	JPN	13.5.90			2 May
5:35.56	Sayaka	Kuwahara	JPN	8.3.93			4 Apr
5:35.60	Ayumi	Hagiwara	JPN	1.6.92			12 Jul
5:35.75	Sabrina	Mockenhaupt	GER	6.12.80			5 Oct
5:35.86	Alia	Gray	USA	12.11.88			3 Apr
5:36.04	Rika	Tokuchi	JPN	2.12.87			16 Jul
5:36.08	Elvin	Kibet	KEN	4.2.90			17 Apr
5:36.10	Moeno	Nakamura	JPN	21.3.90			2 Oct
5:36.18	Renata	Plis	POL	5.2.85			19 Jul
5:36.27	Doricah	Obare	KEN	10.1.90			18 Apr
5:36.32	Jip	Vastenburg	NED	21.3.94			21 Jun
5:36.33	Rachele	Schulist	USA	26.4.94			18 Apr
5:36.49	Beth	Potter	GBR	27.12.91			25 Jul
5:36.66	Silvia	Weissteiner	ITA	13.7.79			17 May
5:36.72	Ann	Mwangi	KEN	8.12.88			30 May
5:36.84	Rachel	Ward	USA	11.10.89			4 Jun
5:36.84	Akane	Yabushita	JPN	6.6.91			16 Jul
5:36.90	Naoko	Koizumi	JPN	14.12.92			19 Dec
5:36.91	Liz	Costello	USA	23.2.88			17 Apr
5:36.96	Shinobu	Koyoshigawa	JPN-J	19.5.97			17 Oct
5:37.17	Brie	Felnagle	USA	9.12.86			13 Jun
5:37.41	Shiho	Takechi	JPN	18.8.90			18 Jul
5:37.56	Michi	Numata	JPN	6.5.89			9 Oct
5:37.58	Natsuko	Goto	JPN	4.8.87			19 Dec
5:37.59	Tomomi	Tanaka	JPN	25.1.88			16 Jul
5:37.64	Saori	Noda	JPN	30.3.93			16 Jul
5:37.68	Yuka	Takashima	JPN	12.5.88			4 Apr
5:37.68	Risa	Kikuchi	JPN	5.2.90			27 Sep
5:37.83	Yui	Fukuda	JPN	1.6.95			16 Jul
5:37.86	Valentyna	Zhudina	UKR	12.3.83			1 Aug
5:38.38	Viktoriya	Kalyuzhna	UKR	11.7.94			12 Jul
5:38.39	Alla	Kulyatina	RUS	9.6.90			28 May
5:38.39	Souad	Aït Salem	ALG	6.1.79			3 Jul
5:38.45	Monica Madalina	Florea	ROU	3.2.93			12 Jul
5:38.47	Giulia	Viola	ITA	24.4.91			2 May
5:38.53	Mao	Kiyota	JPN	12.9.93			2 Oct
5:39.05	Yukari	Abe	JPN	21.8.89			16 Jul
15:39.20	Mai	Nishiwaki	JPN	9.2.93			5 Dec
15:39.27	Kaitlin	Goodman	USA	31.1.87			4 Jun
15:39.6A	Nancy	Nzisa	KEN	.90			11 Jul
15:39.83	Hajiba	Hasnaoui	MAR	28.4.88			9 May
15:39.83	Letesenbet	Gidey	ETH-Y	20.3.98			21 Jun
15:39.90+	Yasemin	Can	TUR-J	11.12.96			8 Aug
15:39.94	Carolina	Tabares	COL	18.7.86			17 Apr
15:40.48	Maddie	Meyers	USA	30.7.94			3 Apr
15:40.64	Sakie	Arai	JPN	3.6.94			19 Dec
15:40.66	Sarah	Pagano	USA	23.7.91			4 Jun
15:40.81	Kara	Goucher	USA	9.7.78			13 Jun
15:40.82	Grace	Kimanzi	KEN	1.3.92			27 Sep
15:41.00	Margarita	Hernández	MEX	3.12.85			17 Apr
15:41.18	Yuki	Hidaka	JPN	22.7.92			28 Jun
15:41.22mx		Xu Qiuzi	CHN	8.2.91			15 Jul
15:41.37	Susan	Wairimu	KEN	11.10.92			25 Apr
15:41.63	Sakiho	Tsutsui	JPN-J	19.1.96			25 Apr
15:41.67	Anna	Fyodorova	RUS	24.1.93			28 May
15:41.68	Kaho	Tanaka	JPN	24.6.91			16 Jul
15:42.22	Tansey	Lystad	USA	27.5.93			2 May
15:42.30+	Meryem	Akda	TUR	5.8.92			8 Aug
15:42.50	Reia	Iwade	JPN	8.12.94			5 Dec
15:42.57	Calli	Thackery	GBR	9.1.93			17 Apr
15:42.82	Daria	Maslova	KGZ	6.5.95			4 Jun
15:43.35	Miho	Shimada	JPN-J	26.8.97			14 Nov
15:43.61	Amanda	Mergaert	USA	4.9.91			2 May
15:43.62	Juliet	Bottorff	USA	21.1.91			3 Apr
15:43.76	Keiko	Nogami	JPN	6.12.85			18 Apr
15:43.77	Genet	Yalew	ETH	31.12.92			13 Sep
15:43.94	Lucie	Sekanová	CZE	5.8.89			10 Jun
15:44.05	Tomona	Omori	JPN-Y	.98			28 Nov
15:44.07	Tomoka	Kimura	JPN	12.11.94			5 Dec
15:44.29	Misaki	Tanabe	JPN	31.8.95			19 Dec
15:44.38	Rui	Aoyama	JPN	15.4.89			19 Dec
15:44.52	Maggie	Montoya	USA	2.5.95			2 May
15:44.59	Ayumi	Uehara	JPN	23.11.94			17 Oct
15:44.72	Honoka	Yuzawa	JPN	11.4.94			19 Dec
15:44.82	Natasha	Wodak	CAN	17.12.81			12 Jul
15:44.85	Monica	Margaret	KEN-Y	.98			5 Dec
15:44.96	Kate	Van Buskirk	CAN	9.6.87			3 Apr
	(192)						

Indoors

4:18.86		Dibaba			1	XL-Galan	Stockholm	19 Feb
5:12.22	Emily	Sisson	USA	12.10.91	1	Big	East New York	28 Feb
5:31.62	Courtney	Frerichs	USA	18.1.93	1		Boston (A)	5 Dec
5:34.15	Birtukan	Adamu	ETH	29.4.92	3	XL-Galan	Stockholm	19 Feb
5:35.71	Dagmawit	Kidane	ETH-J	2.12.96				19 Feb
15:40.35	Rachel	Johnson	USA	30.4.93				13 Mar

JUNIORS

See main list for top 10 juniors. 11 performances by 8 women to 15:30.0. Additional marks and further juniors:

awi	15:17.52				11	DL	Shanghai	17 May
umi	15:21.07				2	NC	Niigata	28 Jun
Mohamed	15:22.06				2		Carquefou	19 Jun
5:35.34	Nao	Yamamoto	JPN	20.10.96	1		Kobe	9 Oct
5:36.96	Shinobu	Koyoshigawa	JPN	19.5.97	2		Oita	17 Oct
5:39.83	Letesenbet	Gidey	ETH-Y	20.3.98	1		Bottrop	21 Jun
5:39.90+	Yasemin	Can	TUR	11.12.96	1		Mersin	8 Aug
5:41.63	Sakiho	Tsutsui	JPN	19.1.96	3		Kobe	25 Apr
5:43.35	Miho	Shimada	JPN	26.8.97	2		Yokohama	14 Nov
5:44.05	Tomona	Omori	JPN-Y	.98	1		Isahaya	28 Nov
5:44.85	Monica	Margaret	KEN-Y	.98	2		Yokohama	5 Dec
5:45.75		Zhang Deshun	CHN	21.2.96	1	NYG	Fuzhou	22 Oct
5:46.09	Kana	Furaya (20)	JPN	.96	5		Oita	17 Oct

10,000 METRES

0:49.68	Gelete	Burka	ETH	15.2.86	1	ETH Ch	Hengelo	17 Jun
0:50.83	Alemitu	Haroye	ETH	9.5.95	2	ETH Ch	Hengelo	17 Jun
0:53.69	Belaynesh	Oljira	ETH	26.6.90	3	ETH Ch	Hengelo	17 Jun
0:55.56	Mamitu	Daska	ETH	16.10.83	4	ETH Ch	Hengelo	17 Jun
0:58.03	Wude	Ayalew	ETH	4.7.87	5	ETH Ch	Hengelo	17 Jun
1:06.53	Netsanet	Gudeta	ETH	12.2.91	6	ETH Ch	Hengelo	17 Jun
1:08.16		Burka			1		Stanford	3 Apr
1:08.82	Genet	Yalew	ETH	31.12.92	7	ETH Ch	Hengelo	17 Jun
1:09.02	Shalane	Flanagan	USA	8.7.81	2		Stanford	3 Apr
1:12.93	Sara	Moreira	POR	17.10.85	1		Huelva	11 Apr
1:13.29	Vivian	Cheruiyot (10)	KEN	11.9.83	1		Bruxelles	5 Jul
1:23.60	Yeshaneh	Ababel	ETH	10.6.90	8	ETH Ch	Hengelo	17 Jun

Mark	Name		Nat	Born	Pos	Meet	Venue	Date
31:24.18	Alice Aprot	Nawowuna	KEN	11.3.94	1	AfG	Brazzaville	16 Se
31:31.97	Susan	Kuijken	NED	8.7.86	1	Jordan	Stanford	2 Ma
31:33.27	Buze	Diriba	ETH	9.2.94	2	Jordan	Stanford	2 Ma
31:34.17	Ana Dulce	Félix	POR	23.10.82	2		Huelva	11 Ap
31:35.48	Jip	Vastenburg	NED	21.3.94	3	Jordan	Stanford	2 Ma
31:36.87	Gladys	Chesire	KEN	20.2.93	2	AfG	Brazzaville	16 Se
31:37.32	Yuka	Takashima	JPN	12.5.88	4	Jordan	Stanford	2 Ma
31:38.03	Emily	Sisson	USA	12.10.91	5	Jordan	Stanford	2 Ma
31:38.33		Burka			3	AfG	Brazzaville	16 Se
31:38.71	Emily	Infeld (20)	USA	21.3.90	6	Jordan	Stanford	2 Ma
31:39.20	Molly	Huddle	USA	31.8.84	1	NC	Eugene	25 Ju
31:39.81		W Ayalew			4	AfG	Brazzaville	16 Se
31:41.31		Cheruiyot			1	WCh	Beijing	24 Au
31:41.44	Kate	Avery	GBR	10.10.91	7	Jordan	Stanford	2 Ma
31:41.59	Natasha	Wodak	CAN	17.12.81	8	Jordan	Stanford	2 Ma
31:41.77		Burka			2	WCh	Beijing	24 Au
31:42.29		Flanagan			2	NC	Eugene	25 Ju
31:42.60		Infeld			3	NC	Eugene	25 Ju
	(30/23)							
31:44.42	Sally	Kipyego	KEN	19.12.85	5	WCh	Beijing	24 Au
31:44.79	Mao	Kiyota	JPN	12.9.93	9	Jordan	Stanford	2 Ma
31:44.86	Rico	Matsuzaki	JPN	24.12.92	1		Abashiri	16 Ju
31:45.16	Brenda	Flores	MEX	4.9.91	10	Jordan	Stanford	2 Ma
31:46.58	Ayumi	Hagiwara	JPN	1.6.92	2		Abashiri	16 Ju
31:46.94	Lanni	Marchant	CAN	11.4.84	11	Jordan	Stanford	2 Ma
31:48.18	Ayuko	Suzuki	JPN	8.10.91	1		Gifu	25 Se
	(30)							
31:48.22	Eri	Makikawa	JPN	22.4.93	12	Jordan	Stanford	2 Ma
31:48.31	Rei	Ohara	JPN	10.8.90	3		Abashiri	16 Ju
31:49.99	Alisha	Williams	USA	5.2.82	13	Jordan	Stanford	2 Ma
31:51.35	Betsy	Saina	KEN	30.6.88	8	WCh	Beijing	24 Au
31:52.29	Alia Mohamed	Saeed	UAE	18.5.91	1	AsiC	Wuhan	7 Ju
31:54.43	Mattie	Suver	USA	10.9.87	14	Jordan	Stanford	2 Ma
31:56.62	Inés	Melchor	PER	30.8.86	1rB	Jordan	Stanford	2 Ma
31:56.92	Yuki	Mitsunobu	JPN	9.11.92	4		Abashiri	16 Ju
31:57.35	Grace	Kimanzi	KEN	1.3.92	1		Fukagawa	9 Ju
31:57.85	Sule	Utura	ETH	8.2.90	9	ETH Ch	Hengelo	17 Ju
	(40)							
31:58.34	Kim	Conley	USA	14.3.86	1		Sacramento	6 De
32:01.79	Liz	Costello	USA	23.2.88	15	Jordan	Stanford	2 Ma
32:02.22	Alexi	Pappas	USA	28.3.90	16	Jordan	Stanford	2 Ma
32:02.61	Eloise	Wellings	AUS	9.11.82	1	NC	Melbourne	5 De
32:03.18	Doricah	Obare	KEN	10.1.90	17	Jordan	Stanford	2 Ma
32:03.95	Amy	Hastings	USA	21.1.84	4	NC	Eugene	25 Ju
32:03.95	Michi	Numata	JPN	6.5.89	5		Abashiri	16 Ju
32:03.96	Selly	Chepyego	KEN	3.10.85	2		Gifu	25 Se
32:05.84	Chelsea	Reilly	USA	9.5.89	2		Sacramento	6 De
32:06.48	Kasumi	Nishihara	JPN	1.3.89	1	NC	Niigata	26 Ju
	(50)							
32:07.37	Yuka	Ando	JPN	16.3.94	2rB	Jordan	Stanford	2 Ma
32:07.43	Yuka	Miyazaki	JPN	21.8.92	2		Fukagawa	9 Ju
32:08.0A	Joyce	Chepkirui	KEN	10.8.88	1	NC	Nairobi	10 Ju
32:08.2A	Jackline	Chepngeno	KEN	16.1.93	2	NC	Nairobi	10 Ju
32:08.74	Tomomi	Tanaka	JPN	25.1.88	3		Fukagawa	9 Ju
32:08.76	Rochelle	Kanuho	USA	4.7.90	3		Sacramento	6 De
32:09.82	Kaitlin	Goodman	USA	31.1.87	3		Stanford	3 Ap
32:10.76	Yuki	Hidaka	JPN	22.7.92	6		Abashiri	16 Ju
32:11.40	Rina	Yamazaki	JPN	6.5.88	5	NC	Niigata	26 Ju
32:11.60	Dominique	Scott	RSA	24.6.92	5		Stanford	3 Ap
	(60)							
32:12.25	Mizuki	Matsuda	JPN	31.5.95	7		Abashiri	16 Ju
32:12.54	Hanami	Sekine	JPN-J	26.2.96	8		Abashiri	16 Ju
32:13.21	Reia	Iwade	JPN	8.12.94	6	NC	Niigata	26 Ju
32:13.28	Emma	Bates	USA	8.7.92	18	Jordan	Stanford	2 Ma
32:13.30	Risa	Yokoe	JPN	12.10.94	1		Yokohama	19 De
32:13.42	Sitora	Khamidova	UZB	12.5.89	1	NC	Tashkent	18 Se
32:13.55	Akane	Yabushita	JPN	6.6.91	2		Yokohama	19 De
32:13.72	Misaki	Kato	JPN	15.6.91	1		Kitakyushu	16 Ma
32:14.0A	Beatrice	Mutai	KEN	19.4.87	4	NC	Nairobi	10 Ju
32:14.33	Darya	Maslova	KGZ	6.5.95	2	NC	Tashkent	18 Se
	(70)							

Mark	Name		Nat	Born	Pos	Meet	Venue	Date
2:14.43	Sayaka	Kuwahara	JPN	8.3.93	3rB	Jordan	Stanford	2 May
2:14.58	Keiko	Nogami	JPN	6.12.85	2		Kitakyushu	16 May
2:14.94	Trihas	Gebre	ESP	29.4.90	1	ECp	Cagliari	6 Jun
2:16.23	Miho	Shimizu	JPN	13.5.90	3		Yokohama	19 Dec
2:16.66	Miyuki	Uehara	JPN	22.11.95	1		Oita	17 Oct
2:17.34	Serena	Burla	USA	29.7.82	4rB	Jordan	Stanford	2 May
2:17.67	Jessica	Trengove	AUS	15.8.87	5rB	Jordan	Stanford	2 May
2:18.49	Gladys	Tejeda #	PER	30.9.85	6rB	Jordan	Stanford	2 May
2:19.36	Hanae	Tanaka	JPN	12.2.90	2		Oita	17 Oct
2:20.77	Lily	Partridge	GBR	9.3.91	3		Huelva	11 Apr
	(80)							
2:20.95	Juliet	Chekwel	UGA	25.5.90	17	WCh	Beijing	24 Aug
2:21.4A	Lucy	Cheruiyot	KEN-J	4.1.97	5	NC	Nairobi	10 Jul
2:22.15	Lindsey	Flanagan	USA	24.1.91	7rB	Jordan	Stanford	2 May
2:22.29	Eunice	Chumba	BRN	23.5.93	2	AsiC	Wuhan	7 Jun
2:22.79	Rhona	Auckland	GBR	11.5.93	2	EU23	Tallinn	10 Jul
2:22.88	Ayumi	Sakaida	JPN	7.11.85	9		Abashiri	16 Jul
2:22.92	Sakiko	Matsumi	JPN	7.8.88	3		Oita	17 Oct
2:23.43	Katie	Matthews	USA	19.11.90	4		Sacramento	6 Dec
2:24.1A	Gladys	Cherono	KEN	12.5.83	6	NC	Nairobi	10 Jul
2:24.24	Carolina	Tabares	COL	18.7.86	20	Jordan	Stanford	2 May
	(90)							
2:25.22	Natalya	Popkova	RUS	21.9.88	1	Znam	Zhukovskiy	19 Jul
2:26.20	Yuko	Mizuguchi	JPN	24.5.85	10		Abashiri	16 Jul
2:26.28	Yelena	Nagovitsyna	RUS	7.12.82	2	Znam	Zhukovskiy	19 Jul
2:26.36	Camille	Buscomb	NZL	11.7.90	2	Zátopek	Melbourne	5 Dec
2:26.38	Shiho	Takechi	JPN	18.8.90	3		Gifu	25 Sep
2:26.41	Marisol	Romero	MEX	26.11.83	21	Jordan	Stanford	2 May
2:26.98	Angela	Bizzarri	USA	15.2.88	6		Stanford	3 Apr
2:28.39	Chelsea	Blaase	USA	10.4.94	7		Stanford	3 Apr
2:28.7		Ding Changqin	CHN	27.11.91	1		Cantalupa	29 Jul
2:29.06	Alia	Gray	USA	12.11.88	5		Sacramento	6 Dec
	(100)							

Mark	Name		Nat	Born	Date
2:29.88	Kellyn	Taylor	USA	22.7.86	2 May
2:29.89	Margo	Malone	USA	3.9.93	3 Apr
2:32.41	Valeria	Straneo	ITA	5.4.76	6 Jun
2:35.87	Sara	Hall	USA	15.4.83	6 Dec
2:36.17	Rachel	Hannah	CAN	2.10.86	2 May
2:36.25	Ayumi	Uehara	JPN	23.11.94	21 Nov
2:36.29	Margarita	Hernández	MEX	3.12.85	2 May
2:37.19	Valentina	Galimova	RUS	11.5.86	19 Jul
2:37.68	Kaho	Tanaka	JPN	24.6.91	9 Jul
2:39.04	Ai	Inoue	JPN	13.1.90	26 Apr
2:39.2A	Veronica	Nyaruai	KEN	29.10.89	10 Jun
2:40.3A	Yebrqual	Melese	ETH	18.4.90	10 Jun
2:40.54	Fuyuka	Kimura	JPN	13.1.95	21 Nov
2:40.81	Yukari	Ishizawa	JPN	16.4.88	16 Jul
2:40.81	Yuri	Karasawa	JPN	25.11.95	21 Nov
2:41.00	Ai	Hosoda	JPN	27.11.95	21 Nov
2:41.44	Lidia	Rodríguez	ESP	26.5.86	11 Apr
2:41.45	Olha	Skrypak	UKR	2.12.90	19 Jul
2:41.5		He Yinli	CHN	20.9.88	29 Jul
2:41.59	Jessica	Coulson	GBR	18.4.90	16 May
2:42.31	Yasemin	Can	TUR-J	11.12.96	8 Aug
2:42.43	Kanayo	Miyata	JPN	14.2.95	16 Jul
2:42.53	Rika	Shintaku	JPN	19.10.85	16 Jul
2:42.67	Catarina	Ribeiro	POR	31.5.90	11 Apr
2:43.1A	Rebecca	Chesire	KEN	.92	10 Jul
2:43.31	Reina	Hayashida	JPN-J	30.3.96	16 Jul
2:43.75	Mari	Ozaki	JPN	16.7.75	16 Jul
2:43.99	Desiree	Linden	USA	26.7.83	23 Jul
2:45.46	Sarah	Pagano	USA	23.7.91	6 Dec
2:45.47	Saki	Fukui	JPN-J	25.3.96	16 Jul
2:45.73	Yukiko	Okuno	JPN	12.9.92	16 Jul
2:46.04	Jordan	Hasay	USA	21.9.91	6 Dec
2:46.20	Mai	Tsuda	JPN	21.2.93	16 Jul
2:46.49	Allison Grace	Morgan	USA	1.12.82	2 May
2:46.57	Alice	Wright	GBR	3.11.94	10 Jul
2:46.75	Carrie	Dimoff	USA	31.5.83	2 May
2:46.90	Brianne	Nelson	USA	27.10.80	9 Aug
2:47.15	Katrina	Allison	CAN	21.2.94	2 May
2:47.37	Eri	Hayakawa	JPN	15.11.81	9 Jul
2:47.62	Almensch	Belete	BEL	26.7.89	24 Aug
2:50.62	Souad	Aït Salem	ALG	6.1.79	12 Jun
2:50.71	Miho	Ihara	JPN	4.2.88	26 Jun
2:51.0		Wang Xueqin	CHN	1.1.91	29 Jul
32:51.02	Natasha	Anzures	CAN	5.8.87	13 Jun
32:51.04	Johanna	Peiponen	FIN	18.12.90	13 Sep
32:51.33	María Balvina	Pastuña ¶	ECU	6.6.89	12 Jun
32:51.48	Hitomi	Nakamura	JPN	23.6.87	9 Jul
32:52.27	Alla	Kulyatina	RUS	9.6.90	8 Jul
32:52.74	Amy	Van Alstine	USA	11.11.87	13 Jun
32:53.07	Albina	Mayorova	RUS	16.5.77	19 Jul
32:54.1A	Shure	Demise	ETH-J	21.1.96	10 Jun
32:54.46	Nao	Isaka	JPN	19.7.94	9 Jul
32:54.70	Rachel	Cliff	CAN	1.4.88	2 May
32:55.08	Monica Madalina	Florea	ROU	3.2.93	10 Jul
32:55.34	Kaho	Nishizawa	JPN	27.4.95	17 Oct
32:55.35	Gulshat	Fazlitdinova	RUS	28.8.92	8 Jul
32:55.36	Alyson	Dixon	GBR	24.9.78	16 May
32:55.41	Agnes	Tirop	KEN	23.10.95	16 Sep
32:56.31	Chieko	Kido	JPN	14.3.90	16 May
32:56.60		Zhang Yingying	CHN	4.1.90	8 Jul
32:57.00	Elvin	Kibet	KEN	4.2.90	3 Apr
32:57.15	Mai	Nagaoka	JPN	.93	19 Dec
32:58.12A	Nancy	Kimaiyo	KEN	.84	20 Jun
32:58.17	Alisa	Vainio	FIN-J	16.11.97	2 Aug
32:58.17		Zhang Deshun	CHN-J	21.2.96	25 Oct
32:58.58	Kotomi	Takayama	JPN	18.2.93	26 Jun
32:59.39	Chiharu	Suzuki	JPN	18.11.93	9 Jul
32:59.91	Naoka	Akutsu	JPN	5.7.94	19 Dec
32:59.92	Jelena	Prokopcuka	LAT	21.9.76	19 Jul
33:00.89	Laura	Batterink	CAN	11.11.84	6 Dec
33:01.15	Wilma	Arizapana	PER	1.10.82	12 Jun
33:01.30A	Visiline	Jepkesho	KEN	.88	20 Jun
33:01.50	Addie	Bracy	USA	4.8.86	2 May
33:01.77	Natsumi	Yoshida	JPN	24.12.92	16 Jul
33:02.0A	Jemima	Jelagat	KEN	21.12.84	10 Jun
33:02.37	Rika	Toguchi	JPN	2.12.87	25 Sep
33:02.98	Kana	Furuya	JPN-J	.96	16 Jul
33:03.03	Rina	Koeda	JPN	29.8.94	25 Apr
33:03.18	Sakie	Arai	JPN	3.6.94	25 Apr
33:03.35		Zheng Zhiling	CHN-J	25.12.96	25 Oct
33:03.80	Mara	Olson	USA	8.3.93	6 Dec
33:03.86		Wu Xufeng	CHN	10.1.93	7 Jun
33:03.91	Orchatteri P.	Jaisha	IND	23.5.83	19 Sep
33:03.92	Mai	Shoji	JPN	9.12.93	19 Dec
33:04.11	Kathya	García	MEX	3.12.87	2 May
33:04.59	Ayako	Mitsui	JPN	17.1.92	16 Jul

Mark	Name		Nat	Born	Date
33:04.68	Iwona	Lewandowska	POL	19.2.85	6 Jun
33:05.03	Jenifer	Rhines	USA	1.7.74	6 Dec
33:05.35	Sandra	López	MEX	16.4.84	3 Apr
33:05.63	Saori	Noda	JPN	30.3.93	19 Dec
33:06.04	Mao	Kuroda	JPN	1.11.89	25 Sep
33:06.94	Natalya	Puchkova	RUS	28.1.87	19 Jul
33:06.98	Nanako	Kanno	JPN	30.12.94	14 May
33:07.27	Joanna	Thompson	USA	24.9.92	3 A
33:07.58	Asami	Kato	JPN	12.10.90	16 Ma
33:08.62	Manami	Kamitanida	JPN	21.12.89	16 Ma
33:09.27	Katja	Goldring	USA	11.8.90	2 Ma
33:09.63	Katy	Moen	USA	20.4.92	2 Ma
33:09.78	Helen	Jepkurgat	KEN	21.2.89	25 Ap
33:09.86	Juliet (200)	Bottorff	USA	21.1.91	6 De

JUNIORS

See main list for top 2 juniors. 11 performances by 10 women to 33:05.0. Additional marks and further juniors:

Cheruiyot 32:35.45A 1 Nairobi 20 Jun

Mark	Name		Nat	Born	Pos	Meet	Venue	Date
32:42.31	Yasemin	Can	TUR-J	11.12.96	1		Mersin	8 Au
32:43.31	Reina	Hayashida	JPN-J	30.3.96	16		Abashiri	16 Ju
32:45.47	Saki	Fukui	JPN-J	25.3.96	18		Abashiri	16 Ju
32:54.1A	Shure	Demise	ETH-J	21.1.96	2		Addis Ababa	10 Ju
32:58.17	Alisa	Vainio	FIN-J	16.11.97	1	NC	Pori	2 Au
32:58.17		Zhang Deshun	CHN-J	21.2.96	1	NYG	Fuzhou	25 Oc
33:02.98	Kana	Furuya	JPN-J	.96	23		Abashiri	16 Ju
33:03.35		Zheng Zhiling (10)	CHN-J	25.12.96	2	NYG	Fuzhou	25 Oc
33:19.12	Maki	Izumida	JPN	22.1.96	2	Univ Ch	Osaka	11 Se
33:20.79	Misaki	Hayashida	JPN	31.1.96	9		Yokohama	19 De
33:32.81	Hinako	Kashio	JPN	28.1.96	2rB		Abashiri	16 Ju
33:37.92		Jun Mingming	CHN	10.12.96	2	NC	Suzhou	22 Se

10 KILOMETRES ROAD

Mark	Name		Nat	Born	Pos	Meet	Venue	Date
30:41	Gladys	Chesire	KEN	20.2.93	1		Berlin	11 Oc
30:55	Peres	Jepchirchir	KEN	27.9.93	1		Praha	5 Se
30:56	Gladys	Cherono	KEN	12.5.83	1		Ottawa	23 Ma
30:58	Genet	Yalew	ETH	31.12.92	1		Tilburg	6 Se
31:00	Malika	Asahssah	MAR	24.9.82	1		Laredo	21 Ma
31:02+	Florence	Kiplagat	KEN	27.2.87	1	in HMar	Barcelona	15 Fe
31:02	Alice Aprot	Nawowuna	KEN	11.3.94	2		Berlin	11 Oc
31:03	Shalane	Flanagan	USA	8.7.81	2		Tilburg	6 Se
31:07+	Mary	Keitany	KEN	18.1.82	1=	in HMar	Ra's Al-Khaymah	13 Fe
31:07+	Mamitu	Daska	ETH	16.10.83	1=	in HMar	Ra's Al-Khaymah	13 Fe
31:07+	Cynthia	Limo	KEN	18.12.89	1=	in HMar	Ra's Al-Khaymah	13 Fe
31:11+		Keitany			1	in HMar	Olomouc	20 Ju
31:11	Sutume	Asefa	ETH	.94	3		Berlin	11 Oc
31:15		Keitany			1		New York	13 Ju
31:18		Jepchirchir			2		Ottawa	23 Ma
31:21	Molly	Huddle	USA	31.8.84	1		Boston	12 Oc
Where better than 10,000m track times								
31:22	Gladys	Yator	KEN	8.8.92	1		Koutobia	17 Ma
31:33+	Worknesh	Degefa	ETH	28.10.90	2	in HMar	Valencia	18 Oc
31:38+	Angela	Tanui	KEN	.92	1	in HMar	Olomouc	20 Ju
31:39+	Rose	Chelimo	KEN	12.7.89	4	in HMar	Valencia	18 Oc
31:41	Karoline	Bjerkeli Grøvdal	NOR	14.6.90	1		Oslo	25 Ap
31:48+	Helah	Kiprop	KEN	7.4.85		in HMar	Olomouc	20 Ju
31:49	Betsy	Saina	KEN	30.6.88	1		Manchester	10 Ma
31:49+	Peninah	Arusei	KEN	23.2.79	5	in HMar	Valencia	18 Oc
31:55	Gemma	Steel	GBR	12.11.85	2		Manchester	10 Ma
31:56	Wude	Ayalew	ETH	4.7.87	1		Cape Elizabeth	1 Au
31:56	Fate	Tola	ETH	22.10.87	1		Bad Liebenzell	6 Se
31:57	Edna	Kiplagat	KEN	15.9.79	3		Manchester	10 Ma
31:58+	Yebrqual	Melese	ETH	18.4.90	2	in HMar	Praha	28 Ma
31:59+	Afera	Godfay	ETH	25.9.91	3	in HMar	Praha	28 Ma
31:59	Caroline	Chepkemoi	KEN	1.3.93	4		Berlin	11 Oc
32:00	Diane	Nukuri	BDI	1.12.84	2		Cape Elizabeth	1 Au
32:00	Clémence	Calvin	FRA	17.5.90	5		Berlin	11 Oc
32:03	Rosemary	Wanjiru	KEN	9.12.94	1		Okayama	23 De
32:05	Priscah	Cherono	KEN	27.6.80	2		Langueux	13 Ju
32:05+	Joyce	Chepkirui	KEN	10.8.88	1=	in 10M	Zaandam	20 Se
32:05+	Jackline	Chepngeno	KEN	16.1.93	1=	in 10M	Zaandam	20 Se
32:07	Mercy	Wacera	KEN	17.12.88	1		Boston	21 Ju
32:07	Zerfie	Limeneh	ETH-J	10.2.97	1		Houilles	27 De
32:08	Linah	Cheruto	KEN	18.3.95	2		Praha	5 Se
32:09	Viola	Jepchumba	KEN	22.9.90	1		Casablanca	7 Ju
32:10	Kidsan	Alema	ETH	.95	3		Praha	5 Se
32:10	Stella	Chesang	UGA-J	1.12.96	2		Houilles	27 De
32:11+	Viola	Jelagat	KEN	20.4.92	4=	in HMar	Praha	28 Ma
32:11+	Lucy	Kabuu	KEN	24.3.84	4=	in HMar	Praha	28 Ma

Mark	Name		Nat	Born	Pos	Meet	Venue	Date
32:11	Dibabe	Kuma	ETH		1		Appingedam	27 Jun
32:11	Vanessa	Fernández	POR	14.9.85	1		Póvoa do Varzim	5 Jul
32:11	Shitaye	Eshete	BRN	21.5.90	4		Praha	5 Sep
32:12	Gwen	Jorgensen	USA	25.4.86	1		Sydney	2 May
32:12	Elizeba	Cherono	KEN	6.6.88	2		Appingedam	27 Jun
32:16	Meskerem	Amare	ETH-J	.97	4		Houilles	27 Dec
32:17	Pauline	Njeru	KEN	.88	5		Ottawa	23 May
32:17	Sentayehu	Ejigu	ETH	21.6.85	3		Cape Elizabeth	1 Aug
32:17	Alyson	Dixon	GBR	24.9.78	1		Middlesbrough	6 Sep
32:18	Caroline	Kilel	KEN	21.3.81	4		Manchester	10 May
32:18+	Purity	Rionoripo	KEN	10.6.93	1=	in HMar	København	13 Sep
32:19	Yelena	Korobkina	RUS	25.11.90	1		Zhukovskiy	26 Apr
32:19	Bekelech	Daba	ETH	29.12.91	3		Langueux	13 Jun
32:21	Maryanne	Wanjiru	KEN	.86	1		Brunssum	29 Mar
32:21	Madeline	Heiner	AUS	5.3.88	1		Sydney	12 Jul
32:22	Hiwot	Gebrekidan	ETH	11.5.95	2		Taroudant	8 Mar
32:22	Ann	Wanjiru	KEN	6.6.86	1		Des Moines	26 Apr
32:23	Ruti	Aga	ETH	16.1.94	2		Des Moines	26 Apr
32:23	Christelle	Daunay	FRA	5.12.74	1		Arras	30 Aug
32:23	Helen	Bekele	ETH	.94	1		Annecy	20 Sep
32:24	Felista	Wanjugu	KEN	18.2.90	2		Okayama	23 Dec
32:25	Svetlana	Kireyeva	RUS	12.6.87	2		Zhukovskiy	26 Apr
32:25	Emily	Chebet ¶	KEN	18.2.86	5		Bangalore	17 May

Mark	Name		Nat	Born	Date
32:26	Yuika	Mori	JPN	25.1.88	15 Feb
32:27	Jane	Onyangi	KEN	21.9.91	29 Mar
32:28dh	Risper	Gesabwa	KEN	10.2.89	19 Apr
32:28	Susan	Tanui	USA	28.3.87	19 Apr
32:28	Nancy	Kiprop	KEN	7.7.79	17 May
32:28	Veerle	Dejaeghere	BEL	1.8.73	6 Sep
32:30	Sakiho	Tsutsui	JPN-J	19.1.96	15 Feb
32:31	Lucy	Macharia	KEN	.91	31 May
32:32+	Esther	Chemtai	KEN	4.6.88	18 Oct
32:33	Jeļena	Prokopcuka	LAT	21.9.76	10 May
32:34	Isabellah	Andersson	SWE	12.11.80	18 Apr
32:34+	Eunice	Jepkirui	BRN	20.5.84	17 May
32:34+	Margaret	Agai	KEN	10.6.88	13 Sep
32:34	Mariam	Waithera	KEN-J	23.12.96	23 Dec
32:36	Urge	Diro	ETH	.94	20 Sep
32:37+	Sultan	Haydar	TUR	23.5.87	4 Jan
32:39	Monicah	Wanjuhi	KEN	7.11.93	28 Mar
32:39+	Pauline	Kamulu	KEN	16.4.95	23 Dec
32:39+	Mirai	Waku	JPN	1.7.95	23 Dec
32:40	Sabrina	Mockenhaupt	GER	6.12.80	1 Mar
32:41+	Isabella	Ochichi	KEN	28.10.79	23 May
32:42+	Leonidah	Mosop	KEN	.91	19 Apr
32:42+	Mulu	Seboka	ETH	24.9.84	23 May
32:44	Etalemahu	Habtewold	ETH	.90	26 Apr
32:44	Sarah	Chepchirchir	KEN	27.7.84	30 Aug
32:45	Nami	Hashimoto	JPN	8.8.91	15 Feb
32:45+	Lisa	Nemec ¶	CRO	18.5.94	28 Mar
32:45	Makida	Wordofa	ETH	.89	28 Mar
32:45	Ivy	Kibet	KEN		29 Mar
32:46	Jane	Kibii	KEN	10.3.85	28 Mar
32:46	Faith	Chepkoech	KEN	.93	4 Apr
32:46	Dominika	Napieraj	POL	12.12.91	26 Apr
32:46	Lineth	Chepkurui	KEN	23.2.88	23 May
32:46+	Sara	Hall	USA	15.4.83	15 Nov
32:46+	Brianne	Nelson	USA	27.10.80	15 Nov
32:47	Leonidah	Mosop	KEN	.91	26 Apr
32:48	Agnieszka	Mierzejewska	POL	22.10.85	26 Apr
32:48+	Jo	Pavey	GBR	20.9.73	25 Oct
32:48+	Hiroko	Miyauchi	JPN	19.6.83	23 Dec
32:49	Stephanie	Twell	GBR	17.8.89	12 Apr
32:49	Gulshat	Fazlitdinova	RUS	28.8.92	26 Apr
32:49	Nancy	Kimaiyo	KEN	.84	27 Dec
32:50	Etaferahu	Temesgen	ETH	.89	13 Jun
32:51	Chaltu	Bedo	ETH	.94	12 Apr
32:51	Charlotta	Fougberg	SWE	19.6.85	18 Apr
32:52	Amane	Beriso	ETH	.91	13 Jun
32:53	Genet	Gashie	ETH	.95	28 Mar
32:53+	Paskalia	Kipkoech	KEN	22.12.88	18 Oct
32:54	Mapaseka	Makhanya	RSA	9.4.85	29 Mar
32:54+	Yenenesh	Tilahun	ETH	.94	20 Sep
32:54+	Risa	Takenaka	JPN	6.1.90	20 Sep
32:56	Fionnuala	McCormack	IRL	24.9.84	10 May
32:57	Tarah	McKay-Korir	CAN	1.5.87	19 Apr
32:57	Dinah Lebo	Phalula	RSA	9.12.83	9 May
32:58	Sarah	Lahti	SWE	18.2.95	4 Apr
32:59	Victoria	Mitchell	AUS	25.4.82	4 Jul
32:59+	Helen	Tola	ETH	.94	13 Sep
33:00	Teresiah	Omosa	KEN-J	.96	8 Mar
33:00	Fabienne	Schlumpf	SUI	17.11.90	28 Mar
33:00	Clara	Santucci	USA	24.3.87	27 Sep

Drugs disqualification

Mark	Name		Nat	Born	Pos	Meet	Venue	Date
31:07	Josephine	Jepkoech	KEN	21.4.89	(1=)	in HMar	Ra's Al-Khaymah	13 Feb

Also many intermediate times in longer races (to 32:45)

Ostia 1 Mar: 32:06 Hirut Alemayehu ETH-J, Amane Beriso ETH, Askale Alemayehu ETH-J, 32:25 Emily Ngetich KEN, 32:26 Sylvia Kibet KEN, 32:27 Sharon Cherop KEN

Milano 29 Mar: 32:23 Rebecca Chseire KEN, 32:42 Lucy Murigi

Yangzhou 19 Apr: 32:39 Guteni Shoine ETH, 32:40 Abebech Afework ETH, Flomena Cheyech KEN

15 KILOMETRES ROAD

See also Half Marathon lists

Mark	Name		Nat	Born	Pos	Meet	Venue	Date
48:33+	Helah	Kiprop	KEN	7.4.85		in HMar	Olomouc	20 Jun
48:49	Mercy	Wacera Ngugi	KEN	17.12.88	1		Utica	11 Jul
49:00+	Viola	Jepchumba	KEN	22.9.90		in HMar	Göteborg	23 May
49:22+	Eunice	Chumba	BRN	23.5.93		in HMar	Karlovy Vary	23 May
49:45	Ruti	Aga	ETH	16.1.94	1		Istanbul	15 Nov
49:46	Gladys	Chemweno	KEN	4.7.88	2		Istanbul	15 Nov

10 MILES ROAD

10M	15k	Name		Nat	Born	Pos	Venue	Date
51:17	47:51	Vivian	Cheruiyot	KEN	11.9.83	1	Portsmouth	25 Oct
51:30	48:07	Joyce	Chepkirui	KEN	10.8.88	1	Zaandam	20 Sep

Mark		Name		Nat	Born	Pos	Meet	Venue	Date
51:34	48:11	Jackline	Chepngeno	KEN	16.1.93	2		Zaandam	20 Sep
51:44		Molly	Huddle	USA	31.8.84	1	NC	Minneapolis	4 Oct
51:49dh	48:16	Mary	Keitany	KEN	18.1.82	1	in HMar	South Shields	13 Sep
52:44	49:17	Jo	Pavey	GBR	20.9.73	2		Portsmouth	25 Oct
52:51	49:17	Doris	Changeywo	KEN	12.12.84	3		Portsmouth	25 Oct
52:52	49:25	Dibabe	Kuma	ETH		3		Zaandam	20 Sep
52:53	49:25	Yenenesh	Tilahun	ETH	.94	4		Zaandam	20 Sep
52:56	49:25	Risa	Takenaka	JPN	6.1.90	5		Zaandam	20 Sep
53:03		Neely	Spence Gracey	USA	16.4.90	2	NC	Minneapolis	4 Oct
53:06		Caroline	Rotich	KEN	13.5.84	1		Flint	22 Aug
53:06	49:24	Gemma	Steel	GBR	12.11.85	4		Portsmouth	25 Oct

Mark	Name		Nat	Born	Date	Mark	Name		Nat	Born	Date
53:10	Alexi	Pappas	USA	28.3.90	4 Oct	53:28	Alisha	Williams	USA	5.2.82	4 Oct
53:14	Laura	Thweatt	USA	17.12.88	4 Oct	53:35	Tigist	Jabore	ETH		3 May
53:27	Aliphine	Tuliamuk-Bolton	KEN	5.4.89	22 Aug	53:40	Askale	Maracchi	ETH	.87	3 May

20 KILOMETRES ROAD

And see below in Half Marathon races

20k	15k	Name		Nat	Born	Pos	Meet	Venue	Date
65:13	49:08+	Flomena	Cheyech	KEN	5.7.82		in HMar	Yangzhou	19 Apr
65:17	48:22+	Rose	Chelimo	KEN	12.7.89		in HMar	Valencia	18 Oct
65:36	49:08+	Gladys	Chesire	KEN	20.2.93		in HMar	Yangzhou	19 Apr
66:03		Nancy	Kimaiyo	KEN	.84	1		Paris	11 Oct
66:05	49:10+	Viola	Jelagat	KEN	20.4.92		in HMar	Praha	28 Mar
66:26		Molly	Huddle	USA	31.8.84	1	NC	New Haven	7 Sep
66:37+		Gladys	Cherono	KEN	12.5.83		in HMar	Berlin	27 Sep
66:40+		Mulu	Seboka	ETH	24.9.84		in Mar	Chicago	11 Oct
66:43+		Tadelech	Bekele	ETH	11.4.91		in Mar	Berlin	27 Sep
66:49		Sutume	Asefa	ETH	.94	1		Lausanne	25 Apr
67:09+		Gladys	Yator	KEN	8.8.92		in HMar	København	13 Sep
67:10+		Hirut	Alemayehu	ETH-J	19.12.93		in HMar	Lille	5 Sep
67:26		Janet	Bawcom	USA	22.8.78	2	NC	New Haven	7 Sep
67:28		Brianne	Nelson	USA	27.10.80	3	NC	New Haven	7 Sep
67:39		Lucy	Njeri	KEN	7.12.87	2		Paris	11 Oct

HALF MARATHON

Slightly downhill course: South Shields 30.5m

Mark	20k	15k	Name		Nat	Born	Pos	Meet	Venue	Date
65:09	61:54	46:14	Florence	Kiplagat	KEN	27.2.87	1		Barcelona	15 Feb
66:02	62:35	46:42	Mary	Keitany	KEN	18.1.82	1		Ra's Al-Khaymah	13 Feb
66:28	62:58	46:42	Mamitu	Daska	ETH	16.10.83	2		Ra's Al-Khaymah	13 Feb
66:38			Gladys	Cherono	KEN	12.5.83	1		Istanbul	26 Apr
66:38		47:18		Keitany			1		Olomouc	20 Jun
67:02	63:34	47:11	Cynthia	Limo	KEN	18.12.89	3		Ra's Al-Khaymah	13 Feb
67:14	63:50	48:11	Worknesh	Degefa	ETH	28.10.90	1		Praha	28 Mar
67:17		47:32	Peres	Jepchirchir	KEN	27.9.93	1		Ústí nad Labem	12 Sep
67:31	63:59	47:27	Netsanet	Gudeta	ETH	12.2.91	1		Valencia	18 Oct
67:32	dh			Keitany			1	GNR	South Shields	13 Sep
67:51	64:15	47:28		Degefa			2		Valencia	18 Oct
68:12	64:33	47:37	Genet	Yalew	ETH	31.12.92	3		Valencia	18 Oct
68:13				Degefa			1		Göteborg	23 May
68:17	64:48	48:34	Selly	Chepyego (10)	KEN	3.10.85	1		Okayama	23 Dec
68:18			Flomena	Cheyech	KEN	5.7.82	1		Luanda	6 Sep
68:21	64:43	48:18	Yebrqual	Melese	ETH	18.4.90	2		Praha	28 Mar
68:21		48:27	Rebecca	Chesire	KEN	.92	1	Stram	Milano	29 Mar
68:21		48:52	Edna	Kiplagat	KEN	15.9.79	1	GSR	Glasgow	4 Oct
68:22	64:47		Rose	Chelimo	KEN	12.7.89	1		Lisboa	22 Mar
68:23			Helah	Kiprop	KEN	7.4.85	2		Istanbul	26 Apr
68:29	65:02	48:44	Purity	Rionoripo	KEN	10.6.93	1		København	13 Sep
68:31	65:03	49:07	Molly	Huddle	USA	31.8.84	1		New York	16 Mar
68:33				Chelimo			2		Olomouc	20 Jun
68:35				Limo			1		New Delhi	29 Nov
68:35				Kiprop			2		New Delhi	29 Nov
68:36				Cheyech			1		Yangzhou	19 Apr
68:36			Gladys	Chesire	KEN	20.2.93	3		New Delhi	29 Nov
68:37				Degefa			2		Yangzhou	19 Apr
68:41		48:13	Angela	Tanui (20)	KEN	27.7.92	3		Olomouc	20 Jun
68:42	65:03	49:06	Joyce	Chepkirui	KEN	10.8.88	2		New York	16 Mar
68:43		48:35	Amane	Beriso	ETH	13.10.91	1		Ostia	1 Mar
			(31/22)							

Mark			Name		Nat	Born	Pos	Meet	Venue	Date
68:47	65:13	48:44	Sutume	Asefa	ETH	.94	2		København	13 Sep
68:51	65:18	48:48	Lucy	Kabuu	KEN	24.3.84	3		København	13 Sep
68:52			Tadelech	Bekele	ETH	11.4.91	5		New Delhi	29 Nov
68:56	65:09	48:24	Peninah	Arusei	KEN	23.2.79	1		Lille	5 Sep
69:11		49:07	Mulu	Seboka	ETH	24.9.84	1		Karlovy Vary	23 May
69:13		49:02	Emily	Ngetich	KEN	.84	2		Ostia	1 Mar
69:13		49:03	Sharon	Cherop	KEN	16.3.84	3		Ostia	1 Mar
69:14	65:41	49:08	Abebech	Afework	ETH	11.12.90	5		Yangzhou	19 Apr
			(30)							
69:17	65:38	48:46	Rei	Ohara	JPN	10.8.90	2		Okayama	23 Dec
69:18	65:42		Sara	Moreira	POR	17.10.85	2		Lisboa	22 Mar
69:21	65:37		Priscah	Jeptoo	KEN	26.6.84	3		Lisboa	22 Mar
69:22			Muluhabt	Tsega	ETH	11.9.89	3		Istanbul	26 Apr
69:27	65:51	49:24	Michi	Numata	JPN	6.5.89	1		Yamaguchi	15 Feb
69:27		49:04	Viola	Jelagat	KEN	20.4.92	1		Piacenza	3 May
69:30			Viola	Jepchumba	KEN	22.9.90	1		Udine	20 Sep
69:32		49:02	Sylvia	Kibet	KEN	28.3.84	5		Ostia	1 Mar
69:33	65:57	49:19	Diane	Nukuri	BDI	1.12.84	3		Praha	28 Mar
69:37	66:04		Eunice	Jepkirui	BRN	20.5.84	1		Gifu	17 May
			(40)							
69:39	65:55	49:06	Sally	Kipyego	KEN	19.12.85	3		New York	16 Mar
69:44	66:20		Kim	Conley	USA	14.3.86	1	NC	Houston	18 Jan
69:44	65:58	48:44	Pauline	Kamulu	KEN	16.4.95	3		Okayama	23 Dec
69:45	66:11	49:20	Isabella	Ochichi	KEN	28.10.79	2		Göteborg	23 May
69:46	66:11	49:02	Beatrice	Mutai	KEN	19.4.87	3		Göteborg	23 May
69:49			Sultan	Haydar	TUR	23.5.87	2		Adana	4 Jan
69:49	66:11	49:11	Misaki	Kato	JPN	15.6.91	2		Osaka	25 Jan
69:49			Aliphine	Tuliamuk-Bolton	KEN	5.4.89	1		Philadelphia	22 Nov
69:50		49:34	Doris	Changeywo	KEN	12.12.84	2	GSR	Glasgow	4 Oct
69:51	66:01	48:55	Afera	Godfay	ETH	25.9.91	5		Praha	28 Mar
			(50)							
69:51			Maegan	Krifchin	USA	8.4.88	1		Philadelphia	31 Oct
69:51	66:24	49:22	Yuka	Ando	JPN	16.3.94	4		Okayama	23 Dec
69:53	66:03	49:08	Caroline	Rotich	KEN	13.5.84	4		New York	16 Mar
69:53			Wude	Ayalew	ETH	4.7.87	2		Lisboa	18 Oct
69:56		49:16	Helen	Jepkurgat	KEN	21.2.89	2		Piacenza	3 May
69:56		49:33	Gemma	Steel	GBR	12.11.85	3	GSR	Glasgow	4 Oct
69:56	66:09	48:49	Eloise	Wellings	AUS	9.11.82	5		Okayama	23 Dec
69:56	66:18	49:04	Mirai	Waku	JPN	1.7.95	6		Okayama	23 Dec
69:57	66:23	49:35	Mai	Ito	JPN	23.5.84	2		Yamaguchi	15 Feb
69:57	66:27	49:48	Margaret	Agai	KEN	10.6.88	4		København	13 Sep
			(60)							
69:57	66:25	49:53	Christelle	Daunay	FRA	5.12.74	5		København	13 Sep
69:58		49:42	Jo	Pavey	GBR	20.9.73	4	GSR	Glasgow	4 Oct
69:59			Neely	Spence Gracey	USA	16.4.90	2		Philadelphia	31 Oct
70:01		49:04	Askale	Alemaheyu	ETH	11.1.96	6		Ostia	1 Mar
70:02	66:03	48:49	Sarah	Chepchirchir	KEN	27.7.84	2		Lille	5 Sep
70:09			Bekelech	Daba	ETH	29.12.91	3		Paris	8 Mar
70:10			Elizeba	Cherono	KEN	6.6.88	1		Breda	4 Oct
70:10	66:35	49:27	Esther	Chemtai	KEN	4.6.88	6		Valencia	18 Oct
70:13	66:35	49:43	Reia	Iwade	JPN	8.12.94	3		Yamaguchi	15 Feb
70:14			Shitaye	Eshete	BRN	21.5.90	2		Ústí nad Labem	12 Sep
			(70)							
70:15		48:52	Hirut	Alemayehu	ETH	19.12.93	7		Ostia	1 Mar
70:15+	66:38		Aberu	Kebede	ETH	12.9.86	1=	in Mar	Berlin	27 Sep
70:16	66:42		Brianne	Nelson	USA	27.10.80	2	NC	Houston	18 Jan
70:18			Leonidah	Mosop	KEN	.91	2		Verbania	19 Apr
70:21			Mercy	Wacera	KEN	17.12.88	1		Boston	11 Oct
70:22		49:07	Linah	Cheruto	KEN	18.3.95	2		Karlovy Vary	23 May
70:23+	66:43		Meseret	Hailu	ETH	12.9.90		in Mar	Berlin	27 Sep
70:24	66:42	49:53	Sairi	Maeda	JPN	7.11.91	1		Sendai	10 May
70:25			Biruktayit	Degefa	ETH	29.9.90	2		Philadelphia	22 Nov
70:26			Monica	Jepkoech	KEN	.85	1		Gaia	20 Sep
			(80)							
70:27	66:43		Ana Dulce	Félix	POR	23.10.82	5		Lisboa	22 Mar
70:27+	66:39	49:42	Kayoko	Fukushi	JPN	25.3.82	1	in Mar	Chicago	11 Oct
70:27	66:49	49:33	Hiroko	Miyauchi	JPN	19.6.83	8		Okayama	23 Dec
70:28+	66:40	49:41	Birhane	Dibaba	ETH	11.9.93	2=	in Mar	Chicago	11 Oct
70:28+	66:40	49:41	Meskerem	Assefa	ETH	20.9.85	2=	in Mar	Chicago	11 Oct
70:28+	66:40	49:40	Amane	Gobena	ETH	1.9.82	2=	in Mar	Chicago	11 Oct
70:28	66:48	49:25	Pauline	Njeru	KEN	.88	7		Valencia	18 Oct

Mark			Name		Nat	Born	Pos	Meet	Venue	Date
70:29			Feyse	Tadese	ETH	19.11.88	4		Lisboa	18 Oct
70:31	66:56	49:51	Mao	Kiyota	JPN	12.9.93	8		Valencia	18 Oct
70:32	66:25		Lily	Partridge	GBR	9.3.91	1		Reading	22 Ma
			(90)							
70:32			Alisha	Williams	USA	5.2.82	3		Philadelphia	31 Oct
70:34			Purity	Changwony	KEN	.90	4		Istanbul	26 Apr
70:36	67:05		Asami	Kato	JPN	12.10.90	1		Matsue	15 Ma
70:37	66:58	49:23	Guteni	Shone	ETH	17.11.91	7		Yangzhou	19 Apr
70:37	67:04		Atsede	Baysa	ETH	16.4.87	2		Gifu	17 Ma
70:39	66:52	49:55	Lisa	Nemec ¶	CRO	18.5.84	7		Praha	28 Ma
70:41	67:08		Jane	Moraa	KEN	21.9.91	1		Venlo	22 Ma
70:41			Belaynesh	Oljira	ETH	26.6.90	3		Boston	11 Oct
70:43			Risper	Chebet	KEN	6.6.92			Troyes	10 Ma
70:43			Filomena	Chepchirchir	KEN	1.12.81	2		Krems	13 Sep
			(100)							
70:45			Ednah	Kimaiyo	KEN	.88	1		Nice	26 Apr
70:46			Janet	Bawcom	USA	22.8.78	3	NC	Houston	18 Jan
70:46			Gladys	Yator	KEN	8.8.92	2		Reading	22 Ma
70:47	67:09		Kotomi	Takayama	JPN	18.2.93	2		Matsue	15 Ma
70:49	67:04		Sara	Hall	USA	15.4.83	2		Gold Coast	5 Jul
70:49			Priscah	Cherono	KEN	27.6.80	6		Lisboa	18 Oct

Mark		Name		Nat	Born	Date
70:50		Eunice	Chumba	BRN	23.5.93	20 Jun
70:50		Agnes	Barsosio	KEN	5.8.82	6 Sep
70:52		Cynthia	Kosgei	KEN	.93	29 Mar
70:52		Lalita	Babar	IND	2.6.89	29 Nov
70:54		Nancy	Kimaiyo	KEN	.84	4 Oct
70:56		Martha	Akeno	KEN	.93	11 Oct
70:57	67:16	Rina	Yamazaki	JPN	6.5.88	15 Feb
70:58	67:11	Annie	Bersagel	USA	30.3.83	18 Jan
71:00		Yoko	Shibui	JPN	14.3.79	15 Feb
71:00		Lisa	Weightman	AUS	16.1.79	18 Oct
71:01		Kellyn	Taylor	USA	22.7.86	31 Oct
71:02		Georgina	Rono	KEN	19.5.84	18 Jan
71:02		Ai	Inoue	JPN	13.1.90	15 Mar
71:02		Parendis	Lekapana	KEN	4.8.91	11 Oct
71:03		Yuko	Mizuguchi	JPN	24.5.85	1 Feb
71:04		Eri	Makikawa	JPN	22.4.93	1 Feb
71:06		Misato	Horie	JPN	10.3.87	1 Feb
71:08		Pauline	Kittu	KEN	4.7.90	25 Jan
71:08		Maja	Neuenschwander	SUI	13.2.80	8 Mar
71:10		Risa	Takenaka	JPN	6.1.90	10 May
71:10		Janet	Rono	KEN	8.12.88	13 Jun
71:10		Kara	Goucher	USA	9.7.78	6 Dec
71:11		Yeshaneh	Ababel	ETH	10.6.90	9 Jan
71:11		Yuka	Yano/Takamoto	JPN	11.6.86	15 Feb
71:12		Kaho	Tanaka	JPN	24.6.91	1 Feb
71:12		Maryanne	Wanjiru	KEN	.86	4 Apr
71:14		Alice	Kimutai	KEN	7.9.92	18 Oct
71:15+		Risa	Shigemoto	JPN	29.8.87	25 Jan
71:15		Sabrina	Mockenhaupt	GER	6.12.80	4 Apr
71:15		Emily	Chebet ¶	KEN	18.2.86	12 Apr
71:16		Ayantu	Abera	ETH	.95	4 Apr
71:17		Geneta	Kabela	ETH		19 Apr
71:17		Anna	Incerti	ITA	19.1.80	20 Sep
71:19		Ayumi	Uehara	JPN	23.11.94	15 Mar
71:19		Lucy	Murigi	KEN	7.7.85	29 Mar
71:20		Natasha	Wodak	CAN	17.12.81	16 Mar
71:20		Yewbdar	Teshome	ETH	.89	19 Apr
71:22		Etaferahu	Temesgen	ETH	.89	16 Mar
71:22		Sayo	Nomura	JPN	18.4.89	23 Dec
71:24		Hanae	Tanaka	JPN	12.2.90	1 Feb
71:24		Nanako	Kanno	JPN	30.12.94	15 Mar
71:26		Maki	Izumida	JPN-J	22.1.96	15 Mar
71:27		Helen	Tola	ETH	.94	4 Apr
71:27		Agnes	Mutune	KEN	26.6.86	21 Jun
71:28		Yurie	Doi	JPN	8.12.88	15 Feb
71:28		Yukiko	Okuno	JPN	12.9.92	15 Mar
71:28		Cassie	Fien	AUS	15.9.85	5 Jul
71:29+		Gulume	Tollesa	ETH	.92	25 Oct
71:29+		Koren	Jelela	ETH	18.1.87	25 Oct
71:29+		Ashete	Bekele	ETH	17.4.88	25 Oct
71:29+		Meseret	Mengistu	ETH	6.3.90	25 Oct
71:29		Ayumi	Kubo	JPN	.95	23 Dec
71:30		Juliet	Bottorff	USA	21.1.91	18 Jan
71:30		Aberta	Sadura	ETH		25 Jan
71:30		Alyson	Dixon	GBR	24.9.78	22 Mar
71:30+		Dinknesh	Mekasha	ETH	.85	25 Oct
71:30+		Meseret	Kitata	ETH	8.11.93	25 Oct
71:31		Isabellah	Andersson	SWE	12.11.80	29 Mar
71:31		Jessica	Trengove	AUS	15.8.87	5 Jul
71:31		Lenah	Cherotich	KEN		4 Oct
71:31+		Sardana	Trofimova	RUS	28.3.88	25 Oct
71:32		Damaris	Kemunto	KEN	.95	4 Oct
71:33		Lucy	Karimi	KEN	24.2.75	20 Jun
71:33		Fionnuala	McCormack	IRL	24.9.84	5 Sep
71:34		Orchatteri P.	Jaisha	IND	23.5.83	29 Nov
71:36		Jessica	Coulson	GBR	18.4.90	4 Oct
71:36		Paskalia	Kipkoech	KEN	22.12.88	18 Oct
71:37		Mami	Onuki	JPN	9.10.91	15 Mar
71:40+		Miho	Ihara	JPN	4.2.88	8 Mar
71:41+		Tiki	Gelana	ETH	22.10.87	22 Feb
71:41		Bezunesh	Getachew	ETH-J	.97	19 Apr
71:42+		Aselefech	Mergia	ETH	23.1.85	26 Apr
71:43+		Tigist	Tufa	ETH	26.1.87	26 Apr
71:43+		Tirfe	Tsegaye	ETH	25.11.84	26 Apr
71:43+		Jemima	Jelagat	KEN	21.12.84	26 Apr
71:44		Sakurako	Fukuchi	JPN	30.8.93	15 Mar
71:45		Caroline	Kilel	KEN	21.3.81	12 Sep
71:45		Abnet	Simegn	ETH	.86	20 Sep
71:45		Alice	Mogire	KEN	27.11.81	25 Oct
71:45		Risper	Gesabwa	KEN	10.2.89	22 Nov
71:46+		Keiko	Nogami	JPN	6.12.85	8 Mar
71:46		Sudha	Singh	IND	25.6.86	29 Nov
71:47		Atsede	Habtamu	ETH	26.10.87	20 Jun
71:48			He Yinli	CHN	20.9.88	19 Apr
71:48		Dorcas	Nzembi	KEN-J	22.12.97	6 Dec
71:49		Zewdnesh	Ayele	ETH	21.11.93	28 Mar
71:49		Hellen	Musyoka	KEN	3.1.87	6 Dec
71:50		Chaltu	Bedo	ETH	.94	19 Apr
71:50		Hana	Abo	ETH		19 Apr
71:50		Jackline	Chepngeno	KEN	16.1.93	4 Oct
71:50		Susan	Jerotich	KEN		18 Oct
71:51		Mattie	Suver	USA	10.9.87	18 Jan
71:52 dh		Jelena	Prokopcuka	LAT	21.9.76	13 Sep
71:54		Dinah Lebo	Phalula	RSA	9.12.83	25 Jul
71:55		Eri	Hayakawa	JPN	15.11.81	15 Feb
71:57		Katie	Matthews	USA	19.11.90	18 Jan
71:57		Roman	Mengistu	ETH	.95	13 Sep
72:00		Workenesh	Edesa	ETH		22 Mar
72:00+		Iwona	Lewandowska	POL	19.2.85	26 Apr
72:00		Bentu	Wodajo	ETH		6 Dec
		(200)				

Excessively downhill

Mark	Name		Nat	Born	Pos	Venue	Date
70:47	Eri	Hayakawa	JPN	15.11.81	1	San Diego (86.5m)	31 May
71:07	Jessica	Trengove	AUS	15.8.87			31 May
71:08	Lanni	Marchant	CAN	11.4.84			28 Jun
71:50	Lindsey	Scherf	USA	18.9.86			31 May

Mark	Name		Nat	Born	Pos	Meet	Venue	Date

Uncertain distance: Mar 8, Nairobi KEN (A): 1. Georgina Rono 68:08, 2. Mercy Kibarus 68:13, 3. Carolina Kilel 68:23, 4. Mercy Jemutai 68:42

Drugs disqualification

Mark			Name		Nat	Born	Pos	Venue	Date
67:32	64:00	47:11	Josephine	Jepkoech ¶	KEN	21.4.89	(4)	Ra's Al-Khaymah	13 Feb
70:14	66:31	49:28	Rkia	El Moukim ¶	MAR	22.2.88	(5)	New York	16 Mar

Mark	Name		Nat	Born	Date	Mark	Name		Nat	Born	Date
71:15+	Tetyana	Hamera ¶	UKR	1.6.83	25 Jan	71:49	Mariya	Konovalova ¶	RUS	14.8.74	12 Sep

JUNIORS

Mark	Name		Nat	Born	Pos	Venue	Date
71:26	Maki	Izumida	JPN	22.1.96	6	Matsue	15 Mar
71:41	Bezunesh	Getachew	ETH-J	.97	1	Vitry-sur-Seine	19 Apr
71:48	Dorcas	Nzembi	KEN-J	22.12.97	1	Pune	6 Dec
72:41A	Lucy	Cheruiyot	KEN	.97	3	Nairobi	25 Oct
73:07		Zhang Deshun	CHN	21.2.96	13	Yangzhou	19 Apr
73:34	Saki	Fukui	JPN	25.3.96	22	Matsue	15 Mar
73:47A	Shure	Demise	ETH	21.1.96	2	Bogotá	26 Jul

25 – 30 KILOMETRES ROAD

In addition to those shown in Marathon listing

25k	30k	Name		Nat	Born	Pos	Meet	Venue	Date
1:21:55		Sutume	Asefa	ETH	.94	1	BIG	Berlin	10 May
1:23:32	1:40:29	Tadelech	Bekele	ETH	11.4.91		in Mar	Berlin	27 Sep
1:24:01	1:41:19+	Mulu	Seboka	ETH	24.9.84		in Mar	Chicago	11 Oct
1:24:00	1:41:20+	Amane	Gobena	ETH	1.9.82		in Mar	Chicago	11 Oct
1:24:40	1:41:43+	Ashete	Bekele	ETH	17.4.88		in Mar	Frankfurt	25 Oct
	1:41:53+	Priscah	Jeptoo	KEN	26.6.84		in Mar	Milano	12 Apr
1:24:40	1:42:02+	Meseret	Mengistu	ETH	6.3.90		in Mar	Frankfurt	25 Oct
	1;42:03+	Lucy	Karimi	KEN	24.2.75		in Mar	Milano	12 Apr
1:25:15+		Rei	Ohara	JPN	10.8.90		in Mar	Nagoya	8 Mar
1:25:27	1:42:55+	Chieko	Kido	JPN	14.3.90		in Mar	Osaka	25 Jan
1:25:34	1:43:34+	Miho	Ihara	JPN	4.2.88		in Mar	Nagoya	8 Mar
1:25:21	1:44:17+	Reia	Iwade	JPN	8.12.94		in Mar	Nagoya	8 Mar

MARATHON

Mark	25k	30k	Name		Nat	Born	Pos	Venue	Date
2:19:25	1:23:13	1:39:40	Gladys	Cherono	KEN	12.5.83	1	Berlin	27 Sep
2:19:52			Mare	Dibaba	ETH	20.10.89	1	Xiamen	3 Jan
2:20:02			Aselefech	Mergia	ETH	23.1.85	1	Dubai	23 Jan
2:20:03				Cherono			2	Dubai	23 Jan
2:20:21			Lucy	Kabuu	KEN	24.3.84	3	Dubai	23 Jan
2:20:48	1:23:13	1:39:40	Aberu	Kebede	ETH	12.9.86	2	Berlin	27 Sep
2:20:59			Shure	Demise	ETH-J	21.1.96	4	Dubai	23 Jan
2:21:17				Kebede			5	Dubai	23 Jan
2:21:56			Mulu	Seboka	ETH	24.9.84	6	Dubai	23 Jan
2:22:08	1:24:15	1:41:10	Eunice	Jepkirui Kirwa	BRN	20.5.84	1	Nagoya	8 Mar
2:22:48	1:24:16	1:41:10	Sairi	Maeda	JPN	7.11.91	2	Nagoya	8 Mar
2:22:51			Tadelech	Bekele (10)	ETH	11.4.91	7	Dubai	23 Jan
2:23:12	1:24:41	1:41:36	Gulume	Tollesa	ETH	.92	1	Frankfurt	25 Oct
2:23:12	1:24:40	1:41:36	Dinknesh	Mekasha	ETH	.85	2	Frankfurt	25 Oct
2:23:15			Birhane	Dibaba	ETH	11.9.93	1	Tokyo	22 Feb
2:23:22	1:25:29	1:42:36	Tigist	Tufa	ETH	26.1.87	1	London	26 Apr
2:23:23			Yebrqual	Melese	ETH	18.4.90	1	Houston	18 Jan
2:23:26			Meseret	Mengistu	ETH	6.3.90	1	Paris	12 Apr
2:23:30			Amane	Gobena	ETH	1.9.82	2	Paris	12 Apr
2:23:32			Guteni	Shone	ETH	17.11.91	2	Houston	18 Jan
2:23:33			Abebech	Afework	ETH	11.12.90	8	Dubai	23 Jan
2:23:33	1:24:00	1:41:19	Florence	Kiplagat (20)	KEN	27.2.87	1	Chicago	11 Oct
2:23:37				Demise			1	Toronto	18 Oct
2:23:40	1:25:31	1:42:36	Mary	Keitany	KEN	18.1.82	2	London	26 Apr
2:23:41	1:25:30	1:42:36	Tirfe	Tsegaye	ETH	25.11.84	3	London	26 Apr
2:23:43			Ashete	Bekele	ETH	17.4.88	9	Dubai	23 Jan
2:23:43	1:24:00	1:41:19		Melese			2	Chicago	11 Oct
2:23:49				Melese			1	Praha	3 May
2:23:51			Biruktayit	Degefa	ETH	29.9.90	3	Houston	18 Jan
2:23:52	1:24:40	1:41:36	Koren	Jelela	ETH	18.1.87	3	Frankfurt	25 Oct
2:23:53	1:25:30	1:42:36		Mergia			4	London	26 Apr
2:24:03	1:25:09	1:42:09	Helah	Kiprop	KEN	7.4.85	2	Tokyo	22 Feb
2:24:07	1:25:27	1:42:15	Jelena	Prokopcuka	LAT	21.9.76	1	Osaka	25 Jan
2:24:11	1:23:27	1:40:15	Joyce	Chepkirui	KEN	10.8.88	1	Amsterdam	18 Oct
2:24:15	1:25:30	1:42:36		F Kiplagat			5	London	26 Apr
2:24:16			Sharon	Cherop	KEN	16.3.84	2=	Toronto	18 Oct
2:24:16			Fatuma	Sado (30)	ETH	11.10.91	2=	Toronto	18 Oct

Mark			Name		Nat	Born	Pos	Meet	Venue	Date
2:24:23	1:25:31	1:42:36	Jemima	Jelagat	KEN	21.12.84	6		London	26 Apr
2:24:24	1:24:00	1:41:19		B Dibaba			3		Chicago	11 Oct
2:24:25	1:24:01	1:41:20	Kayoko	Fukushi	JPN	25.3.82	4		Chicago	11 Oct
2:24:25				Keitany			1		New York	1 Nov
			(41/32)							
2:24:26	1:25:08	1:42:10	Tiki	Gelana	ETH	22.10.87	3		Tokyo	22 Feb
2:24:29			Betelhem	Moges	ETH	3.5.91	10		Dubai	23 Jan
2:24:33	1:23:33	1:41:19	Meseret	Hailu	ETH	12.9.90	3		Berlin	27 Sep
2:24:38	1:23:29	1:40:21	Flomena	Cheyech	KEN	5.7.82	2		Amsterdam	18 Oct
2:24:38	1:24:41	1:41:37	Sardana	Trofimova	RUS	28.3.88	4		Frankfurt	25 Oct
2:24:42	1:24:16	1:41:24	Mai	Ito	JPN	23.5.84	3		Nagoya	8 Mar
2:24:44			Sultan	Haydar	TUR	23.5.87	11		Dubai	23 Jan
2:24:44			Visiline	Jepkesho	KEN	.88	3		Paris	12 Apr
			(40)							
2:24:49	1:25:40		Sara	Moreira	POR	17.10.85	2		Praha	3 May
2:25:01	1:25:31	1:42:36	Priscah	Jeptoo	KEN	26.6.84	7		London	26 Apr
2:25:09			Purity	Rionoripo	KEN	10.6.93	1		Lisboa	18 Oct
2:25:11	1:24:00	1:41:19	Meskerem	Assefa	ETH	20.9.85	6		Chicago	11 Oct
2:25:15	1:25:31	1:42:36	Ana Dulce	Félix	POR	23.10.82	8		London	26 Apr
2:25:22			Rebecca	Chesire	KEN	.92	12		Dubai	23 Jan
2:25:24	1:25:40		Letebrhan	Gebreslasea	ETH	29.10.90	3		Praha	3 May
2:25:30			Aberu	Mekuria	ETH	24.12.83	1		Ottawa	24 May
2:25:36		1:44:37	Olga	Mazurenok	BLR	14.4.89	9		London	26 Apr
2:25:42			Melkaw	Gizaw	ETH	17.9.90	1		Ljubljana	25 Oct
			(50)							
2:25:44			Atsede	Baysa	ETH	16.4.87	1		Saitama	15 Nov
2:25:46			Agnes	Kiprop	KEN	12.12.79	1		Hengshui	26 Sep
2:25:59			Marta	Lema	ETH	.90	2		Hengshui	26 Sep
2:26:14			Fantu	Eticha	ETH	11.9.87	14		Dubai	23 Jan
2:26:16			Sylvia	Kibet	KEN	28.3.84	2		Hamburg	26 Apr
2:26:23			Rael	Kiyara	KEN	4.4.84	1		Shanghai	8 Nov
2:26:30	1:25:17	1:42:36	Asami	Kato	JPN	12.10.90	1		Rotterdam	12 Apr
2:26:31	1:25:21		Janet	Rono	KEN	8.12.88	4		Praha	3 May
2:26:39	1:24:39	1:42:14	Risa	Shigemoto	JPN	29.8.87	2		Osaka	25 Jan
2:26:43	1:25:08	1:42:08	Selly	Chepyego	KEN	3.10.85	4		Tokyo	22 Feb
			(60)							
2:26:45			Meselech	Melkamu	ETH	27.4.85	5		Ottawa	24 May
2:26:46		1:44:34	Andrea	Deelstra	NED	6.3.85	5		Berlin	27 Sep
2:26:49		1:44:37	Maja	Neuenschwander	SUI	13.2.80	6		Berlin	27 Sep
2:26:54				Ding Changqin	CHN	27.11.91	1	NC	Chongqing	22 Mar
2:26:57			Christelle	Daunay	FRA	5.12.74	5		New York	1 Nov
2:26:57			Beata	Naigambo	NAM	11.3.80	1		Valencia	15 Nov
2:27:06			Mercy	Kibarus	KEN	25.2.84	2		Warszawa	26 Apr
2:27:08			Lucy	Karimi	KEN	24.2.75	15		Dubai	23 Jan
2:27:12			Sechale	Delasa	ETH	20.9.91	4		Houston	18 Jan
2:27:14			Yeshi	Esayias	ETH	28.12.85	6		Ottawa	24 May
			(70)							
2:27:14			Netsanet	Achano	ETH	14.12.87	1		Rennes	25 Oct
2:27:16	1:25:31	1:42:39	Edna	Kiplagat	KEN	15.9.79	11		London	26 Apr
2:27:17	1:24:52	1:43:05	Meseret	Kitata	ETH	8.11.93	5		Frankfurt	25 Oct
2:27:21			Souad	Aït Salem	ALG	6.1.79	1		Hannover	19 Apr
2:27:26			Mona	Jaber Salem	BRN	.83	4		Toronto	18 Oct
2:27:28			Meseret	Legesse	ETH	28.8.87	7		Paris	12 Apr
2:27:29			Shuko	Genemo	ETH		3		Hengshui	26 Sep
2:27:34			Nancy	Kiprop	KEN	79	2		Valencia	15 Nov
2:27:35				He Yinli	CHN	20.9.88	2	NC	Chongqing	22 Mar
2:27:45			Jessica	Trengove	AUS	15.8.87	1		Melbourne	18 Oct
			(80)							
2:27:47	1:25:31	1:43:22	Iwona	Lewandowska	POL	19.2.85	12		London	26 Apr
2:27:47			Deena	Kastor	USA	14.2.73	7		Chicago	11 Oct
2:27:50	1:25:32	1:42:38	Diane	Nukuri	BDI	1.12.84	13		London	26 Apr
2:27:52			Agnes	Barsosio	KEN	5.8.82	3		Chongqing	22 Mar
2:27:53			Miriam	Wangari	KEN	22.2.79	3		Xiamen	3 Jan
2:27:57		1:44:13	Lisa	Nemec ¶	CRO	18.5.84	7		Berlin	27 Sep
2:28:00			Filomena	Costa	POR	22.2.85	1		Sevilla	22 Feb
2:28:00		1:44:17	Tomomi	Tanaka	JPN	25.1.88	8		Berlin	27 Sep
2:28:01			Malika	Asahssah	MAR	24.9.82	3		Valencia	15 Nov
2:28:02			Tizita	Terecha	ETH	.92	1		Guangzhou	6 Dec
			(90)							
2:28:04		1:44:50	Sonia	Samuels	GBR	16.5.79	9		Berlin	27 Sep
2:28:09	1:24:56	1:42:38	Risa	Takenaka	JPN	6.1.90	4		Nagoya	8 Mar

Mark			Name		Nat	Born	Pos	Meet	Venue	Date
2:28:09			Lanni	Marchant	CAN	11.4.84	5		Toronto	18 Oct
2:28:12	1:25:57	1:43:32	Gladys	Tejeda #	PER	30.9.85	2		Rotterdam	12 Apr
2:28:18			Aynalem	Kassahun	ETH		1		Barcelona	15 Mar
2:28:18			Inés	Melchor	PER	30.8.86	1		Santiago de Chile	12 Apr
2:28:19	1:25:34	1:43:33	Keiko	Nogami	JPN	6.12.85	5		Nagoya	8 Mar
2:28:20				Kim Sung-eun	KOR	24.2.89	2		Seoul	15 Mar
2:28:23			Laura	Thweatt	USA	17.12.88	7		New York	1 Nov
2:28:24		1:44:12	Fate (100)	Tola	ETH	22.10.87	10		Berlin	27 Sep

Mark	Name		Nat	Born	Date
2:28:29	Annie	Bersagel	USA	30.3.83	26 Apr
2:28:35		Liu Ruihuan	CHN	29.6.92	26 Sep
2:28:36	Yuko	Watanabe	JPN	3.11.87	25 Jan
2:28:39		Wang Xueqin	CHN	1.1.91	15 Mar
2:28:39	Lisa	Hahner	GER	20.11.89	25 Oct
2:28:40	Kellyn	Taylor	USA	22.7.86	18 Jan
2:28:42	Tatyana	Arkhipova	RUS	8.4.83	26 Apr
2:28:43	Kaori	Yoshida	JPN	4.8.81	15 Nov
2:28:57	Diana	Lobacevske	LTU	7.8.80	26 Apr
2:29:07	Milly	Clark	AUS	1.3.89	18 Oct
2:29:08	Chieko	Kido	JPN	14.3.90	25 Jan
2:29:10	Anna	Incerti	ITA	19.1.80	8 Mar
2:29:10	Mulu	Diro	ETH	.94	15 Mar
2:29:12		Kim Hye-song	PRK	9.3.93	12 Apr
2:29:12	Margaret	Agai	KEN	10.6.88	18 Oct
2:29:13	Olha	Kotovska	UKR	5.12.83	19 Apr
2:29:16	Reia	Iwade	JPN	8.12.94	8 Mar
2:29:18	Alina	Prokopyeva	RUS	16.8.85	26 Apr
2:29:24	Etaferahu	Temesgen	ETH	.89	24 May
2:29:26		Yue Chao	CHN	5.1.91	15 Mar
2:29:27	Rika	Shintaku	JPN	19.10.85	25 Jan
2:29:28	Monika	Stefanowicz	POL	15.5.80	19 Apr
2:29:30	Chaltu	Waka	ETH	.85	26 Apr
2:29:30	Alyson	Dixon	GBR	24.9.78	27 Sep
2:29:32A	Elizabeth	Rumokol	KEN	26.3.83	25 Oct
2:29:37	Askale	Tafa	ETH	27.9.84	23 Jan
2:29:38	Krista	Duchene	CAN	9.1.77	12 Apr
2:29:39	Ruth	Wanjiru	KEN	11.9.81	27 Sep
2:29:40	Atsede	Habtamu	ETH	26.10.87	18 Oct
2:29:41	Katarzyna	Kowalska	POL	7.4.85	27 Sep
2:29:45	Olena	Burkovska	UKR	9.8.81	8 Mar
2:29:45	Alessandra	Aguilar	ESP	1.7.78	26 Apr
2:29:45	Isabella	Ochichi	KEN	28.10.79	13 Dec
2:29:46	Workitu	Ayanu	ETH	19.4.87	18 Oct
2:29:49	Ayelu	Lemma	ETH		12 Apr
2:29:56	Mari	Ozaki	JPN	16.7.75	25 Jan
2:30:07	Halima	Hassen	ETH	10.11.92	22 Mar
2:30:07	Maryna	Domantsevich	BLR	6.6.85	26 Apr
2:30:07	Jess	Draskau-Petersson	DEN	8.9.77	11 Oct
2:30:11	Racheal Jemutai Mutgaa		KEN		6 Dec
2:30:13	Agnes	Mutune	KEN	26.6.86	25 Oct
2:30:18	Natalya	Starkova	RUS	8.11.87	25 Oct
2:30:19	Goitetom	Haftu	ETH	.87	12 Apr
2:30:19	Anna	Hahner	GER	20.11.89	27 Sep
2:30:21	Eri	Hayakawa (1:25:55)	JPN	15.11.81	8 Mar
2:30:24	Aki	Otagiri	JPN	20.8.90	8 Mar
2:30:25	Madoka	Ogi	JPN	26.10.83	22 Feb
2:30:25	Pamela	Rotich	KEN		19 Apr
2:30:25	Nancy	Koech	KEN	.86	6 Sep
2:30:28	Chaltu	Chimdesa	ETH	.95	15 Mar
2:30:32	Esther	Chemtai	KEN	4.6.88	12 Apr
2:30:33	Abeba	Gebremeskel	ETH	.89	11 Oct
2:30:35	Beatrice	Toroitich	KEN	15.12.81	11 Oct
2:30:36	Caroline	Chepkwony	KEN	18.4.84	12 Apr
2:30:36	Rebecca	Jepchirchir	KEN	.89	25 Oct
2:30:39	Ayumi	Sakaida	JPN	7.11.85	5 Apr
2:30:44	Sabrina	Mockenhaupt	GER	6.12.80	15 Nov
2:30:47	Emily	Ngetich	KEN	.84	12 Apr
2:30:49	Risper	Gesabwa (1:25:27)	KEN	10.2.89	25 Oct
2:30:50	Fatna	Maraoui	ITA	10.7.77	15 Nov
2:30:52	Miho	Ihara	JPN	4.2.88	8 Mar
2:30:55	Agnieszka	Mierzejewska	POL	22.10.85	19 Apr
2:30:56	Kumeshi	Sichala	ETH	.95	18 Jan
2:30:58	Damte	Hirut	ETH		22 Mar
2:30:58		Hua Shaoqing	CHN	12.2.94	26 Sep
2:30:59		Kim Kum-ok	PRK	12.9.88	12 Apr
2:31:01	Alem	Fikre	ETH	22.10.88	22 Mar
2:31:02	Mapaseka	Makhanya	RSA	9.4.85	19 Apr
2:31:02	Alem	Mokonnin	ETH	19.6.94	25 Oct
2:31:06	Worknesh	Edesa	ETH		25 Jan
2:31:06	Serena	Burla	USA	29.7.82	30 Aug
2:31:06	Yoko	Shibui	JPN	14.3.79	15 Nov
2:31:08	Belaynesh	Shifera	ETH	.88	15 Mar
2:31:08	Nataliya	Lehonkova	UJR	27.2.82	26 Oct
2:31:14	Sara	Hall	USA	15.4.83	11 Oct
2:31:18	Shiho	Takechi	JPN	18.8.90	8 Mar
2:31:20	Mary	Chemutai	KEN		19 Apr
2:31:23	Haruna	Takada	JPN	17.2.90	8 Mar
2:31:23	Rasa	Drazdauskaité	LTU	20.3.81	30 Aug
2:31:25	Helen	Tola	ETH	.94	25 Oct
2:31:25	Ednah	Kimaiyo	KEN	.88	25 Oct
2:31:25	Vanessa	Fernández	POR	14.9.85	15 Nov
2:31:28	Deborah	Toniolo	ITA	24.4.77	27 Sep
2:31:31		Sin Yong-sun	PRK	20.5.90	20 Sep
2:31:31	Susan	Partridge	GBR	4.1.80	11 Oct
2:31:34	Priscah	Cherono	KEN	27.6.80	29 Nov
2:31:38	Helena	Kiprop	KEN	9.9.76	26 Apr
2:31:38		Zhang Yingying	CHN	4.1.90	26 Sep
2:31:40		Ma Yugui	CHN	4.3.95	11 Oct
2:31:40	Serkalem	Abrha	ETH	8.3.87	4 Oct
2:31:44	Jane	Kibii	KEN	10.3.85	4 Oct
2:31:46		Kim Hye-gyong	PRK	9.3.93	25 Jan
2:31:53	Natalya	Sokolova	RUS	12.3.82	11 May
2:31:56	Veerle	Dejaeghere	BEL	1.8.73	27 Sep
2:31:57	Valary	Aiyabei	KEN	.91	25 Jan
2:32:01	Vianney	De La Rosa	MEX	4.8.86	18 Jan
2:32:06	Georgina	Rono	KEN	19.5.84	14 Jun
2:32:08	Winfridah	Kebaso	KEN	16.4.85	15 Nov
2:32:10	Yui	Okada	JPN	15.3.94	30 Aug
2:32:11	Bekelech (200)	Daba	ETHJ	29.12.91	29 Nov

Downhill

Mark	Name		Nat	Born	Pos	Venue	Date
2:24:55	Caroline	Rotich	KEN	13.5.84	1	Boston (136m dh)	20 Apr
2:25:09	Buzunesh	Deba	ETH	8.9.87	3	Boston	20 Apr
2:25:39	Desiree	Linden	USA	26.7.83	4	Boston	20 Apr
2:26:40	Caroline	Kilel	KEN	21.3.81	6	Boston	20 Apr
2:27:47	Shalane	Flanagan	USA	8.7.81	9	Boston	20 Apr

Drugs disqualification

Mark			Name		Nat	Born	Pos	Venue	Date
2:22:09	1:24:15	1:41:08	Tetyana	Hamera ¶	UKR	1.6.83	(1)	Osaka	25 Jan
2:22:27	1:24:16	1:41:10	Mariya	Konovalova ¶	RUS	14.8.74	(2)	Nagoya	8 Mar
2:23:06			Aleksandra	Duliba ¶	BLR	9.1.88	(8)	Dubai	23 Jan
2:26:33	1:25:31	1:42:36	Rkia	El Moukim ¶	MAR	22.2.88	(10)	London	26 Apr
2:31:34			Tetyana	Vernyhor	UKR	23.1.83	(3)	Lódz	19 Apr

JUNIORS

Mark	Name		Nat	Born	Pos	Venue	Date
2:20:59	Shure	Demise	ETH-J	21.1.96	4	Dubai	23 Jan
	2:23:37 1 Toronto 18 Oct	2:27:14dh 8 Boston 20 Apr					
2:33:24	Alisa	Vainio	FIN	16.11.97	1	Lappeenranta	19 Sep
2:33:49	Abebech	Tsegaye	ETH	.96	2	Sevilla	22 Sep

Mark	Name		Nat	Born	Pos	Meet	Venue	Date
2:35:25		Lee Suk-jeong	KOR-Y	24.2.99	9		Seoul	15 Mar

100 KILOMETRES

Mark	Name		Nat	Born	Pos	Meet	Venue	Date
7:08:35	Camille	Herron	USA	25.12.81	1	WCh	Winschoten	12 Sep
7:20:48	Kajsa	Berg	SWE	16.1.79	2	WCh	Winschoten	12 Sep
7:26:24		Herron			1		Madison	11 Apr
7:27:11	Marija	Vrajic Trosic	CRO	22.9.76	3	WCh	Winschoten	12 Sep
7:29:01	Sarah	Bard	USA	20.6.84	4	WCh	Winschoten	12 Sep
7:31:33	Joasia	Zakrzewski	GBR	19.1.76	5	WCh	Winschoten	12 Sep
7:34:09	Marina	Zhalybina	RUS	18.12.75	6	WCh	Winschoten	12 Sep
7:36:39	Chiyuki	Mochizuki	JPN	29.9.86	1		Yubetsu	28 Jun
7:37:09		Vrajic Trosic			1		Stockholm	8 Aug
7:38:15	Stina	Svensson	SWE	11.6.73	7	WCh	Winschoten	12 Sep
7:39:28	Kirstin	Bull	AUS	2.8.81	8	WCh	Winschoten	12 Sep
7:39:42	Irina	Antropova (10)	RUS	2.6.82	9	WCh	Winschoten	12 Sep
7:39:50	Susan	Harrison	GBR	6.8.71	10	WCh	Winschoten	12 Sep
7:41:42	Nikolina	Sustic	CRO	24.7.87	1		Firenze	31 May
7:41:46		Sustic			2		Stockholm	8 Aug
7:43:16	Hisayo	Matsumoto	JPN	.78	2		Yubetsu	28 Jun
7:44:31	Shiho	Katayama	JPN	18.12.77	3		Yubetsu	28 Jun
7:44:45	Veronika	Jurisic	CRO	6.4.77	11	WCh	Winschoten	12 Sep
7:51:19		Svensson			3	1 NC	Stockholm	8 Aug
7:52:05	Frida (20/16)	Södermark	SWE	5.8.78	12	WCh	Winschoten	12 Sep
7:52:39	Mikiko	Ota	JPN	28.4.75	13	WCh	Winschoten	12 Sep
7:53:56	Mai	Fujisawa	JPN	21.9.74	4		Yubetsu	28 Jun
7:56:24	Laurence	Klein	FRA	22.1.69	14	WCh	Winschoten	12 Sep
7:57:05	Mieke	Dupont	BEL	28.6.73	16	WCh	Winschoten	12 Sep
7:58:22	Caroline	Dubois	FRA	8.5.83	1		Chavagnes-en-Paillers	16 May

Mark	Name		Nat	Born	Date
8:00:43	Marita	Eisler	AUS	7.3.80	7 Jun
8:00:56t	Patrycja	Bereznowska	POL	17.10.75	8 Nov
8:01:41	Dominika	Stelmach	POL	28.2.82	7 Nov
8:02:01	Meghan	Arbogast	USA	16.4.61	12 Sep
8:02:09	Pamela	Veith	GER	10.7.73	11 Apr
8:05:48	Barbara	Cimmarusti	ITA	18.12.71	12 Sep
8:06:09	Aiko	Kanematsu	JPN	.80	28 Jun
8:07:06	Gwenaelle	Guillou	FRA	25.9.70	16 May
8:07:47	Mina	Nagaoka	JPN	.69	28 Jun
8:09:20	Olivia	Hartweg (31)	FRA	29.9.71	12 Sep
Indoors					
8:07:40	Alsu	Asanova	RUS	21.9.86	14 Feb

24 HOURS

Mark		Name		Nat	Born	Pos	Meet	Venue	Date
244.495		Katalin	Nagy	USA	5.5.79	1	WCh	Torino	12 Apr
239.740		Traci	Falbo	USA	12.11.71	2	WCh	Torino	12 Apr
238.964		Maria	Jansson	SWE	10.7.85	3	WCh	Torino	12 Apr
235.811		Maggie	Guterl	USA	20.8.80	4	WCh	Torino	12 Apr
233.395		Patrycja	Bereznowska	POL	17.10.75	5	WCh	Torino	12 Apr
230.244		Jodie	Oborne	AUS	9.5.71	6	WCh	Torino	12 Apr
230.088	t	Beth	Pascall	GBR	15.9.87	1		London (BP)	20 Sep
230.054		Annika	Nilrud	SWE	7.12.75	7	WCh	Torino	12 Apr
227.429	t		Oborne			1		Soochow	22 Nov
227.090		Isobel	Wykes	GBR	24.4.78	8	WCh	Torino	12 Apr
226.002		Julia	Fatton (10)	GER	24.4.72	9	WCh	Torino	12 Apr
225.989		Aleksandra (12/11)	Niwinska	POL	23.1.86	10	WCh	Torino	12 Apr
223.650		Ruthann	Sheahan	IRL	30.4.75	11	WCh	Torino	12 Apr
223.497		Antje	Krause	GER	1.5.72	1		Reichenbach	28 Jun
222.694		Jennifer	Hoffman	USA	1.7.78	1		Cleveland	20 Sep
221.714		Debbie	Martin-Consani	GBR	4.4.75	12	WCh	Torino	12 Apr
221.414		Denise	Zimmermann	SUI	25.11.75	1		Basel	10 May
221.113	t	Nikki	Wynd	AUS	22.6.72	1		Coburg	19 Apr
220.686	t		Ying Shan	CHN	.82	1		Soochow	22 Nov
219.501		Sharon	Law	GBR	9.3.75	13	WCh	Torino	12 Apr
219.084		Agata	Matejczuk	POL	27.11.81	14	WCh	Torino	12 Apr
218.624		Sigrid (20)	Hoffmann	GER	11.9.65	15	WCh	Torino	12 Apr
218.600		Veronika	Jurisic	CRO	6.4.77	16	WCh	Torino	12 Apr
218.156		Ninette	Banoun	NOR	13.10.64	17	WCh	Torino	12 Apr
218.070		Laurie	Dymond	USA	30.11.65	2		Cleveland	20 Sep

Mark	Name		Nat	Born	Date
217.639 t	Alison	Young	GBR	26.11.73	20 Sep
217.292	Luisa	Zecchino	ITA	11.12.67	12 Apr
215.992	Antje	Schuhaj	GER	11.4.68	12 Apr
215.963	Torill	Fonn	SWE	1.11.67	12 Apr
215.782		Chou Ling-Chun	TPE	28.2.72	14 Feb
214.556	Patricia	Verschuere	BEL	25.1.68	12 Apr
213.675	Gabriele	Werthmüller	SUI	31.3.74	12 Apr
213.573 t	Nicole	Barker	AUS	16.7.71	19 Apr
213.177	Linda	Voets	NED	17.8.81	12 Apr
212.556	Veerle	Beernaert	BEL	2.7.69	12 Apr
212.280	Heike	Bergmann	GER	16.12.62	12 Apr
212.234	Anne-Marie	Vernet	FRA	15.12.67	13 Sep
211.177	Tatyana	Maslova	RUS	23.6.75	12 Apr
211.100 t	Wilma	Dierx	NED	11.5.66	20 Dec
211.041 t	Åsa	Hällstorp	SWE	20.7.73	1 Aug
210.824	Megan	Stegemiller	USA	29.8.88	26 Apr

Mark	Name		Nat	Born	Pos	Meet	Venue	Date
Indoors								
20.198	Sumie	Inagaki	JPN	6.4.66	1		Espoo	22 Feb

Mark	Name		Nat	Born	Date
16.456	Torill	Fonn	SWE	1.11.67	22 Feb
10.764	Therese	Falk	NOR	5.8.75	22 Nov

Best track times

Mark	Name		Nat	Born	Date
215.257	Torill	Fonn	SWE	1.11.67	1 Aug
212.547	Antje	Krause	GER	1.5.72	20 Dec

2000 METRES STEEPLECHASE

Mark	Name		Nat	Born	Pos	Meet	Venue	Date
:02.16	Virginia	Nyambura	KEN	20.7.93	1	ISTAF	Berlin	6 Sep
:02.47	Beatrice	Chepkoech	KEN	6.7.91	2	ISTAF	Berlin	6 Sep
:04.20	Gesa-Felicitas	Krause	GER	3.8.92	3	ISTAF	Berlin	6 Sep
:10.82	Magdalene	Masai	KEN	4.4.93	4	ISTAF	Berlin	6 Sep
:14.34	Tigist	Mekonen	BRN-J	7.7.97	5	ISTAF	Berlin	6 Sep
:15.52		Krause			1		Pliezhausen	17 May
:16.19A	Sandra Felis	Tuei	KEN-Y	20.1.98	1	NC-y	Nairobi	17 Jun
:16.25	Birtukan	Fente	ETH	18.6.89	6	ISTAF	Berlin	6 Sep
:16.86	Genevieve	LaCaze	AUS	4.8.89	7	ISTAF	Berlin	6 Sep
:17.15A	Celphine	Chespol	KEN-Y	23.3.99	1	WY	Cali	17 Jul
:18.12	Ann	Gathoni	KEN-Y	5.3.98	8	ISTAF	Berlin	6 Sep
:22.30	Natalya	Vlasova	RUS	19.7.88	9	ISTAF	Berlin	6 Sep
:22.3	Aleksandra	Pavlyutenkova	RUS	21.3.90	1		Yerino	25 Jul

Mark	Name		Nat	Born	Date
:24.21	Ophélie	Claude-Boxberger	FRA	18.10.88	17 May
:25.28	Jessica	Furlan	CAN	15.3.90	21 Mar
:26.79	Racheal	Bamford	GBR	4.8.89	25 Aug
6:27.27	Marusa	Mismas	SLO	24.10.94	18 Sep
6:27.95	Charlotta	Fougberg	SWE	19.6.85	1 Jul
6:28.49	Sanaa	Koubaa	GER	6.1.85	6 Sep

JUNIORS

See main list for top 4 juniors. 6 performances by 4 women to 6:24.0. Additional marks and further juniors:

Tuei 6:19.612 WY Cali 17 Jul 6:20.47 1 Af-Y Réduit 25 Apr

Mark	Name		Nat	Born	Pos	Meet	Venue	Date
:32.0A	Betty	Sigei	KEN-Y	30.9.98	3		Nairobi	1 Apr
:32.9A	Agrie	Belachew	ETH-Y	20.1.99	1		Assela	15 May
:33.3A	Beletu	Haile	ETH-Y	8.5.99	2		Assela	15 May
:33.8A	Asmerech	Nega	ETH-Y		3		Assela	15 May
:34.23	Bezuayeh	Mohamed	ETH	4.1.96	11	ISTAF	Berlin	6 Sep

3000 METRES STEEPLECHASE

Mark	Name		Nat	Born	Pos	Meet	Venue	Date
:05.36	Habiba	Ghribi	TUN	9.4.84	1	VD	Bruxelles	11 Sep
:10.15	Hyvin	Jepkemoi	KEN	13.1.92	2	VD	Bruxelles	11 Sep
:11.28		Ghribi			1	Herc	Monaco	17 Jul
:12.51		Jepkemoi			2	Herc	Monaco	17 Jul
:12.63	Sofia	Assefa	ETH	14.11.87	3	VD	Bruxelles	11 Sep
:13.85	Virginia	Nyambura	KEN	20.7.93	3	Herc	Monaco	17 Jul
:14.73	Hiwot	Ayalew	ETH	6.3.90	4	VD	Bruxelles	11 Sep
:14.98		Ayalew			4	Herc	Monaco	17 Jul
:15.08		Jepkemoi			1	GGala	Roma	4 Jun
:15.59	Emma	Coburn	USA	19.10.90	1	NC	Eugene	27 Jun
:15.75		Nyambura			2	GGala	Roma	4 Jun
:16.87		Ayalew			3	GGala	Roma	4 Jun
:16.99		Nyambura			1	Athl	Lausanne	9 Jul
:17.22		Ayalew			2	Athl	Lausanne	9 Jul
:17.74	Purity	Kirui	KEN	13.8.91	5	VD	Bruxelles	11 Sep
:17.89		Kirui			5	Herc	Monaco	17 Jul
:19.11		Jepkemoi			1	WCh	Beijing	26 Aug
:19.24		Ghribi			2	WCh	Beijing	26 Aug
:19.25	Gesa-Felicitas	Krause	GER	3.8.92	3	WCh	Beijing	26 Aug
:20.01		Assefa			4	WCh	Beijing	26 Aug
:20.15		Krause			1	Herc	Monaco	17 Jul
:20.38		Nyambura			6	VD	Bruxelles	11 Sep
:20.44	Lydia	Chepkurui	KEN	23.8.84	4	GGala	Roma	4 Jun
:20.64	Salima Alami	El Ouali (10)	MAR	29.12.83	7	Herc	Monaco	17 Jul
:20.65	Tigist	Mekonen	BRN-J	7.7.97	8	Herc	Monaco	17 Jul
:20.67		Coburn			3	Athl	Lausanne	9 Jul
:21.40	Ruth	Chebet	BRN-J	17.11.96	9	Herc	Monaco	17 Jul
:21.51		Nyambura			1	DL	Doha	15 May
:21.54		Ayalew			2	DL	Doha	15 May
:21.56	Madeline	Heiner	AUS	5.3.88	5	GGala	Roma	4 Jun
	(30/13)							
:21.78		Coburn			5	WCh	Beijing	26 Aug
:23.48	Stephanie	Garcia	USA	3.5.88	2	NC	Eugene	27 Jun
:24.91	Birtukan	Fente	ETH	18.6.89	7	GGala	Roma	4 Jun
:24.92	Colleen	Quigley	USA	20.11.92	3	NC	Eugene	27 Jun
:25.77	Yekaterina	Sokolenko	RUS	13.9.92	1	WUG	Gwangju	10 Jul

Mark	Name		Nat	Born	Pos	Meet	Venue	Date
9:25.91	Rosefline	Chepngetich	KEN-J	17.6.97	3h2	WCh	Beijing	24 Au
9:27.86	Lalita	Babar	IND	2.6.89	4h2	WCh	Beijing	24 Au
9:27.87	Fadwa	Sidi Madane	MAR	20.11.94	4h3	WCh	Beijing	24 Au
	(20)							
9:29.10	Etenesh	Diro	ETH	10.5.91	1		Sotteville-lès-Rouen	6 Ju
9:29.16	Magdalene	Masai	KEN	4.4.93	5	DL	Birmingham	7 Ju
9:30.23	Özlem	Kaya	TUR	20.4.90	7h2	WCh	Beijing	24 Au
9:30.89	Hanane	Ouhaddou	MAR	1.1.82	1		Ninove	1 Au
9:31.03	Leah	O'Connor	USA	30.8.92	4	NC	Eugene	27 Ju
9:31.32	Ashley	Higginson	USA	17.3.89	2	adidas	New York	13 Ju
9:31.36	Courtney	Frerichs	USA	18.1.93	2	NCAA	Eugene	13 Ju
9:31.70	Svetlana	Kudzelich	BLR	7.5.87	3	adidas	New York	13 Ju
9:33.34	Tugba	Güvenç	TUR	9.7.94	1		Istanbul	14 Ju
9:33.41	Silvia	Danekova	BUL	7.2.83	1	BalkC	Pitesti	1 Au
	(30)							
9:34.15	Caroline	Chepkurui	KEN	12.3.90	7	Athl	Lausanne	9 Ju
9:35.07	Natalya	Aristarkhova	RUS	31.10.89	1	NC	Cheboksary	5 Au
9:35.10	Marusa	Mismas	SLO	24.10.94	1		Bratislava	9 Ma
9:35.17	Genevieve	LaCaze	AUS	4.8.89	4	adidas	New York	13 Ju
9:35.56	Ophélie	Claude-Boxberger	FRA	18.10.88	2		Ninove	1 Au
9:35.69	Geneviève	Lalonde	CAN	5.9.91	5	adidas	New York	13 Ju
9:35.99	Natalya	Vlasova	RUS	19.7.88	2	WUG	Gwangju	10 Ju
9:36.10	Amina	Bettiche	ALG	14.12.87	5h1	WCh	Beijing	24 Au
9:36.52	Victoria	Mitchell	AUS	25.4.82	3		Ninove	1 Au
9:36.56	Lyudmila	Lebedeva	RUS	23.5.90	2	NC	Cheboksary	5 Au
	(40)							
9:36.63	Aisha	Praught	USA/JAM	14.12.89	3		Sotteville-lès-Rouen	6 Ju
9:36.72	Bezuayehu	Mohamed	ETH-J	4.1.96	1		Montbéliard	5 Ju
9:36.79	Yekaterina	Ivonina	RUS	14.6.94	1		Sochi	28 Ma
9:36.87	Mariya	Shatalova	UKR	3.3.89	8h2	WCh	Beijing	24 Au
9:36.88	Bridget	Franek	USA	8.11.87	6	adidas	New York	13 Ju
9:36.90	Sandra	Eriksson	FIN	4.6.89	1	NC	Pori	2 Au
9:37.09	Shalaya	Kipp	USA	19.8.90	6	NC	Eugene	27 Ju
9:37.12	Eunice	Jepkorir	KEN	17.2.82	10	VD	Bruxelles	11 Se
9:37.84	Marisa	Howard	USA	9.8.92	4	NCAA	Eugene	13 Ju
9:38.16	Daisy	Jepkemei	KEN-J	13.2.96	8	DL	Doha	15 Ma
	(50)							
9:39.20	Jessica	Furlan	CAN	15.3.90	3	Jordan	Stanford	2 Ma
9:39.37	Yekaterina	Doseykina	RUS	30.3.90	1	Znam	Zhukovskiy	19 J
9:40.07	Erin	Teschuk	CAN	25.10.94	10h2	WCh	Beijing	24 Au
9:40.21	Klara	Bodinson	SWE	11.6.90	4		Ninove	1 Au
9:40.39	Lennie	Waite	GBR	4.5.86	1		Karlstad	22 J
9:40.63	Fabienne	Schlumpf	SUI	17.11.90	1		Oordegem	23 Ma
9:40.69	Agnes	Chesang	KEN	1.4.86	2	WMilG	Mungyeong	4 Oc
9:40.89	Maëva	Danois	FRA	10.3.93	2	EU23	Tallinn	11 J
9:40.99	Jamie	Cheever	USA	28.2.87	1		Letterkenny	10 J
9:41.40	Ann	Gathoni	KEN-Y	5.3.98	4		Sotteville-lès-Rouen	6 Ju
	(60)							
9:41.42	Rosa	Flanagan	NZL-J	28.2.96	4		Melbourne	21 Ma
9:41.43		Li Zhenzhu	CHN	13.12.85	2	AsiC	Wuhan	6 Ju
9:41.84	Lucie	Sekanová	CZE	5.8.89	1	ECCp	Mersin	30 Ma
9:41.91	Birtukan	Adamu	ETH	29.4.92	13	DL	Doha	15 Ma
9:42.14	Diana	Martín	ESP	1.4.81	12	Herc	Monaco	17 J
9:42.61	Kerry	O'Flaherty	IRL	15.7.81	2		Letterkenny	10 J
9:42.77	Joan	Chepkemoi	KEN	24.11.93	14	DL	Doha	15 Ma
9:42.93	Rachel	Johnson	USA	30.4.93	6	NCAA	Eugene	13 Ju
9:43.34	Michele	Finn	IRL	16.12.89	3		Letterkenny	10 J
9:44.14	Sara	Treacy	IRL	22.6.89	4		Letterkenny	10 J
	(70)							
9:44.68	Nicole	Bush	USA	4.4.86	8	adidas	New York	13 Ju
9:44.74	Emma	Oudiou	FRA	2.10.95	3	EU23	Tallinn	11 J
9:45.05	Svetlana	Shestakova	RUS	30.4.92	2	Znam	Zhukovskiy	19 J
9:45.75	Valeriya	Mara	RUS	22.2.83	3	Znam	Zhukovskiy	19 J
9:46.00A	Stella	Ruto	KEN-J	12.12.96	5	NC	Nairobi	11 J
9:46.06	Charlotta	Fougberg	SWE	19.6.85	1		Göteborg	5 Se
9:46.29A	Marion	Kibor	KEN	27.9.94	6	NC	Nairobi	11 J
9:46.34	Camilla	Richardsson	FIN	14.9.93	4	EU23	Tallinn	11 J
9:46.66	Sarah	Pease	USA	9.11.87	4		Karlstad	22 J
9:46.81	Sanaa	Koubaa	GER	6.1.85	2		Oordegem	23 Ma
	(80)							
9:46.82		Zhang Xinyan	CHN	9.2.94	3	AsiC	Wuhan	6 Ju

Mark	Name		Nat	Born	Pos	Meet	Venue	Date
:46.82	Viktoriya	Ivanova	RUS	21.11.91	4	NC	Cheboksary	5 Aug
:47.16	Rolanda	Bell	PAN	27.10.87	9	adidas	New York	13 Jun
:47.31	Sudha	Singh	IND	25.6.86	2	NC	Kolkata	17 Sep
:47.4A	Nancy	Kimaiyo	KEN	.84	1		Nairobi	20 Jun
:48.01	Juliet	Chekwel	UGA	25.5.90	1		Watford	27 Jun
:48.33	Ana Cristina	Narvaez	MEX	12.8.91	5		Los Angeles (ER)	14 May
:48.48	Elif	Karabulut	TUR	8.8.91	1		Mersin	2 May
:48.75	Eva	Krchová	CZE	10.9.89	6	Jordan	Stanford	2 May
:48.89	Ingeborg (90)	Løvnes	NOR	5.9.92	7	Jordan	Stanford	2 May
:49.88	Maya	Rehberg	GER	28.4.94	1		Kessel-Lo	8 Aug
:50.10A	Jackline	Cherono	KEN-Y	25.6.98	7	NC	Nairobi	11 Jul
:50.47	Collier	Lawrence	USA	4.10.86	1rB	Jordan	Stanford	2 May
:50.57	Madelin	Talbert	USA	23.4.94	2h1	NCAA-E	Jacksonville	29 May
:51.21	Zita	Kácser	HUN	2.10.88	1		Debrecen	5 Sep
:51.63	Viktoriya	Voronko	RUS	15.5.91	1h2	NCAA-E	Jacksonville	29 May
:51.89A	Lydia	Rotich	KEN	8.8.88	2h2	NC	Nairobi	9 Jul
:52.14	Elena	Panaet	ROU	5.6.93	1	NC	Pitesti	25 Jul
:52.23	Natalya	Gorchakova	RUS	17.4.83	2	NCp	Yerino	9 Jul
:52.62	Ann (100)	Ndungu	KEN	.95	1		Rehlingen	25 May

Mark	Name		Nat	Born	Date
:52.66	Sofie	Gallein	BEL	7.8.92	29 May
:52.73	Mekdes	Bekele	ETH	20.1.87	6 Jul
:52.85	Olga	Vovk	RUS	13.2.93	5 Aug
:53.03	Olga	Dereveva	RUS	5.4.85	28 May
:53.1	Muriel	Coneo	COL	15.3.87	14 Jun
:53.45	Mary	Goldkamp	USA	4.10.88	14 May
:53.53	Elinor	Purrier	USA	20.2.95	15 May
:53.65	Irene	Sánchez	ESP	25.9.92	1 Aug
:53.71	Maria	Bernard	CAN	6.4.93	17 Apr
:53.72	Rebeka	Stowe	USA	9.3.90	14 May
:53.72	Anju	Takamizawa	JPN-J	6.3.96	13 Sep
:53.76	Beverly	Ramos	PUR	24.8.87	17 Apr
:53.81	Megan	Rolland	USA	30.8.88	14 May
:53.92	Woynshet	Ansa	ETH-J	9.4.96	6 Jul
:53.98	Tori	Gerlach	USA	2.6.94	29 May
:54.34	Emily	Ritter	USA	28.12.92	29 May
:54.38	Eliane	Sahalinirina	MAD	20.3.82	6 Jul
:54.42	Maddie	Van Beek	USA	20.8.91	13 Jun
:54.43	Emily	Oren	USA	20.9.93	22 May
:54.43	Elena	García	ESP	19.6.86	1 Aug
:54.76	Elizabeth	Bird	GBR	4.10.94	29 May
:54.77	Betsy	Graney	USA	23.10.89	9 May
:55.12	Katarzyna	Kowalska	POL	7.4.85	4 Jun
:55.44	Norah	Tanui	KEN	2.10.95	23 May
:55.54	Diana	Martín	ESP	31.7.90	1 Aug
:55.92	Juliana Paula	dos Santos	BRA	12.6.83	25 May
:56.06	Sabahat	Akpinar	TUR	20.7.93	23 May
:56.64	Iona	Lake	GBR	15.1.93	27 Jun
:56.8	Tatiana Raquel	da Silva	BRA	10.6.90	14 Jun
:56.80	Jana	Sussmann	GER	12.10.90	8 Aug
:57.10	Addie	Bracy	USA	4.8.86	6 Jun
:57.1	Belén	Casetta	ARG	26.9.94	14 Jun
:57.17	Jessica	Kamilos	USA	3.8.93	17 Apr
:57.62	Meryem	Akda	TUR	5.8.92	4 Sep
:57.75	Cornelia	Griesche	GER	28.8.93	9 Jul
:57.81	Mariya	Bykova	RUS	7.11.89	28 May
:58.15	Valeria	Roffino	ITA	9.4.90	2 May
:58.28	Nataliya	Soltan	UKR	6.3.95	31 Jul
:58.29	Anastasiya	Puzakova	BLR	12.12.93	9 Jul
:58.42A	Ruth	Bisibori	KEN	2.1.88	9 Jul
:58.95	Rosie	Donegan	AUS	1.7.93	11 Jun
:58.99	Erika	Lima	BRA	13.8.93	26 Sep
:59.17	Matylda	Kowal	POL	11.1.89	23 Jul
:59.42	Jennifer	Agnew	USA	7.12.90	17 Apr
:59.67	Erin	Clark	USA	25.10.94	29 May
:59.68	Kimber	Mattox	USA	27.11.88	2 May
:59.89	María José	Pérez	ESP	12.6.92	25 Jul
10:00.02	Lyudmila	Remeslova	RUS	13.8.87	5 Aug
10:00.17	Cristina	Casandra	ROU	1.2.77	20 Jun
10:00.77	Katelyn	Greenleaf	USA	9.3.94	29 May
10:00.77	Aleksandra	Pavlyutenkova	RUS	21.3.90	5 Aug
10:01.3	Ángela	Figueroa	COL	28.6.84	14 Jun
10:01.31	Tansey	Lystad	USA	27.5.93	3 Apr
10:01.58	Bret	McDaniel	USA	18.10.91	29 May
10:01.68	Heather	Demorest	USA	12.7.92	13 Jun
10:02.45	Alisa	Vainio	FIN-J	16.11.97	30 Aug
10:02.63	Natalie	Schudrowitz	USA	14.9.95	29 May
10:02.82	Carmen	Graves	USA	27.1.91	6 Jun
10:02.92		Zhong Xiaoqian	CHN-J	24.10.97	23 Oct
10:03.06	Seyran	Adanir	TUR	12.1.93	11 Jul
10:03.22	Mackenzie	Chojnacky	USA	7.10.92	29 May
10:03.4A	Veronica	Jepkosgei	KEN	.93	5 Jun
10:04.04	Liz	Weiler	USA	22.2.93	29 May
10:04.12	Chikako	Mori	JPN	25.11.92	28 Jun
10:04.33	Amber	Schulz	USA	27.12.90	22 Jul
10:05.04	Mel	Lawrence	USA	29.8.89	14 Jun
10:05.34	Jekaterina	Patjuk	EST	6.4.83	5 Sep
10:05.45	Ronja	Fjellner	SWE	22.9.89	23 May
10:05.84	Martina	Merlo	ITA	19.2.93	23 May
10:05.94	Misaki	Mishima	JPN	14.6.94	13 Sep
10:06.14	Regan	Yee	CAN	4.7.95	8 Jun
10:06.14	Fabiana	Lafuente	ESP	6.2.87	1 Aug
10:06.37	Moeno	Shimizu	JPN-J	20.3.97	13 Sep
10:06.50		Yu Xiaoxia	CHN-J	29.3.96	23 Oct
10:07.08	Pippa	Woolven	GBR	26.7.93	29 May
10:07.09		Sun Ran	CHN	10.5.91	22 Sep
10:07.19	Marie	Bouchard	FRA	7.12.93	5 Jun
10:07.24	Katie	Landwehr	USA	23.1.93	17 Apr
10:07.36	Racheal	Bamford	GBR	4.8.89	16 May
10:07.62	Shannon	Klenke	USA	1.2.93	3 Apr
10:08.10	Kira	Garry	USA	4.3.93	29 May
10:08.18	Jordan	O'Dea	USA	29.12.93	15 May
10:08.64	Yekaterina	Rogozina	RUS	21.12.89	5 Aug
10:08.75	Anna	Petrova	RUS	15.7.94	19 Jul
10:08.92	Misaki	Sango	JPN	21.4.89	2 May
10:08.99	Courtney	Heiner	USA	7.9.91	3 Apr
10:09.02	Danielle	Winslow	USA	2.9.93	15 May
10:09.08A	Jane	Murage	KEN	.87	9 Jul
10:09.49	U.K. Nilani	Rathnayake	SRI		24 Jul
10:09.55	Erika	Barr	USA		17 Apr
10:09.58	Anna Emilie	Møller	DEN-J	28.7.97	22 Aug
10:09.60	Gulnara	Galkina	RUS	9.7.78	5 Aug
10:09.94	Frida	Berge	NOR	13.3.94	16 May
10:09.99	Carolina (194)	Lozano	ARG-J	27.2.96	25 Apr

JUNIORS

ee main list for top 9 juniors. 12 performances by 4 women to 9:38.0. Additional marks and further juniors:

	Mark	Pos	Meet	Venue	Date	Mark	Pos	Meet	Venue	Date
lekonen	9:27.07	4	DL	Doha	15 May	9:31.53	5	Athl	Lausanne	9 Jul
hebet	9:26.87	4	Athl	Lausanne	9 Jul	9:30.24	1	WMilG	Mungyeong	4 Oct
	9:27.93	5h3	WCh	Beijing	24 Aug	9:33.41	11	WCh	Beijing	26 Aug
hepngetich	9:35.75A	3	WCT	Nairobi	1 Aug	9:36.77A	3	NC	Nairobi	11 Jul

Mark	Name		Nat	Born	Pos	Meet	Venue	Date
:53.72	Anju	Takamizawa (10)	JPN	6.3.96	4	Déca	Paris (C)	13 Sep
:53.92	Woynshet	Ansa	ETH	9.4.96	6		Sotteville-lès-Rouen	6 Jul

WOMEN 2015

Mark	Name		Nat	Born	Pos	Meet	Venue	Date
10:02.45	Alisa	Vainio	FIN-	16.11.97	1	Nordic-J	Espoo	30 Au
10:02.92		Zhong Xiaoqian	CHN	24.10.97	1	NYG	Fuzhou	23 Oc
10:06.37	Moeno	Shimizu	JPN	20.3.97	2	Univ Ch	Osaka	13 Se
10:06.50		Yu Xiaoxia	CHN	29.3.96	2	NYG	Fuzhou	23 Oc
10:09.58	Anna Emilie	Møller	DEN	28.7.97	1	NC-j	Hvidovre	22 Au
10:09.99	Carolina	Lozano	ARG	27.2.96	1		Rosario	25 Ap
10:10.67	Maki	Izumida	JPN	22.1.96	1		Inba	24 Oc
10:11.1A	Dorcas	Nzembi	KEN	22.12.97	2		Nairobi	17 Fe
10:11.15	Amy	McCormick (20)	AUS	7.7.96	1		Melbourne	1 Ma

60 METRES HURDLES INDOORS

Mark	Name		Nat	Born	Pos	Meet	Venue	Date
7.83	Sharika	Nelvis	USA	10.5.90	1		Malmö	25 Fe
7.84	Jasmin	Stowers	USA	23.9.91	1	NC	Boston (R)	1 Ma
7.85	Alina	Talay	BLR	14.5.89	1	EI	Praha (O2)	6 Ma
7.87		Nelvis			1	GP	Birmingham	21 Fe
7.87	Kendra	Harrison	USA	18.9.92	1	NCAA	Fayetteville	14 Ma
7.88		Talay			1		Wien	14 Fe
7.88		Talay			1	NC	Mogilyov	21 Fe
7.88	Bridgette	Owens	USA	14.3.92	2	NCAA	Fayetteville	14 Ma
7.89		Stowers			1h1	NC	Boston (R)	1 Ma
7.89		Talay			1s1	EI	Praha (O2)	6 Ma
	(10/5)							
7.90	Lucy	Hatton	GBR	8.11.94	2	EI	Praha (O2)	6 Ma
7.93	Serita	Solomon	GBR	1.3.90	3	EI	Praha (O2)	6 Ma
7.93	Cindy	Roleder	GER	21.8.89	4	EI	Praha (O2)	6 Ma
7.95	Eline	Berings	BEL	28.5.86	1	NC	Gent	21 Fe
7.95	Isabelle	Pedersen	NOR	27.1.92	3s1	EI	Praha (O2)	6 Ma
	(10)							
7.97	Andrea	Ivancevic	CRO	21.8.84	4s1	EI	Praha (O2)	6 Ma
7.97	Nooralotta	Neziri	FIN	9.11.92	6	EI	Praha (O2)	6 Ma
7.98	Tiffany	Porter	GBR	13.11.87	2h2		Malmö	25 Fe
7.99	Hanna	Plotitsyna	UKR	1.1.87	1h1	Pedro	Lódz	17 Fe
8.01	Josephine	Onyia ¶	ESP	15.7.86	1	NC	Antequera	22 Fe
8.01	Dior	Hall	USA-J	2.1.96	1h2	NCAA	Fayetteville	13 Ma
8.02	Danielle	Williams	JAM	14.9.92	1		University Park	30 Ja
8.02	Yvette	Lewis	PAN	16.3.85	1		Eaubonne	10 Fe
8.03	Anne	Zagré	BEL	13.3.90	2	NC	Gent	21 Fe
8.03	Erica	Bougard	USA	26.7.93	1h3	SEC	Lexington KY	27 Fe
	(20)							
8.03	Tenaya	Jones	USA	22.3.89	2	NC	Boston (R)	1 Ma
8.05	Kseniya	Medvedzeva	BLR	24.10.94	1h	Univ Ch	Minsk	23 Ja
8.05A	Lindsay	Lindle	NGR	6.10.89	1		Flagstaff	20 Fe
8.05	Nina	Morozova	RUS	15.9.89	6s1	EI	Praha (O2)	6 Ma
8.05	Karolina	Koleczek	POL	15.1.93	7s1	EI	Praha (O2)	6 Ma
8.06	Tiffani	McReynolds	USA	4.12.91	3	NC	Boston (R)	1 Ma
8.07	Morgan	Snow	USA	26.7.93	2	Tyson	Fayetteville	13 Fe
8.07	Yekaterina	Galitskaya	RUS	24.2.87	1s1	NC	Moskva	18 Fe
8.07	Alice	Decaux	FRA	10.4.85	1h1	NC	Aubière	22 Fe
8.07	Pamela	Dutkiewicz	GER	28.9.91	2	NC	Karlsruhe	22 Fe
	(30)							
8.07	Kristi	Castlin	USA	7.7.88	4	NC	Boston (R)	1 Ma
8.08	Nadine	Visser	NED	9.2.95	3	ISTAF	Berlin	14 Fe
8.08	Giulia	Pennella	ITA	27.10.89	1	NC	Padova	21 Fe
8.08	Marina	Tomic	SLO	30.4.83	8s1	EI	Praha (O2)	6 Ma
8.09	Yekaterina	Poplovskaya	BLR	7.5.87	h	Univ Ch	Minsk	23 Ja
8.09	Beate	Schrott	AUT	15.4.88	1h1	Gugl	Linz	6 Fe
8.10	Cindy	Ofili	GBR	5.8.94	2		Notre Dame	7 Fe
8.10	Brianne	Theisen-Eaton	CAN	18.12.88	3	Mill	New York (Arm)	14 Fe
8.10	Svetlana	Topylina	RUS	6.1.85	3	NC	Moskva	18 Fe
8.10	Sandra	Gomis	FRA	21.11.83	1	NC	Aubière	22 Fe
	(40)							
8.10	LeTristan	Pledger	USA	27.8.93	2h1	NCAA	Fayetteville	13 Ma
8.10	Kendell	Williams	USA	14.6.95	1P	NCAA	Fayetteville	14 Ma
8.11	Yuliya	Kondakova	RUS	4.12.81	1		Sankt-Peterburg	10 Fe
8.11	Noemi	Zbären	SUI	12.3.94	3h2	EI	Praha (O2)	6 Ma
8.12	Kaylon	Eppinger	USA	17.9.89	3h1	NC	Boston (R)	1 Ma
8.13	Anastasiya	Mokhnyuk	UKR	1.1.91	1P		Zaporizhzhya	27 Ja
8.13	Marzia	Caravelli	ITA	23.10.81	1		Roma	1 Fe
8.13	Stephanie	Bendrat	GER	5.3.91	2h2	Gugl	Linz	6 Fe
8.13	Katerina	Cachová	CZE	26.2.90	1	NC	Praha (Strom)	21 Fe

Mark		Name		Nat	Born	Pos	Meet	Venue	Date
8.13		Rosina (50)	Hodde	NED	10.2.83	2	NC	Apeldoorn	22 Feb
8.13			Wu Shuijiao	CHN	19.6.91	1h2	NGP	Shanghai	2 Mar
8.14		Christina	Manning	USA	29.5.90	2		Birmingham	24 Jan
8.14		Shermaine	Williams	JAM	4.2.90	2		University Park	30 Jan
8.14		Susanna	Kallur	SWE	16.2.81	2h2		Karlsruhe	31 Jan
8.14		Akela	Jones	BAR	21.4.95	3	Big 12	Ames	28 Feb
8.14		Janay	DeLoach	USA	12.10.85	1h1		Golden	12 Dec
8.15A		Sasha	Wallace	USA	21.9.95	3	Kirby	Albuquerque	14 Feb
8.15		Caridad	Jerez	ESP	23.1.91	2	NC	Antequera	22 Feb

100 METRES HURDLES

Mark	Wind	Name		Nat	Born	Pos	Meet	Venue	Date
12.34	1.9	Sharika	Nelvis	USA	10.5.90	1h3	NC	Eugene	26 Jun
12.35	0.9	Jasmin	Stowers	USA	23.9.91	1	DL	Doha	15 May
12.37	2.0		Nelvis			1s1	NC	Eugene	27 Jun
12.39	2.0		Stowers			1		Kingston	9 May
12.40	1.5		Stowers			1	DrakeR	Des Moines	25 Apr
12.46	-0.3		Nelvis			1	Herc	Monaco	17 Jul
12.47	-1.2		Stowers			1	DL	London (OS)	24 Jul
12.48	1.9	Dawn	Harper Nelson	USA	13.5.84	2h3	NC	Eugene	26 Jun
12.50	1.8	Kendra	Harrison	USA	18.9.92	1	SEC	Starkville	16 May
12.52	-0.3		Nelvis			1	GGala	Roma	4 Jun
12.52	1.4	Queen	Harrison	USA	10.9.88	1	PAm	Toronto	21 Jul
12.52	-0.3		K Harrison			2	Herc	Monaco	17 Jul
12.54	0.9		Nelvis			2	DL	Doha	15 May
12.54	1.2		Stowers			1s2	NC	Eugene	27 Jun
12.55	-1.7		Nelvis			1	GS	Ostrava	26 May
12.55	1.7		K Harrison			1	NCAA	Eugene	13 Jun
12.55	-0.1		Harper Nelson			1	NC	Eugene	27 Jun
12.55	1.7		Harper Nelson			1	Athl	Lausanne	9 Jul
12.56	1.8	Tiffany	Porter	GBR	13.11.87	1		Clermont	18 Apr
12.56	-0.1		K Harrison			2	NC	Eugene	27 Jun
12.56	-0.3	Brianna	Rollins	USA	18.8.91	3	Herc	Monaco	17 Jul
12.56	-0.3		Stowers			4	Herc	Monaco	17 Jul
12.57	-0.3	Danielle	Williams	JAM	14.9.92	1	WCh	Beijing	28 Aug
12.58	1.5		Harper Nelson			1	DL	Birmingham	7 Jun
12.58	1.7		Stowers			2	Athl	Lausanne	9 Jul
12.58	-0.3		Harper Nelson			5	Herc	Monaco	17 Jul
12.58	-0.3		Williams			1s1	WCh	Beijing	28 Aug
12.59	1.3	Sally	Pearson	AUS	19.9.86	1	NC	Brisbane	29 Mar
12.59	1.0		Harper Nelson			2	GGala	Roma	4 Jun
12.59	2.0		Harper Nelson			2s1	NC	Eugene	27 Jun
12.59	1.2		K Harrison			2s2	NC	Eugene	27 Jun
12.59	-0.1		Nelvis			3	NC	Eugene	27 Jun
12.59	-0.3	Cindy	Roleder	GER	21.8.89	2	WCh	Beijing	28 Aug
12.59	-0.3		Nelvis			2s1	WCh	Beijing	28 Aug
		(34/10)							
12.60	1.7	Cindy	Ofili	GBR	5.8.94	2	NCAA	Eugene	13 Jun
12.65	0.4	Lolo	Jones	USA	5.8.82	2		Bellinzona	21 Jul
12.66	-0.3	Alina	Talay	BLR	14.5.89	3	WCh	Beijing	28 Aug
12.71	1.7	Kristi	Castlin	USA	7.7.88	6	Athl	Lausanne	9 Jul
12.71	-0.2	Noemi	Zbären	SUI	12.3.94	1	EU23	Tallinn	11 Jul
12.71	1.4	Anne	Zagré	BEL	13.3.90	1	NA	Heusden-Zolder	18 Jul
12.72	2.0	Tenaya	Jones	USA	22.3.89	4s1	NC	Eugene	27 Jun
12.73	1.5	Bridgette	Owens	USA	14.3.92	1h2	SEC	Starkville	15 May
12.74	1.7	Dior	Hall	USA-J	2.1.96	3	NCAA	Eugene	13 Jun
12.78	1.2	Morgan (20)	Snow	USA	26.7.93	5s2	NC	Eugene	27 Jun
12.78	-0.4	Shermaine	Williams	JAM	4.2.90	2h4	WCh	Beijing	27 Aug
12.79	-1.2	Jessica	Ennis-Hill	GBR	28.1.86	5	DL	London (OS)	24 Jul
12.80	1.5	Nina	Morozova	RUS	15.9.89	1r1		Joensuu	23 Jul
12.81	0.4	Virginia	Crawford	USA	7.9.83	3		Bellinzona	21 Jul
12.81	-0.7	Nadine	Visser	NED	9.2.95	1H	WCh	Beijing	22 Aug
12.82	1.3	Michelle	Jenneke	AUS	23.6.93	2	NC	Brisbane	29 Mar
12.83	0.0	Cindy	Billaud	FRA	11.3.86	1h2	NC	Villeneuve d'Ascq	11 Jul
12.84	1.8	Lucy	Hatton	GBR	8.11.94	2		Clermont	18 Apr
12.84	1.8	Monique	Morgan	JAM	14.10.85	1		Charlottesville	8 May
12.84	0.4	Janay (30)	DeLoach	USA	12.10.85	4		Bellinzona	21 Jul

Mark		Name		Nat	Born	Pos	Meet	Venue	Date
12.85	1.5	Jackie	Coward	USA	5.11.89	1h2		Clermont	18 Ap
12.85	0.8		Wu Shuijiao	CHN	19.6.91	1		Beijing	20 May
12.85	1.7	Jade	Barber	USA	4.4.93	4	NCAA	Eugene	13 Jun
12.85	1.4	Nikkita	Holder	CAN	7.5.87	3	PAm	Toronto	21 Ju
12.86	-0.3	Isabelle	Pedersen	NOR	27.1.92	4s1	WCh	Beijing	28 Aug
12.87	1.5	Serita	Solomon	GBR	1.3.90	5	DL	Birmingham	7 Jun
12.87	-0.1	Andrea	Ivancevic	CRO	21.8.84	3	Gyulai	Székesfehérvár	7 Ju
12.87	-0.3	Phylicia	George	CAN	16.11.87	5s1	WCh	Beijing	28 Aug
12.88	-1.0	Kierre	Beckles	BAR	21.5.90	2h3	WCh	Beijing	27 Aug
12.89	-1.1	Kimberley	Laing	JAM	8.1.89	3	NC	Kingston	28 Jun
		(40)							
12.91	2.0	Megan	Simmonds	JAM	18.3.94	1		Kingston	1 Ap
12.91	1.7	Karolina	Koleczek	POL	15.1.93	1	EAF	Bydgoszcz	14 Jun
12.92	0.4	Beate	Schrott	AUT	15.4.88	5		Bellinzona	21 Ju
12.92	-2.7	Yekaterina	Galitskaya	RUS	24.2.87	2	NC	Cheboksary	4 Aug
12.93	-0.4	Tiffani	McReynolds	USA	4.12.91	1	Johnson	Waco	18 Ap
12.94	1.4	Caridad	Jerez	ESP	23.1.91	1	Gil	Salamanca	6 Jun
12.95	1.7	Chanice	Taylor-Chase	CAN	6.8.93	6	NCAA	Eugene	13 Jun
12.97	1.3	Lindsay	Lindley	NGR	6.10.89	1rB	MSR	Walnut	18 Ap
12.97	1.3	Lutisha	Bowen	USA	9.7.90	1		Jacksonville	8 May
12.97	-1.1	Daeshon	Gordon	JAM-J	8.11.96	4	NC	Kingston	28 Jun
		(50)							
12.98	0.8	Yvette	Lewis	PAN	16.3.85	4		Beijing	20 May
12.98	1.5	Josephine	Onyia ¶	ESP	15.7.86	1		Lisboa	25 Jun
12.98	-0.7	Brianne	Theisen-Eaton	CAN	18.12.88	3H	WCh	Beijing	22 Aug
12.99	1.2	Erica	Bougard	USA	26.7.93	2q2	NCAA-E	Jacksonville	30 May
13.00	-0.4	Sasha	Wallace	USA	21.9.95	2	Pac 12	Los Angeles (Ww)	17 May
13.00	-0.1	Anastasiya	Mokhnyuk	UKR	1.1.91	1H	Hypo	Götzis	30 May
13.00	1.7	Devynne	Charlton	BAH	26.11.95	7	NCAA	Eugene	13 Jun
13.00	-0.1	Adanaca	Brown	BAH	23.10.93	1	NC	Nassau	27 Jun
13.00	0.0	Hanna	Plotitsyna	UKR	1.1.87	1		Kyiv	21 Ju
13.00A	1.2	Lina Marcela	Florez	COL	1.11.84	1	NG	Cali	16 Nov
		(60)							
13.01	1.5	Nooralotta	Neziri	FIN	9.11.92	2r1		Joensuu	23 Ju
13.02	-1.0	Alice	Decaux	FRA	10.4.85	2	NC	Villeneuve d'Ascq	11 Ju
13.02	1.4	Sara	Aerts	BEL	25.1.84	2h1		Ninove	1 Aug
13.03	1.1	Danielle	Demas	USA	28.8.93	1h3		Hammond	9 May
13.03	1.9	Evonne	Britton	USA	10.10.91	5h3	NC	Eugene	26 Jun
13.04	1.8	Christina	Manning	USA	29.5.90	4		Clermont	18 Ap
13.04	-4.4	Irina	Reshetkina	RUS	30.1.89	2h2	NC	Cheboksary	4 Aug
13.05	0.9	Lavonne	Idlette	DOM	31.10.85	5		Kawasaki	10 May
13.05	-1.1	Sandra	Gomis	FRA	21.11.83	1r1		La Roche-sur-Yon	22 Ju
13.06	1.0	Adelly	Santos	BRA	8.7.87	1	NC	São Bernardo do Campo	15 May
		(70)							
13.06A	1.2	Briggit	Merlano	COL	29.4.82	2	NG	Cali	16 Nov
13.07	2.0	Andrea	Bliss	JAM	5.10.80	6		Kingston	9 May
13.07	1.9	Jacklyn	Howell	USA-J	3.10.96	2h3	SEC	Starkville	15 May
13.07	0.0	Kaylon	Eppinger	USA	17.9.89	2H	NC	Eugene	27 Jun
13.08	1.0	Kendell	Williams	USA	14.6.95	1H	NCAA	Eugene	10 Jun
13.09	-1.5	Yuliya	Kondakova	RUS	4.12.81	3		Sochi	28 May
13.09	1.2	Tiana	Davis	USA	12.8.89	7s2	NC	Eugene	27 Jun
13.09	0.1	Eefje	Boons	NED	18.7.94	2s1	EU23	Tallinn	10 Ju
13.10	-0.3	Le'Tristan	Pledger	USA	27.8.93	2h1	Big 12	Ames	16 May
13.10	0.3	Eva	Strogies	GER	21.3.91	1		Weinheim	30 May
		(80)							
13.10	0.9	Akela	Jones	BAR	21.4.95	1H	NCAA	Eugene	10 Jun
13.10	0.2	Raven	Clay	USA	5.10.90	5		Edmonton	12 Ju
13.11	1.2	Leah	Nugent	USA	23.11.92	1rC	Jones	Gainesville	24 Ap
13.11	0.4	Samantha	Elliott	JAM	3.2.92	2h4	NCAA-E	Jacksonville	29 May
13.11	0.0	Amusan	Oluwatobeloba	NGR-J	23.4.97	1h2	AfG	Brazzaville	14 Sep
13.12			Kang Ya	CHN	16.3.90	1	NGPF	Beijing	29 Jun
13.12	0.2	Jessica	Zelinka	CAN	3.9.81	1H	PAm	Toronto	24 Ju
13.13	-0.7	Fabiana	Moraes	BRA	5.6.86	3		La Chaux-de-Fonds	5 Ju
13.13	0.3	Vashti	Thomas	PAN	21.4.90	5	Spitzen	Luzern	14 Ju
13.14	0.5	Kendra	Newton	USA	3.8.87	2		Greensboro NC	17 May
		(90)							
13.14	1.7	Giulia	Tessaro	ITA	1.11.85	1	NC	Torino	25 Ju
13.14A	-0.3	Christie	Gordon	CAN	5.10.86	2h1	NACAC	San José, CRC	7 Aug
13.14	0.6	Giulia	Pennella	ITA	27.10.89	2		Rieti	13 Sep
13.15	2.0	Alex	Gochenour	USA	17.2.93	1H	TexR	Austin	25 Mar
13.15	1.8	Indira	Spence	JAM	8.9.86	3	MSR	Walnut	18 Ap

Mark	Wind	Name		Nat	Born	Pos	Meet	Venue	Date
13.15	0.9	Nikki	Larch-Miller	USA	13.8.94	2H	NCAA	Eugene	10 Jun
13.15	1.9	Rosina	Hodde	NED	10.2.83	2		Bruxelles	5 Jul
13.16	1.2	Alexis	Perry	USA	8.8.94	3q2	NCAA-E	Jacksonville	30 May
13.16	1.3	Sirena	Alise Williams	USA	26.12.87	1		Chula Vista	13 Jun
13.17	2.0	Chrisdale	McCarthy	JAM	12.4.94	2		Kingston	1 Apr
		(100)							
13.17	1.4	Jasmyne	Graham	USA-J	6.5.97	1		Clovis	6 Jun
13.17	-0.2	Franziska	Hofmann	GER	27.3.94	4	EU23	Tallinn	11 Jul

Mark	Wind	Name		Nat	Born	Date
13.18	1.8	Brianna	Beahan	AUS	1.11.91	20 Feb
13.18	1.9	Samantha	Scarlett	JAM	7.4.93	15 May
13.18	1.7	Yekaterina	Poplovskaya	BLR	7.5.87	26 May
13.18	1.2	Shanique	Walker	USA	20.11.93	30 May
13.18	1.4	Mecca	McGlaston	USA-Y	23.7.98	6 Jun
13.19	1.4	Aisseta	Diawara	FRA	29.6.89	21 Jun
13.19	-1.1	Rosvitha	Okou	CIV	5.9.86	22 Jul
13.20	1.7	Elvira	German	BLR-J	19.6.97	26 May
13.20	0.1	Lilla	Juhász	HUN	8.11.93	10 Jul
13.20	-1.1	Gnima	Faye	SEN	17.11.84	22 Jul
13.21	-0.4	Anna	Cockrell	USA-J	28.8.97	6 Jun
13.21	1.8	Angela	Whyte	CAN	22.5.80	4 Jul
13.21	1.2	Meghan	Beesley	GBR	15.11.89	18 Jul
13.21	0.6	Laura	Ikauniece-Admidina	LAT	31.5.92	22 Aug
13.22	1.8	Ricarda	Lobe	GER	13.4.94	14 Jun
13.23		Kim	Francis	USA	6.1.92	25 Apr
13.23	1.9	Taliyah	Brooks	USA	8.2.95	15 May
13.23	1.3	LaTisha	Holden-Palmer	USA	29.8.89	13 Jun
13.23	- 4.4	Valentina	Kibalnikova	UZB	16.10.90	4 Aug
13.24	-0.8	Janice	Jackson	JAM	30.10.91	11 Apr
13.24	1.3	Ayako	Kimura	JPN	11.6.88	18 Apr
13.24	-0.1	Brianna	McGhee	USA	8.11.93	30 May
13.24	0.1	Melia	Cox	USA	23.11.92	30 May
13.25	1.5	Ebony	Morrison	USA	28.12.94	15 May
13.25	2.0	Anastasiya	Nikolayeva	RUS	24.9.95	6 Jun
13.25	0.5	Anastasiya	Pilipenko	KAZ	13.9.86	22 Jun
13.26	0.5	Ann-Marie	Duffus	JAM	18.12.90	17 May
13.26	2.0	Yekaterina	Voronkova	RUS	24.11.88	6 Jun
13.26			Sun Minjing	CHN	22.4.88	29 Jun
13.26	0.1	Lucie	Koudelová	CZE	6.7.94	10 Jul
13.27	-2.7	Melaine	Walker	JAM	1.1.83	11 Apr
13.27	-0.5		Jung Hye-lim	KOR	1.7.87	15 May
13.27	0.0	Amber	Hughes	USA	23.8.94	16 May
13.27	-0.2	Martha	Koala	BUR	8.3.94	12 Jun
13.27	-0.2	Hitomi	Shimura	JPN	8.11.90	27 Jun
13.27	1.6	Clélia	Reuse	SUI	1.8.88	9 Jul
13.28	1.0	Dafne	Schippers	NED	15.6.92	24 Apr
13.28	1.3	Steyce	McNeil	USA	28.1.94	15 May
13.28	0.7	Masumi	Aoki	JPN	16.4.94	7 Jun
13.29	1.8	Kori	Carter	USA	3.6.92	18 Apr
13.29	1.5	Mobolaji	Adeokun	USA	14.1.94	2 May
13.29	0.8	Ivana	Loncarek	CRO	8.4.91	4 Jun
13.30	1.8	Alyssa	Monteverde-Dalton	USA	15.1.93	2 May
13.30	-0.2	Anri	Tanaka	JPN	10.7.94	27 Jun
13.30	0.9	Matilda	Bogdanoff	FIN	8.10.90	31 Jul
13.31	-2.1	Layne	Baggett	USA	1.10.90	2 May
13.31	1.2	Sade-Mariah	Greenidge	BAR	14.10.93	29 May
13.31	1.6	Elisávet	Pesirídou	GRE	12.2.92	6 Jun
13.31	-0.2	Hanna	Kasyanova	UKR	24.4.83	12 Jun
13.31	-1.3	Katerina	Cachová	CZE	26.2.90	14 Jun
13.31	0.0	Sharon	Day-Monroe	USA	9.6.85	27 Jun
13.31	-0.1		Wang Dou	CHN	18.5.93	23 Sep
13.32	1.0	Abbie	Taddeo	AUS	8.2.94	27 Feb
13.32	1.6	Giada	Carmassi	ITA	15.5.94	9 May
13.32	-0.5	Ladonna	Richards	JAM	.92	23 May
13.32	1.0	Demeteria	Edgecombe	BAH	10.12.92	29 May
13.32	0.6	Shavon	Briscoe	USA	2.6.92	30 May
13.32	1.1	Linda	Züblin	SUI	21.3.86	8 Aug
13.33	2.0	Yanique	Thompson	JAM-J	12.3.96	1 Apr
13.33	0.2	Karelle	Edwards	CAN	30.3.90	19 Jun
13.34	-2.4	Alexia	Fortenberry	USA	19.9.93	21 Mar
13.34	1.7	Cheyenne	Hutchinson	USA	21.4.94	11 Apr
13.34	1.3	Cassandra	Lloyd	USA	27.1.90	8 May
13.34	0.5	Awa	Sène	FRA	24.7.94	18 Jun
13.34	1.6	Yasmin	Miller	GBR	24.5.95	21 Jun
13.34	0.9	Grit	Sadeiko	EST	29.7.89	8 Aug
13.34	2.0	Airi	Ito	JPN	5.7.89	5 Oct
13.36	0.9	Claudia	Heunis	RSA	1.5.89	18 Apr
13.36	1.9	Angelita	Broadbelt-Blake	GBR	12.9.85	18 Apr
13.36	1.7	Krystsina	Gachko	BLR	26.10.91	26 May
13.36	-0.1	Krystal	Bodie	BAH	3.1.90	27 Jun
13.37	0.8		Deng Ru	CHN	21.11.89	20 May
13.37	1.8	Monika	Zapalska	GER	24.5.94	14 Jun
13.37	0.6	Katarina	Johnson-Thompson	GBR	9.1.93	22 Aug
13.38	0.9	Jamika	Glades	USA	27.10.93	2 Apr
13.38	0.6	Barbara	Nwaba	USA	18.1.89	3 Apr
13.38	1.2	Ja'Mesha	Richard	USA		24 Apr
13.38	-1.6	Mary	Young	USA-J	6.5.96	2 May
13.38	-2.1	Breeana	Coleman	USA	19.6.92	2 May
13.38	0.7	Stephanie	Bendrat	GER	5.3.91	4 Jun
13.38	1.4	Funlayo	Oluwole	USA-J	19.6.97	6 Jun
13.38	1.5	Génesis	Romero	VEN	6.11.95	25 Jun
13.38A	-0.4	Eliecit	Palacios	COL	15.8.87	16 Nov
13.39	1.7	Alexis	Franklin	USA	9.10.93	18 Apr
13.39	1.5	Antonisha	Stewart	USA		2 May
13.39	1.1	Jessica	Gelibert	HAI	8.11.94	16 May
13.39	1.9	Adja Arette	Ndiaye	SEN	26.2.84	7 Jun
13.39	0.9	Mathilde	Raibaut	FRA	18.4.92	18 Jun
13.39	-0.1	Petra	Répási	HUN-J	30.1.96	7 Jul
		(191)				

Wind assisted

Mark	Wind	Name		Nat	Born	Pos	Meet	Venue	Date
12.46	2.3	Kendra	Harrison	USA	18.9.92	1h1	NC	Eugene	26 Jun
12.47	2.6		Stowers			1h2	NC	Eugene	26 Jun
12.50	2.3	Queen	Harrison	USA	10.9.88	2h1	NC	Eugene	26 Jun
12.54	3.1		Stowers			1		Baton Rouge	18 Apr
12.62	2.6	Lolo	Jones	USA	5.8.82	2h2	NC	Eugene	26 Jun
12.68A	4.1	Tenaya	Jones	USA	22.3.89	2	NACAC	San José, CRC	8 Aug
12.70	3.8	Tiffani	McReynolds	USA	4.12.91	1	Big 12	Ames	17 May
12.70	3.7	Jade	Barber	USA	4.4.93	1s2	NCAA	Eugene	11 Jun
12.71	2.8	Kimberley	Laing	JAM	8.1.89	1h3		Clermont	16 May
12.71	3.3	Bridgette	Owens	USA	14.3.92	1s3	NCAA	Eugene	11 Jun
12.78	2.2	Lavonne	Idlette	DOM	31.10.85	1h1		Clermont	16 May
12.79	2.2	Nina	Morozova	RUS	15.9.89	1r2		Joensuu	23 Jul
12.85	3.2	Yekaterina	Galitskaya	RUS	24.2.87	1	Odlozil	Praha	8 Jun
12.87	3.7	Devynne	Charlton	BAH	26.11.95	3s2	NCAA	Eugene	11 Jun
12.87	2.6	Karolina	Koleczek	POL	15.1.93	1	Kuso	Szczecin	9 Aug
12.91A	4.1	Christie	Gordon	CAN	5.10.86	4	NACAC	San José, CRC	8 Aug
12.92	2.2	Evonne	Britton	USA	10.10.91	2h1		Clermont	16 May
12.92	2.6	Yvette	Lewis	PAN	16.3.85	3h1	PAm	Toronto	21 Jul
12.93	2.2	Sandra	Gomis	FRA	21.11.83	1		Castres	29 Jul
12.94	2.9	Raven	Clay	USA	5.10.90	3		Clermont	16 May
12.94	2.3	Sirena	Alise Williams	USA	26.12.87	5h1	NC	Eugene	26 Jun

Mark	Wind	Name		Nat	Born	Pos	Meet	Venue	Date
12.94	2.2	Nooralotta	Neziri	FIN	9.11.92	2r2		Joensuu	23 Ju
12.96	3.7	Shanique	Walker	USA	20.11.93	5s2	NCAA	Eugene	11 Ju
12.96	2.3	Tiana	Davis	USA	12.8.89	6h1	NC	Eugene	26 Ju
12.99	3.7	Le'Tristan	Pledger	USA	27.8.93	3	TexR	Austin	28 Ma
13.00	2.2	Alice	Decaux	FRA	10.4.85	2		Castres	29 Ju
13.01	3.5	Janice	Jackson	JAM	30.10.91	2	TexR	Austin	28 Ma
13.01	2.6	Briggit	Merlano	COL	29.4.82	5h1	PAm	Toronto	21 Ju
13.02	2.6	Danielle	Demas	USA	28.8.93	1h5	NCAA-W	Austin	29 Ma
13.03	3.2	Yuliya	Kondakova	RUS	4.12.81	3	Odlozil	Praha	8 Ju
13.07	2.6	LaTisha	Holden-Palmer	USA	29.8.89	6h2	NC	Eugene	26 Ju
13.08	3.8	Nikki	Larch-Miller	USA	13.8.94	1		Normal	17 Ma
13.08	2.5	Tia	Jones	USA-Y	8.9.00	1		Greensboro NC	20 Ju
13.08A	4.1	Akela	Jones	BAR	21.4.95	7	NACAC	San José, CRC	8 Au
13.10	2.8	Ebony	Morrison	USA	28.12.94	2h1	NCAA-E	Jacksonville	29 Ma
13.10	3.7	Brianna	McGhee	USA	8.11.93	2h4	NCAA-W	Austin	29 Ma
13.10	2.5		Kang Ya	CHN	16.3.90	1	Nambu	Sapporo	12 Ju
13.12	2.8	Taliyah	Brooks	USA	8.2.95	2h3	NCAA-W	Austin	29 Ma
13.12	3.2	Lucie	Koudelová	CZE	6.7.94	5	Odlozil	Praha	8 Ju
13.12	2.5	Tonea	Marshall	USA-Y	17.12.98	2		Greensboro NC	20 Ju
13.13	2.5	Hitomi	Shimura	JPN	8.11.90	2	Nambu	Sapporo	12 Ju

Mark	Wind	Name		Nat	Born	Date
13.14	2.4	Alexia	Fortenberry	USA	19.9.93	10 May
13.14	3.7	Alexis	Perry	USA	8.8.94	11 Jun
13.15	2.6	Elvira	German	BLR-J	19.6.97	18 Jul
13.17	3.1	Melia	Cox	USA	23.11.92	29 May
13.18	3.1	Kim	Francis	USA	6.1.92	18 Apr
13.18	2.9	Yvana	Hepburn-Bailey	BAH	9.11.87	16 May
13.19	2.9	Taylor	Larch-Miller	USA	13.8.94	2 May
13.20	2.5	Ayako	Kimura	JPN	11.6.88	12 Jul
13.20	2.6	Luca	Kozák	HUN	1.6.96	18 Jul
13.21	4.8	Yanique	Thompson	JAM-J	12.3.96	6 Apr
13.21	2.6	Laura	Valette	FRA-J	16.2.97	18 Jul
13.21	2.7	Rochelle	Coster	NZL	6.6.88	19 Dec
13.22	2.9	Ladonna	Richards	JAM	.92	3 May
13.23	3.8	Eliecít	Palacios	COL	15.8.87	16 May
13.23	2.5	Anri	Tanaka	JPN	10.7.94	12 Jul
13.24	4.0	Courtney	Robinson	USA	18.4.95	15 May
13.24	2.9	Karelle	Edwards	CAN	30.3.90	16 May
13.24	2.7	Mobolaji	Adeokun	USA	14.1.94	11 Jun
13.24	2.6	Petra	Répási	HUN-J	30.1.96	18 Ju
13.25	2.3	Alexis	Duncan	USA-Y	16.8.98	16 Ma
13.25	4.0	Mathilde	Raibaut	FRA	18.4.92	21 Ju
13.25	2.5		Jung Hye-lim	KOR	1.7.87	12 Ju
13.26	2.1	Amber	Hughes	USA	23.8.94	15 Ma
13.26	2.3	Breanna	Leslie	USA	11.8.91	22 Ma
13.28	2.4	Kalena	Franklin	USA	21.4.92	4 Ap
13.28	3.0	Miki	Fujiwara	JPN	7.12.92	6 Ju
13.30	3.8	Mary	Young	USA-J	6.5.96	17 Ma
13.30	3.1	Je'Rica	Sanders	USA	11.8.93	29 Ma
13.30	3.1	Ja'Mesha	Richard	USA		29 Ma
13.30	2.6	Anna	Kielbasinska	POL	26.6.90	9 Au
13.31	2.3	Cheyenne	Hutchinson	USA	21.4.94	17 Ma
13.32	3.8	Micha	Auzenne	USA	10.6.95	25 Ap
13.34	2.8	Traci	Hicks	USA	29.1.94	29 Ma
13.35	3.0	Kristen	Brown	USA	26.5.92	29 Ma
13.37	2.5	Deborah	John	TTO	10.4.90	27 Ju
13.37	2.3	Génesis	Romero	VEN	6.11.95	21 Ju

Best at low altitude

13.14 -0.7 Merlano 1 Ponce 23 May
13.16 0.2 C Gordon 7 Edmonton 12 Ju
13.37 0.9 Florez 1 Cartagena 26 Sep

JUNIORS

See main list for top 5 juniors. 10 performances by 4 women to 13.14. Additional marks and further juniors:

Hall	12.89	1.8	1	MSR	Walnut	18 Apr	13.14	1.0	1h1	Pac12	Los Angeles (Ww)	16 Ma
	12.99	-0.4	1	Pac12	Los Angeles (Ww)	17 May						
Howell	13.08	0.1	1rB	FlaR	Gainesville	2 Apr	13.14	1.8	5	SEC	Starkville	16 Ma
Gordon	13.10	0.6	3q1	NCAAe	Jacksonville	30 May						

Mark	Wind	Name		Nat	Born	Pos	Meet	Venue	Date
13.18	1.4	Mecca	McGlaston	USA-Y	23.7.98	2		Clovis	6 Ju
13.20	1.7	Elvira	German	BLR	19.6.97	2	NCp	Brest	26 Ma
13.21	-0.4	Anna	Cockrell	USA	28.8.97	1		Waxhaw	6 Ju
13.33	2.0	Yanique	Thompson	JAM-J	12.3.96	3		Kingston	1 Ap
13.38	-1.6	Mary	Young (10)	USA-J	6.5.96	1	Botts	Columbia	2 Ma
13.38	1.4	Funlayo	Oluwole	USA-J	19.6.97	1		Newport News	6 Ju
13.39	-0.1	Petra	Répási	HUN-J	30.1.96	6	Gyulai	Székesfehérvár	7 Ju
13.44	1.3	Tonea	Marshall	USA-Y	17.10.98	1		Arlington	2 Ma
13.44	1.1	Ebony	Williams	USA	10.10.96	1		Greensboro	9 Ma
13.45	1.6	Alexis	Duncan	USA-Y	16.8.98	1h2		Arlington	1 Ma
13.45	-0.5	Tia	Jones	USA-Y	8.9.00	1s2		Jacksonville	31 Ju
13.45	-1.7	Maribel	Caicedo	ECU-Y	1.4.98	2	PAm-J	Edmonton	31 Ju
13.46	-0.9	Luca	Kozák	HUN	1.6.96	1s2	EJ	Eskilstuna	17 Ju
13.47	-0.1	Reonna	Collier	USA-Y	10.7.98	2		Shoreline	20 Ju
13.48	1.3	Ashley	Miller	USA-Y	16.2.98	1		Orlando	23 Ma
13.48A	-0.4	Clara	Marín (20)	CHI	17.3.97	1	SAm-J	Cuenca	30 Ma
13.48	-0.2	Tara	Davis	USA-Y	20.5.99	2h1		Clovis	5 Ju

Wind assisted see main lists for 3 juniors. 8 performances by 4 women to 13.12

Hall	12.95	3.7	4s2	NCAA	Eugene	11 Jun	13.01	3.1	1h6	NCAAw	Austin	29 Ma
	13.00	2.1	3	FlaR	Gainesville	2 Apr	13.02	2.6	1	NC-j	Eugene	25 Ju
Gordon	13.04	2.7	2s1	NCAA	Eugene	11 Jun	13.09	2.7	4	TexR	Austin	28 Ma

Mark	Wind	Name		Nat	Born	Pos	Meet	Venue	Date
13.15	2.6	Elvira	German	BLR	19.6.97	1	EJ	Eskilstuna	18 Ju
13.21	4.8	Yanique	Thompson	JAM	12.3.96	1	Carifta	Basseterre	6 Ap
13.21	2.6	Laura	Valette	FRA	16.2.97	3	EJ	Eskilstuna	18 Ju
13.30	3.8	Mary	Young	USA	6.5.96	3		Normal	17 Ma
13.40	4.8	Jeanine	Williams	JAM	28.1.97	2	Carifta	Basseterre	6 Ap

Mark	Wind	Name		Nat	Born	Pos	Meet	Venue	Date
13.46	3.3	Megumi	Henpuhiru	JPN	23.5.96	1H		Wakayama	25 Apr

200 METRES HURDLES

Mark	Wind	Name		Nat	Born	Pos	Meet	Venue	Date
26.33	-0.7	Ayomide	Folorunso	ITA-J	17.10.96			Milano	16 Sep
26.72	-0.8	Noemi	Zbären	SUI	12.3.94	1		Basel	9 May
27.07	-0.8	Robine	Schürmann	SUI	31.1.89	2		Basel	9 May
Straight track									
25.28	0.5	Meghan	Beesley	GBR	15.11.89	1		Manchester	9 May
25.31	0.5	Katarina	Johnson-Thompson	GBR	9.1.93	2		Manchester	9 May
26.06	0.5	Yadisleidy	Pedroso	ITA	28.1.87	3		Manchester	9 May
26.23	0.5	Eilidh	Child	GBR	20.2.87	4		Manchester	9 May

300 METRES HURDLES

Mark	Wind	Name		Nat	Born	Pos	Meet	Venue	Date
38.94		Zuzana	Hejnová	CZE	19.12.86	1		Cheb	12 Aug
38.99		Denisa	Rosolová	CZE	21.8.86	1		Susice	12 May

400 METRES HURDLES

Mark	Name		Nat	Born	Pos	Meet	Venue	Date
53.50	Zuzana	Hejnová	CZE	19.12.86	1	WCh	Beijing	26 Aug
53.74	Shamier	Little	USA	20.3.95	1	NCAA	Eugene	13 Jun
53.76		Hejnová			1	DL	Saint-Denis	4 Jul
53.83		Little			1	NC	Eugene	28 Jun
53.94		Little			2	WCh	Beijing	26 Aug
53.99	Sara Slott	Petersen	DEN	9.4.87	2	DL	Saint-Denis	4 Jul
53.99		Hejnová			1	DL	London (OS)	24 Jul
54.01	Cassandra	Tate	USA	11.9.90	2	NC	Eugene	28 Jun
54.02		Tate			3	WCh	Beijing	26 Aug
54.09	Kendra	Harrison	USA	18.9.92	2	NCAA	Eugene	13 Jun
54.12	Kemi	Adekoya	BRN	16.1.93	3	DL	Saint-Denis	4 Jul
54.14		Little			1s2	NC	Eugene	27 Jun
54.15	Kaliese	Spencer	JAM	6.5.87	1	Bisl	Oslo	11 Jun
54.20		Petersen			4	WCh	Beijing	26 Aug
54.24	Georganne	Moline	USA	6.3.90	2	DL	London (OS)	24 Jul
54.24		Hejnová			1s3	WCh	Beijing	24 Aug
54.27	Tiffany	Williams	USA	5.2.83	1s1	NC	Eugene	27 Jun
54.27		Tate			1h3	WCh	Beijing	23 Aug
54.28		Moline			2s2	NC	Eugene	27 Jun
54.29		Moline			2	Bisl	Oslo	11 Jun
54.31		Adekoya			1	AsiC	Wuhan	6 Jun
54.33		Williams			1		Edmonton	12 Jun
54.33		Tate			1s1	WCh	Beijing	24 Aug
54.34		Petersen			1s2	WCh	Beijing	24 Aug
54.35A		Williams			1	NACAC	San José	9 Aug
54.36		Tate			3	DL	London (OS)	24 Jul
54.37	Wenda	Nel (10)	RSA	30.7.88	1		Beijing	20 May
54.37		Hejnová			1	DL	Stockholm	30 Jul
54.41	Kori	Carter	USA	3.6.92	3	NC	Eugene	28 Jun
54.42		Petersen			2	DL	Stockholm	30 Jul
	(30/11)							
54.44	Lashinda	Demus	USA	10.3.83	4	NC	Eugene	28 Jun
54.46	Eilidh	Child	GBR	20.2.87	1	ET	Cheboksary	20 Jun
54.52	Meghan	Beesley	GBR	15.11.89	3h3	WCh	Beijing	23 Aug
54.64	Janeive	Russell	JAM	14.11.93	5	WCh	Beijing	26 Aug
54.75	Anna	Titimets	UKR	5.3.89	2	ET	Cheboksary	20 Jun
55.15	Denisa	Rosolová	CZE	21.8.86	5	DL	Birmingham	7 Jun
55.16	Anna	Ryzhykova	UKR	24.11.89	4s1	WCh	Beijing	24 Aug
55.18	Yadisleidy	Pedroso	ITA	28.1.87	3	ET	Cheboksary	20 Jun
55.28	Sydney	McLaughlin	USA-Y	7.8.99	1	NC-y	Lisle	1 Jul
	(20)							
55.29	Shevon	Stoddart	JAM	21.11.82	2	NC	Kingston	26 Jun
55.41A	Sparkle	McKnight	TTO	21.12.91	2	NACAC	San José, CRC	9 Aug
55.45	Ristananna	Tracey	JAM	9.5.92	3	NC	Kingston	26 Jun
55.51	Aurélie	Chaboudez	FRA	9.5.93	2		Marseille	6 Jun
55.51	Samantha	Elliott	JAM	3.2.92	4	NC	Kingston	26 Jun
55.55	Vera	Rudakova	RUS	20.3.92	1		Sochi	29 May
55.56	Stina	Troest	DEN	17.1.94	4h3	WCh	Beijing	23 Aug
55.58	Turquoise	Thompson	USA	31.7.91	6	NC	Eugene	28 Jun
55.60	Léa	Sprunger	SUI	5.3.90	1		La Chaux-de-Fonds	5 Jul
55.62	Joanna	Linkiewicz	POL	2.5.90	3		Marseille	6 Jun
	(30)							

Mark	Name		Nat	Born	Pos	Meet	Venue	Date
55.63	Leah	Nugent	USA	23.11.92	1		Atlanta	1 Au
55.65	Sarah	Wells	CAN	10.11.89	3		Edmonton	12 Ju
55.65	Lauren	Wells	AUS	3.8.88	2h4	WCh	Beijing	23 Au
55.68	Janeil	Bellille	TTO	18.6.89	1		Port of Spain	11 Ju
55.69	Darya	Korableva	RUS	23.5.88	1	NC	Cheboksary	4 Au
55.76	Dalilah	Muhammad	USA	7.2.90	1		Los Angeles (ER)	9 Ma
55.77	Amaka	Ogoegbunam	NGR	3.3.90	2		La Chaux-de-Fonds	5 Ju
55.82A	Francisca	Koki ¶	KEN	30.10.93	1	NC	Nairobi	11 Ju
55.82	Axelle	Dauwens	BEL	1.12.90	5s1	WCh	Beijing	24 Au
55.83	Jaide	Stepter	USA	25.4.94	1rB	FlaR	Gainesville	2 Ap
	(40)							
55.88	Elise	Malmberg	SWE	13.7.95	1	EU23	Tallinn	12 Ju
55.92	Amalie	Iuel	DEN/NOR	17.4.94	2rB	FlaR	Gainesville	2 Ap
55.92	Natalya	Antyukh	RUS	26.6.81	1h2	NC	Cheboksary	3 Au
55.94	Hayat	Lambarki	MAR	18.5.88	3		Rabat	14 Ju
55.97	Sage	Watson	CAN	20.6.94	4	NCAA	Eugene	13 Ju
55.97A	Zurian	Hechavarría	CUB	10.8.95	3	NACAC	San José, CRC	9 Au
55.98A	Noelle	Montcalm	CAN	3.4.88	4	NACAC	San José, CRC	9 Au
56.03	Maeva	Contion	FRA	31.5.92	1	NC	Villeneuve d'Ascq	12 Ju
56.04	Jernail	Hayes	USA	8.7.88	1		Greensboro NC	17 Ma
56.05	Shona	Richards	GBR	1.9.95	4	EU23	Tallinn	12 Ju
	(50)							
56.09	Petra	Fontanive	SUI	10.10.88	1h4	NC	Zug	7 Au
56.15		Nguyen Thi Huyen	VIE	19.8.93	1	SEAG	Singapore	10 Ju
56.17	Egle	Staisiunaite	LTU	30.9.88	4h1	WCh	Beijing	23 Au
56.25	Viktoriya	Tkachuk	UKR	8.11.94	1	NC-23	Kirovohrad	28 Ma
56.26	Danielle	Dowie	JAM	5.5.92	2		Los Angeles (ER)	9 Ma
56.29	Rushell	Clayton	JAM	18.10.92	5	NC	Kingston	26 Ju
56.30	Déborah	Rodríguez	URU	2.12.92	6h3	WCh	Beijing	23 Au
56.36	Yekaterina	Artyukh	BLR	14.1.91	2rB	ET	Cheboksary	20 Ju
56.43	Nnenya	Hailey	USA	23.2.94	2h1	NC	Eugene	26 Ju
56.46	Fawn	Dorr	CAN	19.4.87	1		Ottawa	19 Ju
	(60)							
56.53	Angela	Morosanu	ROU	26.7.86	1	NC	Pitesti	26 Ju
56.54	T'Erea	Brown	USA	24.10.89	4	DrakeR	Des Moines	25 Ap
56.55	Christiane	Klopsch	GER	21.8.90	1		Regensburg	6 Ju
56.55	Emilia	Ankiewicz	POL	22.11.90	2	WUG	Gwangju	10 Ju
56.56	Joke	Odumosu	NGR	27.10.87	2	NC	Warri	31 Ju
56.57	Irina	Takuntseva	RUS	14.11.90	3	WUG	Gwangju	10 Ju
56.60	Yelena	Churakova	RUS	16.12.86	1h1	NC	Cheboksary	3 Aug
56.62	Jackie	Baumann	GER	24.8.95	2s2	EU23	Tallinn	11 Ju
56.63	Marzia	Caravelli	ITA	23.10.81	1		Matera	27 Se
56.64	Lamiae	Lhabz	MAR	19.5.84	1	ArabC	Manama	27 Ap
	(70)							
56.64A	Zudikey	Rodriguez	MEX	14.3.87	7	NACAC	San José, CRC	9 Aug
56.65	Robine	Schürmann	SUI	31.1.89	4		Genève	6 Ju
56.65	Magdalena	Mendoza	VEN	20.10.90	2	SAmC	Lima	13 Ju
56.65	Francesca	Doveri	ITA	21.12.82	3		La Chaux-de-Fonds	5 Ju
56.67	Anna	Cockrell	USA-J	28.8.97	1	NC-j	Eugene	27 Ju
56.67	MacKenzie	Hill	USA	5.1.86	5s2	NC	Eugene	27 Ju
56.68	Ellen	Wortham	USA	5.1.90	1		Baton Rouge	18 Ap
56.68	Jade	Miller	USA	13.1.95	5	NCAA	Eugene	13 Ju
56.69	Ashante	Little	GBR	24.8.92	2	SunAngel	Tempe	11 Ap
56.71	Phara	Anacharsis	FRA	17.12.83	1		Chambéry	5 Ju
	(80)							
56.72	Rhonda	Whyte	JAM	6.11.90	1		Kingston	6 Ju
56.76	Symone	Black	USA	26.10.95	1	Big 10	East Lansing	17 May
56.76	Josanne	Lucas	TTO	14.5.84	1	NC	Port of Spain	28 Ju
56.77	Liga	Velvere	LAT	10.2.90	1	NC	Ventspils	9 Aug
56.78	Alexis	Franklin	USA	9.10.93	2	Big 10	East Lansing	17 May
56.79A	Xahria	Santiago	CAN-Y	9.10.99	2	WY	Cali	18 Ju
56.80	Kelsey	Balkwill	CAN	19.9.92	1q2	NCAA-E	Jacksonville	29 May
56.82	Valeriya	Khramova	RUS	13.8.92	2h2	NC	Cheboksary	3 Aug
56.83	Olena	Kolesnychenko	UKR	3.6.93	6	EU23	Tallinn	12 Ju
56.91	Jen	Cotten	CAN	14.10.87	4		Guelph	30 May
	(90)							
56.91	Sharolyn	Scott	CRC	27.10.84	2		Chambéry	5 Ju
56.92	Abigail	Lewis	JAM	7.5.93	1	NC-23	Brügge	13 Sep
56.94	Manami	Kira	JPN	23.10.91	1		Kumagaya	16 May
56.94	Faith	Washington	USA	11.10.93	2h6	NCAA-E	Jacksonville	28 May
56.97	Anastasiya	Lebid	UKR	30.10.93	4s1	EU23	Tallinn	11 Ju

Mark	Name		Nat	Born	Pos	Meet	Venue	Date
56.99	Nadezhda	Alekseyeva	RUS	16.7.88	1	NCp	Yerino	10 Jul
57.01	Chanice	Taylor-Chase	CAN	6.8.93	4	SEC	Starkville	16 May
57.01	Anastasiya	Korshunova	RUS	17.5.92	2	NCp	Yerino	10 Jul
57.02	Evann	Thompson	USA	9.10.94	2q1	NCAA-E	Jacksonville	29 May
57.08	Ariel	Jones	USA	18.7.95	3h1	NC	Eugene	26 Jun
	(100)							

Mark	Name		Nat	Born	Date
57.09	Haruko	Ishizuka	JPN-J	2.6.97	31 Jul
57.12	Joanna	Banach	POL	28.8.92	19 Jul
57.13	Tina	Matusinska	POL	12.7.88	20 Jul
57.16	Satomi	Kubokura	JPN	27.4.82	29 Mar
57.17	Kiah	Seymour	USA	11.1.94	6 Jun
57.18	Yelena	Zuykevich	RUS	26.2.90	6 Jun
57.19	Autumne	Franklin	USA	20.7.94	29 May
57.19	Erica	Twiss	USA	17.6.92	26 Jun
57.19	Ayomide	Folorunso	ITA-J	17.10.96	1 Jul
57.19	Nenah	De Coninck	BEL-J	2.9.96	26 Jul
57.22	LaTosha	Wallace	USA	25.3.85	17 May
57.24	Daeshon	Gordon	JAM-J	8.11.96	11 Jun
57.26	Aisha	Naibe-Wey	GBR	3.8.93	25 May
57.27	Reonna	Collier	USA-Y	10.7.98	27 Jun
57.30	Fanny	Lefèvre	FRA	12.2.92	5 Jul
57.30	Svetlana	Karmalita	RUS	11.12.85	19 Jul
57.30		Wang Huan	CHN	21.9.94	24 Sep
57.31A	Annerie	Ebersohn	RSA	9.8.90	28 Feb
57.31	Liz	Harper	USA	1.5.95	17 May
57.34	Sashel	Brown	JAM	20.1.94	29 May
57.37	Yelizaveta	Anikiyenko	RUS	30.6.94	16 Jun
57.43	Jessica	Turner	GBR	8.8.95	13 Jun
57.44	Glory	Nathaniel	NGR-J	23.1.96	31 Jul
57.45	Tia Adana	Belle	BAR-J	16.6.96	23 May
57.45	Alena	Siseva	RUS	8.2.93	16 Jun
57.45	Alena	Klimentyova	RUS	12.11.94	16 Jun
57.45	Vania	Stambolova	BUL	28.11.83	6 Oct
57.47A	Brandeé	Johnson	USA-Y	3.4.98	18 Jul
57.49	Anna	Raukuc	GER	7.1.90	6 Jun
57.49	Gianna	Woodruff	USA	18.11.93	11 Jun
57.51	Jamika	Glades	USA	27.10.93	11 Apr
57.58	Maris	Mägi	EST	11.8.87	8 Jul
57.58	Jessica	Gelibert	HAI	8.11.94	21 Jul
57.60	Arna Stefanía	Gudmundsdóttir	ISL	1.9.95	22 Aug
57.61		Xiao Xia	CHN	6.6.91	17 May
57.63	Nikita	Tracey	JAM	18.9.90	9 May
57.64	Viktoriya	Nikolenko	UKR	15.6.91	8 Jun
57.66	Aleksandra	Kurakina	RUS	15.8.87	10 Jul
57.69	Anna	Punich	RUS	28.8.87	3 Aug
57.71	Alethia	Marrero	PUR	13.5.95	2 May
57.71	Miku	Fujiwara	JPN	7.12.92	13 Sep
57.73	Katrina	Seymour	BAH	7.1.93	26 Jun
57.73	Elif	Yildirim	TUR	11.2.90	1 Aug
57.74	Viivi	Lehikoinen	FIN-Y	27.8.99	30 Jul
57.75	Jen	Esposito	USA	22.7.94	7 May
57.75	Merryl	Mbeng	FRA	5.11.91	12 Jul
57.75A	Ilaria	Verderio	ITA-Y	22.4.98	18 Jul
57.76	Bianca	Baak	NED	25.1.92	17 May
57.78	Melissa	Gonzalez	USA	24.6.94	11 Jun
57.78	Venla	Paunonen	FIN	24.7.90	2 Aug
57.79	Yekaterina	Khairullina	BLR	13.10.92	16 May
57.79	Anu	Raghavan	IND	20.4.93	6 Jun
57.80	Shantely	Scott	CRC	17.4.91	25 Jun
57.80	Anniina	Laitinen	FIN	18.11.89	2 Aug
57.81	Agnieszka	Karczmarczyk	POL	27.4.93	6 Sep
57.81	Akiko	Ito	JPN	26.5.95	13 Sep
57.85	Anna	Simone	USA		28 May
57.87	Taysia	Radoslav	CAN-J	17.9.96	29 May
57.87		Huang Yan	CHN-J	12.1.96	24 Sep
57.88A	Anne Sofie	Kirkegaard	DEN-Y	3.2.98	18 Jul
57.88	Inge	Drost	NED-J	15.1.96	19 Jul
57.90A	Evelyn	Aguilar	COL	3.1.93	1 Aug
57.92	Yanique	Bennett	CAN	17.10.94	16 May
57.93	Margaux	Soriano	FRA	23.4.93	27 Jun
57.94	Merjen	Ishanguliyeva	KAZ	21.1.88	25 Jul
57.99	Tatyana	Veshkurova	RUS	23.9.81	29 May
58.01	Ayaka	Nishida	JPN	15.7.93	13 Sep
58.02	Betty	Burua	PNG	24.11.86	29 Mar
58.02	Michaela	Pesková	SVK-J	22.10.97	2 Aug
58.02	Satsuki	Umehara	JPN	22.5.94	13 Sep
58.03	Aleksandra	Romanova	KAZ	26.12.90	6 Jun
58.04	Frida	Persson	SWE	14.12.89	13 Jun
58.05	Sarah	Sanford	USA-J	20.8.96	27 Jun
58.05	Christine	McMahon	IRL	6.7.92	18 Jul
58.05	Marina	Reznikova	RUS	10.6.91	3 Aug
58.07	Junelle	Bromfield	JAM-Y	8.2.98	23 May
58.07	Faith	Ross	USA-Y	7.3.98	30 Jun
58.08	Ilaria	Vitale	ITA	25.5.90	26 Jul
58.09	Joan	Medjid	FRA	29.9.95	6 Jun
58.09		Kim Kyong-hwa	KOR	21.8.91	19 Oct
58.10	Raphaela	Boaheng Lukudo	ITA	29.7.94	28 Jun
58.10		Wu Xueting	CHN	20.8.95	28 Jun
58.11	Paulo	Morán	MEX-J	25.2.97	21 May
58.13	Jessica	Tappin	GBR	17.5.90	2 Aug
58.14	Jaílma	de Lima	BRA	31.12.86	17 May
58.14	Kymber	Payne	USA-J	4.6.96	29 May
58.15A	Jennifer	Rockwell	ITA	18.5.83	25 Apr
58.16	Paige	Squire	USA	23.9.92	16 May
58.17	Audrey	Nkamsao	CMR	28.7.89	6 Jun
58.18	Tanaya	Yarde	USA	2.4.94	2 May
58.19	Tia	Gamble	USA	23.9.93	29 May
58.20	Amina	Youssef	BRN-J	27.6.97	6 Oct
58.21	Laura	Sotomayor	ESP	22.4.86	13 Jun
58.21A	Lea	Ahrens	GER-Y	.98	18 Jul
58.22	Kyra	Johnson	USA	15.1.94	16 May
58.22	Mariya	Mykolenko	UKR	4.4.94	27 May
58.22	Andreia	Crespo	POR	9.4.93	25 Jun
58.24	Salsa	Slack	JAM	10.12.89	23 May
58.26	Débora	dos Santos	BRA	13.1.92	31 May
58.27	Lucimar	Teodoro	BRA	1.5.81	31 May
	(200)				

Best at low altitude

55.77	McKnight	2h1	WCh	Beijing	23 Aug
56.33	Hechavarría	1		La Habana	20 Jun
56.53	Montcalm	2	FlaR	Gainesville	2 Apr
57.64	Z Rodriguez				21 Jul
57.67	Santiago				15 Jun
57.79	Ebersohn				18 Apr

JUNIORS

See main list for top 3 juniors. 10 performances by 4 women to 57.10. Additional marks and further juniors:

McLaughlin	55.87	1		Greensboro	21 Jun
	55.94A	1	WY	Cali	18 Jul
	56.66	1h1	NC-y	Lisle	30 Jun
	56.79A	1s1	WY	Cali	16 Jul
	56.81A	1h1	WY	Cali	15 Jul
Cockrell	57.10	1	PAm-J	Edmonton	2 Aug

Mark	Name		Nat	Born	Pos	Meet	Venue	Date
57.09	Haruko	Ishizuka	JPN	2.6.97	1		Wakayama	31 Jul
57.19	Ayomide	Folorunso	ITA	17.10.96	1		Boissano	1 Jul
57.19	Nenah	De Coninck	BEL	2.9.96	3	NC	Bruxelles	26 Jul
57.24	Daeshon	Gordon	JAM	8.11.96	5s2	NCAA	Eugene	11 Jun
57.27	Reonna	Collier	USA-Y	10.7.98	2	NC-j	Eugene	27 Jun
57.44	Glory	Nathaniel	NGR	23.1.96	3	NC	Warri	31 Jul
57.45	Tia Adana	Belle (10)	BAR	16.6.96	1	NCAA-II	Allendale	23 May
57.47A	Brandeé	Johnson	USA-Y	3.4.98	3	WY	Cali	18 Jul
57.74	Viivi	Lehikoinen	FIN-Y	27.8.99	1	EYOF	Tbilisi	30 Jul
57.75A	Ilaria	Verderio	ITA-Y	22.4.98	4	WY	Cali	18 Jul

Mark	Name		Nat	Born	Pos	Meet	Venue	Date
57.87	Taysia	Radoslav	CAN	17.9.96	5q2	NCAA-E	Jacksonville	29 Ma
57.87		Huang Yan	CHN	12.1.96	2	NC	Suzhou	24 Se
57.88A	Anne Sofie	Kirkegaard	DEN-Y	3.2.98	5	WY	Cali	18 Ju
57.88	Inge	Drost	NED	15.1.96	2	EJ	Eskilstuna	19 Ju
58.02	Michaela	Pesková	SVK	22.10.97	1	NC	Banská Bystrica	2 Au
58.05	Sarah	Sanford	USA	20.8.96	3	NC-j	Eugene	27 Ju
58.07	Junelle	Bromfield (20)	JAM-Y	8.2.98	3		Kingston	23 Ma
58.07	Faith	Ross	USA-Y	7.3.98	1h3	NC-y	Lisle	30 Ju

HIGH JUMP

2.03 Anna Chicherova RUS 22.7.82 1 Athl Lausanne 9 Ju
1.85/1 1.91/1 1.94/2 1.97/1 2.00/1 2.03/3
2.01 3 WCh Beijing 29 Aug 1.88/1 1.95/1 1.97/2 1.99/1 2.01/2 2.03/xxx
2.00 1 NC Cheboksary 3 Aug 1.84/1 1.91/1 1.94/1 1.97/1 2.00/1 2.04/xxx
2.02i Kamila Licwinko POL 22.3.86 1 NC Torun 21 Fe
1.85/1 1.90/1 1.94/1 1.98/1 2.02/3 2.04/x
2.01i 1 Winter Moskva 1 Feb 1.85/1 1.90/1 1.94/1 1.97/1 2.01/1 2.03/xxx
2.00i 1 Cottbus 27 Jan 1.84/1 1.88/1 1.92/2 1.94/1 1.96/1 1.98/1 2.00/1 2.02/x
1.99 4 WCh Beijing 29 Aug 1.88/1 1.92/1 1.95/1 1.97/1 1.99/1 2.01/xxx
1.98i 1 Pedros Lódz 17 Feb 1.84/1 1.90/1 1.94/1 1.98/1 2.02/xxx
1.98 1 NC Kraków 20 Jul 1.82/1 1.89/1 1.93/1 1.98/3 2.00/xxx
2.01 Mariya Kuchina RUS 14.1.93 1 WCh Beijing 29 Au
1.88/1 1.92/1 1.95/1 1.97/1 1.99/1 2.01/1 2.03/xxx
2.01 1 VD Bruxelles 11 Sep 1.85/1 1.90/1 1.93/1 1.95/1 1.97/1 1.99/1 2.01/1 2.04/xxx
2.00 1 Herc Monaco 17 Jul 1.80/1 1.86/1 1.91/1 1.94/1 1.97/1 2.00/2 2.02/xx
2.00 1 Hanz Zagreb 8 Sep 1.80/1 1.85/1 1.88/1 1.91/1 1.94/1 2.00/2 2.04/xxp
1.99i 2 Winter Moskva 1 Feb 1.80/1 1.85/1 1.90/1 1.94/1 1.97/3 1.99/2 2.01/xxx
1.99 1 ET Cheboksary 21 Jun 1.80/1 1.84/1 1.88/2 1.91/1 1.94/1 1.97/1 1.99/1 2.01/xxx
1.98i 1 Trinec 8 Feb 1.82/1 1.86/1 1.89/1 1.92/2 1.95/2 1.98/3 2.02/xx
2.01 Blanka Vlasic CRO 8.11.83 2 WCh Beijing 29 Au
1.88/1 1.92/2 1.95/1 1.97/1 1.99/1 2.01/1 2.03/xxx
2.00 Ruth Beitia ESP 1.4.79 1 GGala Roma 4 Ju
1.80/1 1.85/1 1.90/1 1.94/1 1.97/2 2.00/3
1.99 5 WCh Beijing 29 Aug 1.88/1 1.92/1 1.95/2 1.97/1 1.99/1 2.01/xxx
1.98 1 NC Castellón 1 Aug 1.85/1 1.90/1 1.95/2 1.98/2 2.03/xxx
1.99 Marie-Laurence Jungfleisch GER 7.10.90 6 WCh Beijing 29 Au
1.88/1 1.92/1 1.95/1 1.97/x 1.99/2 2.01/xxx
1.98i Airiné Palsyté LTU 13.7.92 2 Cottbus 27 Ja
1.80/1 1.84/1 1.88/1 1.90/1 1.94/3 1.96/1 1.98/2 2.00/xxx
1.98i 1 NC Klaipeda 20 Feb 1.85/1 1.90/1 1.95/2 1.98/1 2.01/xxx
(23/7)

Mark	Name		Nat	Born	Pos	Meet	Venue	Date
1.97i	Katarina	Johnson-Thompson	GBR	9.1.93	1	NC	Sheffield	14 Fe
1.97i	Alessia	Trost	ITA	8.3.93	2	EI	Praha (O2)	7 Ma
1.97	Erika	Kinsey (10)	SWE	10.3.88	4	ET	Cheboksary	21 Ju
1.97	Isobel	Pooley	GBR	21.12.92	1	NC	Birmingham	4 Ju
	more performances at 1.97: Licwinko 4, Beitia 3, Vlasic, Chicherova 2, Kuchina 1+1i							
1.96i	Irina	Gordeyeva	RUS	9.10.86	1		Sankt-Peterburg	22 Fe
1.96	Eleanor	Patterson	AUS-J	22.5.96	1	NC-j	Sydney	15 Ma
1.96	Jeannelle	Scheper	LCA	21.11.94	1	SEC	Starkville	15 Ma
1.96	Vashti	Cunningham	USA-Y	18.1.98	1	PAm-J	Edmonton	1 Au
1.95i	Svetlana	Shkolina	RUS	9.3.86	1		Novocheboksarsk	15 Ja
1.95i	Yana	Maksimova	BLR	9.1.89	1	Univ Ch	Minsk	23 Ja
1.95i	Ana	Simic	CRO	5.5.90	3		Trinec	8 Fe
1.94i	Daniela	Stanciu	ROU	15.10.87	1	NC	Bucuresti	14 Fe
1.94i	Morgan	Lake	GBR-J	12.5.97	2	NC	Sheffield	14 Fe
	(20)							
1.94i	Venelina	Veneva-Mateeva	BUL	13.6.74	1	NC	Dobrich	15 Fe
1.94i	Justyna	Kasprzycka	POL	20.8.87	Q	EI	Praha (O2)	6 Ma
1.94	Doreen	Amata	NGR	6.5.88	1		Dakar	23 Ma
1.94	Iryna	Herashchenko	UKR	10.3.95	1		Kirovohrad	8 Ju
1.94	Svetlana	Radzivil	UZB	17.1.87	2=		Madrid	11 J
1.94	Levern	Spencer	LCA	23.6.84	2=		Madrid	11 J
1.94	Mirela	Demireva	BUL	28.9.89	4		Madrid	11 J
1.94	Barbara	Szabó	HUN	17.2.90	1		Budapest	28 J
1.93i	Leontia	Kallenou	CYP	5.10.94	1	NCAA	Fayetteville	13 M
1.92i	Oksana	Okuneva	UKR	14.3.90	1		Lviv	17 Ja
	(30)							
1.92Ai		Zheng Xingjuan	CHN	20.3.89	1		Albuquerque	24 Ja
1.92i	Urszula	Gardzielewska	POL	21.7.88	1=		Torun	3 Fe
1.92i	Oldriska	Maresová	CZE	14.10.86	1		Valasské Mezirící	14 M
1.92	Hannah	Joye	AUS-J	4.1.96	2	NC-j	Sydney	15 M

Mark	Name		Nat	Born	Pos	Meet	Venue	Date
1.92A	Lissa	Labiche	SEY	18.2.93	1		Potchefstroom	9 May
1.92	Nafissatou	Thiam	BEL	19.8.94	1H	Hypo	Götzis	30 May
1.92	Irina	Iliyeva	RUS	22.12.95	1	NC-23	Saransk	16 Jun
1.92	Yuliya	Levchenko	UKR-J	28.11.97	1	NC-j	Kharkiv	16 Jun
1.92	Yuliya	Chumachenko	UKR	2.10.94	1		Berdychiv	27 Jun
1.92	Valentina	Liashenko	GEO	30.1.81	2		Berdychiv	27 Jun
	(40)							
1.92	Sofie	Skoog	SWE	7.6.90	1	NC	Söderhamn	9 Aug
1.91i	Tatyana	Mnatsakanova	RUS	25.5.83	2=		Volgograd	24 Jan
1.91i	Oksana	Krasnokutskaya	RUS	24.9.93	2=		Volgograd	24 Jan
1.91i	Desirée	Rossit	ITA	19.3.94	2		Pordenone	31 Jan
1.91i	Michaela	Hrubá	CZE-Y	21.2.98	8q	EI	Praha (O2)	6 Mar
1.91	Chaunté	Lowe	USA	12.1.84	5	adidas	New York	13 Jun
1.91	Eleriin	Haas	EST	4.7.92	5		Madrid	11 Jul
1.91	Priscilla	Frederick	ANT	14.2.89	2	PAm	Toronto	22 Jul
1.91	Akela	Jones	BAR	21.4.95	3	PAm	Toronto	22 Jul
1.91	Kristina	Korolyova	RUS	6.11.90	1	Déca	Paris (C)	13 Sep
	(50)							
1.90i	Taisya	Roslova	BLR	7.2.92	1		Minsk	16 Jan
1.90	Maayan	Shahaf	ISR	9.11.86	1		Tel Aviv	14 Feb
1.90i	Clàudia	García	ESP	30.9.92	2	NCAA	Fayetteville	13 Mar
1.90	Kimberly	Williamson	JAM	2.10.93	2	NCAA	Eugene	13 Jun
1.90	Katarina	Mögenburg	NOR	16.6.91	2		Bühl	28 Jun
1.90	Anna	Gorodskaya	BLR	31.1.93	1H	ECp	Aubagne	4 Jul
1.90	Hannelore	Desmet	BEL	25.2.89	1		Ninove	1 Aug
1.90i	Ulyana	Aleksandrova	RUS	1.1.91	1		Moskva	18 Dec
1.89	Brianne	Theisen-Eaton	CAN	18.12.88	2H	Hypo	Götzis	30 May
1.89	Liz	Patterson	USA	9.6.88	1		San Mateo	14 Jun
	(60)							
1.89	Imke	Onnen	GER	17.8.94	5		Eberstadt	31 Jul
1.88i	Marina	Smolyakova	RUS	20.6.89	1		Irkutsk	18 Jan
1.88i	Yevgeniya	Kononova	RUS	28.9.89	2		Sankt-Peterburg	10 Feb
1.88i	Eliska	Klucinová	CZE	14.4.88	2	NC	Praha (Strom)	21 Feb
1.88	Nicola	McDermott	AUS-J	28.12.96	3	NC-j	Sydney	15 Mar
1.88	Amy	Acuff	USA	14.7.75	1	TexR	Austin	28 Mar
1.88	Cassie	Purdon	AUS-J	24.10.96	2	NC	Brisbane	29 Mar
1.88	Margarita	Mazina	RUS	7.7.95	1		Moskva	3 Jun
1.88		Wang Yang	CHN	14.2.89	2	AsiC	Wuhan	3 Jun
1.88	Burcu	Yüksel	TUR	3.5.90	2	ET-1	Iráklio	21 Jun
	(70)							
1.88	Natalya	Aksyonova	RUS-J	6.6.97	1	NC-j	Cheboksary	26 Jun
1.88	Nawal	Meniker	FRA-J	9.12.97	1		Albi	27 Jun
1.88	Erica	Bougard	USA	26.7.93	1H	NC	Eugene	27 Jun
1.88	Maya	Pressley	USA	1.2.91	4	PAm	Toronto	22 Jul
1.88	Cristina	Ferrando	ESP	12.1.92	2	NC	Castellón	1 Aug
1.88	Monika	Gollner	AUT	23.10.74	1		Pottenstein	16 Aug
1.88i	Tynita	Butts	USA	10.6.90	1		Allendale	4 Dec
1.87i	Agnieszka	Borowska	POL	21.10.91	1P		Tallinn	7 Feb
1.87i	Laura	Rautanen	FIN	13.2.88	1	NC	Tampere	22 Feb
1.87i	Tatiána	Goúsin	GRE	26.1.94	2	SEC	Lexington KY	28 Feb
	(80)							
1.87i	Deandra	Daniel	TTO	12.12.92	1	ECAC	Boston	7 Mar
1.87	Nicole	Greene	USA-J	2.5.97	1		Greensboro NC	21 Jun
1.87	Sofia	Linde	SWE	12.1.95	1		Halmstad	28 Jun
1.87	Alina	Fyodorova	UKR	31.7.89	3H	ECp	Aubagne	4 Jul
1.87	Svetlana	Nikolenko	RUS	26.9.91	2	NCp	Yerino	10 Jul
1.87	Bethan	Partridge	GBR	11.7.90	1		Birmingham	12 Jul
1.87	Marija	Vukovic	MNE	21.1.92	1	SRB Ch	Sremska Mitrovica	26 Jul
1.87	Uhunoma	Osazuwa	NGR	23.11.87	1H	NC	Warri	30 Jul
1.87	Ebba	Jungmark	SWE	10.3.87	1		Umeå	16 Aug
1.86i	Saniel	Atkinson Grier	JAM	2.7.91	1		Birmingham	17 Jan
	(90)							
1.86i	Amber	Melville	USA	20.12.92	1		Landover	17 Jan
1.86i	Marusa	Cernjul	SLO	30.6.92	1		Lincoln	24 Jan
1.86i	Elena	Vallortigara	ITA	21.9.91	3		Pordenone	31 Jan
1.86i	Grete	Udras	EST	11.3.88	1		Tallinn	1 Feb
1.86i	Eleonora	Omoregie	ITA-J	22.5.96	1	NC-j	Ancona	8 Feb
1.86i	Alexandra	Plaza	GER	10.8.94	3		Dessau	11 Feb
1.86i	Yekaterina	Kuntsevich	RUS	13.7.84	1	NC	Linz	22 Feb
1.86	Zibby	Boyer	USA	23.9.92	1		Los Angeles (Ww)	24 Mar
1.86A	Ximena	Esquivel	MEX-J	22.8.97	1		Querétaro	11 Apr

Mark	Name		Nat	Born	Pos	Meet	Venue	Date
1.86	Wanida (100)	Boonwan	THA	30.8.86	1		Taipei	15 Ma
1.86	Vanessa	Jules	USA	21.3.91	1H		Chula Vista	22 Ma
1.86	Vita	Palamar	UKR	12.10.77	3		Dakar	23 Ma
1.86	Natalya	Yakovleva	RUS-J	11.10.96	1J		Krasnodar	24 Ma
1.86	Alesya	Blashkevich	BLR	20.6.90	1	NCp	Brest	26 Ma
1.86A	Ana Paula	de Oliveira	BRA-J	8.8.96	1	SAm-J	Cuenca	29 Ma
1.86	Yorgelis	Rodríguez	CUB	25.1.95	H	Hypo	Götzis	30 Ma
1.86	Jessica	Ennis-Hill	GBR	28.1.86	3H	Hypo	Götzis	30 Ma
1.86	Mona	Gottschämmer	GER-Y	11.5.98	1		Regensburg	6 Ju
1.86A	Natasha	Jackson	CAN	10.6.89	1		Calgary	20 Ju
1.86	Jossie	Graumann	GER	18.3.94	4		Bühl	28 Ju
1.86		Wang Lin	CHN	8.1.95	1	AsiGP	Chanthaburi	29 Ju
1.86	Alyx	Treasure	CAN	15.5.92	1	NC	Edmonton	4 Ju
1.86	Izabela	Mikolajczyk	POL	4.9.90	2	NC	Kraków	20 Ju
1.86	Aneta	Rydz	POL	30.3.94	3	NC	Kraków	20 Ju
1.86	Györgyi	Zsivoczky-Farkas	HUN	13.2.85	3=H	WCh	Beijing	22 Au
1.86	Nadine	Broersen	NED	29.4.90	5=H	WCh	Beijing	22 Au

Mark	First	Last	Nat	Born	Date
1.85i	Raffaella	Lamera	ITA	13.4.83	11 Jan
1.85i	Elena	Brambilla	ITA	23.4.83	22 Jan
1.85i	Lauren	Crockett	USA	12.4.92	23 Jan
1.85i	Kendell	Williams	USA	14.6.95	23 Jan
1.85i	Lara	Omerzu	SLO-Y	10.2.98	7 Feb
1.85i	Anastasiya	Muzankova	RUS	11.1.92	19 Feb
1.85i	Yekaterina	Fedotova	RUS	3.7.92	19 Feb
1.85i	Mélanie	Skotnik	FRA	8.11.82	21 Feb
1.85i	Lada	Pejchalová	CZE-Y	15.11.98	21 Feb
1.85i	Sietske	Noorman	NED	16.7.91	22 Feb
1.85i	Gema	Martín-Pozuelo	ESP	21.6.87	22 Feb
1.85i	My	Nordström	SWE	27.4.90	22 Feb
1.85	Megan	Glisar	USA	30.3.91	28 Mar
1.85	Keeley	O'Hagan	NZL	11.3.94	29 Mar
1.85	Elizabeth	Lamb	NZL	12.5.91	29 Mar
1.85	Thea	LaFond	DMA	5.4.94	3 Apr
1.85	Colleen	O'Brien	USA	.93	17 Apr
1.85	Taylor	Burke	USA	4.6.93	24 Apr
1.85	Regina	Sarsekova	KAZ	7.4.93	12 May
1.85	Amina	Smith	USA	10.1.92	17 May
1.85	Megan	Tice	IRL	6.12.89	23 May
1.85	Tonje	Angelsen	NOR	17.1.90	6 Jun
1.85	Emma	Kimoto	CAN	31.7.91	13 Jun
1.85	Sandrine	Champion	FRA	29.8.80	11 Jul
1.85	Zoe	Timmers	AUS	25.5.89	11 Dec
1.85i	Elizabeth	Evans	USA	1.12.90	11 Dec
1.84i	Oksana	Starostina	RUS	1.4.88	9 Jan
1.84i	Iryna	Kovalenko	UKR	17.6.86	3 Feb
1.84i	Elodie	Tshilumba	LUX-Y	1.5.98	7 Fe
1.84i	Erika	Furlani	ITA-J	2.1.96	8 Fe
1.84i	Dior	Delophont	FRA	19.10.94	21 Fe
1.84i	Natalya	Galagoza	RUS	27.4.94	27 Fe
1.84i	Selina	Schulenburg	GER-Y	22.8.98	28 Fe
1.84i	Julisa	Tindall	USA	28.3.95	7 Ma
1.84	Michelle	Sng Suat Li	SIN	19.5.87	19 Ma
1.84	Jailah	Mason	USA-J	12.9.96	23 Ap
1.84		Zhang Luyu	CHN	18.8.94	1 Ma
1.84	Kandie	Bloch-Jones	USA	21.4.95	2 Ma
1.84	Erika	Hurd	USA	8.4.94	8 Ma
1.84	Chanice	Porter	JAM	25.5.94	9 Ma
1.84	Leonie	Reuter	GER-Y	6.1.98	16 Ma
1.84	Lisa	Maihöfer	GER-J	28.10.98	6 Ju
1.84	Marina	Aitova	KAZ	13.9.82	15 Ju
1.84	Sini	Lällä	FIN	12.3.94	21 Ju
1.84	Alisa	Presnyakova	RUS-Y	7.3.98	24 Ju
1.84	Tatyana	Yermachenkova	RUS-Y	9.9.98	24 Ju
1.84	Jennifer	Oeser	GER	29.11.83	27 Ju
1.84	Carolin	Schäfer	GER	5.12.91	27 Ju
1.84		Liu Jingyi	CHN	27.10.94	29 Ju
1.84	Anastasiya	Belyakova	RUS	4.12.90	4 J
1.84	Alesya	Paklina	RUS	27.7.85	10 J
1.84	Noelia	Ruiz	ESP	5.2.88	11 J
1.84	Gintare	Nesteckyte	LTU	30.12.95	21 J
1.84	Yuki	Watanabe	JPN	12.8.88	26 J
1.84	Moe	Sasegbon	NGR	16.9.91	30 J
1.84	Yekaterina (173)	Stepanova	RUS	24.7.94	15 Au

Best outdoors

Mark	Name	Pos	Meet	Venue	Date
1.99	Licwinko	4	WCh	Beijing	29 Aug
1.95	Palsyté	1	NC	Palanga	7 Aug
1.94	Gordeyeva	2	DL	Doha	15 May
1.94	Kasprzycka	2		Rehlingen	25 May
1.94	Simic	5	GGala	Roma	4 Jun
1.94	Shkolina	7	GGala	Roma	4 Jun
1.94	Lake	1	NC-j	Bedford	21 Jun
1.94	Trost	8	ET	Cheboksary	21 Jun
1.93	Kallenou	2	SEC	Starkville	15 May
1.92	Okuneva	1	NC	Kirovohrad	31 Jul
1.91	Maresová	1		Praha	3 Jul
1.90	Hrubá	1	v4N-y	Trnava	6 Jun
1.90	Krasnokutskaya	2	NC-23	Saransk	16 Jun
1.90	Mnatsakanova	1	NCp	Yerino	10 Jul
1.90	Veneva-Mateeva	1	Pavlov	Sofia	11 Ju
1.89	Aleksandrova	1H		Adler	11 Ma
1.89	Gardzielewska	2		Dakar	23 Ma
1.89	Rossit	1		Gorizia	27 Ju
1.89	C García	1		Barcelona	1 Ju
1.89	Johnson-Thompson	1H	WCh	Beijing	22 Au
1.88	Zheng Xingjuan	1	NGPF	Beijing	29 Ju
1.87	Daniel	1		Baltimore	18 Ap
1.86	Cernjul	1		Lincoln	11 Ap
1.86	Kuntsevich	4		Dakar	23 Ma
1.86	Plaza	4		Rehlingen	25 Ma
1.86	Roslova	2	NCp	Brest	26 Ma
1.86	Maksimova	3=H		Götzis	30 Ma
1.86	Klucinová	3=H		Götzis	30 Ma

Mark	Name	Date
1.85	Borowska	11 Apr
1.85	Atkinson Grier	18 Apr
1.85	Skotnik	24May
1.85	Fedotova	7 Jun
1.85	Kononova	9 Jun
1.85	Goúsin	21 Jun
1.85	Stanciu	26 Jul
1.85	Udras	22 Aug
1.85	Pejchalová	29 Aug
1.84	E Evans	10 Apr
1.84	Melville	18 Apr
1.84	Rautanen	19 Jun
1.84	Delophont	28 Ju
1.84	Nordström	3 J
1.84	Vallortigara	25 J
1.84	Smolyakova	15 Au

JUNIORS

See main list for top 16 juniors. 11 performances (inc. 1 indoors) by 5 women to 1.92. Additional marks and further juniors:

Name	Mark	Pos	Meet	Venue	Date	Mark	Pos	Meet	Venue	Date
Patterson	1.94	1		Sunshine Coast	26 Jul	1.92	8	WCh	Beijing	29 Au
	1.92	Q	WCh	Beijing	27 Aug					
Cunningham	1.94	1	MSR-HS	Walnut	18 Apr					
Lake 2+	1.94	3		Eberstadt	31 Jul					

Mark	Name		Nat	Born	Pos	Meet	Venue	Date
1.85i	Lara	Omerzu	SLO-Y	10.2.98	1	NC-j	Celje	7 Fe

Mark	Name		Nat	Born	Pos	Meet	Venue	Date
1.85i	Lada	Pejchalová	CZE-Y	15.11.98	3	NC	Praha (Strom)	21 Feb
	1.85				1	NC-23	Hodonín	29 Aug
.84i	Elodie	Tshilumba	LUX-Y	1.5.98	1		Luxembourg	7 Feb
1.84i	Erika	Furlani (20)	ITA-	2.1.96	2		Ancona	8 Feb
1.84i	Selina	Schulenburg	GER-Y	22.8.98	2		Lyon	28 Feb
1.84	Jailah	Mason	USA	12.9.96	1	PennR	Philadelphia	23 Apr
1.84	Leonie	Reuter	GER-Y	6.1.98	1cB		Eppingen	16 May
1.84	Lisa	Maihöfer	GER	28.10.98	1H		Filderstadt	6 Jun
1.84	Alisa	Presnyakova	RUS-Y	7.3.98	1		Smolensk	24 Jun
.84	Tatyana	Yermachenkova	RUS-Y	9.9.98	2		Smolensk	24 Jun

POLE VAULT

Mark	Name		Nat	Born	Pos	Meet	Venue	Date
4.91	Yarisley	Silva	CUB	1.6.87	1		Beckum	2 Aug
			4.50/2 4.60/1 4.70/1 4.75/x 4.83/2 4.91/3					
	4.90 1 WCh	Beijing 26 Aug	4.50/1 4.60/1 4.70/3 4.80/2 4.85/1 4.90/3 5.01/xxx					
	4.85 1 PAm	Toronto 23 Jul	4.50/1 4.60/1 4.70/1 4.75/2 4.80/1 4.85/3 4.91/x					
	4.81 1 DL	Stockholm 30 Jul	4.46/1 4.56/1 4.66/1 4.76/3 4.81/2 4.86/xx					
	4.73 2 DL	Saint-Denis 4 Jul	4.53/1 4.63/1 4.73/1 4.78/xxx					
4.85	Fabiana	Murer	BRA	16.3.81	2	WCh	Beijing	26 Aug
			4.50/1 4.60/1 4.70/1 4.80/2 4.85/1 4.90/xxx					
	4.83i 1	Nevers 7 Feb	4.40/1 4.50/1 4.58/1 4.70/1 4.83/1 4.90/xxx					
	4.80 1 adidas	New York 13 Jun	4.54/1 4.64/3 4.74/x 4.80/1 4.86/xxx					
	4.80 2 PAm	Toronto 23 Jul	4.50/1 4.60/1 4.70/1 4.75/xx 4.80/1 4.85/xxx					
4.83	Nikoléta	Kiriakopoúlou	GRE	21.3.86	1	DL	Saint-Denis	4 Jul
			4.53/1 4.63/1 4.73/1 4.83/1 4.90/xxx					
	4.80i 1 GP	Birmingham 21 Feb	4.50/1 4.60/1 4.70/3 4.80/3					
	4.80 2 adidas	New York 13 Jun	4.54/3 4.64/3 4.74/1 4.80/1 4.86/xxx					
	4.80 3 WCh	Beijing 26 Aug	4.50/1 4.60/2 4.70/2 4.80/1 4.85/x 4.90/xx					
	4.79 1 DL	London (OS) 25 Jul	4.52/1 4.62/1 4.72/1 4.79/1 4.86/xxx					
	4.77 1 WK	Zürich 3 Sep	4.47/1 4.57/3 4.67/2 4.72/x 4.77/1 4.82/xxx					
	4.76i 1 XLG	Stockholm 19 Feb	4.50/2 4.65/2 4.76/1 4.81/xxx					
	4.76 2 DL	Stockholm 30 Jul	4.56/1 4.66/1 4.76/1 4.81/xxx					
	4.73 1 DL	Shanghai 17 May	4.48/1 4.58/3 4.68/3 4.73/2					
.82	Jenn	Suhr	USA	5.2.82	1	NC	Eugene	28 Jun
			4.55/2 4.60/1 4.70/1 4.82/2 4.93/xxx					
	4.81 1	Churchville 24 May						
	4.80i 1	Brockport 5 Dec	4.55/2 4.80/1 4.90/xxx					
4.80i	Anzhelika	Sidorova	RUS	28.6.91	1	EI	Praha (O2)	8 Mar
			4.50/1 4.60/1 4.70/1 4.75/1 4.80/1 4.85/xxx					
	4.79 2 DL	London (OS) 25 Jul	4.52/1 4.62/3 4.72/1 4.79/2 4.86/xxx					
	4.76 1 NA	Heusden-Zolder 18 Jul	4.52/1 4.61/2 4.66/1 4.71/1 4.76/2 4.81/xxx					
	4.75i 1 NC	Moskva 17 Feb	4.40/1 4.50/1 4.60/2 4.70/1 4.75/1 4.80/xx					
.77Ai	Ekateríni	Stefanídi	GRE	4.2.90	1		Flagstaff	20 Feb
			4.40/2 4.57/1 4.67/1 4.77/3 4.84/xxx					
	4.75i 2 EI	Praha (O2) 8 Mar	4.40/1 4.60/2 4.70/1 4.75/2 4.85/xxx					
.76	Sandi	Morris	USA	8.7.92	2	NA	Heusden-Zolder	18 Jul
			4.42/1 4.52/2 4.61/1 4.71/x 4.76/2 4.81/xxx					
.75Ai	Demi	Payne	USA	30.9.91	1		Albuquerque	24 Jan
			4.22/1 4.42/1 4.52/1 4.65/1 4.75/1					
.75	Silke	Spiegelburg	GER	17.3.86	1	ET	Cheboksary	20 Jun
	(30/9)		4.25/1 4.40/1 4.50/1 4.60/2 4.70/x 4.75/2 4.85/xxx					
.72i	Elizaveta 'Lisa'	Ryzih (10)	GER	27.9.88	1		Metz	25 Feb
.72	Jirina	Ptácníková	CZE	20.5.86	1		Praha	1 Jul
.71i	Marion	Fiack	FRA	13.10.92	1		Aubière	10 Jan
.71	Nicole	Büchler	SUI	17.12.83	1	NC	Zug	8 Aug
.70i	Angelica	Bengtsson	SWE	8.7.93	3	EI	Praha (O2)	8 Mar
.70	Holly	Bradshaw	GBR	2.11.91	7	WCh	Beijing	26 Aug
.67i	Angelina	Krasnova	RUS	7.2.91	2		Metz	25 Feb
.66		Li Ling	CHN	6.7.89	1	AsiC	Wuhan	6 Jun
.65i	Becky	Holliday	USA	12.3.80	1		Jonesboro	16 Apr
.65	Alana	Boyd	AUS	10.5.84	1		Mannheim	27 Jun
.65	Martina	Strutz	GER	4.11.81	3		Rottach-Egern	11 Jul
	(20)							
.65	Katharina	Bauer	GER	12.6.90	3		Beckum	2 Aug
.64	Eliza	McCartney	NZL-J	11.12.96	1		Auckland	19 Dec
.62	Mary	Saxer	USA	21.6.87	2=	DL	Birmingham	7 Jun
.61	Alyona	Lutkovskaya	RUS-J	15.3.96	1		Irkutsk	21 May
.60i	Anastasiya	Savchenko	RUS	15.11.89	2	NC	Moskva	17 Feb
.60i	Olga	Mullina	RUS	1.8.92	4	NC	Moskva	17 Feb
.60	Melinda	Withrow	USA	30.10.84	1		Phoenix	8 May
.60	Robeilys	Peinado	VEN-J	26.11.97	1		Barquisimeto	20 May

Mark	Name		Nat	Born	Pos	Meet	Venue	Date
4.60	Marion	Lotout	FRA	19.11.89	1		Pézenas	30 Ma
4.60	Minna	Nikkanen	FIN	9.4.88	1		Kuortane	8 Au
	(30)							
4.59	Nina	Kennedy	AUS-J	5.4.97	1		Perth	14 Fe
4.55i	Michaela	Meijer	SWE	30.7.93	9q	EI	Praha (O2)	6 Ma
4.55i	Tina	Sutej	SLO	7.11.88	10q	EI	Praha (O2)	6 Ma
4.55	April	Steiner Bennett	USA	22.4.80	2	TexR	Austin	28 Ma
4.55	Katie	Nageotte	USA	30.6.91	4	NC	Eugene	28 Ju
4.55	Malin	Dahlström	SWE	26.8.89	5		Rottach-Egern	11 Ju
4.55	Femke	Pluim	NED	10.5.94	1	NC	Amsterdam	1 Au
4.53i	Melissa	Gergel	USA	24.4.89	2		Lexington KY	23 Ja
4.51i	Victoria	von Eynatten	GER	6.10.91	1		Dortmund	1 Fe
4.51	Leslie	Brost	USA	28.9.89	1		Veracruz	8 Au
	(40)							
4.50i	Natalya	Demidenko	RUS	7.8.93	1		Volgograd	17 Ja
4.50i	Tatyana	Shvydkina	RUS	8.5.90	2	Mosc Ch	Moskva	7 Fe
4.50i	Megan	Clark	USA	10.6.94	2	NCAA	Fayetteville	14 Ma
4.50i	Kayla	Caldwell	USA	19.6.91	2		Jonesboro	16 Ap
4.50		Ren Mengqian	CHN	4.10.93	1	NGP	Taiyuan	12 Ma
4.50	Carolina	Carmichael	USA	28.4.94	1		Storrs	15 Ma
4.50	Kristen	Hixson	USA	1.7.92	5	NC	Eugene	28 Ju
4.50	Tori	Pena	IRL	30.7.87	8		Rottach-Egern	11 Ju
4.50	Mélanie	Blouin	CAN	14.7.90	1		Bolton	11 Ju
4.50	Kelsie	Ahbe	CAN	6.7.91	1		Knoxville	15 Au
	(50)							
4.46	Vanessa	Boslak	FRA	11.6.82	4		Sotteville-lès-Rouen	6 Ju
4.46	Lexi	Weeks	USA-J	20.11.96	1		Black Springs	4 Ju
	(facility with 75mm pegs; best on USATF-legal facility 4.30 1 Fayetteville 11 Apr)							
4.46A	Naroa	Agirre	ESP	15.5.79	1		Monachil	8 Au
4.45i	Anastasiya	Sadovnikova	RUS	22.6.95	1		Tartu	14 Fe
4.45i	Kira	Grünberg	AUT	13.8.93	15q	EI	Praha (O2)	6 Ma
4.45i	Stephanie	Richartz	USA	21.1.92	3	NCAA	Fayetteville	14 Ma
4.45	Annika	Roloff	GER	10.3.91	4		Mannheim	27 Ju
4.45i	Wilma	Murto	FIN-Y	11.6.98	1		Somero	27 De
4.43	Elizabeth	Parnov	AUS	9.5.94	2		Perth	14 Fe
4.43	Kaitlin	Petrillose	USA	10.12.92	1	Big 12	Ames	15 Ma
	(60)							
4.42	Anjuli	Knäsche	GER	18.10.93	1		Jockgrim	4 Au
4.42	Chloé	Henry	BEL	5.3.87	1		Waremme	22 Au
4.41	Alexis	Paine	USA	12.10.90	1		Baton Rouge	2 Ma
4.41	Angelica	Moser	SUI-J	9.10.97	1		Basel	25 Ma
4.41	Jenny	Wartinbee	USA	1.3.87	1		Chula Vista	29 De
4.40i	Yekaterina	Kazeka	RUS	7.10.90	1		Chelyabinsk	9 Ja
4.40i	Lyudmila	Yeryomina	RUS	8.8.91	1		Irkutsk	17 Ja
4.40i	Desiree	Singh	GER	17.8.94	1	Univ Ch	Frankfurt-Kalbach	4 Fe
4.40i	Stélla-Iró	Ledáki	GRE	18.7.88	2	NC	Pireás	15 Fe
4.40i	Hanna	Shelekh	UKR	14.7.93	1		Kyiv	20 Fe
	(70)							
4.40	Kylie	Hutson	USA	27.11.87	3		Phoenix	8 Ma
4.40	Tatyana	Stetsyuk	RUS	27.8.92	1		Moskva	2 Ju
4.40	Anna	Felzmann	GER	18.1.92	1		Leverkusen	5 Ju
4.40	Loréla	Mánou	GRE	20.12.90	1		Haniá	6 Ju
4.40	Martina	Schultze	GER	12.9.90	1		Zweibrücken	7 Ju
4.40	Kristina	Owsinski	USA	16.2.93	4	NCAA	Eugene	11 Ju
4.40	Sonia	Malavisi	ITA	31.10.94	1		Rieti	28 Ju
4.40	Alysha	Newman	CAN	29.6.94	1		Bolton	16 J
4.40	Carolin	Hingst	GER	18.9.80	1		Püttlingen	19 Ju
4.40	Rianna	Galiart	NED	22.11.85	1		Kessel-Lo	8 Au
	(80)							
4.38	Karla Rosa	da Silva	BRA	12.11.84	1		Porto Alegre	11 Ap
4.38	Annie	Rhodes	USA	13.5.95	2	Big 12	Ames	15 Ma
4.37i	Morgann	LeLeux	USA	14.11.92	3		Blacksburg	7 Fe
4.37i	Heather	Hamilton	CAN	31.3.88	1		Seattle	14 Fe
4.37i	Tori	Weeks	USA-J	20.11.96	1		Black Springs	14 Ju
	(facility with 75mm pegs; best on USATF-legal facility 4.29A 1 Albuquerque 6 Jun)							
4.36i	Robin	Bone	CAN	13.2.94	1		Windsor	14 Fe
4.36	Marta	Onofre	POR	28.1.91	1		Fatimá	9 Au
4.35i	Caroline Bonde	Holm	DEN	19.7.90	5		Potsdam	6 Fe
4.35i	Romana	Malácová	CZE	15.5.87	3		Praha	25 Fe
4.35	Emma	Philippe	AUS-J	6.6.97	2		Perth	14 Ma
	(90)							

ark	Name		Nat	Born	Pos	Meet	Venue	Date
.35i	Diamara	Planell	PUR	16.2.93	4	NCAA	Fayetteville	14 Mar
.35	Sophie	Gutermuth	USA	2.11.92	5	TexR	Austin	28 Mar
.35	Desiree	Freier	USA-J	24.7.96	6	TexR	Austin	28 Mar
.35	Jessie	Johnson	USA	21.11.93	1		Auburn	18 Apr
.35	Kat	Majester	USA	22.5.87	5		Louisville	6 Jun
.35	Ninon	Guillon-Romarin	FRA	15.4.95	1	NC-23	Tomblaine	26 Jul
.34	Ariel	Voskamp	USA	8.3.92	2	SEC	Starkville	15 May
.34	Hulda	Thorsteinsdóttir	ISL	10.6.91	1		Akureyri	2 Aug
.33	Maria Eleonor	Tavares	POR	24.9.85	1		Aulnay-sous-Bois	15 Jul
.32i	Elina (100)	Lampela	FIN-Y	18.2.98	1		Oulu	1 Feb
.32i	Fanny	Smets	BEL	21.4.86	6		Metz	25 Feb
.32	Allie	Koressel	USA	2.3.91	1		Chula Vista	23 Apr
.32	Janice	Keppler	USA	22.3.87	2		London ON	3 Jun
.32	Joana	Costa	BRA	15.8.81	1		Rock Hill	22 Jul

31Ai	Lakan	Taylor	USA	21.6.95	31 Jan
30i	Valeriya	Novikova	RUS	25.8.94	9 Jan
30	Vicky	Parnov	AUS	24.10.90	30 Jan
30i	Lindsey	Murray	USA-J	22.7.96	6 Feb
30i	Roberta	Bruni	ITA	8.3.94	7 Feb
30i	Alina	Kakoshinskaya	RUS	16.11.86	10 Feb
.30i	Aneta	Morysková	CZE	19.9.92	21 Feb
30i	Gina	Reuland	LUX	28.8.92	6 Mar
.30	Jamie	Scroop	AUS	29.3.88	7 Mar
30	Samantha	Sonnenberg	USA	10.2.88	2 May
30	Patrícia	dos Santos	BRA	13.6.84	2 May
30	Maryna	Kylypko	UKR	10.11.95	12 May
30		Xu Huiqin	CHN	4.9.93	12 May
30	Tomomi	Abiko	JPN	17.3.88	23 May
.30	Anginae	Monteverde	USA	15.1.93	11 Jun
.30	Kamila	Przybyla	POL-J	3.5.96	14 Jun
30		Song Tingting	CHN	8.10.93	28 Jun
30	Vera	Schmitz	USA	3.12.87	25 Jul
28	Anicka	Newell	USA	5.8.93	8 May
28	Kristen	Brown	USA	26.5.92	15 May
27	Cimran	Virdi	CAN	14.10.94	2 May
27	Kimyanna	Rudolph	USA	27.5.94	8 May
27	Leanna	Carrière	CAN	3.4.85	22 May
26i	Kristine	Felix	USA	1.5.94	24 Jan
26i	Kally	Long	USA	28.8.95	31 Jan
26	Angela	Wald	GER	8.9.92	12 Jun
26A	Elienor	Werner	SWE-Y	5.5.98	18 Jul
25i	Catia	Pereira	POR	5.7.89	11 Jan
25i	Sally	Peake	GBR	8.2.86	14 Feb
25i	Lilli	Schnitzerling	GER	5.12.93	27 Feb
25	Lindsey	Bergevin	CAN	14.1.89	28 Mar
25	Irina	Yakoltsevich	BLR	26.1.93	16 May
25	Erica	Hjerpe	FIN	20.8.93	14 Jun
25	Kristina	Bondarenko	RUS	10.8.95	15 Jun
25	Katrine	Haarklau	NOR	21.2.91	20 Jun
25	Lisa	Gunnarsson	SWE-Y	20.8.99	1 Jul
25	Regine	Kramer	GER	5.4.93	7 Jul
25	Henrietta	Paxton	GBR	19.9.83	18 Jul
25	Aino	Siitonen	FIN	29.9.94	2 Aug
24i	Cameron	Overstreet	USA	30.9.92	21 Feb
24	Hunter	Wilkes	USA	17.8.94	29 May
22i	Alexandra	Wasik	USA	6.12.92	16 Jan
22	Natasha	Kolbo	USA	5.4.92	23 Apr
21i	Claire	Lucas	USA	20.2.93	20 Feb
21	Karleigh	Parker	CAN	10.5.92	2 May
21	Samantha	Becker	USA	21.8.92	16 May
21	Demet	Parlak	TUR-J	26.7.96	13 Jun
20i	Mariya	Zakharutkina	RUS-J	14.8.96	20 Jan
20i	Franziska	Kappes	GER	6.5.94	1 Feb
20i	Rebeka	Silhanová	CZE	22.3.95	7 Feb

4.20i	Sophie	Dangla	FRA	19.10.87	7 Feb
4.20i	Gil	Le Bris-Finot	FRA	29.11.95	7 Feb
4.20i	Giorgia	Benecchi	ITA	9.7.89	14 Feb
4.20i	Giulia	Cargnelli	ITA	18.3.88	22 Feb
4.20	Brysun	Stately	USA	22.11.86	21 Mar
4.20	Caroline	Hasse	GER	8.3.91	17 Apr
4.20	Jamie	House	USA	12.12.92	17 Apr
4.20	Bonnie	Draxler	USA	13.10.95	17 Apr
4.20	Madison	Heath	USA	3.11.95	17 Apr
4.20	Paula	Andrie	USA	26.1.93	25 Apr
4.20	Rebecca	Preisler	USA		2 May
4.20		Choi Yea-eun	KOR	22.12.94	23 May
4.20	Alix	Dehaynain	FRA-J	7.12.97	24 May
4.20A	Caitlin	Maulin	USA	28.1.92	25 May
4.20	Justyna	Smietanka	POL	24.9.94	30 May
4.20	Megumi	Nakata	JPN	6.12.88	31 May
4.20	Miho	Imano	JPN	25.1.90	31 May
4.20	Sara	Bercan	SLO	31.5.92	14 Jun
4.20	Sara	Stevens	USA-J	16.4.96	27 Jun
4.20	Lucy	Bryan	GBR	22.5.95	4 Jul
4.20	Giorgia	Benecchi	ITA	9.7.89	11 Jul
4.20		Lim Eun-ji	KOR	2.4.89	12 Jul
4.20	Yelizaveta	Bondarenko	RUS-Y	1.7.99	1 Aug
4.20	Fanni	Juhász	HUN	31.3.81	1 Aug
4.20i	Megumi	Hamana	JPN	10.7.84	2 Aug
4.20A	Martha	Villalobos	MEX	20.3.90	2 Aug
4.20A	Carmelita	Correa	MEX	5.12.88	7 Aug
4.20	Olga	Frackowiak	POL	14.2.90	30 Aug
4.20i	Mallaury	Sautereau	FRA-J	1.8.96	5 Dec
4.20i	Anais	Poumarat	FRA	25.2.89	5 Dec
4.19i	Megan	Zimlich	USA	30.9.93	13 Feb
4.19	Meagan	Gray	USA-J	15.8.97	9 Apr
4.19	Mackenzie	Shell	USA-J	6.1.97	15 May
4.18i	Kristen	Denk	USA-J	15.2.97	15 Mar
4.18	Sarah	Birkmeier	USA	9.11.91	28 May
4.18	Chanel	Krause	USA	31.10.94	28 May
4.18	Sabrina	Hochreuther	GER	2.8.90	28 May
4.18	Katie	Adair	USA	30.6.93	28 May
4.17i	Lauren	Chorny	USA	22.6.93	7 Feb
4.17i	Ellie	Braidic	USA	12.2.94	7 Feb
4.17i	Elizabeth	Powell	USA	3.6.92	13 Feb
4.17	Sarah	Bell	USA	20.9.94	2 May
4.17	Kara	Whitson	USA		8 May
4.17	Nicole	Casper	USA	29.6.94	8 May
4.17	Morgan	Estes	USA		9 May
4.17	Maéva	Alves	FRA	5.3.94	25 Jun
4.17	Lene (201)	Retzius	NOR-J	4.1.96	29 Aug

Exhibition – downhill

4.21	Aneta	Morysková	CZE	19.9.92	22 May

est outdoors

79	Sidorova	2	DL	London (OS)	25 Jul
71	Stefanídi	1	DrakeR	Des Moines	24 Apr
71	D Payne	1		Hammond	8 May
70	Ryzih	1		Rottach-Egern	11 Jul
70	Bengtsson	4=	WCh	Beijing	26 Aug
60	Krasnova	1		Sochi	28 May
60	Holliday	1		Louisville	6 Jun
55	Mullina	2		Kuortane	8 Aug
55	Meijer	Q	WCh	Beijing	24 Aug
50	Clark	1		Durham	11 Apr
50	Gergel	2		Chula Vista	23 May

4.45	Richartz	3	NCAA	Eugene	11 Jun
4.45	Shvydkina	2		Baku	24 Jun
4.40	Sadovnikova	1	NC-23	Saransk	15 Jun
4.40	Grünberg	1		Innsbruck	4 Jul
4.38	Sutej	8	DL	Shanghai	17 May
4.35	LeLeux	1	Towns	Athens GA	11 Apr
4.35	Malácová	2		Praha	4 Jun
4.35	Demidenko	3	EU23	Tallinn	10 Jul
4.30	Planell				18 Apr
4.30	Bruni				22 May
4.30	Reuland				4 Jun
4.30	Kazeka				24 Jul
4.30	Murto				8 Aug

WOMEN 2015

Mark	Wind	Name		Nat	Born	Pos	Meet	Venue	Date

4.30 Smets 9 Sep	4.25 Schnitzerling 25 May	4.22 Bone 3 Jun	4.20 Cargnelli 4 Ju
4.29AT Weeks 6 Jun	4.25 Peake 20 Jun	4.20 Hamilton 18 Apr	4.20 Savchenko 15 Ju
4.27 L Taylor 10 Apr	4.22 Murray 25 Apr	4.20 Benecchi 11 Jul	4.20 Kappes 7 Aug
4.25 Shelekh 24 May			4.18 Felix 28 Mar

JUNIORS

See main list for top 11 juniors. 12 performances (inc. 3 indoors) by 6 women to 4.41. Additional marks and juniors:

McCartney	4.50	1		Auckland	14 Nov					
Lukovskaya	4.60	1		Irkutsk	21 May	4.44	6	adidas	New York	13 Jun
	4.54i	1		Zweibrücken	28 Feb	4.42	1		Montreuil-sous-Bois	9 Jun
	4.50i	5	NC	Moskva	17 Feb					
Kennedy	4.50	1	NC-j	Sydney	13 Mar	4.41	1		Perth	22 Jan

Mark	Name		Nat	Born	Pos	Meet	Venue	Date
4.30i	Lindsey	Murray	USA	22.7.96	1		Carbondale	6 Feb
	4.22				2		Jonesboro	25 Ap
4.30	Kamila	Przybyla	POL	3.5.96	1	EAF	Bydgoszcz	14 Jun
4.26A	Elienor	Werner	SWE-Y	5.5.98	1	WY	Cali	18 Ju
4.25	Lisa	Gunnarsson	SWE-Y	20.8.99	1		Blois	1 Ju
4.21	Demet	Parlak	TUR	26.7.96	1		Istanbul	13 Jun
4.20i	Mariya	Zakharutkina	RUS	14.8.96	1		Moskva	20 Jan
4.20	Alix	Dehaynain	FRA	7.12.97	1		Tourcoing	24 May
4.20	Sara	Stevens	USA	16.4.96	1	NC-j	Eugene	27 Jun
4.20	Yelizaveta	Bondarenko (20)	RUS-Y	1.7.99	1	EYOF	Tbilisi	1 Aug
4.20i	Mallaury	Sautereau	FRA	1.8.96	1		Aubière	5 Dec
Best outdoors								
4.30	Wilma	Murto	FIN-Y	11.6.98	3		Kuortane	8 Aug
4.29A	Tori	Weeks	USA-J	20.11.96	1		Albuquerque	6 Jun

LONG JUMP

Mark	Wind	Name		Nat	Born	Pos	Meet	Venue	Date
7.14	1.2	Tianna	Bartoletta	USA	30.8.85	1	WCh	Beijing	28 Aug
		x	6.95/1.3	6.87/0.1	6.62	6.94/0.6	7.14		
7.12	-0.4	1 NC	Eugene	27 Jun	7.02w/2.3	7.12	x	x	x 6.90/0.3
6.99	0.6	1 DL	Doha	15 May	6.96/1.4	6.73/0.6	6.88/0.7	6.75/0.7	x 6.99
6.97	1.0	2 WK	Zürich	3 Sep	6.67	p	6.72/-0.4	p	p 6.97
6.89	-0.7	2 adidas	New York	13 Jun	6.45	6.49	x	6.56	6.73/-0.5 6.89
7.07	0.4	Shara	Proctor	GBR	16.9.88	2	WCh	Beijing	28 Aug
		x	6.87/0.9	7.07	7.01/0.6	x	x		
6.98	0.5	1 DL	London (OS)	25 Jul	6.67	6.49	x	x	x 6.98
6.95	0.7	2 DL	Doha	15 May	6.57	6.69	6.83/1.1	6.87/0.7	6.77 6.95
7.02	0.5	Ivana	Spanovic	SRB	10.5.90	1	WK	Zürich	3 Sep
		x	x	6.93/0.4	6.90/-0.2	6.66	7.02		
7.01	0.8	3 WCh	Beijing	28 Aug	7.01/0.8	x	x	6.86/0.9	6.98/1.0 7.01/0.6
6.98i		1 EI	Praha (O2)	7 Mar	6.80	x	6.98	6.89	6.71 6.81
6.91	0.7	Q WCh	Beijing	27 Aug	6.91		only jump		
6.87	0.2	1 Herc	Monaco	17 Jul	6.87	6.79	x	6.63	x x
6.99i		Christabel	Nettey	CAN	2.6.91	1	XL-Galan	Stockholm	19 Feb
		6.81	5.19	6.99	p	p	p		
6.99	0.8	1 Pre	Eugene	29 May	6.69	6.83/0.2	6.80/0.7	6.96/1.1	6.81/1.3 6.99
6.95	0.9	4 WCh	Beijing	28 Aug	6.95	6.85/1.0	x	6.69/0.8	6.84/0.9 x
6.93	0.5	3 DL	Doha	15 May	6.74	6.93	x	6.84/1.3	x x
6.92	-1.3	1 adidas	New York	13 Jun	6.28	6.50	6.59	6.87/-0.8	6.92 p
6.90	1.1	1 PAm	Toronto	24 Jul	6.81/1.6	6.56	6.61	6.80/-0.2	6.90 6.84/1.0
6.97	-0.1	Brittney	Reese	USA	9.9.86	2	NC	Eugene	27 Ju
		6.97	6.43	x	x	6.93/0.7	x		
6.95	1.6	Darya	Klishina	RUS	15.1.91	1	ET	Cheboksary	21 Ju
		6.75w/2.1	6.79/0.5	6.95	x				
6.89	2.0	1 GGala	Roma	4 Jun	x	6.89	6.59	x	x 6.70
6.95	1.1	Janay	DeLoach	USA	12.10.85	3	NC	Eugene	27 Ju
		6.61	6.41	6.95	5.32w	6.71/2.0	4.93w		
6.94	0.7	Lena	Malkus	GER	6.8.93	1		Weinheim	30 Ma
		x	6.50	x	x	6.94	6.80/0.1		
6.94	-1.0	Sosthene	Moguenara	GER	17.10.89	1		Bad Langensalza	4 Ju
		6.94	x	x	x	p	6.83/0.8		
6.93i		Katarina (10)	Johnson-Thompson	GBR	9.1.93	1	GP	Birmingham	21 Feb
		6.67	x	6.93	6.85	x	6.71		
6.89i		1P EI	Praha (O2)	6 Mar	6.89	x	x		
6.93A	2.0	Quanesha	Burks	USA	15.3.95	1	NACAC	San José, CRC	9 Au
		6.69	6.27	6.93	x	6.68	6.66		
6.92	0.3	Lorraine	Ugen	GBR	22.8.91	4	DL	Doha	15 Ma
		6.79/0.8	6.68	6.68	6.92	6.88/0.0	x		
6.87	0.1	Q WCh	Beijing	27 Aug	6.29	6.61	6.87		
6.87	0.0	Yuliya	Pidluzhnaya	RUS	1.10.88	1	NC	Cheboksary	4 Au
		(31/13)		6.50	6.46	6.61	6.57	x	6.87

Mark	Wind	Name		Nat	Born	Pos	Meet	Venue	Date
.86	0.6	Olga	Sudareva	BLR	22.2.84	2	ET	Cheboksary	21 Jun
.84	1.2	Jasmine	Todd	USA	23.12.93	4	NC	Eugene	27 Jun
.84	0.2	Malaika	Mihambo	GER	3.2.94	Q	WCh	Beijing	27 Aug
.84	1.2	Konomi	Kai	JPN	10.7.93	1		Konosu	24 Oct
.83		Anastasiya	Mironchik-Ivanova	BLR	13.4.89	1		Minsk	19 May
.83	1.7	Kate	Hall	USA-J	12.1.97	1		Greensboro NC	21 Jun
.83	0.3	Bianca	Stuart	BAH	17.5.88	1	NC	Nassau	26 Jun
		(20)							
.82i		Yekaterina	Koneva	RUS	25.9.88	1	Winter	Moskva	1 Feb
.82i		Aiga	Grabuste	LAT	24.3.88	1		Tbilisi	8 Feb
.81	1.1	Krystyna	Hryshutyna	UKR	21.3.92	1		Kirovohrad	8 Jun
.80	1.7	Jenna	Prandini	USA	20.11.92	2	NCAA	Eugene	11 Jun
.79i		Florentina	Marincu	ROU-J	8.4.96	3	EI	Praha (O2)	7 Mar
.78	1.5	Olga	Kucherenko	RUS	5.11.85	1		Krasnodar	6 Jun
.78A	1.5	María del Mar	Jover	ESP	21.4.88	1		Monachil	8 Aug
.78	1.9	Khaddi	Sagnia	SWE	20.4.94	1	NC	Söderhamn	9 Aug
.75	1.8	Sha'Keela	Saunders	USA	18.12.93	3	NCAA	Eugene	11 Jun
.75	1.7	Alina	Rotaru	ROU	5.6.93	1	NC	Pitesti	26 Jul
		(30)							
.74i		Funmi	Jimoh	USA	29.5.84	1	ISTAF	Berlin	14 Feb
.74i		Éloyse	Lesueur	FRA	15.7.88	3		Malmö	25 Feb
.74	2.0	Chelsea	Hayes	USA	9.2.88	1		Fort Worth	2 May
.74	1.5	Xenia	Stolz	GER	14.1.89	3		Bad Langensalza	4 Jul
.73i		Abigail	Irozuru	GBR	3.1.90	1	NC	Sheffield	15 Feb
.73	0.0	Brooke	Stratton	AUS	12.7.93	1		Adelaide	21 Feb
.73	1.5	Claudia	Rath	GER	25.4.86	1H	Hypo	Götzis	31 May
.72	0.9	Brianne	Theisen-Eaton	CAN	18.12.88	2H	Hypo	Götzis	31 May
.71	0.6	Jazmin	Sawyers	GBR	21.5.94	2	EU23	Tallinn	12 Jul
.70A	-0.1	Yariagnis	Argüelles	CUB	18.4.84	1		Medellín	10 May
		(40)							
.70	1.3	Keila	Costa	BRA	6.2.83	1	NC	São Bernardo do Campo	15 May
.70	2.0	Tori	Polk	USA	21.9.83	1		Chula Vista	23 May
.70	0.0	Maria Natalia	Londa	INA	29.10.90	1	SEAG	Singapore	10 Jun
.70	1.8	Yelena	Sokolova	RUS	23.7.86	2	NC	Cheboksary	4 Aug
.70	0.4	Erica	Jarder	SWE	2.4.86	Q	WCh	Beijing	27 Aug
.69	2.0	Háido	Alexoúli	GRE	29.3.91	1		Haniá	6 Jun
.69A	0.0	Chantel	Malone	IVB	2.12.91	2	NACAC	San José, CRC	9 Aug
.68	0.4	Eliane	Martins	BRA	26.5.86	*		Santiago de Chile	11 Apr
.68	1.3	Tânia	da Silva	BRA	17.12.86	2	NC	São Bernardo do Campo	15 May
.68	1.8	Julienne	McKee	USA	6.12.91	1		Atlanta	6 Jun
		(50)							
.68	0.9	Jana	Veldáková	SVK	3.6.81	1	ET-3	Baku	22 Jun
.67	1.3	Yelena	Mashinistova	RUS	29.3.94	1		Athí	27 May
.66	0.6	Karin	Melis Mey	TUR	31.5.84	1		Mersin	24 May
.66	1.1	Blessing	Okagbare	NGR	9.10.88	4	Athl	Lausanne	9 Jul
.66	0.4	Ksenija	Balta	EST	11.1.86	1	NC	Tallinn	9 Aug
.65	0.2	Bui	Thi Thu Thao	VIE	29.4.92	2	SEAG	Singapore	10 Jun
.64i		Akela	Jones	BAR	21.4.95	1	Tyson	Fayetteville	13 Feb
.63	0.3	Chelsea	Jaensch	AUS	6.1.85	2		Canberra	7 Feb
.63	0.6	Shanieka	Thomas	JAM	2.2.92	1		Kingston	28 Feb
.63	1.0	Keturah	Orji	USA-J	5.3.96	3		Athens GA	9 May
		(60)							
.63	1.7	Maryna	Bekh	UKR	18.7.95	1		Kharkiv	21 May
.63A	1.1	Caterine	Ibargüen	COL	12.2.84	*	NG	Cali	16 Nov
.62	1.7	Nektaria	Panagi	CYP	20.3.90	1		Larnaca	12 Jun
.61i		Melanie	Bauschke	GER	14.7.88	3	ISTAF	Berlin	14 Feb
.61	1.9	Anna	Yermakova	UKR	1.10.91	2		Kirovohrad	8 Jun
.61	1.2	Ese	Brume	NGR-J	20.1.96	1		Akure	11 Jul
.59	2.0	Andrea	Geubelle	USA	21.6.91	*		Chula Vista	23 May
.59	0.5	Tania	Vicenzino	ITA	1.4.86	3		Weinheim	30 May
.59	0.0		Xu Xiaoling	CHN	13.5.92	1	NGPF	Beijing	27 Jun
.59		Yekaterina	Levitskaya	RUS	2.1.87	4	NC	Cheboksary	4 Aug
		(70)							
.59	0.0	Alexandra	Wester	GER	21.3.94	1		Kassel	12 Aug
.58	0.0	Shanice	Stewart	USA	2.12.93	1		Lubbock	30 Apr
.58		Anna	Misochenko	RUS	15.4.92	5	NC	Cheboksary	4 Aug
.57i		Olga	Balayeva	RUS	31.7.84	1		Novocheboksarsk	16 Jan
.57	0.0	Yulimar	Rojas	VEN	21.10.95	1	NC	Barinas	17 Apr
.57	-1.1	Anna	Jagaciak	POL	10.2.90	2	WUG	Gwangju	9 Jul
.56	0.0	Euphemia	Edem	NGR	3.3.89	1	NCAA-II	Allendale	21 May
.56	1.9	Tatyana	Akmukhamedova	RUS	14.7.93	1	NC-23	Saransk	16 Jun

Mark	Wind	Name		Nat	Born	Pos	Meet	Venue	Date
6.56	0.7	Nadja	Käther	GER	29.9.88	3	NC	Nürnberg	24 Ju
6.56	1.7	Hafdís	Sigurdardóttir	ISL	12.2.87			Akureyri	1 Au
		(80)							
6.55i		Jessie	Gaines	USA	12.8.90	1		South Huntington	13 Fe
6.55	0.6		Zhou Xiaoxue	CHN	19.6.92	1	NGP	Jinan	29 Ap
6.55	1.2	Irisdaymi	Herrera	CUB	18.4.92	3		Baie Mahault	2 Ma
6.55	0.0	Lisa	Steinkamp	GER	17.8.90	2		Oberteuringen	6 Ju
6.55	1.9	Toni	Smith	USA	13.10.84	2		Chula Vista	13 Ju
6.55	1.3	Naa	Anang	AUS	10.3.95	3	WUG	Gwangju	9 Ju
6.55	0.6	Marharyta	Tverdohlib	UKR	2.6.91	2	NC	Kirovohrad	31 Ju
6.54i		Kendell	Williams	USA	14.6.95	1	Hale	Blacksburg	7 Fe
6.54	1.0	Yilian	Durruty	CUB	30.1.90	1		La Habana	8 Ma
6.54	-0.2	Anastasiya	Mokhnyuk	UKR	1.1.91	3H	Hypo	Götzis	31 Ma
		(90)							
6.53i		Laura	Strati	ITA	3.10.90	1	NC	Padova	22 Fe
6.53	0.8	Jessica	Penney	AUS	21.12.87	1		Canberra	7 Ma
6.53	0.0	Marestella	Torres	PHI	20.2.81	1		Taipei	16 Ma
6.52	1.5	Shanice	McPherson	JAM	12.3.94	2	NCAA-II	Allendale	21 Ma
6.52	-0.4		Lu Minjia	CHN	29.12.92	1	AsiC	Wuhan	3 Ju
6.52	0.6	Dariya	Derkach	ITA	27.3.93	1	NC-23	Rieti	12 Ju
6.51	1.2	Maurren	Maggi	BRA	25.6.76	1		Campinas	28 Ma
6.50A	0.6	Yuliana	Angulo	ECU	6.7.94	2		Medellín	10 Ma
6.50	1.3	Kenyattia	Hackworth	USA	15.9.93	9	NC	Eugene	27 Ju
6.49i		Concepción	Montaner	ESP	14.1.81	1		Valencia	25 Fe
		(100)							
6.49	1.1	Munich	Tovar	VEN	25.10.89	1		São Bernardo do Campo	15 Ma
6.49	1.6	Romaissa	Belbiod	ALG	28.2.91	1		Moulins	26 Ju
6.49	0.2	Martina	Lorenzetto	ITA	18.4.92	1	NC	Torino	25 J

Mark	Wind	Name		Nat	Born	Date
6.48i		Dafne	Schippers	NED	15.6.92	21 Feb
6.48i		Lisa	Kurschilgen	GER	27.3.91	22 Feb
6.48	1.4	Sydney	Conley	USA	11.12.93	28 May
6.48	1.1	Nadine	Visser	NED	9.2.95	31 May
6.48	1.3	Paola	Mautino	PER	1.7.90	13 Jun
6.48	1.0	Nadia	Akpana Assa	NOR	22.12.95	11 Jul
6.47i		Nina	Djordjevic	SLO	15.5.88	14 Feb
6.47	1.0	Jéssica Carolina dos Reis		BRA	17.3.93	28 Mar
6.47	0.8		Jung Soon-ok	KOR	23.4.83	3 Jun
6.47	0.1	Anna	Bühler	GER-J	3.6.97	6 Jun
6.46i		Kristin	Gierisch	GER	20.8.90	17 Jan
6.46	1.5	Fátima	Diame	ESP-J	22.9.96	4 Jun
6.46	1.8	Whitney	Gipson	USA	20.9.90	27 Jun
6.46	0.6	Gabriela	Petrova	BUL	29.6.92	18 Jul
6.45	0.9	Haoua	Kessely	FRA	2.2.88	26 Jun
6.45	1.5	Milena	Mitkova	BUL	26.1.90	28 Jun
6.45	-0.6	Irène	Pusterla	SUI	21.6.88	1 Jul
6.45		Violetta	Skvortsova	BLR-Y	15.4.98	2 Jul
6.45	1.0	Annika	Gärtz	GER	24.8.94	11 Jul
6.45	1.5	Martha	Traoré	DEN	8.1.95	12 Jul
6.45	1.7	Bohdana	Melnyk	UKR	25.10.94	31 Jul
6.44i		Alexis	Perry	USA	8.8.94	23 Jan
6.44i		Elena	Panturoiu	ROU	24.2.95	15 Feb
6.44	1.3	Yana	Nikulina	RUS	2.7.90	28 May
6.44		Veronika	Mosina/Semashko	RUS	17.10.90	17 Jun
6.43	1.9	Chanice	Porter	JAM	25.5.94	15 May
6.43	2.0	Malaina	Payton	USA	16.10.91	23 May
6.43	0.6	Andriana	Bânova	BUL	1.5.87	30 May
6.43	0.3		Wang Wupin	CHN	18.1.91	27 Jun
6.43	1.1	Malin	Marmbrandt	SWE	29.4.85	4 Jul
6.43	0.5	Nafissatou	Thiam	BEL	19.8.94	15 Jul
6.43	0.2	Teresa	Dobija	POL	9.10.82	21 Jul
6.43	1.9	Yekaterina	Khalyutina	RUS	16.1.91	4 Aug
6.43	0.8	Jessica	Ennis-Hill	GBR	28.1.86	23 Aug
6.43	1.2	N.C.D.	Priyadharshani	SRI	15.9.79	19 Dec
6.42i		Karolina	Zawila	POL	21.11.86	7 Feb
6.42	1.7	Yurina	Hiraka	JPN	4.6.91	4 Apr
6.42	0.6	Macarena	Reyes	CHI	30.3.84	11 Apr
6.42	1.7	Lisa	Maihöfer	GER-Y	28.10.98	10 May
6.42	-0.5	Nataliyah	Friar	USA	3.4.95	9 Jul
6.42	0.3	Mara	Griva	LAT	4.8.89	1 Aug
6.41i		Olga	Rypakova	KAZ	30.11.84	14 Feb

Mark	Wind	Name		Nat	Born	Date
6.41i		Ilona	Kyrychenko	UKR	23.6.95	14 Fe
6.41A	0.3	Tara	Davis	USA-Y	20.5.99	19 Ju
6.40i		Erica	Bougard	USA	26.7.93	30 Ja
6.40	0.0	Susana	Hernández	MEX-Y	18.1.99	21 Ma
6.40	-0.2	Catherine	Kay Santos	PHI	29.10.90	4 Ap
6.40A	1.0	Gloria	Maldonado	MEX	18.4.92	1 Ma
6.40	2.0	Der'Renae	Freeman	USA	15.4.94	2 Ma
6.40	0.0	Klaudia	Kaczmarek	GER	13.3.90	30 Ma
6.39	1.7	Narayanan	V. Neena	IND	2.5.91	11 Fe
6.39i		Giulia	Liboà	ITA	3.6.93	22 Fe
6.39	1.9	Skye	Morrison	USA	5.8.90	13 Ju
6.39	0.7	Lyudmila	Yeryomina	RUS	8.8.91	16 Au
6.38	0.6	Génesis	Romero	VEN	6.11.95	17 Ap
6.38	1.9	Gabriela	dos Santos	BRA	23.2.95	15 Ma
6.38	0.2	Maryse	Luzolo	GER	13.3.95	30 Ma
6.38	0.7	Fatim	Affessi	SUI	8.7.93	31 Ma
6.38	0.0	Rebecca	Camilleri	MLT	6.7.85	22 Ju
6.38	0.7	Darlene	Mazeau	FRA	27.4.92	26 Ju
6.38	0.2	Chinazor	Amadi ¶	NGR	9.12.87	27 Ju
6.38		Shraddha	Bhaskar Ghule	IND	6.3.91	16 Se
6.37i		Sarah	Warnock	GBR	5.6.91	15 Fe
6.37i		Abie	Ehimwenman	USA	2.5.93	27 Fe
6.37		Kristina	Aleynikova	BLR	31.3.92	2 Ju
6.37	2.0	Courtney	Corrin	USA-J	12.12.97	23 Ma
6.37		Krystsina	Aleynikova	BLR	31.3.92	2 J
6.36i		Nathalie	Buschung	GER-J	2.3.96	15 Fe
6.36i		Agnieszka	Borowska	POL	21.10.91	21 Fe
6.36i		Gabrielle	Farquharson	USA		27 Fe
6.36	0.0	Mariah	Ririnui	NZL	29.6.92	10 Ap
6.36	1.5	Jhaanmy	Luque	VEN	20.12.95	28 Ma
6.36	1.0	Anna	Kornuta	UKR	10.11.88	8 Ju
6.36	0.0	Ulyana	Aleksandrova	RUS	1.1.91	9 Ju
6.36	1.8	Tierra	Williams	USA	10.6.95	11 Ju
6.36	1.7	Dana	Veldáková	SVK	3.6.81	14 Ju
6.35i		Alina	Fyodorova	UKR	31.7.89	12 Fe
6.35	0.8	Xenia	Rahn	GER	9.3.91	9 Ap
6.35		Darya	Reznichenko	UZB	3.4.91	29 Ap
6.35	1.5	Yekaterina	Ektova	KAZ	30.8.92	19 Ma
6.35	-1.6	Aleksandra	Yevstyunina	RUS	8.7.93	18 J
6.35	1.9	Jessamyn	Sauceda	MEX	22.5.89	25 J
6.35	0.4	Margrethe	Renstrøm	NOR	21.3.85	8 Au
		(186)				

Wind assisted

Mark	Wind	Name	Pos	Meet	Venue	Date
7.11	2.5	Bartoletta	1	Pre	Eugene	29 M
		6.61	6.70	7.11w	6.83/1.5 p	p
6.98		Nettey	1	MSR	Walnut	18 A
		6.74w	6.98w	6.89w	x x	6.54

Mark	Wind	Name		Nat	Born	Pos	Meet	Venue	Date
6.96	5.8	Lorraine	Ugen	GBR	22.8.91	1	TexR	Austin	28 Mar
					6.71w	6.96w	6.84w/3.8	6.73w	p p
	6.89	2.8 3 Pre	Eugene	29 May	6.54w	6.89w	6.71	x 6.69	6.81/0.1
6.91	2.6		Burks			1	NCAA	Eugene	11 Jun
		best at low altitude			6.70w	6.74w/2.4	6.61w	6.51w 6.91w	6.75w/2.2
6.84	2.2	Claudia	Rath	GER	25.4.86	2		Bad Langensalza	4 Jul
6.82A	4.6	Chioma	Agwunobi	USA	.95	1	Conf USA	El Paso	17 May
6.74	3.2	Chelsea	Jaensch	AUS	6.1.85	1	NC	Brisbane	29 Mar
6.73	2.1	Eliane	Martins	BRA	26.5.86	1		Santiago de Chile	11 Apr
6.73	2.5	Tânia	da Silva	BRA	17.12.86	2		Santiago de Chile	11 Apr
6.71	3.6	Susana	Hernández	MEX-Y	18.1.99	1	MSR	Walnut	18 Apr
6.70	2.1	Julienne	McKee	USA	6.12.91	2		Athens GA	9 May
6.70	2.6	Andrea	Geubelle	USA	21.6.91	2		Chula Vista	23 May
6.67	2.5	Nataliyah	Friar	USA	3.4.95	2	SEC	Starkville	15 May
6.66A	2.1	Caterine	Ibargüen	COL	12.2.84	1	NG	Cali	16 Nov
6.60	3.4	Sydney	Conley	USA	11.12.93	5	NCAA	Eugene	11 Jun
6.59	2.9	Der'Renae	Freeman	USA	15.4.94	6	NCAA	Eugene	11 Jun
6.56	2.5	Courtney	Corrin	USA-J	12.12.97	1	NC-j	Eugene	25 Jun
6.55	2.9	Paola	Mautino	PER	1.6.90	3		Santiago de Chile	11 Apr
6.55	5.4	Lynique	Prinsloo	RSA	30.3.91	1	NC	Stellenbosch	17 Apr
6.55	3.0	Anna	Bühler	GER-J	3.6.97	2	EJ	Eskilstuna	19 Jul
6.55	4.0	Fátima	Diame	ESP-J	22.9.96	3	EJ	Eskilstuna	19 Jul
6.54	2.3		Lu Minjia	CHN	29.12.92	1	Nambu	Sapporo	12 Jul

Mark	Wind	Name		Nat	Born	Date
6.53	2.3	Carla	Marais	RSA	10.12.87	17 Apr
6.53	2.7	Chanice	Porter	JAM	25.5.94	15 May
6.53	2.7	Skye	Morrison	USA	5.8.90	13 Jun
6.52	4.0	Diane	Barras	FRA	21.8.85	21 Jun
6.51	2.6	Dana	Veldáková	SVK	3.6.81	9 May
6.50	3.8	Laura	Rombach Rau	USA	8.1..85	14 Jun
6.47	2.4	Sonnisha	Williams	USA	20.4.91	8 May
6.47	2.8	Shakinah	Brooks	USA	23.6.95	21 May
6.46	2.2	Erika	Kinsey	SWE	10.3.88	21 May
6.43	2.4	Uhunoma	Osazuwa	NGR	23.11.87	16 Apr
6.42	3.7	Alexis	Faulknor	USA	22.9.94	16 May
6.42	3.4	Allie	Saunders	USA	8.1.93	28 May
6.42	2.5	Petya	Dacheva	BUL	10.3.85	18 Jul
6.41A	2.4	Zoila	Flores	MEX	29.8.89	29 Mar
6.37	2.6	Sanna	Nygård	FIN	22.3.88	13 Sep
6.37	4.3	Saeko	Okayama	JPN	12.4.82	4 Oct
6.35	3.1	Rougui	Sow	FRA	7.6.95	21 Jun

Best outdoors plus 6.99 Nettey

Mark	Wind	Name	Pos	Meet	Venue	Date
6.79	0.2	Johnson-Thompson	Q	WCh	Beijing	27 Aug
6.72	0.7	Jimoh	5	GGala	Roma	4 Jun
6.66	0.4	Marincu	1	BalkJ	Pitesti	5 Jul
	6.78w	3.8	1	EJ	Eskilstuna	19 Jul
6.62	1.6	Grabuste	1		Riga	28 May
6.63w	2.6	Grabuste	1	Sule	Tartu	9 Jun
6.61	1.5	Irozuru	1		Phoenix	8 May
6.60	1.2	AJones	6	PAm	Toronto	24 Jul
6.59	0.7	Bauschke	6	GGala	Roma	4 Jun
6.53	1.3	Gaines	1	PennR	Philadelphia	25 Apr

6.48A 0.0 Montaner 8 Aug | 6.39 -2.1 Koneva 8 Oct | Strati 6.43w 5.4 27 Sep
6.46 0.1 K Williams 9 May | 6.37 -0.5 Zawila 21 Jul | 6.36 -0.1 Perry 7 May
6.43 -0.4 Schippers 31 May | 6.37 2.0 Strati 27 Sep | 6.35 0.7 Liboà 2 Jun

Best at low altitude

Mark	Wind	Name	Pos	Meet	Venue	Date
6.84	1.9	Burks	1	SEC	Starkville	15 May
	6.91w	2.6	1	NCAA	Eugene	11 Jun
6.66	0.9	Argüelles	1		Ponce	23 May
6.62	0.9	Malone	5	PAm	Toronto	24 Jul
6.42	1.1	Jover				1 Aug
	6.48w	2.9				4 Jun
6.38	1.2	Angulo				24 Apr
6.39w	2.6	Bougard				15 May

JUNIORS

See main list for top 4 juniors. 11 performances (inc. 3 indoors) by 4 women to 6.58. Additional marks and further juniors:

Marincu 2+ 6.67i 1 NC-j Bucuresti 28 Feb | 6.65 0.8 1 BalkC Pitesti 26 Jul
6.66i 1 Bacau 25 Jan | 6.63 1.3 2 NC Pitesti 26 Jul
Orji 6.62 0.0 1 Towns Athens GA 11 Apr | 6.61 1.4 3 SEC Starkville 15 May

Mark	Wind	Name		Nat	Born	Pos	Meet	Venue	Date
6.47	0.1	Anna	Bühler	GER	3.6.97	3		Oberteuringen	6 Jun
6.46	1.5	Fátima	Diame	ESP	22.9.96	1		Castellón	4 Jun
6.45		Violetta	Skvortsova	BLR-Y	15.4.98	1		Minsk	2 Jul
6.42	1.7	Lisa	Maihöfer	GER-Y	28.10.98	1		Ulm	10 May
6.41A	0.3	Tara	Davis	USA-Y	20.5.99	1	WY	Cali	19 Jul
6.40	0.0	Susana	Hernández (10)	MEX-Y	18.1.99	1		San Luis Potosi	21 Mar
6.37	2.0	Courtney	Corrin	USA	12.12.97	1		Norwalk	23 May
6.36i		Nathalie	Buschung	GER	2.3.96	1	NC-j	Neubrandenburg	15 Feb
6.33i		Abigail	Adjei	GER	10.1.97	2	NC-j	Neubrandenburg	15 Feb
6.33	1.3	Anastasiya	Seleznyova	RUS	15.4.97	1		Krasnodar	23 May
6.32i			Wang Rong	CHN	1.7.96	3		Xianlin	8 Mar
		6.30 0.2				1	NC-j	Fuzhou	28 May
6.32	0.1	Beatrice	Floresе	ITA	9.2.97	1		Castelnovo Monti	2 Jul
6.32	0.9	Jessie	Maduka	GER	23.4.96	Q	EJ	Eskilstuna	18 Jul
6.31	0.6	Sarah	Lagger	AUT-Y	3.9.99	1	NC	Kapfenburg	8 Aug
6.30i		Darrielle	McQueen	USA	29.5.96	5	SEC	Lexington	27 Feb
6.29	1.5	Holly	Mills (2)	GBR-Y	15.4.00	1		Ashford	16 Aug

Wind assisted 3 performances by 2 women to 6.58. See main list for top 4 juniors, additional performers to 6.30

Mark	Wind	Name		Nat	Born	Pos	Meet	Venue	Date
Marincu		6.62	2.6 1					Pitesti	7 Jun
6.32	4.2	Zinzi	Chanbangu	RSA	28.9.96	3	NC	Stellenbosch	17 Apr
6.31A	3.4	Maya	Evans	USA-Y	12.6.99	1		Albuquerque	6 Jun

WOMEN 2015

Mark	Wind	Name		Nat	Born	Pos	Meet	Venue	Date
6.30	2.5	Domique	Bullock	USA	14.5.96	2		Auburn	4 Ap
6.30		Carsyn	Spurgeon	USA	8.10.97	1		Tulsa	12 Ju

TRIPLE JUMP

Mark	Wind	Name		Nat	Born	Pos	Meet	Venue	Date
15.04	1.7	Yekaterina	Koneva	RUS	25.9.88	2	Pre	Eugene	30 Ma
					14.28 15.04 14.81/1.6 14.69 p p				
14.87	1.2	* ET	Cheboksary	20 Jun	14.41w/2.8 14.98w 14.72/1.2 14.87/1.7				
14.84		*	Krasnodar	23 May	14.18 14.92w 14.84/1.6				
14.72	-0.5	2 DL	Saint-Denis	4 Jul	14.60/0.0 14.08/2.0 14.72 14.33/0.2 p 14.45/-0.3				
14.69i		1 EI	Praha (O2)	8 Mar	14.42 14.28 14.69 14.40 p 14.32				
14.68i		1	Volgograd	24 Jan	14.34 14.53 14.68 14.29				
14.60	0.3	1 WUG	Gwangju	11 Jul	14.17 14.41 14.28 14.60 p p				
14.57i		Q NC	Moskva	19 Feb	14.57				
14.90	0.1	Caterine	Ibargüen	COL	12.2.84	1	WCh	Beijing	24 Au
					14.47/-0.1 14.80/-0.5 14.54/0.2 14.90 13.93 14.70/0.4				
14.88	0.9	* Pre	Eugene	30 May	14.83/0.2 14.88 x 14.82/0.9 15.01w/2.4 15.18w				
14.87	0.3	1	Kingston	9 May					
14.87	0.3	1 DL	Saint-Denis	4 Jul	14.65/0.8 14.86/0.4 14.71/1.1 14.87 14.84/0.0 14.85/0.				
14.85	1.2	1 DL	Shanghai	17 May	14.68/-1.5 14.70/1.3 14.68/0.7 14.71/-0.7 14.85 x				
14.69	0.4	1 DL	Stockholm	30 Jul	14.59/1.3 14.51/1.2 14.49/0.0 14.60/-0.5 14.69 p				
14.68	-0.1	1 Bisl	Oslo	11 Jun	14.40/-1.3 14.17 14.33 14.68 14.45/-0.4 14.58/0.2				
14.60	0.2	1 VD	Bruxelles	11 Sep	13.94 14.26 14.13 14.34 14.33 14.60				
14.78	-0.1	Hanna	Minenko	ISR	25.9.89	2	WCh	Beijing	24 Au
					x 14.78 14.53/0.3 x x x				
14.61	1.4	2 Odlozil	Praha	8 Jun	14.21w 14.39w 14.32 14.61 14.21 14.43				
14.56	1.3	3 DL	Saint-Denis	4 Jul	x 14.24 14.30 x 14.56 14.01				
14.49i		3 EI	Praha (O2)	8 Mar	14.49 14.48 14.46 14.20 14.18 13.93				
14.77	0.1	Olga	Rypakova	KAZ	30.11.84	3	WCh	Beijing	24 Au
					14.23 x x 14.59/0.3 x 14.77				
14.48	0.0	1	Almaty	12 May	14.34/-1.0 only other valid jump				
14.66	0.4	Gabriela	Petrova	BUL	29.6.92	4	WCh	Beijing	24 Au
					14.52/0.0 14.33 14.47/0.5 14.23 14.66 14.44/-0.1				
14.64	1.6	1 Odlozil	Praha	8 Jun	14.50/0.6 14.57w/2.3 x 14.64 x x				
14.57	-0.9	2 Bisl	Oslo	11 Jun	13.78 14.32 14.57 14.40/-0.6 x x				
14.55i		1 NC	Dobrich	15 Feb	x 14.20 p x 14.55 p				
14.53	0.0	* ET-2	Stara Zagora	20 Jun	x 14.41/0.0 14.53/0.4 14.85w				
14.53	-0.1	*	Madrid	11 Jul	x 14.11 14.17 14.51/1.7 14.53/0.7 14.54w				
14.52i		2 EI	Praha (O2)	8 Mar	14.21 x x 14.33 14.37 14.52				
14.62	0.5	Olha	Saladukha	UKR	4.6.83	2	DL	Shanghai	17 Ma
					14.53 x x 14.57 14.49 14.62				
14.48	1.5	3 Pre	Eugene	30 May	14.27w 14.26 14.21 14.48 x 13.99				
	(31/6)								
14.46i		Kristin	Gierisch	GER	20.8.90	4	EI	Praha (O2)	8 Ma
14.45	0.0	Kimberly	Williams	JAM	3.11.88	5	WCh	Beijing	24 Au
14.32i		Patrícia	Mamona	POR	21.11.88	5	EI	Praha (O2)	8 Ma
14.32	1.9	Susana	Costa (10)	POR	22.9.84	3		Madrid	11 J
14.32	0.0	Irina	Ektova	KAZ	8.1.87	1		Almaty	17 J
14.29	?	Kseniya	Detsuk	BLR	23.4.86	1		Minsk	2 J
14.28i		Cristina	Bujin	ROU	12.4.88	1	NGP	Bucuresti	31 Ja
14.27	1.2	Dana	Veldáková	SVK	3.6.81	1	NC	Banská Bystrica	1 Au
14.24	1.4	Jeanine	Assani Issouf	FRA	17.8.92	1		Forbach	31 Ma
14.23	1.9	Dovilé	Dzindzaletaité	LTU	14.7.93	1	EU23	Tallinn	10 J
14.23A	1.3	Shanieka	Thomas	JAM	2.2.92	1	NACAC	San José, CRC	7 Au
14.22	2.0	Simona	La Mantia	ITA	14.4.83	3	ET	Cheboksary	20 Ju
14.22	1.8	Yosiri	Urrutia	COL	26.6.86	*	PAm	Toronto	21 J
14.21i		Natalya	Vyatkina	BLR	10.2.87	Q	EI	Praha (O2)	7 Ma
		(20)							
14.21i			Li Yanmei	CHN	6.2.90	1	NGP	Xianlin	9 Ma
14.20i		Kristiina	Mäkelä	FIN	20.11.92	1		Mustasaari	4 Fe
14.20	1.6		Li Xiaohong	CHN	8.1.95	1	AsiGP	Chanthaburi	29 Ju
14.20	2.0	Yulimar	Rojas	VEN	21.10.95	*	PAm	Toronto	21 J
14.17	1.5	Anna	Jagaciak	POL	10.2.90	2		Marseille	6 Ju
14.17	-0.2	Keila	Costa	BRA	6.2.83	3		Marseille	6 Ju
14.16i		Katja	Demut	GER	21.12.83	2		Chemnitz	7 Fe
14.16	1.9	Jenny	Elbe	GER	18.4.90	1		Lahti	14 Ju
14.16		Joëlle	Mbumi	CMR	25.5.86	1		Yaoundé	12 J
14.15	1.8	Keturah	Orji	USA-J	5.3.96	1	NCAA	Eugene	13 Ju
		(30)							
14.13	1.8	Elena Andreea	Panturoiu	ROU	24.2.95	2	EU23	Tallinn	10 J
14.11i		Irina	Gumenyuk	RUS	6.1.88	1		Sankt-Peterburg	10 Fe
14.10i		Andriana	Bânova	BUL	1.5.87	1		Dobrich	11 Fe

Mark	Wind	Name		Nat	Born	Pos	Meet	Venue	Date
4.10	0.6		Wang Wupin	CHN	18.1.91	1	NGP	Beijing	8 May
4.09	1.1	Christina	Epps	USA	20.6.91	1	NC	Eugene	26 Jun
4.09	1.7	Viktoriya	Prokopenko	RUS	17.4.91	*	NC	Cheboksary	5 Aug
4.08i		Natalya	Alekseyeva	RUS	27.5.86	2	NC	Moskva	19 Feb
4.08	1.1	Tetyana	Ptashkina	UKR	10.1.93	Q	EU23	Tallinn	9 Jul
4.08	0.0	Liadagmis	Povea	CUB-J	6.2.96	2	PAm-J	Edmonton	2 Aug
4.06	0.5	Laura	Samuel	GBR	19.2.91	4	ET	Cheboksary	20 Jun
		(40)							
4.03i		Olesya	Zabara	RUS	6.10.82	3	NC	Moskva	19 Feb
4.03	0.0	Dailenis	Alcántara	CUB	10.8.91	1	Barr	La Habana	28 May
4.03	-0.1	Anastasiya	Potapova	RUS	6.9.85	1		Krasnodar	7 Jun
4.03	2.0	Ana	Peleteiro	ESP	2.12.95	5	ET	Cheboksary	20 Jun
4.03A	0.9	Ana José	Tima	DOM	10.10.89	*	NACAC	San José, CRC	7 Aug
4.01i		Ciarra	Brewer	USA	12.3.93	1	NCAA	Fayetteville	14 Mar
3.99	1.5	Paraskeví	Papahrístou	GRE	17.4.89	1		Haniá	6 Jun
3.98	1.5	Olesya	Tikhonova	RUS	22.1.90	3	NC	Cheboksary	5 Aug
3.98		Viktoriya	Gurova	RUS	22.5.82	4	NC	Cheboksary	5 Aug
3.97i		Cristina	Sandu	ROU	4.3.90	9q	EI	Praha (O2)	7 Mar
		(50)							
3.96	1.3	Ayanna	Alexander	TTO	20.7.82	1		Alexandria	30 May
3.94i		Patricia	Sarrapio	ESP	16.11.82	1	NC	Antequera	21 Feb
3.92	0.0	Ruslana	Tsyhotska	UKR	23.3.86	1		Kyiv	21 Jul
3.91	?	Iryna	Vaskovskaya	BLR	2.4.91	2		Minsk	2 Jul
3.89	1.6		Deng Linuo	CHN	16,3.92	3	AsiGP	Chanthaburi	29 Jun
3.88	1.9	Natalya	Yevdokimova	RUS	7.9.93	4	NCp	Yerino	10 Jul
3.87	1.7	Amanda	Smock	USA	27.7.82	1	MSR	Walnut	18 Apr
3.87	1.8	Alsu	Murtazina	RUS	12.12.87	6	NC	Cheboksary	5 Aug
3.85i		Ruth	Ndoumbe	ESP	1.1.87	2	NC	Antequera	21 Feb
3.85	1.7	Kristina	Malaya	RUS-J	8.10.96	2		Krasnodar	23 May
		(60)							
3.84i		Dariya	Derkach	ITA	27.3.93	1	NC	Padova	21 Feb
3.84	0.0		Tran Hue Hoa	VIE	8.8.91	1		Taipei	15 May
3.83i		Rouguy	Diallo	FRA	5.2.95	2		Eaubonne	8 Feb
3.83	1.5	April	Sinkler	USA	1.9.89	2	NC	Eugene	26 Jun
3.83A	1.8	Lynnika	Pitts	USA	19.5.92	*	NACAC	San José, CRC	7 Aug
3.82i		Snezana	Vukmirovic	SLO	19.8.82	1		Zagreb	24 Jan
3.81i		Veronika	Semashko	RUS	17.10.90	2		Sankt-Peterburg	27 Dec
3.80	-0.8	Yarianna	Martínez	CUB	20.9.84	2		La Habana	14 Feb
3.80	0.9	Tânia	da Silva	BRA	17.12.86	1		São Bernardo do Campo	19 Apr
3.80	0.6	Lucie	Májková	CZE	9.7.88	4	Odlozil	Praha	8 Jun
		(70)							
3.79	0.5	Biljana	Topic	SRB	17.10.77	1		Kragujevac	6 Jun
3.78		Mayookha	Johny	IND	9.4.88	1	NC	Kolkata	18 Sep
3.77	0.5	Danellys	Dutil	CUB	12.2.95	2		La Habana	19 Jun
3.76	0.4	Aleksandra	Kotlyarova	UZB	10.10.88	2	AsiGP	Bangkok	22 Jun
3.76	1.9	Ottavia	Cestonaro	ITA	12.1.95	1	NC	Torino	26 Jul
3.75	0.0	Maria Natalia	Londa	INA	29.10.90	1	SEAG	Singapore	11 Jun
3.73	0.0		Wang Rong	CHN-J	1.7.96	1	NGP	Jinan	30 Apr
3.73	-0.5	Benedetta	Cuneo	ITA-J	11.3.96	1	NC-j	Rieti	14 Jun
3.73	1.5	Sanna	Nygård	FIN	22.3.88	1		Umeå	16 Aug
3.72	1.5	Carmen	Toma	ROU	28.3.89	3	NC	Pitesti	25 Jul
		(80)							
3.70	-0.6	Claudine	de Jesus	BRA	9.9.94	3	NC	São Bernardo do Campo	17 May
3.70	1.7	Hanna	Krasutska	UKR	20.7.95	1		Kharkiv	22 May
3.70	1.6	Sasa	Babsek	SLO	27.3.92	*	NCp	Celje	13 Jun
3.70	1.7	Darya	Nidbaykina	RUS	26.12.94	1	NC-23	Saransk	17 Jun
3.70			Vu Thi Men	VIE	10.7.90	1	NC	Ho Chi Minh	13 Oct
3.69i		Teresa	Nzola Meso Ba	FRA	30.11.83	2	NC	Aubière	21 Feb
3.68	1.8	Madara	Apine	LAT	2.3.89	1		Kaunas	6 Jun
3.67	0.4		Wang Xiaofang	CHN	20.1.92	1	NGP	Taiyuan	12 May
3.67	0.1	Petya	Dacheva	BUL	10.3.85	1	BalkC	Pitesti	1 Aug
3.65	0.9	Nneka	Okpala	NZL	27.4.88	1		Canberra	7 Feb
		(90)							
3.65	0.6		Bae Chan-mi	KOR	24.3.91	1		Yecheon	22 Apr
3.65	1.0	Yanis	David	FRA-J	12.12.97	2	Hampton	Port of Spain	23 May
3.65	0.2	Irina	Kosko	RUS	1.3.90	1		Sochi	29 May
3.65	0.0	Iryna	Nikolayeva	UKR	20.1.84	2		Kirovohrad	9 Jun
3.65	0.1	Thitima	Muangjan	THA	13.4.83	3	SEAG	Singapore	11 Jun
3.65	-0.5	Blessing	Ibrahim	NGR	4.4.90	1		Akure	11 Jul
3.64	-2.3	Allie	Saunders	USA	8.1.93	1q	NCAA-W	Austin	29 May
3.64	1.7	Amy	Zongo-Filet	FRA	4.10.80	1		Nogent-sur-Marne	28 Jun

Mark	Wind	Name		Nat	Born	Pos	Meet	Venue	Date
13.63	1.0	Toni	Smith	USA	13.10.84	2		Chula Vista	25 Ju
13.62	1.9	Nathalie (100)	Marie-Nély	FRA	24.11.86	1		Castres	29 Ju

Mark	Wind	Name		Nat	Born	Date
13.61i		Valeriya	Fyodorova	RUS-J	9.4.96	6 Feb
13.60i		Georgiana	Anitei	ROU-Y	26.3.99	14 Feb
13.60	1.2	Dilyara	Abuova	KAZ	6.1.94	17 Jul
13.60	0.0	Andrea	Calleja	ESP	3.10.92	18 Jul
13.59		Violetta	Maksimchuk	RUS	1.12.90	5 Jul
13.56	1.5	Yekaterina	Sariyeva	AZE	18.12.95	6 Jun
13.55	0.5	Anastasiya	Leonova	BLR	15.2.94	15 May
13.55	1.8	Yargelis	Savigne	CUB	13.11.84	28 May
13.55	1.4	Anna	Zych	POL	15.5.88	20 Jun
13.55	0.9	Eleonora	D'Elicio	ITA	28.5.89	26 Jul
13.54	1.2	Sineade	Gutzmore	GBR	9.10.86	24 Jul
13.53	1.0	Chioma	Matthews	GBR	12.3.81	17 May
13.53	1.3	Florentina	Marincu	ROU-J	8.4.96	6 Jun
13.53	1.5	Marshay	Ryan	USA	4.2.95	13 Jun
13.52	1.8	Ellen	Pettitt	AUS	13.5.86	7 Feb
13.52i			Sun Yan	CHN	30.3.91	9 Mar
13.52	-0.8	Núbia	Soares	BRA-J	26.3.96	22 Aug
13.51	1.3	Jamaa	Chnaïk	MAR	28.7.84	27 Apr
13.50A	0.6	Sandisha	Antoine	LCA	5.11.91	7 Aug
13.49	0.0	Yanna Anay	Armenteros	CUB-Y	2.10.99	14 Feb
13.49	1.6	Alitta	Boyd	USA	7.12.91	23 Apr
13.49	0.9	H.D.Vidusha	Lakshani	SRI-J	28.12.96	28 Jun
13.48	1.0	Kenna	Wolter	USA	21.9.89	18 Apr
13.47	1.3	Blessing	Ufodiama	USA	28.11.81	4 Apr
13.46	-0.4	Malgorzata	Trybanska-Stronska	POL	21.6.81	19 Jul
13.44	2.0	Aleksandra	Nikitsina	BLR	11.1.93	6 Jun
13.44	1.2	Essi	Lindgren	FIN	10.4.90	27 Jun
13.43i			Chen Mudan	CHN	4.10.93	2 Mar
13.43	1.8	Paetyn	Revell	USA	24.2.95	30 Apr
13.43	0.2	Julienne	McKee	USA	6.12.91	30 May
13.43	0.3	Klaudia	Kaczmarek	GER	13.3.90	21 Jun
13.43	1.1	Keri	Emanuel	USA	30.6.92	26 Jun
13.43	1.6	Valentina	Kosolapova	RUS-J	11.7.97	27 Jun
13.42	0.3		Zeng Tingchao	CHN-J	29.1.96	28 Jun
13.41	1.8	Tamara	Myers	BAH	27.7.93	11 Apr
13.41	-0.2	Liliana	Breto	CUB-J	4.2.97	19 Jun
13.40	0.5	Hope	Idhe	NGR	29.1.87	27 Jun
13.40	0.4		Wei Mingchen	CHN	4.1.91	28 Jun
13.40	0.9		Li Sirui	CHN-J	17.2.96	21 Jul
13.40	-0.1	Nadia	Eke	GHA	11.1.93	13 Sep
13.38i		Anastasiya	Mironchik-Ivanova	BLR	13.4.89	23 Jan
13.38i		Tori	Franklin	USA	7.10.92	7 Feb
13.38i		Sokhna	Galle	FRA	23.4.94	8 Feb
13.38	-2.0	Liliana	Hernández	MEX	22.8.90	17 Apr
13.38	1.9	Asta	Dauksaité	LTU	3.4.88	6 Jun
13.38	0.4	Kateryna	Kravchenko	UKR	29.1.92	1 Aug
13.36i		Haoua	Kessely	FRA	2.2.88	3 Jan
13.36	1.4	Chardaé	Greenlee	USA	14.8.95	2 May
13.36	0.9	Nataliyah	Friar	USA	3.4.95	16 May
13.36	2.0	Thomaida	Polydorou	CYP	7.11.86	6 Jun
13.36	0.9		Diao Limin	CHN	12.6.92	21 Jul
13.35	1.3	Giselly Andrea	Landázuri	COL	8.8.92	12 Jun
13.35	0.8	Darya	Dyachenko	UKR-J	15.2.96	16 Jun
13.35	1.5	Thea	Lafond	DMA	5.4.94	21 Jul
13.35	-2.9	Norka	Moretic	CHI-Y	26.3.98	6 Nov
13.34i		Neele	Eckhardt	GER	2.7.92	25 Jan
13.34	2.0	Brianna	Richardson	USA	9.9.94	3 Apr
13.34	0.3	Silvia	La Tella	ITA	11.8.95	10 Jul
13.34	0.4	Martyna	Bielawska	POL	15.11.90	9 Aug
13.33	-0.1	Gabriela	dos Santos	BRA	23.2.95	17 May
13.33	1.3		Chen Liwen	CHN-Y	3.1.98	30 May
13.33	-0.1	Ivonne	Rangel	MEX	24.8.93	12 Jun
13.33	0.0	Maliakkal	Prajusha	IND	20.5.87	12 Jul
13.33	0.2		Rao Fan	CHN-J	1.1.96	25 Oct
13.32	1.0	Patience	Ntshingila	RSA	26.8.89	18 Apr
13.32	1.9	Mary Amiata	Otuorah	BRN	18.4.94	27 Apr
13.32	1.2	Simone	Charley	USA	4.2.95	13 Jun
13.32	1.0	Barbara	Leuthard	SUI	4.12.81	8 Aug
13.30	0.2	Anna (169)	Kornuta	UKR	10.11.88	10 Jul

Wind assisted

Mark	Wind	Name		Nat	Born	Pos	Meet	Venue	Date
15.18w	2.1	Caterine	Ibargüen	COL	12.2.84	1	Pre	Eugene	30 May
					14.83/0.2 14.88/0.9 x 14.82/0.9 15.01w/2.4 15.18w				
	15.08w 2.3	1 PAm	Toronto	21 Jul	14.37w 14.38w 14.74w/3.5 14.59w/2.1 14.88w/2.1 15.08w				
14.98w	2.3		Koneva			1	ET	Cheboksary	20 Jun
					14.41w 14.98w 14.72/1.2 14.87/1.7				
	14.92w 2.3	1	Krasnodar	23 May	14.18 14.92w 14.84/1.6				
14.85	2.5	Gabriela	Petrova	BUL	29.6.92	1	ET-2	Stara Zagora	20 Jun
					x 14.41/0.0 14.53/0.4 14.85w				
	14.54w 2.1	1	Madrid	11 Jul	x 14.11 14.17 14.51/1.7 14.53/0.7 14.54w				
14.50w	2.9	Keila	Costa	BRA	6.2.83	2	PAm	Toronto	21 Jul
					13.59w 14.08w 14.19w 14.21w 14.50w x				
14.46	3.5	Kristin	Gierisch	GER	20.8.90	2	ET	Cheboksary	20 Jun
14.41	3.0	Simona	La Mantia	ITA	14.4.83	1		Palermo	9 May
14.38	2.2	Jenny	Elbe	GER	18.4.90	1		Marseille	6 Jun
14.38	3.3	Yosiri	Urrutia	COL	26.6.86	3	PAm	Toronto	21 Jul
14.37	2.2	Yulimar	Rojas	VEN	21.10.95	4	PAm	Toronto	21 Jul
14.21A	3.3	Ana José	Tima	DOM	10.10.89	2	NACAC	San José, CRC	7 Aug
14.20	3.0	Paraskeví	Papahrístou	GRE	17.4.89	1	Veniz	Haniá	1 Jun
14.16	3.0	Núbia	Soares	BRA-J	26.3.96	1	PAm-J	Edmonton	2 Aug
14.10	2.1	Viktoriya	Prokopenko	RUS	17.4.91	2	NC	Cheboksary	5 Aug
14.07	3.1	Anastasiya	Potapova	RUS	6.9.85	1		Krasnodar	6 Jun
14.04	3.5	Dailenis	Alcántara	CUB	10.8.91	5	PAm	Toronto	21 Jul
14.02	3.4	Sasa	Babsek	SLO	27.3.92	1	NCp	Celje	13 Jun
14.02A	4.2	Lynnika	Pitts	USA	19.5.92	3	NACAC	San José, CRC	7 Aug
13.92	6.8	Tamara	Moncrieffe	JAM-J	16.5.96	1	NSch	Kingston	27 Ma
13.88	2.6	Dariya	Derkach	ITA	27.3.93	4	EU23	Tallinn	10 Ju
13.85	2.2	Blessing	Ufodiama	USA	28.11.81	1		Claremont	4 Ap
13.79	2.1	Teresa	Nzola Meso Ba	FRA	30.11.83	1		Montélimar	21 Jun
13.78A	3.4	Tamara	Myers	BAH	27.7.93	4	NACAC	San José, CRC	7 Aug
13.66	2.9	Jamaa	Chnaïk	MAR	28.7.84	1		Rabat	9 May

Mark	Wind	Name		Nat	Born	Date
13.63	2.2	Andrea	Calleja	ESP	3.10.92	2 Aug
13.61	2.5	Liliana	Hernández	MEX	22.8.90	30 May
13.60A	2.5	Thea	LaFond	DMA	5.4.94	7 Aug
13.53A	2.4	Sandisha	Antoine	LCA	5.11.91	7 Aug
13.49	2.7	Simone	Charley	USA	4.2.95	13 Jun
13.49	2.4	Ariadna	Ramos	ESP	5.1.94	28 Jun
13.48A	2.3	Ivonne	Rangel	MEX	24.8.93	1 May
13.47	2.4	Chardaé	Greenlee	USA	14.8.95	17 May
13.46	3.1	Nadia	Eke	GHA	11.1.93	13 Jun
13.44	?	Arianna	Gutiérrez	VEN	11.10.92	28 Feb
13.44	2.9	Keri	Emanuel	USA	30.6.92	26 Jun
13.38	5.3	Tori	Franklin	USA	7.10.92	13 Jun
13.30	4.9	Sokhna	Galle	FRA	23.4.94	21 Jun
13.30	2.1	Sonya	Kussekala	UKR	5.5.00	29 Ju

Mark	Wind	Name	Nat	Born	Pos	Meet	Venue	Date

Best outdoors

4.38 0.6 Gierisch 1 NC Nürnberg 26 Jul
4.19 0.0 Bujin 1 IntC Pitesti 23 May
4.19 -0.8 Mamona 6 Bisl Oslo 11 Jun
4.06 0.5 Mäkelä 2 Lahti 14 Jun
3.95 0.6 Bânova 1 Sofia 25 Jun
14.06w 2.2 1 NC Sofia 11 Jun
3.59 0.2 Sandu 23 May
3.56 -1.1 Demut 25 May
13.70w 4.0 31 May

13.53 -0.7 Derkach 13 Jun
13.49 0.0 Brewer 4 Apr
13.49A 0.3 Anitei 18 Jul
13.50w 2.9 29 Jul

13.94 0.6 Vyatkina 2 NC Grodno 24 Jul
13.93 1.7 Alekseyeva 3 NCp Yerino 10 Jul
13.83 0.3 Li Yanmei 6 DL Shanghai 17 May
13.80 0.7 Diallo 7 DL Shanghai 17 May
13.76 -1.6 Sarrapio 1 Salamanca 6 Jun
13.69 1.2 Nzola Meso Ba 1 NC Villeneuve d'A10 Jul
13.68 -0.8 Gumenyuk 8 DL Shanghai 17 May

13.44 -1.3 Ndoumbe 6 Jun
13.39 0.2 Chen Mudan 28 Jun
13.37 0.6 Sun Yan 28 Jun
13.30 1.1 Franklin 2 May

Best at low altitude

4.08 0.2 Thomas 11 WCh Beijing 24 Aug
3.80 1.5 Tima 3 WMilG Mugyeong 6 Oct
3.79 1.9 Pitts 4 NC Eugene 26 Jun

13.67w 2.6 Vukmirovic 2 NCp Celje 13 Jun
13.57w 2.3 Myers 21 Jul
13.48w 2.4 Lafond 17 May

JUNIORS

See main list for top 6 juniors (and 2 wa). 11 performances (inc. 2 Indoors) by 3 women to 13.79. Additional marks and further juniors:

Orji 13.98i 1 Lexington 24 Jan; 13.84 1.4 * SEC Starkville 16 May
13.91i 1 Tyson Fayetteville 14 Feb; 13.81 0.3 3 NC Eugene 25 Jun
Povea 14.07 0.0 1 La Habana 7 Mar; 13.94 0.0 1 La Habana 19 Jun
14.00 0.0 2 Barr La Habana 26 May; 13.79 1.5 1 La Habana 28 Feb

Mark	Wind	First name	Name	Nat	Born	Pos	Meet	Venue	Date
3.61i		Valeriya	Fyodorova	RUS	9.4.96	1	NC-j	Novocheboksarsk	6 Feb
3.60i		Georgiana	Anitei	ROU-Y	26.3.99	4	NC	Bucuresti	14 Feb
3.53	1.3	Florentina	Marincu	ROU	8.4.96	3	NGP	Pitesti	6 Jun
3.52	-0.8	Núbia	Soares (10)	BRA	26.3.96	22q	WCh	Beijing	22 Aug
3.49	0.0	Yanna Anay	Armenteros	CUB-Y	2.10.99	3		La Habana	14 Feb
3.49	0.9	H.D.Vidusha	Lakshani	SRI	28.12.96	1		Diyagama	28 Jun
3.43	1.6	Valentina	Kosolapova	RUS	11.7.97	1	NC-j	Cheboksary	27 Jun
3.42	0.3		Zeng Tingchao	CHN	29.1.96	4	NGPF	Beijing	28 Jun
3.41	-0.2	Liliana	Breto	CUB	4.2.97	3		La Habana	19 Jun
3.40	0.9		Li Sirui	CHN	17.2.96	1	Univ Ch	Guilin	21 Jul
3.35	0.8	Darya	Dyachenko	UKR	15.2.96	1	NC-j	Kharkiv	16 Jun
3.35	-2.9	Norka	Moretic	CHI-Y	26.3.98	1		Santiago de Chile	6 Nov
3.33	1.3		Chen Liwen	CHN-Y	3.1.98	2	NC-j	Fuzhou	30 May
3.33	0.2		Rao Fan (20)	CHN	1.1.96	2	NYG	Fuzhou	25 Oct

Wind assisted 6 performances by 4 women to 13.79

Orji 14.13 2.7 1 SEC Starkville 16 May
Povea 14.07 3.2 1 La Habana 14 Feb; 13.83 3.7 2 Saint-Martin 9 May
13.97 2.6 6 PAm Toronto 21 Jul

SHOT

WOMEN 2015

20.77 Christina Schwanitz GER 24.12.85 1 Beijing 20 May — 19.86 20.22 x 20.38 20.77 20.13

Mark	Pos	Meet	Venue	Date	1	2	3	4	5	6
20.60	1		Biberach	13 Jul	19.73	20.47	x	19.78	20.60	20.22
20.37	1	WCh	Beijing	22 Aug	19.80	20.00	20.37	x	20.10	x
20.36	1		Schönebeck	26 Jun	20.33	x	20.36	x	x	20.21
20.31	1	DL	Saint-Denis	4 Jul	19.76	x	20.17	19.68	20.18	20.31
20.14	1	Bisl	Oslo	11 Jun	20.14	x	19.62	19.66	19.54	19.48
20.13	1	DL	Stockholm	29 Jul	19.90	20.13	19.94	x	19.66	19.24
20.08	2		Gotha	19 Jul	18.79	19.77	19.96	19.35	20.08	x
20.00	1	NC	Nürnberg	25 Jul	20.00	19.81	x	19.59	x	19.23
19.97	1		Thum	4 Sep	19.29	19.97	x	x	x	x
19.94	2	DL	Shanghai	17 May	18.89	19.94	x	19.41	x	19.37
19.91	1	WK	Zürich	3 Sep	19.55	19.91	x	19.51	x	x
19.85	1		Rehlingen	25 May	x	19.51	19.54	19.85	x	19.59
19.82	1	ET	Cheboksary	21 Jun	18.85	19.82	19.34	x		
19.77	1		Bad Köstritz	13 Sep	x	19.72	x	19.77	19.69	x
19.68	1	DL	Birmingham	7 Jun	19.10	19.68	19.26	x	19.32	18.95
19.66	1	ISTAF	Berlin	6 Sep	19.23	x	19.46	19.66	x	19.54
19.39	Q	WCh	Beijing	22 Aug	19.39					

20.34 Gong Lijiao CHN 24.1.89 1 Gotha 19 Jul — 19.57 20.03 20.34 19.61 19.63 x

Mark	Pos	Meet	Venue	Date	1	2	3	4	5	6
20.30	2	WCh	Beijing	22 Aug	20.30	20.05	20.25	x	x	19.91
20.24	2		Schönebeck	26 Jun						
20.23	1	DL	Shanghai	17 May	19.82	20.23	19.48	x	19.27	19.35
19.75	2	DL	Saint-Denis	4 Jul	19.55	19.75	19.74	19.65	19.48	19.55
19.54	1		Neubrandenburg	1 Jul	18.82	19.33	19.30	19.34	19.54	19.48
19.50	2		Beijing	20 May	x	19.50	x	19.28	19.35	x

20.02 Michelle Carter USA 12.10.85 1 NC Eugene 25 Jun — 20.02 x 18.86 x 18.90 x

Mark		Name	Nat	Born	Pos	Meet	Venue	Date
	19.76 3 WCh	Beijing	22 Aug	19.45	19.76	18.57	18.85 19.48	19.71
	19.74 1 DL	London (OS)	7 Jun	19.74	19.45	19.59	19.11 18.90	19.30
	19.45i 1 NC	Boston (Roxbury)	1 Mar	17.93	19.32	18.65	19.39 18.99	19.45
19.48	Anita	Márton	HUN	15.1.89	4	WCh	Beijing	22 Aug
	(30/4)			18.02	18.23	18.06	19.48 18.89	19.11
19.26	Cleopatra	Borel	TTO	3.10.79	1	Gyulai	Székesfehérvár	7 Ju
19.04		Gao Yang	CHN	1.3.93	5	WCh	Beijing	22 Aug
19.01i	Brittany	Smith	USA	25.3.91	1		Bloomington	17 Jan
19.00i	Yuliya	Leontyuk	BLR	31.1.84	1	NC	Mogilyov	20 Feb
19.00	Tia	Brooks	USA	2.8.90	2		Bad Köstritz	13 Sep
18.89	Dani	Bunch (10)	USA	16.5.91	1		Tucson	23 May
18.88	Alyona	Dubitskaya	BLR	25.1.90	1	NC	Grodno	24 Ju
18.84	Jeneva	Stevens	USA	28.10.89	3	NC	Eugene	25 Jun
18.79	Valerie	Adams	NZL	6.10.84	5	DL	Saint-Denis	4 Ju
18.73	Felisha	Johnson	USA	24.7.89	3		Beijing	20 May
18.71	Jill	Camarena-Williams	USA	2.8.82	4	NC	Eugene	25 Jun
18.71		Bian Ka	CHN	5.1.93	1	NC	Suzhou	25 Sep
18.62i	Raven	Saunders	USA-J	15.5.96	1	NCAA	Fayetteville	14 Mar
18.60	Natalya	Mikhnevich	BLR	25.5.82	1		Minsk	6 Jun
18.59		Guo Tianqian	CHN	1.6.95	1	AsiC	Wuhan	7 Jun
18.53	Irina	Tarasova	RUS	15.4.87	1		Yerino	6 Jun
	(20)							
18.49	Tori	Bliss	USA	1.12.92	1		Baton Rouge	2 May
18.42	Jessica	Ramsey	USA	26.7.91	6	NC	Eugene	25 Jun
18.40	Emel	Dereli	TUR-J	25.2.96	1	EJ	Eskilstuna	18 Ju
18.34i	Radoslava	Mavrodieva	BUL	13.3.87	1		Dobrich	11 Feb
18.34i	Rebecca	O'Brien	USA	30.4.90	2	NC	Boston (R)	1 Mar
18.31i	Yelena	Abramchuk	BLR	14.2.88	2	Blr	Gomel	7 Feb
18.29	Natalia	Ducó	CHI	31.1.89	Q	WCh	Beijing	22 Aug
18.21i	Chiara	Rosa	ITA	28.1.83	1		Padova	31 Jan
18.16	Olesya	Sviridova	RUS	28.10.89	1	NCp	Yerino	10 Ju
18.04	Leyla	Rajabi	IRI	18.4.83	1	Kosanov	Almaty	25 Ju
	(30)							
18.00	Lena	Urbaniak	GER	31.10.92	1	WUG	Gwangju	11 Ju
17.97i	Julaika	Nicoletti	ITA	20.3.88	1		Ancona	24 Jan
17.97i	Anastasiya	Podolskaya	RUS	18.8.90	1	Mosc Ch	Moskva	8 Feb
17.96	Kelsey	Card	USA	20.8.92	2	NCAA	Eugene	11 Jun
17.96	Manpreet	Kaur	IND	6.7.90	1	NC	Kolkata	16 Sep
17.95i	Claire	Uke	NGR	31.12.92	1	Conf USA	Birmingham	26 Feb
17.95	Paulina	Guba	POL	14.5.91	4	ISTAF	Berlin	6 Sep
17.94i	Halyna	Obleshchuk	UKR	23.2.89	1	NC	Sumy	13 Feb
17.90	Ahymara	Espinoza	VEN	28.5.85	1		Brezice	2 Ju
17.85	Sandra	Lemus	COL	1.1.89	1		Cartagena	29 Ju
	(40)							
17.82	Irina	Kirichenko	RUS	18.5.87	1		Sochi	29 May
17.78	Yaniuvis	López	CUB	1.2.86	4	PAm	Toronto	22 Jul
17.76i	Denise	Hinrichs	GER	7.6.87	2	NC	Karlsruhe	21 Feb
17.76	Geisa	Arcanjo	BRA	19.9.91	1	SAmC	Lima	14 Jun
17.76	Danniel	Thomas	JAM	11.11.92	5	PAm	Toronto	22 Jul
17.75	Dani	Winters	USA	18.2.93	1	Big 12	Ames	16 May
17.75	Melissa	Boekelman	NED	11.5.89	1		Brasschaat	2 Aug
17.74i	Olha	Holodna	UKR	14.11.91	2	NC	Sumy	13 Feb
17.72	Jill	Rushin	USA	18.7.91	1		Columbia	2 May
17.68i	Úrsula	Ruiz	ESP	11.8.83	1		Zaragoza	7 Feb
	(50)							
17.67	Yanina	Provalinskaya-Korolchik	BLR	26.12.76	1		Minsk	12 Jun
17.64	Auriole	Dongmo	CMR	3.8.90	3	WMilG	Mungyeong	4 Oct
17.61	Taryn	Suttie	CAN	7.12.90	1	SunAngel	Tempe	11 Apr
17.57	Monique	Riddick	USA	8.11.89	2		Bloomington	2 May
17.52i	Josephine	Terlecki	GER	17.2.86	1		Rochlitz	1 Feb
17.50	Saily	Viart	CUB	10.9.95	7	PAm	Toronto	22 Jul
17.49	Yevgeniya	Smirnova	RUS	16.3.91	1		Cheboksary	3 Jul
17.48	Vera	Kunova	RUS	2.4.90	2		Sochi	29 May
17.47	Viktoryia	Kolb	BLR	26.10.93	1	EU23	Tallinn	9 Ju
17.45	Christina	Hillman	USA	6.10.93	2	Big 12	Ames	16 May
	(60)							
17.42	Rachel	Wallader	GBR	1.9.89	1	NC	Birmingham	4 Ju
17.40i	Brittany	Mann	USA	16.4.94	3	NCAA	Fayetteville	14 Mar
17.39	Chase	Ealey	USA	20.7.94	3	Big 12	Ames	16 May
17.37i		Meng Qianqian	CHN	6.1.91	2	NGP	Shanghai	2 Mar
17.32	Nikki	Okwelogu	NGR	5.5.95	1		Philadelphia	10 May

Mark	Name		Nat	Born	Pos	Meet	Venue	Date
17.29	Shanice	Craft	GER	15.5.93	2	EU23	Tallinn	9 Jul
17.29	Jessica	Cérival	FRA	20.1.82	1	NC	Villeneuve d'Ascq	11 Jul
17.27	Ányela	Rivas	COL	13.8.89	1		Medellín	9 May
17.27	Brittany	Crew	CAN	3.6.94	3	WUG	Gwangju	11 Jul
17.26	Sara	Gambetta	GER	18.2.93	4		Thum	4 Sep
	(70)							
17.23	Yelena	Bezruchenko	RUS-J	23.7.96	1	NC-j	Cheboksary	25 Jun
17.21	Nia	Henderson	USA	21.10.86	1		Ashland	5 Jun
17.19	Anna	Omarova	RUS	3.10.81	3	NC	Cheboksary	5 Aug
17.18	Kearsten	Peoples	USA	20.12.91	12	NC	Eugene	25 Jun
17.16i	Casandra	Wertman	USA	14.6.93	3	SEC	Lexington KY	27 Feb
17.16		Geng Shuang	CHN	9.7.93	4	NGP	Jinan	1 May
17.15	Rachel	Fatherly	USA	20.4.94	2	Big 10	East Lansing	17 May
17.15i	Yekaterina	Burmistrova	RUS	18.8.90	1		Sankt-Peterburg	26 Dec
17.14	Anna	Avdeyeva	RUS	6.4.85	5	NC	Cheboksary	5 Aug
17.13	Claudine	Vita	GER-J	19.9.96	2	EJ	Eskilstuna	18 Jul
	(80)							
17.09	Emmonie	Henderson	USA	5.11.94	1	ACC	Tallahassee	15 May
17.08	Anna	Rüh	GER	17.6.93	1	U23 Werfer	Halle	17 May
17.05	Fanny	Roos	SWE	2.1.95	2	GS	Leiden	13 Jun
17.04		Lee Mi-young	KOR	19.8.79	1	NG	Gangneung	18 Oct
17.03i	Agnieszka	Maluskiewicz	POL	18.3.89	1		Spala	1 Feb
17.03i		Dong Yangzi	CHN	22.10.92	2	NGP	Beijing	16 Mar
17.02i	Natalya	Troneva	RUS	24.3.93	1	NC-23	Volgograd	26 Feb
16.99	Sarah	Howard	USA/CAN	11.10.93	1		Tallahassee	28 Mar
16.99	Jianna	Williams	USA	20.8.93	2		Madison	8 May
16.98	Alyona	Bugakova	RUS-J	24.4.97	4		Sochi	29 May
	(90)							
16.97i	Yevgeniya	Solovyova	RUS	28.6.86	3	NC	Moskva	18 Feb
16.95	Aaliyah	Pete	USA	15.3.95	1	MWC	San Diego	16 May
16.94i	Eden	Francis	GBR	19.10.88	1		Wien	31 Jan
16.93	Torie	Owers	NZL	6.3.94	2	Pac 12	Los Angeles (Ww)	16 May
16.91i	Amelia	Strickler	USA	24.1.94	1		Allendale	13 Feb
16.88	Vera	Yepimashko	BLR	10.7.76			Minsk	19 May
16.87i	Jamie	Sindelar	USA		1		Saginaw	1 Mar
16.86i	Ashley	Gaston	USA	1.1.93	2		Nashville	24 Jan
16.85	Itohan	Aikhonbare	USA	29.3.94	1		Norwalk	18 Apr
16.84i	Raisa	Blinova	RUS	22.11.94	4	NC	Moskva	18 Feb
	(100)							
16.84		Liu Xiangrong	CHN	6.6.88	2	NGPF	Beijing	29 Jun

Mark	Name		Nat	Born	Date
16.80	Julie	Labonté	CAN	12.1.90	11 Apr
16.80	Trine	Mulbjerg	DEN	23.4.90	23 May
16.80	Klaudia	Kardasz	POL-J	2.5.96	18 Jul
16.79	Alexis	Cooks	USA	11.9.93	11 Jun
16.76	Rachel	Dincoff	USA	24.12.93	11 Jun
16.75i	Jana	Kárníková	CZE	14.2.81	1 Feb
16.73i	Kendra	Averesch	USA	4.3.93	30 Jan
16.73	Christine	Bohan	USA	14.7.95	28 May
16.69	Cion	Hicks	USA	14.10.94	18 Apr
16.66	Alex	Hartig	USA	5.9.91	2 May
16.63	Brittany	Cox	USA	18.4.88	18 Apr
16.62	Megan	Smith	USA	31.3.93	11 Apr
16.62	Ivanna	Gallardo	CHI	20.7.93	14 Jun
16.60	Danielle	Frere	USA	27.4.90	2 May
16.59	Anna	Wloka	POL	14.3.93	9 Jul
16.58i	Alyssa	Wilson	USA-Y	20.2.99	19 Dec
16.54	Breana	Jemison	USA		25 Apr
16.53i	Sara	Wells	USA	11.8.92	14 Mar
16.53		Cai Yilin	CHN	27.11.90	5 May
16.53	Tremanisha	Taylor	USA	10.3.92	15 May
16.51i	Magdalena	Zebrowska	POL	11.1.91	7 Feb
16.51	Emily	Lesser	USA		14 May
16.51	Valeriya	Zyryanova	RUS	12.8.90	29 May
16.47	Jolien	Boumkwo	BEL	27.8.93	9 Jul
16.44		Lin Chia-Ying	TPE	5.11.82	16 May
16.44i	Adriana	Brown	USA-J	15.5.96	11 Dec
16.41	Sophie	McKinna	GBR	31.8.94	20 Jun
16.38i	Lenuta	Burueana	ROU-J	29.4.96	14 Feb
16.36i	Annastasia	Muchkaev	ISR	18.7.91	9 Jan
16.36	Izabela	da Silva	BRA	2.8.95	17 May
16.33	Maggie	Ewen	USA	23.9.94	2 May
16.31i	Brea	Garrett	USA	27.6.93	7 Feb
16.31i	Kätlin	Piirimäe	EST	8.11.95	21 Feb
16.31	María Belén	Toimil	ESP	5.5.94	27 Jun

Mark	Name		Nat	Born	Date
16.30	DeAnna	Price	USA	8.6.93	18 Apr
16.30	Sophia	Rivera	USA-Y	17.10.98	26 Jun
16.29	Elena	Bruckner	USA-Y	19.4.98	29 May
16.26	Angelika	Kalinowska	POL	4.2.93	9 Jul
16.24i	Valentina	Muzaric	CRO	23.7.92	27 Feb
16.23i	Carlie	Pinkelman	USA	21.11.91	17 Jan
16.23	Janeah	Stewart	USA-J	21.7.96	15 May
16.22i		Wang Xiaoyun	CHN	7.12.93	16 Mar
16.21	Austra	Skujyté	LTU	12.8.79	21 Jul
16.20	Evaggelía	Sofáni	GRE	28.1.85	26 Jul
16.20	Portious	Warren	TTO-J	2.3.96	5 Dec
16.19		Xu Yang	CHN	22.4.91	1 May
16.16	Pamela	Kiel	NED	9.4.91	25 Apr
16.16	Devene	Brown	JAM	16.3.93	15 May
16.15	Yiliena	Otamendi	CUB-J	12.4.96	27 May
16.13	Alina	Kenzel	GER-J	10.8.97	27 Jun
16.12	Keely	Medeiros	BRA	30.4.87	18 Apr
16.12		Xu Jiaqi	CHN	3.2.95	5 May
16.11		Lee Su-kyung	KOR	15.2.93	18 Oct
16.11i	Emmaline	Berg	USA		5 Dec
16.10i	Avione	Allgood	USA	14.12.93	17 Jan
16.10	Chioma	Onyekwere	USA	28.6.94	17 May
16.09i	Alexus	Scott	USA	18.11.93	5 Dec
16.08		Yang Mingyue	CHN	23.1.93	1 Apr
16.07	Frida	Åkerström	SWE	29.11.90	17 May
16.05i	Chamaya	Turner	USA	28.2.95	31 Jan
16.05	Jasmine	Burrell	USA	27.2.92	16 May
16.05	Sarah	Schmidt	GER-J	9.7.97	27 Jun
16.04	Alex	Porlier-Langlois	CAN	16.7.93	21 Mar
16.04	Markéta	Cervenková	CZE	20.8.91	27 Jun
16.03	Sonia	Smuts	RSA	5.10.91	28 Feb
16.03i	Mackenna	Howard	USA-J	25.1.96	28 Feb
16.02i	Talore	Kelly	USA	11.3.94	7 Feb
16.02i	Kiah	Hicks	USA	21.2.93	14 Feb

Mark		Name	Nat	Born	Pos	Meet	Venue	Date
16.02	Julie	Lange	USA	21.7.95				3 Apr
16.02		Lee Mi-na	KOR	25.10.95				18 Oct
16.01i	LaPorscha	Wells	USA					10 Jan
16.01	Anu	Teesaar	EST	15.2.83				3 Jun
16.00i	Emily	Morris	USA					24 Jan
16.00i	Giedré	Kupstyté	LTU	9.3.92				20 Feb
16.00	Obeng	Marfo	CAN-J	11.4.96				17 May
15.99	Rose Sharon	Pierre-Louis	FRA	7.9.94				26 Jul
15.97	Andreea	Huzum-Vitan	ROU	15.4.93				27 Jun
15.94	Geraldine	Duvenage	RSA	17.8.95				24 Jan
15.94	Madison	McLaughlin	USA-J	14.11.96				25 Apr
15.92i	Michaela	Dendinger	USA	9.5.95				31 Jan
15.92		Chen Xiarong	CHN-Y	21.12.98				26 Oct
15.91i	Laura	Jokeit	GER	16.8.95				11 Jan
15.91		Song Jiayuan	CHN-J	15.9.97				5 May
15.91	Yekaterina	Kuznetsova	RUS	8.1.91				10 Jun
15.90i	Aleksandra	Butvina	RUS	14.2.86				13 Feb
15.90i	Megan	Tomei	USA					20 Feb
15.90	Tiffany	Okieme	USA	8.1.94				2 May
	(188)							

Best outdoors

Mark	Name	Pos	Meet	Venue	Date
18.96	B Smith	1		Chula Vista	23 Apr
18.86	Leontyuk	1	PNG	Turku	25 Jun
18.35	Saunders	1	NCAA	Eugene	11 Jun
18.21	O'Brien	1	FlaR	Gainesville	4 Apr
18.21	Abramchuk	1		Brest	30 Jun
18.13	Rosa	1		Caprino Veronese	27Jun
17.84	Mavrodieva	2	ET-2	Stara Zagora	21 Jun
17.79	Obleshchuk	1		Kyiv	22 May
17.47	Ruiz	1	Gil	Salamanca	6 Jun
17.43	Terlecki	2	Werfer	Halle	16 May
17.39	Podolskaya	3		Yerino	6 Jun
17.33	Uke	22		Houston	4 Apr
17.25	Mann	11	NC	Eugene	25 Jun
17.23	Meng Qianqian	2	AsiGP	Chanthaburi	29 Jun
17.20	Hinrichs	5		Schönebeck	26 Jun
17.05	Nicoletti	1		Serravalle	10 Jun
16.84	Francis	4	Werfer	Halle	16 May

Mark	Name	Date	Mark	Name	Date
16.81	Troneva	14 Mar	16.63	Kárníková	16 Jun
16.75	Blinova	15 Jun	16.54	Dong Yangzi	25 Sep
16.74	Maluskiewicz	2 May	16.47	S Wells	9 May
16.74	Gaston	15 May	16.23	Burmistrova	5 Aug
16.72	Strickler	2 May	16.21	Wang Xiaoyun	1 Apr
16.12	Sindelar	11 Apr	16.05	Pinkelman	2 May
16.12	Piirimäe	24 May	16.03	Garrett	11 Apr
16.12	Zebrowska	30 May	16.00	L Wells	9 May
16.10	Muchkaev	16 May	15.97	Burueana	26 Jul
			15.95	Kupstyté	7 Aug

JUNIORS

See main list for top 5 juniors. 11 performances (3 indoors) by 2 women to 17.85. Additional marks and further juniors:

Name	Mark	Pos	Meet	Venue	Date	Mark	Pos	Meet	Venue	Date
Saunders 2+	18.27	1	PAm-J	Edmonton	31 Jul	17.99i	1		West Lafayette	14 Feb
	18.23	3	MSR	Walnut	18 Apr	17.98i	1		Cedar Falls	1 Ma
	18.12	1		Normal	15 May	17.85	8	NC	Eugene	25 Ju
Dereli	18.03	1		Mersin	23 May	17.85	1		Istanbul	9 Ju
	17.91	1		Istanbul	13 Jun					

Mark		Name	Nat	Born	Pos	Meet	Venue	Date
16.80	Klaudia	Kardasz	POL	2.5.96	4	EJ	Eskilstuna	18 Ju
16.58i	Alyssa	Wilson	USA-Y	20.2.99	1		Staten Island	19 De
16.44i	Adriana	Brown	USA	15.5.96	2		Bloomington IN	11 De
	15.89				5	SEC	Starkville	16 Ma
16.38i	Lenuta	Burueana	ROU	29.4.96	1	NC	Bucuresti	14 Fe
	15.97				1	NC	Pitesti	26 Ju
16.30	Sophia	Rivera (10)	USA-Y	17.10.98	2	NC-j	Eugene	26 Ju
16.29	Elena	Bruckner	USA-Y	19.4.98	1		San Jose	29 Ma
16.23	Janeah	Stewart	USA	21.7.96	1	JUCO	Hutchinson	15 Ma
16.20	Portious	Warren	TTO	2.3.96	1		Phoenix	5 De
16.15	Yiliena	Otamendi	CUB	12.4.96	3	Barr	La Habana	27 Ma
16.13	Alina	Kenzel	GER	10.8.97	2		Mannheim	27 Ju
16.05	Sarah	Schmidt	GER	9.7.97	3J		Mannheim	27 Ju
16.03i	Mackenna	Howard	USA	25.1.96	2	MWC	Albuquerque	28 Fe
16.00	Obeng	Marfo	CAN	11.4.96	4	Big 10	East Lansing	17 Ma
15.94	Madison	McLaughlin	USA	14.11.96	2		Fort Collins	25 Ap
15.92		Chen Xiarong (20)	CHN-Y	21.12.98	1		Fuzhou	26 Oc

DISCUS

Mark			Name / Venue	Nat / Date						
70.65	Denia		Caballero	CUB	13.1.90	1		Bilbao		20 Ju
					65.88	70.65	63.50	64.74	x	64.92
69.51	1	Barr	La Habana	26 May	68.52	x	p	69.51	p	67.24
69.28	1	WCh	Beijing	25 Aug	69.28	63.83	x	65.97	66.55	66.58
67.87	1		La Habana	8 May	x	66.63	62.24	64.12	67.87	67.52
67.25	1		Sotteville-lès-Rouen	6 Jul	x	x	67.25	p	p	p
66.04	3	Athl	Lausanne	9 Jul	66.00	66.04	x	x	x	64.04
65.77	2	VD	Bruxelles	11 Sep	60.58	64.55	65.77	63.90	x	64.65
65.46	1	FBK	Hengelo	24 May	57.68	65.46	63.38	63.56	64.97	x
70.08	Sandra		Perkovic	CRO	21.6.90	1	NC-w	Split		8 Ma
					69.43	x	65.39	x	x	70.08
69.88	1	Hanz	Zagreb	8 Sep	62.30	62.28	69.77	x	68.95	69.88
69.23	1	DL	Birmingham	7 Jun	69.23	68.54	x	x	68.32	x
68.44	1	adidas	New York	13 Jun	68.44	64.40	x	66.34	x	x
68.10	1	DL	Doha	15 May	x	68.07	67.54	68.10	65.45,	
67.92	1	GGala	Roma	4 Jun	66.21	67.92	x	65.27	65.68	x
67.50	1	VD	Bruxelles	11 Sep	64.46	x	64.97	67.50	x	66.81
67.39	2	WCh	Beijing	25 Aug	x	65.35	x	65.37	x	67.39
67.23	1		Velenje	1 Jul	63.01	65.67	x	62.59	x	67.23
67.06	2	Athl	Lausanne	9 Jul	64.72	63.74	67.06	x	x	x
66.80	1	Herc	Monaco	17 Jul	62.37	x	x	x	66.80	62.82

Mark	Name		Nat	Born	Pos	Meet	Venue		Date
67.13	Yaimé	Pérez	CUB	29.5.91	1	Athl	Lausanne		9 Jul
				65.40	67.06	65.89	x	67.13	x
66.42	2	Sotteville-lès-Rouen	6 Jul	64.63	61.84	64.11	63.04	63.33	66.42
66.23	2 Barr	La Habana	26 May	x	66.23	x	x	64.95	64.50
65.86	2 adidas	New York	13 Jun	63.86	65.85	x	64.45	65.86	64.11
65.46	4 WCh	Beijing	25 Aug	x	62.63	59.63	64.60	64.31	65.46
66.21	Dani	Samuels	AUS	26.5.88	1		Sydney		14 Mar
				x	63.54	65.36	62.14	66.21	61.97
65.47	2 GGala	Roma	4 Jun	65.47	64.03	65.24	62.54	62.08	63.95
66.14	Anna	Rüh	GER	17.6.93	1		Wiesbaden		10 May
				65.84	64.25	x	64.06	64.02	66.14
65.98	Julia	Fischer	GER	1.4.90	1	NC	Nürnberg		25 Jul
				x	62.78	63.14	63.51	65.98	x
65.72	Nadine	Müller	GER	21.11.85	2	NC	Nürnberg		25 Jul
				65.72	x	62.82	61.95	60.82	x
65.53	3 WCh	Beijing	25 Aug	65.53	x	60.85	x	x	62.67
	(30/7)								
65.04	Mélina	Robert-Michon	FRA	18.7.79	2		Montreuil-sous-Bois		9 Jun
64.80	Whitney	Ashley	USA	18.2.89	1		Claremont		7 Jun
64.79	Shanice	Craft	GER	15.5.93	3	NC	Nürnberg		25 Jul
	(10)								
64.52	Shelbi	Vaughan	USA	24.8.94	1	SEC	Starkville		15 May
64.33	Yekaterina	Strokova	RUS	17.12.89	4	DL	Doha		15 May
64.27		Su Xinyue	CHN	8.11.91	1	NGP	Jinan		30 Apr
64.15	Andressa	de Morais	BRA	21.12.90	1	NC	São Bernardo do Campo		15 May
64.01	Gia	Lewis-Smallwood	USA	1.4.79	1		Naperville		11 Jul
63.87	Liz	Podominick	USA	5.12.84	2		Claremont		7 Jun
63.48	Yuliya	Maltseva	RUS	30.11.90	3		Montreuil-sous-Bois		9 Jun
63.25	Irina	Rodrigues	POR	5.2.91	3	ECp-w	Leiria		15 Mar
63.22	Yelena	Panova	RUS	2.3.87	1	NC	Cheboksary		4 Aug
62.97		Tan Jian	CHN	20.1.88	2	AsiC	Wuhan		4 Jun
	(20)								
62.80	Fernanda Raquel	Borges	BRA	26.7.88	1		Los Angeles (Ww)		11 Apr
62.61	Kristin	Pudenz	GER	9.2.93	3		Schönebeck		26 Jun
62.31	Claudine	Vita	GER-J	19.9.96	1		Neubrandenburg		30 May
62.30		Lu Xiaoxin	CHN	22.2.89	3	AsiC	Wuhan		4 Jun
62.20		Weng Chunxia	CHN	29.8.92	1	AsiGP	Pathumthani		25 Jun
62.15	Zaneta	Glanc	POL	11.3.83	6	DL	Doha		15 May
62.07		Feng Bin	CHN	3.4.94	1	WMilG	Mungyeong		7 Oct
61.85	Svetlana	Saykina	RUS	10.7.85	1	NCp	Yerino		10 Jul
61.84	Rocío	Comba	ARG	14.7.87	1		Río Tercero		23 May
61.47	Dragana	Tomasevic	SRB	4.6.82	1		Szentes		1 Aug
	(30)								
61.40	Hrisoúla	Anagnostopoúlou	GRE	27.8.91	1		Haniá		6 Jun
61.37	Zinaida	Sendriuté	LTU	20.12.84	1		Rabat		14 Jun
61.36	Sabina	Asenjo	ESP	3.8.86	1	NC	Castellón		2 Aug
61.23	Summer	Pierson	USA	3.9.78	2		Claremont		6 Jun
61.21	Jessica	Maroszek	USA	26.2.92	1		Emporia		28 Mar
61.16		Chen Yang	CHN	10.7.91	3	NGPF	Beijing		28 Jun
61.10	Karen	Gallardo	CHI	6.3.84	2	NC	Castellón		2 Aug
61.09	Nataliya	Semenova	UKR	7.7.82	3	FBK	Hengelo		24 May
61.07	Sanna	Kämäräinen	FIN	8.2.86	5	ECp-w	Leiria		15 Mar
60.90		Yang Yanbo	CHN	9.3.90	1	MSR	Walnut		17 Apr
	(40)								
60.78	Te Rina	Keenan	NZL	29.9.90	1		Hamilton		21 May
60.23	Daria	Zabawska	POL	16.4.95	Q	EU23	Tallinn		11 Jul
60.16	Kelsey	Card	USA	20.8.92	4	NC	Eugene		27 Jun
60.09	Subenrat	Insaeng	THA	10.2.94	1		Taipei		15 May
60.01	Jade	Lally	GBR	30.3.87	6		Sotteville-lès-Rouen		6 Jul
59.93	Pauline	Pousse	FRA	17.9.87	6		Montreuil-sous-Bois		9 Jun
59.92	Kiah	Hicks	USA	21.2.93	1	MWC	San Diego		15 May
59.81	Siositina	Hakeai	NZL	1.3.94	3		Chula Vista		23 Apr
59.43	Joanna	Wisniewska	POL	24.5.72	1		Lódz		7 Jun
59.25	Sofia	Larsson	SWE	22.7.88	1		Södertälje		6 Jun
	(50)								
59.12	Tera	Novy	USA	10.2.94	1		Los Angeles		16 Apr
59.06	Katelyn	Daniels	USA	11.4.95	1	Big 10	East Lansing		16 May
59.03	Marike	Steinacker	GER	4.3.92	1cB	Werfer	Wiesbaden		10 May
58.81	Izabela	da Silva	BRA	2.8.95	2	NC	São Bernardo do Campo		15 May
58.80	Anita	Márton	HUN	15.1.89	1		Szeged		20 Sep
58.79	Stephanie	Brown Trafton	USA	1.12.79	4		Claremont		6 Jun

Mark	Name		Nat	Born	Pos	Meet	Venue	Date
58.77	Danniel	Thomas	JAM	11.11.92	1		Muncie	16 May
58.66	Eliska	Stanková	CZE	11.11.84	1	NC	Plzen	28 Jun
58.55	Tara-Sue	Barnett	JAM	9.10.93	1	UWI	Mona	21 Mar
58.55	Valentina	Aniballi	ITA	19.4.84	1		Tarquinia	21 May
	(60)							
58.53	Natalya	Shirobokova	RUS	18.1.94	3		Sochi	28 May
58.50	Samantha	Hall	JAM	19.4.93	3q	NCAA-W	Austin	29 May
58.43		Jiang Fengjing	CHN	28.8.87	1	NGP	Taiyuan	12 May
58.41	Natalia	Stratulat	MDA	24.7.87	1	NC	Chisinau	30 May
58.37	Sabine	Rumpf	GER	18.3.83	2cB	Werfer	Wiesbaden	10 May
58.34	Emmonie	Henderson	USA	5.11.94	3	NCAA	Eugene	13 Jun
58.30		Gu Siyu	CHN	11.2.93	5	NC	Suzhou	24 Sep
58.22	Stefania	Strumillo	ITA	14.10.89	3	WUG	Gwangju	9 Jul
58.19	Suzanne	Kragbé	CIV	22.12.81	1		Romans	23 Jun
58.10	Rachel	Longfors	USA	6.6.83	6	NC	Eugene	27 Jun
	(70)							
58.04	Gleneve	Grange	JAM	6.7.95	1		Kingston	14 Mar
58.01	Viktoriya	Klochko	UKR	2.9.92	1		Uman	3 Jul
57.94		Liang Yan	CHN	2.1.95	4	NGP	Jinan	30 Apr
57.82		Yang Fei	CHN	20.7.87	7	NGP	Chengdu	5 Apr
57.82	Alex	Collatz	USA	25.5.93	2		Los Angeles	16 Apr
57.55	Rachel	Varner	USA	20.7.83	3		Claremont	7 Jun
57.54	Chinwe	Okoro	NGR	20.6.89	1		Louisville	28 Mar
57.48	Valarie	Allman	USA	23.2.95	1		Stanford	11 Apr
57.44	Maggie	Ewen	USA	23.9.94	2		Chula Vista	23 Apr
57.41	Taryn	Gollshewsky	AUS	18.5.93	2		Brisbane	5 Mar
	(80)							
57.39	Rosalía	Vázquez	CUB	11.10.95	1		Las Tunas	15 May
57.37	Julia	Bremser	GER	27.4.82	1		Eppstein	7 Jul
57.32	Yekaterina	Burmistrova	RUS	18.8.90	4	NC-w	Adler	23 Feb
57.24	Olha	Abramchuk	UKR	12.4.91	1		Kyiv	22 May
57.13	Becky	Famurewa	USA	24.2.94	2	SEC	Starkville	15 May
57.09	Megan	Smith	USA	31.3.93	1		Abilene	11 Apr
57.08		Xie Yuchen	CHN-J	12.5.96	1	NYG	Fuzhou	22 Oct
57.07	Julia	Viberg	SWE	8.1.92	2	TexR	Austin	28 Mar
57.06	Eden	Francis	GBR	19.10.88	1		Birmingham	14 Jun
56.74	Anastasiya	Kashtanova	BLR	14.1.89	1		Minsk	6 Jun
	(90)							
56.63	Veronika	Domjan	SLO-J	3.9.96	2	EJ	Eskilstuna	17 Jul
56.58	Laura	Bordignon	ITA	26.3.81	2		Tarquinia	21 May
56.55	Sarah	Thornton	USA	29.8.86	1		New York	14 Jun
56.45	Lidiane	Cansian	BRA	8.1.92	2		São Bernardo do Campo	19 Apr
56.43A	Johana	Martínez	COL	9.9.86	1	NG	Cali	19 Nov
56.41	Kree	Clark	USA	.94	1		Jacksonville	10 Apr
56.40	Anna	Jelmini	USA	15.7.90	7		La Jolla	24 Apr
56.37	Vera	Ganeyeva	RUS	6.11.88	5	NC	Cheboksary	4 Aug
56.30	Tatyana	Zhuravlyova	RUS	27.5.89	1		Muncie	17 Apr
56.26	Katarzyna	Mos	POL	20.12.94	1		Chorzów	29 Aug
	(100)							

Mark	Name		Nat	Born	Date
56.22	Alexa	Evans	USA	27.11.93	15 May
56.14	Madison	Jacobs	USA	2.8.95	23 Apr
56.09	Jeré	Summers	USA	21.5.87	23 May
56.04	Karolina	Makul	POL	23.8.94	15 Mar
56.03	Kirsty	Law	GBR	11.10.86	17 May
56.00	Josie	Natrasevschi	USA-J	13.8.96	24 Apr
56.00	Jitka	Kubelová	CZE	2.10.91	1 May
55.97	Sam	Lockhart	USA	25.8.91	17 Apr
55.92	Alissa	Rausch	USA		2 May
55.91	Alison	Szykowny	USA	17.8.93	2 May
55.80		Li Tsai-Yi	TPE	3.12.89	15 May
55.80	Rachel	Dincoff	USA	24.12.93	15 May
55.72	Androniki	Lada	CYP	19.4.91	15 May
55.68	Elena	Bruckner	USA-Y	19.4.98	15 May
55.67	Lidia	Augustyniak	POL	14.5.94	6 Sep
55.65i	Heidi	Schmidt	SWE	13.11.93	31 Jan
55.65A	Geraldine	Duvenage	RSA	17.8.95	24 Mar
55.65	Rebecca	Hammar	USA	28.1.93	4 Apr
55.54	Katri	Hirvonen	FIN	25.6.90	28 Apr
55.51	Alexis	Cooks	USA	11.9.93	13 Jun
55.26		Wang Lan	CHN	8.7.93	5 Apr
55.23	Corinne	Nugter	NED	28.3.92	23 May
55.19	Jaleesa	Williams	TTO	6.4.91	27 Jun
55.16	Yelena	Abramchuk	BLR	14.2.88	25 Jul
55.13	Kellion	Knibb	JAM	25.12.93	8 May
55.00A	Aixa	Middleton	PAN	6.2.88	27 Jun
54.98	Hannah	Carson	USA	26.1.93	11 Apr
54.98	Heavin	Warner	USA	4.3.93	9 May
54.94	Erica	Brand	USA	1.8.92	29 May
54.90A	Rachel	Andres	CAN	21.4.87	15 Ju
54.79	Natalina	Capoferri	ITA	6.11.92	11 Ju
54.73	Bogna	Szyczewska	POL	28.7.94	29 Aug
54.66	Annelies	Peetroons	BEL	4.5.87	6 Jun
54.56	Salla	Sipponen	FIN	13.3.95	2 Aug
54.54	Mélanie	Pingeon	FRA	4.11.86	17 May
54.50	And⊠elika	Przybylska	POL	14.10.92	23 May
54.46	Ivana	Gallardo	CHI	20.7.93	15 May
54.45	Laura	Bobek	USA	16.2.91	10 Ap
54.45	Devene	Brown	JAM	16.3.93	13 Jun
54.38	Agnes	Esser	CAN	22.8.95	2 May
54.37	Tori	Bliss	USA	1.12.92	28 Ma
54.34	Christie	Baker	AUS	9.6.89	14 Ma
54.34	Michaela	Dendinger	USA	9.5.95	22 Ma
54.31	Julie	Hartwig	GER	30.6.94	10 Ma
54.30	Tanja	Komulainen	FIN	2.3.80	22 Au
54.25	Claire	Uke	NGR	31.12.92	16 Sep
54.24	Devin	Stanford	USA	12.11.92	24 Ap
54.21	Anastasiya	Vityugova	RUS-J	13.3.97	17 Ju

ʌark	Name		Nat	Born	Pos Meet	Venue	Date				
4.14	Itohan	Aikhonbare	USA	29.3.94	4 Apr	53.78	Nikki	Okwelogu	NGR	5.5.95	10 May
4.13	Ieva	Zarankaité	LTU	23.11.94	26 Mar	53.78	Corina	Cox	USA	5.1.95	29 May
4.03	Aaliyah	Pete	USA	15.3.95	15 May	53.74	Julie	Lange	USA	21.7.95	26 Mar
3.98	Kearsten	Peoples	USA	20.12.91	2 May	53.73	Daina	Levy	JAM	27.5.93	29 May
3.96	Katrine	Bebe	DEN	27.1.91	15 Mar	53.72	Miranda	Daucher	USA		2 Apr
3.96	Gabriella	Dixson	USA	24.8.81	17 Apr	53.70	Krisztina	Váradi	HUN	21.10.93	16 May
3.91	Kristina	Rakocevic	MNE-Y	13.6.98	21 Jun	53.70	Ashley	Gaston	USA	1.1.93	17 May
3.84	Jessica	Woodard	USA	4.2.95	29 May		(165)				
3.82	Dasha	Tsema	USA	10.8.94	17 Apr	**Best outdoors**					
3.80	Lucie	Catouillart	FRA	21.10.91	22 Feb	55.14	Heidi	Schmidt	SWE	13.11.93	23 May

JUNIORS

See main list for top 3 juniors. 11 performances by 1 women to 57.45. Additional marks and further juniors:

ita	60.02	1	NC-23	Wetzlar	13 Jun	58.32	5	NC	Nürnberg	25 Jul
	59.85	5		Schönebeck	26 Jun	57.75	1		Osterode	19 Jun
	59.23	1		Wiesbaden	10 May	57.56	1	v2N-23	Vénissieux	28 Feb
	58.54	1		Mannheim	28 Jun	57.52	2-23	Werfer	Halle	17 May
	58.38	1J	Werfer	Halle	16 May	57.47	1	EJ	Eskilstuna	17 Jul

6.00	Josie	Natrasevschi	USA	13.8.96	1	PennR	Philadelphia	24 Apr
5.68	Elena	Bruckner	USA-Y	19.4.98	1		Mountain View	15 May
4.21	Anastasiya	Vityugova	RUS	13.3.97	3	EJ	Eskilstuna	17 Jul
3.91	Kristina	Rakocevic	MNE-Y	13.6.98	2	ET-3	Baku	21 Jun
3.56	Kirsty	Williams	AUS	13.1.97	4		Sydney	14 Mar
3.42	Lara	Kempka	GER	6.9.97	2		Leipzig	6 Jun
3.38	Kennedy	Blahnik (10)	USA	6.3.96	3		Madison	8 May
3.12		Sun Kangping	CHN-Y	7.3.97	4		Lianyungang	5 May
2.92	Jennifer	Prestel	GER	5.7.96	2J	Werfer	Halle	16 May
2.78A	Alexandra	Emelianov	MDA-Y	19.9.99	1	WY	Cali	15 Jul
2.77	Alex	Meyer	USA	8.4.96	2		Iowa City	2 May
2.72		Liang Xingyun	CHN	4.6.96	2	NC-j	Fuzhou	30 May
2.65	Kiana	Phelps	USA	22.7.97	1		Correctionville	1 May
2.17		Lin Aoxue	CHN	5.10.97	3	NYG	Fuzhou	22 Oct
2.01	Lloydricia	Cameron	USA	8.4.96	2	NC-j	Eugene	25 Jun
1.96	Paul-Ann	Gayle	JAM	3.11.96	1J	PennR	Philadelphia	23 Apr
1,91	Alena	Belyakova (20)	RUS-Y	21.12.98	1		Krasnodar	7 Jun

HAMMER

1.08		Anita	Wlodarczyk	POL	8.8.85	1	Skol	Cetniewo			1 Aug
					x	81.08	79.07	78.53	76.61	77.83	
80.85	1	WCh	Beijing	27 Aug	74.40	78.52	80.27	80.85	79.31	x	
78.28	1	ET	Cheboksary	21 Jun	x	74.38	x	78.28			
78.24	1	NC	Kraków	21 Jul	73.63	78.24	76.37	76.76	p	p	
78.16	1	Skol	Warszawa	13 Sep	x	77.06	x	75.49	78.16	77.65	
77.73	1		Beijing	20 May	74.14	77.73	74.54	76.23	75.59	75.61	
76.70	1	Kuso	Szczecin	9 Aug	70.56	76.37	75.75	71.77	76.66	76.70	
76.61	1	GS	Ostrava	25 May	70.17	75.48	76.61	x	75.65	74.12	
75.48	1	Gyulai	Székesfehérvár	7 Jul	73.99	x	74.62	75.48	x	74.29	
75.01	Q	WCh	Beijing	26 Aug	75.01						
74.29	1	EAF	Bydgoszcz	14 Jun	72.36	x	74.29	x	72.96	73.38	
6.33			Zhang Wenxiu	CHN	22.3.86	2	WCh	Beijing			27 Aug
					73.47	75.92	73.65	76.33	69.93	72.99	
74.87	1	WMilG	Mungyeong	7 Oct	70.35	71.21	x	74.87	x	74.68	
74.08	1	NC	Suzhou	24 Sep							
5.73		Betty	Heidler	GER	14.10.83	2	ET	Cheboksary			21 Jun
					68.28	68.16	72.18	75.73			
75.46	1		Zeulenroda	10 Jul							
75.41	1		Schönebeck	26 Jun	72.49	x	72.27	71.98	75.41	71.59	
75.34	1	NC	Nürnberg	25 Jul	68.44	71.44	73.86	x	75.34	72.20	
75.00	2	GS	Ostrava	25 May	72.25	70.85	72.64	72.73	75.00	73.93	
73.91	2	Gyulai	Székesfehérvár	7 Jul	70.54	x	69.52	73.91	73.38	73.15	
4.92			Wang Zheng	CHN	14.12.87	1	NGP	Chengdu			1 Apr
73.99	2		Beijing	20 May	71.03	73.99	73.21	73.75	72.54	73.54	
73.83	5	WCh	Beijing	27 Aug	72.92	68.80	x	x	71.50	73.83	
4.39		Alexandra	Tavernier	FRA	13.12.93	Q	WCh	Beijing			26 Aug
					74.39	only throw					
74.05	3	ET	Cheboksary	21 Jun	74.05	x	72.13	x			
74.02	3	WCh	Beijing	27 Aug	74.02	69.59	x	67.83	69.93	70.60	
4.27		Martina	Hrasnová	SVK	21.3.83	1		Kawasaki			10 May
					x	70.91	71.96	70.12	70.77	74.27	
74.13	3	GS	Ostrava	25 May	68.26	68.08	68.65	71.98	73.53	74.13	

Mark	Name		Nat	Born	Pos	Meet	Venue	Date
73.97	Zalina	Marghieva	MDA	5.2.88	1	BalkC	Pitesti	2 Au
				71.19	73.97	73.70	69.94 72.03	73.31
73.86	Sophie	Hitchon	GBR	11.7.91	4	WCh	Beijing	27 Au
	(30/8)			71.20	71.44	73.65	71.06 72.10	73.86
73.74	Mariya	Bespalova ¶	RUS	21.5.86	1		Zhukovskiy	24 Ju
73.66	Sultana	Frizell (10)	CAN	24.10.84	3		Kawasaki	10 Ma
73.26	Oksana	Menkova	BLR	28.3.82	1	NCp	Brest	27 Ma
73.18	Kathrin	Klaas	GER	6.2.84	6	WCh	Beijing	27 Au
73.06	Rosa	Rodríguez	VEN	2.7.86	1		Zagreb	16 Ma
72.86	Yelena	Soboleva	BLR	11.5.93	4	ET	Cheboksary	21 Ju
72.81	Amber	Campbell	USA	5.6.81	1		Myrtle Beach	20 Ma
72.69	Jeneva	Stevens	USA	28.10.89	1		Tucson	23 Ma
72.67	Joanna	Fiodorow	POL	4.3.89	1		Bialystok	20 Ju
72.53	Marina	Nikisenko	MDA	28.6.86	2	NC	Chisinau	30 Ma
72.40	Yirisleyidi L.	Ford	CUB	18.8.91	1	Barr	La Habana	28 Ma
72.35	Amanda	Bingson	USA	20.2.90	9	WCh	Beijing	27 Au
	(20)							
72.31	Hanna	Skydan	AZE	14.5.92	2		Chisinau	30 Ma
72.30	Deanna	Price	USA	8.6.93	2	NC	Eugene	27 Ju
72.26	Gwen	Berry	USA	29.6.89	4		Beijing	20 Ma
72.15	Anna	Bulgakova	RUS	17.1.88	1	NC-w	Adler	24 Fe
72.06	Yelena	Krechik	BLR	20.7.87	3		Brest	29 Ap
72.01	Oksana	Kondratyeva	RUS	22.11.85	1		Sochi	28 Ma
72.01	Jennifer	Dahlgren	ARG	27.8.84	1		Buenos Aires	8 Au
71.95	Iryna	Novozhylova	UKR	7.1.86	1		Jablonec	20 Ma
71.40		Liu Tingting	CHN	29.10.90	1	Werfer	Halle	16 Ma
71.37	Kivilcim	Salman-Kaya	TUR	27.3.92	1		Eskisehir	4 Ju
	(40)							
71.35	Yelizaveta	Tsareva	RUS	15.3.93	1		Adler	11 Fe
71.27	Malwina	Kopron	POL	16.11.94	1		Kielce	9 Ma
71.08	Britney	Henry	USA	17.10.84	3	MSR	Walnut	18 Ap
70.77	Alexia	Sedykh	FRA	13.9.93	1		Amiens	27 Ju
70.42	Silvia	Salis	ITA	17.9.85	1		Rieti	13 Ju
70.39	Réka	Gyurátz	HUN-J	31.5.96	1		Budapest	23 Ma
70.22	Carolin	Paesler	GER	16.12.90	2cB	Werfer	Halle	16 Ma
70.14	Éva	Orbán	HUN	29.11.84	8		Beijing	20 Ma
70.12	Tereza	Králová	CZE	22.10.89	1	ECCp	Mersin	30 Ma
69.92	Tugçe	Sahutoglu	TUR	1.5.88	1		Mersin	24 Ju
	(40)							
69.92	Ariannis	Vichy	CUB	18.5.89	1		La Habana	26 Ju
69.72	Brooke	Pleger	USA	21.6.92	1		Muncie	14 Ma
69.61	Nina	Volkova	RUS	26.8.84	3		Adler	11 Fe
69.47	Jessica	Ramsey	USA	26.7.91	2		Tucson	21 Ma
69.29	Maryia	Smolyachkova	BLR	10.2.85	1		Minsk	26 Ju
69.28	Amy	Haapanen	USA	23.3.84	1		San Mateo	14 Ju
69.25	Audrey	Ciofani	FRA-J	13.3.96	1		Gagny	10 Ma
69.23	Tracey	Andersson	SWE	5.12.84	1		Växjö	29 Ju
69.07	Laura	Redondo	ESP	3.7.88	1		Barcelona	1 Fe
69.01	Daina	Levy	JAM	27.5.93	1q	NCAA-W	Austin	28 Ma
	(50)							
68.97	Sarah	Holt	GBR	17.4.87	1		Nové Mesto nad Metují	25 Ju
68.96	Alyona	Shamotina	UKR	27.12.95	2-22	ECp-w	Leiria	15 Ma
68.90	Kristin	Smith	USA	23.12.87	2		Naperville	11 Ju
68.76	Eleni	Larsson	SWE	4.4.93	8	ET	Cheboksary	21 Ju
68.62	Fruzsina	Fertig	HUN	2.9.93	1		Veszprém	7 Ju
68.59	Berta	Castells	ESP	24.1.84	2	ECCp	Mersin	30 Ma
68.53	Julia	Ratcliffe	NZL	14.7.93	1	ECAC	Princeton	16 Ma
68.52	Alena	Lysenko	RUS	3.2.88	2	NC	Cheboksary	5 Au
68.50	Aubrey	Baxter	USA	7.11.85	1		Seward	11 Ap
68.48	Heather	Steacy	CAN	14.4.88	3		Tucson	21 Ma
	(60)							
68.43	Merja	Korpela	FIN	15.5.81	1		Äänekoski	4 Ju
68.43	Katerina	Safránková	CZE	8.6.89	1		Kolín	30 Ju
68.25	Inga	Linna	FIN	21.2.95	1		Kaustinen	27 Ju
68.16	Alina	Kostrova	BLR	2.3.90	1		Minsk	10 Ap
68.11	Barbara	Spiler	SLO	2.1.92	2		Domzale	12 Ap
68.07		Wang Lu	CHN	22.12.91	3	NGP	Chengdu	1 Ap
68.05	Charlene	Woitha	GER	21.8.93	1-22		Fränkisch-Crumbach	24 Ma
67.86	Amy	Sène	SEN	6.4.85	2		Amiens	27 Ju
67.67	Natalya	Polyakova	RUS	9.12.90	2	NC-w	Adler	24 Fe

Mark	Name		Nat	Born	Pos	Meet	Venue	Date
7.67	Gulfiya (70)	Agafonova	RUS	4.6.82	3		Zhukovskiy	24 Jul
7.60	Iryna	Sekachyova	UKR	21.7.76	2	NC	Kirovohrad	30 Jul
7.57	Jessika	Guéhaseim	FRA	23.8.89	1		Aulnay-sous-Bois	15 Jul
7.56	Lauren	Stuart	CAN	16.11.91	1	SunAngel	Tempe	11 Apr
7.37	Anastasiya	Kolomoyets	BLR	15.7.94	2		Minsk	26 Jun
7.26	Kati	Ojaloo	EST	31.1.90	2		Kaustinen	27 Jun
7.24	Heavin	Warner	USA	4.3.93	1		Warrensburg	17 Apr
7.15	Jillian	Weir	CAN	9.2.93	3q	NCAA-W	Austin	28 May
7.11		Luo Na	CHN	8.10.93	4	WUG	Gwangju	11 Jul
7.05	Beatrice Nedberge	Llano	NOR-J	14.12.97	1	NC	Haugesund	2 Aug
7.04	Nikola (80)	Lomnická	SVK	16.9.88	1		Szombathely	24 Jun
7.03	Elisa	Palmieri	ITA	18.9.83	2	NC	Torino	25 Jul
6.91	Laëtitia	Bambara	BUR	30.3.84	1	AfG	Brazzaville	14 Sep
6.87	Zsófia	Bácskay	HUN-J	18.3.97	3	NC	Székesfehérvár	8 Aug
6.86	Ida	Storm	SWE	26.12.91	3	NC	Söderhamn	8 Aug
6.50	Anna	Zinchuk	BLR	4.2.94	2	Univ Ch	Brest	15 May
6.47	Iliána	Korosídou	GRE	14.1.95	1	NC	Athína	26 Jul
6.41	Sara	Savatovic	SRB	5.10.93	1	Big 12	Ames	15 May
6.38	Masumi	Aya	JPN	1.1.80	1		Wakayama	11 Jul
6.37	Lara	Nielsen	AUS	19.12.92	1	NC	Brisbane	27 Mar
6.36	Carys (90)	Parry	GBR	24.7.81	2	LI	Loughborough	17 May
6.25		Yan Ni	CHN	7.2.93	5	WMilG	Mungyeong	7 Oct
6.17	Kearsten	Peoples	USA	20.12.91	1		Columbia	1 May
6.15	Lisa	Wilson	USA	29.3.88	1		West Long Branch	6 Jun
6.11	Daniela	Manz	GER	19.9.86	3		Schönebeck	26 Jun
6.06	Johana	Moreno	COL	15.4.85	1		Medellín	9 May
5.96	Laura	Igaune	LAT	2.10.88	1		Allendale	9 May
5.92	Cintia	Gergelics	HUN	16.11.91	4		Székesfehérvár	13 Sep
5.83	Johanna	Salmela	FIN	6.11.90	2		Raasepori	7 Jun
5.77	Veronika	Kanuchová	SVK	19.4.93	2	NC	Banská Bystrica	1 Aug
5.67	Marinda (100)	Petersson	SWE	3.2.95	3cB	Werfer	Halle	16 May

Mark	Name		Nat	Born	Date
5.65	Micaela	Mariani	ITA	11.2.88	25 Jul
5.63	Rachel	Hunter	GBR	30.8.93	17 May
5.47	Carly	Fehringer	USA	9.11.91	11 Apr
5.38	Bianca	Lazar	ROU	24.2.93	2 Aug
5.33	Jenni	Penttilä	FIN	9.3.91	5 Sep
5.27	Taylor	Bush	USA	26.11.89	11 Apr
5.22	Irina	Sarvilova	RUS	11.11.91	24 Feb
5.21	Iryna	Klymets	UKR	4.10.94	21 Apr
5.20	Jolien	Boumkwo	BEL	27.8.93	15 Mar
5.17	Cynthia	Watt	USA	8.12.93	18 Apr
5.04	Josefin	Berg	SWE	27.12.85	25 Feb
5.03	Sarah	Bensaad	TUN	27.1.87	27 Jun
5.03	Trude	Raad	NOR	27.4.90	2 Aug
4.92	Akane	Watanabe	JPN	13.8.91	27 Sep
4.83	Katarzyna	Furmanek	POL-J	19.2.96	29 Jun
4.64	Alina	Duran	USA	28.3.90	17 Apr
4.59		Dan Dongxue	CHN	23.3.92	27 Jun
4.55	Crystal	Bourque	USA	7.1.89	3 Apr
4.54	Lenka	Valesová	CZE	11.8.85	14 Jun
4.52	Shelby	Ashe	USA	13.3.93	4 Apr
4.41	Julia	Reedy	USA	27.1.93	11 Jun
4.38	Brittany	Funk	USA	13.5.92	8 May
4.20	Viktoriya	Sadova	RUS	18.3.93	11 Feb
4.08	Zlata	Tarasova	RUS	2.12.86	24 Feb
4.04	Aline	Salut	FRA	30.7.92	24 May
4.00	Susen	Küster	GER	27.7.94	26 Jun
3.98	Christina	Jones	GBR	5.4.90	25 Apr
3.93	Alexis	Cooks	USA	11.9.93	24 Apr
3.89	Krista	Tervo	FIN-J	15.11.97	9 Jul
3.85	Marthaline	Cooper	USA	10.11.94	16 May
3.85	Jianna	Williams	USA	20.8.93	28 May
3.81	Tatyana	Beloborodova	RUS	9.10.83	24 Jul
3.74	Vanessa	Sterckendries	BEL	15.9.95	10 Oct
3.66	Ashley	Jenkins	USA	10.12.93	4 Apr
3.65	Alex	Hulley	AUS-J	24.7.97	26 Jan
3.65	Becky	Famurewa	USA	24.2.94	24 Apr
3.55	Natalya	Pospelova	RUS-J	28.6.96	26 Jun
3.50	Anastasiya	Maslovskaya	BLR-J	7.1.96	10 Apr
3.38	Paraskevi	Theodorou	CYP	15.3.86	16 May
3.31		Xu Xinying	CHN-J	17.2.97	10 Jul
63.30	Brooke	Andersen	USA	23.8.95	11 Apr
63.27	Kiah	Hicks	USA	21.2.93	10 Apr
63.24	Carla	Michel	BRA	18.1.88	13 Jun
63.20	Anastasiya	Maslova	BLR-J	16.10.97	7 Jun
63.20	Marika	Kaczmarek	POL-J	25.4.96	21 Jul
63.10		Xia Youlian	CHN	4.8.93	29 Apr
63.08	Anna	Zayanchkovskaya	BLR-J	9.7.96	7 Jun
63.04	Suvi	Koskinen	FIN-J	24.4.97	14 Jul
62.99	Emma	Thor	SWE-J	20.11.97	17 Jul
62.96	Hitomi	Katsuyama	JPN	21.5.94	8 Aug
62.94		Li Yumao	CHN	28.3.93	24 Sep
62.91	Wendy	Koolhaas	NED	2.1.80	1 Aug
62.90	Monique	Griffiths	USA	10.8.94	28 May
62.86	Valeria	Chiliquinga	ECU	27.2.92	3 Oct
62.80	Camille	Sainte-Luce	FRA-J	18.4.96	27 Jun
62.72	Susan	McKelvie	GBR	15.6.85	14 Jun
62.61	Nicole	Zihlmann	SUI	30.7.86	14 Jul
62.58		Shang Ningyu	CHN-Y	26.5.98	5 Apr
62.55	Heli	Rinnekari	FIN	30.9.94	25 Jun
62.54	Emily	Hunsucker	USA	20.4.91	24 Apr
62.48	Jade	Grace	USA	22.9.88	18 Apr
62.47	Milja	Jylhänniska	FIN	5.1.95	27 Jun
62.33	Sophie	Gimmler	GER-J	18.3.96	4 Jul
62.32	Hassana	Divó	CUB	15.8.95	12 Mar
62.32	Nicole	Bradley	NZL	23.4.92	8 May
62.32	Anna Maria	Orel	EST-J	11.12.96	12 Dec
62.29	Nicky	Grant	JAM	25.5.81	27 Jun
62.23	Mariana	Marcelino	BRA	16.7.92	27 Mar
62.20	Celina	Julin	DEN	12.8.94	1 Feb
62.17	Shaunagh	Brown	GBR	15.3.90	31 May
62.13	Jennifer	Batu	CGO	24.10.93	14 Sep
62.06	Kristyna	Krouzková	CZE	5.3.90	16 May
62.02	Hayli	Bozarth	USA	10.6.91	1 May
62.00	Zuleima	Mina	ECU	5.6.90	18 Apr
61.98	Odette	Palma	CHI	7.8.82	18 Apr
61.98	Ami	Schimanski	CAN	23.8.90	3 Jun
61.92	Zeliha	Uzunbilek	TUR	10.6.91	23 May
61.90	Francesca	Massobrio	ITA	9.7.93	28 Feb
61.82	Devin	Stanford	USA	12.11.92	2 May
61.82		Kang Na-ru	KOR	25.4.83	27 Jun

Mark	Name		Nat	Born	Date
61.75	Mona	Holm Solberg	NOR	5.8.83	27 Aug
61.75	Sara	Fantini	ITA-J	16.9.97	26 Sep
61.71	Meagan	McKee	USA	6.12.91	20 Mar
61.61	Sandra	Malinowska	POL	31.7.93	6 Sep
61.56	Gabi	Wolfarth	GER	6.9.89	6 Jun
61.53	Vânia	Silva	POR	8.6.80	25 Jul
61.50	Katerina	Chlupová	CZE	22.10.86	27 Jun
61.47	Jackie	Leppelmeier	USA	13.10.92	14 May
61.46	Tiina	Rinnekari	FIN-J	24.10.96	10 Jun
61.43	Roxana	Perie	ROU	6.9.95	25 Jul
61.42	Kayla	Kovar	USA	11.8.91	28 May
61.39	Katja	Vangsnes	NOR	16.11.91	27 Ma
61.38	Galina	Mityayeva	TJK,CAN	29.4.91	1 Aug
61.31		Zong Dan	CHN	19.1.95	24 Sep
61.30	Maci	Bingham	USA	30.12.92	15 May
61.24	Adrienne	Quillin	USA		28 May
61.22		Wang Lamei	CHN	15.1.90	1 Ap
61.21	Jocelyn	Williams	USA	23.1.9?	16 May
61.20	Jenny	Mina	ECU-J	4.1.97	2 May
61.17	Precious	Ogunleye (200)	USA	21.8.93	27 Ma

Irregular: Wroclaw 27 Jun: 79.83 Wlodarczyk (1) 73.15 69.63 77.26 76.95 77.71 79.83

JUNIORS

See main list for top 4 juniors. 11 performances by 2 women to 68.00. Additional marks and further juniors:

Name	Mark	Pos	Meet	Venue	Date	Mark	Pos	Meet	Venue	Date
Gyurátz	69.63	1		Budapest	13 Jun	68.36	1		Szombathely	17 Ju
	69.55	1		Székesfehérvár	13 Sep	68.26	19q	WCh	Beijing	26 Au
	69.44	1J	Werfer	Halle	16 May	68.25	1		Szombathely	10 Ma
	68.50	2		Veszprém	7 Jun	68.21	1		Szombathely	16 Se
Ciofani	68.20	1cB	ECp-w	Leiria	15 Mar					

Mark	Name		Nat	Born	Pos	Meet	Venue	Date
64.83	Katarzyna	Furmanek	POL	19.2.96	1	NC-j	Biala Podlaska	29 Ju
63.89	Krista	Tervo	FIN	15.11.97	9	Jul		
63.65	Alex	Hulley	AUS	24.7.97	1c2		Hobart	26 Ja
63.55	Natalya	Pospelova	RUS	28.6.96	1	NC-j	Cheboksary	26 Ju
63.50	Anastasiya	Maslovskaya	BLR	7.1.96	1		Minsk	10 Ap
63.31		Xu Xinying (10)	CHN	17.2.97	3		Minsk	10 Ju
63.20	Anastasiya	Maslova	BLR	16.10.97	1		Grodno	7 Ju
63.20	Marika	Kaczmarek	POL	25.4.96	5	NC	Kraków	21 Ju
63.08	Anna	Zayanchkovskaya	BLR	9.7.96	2		Grodno	7 Ju
63.04	Suvi	Koskinen	FIN	24.4.97	1		Kauhajoki	14 Ju
62.99	Emma	Thor	SWE	20.11.97	Q	EJ	Eskilstuna	17 Ju
62.80	Camille	Sainte-Luce	FRA	18.4.96	3		Mannheim	27 Ju
62.58		Shang Ningyu	CHN-Y	26.5.98	1cB	NGP	Chengdu	5 Ap
62.33	Sophie	Gimmler	GER	18.3.96	1		Kaiserslautern	4 Ju
62.32	Anna Maria	Orel	EST	11.12.96	1		Tallinn	12 De
61.75	Sara	Fantini (20)	ITA	16.9.97	1		Jesolo	26 Se

JAVELIN

Mark	Name		Nat	Born	Pos	Meet	Venue	Date	Series
67.69	Katharina	Molitor	GER	8.11.83	1	WCh	Beijing	30 Au	60.84 61.37 64.74 61.86 62.13 67.69
66.40					1	Spitzen	Luzern	14 Jul	65.40 x 58.80 59.91 x 66.40
65.40					1	NC	Nürnberg	26 Jul	63.37 60.64 65.40 61.38 x 60.47
66.62	Sunette	Viljoen	RSA	6.1.83	1		Melbourne	21 Ma	60.57 66.62 62.04 62.93 60.94 59.57
65.79					3	WCh	Beijing	30 Aug	60.18 63.09 62.93 65.79 62.11 60.11
64.36					2	Bisl	Oslo	11 Jun	58.02 64.36 x 63.66 58.03 x
64.14					1	NC	Stellenbosch	18 Apr	61.25 61.50 61.19 63.18 64.14 60.42
66.57	Kim	Mickle	AUS	28.12.84	2		Melbourne	21 Ma	x 62.04 66.57 x 61.17 64.45
66.47	Kara	Winger	USA	10.4.86	1		Austin	2 Ma	x 66.47 63.51 63.42 63.21 59.15
64.94					1	NC	Eugene	26 Jun	64.94 61.38 x 61.42 x 64.45
66.13		Lu Huihui	CHN	26.6.89	2	WCh	Beijing	30 Au	63.80 x 64.72 59.65 66.13 63.72
64.59					3		Melbourne	21 Mar	x 61.01 x 58.85 64.59 62.11
65.92	Christin	Hussong	GER	17.4.94	Q	WCh	Beijing	28 Au	60.27 61.00 65.92
65.60					1	EU23	Tallinn	11 Jul	62.07 x 59.40 65.60 x x
65.75	Martina	Ratej	SLO	2.11.81	1	NC-w	Ptuj	28 Fe	59.61 59.36 58.11 63.02 58.71 65.75
65.66	Barbora	Spotáková	CZE	30.6.81	1	DL	Stockholm	30 Ju	64.62 61.67 65.66 x 64.02 x
65.02					Q	WCh	Beijing	28 Aug	60.62 65.02
65.00					2	DL	London (OS)	25 Jul	60.69 65.00 x x x 62.23
64.42					1	DL	Saint-Denis	4 Jul	62.62 x x x 64.42 61.89
64.31					1	WK	Zürich	3 Sep	59.70 61.44 62.59 64.31 x 57.24
65.07		Li Lingwei	CHN	26.1.89	Q	WCh	Beijing	28 Au	65.07
65.01	Madara	Palameika (10)	LAT	18.6.87	1	DL	London (OS)	25 J	61.91 59.50 65.01 x x x
64.93	Vera	Rebrik	RUS	25.2.89	1	NC	Cheboksary	5 Au	64.68 x 59.39 x 64.93 x

Mark	Name		Nat	Born	Pos	Meet	Venue		Date
4.83	Liz	Gleadle	CAN	5.12.88	1		Kawasaki		10 May
				63.71	63.43	64.83	x	62.00	59.52
64.34	1	JeromeBurnaby	8 Jun	64.34	60.26	63.78	x	p	p
4.75	Brittany	Borman	USA	1.7.89	2		Kawasaki		10 May
				64.75	x	56.92	60.70	61.25	57.90
64.22	Q	WCh Beijing	28 Aug	58.24	x	64.22			
4.65	Linda	Stahl	GER	2.10.85	2	Spitzen	Luzern		14 Jul
				60.70	61.36	59.13	58.19	x	64.65
4.61	Christina	Obergföll	GER	22.8.81	4	WCh	Beijing		30 Aug
				x	61.04	64.61	x	62.51	x
4.56	Margaryta	Dorozhon	ISR	4.9.87	1	Bisl	Oslo		11 Jun
	(30/16)			53.29	64.56	p	55.27	p	x
3.86	Yulenmis	Aguilar	CUB-J	3.8.96	1	PAm-J	Edmonton		2 Aug
3.80	Yuki	Ebihara	JPN	28.10.85	4		Kawasaki		10 May
3.78	Kelsey-Lee	Roberts	AUS	21.9.91	1		Canberra		7 Feb
3.70	Kathryn	Mitchell	AUS	10.7.82	2		Canberra		7 Feb
	(20)								
3.03	Sanni	Utriainen	FIN	5.2.91	1		Kuortane		8 Aug
2.95		Zhang Li	CHN	17.1.89	1	WMilG	Mungyeong		4 Oct
2.81	Sinta	Ozolina	LAT	26.2.88	Q	WCh	Beijing		28 Aug
2.78	Viktoriya	Sudarushkina	RUS	2.9.90	1	NC-w	Adler		24 Feb
2.77		Liu Shiying	CHN	24.9.93	1	NGP	Chengdu		1 Apr
2.14	Ásdís	Hjálmsdóttir	ISL	28.10.85	1		Riga		28 May
2.11	Maria	Andrejczyk	POL-J	9.3.96	1	Skol	Cetniewo		1 Aug
2.09	Goldie	Sayers	GBR	16.7.82	6	DL	London (OS)		25 Jul
2.00	Tatyana	Kholodovich	BLR	21.6.91	1		Tel Aviv		2 Jul
1.92		Yang Xinli	CHN	7.2.88	2	NGP	Chengdu		1 Apr
	(30)								
1.90	Kateryna	Derun	UKR	24.9.93	1	NC	Kirovohrad		1 Aug
1.41	Hanna	Hatsko-Fedusova	UKR	3.10.90	15q	WCh	Beijing		28 Aug
1.27	Mariya	Abakumova	RUS	15.1.86	1		Yerino		25 Jul
1.23	Jucilene	de Lima	BRA	14.9.90	1		Los Angeles (Ww)		11 Apr
0.67	Matilde	Andraud	FRA	28.4.89	1		Salon-de-Provence		10 Oct
0.54	Yevgeniya	Ananchenko	RUS	7.11.92	1		Krasnodar		17 Jan
0.48	Lina	Muze	LAT	4.12.92	1		Dakar		23 May
0.01	Anete	Kocina	LAT-J	5.2.96	2	NC	Ventspils		8 Aug
9.89	Irena	Sedivá	CZE	19.1.92	3	WUG	Gwangju		12 Jul
9.86	Flor Dennis	Ruiz	COL	29.1.91	2	SAmC	Lima		14 Jun
	(40)								
9.86	Heidi	Nokelainen	FIN	30.9.90	2		Joensuu		23 Jul
9.84	Ariana	Ince	USA	14.3.89	1	MSR	Walnut		18 Apr
9.73	Margaux	Nicollin	FRA	1.5.95	1	NC-23	Tomblaine		25 Jul
9.57	Hannah	Carson	USA	26.1.93	3	NC	Eugene		26 Jun
9.26A	Abigail	Gómez	MEX	30.6.91	1	NC	Morelia		13 Jun
9.15	Laila	Ferrer e Silva	BRA	30.7.82	2		Dakar		23 May
9.05	Kim	Hamilton	USA	28.11.85	4	NC	Eugene		26 Jun
9.03	Lidia	Parada	ESP	11.6.93	1	NC	Castellón		1 Aug
9.00	Nadeeka	Lakmali	SRI	18.9.81	1		Diyagama		14 Jul
8.90	Haruka	Kitaguchi	JPN-Y	16.3.98	1	NC-j	Nagoya		16 Oct
	(50)								
8.85	Annu	Rani	IND	29.8.92	1	NC	Kolkata		18 Sep
8.81	Oona	Sormunen	FIN	2.8.89	3		Joensuu		23 Jul
8.77	Mercedes	Chilla	ESP	19.1.80	1	ECCp	Mersin		30 May
8.77		Kim Kyung-ae	KOR	5.3.88	1	NG	Gangneung		19 Oct
8.76	Ai	Yamauchi	JPN	6.12.94	1		Osaka		17 May
8.74		Suh Hae-an	KOR	1.7.85	1		Goseng		18 Jun
8.70	Liina	Laasma	EST	13.1.92	1		Türi		9 Oct
8.61	Anastasiya	Svechnikova	UZB	20.9.92	1		Bishkek		20 Jun
8.59	Mikako	Yamashita	JPN-J	3.5.97	1		Kyoto		11 Jul
8.58		Du Xiaowei	CHN	11.8.87	2	NGPF	Beijing		28 Jun
	(60)								
8.51	Hitomi	Sukenaga	JPN	4.5.88	2	NC	Niigata		26 Jun
8.43	Marta	Kakol	POL	25.2.92	1		Warszawa		26 Jul
8.34	Anna	Wessman	SWE	9.10.89	4	WUG	Gwangju		12 Jul
8.12	Marcelina	Witek	POL	2.6.95	2		Warszawa		26 Jul
7.91	Risa	Miyashita	JPN	26.4.84	1		Kitakyushu		3 Nov
7.90	Marina	Saito	JPN	15.10.95	1		Tokyo		23 Mar
7.77	Elizabeth	Herrs	USA	20.12.93	1		Norman		18 Apr
7.64	Karlee	McQuillen	USA	31.5.89	2	FlaR	Gainesville		3 Apr
7.56		Zhu Dandan	CHN	1.3.94	1cB	NGP	Chengdu		1 Apr

Mark	Name		Nat	Born	Pos	Meet	Venue	Date
57.50	Sofía (70)	Ifantídou	GRE	5.1.85	1H		Náxos	7 Ju
57.39	Izzy	Jeffs	GBR	3.2.92	2	LEAP	Loughborough	18 Ju
57.35	Haruka	Matoba	JPN	24.4.87	1		Osaka	24 May
57.20	Sara	Jemai	ITA	12.4.92	1		Busto Arsizio	28 Ju
57.15	Suman	Devi	IND	15.7.85	2	NC	Kolkata	18 Sep
57.13	Indré	Jakubaityté	LTU	24.1.76	1	NC-w	Kaunas	9 May
56.89	Sarah	Leidl	GER	5.3.87	5	NC	Nürnberg	26 Ju
56.78	Sarah	Mayer	GER	20.5.91	6	NC	Nürnberg	26 Ju
56.77	Lilian	Seibert	BRA	23.7.89	3	NC	São Bernardo do Campo	16 May
56.77		He Daixian	CHN	1.9.94	4	NC	Suzhou	23 Sep
56.76	Arantxa	Moreno	ESP	16.1.95	1		Pamplona	23 May
56.76	Sofi	Flink	SWE	8.7.95	9	DL	Stockholm	30 Ju
56.74	Tatyana	Korzh	BLR	17.3.93	2	NCp	Brest	26 May
56.60	Yekaterina	Starygina	RUS	26.8.95	1-23		Adler	11 Feb
56.60	Madison	Wiltrout	USA-Y	4.6.99	1		North Huntington	7 May
56.56	Jenni	Kangas	FIN	3.7.92	1		Alavus	13 Jun
56.54	Mizuki	Kato	JPN	27.10.93	1		Kyoto	12 Ap
56.52	Eda	Tugsuz	TUR-J	1.3.97	1		Mersin	28 Feb
56.48	Leigh	Petranoff	USA	16.5.89	5		Melbourne	21 Ma
56.43	Lisanne	Schol	NED	22.6.91	2	GS	Leiden	13 Jun
56.37	Dilhani	Lekamge	SRI	14.1.87	2	Army Ch	Colombo	26 Aug
56.34		Chang Chunfeng	CHN	4.5.88	2	NGP	Chengdu	5 Ap
56.30	Nikola	Ogrodníková	CZE	18.8.90	9	ECp-w	Leiria	14 Ma
56.29		Chen Jiajia	CHN-Y	14.10.98	4	NGPF	Beijing	28 Jun
56.27	Petra	Andrejsková	CZE	25.6.92	1		Kladno	14 Jun
56.24	Aleksandra	Ostrowska	POL-J	19.12.97	3	EJ	Eskilstuna	19 Ju
56.16	Eliza	Toader	ROU	12.5.90	1	IntC	Pitesti	23 May
56.15	Sarah	Firestone	USA	16.2.95	1	Big 10	East Lansing	16 May
56.01	Fawn	Miller	USA	10.5.92	1		Baton Rouge	2 May
55.97	Marina	Maksimova	RUS	20.5.85	1		Cheboksary	4 Ju
55.95	Annabella (100)	Bogdán	HUN	7.4.92	1		Szekszárd	1 Ju

55.91	Réka	Szilágyi	HUN-J	19.1.96	19 Jul
55.90	Shiori	Toma	JPN-J	7.2.96	18 Jul
55.85	Tetyana	Fetiskina	UKR	11.9.94	13 May
55.77	Liveta	Jasiunaité	LTU	26.7.94	11 Jul
55.72	Sigrid	Borge	NOR	3.12.95	11 Jul
55.52	Nicoleta Madalina Anghelescu		ROU	13.1.92	3 Mar
55.43	Allison	Updike	USA	16.10.92	23 May
55.42	Coralys B.	Ortiz	PUR	16.4.85	19 Dec
55.37	Jelena	Jaakkola	FIN	7.3.89	8 Aug
55.33	Rafaela	Gonçalves	BRA	27.11.91	16 May
55.29	Gundega	Griva	LAT	8.4.91	9 May
55.25	Kiho	Kuze	JPN	28.3.95	15 May
55.16	Estefany	Chacón	VEN-J	1.11.97	28 Mar
55.16	Edivania	Araújo	BRA	27.8.95	19 Apr
55.14	Tori	Peeters	NZL	17.5.94	21 Mar
55.13	Nora Aïda	Bicet	ESP	29.10.77	1 Aug
54.98	Marie-Therese Obst		NOR-J	7.1.96	30 Aug
54.91	Jarmila	Jurkovicová	CZE	9.2.81	14 Jun
54.87	Melissa	Fraser	CAN	26.5.89	14 Jun
54.85	Rebekah	Wales	USA	2.10.95	28 May
54.72		Lee Hye-lim	KOR	6.3.89	22 Apr
54.68	Monika	Gruszecki	USA	3.12.87	3 Jun
54.57	Eleonora	Bacciotti	ITA	13.12.89	25 Jan
54.57	Joanna	Blair	GBR	1.3.86	19 Jul
54.52	Daniella Mieko Nisimura		BRA	26.3.94	29 Mar
54.52	Olga	Shestakova	RUS	4.12.93	17 Jun
54.48	Andrea	Enerstad Bolle	NOR	8.3.92	12 Jul
54.47	Lyubov	Zhatkina	RUS	30.3.90	23 Apr
54.47	Angéla	Moravcsik	HUN-J	13.5.96	8 Aug
54.42		Huang Mingyue	CHN	8.1.95	23 Sep
54.39	Sílvia	Cruz	POR	29.12.80	20 Jun
54.38	Nuttha	Nacharn	THA	4.6.90	10 Jun
54.35	Andrea	Lindenthaler	AUT	7.9.87	4 Jun
54.30	Melissa	Dupré	BEL	5.11.86	26 Jul
54.26		Liu Beibei	CHN	5.10.90	5 Apr
54.22	Reina	Kojima	JPN	30.6.95	15 May
54.17		Chang Chu	TPE-J	11.9.97	21 Oct
54.15	Laura	Whittingham	GBR	6.6.86	2 Aug
54.13	Barbara	Madejczyk	POL	30.9.76	24 Ma
54.11	Freya	Jones	GBR	13.11.93	11 Ju
54.10	Kseniya	Zybina	RUS	1.2.89	5 Au
54.07	Laura	Henkel	GER	29.2.92	14 Ma
54.06	Avione	Allgood	USA	14.12.93	21 Ma
54.05	Séphora	Bissoly	FRA	6.11.81	24 Ma
54.04	Kisumi	Miyamoto	JPN	4.5.91	26 Ju
54.01		Ge Lijuan	CHN-J	17.7.97	5 Ap
53.96	Megan	Glasmann	USA	3.1.95	26 Ju
53.95		Peng Juanhong	CHN	8.8.93	30 Ap
53.91	Marija	Vucenovic	SRB	3.4.93	2 Au
53.76	Natálie	Durcáková	CZE-J	5.6.97	20 Ju
53.74	Nagisa	Mori	JPN-J	5.2.97	12 Se
53.71A	Merly	Cabrera	COL	29.8.96	25 Se
53.67	Laura	Ikauniece-Admidina	LAT	31.5.92	23 Au
53.65	Nadine	Broersen	NED	29.4.90	31 Ma
53.64	Alexia	Kogut Kubiak	FRA	22.1.88	10 Ju
53.63	Nathalie	Meier	SUI	30.3.93	9 Ma
53.60	Sophia	Rivera	USA-Y	17.10.98	21 Ap
53.56	Nicolle	Murphy	USA	19.10.94	11 Ju
53.50	Viktoriya	Abakumova	RUS	12.10.89	5 Au
53.49	Eloah Caetano Scramin		BRA-J	8.6.96	5 Ju
53.47	Prescilla	Lecurieux	FRA	1.12.92	21 Fe
53.44	Christine	Winkler	GER	4.5.95	17 Ma
53.33	Margarita	Shevyakova	RUS-J	20.12.96	11 Fe
53.32A	Lucy	Kibet	KEN		17 Ap
53.32		Park Ju-hyun	KOR	22.6.94	22 Ap
53.30	Anastasiya	Kregleva	RUS	3.6.92	23 Ap
53.29	Brianna	Bain	USA	23.6.93	27 Ma
53.29	Jessie	Merckle	USA	13.7.94	11 Ju
53.22	Tiffany	Mattaezzi	CAN	13.9.91	8 Ju
53.17	Mackenzie	Little	AUS-J	22.12.96	28 Ma
53.17	Urszula	Jakimowicz	POL	11.6.88	19 Ju
53.08		Hu Hyo-jung	KOR	19.12.94	5 Ju
53.08	Janette	Lepistö	FIN	20.10.93	25 Ju
53.06	Bernarda	Letnar	SLO	26.12.89	27 Ma
53.01	Azize	Altun	TUR-J	3.7.97	19 Ju
53.00	María Paz (176)	Ríos	CHI	13.10.89	24 Ap

Symbols/Abbreviations
+ intermediate time in longer race, A made at an altitude of 1000m or higher, D made in a decathlon, h made in a heat
qf quarter-final, sf semi-final, i indoors, Q qualifying round, r race number, -J juniors, -Y youths (b. 1998 or later)

ʼlark	Name		Nat	Born	Pos	Meet	Venue	Date

JUNIORS

ee main list for top 9 juniors. 13 performances by 5 women to 58.00. Additional marks and further juniors:

guilar	60.52	18q	WCh	Beijing	28 Aug	59.18	1	Barr	La Habana	28 May
ndrejczyk	60.77	1		Skupsk	19 Sep	59.54	1		Kolobrzeg	18 Sep
	59.73	1	EJ	Eskilstuna	19 Jul	58.72	3		Bottrop	21 Jun
ocina	58.88	2	EJ	Eskilstuna	19 Jul	58.84	2		Valmiera	31 Jul

Mark	Name		Nat	Born	Pos	Meet	Venue	Date
5.91	Réka	Szilágyi (10)	HUN	19.1.96	4	EJ	Eskilstuna	19 Jul
5.90	Shiori	Toma	JPN	7.2.96	1		Fukuoka	18 Jul
5.16	Estefany	Chacón	VEN	1.11.97	1		Caracas	28 Mar
4.98	Marie-Therese	Obst	NOR	7.1.96	1	Nordic-J	Espoo	30 Aug
4.47	Angéla	Moravcsik	HUN	13.5.96	2	NC	Székesfehérvár	8 Aug
4.17		Chang Chu	TPE	11.9.97	1	NG	Kaohsiung	21 Oct
4.01		Ge Lijuan	CHN	17.7.97	2cB	NGP	Chengdu	5 Apr
3.76	Natálie	Durcáková	CZE	5.6.97	1	NC-j	Ostrava	20 Jun
3.74	Nagisa	Mori	JPN	5.2.97	3q	Univ Ch	Osaka	12 Sep
3.60	Sophia	Rivera	USA-Y	17.10.98	1		Brentwood	21 Apr
3.49	Eloah Caetano	Scramin (20)	BRA	8.6.96	1	NC-j	São Bernardo do Campo	5 Jul

INDOOR PENTATHLON

Mark	Name		Nat	Born	Pos	Meet	Venue	Date
)00	Katarina	Johnson-Thompson	GBR	9.1.93	1	EI	Praha (O2)	6 Mar
	8.18 1.95 12.32 6.89 2:12.78							
ʼ742	Yana	Maksimova	BLR	9.1.89	1	NC	Gomel	6 Feb
	8.66 1.92 14.95 6.07 2:14.57							
ʼ707	Anastasiya	Mokhnyuk	UKR	1.1.91	1		Zaporizhzhya	27 Jan
	8.13 1.80 13.73 6.53 2:19.05							
696	Nafissatou	Thiam	BEL	19.8.94	2	EI	Praha (O2)	6 Mar
	8.42 1.89 14.80 6.33 2:24.23							
691	Györgyi	Zsivoczky-Farkas	HUN	13.2.85	1	NC	Budapest	14 Feb
	8.44 1.85 14.34 6.20 2:15.10							
687	Eliska	Klucinová	CZE	14.4.88	3	EI	Praha (O2)	6 Mar
	8.53 1.86 15.07 6.15 2:17.26							
678	Kendell	Williams	USA	14.6.95	1	NCAA	Fayetteville	14 Mar
	8.10 1.83 12.24 6.53 2:17.30							
654	Sharon	A	USA	9.6.85	1	NC	Boston (R)	27 Feb
	8.56 1.83 15.41 5.94 2:13.45							
609	Alina	Fyodorova	UKR	31.7.89	1	NC	Sumy	12 Feb
	8.70 1.83 15.76 6.35 2:25.71							
591	Antoinette	Nana Djimou (10)	FRA	2.8.85	5	EI	Praha (O2)	6 Mar
	8.25 1.80 15.05 6.13 2:22.78							
566	Erica	Bougard	USA	26.7.93	2	NCAA	Fayetteville	14 Mar
	8.16 1.83 12.46 6.16 2:16.93							
548	Anouk	Vetter	NED	4.2.93	8	EI	Praha (O2)	6 Mar
	8.33 1.77 14.80 6.29 2:24.48							
527	Morgan	Lake	GBR	12.5.97	9	EI	Praha (O2)	6 Mar
	8.81 1.92 13.91 6.10 2:23.44							
518	Aleksandra	Butvina	RUS	14.2.86	10	EI	Praha (O2)	6 Mar
	8.74 1.77 14.96 6.03 2:14.84							
489	Yekaterina	Netsvetayeva	BLR	26.6.89	2	NC	Gomel	6 Feb
	8.57 1.77 14.91 5.79 2:14.10							
489	Anna	Blank	RUS	12.1.90	11	EI	Praha (O2)	6 Mar
	8.73 1.77 14.11 6.03 2:13.04							
478	Xénia	Krizsán	HUN	13.1.93	2	NC	Budapest	14 Feb
	8.38 1.76 14.09 5.95 2:16.51							
450	Xenia	Rahn	GER	9.3.91	3	NCAA	Fayetteville	14 Mar
	8.39 1.77 12.98 6.23 2:20.17							
430	Alex	Gochenour	USA	17.2.93	4	NCAA	Fayetteville	14 Mar
	8.41 1.80 12.37 6.04 2:16.85							
404	Lindsay	Vollmer (20)	USA	10.9.92	1	Big 12	Ames	27 Feb
	8.35 1.78 13.12 6.09 2:22.56							
402	Akela	Jones	BAR	21.4.95	1		Lawrence	30 Jan
	8.21 1.82 12.78 6.38 2:34.75							

HEPTATHLON

Mark	Name		Nat	Born	Pos	Meet	Venue	Date
308	Brianne	Theisen-Eaton	CAN	18.12.88	1	Hypo	Götzis	31 May
	13.05/-0.2 1.89 13.73 23.34/1.4			6.72/0.9		42.96	2:09.37	
369	Jessica	Ennis-Hill	GBR	28.1.86	1	WCh	Beijing	23 Aug
	12.91/-0.7 1.86 13.73 23.42/0.2			6.43/0.8		42.51	2:10.13	
554		Theisen-Eaton			2	WCh	Beijing	23 Aug
	12.98/-0.7 1.80 13.70 23.94/0.2			6.55/1.2		42.94	2:11.52	

WOMEN 2015

Mark	Name				Nat	Born	Pos	Meet	Venue	Date
6547	Carolin	Schäfer			GER	5.12.91	2	Hypo	Götzis	31 Ma
	13.58/-0.1	1.83	14.06	23.53/0.1		6.23/-0.4		49.08	2:14.10	
6531	Nadine	Broersen			NED	29.4.90	3	Hypo	Götzis	31 Ma
	13.59/-0.1	1.80	14.82	24.85/-1.2		6.25/-0.3		53.65	2:13.92	
6520		Ennis-Hill					4	Hypo	Götzis	31 Ma
	13.24/-0.2	1.86	13.95	23.86/1.4		6.16/1.1		42.60	2:09.21	
6516	Laura	Ikauniece-Admidina			LAT	31.5.92	3	WCh	Beijing	23 Au
	13.21/0.6	1.77	12.71	23.97/0.8		6.32/0.9		53.67	2:13.79	
6500	Barbara	Nwaba			USA	18.1.89	1	NC	Eugene	28 Ju
	13.49/0.0	1.82	13.77	23.76/0.0		6.23/1.5		43.48	2:07.13	
6491		Broersen					4	WCh	Beijing	23 Au
	13.55/0.6	1.86	14.59	25.41/0.4		6.20/0.5		53.52	2:16.58	
6470		Ikauniece-Admidina					1	ECp-1	Inowroclaw	5 J
	13.51/0.1	1.81	13.22	23.95/-0.4		6.27/1.0		49.97	2:13.95	
6467	Nadine	Visser			NED	9.2.95	5	Hypo	Götzis	31 Ma
	13.04/-0.2	1.77	13.15	23.62/1.4		6.48/1.1		44.01	2:13.88	
6458	Anouk	Vetter			NED	4.2.93	6	Hypo	Götzis	31 Ma
	13.53/-1.1	1.77	15.41	23.82/0.1		6.21/1.2		50.09	2:21.18	
6458	Claudia	Rath			GER	25.4.86	7	Hypo	Götzis	31 Ma
	13.56/-0.1	1.80	12.42	23.92/-1.2		6.73/1.5		41.92	2:09.24	
6458	Sharon	Day-Monroe (10)			USA	9.6.85	2	NC	Eugene	28 Ju
	13.31/0.0	1.76	15.62	24.32/0.0		6.05/0.9		44.90	2:09.41	
6441		Rath					5	WCh	Beijing	23 Au
	13.44/0.6	1.80	13.09	24.15/0.8		6.61/-0.1		41.31	2:09.66	
6436		Ikauniece-Admidina					8	Hypo	Götzis	31 Ma
	13.66/-0.1	1.83	12.80	24.06/0.1		6.18/0.3		50.84	2:12.85	
6412	Nafissatou	Thiam			BEL	19.8.94	9	Hypo	Götzis	31 Ma
	13.79/-0.4	1.92	14.69	24.88/0.6		6.06/-0.2		52.03	2:24.20	
6389	Györgyi	Zsivoczky-Farkas			HUN	13.2.85	6	WCh	Beijing	23 Au
	13.85/-0.5	1.86	14.13	25.43/0.4		6.29/0.6		49.30	2:14.71	
6387		Vetter					1		Ratingen	28 Ju
	13.55/-0.3	1.72	15.50	24.12/-1.4		6.07/0.5		52.75	2:20.38	
6371(w)	Akela	Jones			BAR	21.4.95	1	NCAA	Eugene	11 Ju
	13.10/0.9	1.84	14.85	23.45w/3.2		6.53w/3.3		38.13	2:29.43	
6359	Anastasiya	Mokhnyuk			UKR	1.1.91	7	WCh	Beijing	23 Au
	13.07/-0.7	1.83	13.83	24.60/-1.3		6.51/1.2		38.93	2:17.00	
6349	Eliska	Klucinová			CZE	14.4.88	10	Hypo	Götzis	31 Ma
	14.11/-0.4	1.86	14.69	24.62/0.6		6.26/-0.6		46.12	2:17.68	
6344		Visser					8	WCh	Beijing	23 Au
	12.81/-0.7	1.80	13.16	23.78/0.2		6.14/1.7		40.07	2:13.72	
6342		Nwaba					11	Hypo	Götzis	31 Ma
	13.55/-0.1	1.80	14.51	23.82/0.1		5.99/0.3		38.89	2:07.37	
6332	Yorgelis	Rodríguez			CUB	25.1.95	1	PAm	Toronto	25 J
	13.81/-1.7	1.83	14.14	24.25/1.5		6.25/-0.4		48.32	2:22.01	
6331		Mokhnyuk					12	Hypo	Götzis	31 Ma
	13.00/-0.1	1.80	14.13	24.42/-1.2		6.54/-0.2		36.18	2:16.55	
6322	Xénia	Krizsán			HUN	13.1.93	9	WCh	Beijing	23 Au
	13.70/-0.6	1.80	14.12	25.27/-1.3		6.16/0.4		49.17	2:13.36	
6308	Jennifer	Oeser			GER	29.11.83	10	WCh	Beijing	23 Au
	13.67/-0.6	1.83	13.81	25.03/0.4		6.17/0.4		46.45	2:13.89	
6306		Oeser					2		Ratingen	28 Ju
	13.88/-0.3	1.84	14.23	24.91/-0.3		6.26/0.4		45.03	2:15.63	
6306		Zsivoczky-Farkas					1	Déca	Talence	20 Se
	13.96/1.4	1.84	13.78	25.21/1.9		6.26/-0.7		45.82	2:11.88	
	(30/18)									
6288	Erica	Bougard			USA	26.7.93	3	NC	Eugene	28 Ju
	13.03/0.0	1.88	9.97	23.40/0.0		6.13/1.4		38.76	2:08.39	
6278	Alina	Fyodorova			UKR	31.7.89	1	ECp	Aubagne	5 J
	13.80/-0.1	1.87	15.01	24.70/0.8		6.31/1.2		35.72	2:14.77	
	(20)									
6277	Hanna	Kasyanova			UKR	24.4.83	1		Kladno	13 Ju
	13.31/-0.2	1.73	13.98	23.99/-2.4		6.25/-0.5		42.50	2:15.09	
6274	Heather	Miller Koch			USA	30.3.87	4	NC	Eugene	28 Ju
	13.47/0.0	1.73	12.72	23.64/0.0		6.19/0.6		41.23	2:07.32	
6223(w)	Kendell	Williams			USA	14.6.95	2	NCAA	Eugene	11 Ju
	13.08/1.0	1.81	12.41	23.67w/3.2		6.43w/3.3		38.74	2:22.43	
6213	Grit	Sadeiko			EST	29.7.89	15	WCh	Beijing	23 Au
	13.36/0.6	1.77	12.05	24.41/-1.3		6.22/0.6		47.78	2:17.32	
6212	Yekaterina	Voronina			UZB	16.2.92	1	NC	Tashkent	19 Se
	14.59/1.8	1.80	13.90	25.10/1.5		6.21/1.3		50.86	2:15.93	

Mark	Name		Nat	Born	Pos	Meet	Venue	Date
174	Karolina	Tyminska	POL	4.10.84	1	ECp-1	Inowroclaw	5 Jul
	13.72/-0.8	1.75	13.99	24.12/0.1	6.28/1.1	36.34	2:11.44	
151	Lyubov	Tkach	RUS	18.2.93	1	NC	Cheboksary	9 Jun
	14.37w/2.6	1.77	14.81	24.22/1.7	5.95/0.0	45.44	2:16.71	
151	Ivona	Dadic	AUT	29.12.93	4	Décastar	Talence	20 Sep
	14.02/1.4	1.69	13.62	24.40/1.1	5.94/-1.3	52.48	2:15.76	
147	Quintunya	Chapman	USA	7.1.93	3	NCAA	Eugene	11 Jun
	13.43/1.0	1.66	14.56	23.62w/3.2	6.07/1.0	43.66	2:19.96	
141	Salsa	Slack	JAM	10.12.89	1	Click	Tucson	10 Apr
	13.68/0.0	1.62	14.99	23.92/0.0	6.06/0.4	43.77	2:14.34	
	(30)							
123	Caroline	Agnou	SUI-J	26.5.96	1	EJ	Eskilstuna	17 Jul
	13.74/1.5	1.74	13.86	25.24/-1.5	6.28/-0.4	49.34	2:23.90	
113	Sofía	Ifantídou	GRE	5.1.85	1	NC	Náxos	7 Jun
	13.82w/3.1	1.65	13.65	25.40/-0.3	6.02/0.7	57.50	2:19.45	
112	Chantae	McMillan	USA	1.5.88	5	Décastar	Talence	20 Sep
	13.65/1.4	1.75	14.00	25.00/0.6	5.74/0.6	49.39	2:16.77	
111	Anna	Maiwald	GER	21.7.90	2		Ulm	28 May
	13.63/0.0	1.72	14.13	24.03/0.0	5.78/0.1	44.84	2:16.09	
106	Uhunoma	Osazuwa	NGR	23.11.87	1	NC	Warri	31 Jul
	13.71/-0.2	1.87	12.72	24.65/-1.0	6.21/1.2	41.23	2:22.84	
103	Vanessa	Spínola	BRA	5.3.90	1		Arona	7 Jun
	14.37/-0.8	1.73	13.82	24.02/0.8	6.03/1.6	43.64	2:12.52	
102	Portia	Bing	NZL	17.4.93	1		Brisbane	11 Jan
	13.65/0.6	1.80	12.30	23.85/0.0	6.20/-0.3	36.74	2:14.28	
057	Xenia	Rahn	GER	9.3.91	1	ACC	Tallahassee	16 May
	13.69/1.7	1.78	12.95	25.39/0.4	6.31/1.5	44.46	2:21.24	
055	Anna	Blank	RUS	12.1.90	1	NCp	Adler	12 May
	14.38/1.8	1.77	14.41	25.13/1.3	6.05/0.3	41.13	2:11.73	
055	Cindy	Roleder	GER	21.8.89	5		Ratingen	28 Jun
	13.05/-0.3	1.66	13.07	23.68/-0.3	6.18w/3.5	36.33	2:15.49	
	(40)							
051	Annett	Fleming	GER	4.5.84	2		Santa Barbara	4 Apr
	14.02/0.8	1.75	14.02	25.83/0.6	5.72/0.0	51.58	2:14.80	
047	Linda	Züblin	SUI	21.3.86	2	ECp-1	Inowroclaw	5 Jul
	13.65/-0.8	1.63	13.30	25.10/0.1	6.33/-0.9	48.12	2:18.38	
042	Valérie	Reggel	SUI	3.1.87	15	Hypo	Götzis	31 May
	13.78/-1.1	1.65	14.06	24.48/0.1	6.10/-0.2	44.76	2:16.98	
027w	Alex	Gochenour	USA	17.2.93	1	TexR	Austin	26 Mar
	13.15/2.0	1.78	13.02	24.08w/4.3	6.27w/3.6	31.14	2:18.95	
023	Lindsay	Lettow	USA	6.6.90	5	NC	Eugene	28 Jun
	13.56/0.0	1.76	11.87	24.63/0.0	5.92/0.4	42.63	2:11.90	
023(w)	Mari	Klaup	EST	27.2.90	1	NC	Rakvere	16 Aug
	13.78w/3.7	1.77	13.06	25.77/1.8	6.00w/3.8	49.87	2:20.59	
022	Yelena	Molodchinina	RUS	16.4.91	2	NCp	Adler	12 May
	13.96/1.8	1.74	13.10	24.76/1.3	6.08/1.3	41.18	2:12.52	
022	Jena	Hemann	USA	16.10.92	6	NC	Eugene	28 Jun
	14.28/0.0	1.79	12.88	25.06/0.0	6.05w/2.1	48.28	2:19.87	
019(w)	Sami	Spenner	USA	21.3.91	1	MSR	Azusa	16 Apr
	14.11w/2.1	1.76	12.17	23.80w/3.1	6.06w/2.5	38.73	2:11.38	
014	Jess	Herauf	USA	17.1.93	1	Big 10	East Lansing	16 May
	14.41/1.6	1.76	12.59	24.97/-0.3	6.00/1.5	45.91	2:11.44	
	(50)							
998	Lindsay	Schwartz	USA	23.4.90	3		Santa Barbara	4 Apr
	13.82/0.0	1.78	13.03	24.27/-0.2	5.82/0.2	39.12	2:13.62	
995	Ulyana	Aleksandrova	RUS	1.1.91	3	NCp	Adler	12 May
	14.20/1.8	1.89	12.98	25.85/1.3	6.17/1.6	49.40	2:32.28	
984	Yana	Maksimova	BLR	9.1.89	16	Hypo	Götzis	31 May
	14.55/-0.4	1.86	13.97	26.51/0.0	5.97/1.2	43.48	2:13.87	
962	Yekaterina	Netsvetayeva	BLR	26.6.89	1	NC	Grodno	25 Jul
	14.03w/2.2	1.77	14.90	25.81/-0.3	5.74w/3.2	43.62	2:16.58	
930	Evelis	Aguilar	COL	3.1.93	4	PAm	Toronto	25 Jul
	14.35/-1.7	1.68	12.55	23.99/0.5	6.15w/3.0	41.02	2:13.95	
918	Yusleidys	Mendieta	CUB	17.2.94	1	SAmGP	Asunción	12 Apr
	14.09/0.9	1.79	13.42	24.20/-1.1	5.99/0.5	41.51	2:27.31	
914	Deanna	Latham	USA	23.2.92	2	Big 10	East Lansing	16 May
	13.49/1.7	1.73	13.46	24.37/1.9	5.93/1.2	37.15	2:19.75	
888	Kaylon	Eppinger	USA	17.9.89	9	NC	Eugene	28 Jun
	13.07/0.0	1.76	13.34	24.70/0.0	5.79/-0.7	35.62	2:20.83	
868	Ida	Marcussen	NOR	1.11.87	4		Kladno	13 Jun
	14.35/-0.5	1.64	13.52	25.60/-0.8	5.82/-1.5	48.74	2:12.38	

Mark	Name		Nat	Born	Pos	Meet	Venue	Date
5864(w)	Breanna	Leslie	USA	11.8.91	1	172/61	Chula Vista	23 Ma
	13.26w/2.3	1.65 11.81	23.97w/2.8	5.85/1.2		38.12	2:13.40	
	(60)							
5852	Marthe	Koala	BUR	8.3.94	5		Kladno	13 Ju
	13.27/-0.2	1.70 12.53	24.28/-2.4	6.16/0.3		38.27	2:27.11	
5848	Gaëlle	Le Foll	FRA	27.4.91	1	NC	Villeneuve d'Ascq	11 J
	14.40/-0.8	1.81 11.97	26.11/-1.5	5.94/0.7		42.27	2:11.34	
5840	Verena	Preiner	AUT	1.2.95	4	EU23	Tallinn	10 Ju
	14.23/-1.1	1.67 13.44	25.44/0.3	5.75/0.7		45.30	2:12.43	
5835	Celina	Leffler	GER-J	9.4.96	1-19		Kreuztal	17 Ma
	13.96	1.73 13.19	24.00/-0.5	5.83/0.1		41.05	2:25.21	
5824	Michelle	Zeltner	SUI	22.12.91	1		Landquart	24 Ma
	13.90w/2.3	1.75 13.36	24.97/0.9	5.76/0.4		39.37	2:18.65	
5823	Izabela	Mikolajczyk	POL	4.9.90	1	NC	Kraków	7 Ju
	14.05/-0.5	1.84 11.84	25.02/-0.7	6.20/1.0NC		38.97	2:27.30	
5817	Marisa	De Aniceto	FRA	11.11.86	2		Arona	7 Ju
	14.40/-0.8	1.73 13.41	25.95/0.8	5.92/1.9		49.40	2:23.83	
5813	Grete	Sadeiko	EST	29.5.93	5	EU23	Tallinn	10 Ju
	14.36/-0.3	1.76 12.61	24.52/2.0	5.78/-0.1		41.37	2:18.26	
5812	Nikki	Larch-Miller	USA	13.8.94	2		Azusa	16 Ap
	13.63/-0.2	1.59 11.59	23.23w/3.5	5.98/1.3		39.54	2:16.92	
5812	Anna	Gorodskaya	BLR	31.1.93	6	ECp	Aubagne	5 Ju
	14.13/-0.1	1.90 13.11	26.43/0.8	5.64/0.0		41.93	2:21.33	
	(70)							
5810	Alysbeth	Félix	PUR	7.3.93	7	PAm	Toronto	25 Ju
	13.96/0.2	1.74 11.12	24.69/0.5	6.17/1.5		39.38	2:18.19	
5807	Anastasiya	Belyakova	RUS	4.12.90	3	NC	Cheboksary	9 Ju
	14.69/0.8	1.83 12.96	25.93/1.7	5.97/0.0		43.96	2:21.98	
5803	Alissa	Brooks-Johnson	USA	1.8.95	1	Pac 12	Los Angeles (Ww)	10 Ma
	13.96/0.3	1.70 11.41	24.91/1.6	5.77/0.2		44.75	2:13.94	
5803	Élodie	Jakob	SUI	8.10.93	1	NC	Lausanne	16 Au
	13.54/-0.5	1.69 11.33	25.04/0.0	5.85/0.0		44.95	2:18.10	
5795	Anna	Petrich	RUS	10.2.92	3	WUG	Gwangju	11 Ju
	14.26/-0.7	1.77 11.61	25.13/-0.5	6.03/-0.7		38.05	2:13.60	
5792	Lecabela	Quaresma	POR	26.12.89	3	ECp-2	Inowroclaw	5 Ju
	13.90/0.1	1.72 11.59	25.35/-0.4	6.13/-0.7		37.25	2:12.65	
5786	Georgia	Ellenwood	CAN	5.8.95	10	NCAA	Eugene	11 Ju
	14.11/0.1	1.75 11.40	24.45w/2.2	6.08/1.8		40.04	2:21.31	
5786	Jessamyn	Sauceda	MEX	22.5.89	8	PAm	Toronto	25 Ju
	14.09/-1.7	1.74 12.16	25.11/1.5	6.35/1.9		38.51	2:23.97	
5784	Lucia	Mokrásová	SVK	27.3.94	6	EU23	Tallinn	10 Ju
	14.01/-0.3	1.70 12.54	24.56/2.0	5.93/-0.6		39.68	2:18.93	
5782	Kiani	Profit	USA	18.2.90	5		Santa Barbara	4 Ap
	13.96/0.6	1.69 12.50	24.75/-0.2	5.64/-1.0		40.80	2:12.53	
	(80)							
5782	Sarah	Chauchard	FRA	13.3.91	11	NCAA	Eugene	11 Ju
	13.88/0.8	1.69 12.86	25.09w/2.1	5.82/1.7		38.04	2:12.88	
5776	Kristina	Korolyova	RUS	6.11.90	4	NCp	Adler	12 Ma
	14.43/0.7	1.89 11.93	25.83/1.3	5.87w/2.1		40.42	2:20.83	
5771(w)	Tatum	Souza	USA	20.4.92	5	MSR	Azusa	16 Ap
	13.89w/2.4	1.64 13.35	25.36w/2.1	5.74w/2.3		44.27	2:16.67	
5767w	Lindsay	Vollmer	USA	10.9.92	1	KansR	Lawrence	16 Ap
	13.63w/2.4	1.70 12.08	24.99w/5.3	6.07		42.58	2:26.34	
5767	Jessica	Taylor	GBR	27.6.88	1	NC	Castellón	2 Au
	13.94/0.9	1.67 12.72	24.10/0.5	6.10/0.2		32.96	2:16.67	
5764	Lisa	Linnell	SWE	30.4.91	1		Dilbeek	2 Au
	14.13/-0.7	1.76 12.28	25.14/0.2	5.78/1.1		38.23	2:14.04	
5760	Giovana	Cavaleti	BRA	13.1.89	2	NC	São Bernardo do Campo	15 Ma
	14.25/0.9	1.73 12.75	24.43/0.5	6.20/0.8		36.23	2:24.18	
5757	Fabia	McDonald	USA	18.4.92	13	NCAA	Eugene	11 Ju
	14.01/0.1	1.69 12.23	25.36w/2.1	5.86w/3.4		42.92	2:16.07	
5751	Odile	Ahouanwanou	BEN	5.1.91	7		Kladno	13 Ju
	13.98/-0.5	1.70 13.66	24.62/0.2	5.78/0.0		42.01	2:26.81	
5751	Lindsey	Hall	USA	25.3.91	10	NC	Eugene	28 Ju
	13.68/0.0	1.70 12.08	25.60/0.0	5.94/1.6		46.65	2:25.79	
	(90)							
5750(w)	Chari	Hawkins	USA	21.5.91	14	NCAA	Eugene	11 Ju
	13.44/1.9	1.69 11.48	24.28w/2.2	6.02w/3.5		39.13	2:24.68	
5747	Louisa	Grauvogel	GER-J	28.9.96	1		Filderstadt	7 Ju
	14.03/0.0	1.69 12.38	24.68/-1.0	5.79/0.0		40.89	2:17.42	

Mark	Name		Nat	Born	Pos	Meet	Venue	Date
5740	Mariya	Gromysheva	RUS	10.1.90	4	NC	Cheboksary	9 Jun
	13.87w/2.6	1.71 12.72	24.77/1.7	6.02/0.0		36.88	2:22.09	
5739	Sandra	Jacmaire	FRA	4.1.91	1		Angoulême	7 Jun
	13.60/1.1	1.81 11.19	25.57/1.5	6.02/-1.9		38.24	2:23.30	
5738	Anaelle	Nyabeu Djapa	FRA	15.9.92	2	NC	Villeneuve d'Ascq	11 Jul
	13.72/0.3	1.69 12.38	25.28/-1.5	5.97/0.4		38.26	2:17.57	
5734(w)	Tiffeny	Parker	USA	8.6.88	3		Chula Vista	23 May
	13.64w/2.3	1.71 12.53	25.15/1.4	5.85w/3.0		45.69	2:30.46	
5724	Vanessa	Jules	USA	21.3.91	4		Chula Vista	23 May
	13.75/1.4	1.86 11.16	24.92/1.4	5.97w/2.3		30.50	2:19.52	
5720	Hanne	Maudens	BEL-J	12.3.97	2	EJ	Eskilstuna	17 Jul
	14.94w/2.5	1.77 10.43	25.29/-1.5	6.21/1.2		42.27	2:15.56	
5717	Taliyah	Brooks	USA	8.2.95	16	NCAA	Eugene	11 Jun
	13.39/1.0	1.66 11.68	24.35w/3.2	6.28/1.4		35.18	2:25.83	
5715	Jutta	Heikkinen	FIN	27.10.94	8	EU23	Tallinn	10 Jul
	14.45/-1.1	1.73 11.83	25.22/0.3	5.83/-0.1		44.06	2:18.20	
	(100)							

Mark	First name	Surname	Nat	Born	Date
5706	Teddi	Maslowski	USA	6.8.93	16 Apr
5695	Magdalena	Sochon	POL	25.2.95	7 Jun
5685	Niki	Oudenaarden	CAN	14.1.94	16 Apr
5678	Megumi	Henpuhiru/Hemphill	JPN-J	23.5.96	26 Apr
5665	Veronica	Torr	NZL	17.5.87	27 Mar
5665(w)	Allison	Reaser	USA	9.9.92	23 May
5663	Ana Camila	Pirelli	PAR	10.1.89	25 Jul
5659	Kaymarie	Jones	JAM	3.3.90	23 Aug
5652	Noor	Vidts	BEL-J	30.5.96	17 Jul
5643	Madelaine	Buttinger	CAN	3.11.89	20 Jun
5615	Jillian	Drouin	CAN	30.9.86	20 Jun
5614	Estefanía	Fortes	ESP	25.4.87	7 Jun
5613	Mariya	Pavlova	RUS-J	21.5.96	17 Jul
5610	Amalie	Iuel	DEN/NOR	17.4.94	10 May
5600	Emma	Stenlöf	SWE-J	25.6.96	17 Jul
5574	Tamara	de Souza	BRA	8.9.93	15 May
5563	Daryna	Sloboda	UKR	19.6.95	31 Jul
5561	Valeriya	Andreyeva	RUS	2.2.93	8 Sep
5559	Maureen	Rots	NED	25.2.93	5 Jul
5556	Jessica	Flax	USA	4.9.90	16 Apr
5554	Liksy	Joseph	IND	17.2.90	4 Jun
5554	Hertta	Heikkinen	FIN	27.10.94	1 Aug
5553	Yelizaveta	Kolokolchikova	RUS-J	7.6.96	13 May
5552	Ryann	Krais	USA	21.3.90	23 May
5551	Sophie	Klumper	NED	4.4.95	5 Jul
5549	Miia	Kurppa	FIN	30.1.88	13 Jun
5548	Lovisa	Östervall	SWE-J	9.3.97	6 Sep
5545	Abrianna	Torres	USA	3.1.93	16 Apr
5545	Jessica	Tappin	GBR	17.5.90	7 Jun
5540	Miia	Sillman	FIN	3.6.95	10 Jul
5536	Chie	Kiriyama	JPN	2.8.91	5 Jul
5535	Laura	Ginés	ESP	11.6.86	31 May
5531	Brittany	Kelly	USA	5.12.95	15 May
5529	Myrte	Goor	NED	3.4.89	5 Jul
5527w	Jallycia	Pearson	USA	1.5.93	26 Mar
5527	Alina	Biesenbach	GER	27.4.92	9 Aug
5512	Ashlee	Moore	USA	21.5.95	10 May
5511	Purnima	Hembram	IND	10.7.93	4 Jun
5506	Madison	Hansen	USA	4.11.93	9 May
5506	Malin	Skogström	SWE	8.4.95	14 Jun
5504(w)	Megan	VanWinkle	USA	25.8.91	16 Apr
5501	Carly	Loeffel	USA	20.8.92	16 May
5499	Silvia	Mrotzek	GER	.90	28 May
5487	Yanira	Soto	ESP	21.8.88	5 Jul
5483		Li Weijian	CHN	19.10.93	29 Jun
5482	Ashtin	Zamzow	USA-J	13.8.96	15 May
5478	Amber	Metoyer	USA	7.9.83	16 Apr
5478	Karen	Ettleman	USA	9.7.93	22 May
5478	Agnieszka	Borowska	POL	21.10.91	23 Aug
5474	Karli	Johonnot	USA	21.8.93	16 May
5473w	Leigha	Brown	USA	19.9.94	26 Mar
5464	Crystiane	Teresa Barroso	BRA	26.8.88	15 May
5461	Carley	McCutchen	USA	10.10.92	16 Apr
5460	Eri	Utsunomiya	JPN	11.4.93	26 Apr
5451	Patricia	Ortega	ESP	18.4.94	17 Jun
5444	Guillercy	González	VEN	7.5.88	14 Jun
5443	Sepideh	Tavakoli	IRI	2.3.89	4 Jun
5440	Natalie	Thompson	USA	30.9.93	16 May
5434	Makeba	Alcide	LCA	24.2.90	20 Jun
5432	Kristin	Tuxford	GER-J	6.5.97	7 Jun
5432	Simone	Mrotzek	GER	7.5.90	28 Jun
5430	Sophie	Hamann	GER-J	12.8.96	16 Aug
5429	Barbora	Zatloukalová	CZE-J	3.6.97	5 Jul
5428	Francis Ruth	Oluwakemi	NGR	7.3.93	16 Sep
5427	Lucija	Cvitanovic	CRO	17.9.91	15 May
5426	Tine Bach	Ejlersen	DEN	25.7.85	5 Jul
5426	Yelena	Yermolina	RUS	2.2.89	8 Sep
5425	Rachel	Peth	USA		17 May
5425	Zoya	Solyanaya	RUS	7.6.95	9 Jun
5422w	Payton	Stumbaugh	USA	29.11.95	26 Mar
5417		Wang Qingling	CHN	14.1.93	23 Sep
5415	Coralie	Arcuby	FRA	7.8.95	28 Jun
5412	Yuliya	Marchenko	UKR	5.8.95	13 May
5407	Houda	Mohamed Atef	EGY	11.5.95	16 Sep
5406	Breanne	Borman	USA	29.12.93	17 May
5406	Andrea	Medina	ESP-J	26.4.96	7 Jun
5404	Inna	Synytsya	UKR	3.4.85	9 Jun
5403	Kaitlyn	Good	USA	12.6.92	15 May
5400	Shianne	Smith	BER	10.10.85	2 May
5400	Anna	Kulinich	BLR	31.10.94	5 Jun
	(180)				

Best without excess wind assistance

Mark	Name		Nat	Born	Pos	Meet	Venue	Date
5892	Alex	Gochenour	USA	17.2.93	3	SEC	Strakville	15 May
	13.41/0.7	1.70 13.09	24.51/1.8	6.05w/2.3		37.69	2:20.19	

JUNIORS

See main list for top 4 juniors. 10 performances by 6 women to 5650. Additional marks and further juniors:

Name	Mark	Pos	Meet	Venue	Date	Mark	Pos	Meet	Venue	Date
Agnou	5866	22	WCh	Beijing	23 Aug	5722	21	Hypo	Götzis	31 May
Grauvogel	5704	3	EJ	Eskilstuna	17 Jul	5653	2		Kreuztal	17 May

Mark	Name		Nat	Born	Pos	Meet	Venue	Date
5678	Megumi	Henpuhiru/Hemphill	JPN	23.5.96	1		Wakayama	26 Apr
	13.46w/3.3	1.63 10.78	24.99/0.0	5.81/0.8		40.49	2:13.54	
5652	Noor	Vidts	BEL	30.5.96	4	EJ	Eskilstuna	17 Jul
	14.13/1.5	1.71 12.35	24.98/-1.5	5.91/0.7		35.14	2:17.62	
5613	Mariya	Pavlova	RUS	21.5.96	5	EJ	Eskilstuna	17 Jul
	14.39/1.5	1.80 11.42	25.56/-1.1	5.80/0.5		39.77	2:21.76	
5600	Emma	Stenlöf	SWE	25.6.96	6	EJ	Eskilstuna	17 Jul
	14.05/1.8	1.74 12.28	26.04/-1.1	5.81/0.7		42.06	2:25.27	
5553	Yelizaveta	Kolokolchikova	RUS	7.6.96	1	NCp-j	Adler	13 May
	14.14/1.3	1.71 12.82	25.24/-0.2	5.88/-2.1		36.40	2:26.64	

Mark	Name		Nat	Born	Pos	Meet	Venue	Date
5548	Lovisa	Östervall (10)	SWE	9.3.97	1	NC	Gävle	6 Sep
	14.24/0.5	1.72 10.69	25.64/-1.9	6.12w/3.5		38.18	2:21.63	
5482	Ashtin	Zamzow	USA	13.8.96	9	SEC	Starkville	15 May
	14.22/0.3	1.70 11.67	25.20/2.0	5.24w/3.0		45.80	2:24.19	
5432	Kristin	Tuxford	GER	6.5.97	3		Filderstadt	7 Jun
	14.40/0.0	1.63 12.45	25.56/0.5	5.70/0.0		43.15	2:27.54	
5430	Sophie	Hamann	GER	12.8.96	1	NC-j	Heidenheim	16 Aug
	14.25/1.6	1.74 9.83	25.18/0.4	5.58/0.0		36.10	2:15.92	
5429	Barbora	Zatloukalová	CZE	3.6.97	17	ECp	Aubagne	5 Ju
	14.46/-0.7	1.72 11.31	25.47/0.5	5.59/-1.0		39.59	2:22.38	
5406	Andrea	Medina	ESP	26.4.96	2J		Arona	7 Jun
	14.57/-0.6	1.67 11.69	24.97/0.0	5.96/1.5		35.57	2:26.49	
5393	Lea	Fleury	FRA	8.2.96	3J		Arona	7 Jun
	14.32/-0.6	1.67 11.16	25.86/0.0	6.14/1.4		35.09	2:24.79	
5386	Swapna	Barman	IND	29.10.96	1	NC-j	Ranchi	25 Nov
	14.42	1.73 10.75	25.59	5.81		38.08	2:24.30	
5383	Anna-Lena	Obermeier	GER	.96	2	NC-j	Heidenheim	16 Aug
	14.27/1.6	1.74 11.27	26.12/0.4	5.33/0.0		40.74	2:21.25	
5379	Paulina	Ligarska	POL	9.4.96	8	EJ	Eskilstuna	17 Ju
	14.77w/2.5	1.68 11.29	25.72/-1.1	5.70/-0.4		39.79	2:20.30	
5374	Inge	Drost (20)	NED	15.1.96	1	NC	Tilburg	24 May
	13.91/-2.1	1.58 11.12	25.14/-1.0	5.79/0.3		32.31	2:15.31	

4 X 100 METRES RELAY

Mark	Nat	Team	Pos	Meet	Venue	Date
41.07	JAM	Campbell-Brown, Morrison, Thompson, Fraser-Pryce	1	WCh	Beijing	29 Aug
41.60	JAM	Simpson, Morrison, Thompson, Fraser-Pryce	1	WK	Zürich	3 Sep
41.68	USA	Gardner, Felix, Prandini, Todd	2	WCh	Beijing	29 Aug
41.83	USA	Pierre, McGrone, Tarmoh, Bowie	2	WK	Zürich	3 Sep
41.84	JAM	Simpson, Morrison, Stewart, Fraser-Pryce	1h1	WCh	Beijing	29 Aug
41.96	USA	Gardner, Felix, Prandini, Whitney	1	Herc	Monaco	17 Ju
42.00	USA	Gardner, Felix, Prandini, Todd	1h2	WCh	Beijing	29 Aug
42.03	TTO	Baptiste, Ahye, Thomas, Hackett	3	WCh	Beijing	29 Aug
42.10	GBR	Philip, Asher-Smith, Jodie Williams, Henry	4	WCh	Beijing	29 Aug
42.14	JAM	Facey, Stewart, Calvert, Campbell-Brown	1	W.Rly	Nassau	3 May
42.24A	USA	Pierre, Lawson, Bryant, Jefferson	1	NACAC	San José, CRC	9 Aug
42.24	TTO	Baptiste, Ahye, Thomas, St. Fort	2h2	WCh	Beijing	29 Aug
42.27	USA	Todd, McGrone, Tarmoh, Jefferson	2	Herc	Monaco	17 Ju
42.32	USA	Bartoletta, Felix, K Duncan, Jeter	2	W.Rly	Nassau	3 May
42.32	USA	Young, Townsend, C Williams, Richards-Ross	1	DL	London (OS)	24 Ju
42.32	NED	Visser, Schippers, Sedney, Samuel	3h2	WCh	Beijing	29 Aug
42.48	GBR	Philip, J Williams, B Williams, Henry	2h1	WCh	Beijing	29 Aug
42.50	JAM	Facey, Stewart, Calvert, Morrison	1h1	W.Rly	Nassau	3 May
42.50	UKR	Strohova, Pohrebnyak, Kashcheyeva, Stuy	1	ET	Cheboksary	20 Jun
42.58	USA	Pierre, Lawson, Akinosun, Whitney	1	PAm	Toronto	25 Ju
42.60	CAN	Emmanuel, Hyacinthe, Fofanah, Bingham	3h1	WCh	Beijing	29 Aug
	(21/7)					
42.64	GER	Haase, Burghardt, Lückenkemper, Sailer	4h2	WCh	Beijing	29 Aug
42.92	BRA	V dos Santos, A C Silva, Krasucki, R Santos	6	W.Rly	Nassau	3 May
42.99	NGR	Asumnu, Okagbare, Duncan, Uko	7	W.Rly	Nassau	3 May
	(10)					
42.99	RUS	Panteleyeva, Ryzhova, Demirova, Smirnova	2	ET	Cheboksary	20 Jun
43.09	CHN	Tao Yujia, Kong Lingwei, Yuan Qiqi, Wei Yongli	1	Nambu	Sapporo	12 Ju
43.10	SUI	Lavanchy, Sprunger, Kambundji, Atcho	4	WK	Zürich	3 Sep
43.20	POL	Forkasiewicz, Kiełbasi⊠ska, Wedler, Jeschke	6h1	WCh	Beijing	29 Aug
43.22	ITA	Riva, Siragusa, Bongiorni, Hooper	7h1	WCh	Beijing	29 Aug
43.30	KAZ	Ivanchukova, Zyabkina, Rakhmanova, Safronova	1	Kosanov	Almaty	25 Ju
43.51A	PUR	Cruz, Morales, Cancel, Rodríguez	2	NACAC	San José, CRC	9 Aug
43.58	FRA	Guion-Firmin, Akakpo, Pare, Distel-Bonnet	7h2	WCh	Beijing	29 Aug
43.61	JPN	Watanabe, Doi, Fukushima, Ichikawa	2		Kawasaki	10 May
43.72	GHA	Owusu-Agyapong, Acheampong, Gyaman, Amponsah	2	AfG	Brazzaville	15 Sep
	(20)					
43.80	GRE	Gátou, Koklóni, Férra, Belibasáki	1	ET-1	Iráklio	20 Jun
43.94	NOR	Pedersen, Bakke Hansen, Slettum, Okparaebo	2rB	ET	Cheboksary	20 Jun
43.98	CIV	Okou, Gouenon, Tryphène Kouamé, Ta Lou	3	AfG	Brazzaville	15 Sep
44.04	SWE	Bamane, Eurenius, Busk, Hjelmer	3rB	ET	Cheboksary	20 Jun
44.11	BAH	Robinson, Carter, Bethel, Ferguson McKenzie	4h1	W.Rly	Nassau	3 May
44.13	VEN	Álvarez, Purica, Vargas, Soto	5	PAm	Toronto	25 Ju
44.14	ECU	Ângulo, Landázuri, de la Cruz, Tenorio	1rB	W.Rly	Nassau	3 May
44.14A	COL	(Antioquia) E Palacios, Rivera, M Palacios, Flores	1	NG	Cali	17 Nov
44.19	ESP	Diez, Furundarena, García, Lara	4rB	ET	Cheboksary	20 Jun

Mark		Name	Nat	Born	Pos	Meet	Venue	Date
4.27	THA	Thipat, Pakdee, Jaksuninkorn, Wannakit (30)			1	SEAG	Singapore	12 Jun

4.35 DOM 4 Apr | 44.58 CUB 24 Jul | 44.75 CYP 20 Jun | 44.83 CHI 13 Jun | 44.95 BEL 20 Jun
4.41 BLR 20 Jun | 44.64 CZE 20 Jun | 44.75 KEN 15 Sep | 44.83 HUN 20 Jun | 44.97 ZAM 15 Sep
4.54 AUS 13 Mar | 44.68 IRL 12 Jul | 44.77 VIE r12 Jun | 44.92 SVK 21 Jun | 44.99 solo IND 27 May
45.06 FIN 20 Jun

est at low altitude

Mark		Name	Pos	Meet	Venue	Date
4.03	PUR	Santana, Cruz, Morales, Cancel	1	CAm	Managua	27 Jun

JUNIORS

Mark		Name	Pos	Meet	Venue	Date
3.79	USA	Daniels, Hobbs, Brisco, D Hill	1	PAm-J	Edmonton	2 Aug
3.79	GER	Kwaiye, Mayer, Lückenkemper, Bützek	1		Mannheim	28 Jun
3.82	GER	Kwaiye, Mayer, Lückenkemper, Bützek	1		Pliezhausen	17 May
4.18	GBR	Malone, S Hylton. McLennaghan, Lansiquot	1	EJ	Eskilstuna	19 Jul
4.31	JAM	Hines, J Smith, A Williams, Forbes	2	PAm-J	Edmonton	2 Aug
4.48	JPN	(Tokyo HS) Saita, Fukuda, Uemura, Edobor	1		Yokohama	24 Oct
4.52	FRA	Challou, Leduc, Paré, Minku-Meye	1r2		Mannheim	28 Jun
4.67A	BRA	R Santos, M da Silva, de Paula, Rosa	1	SAm-J	Cuenca	31 May
4.83A	NGR	Alphonus, Abolaji, Adaikerehwa, Brume	1	Af-J	Addis Ababa	7 Mar
4.86	NED	Boogerd, Hovenkamp, Kalver, Jiya	2h1	EJ	Eskilstuna	19 Jul
4.88A	ECU	Ferrín, Caicedo, Quiñonez, Tenorio	2	SAm-J	Cuenca	31 May
5.08	IRL	Murphy, Neville, Harrison. Mawdsley	1		Mannheim	27 Jun
5.20	CHN	(Xiamen) Huang Guifen, Wang Xuan, Ge Manqi, Lin Yuwei	1	NYG	Fuzhou	25 Oct
5.28	POL	Blazek, Kaniecka, Ciesielska, Swoboda	2	EJ	Eskilstuna	19 Jul

4 X 200 METRES RELAY

Mark		Name	Pos	Meet	Venue	Date
:30.52	NGR	Okagbare, R George, Duncan, Udoh	1	W.Rly	Nassau	2 May
:30.80	JAM	(U.Tech)	1	PennR	Philadelphia	24 Apr
:31.17	USA	Texas A&M Univ. Purvis, A.Brown, Little,, K.Brown	2	PennR	Philadelphia	24 Apr

4 X 400 METRES RELAY

Mark		Name	Pos	Meet	Venue	Date
:19.13	JAM	Day 50.5, Jackson 49.4, McPherson 50.19, Williams-Mills 49.14	1	WCh	Beijing	30 Aug
:19.39	USA	Francis 51.40, Hastings 49.93, Richards-Ross 48.79, McCorory 49.27	1	W.Rly	Nassau	3 May
:19.44	USA	Richards-Ross 51.5, Hastings 50.4, Felix 47.72, McCorory 49.93	2	WCh	Beijing	30 Aug
:22.49	JAM	Le-Roy 51.88, Williams-Mills 50.02, Day 50.46, McPherson 50.13	2	W.Rly	Nassau	3 May
:23.05	USA	Francis 51.3, Beard 50.5, Richards-Ross 50.45, McCorory 50.83	1h2	WCh	Beijing	29 Aug
:23.27	NGR	R George 51.3, Oladoye 50.6, Adeloye 50.96, P George 50.51	1h1	WCh	Beijing	29 Aug
23.62	JAM	Le-Roy 52.2, Jackson 49.9, Gordon 51.71, Day 49.86	2h1	WCh	Beijing	29 Aug
:23.62	GBR	Ohuruogu 51.3, Onuora 51.0, Child 50.61, Bundy-Davies 50.84	3	WCh	Beijing	30 Aug
:23.75	RUS	Mikhailyuk 51.9, Zadorina 50.3, Renzhina 51.25, Aksyonova 50.43	3h1	WCh	Beijing	29 Aug
:23.90	GBR	Child 51.8, Onuora 50.5, McAslan 51.02, Bundy-Davies 50.63	2h2	WCh	Beijing	29 Aug
:24.05	USA	Trotter 52.16, Hastings 50.73, Francis 49.74, Beard 51.42	1h3	W.Rly	Nassau	2 May
:24.84	RUS	Kotlyarova 51.8, Zadorina 51.2, Ryzhova 51.12, Aksyonova 50.82	4	WCh	Beijing	30 Aug
24.86	FRA	Perrossier 52.5, Gayot 50.6, Raharolahy 52.02, Guei 49.85	3h2	WCh	Beijing	29 Aug
:24.98	RUS	Mamina 51.8, Zadorina 51.2, Ryzhova 50.79, Mikhailyuk 51.10	1	ET	Cheboksary	21 Jun
:25.11	NGR	R George 52.4, Oladoye 50.9, Adeloye 51.14, P George 50.76	5	WCh	Beijing	30 Aug
:25.39A	USA	Funderburk, C Williams, T Williams, Okolo	1	NACAC	San José,CRC	9 Aug
:25.68	USA	Little 50.83, Jefferson 51.52, Wimbley 51.07, Baisden 52.26	1	PAm	Toronto	25 Jul
:25.94	UKR	Zemlyak 52.1, Lupu 51.6, Pyhyda 51.47, Lyakhova 50.89	6	WCh	Beijing	30 Aug
.26.01	UKR	Olishevska 53.2, Bibik 51.5, Zemlyak 51.56, Lyakhova 49.87	4h2	WCh	Beijing	29 Aug
26.14	CAN (20/8)	Muir 51.4, Stiverne 51.3, Watson 51.36, Sassine 52.16	4h1	WCh	Beijing	29 Aug
27.07	ITA	Chigbolu 53.4, Bonfanti 50.9, Folorunso 51.99, Bazzoni 51.43	5h2	WCh	Beijing	29 Aug
28.15	CUB (10)	Veitía, Borlot, Casanova, Bonne	1h1	PAm	Toronto	24 Jul
28.46	BAH	Clarke 53.5, Amertil 50.5, Seymour 53.22, Miller 51.33	6h2	WCh	Beijing	29 Aug
.28.60	ROU	Grecu 53.2, Ionitâ 52.7, Belgyan 52.39, Râzor 50.41	5h1	WCh	Beijing	29 Aug
28.61	AUS	Rubie 52.3, Gulli 52.2, Wells 52.63, Mitchell 51.62	6h1	WCh	Beijing	29 Aug
:28.91	JPN	Aoyama 52.8, Ichikawa 51.6, Chiba 51.21, Aoki 52.41	7h2	WCh	Beijing	29 Aug
29.08	IND	Mathew 53.6, Luka 51.7, Majumdar 51.98, Poovamma 51.87	8h2	WCh	Beijing	29 Aug
:29.30	POL	Ptak 52.98, Holub 51.75, Linkiewicz 52.23, Swiety 52.34	5	W.Rly	Nassau	3 May
29.38	BRA	J Souza 52.77, J de Lima 54.02, Barbosa 52.86, Coutinho 51.24	3h2	W.Rly	Nassau	2 May
.29.86	GER	Spelmeyer 52.9, Möhlenkamp 52.9, Klopsch 52.43, Hering 52.34	4	ET	Cheboksary	21 Jun
:31.21	TTO	Bellille, Modeste, Brooks, McKnight	4h2	PAm	Toronto	24 Jul
31.46	VIE (20)	Nguyen Thi Oanh, Nguyen Thi Thuy, Quach Thi Lan, Nguyen Thi Huyen	1	SEAG	Singapore	11 Jun
.31.72	BAR	Cummins, Williams, Sealy, Belle	3h1	PAm	Toronto	24 Jul
:32.04	PUR	Rodríguez, Marrero, Claxton, García	4h1	PAm	Toronto	24 Jul
:32.29	MEX	Brito, Medina, Morán, Z Rodriguez	5h2	PAm	Toronto	24 Jul
:32.33	BLR	Kievich 52.6, Arzamasova 53.8, Yurenya 52.79, I Usovich 53.01	2rB	ET	Cheboksary	21 Jun
:32.37	CZE	Rosolová, Masná, Seidlová, Hejnová	1	ET-1	Iráklio	21 Jun

Mark		Name	Pos	Meet	Venue	Date
3:32.62	BRN	Nasser, Odiong, Jassim, Adekoya	3	WMilG	Mungyeong	6 Oc
3:32.84	BOT	Jele, Seleka, Galefele, Botlogetswe	2	AfG	Brazzaville	17 Se
3:33.18	SUI	Fontanive, L Sprunger, Schürmann, Büchel	1rB	ET-1	Iráklio	21 Ju
3:33.30	NED	Laura de Witte, Lisanne de Witte, van Schagen, van Leuveren	2	ET-1	Iráklio	21 Ju
3:33.44	CHN	Huang Guifen, Cheng Chong, Chen Jingwen, Yang Huizhen	1	AsC	Wuhan	7 Ju
	(30)					

3:33.69	BEL	21 Jun	3:35.57	RSA	18 Apr	3:36.22	NOR	21 Jun	3:37.26	GRE	21 Jun	3:37.90	SRB	2Aug
3:35.03	SVK	22 Jun	3:35.80	SWE	21 Jun	3:36.82	THA	11 Jun	3:37.45	POR	21 Jun	**Best at low altitude**		
3:35.14	KAZ	7Jun	3:35.83A	KEN	10 Apr	3:37.05	VEN	14 Jun	3:37.51	AUT	22 Jun	3:35.91	KEN	17Se
3:35.48	ESP	21 Jun	3:36.07	CRO	2Aug	3:37.25	LTU	21 Jun	3:37.56A	COL (B	21 Nov			

JUNIORS

Mark		Name	Pos	Meet	Venue	Date
3:31.49	USA	Golden, Baker, Ellis, Rogers	1	PAm-J	Edmonton	2 Au
3:34.36	GBR	C Hylton 53.8, Lina Nielsen 53.7, Beckford 54.31, Laviai Neilsen 52.57	1	EJ	Eskilstuna	19 Ju
3:35.78	JAM	St. Jago HS	1	N.Sch	Kingston	28 Ma
3:37.45	ITA	Mangione, Troiani, Putti, Folorunso	2	EJ	Eskilstuna	19 Ju
3:37.57	RUS	Kudryatvtseva, Kondrashkina, Tsaplina, Bednova	3	EJ	Eskilstuna	19 Ju
3:38.39	NOR	Norum, Daland, Nordahl, Jensen,	1	Nord-J	Espoo	30 Au
3:38.69	JPN	(Higashiosaka HS) Osaka, Murakami, Sasaki, Ishizuka	1		Osaka	31 Ma
3:38.94A	NGR	Asamun, Ajayi, Idamadudu, Adeloye	1	Af-J	Addis Ababa	7 Ma
3:39.11	GER	Richter, Mergenthaler, Hochkeppler, Jacoby	5	EJ	Eskilstuna	19 Ju
3:39.76	FRA	Peltier, Gruffaz, Carti, Chatelle	6	EJ	Eskilstuna	19 Ju
3:40.00	CAN	Stenman-Fahey, Guay, Sharpe, Radoslav	3	PAm-J	Edmonton	2 Au

4 X 800 METRES RELAY

Mark		Name	Pos	Meet	Venue	Date
8:00.62	USA	Price 2:01.30, Vessey 2:00.92, Ludlow 1:59.50, Montaño 1:58.90	1	W.Rly	Nassau	3 Ma
8:11.36	POL	Ellward 2:02.44, Broniatowska 2:03.64, Cichocka 2:00.90, Ennaoui 2:04.38	2	W.Rly	Nassau	3 Ma
8:13.97	AUS	de la Motte 2:02.43, Hetherington 2:03.49, Kajan 2:05.68, McGowan 2:02.37	3	W.Rly	Nassau	3 Ma
8:15.84	CUB	Almanza 2:00.45, Thaureaux J, Casanova, Diago 2:02.42	4	W.Rly	Nassau	3 Ma
8:16.04	JAM	McDonald, Campbell, Goule 2:01.43, James	5	W.Rly	Nassau	3 Ma
8:16.27	CAN	Belleau-Béliveau 2:02.57, Francois 2:03.18, Whelan, Aubry	6	W.Rly	Nassau	3 Ma

DISTANCE MEDLEY RELAY

Mark		Name	Pos	Meet	Venue	Date
10:36.50	USA	Moser 3:18.38, Richards-Ross 50.12, Wilson 2:00.08, Rowbury 4:27.92	1	W.Rly	Nassau	2 Ma
10:43.35	KEN	Busienei 3:18.96, Zakari 52.59, Chesebe 2:03.32, Nyambura 4:28.48	2	W.Rly	Nassau	2 Ma
10:45.32	POL	Broniatowska 3:19.87, Szczesna 54.12, Cichocka 2:01.06, Ennaoui 4:30.27	3	W.Rly	Nassau	2 Ma
10:46.94	AUS	M Duncan 3:19.78, Lind 53.31, McGowan 2:03.15, See 4:30.70	4	W.Rly	Nassau	2 Ma
Indoors						
10:42.57	USA	New Balance S Brown 3:15.54, M Jones 53.59, Krumpoch 2:05.68, Martinez 4:27.77	1		Boston (R)	7 Fe
10:42.79		New York All Stars	2		Boston (R)	7 Fe
10:51.89		U of Arkansas Kamilos 3:22.87, McKnight TTO 52.84, Haiss 2:07.29, Scott RSA 4:28.89	1	NCAA	Fayetteville	13 M

4 X 100 METRES HURDLES

Mark	Name	Pos	Meet	Venue	Date
50.50	USA Blue (Castlin, Q Harrison, Harper Nelson, Rollins)	1	DrakeR	Des Moines	24 A
50.50	USA White (Coward, Nelvis, Porter GBR, Stowers)	2	DrakeR	Des Moines	24 A
52.32	Drake Red (DeLoach, Jones, Clay, Thomas PAN)	3	DrakeR	Des Moines	24 A
52.62	Elite Athletes Manning, Nelvis, Clay, C Jones	1	FlaR	Gainesville	4 A
52.97	JAM Bliss, D Williams, ?, Sher. Williams	2	FlaR	Gainesville	4 A

3000 METRES WALK

Mark	Name		Nat	Born	Pos	Meet	Venue	Date
11:52.38	Anezka	Drahotová	CZE	22.7.95	1	GS	Ostrava	26 Ma
12:07.41	Eleonora	Giorgi	ITA	14.9.89			San Diego	17 Ja
12:11.12	Brigita	Virbalyté-Dimsiené	LTU	1.2.85	2	GS	Ostrava	26 Ma
12:20.09	Julia	Takács	ESP	29.6.89	1		Huelva	10 Ju
12:24.51	Raquel	González	ESP	16.11.89	2		Huelva	10 Ju
12:29.38	Laura	García-Caro	ESP	16.4.95	3		Huelva	10 Ju
12:33.51	Viktória	Madarász	HUN	12.5.85	3	GS	Ostrava	26 Ma
12:35.47	Emilie	Menuet	FRA	27.11.91	1		Vineuil	10 Ma
Indoors								
12:05.68	Antonella	Palmisano	ITA	6.8.91	1	NC	Padova	21 Fe
12:17.93	Ana	Cabecinha	POR	29.4.84	1	NC	Pombal	14 Fe
12:21.17	Inna	Kashyna	UKR	27.9.91	1	NC	Sumy	12 Fe
12:21.19	Alyona	Khramova	RUS	18.8.93	1		Novocheboksarsk	15 Ja
12:33.03	Rachel	Seaman	CAN	14.1.86	1	NC	Montréal	22 Fe
12:34.67	Agnieszka	Szwarnóg	POL	28.12.86	1	NC	Torun	22 Fe
12:35.55	Valentina	Trapletti	ITA	12.7.85	2	NC	Padova	21 Fe

5000 METRES WALK

Mark	Name		Nat	Born	Pos	Meet	Venue	Date
21:03.59	Julia	Takács	ESP	29.6.89	1		Gijón	25 Jul
21:07.51	Raquel	González	ESP	16.11.89	1	Univ Ch	Cartagena	29 Apr
21:17.00+	Viktória	Madarász	HUN	12.5.85	1	in 10000	Székesfehérvár	13 Sep
21:17.97	Kumiko	Okada	JPN	17.10.91	1		Kumagaya	16 May
21:22.23	Ana	Cabecinha	POR	29.4.84	1		Faro	21 Mar
21:24.73	Eleonora	Giorgi	ITA	14.9.89	1		Milano	23 Apr
21:25.06		Liu Hong	CHN	12.5.87	1		Torino	9 May
21:25.11		Qieyang Shenjie	CHN	11.11.90	2		Torino	9 May
21:27.39	Rachel	Seaman	CAN	14.1.86	1		Chula Vista	13 Jun
21:32.1+	Elisa	Rigaudo	ITA	17.6.80	1	in 10000	Rieti	13 Jun
	(10)							

Mark	Name		Nat	Born	Date
21:41.72	Emilie	Menuet	FRA	27.11.91	1 Jul
21:41.99	Miranda	Melville	USA	20.3.89	13 Jun
21:44.71		Wang Yingliu	CHN	1.3.92	20 Jul
21:46.19	Amanda	Cano	ESP	19.8.94	25 Jul
21:46.37	Sae	Matsumoto	JPN	15.3.93	12 Dec
21:49.09	Laura	García-Caro	ESP	16.4.95	13 Jun
21:49.33mx	Kelly	Ruddick	AUS	19.4.73	1 Mar
21:50.15	Maria	Michta-Coffey	USA	23.6.86	25 Apr
21:51.90	Ai	Michiguchi	JPN	3.6.88	12 Jul
21:52.10	Inês	Henriques	POR	1.5.80	30 May
21:53.2	Agnese	Pastare	LAT	27.10.88	1 Aug
21:53.75	María José	Poves	ESP	16.3.78	13 Jun
Indoors					
21:46.21	Inna	Kashyna	UKR	27.9.91	19 Dec

JUNIORS

Mark	Name		Nat	Born	Pos	Meet	Venue	Date
21:58.51	Taika	Nummi	FIN	12.10.97	1	vSWE	Stockholm	12 Sep
22:01.33	Lidia	Sánchez-Puebla	ESP	17.7.96	1		Plasencia	24 Jun
22:04.29mx	Jemima	Montag	AUS-Y	15.2.98	1		Brisbane	14 Jun

See also 20km list for many intermediate times.

10 KILOMETRES WALK

Mark	Name		Nat	Born	Pos	Meet	Venue	Date
42:43	Brigita	Virbalyté-Dimsiené	LTU	1.2.85	1		Katowice	5 Sep
42:55.35t	Elisa	Rigaudo	ITA	17.6.80	1		Rieti	13 Jun
43:08		Rigaudo			1	NC	Torino	24 Jul
43:18.99t	Viktória	Madarász	HUN	12.5.85	1		Debrecen	5 Sep
43:19		Yang Jiayu	CHN-J	18.2.96	1	NC-j	Changbaishan	5 Sep
43:19.12t	Ana	Cabecinha	POR	29.4.84	1	NC	Leiria	25 Jul
43:26.13t	Kumiko	Okada	JPN	17.10.91	1		Abashiri	16 Jul
43:32		Okada			1		Wajima	18 Apr
43:36.88 t	Klavdiya	Afanasyeva	RUS-J	15.1.96	1	EJ	Eskilstuna	16 Jul
43:39	Beatriz	Pascual	ESP	9.5.82	1		Viladecans	25 Jan
43:40.68t	Inês	Henriques	POR	1.5.80	2	NC	Leiria	25 Jul
43:53+	Natalya	Serezhkina (10)	RUS	7.5.92		in 20k	Sochi	27 Feb
43:55.05t		Okada			1		Gifu	5 Oct
44:00.36t	Julia	Takacs	ESP	29.6.89	1		Castellón	1 Aug
44:01.08 t	Olga	Shargina	RUS-J	24.7.96	2	EJ	Eskilstuna	16 Jul
44:05	Mirna	Ortiz	GUA	28.2.87	2		Katowice	5 Sep
44:07.44 t	Mariya	Losinova	RUS-J	2.3.97	3	EJ	Eskilstuna	16 Jul
44:09	Neringa	Aidietyté	LTU	5.6.83	3		Katowice	5 Sep
44:14+	Anezka	Drahotová	CZE	22.7.95	7	in 20k	Murcia	17 May
44:16.98t	Rachel	Seaman	CAN	14.1.86	1	NC	Edmonton	4 Jul
44:17.21t	María José	Poves	ESP	16.3.78	2		Castellón	1 Aug
44:19	Nadiya	Borovska	UKR	25.2.81	1		Lutsk	28 Jun
44:19.05t	Mária	Pérez	ESP-J	29.4.96	4	EJ	Eskilstuna	16 Jul
44:22.19t	Ai	Michiguchi	JPN	3.6.88	2		Abashiri	16 Jul
44:24	Beki	Smith	AUS	25.11.86	1		Sydney	24 May
44:25		Caixiang Zhuoma	CHN-J	2.6.96	2	NC-j	Changbaishan	5 Sep
44:33+	Kimberley	García	PER	19.10.93		in 20k	Toronto	19 Jul
44:35+	Alyona	Khramova	RUS	18.8.93		in 20k	Sochi	27 Feb
44:43.78t	Noemi	Stella	ITA-J	2.2.97	5	EJ	Eskilstuna	16 Jul
44:45+		Hou Yongbo	CHN	15.9.94	2	in 20k	Nomi	15 Mar
44:45.76t		Wang Yingliu	CHN	1.3.92	1		Guilin	23 Jul
44:49		Ji Yefang	CHN-J	4.3.96	3	NC-j	Changbaishan	5 Sep
44:50.19t	Susana	Feitor	POR	28.1.75	3	NC	Leiria	25 Jul
44:51		Zhao Wenli	CHN-J	11.12.96	4	NC-j	Changbaishan	5 Sep
44:53	Monika	Kapera	POL	15.2.90	2		Voronovo	13 Sep
44:56.44t	Tanya	Holliday	AUS	21.9.88	1	NC	Brisbane	27 Mar
44:58	Agnieszka	Szwarnóg	POL	28.12.86	3		Voronovo	13 Sep
44:58.49t	Katarzyna	Golba	POL	21.12.89	1		Sosniwicz	30 May
45:01.0At	Lorena	Arenas	COL	17.9.93	1		Medellín	11 Apr
45:01		Yin Hang	CHN-J	7.2.97	5	NC-j	Changbaishan	5 Sep
45:04	Paulina	Buziak	POL	16.12.86	4		Katowice	5 Sep
45:05		Zhang Lifang	CHN-J	6.12.97	6	NC-j	Changbaishan	5 Sep
45:06.18t	Emilie	Menuet	FRA	27.11.91	1	NC	Villeneuve d'Ascq	11 Jul
45:08		Xue Ke	CHN-Y	14.3.98	1	NC-y	Changbaishan	5 Sep
45:09.13t	Rei	Inoue	JPN	23.7.91	3		Abashiri	16 Jul

Mark		Name	Nat	Born	Pos	Meet	Venue	Date
45;10+	Alejandra	Ortega	MEX	8.7.94		in 20k	Toronto	19 Ju
45:10	Nadezhda	Dorozhuk	BLR	23.1.90	1		Grodno	3 Oc
45:11	Vasylyna	Vitovshchyk	UKR	30.4.90	2		Lutsk	28 Ju
45:13.53t	Rena	Goto	JPN	6.9.95	4		Abashiri	16 Ju
45:20		La Mao	CHN-J	17.12.96	2	WCT-j	Beijing	20 Ma
45:23	Masumi	Fuchise	JPN	2.9.86	1		Tokyo	1 Ja
45:26+	Olena	Shumkina	UKR	24.1.88		in 20k	Murcia	17 Ma
45:26.93t		Ni Yuanyuan	CHN	6.4.95	2		Guilin	23 Ju
45:28.5t	Laura	Polli	SUI	7.9.83	1	NC	Tesserete	26 Ju
45:35+	Regan	Lamble	AUS	14.10.91	1	in 20k	Melbourne	39 Au
45:36+	Ainhoa	Pinedo	ESP	17.2.83	7	in 20k	La Coruña	6 Jur
45:38+	Paola	Pérez	ECU	21.12.89		in 20k	Beijing	28 Au
45:39	Andreea	Arsine	ROU	14.9.88	1		Pitesti	7 Ju
45:39+	Lina	Kalutskaya	RUS	1.10.88		in 20k	Sochi	27 Fe
45:41	Anna	Tropareva	RUS	20.8.88	2		Podolsk	9 Ma

Mark		Name	Nat	Born	Date
45:44.53t	Taika	Nummi	FIN-J	12.10.97	16 Jul
45:46	Mar	Juárez	ESP	27.9.93	25 Jan
45:47.88t	Lidia	Sánchez-Puebla	ESP-J	17.7.96	16 Jul
45:48	Yana	Smerdova	RUS-Y	7.2.98	9 May
45:50+	Kristina	Mikhaylova	RUS	16.10.92	27 Feb
45:50		Mao Yanqiu	CHN-J	7.10.96	5 Sep
45:51	Valentina	Trapletti	ITA	12.7.85	24 Jul
45:52.22t	Federica	Curiazzi	ITA	14.8.92	19 Apr
45:57		Yang Liujing	CHN-Y	22.8.98	1 May
45:59		Xiao Xianghua	CHN-J	19.2.97	5 Sep
46:00	Darya	Bolkunets	BLR	4.3.93	3 Oct
46:03+	Mária	Czaková	SVK	2.10.88	15 Mar
46:04.0t	Lucie	Pelantová	CZE	7.5.86	29 Mar
46:04	Katarzyna	Zdzieblo	POL-J	28.11.96	18 Apr
46:05.10t	Amanda	Cano	ESP	19.8.94	1 Aug
46:06		Xiao Han	CHN-Y	12.11.98	1 May
46:07.73t	Sae	Matsumoto	JPN	15.5.93	19 Ju
46:11		Ma Yiming	CHN-J	10.9.97	5 Sep
46:13.23t	Zivile	Vaiciukeviciute	LTU-J	3.4.96	16 Ju
46:14.23t	Anastasiya	Taushkanova	RUS-J	25.3.96	12 Jur
46:16+	Maritza Rafaela	Poncio	GUA	3.12.94	28 Aug
46:20	Halyna	Yakovchuk	UKR	21.2.92	28 Jur
46:21.49t	Eleonora	Dominici	ITA	22.2.96	16 Ju
46:21.6t	Maria	Polli	SUI	28.11.80	26 Ju
46:28	Yevdokiya	Korotkova	RUS	28.2.79	9 May
46:30+	Viktoriya	Rashchupkina	BLR	23.5.95	10 Ju

Best track times

Mark		Name	Nat	Born	Pos	Venue	Date
44:45.76t		Wang Yingliu	CHN	1.3.92	1	Guilin	23 Ju
44:47.51t	Raquel	González	ESP	16.11.89	3	Castellón	1 Au

Mark		Name	Nat	Born	Date
45:59.17t	Ainhoa	Pinedo	ESP	17.2.83	1 Aug
46:01.71t		Yang Liujing	CHN-Y	22.8.98	24 Oct
46:07.14t		Zhao Wenli	CHN-J	11.12.96	24 Oct
46:10.09t		Ji Yefang	CHN-J	4.3.96	24 Oct
46:18.09t	Agnieszka	Szwarnóg	POL	28.12.86	30 May
46:18.3t	hiaki	Asada	JPN	21.1.91	29 Nov
46:18.70t		Xue Ke	CHN-Y	14.3.98	24 Oc
46:19.90t	Masumi	Fuchise	JPN	2.9.86	5 Oc
46:20.48t		La Mao	CHN-J	17.12.96	24 Oc
46:25.37t		Yang Liujing	CHN-Y	22.8.98	24 Oc
46:25.92		Caixiang Zhuoma	CHN	2.6.96	24 Oc

Indoors

Mark		Name	Nat	Born	Pos	Meet	Venue	Date
43:55.51		Cabecinha			1		Vila Real de S.Antonio	11 Ja
45:59.61	Darya	Bolkunets	BLR	4.3.93	1	NC	Mogilyov	20 Fe

JUNIORS

See main list for top 13 juniors. 11 performances by 6 women to 44:51. Additional marks and further juniors:

Yang	44:18	1	Taicang	9 May
Ji	44:50	9r2	Suzhou	27 Sep

Mark		Name	Nat	Born	Pos	Meet	Venue	Date
45:44.53 t	Taika	Nummi	FIN-J	12.10.97	6	EJ	Eskilstuna	16 Ju
45:47.88t	Lidia	Sánchez-Puebla	ESP-J	17.7.96	7	EJ	Eskilstuna	16 Ju
45:48	Yana	Smerdova	RUS-Y	7.2.98	3		Podolsk	9 Ma
45:50		Mao Yanqiu	CHN-J	7.10.96	7	NC-j	Changbaishan	5 Se
45:57		Yang Liujing	CHN-Y	22.8.98	1Y	NGP	Taicang	1 Ma
45:59		Xiao Xianghua	CHN-J	19.2.97	8	NC-j	Changbaishan	5 Se
46:04	Katarzyna	Zdzieblo	POL-J	28.11.96	1		Zaniemysl	18 Ap

20 KILOMETRES WALK

10 kilometre times in second column

Mark	10k		Name	Nat	Born	Pos	Meet	Venue	Date
1:24:38	42:39		Liu Hong	CHN	12.5.87	1		La Coruña	6 Ju
1:24:47	42:12	Elmira	Alembekova	RUS	30.6.90	1	NC-w	Sochi	27 Fe
1:25:03	42:12	Marina	Pandakova	RUS	1.3.89	2	NC-w	Sochi	27 Fe
1:25:04	42:12	Svetlana	Vasilyeva	RUS	24.7.92	3	NC-w	Sochi	27 Fe
1:25:12	43:19		Lu Xiuzhi	CHN	26.10.93	1	WCT	Beijing	20 Ma
1:25:38	42:38	Vera	Sokolova	RUS	8.6.87	4	NC-w	Sochi	27 Fe
1:26:15	44:14		Alembekova			1	ECp	Murcia	17 Ma
1:26:17	44:14	Eleonora	Giorgi	ITA	14.9.89	2	ECp	Murcia	17 Ma
1:26:17	43:45		Sokolova			1	NC	Cheboksary	13 Ju
1:26:31	44:14		Vasilyeva			3	ECp	Murcia	17 Ma
1:26:44	43:45	Anisya	Kirdyapkina	RUS	23.10.89	2	NC	Cheboksary	13 Ju
1:26:46	43:16		Giorgi			1		Dudince	21 Ma
1:26:53	44:14	Anezka	Drahotová	CZE	22.7.95	4	ECp	Murcia	17 Ma
1:26:58	44:15		Pandakova			5	ECp	Murcia	17 Ma
1:27:08	44:15		Sokolova			6	ECp	Murcia	17 Ma
1:27:09	44:12	Lyudmyla	Olyanovska (10)	UKR	20.2.93	7	ECp	Murcia	17 Ma
1:27:17	44:45	Mariya	Ponomaryova	RUS	18.6.95	1	EU23	Tallinn	10 Ju
1:27:22	44:41		Liu Hong			1		Rio Maior	18 Ap
1:27:25	44:46		Drahotová			2	EU23	Tallinn	10 Ju

Mark		Name		Nat	Born	Pos	Meet	Venue	Date
1:27:39	43:57		Liu Hong			2	WCT	Beijing	20 Mar
1:27:44	43:23		Qieyang Shenjie	CHN	11.11.90	2		La Coruña	6 Jun
1:27:45	44:19		Liu Hong			1	WCh	Beijing	28 Aug
1:27:45	44:19		Lu Xiuzhi			2	WCh	Beijing	28 Aug
1:27:51	43:58		Nie Jingjing	CHN	1.3.88	3	WCT	Beijing	20 Mar
1:28:01	44:16	Elisa	Rigaudo	ITA	17.6.80	8	ECp	Murcia	17 May
1:28:12	44:47		Giorgi			2		Rio Maior	18 Apr
1:28:13	44:45		Olyanovska			3	WCh	Beijing	28 Aug
1:28:18	43:15		Olyanovska			2		Dudince	21 Mar
1:28:18	44:09		Kirdyapkina			1	WUG	Gwangju	10 Jul
1:28:24	43:22		Kirdyapkina			5	NC-w	Sochi	27 Feb
		(30/14)							
1:28:28	44:14	Ana	Cabecinha	POR	29.4.84	9	ECp	Murcia	17 May
1:28:30			Hou Yongbo	CHN	15.9.94	2	NC	Changbaishan	6 Sep
1:28:40	44:18	Antonella	Palmisano	ITA	6.8.91	3		Dudince	21 Mar
1:29:14	43:58		Xie Lijuan	CHN	14.5.93	5	WCT	Beijing	20 Mar
1:29:21	43:49	María Guadalupe	González	MEX	9.1.89	1	PAmCp	Arica	9 May
1:29:22			Liang Rui	CHN	18.6.94	3	NC	Changbaishan	6 Sep
		(20)							
1:29:32	44:57		Ding Huiqin	CHN	5.2.90	6	WCT	Beijing	20 Mar
1:29:32	44:35	Laura	García-Caro	ESP	16.4.95	10	ECp	Murcia	17 May
1:29:32	45:27	Yekaterina	Medvedyeva	RUS	29.3.94	3	NC	Cheboksary	13 Jun
1:29:34	44:14	Raquel	González	ESP	16.11.89	11	ECp	Murcia	17 May
1:29:37	44:22	Érica	de Sena	BRA	3.5.85	4		Dudince	21 Mar
1:29:46	44:06	Kumiko	Okada	JPN	17.10.91	2	AsiC	Nomi	15 Mar
1:29:47	45:33		Mao Yanxue	CHN	15.2.94	7	WCT	Beijing	20 Mar
1:29:52	45:26	Inês	Henriques	POR	1.5.80	5		Rio Maior	18 Apr
1:29:54	44:46	Rachel	Seaman	CAN	14.1.86	3		Nomi	15 Mar
1:30:02		Neringa	Aidietyté	LTU	5.6.83	1	NC	Alytus	12 Jun
		(30)							
1:30:19	45:19		Wang Na	CHN	29.5.95	8	WCT	Beijing	20 Mar
1:30:20	45:10		Wang Yingliu	CHN	1.3.92	9	WCT	Beijing	20 Mar
1:30:20	45:17	Brigita	Virbalyté-Dimsiené	LTU	1.2.85	7	WCh	Beijing	28 Aug
1:30:21			Sun Huanhuan	CHN	15.3.90	4	NC	Changbaishan	6 Sep
1:30:23	45:04	Vera	Santos	POR	3.12.81	2		Lugano	15 Mar
1:30:24		Beki	Smith	AUS	25.11.86	1		Sydney	26 Jul
1:30:35	44:56		Jeon Yang-eun	KOR	24.5.88	3	AsiC	Nomi	15 Mar
1:30:38	44:42	Agnieszka	Dygacz	POL	18.7.85	3		Lugano	15 Mar
1:30:38	44:43	Nadiya	Borovska	UKR	25.2.81	15	ECp	Murcia	17 May
1:30:45		Regan	Lamble	AUS	14.10.91	1		Melbourne	13 Dec
		(40)							
1:30:48	43:52	Tatyana	Sibileva	RUS	17.5.80	7	NC-w	Sochi	27 Feb
1:30:52	45:32	Inna	Kashyna	UKR	27.9.91	17	ECp	Murcia	17 May
1:31:02.25	t	Sandra Lorena	Arenas	COL	17.9.93	1	SACh	Lima	13 Jun
1:31:04	45:17	Alejandra	Ortega	MEX	8.7.94	9	WCh	Beijing	28 Aug
1:31:06	45:29	María José	Poves	ESP	16.3.78	10	WCh	Beijing	28 Aug
1:31:13		Kimberley	García	PER	19.10.93	2	PAmCp	Arica	9 May
1:31:23	45:39	Julia	Takacs	ESP	29.6.89	7		Rio Maior	18 Apr
1:31:25	45:31	Paulina	Buziak	POL	16.12.86	1		Zaniemysl	18 Apr
1:31:25		Mirna	Ortiz	GUA	28.2.87	8		Rio Maior	18 Apr
1:31:28	44:57	Chiaki	Asada	JPN	21.1.91	5		Nomi	15 Mar
		(50)							
1:31:31		Viktória	Madarász	HUN	12.5.85	1	NC	Békéscsaba	25 Apr
1:31:36			Ni Yuanyuan	CHN	6.4.95	8	NC	Changbaishan	6 Sep
1:31:42	45:21	Mária	Galíková	SVK	21.8.80	8		Dudince	21 Mar
1:31:44	46:04	Valentina	Trapletti	ITA	12.7.85	5		La Coruña	6 Jun
1:31:49			Li Leilei	CHN	18.8.89	9	NC	Changbaishan	6 Sep
1:31:51		Beatriz	Pascual	ESP	9.5.82	2		Igualada	8 Feb
1:31:53		Paola	Pérez	ECU	21.12.89	3	PAm	Toronto	19 Jul
1:31:58		Ainhoa	Pinedo	ESP	17.2.83	10		Rio Maior	18 Apr
1:31:58		Susana	Feitor	POR	28.1.75	11		Rio Maior	18 Apr
1:32:01			Weon Aseas-byeol	KOR	8.4.90	2	NG	Gangneung	20 Oct
		(60)							
1:32:02	45:26	Sofiya	Brodatskaya	RUS	4.10.95	8	NC-w	Sochi	27 Feb
1:32:13	45:21	Nadezhda	Sergeyeva	RUS	6.11.94	5	EU23	Tallinn	10 Jul
1:32:16		Agnieszka	Szwarnóg	POL	28.12.86	2		Zaniemysl	18 Apr
1:32:20		Emilie	Menuet	FRA	27.11.91	21	ECp	Murcia	17 May
1:32:21	45:26	Tatyana	Mineyeva	RUS	10.8.90	9	NC-w	Sochi	27 Feb
1:32:21			Duan Dandan	CHN	23.5.95	1		Taicang	1 May
1:32:21		Alyona	Khramova	RUS	18.8.93	1	NCp	Cheboksary	6 Sep
1:32:22		Stephanie	Stigwood	AUS	21.10.90	2		Melbourne	13 Dec

Mark		Name		Nat	Born	Pos	Meet	Venue	Date
1:32:23	46:23	Mária	Czaková	SVK	2.10.88	2		Podébrady	11 Ap
1:32:27			Zhou Kang	CHN	24.12.89	2	NGP	Taicang	1 May
		(70)							
1:32:29		Monika	Kapera	POL	15.2.90	3		Zaniemysl	18 Ap
1:32:32	45:43	Katarzyna	Golba	POL	21.12.89	9		Dudince	21 Ma
1:32:34			He Qin	CHN	23.3.92	11	NC	Changbaishan	6 Sep
1:32:36	45:28	Darya	Bolkunets	BLR	4.3.93	6	EU23	Tallinn	10 Ju
1:32:38	45:32		Pei Mowen	CHN	17.9.95	12	WCT	Beijng	20 Ma
1:32:46	45:47	Sandra	Galvis	COL	28.6.86	12		Rio Maior	18 Ap
1:32:50		Alana	Barber	NZL	8.7.87	3		Melbourne	13 Dec
1:32:34		Ai	Michiguchi	JPN	3.6.88	1		Takahata	25 Oc
1:33:00		Lina	Kalutskaya	RUS	1.10.88	6	NC	Cheboksary	13 Jun
1:33:04		Rei	Inoue	JPN	23.7.91	6		Nomi	15 Ma
		(80)							
1:33:07	46:09	Déspina	Zapounídou	GRE	5.10.85	3		Alytus	12 Jun
1:33:07		Maria	Michta-Coffey	USA	23.6.86	7	PAm	Toronto	19 Ju
1:33:09	45:25		Lee Jeong-eun	KOR	13.9.94	7		Nomi	15 Ma
1:33:10		Federica	Ferraro	ITA	18.8.88	1		Riposto	1 Feb
1:33:27		Olena	Shumkina	UKR	24.1.88	2	NC	Oleksandriya	13 Jun
1:33:28	45:26	Anastasiya	Yatsevich	BLR	18.1.85	11	NC-w	Sochi	27 Feb
1:33:39			Li Ping	CHN	7.1.94	13	NC	Changbaishan	6 Sep
1:33:39			Ma Faying	CHN	30.8.93	14	NC	Changbaishan	6 Sep
1:33:43			Wang Di	CHN	30.8.92	15	NC	Changbaishan	6 Sep
1:33:43	46:25	Johanna	Atkinson	GBR	17.1.85	1		Hillingdon	4 Oc
		(90)							
1:33:49			Yang Mingxia	CHN	13.1.90	5	NGP	Taicang	1 May
1:33:50	45:50	Olga	Chudayeva	RUS	8.11.88	12	NC-w	Sochi	27 Feb
1:33:51	46:32	Antigóni	Drisbióti	GRE	21.3.84	6		Lugano	15 Ma
1:33:55			Li Maocuo	CHN	20.10.92	6	NGP	Taicang	1 May
1:33:58	46:05	Khushbir	Kaur	IND	9.7.93	13		Rio Maior	18 Ap
1:34:05		Tanya	Holliday	AUS	21.9.88	1	OCE Ch	Adelaide	22 Feb
1:34:12	46:02	Wendy	Cornejo	BOL	7.1.93	22	WCh	Beijing	28 Aug
1:34:13			Su Yingqiu	CHN	1.2.95	13	WCT	Beijing	20 Ma
1:34:16		Rachel	Tallent	AUS	20.2.93	4		Melbourne	13 Dec
1:34:18		Viktoriya	Rashchupkina	BLR	23.5.95	2	NC	Grodno	24 Ju
		(100)							

Mark	Name		Nat	Born	Date
1:34:20	Kristina	Saltanovic	LTU	20.2.75	18 Apr
1:34:21	Cisiane	Lopes	BRA	17.2.83	25 Oct
1:34:22	Maritza Rafaela	Poncio	GUA	3.12.94	9 May
1:34:29	Mariavittoria	Becchetti	ITA	12.12.94	29 Mar
1:34:29		Zhao Huimin	CHN	12.10.93	6 Sep
1:34:31	Claudia	Stef	ROU	25.2.78	17 May
1:34:31		Chen Zhen	CHN	3.11.94	6 Sep
1:34:34	Marina	Ignatova	RUS	6.6.95	27 Feb
1:34:41	Claudia	Balderrama	BOL	13.11.83	21 Mar
1:34:42	Tatyana	Gabellone	ITA	20.10.84	29 Mar
1:34:46	Miranda	Melville	USA	20.3.89	12 Apr
1:34:46	Lucie	Pelantová	CZE	7.5.86	17 May
1:34:47	Mayra Carolina	Herrera	GUA	20.12.88	18 Apr
1:34:48	Florida	Miniyanova	KAZ	1.7.92	13 Jun
1:34:50		Wang Yalan	CHN	19.2.93	6 Sep
1:34:53	Andreea	Arsine	ROU	14.9.88	26 Jul
1:34:55	Galina	Kichigina	KAZ	14.7.88	27 Feb
1:34:56	Anna	Tropareva	RUS	20.8.88	27 Feb
1:34:58		Kang Jinzi	CHN	25.1.90	1 May
1:34:58	Lidia	Sánchez-Puebla	ESP-J	17.7.96	6 Jun
1:35:04	Masumi	Fuchise	JPN	2.9.86	25 Oct
1:35:06	Rena	Goto	JPN	6.9.95	15 Mar
1:35:08	Magaly	Bonilla	ECU	8.2.92	25 Oct
1:35:14	Mária	Pérez	ESP-J	29.4.96	22 Mar
1:35:14	Amanda	Cano	ESP	19.8.94	6 Jun
1:35:18	Mami	Urabe (46:29)	JPN	18.1.88	15 Mar
1:35:22.4t	Violaine	Averous	FRA	15.3.85	15 Nov
1:35:32	Federica	Curiazzi	ITA	14.8.92	29 Mar
1:35:32	Kristina	Mikhaylova	RUS	16.10.92	13 Jun
1:35:34	Vasylyna	Vitovshchyk	UKR	30.4.90	19 Apr
1:35:36		Sapna	IND	2.1.88	15 Mar
1:35:37	Ayako	Fukuda	JPN	8.5.93	15 Mar
1:35:43	Daniela	Cardoso	POR	15.12.91	18 Apr
1:35:50		Yang Peili	CHN	7.8.94	6 Sep
1:36:02	Janeth	Guamán	ECU	15.1.88	25 Oct
1:36:04	Inès	Pastorino	FRA	20.10.92	8 Mar
1:36:07	Bethan	Davies	GBR	7.11.90	4 Oct
1:36:08	Corinne	Baudoin	FRA	22.2.80	17 May
1:36:14.0t	Jéssica	Hancco	PER	10.9.95	3 Oct
1:36:17	Kelly	Ruddick	AUS	19.4.73	22 Feb
1:36:18		Zhang Xuhong	CHN	2.1.94	20 Ma
1:36:24	Mariya	Volkova	RUS	25.5.95	27 Feb
1:36:26	Laura	Polli	SUI	7.9.83	28 Aug
1:36:29		Chen Chen	CHN	25.8.95	20 Ma
1:36:30	Kristina	Osipova	RUS	9.11.92	27 Feb
1:36:32	Mar	Juárez	ESP	27.9.93	22 Ma
1:36:33A	Lizbeth	Silva	MEX	30.9.89	7 Ma
1:36:36	Kaori	Kawazoe	JPN	30.5.95	25 Oc
1:36:42.1t	Ingrid	Hernández	COL	21.3.88	13 Jun
1:36:43	Serena	Pruner	ITA	21.5.86	15 Ma
1:36:49	Ana Veronica	Rodean	ROU	23.6.84	26 Ju
1:36:50	Tomomi	Maekawa	JPN	28.9.91	15 Feb
1:36:50		Yang Jiayu	CHN-J	18.2.96	10 Ju
1:36:56	Justyna	Swierczynska	POL	26.2.87	31 May
1:37:00	Agnese	Pastare	LAT	27.10.88	17 May
1:37:07	Nami	Kumagai	JPN-J	.96	25 Oc
1:37:18	Chahinez	Nasri	TUN-J	3.6.96	6 Jun
1:37:18		Dong Genmiao	CHN	16.7.94	6 Sep
1:37:19	Marie	Polli	SUI	28.10.80	25 Ap
1:37:27		Zhao Qianyuan	CHN	11.3.95	6 Sep
1:37:32		Xu Liqin	CHN	6.2.90	6 Sep
1:37:39		Zhang Xin	CHN	17.8.89	6 Sep
1:37:48		Tong Lingling	CHN	25.1.92	22 Ma
1:37:50	Mari	Olsson	SWE	27.4.86	19 Ap
1:37:50		Wang Chen	CHN	18.2.94	6 Sep
1:37:53	Olga	Ravayeva	RUS	13.4.95	27 Feb
1:37:56	Halyna	Yakovchuk	UKR	21.2.92	13 Jun
1:37:57	Regina	Rykova	KAZ	19.12.91	27 Feb
1:37:57		Ma Yue	CHN	2.2.94	6 Sep
1:37:58	Anna	Krakhmaleva	RUS	1.5.92	27 Feb
1:37:58	Fumiko	Okabe	JPN	8.7.90	15 Ma
1:37:58	Monica	Equihua	MEX	23.9.82	1 May
1:37:58	Ángela	Castro	BOL	21.2.93	6 Jun
1:37:59	Jessica	Ching Siu Nga	HKG	11.2.87	19 Ap
1:37:59	Nicole	Fagan	AUS	24.7.89	13 Dec
	(175)				

Continued on page 592

Name		Nat	Born	Ht/Wt	Event	2015 Mark	Pre-2015 Best

MEN'S INDEX 2015

thletes included are those ranked in the top 100s at standard (World Championships) events (plus shorter lists for 000m, 1M, 2000m and 3000m). Those with detailed biographical profiles are indicated in first column by:
* in this year's Annual, ^ featured in a previous year's Annual.

Name		Nat	Born	Ht/Wt	Event	2015 Mark	Pre-2015 Best
Abadía	Antonio	ESP	2.7.90	181/70	5000	13:26.98	13:30.91- 14
Abaraghi	Mohamed Hussein	IRI	5.1.95	175/70	200	20.47	20.63- 14
Abda	Harun	USA	1.1.90	178/64	800	1:46.33	1:45.55- 14
Abdelrahman	Ihab	EGY	1.5.89	194/96	JT	88.99	89.21- 14
Abdi	Bashir	BEL	10.2.89	178/64	3000	7:40.44	7:44.12- 14
					5000	13:06.10	13:20.61- 14
					10k	27:47.55	27:36.40- 14
Abera	Melaku	ETH	20.4.94	177/61	10k	27:55.19	27:42.35- 14
Abinet	Abiyot	ETH	10.5.89	168/54	5000	13:22.42	-0-
Abraham	Tadesse	SUI	12.8.82		HMar	60:42	61:25- 09
Abramchuk	Mikhail	BLR	15.11.92		SP	19.79	19.88- 14
Abromavicius	Aleksas	LTU	6.12.84	197/115	DT	62.75	63.32- 10
Abshero	Ayele	ETH	28.12.90	167/52	Mar	2:08:53	2:04:23- 12
Abubaker	Abbas	BRN-J	17.5.96	175/64	400	45.15	45.17- 14
Acea	Raidel	CUB	31.10.90	188/87	400	45.18	45.36A- 14, 45.90- 13
Acy	Tremayne	USA	21.1.95	173/70	100	10.16, 10.12w	10.41- 12, 10.20w -14
					200	20.17, 20.04w	21.01i, 20.90w- 14
Adams	Antoine	SKN	31.8.88	180/79	100	10.03	10.01, 10.00w- 13
					200	20.47A, 20.63, 20.24w	20.08- 14
Adams	Harry	USA	27.11.89	182/81	100	10.08	9.96- 12
					200	20.25	20.10- 12
Adams	Lyukman	RUS	24.9.88	194/87	LJ	8.01	7.47i- 05, 7.42- 07
					TJ	17.34	17.53- 12
Adams	Spencer	USA	10.9.89	188/84	110h	13.48	13.33- 14, 13.24w- 13
Addison	Jonathan	USA	27.2.95		LJ	7.87, 7.99w	7.74- 14
Adhana	Gebretsadik	ETH	16.7.92		Mar	2:08:38	2:06:21- 12
Adkins	Bradley	USA	30.12.93	190/79	HJ	2.29i, 2.25	2.23i, 2.21- 14
Adola	Guye	ETH	20.10.90	180/60	HMar	60:45	59:06- 14
Afewerki	Berhane	ERI	6.5.96		10k	28:04.07	28:45.83- 14
Afonin	Maksim	RUS	6.1.92		SP	20.06	19.30- 12
Ahmed	Mohammed	CAN	5.1.91	175/61	5000	13:10.00	13:18.88- 14
					10k	27:46.90	27:34.64- 12
Ahmed Hassan	Mustafa Amer	EGY	16.12.95	196/125	SP	20.57	19.19- 14
Aikines-Aryeetey	Harry	GBR	29.8.88	180/87	100	10.16	10.08- 13
Akamatsu	Ryoichi	JPN	2.5.95	182/60	HJ	2.25	2.18- 14
Akdag	Tarik Langat	TUR	16.6.88	176/60	3kSt	8:21.59	8:08.59- 11
Akins	Tyrone	NGR	6.1.86	180/79	110h	13.54	13.25- 08, 13.2w- 10
Akkas	Halil	TUR	1.7.83	174/60	3kSt	8:22.49	8:18.43- 07
Al-Amri	Tariq	KSA	23.12.90	174/57	5000	13:25.00	13:31.13- 14
Al-Daran	Ali Saad	KSA	17.4.90	185/65	800	1:45.50	1:46.08- 09
Al-Dawoodi	Sultan M.	KSA	16.6.77	180/110	DT	60.43	65.08- 12
Al-Dosari	Ahmad Fayez	KSA	6.9.79	180/75	LJ	8.11	8.12- 02
Al-Gamal	Mostafa	EGY	1.10.88	191/105	HT	79.90	81.27- 14
Al-Garni	Mohamed	QAT	2.7.92	178/66	1500	3:35.78	3:34.61- 11
Al-Haddad	Saleh Abdelaziz	KUW	7.4.86	179/65	LJ	7.90, 7.96w	8.02- 09, 8.05w- 07
Al-Harthi	Barakat	OMA	15.6.88	172/64	100	10.16, 10.05w	10.17- 11
Al-Hayrani	Jamal	QAT	26.5.93		800	1:46.16	1:47.61- 12
Al-Mandeel	Abdulaziz	KUW	22.5.89	175/66	110h	13.61, 13.32w	13.49- 14
Al-Mannai	Rashid Ahmed	QAT	18.6.88	187/75	TJ	16.47, 16.58w	16.40 -13
Al-Masrahi	Youssef	KSA	31.12.87	176/76	400	43.93	44.43- 14
Al-Mutairi	Meshal Khalifa	KUW-J	16.3.97	176/65	100	10.27, 10.06w	10.61 -14
Al-Yoha	Yacoub	KUW	31.1.93	185/70	110h	13.58, 13.37w	13.64- 14
Al-Zankawi	Essa Mohamed	KUW	17.10.92	179/100	DT	63.22	59.13 -13
Alaiz	Roberto	ESP	20.7.90	182/63	3kSt	8:19.85	8:24.53- 12
Alamirew	Yenew	ETH	27.5.90	175/57	3000	7:36.39	7:27.26- 11
					5000	13:05.53	12:48.77- 12
Alejandro	Eric	PUR	15.4.86	180/70	400h	49.23	49.07- 14
Alexander	Colby	USA	13.6.91	183/64	1500	3:36.56	3:41.45- 14
Ali	Ahmed	USA/SUD	15.11.93	180/80	200	20.46	20.66- 14
Alic	Hamza	BIH	20.1.79	186/127	SP	20.67	20.73- 13
Alkana	Antonio	RSA	12.4.90	185/77	110h	13.32	13.98A- 14, 14.00, 13.78Aw- 13
Allen	Nathon	JAM	28.10.95	178/68	400	45.30	46.11- 14
Almgren	Andreas	SWE	12.6.95	177/66	800	1:45.59	1:45.65 -14
Alowonle	Rilwan	NGR	12.12.93	175/66	400h	50.02	50.11- 14
Alves	Higor	BRA	23.2.94	181/75	LJ	8.07	8.18- 14
Aman	Mohammed	ETH	10.1.94	169/55	800	1:43.56	1:42.37- 13
Amankwah	Alex	USA/GHA	2.3.92	179/61	800	1:45.91	1:47.89- 14

Name		Nat	Born	Ht/Wt	Event	2015 Mark	Pre-2015 Best
Amare	Hailemariyam	ETH-J	22.2.97	165/50	3kSt	8:24.19	8:42.00- 14
* Amb	Kim	SWE	31.7.90	180/85	JT	82.40	84.61- 13
Amdouni	Mourad	FRA	21.1.88	175/60	1500	3:34.05	3:42.84- 07
Amezcua	Luis Alberto	ESP	1.5.92	183/67	20kW	1:22:03	1:22:19- 14
* Amos	Nijel	BOT	15.3.94	179/60	800	1:42.66	1:41.73- 12
Ampomah	John	GHA	11.7.90	187/90	JT	82.94	75.99- 14
Anastasákis	Mihaíl	GRE	3.12.94	183/92	HT	73.23	70.63- 14
^ Anderson	Jeshua	USA	22.6.89	187/84	400h	48.95	47.93- 11
Anderson	Nick	USA	28.4.95	186/77	110h	13.60	13.91, 13.82w- 14
André	Thiago	BRA	4.8.95	177/62	800	1:46.36	1:45.99 -14
					1500	3:35.90	3:40.59- 14
Andrade	Jordin	USA	5.5.92	183/73	400h	49.24	50.03- 14
Andrews	Robby	USA	29.3.91	177/68	800	1:45.98	1:44.71- 11
					1500	3:35.52	3:34.78- 12
Anichkin	Vitaliy	KAZ	11.11.88	176/60	20kW	1:23:16	1:25:39- 11
Anne	Mame-Ibra	FRA	7.11.89	184/70	400	45.26	45.44- 14
Aouad	Zouhaïr	BRN	7.4.89		5000	13:26.19	
^ Apak	Esref	TUR	3.1.82	186/105	HT	76.82	81.45- 05
Apolloni	Federico	ITA	14.3.87	187/90	DT	61.78	60.64- 14
Appier	Garrett	USA	15.10.92		SP	19.55i	18.15- 14
Arai	Hiroki	JPN	18.5.88	179/61	20kW	1:20:35	1:20:38- 14
					50kW	3:40:20	3:40:34- 14
* Arai	Ryohei	JPN	23.6.91	183/92	JT	84.66	86.83- 14
Araya	Edward	CHI	14.2.86	177/58	50kW	4:00:56A	4:00:31- 13
Arents	Mareks	LAT	6.8.86	190/90	PV	5.65	5.62- 13
* Arévalo	Eider	COL	9.3.93	165/58	20kW	1:20:41	1:19:45- 13
^ Arikan	Polat Kemboi	TUR	12.12.90	173/62	10k	28:05.64	27:38.81- 12
Arita	Stephen	KEN	26.6.88	165/54	10k	27:55.17A	29:43.5A- 14
					HMar	60:52	64:29- 10
Armbrust	Jacob	USA	22.2.94	203/109	DT	63.17	52.59- 14
Arnaudov	Tsanko	POR	14.3.92	192/118	SP	21.06	18.80- 14
Arnold	Mike	USA	13.8.90	190/84	PV	5.72A	5.70- 13
Arnold	Seth	USA	29.7.92	185/82	PV	5.50	5.51- 12
Arnos	Zacharias	CYP	24.11.86	186/77	TJ	16.26, 16.45w	16.72, 16.73w- 12
de Araújo	Luiz Alberto	BRA	27.9.87	190/90	Dec	8179(w)	8276- 12
Arrhenius	Leif	SWE	15.7.86	192/120	SP	20.21	20.50- 13
					DT	60.36	64.46- 11
Arrhenius	Niklas	SWE	10.9.82	192/125	DT	63.85A	66.22- 11
Arroyo	Andrés	PUR	7.6.95	171/61	800	1:46.49	1:47.57- 14
Art	Arnaud	BEL	28.1.93	185/83	PV	5.65	5.55- 14
Arteaga	Mauricio	ECU	8.8.88	173/65	20kW	1:22:37	1:21:46- 14
Asekun	Olabanji	USA	15.7.92		LJ	8.04w	7.80w- 14
* Ash	Ronnie	USA	2.7.88	188/86	110h	13.13	12.99- 14, 12.98w- 10
* Ashmeade	Nickel	JAM	7.4.90	184/87	100	9.91	9.90- 13
					200	20.18	19.85- 12
Atanasov	Zlatozar	BUL	12.12.89	191/77	TJ	16.59i, 16.46	17.09- 13
Atnafu	Yitayal	ETH	20.1.93	172/55	10k	27:50.70	
Augustyn	Rafal	POL	14.5.84	178/71	50kW	3:43:55	3:45:32- 14
Auzeil	Bastien	FRA	22.10.89	190/82	Dec	8147	8022- 13
^ Avan	Fatih	TUR	1.1.89	183/90	JT	81.45	85.60- 12
Ayalew	Aweke	BRN	23.2.93	170/54	5000	13:19.80	13:05.00- 13
Ayele	Abayneh	ETH	4.11.87	175/57	Mar	2:07:16	-0-
Baaru	Philemon	KEN	20.5.81		Mar	2:09:08	2:07:49- 12
* Bába	Jaroslav	CZE	2.9.84	196/82	HJ	2.31	2.37i, 2.36- 05
Babayev	Nazim	AZE-J	8.10.97	185/70	TJ	17.04	16.18- 14
Babicz	Matt	USA	.92	183/123	SP	19.96i, 19,52	19.43i, 19.27- 14
Bachir	Youssouf Hiss	DJI	.87	178/70	1500	3:36.96	3:38.70- 14
Bacon	Jaylen	USA-J	5.8.96	183/75	100	10.10	10.51- 14
Baden	Joel	AUS-J	1.2.96		HJ	2.26	2.29- 14
Badji	Ndiss Kaba	SEN	21.9.83	192/79	LJ	8.00	8.32- 09
Bailey	Aldrich	USA	6.2.94	183/70	200	20.30, 20.16w	20.66Ai- 14, 20.78, 20.49w- 12
					400	45.38	45.19- 12
Bailey	Daniel	ANT	9.9.86	173/70	100	10.11	9.91- 09
* Bailey	Ryan	USA	13.4.89	193/98	100	9.93, 9.89w	9.88- 10
Bailey	Tavis	USA	6.1.92	190/134	DT	62.20	64.51- 14
* Bailey-Cole	Kemar	JAM	10.1.92	195/84	100	9.92	9.93- 13
Baillio	Hayden	USA	22.7.91	186/141	SP	19.55	20.06- 14
Baines	Sam	AUS	8.2.91	188/82	110h	13.54	13.69- 14
Baji	Balázs	HUN	9.6.89	192/84	110h	13.44	13.29- 14
Baker	Ronnie	USA	15.10.93	178/73	100	10.05, 9.94w	10.21, 10.14w -14
Bakharev	Viktor	RUS	5.5.94	184/70	3kSt	8:32.45	8:37.26 -14

Name		Nat	Born	Ht/Wt	Event	2015 Mark	Pre-2015 Best
Balla	Abdulrahman Musaeb	QAT	19.3.89	175/60	800	1:43.82	1:43.93- 13
Balner	Michal	CZE	12.9.82	193/78	PV	5.82	5.76i, 5.73- 10, 5.75ex- 14
Balnuweit	Erik	GER	21.9.88	189/75	110h	13.56, 13.55w	13.44, 13.32w-13
Baloyes	Bernardo	COL	6.1.94	177/66	200	20.37A	20.43, 20.35Aw- 14
Baltaci	äïzkan	TUR	13.2.94	187/111	HT	70.74	72.89- 14
Baltadoúros	Dimítrios	GRE	1.10.89	180/70	TJ	16.60	16.45- 14
Banevicius	Sarunas	LTU	23.1.91	188/105	SP	19.63i	19.50- 13
Baniótis	Konstadínos	GRE	6.11.86	202/80	HJ	2.31	2.34- 13
Banks	Tremayne	USA	29.7.92	178/70	110h	13.62, 13.57w	13.68- 14
Banzeruk	Ivan	UKR	9.2.90	177/65	20kW	1:22:08	1:23:42- 13
					50kW	3:49:02	3:44:49- 14
Barber	Shawn	CAN	27.5.94	190/82	PV	5.93	5.75Ai- 14, 5.71- 13
Barnes	Will	USA	17.3.94	188/77	110h	13.56	13.86- 14
Barr	Thomas	IRL	24.7.92	183/73	400h	48.65	48.90- 14
Barras	Romain	FRA	1.8.80	193/84	Dec	8007	8453- 10
Barrineau	Tommy	FIN	28.8.88	188/82	Dec	7762	7654- 11
Barrios	Juan Luis	MEX	24.6.83	175/63	5000	13:15.71	13:09.81- 11
10k	28:12.91		27:28.82- 12		HMar	60:46	61:21- 13
Barroilhet	Gonzalo	CHI	19.8.86	196/96	Dec	7805	8065- 12
Barrondo	Erick	GUA	14.6.91	172/60	20kW	1:21:25	1:18:25- 12
					50kW	3:55:57	3:41:09- 13
de Barros	Bruno	BRA	7.1.87	178/70	200	20.41	20.16- 11
Barry	Trevor	BAH	14.6.83	190/77	HJ	2.29	2.32- 11
Barshim	Muamer Aissa	QAT	3.1.94	191/68	HJ	2.25i	2.28- 14
Barshim	Mutaz Essa	QAT	24.6.91	192/70	HJ	2.41i, 2.41	2.43- 14
Barsoton	Leonard	KEN	21.10.94	166/56	5000	13:16.25	13:19.04- 13
					10k	27:27.55	27:20.74- 14
Bascou	Dimitri	FRA	20.7.87	182/79	110h	13.16	13.25- 14
Bashan	Mikalay	RUS	18.11.92		HT	72.04	71.61- 14
Bates	Keandre	USA-J	24.5.96	181/75	LJ	8.02i, 7.97w	7.45- 14
Batson	Diondre	USA	13.7.92	188/75	100	9.94, 9.86w	10.04 -14, 10.01w- 13
Batzávalis	Paraskevás	GRE	25.11.94	185/85	JT	81.04	74.86- 14
Bayer	Andrew	USA	3.2.90	180/60	1500	3:36.77	3:34.47- 13
3000	7:48.59		7:43.84- 13		3kSt	8:18.08	8:25.71- 14
Baymukhambetov	Batyrkhan	KAZ	7.9.92	182/71	HJ	2.25	2.20- 14
Beach	Curtis	USA	22.7.90	183/75	Dec	8081	8083- 11
Bednarek	Sylwester	POL	28.4.89	198/75	HJ	2.30	2.32- 09
Beer	Lukás	SVK	23.8.89	186/73	HJ	2.25i, 2.20	2.26- 14
Behrenbruch	Pascal	GER	19.1.85	196/96	Dec	7826	8558- 12
Belferrar	Mohamed Amine	ALG	6.2.91	180/69	800	1:46.46	1:46.07- 13
Belhanbel	Nader	MAR	1.7.94	175/61	800	1:44.64	1:45.37- 14
Bell	Javere	JAM	20.9.92	184/73	400	45.56	45.08- 13
Belocian	Wilhem	FRA	22.6.95	178/78	110h	13.28	13.54- 14
Benard	Chris	USA	4.4.90	190/79	TJ	16.95	17.10- 14
Benedetti	Giordano	ITA	22.5.89	189/67	800	1:45.07	1:44.67- 13
Benjamin	Rai	ANT-J	27.7.97	191/77	400h	49.97	52.12- 14
Benmahdi	Khaled	ALG	22.10.88	180/68	800	1:46.06	1:46.59- 12
Bennett	Chris	GBR	17.12.89	188/115	HT	74.66	72.58- 14
Bensghir	Yassine	MAR	3.1.83	170/68	1500	3:34.29	3:33.04- 07
Benyahia	Amor	TUN	1.7.85	176/54	3kSt	8:19.30	8:14.05- 13
Berdeja	Cristian	MEX	21.6.81	169/58	50kW	3:50:19	3:52:18A- 12
Berian	Boris	USA	19.12.92	180/73	800	1:43.34	1:48.89- 13
Berry	Michael	USA	10.12.91	184/73	400	45.13	44.75- 12
Bertemes	Bob	LUX	24.5.93	187/118	SP	20.56i, 19,87	19.45i, 19.36- 14
Bertolini	Roberto	ITA	9.10.85	187/100	JT	80.97	78.10- 08
Beshr	Anas	EGY	19.7.93	188/77	400	45.61	45.59A, 45.60- 14
Bett	Bernard	KEN	4.1.93		HMar	60:43	60:46- 14
Bett	David	KEN	18.10.92	160/52	10k	28:07.4A	-0-
Bett	Emmanuel	KEN	30.3.83	170/55	5000	13:22.0+	13:08.35- 12
10k	27:22.34		26:51.16- 12		HMar	60:08	60:56- 12
Bett	Josphat	KEN	12.6.90	173/60	10k	27:40.20	26:48.99- 11
Bett	Kipyegon	KEN-Y	2.1.98		800	1:44.55A	1:52.45A -14
Bett	Nicholas	KEN-J	20.12.96	172/52	3kSt	8:19.26	8:28.83- 14
Bett	Nicholas	KEN	14.6.92	186/77	400h	47.79	49.03- 14
Beukes	Adriaan	BOT	14.7.94	183/82	JT	80.49A	76.52- 14
Beyo	Chala	ETH-J	18.1.96	174/57	3kSt	8:25.82	8:25.45- 14
Bezabeh	Alemayehu	ESP	22.9.86	182/53	5000	13:16.98	12:57.25- 10
Bian Tongda		CHN	1.4.91	170/58	50kW	3:59:30	4:15:02- 14
Bilderback	Zack	USA	27.8.93	193/80	400	45.53	45.66- 14
Bilodeau	Mathieu	CAN	27.11.83	185/73	50kW	4:01:35	3:59:48- 14
Bird-Smith	Dane	AUS	15.7.92	178/66	20kW	1:20:05	1:20:27- 14

	Name		Nat	Born	Ht/Wt	Event	2015 Mark	Pre-2015 Best
*	Birech	Jairus	KEN	14.12.92	167/56	3kSt	7:58.83	7:58.41- 14
*	Birgen	Bethwel	KEN	6.8.88	178/64	1500	3:34.62i	3:30.77- 13
						3000	7:43.77i	7:37.15- 13
	Birkinhead	Damien	AUS	8.4.93	190/130	SP	20.40	19.69- 14
	Birmingham	Collis	AUS	27.12.84	189/71	3000	7:39.85	7:35.45- 12
						5000	13:17.49	13:09.57- 12
*	Biwott	Robert	KEN-J	28.1.96	180/68	800	1:43.56	1:44.69- 14
						1500	3:30.10	3:36.77- 13
*	Biwott	Stanley	KEN	21.4.86	176/60	HMar	59:20	58:56- 13
						Mar	2:06:41	2:04:55- 14
	Blair-Sanford	Donald	ISR	5.2.87	193/84	400	45.04	45.21- 10
*	Blake	Yohan	JAM	26.12.89	181/79	100	10.12	9.69- 12
	Blankenship	Ben	USA	15.12.89	173/61	1500	3:35.48, 3:25.28i	3:37.03- 13
	1M 3:53.13i 3:54.10- 11		3000 7:38.08 7:46.55i- 14, 7:47.07- 13			2M	8:16.53i	
	Blankenship	Jacob	USA	15.3.94	183/79	PV	5.80i, 5.80	5.64- 14
*	Bledman	Keston	TTO	8.3.88	183/75	100	9.86	9.86, 9.85w- 12
	Blocki	Adrian	POL	11.4.90	173/63	50kW	3:49:11	3:50:48- 13
	Blocki	Damian	POL	28.4.89	180/65	50kW	3:53:55	3:51:32- 13
	Bloomfield	Akeem	JAM-J	10.11.97	188/77	400	44.93	
	Blum	Christian	GER	10.3.87	179/62	100	10.05w	10.20- 14, 10.19w- 10
	Blundell	Theo	GBR	30.11.95	181/70	800	1:46.43	1:48.20- 14
	Bocchi	Tobia	ITA-J	7.4.97	187/80	TJ	16.54	16.04- 14
	Bodie	Patrick	BAH	27.3.92	186/77	400h	49.63	52.70 -14
	Bohdan	Maksym	UKR	27.2.94	184/84	JT	81.83	83.41- 14
	Boirie	Baptiste	FRA	26.12.92	171/65	PV	5.50i, 5.50	5.50- 12
	Bol	Peter	AUS	22.2.94	168/57	800	1:46.51	1:47.97- 14
*	Bolt	Usain	JAM	21.8.86	196/88	100	9.79	9.58- 09
						200	19.55	19.19--09
	Bondarenko	Artyom	BLR	19.6.91			16.26, 16.74w?	
*	Bondarenko	Bogdan	UKR	30.8.89	197/80	HJ	2.37	2.42- 14
	Bondarenko	Krystian	POL	22.10.91	187/86	JT	78.06	73.14- 13
	Bonevacia	Liemarvin	NED	5.4.89	180/81	400	44.72	45.41- 14
*	Bonfim	Caio	BRA	19.3.91	170/58	20kW	1:20:44	1:20:28- 14
						50kW	4:02:20	-0-
	Bonvecchio	Norbert	ITA	14.8.85	183/82	JT	79.45	80.37- 14
	Bor	Nicholas	KEN	27.4.88		HMar	60:09	61:03- 14
	Bore	Ambrose	KEN	8.8.95		5000	13:23.80	13:31.64- 14
	Boreysha	Pavel	BLR	16.2.91	193/105	HT	77.03	76.86- 14
	Borichevskiy	Konstantin	BLR	29.5.90		LJ	8.17, 8.22w	7.90- 14
	Borlée	Dylan	BEL	20.9.92	190/77	400	45.57	45.80- 13
*	Borlée	Jonathan	BEL	22.2.88	180/70	200	20.45	20.31- 12
						400	44.67	44.43- 12
*	Borlée	Kévin	BEL	22.2.88	180/71	400	44.74	44.56- 12
	Bortolato	Marco	ITA	11.2.94	189/107	HT	70.85	70.15- 14
	Bortoluzzi	Jérôme	FRA	20.5.82	180/111	HT	74.01	78.26- 12
*	Bosse	Pierre-Ambroise	FRA	11.5.92	185/68	800	1:43.88	1:42:53- 14
	Bosworth	Tom	GBR	17.1.90	184/54	20kW	1:22:33	1:22:20- 14
	Bouchicha	Hichem	ALG	19.5.89	183/70	3kSt	8:24.65	8:20.11- 13
	Boukamouche	Saber	ALG	20.4.92	194/79	400h	49.43	49.90- 14
*	Bouraada	Larbi	ALG	10.5.88	187/84	Dec	8461	8332dq- 12, 8311- 14
	Boyce	Brendan	IRL	15.10.86	183/76	50kW	3:48:55	3:51:34- 14
	Boyez	Antonin	FRA	9.11.84	185/72	20kW	1:23:24	1:22:21- 14
*	Bracy	Marvin	USA	15.12.93	175/74	100	9.93	10.08- 14, 10.05w- 11
	Bramble	Daniel	GBR	14.10.90	178/76	LJ	8.21	7.91- 13
	Branch	Drew	USA	13.5.93	186/79	400h	49.53	50.41- 14
	Brannen	Nathan	CAN	8.9.82	175/59	1500	3:35.42	3:34.22- 12
*	Brathwaite	Shane	BAR	8.2.90	185/75	110h	13.21	13.24- 14
	Braun	Pieter	NED	21.1.93	182/80	Dec	8197	7892- 14
	Bravo	Albert	VEN	29.8.87	198/85	400	45.26	45.21A- 14, 45.61- 12
*	Braz da Silva	Thiago	BRA	16.12.93	193/84	PV	5.92	5.83- 13
	Brembach	Nils	GER	23.2.93	184/68	20kW	1:21:21	1:23:44- 14
^	Brenes	Nery	CRC	25.9.85	174/62	400	44.80A, 44.85	44.65A- 11, 44.84- 10
	Brock	David	AUS	8.6.94	186/85	Dec	7733	7341- 14
	Brockman	Martin	GBR	13.11.87	197/92	Dec	7630	7712- 10
*	Bromell	Trayvon	USA	10.7.95	175/71	100	9.84, 9.76w	9.97, 9.77w -14
						200	20.03, 19.86w	20.59, 20.23w- 14
	Brondyke	Kurtis	USA	24.1.89	198/93	Dec	7689(w)	7613- 14
	Brookins	Ronald	USA	5.7.89	185/75	110h	13.57	13.42- 11
						LJ	8.08w	7.74, 7.87w- 13
	Brooks	Lance	USA	1.1.84	198/123	DT	61.00A	65.15- 12
	Brown	Aaron	CAN	27.5.92	185/79	100	10.10, 10.03w	10.05, 10.01w- 13
						200	20.30, 20.11w	20.16, 20.02w- 14

Name		Nat	Born	Ht/Wt	Event	2015 Mark	Pre-2015 Best
Brown	Chris	BAH	15.10.78	178/68	400	44.54	44.40- 08
Brown	Jermaine	JAM	4.7.91	183/80	200	20.51	20.28A, 20.29- 14
Brown	Kemarley	JAM	20.7.92	180/72	100	10.11	9.93 -14
Brown	Rodney	USA	21.5.93	183/109	DT	65.04	64.68- 14
Brown	Trevor	USA	24.3.92	183/79	400h	49.67A, 49.79	49.64A, 49.89- 14
Brugger	Mathias	GER	6.8.92	192/93	Dec	8009	7942- 12
Bruintjies	Henricho	RSA	16.7.93	182/73	100	9.97	10.26, 10.17A -14, 10.06Aw-dt- 13
Bryan	Christoffe	JAM-J	26.4.96	193/75	HJ	2.28i, 2.24	2.24- 14
Brzozowski	Krzysztof	POL	15.7.93	190/115	SP	19.57	19.18- 11
Bube	Andreas	DEN	13.7.87	178/65	800	1:45.78	1:44.89- 12
Bubeník	Matús	SVK	14.11.89	197/78	HJ	2.31i, 2.29	2.27- 14
Bucki	Gaëtan	FRA	9.5.80	195/135	SP	20.18	20.39i- 11, 20.21- 14
Budza	Sergiy	UKR	6.12.84	180/75	50kW	3:51:33	3:47:36- 13
Bühler	Matthias	GER	2.9.86	189/74	110h	13.34	13.34- 12, 13.20w- 14
Bukowiecki	Konrad	POL-J	17.3.97	191/129	SP	20.78	17.29i- 14
Bulanov	Aleksandr	RUS	26.12.89	193/120	SP	19.99	19.92i ,19.81-13
Bultheel	Michaël	BEL	30.6.86	189/81	400h	49.04	49.10- 12
Buraas	Sindre	NOR	8.5.89	183/64	5000	13:11.96	13:15.91- 13
Burka	Gebo	ETH	27.9.87		Mar	2:08:12	2:10:18- 09
Burrell	Cameron	USA	11.9.94	173/68	LJ	8.06A, 7.82, 8.17w	7.73- 14
Burton	Tom	GBR	29.10.88	178/68	400h	49.36	49.66- 14
Burya	Artem	RUS	11.4.86	185/82	PV	5.65	5.61- 14
Busendich	Ishmael	KEN	7.7.91		Mar	2:09:00	2:08:25- 14
Bush	Darrell	USA	13.5.93	175/70	400	45.49	46.15- 13
Bustamante	Luis	MEX	10.6.84		50kW	3:52:17A	3:54:00A- 14
Bustos	David	ESP	25.8.90	182/65	1500	3:35.97	3:34.77- 12
Butenko	Viktor	RUS	10.3.93	196/116	DT	65.44	65.97- 13
Butler	Quentin	USA	18.9.92	175/70	100	9.96	10.33, 10.24w- 13
Butrym	Vitaliy	UKR	10.1.91	180/75	400	45.01	45.88- 13
Bychkov	Igor	ESP	7.3.87	189/80	PV	5.55	5.65- 13
Cabral	Donn	USA	12.12.89	175/60	3kSt	8:13.37	8:19.14- 12
Cabral	Johnathan	CAN	31.12.92	193/82	110h	13.37, 13.22w	13.45- 12, 13.33w- 13
Cáceres	Eusebio	ESP	10.9.91	175/68	LJ	8.16i, 8.06	8.37- 13
Cáceres	Jonathan	ECU	20.1.90		50kW	4:00:58	3:50:52- 14
Cadée	Erik	NED	15.2.84	201/120	DT	64.57	67.30- 12
Cadogan	Levi	BAR	8.11.95	171/68	100	10.06, 10.01Aw	10.25, 10.24w -14
Caesa	Leslie	CUB-J	14.1.97		TJ	16.48, 16.83w	15.76, 15.91w- 14
Cai Zelin		CHN	11.4.91	172/55	20kW	1:19:45	1:18:47- 12
Cairoli	Simone	ITA	12.9.90		Dec	7611	7322- 14
Cakss	Gatis	LAT	13.6.95	185/83	JT	80.06	77.26- 14
Caldwell	Chris	USA	5.4.94	188/88	110h	13.56	13.84, 13.69w- 14
Callahan	Peter	USA	1.6.91	183/68	1500	3:37.88	3:39.27- 14
Camara	Alyn	GER	31.3.89	195/85	LJ	8.22	8.29- 13
Campbell	Kemoy	JAM	14.1.91	165/57	5000	13:20.39	13:32.82- 13
Campion	Kevin	FRA	23.5.88	183/63	20kW	1:21:34	1:20:39- 14
Cantero	Bryan	FRA	28.4.91	178/64	1500	3:36.84	3:36.08- 14
Cantwell	Christian	USA	30.9.80	193/154	SP	21.64	22.54- 04
Cao Shuo		CHN	8.10.91	183/69	TJ	16.77, 16.98w	17.35- 12
Caporaso	Teodorico	ITA	14.9.87	166/60	50kW	3:51:44	3:56:45- 13
Capotosti	Leonardo	ITA	24.7.88	192/78	400h	49.93	50.05- 14
Carbonell	Julio César	CUB-Y	16.5.99		TJ	16.21, 16.60w	15.07, 15.35w- 14
Carnes	Brandon	USA	-.3.95	175/73	100	10.10w	10.42 -14
					200	20.31w	20.98, 20.97w- 14
Carper	Chris	USA	19.4.92	186/86	JT	78.08	73.09- 14
Carrere	Martin	FRA	31.10.90	184/74	400h	50.05	51.12- 14
Carro	Fernando	ESP	1.4.92	175/67	3kSt	8:21.78	8:35.51- 12
Carter	Chris	USA	11.3.89	186/80	TJ	16.71i, 16.70	17.15Ai, 17.09- 14
Carter	Deuce	JAM	28.9.90	182/75	110h	13.49A, 13.53	13.51A- 14, 13.53- 13
Carter	Nesta	JAM	10.11.85	178/70	100	9.98	9.78- 10
Casañas	Frank	ESP	18.10.78	187/115	DT	61.49	67.91- 08
Caspari	Marvin	GER	9.8.91	179/78	PV	5.53	5.45- 14
Castillo	Maurys Surel	CUB	19.10.84	182/60	800	1:46.04	1:44.89- 12
Cato	Roxroy	JAM	1.5.88	183/76	400h	48.72	48.48- 14
Cedenio	Machel	TTO	6.9.95	183/70	400	44.36	45.13- 14
Centrowitz	Matthew	USA	18.10.89	175/61	800	1:44.62	1:45.86- 13
1000	2:17.00i 2:19.56i- 13	1500	3:30.40	3:31.09- 14	1M	3:51.20	3:50.53- 14
Chacha	Joseph	KEN	4.9.92		5000	13:26.25	13:52.16- 13
Chala	Regasa	ETH-J	.97		1500	3:37.24	3:38.06- 14
Chalyy	Timofey	RUS	7.4.94	190/79	400h	48.69	48.69- 14
Chambers	Marcus	USA	3.11.94	178/75	400	44.95	46.55- 13
Chambers	Ricardo	JAM	7.10.84	177/73	400	44.93A, 45.56	44.54- 10

Name		Nat	Born	Ht/Wt	Event	2015 Mark	Pre-2015 Best
Chang Ming-Huang		TPE	7.8.82	194/130	SP	19.56	20.58- 11
Chapelle	Axel	FRA	24.4.95	180/79	PV	5.55	5.55- 14
^ Charfreitag	Libor	SVK	11.9.77	191/117	HT	73.82	81.81- 03
Chatbi	Jamal	ITA	30.4.84	178/62	3kSt	8:30.35	8:08.86- 09
Chavez	Richard	USA	30.7.92	178/115	SP	19.61i, 19.37	20.06i- 13, 18.43- 12
Chavkin	Nikolay	RUS	24.4.84	183/70	3kSt	8:23.0	8:22.81- 12
Chebet	Evans Kiplagat	KEN	5.3.88		Mar	2:08:50	2:07:46- 14
Chebet	Wilson	KEN	12.7.85	174/59	Mar	2:08:45	2:05:27- 11
Chebii	Ezekiel	KEN	3.1.91		Mar	2:07:18	2:09:15- 14
Chebogut	Stephen	KEN	.85		HMar	60:19	62:41- 12
					Mar	2:05:52	2:08:02- 11
* Cheboi	Collins	KEN	25.9.87	175/64	1500	3:30.34	3:31.53- 13
					1M	3:52.63	3:49.56- 14
Chematot	Evans	BRN-J	19.3.96	174/70	3kSt	8:33.52	8:32.61- 14
Chemlal	Hicham	MAR-J	2.12.97		3kSt	8:28.78	8:41.0- 14
Chemlal	Jaouad	MAR	11.4.94	177/59	3kSt	8:31.10	8:19.22- 13
Chemlany	Stephen	KEN	9.8.82	175/64	Mar	2:08:21	2:06:24- 14
Chemosin	Robert	KEN	1.2.89		HMar	59:37	59:19- 13
					Mar	2:08:05	-0-
Chen Chieh		TPE	8.5.92	174/55	400h	49.05	49.68- 12
* Chen Ding		CHN	5.8.92	180/62	20kW	1:18:44	1:17:40- 12
Cheng Chao-Tsun		TPE	17.10.93	182/88	JT	81.78	81.61- 14
Cheng Wen		CHN	18.3.92	187/77	400h	49.56	49.28- 11
Cheprot	Simon	KEN	2.7.93	183/62	HMar	59:32	59:20- 13
^ Chepseba	Nixon	KEN	12.12.90	185/66	1500	3:36.37, 3:35.28i	3:29.77- 12
3000	7:42.65i		7:37.64i- 11		5000	13:30.20	13:26.28- 14
* Cheptegei	Joshua	UGA-J	12.9.96	167/52	10k	27:27.57	27:56.26- 14
Cherabi	Hicham	ALG	30.3.93	185/75	PV	5.50	5.20- 14
^ Cherkos	Abreham	ETH	23.9.89	163/52	Mar	2:08:14	2:07:08- 14, 2:06:13wdh- 11
Chernov	Yevgeniy	RUS	9.11.91		Dec	7600	7231- 13
Cheroben	Abreham	KEN	10.11.92	174/58	HMar	59:10	58:48- 14
Cherry	Michael	USA	23.3.95	186/75	400	45.43	45.37- 14
* Cheruiyot	Ferguson	KEN	30.11.89	183/73	800	1:43.60A	1:42.84- 14
Cheruiyot	John	KEN	5.7.90	167/55	Mar	2:08:56	-0-
* Cheruiyot	Timothy	KEN	20.11.95	178/64	1500	3:34.86A	-0-
Chesani	Silvano	ITA	17.7.88	190/75	HJ	2.31i	2.33i, 2.31 -13
Chesebe	Abednego	KEN	20.6.82	174/62	1500	3:37.4A	3:35.02A- 12
Cheserek	Edward	KEN	2.2.94	168/57	1500	3:37.08	3:36.50 -14
Chiaraviglio	Germán	ARG	16.4.87	192/77	PV	5.75	5.71- 06
Chiari	Andrea	ITA	12.2.91	186/70	TJ	16.49	16.85i, 16.83- 12
* Chimsa	Deressa	ETH	21.11.86	175/62	Mar	2:07:56	2:05:42- 12
* Chizhikov	Dmitriy	RUS	6.12.93		TJ	17.20	16.51- 14
Chmielak	Hubert	POL	19.6.89	188/88	JT	82.28	82.58- 14
* Chocho	Andrés	ECU	4.11.83	167/67	20kW	1:20:40	1:21:26- 13
					50kW	3:46:00	3:49:26- 12
Chopra	Neeraj	IND-J	24.12.97	188/86	JT	81.04	70.19- 14
* Chumba	Dickson	KEN	27.10.86	167/50	Mar	2:06:34	2:04:32- 14
Chumo	Victor	KEN	1.1.87	175/59	5000	13:20.34	13:12.67- 12
Churkor	Patrick	KEN	17.2.91	177/58	3kSt	8:25.54	8:42.3A- 11
Churyla	Andrey	BLR	19.5.93	190/72	HJ	2.26i, 2.20	2.30- 14
Cienfuegos	Javier	ESP	15.7.90	193/134	HT	74.76	76.71- 13
^ Cisneros	Omar	CUB	19.11.89	186/80	400h	49.26	47.93- 13
Clark	Ryan	USA-J	14.9.96	185/77	200	20.46	20.98- 14
Clarke	Andre	JAM	6.6.92		400h	49.87	51.17- 13
* Clarke	Jordan	USA	10.7.90	193/125	SP	21.49	21.37- 14
* Clarke	Lawrence	GBR	12.3.90	187/78	110h	13.39	13.31, 13.14w- 12
^ Clavier	Jérôme	FRA	3.5.83	185/73	PV	5.61i, 5.50	5.81i- 11, 5.75- 08
* Claye	Will	USA	13.6.91	180/68	LJ	8.07, 8.11w	8.29- 11
					TJ	17.48, 17.50w	17.75- 14
Clemens	Daniel	GER	28.4.92	181/74	PV	5.55i, 5.52	5.60- 13
* Clement	Kerron	USA	31.10.85	188/84	400h	48.18	47.24- 05
Clemons	Kyle	USA	27.8.90	181/73	400	44.84	45.00- 14
Cochrane	Michael	NZL	13.8.91	188/82	400h	49.58	49.72- 14
Cocioran	Marius	ROU	10.7.83	178/66	50kW	3:55:59	3:57:52- 12
* Coertzen	Willem	RSA	30.12.82	186/80	Dec	8398	8343- 13
Coleman	Greg	USA	24.7.93	190/79	400h	49.70	49.60- 14
Collie-Minns	Latario	BAH	10.3.94	173/64	TJ	17.18, 17.25w	16.91, 17.12w- 14
* Collins	Kim	SKN	5.4.76	175/64	100	9.98, 9.94w	9.96- 14, 9.92w- 03
* Compaoré	Benjamin	FRA	5.8.87	189/86	TJ	17.01	17.48- 14
Contreras	Yidiel	ESP	27.11.92	186/73	110h	13.35	13.71- 14, 13.5- 11
Coover	Jeff	USA	1.12.87	185/77	PV	5.68i, 5.50	5.60- 13

Name		Nat	Born	Ht/Wt	Event	2015 Mark	Pre-2015 Best
Copello	Alexis	ex-CUB	12.8.85	185/80	TJ	17.15,17.24w	17.68A- 11, 17.65,17.69w- 09
Copello	Yasmani	TUR	15.4.87	196/86	400h	48.46	49.56- 09
Corchete	Luis Manuel	ESP	14.5.84	185/74	50kW	4:02:29	3:59:58- 12
Corréa	Harold	FRA	26.6.88	190/78	TJ	16.81, 16.87w	16.94i, 16.92- 13
Corrales	Víctor José	ESP	12.3.89	186/65	1500	3:37.70	3:38.91- 13
Cortéz	Alvaro	CHI	27.10.95	188/82	TJ	16.52	15.88, 15.97w- 14
Cotton	Terrel	USA	19.7.88	182/73	200	20.16	20.48A,20.39Aw,20.66- 12,20.41w- 13
Couto	Kurt	MOZ	14.5.85	180/67	400h	49.15	49.02- 12
Cowart	Donnie	USA	24.10.85	170/60	3kSt	8:27.86	8:26.38- 11
Craddock	Kevin	USA	25.6.87	193/84	110h	13.48	13.42- 12, 13.41w- 08
Craddock	Omar	USA	26.4.91	178/79	TJ	17.53	16.98, 17.26w- 14
Cranston	Kyle	AUS	3.9.92		Dec	7629	7394- 13
Cray	Eric	PHI	6.11.88	176/73	400h	49.12	50.00- 14
Cremona	Orazio	RSA	1.7.89	192/130	SP	20.49	20.63- 14
Crittenden	Freddie	USA	3.8.94	183/73	110h	13.62	13.73- 14
Cronje	Johan	RSA	13.4.82	182/69	1500	3:36.34	3:31.93- 13
					1M	3:53.02	3:50.70- 14
Crouser	Ryan	USA	18.12.92	201/120	SP	21.14i. 21.11	21.39- 14
Crouser	Sam	USA	31.12.91	196/102	JT	83.33	80.80- 12
Crowther	Robert	AUS	2.8.87	188/77	LJ	8.05	8.12- 11, 8.15w- 07
Cuesta	Gustavo	DOM	14.11.88	183/80	400	45.09A, 45.33	45.45A- 13, 45.78- 10
Cuesta	Pedro José	ESP	22.8.83	187/108	DT	60.59	61.95- 11
Culson	Javier	PUR	25.7.84	198/79	400h	48.48	47.72- 10
Curtis	Bobby	USA	28.11.84	182/68	10k	27:56.59	27:24.67- 11
Cutts	Luke	GBR	13.2.88	192/82	PV	5.60i, 5.60	5.83i- 14, 5.70- 13
Czajkowski	Przemyslaw	POL	26.10.88	197/108	DT	62.70	65.61- 12
Czerwinski	Przemyslaw	POL	28.7.83	185/80	PV	5.56	5.82i- 10, 5.80- 06
Dacres	Fedrick	JAM	28.2.94	191/97	DT	66.40	66.75- 14
Dagée	Frédéric	FRA	11.12.92	192/103	SP	19.87	19.05- 14
Dagher	Mustapha Katem	IRQ	29.11.95	180/81	DT	60.60	59.52- 14
Dahm	Tobias	GER	23.5.87	203/117	SP	19.97i, 19.93	19.96- 13
Dahmani	Samir	FRA	3.4.91	183/65	800	1:45.62	1:46.74- 10
					1500	3:37.05	3:38.01- 10
Dairokuno	Shuho	JPN	23.12.92	168/51	10k	27:46.55	28:40.88- 13
Dangel	Josh	USA	21.1.91	184/79	PV	5.50i, 5.42	5.44- 14
Darien	Garfield	FRA	22.12.87	187/76	110h	13.17	13.15- 12
Dasaolu	James	GBR	5.9.87	180/75	100	10.12	9.91- 13
Dasor	Emmanuel	GHA	14.9.95	180/68	400	45.61A	
Dauphin	Tumatai	FRA/PYF	12.1.88	188/138	SP	20.10i, 19.82	19.76- 13
Davis	Wayne	TTO	22.8.91	178/72	110h	13.59	13.20- 14, 13.14w- 13
Days	Braheme	USA	18.1.95	185/136	SP	19.61	18.99- 14
De Borger	Dario	BEL	20.3.92	179/70	110h	13.56	13.59- 13
De Grasse	Andre	CAN	10.11.94	180/73	100	9.92, 9.75w	10.15 -14, 9.96w- 13
					200	19.88, 19.58w	20.38- 14
De Luca	Marco	ITA	12.5.81	189/72	20kW	1:22:13	1:22:38- 10
					50kW	3:46:21	3:45:25- 14
de Sá	Mateus Daniel	BRA	21.11.95	183/73	TJ	16.46	16.47- 14
de Souza	Éder Antônio	BRA	15.10.86	189/85	110h	13.46	13.58 -07
Dean	Genki	JPN	30.12.91	182/88	JT	77.51	84.28- 12
Debela	Dejene	ETH	.94	180/62	3000	7:43.94	
					5000	13:25.70	13:26.67- 14
DeChant	Matt	USA	31.5.89	195/115	SP	19.74	19.82i- 11, 19.57- 12
Dechasa	Shumi	BRN	28.5.89	172/54	Mar	2:07:20	2:06:43- 14
Dechase	Chala	ETH	13.6.84	167/52	Mar	2:08:11	2:06:33- 10
Dedewo	Paul	USA	5.6.91	185/73	400	45.41	48.17- 11
Dei Tos	Leonardo	ITA	27.4.92	175/56	20kW	1:22:58	1:27:10- 14
Demczyszak	Mateusz	POL	18.1.86	176/62	3kSt	8:31.82	8:22.38 -14
Dendy	Marquis	USA	17.11.92	190/75	LJ	8.39, 8.68w	8.28i, 8.10, 8.29w- 13
					TJ	17.50, 17.71w	16.52, 17.05w- 14
Dennis	Thurgood	USA	30.9.92	183/81	100	10.12w	10.28, 10.27w- 14
Denny	Matthew	AUS-J	2.6.96	195/115	DT	62.58	59.04- 14
Derrick	Chris	USA	17.10.90	180/64	3000	7:43.77	7:44.01- 13
					5000	13:19.56	13:08.04- 13
Desisa	Lelisa	ETH	14.1.90	170/52	Mar	2:05:52	2:04:45- 13
Dheeb	Ahmed Mohamed	QAT	29.9.85	195/113	DT	63.01	63.70. 64.56dq- 10
D'Hoedt	Jeroen	BEL	10.1.90	182/59	3kSt	8:30.03	8:46.96- 11
Dia	Mamadou Cherif	MLI	13.3.85	182/70	TJ	16.55	16.46 -13
Diarra	Abdoulaye	MLI	27.5.88	184/82	HJ	2.25	2.27i- 09, 2.25- 12
Diaz	Andy	CUB	25.12.95	180/68	TJ	16.81	16.38, 16.43w- 14
Díaz	Carlos	CHI	9.7.93	174/58	1500	3:37.86	3:40.24- 14
Díaz	Junior	CUB	28.4.87	193/80	LJ	7.94	8.02- 13, 8.10w- 14

MEN'S INDEX

Name		Nat	Born	Ht/Wt	Event	2015 Mark	Pre-2015 Best
Dibaba Tola	Seboka	ETH	10.11.87	172/53	Mar	2:07:33	2:06:17- 12
Dida	Bonse	ETH	21.1.95		HMar	60:19	61:12- 14
Dilla	Karsten	GER	17.7.89	189/80	PV	5.60	5.73i, 5.72- 11
Dimitrov	Rumen	BUL	19.9.86	175/77	TJ	16.87	16.69, 16.77w- 14
* Diniz	Yohann	FRA	1.1.78	185/69	20kW	1:17:02	1:17:43- 12
^ Dix	Walter	USA	31.1.86	178/84	100	10.17, 10.13w	9.88- 10, 9.80w- 08
					200	20.59, 20.41w	19.53- 11
Djouhan	Lolassonn	FRA	18.5.91	188/118	DT	61.52	61.70- 13
Djoumessi	Fernand	CMR	5.9.89	189/75	HJ	2.25	2.28- 14
* Dmitrik	Aleksey	RUS	12.4.84	191/69	HJ	2.32	2.40i- 14, 2.36- 11
* Dmytrenko	Ruslan	UKR	22.3.86	180/62	20kW	1:21:25	1:18:37- 14
* Dobek	Patryk	POL	13.2.94	183/75	400h	48.40	49.13- 14
Dodson	Jeremy	SAM	30.8.87	184/75	200	20.31	20.33, 20.07w- 11
Doerflein	Cody	USA	11.6.90	181/82	PV	5.50	5.35- 12
Dohmann	Carl	GER	18.5.90	182/60	20kW	1:22:24	1:21:42- 14
					50kW	3:50:12	3:51:27- 14
Dolezal	Riley	USA	16.11.85	188/100	JT	81.62	83.50- 13
Dolve	Eirik Greibrokk	NOR	5.5.95	185/80	PV	5.50	5.35 -14
Domingos	Wágner	BRA	23.6.83	183/126	HT	74.20	75.47- 14
* Donato	Fabrizio	ITA	14.8.76	189/82	TJ	16.91,17.11w	17.73i- 11, 17.60- 00, 17.63w- 12
* Dong Bin		CHN	22.11.88	179/67	TJ	17.12, 17.21w	17.38- 12
Donisan	Mihai	ROU	24.7.88	193/74	HJ	2.29	2.32i- 14, 2.31- 13
^ Dossévi	Damiel	FRA	3.2.83	182/82	PV	5.60i	5.75- 05
^ Doucouré	Ladji	FRA	28.3.83	183/75	110h	13.70, 13.59w	12.97- 05
^ Douglas	Nathan	GBR	4.12.82	183/71	TJ	16.94	17.64- 05
Douvalídis	Konstadínos	GRE	10.3.87	184/78	110h	13.33	13.34- 13
Downing	Quincy	USA	16.1.93	185/75	400h	49.63	49.97- 14
Drack	Jonathan	MRI	6.11.88	184/77	TJ	16.96,17.05w	16.11- 13, 16.25w- 14
* Drouin	Derek	CAN	6.3.90	195/80	HJ	2.37	2.38- 13
Dry	Mark	GBR	11.10.87	184/110	HT	76.93	74.82- 12
Dubitskiy	Oleg	BLR	14.10.90	184/100	HT	76.67	75.56- 14
Dudas	Mihail	SRB	1.11.89	182/85	Dec	7720	8275- 13
Duffield	Jacorian	USA	2.9.92	190/79	HJ	2.34	2.27- 14
* Dukes	Dedric	USA	2.4.92	180/70	200	19.99, 19.86w	19.97, 19.91w- 14
Dunbar	Colin	USA	27.6.88	190/115	HT	73.56	70.44 -13
Duncan	Marcus	TTO	4.12.86	170/62	100	10.15	10.26- 10, 10.18w- 04
* Dunfee	Evan	CAN	28.9.90	186/68	20kW	1:21:48	1:20:13- 14
					50kW	3:43:45	3:58:34- 14
Dunkerley-Offor	Spencer	USA	6.1.95	196/88	110h	13.58, 13.45w	13.83- 14
Dunn	Jarryd	GBR	30.1.92	183/75	400	45.09	46.00- 12
Durañona	Yordanys	DMA	16.6.88	188/75	TJ	16.98A, 16.73	17.20A- 14, 17.02, 17.28w- 09
Durham	Adam	USA	30.8.85	186/79	400h	49.20	49.88- 13
* Dutch	Johnny	USA	20.1.89	180/82	400h	48.13	47.63- 10
* Dutra de Oliveira	Augusto	BRA	16.7.90	180/70	PV	5.81	5.82- 13
Duvio	Dylan	USA	6.4.95	186/80	PV	5.53	5.35- 14
Dvornikov	Mikhail	RUS	15.8.89		DT	61.28	60.65- 12
* Dwyer	Rasheed	JAM	29.1.89	188/80	100	10.16	10.20- 13
					200	19.80	19.98- 14
Dykstra	Raymond	CAN	18.6.92	188/93	JT	77.63	78.58- 14
Dyldin	Maksim	RUS	19.5.87	185/78	400	45.56	45.01- 12
Eaddy	Maurice	USA	1.6.95	175/70	100	10.11	10.61, 10.57w -13
* Eaton	Ashton	USA	21.1.88	186/86	400	45.00	45.64- 13
					110h	13.38	13.35- 11, 13.34w- 12
					LJ	8.03	8.23- 12
					Dec	9045	9039- 12
Eaton	Jarret	USA	24.6.89	183/82	110h	13.41, 13.40w	13.44- 12
Eaves	Max	GBR	31.5.88	186/84	PV	5.50i	5.62- 14
Echevarría	Juan Miguel	CUB-Y	11.8.98		LJ	8.05	7.47- 14
Echols	Dondre	USA	6.7.93	178/77	110h	13.46	13.82- 14
Echols-Luper	Cameron	USA	9.4.95	183/86	200	20.39	21.07- 13, 20.61w- 14
					LJ	7.91i, 7.96w	7.48- 13
* Edris	Muktar	ETH	14.1.94	172/57	3000	7:47+	7:46.0- 14
					5000	13:00.30	12:54.83- 14
					10k	27:17.18	28:44.95- 11
* Edward	Alonso	PAN	8.12.89	183/73	200	19.87	19.81- 09
Edwards	Mike	GBR	11.7.90		HJ	2.25	2.22i- 14, 2.18- 11
Ehrhardt	Tim	USA	16.3.95	186/90	Dec	7677	-0-
* El Abbassi	El Hassan	BRN	15.7.79	171/54	10k	27:25.02	27:32.96- 14
El Amine	Mouhcine	MAR	8.1.82	175/64	800	1:46.45	1:45.62- 11
El Bakkali	Soufiane	MAR-J	7.1.96	186/73	3kSt	8:27.79	8:32.66- 14
El Goumri	Othmane	MAR	28.5.92	171/57	1500	3:36.21	3:37.79- 13
					3000	7:36.71	7:44.73i- 14, 7:48.95- 13
					5000	13:13.90	13:13.72- 13
					10k	27:46.34	-0-
El Guers	Abdellatif	MAR	27.2.93		800	1:45.78	1:47.91- 14
El Kaam	Fouad	MAR	27.5.88	177/62	1500	3:34.53, 3:33,27 short	3:33.71- 13

Name		Nat	Born	Ht/Wt	Event	2015 Mark	Pre-2015 Best
El Manaoui	Amine	MAR	20.11.91	183/65	800	1:45.20	1:44.96- 13
El-Ashry	Alaa El-Din M.	EGY	6.1.91	183/95	HT	75.41	73.60 -13
El-Seify	Ashraf Amjad	QAT	20.2.95	183/100	HT	78.04	76.37- 13
Elemba	Frank	CGO	21.7.90	200/115	SP	20.25	19.72- 14
Ellenson	Wally	USA	4.5.94	193/91	HJ	2.28i, 2.20	2.25- 14
Ellington	James	GBR	6.9.85	180/75	100	10.19, 10.10w	10.13- 14, 10.12w- 11
					200	20.49	20.42- 13
Emanuel	Lee	GBR	24.1.85	178/64	1500	3:36.35, 3:35.66i	3:36.55- 13
3000	7:44.48i		7:45.12i- 14		2M	8:21.24i	8:50.18- 14
Embaye	Abadi	ETH-Y	99?		5000	13:13.17	
Emilianov	Ivan	MDA	19.2.77	202/160	SP	20.25i, 19.92	20.64- 11
Enekwechi	Chukwuewuka	USA	28.1.93	181/107	HT	72.77	68.53- 14
Engel	Roscoe	RSA	6.3.89	178/72	100	10.24A, 10.12w	10.19- 11, 10.17Aw- 14
					200	20.51A	20.64A- 12, 20.63w- 11
Engelbrecht	Jaco	RSA	8.3.87	200/125	SP	20.45	20.31- 13
Engels	Craig	USA	1.5.94	187/73	800	1:46.13	1:51.03- 13
English	Mark	IRL	18.3.93	187/76	800	1:45.49	1:44.84- 13
Eradiri	Denis	BUL	24.10.83	183/93	LJ	8.01	7.95, 7.97w- 12
Erayokan	Orukpe	NGR	20.12.93	175/70	400	44.95	46.27- 12
Erewa	Robin	GER	24.6.91	184/77	200	20.49	20.75- 13
Erickson	Chris	AUS	1.12.81	175/62	20kW	1:22:08	1:22:19- 14
					50kW	3:51:26	3:49:33- 14
Ernest	Aaron	USA	8.11.93	183/75	100	10.12, 10.09w	10.17- 12, 10.04w- 13
					200	20.22, 20.11w	20.38, 20.36w- 13
^ España	Jesús	ESP	21.8.78	173/56	3000	7:46.53	7:38.26- 06
					5000	13:22.92	13:04.73- 11
Essalhi	Younès	MAR	20.2.93	181/68	1500	3:35.82	3:35.52- 13
					5000	13:18.95	13:16.07- 13
^ Esser	Markus	GER	3.2.80	180/105	HT	74.06	81.10- 06
Estefani	Hederson	BRA	11.9.91	184/75	400	45.36	45.25- 12
					400h	49.40	49.59- 14
Estrada	Diego	USA	12.12.89	180/61	5000	13:17.30	13:15.33- 13
10k	27:30.53		27:32.90- 12		HMar	60:51	-0-
Eto	Takashi	JPN	5.2.91	183/67	HJ	2.28	2.28- 14
Evans	Andrew	USA	25.1.91	198/105	DT	63.91	66.37- 14
Évora	Nelson	POR	20.4.84	181/70	TJ	17.52	17.74- 07, 17.82w- 09
Ezzaydouny	Ibrahim	MAR	28.4.91		3kSt	8:27.43	8:38.61- 13
Ezzine	Hamid	MAR	5.10.83	174/60	3kSt	8:18.78	8:09.72- 07
Fajdek	Pawel	POL	4.6.89	186/118	HT	83.93	83.48- 14
Falloni	Simone	ITA	26.9.91	190/108	HT	73.29	72.43- 13
Faloci	Giovanni	ITA	13.10.85	193/108	DT	62.50	64.77- 13
Fang Yaoqing		CHN-J	20.4.96	182/70	LJ	7.91	7.68- 12
					TJ	16.55	16.48- 13
Farah	Mohamed	GBR	23.3.83	175/65	1500	3:28.93	3:28.81- 13
3000	7:34.66, 7:33.1i		7:34.47i- 09, 7:36.8+- 14		HMar	59:22dh, 59:32	60:23- 11, 60:00dh- 14
2M	8:03.40i	8:07.85- 14	5000	13:11.77	12:53.11- 11	10k	26:50.97 26:46.57- 11
^ Farquhar	Stuart	NZL	15.3.82	187/98	JT	82.75	86.31- 12
Farrell	Thomas	GBR	23.3.91	174/61	5000	13:10.48	13:15.31- 12
Fassinotti	Marco	ITA	29.4.89	190/71	HJ	2.34i, 2.33	2.34i, 2.30- 14
Fatecha	Víctor	PAR	10.3.88	190/98	JT	77.69	79.03- 13
Faust	Tim	USA	11.8.92	180/73	200	20.34	20.64- 14
Feeney	Patrick	USA	29.12.91	188/82	400	45.51	45.56- 14
Feger	Alexandre	FRA	22.1.90	179.74	PV	5.55	5.60- 14
Feleke	Getu	ETH	28.11.86		HMar	60:45	59:56- 10
					Mar	2:08:31	2:04:50- 12
Felix	Kurt	GRN	4.7.88	190/88	Dec	8302	8070- 14
Ferguson	Emeilo	JAM	16.4.93	171/64	100	10.15w	10.69- 10
Fernández	Jorge	CUB	2.10.87	190/100	DT	62.35	66.50- 14
Fernández	Sergio	ESP	1.4.93	188/70	400h	50.00A, 50.18	49.90- 14
Fernandes	Nélson	BRA	9.7.94	188/105	SP	19.60	18.87- 14
Ferreira	Diogo	POR	30.7.90	175/77	PV	5.60i, 5.55	5.67- 14
Ferreira	Fernando	BRA	13.12.94	188/57	HJ	2.26	2.24- 14
Fifa	Illias	MAR/ESP	16.5.89	174/55	3000	7:47+	7:49.13- 14
					5000	13:05.61	13:14.91- 14
Filip	Scott	USA	28.1.95	188/85	Dec	7647	7045w- 14
Filipovic	Predrag	SRB	5.10.78	182/75	50kW	4:00:26	3:57:22- 10
Filippídis	Konstadinos	GRE	26.11.86	188/73	PV	5.91	5.83i, 5.82- 13
Filippov	Nikita	KAZ	7.10.91	191/84	PV	5.65	5.60- 12
Finley	Mason	USA	7.10.90	203/150	DT	64.80A	64.17A- 14
Firfirica	Alin Alexandru	ROU	3.11.95	196/108	DT	61.04	56.45- 14
Fisher	Andrew	JAM	15.12.91	168/64	100	9.94	10.07A- 13, 10.09- 14

	Name		Nat	Born	Ht/Wt	Event	2015 Mark	Pre-2015 Best
	FitzSimons	Thomas	USA	8.3.89	188/83	Dec	7791	7645- 14
	Flannery	Niall	GBR	26.4.91	178/70	400h	48.90	48.80- 14
	Florant	Fabian	NED	1.2.83	176/73	TJ	16.65	16.75i- 12, 16.65- 09, 16.85w- 13
	Floriani	Yuri	ITA	25.12.81	180/64	3kSt	8:33.37	8:22.62- 12
	Fofana	Hassane	ITA	28.4.92	187/77	110h	13.59, 13.60w	13.55- 14
^	Forbes	Damar	JAM	18.9.90	185/77	LJ	8.17	8.25, 8.35w- 13
	Forbes	Ronald	CAY	5.4.85	192/86	110h	13.47	13.50, 13.24w- 11
	Forte	Julian	JAM	1.7.93	186/73	100	10.06	10.03- 14, 9.98w- 13
						200	20.04	20.38- 12, 20.22w- 13
^	Fortes	Marco	POR	26.9.82	189/139	SP	19.75	21.02- 12
	Fox	Nathan	GBR	21.10.90	186/84	TJ	16.65	16.69- 14
	François	Mickaël	FRA	12.3.88	182/72	400h	49.58	49.35- 13
*	Francis	Javon	JAM	14.12.94	183/73	400	44.50	45.00- 14
	Francis	Miguel	ANT	28.2.95	186/75	200	20.05, 19.76dt	20.60, 20.58w- 13
	Frater	Michael	JAM	6.10.82	170/67	100	10.14	9.88, 9.86w- 11
	Frauen	Michael	GER	19.1.86	179/76	PV	5.50	5.55- 13
*	Fredericks	Cornel	RSA	3.3.90	178/70	400h	49.50	48.14- 11
	Freeman	Jake	USA	5.11.80	193/129	HT	74.31	76.86- 09
	Freeman	Josh	USA	22.8.94	193/134	SP	20.15	19.86- 14
*	Freimuth	Rico	GER	14.3.88	196/92	Dec	8561	8488w, 8382- 13
	French	Cameron	NZL	17.5.92	180/73	400h	49.72	50.16- 14
	Frolov	Aleksandr	RUS	5.3.87		Dec	7793	7675- 13
	Frolov	Kirill	RUS	29.9.93		20kW	1:21:11	1:22:16- 13
^	Frydrych	Petr	CZE	13.1.88	198/99	JT	85.52	88.23- 10
	Fryman	Andy	USA	3.2.85	188/130	HT	71.83	73.90- 14
	Fu Haitao		CHN	1.11.93		TJ	16.79	16.56- 11
	Fueki	Yasuhiro	JPN	20.12.85	181/73	400h	49.92	49.31- 13
	Fujimitsu	Kenji	JPN	1.5.86	182/70	100	10.24, 10.14w	10.28, 10.27w- 14
						200	20.13	20.38- 10
	Fujisawa	Isamu	JPN	12.10.87	165/53	20kW	1:19:08	1:20:03- 14
	Fukasawa	Hiroyuki	JPN	10.12.92		LJ	7.88, 8.01w	7.66- 12
	Furey	Sean	USA	31.8.82	190/95	JT	83.08	82.73- 12
	Furtula	Danijel	MNE	31.7.92	195/115	DT	63.33	64.60- 13
	Futch	Eric	USA	25.4.93	175/70	400h	49.45	50.24- 12
*	Fyodorov	Aleksey	RUS	25.5.91	184/73	TJ	17.42	17.19- 12
	Gabius	Arne	GER	22.3.81	188/68	5k	13:32.68, 13:27.53i,	13:12.50- 13
	10k	27:43.93		27:55.35- 14		Mar	2:08:33	2:09:32- 14
	Gado	Ruben	FRA	13.12.93	180/73	Dec	7610	7323- 13
*	Gag	Andrei	ROU	27.4.91	195/118	SP	20.96	20.17i, 19.64- 14
^	Gaisah	Ignisious	NED	20.6.83	185/75	LJ	8.19	8.43, 8.51w- 06
	Gakémé	Antoine	BDI	24.12.91	170/57	800	1:44.09	1:45.39- 13
	Gallimore	Javan	JAM	7.8.93	183/75	400h	49.94	49.76- 13
	Gandou	Adil	FRA	18.8.93	187/69	TJ	16.55	16.28- 14
	Gandu	Benjamin	KEN	21.5.90	169/57	HMar	60:20	61:06- 12
	Gao Wenkui		CHN	28.7.95		20kW	1:23:15	1:25:19- 14
*	Gao Xinglong		CHN	12.3.94	181/65	LJ	8.34	8.18, 8.21w- 14
	García	Diego	ESP-J	19.1.96	174/60	20kW	1:21:45	-0-
*	García	Jesús Ángel	ESP	17.10.69	172/64	50kW	3:46:43	3:39:54- 97
	García	Víctor	ESP	13.3.85	173/57	3kSt	8:22.46	8:15.20- 12
^	García	Yordani	CUB	21.11.88	193/88	Dec	8186	8496- 09
*	Gardiner	Steven	BAH	12.9.95	188/75	400	44.27	47.78- 13
	Gardner	Jonathan	USA	10.12.91	180/77	TJ	16.45i	16.15- 14
	Garrett	Richard	USA	21.12.90	186/118	SP	19.65	20.35- 14
	Garrido	Iván	COL	25.1.94		20kW	1:21:39	1:22:13.74t- 14
	Gaspar	José Luis	CUB	25.8.95	188/72	400h	49.67A, 50.12	49.88- 14
	Gastaldi	Román Andrés	ARG	25.9.89	187/86	Dec	7882w, 7447	7826A- 11
	Gathimba	Samuel	KEN			20kW	1:23:12A	1:23:59A- 14
*	Gatlin	Justin	USA	10.2.82	185/79	100	9.74	9.77, 9.76w -14
						200	19.57	19.68- 14
	Gaul	Florian	GER	21.9.91	182/78	PV	5.53	5.50- 13
*	Gay	Tyson	USA	9.8.82	180/73	100	9.87, 9.79w	9.69- 09, 9.68w- 08
^	Gaymon	Justin	USA	13.12.86	175/70	400h	49.58	48.46- 08
	Gdula	Lukás	CZE	6.12.91	178/65	50kW	3:59:03	4:01:52- 14
*	Gebremedhin	Mekonnen	ETH	11.10.88	180/64	1500	3:35.67	3:31.45- 12
*	Gebremeskel	Dejen	ETH	24.11.89	178/53	3000	7:47+	7:34.14i- 12, 7:45.9- 10
						5000	13:00.49	12:46.81- 12
*	Gebrhiwet	Hagos	ETH	11.5.94	167/65	3000	7:38.08	7:30.36- 13
						5000	12:54.70	12:47.53- 12
	Gebrselassie	Ghirmay	ERI	14.11.95		Mar	2:07:47	2:09:08- 14
	Gebrselassie	Leul	ETH	20.9.93	170/55	5000	13:15.07	13:14.59- 14
	10k	27:22.89		28:05.66 -13		HMar	60:34	61:00- 14

Name		Nat	Born	Ht/Wt	Event	2015 Mark	Pre-2015 Best
Gebru	Birhanu	ETH	22.11.86		Mar	2:07:26	2:05:49- 14
Gedefa	Berhanu	ETH	.94		Mar	2:08:03	-0-
Geffrouais	Florian	FRA	5.12.88	183/78	Dec	7970	8164- 14
Gelant	Elroy	RSA	25.8.86	174/55	1500	3:37.97	3:38.59- 09
3000	7:47.35	7:39.55i- 14, 7:41.38- 12			5000	13:28.69	13:15.87- 13
Gelmanov	Mikhail	RUS	18.3.90		PV	5.50i	5.40- 12
Gemili	Adam	GBR	6.10.93	178/73	100	9.97	10.04- 14
Genest	Alexandre	CAN	30.6.86	175/57	3kSt	8:24.84	8:19.33- 11
Geneti	Markos	ETH	30.5.84	175/55	Mar	2:07:25	2:04:54- 12
Geoghegan	Will	USA	15.7.92	179/61	3000	7:45.71i, 7:48.79	7:51.57i- 14
					5000	13:17.85	13:55.92- 13
George	Winston	GUY	19.5.87	174/66	100	9.9	
200	20.62, 20.4	20.59- 13, 20.4- 14			400	45.25	45.57- 14
Geraghty	Peter	USA	11.6.91	183/73	PV	5.64	5.56- 14
Geremew	Mosinet	ETH	12.2.92	174/57	10k	27:18.86	
					HMar	59:21	59:11- 14
Gertleyn	Ivan	RUS	25.9.87	184/75	PV	5.70	5.55- 10
Getachew	Limenih	ETH	30.4.90		Mar	2:08:19	2:06:49- 14
Getahun	Birhan	ETH	5.9.91	181/64	3kSt	8:27.7	8:17.36- 11
Gföhler	Benjamin	SUI	27.1.94	178/	LJ	7.93	7.52- 14
Ghalenouei	Peyman	IRI	29.1.92		HT	73.07	70.73- 14
Ghanbarzadeh	Keyvan	IRI	26.5.90	193/78	HJ	2.26	2.26- 12
Ghasemi	Reza	IRI	24.7.87	179/76	100	10.12	10.16- 13
Ghazal	Majed El Dein	SYR	21.4.87	193/70	HJ	2.31	2.28- 11
Gibson	Jeffery	BAH	15.8.90	186/79	400h	48.17	48.78- 14
Gill	Jacko	NZL	20.12.94	190/118	SP	20.75	20.70- 14
Gimeno	Jorge	ESP	16.2.90	179/64	TJ	16.67i, 16.38A	16.61- 14
Giraldo	Gerald	COL	21.3.89	177/61	3kSt	8:29.53	8:28.6 -13
Gittens	Ramon	BAR	20.7.87	180/77	100	10.02, 10.10Aw	10.02- 13
Giupponi	Matteo	ITA	8.10.88	190/65	50kW	3:49:52	3:51:49- 14
Givans	Senoj-Jay	JAM	30.12.93	178/73	100	10.03, 9.97w	10.10, 9.90w- 14
					200	20.47	20.67, 20.28w- 14
Glass	Najee	USA	12.6.94	183/73	400	44.79	45.40- 14
Gloger	Nils Christopher	GER	6.8.90	178/66	20kW	1:22:50	1:21:49- 14
Glover	Tim	USA	1.11.90	185/86	JT	84.09	84.01- 14
Gomes	Hélio	POR	27.12.84	191/73	1500	3:37.75	3:37.50- 13
Gómez	Iñaki	CAN	16.1.88	172/58	20kW	1:21:55	1:20:18- 14
Gomis	Kafétien	FRA	23.3.80	183/67	LJ	8.26	8.24- 10
González	Andy	CUB	17.10.87	183/70	800	1:46.28	1:45.3- 08, 1:45.40- 10
González	Erwin	MEX	7.2.94		20kW	1:23:18A	1:22:36- 14
Goodwin	Marquise	USA	19.11.90	177/83	LJ	8.13, 8.37w	8.33- 12
Gordon	Jehue	TTO	15.12.91	190/80	400h	49.22	47.69- 13
Gordon	Lalonde	TTO	25.11.88	188/83	400	44.64A, 44.70	44.52- 12
Gordon	Nick	JAM	17.9.88	174/73	LJ	7.95	8.11- 09, 8.14w- 11
Gorokhov	Georgiy	RUS	20.4.93		PV	5.65	5.50i, 5.41- 14
Goss	Angelo	USA	.94	193/75	110h	13.51	13.89, 13.79w- 14
Gotch	Jarvis	USA	25.3.92	185/73	LJ	8.12i	8.09A, 8.18Aw- 13
Goto	Shuto	JPN	26.2.94		50kW	3:59:23	4:06:53- 14
Gowda	Vikas	IND	5.7.83	196/115	DT	65.75	66.28- 12
Grabarz	Robbie	GBR	3.10.87	192/87	HJ	2.28	2.37- 12
Grace	Bobby	USA	10.10.90	193/118	SP	20.51	19.90i, 19.56- 14
Grau	Martin	GER	26.3.92	176/64	3kSt	8:31.55	8:24.29- 14
Greaux	Kyle	TTO	26.4.88	190/80	200	20.42	20.57- 13
Greeley	Mitch	USA	5.5.86	185/74	PV	5.50	5.56- 08
Green	Jack	GBR	6.10.91	187/82	400h	49.31	48.60- 12
Green	Jeremiah	USA	9.2.94	173/70	TJ	16.50w	16.29i- 14
Green	Leford	JAM	14.11.86	186/79	400h	49.22	48.47- 10
Greene	David 'Dai'	GBR	11.4.86	183/75	400h	49.85	47.84- 12
Gregg	Brendan	USA	15.5.89	183/64	10k	28:03.27	28:28.54- 14
Gregson	Ryan	AUS	26.4.90	184/68	1500	3:36.51	3:31.06- 10
Grey	Jonathan	USA	13.2.88	175/61	10k	27:59.88	28:26.44- 12
Grice	Charlie	GBR	7.11.93	182/68	1500	3:35.29	3:35.59 -14
Grigoryev	Sergey	KAZ	24.6.92	178/65	PV	5.50	5.50- 14
Gripich	Aleksandr	RUS	21.9.86	190/80	PV	5.85i, 5,71	5.75- 09
Gruber	Hendrik	GER	28.9.86	192/82	PV	5.55	5.75i- 13, 5.70- 10
Gudnason	Gudni Valur	ISL	11.10.95	198/115	DT	63.50	47.05- 14
Gudzius	Andrius	LTU	14.2.91	200/130	DT	65.51	66.11- 14
Guèye	Mamadou	SEN	1.4.86	178/71	LJ	7.86, 8.12w	7.76- 12
					TJ	16.50	16.37- 14
Guliyev	Ramil	TUR	29.5.90	187/73	100	10.12	10.08- 09
					200	19.88	20.04- 09

Name		Nat	Born	Ht/Wt	Event	2015 Mark	Pre-2015 Best
Günther	Martin	GER	8.10.86	188/74	HJ	2.25	2.30i- 10, 2.24- 08
Gutema	Bekele	ETH	.94	173/60	1500	3:39.91, 3:34.90 short	3:38.99- 14
Haapala	Eero	FIN	10.7.89	193/87	LJ	7.95	8.11i, 7.90- 13
^ Haatainen	Harri	FIN	5.1.78	186/85	JT	77.95	86.63- 01
* Hadadi	Ehsan	IRI	21.1.85	193/125	DT	65.22	69.32- 08
Hadj Lazib	Othman	ALG	10.5.83	186/85	110h	13.76, 13.60w	13.46- 11
Hague	Adam	GBR-J	29.8.97	188/73	PV	5.60	5.46i, 5.35- 14
Haji	Yasin	ETH-J	22.1.96	168/52	3000	7:41.74	
					5000	13:10.67	13:26.21- 14
Håkansson	Elias	SWE	29.2.92	190/104	HT	71.31	71.38- 14
Hall	Cameron	USA	12.5.93	190/100	110h	13.61	13.89- 13
Hall	David	GBR	25.4.95	185/84	Dec	7651	-0-
Halleselassie	Yemane	ERI-Y	21.2.98			8:32.05	
Hamann	Lars	GER	4.4.89	187/88	JT	84.26	84.20- 13
Hamza	Mohamed	EGY-J	30.8.96		SP	19.78	17.64- 14
Han Do-hyun		KOR	28.7.94	184/73	PV	5.51	5.45- 14
Han Yucheng		CHN	16.12.78	177/59	50kW	3:55:44	3:36:20- 05
Hanßen	Jonas	GER	15.7.95	180/76	400h	49.87	50.68- 14
Hanany	Mickaël	FRA	25.3.83	198/84	HJ	2.25	2.34- 14
Hanekom	Lindsay	RSA	15.5.93	176/65	400h	50.00	51.56- 14
Hanne	Mamadou-Elimane	FRA	6.3.88	186/72	400	45.56	46.09- 13
Hannes	Pieter Jan	BEL	30.10.92	186/72	1500	3:35.95	3:34.49 -14
1M	3:51.84		3:55.33- 14		3000	7:47.55i	7:54.06- 13
Hara	Shota	JPN	18.7.92	180/75	200	20.65, 20.49w	20.41- 14
Haratyk	Michael	POL	10.4.92	187/90	SP	20.10i, 19.95	19.95- 14
* Hardee	Trey	USA	7.2.84	196/95	Dec	8725(w)	8790- 09
Harmse	Chris	RSA	31.5.73	184/118	HT	74.00	80.63- 05
* Haroun	Abdelilah	QAT-J	1.1.97		400	44.27	45.74- 14
* Harradine	Benn	AUS	14.10.82	198/115	DT	66.75	68.20- 13
Harrell	Jason	USA	10.1.91	188/109	DT	61.74	58.46- 14
Harrington	James	USA	3.7.93	174/70	200	20.50	21.16- 14
Harris	Adam	GUY	21.7.87	178/77	100	9.99w	10.12, 9.90w -14
* Harris	Aleec	USA	31.10.90	185/77	110h	13.11	13.14- 14
Harris	James	USA	18.9.91	196/88	400	45.24A, 45.53	45.23- 13
Harris	Kevin	USA	4.12.95	188/82	200	20.49	20.92, 20.68w- 14
Härstedt	Axel	SWE	28.2.87	197/130	DT	64.72	62.43- 14
Hart	Shavez	BAH	6.9.92	176/70	100	10.10	10.11- 14, 10.08w- 13
					200	20.23	20.35- 14, 20.24w- 12
* Hartfield	Mike	USA	29.3.90	190/77	LJ	8.27, 8.42w	8.15- 13, 8.17w- 14
* Harting	Christophe	GER	4.10.90	205/117	DT	67.93	64.99- 13
Hartling	Nicolai	DEN	17.1.94	181/67	400h	50.02	50.94- 14
Harvey	Jak Ali	TUR	5.4.89	182/73	100	10.01	10.04- 13, 10.03w- 11
					200	20.38	20.44- 13
Hasegawa	Daigo	JPN	27.2.90	172/56	TJ	16.49	16.36- 13
Hashimoto	Akiyuki	JPN	18.11.94	175/60	200	20.71, 20.43w	20.35- 13
Hashimoto	Takaoki	JPN	18.7.92	181/64	400h	49.89	50.37- 13
Hassi	Juuso	FIN	4.4.93	185/79	Dec	7621	7569- 14
Hathat	Yassine	ALG	30.7.91	180/68	800	1:45.79	1:46.09- 13
					1500	3:36.54	3:35.68 -14
Haukenes	Håvard	NOR	22.4.90	180/68	50kW	3:56:50	3:56:38- 12
Hayakawa	Tsubasa	JPN	2.7.90	168/48	10k	28:06.10	28:15.36- 14
Hayes	Keyunta	USA	15.2.92	183/73	400h	49.48	49.38- 12
Haynes	Akeem	CAN	3.11.92	170/66	100	10.15, 10.06w	10.23A, 10.27, 10.18w- 12
Hearn	Scottie	USA	3.1.94	173/68	400h	49.39	50.56- 13
Heath	Garrett	USA	3.11.85	183/65	1500	3:34.13	3:34.12- 13
3000	7:37.97		7:37.40i- 14, 7:51.34- 12		5000	13:16.31	13:16.65- 14
* Heffernan	Robert	IRL	20.2.78	173/55	50kW	3:44:17	3:37:54- 12
Heinle	Fabian	GER	14.5.94	188/70	LJ	8.25	7.91- 13
Helcelet	Adam	CZE	27.10.91	187/86	Dec	8234	8252- 13
Helebrandt	Máté	HUN	12.1.89	174/60	20kW	1:23:04	1:22:39- 13
* Henderson	Jeff	USA	19.2.89	178/82	LJ	8.52, 8.54w	8.43, 8.52w- 14
Henderson	Khalil	USA	18.11.94	188/75	200	20.29	20.63, 20.61w- 14
Henriksen	Eivind	NOR	14.9.90	191/116	HT	71.84	75.57- 12
Henry	Eldred	IVB	18.9.94	196/159	SP	20.00	17.34- 14
Hering	Robert	GER	14.6.90	178/73	100	10.15w	10.34- 09
Herman	Chad	RSA	25.5.92		JT	77.67A	75.83A- 13
Hernández	Diego Alí	VEN	21.2.95	176/60	LJ	7.82, 7.99w	7.82- 13
Herrera	José Carlos	MEX	5.2.86	187/77	200	20.33A	20.35- 14
* Hess	Max	GER-J	13.7.96	185/77	LJ	8.03i	7.52- 14
Hesselbjerg	Ole	DEN	23.4.90	183/70	3kSt	8:33.22	8:38.75- 14
Hester	Tevin	USA	10.1.94	170/66	100	10.05, 9.87w	10.16- 14
					200	20.14	20.90- 13

Name		Nat	Born	Ht/Wt	Event	2015 Mark	Pre-2015 Best
Hicks ¶	Jeremy	USA	19.9.86	178/75	LJ	8.30	8.11- 12, 8.31w- 13
Hill	Darrell	USA	17.8.93	193/135	SP	20.86	20.57- 14
Hill	Ryan	USA	31.1.90	173/61	5000	13:05.69	13:14.22- 13
Hinch	Derick	USA	2.2.91	186/80	PV	5.50Ai, 5.50	5.50- 12
Hiramatsu	Yuji	JPN-J	11.1.97	185/64	HJ	2.28	2.20- 14
Hirsuato	Nuguse	ETH	31.2.82	180/58	10k	27:40.78	
Hlaselo	Dumisani	RSA	8.6.89	168/56	1500	3:36.36	3:38.15- 08
Hlavan	Igor	UKR	25.9.90	172/62	20kW	1:20:29	1:19:59- 14
Hoffa	Reese	USA	8.10.77	181/133	SP	21.30	22.43- 07
Hofmann	Andreas	GER	16.12.91	195/108	JT	86.14	86.13- 14
Hogan	Victor	RSA	25.7.89	198/108	DT	64.56	65.33- 13
Hollis	Mark	USA	1.12.84	190/84	PV	5.60	5.83- 14
Holloway	Trey	USA	7.7.94	188/75	110h	13.57	13.70- 14
Holusa	Jakub	CZE	20.2.88	183/72	800	1:45.81	1:45.12- 12
1500	3:34.26		3:35.26- 14		1M	3:53.46	3:56.75- 10
Holzdeppe	Raphael	GER	28.9.89	181/78	PV	5.94	5.91- 12
Homo	Nicolas	FRA	24.11.88	186/80	PV	5.60i	5.50i, 5.50- 14
Hondrokoukis	Dimitrios	CYP	26.1.88	193/72	HJ	2.32i, 2.31	2.33i- 12, 2.32- 11
Honeycutt	Josh	USA	7.3.89	182/73	TJ	16.79	16.83- 14
Hontsovskyy	Volodymyr	UKR	23.8.91	183/67	50kW	3:57:56	4:08:21- 14
Hooper (Hou Yubo)	Ted	TPE	31.1.91	173/66	LJ	8.08	7.88- 14
Horsley	Carl	USA	17.6.92	178/73	100	10.22, 10.03w	10.22- 13
Horvat	Ivan	CRO	17.8.93	188/77	PV	5.70	5.62- 13
Houdadi	Mustapha	MAR	5.8.86		3kSt	8:30.0	8:35.66- 14
Hough	Nick	AUS	20.10.93	191/86	110h	13.42	13.57- 14
Houston	Scott	USA	11.6.90	193/79	PV	5.65	5.40i -13, 5.30- 10
Howard	Julian	GER	3.4.89	176/75	LJ	8.04i, 7.97	8.07, 8.13w- 13
Howell	Renard	USA	3.3.95	188/82	200	20.46w	20.62- 14
Hrechkovskyy	Andrey	UKR	30.8.93	174/55	50kW	3:53:53	3:49:06- 14
Hsiang Chun-Hsien		TPE	4.9.93	186/70	HJ	2.29	2.20- 11
Hu Wanli		CHN	27.5.92		50kW	3:56:16	4:04:05- 14
Hu Yufei		CHN	9.11.93		Dec	7664	7582- 14
Huang Bokai		CHN-J	26.9.96	183/75	PV	5.50i, 5.50	5.45- 14
Huang Changzhou		CHN	20.8.94	183/64	LJ	8.17	8.12- 14
Huang Shih-Feng		TPE	2.3.92	181/88	JT	81.48	82.11- 13
Hudi	Ákos	HUN	10.8.91	185/95	HT	74.53	76.93- 13
Hudson-Smith	Matthew	GBR	26.10.94	192/79	400	45.09	44.75- 14
Hughes	Matt	CAN	3.8.89	180/64	5000	13:19.56	13:28.36- 14
					3kSt	8:18.63	8:11.64- 13
Hughes	Zharnel	AIA/GBR	13.7.95	190/79	100	10.15	10.12- 14
					200	20.02	20.32- 14
Huling	Dan	USA	16.7.83	185/70	3kSt	8:14.11	8:13.29- 10
Hunegnaw	Fentahun	ETH			HMar	60:10	61:35A- 14
Hunt	Leon	ISV	17.5.87	186/77	LJ	7.93	8.11- 11
Hussein	Kariem	SUI	1.4.89	190/77	400h	48.45	48.47- 14
Huszák	János	HUN	5.2.92	197/118	DT	61.30	59.01- 14
Hyde	Jaheel	JAM-J	2.2.97	180/73	400h	49.01	49.29- 14
Hyman	Kemar	CAY	11.10.89	178/74	100	10.07, 9.85Aw	9.95- 12
Ibáñez	Anatole	SWE	14.11.85	177/69	20kW	1:22:48	1:22:36- 12
Ibargüen	Arley	COL	4.12.82	182/85	JT	80.67A	81.07- 09
Ibrahim	Mohamed Ismail	DJI-J	.97	171/60	1500	3:37.08	3:45.72- 14
					3kSt	8:24.58	
Ibrahimov	Hayle	AZE	18.1.90	168/58	5000	13:22.11	13:09.17- 14
Idiata	Samson	NGR	28.2.82	186/75	LJ	7.89, 8.04w	8.00- 13, 8.02w- 12
Iguider	Abdelaati	MAR	25.3.87	170/52	1500	3:28.79	3:29.83 -14
1M	3:53.21		3:49.09- 14		5000	12:59.25	13:09.17- 12
Iizuka	Shota	JPN	25.6.91	185/80	200	20.42	20.21- 13
Ijah/Simmons	Solomon	USA	26.9.93	196/91	Dec	7862	7312w- 14
Ikonnikov	Kirill	RUS	5.3.84	187/115	HT	77.15	80.71- 12
Imai	Masato	JPN	2.4.84	169/56	Mar	2:07:39	2:09:30- 14
Ingebrigtsen	Henrik	NOR	24.2.91	180/69	1500	3:32.85	3:31.46- 14
1M	3:53.43		3:50.72- 14		3000	7:46.59, 7:45.54i	7:42.19- 13
					5000	13:27.10	14:19.39- 13
Ingraham	Ryan	BAH	2.11.93	191/70	HJ	2.28	2.30- 13
Ioannou	Kyriakos	CYP	26.7.84	193/66	HJ	2.29	2.35- 07
Iordan	Valeriy	RUS	14.2.92	192/95	JT	83.00	83.56- 13
Irwin	Andrew	USA	23.1.93	190/84	PV	5.75i, 5.65	5.72- 12
Irwin	Willy	USA	2.6.92	188/107	SP	20.13	20.13- 14
Isidro	Pedro	POR	17.7.85	175/58	50kW	3:55:44	3:56:15- 14
Ismail	Muhammad Hakimi	MAS	8.4.91	188/80	TJ	16.76	16.44- 13
Israel	Märt	EST	23.9.83	190/119	DT	62.19	66.98- 11
Ito	Yuki	JPN	12.4.92		50kW	3:55:54	4:01:10- 14

	Name		Nat	Born	Ht/Wt	Event	2015 Mark	Pre-2015 Best
	Ivakin	Anton	RUS	3.2.91	178/73	PV	5.70i, 5.562	5.65i- 13, 5.65- 14
*	Ivanov	Aleksandr	RUS	25.4.93	182/68	20kW	1:20:06	1:19:45- 14
^	Ivanov	Georgi	BUL	13.3.85	187/130	SP	20.54	21.09- 13
	Ivanov	Tihomir	BUL	11.7.94	198/77	HJ	2.25i, 2.25	2.28- 14
	Ivanyuk	Ilya	RUS	9.3.93	183/75	HJ	2.30	2.27i, 2.26- 13
	Ivashko	Pavel	RUS	16.11.94	185/75	400	45.25	45.46- 14
	Jackson	Adoreé	USA	18.9.95	178/78	LJ	7.91	7.75- 12
*	Jackson	Bershawn	USA	8.5.83	173/69	400h	48.09	47.30- 05
	Jackson	Marcus	USA	8.7.91	201/82	HJ	2.28	2.29i, 2.27- 13
	Jackson	Mark	USA	12.10.91	175/82	TJ	16.46	16.38Ai- 14
	Jacobs	Lamont Marcell	ITA	26.9.94	184/73	LJ	8.03i	7.75i, 7.68- 13
*	Jager	Evan	USA	8.3.89	186/66	1500	3:32.97	3:36.34- 13
	1M	3:55.25i		3:53.33- 14		3kSt	8:00.45	8:04.71- 14
	Jagers	Reggie	USA	13.8.94	185/100	DT	61.00	59.19- 14
	Jagor	Jaak-Heinrich	EST	11.5.90		400h	49.37	50.69- 14
	Jagusch	Christian	GER	13.7.92	190/110	SP	20.10	19.74- 14
	Jakubczyk	Lucas	GER	28.4.85	183/73	100	10.09w	10.07, 10.01w- 14
	James	Antonio	USA	7.4.92	190/116	DT	60.99	60.15- 14
	James	Jamol	TTO	16.7.92	175/70	100	10.15	10.17- 12, 10.08w -13
*	James	Kirani	GRN	1.9.92	185/74	400	43.78	43.74- 14
*	Janet	Roberto	CUB	29.8.86	187/106	HT	78.02	77.08- 12
	Janezic	Luka	SLO	14.11.95	192/83	400	45.28	47.06- 13
	Jasinski	Daniel	GER	5.8.89	207/125	DT	65.93	65.98- 14
	Jaszczuk	Tomasz	POL	9.3.92	195/83	LJ	8.05, 8.08w	8.15, 8.16w- 14
^	Jelks	Mark	NGR	10.4.84	170/66	100	9.96w	9.99- 08, 9.8w- 05
	Jenkins	Eric	USA	24.11.91	170/61	3000	7:41.79	7:50.44i- 13
						5000	13:07.33	13:18.57- 13
^	Jeylan	Ibrahim	ETH	12.6.89	168/57	5000	13:20.21	13:09.16- 13
	Jiang Fan		CHN	16.9.89	188/75	110h	13.61	13.47- 11
	Jílek	Jaroslav	CZE	22.10.89	183/85	JT	81.45	74.15- 13
	Jin Min-sub		KOR	2.9.92	185/77	PV	5.53	5.65- 14
*	Jobodwana	Anaso	RSA	30.7.92	187/71	100	10.13	10.10- 13
						200	19.87	20.13, 20.00w- 13
	Jock	Charles	USA	23.11.89	188/73	800	1:45.40	1:44.67- 11
	John	Alexander	GER	3.5.86	185/77	110h	13.46, 13.42w	13.35- 09
	John	Jeffrey	FRA	6.6.92	184/67	200	20.38	20.63- 14
	Johnson	Justin	USA	25.10.92	188/79	110h	13.52	13.79- 12
^	Johnson	Kibwé	USA	17.7.81	189/108	HT	76.95	80.31- 11
	Johnson	Taffawee	JAM	10.3.88	180/73	100	10.13	10.20, 10.19w- 13
^	Jonas	Dusty	USA	19.4.86	198/84	HJ	2.28	2.36A- 08, 2.35- 14
	Jones	Avion	USA	31.1.94		HJ	2.25	2.21- 14
	Jones	Jonathan	USA	23.4.91	183/127	SP	20.92	20.75- 14
	Jordan	Alphonso	USA	1.11.87	190/75	TJ	16.89	16.74- 11, 16.88w- 12
	Jordier	Thomas	FRA	12.8.94	170/65	400	45.50	46.00- 14
	Jorgensen	Jesse	USA	1.9.91	180/68	800	1:45.76	1:48.62- 14
	Jørgensen	Rasmus	DEN	23.1.89	180/75	PV	5.53	5.65- 13
	Joseph	Stanley	FRA	24.10.91	181/66	PV	5.55	5.62i- 13, 5.55- 12
	Julião	Ronald	BRA	16.6.85	194/113	DT	64.65	65.55- 13
	Juska	Radek	CZE	8.3.93	195/82	LJ	8.15	7.94- 14
	Kaba	Sekou	CAN	25.8.90	190/82	110h	13.43	13.68- 14
	Kafia	Louhab	ALG	24.2.87	192/77	TJ	16.76	16.63- 14
	Kamais	Paul	KEN-J	24.10.96	178/62	5000	13:21.52	13:41.62- 14
	Kamathi	Joseph	KEN-J	23.11.96	175/56	10k	27:49.46	27:38.18- 14
*	Kamworor	Geoffrey	KEN	28.11.92	168/54	5000	13:13.28A	13:12.23- 11
						10k	26:52.65	27:06.35- 11
	Kanda	Luka	KEN	.87		Mar	2:07:20	2:08:02- 14
	Kandie	Felix	KEN	10.4.87	178/62	HMar	60:42	62:46- 11
						Mar	2:07:07	2:10:37- 14
	Kandu	Chris	GBR	10.9.95	197/79	HJ	2.26i, 2.21	2.24- 14
	Kanemaru	Yuzo	JPN	18.9.87	177/77	400	45.22	45.16- 09
	Kanervo	Jussi	FIN	1.2.93	180/63	400h	49.66	50.35- 14
	Kangas	Arttu	FIN	13.7.93	186/108	SP	20.09i, 19.79	19.74- 14
	Kangogo	Cornelius	KEN	31.12.93	166/62	3000	7:47.21	7:39.73- 12
	Kangogo	Philip	KEN			Mar	2:08:16	-0
	Kankaanpää	Mikko	FIN	17.4.87	183/75	JT	77.68	83.33- 10
	Kanno	Tomofumi	JPN	25.4.93		50kW	3:54:24	-0
*	Kanter	Gerd	EST	6.5.79	196/125	DT	66.02	73.38- 06
^	Karailiev	Momchil	BUL	21.5.82	188/75	TJ	16.58	17.41- 09
	Karavayev	Pavel	RUS	27.8.88	185/74	LJ	7.95	8.08- 11
	Karlström	Perseus	SWE	2.5.90	184/73	20kW	1:22:44	1:21:54- 14

Name		Nat	Born	Ht/Wt	Event	2015 Mark	Pre-2015 Best
Karoki	Bidan	KEN	21.8.90	169/53	5000	13:21.26	13:15.25- 14
10k	27:04.77	26:52.36- 14			HMar	59:14	59:23- 14
Kasongor	Abraham	KEN	.93		HMar	60:25	61:27- 14
Kasyanov	Oleksiy	UKR	26.8.85	191/87	Dec	8262	8479- 09
Katsuki	Hayato	JPN	28.11.90	168/58	50kW	3:59:03	-0-
Kawasaki	Kazuya	JPN	2.9.92		Dec	7679	7515- 14
Kaya	Ali	TUR	20.4.94	171/55	3000	7:38.65, 7:38.42i	7:43.61i -14, 7:58.76- 13
5000	13:00.31	13:31.39- 13			10k	27:24.09	28:08.72- 14
Kazmirek	Kai	GER	28.1.91	189/91	Dec	8462	8471- 14
Kebede	Tsegaye	ETH	15.1.87	158/50	Mar	2:07:58	2:04:38- 12
Kebenei	Stanley	USA	6.11.89	170/61	3kSt	8:23.93	8:24.45- 13
Keddar	Salim	ALG	23.11.93		1500	3:35.92	3:45.64- 14
Kedi	Aman	ETH	16.9.94		1500	3:36.73	3:37.54- 13
						7:45.99	
Keiner	Sebastian	GER	22.8.89	183/65	1500	3:36.46	3:37.75 -13
Kejelcha	Yomif	ETH-Y	1.8.97	186/58	3000	7:39.99	7:36.28- 14
					5000	12:53.98	13:25.19- 14
Kemboi	Clement	KEN	1.2.92	180/65	3kSt	8:12.68	8:16.96- 14
Kemboi	Edward	KEN	12.12.91	170/57	800	1:45.58	1:45.98i -14, 1:46.06- 11
Kemboi	Edwin	KEN	22.8.86		800	1:45.4A	1:45.5A- 14
Kemboi	Elijah	KEN	10.9.84		Mar	2:08:29	2:07:34- 13
Kemboi	Ezekiel	KEN	25.5.82	175/62	3kSt	8:01.71	7:55.76- 11
Kemboi	Hillary	KEN	.86		3kSt	8:22.96	8:22.26- 14
Kemboi	Lawrence	KEN	15.6.93	170/57	3kSt	8:18.51	8:19.59- 14
Kemboi	Mike	KEN	.89			1:46.3A	
Kendagor	Jacob	KEN	24.8.84	158/50	Mar	2:07:47	2:07:53- 14
Kendricks	Sam	USA	7.9.92	189/79	PV	5.86Ai, 5.82	5.81- 13
Kendziera	David	USA	9.9.94	190/84	110h	13.67, 13.56w	13.93- 14
					400h	49.56	51.10- 14
Keny	Felix	KEN	25.12.85	181/58	Mar	2:09:05	2:07:14- 13
Kesete	Merhawi	ERI	.86		HMar	60:52	-0-
Keys	Dakotah	USA	27.9.91	188/79	Dec	7863(w)	8068- 14
Kgosiemang	Kabelo Mmono	BOT	7.1.86	188/74	HJ	2.25	2.34A- 08, 2.30- 06
Khodjayev	Sukhrob	UZB	21.5.93	186/105	HT	78.22	74.20- 12
Khorava	Bachana	GEO	15.3.93	172/67	LJ	8.01	7.51- 13
Khudyakov	Aleksey	RUS	31.3.95		DT	61.25	55.64- 14
Kibet	Alex	KEN	20.10.90	172/52	3kSt	8:28.41	8:33.18- 13
Kibet	Edwin	KEN-J	7.7.96		Mar	2:08:17	-0-
Kibet	Moses	KEN	20.11.94	177/60	800	1:46.5A	1:45.83- 13
Kibet	Raymond	KEN-J	4.2.96	188/80	400	45.39A, 45.66	47.91- 14
Kibet	Stephen	KEN	9.11.86	172/55	HMar	59:58	58:54- 12
Kibet	Vincent	KEN	6.5.91	170/57	1500	3:36.80, 3:34.91i	3:31.96 -14
Kibitok	Amos	KEN	4.4.94		5000	13:23.91	13:52.89- 14
					10k	27:48.53	28:29.69- 14
Kibiwot	Abraham	KEN-J	4.6.96	175/55	3kSt	8:22.10	8:52.36A- 14
Kibor	William	KEN	10.1.85		HMar	60:55	60:51- 14
Kidder	Brannon	USA	18.11.93	183/66	800	1:45.58	1:46.87- 13
Kiecana	Szymon	POL	26.3.89	193/67	HJ	2.25	2.31- 13
Kifle	Aron	ERI-Y	20.2.98		5000	13:17.62	-0-
Kigen	Mike	KEN	15.1.86	170/54	HMar	60:10dh	59:58- 11
(Kaan Kigen Özbilen TUR)					Mar	2:07:42	2:06:59- 14
Kigen	Norbert	KEN	24.1.93		HMar	60:35	62:52- 14
Kikuchi	Masato	JPN	18.9.90	172/56	HMar	60:32	61:17- 14
Kilty	Richard	GBR	2.9.89	184/79	100	10.05	10.10- 13
Kim Byung-jun		KOR	15.8.91	190/80	110h	13.53, 13.49w	13.43- 14
Kim Duk-hyung		KOR	8.12.85	180/70	LJ	7.92	8.20, 8.41w- 09
					TJ	17.00, 17.07w	17.10- 09
Kim Hyun-sub		KOR	31.5.85	175/53	20kW	1:19:13	1:19:24- 14
Kim Jang-jun		KOR	10.5.87	186/77	LJ	7.84, 7.91w	7.89- 09
Kim Kuk-young		KOR	19.4.91	172/60	100	10.16	10.23, 10.17w- 10
Kimani	Bernard	KEN	10.9.93	172/54	5000	13:10.83	13:14.64- 14
10k	27:39.76	27:36.60- 14			HMar	60:05	-0-
Kimetto	Dennis	KEN	22.1.84	172/57	Mar	2:05:50	2:02:57- 14
Kimitei	Elijah	KEN	25.12.86	183/81	TJ	16.63A	16.66A, 16.28- 12
Kimmons	Trell	USA	13.7.85	178/77	100	10.07, 10.01w	9.95, 9.92w- 10
Kimurer	Joel	KEN	21.1.88		HMar	60:58	59:36- 12
					Mar	2:08:11	2:07:48- 13
Kimutai	Marius	KEN	.89		Mar	2:09:14	?
King	David	GBR	13.6.94	187/79	110h	13.69, 13.61w	13.80, 13.70w- 14
King	Dominic	GBR	30.5.83	179/60	50kW	3:59:22	4:06:34- 12
King	Kyree	USA	9.7.94	181/68	100	10.23, 10.11w	10.38, 10.30w- 14
					200	20.51	20.93, 20.66w- 14

Name		Nat	Born	Ht/Wt	Event	2015 Mark	Pre-2015 Best
Kinnunen	Jarkko	FIN	19.1.84	187/69	50kW	4:02:07	3:46:25- 12
Kinsley	Craig	USA	19.1.89	186/82	JT	77.85	82.31- 12
Kinyor	Job	KEN	2.9.90	176/68	800	1:43.92	1:43.76- 12
Kipchoge	Cosmas	KEN	21.3.86		HMar	60:23	-0-
* Kipchoge	Eliud	KEN	5.11.84	167/52	HMar	60:50	59:25- 12
					Mar	2:04:00	2:04:05- 13
Kipkemoi	Daniel	KEN-J	5.7.96	170/52	10k	27:53.19	28:23.99- 14
Kipkemoi	Kenneth	KEN	2.8.84	165/54	HMar	60:17	59:01- 14
* Kipketer	Alfred	KEN-J	26.12.96	169/61	800	1:44.07A	1:43.95 -14
Kipketer	Gideon	KEN	10.11.92	178/57	Mar	2:09:01	2:08:14- 12
Kipkoech	Nicholas	KEN	22.10.92	168/57	800	1:44.9A	1:45.01- 12
Kipkosgei	Fredrick	KEN-J	13.11.96	170/57	3000	7:46.80	
					5000	13:23.66	13:33.6A- 14
Kipkosgei	Nelson	BRN	9.3.93	170/55	3kSt	8:31.35	8:22.24- 12
Kiplagat	Benjamin	UGA	4.3.89	186/61	3kSt	8:29.83	8:03.81- 10
Kiplagat	Evans	KEN	5.3.88		HMar	60:13	59:56- 09
* Kiplagat	Silas	KEN	20.8.89	170/57	1500	3:30.12	3:27.64 -14
					800	1:46.75A	1:44.8A- 12
					1M	3:51.72	3:47.88- 14
Kiplimo	Joash	KEN	.91		3kSt	8:24.26A	8:27.0A- 14
Kiprono	Festus	KEN	29.12.95	175/57	3kSt	8:26.24	8:36.4A- 13
* Kiprop	Asbel	KEN	30.6.89	186/70	800	1:44.4A	1:43.15- 11
					1000	2:17.38	-0-
					1500	3:26.69	3:27.72- 13
					1M	3:51.25	3:48.50- 09
Kiprotich	Alex	KEN	10.10.94	185/84	JT	78.84A	75.56A- 13
Kiprotich	Felix	KEN	.88		Mar	2:06:59	2:08:05- 14
Kiprotich	John	KEN	30.3.89		HMar	60:13	59:23- 09
Kiprotich Sigei	Richard	KEN	11.5.84		Mar	2:08:28	2:10:23- 13
* Kiprotich	Stephen	UGA	18.4.89	172/56	Mar	2:06:33	2:07:20- 11
* Kipruto	Brimin	KEN	31.7.85	176/54	3kSt	8:10.09	7:53.64- 11
* Kipruto	Conseslus	KEN	8.12.94	171/55	3kSt	8:05.20	8:01.16- 13
Kipruto	Vincent	KEN	13.9.87	172/57	HMar	60:19	60:39- 13
Kipsang	Asbel	KEN	10.9.93		HMar	60:37	63:49- 12
Kipsang	Emmanuel	KEN	13.6.91	171/62	3000	7:37.05	
					5000	13:08.55	
					10k	28:03.86	27:59.7A- 13
Kipsang	Wilson	KEN	15.3.82	178/59	Mar	2:04:47	2:03:23- 13
* Kipsiro	Moses	UGA	2.9.86	174/59	HMar	60:41	63:15A- 14
* Kiptanui	Eliud	KEN	6.6.89	169/55	Mar	2:05:21	2:05:39- 10
Kiptanui	Mathew	KEN	.94		1500	3:37.91	3:39.91- 13
Kiptarus	Dominic	KEN-J	3.8.96	168/52	3kSt	8:33.40	8:29.28A- 14
Kiptis	Josphat	KEN	16.11.93		HMar	60:21	61:25- 14
Kiptoo	Anthony	KEN-J	19.8.97	174/61	1500	3:35.33	-0-
Kiptoo	Edwin Kibet	KEN	28.12.87		HMar	60:11	61:19- 13
Kiptoo	Edwin Kiprop	KEN	14.8.93		HMar	59:26	61:13- 14
Kiptoo	Elijah	KEN	9.6.86	171/53	1500	3:35.84, 3:33.98 short	3:33.81- 12
* Kiptoo	Mark	KEN	21.6.76	175/64	Mar	2:06:00	2:06:16- 13
Kiptum	Joseph	KEN	25.9.87		10k	28:06.5A	28:11.47- 08
					HMar	60:17	60:26- 12
Kipyatich	Abraham	KEN	.93		HMar	60:03	-0-
Kipyego	Barnabas	KEN	12.6.95	176/57	3kSt	8:21.93	8:17.03- 14
Kipyego	Barselius	KEN	.93		HMar	60:51	63:12A- 14
* Kipyego	Bernard	KEN	16.7.86	160/50	Mar	2:06:19	2:06:22- 14
Kipyego	Edwin	KEN	16.11.90		HMar	59:30	60:04- 13
Kipyegon	Bernard	KEN	.94	181/65	800	1:45.68	1:46.0A- 13
Kipyeko	Kennedy	KEN	.91		HMar	60:39	61:31- 14
Kipyeko	Phillip	UGA	10.1.95	168/55	5000	13:10.69	13:16.92- 13
Kirchler	Hannes	ITA	22.12.78	191/105	DT	62.56	65.01- 07
Kiriazis	Ioannis	GRE-J	19.1.96	192/84	JT	78.41	73.66- 14
Kirongo	Sammy	KEN	4.2.94	176/62	800	1:45.5A	1:45.3A- 14, 1:45.38 -14
Kirt	Magnus	EST	10.4.90	192/89	JT	86.65	79.82- 13
Kirui	Geoffrey	KEN	16.2.93	158/50	5000	13:21.6+	13:16.68- 13
					10k	27:17.91	26:55.73- 11
					HMar	59:38	60:51- 14
Kirui	Gilbert	KEN	22.1.94	172/55	3kSt	8:31.04	8:06.96- 13
Kirwa	Gilbert	KEN	20.12.85	178/59	Mar	2:07:44	2:06:14- 09
Kiryu	Yoshihide	JPN	15.12.95	175/69	100	10.09, 9.87w	10.01- 13
Kiselkov	Fyodor	RUS	3.6.95		TJ	16.50	
Kishimoto	Takayuki	JPN	6.5.90	171/61	400h	49.17	48.41- 12
Kishoyan	Alphas	KEN	12.10.94	164/60	400	44.75A, 45.81	45.64A, 46.19- 12
^ Kisorio	Mathew	KEN	16.5.89	178/62	HMar	59:52	58:46- 11
					Mar	2:06:33	2:10:58- 11
Kitagawa	Takamasa	JPN-J	5.9.96	177/68	400	45.52	46.46- 14
Kitilit	Jonathan	KEN	24.4.94	171/61	800	1:45.0A	1:47.8A- 12
					1000	2:15.78	-0-

Name		Nat	Born	Ht/Wt	Event	2015 Mark	Pre-2015 Best
Kitum	Timothy	KEN	20.11.94	172/60	800	1:45.0A	1:42.53- 12
					1000	2:17.62	2:17.96- 12
Kitwara	Sammy	KEN	26.11.86	177/54	HMar	60:25	58:47- 11
					Mar	2:07:43	2:04:28- 14
Kivalov	Leonid	RUS	1.4.88	183/75	PV	5.56	5.71i- 08, 5.61- 14
Kivistik	Kaur	EST	29.4.91	179/68	3kSt	8:32.23	8:36.10- 12
Kivuva	Jackson	KEN	11.8.88	172/59	800	1:44.56A	1:43.72- 10
Kling-Baptiste	Tom	SWE	29.8.90	170/65	100	10.13w	10.29- 14
Kloptsov	Yuriy	RUS	22.12.89	176/64	3kSt	8:33.09	8:28.03- 14
Knipphals	Sven	GER	20.9.85	190/85	100	10.13, 10.07w	10.20- 13
Kniya	Younès	MAR	15.8.95		3kSt	8:29.7	8:58.42- 14
Knobel	Jan Felix	GER	16.1.89	189/89	Dec	8045	8396- 13
Kobayashi	Kai	JPN	28.2.93	164/52	20kW	1:19:12	1:21:13- 14
Kobelev	Leonid	RUS	24.6.95	183/75	PV	5.55	5.45- 14
Koech	Bernard	KEN	31.1.88	165/50	HMar	60:09	59:10- 12, 58:42dh- 13
					Mar	2:08:02	2:04:53- 13
Koech	Edwin	KEN	.87		HMar	59:54	60:13- 14
Koech	Haron	KEN	27.1.90	188/79	400h	49.38	51.96A- 14
Koech	Isiah	KEN	19.12.93	178/60	3000	7:37.16	7:30.43- 12
					5000	13:07.33	12:48.64- 12
Koech	John	BRN	23.8.95	174/59	3kSt	8:14.75	8:16.96- 13
Koech	Moses	KEN-J	5.4.97	168/52	3000	7:47.48	8:06.33- 14
					5000	13:15.56	13:34.0A- 14
Koech	Paul Kipsiele	KEN	10.11.81	168/57	3000	7:39.68i	7:32.78i- 10, 7:33.93- 05
2M	8:13.46i	8:06.48i, 8:13.31- 08			5000	13:07.74	13:02.69i- 12, 13:05.18- 10
3kSt	8:10.24	7:54.31- 12					
Koekemoer	Barend	RSA	12.6.95	176/70	400	45.42A	45.97A- 14
Koffi	Hua Wilfried	CIV	24.9.89	186/80	100	10.09	10.05- 14
					200	20.39	20.25- 14
Kogei	David	KEN	5.5.85	174/58	HMar	59:46	60:50- 13
Kogo	Micah	KEN	3.6.86	170/60	HMar	59:33	59:07dh- 12
Koivu	Joachim	FIN	5.9.88	195/104	HT	71.07	71.67- 14
Kolasinac	Asmir	SRB	15.10.84	186/137	SP	21.58	20.85- 12
Kolesnikov	Maksim	RUS	28.2.91		LJ	7.87, 7.95w	7.80- 13
Kolomoyets	Sergey	BLR	11.8.89	191/110	HT	77.43	77.52- 11
Komarov	German	RUS	14.12.94		JT	79.60	76.61- 13
Kombe	Saviour	ZAM	3.8.91	174/66	400	45.57	46.49- 12
Kombich	Ismael	KEN	16.10.85	183/73	1500	3:36.86	3:33.31- 10
Komen	Willy	KEN	22.12.87	168/55	3kSt	8:31.8A	8:11.18- 07
Komon	Leonard Patrick	KEN	10.1.88	175/52	HMar	59:57	59:14- 14
Konchellah	Felix	KEN	15.11.90		800	1:46.5A	1:48.56- 12
Kondratyev	Roman	RUS	15.5.95	183/77	Dec	7752	
Konishi	Yuta	JPN	31.7.90	182/70	400h	49.58	49.41- 11
Konstantinou	Vasilios	CYP	13.9.92	173/60	HJ	2.26	2.20- 14
Koorep	Ranno	EST	24.1.90		JT	77.81	76.96- 14
Kopeykin	Vasiliy	RUS	9.3.88	176/73	LJ	8.00i, 7.96, 8.01w	8.00, 8.06w- 13
Korchmid	Oleksandr	UKR	22.1.82	188/89	PV	5.55i	5.81- 05
Korir	Fredrick	KEN	17.4.87		800	1:45.2A	1:46.30A- 13
Korir	Geoffrey	KEN-J	2.5.96	175/60	10k	28:06.8A	28:52.41A- 14
Korir	Laban	KEN	30.12.85		Mar	2:07:54	2:06:05- 11
Korir	Mark	KEN	10.1.85	175/59	HMar	60:48	60:49- 13
					Mar	2:05:49	2:07:08- 13
Korme	Sisay	ETH	9.1.85	170/62	3kSt	8:32.54	8:20.72- 11
Kornhardt	Marcel	GER	3.8.93	182/75	TJ	16.21i, 16.56w	15.86i- 14, 15.84- 13
Korolyov	Aleksey	RUS	5.4.82	190/118	HT	76.42	79.36- 08
Korotovskiy	Yevgeniy	RUS	21.6.92	184/102	HT	71.39	72.16- 14
Korshunov	Yevgeniy	RUS	11.4.86		HJ	2.26	2.29i, 2.23- 14
Kosgei	Kiprono	KEN			400h	49.84A	50.41A- 14
Kosgei	Samuel Kiplimo	KEN	20.1.86	173/55	Mar	2:07:07	2:07:47- 11
Kostoglídis	Konstadínos	GRE	10.8.90	181/85	HT	71.16	68.52- 14
Kosynskyy	Dmytro	UKR	31.3.89	198/105	JT	79.00	83.39- 11
Kotov	Danyil	RUS	14.11.95	183/73	PV	5.50	5.50- 14
Kotut	Cyprian	KEN	.92		HMar	59:28	59:12- 14
					Mar	2:08:55	-0-
Koumi	Sadam	SUD	6.4.94	173/68	400	45.41	46.06- 14
Kovacs	Joe	USA	28.6.89	185/114	SP	22.56	22.03- 14
Kövágó	Zoltán	HUN	10.4.79	204/127	DT	67.39	69.95- 06
Kovalenko	Nazar	UKR	9.2.89	178/68	20kW	1:23:03	1:19:46- 14
Kovals	Ainars	LAT	21.11.81	192/105	JT	78.90	86.64- 08
Kovalyov	Andriy	UKR	11.6.92	198/67	HJ	2.28i, 2.25	2.25i- 14, 2.24- 13
Kovenko	Andriy	UKR	25.11.73	174/68	20kW	1:22:44	1:20:20- 14

	Name		Nat	Born	Ht/Wt	Event	2015 Mark	Pre-2015 Best
^	Kowal	Yoann	FRA	28.5.87	174/58	3kSt	8:18.38	8:12.53- 13
	Kownatke	Rafal	POL	24.3.85	189/133	SP	20.07i, 19.91	20.13- 13
	Kranjc	Matija	SLO	12.6.84	181/81	JT	78.35	80.46- 14
	Krauss	Simon	FRA	12.2.92	182/75	110h	13.59, 13.52w	13.50- 14, 13.41w- 13
	Kravtsov	Aleksey	RUS	8.5.93		Dec	7894	7764- 14
^	Krivitskiy ¶	Pavel	BLR	17.4.84	184/110	HT	74.80, 76.20dq	80.67- 11
*	Krivov	Andrey	RUS	14.11.85	185/72	20kW	1:20:43	1:18:25- 12
	Kroyter	Dmitriy	ISR	18.2.93	189/71	HJ	2.29	2.28- 11
	Kruger	A.G.	USA	18.2.79	193/118	HT	76.87	79.26- 04
	Krukowski	Marcin	POL	14.6.92	182/92	JT	85.20	83.04- 13
	Krymarenko	Yuriy	UKR	11.8.83	187/65	HJ	2.28	2.34i- 07, 2.34- 13
*	Kszczot	Adam	POL	2.9.89	178/64	800	1:43.45	1:43.30- 11
	Kubota	Shinobu	JPN	12.12.91	167/53	10k	28:06.44	27:54.25- 14
	Kuciapski	Artur	POL	26.12.93	183/65	800	1:45.21	1:44.89 -14
*	Kudlicka	Jan	CZE	29.4.88	184/76	PV	5.75	5.80i- 14, 5.76,5.83ex/dh- 13,5.81ex- 11,
*	Kudryavtsev	Denis	RUS	13.4.92	187/77	400h	48.05	48.95- 14
	Kuira	Paul	KEN	25.1.90	172/53	10k	27:50.81	27:40.43- 14
						HMar	59:47	-0-
*	Kuma	Abera	ETH	31.8.90	160/50	Mar	2:06:47	2:05:56- 14
	Kumar Sangwan	Sandeep	IND	16.12.86	178/79	20kW	1:22:16	1:26:07- 13
						50kW	3:57:03	3:56:22- 14
	Kupers	Thijmen	NED	4.10.91	180/65	800	1:45.28	1:45.68 -14
	Kupper	Martin	EST	31.5.89	195/108	DT	66.67	65.03- 13
	Kusuro	Geoffrey	UGA	12.2.89	169/55	HMar	59:43	60:41- 14
	Kwambai	Robert	KEN	22.11.85		Mar	2:08:18	2:08:48- 14
	Kwemboi	Gilbert	KEN-J	3.10.97	180/64	1500	3:40.47, 3:35.68 short	3:41.99- 14
*	Kwemoi	Ronald	KEN	19.9.95	180/68	1500	3:30.43	3:28.81 -14
	1M	3:52.57			-0-	5000	13:16.14	13:21.53- 14
	Kwemoi Chumo	Ronald	KEN-J	3.3.97	165/49	10k	27:42.09	
*	Kynard	Eric	USA	3.2.91	193/86	HJ	2.37	2.37- 14
^	Laâlou ¶	Amine	MAR	13.5.82	178/57	800	1:45.92	1:43.25 -06
						1500	3:35.71	3:29.53- 10
	Laanmäe	Tanel	EST	29.9.89	183/94	JT	83.82	81.96- 09
	Labali	Abdelhadi	MAR	26.4.93	174/62	1500	3:37.89	3:35.95- 13
	Lagat	Alfers	KEN	7.8.86		HMar	60:33	61:34- 13
						Mar	2:06:48	2:07:11- 14
*	Lagat	Bernard	USA	12.12.74	174/61	3000	7:42.75, 7:37.92i	7:29.00- 10
	2M	8:17.05i	8:09.49i- 13, 8:12.45- 08			5000	13:14.97	12:53.60- 11
	Lagat	Haron	KEN	15.8.83	185/72	3kSt	8:25.04	8:15.80- 11
	Lagat	Justus	KEN-J	20.5.96	168/55	3kSt	8:26.37	
	Lahoulou	Abdelmalik	ALG	7.5.92	180/70	400h	48.67	50.15- 14
^	Lalang	Lawi	KEN	15.6.91	170/58	5000	13:16.11	13:00.95- 13
	Lambert	James JC	USA	12.4.90	186/107	HT	72.49	67.64- 14
	Lancashire	Tom	GBR	2.7.85	179/63	1500	3:38.02	3:33.96- 10
	Landry	Christopher	USA	29.4.86	175/61	10k	27:55.19	27:59.22- 13
	Lane	John	GBR	29.1.89	186/88	Dec	7798	7922- 14
	Langat	Leonard	KEN	7.8.90		HMar	60:06	59:52- 11
	Langat	Philip	KEN	23.4.90	176/66	HMar	60:04	61:05- 12
	Langford	Kyle	GBR-J	2.2.96	183/66	800	1:45.78	1:47.41 -14
	Langowski	Artur	BRA	8.5.91	183/77	400h	49.73	49.77- 13
	Langton-Burnell	Ben	NZL	10.7.92	183/82	JT	77.97	74.69- 14
*	Lapierre	Fabrice	AUS	17.10.83	179/66	LJ	8.29	8.40, 8.78w- 10
	Lasa	Emiliano	URU	25.1.90	180/75	LJ	8.09, 8.17w	7.94- 14
*	Lauro	Germán	ARG	2.4.84	185/127	SP	20.77	21.26- 13
*	Lavillenie	Renaud	FRA	18.9.86	177/69	PV	6.05	6.16i- 14, 6.02- 13
	Lavillenie	Valentin	FRA	16.7.91	170/65	PV	5.80i, 5.70	5.70i, 5.65- 13
	Lawal	Biliaminu	USA	12.3.85		LJ	8.02w	
	Lawrence	Brijesh BJ	SKN	27.12.89	181/75	100	10.15	10.12- 12, 10.11w- 14
*	Lawson	Jarrion	USA	6.5.94	188/75	100	10.04, 9.90w	-
						LJ	8.34, 8.36w	8.39Ai, 7.92, 8.13w- 14
	Lazas	Kevin	USA	25.1.92	178/84	Dec	7594	7955- 12
	Le Coz	Xavier	FRA	30.12.79	182/62	50kW	3:58:20	4:01:21- 14
	le Roux	Wouter	RSA	17.1.86	186/77	400h	49.87A	49.25A- 05, 49.54- 04
	Lee	Beejay	USA	5.3.93	168/72	100	9.99, 9.94w	10.07- 13
						200	20.11	20.83- 14
	Lefete	Tshepo	RSA	2.2.92	182/73	110h	13.57A	13.96A, 14.18, 13.99w- 13
	Legesse	Berhanu	ETH	11.9.94	168/55	5000	13:23.26	13:08.88- 14
						HMar	59:20	
	Legesse	Frezer	USA	4.6.90	181/64	1500	3:36.93	3:41.14- 12
	Lehata	Mosito	LES	8.4.89	177/69	100	10.11	10.13 -14
						200	20.42	20.36- 14

Name		Nat	Born	Ht/Wt	Event	2015 Mark	Pre-2015 Best
Lehto	Jesse	FIN	12.2.93	180/85	HT	72.31	71.81- 14
Lekopa	Dikotsi	RSA	7.7.88	168/52	3kSt	8:32.17	8:41.93- 11
Lemaitre	Christophe	FRA	11.6.90	189/74	100	10.07	9.92- 11
					200	20.21	19.80- 11
Lemi	Hayle	ETH	13.9.94	172/56	Mar	2:05:28	2:10:40- 14
Lemma	Sisay	ETH	12.12.90		Mar	2:06:26	2:09:02- 14
Lemmi	Andrea	ITA	12.5.84	190/70	HJ	2.26i, 2.26	2.25- 03
Lendore	Deon	TTO	28.10.92	179/75	400	44.41	44.36- 14
Lescay	Yoandys	CUB	5.1.94	181/77	400	45.13A, 45.84	45.29- 13
Leslie	Cory	USA	24.10.89	175/60	1500	3:35.36	3:34.93- 13
					3kSt	8:25.74	8:20.08- 13
Lesnoy	Aleksandr	RUS	28.7.88	194/116	SP	20.70i, 20.55	21.40- 14
Letnicov	Vladimir	MDA	7.10.81	178/70	TJ	16.55	17.06- 02
Levins	Cameron	CAN	28.3.89	181/68	3000	7:45.21+i	7:41.59i- 14, 7:45.75i- 12
					2M	8:15.38i	
					5000	13:20.68	13:15.19- 13
					10k	27:07.51	27:27.96- 12
Lewandowski	Marcin	POL	13.6.87	180/64	800	1:43.72	1:43.79- 13
					1000	2:17.25	2:15.76- 11
Lewis	Steve	GBR	20.5.86	191/83	PV	5.71Ai, 5.50	5.82- 12
Leyver	José	MEX	12.11.85	164/52	50kW	3:50:14A	3:49:16A- 11
Li Jialei		CHN	14.9.94		TJ	16.78	16.01- 14
Li Jinzhe		CHN	1.9.89	188/64	LJ	8.26	8.47- 14
Li Tianlei		CHN	13.1.95	173/63	20kW	1:20:57	1:21:01- 12
Li Zhipeng		CHN	1.5.95		LJ	7.92i	7.76- 14
Licht	Dennis	NED	30.5.84	182/67	5000	13:23.00	13:29.83- 12
Lihrman	Michael	USA	6.12.91	196/114	HT	75.29	71.24- 14
Likhanov	Yevgeniy	RUS	10.1.95	187/82	Dec	7869	
Lilesa	Feyisa	ETH	1.2.90	158/50	Mar	2:06:35	2:04:52- 12
Limo	Daniel Kiprop	KEN	1.1.93		HMar	60:52	59:55- 12
Limo	Silah	KEN	1.2.92	172/68	Mar	2:08:54	2:09:14- 14
Lingua	Marco	ITA	4.6.78	179/112	HT	78.29	79.97- 08
Linke	Christopher	GER	24.10.88	191/64	20kW	1:20:37	1:20:41- 12
Linnik	Aleksandr	BLR	28.1.91	176/66	400	45.43	47.02- 14
Lipsanen	Simo	FIN	13.9.95	191/72	TJ	16.62w	15.64- 14
Lipsey	Javonte	USA	17.10.92	175/78	400h	49.65	50.65- 14
Lisek	Piotr	POL	16.8.92	188/85	PV	5.90i, 5.82	5.82- 14
Listenbee	Kolby	USA	25.1.94	186/83	100	10.04, 10.03w	10.23, 10.12w- 14
Litvinov	Sergey	RUS	27.1.86	185/105	HT	77.24	80.98- 12
Litzell	Simon	SWE-J	11.2.97	189/90	JT	78.73	74.01- 14
Liu Jian		CHN	19.5.95		50kW	3:56:25	-0-
Liu Yang		CHN	29.10.86	190/110	SP	19.69	19.77- 13
Livermore	Jason	JAM	25.4.88	178/77	100	10.06, 10.10Aw	10.05 -14
Lokomwa	Thomas	KEN	.87		HMar	60:33	60:56- 14
Lomnicky	Marcel	SVK	6.7.87	177/106	HT	77.63	79.16- 14
Lomong	Lopez	USA	1.1.85	178/67	3000	7:42.19	7:39.81- 14
					5000	13:21.32	13:07.00i- 13, 13:07.95- 14
Longosiwa	Thomas	KEN	14.1.82	175/57	3000	7:39.22	7:30.09- 09
					5000	12:59.72	12:49.04- 12
Lonyangata	Paul	KEN	12.12.92	170/55	HMar	60:01	59:53- 12
					Mar	2:07:14	2:07:44- 13
López	Francisco Javier	ESP	29.12.89	181/70	110h	13.62	13.64- 13, 13.62w- 13
López	Kevin	ESP	12.6.90	172/60	800	1:45.25	1:43.74- 12
López	Luis Fernando	COL	3.6.79	173/60	50kW	3:55:43	4:05:14- 14
López	Miguel Ángel	ESP	3.7.88	181/70	20kW	1:19:14	1:19:21- 14
López	Yeimer	CUB	20.8.82	184/73	800	1:46.13	1:43.07- 08
Losev	Ivan	UKR	26.1.86	177/69	20kW	1:22:37	1:19:33- 14
Lovett	Eddie	ISV	25.6.92	181/73	110h	13.31A, 13.41	13.39, 13.29w- 13
Loxsom	Casimir	USA	17.3.91	183/64	800	1:44.92	1:45.28- 11
Loyanae	Wilson	KEN	20.11.88		Mar	2:06:11	2:05:37- 12
Lu Zhiwei		CHN-J	4.4.96		TJ	16.45	15.59, 15.91w- 14
Lukás	Marek	CZE	16.7.91	180/75	Dec	7892	7829- 14
Lukyanenko	Artem	RUS	30.1.90	193/84	Dec	7728	8177- 13
Lukyanov	Denis	RUS	11.7.89	190/115	HT	73.94	79.61- 13
Lundgren	Daniel	SWE	4.7.85	181/65	3kSt	8:33.51	8:38.75- 14
Luo Dongpo		CHN	23.6.95		50kW	3:56:46	-0-
Luo Yadong		CHN	15.1.92		50kW	3:48:48	4:04:26- 14
Luron	Kevin	FRA	8.11.91	184/80	TJ	16.63, 16.83w	16.56- 14
Lyadusov	Konstantin	RUS	2.3.88	190/125	SP	20.57	20.54- 14
Lyakhovich	Aleksandr	BLR	4.7.89	171/65	20kW	1:21:49	1:22:50- 14
Lyles	Josephus	USA-Y	22.7.98	184/73	400	45.46A, 45.77	46.23- 14
Lyles	Noah	USA-J	18.7.97	182/73	100	10.14, 10.07w	10.45- 14
					200	20.18	20.71- 14

Name		Nat	Born	Ht/Wt	Event	2015 Mark	Pre-2015 Best
Lynsha	Maksim	BLR	6.4.85	190/72	110h	13.59	13.36- 12
Lyzhyn	Pavel	BLR	24.3.81	189/110	SP	20.19	21.21- 10
Ma Qun		CHN	8.2.94		JT	79.39	76.41- 14
Maazouzi	Zakaria	MAR	15.6.85	171/62	1500	3:37.76	3:31.94- 13
Madison	Chase	USA	13.9.85	192/130	DT	65.42	62.85- 08
* Mägi	Rasmus	EST	4.5.92	188/74	400h	48.65	48.54- 14
Magnini	Stefano	ITA	17.11.88		TJ	16.55	16.08i- 12, 15.98- 11
Magour	Ahmed Bader	QAT-J	3.3.96		JT	77.88	
* Magut	James	KEN	20.7.90	180/64	1500	3:31.76	3:30.61- 14
					1M	3:52.33	3:49.43- 14
Maheswary	Renjith	IND	30.1.86	177/72	TJ	16.66	17.07- 10, 17.19w- 07
Mahler	Wolf	USA	26.9.94	180/77	Dec	7650	7602- 14
Mahoney	Travis	USA	25.7.90	172/61	3kSt	8:27.08	8:30.87- 13
Maia	Edi	POR	10.11.87	176/75	PV	5.60i, 5.55	5.70- 13
Maiau	Raihau	PYF	1.8.92	184/77	LJ	7.99i, 7.98, 8.14w	7.96- 14
Maina	Johana	KEN	25.12.90	170/54	5000	13:25.24	13:38.98- 13
					10k	27:26.92	28:02.87- 14
Maina	John	KEN	14.7.93	179/53	5000	13:24.21	13:37.09- 11
Maina	John	KEN	3.8.94	179/53	10k	27:35.54	29:25.68- 14
Maiyo	Hillary	KEN	2.10.93	174/61	1500	3:35.20	3:35.43A- 11
					3000	7:39.70	
Maiyo	Jonathan	KEN	5.5.88	175/52	HMar	59:26	59:02- 12
Majdán	Dusan	SVK	8.9.87	180/67	50kW	3:58:57	3:53:26- 14
* Majewski	Tomasz	POL	30.8.81	204/140	SP	20.82	21.95- 09
Makau	Patrick	KEN	2.3.85	173/57	Mar	2:08:18	2:03:38- 11
* Makhloufi	Taoufik	ALG	29.4.88	181/66	800	1:44.24	1:43.53 -14
1000	2:13.08		-0-		1500	3:28.75	3:30.40- 14
Makhrosenko	Zakhar	BLR	10.10.91	182/105	HT	74.28	76.08- 13
* Makwala	Isaac	BOT	29.9.86	183/79	200	20.44A	19.96, 19.7A- 14
					400	43.72	44.01- 14
* Malachowski	Piotr	POL	7.6.83	194/135	DT	68.29	71.84- 13
Malel Sitonik	William	KEN	1.3.94	165/52	5000	13:22.36	13:19.83- 13
					10k	27:22.12	27:25.56- 14
Mallett	Aaron	USA	26.9.94	188/79	110h	13.59, 13.40w	13.86- 14
Malone	Casey	USA	6.4.77	203/109	DT	61.96	68.49A- 09
Mamedov	Mergen	TKM	24.12.90		HT	71.08	74.01- 13
* Manangoi	Elijah	KEN	5.1.93	181/65	1500	3:29.67	3:35.0A- 14
* Mannio	Ari	FIN	23.7.87	185/104	JT	86.82	85.70- 09
Mansilla	Humberto	CHI-J	22.5.96	180/100	HT	71.01	66.91- 14
* Manzano	Leonel	USA	12.9.84	165/57	800	1:45.24	1:44.56- 10
1500	3:36.16		3:30.98- 14		1M	3:53.55	3:50.64- 10
Maraba	Wilson	KEN	2.12.86		3kSt	8:25.99A	8:16.96- 12
Marcell	Jan	CZE	4.6.85	197/111	SP	20.71i, 20.32	20.93- 14
					DT	60.45	66.00- 11
Marghiev	Serghei	MDA	6.11.92	194/96	HT	78.72	78.27- 14
Markov	Nikolay	RUS	1.2.95		20kW	1:23:19	-0-
Markovic	Martin	CRO-J	13.1.96	190/110	DT	62.43	57.54- 14
Márquez	Dayron	COL	19.11.83	181/93	JT	80.17A	80.61A- 12, 82.20Au- 08
Marshin	Dmitriy	AZE	24.2.72	186/115	HT	78.52	79.56- 12
Martín	Álvaro	ESP	18.6.94	181/62	20kW	1:20:19	1:20:39- 14
* Martin	Cory	USA	22.5.85	196/125	SP	20.74	22.10- 10
Martin	Romain	FRA	12.7.88	198/86	Dec	7825	8104 -14
Martin	Ryan	USA	23.3.89	185/68	800	1:45.79A	1:44.77- 12
* Martina	Churandy	NED	3.7.84	178/675	100	10.06	9.91- 12, 9.76Aw- 06
					200	20.20	19.85- 12
^ Martínez	Guillermo	CUB	28.6.81	185/106	JT	78.15A	87.20A- 11
Martínez	Jorge	MEX	25.10.90		50kW	3:55:21A	4:06:04A- 14
Martínez	José Ernesto	CUB	1.1.91	175/73	TJ	16.78	16.56- 13
* Martínez	Lázaro	CUB-J	3.11.97	192/83	TJ	17.02	17.24- 14
Martínez	Lois Maikel	CUB/ESP	3.6.81	185/90	DT	65.30	67.45- 05
^ Martínez	Wilfredo	ex-CUB	9.1.85	180/82	LJ	8.04	8.31A- 08, 8.20- 10
Martínez	Yancarlos	DOM	8.7.92	167/61	100	10.14	10.29A- 14
					200	20.22	
* Martinot Lagarde	Pascal	FRA	22.9.91	190/80	110h	13.06	12.95- 14
Martinot Lagarde	Thomas	FRA	7.2.88	186/78	110h	13.49	13.26- 13
Martinsen	Andreas	DEN	17.7.90	190/82	110h	13.55	13.68- 13
Martos	Sebastián	ESP	20.6.89	178/63	3kSt	8:22.38	8:18.31- 14
Martynyuk	Andriy	UKR	25.9.90	184/100	HT	72.04	77.70- 12
Maruo	Satoshi	JPN	28.11.91		20kW	1:19:42	1:24:42- 13
* Maslák	Pavel	CZE	21.2.91	176/67	400	45.09	44.79- 14
Maslov	Stanislav	UKR	19.1.89	183/72	1500	3:38.02	3:38.61- 14
					3000	7:47.22	8:05.93i, 8:07.70- 13

Name		Nat	Born	Ht/Wt	Event	2015 Mark	Pre-2015 Best
Mason	Michael	CAN	30.9.86	188/67	HJ	2.33	2.31- 12
Mason	Tyler	JAM	15.1.95	183/73	110h	13.32A, 13.39	-0-
Massó	Maykel	CUB-Y	8.5.99	176/65	LJ	8.12	
Masters	Riley	USA	5.4.90	185/73	1500	3:36.49	3:37.19- 12
1M	3:56.15i, 3:57.48	3:56.25i- 13, 3:56.75- 14			5000	13:17.97	13:39.47- 14
Mástoras	Adónios	GRE	6.1.91	198/77	HJ	2.31i, 2.30	2.30- 14
Mätas	Risto	EST	30.4.84	189/91	JT	82.06	83.48- 13
Mathenge	Patrick Wambui	KEN-J	2.11.96	169/53	10k	27:54.98	
Mathieu	Michael	BAH	24.6.83	180/78	200	20.40	20.16- 12
					400	45.00	45.06- 12
Matsumoto	Aoi	JPN	7.9.87	177/60	3kSt	8:33.69	8:30.49- 10
Matsunaga	Daisuke	JPN	24.3.95	174/60	20kW	1:19:08	1:21:17- 14
Matsushita	Yuki	JPN	9.9.91	176/64	400h	49.14	49.71- 13
Matthews	Julian	NZL	21.7.88	178/66	1500	3:37.37	3:38.20- 14
Matthews	Peter	JAM	13.11.89	189/77	400	44.69	45.62- 11
Mattis	Sam	USA	19.3.94	185/100	DT	62.48	62.13- 14
Matusevicius	Edis	LTU-J	30.6.96	184/79	JT	78.82	71.52- 14
Maugein	Maxime	FRA	27.9.92	182/80	Dec	7801	7764- 14
Mayer	Gerhard	AUT	20.5.80	191/100	DT	67.20	65.24- 10
Mayer	Kevin	FRA	10.2.92	186/77	Dec	8469	8521- 14
Mayers	Emanuel	TTO	9.3.89	178/70	400h	49.80	49.57- 14
Mbishei	Titus	KEN	28.10.90	178/59	10k	27:31.48	26:59.81- 11
					HMar	60:18	59:55- 14
McBride	Brandon	CAN	15.6.94	195/75	800	1:45.87	1:45.35- 14
McBride	Bryan	USA	10.12.91	188/77	HJ	2.30	2.28- 14
McClain	Remontay	USA	21.9.92	188/85	100	10.07, 9.82w	10.14- 14
					200	20.12	20.27- 14
McCullough	Conor	IRL/USA	31.1.91	186/102	HT	76.91	77.20- 14
McDonald	Rusheen	JAM	17.8.92	175/73	400	43.93	45.10- 12
McLean	Sean	USA	23.3.92	185/79	100	10.01	10.13- 14
					200	20.37	20.41, 20.38w- 14
McLeod	Omar	JAM	25.4.94	180/73	110h	12.97	13.44- 14
McNamara	Jordan	USA	7.3.87	178/64	1500	3:37.20	3:34.00- 13
McNeill	David	AUS	6.10.86	175/59	10k	27:45.01	28:03.02- 08
McQuay	Tony	USA	16.4.90	180/70	400	44.81	44.40- 13
Mead	Hassan	USA	28.8.89	174/61	5000	13:10.38	13:02.80- 14
					10k	27:33.04	27:59.04 -12
Mechaal	Adel	ESP	5.12.90	184/67	1500	3:36.55	3:36.78- 13
					3000	7:52.16, 7:46.92i	7:52.29i- 14, 8:03.38- 12
Meité	Ben Youssef	CIV	11.11.86	179/70	100	10.04	10.06- 12
Mejias	Reinier	CUB	22.9.90	178/98	HT	73.18	75.98- 13
Mekashaw	Kassa	ETH	19.3.84	167/54	5000	13:24.87	13:26.07- 14
					10k	27:45.92	27:38.93- 14
Mekonen	Teshome	ETH	5.8.95		HMar	60:27	61:21- 14
Meleshko	Pavel	BLR	24.11.92	187/90	JT	80.96	80.68- 14
Melich	Lukás	CZE	16.9.80	186/110	HT	76.21	80.28- 13
Melly	Edwin	KEN	23.4.94	178/60	800	1:44.50	1:43.81- 12
					1000	2:17.51	-0-
Melnykov	Stanislav	UKR	26.2.87	184/70	400h	49.62	49.09- 10
Melo	Aleksandro	BRA	26.9.95	179/56	LJ	8.12	7.46- 13
Mena	Reynier	CUB-J	21.11.96	174/79	100	10.17, 10.08w	10.26- 14
					200	20.32	20.50A- 14, 20.72- 13, 20.63w- 12
Menaldo	Kévin	FRA	12.7.92	176/66	PV	5.81	5.75i, 5.72- 14
Mendes	Jonathan	BRA	14.4.90	187/80	110h	13.54	13.53- 14, 13.5- 13
Mendieta	José Angel	CUB	16.10.91	187/84	Dec	7771	7967h- 13
Mengich	Richard	KEN	.89	185/68	HMar	59:59	60:11- 14
Mengistu	Azmeraw	ETH	15.9.92	166/52	10k	27:33.82	
					HMar	60:48	-0-
Menkov	Aleksandr	RUS	7.12.90	178/74	LJ	8.27	8.56- 13
Merber	Kyle	USA	19.11.90	180/64	1500	3:34.54	3:35.59- 12
Merga	Imane	ETH	15.10.88	174/61	3000	7:39.96	7:43.59- 14
5000	12:59.04	12:53.58- 10			10k	27:17.63	26:48.35- 11
Merritt	Aries	USA	24.7.85	182/70	110h	13.04	12.80- 12
Merritt	LaShawn	USA	27.6.86	188/82	400	43.65	43.74- 13
Merzougui	Abdelaziz	ESP	30.8.91	177/62	3kSt	8:26.34	8:18.03- 12
Mesel	Amanuel	ERI	29.12.90	175/57	HMar	60:26	60:10- 13
				7	Mar	2:08:18	2:08:17- 13
Mesic	Kemal	BIH	4.8.85	196/110	SP	20.49	20.71- 12
Mezones	Freddy	VEN	24.9.87	176/68	400	45.53	45.55- 14
Mihaljevic	Filip	CRO	31.7.94	201/113	SP	20.16	19.65- 14
					DT	63.11	60.45- 14

	Name		Nat	Born	Ht/Wt	Event	2015 Mark	Pre-2015 Best
	Mikhou	Sadik	MAR	25.7.90	174/61	1500	3:33.45	3:33.31- 13
	Mikos	Mateusz	POL	10.4.87	196/107	SP	20.06	19.62- 13
*	Milanov	Philip	BEL	6.7.91	191/118	DT	66.90	66.02- 14
	Milaw	Abrha	ETH	3.1.88		Mar	2:08:09	2:07:46- 14
	Mileusnic	Dejan	BIH	16.11.91	183/84	JT	78.05	80.40- 14
	Miller	Ashinia	JAM	6.6.93	189/100	SP	20.31i, 19.84	19.54- 14
	Miller	Jalen	USA	17.6.95	175/77	100	10.12	10.19- 14
*	Miller	Nick	GBR	1.5.93	188/112	HT	77.55	74.38- 14
	Miller	Ramon	BAH	17.2.87	180/73	400	45.36	44.87- 12
	Milne	Taylor	CAN	14.6.81	180/66	3kSt	8:19.90	8:27.81- 14
	Minemura	Kota	JPN	22.12.92	176/62	LJ	7.88, 8.08w	7.94- 14
	Minor	Eli	USA-J	.96	175/61	100	10.15w	10.75- 14
	Misans	Elvijs	LAT	8.4.89	182/73	LJ	7.97i, 7.88	8.05- 14
	Missirov	Lev	RUS	4.8.90	194/75	HJ	2.26i	2.33i- 14, 2.26- 13
*	Mitchell	Curtis	USA	11.3.89	188/79	200	20.36	19.97- 13
^	Mitchell	Maurice	USA	22.12.89	178/73	200	20.46, 20.42w	20.13- 12, 19.99w- 11
	Mitchell	Sheldon	JAM	19.7.90	181/75	100	10.07A	10.11- 13
	Mogawane	Ofentse	RSA	20.2.82	179/63	400	45.51A, 45.63	45.11- 06
	Moghaddam	Reza	IRI	17.11.88	197/128	HT	73.08	71.82- 11
	Möhsner	Sven	GER	30.1.86	190/115	HT	71.20	73.82- 09
	Mokdel	Lyès	ALG	20.6.90	195/84	110h	13.49	13.48- 14
*	Mokoena	Khotso	RSA	6.3.85	190/73	LJ	8.16	8.50- 09
						TJ	16.85	17.35- 14
	Mokoka	Stephen	RSA	31.1.85	156/50	5000	13:11.44	13:25.94- 13
						10k	27:43.73	27:40.73- 12
						HMar	60:40dh	60:47- 14
						Mar	2:07:40	2:08:33- 10
	Monnatlala	Tumisang	RSA	31.1.95	180/62	3kSt	8:33.02	8:38.70- 14
	Montaña	José Leonardo	COL	21.3.92	168/61	20kW	1:22:45	1:22:03- 14
	Moore	Jordan	USA	13.12.93	190/101	110h	13.47	13.72, 13.64w- 14
	Morgan	Jason	JAM	6.10.82	186/114	DT	68.19	67.15- 12
	Morgunov	Timur	RUS-J	12.10.96		PV	5.50	5.20- 14
^	Morioka	Koichiro	JPN	2.4.85	184/70	20kW	1:22:43	1:20:14- 13
						50kW	3:44:27	3:43:14- 12
	Morris	Joe	USA	4.10.89	180/68	100	10.19, 9.98w	10.24, 10.09Aw- 13
						200	20.43	20.45- 14
	Morris	Julius	MNT	14.4.94	178/68	100	10.23A, 10.06Aw	10.41, 10.31w- 14
						200	20.45A, 20.56	20.52- 14
	Morse	Brett	GBR	11.2.89	191/114	DT	63.42	66.84- 13
	Morse	Mikese	USA	30.10.87	185/73	LJ	7.86, 8.02w	7.90i- 09, 7.89, 8.08w- 14
*	Mosop	Moses	KEN	17.7.85	172/57	Mar	2:06:19	2:03:06w dh- 11, 2:05:03- 12
	Moss	Miller	USA	14.3.88	193/86	Dec	7743(w)	7996- 11
	Mossberg	Nick	USA	5.4.86	178/77	PV	5.56	5.60- 13
	Mouhyadin	Abdi Waiss	DJI-J	3.7.96	168/52	1500	3:36.09	3:40.02- 14
	Moulinet ¶	Bertrand	FRA	6.1.87	178/63	20kW	1:19:18	1:20:12- 12
	Mousavi	Kaveh	IRI	27.5.85	196/105	HT	74.30	75.26- 11
	Mozia	Stephen	NGR	16.8.93	190/102	SP	20.18	20.79i, 20.46- 14
						DT	61.34	62.80- 14
*	Mucheru	Boniface Tumuti	KEN	2.5.92	185/75	400h	48.29	49.25A- 14, 49.45- 12
	Mudrov	Ilya	RUS	17.11.91	190/79	PV	5.78i, 5.51	5.70- 14
^	Mudrov	Sergey	RUS	8.9.90	190/79	HJ	2.25	2.35i- 13, 2.31- 12
	Muhar	Matija	SLO-J	22.7.96	182/82	JT	79.20	75.38- 14
^	Mulabegovic	Nedzad	CRO	4.2.81	190/120	SP	20.25	20.67- 14
	Mulder	Nils	NED	25.6.87	192/84	PV	5.50	5.36- 12
	Mullera	Ángel	ESP	20.4.84	175/62	3kSt	8:27.95	8:13.71- 12
	Mullett	Rob	GBR	31.7.87	183/68	3kSt	8:31.32	8:31.62- 12
	Münch	Markus	GER	13.6.86	207/117	DT	64.30	66.87- 11
	Mundell	Marc	RSA	7.7.83	189/86	50kW	3:54:12	3:55:32- 12
	Mungara	Kenneth	KEN	7.9.73	170/52	Mar	2:08:42	2:07:36- 11
^	Murakami	Yukifumi	JPN	23.12.79	186/102	JT	79.05	85.96- 13
	Murasky	JC	USA	6.2.93	203/123	SP	20.16	19.13- 14
	Murayama	Kenta	JPN	23.2.93	176/55	10k	27:39.95	27:49.94- 14
	Murayama	Kota	JPN	23.2.93	174/53	5000	13:19.62	13:34.57- 14
						10k	27:29.69	28:42.09- 14
	Murgor	Wilfred	KEN	12.12.88	178/65	HMar	59:57	61:02- 12
	Murillo	Jhon Freddy	COL	13.6.84	183/84	TJ	16.55	16.58, 16.82Aw- 13
	Murphy	Clayton	USA	26.2.95	182/68	800	1:45.59	1:50.03- 14
	Murray	Ross	GBR	8.10.90	180/70	1500	3:37.76	3:34.76- 12
	Musagala	Ronald	UGA	16.12.94	176/61	1500	3:35.02	3:37.75- 14
						5000	13:24.41	-0
	Muskwe	Osman	GBR	24.11.85	192/86	Dec	7597	7565- 14
*	Mutai	Abel	KEN	2.10.88	172/73	3kSt	8:20.38	8:01.67- 12
	Mutai	Benjamin	KEN	13.7.82		Mar	2:08:45	2:11:01- 09

Name		Nat	Born	Ht/Wt	Event	2015 Mark	Pre-2015 Best
Mutai	Emmanuel	KEN	12.10.84	168/54	Mar	2:07:46	2:03:13- 14
Mutai	Jeremiah	KEN	27.12.92	173/60	800	1:45.50	1:43.9A- 13
Mutai	Vincent	KEN	3.11.94	174/61	1500	3:38.62, 3:35.81 short	3:35.45- 12
Mutiso	Alexander	KEN-J	10.9.96		10k	27:56.87	
Mutisya	Boniface	KEN			800	1:45.6A	1:49.5A -11
Mutunga	William	KEN	17.9.93	178/70	400h	49.43	49.82A. 51.3- 13
Mwaka	Patrick	KEN	2.11.92	165/45	10k	27:58.58	27:33.14- 11
Mwangangi	John	KEN	1.11.90		Mar	2:06:13	2:07:28- 14
Mwangi	James	KEN	23.6.84	175/58	5000	13:24.50	13:16.06- 14
					10k	27:43.25	27:23.66- 14
Mwangi	Samuel	KEN-J	19.9.97	169/51	10k	27:50.93	
Mwaniki	Samuel	KEN	.84		Mar	2:08:56	2:16:51- 12
Mweresa	Boniface	KEN	13.11.93	170/70	400	45.01	46.00A- 12
Mzazi	Gladwin	RSA	28.8.88	160/48	10k	27:56.9	28:09.33- 11
Nabokov	Dmitriy	BLR-J	20.1.96		HJ	2.25	2.24- 14
Nakamura	Akihiko	JPN	23.10.90	180/73	Dec	8043	8035- 14
Nápoles	Cristian	CUB-Y	27.11.98		TJ	16.45	15.42- 14
Nascimento	Yazaldes	POR	17.4.86	178/73	100	10.16	10.21- 14
Naumovich	Artyom	BLR	19.2.91		HJ	2.25	2.25- 13
Nava	Horacio	MEX	20.1.82	175/62	50kW	3:45:41	3:42:51- 14
Nazarov	Dilshod	TJK	6.5.82	187/115	HT	79.36	80.71- 13
Ndiema	Eric Leon	KEN	1.1.90	174/58	HMar	60:45	61:21- 14
Ndiku	Caleb	KEN	9.10.92	183/68	1500	3:38.13	3:29.50- 13
3000	7:35.13		7:30.99- 12		5000	13:05.30	12:59.17- 14
Ndiku	Jonathan	KEN	18.9.91	173/60	5000	13:13.16	13:11.99- 09
10k	27:40.64		27:37.72- 09		3kSt	8:11.64	8:07.75- 11
Ndirangu	Charles	KEN	8.2.93	170/50	HMar	60:18	-0-
Ndirangu	Joseph	KEN	9.9.94	168/49	10k	28:01.87	27:59.11- 13
					HMar	60:30	62:54- 14
Ndungu	Samuel	KEN	4.4.88	166/53	Mar	2:09:08	2:07:04- 12
Nebebew	Birhan	ETH	14.8.94	172/55	5000	13:19.14	13:14.60- 13
Nedow	Tim	CAN	16.10.90	198/125	SP	20.98i, 20.78	20.98- 14
					DT	61.49	59.24- 12
Negesse	Endeshaw	ETH	13.3.88		Mar	2:06:00	2:04:52- 13
Nellum	Bryshon	USA	1.5.89	183/79	200	20.39	20.23, 19.99w- 13
					400	44.65	44.73- 12
Németh	Kristóf	HUN	17.9.87	190/97	HT	70.97	76.45- 10
Nesterenko	Maksim	BLR	1.9.92		TJ	16.66i, 16.59	16.46i,16.40w- 14, 16.35- 13
Nesterenko	Mykyta	UKR	15.4.91	206/115	DT	63.34	65.31- 08
Newman	Calesio	USA	20.8.86	172/66	100	10.04	10.07- 12, 9.96w- 14
					200	20.37w	20.28, 20.17w- 12
Nganga	Bernard Mbugua	KEN	17.1.85	178/59	3kSt	8:15.66	8:05.88- 11
Ngatia	Hiram	KEN-J	1.1.96	170/56	5000	13:13.66	13:22.08- 14
					10k	27:41.74	28:25.25- 14
Ngatuny	Emmanuel	KEN	10.10.92		10k	28:08.4A	
					HMar	60:58	61:51- 13
Ngeno	Alfred	KEN-J	2.5.97	170/52	5000	13:22.04	13:58.1A
Ngeno	Ernest	KEN	20.5.95		Mar	2:07:57	2:09:57- 14
Ngeno	Geoffrey	KEN	11.1.94	177/60	3kSt	8:24.81A	8:40.2A- 10
Ngetich	Hillary	KEN	15.9.95	171/57	1500	3:35.40, 3:35.26i	3:35.87- 13
Nigusse	Siboke	ETH	.84		Mar	2:09:14	2:13:14- 14
Nilsson	Marcus	SWE	3.5.91	185/90	Dec	7663	8104(w)- 13
Nima	Issam	ALG	8.4.79	187/75	TJ	16.58, 16.78w	16.89, 17.02w- 12
Niskala	Pyry	FIN	6.11.90	191/105	DT	61.17	60.71- 14
Niu Wenbin		CHN	20.1.91		50kW	3:51:00	3:54:19- 11
Njuguna	David	KEN	6.9.89	176/60	5000	13:24.69	13:23.89- 14
Nkanata	Carvin	KEN	6.5.91	183/73	200	20.14	20.17- 14
Nkobolo	Onkabetse	BOT	22.7.93	183/74	400	45.10	46.21- 14
Noda	Tomohiro	JPN-J	24.1.96		20kW	1:20:08	1:22:37- 14
Noga	Artur	POL	2.5.88	195/82	110h	13.37	13.26- 13, 13.20w- 10
Noguchi	Hiroshi	JPN	3.5.83	177/114	HT	71.98	72.43- 13
Noguchi	Naoto	JPN	27.5.94		400h	50.06	50.98- 12
Nolf	Cedric	BEL	18.6.89	182/82	LJ	7.91i, 7.83w	7.89- 14
Nopper	David	GER	25.1.95	201/82	HJ	2.25	2.21- 14
Norman	Michael	USA-J	3.12.97	183/73	200	20.24	20.82- 14
					400	45.19	46.94- 14
Norwood	Vernon	USA	10.4.92	187/77	400	44.44	45.02- 14
Noskov ¶	Ivan	RUS	16.7.88	177/62	50kW	3:43:57	3:37:41- 14
Novák	Martin	CZE	5.10.92	196/115	SP	19.70	19.69- 14
Nowak	Lukasz	POL	18.12.88	194/77	50kW	3:44:53	3:42:47- 12
Nowak	Tim	GER	13.8.95	183/78	Dec	7827	

	Name		Nat	Born	Ht/Wt	Event	2015 Mark	Pre-2015 Best
*	Nowicki	Wojciech	POL	22.2.89	196/112	HT	78.71	76.14- 14
	Nozawa	Keisuke	JPN	7.6.91	175/63	400h	49.08	49.15- 12
	Nurgi	Tolossa	ETH	29.3.90	183/65	3kSt	8:22.9	8:28.97- 14
	Nyakora	Teressa	ETH	26.2.95		10k	27:38.93	
	Nyangau	Mike	KEN	28.8.94	171/75	100	10.23A, 9.9A	10.56A- 12
						200	20.48A, 20.51, 20.2A	20.69- 13
	Nychyporchuk	Oleksandr	UKR	14.4.92	185/86	JT	81.80	81.65- 12
	Occin	Louis-Grégory	FRA	2.6.89	170/69	TJ	16.61, 167.63w	16.31- 14
	Oduduru	Divine	NGR-J	7.10.96	175/70	200	20.45	20.66, 20.25w- 14
*	O'Farrill	Yordan	CUB	9.2.93	183/72	110h	13.23	13.19- 14
	Ogho-Oghene	Egweru	NGR	26.11.88	171/66	100	10.06	10.06- 11, 10.0- 08
	Ogita	Hiroki	JPN	30.12.87	186/80	PV	5.65i, 5.65	5.70- 13
*	Ogunode	Femi Seun	QAT	15.5.91	183/79	100	9.91	9.93- 14
						200	19.97	20.06- 14
	O'Hara	Michael	JAM-J	29.9.96	185/73	200	20.59, 20.46Aw	20.45, 20.31w- 14
	O'Hare	Chris	GBR	23.11.90	174/60	1500	3:34.83	3:35.06- 14
	Oiglane	Janek	EST	25.4.94	182/78	Dec	7945	7815-14
	Oikawa	Fumitaka	JPN	5.4.95		20kW	1:23:01	1:22:06- 14
	Oishi	Minato	JPN	19.5.88	162/48	10k	28:04.65	28:18.73- 13
	Oiwa	Yuhi	JPN	17.2.91	173/62	LJ	7.91, 7.98w	7.90- 14
	Ojala	Aleksi	FIN	9.12.92	180/62	50kW	3:57:14	-0-
*	Oke	Tosin	NGR	1.10.80	178/77	TJ	17.00	17.23- 12
	Okorie	Henry	NGR	11.4.87		400h	50.01	51.30- 13
	Okpara	Tadius	NGR-J	7.7.96		LJ	7.90	7.31- 14
	Okuma	Takeshi	JPN	14.12.83		50kW	3:55:06	4:20:26- 13
	Okutu	Jean Marie	ESP	4.8.88	179/68	LJ	8.04A,7.96i, 7.90,7.99w	8.01- 14, 8.05w- 12
	Olamigoke	Olu	NGR	19.9.90	178/68	TJ	16.98	16.73- 14
	Oleitiptip	Alex	KEN	22.9.82	176/58	HMar	59:28	59:58- 14
	Oleszczuk	Kacper	POL	15.5.94	182/78	JT	82.29	77.46- 14
	Olgundeniz	Ercüment	TUR	7.7.76	203/120	DT	63.07	67.50- 12
	de Oliveira	João Vitor	BRA	15.5.92	192/86	110h	13.45	13.81- 12
	de Oliveira	Júlio César	BRA	4.2.86	185/97	JT	83.67	80.05, 80.29 irreg- 09
	Oliveira	Paulo Sérgio	BRA	1.6.93	185/65	LJ	7.95w	8.13- 14
*	Oliver	David	USA	24.4.82	188/93	110h	12.98	12.89- 10
*	Olivier	André	RSA	29.12.89	192/72	800	1:45.73	1:44.29- 12
	Omoregie	David	GBR	1.11.95	185/84	110h	13.50	13.53- 14
	Omuro	Hideki	JPN	25.7.90	180/67	110h	13.54	13.54- 12
	Omwamba	Enoch	KEN	4.4.93	168/55	1500	3:35.69	3:39.01- 14
	5000	13:28.41		13:31.54- 13		10k	28:00.41	28:00.33- 14
	O'Neal	Matthew	USA	10.6.94	185/74	TJ	16.44i, 16.37	16.23- 14
^	Onnen	Eike	GER	3.8.82	194/83	HJ	2.32	2.34- 07
	Ono	Hiroyuki	JPN	10.3.86	170/56	10k	27:57.85	28:06.35- 11
*	Oprea	Marian	ROU	6.6.82	190/80	TJ	17.07	17.81- 05
	Ortega	Mauricio	COL	4.8.94	184/102	DT	64.47A	62.30A- 14
*	Ortega	Orlando	CUB/ESP	29.7.91	185/70	110h	12.94	13.01- 14
	Orth	Florian	GER	24.7.89	181/64	1500	3:36.05	3:34.54- 14
*	Osaghae	Omo	USA	18.5.88	184/75	110h	13.56, 13.34w	13.01- 13
	Osako	Suguru	JPN	23.5.91	170/53	3000	7:46.14, 7:45,62+i	7:40.09- 14
	2M	8:16.47i		5000	13:08.40	13:20.80- 13	10k 27:45.24	27:38.31- 13
	Osei	Philip	CAN	30.10.90	173/65	400	45.23A, 45.80	45.51A- 12, 45.71- 13
	Osewski	Bartosz	POL	20.3.91	194/104	JT	78.86	83.89- 12
*	Osman	Abrar	ERI	1.1.94	173/55	3000	7:44.59	7:39.70- 13
	5000	13:14.00	13:16.45- 14	10k	27:41.69	HMar	60:39	-0-
	Osmanoglu	Seref	TUR	2.1.89	176/58	TJ	16.74	17.72- 11
	Ost	Noël	FRA	15.11.89	189/82	PV	5.51i, 5.50	5.45i, 5.38- 14
	Otobe	Takumi	JPN	22.4.89	183/76	Dec	7725	7604- 14
	Otterling	Andreas	SWE	25.5.86	183/80	LJ	8.06i, 8.06, 8.13w	8.03- 12
	Otuonye	Ifeanyi	TKS	27.6.94	184/73	LJ	7.87, 7.98w	7.50i- 13, 7.47- 14
	Ouhadi	Aziz	MAR	24.7.84	175/73	100	10.16, 10.07w	10.09- 11, 9.9- 09
	Outzen	Matthew	AUS	12.10.87	185/100	JT	81.80	79.41- 10
*	Özbilen	Ilham Tanui	TUR	5.3.90	177/60	800	1:46.14	1:44.00- 13
						1500	3:32.68	3:31.30- 13
	Paech	Carlo	GER	18.12.92	190/84	PV	5.80	5.53i, 5.52 -13
	Palma	Isaac	MEX	26.10.90	174/59	20kW	1:23:11A	1:21:13- 13
	Palmer	Desmond	USA	30.7.95	196/84	400h	49.41	50.73- 14
	Palmer	Ford	USA	6.10.90	180/64	1500	3:36.98	3:38.58- 14
	Palomeque	Diego	COL	5.12.93	176/68	100	10.22A, 10.11Aw	10.41A,10.45 -14
						200	20.50A	20.69A, 20.99- 12?
	Panasyuk	Ivan	UKR	8.10.91	188/115	DT	61.23	63.39- 14
	Papamihaíl	Aléxandros	GRE	18.9.88	178/63	20kW	1:22:43	1:21:12- 12
						50kW	3:51:38	3:49:56- 12

Name		Nat	Born	Ht/Wt	Event	2015 Mark	Pre-2015 Best
Parchment	Hansle	JAM	17.6.90	196/90	110h	13.03	12.94- 14
Parellis	Apostolos	CYP	24.7.85	186/110	DT	65.04	65.36- 12
Park Chil-sung		KOR	8.7.82	173/61	50kW	3:56:42	3:45:55- 12
Parker	Julian	USA	20.7.91	183/70	800	1:46.17	1:49.72- 14
Parros	Clayton	USA	11.12.90	178/70	400	45.25	45.42- 14
Pars	Krisztián	HUN	18.2.82	188/113	HT	79.91	82.69- 14
Parshin	Pavel	RUS	2.1.94	171/55	20kW	1:22:38	1:21:55- 14
Partanen	Veli-Matti	FIN	28.10.91	178/62	50kW	3:49:02	3:52:58- 14
Pasinski	Pawel	POL	6.3.93	196/115	DT	61.46	60.38- 14
Pásztor	Bence	HUN	5.2.95	186/84	HT	75.74	71.50- 14
Peña	José Gregorio	VEN	12.1.87	163/60	3kSt	8:31.47	8:20.87- 13
Peacock	Hamish	AUS	15.10.90	186/96	JT	83.31	82.24- 14
Peltomäki	Sami	FIN	11.1.91	180/87	JT	79.55	80.36- 14
Pérez	Kenny	COL	19.11.94		20kW	1:22:21	1:27:38- 14
Pervan	Dino	CRO	12.1.91	192/75	LJ	7.90	7.99i- 14, 7.95- 11
Pestano	Mario	ESP	8.4.78	195/120	DT	61.70	69.50- 08
Petrov	Aleksandr	RUS	9.8.86	187/79	LJ	8.01	8.20- 11
Pezer	Mesud	BIH	27.8.94	198/120	SP	19.99	19.37- 14
Philibert-Thiboutot	Charles	CAN	31.12.90	176/62	1500	3:34.23	3:38.33- 14
Phiri	Gerald	ZAM	6.10.88	184/80	100	10.17, 10.00w	10.03- 14, 10.00w- 13
Pichardo	Pedro Pablo	CUB	30.6.93	185/71	TJ	18.08	17.76- 14
Pienaar	Roelf	RSA	23.12.93	183/76	LJ	8.01, 8.13w	7.87A. 7.71- 11, 7.97w- 14
Pierson	Sam	USA	7.4.88	180/75	PV	5.55Ai	5.45Ai- 14, 5.37A- 10
Pillow	Chris	USA	8.7.93	190/82	PV	5.60i	5.50- 14
Pineda	Daniel	CHI	19.9.85	178/72	LJ	7.97A, 7.92	8.08- 12
Pitkämaki	Tero	FIN	19.12.82	195/92	JT	89.09	91.53- 05
Pittomvils	Niels	BEL	18.7.92	198/88	Dec	8049	8000- 14
Plesko	Nejc	SLO	9.10.92	186/97	HT	73.63	69.67- 14
Pless	David W.	USA	19.11.90	191/109	SP	19.83	18.80- 14
Plotnitskiy	Dmitriy	BLR	26.8.88	189/80	TJ	16.65i	16.91- 10
Pohle	Hagen	GER	5.3.92	177/64	20kW	1:21:34	1:21:29- 14
					50kW	3:51:18	-0-
Pollitt	Don	USA	1.10.91	181/75	110h	13.59	13.64, 13.52w- 13
Poluboyarov	Vladislav	RUS	17.4.94		TJ	16.63	15.40- 12
Polyanskiy	Sergey	RUS	29.10.89	180/75	LJ	8.20	8.16- 13, 8.18w- 11
Pontvianne	Jean Marc	FRA	6.8.94	170/60	TJ	16.81	16.48i, 16.09- 14
Porter	Garland	USA	10.2.82	193/118	HT	72.99	72.99- 11
Porter	Jeff	USA	27.11.85	183/84	110h	13.25	13.08- 12
Portilla	Jhoanis	CUB	24.7.90	182/76	110h	13.30	13.41- 14, 13.1w- 11, 13.3- 10
Postema	Tomás	USA	17.7.89	185/111	HT	71.70	65.80- 13
Potaptsev	Ilya	RUS	19.4.93		TJ	16.90	16.45- 14
Pouzy	Frédéric	FRA	18.2.83	184/88	HT	73.08	77.05- 12
Powell	Asafa	JAM	23.11.82	190/88	100	9.81	9.72- 08
Pozdnyakov	Anatoliy	RUS	1.2.87	184/101	HT	76.38	79.06- 13
Pozzi	Andrew	GBR	15.5.92	186/79	110h	13.62	13.34- 12
Prásil	Ladislav	CZE	17.5.90	198/125	SP	20.66i	21.47- 13
Prüfer	Henning	GER-J	7.3.96	201/125	DT	60.39	57.04- 14
Premeru	Marin	CRO	29.8.90	186/115	SP	20.58	20.59- 13
					DT	60.70	63.38- 10
Premkumar	Kumaravel	IND	6.2.93		LJ	8.04	8.09, 8.12w- 13
Presson	Isaac	USA	7.2.92	190/73	1500	3:37.06	3:40.16- 12
Pretorius	Friedrich	RSA	4.8.95	187/84	Dec	7764	7730A- 14
Price	Tim	USA	26.12.87	183/84	200	20.48w	20.75- 14, 20.46Aw- 12
Pronkin	Valeriy	RUS	15.6.94	195/115	HT	76.80	73.50- 13
Protsenko	Andriy	UKR	20.5.88	194/65	HJ	2.33i, 2.32	2.40- 14
Prugovecki	Marko	CRO	1.1.87	180/75	LJ	7.92	8.00- 12
Przybylko	Mateusz	GER	9.3.92	194/72	HJ	2.30	2.24- 13
Pujats	Pauls	LAT	6.8.91	184/73	PV	5.55	5.54- 14
Pyatnytsya	Oleksandr	UKR	14.7.85	187/92	JT	81.63	86.12- 12
Quérin	Gaël	FRA	26.6.87	182/76	Dec	7914	8194- 14
Quiyuch	Jaime	GUA	24.4.88	178/59	50kW	3:57:41	3:50:33A- 11
Quow	Renny	TTO	25.8.87	170/66	400	44.54	44.53- 09
Rae	Jeremy	CAN	19.5.91	178/64	1500	3:36.85	3:38.29- 13
Rahmouni	Miloud	ALG	13.12.83	175/70	400h	49.24	49.34- 13
Rajiv	Arokia	IND	22.5.91	172/64	400	45.57	46.54- 13
Ralph	Joshua	AUS	27.10.91	185/70	800	1:45.79	1:45.81 -14
Ramsay	Liam	GBR	18.11.92	188/82	Dec	7857(w)	7822- 14
Ramsey	Jalen	USA	24.10.94	186/92	LJ	7.97i, 7.96	7.62- 14
Ramzi	Rashid	BRN	17.7.80	172/65	1500	3:37.59	3:29.14- 06
Ranasinghe	R.M.Sumedha	SRI	10.2.91		JT	83.04	72.42- 14
Raymundo	José Maria	GUA	1.9.93	156/49	20kW	1:22:49	

Name		Nat	Born	Ht/Wt	Event	2015 Mark	Pre-2015 Best
Rayson	Ian	AUS	4.2.88	185/75	50kW	3:55:17	3:57:55- 11
Reading	Brendon	AUS	26.1.89		50kW	3:55:03	4:19:30- 14
del Real	Alan Diego	MEX	6.3.94	185/103	HT	72.66	69.84- 14
Reed	Hayden	USA	4.4.94	190/102	DT	60.70	63.74- 14
Regassa	Tilahun	ETH	18.1.90	170/54	Mar	2:06:54	2:05:27- 12
Registe	David	DMA	2.5.88	180/80	LJ	7.85, 8.29w	8.06A, 7.84- 14
Reheda	Serhiy	UKR	6.2.94	190/100	HT	71.86	67.44- 12
Reid	Jonathan	JAM	9.5.92	190/82	TJ	16.52w	16.32i- 14
Reid	Julian	GBR	23.9.88	186/77	LJ	8.07, 8.08w	8.08- 11, 8.18w- 09
					TJ	16.95	16.98, 17.10w- 09
Reina	Antonio Manuel	ESP	13.6.81	186/71	800	1:46.27	1:43.83- 02
Rendón	James	COL	7.7.85	155/55	50kW	3:50:47	3:47:41- 14
Renner	Robert	SLO	8.3.94	182/75	PV	5.70	5.62i -13, 5.50- 12
Repcík	Jozef	SVK	3.8.86	186/72	800	1:45.40	1:44.94- 08
Reus	Julian	GER	29.4.88	177/73	100	10.09, 10.07w	10.05- 14, 10.00w- 13
					200	20.42	20.36- 13
* Revé	Ernesto	CUB	26.2.92	182/70	TJ	17.02	17.58- 14
Revenko	Vladislav	UKR	15.11.84	181/77	PV	5.65	5.80- 05
Rew	Quentin	NZL	16.7.84	175/63	20kW	1:22:18	1:22:11- 14
					50kW	3:48:48	3:50:22- 14
Reynolds	Albert	STL	28.3.88	178/82	JT	77.71A	72.86- 12
Reynolds	Ben	IRL	26.9.90	188/77	110h	13.48	13.49- 13
Reynolds	Maalik	USA	26.4.92	193/73	HJ	2.25	2.28- 11
Richards	Joseph	USA	14.10.93	186/75	400	45.61	45.80- 14
* Richards	O'Dayne	JAM	14.12.88	178/117	SP	21.69	21.61- 14
* Richardson	Jason	USA	4.4.86	186/73	110h	13.12	12.98- 12
Ricks	Keith	USA	9.10.90	183/75	100	10.15, 10.13w	10.13- 13
* Riley	Andrew	JAM	6.9.88	188/80	110h	13.28	13.14- 13
Riley	Jake	USA	11.2.88	173/61	10k	27:59.37	28:08.36- 12
^ Rimmer	Michael	GBR	3.2.86	180/71	800	1:45.67	1:43.89- 10
Ringer	Richard	GER	27.2.89	180/62	3000	7:46.18i	7:50.99- 14
					5000	13:10.94	13:25.24- 14
Riparelli	Jacques	ITA	27.3.83	183/75	100	10.11	10.21- 12
Rise	Lars Vikan	NOR	23.11.88	184/86	Dec	7742	7942- 11
Riseley	Jeff	AUS	11.11.86	192/74	800	1:44.99	1:44.48- 12
					1500	3:36.87	3:32.93- 09
Ristic	Milan	SRB	8.8.91	186/72	110h	13.50	13.63, 13.59w- 14
Riva	Thomas	CAN	31.1.92	177/64	1500	3:37.34	3:45.66- 14
Rivas	Yeison	COL	24.9.87	175/64	400h	49.90A, 50.88	50.12- 11
Rivera	Edgar	MEX	13.2.91	191/80	HJ	2.25	2.28- 11
* Roberts	Gil	USA	15.3.89	188/81	400	45.29	44.53- 14
* Roberts	Kurt	USA	20.2.88	191/127	SP	20.45	21.50i, 21.47- 14
Roberts	Matthew	GBR	22.12.84		HJ	2.25	2.26- 10
Robertson	Josef	JAM	14.5.87	176/63	400h	49.68	49.04A- 14, 49.16-12
Robertson	Ricky	USA	19.9.90	178/70	HJ	2.31i, 2.25	2.32- 12
* Robertson	Zane	NZL	14.11.89	180/65	5000	13:25.41	13:13.83- 13
10k	27:46.82		-0-		HMar	59:47	-0-
Robi	Deribe	ETH	26.9.84		Mar	2:05:58	2:07:16- 14
Robinson	Brett	AUS	8.5.91	173/57	3000	7:45.97	7:51.99- 13
					5000	13:21.23	13:18.96- 13
Robinson	Bryce	USA	13.11.93	178/75	100	9.99, 9.96w	10.18, 10.15w- 14
					200	20.30, 20.29w	20.48, 20.30w- 14
Robinson	Jeron	USA	30.4.91	193/73	HJ	2.31	2.30- 14
* Robles	Dayron	CUB	19.11.86	191/91	110h	13.32	12.87- 08
Rocha	Matheus	BRA	19.12.94		110h	13.2	14.17, 14.13w- 14
Rodger	Sebastian	GBR	29.6.91	181/73	400h	49.84	49.19- 13
* Rodgers	Michael	USA	24.4.85	178/73	100	9.86	9.85- 11, 9.80w- 14
Rodhe	Justin	CAN	17.10.84	186/118	SP	19.99i, 19,73	21.29- 13
Rodney	Brendon	CAN	9.4.92	190/84	200	20.18	20.41- 14
Rodríguez	Álvaro	ESP	25.5.87	179/66	1500	3:37.30	3:34.10- 12
Rodríguez	Rafith	COL	1.6.89	187/73	800	1:45.53	1:44.31- 11
Roe	Martin	NOR	1.4.92	187/86	Dec	7875	7563- 13
Rogers	Jason	SKN	31.8.91	173/66	100	10.17, 9.98Aw	10.01- 13
Rogowski	Arkadiusz	POL	30.3.93	182/90	HT	73.10	72.21- 14
* Röhler	Thomas	GER	30.9.91	195/83	JT	89.27	87.63- 14
Rolnin	Basile	FRA	21.1.94	194/83	Dec	7679	7170- 14
Romani	Darlan	BRA	9.4.91	183/127	SP	20.90	20.84- 14
Rono	Festus	KEN	28.12.93		3kSt	8:27.93	8:40.1A- 12
Rono	Patrick Kiprotich	KEN-J	9.4.96	175/68	800	1:45.2A	1:46.3A- 14
Rono	Philemon	KEN	8.2.91		Mar	2:08:18	2:07:07- 14
Rono	Vincent	KEN	22.12.90	165/55	3000	7:43.26	7:41.18- 10, 7:37.87i- 11
					HMar	60:52	61:43- 14

Name		Nat	Born	Ht/Wt	Event	2015 Mark	Pre-2015 Best
Ronoh	Geoffrey	KEN	29.11.82	182/62	HMar	60:28	59:45- 14
Rooney	Martyn	GBR	3.4.87	198/78	400	44.45	44.60- 08
Rop	Albert	BRN	17.7.92	176/55	3000	7:46.36	7:35.53- 13
					5000	13:06.74	12:51.96- 13
Roper	Darcy	AUS-Y	31.3.98	183/70	LJ	8.01A, 7.91	7.52w- 14
Rosa	Jean	BRA	1.2.90	188/78	TJ	16.80	16.53- 12, 16.82w- 13
Rose	Alex	SAM	7.11.91	188/127	DT	61.35	59.83 -13
Rosenberg	Kristjan	EST	16.5.94		Dec	7668	7164- 14
Ross	Nick	USA	8.8.91	188/75	HJ	2.29Ai, 2.26	2.31Ai, 2.30- 14
Rosser	Khallifah	USA	13.7.95	188/73	400h	49.96	50.62- 14
Rossi	Eugenio	SMR	6.3.92	192/72	HJ	2.27	2.24- 14
Rotich	Abraham	BRN	26.6.93	183/64	800	1:45.33	1:43.13- 12
Rotich	Lucas	KEN	16.4.90	171/57	Mar	2:07:17	2:07:18- 14
Roulhac	Brandon	USA	13.12.83	188/73	TJ	16.75	17.26, 17.44w- 09
Rowe	Alex	AUS	8.7.92	181/70	800	1:45.38	1:44.40 -14
Rubino	Giorgio	ITA	15.4.86	174/56	20kW	1:21:38	1:19:37- 09
Rudisha	David	KEN	17.12.88	189/73	800	1:43.58	1:40.91- 12
Rudnev	Pavel	RUS	26.10.92		Dec	7659	7620- 12
Rudolf	Zan	SLO	9.5.93	182/68	800	1:46.00	1:46.79- 12
Ruiz	Jorge	COL	17.5.89	167/57	50kW	3:58:23	3:58:58- 14
Rungaru	James	KEN	14.1.93	174/58	10k	27:50.09A	27:22.53- 11
					HMar	60:12	61:04- 14
Rupp	Galen	USA	8.5.86	180/62	3000	7:44.97+i	7:30.16i- 13, 7:43.24- 10
2M 8:17.24i 8:07.41i- 14 5000 13:08.38 12:58.90- 12 10k 27:08.91 26:44.36- 14							
Ruskys	Eligijus	LTU	1.12.90	198/115	DT	63.21	60.45- 14
Rutherford	Greg	GBR	17.11.86	188/84	LJ	8.41	8.51- 14
Ruto	Evans	KEN	14.1.84		Mar	2:08:55	2:07:49- 12
Rutt	Michael	USA	28.10.87	175/64	800	1:45.47	1:45.08- 13
Rutto	Cyrus	KEN	21.4.92	173/52	5000	13:25.00	13:12.91- 13
Rutto	Samuel	KEN	.95		Mar	2:08:59	2:10:00- 14
Rutto	Lani	KEN	29.3.89		Mar	2:06:34	2:10:01- 13
Ruuskanen	Antti	FIN	21.2.84	189/86	JT	88.98	88.01- 14
Ryapolov	Anatoliy	RUS-J	31.1.97		LJ	7.96	7.90- 13
Ryzhov ¶	Mikhail	RUS	17.12.91	180/65	50kW	3:43:32	3:38:58- 13
Saarikoski	Juho	FIN	19.5.93	180/95	HT	71.57	71.52- 14
Sabino	Jefferson	BRA	4.11.82	192/94	TJ	16.62	17.28- 08
Sáenz	Stephen	MEX	23.8.90	188/116	SP	19.67	20.35- 14
Safiulin	Ilgizar	RUS	9.12.92	183/64	3kSt	8:18.49	8:20.29- 14
Safo-Antwi	Sean	GBR/GHA	31.10.90	171/69	100	10.16	10.14, 10.07w- 14
Saharuk	Igor	UKR	3.6.88	179/63	50kW	3:55:34	3:50:49- 14
Saito	Takumi	JPN	23.3.93	178/61	20kW	1:21:15	1:20:05- 13
Salah	Mohamed Hashim	QAT	15.4.94		3kSt	8:33.25	8:51.35- 12
Salas	Dídac	ESP	19.5.93	187/75	PV	5.60i, 5.40	5.60- 14
Salazar	Julio César	MEX	8.7.93		20kW	1:21:43	1:21:58- 14
Salel	Daniel	KEN	11.12.90	173/57	HMar	60:56	60:41- 13
Samaai	Rushwal	RSA	25.9.91	178/73	LJ	8.38	8.13A, 8.08- 14
Samac	Vedran	SRB	22.1.90	183/90	JT	80.90	79.22- 14
Sambu	Stephen	KEN	7.7.88	169/55	5000	13:25.13	13:13.74i- 12, 13:26.44+-14
Samimi	Mahmoud	IRI	18.9.88	190/105	DT	63.08A	64.67- 09
Samimi	Mohammed	IRI	29.3.87	188/104	DT	60.42A	65.46- 14
Sampao	Alex	KEN-J	31.12.96	180/64	400	45.22A, 45.31	46.78- 13
Samuelsson	Fredrik	SWE	16.2.95	185/80	Dec	7884	
Sánchez	Benjamin	ESP	10.3.85	185/72	50kW	3:55:45	3:58:51- 12
Sánchez	Eder	MEX	21.5.86	176/67	20kW	1:21:56	1:18:34- 08
Sánchez	Luis Angel	GUA	15.12.93		50kW	4:01:48	-0-
Sancho	Miguel Ángel	ESP	24.4.90	180/67	HJ	2.25	2.27i- 09, 2.26- 11
Sands	Leevan	BAH	16.8.81	190/73	TJ	16.99	17.59- 08
Sang	Ezra	KEN	8.6.94		HMar	60:36	61:03- 14
Sani Brown	Abdul Hakim	JPN-Y	6.3.99	187/72	200	20.34A, 20.35	21.09- 14
Sano	Hiroaki	JPN	28.2.88	173/50	Mar	2:09:12	2:10:29- 13
dos Santos	Felipe	BRA	30.7.94	181/80	Dec	8019	7952- 14
Santos	Luguelín	DOM	12.11.92	173/61	400	44.11	44.45- 12
dos Santos	Mário José	BRA	10.9.79	172/59	50kW	3:55:36	3:57:29- 14
Sarantsev	Yevgeniy	RUS	5.8.88	188/85	Dec	8059	8123- 14
Sasaki	Satoru	JPN	16.10.85	171/56	Mar	2:08:56	2:09:47- 14
Sasase	Hiroki	JPN	17.8.89	166/53	PV	5.51	5.50- 09
Sato	Kentaro	JPN	16.11.94	173/62	400	45.58	46.85- 14
Sato	Yuki	JPN	26.11.86	179/60	10k	27:57.13	27:38.25- 09
Savanovic	Vladimir	SRB	12.6.85	179/67	50kW	3:59:11	4:02:07- 11
Savola	Elmo	FIN	10.3.95	189/77	Dec	7743	
Sawe	Jonathan	KEN	22.5.95	176/64	1500	3:38.51, 3:34.68 short	3:38.61- 13

	Name		Nat	Born	Ht/Wt	Event	2015 Mark	Pre-2015 Best
	Sawe	Matthew	KEN	2.7.88		HJ	2.25A	2.15- 12
	Sawyers	Roberto	CRC	17.10.86	189/107	HT	76.37	73.85- 14
	Sbaï	Hassanine	TUN	21.1.84	176/60	20kW	1:23:14	1:20:19- 11
	Scantling	Garrett	USA	19.5.93	190/86	Dec	8232	8169- 14
	Schembera	Robin	GER	1.10.88	186/67	800	1:45.48	1:45.63- 09
	Schembri	Fabrizio	ITA	27.1.81	183/74	TJ	16.86, 16.94w	17.27- 09
*	Scherbarth	Tobias	GER	17.8.85	195/84	PV	5.70i, 5.70	5.76i- 09, 5.73- 14
	Scherfose	Patrick	GER	28.11.91	186/86	Dec	7693	7611- 13
	Schirrmeister	Silvio	GER	7.12.88	195/80	400h	50.06	49.15- 13
	Schmitt	Thomas	GER	23.1.89	203/119	SP	21.35irr	19.07- 13
*	Schrader	Michael	GER	1.7.87	183/83	Dec	8419	8670- 13
	Schuurmans	Jared	USA	20.8.87	198/118	DT	66.10	64.42- 14
	Scott	Donald	USA	23.2.92	183/84	TJ	16.84i, 16.71, 16.83w	16.34w -14
	Scott	Jordan	USA	22.2.88	188/84	PV	5.60A	5.72- 12
^	Sdiri	Salim	FRA	26.10.78	185/80	LJ	7.91	8.42- 09
	Sears	Ventavius	USA	14.5.95	183/64	LJ	7.84, 7.98Aw	7.49, 7.63w- 14
	Sebisibe	Wogene	ETH-Y	23.6.98			8:26.62	
	Secci	Daniele	ITA	9.3.92	193/110	SP	19.56i, 19.18	19.28i, 19.03- 14
	Sedoc	Gregory	NED	16.10.81	179/74	110h	13.56	13.37- 07, 13.1w- 10
	Sedyuk	Nikolay	RUS	29.4.88	198/115	DT	62.79	64.72- 08
	See	Jeff	USA	6.6.86	186/72	1500	3:36.70	3:35.21- 12
						5000	13:21.16	13:29.08- 13
	Seifert	Bernhard	GER	15.2.93	190/88	JT	80.57	82.42- 13
	Selmon	Kenny	USA-J	27.8.96	188/82	400h	49.60	50.13- 14
	Selmouni	Sofiane	FRA	22.9.89	190/73	800	1:45.97	1:45.94 -14
	Semenov	Oleksiy	UKR	27.6.82	198/120	DT	62.35	65.96- 12
	Semyonov	Dmitriy	RUS	2.8.92	195/77	HJ	2.31i, 2.26	2.30i- 13, 2.28- 14
	Seppänen	Tuomas	FIN	16.5.86	180/107	HT	74.74	75.31- 11
	Seres	András	HUN	31.1.89	195/115	DT	60.36	62.27- 14
	Seribe	Pako	BOT	7.4.91	183/68	200	20.17A	20.57A- 14, 20.97- 13
	Seurei	Benson	BRN	27.3.84	172/62	1500	3:35.14, 3:34.32 short	3:31.61- 12
						3000	7:42.03	7:40.56- 13
	Sghaier	Mohamed	TUN	18.7.88	188/77	400h	49.22	49.71- 14
	Shabanov	Konstantin	RUS	17.11.89	184/75	110h	13.57	13.35- 11
	Shablyuyev	Ivan	RUS	17.4.88	189/82	400h	49.04	49.65- 13
	Shalin	Pavel	RUS	15.3.87	175/73	LJ	8.01, 8.29w	8.25- 10, 8.33w- 11
	Shama	Mykola	UKR	5.4.91	184/94	JT	79.29	76.88- 13
	Shange	Lebogang	RSA	1.8.90		20kW	1:21:43, 1:23:20.86t	1:24:09- 14
	Sharipov	Sergey	RUS	14.4.92		20kW	1:23:10	1:23:50- 14
						50kW	3:57:40	4:12:57- 13
	Sharma	Ankit	IND	20.7.92		LJ	8.04	7.91- 13
*	Sharman	William	GBR	12.9.84	188/82	110h	13.53	13.16- 14, 12.9w- 10
^	Shayunov	Yuriy	BLR	22.10.87	189/120	HT	76.85	80.72- 09
	Sheyko	Georgiy	KAZ	24.8.89	183/70	20kW	1:21:34	1:21:44- 14
	Shimizu	Tsuyoshi	JPN	21.12.93	175/68	Dec	7697	7413- 13
	Shimono	Shin-ichiro	JPN	10.10.90	177/64	LJ	8.11	8.08- 12
	Shitara	Keita	JPN	18.12.91	169/50	10k	28:05.28	27:51.54- 13
	Shitara	Yuta	JPN	18.12.91	170/48	10k	27:42.71	27:54.82- 13
*	Shkurenyov	Ilya	RUS	11.1.91	191/82	Dec	8538	8498- 14
	Shokirjanov	Bobur	UZB	5.12.90	193/99	JT	84.24	79.83- 14
*	Shubenkov	Sergey	RUS	4.10.90	190/75	110h	12.98	13.09- 12
	Shunikhin	Aleksandr	RUS	29.11.92		50kW	4:02:23	-0-
	Shura	Tola	ETH-J	.96		Mar	2:08:53	-0-
*	Shustov	Aleksandr	RUS	29.6.84	188/80	HJ	2.30	2.36- 11
	Sicard	Lloyd	USA	31.5.95	178/73	110h	13.60	14.01- 14
	Sidorchenko	Gleb	RUS	15.5.86	197/110	DT	61.34	62.55- 13
^	Sidorov	Maksim	RUS	13.5.86	190/126	SP	20.58	21.51- 12
	Siegmeier	Zachary	USA	8.1.91	183/77	PV	5.50Ai, 5.50	5.51- 14
	Sigueni	Hicham	MAR	30.1.93	172/51	3kSt	8:16.54	8:21.78- 12
	Sikora	Rafal	POL	17.2.87	187/76	50kW	4:01:14	3:46:16- 11
^	Silmon	Charles	USA	4.7.91	175/72	100	10.02, 9.91w	9.98, 9.85w- 13
	da Silva	Aldemir G.	BRA	8.6.92	179/67	200	20.44, 20.36w	20.32- 14
	Silva #	Andrés	URU	27.3.86	180/76	400h	49.43dq	48.65- 14
	Silva	Jonathan	BRA	21.7.91	185/75	TJ	16.43, 16.46w	17.39- 12
*	da Silva	Mauro Vinícius	BRA	26.12.86	183/69	LJ	8.03	8.31- 13
	Silva	Talles	BRA	20.8.91	190/78	HJ	2.28	2.25- 14
	da Silva	Tiago	BRA	23.10.93	176/73	LJ	7.91	8.09- 14
	Simanovich	Denis	BLR	20.4.87	179/58	20kW	1:21:11	1:20:42- 12
	Simbine	Akani	RSA	21.9.93	174/67	100	9.97	10.02A, 10.18- 14
						200	20.23	20.37- 14
	Simmons	Cale	USA	5.2.91	178/70	PV	5.60Ai	5.61- 13

Name		Nat	Born	Ht/Wt	Event	2015 Mark	Pre-2015 Best
Simon	Dillon	DMA	5.3.92	200/109	SP	19.87	18.81i- 14
Simotwo	Charles	KEN	6.5.95			3:35.86A	
Simotwo	Suleiman	KEN	21.4.80	182/65	Mar	2:08:49	-0-
Simpson	Damarcus	USA	14.7.93	175/68	LJ	8.02, 8.03w	7.28- 12
Singh	Amarender	IND	15.8.91		JT	77.75	
Singh	Baljinder	IND	18.9.86		20kW	1:22:58	1:22:12- 12
Singh	Chandan	IND	8.6.87		20kW	1:23:12	1:23:28- 13
Singh	Devender	IND	18.12.88	178/92	JT	79.65	78.57- 14
Singh	Gurmeet	IND	1.7.85		20kW	1:21:36	1:20:22.52t- 12
Singh	Inderjeet	IND	19.4.88	191/125	SP	20.65	19.89- 14
Singh	Kamalpreet	IND	3.11.87		HT	72.86	70.37- 14
Singh Dalvir	Rajender	IND	5.4.89	175/89	JT	82.23	79.32-14
Singh Rawat	Manish	IND	5.5.91		20kW	1:22:50	1:26:24- 14
					50kW	3:57:11	4:02:08- 14
Sintnicolaas	Eelco	NED	7.4.87	186/81	Dec	8298	8506- 12
Sirmais	Zigismunds	LAT	6.5.92	191/90	JT	79.37	86.61- 14
Sirviö	Toni	FIN	8.1.92	190/93	JT	81.62	79.90- 14
Sitkovskiy	Oleksandr	UKR	9.6.78	184/68	Mar	2:09:11	2:09:14- 13
Skagestad	Sven Martin	NOR	13.1.95	201/118	DT	61.53	57.36- 14
Skarvélis	Nicholas	USA/GRE	2.2.93	185/121	SP	19.82	19.62- 14
Skipper	Greg	USA	26.3.93	193/105	HT	71.25	70.57- 14
Skyers	Roberto	CUB	12.11.91	187/83	100	10.17, 10.13w	10.29- 10, 9.9dt- 10
					200	20.02	20.24- 09
Smaliós	Jiannis	SWE	17.2.87	192/90	JT	79.85	80.77- 10
Smellie	Gavin	CAN	26.6.86	180/75	100	10.09, 10.05w	10.14- 12, 10.11w- 11
					200	20.69, 20.16w	20.45- 09, 20.33w- 14
Smelyk	Sergiy	UKR	19.4.87	178/74	200	20.45	20.30- 14
Smet	Koen	NED	9.8.92	186/74	110h	13.60	13.58, 13.52w- 13
Smith	Allan	GBR	6.11.92	198/84	HJ	2.29i, 2.24	2.26- 13
Smith	Antwon	USA	18.6.95	183/80	200	20.40w	
Smith	Aubrey	CAN	30.6.88	175/73	LJ	7.94	7.80- 14
Smith	Blake	USA	28.5.93	183/75	100	10.25, 10.11w	10.45, 10.42w- 14
Smith	Calvin	USA	10.12.87	180/75	400	45.41	44.81- 10
Smith	David	GBR	14.7.91	188/77	HJ	2.26i, 2.24	2.25- 14
Smith	Rutger	NED	9.7.81	197/129	DT	63.90	67.77- 11
Smith	Teray	BAH	28.9.94	185/77	200	20.34	20.57 -14
Smith	Terrell	USA	10.10.94	182/75	200	20.51	21.03, 20.82w- 14
Smith	Tyrone	BER	7.8.86	183/70	LJ	8.20	8.22- 10
Sobera	Robert	POL	19.1.91	190/77	PV	5.81i, 5.70	5.75i, 5.70, 5.80ex- 14
Soboka	Tafese	ETH	29.9.93		3kSt	8:25.56	8:26.33- 12
Söderberg	David	FIN	11.8.79	185/100	HT	76.92	78.83- 03
Soerens	Stephen	USA	18.6.93	188/87	Dec	7669(w)	7291- 14
Soi	Edwin	KEN	3.3.86	172/55	3000	7:37.85	7:27.55- 11
					5000	13:11.97	12:51.34- 13
Sokirskiy	Aleksey	RUS	16.3.85	185/108	HT	75.29	78.91- 12
Sokolovs	Igors	LAT	17.8.74	187/110	HT	76.18	80.14- 09
Solanas	Sergio	ESP	28.4.87	194/83	TJ	16.68A, 16.52	16.14- 14
Solomon	Duane	USA	28.12.84	191/77	800	1:45.56	1:42.82- 12
Solomon	Jarrin	TTO	11.1.86	173/73	400	45.15	44.98- 14
Some	Peter	KEN	5.6.90		Mar	2:07:22	2:05:38- 13
Sorokin	Dmitriy	RUS	27.9.92	176/73	TJ	17.29	16.96- 14
Sorrillo	Rondell	TTO	21.1.86	178/62	100	10.16	10.03- 12, 9.99w- 13
					200	20.46	20.16- 11
Souleiman	Ayanleh	DJI	3.12.92	172/60	800	1:42.97	1:43.63- 13
1500 3:30.17 3:29.58 -14 1M 3:51.10 3:47.32- 14 5000 13:17.97 -0-							
Souza	Hugo	BRA	5.3.87	188/77	400	45.42	45.09- 14
Sowinski	Erik	USA	21.12.89	186/70	800	1:44.84	1:44.58 -14
Spasovkhodskiy	Igor	RUS	1.8.79	191/91	TJ	16.44	17.44- 01
Spearmon	Wallace	USA	24.12.84	190/80	200	20.03	19.65- 06
Spears	Ro'Derick	USA	14.8.94	188/77	110h	13.77, 13.45w	
Sperlich	Martin	GER	28.8.91	189/70	1500	3:37.81	3:38.69- 13
Spratling	Brycen	USA	10.3.92	175/68	400	45.46	45.09- 14
Srp	Miklós	HUN	6.3.93		50kW	4:01:44	-0-
St. Lawrence	Ben	AUS	7.11.81	176/62	10k	27:44.24	27:24.95 -11
Ståhl	Daniel	SWE	27.8.92	200/145	DT	64.73	66.89- 14
Stanek	Tomás	CZE	13.6.91	190/127	SP	20.94i, 20.64	20.93- 14
Stano	Massimo	ITA	27.2.92	180/60	20kW	1:22:16	1:23:01- 14
Stanys	Raivydas	LTU	3.2.87	184/77	HJ	2.28i, 2.24	2.31- 12
Starc	Brandon	AUS	24.11.93	188/73	HJ	2.31	2.28- 13
Stathelakos	Constantinos	CYP	30.12.87	181/105	HT	75.32	74.38- 11
Stauß	René	GER	17.9.87	190/75	Dec	7907	7819- 14

Name		Nat	Born	Ht/Wt	Event	2015 Mark	Pre-2015 Best
Steacy	James	CAN	29.5.84	189/115	HT	71.60	79.13- 08
Stecchi	Claudio Michel	ITA	23.11.91	184/82	PV	5.55	5.60- 12
Steele	Edino	JAM	6.1.87	178/72	400	45.19	45.38- 12
Stevens	Tabor	USA	21.6.91	196/79	3kSt	8:26.81	8:35.05- 14
Stewart	Ray	USA	5.4.89	183/79	110h	13.34	13.35- 14
Stewart	Tyron	USA	8.7.89	180/70	LJ	7.96	8.39- 14
Stigler	Michael	USA	5.4.92	178/70	400h	48.44	49.19- 13
Stinson	Parker	USA	3.3.92	173/61	10k	27:54.98	28:34.71- 13
Storl	David	GER	27.7.90	199/122	SP	22.20	21.97- 14
^ Strelkov ¶	Denis	RUS	26.10.90	185/75	20kW	1:20:04	1:19:46- 14
Strobinders	Rolands	LAT	14.4.92	193/90	JT	83.37	83.10- 14
Strzalkowski	Adrian	POL	28.3.90	178/64	LJ	7.97i, 7.88	8.18i, 8.02- 14
* Su Bingtian		CHN	29.8.89	172/64	100	9.99	10.06- 13, 10.04w- 12
Su Xianzhen		CHN	26.2.95		20kW	1:22:58	-0-
* Suárez	Leonel	CUB	1.9.87	181/76	Dec	8027	8654- 09
^ Sudol	Grzegorz	POL	28.8.78	174/60	50kW	3:51:48	3:41:20- 13
Sugai	Yohei	JPN	30.8.85	180/77	LJ	8.18	8.10- 10, 8.16w- 14
Suguimati	Mahau	BRA	13.11.84	184/78	400h	49.59	48.67- 09
Sukharev	Kirill	RUS	24.5.92	183/75	LJ	7.98i, 7.96	8.13- 14
Sun Chenggang		CHN	11.3.91		20kW	1:22:22	1:19:55- 13
Suskevicius	Tadas	LTU	22.5.85	175/65	50kW	3:56:27	3:51:58- 14
* Suzuki	Yusuke	JPN	2.1.88	171/58	20kW	1:16:36	1:18:17- 14
Sviridov	Sergey	RUS	20.10.90	192/85	Dec	7693	8365- 12
^ Svoboda	Petr	CZE	10.10.84	195/83	110h	13.44	13.27- 10
Svyatokho	Valeriy	BLR	20.7.81	186/112	HT	72.84	81.49- 06
Swiderski	Adrian	POL	26.9.86	188/74	TJ	16.81	16.73- 14
Swift	Greggmar	BAR	16.2.91	183/68	110h	13.28	13.35- 14
Sykora	Jiri	CZE	20.1.95	184/79	Dec	7832	7927- 14
* Symmonds	Nick	USA	30.12.83	178/73	800	1:44.53	1:42.95- 12
Szikszai	Robert	HUN	30.9.94	200/118	DT	61.31	63.20- 14
Szypka	Brad	USA	13.2.93	188/111	SP	19.68i, 19.49	19.85- 14
Szyszkowski	Jakub	POL	21.8.91	193/145	SP	20.55i, 20.55	20.32- 13
Tabti	Bilal	ALG	7.6.93	175/60	3kSt	8:21.15	8:32.32- 13
Tadese	Tsegay	ETH	30.11.96		10k	28:04.57	
* Tadese	Zersenay	ERI	8.2.82	158/52	10k	28:05.34	26:37.25- 06
					HMar	59:24	58:23- 10
Taftian	Hasan	IRI	4.5.93	178/75	100	10.10	10.15- 13
Taiwo	Jeremy	USA	15.1.90	196/85	Dec	8303	8239 -13
Takahari	Hiromi	JPN	13.11.87	182/64	HJ	2.28	2.25- 13
* Takahashi	Eiki	JPN	19.11.92	175/56	20kW	1:18:03	1:18:41- 14
Takamasa	Tomoya	JPN	13.6.93		LJ	8.03	7.78, 7.79w- 14
Takase	Kei	JPN	25.11.88	179/67	100	10.09	10.13- 14
					200	20.14, 20.09w	20.34- 14
Takezawa	Kensuke	JPN	11.10.86	170/54	10k	28:02.70	27:45.59- 07
Taki	Kumari	KEN-Y	6.5.99		800	1:46.2A	1:48.0A- 14
Talam	Festus	KEN	20.10.94		HMar	60:56	61:47- 14
Talbot	Danny	GBR	1.5.91	184/73	200	20.27	20.36- 14
* Taleb	Brahim	MAR	16.2.85	182/70	3kSt	8:16.56	8:07.02- 07
* Tallent	Jared	AUS	17.10.84	178/60	50kW	3:42:17	3:36:53- 12
* Tamberi	Gianmarco	ITA	1.6.92	192/77	HJ	2.37	2.31- 12
* Tamgho	Teddy	FRA	15.6.89	187/82	TJ	17.24	18.04 -13
Tamire	Getaneh	ETH	.94	171/55	5000	13:21.88	13:13.04- 14
Tammert	Aleksander	EST	2.2.73	196/125	DT	60.93	70.82- 06
Tang Gongchen		CHN	24.4.89	185/71	LJ	8.17	8.09- 14
* Tanii	Takayuki	JPN	14.2.83	167/57	50kW	3:42:01	3:40:19- 14
Tanui	Collins	KEN	.92		Mar	2:08:08	-0-
* Tanui	Paul	KEN	22.12.90	172/54	3000	7:46.83+	7:50.88- 11
5000	12:58.69	13:00.53- 14			10k	26:51.86	26:50.63- 11
Taplin	Bralon	GRN	8.5.92	180/73	400	44.89	45.18- 14
* Tarabin	Dmitriy	RUS	29.10.91	176/85	JT	84.70	88.84- 13
Tarbei	Willy	KEN-Y	30.5.98	180/64	800	1:44.51A	-0-
Tarus	Eliud	KEN	3.3.93		HMar	60:04	62:08- 13
Tayala	Matthias	USA	27.4.93	183/100	HT	71.94	73.57- 14
* Taylor	Christian	USA	18.6.90	190/75	LJ	8.18	8.19- 10
					TJ	18.21	17.96- 11
Taylor	Christopher	JAM-Y	29.9.99	178/70	400	45.27A, 45.55	48.80- 14
Taylor	Joshua	USA	19.6.92	183/82	400h	50.03	50.17- 14
Taylor	Logan	USA	3.4.86	183/70	110h	13.56	13.65, 13.48w- 14
Taylor	Ronald	USA	13.8.90	182/73	LJ	7.94w	8.19- 13
Teeters	John	USA	19.5.93	183/77	100	10.07, 9.95w	10.14, 9.91w- 14
Tega	Odele	NGR	12.6.95	186/75	200	20.45	21.12- 14

Name		Nat	Born	Ht/Wt	Event	2015 Mark	Pre-2015 Best
Tekele	Adugna	ETH	26.2.89	170/55	10k	27:19.34	28:12.27- 14
HMar	60:26		60:15- 14		Mar	2:09:39	2:08:41- 14
Tesfaldet	Nguse	ERI	10.11.86	180/56	10k	27:50.14	27:28.10- 12
					HMar	59:55	59:39- 14
Tesfaye	Homiyu	GER	23.6.93	183/66	1500	3:34.13i	3:31.98- 14
Tewelde	Hiskel	ERI	15.9.86		HMar	60:29	-0-
Theiner	Wojciech	POL	25.6.86	187/74	HJ	2.26	2.32- 14
Thoirs	Jax	GBR	7.4.93	195/90	PV	5.65	5.61i, 5.60- 14
Thomas	Donald	BAH	1.7.84	190/75	HJ	2.34	2.35- 07
Thomas	Dwight	JAM	23.9.80	185/82	110h	13.42	13.15- 11
Thomas	Mikel	TTO	23.11.87	182/77	110h	13.17	13.19- 13
Thompson	Josh	USA	16.1.93	181/75	110h	13.55, 13.34w	13.80- 12
Thompson	Richard	TTO	7.6.85	187/79	100	10.04	9.82, 9.74w- 14
Thorne	Benjamin	CAN	19.3.93	180/57	20kW	1:19:57	1:20:19- 14
Thuku	Karemi Jeremiah	KEN	7.7.94	176/62	10k	27:43.59	27:28.27- 14
Thymes	Just'n	USA	24.1.94	180/70	200	20.46	20.61, 20.52w -14
Tian Zhizhong		CHN	15.12.92	196/128	SP	19.61	19.13- 14
Tikhomirov	Anton	RUS	29.4.88	191/118	SP	19.67i, 19.10	21.10- 14
Tikhon ¶	Ivan	BLR	24.7.76	186/110	HT	77.46	84.51- 08, 86.73dq- 05
Timshin	Sergey	RUS	25.11.92	183/79	Dec	7984	7794- 14
Tinsley	Michael	USA	21.4.84	185/74	400h	48.34	47.70- 13
Tirop	Elijah	KEN	1.1.92		HMar	60:55	-0-
Tiruneh	Workneh	ETH	.84		Mar	2:08:51	2:10:26- 13
Tistan	Martin	SVK	12.11.92	173/65	50kW	4:02:26	4:06:11- 14
Tobalina	Carlos	ESP	2.8.85	187/127	SP	20.13	20.32- 14
Tobe	Naoto	JPN	31.3.92	194/74	HJ	2.29	2.31- 14
Toboc	Valentin	ROU	17.3.92	188/73	LJ	7.99	7.98i, 7.92- 13
Tola	Tamirat	ETH	11.8.91		10k	27:22.64	
					HMar	60:08	61:27- 13
Toledo	Braian	ARG	8.9.93	187/100	JT	83.32	79.87- 12
Toledo	Yoiser	ESP	24.4.83	196/126	SP	20.23	20.25- 14
Tolokonnikov	Konstantin	RUS-J	26.2.96		800	1:45.76	1:48.29- 13
Tolossa	Debebe	ETH	7.7.91		Mar	2:09:07	2:07:41- 12
Tomlinson	Chris	GBR	15.9.81	197/84	LJ	7.96	8.35- 11
Tonnesen	Pau Gaspar	ESP	24.10.92	196/89	Dec	8247	7303- 13
Tontodonati	Federico	ITA	30.10.89	169/55	20kW	1:22:33	1:22:00- 12
					50kW	3:49:27	3:51:37- 12
Torgvaidze	Lasha	GEO	26.5.93	174/65	TJ	16.58	16.31- 12
Torie	Mike	USA	12.3.86	186/110	DT	61.54	63.12- 13
Tornéus	Michel	SWE	26.5.86	184/70	LJ	8.30i, 7.83, 8.07w	8.29i- 13, 8.22- 12
Toroitich	Timothy	UGA	10.10.91	169/57	10k	27:39.71	27:31.07- 13
Torrijos	Pablo	ESP	12.5.92	187/78	TJ	17.04i, 16.61	16.87- 14
Tóth	Matej	SVK	10.2.83	185/72	20kW	1:20:21	1:19:48- 14
					50kW	3:34:38	3:36:21- 14
Touil	Imad	ALG	11.2.89	172/62	1500	3:39.42, 3:37.12 short	3:35.82- 12
Tovarnov	Aleksey	RUS	21.1.85	183/86	JT	77.95	82.54- 13
Traber	Gregor	GER	2.12.92	189/77	110h	13.32	13.43, 13.23w- 14
Tracey	Tyquendo	JAM	10.6.93	179/75	100	10.14	10.21- 14
					200	20.39	20.92- 14
Traoré	Bano	MLI	25.4.85	180/65	110h	13.62,13.54w	13.49A, 13.50- 08, 13.51w- 11
Trofimov	Pyotr	RUS	28.11.83	174/63	20kW	1:20:53	1:18:28- 13
True	Ben	USA	29.12.85	183/70	5000	13:05.54	13:02.74- 14
					10k	27:43.79	27:41.17 -12
Tsákonas	Likoúrgos-Stéfanos	GRE	8.3.90	184/67	200	20.09	20.40 -14
Tsátoumas	Loúis	GRE	12.2.82	187/76	LJ	8.09	8.66- 07
Tsapik	Aleksey	BLR	4.8.88		TJ	16.77i	16.86i, 16.82, 16.97w- 12
Tsegay Adhane	Yemane	ETH	8.4.85		Mar	2:09:48dh	2:04:48- 12
Tsenov	Mitko	BUL	13.6.93	185/64	3kSt	8:21.89	8:20.87- 14
Tsernjavski	Taavi	EST	4.3.95	196/86	Dec	7744	7487- 14
Tsiámis	Dimítrios	GRE	12.1.82	178/67	TJ	16.45i	17.55- 06
Tsonov	Georgi	BUL	2.5.93	172/66	TJ	17.03, 17.11w	16.58i, 16.85w- 13, 16.35- 14
Tsuetaki	Hironori	JPN	8.5.93	175/60	3kSt	8:32.89	8:39.54- 14
Tsumba	Tatenda	ZIM	12.11.91	175/73	200	20.46A	
Tsvetkov	Mikhail	RUS	4.5.80	194/74	HJ	2.28	2.30i- 02, 2.30- 03
Tsyplakov	Daniyil	RUS	29.7.92	190/75	HJ	2.33	2.34i, 2.33- 14
Tucker	Russel	RSA	4.11.90	197/115	DT	62.74	62.15- 14
Tudor	Macklin	USA	13.6.94	188/109	DT	61.41	59.37- 14
Tuka	Amel	BIH	9.1.91	187/77	800	1:42.51	1:46.12- 14
Tulácek	Vladislav	CZE	9.7.88	193/115	SP	19.74i	19.51- 12
Turner	James	CAN	4.8.93	183/82	Dec	7773(w)	7536- 14
Tysse	Erik	NOR	4.12.80	184/59	20kW	1:20:52	1:19:11- 08

	Name		Nat	Born	Ht/Wt	Event	2015 Mark	Pre-2015 Best
	Ugachi	Tsuyoshi	JPN	27.4.87	163/49	10k	27:55.02	27:40.69- 11
	Uhle	Chris	USA	14.11.92	185/82	PV	5.52i, 5.41	5.35- 14
	Uhle	Joseph	USA	14.11.92	185/82	PV	5.55Ai	5.51- 13
*	Uibo	Maicel	EST	27.12.92	188/86	Dec	8356	8223- 13
*	Ujah	Chijindu	GBR	5.3.94	180/75	100	9.96	9.96- 14
						200	20.47	20.63- 14
	Ukaoma	Miles	NGR	21.7.92	183/75	400h	48.84	49.23- 12
*	Ukhov	Ivan	RUS	29.3.86	192/83	HJ	2.32	2.42i, 2.41- 14
	Umar	Jena	ETH	24.12.95	174/60	800	1:46.0A, 1:46.07	1:46.23- 14
	Unterberger	Aaron	USA	12.7.89	193/82	PV	5.50	5.44i, 5.35- 13
*	Urbanek	Robert	POL	29.4.87	200/120	DT	66.31	66.93- 12
	Ureña	Jorge	ESP	8.10.93	178/75	Dec	7983	7656- 14
^	Urtans	Maris	LAT	9.2.81	188/123	SP	20.37i, 20.23	21.63- 10
	Ushiro	Keisuke	JPN	24.7.86	196/95	Dec	8058	8308- 14
	Vadlejch	Jakub	CZE	10.10.90	190/93	JT	86.21	84.47- 10
	Vail	Ryan	USA	19.3.86	173/59	10k	28:04.60	27:44.05- 13
	Valiyev	Roman	KAZ	27.3.84	190/73	TJ	17.00i, 16.74	17.20- 12
	Vallés	Adrián	ESP	16.3.95	190/76	PV	5.65	5.31- 14
	Van Alphen	Hans	BEL	12.1.82	192/90	Dec	7876	8519- 12
^	Van Der Plaetsen	Thomas	BEL	24.12.90	188/82	Dec	8035	8255- 13
	van der Wath	Strydom	NAM	25.9.91	185/89	JT	78.32A	69.58- 09
	van Liew	Tim	USA	25.5.90	190/95	JT	79.49	75.55- 13
*	van Niekerk	Wayde	RSA	15.7.92	183/73	200	19.94	20.19- 14
						400	43.48	44.38- 14
	van Rensburg	Rynhardt	RSA	23.3.92	184/70	800	1:45.40	1:46.36 -12
	van Rooyen	Rocco	RSA	23.12.92	188/93	JT	85.39	80.10 -14
*	van Zyl	Louis 'L.J'	RSA	20.7.85	186/75	400h	48.78	47.66- 11
^	Varga	Roland	CRO	22.10.77	196/125	DT	63.01	67.38- 02
	Vargas	Richard	VEN	28.12.94	178/70	20kW	1:22:24	1:23:25.6t- 14
	Vasilchenko ¶	Yuriy	BLR	4.1.94	194/115	HT	73.21	69.51- 14
	Vaughn	Clayton	USA	15.5.92	173/77	100	9.93	10.13, 10.07w- 14
	Väyrynen	Henri	FIN	16.10.91	185/75	LJ	7.93	7.85i, 8.05w- 14
	Velikopolskiy	Dmitriy	RUS	27.11.84	188/110	HT	71.28	78.76- 08
	Vena	Nick	USA	16.4.93	194/120	SP	19.99i, 19.80	20.39- 14
	Venhlovskyy	Oleksandr	UKR	5.8.85	184/70	50kW	4:00:57	3:56:07- 13
*	Verburg	David	USA	14.5.91	168/64	400	44.41	44.75- 13
	Vernon	Andrew	GBR	7.1.86	178/65	5000	13:20.34	13:11.50- 14
						10k	27:42.62	27:53.65- 12
	Veryovkin	Mikhail	RUS	28.6.91		HJ	2.29i, 2.20	2.25i- 13, 2.23- 14
*	Vesely	Vitezslav	CZE	27.2.83	186/94	JT	88.18	88.34- 12
	Vestlund	Oscar	SWE	27.4.93	189/110	HT	72.20	67.69- 14
*	Vetter	Johannes	GER	26.3.93	188/105	JT	85.40	79.75- 14
*	Vicaut	Jimmy	FRA	27.2.92	188/83	100	9.86	9.95- 13, 9.89w- 14
						200	20.42	20.30- 13
	Vicente	Isaac	ESP	30.4.87	184/87	HT	71.25	70.77- 14
^	Vieira	João	POR	20.2.76	174/58	20kW	1:21:51	1:20:09- 06
	Vieira	Sérgio	POR	20.2.76	174/58	20kW	1:21:51	1:20:58- 97
	Villanueva	Claudio	ECU	3.8.88	168/55	50kW	4:02:14	3:50:29- 13
	Villar	Paulo César	COL	28.7.78	175/64	110h	13.62A, 13.81	13.27A- 11, 13.29- 06
	Viney	Cam	USA	6.9.93	185/75	400h	49.92	50.09- 14
	Viney	Cameron	USA	6.9.93	185/75	110h	13.64, 13.52w	14.09- 14
	Vinichenko	Igor	RUS	11.4.84	196/119	HT	73.72	80.00- 07
*	Visser	Zarck	RSA	15.9.89	178/70	LJ	8.41	8.32- 13
^	Vivas	Borja	ESP	26.5.84	203/140	SP	20.66i, 20.28	21.07- 14
	Vloon	Menno	NED	11.5.94	177/77	PV	5.55	5.41- 14
	Vonavka	Tomás	CZE	4.6.90	197/109	DT	60.73	62.10- 14
	Vos	Ingmar	NED	28.5.86	186/80	Dec	7852	8224- 12
	de Vries	Ruan	RSA	1.2.86	187/88	110h	13.60A, 13,72, 13.57Aw	13.59A, 13.67- 13
	Vrublevskiy	Vadim	RUS	18.3.93		HJ	2.26	2.24- 13
	Vynogradov	Yevgen	UKR	30.4.84	195/105	HT	79.25	80.58- 08
*	Walcott	Keshorn	TTO	2.4.93	188/90	JT	90.16	85.77- 14
^	Walker	Brad	USA	21.6.81	188/86	PV	5.72	6.04- 08
	Walker	Justin	USA	30.11.90	175/70	100	10.12, 10.06w	10.12, 9.95w- 14
						200	20.29	20.47, 20.13w- 14
	Walker	Shaquille	USA	24.6.93	178/70	800	1:45.58	1:49.39- 12
	Wallin	Gabriel	SWE	14.10.81	193/93	JT	79.16	83.23- 13
*	Walsh	Tom	NZL	1.3.92	186/123	SP	21.62	21.26i, 21.24- 14
	Walters	Ruebin	TTO	2.4.95	184/70	110h	13.82, 13.53w	14.13- 14
	Wamer	Michael	USA	21.12.94	188/85	TJ	16.47	15.25i, 15.00- 14
	Wami	Mulugeta	ETH	12.7.82		Mar	2:08:37	2:07:11- 12
	Wan Yong		CHN	22.7.87	188/107	HT	74.74	73.49- 13

Name		Nat	Born	Ht/Wt	Event	2015 Mark	Pre-2015 Best
Wang Guangfu		CHN	15.11.87	192/110	SP	19.55	20.20- 12
Wang Jianan		CHN-J	27.8.96	178/61	LJ	8.25	8.10- 14
Wang Kaihua		CHN	16.2.94		20kW	1:19:49	1:23:35- 13
Wang Qin		CHN	8.5.94		20kW	1:22:56	1:22:50- 14
Wang Shizhu		CHN	20.2.89	184/100	HT	74.61	75.20- 13
Wang Yu		CHN	18.8.91	192/73	HJ	2.31	2.33- 13
Wang Zhen		CHN	24.8.91	180/62	20kW	1:18:00	1:17:36- 12
Wanjiru	Daniel	KEN	25.5.92	174/58	HMar	59:51	59:58- 14
Wanjuki	Jacob	KEN	16.1.86	178/52	HMar	60:48	60:32- 10
Ward	Laderrick	USA	28.12.92	173/68	LJ	8.14w	8.00- 14
Wariner	Jeremy	USA	31.1.84	183/70	400	45.42	43.45- 07
Warner	Damian	CAN	4.11.89	185/83	110h	13.27	13.50- 14
					Dec	8695	8512- 13
Warner	Justyn	CAN	28.6.87	174/70	100	10.16, 10.08w	10.09- 12
Washington	Adarius	USA	19.10.92	183/73	110h	13.58	13.74- 14
Wasihun	Mule	ETH	20.10.93		HMar	60:42	60:08- 14
Watanabe	Yoshihiro	JPN-J	7.1.97		400h	49.97	51.35- 14
Watson	Reese	USA	8.10.93	188/85	PV	5.60	5.51- 14
Ways	Ceolamar	USA	22.11.94	182/73	400	45.49	45.93- 14
Webb	Ameer	USA	19.3.91	175/75	100	10.04	10.14- 13, 10.05w- 12
					200	20.02	20.20, 20.05w- 13
Weber	Julian	GER	29.8.94	190/94	JT	81.15	80.72- 14
Weißhaidinger	Lukas	AUT	20.2.92	192/115	DT	67.24	60.68- 14
Weir	Warren	JAM	31.10.89	178/75	200	20.24	19.79- 13
Weirich	Victor	USA	25.10.87	188/86	PV	5.66Ai, 5.50	5.60- 14
Weldesilasie	Dawit	ERI	10.12.94		HMar	60:26	61:07- 13
Werskey	Eric	USA	17.7.87	188/120	SP	20.13	20.13- 13
Wesh	Darrell	HAI	21.1.92	173/70	100	10.16	10.14- 13
Whiting	Ryan	USA	24.11.86	191/134	SP	21.80i, 21.37	22.28- 13
Whitt	Jack	USA	12.4.90	193/84	PV	5.70A	5.72i- 12, 5.70- 13
Whyte	Annsert	JAM	10.4.87	185/75	400h	48.90	48.58- 14
Wieczorek	Mark	USA	25.12.84	178/68	800	1:45.89	1:45.36- 13
Wieland	Luca	GER	7.12.94	185/82	Dec	7635	6120- 14
Wierig	Martin	GER	10.6.87	202/108	DT	65.94	68.33- 12
Wiesiolek	Pawel	POL	13.8.91	194/84	Dec	8140	7727- 13
Williams	Ben	GBR	25.1.92	183/73	TJ	16.74	16.46- 14
Williams	Conrad	GBR	20.3.82	182/76	400	45.06	45.08- 12
Williams	Delano	GBR	23.12.93	183/72	200	20.40	20.27- 13
					400	45.42	47.51- 14
Williams	Harrison	USA-J	7.3.96	190/82	Dec	7806	
Williams	Isaac	USA	30.11.93	188/80	110h	13.56, 13.13w	13.81, 13.44w- 14
Williams	Ivory	USA	2.5.85	173/77	100	10.12w	9.93 -09, 9.88w -10
Williams	Jesse	USA	27.12.83	184/75	HJ	2.31i, 2.31	2.37- 11
Williams	Kendal	USA	23.9.95	180/73	100	10.07, 9.98w	10.21- 14, 10.18w- 13
					200	20.26	20.55, 20.46w- 14
Williams	LaToy	BAH	28.5.88	190/77	400	45.30	44.73- 09
Williams	Marvin	JAM-J	13.6.96	175/66	400h	49.90	51.01- 14
Williams	Will	USA	31.1.95	183/79	LJ	8.03	7.77i, 7.62, 7.68w- 14
Willis	Nick	NZL	25.4.83	183/68	1500	3:29.66	3:29.91- 14
1M	3:51.46i		3:49.83- 14		5000	13:22.11	13:20.33- 04
Wilson	Ryan	USA	19.12.80	188/81	110h	13.54	13.02- 07
Winger	Russ	USA	2.8.84	191/120	DT	64.34	66.04- 11
Winn	Daniel	USA	30.7.91	188/68	1500	3:37.56	3:42.95- 14
Winter	Chris	CAN	22.7.86	188/75	3kSt	8:26.55	8:28.46- 12
Wirkkala	Teemu	FIN	14.1.84	187/85	JT	84.39	87.23- 09
Witt	Jason	USA	9.12.89	193/73	10k	27:54.25	28:36.64- 14
Woepse	Mike	USA	29.5.91	185/79	PV	5.55Ai, 5.46	5.62- 14
Wojciechowski	Pawel	POL	6.6.89	190/81	PV	5.84	5.91- 11
Wolde	Dawit	ETH	19.5.91	169/54	1500	3:35.87	3:33.82- 12
Wolfle	Chase	USA	9.10.92	185/84	PV	5.50i, 5.40	5.56- 14
Wolski	Allan	BRA	18.1.90	185/110	HT	73.52	71.93- 14
Woodruff	Ben	USA	9.5.89	183/91	JT	78.67	78.03- 14
Woodson	Markesh	USA	6.9.93	168/64	100	10.18, 10.14w	10.18, 10.11w -13
Worku	Bazu	ETH	15.9.90	170/52	Mar	2:07:09	2:05:25- 10
Wöschler	Till	GER	9.6.91	196/110	JT	80.41	84.38- 11
Wote	Aman	ETH	18.4.84	181/64	1500	3:30.29	3:29.91- 14
Wright	Alex	IRL	19.12.90	173/64	20kW	1:22:09	1:23:05- 13
Wright	Chad	JAM	25.3.91	188/110	DT	65.03	63.96- 14
Wrobel	David	GER	13.2.91	195/100	DT	62.66	62.72- 14
Wruck	Julian	AUS	6.7.91	198/125	DT	63.88	68.16- 13
Wu Qianlong		CHN	30.1.90	176/62	50kW	3:47:35	3:50:51- 14

Name		Nat	Born	Ht/Wt	Event	2015 Mark	Pre-2015 Best
Wu Ruiting		CHN	29.11.95		TJ	16.83	15.48- 14
Wyatt	Audie	USA-J	30.4.96	190/84	PV	5.50	5.18- 14
Xia Xiang		CHN	28.3.91	181/64	PV	5.50i, 5.50	5.35- 10
Xie Sichao		CHN	28.2.93		20kW	1:22:08	1:22:34- 12
					50kW	3:49:57	4:10:37- 14
* Xie Wenjun		CHN	11.7.90	188/77	110h	13.36	13.23- 14
Xu Faguang		CHN	17.5.87	178/69	50kW	3:52:29	3:42:20- 11
Xu Xiaolong		CHN	20.12.92		TJ	16.93	16.82- 14
Yakovenko	Dmytro	UKR	17.9.92	191/72	HJ	2.30	2.25i, 2.24- 14
Yamagata	Ryota	JPN	10.6.92	176/70	100	10.15w	10.07- 12, 10.04w- 13
Yamamoto	Hiroyuki	JPN	30.4.86	172/54	10k	27:55.40	28:24.93- 14
Yamamoto	Seito	JPN	11.3.92	181/70	PV	5.70	5.75- 13
Yamanishi	Toshikazu	JPN-J	15.2.96	164/51	20kW	1:21:20	-0-
Yamashita	Yuga	JPN-J	6.2.96		20kW	1:23:16.34	1:23:06- 14
Yamazaki	Yuki	JPN	16.1.84	179/65	50kW	3:43:40	3:40:12- 09
Yami	Dadi	ETH	.82		Mar	2:08:05	2:05:41- 12
Yáñez	Eure	VEN	20.5.93	194/77	HJ	2.25	2.27- 14
Yao Jie		CHN	21.9.90	188/85	PV	5.65	5.60- 14
Yargunkin	Aleksandr	RUS	6.1.81	182/68	50kW	3:45:41	3:42:26- 14
Yashin Hasen	Agato	ETH	19.1.86	175/58	10k	27:46.21	27:46.35- 13
Yastrebov	Viktor	UKR	13.1.82	185/79	TJ	16.37, 16.49w	17.32- 04
Yator	Vincent	KEN	11.7.89	172/55	10k	27:33.45A	
					HMar	59:55	61:02- 12
* Yego	Hillary	KEN	2.4.92	178/60	3kSt	8:13.10	8:03.57- 13
Yego	Isaac	KEN	.89		3kSt	8:32.48A	8:37.5A- 14
* Yego	Julius	KEN	4.1.89	175/90	JT	92.72	85.40- 13
Yego	Philip	KEN	79		3kSt	8:27.99A	8:34.4A- 12
Yego	Solomon	KEN	.87		HMar	60:04	61:59- 14
^ Yemelyanov ¶	Stanislav	RUS	23.10.90	175/62	20kW	1:20:10	1:19:43- 10
Yeremich	Yuriy	BLR	24.10.95	178/74	Dec	7817	7237- 14
Yevstifeyev	Roman	RUS	19.9.92		20kW	1:22:21	1:26:26- 13
					50kW	3:51:00	3:45:41- 14
Yokote	Ken	JPN	27.4.93	165/54	10k	27:58.40	28:38.73- 14
Yoon Seung-hyun		KOR	1.6.94	194/74	HJ	2.32	2.26- 14
Yoroizaka	Tetsuya	JPN	20.3.90	166/53	5000	13:12.63	13:29.03- 14
					10k	27:29.74	27:38.99- 14
Yosei	Charles	KEN-J	.96		10k	27:54.6A	
Yoshida	Kazuaki	JPN	31.8.87	180/73	400h	49.95	49.45- 09
Yoshida	Takuya	JPN	10.8.90		50kW	3:46:07	3:43:02- 14
Younes Idris	Ali Mohamed	SUD	15.9.89	191/75	HJ	2.28	2.28i, 2.26- 14
* Young	Isiah	USA	5.1.90	183/75	100	10.00, 9.82w	9.99, 9.93w- 13
					200	19.93, 19.75w	19.86- 13
Young	Jordan	CAN	21.6.93	190/113	SP	19.80	17.93- 13
DT	62.27		56.74- 12		HT	70.73	68.28- 14
* Yousif	Rabah	GBR	11.12.86	183/75	400	44.54	45.13- 11
Yu Chia-Hsuan		TPE	22.1.95	178/66	400h	50.04	50.49- 14
Yu Shisuo		CHN	20.2.90	188/65	HJ	2.25	2.20- 12
* Yu Wei		CHN	11.9.87	180/60	50kW	3:45:21	3:51:46- 11
Yurchenko	Aleksandr	RUS	30.7.92		TJ	16.81i, 16.57	16.67- 13
Zaghou	Montacer	MAR	1.1.89		3kSt	8:29.5	8:23.84- 13
Zahn	D.J.	USA	31.1.93	178/80	200	20.37	21.10- 14
					400	45.51	45.69- 14
Zakalnytskyy	Maryan	UKR	19.8.94	180/65	50kW	3:57:18	4:07:08- 14
Zalewski	Karol	POL	7.8.93	189/86	200	20.45	20.41- 13
Zalewski	Krystian	POL	11.4.89	185/67	3kSt	8:21.22	8:16.20- 14
Zango	Fabrice	BUR	25.6.93	180/75	TJ	16.76	15.97- 13
* Zawude	Tebalu	ETH	2.11.87	184/65	10k	27:20.54	28:03.16- 12
					Mar	2:08:46	2:07:10- 14
Zaytsev	Artyom	BLR	7.12.84	202/75	HJ	2.25	2.28- 09
Zenúch	Patrik	SVK	30.12.90	184/86	JT	82.51	84.83- 14
Zepeda	Omar	MEX	8.7.77	177/68	50kW	3:55:02A	3:47:35- 14
Zernikel	Oleg	GER	16.4.95	184/72	PV	5.51	5.50- 14
Zerrifi	Abdelhamid	ALG	20.6.86		3kSt	8:31.08	8:25.96- 13
* Zhang Guowei		CHN	4.6.91	200/77	HJ	2.38	2.34- 14
Zhang Hang		CHN	28.10.91		50kW	3:50:01	4:03:40- 12
Zhang Honglin		CHN	12.1.94		110h	13.53	13.69- 14
Zhang Kuo		CHN	12.12.89		50kW	3:58:47	4:08:02- 12
* Zhang Lin		CHN	11.11.93	175/55	50kW	3:44:39	3;48:49- 14
Zhang Peimeng		CHN	13.3.87	186/78	100	10.13	10.00- 13
Zhang Wei		CHN	22.3.94	188/77	PV	5.65	5.62i- 13, 5.60- 14
Zhang Yaoguang		CHN	21.6.93		LJ	7.98, 8.01w	7.99- 13

Name		Nat	Born	Ht/Wt	Event	2015 Mark	Pre-2015 Best
Zhao Qi		CHN	14.1.93		50kW	3:57:53	3:51:47- 14
Zhao Qinggang		CHN	24.7.85	184/93	JT	79.47	89.15- 14
Ziólkowski	Szymon	POL	1.7.76	188/120	HT	73.15	83.38- 01
Ziegler	Alexander	GER	7.7.87	180/98	HT	74.73	76.29- 14
Ziegler	Manuel	GER	28.7.90	183/75	TJ	16.61i	16.54- 14
Ziemek	Zach	USA	23.2.93	190/77	Dec	8107	7981- 14
Zunic	Stipe	CRO	13.12.90	188/115	SP	21.11i, 20.38	20.68- 14

WOMEN'S INDEX 2015

Athletes included are those ranked in the top 100s at standard (World Champs) events (plus shorter lists for 1000m, M, 2000m and 3000m). Those with detailed biographical profiles are indicated in first column by:
in this year's Annual, ^ featured in a previous year's Annual

Name		Nat	Born	Ht/Wt	Event	2015 Mark	Pre-2015 Best
Ababel	Yeshaneh	ETH	10.6.90	157/42	10000	31:23.60	30:35.91- 13
Abakumova	Mariya	RUS	15.1.86	178/85	JT	61.27	71.99- 11
Abramchuk	Olha	UKR	12.4.91	180/78	DT	57.24	56.55- 14
Abramchuk	Yelena	BLR	14.2.88	178/72	SP	18.31i, 18.21	19.24- 13
Achano	Netsanet	ETH	14.12.87	167/53	Mar	2:27:14	2:24:12- 12
Acuff	Amy	USA	14.7.75	188/66	HJ	1.88	2.01- 03
Adams	Valerie	NZL	6.10.84	193/123	SP	18.79	21.24- 11
Adamu	Birtukan	ETH	29.4.92	164/49	3kSt	9:41.91	9:20.37- 11
Addison	Rebecca	USA	28.5.91	165/52	1500	4:08.93	4:15.81- 13
Adekoya	Kemi	BRN	16.1.93	168/57	400	50.86	51.11- 14
					400h	54.12	54.59- 14
Adeloye	Tosin	NGR-J	7.2.96	170/60	400	51.24	53.14- 12
Adeoye	Margaret	GBR	27.4.85	175/64	200	22.92	22.88- 13
					400	52.07	51.93- 13
Aerts	Sara	BEL	25.1.84	182/64	100h	13.02	12.90- 13
Afework	Abebech	ETH	11.12.90	152/42	HMar	69:14	69:57+- 14
					Mar	2:23:33	2:23:59- 13
Agafonova	Gulfiya	RUS	4.6.82	183/83	HT	67.67	77.26- 06
Agai	Margaret	KEN	10.6.88	154/44	HMar	69:57	
Agirre	Naroa	ESP	15.5.79	177/64	PV	4.46A	4.56i- 07. 4.51- 14
Agnou	Caroline	SUI-J	26.5.96	171/65	Hep	6123	5540- 14
Aguilar	Evelis	COL	3.1.93	170/62	Hep	5930	5707A, 5518- 14
Aguilar	Yulenmis	CUB-J	3.8.96	167/70	JT	63.86	54.50A- 14
Agwunobi	Chioma	USA	.95	173/55	200	22.68	23.93, 23.75w- 14
					LJ	6.82Aw	5.95- 13
Ahbe	Kelsie	CAN	6.7.91	170/63	PV	4.50	4.40- 14
Ahouanwanou	Odile	BEN	5.1.91	178/71	Hep	5751	4983- 12
Ahouré	Murielle	CIV	23.8.87	167/57	100	10.81	10.91- 13, 10.86w- 11
					200	22.29	22.24- 13
Ahye	Michelle-Lee	TTO	10.4.92	168/59	100	10.97, 10.87w	10.85- 14
					200	23.19i, 22.01w	22.77- 14
Aidietyté	Neringa	LTU	5.6.83	177/64	20kW	1:30:02	1:29:01- 14
Aikhonbare	Itohan	USA	29.3.94		SP	16.85	16.38- 14
Aït Salem	Souad	ALG	6.1.79	158/51	Mar	2:27:21	2:25:08- 07
Akinosun	Morolake	USA	17.5.94	163/61	100	11.29, 10.94w	11.04, 10.96w- 14
					200	22.52	22.68, 22.17w- 14
Akkaoui	Malika	MAR	25.12.87	160/46	800	1:59.03	1:57.64- 13
					1500	4:04.49	4:04.96- 11
Akmukhamedova	Tatyana	RUS	14.7.93		LJ	6.56	6.25- 14, 6.52w- 12
Aksyonova	Kseniya	RUS	14.1.88	177/60	400	51.44	49.92- 10
Aksyonova	Natalya	RUS-J	6.6.97		HJ	1.88	1.86i- 14, 1.77- 13
Alcántara	Dailenis	CUB	10.8.91	163/56	TJ	14.03, 14.04w	14.58- 12
Aleksandrova	Ulyana	RUS	1.1.91	182/63	HJ	1.90i, 1.89	1.86i, 1.84- 13
					Hep	5995	5932- 14
Alekseyeva	Nadezhda	RUS	16.7.88		400h	56.99	57.39- 13
Alekseyeva	Natalya	RUS	27.5.86		TJ	14.08i, 13.93	
Alemaheyu	Askale	ETH	11.1.96		HMar	70:01	73:18- 14
Alemayehu	Hirut	ETH	19.12.93		HMar	70:15	70:25- 14
Alembekova	Elmira	RUS	30.6.90		20kW	1:24:47	1:25:27- 12
Alemu	Habitam	ETH-J	9.7.97	167/52	800	2:01.27	2:09.6A- 14
Alexander	Ayanna	TTO	20.7.82	172/65	TJ	13.96	14.40- 14
Alexander	Kineke	VIN	21.2.86	178/65	200	23.25, 22.99w	23.00- 13
					400	51.49	51.23, 50.8- 14
Alexoúli	Háido	GRE	29.3.91	179/59	LJ	6.69	6.31- 12, 6.38w- 14
Alise Williams	Sirena	USA	26.12.87	163/	100h	13.16, 12.94w	13.27, 13.13w- 14
Allman	Valarie	USA	23.2.95	183/70	DT	57.48	57.45- 14
Almanza	Rose Mary	CUB	13.7.92	166/53	800	1:57.70	1:59.4- 13, 1:59.48- 14
Amata	Doreen	NGR	6.5.88	185/55	HJ	1.94	1.95- 08

Name		Nat	Born	Ht/Wt	Event	2015 Mark	Pre-2015 Best
Amponsah	Janet	GHA	12.4.93	167/52	100	11.29, 11.12w	11.36, 11.09w- 14
					200	23.04	23.05- 14
Anacharsis	Phara	FRA	17.12.83	177/60	400h	56.71	55.94- 13
Anagnostopoúlou	Hrisoúla	GRE	27.8.91	176/79	DT	61.40	57.20- 14
Ananchenko	Yevgeniya	RUS	7.11.92	178/73	JT	60.54	56.44- 14
Anang	Naa	AUS	10.3.95	165/54	LJ	6.55	6.27- 14
^ Anderson	Alexandra	USA	28.1.87	175/60	100	11.16, 11.10w	10.91- 13
Andersson	Tracey	SWE	5.12.84	167/87	HT	69.23	70.82- 13
Ando	Yuka	JPN	16.3.94	160/43	5000	15:32.67	15:33.72- 12
10000	32:07.37		32:24.50- 14		HMar	69:51	-0-
Andraud	Matilde	FRA	28.4.89	172/68	JT	60.67	59.80- 14
Andrejczyk	Maria	POL-J	9.3.96	172/71	JT	62.11	56.53- 14
Andrejsková	Petra	CZE	25.6.92	167/64	JT	56.27	57.48- 14
Ângulo	Yuliana	ECU	6.7.94	162/55	LJ	6.50A, 6.38	6.33- 14
Aniballi	Valentina	ITA	19.4.84	176/85	DT	58.55	57.73- 13
Ankiewicz	Emilia	POL	22.11.90	178/64	400h	56.55	56.73- 14
^ Antyukh	Natalya	RUS	26.6.81	182/73	400h	55.92	52.70- 12
Apine	Madara	LAT	2.3.89		TJ	13.68	13.22- 07
Arcanjo	Geisa	BRA	19.9.91	180/92	SP	17.76	19.02- 12
* Aregawi ¶?	Abeba	SWE	5.7.90	169/48	800	1:59.98	1:59.20- 13
1500	4:01.97		3:56.54- 12		1M	4:23.07	
Arenas	Lorena	COL	17.9.93	160/50	20kW	1:31:02.25t	1:30:18- 14
Argüelles	Yariagnis	CUB	18.4.84	173/55	LJ	6.70A, 6.66	6.66- 09
Aristarkhova	Natalya	RUS	31.10.89	163/46	3kSt	9:35.07	9:30.64- 13
* Arrafi	Rabab	MAR	12.1.91	167/54	800	1:58.55	2:00.58- 13
1500	4:02.94		4:02.71- 14		1M	4:23.50	
Artyukh	Yekaterina	BLR	14.1.91		400h	56.36	56.63- 14, 56.16dq- 10
Arusei	Peninah	KEN	23.2.79	165/51	HMar	68:56	67:48- 10
* Arzamasova	Marina	BLR	17.12.87	173/57	800	1:57.54	1:58.15- 14
Asada	Chiaki	JPN	21.1.91		20kW	1:31:28	1:32:27- 10
Asahssah	Malika	MAR	24.9.82	173/56	Mar	2:28:01	2:30:23- 12
Asefa	Sutume	ETH	.94	153/42	HMar	68:47	
Asenjo	Sabina	ESP	3.8.86	181/95	DT	61.36	58.65- 13
* Asher-Smith	Dina	GBR	4.12.95	165/55	100	10.99	11.14, 11.03w- 14
					200	22.07	22.61- 14
Ashley	Whitney	USA	18.2.89	178/80	DT	64.80	63.78- 14
Assani Issouf	Jeanine	FRA	17.8.92	169/57	TJ	14.24	13.95- 14
Assefa	Meskerem	ETH	20.9.85	155/43	HMar	70:28+	69:10- 14
					Mar	2:25:11	2:25:17- 13
* Assefa	Sofia	ETH	14.11.87	171/58	3kSt	9:12.63	9:09.00- 12
Atkinson	Johanna	GBR	17.1.85	168/54	20kW	1:33:43	1:30:41- 10
Aubry	Rachel	CAN	18.5.90	172/57	800	2:01.56	2:02.05- 14
Auckland	Rhona	GBR	11.5.93	160/45	5000	15:27.60	15:58.95- 14
					10000	32:22.79	33:09.58- 14
Avdeyeva	Anna	RUS	6.4.85	171/100	SP	17.14	20.07- 09
* Avery	Kate	GBR	10.10.91	175/50	3000	8:53.12i	8:56.20i, 8:56.24- 14
5000	15:25.63		15:27.90- 14		10000	31:41.44	32:33.35- 14
Aya	Masumi	JPN	1.1.80	165/75	HT	66.38	67.26- 06
* Ayalew	Hiwot	ETH	6.3.90	173/51	3kSt	9:14.73	9:09.61- 12
* Ayalew	Wude	ETH	4.7.87	150/44	10000	30:58.03	30:11.87- 09
					HMar	69:53	67:58- 09
* Ayana	Almaz	ETH	21.11.91	165/50	2000	5:35.10+	5:37.5+- 14
3000	8:22.22		8:24.58- 14		5000	14:14.32	14:25.84- 13
Babar	Lalita	IND	2.6.89	162/55	3kSt	9:27.86	9:35.37- 14
Babsek	Sasa	SLO	27.3.92	172/65	TJ	13.70, 14.02w	13.17- 13
Bácskay	Zsófia	HUN-J	18.3.97		HT	66.87	64.79- 14
Bae Chan-mi		KOR	24.3.91	175/62	TJ	13.65	13.65- 14
* Bahta	Meraf	SWE	24.6.89	177/51	1500	4:06.42i	4:01.34- 14
* Baisden	Kendall	USA	5.3.95	180/61	100	11.12w	11.73- 09, 11.33w- 14
200	22.80		23.15, 22.99w- 14		400	50.50	50.46- 14
Balayeva	Olga	RUS	31.7.84		LJ	6.57i	6.89- 11
Balciunaité	Eglé	LTU	31.10.88	175/60	800	2:00.21	1:59.29- 10
Balkwill	Kelsey	CAN	19.9.92	175/62	400h	56.80	57.94- 10
Balta	Ksenija	EST	11.1.86	168/53	LJ	6.66	6.87i- 09, 6.87- 10
Bambara	Laëtitia	BUR	30.3.84	180/75	HT	66.91	68.53- 11
Bamgbose	Margaret	USA	19.10.93	162/52	400	51.37	51.72- 14
Bânova	Andriana	BUL	1.5.87	178/64	TJ	14.10i, 13.95, 14.06w	14.34- 11
* Baptiste	Kelly-Ann	TTO	14.10.86	160/54	100	10.84	10.83- 13
					200	22.91w	22.36- 13, 22.33w- 12
Barber	Alana	NZL	8.7.87	163/52	20kW	1:32:50	1:39:01- 14
Barber	Jade	USA	4.4.93	170/64	100h	12.85, 12.70w	12.97- 14, 12.93w- 13

Name		Nat	Born	Ht/Wt	Event	2015 Mark	Pre-2015 Best
^ Barber	Mikele	USA	4.10.80	159/50	100	11.17	11.02- 07, 10.96w- 11
Barnett	Sharrika	USA-J	16.4.97	168/52	400	52.25	53.43- 14
Barnett	Tara-Sue	JAM	9.10.93	178/81	DT	58.55	54.91A- 14
Barras	Diane	FRA	21.8.85	177/62	LJ	6.52w	6.09- 10
Barsosio	Agnes	KEN	5.8.82	159/44	Mar	2:27:52	2:24:03- 13
Bartoletta	Tianna	USA	30.8.85	168/60	100	10.94, 10.89w	10.85- 12
					LJ	7.14	7.02- 14
Bates	Emma	USA	8.7.92	166/54	5000	15:32.46	15:33.42- 14
					10000	32:13.28	32:20.83- 14
Bauer	Katharina	GER	12.6.90	179/68	PV	4.65	4.55- 14
Baumann	Jackie	GER	24.8.95	172/57	400h	56.62	58.42- 14
Baumgart	Iga	POL	11.4.89	178/57	400	52.02	52.75- 12
Bauschke	Melanie	GER	14.7.88	179/63	LJ	6.61i, 6.59	6.83- 09
Bawcom	Janet	USA	22.8.78	170/52	HMar	70:46	69:55- 12
Baxter	Aubrey	USA	7.11.85	173/84	HT	68.50	70.90- 12
^ Baysa	Atsede	ETH	16.4.87	160/42	HMar	70:37	67:34- 13
					Mar	2:25:44	2:22:03- 12
Bazdyreva	Anastasiya	RUS	6.3.92	168/55	800	1:58.75	2:00.90- 14
Beard	Jessica	USA	8.1.89	168/57	200	23.08	22.81- 13
					400	50.68	50.56- 09
Beckles	Kierre	BAR	21.5.90	169/54	100h	12.88	12.98- 14, 12.97w- 12
Beesley	Meghan	GBR	15.11.89	167/63	400h	54.52	54.97- 13
Beitia	Ruth	ESP	1.4.79	192/71	HJ	2.00	2.02- 07
Bekele	Ashete	ETH	17.4.88	169/52	Mar	2:23:43	2:24:59- 14
Bekele	Tadelech	ETH	11.4.91	156/42	HMar	68:52	68:38- 13
					Mar	2:22:51	2:23:02- 14
Bekh	Maryna	UKR	18.7.95	172/61	LJ	6.63	6.78- 13
Belete	Mimi	BRN	9.6.88	164/62	1500	4:05.37	4:00.08- 14
3000 8:53.96 8:30.00- 14					5000	14:54.71	15:00.87- 14
Bell	Alexandra	GBR	4.11.92	166/55	800	2:01.82	2:03.16- 14
Bell	Rolanda	PAN	27.10.87	160/48	3kSt	9:47.16	9:52.07- 13
Bellamy	J'Nea	USA	5.11.94	165/54	200	23.06	23.38- 14
Bellille	Janeil	TTO	18.6.89	172/60	400h	55.68	55.41- 14
Belyakova	Anastasiya	RUS	4.12.90		Hep	5807	6010- 11
Bengtsson	Angelica	SWE	8.7.93	163/51	PV	4.70i, 4.70	4.63i- 11, 4.58- 12
Benson	Fiona	CAN	25.5.92	178/68	800	1:59.59	2:09.50- 12
1500 4:05.24 4:22.97- 12					1M	4:25.79	
Beriso	Amane	ETH	13.10.91	163/60	HMar	68:43	71:51- 14
Berry	Gwen	USA	29.6.89	1.80/	HT	72.26	73.81- 13
^ Bespalova ¶	Mariya	RUS	21.5.86	183/85	HT	73.74	76.72- 12
Bettiche	Amina	ALG	14.12.87	161/44	3kSt	9:36.10	9:29.20- 14
Bezruchenko	Yelena	RUS-J	23.7.96		SP	17.23	16.24- 14
Bian Ka		CHN	5.1.93		SP	18.71	17.71- 14
Billaud	Cindy	FRA	11.3.86	165/59	100h	12.83	12.56- 14
Bing	Portia	NZL	17.4.93	179/65	Hep	6102	5774(w)- 13, 5695- 14
Bingham	Khamica	CAN	15.6.94	163/59	100	11.13, 11.00w	11.32- 14
					200	22.84, 22.83w	23.46- 11
Bingson	Amanda	USA	20.2.90	170/89	HT	72.35	75.73- 13
Bishop	Melissa	CAN	5.8.88	173/57	800	1:57.52	1:59.70- 14
Bizzarri	Angela	USA	15.2.88	162/48	5000	15:30.00	15:16.04- 11
					10000	32:26.98	
Blaase	Chelsea	USA	10.4.94	165/52	10000	32:28.39	33:13.94- 14
Black	Symone	USA	26.10.95	158/50	400h	56.76	60.06- 13
Blank	Anna	RUS	12.1.90	174/65	Hep	6055	6067- 14
Blinova	Raisa	RUS	22.11.94		SP	16.84i, 16.75	15.82- 14
Bliss	Andrea	JAM	5.10.80	173/63	100h	13.07	12.82- 13
Bliss	Tori	USA	1.12.92	183/100	SP	18.49	17.48- 14
Blouin	Mélanie	CAN	14.7.90	175/64	PV	4.50	4.40- 12
Bodinson	Klara	SWE	11.6.90	164/56	3kSt	9:40.21	9:53.23- 14
Boekelman	Melissa	NED	11.5.89	177/82	SP	17.75	18.17- 10
Bogdán	Annabella	HUN	7.4.92		JT	55.95	54.01- 14
Bokesa	Aauri Lorena	ESP	14.12.88	183/68	400	52.20A, 52.26	51.66- 14
Bolkunets	Darya	BLR	4.3.93		20kW	1:32:36	1:32:43- 13
Bone	Robin	CAN	13.2.94	172/54	PV	4.36i, 4.22	4.22- 13
Bonne	Daysiurami	CUB	9.3.88	173/58	400	52.22	51.69A- 11, 51.81- 09
Boons	Eefje	NED	18.7.94	176/68	100h	13.09	13.76- 14
Bordignon	Laura	ITA	26.3.81	180/78	DT	56.58	59.21- 08
Borel	Cleopatra	TTO	3.10.79	168/93	SP	19.26	19.48i- 04, 19.42- 11
Borges	Fernanda Raquel	BRA	26.7.88	165/65	DT	62.80	64.01- 14
Borman	Brittany	USA	1.7.89	180/77	JT	64.75	62.05- 14
Borovska	Nadiya	UKR	25.2.81	163/50	20kW	1:30:38	1:30:03- 12

Name		Nat	Born	Ht/Wt	Event	2015 Mark	Pre-2015 Best
Borowska	Agnieszka	POL	21.10.91	187/64	HJ	1.87i, 1.85	1.87i- 13, 1.87- 14
^ Boslak	Vanessa	FRA	11.6.82	170/57	PV	4.46	4.70- 06
Bouaasayriya	Kaltoum	MAR	23.8.82	157/46	5000	15:32.44	16:09.72- 11
Bougard	Erica	USA	26.7.93	168/57	100h	12.99	13.28- 14
HJ	1.88		1.81- 13		Hep	6288	6118- 14
Bowen	Lutisha	USA	9.7.90	159/52	100h	12.97	13.15- 13, 13.10w- 14
* Bowie	Tori	USA	27.8.90	175/61	100	10.81,10.72w	10.80- 14
					200	22.23	22.18- 14
* Boyd	Alana	AUS	10.5.84	171/61	PV	4.65	4.76- 12
* Bradshaw	Holly	GBR	2.11.91	175/68	PV	4.70	4.87i, 4.71- 12
Breen	Melissa	AUS	17.9.90	174/66	100	11.26	11.11- 14
Bremser	Julia	GER	27.4.82	176/78	DT	57.37	59.84- 11
Brewer	Ciarra	USA	12.3.93	158/52	TJ	14.01i, 13.49	13.91- 14
Brichacek	Emily	AUS	7.7.90	166/52	5000	15:19.06	15:30.00- 12
Brisco	Mikiah	USA-J	14.7.96	165/54	100	11.31, 11.24w	11.61A,11.53w- 14,11.69- 13
Britton	Evonne	USA	10.10.91	173/59	100h	13.03, 12.92w	13.03- 14
Brodatskaya	Sofiya	RUS	4.10.95		20kW	1:32:02	1:36:07- 14
* Broersen	Nadine	NED	29.4.90	171/62	Hep	6531	6539- 14
Broniatowska	Katarzyna	POL	22.2.90	167/53	1500	4:10.45, 4:09.22i	4:08.79- 14
Brooks	Taliyah	USA	8.2.95		100h	13.23, 13.12w	14.17- 12
					Hep	5717	
* Brooks	Tia	USA	2.8.90	183/109	SP	19.00	19.22i, 18.96- 13
Brooks-Johnson	Alissa	USA	1.8.95	175/64	Hep	5803	5325- 14
Brost	Leslie	USA	28.9.89	163/57	PV	4.51	4.35i- 12, 4.30- 10
Brown	Aaliyah	USA	6.1.95	173/60	100	11.08	11.31, 11.20w- 14
					200	22.76, 22.66w	23.12- 14
Brown	Adanaca	BAH	23.10.93	172/62	100h	13.00	13.66, 13.64w- 14
Brown	Brittany	USA	18.4.95	164/55	200	22.89	22.95- 14
Brown	Felicia	USA	27.10.93	168/57	200	22.76	23.19, 23.04w- 13
Brown	Kamaria	USA	21.12.92	164/55	200	22.24	22.50i- 14, 22.58- 13
					400	51.76	50.94i- 14, 52.10- 13
Brown	Sarah	USA	15.10.86	170/52	800	2:01.56	2:02.25- 10
					1500	4:03.20	4:05.27- 13
Brown	Stephanie	USA	29.7.91	163/50	1500	4:07.55	4:11.06- 14
Brown	T'Erea	USA	24.10.89	178/59	400h	56.54	54.21- 12
^ Brown Trafton	Stephanie	USA	1.12.79	193/102	DT	58.79	67.74- 12
Brume	Ese	NGR-J	20.1.96	169/55	LJ	6.61	6.68- 14
* Bryant	Dezerea	USA	27.4.93	157/50	100	11.00, 10.99w	11.20- 13, 10.96w- 14
					200	22.18	22.68- 14, 22.54w- 13
* Büchel	Selina	SUI	26.7.91	168/55	800	1:57.95	2:00.93i, 2:01.42- 14
* Büchler	Nicole	SUI	17.12.83	162/55	PV	4.71	4.67- 14
^ Buckman	Zoe	AUS	21.12.88	172/55	1500	4:06.30	4:04.09- 14
Bugakova	Alyona	RUS-J	24.4.97		SP	16.98	16.94- 14
Bühler	Anna	GER-J	3.6.97		LJ	6.47, 6.55w	6.26- 14
^ Bujin	Cristina	ROU	12.4.88	171/52	TJ	14.28i, 14.19	14.42- 09
Bulgakova	Anna	RUS	17.1.88	173/90	HT	72.15	76.17- 13
Bunch	Dani	USA	16.5.91	178/95	SP	18.89	17.39- 14
Bundy-Davies	Seren	GBR	30.12.94	171/59	400	51.48	52.50- 14
Burchell	Remona	JAM	15.9.91	166/52	100	11.04	11.03, 10.95w- 14
* Burka	Gelete	ETH	15.2.86	165/45	5000	14:40.50	14:31.20- 07
					10000	30:49.68	-0-
Burks	Quanesha	USA	15.3.95	160/55	LJ	6.93A, 6.84, 6.91w	6.38- 14
Burla	Serena	USA	29.7.82	158/45	10000	32:17.34	32:47.48- 08
Burmistrova	Yekaterina	RUS	18.8.90		SP	17.15i, 16.23	16.51- 14
					DT	57.32	54.44- 13
Buscomb	Camille	NZL	11.7.90	164/51	5000	15:28.78	15:38.74mx- 14
					10000	32:26.36	-0-
Bush	Nicole	USA	4.4.86	159/50	3kSt	9:44.68	9:24.59- 14
Busienei	Selah	KEN	27.12.91	177/57	1500	4:07.58	4:08.85- 14
					3000	8:54.15	
Butts	Tynita	USA	10.6.90	179/60	HJ	1.88i	1.91- 14
Buziak	Paulina	POL	16.12.86	170/52	20kW	1:31:25	1:29:41- 14
* Caballero	Denia	CUB	13.1.90	175/73	DT	70.65	65.60- 12
* Cabecinha	Ana	POR	29.4.84	168/52	20kW	1:28:28	1:27:46- 08
* Cain	Mary	USA-J	3.5.96	170/50	1000	2:38.57, 2:38.25i	2:35.80i- 14
1500	4:09.08		4:04.62- 13		1M	4:31.31i	4:24.11i- 14, 4:39.28- 12
Caldwell	Kayla	USA	19.6.91	163/57	PV	4.50i, 4.35?	4.40A- 13, 4.40i- 14
Calleja	Andrea	ESP	3.10.92		TJ	13.60, 13.63w	13.60- 14
^ Calvert	Schillonie	JAM	27.7.88	166/57	100	11.23	11.05- 11
* Camarena-Williams	Jill	USA	2.8.82	180/91	SP	18.71	20.18- 11

Name		Nat	Born	Ht/Wt	Event	2015 Mark	Pre-2015 Best
Campbell	Amber	USA	5.6.81	170/91	HT	72.81	73.61- 14
Campbell	Simoya	JAM	1.3.94	167/54	800	1:59.26	2:02.43- 14
Campbell-Brown	Veronica	JAM	15.5.82	163/61	100	10.89	10.76- 11
					200	21.97	21.74- 08
Cansian	Lidiane	BRA	8.1.92		DT	56.45	56.77- 14
Caravelli	Marzia	ITA	23.10.81	176/64	400h	56.63	
Card	Kelsey	USA	20.8.92	178/115	SP	17.96	17.77- 14
					DT	60.16	58.94- 14
Carmichael	Carolina	USA	28.4.94	165/52	PV	4.50	4.20- 14
Carson	Hannah	USA	26.1.93	160/66	JT	59.57	56.43- 14
Carter	Destiny	USA			100	11.28w	11.70, 11.39w- 14
Carter	Kori	USA	3.6.92	165/47	400h	54.41	53.21- 13
Carter	Michelle	USA	12.10.85	175/110	SP	20.02	20.24- 13
Carton	Louise	BEL	16.4.94	172/57	5000	15:23.82	
Castells	Berta	ESP	24.1.84	174/79	HT	68.59	69.59- 12
Castlin	Kristi	USA	7.7.88	170/75	100h	12.71	12.56, 12.48w- 12
Cavaleti	Giovana	BRA	13.1.89	181/70	Hep	5760	5477- 14
Cavin	Aisha	USA	3.12.92	168/55	200	22.86	23.46- 12
Cérival	Jessica	FRA	20.1.82	187/120	SP	17.29	17.99i- 11, 17.87- 09
Cestonaro	Ottavia	ITA	12.1.95	162/55	TJ	13.76	13.69- 13
Chaboudez	Aurélie	FRA	9.5.93	173/60	400h	55.51	56.53- 14
Chambers	Kendra	USA	11.9.90	161/48	800	2:01.93	2:03.91- 12
Chang Chunfeng		CHN	4.5.88	179/75	JT	56.34	61.61- 07
Changeywo	Doris	KEN	12.12.84	168/52	HMar	69:50	68:49- 11
Changwony	Purity	KEN	.90		HMar	70:34	
Chapman	Quintunya	USA	7.1.93	173/66	Hep	6147	5659- 14
Charlton	Devynne	BAH	26.11.95	161/54	100h	13.00, 12.87w	13.56, 13.36w- 14
Charnigo	Stephanie	USA	25.7.88	163/52	1M	4:28.02i	4:33.26- 14
Chauchard	Sarah	FRA	13.3.91	176/62	Hep	5782	5638- 14
Chebet	Risper	KEN	6.6.92		HMar	70:43	71:40- 14
Chebet	Ruth	BRN-J	17.11.96	165/49	3kSt	9:21.40	9:20.55- 14
Cheever	Jamie	USA	28.2.87	175/55	3kSt	9:40.99	9:29.13- 13
Chekwel	Juliet	UGA	25.5.90	165/52	10000	32:20.95	32:57.02- 13
					3kSt	9:48.01	
Chelimo	Margaret	KEN-J	2.8.97	168/55	5000	15:28.6A	16:02.19- 14
Chelimo	Rose	KEN	12.7.89	162/45	HMar	68:22	68:40- 14
Chemtai	Esther	KEN	4.6.88	156/44	HMar	70:10	69:49- 14
Chen Jiajia		CHN-Y	14.10.98		JT	56.29	51.95- 14
Chen Yang		CHN	10.7.91		DT	61.16	58.53- 14
Chepchirchir	Filomena	KEN	1.12.81	165/43	HMar	70:43	68:06- 12
Chepchirchir	Sarah	KEN	27.7.84	162/42	HMar	70:02	68:07- 11
Chepkemoi	Caroline	KEN	1.3.93	158/45	1500	4:05.31	4:13.59- 14
					3000	8:49.04	
Chepkemoi	Joan	KEN	24.11.93	163/48	3kSt	9:42.77	10:07.1A- 09
Chepkirui	Joyce	KEN	10.8.88	152/48	10000	32:08.0A	31:26.10- 11
					HMar	68:42	66:19- 14
					Mar	2:24:11	2:30:23- 14
Chepkoech	Beatrice	KEN	6.7.91	171/57	1500	4:03.28	4:12.37- 14
Chepkurui	Caroline	KEN	12.3.90	169/52	3kSt	9:34.15	9:40.95- 06
Chepkurui	Lydia	KEN	23.8.84	170/52	3kSt	9:20.44	9:12.55- 13
Chepkwemoi	Nancy	KEN	8.10.93	162/48	1500	4:03.09	4:07.63- 11
					1M	4:28.66	
Chepngeno	Jackline	KEN	16.1.93	164/48	10000	32:08.2A	34:04.4A- 13
Chepngetich	Rosefline	KEN-J	17.6.97	166/55	3kSt	9:25.91	9:40.28- 14
Cheptai	Irene	KEN	4.2.92	160/45	3000	8:48.03	8:56.20- 13
					5000	14:53.32	14:50.99- 13
Chepyego	Selly	KEN	3.10.85	160/42	5000	15:15.73	15:06.26- 06
					10000	32:03.96	31:22.11- 13
					HMar	68:17	67:52- 14
					Mar	2:26:43	-0-
Cherono	Elizeba	KEN	6.6.88	160/50	HMar	70:10	70:15- 14
Cherono	Gladys	KEN	12.5.83	166/50	10000	32:24.1A	30:29.23- 13
					HMar	66:38	66:48- 13
					Mar	2:19:25	-0-
Cherono	Jackline	KEN-Y	25.6.98		3kSt	9:50.10A	
Cherono	Mercy	KEN	7.5.91	168/54	1500	4:01.26	4:02.31- 11
					1M	4:22.67	
					3000	8:35.48	8:21.14- 14
					5000	14:34.10	14:35.13- 11
Cherop	Sharon	KEN	16.3.84	157/45	HMar	69:13	67:08- 11
					Mar	2:24:16	2:22:28- 13
Cheruiyot	Lucy	KEN-J	4.1.97		10000	32:21.4A	
Cheruiyot	Vivian	KEN	11.9.83	155/38	1500	4:09.88A	4:06.6A- 12, 4:06.65- 07
					3000	8:38.91	8:28.66- 07
					5000	14:46.69	14:20.87- 11
					10000	31:13.29	30:30.44- 12
Cheruto	Linah	KEN	18.3.95		HMar	70:22	72:08A- 14
Chesang	Agnes	KEN	1.4.86	171/53	3kSt	9:40.69	9:34.33- 13
Chesang	Stella	UGA-J	1.12.96	161/47	3000	8:52.39	9:11.03- 13
					5000	15:25.01	15:53.85- 14

Name		Nat	Born	Ht/Wt	Event	2015 Mark	Pre-2015 Best
Chesebe	Sylivia	KEN	17.5.87	167/52	800	2:02.06A	2:00.76A- 13
Chesire	Gladys	KEN	20.2.93	162/47	10000	31:36.87	
					HMar	68:36	
Chesire	Rebecca	KEN	.92	161/45	HMar	68:21	70:45- 12
					Mar	2:25:22	2:27:16- 14
* Cheyech	Flomena	KEN	5.7.82	168/49	HMar	68:18	67:39- 13
					Mar	2:24:38	2:22:44- 14
* Chicherova	Anna	RUS	22.7.82	180/57	HJ	2.03	2.07- 11
Chigbolu	Maria Benedicta	ITA	27.7.89	172/53	400	51.67	52.39- 14
* Child (now Doyle)	Eilidh	GBR	20.2.87	172/59	400h	54.46	54.22- 13
Chilla	Mercedes	ESP	19.1.80	170/60	JT	58.77	64.07- 10
Chnaïk	Jamaa	MAR	28.7.84	177/60	TJ	13.51, 13.66w	13.75- 12, 14.02w- 10
Chudayeva	Olga	RUS	8.11.88		20kW	1:33:50	1:36:38- 14
Chumachenko	Yuliya	UKR	2.10.94	185/65	HJ	1.92	1.85- 10
Chumba	Eunice	BRN	23.5.93	160/46	10000	32:22.29	32:27.69- 14
Churakova	Yelena	RUS	16.12.86	175/56	400h	56.60	54.78- 12
Cichocka	Angelika	POL	15.3.88	169/54	800	1:59.55	2:00.20- 11
1000	2:36.50		2:37.01- 09		1500	4:03.06	4:06.50- 11
Ciofani	Audrey	FRA-J	13.3.96	174/70	HT	69.25	63.30- 14
Clark	Kree	USA	.94	170/	DT	56.41	52.26- 14
Clark	Megan	USA	10.6.94	167/57	PV	4.50i, 4.50	4.45- 14
Claude-Boxberger	Ophélie	FRA	18.10.88	169/54	3kSt	9:35.56	9:56.25- 14
Clay	Raven	USA	5.10.90	168/59	100h	13.10, 12.94w	13.05A, 13.19- 12
Clayton	Rushell	JAM	18.10.92	175/61	400h	56.29	56.41- 14
* Coburn	Emma	USA	19.10.90	173/55	1500	4:05.10	4:05.29- 14
2000	5:41.11i		5:47.20i- 14		3kSt	9:15.59	9:11.42- 14
Cockrell	Anna	USA-J	28.8.97	178/	400h	56.67	59.69- 14
Cole	Leslie	USA	16.2.87	170/60	200	22.99	22.63- 12
Collatz	Alex	USA	25.5.93	173/77	DT	57.82	57.15- 14
Comba	Rocío	ARG	14.7.87	175/78	DT	61.84	62.77- 13
Coneo	Muriel	COL	15.3.87	160/49	1500	4:08.31	4:09.79- 13
Conley	Kim	USA	14.3.86	160/49	10000	31:58.34	31:48.71- 14
					HMar	69:44	75:41- 14
Conley	Sydney	USA	11.12.93	176/60	100	11.28w	11.63, 11.39w- 14
					LJ	6.48, 6.60w	6.35- 13, 6.50w- 14
Contion	Maeva	FRA	31.5.92	167/55	400h	56.03	57.68- 14
Cornejo	Wendy	BOL	7.1.93	162/53	20kW	1:34:12	1:35:37A- 13
Corrin	Courtney	USA-J	12.12.97		LJ	6.37, 6.56w	6.40- 13
Costa	Filomena	POR	22.2.85	160/46	Mar	2:28:00	2:31:08- 14
* Costa	Keila	BRA	6.2.83	170/62	LJ	6.70	6.88- 07
					TJ	14.17, 14.50w	14.58- 13, 15.10w- 07
Costa	Susana	POR	22.9.84	178/65	TJ	14.32	14.19- 12
Costello	Liz	USA	23.2.88	160/45	10000	32:01.79	32:40.55- 12
Cotten	Jen	CAN	14.10.87	173/60	400h	56.91	56.86- 14
Coulson	Jessica	GBR	18.4.90	167/48	5000	15:29.50	15:44.85- 14
Courtney	Melissa	GBR	30.8.93	170/54	1500	4:09.74	4:11.41- 14
Coutinho	Geisa	BRA	1.6.80	160/53	400	51.43	51.08- 11
Coward	Jackie	USA	5.11.89	167/55	100h	12.85	12.73- 14, 12.67w- 13
* Craft	Shanice	GER	15.5.93	185/89	SP	17.29	17.75- 14
					DT	64.79	65.88- 14
Cragg (Hastings)	Amy	USA	21.1.84	163/46	5000	15:30.43	15:09.59- 13
^ Crawford	Virginia 'Ginnie'	USA	7.9.83	178/63	100h	12.81	12.45- 07
Crew	Brittany	CAN	3.6.94	178/111	SP	17.27	16.59- 14
Cullen	Mary	IRL	17.8.82	165/54	5000	15:26.46	15:19.04- 07
Cuneo	Benedetta	ITA-J	11.3.96	172/56	TJ	13.73	13.27- 13
* Cunningham	Vashti	USA-Y	18.1.98	185/66	HJ	1.96	1.90- 14
Czaková	Mária	SVK	2.10.88	165/60	20kW	1:32:23	1:34:13- 14
D'Agostino	Abbey	USA	25.5.92	159/48	1500	4:08.04	4:09.77i- 14, 4:11.94- 13
3000	8:58.39		8:51.91i, 9:14.57- 14		5000	15:03.85	15:11.35- 13
Daba	Bekelech	ETH	29.12.91		HMar	70:09	70:54- 12
Dabrowska	Martyna	POL	5.4.94	174/50	400	52.23	53.81- 14
Dacheva	Petya	BUL	10.3.85	168/52	TJ	13.67	14.45- 10
Dadic	Ivona	AUT	29.12.93	183/60	Hep	6151	5959- 12
^ Dahlgren	Jennifer	ARG	27.8.84	180/95	HT	72.01	73.74- 10
Dahlström	Malin	SWE	26.8.89	171/60	PV	4.55	4.52i- 14, 4.50- 12
Danekova	Silvia	BUL	7.2.83	165/50	3kSt	9:33.41	9:35.66- 13
Daniel	Deandra	TTO	12.12.92	180/64	HJ	1.87i, 1.87	1.83- 14
Daniels	Katelyn	USA	11.4.95		DT	59.06	53.26- 14
Daniels	Teahna	USA-J	25.3.97	165/55	100	11.24, 11.15w	11.31- 14
Danois	Maëva	FRA	10.3.93	165/53	3kSt	9:40.89	9:54.91- 14

Name		Nat	Born	Ht/Wt	Event	2015 Mark	Pre-2015 Best
Daska	Mamitu	ETH	16.10.83	164/45	10000	30:55.56	31:36.88- 09
					HMar	66:28	68:07- 09
Daunay	Christelle	FRA	5.12.74	163/43	HMar	69:57	68:34- 10
					Mar	2:26:57	2:24:22- 10
Dauwens	Axelle	BEL	1.12.90	171/62	400h	55.82	55.56- 14
David	Yanis	FRA-J	12.12.97	169/58	TJ	13.65	13.33- 14
Davis	Tiana	USA	12.8.89	168/57	100h	13.09, 12.96w	13.49- 13, 13.43w- 11
Day	Christine	JAM	23.8.86	168/51	400	50.14	50.16- 14
Day-Monroe	Sharon	USA	9.6.85	175/70	Hep	6458	6550- 13
De Aniceto	Marisa	FRA	11.11.86	162/57	Hep	5817	6182- 12
Deba	Buzunesh	ETH	8.9.87	162/45	Mar	2:25:09dh	2:19:59- 14
Decaux	Alice	FRA	10.4.85	165/65	100h	13.02, 13.00w	12.85- 13
Deelstra	Andrea	NED	6.3.85	169/57	Mar	2:26:46	2:32:39- 14
Degefa	Biruktayit	ETH	29.9.90		HMar	70:25	
					Mar	2:23:51	2:26:22- 14
Degefa	Worknesh	ETH	28.10.90	159/42	HMar	67:14	67:49- 13
Del Buono	Federica	ITA	12.12.94	164/48	1500	4:08.87i	4:05.52- 14
Delasa	Sechale	ETH	20.9.91		Mar	2:27:12	2:26:27- 12
DeLoach	Janay	USA	12.10.85	165/59	100h	12.84	12.97- 13
					LJ	6.95	7.03, 7.15w- 12
Demas	Danielle	USA	28.8.93	165/55	100h	13.03, 13.02w	13.36- 14
Demidenko	Natalya	RUS	7.8.93	164/59	PV	4.50i, 4.35	4.40- 11
Demireva	Mirela	BUL	28.9.89	180/50	HJ	1.94	1.95- 12
Demirova	Yelizaveta	RUS	14.8.87	176/65	100	11.22	11.30- 11
Demise	Shure	ETH-J	21.1.96	159/45	Mar	2:20:59	-0-
Demus	Lashinda	USA	10.3.83	170/62	400h	54.44	52.47- 11
Demut	Katja	GER	21.12.83	176/55	TJ	14.16i, 13.56, 13.70w	14.57- 11
Deng Linuo		CHN	16,3.92	165/44	TJ	13.89	13.92- 13
Dereli	Emel	TUR-J	25.2.96	167/90	SP	18.40	18.04- 13
Derkach	Dariya	ITA	27.3.93	167/56	LJ	6.52	6.67- 13
					TJ	13.84i, 13.53, 13.88w	13.92- 13
Derun	Kateryna	UKR	24.9.93	168/71	JT	61.90	60.32- 14
Desalegn	Betlhem	UAE	13.11.91	164/52	1500	4:05.41	4:05.13- 13
3000	8:53.75		8:46.54i- 14		5000	15:25.15	15:12.84- 13
Desmet	Hannelore	BEL	25.2.89	167/48	HJ	1.90	1.89- 10
Detsuk	Kseniya	BLR	23.4.86	177/56	TJ	14.29	14.76, 14.81w- 12
Devi	Suman	IND	15.7.85	164/65	JT	57.15	56.92- 14
Diago	Sahily	CUB	26.8.95	168/49	800	1:59.91	1:57.74- 14
Diallo	Rouguy	FRA	5.2.95	168/52	TJ	13.83i, 13.80	14.20, 14.44w- 14
Diame	Fátima	ESP-J	22.9.96	170/52	LJ	6.46, 6.55w	6.38- 13, 6.43w- 14
Dibaba	Birhane	ETH	11.9.93	159/44	HMar	70:28+	69:34- 14
					Mar	2:23:15	2:22:30- 14
Dibaba	Genzebe	ETH	8.2.91	168/52	1000	2:35.6+	
1500	3:50.07		3:57.54- 13		2000	5:35.5+	5:27.50- 14
3000	8:26.54		8:16.60i, 8:26.21- 14		5000	14:15.41	14:28.88- 14
Dibaba	Mare	ETH	20.10.89	152/40	Mar	2:19:52	2:19:52- 12
Dida	Dera	ETH-J	26.10.96	155/42	5000	15:28.81	16:26.2A- 14
Ding Changqin		CHN	27.11.91	160/50	5000	15:25.21	15:12.51- 14
10000	32:28.7		31:53.09- 14		Mar	2:26:54	2:30:20- 13
Ding Huiqin		CHN	5.2.90		20kW	1:29:32	1:29:17- 14
Diriba	Buze	ETH	9.2.94	160/43	3000	8:47.52	8:39.65- 12
2M	9:29.03i				10000	31:33.27	-0-
Diro	Etenesh	ETH	10.5.91	169/47	3kSt	9:29.10	9:14.07- 12
Domjan	Veronika	SLO-J	3.9.96	178/94	DT	56.63	53.54- 14
Dong Yangzi		CHN	22.10.92		SP	17.03i, 16.54	16.70- 11
Dongmo	Auriole	CMR	3.8.90	173/95	SP	17.64	16.84- 14
Donohue	Erin	USA	8.5.83	173/66	1000	2:37.42	2:39.50- 07
Dorozhon	Margaryta	ISR	4.9.87	180/75	JT	64.56	62.01- 13
Dorr	Fawn	CAN	19.4.87	162/52	400h	56.46	55.57- 10
Doseykina	Yekaterina	RUS	30.3.90	162/50	3kSt	9:39.37	9:35.28- 14
Doveri	Francesca	ITA	21.12.82	179/64	400h	56.65	56.65- 13
Dowie	Danielle	JAM	5.5.92	173/60	400h	56.26	54.94- 13
Drabenya ¶	Anna	BLR	15.8.87	153/46	20kW	1:32:27 dq	1:29:39- 14
Drahotová	Anezka	CZE	22.7.95	183/63	20kW	1:26:53	1:28:08- 14
Drisbióti	Antigóni	GRE	21.3.84	162/52	20kW	1:33:51	1:33:42- 13
Du Xiaowei		CHN	11.8.87	180/72	JT	58.58	61.89- 12
Duan Dandan		CHN	23.5.95		20kW	1:32:21	1:32:45- 13
Dubitskaya	Alyona	BLR	25.1.90	182/77	SP	18.88	19.03- 14
Ducó	Natalia	CHI	31.1.89	177/95	SP	18.29	18.80- 12
Dudgeon	Emily	GBR	3.3.93	174/59	800	2:01.97	2:01.89- 14
Duliba ¶	Aleksandra	BLR	9.1.88	168/54	Mar	2:23:06dq	2:21:29- 14

Name		Nat	Born	Ht/Wt	Event	2015 Mark	Pre-2015 Best
* Duncan	Kimberlyn	USA	2.8.91	173/59	100	11.13, 11.08w	10.96, 10.94w- 12
					200	22.83	22.19- 12, 21.80w- 13
Duncan	Melissa	AUS	30.1.90	170/55	1500	4:05.56	4:05.76- 14
Durant	Kamaria	TTO	24.2.91	170/59	200	22.74	23.35- 13, 23.11w- 14
Durruty	Yilian	CUB	30.1.90	176/77	LJ	6.54	6.59- 12
Dutil	Danellys	CUB	12.2.95	171/57	TJ	13.77	
Dygacz	Agnieszka	POL	18.7.85	160/51	20kW	1:30:38	1:28:58- 14
Dzindzaletaitė	Dovilė	LTU	14.7.93	168/58	TJ	14.23	14.17- 12, 14.26w- 14
Ealey	Chase	USA	20.7.94	178/84	SP	17.39	16.01- 13
Ebihara	Yuki	JPN	28.10.85	164/68	JT	63.80	62.83- 13
Eccleston	Amanda	USA	18.6.90		1M	4:29.06	4:30.42- 14
Edem	Euphemia	NGR	3.3.89	160/52	LJ	6.56	6.04- 12
Efraimson	Alexa	USA-J	20.2.97	170/57	800	2:01.11	2:03.26- 14
					1500	4:03.39	4:07.05- 14
Eid Nasser	Salwa	BRN-Y	23.5.98	167/50	200	23.03	24.61- 14
^ Ejigu	Sentayehu	ETH	21.6.85	160/45	2M	9:27.05i	9:12.68i- 10
Ektova	Irina	KAZ	8.1.87	173/61	TJ	14.32	14.48- 11
El Moukim ¶	Rkia	MAR	22.2.88	157/44	HMar	70:14dq	70:03- 14
					Mar	2:26:33dq	2:28:12- 14
* El Ouali	Salima Alami	MAR	29.12.83	167/53	1500	4:08.53	4:12.25- 12
3000	8:50.12		8:55.51- 13		3kSt	9:20.64	9:21.24- 14
Elbe	Jenny	GER	18.4.90	180/60	TJ	14.16, 14.38w	14.20, 14.24w- 14
Ellenwood	Georgia	CAN	5.8.95	170/63	Hep	5786	5594- 14
Ellington	Yanique	JAM	3.9.92		200	23.01w	23.63- 14
Elliott	Samantha	JAM	3.2.92	166/52	100h	13.11	13.05- 14
					400h	55.51	56.38A, 56.44- 13
Ellis-Watson	Taylor	USA	6.5.93	183/64	200	22.93	23.58- 14
					400	51.18	51.78- 14
* Embaye	Axumawit	ETH	18.10.94	160/50	1000	2:37.43	
1500	4:03.00, 4:02.92i	4:02.35- 14	1M	4:26.84, 4:23.50i	3000	8:51.82	
Emmanuel	Crystal	CAN	27.11.91	170/50	100	11.27, 11.26w	11.34- 12, 11.16w- 13
					200	22.92, 22.83w	22.89- 13
Ennaoui	Sofia	POL	30.8.95	158/40	800	2:00.11	2:02.72- 13
1500	4:04.26	4:07.34- 14	1M	4:27.32	3000	8:53.22i	8:59.44- 14
* Ennis-Hill	Jessica	GBR	28.1.86	164/57	100h	12.79	12.54- 12
					Hep	6669	6955- 12
Eppinger	Kaylon	USA	17.9.89	173/70	100h	13.07	13.49- 12
					Hep	5888	5560- 12
Epps	Christina	USA	20.6.91	175/63	TJ	14.09	13.40- 14
Eriksson	Sandra	FIN	4.6.89	163/48	3000	8:54.06i	8:55.13- 14
					3kSt	9:36.90	9:24.70- 14
Esayias	Yeshi	ETH	28.12.85	160/48	Mar	2:27:14	2:24:06- 13
^ Eshete	Shitaye	BRN	21.5.90	159/56	HMar	70:14	-0-
Espinoza	Ahymara	VEN	28.5.85	170/80	SP	17.90	18.15- 13
Eticha	Fantu	ETH	11.9.87		Mar	2:26:14	2:27:31- 14
Everard	Ciara	IRL	10.7.90	169/54	800	2:01.21	2:02.54i, 2:02.96- 13
Ewen	Maggie	USA	23.9.94	178/79	DT	57.44	55.07- 14
^ Facey	Simone	JAM	7.5.85	162/53	100	11.10, 11.04w	10.95A- 08,11.09- 14,11.0- 04
					200	22.55	22.25- 08
Famurewa	Becky	USA	24.2.94	180/86	DT	57.13	57.09- 13
Fatherly	Rachel	USA	20.4.94	180/86	SP	17.15	16.10- 14
Faulknor	Alexis	USA	22.9.94	165/52	100	11.26, 11.18w	11.42, 11.33w- 13
					200	22.97	23.48- 14
Fazlitdinova	Gulshat	RUS	28.8.92	165/48	5000	15:18.88	15:32.07- 14
^ Feitor	Susana	POR	28.1.75	160/52	20kW	1:31:58	1:27:55- 01
* Felix	Allyson	USA	18.11.85	168/57	100	11.09	10.89- 12
200	21.98		21.69- 12		400	49.26	49.59- 11
Félix	Alysbeth	PUR	7.3.93	170/57	Hep	5810	5721A- 14
Félix	Ana Dulce	POR	23.10.82	165/53	10000	31:34.17	31:30.90*- 09, 31:33.42- 11
HMar	70:27		68:33- 11		Mar	2:25:15	2:25:40- 11
Felnagle	Brie	USA	9.12.86	170/57	3000	8:54.77i	8:51.38- 12
Felzmann	Anna	GER	18.1.92	166/49	PV	4.40	4.30- 13
Feng Bin		CHN	3.4.94	184/95	DT	62.07	59.73- 14
Fente	Birtukan	ETH	18.6.89	166/50	5000	15:16.69	16:02.29- 10
					3kSt	9:24.91	9:28.27- 11
Ferguson	Sheniqua	BAH	24.11.89	170/57	100	11.21	11.07- 12
					200	23.03	22.64- 12
Ferrando	Cristina	ESP	12.1.92	175/59	HJ	1.88	1.84- 13
Ferraro	Federica	ITA	18.8.88	168/51	20kW	1:33:10	1:31:20- 13
Fertig	Fruzsina	HUN	2.9.93	175/80	HT	68.62	67.02- 13

Name		Nat	Born	Ht/Wt	Event	2015 Mark	Pre-2015 Best
Feyne	Gemeda	ETH	28.6.92	157/45	1500	4:08.54/4:06.62 short	4:06.66- 12
					3000	8:48.76	8:57.52- 14
Fiack	Marion	FRA	13.10.92	170/60	PV	4.71i	4.61i, 4.55- 14
Finn	Michele	IRL	16.12.89	160/52	3kSt	9:43.34	9:54.00- 13
Fiodorow	Joanna	POL	4.3.89	169/89	HT	72.67	74.39- 14
Firestone	Sarah	USA	16.2.95	167/	JT	56.15	50.49- 14
Fischer	Julia	GER	1.4.90	192/95	DT	65.98	66.46- 14
Flanagan	Lindsey	USA	24.1.91	162/46	10000	32:22.15	33:15.12- 14
Flanagan	Rosa	NZL-J	28.2.96	159/44	3kSt	9:41.42	9:56.98- 14
Flanagan	Shalane	USA	8.7.81	165/50	5000	15:10.02	14:44.80- 07
10000 31:09.02			30:22.22- 08		Mar	2:27:47dh	2:21:14- 14
Fleming	Annett	GER	4.5.84	178/66	Hep	6051	5918- 14
Flink	Sofi	SWE	8.7.95	168/71	JT	56.76	61.96- 13
Flores	Brenda	MEX	4.9.91	160/51	5000	15:31.82	15:30.87- 14
					10000	31:45.16	32:49.09- 14
Florez	Lina Marcela	COL	1.11.84	165/55	100h	13.00A, 13.37	12.94- 11
Fontanive	Petra	SUI	10.10.88	170/60	400h	56.09	56.21- 14
Ford	Yirisleyidi L.	CUB	18.8.91	168/69	HT	72.40	70.46- 14
Fortenberry	Alexia	USA	19.9.93	162/60	100h	13.34, 13.14w	13.68, 13.45w- 14
Fougberg	Charlotta	SWE	19.6.85	165/51	3kSt	9:46.06	9:23.96- 14
Francis	Eden	GBR	19.10.88	178/85	SP	16.94i, 16.84	17.24- 12
					DT	57.06	59.78- 11
Francis	Phyllis	USA	4.5.92	178/61	200	22.70	22.77- 13
					400	50.50	50.46Ai, 50.59- 14
Francis	Zaria	USA-Y	22.3.98	158/52	100	11.26, 11.24w	11.87, 11.85w- 14
Franek	Bridget	USA	8.11.87	160/50	3kSt	9:36.88	9:29.53- 12
Franklin	Alexis	USA	9.10.93		400h	56.78	56.55- 14
Fraser-Pryce	Shelly-Ann	JAM	27.12.86	160/52	100	10.74	10.70- 12
					200	22.37	22.09- 12
Frederick	Priscilla	ANT	14.2.89	178/68	HJ	1.91	1.85- 13
Freeman	Der'Renae	USA	15.4.94		LJ	6.40, 6.59w	6.38i, 6.34- 14
Freese	Anna-Lena	GER	21.1.94	175/58	100	11.30	11.46- 13
					200	23.08	23.28- 13
Freier	Desiree	USA-J	24.7.96	152/52	PV	4.35	4.45- 14
Frerichs	Courtney	USA	18.1.93	167/52	5000	15:31.62i	16:19.67i- 14, 16:22.98- 13
					3kSt	9:31.36	9:43.07- 14
Friar	Nataliyah	USA	3.4.95	173/61	LJ	6.42, 6.67w	6.30i, 6.24- 14
Fricker	McKayla	USA	19.4.92	167/52	800	2:00.81	2:06.18- 14
Frizell	Sultana	CAN	24.10.84	183/110	HT	73.66	75.73- 14
Fukushi	Kayoko	JPN	25.3.82	160/45	HMar	70:27+	67:26- 06
					Mar	2:24:25	2:24:21- 13
Fukushima	Chisato	JPN	27.6.88	166/50	100	11.23	11.21- 10, 11.16w- 11
Fullerton	Faye	GBR	31.5.84	175/54	1500	4:10.24	4:10.45- 08
Funderburk	Kala	USA	14.9.92	174/59	400	51.09	51.87- 14
Furlan	Jessica	CAN	15.3.90	165/54	3kSt	9:39.20	9:33.45- 14
Fyodorova	Alina	UKR	31.7.89	175/70	HJ	1.87	1.90- 13
					Hep	6278	6126- 12
Gaines	Jessie	USA	12.8.90	164/52	LJ	6.55i, 6.53	6.55- 14
Gaither	Tynia	BAH	16.3.93	158/50	100	11.27	11.41- 11, 11.23w- 14
					200	22.97	22.88, 22.80w- 14
Galiart	Rianna	NED	22.11.85	168/56	PV	4.40	4.35i- 13, 4.32- 12
Galíková	Mária	SVK	21.8.80	161/55	20kW	1:31:42	1:32:03- 14
Galitskaya	Yekaterina	RUS	24.2.87	174/63	100h	12.92, 12.85w	12.78- 12
Gallagher	Kerri	USA	31.5.89	168/52	1500	4:03.56	4:09.64- 13
					1M	4:30.24	4:39.30- 13
Gallardo	Karen	CHI	6.3.84	175/95	DT	61.10	60.48- 11
Galvis	Sandra	COL	28.6.86	165/60	20kW	1:32:46	1:31:15- 14
Gambetta	Sara	GER	18.2.93	183/70	SP	17.26	16.83- 14
Gandulla	Arialis	CUB	22.6.95	170/65	200	23.08	23.19, 23.14w- 14
Ganeyeva	Vera	RUS	6.11.88	172/87	DT	56.37	64.30- 13
Gao Yang		CHN	1.3.93	178/110	SP	19.04	17.76- 13
Garcia	Stephanie	USA	3.5.88	168/52	1500	4:05.39	4:13.33- 13
1M 4:28.84 4:31.25- 14		5000	15:19.50	15:43.47- 14	3kSt	9:23.48	9:24.28- 14
García	Clàudia	ESP	30.9.92	169/54	HJ	1.90i, 1,89	1.85- 11
García	Kimberley	PER	19.10.93	167/44	20kW	1:31:13	1:29:44- 14
García-Caro	Laura	ESP	16.4.95	165/56	20kW	1:29:32	1:34:50- 14
Gardner	English	USA	22.4.92	162/50	100	10.79, 10.76w	10.85- 13
					200	22.74	22.62- 13
Gardzielewska	Urszula	POL	21.7.88	177/55	HJ	1.92i, 1.89	1.90i- 14, 1.89- 12
Gashaw	Tigist	BRN-J	25.12.96	172/54	1500	4:05.58	4:08.62- 14
Gaston	Ashley	USA	1.1.93		SP	16.86i, 16.74	16.22- 14

Name		Nat	Born	Ht/Wt	Event	2015 Mark	Pre-2015 Best
Gathoni	Ann	KEN-Y	5.3.98	163/48	3kSt	9:41.40	
Gause	Destinee	USA	4.4.94	163/55	200	22.93, 22.68w	23.19- 13
					400	52.01	52.36- 14
Gayot	Marie	FRA	18.12.89	171/58	400	50.97	51.54- 13
Gebre	Trihas	ESP	29.4.90	163/46	5000	15:27.94	15:35.96- 13
					10000	32:14.94	32:03.39- 13
Gebreselassie	Goytatom	ETH	15.1.95		3000	8:45.05i	8:46.01i- 12, 8:57.23- 14
2M	9:31.41i		9:49.08i- 14		5000	14:57.33	15:11.12- 13
Gebreslasea	Letebrhan	ETH	29.10.90	155/40	Mar	2:25:24	
Gebru	Azmera	ETH	5.5.92	160/45	5000	15:15.77	14:58.23- 12
Gega	Luiza	ALB	5.11.88	166/56	1500	4:02.63	4:03.12- 14
* Gelana	Tiki	ETH	22.10.87	165/48	Mar	2:24:26	2:18:58- 12
Genemo	Shuko	ETH			Mar	2:27:29	2:31:09- 14
Geng Shuang		CHN	9.7.93		SP	17.16	16.67- 13
George	Patience	NGR	25.11.91	176/61	400	50.71	51.29- 14
George	Phylicia	CAN	16.11.87	178/65	100h	12.87	12.65- 12
George	Regina	NGR	17.2.91	168/53	400	51.30	50.84- 13
Gergel	Melissa	USA	24.4.89	170/62	PV	4.53i, 4.50	4.50- 13
Gergelics	Cintia	HUN	16.11.91		HT	65.92	64.83- 12
German	Elvira	BLR-J	19.6.97	19.6.97	100h	13.20, 13.15w	
Getachew	Bezunesh	ETH-J	.97	164/48	5000	15:25.20	16:37.4A- 12
Geubelle	Andrea	USA	21.6.91	165/57	LJ	6.59, 6.70w	6.69i, 6.53- 13
* Ghribi	Habiba	TUN	9.4.84	170/57	3000	8:46.61i	8:49.5+- 13
					3kSt	9:05.36	9:08.37- 12
* Gierisch	Kristin	GER	20.8.90	178/59	TJ	14.46i, 14.38, 14.46w	14.31, 14.34w- 14
* Giorgi	Eleonora	ITA	14.9.89	163/52	20kW	1:26:17	1:27:05- 14
Gizaw	Melkaw	ETH	17.9.90		Mar	2:25:42	2:26:24- 13
Glanc	Zaneta	POL	11.3.83	187/86	DT	62.15	65.34- 12
* Gleadle	Liz	CAN	5.12.88	183/95	JT	64.83	64.50- 14
^ Gobena	Amane	ETH	1.9.82	163/48	Mar	2:23:30	2:23:50- 13
Gochenour	Alex	USA	17.2.93	183/70	100h	13.15	13.63, 13.48w- 14
					Hep	6027w, 5892	5522- 14
Godfay	Afera	ETH	25.9.91	156/42	HMar	69:51	69:52- 14
Goggins	Aiesha	USA	13.9.91	164/55	400	51.48	51.94- 11
Golba	Katarzyna	POL	21.12.89	160/52	20kW	1:32:32	1:32:37- 13
Gollish	Sasha	CAN	27.12.81	165/52	1500	4:07.08	4:13.63- 14
Gollner	Monika	AUT	23.10.74	180/61	HJ	1.88	1.92- 96
Gollshewsky	Taryn	AUS	18.5.93	184/80	DT	57.41	58.24- 14
Gómez	Abigail	MEX	30.6.91	164/69	JT	59.26A	57.28A- 14
Gomis	Sandra	FRA	21.11.83	165/53	100h	13.05, 132.93w	12.89- 12
* Gong Lijiao		CHN	24.1.89	174/110	SP	20.34	20.35- 09
González	María Guadalupe	MEX	9.1.89	162/48	20kW	1:29:21	1:28:48- 14
González	Raquel	ESP	16.11.89	176/55	20kW	1:29:34	1:28:36- 14
Goodman	Kaitlin	USA	31.1.87	158/42	10000	32:09.82	33:01.03- 12
Gorchakova	Natalya	RUS	17.4.83	167/55	3kSt	9:52.23	9:35.55- 12
* Gordeyeva	Irina	RUS	9.10.86	185/55	HJ	1.96i, 1.94	2.04- 12
Gordon	Chris-Ann	JAM	18.9.94	164/52	400	51.52	51.39- 14
Gordon	Christie	CAN	5.10.86	172/62	100h	13.14A, 13.16, 12.91Aw	13.20A- 11, 13.21, 13.00w-13
Gordon	Daeshon	JAM-J	8.11.96	168/60	100h	12.97	13.61, 13.46w- 14
Gorodskaya	Anna	BLR	31.1.93		HJ	1.90	1.88- 14
					Hep	5812	5504- 14
Goule	Natoya	JAM	30.3.91	160/50	800	1:59.63	1:59.93- 13
Goúsin	Tatiána	GRE	26.1.94	188/63	HJ	1.87i, 1.85	1.86- 14
^ Grabuste	Aiga	LAT	24.3.88	178/67	LJ	6.82i, 6.62, 6.63w	6.69, 6.75w- 14
Graham	Jasmyne	USA-J	6.5.97	160/	100h	13.17	13.66, 13.60w- 14
Grange	Gleneve	JAM	6.7.95	170/75	DT	58.04	54.29- 13
Grauvogel	Louisa	GER-J	28.9.96	171/58	Hep	5747	5621- 14
Gray	Alia	USA	12.11.88	160/52	10000	32:29.06	32:57.85- 14
Green	Hanna	USA	16.10.94	168/59	800	2:01.17	2:04.46- 14
Greene	Nicole	USA-J	2.5.97		HJ	1.87	1.78- 12
* Grenot	Libania	ITA	12.7.83	175/61	400	51.07	50.30- 09
Gromysheva	Mariya	RUS	10.1.90		Hep	5740	5885- 12
Grøvdal	Karoline Bjerkeli	NOR	14.6.90	167/52	3000	8:52.83	8:55.95- 12
					5000	15:15.18	15:16.27mx- 13, 15:24.86- 12
Grünberg	Kira	AUT	13.8.93	169/56	PV	4.45i, 4.40	4.45- 14
Grunewald	Gabe	USA	25.6.86	168/55	800	2:01.23	2:01.38- 13
1500 4:04.26 4:01.48- 13	1M 4:30.43 4:27.94- 12				5000	15:19.01	15:33.64- 14
^ Gu Siyu		CHN	11.2.93	183/90	DT	58.30	67.86- 13
Guba	Paulina	POL	14.5.91	184/90	SP	17.95	17.79i, 17.47- 12

Name		Nat	Born	Ht/Wt	Event	2015 Mark	Pre-2015 Best
Gudeta	Netsanet	ETH	12.2.91	162/47	5000	15:31.25	
10000 31:06.53					HMar	67:31	68:46- 14
Guéhaseim	Jessika	FRA	23.8.89	175/79	HT	67.57	70.44- 12
Guei	Floria	FRA	2.5.90	166/53	200	23.06w	23.39i- 14, 23.60- 12
					400	50.89	51.30- 14
Guerrero	Esther	ESP	7.2.90	160/57	800	2:01.43	2:03.88- 14
Guillon-Romarin	Ninon	FRA	15.4.95	163/53	PV	4.35	4.20- 14
Gumenyuk	Irina	RUS	6.1.88	176/59	TJ	14.11i, 13.68	14.58- 13
Guo Tianqian		CHN	1.6.95	180/110	SP	18.59	18.08- 14
Gurova	Viktoriya	RUS	22.5.82	178/63	TJ	13.98	14.85- 08
Guster	Elexis	USA	7.7.94	171/60	400	52.19	52.77- 14
Gutermuth	Sophie	USA	2.11.92		PV	4.35	4.30- 14
Güvenç	Tugba	TUR	9.7.94	166/50	3kSt	9:33.34	
Gyurátz	Réka	HUN-J	31.5.96	175/70	HT	70.39	67.32- 14
Haapanen	Amy	USA	23.3.84	172/79	HT	69.28	70.63- 12
Haas	Eleriin	EST	4.7.92	180/60	HJ	1.91	1.94- 14
Haase	Rebekka	GER	2.1.93	170/57	100	11.21	11.32, 11.21w- 14
					200	22.95	23.01- 14
Hackett	Semoy	TTO	27.11.88	173/70	100	11.13	11.10- 12, 10.98w- 11, 11.04dq- 12
					200	22.51A, 22.75	22.55- 12, 22.14w- 11
Hackworth	Kenyattia	USA	15.9.93	168/55	LJ	6.50	6.31- 13
Hadley	Sabria	USA	1.1.95	157/50	100	11.28	11.75, 11.71w- 12
					200	23.04	23.78- 12
Hagiwara	Ayumi	JPN	1.6.92	155/41	10000	31:46.58	31:41.80- 14
Hailey	Nnenya	USA	23.2.94	165/54	400h	56.43	56.99- 14
Hailu	Meseret	ETH	12.9.90	168/54	HMar	70:23+	66:56- 13
					Mar	2:24:33	2:21:09- 12
Hakeai	Siositina	NZL	1.3.94	182/105	DT	59.81	59.65- 14
Hall	Dior	USA-J	2.1.96	168/55	100h	12.74	12.92- 14
Hall	Kate	USA-J	12.1.97	173/64	LJ	6.83	6.08i, 5.90- 14
Hall	Lindsey	USA	25.3.91	173/64	Hep	5751	5603- 14
Hall	Marielle	USA	28.1.92	160/52	5000	15:06.45	15:12.79- 14
Hall	Samantha	JAM	19.4.93	178/77	DT	58.50	52.49- 14
Hall-Pritchett	Patricia	JAM	16.10.82	165/58	400	51.95	50.71- 12
Hamblin	Nikki	NZL	20.5.88	165/52	1500	4:05.03	4:04.82- 11
					5000	15:18.02	16:30.46- 13
Hamera ¶	Tetyana	UKR	1.6.83	165/52	Mar	2:22:09dq	2:23:58- 13
Hamilton	Heather	CAN	31.3.88	178/68	PV	4.37i, 4.20	4.40- 13
Hamilton	Kim	USA	28.11.85	170/70	JT	59.05	58.04- 12
Haroye	Alemitu	ETH	9.5.95	160/44	2000	5:36+e	
3000 8:39.85+ 8:36.87- 14 5000 14:43.28 14:52.67- 14 10000 30:50.83 -0-							
Harper Nelson	Dawn	USA	13.5.84	168/61	100h	12.48	12.37- 12, 12.36w- 09
Harrer	Corinna	GER	19.1.91	167/55	1500	4:10.04	4:04.30- 12
Harrigan	Tahesia	IVB	15.2.82	157/54	100	11.14	11.13, 11.02w- 06, 10.89wdq- 11
Harrison	Kendra	USA	18.9.92	163/52	100h	12.50, 12.46w	12.71, 12.68w- 14
					400h	54.09	54.76- 14
Harrison	Queen	USA	10.9.88	170/60	100h	12.52, 12.50w	12.43- 13
Hasay	Jordan	USA	21.9.91	163/45	1500	4:07.93+i	4:07.70- 14
1M 4:28.27i 4:28.37i- 14, 4:42.21- 06					3000	8:50.21i	8:46.89- 13
Hassan	Sifan	NED	1.1.93	170/49	800	1:58.50	1:59.95- 14
1000 2:34.68 2:41.43- 13 1500 3:56.05 3:57.00- 14 1M 4:18.20 4:29.85- 12							
Hastings/Cragg	Amy	USA	21.1.84	163/46	10000	32:03.95	31:10.69- 12
Hastings	Natasha	USA	23.7.86	173/63	200	22.76	22.61- 07
					400	50.24	49.84- 07
Hatsko-Fedusova	Hanna	UKR	3.10.90	174/73	JT	61.41	67.29- 14
Hatton	Lucy	GBR	8.11.94	168/62	100h	12.84	13.20, 13.17w- 14
Hawi	Alemitu	ETH-J	14.11.96	168/52	3000	8:51.23	
					5000	15:13.16	15:10.46- 14
Hawkins	Chari	USA	21.5.91	170/57	Hep	5750(w)	5598(w)- 13, 5552- 14
Haydar	Sultan	TUR	23.5.87	170/55	HMar	69:49	70:02- 11
					Mar	2:24:44	2:25:09- 12
Hayes	Chelsea	USA	9.2.88	168/55	LJ	6.74	7.10- 12
Hayes	Jernail	USA	8.7.88	163/55	400h	56.04	55.60- 14
Hayes	Quanera	USA	7.3.92	172/59	200	23.29, 22.81w	23.30A, 22.91Aw- 13
					400	50.84	51.54A- 13, 51.91- 14
He Daixian		CHN	1.9.94		JT	56.77	53.49- 14
He Qin		CHN	23.3.92		20kW	1:32:34	1:27:42- 13
He Yinli		CHN	20.9.88		Mar	2:27:35	2:28:31- 12
Hechavarría	Zurian	CUB	10.8.95	164/58	400h	55.97A, 56.33	56.54- 14
Heidler	Betty	GER	14.10.83	175/80	HT	75.73	79.42- 11
Heikkinen	Jutta	FIN	27.10.94	168/63	Hep	5715	5393- 14

	Name		Nat	Born	Ht/Wt	Event	2015 Mark	Pre-2015 Best
	Heiner/Hills	Madeline	AUS	5.3.88	174/51	3000	8:44.20	9:07.73- 14
	5000	15:11.17		15:27.75- 14		3kSt	9:21.56	9:34.01- 14
*	Hejnová	Zuzana	CZE	19.12.86	170/54	400h	53.50	52.83- 13
	Hemann	Jena	USA	16.10.92	165/59	Hep	6022	5531w- 13, 5471- 14
	Henderson	Emmonie	USA	5.11.94	188/84	SP	17.09	15.71- 14
						DT	58.34	50.51- 14
	Henderson	Nia	USA	21.10.86	168/93	SP	17.21	17.38- 13
^	Henriques	Inês	POR	1.5.80	158/46	20kW	1:29:52	1:29:30- 13
	Henry	Britney	USA	17.10.84	178/84	HT	71.08	71.27- 10
	Henry	Chloé	BEL	5.3.87	170/58	PV	4.42	4.41- 14
	Henry	Desiree	GBR	26.8.95	172/60	100	11.11	11.21, 11.04w- 14
						200	22.94	23.25- 11, 23.16w- 14
	Henry-Robinson	Samantha	JAM	25.9.88	160/52	100	11.01A,11.08, 10.99w	11.00- 14, 10.94w- 12
						200	22.95, 22.75w	22.77, 22.50w- 12
	Herashchenko	Iryna	UKR	10.3.95	181/61	HJ	1.94	1.95i, 1.92- 14
	Herauf	Jess	USA	17.1.93	173/61	Hep	6014	5490- 14
	Hering	Christina	GER	9.10.94	185/62	800	1:59.54	2:01.25- 14
	Hernández	Liliana	MEX	22.8.90		TJ	13.61w	13.50- 14
	Hernández	Susana	MEX-Y	18.1.99		LJ	6.40, 6.71w	6.25A- 14
	Herrera	Irisdaymi	CUB	18.4.92	167/66	LJ	6.55	6.56- 14
	Herrs	Elizabeth	USA	20.12.93	176/73	JT	57.77	57.73- 14
	Herunga	Tjipekapora	NAM	1.1.88	167/51	400	51.51	51.24A- 12, 51.84- 11
	Hicks	Kiah	USA	21.2.93	178/82	DT	59.92	55.13- 13
	Hidaka	Yuki	JPN	22.7.92	156/41	10000	32:10.76	32:40.80- 13
	Higginson	Ashley	USA	17.3.89	167/62	5000	15:18.53	15:34.85- 14
						3kSt	9:31.32	9:27.59- 14
	Hilali	Siham	MAR	2.5.86	161/58	1500	4:04.66	4:01.33- 11
*	Hill	Candace	USA-Y	11.2.99	175/59	100	10.98	11.44, 11.34w- 14
						200	22.43A, 23.05	23.12- 14
	Hill	Deanna	USA-J	13.4.96	168/55	100	11.41, 11.25w	11.63- 13, 11.59w- 12
						200	22.88	23.65- 13
	Hill	MacKenzie	USA	5.1.86	166/54	400h	56.67	56.25- 14
	Hillman	Christina	USA	6.10.93	178/84	SP	17.45	18.15i,17.73- 14
^	Hingst	Carolin	GER	18.9.80	174/60	PV	4.40	4.72- 10
	Hinrichs	Denise	GER	7.6.87	181/81	SP	17.76i, 17.20	19.63i, 19.47- 09
	Hinriksdóttir	Aníta	ISL-J	13.1.96	161/50	800	2:01.01	2:00.49- 13
						1000	2:36.63	
*	Hitchon	Sophie	GBR	11.7.91	170/74	HT	73.86	72.97- 13
	Hixson	Kristen	USA	1.7.92	170/60	PV	4.50	4.50- 14
	Hjálmsdóttir	Ásdís	ISL	28.10.85	175/65	JT	62.14	62.77- 12
	Hobbs	Aleia	USA-J	24.2.96	172/59	100	11.13	11.49- 14
	Hodde	Rosina	NED	10.2.83	169/60	100h	13.15	12.89- 14
	Hofmann	Franziska	GER	27.3.94	175/69	100h	13.17	12.87- 14
	Holden-Palmer	LaTisha	USA	29.8.89		100h	13.23, 13.07w	12.95- 12
	Holder	Nikkita	CAN	7.5.87	170/59	100h	12.85	12.80- 12
	Holliday	Becky	USA	12.3.80	160/52	PV	4.65i, 4.60	4.60- 10, 4.61dh- 11
	Holliday	Tanya	AUS	21.9.88		20kW	1:34:05	1:31:28- 12
	Holm	Caroline Bonde	DEN	19.7.90	178/68	PV	4.35i	4.43i- 14, 4.36- 12
	Holodna	Olha	UKR	14.11.91	183/95	SP	17.74i	18.72- 13
	Holt	Sarah	GBR	17.4.87	185/80	HT	68.97	68.50- 12
	Holub	Malgorzata	POL	30.10.92	168/56	400	51.74	51.84- 14
^	Hooker	Marshevet	USA	25.9.84	175/67	100	11.21w	10.86- 11, 10.76w- 08
	Hooper	Gloria	ITA	3.3.92	175/63	200	22.92	22.95- 12
	Horn	Carina	RSA	9.3.89	169/56	100	11.06	11.17, 11.16w- 14
	Hou Yongbo		CHN	15.9.94		20kW	1:28:30	1:30:27- 14
	Houlihan	Shelby	USA	8.2.93	160/54	800	2:01.92	2:01.12- 14
	1500	4:09.62		4:10.89- 14		1M	4:28.71i, 4:31.79	4:33.52- 14
	Howard	Marisa	USA	9.8.92	160/53	3kSt	9:37.84	9:43.82- 14
	Howard	Sarah	USA/CAN	11.10.93	174/73	SP	16.99	16.98i, 16.49- 14
	Howell	Jacklyn	USA-J	3.10.96	160/52	100h	13.07	13.68, 13.52w- 14
*	Hrasnová	Martina	SVK	21.3.83	177/88	HT	74.27	76.90- 09
	Hrubá	Michaela	CZE-Y	21.2.98	191/75	HJ	1.91i, 1.90	1.91- 14
	Hryshutyna	Krystyna	UKR	21.3.92	176/59	LJ	6.81	6.65- 12
*	Huddle	Molly	USA	31.8.84	163/48	5000	14:57.23	14:42.64- 14
	10000	31:39.20		30:47.59- 14		HMar	68:31	69:04- 14
*	Hussong	Christin	GER	17.4.94	187/82	JT	65.92	63.34- 14
^	Hutson	Kylie	USA	27.11.87	165/57	PV	4.40	4.75Ai, 4.70- 13
	Hyacinthe	Kimberly	CAN	28.3.89	179/62	100	11.31, 11.24w	11.41, 11.33w- 14
						200	22.86, 22.56w	22.78- 13
	Hylton	Shannon	GBR-J	19.12.96	168/52	200	22.94, 22.73w	23.24i, 23.30, 23.25w- 14
*	Ibargüen	Caterine	COL	12.2.84	181/65	LJ	6.63A, 6.66Aw	6.73A,6.87Aw,6.63, 6.66w- 12
						TJ	14.90, 15.18w	15.31- 14

	Name		Nat	Born	Ht/Wt	Event	2015 Mark	Pre-2015 Best
	Ibrahim	Blessing	NGR	4.4.90		TJ	13.65	13.82- 12
	Idlette	Lavonne	DOM	31.10.85	167/54	100h	13.05, 12.78w	12.77- 13
	Ifantídou	Sofía	GRE	5.1.85	164/53	JT	57.50	56.96- 12
						Hep	6113	6109- 12
	Igaune	Laura	LAT	2.10.88	170/70	HT	65.96	68.94- 12
*	Ikauniece-Admidina	Laura	LAT	31.5.92	179/60	Hep	6516	6414- 12
	Iliyeva	Irina	RUS	22.12.95	180/58	HJ	1.92	1.90- 14
	Ince	Ariana	USA	14.3.89	180/75	JT	59.84	57.90- 14
*	Infeld	Emily	USA	21.3.90	163/48	3000	8:52.02	8:41.43- 13
	5000	15:07.18		15:28.60- 12		10000	31:38.71	-0-
	Inoue	Rei	JPN	23.7.91	155/41	20kW	1:33:04	1:31:48- 14
	Insaeng	Subenrat	THA	10.2.94	183/105	DT	60.09	56.85- 14
	Irby	Lynna	USA-Y	6.12.98	168/55	400	51.79A	54.16- 13
	Irozuru	Abigail	GBR	3.1.90	170/61	LJ	6.73i, 6.61	6.80- 12
	Ito	Mai	JPN	23.5.84	156/40	HMar	69:57	70:00- 13
						Mar	2:24:42	2:25:26- 12
	Iuel	Amalie	DEN/NOR	17.4.94	180/59	400h	55.92	58.10- 14
	Ivancevic	Andrea	CRO	21.8.84	167/59	100	11.30	11.83- 04
						100h	12.87	13.26- 08
	Ivanova	Viktoriya	RUS	21.11.91		3kSt	9:46.82	9:40.78- 14
	Ivonina	Yekaterina	RUS	14.6.94	164/52	3kSt	9:36.79	10:15.54- 14
	Iwade	Reia	JPN	8.12.94	154/42	10000	32:13.21	32:24.38- 14
						HMar	70:13	69:45- 13
	Jaber Salem	Mona	BRN	.83		Mar	2:27:26	2:30:53- 14
	Jackson	Janice	JAM	30.10.91	173/55	100h	13.24, 13.01w	12.98- 14
*	Jackson	Shericka	JAM	15.7.94	174/59	200	22.87	22.84- 13
						400	49.99	51.32- 14
	Jacmaire	Sandra	FRA	4.1.91	174/58	Hep	5739	5547(w)- 13, 5466- 14
	Jaensch	Chelsea	AUS	6.1.85	168/55	LJ	6.63, 6.74w	6.37- 14
	Jagaciak	Anna	POL	10.2.90	177/59	LJ	6.57	6.74- 10
						TJ	14.17	14.25- 11
	Jaisha	Orchatteri P.	IND	23.5.83	156/48	5000	15:31.37	15:18.30- 14
	Jakob	Élodie	SUI	8.10.93	165/54	Hep	5803	5657- 11
	Jakubaityté	Indré	LTU	24.1.76	177/70	JT	57.13	63.65- 07
	Jamal	Maryam	BRN	16.9.84	170/54	1500	4:09.63	3:56.18- 06
*	Jarder	Erica	SWE	2.4.86	173/59	LJ	6.70	6.68, 6.84w- 14
	Jean-Baptiste	Audrey	CAN	15.7.91	164/54	400	51.93	53.07- 14
*	Jefferson	Kyra	USA	23.9.94	165/57	200	22.24	22.78- 14
						400	51.50	
	Jeffs	Izzy	GBR	3.2.92	178/74	JT	57.39	58.63- 14
*	Jelagat	Irene	KEN	10.12.88	162/45	1500	4:07.75	4:02.59- 11
	3000	8:36.90		8:28.51- 14		5000	14:55.49	15:01.73- 14
*	Jelagat	Jemima	KEN	21.12.84	161/47	Mar	2:24:23	2:20:41dh- 14, 2:20:48- 13
	Jelagat	Viola	KEN	20.4.92	154/42	HMar	69:27	71:27- 14
^	Jelela	Koren	ETH	18.1.87	165/50	Mar	2:23:52	2:22:43- 11
	Jelmini	Anna	USA	15.7.90	176/86	DT	56.40	60.80- 10
	Jemai	Sara	ITA	12.4.92	178/65	JT	57.20	56.55- 14
	Jenneke	Michelle	AUS	23.6.93	172/63	100h	12.82	13.23- 14
	Jeon Yang-eun		KOR	24.5.88	157/43	20kW	1:30:35	1:33:18- 14
*	Jepchirchir	Peres	KEN	27.9.93	153/40	HMar	67:17	69:12- 14
	Jepchumba	Viola	KEN	22.9.90	172/52	HMar	69:30	73:20- 14
	Jepkemei	Daisy	KEN-J	13.2.96	167/50	3kSt	9:38.16	9:47.22- 12
*	Jepkemoi	Hyvin	KEN	13.1.92	156/45	3kSt	9:10.15	9:22.05- 13
	Jepkesho	Visiline	KEN	.88	160/45	Mar	2:24:44	2:26:47- 14
*	Jepkirui Kirwa	Eunice	BRN	20.5.84	165/52	HMar	69:37	68:31- 14
						Mar	2:22:08	2:21:41- 12
	Jepkoech	Monica	KEN	.85	160/48	HMar	70:26	69:12- 12
	Jepkoech ¶	Josephine	KEN	21.4.89		HMar	67:32dq	68:53- 13
	Jepkorir	Eunice	KEN	17.2.82	164/48	3kSt	9:37.12	9:07.41- 08
*	Jepkosgei	Janeth	KEN	13.12.83	167/47	800	1:59.37	1:56.04- 07
	Jepkurgat	Helen	KEN	21.2.89	172/52	HMar	69:56	70:42- 14
	Jeptoo	Priscah	KEN	26.6.84	165/49	HMar	69:21	65:45- 13
						Mar	2:25:01	2:20:14- 12
	Jerez	Caridad	ESP	23.1.91	170/57	100h	12.94	13.09- 14
	de Jesus	Claudine	BRA	9.9.94		TJ	13.70	13.51- 13
	Jeter	Carmelita	USA	24.11.79	163/63	100	11.01, 10.76w	10.64- 09
						200	22.88, 22.84w	22.11- 12
	Jiang Fengjing		CHN	28.8.87	180/75	DT	58.43	62.56- 11
	Jiménez	Isidora	CHI	10.8.93	170/54	200	22.95	23.19A- 13, 23.42- 12
	Jimoh	Funmi	USA	29.5.84	173/64	LJ	6.74i, 6.72	6.96- 09
	Johnson	Felisha	USA	24.7.89	185/105	SP	18.73	19.18- 14

Name		Nat	Born	Ht/Wt	Event	2015 Mark	Pre-2015 Best
Johnson	Jessie	USA	21.11.93		PV	4.35	4.11- 12
Johnson	Kortnei	USA-J	11.8.97	165/52	100	11.26w	11.51- 14, 11.35w- 13
Johnson	Lauren	USA	4.5.87	170/52	800	2:02.02	2:02.19- 14
					1500	4:04.17	4:10.67- 14
Johnson	Rachel	USA	30.4.93	165/52	3kSt	9:42.93	9:41.56- 14
Johnson	Tristie	USA	20.11.93	163/50	100	11.26	11.29- 14, 11.28w- 12
* Johnson-Thompson	Katarina	GBR	9.1.93	183/70	200	23.08	22.89- 14
HJ	1.97i, 1.89	1.96i, 1.90- 14			LJ	6.93i, 6.79	6.92- 14
Johny	Mayookha	IND	9.4.88	171/55	TJ	13.78	14.11- 14
* Jones	Akela	BAR	21.4.95	186/77	100h	13.10, 13.08Aw	13.35- 14
HJ	1.91	1.87i- 14, 1.85- 10	LJ	6.64i, 6.60	6.55- 14	Hep 6371(w)	-0-
Jones	Ariel	USA	18.7.95		400h	57.08	
* Jones	Lolo	USA	5.8.82	175/59	100	11.30	11.24- 06
					100h	12.65, 12.62w	12.43, 12.29w- 08
Jones	Tenaya	USA	22.3.89	162/53	100h	12.72, 12.68Aw	12.75- 14, 12.65w- 13
Jones	Tia	USA-Y	8.9.00		100h	13.45, 13.08w	
Jones	Vanessa	USA	1.1.93	170/61	400	51.50	52.15- 14
^ Jones-Ferrette	Laverne	ISV	16.9.81	173/66	100	11.14w	11.07, 10.91w- 12
Jover	María del Mar	ESP	21.4.88	161/51	LJ	6.78A,6.42, 6.48w	6.78A,6.59- 14, 6.78w- 13
Joye	Hannah	AUS-J	4.1.96	177/63	HJ	1.92	1.89- 14
* Józwik	Joanna	POL	30.1.91	167/52	800	1:58.35	1:59.63- 14
					1500	4:09.56	4:09.93- 12
Jules	Vanessa	USA	21.3.91	180/62	Hep	5724	5865(w)- 13
* Jungfleisch	Marie-Laurence	GER	7.10.90	181/68	HJ	1.99	1.97- 14
^ Jungmark	Ebba	SWE	10.3.87	179/57	HJ	1.87	1.96i, 1.94- 11
* Kabuu	Lucy	KEN	24.3.84	155/42	HMar	68:51	66:09- 13
					Mar	2:20:21	2:19:34- 12
Kácser	Zita	HUN	2.10.88		3kSt	9:51.21	10:04.36- 14
Kai	Konomi	JPN	10.7.93	153/50	LJ	6.84	6.07- 14
Kakol	Marta	POL	25.2.92	174/68	JT	58.43	56.02- 14
Kalina	Anastasiya	RUS	16.2.94	162/50	800	2:02.06	2:04.14- 14
					1500	4:07.37	4:13.27- 14
Kallenou	Leontia	CYP	5.10.94	183/68	HJ	1.93i, 1.93	1.92- 14
Kalutskaya	Lina	RUS	1.10.88		20kW	1:33:00	1:28:12- 14
Kämäräinen	Sanna	FIN	8.2.86	182/82	DT	61.07	60.94- 14
Kambundji	Mujinga	SUI	17.6.92	168/59	100	11.07	11.20- 14
					200	22.64	22.83- 14
Kampf	Heather	USA	19.1.87	162/53	1500	4:04.50	4:06.16- 14
					1M	4:30.37, 4:30.07i	4:30.14i- 14
Kamulu	Pauline	KEN	16.4.95		HMar	69:44	75:20- 11
Kang Ya		CHN	16.3.90	168/50	100h	13.12, 13.10w	13.13- 14
Kangas	Jenni	FIN	3.7.92	178/74	JT	56.56	55.62- 13
Kanuchová	Veronika	SVK	19.4.93	170/69	HT	65.77	64.12- 14
Kanuho	Rochelle	USA	4.7.90	160/44	10000	32:08.76	34:20.69- 13
Kapera	Monika	POL	15.2.90	170/52	20kW	1:32:29	1:34:20- 14
Karabulut	Elif	TUR	8.8.91	170/55	3kSt	9:48.48	9:58.28- 14
Karimi	Lucy	KEN	24.2.75		Mar	2:27:08	2:33:36- 13
Kashtanova	Anastasiya	BLR	14.1.89	173/70	DT	56.74	61.13- 13
Kashyna	Inna	UKR	27.9.91	165/50	20kW	1:30:52	1:30:17- 14
* Kasprzycka	Justyna	POL	20.8.87	183/62	HJ	1.94i, 1.94	1.99- 14
Kassahun	Aynalem	ETH			Mar	2:28:18	2:47:48- 13
^ Kastor	Deena	USA	14.2.73	163/47	Mar	2:27:47	2:19:36- 06
Kasyanova	Hanna	UKR	24.4.83	178/67	Hep	6277	6586- 13
Käther	Nadja	GER	29.9.88	178/62	LJ	6.56	6.66- 10
Kato	Asami	JPN	12.10.90	156/38	HMar	70:36	70:21- 13
					Mar	2:26:30	2:28:51- 14
Kato	Misaki	JPN	15.6.91	155/40	10000	32:13.72	32:05.87- 14
					HMar	69:49	70:44- 13
Kato	Mizuki	JPN	27.10.93		JT	56.54	54.14- 14
Kaur	Khushbir	IND	9.7.93	155/49	20kW	1:33:58	1:31:40- 14
Kaur	Manpreet	IND	6.7.90		SP	17.96	16.39- 14
Kaya	Özlem	TUR	20.4.90	160/49	3kSt	9:30.23	9:38.32- 12
Kazeka	Yekaterina	RUS	7.10.90		PV	4.40i, 4.30	4.45- 14
* Kebede	Aberu	ETH	12.9.86	163/50	HMar	70:15+	67:39- 09
					Mar	2:20:48	2:20:30- 12
Keenan	Te Rina	NZL	29.9.90	180/84	DT	60.78	58.25- 13
* Keitany	Mary	KEN	18.1.82	158/45	HMar	66:02	65:39- 14
					Mar	2:23:40	2:18:37- 12
Kennedy	Nina	AUS-J	5.4.97	166/57	PV	4.59	4.40- 14
Khamidova	Sitora	UZB	12.5.89	166/50	10000	32:13.42	32:12.54- 14
Kholodovich	Tatyana	BLR	21.6.91	181/81	JT	62.00	63.61- 14

Name		Nat	Born	Ht/Wt	Event	2015 Mark	Pre-2015 Best
Khramova	Alyona	RUS	18.8.93		20kW	1:32:21	1:32:07- 14
Khramova	Valeriya	RUS	13.8.92	170/60	400h	56.82	55.80- 14
Kibarus	Mercy	KEN	25.2.84		Mar	2:27:06	2:31:14- 13
Kibet	Sylvia	KEN	28.3.84	157/44	HMar	69:32	69:51- 09
					Mar	2:26:16	-0-
Kibiwot	Viola	KEN	22.12.83	157/45	1500	4:01.41	3:59.25- 12
					1M	4:24.31	
					3000	8:37.2+e, 8:41.93	8:24.41- 14
					5000	14:34.22	14:33.48- 13
Kibor	Marion	KEN	27.9.94	158/52	3kSt	9:46.29A	10:02.46- 13
Kielbasinska	Anna	POL	26.6.90	170/55	200	22.94	23.23- 11
Kilel	Caroline	KEN	21.3.81	152/47	Mar	2:26:40dh	2:22:34- 13
Kim Kyung-ae		KOR	5.3.88	163/62	JT	58.77	58.76- 08
Kim Sung-eun		KOR	24.2.89	164/47	Mar	2:28:20	2:27:20- 13
Kimaiyo	Nancy	KEN	.84		3kSt	9:47.4A	9:52.2A- 14
Kimanzi	Grace	KEN	1.3.92	162/46	10000	31:57.35	32:22.14- 14
Kinsey	Erika	SWE	10.3.88	185/68	HJ	1.97	1.91- 08
Kiplagat	Edna	KEN	15.9.79	171/54	HMar	68:21	67:41- 12
					Mar	2:27:16	2:19:50- 12
Kiplagat	Florence	KEN	27.2.87	155/42	HMar	65:09	65:12- 14
					Mar	2:23:33	2:19:44- 11
Kipp	Shalaya	USA	19.8.90	170/58	3kSt	9:37.09	9:35.73- 12
Kiprop	Agnes	KEN	12.12.79	171/51	Mar	2:25:46	2:23:54- 11
Kiprop	Helah	KEN	7.4.85	164/48	HMar	68:23	67:39- 13
					Mar	2:24:03	2:27:14- 14
Kiprop	Nancy	KEN	79		Mar	2:27:34	
Kipyego	Sally	KEN	19.12.85	168/52	2000	5:40.35i	5:35.20- 09
					3000	8:41.72i, 8:50.07+	8:34.18- 14
					5000	14:47.75	14:30.42- 11
					10000	31:44.42	30:26.37- 12
					HMar	69:39	68:31- 14
Kipyegon	Faith	KEN	10.1.94	157/42	800	1:58.02	2:02.8A- 13
					1500	3:59.32+	3:56.98- 13
					1M	4:16.71	
					3000	8:38.91+	8:23.55- 14
					5000	14:31.95	-0-
Kira	Manami	JPN	23.10.91	174/61	400h	56.94	56.63- 14
Kirdyapkina	Anisya	RUS	23.10.89	165/51	20kW	1:26:44	1:25:09- 11
Kireyeva	Svetlana	RUS	12.6.87	170/55	5000	15:19.85	15:08.36- 12
Kiriakopoúlou	Nikoléta	GRE	21.3.86	167/56	PV	4.83	4.72i- 14, 4.71- 11
Kirichenko	Irina	RUS	18.5.87		SP	17.82	17.48- 14
Kirui	Purity	KEN	13.8.91	162/47	3kSt	9:17.74	9:19.42- 13
Kisa	Janet	KEN	5.3.92	160/48	5000	15:02.68	14:52.59- 14
Kitaguchi	Haruka	JPN-Y	16.3.98	178/80	JT	58.90	53.15- 14
Kitata	Meseret	ETH	8.11.93		Mar	2:27:17	2:27:26- 14
Kiyara	Rael	KEN	4.4.84		Mar	2:26:23	2:25:23- 11
Kiyota	Mao	JPN	12.9.93	153/44	10000	31:44.79	32:12.27- 14
					HMar	70:31	71:50- 14
Klaas	Kathrin	GER	6.2.84	168/72	HT	73.18	76.05- 12
Klaup	Mari	EST	27.2.90	180/58	Hep	6023(w)	6002- 13
Klein	Hanna	GER	6.4.93	172/55	800	2:01.60	2:03.84- 14
					1500	4:09.91	4:15.49- 14
Klishina	Darya	RUS	15.1.91	180/57	LJ	6.95	7.05- 11
Klochko	Viktoriya	UKR	2.9.92	187/115	DT	58.01	57.17- 14
Klocová	Lucia	SVK	20.11.83	170/56	800	1:59.14	1:58.51- 08
Klopsch	Christiane	GER	21.8.90	175/58	400h	56.55	56.02- 14
Klosterhalfen	Konstanze	GER-J	18.2.97	169/52	1500	4:09.58	4:19.97- 14
					3000	8:53.21	9:39.65- 14
Klucinová	Eliska	CZE	14.4.88	177/69	HJ	1.88i, 1.86	1.90- 14
					Hep	6349	6460- 14
Knäsche	Anjuli	GER	18.10.93	169/61	PV	4.42	4.45- 13
Koala	Marthe	BUR	8.3.94	174/68	Hep	5852	5454- 14
Kocina	Anete	LAT-J	5.2.96		JT	60.01	55.56- 14
Kock	Maren	GER	22.6.90	173/55	1500	4:07.56	4:10.28- 14
Kohlmann	Fabienne	GER	6.11.89	170/57	800	1:58.34	2:00.72- 10
Koki ¶	Francisca	KEN	30.10.93	170/60	400h	55.82A	55.84- 14
Kolb	Viktoryia	BLR	26.10.93		SP	17.47	16.91i, 16.81- 14
Koleczek	Karolina	POL	15.1.93	169/49	100h	12.91, 12.87w	12.94- 14
Kolesnychenko	Olena	UKR	3.6.93	172/58	400h	56.83	56.55- 14
Kolomoyets	Anastasiya	BLR	15.7.94		HT	67.37	67.23- 14
Kondakova	Yuliya	RUS	4.12.81	170/64	100h	13.09, 13/.03w	12.73- 13
Kondratyeva	Oksana	RUS	22.11.85	180/80	HT	72.01	77.13- 13
Koneva	Yekaterina	RUS	25.9.88	169/55	LJ	6.82i, 6.39	6.70, 6.80w- 11
					TJ	15.04	14.89- 14
Kononova	Yevgeniya	RUS	28.9.89	175/53	HJ	1.88i	1.92- 12
Konovalova ¶	Mariya	RUS	14.8.74	179/58	Mar	2:22:27dq	2:22:46- 13
Kopron	Malwina	POL	16.11.94	170/63	HT	71.27	69.30- 14

Name		Nat	Born	Ht/Wt	Event	2015 Mark	Pre-2015 Best
Korableva	Darya	RUS	23.5.88	177/64	400h	55.69	56.01- 09
^ Korikwiang	Pauline	KEN	1.3.88	163/39	5000	15:23.85	14:41.28- 11
Korobkina	Yelena	RUS	25.11.90	163/47	1500	4:06.55	4:05.18- 13
3000 8:54.27, 8:47.61i	8:50.42i- 13, 8:51.00- 14				5000	15:18.80	15:14.67- 14
Korolyova	Kristina	RUS	6.11.90	183/68	HJ	1.91	1.85- 11
					Hep	5776	5797- 14
Korosídou	Iliána	GRE	14.1.95	175/72	HT	66.47	65.34- 14
Korpela	Merja	FIN	15.5.81	170/75	HT	68.43	69.56- 09
Korshunova	Anastasiya	RUS	17.5.92	168/60	400h	57.01	55.12- 13
Korzh	Tatyana	BLR	17.3.93		JT	56.74	53.85- 14
Kosko	Irina	RUS	1.3.90		TJ	13.65	14.11- 14
Koster	Maureen	NED	3.7.92	176/56	1500	3:59.79	4:04.92- 14
3000 8:51.10i	9:23.20- 11				5000	15:07.73	
Kostrova	Alina	BLR	2.3.90	181/79	HT	68.16	70.31- 12
Kotlyarova	Aleksandra	UZB	10.10.88	170/64	TJ	13.76	14.35- 11
Kotlyarova	Nadezhda	RUS	12.6.89	176/64	400	51.42	51.93- 13
Koubaa	Sanaa	GER	6.1.85	168/58	3kSt	9:46.81	9:43.08- 12
Koudelová	Lucie	CZE	6.7.94	170/64	100h	13.26, 13.12w	13.15- 14
Kragbé	Suzanne	CIV	22.12.81	179/92	DT	58.19	59.61- 14
Králová	Tereza	CZE	22.10.89	175/85	HT	70.12	70.21- 13
Krasnokutskaya	Oksana	RUS	24.9.93	185/64	HJ	1.91i, 1.90	1.90- 13
* Krasnova	Angelina	RUS	7.2.91	168/55	PV	4.67i, 4.60	4.70- 13
Krasutska	Hanna	UKR	20.7.95	180/65	TJ	13.70	13.61- 14
* Krause	Gesa-Felicitas	GER	3.8.92	167/55	3kSt	9:19.25	9:23.52- 12
Krchová	Eva	CZE	10.9.89	182/67	3kSt	9:48.75	9:52.69- 13
Krechik	Yelena	BLR	20.7.87	174/73	HT	72.06	69.92- 14
Krifchin	Maegan	USA	8.4.88		HMar	69:51	70:56- 12
Krizsán	Xénia	HUN	13.1.93	171/62	Hep	6322	6317(w)- 14
* Kucherenko	Olga	RUS	5.11.85	172/59	LJ	6.78	7.13- 10
* Kuchina	Mariya	RUS	14.1.93	182/60	HJ	2.01	2.01i, 2.00- 14
Kudzelich	Svetlana	BLR	7.5.87	170/52	3000	8:46.83	9:00.06- 11
					3kSt	9:31.70	9:27.95- 14
Kuijken	Susan	NED	8.7.86	170/54	1500	4:06.37	4:05.38- 13
5000 15:07.38	15:04.36- 13				10000	31:31.97	-0-
Kunova	Vera	RUS	2.4.90		SP	17.48	16.99- 11
Kuwahara	Sayaka	JPN	8.3.93	162/45	10000	32:14.43	
Kwadwo	Yasmin	GER	9.11.90	171/62	100	11.30, 11.16w	11.29- 11
^ La Mantia	Simona	ITA	14.4.83	177/65	TJ	14.22, 14.14w	14.69- 05, 14.71w- 04
Laasma	Liina	EST	13.1.92	178/77	JT	58.70	63.17- 14
Labiche	Lissa	SEY	18.2.93	172/52	HJ	1.92A	1.88- 12
LaCaze	Genevieve	AUS	4.8.89	168/54	3kSt	9:35.17	9:33.19- 14
Lagat	Violah	KEN	13.3.89	165/49	800	2:02.05	2:02.61- 14
					1500	4:04.10	4:05.66- 13
Laing	Kimberley	JAM	8.1.89	167/55	100h	12.89, 12.71w	12.97- 12, 12.92w- 10
* Lake	Morgan	GBR-J	12.5.97	178/64	HJ	1.94i, 1.94	1.94- 14
Lakmali	Nadeeka	SRI	18.9.81	165/60	JT	59.00	60.64- 13
Lally	Jade	GBR	30.3.87	183/81	DT	60.01	60.76- 11
Lalonde	Geneviève	CAN	5.9.91	167/47	3kSt	9:35.69	9:50.79- 14
* Lalova-Collio	Ivet	BUL	18.5.84	168/56	100	11.09	10.77- 04
					200	22.32	22.51, 22.36w- 04
Lambarki	Hayat	MAR	18.5.88	168/62	400h	55.94	55.27- 13
Lamble	Regan	AUS	14.10.91	173/55	20kW	1:30:45	1:30:08- 12
* Lamote	Renelle	FRA	26.12.93	168/57	800	1:58.86	2:00.06- 14
Landázuri	Narcisa	ECU	25.11.92	160/52	100	11.30A, 11.48, 11.33w	11.57, 11.41Aw- 14
Lara	Geena	USA	18.1.87	167/57	800	2:01.87	1:59.24- 12
Larch-Miller	Nikki	USA	13.8.94	165/55	100h	13.15, 13.08w	13.50- 14
				Hep	5812	5281- 14	
Larsson	Eleni	SWE	4.4.93	186/100	HT	68.76	67.13- 13
Larsson	Sofia	SWE	22.7.88	174/82	DT	59.25	58.65- 09
Latham	Deanna	USA	23.2.92	168/59	Hep	5914	5745- 14
Latiseva-Cudare	Gunta	LAT	9.3.95	179/68	400	52.17	52.76- 13
Lawrence	Collier	USA	4.10.86	163/52	3kSt	9:50.47	9:53.79- 12
Lawson	LeKeisha	USA	3.6.87	168/57	100	11.06	11.07- 14
					200	22.99, 22.88w	23.09- 14, 22.75w- 13
Le Foll	Gaëlle	FRA	27.4.91	170/63	Hep	5848	5365- 13
Le-Roy	Anastasia	JAM	11.9.87	168/55	400	51.28	50.84- 14
Lebedeva	Lyudmila	RUS	23.5.90	165/48	3kSt	9:36.56	9:39.98- 13
Lebid	Anastasiya	UKR	30.10.93	166/50	400h	56.97	56.91- 13
Leblanc	Annie	CAN	29.4.92	170/57	800	2:01.87	2:03.41- 12
Ledáki	Stélla-Iró	GRE	18.7.88	170/58	PV	4.40i	4.50- 12

Name		Nat	Born	Ht/Wt	Event	2015 Mark	Pre-2015 Best
Lee	Muna	USA	30.10.81	173/50	100	11.02	10.85- 08, 10.78w- 09
					200	22.60	22.01, 21.91w- 08
Lee Jeong-eun		KOR	13.9.94		20kW	1:33:09	1:35:30- 14
Lee Mi-young		KOR	19.8.79	174/81	SP	17.04	17.62- 05
Leffler	Celina	GER-J	9.4.96	174/61	Hep	5835	5846- 14
Legesse	Meseret	ETH	28.8.87		Mar	2:27:28	2:26:15- 13
Leidl	Sarah	GER	5.3.87	173/65	JT	56.89	55.78- 14
Leinert	Shannon	USA	30.6.87	170/60	800	2:01.62	2:01.65- 12
Lekamge	Dilhani	SRI	14.1.87		JT	56.37	55.87- 14
LeLeux	Morgann	USA	14.11.92	170/62	PV	4.37i, 4.35	4.50i- 13, 4.44- 12
Lema	Marta	ETH	.90		Mar	2:25:59	2:28:02- 13
Lemus	Sandra	COL	1.1.89	170/102	SP	17.85	18.03- 13
Leonard	Alison	GBR	17.3.90	168/56	800	2:00.50	2:00.08- 14
Leontyuk	Yuliya	BLR	31.1.84	185/80	SP	19.00i, 18.86	19.79- 08
Leslie	Breanna	USA	11.8.91	172/61	Hep	5864(w)	5893- 14
Lesueur	Éloyse	FRA	15.7.88	179/65	LJ	6.74i	6.92- 14, 7.04w- 12
Lettow	Lindsay	USA	6.6.90	175/62	Hep	6023	5859- 14
Levchenko	Yuliya	UKR-J	28.11.97	179/60	HJ	1.92	1.89- 14
Levitskaya	Yekaterina	RUS	2.1.87		LJ	6.59	6.70- 14
Levy	Daina	JAM	27.5.93	170/82	HT	69.01	64.30- 13
Lewandowska	Iwona	POL	19.2.85	158/47	Mar	2:27:47	2:28:32- 12
Lewetegn	Sintayehu	ETH-J	9.5.96		5000	15:25.78	
Lewis	Abigail	JAM	7.5.93		400h	56.92	59.20- 14
Lewis	Yvette	PAN	16.3.85	173/62	100h	12.98, 12.92w	12.67, 12.43w- 13
Lewis-Smallwood	Gia	USA	1.4.79	183/93	DT	64.01	69.17- 14
Lhabz	Lamiae	MAR	19.5.84	178/59	400h	56.64	55.51- 13
Li Leilei		CHN	18.8.89	160/46	20kW	1:31:49	1:33:23- 14
Li Ling		CHN	6.7.89	180/65	PV	4.66	4.65- 13
Li Lingwei		CHN	26.1.89	172/75	JT	65.07	65.11- 12
Li Maocuo		CHN	20.10.92		20kW	1:33:55	1:31:55- 14
Li Ping		CHN	7.1.94		20kW	1:33:39	1:35:10- 13
Li Xiaohong		CHN	8.1.95	161/50	TJ	14.20	14.06i, 13.85- 12, 14.03w- 12
Li Yanmei		CHN	6.2.90	171/56	TJ	14.21i, 13.83	14.35- 13
Li Zhenzhu		CHN	13.12.85	168/45	3kSt	9:41.43	9:32.35- 07
Liang Rui		CHN	18.6.94		20kW	1:29:22	1:37:21- 12
Liang Yan		CHN	2.1.95		DT	57.94	62.01- 13
Liashenko	Valentina	GEO	30.1.81	176/58	HJ	1.92	1.91- 12
Licwinko	Kamila	POL	22.3.86	184/65	HJ	2.02i, 1.99	2.00i- 14, 1.99- 13
de Lima	Flávia	BRA	1.7.93	176/65	800	2:00.40	2:02.94- 13
de Lima	Jucilene	BRA	14.9.90	174/63	JT	61.23	62.89- 14
Limo	Cynthia	KEN	18.12.89	167/52	HMar	67:02	68:24- 14
Linde	Sofia	SWE	12.1.95	174/66	HJ	1.87	1.80- 13
Linden	Desiree	USA	26.7.83	157/44	5000	15:27.13	15:08.64- 11
10000	32:43.99		31:37.14- 11		Mar	2:25:39dh	2:22:38dh- 11
Lindley	Lindsay	NGR	6.10.89	173/63	100h	12.97	13.21, 13.11w- 14
Linkiewicz	Joanna	POL	2.5.90	172/55	400h	55.62	55.89- 14
Linna	Inga	FIN	21.2.95	172/72	HT	68.25	60.63- 14
Linnell	Lisa	SWE	30.4.91	175/66	Hep	5764	5888- 13
Lipsey	Charlene	USA	16.7.91	168/57	800	2:00.60	2:00.91- 14
Little	Ashante	GBR	24.8.92		400h	56.69	58.51- 14
Little	Shamier	USA	20.3.95	163/53	400	51.77, 51.37i	51.06- 14
					400h	53.74	55.07- 14
Liu Hong		CHN	12.5.87	161/48	20kW	1:24:38	1:25:46- 12
Liu Shiying		CHN	24.9.93		JT	62.77	62.72- 14
Liu Tingting		CHN	29.10.90	174/75	HT	71.40	73.06- 14
Llano	Beatrice Nedberge	NOR-J	14.12.97		HT	67.05	63.67- 14
Lohvynenko	Alina	UKR	18.7.90	180/70	400	52.23	51.19- 12
Lomnická	Nikola	SVK	16.9.88	166/70	HT	67.04	71.58- 14
Londa	Maria Natalia	INA	29.10.90	167/59	LJ	6.70	6.55- 12
					TJ	13.75	14.17- 13
Longfors	Rachel	USA	6.6.83	183/82	DT	58.10	59.67- 14
López	Yaniuvis	CUB	1.2.86	180/71	SP	17.78	18.81- 09
Lotout	Marion	FRA	19.11.89	165/54	PV	4.60	4.60- 13
Love	Alexis	USA	24.4.91	168/57	200	22.98w	23.03- 12
Løvnes	Ingeborg	NOR	5.9.92	165/52	3kSt	9:48.89	10:00.73- 14
Lowe	Chaunté	USA	12.1.84	175/60	HJ	1.91	2.05- 10
Lu Huihui		CHN	26.6.89	171/68	JT	66.13	64.95- 12
Lu Minjia		CHN	29.12.92	172/58	LJ	6.52, 6.54w	6.74- 09
Lu Xiaoxin		CHN	22.2.89	184/90	DT	62.30	63.27- 13
Lu Xiuzhi		CHN	26.10.93	167/52	20kW	1:25:12	1:27:01- 12
Lucas	Josanne	TTO	14.5.84	170/55	400h	56.76	53.20- 09

Name		Nat	Born	Ht/Wt	Event	2015 Mark	Pre-2015 Best
Lucas	Porscha	USA	18.6.88	170/56	200	22.89	22.29A- 08, 22.38- 09
Lückenkemper	Gina	GER-J	21.11.96	170/58	100	11.25	11.54, 11.34w- 14
					200	23.04, 22.41w	23.26- 14
Ludlow	Molly	USA	4.8.87	173/59	800	1:58.68	1:59.12- 11
Luka	Tintu	IND	26.4.89	164/51	800	2:00.56	1:59.17- 10
Luo Na		CHN	8.10.93		HT	67.11	69.81- 14
^ Lupu	Nataliya ¶?	UKR	4.11.87	172/62	800	1:58.57	1:58.46- 12
Lutkovskaya	Alyona	RUS-J	15.3.96	164/55	PV	4.61	4.50- 14
Lyakhova	Olha	UKR	18.3.92	174/57	800	1:58.64	1:59.92- 14
Lysenko	Alena	RUS	3.2.88		HT	68.52	69.01- 14
Ma Faying		CHN	30.8.93		20kW	1:33:39	1:35:22- 13
Macías	Isabel	ESP	11.8.84	165/53	1500	4:09.99	4:04.84- 12
Mackey	Katie	USA	12.11.87	165/53	800	2:01.20	2:02.00- 13
					1500	4:03.81	4:04.60- 13
					3000	8:52.99	8:59.41- 13
					5000	15:16.60	15:04.74- 14
Madarász	Viktória	HUN	12.5.85	153/46	20kW	1:31:31	1:30:57- 14
Madu	Jennifer	USA	23.9.94	160/52	100	11.16, 11.12w	11.23- 14, 11.18w- 13
Maeda	Sairi	JPN	7.11.91	159/45	HMar	70:24	
					Mar	2:22:48	2:26:46- 14
Mageean	Ciara	IRL	12.3.92	168/56	1500	4:06.49	4:07.45- 11
					1M	4:30.64	4:38.81i- 11
					3000	8:55.09i	9:39.48- 07
^ Maggi	Maurren Higa	BRA	25.6.76	173/62	LJ	6.51	7.26A- 99, 7.06- 03, 7.17w- 02
Magnani	Margherita	ITA	26.2.87	161/45	1500	4:06.81	4:06.05- 14
Mahan	Shayla	USA	18.1.89	160/50	100	11.39, 11.13w	11.20- 11
Maiwald	Anna	GER	21.7.90	176/62	Hep	6111	5894- 14
Maiyo	Maureen	KEN	28.5.85	167/59	400	51.40	51.63A- 13, 52.62- 14
Majester	Kat	USA	22.5.87	173/59	PV	4.35	4.51Ai- 14, 4.40- 12
Májková	Lucie	CZE	9.7.88	182/66	TJ	13.80	13.71, 13.85w- 14
Mäkelä	Kristiina	FIN	20.11.92	184/71	TJ	14.20i, 14.06	13.70, 13.81w- 14
Makikawa	Eri	JPN	22.4.93	158/45	10000	31:48.22	32:00.25- 14
Maksimova	Marina	RUS	20.5.85	177/80	JT	55.97	60.73- 11
Maksimova	Yana	BLR	9.1.89	182/70	HJ	1.95i, 1.86	1.93i- 14, 1.91- 12
					Hep	5984	6198- 12
Malácová	Romana	CZE	15.5.87	164/57	PV	4.35i, 4.35	4.50- 14
Malanova	Ayvika	RUS	28.11.92	167/55	800	2:01.71i	1:59.61- 13
Malavisi	Sonia	ITA	31.10.94	172/65	PV	4.40	4.42- 13
Malaya	Kristina	RUS-J	8.10.96		TJ	13.85	13.18- 13
* Malkus	Lena	GER	6.8.93	180/74	LJ	6.94	6.88- 14
Malmberg	Elise	SWE	13.7.95	170/61	400h	55.88	58.42- 14
Malone	Chantel	IVB	2.12.91	175/62	LJ	6.69A, 6.62	6.65i- 11, 6.65- 13, 6.66w- 12
Maltseva	Yuliya	RUS	30.11.90	187/84	DT	63.48	63.39- 14
Maluskiewicz	Agnieszka	POL	18.3.89	175/83	SP	17.03i, 16.74	17.20- 14
Mamina	Alena	RUS	30.5.90	168/58	400	51.36	51.17- 13
* Mamona	Patrícia	POR	21.11.88	168/53	TJ	14.32i, 14.19	14.52- 12
^ Mang	Véronique	FRA	15.12.84	173/63	100	11.29	11.11- 11, 11.06w- 10
Mann	Brittany	USA	16.4.94	173/89	SP	17.40i, 17.25	17.07- 14
Manning	Christina	USA	29.5.90	163/54	100h	13.04	12.68- 12
Mánou	Loréla	GRE	20.12.90	167/52	PV	4.40	4.45- 13
Manz	Daniela	GER	19.9.86	164/72	HT	66.11	66.42- 14
Mao Yanxue		CHN	15.2.94	162/44	20kW	1:29:47	1:30:25- 12
Mara	Valeriya	RUS	22.2.83	163/50	3kSt	9:45.75	9:38.91- 10
Marais	Carla	RSA	10.12.87	166/55	LJ	6.53w	6.64- 13
Marchant	Lanni	CAN	11.4.84	155/45	10000	31:46.94	32:29.61- 14
					Mar	2:28:09	2:28:00- 13
Marcussen	Ida	NOR	1.11.87	173/67	Hep	5868	6226- 07
Maresová	Oldriska	CZE	14.10.86	187/67	HJ	1.92i, 1.91	1.92- 12
* Marghieva	Zalina	MDA	5.2.88	174/90	HT	73.97	71.56- 09, 74.47dq- 12
Marie-Nély	Nathalie	FRA	24.11.86	175/66	TJ	13.62	14.03- 12, 14.18w- 1
^ Marincu	Florentina	ROU-J	8.4.96	178/60	LJ	6.79i, 6.66, 6.78w	6.71, 6.73w- 14
Markelova	Tatyana	RUS	19.12.88	166/59	800	2:01.61	1:58.55- 12
Maroszek	Jessica	USA	26.2.92	175/91	DT	61.21	60.18- 14
Marshall	Ashley	USA	10.9.93	160/52	100	11.37, 11.22w	11.34- 13, 11.22w- 14
Marshall	Tonea	USA-Y	17.12.98		100h	13.12w	14.07, 13.73w- 14
Martin	Jada	USA	8.6.95	170/55	100	11.34, 11.27w	11.35- 14
					200	22.76	23.02, 22.96w- 14
Martín	Diana	ESP	1.4.81	162/50	3kSt	9:42.14	9:30.70- 14
* Martinez	Brenda	USA	8.9.87	163/52	800	1:59.06	1:57.91- 13
Martínez	Johana	COL	9.9.86	180/84	DT	56.43A	56.27A- 14
Martínez	Yarianna	CUB	20.9.84	167/56	TJ	13.80	14.42- 1
Martins	Eliane	BRA	26.5.86	160/49	LJ	6.68, 6.73w	6.66A- 07, 6.61- 0
* Márton	Anita	HUN	15.1.89	171/84	SP	19.48	19.04- 14
					DT	58.80	59.27- 14

Name		Nat	Born	Ht/Wt	Event	2015 Mark	Pre-2015 Best
Masai	Magdalene	KEN	4.4.93	160/48	5000	14:58.54	15:17.51- 13
					3kSt	9:29.16	9:52.97- 14
Mashinistova	Yelena	RUS	29.3.94		LJ	6.67	6.33- 14
Maslova	Darya	KGZ	6.5.95	170/50	10000	32:14.33	
Masná	Lenka	CZE	22.4.85	170/56	800	2:01.93	1:59.56- 13
Mathias	Charline	LUX	23.5.92	173/61	800	2:01.30	2:02.53- 14
Matoba	Haruka	JPN	24.4.87	163/60	JT	57.35	58.93- 12
Matsuda	Mizuki	JPN	31.5.95	158/46	10000	32:12.25	
Matsumi	Sakiko	JPN	7.8.88	159/41	10000	32:22.92	32:37.60- 14
Matsuzaki	Rico	JPN	24.12.92	157/44	5000	15:25.54	15:18.95- 14
					10000	31:44.86	
Matthews	Katie	USA	19.11.90		10000	32:23.43	32:44.58- 12
Maudens	Hanne	BEL-J	12.3.97		Hep	5720	-0-
Mautino	Paola	PER	1.6.90	170/60	LJ	6.48, 6.55w	6.32- 13
Mavrodieva	Radoslava	BUL	13.3.87	178/86	SP	18.34i, 17.84	18.67- 13
Mayer	Lisa	GER-J	2.5.96	171/57	100	11.31	11.63- 13
Mayer	Sarah	GER	20.5.91	170/60	JT	56.78	59.29- 11
Mazina	Margarita	RUS	7.7.95		HJ	1.88	1.85- 14
Mazurenok	Olga	BLR	14.4.89	176/56	Mar	2:25:36	2:33:33- 14
Mbumi	Joëlle	CMR	25.5.86	170/54	TJ	14.16	14.02- 14
McAslan	Kirsten	GBR	1.9.93	168/54	400	52.13	52.85- 13
McCarthy	Chrisdale	JAM	12.4.94		100h	13.17	13.38- 14
McCartney	Eliza	NZL-J	11.12.96	179/65	PV	4.64	4.45- 14
McCorory	Francena	USA	20.10.88	170/60	200	23.07	22.92- 10
					400	49.83	49.48- 14
McDermott	Nicola	AUS-J	28.12.96	186/63	HJ	1.88	1.86- 14
McDonald	Fabia	USA	18.4.92	170/57	Hep	5757	5563- 12
McGee	Cory	USA	29.5.92	168/52	1500	4:09.65	4:06.67- 13
McGhee	Brianna	USA	8.11.93		100h	13.24, 13.10w	13.33, 13.26Aw- 13
McGrone	Candyce	USA	24.3.89	168/59	100	11.00, 10.91w	11.08, 11.07w- 11
					200	22.01	22.81- 11
McKee	Julienne	USA	6.12.91		LJ	6.68, 6.70w	6.30- 12, 6.32w- 13
McKnight	Sparkle	TTO	21.12.91	165/55	400h	55.41A, 55.77	55.71- 13
McLaughlin	Sydney	USA-Y	7.8.99	174/61	400h	55.28	55.63- 14
McMillan	Chantae	USA	1.5.88	173/69	Hep	6112	6188- 12
McMillan	Lilla	USA	31.8.94	163/52	400	51.86	53.88- 14
McPherson	Shanice	JAM	12.3.94	163/52	LJ	6.52	6.14, 6.17w- 14
McPherson	Stephenie Ann	JAM	25.11.88	168/55	400	50.32	49.92- 13
McQuillen	Karlee	USA	31.5.89	170/74	JT	57.64	55.73- 12
McReynolds	Tiffani	USA	4.12.91	153/50	100	11.29w	11.32, 11.21w- 14
					100h	12.93, 12.70w	12.77- 14
Meadows	Jennifer	GBR	17.4.81	156/48	800	2:00.53, 1:59.12i	1:57.93- 09
					1000	2:36.13	2:39.84- 07
Meadows	Tawanna	USA	4.8.86	168/55	100	11.22	11.11- 14
Mecke	Dana	USA	20.9.87	158/48	800	2:00.76	2:02.85- 14
1000 2:37.89					1M	4:32.7	4:39.53i- 13
Medvedyeva	Yekaterina	RUS	29.3.94		20kW	1:29:32	
Meijer	Michaela	SWE	30.7.93	172/63	PV	4.55i, 4.55	4.28- 14
Mekasha	Dinknesh	ETH	.85	160/48	Mar	2:23:12	2:25:09- 13
Mekonen	Tigist	BRN-J	7.7.97	171/70	3kSt	9:20.65	9:28.36- 14
Mekuria	Aberu	ETH	24.12.83		Mar	2:25:30	2:26:07- 13
Melchor	Inés	PER	30.8.86	158/55	10000	31:56.62	33:07.75- 13
					Mar	2:28:18	2:26:48- 14
Melese	Yebrqual	ETH	18.4.90	164/55	HMar	68:21	69:02- 13
					Mar	2:23:23	2:26:21- 14
Melis Mey	Karin	TUR	31.5.84	173/57	LJ	6.66	6.93- 07
Melkamu	Meselech	ETH	27.4.85	158/48	Mar	2:26:45	2:21:01- 12
Mendieta	Yusleidys	CUB	17.2.94	180/66	Hep	5918	6024- 13
Mendoza	Magdalena	VEN	20.10.90	168/58	400h	56.65	56.87A- 14, 57.86- 12
Meng Qianqian		CHN	6.1.91	178/85	SP	17.37i, 17.23	18.31- 13
Mengistu	Meseret	ETH	6.3.90	161/47	Mar	2:23:26	2:29:22- 13
Meniker	Nawal	FRA-J	9.12.97	173/55	HJ	1.88	1.87- 14
Menkova	Oksana	BLR	28.3.82	183/91	HT	73.26	78.69- 12
Menuet	Emilie	FRA	27.11.91	155/44	20kW	1:32:20	1:35:16- 14
Mergia	Aselefech	ETH	23.1.85	168/51	Mar	2:20:02	2:19:31- 12
Merlano	Briggit	COL	29.4.82	174/65	100h	13.06A, 13.14, 13.01w	12.89- 11
Michiguchi	Ai	JPN	3.6.88	159/53	20kW	1:32:34	1:32:41- 14
Michta-Coffey	Maria	USA	23.6.86	165/51	20kW	1:33:07	1:30:49- 14
Mickle	Kim	AUS	28.12.84	169/69	JT	66.57	66.83- 14
Mihalinec	Maja	SLO	17.12.89	175/65	200	23.04	23.83- 14
Mihambo	Malaika	GER	3.2.94	170/52	LJ	6.84	6.90- 14

Name		Nat	Born	Ht/Wt	Event	2015 Mark	Pre-2015 Best
Mikhailyuk	Mariya	RUS	29.1.91	159/55	400	51.45	52.21- 14
* Mikhnevich	Natalya	BLR	25.5.82	180/81	SP	18.60	20.70- 08
Mikolajczyk	Izabela	POL	4.9.90	177/60	Hep	5823	5968- 12
Miller	Fawn	USA	10.5.92	174/80	JT	56.01	58.13- 14
Miller	Jade	USA	13.1.95	168/57	400h	56.68	56.22- 14
* Miller	Shaunae	BAH	15.4.94	185/69	200	22.14	22.45, 22.41w- 13
					400	49.67	50.70- 13
Miller Koch	Heather	USA	30.3.87	173/63	Hep	6274	6100- 14
* Minenko	Hanna	ISR	25.9.89	178/61	TJ	14.78	14.71- 12
Mineyeva	Tatyana	RUS	10.8.90		20kW	1:32:21	1:28:09- 11
* Mironchik-Ivanova	Anastasiya	BLR	13.4.89	171/54	LJ	6.83	7.08, 7.22w- 12
^ Mishchenko ¶	Anna	UKR	25.8.83	166/51	1500	4:01.95dq	4:01.16- 12
Mismas	Marusa	SLO	24.10.94	161/50	3kSt	9:35.10	9:40.49- 14
Misochenko	Anna	RUS	15.4.92		LJ	6.58	6.53- 13
Mitchell	A'Keyla	USA	25.11.95	168/52	200	22.95, 22.84w	23.73, 23.31w- 14
* Mitchell	Kathryn	AUS	10.7.82	168/75	JT	63.70	66.10- 14
^ Mitchell	Victoria	AUS	25.4.82	164/48	3kSt	9:36.52	9:30.84- 06
Mitsunobu	Yuki	JPN	9.11.92	162/46	10000	31:56.92	32:15.45- 13
Miyashita	Risa	JPN	26.4.84	171/71	JT	57.91	60.08- 11
Miyauchi	Hiroko	JPN	19.6.83	154/40	HMar	70:27	69:54- 08
Miyazaki	Yuka	JPN	21.8.92	160/41	5000	15:26.18	15:27.49- 14
					10000	32:07.43	
Mizuguchi	Yuko	JPN	24.5.85	164/45	10000	32:26.20	32:10.15- 13
Mjåland	Trine	NOR	30.6.90	161/54	800	2:01.69	2:02.40- 14
Mnatsakanova	Tatyana	RUS	25.5.83	181/64	HJ	1.91i, 1.90	1.95- 11
Mögenburg	Katarina	NOR	16.6.91	191/65	HJ	1.90	1.86i- 12, 1.84- 14
Moges	Betelhem	ETH	3.5.91	157/42	Mar	2:24:29	2:26:42- 14
* Moguenara	Sosthene	GER	17.10.89	182/68	LJ	6.94	7.04- 13
Mohamed	Bezuayehu	ETH-J	4.1.96	160/50	5000	15:19.30	
					3kSt	9:36.72	9:40.26- 14
* Mokhnyuk	Anastasiya	UKR	1.1.91	175/67	100h	13.00	13.08- 14
LJ	6.54	6.62i, 6.57- 13			Hep	6359	6220- 14
Mokrásová	Lucia	SVK	27.3.94	178/68	Hep	5784	5789- 14
* Moline	Georganne	USA	6.3.90	178/59	400	52.08	52.09i- 13, 52.92- 12
					400h	54.24	53.72- 13
* Molitor	Katharina	GER	8.11.83	182/76	JT	67.69	64.67- 11
Molodchinina	Yelena	RUS	16.4.91	174/65	Hep	6022	5796- 13
Moncrieffe	Tamara	JAM-J	16.5.96		TJ	13.92w	13.51- 14
* Montaño	Alysia	USA	26.4.86	170/61	800	1:59.15	1:57.34- 10
Montcalm	Noelle	CAN	3.4.88	166/53	400h	55.98A, 56.53	55.81- 14
^ Moore	Lashauntea	USA	31.7.83	170/56	100	11.19w	10.97- 10, 10.93w- 12
Moraa	Jane	KEN	21.9.91		HMar	70:41	70:27- 13
Moraes	Fabiana	BRA	5.6.86	170/56	100h	13.13	12.98- 14
de Morais	Andressa	BRA	21.12.90	178/100	DT	64.15	64.21- 12
Morales	Celiangely	PUR	2.11.85	164/65	200	23.03A, 23.34	23.69- 08
* Moreira	Sara	POR	17.10.85	168/51	10000	31:12.93	31:16.44- 12
HMar	69:18	70:08- 10			Mar	2:24:49	2:26:00- 14
Moreno	Arantxa	ESP	16.1.95	173/67	JT	56.76	53.72- 13
Moreno	Johana	COL	15.4.85	175/78	HT	66.06	69.80- 09
Morgan	Monique	JAM	14.10.85	168/60	100h	12.84	12.94- 14, 12.93w- 13
Mori	Yuika	JPN	25.1.88	158/46	5000	15:20.21	15:25.58- 14
^ Morosanu	Angela	ROU	26.7.86	178/57	400h	56.53	53.85- 13
Morozova	Nina	RUS	15.9.89	172/63	100h	12.80, 12.79w	13.01- 13
* Morris	Sandi	USA	8.7.92	163/54	PV	4.76	4.55- 14
Morrison	Ebony	USA	28.12.94	165/	100h	13.25, 13.10w	13.06- 14
* Morrison	Natasha	JAM	17.11.92	170/57	100	10.96	11.06- 14
Morrison	Skye	USA	5.8.90		LJ	6.53w	6.49- 12
Mos	Katarzyna	POL	20.12.94	184/94	DT	56.26	52.96- 14
Moser	Angelica	SUI-J	9.10.97	168/63	PV	4.41	4.36- 14
Moser	Treniere	USA	27.10.81	159/50	800	2:00.42	1:59.15- 07
1000 2:37.53 2:37.88i- 14	1500 4:04.26 4:02.85- 13				1M	4:27.49i	4:28.86i- 14, 4:35.07- 05
Mosop	Leonidah	KEN	.91		HMar	70:18	70:11- 14
Muangjan	Thitima	THA	13.4.83	168/53	TJ	13.65	14.16- 13
Muhammad	Dalilah	USA	7.2.90	170/62	400h	55.76	53.83- 13
Muir	Carline	CAN	1.10.87	170/65	400	51.70	51.55- 08, 51.1- 14
* Muir	Laura	GBR	9.5.93	162/54	800	2:00.42	2:00.67- 14
1500	3:58.66	4:00.07- 14			3000	8:38.47	9:02.35i- 13, 9:12.80- 12
Mukai	Yuka	JPN-Y	10.12.98	155/37	5000	15:31.92	16:20.49- 14
* Müller	Nadine	GER	21.11.85	193/90	DT	65.72	68.89- 12
Mullina	Olga	RUS	1.8.92	166/60	PV	4.60i, 4.55	4.40- 14
* Mupopo	Kabange	ZAM	21.9.92	170/57	400	50.22	50.87- 14

Name		Nat	Born	Ht/Wt	Event	2015 Mark	Pre-2015 Best
Muratova	Olesya	RUS	25.10.92		1500	4:09.10	4:21.86- 14
Murer	Fabiana	BRA	16.3.81	172/64	PV	4.85	4.85- 10
Murray	Madeleine	GBR	19.10.93	163/47	1500	4:10.17	4:20.86- 14
Murtazina	Alsu	RUS	12.12.87	175/59	TJ	13.87	14.55- 11, 14.63w- 10
Murto	Wilma	FIN-Y	11.6.98	180/62	PV	4.45i, 4.30	4.05- 14
Muscaro	Carly	USA	18.5.95	164/54	400	51.83	53.43- 14
Mutai	Beatrice	KEN	19.4.87	152/38	10000	32:14.0A	32:24+- 14
					HMar	69:46	69:30- 14
Muze	Lina	LAT	4.12.92	182/75	JT	60.48	61.97- 13
Mwangi	Ann	KEN	8.12.88	172/51	1500	4:06.36	4:05.23- 14
					3000	8:52.29	8:43.54- 09
Mwanzi	Annet	KEN	21.7.87	159/48	800	2:01.46A	2:00.96- 11
Myers	Tamara	BAH	27.7.93	173/	TJ	13.41, 13.78Aw, 13.57w	13.36i, 13.28- 13
Nageotte	Katie	USA	30.6.91	168/59	PV	4.55	4.50dh?, 4.48- 14
Nagovitsyna	Yelena	RUS	7.12.82	169/55	5000	15:24.58	15:02.80- 12
					10000	32:26.28	32:02.99- 13
Naigambo	Beata	NAM	11.3.80	160/47	Mar	2:26:57	2:27:54- 13
Nanyondo	Winnie	UGA	23.8.93	164/48	800	2:01.97	1:58.63- 14
Narvaez	Ana Cristina	MEX	12.8.91	168/56	3kSt	9:48.33	10:11.22A- 14
Naser	Salwa Eid	BRN-Y	23.5.98	167/50	400	51.39	52.74- 14
Nawowuna	Alice Aprot	KEN	11.3.94	174/55	5000	15:31.82	15:16.74- 10
					10000	31:24.18	
Ndoumbe	Ruth	ESP	1.1.87	173/59	TJ	13.85i, 13.44	14.15- 14
Ndungu	Ann	KEN	.95		3kSt	9:52.62	
Nel	Wenda	RSA	30.7.88	169/52	400	52.09A	52.53A- 14, 53.93- 11
					400h	54.37	54.82- 14
Nelson	Brianne	USA	27.10.80	159/50	HMar	70:16	72:23- 13
Nelson	Ella	AUS	10.5.94	169/56	200	23.04	23.26, 23.10w- 14
Nelvis	Sharika	USA	10.5.90	178/64	100h	12.34	12.71, 12.52w- 14
Nemec	Lisa	CRO	18.5.84	158/44	HMar	70:39	69:16- 14
					Mar	2:27:57	2:25:44- 13
Nengampi	Perine	KEN	1.1.89	167/49	3000	8:46.17	8:45.15- 14
					5000	15:08.39	15:16.50- 14
Netsvetayeva	Yekaterina	BLR	26.6.89	174/64	Hep	5962	6121- 14
Nettey	Christabel	CAN	2.6.91	162/59	LJ	6.99i, 6.99	6.75- 14
Neuenschwander	Maja	SUI	13.2.80	168/55	Mar	2:26:49	2:29:42- 13
Newman	Alysha	CAN	29.6.94	175/63	PV	4.40	4.41- 14
Newton	Kendra	USA	3.8.87		100h	13.14	13.12- 14, 12.92w- 13
Neziri	Nooralotta	FIN	9.11.92	174/60	100h	13.01, 12.94w	12.98- 14
Ngetich	Emily	KEN	.84	160/48	HMar	69:13	71:34+- 14
Nguyen Thi Huyen		VIE	19.8.93	162/52	400	52.00	52.76- 14
					400h	56.15	56.49- 14
Ni Yuanyuan		CHN	6.4.95		20kW	1:31:36	1:31:56- 11
Nicoletti	Julaika	ITA	20.3.88	178/90	SP	17.97i, 17.05	17.17i- 13, 17.09- 12
Nicollin	Margaux	FRA	1.5.95	185/72	JT	59.73	53.44- 14
Nidbaykina	Darya	RUS	26.12.94		TJ	13.70	13.35, 13.58w- 13
Nie Jingjing		CHN	1.3.88	168/45	20kW	1:27:51	1:28:26- 12
Nielsen	Lara	AUS	19.12.92	168/80	HT	66.37	63.11- 14
Nielsen	Laviai	GBR-J	13.3.96	168/54	400	52.25	53.86- 14
Nikisenko	Marina	MDA	28.6.86	185/85	HT	72.53	72.53- 09
Nikkanen	Minna	FIN	9.4.88	169/53	PV	4.60	4.60i- 11, 4.52- 14
Nikolayeva	Iryna	UKR	20.1.84	170/58	TJ	13.65	13.93- 13, 13.97w- 14
Nikolenko	Svetlana	RUS	26.9.91		HJ	1.87	1.80- 14
Nishihara	Kasumi	JPN	1.3.89	162/46	5000	15:20.20	15:23.80- 11
					10000	32:06.48	31:53.69- 14
Niyonsaba	Francine	BDI	5.5.93	161/56	800	1:57.62	1:56.59- 12
Njeru	Pauline	KEN	.88		HMar	70:28	69:06- 14
Nogami	Keiko	JPN	6.12.85	160/46	10000	32:14.58	32:30.10- 08
					Mar	2:28:19	
Nokelainen	Heidi	FIN	30.9.90	170/68	JT	59.86	57.28- 14
Novozhylova	Iryna	UKR	7.1.86	175/90	HT	71.95	74.10- 12
Novy	Tera	USA	10.2.94	183/84	DT	59.12	54.60- 14
Nowakowska	Dominika	POL	25.1.85	172/56	5000	15:29.26	15:16.11- 13
Nugent	Leah	USA	23.11.92	168/62	100h	13.11	13.29, 13.27w- 14
					400h	55.63	56.97- 14
Nukuri	Diane	BDI	1.12.84	175/54	HMar	69:33	69:12- 13
					Mar	2:27:50	2:29:35- 14
Numata	Michi	JPN	6.5.89	155/45	10000	32:03.95	32:45.86- 12
					HMar	69:27	72:47- 13
Nwaba	Barbara	USA	18.1.89	175/64	Hep	6500	6307- 14
Nyabeu Djapa	Anaelle	FRA	15.9.92	174/63	Hep	5738	5817- 14

	Name		Nat	Born	Ht/Wt	Event	2015 Mark	Pre-2015 Best
*	Nyambura	Virginia	KEN	20.7.93	165/48	1500	4:10.0A	4:16.07- 13
						3kSt	9:13.85	9:58.08- 13
	Nyaruai	Veronica	KEN	29.10.89	165/43	5000	15:21.10	14:44.82- 12
	Nygård	Sanna	FIN	22.3.88	176/60	TJ	13.73	13.63- 13
^	Nzola Meso Ba	Teresa	FRA	30.11.83	170/53	TJ	13.79i, 13.69, 13.79w	14.69- 07
	O'Brien	Rebecca	USA	30.4.90	173/86	SP	18.34i, 18.21	17.85- 14
	O'Connell	Jessica	CAN	10.2.89	158/48	3000	8:51.37	8:54.87- 14
						5000	15:06.44	15:13.21- 14
	O'Connor	Leah	USA	30.8.92	171/55	1500	4:11.04	4:15.13- 14
	1M 4:27.18i 4:34.35i- 14					3kSt	9:31.03	9:36.43- 14
	O'Flaherty	Kerry	IRL	15.7.81	167/52	3kSt	9:42.61	9:52.94- 14
	Obare	Dorichah	KEN	10.1.90	162/48	10000	32:03.18	31:37.07- 10
*	Obergföll	Christina	GER	22.8.81	175/79	JT	64.61	70.20- 07
	Obleshchuk	Halyna	UKR	23.2.89	177/94	SP	17.94i, 17.79	19.40- 14
^	Ochichi	Isabella	KEN	28.10.79	162/48	HMar	69:45	68:38- 01
	Odiong	Ofonime	BRN-J	13.3.97	168/60	200	22.98w	23.97- 14
	Odumosu	Joke	NGR	27.10.87	168/59	400h	56.56	54.40- 12
*	Oeser	Jennifer	GER	29.11.83	176/65	Hep	6308	6683- 10
	Ofili	Cindy	GBR	5.8.94	172/60	100h	12.60	12.93- 14
	Ogoegbunam	Amaka	NGR	3.3.90	168/60	400h	55.77	55.46- 14
	Ogrodníková	Nikola	CZE	18.8.90	175/73	JT	56.30	60.04- 14
	Ohara	Rei	JPN	10.8.90	165/47	10000	31:48.31	32:08.73- 13
						HMar	69:17	69:45- 13
*	Ohuruogu	Christine	GBR	17.5.84	175/70	400	50.16	49.41- 13
	Ojaloo	Kati	EST	31.1.90	165/72	HT	67.26	65.07- 14
	Okada	Kumiko	JPN	17.10.91	158/47	20kW	1:29:46	1:32:22- 13
*	Okagbare	Blessing	NGR	9.10.88	180/68	100	10.80	10.79, 10.75w- 13, 10.7Aw- 10-
	200 22.67 22.23- 14					LJ	6.66	7.00, 7.14w- 13
*	Okolo	Courtney	USA	15.3.94	168/54	200	22.93	23.17, 23.04w- 14
						400	50.82A, 50.99	50.03- 14
	Okoro	Chinwe	NGR	20.6.89	184/84	DT	57.54	59.79- 14
	Okpala	Nneka	NZL	27.4.88	175/63	TJ	13.65	13.55- 14
	Okparaebo	Ezinne	NOR	3.3.88	164/56	100	11.12, 11.0	11.10- 12
*	Okuneva	Oksana	UKR	14.3.90	175/61	HJ	1.92i, 1.92	1.98- 14
	Okwelogu	Nikki	NGR	5.5.95	179/90	SP	17.32	16.05- 14
*	Oljira	Belaynesh	ETH	26.6.90	165/49	5000	15:05.19	14:58.16- 10
	10000 30:53.69 30:26.70- 12					HMar	70:41	67:27- 11
	Oluwatobeloba	Amusan	NGR-J	23.4.97		100h	13.11	13.89- 14
	Oluwole	Funlayo	USA-J	19.6.97		100	11.27w	
*	Olyanovska	Lyudmyla	UKR	20.2.93	172/57	20kW	1:27:09	1:27:27- 14
^	Omarova	Anna	RUS	3.10.81	180/108	SP	17.19	19.69- 07
	Omori	Natsuki	JPN	22.6.94	162/46	5000	15:28.32	15:39.96- 14
	Onishi	Misaki	JPN	24.2.85	164/46	5000	15:16.82	15:21.73- 13
	Onnen	Imke	GER	17.8.94	190/66	HJ	1.89	1.84- 13
	Onofre	Marta	POR	28.1.91	171/65	PV	4.36	4.35A- 14
	Onuora	Anyika	GBR	28.10.84	175/69	200	23.19, 22.88w	22.64- 14
						400	50.87	51.38- 13
^	Onyia ¶	Josephine	ESP	15.7.86	166/60	100h	12.98	12.50- 08
^	Orbán	Éva	HUN	29.11.84	173/75	HT	70.14	73.44- 13
	Orji	Keturah	USA-J	5.3.96	165/52	LJ	6.63	6.39- 13
						TJ	14.15	13.69- 13
	Ortega	Alejandra	MEX	8.7.94	164/56	20kW	1:31:04	1:36:04u- 13
	Ortiz	Mirna	GUA	28.2.87	158/44	20kW	1:31:25	1:28:32- 13
	Osazuwa	Uhunoma	NGR	23.11.87	178/68	HJ	1.87	1.85- 12
						Hep	6106	6049- 12
*	Oskan-Clarke	Shelayna	GBR	20.1.90		800	1:58.86	2:01.94- 14
	Ostrowska	Aleksandra	POL-J	19.12.97		JT	56.24	51.06- 14
	Oudiou	Emma	FRA	2.10.95	172/54	3kSt	9:44.74	10:12.69- 14
	Ouhaddou	Hanane	MAR	1.1.82	158/46	3kSt	9:30.89	9:22.12- 09
	Owens	Bridgette	USA	14.3.92	163/52	100h	12.73, 12.71w	12.71- 12, 12.62w- 14
	Owers	Torie	NZL	6.3.94	170/80	SP	16.93	16.11i- 13, 16.00- 12
	Owsinski	Kristina	USA	16.2.93	172/60	PV	4.40	4.12i- 14, 4.07- 13
	Owusu-Agyapong	Flings	GHA	16.10.88	168/55	100	11.42, 11.16w	11.39- 13
	Ozolina	Sinta	LAT	26.2.88	185/72	JT	62.81	64.38- 13
	Paesler	Carolin	GER	16.12.90	167/72	HT	70.22	70.76- 14
	Paine	Alexis	USA	12.10.90	168/60	PV	4.41	4.45- 13
*	Palameika	Madara	LAT	18.6.87	185/76	JT	65.01	66.15- 14
	Palframan	Justine	RSA	4.11.93	165/60	200	22.96, 22.92w	23.02A, 23.27- 14
						400	51.27	51.87- 12
	Palmieri	Elisa	ITA	18.9.83	169/85	HT	67.03	67.33- 11
*	Palmisano	Antonella	ITA	6.8.91	166/49	20kW	1:28:40	1:27:51- 14

Name		Nat	Born	Ht/Wt	Event	2015 Mark	Pre-2015 Best
Palsyté	Airiné	LTU	13.7.92	186/62	HJ	1.98i, 1.95	1.98- 14
Panaet	Elena	ROU	5.6.93		3kSt	9:52.14	10:16.61- 14
Panagi	Nektaria	CYP	20.3.90	165/48	LJ	6.62	6.56- 12
Pandakova	Marina	RUS	1.3.89		20kW	1:25:03	1:27:39- 13
Panova	Yelena	RUS	2.3.87	185/95	DT	63.22	61.02- 13
Panturoiu	Elena Andreea	ROU	24.2.95		TJ	14.13	13.93i, 13.81, 14.20w- 14
Papahrístou	Paraskeví	GRE	17.4.89	170/53	TJ	13.99, 14.20w	14.72- 11, 14.77w- 12
Papaioannou	Ramona	CYP	15.6.89		100	11.36, 11.29w	11.45- 14
Pappas	Alexi	USA	28.3.90	165/48	10000	32:02.22	
Parada	Lidia	ESP	11.6.93	174/70	JT	59.03	54.52- 13
Pare	Maroussia	FRA-J	18.7.96	162/52	200	23.29, 23.05w	24.04, 23.89w- 14
Parker	Tiffeny	USA	8.6.88	170/60	Hep	5734(w)	5562- 14
Parnov	Elizabeth	AUS	9.5.94	175/57	PV	4.43	4.50- 12
Parry	Carys	GBR	24.7.81	173/72	HT	66.36	66.80- 14
Partridge	Bethan	GBR	11.7.90	178/60	HJ	1.87	1.83i, 1.82- 14
Partridge	Lily	GBR	9.3.91	160/45	10000	32:20.77	32:51.26- 14
					HMar	70:32	74:55- 13
Pascual	Beatriz	ESP	9.5.82	163/53	20kW	1:31:51	1:27:44- 08
Patterson	Eleanor	AUS-J	22.5.96	182/66	HJ	1.96	1.96- 13
Patterson	Liz	USA	9.6.88	183/65	HJ	1.89	1.91- 10
Pavey	Jo	GBR	20.9.73	168/48	HMar	69:58	68:53- 08
Payne	Demi	USA	30.9.91	182/65	PV	4.75Ai, 4.71	4.25i- 13, 4.21, 4.29irr- 14
Pearson	Sally	AUS	19.9.86	166/60	100	11.16	11.14- 07
200	22.97	23.02, 22.66w- 09			100h	12.59	12.28- 11
Pease	Sarah	USA	9.11.87	166/52	3kSt	9:46.66	9:48.94- 14
Pedersen	Isabelle	NOR	27.1.92	170/64	100h	12.86	13.04- 13
Pedroso	Yadisleidy	ITA	28.1.87	168/51	400h	55.18	54.54- 13
Pei Mowen		CHN	17.9.95		20kW	1:32:38	1:30:33- 13
Peinado	Robeilys	VEN-J	26.11.97	168/62	PV	4.60	4.40A- 13
Peleteiro	Ana	ESP	2.12.95	171/52	TJ	14.03	14.17- 12
Pena	Tori	IRL	30.7.87	167/57	PV	4.50	4.60- 13
Pennella	Giulia	ITA	27.10.89	169/53	100h	13.14	13.03- 14
Penney	Jessica	AUS	21.12.87	179/63	LJ	6.53	6.54- 14
Peoples	Kearsten	USA	20.12.91	183/105	SP	17.18	18.22- 12
					HT	66.17	62.38- 12
Pérez	Paola	ECU	21.12.89	148/55	20kW	1:31:53	1:32:01- 12
Pérez	Yaimé	CUB	29.5.91	174/78	DT	67.13	66.03- 14
Périz	Élian	ESP	1.4.84	171/56	800	2:01.72	2:02.1- 10
Perkovic	Sandra	CRO	21.6.90	183/80	DT	70.08	71.08- 14
Perrossier	Estelle	FRA	12.1.90	163/52	400	52.25	52.09- 14
Perry	Alexis	USA	8.8.94	173/63	100h	13.16, 13.14w	13.24- 14
Pete	Aaliyah	USA	15.3.95		SP	16.95	16.68- 14
Petersen	Sara Slott	DEN	9.4.87	171/57	400h	53.99	55.68- 12
Petersson	Marinda	SWE	3.2.95	165/74	HT	65.67	61.97- 14
Petranoff	Leigh	USA	16.5.89	170/65	JT	56.48	58.37- 14
Petrich	Anna	RUS	10.2.92		Hep	5795	5791- 14
Petrillose	Kaitlin	USA	10.12.92	168/57	PV	4.43	4.60Ai, 4.50- 14
Petrova	Gabriela	BUL	29.6.92	167/61	TJ	14.66, 14.85w	14.14i- 13, 14.13- 14
Petty	Angela	NZL	16.8.91	164/55	800	1:59.06	2:00.03- 13
1500	4:08.54		4:11.72- 13		1000	2:37.28	
Philip	Asha	GBR	25.10.90	163/54	100	11.10	11.18, 11.11w- 14
Philippe	Emma	AUS-J	6.6.97		PV	4.35	4.25- 14
Pidluzhnaya	Yuliya	RUS	1.10.88	180/63	LJ	6.87	6.84- 10, 6.85w- 11
Pierdevarâ	Florina	ROU	29.3.90	169/58	800	2:00.91	2:02.53- 14
					1500	4:07.95	4:13.47- 14
Pierre	Barbara	USA	28.4.87	175/60	100	10.92	10.85- 13
Pierson	Summer	USA	3.9.78	180/84	DT	61.23	61.19, 61.25dh- 09
Piliusina	Natalija	LTU	22.10.90	170/60	800	2:01.93	2:01.59- 13
Pinedo	Ainhoa	ESP	17.2.83	171/60	20kW	1:31:58	1:32:20- 13
Pinto	Tatjana	GER	2.7.92	170/56	100	11.23, 11.07w	11.19- 12, 11.11w- 14
					200	23.02	
Pitts	Lynnika	USA	19.5.92	173/61	TJ	13.83A, 13.70, 14.02Aw	13.44, 13.57w- 14
Planell Cruz	Diamara	PUR	16.2.93	172/59	PV	4.35i, 4.30	4.28- 14
Plaza	Alexandra	GER	10.8.94		HJ	1.86	
Pledger	Le'Tristan	USA	27.8.93	166/55	100h	13.10, 12.99w	12.93, 12.85w- 14
Pleger	Brooke	USA	21.6.92	171/77	HT	69.72	67.97- 14
Plis	Renata	POL	5.2.85	165/51	1500	4:04.74	4:03.50- 11
1M	4:25.32				3000	8:45.93	8:39.18- 14
Plotitsyna	Hanna	UKR	1.1.87	182/68	100h	13.00	12.93- 14, 12.91w- 13
Pluim	Femke	NED	10.5.94	180/62	PV	4.55	4.30- 13
Podolskaya	Anastasiya	RUS	18.8.90		SP	17.97i, 17.39	17.71- 14

Name		Nat	Born	Ht/Wt	Event	2015 Mark	Pre-2015 Best
Podominick	Liz	USA	5.12.84	188/86	DT	63.87	63.32- 13
Pohrebnyak	Nataliya	UKR	19.2.88	171/62	100	11.09	11.17- 11
					200	22.75	22.89- 14
^ Poistogova	Yekaterina	RUS	1.3.91	175/65	800	2:00.03	1:57.53- 12
^ Polk	Tori	USA	21.9.83	173/62	LJ	6.70	6.75- 11, 6.80w- 13
Polyakova	Natalya	RUS	9.12.90		HT	67.67	70.04- 14
Ponomaryova	Mariya	RUS	18.6.95		20kW	1:27:17	
* Pooley	Isobel	GBR	21.12.92	191/70	HJ	1.97	1.96- 14
Popkova	Natalya	RUS	21.9.88	165/50	10000	32:25.22	31:55.83- 12
Popowicz	Marika	POL	28.4.88	163/53	100	11.28, 11.27w	11.29- 13
Porter	Chanice	JAM	25.5.94	170/	LJ	6.43, 6.53w	6.58, 6.78w- 12
Porter	Kiara	USA	22.10.93	158/52	400	51.42	51.72- 14
* Porter	Tiffany	GBR	13.11.87	172/62	100h	12.56	12.51- 14, 12.47w- 12
Potapova	Anastasiya	RUS	6.9.85	178/61	TJ	14.03, 14.07w	14.68i, 14.40- 09
Pousse	Pauline	FRA	17.9.87	184/84	DT	59.93	57.15- 14
Povea	Liadagmis	CUB-J	6.2.96	165/61	TJ	14.08	14.02, 14.07w- 14
Poves	María José	ESP	16.3.78	168/52	20kW	1:31:06	1:28:15- 12
* Prandini	Jenna	USA	20.11.92	172/59	100	10.92, 10.90w	11.11- 14
200	22.20, 22.18w		22.60- 14		LJ	6.80	6.55- 14
Praught	Aisha	USA/JAM	14.12.89	173/55	1500	4:05.52	4:08.92- 14
					3kSt	9:36.63	9:34.69- 14
Preiner	Verena	AUT	1.2.95	177/64	Hep	5840	5530- 14
Pressley	Maya	USA	1.2.91	175/60	HJ	1.88	1.92- 13
* Price	Chanelle	USA	22.8.90	166/53	800	1:59.10	1:59.75- 14
Price	Deanna	USA	8.6.93	172/109	HT	72.30	65.18- 13
Price	Rhianwedd	GBR	11.8.94	163/52	1500	4:09.56	4:16.11- 14
Prinsloo	Lynique	RSA	30.3.91	165/54	LJ	6.55w	6.81- 13
* Proctor	Shara	GBR	16.9.88	174/56	LJ	7.07	6.95- 12
Profit	Kiani	USA	18.2.90	163/55	Hep	5782	6133- 13
^ Prokopcuka	Jelena	LAT	21.9.76	168/51	Mar	2:24:07	2:22:56- 05
Prokopenko	Viktoriya	RUS	17.4.91	174/60	TJ	14.09, 14.10w	14.41i- 13, 14.35- 12
^ Provalinskaya-Korolchik	Yanina	BLR	26.12.76	186/87	SP	17.67	20.61- 01
Pryshchepa	Nataliya	UKR	11.9.94	163/50	1500	4:06.29	4:08.89- 14
* Ptácníková	Jirina	CZE	20.5.86	175/69	PV	4.72	4.76- 13
Ptashkina	Tetyana	UKR	10.1.93	183/63	TJ	14.08	13.70- 14
Pudenz	Kristin	GER	9.2.93	180/92	DT	62.61	60.89- 14
Purdon	Cassie	AUS-J	24.10.96		HJ	1.88	1.86- 14
Purvis	Ashton	USA	12.7.92	173/60	100	11.30w	11.17- 10
					200	23.23, 22.88w	22.86- 12, 22.70i- 13
Putalová	Iveta	SVK	24.3.88	173/60	400	52.18	53.25- 14
Pyhyda	Nataliya	UKR	30.1.81	171/62	400	50.62	50.86- 13
* Qieyang Shenjie		CHN	11.11.90	160/50	20kW	1:27:44	1:25:16- 12
Quaresma	Lecabela	POR	26.12.89	172/67	Hep	5792	5744- 14
Quigley	Colleen	USA	20.11.92	173/59	1500	41:11.61	4:15.05- 13
1M	4:29.67i		4:34.80i- 14		3kSt	9:24.92	9:38.23- 13
* Radzivil	Svetlana	UZB	17.1.87	184/61	HJ	1.94	1.97- 12
Raharolahy	Agnes	FRA	7.11.92	167/56	400	52.23	52.48- 14
Rahn	Xenia	GER	9.3.91	173/65	Hep	6057	5558- 14
Rajabi	Leyla	IRI	18.4.83	185/95	SP	18.04	18.18- 13
Ramsey	Jessica	USA	26.7.91	165/85	SP	18.42	17.49- 14
					HT	69.47	61.45- 14
Rani	Annu	IND	29.8.92	165/63	JT	58.85	59.53- 14
Ratcliffe	Julia	NZL	14.7.93	171/66	HT	68.53	70.28- 14
* Ratej	Martina	SLO	2.11.81	178/69	JT	65.75	67.16- 10
* Rath	Claudia	GER	25.4.86	175/65	LJ	6.73, 6.84w	6.67- 13
					Hep	6458	6462- 13
Rautanen	Laura	FIN	13.2.88	173/60	HJ	1.87i, 1.84	1.86- 13
Ray	Shannon	USA	31.12.95		200	23.15, 23.03w	23.89- 13
* Rebrik	Vera	RUS	25.2.89	176/65	JT	64.93	66.86- 12
Redondo	Laura	ESP	3.7.88	165/80	HT	69.07	69.59- 13
* Reese	Brittney	USA	9.9.86	173/64	LJ	6.97	7.25- 13
Reggel	Valérie	SUI	3.1.87	174/64	Hep	6042	6091- 14
Rehberg	Maya	GER	28.4.94	170/58	3kSt	9:49.88	9:55.73- 14
Reid	Catherine	GBR-Y	21.4.98	178/63	400	52.25A	57.0- 14
Reid	Sheila	CAN	2.8.89	166/52	1500	4:06.97	4:02.96- 13
Reilly	Chelsea	USA	9.5.89	167/52	10000	32:05.84	-0-
Ren Mengqian		CHN	4.10.93	175/62	PV	4.50	4.40- 13
Renzhina	Yekaterina	RUS	18.10.94	172/57	100	11.31, 11.21w	11.80- 11
200	23.11		22.61- 14		400	51.49	51.67- 14
Reshetkina	Irina	RUS	30.1.89		100h	13.04	13.31- 14
Reynolds	Robin	USA	22.2.94	162/50	400	51.93	51.36- 14

Name		Nat	Born	Ht/Wt	Event	2015 Mark	Pre-2015 Best
Rhobas	Annie	USA	13.5.95	173/64	PV	4.38	4.27- 14
Rhone	Raena	USA	27.9.93	175/64	400	52.05	52.57- 14
Richards	Shona	GBR	1.9.95	165/50	400h	56.05	56.16- 14
Richards-Ross	Sanya	USA	26.2.85	173/61	100	11.28	10.97- 07, 10.89w- 12
200 22.87			22.09- 12		400	49.95	48.70- 06
Richardsson	Camilla	FIN	14.9.93	165/48	3kSt	9:46.34	9:56.44- 14
Richartz	Stephanie	USA	21.1.92	175/64	PV	4.45i, 4.45	4.34- 12
Riddick	Monique	USA	8.11.89	168/84	SP	17.57	16.64i, 16.51- 14
Rigaudo	Elisa	ITA	17.6.80	168/56	20kW	1:28:01	1:27:12- 08
Rionoripo	Purity	KEN	10.6.93	165/48	HMar	68:29	70:40- 14
					Mar	2:25:09	
Rivas	Ányela	COL	13.8.89	180/82	SP	17.27	17.53- 12
Roberson	Daye Shon	USA	3.7.95	168/52	400	51.37	53.77- 13
Robert-Michon	Mélina	FRA	18.7.79	180/85	DT	65.04	66.28- 13
Roberts	Kelsey-Lee	AUS	21.9.91	175/72	JT	63.78	63.92- 14
Rodrigues	Irina	POR	5.2.91	182/81	DT	63.25	62.91- 12
Rodriguez	Zudikey	MEX	14.3.87	168/56	400h	56.64A, 57.64	55.78A- 14, 56.10- 10
Rodríguez	Déborah	URU	2.12.92	174/61	800	2:01.46	2:05.67- 14
					400h	56.30	56.60- 14
Rodríguez	Lidia	ESP	26.5.86	171/59	5000	15:24.25	15:35.13- 12
Rodríguez	Rosa	VEN	2.7.86	180/85	HT	73.06	73.64- 13
Rodríguez	Yorgelis	CUB	25.1.95	173/60	Hep	6332	6231- 14
Rogers	Raevyn	USA-J	7.9.96	171/64	800	1:59.71	2:03.32- 13
Rojas	Yulimar	VEN	21.10.95	189/75	LJ	6.57	6.48, 6.53Aw- 14
					TJ	14.20, 14.37w	13.65- 14
Roleder	Cindy	GER	21.8.89	178/68	100h	12.59	12.80- 14
					Hep	6055	5728- 14
Rollins	Brianna	USA	18.8.91	164/55	100h	12.56	12.26- 13
Roloff	Annika	GER	10.3.91	166/54	PV	4.45	4.45Ai- 14, 4.41- 13
Romero	Marisol	MEX	26.11.83	155/48	10000	32:26.41	31:46.43- 13
Romero	Shapri	USA	13.11.91	158/50	400	51.93	51.96- 14
Rono	Janet	KEN	8.12.88	172/58	Mar	2:26:31	2:26:03- 14
Roos	Fanny	SWE	2.1.95	173/78	SP	17.05	16.29- 14
Rosa	Chiara	ITA	28.1.83	178/112	SP	18.21i, 18.13	19.15- 07
Roslova	Taisya	BLR	7.2.92		HJ	1.90i, 1.86	1.88- 14
Rosolová	Denisa	CZE	21.8.86	175/63	400h	55.15	54.24- 12
Rossit	Desirée	ITA	19.3.94	181/53	HJ	1.91i, 1.89	1.88- 14
Rotaru	Alina	ROU	5.6.93	175/54	LJ	6.75	6.74- 14
Rotich	Caroline	KEN	13.5.84	161/45	HMar	69:53	68:52- 11
					Mar	2:24:55dh	2:23:22- 12
Rotich	Lydia	KEN	8.8.88	158/45	3kSt	9:51.89A	9:18.03- 10
Rowbury	Shannon	USA	19.9.84	165/52	800	2:00.03	2:00.47- 10
1500 3:56.29 3:59.49- 14			1M 4:22.10	4:20.34- 08	3000	8:39.92	8:29.93- 14
Rubie	Anneliese	AUS	22.4.92	172/56	400	51.69	52.35- 14
Rudakova	Vera	RUS	20.3.92	175/57	400h	55.55	55.92- 13
Rüh	Anna	GER	17.6.93	186/78	SP	17.08	16.01- 11
					DT	66.14	64.33- 13
Ruiz	Úrsula	ESP	11.8.83	170/83	SP	17.68i, 17.47	17.99- 12
Ruiz	Flor Dennis	COL	29.1.91	171/67	JT	59.86	63.80A- 14
Rumpf	Sabine	GER	18.3.83	176/95	DT	58.37	62.21- 10
Rushin	Jill	USA	18.7.91	183/93	SP	17.72	17.62- 14
Russell	Janeive	JAM	14.11.93	175/63	400	51.88	51.49- 14
					400h	54.64	54.75- 14
Ruto	Stella	KEN-J	12.12.96		3kSt	9:46.00A	9:50.58- 12
Rypakova	Olga	KAZ	30.11.84	183/62	TJ	14.77	15.25- 10
Ryzhova	Kseniya	RUS	19.4.87	172/62	100	11.27, 11.24w	11.55- 08
					400	51.97	49.80- 13
Ryzhykova	Anna	UKR	24.11.89	176/67	400h	55.16	54.35- 12
Ryzih	Elizaveta 'Lisa'	GER	27.9.88	179/59	PV	4.72i, 4.70	4.71- 14
Sadeiko	Grete	EST	29.5.93	178/	Hep	5813	5706- 14
Sadeiko	Grit	EST	29.7.89	172/62	Hep	6213	6221- 13
Sado	Besu	ETH-J	12.1.96	165/50	1000	2:37.73	
					1500	4:00.65	4:07.59- 14
Sado	Fatuma	ETH	11.10.91	165/48	Mar	2:24:16	2:25:39sh- 12, 2:27:35- 13
Sadovnikova	Anastasiya	RUS	22.6.95	174/61	PV	4.45i, 4.40	4.35- 14
Saeed	Alia Mohamed	UAE	18.5.91	164/53	3000	8:55.40	8:48.27i- 14.9:07.42- 13
5000 15:28.74			15:24.94- 14		10000	31:52.29	31:51.86- 14
Safránková	Katerina	CZE	8.6.89	191/105	HT	68.43	71.16- 12
Safronova	Olga	KAZ	5.11.91	171/62	100	11.20	11.12- 12
Sagnia	Khaddi	SWE	20.4.94	173/63	LJ	6.78	6.55- 14
Sahutoglu	Tugçe	TUR	1.5.88	180/115	HT	69.92	74.17- 12

Name		Nat	Born	Ht/Wt	Event	2015 Mark	Pre-2015 Best
^ Sailer	Verena	GER	16.10.85	166/50	100	11.10, 10.91w	11.02- 13
* Saina	Betsy	KEN	30.6.88	163/48	3000	8:43.19i	8:38.01- 14
5000	15:00.48		14:39.49- 14		10000	31:51.35	30:57.30- 14
Saito	Marina	JPN	15.10.95	164/64	JT	57.90	56.76- 13
Sakaida	Ayumi	JPN	7.11.85	157/44	10000	32:22.88	32:24.55- 14
* Saladukha	Olha	UKR	4.6.83	175/55	TJ	14.62	14.99- 12, 15.06w- 11
Salerno	Melissa	USA	22.11.86	167/54	1500	4:09.49	4:12.35- 14
Salis	Silvia	ITA	17.9.85	179/74	HT	70.42	71.93- 11
Salman-Kaya	Kivilcim	TUR	27.3.92	166/85	HT	71.37	72.55- 12
Salmela	Johanna	FIN	6.11.90	172/76	HT	65.83	65.81- 13
Samuel	Jamile	NED	24.4.92	168/54	100	11.25	11.12- 14
					200	22.95	22.72- 14
Samuel	Laura	GBR	19.2.91	165/65	TJ	14.06	14.09- 14
* Samuels	Dani	AUS	26.5.88	182/82	DT	66.21	67.99- 14
Samuels	Sonia	GBR	16.5.79		Mar	2:28:04	2:30:56- 12
Sananes	Deborah	FRA	26.10.95	171/52	400	52.09	53.96- 13
Sanders	Shayla	USA	6.1.94	168/55	100	11.30, 11.13w	11.20, 11.12w- 14
Sandu	Cristina	ROU	4.3.90	172/58	TJ	13.97i, 13.59	13.99- 14
Santiago	Xahria	CAN-Y	9.10.99	165/50	400h	56.79A, 57.67	
Santos	Adelly	BRA	8.7.87	176/68	100h	13.06	13.42- 13
Santos	Rosângela	BRA	20.12.90	165/55	100	11.04, 11.01w	11.17, 11.07w- 12
					200	22.77	22.92- 12
^ Santos	Vera	POR	3.12.81	164/57	20kW	1:30:23	1:28:02- 14
Sarrapio	Patricia	ESP	16.11.82	168/58	TJ	13.94i, 13.76	14.10- 10, 14.30w- 12
Sassine	Nicole	CAN	24.11.89	170/61	400	52.25	53.81- 14
Sauceda	Jessamyn	MEX	22.5.89	173/59	Hep	5786	5606A, 5528- 14
Saunders	Allie	USA	8.1.93	161/50	TJ	13.64	12.77- 14
Saunders	Claudia	USA	19.5.94	159/50	800	2:00.63	2:02.68- 14
* Saunders	Raven	USA-J	15.5.96	165/89	SP	18.62i, 18.35	17.28- 14
Saunders	Sha'Keela	USA	18.12.93	168/59	LJ	6.75	6.43- 14
Savatovic	Sara	SRB	5.10.93	169/87	HT	66.41	65.19- 14
* Savchenko	Anastasiya	RUS	15.11.89	175/65	PV	4.60i	4.73- 13
Sawyers	Jazmin	GBR	21.5.94	167/52	LJ	6.71	6.67- 12
* Saxer	Mary	USA	21.6.87	169/57	PV	4.62	4.71Ai- 14, 4.70- 13
^ Sayers	Goldie	GBR	16.7.82	171/70	JT	62.09	66.17- 12
Saykina	Svetlana	RUS	10.7.85	177/82	DT	61.85	63.42- 08
* Schäfer	Carolin	GER	5.12.91	178/64	Hep	6547	6395- 14
Scheper	Jeannelle	LCA	21.11.94	175/60	HJ	1.96	1.92A- 13
* Schippers	Dafne	NED	15.6.92	179/68	100	10.81	11.03- 14
LJ	6.48i, 6.43		6.78- 14		200	21.63	22.03- 14
Schlumpf	Fabienne	SUI	17.11.90	183/62	3kSt	9:40.63	9:37.81- 14
Schmidt	Sarah	GER-J	4.10.96	175/56	800	2:01.44	2:05.00- 14
Schneider	Rachel	USA	18.7.91	168/52	1500	4:06.90	4:10.53- 13
Schol	Lisanne	NED	22.6.91	176/73	JT	56.43	57.50- 11
^ Schrott	Beate	AUT	15.4.88	177/68	100h	12.92	12.82- 12
Schultze	Martina	GER	12.9.90	172/59	PV	4.40	4.50- 13
Schürmann	Robine	SUI	31.1.89	165/56	400h	56.65	57.51- 14
* Schwanitz	Christina	GER	24.12.85	180/103	SP	20.77	20.41- 13
Schwartz	Lindsay	USA	23.4.90	178/64	Hep	5998	5980- 13
Scott	Dominique	RSA	24.6.92	160/50	1500	4:08.65	4:14.33- 14
3000	8:52.57i	9:02.33i- 14, 9:45.28- 09	5000 15:32.55	15:42.42- 14	10000	32:11.60	33:51.84- 14
Scott	Sharolyn	CRC	27.10.84	167/64	400h	56.91	56.19- 12
Seaman	Rachel	CAN	14.1.86	173/59	20kW	1:29:54	1:30:43- 14
* Seboka	Mulu	ETH	24.9.84	158/45	HMar	69:11	69:53+- 12
					Mar	2:21:56	2:23:15- 14
Sedivá	Irena	CZE	19.1.92	173/70	JT	59.89	57.41- 12
Sedykh	Alexia	FRA	13.9.93	173/70	HT	70.77	68.35- 13
See	Heidi	AUS	8.9.89	168/52	1500	4:08.15	4:11.66- 14
2000	5:43.82i				3000	8:55.20i	9:27.11i- 12
Seibert	Lilian	BRA	23.7.89	176/78	JT	56.77	55.45- 14
^ Sekachyova	Iryna	UKR	21.7.76	163/70	HT	67.60	74.52- 08
Sekanová	Lucie	CZE	5.8.89	169/51	3kSt	9:41.84	9:50.84- 10
Sekine	Hanami	JPN-J	26.2.96	156/43	10000	32:12.54	33:09.61- 14
Semashko (Mosina)	Veronika	RUS	17.10.90	172/57	TJ	13.81i	14.50- 12
^ Semenova	Nataliya	UKR	7.7.82	178/85	DT	61.09	64.70- 08
^ Semenya	Caster	RSA	7.1.91	170/64	800	1:59.59	1:55.45- 09
* de Sena	Érica	BRA	3.5.85	168/55	20kW	1:29:37	1:30:43- 14
* Sendriuté	Zinaida	LTU	20.12.84	188/89	DT	61.37	65.97- 13
Sène	Amy	SEN	6.4.85	174/70	HT	67.86	69.70- 14
Sergeyeva	Nadezhda	RUS	6.11.94		20kW	1:32:13	

Name		Nat	Born	Ht/Wt	Event	2015 Mark	Pre-2015 Best
Seyaum	Dawit	ETH-J	27.7.96	158/45	1500	3:59.76	3:59.53- 14
					2000	5:35.46i	
Shahaf	Maayan	ISR	9.11.86	184/62	HJ	1.90	1.92- 11
Shamotina	Alyona	UKR	27.12.95	178/87	HT	68.96	68.43- 14
Sharmina	Yekaterina	RUS	6.8.86	172/59	800	2:00.14	1:59.17- 11
					1500	4:05.87	3:59.49- 12
Sharp	Lynsey	GBR	11.7.90	175/60	800	1:57.71	1:58.80- 14
Shatalova	Mariya	UKR	3.3.89	169/56	3kSt	9:36.87	9:44.91- 12
Shchagina	Anna	RUS	7.12.91	166/54	1500	4:01.46	4:05.58- 14
Shelekh	Hanna	UKR	14.7.93	167/60	PV	4.40i, 4.25	4.60i- 12, 4.50- 14
Shestakova	Svetlana	RUS	30.4.92		3kSt	9:45.05	10:35.25- 12
Shigetomo	Risa	JPN	29.8.87	168/50	Mar	2:26:39	2:23:23- 12
Shimizu	Miho	JPN	13.5.90	158/52	10000	32:16.23	32:14.44- 14
Shimura	Hitomi	JPN	8.11.90	167/53	100h	13.27, 13.13w	13.02- 13
Shirobokova	Natalya	RUS	18.1.94		DT	58.53	55.42- 13
Shkolina	Svetlana	RUS	9.3.86	187/66	HJ	1.95i, 1.94	2.03- 12
Shone	Guteni	ETH	17.11.91	166/50	HMar	70:37	68:31- 14
					Mar	2:23:32	2:30:23- 14
Shume	Chaltu	ETH-J	.96	162/48	800	2:01.59	
Shumkina	Olena	UKR	24.1.88	160/46	20kW	1:33:27	1:25:32- 09
Shvydkina	Tatyana	RUS	8.5.90	171/62	PV	4.50i, 4.45	4.40i- 14
Sibileva	Tatyana	RUS	17.5.80	159/42	20kW	1:30:48	1:25:52- 10
Sidi Madane	Fadwa	MAR	20.11.94	162/50	3kSt	9:27.87	9:51.50- 13
Sidorova	Anzhelika	RUS	28.6.91	170/52	PV	4.80i, 4.79	4.72i, 4.70- 14
Sifuentes	Nicole	CAN	30.6.86	173/57	1500	4:06.44	4:04.65- 13
1M	4:32.36i	4:28.97i- 14, 4:31.98- 11			5000	15:19.15	15:27.58- 13
Sigurdardóttir	Hafdís	ISL	12.2.87		LJ	6.56	6.41, 6.72w- 14
Silva	Ana Cláudia ¶?	BRA	6.11.88	158/55	100	11.01, 10.96w	11.05, 10.93w- 13
					200	23.08, 22.84w	22.48- 11
Ferrer e Silva	Laila	BRA	30.7.82	180/80	JT	59.15	60.33- 14
da Silva	Izabela	BRA	2.8.95	178/95	DT	58.81	58.70- 14
da Silva	Karla Rosa	BRA	12.11.84	168/58	PV	4.38	4.53- 13
da Silva	Tânia	BRA	17.12.86	178/59	LJ	6.68, 6.73w	6.52- 14
					TJ	13.80	14.11- 07
Silva	Yarisley	CUB	1.6.87	169/68	PV	4.91	4.90- 13
Simic	Ana	CRO	5.5.90	177/58	HJ	1.95i, 1.94	1.99- 14
Simmonds	Megan	JAM	18.3.94	159/48	100h	12.91	13.07, 13.06w- 14
Simpson	Jennifer	USA	23.8.86	165/50	800	2:00.79	2:00.45- 13
1500	3:57.30		3:57.22- 14		1M	4:22.18	4:25.91i- 09
3000	8:34.43		8:29.58- 14		2M	9:18.35i	9:26.19i- 14
Simpson	Sherone	JAM	12.8.84	175/59	100	10.95	10.82- 06
					200	22.50	22.00- 06
Sindelar	Jamie	USA			SP	16.87i, 16.12	16.46- 14
Singh	Desiree	GER	17.8.94	166/54	PV	4.40i	4.36- 14
Singh	Sudha	IND	25.6.86	163/52	3kSt	9:47.31	9:35.64- 14
Sinkler	April	USA	1.9.89	170/57	TJ	13.83	13.89- 13
Sisson	Emily	USA	12.10.91	165/47	3000	8:52.60i	9:00.76i- 14, 9:16.80- 10
5000	15:25.84, 15:12.22i	15:21.84i, 15:33.16- 14			10000	31:38.03	32:31.06- 14
Skoog	Sofie	SWE	7.6.90	181/65	HJ	1.92	1.90- 13
Skydan	Hanna	AZE	14.5.92	183/114	HT	72.31	74.21- 12
Slack	Salsa	JAM	10.12.89	180/77	Hep	6141	5833A, 5718- 14
Smirnova	Yekaterina	RUS	8.9.88	168/52	100	11.24	11.35- 12
					200	23.04	23.02- 12
Smirnova	Yevgeniya	RUS	16.3.91		SP	17.49	16.77- 10
Smith	Beki	AUS	25.11.86	165/46	20kW	1:30:24	1:32:14- 12
Smith	Brittany	USA	25.3.91	178/89	SP	19.01i, 18.96	18.57- 14
Smith	Jessica	CAN	11.10.89	172/54	800	2:01.07	1:59.86- 12
Smith	Kristin	USA	23.12.87	168/75	HT	68.90	68.40- 14
Smith	Megan	USA	31.3.93		DT	57.09	55.42- 14
Smith	Rochene	JAM	.95	170/57	100	11.18w	11.86- 14
Smith	Toni	USA	13.10.84	168/59	LJ	6.55	6.40, 6.58w- 14
					TJ	13.63	13.99- 08, 14.02w- 10
Smock	Amanda	USA	27.7.82	170/57	TJ	13.87	14.18- 11
Smolyachkova	Maryia	BLR	10.2.85	177/78	HT	69.29	74.65- 08
Smolyakova	Marina	RUS	20.6.89	188/65	HJ	1.88i	1.90- 13
Snow	Morgan	USA	26.7.93	161/52	100h	12.78	12.88- 13, 12.81w- 14
Snowden	Katie	GBR	9.3.94	167/52	800	2:01.77	2:03.46- 14
Soares	Núbia	BRA-J	26.3.96		TJ	14.16w	14.22- 14
Soboleva	Yelena	BLR	11.5.93	180/96	HT	72.86	68.96- 14
Sokolenko	Yekaterina	RUS	13.9.92	164/50	3kSt	9:25.77	9:34.12- 14
Sokolova	Vera	RUS	8.6.87	151/51	20kW	1:25:38	1:25:08- 11

	Name		Nat	Born	Ht/Wt	Event	2015 Mark	Pre-2015 B
	Sokolova	Yekaterina	RUS	16.12.95		1500	4:09.15	4:18.98
*	Sokolova	Yelena	RUS	23.7.86	170/61	LJ	6.70	7.07
	Solomon	Serita	GBR	1.3.90	167/62	100h	12.87	13.09
*	Solomon	Shalonda	USA	19.12.85	169/56	100	11.06, 10.97w	10.90
						200	22.56, 22.44w	22.15
	Solovyova	Yevgeniya	RUS	28.6.86	185/90	SP	16.97i	18.71i, 18.03
	Sormunen	Oona	FIN	2.8.89	165/72	JT	58.81	60.56
	Soto	Nercely	VEN	23.8.90	169/55	200	22.99	22.53
	Souza	Tatum	USA	20.4.92	175/66	Hep	5771(w)	5691(w)
*	Spanovic	Ivana	SRB	10.5.90	176/65	LJ	7.02	6.92i, 6.88
	Speight	Montené	GBR	5.11.92	165/48	400	52.21	52.67
	Spelmeyer	Ruth Sophia	GER	19.9.90	175/57	400	52.04	52.63
	Spence	Indira	JAM	8.9.86	178/68	100h	13.15	12.92, 12.80w
	Spence Gracey	Neely	USA	16.4.90	163/50	5000	15:25.34	15:26.51
						HMar	69:59	
*	Spencer	Ashley	USA	8.6.93	168/54	400	51.72	50.28
*	Spencer	Kaliese	JAM	6.5.87	175/63	400	51.14	50.19
						400h	54.15	52.79
*	Spencer	Levern	LCA	23.6.84	180/54	HJ	1.94	1.98
	Spenner	Sami	USA	21.3.91	168/59	Hep	6019(w)	6003
*	Spiegelburg	Silke	GER	17.3.86	173/64	PV	4.75	4.82
	Spiler	Barbara	SLO	2.1.92	184/79	HT	68.11	71.25
	Spínola	Vanessa	BRA	5.3.90	178/68	Hep	6103	6015
*	Spotáková	Barbora	CZE	30.6.81	182/80	JT	65.66	72.28
	Sprunger	Léa	SUI	5.3.90	183/69	400h	55.60	
	St.Fort	Khalifa	TTO-Y	13.2.98	168/52	100	11.19A, 11.31	11.51
	Stafford	Gabriela	CAN	13.9.95	165/53	1500	4:07.44	4:17.00
*	Stahl	Linda	GER	2.10.85	174/72	JT	64.65	67.32
	Staisiunaite	Egle	LTU	30.9.88	175/65	400h	56.17	56.39
	Stanciu	Daniela	ROU	15.10.87	175/57	HJ	1.94i, 1.85	1.94
	Stanková	Eliska	CZE	11.11.84	181/82	DT	58.66	59.34
	Starygina	Yekaterina	RUS	26.8.95	177/73	JT	56.60	58.59
	Steacy	Heather	CAN	14.4.88	175/73	HT	68.48	72.16
	Steel	Gemma	GBR	12.11.85	167/50	HMar	69:56	68:13dh
*	Stefanídi	Ekateríni	GRE	4.2.90	172/63	PV	4.77Ai, 4.71	4.71
	Steinacker	Marike	GER	4.3.92	184/80	DT	59.03	57.36
	Steiner Bennett	April	USA	22.4.80	175/61	PV	4.55	4.63
	Steinkamp	Lisa	GER	17.8.90	178/58	LJ	6.55	6.58
	Stepanova	Yuliya	RUS	3.7.86	161/50	800	2:01.31	1:58.99
	Stepter	Jaide	USA	25.4.94	173/64	400h	55.83	56.99
	Stetsyuk	Tatyana	RUS	27.8.92	174/62	PV	4.40	4.40
*	Stevens	Jeneva	USA	28.10.89	178/102	SP	18.84	19.10i- 12, 18.47
						HT	72.69	74.77
*	Stewart	Kerron	JAM	16.4.84	175/61	100	11.17	10.75
						200	22.72	21.99
	Stewart	Shanice	USA	2.12.93	165/55	LJ	6.58	6.30i, 6.26
	Stigwood	Stephanie	AUS	21.10.90	165/55	20kW	1:32:22	1:37:39
	Stoddart	Shevon	JAM	21.11.82	165/52	400h	55.29	54.47
	Stolz	Xenia	GER	14.1.89	174/58	LJ	6.74	6.66- 13, 6.72w
	Storm	Ida	SWE	26.12.91	189/90	HT	66.86	69.13
*	Stowers	Jasmin	USA	23.9.91	175/64	100h	12.35	12.71, 12.54w
*	Strachan	Anthonique	BAH	22.8.93	168/57	200	22.69	22.32
	Strati	Laura	ITA	3.10.90	171/58	LJ	6.53i, 6.37, 6.43w	6.36
*	Stratton	Brooke	AUS	12.7.93	168/58	LJ	6.73	6.70
	Stratulat	Natalia	MDA	24.7.87	178/82	DT	58.41	62.13
	Strickler	Amelia	USA	24.1.94		SP	16.91i, 16.72	15.34i, 15.11
	Strogies	Eva	GER	21.3.91	174/55	100h	13.10	13.32
	Strohova	Nataliya	UKR	26.12.92	170/62	100	11.41, 11.27w	11.41
	Strokova	Yekaterina	RUS	17.12.89	184/80	DT	64.33	65.78
	Strumillo	Stefania	ITA	14.10.89	182/80	DT	58.22	55.07
*	Strutz	Martina	GER	4.11.81	160/57	PV	4.65	4.80
	Stuart	Bianca	BAH	17.5.88	168/52	LJ	6.83	6.81, 6.91w
	Stuart	Lauren	CAN	16.11.91	168/79	HT	67.56	65.05
*	Su Xinyue		CHN	8.11.91	179/70	DT	64.27	61.67
	Su Yingqiu		CHN	1.2.95		20kW	1:34:13	1:32:07
	Subbotina	Yevgeniya	RUS	30.10.89	171/55	800	2:00.83	2:01.05
*	Sudareva	Olga	BLR	22.2.84	176/63	LJ	6.86	6.85
	Sudarushkina	Viktoriya	RUS	2.9.90	176/76	JT	62.78	62.77
	Suh Hae-an		KOR	1.7.85	181/93	JT	58.74	57.61
*	Suhr	Jenn	USA	5.2.82	180/64	PV	4.82	5.02Ai- 13, 4.92
	Sujew	Elina	GER	2.11.90	164/51	1500	4:09.28	4:07.36

Name		Nat	Born	Ht/Wt	Event	2015 Mark	Pre-2015 Best
Sukenaga	Hitomi	JPN	4.5.88	168/76	JT	58.51	55.59- 13
Sum	Eunice	KEN	2.9.88	172/53	800	1:56.99	1:57.38- 13
					1500	4:09.7A	4:01.54- 14
Sumi	Azusa	JPN-J	12.8.96	166/49	5000	15:17.62	
Sun Huanhuan		CHN	15.3.90	161/50	20kW	1:30:21	1:27:36- 13
Sutej	Tina	SLO	7.11.88	173/58	PV	4.55i, 4.38	4.71i- 14, 4.61- 11
Suttie	Taryn	CAN	7.12.90	182/95	SP	17.61	16.48- 14
Suver	Mattie	USA	10.9.87	163/48	10000	31:54.43	32:29.14- 13
Suzuki	Ayuko	JPN	8.10.91	154/38	5000	15:08.29	15:14.96- 14
					10000	31:48.18	32:49.02- 13
Svechnikova	Anastasiya	UZB	20.9.92	165/60	JT	58.61	61.17- 12
Sviridova	Olesya	RUS	28.10.89	176/94	SP	18.16	19.72- 12
Swoboda	Ewa	POL-J	26.7.97	164/55	100	11.24, 11.21w	11.30- 14
Szabó	Barbara	HUN	17.2.90	175/59	HJ	1.94	1.92Ai- 13, 1.91- 14
Szwarnóg	Agnieszka	POL	28.12.86	167/59	20kW	1:32:16	1:30:56- 12
Ta Lou Gonerie	Marie Josée	CIV	18.11.88	159/57	100	11.02, 10.95w	11.20- 14
					200	22.56	22.78- 14
Tabares	Carolina	COL	18.7.86	162/50	10000	32:24.24	32:39.13- 14
Tadese	Feyse	ETH	19.11.88	167/53	HMar	70:29	68:35- 13
Takacs	Julia	ESP	29.6.89	171/55	20kW	1:31:23	1:28:44- 13
Takashima	Yuka	JPN	12.5.88	153/39	10000	31:37.32	31:55.81- 14
Takechi	Shiho	JPN	18.8.90	159/44	10000	32:26.38	32:26.53- 14
Takenaka	Risa	JPN	6.1.90	159/41	Mar	2:28:09	
Takuntseva	Irina	RUS	14.11.90	169/60	400h	56.57	57.02- 13
Talay	Alina	BLR	14.5.89	164/54	100h	12.66	12.71- 12
Talbert	Madelin	USA	23.4.94	155/45	3kSt	9:50.57	10:08.21- 14
Tallent	Rachel	AUS	20.2.93	167/53	20kW	1:34:16	1:34:53- 13
Tan Jian		CHN	20.1.88	179/80	DT	62.97	64.45- 12
Tanaka	Hanae	JPN	12.2.90	160/48	10000	32:19.36	32:00.15- 14
Tanaka	Tomomi	JPN	25.1.88	154/40	10000	32:08.74	32:27.70- 12
					Mar	2:28:00	2:26:05- 14
Tanui	Angela	KEN	27.7.92	155/42	HMar	68:41	71:55- 14
Tarasova	Irina	RUS	15.4.87	183/110	SP	18.53	19.35- 12
Tarmoh	Jeneba	USA	27.9.89	167/59	100	10.93	10.93- 13
					200	22.23	22.28- 11, 22.06w- 14
Tate	Brianna	USA	4.4.95	168/55	400	51.66	52.32- 14
Tate	Cassandra	USA	11.9.90	174/64	400h	54.01	54.70- 14
Tavares	Maria Eleonor	POR	24.9.85	164/55	PV	4.33	4.50- 11
Tavernier	Alexandra	FRA	13.12.93	170/82	HT	74.39	71.17- 14
Taylor	Jessica	GBR	27.6.88	172/63	Hep	5767	5826- 14
Taylor	Kellyn	USA	22.7.86	167/52	5000	15:32.04	15:21.93- 14
Taylor-Chase	Chanice	CAN	6.8.93	172/61	100h	12.95	13.20- 14
					400h	57.01	56.27- 14
Teferi	Senbere	ETH	3.5.95	159/45	1500	4:01.86	4:04.55- 13
3000	8:34.32		8:41.54- 14		5000	14:36.44	16:21.0A- 13
Tejeda #	Gladys	PER	30.9.85	162/46	10000	32:18.49	33:01.99- 14
					Mar	2:28:12	2:31:48- 13
Tenorio	Ángela	ECU-J	27.1.96	167/59	100	10.99	11.25A, 11.27- 14, 11.24w- 13
					200	22.84A, 22.86, 22.59w	23.13- 13,22.82Aw- 14
Terecha	Tizita	ETH	.92		Mar	2:28:02	2:34:36- 14
Terlecki	Josephine	GER	17.2.86	183/84	SP	17.52i, 17.43	18.87- 12
Terzic	Amela	SRB	2.1.93	169/51	800	1:59.90	2:04.67- 13
					1500	4:04.77	4:05.69- 13
Teschuk	Erin	CAN	25.10.94	168/54	3kSt	9:40.07	10:23.75- 14
Tesfay	Haftamnesh	ETH	28.4.94	162/48	3000	8:55.19	8:59.50i- 13, 9:10.02- 12
					5000	15:20.52	15:22.79- 13
Tesfaye	Kokebe	ETH-J	5.5.97	160/50	800	2:01.60	2:04.1A- 13
					1500	4:07.44	4:07.34- 14
Tessaro	Giulia	ITA	1.11.85	164/49	100h	13.14	13.50- 14
Theisen-Eaton	Brianne	CAN	18.12.88	180/64	100h	12.98	13.00- 14
HJ	1.891.88i- 12, 1.87- 14	LJ	6.72			6.59- 14 Hep 6808	6641- 14
Thi Thu Thao	Bui	VIE	29.4.92	162/53	LJ	6.65	6.46- 14
Thiam	Nafissatou	BEL	19.8.94	184/69	HJ	1.92	1.97- 14
					Hep	6412	6508- 14
Thomas	Charlene	GBR	6.5.82	166/52	1500	4:08.92	4:03.74- 13
Thomas	Danniel	JAM	11.11.92	166/89	SP	17.76	16.97i, 16.82- 14
					DT	58.77	59.38- 14
Thomas	LaTavia	USA	17.12.88	173/57	800	2:00.95	1:59.67- 11
Thomas	Reyare	TTO	23.11.87	168/60	100	11.22	11.30A- 12, 11.33, 11.16w- 14
					200	22.82	23.17, 22.57w- 14
Thomas	Shanieka	JAM	2.2.92	180/64	LJ	6.63	6.06- 14, 6.28w- 13
					TJ	14.23A, 14.08	14.15- 13

Name		Nat	Born	Ht/Wt	Event	2015 Mark	Pre-2015 Best
Thomas	Vashti	PAN	21.4.90	175/60	100h	13.13	12.61, 12.56w- 13
* Thompson	Elaine	JAM	28.6.92	169/57	100	10.84	11.17- 14
					200	21.66	23.23- 14
Thompson	Evann	USA	9.10.94		400h	57.02	56.87- 14
Thompson	Turquoise	USA	31.7.91	178/66	400h	55.58	54.99- 13
Thornton	Sarah	USA	29.8.86	174/79	DT	56.55	55.66- 12
Thorsteinsdóttir	Hulda	ISL	10.6.91		PV	4.34	4.00i- 12. 3.88- 10
Thweatt	Laura	USA	17.12.88	163/	Mar	2:28:23	-0-
Tikhonova	Olesya	RUS	22.1.90		TJ	13.98	13.89- 12, 14.11w- 14
Tima	Ana José	DOM	10.10.89		TJ	14.03A, 13.80, 14.21Aw	13.73- 10
* Titimets	Anna	UKR	5.3.89	173/62	400h	54.75	54.56- 14
Tkach	Lyubov	RUS	18.2.93	176/65	Hep	6151	5903- 14
Tkachuk	Anastasiya	UKR	20.4.93	168/57	800	2:00.21	2:00.37- 11
Tkachuk	Viktoriya	UKR	8.11.94	178/69	400h	56.25	58.25- 14
Toader	Eliza	ROU	12.5.90		JT	56.16	60.80- 13
* Todd	Jasmine	USA	23.12.93	165/55	100	10.92, 10.86w	11.25- 14
					200	22.89	23.60w- 14
					LJ	6.84	6.50Ai, 6.23w- 14, 6.13- 12
Tola	Fate	ETH	22.10.87		Mar	2:28:24	2:25:14- 12
Tollesa	Gulume	ETH	.92	155/42	Mar	2:23:12	2:34:26- 14
Toma	Carmen	ROU	28.3.89	168/50	TJ	13.72	14.29- 09, 14.56w- 13
^ Tomasevic	Dragana	SRB	4.6.82	175/80	DT	61.47	63.63- 06
^ Tomashova	Tatyana	RUS	1.7.75	165/52	1500	4:04.48	3:56.91- 06
Tonn	Jessica	USA	15.2.92	164/48	5000	15:18.85	15:32.26- 14
^ Topic	Biljana	SRB	17.10.77	180/60	TJ	13.79	14.56- 09
Torres	Marestella	PHI	20.2.81	164/53	LJ	6.53	6.71- 11
Townsend	Tiffany	USA	14.6.89	163/50	100	11.08	11.13- 09, 11.09w- 11
					200	22.62	22.26- 13
Tracey	Adele	GBR	27.5.93	164/50	800	2:01.10	2:02.01- 14
Tracey	Ristananna	JAM	9.5.92	170/61	400h	55.45	54.52- 13
Tran Hue Hoa		VIE	8.8.91	170/55	TJ	13.84	14.12- 13
Trapletti	Valentina	ITA	12.7.85	172/56	20kW	1:31:44	1:32:53- 08
Treacy	Sara	IRL	22.6.89	168/59	3kSt	9:44.14	9:47.92- 14
Trengove	Jessica	AUS	15.8.87	168/54	10000	32:17.67	33:06.48- 14
					Mar	2:27:45	2:30:12- 14
Troest	Stina	DEN	17.1.94	169/57	400h	55.56	56.55- 14
Trofimova	Sardana	RUS	28.3.88	164/50	Mar	2:24:38	2:28:18- 14
Troneva	Natalya	RUS	24.3.93	181/84	SP	17.02i, 16.81	17.25- 13
* Trost	Alessia	ITA	8.3.93	188/68	HJ	1.97i, 1.94	2.00i, 1.98- 13
^ Trotter	DeeDee	USA	8.12.82	178/60	400	51.24	49.64- 07
Tsareva	Yelizaveta	RUS	15.3.93	177/82	HT	71.35	68.14- 14
Tsega	Muluhabt	ETH	11.9.89	156/47	HMar	69:22	72:23- 14
* Tsegay	Gudaf	ETH-J	23.1.97	159/45	1500	4:03.09	4:02.83- 14
					1M	4:26.84i	
* Tsegaye	Tirfe	ETH	25.11.84	165/54	Mar	2:23:41	2:20:18- 14
Tsyhotska	Ruslana	UKR	23.3.86	170/58	TJ	13.92	14.53- 12
* Tufa	Tigist	ETH	26.1.87	155/40	Mar	2:23:22	2:21:52- 14
Tugsuz	Eda	TUR-J	1.3.97	172/70	JT	56.52	52.53- 14
Tuliamuk-Bolton	Aliphine	KEN	5.4.89	161/47	HMar	69:49	69:16dh- 13, 70:38- 14
Tully	Nicole	USA	30.10.86	156/45	1500	4:05.89	4:06.87- 12
					5000	15:05.58	
Tverdohlib	Marharyta	UKR	2.6.91	179/70	LJ	6.55	6.80- 12
^ Twell	Stephanie	GBR	17.8.89	168/54	3000	8:50.70mx,9:03.55i	8:42.75mx-10,8:50.89- 08
					5000	15:13.82	14:54.08- 10
* Tyminska	Karolina	POL	4.10.84	178/64	Hep	6174	6544- 11
Tyson	Keilah	USA	6.11.92	170/60	100	11.09	11.32, 11.14w- 14
^ Uceny	Morgan	USA	10.3.85	168/57	1500	4:09.31	4:00.06- 11
					1M	4:29.39i, 4:34.02	4:39.61- 14
Uehara	Miyuki	JPN	22.11.95	153/38	5000	15:21.40	15:33.21- 13
					10000	32:16.66	32:56.38- 14
Ufodiama	Blessing	USA	28.11.81	178/61	TJ	13.47, 13.85w	14.06- 11
* Ugen	Lorraine	GBR	22.8.91	178/64	LJ	6.92, 6.96w	6.77- 13, 6.83w- 12
Uke	Claire	NGR	31.12.92	179/80	SP	17.95i, 17.33	17.18- 14
Uko	Peace	NGR	26.12.95	160/48	100	11.27	11.39- 12, 11.2A, 11.38w- 13
Uloga	Svetlana	RUS	23.11.86	162/55	800	2:01.61	2:01.35- 14
Urbaniak	Lena	GER	31.10.92	175/95	SP	18.00	17.84- 14
* Urrutia	Yosiri	COL	26.6.86	175/61	TJ	14.22, 14.38w	14.58- 14
Utriainen	Sanni	FIN	5.2.91	107/64	JT	63.03	59.35- 13
Utura	Sule	ETH	8.2.90	169/50	10000	31:57.85	30:55.50- 13
Van Buskirk	Kate	CAN	9.6.87	178/60	1500	4:08.47	4:05.38- 14
van Leuveren	Nicky	NED	25.5.90	165/55	400	52.04	52.14- 13
Varner	Rachel	USA	20.7.83	176/82	DT	57.55	59.06- 14

Name		Nat	Born	Ht/Wt	Event	2015 Mark	Pre-2015 Best
Vasilyeva	Svetlana	RUS	24.7.92		20kW	1:25:04	1:28:30- 12
Vaskovskaya	Iryna	BLR	2.4.91		TJ	13.91	13.79- 14
Vastenburg	Jip	NED	21.3.94	181/59	3000	8:49.50	9:04.67- 13
					10000	31:35.48	32:11.90- 14
Vaughan	Shelbi	USA	24.8.94	185/91	DT	64.52	63.60- 14
Vázquez	Rosalía	CUB	11.10.95	175/75	DT	57.39	55.17- 13
Veit	Sabina	SLO	2.12.85	166/56	200	23.08, 23.02w	22.74- 08
Veitía	Lisneidy Inés	CUB	29.4.94	169/57	400	52.11A. 52.25	51.72A, 53.29- 14
Veldáková	Dana	SVK	3.6.81	182/68	LJ	6.36, 6.51w	6.56- 08
					TJ	14.27	14.51- 08, 14.59w- 10
Veldáková	Jana	SVK	3.6.81	177/59	LJ	6.68	6.72- 08, 6.88w- 10
Velvere	Liga	LAT	10.2.90	171/59	400h	56.77	56.87- 14
Veneva-Mateeva	Venelina	BUL	13.6.74	179/61	HJ	1.94i, 1.90	2.04- 01
Veshkurova	Tatyana	RUS	23.9.81	180/70	400	52.22	49.99- 06
Vessey	Maggie	USA	23.12.81	170/58	800	2:00.05	1:57.84- 09
Vetter	Anouk	NED	4.2.93	177/62	Hep	6458	6316- 14
Viart	Saily	CUB	10.9.95	169/97	SP	17.50	17.21- 14
Viberg	Julia	SWE	8.1.92	175/80	DT	57.07	56.37- 14
Vicenzino	Tania	ITA	1.4.86	167/61	LJ	6.59	6.65- 14
Vichy	Ariannis	CUB	18.5.89	170/70	HT	69.92	71.50- 12
Viljoen	Sunette	RSA	6.1.83	170/70	JT	66.62	69.35- 12
Virbalyté-Dimsiené	Brigita	LTU	1.2.85	165/50	20kW	1:30:20	1:30:55- 13
Visser	Nadine	NED	9.2.95	175/63	100h	12.81	12.99- 14
					Hep	6467	6110- 14
Vita	Claudine	GER-J	19.9.96	177/66	SP	17.13	15.14i- 14
					DT	62.31	56.98- 14
Vlasic	Blanka	CRO	8.11.83	192/75	HJ	2.01	2.08- 09
Vlasova	Natalya	RUS	19.7.88	164/48	3kSt	9:35.99	9:34.16- 14
Volkova	Nina	RUS	26.8.84	168/70	HT	69.61	68.30- 14
Vollmer	Lindsay	USA	10.9.92	168/59	Hep	5767w	6086- 13
von Eynatten	Victoria	GER	6.10.91	174/54	PV	4.51i	4.40i- 13, 4.30- 11
Voronina	Yekaterina	UZB	16.2.92	175/65	Hep	6212	5912- 14
Voronko	Viktoriya	RUS	15.5.91	170/55	3kSt	9:51.63	10:04.89- 14
Voskamp	Ariel	USA	8.3.92	170/62	PV	4.34	4.30i, 4.25- 14
Vu Thi Men		VIE	10.7.90	170/57	TJ	13.70	13.60- 13
Vukmirovic	Snezana	SLO	19.8.82	180/66	TJ	13.82i, 13.67w	14.58- 13
Vukovic	Marija	MNE	21.1.92	194/69	HJ	1.87	1.91- 10
Vyatkina	Natalya	BLR	10.2.87	176/50	TJ	14.21i, 13.94	14.40- 13
Wacera Ngugi	Mercy	KEN	17.12.88	155/	HMar	70:21	67:44- 14
Waite	Lennie	GBR	4.5.86	172/59	3kSt	9:40.39	9:48.17- 14
Waithera	Mariam	KEN-J	23.12.96	162/44	5000	15:32.53	15:33.47- 14
Waku	Mirai	JPN	1.7.95	156/37	HMar	69:56	
Walker	Shanique	USA	20.11.93	170/	100h	13.18, 12.96w	13.16- 13, 13.11w- 14
Walker	Sonikqua	JAM	24.9.94	173/61	400	51.53	53.10- 14
Wallace	Lauren	USA	19.12.88	160/50	800	2:00.48	2:02.16- 14
Wallace	Sasha	USA	21.9.95	175/64	100h	13.00	13.23, 13.06w- 14
Wallader	Rachel	GBR	1.9.89	180/87	SP	17.42	16.83- 14
Wambui	Margaret	KEN	15.9.95	171/57	800	2:01.32	2:00.49- 14
Wang Di		CHN	30.8.92		20kW	1:33:43	1:30:44- 14
Wang Lu		CHN	22.12.91	178/83	HT	68.07	69.39- 13
Wang Na		CHN	29.5.95		20kW	1:30:19	1:39:51- 13
Wang Rong		CHN-J	1.7.96	169/59	TJ	13.73	14.09i- 13, 13.98- 14
Wang Wupin		CHN	18.1.91		TJ	14.10	13.67- 14
Wang Xiaofang		CHN	20.1.92		TJ	13.67	13.21- 14
Wang Yang		CHN	14.2.89	185/65	HJ	1.88	1.92- 12
Wang Yingliu		CHN	1.3.92		20kW	1:30:20	1:30:51- 14
Wang Zheng		CHN	14.12.87	174/108	HT	74.92	77.68- 14
Wangari	Miriam	KEN	22.2.79		Mar	2:27:53	2:28:20- 14
Wanjiru	Rosemary	KEN	9.12.94	158/45	5000	15:15.42	15:19.00- 14
Wanjugu	Felista	KEN	18.2.90	158/46	5000	15:31.69	15:02.28mx- 08, 15:21.57- 13
Warner	Heavin	USA	4.3.93	180/86	HT	67.24	64.05- 14
Wartinbee	Jenny	USA	1.3.87	175/61	PV	4.41	4.36- 10
Washington	Ariana	USA	4.9.96	175/59	200	23.07i	22.96- 14
Washington	Faith	USA	11.10.93	170/60	400h	56.94	58.44- 13
Watson	Sage	CAN	20.6.94	175/62	400h	55.97	56.81- 13
Weeks	Alexis 'Lexi'	USA-J	20.11.96	167/	PV	4.46, 4.30	4.26irr- 14
Weeks	Victoria 'Tori'	USA-J	20.11.96	167/	PV	4.37i, 4.29A	4.01- 14
Wei Yongli		CHN	11.10.91	166/54	100	11.27	11.29- 13
Weightman	Laura	GBR	1.7.91	172/58	1500	4:04.70	4:00.17- 14
Weir	Jillian	CAN	9.2.93	177/78	HT	67.15	67.43- 14

	Name		Nat	Born	Ht/Wt	Event	2015 Mark	Pre-2015 Best
	Wellings	Eloise	AUS	9.11.82	167/44	5000	15:09.62	14:54.11- 06
	10000 32:02.61			31:41.31- 11		HMar	69:56	-0-
	Wells	Lauren	AUS	3.8.88	179/86	400h	55.65	55.08- 13
	Wells	Sara	USA	11.8.92		SP	16.47	
	Wells	Sarah	CAN	10.11.89	163/56	400h	55.65	55.65- 13
	Weng Chunxia		CHN	29.8.92		DT	62.20	58.89- 14
	Wenth	Jennifer	AUT	24.7.91	166/48	5000	15:16.12	15:36.96mx, 15:45.50- 14
	Weon Aseas-byeol		KOR	8.4.90	159/48	20kW	1:32:01	1:34:30- 12
	Wertman	Casandra	USA	14.6.93	176/	SP	17.16i	17.26- 14
	Wessman	Anna	SWE	9.10.89	164/70	JT	58.34	57.75i- 12, 57.09- 11
	Westbrook	Ky	USA-J	25.2.96	175/64	100	11.17, 11.11w	11.33- 13
						200	23.22, 23.01w	23.37- 13
*	Wester	Alexandra	GER	21.3.94	173/59	LJ	6.59	6.29- 13
	Westphal	Liv	FRA	22.12.93	168/51	5000	15:28.71	15:31.62i- 14. 16:03.69- 13
	White	Cierra	USA	29.4.93	165/52	100	11.33, 11.07w	11.09- 13
						200	22.84, 22.65w	22.89- 13, 22.61w- 14
*	Whitney	Kaylin	USA-Y	9.3.98	167/57	100	11.37, 11.01w	11.10- 14
						200	22.47	22.49- 14
	Whittle	Laura	GBR	27.6.85	169/55	5000	15:22.00	15:20.92- 14
	Whyte	Rhonda	JAM	6.11.90	170/55	400h	56.72	58.41- 13
	Wilkins-Gooden	Bobby-Gaye	JAM	10.9.88	160/53	400	51.79A, 52.08	50.87- 08
	Williams	Alisha	USA	5.2.82	167/52	5000	15:19.42	15:09.73- 13
	10000 31:49.99			32:03.07- 12		HMar	70:32	72:39- 14
	Williams	Bianca	GBR	18.12.93	167/55	200	22.85	22.58- 14
*	Williams	Charonda	USA	27.3.87	167/55	100	11.14, 11.06w	11.07- 13, 10.95w- 12
						200	22.32	22.52- 12, 22.39w- 09
	Williams	Chrishuna	USA	31.3.93	161/54	800	2:01.61	2:06.48- 14
	Williams	Christania	JAM	17.10.94	157/52	100	11.11	11.19- 14
*	Williams	Danielle	JAM	14.9.92	168/59	100h	12.57	12.69- 13
	Williams	Jianna	USA	20.8.93		SP	16.99	15.75- 14
	Williams	Jodean	JAM	11.11.93	175/65	200	23.05	23.66- 13
*	Williams	Jodie	GBR	28.9.93	174/65	200	22.88	22.46- 14
	Williams	Kendell	USA	14.6.95	173/64	100h	13.08	12.87- 14
	LJ 6.54i, 6.46			6.32Ai- 14, 6.26, 6.32w- 12		Hep	6223(w)	6018- 14
*	Williams	Kimberly	JAM	3.11.88	169/66	TJ	14.45	14.62, 14.78w- 13
	Williams	Lauren Rain	USA-Y	25.7.99	170/57	200	22.90A, 23.16, 22.68w	23.95- 13
	Williams	Shermaine	JAM	4.2.90	174/62	100h	12.78	12.78, 12.65w- 12
*	Williams	Tiffany	USA	5.2.83	158/57	400h	54.27	53.28- 07
*	Williams-Mills	Novlene	JAM	26.4.82	170/57	400	50.47	49.63- 06
	Williamson	Kimberly	JAM	2.10.93	168/57	HJ	1.90	1.88- 14
*	Wilson	Ajee'	USA	8.5.94	169/55	800	1:57.87	1:57.67- 14
	Wilson	Heather	USA	13.6.90	169/55	1500	4:09.57	4:07.47- 14
						1M	4:29.39	4:33.45i- 14, 4:38.12- 13
	Wilson	Lisa	USA	29.3.88	170/	HT	66.15	64.28- 14
	Wiltrout	Madison	USA-Y	4.6.99	178/75	JT	56.60	46.05- 14
	Wimbley	Shakima	USA	23.4.95	178/61	200	22.43	23.12- 14
						400	50.84	51.68- 14
*	Winger	Kara	USA	10.4.86	183/84	JT	66.47	66.67- 10
	Winters	Dani	USA	18.2.93	182/91	SP	17.75	15.93- 14
	Wise	Katie	USA	15.10.93	165/54	100	11.38, 11.15w	11.23, 11.18w- 14
^	Wisniewska	Joanna	POL	24.5.72	178/64	DT	59.43	63.97- 99
	Witek	Marcelina	POL	2.6.95	168/58	JT	58.12	61.24- 14
	Withrow	Melinda	USA	30.10.84	165/52	PV	4.60	4.55Ai- 11, 4.52- 10
*	Wlodarczyk	Anita	POL	8.8.85	178/95	HT	81.08	79.58- 14
	Wodak	Natasha	CAN	17.12.81	160/45	10000	31:41.59	33:09.57- 13
	Woitha	Charlene	GER	21.8.93	178/77	HT	68.05	65.92- 14
	Woodall	Kenya	USA	17.7.94	169/60	400	51.78	53.26- 14
	Wortham	Ellen	USA	5.1.90	174/61	400h	56.68	55.55- 12
	Wright	Phoebe	USA	30.8.88	170/57	800	2:00.61	1:58.22- 10
	Wu Shuijiao		CHN	19.6.91	159/48	100h	12.85	12.72- 14
	Wyciszkiewicz	Patrycja	POL	8.1.94	169/50	400	51.31	51.56- 13
	Xie Lijuan		CHN	14.5.93		20kW	1:29:14	1:31:19- 14
	Xie Yuchen		CHN-J	12.5.96	179/79	DT	57.08	56.34- 13
	Xu Xiaoling		CHN	13.5.92		LJ	6.59	6.63- 12
	Yabushita	Akane	JPN	6.6.91	154/44	10000	32:13.55	0
	Yalew	Genet	ETH	31.12.92	156/42	10000	31:08.82	32:05.90- 11
						HMar	68:12	69:15- 14
	Yamashita	Mikako	JPN-J	3.5.97		JT	58.59	49.45- 14
	Yamauchi	Ai	JPN	6.12.94	169/66	JT	58.76	56.55- 14
	Yamazaki	Rina	JPN	6.5.88	162/50	10000	32:11.40	31:56.11- 14
	Yan Ni		CHN	7.2.93	176/62	HT	66.25	64.24- 14

Name		Nat	Born	Ht/Wt	Event	2015 Mark	Pre-2015 Best
Yang Fei		CHN	20.7.87	186/90	DT	57.82	60.43- 12
Yang Huizhen		CHN	13.8.92	168/55	400	51.98	52.60- 14
Yang Mingxia		CHN	13.1.90	163/44	20kW	1:33:49	1:28:56- 08
Yang Xinli		CHN	7.2.88		JT	61.92	61.37- 13
Yang Yanbo		CHN	9.3.90		DT	60.90	63.32- 12
Yarigo	Noélie	BEN	26.12.85	165/52	800	2:00.97	2:00.51- 14
Yator	Gladys	KEN	.92		HMar	70:46	72:39- 14
Yatsevich	Anastasiya	BLR	18.1.85		20kW	1:33:28	1:29:30- 11
Yepimashko	Vera	BLR	10.7.76	181/74	SP	16.88	18.95- 10
Yermakova	Anna	UKR	1.10.91	175/59	LJ	6.61	6.58- 14
Yeryomina	Lyudmila	RUS	8.8.91	171/60	PV	4.40i	4.56i- 14. 4.45- 13
Yevdokimova	Natalya	RUS	7.9.93		TJ	13.88	13.39- 14
Yokoe	Risa	JPN	12.10.94	164/40	10000	32:13.30	0
Young	Jessica	USA	6.4.87	160/50	100	11.20, 11.06w	11.13- 14, 11.06w- 09
Yüksel	Burcu	TUR	3.5.90	182/58	HJ	1.88	1.94- 11
Zabara	Olesya	RUS	6.10.82	165/56	TJ	14.03i	14.54i- 08, 14.50- 06
Zabawska	Daria	POL	16.4.95	185/70	DT	60.23	54.58- 14
Zadorina	Kseniya	RUS	2.3.87	173/59	400	51.85	50.55- 13
Zagré	Anne	BEL	13.3.90	178/69	100h	12.71	12.79- 12
Zakari ¶	Joyce	KEN	6.6.86	170/60	400	22.4A	23.74- 09
					400	51.14A, 50.71dq	51.56- 09
Zang Milama	Ruddy	GAB	6.6.87	156/46	100	11.08	11.03- 12
Zapounídou	Déspina	GRE	5.10.85	166/55	20kW	1:33:07	1:31:08- 12
Zbären	Noemi	SUI	12.3.94	177/65	100h	12.71	12.92- 14
Zelinka	Jessica	CAN	3.9.81	172/62	100h	13.12	12.65- 12
Zeltner	Michelle	SUI	22.12.91	184/72	Hep	5824	5717- 13
Zemlyak	Olha	UKR	16.1.90	165/55	400	51.61	51.00- 14
Zhang Li		CHN	17.1.89	175/75	JT	62.95	65.47- 14
Zhang Wenxiu		CHN	22.3.86	182/108	HT	76.33	77.33- 14
Zhang Xinyan		CHN	9.2.94		3kSt	9:46.82	10:01.00- 14
Zheng Xingjuan		CHN	20.3.89	184/60	HJ	1.92Ai, 1.88	1.96- 14
Zhou Kang		CHN	24.12.89	165/54	20kW	1:32:27	1:30:58- 13
Zhou Xiaoxue		CHN	19.6.92		LJ	6.55	6.46- 14
Zhu Dandan		CHN	1.3.94		JT	57.56	55.44- 12
Zhuravlyova	Tatyana	RUS	27.5.89		DT	56.30	56.10- 14
Zinchuk	Anna	BLR	4.2.94		HT	66.50	67.53- 14
Zongo-Filet	Amy	FRA	4.10.80	165/52	TJ	13.64	14.08i- 09, 14.03- 08, 14.16w- 12
Zsivoczky-Farkas	Györgyi	HUN	13.2.85	170/58	Hep	6389	6269- 13
Züblin	Linda	SUI	21.3.86	171/60	Hep	6047	6057- 13
Zyabkina	Viktoriya	KAZ	4.9.92	174/62	100	11.19	11.42- 11
					200	22.77	22.92- 12

inal late amendments

he IAAF published its latest list of doping bans at the end of March 2016 (add to page 113):

rugs bans in 2016: 4y: Saad Musleh Al-Bishim Nawaf Al-Yami, Naif Daak, Khalid Ogby all KSA (6 Feb)

dd to Drugs Bans 2015

len: Daniel Chebii Kosgei KEN 8 Feb 6m; **Women**: Hanna Drabenya BLR 11 Apr 2y; Lisa Nemec CRO 6 Oct 4y

y: Ankit Dahiya IND (7 Aug), Maksim Kosyukov RUS (23 Jun), Faishal Shah IND (18 Apr); **2y**: André Leal POR (24 ug), Sandile Ngunuza RSA (31 May); **6m**: Thomas Ginger GER (12 Jul); **W**: Rodrigo Sagaon MEX (28 Mar)

014: **4y**: Ali Benali MAR (12 Oct); **2y**: Satyajit Buragohain IND (12 Dec), Judy Kimuge KEN (1 Jun)

013: **2y**: Kim Mottrom AUS (15 Dec); **6m**: Lina Pantoja COL (19 May)

011: **8y**: Vladimir Kanaykin* RUS (25 Feb); **3y 2m**: Sergey Bakulin* RUS (25 Feb); **2y 6m**: Yuliya Zaripova* RUS (20 Jul).

009: **8y**: Valeriy Borchin* RUS (14 Aug); **4y**: Cristina Amigoni ITA (19 Jun); **3y 2m**: Olga Kaniskina* RUS (15 Aug), ergey Kirdyapkin* RUS (20 Aug); **2y 4m**: Ana Tollumi ITA. (1 Feb)

---

ontinuation of Women 20 Kilometres Walk (from page 526)

est track times

:36:34.0	Miranda	Melville	USA	20.3.89	28	Jun
1:36:39.70	Bethan	Davies	GBR	7.11.90	21	Jun
1:37:08.0	Florida	Miniyanova	KAZ	1.7.92	28	Mar

JUNIORS

:34:58	Lidia	Sánchez-Puebla	ESP	17.7.96	10		La Coruña	6	Jun
:35:14	Mária	Pérez	ESP	29.4.96	5	NC	Renteria	22	Mar
:36:50		Yang Jiayu	CHN	18.2.96	5	WUG	Gwangju	10	Jul
:37:07	Nami	Kumagai	JPN	.96	6		Takahata	25	Oct
:37:18	Chahinez	Nasri	TUN	3.6.96	17		La Coruña	6	Jun
:38:32	Katarzyna	Zdzieblo	POL	28.11.96	1		Gdansk	29	Aug
:39:58	Ilaria	Galli	ITA	20.6.97	6	NC	Cassino	29	Mar

rugs disqualification: 1:32:27 Hanna Drabenya ¶ BLR 15.8.87 1 NCp Brest 11 Apr

ussians – Alembekova and Sokolova suspended pending investigation

WORLD INDOOR LISTS 2016 – MEN

60 METRES

Note: including some marks froim December 2015, # Oversized track

Mark	First name	Last name	Nat	Born	Pos	Meet	Venue	Date
6.44	Asafa	Powell	JAM	23.11.82	1h5	WI	Portland	18 M
6.47	Ronnie	Baker	USA	15.10.93	1	NCAA	Birmingham	12 M
6.47	Trayvon	Bromell	USA	10.7.95	1	WI	Portland	18 M
6.48	Cameron	Burrell	USA	11.9.94	2	NCAA	Birmingham	12 M
6.49	Kim	Collins	SKN	5.4.76	1s2	WI	Portland	18 M
6.50	Richard	Kilty	GBR	2.9.89	1		Jablonec nad Nisou	5 M
6.50		Su Bingtian	CHN	29.8.89	2s3	WI	Portland	18 M
6.51	Marvin	Bracy	USA	15.12.93	1	NC	Portland	12 M
6.51	Mike	Rodgers	USA	24.4.85	2s2	WI	Portland	18 M
6.51	Ramon	Gittens	BAR	20.7.87	3	WI	Portland	18 M
6.52	Julian	Reus	GER	29.4.88	1	NC	Leipzig	27 Fe
6.52	Christian	Coleman	USA	6.3.96	3	NCAA	Birmingham	12 M
6.53	Yunier	Pérez	CUB	16.2.85	1	Pedros	Lódz	5 Fe
6.53	James	Dasaolu	GBR	5.9.87	1	NC	Sheffield	27 Fe
6.53	John	Teeters	USA	19.5.93	4	NCAA	Birmingham	12 M
6.53		Xie Zhenye	CHN	17.8.93	4	WI	Portland	18 M
6.54	Andrew	Robertson	GBR	17.12.90	2	NC	Sheffield	27 Fe
6.55	Sean	Safo-Antwi	GBR/GHA	31.10.90	1		Mondeville	6 Fe
6.55		Yang Yang	CHN	26.6.91	1	NGP	Nanjing	3 M
6.55	Trell	Kimmons	USA	13.7.85	2s1	NC	Portland	12 M
6.56	Joe	Morris	USA	4.10.89	1		Torun	12 Fe
6.56	Hassan	Taftian	IRI	4.5.93	1	AsiC	Doha	19 Fe
6.56		Tang Xingqiang	CHN	11.8.95	2	NGP	Nanjing	3 M
6.56	Theo	Etienne	GBR	3.9.96	2		Jablonec nad Nisou	5 M
6.56	Kenzo	Cotton	USA	13.5.96	2h1	NCAA	Birmingham	11 M
6.56	Yoshihide	Kiryu	JPN	15.12.95	3s1	WI	Portland	18 M
6.57	Eric	Cray	PHI	6.11.88	1s1	AsiC	Doha	19 Fe
6.57	Bolade	Ajomale	CAN	31.8.95	1	NCAA-II	Pittsburg	12 M
6.57	D'Angelo	Cherry	USA	1.8.90	4	NC	Portland	12 M
6.58	Emmanuel	Matadi	LBR	15.4.91	1		Mankato	22 Ja
6.58	Antoine	Adams	SKN	31.8.88	1		Houston	12 Fe
6.58	Jeffrey	Henderson	USA	19.2.89	2h1	NC	Portland	11 M

Mark	First name	Last name	Nat	Born	Date
6.59	Warren	Fraser	BAH	8.7.91	29 Jan
6.59	Chevaughn	Walsh	ANT	29.12.87	30 Jan
6.59	Adam	Gemili	GBR	6.10.93	31 Jan
6.59	Keitavious	Walter	USA		31 Jan
6.59	Christophe	Lemaitre	FRA	11.6.90	6 Feb
6.59	Markesh	Woodson	USA	6.9.93	12 Feb
6.60	Adrian	Griffith	BAH	11.11.84	31 Jan
6.60	Kevaughn	Rattray	JAM	16.4.96	5 Feb
6.60	Churandy	Martina	NED	3.7.84	6 Feb
6.60A	Ameer	Webb	USA	19.3.91	13 Feb
6.60	Daveon	Collins	USA	3.10.92	13 Feb
6.60 dt?	Qawatvis	Johnson	USA		19 Feb
6.60	Christian	Blum	GER	10.3.87	27 Feb
6.60	Bryce	Robinson	USA	13.11.93	11 Mar
6.60	Jarrion	Lawson	USA	6.5.94	12 Mar
6.61	Rondell	Sorrillo	TTO	21.1.86	23 Jan
6.61	Quentin	Butler	USA	18.9.92	30 Jan
6.61	Diondre	Batson	USA	13.7.92	30 Ja
6.61	Andre	De Grasse	CAN	10.11.94	20 Fe
6.61	Tevin	Hester	USA	10.1.94	27 Fe
6.61	Kyle	De Escofet	GBR	4.10.96	27 Fe
6.61	Sean	McLean	USA	23.3.92	11 M
6.61	Albert	Huntley	USA	3.1.90	12 M
6.61	Kemar	Hyman	CAY	11.10.89	18 M
6.62	Keenan	Brock	USA	1.6.92	15 Ja
6.62	Odean	Skeen	JAM	28.8.94	16 Ja
6.62A	Wilfried	Koffi	CIV	12.10.87	30 Ja
6.62	Levi	Cadogan	BAR	8.11.95	6 Fe
6.62	Likoúrgos-Stéfanos	Tsákonas	GRE	8.3.90	13 Fe
6.62	Henricho	Bruintjies	RSA	16.7.93	13 Fe
6.62	Odain	Rose	SWE	19.7.92	17 Fe
6.62	Darrell	Wesh	HAI	21.1.92	19 Fe
6.62	Lamar	Hargrove	USA	21.4.94	28 Fe
6.62	Remigiusz	Olszewski	POL	20.9.92	5 M

200 METRES

Mark	First name	Last name	Nat	Born	Pos	Meet	Venue	Date
20.43	Christophe	Lemaitre	FRA	11.6.90	1	NC	Aubière	28 Fe
20.46	Brendon	Rodney	CAN	9.4.92	1		Staten Island	20 Fe
20.51	Nethaneel	Mitchell-Blake	GBR	2.4.94	1h1	SEC	Fayetteville	26 Fe
20.54	Christian	Coleman	USA	6.3.96	1rB	SEC	Fayetteville	27 Fe
20.54	Mickael-Meba	Zeze	FRA	19.5.94	2	NC	Aubière	28 Fe
20.55	Arman	Hall	USA	12.2.94	2rB	SEC	Fayetteville	27 Fe
20.55	Julian	Reus	GER	29.4.88	1	NC	Leipzig	28 Fe
20.58	Devin	Jenkins	USA	16.2.94	1		College Station	6 Fe
20.58	Cameron	Williams	USA	.95	1		Boston (All)	21 Fe

Mark	First name	Last name	Nat	Born	Date
20.60A	Ronnie	Baker	USA	15.10.93	30 Jan
20.60	Sam	Watts	GBR	14.2.92	13 Feb
20.61	David	Winters	USA	19.2.94	26 Feb
20.63	Noah	Lyles	USA-J	18.7.97	13 Mar
20.64	Trayvon	Bromell	USA	10.7.95	6 Feb
20.66	Kenzo	Cotton	USA	13.5.96	27 Fe
20.69A	Bryce	Robinson	USA	13.11.93	12 Fe
20.71	Tevin	Hester	USA	10.1.94	13 Fe
20.73A	Parker	Bluth	USA	1.1.92	30 Ja
20.71#	Nick	Gray	USA-J	2.6.97	2 Fe

400 METRES

Mark	First name	Last name	Nat	Born	Pos	Meet	Venue	Date
45.20	Bralon	Taplin	GRN	8.5.92	1		College Station	16 Ja
45.44	Pavel	Maslák	CZE	21.2.91	1	WI	Portland	19 M
45.51	Lalonde	Gordon	TTO	25.11.88	2	Mill	New York (Arm)	20 Fe
45.56	Deon	Lendore	TTO	28.10.92	1		Fayetteville	19 Fe
45.59	Abdelilah	Haroun	QAT-J	1.1.97	2	WI	Portland	19 M
45.61	Michael	Cherry	USA	23.3.95	1h1	SEC	Fayetteville	26 Fe

45.72	Marqueze	Washington	USA	.94	2		Fayetteville	19 Feb
45.78	Kahmari	Montgomery	USA		1	SEC	Fayetteville	27 Feb
45.79	Arman	Hall	USA	12.2.94	2	SEC	Fayetteville	27 Feb
45.80	Vernon	Norwood	USA	10.4.92	1	NC	Portland	12 Mar
45.86	Calvin	Smith	USA	10.12.87	1		Birmingham AL	31 Jan
45.91	Neil	Braddy	USA	18.10.91	3		Fayetteville	19 Feb
45.95	Kyle	Clemons	USA	27.12.90	1rB	NC	Portland	12 Mar

46.03	Zack	Bilderback	USA	27.8.93	12 Mar
46.04	Fitzroy	Dunkley	JAM	20.5.93	27 Feb
46.05	Michael	Mathieu	BAH	24.6.84	31 Jan
46.09	Mike	Berry	USA	10.12.91	28 Feb
46.11	Najee	Glass	USA	12.6.94	26 Feb
46.20	Yavuz	Can	TUR	23.2.87	25 Feb
46.21	Emmanuel	Dasor	GHA	14.9.95	25 Feb
46.22	Elvyonn	Bailey	USA	28.9.91	12 Mar

Oversized track

45.27	Zack	Bilderback	USA	27.8.93	1	Big 12	Ames	27 Feb
45.62	Izaiah	Brown	USA-J	.97	1	Big 10	Geneva OH	27 Feb

46.11	Aldrich	Bailey	USA	6.2.94	27 Feb
46.13	Alfred	Larry	USA	9.4.93	20 Feb

500 METRES

59.83	Abdelilah	Haroun	QAT-J	1.1.97	1	Globen	Stockholm	17 Feb
1:00.71	Onkabetse	Nkobolo	BOT	22.7.93	2	Globen	Stockholm	17 Feb

600 METRES

1:15.51	Boris	Berian	USA	19.12.92	1		Boston (R)	14 Feb
1:16.02#	Daniel	Kuhn	USA	11.8.95	1	Big 10	Geneva	27 Feb

1:16.12#	Jermaine	Griffith	USA	28.5.95	27 Feb
1:16.21#	Mitch	Hechsel	USA		27 Feb
1:16.29#	Nate	Roese	USA		27 Feb
1:16.65	Edward	Kemboi	KEN	9.12.93	6 Feb
1:16.67	Erik	Sowinski	USA	21.12.89	16 Jan

800 METRES

1:45.63	Adam	Kszczot	POL	2.9.89	1	Globen	Stockholm	17 Feb
1:45.83	Boris	Berian	USA	19.12.92	1	WI	Portland	19 Mar
1:45.93	Donavan	Brazier	USA-J	15.4.97	1		College Station	16 Jan
1:45.93	Abdulrahman	Musaeb Balla	QAT	19.3.89	2	Globen	Stockholm	17 Feb
1:46.13#	Clayton	Murphy	USA	26.2.95	1		Ames	13 Feb
1:46.20	Andrés	Arroyo	PUR	7.6.95	2	SEC	Fayetteville	27 Feb
1:46.21	Thijmen	Kupers	NED	4.10.91	1	NC	Apeldoorn	28 Feb
1:46.24#	Isaiah	Harris	USA	18.10.96	1	Big 10	Geneva OH	27 Feb
1:46.25	Pierre-Ambroise	Bosse	FRA	11.5.92	2		Karlsruhe	6 Feb
1:46.26	Kevin	López	ESP	12.6.90	1		Sabadell	19 Feb
1:46.32	Hector	Hernandez	PUR	30.9.94	3	SEC	Fayetteville	27 Feb
1:46.50	Mostafa	Smaili	MAR-J	9.1.97	1		Gent	13 Feb
1:46.63	Álvaro	de Arriba	ESP	2.6.94	1		Valencia	13 Feb
1:46.65	Antoine	Gakeme	BDI	24.12.91	2	WI	Portland	19 Mar

1:46.72	Timothy	Kitum	KEN	20.11.94	12 Feb
1:46.79#	Edward	Kemboi	KEN	9.12.93	13 Feb
1:46.81	Eliud	Rutto	KEN	13.3.94	12 Mar
1:46.93	Nicholas	Kipkoech	KEN	22.10.92	17 Feb
1:46.97#	Shaquille	Walker	USA	24.6.93	30 Jan
1:46.97+	Ayanleh	Souleiman	DJI	3.12.92	17 Feb
1:46.98	Robby	Andrews	USA	29.3.91	27 Feb
1:46.99	Mark	English	IRL	18.3.93	20 Feb
1:47.01	Brannon	Kidder	USA	18.11.93	30 Jan
1:47.11	Erik	Sowinski	USA	21.12.89	20 Feb
1:47.13#	Goaner	Deng	USA	30.6.93	27 Feb
1:47.21	Jeremiah	Mutai	KEN	27.12.92	19 Feb
1:47.24	Mohamed	Aman	ETH	10.1.94	12 Feb
1:47.28	Drew	Piazza	USA	28.1.95	30 Jan
1:47.35	Guy	Learmonth	GBR	20.4.92	30 Jan
1:47.35	Robert	Heppenstall	CAN	28.2.97	27 Feb
1:47.37	Ryan	Manahan	USA	14.7.94	30 Jan
1:47.38	Carlton	Orange	USA-J	11.3.97	30 Jan
1:47.44	Joseph	White	USA	16.11.95	30 Jan
1:47.52	Duane	Solomon	USA	28.12.84	20 Feb

1000 METRES

2:14.20	Ayanleh	Souleiman	DJI	3.12.92	1	Globen	Stockholm	17 Feb
2:17.02	Thijmen	Kupers	NED	4.10.91	2	Globen	Stockholm	17 Feb
2:17.09	Elijah	Manangoi	KEN	5.1.93	3	Globen	Stockholm	17 Feb

2:18.24	Manuel	Olmedo	ESP	17.5.83	16 Jan
2:18.26	Brannon	Kidder	USA	18.11.93	16 Jan
2:18.27	Jakub	Holusa	CZE	20.2.88	17 Feb
2:18.68	Andrew	Wheating	USA	21.11.87	14 Feb

1500 METRES

3:34.94	Abdelaati	Iguider	MAR	25.3.87	1	GP	Glasgow	20 Feb
3:35.91+	Matthew	Centrowitz	USA	18.10.89	1	in 1M	New York (Arm)	20 Feb
3:36.12+	Nick	Willis	NZL	25.4.83	2	in 1M	New York (Arm)	20 Feb
3:36.30	Ayanleh	Souleiman	DJI	3.12.92	2	GP	Glasgow	20 Feb
3:36.35	Mohamed	Al-Garni	QAT	2.7.92	1	AsiC	Doha	20 Feb
3:37.08	Benson	Seurei	BRN	27.3.84	2	AsiC	Doha	20 Feb
3:37.29	Said	Aden Said	QAT	1.1.93	3	AsiC	Doha	20 Feb
3:37.30	Adam Ali	Musaab	QAT	17.4.95	4	AsiC	Doha	20 Feb
3:37.55	Bethwel	Birgen	KEN	6.8.88	3	GP	Glasgow	20 Feb
3:37.55	Vincent	Kibet	KEN	6.5.91	4	GP	Glasgow	20 Feb
3:37.67+	Cory	Leslie	USA	24.10.89	3	in 1M	New York (Arm)	20 Feb
3:37.86+	Dawit	Wolde	ETH	19.5.91	1	in 1M	Athlone	17 Feb
3:37.88+	Chris	O'Hare	GBR	23.11.90	4	in 1M	New York (Arm)	20 Feb
3:38.04	Aman	Wote	ETH	18.4.84	1		Reims	17 Feb
3:38.09+	Robby	Andrews	USA	29.3.91	5	in 1M	New York (Arm)	20 Feb
3:38.25	Manuel	Olmedo	ESP	17.5.83	1		Sabadell	7 Feb

3:38.48+	Garrett	Heath	USA	3.11.85	20	Feb
3:38.68	Lee	Emanuel	GBR	24.1.85	20	Feb
3:39.33	Marc	Alcalá	ESP	7.11.94	7	Feb
3:39.39	Iván	López	CHI	10.3.90	19	Feb
3:39.77	Elijah	Manangoi	KEN	5.1.93	3	Feb
3:39.82	Andrew	Wheating	USA	21.11.87	22	Jan
3:39.89	Cornelius	Kiplangat	KEN	21.12.92	17	Feb
3:39.89	Yassine	Bensghir	MAR	3.1.83	19	Feb

1 MILE

3:50.63	Matthew	Centrowitz	USA	18.10.89	1	Mill	New York (Arm)	20 Feb
3:51.06	Nick	Willis	NZL	25.4.83	2	Mill	New York (Arm)	20 Feb
3:52.91	Chris	O'Hare	GBR	23.11.90	3	Mill	New York (Arm)	20 Feb
3:53.16	Robby	Andrews	USA	29.3.91	4	Mill	New York (Arm)	20 Feb
3:53.87	Cory	Leslie	USA	24.10.89	5	Mill	New York (Arm)	20 Feb
3:53.89#	Izaic	Yorks	USA	17.4.94	1		Seattle	27 Feb
3:53.95#	Sean	McGorty	USA	8.3.95	2		Seattle	27 Feb
3:54.02	Dawit	Wolde	ETH	19.5.91	1		Athlone	17 Feb
3:55.10	Garrett	Heath	USA	3.11.85	6	Mill	New York (Arm)	20 Feb
3:55.41	Bethwel	Birgen	KEN	6.8.88	2		Boston (R)	14 Feb

3:56.05	Cristian	Soratos	USA	26.9.92	20	Feb
3:56.36	Blake	Haney	USA	29.3.96	20	Feb
3:56.57	Johnny	Gregorek	USA	7.12.91	20	Feb
3:56.87	Justyn	Knight	CAN	19.7.96	30	Jan
3:56.91	Julian	Matthews	NZL	21.7.88	20	Feb
3:57.03	Thomas	Awad	USA	27.5.94	20	Feb
3:57.11#	Clayton	Murphy	USA	26.2.95	6	Feb
3:57.29	Sam	Penzenstadler	USA	11.9.92	6	Feb

3000 METRES

7:38.03	Dejen	Gebremeskel	ETH	24.11.89	1		Boston (All)	28 Feb
7:38.60	Ryan	Hill	USA	31.1.90	1	NC	Portland	11 Mar
7:38.85	Hassan	Mead	USA	28.8.89	2	Mill	New York (Arm)	20 Feb
7:39.00	Paul	Chelimo	USA	27.10.90	2	NC	Portland	11 Mar
7:39.04	Abdelaati	Iguider	MAR	25.3.87	1	Globen	Stockholm	17 Feb
7:39.11	Yomif	Kejelcha	ETH-J	1.8.97	2	Globen	Stockholm	17 Feb
7:39.23	Augustine	Choge	KEN	21.1.87	1		Düsseldorf	3 Feb
7:39.23	Mohamed	Al-Garni	QAT	2.7.92	1	AsiC	Doha	21 Feb
7:39.43	Eric	Jenkins	USA	24.11.91	3	Mill	New York (Arm)	20 Feb
7:39.55	Mohamed	Farah	GBR	23.3.83	1	GP	Glasgow	20 Feb
7:39.82	Caleb	Ndiku	KEN	9.10.92	2		Düsseldorf	3 Feb
7:40.10	Evan	Jager	USA	8.3.89	4	Mill	New York (Arm)	20 Feb
7:40.11	Mohammed	Ahmed	CAN	5.1.91	5	Mill	New York (Arm)	20 Feb
7:40.24	Yenew	Alamirew	ETH	27.5.90	3		Düsseldorf	3 Feb
7:40.27	Albert	Rop	BRN	17.7.92	2	AsiC	Doha	21 Feb
7:40.51	Edward	Cheserek	KEN	2.2.94	6	Mill	New York (Arm)	20 Feb
7:40.74	Matthew	Centrowitz	USA	18.10.89	1		Portland	5 Feb
7:40.79	Kemoy	Campbell	JAM	14.1.91	7	Mill	New York (Arm)	20 Feb
7:41.25	Bernard	Lagat	USA	12.12.74	4	NC	Portland	11 Mar
7:41.26	Garrett	Heath	USA	3.11.85	5	NC	Portland	11 Mar
7:41.69	Dawit	Wolde	ETH	19.5.91	3	GP	Glasgow	20 Feb
7:42.18	Yasin	Haji	ETH	22.1.96	5		Düsseldorf	3 Feb
7:42.33	Andy	Bayer	USA	3.2.90	8	Mill	New York (Arm)	20 Feb
7:42.47	Thomas	Farrell	GBR	23.3.91	3		Portland	5 Feb
7:42.53	Isiah	Koech	KEN	19.12.93	6		Düsseldorf	3 Feb
7:43.01	Lopez	Lomong	USA	1.1.85	9	Mill	New York (Arm)	20 Feb
7:43.04	Vincent	Rono	KEN	11.11.90	7		Düsseldorf	3 Feb
7:43.33	Trevor	Dunbar	USA	29.4.91	4		Portland	5 Feb
7:43.44	Youssouf	Hiss Bachir	DJI	.87	4	Globen	Stockholm	17 Feb
7:43.49	Bethwel	Birgen	KEN	6.8.88	3		Karlsruhe	6 Feb
7:44.29	Brett	Robinson	AUS	8.5.91	2		Boston (R)	14 Feb
7:44.50	Leul	Gebrselassie	ETH	20.9.93	1		Sabadell	19 Feb
7:44.69	Said	Aden Said	QAT	1.1.93	3	AsiC	Doha	21 Feb
7:44.87	Vincent	Kibet	KEN	6.5.91	5		Karlsruhe	6 Feb
7:44.96	Ben	Blankenship	USA	15.12.89	4	GP	Glasgow	20 Feb

7:45.07	Lawi	Lalang	KEN	15.6.91	14	Feb
7:45.09	Paul Kipsiele	Koech	KEN	10.11.81	3	Feb
7:45.15	Soufiyan	Bouqantar	MAR	30.8.93	19	Feb
7:45.44	Cam	Levins	CAN	28.3.89	20	Feb
7:46.15	Birhanu	Yemataw	BRN	27.2.96	19	Feb
7:46.24	Dejene	Debela	ETH	.95	19	Feb
7:46.72#	Jeff	See	USA	6.6.86	13	Feb
7:47.18	Donn	Cabral	USA	12.12.89	20	Feb
7:47.70	Mourad	Amdouni	FRA	21.1.88	21	Feb
7:48.34	Galen	Rupp	USA	8.5.86	11	Mar
7:48.55	Patrick	Tiernan	AUS	11.9.94	12	Feb
7:48.71#	Justyn	Knight	CAN	19.7.96	12	Feb
7:48.79#	Sean	McGorty	USA	8.3.95	12	Feb
7:48.89	William	Kincaid	USA		22	Jan
7:49.53	Antonio	Abadía	ESP	2.7.90	6	Feb

60 METRES HURDLES

7.41	Dimitri	Bascou	FRA	20.7.87	1	ISTAF	Berlin	13 Feb
7.41	Omar	McLeod	JAM	25.4.94	1	WI	Portland	20 Mar
7.46	Pascal	Martinot-Lagarde	FRA	22.9.91	2	WI	Portland	20 Mar
7.49	Orlando	Ortega	ESP	29.7.91	1		Düsseldorf	3 Feb
7.50	Jarret	Eaton	USA	24.6.89	4	WI	Portland	20 Mar
7.53	Ashton	Eaton	USA	21.1.88	2	Mill	New York (Arm)	20 Feb
7.53	Myles	Hunter	USA	16.8.95	1	NCAA-II	Pittsburg KS	12 Mar
7.55	Balázs	Baji	HUN	9.6.89	1h1	NC	Budapest	21 Feb
7.56	Devon	Allen	USA	12.12.94	1	NCAA	Birmingham	12 Mar
7.57	Jeff	Porter	USA	27.11.85	3		Jablonec nad Nisou	5 Mar

7.58	Greggmar	Swift	BAR	16.2.91	2	Pedros	Lódz	5 Feb
7.58A	Aries	Merritt	USA	24.7.85	1h3		Flagstaff	13 Feb
7.58	Jordan	Moore	USA	13.12.93	1h1	NCAA	Birmingham	11 Mar
7.58	Spencer	Adams	USA	10.9.89	2	NC	Portland	12 Mar
7.59	Terence	Somerville	USA	5.11.89	1		Bloomington, IN	30 Jan
7.60	Abdulaziz	Al-Mandeel	KUW	22.5.89	1	AsiC	Doha	21 Feb
7.61	Andy	Pozzi	GBR	15.5.92	1h1	South	London (LV)	17 Jan
7.61	Yordan	O'Farrill	CUB	9.2.93	2		Mondeville	6 Feb
7.61	Erik	Balnuweit	GER	21.9.88	1	NC	Leipzig	27 Feb
7.62	Garfield	Darien	FRA	22.12.87	3		Düsseldorf	3 Feb

7.63	Damian	Warner	CAN	4.11.89	30	Jan
7.63		Xie Wenjun	CHN	11.7.90	20	Feb
7.63	Eddie	Lovett	ISV	25.6.92	19	Mar
7.64	Yidiel	Contreras	ESP	27.11.91	5	Feb
7.64	Alexander	John	GER	3.5.86	27	Feb
7.64	Freddie	Crittenden	USA	3.8.94	12	Mar
7.64	Shane	Brathwaite	BAR	8.2.90	20	Mar
7.65	Aleec	Harris	USA	31.10.90	30	Jan
7.65	Lawrence	Clarke	GBR	12.3.90	13	Feb
7.65	Yaqoub	Al-Yoha	KUW	31.1.93	21	Feb
7.65	Ronald	Forbes	CAY	5.4.85	4	Mar
7.65	Artur	Noga	POL	2.5.88	6	Mar
7.66	David	King	GBR	13.6.94	13	Feb
7.66		Zhang Honglin	CHN	12.1.94	17	Feb
7.67	Koen	Smet	NED	9.8.92	6	Feb
7.67	Will	Barnes	USA	17.3.94	20	Feb
7.67	Konstantin	Shabanov	RUS	17.11.89	24	Feb
7.67	Martin	Vogel	GER	16.3.92	27	Feb
7.67	Mikel	Thomas	TTO	23.11.87	4	Mar
7.68	Simon	Krauss	FRA	12.2.92	16	Jan
7.68	Kevin	Craddock	USA	25.6.87	3	Feb
7.68	David	Omoregie	GBR	1.11.95	6	Feb
7.68	Dominik	Bochenek	POL	14.5.87	20	Feb
7.68	Fabio	dos Santos	BRA	11.10.83	27	Feb
7.69	Israel	Nelson	USA		29	Jan
7.69	Konstadínos	Douvalídis	GRE	10.3.87	3	Feb
7.69	Dondre	Echols	USA	6.7.93	12	Feb
7.69	Chad	Zallow	USA-J	25.4.97	19	Feb
7.69	Damien	Broothaerts	BEL	13.3.83	20	Feb
7.69	Andreas	Martinsen	DEN	17.7.90	21	Feb
7.69	Aaron	Mallett	USA	26.9.94	27	Feb
7.69	Francisco Javier	López	ESP	8.4.89	12	Mar

HIGH JUMP

2.38	Gianmarco	Tamberi	ITA	1.6.92	1		Hustopece	13 Feb
2.36	Mutaz Essa	Barshim	QAT	24.6.91	1		Malmö	13 Feb
2.36	Chris	Baker	GBR	2.2.91	2		Hustopece	13 Feb
2.35	Marco	Fassinotti	ITA	29.4.89	2		Banská Bystrica	4 Feb
2.33	Donald	Thomas	BAH	1.7.84	3		Banská Bystrica	4 Feb
2.33	Robbie	Grabarz	GBR	3.10.87	4		Banská Bystrica	4 Feb
2.33	Konstadínos	Baniótis	GRE	6.11.86	1	NC	Pireás	13 Feb
2.33	Erik	Kynard	USA	3.2.91	3	WI	Portland	19 Mar
2.32	Kyriakos	Ioannou	CYP	26.7.84	3		Hustopece	13 Feb
2.31	Eike	Onnen	GER	3.8.82	1		Hannover	22 Jan
2.31	Danyil	Lysenko	RUS-J	19.5.97	1		Moskva	29 Jan
2.31	Jamal	Wilson	BAH	1.9.88	1	Gugl	Linz	12 Feb
2.30	Daniyil	Tsyplakov	RUS	29.7.92	1		Volgograd	19 Jan
2.30	Matús	Bubeník	SVK	14.11.89	5		Banská Bystrica	4 Feb
2.30	Andrey	Churylo	BLR	19.5.93	1	NCp	Minsk	7 Feb
2.30	Edgar	Rivera	MEX	13.2.91	1		Brno	9 Feb
2.30	Silvano	Chesani	ITA	17.7.88	4		Hustopece	13 Feb
2.30A		Zhang Guowei	CHN	4.6.91	1		Flagstaff	19 Feb
2.30	Andrii	Protsenko	UKR	20.5.88	1		Metz	21 Feb
2.29	Mikhail	Veryovkin	RUS	28.6.91	1		Kineshma	6 Dec
2.29	Mateusz	Przybylko	GER	9.3.92	1		Leverkusen	16 Jan
2.29	Bradley	Adkins	USA	30.12.93	1	Tyson	Fayetteville	13 Feb
2.29	Jeron	Robinson	USA	30.4.91	1		Alamosa	20 Feb
2.29	Dmitriy	Nabokov	BLR	20.1.96	1	NC	Mogilyov	20 Feb
2.28	Dmitriy	Semyonov	RUS	2.8.92	2		Chelyabinsk	9 Jan
2.28	Aleksey	Dmitrik	RUS	12.4.84	1		Volgograd	6 Feb
2.28	Trevor	Barry	BAH	14.6.83	5		Hustopece	13 Feb
2.28	Sylwester	Bednarek	POL	28.4.89	6=		Hustopece	13 Feb
2.28	Jaroslav	Bába	CZE	2.9.84	6=		Hustopece	13 Feb
2.28	Vasilios	Constantinou	CYP	13.9.92	8		Hustopece	13 Feb
2.28	Majed El Dein	Ghazal	SYR	21.4.87	2	AsiC	Doha	19 Feb

2.27	Sergey	Mudrov	RUS	8.9.90	7	Jan
2.27A	Deante	Kemper	USA	27.3.93	19	Feb
2.27		Sun Zhao	CHN	8.2.90	8	Mar
2.26	Barry	Pender	IRL	2.4.90	10	Jan
2.26	Randall	Cunningham	USA	4.1.96	22	Jan
2.26	Allan	Smith	GBR	6.11.92	23	Jan
2.26	Wojciech	Theiner	POL	25.6.86	23	Jan
2.26	Marius	Dumitrache	ROU	15.6.89	30	Jan
2.26	Yuriy	Dergachev	KAZ	8.11.94	31	Jan
2.26A	Bryan	McBride	USA	10.12.91	5	Feb
2.26	Hiromi	Takahari	JPN	13.11.87	7	Feb
2.26	Mihai	Donisan	ROU	24.7.88	20	Feb
2.26	Yuriy	Krymarenko	UKR	11.8.83	27	Feb
2.25	Avion	Jones	USA	31.1.94	15	Jan
2.25	Ali Mohamed	Younes Idris	SUD	15.9.89	16	Jan
2.25		Yun Seung-hyun	KOR	1.6.94	23	Jan
2.25	Christoffe	Bryan	JAM	26.4.96	13	Feb
2.25	Ilya	Ivanyuk	RUS	9.3.93	14	Feb
2.25	Joel	Castro	PUR	28.1.91	21	Feb
2.25	Ivan	Ilyichev	RUS	14.10.86	24	Feb
2.25	Kyle	Landon	USA	16.10.94	28	Feb
2.25	Mikhail	Akimenko	RUS	6.12.95	2	Mar

POLE VAULT

6.03	Renaud	Lavillenie	FRA	18.9.86	1		Jablonec nad Nisou	5 Mar
6.00A	Shawnacy	Barber	CAN	27.5.94	1		Reno	15 Jan
5.93	Thiago Braz	da Silva	BRA	16.12.93	1	ISTAF	Berlin	13 Feb
5.90	Sam	Kendricks	USA	7.9.92	1	NC	Portland	11 Mar

5.84	Raphael	Holzdeppe	GER	28.9.89	1		Rouen	23 Jan
5.84	Konstadínos	Filippídis	GRE	26.11.86	3=		Clermont-Ferrand	21 Feb
5.84	Pawel	Wojciechowski	POL	6.6.89	5		Clermont-Ferrand	21 Feb
5.81		Xue Changrui	CHN	31.5.91	1		Orléans	16 Jan
5.80	Timur	Morgunov	RUS	27.10.96	1	NC-23	Volgograd	2 Mar
5.77A	Seito	Yamamoto	JPN	11.3.92	2		Reno	15 Jan
5.77	Kévin	Menaldo	FRA	12.7.92	3		Rouen	23 Jan
5.77	Carlo	Paech	GER	18.12.92	1		Potsdam	6 Feb
5.77	Jérôme	Clavier	FRA	3.5.83	2		Potsdam	6 Feb
5.77	Robert	Sobera	POL	19.1.91	1		Torun	12 Feb
5.77	Piotr	Lisek	POL	16.8.92	2		Torun	12 Feb
5.77A	Mike	Arnold	USA	13.8.90	1		Flagstaff	13 Feb
5.77	Jan	Kudlicka	CZE	29.4.88	1	NC	Ostrava	28 Feb
5.75		Huang Bokai	CHN	26.9.96	1	AsiC	Doha	20 Feb
5.72	Jake	Blankenship	USA	15.3.94	1		Blacksburg	6 Feb
5.70	Michal	Balner	CZE	12.9.82	3		Cottbus	27 Jan
5.70	Luke	Cutts	GBR	13.2.88	1		Cardiff	7 Feb
5.70	Georgiy	Gorokhov	RUS	20.4.93	1	Mosc Ch	Moskva	10 Feb
5.70	Pauls	Pujats	LAT	6.8.91	1		Black Springs	28 Feb
5.67	Jason	Colwick	USA	25.1.88	1		Houston	12 Feb
5.65A	Cale	Simmons	USA	5.2.91	1		Air Force Academy	23 Jan
5.65	Yevgeniy	Lukyanenko	RUS	23.1.85	1		Slavyansk-na-Kubani	31 Jan
5.65	Adam	Bragg	USA	18.4.93	1		Staten Island	12 Feb
5.64	Stanley	Joseph	FRA	24.10.91	3		Jablonec nad Nisou	5 Mar
5.64	Max	Eaves	GBR	31.5.88	4		Jablonec nad Nisou	5 Mar
5.63	Ivan	Horvat	CRO	17.8.93	1		Beograd	1 Mar
5.62	Valentin	Lavillenie	FRA	16.7.91	1		Lyon	6 Feb
5.62	Torben	Laidig	GER	13.3.94	2		Blacksburg	6 Feb
5.62	Drew	Volz	USA	20.11.92	1		Blacksburg	20 Feb
5.60	Scott	Houston	USA	11.6.90	2		Akron	9 Jan
5.60	Dimítrios	Patsoukákis	GRE	18.3.87	1		Pireás	30 Jan
5.60		Yao Jie	CHN	21.9.90	4		Karlsruhe	6 Feb
5.60	Baptiste	Boirie	FRA	26.12.92	1		Clermont-Ferrand	20 Feb
5.60	Florian	Gaul	GER	21.9.91	2		Chemnitz	20 Feb
5.60	Germán	Chiaraviglio	ARG	16.4.87	4	GP	Glasgow	20 Feb

5.57	Augusto	Dutra de Oliveira	BRA	16.7.90	21	Feb
5.56A	Dylan	Bell	USA	21.7.93	5	Feb
5.55A	Mark	Hollis	USA	1.12.84	15	Jan
5.55A	Hiroki	Ogita	JPN	30.12.87	15	Jan
5.55A	Victor	Weirich	USA	25.10.87	15	Jan
5.55	Menno	Vloon	NED	11.5.94	23	Jan
5.55A	Sam	Pierson	USA	7.4.88	23	Jan
5.55	Anton	Ivakin	RUS	3.2.91	31	Jan
5.55A	John	Prader	USA	10.2.91	19	Feb
5.54	Emmanouíl	Karális	GRE	20.10.99	5	Mar
5.53	Adam	Hague	GBR-J	29.8.97	7	Feb
5.53	Igor	Bychkov	ESP	7.3.87	26	Feb
5.53	Diogo	Ferreira	POR	30.7.90	26	Feb
5.53	Pau	Tonnesen	ESP	24.10.92	27	Feb
5.52	Jeff	Coover	USA	1.12.87	26	Feb
5.52	Luke	Winder	USA	2.8.95	11	Mar
5.51	Noël	Ost	FRA	15.11.89	18	Dec
5.51	Tobias	Scherbarth	GER	17.8.85	31	Jan
5.51	Daniel	Clemens	GER	28.4.92	31	Jan
5.51	João Gabriel	Sousa	BRA	6.11.84	13	Feb
5.51	Audie	Wyatt	USA	30.4.96	27	Feb
5.51	Tom	Konrad	GER	30.3.91	5	Mar
5.50	Ilya	Mudrov	RUS	17.11.91	26	Dec
5.50	Mikhail	Gelmanov	RUS	18.3.90	9	Jan
5.50	Anatoliy	Bednyuk	RUS	30.1.89	22	Jan
5.50	Leonid	Kivalov	RUS	1.4.88	22	Jan
5.50	Sergey	Grigoryev	KAZ	24.6.92	23	Jan
5.50	Aleksandr	Gripich	RUS	21.9.86	7	Feb
5.50	Edi	Maia	POR	10.11.87	20	Feb
5.50	Karsten	Dilla	GER	17.7.89	20	Feb
5.50	Leonid	Kobelev	RUS	24.6.95	24	Feb
5.50	Artem	Burya	RUS	11.4.86	24	Feb
5.50	Jax	Thoirs	GBR	7.4.93	11	Mar
5.50	Darren	Niedermeyer	USA	2.4.82	11	Mar
5.50	Joey	Uhle	USA	14.11.92	11	Mar
5.50	Zach	Siegmeier	USA	8.1.91	11	Mar

LONG JUMP

8.41	Marquis	Dendy	USA	17.11.92	1	NC	Portland	11 Mar
8.26A	Greg	Rutherford	GBR	17.11.86	1		Albuquerque	5 Feb
8.25	Bachana	Khorava	GEO	15.3.93	1	NC	Tbilisi	7 Feb
8.25	Fabrice	Lapierre	AUS	17.10.83	2	WI	Portland	20 Mar
8.23	Kafétien	Gomis	FRA	23.3.80	1	NC	Aubière	28 Feb
8.21		Huang Changzhou	CHN	20.8.94	3	WI	Portland	20 Mar
8.19	Jeffrey	Henderson	USA	19.2.89	4	WI	Portland	20 Mar
8.18		Wang Jianan	CHN	27.8.96	2	NGP	Nanjing	3 Mar
8.18	Rushwal	Samaai	RSA	25.9.91	5	WI	Portland	20 Mar
8.17	Jarrion	Lawson	USA	6.5.94	1		Fayetteville	29 Jan
8.17	Jonathan	Addison	USA	27.2.95	1		Blacksburg	5 Feb
8.14	Dan	Bramble	GBR	14.10.90	6	WI	Portland	20 Mar
8.12	Andreas	Otterling	SWE	25.5.86	1	Globen	Stockholm	17 Feb
8.09		Zhang Yaoguang	CHN	21.6.93	3	NGP	Nanjing	3 Mar
8.08	Vasiliy	Kopeykin	RUS	9.3.88	Q	NC	Moskva	24 Feb
8.08	Ashton	Eaton	USA	21.1.88	1H	WI	Portland	18 Mar
8.07	Kirill	Sukharev	RUS	24.5.92	1		Moskva	10 Jan
8.05	Marquise	Goodwin	USA	19.11.90	3	NC	Portland	11 Mar
8.03	Julian	Howard	GER	3.4.89	1		Karlsruhe	6 Feb
8.03	Radek	Juska	CZE	8.3.93	1		Jablonec nad Nisou	5 Mar

.02	Raihau	Maiau	PYF	1.8.92	1		Nantes	4 Feb
.01		Tang Gongchen	CHN	24.4.89	3	NGP	Nanjing	28 Feb
.01		Zhong Peifeng	CHN	3.3.97	4	NGP	Nanjing	3 Mar

.99		Li Chengbin	CHN	22.2.90	28 Feb
.98	Bilal	Abdullah	USA	6.10.93	16 Jan
.98	Damar	Forbes	JAM	11.9.90	19 Feb
.98		Gao Xinglong	CHN	12.3.94	20 Feb
.97	Sadeekie	Edie	JAM	28.10.93	11 Mar
.96	Pavel	Shalin	RUS	6.3.87	10 Jan
.96	Sergey	Polyanskiy	RUS	29.10.89	31 Jan
.94	Stefano	Tremigliozzi	ITA	7.5.85	24 Jan
.94	Dmitriy	Sorokin	RUS	27.9.92	31 Jan
.94	Emiliano	Lasa	URU	25.1.90	20 Mar
.93	KeAndre	Bates	USA	24.5.96	29 Jan
.93	Pavel	Karavayev	RUS	27.8.88	9 Feb
7.93	Tomasz	Jaszczuk	POL	9.3.92	17 Feb
7.93	Rayvon	Grey	USA	2.12.97	12 Mar
7.92	Steven	Barze	USA	.95	8 Jan
7.92	Kumaravel	Premkumar	IND	6.2.93	21 Feb
7.91	Aleksandr	Petrov	RUS	19.8.86	10 Jan
7.91	Grant	Holloway	USA-J	19.11.97	30 Jan
7.91	Lutalo	Boyce	USA	11.8.91	13 Feb
7.91	Maksim	Kolesnikov	RUS	28.2.91	25 Feb
7.91	Serhiy	Nykyforov	UKR	6.2.94	26 Feb
7.90	Maksim	Yunyakin	RUS	13.2.96	2 Mar
7.90	Damarcus	Simpson	USA	14.7.93	11 Mar

TRIPLE JUMP

7.41		Dong Bin	CHN	22.11.88	1	NGP	Nanjing	29 Feb
7.14	Max	Hess	GER	13.7.96	2	WI	Portland	19 Mar
7.12	Lyukman	Adams	RUS	24.9.88	1		Orenburg	16 Mar
7.09	Benjamin	Compaoré	FRA	5.8.87	3	WI	Portland	19 Mar
7.06	Chris	Carter	USA	11.3.89	1	NC	Portland	12 Mar
7.05	Dmitriy	Sorokin	RUS	27.9.92	1		Sankt Peterburg	7 Feb
7.03	Eric	Sloan	USA	20.6.94	1	Tyson	Fayetteville	13 Feb
6.99	Alexis	Copello	CUB	12.8.85	1		Karlsruhe	6 Feb
6.98	Teddy	Tamgho	FRA	15.6.89	1	NC	Aubière	28 Feb
6.96	Omar	Craddock	USA	26.4.91	2	NC	Portland	12 Mar
6.93	Chris	Benard	USA	4.4.90	3	NC	Portland	12 Mar
6.91	Harold	Correa	FRA	26.6.88	2	NC	Aubière	28 Feb
6.89	Nelson	Évora	POR	20.4.84	4	WI	Portland	19 Mar
6.87	Roman	Valiyev	KAZ	27.3.84	1	NC	Ust-Kamenogorsk	31 Jan
6.85	Dmitriy	Chizhikov	RUS	6.12.93	2		Sankt Peterburg	7 Feb
6.82	Marian	Oprea	ROU	6.6.82	1	NC	Bucuresti	20 Feb
6.82	Fabrizio	Schembri	ITA	27.1.81	1	NC	Ancona	5 Mar
6.80	Donald	Scott	USA	23.2.92	1		Notre Dame	6 Feb
6.75	Troy	Doris	USA	12.4.89	1		New York (Arm)	4 Mar
6.74	Fabrizio	Donato	ITA	14.8.76	2	NC	Ancona	5 Mar
6.73	Tosin	Oke	NGR	1.10.80	6	WI	Portland	19 Mar
6.72	Aleksey	Fyodorov	RUS	25.5.91	4		Sankt Peterburg	7 Feb
6.71		Liu Ruihai	CHN	23.12.96	2	NGP	Nanjing	29 Feb
6.68	Pablo	Torrijos	ESP	12.5.92	1		Valencia	13 Feb
6.68	Jeremiah	Green	USA	9.2.94	2		Fayetteville	13 Feb
6.67	Jonathan	Drack	MRI	6.11.88	2		Karlsruhe	6 Feb
6.66	Matthew	O'Neal	USA	10.6.94	1		Boston (R)	22 Jan
6.64	Clive	Pullen	JAM	18.10.94	1	NCAA	Birmingham	12 Mar
6.62	Lasha	Torgvaidze	GEO	26.5.93	1		Tbilisi	24 Jan
6.62	Simone	Forte	ITA	20.1.96	3	NC	Ancona	5 Mar
6.61	Seref	Osmanoglu	TUR	2.1.89	1	NC	Sumy	27 Feb

6.59	Rumen	Dimitrov	BUL	19.9.86	31 Jan
6.59	Karol	Hoffmann	POL	1.6.89	20 Feb
6.58	Jean-Marc	Pontvianne	FRA	6.8.94	21 Feb
6.56		Cao Shuo	CHN	8.10.91	29 Feb
6.55	Yevgeniy	Ektov	KAZ	1.9.86	31 Jan
6.54	Sergey	Laptev	RUS	7.2.91	16 Mar
16.51		Wu Ruiting	CHN	29.11.95	29 Feb
16.50	Nazim	Babayev	AZE-J	8.10.97	29 Jan
16.47	Adrian	Swiderski	POL	27.9.86	27 Feb
16.46		Xu Xiaolong	CHN	20.12.92	29 Feb
16.45	Kevin	Luron	FRA	8.11.91	7 Feb
16.45	Maksim	Nesterenko	BLR	1.9.92	20 Feb

SHOT

21.78	Tom	Walsh	NZL	1.3.92	1	WI	Portland	18 Mar
21.73	Ryan	Crouser	USA	18.12.92	1	Big 12	Ames	27 Feb
21.57	Kurt	Roberts	USA	20.2.88	1		Boston (R)	14 Feb
21.35	Michal	Haratyk	POL	10.4.92	1	Pedros	Lódz	5 Feb
21.33	Tim	Nedow	CAN	16.10.90	1	Globen	Stockholm	17 Feb
21.30	Tomás	Stanek	CZE	13.6.91	1		Jablonec nad Nisou	5 Mar
21.11	Stephen	Mozia	NGR	16.8.93	1		Nashville	30 Jan
21.02	Reese	Hoffa	USA	8.10.77	2		Boston (R)	14 Feb
20.89	Andrei	Gag	ROU	27.4.91	2	WI	Portland	18 Mar
20.88	Konstantin	Lyadusov	RUS	2.3.88	1	NC	Moskva	24 Feb
20.87	Filip	Mihaljevic	CRO	31.7.94	3	WI	Portland	18 Mar
20.82	Jon	Jones	USA	23.4.91	1		University Park	30 Jan
20.70	Pavel	Lyzhyn	BLR	24.3.81	1		Mogilyov	22 Jan
20.62	Ivan	Emilianov	MDA	19.2.77	1	NC	Chisinau	6 Feb
20.61	Stipe	Zunic	CRO	13.12.90	1		Slovenska Bistrica	13 Jan
20.61	Konrad	Bukowiecki	POL-J	17.3.97	2		Madrid	26 Feb
20.56	Tobias	Dahm	GER	23.5.87	1		Sassnitz	14 Feb
20.53	Frank	Elemba	CGO	21.7.90	3		Karlsruhe	6 Feb
20.53	Maksim	Sidorov	RUS	13.5.86	1		Moskva	14 Feb
20.51	Ivan	Ivanov	KAZ	3.1.92	1	NC	Ust-Kamenogorsk	30 Jan

20.50	Carlos	Tobalina	ESP	2.8.85	1	NC	Madrid	5 Ma
20.46	Mustafa Amer	Ahmed Hassan	EGY	16.12.95	1		Golden	12 De
20.41	Tomasz	Majewski	POL	30.8.81	3		Torun	12 Fe
20.37	Rafał	Kownatke	POL	24.3.85	1	NC	Torun	6 Ma
20.36	Nikólaos	Skarvélis	GRE	2.2.93	1		Flagstaff	16 Ja
20.29	Germán	Lauro	ARG	2.4.84	4		Madrid	26 Fe
20.26	Aleksandr	Lesnoy	RUS	28.7.88	1		Volgograd	19 Ja
20.22	Tsanko	Arnaudov	POR	14.3.92	1		Pombal	7 Fe
20.22	Mesud	Pezer	BIH	27.8.94	2	BalkC	Istanbul	27 Fe
20.19	JC	Murasky	USA	6.2.93	1	Big 10	Geneva	26 Fe
20.19	Borja	Vivas	ESP	26.5.84	2	NC	Madrid	5 Ma
20.18	Mikalai	Abramchuk	BLR	22.9.92	1		Minsk	28 Ja
20.07	Jacob	Thormaehlen	USA	13.2.90	1		Houston	15 Ja
20.06	Ashinia	Miller	JAM	6.6.93	1	SEC	Fayetteville	27 Fe
20.00	Leif	Arrhenius	SWE	15.7.86	1		Ogden	29 Ja

19.96	Rob	Golabek	USA	27.4.89	19 Feb
19.95	Chuk	Enekwechi	USA	28.1.93	12 Mar
19.93	Curtis	Jensen	USA	1.11.90	9 Jan
19.93	Jacko	Gill	NZL	20.12.94	18 Mar
19.87	Nick	Vena	USA	16.4.93	11 Dec
19.81	Paul	Davis	USA	11.9.90	29 Jan
19.80	Andrei	Toader	ROU-J	26.5.97	9 Jan
19.67	Josh	Freeman	USA	22.8.94	16 Jan
19.64	Jordan	Clarke	USA	10.7.90	19 Feb
19.56	Aleksandr	Bulanov	RUS	26.12.89	14 Feb
19.55	Garrett	Appier	USA	15.10.92	5 Dec
19.54	Arttu	Kangas	FIN	13.7.93	13 Feb
19.48	Luke	Johnson	USA	10.7.92	13 Feb
19.48	Matt	DeChant	USA	31.5.89	12 Mar
19.48	Bob	Bertemes	LUX	24.5.93	18 Mar
19.45	Aleksey	Nichypor	BLR	10.4.93	25 Feb
19.45	Braheme	Days	USA	18.1.95	27 Feb
19.44	Soslan	Tsirikhov	RUS	24.11.84	14 Feb
19.44	Georgi	Ivanov	BUL	13.3.85	27 Feb
19.43	Nick	Ponzio	USA	4.1.95	16 Jan
19.42	Sergey	Dementyev	UZB	1.6.90	11 Feb
19.40	Sebastiano	Bianchetti	ITA	20.1.96	6 Feb
19.39	Frederic	Dagee	FRA	11.12.92	5 Mar
19.37	Richard	Garrett	USA	21.12.90	29 Jan
19.36	Martin	Novák	CZE	5.10.92	28 Feb
19.35	Daniele	Secci	ITA	9.3.92	6 Mar
19.34	Colt	Feltes	USA	8.4.93	12 Mar
19.30		Liu Yang	CHN	29.10.86	21 Feb
19.30	Gaëtan	Bucki	FRA	9.5.80	27 Feb
19.29	Nick	Baatz	USA	4.1.90	4 Dec
19.29		Tian Zhizhong	CHN	15.12.92	28 Jan
19.29	Denzel	Comenentia	NED	25.11.95	12 Mar
19.28	Jan Josef	Jeuschede	GER	23.4.93	27 Feb
19.25	Nicolai	Ceban	MDA	4.2.95	13 Feb
19.20	Luke	Pinkelman	USA	5.5.88	6 Feb
19.20	Coy	Blair	USA	10.6.94	20 Feb

DISCUS

64.91	Robert	Harting	GER	18.10.84	1	ISTAF	Berlin	13 Feb
64.34	Christoph	Harting	GER	4.10.90	2	ISTAF	Berlin	13 Feb
64.16	Philip	Milanov	BUL	6.7.91	3	ISTAF	Berlin	13 Feb
63.60	Axel	Härstedt	SWE	28.2.87	1		Växjö	5 Ma
63.40	Fedrick	Dacres	JAM	28.2.94	4	ISTAF	Berlin	13 Feb

61.45	Martin	Wierig	GER	10.6.87	3 Feb
61.09	Daniel	Ståhl	SWE	27.8.92	6 Feb

35 LB WEIGHT

23.96	Colin	Dunbar	USA	27.6.88	1	NC	Portland	11 Ma
23.89	Chuk	Enekwechi	USA	28.1.93	1		West Lafayette	13 Feb
23.80	Alex	Young	USA	1.9.94	1	NCAA	Birmingham	11 Ma
23.69	Michael	Lihrman	USA	6.12.91	9		Madison	19 Feb
23.65	A.G.	Kruger	USA	18.2.79	1		Ames	12 Feb
23.54	Cameron	Brown	USA	15.3.94	3	NCAA	Birmingham	11 Ma
23.05	Sean	Donnelly	USA	1.4.93	3	NC	Portland	11 Ma
22.82	Rudy	Winkler	USA	6.12.94	1		University Park	5 Feb
22.59	Tom	Postema	USA	17.7.89	1		Findlay	12 Feb
22.55	Greg	Skipper	USA	26.3.93	4	NCAA	Birmingham	11 Ma
22.42	Darien	Thornton	USA	14.7.94	1		Allendale	30 Jan

22.06	Bradley	Sauer	USA	21.5.93	29 Jan
21.92	Andrew	Wells	CAN	6.8.91	25 Feb
21.88	Joe	Frye	USA	20.7.88	11 Mar
21.85	Brian	Waterfield	USA	25.2.93	19 Feb
21.84	Jordan	Crayon	USA		12 Feb
21.84	Anthony	Jones	USA		12 Feb
21.84	Paul	Wagner	USA	23.2.88	4 Mar
21.80	Rob	Klenk	USA	25.2.85	11 Mar

HEPTATHLON

6470	Ashton	Eaton	USA	21.1.88	1	WI	Portland	19 Ma
	6.81	8.08	14.16	1.99	7.78	5.10	2:35.22	
6182	Oleksiy	Kasyanov	UKR	26.8.85	2	WI	Portland	19 Ma
	6.86	7.49	14.53	1.99	7.91	4.90	2:39.64	
6173	Zach	Ziemek	USA	23.2.93	1	NCAA	Birmingham	12 Ma
	6.75	7.48	14.53	2.04	8.31	5.40	2:53.53	
6126	Mathias	Brugger	GER	6.8.92	3	WI	Portland	19 Ma
	7.15	7.30	14.47	2.05	8.24	5.10	2:34.10	
6118	Curtis	Beach	USA	22.7.90	4	WI	Portland	19 Ma
	7.04	7.65	13.12	2.02	8.45	5.00	2:29.04	
6111	Kai	Kazmirek	GER	28.1.91	1		Tallinn	14 Feb
	7.04	7.47	14.53	2.08	8.02	4.85	2:43.47	
6076	Jorge	Ureña	ESP	8.10.93	1	v3N	Reims	30 Jan
	7.01	7.21	13.52	2.03	7.83	5.02	2:41.10	
6037	Ilya	Shkurenyov	RUS	11.1.91	1	NC	Smolensk	20 Feb
	7.14	7.36	14.12	2.04	8.06	5.30	2:50.85	

Mark	First name	Surname	Nat	Born	Pos	Meet	Venue	Date
6027	Pau	Tonnesen	ESP	24.10.92	2	NCAA	Birmingham	12 Mar
	7.25	7.54 14.57	2.01	8.24		5.30	2:48.29	
6020	Garrett	Scantling	USA	19.5.93	1		Fayetteville	30 Jan
	6.99	7.10 15.54	2.02	7.96		5.10	2:54.57	
6015	Mihail	Dudas	SRB	1.11.89	1	NC	Beograd	6 Mar
	7.11	7.52 14.10	2.04	8.08		4.80	2:42.51	
6003	Adam Sebastian	Helcelet	CZE	27.10.91	5	WI	Portland	19 Mar
	7.05	7.19 14.96	2.02	8.04		4.90	2:45.06	
5986	Kurt	Felix	GRN	4.7.88	6	WI	Portland	19 Mar
	7.00	7.45 15.02	2.11	8.34		4.50	2:44.23	
5965	Jérémy	Lelièvre	FRA	8.2.91	1	NC	Aubière	28 Feb
	6.99	7.32 15.02	1.96	8.24		4.65	2:37.28	
5964A	Japheth	Cato	USA	25.12.90	1		Albuquerque	6 Feb
	7.07	7.51 13.03	2.13	8.20		5.10	2:56.16	
5958	Sergey	Timshin	RUS	25.11.92	2	NC	Smolensk	20 Feb
	7.04	7.13 14.58	2.10	8.13		4.90	2:50.95	
5937	Harrison	Williams	USA	7.3.96	4	NCAA	Birmingham	12 Mar
	6.96	6.89 13.51	1.98	8.12		5.10	2:39.75	
5919	Luca	Wieland	GER	7.12.94	5	NCAA	Birmingham	12 Mar
	6.87	7.53 13.90	1.98	8.23		5.00	2:55.77	
5900	Bilal	Abdullah	USA	6.10.93	6	NCAA	Birmingham	12 Mar
	6.92	7.43 12.27	2.10	7.86		4.70	2:54.85	
5889	Yevgeniy	Sarantsev	RUS	5.2.88	3	NC	Smolensk	20 Feb
	7.24	7.07 15.52	2.07	8.29		5.10	2:54.53	
5889	Samuel	Remédios	POR	24.2.92	1	NC	Pombal	21 Feb
	6.91	7.37 13.11	1.96	8.09		4.85	2:46.15	

Mark	First name	Surname	Nat	Born	Date	Mark	First name	Surname	Nat	Born	Date
5856	Karl-Robert	Saluri	EST	6.8.93	12 Mar	5820	Axel	Martin	FRA	13.4.94	7 Feb
5854	Maicel	Uibo	EST	27.12.92	30 Jan	5811	Maxime	Maugein	FRA	27.9.92	28 Feb
5852	Artem	Lukyanenko	RUS	30.1.90	20 Feb	5810	Steven	Bastien	USA	4.3.94	12 Mar
5837	Petter	Olson	SWE	14.2.91	14 Feb	5808	Mikk	Meerents	EST	26.7.91	14 Feb
5832	Tim	Nowak	GER	13.8.95	19 Mar	5783#	Steele	Wasik	USA	8.12.95	27 Feb
5831	Akihiko	Nakamura	JPN	23.10.90	21 Feb	5776	Lindon	Victor	GRN	28.2.93	27 Feb
5829	Ruben	Gado	FRA	13.12.93	28 Feb	5762	Dylan	Anderson	USA	25.7.92	12 Mar
5825	Basile	Rolnin	FRA	21.1.94	7 Feb	5758	Liam	Ramsay	GBR	18.11.92	10 Jan
5824	Roman	Kondratyev	RUS	15.5.95	20 Feb	5745		Hu Yufei	CHN	9.11.93	21 Feb

3000 METRES WALK

Mark	First name	Surname	Nat	Born	Pos	Meet	Venue	Date
10:58.21	Tom	Bosworth	GBR	17.1.90	1	NC	Sheffield	28 Feb
11:25.57+	Grzegorz	Sudol	POL	28.8.78	3	in 5k	Bratislava	31 Jan

5000 METRES WALK

Mark	First name	Surname	Nat	Born	Pos	Meet	Venue	Date
18:44.32	Christopher	Linke	GER	24.10.88	1	NC	Erfurt	14 Feb
18:46.77	Nils	Brembach	GER	23.2.93	2	NC	Erfurt	14 Feb
18:47.55	Ruslan	Dmytrenko	UKR	22.3.86	1		Kyiv	8 Jan
18:51.9	Vasiliy	Mizinov	RUS-J	29.12.97	1		Chelyabinsk	6 Jan
18:54.18	Tom	Bosworth	GBR	17.1.90	1		Bratislava	31 Jan
18:54.32	Hagen	Pohle	GER	5.3.92	3	NC	Erfurt	14 Feb
19:08.74	Aléxandros	Papamihaíl	GRE	18.9.88	1	NC	Pireás	13 Feb
19:09.62	Grzegorz	Sudol	POL	28.8.78	2		Bratislava	31 Jan
19:12.00	Francesco	Fortunato	ITA	13.12.94	1	NC	Ancona	5 Mar

Mark	First name	Surname	Nat	Born	Date	Mark	First name	Surname	Nat	Born	Date
19:13.25	Ihor	Hlavan	UKR	25.9.90	8 Jan	19:23.07	Leonardo	Dei Tos	ITA	27.4.92	20 Feb
19:19.83	Robert	Heffernan	IRL	20.2.78	31 Jan	19:25.42	Matej	Tóth	SVK	10.2.83	31 Jan

10,000m Walk: 40:12.56 Aleksandr Lyakhovich BLR 4.7.89 1 NC Mogilyov 20 Feb

WORLD INDOOR LISTS 2016 – WOMEN

60 METRES

Mark	First name	Surname	Nat	Born	Pos	Meet	Venue	Date
7.00	Dafne	Schippers	NED	15.6.92	1	ISTAF	Berlin	13 Feb
7.00	Barbara	Pierre	USA	28.4.87	1	NC	Portland	12 Mar
7.04	Elaine	Thompson	JAM	28.6.92	1s3	WI	Portland	19 Mar
7.06	Marie Josée	Ta Lou	CIV	18.11.88	2	ISTAF	Berlin	13 Feb
7.07	Ewa	Swoboda	POL-J	26.7.97	1		Torun	12 Feb
7.07	Tatjana	Pinto	GER	2.7.92	1	NC	Leipzig	27 Feb
7.09	Michelle-Lee	Ahye	TTO	10.4.92	1h4	WI	Portland	19 Mar
7.10	Asha	Philip	GBR	25.10.90	1	NC	Sheffield	27 Feb
7.11	Dina	Asher-Smith	GBR	4.12.95	3		Karlsruhe	6 Feb
7.11	Teahna	Daniels	USA-J	27.3.97	1	NCAA	Birmingham	12 Mar
7.11	Tori	Bowie	USA	27.8.90	2s2	WI	Portland	19 Mar
7.12	Stella	Akakpo	FRA	28.2.94	2		Metz	21 Feb
7.12	Hannah	Cunliffe	USA	9.1.96	1h2	NCAA	Birmingham	11 Mar
7.14	Simone	Facey	JAM	7.5.85	1		Eaubonne	9 Feb
7.14	Jamile	Samuel	NED	24.4.92	2h2	ISTAF	Berlin	13 Feb
7.15	Natasha	Morrison	JAM	17.11.92	1s1		Houston	12 Feb
7.15	English	Gardner	USA	22.4.92	1		Boston (R)	14 Feb
7.15	Allyson	Felix	USA	18.11.85	1	Mill	New York (Arm)	20 Feb

7.16	Rebekka	Haase	GER	2.1.93	1		Leipzig	13 Feb
7.16	Kelly-Ann	Baptiste	TTO	14.10.86	4s1	WI	Portland	19 Mar
7.17	Shayla	Sanders	USA	6.1.94	1		Fayetteville	30 Jan
7.17	Rosângela	Santos	BRA	20.12.90	4	ISTAF	Berlin	13 Feb
7.17		Wei Yongli	CHN	11.10.91	1	NGP	Nanjing	28 Feb
7.17	Ezinne	Okparaebo	NOR	3.3.88	1	NC	Rud	5 Mar
7.17	Mikiah	Brisco	USA	14.7.96	3	NCAA	Birmingham	12 Mar
7.17	Tianna	Bartoletta	USA	30.8.85	3	NC	Portland	12 Mar
7.18	Nataliya	Pohrebnyak	UKR	19.2.88	1		Zaporizhzhya	27 Jan
7.18	Carole	Zahi	FRA	12.6.94	2	NC	Aubière	27 Feb
7.18	Jenna	Prandini	USA	20.11.92	4	NC	Portland	12 Mar
7.19	Carina	Horn	RSA	9.3.89	5	ISTAF	Berlin	13 Feb
7.19	Morolake	Akinosun	USA	17.5.94	4h2	NCAA	Birmingham	11 Mar
7.19	Jasmine	Todd	USA	23.12.93	4	NCAA	Birmingham	12 Mar
7.19	Mikele	Barber	USA	4.10.80	5	NC	Portland	12 Mar

7.20	Kristina	Sivkova	RUS-J	28.2.97	7 Jan
7.20	Olesya	Povh	UKR	18.10.87	16 Jan
7.20	Viktoriya	Zyabkina	KAZ	4.9.92	29 Jan
7.20	Kerron	Stewart	JAM	16.4.84	28 Feb
7.20	Tahesia	Harrigan	IVB	15.2.82	4 Mar
7.20	Marika	Popowicz-Drapala	POL	28.4.88	5 Mar
7.20	Javianne	Oliver	USA	26.12.94	11 Mar
7.21	Mujinga	Kambundji	SUI	17.6.92	27 Feb
7.21	Angela	Tenorio	ECU	27.1.96	19 Mar
7.22	Alex	Anderson	USA	28.1.87	30 Jan
7.22	Dezerea	Bryant	USA	27.4.93	12 Mar
7.23	Tawanna	Meadows	USA	4.8.86	9 Feb
7.23	Crystal	Emmanuel	CAN	27.11.91	12 Feb
7.23	Flings	Owusu-Agyapong	GHA	16.10.88	20 Feb
7.23	Felicia	Brown	USA	27.10.93	26 Feb
7.23		Liang Xiaojing	CHN-J	7.4.97	3 Mar
7.24	Myasia	Jacobs	USA	8.1.94	27 Feb
7.24	Maja	Mihalinec	SLO	17.12.89	5 Mar
7.25	Khamica	Bingham	CAN	15.6.94	20 Feb

200 METRES

22.45	Felicia	Brown	USA	27.10.93	1	SEC	Fayetteville	27 Feb
22.72	Kyra	Jefferson	USA	23.9.94	1		Fayetteville	29 Jan
22.85	Hannah	Cunliffe	USA	9.1.96	2	NCAA	Birmingham	12 Mar
22.92	Jada	Martin	USA	8.6.95	1rB	SEC	Fayetteville	27 Feb
22.98	Deajah	Stevens	USA	19.5.95	1h3	NCAA	Birmingham	11 Mar
22.99	Taylor	Ellis-Watson	USA	6.5.93	1h5	SEC	Fayetteville	26 Feb
23.03A	Deanna	Hill	USA	13.4.96	2		Albuquerque	5 Feb
23.05	Daye Shon	Roberson	USA	3.7.95	3rB	NCAA	Birmingham	12 Mar
23.08	Kali	Davis-White	USA	27.10.94	4rB	NCAA	Birmingham	12 Mar
23.10	Robin	Reynolds	USA	22.2.94	2rC		Fayetteville	13 Feb
23.10	Rebekka	Haase	GER	2.1.93	1	NC	Leipzig	28 Feb
23.11	Tynia	Gaither	BAH	16.3.93	1		Fayetteville	13 Feb

23.19	Michelle-Lee	Ahye	TTO	10.4.92	12 Dec
23.19	Ashley	Spencer	USA	8.6.93	6 Feb
23.19	Diamond	Spaulding	USA	29.9.96	27 Feb
23.20	Shakima	Wimbley	USA	23.4.95	13 Feb
23.23	Floria	Guei	FRA	2.5.90	31 Jan
23.23	LaurenRain	Williams	USA-Y	25.7.99	13 Mar
23.24	Taylor	Bennett	USA-J	15.1.97	19 Feb
23.25	Viktoriya	Zyabkina	KAZ	4.9.92	30 Jan
23.26	A'Keyla	Mitchell	USA	25.11.95	11 Mar
23.27	Stella	Akakpo	FRA	28.2.94	28 Feb
23.28	Phyllis	Francis	USA	4.5.92	6 Feb
23.28	Léa	Sprunger	SUI	5.3.90	28 Feb
23.30	Aaliyah	Brown	USA	6.1.95	6 Feb
23.30	Quanera	Hayes	USA	7.3.92	12 Feb
23.30	Lisa	Mayer	GER	2.5.96	28 Feb

Oversized track

Big 12 Ames 27 Feb: 1. Courtney Okolo 22.79, 2. Taylor Bennett USA-J 15.1.97 23.08, 3. A'Keyla Mitchell USA 23.16

300 METRES

36.25	Natasha	Hastings	USA	23.7.86	1		Boston (R)	14 Feb
36.46	Floria	Guei	FRA	2.5.90	1		Metz	21 Feb

36.94	Jessica	Beard	USA	8.1.89	14 Feb
37.12	Felicia	Brown	USA	27.10.93	11 Dec
37.47	Brianne	Theisen-Eaton	CAN	18.12.88	14 Feb
37.47	Justyna	Swiety	POL	3.12.92	27 Feb

400 METRES

50.69	Courtney	Okolo	USA	15.3.94	1	NCAA	Birmingham	12 Mar
51.09	Quanera	Hayes	USA	7.3.92	1	NC	Portland	12 Mar
51.29	Ashley	Spencer	USA	8.6.93	2	NC	Portland	12 Mar
51.34	Natasha	Hastings	USA	23.7.86	3	NC	Portland	12 Mar
51.45	Kemi	Adekoya	BRN	16.1.93	1	WI	Portland	19 Mar
51.51	Taylor	Ellis-Watson	USA	6.5.93	1rB	NCAA	Birmingham	12 Mar
51.60	Seren	Bundy-Davies	GBR	30.12.94	1		Wien	30 Jan
51.69	Chris-Ann	Gordon	JAM	18.9.94	2	NCAA	Birmingham	12 Mar
51.70	Antonina	Krivoshapka	RUS	21.7.87	1		Volgograd	6 Feb
51.74	Shamier	Little	USA	20.3.95	3	NCAA	Birmingham	12 Mar
51.84	Sydney	McLaughlin	USA-Y	7.8.99	1	N.Sch	New York (Arm)	13 Mar
51.91	Stephenie Ann	McPherson	JAM	25.11.88	3s2	WI	Portland	18 Mar
52.08	Phyllis	Francis	USA	4.5.92	4	NC	Portland	12 Mar
52.12	Margaret	Bamgbose	USA	19.10.93	2rB	NCAA	Birmingham	12 Mar
52.19	Kyra	Jefferson	USA	23.9.94	1rB		Fayetteville	12 Feb
52.22	Jaide	Stepter	USA	25.4.94	3rB	NCAA	Birmingham	12 Mar

52.27	Robin	Reynolds	USA	22.2.94	12 Feb
52.30	Justyna	Swiety	POL	3.12.92	6 Mar
52.34	Briana	Haith	USA	8.6.94	27 Feb
52.34	Zuzana	Hejnová	CZE	19.12.86	28 Feb
52.34	Lilla	McMillan	USA	31.8.94	29 Feb
52.36	Léa	Sprunger	SUI	5.3.90	31 Jan
52.39	Claudia	Francis	USA	14.11.93	12 Feb
52.40	Jasmine	Blocker	USA	8.3.95	29 Feb
52.43	Carly	Muscaro	USA	18.5.95	27 Feb
52.49	Lisanne	de Witte	NED	10.9.92	20 Feb

2.49	Felicia	Majors	USA	2.12.95	27	Feb
2.52	Amalie	Iuel	NOR	17.4.94	12	Feb
2.59	Sara Slott	Petersen	DEN	9.4.87	13	Feb
2.59	Kiara	Porter	USA	22.10.93	28	Feb
2.60	Aliyah	Abrams	USA-J	3.4.97	26	Feb
2.62	Daye Shon	Roberson	USA	3.7.95	23	Jan
2.63	Shakima	Wimbley	USA	23.4.95	27	Feb
2.68	Mupopo	Kabange	ZAM	21.9.92	18	Mar
52.69	Daina	Harper	USA	26.6.95	27	Feb
52.73	Malgorzata	Holub	POL	30.10.92	18	Mar
52.75	Marie	Gayot	FRA	18.12.89	21	Feb

Oversized track

52.34	Carly	Muscaro	USA	18.5.95	12	Mar
52.36	Elexis	Guster	USA	7.7.94	27	Feb
52.48	Brionna	Thomas	USA	21.3.96	27	Feb
52.56	Micha	Powell	CAN	.95	27	Feb

500 METRES

:09.35	Carly	Muscaro	USA	18.5.95	1		Boston (All)	6 Feb
:09.44	Georganne	Moline	USA	6.3.90	1		New York (Arm)	5 Feb

600 METRES

:26.34#	Raevyn	Rogers	USA	7.9.96	1		Seattle	16 Jan
:26.70A	Georganne	Moline	USA	6.3.90	1		Albuquerque	12 Feb

800 METRES

:00.01	Francine	Niyonsaba	BDI	5.5.93	1	WI	Portland	20 Mar
:00.09	Ajee'	Wilson	USA	8.5.94	1	Mill	New York (Arm)	20 Feb
:00.12	Joanna	Józwik	POL	30.1.91	1		Torun	12 Feb
:00.14	Brenda	Martinez	USA	8.9.87	2	Mill	New York (Arm)	20 Feb
:00.19	Melissa	Bishop	CAN	5.8.88	1	GP	Glasgow	20 Feb
:00.30	Lynsey	Sharp	GBR	11.7.90	1		Boston (All)	12 Feb
:00.36	Nataliya	Lupu	UKR	4.11.87	2		Torun	12 Feb
:00.44	Margaret	Wambui	KEN	15.9.95	3	WI	Portland	20 Mar
:00.49	Laura	Roesler	USA	19.12.91	3	Mill	New York (Arm)	20 Feb
:00.70	Laura	Muir	GBR	9.5.93	2	GP	Glasgow	20 Feb
:00.90	Raevyn	Rogers	USA	7.9.96	4	Mill	New York (Arm)	20 Feb
:00.93	Christina	Hering	GER	9.10.94	4	GP	Glasgow	20 Feb
:00.96	Malika	Akkaoui	MAR	25.12.87	2		Metz	21 Feb
:01.31	Habitam	Alemu	ETH-J	9.7.97	1		Eaubonne	9 Feb
:01.31	Selina	Büchel	SUI	26.7.91	5	GP	Glasgow	20 Feb
:01.59	Aníta	Hinriksdóttir	ISL	13.1.96	1	v3N	Växjö	13 Feb
:01.61	Jennifer	Meadows	GBR	17.4.81	3		Torun	12 Feb
:01.82	Hedda	Hynne	NOR	13.3.90	2	v3N	Växjö	13 Feb

:02.01	Tigist	Assefa	ETH	28.3.94	21	Feb
:02.15	Adele	Tracey	GBR	27.5.93	30	Jan
:02.33	Lovisa	Lindh	SWE	9.7.91	13	Feb
:02.44	Anastasiya	Tkachuk	UKR	20.4.93	17	Feb
:02.51	Phoebe	Wright	USA	30.8.88	12	Mar
2:02.62	Sifan	Hassan	NED	1.1.93	28	Feb
2:02.66	Shelayna	Oskan-Clarke	GBR	20.1.90	13	Feb
2:02.75	Treniere	Moser	USA	27.10.81	5	Feb
2:02.81	Stina	Troest	DEN	17.1.94	30	Jan
2:02.84	McKayla	Fricker	USA	19.4.92	12	Mar

000 Metres: 2:39.22 Renata Plis POL 5.2.85 1 Spala 6 Feb

1500 METRES

:56.46+	Genzebe	Dibaba	ETH	8.2.91	1	in 1M	Stockholm	17 Feb
:00.28	Dawit	Seyaum	ETH	27.7.96	1		Boston (All)	28 Feb
:01.40	Sifan	Hassan	NED	1.1.93	1	GP	Glasgow	20 Feb
:01.81	Gudaf	Tsegay	ETH-J	23.1.97	2	GP	Glasgow	20 Feb
:04.58	Brenda	Martinez	USA	8.9.87	2		Boston (R)	14 Feb
:06.11	Axumawit	Embaye	ETH	18.10.94	3	GP	Glasgow	20 Feb
:06.75	Kate	Grace	USA	24.10.88	3		Boston (R)	14 Feb
:06.89	Luiza	Gega	ALB	5.11.88	1	BalkC	Istanbul	27 Feb
:06.93	Melissa	Duncan	AUS	30.1.90	4		Boston (R)	14 Feb
:07.30+	Shannon	Rowbury	USA	19.9.84	1	in 1M	New York (Arm)	20 Feb
:07.38	Renata	Plis	POL	5.2.85	1		Torun	12 Feb
:08.38	Konstanze	Klosterhalfen	GER-J	18.2.97	2		Karlsruhe	6 Feb
:08.46	Nancy	Chepkwemoi	KEN	8.10.93	1		Athlone	17 Feb
:08.53+	Kerri	Gallagher	USA	31.5.89	2	in 1M	New York (Arm)	20 Feb
:08.66	Ciara	Mageean	IRL	12.3.92	3		Karlsruhe	6 Feb
:08.91	Gesa-Felicitas	Krause	GER	3.8.92	4		Karlsruhe	6 Feb
:08.95	Selina	Büchel	SUI	26.7.91	5		Karlsruhe	6 Feb
:09.12+	Amanda	Eccleston	USA	18.6.90	4	in 1M	New York (Arm)	20 Feb
:09.20+	Alexa	Efraimson	USA-J	20.2.97	5	in 1M	New York (Arm)	20 Feb
:09.21+	Morgan	Uceny	USA	10.3.85	6	in 1M	New York (Arm)	20 Feb
:09.27	Rabab	Arrafi	MAR	12.1.91	4	GP	Glasgow	20 Feb
:09.41	Danuta	Urbanik	POL	24.12.89	3h2	WI	Portland	18 Mar
:09.50	Yelena	Korobkina	RUS	25.11.90	1	NC	Moskva	25 Feb
:09.54+	Heather	Kampf	USA	19.1.87	7	in 1M	New York (Arm)	20 Feb
:09.64	Claudia	Bobocea	ROU	11.6.92	1		Luxembourg (K)	30 Jan
:09.69	Hannah	England	GBR	6.3.87	5	GP	Glasgow	20 Feb
:09.81	Anastasiya	Kalina	RUS	16.2.94	2	NC	Moskva	25 Feb

:09.97+	Stephanie	Garcia	USA	3.5.88	24	Jan
:09.97	Cory	McGee	USA	29.5.92	12	Mar
:10.45	Violah	Lagat	KEN	13.3.89	19	Mar
:10.66+	Kim	Conley	USA	14.3.86	24	Jan
:10.68	Maureen	Koster	NED	3.7.92	6	Feb
4:10.69+	Katie	Mackey	USA	12.11.87	20	Feb
4:10.77	Alison	Leonard	GBR	17.3.90	20	Feb
4:11.02	Aleksandra	Gulyayeva	RUS	30.4.94	14	Feb
4:11.07	Rose-Anne	Galligan	IRL	9.12.87	17	Feb
4:11.28	Kristiina	Mäki	CZE	22.9.91	18	Mar

4:11.42+	Heather	Wilson	USA	13.6.90	20	Feb
4:11.46	Gabriela	Stafford	CAN	13.9.95	18	Mar
4:11.53+	Leah	O'Connor	USA	30.8.92	20	Feb
4:11.59+	Ashley	Higginson	USA	17.3.89	6	Feb
4:11.68	Sarah	Lahti	SWE	18.2.95	18	Ma
4:11.76+	Erin	Donohue	USA	8.5.83	6	Feb
4:12.14	Besu	Sado	ETH	12.1.96	19	Feb
4:12.68	Yekaterina	Sokolova	RUS	16.12.95	3	Ma
4:12.72	Olga	Vovk	RUS	13.2.93	14	Fe

1 MILE

4:13.31	Genzebe	Dibaba	ETH	8.2.91	1	Globen	Stockholm	17 Fe
4:24.39	Shannon	Rowbury	USA	19.9.84	1	Mill	New York (Arm)	20 Fe
4:24.98	Gudaf	Tsegay	ETH-J	23.1.97	2	Globen	Stockholm	17 Fe
4:26.18	Kerri	Gallagher	USA	31.5.89	2	Mill	New York (Arm)	20 Fe
4:26.63	Amanda	Eccleston	USA	18.6.90	3	Mill	New York (Arm)	20 Fe
4:27.26	Heather	Kampf	USA	19.1.87	4	Mill	New York (Arm)	20 Fe
4:27.57	Sheila	Reid	CAN	2.8.89	1		Boston (All)	28 Fe
4:27.75	Axumawit	Embaye	ETH	18.10.94	3	Globen	Stockholm	17 Fe
4:27.88	Kim	Conley	USA	14.3.86	1		New York (Arm)	24 Ja
4:27.93	Nicole	Sifuentes	CAN	30.6.86	2		Boston (All)	12 Fe
4:27.99	Morgan	Uceny	USA	10.3.85	5	Mill	New York (Arm)	20 Fe
4:28.30	Kate	Grace	USA	24.10.88	2		New York (Arm)	24 Ja
4:28.40	Ciara	Mageean	IRL	12.3.92	6	Mill	New York (Arm)	20 Fe
4:28.47	Stephanie	Garcia	USA	3.5.88	2		Winston-Salem	29 Ja
4:28.50	Rachel	Schneider	USA	18.7.91	2		Boston (All)	28 Fe
4:28.84	Katie	Mackey	USA	12.11.87	7	Mill	New York (Arm)	20 Fe
4:28.91	Alexa	Efraimson	USA-J	20.2.97	8	Mill	New York (Arm)	20 Fe
4:29.07	Gabriela	Stafford	CAN	13.9.95	1		New York (Arm)	6 Fe
4:29.07	Erin	Donohue	USA	8.5.83	3		Boston (All)	12 Fe
4:29.71	Elinor	Purrier	USA	20.2.95	4		Boston (All)	12 Fe
4:29.87	Violah	Lagat	KEN	13.3.89	3		New York (Arm)	6 Fe

4:30.10	Rabab	Arrafi	MAR	12.1.91	17	Feb
4:30.16	Ashley	Higginson	USA	17.3.89	6	Feb
4:30.42	Sarah	Lahti	SWE	18.2.95	17	Feb
4:30.43	Sofia	Ennaoui	POL	30.8.95	17	Feb
4:30.65	Heather	Wilson	USA	13.6.90	12	Feb
4:30.91	Sandra	Eriksson	FIN	4.6.89	17	Feb
4:30.93	Cory	McGee	USA	29.5.92	24	Jan
4:31.50	Abbey	D'Agostino	USA	25.5.92	29	Jan
4:31.53	Hannah	England	GBR	6.3.87	17	Fe
4:31.57	Dominique	Scott	RSA	24.6.92	20	Fe
4:31.68	Emily	Lipari	USA	19.11.92	12	Fe
4:31.83	Leah	O'Connor	USA	30.8.92	20	Fe
4:32.05	Brenda	Martinez	USA	8.9.87	29	Ja
4:32.14	Kaela	Edwards	USA	8.12.93	30	Ja
4:32.71#	Rebecca	Tracy	USA	20.2.91	20	Fe

2000 Metres: c.5:39 Genzebe Dibaba ETH 8.2.91 1 in 3000 Sabadell 19 Fe

3000 METRES

8:22.50	Genzebe	Dibaba	ETH	8.2.91	1		Sabadell	19 Fe
8:30.83	Meseret	Defar	ETH	19.11.83	1		Boston (R)	14 Fe
8:33.76	Gelete	Burka	ETH	23.1.86	2		Sabadell	19 Fe
8:44.59	Betlhem	Desalegn	UAE	13.11.91	1	AsiC	Doha	20 Fe
8:47.24	Ruth	Chebet	BRN	17.11.96	2	AsiC	Doha	20 Fe
8:48.62	Alia Mohamed	Saeed	UAE	18.5.91	3	AsiC	Doha	20 Fe
8:49.06	Nancy	Chepkwemoi	KEN	8.10.93	1	GP	Glasgow	20 Fe
8:49.07	Sofia	Ennaoui	POL	30.8.95	2	GP	Glasgow	20 Fe
8:49.18	Maureen	Koster	NED	3.7.92	3	GP	Glasgow	20 Fe
8:49.43	Gesa-Felicitas	Krause	GER	3.8.92	4	GP	Glasgow	20 Fe
8:50.24	Stephanie	Twell	GBR	17.8.89	5	GP	Glasgow	20 Fe
8:50.75	Renata	Plis	POL	5.2.85	6	GP	Glasgow	20 Fe
8:51.88 mx	Abbey	D'Agostino	USA	25.5.92	1		Boston (All)	3 Ja

8:53.20i	Stephanie	Garcia	USA	3.5.88	20	Feb
8:53.52	Shannon	Rowbury	USA	19.9.84	15	Jan
8:54.27#	Allie	Ostrander	USA	24.12.96	13	Feb
8:54.65	Goytatom	Gebreselassie	ETH	15.1.95	19	Feb
8:54.70	Marielle	Hall	USA	28.1.92	6	Feb
8:54.87#	Gabriela	Stafford	CAN	13.9.95	13	Feb
8:55.89	Tigist	Gashaw	BRN	25.12.96	6	Feb
8:56.36	Konstanze	Klosterhalfen	GER-J	18.2.97	28	Feb
8:56.50	Sheila	Reid	CAN	2.8.89	6	Feb
8:56.52	Kerri	Gallagher	USA	31.5.89	30	Jan
8:56.55	Gemeda	Feyne	ETH	28.6.92	6	Feb
8:56.58	Jessica	O'Connell	CAN	10.2.89	12	Feb
8:57.11	Laura	Thweatt	USA	17.12.88	14	Feb
8:57.13#	Molly	Seidel	USA	12.7.94	6	Fe
8:57.14 mx	Josephine	Moultrie	GBR	19.11.90	3	Ja
	8:58.78				28	Fe
8:57.17	Nicole	Sifuentes	CAN	30.6.86	14	Fe
8:57.66	Heidi	See	AUS	8.9.89	14	Fe
8:57.78#	Lauren	Paquette	USA	27.6.86	13	Fe
8:58.34	Heather	Kampf	USA	19.1.87	6	Fe
8:58.84	Rachel	Schneider	USA	18.7.91	30	Ja
8:59.04	Sara	Moreira	POR	17.10.85	21	Fe
8:59.06	Nicole	Tully	USA	30.10.86	4	Ma
8:59.44#	Leah	O'Connor	USA	30.8.92	22	Ja
8:59.69	Amanda	Eccleston	USA	18.6.90	6	Fe
8:59.77#	Sandra	Eriksson	FIN	4.6.89	28	Fe
8:59.85	Shalaya	Kipp	USA	19.8.90	11	Ma

5000 METRES

14:57.18	Betsy	Saina	KEN	30.6.88	1	Mill	New York (Arm)	20 Fe
14:57.31	Molly	Huddle	USA	31.8.84	2	Mill	New York (Arm)	20 Fe
15:00.91	Emily	Infeld	USA	21.3.90	3	Mill	New York (Arm)	20 Fe
15:06.05	Marielle	Hall	USA	28.1.92	4	Mill	New York (Arm)	20 Fe
15:06.22	Shelby	Houlihan	USA	8.2.93	5	Mill	New York (Arm)	20 Fe
15:08.46	Yasemin	Can	TUR	11.12.96	1	NC	Istanbul	20 Fe
15:09.31#	Kim	Conley	USA	14.3.86	1		Seattle	29 Ja
15:15.21	Molly	Seidel	USA	12.7.94	1	NCAA	Birmingham	11 Ma
15:19.27	Meryem	Akda	TUR	5.8.92	2	NC	Istanbul	20 Fe

15:21.85#	Allie	Ostrander	USA	24.12.96	29	Jan
15:23.16	Erin	Finn	USA	19.11.94	11	Mar
15:24.44	Abbey	D'Agostino	USA	25.5.92	20	Fe
15:28.95	Yelena	Sedova	RUS	1.3.90	25	Fe

60 METRES HURDLES

.76	Brianna	Rollins	USA	18.8.91	1	NC	Portland	12 Mar
.77	Keni	Harrison	USA	18.9.92	2	NC	Portland	12 Mar
.81	Nia	Ali	USA	23.10.88	1	WI	Portland	18 Mar
.83	Queen	Harrison	USA	10.9.88	3	NC	Portland	12 Mar
.85	Janay	DeLoach	USA	12.10.85	1	Mill	New York (Arm)	20 Feb
.88	Cindy	Roleder	GER	21.8.89	1	NC	Leipzig	27 Feb
.89	Tiffany	Porter	GBR	13.11.87	1		Jablonec nad Nisou	5 Mar
.89	Cindy	Ofili	GBR	5.8.94	1	NCAA	Birmingham	12 Mar
.90	Christina	Manning	USA	29.5.90	1		Montréal	20 Feb
.90	Sharika	Nelvis	USA	10.5.90	1h2	NC	Portland	11 Mar
.91	Sasha	Wallace	USA	21.9.95	2	NCAA	Birmingham	12 Mar
.91	Andrea	Ivancevic	CRO	21.8.84	2h3	WI	Portland	18 Mar
.92	Kristi	Castlin	USA	7.7.88	1		Athlone	17 Feb
.93	Jackie	Coward	USA	5.11.89	2		Montréal	20 Feb
.93	Jasmin	Stowers	USA	23.9.91	3	Mill	New York (Arm)	20 Feb
.95A	Lolo	Jones	USA	5.8.82	1		Albuquerque	6 Feb
.96	Alina	Talay	BLR	14.5.89	2h1	WI	Portland	18 Mar
.97	Devynne	Charlton	BAH	26.11.95	1	Big 10	Geneva OH	27 Feb
.99	Angela	Whyte	CAN	22.5.80	5	WI	Portland	18 Mar
.00	Akela	Jones	BAR	21.4.95	1	Big 12	Ames	27 Feb

.01	Lucy	Hatton	GBR	8.11.94	6 Feb
.01	Sandra	Gomis	FRA	21.11.83	13 Feb
01	Nadine	Hildebrand	GER	20.9.87	27 Feb
02	Serita	Solomon	GBR	1.3.90	5 Mar
02	Tonea	Marshall	USA-J	17.12.98	13 Mar
.03	Bridgette	Owens	USA	14.3.92	9 Feb
.03	Dawn	Harper Nelson	USA	13.5.84	14 Feb
.04	Cindy	Billaud	FRA	11.3.86	21 Feb
.04	Daeshon	Gordon	JAM	8.11.96	12 Mar
04	Mikiah	Brisco	USA	14.7.96	12 Mar
04	Brianne	Theisen-Eaton	CAN	18.12.88	18 Mar
05	Karolina	Koleczek	POL	15.1.93	12 Feb
.05	Kaila	Barber	USA	4.4.93	11 Mar
.06	Jade	Barber	USA	4.4.93	6 Feb
.06	Hanna	Plotitsyna	UKR	1.1.87	5 Mar
.07	Danielle	Williams	JAM	14.9.92	30 Jan
.07	Anastasiya	Soprunova	KAZ	14.1.86	31 Jan
.08	Pamela	Dutkiewicz	GER	28.9.91	6 Feb
8.08	Fabiana	Moraes	BRA	5.6.86	13 Feb
8.08	Mulern	Jean	USA	25.9.92	26 Feb
8.08	Alaysha	Johnson	USA	.96	11 Mar
8.09	Candice	Davis-Price	USA		6 Feb
8.09	Ginnie	Crawford	USA	7.9.83	12 Feb
8.09	Nina	Morozova	RUS	15.9.89	24 Feb
8.09	Payton	Stumbaugh	USA	29.11.95	11 Mar
8.09	Kendell	Williams	USA	14.6.95	11 Mar
8.10	Nikkita	Holder	CAN	7.5.87	8 Jan
8.10A	Kaylon	Eppinger	USA	17.9.89	23 Jan
8.10	Anastasiya	Pilipenko	KAZ	13.9.86	31 Jan
8.10	Aisseta	Diawara	FRA	29.6.89	13 Feb
8.10	Raven	Clay	USA	5.10.90	19 Feb
8.10	Ricarda	Lobe	GER	13.4.94	27 Feb
8.10	Nooralotta	Neziri	FIN	9.11.92	28 Feb
8.10	LaTisha	Holden-Palmer	USA	29.8.89	11 Mar
8.10	Michelle	Jenneke	AUS	23.6.93	18 Mar

HIGH JUMP

.99	Vashti	Cunningham	USA	18.1.98	1	NC	Portland	12 Mar
.98	Mariya	Kuchina	RUS	14.1.93	1		Moskva	14 Feb
.98	Ruth	Beitia	ESP	1.4.79	1	NC	Madrid	6 Mar
.98	Akela	Jones	BAR	21.4.95	1P	NCAA	Birmingham	11 Mar
.97	Airine	Palsyte	LTU	13.7.92	1		Cottbus	27 Jan
.97	Kamila	Licwinko	POL	22.3.86	1	Pedros	Lódz	5 Feb
.95	Blanka	Vlasic	CRO	8.11.83	1		Split	29 Jan
.95A	Chaunté	Lowe	USA	12.1.84	2		Albuquerque	6 Feb
.95	Levern	Spencer	LCA	23.6.84	1		Hustopece	13 Feb
.95	Michaela	Hrubá	CZE-J	21.2.98	1	NC-j	Praha (Strom)	20 Feb
.95	Alessia	Trost	ITA	8.3.93	1		Madrid	26 Feb
.95	Marie-Laurence	Jungfleisch	GER	7.10.90	1	NC	Leipzig	28 Feb
.94	Sofie	Skoog	SWE	7.6.90	1	v3N	Växjö	13 Feb
.94	Irina	Gordeyeva	RUS	9.10.86	1	NC	Moskva	25 Feb
.93	Oksana	Okuneva	UKR	14.3.90	1		Lviv	16 Jan
.93	Daniela	Stanciu	ROU	15.10.87	1		Bucuresti	31 Jan
.93	Doreen	Amata	NGR	6.5.88	1		Banská Bystrica	4 Feb
.93	Isobel	Pooley	GBR	21.12.92	3	GP	Glasgow	20 Feb
.93	Morgan	Lake	GBR-J	12.5.97	1P	v2N23	Salamanca	20 Feb
.93	Yuliya	Chumachenko	UKR	2.10.94	1		Kherson	5 Mar
.93	Urszula	Gardzielewska	POL	21.7.88	1P	NC	Torun	5 Mar
.93	Liz	Patterson	USA	9.6.88	2	NC	Portland	12 Mar
.93	Erika	Kinsey	SWE	10.3.88	8	WI	Portland	20 Mar
.92	Svetlana	Radzivil	UZB	17.1.87	1	AsiC	Doha	21 Feb

.91	Kristina	Korolyova	RUS	6.11.90	22 Jan
.91	Nafissatou	Thiam	BEL	19.8.94	7 Feb
.91	Tatyana	Mnatsakanova	RUS	25.5.83	25 Feb
.90	Ulyana	Aleksandrova	RUS	1.1.91	19 Dec
.90	Marusa	Cernjul	SLO	30.6.92	6 Feb
.90	Priscilla	Frederick	ANT	14.2.89	27 Feb
.90	Raquel	Álvarez	ESP	13.6.83	6 Mar
.90	Zibby	Boyer	USA	23.9.93	12 Mar
.89	Yuliya	Levchenko	UKR-J	28.11.97	9 Jan
.89	Yana	Maksimova	BLR	9.1.89	7 Feb
.89	Abby	Ward	GBR-Y	19.4.99	7 Feb
1.89	Jeannelle	Scheper	LCA	21.11.94	17 Feb
1.89	Lissa	Labiche	SEY	18.2.93	20 Mar
1.88	Ty	Butts	USA	10.6.90	4 Dec
1.88	Margarita	Mazina	RUS	7.7.95	22 Jan
1.88	Katarina	Mögenburg	NOR	16.6.91	27 Jan
1.88	Ariane	Friedrich	GER	10.1.84	27 Jan
1.88	Nadezhda	Dusanova	UZB	17.11.87	29 Jan
1.88	Claudia	García	ESP	30.9.92	30 Jan
1.88	Svetlana	Nikolenko	RUS	26.9.91	25 Feb
1.88		Wang Yang	CHN	14.2.89	4 Mar
1.88	Michalina	Kwasniewska	POL	22.10.91	6 Mar

POLE VAULT

5.03	Jenn	Suhr	USA	5.2.82	1		Brockport	30 Ja
4.95	Sandi	Morris	USA	8.7.92	1	NC	Portland	12 Ma
4.90	Ekateríni	Stefanídi	GRE	4.2.90	1	Mill	New York (Arm)	20 Fe
4.90	Demi	Payne	USA	30.9.91	2	Mill	New York (Arm)	20 Fe
4.81	Nikoléta	Kiriakopoúlou	GRE	21.3.86	1	Globen	Stockholm	17 Fe
4.80	Nicole	Büchler	SUI	17.12.83	4	WI	Portland	17 Ma
4.75	Anzhelika	Sidorova	RUS	28.6.91	1		Moskva	22 Ja
4.71A	Mary	Saxer	USA	21.6.87	3		Reno	15 Ja
4.71	Wilma	Murto	FIN-J	11.6.98	1		Zweibrücken	31 Ja
4.71	Fabiana	Murer	BRA	16.3.81	2	Globen	Stockholm	17 Fe
4.70		Li Ling	CHN	6.7.89	1	AsiC	Doha	19 Fe
4.70	Eliza	McCartney	NZL	11.12.96	5	WI	Portland	17 Ma
4.66	Angelica	Bengtsson	SWE	8.7.93	1	v3N	Växjö	13 Fe
4.66	Angelina	Krasnova	RUS	7.2.91	2		Moskva	14 Fe
4.66	Jirina	Ptácníková	CZE	20.5.86	1		Praha	17 Fe
4.65	Kristen	Hixson	USA	1.7.92	4	NC	Portland	12 Ma
4.63	Katie	Nageotte	USA	30.6.91	1	Starks	Columbus OH	4 Ma
4.63	Lexi	Weeks	USA	20.11.96	1	NCAA	Birmingham	12 Ma
4.62	Lisa	Ryzih	GER	27.9.88	4=		Clermont-Ferrand	21 Fe
4.62	Romana	Malácová	CZE	15.5.87	4=		Clermont-Ferrand	21 Fe
4.61	Minna	Nikkanen	FIN	9.4.88	2	v3N	Växjö	13 Fe
4.60	Megan	Clark	USA	10.6.94	1		New York (Arm)	6 Fe
4.60	Olga	Mullina	RUS	1.8.92	3	NC	Moskva	23 Fe
4.60	Vanessa	Boslak	FRA	11.6.82	1	NC	Aubière	28 Fe
4.60	Michaela	Meijer	SWE	30.7.93	1	NC	Rud	5 Ma
4.56	Silke	Spiegelburg	GER	17.3.86	1	NC	Leipzig	27 Fe
4.55A	Melinda	Withrow	USA	30.10.84	1		Air Force Academy	23 Ja
4.52	Rosbeilys	Peinado	VEN-J	26.11.97	6		Clermont-Ferrand	21 Fe
4.51	Martina	Strutz	GER	4.11.81	2	NC	Leipzig	27 Fe
4.51	Marta	Onofre	POR	28.1.91	1		Pombal	6 Ma
4.50A	Kylie	Hutson	USA	27.11.87	4		Reno	15 Ja
4.50	Femke	Pluim	NED	10.5.94	1		Gent	16 Ja
4.50	Alysha	Newman	CAN	6.6.94	2		New York (Arm)	6 Fe
4.50	Emily	Grove	USA	22.5.93	1		Ames	13 Fe
4.50	Angelica	Moser	SUI-J	9.10.97	1		Dornbirn	14 Fe
4.50	Leslie	Brost	USA	28.9.89	6	NC	Portland	12 Ma
4.49	Lisa	Gunnarsson	SWE-Y	20.8.99	4	Globen	Stockholm	17 Fe

4.46	Annika	Roloff	GER	10.3.91	27 Feb
4.45	Diamara	Planell	PUR	16.2.93	12 Mar
4.45	Annie	Rhodes	USA	13.5.95	26 Mar
4.43	Anjuli	Knäsche	GER	18.10.93	30 Jan
4.42A	Kristen	Brown	USA	26.5.92	13 Feb
4.41	Sophie	Gutermuth	USA	2.11.92	12 Feb
4.41A	Carmelita	Correa	MEX	5.12.88	13 Feb
4.41	Melissa	Gergel	USA	24.4.89	20 Feb
4.41	Kaitlin	Petrillose	USA	10.12.92	26 Feb
4.40	Maryna	Kylypko	UKR	10.11.95	14 Jan
4.40	Kayla	Caldwell	USA	19.6.91	31 Jan
4.40	Sonia	Malavisi	ITA	31.10.94	6 Feb
4.40A	Tori	Pena	IRL	30.7.87	6 Feb
4.40	Irina	Yakoltsevich	BLR	26.1.93	7 Feb
4.40	Rianna	Galiart	NED	22.11.85	13 Feb
4.40	April	Steiner Bennett	USA	22.4.80	13 Feb
4.40	Annie	Rhodes	USA	13.5.95	13 Fe
4.40	Tori	Weeks	USA	20.11.96	19 Fe
4.40	Maria Eleanor	Tavares	POR	24.9.85	21 Fe
4.40	Natalya	Demidenko	RUS	7.8.93	23 Fe
4.40	Yelizaveta	Bondarenko	RUS-Y	1.7.99	23 Fe
4.40	Jessie	Johnson	USA	21.11.93	27 Fe
4.39	Becky	Holliday	USA	12.3.80	9 Ja
4.38	Marion	Fiack	FRA	13.10.92	23 Ja
4.35	Karla	da Silva	BRA	12.11.84	23 Ja
4.35	Elienor	Werner	SWE-J	5.5.98	30 Ja
4.35	Marion	Lotout	FRA	19.11.89	31 Ja
4.35	Tatyana	Shvydkina	RUS	8.5.90	7 Fe
4.35	Elizabeth	Quick	USA	.94	13 Fe
4.35	Anastasiya	Savchenko	RUS	15.11.89	14 Fe
4.35	Tatyana	Stetsyuk	RUS	27.8.92	14 Fe
4.35	Sydney	Clute	USA	15.11.93	26 Fe
4.35	Ninon	Guillon-Romarin	FRA	15.4.95	28 Fe

LONG JUMP

7.22	Brittney	Reese	USA	9.9.86	1	WI	Portland	18 Ma
7.07	Ivana	Spanovic	SRB	10.5.90	2	WI	Portland	18 Ma
6.95	Alexandra	Wester	GER	21.3.94	1	ISTAF	Berlin	13 Fe
6.93	Lorraine	Ugen	GBR	22.8.91	3	WI	Portland	18 Ma
6.91	Shara	Proctor	GBR	16.9.88	2	ISTAF	Berlin	13 Fe
6.89	Janay	DeLoach	USA	12.10.85	4	WI	Portland	18 Ma
6.84	Anastasiya	Mironchik-Ivanova	BLR	13.4.89	1	NCp	Minsk	7 Fe
6.80	Quanesha	Burks	USA	15.3.95	1	NCAA	Birmingham	11 Ma
6.80	Akela	Jones	BAR	21.4.95	1P	NCAA	Birmingham	11 Ma
6.76	Anna	Misochenko	RUS	15.4.92	1		Slavyansk-na-Kubani	31 Ja
6.76	Ksenija	Balta	EST	1.11.86	1	Globen	Stockholm	17 Fe
6.75	Yuliya	Pidluzhnaya	RUS	1.10.88	1	NC	Moskva	24 Fe
6.75	Brooke	Stratton	AUS	12.7.93	5	WI	Portland	18 Ma
6.71	Veronika	Semashko	RUS	17.10.90	2	NC	Moskva	24 Fe
6.70	Yekaterina	Koneva	RUS	25.9.88	2		Slavyansk-na-Kubani	31 Ja
6.69A	Lynique	Prinsloo	RSA	30.3.91	1		Germiston	27 Fe
6.67	Jazmin	Sawyers	GBR	21.5.94	1	NC	Sheffield	28 Fe
6.66		Xu Xiaoling	CHN	13.5.92	1	NGP	Nanjing	28 Fe
6.66	Anastasiya	Mokhnyuk	UKR	1.1.91	1P	WI	Portland	18 Ma

6.64	Chanice	Porter	JAM	25.5.94	2	SEC	Fayetteville	26 Feb
6.63	Xenia	Stolz	GER	14.1.89	3	ISTAF	Berlin	13 Feb
6.61	Khaddi	Sagnia	SWE	20.4.94	1		Malmö	31 Jan
6.61		Jiang Yanfei	CHN	5.7.92	2	NGP	Nanjing	3 Mar
6.61A	Jana	Veldáková	SVK	3.6.81	1	ACNW Ch	Potchefstroom	12 Mar
6.60	Alina	Rotaru	ROU	5.6.93	1	NC	Bucuresti	21 Feb

6.59	Sha'Keela	Saunders	USA	18.12.93	26 Feb	6.52	Veranika	Shutkova	BLR	26.5.86	7 Feb
6.57	Andrea	Geubelle	USA	21.6.91	12 Mar	6.51	Keturah	Orji	USA	5.3.96	29 Jan
6.56	Chantel	Malone	IVB	2.12.91	13 Feb	6.51	Paraskeví	Papahrístou	GRE	17.4.89	31 Jan
6.55	Funmi	Jimoh	USA	29.5.84	12 Mar	6.51	Bianca	Stuart	BAH	17.5.88	12 Feb
6.54	Hafdís	Sigurdardóttir	ISL	12.2.87	23 Jan	6.51	Melanie	Bauschke	GER	14.7.88	13 Feb
6.54	Kate	Hall	USA-J	12.1.97	29 Jan	6.51	Nafissatou	Thiam	BEL	19.8.94	20 Feb
6.54	Jana	Veldáková	SVK	3.6.81	16 Feb	6.51	Darrielle	McQueen	USA	29.5.96	26 Feb
6.53	Erica	Jarder	SWE	2.4.86	17 Feb	6.51	Maryse	Luzolo	GER	13.3.95	28 Feb

TRIPLE JUMP

14.69	Yulimar	Rojas	VEN	21.10.95	1		Madrid	23 Jan
14.32	Olga	Rypakova	KAZ	30.11.84	1	AsiC	Doha	20 Feb
14.32	Yekaterina	Koneva	RUS	25.9.88	1	NC	Moskva	25 Feb
14.32	Gabriela	Petrova	BUL	29.6.92	1	BalkC	Istanbul	27 Feb
14.30	Kristin	Gierisch	GER	20.8.90	2	WI	Portland	19 Mar
14.23	Irina	Vaskovskaya	BLR	2.4.91	1	NC	Mogilyov	20 Feb
14.21	Paraskeví	Papahrístou	GRE	17.4.89	1	NC	Bucuresti	20 Feb
14.20	Kristiina	Mäkelä	FIN	20.11.92	1		Mustasaari	6 Feb
14.17	Jeanine	Assani Issouf	FRA	17.8.92	1	NC	Aubière	27 Feb
14.16	Rouguy	Diallo	FRA	5.2.95	2	NC	Aubière	27 Feb
14.15	Jenny	Elbe	GER	18.4.90	1	NC	Leipzig	27 Feb
14.15	Elena	Panturoiu	ROU	24.2.95	1		Bucuresti	5 Mar
14.14	Keturah	Orji	USA	5.3.96	4	WI	Portland	19 Mar
14.08	Anna	Jagaciak	POL	10.2.90	3		Chemnitz	20 Feb
14.05	Christina	Epps	USA	20.6.91	1	NC	Portland	11 Mar
14.00	Mayookha	Johny	IND	9.4.88	2	AsiC	Doha	20 Feb
13.96	Natalya	Alekseyeva	RUS	27.5.86	1		Moskva	10 Feb
13.95	Shanieka	Thomas	JAM	2.2.92	8	WI	Portland	19 Mar

13.94	Carmen	Toma	ROU	28.3.89	30 Jan	13.84	Susana	Costa	POR	22.9.84	27 Feb
13.94	Keila	Costa	BRA	6.2.83	19 Mar	13.83	Olesya	Zabara	RUS	6.10.82	19 Jan
13.91	Patrícia	Mamona	POR	21.11.88	20 Feb	13.83	Petia	Dacheva	BUL	10.3.85	27 Feb
13.91	Ana	Peleteiro	ESP	2.12.95	26 Feb	13.81	Veronika	Semashko	RUS	17.10.90	27 Dec
13.91	Andrea	Geubelle	USA	21.6.91	27 Feb	13.76	Neele	Eckhardt	GER	2.7.92	27 Feb
13.91		Chen Mudan	CHN	4.10.93	29 Feb	13.75	Anastasiya	Mironchik-Ivanova	BLR	13.4.89	23 Jan
13.91		Wang Wupin	CHN	18.1.91	29 Feb	13.74	Dana	Veldáková	SVK	3.6.81	20 Feb
13.90	Viktoriya	Prokopenko	RUS	17.4.91	27 Dec	13.72	Natalya	Vyatkina	BLR	10.2.87	20 Feb
13.90	Ksenia	Detsuk	BLR	23.4.86	20 Feb	13.72	Darya	Nidbaykina	RUS	26.12.94	3 Mar
13.89	Olesya	Tikhonova	RUS	22.1.90	25 Feb	13.71	Ruslana	Tsyhotska	UKR	23.3.86	9 Jan
13.89	Kimberly	Williams	JAM	3.11.88	26 Feb	13.70	Martyna	Bielawska	POL	15.11.90	20 Feb
13.86	Hanna	Minenko	ISR	25.9.89	12 Feb	13.70	Ayanna	Alexander	TTO	20.7.82	20 Feb
13.84	Patricia	Sarrapio	ESP	16.11.82	23 Jan						

SHOT

20.21	Michelle	Carter	USA	12.10.85	1	WI	Portland	19 Mar
19.43	Valerie	Adams	NZL	6.10.84	1	NC	Dunedin	6 Mar
19.37		Gong Lijiao	CHN	24.1.89	1		Beijing	28 Jan
19.33	Anita	Márton	HUN	15.1.89	2	WI	Portland	19 Mar
19.25	Valerie	Adams	NZL	6.10.84	3	WI	Portland	19 Mar
19.23	Raven	Saunders	USA	15.5.96	1		Ames	13 Feb
18.87	Dani	Bunch	USA	16.5.91	1		Notre Dame	20 Feb
18.68	Yuliya	Leontyuk	BLR	31.1.84	1		Mogilyov	22 Jan
18.64	Jill	Camarena-Williams	USA	2.3.82	2	NC	Portland	11 Mar
18.63	Paulina	Guba	POL	14.5.91	1	NC	Torun	5 Mar
18.57	Brittany	Smith	USA	25.3.91	1		Allendale	12 Feb
18.56	Jeneva	Stevens	USA	28.10.89	3	NC	Portland	11 Mar
18.38	Cleopatra	Borel	TTO	10.3.79	4	WI	Portland	19 Mar
18.36	Felisha	Johnson	USA	24.7.89	1		Indianapolis IN	30 Jan
18.36	Emel	Dereli	TUR	25.2.96	1		Istanbul	25 Feb
18.35	Irina	Kirichenko	RUS	18.5.87	1		Irkutsk	19 Jan
18.32	Lena	Urbaniak	GER	31.10.92	1	NC	Leipzig	27 Feb
18.28	Jessica	Ramsey	USA	26.7.91	3		Nashville	30 Jan
18.25		Gao Yang	CHN	1.3.93	1		Neubrandenburg	19 Dec
18.19	Alyona	Dubitskaya	BLR	25.1.90	2	NC	Mogilyov	20 Feb
18.12		Bian Ka	CHN	5.1.93	2		Beijing	28 Jan
18.06		Geng Shuang	CHN	9.7.93	1	AsiC	Doha	19 Feb
18.02	Alena	Abramchuk	BLR	14.2.88	1		Minsk	16 Jan
18.00	Yevgeniya	Solovyova	RUS	28.6.86	1	NC	Moskva	24 Feb
18.00	Radoslava	Mavrodieva	BUL	13.3.87	6	WI	Portland	19 Mar
17.97	Dani	Winters	USA	18.2.93	1	NCAA	Birmingham	12 Mar
17.93	Christina	Hillman	USA	6.10.93	1	Big 12	Ames	27 Feb
17.90	Chiara	Rosa	ITA	28.1.83	1		Padova	20 Feb

17.87	Olesya	Sviridova	RUS	28.10.89	2	NC	Moskva	24 Fe
17.85	Kelsey	Card	USA	20.8.92	1		Minneapolis	22 Ja

17.78	Brittany	Crew	CAN	3.6.94	30 Jan
17.77	Irina	Tarasova	RUS	15.4.87	24 Feb
17.74	Anastasiya	Podolskaya	RUS	18.8.90	10 Jan
17.71		Guo Tianqian	CHN	1.6.95	28 Jan
17.68	Melissa	Boekelman	NED	11.5.89	27 Feb
17.68	Anna	Rüh	GER	17.6.93	27 Feb
17.68	Cassie	Wertman	USA	14.6.93	12 Mar
17.66	Taryn	Suttie	CAN	7.12.90	12 Feb
17.66	Monique	Riddick	USA	8.11.89	27 Feb
17.66	Nikki	Okwelogu	NGR	5.5.95	12 Mar
17.63	Chase	Ealey	USA	20.7.94	13 Feb
17.62	Whitney	Ashley	USA	18.2.89	29 Jan
17.62		Liu Xiangrong	CHN	6.6.88	4 Mar
17.58	Alyona	Bugakova	RUS-J	24.4.97	9 Feb
17.39	Cion	Hicks	USA	14.10.94	13 Feb
17.35	Rachel	Wallader	GBR	1.9.89	30 Jan
17.33	Jill	Rushin	USA	18.7.91	19 Feb
17.31	Úrsula	Ruiz	ESP	11.8.83	19 Feb
17.30	Jessica	Cérival	FRA	20.1.82	27 Feb
17.29	Alexis	Cooks	USA	11.9.93	19 Feb
17.28		Meng Qianqian	CHN	6.1.91	4 Mar
17.27	Rachel	Fatherly	USA	20.4.94	6 Feb
17.22	Vera	Kunova	RUS	2.4.90	24 Feb
17.20	Fanny	Roos	SWE	2.1.95	20 Feb
17.20	Viktoryia	Kolb	BLR	26.10.93	20 Feb
17.20	Yanina	Provalinskay-Karolchik	BLR	26.12.76	20 Feb

20 LB WEIGHT

24.51	Gwen	Berry	USA	29.6.89	1		Carbondale	6 Fe
24.33	Amber	Campbell	USA	5.6.81	1		Columbia SC	20 Fe
23.75	Jeneva	Stevens	USA	28.10.89	1		Akron	6 Fe
23.53	Felisha	Johnson	USA	24.7.89	3	NC	Portland	11 Ma
23.22	Jessica	Ramsey	USA	26.7.91	3		Nashville	29 Ja
22.70	Kaitlyn	Long	USA	25.4.96	1	NCAA-II	Pittsburg	11 Ma
22.42	Vesta	Bell	USA		1	NCAA	Birmingham	11 Ma
22.29	Ida	Storm	SWE	26.12.91	1	NC	Malmö	27 Fe
22.21	Dolly	Nyemah	USA		2	NCAA	Birmingham	11 Ma
22.14	Kelsey	Card	USA	20.8.92	1	Big 10	Geneva OH	27 Fe
22.05	Amanda	Bingson	USA	20.2.90	5	NC	Portland	11 Mar

21.93	Marthaline	Cooper	USA		19 Feb
21.91	Nicole	Chavis	USA	11.1.93	29 Jan
21.67	Deanna	Price	USA	8.6.93	6 Fe
21.65	Ashley	Jenkins	USA	10.12.93	22 Ja

PENTATHLON

4881	Brianne	Theisen-Eaton	CAN	18.12.88	1	WI	Portland	18 Ma
	8.04	1.85	13.70	6.42	2:09.99			
4847	Anastasiya	Mokhnyuk	UKR	1.1.91	2	WI	Portland	18 Ma
	8.11	1.85	15.01	6.66	2:23.19			
4770	Alina	Fyodorova	UKR	31.7.89	3	WI	Portland	18 Ma
	8.27	1.85	15.44	6.33	2:20.42			
4703	Kendell	Williams	USA	14.6.95	1	NCAA	Birmingham	11 Ma
	8.09	1.86	13.55	6.35	2:20.47			
4688	Claudia	Rath	GER	25.4.86	1		Tallinn	14 Fe
	8.45	1.81	12.85	6.40	2:09.19			
4678	Nafissatou	Thiam	BEL	19.8.94	1	NC	Gent	7 Fe
	8.49	1.91	14.60	6.23	2:22.84			
4661	Barbara	Nwaba	USA	18.1.89	4	WI	Portland	18 Ma
	8.43	1.82	15.00	5.84	2:10.07			
4656	György	Zsivoczky-Farkas	HUN	13.2.85	5	WI	Portland	18 Ma
	8.56	1.85	14.54	6.28	2:18.48			
4643	Akela	Jones	BAR	21.4.95	1		Manhattan KS	22 Ja
	8.25	1.85	12.99	6.64	2:25.63			
4535	Ulyana	Aleksandrova	RUS	1.1.91	1	NC	Smolensk	19 Fe
	8.57	1.90	12.79	6.27	2:23.25			
4519	Morgan	Lake	GBR-J	12.5.97	1	v2N-23	Salamanca	20 Fe
	8.63	1.93	12.97	5.89	2:18.53			
4506	Katerina	Cachová	CZE	26.2.90	1	NC	Praha (Strom)	13 Fe
	8.30	1.84	11.67	6.28	2:18.78			
4482	Lyubov	Tkach	RUS	18.2.93	2	NC	Smolensk	19 Fe
	9.07	1.81	14.86	6.03	2:15.52			
4470	Yana	Maksimova	BLR	9.1.89	1	NC	Gomel	17 Fe
	8.92	1.86	14.27	5.91	2:17.70			
4457	Taliyah	Brooks	USA	8.2.95	2		Fayetteville	29 Ja
	8.18	1.78	11.40	6.35	2:19.06			
4444#	Amalie	Iuel	NOR	17.4.94	1		Seattle	26 Fe
	8.48	1.78	11.07	6.03	2:06.88			
4434	Mariya	Gromysheva	RUS	10.1.90	1		Volgograd	20 Ja
	8.63	1.74	13.37	6.42	2:21.05			

4393#	Jess	Lehman	USA	17.1.93	26 Feb
4392#	Georgia	Ellenwood	CAN	5.8.95	26 Feb
4380A	Makeba	Alcide	LCA	24.2.90	5 Feb
4373	Lisa	Maihöfer	GER	28.10.98	31 Jan
4371	Payton	Stumbaugh	USA	29.11.95	11 Mar
4369	Michelle	Zeltner	SUI	22.12.91	14 Feb
4363	Annie	Kunz	USA	16.2.93	5 Feb
4354	Alina	Shukh	UKR	12.2.99	27 Jan
4347	Celina	Leffler	GER	9.4.96	31 Jan
4341	Aleksandra	Butvina	RUS	14.2.86	19 Feb
4336	Alex	Gochenour	USA	17.2.93	11 Mar
4322	Daryna	Sloboda	UKR	19.6.95	25 Feb
4320	Lisa	Linnell	SWE	30.4.91	21 Feb
4292	Anna	Gorodskaya	BLR	31.1.93	28 Jan
4292	Vanessa	Spínola	BRA	5.3.90	14 Feb
4291	Austra	Skujyte	LTU	12.8.79	14 Feb
4285	Kaylon	Eppinger	USA	17.9.89	27 Feb
4282	Karl	Johonnot	USA	21.8.93	21 Jan
4268	Xenia	Rahn	GER	9.3.91	11 Ma
4260	Ivona	Dadic	AUT	29.12.93	14 Feb
4250	Lecabela	Quaresma	POR	26.12.89	27 Feb
4245	Beatrice	Puiu	ROU	1.1.86	30 Ja